Hoover's Handbook of Private Companies 2005

Hoover's Business Press

Austin, Texas

Hoover's Handbook of Private Companies 2005 is intended to provide readers with accurate and authoritative information about the enterprises covered in it. Hoover's asked all companies and organizations profiled to provide information. Many did so; a number did not. The information contained herein is as accurate as we could reasonably make it. In many cases we have relied on third-party material that we believe to be trustworthy, but were unable to independently verify. We do not warrant that the book is absolutely accurate or without error. Readers should not rely on any information contained herein in instances where such reliance might cause loss or damage. The publisher, the editors, and their data suppliers specifically disclaim all warranties, including the implied warranties of merchantability and fitness for a specific purpose. This book is sold with the understanding that neither the publisher, the editors, nor any content contributors are engaged in providing investment, financial, accounting, legal, or other professional advice.

The financial data (Historical Financials sections) in this book are from the companies profiled or from trade sources deemed to be reliable. Hoover's, Inc., is solely responsible for the presentation of all data.

Many of the names of products and services mentioned in this book are the trademarks or service marks of the companies manufacturing or selling them and are subject to protection under US law. Space has not permitted us to indicate which names are subject to such protection, and readers are advised to consult with the owners of such marks regarding their use. Hoover's is a trademark of Hoover's, Inc.

Copyright © 2005 by Hoover's, Inc. All rights reserved. No part of this book may be reproduced or transmitted in any form or by any means, electronic or mechanical, including by photocopying, facsimile transmission, recording, rekeying, or using any information storage and retrieval system, without permission in writing from Hoover's, except that brief passages may be quoted by a reviewer in a magazine, in a newspaper, online, or in a broadcast review.

10 9 8 7 6 5 4 3 2 1

Publishers Cataloging-in-Publication Data

Hoover's Handbook of Private Companies 2005

    Includes indexes.

    ISBN 1-57311-102-3

    ISSN 1073-6433

    1. Business enterprises — Directories. 2. Corporations — Directories.

HF3010 338.7

Hoover's Company Information is also available on the Internet at Hoover's Online (www.hoovers.com). A catalog of Hoover's products is available on the Internet at www.hooversbooks.com.

The Hoover's Handbook series is edited by George Sutton and is produced for Hoover's Business Press by:

Sycamore Productions, Inc.
5808 Balcones Drive, Suite 205
Austin, Texas 78731
info@sycamoreproductions.com

Cover design is by John Baker. Electronic prepress and printing are by Sheridan Books, Inc., Ann Arbor, Michigan.

U.S. AND WORLD BOOK SALES

Hoover's, Inc.
5800 Airport Blvd.
Austin, TX 78752
Phone: 512-374-4500
Fax: 512-374-4538
e-mail: orders@hoovers.com
Web: www.hooversbooks.com

EUROPEAN BOOK SALES

William Snyder Publishing Associates
5 Five Mile Drive
Oxford OX2 8HT
England
Phone & fax: +44-186-551-3186
e-mail: snyderpub@aol.com

Hoover's, Inc.

Founder: Gary Hoover
President: Dwayne H. Spradlin
EVP International: Russell Secker
VP Advertising and Large Accounts: Jonathan Cherins
VP Enterprise Subscription Sales: John Lysinger
VP Finance and Administration: Jeffrey A. Cross
VP Human Resources: James M. (Mike) Smith
VP Marketing: Paul Pellman
VP Product Management: Michael Reiff
VP Technology and CTO: Thomas M. (Tom) Ballard

EDITORIAL

VP, Managing Editor: Rachel Brush
Director of Quality: Valerie Pearcy
Senior Editors: Margaret Claughton, Kathleen Kelly, Laurie Najjar, Barbara Redding, Dennis Sutton
Research Manager: Amy Degner
Editors: Sally Alt, Linnea Anderson, Lisa Baehr, Alex Biesada, Larry Bills, Angela Boeckman, Joe Bramhall, James Bryant, Troy Bryant, Ryan Caione, Jason Cella, Jannell Chester, Catherine Colbert, Elizabeth Cornell, Danny Cummings, Amy Davison, Lesley Dings, Jeff Dorsch, Michaela Drapes, Bobby Duncan, Adriane Foster, David Hamerly, Stuart Hampton, Jeanette Herman, Kenny Jones, Julie Krippel, Anne Law, Josh Lower, John MacAyeal, Michael McLellan, Rachel Meyer, Barbara Murray, Nell Newton, Peter Partheymuller, Greg Perliski, Anna Porlas, Jennifer Powers, David Ramirez, Kcevin Rob, Melanie Robertson, Matt Saucedo, Amy Schein, Seth Shafer, Joe Simonetta, Diane Stimets, Daysha Taylor, Vanita Trippe, Tim Walker, Josh Wardrip, Kathi Whitley, Randy Williams, David Woodruff
QA Editors: Jason Cother, Emily Domaschk, Carrie Geis, Allan Gill, Diane Lee, John Willis
Financial Editors: Adi Anand, Jim Harris, Chris Huston, Anthony Staats
Editorial Projects Manager: Karin Marie
Editorial Customer Advocate: Alison Stoeltje
Library Coordinator: Kris Stephenson
Library Assistant: Makiko Schwartz

HOOVER'S BUSINESS PRESS

Director, Hoover's Business Press: Dana Smith
Distribution Manager: Rhonda Mitchell
Fulfillment and Shipping Manager: Michael Febonio
Shipping Clerk: Paul Olvera

ABOUT HOOVER'S, INC. — THE BUSINESS INFORMATION AUTHORITY™

Hoover's, Inc., a subsidiary of D&B (NYSE: DNB), is a leading provider of business information. Hoover's provides authoritative, updated information for sales, marketing, business development, and other professionals who need intelligence on U.S. and global companies, industries, and the people who shape them. This information, along with powerful tools to search, sort, download, and integrate the content, is available through Hoover's Online (www.hoovers.com), the company's premier online service. Hoover's business information is also available through corporate intranets and distribution agreements with licensees, as well as via print from Hoover's Business Press. Hoover's is headquartered in Austin, Texas.

Abbreviations

AFL-CIO – American Federation of Labor and Congress of Industrial Organizations
AMA – American Medical Association
AMEX – American Stock Exchange
ARM – adjustable-rate mortgage
ASP – application services provider
ATM – asynchronous transfer mode
ATM – automated teller machine
CAD/CAM – computer-aided design/computer-aided manufacturing
CD-ROM – compact disc – read-only memory
CD-R – CD-recordable
CEO – chief executive officer
CFO – chief financial officer
CMOS – complimentary metal oxide silicon
COO – chief operating officer
DAT – digital audiotape
DOD – Department of Defense
DOE – Department of Energy
DOS – disk operating system
DOT – Department of Transportation
DRAM – dynamic random-access memory
DSL – digital subscriber line
DVD – digital versatile disc/digital video disc
DVD-R – DVD-recordable
EPA – Environmental Protection Agency
EPROM – erasable programmable read-only memory
EPS – earnings per share
ESOP – employee stock ownership plan
EU – European Union
EVP – executive vice president
FCC – Federal Communications Commission
FDA – Food and Drug Administration
FDIC – Federal Deposit Insurance Corporation
FTC – Federal Trade Commission
FTP – file transfer protocol
GATT – General Agreement on Tariffs and Trade
GDP – gross domestic product
HMO – health maintenance organization
HR – human resources
HTML – hypertext markup language
ICC – Interstate Commerce Commission
IPO – initial public offering
IRS – Internal Revenue Service
ISP – Internet service provider
kWh – kilowatt-hour
LAN – local-area network
LBO – leveraged buyout
LCD – liquid crystal display
LNG – liquefied natural gas
LP – limited partnership
Ltd. – limited
mips – millions of instructions per second
MW – megawatt
NAFTA – North American Free Trade Agreement
NASA – National Aeronautics and Space Administration
NASDAQ – National Association of Securities Dealers Automated Quotations
NATO – North Atlantic Treaty Organization
NYSE – New York Stock Exchange
OCR – optical character recognition
OECD – Organization for Economic Cooperation and Development
OEM – original equipment manufacturer
OPEC – Organization of Petroleum Exporting Countries
OS – operating system
OSHA – Occupational Safety and Health Administration
OTC – over-the-counter
PBX – private branch exchange
PCMCIA – Personal Computer Memory Card International Association
P/E – price to earnings ratio
RAID – redundant array of independent disks
RAM – random-access memory
R&D – research and development
RBOC – regional Bell operating company
RISC – reduced instruction set computer
REIT – real estate investment trust
ROA – return on assets
ROE – return on equity
ROI – return on investment
ROM – read-only memory
S&L – savings and loan
SCSI – Small Computer System Interface
SEC – Securities and Exchange Commission
SEVP – senior executive vice president
SIC – Standard Industrial Classification
SOC – system on a chip
SVP – senior vice president
USB – universal serial bus
VAR – value-added reseller
VAT – value-added tax
VC – venture capitalist
VoIP – Voice over Internet Protocol
VP – vice president
WAN – wide-area network
WWW – World Wide Web

Contents

Companies Profiled vi
About *Hoover's Handbook of Private Companies 2005* xi
Using Hoover's Handbooks xii
A List-Lover's Compendium 1

    The 300 Largest Companies by Sales in *Hoover's Handbook of
    Private Companies 2005* 2

    The 300 Largest Employers in *Hoover's Handbook of
    Private Companies 2005* 4

    The *Inc.* 500 Fastest-Growing Private Companies in America 6

    The *Forbes* Largest Private Companies in the US 11

    Top 20 Universities 14

    Top 20 US Foundations 14

    American Lawyer's Top 20 US Law Firms 14

    Top 20 Tax & Accounting Firms 14

The Companies 15
The Indexes 543

    Index of Companies by Industry 544

    Index of Companies by Headquarters Location 549

    Index of Company Executives 556

Companies Profiled

24 Hour Fitness Worldwide Inc. 16
84 Lumber Company 16
A&E Television Networks 17
AARP 17
ABC Supply (American Builders
   & Contractors Supply Co., Inc.) 18
Academy Sports & Outdoors, Ltd. 19
Ace Hardware Corporation 19
ACF Industries, Inc. 20
Acosta Sales Company, Inc. 21
Advance Publications, Inc. 21
Advantage Sales and Marketing, LLC 22
Adventist Health 22
Adventist Health System 23
Adventist HealthCare, Inc. 23
Advocate Health Care 23
AECOM Technology Corporation 24
Aera Energy LLC 25
The Aerospace Corporation 25
Affiliated Foods Incorporated 25
AFL-CIO 26
Ag Processing Inc 27
A. G. Spanos Companies 28
AgFirst Farm Credit Bank 28
AgriBank, FCB 29
Agri-Mark, Inc. 29
Akin Gump Strauss Hauer & Feld LLP 29
Alberici Corporation 30
Alegent Health 30
Alex Lee, Inc. 31
Allegis Group, Inc. 31
Alliance Capital Management L.P. 31
Alliance Entertainment Corp. 33
Allina Hospitals and Clinics 33
Alticor 33
A-Mark Financial Corporation 34
American Cancer Society, Inc. 35
American Cast Iron Pipe Company 36
American Crystal Sugar Company 36
American Family Insurance Group 37
American Foods Group, Inc. 38
American Golf Corporation 38
American Heart Association 39
American Plumbing & Mechanical, Inc. 39
The American Red Cross 39
American Tire Distributors, Inc. 41
American United Mutual
   Insurance Holding Company 41
Amerisure Mutual Insurance Company 42
AMF Bowling Worldwide, Inc. 42
Amica Mutual Insurance Company 43
Amsted Industries Incorporated 43
AMTRAK (National Railroad
   Passenger Corporation) 44
ANCIRA 45
Andersen Corporation 45
The Angelo Iafrate Companies 46
Apex Oil Company, Inc. 47
APi Group, Inc. 47
Appleton Papers Inc. 48
Arctic Slope Regional Corporation 48
Ardent Health Services LLC 49
Arkansas Blue Cross and Blue Shield 49

Army and Air Force Exchange Service 50
ASCAP (American Society of Composers,
   Authors and Publishers) 51
Ascension Health 51
Ash Grove Cement Company 52
Ashley Furniture Industries, Inc. 53
ASI Corp. 53
Asplundh Tree Expert Co. 54
Associated Electric Cooperative Inc. 54
Associated Food Stores, Inc. 55
Associated Grocers, Inc. 55
Associated Materials Incorporated 56
Associated Milk Producers Inc. 56
The Associated Press 57
Associated Wholesale Grocers, Inc. 57
Associated Wholesalers, Inc. 59
Atlantic Mutual Companies 59
Atrium Companies, Inc. 59
Austin Industries, Inc. 60
Auto-Owners Insurance Group 61
Averitt Express, Inc. 61
Avondale Incorporated 61
Bain & Company, Inc. 62
Baker & McKenzie 62
Baker & Taylor Corporation 63
Banner Health 64
Baptist Health South Florida 64
Barnes & Noble
   College Bookstores, Inc. 65
Bartlett and Company 65
Barton Malow Company 66
Bashas' Inc. 66
Basin Electric Power Cooperative 67
Bass Pro Shops, Inc. 67
Battelle Memorial Institute 68
Baystate Health Systems, Inc. 69
BE&K, Inc. 69
Beaulieu of America, LLC 70
Bechtel Group, Inc. 70
The Beck Group 71
Belk, Inc. 72
Bellco Health Corp. 73
Ben E. Keith Company 73
Berwind Group 73
Big Y Foods, Inc. 74
Bill & Melinda Gates Foundation 74
Bill Blass Ltd. 75
Bill Heard Enterprises 75
Birds Eye Foods, Inc. 76
BJC HealthCare 76
Black & Veatch Holding Company 77
Bloomberg L.P. 78
Blue Cross
   and Blue Shield Association 78
Blue Cross and Blue Shield
   of Massachusetts, Inc. 79
Blue Cross Blue Shield of Michigan 80
Blue Shield Of California 81
BlueCross
   and BlueShield of Mississippi 82
BMI (Broadcast Music, Inc.) 82
Bob Rohrman Auto Group 83
Bon Secours Health System, Inc. 83

Bonneville Power Administration 84
Booz Allen Hamilton Inc. 84
Borden Chemical, Inc. 85
Boscov's Department Store 86
Bose Corporation 86
The Boston Consulting Group 87
Bozzuto's Inc. 88
BPC Holding Corp. 88
Bradco Supply Corp. 89
Braman Management Association 89
Brasfield & Gorrie, LLC 90
Brazos Electric Power Cooperative, Inc. ...90
Brightstar Corp. 90
Brookshire Brothers, Ltd. 91
Brookshire Grocery Company 91
Brown Brothers Harriman & Co. 92
Buffets Holdings, Inc. 92
Builders FirstSource 93
Burger King Corporation 93
Burlington Industries, Inc. 94
Burt Automotive Network 95
BWAY Corporation 95
California Dairies Inc. 96
Trustees of the
   California State University 96
California Steel Industries, Inc. 97
CalPERS (California Public Employees'
   Retirement System) 98
C&S Wholesale Grocers, Inc. 99
Cargill, Incorporated 100
Carilion Health System 101
Carlson Companies, Inc. 102
Carlson Wagonlit Travel, Inc. 103
The Carlyle Group 104
Carpenter Co. 105
CARQUEST Corporation 105
Carrols Holdings Corporation 106
Catholic Health East 107
Catholic Health Initiatives 108
Catholic Health Services
   of Long Island 109
Catholic Healthcare Partners 109
Catholic Healthcare West 110
CCA Global Partners 111
Center Oil Company 111
Central Grocers Cooperative, Inc. 112
Central National-Gottesman Inc. 112
Certified Grocers Midwest, Inc. 113
CF Industries, Inc. 113
CH2M HILL Companies, Ltd. 113
Chapman Automotive Group, LLC 114
Chas. Levy Company LLC 115
Charmer Industries, Inc. 115
The Charmer-Sunbelt Group 115
CHEMCENTRAL Corporation 116
Chevron Phillips
   Chemical Company LLC 116
Chevy Chase Bank, F.S.B. 117
Chick-fil-A Inc. 117
The Children's Hospital
   of Philadelphia 118
Choice Homes, Inc. 118
CHRISTUS Health 119

Companies Profiled (continued)

CIC International Ltd....119
Cincinnati Children's Hospital Medical Center....120
Cinemark, Inc....120
Cingular Wireless LLC....121
Citation Corporation....122
The City University of New York....122
Clarian Health Partners, Inc....123
Clark Enterprises, Inc....124
Cleary, Gottlieb, Steen & Hamilton....124
ClubCorp, Inc....124
Coca-Cola Bottling Co. United, Inc....125
Coinmach Service Corp....126
Colliers International Property Consultants Inc....126
Colson & Colson Construction Company....127
Colt's Manufacturing Company, LLC....127
Columbia Forest Products Inc....128
Columbia House Company....128
Columbia University....129
Community Hospitals of Indiana, Inc....130
Community Medical Centers....130
CompuCom Systems, Inc....130
Conair Corporation....131
Concentra Inc....132
Conemaugh Health System....132
ConnectiCare Inc....133
Connecticut Lottery Corporation....133
The Connell Company....134
Connell Limited Partnership....134
Conrail Inc....134
Consolidated Electrical Distributors, Inc....135
Consumers Union of United States, Inc....135
ContiGroup Companies, Inc....136
Contran Corporation....137
Cook Inlet Energy Supply L.L.C....137
The Copley Press, Inc....138
Cornell University....138
Cornerstone Brands, Inc....139
Cornerstone Propane Partners, L.P....139
Corporation for Public Broadcasting....140
Cox Enterprises, Inc....140
Cox Health Systems....142
Crete Carrier Corporation....142
CROSSMARK....142
Crowley Maritime Corporation....143
Crown Central Petroleum Corporation....143
Crown Equipment Corporation....143
Culligan International Company....144
Cumberland Farms, Inc....144
CUNA Mutual Group....145
Cushman & Wakefield, Inc....145
Dairy Farmers of America, Inc....146
Dairylea Cooperative Inc....147
D&H Distributing Co., Inc....147
Darcars Automotive Group....148
Dart Container Corporation....148
David McDavid Auto Group....149
David Weekley Homes....149
David Wilson's Automotive Group....150
Davis Polk & Wardwell....150
Dawn Food Products, Inc....151
The Day & Zimmermann Group, Inc....151
The DeBartolo Corporation....151
DeBruce Grain, Inc....152
Delaware North Companies, Inc....153
Deloitte Touche Tohmatsu....153
Delta Dental of California....154
Delta Dental Plan of Michigan Inc....155
Demoulas Super Markets Inc....155
The Depository Trust & Clearing Corporation....155
Detroit Medical Center....156
Di Giorgio Corporation....157
Dick Corporation....157
Dierbergs Markets Inc....158
Discount Drug Mart Inc....158
Discount Tire Co. Inc....158
Discovery Communications, Inc....159
Do it Best Corp....160
Doane Pet Care Company....160
Doctor's Associates Inc....161
Dole Food Company, Inc....162
Dot Foods, Inc....163
Dow Corning Corporation....163
DPR Construction, Inc....165
Dr Pepper/Seven Up Bottling Group, Inc....165
DreamWorks L.L.C....166
The Drees Co....167
Dresser, Inc....167
DriveTime Automotive Group, Inc....168
Drummond Company, Inc....168
Duane Reade Inc....168
Duchossois Industries, Inc....169
Duke Energy Field Services, LLC....170
Dunavant Enterprises, Inc....170
Dunn Industries, Inc....170
The Dyson-Kissner-Moran Corporation....171
Eagle-Picher Industries, Inc....171
E. & J. Gallo Winery....172
Earle M. Jorgensen Company....173
Earnhardt's Auto Centers....173
EBSCO Industries Inc....174
Eby-Brown Company....174
Educational Testing Service....175
Elder Automotive Group....175
Elkay Manufacturing Company....176
Encyclopaedia Britannica, Inc....176
Enterprise Rent-A-Car Company....177
Equistar Chemicals, LP....178
Equity Group Investments, L.L.C....178
Ergon, Inc....179
Ernst & Young International....180
ESPN, Inc....181
Esselte....181
Estes Express Lines, Inc....182
ETMC Regional Healthcare....182
Euromarket Designs Inc....183
Evanston Northwestern Healthcare Corporation....183
Everett Smith Group, Ltd....184
Evergreen International Aviation, Inc....184
Express Personnel Services....185
Extended Stay America, Inc....185
The F. Dohmen Co....186
Fallon Community Health Plan Inc....186
The Faulkner Organization....186
Federal Prison Industries, Inc....187
Federal Reserve System....188
Federated Insurance Companies....189
Feld Entertainment, Inc....189
Fellowes, Inc....190
The Ferolie Group....191
FHC Health Systems, Inc....191
Findlay Industries, Inc....191
Fletcher Jones Management Group....192
Flint Ink Corporation....192
Florida's Natural Growers....193
Flying J Inc....193
FM Global....193
FMR Corp....194
Follett Corporation....195
The Ford Foundation....196
Foremost Farms USA, Cooperative....197
Forever Living Products International, Inc....197
Foster Poultry Farms....198
Foundation Coal Holdings, Inc....198
Foxworth-Galbraith Lumber Company....198
Frank Consolidated Enterprises....199
Freedom Communications, Inc....199
Fry's Electronics, Inc....200
Galpin Motors, Inc....201
Gate Petroleum Company....201
General Parts, Inc....202
Genlyte Thomas Group LLC....202
Genmar Holdings, Inc....202
GeoLogistics Corporation....203
George E. Warren Corporation....203
Georgia Crown Distributing Company....204
Georgia Lottery Corporation....204
G-I Holdings Inc....204
Giant Eagle, Inc....205
Gibson, Dunn & Crutcher LLP....206
Gilbane, Inc....206
Glazer's Wholesale Drug Company, Inc....207
Global Companies LLC....207
Golden State Foods....207
The Golub Corporation....208
Goodman Manufacturing Company, L.P....208
Goodwill Industries International, Inc....209
Gordon Food Service....209
Gores Technology Group, LLC....210
Gould Paper Corporation....210
Goya Foods, Inc....210
Graham Packaging Company, Inc....211
Grant Thornton International....212
Graybar Electric Company, Inc....213
Great Dane Limited Partnership....214
Great Lakes Cheese Company, Inc....214
Green Bay Packaging Inc....215
The Green Bay Packers, Inc....215
Greenberg Traurig, LLP....216
Greenville Hospital System....217
The Grocers Supply Co., Inc....217
Group Health Cooperative of Puget Sound....217
GROWMARK, Inc....218
Guardian Industries Corp....218
The Guardian Life Insurance Company of America....219
Gulf Oil Limited Partnership....220
Gulf States Toyota, Inc....221
Guthy-Renker Corp....221
H Group Holding Inc....221
Haggen, Inc....222
Hallmark Cards, Inc....222
Hampton Affiliates....223
Harbour Group Industries, Inc....224
Harpo, Inc....224
Harvard University....225
The Haskell Company....226
Haworth, Inc....227
HBE Corporation....227
H. E. Butt Grocery Company....228
Health Care Service Corporation....229
Health Insurance Plan of Greater New York....230
The Hearst Corporation....230
Helmsley Enterprises, Inc....232
Hendrick Automotive Group....232
Henry Ford Health System....233
Hensel Phelps Construction Co....233
The Herb Chambers Companies....234
Herbalife International, Inc....234
Hicks, Muse, Tate & Furst Incorporated....235
Highmark Inc....236
Hines Interests L.P....237
Hitachi Global Storage Technologies....237
Hobby Lobby Stores, Inc....238
Hogan & Hartson....238
Holiday Companies....239
Holland & Knight LLP....239
Holman Enterprises....240
The Holmes Group, Inc....240
Home Interiors & Gifts, Inc....240
Honickman Affiliates....241
Horizon Blue Cross Blue Shield of New Jersey....241
Horizon Natural Resources Company....242
Horseshoe Gaming Holding Corp....242
Houchens Industries Inc....243
Houghton Mifflin Company....243
HP Hood Inc....244
H.T. Hackney Company....244

Companies Profiled (continued)

Hunt Consolidated Inc.	244
Huntsman International LLC	245
Hyatt Corporation	246
Hy-Vee, Inc.	247
IASIS Healthcare Corporation	247
ICON Health & Fitness, Inc.	248
IGA, Inc.	248
Illinois Department of the Lottery	249
IMG	250
Indiana University	251
Inductotherm Industries, Inc.	251
Information Resources, Inc.	252
Ingram Entertainment Holdings Inc.	253
Ingram Industries Inc.	253
Inova Health System	254
Inserra Supermarkets, Inc.	254
Integris Metals Corporation	255
Intelsat, Ltd.	255
Interactive Brokers Group LLC	256
Interbond Corporation of America	256
Inter-Con Security Systems, Inc.	257
Interline Brands, Inc.	257
Intermountain Health Care, Inc.	257
International Data Group	258
International Specialty Products Inc.	259
Interstate Battery System of America, Inc.	260
The Irvine Company Inc.	260
J. Crew Group, Inc.	261
Jefferson Health System Inc.	262
JELD-WEN, inc.	262
J.F. Shea Co., Inc.	262
Jim Koons Automotive Companies, Inc.	263
JM Family Enterprises, Inc.	263
J.M. Huber Corporation	264
Jockey International, Inc.	265
John Paul Mitchell Systems	265
John Wieland Homes and Neighborhoods, Inc.	266
Johns Hopkins Medicine	266
Johnson Brothers Liquor Company	267
Johnson Publishing Company, Inc.	267
JohnsonDiversey, Inc.	268
Jones Day	268
The Jones Financial Companies, L.L.L.P.	269
Jordan Industries, Inc.	270
Jostens, Inc.	271
J.R. Simplot Company	271
Kaiser Foundation Health Plan, Inc.	272
Kaleida Health	273
KB Toys, Inc.	273
W.K. Kellogg Foundation	274
Kentucky Lottery Corporation	275
Key Safety Systems, Inc.	275
Keystone Foods LLC	276
KI	276
Kimball Hill Homes	277
Kinetics Group, Inc.	277
King Kullen Grocery Company, Inc.	278
Kingston Technology Company, Inc.	278
Kinray Inc.	279
Kirkland & Ellis LLP	279
Klaussner Furniture Industries, Inc.	280
Knoll, Inc.	280
Koch Enterprises, Inc.	280
Koch Industries, Inc.	281
Kohlberg Kravis Roberts & Co.	282
Kohler Co.	283
Koppers Inc.	284
KPMG International	285
KRATON Polymers LLC	286
K-VA-T Food Stores, Inc.	286
Land O'Lakes, Inc.	287
Landmark Communications, Inc.	288
The Lane Construction Corporation	289
Lane Industries, Inc.	289
Lanoga Corporation	289
Larry H. Miller Group	290
Las Vegas Sands, Inc.	290
Latham & Watkins LLP	291
The Lefrak Organization	291
Lenox Hill Hospital	292
Leprino Foods Company	292
Les Schwab Tire Centers	293
Levi Strauss & Co.	293
Levitz Home Furnishings, Inc.	294
Liberty Mutual Insurance Company	295
Life Care Centers of America	296
LifeBridge Health, Inc.	296
Lifetime Entertainment Services	297
Lincoln Property Company	297
L.L. Bean, Inc.	298
Loews Cineplex Entertainment Corporation	299
The Longaberger Company	299
The Louis Berger Group, Inc.	300
Love's Travel Stops & Country Stores, Inc.	300
Lucasfilm Ltd.	301
Lumbermens Merchandising Corporation	302
M. Fabrikant & Sons, Inc.	302
MA Laboratories, Inc.	302
M. A. Mortenson Company	303
MacAndrews & Forbes Holdings Inc.	303
Madison Square Garden, L.P.	304
MAGNATRAX Corporation	305
Main Street America Group	305
Major League Baseball	306
Marc Glassman, Inc.	307
Marian Health System	307
Maritz Inc.	308
Mark IV Industries, Inc.	308
The Marmon Group, Inc.	309
Mars, Incorporated	310
The Martin-Brower Company, L.L.C.	311
Marty Franich Auto Center	312
Mary Kay Inc.	312
Maryland State Lottery Agency	313
Mashantucket Pequot Gaming Enterprise Inc.	313
Massachusetts Mutual Life Insurance Company	314
MasterCard Incorporated	315
Mayer, Brown, Rowe & Maw	317
Mayo Foundation for Medical Education and Research	317
MBM Corporation	318
McCarthy Building Companies, Inc.	319
McDermott, Will & Emery	319
McJunkin Corporation	319
McKee Foods Corporation	320
McKinsey & Company	321
McWane Corp.	322
MediaNews Group, Inc.	322
Medical Mutual of Ohio	323
Medline Industries, Inc.	324
MedStar Health	324
Meijer, Inc.	324
Memec Group Holdings Limited	326
Memorial Hermann Healthcare System	326
Memorial Sloan-Kettering Cancer Center	327
Menard, Inc.	327
Menasha Corporation	328
Meridian Automotive Systems, Inc.	329
Merrill Corporation	329
Mervyn's	330
Metaldyne Corporation	330
Metromedia Company	331
Metromedia Restaurant Group	332
Metropolitan Transportation Authority	332
MFA Incorporated	333
Michael Foods, Inc.	333
Michigan State University	334
MidAmerican Energy Holdings Company	334
Milliken & Company Inc.	336
Minnesota Mutual Companies, Inc.	336
Minyard Food Stores, Inc.	337
MIT (Massachusetts Institute of Technology)	337
The MITRE Corporation	338
Modern Continental Companies, Inc.	338
Mohegan Tribal Gaming Authority	339
Morgan, Lewis & Bockius LLP	339
Morris Communications Company LLC	340
Morrison & Foerster LLP	341
Motiva Enterprises LLC	341
MPC Computers, LLC	342
MSX International, Inc.	342
MTS, Incorporated	343
The Musicland Group, Inc.	343
Mutual of America Life Insurance Company	344
The Mutual of Omaha Companies	344
Muzak LLC	345
MWH Global, Inc.	346
Nalco Holding Company	347
NASCAR (National Association for Stock Car Auto Racing)	347
NASD	348
National Basketball Association	349
National Cooperative Refinery Association	350
National Distributing Company, Inc.	351
National Envelope Corporation	351
National Football League Inc.	352
National Geographic Society	353
National Grape Cooperative Association, Inc.	354
National Hockey League	354
National Life Insurance Company	356
National Rural Utilities Cooperative Finance Corporation	356
National Service Industries, Inc.	357
National Textiles, L.L.C.	357
National Waterworks, Inc.	358
National Wine & Spirits, Inc.	358
Nationwide	359
Navy Exchange Service Command	360
Navy Federal Credit Union	360
NCH Corporation	360
NESCO, Inc.	361
New Balance Athletic Shoe, Inc.	361
New NGC, Inc.	362
New United Motor Manufacturing, Inc.	362
New York City Health and Hospitals Corporation	363
New York Life Insurance Company	364
Power Authority of the State of New York	365
New York State Lottery	366
New York Stock Exchange, Inc.	367
New York University	368
The Newark Group, Inc.	368
NewYork-Presbyterian Healthcare System	369
NextiraOne, LLC	369
Nikken Global Inc.	370
Nortek Holdings, Inc.	370
North Carolina Electric Membership Corporation	371
North Pacific Group, Inc.	371
The Northwestern Mutual Life Insurance Company	372
Northwestern University	373
Novant Health, Inc.	374
Nypro Inc.	374
Ocean Spray Cranberries, Inc.	375
Oglethorpe Power Corporation	376
Ohio Lottery Commission	377
Ohio National Financial Services	377
The Ohio State University	378
OhioHealth Corporation	378
O'Melveny & Myers LLP	379
OmniSource Corporation	379

Companies Profiled (continued)

O'Neal Steel, Inc. 380
Opus Corporation 380
Ormet Corporation 381
Ourisman Automotive Enterprises 381
Outsourcing Solutions Inc. 382
Oxbow Corporation 382
Oxford Automotive, Inc. 383
Pabst Brewing Company 383
Pacific Mutual Holding Company 383
Packard Foundation 385
PanAmSat Corporation 385
Park Nicollet Health Services 386
Parkdale Mills, Inc. 386
Parsons Corporation 387
Parsons & Whittemore, Incorporated 388
Parsons Brinckerhoff Inc. 388
Partners HealthCare System, Inc. 389
Paul, Hastings, Janofsky & Walker LLP 389
Paul, Weiss, Rifkind, Wharton & Garrison LLP 390
P.C. Richard & Son 390
PeaceHealth 390
Peerless Importers, Inc. 391
Pella Corporation 391
The Penn Mutual Life Insurance Company 392
The Pennsylvania Lottery 392
Penske Corporation 393
Pepper Construction Group, LLC 394
Perdue Farms Incorporated 394
Peter Kiewit Sons', Inc. 395
Petro Stopping Centers, L.P. 396
Phil Long Dealerships, Inc. 397
Philip Services Corporation 397
Pilot Travel Centers, LLC 398
Pinnacle Foods Group, Inc. 398
Plains Cotton Cooperative Association 398
Planet Automotive Group, Inc. 399
Plastipak Holdings, Inc. 399
Platinum Equity, LLC 400
Pliant Corporation 400
PMC Global, Inc. 401
Polaroid Corporation 401
The Port Authority of New York and New Jersey 402
PricewaterhouseCoopers 403
Primus, Inc. 404
Princeton University 405
Printpack, Inc. 405
Provena Health 406
Providence Health System 406
Publix Super Markets, Inc. 407
Purdue Pharma L.P. 408
Purity Wholesale Grocers, Inc. 408
Quad/Graphics, Inc. 409
Quality King Distributors Inc. 409
Quexco Incorporated 410
QuikTrip Corporation 410
Quintiles Transnational Corp. 411
RaceTrac Petroleum, Inc. 412
Raley's Inc. 412
Rand McNally & Company 413
R. B. Pamplin Corporation 413
RDO Equipment Co. 414
Red Apple Group, Inc. 414
Red Chamber Co. 415
The Regence Group 415
REI (Recreational Equipment, Inc.) 415
Remy International, Inc. 416
Renco Group, Inc. 417
Republic Engineered Products Inc. 417
Resolution Performance Products LLC 418
Retail Brand Alliance, Inc. 418
Reyes Holdings LLC 419
Riceland Foods, Inc. 419
Rich Products Corporation 419
Ritz Camera Centers, Inc. 420
Robert Wood Johnson University Hospital 421
The Rockefeller Foundation 421
Rockwood Specialties Group, Inc. 422
Roll International Corporation 422
Rooms To Go, Inc. 423
Rooney Holdings, Inc. 423
Roseburg Forest Products Co. 424
Rosen's Diversified, Inc. 424
Rosenthal Automotive Organization 425
Rotary International 425
Roundy's, Inc. 426
Royster-Clark, Inc. 427
RTM Restaurant Group 428
Rudolph and Sletten, Inc. 428
Safelite Group, Inc. 428
Safety-Kleen Holdco, Inc. 429
St. Joseph Health System 429
The Salvation Army National Corporation 430
Sammons Enterprises, Inc. 431
Santa Monica Ford 431
Sargento Foods Inc. 432
SAS Institute Inc. 432
Sauder Woodworking Co. 433
Save Mart Supermarkets 433
S.C. Johnson & Son, Inc. 434
Schneider National, Inc. 435
Schnuck Markets, Inc. 436
Schreiber Foods, Inc. 436
The Schwan Food Company 436
Science Applications International Corporation 438
Scott & White 439
The Scoular Company 439
Scripps 440
Sealy Corporation 440
The Security Benefit Group of Companies 440
SEMATECH, Inc. 441
Seminole Electric Cooperative, Inc. 442
Sentara Healthcare 442
Sentry Insurance, a Mutual Company 443
Serta, Inc. 443
Services Group of America 444
Shamrock Foods Company 444
Shapell Industries, Inc. 444
Shearman & Sterling 445
Sheehy Auto Stores, Inc. 445
Sheetz, Inc. 445
Sherwood Food Distributors 446
Sidley Austin Brown & Wood LLP 446
Siegel-Robert Inc. 447
Sierra Pacific Industries 447
Sigma Plastics Group 448
Simpson Investment Company 448
Simpson Thacher & Bartlett LLP 449
Sinclair Oil Corporation 449
Sisters of Mercy Health System 449
Sithe Energies, Inc. 450
Skadden, Arps, Slate, Meagher & Flom LLP 450
Smithsonian Institution 451
Software House International, Inc. 452
Solo Cup Company 453
Sony BMG Music Entertainment 453
Southern States Cooperative, Incorporated 454
Southern Wine & Spirits of America, Inc. 454
Southwire Company 455
Spectrum Health 455
Springs Industries, Inc. 456
SRI International 457
SSA Marine 458
SSM Health Care System Inc. 458
Stanford University 458
Staple Cotton Cooperative Association 459
State Farm Insurance Companies 460
State University of New York 461
Stater Bros. Holdings Inc. 462
Stewart's Shops Corp. 463
The Structure Tone Organization 463
Suffolk Construction Company, Inc. 464
Sullivan & Cromwell LLP 464
Sunkist Growers, Inc. 464
Superior Group, Inc. 465
Sutter Health 466
Swagelok Company 466
Swedish Health Services 467
Swinerton Incorporated 467
Tang Industries, Inc. 468
TAP Pharmaceutical Products Inc. 468
Taylor Corporation 469
Team Health, Inc. 469
Teamsters 470
Tekni-Plex, Inc. 470
Tenaska, Inc. 471
The Texas A&M University System 472
Texas Health Resources Inc. 473
Texas Lottery Commission 473
Texas Pacific Group 474
Thrivent Financial for Lutherans 475
TIAA-CREF 475
TIC Holdings, Inc. 476
Timex Corporation 477
Tishman Realty & Construction Co. Inc. 478
TNP Enterprises, Inc. 478
Topa Equities, Ltd. 479
Topco Associates LLC 479
Towers Perrin 480
Trader Joe's Company, Inc. 481
Trader Publishing Company 481
Trammell Crow Residential 482
Transammonia, Inc. 482
TravelCenters of America, Inc. 483
TriMas Corporation 483
Trinity Health 484
Tri-State Generation and Transmission Association, Inc. 484
Truman Arnold Companies 485
The Trump Organization 485
TruServ Corporation 486
Trustmark Insurance Company 487
TTI, Inc. 488
TTX Company 488
Tube City, LLC 489
Tufts Associated Health Plans, Inc. 489
Turner Industries, Ltd. 490
Tuttle-Click Automotive Group 490
TVA (Tennessee Valley Authority) 491
Ty Inc. 492
UAP Holding Corp. 492
UIS, Inc. 493
Ukrop's Super Markets, Inc. 493
Underwriters Laboratories Inc. 494
UNICCO Service Company 494
Unified Western Grocers, Inc. 495
UniGroup, Inc. 496
Unimin Corporation 496
The Union Central Life Insurance Company 496
Unisource Worldwide, Inc. 497
United Industries Corporation 497
United Space Alliance 498
United Supermarkets, Ltd. 498
United Way of America 499
University of California 500
The University of Chicago 500
University of Florida 501
University of Illinois 502
The University of Iowa 502
University System of Maryland 503
The University of Michigan 503
University of Minnesota 504
University of Missouri System 504
The University of Nebraska 505
The University of Pennsylvania 505
University of Pittsburgh 506
University of Rochester 506
The University of Southern California 507
University of Tennessee 507
The University of Texas System 508

Companies Profiled (continued)

University of Washington..........................509
The University of Wisconsin System........509
The University of Wisconsin
    Hospital & Clinics Authority................510
UOP LLC..510
U.S. Can Corporation................................511
U.S. Central Credit Union........................511
U.S. Oil Co., Inc......................................512
US Oncology, Inc.....................................512
United States Postal Service.....................513
USAA..514
Utica Mutual Insurance Company............515
Utility Trailer Manufacturing Co...............515
ValleyCrest Companies.............................516
Vanderbilt University................................516
The Vanguard Group, Inc........................517
Vanguard Health Systems, Inc.................518
Variety Wholesalers, Inc..........................518
VarTec Telecom, Inc................................519
Venture Industries....................................519
Verizon Wireless (Cellco Partnership).....520
Vermeer Manufacturing Company...........520
Vertis Inc..521

Viasystems Group, Inc.............................521
ViewSonic Corporation............................522
Visa International.....................................523
Vision Service Plan..................................524
Vistar/VSA Corporation...........................524
Volunteers of America, Inc......................524
Vought Aircraft Industries, Inc.................524
VT Inc..525
Vulcan Inc...525
Wakefern Food Corporation....................526
Walbridge Aldinger Company..................527
The Walsh Group...................................528
Warner Music Group................................528
Warren Equities, Inc................................529
Watkins Associated Industries, Inc..........529
Wawa, Inc..530
The WB Television Network....................530
Webcor Builders, Inc...............................531
Wegmans Food Markets, Inc...................531
Weil, Gotshal & Manges LLP..................532
The Weitz Group, LLC............................532
Wells' Dairy, Inc.....................................533
Westcon Group, Inc................................533

Western Family Foods, Inc......................534
Westfield Group......................................534
White & Case LLP..................................535
The Whiting-Turner
    Contracting Company.........................535
Wilbur-Ellis Company..............................536
Wilmer Cutler Pickering
    Hale and Dorr LLP..............................536
WinCo Foods, Inc...................................537
Wirtz Corporation...................................537
WKI Holding Company, Inc....................538
W. L. Gore & Associates, Inc..................538
WL Homes LLC......................................539
WorldTravel BTI.....................................539
Yale University..540
The Yates Companies, Inc......................540
Young's Market Company, LLC...............540
The Yucaipa Companies LLC..................541
Zachry Construction Corporation............541

About Hoover's Handbook of Private Companies 2005

With this 2005 edition, *Hoover's Handbook of Private Companies* celebrates its 10th year as one of the premier sources of business information on privately held enterprises in the US.

Publishing current, relevant information about nonpublic companies can be a challenge, as many of them see secrecy as a competitive strategy, but we continue to do the hard work of compiling the hard-to-find facts.

In this edition we bring you the facts on 900 of the largest and most influential enterprises in the US. As we did last year, we have dropped the past distinction between companies with in-depth profiles and those with shorter, capsule profiles. Some larger and more visible companies will continue to have an additional History section, but now all companies will have up to 10 years of financial information, product information where available, and a longer list of company executives.

By doing this, we achieve our goal of adding even more value to this already valuable resource.

HOOVER'S ONLINE FOR BUSINESS NEEDS

In addition to the 2,550 companies featured in our handbooks, coverage of some 40,000 business enterprises is available in electronic format on our Web site, Hoover's Online (www.hoovers.com). Our goal is to provide one site that offers authoritative, updated intelligence on US and global companies, industries, and the people who shape them. Hoover's has partnered with other prestigious business information and service providers to bring you all the right business information, services, and links in one place.

We welcome the recognition we have received as the premier provider of high-quality company information — online, electronically, and in print — and continue to look for ways to make our products more available and more useful to you.

Hoover's Handbook of Private Companies is one of our four-title series of handbooks that covers, literally, the world of business. The series is available as an indexed set, and also includes *Hoover's Handbook of American Business*, *Hoover's Handbook of World Business*, and *Hoover's Handbook of Emerging Companies*. This series brings you information on the biggest, fastest-growing, and most influential enterprises in the world.

We believe that anyone who buys from, sells to, invests in, lends to, competes with, interviews with, or works for a company should know all there is to know about that enterprise. Taken together, this book and the other Hoover's products and resources represent the most complete source of basic corporate information readily available to the general public.

HOW TO USE THIS BOOK

This book has four sections:

1. "Using Hoover's Handbooks" describes the contents of our profiles and explains the ways in which we gather and compile our data.

2. "A List-Lover's Compendium" contains lists of the largest and fastest-growing private companies. The lists are based on the information in our profiles, or compiled from well-known sources.

3. The company profiles section makes up the largest and most important part of the book — 900 profiles of major private enterprises, arranged alphabetically.

4. Three indexes complete the book. The first sorts companies by industry groups, the second by headquarters location. The third index is a list of all the executives found in the Executives section of each company profile.

As always, we hope you find our books useful. We invite your comments via phone (512-374-4500), fax (512-374-4538), mail (5800 Airport Boulevard, Austin, Texas 78752), or e-mail (custsupport@hoovers.com).

The Editors,
Austin, Texas,
December 2004

Using Hoover's Handbooks

SELECTION OF THE COMPANIES PROFILED

The 900 enterprises profiled in this book include the largest and most influential private enterprises in America. Among them are:
- private companies, from the giants (Cargill and Koch) to the colorful and prominent (Helmsley Enterprises and L.L. Bean)
- mutuals and cooperative organizations owned by their customers (State Farm Insurance, Ace Hardware, Ocean Spray Cranberries)
- not-for-profits (American Red Cross, Kaiser Foundation Health Plan, Smithsonian Institution)
- joint ventures (Motiva Enterprises, Dow Corning)
- partnerships (Baker & McKenzie, Kohlberg Kravis Roberts & Co.)
- universities (Columbia, Harvard, University of California)
- government-owned corporations (US Postal Service and New York City's Metropolitan Transportation Authority)
- and a selection of other enterprises (National Basketball Association, AFL-CIO, Texas Lottery Commission).

ORGANIZATION

The profiles are presented in alphabetical order. You will find the commonly used name of the enterprise at the beginning of the profile; the full, legal name is found in the Locations section. If a company name is also a person's name, such as Henry Ford Health System or Mary Kay, it will be alphabetized under the first name; if the company name starts with initials, for example, L.L. Bean or S.C. Johnson, look for it under the combined initials (in the above examples, LL and SC, respectively).

Basic financial data are listed under the heading Historical Financials. The annual financial information contained in the profiles is current through fiscal year-ends occurring as late as October 2004. We have included certain nonfinancial developments, such as officer changes, through November 2004.

OVERVIEW

In the first section of the profile, we have tried to give a thumbnail description of the company and what it does. The description will usually include information on the company's strategy, reputation, and ownership. We recommend that you read this section first.

HISTORY

This extended section, which is available for some of the larger and more well-known companies, reflects our belief that every enterprise is the sum of its history and that you have to know where you came from in order to know where you are going. While some companies have limited historical awareness and were unable to help us much and other companies are just plain boring, we think the vast majority of the enterprises in this book have colorful backgrounds. We have tried to focus on the people who made the enterprises what they are today. We have found these histories to be full of twists and ironies; they make fascinating reading.

EXECUTIVES

Here we list the names of the people who run the company, insofar as space allows. In the few cases where available, we have shown the ages and pay of key officers. In some instances the published data is for the previous year although the company has announced promotions or retirements since year-end. The pay represents cash compensation, including bonuses, but excludes stock option programs.

Although companies are free to structure their management titles any way they please, most modern corporations follow standard practices. The ultimate power in any corporation lies with the shareholders, who elect a board of directors, usually including officers or "insiders" as well as individuals from outside the company. The chief officer, the person on whose desk the buck stops, is usually called the chief executive officer (CEO). Often, he or she is also the chairman of the board.

As corporate management has become more complex, it is common for the CEO to have a "right-hand person" who oversees the day-to-day operations of the company, allowing the CEO plenty of time to focus on strategy and long-term issues. This right-hand person is usually designated the chief operating officer (COO) and is often the president of the company. In other cases one person is both chairman and president.

A multitude of other titles exists, including chief financial officer (CFO), chief administrative officer, and vice chairman. We have always tried to include the CFO, the chief legal officer, and the chief human resources or personnel officer.

The people named in the Executives section are indexed at the back of the book.

The Executives section also includes the name of the company's auditing (accounting) firm, where available.

LOCATIONS

Here we include the company's full legal name and its headquarters, street address, telephone and fax numbers, and Web site, as available. The back of the book includes an index of companies by headquarters locations.

In some cases we have also included information on the geographic distribution of the company's business, including sales and profit data. Note that these profit numbers, like those in the Products/Operations section below, are usually operating or pretax profits rather than net profits. Operating profits are generally those before financing costs (interest income and payments) and before taxes, which are considered costs attributable to the whole company rather than to one division or part of the world. For this reason the net income figures (in the Historical Financials section) are usually much lower, since they are after interest and taxes. Pretax profits are after interest but before taxes.

Headquarters for companies that are incorporated in Bermuda, but whose operational headquarters are in the US, are listed under their US address. The same applies for companies with joint US and non-US headquarters (such as KPMG International).

PRODUCTS/OPERATIONS

This section lists as many of the company's products, services, brand names, divisions, subsidiaries, and joint ventures as we could fit. We have tried to include all of its major lines and all familiar brand names.

The nature of this section varies by company and the amount of information available. If the company publishes sales and profit information by type of business, we have included it.

COMPETITORS

In this section we have listed companies that compete with the profiled company. This feature is included as a quick way to locate similar companies and compare them. The universe of competitors includes all public companies and all private companies with sales in excess of $500 million. In a few instances we have identified smaller private companies as key competitors.

HISTORICAL FINANCIALS

Here we have tried to present as much data about each enterprise's financial performance as we could compile in the allocated space. The information varies somewhat from industry to industry and is less complete in the case of private companies that do not release data (although we have always tried to provide annual sales and employment). There are a few industries, venture capital and investment banking, for example, for which revenue numbers are not reported as a rule. In the case of private companies that do not publicly disclose financial information, we have gathered estimates of sales and other statistics from numerous sources.

The following information is generally present.

A 10-year table, with relevant annualized compound growth rates, covers:
- Sales — fiscal year sales (year-end assets for most financial companies)
- Net income — fiscal year net income (before accounting changes)
- Income as a percent of sales — fiscal year net income as a percent of sales (as a percent of assets for most financial firms)
- Employees — fiscal year-end or average number of employees

The information on the number of employees is intended to aid the reader interested in knowing whether a company has a long-term trend of increasing or decreasing employment. As far as we know, we are the only company that publishes this information in print format.

The numbers on the left in each row of the Historical Financials section give the month and the year in which the company's fiscal year actually ends. Thus, a company with a February 29, 2004, year-end is shown as 2/04. The last item in the Financials section is a graph, which for private companies shows net income, or, if that is unavailable, sales.

Key year-end statistics are included in this section for insurance companies and companies required to file reports with the SEC. They generally show the financial strength of the enterprise, including:
- Debt ratio (long-term debt as a percent of shareholders' equity)
- Return on equity (net income divided by the average of beginning and ending common shareholders' equity)
- Cash and cash equivalents
- Current ratio (ratio of current assets to current liabilities)
- Total long-term debt (including capital lease obligations)
- Fiscal year sales for financial institutions.

Hoover's Handbook of Private Companies

A List-Lover's Compendium

The 300 Largest Companies by Sales in *Hoover's Handbook of Private Companies 2005*

Rank	Company	Sales ($ mil.)
1	Blue Cross	182,700
2	U.S. Postal Service	68,529
3	Cargill	62,907
4	State Farm	56,100
5	Koch	40,000
6	Nationwide	29,421
7	Federal Reserve	26,847
8	New York Life	25,700
9	Kaiser Foundation	25,300
10	Verizon Wireless	22,489
11	IGA	21,000
12	Motiva Enterprises	19,300
13	MassMutual	17,947
14	Mars	17,000
15	Publix	16,946
16	Liberty Mutual	16,618
17	Northwestern Mutual	16,545
18	Bechtel	16,300
19	Cingular Wireless	15,483
20	Deloitte	15,100
21	PricewaterhouseCoopers	14,683
22	University of California	14,166
23	Penske	14,000
24	Blue Cross (MI)	13,716
25	Ernst & Young	13,136
26	TIAA-CREF	12,815
27	KPMG	12,160
28	Carlson Wagonlit	11,500
29	C&S Wholesale	11,300
30	Meijer	11,100
31	Cox Enterprises	10,700
32	H-E-B	10,700
33	USAA	10,593
34	Adventist Health System	10,123
35	FMR	9,200
36	Ascension Health	9,054
37	Duke Energy Field Services	8,819
38	Trump	8,500
39	Health Care Service	8,190
40	Highmark	8,105
41	CCA Global	8,000
42	Sony BMG	8,000
43	Army and Air Force Exchange	7,905
44	JM Family Enterprises	7,700
45	Chevron Phillips Chemical	7,018
46	TVA	6,952
47	Dairy Farmers of America	6,933
48	Enterprise Rent-A-Car	6,900
49	Carlson	6,800
50	Guardian Life	6,732
51	SAIC	6,720
52	Regence Group	6,700
53	NewYork-Presbyterian Healthcare	6,580
54	Wakefern Food	6,578
55	Equistar Chemicals	6,545
56	Land O'Lakes	6,321
57	Blue Shield Of California	6,203
58	MidAmerican Energy	6,145
59	Catholic Health Initiatives	6,072
60	American Family Insurance	6,065
61	Advance Publications	5,909
62	New York State Lottery	5,848
63	MacAndrews & Forbes	5,700
64	Sutter Health	5,672
65	Flying J	5,600
66	Menard	5,600
67	Marmon Group	5,560
68	Pilot Travel Centers	5,500
69	Visa	5,400
70	S.C. Johnson	5,370
71	Huntsman	5,246
72	Adventist Health	5,237
73	University of Texas	5,235
74	VT Inc.	5,229
75	Horizon Blue Cross Blue Shield of New Jersey	5,082
76	Catholic Healthcare West	4,989
77	Trinity Health (Novi)	4,957
78	Alticor	4,900
79	Mayo Foundation	4,822
80	Dole Food	4,773
81	Unisource	4,755
82	Giant Eagle	4,739
83	Pacific Mutual	4,668
84	KPMG L.L.P.	4,630
85	Topco Associates	4,600
86	Partners HealthCare	4,561
87	MTA	4,523
88	California State University	4,499
89	Blue Cross (MA)	4,497
90	Southern Wine & Spirits	4,400
91	Roundy's	4,383
92	Hallmark	4,300
93	Delta Dental Plan	4,300
94	MBM	4,236
95	Hy-Vee	4,230
96	Thrivent Financial	4,219
97	NFL	4,200
98	New York City Health and Hospitals	4,200
99	Hitachi Global Storage	4,200
100	Reyes Holdings	4,180
101	Auto-Owners Insurance	4,141
102	Hearst	4,100
103	Levi Strauss	4,091
104	Bill & Melinda Gates Foundation	4,010
105	Platinum Equity	4,000
106	Schwan's	4,000
107	Guardian Industries	4,000
108	TAP Pharmaceutical Products	3,980
109	Graybar Electric	3,803
110	WorldTravel	3,800
111	Major League Baseball	3,800
112	University of Pennsylvania	3,786
113	Providence Health System	3,780
114	AWG	3,721
115	Mutual of Omaha	3,719
116	Martin-Brower	3,700
117	Gulf States Toyota	3,700
118	Eby-Brown	3,670
119	Bonneville Power	3,612
120	Hyatt	3,600
121	Mervyn's	3,553
122	Warner Music	3,500
123	H.T. Hackney	3,500
124	SUNY	3,461
125	Center Oil	3,400
126	Milliken	3,400
127	Peter Kiewit Sons'	3,375
128	Health Insurance of New York	3,370
129	Wegmans	3,300
130	University of Wisconsin	3,273
131	Intermountain Health Care	3,267
132	Raley's	3,200
133	Racetrac Petroleum	3,200
134	Ace Hardware	3,159
135	University of Michigan	3,157
136	J.R. Simplot	3,100
137	Ohio State University	3,060
138	Salvation Army	3,040
139	Red Cross	3,034
140	Kohler	3,005
141	NASCAR	3,000
142	Gordon Food Service	3,000
143	McKinsey & Company	3,000
144	Bloomberg	3,000
145	Security Benefit Group	2,969
146	Texas Lottery	2,966
147	Cook Inlet Energy Supply	2,950
148	JohnsonDiversey	2,948
149	Stanford University	2,940
150	University of Illinois	2,900

SOURCE: HOOVER'S, INC., DATABASE, OCTOBER 2004

The 300 Largest Companies by Sales in
Hoover's Handbook of Private Companies 2005 (continued)

Rank	Company	Sales ($ mil.)
151	Schneider National	2,900
152	Catholic Healthcare Partners	2,874
153	Dow Corning	2,873
154	ESPN	2,869
155	Unified Western Grocers	2,819
156	Wawa, Inc.	2,819
157	Marian Health System	2,805
158	QuikTrip	2,800
159	Apex Oil	2,800
160	Harbour Group	2,800
161	Lefrak Organization	2,800
162	FM Global	2,789
163	Hendrick Automotive	2,783
164	Gilbane	2,771
165	Nalco	2,767
166	Port Authority of NY & NJ	2,764
167	Stater Bros.	2,754
168	Swinerton	2,751
169	Clark Enterprises	2,750
170	Alliance Capital Management	2,733
171	University of Maryland	2,729
172	Sisters of Mercy Health System	2,722
173	Advocate Health Care	2,716
174	Perdue	2,700
175	Booz Allen	2,700
176	University of Florida	2,646
177	Georgia Lottery	2,604
178	Henry Ford Health System	2,600
179	Keystone Foods	2,600
180	George Warren	2,586
181	84 Lumber	2,584
182	Yale University	2,565
183	Jones Financial Companies	2,539
184	Bon Secours Health	2,523
185	Springs Industries	2,500
186	Memorial Hermann Healthcare	2,500
187	Global Companies	2,500
188	BJC HealthCare	2,500
189	Kinray	2,500
190	Vistar Corporation	2,500
191	Trader Joe's Co	2,500
192	Jefferson Health System	2,500
193	Harvard University	2,473
194	UAP Holding	2,452
195	Quality King	2,450
196	CUNA Mutual	2,416
197	International Data Group	2,410
198	Pennsylvania Lottery	2,352
199	Do it Best	2,334
200	Transammonia	2,309
201	CHRISTUS Health	2,302
202	Lumbermens Merchandising	2,300
203	Tufts Health Plan	2,300
204	Consolidated Electrical	2,300
205	New York Power Authority	2,292
206	Sinclair Oil	2,290
207	Bill Heard	2,279
208	Belk	2,265
209	MedStar Health	2,250
210	Aera Energy	2,234
211	MasterCard	2,231
212	Goodwill	2,210
213	Services Group	2,200
214	Sunbelt Beverage	2,200
215	Ferolie Group	2,200
216	Schnuck Markets	2,200
217	ContiGroup	2,200
218	A-Mark Financial	2,200
219	Ingram Industries	2,200
220	TravelCenters of America	2,176
221	NBA	2,164
222	CH2M HILL	2,154
223	Alex Lee	2,140
224	Ag Processing	2,127
225	Clarian Health Partners	2,102
226	Red Apple Group	2,100
227	Renco	2,100
228	Golub	2,100
229	Banner Health	2,100
230	Navy Exchange	2,100
231	Gulf Oil	2,100
232	NHL	2,100
233	Sentry Insurance	2,088
234	Ohio Lottery	2,078
235	Amtrak	2,077
236	Columbia University	2,074
237	University of Washington	2,050
238	H Group Holding	2,047
239	Quintiles Transnational	2,046
240	Vanguard Group	2,044
241	Holman Enterprises	2,042
242	Allegis Group	2,035
243	TruServ	2,024
244	DeBruce Grain	2,018
245	Forever Living	2,012
246	NYU	2,005
247	Cumberland Farms	2,000
248	Gores Technology	2,000
249	Quexco	2,000
250	Irvine Company	2,000
251	NextiraOne	2,000
252	Schreiber Foods	2,000
253	Grant Thornton International	2,000
254	Quad/Graphics	2,000
255	WinCo Foods	2,000
256	Golden State Foods	2,000
257	Andersen Corporation	2,000
258	KB Toys	2,000
259	Fry's Electronics	2,000
260	J.F. Shea	1,994
261	Tishman	1,980
262	Vanderbilt University	1,971
263	Vision Service Plan	1,970
264	Sammons Enterprises	1,969
265	Group Health	1,966
266	US Oncology	1,966
267	Allina Hospitals	1,940
268	Hunt Consolidated	1,930
269	California Dairies Inc.	1,916
270	Houchens	1,913
271	Cornell University	1,903
272	Texas Health Resources	1,900
273	Sheetz	1,900
274	Scoular	1,900
275	Brookshire Grocery	1,900
276	SSM Health Care	1,900
277	Leprino Foods	1,900
278	DeMoulas Super Markets	1,900
279	Westcon	1,885
280	JELD-WEN	1,878
281	Whiting-Turner	1,874
282	Hensel Phelps Construction	1,872
283	Spectrum Health	1,868
284	University of Iowa	1,857
285	Follett	1,851
286	Minnesota Mutual	1,827
287	Dr Pepper/Seven Up Bottling	1,820
288	UniGroup	1,809
289	CARQUEST	1,800
290	Kingston Technology	1,800
291	Gallo	1,800
292	Mary Kay	1,800
293	Rich Products	1,800
294	Illinois Lottery	1,799
295	Memec	1,798
296	Software House	1,797
297	Metaldyne	1,793
298	Evanston Northwestern Healthcare	1,793
299	ABC Supply	1,793
300	Loews Cineplex	1,772

The 300 Largest Employers in
Hoover's Handbook of Private Companies 2005

Rank	Company	Employees
1	U.S. Postal Service	826,955
2	Burger King	349,600
3	Express Personnel	224,000
4	Carlson	190,000
5	Blue Cross	150,000
6	Publix	125,000
7	PricewaterhouseCoopers	122,820
8	Deloitte	119,237
9	University of California	118,533
10	Ernst & Young	103,000
11	Cargill	101,000
12	KPMG	100,000
13	IGA	92,000
14	Ascension Health	87,469
15	Goodwill	82,370
16	State Farm	79,000
17	Cox Enterprises	77,000
18	Meijer	75,000
19	Catholic Health Initiatives	67,000
20	University of Texas	66,845
21	Dole Food	59,000
22	H-E-B	56,000
23	Kaiser Foundation	54,300
24	Enterprise Rent-A-Car	53,500
25	NewYork-Presbyterian Healthcare	53,268
26	Wakefern Food	50,000
27	Army and Air Force Exchange	47,323
28	Chick-fil-A	46,500
29	Hy-Vee	46,000
30	Adventist Health System	44,000
31	Bechtel	44,000
32	Trinity Health (Novi)	43,900
33	Verizon Wireless	43,900
34	Catholic Health East	43,000
35	SAIC	42,700
36	Mayo Foundation	42,620
37	Salvation Army	42,530
38	H Group Holding	41,000
39	Sutter Health	41,000
40	California State University	40,000
41	Red Cross	40,000
42	Hyatt	40,000
43	Cingular Wireless	39,400
44	Texas A&M	38,500
45	Liberty Mutual	38,000
46	CARQUEST	36,500
47	Penske	36,000
48	Catholic Healthcare West	36,000
49	Bon Secours Health	34,512
50	Ohio State University	34,000
51	Providence Health System	32,526
52	Wegmans	32,000
53	Mars	31,000
54	Catholic Healthcare Partners	30,524
55	Koch	30,000
56	Nationwide	30,000
57	Life Care Centers	30,000
58	CUNY	30,000
59	Metromedia	29,500
60	FMR	29,424
61	Jones Financial Companies	29,200
62	University of Washington	29,077
63	Mervyn's	29,000
64	University of Wisconsin	28,030
65	Delaware North	28,000
66	Marmon Group	28,000
67	Advance Publications	28,000
68	Asplundh	27,978
69	Jefferson Health System	27,000
70	University of Missouri	26,246
71	Sisters of Mercy Health System	26,000
72	Giant Eagle	26,000
73	BJC HealthCare	25,525
74	Advocate Health Care	25,000
75	Kohler	25,000
76	Johns Hopkins Medicine	25,000
77	Inter-Con Security	25,000
78	RTM Restaurant Group	25,000
79	Schwan's	24,000
80	KB Toys	24,000
81	University of Illinois	23,483
82	SSM Health Care	23,300
83	Buffets Holdings	23,000
84	Allina Hospitals	22,583
85	Viasystems	22,400
86	Amtrak	22,000
87	MedStar Health	22,000
88	Banner Health	22,000
89	Grant Thornton International	21,500
90	USAA	21,000
91	JELD-WEN	21,000
92	Hitachi Global Storage	21,000
93	Schneider National	20,733
94	UNICCO Service	20,500
95	Federal Reserve	20,448
96	UNICOR	20,274
97	Hearst	20,000
98	Day & Zimmermann	20,000
99	Golub	20,000
100	Roundy's	19,999
101	MacAndrews & Forbes	19,800
102	Perdue	19,000
103	Guardian Industries	19,000
104	ClubCorp	19,000
105	Vanderbilt University	18,551
106	Adventist Health	18,352
107	St. Joseph Health System	18,157
108	AECOM	18,000
109	Hallmark	18,000
110	KPMG L.L.P.	18,000
111	Belk	17,200
112	University of Minnesota	17,014
113	Springs Industries	17,000
114	Texas Health Resources	16,800
115	Schnuck Markets	16,500
116	Raley's	16,200
117	Lefrak Organization	16,200
118	University of Rochester	16,040
119	Platinum Equity	16,000
120	American Golf	16,000
121	24 Hour Fitness	16,000
122	Quintiles Transnational	15,991
123	Carrols	15,900
124	ContiGroup	15,500
125	Navy Exchange	15,500
126	NYU	15,010
127	Peter Kiewit Sons'	15,000
128	Wawa, Inc.	15,000
129	Indiana University	15,000
130	Sentara Healthcare	15,000
131	OhioHealth	15,000
132	Trump	15,000
133	Booz Allen	14,800
134	Taylor Corporation	14,350
135	Detroit Medical Center	14,311
136	Novant Health	14,060
137	CH2M HILL	14,000
138	Volunteers of America	14,000
139	Milliken	14,000
140	USC	14,000
141	Spectrum Health	14,000
142	AMF Bowling	13,800
143	Cornell University	13,517
144	Renco	13,500
145	Inova	13,500
146	Stater Bros.	13,500
147	Hobby Lobby	13,500
148	Vanguard Health Systems	13,500
149	General Parts	13,500
150	Catholic Health Services of Long Island	13,500

SOURCE: HOOVER'S, INC., DATABASE, OCTOBER 2004

The 300 Largest Employers in
Hoover's Handbook of Private Companies 2005 (continued)

Rank	Company	Employees
151	International Data Group	13,450
152	Bashas'	13,200
153	JohnsonDiversey	13,000
154	Memorial Hermann Healthcare	13,000
155	Health Care Service	13,000
156	TVA	13,000
157	Pilot Travel Centers	13,000
158	Henry Ford Health System	12,700
159	Cinemark	12,700
160	DeMoulas Super Markets	12,700
161	University of Chicago	12,623
162	Advantage Sales and Marketing	12,500
163	Princeton University	12,497
164	Levi Strauss	12,300
165	New York Life	12,100
166	Flying J	12,000
167	Zachry	12,000
168	Quad/Graphics	12,000
169	Brookshire Grocery	12,000
170	J.R. Simplot	12,000
171	McKinsey & Company	12,000
172	Turner Industries	12,000
173	S.C. Johnson	12,000
174	University of Florida	11,996
175	University of Pennsylvania	11,949
176	Alticor	11,500
177	Mashantucket Pequot Gaming	11,500
178	MidAmerican Energy	11,440
179	Bass Pro Shops	11,400
180	Mohegan Tribal Gaming	11,100
181	Clarian Health Partners	11,088
182	Harvard University	11,000
183	Cushman & Wakefield	11,000
184	Nypro	11,000
185	Highmark	11,000
186	Ritz Camera Centers	10,800
187	University of Tennessee	10,787
188	Venture Industries	10,700
189	TravelCenters of America	10,500
190	Michigan State University	10,500
191	Boscov's	10,500
192	Menard	10,500
193	Nalco	10,500
194	Ardent Health	10,100
195	Retail Brand Alliance	10,036
196	Estes Express	10,027
197	University of Pittsburgh	10,000
198	Gores Technology	10,000
199	Musicland	10,000
200	MediaNews	10,000
201	C&S Wholesale	10,000
202	Scripps	10,000
203	Sony BMG	10,000
204	CROSSMARK	10,000
205	Vanguard Group	10,000
206	Key Safety Systems	10,000
207	Unisource	10,000
208	MassMutual	10,000
209	SSA Marine	10,000
210	Follett	10,000
211	Concentra	10,000
212	United Space Alliance	10,000
213	Acosta Sales	10,000
214	Provena Health	10,000
215	Texas Pacific Group	9,900
216	Parsons	9,800
217	Kaleida Health	9,724
218	Group Health	9,708
219	Barnes & Noble College Bookstores	9,700
220	Alex Lee	9,500
221	MIT	9,500
222	K-VA-T Food Stores	9,500
223	NESCO	9,500
224	Carilion Health System	9,498
225	Discount Tire	9,430
226	Trader Publishing Company	9,400
227	SAS Institute	9,306
228	Amsted	9,200
229	Sheetz	9,000
230	NextiraOne	9,000
231	Watkins Associated Industries	9,000
232	Towers Perrin	9,000
233	Parsons Brinckerhoff	8,975
234	Battelle Memorial	8,900
235	Colliers International	8,823
236	Dr Pepper/Seven Up Bottling	8,800
237	UIS	8,800
238	Cox Health Systems	8,799
239	Baptist Health South Florida	8,616
240	Haworth	8,525
241	Community Hospitals of Indiana	8,500
242	Blue Cross (MI)	8,500
243	Big Y Foods	8,500
244	Baker & McKenzie	8,400
245	Dresser	8,300
246	Memorial Sloan-Kettering	8,255
247	BE&K	8,212
248	Iasis Healthcare	8,200
249	Dow Corning	8,200
250	American Family Insurance	8,100
251	US Oncology	8,096
252	Yale University	8,071
253	CHRISTUS Health	8,000
254	Scott & White	8,000
255	Vertis	8,000
256	ValleyCrest Companies	8,000
257	Duchossois Industries	8,000
258	Andersen Corporation	8,000
259	Land O'Lakes	8,000
260	Bose	8,000
261	Graybar Electric	7,900
262	Houchens	7,760
263	Evanston Northwestern Healthcare	7,665
264	Extended Stay America	7,600
265	Burlington Industries	7,600
266	Horseshoe Gaming	7,562
267	Red Apple Group	7,500
268	Park Nicollet Health Services	7,500
269	Timex	7,500
270	Holmes Group	7,500
271	Alegent Health	7,500
272	Mark IV	7,500
273	Beaulieu of America	7,500
274	Variety Wholesalers	7,500
275	Save Mart	7,400
276	Longaberger	7,350
277	Colson & Colson	7,300
278	Contran	7,300
279	Cincinnati Children's Hospital	7,207
280	Oxford Automotive	7,200
281	Metaldyne	7,100
282	Pella	7,100
283	Swedish Health Services	7,100
284	National Service Industries	7,100
285	Southern Wine & Spirits	7,100
286	Carlson Wagonlit	7,047
287	Lanoga	7,009
288	United Supermarkets	7,000
289	Adventist HealthCare	7,000
290	Quexco	7,000
291	TIC Holdings	7,000
292	WinCo Foods	7,000
293	Port Authority of NY & NJ	7,000
294	FHC Health Systems	7,000
295	Klaussner Furniture	7,000
296	Holiday Companies	6,993
297	Cumberland Farms	6,976
298	Ingram Industries	6,900
299	Sinclair Oil	6,900
300	Keystone Foods	6,700

The *Inc.* 500 Fastest-Growing Private Companies in America

Rank	Company	Headquarters	Sales Growth Increase (%)*
1	InPhonic	Washington, DC	5,958
2	uSight	Orem, UT	3,283
3	VCustomer	Seattle, WA	2,955
4	SeamlessWeb	New York, NY	2,608
5	Liquidnet	New York, NY	2,602
6	METI	El Paso, TX	2,461
7	Sullivan International Group	San Diego, CA	1,977
8	Go Daddy Group	Scottsdale, AZ	1,882
9	Stentor	Brisbane, CA	1,810
10	Coventry First	Fort Washington, PA	1,675
11	Enterprise Information Management	Lanoka Harbor, NJ	1,642
12	NetSuite	San Mateo, CA	1,441
13	DSL Extreme	Canoga Park, CA	1,215
14	SecureInfo	San Antonio, TX	1,203
15	Zappos.com	Las Vegas, NV	1,115
16	Commodity Sourcing Group	Detroit, MI	1,110
17	C&S Marketing	Sacramento, CA	968
18	CodeCorrect	Yakima, WA	897
19	Telesis	Rockville, MD	871
20	Atrilogy Solutions Group	Irvine, CA	866
21	Red F	Charlotte, NC	864
22	ScripNet	Las Vegas, NV	855
23	Lydian Trust	Palm Beach, FL	816
24	Khimetrics	Scottsdale, AZ	803
25	PaySource	Dayton, OH	795
26	2Wire	San Jose, CA	783
27	Atlantic Credit & Finance	Roanoke, VA	763
28	New Edge Networks	Vancouver, WA	763
29	Preferred Systems Solutions	Fairfax, VA	741
30	Edge Products	Ogden, UT	734
31	Catapult Technology	Bethesda, MD	732
32	180s	Baltimore, MD	729
33	Configuresoft	Colorado Springs, CO	718
34	Intellimar	Sykesville, MD	680
35	STOPS	Titusville, FL	663
36	Clover Technologies Group	Ottawa, IL	642
37	Family First Mortgage	Palm Coast, FL	635
38	Kara Homes	East Brunswick, NJ	616
39	180solutions	Bellevue, WA	611
40	ProSight	Portland, OR	600
41	ATI	Trabuco Canyon, CA	594
42	Guy Brown Products	Brentwood, TN	557
43	The Outsource Group	Walnut Creek, CA	554
44	Tastefully Simple	Alexandria, MN	534
45	Hobbytron.com	Orem, UT	532
46	Garden of Life	W. Palm Beach, FL	523
47	Genscape	Louisville, KY	523
48	iboats.com	Draper, UT	515
49	ExecuTrain	Alpharetta, GA	496
50	iSqFt	Cincinnati, OH	496
51	Sauna Warehouse	Lake Forest, CA	481
52	Paloma Systems	Annandale, VA	476
53	Logic Trends	Atlanta, GA	475
54	GamePlan Financial Marketing	Woodstock, GA	462
55	Premiere Credit of North America	Indianapolis, IN	455
56	Unipro Group	Miami, FL	454
57	Ark-La-Tex Financial Services	Frisco, TX	447
58	Magnetech Industrial Services	South Bend, IN	446
59	Websurveyor.com	Herndon, VA	430
60	ServiceMagic	Golden, CO	422
61	Dynarand	San Francisco, CA	418
62	Global Solutions Network	Alexandria, VA	414
63	Call Inc.	Doylestown, PA	413
64	Alere Medical	Reno, NV	411
65	Barlovento	Dothan, AL	393
66	Appian	Vienna, VA	391
67	Infoglide Software	Austin, TX	387
68	Intercosmos Media Group	New Orleans, LA	384
69	JLT Mobile Computers	Chandler, AZ	383
70	USA Lending	Salt Lake City, UT	380
71	Dynetech	Orlando, FL	379
72	Micah Group	Lexington, KY	376
73	Vesta	Portland, OR	374
74	Carteret Mortgage	Centreville, VA	374
75	Intuitive Research and Technology	Grand Prairie, TX	373
76	HouseValues	Bellevue, WA	369
77	Columbia Data Products	Altamonte Springs, FL	366
78	EveryTicket.com	Miami Beach, FL	358
79	Nobel	Carlsbad, CA	357
80	Contours Express	Nicholasville, KY	355
81	Maverick Technologies	Columbia, IL	354
82	The Diamond Group	Dallas, TX	351
83	Mindbridge Software	Norristown, PA	349
84	StarMine	San Francisco, CA	339
85	Xodiax Data Centers	Louisville, KY	336
86	iDirect Technologies	Herndon, VA	326
87	Elan Development	Houston, TX	325
88	Intelligence Data Systems	Reston, VA	324
89	Evolve Manufacturing Technologies	Mountain View, CA	322
90	iDirect Marketing	Irvine, CA	318
91	SP Systems	Greenbelt, MD	313
92	eCopy	Nashua, NH	311
93	Backcountry.com	Heber City, UT	306
94	HRsmart	Richardson, TX	304
95	Gratis Internet	Washington, DC	293
96	Summit Energy	Park City, UT	292
97	ComScore Networks	Reston, VA	290
98	Tripwire	Portland, OR	290
99	Active Network	La Jolla, CA	284
100	Nexstar Financial	Creve Coeur, MO	283

*Average annual sales growth measured over a four- or five-year period.

SOURCE: *INC.*; FALL, 2004

The *Inc.* 500 Fastest-Growing Private Companies in America (continued)

Rank	Company	Headquarters	Sales Growth Increase (%)
101	Panther Technologies	Medford, NJ	283
102	Global Brand Marketing	Santa Barbara, CA	280
103	Ace Mortgage Funding	Indianapolis, IN	276
104	STSN	Salt Lake City, UT	276
105	Forex Capital Markets	New York, NY	274
106	Red Hawk Industries	Denver, CO	273
107	HC Oregon	Portland, OR	270
108	Dynamic Corporate Solutions	Orange Park, FL	269
109	Starmark International	Ft. Lauderdale, FL	268
110	DSR Management	Evanston, IL	268
111	iMortgage Services	Pittsburgh, PA	266
112	Concentrek	Jenison, MI	265
113	Comfort Research	Grand Rapids, MI	261
114	Health Dialog Services	Boston, MA	259
115	Millennium Rugs	Chatsworth, CA	259
116	BondDesk	Mill Valley, CA	254
117	Wholesale Carrier Services	Boca Raton, FL	253
118	Ellie Mae	Dublin, CA	253
119	LTM	Havelock, NC	253
120	Passport Health Communications	Franklin, TN	253
121	Pathwayz Communications	Amarillo, TX	253
122	Forerunner	Lakewood, CO	244
123	Broadlane	San Francisco, CA	243
124	ScriptLogic	Boca Raton, FL	243
125	Arbitech	Laguna Beach, CA	241
126	Prism Innovations	Deerfield, IL	240
127	MegaPath Networks	Pleasanton, CA	239
128	Long Wave	Oklahoma City, OK	239
129	HealthEssentials	Louisville, KY	235
130	Treetop Technologies	Boise, ID	232
131	Alienware	Miami, FL	232
132	Ikano Communications	Salt Lake City, UT	231
133	Counsel On Call	Brentwood, TN	231
134	VNUS Medical Technologies	San Jose, CA	228
135	Smooth	Bellevue, WA	225
136	Global Home Loans and Finance	Melville, NY	225
137	Sunlight Systems	Allendale, NJ	225
138	Noodles & Co.	Boulder, CO	225
139	Commtech Solutions	Grafton, OH	225
140	Optistreams	Fresno, CA	221
141	Ambient Weather	Chandler, AZ	220
142	Star Software Systems	Warner Robins, GA	220
143	Netspoke	Woburn, MA	218
144	BankServ	San Francisco, CA	218
145	The Scooter Store	New Braunfels, TX	217
146	Velocity11	Palo Alto, CA	217
147	Rowland Express	Elkhorn, WI	217
148	Chadco Enterprises	Sarasota, FL	217
149	Distant Replays	Atlanta, GA	216
150	Premier Environmental Services	Marietta, GA	216
151	Quality Assured Services	Orlando, FL	215
152	Serralta Rebull Serig	Miami Lakes, FL	214
153	Network Management	North Highlands, CA	213
154	FNC	Oxford, MS	213
155	Apex Document Solutions	Austin, TX	211
156	Vitacost.com	Boynton Beach, FL	211
157	InSource	King of Prussia, PA	209
158	The Works Corp.	Boise, ID	208
159	Silver State Financial Services	Henderson, NV	206
160	VIPdesk	Alexandria, VA	206
161	First Magnus Financial	Tucson, AZ	206
162	HTP	Columbus, OH	205
163	VisionIT	Detroit, MI	203
164	Red Peacock International	Glendale, CA	203
165	Netuno USA	Miami, FL	202
166	AnswerNet Network	Princeton, NJ	202
167	Liberty Tax Service	Virginia Beach, VA	202
168	ReQuest Multimedia	Ballston Spa, NY	202
169	POS World	Atlanta, GA	202
170	Apartment Express Corporate Housing	Tampa, FL	200
171	Specialty Bottle	Seattle, WA	197
172	Conduant	Longmont, CO	196
173	Edocs	Natick, MA	195
174	Lendia	Worcester, MA	195
175	Maui Wowi	Greenwood Village, CO	194
176	Ameritac	Concord, CA	194
177	Co-Advantage Resources	Orlando, FL	193
178	Neumann Enterprises	Nashotah, WI	192
179	CompressorWorks	Dallas, TX	191
180	Exstream Software	Lexington, KY	189
181	American Teleconnect	Southampton, NY	189
182	TTXE	Rossford, OH	187
183	PrintingForLess.com	Livingston, MT	187
184	Gray Hawk Systems	Alexandria, VA	186
185	Network Telephone	Pensacola, FL	185
186	Mimeo	New York, NY	183
187	Mont Blanc Gourmet	Denver, CO	183
188	Click Wine Group	Seattle, WA	182
189	FatPipe Networks	Salt Lake City, UT	182
190	Cokem International	Plymouth, MN	181
191	Earth Sun Moon Trading	Grove City, PA	180
192	Gartner Studios	Stillwater, MN	180
193	D&D Consulting	Albany, NY	180
194	DataCert	Houston, TX	180
195	Homefield Financial	Irvine, CA	179
196	ISS	Colorado Springs, CO	179
197	IntelliClaim	Norwalk, CT	179
198	NFM	Baltimore, MD	179
199	Pro Look Sports	Provo, UT	177
200	Underground Technologies	Houston, TX	175

The *Inc.* 500 Fastest-Growing Private Companies in America (continued)

Rank	Company	Headquarters	Sales Growth Increase (%)
201	Mansell Group	Atlanta, GA	175
202	Prometheus Laboratories	San Diego, CA	175
203	AdminServer	Chester, PA	175
204	Capella Education	Minneapolis, MN	175
205	Excel Archives of Virginia	Sterling, VA	174
206	PureSafety	Nashville, TN	173
207	Brownwood Acres Foods	Eastport, MI	173
208	Innovative Lighting	Roland, IA	171
209	Integrity Sales	Castro Valley, CA	170
210	PTO Today	Wrentham, MA	170
211	On Target Promotions	Warrensville Hts., OH	170
212	Managed Care Network	Niagara Falls, NY	169
213	Real Foundations	Addison, TX	169
214	Radiance Technologies	Huntsville, AL	168
215	Carbolite Foods	Evansville, IN	168
216	Allied Home Medical	Cookeville, TN	168
217	FlavorX	Bethesda, MD	168
218	Partners Human Resources	Oklahoma City, OK	166
219	Diagnostic Hybrids	Athens, OH	166
220	National Logistics Management	Detroit, MI	165
221	Franklin Financial	Southfield, MI	165
222	E.A. Technologies	Hauppauge, NY	165
223	Zyman Group	Atlanta, GA	164
224	Spectorsoft	Vero Beach, FL	163
225	Cultural Experiences Abroad	Tempe, AZ	163
226	Palm Beach Tan	Carrollton, TX	163
227	Packaging Resources	Lyons, IL	162
228	DieCuts with a View	Provo, UT	162
229	Milestone Group	Arlington, VA	162
230	PowerLight	Berkeley, CA	162
231	iProspect	Watertown, MA	161
232	Argotek	South Riding, VA	160
233	HRS/Erase	Independence, MO	159
234	Print Inc.	Kirkland, WA	159
235	TurnKey	Temecula, CA	157
236	InMotion Pictures	Jacksonville, FL	157
237	Thomas & Herbert Consulting	Silver Spring, MD	156
238	Advanced Health Media	Union, NJ	156
239	TruStar Solutions	Fishers, IN	156
240	Günther Douglas	Denver, CO	156
241	New Heights Manufacturing	Marietta, GA	156
242	SecureUSA	Cumming, GA	153
243	Metronome	Santa Ana, CA	152
244	Pacific Property Assets	Irvine, CA	152
245	Digital Management Systems	Absecon, NJ	151
246	Access Systems	Reston, VA	151
247	theprinters.com	State College, PA	148
248	Plateau Systems	Arlington, VA	147
249	Publishing Group of America	Franklin, TN	146
250	Back to Basics	Bluffdale, UT	145
251	Portage Environmental	Espanola, NM	145
252	UpStream Software	Rochester, MI	144
253	The Experts	Ft. Lauderdale, FL	144
254	WorldNet Technology Consultants	Wyomissing, PA	144
255	Zentech Manufacturing	Baltimore, MD	144
256	DataStream Market Intelligence	Owasso, OK	143
257	C&A Industries	Omaha, NE	143
258	AuthenTec	Melbourne, FL	143
259	Quantech Services	Bedford, MA	141
260	New Media Strategies	Arlington, VA	140
261	Rochester MicroSystems	Rochester, NY	139
262	PlayNetwork	Redmond, WA	138
263	Franklin American Mortgage	Franklin, TN	138
264	Enlightened	Washington, DC	138
265	Patchlink	Scottsdale, AZ	138
266	The Good Home Co.	New York, NY	136
267	FirsTrust Mortgage	Olathe, KA	135
268	Softscape	Wayland, MA	135
269	The Newberry Group	St. Charles, MO	135
270	Financial Recovery Services	Edina, MN	133
271	Mosso's Medical Supply Company	Latrobe, PA	133
272	Casabyte	Renton, WA	132
273	Handango	Hurst, TX	132
274	TechDisposal.com	Columbus, OH	132
275	Global Performance	Greenville, SC	132
276	Computer System Designers	Oklahoma City, OK	132
277	American Capital Financial Services	Gold River, CA	130
278	Postfuture	Richardson, TX	130
279	Refinery	Huntingdon Valley, PA	129
280	MorNorth Mortgage	Brainerd, MN	129
281	Fetch Logistics	Amherst, NY	129
282	Insulair	Vernalis, CA	128
283	Just Marketing	Indianapolis, IN	127
284	Directed Energy Solutions	Colorado Springs, CO	127
285	eMarket Group	Portland, OR	126
286	Joseph Sheairs Associates	Shamong, NJ	126
287	Sedona Staffing Services	Frankfort, IL	125
288	Trios Associates	Lanham, MD	125
289	Phase Forward	Waltham, MA	125
290	RxUSA	Port Washington, NY	124
291	Ameripay Payroll	Elk Grove Village, IL	124
292	Mobile Homes Central	Lake Worth, FL	124
293	CapAdvisory	Vienna, VA	124
294	Intelliseek	Cincinnati, OH	123
295	TPi Billing Solutions	Tulsa, OK	123
296	Wyant Data Systems	Louisville, CO	122
297	Cardtronics	Houston, TX	122
298	Trilogy Health Services	Louisville, KY	122
299	3t Systems	Denver, CO	122
300	Stinger Industries	Murfreesboro, TN	122

The *Inc.* 500 Fastest-Growing Private Companies in America (continued)

Rank	Company	Headquarters	Sales Growth Increase (%)
301	Clubfurniture.com	Charlotte, NC	121
302	ArchivesOne	Waterbury, CT	121
303	Skoda, Minotti & Co.	Mayfield Village, OH	120
304	Advanced Data Services	Charleston, SC	120
305	MicroPact Engineering	Herndon, VA	119
306	Barton Medical	Austin, TX	119
307	Tourico Holiday Flights	Altamonte Springs, FL	119
308	Solid Earth	Huntsville, AL	118
309	First Financial Network	Oklahoma City, OK	118
310	Mortgage Partners	Dracut, MA	118
311	PremierGarage	Phoenix, AZ	118
312	FastBucks	Dallas, TX	117
313	SEI Group	Huntsville, AL	117
314	Advantage Data	Boston, MA	117
315	ecfirst.com	Clive, IA	116
316	KeyLogic Systems	Morgantown, WV	116
317	Resource Options	Needham, MA	116
318	Portraits International of the Southwest	Houston, TX	115
319	AFMS	Portland, OR	115
320	Milestone Construction Services	Sterling, VA	115
321	Smarts	White Plains, NY	114
322	US Script	Fresno, CA	114
323	The BMC Group	Seattle, WA	114
324	ATM Express	Billings, MT	113
325	Authsec	Columbia, MD	112
326	KSJ & Associates	Falls Church, VA	112
327	IVCi	Hauppauge, NY	112
328	The Prosthetic Center	Houston, TX	112
329	Pacific Data Designs	San Francisco, CA	111
330	Innovative Marketing	Minnetonka, MN	111
331	BCS Industries	Memphis, TN	111
332	TheZeb.com	Statesville, NC	111
333	Money Marketing	Ridgefield Park, NJ	110
334	Virtual-Agent Services	Schaumburg, IL	110
335	Access Integrated Networks	Macon, GA	110
336	Marlabs	Edison, NJ	109
337	Digital Visual Display Technologies	Atlanta, GA	109
338	Kaizen Direct	Rochester, NY	109
339	Information Transport Solutions	Wetumpka, AL	109
340	S2F Engineering	Blissfield, MI	109
341	Quickparts.com	Atlanta, GA	109
342	3D Research	Huntsville, AL	108
343	The Ultimate Backrub Store	Glenview, IL	108
344	Integra Telecom	Portland, OR	108
345	Switch and Data	Tampa, FL	108
346	Newcastle Construction	Bessemer, AL	108
347	EM-Assist	Folsom, CA	108
348	Legal Network	Pittsburgh, PA	107
349	Automation Technologies	Vienna, VA	107
350	Republic Trust & Mortgage	Largo, FL	107
351	Pacific Dental Services	Costa Mesa, CA	106
352	Strategic Data Systems	San Diego, CA	105
353	Gray Research	Huntsville, AL	105
354	EnvoyWorldWide	Bedford, MA	104
355	TUI Consulting	Tacoma, WA	104
356	Perseus Development	Braintree, MA	104
357	Creating Results	Occoquan, VA	104
358	iPlacement	Orlando, FL	104
359	Peripheral Imaging	San Jose, CA	103
360	Navarro Research and Engineering	Oak Ridge, TN	102
361	USA Funding	Brookfield, WI	102
362	The Christmas Light Co.	Mesa, AZ	102
363	G&A Partners	Houston, TX	101
364	Tesoro	Virginia Beach, VA	101
365	Beacon Technologies	Nashville, TN	101
366	DDM Direct	Buffalo, NY	100
367	GeoLearning	W. Des Moines, IA	100
368	Café Rio	Provo, UT	100
369	Amity Technology	Fargo, ND	99
370	Risk Management Services	Louisville, KY	99
371	Métier	Washington, DC	99
372	Cherokee Information Services	Arlington, VA	99
373	Gracar	Dayton, OH	98
374	Vosges Haut-Chocolat	Chicago, IL	98
375	Blue Ridge Numerics	Charlottesville, VA	98
376	ath Power Consulting	Andover, MA	98
377	All Action Architectural Metal & Glass	Edison, NJ	98
378	Capitol	Sacramento, CA	97
379	TicketsNow.com	Crystal Lake, IL	97
380	GTCI	Allen, TX	97
381	Proven Direct	Menomonee Falls, WI	97
382	Melton Franchise Systems	Carpinteria, CA	97
383	One Stop Shop	Chatsworth, CA	96
384	National Bankcard Systems	Austin, TX	96
385	Database Marketing Group	Santa Ana, CA	96
386	Color Kinetics	Boston, MA	95
387	Alpine Access	Golden, CO	95
388	Odyssey Systems Consulting Group	Wakefield, MA	94
389	iHomeowners	Calabasas, CA	94
390	IncorporateTime.com	Islip Terrace, NY	94
391	Innovative Technical Solutions	Honolulu, HI	94
392	MagnaDrive	Bellevue, WA	94
393	MV Transportation	Fairfield, CA	94
394	S2Tech	Chesterfield, MO	94
395	Rackspace Managed Hosting	San Antonio, TX	94
396	The Astra Group	Overland Park, KS	93
397	Auction Systems Auctioneers and Appraisers	Phoenix, AZ	93
398	Valco Data Systems	Salem, NH	93
399	Keystrokes Transcription	Bolingbrook, IL	93
400	WRG Services	Willoughby, OH	93

The *Inc.* 500 Fastest-Growing Private Companies in America (continued)

Rank	Company	Headquarters	Sales Growth Increase (%)
401	The Spa Depot	Olympia, WA	93
402	Axis Healthcare Communications	Yardley, PA	93
403	Pacific Pavingstone	La Crescenta, CA	93
404	StoneTech Professional	Walnut Creek, CA	92
405	CourtSmart Digital Systems	N. Chelmsford, MA	92
406	New Era Builders	Cleveland	92
407	Data Warehouse	Boca Raton, FL	92
408	Educational Outfitters	Chattanooga, TN	92
409	Budget Blinds	Orange, CA	92
410	WorthGroup	Reno, NV	91
411	The White Stone Group	Knoxville, TN	91
412	L.E.M. Products	Harrison, OH	91
413	Schaller Anderson	Phoenix, AZ	91
414	Car Wash Technologies	Cranberry Township, PA	91
415	Applied Global Technologies	Rockledge, FL	91
416	BurstNet Technologies	Scranton, PA	91
417	McKeough Land Co.	Grand Haven, MI	91
418	RiskMetrics	New York, NY	90
419	Barcoding	Baltimore, MD	90
420	Market Technologies	Wesley Chapel, FL	90
421	Resolution Consulting	Broomfield, CO	90
422	Amtrust Mortgage	Atlanta, GA	90
423	Lenco Marine	Stuart, FL	89
424	Communispace	Watertown, MA	89
425	TechTarget	Needham, MA	89
426	Mosaica Education	New York, NY	88
427	Vedicsoft Solutions	Iselin, NJ	87
428	ComFrame Software	Birmingham, AL	87
429	Integrated Science Solutions	Walnut Creek, CA	87
430	SupplyCore	Rockford, IL	87
431	Southern Development	Jacksonville, FL	87
432	Integrated Management Services	Jackson, MS	86
433	Foundstone	Mission Viejo, CA	86
434	Valley Oak Systems	San Ramon, CA	86
435	Info-X	Rockleigh, NJ	86
436	LocalNet	Williamsville, NY	85
437	Synergis	Alpharetta, GA	85
438	NovaCopy	Memphis, TN	85
439	Round Table Group	Chicago, IL	85
440	CHE Consulting	Fenton, MO	84
441	Cold Stone Creamery	Scottsdale, AZ	84
442	Trinity Healthcare Staffing	Florence, SC	84
443	ACS International Resources	Newark, DE	84
444	Resulté Universal	Dallas, TX	84
445	ChartLogic	Salt Lake City, UT	84
446	CyraCom International	Tucson, AZ	84
447	Carousel Industries	Charlestown, RI	83
448	Residential Loan Centers of America	Des Plaines, IL	83
449	eCompanyStore	Alpharetta, GA	83
450	CaseCentral	San Francisco, CA	82
451	Intranets.com	Woburn, MA	82
452	ProClarity	Boise, ID	82
453	Micro Solutions Enterprises	Chatsworth, CA	82
454	Weather Decision Technologies	Norman, OK	82
455	FirstComp Insurance	Omaha, NE	81
456	O1 Communications	Sacramento, CA	81
457	Electronic Data Resources	W. Palm Beach, FL	81
458	Quotable Cards	New York, NY	81
459	Signature Mortgage	Canton, OH	81
460	Angie's List	Indianapolis, IN	80
461	Great Works Internet	Biddeford, ME	80
462	Freightquote.com	Overland Park, KA	80
463	High Power Technical Services	Louisville, KY	80
464	IntegriNautics	Menlo Park, CA	80
465	ActioNet	Fairfax, VA	79
466	New Territories	N. Kingstown, RI	79
467	Xtiva Financial Systems	San Francisco, CA	79
468	icruise.com	New York, NY	79
469	PowerNet Global	Fairfield, OH	79
470	Y2Marketing	Irving, TX	79
471	Liberty Threads N.A.	Winsted, CT	79
472	Landmark Protection	San Jose, CA	79
473	Smart Carpet	Point Pleasant, NJ	78
474	Studeo	Salt Lake City, UT	77
475	MD On-Line	Parsippany, NJ	77
476	Human Resource Staffing	Saint Peters, MO	77
477	Collaborative Consulting	Woburn, MA	77
478	Appletree Answering Services	Wilmington, DE	77
479	ReNew Life Formulas	Clearwater, FL	77
480	Trancentrix	Omaha, NE	77
481	Jackson Healthcare Solutions	Alpharetta, GA	76
482	AmeriMex Communications	Roswell, GA	76
483	Vocollect	Pittsburgh, PA	76
484	Honest Tea	Bethesda, MD	76
485	Communication Technologies	Chantilly, VA	76
486	Headsets.com	San Francisco, CA	76
487	Esys	Auburn Hills, MI	76
488	A.M.E.'s Uniforms	Ft. Lauderdale, FL	75
489	OnlineBenefits	Uniondale, NY	75
490	Cairo	Chantilly, VA	75
491	CoreMedical Group	Windham, NH	75
492	Questar Capital	Ann Arbor, MI	75
493	Technology Ventures	Warren, MI	74
494	National Heritage Academies	Grand Rapids, MI	74
495	The Custom Shop Clothiers	Maumee, OH	74
496	Buck Wear	Baltimore, MD	74
497	Adenna	Santa Fe Springs, CA	74
498	Movex	Tampa, FL	74
499	SNVC	Fairfax, VA	73
500	Topaz Systems	Simi Valley, CA	73

The *Forbes* Largest Private Companies in the US

Rank	Company	Sales ($ mil.)
1	Cargill	62,900
2	Koch Industries	50,000
3	Mars	18,200
4	Publix Super Markets	16,946
5	Bechtel	16,337
6	PricewaterhouseCoopers	15,900
7	Ernst & Young	14,547
8	C&S Wholesale Grocers	13,500
9	Meijer	11,900
10	H.E. Butt Grocery	11,500
11	Swift & Co.	9,879
12	Huntsman Companies	9,252
13	Fidelity Investments	9,224
14	SemGroup	8,335
15	JM Family Enterprises	7,700
16	Enterprise Rent-A-Car	7,400
17	Science Applications Intl.	6,720
18	S.C. Johnson & Son	6,500
19	Alticor	6,200
20	Menard	6,065
21	Unisource Worldwide	5,900
22	Advance Publications	5,890
23	MDFC Holding	5,607
24	Tenaska Energy	5,591
25	Capital Group Companies	5,590
26	Marmon Group	5,560
27	Southern Wine & Spirits	5,400
28	Giant Eagle	5,100
29	MBM	4,744
30	Reyes Holdings	4,630
31	Hy-Vee	4,525
32	Platinum Equity	4,500
33	Cox Enterprises	4,474
34	Roundy's	4,383
35	Flying J	4,297
36	Hallmark Cards	4,092
37	Levi Strauss & Co.	4,091
38	QuikTrip	4,051
39	Transammonia	3,967
40	Gulf States Toyota	3,835
41	Graybar Electric	3,802
42	Stater Bros. Markets	3,800
43	Hearst	3,723
44	Schwan Food	3,700
45	Gulf Oil	3,600
46	Guardian Industries	3,560
47	Mervyn's	3,553
48	Gordon Food Service	3,450
49	Warner Music Group	3,400
50	Milliken & Co.	3,390
51	Peter Kiewit Sons'	3,375
52	Wegmans Food Markets	3,300
53	Bloomberg	3,250
54	Kohler	3,200
55	OSI Group	3,200
56	Raley's	3,200
57	Eby-Brown	3,100
58	HT Hackney	3,100
59	J.R. Simplot	3,100
60	McKinsey & Co.	3,000
61	JohnsonDiversey	2,948
62	Kinray	2,910
63	Schneider National	2,905
64	Sinclair Oil	2,900
65	A-Mark Financial	2,800
66	Perdue Farms	2,800
67	RaceTrac Petroleum	2,771
68	Nalco	2,767
69	Allegis Group	2,750
70	Keystone Foods	2,750
71	Grocers Supply	2,729
72	Booz Allen Hamilton	2,700
73	Clark Enterprises	2,700
74	Wawa	2,691
75	JF Shea	2,597
76	Golub	2,540
77	Edward Jones	2,539
78	84 Lumber	2,538
79	Colonial Group	2,500
80	Leprino Foods	2,500
81	Rockwood Specialties	2,500
82	Vistar	2,500
83	International Data Group	2,460
84	Consolidated Elec. Distributors	2,340
85	Alex Lee	2,320
86	Quality King Distributors	2,300
87	Sheetz	2,300
88	Belk	2,265
89	Hunt Consolidated/Hunt Oil	2,250
90	ContiGroup Cos.	2,200
91	Glazer's Wholesale Drug	2,200
92	H Group Holding	2,200
93	HP Hood	2,200
94	Schnuck Markets	2,200
95	Schreiber Foods	2,200
96	Services Group of America	2,200
97	Save Mart Supermarkets	2,194
98	Jeld-Wen	2,189
99	Solo Cup	2,189
100	TravelCenters of America	2,176
101	Ingram Industries	2,164
102	Springs Industries	2,162
103	CH2M Hill Companies	2,154
104	Andersen	2,150
105	F. Dohmen	2,141

SOURCE: *FORBES*; NOVEMBER 29, 2004

The *Forbes* Largest Private Companies in the US (continued)

Rank	Company	Sales ($ mil.)	Rank	Company	Sales ($ mil.)	Rank	Company	Sales ($ mil.)
106	WinCo Foods	2,139	141	Mary Kay	1,800	176	Ben E. Keith	1,515
107	Fry's Electronics	2,100	142	ABC Supply	1,793	177	Nortek Holdings	1,515
108	Gilbane	2,100	143	Vanguard Health Systems	1,783	178	Metaldyne	1,508
109	Golden State Foods	2,100	144	Hensel Phelps Construction	1,767	179	McWane	1,505
110	Carlson Cos.	2,050	145	General Parts	1,754	180	Maines Paper & Food Service	1,500
111	Cumberland Farms	2,050	146	Software House Intl.	1,739	181	Metromedia	1,500
112	Grant Thornton International	2,050	147	Walsh Group	1,725	182	National Gypsum	1,500
113	Quintiles Transnational	2,046	148	Bose	1,700	183	Southwire	1,500
114	Tishman Realty & Construction	2,035	149	Delaware North Cos.	1,700	184	Dunn Industries	1,484
115	Ergon	2,025	150	Purdue Pharma	1,700	185	Heico Cos.	1,470
116	DeBruce Grain	2,018	151	AG Spanos Cos.	1,700	186	McCarthy Building Cos.	1,459
117	Houchens Industries	2,005	152	Ashley Furniture Industries	1,680	187	Rooney Holdings	1,457
118	Aecom Technology	2,000	153	Builders FirstSource	1,675	188	Flint Ink	1,450
119	E&J Gallo Winery	2,000	154	Dunavant Enterprises	1,664	189	Purity Wholesale Grocers	1,450
120	InterTech Group	2,000	155	Sunbelt Beverage	1,660	190	Battelle Memorial Institute	1,440
121	Scoular	2,000	156	Dresser	1,657	191	Borden Chemical	1,435
122	Sammons Enterprises	1,971	157	Parsons	1,651	192	GNC	1,430
123	US Oncology	1,966	158	Hunt Construction Group	1,650	193	Black & Veatch	1,400
124	Lanoga	1,952	159	Swinerton	1,617	194	Musicland Group	1,400
125	DeMoulas Super Markets	1,950	160	Bass Pro	1,610			
						195	Rooms to Go	1,400
126	Quad/Graphics	1,950	161	G-I Holdings	1,608	196	Sierra Pacific Industries	1,400
127	Structure Tone	1,950	162	Frank Consolidated Enterprises	1,600	197	Taylor	1,400
128	Brookshire Grocery	1,944	163	Medline Industries	1,600	198	Young's Market	1,400
129	Rich Products	1,910	164	Red Apple Group	1,600	199	Wilbur-Ellis	1,366
130	Central National-Gottesman	1,900	165	Reinhart FoodService	1,600	200	National Distributing	1,360
131	Dr Pepper/7 Up Bottling Group	1,900	166	Renco Group	1,600	201	Shamrock Foods	1,354
132	Love's Travel Stops	1,900	167	Life Care Centers of America	1,598	202	Parsons Brinckerhoff	1,350
133	Follett	1,899	168	Vertis	1,586	203	Day & Zimmermann	1,346
134	Whiting-Turner Contracting	1,876	169	W.L. Gore & Associates	1,579	204	SAS Institute	1,340
135	Asplundh Tree Expert	1,838	170	Dot Foods	1,573	205	Skadden, Arps	1,330
136	UniGroup	1,809	171	Amsted Industries	1,560	206	Michael Foods	1,325
137	JM Huber	1,805	172	Di Giorgio	1,544	207	Ardent Healthcare Services	1,320
138	Bashas'	1,800	173	Discount Tire	1,541	208	CC Industries	1,320
139	Ebsco Industries	1,800	174	Foster Farms	1,520	209	Baker & Taylor	1,300
140	Kingston Technology	1,800	175	Towers Perrin	1,520	210	Burger King	1,300

The *Forbes* Largest Private Companies in the US (continued)

Rank	Company	Sales ($ mil.)
211	FHC Health Systems	1,300
212	Goodman Manufacturing	1,300
213	Pinnacle Foods Group	1,300
214	Republic Beverage	1,300
215	Hobby Lobby Stores	1,297
216	Barnes & Noble College Bookstores	1,284
217	TIC Holdings	1,281
218	National Waterworks	1,278
219	Conair	1,277
220	DPR Construction	1,270
221	Houghton Mifflin	1,264
222	Bartlett & Co.	1,260
223	KB Toys	1,250
224	SSA Marine	1,244
225	Haworth	1,230
226	Baker & McKenzie	1,228
227	Maritz	1,228
228	North Pacific Group	1,227
229	Bellco Health	1,215
230	Big Y Foods	1,210
231	Vought Aircraft Industries	1,209
232	Carpenter	1,207
233	Brightstar	1,205
234	Truman Arnold Cos.	1,205
235	Austin Industries	1,203
236	ASI	1,200
237	Boar's Head Provisions	1,200
238	Esselte	1,200
239	Holiday Cos.	1,200
240	Primus	1,200
241	Rosen's Diversified	1,200
242	Sealy	1,190
243	K-VA-T Food Stores	1,181
244	Dart Container	1,180
245	Herbalife International	1,159
246	L.L. Bean	1,150
247	Ritz Camera Centers	1,135
248	Boston Consulting Group	1,120
249	Watkins Associated Industries	1,118
250	American Tire Distributors	1,113
251	Plastech Engineered Products	1,105
252	M. A. Mortenson	1,103
253	Yates Cos.	1,101
254	D&H Distributing	1,100
255	DreamWorks SKG	1,100
256	Honickman Affiliates	1,100
257	Key Safety Systems	1,100
258	New Balance Athletic Shoe	1,100
259	World Wide Technology	1,100
260	Icon Health & Fitness	1,096
261	Printpack	1,091
262	Crown Equipment	1,090
263	Iasis Healthcare	1,088
264	Gould Paper	1,087
265	Anderson News	1,080
266	Barton Malow	1,080
267	ViewSonic	1,075
268	Soave Enterprises	1,074
269	GSC Enterprises	1,073
270	Wirtz	1,070
271	Oxbow	1,060
272	Pella	1,060
273	Academy Sports & Outdoors	1,059
274	Topa Equities	1,056
275	Remy International	1,053
276	Berwind Group	1,051
277	Boscov's Department Store	1,051
278	Concentra Operating	1,051
279	McKee Foods	1,050
280	Brasfield & Gorrie	1,046
281	Connell Limited Partnership	1,040
282	Earle M. Jorgensen	1,040
283	Jones Day	1,034
284	Ingram Entertainment Holdings	1,030
285	Arctic Slope Regional	1,029
286	Menasha	1,025
287	Meridian Automotive Systems	1,025
288	Warren Equities	1,025
289	Alsco	1,022
290	Klein Wholesale Distributors	1,022
291	MWH	1,021
292	BE&K	1,020
293	Swagelok	1,020
294	Walbridge Aldinger	1,015
295	Oxford Automotive	1,007
296	Zachry Construction	1,007
297	Columbia House	1,000
298	Genmar Holdings	1,000
299	Koch Foods	1,000
300	Levitz Home Furnishings	1,000
301	Micro Electronics	1,000
302	MTD Products	1,000
303	Peerless Importers	1,000
304	Red Chamber Group	1,000
305	Team Health	

Top 20 Universities

Rank	School
1	Harvard University
1	Princeton University
3	Yale University
4	University of Pennsylvania
5	Duke University
5	Massachusetts Institute of Technology
5	Stanford University
8	California Institute of Technology
9	Columbia University
9	Dartmouth College
11	Northwestern University
11	Washington University in St. Louis
13	Brown University
14	Cornell University
14	Johns Hopkins University
14	University of Chicago
17	Rice University
18	University of Notre Dame
18	Vanderbilt University
20	Emory University

Ranked by composite score, including such factors as graduation and retention rates, faculty resources, and student-to-faculty ratio.

SOURCE: U.S. NEWS AND WORLD REPORT, SEPTEMBER 1, 2004

Top 20 US Foundations

Rank	Name	State	Assets ($ mil.)
1	Bill & Melinda Gates Foundation	WA	26,810.5
2	Lilly Endowment Inc.	IN	10,849.4
3	The Ford Foundation	NY	10,015.6
4	J. Paul Getty Trust	CA	8,623.8
5	The Robert Wood Johnson Foundation	NJ	7,933.8
6	The David and Lucile Packard Foundation	CA	5,982.5
7	W. K. Kellogg Foundation	MI	5,729.3
8	The William and Flora Hewlett Foundation	CA	5,144.3
9	The Andrew W. Mellon Foundation	NY	4,719.6
10	John D. and Catherine T. MacArthur Foundation	IL	3,836.6
11	The Pew Charitable Trusts	PA	3,753.4
12	The Starr Foundation	NY	3,322.1
13	The Annie E. Casey Foundation	MD	3,106.5
14	The Rockefeller Foundation	NY	2,801.5
15	The California Endowment	CA	2,762.6
16	The Annenberg Foundation	PA	2,676.0
17	The Kresge Foundation	MI	2,504.6
18	Robert W. Woodruff Foundation, Inc.	GA	2,464.4
19	Charles Stewart Mott Foundation	MI	2,376.1
20	The Duke Endowment	NC	2,307.7

SOURCE: THE FOUNDATION CENTER (WWW.FOUNDATIONCENTER.ORG), OCTOBER 26, 2004

Top 20 US Law Firms

Rank	Law Firm	Gross Revenue ($ mil.)	Number of lawyers
1	Skadden, Arps, Slate, Meagher & Flom	1,330.0	1,650
2	Baker & McKenzie	1,134.0	3,053
3	Jones Day	1,035.0	1,970
4	Latham & Watkins	1,033.0	1,513
5	Sidley Austin Brown & Wood	926.0	1,421
6	Mayer, Brown, Rowe & Maw	813.0	1,249
7	White & Case	811.0	1,552
8	Weil, Gotshal & Manges	801.0	1,015
9	Shearman & Sterling	730.5	988
10	Kirkland & Ellis	725.0	854
11	Sullivan & Cromwell	687.0	647
12	McDermott, Will & Emery	668.0	901
13	O'Melveny & Myers	658.0	909
14	Gibson, Dunn & Crutcher	645.5	747
15	Morgan, Lewis & Bockius	631.0	1,063
16	Davis Polk & Wardwell	587.0	581
17	Akin Gump Strauss Hauer & Feld	585.0	832
18	Cleary, Gottlieb, Steen & Hamilton	580.0	758
19	Simpson Thacher & Bartlett	576.5	637
20	Greenberg Traurig	572.5	952

SOURCE: AMERICAN LAWYER, JULY 2004

Top 20 Tax & Accounting Firms by US Revenue

Rank	Firm	Headquarters	2003 US Revenue ($ mil.)
1	Deloitte & Touche	New York	6,511.0
2	Ernst & Young	New York	5,260.0
3	PricewaterhouseCoopers	New York	4,850.0
4	KPMG	New York	3,703.0
5	H&R Block Inc.	Kansas City, MO	3,694.5
6	RSM McGladrey/ McGladrey & Pullen	Bloomington, MN	595.9
7	Grant Thornton	Chicago	484.8
8	Jackson Hewitt Inc.	Parsippany, NJ	397.3
9	American Express Tax & Business Services	New York	367.5
10	Century Business Services	Cleveland	354.4
11	BDO Seidman	Chicago	350.0
12	Crowe Group	Indianapolis	247.3
13	BKD	Springfield, MO	215.7
14	Moss Adams	Seattle	181.0
15	Plante & Moran	Southfield, MI	174.0
16	Centerprise Advisors Inc.	Chicago	151.5
17	Clifton Gunderson	Peoria, IL	145.1
18	Virchow, Krause & Co.	Madison, WI	104.1
19	Fiducial Inc.	New York	94.5
20	Larson, Allen, Weishair	Minneapolis	90.6

SOURCE: ACCOUNTING TODAY, MARCH-APRIL 2004

Hoover's Handbook of Private Companies

The Companies

24 Hour Fitness

If you're holding too much weight, 24 Hour Fitness Worldwide has the solution. It owns and operates more than 300 fitness centers that offer aerobic, cardiovascular, and weight lifting activities. Some facilities also feature squash, racquetball, and basketball courts; swimming pools; steam and sauna rooms; tanning rooms; and whirlpools. The centers are located in 16 states in the US, as well as in Europe and Asia. Investment partnership McCown De Leeuw & Co. is the leading investor in the firm, which was founded in 1983 by CEO Mark Mastrov. The company has bought the Q Clubs and Hart's Athletic Clubs chains, which it converted to 24 Hour Fitness locations.

EXECUTIVES

Chairman and CEO: Mark S. Mastrov
EVP and CFO: Colin Heggie
VP Human Resources: Dan Abfalter
VP Sports Marketing: Kevin Steele
VP and Assistant General Counsel: Joseph Freschi
CIO: Lee Kennedy
President, 24 Hour Fitness USA: Brian Bouma
Corporate Director, Group Exercise: Donna Meyer
Director of Corporate Group Sales, Central Midwest Division: Eric Frazier
Director of Corporate Group Sales, Northern California Division: Ben Midgley
Director of Corporate Group Sales, Pacific Northwest Division: Michelle Briede
Director of Corporate Group Sales, Southern California Division: Daryl Hawkins
Corporate Account Director, Central California Division: Jad Hassan
Director of Team Sports Marketing: Chris Feder
Public Relations Manager: Shannon May
Auditors: Deloitte & Touche

LOCATIONS

HQ: 24 Hour Fitness Worldwide Inc.
12647 Alcosta Blvd., 5th Fl., San Ramon, CA 94583
Phone: 925-543-3100 **Fax:** 925-543-3229
Web: www.24hourfitness.com

24 Hour Fitness Worldwide operates clubs in China, Denmark, Germany, Norway, Singapore, South Korea, Spain, Sweden, Taiwan, Thailand, and the US.

COMPETITORS

Bally Total Fitness
Bannatyne Fitness
Curves International
Gold's Gym
Jazzercise
Lift Club
Physical Spa & Fitness
The Sports Club
World Gym
YMCA
YWCA

HISTORICAL FINANCIALS
Company Type: Private

Income Statement
FYE: December 31

	REVENUE ($ mil.)	NET INCOME ($ mil.)	NET PROFIT MARGIN	EMPLOYEES
12/03	1,000	—	—	16,000
12/02	1,000	—	—	20,000
12/01	1,029	—	—	27,000
12/00	911	—	—	26,794
12/99	736	—	—	19,500
12/98	330	—	—	15,000
12/97	262	—	—	11,500
12/96	180	—	—	—
12/95	98	—	—	—
12/94	41	—	—	—
Annual Growth	42.5%	—	—	5.7%

Revenue History

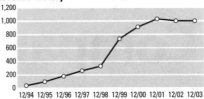

84 Lumber

With its no-frills stores (most don't have air conditioning or heating), 84 Lumber has built itself to be a low-cost provider of lumber and building materials. Through more than 450 stores, the company, which is the nation's largest privately held building-materials supplier, sells lumber, siding, drywalls, windows, and other supplies, as well as kits to make barns, play sets, decks, and even homes. Its stores are in about 35 states, mainly in the East, Southeast, and Midwest; 84 Lumber also sells products internationally. CEO Joseph Hardy Sr. founded 84 Lumber in 1956.

Founded to serve professionals, 84 Lumber expanded its product offering to attract more DIY consumers. It has since re-shifted its focus to professional builders and remodelers, who account for about 80% of sales. A sister company, 84 Components, operates 10 truss and wall-panel plants in eight states with plans to build another 10. While the professional market is less profitable and more cyclic than the DIY segment, it has the advantage of being less crowded with heavy competitors such as The Home Depot and Lowe's.

HISTORY

In 1956 Joseph Hardy Sr. opened the first 84 Lumber store in Eighty Four, Pennsylvania, a town near Pittsburgh. Hardy epitomized the bare-bones approach, keeping a tight rein on his company and paying cash for new building sites.

The strategy was successful, and for the next two decades 84 Lumber prospered, growing steadily to more than 350 stores in the early 1980s. But the 1980s brought trouble, not only for 84 Lumber but also within the Hardy family. Paul Hardy, the second-eldest son, left the company after continued sparring with Hardy Sr. Another son, Joe Hardy Jr., seemed to be his father's handpicked successor: He had worked for 84 Lumber since 1967, rising to the level of COO. However, Joe Jr. and Joe Sr. clashed and under pressure from his father, Joe Jr. resigned in 1988.

Joe Sr. also underwent a transformation during this time, opening his once-tight purse strings to buy himself an honorary English title — lord of the manor of Henley-in-Arden — for about $170,000. In 1987 he paid $3.1 million to purchase a retreat in southwestern Pennsylvania, the Nemacolin Woodlands. He placed the renovation of the resort (at the cost of some $100 million) in the hands of his daughter Maggie, who was in her early twenties at the time.

While Hardy was transforming, so was 84 Lumber. The company started moving away from its traditional approach in an attempt to gain a piece of the budding yuppie market. This approach, along with an ill-timed expansion, led to a loss of customers and falling profits. Earnings fell from $52 million in 1987 to $22 million in 1989.

84 Lumber started to right itself in 1991. Hardy transferred stock to Maggie, his heir apparent. While running luxury resort Nemacolin Woodlands, Maggie strove to emulate her father's business style, including obscenity-laced staff meetings. 84 Lumber shut stores and returned to its basic operating scheme as a low-cost provider of lumber in small towns. The company also added do-it-yourself (DIY) building kits for kitchens and baths that year, and it expanded that DIY concept a year later in 1992, with home building kits.

Under new president Maggie, 84 Lumber's sales topped the $1 billion mark in 1993 and the company refocused on its professional contractor customers. The company first shipped its building materials internationally in 1996 (to New Zealand) and added customers in China, Korea, Switzerland, and Australia in the late 1990s.

In 1997 84 Lumber opened Maggie's Building Solutions Showroom, a 7,500-sq.-ft. remodeling center featuring upscale home products. By 1997 84 Lumber was the US's largest dealer of building supplies to professional contractors.

In a further effort to attract contractors' business, 84 Lumber introduced a builder financing program in 1999 and began converting some of its stores to an 84-Plus store format, in which its traditional lumberyard setup is matched with a 10,000-sq.-ft. hardware store.

In an effort to reach more professionals, the company increased outside sales staff by 25% in 2000. The next year the company bought 15 stores from Payless Cashways, which went out of business, a move that extended 84 Lumber's operations to Oklahoma, Nevada, and Nebraska.

The company added two red-letter dates to its company history in 2002. On April 3 of that year, 84 Lumber opened 20 new stores throughout the US, increasing its store count by 5%. Thanks in part to added revenue from those stores, on December 7, 2002, company cash registers went past the $2 billion mark in sales for the year.

In June 2004, 84 Lumber opened a distribution center in Auburn, New York. The facility supplies vinyl siding and roofing materials to stores in Rochester and Syracuse.

EXECUTIVES

CEO: Joseph A. Hardy Sr., age 81
President: Maggie Hardy Magerko, age 38
COO: Bill Myrick
CFO: Dan Wallach
VP Human Resources: Steve Cherry

LOCATIONS

HQ: 84 Lumber Company
1019 Rte. 519, Eighty Four, PA 15330
Phone: 724-228-8820   **Fax:** 724-228-8058
Web: www.84lumber.com

84 Lumber operates stores in about 35 states and sells its products in Australia, China, South Korea, and Switzerland.

PRODUCTS/OPERATIONS

Selected Products
Doors
Drywall
Flooring
Insulation
Lumber
Plywood
Project kits
  Barns
  Decks
  Garages
  Houses
  Kitchens
  Play sets
Roofing
Siding
Skylights
Trim
Trusses
Ventilation
Windows

COMPETITORS

Ace Hardware
Builders FirstSource
Building Materials Holding
Carter Lumber
Contractors' Warehouse
Cox Lumber
Do it Best
Foxworth-Galbraith Lumber
Futter Lumber
Grossman's
Home Depot
Lanoga
Lowe's
McCoy
Menard
Stock Building Supply
Sutherland Lumber
TruServ
Wolohan Lumber

HISTORICAL FINANCIALS

Company Type: Private

Income Statement   FYE: December 31

	REVENUE ($ mil.)	NET INCOME ($ mil.)	NET PROFIT MARGIN	EMPLOYEES
12/03	2,584	—	—	6,500
12/02	2,177	—	—	5,800
12/01	1,904	—	—	5,400
12/00	1,850	—	—	5,000
12/99	1,800	—	—	4,500
12/98	1,625	—	—	4,400
12/97	1,600	—	—	4,815
12/96	1,590	—	—	4,500
12/95	1,275	—	—	3,500
12/94	1,275	—	—	3,500
Annual Growth	8.2%	—	—	7.1%

Revenue History

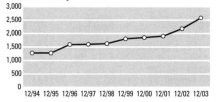

A&E Television

A&E Television Networks is defying the notion that TV rots the brain. It offers a smorgasbord of programming in history, the arts, current events, popular culture, reality, and nature through its two main cable networks: A&E (more than 88 million subscribers) and The History Channel (more than 86 million subscribers). A&E Television also operates three digital cable channels (Biography Channel, History Channel International, and The History Channel en Español) and a handful of Web sites. Internationally, A&E's channels reach about 100 million subscribers. A&E is a joint venture of media giants Hearst (37.5%), Walt Disney's Disney ABC Cable (37.5%), and General Electric's NBC (25%).

A&E has turned its *Biography* into a media juggernaut, expanding into videos, books, and magazines. In addition, the company plans to expand its Internet-related activities, which include a handful of Web sites (biography.com, mysteries.com, historytravel.com); it acquired Genealogy.com in 2001.

In spite of its success with *Biography*, A&E's flagship cable channel has suffered from lagging ratings. It lost its stable *Law and Order* syndicated program to competitor TNT and replaced it with rescue drama *Third Watch*, which has attracted less than stellar ratings. The network has also been unsuccessful with its original programming (*Nero Wolf*, *100 Centre Street*), which won critical acclaim but few viewers. It plans to push further into more contemporary, lifestyle programming with about 30 new shows including *Airline*, a reality show about Southwest Airlines, and *Growing Up Gotti*, about the late mafia kingpin John Gotti's family.

EXECUTIVES

President and CEO: Nickolas Davatzes
EVP Advertising Sales: Mel Berning
EVP Sales and Marketing: Whitney Goit II
EVP Finance and CFO: Gerard Gruosso
President, A&E Network: Abbe Raven
President, The History Channel: Daniel E. Davids
SVP and General Manager, The Biography Channel: Thomas Heymann
SVP and General Manager, International: Maria Komodikis
SVP Enterprises: Steve Ronson
SVP Human Resources: Rosalind Clay Carter
SVP Marketing, A&E Network: Artie Scheff
SVP Marketing, The History Channel: Michael Mohamad
SVP Programming, A&E Network: Robert DiBitetto, age 46
SVP Programming, The History Channel: Charles Maday
SVP and General Counsel: Anne Atkinson
VP Financial Planning: Art Vomvas
VP Legal and Business Affairs: Stephen Stander
VP Public Affairs and Communication: Michael Feeney

LOCATIONS

HQ: A&E Television Networks
235 E. 45th St., New York, NY 10017
Phone: 212-210-1400   **Fax:** 212-850-9370
Web: www.aande.com

PRODUCTS/OPERATIONS

Operating Units
A&E Network
AETN Consumer Products (home videos, magazines, CDs, and e-commerce)
AETN International
The Biography Channel
The History Channel
The History Channel en Español
History Channel International

COMPETITORS

ABC
Advance Publications
CPB
Crown Media
Discovery Communications
Fox Entertainment
HBO
Lifetime
National Geographic
NBC
NBC Universal
PBS
Rainbow Media
Turner Broadcasting
Viacom

HISTORICAL FINANCIALS

Company Type: Joint venture

Income Statement   FYE: December 31

	REVENUE ($ mil.)	NET INCOME ($ mil.)	NET PROFIT MARGIN	EMPLOYEES
12/03	886	—	—	500
12/02	814	—	—	500
12/01	772	—	—	600
12/00	753	—	—	600
12/99	499	—	—	570
12/98	394	—	—	450
12/97	349	—	—	425
12/96	304	—	—	400
12/95	284	—	—	315
12/94	214	—	—	260
Annual Growth	17.1%	—	—	7.5%

Revenue History

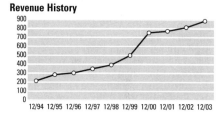

AARP

AARP is gearing up for the geezer boom. Open to anyone age 50 or older (dues are $12.50 per year), the not-for-profit organization is the largest organization of older adults in the US with more than 35 million members and is also the largest lobbyist for the elderly (it spends about $57 million on lobbying and related activities). On a mission to enhance the quality of life for older Americans, AARP is active in four areas: information and education, community service, advocacy, and member services. It also publishes the monthly *AARP Bulletin* and has combined its bimonthly *Modern Maturity* and *My Generation* magazines into a single publication, *AARP The Magazine*.

AARP may not be the most exclusive club around, but it is one of the most powerful. As the largest advocacy group in the US, the organization has a loud (and sometimes feared) voice on Capitol Hill. Its policy recommendations address such issues as the national budget, Medicare, elder abuse, and Social Security.

AARP is attempting to transform itself by adapting to its changing demographics. The organization has initiated a $100 million, five-year marketing plan to attract aging baby boomers who are becoming eligible for membership.

AARP disseminates information in a variety of formats (a Web site, public policy agendas, and radio and TV spots) and pursues educational and research efforts through the AARP Andrus Foundation, the Research Information Center, and the Public Policy Institute. Members are eligible for services including savings on prescription drugs, travel, investment opportunities, and health, life, and auto insurance. Retired educators who join the National Retired Teachers Association (a division of AARP) can receive both AARP services and other benefits designed specifically for them.

HISTORY

Ethel Andrus, a retired Los Angeles high school principal who founded the National Retired Teachers Association (NRTA) in 1947, founded the American Association of Retired Persons (AARP) in 1958 with the help of Leonard Davis, a New York insurance salesman who had helped her find an underwriter for the NRTA. The new organization's goal: to "enhance the quality of life" for older Americans and "improve the image of aging."

Andrus offered members the same low rates for health and accident insurance provided to NRTA members. She also started publishing AARP's bimonthly magazine, *Modern Maturity*, in 1958. The organization's first local chapter opened in Youngstown, Arizona, in 1960. Still an insurance man, Davis formed Colonial Penn Insurance in 1963 to take over the AARP account. Andrus led AARP and its increasingly powerful lobby for the elderly until her death in 1967.

With criticism of Colonial Penn mounting in the 1970s (critics charged the organization was little more than a front for the insurance company), Prudential won AARP's insurance business in 1979. The NRTA merged with AARP in 1982, and the following year it lowered the membership eligibility age from 55 to 50. The organization continued to expand its offerings, adding an auto club and financial products such as mutual funds and expanded insurance policies. The organization also started a federal credit union for members in 1988, but despite rosy projections, it ceased operations two years later.

AARP forked over $135 million to the IRS in 1993 as part of a settlement regarding the tax status of profits from some of its activities, but the dispute remained unresolved. AARP switched insurance providers again in 1996 (New York Life) and started offering discounted legal services. Also that year, AARP said it would let HMOs offer managed-care services to members. The plan drew objections over its potential violation of Medicare anti-kickback laws, and AARP developed a revised payment plan in 1997.

AARP's image was bruised in 1998 when Dale Van Atta wrote a scathing account of the organization, *Trust Betrayed: Inside the AARP*. The book accused the organization of operating out of lavish accommodations, acting as a shill for businesses to hawk their wares, and concealing a drop in membership. Also in 1998, recognizing that nearly a third of its members were working, the organization dropped the American Association of Retired Persons moniker and began to refer to itself by the AARP abbreviation.

To end the long-running dispute with the IRS, AARP reached a settlement over its alleged profit-making enterprises by creating a new taxable subsidiary called AARP Services in 1999. The following year AARP initiated a five-year plan to attract aging baby boomers. AARP launched its new *My Generation* magazine 2001. In 2003 the organization combined *My Generation* with its *Modern Maturity* magazine to form a single publication: *AARP The Magazine*.

EXECUTIVES

CEO: William D. (Bill) Novelli
President: Marie F. Smith
COO: Thomas C. Nelson
CFO: Robert R. Hagans Jr., age 49
VP Membership and Member Services:
  Charles J. Mendoza
President, AARP Services: Dawn Sweeney
CIO: John Sullivan
Chief Communications Officer: Christine Donohoo
Associate Executive Director Operations:
  Richard Henry
Associate Executive Director State and National Initiatives: Christopher W. (Chris) Hansen
Director Policy and Strategy: John Rother
General Counsel: Joan Wise
Chief Sponsor and Champion, People Strategy:
  Ellie Hollander

LOCATIONS

HQ: AARP
  601 E. St. NW, Washington, DC 20049
Phone: 202-434-2277   **Fax:** 202-434-6548
Web: www.aarp.org

AARP has offices in all 50 states, the District of Columbia, Puerto Rico, and the Virgin Islands.

PRODUCTS/OPERATIONS

2003 Sales

	$ mil.	% of total
Royalties	300.4	39
Membership dues	210.8	27
Advertising	77.6	10
Federal & other grants	76.2	10
Investment income	60.3	8
Program income	20.8	3
Other	23.5	3
Total	**769.6**	**100**

Selected Operations and Programs
55 ALIVE/Mature Driving
AARP Andrus Foundation (gerontology research)
AARP Bulletin (monthly news update)
AARP Legal Services Network
AARP Services (taxable product management, marketing & e-commerce subsidiary)
AARP The Magazine (bimonthly magazine)
Financial Planning
Mature Focus Radio (daily news program)
National Retired Teachers Association
Public Policy Institute
Research Information Center
Senior Community Service Employment Program
Tax-Aide

HISTORICAL FINANCIALS
Company Type: Association

Income Statement
FYE: December 31

	REVENUE ($ mil.)	NET INCOME ($ mil.)	NET PROFIT MARGIN	EMPLOYEES
12/03	770	—	—	—
12/02	636	—	—	1,800
12/01	595	—	—	1,800
12/00	580	—	—	2,000
12/99	486	—	—	2,000
12/98	541	—	—	2,000
12/97	529	—	—	1,900
12/96	475	—	—	1,850
12/95	506	—	—	1,800
12/94	469	—	—	1,752
Annual Growth	5.7%	—	—	0.3%

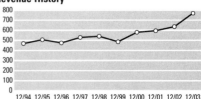

Revenue History

ABC Supply

American Builders & Contractors Supply Co. (which operates as ABC Supply) has put roofs over millions of heads. A leading supplier of roofing, siding, windows, and related builder's supplies, ABC Supply has more than 250 outlets in some 45 states. It carries its own brand of products, Amcraft, and it offers doors, windows, tools and such from vendors. In 2002 the company purchased about 30 distribution centers, primarily in the Western US, from Wm. Cameron & Co. ABC Supply, which markets its products mostly to small and medium-sized professional contractors, was founded in 1982 by CEO Kenneth Hendricks. Hendricks and his wife, EVP Diane, own the company.

In July 2004 ABC Supply acquired Paco Building Supply, which distributes exterior siding and windows in Missouri, and Mansion Supply, a New Jersey window company.

EXECUTIVES

Chairman and CEO: Kenneth A. (Ken) Hendricks, age 63, $1,861,538 pay
President, COO, and Director: David A. Luck, age 54, $1,230,506 pay
CFO, Treasurer, and Director: Kendra A. Story, age 44, $502,273 pay
EVP, Secretary, and Director: Diane M. Hendricks, age 56, $385,577 pay
SVP Manufacturing Operations: Robert Bartels, age 55, $481,504 pay
VP Branch Operations: Kevin Hendricks, age 39
VP Strategic Marketing and Planning: Keith Rozolis, age 44
MIS Director: Kathy Murray
Director Human Resources: Lisa Indgjer, age 40
Development Supervisor: John Homer
Auditors: Ernst & Young LLP

LOCATIONS

HQ: American Builders & Contractors Supply Co., Inc.
1 ABC Pkwy., Beloit, WI 53511
Phone: 608-362-7777 **Fax:** 608-362-2717
Web: www.abc-supply.com

PRODUCTS/OPERATIONS

2003 Sales

	$ mil.	% of total
Steep slope	1,068.3	60
Low slope	324.5	18
Siding	259.9	14
Windows	80.1	5
Other	59.7	3
Total	**1,792.5**	**100**

COMPETITORS

Bradco Supply
Eagle Supply Group
Emco Corporation
Georgia-Pacific Corporation
Guardian Building Products
Huttig Building Products
North Pacific Group
Pacific Coast Building Products
PrimeSource Building

HISTORICAL FINANCIALS

Company Type: Private

Income Statement
FYE: December 31

	REVENUE ($ mil.)	NET INCOME ($ mil.)	NET PROFIT MARGIN	EMPLOYEES
12/03	1,793	67	3.8%	4,128
12/02	1,425	41	2.9%	3,711
12/01	1,382	42	3.1%	3,188
12/00	1,239	14	1.1%	3,121
12/99	1,198	7	0.6%	3,239
12/98	1,162	(3)	—	3,100
Annual Growth	**9.1%**	**—**	**—**	**5.9%**

2003 Year-End Financials

Debt ratio: 205.1% Current ratio: 2.39
Return on equity: 57.1% Long-term debt ($ mil.): 275
Cash ($ mil.): 6

Net Income History

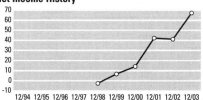

Academy

Academy Sports & Outdoors is near the head of the class among sporting goods retailers. The company is one of the top full-line sporting goods chains in the US with over 70 stores located throughout the South and Southwest. Academy's low-frills stores carry clothing, shoes, and equipment for almost any sport and outdoor activity, including camping, hunting, fishing, and boating. The company dates back to a San Antonio tire shop opened by Max Gochman in 1938. The business moved into military surplus items and during the 1980s began focusing on sports and outdoor merchandise. The Gochman family still owns Academy.

EXECUTIVES

Chairman, President, and CEO: David Gochman
EVP and COO: James Pierce
EVP, Apparel: Robert Frennea
EVP, Footwear: Beth Menuet
EVP, Hardgoods: A. J. Blanchard
VP and CFO: Michael Ondruch
VP and General Counsel: Elise Neal
VP, Administrative Resources: Sylvia Barrera-Moses
VP, Information Technology: Mike Marrie
VP, Logistics and Distribution: Kal Patel
VP, Marketing: Casey Ramm
VP, Risk Management and Chief Risk Officer: David Pittman
VP, Store Operations: Allen McConnell
Senior Controller: Gary Winkler

LOCATIONS

HQ: Academy Sports & Outdoors, Ltd.
1800 N. Mason Rd., Katy, TX 77449
Phone: 281-646-5200 **Fax:** 281-646-5204
Web: www.academy.com

Academy Sports & Outdoors operates stores in Alabama, Arkansas, Florida, Louisiana, Mississippi, Oklahoma, Tennessee, and Texas.

COMPETITORS

Athlete's Foot
Bass Pro Shops
Finish Line
Foot Locker
Hibbett Sporting Goods
Kmart
REI
Sears
Sports Authority
Target
Wal-Mart

HISTORICAL FINANCIALS

Company Type: Private

Income Statement
FYE: January 31

	REVENUE ($ mil.)	NET INCOME ($ mil.)	NET PROFIT MARGIN	EMPLOYEES
1/02	775	—	—	5,000
1/01	720	—	—	4,748
1/00	612	—	—	4,745
1/99	499	—	—	4,500
1/98	435	—	—	3,200
1/97	367	—	—	2,800
1/96	315	—	—	2,500
1/95	268	—	—	1,700
1/94	210	—	—	1,700
1/93	154	—	—	—
Annual Growth	**19.7%**	**—**	**—**	**14.4%**

Revenue History

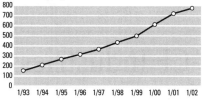

Ace Hardware

Luckily, Ace has John Madden up its sleeve. Despite the growth of warehouse-style competitors, Ace Hardware has remained a household name, thanks to ads featuring Madden, a former Oakland Raiders football coach and TV commentator. By sales the company is the #1 hardware cooperative in the US, ahead of Do It Best, which operates about 4,400 member-owned stores in the US and more than 40 other countries. Ace dealer-owners operate more than 4,800 Ace Hardware stores throughout the US and in about 70 other countries. From about 25 warehouses Ace distributes such products as electrical and plumbing supplies, garden equipment, hand tools, housewares, and power tools.

It also makes its own brand of paint and offers thousands of other Ace-brand products. Ace additionally provides training programs and advertising campaigns for its dealers.

Challenged by big-box chains such as The Home Depot and Lowe's, Ace has unveiled its Next Generation store concept, which calls for signage with detailed product descriptions and different flooring to set off departments, among other features. Ace dealers own the company and receive dividends from Ace's profits.

In its most ambitious expansion plan to date, Ace Hardware will add 150 to 200 stores. The company is also increasing the size of its stores. The average store is 10,000 square feet, but newer stores are about 14,000 square feet.

HISTORY

A group of Chicago-area hardware dealers — William Stauber, Richard Hesse, Gern Lindquist, and Oscar Fisher — decided in 1924 to pool their hardware buying and promotional costs. In 1928 the group incorporated as Ace Stores, named in honor of the superior WWI fliers dubbed aces. Hesse became president the following year, retaining that position for the next 44 years. The company also opened its first warehouse in 1929, and by 1933 it had 38 dealers.

The organization had 133 dealers in seven states by 1949. In 1953 Ace began to allow dealers to buy stock in the company through the Ace Perpetuation Plan. During the 1960s Ace expanded into the South and West, and by 1969 it had opened distribution centers in Georgia and California — its first such facilities outside Chicago. In 1968 it opened its first international store in Guam.

By the early 1970s the do-it-yourself market began to surge as inflation pushed up plumber and electrician fees. As the market grew, large home center chains gobbled up market share from independent dealers such as those franchised through Ace. In response, Ace and its dealers became a part of a growing trend in the hardware industry — cooperatives.

Hesse sold the company to its dealers in 1973 for $6 million (less than half its book value), and the following year Ace began operating as a cooperative. Hesse stepped down in 1973. In 1976 the dealers took full control when the company's first Board of Dealer-Directors was elected.

After signing up a number of dealers in the eastern US, Ace had dealers in all 50 states by 1979. The co-op opened a plant to make paint in Matteson, Illinois, in 1984. By 1985 Ace had reached $1 billion in sales and had initiated its Store of the Future Program, allowing dealers to borrow up to $200,000 to upgrade their stores and conduct market analyses. Former head coach John Madden of the National Football League's Oakland Raiders signed on as Ace's mouthpiece in 1988.

A year later the co-op began to test ACENET, a computer network that allowed Ace dealers to check inventory, send and receive e-mail, make special purchase requests, and keep up with prices on commodity items such as lumber. In 1990 Ace established an International Division to handle its overseas stores. (It had been exporting products since 1975.) EVP and COO David Hodnik became president in 1995. That year the co-op added a net of 67 stores, including a three-store chain in Russia. Expanding further internationally, Ace signed a five-year joint-supply agreement in 1996 with Canadian lumber and hardware retailer Beaver Lumber. Hodnik added CEO to his title in 1996.

Ace fell further behind its old rival, True Value, in 1997 when ServiStar Coast to Coast and True Value merged to form TruServ, a hardware giant that operated more than 10,000 outlets at the completion of the merger.

Late in 1997 Ace launched an expansion program in Canada. (The co-op already operated distribution centers in Ontario and Calgary.) In 1999 Ace merged its lumber and building materials division with Builder Marts of America to form a dealer-owned buying group to supply about 2,700 retailers. In 2000, Ace gained 208 member outlet stores, but saw 279 member outlets terminated. The next year it gained 220, but lost 255.

Sodisco-Howden bought all the shares of Ace Hardware Canada in February 2003. To better serve international members, Ace opened its first international buying office, in Hong Kong, in April 2004.

EXECUTIVES

Chairman: J. Thomas Glenn
President and CEO: David F. Hodnik
EVP: Rita D. Kahle
EVP, Retail: Ray A. Griffith
SVP, International and Technology: Paul M. Ingevaldson
SVP, Retail Support and Logistics: David F. Myer
VP and Controller: Ronald J. (Ron) Knutson, age 39
VP, Human Resources: Jimmy Alexander
VP, Information Technology: Michael J. Altendorf
VP, Marketing, Advertising, Retail Development, and Company Stores: Michael C. Bodzewski, age 53
VP, Merchandising: Lori L. Bossmann
VP, Retail Operations: Kenneth L. (Ken) Nichlos
VP, Retail Support - East: Daniel C. Prochaska
VP, Retail Support - West: William J. Bauman
Treasurer: Sandy Brandt
Managing Director, International Department: Murray Armstrong
Director, Application Development: Jay Heubner
Director, International Licensees: Maurice Ademe
Director, People Development and Learning Systems: Ron Wagner
Director, Retail Operations - Midwest Division: Bob Guido
Manager, Advertising: Frank Rothing
Manager, Corporate Communications and Public Relations: Paula Erickson, age 34
General Counsel: Donna Flenard
Customer Service: Tim Schubert

LOCATIONS

HQ: Ace Hardware Corporation
2200 Kensington Ct., Oak Brook, IL 60523
Phone: 630-990-6600   **Fax:** 630-990-6838
Web: www.acehardware.com

PRODUCTS/OPERATIONS

2003 Sales

	$ mil.	% of total
Wholesale	3,094	98
Paint manufacturing	17	1
Other	48	1
Total	**3,159**	**100**

COMPETITORS

84 Lumber	Lowe's
Akzo Nobel	McCoy
Benjamin Moore	Menard
Building Materials Holding	Northern Tool
	Réno-Dépôt
Costco Wholesale	Sears
Do it Best	Sherwin-Williams
Fastenal	Stock Building Supply
Grossman's	Sutherland Lumber
Handy Hardware Wholesale	TruServ
	United Hardware Distributing
Home Depot	
ICI American	Wal-Mart
Kmart	Wolohan Lumber
Lanoga	

HISTORICAL FINANCIALS

Company Type: Cooperative

Income Statement
FYE: Saturday nearest December 31

	REVENUE ($ mil.)	NET INCOME ($ mil.)	NET PROFIT MARGIN	EMPLOYEES
12/03	3,159	101	3.2%	5,100
12/02	3,029	82	2.7%	5,268
12/01	2,894	73	2.5%	5,229
12/00	2,945	80	2.7%	5,513
12/99	3,182	93	2.9%	5,180
12/98	3,120	88	2.8%	4,672
12/97	2,907	76	2.6%	4,685
12/96	2,743	72	2.6%	4,352
12/95	2,436	64	2.6%	3,917
12/94	2,326	65	2.8%	3,664
Annual Growth	3.5%	5.1%	—	3.7%

2003 Year-End Financials

Debt ratio: 54.3%   Current ratio: 1.38
Return on equity: 35.2%   Long-term debt ($ mil.): 159
Cash ($ mil.): 42

Net Income History

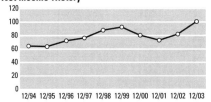

ACF Industries

ACF Industries (ACF) has been around for more than a century, but it is still on track. The company makes railroad tank and covered hopper cars (a category that it revolutionized with its Center Flow design). Through ACF Acceptance, the company also provides financing for its customers. ACF Industries has manufacturing operations in Pennsylvania and West Virginia. Formed in 1899 and originally known as American Car & Foundry, ACF is the oldest builder of railcars in the US and is owned by billionaire financier Carl Icahn, who also is ACF's chairman.

EXECUTIVES

Chairman: Carl C. Icahn, age 68
President: Roger Wynkoop
VP and Controller: Harry McKinstry
VP, Finance: Laura Parli
VP, Marketing: Brian Evdoe
Senior Director of Human Resources: Gary Rager

LOCATIONS

HQ: ACF Industries, Inc.
620 N. 2nd St., St. Charles, MO 63301
Phone: 636-940-5000   **Fax:** 636-940-5020
Web: www.acfindustries.com

ACF Industries has manufacturing plants in Milton, Pennsylvania and Huntington, West Virginia.

PRODUCTS/OPERATIONS

Selected Products
Covered hopper cars
Tank cars

COMPETITORS

Duchossois Industries
GATX
Greenbrier
Johnstown America
L. B. Foster
Marmon Group
Meridian Rail
Miner Enterprises
Pioneer Railcorp
Siemens Transportation Systems
Trinity Industries

HISTORICAL FINANCIALS

Company Type: Private

Income Statement
FYE: December 31

	REVENUE ($ mil.)	NET INCOME ($ mil.)	NET PROFIT MARGIN	EMPLOYEES
12/02	600	—	—	2,800
12/01	620	—	—	3,000
12/00	623	—	—	2,900
12/99	604	—	—	2,700
12/98	638	—	—	2,700
12/97	891	—	—	2,600
12/96	720	—	—	2,200
12/95	550	—	—	2,400
12/94	430	—	—	2,200
Annual Growth	4.3%	—	—	3.1%

Revenue History

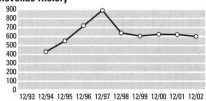

Acosta Sales

Acosta Sales Company helps food service and grocery businesses jockey for position. Some 1,600 US consumer products manufacturers call on Acosta to help them position their products in grocery and convenience stores, drug stores, and mass merchandisers in the US, and food service distributors and operators in Canada. Acosta specializes in inventory and merchandising services and business consulting for promotions, marketing campaigns, and sales.

EXECUTIVES

Chairman and CEO: Gary Chartrand
President and Chief Customer Officer: Jack Laurendeau
CFO: Gregory Delaney
EVP, Business Development: Nick Mills
EVP, Strategic Initiatives: Jack Parker
EVP, Marketing and Client Services: John Streurer
President, Operations: Robert Hill
General Counsel: Drew Prusiecki

LOCATIONS

HQ: Acosta Sales Company, Inc.
6600 Corporate Center Pkwy.,
Jacksonville, FL 32216
Phone: 904-281-9800   **Fax:** 904-281-9966
Web: www.acosta.com

Advance Publications

Advance Publications gets its marching orders from the printed page. A leading US newspaper publisher, Advance owns some 25 daily newspapers around the country, including *The Star-Ledger* (New Jersey), *The Cleveland Plain Dealer,* and its namesake *Staten Island Advance.* It also owns American City Business Journals (more than 40 weekly papers) and Parade Publications (*Parade Magazine* Sunday insert). Advance is a top magazine publisher in the US (along with Time, Inc.) through units Condé Nast Publications, with its popular titles such as *Allure, Glamour,* and *Vanity Fair,* and trade journal publisher Fairchild Publications (*Women's Wear Daily*). Samuel "Si" Newhouse Jr. and his brother, Donald, own the company.

Aside from print publishing, Advance is a major online publisher with 10 regional news Web sites. Its CondéNet unit runs Web versions of Condé Nast's magazines and other Internet properties, including Epicurious (food and dining) and Concierge (travel). The company also has stakes in cable TV systems (33%, with Time Warner), broadband ISP Road Runner (9%), and cable broadcaster Discovery Communications (about 25%).

Advance has boosted its magazine portfolio, acquiring The New York Times Company's Golf Properties unit (*Golf Digest*), Miami-based Condé Nast Americas (Spanish language versions of US magazines), and PRIMEDIA's *Modern Bride.*

HISTORY

Solomon Neuhaus (later Samuel I. Newhouse) got started in the newspaper business after dropping out of school at age 13. He went to work at the *Bayonne Times* in New Jersey and was put in charge of the failing newspaper in 1911; he managed to turn the paper around within a year. In 1922 he bought the *Staten Island Advance* (founded in 1886) and formed the Staten Island Advance Company in 1924. After buying up more papers, he changed the name of the company to Advance Publications in 1949. By the 1950s the company had local papers in New York, New Jersey, and Alabama.

In 1959 Newhouse bought magazine publisher Condé Nast as an anniversary gift for his wife. (He joked that she had asked for a fashion magazine, so he bought her *Vogue.*) His publishing empire continued to grow with the addition of the *Times-Picayune* (New Orleans) in 1962 and *The Cleveland Plain Dealer* in 1967. In 1976 the company paid more than $300 million for Booth Newspapers, publisher of eight Michigan papers and *Parade Magazine.*

Newhouse died in 1979, leaving his sons Si and Donald to run the company, which encompassed more than 30 newspapers, a half-dozen magazines, and 15 cable systems. The next year Advance bought book publishing giant Random House from RCA. Si resurrected the Roaring Twenties standard *Vanity Fair* in 1983 and added *The New Yorker* under the Condé Nast banner in 1985. The Newhouses scored a victory over the IRS in 1990 after a long-running court battle involving inheritance taxes. Condé Nast bought Knapp Publications (*Architectural Digest*) in 1993 and Advance later acquired American City Business Journals in 1995.

In 1998 the company sold the increasingly unprofitable Random House to Bertelsmann for about $1.2 billion. It later bought hallmark Internet magazine *Wired* (though it passed on Wired Ventures' Internet operations). That year revered *New Yorker* editor Tina Brown, credited with jazzing up the publication's content and increasing its circulation, left the magazine; staff writer and Pulitzer Prize winner David Remnick was named as Brown's replacement.

In 1999 Advance joined Donrey Media Group (now called Stephens Media Group), E.W. Scripps, Hearst Corporation, and MediaNews Group to purchase the online classified advertising network AdOne (later named PowerOne Media). It also bought Walt Disney's trade publishing unit, Fairchild Publications, for $650 million. In 2000 the company shifted *Details* from Condé Nast to Fairchild and relaunched the magazine as a fashion publication. Later that year the company announced it would begin creating Web versions of its popular magazine titles.

In 2001 Condé Nast bought a majority stake in Miami-based Ideas Publishing Group (Spanish language versions of US magazines; its name was later changed to Condé Nast Americas). Also that year Advance bought four golf magazines, including *Golf Digest,* from the New York Times Company for $430 million. Condé Nast picked up *Modern Bride* magazine from PRIMEDIA in 2002 for $52 million.

Richard Diamond, a Newhouse relative who'd been publisher of the *Staten Island Advance* since 1979, died in 2004.

EXECUTIVES

Chairman and CEO; Chairman, Condé Nast Publications: Samuel I. (Si) Newhouse Jr., age 74
President: Donald E. Newhouse, age 72
COO; CEO, Condé Nast: Charles H. (Chuck) Townsend, age 59
CFO, Advance Media Group; EVP and COO, Condé Nast: John Bellando, age 47
EVP and President, Condé Nast Media Group: Richard D. Beckman, age 42
Chairman and Editorial Director, Golf Digest Companies: Jerry Tarde
Chairman and CEO, American City Business Journals: Ray Shaw
Chairman, CEO, and Publisher, Parade Publications: Walter Anderson
President and CEO, Golf Digest Companies: Mitchell Fox
President and CEO, Fairchild Publications: Mary G. Berner
President and Creative Director, Advance.net: Jeff Jarvis
President, Advance Internet: Peter Weinberger
President, CondéNet: Sarah Chubb
Publisher, Style.com: Catherine Jaccodine
SVP Consumer Marketing; SVP Circulation, Condé Nast Publications: Peter A. Armour
VP Marketing, Staten Island Advance: Jack Furnari
Comptroller, Staten Island Advance: Arthur Silverstein
Director of Retail, Classified, and National Sales, Staten Island Advance: Gary Cognetta

LOCATIONS

HQ: Advance Publications, Inc.
950 Fingerboard Rd., Staten Island, NY 10305
Phone: 212-286-2860   **Fax:** 718-981-1456
Web: www.advance.net

PRODUCTS/OPERATIONS

Broadcasting and Communications
Cartoonbank.com (database of cartoons from *The New Yorker*)
Discovery Communications (25%, cable TV channel)
Newhouse Broadcasting (33%, cable TV joint venture with Time Warner)
Newhouse News Service
Religion News Service
Road Runner (9%, broadband Internet service)

Magazine Publishing
Condé Nast Publications
  Allure
  Architectural Digest
  Bon Appetit
  Bride's
  Condé Nast Traveler
  Glamour
  Gourmet
  GQ
  House & Garden
  Lucky
  Modern Bride
  The New Yorker
  Self
  Teen Vogue
  Vanity Fair
  Vogue
  Wired
Fairchild Publications
  Details
  Jane
  Supermarket News
  W
  Women's Wear Daily
The Golf Digest Companies
  Golf Digest
  Golf for Women
  Golf World
  Golf World Business

Newspaper Publishing
American City Business Journals (41 weekly titles in 22 states)
  Street & Smith's Sports Business Group
Newhouse Newspapers (25 papers across the US)
  The Birmingham News (Alabama)
  The Oregonian (Portland)
  The Plain Dealer (Cleveland)
  The Star-Ledger (Newark, NJ)
  Staten Island Advance (New York)
  The Times-Picayune (New Orleans)
Parade Publications

Online Publishing
Advance Internet
  al.com (Alabama)
  cleveland.com
  MassLive.com (Massachusetts)
  MLive (Michigan)
  NJ.com (New Jersey)
  NOLA.com (New Orleans)
  OregonLive.com
  PennLive.com (Pennsylvania)
  SILive (New York)
  Syracuse.com (New York)
CondéNet
  Concierge (travel information)
  Epicurious (recipes and fine dining)
  Style.com (fashion and beauty)

COMPETITORS

American Express	Martha Stewart Living
American Media	McClatchy Company
Crain Communications	Meredith
Dow Jones	New York Times
E. W. Scripps	News Corp.
Essence Communications	Newsweek
F+W Publications	North Jersey Media
Forbes	PRIMEDIA
Freedom Communications	Reader's Digest
Gannett	Reed Elsevier Group
Gruner + Jahr	Rodale
Hachette Filipacchi Médias	Time
Hearst	Tribune
Johnson Publishing	Washington Post
Knight-Ridder	Wenner Media

HISTORICAL FINANCIALS
Company Type: Private

Income Statement
FYE: December 31

	REVENUE ($ mil.)	NET INCOME ($ mil.)	NET PROFIT MARGIN	EMPLOYEES
12/03	5,909	—	—	28,000
12/02	5,565	—	—	27,585
12/01	4,200	—	—	22,785
12/00	4,542	—	—	23,000
12/99	4,228	—	—	26,300
12/98	3,859	—	—	24,000
12/97	3,669	—	—	24,000
12/96	4,250	—	—	24,000
12/95	5,349	—	—	24,000
12/94	4,855	—	—	19,000
Annual Growth	2.2%	—	—	4.4%

Revenue History
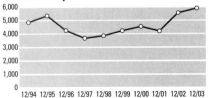

Advantage Sales and Marketing

Advantage Sales & Marketing provides outsourced sales, merchandising, and marketing services to consumer goods and food product manufacturers and suppliers. The company's services include retail distribution, positioning, and auditing in supermarkets, drug stores, and mass marketers. Advantage Sales & Marketing counts Del Monte, Gillette, Mars, and Unilever among its more than 1,200 clients.

EXECUTIVES
Chairman and CEO: Sonny King
President and COO: Mike Sunderland
President, Client Services: Mark Meyer
Human Resources: Stephanie Neuvirth

LOCATIONS
HQ: Advantage Sales and Marketing, LLC
  19100 Von Karman Ave., Ste. 600, Irvine, CA 92612
Phone: 949-797-2900   **Fax:** 949-797-9112
Web: www.asmnet.com

COMPETITORS
DCI Marketing

HISTORICAL FINANCIALS
Company Type: Private

Income Statement

	ESTIMATED REVENUE ($ mil.)	NET INCOME ($ mil.)	NET PROFIT MARGIN	EMPLOYEES
2003	700	—	—	12,500

Adventist Health

Adventist Health is the West Coast wing of an international organization with strong ties to the Seventh-Day Adventist Church that operates more than 160 Adventist health care providers around the globe.

Adventist Health runs 20 hospitals (with some 3,100 beds), almost 20 home health services agencies, and various other outpatient facilities and hospices in California, Hawaii, Oregon, and Washington. The organization also works with its own churches and those of other denominations to offer such preventative health services as medical screenings, immunizations, and health education.

Adventist Health has joint ventures to operate independent and assisted-living centers in California and Oregon. With Loma Linda University Medical Center, the health system has a behavioral care provider and a managed care organization.

EXECUTIVES
Chairman: Thomas J. Mostert Jr.
President and CEO: Donald R. Ammon
EVP and COO: Robert G. Carmen
SVP: Larry D. Dodds
SVP and CFO: Douglas E. Rebok
SVP: Alan J. Rice
VP, Hospital Finance Region III: Stan Adams
VP, Finance: James Brewster
VP, Hospital Finance Region I: Teresa M. Day
VP, Government Relations: Everett Gooch
VP, Delivery of Care: Wynelle J. Huff
VP, Marketing and Business Development, Adventist Health and Adventist Health System: Monty Knittel
VP, Rural Health Clinics: Darwin Remboldt
VP and CIO: Brett Spenst
VP and Treasurer: Rodney Wehtje
VP, Hospital Finance Region II: Harry Weis
Assistant VP, Human Resources: Roger Ashley
Assistant VP, Corporate Communication: Rita Waterman
Auditors: Ernst & Young LLP

LOCATIONS
HQ: Adventist Health
  2100 Douglas Blvd., Roseville, CA 95661
Phone: 916-781-2000   **Fax:** 916-783-9909
Web: www.adventisthealth.org

Selected Facilities
California
  San Joaquin Community Hospital (Bakersfield)
  Redbud Community Hospital (Clearlake)
  St. Helena Hospital (Deer Park)
  Glendale Adventist Medical Center (Glendale)
  Central Valley General Hospital (Hanford)
  Hanford Community Medical Center (Hanford)
  South Coast Medical Center (Laguna Beach)
  White Memorial Medical Center (Los Angeles)
  Paradise Valley Hospital (National City)
  Feather River Hospital (Paradise)
  Selma Community Hospital (Selma)
  Simi Valley Hospital (Simi Valley)
  Sonora Regional Medical Center (Sonora)
  Ukiah Valley Medical Center (Ukiah)
  Frank R. Howard Memorial Hospital (Willits)
Hawaii
  Castle Medical Center (Kailua)
  North Hawaii Community Hospital (Kamuela)
Oregon
  Adventist Medical Center (Portland)
  Tillamook County General Hospital (Tillamook)
Washington
  Walla Walla General Hospital (Walla Walla)

COMPETITORS
Catholic Healthcare West
HCA
Kaiser Foundation
Legacy Health System
LifePoint
Los Angeles County Health Department
Memorial Health Services
PacifiCare
Providence Health System
Province Healthcare
Sisters of Charity of Leavenworth
Sutter Health
Tenet Healthcare
Triad Hospitals
Trinity Health (Novi)
Vitas Healthcare

HISTORICAL FINANCIALS

Company Type: Not-for-profit

Income Statement				FYE: December 31
	REVENUE ($ mil.)	NET INCOME ($ mil.)	NET PROFIT MARGIN	EMPLOYEES
12/03	5,237	—	—	18,352
12/02	3,822	—	—	17,200
12/01	2,869	—	—	16,500
12/00	2,510	—	—	16,500
12/99	2,045	—	—	16,477
12/98	1,740	—	—	17,129
12/97	1,090	—	—	16,567
12/96	980	—	—	15,351
12/95	981	—	—	14,610
12/94	952	—	—	13,799
Annual Growth	20.9%	—	—	3.2%

Revenue History

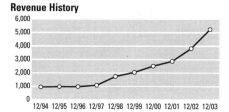

Adventist Health System

Adventist Health System (AHS) operates nearly 40 hospitals and about two dozen long-term care facilities located in a dozen states, mostly in the midwestern and southeastern US. Its acute care hospitals have more than 6,200 beds combined, and its nursing homes offer about 2,500 beds total. Florida is a key market: Its Florida Hospital system serves residents of the central part of the state and has nearly 1,800 beds. The AHS system includes about two dozen home health care agencies. The health system is sponsored by the Seventh-Day Adventist Church.

EXECUTIVES

President and CEO: Thomas L. (Tom) Werner
EVP, Florida Division: Des D. Cummings Jr.
EVP; COO, Florida Hospital: Lars D. Houmann
EVP; President and CEO, Florida Division and Florida Hospital: Donald L. Jernigan
SVP, Administration: Robert R. Henderschedt
SVP and CFO: Terry D. Shaw
SVP, Information Services and Senior Financial Officer; CFO, Multistate Hospital Division: Brent G. Snyder
VP, Home Care Services: La Donna R. Blom-Antonio
VP, Finance: Dan E. Enderson
VP, Medical Affairs and Chief Medical Officer: Loran D. Hauck
VP, Business Development, Risk Management, and Compliance: Sandra K. Johnson
VP, Human Resources: Donald G. (Don) Jones
VP, Finance and Senior Financial Officer: Paul C. Rathbun
VP, Mission and Ministries: Benjamin F. Reaves
VP: Womack H. Rucker Jr.
VP and Treasurer: Gary C. Skilton
VP, Legal Services: T. L. Trimble

LOCATIONS

HQ: Adventist Health System
  111 N. Orlando Ave., Winter Park, FL 32789
Phone: 407-647-4400   **Fax:** 407-975-1469
Web: www.ahss.org

Hospitals

Colorado
  Porter Adventist Hospital (Denver)
  Littleton Adventist Hospital (Littleton)
  Avista Adventist Hospital (Louisville)
Florida
  Florida Hospital Altamonte (Altamonte Springs)
  Florida Hospital Apopka (Apopka)
  Florida Hospital Celebration Health (Celebration)
  Florida Hospital DeLand (DeLand)
  Florida Hospital Kissimmee (Kissimmee)
  Florida Hospital Lake Placid (Lake Placid)
  Florida Hospital Fish Memorial (Orange City)
  Florida Hospital East Orlando (Orlando)
  Florida Hospital Orlando (Orlando)
  Florida Hospital – Oceanside (Ormond Beach)
  Florida Hospital – Ormond Memorial (Ormond Beach)
  Florida Hospital – Flagler (Palm Coast)
  Florida Hospital Heartland Medical Center (Sebring)
  Florida Hospital Waterman (Tavares)
  Florida Hospital Wauchula (Wauchula)
  Winter Park Memorial Hospital (Winter Park)
  East Pasco Medical Center (Zephyrhills)
Georgia
  Gordon Hospital (Calhoun)
  Emory-Adventist Hospital (Smyrna)
Illinois
  Bolingbrook Medical Center (Bolingbrook)
  GlenOaks Hospital (Glendale Heights)
  Hinsdale Hospital (Hinsdale)
  La Grange Memorial Hospital (La Grange)
Kansas
  Shawnee Mission Medical Center (Shawnee Mission)
Kentucky
  Manchester Memorial Hospital (Manchester)
North Carolina
  Park Ridge Hospital (Fletcher)
Tennessee
  Takoma Adventist Hospital (Greeneville)
  Jellico Community Hospital (Jellico)
  Tennessee Christian Medical Center – Madison (Madison)
  Tennessee Christian Medical Center – Portland (Portland)
Texas
  Huguley Memorial Medical Center (Fort Worth)
  Metroplex Hospital (Killeen)
  Rollins-Brook Community Hospital (Lampasas)
  Central Texas Medical Center (San Marcos)
Wisconsin
  Chippewa Valley Hospital (Durand)

HISTORICAL FINANCIALS

Company Type: Not-for-profit

Income Statement				FYE: December 31
	REVENUE ($ mil.)	NET INCOME ($ mil.)	NET PROFIT MARGIN	EMPLOYEES
12/03	10,123	—	—	44,000
12/02	8,433	—	—	42,000
12/01	6,655	—	—	—
12/00	5,285	—	—	—
Annual Growth	24.2%	—	—	4.8%

Revenue History

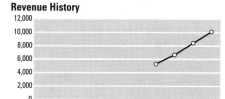

Adventist HealthCare

Adventist HealthCare (unrelated to Adventist Health) serves the state of Maryland, as well as portions of New Jersey, through a network that includes three acute care hospitals (Shady Grove Adventist Hospital, Washington Adventist Hospital, and Hackettstown Community Hospital); two rehabilitation hospitals (operating as the Adventist Rehabilitation Hospital of Maryland); and a number of home care services, long-term care centers, and independent and assisted living facilities. Combined, the health care network has more than 1,600 beds.

EXECUTIVES

President and CEO; Interim President, Washington Adventist Hospital: William G. (Bill) Robertson, age 44
EVP and Chief Administrative Officer: Edmund F. (Ed) Hodge
EVP and CFO: Jack W. Wagner
VP, Adventist Home Health: Keith Ballenger
VP, Adventist Senior Living Services: George L. Child
VP, Financial Services: Thomas Chan
VP and General Counsel: Kenneth B. DeStefano
VP, System Quality: Susan L. Glover
VP, System Strategy: Paula S. Widerlite
President, Hackettstown Community Hospital: Gene C. Milton
CEO, Adventist Rehabilitation Hospital of Maryland: Kenneth Aitchison
President and COO, Potomac Ridge Behavioral Health Center: Craig S. Juengling
President, Shady Grove Adventist Hospital: Deborah A. Yancer
CIO: Edna V. Bruehl

LOCATIONS

HQ: Adventist HealthCare, Inc.
  1801 Research Blvd. #300, Rockville, MD 20850
Phone: 301-315-3030   **Fax:** 301-315-3110
Web: www.adventisthealthcare.com

HISTORICAL FINANCIALS

Company Type: Not-for-profit

Income Statement				FYE: December 31
	REVENUE ($ mil.)	NET INCOME ($ mil.)	NET PROFIT MARGIN	EMPLOYEES
12/03	568	—	—	7,000

Advocate Health Care

Advocating wellness in Chicagoland from Palos Heights to Palatine, Advocate Health Care is an integrated health care network with more than 200 sites serving the Chicago area. Advocate's operations include eight acute care hospitals (including Christ Medical Center and Lutheran General Hospital) with more than 3,000 beds, and two children's hospitals, as well as home health care and ambulatory care services. Advocate also has teaching affiliations with area medical schools such as the University of Illinois at Chicago. The health system's Advocate Medical Group has nearly 200 physician members serving northwest Chicago.

Advocate Health Care has ties to both the United Church of Christ and the Evangelical Lutheran Church in America.

EXECUTIVES

President and CEO: James H. (Jim) Skogsbergh
EVP and COO: William P. (Bill) Santulli
EVP and CFO: Lawrence J. Majka
EVP and Chief Medical Officer; President, Advocate Health Partners: Lee B. Sacks
SVP, Human Resources: Ben Grigaliunas
SVP, Strategy and Business Development:
  Gregory K. Morris
SVP and CIO: Bruce Smith
SVP, Mission and Spiritual Care:
  Rev Jerry A. Wagenknecht
VP, Finance and Corporate Controller: Dominic J. Nakis
VP, Public Relations: Daniel Parker
VP, System Business Development:
  Kenneth J. (Ken) Rojek
Chief Development Officer; President, Advocate Charitable Foundation: Heather T. Hutchison
Chief Ethics Officer; President and CEO, The Park Ridge Center for the Study of Health, Faith and Ethics: Laurence J. O'Connell
Chief Legal Officer and General Counsel:
  Gail D. Hasbrouck
Director, System Public Relations:
  Edward C. (Ed) Domansky
Auditors: Ernst & Young

LOCATIONS

HQ: Advocate Health Care
  2025 Windsor Dr., Oak Brook, IL 60523
Phone: 630-572-9393   **Fax:** 630-572-9139
Web: www.advocatehealth.com

PRODUCTS/OPERATIONS

Selected Operations

Advocate Bethany Hospital
Advocate Christ Medical Center
Advocate Good Samaritan Hospital
Advocate Good Shepherd Hospital
Advocate Health Centers
Advocate Home Health Services
Advocate Hope Children's Hospital
Advocate Illinois Masonic Medical Center
Advocate Lutheran General Hospital
Advocate Lutheran General Children's Hospital
Advocate Medical Group
Advocate South Suburban Hospital
Advocate Trinity Hospital
Dreyer Clinic, Inc.

COMPETITORS

Alexian Brothers Health System
Ancilla Systems
Covenant Ministries
HCA
Provena Health
Rush System for Health
SSM Health Care

HISTORICAL FINANCIALS

Company Type: Not-for-profit

Income Statement

FYE: December 31

	REVENUE ($ mil.)	NET INCOME ($ mil.)	NET PROFIT MARGIN	EMPLOYEES
12/03	2,716	124	4.6%	25,000
12/02	2,604	(7)	—	25,293
12/01	2,467	108	4.4%	24,500
12/00	1,675	(7)	—	24,500
12/99	1,600	—	—	23,000
12/98	1,390	—	—	21,000
12/97	1,636	—	—	21,000
12/96	1,522	—	—	21,054
12/95	1,421	—	—	21,145
12/94	1,340	—	—	20,400
Annual Growth	8.2%	—	—	2.3%

2003 Year-End Financials

Debt ratio: 36.7%   Current ratio: 0.98
Return on equity: 8.5% Long-term debt ($ mil.): 590
Cash ($ mil.): —

Net Income History

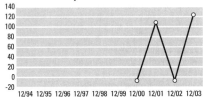

AECOM

AECOM Technology means never having to say Architecture, Engineering, Consulting, Operations, and Maintenance. One of the world's leading engineering and design groups, AECOM offers a range of professional technical services, mostly to government agencies and large corporations. It is a top design firm in Asia and the Middle East and a global leader in the water, transportation, and wastewater sectors. It has expanded in Europe by acquiring UK-based companies such as transportation infrastructure groups Maunsell and Oscar Faber and water and wastewater construction firm Metcalf & Eddy UK. When AECOM withdrew its IPO in 2002, chairman Richard Newman and vice chairman Joseph Incaudo were major shareholders.

The group is a recipient of one of the management contracts awarded to US and UK engineering and construction companies to assist in the reconstruction of Iraq. AECOM won a $21.6 million contract to support management activities of several public works and other facilities being constructed. The company is helping the Pentagon in buying goods and services and is assisting in auditing projects of other contractors working on Iraq's reconstruction.

The group expanded even more in 2004 with the addition of Australian mechanical and electrical engineering firm Bassett, which joined the Maunsell group to become part of AECOM.

EXECUTIVES

Chairman and CEO: Richard G. Newman, age 69
Vice Chairman; Treasurer, DMJM: Joseph A. Incaudo
President; CEO, Americas Group:
  Raymond W. Holdsworth
EVP and COO; Chairman, DMJM + HARRIS:
  John M. Dionisio
SVP and CFO: Glenn R. Robson
SVP, Chief Administrative Officer, and Corporate Secretary: Stephanie A. Hunter
SVP Corporate Finance and General Counsel: Eric Chen
Executive Chairman, Asia: Francis S. Y. Bong
CEO, Global Group: David N. Odgers
CEO, Americas Environmental and Transportation Group: Robert H. Fischer
CEO, Americas Facilities and Government Services Groups: James R. Royer
CEO, United Kingdom Group: Ken F. Dalton
Director of Corporate Communications: Jill Groswirth
Auditors: Ernst & Young LLP

LOCATIONS

HQ: AECOM Technology Corporation
  555 S. Flower St., Ste. 3700, Los Angeles, CA 90071
Phone: 213-593-8000   **Fax:** 213-593-8729
Web: www.aecom.com

AECOM Technology has 25 major operating offices worldwide.

PRODUCTS/OPERATIONS

Selected Operations

Consoer Townsend Envirodyne (CTE, transportation and environmental engineering)
DMJM Aviation (consulting and engineering for aviation industry)
Daniel, Mann, Johnson, Mendenhall, Holmes & Narver (architecture, engineering, construction services)
DMJM + Harris (construction and engineering)
Maunsell Ltd. (transportation infrastructure, water and wastewater facilities, engineering, UK)
McClier Corporation (architectural engineering, construction, and consulting)
Metcalf & Eddy Ltd. (wastewater engineering and environmental consulting, UK)
Turner Collie & Braden Inc. (engineering and project management)

COMPETITORS

ABB
AMEC
Bechtel
Black & Veatch
Earth Tech
Fluor
Foster Wheeler
Henkels & McCoy
Jacobs Engineering
Lockwood Greene
Louis Berger
MWH Global
Parsons
Parsons Brinckerhoff
Perini
Skidmore Owings
STV
Thornton-Tomasetti
URS

HISTORICAL FINANCIALS

Company Type: Private

Income Statement

FYE: September 30

	REVENUE ($ mil.)	NET INCOME ($ mil.)	NET PROFIT MARGIN	EMPLOYEES
9/04	2,000	—	—	18,000
9/03	1,850	—	—	17,100
9/02	1,700	—	—	15,500
9/01	1,530	—	—	12,700
9/00	1,402	—	—	12,100
Annual Growth	9.3%	—	—	10.4%

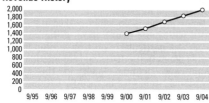
Revenue History

Aera Energy

Aera Energy covers a large area, California. The state's leading oil and gas producer, Aera Energy's properties extend from the Los Angeles Basin in the south to Coalinga in the north. It has daily production of 250,000 barrels of oil and 90 million cu. ft. of natural gas and boasts proved onshore and offshore reserves of about 1 billion barrels of oil equivalent. Aera Energy also has interests in a soil management company (Terrain Technology), and in real estate operations. The exploration and production company is a joint venture of Exxon Mobil and the Royal Dutch/Shell Group.

EXECUTIVES
President and CEO: Eugene J. (Gene) Voiland
VP: George Basye
CFO: Len Fox
CIO: David Walker
Manager Operations: Frank Dominguez
Auditors: PricewaterhouseCoopers LLP

LOCATIONS
HQ: Aera Energy LLC
10000 Ming Ave., Bakersfield, CA 93311
Phone: 661-665-5000   **Fax:** 661-665-5042
Web: www.aeraenergy.com

COMPETITORS
Berry Petroleum Company
BP
ChevronTexaco
Occidental Petroleum
PYR Energy

HISTORICAL FINANCIALS
Company Type: Joint venture

Income Statement
FYE: December 31

	REVENUE ($ mil.)	NET INCOME ($ mil.)	NET PROFIT MARGIN	EMPLOYEES
12/03	2,234	—	—	1,100
12/02	1,807	—	—	1,100
Annual Growth	23.6%	—	—	0.0%

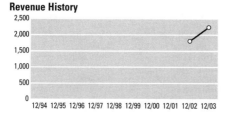
Revenue History

Aerospace Corporation

The Aerospace Corporation definitely knows its space from its aero. Established in 1960, the not-for-profit organization provides research, development, and advisory services to space-related programs of the US government, international organizations, and commercial businesses. Its primary customers are the US Air Force's Space and Missile Systems Center and the National Reconnaissance Office, but it also works with NASA and other international space organizations. The Aerospace Corporation also runs a federally funded research and development center for the Department of Defense. Its areas of expertise include launch certification, systems engineering, process implementation, and satellite control systems.

EXECUTIVES
Chairman: Bradford W. Parkinson, age 69
Vice Chairman: Howell M. Estes III
President and CEO: Wiliam F. Ballhaus Jr.
EVP: Joe M. Straus
SVP, General Counsel, and Secretary: Gordon J. Louttit
SVP Engineering and Technology Group: John R. Parsons
SVP National Systems Group: Wanda M. Austin
SVP Systems Planning and Engineering: Donald R. Walker
VP, CFO, and Treasurer: Dale E. Wallis
VP Human Resources and Administration: Marlene M. Dennis
VP Laboratory Operations: Lawrence T. Greenberg
VP Program Assessment: John R. Wormington
VP Space Launch Operations: Ray F. Johnson
VP Space Operations, Requirements, and Technology: Jerry M. (Mike) Drennan
VP Space Program Operations: Stephen E. Burrin
General Manager, Satellite and Launch Control Division: Linda R. Drake
General Manager, Space Support Division: Dennis A. Plunkett
Associate General Manager, Space Support Division: Rami R. Razouk
Assistant Secretary: Roberta L. Ackley
Auditors: Deloitte & Touche LLP

LOCATIONS
HQ: The Aerospace Corporation
2350 E. El Segundo Blvd., El Segundo, CA 90245
Phone: 310-336-5000   **Fax:** 310-336-7055
Web: www.aero.org

The Aerospace Corporation has operations in California, Colorado, Florida, Maryland, Nebraska, New Mexico, Pennsylvania, Texas, Virginia, and Washington, DC.

PRODUCTS/OPERATIONS

Selected Services
Launch certification
Process implementation
Systems development and acquisition
Systems engineering
Task integration
Technology application

Selected Programs
Control systems
  Air Force Satellite Control Network (AFSCN)
  MILSATCOM Integrated Satellite Control System
  Range Safety
  Spacelift Operations Telemetry Acquisition and Reporting System (STARS)
Launch vehicles
  Atlas
  Delta
  Evolved Expendable Launch Vehicle (EELV)
  Space Maneuvering Vehicle (SMV)
  Titan
Satellites
  Air Force Satellite Communications (AFSATCOM)
  Defense Meteorological Satellite Program (DMSP)
  Defense Satellite Communications System (DSCS)
  Defense Support Program (DSP)
  Global Positioning System (GPS)
  MightySat Small Satellite Program
  MILSATCOM Advanced Programs
  Milstar
  National Polar-Orbiting Operational Environment Satellite System (NPOESS)
  Space Based Infrared System (SBIRS)

COMPETITORS
Alliant Techsystems
Altran Technologies
Battelle Memorial
Boeing
Booz Allen
CACI International
Charles Stark Draper Laboratory
Computer Sciences
EDS
General Dynamics
Honeywell International
Lockheed Martin
MITRE
Northrop Grumman
Orbital Research
Orbital Sciences
QinetiQ
Raytheon
Research Triangle Institute
SAIC
Southwest Research Institute
SRI International
United Technologies

HISTORICAL FINANCIALS
Company Type: Not-for-profit

Income Statement
FYE: September 30

	REVENUE ($ mil.)	NET INCOME ($ mil.)	NET PROFIT MARGIN	EMPLOYEES
9/03	581	—	—	3,260
9/02	506	—	—	3,000
9/01	476	—	—	3,000
9/00	434	—	—	3,000
9/99	350	—	—	3,000
9/98	339	—	—	3,000
9/97	346	—	—	3,000
9/96	327	—	—	—
Annual Growth	8.6%	—	—	1.4%

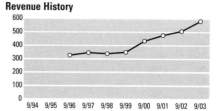
Revenue History

Affiliated Foods

Affiliated Foods distributes food and grocery items to its member-owners' stores in Arizona, Colorado, Kansas, New Mexico, Oklahoma, Texas, and Wyoming. Founded in 1946 as Panhandle Associated Grocers, Affiliated Foods also helps retailers implement computer systems and software. In addition, the co-op operates Tri-State Baking (TenderCrust and Always Fresh brands) and owns the Plains Dairy, which produces

60,000 gallons of milk a day and bottles water, juice, tea, and fruit drinks. It also owns a stake in private-label products supplier Western Family Foods (Western Family and Shurfine brands).

EXECUTIVES

President: George Lankford
CFO: Tammie Coffee
VP: Mark Griffin
President, Plains Dairy: Dub Garlington
President, Tri State Baking Company: Jim Ravenscraft
Director, Advertising: Bob Mitchusson
Director, Corporate Purchasing: Joe Self
Director, Grocery Purchasing: Richard Splayt
Director, Human Resources: Gene Blackburn
Director, IT: Michael Lindley
Director, Meat: Bob Cota
Director, New Accounts: Dale Thomson
Director, Non-Foods: George Satterwhite
Director, Produce: Harold Callaway
Business Manager, Plains Dairy: Deborah Giles
General Manager, Food Service: Jamey Williams
Manager, Advertising: David Campsey
Manager, Retail Systems: Tim Terry
Manager, Sales Foodservice: David Beal
Supervisor, Operations: Kevin Fortenberry
Customer Service: Debbie Carnes
Director, New Accounts: Dale Thompson
Auditors: Johnson Moore & Associates, PC

LOCATIONS

HQ: Affiliated Foods Incorporated
1401 Farmers Ln., Amarillo, TX 79118
Phone: 806-372-3851 **Fax:** 806-372-3647
Web: www.afiama.com

COMPETITORS

AWG
GSC Enterprises
IGA
Nash Finch
SUPERVALU

HISTORICAL FINANCIALS

Company Type: Cooperative

Income Statement				FYE: September 30
	REVENUE ($ mil.)	NET INCOME ($ mil.)	NET PROFIT MARGIN	EMPLOYEES
9/03	905	—	—	1,000
9/02	854	—	—	1,000
9/01	700	—	—	962
9/00	697	—	—	1,100
9/99	671	—	—	1,100
9/98	655	—	—	1,000
9/97	640	—	—	920
9/96	608	—	—	875
9/95	570	—	—	840
9/94	530	—	—	850
Annual Growth	6.1%	—	—	1.8%

Revenue History

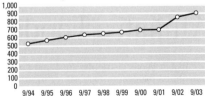

AFL-CIO

Talk about spending a long time in labor: The AFL-CIO (American Federation of Labor and Congress of Industrial Organizations) has been at it for more than a century. The AFL-CIO is an umbrella organization for 65 autonomous national and international unions representing more than 13 million workers — ranging from actors and airline pilots to teachers and Teamsters — and works to improve wages and working conditions. The organization charters 51 state federations and nearly 580 central labor councils. Union members generally receive about 33% higher pay and more benefits than nonmembers.

The organization's membership has been decreasing because of the decline in manufacturing jobs and the increased use of temporary workers and automation. However, the AFL-CIO is reviving under the leadership of John Sweeney, primarily because of his aggressive emphasis on recruiting.

HISTORY

The American Federation of Labor (AFL) was formed in 1886 in Columbus, Ohio, by the merger of six craft unions and a renegade craft section of the Marxist-oriented Knights of Labor. Samuel Gompers, a New York cigar factory worker who headed the AFL until his death in 1924, initiated the AFL's pragmatic focus: to work within the economic system to increase wages, improve working conditions, and abolish child labor.

Gompers' successes incensed employers, whose arsenal, supported by the US courts and public opinion, included injunctions, government-backed police forces to crush strikes, and the Sherman Anti-Trust Act (used to assail union monopoly powers).

WWI's production needs boosted AFL membership to 4 million by 1919. Labor clashes with management were widespread in the 1920s amid the fear of Bolsheviks. As part of open-shop drives, employers replaced strikers with southern African-Americans and Mexican workers.

The Great Depression brought more supportive public and pro-labor laws, including the National Industrial Recovery Act (NIRA, 1933), which allowed union organizing and collective bargaining. After NIRA was declared unconstitutional, the Wagner Act (1936) restated many of NIRA's provisions and established the legal basis for unions.

Union power split in 1935 when AFL coal miner John L. Lewis began organizing unskilled workers. Lewis and his allies, expelled from the AFL, formed the Congress of Industrial Organizations (CIO, 1938) and enjoyed success in unionizing the auto, steel, textile, and other industries. By 1946 the AFL and CIO had 9 million and 5 million members, respectively.

Amid postwar concern over rising prices, communist infiltration, and union corruption, Congress passed the Taft-Hartley Act in 1947 (which outlawed closed shops). The new climate of hostility led the AFL (headed by plumber George Meany) and the CIO (headed by autoworker Walter Reuther) to merge in 1955. The AFL-CIO soon expelled the Teamsters and other unions on charges of corruption. (The Teamsters reaffiliated in 1987.)

AFL-CIO membership jumped after President Kennedy gave federal employees the right to unionize (1962); state, county, and municipal workers soon followed.

Union membership, which peaked in the mid-1940s with more than a third of the US labor force, was particularly hurt by a jump in imported goods in the 1970s and automation's triumph over manual labor in the 1980s. Legislation supported by the AFL-CIO included a law requiring 60 days' notice for plant closings (1988) and the Family Leave Act (1993). But labor lost its battle against NAFTA (North American Free Trade Agreement), which it feared would export jobs to Mexico.

In 1995 John Sweeney, former head of the Service Employees International Union, became president of the AFL-CIO in its first contested election. Under Sweeney the union spent $35 million in advertising in 1996 to draw attention to issues. After years with little focus on organizing, in 1997 the AFL-CIO launched a massive campaign to organize construction, hospital, and hotel workers in Las Vegas, and committed a third of its budget to recruiting and reorganizing. It supported the Teamsters' successful strike against UPS in 1997 and in 1998 threw its weight behind the Air Line Pilots Association's walkout on Northwest Airlines. It approved a restructuring plan in 1999 and the next year spent significant time and money rallying members all across the US in support of losing presidential candidate Al Gore. In 2002 AFL-CIO announced its pledge of $750 million to create affordable housing in New York City.

EXECUTIVES

President: John J. Sweeney, age 70
EVP: Linda Chavez-Thompson, age 60
Secretary and Treasurer: Richard L. Trumka, age 55
VP; President, International Association of Machinists and Aerospace Workers: R. Thomas Buffenbarger
VP; President, International Brotherhood of Teamsters: James P. Hoffa
VP; President, International Brotherhood of Electrical Workers: Edwin D. Hill
VP; President Sheet Metal Workers Union: Mike Sullivan
Director Corporate Affairs: Ron Blackwell
Director International Affairs: Barbara Shailor
Director Human Resources: Karla Garland
General Counsel: Jonathan Hiatt
Director, Legislative: Bill Samuel

LOCATIONS

HQ: AFL-CIO
815 16th St. NW, Washington, DC 20006
Phone: 202-637-5000 **Fax:** 202-637-5058
Web: www.aflcio.org

The AFL-CIO encompasses 65 national and international unions.

PRODUCTS/OPERATIONS

Selected Trades and Workers Represented

Acting	Industrial trades
Airline pilots	Maritime trades
Broadcasting	Metal trades
Building trades	Mining
Education	Music
Electrical trades	Office employees
Engineering	Police
Farmworkers	Postal employees
Firefighters	Restaurant employees
Flight attendants	Teachers
Food trades	Transportation trades
Government workers	Utility workers
Hotel employees	Writers

HISTORICAL FINANCIALS

Company Type: Labor union

Income Statement			FYE: June 30
	REVENUE ($ mil.)	NET INCOME ($ mil.)	NET PROFIT MARGIN	EMPLOYEES
6/03	145	—	—	480

Ag Processing

Soy far, soy good for Ag Processing (AGP), one of the largest soybean processors in the US. AGP's chief soybean products include vegetable oil and commercial animal feeds. It also provides grain marketing and transportation services. The co-operative is promoting its corn-based ethanol and soybean oil-based bio-fuels, fuel additives, and solvents. AGP processes some 15,000 acres of soybeans a day from its members' farms. The co-op's owners include 200,000 members from 16 US states and Canada. The members, mostly in the Midwest, are represented through 238 local co-ops and eight regional co-ops.

AGP also turns its products into food ingredients, such as lethicin and meat extenders for ground beef. To capitalize on new EPA emission limits and mandates, the co-op is lobbying to increase retail demand for ethanol. Additionally, AGP is promoting methyl ester, a by-product of soy oil refining, for use as a clean fuel and fuel additive, agricultural spray, and non-toxic solvent to replace petroleum-based products.

HISTORY

Seeking strength in numbers, Ag Processing (AGP) was formed in 1983 when agricultural cooperatives Land O' Lakes and Farmland Industries merged their money-losing soybean operations into similarly struggling Boone Valley Cooperative.

Separately, AGP's six soybean mills had been unable to compete successfully against each other and larger corporations. The entire industry had been hampered by the Soviet grain embargoes imposed by the US in 1973 and 1979, and US government policies had contributed to increased competition from heavily subsidized soy producers in Argentina and Brazil. Soy exports from the US had fallen dramatically, leading to a production capacity surplus.

Collectively, AGP was able to attract a stronger management staff than its predecessors had; it hired 21-year Archer Daniels Midland (ADM) veteran James Lindsay as CEO and general manager. With operations scattered over four states, AGP placed its headquarters in Omaha, Nebraska — chosen for its central location and close proximity to the co-op's main bank.

In its first two years, AGP cut employee rolls by 20% and scaled back production, thus trimming costs and squeezing higher prices for finished products. A turnaround came quickly, and in 1985 members received a dividend from the co-op's $8 million pretax profit. That year AGP purchased two Iowa plants from AGRI Industries.

AGP dismantled two plants in 1987. By the next year the co-op witnessed an increase in domestic demand and had resumed selling to the Soviet Union. It generated additional sales by further processing soybean oil into food-grade products like hydrogenated oil and lecithin.

With an eye on diversification and value-added products, by 1991 AGP had expanded to eight soybean plants and two vegetable oil refineries; it also acquired the feed and grain business of International Multifoods that year through an 80%-owned joint venture with ADM. The acquisition included 29 feed plants in the US and Canada, 26 retail centers, 18 grain elevators, and the brands Supersweet and Masterfeeds. In 1994 AGP formed feed manufacturer Consolidated Nutrition, a 50-50 joint-venture with ADM.

Consolidated Nutrition introduced a Swine Operations program in 1996. The program quickly grew through the development of PORK PACT, a partnership to serve pork producers. (The co-op has since exited the swine business.) The next year AGP's grain division sold nine grain elevators in Ohio and Indiana to Cargill. That year the co-op gained control of Venezuelan feed manufacturer Proagro.

By 1998 passage of the Freedom to Farm Act and growing demand had spurred soybean planting. The co-op in 1998 opened an additional processing plant in Emmetsburg, Iowa, followed by another in Eagle Grove, Iowa. AGP sold off its pet food operations in 1998 to Windy Hill, which was later acquired by Doane Pet Care Enterprises. Also that year Consolidated Nutrition combined its Master Mix and Supersweet feed brands into the Consolidated Nutrition label.

In 1999 the company added the Garner-Klemme-Meservey cooperative to its grain operations. It opened a new plant late that year in St. Joseph, Missouri, to make value-added products such as hardfat (used in emulsifiers).

In June 2001 AGP sold its 50% share of Consolidated Nutrition to ADM. In 2002 the co-op's Masterfeeds business acquired four feed mills and a merchandising operation from Saskatchewan Wheat Pool. In 2003 AGP opened the Port of Grays Harbor vessel-loading terminal in Aberdeen, Washington, that year.

EXECUTIVES

Chairman: Bradley T. Davis
Vice Chairman: Lowell D. Wilson
CEO and General Manager: Martin P. Reagan
SVP and Corporate Controller: Tim E. Witty
SVP, Corporate & Member Relations: Michael L. Maranell
SVP, Engineering and Environment: Charles A. Janiszewski
SVP, Human Resources: Judith V. Ford
SVP, Transportation: Terry J. Voss
Group VP, Animal Nutrition; President, Masterfeeds: Robert J. Flack
Group VP, Finance; CFO; Assistant Secretary; and Assistant Treasurer: J. Keith Spackler
Group VP, Food and Industrial: George L. Hoover
Group VP, Grain: Michael J. Knobbe
Group VP, Processing Soybean and Corn: Calvin J. Meyer
VP, Corporate General Counsel, and Assistant Secretary: Larry J. Steier
VP, Government Relations and Industrial Products: John B. Campbell
VP, Information Systems: Michael C. Reed
VP, Technology Marketing and Applications: W. Blake Hendrix
Treasurer, Secretary, and Director: Dean B. Isaacson
Manager, Communications: Ed Woll
Auditors: Deloitte & Touche LLP

LOCATIONS

HQ: Ag Processing Inc
12700 W. Dodge Rd., Omaha, NE 68154
Phone: 402-496-7809 **Fax:** 402-498-2215
Web: www.agp.com

PRODUCTS/OPERATIONS

Selected Brands
AMINOPLUS (dairy feed additive)
Masterfeeds (feeds, Canada)
Progtinal/Proagro (poultry and feed, Venezuela)
SOYGOLD (bio-diesel, solvents, fuel additives)

Selected Subsidiaries
Ag Environmental Products (soybean methyl ester products)
AGP Grain, Ltd.
AGP Grain Marketing, Inc.
Intellectual Property Holdings LLC

COMPETITORS

Abengoa Bioenergy
ADM
Andersons
Bunge Limited
Cargill
CHS
ConAgra
Corn Products International
DeBruce Grain
Griffin Industries
MFA
Riceland Foods
Southern States
SunOpta

HISTORICAL FINANCIALS

Company Type: Cooperative

Income Statement			FYE: August 31
	REVENUE ($ mil.)	NET INCOME ($ mil.)	NET PROFIT MARGIN	EMPLOYEES
8/03	2,127	11	0.5%	1,500
8/02	1,802	32	1.8%	2,500
8/01	1,789	27	1.5%	2,500
8/00	1,962	—	—	2,500
8/99	2,095	—	—	2,500
8/98	2,615	—	—	2,550
8/97	2,948	—	—	3,000
8/96	2,765	—	—	3,050
8/95	2,132	—	—	—
8/94	1,377	—	—	—
Annual Growth	4.9%	(36.1%)	—	(9.6%)

2003 Year-End Financials

Debt ratio: 19.5% Current ratio: 1.62
Return on equity: 2.7% Long-term debt ($ mil.): 79
Cash ($ mil.): 7

Net Income History

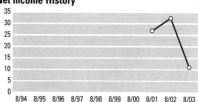

A. G. Spanos

Spanning the land from California to Florida, A.G. Spanos Companies bridges many operations: from building, managing, and selling multi-family housing units to constructing master-planned communities, to developing land. The firm has built more than 100,000 apartments in 18 states since its founding in 1960. Major projects include Spanos Park, a $1 billion master-planned community on 3,000 acres in founder and chairman Alex Spanos' hometown of Stockton, California, as well as the construction of luxury apartments across the nation. Alex Spanos, owner of the NFL's San Diego Chargers, operates the company with his sons Dean (president and CEO) and Michael Spanos (EVP).

EXECUTIVES

Chairman: Alexander Gus (Alex) Spanos, age 81
President and CEO: Dean A. Spanos, age 54
EVP: Michael A. Spanos, age 45
CFO: Jeremiah T. Murphy
Financial Officer and CTO: Steven L. Cohen
VP Marketing and Sales: Nick Faklis
Director, Public Relations: Natalia Orfanos
Manager, Human Resources: Charlene Flynn
Manager, Land Development Division:
 Jim Panagopoulos
Manager, Florida and Texas Division: Charlie Raffo
Manager, Georgia Division: Jim Kourafas
Manager, Nevada Division: George Filios
Manager, Southern California, Arizona, and New Mexico Division: Ray Hanes
Manager, Property Management Division:
 Jean Lobsinger
Manager, Property Management Division:
 Michael Meath
Manager, Property Management Division: Betty Wells

LOCATIONS

HQ: A. G. Spanos Companies
 10100 Trinity Pkwy., Stockton, CA 95219
Phone: 209-478-7954 **Fax:** 209-473-3703
Web: www.agspanos.com

The A.G. Spanos Companies operates offices in Arizona (Phoenix/Tempe), California (Fairfield, Riverside, and Stockton), Florida (Tampa), Georgia (Atlanta/Marietta), Indiana (Fishers), Kansas (Overland), Nevada (Las Vegas), North Carolina (Charlotte), and Texas (Austin, Dallas/Irving).

PRODUCTS/OPERATIONS

Selected Subsidiaries
A. G. Spanos Construction
A. G. Spanos Development, Inc.
A. G. Spanos Enterprises, Inc.
A. G. Spanos Management, Inc.
A. G. Spanos Realty, Inc.
A. G. Spanos Securities
A. G. Spanos Ventures
AGS Financial Corporation
AGS International Corporation
The Spanos Corporation

Other Ownership Interests
A. G. Spanos Aviation (Stockton, California)
San Diego Chargers National Football League Team

COMPETITORS

Barratt Developments
Calprop
Centex
Del Webb
Edward Rose
Irvine Company
Lennar
Morrison Homes
Perini
Pinnacle West
Pulte Homes
Schuler Homes
William Lyon Homes

HISTORICAL FINANCIALS
Company Type: Private

Income Statement
FYE: September 30

	REVENUE ($ mil.)	NET INCOME ($ mil.)	NET PROFIT MARGIN	EMPLOYEES
9/04	1,700	—	—	600
9/03	1,700	—	—	600
9/02	1,400	—	—	600
9/01	1,560	—	—	600
9/00	1,590	—	—	600
9/99	1,440	—	—	600
9/98	1,175	—	—	600
9/97	964	—	—	600
9/96	950	—	—	600
9/95	947	—	—	—
Annual Growth	6.7%	—	—	0.0%

Revenue History

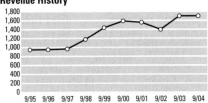

AgFirst

AgFirst puts farmers first. A large and growing agricultural lender, AgFirst Farm Credit Bank operates in 15 eastern states and Puerto Rico, offering more than $10 billion in loans to some 80,000 farmers, ranchers, rural homeowners, and agribusiness owners. The lender originates real estate, operating, and rural home mortgage loans. Additionally, it offers crop, life, and timber insurance; equipment leasing; tax services; record keeping; and other products and services designed to meet customers' business and personal needs. The bank does not accept deposits; it raises money by selling bonds and notes on the capital markets.

AgFirst is a member of the largest agricultural lending organization in the US, Farm Credit System (FCS), with assets eclipsing $100 billion. The bank finances farmers, agribusiness owners and rural homeowners through affiliated retail lenders. Through its Capital Markets unit, it arranges and participates in loans for agribusinesses. Its Secondary Mortgage Market unit buys, sells, and services agricultural and rural home loans.

EXECUTIVES

Chairman: Paul Lemoine
President and CEO: F. A. (Andy) Lowrey
CFO: Leon T. (Timmy) Amerson
EVP: Thomas S. Welsh
SVP and Chief Lending and Operations Officer:
 William R. Clayton
VP, Capital Markets: Felicia Morant
VP, Marketing: Joy M. Upchurch
Director, Advertising and Communications:
 Donna J. Camacho
Senior Specialist, Human Resources: Pat N. Roche
Auditors: PricewaterhouseCoopers LLP

LOCATIONS

HQ: AgFirst Farm Credit Bank
 1401 Hampton St., Columbia, SC 29202
Phone: 803-799-5000 **Fax:** 803-254-1776
Web: www.agfirst.com

AgFirst Farm Credit Bank operates in Alabama, Delaware, Florida, Georgia, Kentucky, Louisiana, Maryland, Mississippi, Ohio, North Carolina, Pennsylvania, Puerto Rico, South Carolina, Tennessee, Virginia, and West Virginia.

PRODUCTS/OPERATIONS

2003 Sales

	$ mil.	% of total
Interest		
Loan interest	469.1	87
Security interest	59.4	11
Noninterest		
Loan fees	8.9	2
Gain on investments	0.2	—
Secondary mortgage operations	(1.4)	—
Other	1.9	—
Total	**538.1**	**100**

COMPETITORS

Acceptance Insurance
AgriBank
Alabama Farmers Cooperative
National Rural Utilities Cooperative
Rabo AgServices

HISTORICAL FINANCIALS
Company Type: Cooperative

Income Statement
FYE: December 31

	ASSETS ($ mil.)	NET INCOME ($ mil.)	INCOME AS % OF ASSETS	EMPLOYEES
12/03	15,880	177	1.1%	—
12/02	14,701	194	1.3%	—
12/01	13,233	131	1.0%	—
12/00	13,522	235	1.7%	—
12/99	12,726	218	1.7%	—
12/98	11,987	218	1.8%	—
12/97	11,053	209	1.9%	—
12/96	10,544	201	1.9%	—
12/95	10,355	172	1.7%	—
Annual Growth	5.5%	0.4%	—	—

2003 Year-End Financials
Equity as % of assets: —
Return on assets: 1.2%
Return on equity: —
Long-term debt ($ mil.): —
Sales ($ mil.): 538

Net Income History

AgriBank

AgriBank puts the "green" in green acres. A financial intermediary, AgriBank provides wholesale lending and business services to Farm Credit System (FCS) associations in America's heartland. Established by Congress, the FCS is a nationwide network of cooperatives that provides loans and financial services for some 200,000 farmers, ranchers, agribusiness owners, timber producers, and rural homeowners. Farm Credit Service's co-ops write loans for land, equipment, and other farm operating costs; they in turn own AgriBank. AgriBank also provides credit to rural electric, water, and telephone systems. The cooperative merged with AgAmerica in 2003.

Located in St Paul, Minnesota, AgriBank serves the Seventh Farm Credit District, which operates in primarily Midwestern states. It is organized along three lines of business: wholesale, business services, and retail. Providing district associations with wholesale products and services is its primary focus; however, it also offers a wide range of business services including information technology, portfolio risk management, retail product and processing support, and human resources.

EXECUTIVES

Chairman: Douglas A. Felton, $25,769 pay
CEO: William J. Collins, $538,000 pay
VP and CFO: Diane M. Cole
VP, Audit: Donald W. Theuninck
VP, Credit: Ross B. Anderson
VP, General Counsel, and Secretary: William J. Thone
VP, Human Resources and Administrative Services:
  John E. Lovstad
VP, Information and Business Services:
  Rodney A. Nelsestuen
Auditors: PricewaterhouseCoopers LLP

LOCATIONS

HQ: AgriBank, FCB
  375 Jackson St., St. Paul, MN 55164
Phone: 651-282-8800 **Fax:** 651-282-8666
Web: www.agribank.com

AgriBank operates in Arkansas, Illinois, Indiana, Iowa, Kentucky, Michigan, Minnesota, Missouri, Nebraska, North Dakota, Ohio, South Dakota, Tennessee, Wisconsin, and Wyoming.

PRODUCTS/OPERATIONS

2003 Sales

	$ mil.	% of total
Loan interest	830.4	85
Securities interest	87.3	9
Business services	24.5	2
Loan prepayment fees & other	36.7	4
Total	**978.9**	**100**

COMPETITORS

Acceptance Insurance
AgFirst
Alabama Farmers Cooperative
CHS
Farmland Mutual Insurance Company
National Rural Utilities Cooperative
Rabo AgServices

HISTORICAL FINANCIALS
Company Type: Cooperative

Income Statement				FYE: December 31
	ASSETS ($ mil.)	NET INCOME ($ mil.)	INCOME AS % OF ASSETS	EMPLOYEES
12/03	33,605	81	0.2%	—
12/02	24,074	180	0.7%	3,300
12/01	21,465	146	0.7%	3,300
12/00	22,767	316	1.4%	3,200
12/99	21,343	218	1.0%	3,200
12/98	21,246	266	1.2%	3,200
12/97	19,416	265	1.4%	3,160
12/96	18,649	256	1.4%	—
12/95	16,253	251	1.5%	—
12/94	15,646	222	1.4%	—
Annual Growth	8.9%	(10.5%)	—	0.9%

2003 Year-End Financials
Equity as % of assets: 5.9% Long-term debt ($ mil.): 31,346
Return on assets: 0.3% Sales ($ mil.): 979
Return on equity: 4.5%

Net Income History

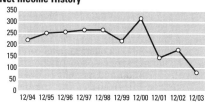

Agri-Mark

Cheese lovers who make a habit of Cabot ought to know Agri-Mark, the northeastern dairy cooperative that makes Cabot-brand cheese, butter, and cultured dairy products, and McCadam-brand cheese. Formed in 1980, Agri-Mark has more than 1,350 member-owners who operate farms throughout New England and New York, producing 2.7 billion pounds of milk a year. The company merged with Cabot Creamery in 1992 and purchased the McCadam Cheese business in 2003. Agri-Mark also sells milk to bottlers and manufacturers in the eastern US. It owns four processing plants: two in Vermont and one each in Massachusetts and New York.

EXECUTIVES

Chairman: Carl Peterson
President and General Manager: Paul P. Johnston
EVP and COO; CEO, Cabot Creamery:
  Richard W. Stammer
EVP Finance and Administration: Margaret H. Bertolino
SVP Economics, Communications, and Legislative Affairs: Robert D. (Bob) Wellington
SVP Sales, Cabot Creamery: Charlie Green
VP Information Services: Ralph Viscomi
VP, Human Resources: Vince Candio
Director of Communications: Douglas (Doug) DiMento

LOCATIONS

HQ: Agri-Mark, Inc.
  100 Milk St., Methuen, MA 01844
Phone: 978-689-4442 **Fax:** 978-794-8304
Web: www.agrimark.net

PRODUCTS/OPERATIONS

Selected Products
Bovine lactoferrin (nutritional whey protein derived from cow's milk)
Butter
Cheese
Condensed skim milk
Condensed whey
Cottage cheese
Cream
Milk powder
Skim milk
Sour cream and dips
Sweet cream
Yogurt

COMPETITORS

Dairy Farmers of America Kraft Foods
Dairylea Land O'Lakes
Great Lakes Cheese Lucille Farms
Keller's Creamery

HISTORICAL FINANCIALS
Company Type: Cooperative

Income Statement				FYE: November 30
	REVENUE ($ mil.)	NET INCOME ($ mil.)	NET PROFIT MARGIN	EMPLOYEES
11/03	600	11	1.9%	700
11/02	550	7	1.2%	700
11/01	570	6	1.0%	600
11/00	520	2	0.4%	600
11/99	556	—	—	500
11/98	575	—	—	500
11/97	462	—	—	—
11/96	479	—	—	—
11/95	396	—	—	—
Annual Growth	5.3%	81.7%	—	7.0%

Net Income History

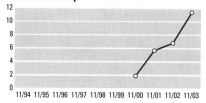

Akin Gump

Lobbying is as lobbying does. Akin Gump Strauss Hauer & Feld is known for its work inside Washington's Beltway and has a staff peppered with political insiders such as Robert Strauss (co-founder and former chairman of the Democratic National Committee) and Vernon Jordan (friend and adviser to former President Clinton). The firm has about 1,000 attorneys in 13 US offices, as well as four international locations. Although known for its prominent lobbying contingent, Akin Gump's expertise ranges from corporate law to white-collar criminal defense.

Over the last few years, the firm has enhanced its intellectual property and technology practices and other standard practice areas. It moved into entertainment law with a 2000 acquisition of Troop Steuber Pasich Reddick & Tobey. The firm expanded its litigation practice by adding attorneys from the Austin office of Brobeck, Phleger & Harrison LLP.

EXECUTIVES
Chairman: R. Bruce McLean
CFO: Janet Campion
CIO: Bradley Christmas
Chief Human Resources Officer: Julie Dressing
Senior Executive Partner: Alan D. Feld, age 67
Senior Executive Partner: James C. Langdon Jr.
Senior Executive Partner: Robert S. Strauss
Communications Manager: Kristin M. White

LOCATIONS
HQ: Akin Gump Strauss Hauer & Feld LLP
Robert S. Strauss Bldg., 1333 New Hampshire Ave. NW, Washington, DC 20036
Phone: 202-887-4000 **Fax:** 202-887-4288
Web: www.akingump.com

Akin Gump Strauss Hauer & Feld has offices in Albany, New York, and New York City; Austin, Dallas, Houston, and San Antonio, Texas; Chicago; McLean, Virginia; Philadelphia; Los Angeles, Riverside, and San Francisco, California; and Washington, DC; as well as in Brussels, London, and Moscow. It also has an affiliate office in Riyadh, Saudi Arabia.

PRODUCTS/OPERATIONS

Selected Practice Areas
Antitrust
Corporate and securities
Energy
Entertainment
Environmental
Government contracts
Health care
Insurance
Intellectual property
International
Investment management
Labor and employment
Litigation
Mergers and acquisitions
Public law and policy
Real estate
Tax
Technology (Akin Gump Technology Ventures)
White-collar criminal defense

COMPETITORS

Arnold & Porter
Covington & Burling
Hogan & Hartson
Howrey Simon Arnold & White
Kaye Scholer
O'Melveny & Myers
Williams & Connolly
Wilson Sonsini

HISTORICAL FINANCIALS
Company Type: Partnership

Income Statement			FYE: December 31	
	REVENUE ($ mil.)	NET INCOME ($ mil.)	NET PROFIT MARGIN	EMPLOYEES
12/03	585	—	—	2,200
12/02	575	—	—	—
12/01	553	—	—	—
12/00	430	—	—	—
12/99	360	—	—	2,000
12/98	301	—	—	1,800
12/97	246	—	—	1,700
12/96	218	—	—	1,550
12/95	190	—	—	1,400
12/94	163	—	—	1,235
Annual Growth	15.3%	—	—	6.6%

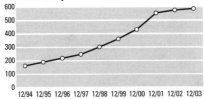

Revenue History

Alberici

Alberici helped shape the St. Louis skyline; it now sets its sights — or its construction sites — across North America. Alberici Corp., parent company of Alberici Constructors (formerly J.S. Alberici Construction Co.), encompasses a group of enterprises with a presence in four US regions, Canada, and Mexico. Operations include construction services, construction equipment, building materials, and steel fabrication and erection units. Alberici offers general contracting, design/build services, construction management, demolition, and specialty contracting. It also offers facilities management. The Alberici family still holds the largest share of the employee-owned firm, founded in 1918 by John S. Alberici.

EXECUTIVES
Chairman: John S. Alberici
President and CEO; President and CEO, Alberici Group: Robert F. (Bob) McCoole
SVP and Contract Review Officer, Alberici Group: James E. (Jim) Frey
VP Corporate Finance, Alberici Group: Gregory T. (Greg) Hesser
VP and Chief Administrative Officer: David E. Pendleton
SVP Business Acquisition and Estimating, Alberici Group: Steven E. (Steve) Olson
President, Alberici Constructors, Inc.: Gregory J. (Greg) Kozicz
COO, Alberici Constructors, Inc.: Leroy J. Stromberg
President, Gunther-Nash: Michael E. (Mike) Stoecker
President, Alberici Constructors, Ltd. (Canada): Sherman Ladner
VP Information Technology, Alberici Group: Frank C. Kropiunik
VP Quality Management, Alberici Group: Ronald T. Rogge
Controller: Gregory (Greg) Hook
Director Employment Resources, Alberici Group: R. Denay Davis
Creative Director, Alberici Group: Scott A. Tripp

LOCATIONS
HQ: Alberici Corporation
2150 Kienlen Ave., St. Louis, MO 63121
Phone: 314-261-2611 **Fax:** 314-261-4225
Web: www.alberici.com

PRODUCTS/OPERATIONS

Selected Subsidiaries and Affiliates
Alberici Global Group, GmbH
Alberici Constructors, Ltd. (industrial and institutional construction services, Canada)
Marhnos-Alberici Construcciones S.A. de C.V. (joint venture, Mexico)

Alberici Group, Inc.
Alberici Constructors, Inc. (construction services)
Alberici Healthcare Constructors (construction services for the health care market)
Alberici Industrial, LLC (construction services)
Alberici Mid-Atlantic, LLC (construction services for petrochemical clients in Ohio Valley)
Gunther-Nash, Inc. (shaft, slope, and tunnel construction for mining industry)
Hillsdale Fabricators (steel fabrication)
Hoffman, LLC (50%, joint venture with Hoffman Corp., design/build services for education and senior living markets)

COMPETITORS

Bechtel
Black & Veatch
DPR Construction
Fluor
Fred Weber
Hensel Phelps Construction
Hoffman Corporation
Hunt Construction
Hyundai Engineering and Construction
Jacobs Engineering
McCarthy Building
Parsons
Perini
Peter Kiewit Sons' Raytheon
TIC Holdings
Walbridge Aldinger
Walsh Group
Washington Group
Zachry

HISTORICAL FINANCIALS
Company Type: Private

Income Statement			FYE: December 31	
	REVENUE ($ mil.)	NET INCOME ($ mil.)	NET PROFIT MARGIN	EMPLOYEES
12/03	608	—	—	—
12/02	763	—	—	—
12/01	837	—	—	480
12/00	837	—	—	430
12/99	866	—	—	1,500
12/98	531	—	—	1,500
12/97	645	—	—	1,500
12/96	563	—	—	1,500
12/95	451	—	—	1,200
12/94	659	—	—	1,500
Annual Growth	(0.9%)	—	—	(15.0%)

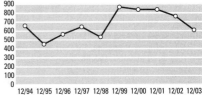

Revenue History

Alegent Health

Alegent Health has pledged its allegiance to the residents of northeast Nebraska and southwest Iowa. The health care system provides patients with seven hospitals and two long-term care facilities that all together have more than 1,800 beds. Alegent Health Clinic is a network of some 40 primary care centers. Other services the organization provides are inpatient and outpatient behavioral health care, rehabilitation, cancer treatment, and Immanuel Fontenelle Home, an assisted-living center. The health care system is a joint venture between Catholic Health Initiatives and Immanuel Healthcare System, which is sponsored by the Nebraska Synod of the Evangelical Lutheran Church in America.

EXECUTIVES
CEO: Wayne A. Sensor, age 47
President: Richard A. Hachten II
CFO: Dwight R. Youngman
VP, Operations: Diane (Di) Smalley
VP, Human Resources: Mark Thomas
VP, Information Technology: Ken Lawonn
Chief Integration Officer: Kevin Nokels
Medical Director of Informatics: Michael Westcott
Operations Leader for Revenue Cycle Operations: Tim Meier

LOCATIONS
HQ: Alegent Health
1010 N. 96th St., Ste. 200, Omaha, NE 68114
Phone: 402-343-4343 **Fax:** 402-343-4316
Web: www.alegent.com

HISTORICAL FINANCIALS
Company Type: Joint venture

Income Statement			FYE: June 30
	REVENUE ($ mil.)	NET INCOME ($ mil.)	NET PROFIT MARGIN	EMPLOYEES
6/03	692	—	—	7,500

Alex Lee

The George family mixed wholesale and retail food well before it was a consolidation trend. Founded by Alex and Lee George in 1931, Alex Lee distributes food to retailers through Merchants Distributors, Inc. (MDI). MDI serves more than 600 retailers in the mid-Atlantic and Southeast, including IGA stores and Galaxy Food Centers. The company became a foodservice supplier in the 1960s with the purchase of Institution Food House. In 1984 it bought the Lowe's Foods chain, which has more than 100 stores in North and South Carolina and Virginia. In 1998 Alex Lee started Consolidation Services to provide logistic services to vendors, distributors, and manufacturers. The George family controls Alex Lee.

EXECUTIVES
Chairman and CEO: Boyd L. George
President: Dennis G. Hatchell
EVP and CFO: Ronald W. Knedlik
VP, Human Resources: Glenn DeBiasi
VP, Information Systems: Jay Schwarz
President, Institution Food House:
  David A. (Dave) Stansfield
President, Lowe's Foods: Curtis Oldenkamp

LOCATIONS
HQ: Alex Lee, Inc.
120 4th St. SW, Hickory, NC 28603
Phone: 828-323-4424 **Fax:** 828-323-4435
Web: www.alexlee.com

COMPETITORS
Ahold USA
ARAMARK
C&S Wholesale
Ingles Markets
Kroger
K-VA-T Food Stores
McLane Foodservice
Nash Finch
Ruddick
SUPERVALU
SYSCO
U.S. Foodservice
Winn-Dixie

HISTORICAL FINANCIALS
Company Type: Private

Income Statement			FYE: September 30
	REVENUE ($ mil.)	NET INCOME ($ mil.)	NET PROFIT MARGIN	EMPLOYEES
9/03	2,140	—	—	9,500
9/02	1,980	—	—	9,000
9/01	1,890	—	—	8,500
9/00	1,690	—	—	8,500
9/99	1,588	—	—	7,154
9/98	1,516	—	—	7,482
9/97	1,315	—	—	6,143
9/96	1,300	—	—	5,400
9/95	1,270	—	—	5,400
9/94	1,159	—	—	3,000
Annual Growth	7.1%	—	—	13.7%

Revenue History

Allegis Group

Clients in need of highly skilled technical and other personnel might want to take the pledge of Allegis. Allegis Group is one of the world's largest staffing and recruitment firms, with more than 230 offices in North America and Europe. Its operating companies include Aerotek (engineering, automotive, and scientific professionals for short- and long-term assignments), Mentor 4 (recruitment for accounting, human resources, and customer support positions), and TEKsystems (IT staffing and consulting). In 1983 CEO Steve Bisciotti and Jim Davis established Aerotek to provide contract engineering personnel to two clients in the aerospace industry; Bisciotti and Davis still control Allegis.

EXECUTIVES
CEO: Steve Bisciotti
CFO: Dave Seandeven
EVP Human Resources: Neil Mann
President, Mentor 4: Mike McSally
CEO, TEKsystems: Mike Salandra
President, Aerotek: Tom Thornton
CIO: Kevin Apperson
General Counsel: Randy Sones

LOCATIONS
HQ: Allegis Group, Inc.
7301 Parkway Dr., Hanover, MD 21076
Phone: 410-579-4800 **Fax:** 410-540-7556
Web: www.allegisgroup.com

PRODUCTS/OPERATIONS
Operating Companies
Aerotek (engineering, automotive, and scientific personnel for short- and long-term assignments)
Mentor 4 (recruitment for accounting, human resources, and customer support positions)
Contacteam
Option One
TEKsystems (IT staffing and consulting)

COMPETITORS
Adecco
CDI
Kelly Services
Manpower
MPS
Randstad
Robert Half
Snelling and Snelling
Spherion
Vedior
Volt Information

HISTORICAL FINANCIALS
Company Type: Private

Income Statement			FYE: December 31
	ESTIMATED REVENUE ($ mil.)	NET INCOME ($ mil.)	NET PROFIT MARGIN	EMPLOYEES
12/02	2,035	—	—	4,600
12/01	2,700	—	—	8,000
12/00	3,700	—	—	8,800
Annual Growth	(25.8%)	—	—	(27.7%)

Revenue History

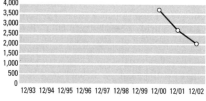

Alliance Capital Management

Alliance Capital Management has tons of funds. As one of the world's largest investment managers, Alliance Capital Management primarily serves such institutional investors as pension funds, foundations, endowments, government entities, and insurers. It offers more than 100 domestic and international mutual funds. It also offers individuals managed accounts, retirement plans, and college savings plans. Alliance Capital owns money manager and research firm Sanford C. Bernstein. French insurer AXA holds nearly 55% of Alliance Capital Management; publicly traded Alliance Capital Management Holding owns about 30% of the firm, which made news in 2003 when it became embroiled in the mutual fund market-timing scandal.

Institutional customers — which include public retirement funds in more than 40 states and for more than 40 of the *FORTUNE* 100 companies — account for more than 55% of Alliance Capital's nearly $490 billion in assets under management.

Alliance Capital and Sanford C. Bernstein utilize in-house research staffs to cover international and domestic stocks and bonds for their own funds and for institutional investors.

Long known as a growth investor, Alliance Capital is trying to cast itself in a more conservative light. But the company took a hit from troubled telecommunications concern WorldCom (now MCI), in which it held a significant stake; Alliance Capital was also one of the largest shareholders of collapsed energy firm Enron.

In 2003 Alliance Capital came under investigation as instances of improper market-timing trades came to light. The firm's president, the head of its mutual fund distribution unit, and some additional employees were ousted amidst the scandal. In late 2003, the company reached a $600 million settlement with regulators, also agreeing to cut its fund fees and freeze the rates at that level for a five-year period.

HISTORY

Alliance Capital Management began in 1962 as the management department of Donaldson, Lufkin & Jenrette, now Credit Suisse First Boston (USA). The company opened its first international office in the UK in 1978. Also that year the company introduced its first money market fund. In 1983 the company debuted its first mutual fund. The Equitable acquired Alliance as part of its DLJ acquisition in 1985.

In an attempt to raise money, cash-strapped Equitable sold 40% of the company in a 1988 public offering of Alliance stock. The company acquired Shields Asset Management in 1994 and bought Cursitor-Eaton two years later. Poor performance of the Cursitor unit forced the company to take a $121 million charge in 1997.

In 1998 the Taxpayer Relief Act of 1997 removed Alliance's Master Limited Partnership tax status and increased the company's tax rate to that of a regular partnership, a 3.5% increase. The next year the company organized a holding company and transferred its operations and old name to a new limited partnership, Alliance Capital Management Holding, to help provide tax relief for parent company The Equitable (renamed AXA Financial in 1999).

The firm continued to bolster its reputation as a global investor, expanding its operations in Asia, Europe, the UK, and South America, where it targeted privatized pension funds. As deregulation opened the Japanese mutual fund market in 1998, the company worked to rapidly establish a major presence there. Alliance's global vision played into the strategy of its ultimate parent, AXA. As one of the world's largest insurers, AXA began building its brand, using Alliance to help establish itself in global financial services.

In 2000 the company bought money manager Sanford C. Bernstein, a firm noted for its research.

EXECUTIVES

Chairman: Bruce W. Calvert, age 57, $285,579 pay
Vice Chairman and CEO: Lewis A. (Lew) Sanders, age 57, $1,340,963 pay
Vice Chairman: Alfred Harrison, age 66
Vice Chairman: Roger Hertog, age 62
EVP, COO, and Director: Gerald M. Lieberman, age 57
EVP: John L. Blundin, age 63
EVP and Chief Investment Officer - Global Value Equities: Sharon E. Fay, age 43, $1,407,692 pay
EVP: Marilyn G. Fedak, age 57
EVP: Mark R. Gordon, age 50
EVP; President, Bernstein Investment Research and Management: Thomas S. Hexner, age 47
EVP: Marc O. Mayer, age 46
EVP: James G. Reilly, age 43
EVP, Director of Global Growth Equity Research, and Portfolio Manager: Paul C. Rissman, age 47
EVP; Chairman and CEO, Sanford C. Bernstein & Co.: Lisa A. Shalett, age 40, $2,203,247 pay
EVP: David A. Steyn, age 44, $1,472,531 pay
EVP: Christopher M. Toub, age 44
SVP and CFO: Robert H. Joseph Jr., age 56
SVP and Acting General Counsel: Mark R. Manley, age 41
SVP: Seth J. Masters, age 44
VP and Director, Investor Relations: Valerie Haertel
Auditors: KPMG LLP

LOCATIONS

HQ: Alliance Capital Management L.P.
1345 Avenue of the Americas, New York, NY 10105
Phone: 212-969-1000   **Fax:** 212-969-2229
Web: www.alliancecapital.com

Alliance Capital Management has offices in Australia, Bahrain, Brazil, Canada, France, Germany, Hong Kong, India, Japan, Luxembourg, New Zealand, Singapore, South Africa, South Korea, Spain, Switzerland, Taiwan, the UK, and the US.

2003 Sales

	% of total
US	82
International	18
Total	**100**

PRODUCTS/OPERATIONS

2003 Sales

	$ mil.	% of total
Investment advisory & service fees		
Retail	746.4	27
Institutional investment management	649.6	24
Private client	486.4	18
Distribution revenues	436.0	16
Institutional research services	267.9	10
Shareholder servicing fees	94.3	3
Other	52.2	2
Total	**2,732.8**	**100**

2003 Assets Under Management

	$ mil.	% of total
Institutional Investment Management	269,465	57
Retail	153,784	32
Private Client	51,550	11
Total	**474,799**	**100**

Selected Mutual Fund Families

Cash Management Funds
CollegeBound Fund
Global & International Stock Funds
Money Market Funds
Select Investor Series
Taxable Bond Funds
Tax-Exempt Bond Funds
US Stock Funds
Value Funds

Selected Subsidiaries and Affiliates

ACAM Trust Company Private Limited (India)
ACM Fund Services (Espana) S.L. (Spain)
ACM Global Investor Services S.A. (Luxembourg)
ACM International (France) SAS
ACM Investments Limited (UK)
ACM New-Alliance (Luxembourg) S.A. (51%)
ACM Software Services Ltd.
Albion Alliance LLC (37%)
Alliance Asset Allocation Limited (UK)
Alliance Capital (Luxembourg) S.A.
Alliance Capital (Mauritius) Private Limited
Alliance Capital Asset Management (India) Private Ltd. (75%)
Alliance Capital Asset Management (Japan) Ltd.
Alliance Capital Australia Limited
Alliance Capital Global Derivatives Corporation
Alliance Capital Latin America Ltda. (Brazil)
Alliance Capital Limited (UK)
Alliance Capital Management (Asia) Ltd.
Alliance Capital Management (Proprietary) Limited (South Africa; 80%)
Alliance Capital Management (Singapore) Ltd.
Alliance Capital Management Australia Limited (50%)
Alliance Capital Management Canada, Inc.
Alliance Capital Management Corporation of Delaware
Alliance Capital Management LLC
Alliance Capital Management New Zealand Limited (50%)
Alliance Capital Oceanic Corporation
Alliance Capital Portfolio and Fund Management Egypt S.A.
Alliance Capital Services Limited (UK)
Alliance Capital Whittingdale Limited (UK)
Alliance Corporate Finance Group Incorporated
Alliance Eastern Europe Inc.
Alliance Global Investor Services, Inc.
Alliance SBS-AGRO Capital Management Company (Russia; 49%)
AllianceBernstein Investment Research and Management, Inc.
Alliance-Cecogest S.A. (France)
Alliance-MBCA Capital (Private) Limited (Zimbabwe; 50%)
Alliance-Odyssey Capital Management (Namibia)(Proprietary) Limited
Cursitor Alliance LLC
Cursitor Holdings Limited (UK)
Cursitor Services Limited (UK)
Dimensional Trust Management Limited (UK)
Far Eastern Alliance Asset Management (Taiwan; 20%)
Hanwha Investment Trust Management Company, Ltd. (Korea; 20%)
Meiji-Alliance Capital Corporation (50%)
New-Alliance Asset Management (Asia) Limited (Hong Kong; 50%)
Sanford C. Bernstein & Co., LLC
Sanford C. Bernstein (CREST Nominees) Limited (UK)
Sanford C. Bernstein Limited (UK)
Sanford C. Bernstein Proprietary Limited (Australia)
Whittingdale Holdings Limited (UK)
Whittingdale Nominees Limited (UK)

COMPETITORS

Affiliated Managers Group	Janus Capital
AIG	Legg Mason
AIG SunAmerica	Merrill Lynch
American Century	MFS
AMVESCAP	Neuberger Berman
BlackRock	Nuveen
Eaton Vance	Principal Financial
Federated Investors	Raymond James Financial
FMR	T. Rowe Price
Franklin Resources	UBS Financial Services
Gabelli Asset Management	Vanguard Group
ING	Waddell & Reed Financial

HISTORICAL FINANCIALS

Company Type: Private

Income Statement

FYE: December 31

	ASSETS ($ mil.)	NET INCOME ($ mil.)	INCOME AS % OF ASSETS	EMPLOYEES
12/03	8,172	330	4.0%	4,096
12/02	7,218	611	8.5%	4,172
12/01	8,175	615	7.5%	4,542
12/00	8,271	669	8.1%	4,438
12/99	1,661	462	27.8%	2,396
Annual Growth	48.9%	(8.1%)	—	14.3%

2003 Year-End Financials

Equity as % of assets: 46.2%   Long-term debt ($ mil.): 405
Return on assets: 4.3%   Sales ($ mil.): 2,733
Return on equity: 8.5%

Net Income History

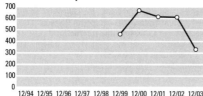

Alliance Entertainment

Alliance Entertainment rolls out the rock 'n' roll. The company distributes more than 265,000 music and video items — CDs, videos, DVDs, games, and related products — to home entertainment retailers (both online retailers and brick-and-mortar stores). Alliance also provides support services (including e-commerce software) and operates the All-Media Guide, an online database of entertainment information with three consumer guides: All-Movie Guide, All-Music Guide, and All-Game Guide. Alliance owns Digital On-Demand, a distributor of digital music, movies, and games, and re-issue record label, One Way Records. Investment firm The Yucaipa Companies owns a majority stake in Alliance.

EXECUTIVES

Chairman and Interim CEO: Tony Schnug
President and COO: Alan Tuchman
CFO: George Campagna
SVP, Corporate Development and Strategic Planning: Lonnie Chenkin
SVP and Legal Counsel: Isabel Barney
SVP, Sales: Mike Donohue
SVP: Karl S. Ryser Jr.
VP, Human Resources: Maureen Linehan
VP, Public Relations: Sue D'Agostino
President, All Media Guide: Vladmir Bogdanov
COO, One Stop Group and Supply Chain Management Division: Peter Blei
SVP, Operations, One Stop Group and Supply Chain Management Division: Bob Keskey
VP, Business Development, On-Demand/RedDotNet: Steve Johnson
VP, Information Services, One Stop Group and Supply Chain Management Division: Laura McLaughlin
General Manager, Innovative Distribution Network: Lou DeBiase
Director, Advertising, Innovative Distribution Network: Jim Freeman
Director, Distribution Center Operations, Innovative Distribution Network: Nelson Perez
Director, Licensing, One Way Record Label: Eddie Wilner

LOCATIONS

HQ: Alliance Entertainment Corp.
4250 Coral Ridge Dr., Coral Springs, FL 33065
Phone: 954-255-4000   **Fax:** 954-255-4078
Web: www.aent.com

COMPETITORS

Baker & Taylor
Diamond Entertainment
Handleman
Image Entertainment
Ingram Entertainment
KOCH Entertainment
Navarre
Rentrak

HISTORICAL FINANCIALS
Company Type: Private

Income Statement   FYE: December 31

	REVENUE ($ mil.)	NET INCOME ($ mil.)	NET PROFIT MARGIN	EMPLOYEES
12/03	870	—	—	1,400
12/02	808	—	—	1,250
12/01	589	—	—	1,200
12/00	466	—	—	1,000
12/99	450	—	—	900
12/98	400	—	—	800
12/97	391	—	—	700
12/96	691	—	—	1,850
12/95	720	—	—	—
12/94	535	—	—	—
Annual Growth	5.5%	—	—	(3.9%)

Revenue History

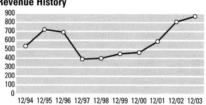

Allina Hospitals

Allina Hospitals and Clinics is a not-for-profit health care system that focuses on protecting people's number one asset — "Their Good Health." Allina Hospitals and Clinics owns and operates 11 hospitals and medical centers, and more than 40 clinics, hospice services, and pharmacies. The Allina network serves Minnesota and western Wisconsin. Allina Hospitals and Clinics also provides disease prevention programs, specialized inpatient and outpatient services, medical equipment, and emergency medical transportation service.

EXECUTIVES

Chairman: Michael E. Dougherty, age 63
Vice Chairman: James Campbell
Vice Chairman: John M. Morrison
President and CEO: Richard R. (Dick) Pettingill, age 55
EVP and CFO: Mark G. Harrison
CIO: Robert Plaszcz
EVP, Compliance and Public Policy, and Chief Compliance Officer: David B. Orbuch
EVP, Hospital & Specialty Operations: Rickie Ressler
EVP, Human Resources and Culture, and Chief Talent Officer: Michael W. Howe
EVP, Safety and Quality Systems: Barbara Balik
Chief Medical Officer: Brian Anderson
Corporate VP, Communications/PR/Marketing: Kendra Calhoun
President, Abbott Northwestern Hospital: Denny DeNarvaez
President, Allina Medical Clinic: Thomas D. Holets
President, Mercy & Unity Hospitals: Venetia Kudrle
President, Phillips Eye Institute: Shari Levy
President, United Hospital: Mark G. Mishek
President, Buffalo Hospital; Interim President, Owatonna Hospital: Mary Ellen Wells
President, Cambridge Medical Center: Dennis Doran
President, New Ulm Medical Center: Lori Wightman
President, River Falls Hospital: Randy Farrow
President, St. Francis Regional Medical Center: Tom O'Connor
Auditors: Deloitte & Touche LLP

LOCATIONS

HQ: Allina Hospitals and Clinics
710 E. 24th St., Minneapolis, MN 55404
Phone: 612-775-5000   **Fax:** 612-863-5667
Web: www.allina.com

PRODUCTS/OPERATIONS

Selected Hospitals
Abbott Northwestern Hospital (Minneapolis, MN)
Buffalo Hospital (Buffalo, MN)
Cambridge Medical Center (Cambridge, MN)
Mercy Hospital (Coon Rapids, MN)
New Ulm Medical Center (New Ulm, MN)
Owatonna Hospital (Owatonna, MN)
Phillips Eye Institute (Minneapolis, MN)
River Falls Area Hospital (River Falls, WI)
St. Francis Regional Medical Center (Shakopee, MN)
United Hospital (St. Paul, MN)
Unity Hospital (Fridley, MN)

COMPETITORS

Alexian Brothers Health System
Catholic Health Initiatives
HCA
Mayo Foundation
SSM Health Care

HISTORICAL FINANCIALS
Company Type: Not-for-profit

Income Statement   FYE: December 31

	REVENUE ($ mil.)	NET INCOME ($ mil.)	NET PROFIT MARGIN	EMPLOYEES
12/03	1,940	—	—	22,583
12/02	1,800	—	—	22,347
12/01	1,700	—	—	22,102
12/00	2,600	—	—	21,500
12/99	2,600	—	—	22,546
12/98	2,550	—	—	22,000
12/97	2,500	—	—	21,200
12/96	2,400	—	—	20,800
12/95	2,100	—	—	20,000
Annual Growth	(1.0%)	—	—	1.5%

Revenue History

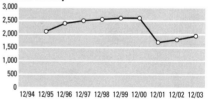

Alticor

At the core of Alticor, there is Amway. Alticor was formed in 2000 as a holding company for four businesses: direct-selling giant Amway, Web-based sales firm Quixtar, Pyxis Innovations (corporate development for Alticor and affiliates), and Access Business Group (manufacturing, logistics services). Access Business' biggest customers are Amway and Quixtar, but Access also serves outsiders. Amway, which accounts for the bulk of Alticor's revenues, sells more than 450 different products through 3 million independent distributors. Quixtar sells Amway and other products online. Alticor is owned by Amway founders, the DeVos and Van Andel families.

EXECUTIVES

Chairman: Steve Van Andel
President and Director; President, Amway; and President, Quixtar: Doug DeVos
COO, Access Business Group LLC: Al Koop
EVP and CFO: Lynn Lyall
VP, Corporate Communications: Mark Bain
VP, Finance and Corporate Controller:
  William J. Viveen Jr.
VP, Human Resources: Robin Horder-Koop
VP, Public Policy: Richard Holwill
VP, Strategic Planning and Mergers and Acquisitions:
  Beto Guajardo
Chief of Staff: William R. (Bill) Payne
Chief Marketing Officer: Bert Crandell
Corporate General Counsel: Michael Mohr

LOCATIONS

HQ: Alticor Inc.
  7575 Fulton St. East, Ada, MI 49355
Phone: 616-787-1000   **Fax:** 616-682-4000
Web: www.alticor.com

Alticor operates in more than 80 countries worldwide. It has manufacturing facilities in the US, China, and South Korea and farming operations in the US, Mexico, and Brazil.

PRODUCTS/OPERATIONS

Selected Amway Products
Catalog Products
  Appliances
  Electronics
  Fashions
  Home furnishings
  Office supplies
  Toys
Home Care Products
  Dishwashing liquid
  Laundry detergent
  Multi-purpose cleaner
Home Living/Home Tech Products
  Cookware
  Water-treatment systems
Nutrition and Wellness Products
  Beverages
  Dietary supplements
  Meals
  Snacks
  Weight-control products
Personal Care Products
  Body washes
  Deodorants
  Hair care products
  Lotions
  Toothpaste
Skin Care and Cosmetics Products
  Cleansers
  Color cosmetics
  Moisturizers
  Toners

Subsidiaries
Access Business Group (manufacturing, distribution, and outsourcing)
Amway (direct sales)
Pyxis (corporate development)
Quixtar (online product sales)

COMPETITORS

Avon
Bath & Body Works
Body Shop
Brown-Forman
CCL Industries
Clorox
Colgate-Palmolive
Daiei
Dial
Estée Lauder
Fingerhut
Forever Living
Gillette
GNC
Henkel
Herbalife
Johnson & Johnson
Kao
L'Oréal
MacAndrews & Forbes
Mary Kay
Newell Rubbermaid
Nikken
Nu Skin
PFSweb
Procter & Gamble
S.C. Johnson
Shaklee
Tom's of Maine
Tupperware
Unilever

HISTORICAL FINANCIALS

Company Type: Private

Income Statement				FYE: August 31
	REVENUE ($ mil.)	NET INCOME ($ mil.)	NET PROFIT MARGIN	EMPLOYEES
8/03	4,900	—	—	11,500
8/02	4,500	—	—	10,500
8/01	3,500	—	—	10,500
8/00	3,500	—	—	10,000
8/99	3,000	—	—	10,000
8/98	2,900	—	—	14,000
8/97	5,780	—	—	13,000
8/96	5,352	—	—	13,000
8/95	4,958	—	—	13,000
8/94	4,309	—	—	12,500
Annual Growth	1.4%	—	—	(0.9%)

Revenue History

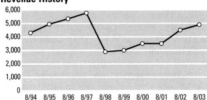

A-Mark Financial

Calling all gold bugs: A-Mark Financial trades, markets, and finances rare coins, precious metals, and collectibles. A-Mark Precious Metals trades in gold, silver, platinum, and palladium coins, bars, ingots, and medallions for central banks, corporations, and individuals around the world. A-Mark Financial distributes coins for government mints, including those of Australia, Canada, South Africa, and the US. Subsidiary Goldline International sells rare and collectible coins and bullion, while A-M Handling provides melting and assay services. Chairman and owner Steven Markoff founded A-Mark Financial in 1965; it is now among the 10 largest privately-held companies in Los Angeles county.

EXECUTIVES

President and CEO: Steven C. Markoff
Chief Administrative Officer: Joseph P. Ozaki
President and CEO, Goldline International:
  Mark Albarian
EVP, Marketing: Joseph C. Battaglia
Auditors: Deloitte & Touche LLP

LOCATIONS

HQ: A-Mark Financial Corporation
  100 Wilshire Blvd., 3rd Fl., Santa Monica, CA 90401
Phone: 310-319-0200   **Fax:** 310-319-0346
Web: www.amark.com

PRODUCTS/OPERATIONS

Selected Services
Deferred pricing transactions
Inventory financing
Leasing and consignment
Market making
Marketing support
New product announcements
Order execution
Platinum market updates
Refining
Storage

COMPETITORS

Anglo American
Degussa
DGSE Companies
Tumba Bruk

HISTORICAL FINANCIALS

Company Type: Private

Income Statement				FYE: July 31
	ESTIMATED REVENUE ($ mil.)	NET INCOME ($ mil.)	NET PROFIT MARGIN	EMPLOYEES
7/02	2,200	—	—	118
7/01	2,600	—	—	102
7/00	1,812	—	—	106
7/99	2,446	—	—	120
7/98	1,000	—	—	100
7/97	1,000	—	—	120
7/96	1,000	—	—	110
7/95	1,000	—	—	121
7/94	1,000	—	—	104
7/93	1,000	—	—	—
Annual Growth	9.2%	—	—	1.6%

Revenue History

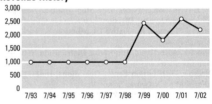

American Cancer Society

The American Cancer Society (ACS) works as a firefighter for your lungs. Dedicated to the elimination of cancer, the not-for-profit organization is staffed by professionals and more than 2 million volunteers at some 3,400 local units across the country. ACS is the largest source of private cancer research funds in the US. Recipients of the society's funding include 32 Nobel Prize laureates. In addition to research, the ACS supports detection, treatment, and education programs. The organization encourages prevention efforts with programs such as the Great American Smokeout. Patient services include moral support, transportation to and from treatment, and camps for children who have cancer.

The ACS has generated considerable income by marketing its name for antismoking nicotine patches and orange juice, and is contemplating even more lucrative deals. Programs account for 73% of expenses; 27% goes to administration and fund raising.

HISTORY

Concerned over the lack of progress in detecting and treating cancer, a group of 10 physicians and five laymen met in New York City in 1913 to form the American Society for the Control of Cancer (ASCC). Because public discussion of cancer was taboo, the group struggled with how to educate people without raising unnecessary fears. Some physicians even preferred keeping knowledge of the disease from the public. In the 1920s the ASCC began sponsoring cancer clinics and collecting statistics on the disease. By 1923 some states reported improvements in early diagnosis and treatment. In 1937 the ASCC started its first nationwide public education program, with the help of volunteers known as the Women's Field Army. President Franklin Roosevelt named April National Cancer Control Month, a practice since followed by every president.

By 1944 some cancer rates were rising but the word "cancer" still couldn't be mentioned on radio. Mary Lasker, wife of prominent ad executive Albert Lasker, was instrumental in getting information about cancer broadcast. At her insistence, in 1945 the newly renamed American Cancer Society began donating at least 25% of its budget to research. The society raised $4 million in its first major national fund-raising campaign.

The link between smoking and lung cancer became known after a study in the early 1950s by ACS medical director Charles Cameron. That information became part of the Surgeon General's Report of 1964. In 1973 an ACS branch in Minnesota held the first Great American Smokeout to encourage people to quit smoking.

The ACS backed the 1971 congressional bill that inaugurated the War on Cancer. The society was attacked in the 1970s for emphasizing cures rather than prevention because, critics claimed, research would reveal environmental causes from industrial products made by companies with connections to ACS directors. In the 1970s and 1980s, the ACS backed tougher restrictions on tobacco and, in response to earlier criticism, directed research toward prevention as well as treatment. The society played a major role in the 1989 airline smoking ban.

John Seffrin, a former Indiana University professor, was named CEO of ACS in 1992. The first of several genetic breakthroughs came in the 1990s when ACS grantees isolated genes believed to be responsible for triggering various types of cancer. In 1995 the ACS accused the tobacco industry of infiltrating its offices in the 1970s and using its papers to aid in the early marketing of low-tar cigarettes.

In 1996 the ACS announced that new data showed a drop in the US cancer death rate for the first time ever. The ACS entered agreements with SmithKline Beecham (NicoDerm antismoking patches) and the Florida Department of Citrus in 1996 to allow the use of the American Cancer Society name in marketing.

The proposed $369 billion settlement between the attorneys general of 40 states and the tobacco industry was big news in 1997. The ACS had wanted more concessions, such as a $2-per-pack tax increase, more power for industry regulation by the FDA, and underage use rate-reduction targets for smokeless tobacco products as stringent as those for cigarettes.

In 1998 the ACS launched a $5 million national advertising campaign to combat what it sees as "misleading" information spread by the tobacco industry. It argued in Supreme Court in 1999 to help the FDA gain control over cigarette production and distribution. In 2000 ACS restructured its $50-million-a-year research program to increase the size of individual grants; it also awarded its largest-ever award, $1.7 million, to study the side effects of cancer treatment. In 2001 ACS filed petitions to the FDA urging them to regulate new tobacco products marketed as being safer than traditional cigarettes. In 2002 ACS and The Robert Wood Johnson Foundation launched the Center for Tobacco Cessation to help people quit smoking. In 2003 ACS published strategic guides to help countries in early stages of tobacco control.

EXECUTIVES

Chairman: David M. Zacks
Chairman-Elect: Gary J. Streit
Vice Chairman: Thomas G. Burish
CEO: John R. Seffrin
President: Mary Simmonds
President-Elect: Ralph B. Vance
CFO: Peter Tartikoff
Chief Medical Officer: Harmon J. Eyre
First VP: Mark Clanton
Second VP: Stephen F. Sener
National VP Corporate Communications:
  A. Gregory Donaldson
National VP Federal and State Governmental Affairs:
  Daniel E. Smith
National VP Human Resources: Aurelia C. Stanley
National VP Strategic Marketing Alliances:
  Cynthia Currence
CIO: Vic Ayers
Chief Counsel: William Dalton
Secretary: Anna Johnson-Winegar
Treasurer: Jean B. McGill

LOCATIONS

HQ: American Cancer Society, Inc.
  1599 Clifton Rd. NE, Atlanta, GA 30345
Phone: 404-320-3333   **Fax:** 404-982-3677
Web: www.cancer.org

PRODUCTS/OPERATIONS

Selected Patient Services Programs
Children's Camps (for children and teens with cancer; some for siblings)
Hope Lodge (housing assistance)
I Can Cope (education and support classes on living with cancer)
Look Good . . . Feel Better (cosmetics and beauty techniques for women experiencing side effects of cancer treatment)
Man To Man Prostate Cancer Support
Pamphlets and brochures for cancer patients and their families
Reach to Recovery (support for women with breast cancer and their families)
Road to Recovery (transportation services)

Selected Public Education Programs and Publications
Great American Smokeout (national stop-smoking-for-a-day event)
Making Strides Against Breast Cancer (fund-raiser)
Relay for Life (fund-raiser)

Selected Research Grants and Awards
Clinical Research Professorships
Clinical Research Training Grants
Institutional research grants
Postdoctoral fellowships
Research Opportunity Grants
Research Professorships

HISTORICAL FINANCIALS

Company Type: Not-for-profit

Income Statement

FYE: August 31

	REVENUE ($ mil.)	NET INCOME ($ mil.)	NET PROFIT MARGIN	EMPLOYEES
8/02	813	—	—	6,500
8/01	822	—	—	6,500
8/00	812	—	—	6,000
8/99	672	—	—	4,500
8/98	677	—	—	4,500
8/97	602	—	—	4,418
8/96	458	—	—	4,500
8/95	420	—	—	4,656
8/94	392	—	—	4,100
8/93	388	—	—	4,200
Annual Growth	8.6%	—	—	5.0%

Revenue History

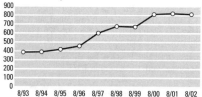

HOOVER'S HANDBOOK OF PRIVATE COMPANIES 2005

American Cast Iron Pipe

American Cast Iron Pipe Co. (ACIPCO) has one of the largest individual ductile iron pipe casting plants in the world. Its divisions — American Centrifugal, American Ductile Iron Pipe, American Flow Control, and American Steel Pipe — make ductile iron pipe and fittings, cast steel tubes, electric resistance welded steel pipes, fire hydrants and fire truck pumps, and valves for water treatment and energy production. ACIPCO's newest subsidiary, American SpiralWeld Pipe, produces spiral-welded steel pipe. John Joseph Eagan founded ACIPCO in 1905, and in 1922 placed all of the company's stock into a beneficial trust for ACIPCO employees. Employees also receive generous quarterly bonuses.

EXECUTIVES
President and CEO: Van L. Richey, age 54
CFO and Treasurer: J. M. Cook
VP, Corporate Communications: Cynthia Lovoy
VP, Human Resources: LeAnn Barr
VP, Sales and Secretary: J. Michael O'Brien
VP Operations, American SpiralWeld Pipe Company: Don Gray
Sales Manager, American Ductile Iron Pipe: Jerry N. Burns
Sales Manager, American Flow Control: Walter L. Cooper
Manager Marketing Services, American Ductile Iron Pipe: Philip A. Selig
Assistant Sales Manager, American Ductile Iron Pipe: W.D. (Skip) Benton
Customer Service Manager, American Ductile Iron Pipe: Maury D. Gaston
Division Manager General Sales, American Steel Pipe: Jon Noland
Manager Field Sales and Eastern Region, American Steel Pipe: Mark Schach
Manager Customer Service, American Steel Pipe: Carol Sparks
Auditors: KPMG LLP

LOCATIONS
HQ: American Cast Iron Pipe Company
1501 N. 31st Ave. North, Birmingham, AL 35202
Phone: 205-325-7701 **Fax:** 205-325-1942
Web: www.acipco.com

American Cast Iron Pipe has operations in Alabama, Minnesota, South Carolina, and Texas.

PRODUCTS/OPERATIONS
Selected Divisions and Products
ACIPCO International
  Coatings and primers
  Ductile iron pipe
  Flanged pipe and fittings
  Joints
  Linings
  Restrained pipe and fittings
American Centrifugal
  Casting
  Fabrication
  Machining
American Ductile Iron Pipe
  Coatings and linings
  Ductile iron pipe and fittings
  Special pipe and fittings
American Flow Control
  Check valves
  Fire hydrants
  Gate valves
  Tapping sleeves and saddles
  Trench adapters
American Steel Pipe
  Electric-resistance weld line pipe

COMPETITORS
AK Steel Holding Corporation
Ameron
CIRCOR International
Dalmine
Darley & Co.
Kubota
Lone Star Technologies
Maverick Tube
McWane
Northwest Pipe
Oregon Steel Mills
Siderca
Valve Research & Manufacturing
Walter Industries
Webco
Wilson Industries

HISTORICAL FINANCIALS
Company Type: Private

Income Statement
FYE: December 31

	REVENUE ($ mil.)	NET INCOME ($ mil.)	NET PROFIT MARGIN	EMPLOYEES
12/02	650	—	—	3,000
12/01	600	—	—	2,313
12/00	600	—	—	2,800
12/99	550	—	—	2,800
12/98	500	—	—	2,800
12/97	405	—	—	3,000
12/96	402	—	—	2,366
Annual Growth	8.3%	—	—	4.0%

Revenue History

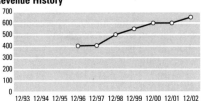

American Crystal Sugar

Call it saccharine, but for American Crystal Sugar, business is all about sharing. The sugar beet cooperative is owned by more than 3,000 growers in the Red River Valley of North Dakota and Minnesota. American Crystal, formed in 1899 and converted into a co-op in 1973, divides the 35-mile-wide valley into five districts, each served by a processing plant. During an annual eight-month "campaign," the plants operate continuously, producing sugar, molasses, and beet pulp. Its products (under the Crystal name, the licensed Pillsbury brand, and private labels) are sold through marketing co-ops United Sugars and Midwest Agri-Commodities. American Crystal also owns 51% of corn sweeteners joint venture ProGold.

EXECUTIVES
Chairman: Robert Vivatson, age 53
President and CEO: James J. Horvath, age 58, $647,062 pay
VP, Administration: Tom Astrup, age 34, $226,348 pay
VP, Factory Operations Crookston: David A. Walden, age 50, $275,628 pay
VP, Finance, and CFO: Joseph J. Talley, age 43, $311,644 pay
VP, Operations: David A. Berg, age 49, $298,969 pay
Corporate Controller, Assistant Secretary, and Assistant Treasurer: Brian F. Ingulsrud, age 40
Director, Business Development, Assistant Treasurer, and Assistant Secretary: David L. Malmskog, age 46
Director, Government Affairs: Kevin Price
Director, Human Resources: Randy Johnson
Manager, Finance Administration: Mark L. Lembke
Manager, Treasury Operations: Lisa M. Maloy
Secretary and General Counsel: Daniel C. Mott, age 44
Treasurer and Assistant Secretary: Samuel S. M. Wai, age 49
Assistant Treasurer and Assistant Secretary: Ronald K. Peterson, age 48
Specialist, Public Relations: Jeff Schweitzer
Superintendent, Production Crookston: Tom Samson
Auditors: Eide Bailly LLP

LOCATIONS
HQ: American Crystal Sugar Company
101 N. Third St., Moorhead, MN 56560
Phone: 218-236-4400 **Fax:** 218-236-4422
Web: www.crystalsugar.com

COMPETITORS
ADM
Alberto-Culver
Alexander & Baldwin
Amalgamated Sugar
C&H Sugar
Cargill
Cumberland Packing
Florida Crystals
Imperial Sugar
M A Patout
Monitor Sugar
Nippon Beet Sugar
NutraSweet
SMBSC
Sterling Sugars
Südzucker
Sugar Cane Growers Cooperative of Florida
Sugar Foods
Tate & Lyle
U.S. Sugar
Western Sugar Cooperative

HISTORICAL FINANCIALS
Company Type: Cooperative

Income Statement
FYE: August 31

	REVENUE ($ mil.)	NET INCOME ($ mil.)	NET PROFIT MARGIN	EMPLOYEES
8/03	829	362	43.6%	1,231
8/02	775	399	51.4%	1,243
8/01	866	389	44.9%	1,250
8/00	731	358	49.0%	1,294
8/99	844	370	43.8%	1,292
8/98	677	306	45.2%	1,263
8/97	677	367	54.2%	1,202
8/96	688	310	45.1%	2,437
8/95	606	321	52.9%	2,000
8/94	563	274	48.6%	—
Annual Growth	4.4%	3.1%	—	(5.9%)

2003 Year-End Financials
Debt ratio: 123.6%
Return on equity: 156.5%
Cash ($ mil.): 1
Current ratio: 1.30
Long-term debt ($ mil.): 287

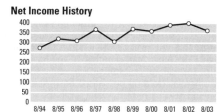

Net Income History

American Family Insurance

Even singles can get insured through American Family Insurance Group. The company specializes in property & casualty insurance, but also offers life, health, and homeowners coverage, as well as investment and retirement-planning products. It is among the largest US mutual companies that concentrates on auto insurance (State Farm is the biggest). American Family also provides coverage for apartment owners, restaurants, contractors, and other businesses. Through the company's consumer finance division, agents can also offer their customers home equity and personal lines of credit.

The company has around 4,000 agents operating primarily in the Midwest. Unlike many of its competitors, American Family has said it has no plans to demutualize.

Benefitting from a rebounding stock market and a favorable insurance market (especially for auto and health lines), American Family Insurance grew its net revenues by some $100 million in 2003.

HISTORY

In 1927 Herman Wittwer founded Farmers Mutual Automobile Insurance to sell coverage to Wisconsin farmers. As farms became mechanized in the 1920s, the insurance market grew. Low-density rural traffic reduced the potential for accidents, a fact that attracted Wittwer and others, such as State Farm (founded in 1922) to serve the similar markets. Wittwer also noted that rural Wisconsin's severe winters made cars unusable for a good part of the year, further reducing risk.

Farmers Mutual grew despite the Depression and WWII, spreading to Minnesota (1933); Missouri (1939); Nebraska and the Dakotas (1940); and Indiana, Iowa, and Kansas (1943). The war years were generous to insurers: Rising incomes allowed people to insure their cars, but rationing programs limited use of the cars. The postwar suburban boom — when cars became a necessity rather than a luxury — also helped auto insurers.

Growing prosperity for single-earner households in the 1950s helped boost the demand for life insurance. In 1958 Farmers Mutual formed American Family Life Insurance. The company wrote $1.6 million in insurance on its first day in the life insurance business. During that decade, Farmers Mutual moved into Illinois.

The 1960s brought growth and change. To capture more auto business, it founded American Standard Insurance to write nonstandard auto insurance. The firm also launched consumer finance operations for insurance customers and noncustomers alike, departing from standard industry practice by selling through agents rather than offices. In 1963, in recognition of its growing diversification, Farmers Mutual changed its name to American Family Mutual Insurance.

During the 1970s and 1980s, the firm strengthened its infrastructure and added regional offices. It moved into Arizona and later formed American Family Brokerage to fill in gaps in its own coverage by obtaining insurance for clients through other insurers.

During this period American Family suffered cultural pains. It moved beyond its traditional rural clientele and into the urban unknown as it sought to increase its market share. In 1981 community groups questioned whether the company was adequately serving racially mixed neighborhoods. In 1988 the US Justice Department began investigating allegations that the firm engaged in redlining (offering inferior or no service for minority neighborhoods); a class-action suit based on similar claims was filed in 1990. The suit went all the way to the Supreme Court, which ruled that insurance sales must comply with the Fair Housing Act.

The company had begun rectifying its practices before the case was decided. Nevertheless, when American Family settled the case in 1995, it agreed to pay a $14.5 million settlement plus about $2 million in court costs. Part of the settlement was to compensate people who had suffered from the company's discrimination. But most of the money went to fund community programs begun in 1996 to promote home ownership among minorities. In 1997 trouble came from within and without: One lawsuit claimed the company falsely promised to shrink premiums as policies earned dividends, and two dissident agents filed a civil complaint for wrongful termination (the latter case was settled the next year).

The company's profits tumbled in 1998 due to severe storms in Minnesota and Wisconsin. The next year American Family expanded its operations in Colorado and moved into Cleveland.

In 2000 Wisconsin was again pounded by hail, high winds, and floods. American Family Insurance announced $100 million in expected losses from the event. Streamlining claims processing, the company closed nine of its offices in 2001.

American Family grew its policy count by almost 10% in 2002 but the volatile stock market hurt the company's net result.

EXECUTIVES

Chairman and CEO: Harvey R. Pierce
President, COO, and Director: David R. Anderson
EVP, Secretary, and Corporate Legal: James F. Eldridge
EVP, Finance and Treasurer: J. Brent Johnson
EVP, Administration: Darnell Moore
EVP, Sales: Daniel R. DeSalvo
SVP, Variable Products: Joseph W. Tisserand
VP and Controller: Daniel R. Schultz
VP, Actuarial: Bradley J. Gleason
VP, American Family Financial Services: R.D. Boschulte
VP, American Family Life Insurance: Jack C. Salzwedel
VP, Claims: Terese A. Taarud
VP, Commercial, Farm/Ranch: Jerry G. Rekowski
VP, Education: Ann M. Hamilton
VP, Government Affairs and Compliance: Mark V. Afable
VP, Human Resources: Vicki L. Chvala
VP, Information Services: Byrne W. Chapman
VP, Investments: Thomas S. King
VP, Legal: Christopher S. Spencer
VP, Marketing: Alan E. Meyer
VP, Office Administration: Richard J. Haas
VP, Personal Lines: Joseph J. Zwettler
VP, Public Relations: Richard A. Fetherston
Auditors: PricewaterhouseCoopers LLP

LOCATIONS

HQ: American Family Insurance Group
6000 American Pkwy., Madison, WI 53783
Phone: 608-249-2111   **Fax:** 608-243-4921
Web: www.amfam.com

American Family Insurance Group operates in Arizona, California, Colorado, Illinois, Indiana, Iowa, Kansas, Minnesota, Missouri, Nebraska, Nevada, North Dakota, Ohio, Oregon, South Dakota, Washington, and Wisconsin.

PRODUCTS/OPERATIONS

2003 Assets

	$ mil.	% of total
Cash	87	1
Bonds	7,546	62
Stocks	1,479	12
Mortgage loans	181	2
Real estate	264	2
Policy loans	175	1
Receivables	1,016	8
Other	1,491	12
Total	**12,239**	**100**

2003 Sales

	$ mil.	% of total
Property & casualty premiums	5,297	87
Investment income	416	7
AFLIC premiums	292	5
Finance charges	11	—
Other	49	1
Total	**6,065**	**100**

Selected Subsidiaries

American Family Mutual Insurance Co.
American Family Financial Services, Inc.
American Family Insurance Co.
American Family Life Insurance Co.
American Standard Insurance Company of Ohio
American Standard Insurance Company of Wisconsin

COMPETITORS

21st Century
AIG
AIG American General
Allstate
American Financial
Berkshire Hathaway
Chubb
CIGNA
Cincinnati Financial
Citigroup
CNA Financial
General Re
The Hartford
Kemper Insurance
Liberty Mutual
Lincoln National
Loews
Mutual of Omaha
Nationwide
Ohio Casualty
Old Republic
Progressive Corporation
Prudential
Safeco
St. Paul Travelers
State Farm
USAA

American Foods

HISTORICAL FINANCIALS
Company Type: Mutual company

Income Statement
FYE: December 31

	ASSETS ($ mil.)	NET INCOME ($ mil.)	INCOME AS % OF ASSETS	EMPLOYEES
12/03	12,239	155	1.3%	8,100
12/02	10,840	58	0.5%	7,500
12/01	10,275	100	1.0%	7,431
12/00	9,970	237	2.4%	7,300
12/99	9,569	282	2.9%	7,247
12/98	8,949	40	0.4%	6,940
12/97	8,348	252	3.0%	6,800
12/96	6,836	55	0.8%	6,506
12/95	6,256	219	3.5%	6,411
12/94	5,706	163	2.9%	6,365
Annual Growth	8.8%	(0.5%)	—	2.7%

2003 Year-End Financials
Equity as % of assets: 29.5%
Return on assets: 1.3%
Return on equity: 4.6%
Long-term debt ($ mil.): 1,980
Sales ($ mil.): 6,065

Net Income History

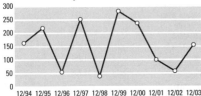

American Foods Group is a bona fide Green Bay packer. It slaughters cattle and produces branded and private label bacon, beef cuts, deli meats, ham, and sausage for sale to the grocery and foodservice industries. Its beef plant cranks out 4 million pounds of ground beef each week. The company operates refrigerated trucking unit America's Service Lines. CEO and owner Carl Kuehne purchased American Foods in 1985 and grew it through acquisitions and product development. After nixing plans to be acquired by Smithfield Foods, American Foods set up a joint venture with an Iowa beef producers cooperative.

EXECUTIVES
President and CEO: Carl W. Kuehne
CFO: Doug Hagen
Chief Sales and Marketing: Joseph P. Baker
VP, Human Resources: Trudy Kamps
President, America's Service Line: Tom McClone
Controller: Dave Schuldt
Director, Case Ready Meats: Mike Zimmerman
Director, Information Technology: LouAnn Bannow
Director, International Sales: Mike Stone
Director, Purchasing: Ron Bouche

LOCATIONS
HQ: American Foods Group, Inc.
544 Acme St., Green Bay, WI 54308
Phone: 920-437-6330 **Fax:** 920-436-6410
Web: www.americanfoodsgroup.com

American Foods Group operates facilities in Iowa, Ohio, South Dakota, and Wisconsin.

PRODUCTS/OPERATIONS

Selected Brands
American Foods Group
American Foods Specialties
Black Angus Reserve Beef
Dakota Supreme
Dakota Valley
Golden Prairie
Golden Superb
Green Bay Dressed Beef
Server's Choice
Sheboygan Deli Superb

Company Divisions
America's Service Line (refrigerated transportation)
American Foods, Kosher Processing
American Foods Specialties

COMPETITORS
Rosen's Diversified
Smithfield Beef Enterprises
Swift
Tyson Fresh Meats
U.S. Premium Beef

American Golf

American Golf Corporation (AGC) is in the rough. The company — one of the largest golf course management firms in the world with about 240 public, private, and resort courses in the US and the UK — is struggling with the weak US economy and increased competition. The firm had fallen behind in rental payments to sister firm National Golf Properties, from which it leased about half its properties. National Golf had agreed to acquire AGC, although some National Golf shareholders challenged the deal on claims that the primary beneficiary would be David Price (chairman of both AGC and National Golf). Instead, an investor group led by GMAC Commercial Holding purchased both National Golf and ACG in 2003.

EXECUTIVES
CEO: Roland C. Smith, age 49
CFO: Neil Miller
EVP: Paul Major
SVP, Eastern Region: Mark Burnett
SVP, Operations Support: Stuart Hayden
SVP, Maintenance: Craig Kniffen
COO, West: Keith Brown
General Counsel: Mark Friedman
VP Human Resources: Tom Norton
Auditors: PricewaterhouseCoopers LLP

LOCATIONS
HQ: American Golf Corporation
2951 28th St., Santa Monica, CA 90405
Phone: 310-664-4000 **Fax:** 310-664-6160
Web: www.americangolf.com

PRODUCTS/OPERATIONS

Selected Properties
Addington Court Golf Course (Surrey, UK)
Arrowhead Country Club (Glendale, AZ)
Bobby Jones Golf Course (Atlanta)
The Classics Country Club (Naples, FL)
Cotgrave Place Golf & Country Club (Nottingham, UK)
The Foothills Golf Club (Phoenix)
Highland Park Country Club (Illinois)
Ivy Hills Country Club (Cincinnati)
Las Vegas Golf Club
Mission Trails Golf Course (San Diego)
Oyster Reef Golf Club (Hilton Head, SC)
Park Hill Golf Club (Denver)
Plantation Country Club (Boise, ID)
Reynolds Park Golf Course (Winston-Salem, NC)
Riverside Golf Course (Austin, TX)
Silver Lake Golf Course (Staten Island, NY)
Skylinks Municipal Golf Course (Long Beach, CA)
Tilden Park Golf Course (Berkeley, CA)
Woodlake Country Club (San Antonio, TX)
World Houston Golf Course

COMPETITORS
ClubCorp
Golf Trust of America

HISTORICAL FINANCIALS
Company Type: Private

Income Statement
FYE: June 30

	REVENUE ($ mil.)	NET INCOME ($ mil.)	NET PROFIT MARGIN	EMPLOYEES
6/04	1,000	—	—	2,000
6/03	850	—	—	2,625
6/02	655	—	—	1,800
6/01	650	—	—	1,500
6/00	580	—	—	1,450
6/99	510	—	—	1,250
6/98	520	—	—	1,450
6/97	600	—	—	2,000
6/96	575	—	—	1,800
6/95	555	—	—	1,800
Annual Growth	6.8%	—	—	1.2%

Revenue History

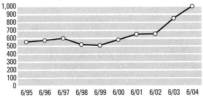

HISTORICAL FINANCIALS
Company Type: Private

Income Statement
FYE: December 31

	REVENUE ($ mil.)	NET INCOME ($ mil.)	NET PROFIT MARGIN	EMPLOYEES
12/03	700	—	—	16,000
12/02	715	—	—	18,000
12/01	731	—	—	20,000
12/00	746	—	—	22,000
12/99	698	—	—	20,000
12/98	576	—	—	20,000
12/97	525	—	—	15,000
12/96	440	—	—	13,000
12/95	359	—	—	10,344
12/94	307	—	—	10,000
Annual Growth	9.6%	—	—	5.4%

American Heart Association

The American Heart Association (AHA) is a non-profit health agency devoted to fight against heart disease, stroke, and other cardiovascular illnesses. In the early part of the 1900s, heart disease patients were prescribed bed rest and not given much chance of survival. The AHA was founded in 1924 by six cardiologists, who recognized the need to widely share their heart disease education and research.

EXECUTIVES

Chairman: Craig T. Beam
CEO: M. Cass Wheeler
President: Robert O. Bonow
COO, Field Operations: Gordon L. McCullough
EVP Corporate Operations and CFO:
  Walter D. Bristol Jr.
EVP Chief Administrative Officer: Nancy A. Brown
Chief Science Officer: Rose Marie Robertson
Corporate Secretary and Counsel: David WM. Livingston

LOCATIONS

HQ: American Heart Association
  7272 Greenville Ave., Dallas, TX 75231
Phone: 800-242-8721   **Fax:** 214-706-1191
Web: www.americanheart.org

HISTORICAL FINANCIALS
Company Type: Not-for-profit

Income Statement
FYE: June 30

	REVENUE ($ mil.)	NET INCOME ($ mil.)	NET PROFIT MARGIN	EMPLOYEES
6/03	536	—	—	—

American Plumbing & Mechanical

American Plumbing & Mechanical (AMPAM) provides contract plumbing services, as well as HVAC and mechanical services, in more than a dozen states. It offers services for single-family and multifamily residential structures, and for commercial and institutional projects. Founded in 1998 to acquire 10 regional contracting companies, AMPAM began operations in 1999 and continued to acquire or create companies in new service areas. The firm's subsidiaries operate as separate entities, with AMPAM providing financial and accounting support. To avoid pulling the plug on its operations, AMPAM went through a bankruptcy restructuring in 2004.

As part of its plan to pay down debt, the company sold off its AMPAM Commercial Sherwood Mechanical division to local management. Also in 2004, the company divested its AMPAM Atlas and AMPAM Riggs divisions. AMPAM has also spun off its Midwest commercial unit as Teepe & Partners Mechanical Contractors. The company sold its AMPAM J.A. Croson Company, too.

EXECUTIVES

Chairman, President, and CEO: Robert A. Christianson, age 58
President and COO, Multifamily Operations; CEO, AMPAM LDI Mechanical: Lloyd C. Smith, age 59
President, Single-Family Plumbing Operations, California, Nevada, and Arizona:
  Robert C. (Bob) Richey
VP and CFO: Terry Reynolds
VP, General Counsel, and Corporate Secretary:
  Carl Wimberley
VP Human Resources: Phil Thompson
VP Materials: David Muir
Controller: Paul Leleux
Treasurer: Steven M. (Steve) Smith
Director Information Systems: Darrell Wolle
Director Sales and Marketing: Greg Rotunno
Corporate Network Manager: Ed Humes
Director, Information Technology: Tony Jimenez
Safety and Risk Manager: Ken Colonna
HR Representative: Susan Fulton
Auditors: Deloitte & Touche

LOCATIONS

HQ: American Plumbing & Mechanical, Inc.
  1950 Louis Henna Blvd., Round Rock, TX 78664
Phone: 512-246-5260   **Fax:** 512-246-5290
Web: www.ampam.com

American Plumbing & Mechanical has operations in Arizona, California, Nevada, New Jersey, and Texas.

PRODUCTS/OPERATIONS

Selected AMPAM Companies
AMPAM Christianson, LP
AMPAM LDI Mechanical, Inc.
AMPAM Parks Mechanical, Inc.
AMPAM Power Plumbing, LP
AMPAM RCR Companies

COMPETITORS
ACCO
American Residential Services
APi Group
Chemed
EMCOR
Integrated Electrical Services
NorthWestern
Southland Industries
TDIndustries

HISTORICAL FINANCIALS
Company Type: Private

Income Statement
FYE: December 31

	REVENUE ($ mil.)	NET INCOME ($ mil.)	NET PROFIT MARGIN	EMPLOYEES
12/02	575	(55)	—	5,500
12/01	606	8	1.3%	5,600
12/00	558	15	2.6%	5,200
12/99	334	3	0.9%	4,000
12/98	322	9	2.8%	2,700
Annual Growth	15.6%	—	—	19.5%

2002 Year-End Financials
Debt ratio: 870.2%   Current ratio: 1.60
Return on equity: —   Long-term debt ($ mil.): 155
Cash ($ mil.): 3

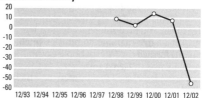

American Red Cross

When it comes to disaster, the Red Cross is the master. The American Red Cross is a member of the International Red Cross and Red Crescent Movement, a not-for-profit organization that offers disaster relief and other humanitarian services through more than 900 chapters nationwide. Chartered by Congress in 1905, the American Red Cross isn't a government agency. Its staff is largely volunteer — more than 1.2 million strong. Aside from helping victims of more than 70,000 disasters each year, the Red Cross teaches CPR, first aid, and AIDS awareness courses; provides counseling for US military personnel; and maintains some of the largest blood, plasma, and tissue banks in the nation.

To fund its activities, the Red Cross relies primarily on its biomedical operation, which supplies blood and tissue to some 3,000 hospitals and accounts for about two-thirds of the organization's revenue. Contributions from organizations such as the United Way, grants, and other sources make up the rest of the Red Cross' operating fund.

The organization was stretched to its limits, however, due to five hurricanes that ravaged coastal areas in Florida and other parts of the Southeast during a two-month period in 2004.

Nearly 26,000 Red Cross disaster workers were called out to help more than 400,000 victims of the storms. To help cover the costs, the group was forced to seek additional money from the federal government.

The mission of the American Red Cross was highlighted after the 2001 terrorist attacks on New York City and Washington, DC, gaining praise for its quick response immediately afterwards. Soon after, however, it drew fire from critics about the handling of donations given for attack victims and their families. In the wake of those critical reports, the Red Cross has revised its methods of accepting donations to ensure those funds and supplies are directed towards the intended victims.

In the years since the terrorist attacks, the organization has been engaged in a campaign to raise the nation's emergency preparedness, both for government agencies and individuals.

HISTORY

The Red Cross traces its start to a trip made in 1859 by Jean-Henri Dunant, a Swiss businessman. Dunant was traveling in northern Italy when he saw the aftermath of the Battle of Solferino — 40,000 dead or wounded troops, left without help. He published a pamphlet three years later calling for the formation of international volunteer societies to aid wounded soldiers.

In 1863 a five-member committee (including Dunant) formed the International Committee of the Red Cross in Geneva. Delegates of 16 countries attended the first conference, which resulted in the formation of national Red Cross societies across Europe. A red cross on a white background (the reverse of the Swiss flag) was chosen as the organization's symbol; the Red Crescent symbol was added in 1876 by Muslim relief workers during the Russo-Turkish War. In 1864 the group's principles were codified into international law — initially signed by 12 nations — through the Geneva Convention.

Clara Barton, famous for her aid to soldiers during the US Civil War, learned about the Red Cross when she assisted with relief efforts during the Franco-Prussian War (1870-71). After the war, Barton returned home and persuaded Congress to support the Geneva Convention. In 1881 she and some friends founded the American Association of the Red Cross, with the first chapter in Dansville, New York. The US signed the Geneva Convention in 1882.

Barton soon expanded the Red Cross' mission to include aiding victims of natural disasters. The group received a congressional charter in 1905, making it responsible for providing assistance to the US military and disaster relief in the US and overseas.

Membership soared during WWI as the number of chapters jumped from 107 to 3,864, and volunteers from the US and other nations served with the armed forces in Europe. After the war, the American Red Cross helped refugees in Europe, recruited thousands of nurses to improve the health and hygiene of rural Americans, and provided food and shelter to millions during the Depression.

The Red Cross established its first blood center, in New York's Presbyterian Hospital, in 1941. During WWII the American Red Cross again mobilized massive relief efforts. At home, volunteers taught nutrition courses, served in hospitals, and collected blood.

In 1956 the Red Cross began research to increase the safety of its blood supply. It also continued to provide assistance during natural disasters, as well as during the Korean and Vietnam Wars and other US military conflicts.

During the 1980s the Red Cross was criticized for moving too slowly to improve testing of its blood supply for the HIV virus. Elizabeth Dole, named the organization's president in 1991, reorganized the blood collection program. (Dole took a leave of absence in 1996 to help her husband, Bob Dole, in his unsuccessful bid for the US presidency.)

In 1996 *Money* magazine reported that the Red Cross spent more than 91 cents of every dollar on programs, the best ratio of any major charity. In 1998 the organization ran up against its costliest year ever, spending more than $162 million to fight some 240 disasters across the US. The next year Dole resigned from the Red Cross and followed in her husband's footsteps by making her own bid for the US presidency in 2000 (she later dropped out of the race). Dole was succeeded by Dr. Bernadine Healy, a former dean of the Ohio State University College of Medicine and the first physician to head the association.

Healy was given her walking papers less than two months after the September 11 attacks amid disagreements with the Red Cross board and ire from critics over a proposal to use some donations for a blood bank reserve instead of it all going to families of those killed and injured in the attacks.

General Counsel Harold Decker was tapped to replace Healy at the end of 2001. That same year the FDA announced that the Red Cross had failed to be in compliance with safety laws in its blood collection program, despite being under a consent decree since 1993. The American Red Cross appointed Marsha Johnson Evans as president and CEO in 2002. In 2003 the organization provided humanitarian aid to military personnel and their families during and after the war in Iraq.

EXECUTIVES

Chair: Bonnie McElveen-Hunter
President and CEO: Marsha J. (Marty) Evans, age 56
COO: R. Alan McCurry
EVP Biomedical Services: John F. (Jack) McGuire III
EVP Chapter Services: James Krueger
EVP Disaster Services: Terry Sicilia
Acting EVP Human Resources: Carol Miller
SVP and CFO: Robert P. McDonald
SVP Communications and Marketing:
 Charles D. Connor
SVP Quality Assurance and Regulatory Affairs:
 C. William Cherry
VP Communications and Marketing: Deborah Daley
CIO: Tom Schwaninger
Chief Diversity Officer: Anthony J. Polk
National Chair of Volunteers: Mary H. DeKuyper
Director of Creative Resources: Carol Robinson
General Counsel and Corporate Secretary:
 Mary S. Elcano
Senior Media Relations Associate: Larry Rockwell
Media Relations Associate: Kelly Donaghy
Media Relations Associate: Jacki Flowers
Media Relations Associate: Stacey Grissom
Media Relations Associate: Lesly Hallman
Media Relations Associate: Ray Steen
Auditors: KPMG LLP

LOCATIONS

HQ: The American Red Cross
 430 17th St., NW, Washington, DC 20006
Phone: 202-737-8300   **Fax:** 202-942-2024
Web: www.redcross.org

The American Red Cross has more than 900 chapters nationwide. In addition the Red Cross has international chapters in Germany, Italy, and Japan.

PRODUCTS/OPERATIONS

2003 Revenue

	$ mil.	% of total
Products & services		
Biomedical	2,017	67
Program materials	149	5
Public support		
United Way & other federated	176	6
Legacies & bequests	94	3
Grants	75	2
Services & materials	61	2
Disaster relief	58	2
Liberty relief	12	—
Other contributions	216	7
Other	176	6
Total	**3,034**	**100**

2003 Program Expenditures

	% of total
Biomedical services	66
Disaster services	12
Health & safety services	7
Liberty disaster (Sept. 11 response)	7
Community services	5
Armed forces emergency services	2
International services	1
Total	**100**

Selected Programs and Services

Biomedical Services
 Blood, plasma, and tissue services
 Clinical services
 Testing
Disaster Relief
Health and Safety Services
 Care giving and babysitting
 CPR training
 First aid
 Lifeguard training
 Swimming lessons
 Youth programs
Community Services
 Food and nutrition
 Homeless shelters
 Hospitals and nursing homes
 Senior services
 Transportation services
Military Services
 Counseling
 Emergency communications
 Financial assistance
 Veterans services
International Services

HISTORICAL FINANCIALS

Company Type: Not-for-profit

Income Statement				FYE: June 30
	REVENUE ($ mil.)	NET INCOME ($ mil.)	NET PROFIT MARGIN	EMPLOYEES
6/03	3,034	—	—	40,000
6/02	4,117	—	—	40,000
6/01	2,743	—	—	35,000
6/00	2,529	—	—	35,000
6/99	2,422	—	—	35,000
6/98	2,080	—	—	30,000
6/97	1,940	—	—	29,850
6/96	1,814	—	—	30,021
6/95	1,724	—	—	31,000
6/94	1,740	—	—	32,169
Annual Growth	6.4%	—	—	2.5%

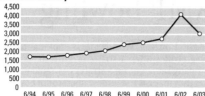

Revenue History

Selected Products and Brands

Equipment	Dunlop	Nitto
Ammco	DynaTrac	Pirelli
Hunter	Firestone	Powermark
Lincoln	General	Regul
Magnum	Gillette	SteelMark
Tires	Goodyear	Titan
BF Goodrich	Kumho	UniRoyal
Bridgestone	Lee	Winston
Carlisle	Michelin	Wynstar
Continental	Modi	Yokohama
	Monarch	

COMPETITORS

BFS Retail & Commercial Operations
Cooper Tire & Rubber
Discount Tire
Sears
TBC

HISTORICAL FINANCIALS

Company Type: Private

Income Statement				FYE: December 31
	REVENUE ($ mil.)	NET INCOME ($ mil.)	NET PROFIT MARGIN	EMPLOYEES
12/03	1,113	16	1.4%	1,894
12/02	1,060	37	3.5%	1,915
12/01	1,108	(31)	—	2,025
12/00	1,087	(43)	—	2,600
12/99	908	(7)	—	—
Annual Growth	5.2%	—	—	(10.0%)

2003 Year-End Financials
Debt ratio: (974.5%)
Return on equity: —
Cash ($ mil.): 3
Current ratio: 1.52
Long-term debt ($ mil.): 180

Net Income History

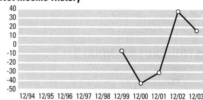

American Tire

American Tire Distributors' business starts where the rubber meets the road. The company, formerly Heafner Tire, is one of the largest independent distributors of tires and related products in the US. Tire brands include industry leaders Michelin and Bridgestone/Firestone as well as Goodyear, which also makes American Tire's Monarch house brand through its Kelly-Springfield subsidiary. American Tire's distribution business is conducted through about 70 distribution centers that serve about 40 states. To focus on national distribution, American Tire sold 130 Winston Tire Centers on the West Coast and about 30 T.O. Haas Tire outlets. Charlesbank Equity Fund IV owns more than 97% of the company.

American Tire Distributors is acquiring Texas Market Tire, which operates in Texas, Oklahoma, and New Mexico as Big State Tire Supply. It acquired Target Tire, which supplies about 1,800 retailers through more than ten distribution centers in Georgia, North Carolina, South Carolina, Tennessee, and Virginia, in September 2004.

EXECUTIVES

Chairman and CEO: Richard P. (Dick) Johnson, age 56, $541,730 pay
President and COO: William E. Berry, age 49, $271,291 pay
SVP, Finance and Administration and Treasurer: Scott A. Deininger, age 41
EVP, General Counsel, and Secretary: J. Michael Gaither, age 51, $317,291 pay
SVP, Procurement: Daniel K. Brown, age 50, $308,767 pay
SVP, Sales and Marketing: Phillip E. Marrett, age 53, $246,291 pay
VP, Credit and Financial Services: Jack Phillips
VP, Equipment and Supply: Gary Reed
VP, Heafner Worldwide: Lee Fishkin
Regional Vice President: James L. Matthews, age 58
Auditors: PricewaterhouseCoopers LLP

LOCATIONS

HQ: American Tire Distributors, Inc.
12200 Herbert Wayne Ct., Ste. 150, Huntersville, NC 28070
Phone: 704-992-2000 **Fax:** 704-992-1384
Web: www.americantiredistributors.com

PRODUCTS/OPERATIONS

2003 Sales

	% of total
Tires	87
Wheels, service equipment & other parts	13
Total	**100**

American United

There are 50 states, but only OneAmerica. American United Mutual Insurance Holding Company, whose operating units do business under the OneAmerica Financial Partners banner, specializes in annuities and individual and group life insurance and disability coverage throughout the US.

Flagship insurer American United Life was formed in the 1936 merger of United Mutual Life Insurance and American Central Life Insurance. The insurer restructured into mutual holding company ownership in 2000, a move that has not only given it a more favorable tax status, but has allowed it to form and acquire stock subsidiaries.

Acquisitions include R.E. Moulton (medical stop-loss insurance) and the group life and disability insurance business of The Union Central Life Insurance Company in 2003, and Pioneer Mutual Life Insurance in 2002. American United sold most of its life reinsurance business in 2002.

EXECUTIVES

Chairman: Jerry D. Semler
Vice Chairman: R. Stephen Radcliffe
President and CEO: Dayton H. Molendorp
SVP, Group Operations: John R. Barton
SVP, Strategic Planning and Corporate Development: J. Scott Davison
SVP, Corporate Finance: Constance E. Lund
SVP, Human Resources: Mark Roller
SVP, Investments: G. David Sapp
General Counsel and Corporate Secretary: Thomas M. Zurek
Auditors: PricewaterhouseCoopers LLP

LOCATIONS

HQ: American United Mutual Insurance Holding Company
1 American Sq., Indianapolis, IN 46206
Phone: 317-285-1111
Web: www.aul.com

PRODUCTS/OPERATIONS

2003 Sales

	% of total
Insurance premiums & other considerations	44
Net investment income	44
Policy & contract charges	11
Other income	1
Total	**100**

Selected Subsidiaries and Affiliates

American United Life Insurance Company (life insurance and annuities)
AUL Reinsurance Management Services, LLC (accident reinsurance)
CNL Financial Corp. (credit-related products)
Cherokee National Life Insurance Company
CNL/Insurance America, Inc.
CNL/Resource Marketing Corporation
OneAmerica Securities, Inc. (broker/dealer and investment advisor)
R.E. Moulton, Inc. (stop-loss insurance; group life, health, and disability insurance)
Pioneer Mutual Life Insurance Company (individual life insurance and annuities)
The State Life Insurance Company (individual life insurance, annuities, and long-term care insurance)

COMPETITORS

Aetna
AXA Financial
Citigroup
CNA Financial
General Re
John Hancock Financial Services
Lincoln National
MassMutual
MetLife
Minnesota Mutual
Nationwide Financial
New York Life
Northwestern Mutual
Ohio National Financial Services
Principal Financial
Prudential
Security Benefit Group

HISTORICAL FINANCIALS

Company Type: Mutual company

Income Statement			FYE: December 31
	ASSETS ($ mil.)	NET INCOME ($ mil.)	INCOME AS % OF ASSETS	EMPLOYEES
12/03	14,041	62	0.4%	1,730
12/02	12,208	9	0.1%	1,700
12/01	12,092	53	0.4%	1,700
12/00	10,933	80	0.7%	1,634
12/99	10,578	68	0.6%	1,400
12/98	9,336	67	0.7%	1,500
12/97	8,598	74	0.9%	1,475
12/96	7,852	52	0.7%	1,300
12/95	7,328	46	0.6%	1,152
Annual Growth	8.5%	3.8%	—	5.2%

2003 Year-End Financials
Equity as % of assets: 8.3%
Return on assets: 0.5%
Return on equity: 5.4%
Long-term debt ($ mil.): 275
Sales ($ mil.): 1,004

Net Income History

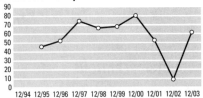

Amerisure

Hoping all businesses rest Amerisured, the Amerisure Insurance Companies provides a range of commercial property and casualty products. The company specializes in workers' compensation programs, primarily for the manufacturing and contracting industries. Coverage includes general and employee benefits liability, property, auto, inland marine, and equipment insurance. Amerisure also sells commercial property policies and provides reinsurance through a Bermuda-based subsidiary. The company operates out of about a dozen offices in the southern and midwestern parts of the US.

Workers' compensation accounts for more than half of Amerisure's business.

EXECUTIVES
Chairman: James B. (Jim) Nicholson
President and CEO: Richard F. Russell
EVP and COO: Thomas E. Hoeg, age 49
SVP, CFO, and Treasurer: R. Douglas Kinnan
SVP and Counsel, Government Relations:
 D. Joseph Olson
VP, General Counsel, and Secretary:
 Susan Gailey Vincent
VP and Chief Actuary: Ted Wagner
VP, Underwriting, and Business and Product Development: David B. Hostetter
VP, Claims, Loss Control, Premium Audit, Quality and Productivity: Don A. Smith
VP, Field Marketing and Underwriting:
 Michael M. Dieterle
VP, Human Resources: Derick W. Adams
VP and Regional Manager, Michigan:
 Douglas R. Roggenbaum
VP and Regional Manager, Florida and North Carolina:
 Todd Ruthruff
VP and Regional Manager, Texas and Tennessee:
 Stephen P. Solimine
VP and Regional Manager, Missouri and Illinois:
 Jim Ziolkowski
Auditors: PricewaterhouseCoopers LLP

LOCATIONS
HQ: Amerisure Mutual Insurance Company
 26777 Halsted Rd., Farmington Hills, MI 48331
Phone: 248-615-9000   **Fax:** 248-615-8548
Web: www.amerisure.com

PRODUCTS/OPERATIONS
2003 Sales
	$ mil.	% of total
Premiums	514.7	90
Investment income	50.0	9
Realized capital gains	6.3	1
Total	**571.0**	**100**

Selected Subsidiaries
Amerisure Insurance Company
Amerisure Partners Insurance Company
Amerisure Re (Bermuda) Ltd.

COMPETITORS
AIG
American Financial
CNA Financial
The Hartford
Liberty Mutual
Nationwide
Prudential
Safeco
St. Paul Travelers

HISTORICAL FINANCIALS
Company Type: Mutual company

Income Statement			FYE: December 31
	REVENUE ($ mil.)	NET INCOME ($ mil.)	NET PROFIT MARGIN	EMPLOYEES
12/03	571	19	3.3%	—
12/02	498	(5)	—	—
12/01	385	16	4.1%	—
12/00	321	28	8.6%	—
Annual Growth	21.2%	(11.5%)	—	—

Net Income History

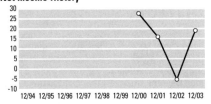

AMF Bowling

AMF Bowling Worldwide is looking to hit some strikes after a string of gutterballs. The company set about on a strategy of rapid expansion that made it the largest operator of bowling centers in the world with about 430 facilities in the US and four other countries. In addition to operating bowling alleys, AMF sells goods such as shoes and ball bags and provides equipment such as pinsetters and ball returns to other bowling centers. The company makes billiard tables under the brands Highland, Renaissance, and PlayMater. It had also owned two Michael Jordan Golf driving ranges, but closed them in 2002. Private investment firm Code Hennessy & Simmons bought AMF in 2004.

The company's expansion spree and an economic slowdown in Asia left AMF with a heap of debt. To avoid rolling a gutter ball, AMF filed for Chapter 11 in 2001, trimmed management, curbed its expansion plans, and focused on improving its existing bowling centers. The company emerged from bankruptcy the following year with help from a $315 million exit financing deal. As a result former majority owner Goldman Sachs' stake in the firm was wiped out.

Two years later AMF was purchased by private investment firm Code Hennessy & Simmons for about $670 million. It named former California Pizza Kitchen bigwig Fred Hipp as AMF's new president and CEO. In 2004 the company exited the UK market by selling its operations in that country to Bourne Leisure. It later signed a deal to exit another international market, this time its 45 bowling centers in Austraila.

EXECUTIVES
Chairman: Philip L. Maslowe, age 56
President and CEO: Frederick R. (Fred) Hipp, age 53, $242,308 pay
SVP, CFO, and Treasurer: Christopher F. Caesar, age 39, $307,043 pay
SVP Marketing: Timothy N. Scott, $228,575 pay
SVP Human Resources: Wayne T. Tennent
VP North America Sales: Jay Buhl
President and COO, AMF Bowling Products: John B. Walker, age 48, $270,003 pay
Auditors: KPMG LLP

LOCATIONS
HQ: AMF Bowling Worldwide, Inc.
 8100 AMF Dr., Richmond, VA 23111
Phone: 804-730-4000   **Fax:** 804-559-6276
Web: www.amf.com

AMF Bowling Worldwide has operations in Australia, France, Japan, Mexico, Puerto Rico, and the US.

PRODUCTS/OPERATIONS
Selected Operations
AMF Bowling Centers
Billiard tables
 Highland
 PlayMaster
 Renaissance
Bowling equipment

COMPETITORS
Bowl America
Brunswick
Dave & Buster's
Haw Par
Jillian's Entertainment
Vulcan International

HISTORICAL FINANCIALS

Company Type: Private

Income Statement
FYE: June 30

	REVENUE ($ mil.)	NET INCOME ($ mil.)	NET PROFIT MARGIN	EMPLOYEES
6/04	679	(67)	—	13,800
6/03	668	3	0.5%	15,361
6/02*	342	(35)	—	14,500
12/01	695	(217)	—	16,500
12/00	715	(201)	—	16,386
12/99	733	(162)	—	15,568
12/98	738	(126)	—	14,489
12/97	714	(56)	—	18,415
12/96	385	(20)	—	13,929
12/95	565	97	17.1%	—
Annual Growth	2.1%	—	—	(0.1%)

*Fiscal year change

2004 Year-End Financials
Debt ratio: 257.1%
Return on equity: —
Cash ($ mil.): 13
Current ratio: 0.85
Long-term debt ($ mil.): 287

Net Income History

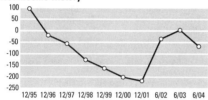

Amica Mutual

Amica is an amicable source for your insurance needs. Amica Mutual Insurance Company provides a variety of personal insurance products, including auto, home, marine, personal liability, and life policies. Amica sells its policies directly to customers through about 70 offices throughout the US. Its roots as an auto insurer go back to 1907 (when fire coverage was a car owner's most important need, due to exploding gas tanks). Amica was formed in 1973 through the consolidation of Automobile Mutual Insurance Company of America and Factory Mutual Liability Insurance Company of America.

EXECUTIVES
President and CEO: Thomas A. (Tom) Taylor, age 62
EVP: Robert A. DiMuccio, age 47
SVP; General Manager, Amica Life:
 James E. McDermott Jr.
SVP and Chief Investment Officer: Robert K. Benson
SVP and Superintendent of Claims: M. Stewart Towsey
SVP Human Resources: Patricia A. Talin
VP and Secretary: Robert MacKenzie
VP Accounting: Maribeth Williamson
Senior Assistant VP, Claims: Mark Divoll
Communications Officer: Patricia Stadnick
Assistant Marketing Manager: Gary Bilotti
Auditors: KPMG LLP

LOCATIONS
HQ: Amica Mutual Insurance Company
 100 Amica Way, Lincoln, RI 02865
Phone: 800-622-6422   **Fax:** 401-334-4241
Web: www.amica.com

PRODUCTS/OPERATIONS

Selected Subsidiaries
Amica Life Insurance Company
Amica Lloyds of Texas

COMPETITORS
ACE Limited
AIG
Allstate
Chubb
CNA Financial
GEICO
The Hartford
Liberty Mutual
Progressive Corporation
Prudential
State Farm
USAA

HISTORICAL FINANCIALS
Company Type: Mutual company

Income Statement
FYE: December 31

	ASSETS ($ mil.)	NET INCOME ($ mil.)	INCOME AS % OF ASSETS	EMPLOYEES
12/03	3,132	42	1.3%	3,200
12/02	2,826	16	0.6%	3,700
12/01	2,909	40	1.4%	3,600
12/00	3,007	78	2.6%	3,300
12/99	2,953	58	2.0%	3,000
12/98	2,787	73	2.6%	3,000
12/97	2,531	82	3.3%	3,000
12/96	2,249	41	1.8%	3,300
12/95	2,093	81	3.9%	—
Annual Growth	5.2%	(7.9%)	—	(0.4%)

2003 Year-End Financials
Equity as % of assets: —
Return on assets: 1.4%
Return on equity: —
Long-term debt ($ mil.): —
Sales ($ mil.): 1,384

Net Income History

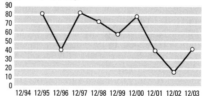

Amsted

Wilbur and Orville Wright's first flight might never have succeeded without an assist from Amsted's Diamond Chain subsidiary. A maker of roller chains for a variety of equipment and machinery, Diamond Chain also produced the propeller chain for the Wright brothers' aircraft. Amsted's other subsidiaries include ASF-Keystone (side frames, bolsters, and cast steel freight car components), Griffin Pipe Products (ductile iron pressure and sewer pipe), and Means Industries (automotive steering and transmission components). Customers include industrial distributors, locomotive and railcar manufacturers, and automotive OEMs. Employee-owned, Amsted has roughly 50 plants worldwide.

EXECUTIVES
Chairman Emeritus: Gordon R. Lohman, age 69
Chairman, President, and CEO: W. Robert Reum, age 61
SVP Finance: Stephen Gregory
VP Finance and CFO; COO of ASF-Keystone:
 Paul F. Fischer
VP, Chief Accounting Officer:
 Richard A. (Rick) Nunemaker
VP, General Counsel, and Secretary: Thomas G. Berg
Corporate VP: Bryon D. Spelce
President ASF-Keystone, North America:
 John Wories Jr.
President, Baltimore Aircoil: Steven S. Duerwachter
President, Burgess-Norton Mfg. Co.: John F. Carroll
President, Brenco Incorporated: J. Craig Rice
President, Consolidated Metco: Ed Oeltjen
President, Diamond Chain Company:
 James E. Humphrey
President, Griffin Pipe Products: Paul T. Ciolino
President, Griffin Wheel Company: William J. Demmert
President, Means Industries, Inc.: D. W. (Bill) Shaw
Treasurer: Matthew J. Hower
Director, Human Resources: Shirley J. Whitesell
Auditors: PricewaterhouseCoopers

LOCATIONS
HQ: Amsted Industries Incorporated
 205 N. Michigan Ave., 44th Fl., Chicago, IL 60601
Phone: 312-645-1700   **Fax:** 312-819-8494
Web: www.amsted.com

Amsted has 47 manufacturing facilities in 11 countries.

PRODUCTS/OPERATIONS

Selected Divisions
ASF-Keystone (cast steel freight car components, hot coiled steel springs and buffers, discharge gates, draft and draw gears, dynamic brake components, valves)
Baltimore Aircoil Company (cooling towers, evaporative condensers, heat exchangers, ice thermal storage systems, industrial fluid coolers)
Brenco, Incorporated (railroad track anchoring systems, tapered roller bearings)
Burgess-Norton Mfg. Co. (gray and ductile iron castings, piston pins, powder metal parts, rocker arms and assemblies)
Consolidated Metco, Inc. (aluminum permanent mold and die castings, axle hubs, door sill assemblies, fifth wheels and assemblies, instrument panels, sleeper cab accessories, spring brake flanges and pistons, structural molded plastic products, suspension components, transmission housings)
Diamond Chain Company (roller chain)
Griffin Pipe Products Co.(ductile iron pressure pipe and fittings, ductile iron sewer pipe)
Griffin Wheel Co. (cast steel railroad wheels)
Means Industries, Inc. (automatic transmission reaction plates, one-way clutches, stamped metal components, steering column components, transmission components)

COMPETITORS
ALSTOM
American Standard
Japan Steel Works
Meridian Rail
Newcor
Trinity Industries

HISTORICAL FINANCIALS

Company Type: Private

Income Statement
FYE: September 30

	REVENUE ($ mil.)	NET INCOME ($ mil.)	NET PROFIT MARGIN	EMPLOYEES
9/03	1,400	—	—	9,200
9/02	1,360	—	—	9,000
9/01	1,650	—	—	10,300
9/00	1,774	—	—	11,200
9/99	1,370	—	—	12,600
9/98	1,252	—	—	9,100
9/97	1,105	—	—	8,500
9/96	1,140	—	—	8,700
9/95	1,165	—	—	9,300
9/94	1,030	—	—	9,000
Annual Growth	3.5%	—	—	0.2%

Revenue History

AMTRAK

Fueled by government dollars, Amtrak keeps on chugging, hoping to operate under its own steam. The National Railroad Passenger Corporation, better known as Amtrak, carries more than 24 million passengers a year in 46 states — Alaska, Hawaii, South Dakota, and Wyoming are excluded. The company's system includes more than 22,000 route miles, nearly all of which are owned by freight railroads. A for-profit company that has never been profitable, Amtrak is almost wholly owned by the US Department of Transportation and receives large subsidies from the federal government. Some government officials have called for Amtrak to be self-sufficient.

Under CEO David Gunn, Amtrak has moved to cut costs by reducing its workforce. Nevertheless, the railroad needs subsidies to maintain its operations. For fiscal 2003, Amtrak asked for $1.8 billion from the federal government and received $1.2 billion. With more cash, Amtrak officials say, the railroad could put more cars on the tracks in high-traffic areas such as the northeastern US.

To improve the on-time performance of its long-distance trains, Amtrak in 2004 announced plans to stop carrying mail shipments for the U.S. Postal Service. The train operator already had been scaling back its small express freight business.

However, Amtrak's efforts to reform itself could be overwhelmed by one or more proposals pending in Washington. One plan — proposed by a commission created by Congress — would divide the company into three parts: a federal agency to oversee national rail programs, a company to manage tracks, and a company to manage rail service. The plan also calls for Amtrak's monopoly on rail passenger service to end. Another proposal would divide Amtrak into a network of regional rail systems supported by state governments.

HISTORY

US passenger train travel peaked in 1929, with 20,000 trains in operation. But the spread of automobiles, bus service, and air travel cut into business, and by the late 1960s only about 500 passenger trains remained running in the country. In 1970 the combined losses of all private train operations exceeded $1.8 billion in today's dollars. That year Congress passed the Rail Passenger Service Act, which created Amtrak to preserve America's passenger rail system. Although railroads were offered stock in the corporation for their passenger equipment, most just wrote off the loss.

Amtrak began operating in 1971 with 1,200 cars, most built in the 1950s. Although the company lost money from the outset ($153 million in 1972), it continued to be bankrolled by Uncle Sam, despite much criticism. Amtrak ordered its first new equipment in 1973, the year it also began taking over stations, yards, and service staff. The company didn't own any track until 1976, when it purchased hundreds of miles of right-of-way track from Boston to Washington, DC.

After a 1979 study showed Amtrak passengers to be by far the most heavily subsidized travelers in the US, Congress ordered the company to better utilize its resources. The 1980s saw Amtrak leasing its rights-of-way along its tracks in the Northeast corridor to telecommunications companies, which installed fiber-optic cables, and beginning mail and freight services for extra revenue.

In the early 1990s Amtrak faced a number of challenges: Midwest flooding, falling airfares, and safety concerns over a number of rail accidents, particularly the 1993 wreck of the Sunset Limited near Mobile, Alabama, in which 47 people were killed (the worst accident in Amtrak's history). In 1994 Amtrak's board of directors (at Congress' behest) adopted a plan to be free of federal support by 2002. In 1995 the company began planning high-speed trains for its heavily traveled East Coast routes.

In 1997 Amtrak finalized agreements to buy the high-speed cars and locomotives central to its self-sufficiency plan. It also began increasing its freight hauling and had its first profitable offering: the Metroliner route between New York and Washington, DC.

Amtrak's board of directors was replaced by Congress in 1997 with a seven-member Reform Board appointed by President Clinton. Chairman and president Thomas Downs resigned that year, and Tommy Thompson, then governor of Wisconsin, took over as chairman. Former Massachusetts governor Michael Dukakis was named vice chairman, and George Warrington stepped in as Amtrak's president and CEO.

Technical problems in 1999 delayed Amtrak's introduction of the Acela high-speed train in the Northeast until late 2000, when service began in the Boston-Washington corridor. In 2001 Amtrak pitched a 20-year plan, involving an annual outlay of $1.5 billion in federal funds, for expanding and modernizing its passenger service to help alleviate highway and airport congestion nationwide.

Thompson left the Amtrak board in 2001 after he was named US secretary of health and human services.

Realizing Amtrak would not meet its end-of-the-year deadline to be self-sufficient, in 2002 the Amtrak Reform Council sent a proposal to Congress that Amtrak be divided into three groups: one to oversee operations and funding, a second to maintain certain Amtrak-owned tracks and properties, and a third to operate trains. It also called for competition to be allowed on some passenger routes within two to three years.

Also in 2002 Warrington resigned and was replaced by David Gunn, who formerly headed the metropolitan transit systems in New York and Toronto. Gunn began moving to cut costs, and he worked to secure new federal money to avert a threatened shutdown of rail service in July 2002.

EXECUTIVES

Chairman: David M. Laney
President and CEO: David L. Gunn
CFO: Deno G. Bokas
SVP Operations: William L. (Bill) Crosbie
VP Business Diversity: Gerri Mason Hall
VP Government Affairs: Joseph H. (Joe) McHugh
VP Human Resources: Lorraine A. Green
VP Labor Relations: Joseph M. Bress
VP Marketing and Sales: Barbara J. Richardson
VP Procurement and Materials Management: Michael J. Rienzi
VP Strategic Planning and Contract Administration: Gilbert O. (Gil) Mallery
Chief of Sales, Distribution, and Customer Service: Matt Hardison
General Counsel and Corporate Secretary: Alicia M. Serfaty
Inspector General: Fred E. Weiderhold
Auditors: KPMG LLP

LOCATIONS

HQ: National Railroad Passenger Corporation
60 Massachusetts Ave. NE, Washington, DC 20002
Phone: 202-906-3000   **Fax:** 202-906-3306
Web: www.amtrak.com

PRODUCTS/OPERATIONS

2003 Sales

	$ mil.	% of total
Passenger-related	1,399.9	67
Commuter	269.2	13
Mail & express	77.1	4
Other	330.4	16
Total	**2,076.6**	**100**

COMPETITORS

America West
AMR Corp.
Burlington Northern Santa Fe
Continental Airlines
CSX
Delta
Greyhound
Norfolk Southern
Northwest Airlines
Southwest Airlines
UAL
Union Pacific
US Airways

HISTORICAL FINANCIALS
Company Type: Government-owned

Income Statement
FYE: September 30

	REVENUE ($ mil.)	NET INCOME ($ mil.)	NET PROFIT MARGIN	EMPLOYEES
9/03	2,077	(1,274)	—	22,000
9/02	2,228	(1,132)	—	22,000
9/01	2,109	(1,248)	—	24,600
9/00	2,111	(768)	—	25,000
9/99	2,042	(702)	—	25,000
9/98	2,285	(353)	—	24,000
9/97	1,674	(762)	—	23,000
9/96	1,555	(764)	—	23,000
9/95	1,497	(808)	—	24,100
9/94	1,413	(986)	—	24,000
Annual Growth	4.4%	—	—	(1.0%)

2003 Year-End Financials
Debt ratio: (53.0%)
Return on equity: —
Cash ($ mil.): 182
Current ratio: 0.45
Long-term debt ($ mil.): 3,773

Net Income History

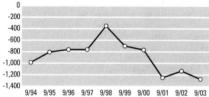

ANCIRA

ANCIRA wants to help Texans hit the road: It sells cars, trucks, and recreational vehicles exclusively in the Lone Star State. The company's dealerships feature new vehicles under the Buick, Chevrolet, Chrysler, Ford, GMC, Jeep, Kia, Nissan, Pontiac, and Volkswagen brands, as well as used cars and trucks. ANCIRA also sells new and used campers, motor homes, and recreational vehicles under the Fleetwood and Winnebago names, among others. The company is one of the nation's top fleet dealers and operates on-site parts and service departments. ANCIRA, which was founded in 1984, is owned by president Ernesto Ancira Jr.

EXECUTIVES
President and CEO: Ernesto Ancira Jr.
CFO: Betty Ferguson
Director of Human Resources: Valerie Tackett

LOCATIONS
HQ: ANCIRA
6111 Bandera Rd., San Antonio, TX 78238
Phone: 210-681-4900 **Fax:** 210-681-9413
Web: www.ancira.com

COMPETITORS

Allen Samuels Enterprises
AutoNation
Coast Distribution
Cruise America
Curtis Gunn
David McDavid Auto Group
Don Davis Auto Group
DriveTime
Gillman
Group 1 Automotive
Gunn Automotive
McCombs Enterprises
Red McCombs Automotive Group

HISTORICAL FINANCIALS
Company Type: Private

Income Statement
FYE: December 31

	REVENUE ($ mil.)	NET INCOME ($ mil.)	NET PROFIT MARGIN	EMPLOYEES
12/03	565	—	—	700
12/02	556	—	—	675
12/01	648	—	—	675
12/00	589	—	—	625
12/99	525	—	—	600
12/98	450	—	—	550
12/97	412	—	—	520
12/96	358	—	—	483
12/95	300	—	—	450
12/94	261	—	—	434
Annual Growth	9.0%	—	—	5.5%

Revenue History

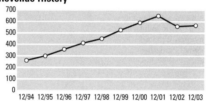

Andersen Corporation

Windows of opportunity open and shut daily for Andersen, a leading and well-known maker of wood-clad windows and patio doors in the US. Andersen offers window designs from hinged, bay, and double-hung to skylight, gliding, and picture windows. It operates 50 Renewal by Andersen window replacement stores in more than 20 states. Andersen's EMCO subsidiary makes storm and screen doors. Through independent and company-owned distributorships, the company sells to architects, general contractors, and building owners throughout the Americas, Europe, Asia, and the Middle East. Andersen Logistics operates in 16 states. The company is owned equally by the Andersen family, company employees, and the Andersen Foundation.

Andersen competes in the marketplace by building strong brand recognition for its products. Acquisitions play an important role in the company's growth strategy, and Andersen has been buying many of the independent distributorships that carry its products, including Morgan Products, the largest US distributor of its products.

Through its Aspen Research Corporation subsidiary, the company analyzes product life-cycle management, composite materials development, and waste elimination and reclamation.

Andersen is building a 150,000-sq.-ft. facility for wood composite profile extrusion in North Branch, Minnesota. It is expected to be operating in the spring of 2004. The company plans to close a plant in White Bear Lake and relocate about 40 jobs to North Branch.

HISTORY

Danish immigrant Hans Andersen and his two sons, Fred and Herbert, founded Andersen in 1903. Andersen's first words in English, "All together, boys," became the company motto. Andersen arrived in Portland, Maine, in 1870 and worked as a lumber dealer and manufacturer. In the 1880s he bought a sawmill in St. Cloud, Minnesota, and later managed one in Hudson, Wisconsin. When the Hudson mill owners asked him to let workers go during the off season, Andersen refused and then resigned. He subsequently launched his own lumber business — Andersen Lumber Company — in 1903 and hired some of the men who had been laid off. He opened a second lumberyard, in Afton, Minnesota, in 1904. Andersen and his sons revolutionized the window industry in the early 1900s by introducing a standardized window frame with interchangeable parts. Buoyed by success, the Andersens sold their lumberyards in 1908 to focus on the window-frame business. (Andersen purchased lumberyards again in 1916 before exiting the lumberyard business for good in the 1930s.) Around 1913 the company moved from Hudson to South Stillwater (now Bayport), Minnesota.

Thrifty Hans launched the company's first (and the US's third) profit-sharing plan shortly before his death in 1914. Herbert became VP, secretary, treasurer, and factory manager, and Fred became president. Herbert died in 1921 (at age 36), but Fred proved to be a versatile and capable successor. Among his accomplishments, Fred came up with the tag line "Only the rich can afford poor windows."

In 1929 the company changed its name to Andersen Frame Corporation. In the following decade Andersen introduced a number of innovations, including Master Frame (a frame with a locked sill joint, 1930); a casement window, the industry's first complete factory-made window unit (1932); and a basement window (1934). The company adopted its current name in 1937.

Andersen introduced the gliding window concept in the early 1940s. It also launched the Home Planners Scrap Book consumer ad campaign in 1943. During the 1950s Andersen's new products included the Flexivent awning window, which featured welded insulating glass that served as an alternative to traditional storm windows. In the 1960s the company produced a gliding door and introduced the Perma-Shield system. The system featured easy-to-maintain vinyl cladding to protect wood frames from weathering. By 1978 Perma-Shield products accounted for three-quarters of sales. Fred, who had run the company as president until 1960 and had subsequently held the positions of chairman and chairman emeritus, died in 1979 at age 92.

Between 1984 and 1994 the company increased its sales threefold by introducing additional customized and state-of-the-art products, including patio doors. In 1995 it launched Renewal by Andersen, a retail window-replacement business that has expanded to about 40 US locations.

Andersen acquired former long-term strategic partner Aspen Research (materials testing, research, and product development) in 1997. Among its jointly developed products is Fibrex, a composite material used in replacement windows. Also in 1997 the company moved its international division office from Bayport, Minnesota, to the Minnesota World Trade Center in St. Paul to help boost its export drive.

In 1998 company veteran Donald Garofalo succeeded Andersen's president and CEO Jerold Wulf, who retired after 39 years with the company. Andersen reinforced its company-owned distributorships in 1999 when it bought millwork distributors Morgan Products and Independent Millwork.

Expanding its product offerings, Andersen purchased privately held EMCO Enterprises (storm doors and accessories, Iowa) in 2001. Other acquisitions from about 1993 to 2003 have included Dashwood Industries (windows, skylights, roof windows, doors; Canada), Aspen Research (product development), and KML Windows (architectural windows and doors, Canada). The company also opened a new production facility in Menomonie, Wisconsin.

At the close of 2002, Andersen's COO James Humphrey was promoted to president, becoming the company's ninth president; he gained the added role of chief executive the next year. Garofalo retained the position of vice chair of the board. Andersen celebrated its 100th year in 2003, publishing a book on its history, and the company kicked off a community project to build 100 Habitat for Humanity homes throughout North America over the next five years.

EXECUTIVES

Board Chair: Sarah J. Andersen
Board Vice Chair: Donald L. Garofalo
President and CEO: James E. (Jim) Humphrey, age 57
SVP and CFO: Philip (Phil) Donaldson
SVP Operations: W. Patrick (Pat) Riley
SVP Human Resources and Corporate Administration: Mary D. Carter
SVP Research, Technology and Engineering: Mary J. Schumacher, age 46
SVP Sales and Marketing: Jay Lund
VP and General Counsel: Alan Bernick
VP Engineering and Quality: James (Jim) Brett
VP Marketing: J. Glasnapp
VP Sales: Steve Mog
President, Renewal by Andersen: Craig Evanich
Director, Corporate Communications: Maureen McDonough
Technology and Business Development Project Manager: Jay Libby
Corporate Planning and Reporting Manager: Tom Pomeroy
Manager, Residential and Commercial Trade Marketing: Sarah Meek

LOCATIONS

HQ: Andersen Corporation
100 4th Ave. North, Bayport, MN 55003
Phone: 651-264-5150 **Fax:** 651-264-5107
Web: www.andersencorp.com

Andersen markets its products in Brazil, the Caribbean, China, Guatemala, Honduras, Ireland, Israel, Japan, Kuwait, Mexico, Poland, Portugal, South Korea, Spain, Taiwan, Turkey, the UK, and the US.

PRODUCTS/OPERATIONS

Selected Products and Brands
Doors
  Patio doors
    Art glass (Frank Lloyd Wright designs)
    Frenchwood Collection (gliding, hinged, and outswing)
    Narroline gliding patio doors
    Perma-Shield gliding patio doors
  Screen doors
  Storm doors
Windows
  Art glass
  Awning
  Basement
  Bay and bow
  Casement
  Double-hung
  Fixed
  Gliding
  Horizontal sliding
  Picture
  Skylights and roof windows
  Transom
  Utility

COMPETITORS

Bocenor
JELD-WEN
Marshfield DoorSystems
Overhead Door
Pella
Royal Group Technologies
Sierra Pacific Industries
Simonton Windows
Thermal Industries
Weru

HISTORICAL FINANCIALS

Company Type: Private

Income Statement				FYE: December 31
	ESTIMATED REVENUE ($ mil.)	NET INCOME ($ mil.)	NET PROFIT MARGIN	EMPLOYEES
12/03	2,000	—	—	8,000
12/02	2,000	—	—	8,000
12/01	1,800	—	—	7,000
12/00	1,700	—	—	6,000
12/99	1,500	—	—	6,000
12/98	1,400	—	—	3,700
12/97	1,300	—	—	3,700
12/96	1,250	—	—	3,700
12/95	1,200	—	—	3,700
12/94	1,100	—	—	3,700
Annual Growth	6.9%	—	—	8.9%

Revenue History

Angelo Iafrate Companies

Included among the largest US private firms, The Angelo Iafrate Companies also ranks among the nation's top environmental construction firms. The group's subsidiaries are engaged in surface paving and heavy civil and highway construction projects, turnkey industrial contracting, underground utility infrastructure installation, site preparation and excavation, and environmental construction and remediation. The company also has a materials division that processes and sells crushed concrete, sand and gravel, limestone, and asphalt. Founded in 1960, the company is owned by the Iafrate family, who developed a state-of-the-art process to crush and recycle concrete.

EXECUTIVES

Vice Chairman: Angelo E. Iafrate Sr.
Vice Chairman: Dominic Iafrate
President: Angelo E. Iafrate Jr.
SVP: Duane Laurila
Treasurer: Michael Kiehnau
VP Engineering/Estimating: Don Statler
VP Operations: Dave Michael
Risk Manager: Craig Chall
Controller: Chris Hamrick

LOCATIONS

HQ: The Angelo Iafrate Companies
26400 Sherwood, Warren, MI 48091
Phone: 586-756-1070 **Fax:** 586-756-0467
Web: www.iafrate.com

PRODUCTS/OPERATIONS

Major Operations
Angelo Iafrate Construction Company
Angelo's Aggregate Materials, LTD
James Construction Group, LLC

COMPETITORS

Bechtel
Earth Tech
Jacobs Engineering
Lane Construction
MWH Global
Shaw Group
Washington Group
Zachry

HISTORICAL FINANCIALS

Company Type: Private

Income Statement				FYE: December 31
	REVENUE ($ mil.)	NET INCOME ($ mil.)	NET PROFIT MARGIN	EMPLOYEES
12/02	700	—	—	4,400
12/01	688	—	—	4,410
12/00	675	—	—	2,000
Annual Growth	1.8%	—	—	48.3%

Revenue History

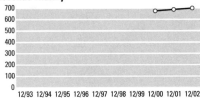

Apex Oil

At the top of its game, Apex Oil is engaged in the wholesale sales, storage, and distribution of petroleum products. Its range of refined products include asphalt, kerosene, fuel oil, diesel fuel, heavy oil, gasoline, and bunker fuels. The company's terminals are located on the East Coast and Gulf Coast, in California, and in the Midwest. Internationally, Apex Oil has a terminal in Caracas, Venezuela, and has additional activities in Bermuda, Monaco, and the Netherlands. The company is also engaged in a tug boat and barge business and has a storage and truck rack operation. Founded in 1932 by Samuel Goldstein, Apex Oil is controlled by CEO Tony Novelly.

EXECUTIVES

CEO: Paul Anthony (Tony) Novelly
CFO: John L. Hank Jr.
Controller: Jeffrey D. Baltz
Terminal Manager: Ken Fenton
Credit: Laura Seymour
Human Resources and Benefits: Julie Cook
Information Technology: John Diderrich
Legal Department: Mary Hockle
Light Oil Bulk Activity: Jeff Call
Midwest Sales: Bob Callahan
Truck Sales, Georgia, Florida, and North and South Carolina Regions: Ken Lommel
Truck Sales, Maryland, Virginia, Pennsylvania, and Delaware Regions: Mark Redel
Truck Sales, Missouri, Illinois, Indiana, and Ohio Regions: Cedrick Pimentel
Truck Sales, New York, Massachusetts, and Vermont Regions: Tom Grimes
Tugs and Barges: Mike Hanneman

LOCATIONS

HQ: Apex Oil Company, Inc.
8235 Forsyth Blvd., Ste. 400, Clayton, MO 63105
Phone: 314-889-9600 **Fax:** 314-854-8539
Web: www.apexoil.com

Apex Oil operates terminals in Arkansas, California, Florida, Illinois, Louisiana, Maryland, Missouri, New York, North Carolina, Tennessee, Texas, Virginia, and West Virginia. It also has operations in Bermuda, Monaco, the Netherlands, and Venezuela.

PRODUCTS/OPERATIONS

Major Products
Asphalt
Bunker fuels
Diesel fuel
Fuel oil
Gasoline
Heavy oil
Kerosene

Subsidiaries and Affiliates
Apex Towing Co. (tug boats and barges)
Clark Oil Trading Co. (wholesale oil trading)
Edgington Oil Co. (asphalt and fuel refinery)
Enjet Incorporated (fuel oil marketing and refinery)
Petroleum Fuel and Terminal Co. (storage and truck racks)

COMPETITORS

Chemoil
Crown Central Petroleum
Getty Petroleum Marketing
Global Companies
Koch
Marathon Oil
Premcor
Tauber Oil
U.S. Oil

HISTORICAL FINANCIALS

Company Type: Private

Income Statement				FYE: September 30
	REVENUE ($ mil.)	NET INCOME ($ mil.)	NET PROFIT MARGIN	EMPLOYEES
9/03	2,800	—	—	260
9/02	1,400	—	—	175
9/01	2,000	—	—	175
9/00	1,700	—	—	—
Annual Growth	18.1%	—	—	21.9%

Revenue History

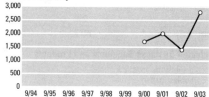

APi Group

Holding company APi Group has a piece of the action in five business sectors: construction services, fire protection, systems, manufacturing, and materials distribution. APi has more than 25 subsidiaries, which operate as independent companies. Services provided by the company's construction subsidiaries include energy conservation; electrical, industrial, and mechanical contracting; industrial insulation; and overhead door installation. Other units install fire protection systems, fabricate structural steel, and distribute building materials. The family-owned company was founded in 1926 by Reuben Anderson, father of CEO Lee Anderson.

EXECUTIVES

Chairman and CEO: Lee R. Anderson Sr., age 64
President: Russell Becker
EVP, CFO, and Treasurer: Loren Rachey
CTO: Brad Bechel
Secretary: William M. Beadie
Sales Manager: Jack Schwartz
Marketing: Kathy Anderson

LOCATIONS

HQ: APi Group, Inc.
2366 Rose Place, St. Paul, MN 55113
Phone: 651-636-4320 **Fax:** 651-636-0312
Web: www.apigroupinc.com

APi Group has US offices primarily in midwestern and western states; through its Vipond Fire Protection subsidiary, APi Group also operates in Canada and the UK.

PRODUCTS/OPERATIONS

Selected Subsidiaries
Fabrication and Manufacturing
 Anco Products, Inc. (flexible air ducts)
 Industrial Fabricators, Inc. (metal fabrication)
 LeJeune Steel Co. (structural steel)
 Wisconsin Structural Steel Co. (steel fabrication)
Fire Protection Systems
 Alliance Fire Protection, Inc.
 Security Fire Protection, Inc.
 United States Fire Protection
 VFP Fire Systems, Inc.
 Viking Automatic Sprinkler Co.
 Vipond Fire Protection, Inc. (Canada)
 Vipond Fire Protection Ltd. (UK)
 Western States Fire Protection
Materials Distribution
 APi Distribution (insulation products)
 ASDCO (wholesale distributor of construction materials)
Specialty Construction Services
 APi Construction Co. (industrial insulation)
 APi Electric (formerly Lakehead Electric and Thompson Electric; electrical contracting)
 APi Supply, Inc. (rental, sales, service of aerial work platforms)
 Doody Mechanical, Inc. (mechanical contracting, including heating, ventilation, and air-conditioning)
 Industrial Contractors, Inc. (ICI; energy industry contracting)
 The Jamar Co. (mechanical and specialty contracting)
 Twin City Garage Door Co. (installation and servicing of overhead doors)
Systems
 API Systems Group (fire and gas detection and security systems provider)
 Communications Systems, Inc. (security systems integration)
 Halon Banking Systems
 Northern Fire & Communication (fire alarm and communications equipment)
 Vipond Systems Group (fire alarm and communications equipment)

COMPETITORS

AMPAM
Comfort Systems USA
EMCOR
Integrated Electrical Services
Irex
John E. Green
TDIndustries
Team Inc
Turner Industries
Tyco Fire and Security Services

HISTORICAL FINANCIALS

Company Type: Private

Income Statement				FYE: December 31
	REVENUE ($ mil.)	NET INCOME ($ mil.)	NET PROFIT MARGIN	EMPLOYEES
12/03	800	—	—	5,000
12/02	675	—	—	5,000
12/01	750	—	—	5,000
12/00	726	—	—	5,000
12/99	535	—	—	4,000
12/98	537	—	—	3,500
12/97	540	—	—	3,000
12/96	530	—	—	3,000
Annual Growth	6.1%	—	—	7.6%

Revenue History

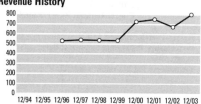

Appleton

Appleton Papers shows that some things don't fall far from the tree. The company manufactures and distributes paper and paperboard products. Its core business is carbonless paper (NCR Paper). Appleton produces thermal paper (Optima) for use with print technology and computer products, uncoated security paper (Docucheck) that protects documents against forgery, and coated paper (Avario) for design and communication printing. Attempting to bolster its presence in the security products market, Appleton is also designing label stock engineered chiefly for radio frequency (RFID) smart labels. The company was acquired from Arjo Wiggins Appleton in 2001 and is 100% owned by its employees.

The company, nearly 100 years old, controls 60% of US carbonless paper sales, and brings in more than $700 million annually, despite the declining market.

Appleton is truly owned by its employees; more than 90% of its employees bought the company from Arjo Wiggins in 2001 by investing roughly 75% of their 401k plans, about $40,000 each.

Appleton Security Products, a division of the company, started out by making paper for checks. Now, galvanized by a renewed interest in security in the wake of the September 11th terrorist attacks, the division is making waves by producing products designed to prevent document fraud. The division's sales are relatively small (around $40 million), but growth is expected to be in the neighborhood of 25% per year. Appleton Security is already producing treasury checks for several states and foreign countries, important documents like birth certificates and marriage licenses, and ownership titles for a number of prominent auto manufacturers.

Appleton strives for further expansion into the relatively new markets of packaging, brand protection, digital products, and labels through development efforts and acquisitions. The company purchased two companies in early 2003: C&H Packaging Company and American Plastics Company. At the end of 2003, Appleton strengthened its international presence by acquiring BemroseBooth, a security product manufacturer located in the UK.

Though the company's legal name remains Appleton Papers Inc., in 2003 it began referring to itself as simply "Appleton" for branding purposes.

EXECUTIVES

Chairman, President, and CEO: Douglas P. (Doug) Buth, age 49, $817,534 pay
VP, Finance; CFO and Director: Dale E. Parker, age 52, $279,707 pay
VP, Human Resources and Law, Secretary, General Counsel, and Director: Paul J. Karch, age 47, $256,484 pay
VP and General Manager, Thermal and Advanced Technical Products: John R. Depies, age 47, $243,745 pay
VP, Coated Solutions Sales and Marketing: James H. (Jim) McDermott, age 47
VP, Operations and Project Venture: Rick J. Fantini, age 49
VP, Market Transformation: Ann M. Whalen, age 45
VP, Performance Packaging: Stephen P. Sakai, age 50, $253,086 pay
VP, Technology: Ted E. Goodwin, age 47
CEO, BemroseBooth Limited: Graham Bennington, age 53
Director, Manufacturing and Mill Manager, West Carrollton Mill: Todd Downey, age 45
Mill Manager, Roaring Spring Mill: René-Paul Forier, age 56
Plant Manager, Appleton Plant: Paul McCann, age 45
Manager, Corporate Communications: Bill Van Den Brandt
Auditors: PricewaterhouseCoopers LLP

LOCATIONS

HQ: Appleton Papers Inc.
825 E. Wisconsin Ave., Appleton, WI 54911
Phone: 920-734-9841 **Fax:** 920-991-8080
Web: www.appletonideas.com

In addition to owning distribution centers throughout the US, Appleton owns facilities in Canada (Ontario) and England (Birmingham).

PRODUCTS/OPERATIONS

2003 Sales

	$ mil.	% of total
Coated	622.6	72
Thermal & advanced technical products	182.1	21
Other	56.8	7
Total	**861.5**	**100**

Selected Business Segments and Products

Coated solutions products
  Carbonless paper
    Credit card receipts
    Invoices
    NCR Paper
  Coated products
    Inkjet printing
    Other design and print applications
    Point-of-sale displays
Performance packaging
  Flexible packaging materials
  Multilayered films
Security products
  Brand protection products
  Business documents
  Checks
  Government documents
  High-integrity mailing and niche publishing
  Mass transit and car parking tickets
  Security printed vouchers and payment cards
Technical products
  Non-thermal products
  Thermal business products
    Point-of-sale receipts and coupons
    Label products
    Lotteries, tote, and gaming tickets
    Tags for airline baggage
    Tickets

COMPETITORS

ArjoWiggins
Boise Cascade
communisis
Curwood
De La Rue
Document Security Systems
Imation
International Paper
Kanzaki Specialty Papers
MeadWestvaco
Mitsubishi Paper Mills
Oji Paper
Pechiney Plastic Packaging
Pliant
Printpack
Ricoh
Temple-Inland
Weyerhaeuser
Winpak

HISTORICAL FINANCIALS

Company Type: Private

Income Statement FYE: Saturday nearest December 31

	REVENUE ($ mil.)	NET INCOME ($ mil.)	NET PROFIT MARGIN	EMPLOYEES
12/03	862	11	1.3%	3,348
12/02	898	10	1.1%	2,500
12/01	956	40	4.2%	—
Annual Growth	(5.1%)	(47.3%)	—	33.9%

2003 Year-End Financials
Debt ratio: 247.8% Current ratio: 1.70
Return on equity: 8.1% Long-term debt ($ mil.): 358
Cash ($ mil.): 30

Net Income History

Arctic Slope Regional

The Inupiat people have survived the Arctic for centuries, and now they're surviving in the business world. The Inupiat-owned Arctic Slope Regional Corporation (ASRC) was set up to manage 5 million acres on Alaska's North Slope after the Alaska Native Claims Settlement Act in 1971 cleared the way for oil development in the area. ASRC gets about two-thirds of sales from its energy services subsidiaries (ASRC Energy Services) and its petroleum refining and marketing units (Petro Star). Other operations include construction, engineering, and governmental services.

EXECUTIVES

Chairman and VP Government Affairs: Oliver Leavitt
Vice Chairman: Rex A. Rock Sr.
President and CEO: Jacob Adams
COO: Conrad Bagne
VP and CFO: Kristin Mellinger
VP and General Counsel: Alma McClellan Upicksoun
VP Administration and Shareholder Relations: Flossie Chrestman
VP Human Resources: Karen Burnell
VP Lands: Richard Glenn
VP Operations: Forrest (Deano) Olemaun
Corporate Secretary: Mary Ellen Ahmaogak
Corporate Treasurer: Patsy Aamodt
Auditors: Deloitte & Touche LLP

LOCATIONS

HQ: Arctic Slope Regional Corporation
3900 C St., Ste. 801, Anchorage, AK 99503
Phone: 907-339-6000 **Fax:** 907-339-6028
Web: www.asrc.com

Arctic Slope Regional Corporation has US offices in Alaska, Arizona, California, Maryland, New Mexico, and Oregon. It also has operations in Mexico and Venezuela.

PRODUCTS/OPERATIONS

Selected Subsidiaries

Energy services
  Alaska Petroleum Contractors
  ASRC Parsons Engineering, LLC.
  Global Power and Communications
  Houston Contracting Company-Alaska, Ltd.
  Natchiq Sakhalin Ltd.
  Omega Service Industries, Inc.
  Tri Ocean Engineering, Ltd.
Engineering and construction
  Arctic Slope Construction, Inc.
  ASCG, Inc.
  ASCG Inspection, Inc.
  ASCG of New Mexico
  McLaughlin Water Engineers, Ltd.
  SKW/Eskimos, Inc.
Manufacturing
  Puget Plastics Corporation
  Puget Plastics S.A. de C.V. (Mexico)
  Triquest Puget Plastics, LLC
Petroleum refining and marketing
  Kodiak Oil Sales Inc. (North Pacific Fuel)
  Petro Star, Inc.
  Petro Star Valdez, Inc. (Valdez refinery)
  Sourdough Fuel, Inc.
  Valdez Petroleum Terminal (North Pacific Fuel)
Technical services
  Arctic Slope World Services, Incorporated
  ASRC Aerospace Corp.
  ASRC Communications, Ltd.
Other operations
  Alaska Growth Capital Bidco Inc.
  Barrow Cable Television
  Eskimos, Inc.
  Tundra Tours, Inc.

COMPETITORS

Alaska Communications Systems
Baker Hughes
Halliburton
Nabors Industries
Noble
Schlumberger
Smith International
Tesoro Alaska
Tesoro Petroleum
T-Mobile USA

HISTORICAL FINANCIALS
Company Type: Private

Income Statement
FYE: December 31

	REVENUE ($ mil.)	NET INCOME ($ mil.)	NET PROFIT MARGIN	EMPLOYEES
12/03	1,029	5	0.5%	—
12/02	974	17	1.7%	—
12/01	1,062	31	2.9%	6,413
12/00	1,035	24	2.3%	5,973
12/99	888	—	—	3,000
12/98	869	—	—	3,000
Annual Growth	3.4%	(41.4%)	—	28.8%

2003 Year-End Financials
Debt ratio: 44.4%
Return on equity: 2.0%
Cash ($ mil.): 77
Current ratio: 1.97
Long-term debt ($ mil.): 110

Net Income History

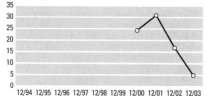

Ardent Health

When you're weary, feeling small, when tears are in your eyes, don't just look for a bridge over troubled water — seek professional help. Ardent Health Services was founded in 1993 as Behavioral Healthcare Corporation (BHC), which had six behavioral treatment centers at the outset. The New York investment firm of Welsh, Carson, Anderson & Stowe acquired majority ownership of BHC in 2001 and renamed the company.

Ardent now has 28 hospitals across the US; 21 are behavioral hospitals, offering services ranging from residential inpatient treatment to outpatient counseling, and seven are acute care hospitals. The company also operates a health plan that serves more than 240,000 members in New Mexico.

Ardent also provides commercial laboratory and behavioral health care management services to acute care hospitals.

The company plans to grow by acquiring additional behavioral and acute care hospitals.

EXECUTIVES

Chairman: Russell L. Carson, age 60
President, CEO, and Manager: David T. Vandewater, age 53, $854,992 pay
COO and Manager: Jamie E. Hopping, age 50, $683,389 pay
CFO and Manager: Dirk Allison, age 48, $733,000 pay (partial-year salary)
EVP, Behavioral Health Group: Vernon (Vern) Westrich, age 53, $558,685 pay
SVP, Finance: William Page Barnes, $350,650 pay
SVP, General Counsel, and Secretary: Steven C. Petrovich, age 37, $306,528 pay
SVP, Human Resources and Administration: Neil Hemphill
VP and Controller: Clint B. Adams
VP and Chief Information Officer: Steve Starkey
VP, Human Resources: Katie Stewart
President, Lovelace Sandia Health System: Norman P. Becker, age 48
Auditors: Ernst & Young LLP

LOCATIONS

HQ: Ardent Health Services LLC
  1 Burton Hills Blvd., Ste. 250, Nashville, TN 37215
Phone: 615-296-3000 **Fax:** 615-296-6004
Web: www.ardenthealth.com

Selected Hospitals
Acute Care Hospitals
  Kentucky (1)
  Louisiana (1)
  New Mexico (5)
Behavioral Hospitals
  Arkansas (1)
  California (4)
  Idaho (1)
  Illinois (1)
  Indiana (4)
  Nevada (3)
  New Mexico (1)
  Ohio (3)
  Pennsylvania (1)
  Virginia (1)
  Washington (1)

PRODUCTS/OPERATIONS

2003 Sales

	$ mil.	% of total
Net patient services	640.9	49
Premiums	592.3	45
Other	86.5	6
Total	**1,319.7**	**100**

COMPETITORS

APS Healthcare
Carilion Health System
Comprehensive Care
FHC Health Systems
Horizon Health
Magellan Health
Mental Health Network
PacifiCare Behavioral Health
PHC
Premier Behavioral Solutions
Psychiatric Solutions
UBH

HISTORICAL FINANCIALS
Company Type: Private

Income Statement
FYE: December 31

	REVENUE ($ mil.)	NET INCOME ($ mil.)	NET PROFIT MARGIN	EMPLOYEES
12/03	1,320	4	0.3%	10,100
12/02	408	5	1.3%	—
12/01	245	21	8.4%	—
Annual Growth	132.3%	(54.3%)	—	—

Net Income History

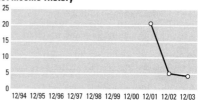

Arkansas Blue Cross and Blue Shield

Arkansas Blue Cross and Blue Shield provides health insurance products and related services for more than 890,000 members in Arkansas. The company's health insurance plans include HMO, PPO, traditional fee-for-service, and supplemental Medicare. Dental, disability, life, and workers compensation insurance are provided through various subsidiaries and affiliates of the company. Arkansas Blue Cross and Blue Shield also provides third-party-administration (TPA) services via its BlueAdvantage Administrators of Arkansas subsidiary. The not-for-profit company is an independent member of the Blue Cross and Blue Shield Association.

Arkansas Blue Cross and Blue Shield has managed to grow by providing a wider range of products and services, such as supplemental insurance products, that complement the company's core health insurance offerings.

Army and Air Force Exchange

EXECUTIVES
Chairman: Hays C. McClerkin
Vice Chairman: George K. Mitchell
CEO: Robert L. Shoptaw
President and COO: Sharon Allen
EVP, CFO, and Treasurer: Mark White
EVP, Legal, Governmental Relations, and Communication Services and Secretary: Robert Cabe
SVP, Customer Service: David Bridges
SVP, Enterprise Networks: Mike Brown
SVP, Public Programs: Dennis Robertson
VP and Chief Medical Officer: James Adamson
VP, Public Programs, Information Systems: Charles Clem
VP, Human Resources: Richard Cooper
VP, Statewide Business: Ron DeBerry
VP, Advertising and Communications: Patrick O'Sullivan
VP, Information Technology Infrastructure: Bob Heard
VP, Enterprise Development Services: Cal Kellogg
VP, Actuarial and Corporate Actuary: Sam Partin
VP, Law and Government Relations: Lee Douglass
VP, Financial Services: Steve Short
VP, Customer Services: Steve Spaulding
Director of Actuarial Services: Samuel C. Vorderstrasse

LOCATIONS
HQ: Arkansas Blue Cross and Blue Shield
601 S. Gaines St., Little Rock, AR 72201
Phone: 501-378-2000   **Fax:** 501-378-3258
Web: www.arkbluecross.com

PRODUCTS/OPERATIONS
Selected Subsidiaries and Affiliates
AHIN, LLC (Information Technology Services)
BlueAdvantage Administrators of Arkansas (Third-Party Administration)
HMO Partners, Inc. (dba Health Advantage)
Ideal Medical Services, Inc. (Federal Medicare Contractor)
USAble Corporation (Group Disability and Life Insurance)

COMPETITORS
Aetna
Baxter Regional Medical Center
CIGNA
Humana
UnitedHealth Group

HISTORICAL FINANCIALS
Company Type: Not-for-profit

Income Statement			FYE: December 31
	REVENUE ($ mil.)	NET INCOME ($ mil.)	NET PROFIT MARGIN	EMPLOYEES
12/03	907	52	5.8%	2,300
12/02	849	—	—	2,300
Annual Growth	6.9%	—	—	0.0%

Revenue History

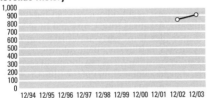

Be all that you can be and buy all that you can buy at the PX (Post Exchange). The Army and Air Force Exchange Service (AAFES) runs more than 12,000 facilities — including PXs and BXs (Base Exchanges) — at US Army and Air Force bases in 35 countries (including about 30 in Iraq) and in all 50 US states. Its outlets range from tents to shopping centers that have retail stores, fast-food outlets (including 180-plus Burger King restaurants worldwide), movie theaters, beauty shops, and gas stations. AAFES serves active-duty military personnel, reservists, retirees, and their family members. A government agency under the Department of Defense (DOD), it receives no funding from the department.

While the AAFES receives no federal money, it pays neither taxes nor rent to occupy US government property. More than 70% of AAFES's profits go into Morale, Welfare, and Recreation Programs for amenities such as libraries and youth centers. Other profits are used to renovate or build stores. Active military personnel head AAFES, but its staff consists mostly of military family members and other civilians.

In May 2003, Deputy Secretary of Defense Paul Wolfowitz proposed a task force to explore a merger of AAFES with the Navy Exchange Service Command and the Marine Corps Personnel Support. The military shops are facing increased competition from Wal-Mart Stores, which is luring soldiers off base with its every day low prices. Texas officials are lobbying members of Congress charged with exploring ways to integrate the three exchange services, to keep the AAFES in Dallas and consolidate shared functions in Texas.

HISTORY

During the American Revolution, peddlers known as sutlers followed the Army, selling items such as soap, razors, and tobacco. The practice lasted until after the Civil War, when post traders replaced sutlers. This system was replaced in 1889 when the War Department authorized canteens at military bases.

The first US military exchanges were established in 1895, creating a system to supply military personnel with personal items on US Army bases around the world. The exchanges were run independently, with each division creating a Post Exchange (PX) to serve its unit. The post commander would assign an officer to run the PX (usually along with other duties) and would decide how profits were spent.

In 1941 the Army Exchange Service was created, and the system was reorganized. A five-member advisory committee made up of civilian merchandisers was created to provide recommendations for the reorganization. The restructuring made the system more like a chain store business. The independent PXs were bought by the War Department from the individual military organizations that ran them. Civilian personnel were brought in to staff the PXs, and a brigadier general was named to head an executive staff made up of Army officers and civilians that provided centralized control of the system. The Army also created a special school to train officers to run the PXs.

Sales at the PXs skyrocketed during WWII; a catalog business was added so soldiers could order gifts to send home to their families. The Department of the Air Force was established in 1947, and the exchange system organization was renamed the Army and Air Force Exchange Service (AAFES) the next year.

In 1960 the government allowed the overseas exchanges to provide more luxury items in an effort to keep soldiers from buying foreign-made goods. By the time the military had been cranked up again for the Vietnam War, big-ticket items such as TVs, cameras, and tape recorders were among the exchanges' best-sellers. In 1967 AAFES moved its headquarters from New York City to Dallas.

By 1991 the exchanges were open to the National Guard and the Reserve; AAFES's customer base had grown to 14 million. When the military began downsizing during the 1990s following the end of the Cold War, AAFES's customer base shrank by 35%.

In 1995 AAFES stores sold more than $12 million of pornographic materials. The House of Representatives passed the Military Honor and Decency Act the next year prohibiting the sale of pornography on US military property, including AAFES stores; this ban was struck down as unconstitutional in 1997. That year AAFES was approved as a provider of medical equipment covered by federal CHAMPUS/TRICARE insurance. It also created a Web site to offer online shopping in 1997.

The Supreme Court upheld the 1996 porn ban in 1998; the Pentagon banned the sale of more than 150 sexually explicit magazines (such as *Penthouse*), while a military board permitted the continued sale of certain publications (including *Playboy*). Maj. Gen. Barry Bates took over as AAFES's Commander and CEO in 1998. To better battle other retailers, that year AAFES announced its stores would offer best-price guarantees, matching prices of local stores and refunding price differences if customers found lower prices within 30 days of buying products.

In 1999 AAFES expanded to Macedonia and Kosovo, providing its services to military personnel in Operation Joint Guardian. In 2000 Bates was replaced as AAFES commander and CEO by Maj. Gen. Charles J. Wax.

Wax stepped down as commander and CEO in August 2002 and was replaced by Maj. Gen. Katherine Frost of the US Army.

EXECUTIVES
Chairman: Lt. Gen. Charles S. Mahan Jr.
Commander: Maj. Gen. Kathryn Frost, USA
Vice Commander and Director, Equal Opportunity: Brig. Gen. Toreraser A. Steele, USAF
COO: Marilyn Iverson
CFO: Jerry Justus
SVP, Europe: Karen Stack
SVP, Human Resources: Ronnie D. Compton
SVP, Management Information Systems: Terry B. Corley
SVP, Sales: Mary Ellen Gillespie
VP, Food and Theater Division: Richard Sheff
VP, Main Store/Soft-lines Division: James Moon
VP, Services: Craig Sewell
Chief of Business Planning: Nick Williams
Chief of Communications: Debra L. Pressley
Chief Technology Officer: Tony Levister
Director, Food Programs: Butch Freed
Director, Planning: Craig Christman
General Counsel: Col. Athena Jones, USAF
Purchasing Manager, Restaurant Operations: Beverly Hopp
AAFES Burger King Restaurant Program Manager: Lee Wiederkeht
Auditors: Ernst & Young LLP

LOCATIONS

HQ: Army and Air Force Exchange Service
3911 S. Walton Walker Blvd., Dallas, TX 75236
Phone: 214-312-2011 **Fax:** 214-312-3000
Web: www.aafes.com

The Army and Air Force Exchange Service has operations in all 50 states and in 35 countries and overseas areas.

PRODUCTS/OPERATIONS

Selected Merchandise and Services
Barber and beauty shops
Books, newspapers, and magazines
Catalog services
Class Six stores
Concessions
Food facilities (mobile units, snack bars, name-brand fast-food franchises, and concession operations)
Gas stations and auto repair
Military clothing stores
Movie theaters
Retail stores
Vending centers

COMPETITORS

7-Eleven
Best Buy
Costco Wholesale
J. C. Penney
Kmart
Kroger
METRO AG
Sears
Target
Wal-Mart

HISTORICAL FINANCIALS

Company Type: Government agency

Income Statement				FYE: January 31
	REVENUE ($ mil.)	NET INCOME ($ mil.)	NET PROFIT MARGIN	EMPLOYEES
1/04	7,905	485	6.1%	47,323
1/03	7,323	416	5.7%	49,861
1/02	7,133	373	5.2%	52,400
1/01	7,369	381	5.2%	52,400
1/00	6,992	362	5.2%	54,000
1/99	6,783	343	5.1%	54,000
1/98	6,620	337	5.1%	53,946
1/97	6,874	348	5.1%	57,583
1/96	6,710	228	3.4%	56,495
1/95	6,746	269	4.0%	58,556
Annual Growth	1.8%	6.8%	—	(2.3%)

2004 Year-End Financials
Debt ratio: 0.0%   Current ratio: 1.97
Return on equity: 12.6%   Long-term debt ($ mil.): 0
Cash ($ mil.): 110

Net Income History

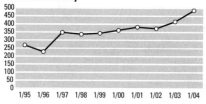

ASCAP

While Frank Sinatra got the glory, Johnny Mercer got some of the money, and his estate still does, thanks to the American Society of Composers, Authors and Publishers (ASCAP). ASCAP is the #1 performance rights organization in the world. The group protects the rights of composers, songwriters, lyricists, and music publishers by licensing and distributing royalties for the public performances of their copyrighted works. Be they played in a stadium, on the radio or Internet, on an airplane, or in a bar, songs of more than 175,000 members are covered.

ASCAP no longer charges annual membership dues. Founded in 1914, the not-for-profit organization is run entirely by members who serve on the board of directors.

EXECUTIVES

Chairman and President: Marilyn Bergman
Vice Chairman: Cy Coleman
Vice Chairman: Jay Morgenstern
CEO: John LoFrumento
VP and CFO: Bob Candela
EVP Membership Group, Los Angeles: Todd Brabec
EVP Performing Rights Group: Al Wallace
SVP Licensing, Performing Rights Group: Vincent Candilora
SVP and Chief Economist, Performing Rights Group: Peter Boyle
SVP Information Services and CIO, Performing Rights Group: Tina Barber
SVP International, Headquarters Group: Roger Greenaway
SVP Marketing, Headquarters Group: Philip Crosland
SVP Creative Affairs, Membership Group, Los Angeles: John Alexander
SVP Industry Affairs and VP and Executive Director, ASCAP Foundation: Karen Sherry
SVP Membership Group, Nashville: Connie Bradley
SVP Director Membership Film and Television Repertory, Membership Group: Nancy Knutsen
SVP Enterprises Group: Chris Amenita
VP Human Resources: Carolyn Jensen
Director Media Relations, Headquarters Group: Jim Steinblatt

LOCATIONS

HQ: American Society of Composers, Authors and Publishers
1 Lincoln Plaza, New York, NY 10023
Phone: 212-621-6000 **Fax:** 212-724-9064
Web: www.ascap.com

PRODUCTS/OPERATIONS

Selected Past and Present Members
Beck
Leonard Bernstein
Garth Brooks
Duke Ellington
George Gershwin
James Horner
Lyle Lovett
Madonna
Henry Mancini
Tito Puente
Stevie Wonder

COMPETITORS

BMI
SESAC

HISTORICAL FINANCIALS

Company Type: Not-for-profit

Income Statement				FYE: December 31
	ESTIMATED REVENUE ($ mil.)	NET INCOME ($ mil.)	NET PROFIT MARGIN	EMPLOYEES
12/03	700	—	—	630
12/02	635	—	—	600
12/01	600	—	—	600
12/00	500	—	—	500
12/99	500	—	—	500
12/98	500	—	—	600
12/97	500	—	—	583
12/96	483	—	—	588
12/95	437	—	—	566
12/94	423	—	—	688
Annual Growth	5.8%	—	—	(1.0%)

Revenue History

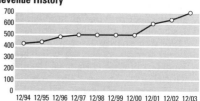

Ascension Health

Ascension Health has ascended to the pinnacle of not-for-profit health care. One of the largest Catholic hospital systems in the US, and thus one of the top providers of charity care in the nation, the organization's health care network consists of some 65 general acute care hospitals along with a dozen long-term care, rehabilitation, and psychiatric hospitals. Ascension Health also operates nursing homes, community clinics, and other health care facilities in about 20 states and the District of Columbia. The organization's facilities have more than 16,700 licensed beds.

Ascension's facilities are primarily located in the southern, midwestern, and northeastern areas of the US.

The system takes to heart the words of St. Vincent de Paul, co-founder of the Daughters of Charity, who advised the order to serve "the poor sick bodily, ministering to them in all their needs, and spiritually also so that they will live and die well."

As such, Nuns from Ascension's sponsoring religious orders sit on its governing board, which is led by non-clergy CEO Douglas French.

In this age of high-cost health care, Ascension realizes the need for fiscal health. In addition to selling money-losing hospitals, Ascension has reorganized its facilities by geographic regions, with each region headed by a VP who controls costs and speeds decision making.

In response to rising health care costs, Ascension merged with national Catholic health care provider Carondelet Health System in 2003.

HOOVER'S HANDBOOK OF PRIVATE COMPANIES 2005

HISTORY

The Daughters of Charity order was formed in France in 1633 when St. Vincent de Paul recruited a rich widow (St. Louise de Marillac) to care for the sick on battlefields and in their homes.

Elizabeth Ann Seton, America's first saint (canonized 1974), brought the order to the US. In 1809 Seton earned the title of Mother and started the Sisters of Charity. The Sisters adopted the vows of the Daughters of Charity, adding "service" to them in 1812.

The Sisters officially became part of the Daughters of Charity in 1850. The Daughters cared for soldiers during the Civil War and were responsible for training Florence Nightingale. In the late 1800s the Daughters pioneered exclusive provider arrangements (similar to today's managed care contracts) with railroads, lumber camps, and the like. During the next 100 years, the order furthered its mission of caring for the sick and the poor by founding hospitals (44 by 1911), schools, and other charity centers.

In 1969 the charity association formed a health care services cooperative, which became the Daughters of Charity National Health System (DCNHS).

DCNHS operated as two regional institutions (one based in Maryland, the other in Missouri) until 1986, when the systems merged. The first task was to balance their holy mission with the need to make money. With competition from managed care companies increasing, DCNHS responded by cutting staff and diversifying into nursing homes and retirement centers.

The Daughters of Charity's western unit combined its six hospitals in California with Mullikin Centers (a physician-owned medical group) in 1993 to form one of the largest health care associations in the state.

DCNHS expanded its network in 1995 by merging its hospitals with and becoming a co-sponsor of San Francisco-based Catholic Healthcare West. That year it joined with Catholic Relief Services to operate a hospital in war-torn Angola.

In 1996 DCNHS dropped a proposed merger of its struggling 221-bed Carney Hospital in Boston with Quincy Hospital because the municipally owned Quincy facility was required by law to provide abortions. Instead, DCNHS sold Carney Hospital to Caritas Christi Health Care System (owned by the Boston Roman Catholic archdiocese), one of about a dozen hospital sales by DCNHS in the mid-1990s.

DCNHS reorganized its leadership in 1997, creating SVP positions for system direction and policy and for program development to strengthen and update its programs. In 1998 Sister Irene Kraus, who had founded DCNHS and led it through its expansion, died.

In 1999 DCNHS merged with fellow Catholic caregiver Sisters of St. Joseph Health System, then Michigan's largest health care system.

In 2000 Ascension saw the collapse of a five-hospital merger in Florida between subsidiary St. Vincent's Health System and Baptist Health System. The organization also launched the Voice for the Voiceless initiative, which combines private monies and federal grants to fund programs for the uninsured in Detroit, New Orleans, and Austin, Texas.

EXECUTIVES

Chairman: John O. (Jack) Mudd
President and CEO: Anthony R. (Tony) Tersigni, age 54
COO: Robert J. (Bob) Henkel, age 50
SVP, Western and Southern States Operating Group: Andrew W. Allen
SVP and Chief Risk Officer: James K. Beckmann Jr.
SVP and CIO: Sherry L. Browne
SVP, Strategic Business Development and Innovation; President, Ascension Health Ventures: John D. Doyle
SVP, Legal Services and General Counsel: Rex P. Killian
SVP, Advocacy and External Relations: Susan Nestor Levy
SVP, Mission Integration: Sister Maureen McGuire
SVP, Clinical Excellence: David B. Pryor
SVP and CFO: Anthony J. (Tony) Speranzo
VP, Advocacy, Ascension Health-Michigan: Sean Gehle
VP, Communications: Steve LeResche
VP and Associate General Counsel: Steven H. Pratt
Director, Communications: Trudy C. Barthels
Manager, Human Resources: Kate Brandt
Auditors: Ernst & Young LLP

LOCATIONS

HQ: Ascension Health
 4600 Edmundson Rd., St. Louis, MO 63145
Phone: 314-733-8000   **Fax:** 314-733-8013
Web: www.ascensionhealth.org

PRODUCTS/OPERATIONS

2003 Sales

	$ mil.	% of total
Patient services	8,597.5	95
Other	456.8	5
Total	9,054.3	100

2003 Payors

	% of total
Managed care	35
Medicare	34
Blue Cross	8
Medicaid	6
Other sources	17
Total	100

2003 Hospitals

	No.
General acute care	63
Long-term acute care	4
Psychiatric	4
Rehabilitation	4
Joint ventures	3
Total	78

COMPETITORS

Beverly Enterprises
Catholic Health East
Catholic Health Initiatives
Catholic Healthcare Partners
HCA
Health Management Associates
HEALTHSOUTH
Kindred
Life Care Centers
Tenet Healthcare
Triad Hospitals
Trinity Health (Novi)
Universal Health Services

HISTORICAL FINANCIALS

Company Type: Not-for-profit

Income Statement FYE: June 30

	REVENUE ($ mil.)	NET INCOME ($ mil.)	NET PROFIT MARGIN	EMPLOYEES
6/03	9,054	—	—	87,469
6/02	7,666	—	—	83,412
6/01	6,853	—	—	83,412
6/00	6,400	—	—	67,000
6/99	6,400	—	—	67,000
6/98	6,170	—	—	65,000
6/97	5,700	—	—	60,000
6/96	5,700	—	—	61,100
6/95	6,200	—	—	62,300
6/94	7,000	—	—	67,400
Annual Growth	2.9%	—	—	2.9%

Revenue History

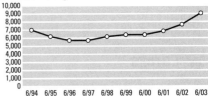

Ash Grove Cement

Ash Grove Cement is a pioneer in the US cement industry. The company, which traces its roots back to 1882, operates nine plants with an annual capacity of more than 7.8 million tons of cement. It's one of the largest cement manufacturers in the country. Ash Grove's products include portland, masonry, and ready-mix cements. It also operates a lime plant in Oregon; a quarry in British Columbia, Canada; and rock quarries in Texas. Other company operations include Ash Grove Packaging (packaged materials); Permanent Paving, Inc.; and Cedar Creek Properties, which develops residential and commercial properties. Lester T. Sunderland joined Ash Grove Cement in 1909; his heirs still own the company.

EXECUTIVES

Honorary Chairman: James P. Sunderland
Chairman and CEO: Charles T. Sunderland
Vice Chairman and Secretary: Kent W. Sunderland
President and COO: Charles T. Wiedenhoft
SVP, General Counsel: John H. Ross III
VP Finance: John H. Woodfill
VP Corporate Maintenance: Kenneth J. Rone Jr.
VP Environmental Affairs: Fran Streitman
VP Manufacturing Services: Stephen Joyce
VP Manufacturing, Midwestern Division: Edwin S. Pierce
VP Marketing, Midwestern Division: Ronald V. Deleenheer
VP Sales, Western Division: David H. Baker

LOCATIONS

HQ: Ash Grove Cement Company
 11011 Cody St., Overland Park, KS 66210
Phone: 913-451-8900 **Fax:** 913-451-8324
Web: www.ashgrove.com

Ash Grove Cement Company has plants in the US in Arkansas, Idaho, Kansas, Montana, Nebraska, Oregon, Texas, Utah, and Washington, and in British Columbia, Canada.

PRODUCTS/OPERATIONS

Selected Products

Cement
  Hydraulic cement
  Masonry cement
  Portland cement
Lime
  Calcium carbonate
  Commercial limestone
  Ground dolomite
  Hydrated lime
  Pebble lime
  Quicklime

Selected Operations

Ash Grove Materials Corporation
  Ash Grove Aggregates
  Ash Grove Packaging Group
    Materials Packaging Corporation
    Precision Packaging, Inc.
  Century Concrete, Inc.
  Fordyce Concrete Company
Cedar Creek Properties, Inc. (residential development, Kansas)
Permanent Paving, Inc.

COMPETITORS

Buzzi Unicem USA
CEMEX
Centex
CRH
Eagle Materials
Essroc
Florida Rock Industries
Holcim (US)
James Hardie
Lafarge Canada
Lafarge North America
St. Lawrence Cement
TXI
U.S. Concrete
Vulcan Materials

HISTORICAL FINANCIALS

Company Type: Private

Income Statement				FYE: December 31
	ESTIMATED REVENUE ($ mil.)	NET INCOME ($ mil.)	NET PROFIT MARGIN	EMPLOYEES
12/03	700	—	—	1,800
12/02	692	—	—	1,800
Annual Growth	1.2%	—	—	0.0%

Revenue History

Ashley Furniture

Furniture buyers took a shine to Ashley Furniture Industries when it added a tough, high-gloss polyester finish to its furniture in 1986. The company is one of the nation's largest furniture manufacturers. Ashley Furniture makes and imports upholstered, leather, and hardwood furniture, as well as bedding. It has manufacturing plants and distribution centers throughout the country and overseas. The company runs nearly 100 Ashley Furniture HomeStores — independently owned shops that sell only Ashley Furniture products. Founded by Carlyle Weinberger in 1945, Ashley Furniture is owned by father-and-son duos Ron and Todd Wanek and Chuck and Ben Vogel.

In 2002 the Vogels (who own 25% of Ashley Furniture) filed a lawsuit against the Waneks (who own 75%), alleging that the Waneks were trying to squeeze the Vogel father and son out of the business.

EXECUTIVES

Chairman: Ronald G. (Ron) Wanek
CEO: Todd Wanek
CFO: Richard (Rich) Barclay
EVP and Chief International Operations Officer: Ben Vogel
EVP Sales: Charles (Chuck) Vogel
CIO: Dwain Jansson
Controller: Dale Barneson
Director of Credit Management: David H. DeLano
Human Resources Manager: Jim Dotta

LOCATIONS

HQ: Ashley Furniture Industries, Inc.
 1 Ashley Way, Arcadia, WI 54612
Phone: 608-323-3377 **Fax:** 608-323-6008
Web: www.ashleyfurniture.com

COMPETITORS

Bassett Furniture
Bombay Company
Brown Jordan International
Ethan Allen
Euromarket Designs
Furniture Brands International
Hooker Furniture
IKEA
Kimball International
Klaussner Furniture
La-Z-Boy
Natuzzi
Pulaski Furniture
Rowe Companies
Williams-Sonoma

HISTORICAL FINANCIALS

Company Type: Private

Income Statement				FYE: December 31
	REVENUE ($ mil.)	NET INCOME ($ mil.)	NET PROFIT MARGIN	EMPLOYEES
12/03	1,700	—	—	6,000
12/02	1,400	—	—	8,000
12/01	1,090	—	—	6,000
12/00	952	—	—	5,000
12/99	816	—	—	5,691
12/98	650	—	—	4,567
12/97	540	—	—	2,100
12/96	450	—	—	—
Annual Growth	20.9%	—	—	19.1%

Revenue History

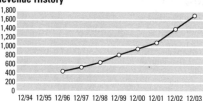

ASI Corp.

ASI has a whole lotta sales going on. The company, a wholesale distributor of computer software, hardware, and accessories, sells more than 3,000 products, including CD-ROM drives, modems, monitors, PCs, networking equipment, and storage devices.

ASI also boasts a dedicated motherboard catalog site, motherboardmaster.com, and offers standard and custom configurations. The company sells to systems integrators and resellers throughout North America. Vendor partners include 3Com, Microsoft, Samsung, and Toshiba. President Christine Liang, who founded ASI in 1987, owns 51% of the company.

EXECUTIVES

Chairman and CEO: Marcel Liang
President: Christine Liang
VP, Marketing: Brian Paterson
Administrator, Human Resources: Crystal Yuan

LOCATIONS

HQ: ASI Corp.
 48289 Fremont Blvd., Fremont, CA 94538
Phone: 510-226-8000 **Fax:** 510-226-8858
Web: www.asipartner.com

ASI has sales offices and warehouses in California, Colorado, Florida, Georgia, Illinois, Kansas, New Jersey, Oregon, and Texas, as well as in Canada.

PRODUCTS/OPERATIONS

Selected Products

Cables
Cameras
CD-ROM drives
Central processing units
Controller cards
Hard drives
Keyboards
Memory
Mice
Modems
Monitors
Motherboards
MP3 players
Multimedia products
Network connectivity products
Notebooks
Optical drives
PCs
Printers
Projectors
Removable drives and media
Scanners
Software
Sound cards
Speakers
Storage devices
Video cards

COMPETITORS

Arrow Electronics
ASCII Group
Avnet
CompuCom
D&H Distributing
Dell
En Pointe
Gateway
Hewlett-Packard
IBM
Ingram Micro
Merisel
Software House
Supercom
Tech Data

HISTORICAL FINANCIALS

Company Type: Private

Income Statement				FYE: December 31
	REVENUE ($ mil.)	NET INCOME ($ mil.)	NET PROFIT MARGIN	EMPLOYEES
12/03	950	—	—	541
12/02	866	—	—	530
12/01	1,000	—	—	500
12/00	818	—	—	500
12/99	730	—	—	610
12/98	730	—	—	560
12/97	540	—	—	400
12/96	426	—	—	350
12/95	326	—	—	300
12/94	300	—	—	250
Annual Growth	13.7%	—	—	9.0%

Revenue History

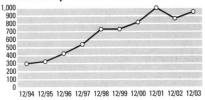

Asplundh

How much wood would a woodchuck chuck, if a woodchuck could chuck wood? A lot, if the woodchuck were named Asplundh. The company is the world's largest tree-trimming business, clearing tree limbs from power lines for utilities and municipalities in Australia, Canada, New Zealand, and the US. The company also offers utility-related services such as meter reading, pipeline maintenance, storm emergency services, street light maintenance and construction, underground pipeline location, and utility pole maintenance. The Asplundh family owns and manages the company, which was founded in 1928.

EXECUTIVES

Chairman and CEO: Christopher B. Asplundh
President: Scott M. Asplundh
EVP: George E. Graham Jr.
Treasurer and Secretary: Joseph P. Dwyer
Director Human Resources: Ryan Swier

LOCATIONS

HQ: Asplundh Tree Expert Co.
 708 Blair Mill Rd., Willow Grove, PA 19090
Phone: 215-784-4200 **Fax:** 215-784-4493
Web: www.asplundh.com

Asplundh has operations in Australia, Canada, New Zealand, and the US.

PRODUCTS/OPERATIONS

Selected Subsidiaries

American Lighting & Signalization (traffic signal services)
Asplundh Construction (utility and heavy construction)
Blume Tree Services (line clearance and vegetation management)
Central Locating Service (locating underground utility pipes and lines)
Compass Equipment Leasing (utility equipment rentals)
Utility Meter Services (meter reading and installation)
Utility Pole Technologies (pole inspection and restoration)

COMPETITORS

Davey Tree
Dow AgroSciences
Wright Tree Service

HISTORICAL FINANCIALS

Company Type: Private

Income Statement				FYE: December 31
	REVENUE ($ mil.)	NET INCOME ($ mil.)	NET PROFIT MARGIN	EMPLOYEES
12/02	1,678	—	—	27,978
12/01	1,557	—	—	26,385
12/00	1,473	—	—	25,500
12/99	1,251	—	—	24,000
12/98	1,026	—	—	25,000
12/97	1,000	—	—	22,000
12/96	936	—	—	18,000
12/95	868	—	—	18,500
12/94	856	—	—	19,200
12/93	560	—	—	14,500
Annual Growth	13.0%	—	—	7.6%

Revenue History

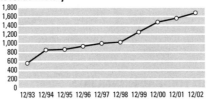

Associated Electric

Associated Electric Cooperative makes the connection between power and cooperatives. The utility provides transmission and generation services to its six member/owner companies, which in turn provide power supply services to 51 distribution cooperatives in three Midwest states. (The distribution cooperatives have a combined customer count of 790,000.)

Associated Electric operates some 9,100 miles of power transmission lines and has 4,000 MW of generating capacity from interests in coal- and gas-fired power plants; it also engages in wholesale energy transactions with other regional utilities.

EXECUTIVES

President of the Board: O. B. Clark
General Manager and CEO: James J. Jura
Director Accounting and Finance and CFO: Michael M. (Mike) Miller
Director Business and Technical Services: Patrick L. Mills
Director Engineering and Operations: Gary L. Fulks
Director Human Resources: David P. Stump
Director Member Services and Corporate Communications: Keith E. Hartner
Director Power Production: Duane D. Highley
Auditors: PricewaterhouseCoopers LLP

LOCATIONS

HQ: Associated Electric Cooperative Inc.
 2814 S. Golden, Springfield, MO 65801
Phone: 417-881-1204 **Fax:** 417-885-9252
Web: www.aeci.org

PRODUCTS/OPERATIONS

2003 Sales

	$ mil.	% of total
Members	459.7	61
Nonmembers	296.1	39
Total	**755.8**	**100**

Member Transmission and Distribution Cooperatives

Central Electric Power Cooperative
KAMO Power
M&A Electric Power Cooperative
Northeast Missouri Electric Power Cooperative
NW Electric Power Cooperative Inc.
Sho-Me Power Electric Cooperative

COMPETITORS

Ameren
Empire District Electric
Great Plains Energy
Westar Energy

HISTORICAL FINANCIALS
Company Type: Cooperative

Income Statement				FYE: December 31
	REVENUE ($ mil.)	NET INCOME ($ mil.)	NET PROFIT MARGIN	EMPLOYEES
12/03	756	11	1.4%	591
12/02	661	16	2.5%	583
12/01	693	7	1.1%	572
12/00	669	—	—	563
12/99	624	—	—	572
12/98	590	—	—	585
12/97	541	—	—	640
12/96	557	—	—	—
12/95	464	—	—	—
12/94	484	—	—	—
Annual Growth	5.1%	20.5%	—	(1.3%)

Net Income History

Associated Food

Associated Food Stores, a regional cooperative wholesale distributor, goes to extremes — mountain cold and desert heat — in supplying more than 500 independent supermarkets. Member stores (and the cooperative's owners) are located in eight western states. Associated owns about 20% of Western Family Foods, a grocery wholesalers' partnership that produces Western Family private-label goods. It acquired three of its four largest customers (Dan's, Lin's, and Macey's) in 1999 to avoid losing them to acquisition-hungry supermarket chains. Associated owns and operates about 20 retail stores. The co-op was formed in 1940 by Donald Lloyd, then president of the Utah Retail Grocers Association, and 34 other retailers.

EXECUTIVES
Chairman: Jack Shaum
President and CEO: Richard A. (Rich) Parkinson
SVP and CFO: S. Neal Berube
SVP, Merchandising: Richard Hardy
VP and Manager, Helena Division: Kelly Atkins
VP, Marketing and Communication: Steve Reich
VP, Operations: Dave Jonckowski
VP, Procurement: Brian Duff
VP, Store Development: Steve Miner
Director, Human Resources: Fred Ferguson
Auditors: Deloitte & Touche LLP

LOCATIONS
HQ: Associated Food Stores, Inc.
1850 W. 2100 South, Salt Lake City, UT 84119
Phone: 801-973-4400 **Fax:** 801-978-8551
Web: www.afstores.com

Associated Food Stores has operations in Idaho, Montana, and Utah.

PRODUCTS/OPERATIONS

2003 Sales
	% of total
Wholesale	70
Retail	29
Other	1
Total	**100**

Selected Services
Buying & category management
Customer service
Market research
Merchandising & space management
Price structuring
Printing
Real estate analysis
Retail accounting
Retail counseling
Retail marketing & advertising
Retail technology
Retail training
Store design & décor
Store engineering
Store insurance & employee benefits programs
Transportation/logistics delivery analysis

COMPETITORS
Albertson's
AMCON Distributing
AWG
Costco Wholesale
IGA
Kroger
Shurfine International
Smith's Food & Drug
SUPERVALU
Unified Western Grocers
Wal-Mart

HISTORICAL FINANCIALS
Company Type: Cooperative

Income Statement				FYE: Saturday nearest March 31
	ESTIMATED REVENUE ($ mil.)	NET INCOME ($ mil.)	NET PROFIT MARGIN	EMPLOYEES
3/03	1,212	10	0.8%	1,400
3/02	1,184	1	0.1%	1,400
3/01	1,190	6	0.5%	1,400
3/00	1,085	2	0.2%	1,400
3/99	925	—	—	1,500
3/98	1,000	—	—	1,500
3/97	925	—	—	1,500
3/96	850	—	—	—
Annual Growth	5.2%	62.0%	—	(1.1%)

2003 Year-End Financials
Debt ratio: 95.4%
Return on equity: 15.3%
Cash ($ mil.): 49
Current ratio: 1.39
Long-term debt ($ mil.): 95

Net Income History

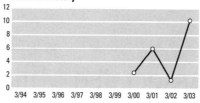

Associated Grocers

Associated Grocers (AG) feeds the ability of its member/owners to remain competitive. The cooperative distributes food and nonfood goods and provides support services to more than 400 independent grocery retailers in the Northwest, Hawaii, Alaska, Guam, and the Pacific Rim. It distributes products under the Western Family, Ovenworks, and Javaworks names. AG (not to be confused with Associated Grocers in other regions) was formed in 1934 to support 11 Seattle-based neighborhood grocers. Financial trouble led to a 15-month-long restructuring effort that resulted in asset sales and the 2002 installation of a new management team led by CEO Robert Hermanns, formerly the COO of Weis Markets.

EXECUTIVES
CEO: Robert P. Hermanns
CFO: John L. Carrosino
VP, Human Resources: Dick Harding
VP, Marketing and Sales: Craig K. Carlton
VP, Perishables: Paul Kennedy
VP, Wholesale Operations: Bob Brewer
VP and General Counsel: Craig Palm
CIO: Gene Puhrmann
Director, Business Development, Oregon and Alaska: John Santos
Director, Sales and Development: Bruce Turner

LOCATIONS
HQ: Associated Grocers, Inc.
3301 S. Norfolk St., Seattle, WA 98118
Phone: 206-762-2100 **Fax:** 206-764-7731
Web: www.agsea.com

COMPETITORS
Albertson's
C&S Wholesale
Kroger
Nash Finch
Safeway
SUPERVALU
Unified Western Grocers
Wal-Mart
Winn-Dixie

HISTORICAL FINANCIALS
Company Type: Private

Income Statement				FYE: Friday nearest September 30
	REVENUE ($ mil.)	NET INCOME ($ mil.)	NET PROFIT MARGIN	EMPLOYEES
9/03	900	—	—	1,000
9/02	900	—	—	1,100
9/01	1,000	—	—	1,100
9/00	1,100	—	—	1,500
9/99	1,100	—	—	1,400
9/98	1,090	—	—	1,300
9/97	1,092	—	—	1,360
9/96	1,090	—	—	1,350
9/95	1,055	—	—	1,340
9/94	1,107	—	—	1,340
Annual Growth	(2.3%)	—	—	(3.2%)

Revenue History

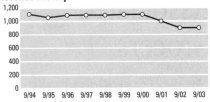

Associated Materials

Associated Materials Incorporated (AMI) is quick to side with its customers. Through its Alside and Gentek divisions, AMI makes and distributes vinyl siding and windows; vinyl fencing, decking, and railing (UltraGuard brand); and aluminum and steel siding, aluminum trim coil, and accessories (Revere and Gentek brands), primarily for the new construction and home remodeling markets (about two-thirds of sales). AMI owns about 125 supply centers that generate roughly 70% of sales. It also distributes building products made by other OEMs. AMI sold its AmerCable division (jacketed electrical cable) in 2002. Investment firm Harvest Partners controls AMI through AMH Holdings, Inc.'s Associated Materials Holdings Inc.

AMI sold its AmerCable division to AmerCable Incorporated and members of AmerCable's management in June 2002.

In 2003 Associated Materials acquired Gentek Holdings, Inc. (vinyl, aluminum, and steel siding and vinyl windows), including its Gentek Building Products, Inc., and Gentek Building Products Limited subsidiaries, for about $118 million.

EXECUTIVES

President, CEO, and Director, Associated Materials Incorporated, AMH Holdings, Inc., and Associated Materials Holdings; CEO and Director, Alside: Michael J. (Mike) Caporale Jr., age 52, $1,500,004 pay
VP, CFO, Secretary, and Treasurer: D. Keith LaVanway, age 39, $550,004 pay
VP Human Resources: John F. Haumesser, age 39, $288,252 pay
President, Alside Siding & Window Company: Kenneth L. Bloom, age 41, $460,005 pay
President, Alside Supply Centers: Robert M. Franco, age 50, $422,505 pay
Auditors: Ernst & Young LLP

LOCATIONS

HQ: Associated Materials Incorporated
3773 State Rd., Cuyahoga Falls, OH 44223
Phone: 330-929-1811   **Fax:** 330-922-2354
Web: www.associatedmaterials.com

Associated Materials has plants in Iowa, New Jersey, North Carolina, Ohio, Texas, Virginia, and Washington in the US, and in Ontario and Quebec, Canada.

2003 Sales

	% of total
US	93
Canada	7
Total	**100**

PRODUCTS/OPERATIONS

2003 Sales

	% of total
Vinyl windows & vinyl siding	60
Other products	40
Total	**100**

Selected Products
Aluminum siding
Aluminum trim coil
Steel siding
Vinyl fencing, decking, and railing
Vinyl siding
Vinyl windows

COMPETITORS

Andersen Corporation
CertainTeed
JELD-WEN
Louisiana-Pacific
MMI Products
Nortek
Owens Corning
Royal Group Technologies
ThermoView Industries

HISTORICAL FINANCIALS
Company Type: Private

Income Statement			FYE: Saturday nearest December 31	
	REVENUE ($ mil.)	NET INCOME ($ mil.)	NET PROFIT MARGIN	EMPLOYEES
12/03	780	25	3.1%	3,173
12/02	630	6	1.0%	2,550
12/01	596	25	4.3%	2,140
12/00	499	24	4.7%	2,000
12/99	453	21	4.5%	1,800
12/98	408	9	2.2%	2,440
12/97	398	13	3.3%	1,500
12/96	357	9	2.5%	2,215
12/95	350	1	0.4%	2,310
12/94	353	8	2.2%	2,400
Annual Growth	9.2%	13.4%	—	3.2%

2003 Year-End Financials
Debt ratio: 148.1%
Return on equity: 12.8%
Cash ($ mil.): 4
Current ratio: 2.05
Long-term debt ($ mil.): 305

Net Income History

Associated Milk Producers

Associated Milk Producers Incorporated might wear a cheesy grin, but it churns up solid sales. Shying away from the liquid stuff, it transforms more than 5 billion pounds of milk into butter, cheese, and other solid milk products each year. A regional cooperative of 4,600 dairy farms from Iowa, Minnesota, Missouri, Nebraska, North and South Dakota, and Wisconsin, AMPI operates 14 manufacturing plants. The co-op produces 60% of all the instant milk sold in the US and is a major cheddar producer. Aside from its own State brand of cheese and butter, AMPI primarily makes private-label products for retailers and foodservice customers.

AMPI has upgraded its 14 plants to produce additional value-added dairy products such as shredded cheese, aseptic-packaged cheese sauces (in coated cardboard containers for stable shelf life), and individually wrapped butter pats. Only one plant produces fluid milk. In addition, AMPI's 93,000-sq.-ft. plant in New Ulm, Minnesota, is the biggest butter barn in the US, whipping up nearly 20,000 pounds of butter per hour.

EXECUTIVES

President of the Board: Paul Toft
General Manager: Mark Furth
CFO: Steve Sorenson
Director of Information Technology: Chip Collum
Director of Marketing: Jim Walsh
Procurement Director: Donn DeVelder
Director of Quality Assurance: Tom Honce
Human Resources Manager: Leigh Heilman

LOCATIONS

HQ: Associated Milk Producers Inc.
315 N. Broadway, New Ulm, MN 56073
Phone: 507-354-8295   **Fax:** 507-359-8651
Web: www.ampi.com

Associated Milk Producers Incorporated has 14 milk processing plants in Iowa, Minnesota, South Dakota, and Wisconsin.

PRODUCTS/OPERATIONS

Selected Products
Butter
Cheese
Cheese Sauce
Dry milk
Fluid milk
Pudding

COMPETITORS

California Dairies Inc.
Dairy Farmers of America
Dairylea
Dean Foods
Foremost Farms
Great Lakes Cheese
Land O'Lakes
Leprino Foods
Marathon Cheese
MMPA
Prairie Farms Dairy
Saputo
Saputo Cheese USA Inc.
Schreiber Foods

HISTORICAL FINANCIALS
Company Type: Cooperative

Income Statement				FYE: December 31
	REVENUE ($ mil.)	NET INCOME ($ mil.)	NET PROFIT MARGIN	EMPLOYEES
12/03	1,057	—	—	1,700
12/02	981	—	—	1,700
12/01	1,200	—	—	1,600
12/00	1,000	—	—	1,600
12/99	1,100	—	—	1,600
12/98	1,100	—	—	1,600
12/97	928	—	—	1,600
12/96	2,189	—	—	4,500
12/95	2,555	—	—	4,500
12/94	2,629	—	—	4,500
Annual Growth	(9.6%)	—	—	(10.3%)

Associated Press

This just in: The Associated Press (AP) is reporting tonight and every night wherever news is breaking. AP is the world's largest newsgathering organization, with about 240 news bureaus serving more than 120 countries. It provides news, photos, graphics, and audiovisual services that reach people daily through print, radio, television, and the Web. In addition to its traditional news services, the not-for-profit cooperative, which is owned by its 1,700 member newspapers, runs several other operations including an international television division (APTN), a digital ad delivery service (AP AdSEND), an ad processing and billing service, photo archives, and a continuous online news service (The WIRE).

AP's news reports are translated into five languages (Dutch, English, French, German, and Spanish) and reach more than 1 billion people daily. Its AP Digital division sells news to the Internet and wireless markets. The cooperative has been in operation for more than 150 years.

In 2003 previous president and publisher of *USA TODAY* and Gannett SVP Tom Curley replaced the retiring Louis Boccardi as president and CEO of AP, becoming the 12th person to lead the news organization since its founding in 1848. Curley's older brother John is AP's vice chairman. AP has moved its headquarters from Manhattan's Rockefeller Plaza (its home for the last 65 years) to 450 W. 33rd St.

HISTORY

The Associated Press was formed in 1848 when six New York City newspapers joined to share news that arrived by telegraph wire. Two years later AP began selling wire reports to other papers and before long started creating regional associations. Adapting to changing technologies and public interests, AP began covering sports, financial, and public interest stories in the 1920s and was selling news reports to radio stations in the 1940s. Advancements during WWII included using transatlantic cable and radio-teletype circuits to deliver news and photos.

In the late 1960s AP and Dow Jones introduced services to improve business and financial reporting. AP improved photo delivery, reception, and storage in the 1970s with the advent of Laserphoto and the Electronic Darkroom. It began transmitting news by satellite and offering color photographs to newspapers in the 1980s. In 1985 Louis Boccardi took over the job as president and CEO of AP.

AP adjusted to the media-heavy culture of the 1990s by launching the APTV international news video service and the All News Radio network in 1994. It then moved onto the Internet with The WIRE in 1996 and began offering online access to its Photo Archive in 1997. It bought Worldwide Television News in 1998, combining it with APTV to form APTN (Associated Press Television News). The following year it purchased the radio news contracts of UPI after the rival organization announced it was getting out of broadcast news.

In 2000 AP created an Internet division, AP Digital, to focus on marketing news to online providers. The cooperative continued its Internet focus the following year, launching AP Online en Español (news for Spanish-language Web sites) and AP Entertainment Online (multimedia entertainment news for Web sites). Also that year AP bought the Newspaper Industry Communication Center from the Newspaper Association of America.

In 2002 the company launched an expanded editorial partnership with Dow Jones Newswires, increasing the amount of financial news distributed on AP wires. Later that year it acquired Capitolwire, a provider of state government news.

EXECUTIVES

Chairman: Burl Osborne
Vice Chairman: Lissa Walls Vahldiek
President and CEO: Tom Curley, age 54
Acting CFO: Kenneth (Ken) Dale
SVP: Jonathan P. Wolman
SVP and Director, Newspaper and New Media Markets: Tom Brettingen
SVP and Executive Editor: Kathleen Carroll, age 46
SVP and General Counsel: John Keitt
SVP, Human Resources and Secretary: James M. (Jim) Donna
SVP, Services and Technology: John Reid
VP: Kelly Smith Tunney
VP and Director, AP Broadcast: James R. William, III
VP and Director, Strategic Planning: James Kennedy
VP and Deputy Director of Human Resources: Jessica Bruce
VP and Deputy Director for Services and Technology: Jeffrey Hastie
VP and Managing Editor: Mike Silverman
VP, New Media Markets: Thomas E. Slaughter
Treasurer: Daniel M. Boruch
Director, Media Relations: Jack Stokes
Director, Corporate Communications: Ellen Hale
Auditors: Ernst & Young

LOCATIONS

HQ: The Associated Press
450 W. 33rd St., New York, NY 10001
Phone: 212-621-1500 **Fax:** 212-621-5447
Web: www.ap.org

The Associated Press has about 240 news bureaus serving 121 countries.

PRODUCTS/OPERATIONS

Selected Products and Services
AP AdVantage (advertising placement)
AP AdSEND (digital transmission of advertisements)
AP Digital (news for Internet and wireless markets)
AP Information Services (news products for corporations, government, and online distributors)
AP Photo Archive (more than 750,000 online photos)
AP Telecommunications (land-based and satellite information networks)
AP Wide World Photos (20th-century historical photos for professional photographers)
APTN (Associated Press Television Network, international television news service)
ENPS (electronic news production system)
The WIRE (24-hour news service for the Internet)

COMPETITORS

Agence France-Presse
Bloomberg
Business Wire
Comtex
Corbis
Dow Jones
E. W. Scripps
Gannett
Getty Images
Knight-Ridder
New York Times
News World Communications
PR Newswire
Reuters
Tribune
UPI

HISTORICAL FINANCIALS

Company Type: Cooperative

Income Statement				FYE: December 31
	REVENUE ($ mil.)	NET INCOME ($ mil.)	NET PROFIT MARGIN	EMPLOYEES
12/03	559	—	—	3,700
12/02	554	—	—	3,500
12/01	575	—	—	3,500
12/00	574	—	—	3,700
12/99	572	—	—	3,500
12/98	495	—	—	3,500
12/97	441	—	—	3,500
12/96	418	—	—	3,000
12/95	390	—	—	3,150
12/94	406	—	—	3,150
Annual Growth	3.6%	—	—	1.8%

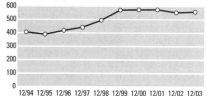

Associated Wholesale Grocers

Associated Wholesale Grocers (AWG) knows its customers can't live by bread and milk alone. The retailer-owned AWG cooperative supplies more than 1,400 member-stores with wholesale grocery sales, advertising and market support, store decorating and design, and selecting appropriate technology. The co-op's territory covers primarily Arkansas, Kansas, Missouri, and Oklahoma, as well as six other midwestern and southern states. The co-op offers its members the use of such banners as Country Mart, Thriftway, Price Chopper, and Sun Fresh. AWG also operates more than 30 of its own Falley's and Food 4 Less stores in Kansas and Missouri, as well as 45 Homeland stores throughout Oklahoma.

AWG acquired Homeland Stores in September 2002 and formed a new subsidiary, Associated Retail Grocers, to oversee Homeland and its Falley's chain. (Wholesaler AWG moved into food retailing in 1998 with its acquisition of Falley's.)

AWG supplies members with brand-name and private-label food (Always Save and Best Choice) and nonfood items; other services the co-op provides include property and casualty insurance, employee benefits packages, loan programs, and real estate lease assistance. It also helps its members appeal to Hispanic customers with its "Authentic Hispanic" product line of more than 300 items.

Other AWG banners include Apple Market, Cash Saver, and Price Mart (a food warehouse format).

HISTORY

About 20 Kansas City, Kansas-area grocers met in a local grocery in 1924 and organized the Associated Grocers Company to get better deals on purchases and advertising. They elected J. C. Harline president, and each chipped in a few hundred dollars to make their first purchases. It took a while to find a manufacturer who would sell directly to them; a local soap maker was finally convinced, and others gradually followed.

In 1926 the group was incorporated as Associated Wholesale Grocers (AWG). It outgrew two warehouses in four years, finally moving to a 16,000-sq.-ft. facility big enough to add new lines and more products. Membership doubled between 1930 and 1932 as grocers moved from ordering products a year ahead to the new wholesale concept, and members took seriously the slogan: "Buy, Sell, Buy Some More." They met every week to plan how to sell their products, and buyer and advertising manager Harry Small gave sales presentations and advertising ideas (his trade-in plan for old brooms sold more than two train-carloads of brooms in two weeks). Heavy newspaper advertising also paid off; AWG topped $1 million in sales in 1933.

The cooperative made its first acquisition in 1936, buying Progressive Grocers, a warehouse in Joplin, Missouri; a second warehouse named Associated Grocers was acquired the next year in Springfield, Missouri. AWG continued building and expanding warehouses, and annual sales were at $11 million by 1951.

Louis Fox became CEO in 1956. Fox maximized year-end rebates for members, led several acquisitions, and formed a new subsidiary for financing stores and small shopping centers where AWG members had a presence (Supermarket Developers). Sales increased nearly fifteen fold to over $200 million in his first 15 years.

James Basha, who succeeded Fox when he retired in 1984, saw sales reach $2.4 billion by his own retirement in 1992. Basha was followed by former COO Mike DeFabis, once a deputy mayor of Indianapolis. DeFabis orchestrated several acquisitions, including 41 Kansas City-area stores — most of which were quickly bought by members — from bankrupt Food Barn Stores in 1994 and 29 Oklahoma stores and a warehouse from Safeway spinoff Homeland Stores in 1995 (members bought all the stores).

AWG's nonfood subsidiary, Valu Merchandisers Co., was established in 1995; its new Kansas warehouse began shipping health and beauty aids and housewares the following year to help members battle big discounters. Members narrowly defeated a proposal in late 1996 to convert the cooperative into a public company. Proponents promptly petitioned for a second vote, which was defeated early the next year.

AWG veteran Doug Carolan succeeded DeFabis in 1998, becoming only the fifth CEO in the cooperative's history. The company bought five Falley's and 33 Food 4 Less stores in Kansas and Missouri from Fred Meyer in 1998 for $300 million. In a break with tradition, AWG is operating the stores rather than selling them to members.

In 2000, after a months-long labor dispute with the Teamsters was resolved, Carolan left AWG. The company's CFO, Gary Phillips, was named president and CEO later that year. In 2001 the company debuted a new format, ALPS (Always Low Price Stores) — small stores that carry a limited selection of grocery top-sellers. Also that year AWG's Kansas City division began distributing to more than 10 new stores that had formerly been served by Fleming, the #1 US wholesale food distributor.

In 2002 supermarket operator Homeland Stores, which operates 43 stores throughout Oklahoma, emerged from bankruptcy as a fully owned subsidiary of AWG.

From the August 2003 sale of Fleming Companies' wholesale distribution business, AWG picked up food distribution centers in Nebraska (two), Oklahoma (one), and Tennessee (two) and general merchandise distribution centers in Tennessee and Kansas.

EXECUTIVES

Chairman: J. Fred Ball
President and CEO: Gary Phillips
EVP and CFO: Robert C. Walker
EVP, Marketing: Jerry Garland
EVP, Operations Wholesale: Mike Rand
SVP, General Counsel, and Corporate Secretary: Frances Pellegrino Puhl
SVP, Perishables: Lucky Hicks
SVP, Procurement: Dennis Kinser
SVP, Real Estate: Scott Wilmoski
Corporate VP, Human Resources: Frank Tricamo
VP, Corporate Sales: Bill Lancaster
VP, Finance: David Carl
VP and CIO: Keith Martin
VP and Corporate Controller: Gary Koch
Auditors: KPMG LLP

LOCATIONS

HQ: Associated Wholesale Grocers, Inc.
5000 Kansas Ave., Kansas City, KS 66106
Phone: 913-288-1000   **Fax:** 913-288-1508
Web: www.awginc.com

Associated Wholesale Grocers serves grocers in Arkansas, Illinois, Iowa, Kansas, Kentucky, Missouri, Nebraska, Oklahoma, Tennessee, and Texas. The cooperative has four distribution centers in Kansas, Missouri, and Oklahoma.

PRODUCTS/OPERATIONS

Selected Operations/Subisidiaries
Benchmark Insurance Co.
Supermarket Developers, Inc. (financing for stores and supermarkets)
Supermarket Insurance Agency Inc.
Valu Merchandisers Company (health and beauty supplies, general merchandise, and pharmacy products)

Selected Private-Label Brands
Always Save
Best Choice

Selected Retail Stores
Apple Market
Cash Saver
Country Mart
Falley's
Food 4 Less
Homeland
Price Chopper
Price Mart
Sun Fresh
Thriftway

Selected Services
Advertising
Category management
Employee training
Financial planning
In-store marketing
Insurance
Market research and analysis
Merchandising advice
Private-label products
Product positioning
Real estate lease assistance
Reclamation
Site acquisition
Store engineering and construction
Store financing
Store franchise formats
Store remodeling

COMPETITORS

Affiliated Foods
Albertson's
Alex Lee
C&S Wholesale
Delhaize America
Grocers Supply
GSC Enterprises
H.T. Hackney
Hy-Vee
IGA
Kroger
Nash Finch
Purity Wholesale Grocers
Roundy's
S. Abraham & Sons
Schnuck Markets
Shurfine International
Spartan Stores
SUPERVALU
Wakefern Food
Wal-Mart

HISTORICAL FINANCIALS

Company Type: Cooperative

Income Statement
FYE: Last Saturday in December

	REVENUE ($ mil.)	NET INCOME ($ mil.)	NET PROFIT MARGIN	EMPLOYEES
12/03	3,721	57	1.5%	6,171
12/02	3,139	53	1.7%	5,727
12/01	3,097	53	1.7%	3,300
12/00	3,267	46	1.4%	3,300
12/99	3,370	65	1.9%	3,300
12/98	3,180	66	2.1%	3,100
12/97	3,129	64	2.0%	3,000
12/96	3,096	—	—	2,797
12/95	2,970	—	—	—
12/94	2,600	—	—	—
Annual Growth	4.1%	(1.8%)	—	12.0%

2003 Year-End Financials
Debt ratio: 642.1%   Current ratio: 1.34
Return on equity: 193.1%   Long-term debt ($ mil.): 204
Cash ($ mil.): 15

Net Income History

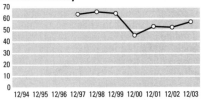

Associated Wholesalers

Being associated with Associated Wholesalers, Inc. (AWI) means having a supplier of food and nonfood items. The retailer-owned cooperative supplies health and beauty-care items, meat, dairy products, produce, bakery products, and canned goods to independent grocers in Delaware, Maryland, New Jersey, New York, Pennsylvania, Virginia, West Virginia, and the New England states. In addition to merchandise, the co-op also provides training and technical services to its members, and it operates nine of its own supermarkets and one cash-and-carry store.

EXECUTIVES

Chairman: Stewart Hartman Jr.
President and CEO: J. Christopher Michael
EVP, Logistics: Robert Rippley
VP, Finance: Thomas C. Teeter
VP, Information Systems: P. Amy Fry
VP, Marketing: Rob Winett
VP, Merchandising: Charles Yahn
VP, Procurement: Donald (Don) Tiesenga
VP, Retail Operations: J. Warren Weaver
VP, Risk: W. Douglas Hager
VP, Store Development and Sales: James Cartin
Advertising: Kevin Pannebaker
Category Merchandising: Mark Semprini
Human Resources: Audrey Hausmann
Auditors: Beard Miller Company LLP

LOCATIONS

HQ: Associated Wholesalers, Inc.
Route 422, Robesonia, PA 19551
Phone: 610-693-3161 **Fax:** 610-693-3171
Web: www.awiweb.com

COMPETITORS

Ahold USA	Kroger
C&S Wholesale	Nash Finch
Di Giorgio	Pathmark
Krasdale Foods	SUPERVALU

HISTORICAL FINANCIALS
Company Type: Cooperative

Income Statement			FYE: July 31	
	REVENUE ($ mil.)	NET INCOME ($ mil.)	NET PROFIT MARGIN	EMPLOYEES
7/03	1,029	—	—	1,100
7/02	1,026	—	—	1,300
7/01	923	—	—	1,500
7/00	879	—	—	1,500
7/99	811	—	—	1,500
7/98	730	—	—	1,400
7/97	752	—	—	1,300
7/96	702	—	—	1,200
7/95	647	—	—	—
Annual Growth	6.0%	—	—	(1.2%)

Atlantic Mutual

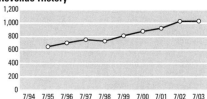

Having set sail as a marine insurer more than 150 years ago, Atlantic Mutual Companies once provided commercial and marine property/casualty insurance to individuals and businesses. Today, the company specializes in providing personal insurance to wealthy or high-asset individuals. Through its subsidiaries (including Atlantic Mutual Insurance, Atlantic Lloyds Insurance Company of Texas, and Centennial Insurance), the company offers personal insurance programs that cover autos, antiques, fine arts, residences, personal property, and yachts. Independent agents and brokers sell the company's products throughout the US.

In order to improve its balance sheet, Atlantic Mutual Companies exited the commercial and marine insurance business, and plans to focus on its personal lines business.

In 2003, the company sold its marine business to Travelers Property Casualty. In 2004, the company divested its commercial business by selling its Atlantic Specialty subsidiary to OneBeacon (part of the White Mountains group of companies).

EXECUTIVES

Chairman and CEO: Klaus G. Dorfi
President: Daniel H. Olmsted
EVP and CFO: Richard J. (Rich) Hertling
VP, Commercial Claims: John K. Shea
VP, Human Resources: Martha Van Hise
VP, Personal Claims: Bill Bernecker
Corporate Marketing and Communications: Peter G. Scott

LOCATIONS

HQ: Atlantic Mutual Companies
140 Broadway, New York, NY 10005
Phone: 212-943-1800 **Fax:** 212-428-6566
Web: www.atlanticmutual.com

PRODUCTS/OPERATIONS

Selected Subsidiaries

Atlantic Companies Holding Corp.
Atlantic Lloyds Insurance Company of Texas
Atlantic Mutual Insurance Company
Atlantic Mutual International Limited (UK)
Atlantic Mutual of Bermuda Limited
Atlantic Risk Services, Inc.
Centennial Insurance Company

COMPETITORS

ACE Limited	Kemper Insurance
AIG	Royal & SunAlliance USA
Capitol Transamerica	St. Paul Travelers
Chubb	W. R. Berkley

HISTORICAL FINANCIALS
Company Type: Mutual company

Income Statement			FYE: December 31	
	ASSETS ($ mil.)	NET INCOME ($ mil.)	INCOME AS % OF ASSETS	EMPLOYEES
12/02	1,845	18	1.0%	1,800
12/01	1,764	(14)	—	1,800
12/00	1,785	11	0.6%	1,800
12/99	1,753	2	0.1%	—
Annual Growth	108.0%	—	—	0.0%

2002 Year-End Financials
Equity as % of assets: 24.7%   Long-term debt ($ mil.): —
Return on assets: 1.0%   Sales ($ mil.): 647
Return on equity: —

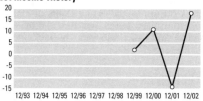

Atrium

Atrium Companies produces aluminum and vinyl windows (more than 75% of sales) and patio doors, and "woodn't" have it any other way after selling its wood window and door business. Customers include retail centers, lumberyards, builders, and wholesalers for both new construction and remodeling markets. Atrium also offers installation and repair services. Since its founding in 1948, Atrium has grown to include window and door making facilities and distribution centers in the US and Mexico, vinyl and aluminum extrusion operations in the US, and joint ventures in North Carolina and China.

Major customers for Atrium's products include retail centers (The Home Depot and Lowe's); national homebuilders (Pulte Homes, D.R. Horton, and Richmond American Homes); and one-step distributors (Owens Corning and Ted Lansing). The company's joint ventures include vinyl compounding operations in North Carolina and a vinyl extrusion operation in China.

Atrium's plan for growth includes maintaining and developing its markets in the US, cross-selling its vinyl products in traditional aluminum markets and vice-versa, leveraging the Atrium brand name across its product lines, increasing operational efficiencies, refining its product offerings, and acquiring complementary businesses.

As part of its plan to vertically integrate its operations, in 2003 Atrium acquired Texas-based zinc die-casting supplier Miniature Die Casting of Texas, LP, for $3.25 million; it operates the company as MD Casting, Inc., a stand-alone operating unit that sells metal hardware to Atrium and to third parties. Also in 2003, Atrium acquired Texas-based aluminum and vinyl window and door maker Danvid Window Company, a subsidiary of American Architectural Products Corporation, for $5.8 million. Atrium formed subsidiary Aluminum Screen Manufacturers, Inc., that year and purchased Aluminum Screen Manufacturing,

Ltd., L.L.P.; Aluminum Screen Products, Inc.; Aztex Screen Products, L.L.C.; and Superior Engineered Products Corporation.

In 2003 GE Investment Private Placement Partners II, owner of about 73% of Atrium, agreed to sell the company's parent, Atrium Corporation, for $658.9 million to an investor group led by KAT Holdings Inc., an affiliate of New York buyout firm Kenner & Co. Inc. (which specializes in home and building products investments) and a management team led by Atrium's president and CEO Jeff Hull. Atrium Companies closed the sale in December 2003 and continues to operate as Atrium Companies, Inc. Hull took on the additional role of chairman at that time.

Atrium acquired Florida-based Robico Shutters, Inc. (hurricane and storm protection systems) and Expert Installation Service, Inc., for $12 million in 2004. Also that year, the company's Atrium Windows and Doors of Florida, LLC subsidiary purchased Kinco, Ltd. (aluminum and vinyl windows) of Jacksonville, Florida for $27 million.

EXECUTIVES

Chairman, President, and CEO: Jeff L. Hull, age 38, $6,107,500 pay
EVP and CFO: Eric W. Long, age 35, $619,692 pay
EVP and Co-COO: Robert E. Burns, age 38, $650,494 pay
EVP and Co-COO: C. Douglas Cross, age 48, $480,892 pay
SVP, General Counsel, and Secretary: Philip J. (Phil) Ragona, age 42, $352,500 pay (partial-year salary)
SVP Human Resources: D. D. (Gus) Agostinelli, age 58
VP, Information Systems: Michael Lynch
Treasurer and Asst. Secretary: Patrick Coffee
President, R. G. Darby Company, Inc., and Total Trim, Inc.: Cliff Darby, age 38, $300,000 pay
President, Superior Engineered Products Corporation: David Oddo
Auditors: Deloitte & Touche LLP

LOCATIONS

HQ: Atrium Companies, Inc.
3890 West Northwest Hwy., Ste. 500, Dallas, TX 75220
Phone: 214-630-5757 **Fax:** 214-951-0642
Web: www.atriumcompanies.com

Atrium Companies has 80 manufacturing and distribution facilities in 23 states; it also operates a distribution center in Mexico City, Mexico.

PRODUCTS/OPERATIONS

2003 Sales

	$ mil.	% of total
New construction	356.7	60
Repair & remodeling	241.1	40
Total	**597.8**	**100**

2003 Sales

	% of total
Windows	76
Patio doors	6
Aluminum & vinyl extrusions & other products & services	18
Total	**100**

2003 Sales

	$ mil.	% of total
Windows & doors	543.2	84
Components	100.9	16
Adjustments	(46.3)	—
Total	**597.8**	**100**

Selected Subsidiaries
Aluminum Screen Manufacturers, Inc.
Atrium Door and Window Company of Arizona
Atrium Door and Window Company of the Northeast
Atrium Door and Window Company of the Northwest
Atrium Door and Window Company of the Rockies
Atrium Door and Window Company West Coast
Atrium Extrusion Systems, Inc.
Atrium Funding Corporation
Atrium Servicios de Mexico
Atrium Shutters, Inc.
Atrium Ventanas de Mexico
Atrium Vinyl, Inc.
Atrium Windows and Doors of Florida, LLC
MD Casting, Inc.
R.G. Darby Company, Inc. (aluminum products)
Superior Engineered Products Corporation
Thermal Industries, Inc.

COMPETITORS

Andersen Corporation
Bocenor
Drew Industries
HW Plastics
International Aluminum
JELD-WEN
Masco
Masonite International
MI Home Products
Milgard Manufacturing
MW Manufacturers
Nortek
Novar
Pella
Ply Gem
Sierra Pacific Industries
Silver Line Building Products
Simonton Windows
Therma-Tru

HISTORICAL FINANCIALS

Company Type: Private

Income Statement
FYE: December 31

	REVENUE ($ mil.)	NET INCOME ($ mil.)	NET PROFIT MARGIN	EMPLOYEES
12/03	598	6	1.1%	6,100
12/02	536	14	2.6%	4,420
12/01	525	(5)	—	4,350
12/00	496	(74)	—	4,100
12/99	499	2	0.4%	4,200
12/98	211	(3)	—	3,200
12/97	187	6	3.3%	1,885
12/96	156	4	2.7%	1,675
12/95	136	2	1.3%	—
12/94	124	9	7.4%	—
Annual Growth	19.1%	(4.1%)	—	20.3%

2003 Year-End Financials
Debt ratio: 329.4% Current ratio: 1.53
Return on equity: 4.9% Long-term debt ($ mil.): 412
Cash ($ mil.): 8

Net Income History

Austin Industries

Paving the way for progress, Austin Industries provides civil, commercial, and industrial construction services. Its oldest subsidiary, Austin Bridge & Road, provides road, bridge, and parking lot construction across Texas. Subsidiary Austin Commercial, known for its high-rises, builds corporate headquarters, technology sites, and hospitals in the central and southwestern US. Austin Commercial tackled its first major sports arena project with American Airlines Center in Dallas. The group's Austin Industrial provides construction, maintenance, and electrical services for the chemical, refining, power, and manufacturing industries, mostly in the US South and Southeast. The employee-owned firm was founded in 1918.

EXECUTIVES

Chairman: William T. (Bill) Solomon, age 61
Vice Chairman: Charles M. Solomon
President and CEO: Ronald J. (Ron) Gafford, age 54
VP Finance and CFO: Paul W. Hill
President, Austin Bridge & Road: James R. (Jim) Andoga
President, Austin Industrial: Henry G. Kelly
President, Austin Commercial: David B. Walls
CIO and Director Corporate Information Systems: Stan Smith
Treasurer and Director Treasury Department: Jim Schranz
Corporate Controller: Dana Bartholomew
Co-General Counsel: Charles Hardy
Co-General Counsel: Elaine E. Nelson
Director Corporate Communications: Lori Elise
Director Human Resources: Brad Brown
Auditors: Ernst & Young LLP

LOCATIONS

HQ: Austin Industries, Inc.
3535 Travis St., Ste. 300, Dallas, TX 75204
Phone: 214-443-5500 **Fax:** 214-443-5581
Web: www.austin-ind.com

Austin Industries and its operating companies have offices in Albuquerque, New Mexico; Augusta, Georgia; Austin, Beaumont, Dallas, Fort Worth, Houston, and San Antonio, Texas; Miami; Phoenix; Richmond, Virginia; and Sulphur, Louisiana.

COMPETITORS

Balfour Beatty	J.F. Shea
Bechtel	JGC
Beck Group	MYR Group
Brasfield & Gorrie	Peter Kiewit Sons'
Choate Construction	Rooney Holdings
Flint Industries	Shaw Group
Fluor	Skanska
Granite Construction	Sundt
Halliburton	Swinerton
Hardin Construction	Turner Corporation
Hensel Phelps Construction	Turner Industries
Hunt Construction	Zachry

Auto-Owners Insurance

HISTORICAL FINANCIALS
Company Type: Private

Income Statement				FYE: December 31
	REVENUE ($ mil.)	NET INCOME ($ mil.)	NET PROFIT MARGIN	EMPLOYEES
12/03	1,200	—	—	6,000
12/02	1,056	—	—	6,000
12/01	1,257	—	—	6,000
12/00	1,217	—	—	6,000
12/99	836	—	—	6,000
12/98	808	—	—	6,300
12/97	619	—	—	6,000
12/96	741	—	—	5,400
12/95	608	—	—	5,100
12/94	613	—	—	5,000
Annual Growth	7.7%	—	—	2.0%

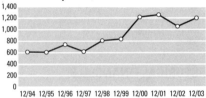

Revenue History

There's more to Auto-Owners Insurance Group than the name implies. In addition to auto coverage, the company provides personal products such as universal and whole life, homeowners, and long-term care insurance through its predictably named subsidiaries (including Home-Owners Insurance Company and Property-Owners Insurance Company). Auto-Owners Insurance Group also sells commercial auto, liability, and workers' compensation policies. With almost 30,000 independent agents in more than 5,000 different locations, the company operates in some 25 states nationwide.

EXECUTIVES
CEO: Roger L. Looyenga
President: John W. Fisher
SVP and Treasurer: Greg L. Cornell
SVP, Personnel: Doug Marsh

LOCATIONS
HQ: Auto-Owners Insurance Group
6101 Anacapri Blvd., Lansing, MI 48917
Phone: 517-323-1200 **Fax:** 517-323-8796
Web: www.auto-owners.com

Auto-Owners Insurance Group has full-service offices in Lansing, MI; Traverse City, MI; White Bear Lake, MN; Peoria, IL; Montgomery, AL; Marion, IN; Lima, OH; Lakeland, FL; Brentwood, TN; West Des Moines, IA; Charlotte, NC; Mesa, AZ; Appleton, WI; Duluth, GA; Columbia, SC; Westminster, CO; and Fargo, North Dakota; with claim offices in 66 cities.

PRODUCTS/OPERATIONS
Selected Subsidiaries
Auto-Owners Insurance Company
Auto-Owners Life Insurance Company
Home-Owners Insurance Company
Owners Insurance Company
Property-Owners Insurance Company
Southern-Owners Insurance Company

COMPETITORS
ACE Limited	Progressive Corporation
AIG	Prudential
Allstate	Safeco
Farmers Group	St. Paul Travelers
GEICO	State Farm
MetLife	

HISTORICAL FINANCIALS
Company Type: Private

Income Statement				FYE: December 31
	REVENUE ($ mil.)	NET INCOME ($ mil.)	NET PROFIT MARGIN	EMPLOYEES
12/03	4,141	—	—	3,200
12/02	3,514	—	—	3,000
12/01	3,016	—	—	3,000
Annual Growth	17.2%	—	—	3.3%

Revenue History

Averitt Express

Averitt Express provides less-than-truckload (LTL), truckload, and expedited freight transportation service. (LTL carriers combine freight from multiple shippers into a single trailer.) The company operates a fleet of about 3,000 tractors and 9,000 trailers from a network of some 80 terminals. Averitt Express operates primarily in the southern US, but it offers service elsewhere in North America through partnerships with other carriers. The company also offers logistics and international freight forwarding services. Affiliate Averitt Air provides chartered passenger transportation services. CEO Gary Sasser owns Averitt Express, which was founded by Thurman Averitt as Livingston Merchants Co-op in 1958.

EXECUTIVES
President and CEO: Gary D. Sasser
EVP and COO: Wayne Spain
EVP and CFO: George Johnson
EVP Sales and Marketing: Phil Pierce

LOCATIONS
HQ: Averitt Express, Inc.
1415 Neal St., Cookeville, TN 38501
Phone: 931-526-3306 **Fax:** 931-520-5603
Web: www.averittexpress.com

COMPETITORS
Arkansas Best	Overnite Transportation
Con-Way	USF
Estes Express	Watkins Associated Industries
FedEx Freight	
Old Dominion Freight	Yellow Roadway

HISTORICAL FINANCIALS
Company Type: Private

Income Statement				FYE: December 31
	REVENUE ($ mil.)	NET INCOME ($ mil.)	NET PROFIT MARGIN	EMPLOYEES
12/03	626	19	3.0%	6,417
12/02	582	18	3.2%	6,485
12/01	553	16	2.9%	6,000
Annual Growth	6.4%	8.3%	—	3.4%

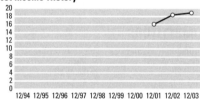

Net Income History

Avondale

Family-owned Avondale has fabric in its genes ... er, jeans. The vertically integrated company makes apparel fabrics (cotton and cotton-blend piece-dyed fabrics, indigo-dyed denim), greige fabrics (undyed, unfinished cotton and cotton blends), specialty fabrics (such as coated materials for awnings, boat covers, and tents), and yarns. Leading apparel makers such as VF Corporation (maker of Lee, Chic, and Wrangler jeans, among others) buy from Avondale. VF accounts for about 15% of sales. The company operates about 20 manufacturing facilities in Alabama, Georgia, and North and South Carolina. Avondale was founded in Georgia in 1895 and is headed by G. Stephen Felker, great-grandson of the founder.

In 2003 the company closed a yarn manufacturing facility in Alabama, after closing two others in North Carolina in 2002.

EXECUTIVES

Chairman, President, and CEO, Avondale and Avondale Mills: G. Stephen Felker, age 52, $800,016 pay
Vice Chairman and CFO, Avondale and Avondale Mills: Jack R. Altherr Jr., age 54, $355,008 pay
VP, Avondale Mills; President, Manufacturing Operations: T. Wayne Spraggins, age 66, $296,016 pay
VP, Avondale Mills; President, Marketing and Sales: Keith M. Hull, age 51, $298,032 pay
VP and Assistant Secretary; VP, Planning and Development, Avondale Mills: Craig S. Crockard, age 61
VP, Secretary, and Controller, Avondale Mills and Avondale: M. Delen Boyd, age 47
VP, Human Resources, Avondale Mills: Sharon L. Rodgers, age 47, $137,088 pay
Auditors: Dixon Hughes PLLC

LOCATIONS

HQ: Avondale Incorporated
506 S. Broad St., Monroe, GA 30655
Phone: 770-267-2226 **Fax:** 770-267-5196
Web: www.avondalemills.com

Avondale operates about 20 manufacturing facilities in Alabama, Georgia, North Carolina, and South Carolina.

PRODUCTS/OPERATIONS

2003 Sales

	$ mil.	% of total
Apparel fabric	502.9	68
Yarns	167.6	23
Other fabric	66.1	9
Adjustments	(145.7)	—
Total	**590.9**	**100**

COMPETITORS

Burlington Industries	Johnston Textiles
Concord Fabrics	Milliken
Cone Mills	Parkdale Mills
Galey & Lord	R. B. Pamplin
Greenwood Mills	Springs Industries
Guilford Mills	

HISTORICAL FINANCIALS
Company Type: Private

Income Statement
FYE: Last Friday in August

	REVENUE ($ mil.)	NET INCOME ($ mil.)	NET PROFIT MARGIN	EMPLOYEES
8/03	591	(8)	—	5,000
8/02	660	(0)	—	5,700
8/01	773	1	0.2%	5,800
8/00	837	33	3.9%	6,600
8/99	881	10	1.1%	6,800
8/98	1,056	34	3.2%	7,000
8/97	1,050	23	2.2%	7,500
8/96	706	14	1.9%	—
8/95	539	21	3.9%	—
8/94	482	14	2.9%	—
Annual Growth	2.3%	—	—	(6.5%)

2003 Year-End Financials
Debt ratio: 141.0% Current ratio: 2.91
Return on equity: — Long-term debt ($ mil.): 164
Cash ($ mil.): 14

Net Income History

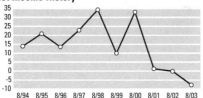

Bain & Company

"Bainies" are always ready when corporate titans need a little direction. One of the world's leading management consulting firms, Bain & Company (whose consultants are called Bainies) offers a wide array of services aimed at increasing efficiency and streamlining business processes. It also offers consulting on strategic business issues, such as mergers and acquisitions, as well as marketing and product development. In addition, Bain offers technology services and IPO preparation work. The firm, founded in 1973 by Boston Consulting Group alumnus Bill Bain, operates through 30 offices in about 20 countries.

Like its rivals, Bain has endured shrinking demand for its consulting work largely due to the slump in the economy. Companies have been less willing to engage consultants unless they can rationalize the cost to their increasingly suspicious and scrutinizing shareholders. A spate of scandals involving other consulting firms have also given the industry a bad name in some circles, causing even more potential clients to shy away from engagements.

As companies have become more savvy to what consulting firms can and cannot do, as well as more sensitive to costs, they have started to demand smaller engagements that will provide specific business improvements and less "big picture" consulting. The business challenge in the future for Bain and other management consulting firms will be to wean themselves off the long-term projects and reorient their businesses towards more numerous, but smaller, engagements.

Although founded by the same individuals, Bain & Company and investment firm Bain Capital are separate entities.

EXECUTIVES

Chairman: Orit Gadiesh, age 53
Worldwide Managing Director: John J. Donahoe
VP and CFO: Leonard C. Banos
Treasurer: Andrew J. Frommer
Director of Human Resources: Elizabeth Corcoran
Worldwide Public Relations Director: Cheryl Krauss

LOCATIONS

HQ: Bain & Company, Inc.
131 Dartmouth St., Boston, MA 02116
Phone: 617-572-2000 **Fax:** 617-572-2427
Web: www.bain.com

Bain & Company has offices in Atlanta; Boston; Chicago; Dallas; Los Angeles, Palo Alto, and San Francisco, California; and New York City. Outside the US, the company operates in Australia, Belgium, Brazil, Canada, China, France, Germany, Italy, Japan, Mexico, the Netherlands, Singapore, South Africa, South Korea, Spain, Sweden, Switzerland, and the UK.

PRODUCTS/OPERATIONS

Selected Consulting Practices
Business processes and organization
Capital management
Customer management and marketing
Information technology
Mergers and acquisitions
Product management
Supply chain management

Selected Industries Served
Aerospace and defense
Business services
Consumer products
Financial services
Government agencies
Healthcare and medical services
Media and entertainment
Non-profit organizations
Retail
Technology
Telecommunications
Transportation
Utilities

COMPETITORS

Accenture	Keane
A.T. Kearney	McKinsey & Company
BearingPoint	Mercer
Booz Allen	PA Consulting
Boston Consulting	Perot Systems
Capgemini	PRTM
Computer Sciences	Roland Berger
Deloitte Consulting	Towers Perrin
IBM	

HISTORICAL FINANCIALS
Company Type: Private

Income Statement
FYE: December 31

	REVENUE ($ mil.)	NET INCOME ($ mil.)	NET PROFIT MARGIN	EMPLOYEES
12/02	761	—	—	2,450
12/01	825	—	—	2,800
12/00	810	—	—	2,700
12/99	700	—	—	2,400
12/98	499	—	—	2,100
12/97	480	—	—	1,700
12/96	450	—	—	1,500
12/95	375	—	—	1,200
12/94	300	—	—	1,000
12/93	213	—	—	900
Annual Growth	15.2%	—	—	11.8%

Revenue History

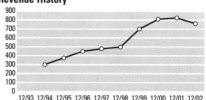

Baker & McKenzie

Baker & McKenzie knows that size has its advantages (and disadvantages). The firm is one of the world's largest law practices with more than 3,000 lawyers and nearly 70 offices in almost 40 countries. It offers expertise in such areas as antitrust law, international trade, mergers and acquisitions, and tax law. Although Baker & McKenzie's size helps attract attorneys as well as clients, the firm also has had to fight the image that it is focused more on franchising than quality legal work. Russell Baker and John McKenzie founded the firm in 1949 with a focus on building an international practice.

The firm is known for the global scale of its practice, with some 80% of Baker & McKenzie attorneys practicing outside the US. However, it is beginning to face new competition on the global scene from firms such as Clifford Chance (which merged with two other practices in 2000 to create a network larger than Baker's). Its global operations have also increased the firm's risk to liability, leading Baker & McKenzie to reorganize itself as a Swiss Verein in 2004. Under the new structure, which is used by accounting firms such as Deloitte Touche Tohmatsu, its member firms operate as separate entities, protecting the parent firm from liability issues. Baker is the first international law firm to organize itself under the Verein structure.

In 2004 John Conroy was selected to replace Christine Lagarde as executive chairman. Elected in 1999, Lagarde was not only one of the first women to lead a major law firm but also one of the youngest partners to reach that high office.

The half-century-old firm has handled the legal affairs of such heavy-duty clients as Chase Manhattan (now J.P. Morgan Chase), Honeywell, and Ingersoll-Rand.

HISTORY

Russell Baker traveled from his native New Mexico to Chicago on a railroad freight car to attend law school. Upon graduation in 1925 he started practicing law with his classmate Dana Simpson under the name Simpson & Baker. Inspired by Chicago's role as a manufacturing and agricultural center for the world and influenced by the international focus of his alma mater, the University of Chicago, Baker dreamed of creating an international law practice. He began developing an expertise in international law, and in 1934 Abbott Laboratories retained him to handle its worldwide legal affairs. Baker was on his way to fulfilling his dream.

Baker joined forces with Chicago litigator John McKenzie in 1949, forming Baker & McKenzie. In 1955 the firm opened its first foreign office in Caracas, Venezuela, to meet the needs of its expanding US client base. Over the next 10 years it branched out into Asia, Australia, and Europe, with offices in London, Manila, Paris, and Tokyo. Baker's death in 1979 neither slowed the firm's growth nor changed its international character. The next year it expanded into the Middle East and opened its 30th office in 1982 (Melbourne). To manage the sprawling law firm, Baker & McKenzie created the position of chairman of the executive committee in 1984.

In late 1991 the firm dropped the Church of Scientology as a client, losing an estimated $2 million in business. It was speculated that pressure from client Eli Lilly (maker of the drug Prozac, which Scientologists actively oppose) influenced the decision. In 1992 Baker & McKenzie was ordered to pay $1 million for wrongfully firing an employee who later died of AIDS. (The case became the basis for the 1993 film *Philadelphia*.) The firm fought the verdict but eventually settled for an undisclosed amount in 1995.

In 1994 Baker & McKenzie closed its Los Angeles office (the former MacDonald, Halsted & Laybourne; acquired 1988) amid considerable rancor. Also that year a former secretary at the firm received a $7.1 million judgment for sexual harassment by a partner. (A San Francisco Superior Court judge later reduced the award to $3.5 million.)

John Klotsche, a senior partner from the firm's Palo Alto, California, office was appointed chairman in 1995. The following year the firm began a major expansion into California's Silicon Valley as part of an initiative to serve technology companies around the world. It also expanded its Warsaw, Poland, office through a merger with the Warsaw office of Dickinson, Wright, Moon, Van Dusen & Freman.

In 1998 Baker & McKenzie formed a special unit in Singapore to deal with business generated by the financial troubles in Asia. The opening of offices in Taiwan and Azerbaijan in 1998 brought the firm's total number of offices to 59. Klotsche stepped down in 1999 as the firm celebrated its 50th anniversary; Christine Lagarde replaced him. In early 2001 Baker & McKenzie created a joint venture practice with Singapore-based associate firm Wong & Leow. Also that year it merged with Madrid-based Briones Alonso y Martin to create the largest independent law firm in Spain.

In 2004 the firm reorganized as a Swiss Verein to protect itself from potential liability issues faced by its growing international operations. Baker & McKenzie was the first international law firm to use the legal structure employed by accounting firms such as Deloitte Touche Tohmatsu. Later that year, John Conroy was elected executive chairman, replacing Lagarde after five years of leading the firm.

EXECUTIVES

Chairman of the Executive Committee: John Conroy
COO: Craig Courter
CFO: Robert S. Spencer, age 57
CTO: Sue Hall
General Counsel: Edward J. Zulkey
Director of Professional Responsibility:
 William J. Linklater
Director of Marketing: David Tabolt
Director of Business Development: Rob Gijsen
Director of Professional Development: Anne Waldron
Chief Global Press Officer: Judith Green
Deputy Global Press Officer: Pamela Ulijasz
Public Relations Coordinator: Kathleen Heffley
Human Resources: Eleonora Nikol
Human Resources: Bethany Phillips

LOCATIONS

HQ: Baker & McKenzie
 130 E. Randolph Dr., Ste. 2500, Chicago, IL 60601
Phone: 312-861-8800 **Fax:** 312-861-8823
Web: www.bakernet.com

Baker & McKenzie has nearly 70 offices throughout Asia, Australia, Europe, Latin America, the Middle East, and North America.

PRODUCTS/OPERATIONS

Selected Practice Areas
Banking and finance
Corporate and securities
E-commerce
International commercial arbitration
International trade
Intellectual property, information technology, and communications
Labor and employment
Tax
US litigation

COMPETITORS

Clifford Chance
Jones Day
Kirkland & Ellis
Latham & Watkins
Mayer, Brown, Rowe & Maw
McDermott, Will

Shearman & Sterling
Sidley Austin Brown & Wood
Skadden, Arps
Sullivan & Cromwell
Weil, Gotshal
White & Case

HISTORICAL FINANCIALS

Company Type: Partnership

Income Statement FYE: June 30

	REVENUE ($ mil.)	NET INCOME ($ mil.)	NET PROFIT MARGIN	EMPLOYEES
6/04	1,228	—	—	8,400
6/03	1,060	—	—	8,401
6/02	1,000	—	—	8,000
6/01	1,000	—	—	8,000
6/00	940	—	—	8,000
6/99	818	—	—	6,900
6/98	785	—	—	6,700
6/97	697	—	—	6,100
6/96	646	—	—	5,680
6/95	594	—	—	5,248
Annual Growth	8.4%	—	—	5.4%

Revenue History

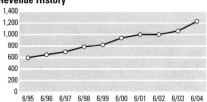

Baker & Taylor

If you've strolled through a library recently, you likely saw a lot of Baker & Taylor (B&T) without knowing it. The #1 book supplier to libraries, B&T maintains three operating units. Its institutional segment distributes books, calendars, music, and DVDs to about 8,000 school, public, and specialty libraries around the world. Its retail unit supplies storefront and Internet retailers, as well as independent booksellers, with some 4 million book titles and more than 135,000 video, DVD, and CD titles. Its product support unit (formerly operated as Informata.com) is B&T's B2B e-commerce arm. The Carlyle Group (who owned about 85% of B&T) sold the company to investment firm Willis Stein & Partners in 2003.

B&T's institutional unit also offers acquisition and collection management support services to libraries through its YBP Library Services subsidiary. In addition, B&T Retail provides fulfillment for companies such as Amazon.com and barnesandnoble.com, as well as handling the company's international operations.

B&T also offers automatic shipping of books and books-on-tape by popular authors (mailed as soon as they are published), and its Replica Books publishes out-of-print and paperback titles on demand.

EXECUTIVES

Chairman, President and CEO: Richard Willis
EVP and CFO: Robert E. Agres
EVP and COO: Marshall A. (Arnie) Wight
SVP and CIO: Matt Carroll
SVP and General Counsel: Bradley D. Murchison
SVP, A/V Library Services: William (Bill) Hartman
SVP, Customized Library Services: Livia Bitner
SVP, Human Resources: Claudette Hampton
SVP, Merchandising: Jean Srnecz
SVP, Operations: James Benjamin
SVP, Retail and International Sales:
  William (Bill) Preston
President, Baker & Taylor Institutional: George Coe
SVP; President and COO, YBP Library Services:
  Gary M. Shirk

LOCATIONS

HQ: Baker & Taylor Corporation
  2550 W. Tyvola Rd., Ste. 300, Charlotte, NC 28217
Phone: 704-998-3100 **Fax:** 704-998-3316
Web: www.btol.com

Baker & Taylor has operations in Georgia, Illinois, Nevada, New Jersey, North Carolina, and Pennsylvania, and sales offices in Australia and Japan.

PRODUCTS/OPERATIONS

Selected Products and Services
Accessories
Audiocassettes
Calendars
Cataloging database (B&T MARC)
CD-ROM and Internet database and ordering software
  (Title Source II)
CDs
DVDs
Hardcover and paperback books
On-demand printing (Replica Books)
Spoken-word audiocassettes
Standing-order service (Compass)
Videos

COMPETITORS

Advanced Marketing
Alliance Entertainment
Book Wholesalers
Chas. Levy
Dawson Holdings
East Texas Distributing
Educational Development
Follett
Handleman
Ingram Industries
Navarre
Rentrak

HISTORICAL FINANCIALS
Company Type: Private

Income Statement			FYE: Last Friday in June	
	REVENUE ($ mil.)	NET INCOME ($ mil.)	NET PROFIT MARGIN	EMPLOYEES
6/02	1,122	—	—	2,750
6/01	1,000	—	—	2,500
6/00	1,130	—	—	2,700
6/99	1,021	—	—	2,500
6/98	883	—	—	—
6/97	829	—	—	—
6/96	751	—	—	—
6/95	784	—	—	—
Annual Growth	5.3%	—	—	3.2%

Revenue History

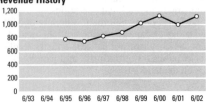

Banner Health

Hoist this Banner high! Banner Health is one of the largest secular not-for-profit health systems in the country. The organization operates 20 hospitals, half a dozen long-term care centers, and family clinics in eight states. Banner Health provides a variety of additional health services, including home care, heart care, cancer care, organ transplantations, and women's health, along with behavioral health and rehabilitation services. Banner Health also participates in medical research in areas such as Alzheimer's disease and spinal cord injuries.

In early 2004, the company ended its contract with Arizona's largest Medicaid plan (which covers about a third of the state's Medicaid recipients). The health system believes the loss of the contract will not have a major impact since demand for hospital beds in its markets is high.

EXECUTIVES

Chairman: Thomas F. Madison, age 68
Vice Chairman: Merlin E. Dewing, age 69
President and CEO: Peter S. Fine
SVP and CFO: Ron Bunnell
SVP, Strategy: Susan Doria
SVP, Quality and Care Management: John Hensing
SVP, People Resources: Gerri Twomey
VP, Corporate Communications: Dan Green
VP, Business Development: Scott Bosch

LOCATIONS

HQ: Banner Health
  1441 N. 12th St., Phoenix, AZ 85006
Phone: 602-495-4000 **Fax:** 602-495-4559
Web: www.bannerhealth.com

Selected Facilities
Alaska
  Fairbanks Memorial Hospital (Fairbanks)
Arizona
  Banner Thunderbird Medical Center (Glendale)
  Banner Baywood Heart Hospital (Mesa)
  Banner Baywood Medical Center (Mesa)
  Banner Desert Medical Center (Mesa)
  Banner Mesa Medical Center (Mesa)
  Page Hospital (Page)
  Banner Good Samaritan Medical Center (Phoenix)
California
  Banner Lassen Community Hospital (Susanville)
Colorado
  East Morgan County Hospital (Brush)
  North Colorado Medical Center (Greeley)
  McKee Medical Center (Loveland)
  Sterling Regional MedCenter (Sterling)
Kansas
  St. Luke Hospital and Living Center (Marion)
Nebraska
  Ogallala Community Hospital (Ogallala)
Nevada
  Banner Churchill Community Hospital (Fallon)
Wyoming
  Washakie Medical Center (Worland)

COMPETITORS

Catholic Healthcare West
HCA
Iasis Healthcare
Presbyterian Healthcare Services
Province Healthcare
Tenet Healthcare
Triad Hospitals
Vanguard Health Systems

HISTORICAL FINANCIALS
Company Type: Not-for-profit

Income Statement			FYE: December 31	
	REVENUE ($ mil.)	NET INCOME ($ mil.)	NET PROFIT MARGIN	EMPLOYEES
12/02	2,100	—	—	22,000
12/01	1,900	—	—	23,000
12/00	1,735	—	—	24,500
12/99	1,561	—	—	22,500
12/98	1,476	—	—	—
Annual Growth	9.2%	—	—	(0.7%)

Revenue History

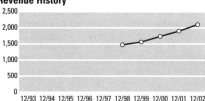

Baptist Health South Florida

Baptist Health South Florida is a not-for-profit health care organization composed of five Miami-area hospitals and a cardiovascular care institute. Baptist Health, which is a provider for about 30 health plans, offers a wide range of services including a comprehensive cancer program, pediatric services, addiction treatment, outpatient services, rehabilitation, and home care. Baptist Health has almost 1,200 hospital beds and more than 1,700 physicians. The system includes a children's hospital, outpatient diagnostic and treatment facilities, and a home health care agency.

EXECUTIVES

President and CEO: Brian E. Keeley
EVP and CFO: Ralph Lawson
VP Human Resources: Carl Gustafson
VP and Administrator, Baptist Childrens Hospital:
  Randy Lee
Director of Marketing: Joanne (Jo) Baxter
President and CEO, Baptist Hospital of Miami:
  Lee Huntley
CEO, Doctors Hospital: Lincoln Mendez
CEO, Homestead Hospital: Bo Boulenger
CEO, Mariners Hospital: Bob Luse
CEO, South Miami Hospital: Wayne Bracken

LOCATIONS

HQ: Baptist Health South Florida
  6855 Red Rd., Coral Gables, FL 33143
Phone: 786-662-7000 **Fax:** 786-662-7334
Web: www.baptisthealth.net

Baptist Health South Florida operates in south Florida, including the Miami area and the Florida Keys.

PRODUCTS/OPERATIONS

Selected Facilities
Baptist Children's Hospital
Baptist Hospital of Miami
Doctors Hospital
Homestead Hospital
Mariners Hospital
Miami Cardiac & Vascular Institute
South Miami Hospital

COMPETITORS

Catholic Health East
HCA
HEALTHSOUTH
North Broward Hospital District

HISTORICAL FINANCIALS

Company Type: Not-for-profit

Income Statement — FYE: September 30

	REVENUE ($ mil.)	NET INCOME ($ mil.)	NET PROFIT MARGIN	EMPLOYEES
9/03	926	—	—	8,616
9/02	900	—	—	8,500
9/01	824	—	—	8,000
9/00	639	—	—	7,500
9/99	538	—	—	7,500
9/98	514	—	—	7,503
Annual Growth	12.5%	—	—	2.8%

Revenue History

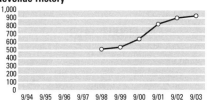

Barnes & Noble College Bookstores

Barnes & Noble College Bookstores is the scholastic sister company of Barnes & Noble (B&N), the US's largest bookseller. Started in 1873, the company operates more than 500 campus bookstores nationwide, selling textbooks, trade books, school supplies, collegiate clothing, and emblematic merchandise. Universities, medical and law schools, and community colleges hire Barnes & Noble College Bookstores to replace traditional campus cooperatives. (The schools get a cut of the sales.) Its College Marketing Network division offers on-campus marketing opportunities to businesses. B&N's chairman, Leonard Riggio, owns a controlling interest in the company.

EXECUTIVES

Chairman; Chairman, Barnes & Noble, Inc.: Leonard S. Riggio, age 63
President and CEO: Max J. Roberts
CFO: Barry Brover
SVP Marketing: Bill Maloney
VP and General Merchandise Manager: Jade Roth
VP, General Merchandise and Stores: Joel Friedman
VP, Marketing: Janine von Juergensonn
Auditors: BDO Seidman, LLP

LOCATIONS

HQ: Barnes & Noble College Bookstores, Inc.
120 Mountain View Blvd., Basking Ridge, NJ 07920
Phone: 908-991-2665   **Fax:** 212-780-1866
Web: www.bkstore.com

COMPETITORS

Amazon.com
Borders
Ecampus.com
Follett
Nebraska Book
Varsity Group
Wal-Mart

HISTORICAL FINANCIALS

Company Type: Private

Income Statement — FYE: April 30

	ESTIMATED REVENUE ($ mil.)	NET INCOME ($ mil.)	NET PROFIT MARGIN	EMPLOYEES
4/03	1,300	—	—	9,700
4/02	1,250	—	—	9,500
4/01	1,200	—	—	9,000
4/00	920	—	—	6,500
4/99	830	—	—	6,000
4/98	800	—	—	5,500
4/97	725	—	—	5,000
4/96	700	—	—	4,000
4/95	700	—	—	—
Annual Growth	8.0%	—	—	13.5%

Revenue History

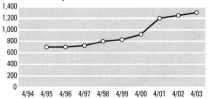

Bartlett and Company

When the cows come home, Bartlett and Company will be ready. The company's primary business is grain merchandising, but it also runs cattle feedlots and mills flour. Bartlett operates grain storage facilities in Kansas City, Kansas; St. Joseph and Waverly, Missouri; and Nebraska City, Nebraska. It has terminal elevators in Iowa, Kansas, and Missouri, as well as more than 10 country elevators. Bartlett's cattle operations are based in Texas; its flour mills are in Kansas, North Carolina, and South Carolina. The Bartlett and Company Grain Charitable Foundation makes financial gifts to local causes. Founded in 1907 as Bartlett Agri Enterprises, the company is still owned by the founding Bartlett family.

EXECUTIVES

Chairman: Paul D. Bartlett Jr., age 84
President and CEO: James B. Heberstreit
CIO: Peter Sorrentino
VP and CFO: Arnie Wheeler
VP, Personnel: Bill Webster

LOCATIONS

HQ: Bartlett and Company
4800 Main St., Ste. 600, Kansas City, MO 64112
Phone: 816-753-6300   **Fax:** 816-753-0062
Web: www.bartlettandco.com

COMPETITORS

ADM	ContiGroup
Ag Processing	DeBruce Grain
AzTx Cattle	Friona Industries
Cactus Feeders	GROWMARK
Cargill	King Ranch
CHS	Scoular

HISTORICAL FINANCIALS

Company Type: Private

Income Statement — FYE: December 31

	ESTIMATED REVENUE ($ mil.)	NET INCOME ($ mil.)	NET PROFIT MARGIN	EMPLOYEES
12/01	800	—	—	600
12/00	810	—	—	575
12/99	705	—	—	600
12/98	720	—	—	575
12/97	750	—	—	575
12/96	866	—	—	560
12/95	825	—	—	525
12/94	700	—	—	525
12/93	708	—	—	525
12/92	758	—	—	—
Annual Growth	0.6%	—	—	1.7%

Revenue History

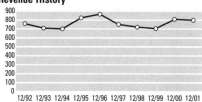

Barton Malow

Barton Malow scores by building end zones and home plates. The construction management and general contracting firm also makes points for its schools, hospitals, offices, and plants. It is a top automotive contractor. Barton Malow's services range from planning to completion on projects located in 37 states and the District of Columbia, including Atlanta's Phillips Arena, Boston's Shriners Hospital, and General Motors' Truck Product Center. Barton Malow Design provides architecture and engineering services, and the company's Barton Malow Rigging unit installs process equipment and machinery. Chairman Ben Maibach III and his family own a majority stake in the company, which was founded in 1924 by C. O. Barton.

EXECUTIVES

Chairman, President, and CEO: Ben C. Maibach III
Vice Chairman: Mark A. Bahr
EVP, Chief Legal Officer, and Secretary:
  Thomas (Tom) Porter
SVP and CFO: Lori R. Howlett
SVP Health Facilities Group: Richard (Dick) Miller
SVP K12 Education, Historic Renovations:
  Richard (Dick) Snider
SVP Sports Facilities: Bob Wyatt
CIO: Phil Go
VP and Treasurer: Edward R. (Ed) Jarchow
VP Sales and Marketing: Sheryl B. Maibach
VP Energy: Bill Mallory
VP Health Facilities: Dave Imesch
VP Higher Education: Todd Ketola
VP Human Resources: Judith Willard
VP and General Counsel: Ronald J. Torbert
Corporate Marketing Director: Donna Jakubowicz
Public Relations Manager: Anne-Marie Poltorak
Auditors: Grant Thornton LLP

LOCATIONS

HQ: Barton Malow Company
  26500 American Dr., Southfield, MI 48034
Phone: 248-436-5000   **Fax:** 248-436-5001
Web: www.bmco.com

Barton Malow has offices in Atlanta; Baltimore; Charlottesville, Virginia; Detroit and Southfield, Michigan; and Phoenix.

PRODUCTS/OPERATIONS

Primary Services
Architecture/planning
Construction management
Design/build
Facility audits
Facility services
General contracting
Interior design
Program management
Rigging/millwright
Technology consulting

Major Units
Barton Malow Concrete Division
Barton Malow Corporate/Industrial Group
Barton Malow Design
Barton Malow Energy Group
Barton Malow Higher Education Group
Barton Malow Health Facilities Group
Barton Malow Interiors Group
Barton Malow Public/Education Group
Barton Malow Rigging Company
Barton Malow Special Events Group
Barton Malow Technology Services

COMPETITORS

Alberici
BE&K
Clark Enterprises
Fluor
Gilbane
Hensel Phelps Construction
H.J. Russell
Hunt Construction
M. A. Mortenson
McCarthy Building
Skanska USA Building
Turner Corporation
Walbridge Aldinger
Walsh Group
Whiting-Turner
Zachry

HISTORICAL FINANCIALS
Company Type: Private

Income Statement
FYE: March 31

	REVENUE ($ mil.)	NET INCOME ($ mil.)	NET PROFIT MARGIN	EMPLOYEES
3/03	1,350	—	—	1,550
3/02	1,251	—	—	1,264
3/01	1,160	—	—	1,640
3/00	1,026	—	—	1,500
3/99	821	—	—	1,350
3/98	727	—	—	1,300
3/97	565	—	—	896
3/96	669	—	—	754
3/95	634	—	—	762
3/94	466	—	—	759
Annual Growth	12.5%	—	—	8.3%

Revenue History

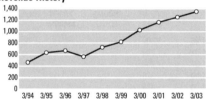

Bashas'

Bashas' has blossomed in the Arizona desert. Founded in 1932 and owned by the Basha family, the food retailer has grown to about 140 stores. These are located primarily throughout Arizona, but with one store each in California and New Mexico. Its holdings include Bashas' traditional supermarkets, AJ's Fine Foods (gourmet-style supermarkets), Bashas' Dine Markets, and Food City supermarkets, which cater to Hispanics in southern Arizona. Bashas' has opened 32 Natural Choice in-store departments that feature natural and organic items. It also operates a handful of supermarkets (including its New Mexico store) in the Navajo Nation. The company offers online grocery shopping through its Groceries On The Go service.

The third-largest grocery retailer in Arizona, Bashas' trails rivals Fry's Food Stores (owned by The Kroger Co.) and Safeway, and is feeling the heat from Wal-Mart Stores, which is rapidly expanding in the state. Bashas' outspoken CEO Eddie Basha has likened the Wal-Mart juggernaut to an economic blitzkrieg. Wal-Mart has 55 locations in Arizona.

EXECUTIVES

Chairman and CEO: Edward N. (Eddie) Basha Jr., age 66
President and COO: Mike Proulx, age 55
SVP, Finance and CFO: James (Jim) Buhr, age 55
SVP, Human Resources: Michael Gantt
SVP, Retail Operations: Ralph Woodward
VP, Food Service: Jay Volk
VP, General Merchandise: Bryon Roberts
VP, Pharmacy: Ed Saba
VP, Produce Director: Bill Romley
VP, Sales Promotions and Customer Loyalty:
  Christie Frazier-Coleman
VP and General Manager, Food City: Tom Swanson
VP and Director of Merchandise, Food City:
  Robert Ortiz
Director, Public Relations: Mimi Meredith
Customer Relations Coordinator: Rob Johnson

LOCATIONS

HQ: Bashas' Inc.
  22402 S. Basha Rd., Chandler, AZ 85248
Phone: 480-895-9350   **Fax:** 480-895-5394
Web: www.bashas.com

COMPETITORS

Albertson's
Fry's Food
Safeway
Smart & Final
SUPERVALU
Trader Joe's Co
Wal-Mart
Whole Foods
Wild Oats Markets

HISTORICAL FINANCIALS
Company Type: Private

Income Statement
FYE: December 31

	ESTIMATED REVENUE ($ mil.)	NET INCOME ($ mil.)	NET PROFIT MARGIN	EMPLOYEES
12/03	1,700	—	—	13,200
12/02	1,600	—	—	12,500
12/01	1,359	—	—	10,500
12/00	1,200	—	—	8,800
12/99	1,210	—	—	8,000
12/98	1,000	—	—	7,600
12/97	870	—	—	7,600
12/96	800	—	—	6,600
12/95	675	—	—	5,600
12/94	650	—	—	5,000
Annual Growth	11.3%	—	—	11.4%

Revenue History

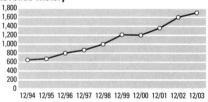

Basin Electric Power

Ranges at home on the range depend on Basin Electric Power Cooperative, as do other electric-powered items in nine states from Montana to Iowa to New Mexico. The regional, consumer-owned power generation and transmission co-op generates about 2,500 MW of capacity (mostly coal-fired) for 125 rural electric member systems, which serve 1.8 million people. It generates an additional 1,000 MW for participants in the Missouri Basin Power Project. Basin Electric's subsidiaries include Dakota Gasification (produces natural gas from coal), Dakota Coal (markets lignite and limestone), Basin Telecommunications (Internet access), Basin Cooperative Services (property management), and Granite Peak Energy (power marketing).

EXECUTIVES

President of the Board of Directors, Basin Electric and Basin Cooperative Services; Chairman, Basin Telecommunications: Wayne L. Child
VP of the Board of Directors, Basin Electric and Basin Cooperative Services; Treasurer, Dakota Gasification: Clifford G. Gjellstad
CEO and General Manager, Basin Electric and Basin Cooperative Services; President and CEO, Dakota Coal, Dakota Gasification, and Basin Telecommunications: Ronald R. (Ron) Harper
SVP and Deputy General Manager: Paul Sukut, age 47
SVP Financial Services and CFO: Clifton T. Hudgins, age 56
SVP Information Systems and Telecommunications and CIO; COO, Basin Telecommunications: Pat Spilman, age 46
SVP, General Counsel, and Assistant Secretary, Basin Electric and Basin Cooperative Services; Secretary, Dakota Gasification, Dakota Coal, and Basin Telecommunications: Claire M. Olson
SVP Administration: Tom Fischer, age 48
SVP External Relations and Communications: Alan Edwards, age 52
SVP Generation: Wayne Backman, age 50
SVP Transmission: Michael Risan
Secretary and Treasurer, Basin Electric and Basin Cooperative Services: Kermit Pearson
Chairman, Dakota Coal: Gary C. Drost
Manager Human Resources: Sharon Klein
Auditors: Deloitte & Touche LLP

LOCATIONS

HQ: Basin Electric Power Cooperative
1717 E. Interstate Ave., Bismarck, ND 58503
Phone: 701-223-0441   **Fax:** 701-224-5336
Web: www.basinelectric.com

Basin Electric Power Cooperative provides electricity in Colorado, Iowa, Minnesota, Montana, Nebraska, New Mexico, North Dakota, South Dakota, and Wyoming.

PRODUCTS/OPERATIONS

2003 Sales

	$ mil.	% of total
Electric		
Non-members	262.9	30
Members	237.5	27
Other	8.7	1
Synthetic gas	161.9	18
Lignite coal	86.9	10
Byproducts & other	125.0	14
Total	**882.9**	**100**

COMPETITORS

Alliant Energy
Aquila
Black Hills
MDU Resources
MidAmerican Energy
Nebraska Public Power
NorthWestern
Omaha Public Power
Otter Tail
Xcel Energy

HISTORICAL FINANCIALS

Company Type: Cooperative

Income Statement
FYE: December 31

	REVENUE ($ mil.)	NET INCOME ($ mil.)	NET PROFIT MARGIN	EMPLOYEES
12/03	883	43	4.9%	1,778
12/02	830	37	4.4%	1,768
12/01	863	27	3.1%	1,775
12/00	512	43	8.3%	1,750
12/99	757	4	0.5%	1,661
12/98	763	(5)	—	1,684
12/97	784	(3)	—	1,790
12/96	774	(3)	—	1,735
12/95	733	—	—	1,761
12/94	783	—	—	—
Annual Growth	1.3%	—	—	0.1%

2003 Year-End Financials
Debt ratio: 146.4%   Current ratio: 1.09
Return on equity: 6.9%   Long-term debt ($ mil.): 963
Cash ($ mil.): 63

Net Income History

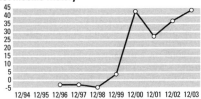

Bass Pro Shops

Bass Pro Shops (BPS) knows how to reel in the shoppers. Each of its 20 Outdoor World stores (in 13 states) covers about 280,000 sq. ft. The cavernous outlets sell boats, campers, equipment, and apparel for most outdoor activities and offer features such as archery ranges, fish tanks, snack bars, and video arcades. The first Outdoor World store, in Missouri, has been one of the state's biggest tourist attractions since it opened in 1981. BPS catches shoppers at home with its seasonal and specialty catalogs and through its TV and radio programs. It owns Tracker Marine (boat manufacturing) and American Rod & Gun (sporting goods wholesale) and runs a resort in the Ozark Mountains. Founder John Morris owns BPS.

EXECUTIVES

Founder: John L. (Johnny) Morris
President and COO: James (Jim) Hagale
VP and CFO: Toni Miller
VP of Human Resources: Mike Roland
Director of Corporate Public Relations: Martin Mac Donald
Manager, Corporate Public Relations: Larry Whitely

LOCATIONS

HQ: Bass Pro Shops, Inc.
2500 E. Kearney, Springfield, MO 65898
Phone: 417-873-5000   **Fax:** 417-873-4672
Web: www.basspro.com

2003 Stores

	No.
Florida	4
Georgia	2
Missouri	2
Tennessee	2
Texas	2
Illinois	1
Louisiana	1
Maryland	1
Michigan	1
North Carolina	1
Ohio	1
Oklahoma	1
Virginia	1
Total	**20**

PRODUCTS/OPERATIONS

Selected Merchandise Categories
Apparel
Camping and auto
Fishing
Fly fishing
Footwear
Gifts and home decor
Hunting
Marine and electronics
Saltwater fishing

Other Operations
American Rod & Gun (sporting goods wholesale)
Bass Pro Shops (sporting goods catalog)
Bass Pro Shops Outdoor World (magazine and radio and TV programs)
Big Creek Lodge (resort)
Outdoor World (retail stores)
Tracker Marine (sport boat manufacturing)

COMPETITORS

Academy
Cabela's
Camping World
Cruise America
Dick's Sporting Goods
Galyan's
Gander Mountain
Hibbett Sporting Goods
Kmart
MarineMax
REI
Sears
Sports Authority
Sportsman's Guide
Travis Boats & Motors
Wal-Mart
West Marine
Winmark

HISTORICAL FINANCIALS

Company Type: Private

Income Statement
FYE: December 31

	ESTIMATED REVENUE ($ mil.)	NET INCOME ($ mil.)	NET PROFIT MARGIN	EMPLOYEES
12/02	1,400	—	—	11,400
12/01	1,100	—	—	8,800
12/00	990	—	—	8,200
12/99	950	—	—	7,900
12/98	311	—	—	—
12/97	270	—	—	—
Annual Growth	39.0%	—	—	13.0%

Revenue History

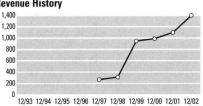

HOOVER'S HANDBOOK OF PRIVATE COMPANIES 2005

Battelle Memorial

When you use a copier, hit a golf ball, or listen to a CD, you're using technologies developed by Battelle Memorial Institute. The not-for-profit trust operates one of the world's largest research enterprises. Originally formed to promote metallurgy and related industries, the institute has diversified into research and development for agriculture, automobiles, chemicals, energy, software, and medicine. Battelle is also a major source of research and development expertise for the US government. It serves the departments of Energy, Defense, and Health and Human Services; the Environmental Protection Agency; and nearly 800 other government organizations.

The institute, which works with corporations and governments in nearly 30 countries, was instrumental in developing the photocopy machine, optical digital recording (used with compact discs), and bar codes. Primarily a contract research provider, the institute continues to explore next-generation technologies including advanced medical products, alternative fuels, and recycling processes.

Battelle is spinning off for-profit companies to benefit its nonprofit cause; it has shed its medical, flat-panel display, and software units as subsidiaries. The institute has also formed Battelle Ventures to commercialize Battelle technologies. Current development projects include lightweight autos, oil spill clean-up, and pulmonary drug delivery devices.

HISTORY

Battelle Memorial Institute was founded with a $1.5 million trust willed by Gordon Battelle, who died in 1923. Battelle was a champion of research for the advancement of humankind, and before taking his father's place as president of several Ohio steel mills, he had funded a former university professor's successful work to extract useful chemicals from mine waste. Battelle's mother, upon her death in 1925, left the institute an additional $2.1 million. The institute opened in 1929.

The institute took on perhaps the most important project in its history in 1944 when it helped an electronics company's patent lawyer, Chester Carlson, find practical uses for his invention, called xerography. Eventually Battelle developed the first photocopy machine, and in 1955 it sold the patent rights for the machine to Haloid (now Xerox) in exchange for royalties.

During WWII Battelle worked on uranium refining for the Manhattan Project, and in the early 1950s it established the world's first private nuclear research facility. The company also set up operations in Germany and Switzerland.

The tax man came knocking in 1961, questioning the tax-free status of some of Battelle's activities. The organization eventually had to pay $47 million. In 1965 Battelle developed a coin with a copper core and a copper-and-nickel-alloy cladding for the US Treasury.

As the result of a ruling that reinterpreted a clause in Gordon Battelle's will, in 1975 the institute gave $80 million to philanthropic enterprises. This ruling, coupled with the taxes that the organization was still unaccustomed to paying, forced Battelle to reexamine its strategy.

Battelle co-developed the Universal Product Code (the bar code symbol found today on nearly all consumer goods packaging) in the 1970s. The institute also landed a lucrative contract from the US Department of Energy (DOE) to manage its commercial nuclear waste isolation program.

In 1987 Battelle chose Douglas Olesen — a 20-year veteran of the institute — to replace retiring CEO Ronald Paul. The company signed an extension with the DOE in 1992 to run its Pacific Northwest Laboratory (which it has operated since 1965).

An Ohio court in 1997 approved a seven-page agreement with the institute outlining the key principles that must be followed according to Gordon Battelle's will. This agreement replaced the 1975 decree and ended more than 20 years of scrutiny by the state attorney general's office.

In 1998 the DOE contracted Brookhaven Science Associates — a partnership between the State University of New York and Battelle — to operate Brookhaven National Laboratory. That year a Battelle contract to dispose of Vietnam War-era napalm drew national attention when subcontractor Pollution Control Industries backed out of the project, citing safety concerns. Under Battelle's direction, Houston-based GNI Group took the 3.4 million gallons of napalm off the US Navy's hands.

Battelle and the University of Tennessee in 1999 won a five-year contract to operate the US government's Oak Ridge National Laboratory. That year the institute made several breakthroughs in cancer research, including FDA approval to test an inhalation delivery system for treating lung cancer.

In 2000 the company spun off OmniViz (data mining software) and Battelle Pulmonary Therapeutics (pulmonary and drug delivery technology) as wholly owned subsidiaries. In 2001 Battelle chose former Kodak EVP and chief technology officer Carl Kohrt to replace Olesen.

EXECUTIVES

Chairman: John B. McCoy Jr.
First Vice Chairman: John J. Hopfield
Second Vice Chairman: W. George Meredith
President and CEO: Carl F. Kohrt, age 60
EVP, Battelle Science & Technology International: Gregory L. (Greg) Frank
EVP, Laboratory Operations: William J. Madia
SVP and CTO, Core Technology Development: Richard C. Adams
SVP, CFO, and Treasurer: Mark W. Kontos
SVP; General Manager, Army/Marines/Office of Secretary of Defense Market Sector: Stephen E. Kelly
SVP; General Manager, Chemical Products Market Sector: Benjamin G. Maiden
SVP; General Manager, Energy Products Market Sector: Henry J. Cialone
SVP, Life Sciences Division: Richard D. Rosen
SVP, Administration, General Counsel, and Secretary: Jerome R. Bahlmann
SVP, National Security Division: Steve Kelly
SVP, Organizational Development: Robert W. Smith Jr.
Media Relations Manager: Katy Delaney

LOCATIONS

HQ: Battelle Memorial Institute
505 King Ave., Columbus, OH 43201
Phone: 614-424-6424   **Fax:** 614-424-5263
Web: www.battelle.org

Battelle Memorial Institute manages programs in nearly 30 countries.

PRODUCTS/OPERATIONS

Selected Inventions

Automobile cruise control (1960s)
Exploded-tip paintbrush (nylon brush for Wooster Brush Co., 1950)
Golf ball coatings (1965)
Heat Seat (microwaveable heated stadium cushion, 1990s)
Holograms (work began in the 1970s)
Insulin injection pen (for Eli Lilly, 1990s)
Oil spill outline monitor (1992)
PCB-cleaning chemical process (1992)
Photocopy machine (with Haloid, 1940s)
Plastic breakdown process (1990s)
"Sandwich" coins (copper/copper and nickel alloy cladding design for US Treasury, 1965)
SenSonic toothbrush (with Teledyne/WaterPik, 1990s)
Smart cards (cards embedded with tiny computer chips that store information, 1980s)
SnoPake (correction fluid, 1955)
Universal Product Code (co-creator; bar code, 1970s)

Subsidiaries

Battelle Pulmonary Therapeutics, Inc.
Geosafe Corporation
Global Transaction Company, Inc.
OmniViz, Inc.
Research Insurance Company Ltd.
Scientific Advances, Inc.
State Science and Technology Institute
Vitex Systems, Inc.

COMPETITORS

Altran Technologies
CDM
Charles Stark Draper Laboratory
Kendle
MIT
MITRE
PAREXEL
Parsons Infrastructure & Technology
Quintiles Transnational
Research Triangle Institute
SAIC
Sandia
Southwest Research Institute
SRI International
University of California

HISTORICAL FINANCIALS

Company Type: Not-for-profit

Income Statement

FYE: September 30

	REVENUE ($ mil.)	NET INCOME ($ mil.)	NET PROFIT MARGIN	EMPLOYEES
9/03	1,350	—	—	8,900
9/02	1,176	—	—	8,700
9/01	1,029	—	—	7,607
9/00	950	—	—	7,100
9/99	901	—	—	7,060
9/98	710	—	—	7,250
9/97	946	—	—	7,060
9/96	945	—	—	7,163
9/95	974	—	—	7,500
9/94	958	—	—	8,583
Annual Growth	3.9%	—	—	0.4%

Revenue History

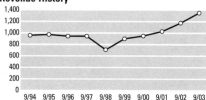

Baystate Health Systems

Patients in need of medical care can dock at this bay. Not-for-profit Baystate Health Systems is the largest health care services provider in western Massachusetts. The system operates four acute-care hospitals with a total of more than 700 beds, including a specialized children's hospital. Baystate Health Systems offers ancillary medical services, including respiratory care, infusion therapy, visiting nurse, hospice, and emergency transportation services. Baystate Health also operates Health New England, a for-profit HMO with some 100,000 members in western Massachusetts and northern Connecticut.

EXECUTIVES
President: Michael J. Daly
CEO; President and CEO, Baystate Medical Center: Mark R. Tolosky
SVP, Finance: Keith McLean-Shinaman
SVP and COO, Baystate Medical Center: Trish Hannon
Director Human Resources: Ann Marie Szmyt
President, Franklin Medical Center: Michael Skinner
EVP, Mary Lane Hospital: Christine (Chris) Shirtcliff
President, Baystate Visiting Nurse Association & Hospice: Ruth Odgren

LOCATIONS
HQ: Baystate Health Systems, Inc.
280 Chestnut St., Springfield, MA 01199
Phone: 413-794-0000   **Fax:** 413-794-8274
Web: baystatehealth.com

Baystate Health Systems operates primarily in Massachusetts.

PRODUCTS/OPERATIONS
Hospitals
Baystate Medical Center (Springfield)
BMC Children's Hospital (Springfield)
Franklin Medical Center (Greenfield)
Mary Lane Hospital (Ware)

COMPETITORS
CareGroup
Catholic Health East
HCA
Partners HealthCare
Tenet Healthcare

HISTORICAL FINANCIALS
Company Type: Not-for-profit

Income Statement				FYE: September 30
	REVENUE ($ mil.)	NET INCOME ($ mil.)	NET PROFIT MARGIN	EMPLOYEES
9/02	874	(29)	—	6,000
9/01	797	6	0.7%	6,000
9/00	628	17	2.8%	6,000
9/99	564	—	—	6,000
9/98	512	—	—	5,900
9/97	534	—	—	5,910
9/96	520	—	—	6,000
9/95	495	—	—	—
9/94	456	—	—	—
9/93	424	—	—	—
Annual Growth	8.4%	—	—	0.0%

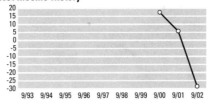

Net Income History

BE&K

A busy bee in the power plant industry, BE&K is a top US engineering and construction contractor. Through a network of subsidiaries, BE&K provides engineering, procurement, and construction and maintenance services worldwide for power plants and other industrial process facilities, including the cement, chemical, petrochemical, pharmaceutical, and pulp and paper industries. It also serves the telecommunications, manufacturing, environmental, and commercial sectors. Founded in 1972 by partners Peter Bolvig, William Edmonds, and Ted Kennedy, the company initially worked primarily for the pulp and paper industry. Overseas operations began in Poland in 1984 through a strategic relationship with International Paper.

EXECUTIVES
Chairman and CEO: T. Michael (Mike) Goodrich, age 58
EVP and COO; President, BE&K Construction Company: John W. Redmon
EVP and CFO: Clyde M. Smith
SVP Human Resources: Kimberly S. Patterson
VP Sales and Marketing: Tom Freeland
VP; General Manager, BE&K Houston: Gerry L. Turner
VP; General Manager, BE&K Raleigh: Paul Turner
VP; Manager, Delaware Operations: Robert Pinson
VP Industrial Services: Susan M. (Sue) Steele
VP Construction Services: Bryson Edmonds
Controller: W. H. Rubar
Director Corporate Communications: Susan Wasley
General Counsel: Ed Cassady
Manager Human Resources: Bruce May
Auditors: Ernst & Young LLP

LOCATIONS
HQ: BE&K, Inc.
2000 International Park Dr., Birmingham, AL 35243
Phone: 205-972-6000   **Fax:** 205-972-6651
Web: www.bek.com

BE&K has offices in Alabama, Delaware, Georgia, New York, North Carolina, Oregon, Pennsylvania, and Texas.

PRODUCTS/OPERATIONS
Selected Services
Bio-pharmaceutical facility design and construction
Boiler and auxiliary equipment installation, repair, and replacement
Computer-aided design (CAD) engineering
Construction design, engineering, and building
Environmental consulting and engineering
Industrial contract maintenance and plant support
International industrial design, engineering, and construction
Process industries design, construction, and maintenance

Selected Subsidiaries
AllStates Technical Services (engineering and information technology outsourcing services)
As Built Data (3D-CAD modeling, including photogrammetry, computer analysis, digitized photography, and surveying)
BE&K's Saginaw Warehouse (small tools, consumables, and construction equipment supply)
BE&K/Terranext (environmental services)
FN Thompson (office, retail, and manufacturing facility construction)
Industra Engineers & Consultants, Inc. (engineering and consulting to pulp and paper industry)
M-E-I Consultants (multidisciplinary engineering company to hydrocarbon industries)
North Star Communications Group, Inc. (data and telecommunications infrastructure consulting, design, installation, and staffing)
QBEK (quality assurance)
Rintekno Group (engineering and contracting companies serving the environmental technology, biochemicals, chemicals, forest industry chemicals, oil refining/petrochemicals, foodstuff/animal feed, and pharmaceuticals industries)
Suitt Construction Company (construction services in chemical, food, general manufacturing, textile, and pharmaceutical industries)
SW&B Construction Corporation (heavy industrial general contractor serving the pulp and paper and non-woven industry)
Tool Specialty, Inc. (TSI, tools and consumables for construction and manufacturing facilities)

COMPETITORS
AMEC
ARCADIS
Bechtel
Black & Veatch
CH2M HILL
Day & Zimmermann
Dick Corporation
E M C Engineers
Eichleay Corporation
Fluor
Foster Wheeler
Gilbane
Halliburton
HOCHTIEF
Jacobs Engineering
McClier
Parsons
Parsons Brinckerhoff
Perini
Peter Kiewit Sons'
Skanska
Tetra Tech
URS
Washington Group

HISTORICAL FINANCIALS
Company Type: Private

Income Statement				FYE: March 31
	REVENUE ($ mil.)	NET INCOME ($ mil.)	NET PROFIT MARGIN	EMPLOYEES
3/03	1,098	—	—	8,212
3/02	1,478	—	—	8,822
3/01	1,776	—	—	10,799
3/00	1,370	—	—	10,525
3/99	960	—	—	8,617
3/98	1,061	—	—	8,159
3/97	960	—	—	7,872
3/96	807	—	—	7,600
3/95	828	—	—	7,303
3/94	580	—	—	6,917
Annual Growth	7.3%	—	—	1.9%

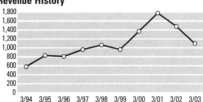

Revenue History

Beaulieu of America

Beaulieu of America (BOA) is rolling into a room near you with products that primarily include berber, commercial, and indoor/outdoor (nonwoven, turf) carpet. Chances are you may have had BOA underfoot at some point; the company is the third-largest carpet manufacturer. Major customers for its carpets include home improvement chains The Home Depot and Lowe's Companies. BOA sold its area rug division to Springs Industries and has closed and consolidated other operations. Chairman and CEO Carl Bouckaert and his wife, Mieke, whose family made carpets in Europe, founded Beaulieu in 1978; the Bouckaerts control BOA.

EXECUTIVES

CEO: Carl M. Bouckaert
President and COO: Ralph Boe
CFO: Tim Devries
Chief Administrative Officer: Clint Hubbard

LOCATIONS

HQ: Beaulieu of America, LLC
1502 Coronet Dr., Dalton, GA 30377
Phone: 706-695-4624   **Fax:** 706-695-6237
Web: www.beaulieu-usa.com

Beaulieu Of America operates facilities in Canada, Mexico, and the US.

PRODUCTS/OPERATIONS

Selected Products
Berber carpet
Cut loops
Cut piles
Indoor/outdoor carpet
Natural nylon BCF nylon fibers
Needle-punched carpet
Nylon intermediates
Outdoor artificial grass
Polypropylene BCF fibers
Polypropylene resin
Polypropylene staple fiber
Solution-dyed nylon BCF fibers

COMPETITORS

Armstrong World Industries
Dixie Group
Interface
Milliken
Mohawk Industries
Shaw Industries

HISTORICAL FINANCIALS
Company Type: Private

Income Statement
FYE: December 31

	ESTIMATED REVENUE ($ mil.)	NET INCOME ($ mil.)	NET PROFIT MARGIN	EMPLOYEES
12/02	1,100	—	—	7,000
12/01	1,400	—	—	10,000
12/00	1,800	—	—	11,000
12/99	1,700	—	—	10,000
12/98	1,130	—	—	9,347
12/97	961	—	—	6,413
12/96	863	—	—	6,617
12/95	868	—	—	6,500
12/94	833	—	—	6,500
12/93	744	—	—	5,900
Annual Growth	4.4%	—	—	1.9%

Revenue History

Bechtel

Whether it's raising an entire city or razing a nuclear power plant, you can bet the Bechtel Group will be there to bid on the business. The firm is the US's #1 contractor (ahead of Fluor). The engineering, construction, and project management firm operates worldwide and has participated in such notable projects as the construction of Hoover Dam and the cleanup of the Chernobyl nuclear plant. Subsidiary Bechtel Enterprises invests in infrastructure projects and arranges financing for its clients. The group is in its fourth generation of leadership by the Bechtel family, with chairman and CEO Riley Bechtel at the helm. The billionaire Bechtel family owns a controlling stake in the firm.

Bechtel has made a name for itself by participating in mega-projects. It completes more than 1,000 projects a year. The services Bechtel offers are as broad as the industries it serves. In addition to providing its core project management and design services, it offers such services as environmental restoration and remediation, telecommunications infrastructure (installing cable-optic networks and constructing data centers), and e-business infrastructure (including design, systems integration, and commissioning).

Among Bechtel's more traditional infrastructure projects has been its involvement in the "Big Dig," Boston's Central Artery/Tunnel project. Bechtel, in a joint venture with Parsons Brinckerhoff, has served as lead contractor on the $14.6 billion project, which has been the subject of much dispute over cost overruns.

Other major projects of the group are its build-outs of both the AT&T Wireless and Cingular Wireless networks. In Europe it is expanding its rail business by participating in the construction of the Channel Tunnel Rail Link, the UK's first major new railroad project in a century. It is also managing the upgrade of the UK's West Coast main line and has joined a consortium to renovate part of London's 140-year-old subway.

The mother of all mega-projects for Bechtel might turn out to be its involvement in the rehabilitation and repair of Iraq's infrastructure system. Its government services company, Bechtel National, Inc. (BNI), has been managing engineering and construction projects for public works in the war-ravaged country, including power systems, water and sanitation systems, roads and bridges, public buildings, airports, and ports. The group's work in Iraq helped contribute to a 40% spike in Bechtel's annual revenues in 2003.

HISTORY

In 1898, 25-year-old Warren Bechtel left his Kansas farm to grade railroads in the Oklahoma Indian territories, then followed the rails west. Settling in Oakland, California, he founded his own contracting firm. Foreseeing the importance of roads, oil, and power, he won big projects such as the Northern California Highway and the Bowman Dam. By 1925, when he incorporated his company as W.A. Bechtel & Co., it ranked as the West's largest construction company. In 1931 Bechtel helped found the consortium that built Hoover Dam.

Under the leadership of Steve Bechtel (president after his father's death in 1933), the company obtained contracts for large infrastructure projects such as the San Francisco-Oakland Bay Bridge. Noted for his friendships with influential people, including Dwight Eisenhower, Adlai Stevenson, and Saudi Arabia's King Faisal, Steve developed projects that spanned nations and industries, such as pipelines in Saudi Arabia and numerous power projects. By 1960, when Steve Bechtel Jr. took over, the company was operating on six continents.

In the next two decades, Bechtel worked on transportation projects — such as San Francisco's Bay Area Rapid Transit (BART) system and the Washington, DC, subway system — and power projects, including nuclear plants. After the 1979 Three Mile Island accident, Bechtel tried its hand at nuclear cleanup. With nuclear power no longer in vogue, it focused on other markets, such as mining in New Guinea (gold and copper, 1981-84) and China (coal, 1984). Bechtel's Jubail project in Saudi Arabia, begun in 1976, raised an entire industrial port city on the Persian Gulf.

The US recession and rising developing-world debt of the early 1980s sent Bechtel reeling. It cut its workforce by 22,000 and stemmed losses by piling up small projects.

Riley Bechtel, great-grandson of Warren, became CEO in 1990. After the 1991 Gulf War, Bechtel extinguished Kuwait's flaming oil wells and worked on the oil-spill cleanup. During the decade it also worked on such projects as the Channel tunnel (Chunnel) between England and France, Hong Kong's new airport, and pipelines in the former Soviet Union.

Bechtel was part of the consortium contracted in 1996 to build a high-speed passenger rail line between London and the Chunnel. International Generating (InterGen), Bechtel's joint venture with Pacific Gas and Electric (PG&E), was chosen to help build Mexico's first private power plant. In 1996 Bechtel bought PG&E's share of InterGen, then sold a 50% stake in InterGen to a unit of Royal Dutch/Shell in early 1997.

That year Bechtel began a venture, Netcon (Thailand), with Lucent to build telecom systems abroad. In 1998 it won a major contract to construct a gas production plant with Technip in Abu Dhabi. That year it joined Battelle and Electricité de France in project management of a long-term plan to stabilize the damaged reactor of the Chernobyl nuclear plant in Ukraine.

In 1999 Bechtel was hired to decommission the Connecticut Yankee nuclear plant. The next year Bechtel teamed up with Shell Oil to build a $400 million power plant in Baja California to meet the high demands of the US-Mexico border region. It also formed Nexant, an energy consulting service for the oil and gas industry and utilities.

Bechtel expanded its telecommunications operations in 2001 to provide turnkey network implementation services in Europe, the Middle East, and Asia. In 2002 Bechtel was once again called on to work on the UK's rail system, taking over management of the upgrade of the West Coast main line from financially troubled Railtrack. As part of a consortium with UK facilities management giants Jarvis and Amey, Bechtel began work that year on a 30-year project to modernize part of London's aging subway system.

In 2003 and 2004, a group led by Bechtel received contracts (worth $1 billion and $1.8 billion respectively) by the U.S. Agency for International Development to manage construction projects for the rebuilding of Iraq's infrastructure.

EXECUTIVES

Chairman Emeritus: Stephen D. (Steve) Bechtel Jr., age 79
Chairman and CEO: Riley P. Bechtel, age 51
President and COO: Adrian Zaccaria
EVP and Deputy COO: Jude Laspa
EVP; President, Bechtel Enterprises Holdings: Tim Statton
EVP and Executive Sponsor of Engineering, Procurement, and Construction Functions: Mike Thiele
EVP; President, Bechtel National, Inc.; President, Bechtel Systems and Infrastructure: Thomas F. (Tom) Hash
EVP; President, Petroleum and Chemical and Pipeline: Bill Dudley
SVP and CFO: Peter Dawson
SVP and General Counsel: Rick Burt
CIO and Manager Information Systems & Technology: Geir Ramleth
Secretary: Foster Wollen
SVP; President, Bechtel Infrastructure: John McDonald
SVP; President, Mining and Metals Global Business Unit: Andy Greig
SVP; President, Power Global Business Unit: Scott Ogilvie
SVP; President, Telecommunications and Industrial Global Business Unit: George Conniff
SVP Human Resources: Chuck Redman
President, Civil Global Business Unit: Mike Adams
President, Bechtel Jacobs Co.: Michael C. (Mike) Hughes
Public Affairs and Information Manager: Jeff H. Berger
Media Relations Manager: Jonathan Marshall
Auditors: PricewaterhouseCoopers LLP

LOCATIONS

HQ: Bechtel Group, Inc.
50 Beale St., San Francisco, CA 94105
Phone: 415-768-1234   **Fax:** 415-768-9038
Web: www.bechtel.com

Bechtel Group operates worldwide from offices in 11 states in the US, along with international offices in Argentina, Australia, Brazil, Canada, Chile, China, Egypt, France, India, Indonesia, Japan, Korea, Malaysia, Mexico, Oman, Peru, the Philippines, Russia, Saudi Arabia, Singapore, Spain, Taiwan, Thailand, Turkey, United Arab Emirates, the UK, and Venezuela.

PRODUCTS/OPERATIONS

Selected Services
Construction
Engineering
Financing and development
Procurement
Project management
Safety
Technology

Selected Markets
Civil infrastructure
Development, financing, and ownership (Bechtel Enterprises)
Federal government
Industrial
Mining and metals
Petroleum and chemicals
Pipelines
Power (fossil and nuclear)
Telecommunications

COMPETITORS

ABB Lummus Global	Kajima
Aker Kværner	Parsons
AMEC	Perini
Black & Veatch	Peter Kiewit Sons'
Bouygues	RWE
Centerline Piping	Schneider
CH2M HILL	Shaw Group
Chiyoda Corp.	Siemens
EIFFAGE	Skanska
Fluor	Technip
Foster Wheeler	URS
Halliburton	VINCI
HOCHTIEF	Vinnell Corporation
Hyundai Engineering and Construction	Washington Group
ITOCHU	Weston
Jacobs Engineering	WFI Government Services

HISTORICAL FINANCIALS

Company Type: Private

Income Statement				FYE: December 31
	REVENUE ($ mil.)	NET INCOME ($ mil.)	NET PROFIT MARGIN	EMPLOYEES
12/03	16,300	—	—	44,000
12/02	11,600	—	—	47,000
12/01	13,400	—	—	50,000
12/00	15,108	—	—	40,000
12/99	12,600	—	—	40,000
12/98	12,645	—	—	30,000
12/97	11,329	—	—	30,000
12/96	8,157	—	—	30,000
12/95	8,504	—	—	29,400
12/94	7,885	—	—	29,200
Annual Growth	8.4%	—	—	4.7%

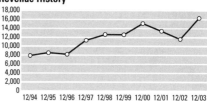

Revenue History

Beck Group

At the beck and call of commercial developers, The Beck Group has built everything from racetracks to runways, retail centers, hotels, and hospitals. The firm provides design/build, general contracting, and construction management services in the US and Mexico. Focusing on commercial and institutional building, Beck offers services such as project management and outsourcing of facilities construction. The company also provides real estate development services. Projects include Dallas' Cotton Bowl, the Texas Motor Speedway outside Fort Worth, the Museum of Contemporary Art in Los Angeles, and California's Beverly Hills Hotel. The company, founded in 1912 by Henry Beck, is owned by the group's managing directors.

EXECUTIVES

CEO and Managing Director; President, Beck Internacional de Mexico: Lawrence A. (Larry) Wilson, age 68
CFO and Managing Director: Patricia P. (Pat) Priest, age 52
COO, Managing Director, and Director: Henry C. (Peter) Beck III
Managing Director, Architecture: Rick del Monte
Managing Director, Realty: Charlie Shelby Jr.
Managing Director, Marketing: Kip Daniel
Marketing Manager: Kent Foster
Director Business Development, Calfiornia: Adrienne Gill
Chief Human Resources Officer: Mark House
Marketing Coordinator: Laura Moyer
Auditors: PricewaterhouseCoopers

LOCATIONS

HQ: The Beck Group
1807 Ross Ave., Ste. 500, Dallas, TX 75201
Phone: 214-303-6200   **Fax:** 214-303-6300
Web: www.beckgroup.com

The Beck Group has offices in Atlanta; Austin, Dallas, Fort Worth, and San Antonio, Texas; Denver; Pasadena and Pleasanton, California; Phoenix; and Tampa, Florida. It also has an office in Mexico City.

COMPETITORS

Austin Industries	Hoffman Corporation
Black & Veatch	Hunt Construction
Centex	Kitchell Corporation
Dick Corporation	McCarthy Building
DPR Construction	Perini
Fluor	Peter Kiewit Sons'
Gilbane	Rudolph & Sletten
Hardin Construction	Skanska USA Building
Hathaway Dinwiddie Construction	Swinerton
	Turner Corporation
Hensel Phelps Construction	Whiting-Turner

HISTORICAL FINANCIALS

Company Type: Private

Income Statement
FYE: December 31

	REVENUE ($ mil.)	NET INCOME ($ mil.)	NET PROFIT MARGIN	EMPLOYEES
3/03*	620	—	—	560
12/02	543	—	—	560
12/01	732	—	—	650
12/00	990	—	—	710
12/99	584	—	—	560
12/98	560	—	—	460
12/97	478	—	—	425
12/96	324	—	—	330
12/95	224	—	—	520
12/94	236	—	—	500
Annual Growth	11.3%	—	—	1.3%

*Fiscal year change

Revenue History

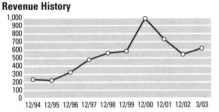

Belk

Belk has shed a lot of bulk. Now a relatively svelte 220-plus-store retailer operating in 13 states, the chain was a confederation of 112 separate companies, formed over the past century, before its 1998 reorganization. Belk stores, located in the Southeast and Mid-Atlantic (primarily in the Carolinas and Georgia), offer mid-priced brand-name and private-label apparel, shoes, cosmetics, gifts, and home furnishings. Its stores usually anchor malls or shopping centers in small to medium-sized markets. The Belk family runs the show and owns most of the company, which is the largest privately owned department store chain in the US.

Larger Belk stores may also contain hair salons, restaurants, and optical centers. In 2003 the company opened eight new stores and completed the renovation of four existing stores. Belk plans to open 14 new stores in 2004. Its first store in Missouri is set to debut in the spring of 2006. Belk is focusing its expansion efforts in medium-sized markets.

While some might say a public offering is the logical next step, former chairman and octogenarian John Belk vowed that would never happen while he is alive. The Belk brood has not always brimmed with brotherly love, but there is no need to call in Richard Dawson to settle the Belk family feud.

After serving over 50 years as the company's CEO and close to 25 years as chairman, John Belk retired in May 2004. Nephew Tim Belk was named the new chairman and CEO, and his brothers McKay and Johnny were promoted to co-presidents of the company.

HISTORY

William Henry Belk didn't mind being known as a cheapskate. At 26 he opened his first store, New York Racket, in 1888 in Monroe, North Carolina. He nicknamed the tiny shop "The Cheapest Store on Earth" and created the slogan "Cheap Goods Sell Themselves." In 1891 Belk convinced his brother John to give up a career as a doctor and join him in the retail business.

The new company, Belk Brothers, opened stores in North and South Carolina, often with partners who were family members or former employees, resulting in many two-family store names such as Belk-Harry and Hudson-Belk.

The Belks formed a partnership with the Leggett family (John's in-laws) in 1920. But feuding between the two families led to a split in 1927. The Leggetts agreed that the Belk family could keep a 20% share of the Leggett stores. John died the next year.

A strict no-credit policy worked in William's favor during the Depression, when he was able to buy out his more lenient competitors for rock-bottom prices. The shrewd businessman grew the chain from 29 stores in 1929 to about 220 stores by 1945, employing concepts such as a no-haggling policy and easy returns. William died in 1952.

That year one of his six children, William Henry Jr., opened a Belk-Lindsey store in Florida using a new format that featured, among other things, an Oriental design. Most of his siblings balked at the store's new look, but William Jr. opened another store in 1953 following the same format.

Two years later four of William Jr.'s siblings — John, Irwin, Tom, and Sarah — cut ties with the Florida stores and formed Belk Stores Services to organize their other stores. Angry at the rebuke, William Jr. and another brother, Henderson, sued the rest of the family, but they later dropped the lawsuit. In 1956 Belk Stores, with John at the helm, bought out 50-store rival chain Effird.

John had political ambitions and was elected mayor of Charlotte, North Carolina, in 1969, despite attempts by his brother William Jr. to foil the campaign. He remained mayor until 1977. Tom became the company's president in 1980.

Belk Stores continued to hold its own in the 1980s against larger department store chains on the prowl for acquisitions, but the company was stung by family discord and a loose ownership structure. Some relatives sold Belk stores to competitors such as Proffitt's (now Saks Inc.) and Dillard's. Irwin and his family, discouraged about the company's direction, sold their stock to John. In 1996 the Leggetts came back into the fold when Belk Stores bought out their 30-store chain.

Tom died in 1997 after complications from gall bladder surgery. His three sons, Tim, Johnny, and McKay, stepped up as co-presidents but continued to answer to their uncle John, the CEO. Also in 1997 Belk Stores closed its struggling 13 Tags off-price outlets.

A year later the firm reorganized and brought all 112 separate corporations under one company, streamlining the company's accounting (previously it had to fill out tax forms for all 112 businesses) and other operations. Soon after, Belk consolidated its 13 divisional offices into four regional units. Also in 1998 it traded several store locations with Dillard's.

In 1999 Belk formed Belk National Bank in Georgia to manage its credit card operations. The company closed four of its distribution centers in 2001, consolidating their operations into its new Blythewood, South Carolina center.

The company opened nine new department stores in 2002 and shut down two others. In 2003 it opened eight stores and completed major renovation on four existing stores.

EXECUTIVES

Chairman and CEO: Thomas M. (Tim) Belk Jr., age 49, $1,047,835 pay
Vice Chairman: B. Frank Matthews II, age 76
Co-President, COO, and Director:
 John R. (Johnny) Belk, age 45, $1,047,835 pay
Co-President, Chief Merchandising Officer, and Director: H. W. McKay Belk, age 47, $1,047,835 pay
EVP, Finance: Brian T. Marley, age 46
EVP, General Counsel and Secretary: Ralph A. Pitts, age 49, $774,549 pay
EVP, Human Resources: Stephen J. Pernotto
EVP, Systems: Robert K. (Roddy) Kerr Jr., age 53
SVP and Controller: Edward J. Record, age 35
President, Merchandising and Marketing: Mary R. Delk, age 53
Auditors: KPMG LLP

LOCATIONS

HQ: Belk, Inc.
 2801 W. Tyvola Rd., Charlotte, NC 28217
Phone: 704-357-1000   **Fax:** 704-357-1876
Web: www.belk.com

2004 Stores

	No.
North Carolina	75
Georgia	40
South Carolina	37
Florida	20
Virginia	19
Tennessee	7
Arkansas	5
Alabama	4
Kentucky	4
Texas	4
Maryland	2
Mississippi	2
West Virginia	2
Total	**221**

PRODUCTS/OPERATIONS

Private Labels
Home Accents
J.Khaki
Kim Rogers
Madison Studio
Meeting Street
Saddlebred

COMPETITORS

Dillard's
Elder-Beerman Stores
Federated
J. C. Penney
Kohl's
May
Saks Inc.
Sears
Stein Mart
Target
TJX Companies
Wal-Mart

Bellco Health

HISTORICAL FINANCIALS
Company Type: Private

Income Statement				FYE: Saturday closest to January 31
	REVENUE ($ mil.)	NET INCOME ($ mil.)	NET PROFIT MARGIN	EMPLOYEES
1/04	2,265	112	4.9%	17,200
1/03	2,242	84	3.7%	17,800
1/02	2,243	63	2.8%	18,500
1/01	2,270	57	2.5%	21,000
1/00	2,145	71	3.3%	21,000
1/99	2,091	57	2.7%	22,000
1/98	1,974	54	2.8%	29,000
1/97	1,773	101	5.7%	25,000
1/96	1,686	44	2.6%	—
1/95	1,694	49	2.9%	—
Annual Growth	3.3%	9.7%	—	(5.2%)

2004 Year-End Financials
Debt ratio: 31.0%
Return on equity: 11.6%
Cash ($ mil.): 166
Current ratio: 3.24
Long-term debt ($ mil.): 301

Net Income History

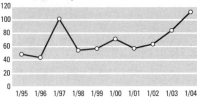

Bellco Health is no baby. The company operates through three divisions. Its Bellco Drug division is an independent drug distributor selling primarily to pharmacies and retailers on Long Island and in New York City. The company distributes various name-brand and generic pharmaceutical products, as well as over-the-counter drugs and sundries. Its American Medical Distributors division sells professional products to specialty clinics and physicians. The company's third division, Dialysis Purchasing Alliance, is a group purchasing organization focusing on dialysis equipment and supplies. The Schuss family, which founded Bellco in 1955, owns the company.

EXECUTIVES
Chairman: Eric Schuss
CEO: Neal Goldstein
President and CFO: Vincent Russo

LOCATIONS
HQ: Bellco Health Corp.
5500 New Horizons Blvd.,
North Amityville, NY 11701
Phone: 631-789-6300 **Fax:** 631-841-6185
Web: www.bellcohealth.com

COMPETITORS
AmerisourceBergen
Cardinal Health
Caremark
McKesson
Quality King

Ben E. Keith

HISTORICAL FINANCIALS
Company Type: Private

Income Statement				FYE: June 30
	REVENUE ($ mil.)	NET INCOME ($ mil.)	NET PROFIT MARGIN	EMPLOYEES
6/02	1,050	—	—	185
6/01	775	—	—	156
6/00	659	—	—	215
6/99	560	—	—	145
6/98	462	—	—	145
6/97	345	—	—	100
6/96	210	—	—	—
Annual Growth	30.8%	—	—	13.1%

Revenue History

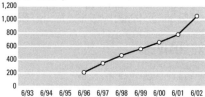

Ben E. Keith is your bud if you like eating out and drinking brew. The firm delivers a full line of foods (produce, dry groceries, frozen food, meat), paper goods, equipment, and supplies to more than 12,000 customers in Arkansas, Kansas, Louisiana, New Mexico, Oklahoma, and Texas. It is one of the world's largest Anheuser-Busch distributors, delivering beer in some 50 Texas counties. Ben E. Keith's customers include restaurants, hospitals, schools, and other institutional businesses. Founded in 1906 as Harkrider-Morrison, the company assumed its current name in 1931 in honor of Benjamin Ellington Keith, who served as the firm's president until 1959. Its owners include executives Robert and Howard Hallam.

EXECUTIVES
Chairman and CEO: Robert Hallam
President and COO: Howard Hallam
CFO: Mel Cockrell
President, Ben E. Keith Beers: Kevin Bartholomew
President, Ben E. Keith Foods: Mike Roach
VP, Produce and Training, Ben E. Keith Foods: Floyd Warner
Corporate Secretary and General Counsel: David Greenlee
Director of Human Resources: Sam Reeves
General Manager, Ben E. Keith Foods, Amarillo: Jeff Yarber
General Manager, Ben E. Keith Foods, Oklahoma Division: Kirk Purnell
District Sales Representative, Ben E. Keith Foods, San Antonio: Bob Daniels

LOCATIONS
HQ: Ben E. Keith Company
601 E. 7th St., Fort Worth, TX 76102
Phone: 817-877-5700 **Fax:** 817-338-1701
Web: www.benekeith.com/main.html

COMPETITORS
Gambrinus
MBM
McLane Foodservice
Morrison Management Specialists
Southern Wine & Spirits
SYSCO
U.S. Foodservice

HISTORICAL FINANCIALS
Company Type: Private

Income Statement				FYE: June 30
	REVENUE ($ mil.)	NET INCOME ($ mil.)	NET PROFIT MARGIN	EMPLOYEES
6/03	1,335	—	—	2,618
6/02	1,185	—	—	2,526
6/01	1,068	—	—	2,347
6/00	959	—	—	2,160
6/99	787	—	—	2,000
6/98	682	—	—	1,800
6/97	630	—	—	1,626
6/96	580	—	—	1,600
6/95	542	—	—	1,513
6/94	513	—	—	1,446
Annual Growth	11.2%	—	—	6.8%

Revenue History

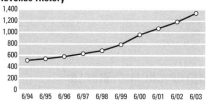

Berwind

Berwind Group isn't workin' in a coal mine anymore. Founded in 1874 to mine Appalachian coal, the firm began leasing its mining operations in 1962 to fund investments in new ventures. Berwind Group gives autonomy to the management teams of its portfolio companies while adding investment fuel to their financial fires. Berwind Property Group owns some $2 billion in commercial, retail, and residential real estate nationwide; Berwind Natural Resources and Berwind Pharmaceutical Services round out the group's operations. The firm sold its financial services and investment banking operations in 2002. The Berwind family owns the company.

The firm has unloaded its investments in Synventive Molding Solutions (plastics) and Zymark Corporation (scientific laboratory automation products), and has acquired glue manufacturer Elmer's Products from Kohlberg Kravis Roberts.

EXECUTIVES

President and CEO: James L. Hamling
CFO: Van Billet, age 50
Director, Human Resources: Catherine Warrin

LOCATIONS

HQ: Berwind Group
3000 Centre Square West, 1500 Market St.,
Philadelphia, PA 19102
Phone: 215-563-2800 **Fax:** 215-563-8347
Web: www.berwind.com

PRODUCTS/OPERATIONS

Selected Operations

Berwind Natural Resources Corp. (land and resource management)
Berwind Pharmaceutical Services, Inc. (pharmaceutical and biotechnology products and services)
Berwind Property Group, Inc. (real estate investment management)
CRC Industries, Inc. (specialty chemical products)
Eureka Growth Capital (investment firm targeting small and mid-sized businesses)
Hunt Corporation (manufacturer and marketer of office supplies and art and framing products)
Perfect Equipment Company, LLC (wheel-balancing weights)
Venture Measurement Company, LLC (instrumentation products)

COMPETITORS

Bosch
Dover
Dow Chemical
DuPont
FMC
Illinois Tool Works
Ingersoll-Rand
Sanofi-Aventis
W.W. Grainger

HISTORICAL FINANCIALS

Company Type: Private

Income Statement
FYE: December 31

	ESTIMATED REVENUE ($ mil.)	NET INCOME ($ mil.)	NET PROFIT MARGIN	EMPLOYEES
12/03	1,000	—	—	3,500
12/02	1,000	—	—	3,500
12/01	1,000	—	—	7,500
12/00	850	—	—	4,150
12/99	1,000	—	—	7,500
12/98	1,300	—	—	4,800
12/97	1,156	—	—	4,500
12/96	850	—	—	5,000
12/95	725	—	—	5,000
12/94	654	—	—	4,000
Annual Growth	4.8%	—	—	(1.5%)

Revenue History

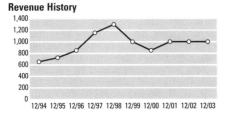

Big Y Foods

Why call it Big Y? Big Y Foods began as a 900-sq.-ft. grocery at a Y intersection in Chicopee, Massachusetts. It now operates about 50 supermarkets in Massachusetts and Connecticut. More than half its stores are Big Y World Class Markets, offering specialty areas such as bakeries and floral shops, as well as banking. The rest consist of Big Y Supermarkets and two gourmet food and wine stores (Table & Vine, Town & Country). Some Big Y stores provide child care, dry cleaning, photo processing, and even propane sales, and their delis and Food Courts offer to-go foods. Big Y is owned and run by the D'Amour family; Paul D'Amour bought the original store in 1936 and was quickly joined by teenage brother Gerald.

EXECUTIVES

Chairman and CEO: Donald H. D'Amour
EVP and COO: Charles L. D'Amour
SVP, CFO: Herbert T. (Herb) Dotterer
SVP, Merchandising: Daniel (Dan) Lescoe
VP, Center Store: Phill Schneider
VP, Corporate Communications:
Claire H. D'Amour-Daley
VP, Employee Services: Jack Henry
VP, Information Systems: John N. Sarno
VP, Store Operations: David Brunelle
VP, Real Estate and Development: Peter J. Thomas
Director, Labor Planning: Jim Killian
Auditors: Deloitte & Touche LLP

LOCATIONS

HQ: Big Y Foods, Inc.
2145 Roosevelt Ave., Springfield, MA 01102
Phone: 413-784-0600 **Fax:** 413-732-7350
Web: www.bigy.com

PRODUCTS/OPERATIONS

Selected Products and Services
Babysitting
Bakery
Banking
Bottle redemption
Coin sorting and counting
Deli
Dry cleaning
Florist
General merchandise
Gourmet food
Knife sharpening
Liquor
Lottery tickets
Meat
Money orders
Phone cards
Photo processing
Postage stamps
Poultry
Produce
Propane
Seafood
Sushi
Western Union
Wine

COMPETITORS

Cumberland Farms
DeMoulas Super Markets
Golub
Hannaford Bros.
Shaw's
Stop & Shop
SUPERVALU
Wal-Mart

HISTORICAL FINANCIALS

Company Type: Private

Income Statement
FYE: June 30

	REVENUE ($ mil.)	NET INCOME ($ mil.)	NET PROFIT MARGIN	EMPLOYEES
6/03	1,190	—	—	8,500
6/02	1,200	—	—	7,850
6/01	1,200	—	—	7,800
6/00	1,083	—	—	7,600
6/99	1,010	—	—	7,000
6/98	1,009	—	—	7,200
6/97	914	—	—	7,173
6/96	789	—	—	6,253
6/95	735	—	—	3,940
6/94	630	—	—	3,305
Annual Growth	7.3%	—	—	11.1%

Revenue History

Bill & Melinda Gates Foundation

You don't have to be one of the richest men in the world to attract attention to your charitable foundation, but it doesn't hurt. Established in 1994, The William H. Gates Foundation was thrust into the spotlight in 1999 after receiving more than $2 billion from Microsoft chairman and foundation namesake Bill Gates. Later that year it combined with affiliate Gates Learning Foundation to form the Bill & Melinda Gates Foundation. Its contributions fund work in the areas of world health (vaccine research) and education; it also supports community service initiatives in the Pacific Northwest. William Gates Sr. runs the foundation, which is the largest in the US, with an endowment of about $27 billion.

The foundation also has the Gates Millennium Scholars Program, which plans to provide scholarships to minority students over the next 20 years. Gates has said he would like to give away most of his fortune while he is still living.

HISTORY

Bill Gates created the William H. Gates Foundation in 1994 with $106 million. During the next four years, he added about $2 billion to the charity. He appointed his father the head of the foundation, and the foundation at first was housed in Bill Gates Sr.'s basement. In 1997 Gates established the Gates Learning Foundation (originally called the Gates Library Foundation), a philanthropic effort to improve library systems. It was

Gates' goal to improve technology and Internet access at libraries, which some critics saw as a way for him to plant Microsoft software at libraries nationwide. Patty Stonesifer, a former executive at Microsoft, ran the organization from an office above a pizza parlor.

Bill and his wife Melinda contributed some $16 billion to the foundation in 1999. That year Gates decided to merge his two charity programs into one entity: the Bill & Melinda Gates Foundation, to be run by the elder Gates and Stonesifer.

In early 2000 Gates made another $5 billion gift of stock to the foundation. That year a federal judge ordered that Microsoft be split up — the effect, if any, on the foundation is unclear. (Most of its donations come in the form of stock that is then converted to cash.) In 2000 the foundation pledged $10 million toward construction of an underground visitors center at Capitol Hill in Washington, DC. The Bill & Melinda Gates Foundation donated another $10 million in 2001 to be awarded over three years to the Hope for African Children Initiative, which will help African children affected by AIDS. In 2002 the Bill & Melinda Gates Foundation pledged more than $100 million over 10 years to reduce the spread of AIDS in India. The foundation awarded a $70 million grant to the departments of genome sciences and bioengineering at the University of Washington in 2003.

EXECUTIVES

Co-Chair: William H. (Bill) Gates III, age 48
Co-Chair and President: Patricia Q. (Patty) Stonesifer, age 47
COO and Executive Director: Sylvia Mathews, age 38
Executive Director, Education: Tom Vander Ark
Executive Director, Global Health: Richard D. Klausner
CFO and Chief Administrative Officer: Allan C. Golston
Program Director, Pacific Northwest Giving: Greg Shaw
Auditors: KPMG LLP

LOCATIONS

HQ: Bill & Melinda Gates Foundation
1551 Eastlake Ave. East, Seattle, WA 98102
Phone: 206-709-3100   **Fax:** 206-709-3180
Web: www.gatesfoundation.org

PRODUCTS/OPERATIONS

Selected Beneficiaries
Alliance for Cervical Cancer Prevention ($3.9 million over two years)
Gay City Health Project ($30,000 over three years)
Global Health Council ($4.8 million over three years)
Helen Keller International ($5 million over five years)
International Planned Parenthood Federation ($8.8 million over five years)
International Tuberculosis Foundation ($1.9 million over five years)
International Vaccine Institute ($40 million over five years)
Library and Information Commission ($4.2 million over one year)
National Institute of Child Health and Human Development ($15 million over five years)
Oxfam ($2.9 million over four years)
Pacific Institute for Women's Health ($1 million over three years)
Population Council ($4 million over two years)
Portland Children's Museum ($600,000 over three years)
United Negro College Fund ($1 billion over 20 years)
US Fund for UNICEF ($15 million over five years)

HISTORICAL FINANCIALS

Company Type: Foundation

Income Statement
FYE: December 31

	REVENUE ($ mil.)	NET INCOME ($ mil.)	NET PROFIT MARGIN	EMPLOYEES
12/03	4,010	—	—	184
12/02	2,048	—	—	—
12/01	1,182	—	—	—
12/00	304	—	—	6
12/99*	276	—	—	4
3/98	128	—	—	2
Annual Growth	99.3%	—	—	147.0%

*Fiscal year change

Revenue History

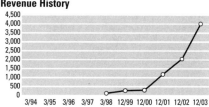

Bill Blass

Bill Blass' signature has marked sophisticated styles for over three decades. His namesake company makes tailored men's and women's clothing known to adorn the upper crust from Barbara Bush to Barbra Streisand. Blass started the company in 1970 and made a name for himself with timeless, tailored designs using fine fabrics. Never yielding to trendy looks such as disco or grunge, the Bill Blass name has acquired a loyal fashion following. Most sales come from more than 40 licenses for items such as furniture, eyewear, and accessories. Blass, who retired in 2000 and died in 2002, sold the firm in 1999 to its jeanswear licensee, Resource Club, and Michael Groveman (CEO).

EXECUTIVES

Co-Chairman: Haresh T. Tharani
Co-Chairman, President, and CEO: Michael Groveman
Controller: Ronald Fetzer, age 40
Design Director: Michael Vollbracht
Director, Licensing: Sheila Marks
Licensing Coordinator: Jean-Claude Huon

LOCATIONS

HQ: Bill Blass Ltd.
550 7th Ave., 12th Fl., New York, NY 10018
Phone: 212-221-6660   **Fax:** 212-302-5166

COMPETITORS

AnnTaylor
Armani
Bernard Chaus
Calvin Klein
Chanel
Christian Dior
Donna Karan
Ellen Tracy
Halston
Jones Apparel
St. John Knits

HISTORICAL FINANCIALS

Company Type: Private

Income Statement
FYE: December 31

	ESTIMATED REVENUE ($ mil.)	NET INCOME ($ mil.)	NET PROFIT MARGIN	EMPLOYEES
12/00*	775	—	—	45
12/99	760	—	—	40
12/98	800	—	—	40
Annual Growth	(1.6%)	—	—	6.1%

*Most recent year available

Revenue History

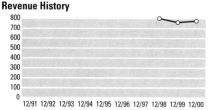

Bill Heard

The Southern hills (and Western deserts) are alive with the sound of Chevys — music to the ears of Bill Heard Enterprises. The nation's leading chain of Chevrolet franchises, Bill Heard has more than 15 dealerships in Alabama, Arizona, Florida, Georgia, Nevada, Tennessee, and Texas. The dealer sells both new and used vehicles and auto supplies and offers repair services; it also owns Oldsmobile and Cadillac franchises in Georgia. William Heard Sr. opened his first dealership in 1919. He switched to selling Chevrolets exclusively in 1932, and his son and grandsons, who now run the family-owned business, continue to focus on Chevy sales.

EXECUTIVES

CEO: William T. Heard
CFO: Ronald A. (Ron) Feldner
Corporate Services Administrator: Jim Matthews
Corporate Accountant: Karen Glisson

LOCATIONS

HQ: Bill Heard Enterprises
200 Brookstone Center Pkwy., Ste. 205, Columbus, GA 31904
Phone: 706-323-1111   **Fax:** 706-321-9488
Web: www.billheard.com

COMPETITORS

AutoNation
CarMax
Charlie Thomas Dealer Group
Gulf States Toyota
Hendrick Automotive
JM Family Enterprises
McCombs Enterprises
Morse Operations
United Auto Group

Birds Eye Foods

Whether from a bird's eye or with eyes on the bottom line, the view is excellent at Birds Eye Foods (formerly Agrilink Foods). As the #1 US maker of store-brand frozen vegetables, company brands include Freshlike, McKenzie's and its flagship brand Birds Eye. The company also makes pie fillings, chili and chili ingredients, salad dressings, and salty snacks. In addition, it produces private-label, food service, and industrial market foods. In 2002 Vestar Holdings acquired control of Birds Eye from Pro-Fac Cooperative. Vestar holds approximately 99% of Birds Eye.

The company has production facilities across the US. Its brands include Comstock and Wilderness canned pie fillings; Brooks and Nalley chili and chili ingredients; Bernstein's salad dressings; and Husman's, Tim's, and Snyder of Berlin snacks. Its Birds Eye brands include Birds Eye Voila! and Birds Eye Simply Grillin'. The Birds Eye brands were named after company founder Clarence Birdseye. The company's name change reflected the company's high visibility of, and continued success with, its Birdseye brands.

Birds Eye's private label and industrial products include frozen vegetables, salad dressings, salsa, fruit fillings and toppings, and frozen vegetable specialty products.

In a move to concentrate on its frozen vegetables, in 2003 the company sold its applesauce business to Knouse Foods and its popcorn business to Gilster-Mary Lee. Also that year, Birds Eye sold its Veg-All canned vegetable unit to Arkansas-based Allen Canning Company for an undisclosed amount. In 2004 the company exited the canned vegetable business entirely with the sale of its Freshlike operations to Allen. Moving into the West Coast market, in 2004 Birds Eye acquired California & Washington Company (C&W), a frozen vegetable and fruit firm based in San Francisco.

EXECUTIVES

Chairman, President, and CEO: Dennis M. Mullen, age 50, $820,000 pay
EVP, Finance, CFO, and Secretary: Earl L. Powers, age 60, $426,473 pay
EVP, Operations: Carl W. Caughran, age 51, $394,000 pay
EVP, Sales, Marketing, and Business Development: David E. (Dave) Hogberg, age 51, $421,244 pay
SVP, Retail Sales: Robert Montgomery
VP, Commodity Management: Paul DeGenova
VP, Corporate Communications: Bea Slizewski
VP, Human Resources: Lois Warlick-Jarvie
VP, Marketing: Randy Zeno
VP and Controller: Linda Nelson
Auditors: PricewaterhouseCoopers LLP

LOCATIONS

HQ: Birds Eye Foods, Inc.
90 Linden Oaks, Rochester, NY 14602
Phone: 585-383-1850 **Fax:** 585-385-2857
Web: www.birdseyefoods.com

PRODUCTS/OPERATIONS

2004 Sales

	$ mil.	% of total
Branded Frozen	334.0	40
Non-Branded	307.0	36
Branded Dry	202.4	24
Total	**843.4**	**100**

Selected Brands

Bernstein's
Birds Eye
Brooks
Chill-Ripe
Comstock
Flavor Destinations
Freshlike
Globe
Gold King
Greenwood
Hearty Spoonfuls
Husman
La Restaurante
McKenzie's
Naturally Good
Pixie
Riviera
Simply Grillin'
Snyder of Berlin
Southern Farms
Southland
Tim's Cascade Style Potato Chips
Wilderness

COMPETITORS

Chiquita Brands
ConAgra
Del Monte Foods
Dole Food
Fyffes
General Mills
Hanover Foods
JR Simplot
Kraft Foods
Michael Foods
Nestlé
Ocean Spray
Seneca Foods
Unilever

HISTORICAL FINANCIALS

Company Type: Private

Income Statement
FYE: December 31

	ESTIMATED REVENUE ($ mil.)	NET INCOME ($ mil.)	NET PROFIT MARGIN	EMPLOYEES
12/03	2,279	—	—	3,500
12/02	2,411	—	—	4,000
12/01	2,600	—	—	4,000
12/00	1,796	—	—	3,100
12/99	1,433	—	—	3,100
12/98	1,200	—	—	2,000
12/97	1,100	—	—	2,000
12/96	950	—	—	1,800
12/95	875	—	—	1,600
12/94	800	—	—	1,600
Annual Growth	12.3%	—	—	9.1%

Revenue History

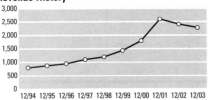

BJC HealthCare

BJC HealthCare brings Jews and Christians together for the good of its patients. The system operates about a dozen hospitals — including Barnes-Jewish Hospital and Christian Hospital — and about 100 primary care and home health facilities in and around St. Louis. BJC HealthCare's facilities have more than 4,300 beds. Specialized services include hospice care, along with long-term care and about half a dozen nursing homes. The company's BarnesCare and OccuMed subsidiaries offer occupational health and workers' compensation services. BJC HealthCare is affiliated with Washington University Medical Center.

After a long, contentious battle with rival SSM Health Care System, the hospital operator in March 2004 won approval to build a new hospital in O'Fallon, one of Missouri's fastest growing cities.

BJC HealthCare is the product of the 1993 merger of Barnes-Jewish, Inc. and Christian Health System.

EXECUTIVES

Chairman: John Dubinsky
President and CEO: Steven H. Lipstein
Senior Executive Officer; President, Barnes-Jewish Hospital: Ronald G. Evens
Senior Executive Officer; President, Boone Hospital Center: Michael B. Shirk
Senior Executive Officer; President, St. Louis Children's Hospital: Lee F. Fetter

HISTORICAL FINANCIALS

Company Type: Private

Income Statement
FYE: Last Saturday in June

	REVENUE ($ mil.)	NET INCOME ($ mil.)	NET PROFIT MARGIN	EMPLOYEES
6/04	843	32	3.8%	2,750
6/03	878	21	2.4%	3,200
6/02	1,011	(131)	—	4,000
6/01	1,303	0	0.0%	4,685
6/00	1,183	6	0.5%	5,289
6/99	1,239	17	1.4%	—
6/98	720	17	2.4%	—
Annual Growth	2.7%	11.0%	—	(15.1%)

2004 Year-End Financials

Debt ratio: 131.8% Current ratio: 2.43
Return on equity: 14.0% Long-term debt ($ mil.): 321
Cash ($ mil.): 73

Net Income History

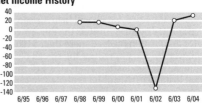

SVP and General Counsel: Michael A. (Mike) DeHaven
VP, Capital Asset Management: Robert W. Cannon
VP and CFO: Patrick Dupuis, age 41
VP, Corporate and Public Communications:
  June McAllister Fowler
VP, Business Development, Planning, and Physician Services: Joan R. Magruder
VP and Chief Human Resources Officer: JoAnn Shaw
VP and CIO: David A. Weiss
Group President: Sandra A. Van Trease, age 43

LOCATIONS
HQ: BJC HealthCare
  4444 Forest Park Ave., St. Louis, MO 63108
Phone: 314-286-2000   **Fax:** 314-286-2060
Web: www.bjc.org

Selected Facilities
Illinois
  Alton Memorial Hospital (Alton)
  Eunice C. Smith Home (Alton)
  Clay County Hospital (Flora)
  Fayette County Hospital (Vandalia)
Missouri
  Boone Hospital Center (Columbia)
  Parkland Health Center (Farmington)
  Village North Manor (Florissant)
  Barnes-Jewish Extended Care (St. Louis)
  Barnes-Jewish Hospital (St. Louis)
  Barnes-Jewish West County Hospital (St. Louis)
  Christian Hospital (St. Louis)
  Missouri Baptist Medical Center (St. Louis)
  St. Louis Children's Hospital
  Barnes-Jewish St. Peters Hospital (St. Peters)
  Missouri Baptist Hospital-Sullivan

COMPETITORS

Alexian Brothers Health System	Sisters of Mercy Health System
Ascension Health	SSM Health Care
Catholic Health Initiatives	Tenet Healthcare
HCA	Universal Health Services

HISTORICAL FINANCIALS
Company Type: Not-for-profit

Income Statement				FYE: December 31
	REVENUE ($ mil.)	NET INCOME ($ mil.)	NET PROFIT MARGIN	EMPLOYEES
12/03	2,500	—	—	25,525
12/02	2,400	—	—	25,993
12/01	2,200	—	—	25,801
12/00	2,100	—	—	26,038
12/99	1,608	—	—	27,071
12/98	1,561	—	—	25,853
12/97	1,587	—	—	25,500
12/96	1,553	—	—	23,696
12/95	1,530	—	—	24,975
12/94	1,413	—	—	—
Annual Growth	6.5%	—	—	0.3%

Revenue History

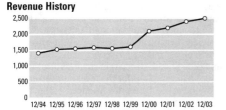

Black & Veatch

From Argentina to Zimbabwe, Black & Veatch provides the ABCs of construction, engineering, and consulting. The international group is one of the largest private companies in the US. Targeting infrastructure development for the energy, water, services, and information markets, the group engages in all phases of building projects, including design and engineering, financing and procurement, and construction. Among its services are environmental consulting, operations and maintenance, security design and consulting, and management consulting. It also offers IT services. Founded in 1915 in Kansas City by engineers E. B. Black and Tom Veatch, the firm is now employee-owned and has more than 90 offices worldwide.

Black & Veatch is involved worldwide in three major market sectors: energy, water, and information. For its part in the energy market, the company claims to have built more gas turbine projects than anyone else in the world. It also says it has been involved in more megawatts of power generation. In addition, it says it is a leader in sulfur recovery and NGL (natural gas liquids) fractionation markets. Supporting those claims is its rankings as one of the top design firms in the power, operations and maintenance, fossil fuel facilities, and transmission and distribution sectors.

The group's operations in the global water markets affect water quality and quantity throughout the water cycle: from source to treatment, to delivery, to wastewater collection and treatment. A key player in water treatment and wastewater treatment design, Black & Veatch's water sector division works with utilities, governments, and industries worldwide. Its expertise has gained it one of the largest design/build/operate contracts in North America for an advanced water treatment plant in Phoenix.

To support its clients' needs for more advanced information technologies and networks, Black & Veatch has an IT division. The company has been involved with the design and construction of wireless, fiber, and integrated networks, as well as mission-critical facilities.

EXECUTIVES
Chairman, President, and CEO:
  Leonard C. (Len) Rodman
Vice Chairman: H. P. Goldfield
EVP and CFO: Karen L. Daniel
EVP, General Counsel, and Secretary:
  G. Christian (Chris) Hedemann
Chief Administrative Officer: Howard G. Withey
Chief Human Resources Officer: Shirley Gaufin
SVP and Treasurer: David E. Kerns
SVP, CTO, and Chief Knowledge Officer:
  John G. Voeller
SVP and Director of Coal Generation Projects: Ron Ott
CIO: Brad Vaughan
VP Brand Management and Communications:
  Corrine Smith
Communications and Media Relations Manager:
  Neal Thurman
Auditors: KPMG LLP

LOCATIONS
HQ: Black & Veatch Holding Company
  8400 Ward Pkwy., Kansas City, MO 64114
Phone: 913-458-2000   **Fax:** 913-458-2934
Web: www.bv.com

Black & Veatch Holding has more than 90 offices worldwide.

PRODUCTS/OPERATIONS
Major Divisions
Energy Sector
  Engineering & Construction
  Energy Services
  Gas, Oil & Chemicals
  Power Delivery
Information Sector
  BV Solutions Group
  Telecommunications
Services Sector
  Construction
  Enterprise Consulting
  Environmental
  US Government
  Startup & Commissioning
  Transportation
Water Sector
  Potable Water
  Research
  Wastewater
  Water Resources

COMPETITORS

AECOM	Malcolm Pirnie
AMEC	McDermott
Bechtel	Michael Baker
Burns and Roe	MWH Global
CH2M HILL	Parsons
EA Engineering	Parsons Brinckerhoff
Fluor	Shaw Group
Foster Wheeler	SNC-Lavalin
Halcrow Group	TIC Holdings
Halliburton	Washington Group
HNTB	Zachry
Louis Berger	

HISTORICAL FINANCIALS
Company Type: Private

Income Statement				FYE: December 31
	REVENUE ($ mil.)	NET INCOME ($ mil.)	NET PROFIT MARGIN	EMPLOYEES
12/03	1,400	—	—	6,200
12/02	2,000	—	—	7,124
12/01	2,224	—	—	8,500
12/00	2,358	—	—	8,500
12/99	2,375	—	—	9,000
12/98	2,100	—	—	9,000
12/97	1,860	—	—	8,000
12/96	1,400	—	—	6,500
12/95	1,102	—	—	4,400
12/94	985	—	—	4,900
Annual Growth	4.0%	—	—	2.6%

Revenue History

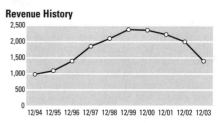

HOOVER'S HANDBOOK OF PRIVATE COMPANIES 2005

Bloomberg

What do you do when you've conquered Wall Street? You become mayor of the city the famous financial district calls home. After leading his financial news and information company to success, founder Michael Bloomberg left Bloomberg to lead the Big Apple. The Bloomberg Professional service's terminals provide real-time, around-the-clock financial news, market data, and analysis. With some 170,000 terminals installed, Bloomberg is among the world's largest providers of such devices. The company also has a syndicated news service; publishes books and magazines; and disseminates business information via TV, radio, and the Web. Michael Bloomberg, inaugurated New York City mayor in 2002, owns about 70% of the company.

Bloomberg serves more than 260,000 customers in more than 125 countries. Although terminals generate most of the company's sales (Bloomberg charges a monthly fee of $1,350 per terminal for multiple system clients), the company distributes financial news and information through many other media channels in an effort to build its brand and keep up with the intense competition. In addition to the company's media products, Bloomberg also offers an order-matching system, the Bloomberg Tradebook. The company's Bloomberg Index License creates and licenses indices to fund managers, stock exchanges, and other clients.

Merrill Lynch also has an ownership stake in the company.

HISTORY

By the mid-1970s Michael Bloomberg had worked his way up to head of equity trading and sales at New York investment powerhouse Salomon Brothers. He left Salomon in 1981, just after the firm went private, cashing out with $10 million for his partnership interest.

Bloomberg founded Innovative Marketing Systems and spent the next year developing the Bloomberg terminal, which allowed users to manipulate bond data. In 1982 he pitched it to Merrill Lynch, which bought 20 machines. Regular production of the terminals began in 1984, and in 1985 Merrill Lynch invested $39 million in the company to gain a 30% stake. The firm prospered during the 1980s boom, and over time the data, not the machines, became the heart of the business, which was renamed Bloomberg L.P. in 1986.

The company weathered the stock market crash of 1987, opening offices in London and Tokyo. Bloomberg made its entry into news-gathering and delivery in 1990 when Bloomberg News began broadcasting on its terminals. The company built its news organization from scratch, hiring away reporters from such publications as *The Wall Street Journal* and *Forbes*. Bloomberg bought a New York radio station in 1992 and converted it to an all-news format. The next year it built an in-house TV studio and created a business news show for PBS. A satellite TV station followed in 1994, along with the *Bloomberg Personal Finance* magazine.

In 1995 Bloomberg began offering business information via its Web site. The company also introduced the Bloomberg Tradebook, an electronic securities-trading venue designed to compete with Reuters' Instinet. (In 1997 Tradebook was approved by the SEC for use in connection with some Nasdaq-listed stocks.) Bloomberg also started offering its services to subscribers in a PC-compatible format and selling its data to other news purveyors, such as LexisNexis (an online information service).

In 1996 the company went further into financial publishing, issuing *Swap Literacy: A Comprehensive Guide* and *A Common Sense Guide to Mutual Funds*. That year Michael Bloomberg bought back 10% of the company from Merrill Lynch for $200 million, giving Bloomberg L.P. an estimated market value of $2 billion. The company agreed in 1997 to supply the daytime programming for Paxson Communications' New York TV station WPXN.

When Bridge Information Systems bought Dow Jones Markets from Dow Jones in 1998, Bridge surpassed Bloomberg in number of financial information terminals installed, bumping Bloomberg from the #2 spot into third place. But Bloomberg continued expanding its offerings through strategic agreements with Internet companies such as America Online and CNET Networks, and through the introduction of new magazines such as *Bloomberg Money* in 1998 as well as *On Investing* and *Bloomberg Wealth Manager* in 1999.

Also in 1999 Bloomberg secured a deal with the Australian stock exchange that would allow its terminals to facilitate international order routing into the Australian market. The company also expanded its presence in the Spanish-language market through its agreement with CBS Telenoticias to produce a TV news program (*Noticiero Financiero*). In 2000 Bloomberg joined with Merrill Lynch to make Merrill Lynch's institutional e-commerce portal available to Bloomberg customers. The company shuttered its *Bloomberg Personal Finance* magazine in early 2003. The next year Bloomberg announced that it would provide financial programming to E! Entertainment Television during the early morning on weekdays in a three-year deal.

EXECUTIVES

Founder: Michael R. (Mike) Bloomberg, age 62
Chairman: Peter T. Grauer, age 58
CEO: Lex Fenwick
Director, Public Relations: Chris Taylor
SVP Media Sales: Michael Rosen
Head, Bloomberg Media and Marketing: David Wachtel
Editor-in-Chief: Matthew Winkler
Global Energy Business Manager: Brad Johnson

LOCATIONS

HQ: Bloomberg L.P.
499 Park Ave., New York, NY 10022
Phone: 212-318-2000   **Fax:** 917-369-5000
Web: www.bloomberg.com

Bloomberg has offices worldwide.

PRODUCTS/OPERATIONS

Selected Products and Services
Bloomberg Custom Publishing Services
Bloomberg Data License (financial database service)
Bloomberg Index License (indices creation and licensing)
Bloomberg Investimenti (financial publication focusing on Italian finance)
Bloomberg Markets (financial magazine)
Bloomberg Money (financial magazine for European investors)
Bloomberg News (syndicated news service)
Bloomberg Portfolio Trading System (asset management tool)
Bloomberg Press (book publishing)
Bloomberg Professional (24-hour, real-time financial information system)
Bloomberg Radio (syndicated radio news service)
Bloomberg Roadshows (presentation service)
Bloomberg Television (24-hour news channel and syndicated reports)
Bloomberg Tradebook (equities trading technology)
Bloomberg Trading System (Bloomberg information combined with trading technology)
Bloomberg Wealth Manager (magazine for financial planners and investment advisers)
Bloomberg.com (Web site)

COMPETITORS

Agence France-Presse	Intuit
Associated Press	MarketWatch
Dow Jones	Media General
FactSet	Reuters
Forbes	TheStreet.com
Interactive Data	Thomson Corporation

HISTORICAL FINANCIALS

Company Type: Private

Income Statement
FYE: December 31

	ESTIMATED REVENUE ($ mil.)	NET INCOME ($ mil.)	NET PROFIT MARGIN	EMPLOYEES
12/03	3,000	—	—	—
12/02	3,000	—	—	8,200
12/01	2,600	—	—	7,200
12/00	2,800	—	—	7,200
12/99	2,300	—	—	5,150
12/98	1,500	—	—	4,900
12/97	1,300	—	—	4,000
12/96	760	—	—	3,000
12/95	650	—	—	2,500
12/94	550	—	—	2,000
Annual Growth	20.7%	—	—	19.3%

Revenue History

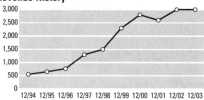

Blue Cross

The rise of managed health care has had some of its members singing the blues, but the Blue Cross and Blue Shield Association still has major market power. The Blue Cross and Blue Shield Association coordinates about 40 chapters that provide health care coverage to nearly 90 million Americans through indemnity insurance, Health Maintenance Organizations (HMOs), preferred provider organizations (PPOs), point-of-service (POS) plans, and fee-for-service plans. Blue Cross and Blue Shield Association chapters also administer Medicare plans for the federal government.

While some Blues always faced competition head-on, most received tax benefits for taking all comers. But as lower-cost plans attracted the hale and hearty, the Blues' customers became older, sicker, and more expensive. With their quasi-charitable status and outdated rate structures, many Blues lost market share.

The Blues have fought back by updating their technology and rate structures, merging among themselves, creating for-profit subsidiaries, forming alliances with for-profit enterprises, or (in some cases) dropping their not-for-profit status and going public — while still using the Blue Cross Blue Shield name. A history of tax breaks complicates these efforts and usually requires the creation of charitable foundations. As a result, the umbrella association is becoming a licensing and brand-marketing entity. The conversion of the Blues to for-profit status is sparking a backlash by consumer organizations and lawmakers due to the rising cost of health care.

The Blues' efforts seem to be paying off as evidenced by increased Blues enrollment and lower administration costs.

HISTORY

Blue Cross was born in 1929, when Baylor University official Justin Kimball offered schoolteachers 21 days of hospital care for $6 a year. A major plan feature was a community rating system that based premiums on the community claims experience rather than members' conditions.

The Blue Cross symbol was devised in 1933 by Minnesota plan executive E. A. van Steenwyck. By 1935 many of the 15 plans in 11 states used the symbol. Many states gave the plans nonprofit status, and in 1936 the American Hospital Association formed the Committee on Hospital Service (renamed the Blue Cross Association in 1948) to coordinate them.

As Blue Cross grew, state medical societies sponsored prepaid plans to cover doctors' fees. In 1946 they united under the aegis of the American Medical Association (AMA) as the Associated Medical Care Plans (later the Association of Blue Shield Plans).

In 1948 the AMA thwarted a Blue Cross attempt to merge with Blue Shield. But the Blues increasingly cooperated on public policy matters while competing for members, and each Blue formed a not-for-profit corporation to coordinate its plan's activities.

By 1960 Blue Cross insured about a third of the US. Over the next decade the Blues started administering Medicare and other government health plans, and by 1970 half of Blue Cross' premiums came from government entities.

In the 1970s the Blues adopted such cost-control measures as review of hospital admissions; many plans even abandoned community rating systems. Most began emphasizing preventive care in HMOs or PPOs. The two Blues finally merged in 1982, but this had little effect on the associations' bottom lines as losses grew.

By the 1990s the Blues were big business. Some of the state associations offered officers high salaries and perks but still insisted on special regulatory treatment.

Blue Cross of California became the first chapter to give up its tax-free status when it was bought by WellPoint Health Networks, a managed care subsidiary it had founded in 1992. In a 1996 deal, WellPoint became the chapter's parent and converted it to for-profit status, assigning all the stock to a public charitable foundation that received the proceeds of its subsequent IPO. WellPoint also bought the group life and health division of Massachusetts Mutual Life Insurance.

The for-profit switches picked up in 1997. Blue Cross of Connecticut merged with insurance provider Anthem, and other mergers followed. Half the nation's Blues formed an alliance called BluesCONNECT, competing with national health plans by offering employers one nationwide benefits organization. The association also pursued overseas licensing agreements in Europe, South America, and Asia, assembling a network of Blue Cross-friendly caregivers aiming for worldwide coverage.

In 1998 Blues in more than 35 states sued the nation's big cigarette companies to recoup costs of treating smoking-related illnesses. In a separate lawsuit, Blue Cross and Blue Shield of Minnesota received nearly $300 million from the tobacco industry. In 1999, Anthem moved to acquire or affiliate with Blues in Colorado, Maine, and New Hampshire.

In 2000, after years of discussions, the New York attorney general permitted Empire Blue Cross and Blue Shield to convert to for-profit status.

In 2003, the Blues had to deal with controversy as former Blues members Anthem and WellPoint announced plans to merge, and become the largest for-profit health insurer in the Nation.

EXECUTIVES

Chairman: Robert L. Shoptaw
President and CEO: Scott P. Serota, $1,307,804 pay
SVP, Corporate Secretary, and General Counsel: Roger G. Wilson
SVP, Strategic Services: Maureen Sullivan
SVP, National Programs: Steve W. Gammarino
SVP, Policy and Representation: Mary Nell Lehnhard
SVP and Chief Medical Officer: Allan M. Korn
VP, Finance and Administration: Ralph Rambach
VP, Human Resources: William (Bill) Colbourne
VP, Deputy General Counsel, and Assistant Corporate Secretary: Paul F. Brown
VP, Plan Programs: Frank Coyne
Chief Information Officer: Robert D. Rosencrans
Executive Director, Branding and Market Intelligence: Kathy Wall
Executive Director, Marketing and Communications: Joe Bogardas
Director, Media Relations: Chris Hamrick
Director, Marketing Support: Wendy Manning
Director, Public Affairs: John Parker
Director, Advertising: Tom Tarr
National Antifraud Director: Byron Hollis
Auditors: PricewaterhouseCoopers LLP

LOCATIONS

HQ: Blue Cross and Blue Shield Association
225 N. Michigan Ave., Chicago, IL 60601
Phone: 312-297-6000 **Fax:** 312-297-6609
Web: www.bcbs.com

The Blue Cross and Blue Shield Association has offices in Chicago and Washington, DC, with licensees operating throughout the US as well as in Africa, Asia, Australia, Canada, Latin America, the Middle East, and Western Europe.

PRODUCTS/OPERATIONS

2003 Health Care Members

	Members (mil.)	% of total
PPO	48.2	54
Traditional Indemnity	17.6	20
HMO	16.6	19
POS (Point of Sale)	6.5	7
Total	**88.9**	**100**

Selected Operations

BlueCard Worldwide (care of US members in foreign countries)
BluesConnect (nationwide alliance)
Federal Employee Health Benefits Program (federal employees and retirees)
Health maintenance organizations
Medicare management
Point-of-service programs
Preferred provider organizations

COMPETITORS

Aetna
CIGNA
Health Net
Humana
Kaiser Foundation
Oxford Health
PacifiCare
Prudential
UniHealth
UnitedHealth Group

HISTORICAL FINANCIALS

Company Type: Association

Income Statement FYE: December 31

	REVENUE ($ mil.)	NET INCOME ($ mil.)	NET PROFIT MARGIN	EMPLOYEES
12/03	182,700	—	—	150,000
12/02	162,800	—	—	150,000
12/01	143,200	—	—	150,000
12/00	126,000	—	—	150,000
12/99	93,700	—	—	150,000
12/98	94,700	—	—	150,000
12/97	76,500	—	—	150,000
12/96	75,200	—	—	150,000
12/95	74,400	—	—	146,000
12/94	71,414	—	—	146,352
Annual Growth	**11.0%**	—	—	**0.3%**

Revenue History

Blue Cross and Blue Shield of Massachusetts

Hobbled by its past, Blue Cross and Blue Shield of Massachusetts has worked its way back into the race. Serving more than 2.4 million members, it offers indemnity insurance, HMOs, preferred provider organizations, and Medicare extension programs. The not-for-profit organization runs HMO Blue, HMO Blue New England, and Blue Choice New England (POS), as well as Medex, a Medicare supplemental plan. Blue Cross and Blue Shield of Massachusetts also teams up with other regional Blues to offer plans HMO Blue New England and Blue Choice New England, which feature discounts at some health clubs.

Blue Cross and Blue Shield of Massachusetts has battled its way back to financial health by selling noncore businesses and reducing staff after spending recent years in the red.

Like Blues nationwide, it has been hit hard by competition. The company is now refocusing on its core business (health insurance) through divestitures and new products. Blue Cross and Blue Shield of Massachusetts also entered the risky business of reinsurance.

HISTORY

The predecessor of the Blue Cross Association was founded in Dallas in 1929 to allow teachers to prepay for hospitalization. The idea spread quickly during the Depression. By 1937, when its 26th affiliate was founded in Massachusetts, the organization had become associated with the Blue Cross logo. Fairly priced by Depression standards, Blue Cross pegged its premiums to care costs in each region rather than underwriting each policyholder or group individually.

Seeing the success of Blue Cross, doctors joined up to offer similar prepayment plans known together as the Blue Shield Association. Doctor participation in Massachusetts was so widespread that members had a nearly unlimited choice of physicians.

Blue Cross and Blue Shield worked almost as one unit in Massachusetts but remained legally separate. At first they limited memberships to groups, but during the 1940s they began accepting individuals. In the 1960s the groups became co-administrators of the state's Medicare program. The Medex program was started in 1966 to supplement Medicare, but later evolved to encompass a state-mandated program for the medically indigent elderly. During the 1970s the companies began creating HMOs, but mostly for rural areas.

The groups continued to dominate Massachusetts health care in the 1980s. By the decade's end, however, the Massachusetts Blues had hit hard times, suffering lost market share, bloated management, and antiquated systems. As Blues in other states merged, competitors repeatedly blocked efforts to join the two Massachusetts organizations. Both Blues lost money from 1986 to 1988.

Efforts to help the situation only made matters worse (a failed upgrade of Blue Cross' information systems was abandoned in 1992 after six years and $100 million). The groups' efforts to drive harder bargains with hospitals led to cries that the plans were trying to force rejected hospitals out of business.

In 1988 the organizations were at last allowed to merge. William Van Faasen became CEO in 1990, charged with reengineering BCBSMA. For five years his efforts seemed to work. But the Medex segment was an earnings vacuum, and the new management drew criticism for hefty pay raises.

Blaming Medex, BCBSMA lost $90 million in 1996, which led the state insurance commissioner to step in and oversee its operations.

To make money like a regular health care company, BCBSMA started acting like a regular health care company — it slashed 16% of its workforce, enforced 10% pay cuts for those executives who survived a year-long purge, sold 10 clinics (to what is now Caremark Rx), and attempted to cancel 7,000 policies.

In 1998 BCBSMA agreed to pay $9.5 million to settle lawsuits that it overcharged Massachusetts subscribers for medical care. It also agreed in 1999 to pay $4.75 million to reimburse the US government for claims paid on people who were actually covered by BCBSMA. In the meantime, it created a new health insurance plan, Access Blue (launched in 2000), that lets patients see specialists without referrals. The plan has met resistance from hospitals and doctors, who consider its premiums too low to be financially viable.

BCBSMA filed to divide its operations into three companies, a move shot down by state legislators in 1998. Meanwhile, for-profit Blues licensees like Anthem continue to buy Blues (including those in Connecticut and New Hampshire). BCBSMA is pursuing affiliation with other not-for-profit regional Blues, although its attempt to do so in Rhode Island was rejected by the state's attorney general. In 2000, BCBSMA got state permission to enter the reinsurance business.

EXECUTIVES

Chairman Emeritus: Milton L. Glass
Chairman and CEO: William C. Van Faasen, age 55
Vice Chairman: Robert J. Haynes
President and COO: Cleve L. Killingsworth Jr., age 51
CFO: Allen P. Maltz
EVP and Chief Legal Officer: Sandra L. Jesse
EVP, Healthcare Services: Sharon L. Smith
EVP, Sales, Marketing, and Services: Stephen R. Booma
EVP, Corporate Affairs: Peter G. Meade
SVP, Corporate Relations: Fredi Shonkoff
SVP, Corporate Planning and Development: Phyllis L. Baron
SVP, Human Resources: Joseph Patrnchak
SVP and Chief Information Officer: Carl J. Ascenzo
Chief Actuary: Bruce W. Butler
Chief Physician Executive: John A. Fallon
Auditors: Ernst & Young LLP

LOCATIONS

HQ: Blue Cross and Blue Shield of Massachusetts, Inc.
LandMark Center, 401 Park Dr., Boston, MA 02215
Phone: 617-246-5000   **Fax:** 617-246-4832
Web: www.bcbsma.com

PRODUCTS/OPERATIONS

Selected Services
Blue Care Elect Preferred (managed care plan)
Blue Choice (managed care plan)
Blue Choice New England (regional managed care)
Comprehensive Major Medical (traditional plan)
Dental Blue
Dental Blue PPO
Direct Blue (nongroup plans)
HMO Blue (statewide managed care)
HMO Blue New England (regional managed care)
Medex (Medicare supplement)

COMPETITORS

Aetna
Anthem
CIGNA
ConnectiCare
Harvard Pilgrim
Prudential
Tufts Health Plan

HISTORICAL FINANCIALS

Company Type: Not-for-profit

Income Statement   FYE: December 31

	REVENUE ($ mil.)	NET INCOME ($ mil.)	NET PROFIT MARGIN	EMPLOYEES
12/03	4,497	265	5.9%	3,545
12/02	4,043	104	2.6%	3,424
12/01	3,725	132	3.5%	3,396
12/00	2,883	110	3.8%	3,045
12/99	2,120	61	2.9%	2,601
12/98	2,041	64	3.1%	2,579
12/97	2,123	13	0.6%	2,756
12/96	3,504	(90)	—	5,500
12/95	3,575	11	0.3%	5,630
12/94	3,595	43	1.2%	5,865
Annual Growth	2.5%	22.4%	—	(5.4%)

2003 Year-End Financials
Debt ratio: 0.0%
Return on equity: 28.5%
Cash ($ mil.): —
Current ratio: —
Long-term debt ($ mil.): 0

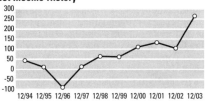

Net Income History

Blue Cross Blue Shield of Michigan

Blue Cross Blue Shield of Michigan is one of the nation's top Blue Cross Blue Shield health insurance associations, serving more than 4.8 million members, including autoworkers for GM and Ford. The company's insurance plans include traditional indemnity, Blue Preferred (PPO), and Blue Care Network (HMO). Blue Cross Blue Shield of Michigan also offers dental, vision, and Medicare supplement coverage, as well as workers' compensation insurance, health assessment, and health care management services. For-profit subsidiary Preferred Provider Organization of Michigan offers private health care management services.

For Blue Cross Blue Shield of Michigan, operating a "profitable" not-for-profit is a constant struggle.

While other Blues have converted to for-profit status or have teamed up with for-profit companies to become more competitive, BCBSM is committed to remaining not-for-profit. Rate hikes have helped get the company's insurance operations back into the black, and it plans to continue raising rates to keep up with the skyrocketing costs of health care.

HISTORY

The history of prepaid medical care began in 1929, when Baylor University Hospital administrator Justin Kimball developed a plan to offer schoolteachers 21 days of hospital care for $6 a year. Fundamental to the plan was a community rating system, which based premiums on the community's claims experience rather than subscribers' conditions.

A similar program was started in Michigan in 1938 when a group of hospitals formed the Michigan Society for Group Hospitalization, which became the Michigan Hospital Service and later became a chapter of the national Blue Cross association. The health care plan was funded by local hospitals and private grants. (A group of private donors, including Oldsmobile automotive founder Ransom Olds, loaned the group $5,000.)

The state insurance commission approved tax-exempt status for the Michigan Blue Cross in 1939. Nine days after opening a three-person office in Detroit, Blue Cross landed its first customer, insurance company John Hancock Mutual Life. John Hancock's Detroit branch manager became the first subscriber, paying $1.90 per month for 21 days of hospitalization coverage for his family of eight.

Due in part to the addition of Chrysler, Ford, and General Motors to its health plans, Blue Cross grew from less than 1 million members in the 1940s to more than 3 million in the 1950s. In 1945 it began to offer coverage for individuals; 14 years later the association started to offer policies to seniors who were ineligible for group coverage. Blue Cross took over operation of Michigan's Medicare program in 1966.

Michigan's Blue Cross merged with longtime partner Blue Shield in 1975 to create Blue Cross Blue Shield of Michigan, with a total of 5 million subscribers. Blue Shield, a prepayment plan that covered doctors' services, had been started in 1939 by the Michigan State Medical Society (a group of Michigan physicians).

As overseas competition forced automakers to cut their employment rolls, Blue Cross Blue Shield of Michigan's membership contracted. BCBSM chairman John McCabe, realizing the need to generate additional revenue, pushed for an end to the company's not-for-profit status in the 1980s but was rejected by the Michigan legislature. This failure was at least partially behind McCabe's resignation in 1987.

The struggling Michigan Blues moved toward profitability in 1994 when the state legislature specially authorized its $291 million purchase of the for-profit State Accident Fund, the state's workers' compensation program. It also lost its large but hard-to-manage state Medicare contract to Blue Cross Blue Shield of Illinois (now Health Care Service Corporation). In 1996 the company reorganized, with a division for Michigan residents and one for nationwide accounts. In 1997 BCBSM continued its efforts to increase revenue by acquiring private health management company Preferred Provider Organization of Michigan, which operates in Michigan and nearby states. BCBSM president and CEO Richard Whitmer announced that he was willing to compete with other Blues in bordering states.

In 1998 Blue Cross Blue Shield of Michigan consolidated four regional HMOs into a single statewide HMO, the Blue Care Network. Costs of the merger and growing losses in drug coverage constrained earnings, but were counterweighted by returns on assets invested in the stock market. In 1999 and 2000 the company rankled Detroit's small business owners with double-digit premium hikes.

EXECUTIVES

Chairman: Greg Sudderth
Vice Chairman: John MacKeigan
President and CEO: Richard E. Whitmer
SVP and CFO: Mark R. Bartlett
SVP and Chief of Staff: Daniel J. Loepp
SVP and Chief Information Officer: William P. Smith
SVP, General Counsel, and Corporate Secretary:
  Lisa S. DeMoss
SVP, Auto/National Business Unit: Leslie A. Viegas
SVP, Health Care Products and Provider Services:
  Marianne Udow
SVP, Human Resources, and Chief Administration Officer: George F. Francis III
SVP, Michigan Sales and Services: J. Paul Austin
SVP, Corporate Communications: Richard T. Cole
VP and Deputy Counsel: Jeffrey P. Rumley
VP and Treasurer: Carolyn Walton
VP, Corporate and Financial Investigations:
  Gregory W. Anderson
VP, Medical Care Management and Provider Inquiry Care Operations: Karen A. Maher
Auditors: Deloitte & Touche LLP

LOCATIONS

HQ: Blue Cross Blue Shield of Michigan
  600 E. Lafayette Blvd., Detroit, MI 48226
Phone: 313-225-9000   **Fax:** 313-225-5629
Web: www.bcbsm.com

PRODUCTS/OPERATIONS

Selected Health Care Plans
Blue Care Network (health maintenance)
Blue Choice (point of service)
Blue MedSave (prescription plan)
Blue Preferred PPO (preferred provider for auto industry workers)
Blue Traditional (prepayment)
Blue Vision PPO
Community Blue PPO
Community Dental
Medicare Blue HMO
Personal Plus HMO
Preferred Rx (prescription plan)
Traditional Dental
Traditional Rx (prescription plan)
Traditional Vision Coverage

COMPETITORS

Aetna
Anthem
CIGNA
Henry Ford Health System
Humana
United American Healthcare
UnitedHealth Group

HISTORICAL FINANCIALS

Company Type: Not-for-profit

Income Statement				FYE: December 31
	REVENUE ($ mil.)	NET INCOME ($ mil.)	NET PROFIT MARGIN	EMPLOYEES
12/03	13,716	368	2.7%	8,500
12/02	12,511	161	1.3%	8,500
12/01	11,883	56	0.5%	8,500
12/00	10,507	65	0.6%	8,500
12/99	9,487	89	0.9%	8,500
12/98	8,432	83	1.0%	8,500
12/97	7,731	43	0.6%	8,827
12/96	7,001	101	1.4%	7,980
12/95	6,926	154	2.2%	6,500
12/94	6,411	71	1.1%	8,415
Annual Growth	8.8%	20.0%	—	0.1%

2003 Year-End Financials
Debt ratio: —   Current ratio: —
Return on equity: —   Long-term debt ($ mil.): —
Cash ($ mil.): 511

Net Income History

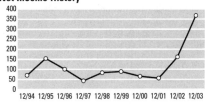

Blue Shield of California

Blue Shield of California (a.k.a. California Physicians' Service) provides health insurance products and related services to more than 2.5 million members in the state of California. The not-for-profit organization's health insurance products include HMO, preferred provider organization (PPO), dental, and a Medicare supplemental plan.

Accidental death and dismemberment, executive medical reimbursement, life insurance, vision, and short-term health plans are provided by the company's Blue Shield of California Life & Health Insurance unit. Blue Shield of California is a Blue Cross and Blue Shield Association member.

A key component of Blue Shield of California's strategy for growth consists of expanding its large group accounts. The company's strategy is paying off as evidenced by its becoming a vendor of CalPERS in 2003.

EXECUTIVES

Chairman, President, and CEO; Chairman, Blue Shield of California Life & Health Insurance:
  Bruce G. Bodaken
EVP and COO: Kenneth F. Wood
EVP and CFO, Blue Shield of California and Blue Shield of California Life & Health Insurance:
  Heidi Kunz, age 49
EVP, Corporate Development: Paul Swenson
SVP and Chief Medical Officer: Eric Book
SVP and Chief Information Officer: David Bowen
SVP; President and CEO, Blue Shield of California Life & Health Insurance: Debra Bowles
SVP, General Counsel, and Corporate Secretary, Blue Shield of California and Blue Shield of California Life & Health Insurance Company: Seth Jacobs
SVP, Network Services: David S. Joyner
SVP and Chief Analytics Officer: Cliff Lange
SVP, Consumer Operations: Bob Novelli
VP, Human Resources, Blue Shield of California and Blue Shield of California Life & Health Insurance:
  Cecily A. Coceo

LOCATIONS

HQ: Blue Shield of California
  50 Beale St., San Francisco, CA 94105
Phone: 415-229-5000   **Fax:** 415-229-5744
Web: www.mylifepath.com

PRODUCTS/OPERATIONS

2003 Membership

	Members	% of total
HMO	1,330,000	50
PPO	1,340,000	50
Total	**2,670,000**	**100**

2003 Sales

	$ mil.	% of total
Dues & premiums	6,125.1	99
Investment & other income	77.6	1
Total	**6,202.7**	**100**

COMPETITORS

Aetna	Kaiser Foundation
CIGNA	PacifiCare
Health Net	WellPoint Health
Health Net of California	Networks

HOOVER'S HANDBOOK OF PRIVATE COMPANIES 2005

HISTORICAL FINANCIALS
Company Type: Not-for-profit

Income Statement				FYE: December 31
	REVENUE ($ mil.)	NET INCOME ($ mil.)	NET PROFIT MARGIN	EMPLOYEES
12/03	6,203	314	5.1%	4,200
12/02	4,624	—	—	4,200
Annual Growth	34.1%	—	—	0.0%

Revenue History

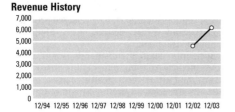

BlueCross BlueShield of Mississippi

BlueCross and BlueShield of Mississippi provides health insurance products and related services to members in Mississippi. The company is the largest health plan provider in Mississippi and is an independent member of the Blue Cross and Blue Shield Association. BlueCross and BlueShield of Mississippi's health plans include HMO, PPO, point-of-service (POS), traditional indemnity, and supplemental Medicare. BlueCross and BlueShield of Mississippi also provides life insurance, third party administration (TPA), and data processing services through its various subsidiaries.

BlueCross and BlueShield of Mississippi has grown by updating its rate structure, developing new health plan products, and enhancing its sales distribution network.

EXECUTIVES
President and CEO: Richard J. (Rick) Hale
CFO: Jeff Leber
EVP: Carol Berry Pigott
VP, Information Services: John Trifone
VP, Marketing: Steve Gregory
VP, Underwriting and Products: John Mansour
VP, Human Resources: John Proctor
Corporate Secretary: Cynthia Gordon
Director, Corporate Communications: John Sewell
Corporate Medical Advisor: Tom Fenter

LOCATIONS
HQ: BlueCross and BlueShield of Mississippi
3545 Lakeland Dr., Jackson, MS 39232
Phone: 601-932-3704   **Fax:** 601-939-7035
Web: www.bcbsms.com

PRODUCTS/OPERATIONS

Selected Subsidiaries
Capstone Corporation
Advanced Health Systems, Inc. (electronic processing services)
Mississippi Insurance Marketing Agency, Inc. (insurance broker)
Employer Benefits Administrator, Inc. (third party administration)
Bluebonnet Life Insurance Company (life insurance)
HMO of Mississippi, Inc.

COMPETITORS
Aetna
CIGNA
UnitedHealth Group

HISTORICAL FINANCIALS
Company Type: Mutual company

Income Statement				FYE: December 31
	REVENUE ($ mil.)	NET INCOME ($ mil.)	NET PROFIT MARGIN	EMPLOYEES
12/03	873	—	—	100
12/02	802	—	—	1,000
Annual Growth	8.9%	—	—	(90.0%)

Revenue History

BMI

The hills may be alive with the sound of music, but all Broadcast Music, Inc. (BMI) hears is "ka-ching!" The not-for-profit organization collects licensing fees from a host of outlets and venues (such as radio stations, TV programs, Web sites, restaurants, and nightclubs) that play the music of the more than 300,000 songwriters, composers, and music publishers it represents. Its catalog of compositions includes more than 4.5 million works by a diverse range of artists including Danny Elfman, Marilyn Manson, Willie Nelson, Sting, and Shania Twain.

Founded in 1940, BMI is working to eliminate online piracy and ensure that its clients get a cut of the proceeds when their music is downloaded on the Internet. The organization monitors music played over the Web and has created a digital licensing center to license music played online.

EXECUTIVES
Chairman: Cecil L. Walker
President and CEO: Del Bryant
President Emeritus: Frances W. Preston
CFO and COO: John Cody
SVP and General Counsel: Marvin Berenson
SVP Government Relations: Fred Cannon
SVP International: Ron Solleveld
SVP Media Licensing: John Shaker
SVP Operations and Information: Robert J. Barone
SVP Performing Rights: Alison Smith
SVP Writer/Publisher Relations: Phillip R. Graham
VP, Controller, and Treasurer: Thomas Curry
VP Business Affairs, Media Licensing: Michael Steinberg, age 38
VP Corporate Relations: Robbin Ahrold
VP General Licensing: Tom Annastas
VP Human Resources: Patricia Wright

LOCATIONS
HQ: Broadcast Music, Inc.
320 W. 57th St., New York, NY 10019
Phone: 212-586-2000   **Fax:** 212-245-8986
Web: www.bmi.com

Broadcast Music, Inc., has offices in Atlanta, London, Los Angeles, Nashville, and New York City.

PRODUCTS/OPERATIONS

Selected BMI Artists
The Beach Boys	Elton John
The Beatles	Kid Rock
Chuck Berry	Little Richard
David Bowie	Marilyn Manson
Brooks & Dunn	Tim McGraw
James Brown	Sarah McLachlan
Dave Brubeck	Moby
Eric Clapton	Willie Nelson
Sheryl Crow	Santana
Dixie Chicks	Sting
Eagles	Shania Twain
Eminem	

COMPETITORS
ASCAP
RIAA
SESAC

HISTORICAL FINANCIALS
Company Type: Not-for-profit

Income Statement				FYE: June 30
	ESTIMATED REVENUE ($ mil.)	NET INCOME ($ mil.)	NET PROFIT MARGIN	EMPLOYEES
6/04	673	—	—	700
6/03	630	—	—	700
6/02	574	—	—	700
6/01	541	—	—	700
6/00	500	—	—	700
6/99	450	—	—	700
6/98	425	—	—	500
6/97	400	—	—	650
6/96	375	—	—	500
6/95	355	—	—	568
Annual Growth	7.4%	—	—	2.3%

Revenue History

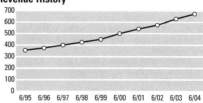

Bob Rohrman Auto

With about 35 dealerships in Indiana and around Chicago, Bob Rohrman Auto Group is after the lion's share of area car sales. The company sells more than 36,000 new and used vehicles annually from its dealerships in Chicago and in Indianapolis, Fort Wayne, and Lafayette, Indiana. Bob Rohrman offers new vehicles from most major auto manufacturers, including Daimler-Chrysler, Ford, Honda, Hyundai, Isuzu, Kia, Mitsubishi, Nissan, and Toyota. It also sells auto parts and offers financing services. Its Web site features an inventory search for new and used cars. President and namesake Bob Rohrman owns the company, which he founded in 1963.

EXECUTIVES
President and CEO: Bob Rohrman
Comptroller and CFO: Tom Hanlan
Director of Fixed Operations: Ryan Turner
Director of Human Resources: Kim Sharp
Director of Operations: Craig Gipson

LOCATIONS
HQ: Bob Rohrman Auto Group
  701 Sagamore Pkwy. South, Lafayette, IN 47905
Phone: 765-448-1000 **Fax:** 765-449-2266
Web: www.rohrman.com

Selected Operations
Chicago Area
  Arlington Acura in Palatine
  Arlington Kia in Palatine
  Arlington Lexus in Palatine
  Arlington Nissan in Buffalo Grove
  Gurnee Hyundai
  Gurnee Oldsmobile
  Gurnee Volkswagen
  Kia of Waukegan
  Libertyville Mitsubishi
  Oakbrook Toyota
  Saturn of Gurnee
  Saturn of Libertyville
  Schaumburg Honda Automobiles
Fort Wayne, Indiana
  Fort Wayne Acura
  Fort Wayne Daewoo
  Fort Wayne Kia
  Fort Wayne Nissan
  Fort Wayne Subaru
  Fort Wayne Toyota
  Infiniti of Fort Wayne
  Lexus of Fort Wayne
Indianapolis
  Indy Honda
  Indy Hyundai
  Indy Isuzu
  Indy Super Store
  Indy Suzuki
Lafayette, Indiana
  Bob Rohrman Collision Center
  Bob Rohrman Daewoo
  Bob Rohrman Honda
  Bob Rohrman Hyundai
  Bob Rohrman Jeep
  Bob Rohrman Kia
  Bob Rohrman Lincoln/Mercury
  Bob Rohrman Mitsubishi
  Bob Rohrman Subaru
  Bob Rorhman Suzuki
  Bob Rohrman Toyota
  Saturn of Lafayette

COMPETITORS
AutoNation
Continental Motors
Jeff Wyler Automotive
Jordan Automotive
Kelley Automotive
Loeber Motors
Motor Werks of Barrington
Patrick Dealer
Rizza Automotive Group
Steve Foley
Wheels
Wolfe Automotive Group

HISTORICAL FINANCIALS
Company Type: Private

Income Statement
FYE: December 31

	REVENUE ($ mil.)	NET INCOME ($ mil.)	NET PROFIT MARGIN	EMPLOYEES
12/03	724	—	—	1,000
12/02	633	—	—	1,000
12/01	694	—	—	1,000
12/00	649	—	—	1,000
12/99	639	—	—	1,000
12/98	509	—	—	900
12/97	494	—	—	1,000
12/96	450	—	—	900
Annual Growth	7.0%	—	—	1.5%

Revenue History

Bon Secours Health

Bon Secours Health System succors the poor and sick. The Roman Catholic health care organization is dedicated to providing health care services to all and is operated by the Sisters of Bon Secours, an international religious order established in 1824 in Paris. Bon Secours Health System is composed of 24 acute-care hospitals, nine long-term-care facilities, and a psychiatric hospital. The organization's facilities are in nine states, primarily on the East Coast. The health care system also operates ambulatory sites, nursing care centers, assisted-living facilities, hospices, and home health care services.

The health system has announced plans to sell two Florida hospitals — St. Joseph Hospital in Port Charlotte and Venice Hospital in Venice — to Health Management Associates.

The system's Detroit-area joint venture, Bon Secours Cottage Health Services, ran afoul of accounting irregularities in early 2004. An audit of the unit revealed it had overstated assets and income for the previous seven years. Bon Secours Cottage Health Services is co-owned by Henry Ford Health System.

EXECUTIVES
Chairperson: Sister Patricia A. Eck
President and CEO: Christopher M. (Chris) Carney, age 57
COO: Stephanie S. McCutcheon
SVP Operations, South Division: Peter J. Bernard
SVP Corporate Services: Edward (Ed) Boyer
SVP Finance and CFO: Michael W. (Mike) Cottrell
SVP Sponsorship: Sister Anne Lutz
SVP Business Development: John T. Shea
SVP Operations, Northeast Division:
  Donald E. (Don) Strange
VP Information Systems and CIO: Skip Hubbard
VP Human Resources: David D. Jones
VP Supply Chain Savings: David McCombs
VP Planning, Marketing, and Communications:
  Peggy Moseley
VP Non Acute Services: Mary Anne Willson
CEO, Bon Secours St. Francis Health System, Greenville, SC: Valinda Rutledge
Director Marketing and Communications: Diana Stager

LOCATIONS
HQ: Bon Secours Health System, Inc.
  1505 Marriottsville Rd., Marriottsville, MD 21104
Phone: 410-442-5511 **Fax:** 410-442-1082
Web: www.bshsi.com

Selected Operations
Florida
  Bon Secours St. Joseph Healthcare Group
  Bon Secours St. Petersburg Health System
  Bon Secours Venice Health Corporation
Kentucky
  Bon Secours Kentucky Health System
Maryland
  Bon Secours Baltimore Health System
Michigan
  Bon Secours Cottage Health Services (80%)
New Jersey
  Bon Secours & Canterbury Partnership for Care
New York
  Bon Secours Charity Health System, Inc.
  Bon Secours New York Health System
Pennsylvania
  Bon Secours Holy Family Regional Health System (Altoona)
South Carolina
  Bon Secours St. Francis Health System, Inc.
  Roper St. Francis Healthcare (Charleston)
Virginia
  Bon Secours Hampton Roads Health System
  Bon Secours Richmond Health System
  Bon Secours St. Mary's Hospital, Inc. (Norton)

COMPETITORS
Carilion Health System
Catholic Health East
Inova
Johns Hopkins Medicine
MedStar Health
North Broward Hospital District
Novant Health
Sentara Healthcare
Trinity Health (Novi)

Bonneville Power

Bonneville Power Administration (BPA) keeps the lights on in the Pacific Northwest. The US Department of Energy power marketing agency operates a 15,000-mile high-voltage transmission grid that delivers about 45% of the electrical power consumed in the region. The electricity that BPA wholesales is generated primarily by 31 federal hydroelectric plants and one private nuclear facility. BPA also purchases power from other hydroelectric, gas-fired, and wind and solar generation facilities in North America. Founded in 1937, the utility sells power primarily to public and investor-owned utilities, as well as some industrial customers.

EXECUTIVES

Administrator and CEO: Stephen J. (Steve) Wright, age 44
Deputy Administrator: Steven G. Hickok
COO: Ruth B. Bennett
EVP, Industry Restructuring: Allen L. Burns
SVP and General Counsel: Randy A. Roach
SVP, Employee and Business Resources: Terence G. (Terry) Esvelt
SVP, Power Business Line: Paul E. Norman
SVP, Transmission Business Line: Mark W. Maher
VP, Finance and CFO: James H. (Jim) Curtis
VP, Environment, Fish, and Wildlife: Therese B. Lamb
VP, Strategic Planning: Pamela J. (Pam) Marshall
VP, National Relations: Jeffrey K. (Jeff) Stier
CIO: Brian Furumasu
Chief Press Officer: Ed Mosey
Chief Risk Officer: Eric Larson
Communications: Dulcy Mahar
Auditors: PricewaterhouseCoopers LLP

LOCATIONS

HQ: Bonneville Power Administration
 905 NE 11th Ave., Portland, OR 97208
Phone: 503-230-3000   **Fax:** 503-230-5884
Web: www.bpa.gov

Bonneville Power Administration carries electricity to California, Idaho, Montana, Nevada, Oregon, Utah, Washington, and Wyoming.

PRODUCTS/OPERATIONS

2003 Sales

	$ mil.	% of total
Power	3,059	85
Transmission	553	15
Total	3,612	100

COMPETITORS

AES	IDACORP
American Electric Power	NW Natural
Avista	PacifiCorp
Black Hills	PG&E
CenterPoint Energy	Portland General Electric
Duke Energy	Puget Energy
Dynegy	Sempra Energy

HISTORICAL FINANCIALS

Company Type: Not-for-profit

Income Statement
FYE: August 31

	REVENUE ($ mil.)	NET INCOME ($ mil.)	NET PROFIT MARGIN	EMPLOYEES
8/03	2,523	—	—	34,512
8/02	2,305	—	—	27,000
8/01	1,998	—	—	20,000
8/00	1,654	—	—	27,000
8/99	1,100	—	—	20,000
8/98	1,190	—	—	20,000
8/97	1,098	—	—	19,000
8/96	761	—	—	19,000
8/95	634	—	—	14,100
8/94	562	—	—	—
Annual Growth	18.2%	—	—	11.8%

Revenue History

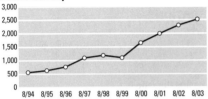

HISTORICAL FINANCIALS

Company Type: Government-owned

Income Statement
FYE: September 30

	REVENUE ($ mil.)	NET INCOME ($ mil.)	NET PROFIT MARGIN	EMPLOYEES
9/03	3,612	555	15.4%	3,121
9/02	3,534	10	0.3%	2,878
9/01	4,279	(169)	—	2,878
9/00	3,041	241	7.9%	2,732
9/99	2,619	123	4.7%	—
9/98	2,313	(49)	—	2,797
9/97	2,273	118	5.2%	2,929
9/96	2,428	96	4.0%	3,152
9/95	2,386	99	4.1%	3,271
9/94	2,196	—	—	—
Annual Growth	5.7%	24.1%	—	(0.6%)

2003 Year-End Financials

Debt ratio: 35.0%
Return on equity: 8.1%
Cash ($ mil.): 503
Current ratio: 1.41
Long-term debt ($ mil.): 2,522

Net Income History

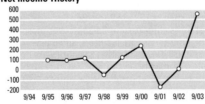

Booz Allen

Consultants at Booz Allen Hamilton serve the needs of big business and big government. One of the world's leading management consulting firms, Booz Allen provides strategic and technology consulting services though nearly 60 offices located around the world. Its commercial sector business provides management consulting and technology integration services to help FORTUNE 500 companies improve their business processes. Booz Allen's government sector business provides similar services for government agencies and organizations, including the Department of Defense and the General Services Administration, as well as foreign governments and institutions. The firm was founded by Edwin Booz in 1914.

One of the largest government prime contractors, Booz Allen has seen an increase in work related to defense and national security in the time since the terrorist attacks of September 11, 2001. The firm has won work related to the reconstruction of Iraq (as a subcontractor on telecommunications projects managed by Lucent), and in 2003 it was awarded a contract from the Health Resources and Services Administration to help establish and operate a bioterrorism technical support center. Outside of the defense and security area, Booz Allen is helping the Department of Energy manage its technology infrastructure and it won a $15 million contract from the National Science Foundation to restructure its human resources operation. Work for US government agencies accounts for about 30% of the firm's business.

In the private sector, Booz Allen has performed work for such companies as Boeing, Ford, and BP. In 2003 it was hired by R.J. Reynolds Tobacco to help the cigarette maker revitalize its struggling business, and was retained by the government of Greece to help that country upgrade its transportation systems in preparation for the 2004 Olympics.

HISTORY

Edwin Booz graduated from Northwestern University in 1914 with degrees in economics and psychology and started a statistical analysis firm in Chicago. After serving in the army during WWI, he returned to his firm, renamed Edwin Booz Surveys. In 1925 Booz hired his first full-time assistant, George Fry, and in 1929 he hired a second, James Allen. By then the company had a long list of clients, including U.S. Gypsum, the *Chicago Tribune*, and Montgomery Ward, which was losing a retail battle with Sears, Roebuck and Co.

In 1935 Carl Hamilton joined the partnership, and a year later it was renamed Booz, Fry, Allen & Hamilton. The firm prospered well into the next decade by providing advice based on "independence that enables us to say plainly from the outside what cannot always be said safely from within," according to a company brochure.

During WWII the firm worked increasingly on government and military contracts. Fry opposed the pursuit of such work for consultants and left in 1942. The firm was renamed Booz, Allen & Hamilton. Hamilton died in 1946, and the following year Booz retired (he died in 1951), leaving Allen as chairman. He successfully steered the firm into lucrative postwar work for clients such as Johnson Wax, RCA, and the US Air Force.

A separate company, Booz, Allen Applied Research, Inc. (BAARINC), was formed in 1955 for technical and government consulting, including missile and weaponry work, as well as consulting with NASA. By the end of the decade, *Time* had dubbed Booz Allen "the world's largest, most prestigious management consultant firm." The partnership was incorporated as a private company in 1962, and in 1967 commissioner Pete Rozelle requested its services for the merger of the National Football League and American Football League.

When Allen retired in 1970, Charlie Bowen became the new chairman, and the company went public. However, as the economy stalled during the energy crisis, spending for consultants plunged. Jim Farley replaced Bowen in 1975, and the company was taken private again in 1976. A turnaround was engineered, and the firm was soon helping Chrysler through its historic bailout and developing strategies for the breakup of AT&T.

Booz Allen again experienced trouble in the 1980s after Farley instituted a competition to select his successor. Michael McCullough was eventually chosen in 1984, but the ten-month election process turned into a dogfight that pitted partner against partner, taking an enormous toll on morale. McCullough began restructuring the firm along industry lines, creating a department store of services in an industry characterized by boutique houses. The turmoil was too much, and by 1988, nearly a third of the partners had quit.

William Stasior became chairman in 1991 and reorganized Booz Allen yet again, splitting it down public and private sector lines. James Allen died in 1992, the same year the firm moved to McLean, Virginia. The company began privatization work in the former Soviet Union and in Eastern Europe in 1992 and continued to emphasize government business, including contracts with the IRS (1995) for technology modernization and with the General Services Administration (1996) to provide technical and management support for all federal telecommunications users.

In 1998 the company won a 10-year, $200 million contract with the US Defense Department to establish a scientific and technical data warehouse. Ralph Shrader was appointed CEO in early 1999; Stasior retired as chairman later that year. Booz Allen acquired Scandinavian consulting firm Carta in 1999 and formed a venture capital firm for startups with Lehman Brothers in 2000. The company announced in late 2000 that it would spin off Aestix, its e-commerce business, but reconsidered amid a general economic slowdown and hostile IPO market. (The unit was integrated back into Booz Allen in 2002.)

EXECUTIVES

Chairman and CEO: Ralph W. Shrader
President, Worldwide Commercial Business: Daniel C. Lewis
President, Worldwide Technology Business: Dennis O. Doughty
CFO: Doug Swenson
SVP and Chief Administrative Officer: Samuel R. Strickland
SVP and General Counsel: C.G. Appleby
VP and CIO: George Tillman
Chief Personnel Officer: Horacio Rozanski
Senior Director of Marketing and Communications: Marie Lerch
Media Relations: Michael Bulger
Media Relations: George Farrar
Auditors: Deloitte & Touche LLP

LOCATIONS

HQ: Booz Allen Hamilton Inc.
8283 Greensboro Dr., McLean, VA 22102
Phone: 703-902-5000   **Fax:** 703-902-3333
Web: www.boozallen.com

PRODUCTS/OPERATIONS

Selected Services

Consulting
  Commercial services
  Corporate strategy
  E-business strategy
  Innovation
  Knowledge management
  Productivity improvement
  Strategic security
Technology services
  Engineering
  Information technology
  Systems development and integration

COMPETITORS

Accenture
Anteon
A.T. Kearney
BAE SYSTEMS
Bain & Company
BearingPoint
Boston Consulting
CACI International
Capgemini
Computer Sciences
Deloitte Consulting
EDS
General Dynamics
IBM
Lockheed Martin
MAXIMUS
McKinsey & Company
Mercer
Northrop Grumman
PA Consulting
PRTM
QinetiQ
Raytheon
SAIC
Titan
Towers Perrin
Unisys

HISTORICAL FINANCIALS

Company Type: Private

Income Statement
FYE: March 31

	REVENUE ($ mil.)	NET INCOME ($ mil.)	NET PROFIT MARGIN	EMPLOYEES
3/04	2,700	—	—	14,800
3/03	2,200	—	—	12,600
3/02	2,038	—	—	11,510
3/01	2,052	—	—	11,045
3/00	1,800	—	—	9,800
3/99	1,600	—	—	9,000
3/98	1,400	—	—	8,000
3/97	1,300	—	—	7,500
3/96	1,100	—	—	6,700
3/95	989	—	—	6,000
Annual Growth	11.8%	—	—	10.6%

Revenue History

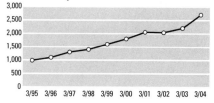

Borden Chemical

A restructured (and renamed) Borden Chemical has moved on from Cracker Jacks and dairy products and turned to the hard stuff: industrial chemicals. After being bought by Kohlberg Kravis Roberts (KKR), the company (formerly just plain Borden) changed its focus. Borden Chemical's operations now consist of the production of formaldehyde, forest product resins, industrial resins, UV coatings, and oilfield products (proppants). Customers include businesses in the forest products, foundry, automotive, construction, and electronics industries. A strong housing market tends to propel Borden Chemical's business (especially formaldehyde production), as it has done in recent years. It is now owned by Apollo Management.

Borden finally gave the last of its edibles the heave-ho late in 2001 when it jettisoned the remainder of its food interests (it had maintained management of certain operations even after their sale) and changed its name to Borden Chemical. It then got out of the consumer products business by selling the remainder of its Elmer's Products division — one of the largest producers of household and school glues (Elmer's and Krazy Glue) in the US — in 2002.

KKR announced its intention to take Borden Chemical public in May 2004 but stepped back from that option in July when it accepted private investment firm Apollo Management's offer of $1.2 billion (including assumption of the company's debt) to buy Borden. Members of Borden Chemical's management are also included in the acquisition group.

Soon after, in October, Borden Chemical made an important move to make its business more international in scope. The company agreed to buy German thermoset resins maker Bakelite from Rütgers for about $315 million. Most of Bakelite's sales (more than $600 million in 2003) come from Europe and Asia, while Borden Chemical does business primarily in North America.

EXECUTIVES

Chairman: C. Robert (Bob) Kidder, age 59
President, CEO, and Director: Craig O. Morrison, age 48, $844,230 pay
EVP, CFO, Treasurer, and Director:
William H. (Bill) Carter, age 50, $1,152,400 pay
EVP, Forest Products and Performance Resins:
Joseph P. (Jody) Bevilaqua, age 49, $393,173 pay
VP, Global Operations: C. Hugh Morton, age 52
VP, Environmental Health and Safety:
Richard L. Monty, age 56
VP, Finance: George F. Knight
VP, Human Resources: Judith A. (Judy) Sonnett, age 47, $313,875 pay
VP, Strategy and Development: Raymond H. Glaser, age 43, $231,757 pay
VP and General Counsel: Nancy G. Brown, age 62
VP, Director of Taxes, and Assistant Controller:
Thomas V. Barr
Secretary: Ellen G. Berndt
Director, Public Affairs and Investor Relations:
Peter Loscocco
Auditors: Deloitte & Touche LLP

LOCATIONS

HQ: Borden Chemical, Inc.
180 E. Broad St., Columbus, OH 43215
Phone: 614-225-4000
Web: www.bordenchem.com

Borden has 48 production and manufacturing facilities in Australia, Canada, Europe, Malaysia, South America, and the US.

2003 Sales

	$ mil.	% of total
US	901	63
Canada	220	15
UK	122	9
Other	192	13
Total	1,435	100

PRODUCTS/OPERATIONS

2003 Sales

	$ mil.	% of total
North American Forest Products	756	53
North American Performance Resins	364	25
International	315	22
Total	1,435	100

Selected Operations

North American Forest Products
    Forest product resins
    Formaldehyde
North American Performance Resins
    Foundry resins
    Industrial resins
    Laminate resins
    Nonwoven resins
    Oilfield resins
    Specialty resins
    UV coatings
International
    Forest product resins
    Formaldehyde
    Performance resins

COMPETITORS

Akzo Nobel	Georgia Gulf
Ashland	Georgia-Pacific
BASF AG	Corporation
Celanese	Huntsman
Dow Chemical	Imperial Chemical
DSM	Industries
DuPont	Rohm and Haas
Dynea	Valspar

HISTORICAL FINANCIALS

Company Type: Private

Income Statement
FYE: December 31

	REVENUE ($ mil.)	NET INCOME ($ mil.)	NET PROFIT MARGIN	EMPLOYEES
12/03	1,435	23	1.6%	2,400
12/02	1,248	(37)	—	2,600
12/01	1,372	(125)	—	2,800
12/00	1,524	34	2.2%	4,000
12/99	1,360	53	3.9%	4,000
12/98	1,400	63	4.5%	4,200
12/97	3,482	278	8.0%	15,000
12/96	5,765	82	1.4%	20,000
12/95	5,944	(366)	—	27,500
12/94	5,626	(598)	—	32,300
Annual Growth	(14.1%)	—	—	(25.1%)

2003 Year-End Financials

Debt ratio: —
Return on equity: —
Cash ($ mil.): 28
Current ratio: 1.35
Long-term debt ($ mil.): 530

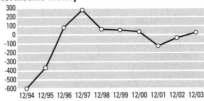

Net Income History

Boscov's

Outlet mall capital Reading, Pennsylvania, has conceived more than bargain shopping. It's given us Boscov's Department Store, which operates about 40 department stores that anchor malls mainly in Pennsylvania, but also in Delaware, Maryland, New Jersey, and New York. The stores sell men's, women's, and children's apparel, shoes, and accessories; also jewelry, cosmetics, housewares, appliances, toys, and sporting goods. Some stores also feature travel agencies, vision centers, hair salons, and restaurants. The firm's charge card services are handled by its Boscov's Receivable Finance subsidiary. Boscov's was founded by Solomon Boscov in 1911 and is owned by the families of Albert Boscov and Edwin Lakin.

EXECUTIVES

Chairman, Boscov's, Inc.: Albert R. (Al) Boscov
President, Boscov's, Inc.: Edwin A. Lakin
Chairman and CEO, Boscov's Department Store, LLC: Kenneth S. Lakin
President and Chief Merchandising Officer, Boscov's Department Store, LLC: Burton C. Krieger
SVP and CIO: Harry Roberts
SVP and Controller: Raymond J. Douglass
SVP and Director of Retail Merchandise Planning: Sam Flamholz
SVP and Director of Stores: Joseph M. Fabrizio
SVP and Treasurer: Russell C. Diehm
SVP, Credit and Customer Relations Management: Dean Sheaffer
SVP, Finance and Administration: Peter Lakin
SVP, Human Resources: Ed Elko
SVP, Marketing and Internet Services: Maralyn Lakin
SVP, Operations: Larry Bergman
SVP, Real Estate and Development: John Hlis
Auditors: PricewaterhouseCoopers LLP

LOCATIONS

HQ: Boscov's Department Store
4500 Perkiomen Ave., Reading, PA 19606
Phone: 610-779-2000   **Fax:** 610-370-3495
Web: www.boscovs.com

COMPETITORS

Bon-Ton Stores
Federated
J. C. Penney
Kmart
Kohl's
May
Sears
Target
Toys "R" Us
Wal-Mart

HISTORICAL FINANCIALS

Company Type: Private

Income Statement
FYE: January 31

	REVENUE ($ mil.)	NET INCOME ($ mil.)	NET PROFIT MARGIN	EMPLOYEES
1/03	1,050	—	—	10,500
1/02	1,000	—	—	12,000
1/01	1,000	—	—	10,000
1/00	958	—	—	10,000
1/99	1,000	—	—	10,000
1/98	846	—	—	9,000
1/97	811	—	—	8,500
1/96	783	—	—	8,500
1/95	750	—	—	6,500
1/94	720	—	—	5,500
Annual Growth	4.3%	—	—	7.4%

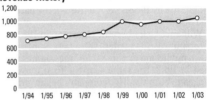

Revenue History

Bose

Bose doesn't subscribe to the theory that bigger is better. One of the world's leading speaker makers, the company may be best known for its compact and critically acclaimed Wave radio, which has continued to be a success despite its $500 price tag. Bose makes a variety of audio products, including sound systems for households, automobiles, and boats. It also makes professional loudspeakers for large venues (auditoriums, retail environments) and stage performers. Bose products are sold at more than 100 of its own "Bose Experience Centers" worldwide, as well as through electronics retailers. Founder Amar Bose, a former MIT professor, owns the company.

True to its commitment to research, Bose reinvests 100% of its profits in product research and development. The company has operations in Asia, Australia, Canada, Europe, South America, and the US.

HISTORY

Music and electronics struck a chord in Amar Bose, the son of an Indian emigrant from Calcutta. As a youngster he studied violin and liked fixing electronic gadgets. A teenaged Bose started a radio repair shop in his basement during WWII that turned out to be the family's main source of income when his father's import business faltered during the war. Bose's interest in electronics led him to college at MIT in 1947.

His quest to develop a better sound system began nearly a decade later when the hi-fi stereo he bought as a reward for doing well in his graduate studies made his violin record sound shrill. MIT allowed Bose to research the topic while he taught there. He formed his namesake company in 1964 and hired as its first employee Sherwin Greenblatt, a former student who later became company president.

Bose discovered that most speaker systems funneled sound directly at the listener, while live concerts sent sound directly and indirectly by bouncing it off walls, floors, and ceilings. He designed a system in which only some speakers are aimed at the listener while others reflect the sounds around the room. Calling the concept "reflected sound," Bose began selling his 901 stereo speakers in 1968.

A feud with *Consumer Reports* showed the arrogant side of the self-made entrepreneur. After the magazine concluded in a 1970 review that Bose speakers created a sound that tended to "wander around the room," Bose sued, claiming product disparagement. (The lawsuit was settled 13 years later when the Supreme Court ruled in favor of *Consumer Reports*.) Bose began making professional loudspeakers in 1972.

After trying and failing to gain market share in Japan throughout the 1970s, in 1978 Bose hired sales executive Sumi Sakura, who convinced 400 Japanese dealers to find space in their jam-packed stores for Bose products. Sales jumped within months. Bose also turned his attention to car stereos in the 1970s. After promising talks with General Motors in 1979, he risked $13 million and four years developing a stereo that could be custom-designed for cars. The first one was offered in 1983 in a Cadillac Seville. Contracts with other major carmakers followed, usually for their top-of-the-line models.

In the 1980s the company took its technology to TVs. With an agreeable guinea pig in Zenith, Bose developed a speaker tube that could coil inside the set without adding much bulk. The set was a hit, even with a price tag of more than $1,400 (in 1987). The firm's speakers were also used in several space shuttle flights, beginning in 1992 with *Endeavour*.

The critically acclaimed Wave radio was introduced in 1993 and has been a huge success ever since. A year later Bose acquired professional loudspeaker maker US Sound from Carver. In 1996 it teamed up with satellite TV firm PRIMESTAR to offer the home theater Companion systems. (The systems were discontinued in 1999, dissolving the partnership.) The next year Bose and IBM paired up to upgrade the quality of PC sound systems.

Bose upped the ante on its retail operations in 1997 when it began opening more upscale showcase stores where audiophiles could test sound systems at in-store music theaters. The company began making its sound systems for more mainstream cars, such as the Chevrolet Blazer, the following year. In 1999 Bose began selling its products online and introduced a new version of its popular Wave radio (with a CD player). In 2001 Bose introduced the Bose Wave/PC interactive system that provides one-touch access to Internet radio, digital audio files, AM/FM radio, and CDs through a personal computer.

EXECUTIVES

Chairman and CEO: Amar G. Bose
President: John Coleman
VP, Engineering: Joseph Veranth
VP, Europe: Nic A. Merks
VP, Finance and CFO: Daniel A. Grady, age 67
VP, Human Resources: John Ferrie
VP, Manufacturing: Thomas Beeson
VP, Research: Thomas Froeschle
VP, Sales: David Wood
VP: Sumiyoshi Sakura

General Manager, India: Ratish Pandey
Secretary: Alexander Bernhard
Assistant Secretary: Mark E. Sullivan
Treasurer: William R. Swanson
Director of Public Relations: Carolyn Cinotti
Director of Retail Development: Linda Pilla
Auditors: PricewaterhouseCoopers LLP

LOCATIONS

HQ: Bose Corporation
 The Mountain, Framingham, MA 01701
Phone: 508-879-7330   **Fax:** 508-766-7543
Web: www.bose.com

PRODUCTS/OPERATIONS

Selected Brands
Acoustic Noise Cancelling (headphones, headsets)
Acoustimass (speaker systems)
Direct/Reflecting (speakers)
Lifestyle (home entertainment systems)
Wave (music systems)

Selected Products
Home entertainment
 Accessories
 Computer speakers
 Custom home installations
 Headphones and headsets
 Home entertainment
 Home theater
 Lifestyle system expansion
 Outdoor and marine speakers
 Stereo speakers
 Wave music systems
Automotive systems
Professional sound systems

COMPETITORS

Aiwa
Altec Lansing Technologies
Bang & Olufsen
Boston Acoustics
Cambridge SoundWorks
Eminence
Harman International
Kenwood
Klipsch
Koss
Mitek
Phoenix Gold
Pioneer
Polk Audio
QSC Audio
Rockford
SpeakerCraft
Stanton Group
Telex Communications

HISTORICAL FINANCIALS

Company Type: Private

Income Statement — FYE: March 31

	REVENUE ($ mil.)	NET INCOME ($ mil.)	NET PROFIT MARGIN	EMPLOYEES
3/03	1,600	—	—	8,000
3/02	1,300	—	—	7,000
3/01	1,250	—	—	7,000
3/00	1,100	—	—	6,000
3/99	950	—	—	4,000
3/98	850	—	—	4,000
3/97	750	—	—	4,000
3/96	700	—	—	3,500
3/95	600	—	—	3,100
3/94	500	—	—	3,100
Annual Growth	13.8%	—	—	11.1%

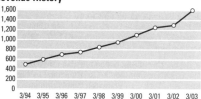

Revenue History

Boston Consulting

Global corporations are willing to give much more than a penny for the thoughts of management consulting firm Boston Consulting Group (BCG). Founded in 1963 by consulting pioneer Bruce Henderson, BCG is one of the world's top ranked consulting practices with about 60 offices in more than 30 countries. The firm's 2,700 consultants offer a wide array of strategic consulting services mainly to blue chip corporate clients. Its practice areas include branding and marketing, corporate development, globalization, and technology. The firm is noted for developing its own original consulting concepts, such as "time-based competition" (rapid response to change) and "deconstruction" (an end to vertical integration).

Although the employee-owned firm is nearly 40 years old, BCG became one of the premier e-commerce consultancies in the 1990s offering services to catapult its clients to the cutting edge of the technology-fueled economy. However, like most firms, BCG has felt the strain of the weakening economy and strategy consultants have taken an even bigger hit as companies have cut consulting from their budgets. As a result BCG has made drastic cuts in its consulting staff.

Against this backdrop, Hans-Paul Bürkner became president in 2003 with the job of distinguishing the firm from competitors such as McKinsey & Company and Bain & Company in an effort to win consulting engagements in this tight economy. One area of focus is the emerging economy of China, where the firm is growing its business. BCG has announced plans to expand its staff there over the next few years.

EXECUTIVES

Co-Chairman: John S. Clarkeson, age 61
Co-Chairman: Carl Stern, age 58
President and CEO: Hans-Paul Bürkner
CFO: Hugh Simons
VP and General Counsel: Lon Povich
Regional Chair of the Americas: Steven H. Gunby
Regional Chair of Asia: John Wong
Regional Chair of Europe: Bjorn Matre
Director of Media Relations: Erol (KC) Munuz

LOCATIONS

HQ: The Boston Consulting Group
Exchange Place, 31st Fl., Boston, MA 02109
Phone: 617-973-1200 **Fax:** 617-973-1399
Web: www.bcg.com

The Boston Consulting Group has about 60 offices in Atlanta, Boston, Chicago, Dallas, Houston, Los Angeles, Miami, New York, San Francisco, and Washington, DC, as well as in more than 30 other countries.

PRODUCTS/OPERATIONS

Selected Practice Areas
Branding and marketing
Consumer products
Corporate development
E-commerce
Energy
Financial services
Healthcare
Industrial goods
Information technology
Organizational practices
Pricing
Retail industry
Strategic operations
Technology and communications
Travel and tourism
Workforce development

COMPETITORS

Accenture
A.T. Kearney
Bain & Company
BearingPoint
Booz Allen
Computer Sciences
Deloitte Consulting
IBM
McKinsey & Company
Mercer
PA Consulting
Perot Systems
PricewaterhouseCoopers
PRTM
Roland Berger
Towers Perrin

HISTORICAL FINANCIALS

Company Type: Private

Income Statement				FYE: December 31
	REVENUE ($ mil.)	NET INCOME ($ mil.)	NET PROFIT MARGIN	EMPLOYEES
12/03	1,120	—	—	—
12/02	1,020	—	—	4,250
12/01	1,050	—	—	4,450
12/00	1,100	—	—	4,300
12/99	948	—	—	4,334
12/98	730	—	—	3,000
12/97	655	—	—	2,000
12/96	600	—	—	1,550
12/95	550	—	—	1,320
12/94	430	—	—	1,246
Annual Growth	11.2%	—	—	16.6%

Revenue History

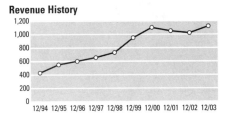

Bozzuto's

Bozzuto's will keep you buzzing. The wholesale food company distributes food and other items to independent supermarkets belonging to the IGA network in New England, New York, New Jersey, Pennsylvania, and Maryland. Bozzuto's Inc. supplies about 700 stores with food, tobacco products, and household items under national brands as well as the IGA and Bestway labels. It also provides store design, administrative, marketing, and inventory management services. Bozzuto's also owns Adams Super Food Stores, a supermarket chain with 11 stores in Connecticut and Massachusetts. Founded in 1945, Bozzuto's serves stores in New England, New York, New Jersey, and Pennsylvania. Founder Adam Bozzuto died in 2002.

EXECUTIVES

Chairman, President, and CEO: Michael A. Bozzuto
EVP, Retail Development: George Motel
SVP, Merchandising, Advertising, and Procurement:
  Steve Heggelke
VP, Deli, Bakery, and Dairy: Robert Cohen
VP, Finance: Robert H. Wood
VP, Meat and Seafood: David Kent
VP, Sales: Dan Brock
Director, Advertising and Marketing: Kristin Manning
VP, Information Technologies: John Keeley
Director, Human Resources: Doug Vaughn
Corporate Secretary and Assistant Treasurer:
  Patricia S. Houle

LOCATIONS

HQ: Bozzuto's Inc.
275 School House Rd., Cheshire, CT 06410
Phone: 203-272-3511 **Fax:** 203-250-2954
Web: www.bozzutos.com

COMPETITORS

C&S Wholesale
Di Giorgio
Krasdale Foods
Nash Finch
Shaw's
Stop & Shop
SUPERVALU
Wakefern Food

HISTORICAL FINANCIALS

Company Type: Private

Income Statement				FYE: September 30
	ESTIMATED REVENUE ($ mil.)	NET INCOME ($ mil.)	NET PROFIT MARGIN	EMPLOYEES
9/03	890	—	—	1,000
9/02	900	—	—	1,050
9/01	850	—	—	1,025
9/00	777	—	—	1,000
9/99	685	—	—	900
9/98	650	—	—	800
Annual Growth	6.5%	—	—	4.6%

Revenue History

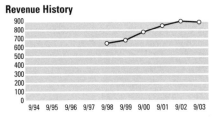

BPC Holding

BPC Holding Corp. is the holding company for Berry Plastics Corporation, a leading maker of injection-molded plastic products. Berry has three business segments: containers (about half of sales), closures, and consumer products such as plastic drink cups and housewares. Its containers package items such as dairy products and pool chemicals. Berry's closures unit makes overcaps for aerosol cans and caps for mouthwash and detergents. Fast-food restaurants, convenience stores, and stadiums use its plastic drink cups. Berry also makes plastic housewares like plates, bowls, pitchers, and flowerpots and has about 12,000 customers, including major retail, beverage, and fast-food companies.

Established in 1967, Berry Plastics has grown primarily through acquisitions. Internationally, the company operates facilities in the UK and Italy. The company acquired Landis Plastics, a leading manufacturer of containers for the yogurt business, for about $230 million in November 2003.

Goldman Sachs owns about 60% of the company; J.P. Morgan Chase & Co. owns about 30%.

EXECUTIVES

Chairman: Joseph H. Gleberman, age 46
President, CEO, and Director: Ira G. Boots, age 50, $583,067 pay
EVP, CFO, Secretary, and Treasurer:
  James M. Kratochvil, age 47, $375,444 pay
EVP and General Manager, Closures:
  William J. (Bill) Herdrich, age 53, $391,952 pay
EVP and President, Containers and Consumer Products: Ralph Brent Beeler, age 51, $425,237 pay
President, Container Division: Gregory (Greg) Landis, age 53, $49,500 pay (partial-year salary)
VP, Mergers, Acquisitions, and Operations Strategy:
  Bimal A. Kalvani
VP and Controller: Mark Miles
VP, Corporate Development: Brett C. Bauer
VP, Finance and Business Planning:
  Rodgers K. Greenwalt
VP, Global Purchasing: Scott Farmer
VP, Human Resources: Marcia C. Jochem
VP, International Division: Antonio Gabriele, age 47
VP, Product Development: David J. Jochem
Auditors: Ernst & Young LLP

LOCATIONS

HQ: BPC Holding Corp.
101 Oakley St., Evansville, IN 47710
Phone: 812-424-2904 **Fax:** 812-424-0128
Web: www.berryplastics.com

The company has facilities throughout the US; foreign facilities include locations in Mexico and the UK.

PRODUCTS/OPERATIONS

2003 Sales

	$ mil.	% of total
Containers	288.5	52
Closures	147.3	27
Consumer products	116.1	21
Total	**551.9**	**100**

Selected Products

Aerosol overcaps
Closures
  Continuous thread
  Child resistant
  Cups and spouts (for liquid laundry detergent)
  Dispensing
  Dropper bulb assemblies
  Fitments and plugs (for medical applications)
  Tamper evident
Consumer products
  Drink cups
  Housewares
Containers
  Dairy
  Industrial Specialty
  Polypropylene
  Pry-off
  Thinwall

COMPETITORS

Berlin Packaging
Dart Container
Dopaco
Huhtamäki
International Paper
Kerr Group
Letica
Owens-Illinois
Polytainers
Portola Packaging
Radnor Holdings
Rexam Beverage Can Americas
Silgan Closures
Sweetheart

HISTORICAL FINANCIALS

Company Type: Private

Income Statement			FYE: Last Saturday in December	
	REVENUE ($ mil.)	NET INCOME ($ mil.)	NET PROFIT MARGIN	EMPLOYEES
12/03	552	13	2.4%	4,700
12/02	494	(33)	—	3,250
12/01	462	(2)	—	3,100
12/00	409	(23)	—	3,100
12/99	329	(9)	—	2,800
12/98	272	(8)	—	2,300
12/97	227	(14)	—	2,100
12/96	151	(3)	—	1,040
12/95	141	6	4.5%	1,100
12/94	106	2	2.1%	930
Annual Growth	20.1%	21.8%	—	19.7%

2003 Year-End Financials

Debt ratio: 486.4%
Return on equity: 11.4%
Cash ($ mil.): 26
Current ratio: 1.76
Long-term debt ($ mil.): 742

Net Income History

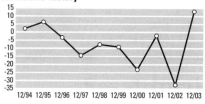

Bradco Supply

Bradco Supply offers construction contractors everything they need to put a roof over their clients' heads. The company distributes roofing, siding, windows, and other building materials through more than 100 locations in more than 25 states. Founded in 1966, Bradco Supply is one of the nation's largest distributors of roofing materials for commercial use. It also exports its construction materials to the Caribbean, Europe, Latin America, and the Middle East. The company has been acquiring smaller roofing material businesses. Bradco has acquired some 20 Wickes locations in the Northeast and Midwest. CEO Barry Segal owns Bradco Supply.

EXECUTIVES

CEO: Barry Segal
President: Bradley (Brad) Segal
CFO and Treasurer: Steven (Steve) Feinberg
Controller: Joe Stacy
Accounting Manager: Susan Biunno
Accounts Payable Manager: Bob Ripp
Facilities and Construction Manager: Skip Roberts
Fleet Manager: Kevin Tremmel
Information Systems Manager: Joe Hradil
Inventory Control Manager: Joe Revello
Marketing Manager: Elaine Ferrie
Marketing Manager: Fran Frank
Marketing Manager: Laurie Henkel
Operations Manager: Chip Halpin
General Counsel: Michael L. Weinberger

LOCATIONS

HQ: Bradco Supply Corp.
    13 Production Way, Avenel, NJ 07001
Phone: 732-382-3400   **Fax:** 732-382-6577
Web: www.bradcosupply.com

COMPETITORS

ABC Supply
CRH
Georgia-Pacific Corporation
Guardian Building Products
Huttig Building Products
North Pacific Group
PrimeSource Building

HISTORICAL FINANCIALS

Company Type: Private

Income Statement			FYE: December 31	
	REVENUE ($ mil.)	NET INCOME ($ mil.)	NET PROFIT MARGIN	EMPLOYEES
12/03	995	—	—	2,000
12/02	850	—	—	1,770
12/01	800	—	—	1,450
12/00	700	—	—	1,425
12/99	600	—	—	1,300
12/98	523	—	—	1,200
12/97	475	—	—	1,100
Annual Growth	13.1%	—	—	10.5%

Revenue History

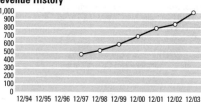

Braman Management

It's no bull to say that Braman Management sells cars fit for Brahmans. Braman Management operates four dealerships in Florida and three in Colorado. The company's dealerships, most of which operate under the Braman name, sell upscale makes such as Acura, Audi, Bentley, BMW, Cadillac, Mercedes, Porsche, and Rolls-Royce; it also sells new Hondas, MINIs, and Mitsubishis and a variety of used cars. Each Braman location offers parts and service departments. Owner and CEO Norman Braman, who once owned the Philadelphia Eagles, formed Braman Management in 1972.

EXECUTIVES

President and CEO: Norman Braman
CFO: Robert E. Bernstein
Director of Human Resources: Linda Brickman

LOCATIONS

HQ: Braman Management Association
    2060 Biscayne Blvd., 2nd Fl., Miami, FL 33137
Phone: 305-576-1889   **Fax:** 305-576-9898
Web: www.braman.com

COMPETITORS

AutoNation
Buchanan Automotive
Ferman Automotive
Germain Motor
Group 1 Automotive
JM Family Enterprises
Kuni Automotive
March/Hodge
Morse Operations
Phil Long Dealerships
Scott-McRae Group

HISTORICAL FINANCIALS

Company Type: Private

Income Statement			FYE: December 31	
	ESTIMATED REVENUE ($ mil.)	NET INCOME ($ mil.)	NET PROFIT MARGIN	EMPLOYEES
12/03	980	—	—	—
12/02	800	—	—	—
12/01	700	—	—	1,100
12/00	600	—	—	950
12/99	500	—	—	900
12/98	500	—	—	850
12/97	536	—	—	806
12/96	480	—	—	800
12/95	423	—	—	750
12/94	392	—	—	750
Annual Growth	10.7%	—	—	5.6%

Revenue History

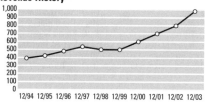

Brasfield & Gorrie

Brasfield & Gorrie holds a healthy share of the health care construction market. One of the top construction companies in the US, as well as a leading regional contractor in the Southeast, Brasfield & Gorrie also works on hotels, industrial plants, multistory offices, retail complexes, schools, and water-treatment plants. Commercial and industrial construction together account for most of its revenues. It provides general contracting, design/build, and construction management services through 12 operating divisions and offices in Alabama, Florida, Georgia, North Carolina, and Tennessee. Founded in 1922 by Thomas C. Brasfield, the company was sold to owner Miller Gorrie (chairman and CEO) in 1964.

EXECUTIVES

Chairman and CEO: M. Miller Gorrie, age 68
President: M. James (Jim) Gorrie
VP and COO: Jeffrey I. (Jeff) Stone
CFO: Randall J. Freeman
CIO: Tom Garrett
VP and General Counsel: Charles (Chip) Grizzle
VP and Manager, Raleigh Division: Mark Jones
Controller: Earl Whatley
Director Marketing: Melissa L. (Missy) Mauk
Director Human Resources: Kelly Crane
Corporate Accounting: Gail Black
Special Projects Coordinator, Marketing: Skip Pennington
Auditors: PricewaterhouseCoopers

LOCATIONS

HQ: Brasfield & Gorrie, LLC
729 S. 30th St., Birmingham, AL 35233
Phone: 205-328-4000 **Fax:** 205-251-1304
Web: www.brasfieldgorrie.com

Brasfield & Gorrie has offices in Atlanta; Birmingham, Alabama; Nashville; Orlando; and Raleigh, North Carolina.

PRODUCTS/OPERATIONS

Major Sectors
Auto and industrial
Commercial
Health care
Institutional
Retail
Treatment plants

COMPETITORS

Alberici
B. L. Harbert
Barton Malow
BE&K
Bechtel
Beck Group
Bovis Lend Lease
Brice Building
Choate Construction
Doster Construction
Hardin Construction
H.J. Russell
Hoar Construction
McCarthy Building
Peter Kiewit Sons'
Skanska USA Building
Turner Corporation
Whiting-Turner

HISTORICAL FINANCIALS
Company Type: Private

Income Statement FYE: December 31

	REVENUE ($ mil.)	NET INCOME ($ mil.)	NET PROFIT MARGIN	EMPLOYEES
12/03	1,040	—	—	2,301
12/02	1,011	—	—	2,088
12/01	943	—	—	2,000
12/00	849	—	—	2,000
12/99	646	—	—	1,765
12/98	566	—	—	1,375
12/97	477	—	—	1,539
Annual Growth	13.9%	—	—	6.9%

Revenue History

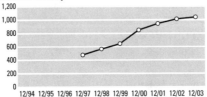

Brazos Electric Power

Brazos means "arms" in Spanish, and the generation and transmission arms of Brazos Electric Power Cooperative reach across 66 Texas counties. Founded in 1941, the utility was the state's first electricity generation and transmission cooperative. It serves 17 member/owner distribution cooperatives, three municipalities, and one university in northern and Central Texas. Brazos Electric Power has 700 MW of fossil-fueled generating capacity. The utility also purchases about 1,300 MW from other utilities and marketers; part of its power supply is procured through ACES Power Marketing.

EXECUTIVES

President, Board of Directors: John Hartgraves
VP, Board of Directors: Ronnie Robinson
EVP and General Manager: Clifton B. Karnei
VP Accounting Services: Khaki Bordovsky
VP Generation: David Murphy
VP Power Supply and Marketing: Hugh F. Lewox
VP Transmission: Johnny A. York
Secretary and Treasurer: Loyd Jackson
Controller: Brent Fox
Director Human Resources: J. Thomas (Tom) Yows Jr.
Administrative Services Manager: Ross Kammlah
Auditors: PricewaterhouseCoopers LLP

LOCATIONS

HQ: Brazos Electric Power Cooperative, Inc.
2404 La Salle Ave., Waco, TX 76710
Phone: 254-750-6500 **Fax:** 254-750-6292
Web: www.brazoselectric.com

Brazos Electric Power Cooperative has operations in 66 counties in northern and Central Texas.

PRODUCTS/OPERATIONS

Member/Owners
Barlett Electric Cooperative
Belfalls Electric Cooperative
Comanche Electric Cooperative
Cooke County Electric Cooperative
CoServ Electric
Fort Belknap Electric Cooperative
Hamilton County Electric Cooperative
HILCO Electric Cooperative
J-A-C Electric Cooperative
McLennan County Electric Cooperative
Mid-South Electric Cooperative
Navarro County Electric Cooperative
Navasota Valley Electric Cooperative
South Plains Electric Cooperative
Tri-County Electric Cooperative
United Cooperative Services
Wise Electric Cooperative

COMPETITORS

American Electric Power
Cap Rock Energy
CenterPoint Energy
El Paso Electric
Entergy
LCRA
TNP Enterprises
TXU

HISTORICAL FINANCIALS
Company Type: Cooperative

Income Statement FYE: December 31

	REVENUE ($ mil.)	NET INCOME ($ mil.)	NET PROFIT MARGIN	EMPLOYEES
12/03	535	—	—	324
12/02	433	—	—	315
12/01	456	—	—	309
12/00	290	—	—	295
12/99	300	—	—	275
12/98	287	—	—	300
12/97	278	—	—	300
12/96	260	—	—	—
12/95	235	—	—	—
12/94	217	—	—	300
Annual Growth	10.5%	—	—	0.9%

Revenue History

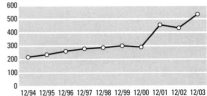

Brightstar

There is a Brightstar in the constellation of wireless products distributors. The company distributes communications products, primarily cell phones, and accessories. It also offers inventory management, logistics, fulfillment, customized packaging, and assembly services. More than half of the phones sold by Brightstar are made by Motorola; other manufacturers include Kyocera, Sagem, Samsung, and Sendo. The company also provides IT services through its Etaris subsidiary. Brightstar's top customers include

América Móvil, BellSouth, Telecom Italia, Telefónica Móviles, and Verizon. Founding chairman and CEO Marcelo Claure owns more than two-thirds of the company.

EXECUTIVES
Chairman, President, and CEO: R. Marcelo Claure, age 33, $246,817 pay
COO and Director; President and COO, Brightstar US: Denise Gibson, age 44, $340,781 pay
CFO, Secretary, Treasurer, and Director: Oscar Fumagali, age 51, $150,562 pay
CTO; President and CEO, Etaris, LLC: David A, (Dave) Stritzinger, age 39
President, Narbitec, LLC: Jaime Narea, age 49, $219,190 pay
VP, Wireless Data and Telecom Solutions: Michael Tate, age 41
VP, Business Development: Javier Villamizar, age 32
General Manager, Brightstar de Mexico: Carlos Lomniczi, age 36
Corporate Controller: Arlene Vargas, age 37
Senior Director, Product Management: Elias J. Kabeche, age 40
Director, Product Management: Diego G. López Carbajal, age 31
Auditors: Deloitte & Touche LLP

LOCATIONS
HQ: Brightstar Corp.
2010 NW 84th Ave., Miami, FL 33122
Phone: 305-477-8676 **Fax:** 305-477-9073
Web: www.brightstarcorp.com

Brightstar has operations in Argentina, Bolivia, Chile, Colombia, Costa Rica, the Dominican Republic, Ecuador, El Salvador, Guatemala, Mexico, Paraguay, Peru, the US, and Venezuela.

2003 Sales

	$ mil.	% of total
Latin America		
Mexico	562.3	47
Other countries	268.8	22
US	373.7	31
Total	**1,204.8**	**100**

COMPETITORS
Axesstel
Brightpoint
CellStar
Phones International
Telular

HISTORICAL FINANCIALS
Company Type: Private

Income Statement   FYE: December 31

	REVENUE ($ mil.)	NET INCOME ($ mil.)	NET PROFIT MARGIN	EMPLOYEES
12/03	1,205	29	2.4%	793
12/02	849	18	2.1%	400
12/01	630	13	2.0%	—
12/00	355	—	—	—
12/99	140	—	—	—
12/98	73	—	—	—
12/97	14	—	—	—
Annual Growth	110.1%	51.4%	—	98.3%

2003 Year-End Financials
Debt ratio: 34.4%
Return on equity: 46.4%
Cash ($ mil.): 43
Current ratio: 1.36
Long-term debt ($ mil.): 29

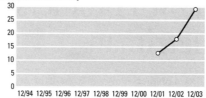

Net Income History

Brookshire Brothers

From its roots in East Texas the Brookshire Brothers supermarket chain now has about 70 locations stretching from Louisiana to Central Texas. The company primarily operates under the Brookshire Brothers banner, although a few fly the B&B Foods, Budget Chopper, and Celebration Foods flags. Nearly all of the stores feature outlets selling Conoco gasoline (the company is one of Conoco's largest distributors). Brookshire Brothers is not affiliated with Brookshire Grocery of Tyler, Texas. The companies share a common ancestry dating back to 1921, but a split between the founding brothers in the late 1930s resulted in separate grocery chains. Formerly family-owned, Brookshire Brothers is now 67%-owned by employees.

EXECUTIVES
President: Jack Gabriel
EVP and CFO: Donny Johnson
EVP and Chief Administrative Officer: Jerry Johnson
VP, Marketing: Kevin Flanagan
Director, Personnel: Emily Watts
Director, Petroleum Marketing: Larry NeGron

LOCATIONS
HQ: Brookshire Brothers, Ltd.
1201 Ellen Trout Dr., Lufkin, TX 75904
Phone: 936-634-8155 **Fax:** 936-633-4611
Web: www.brookshirebrothers.com

2004 Stores

	No.
Texas	66
Louisiana	5
Total	**71**

PRODUCTS/OPERATIONS

2004 Stores

	No.
Brookshire Brothers	59
B&B	9
Budget Chopper	1
Celebration Foods	1
Petro Barn	1
Total	**71**

Selected Departments
Bakery
Deli
Floral
Gasoline
Grocery
Health and beauty
Meat and seafood
Pharmacy
Photo
Produce
Tobacco Barn

COMPETITORS
Albertson's
Fiesta Mart
Foodarama Supermarkets
Gerland's Food Fair
H-E-B
Kroger
Randall's
Wal-Mart

HISTORICAL FINANCIALS
Company Type: Private

Income Statement   FYE: April 30

	ESTIMATED REVENUE ($ mil.)	NET INCOME ($ mil.)	NET PROFIT MARGIN	EMPLOYEES
4/03	800	—	—	6,000
4/02	700	—	—	6,000
4/01	750	—	—	6,000
4/00	700	—	—	5,500
4/99	675	—	—	5,500
4/98	700	—	—	5,500
4/97	725	—	—	5,563
4/96	690	—	—	5,300
4/95	675	—	—	5,200
4/94	650	—	—	5,000
Annual Growth	2.3%	—	—	2.0%

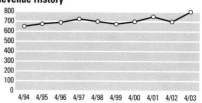

Revenue History

Brookshire Grocery

By selling staples, specialties, and Southern hospitality, Brookshire Grocery Co. has grown into a chain of about 150 Brookshire's, Super 1 Food, and Olé Foods supermarkets in Texas, Arkansas, Louisiana, and Mississippi. The company also owns two distribution centers, a dairy, a fleet of nearly 350 trucks, and SouthWest Foods, its private label manufacturing unit. Brookshire's stores average about 40,000 sq. ft., while its warehouse-style Super 1 Foods stores average 80,000 sq. ft. More than 40 of Brookshire Grocery's stores sell gasoline. Originally part of the Brookshire Brothers grocery chain (dating back to 1921), the company split from it in 1939. The Brookshire family is still among the company's owners.

Super 1 Foods has nearly 30 stores in Louisiana and Texas.

The grocery chain opened its second Olé Foods store, which caters to Hispanic shoppers, in Corsicana, Texas in August 2004.

EXECUTIVES

Chairman: Bruce G. Brookshire
President Corporate Development Group:
 Brad Brookshire
President Human Resources and Finance Group:
 Tim Brookshire
President Marketing Group: Mark Brookshire
President Retail Operations Group: Britt Brookshire
EVP and CFO: Marvin Massey
EVP, Director, Retail Operations: Johnny Skelton
EVP, Distribution and Manufacturing: Rick Rayford
VP and Controller: Tim King
VP and Director, Market Operations: Art McCullars
VP, Merchandising, Olé Foods: Roger Story
Chief Information Officer: Gary Butler
Director, Grocery Purchasing: Jim McCarty
Director, Marketing Operations: James (Jim) Pitner

LOCATIONS

HQ: Brookshire Grocery Company
 1600 W. South West Loop 323, Tyler, TX 75701
Phone: 903-534-3000 **Fax:** 903-534-2206
Web: www.brookshires.com

COMPETITORS

Albertson's
E-Z Mart Stores
Fiesta Mart
H-E-B
Kmart
Kroger
Minyard Food Stores
Randall's
Safeway
SUPERVALU
Target
Wal-Mart
Whole Foods
Winn-Dixie

HISTORICAL FINANCIALS

Company Type: Private

Income Statement
FYE: September 30

	ESTIMATED REVENUE ($ mil.)	NET INCOME ($ mil.)	NET PROFIT MARGIN	EMPLOYEES
9/03	1,900	—	—	12,000
9/02	1,700	—	—	11,500
9/01	1,700	—	—	10,750
9/00	1,600	—	—	10,500
9/99	1,650	—	—	10,700
9/98	1,550	—	—	10,700
9/97	1,500	—	—	10,500
9/96	1,300	—	—	9,500
9/95	1,200	—	—	8,500
9/94	800	—	—	8,000
Annual Growth	10.1%	—	—	4.6%

Revenue History

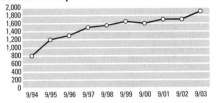

Brown Brothers Harriman

Brown Brothers Harriman is one of the largest, most prestigious private banks in the US. As a private partnership, the bank is not insured by the FDIC, and each of its some 40 partners has unlimited liability. The company provides investment management, brokerage, banking, mutual funds, and trust services to financial institutions, corporations, and well-off families and individuals around the world. It also performs merger and acquisition advisory, securities lending, foreign exchange, alternative investment, and corporate financing services. Founded in 1818 and known for its conservative investment approach, Brown Brothers Harriman has nearly $3 billion in assets.

EXECUTIVES

Managing Partner: Michael W. (Mike) McConnell, age 60
Partner and Head of Systems: J. William Anderson
Managing Director and Equity Strategist:
 Charles H. Blood
Managing Director: Joseph P. Donlan, age 56
Managing Director, Private Equity: Walter W. Grist, age 63
Managing Director, Banking: J. Edward (Jed) Hall
Managing Director, Alternative Investments Group:
 John R. Hass
Managing Director and General Counsel:
 James I. Kaplan, age 50
Managing Director, Private Equity: Mark W. Johnson
Managing Director: James R. Kent
Managing Director and Controller: Maroa Velez
Auditors: PricewaterhouseCoopers

LOCATIONS

HQ: Brown Brothers Harriman & Co.
 140 Broadway, New York, NY 10005
Phone: 212-483-1818 **Fax:** 212-493-8545
Web: www.bbh.com

PRODUCTS/OPERATIONS

Selected Mutual Funds
BBH Broad Market Fund
BBH Inflation-Indexed Securities Fund
BBH International Equity Fund
BBH Money Market Fund
BBH Tax-Efficient Equity Fund
BBH Tax Exempt Money Market Fund
BBH Tax Free Short/Intermediate Fixed Income Fund
BBH US Treasury Money Market Fund

COMPETITORS

Bank of New York
Bear Stearns
Citigroup Global Markets
Citigroup Private Bank
Credit Suisse First Boston (USA), Inc.
Deutsche Bank
Goldman Sachs
J.P. Morgan Private Bank
Lehman Brothers
Mellon Financial
Northern Trust
Pequot Capital

Buffets Holdings

Corn bread dressing, fish patties, baked beans, hot wings... kneel and pray to the almighty buffet. Buffets Holdings operates one of the country's largest portfolios of buffet restaurants, with about 360 locations in 38 states. Operating mostly under the Old Country Buffet and HomeTown Buffet brands, the company's locations are self-service buffets featuring entrees, sides, and desserts for an all-inclusive price. Its other brands include Granny's Buffet, Country Roadhouse Buffet & Grill, and Tahoe Joe's Famous Steakhouse. In addition to its company-owned restaurant operations, Buffets franchises about 20 locations. Private equity firm Caxton-Iseman Capital owns 79% of the company.

Once a public company, Buffets Holdings was taken private in 2000 by a management group led by CEO Kerry Kramp and backed by Caxton-Iseman. Since the $643 million buyout, the company has reorganized its operations, closing or selling several underperforming locations, and has paid down a substantial part of its debt. It is also revamping and updating many of its existing restaurants. As the company starts to see signs of success and a return of profits, it is gearing up for expansion once again.

Sentinel Capital owns an additional 7% of Buffets Holdings; vice chairman and co-founder Roe Hatlen has a 5% stake.

EXECUTIVES

Chairman: Frederick J. (Fred) Iseman, age 51
Vice Chairman: Roe H. Hatlen, age 60
President, CEO, and Director: Kerry A. Kramp, age 48, $491,400 pay
EVP and CFO: R. Michael Andrews Jr., age 39, $224,640 pay
EVP, General Counsel, and Secretary:
 H. Thomas Mitchell, age 46, $194,324 pay
EVP Human Resources: K. Michael Shrader
EVP Marketing: Glenn D. Drasher, age 53, $224,786 pay
VP Development: Janet Astor
VP Workforce Excellence: Nancy Rich
Senior Director of Field Training: Linda Allison
Auditors: Deloitte & Touche

LOCATIONS

HQ: Buffets Holdings, Inc.
 1460 Buffet Way, Eagan, MN 55121
Phone: 651-994-8608 **Fax:** 651-365-2356
Web: www.buffet.com

2004 Locations

	No.
California	96
Illinois	32
Michigan	20
Ohio	20
Pennsylvania	20
New York	16
Washington	16
Minnesota	15
Colorado	14
Arizona	12
Wisconsin	12
Indiana	11
Missouri	11
Virginia	9
Massachusetts	9
New Jersey	8
Maryland	7
Oregon	7
Other states	45
Total	**380**

Builders FirstSource

Builders FirstSource sells hardware and doors, windows, lumber, and other structural building products primarily to new home builders. Since its founding in 1997 as Stonegate Resources, the company has grown, primarily through acquisitions, to include about 60 distribution centers and more than 80 manufacturing plants in more than 10 states. Builders FirstSource was founded by a management team headed by former CEO John Roach and private investment firm JLL Partners (formerly Joseph, Littlejohn & Levy). Builders FirstSource has put itself up for sale.

EXECUTIVES

Chairman and CEO: Floyd F. Sherman
COO: Kevin P. O'Meara
SVP and CFO: Charles L. Horn
SVP and General Counsel: Donald F. McAleenan
VP, Information Technology: Tom McLean
VP, Logistics: Salim Baltagi
VP, Manufacturing: Fred Schenkel
VP, National Sales and Marketing: David M. Snyder
VP, Process Improvement: Rich TerHaar
VP, Purchasing: Dan Carver
Director, Human Resources: Bobby Quinten
Auditors: PricewaterhouseCoopers LLP

LOCATIONS

HQ: Builders FirstSource
2001 Bryan St., Ste. 1600, Dallas, TX 75201
Phone: 214-880-3500 **Fax:** 214-880-3599
Web: www.buildersfirstsource.com

Builders FirstSource has plants and distribution facilities in Colorado, Florida, Georgia, Kentucky, Maryland, New Jersey, North Carolina, Ohio, Tennessee, Texas, South Carolina, and Virginia.

PRODUCTS/OPERATIONS

Selected Products
Building Materials
Interior Items
Lumber and Related Products
Manufactured Components
Millwork
Tools

COMPETITORS

84 Lumber
Ace Hardware
Building Materials Holding
Carter Lumber
CertainTeed
Home Depot
Lanoga
Lowe's
McCoy
Menard
TruServ
Wolohan Lumber

PRODUCTS/OPERATIONS

2004 Locations

	No.
Company-owned	360
Franchised	20
Total	**380**

COMPETITORS

Applebee's
Barnhill's Buffet
Bob Evans
Boston Market
Buffet Partners
Carlson Restaurants
CBRL Group
CiCi Enterprises
Denny's
Frisch's
Garden Fresh Restaurants
Golden Corral
Luby's
Metromedia Restaurant Group
Pancho's Mexican Buffet
Piccadilly Cafeterias
Ryan's
Shoney's
Star Buffet
VICORP Restaurants
Western Sizzlin
Worldwide Restaurant Concepts

HISTORICAL FINANCIALS

Company Type: Private

Income Statement			FYE: Wednesday nearest June 30	
	REVENUE ($ mil.)	NET INCOME ($ mil.)	NET PROFIT MARGIN	EMPLOYEES
6/04	943	8	0.8%	23,000
6/03	985	13	1.3%	23,000
6/02*	527	(7)	—	24,000
12/01	1,045	13	1.2%	25,000
12/00	1,021	32	3.1%	25,200
12/99	937	42	4.5%	25,000
12/98	869	39	4.5%	24,350
12/97	809	29	3.5%	24,830
12/96	751	(7)	—	24,100
12/95	510	27	5.3%	15,540
Annual Growth	**7.1%**	**(12.6%)**	—	**4.5%**

*Fiscal year change

2004 Year-End Financials
Debt ratio: — Current ratio: 0.75
Return on equity: — Long-term debt ($ mil.): 496
Cash ($ mil.): 42

Net Income History

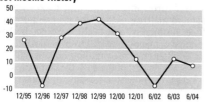

HISTORICAL FINANCIALS

Company Type: Private

Income Statement			FYE: December 31	
	REVENUE ($ mil.)	NET INCOME ($ mil.)	NET PROFIT MARGIN	EMPLOYEES
12/03	1,500	—	—	6,100
12/02	1,500	—	—	6,100
12/01	1,561	—	—	6,800
12/00	1,710	—	—	6,800
12/99	1,900	—	—	5,160
12/98	1,220	—	—	5,200
Annual Growth	**4.2%**	—	—	**3.2%**

Revenue History

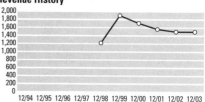

Burger King

This king commands a whopper of a fast food empire. Burger King operates the #2 hamburger chain (behind McDonald's) with more than 11,200 restaurants across the US and in about 55 other countries. In addition to its popular Whopper sandwich, the chain offers a variety of burgers, chicken sandwiches, salads, and breakfast items. Most of Burger King's free-standing units offer drive-through service as well as dine-in seating; about 90% of its restaurants are operated by franchisees. Founded by James McLamore and David Edgerton in 1954, Burger King was owned by UK-based Diageo until 2002 when an investment group led by Texas Pacific Group bought the company for about $1.5 billion and took it private.

The fast food giants have been embroiled in a down-and-dirty price war trying to steal market share while consumers have started to abandon greasy menus in search of healthier alternatives. And while all the big chains have experienced declining same-store sales, Burger King has also suffered from several failed attempts to redesign its brand and, worst of all, a revolving door in the board room.

The company has welcomed nine CEOs since 1989, with the latest CEO to come and go being Brad Blum, former Darden Restaurants vice chairman. Appointed late in 2002, Blum attempted to turn the chain around through a focus on quality and by introducing new products, such as the Angus Steak Burger and Fire-Grilled Salads. Despite some improvement in sales, he resigned the post after just 18 months, citing strategic differences with the company's board. Later, Bob Nilsen, a veteran of the Taco Bell chain brought in to be president of the company, also unexpectedly resigned. Shortly after, the company announced Greg Brenneman as its latest CEO; he is best known for his turnaround work at Continental Airlines.

The company switched its $350 million advertising business from Deutsch to Young & Rubicam in 2003 but promptly fired Y&R in 2004 after results from its "fire-grilled" campaign were weaker than Burger King had hoped. Miami-based Crispin Porter Bogusky took over creative work for the hamburger chain and have created a series of successful advertisements for Burger King, which target the male mid-to-late-20s demographic. Its "subservient chicken" Internet campaign, in which a person dressed a chicken would obey commands, was a gross yet popular illustration of the chain's "Have It Your Way" slogan. The ad company also created "Dr. Angus", a fake motivational speaker who hawked his Atkins-inspired, all-Angus beef diet.

2004 has been a year of consistent sales growth for Burger King, and Brenneman's presence has been a boost for the company. In October 2004 the company signed a deal (with rancher Luiz Eduardo Batalha) to develop about 50 restaurants in Brazil over a five-year period.

HISTORY

In 1954 restaurant veterans James McLamore and David Edgerton opened the first Burger King in Miami. Three years later the company added the Whopper sandwich (which then sold for 37 cents) to its menu of hamburgers, shakes, and sodas. Burger King used television to help advertise the Whopper (its first TV commercial appeared in 1958). During its infancy Burger King was the first chain to offer dining rooms.

Looking to expand nationwide, Burger King turned to franchising in 1959. McLamore and Edgerton took a hands-off approach, allowing franchises to buy large territories and operate with autonomy. Although their technique spurred growth, it also created large service inconsistencies among Burger Kings across the US; this gaffe would haunt the company for years. Having grown to 274 stores in the US and abroad, Burger King was sold to Pillsbury in 1967.

During the early 1970s Burger King continued to add locations. The company did well during this time, launching its successful "Have It Your Way" campaign in 1974 and introducing drive-through service a year later. Yet parent Pillsbury had to fight to rein in large franchisees who argued they could run their Burger Kings better than a packaged-goods company. In 1977 Pillsbury handed control of Burger King to Donald Smith, a McDonald's veteran, who soon silenced the insurrection. Smith tightened franchising regulations, created 10 regional management offices, and instituted annual visits.

Smith left for Pizza Hut in 1980, and by 1982 Burger King had reached the #2 hamburger chain plateau, trailing only McDonald's. The company struggled through the rest of the 1980s, hurt by high management turnover and a string of unsuccessful ad campaigns (such as the ill-fated 1986 NFL Super Bowl "Herb the Nerd" concept). Pillsbury became the target of a hostile takeover by UK-based Grand Metropolitan, and in 1988 Grand Met acquired Pillsbury along with its 5,500 Burger King restaurants.

Grand Met bolstered Burger King's foreign operations in 1990 by converting about 200 recently acquired UK-based Wimpey hamburger stores into Burger Kings. International expansion increased with new restaurants in Mexico (1991), Saudi Arabia (1993), and Paraguay (1995). In 1997 Grand Met and Guinness combined their operations to form Diageo, making Burger King a subsidiary. That year Dennis Malamatinas left Grand Met's Asian beverage division to become Burger King's CEO. In 1999 the company joined rival TRICON (now YUM! Brands) in shucking out $150 million to help food distributor AmeriServe stay afloat following AmeriServe's filing for bankruptcy.

Late in 2000 Diageo announced plans to spin off Burger King, but the burger chain's slow sales delayed action. Malamatinas resigned as CEO and was replaced in 2001 by John Dasburg, former CEO of Northwest Airlines. Late that year Burger King took its cue from McDonald's popular New Tastes Menu and introduced 14 new items to its menu, including a vegetarian burger.

An investment group led by Texas Pacific Group acquired Burger King for $1.5 billion in 2002. Earlier that year Texas Pacific had agreed to pay $2.26 billion but renegotiated amid falling sales and a downturn in the burger market. Shortly after the purchase, Dasburg was ousted and Brad Blum, vice chairman of Darden Restaurants, was named as his replacement.

In May 2004 Burger King began serving its Angus Steak Burger, which includes one-third of a pound of Angus beef. The next month Steak n Shake sued Burger King for allegedly infringing on its trademark by using the words "steak burger" in its advertising. After just 18 months on the job, Blum resigned his post as CEO in 2004, citing differences with the company's board.

EXECUTIVES

CEO: Gregory D. (Greg) Brenneman, age 42
EVP and CFO: Cedric W. Burgher
EVP, Chief Marketing Officer, and President, Burger King Brands: Russ Klein, age 45
EVP and Chief Human Resources Officer: Pete Smith
EVP US Franchise Operations: Jim Hyatt
SVP Corporate Communications: Steven C. DeSutter, age 50
SVP Diversity and Chief of Staff: Clyde Rucker
SVP Restaurant Operations, US: Dave Gagnon
SVP Franchise Operations, Eastern Division: Enrique (Rick) Silva
SVP Franchise Operations, Western Division: Joe Soraci
VP and Corporate Counsel: Elsie Romero
VP Asset Management, Design, and Construction: Amy Knights
VP Audit and Risk Management: Betty Ann Blandon
VP Consumer Insights and Strategic Planning: Mike Kappitt
VP Development, North America: Suk Singh
VP Franchising: Michael Deegan
VP Training: James (Jim) McLaughlin
CIO: Rafael Sanchez
General Counsel: Anne Chwat

LOCATIONS

HQ: Burger King Corporation
5505 Blue Lagoon Dr., Miami, FL 33126
Phone: 305-378-3000   **Fax:** 305-378-7262
Web: www.burgerking.com

2004 Locations

	No.
US	7,679
International	3,544
Total	**11,223**

PRODUCTS/OPERATIONS

2004 Locations

	No.
Franchised	10,144
Company-owned	1,079
Total	**11,223**

COMPETITORS

AFC Enterprises	McDonald's
Chick-fil-A	Papa John's
CKE Restaurants	Subway
Dairy Queen	Triarc
Domino's	Wendy's
Jack in the Box	Whataburger
Little Caesar's	YUM!

HISTORICAL FINANCIALS

Company Type: Private

Income Statement
FYE: June 30

	REVENUE ($ mil.)	NET INCOME ($ mil.)	NET PROFIT MARGIN	EMPLOYEES
6/04	1,110	—	—	349,600
6/03	1,110	—	—	320,000
6/02	1,721	—	—	310,000
6/01	1,474	—	—	30,166
6/00	1,427	—	—	28,432
6/99	1,379	—	—	26,000
6/98	1,449	—	—	27,149
6/97	1,396	—	—	29,590
6/96	1,342	—	—	
Annual Growth	(2.3%)	—	—	42.3%

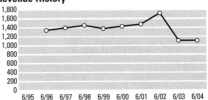

Revenue History

Burlington Industries

Burlington Industries could be considered a fabricator for the fashion industry. The company is one of the largest US fabric makers, along with Milliken and Springs Industries. It makes wool worsted and worsted-blend fabrics, denim, cotton and cotton-blend fabrics, and waterproof synthetics for the apparel market. Burlington's interior furnishing fabrics unit makes woven jacquard mattress ticking and jacquard used in office, hospitality, and health care goods. The troubled company emerged from bankruptcy in late 2003 after a $614 million buyout by W.L. Ross & Co. As part of the deal, the company sold its Lees Carpet division to Mohawk Industries.

Burlington is undergoing an extensive reorganization process in response to an influx of low-priced textiles from Asia, overcapacity in the industry, and the downturn in the economy. The company has most recently sold the consumer products portion of its interior furnishings businesses along with its bathroom accessories unit, shuttering many plants in the U.S. and Mexico.

Burlington has a controlling interest in Nano-Tex, which employs nanotechnology to develop water and wrinkle resistant textiles. The company is looking to its successful Lees carpet division and emerging Nano-Tex unit to help

Burlington return to profitability. It is also shifting manufacturing to contract mills in Asia, while producing more lucrative specialty textiles.

Berkshire Hathaway agreed to acquire the struggling company in early 2003, but dropped its offer after the bankruptcy court rejected certain Berkshire conditions. W.L. Ross & Co., led by chairman Wilbur Ross, was later named the highest bidder for Burlington following a 2003 auction of its assets.

EXECUTIVES

Chairman: Wilbur L. Ross Jr., age 66
CEO and President: Joseph L. Gorga, age 50
CFO: Carl J. Hawk, age 61
Chief Information Officer: Barbara Sorkin
EVP, Global Product Development: Joel Futterman
EVP, Manufacturing: Michael Ambler
VP, Human Resources: Bob Garren
President, Burlington Apparel Fabrics: Ken Kunberger
Auditors: Ernst & Young LLP

LOCATIONS

HQ: Burlington Industries, Inc.
  3330 W. Friendly Ave., Greensboro, NC 27410
Phone: 336-379-2000   **Fax:** 336-332-0815
Web: www.burlington.com

Burlington Industries has manufacturing plants in Mexico and the US.

PRODUCTS/OPERATIONS

Selected Products and Brands

Apparel Fabrics
  Denim
  Woven worsted and worsted blend fabrics
  Woven synthetic fabrics, made with nylon and polyester blends
Carpet
  Tufted synthetic commercial carpet (Lees Carpet, sold in 2003)
Interior Furnishings
  Woven jacquard (mattress ticking, residential bedding and window products, and office, hospitality and healthcare products)

COMPETITORS

Avondale Incorporated
Cone Mills
Culp
Dan River
Delta Woodside
Fab Industries
Galey & Lord
Greenwood Mills
Guilford Mills
Malden Mills
Milliken
Mount Vernon Mills
Quaker Fabric
R. B. Pamplin
Shaw Industries
Springs Industries
Unifi
WL Gore

HISTORICAL FINANCIALS

Company Type: Private

Income Statement			FYE: Saturday nearest September 30	
	REVENUE ($ mil.)	NET INCOME ($ mil.)	NET PROFIT MARGIN	EMPLOYEES
9/02	993	(101)	—	7,600
9/01	1,404	(91)	—	13,700
9/00	1,620	(527)	—	17,900
9/99	1,652	(32)	—	18,500
9/98	2,010	81	4.0%	18,900
9/97	2,091	59	2.8%	20,100
9/96	2,182	41	1.9%	21,000
9/95	2,209	68	3.1%	22,500
9/94	2,127	95	4.5%	23,800
9/93	2,058	85	4.1%	23,600
Annual Growth	(7.8%)	—	—	(11.8%)

2002 Year-End Financials

Debt ratio: —   Current ratio: 0.83
Return on equity: —   Long-term debt ($ mil.): 0
Cash ($ mil.): 165

Net Income History

Burt Automotive

John Elway may have retired, but Burt Automotive Network is still trying to sack him. In Denver Burt goes head-to-head with the John Elway AutoNation dealerships once owned (and still named for) the former Broncos star. Burt operates seven dealerships in Colorado that sell new cars from Ford, GM, Mazda, Toyota, and Subaru. It also sells commercial trucks and used cars and offers parts and repair services. With Kuni Automotive, Burt operates Burt Kuni Honda in Centennial, Colorado. Burt, owned by CEO Lloyd G. Chavez, is one of the largest Hispanic-owned businesses in the US. A salesman with Burt since 1950, Chavez became the majority owner in 1982 and bought the rest of the company in 1987.

EXECUTIVES

Chairman: Lloyd G. Chavez Sr.
President and CEO: Lloyd G. Chavez Jr., age 54
CFO: Robin Helms
SVP, General Manager, and Corporate Legal Counsel: John Held
Marketing Director: Deborah Brown Garrity
Human Resources Manager: Todd van Maldeghem
Executive Administrative Assistant: Patty Hara

LOCATIONS

HQ: Burt Automotive Network
  10301 E. Arapahoe Rd., Centennial, CO 80112
Phone: 303-789-6700   **Fax:** 303-789-6706
Web: www.burt.com

COMPETITORS

AutoNation
Larry H. Miller Group
MNL, Inc.
Phil Long Dealerships

HISTORICAL FINANCIALS

Company Type: Private

Income Statement			FYE: December 31	
	REVENUE ($ mil.)	NET INCOME ($ mil.)	NET PROFIT MARGIN	EMPLOYEES
12/03	1,575	—	—	1,000
12/02	1,478	—	—	1,032
12/01	1,317	—	—	1,350
12/00	1,130	—	—	1,200
12/99	1,004	—	—	1,184
12/98	838	—	—	1,019
12/97	867	—	—	875
12/96	813	—	—	849
12/95	576	—	—	790
12/94	423	—	—	719
Annual Growth	15.7%	—	—	3.7%

Revenue History

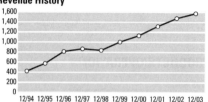

BWAY

BWAY helps keep coffee fresh and ammo dry. The company manufactures steel containers such as aerosol cans, pails, specialty cans, oblong cans, and ammunition boxes. Its products package items from paints, lubricants, and roof and driveway sealants to food, coffee, vegetable oil, and aerosol products. The company also provides material center services such as coating, lithography, and metal shearing. BWAY Manufacturing is the company's main subsidiary. Private investment firm Kelso & Company bought the company in 2002 in partnership with BWAY's chairman and CEO Jean-Pierre Ergas, vice chairman Warren Hayford, and other members of management.

The company has shut down some facilities in Ohio and Illinois in an effort to concentrate on reducing its debt and revitalizing its material center operations (coating and lithography services). The US accounts for the more than 95% of sales.

BWAY has moved into the plastic container manufacturing industry through the acquisition of SST Industries. It also acquired North America Packaging Corporation (NAMPAC), a provider of molded plastic pails, tighthead containers, plastic bottles, and drums in mid 2004. BWAY plans to form a NAMPAC Packaging division by merging NAMPAC with its newly acquired SST Industries subsidiary.

EXECUTIVES

Chairman and CEO: Jean-Pierre M. Ergas, age 64, $1,512,500 pay
Vice Chairman: Warren J. Hayford, age 74
COO: Kenneth M. (Ken) Roessler, age 39, $675,000 pay
EVP, Manufacturing and Engineering:
  Thomas (Tom) Eagleson, age 61, $589,229 pay

VP and Treasurer: Jeffrey M. (Jeff) O'Connell, age 50, $302,400 pay
VP, Administration and CFO: Kevin C. Kern, age 42, $480,000 pay
VP, Marketing and National Accounts: Robert C. (Bob) Coleman
VP, Human Resources: Joe Frabotta
VP, Sales, Aerosols: Sean Fitzgerald
President and COO, NAMPAC Packaging Division: Tom Linton
Director, Engineering: Dennis Dettmer
Director, Information Tech Services: Dennis Strobel
Director, Operations Analysis: Les Bradshaw
Auditors: Deloitte & Touche LLP

LOCATIONS

HQ: BWAY Corporation
8607 Roberts Dr., Ste. 250, Atlanta, GA 30350
Phone: 770-645-4800   **Fax:** 770-645-4810
Web: www.bwaycorp.com

BWAY has manufacturing facilities in California, Georgia, Illinois, Mississippi, New Jersey, Ohio, Pennsylvania, Tennessee, and Texas.

PRODUCTS/OPERATIONS

2003 Sales

	$ mil.	% of total
General line containers	463.6	84
Material center services	64.5	12
Ammunition boxes	20.2	4
Plastic containers	2.8	0
Total	**551.1**	**100**

Selected Products and Services

Aerosol cans
Ammunition boxes
Coffee cans
Material centers (cut, coil, coat, and lithograph sheets of steel)
Oblong cans
Pails
Paint cans
Specialty cans (utility cans with screw-cap tops and applicator brushes; cone top cans)

Selected Subsidiaries

Armstrong Containers, Inc.
BWAY Manufacturing, Inc.

COMPETITORS

Amcor
Ball Corporation
CLARCOR
Consolidated Container
Crown
Jarden
Pechiney
Silgan
U.S. Can

HISTORICAL FINANCIALS

Company Type: Private

Income Statement   FYE: Sunday nearest September 30

	REVENUE ($ mil.)	NET INCOME ($ mil.)	NET PROFIT MARGIN	EMPLOYEES
9/03	551	(3)	—	1,993
9/02	528	12	2.3%	1,868
9/01	475	(17)	—	1,726
9/00	461	(3)	—	1,954
9/99	467	6	1.2%	2,176
9/98	401	2	0.4%	1,898
9/97	402	13	3.3%	2,097
9/96	283	1	0.4%	1,695
9/95	248	9	3.6%	1,155
9/94	225	5	2.3%	1,145
Annual Growth	10.5%	—	—	6.4%

2003 Year-End Financials

Debt ratio: 273.2%
Return on equity: —
Cash ($ mil.): 0
Current ratio: 1.17
Long-term debt ($ mil.): 217

Net Income History

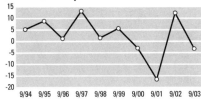

California Dairies

Herding dairies to give them greater "ag"-gregate strength has made California Dairies one of the largest dairy cooperatives in the US. Formed from the 1999 merger of three California dairy cooperatives (California Milk Producers, Danish Creamery Association, and San Joaquin Valley Dairymen), California Dairies' nearly 700 members account for more than 40% of its home state's milk production. The co-op's five plants process milk, cheese, butter, and powdered milk. California Dairies' subsidiaries includes Challenge Dairy Products (retail and foodservice butter products) and Los Banos Foods (cheddar cheese for food manufacturing).

EXECUTIVES

Chairman: George Borba
President and CEO: Gary L. Korsmeier
SVP, CFO: Joe Heffington
SVP, COO: Keith Gomes
SVP of Marketing and Sales: Jim Gomes
SVP of Producer and Government Relations: Richard Cotta
VP, Human Resources: Holly Misenhimer
MIS Director: Scott McDonald

LOCATIONS

HQ: California Dairies Inc.
11709 E. Artesia Blvd., Artesia, CA 90701
Phone: 562-865-1291   **Fax:** 562-860-8633
Web: www.californiadairies.com

COMPETITORS

AMPI
Dairy Farmers of America
Dean Foods
Foremost Farms
Foster Dairy Farms
Land O'Lakes
Northwest Dairy

HISTORICAL FINANCIALS

Company Type: Cooperative

Income Statement   FYE: April 30

	REVENUE ($ mil.)	NET INCOME ($ mil.)	NET PROFIT MARGIN	EMPLOYEES
4/04	1,916	—	—	600
4/03	1,870	—	—	565
4/02	2,240	—	—	560
4/01	2,000	—	—	530
4/00	1,832	—	—	550
4/99	1,900	—	—	550
4/98	1,680	—	—	500
4/97	962	—	—	150
4/96	800	—	—	150
4/95	800	—	—	138
Annual Growth	10.2%	—	—	17.7%

Revenue History

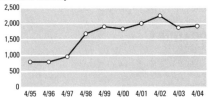

California State University

California State University (CSU) turns students into teachers. The university traces its roots to the state's teaching colleges and trains some 60% of California's teachers. CSU is also neck and neck with the State University of New York (SUNY) as the nation's largest university system. With some baby boomers' children reaching college age and college participation increasing among adults, CSU's student body has grown to about 409,000. The system has campuses in 23 cities, including Bakersfield, Los Angeles, San Francisco, and San Jose. The university primarily awards bachelor's and master's degrees in about 240 subject areas, leaving higher levels of study to the University of California (UC) system.

CSU is developing strategies to cope with an expected enrollment increase of about 40% through 2010 — what it calls Tidal Wave II. The first waves started with more than 20,000 additional students flooding the system in the fall of 2001. To battle the crippling influx of new students, CSU has begun offering distance-education programs in which students are taught via teleconferencing and the Internet. Other strategies involve adding a summer semester to create year-long schooling, and expanding the use of off-campus centers.

HISTORY

In 1862 San Francisco's Normal School, a training center for elementary teachers, became California's first state-founded school for higher education. Six students attended its first classes, but there were 384 by 1866. It later moved to San Jose to escape the bustle of San Francisco.

In the late 1880s State Normal Schools opened in Chico, San Diego, and San Francisco, followed in 1901 by California State Polytechnic Institute, which offered studies in agriculture, business, and engineering. Other new colleges included Fresno State (1911) and Humboldt State (1913). Most of the schools offered four-year programs and admitted any student with eight years of grammar school education.

The Normal Schools were renamed Teachers Colleges in 1921 to reflect their role in teacher education. Two years later the colleges began awarding bachelor of arts degrees in education.

In 1935 the schools were renamed State Colleges and expanded into liberal arts. In 1947 they were authorized to confer master's degrees in education.

After WWII, students on the GI Bill helped increase enrollment, and campuses opened in Los Angeles, Sacramento, and Long Beach. The prospect of the first baby boomers reaching college age prompted the founding of more campuses in the late 1950s. Russia's 1957 launch of Sputnik spurred additional focus on science and math at all education levels. The next year the colleges began awarding master's degrees in subjects unrelated to teacher education.

During the Red Scare, the system's first chancellor, Buell Gallagher, was accused by the press of being soft on communism. Other faculty were subpoenaed to appear before the House Committee on Un-American Activities.

In 1961 the system became the California State Colleges (CSC) and the board of trustees was created, giving the schools more independence from state government. In 1969 student and faculty groups seeking ethnic studies departments went on strike in San Francisco; the unrest closed the campus.

In 1972 CSC became known as the California State University and Colleges. Ten years later it adopted the name California State University.

Barry Munitz became chancellor in 1991, taking over a system that had become oppressive due to a heavy-handed administration. Munitz, who came from corporate America, brought his business sense to the university and increased private fund raising, among other activities. He used words like "consumer" and "product" to describe his job. Munitz also increased tuition, which caused enrollments to drop from 1991-1995.

CSU added two new campuses in 1995, including CSU Monterey Bay, the first military base to be converted into a university since the end of the Cold War.

In 1997 Charles Reed was named to replace Munitz as chancellor, effective the following year. That year CSU proposed the California Educational Technology Initiative (CETI), a plan to build high-speed computer and telephone networks linking its campuses. CETI failed in 1998 after Microsoft and other investors pulled out. In 1999, after lengthy contract negotiations between Reed and faculty members failed to produce accord over teacher salaries and employment conditions, Reed imposed his own merit-based plan. The faculty responded with official rebukes and a vote of no confidence in Reed. The two sides eventually settled on a new three-year contract with provisions that salary and benefits may be negotiated annually.

The rancor over pay continued in 2000 when the California Faculty Association issued a report claiming women were discriminated against and the merit system was inherently unfair. CSU issued its own report denying the charges. In 2001 Reed, stirring up more controversy, began a new quest that would allow CSU to offer doctorate degrees. The move is bitterly opposed by the competing University of California system. In 2002 CSU started a program funded by a federal grant to reduce the harmful effects of alcohol on its students. CSU received a nearly $24 million budget cut in 2003, which led to a reduction in its enrollment growth.

EXECUTIVES

Chair: Murray L. Galinson
Vice Chair: Roberta Achtenberg
Chancellor: Charles B. Reed, age 63
Executive Vice Chancellor and CFO: Richard P. West
Executive Vice Chancellor and Chief Academic Officer: David S. Spence
Vice Chancellor Human Resources: Jackie McClain
Vice Chancellor University Advancement; President, CSU Foundation: Louis E. Caldera, age 48
General Counsel: Christine Helwick, age 57
Auditors: KPMG LLP

LOCATIONS

HQ: Trustees of the California State University
401 Golden Shore, Long Beach, CA 90802
Phone: 562-951-4000   **Fax:** 562-951-4949
Web: www.calstate.edu

California State University has campuses in 23 cities.

California State University Campuses
California Maritime Academy
California Polytechnic State University, San Luis Obispo
California State Polytechnic University, Pomona
California State University
  Bakersfield
  Channel Islands
  Chico
  Dominguez Hills
  Fresno
  Fullerton
  Hayward
  Long Beach
  Los Angeles
  Monterey Bay
  Northridge
  Sacramento
  San Bernardino
  San Marcos
  Stanislaus
Humboldt State University
San Diego State University
San Francisco State University
San Jose State University
Sonoma State University

PRODUCTS/OPERATIONS

Selected Majors
Agriculture
Anthropology
Asian studies
Business administration
Chemistry
Communications
Computer science
Economics
Education
History
Latin American studies
Mathematics
Nursing
Philosophy
Physics
Psychology
Public administration
Theater arts

HISTORICAL FINANCIALS

Company Type: School

Income Statement
FYE: June 30

	REVENUE ($ mil.)	NET INCOME ($ mil.)	NET PROFIT MARGIN	EMPLOYEES
6/03	4,499	—	—	40,000
6/02	4,286	—	—	40,000
6/01	4,050	—	—	40,000
6/00	3,804	—	—	40,000
6/99	3,272	—	—	40,323
6/98	2,612	—	—	39,000
6/97	2,522	—	—	38,512
6/96	3,889	—	—	37,360
6/95	3,121	—	—	33,000
6/94	2,121	—	—	34,779
Annual Growth	8.7%	—	—	1.6%

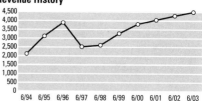

Revenue History

California Steel

California Steel Industries (CSI) is into slab and steel slab. The company uses steel slab produced by third parties to manufacture steel products such as hot-rolled and cold-rolled steel, galvanized coils and sheets, and electric resistance weld (ERW) pipe. Its customers include construction and building suppliers, oil and gas producers, wheel and rim manufacturers, and packaging and container companies. CSI serves the western region of the US; about half of its flat-rolled steel is consumed by customers in Las Vegas, Phoenix, and Southern California. JFE Steel USA, a subsidiary of Japan's JFE Holdings and Brazilian iron ore miner Companhia Vale do Rio Doce (CVRD) each own 50% of CSI.

The majority of sales come from within the US; CSI does sell to foreign customers, primarily in Canada and Mexico (about 1% of tons).

CSI also offers additional services like engineering and metallurgical advice. The company operates slitting, shearing, coating and single-billing services for third parties.

EXECUTIVES

Chairman: Vicente Wright, age 51, $262,370 pay (prior to promotion)
President and CEO: Masakazu Kurushima
EVP and CFO: Ricardo Bernandes, age 41
EVP, Operations: Tashiyuki (Ted) Tamai, age 52, $282,149 pay
VP, Administration and Corporate Secretary: Brett Guge, age 49, $260,050 pay
VP, Sales: James Wilson, age 56, $223,650 pay
Controller and Treasurer: Robert McPherson
Communications Manager: Kyle Schulty

Manager Customer Service, ERW Pipe Products: Martha Martinez
Manager, ERW Pipe Products: Ray Dubreuil
Manager, Manufacturing & OEM Industries: Randy Fox
Manager, Northern Locale Service Centers: Jim Marovich
Manager, Southern Locale Service Center: Al Plummer
Manager, Tubing, Pipe & Culvert: Bill Bender
Auditors: PricewaterhouseCoopers LLP

LOCATIONS

HQ: California Steel Industries, Inc.
14000 San Bernardino Ave., Fontana, CA 92335
Phone: 909-350-6200   **Fax:** 909-350-6223
Web: www.californiasteel.com

California Steel Industries sells steel products in 11 US states located west of the Rocky Mountains.

PRODUCTS/OPERATIONS

2003 Sales

	$ mil.	% of total
Hot-rolled coil & sheet	328.3	43
Galvanized coil & sheet	290.2	38
Cold-rolled coil & sheet	83.9	11
Electric resistance weld (ERW) pipe	61.1	8
Total	**763.5**	**100**

COMPETITORS

AK Steel Holding Corporation
Earle M. Jorgensen
Imsa
Nucor
O'Neal Steel
Reliance Steel
Slater Steel
Steel Dynamics

HISTORICAL FINANCIALS

Company Type: Joint venture

Income Statement   FYE: December 31

	REVENUE ($ mil.)	NET INCOME ($ mil.)	NET PROFIT MARGIN	EMPLOYEES
12/03	764	5	0.6%	921
12/02	754	35	4.6%	929
12/01	640	(4)	—	952
12/00	721	35	4.8%	973
12/99	687	47	6.8%	952
12/98	673	20	2.9%	—
12/97	723	29	4.0%	—
Annual Growth	0.9%	(26.6%)	—	(0.8%)

2003 Year-End Financials

Debt ratio: 71.2%
Return on equity: 2.0%
Cash ($ mil.): 43
Current ratio: 3.78
Long-term debt ($ mil.): 150

Net Income History

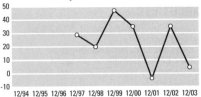

CalPERS

California's public-sector retirees already have a place in the sun; CalPERS gives them the money to enjoy it. CalPERS is the California Public Employees' Retirement System, one of the largest public pension systems in the US. It manages retirement and health plans for more than 1.4 million beneficiaries (employees, retirees, and their dependents) from more than 2,500 government agencies and school districts. Even though the system's beneficiaries are current or former employees of the Golden State, CalPERS brings its influence to bear in all 50 states and beyond.

With more than $165 billion in assets, CalPERS uses its clout to sway such corporate governance issues as company performance, executive compensation, and even social policy. In the absence of a strong federal effort to purge corporations of corruption, CalPERS has often acted as a force for reform; urging companies to remove conflicts of interest and make themselves more accountable to shareholders, employees, and the public.

CalPERS found itself on the receiving end of a corporate governance issue in 2004 when a media group sued, demanding CalPERS make public the fees it pays to venture capital firms and hedge funds.

CalPERS is also a powerful negotiator for such services as insurance; rates established by the system serve as benchmarks for employers throughout the nation.

Most of CalPERS' revenue comes from its enormous investment program: It has interests in US and foreign securities, real estate development and investment, and even hedge funds and venture capital activities. CalPERS has steadily increased its investments in private equity, looking to take ownership stakes in more firms. (It owns a significant stake in investment bank Thomas Weisel.)

During the coming years CalPERS may be forced to sell assets, as it is expected to be hit with a wave of early retirements by middle-aged workers. In the meantime it is eyeing more short-term investments with higher returns.

CalPERS' board consists of six elected, three appointed, and four designated members (the director of the state's Department of Personnel Administration, the state controller, the state treasurer, and a member of the State Personnel Board). The board has seen its share of disputes, on issues ranging from staff salaries to how to invest assets. The public and sometimes nasty donnybrooks have led to the exodus of several key personnel, including a CEO and a chief investment officer.

HISTORY

The state of California founded CalPERS in 1931 to administer a pension fund for state employees. By the 1940s the system was serving other public agencies and educational institutions on a contract basis.

When the Public Employees' Medical and Hospital Care Act was passed in 1962, CalPERS added health coverage. The fund was conservatively managed in-house, with little exposure to stocks. Despite slow growth, the state used the system's funds to meet its own cash shortfalls.

CalPERS became involved in corporate governance issues in the mid-1980s, when California treasurer Jesse Unruh became outraged by corporate greenmail schemes. In 1987 he hired as CEO Wisconsin pension board veteran Dale Hanson, who led the movement for corporate accountability to institutional investors.

In the late 1980s CalPERS moved into real estate and Japanese stocks. When both crashed around 1990, Hanson came under pressure. CalPERS was twice forced to take major writedowns for its real estate holdings and turned to expensive outside fund managers, but its investment performance deteriorated and member services suffered.

Legislation in 1990 enabled CalPERS to offer long-term health insurance. Governor Pete Wilson's 1991 attempt to use $1.6 billion from CalPERS to help meet a state budget shortfall resulted in legislation banning future raids. CalPERS made its first direct investment in 1993, an energy-related infrastructure partnership with Enron.

CalPERS suffered in the 1994 bond crash. That year Hanson resigned amid criticism that his focus on corporate governance had depressed fund performance. The system moved to an indexing strategy. CalPERS eased its corporate relations stance, creating a separate office to handle investor issues and launching an International Corporate Governance Program. However, the next year CalPERS was uninvited from a KKR investment pool because of criticism of its fund management and fee structure.

In 1996 the system teamed with the Asian Development Bank to invest in the Asia/Pacific region; it took a major hit in the Asian financial crisis the next year, but used the downturn as an opportunity to expand its position there in undervalued stocks. In 1998 CalPERS pressured foreign firms to adopt more transparent financial reporting methods.

In 2000 the system raised health care premiums almost 10% to keep up with rising care costs. It widened the scope of its direct investments with stakes in investment bank Thomas Weisel Partners (10%) and asset manager Arrowstreet Capital (15%); it also moved into real estate development, buying Genstar Land Co. with Newland Communities. CalPERS said that year it would sell off more than $500 million in tobacco holdings.

In 2001 California state controller and CalPERS board member Kathleen Connell successfully sued the system for not following state-sanctioned rules regarding pay increases. CalPERS was forced to cut salaries for investment managers, a move that prompted chief investment officer Daniel Szente to resign.

In 2003 CalPERS agreed to a record $250 million settlement relating to an age-discrimination suit brought by the Equal Employment Opportunity Commission. Also in 2003, CalPERS clamored for (and got) the resignation of New York Stock Exchange chairman Richard Grasso. CalPERS and others claimed Grasso's pay of $140 million a year made it impossible for him to effectively monitor the exchange's member companies for corruption.

EXECUTIVES

CEO: Fred R. Buenrostro Jr., age 52
President, Board of Administration; Director: Sean Harrigan
VP, Board of Administration; Director: Rob Feckner
Chief Investment Officer: Mark J.P. Anson
Chief, Human Resources: Patricia Chappie

Chief, Office of Business Solutions, Planning and Organizational Development Branch: Tim Garza
Chief, Fiscal Services Division: Holly Fong
Chief, Customer Service Center: Ron Kraft
Assistant Executive Officer, Financial and Administration Services: Vincent P. Brown
Assistant Executive Officer, Planning and Organizational Development: Allen P. Goldstein
Assistant Executive Officer, Health Benefits Services: Jarvio A. Grevious
Assistant Executive Officer, Information Technology Services: Ronald E. (Gene) Reich
Assistant Executive Officer, Investment Operations: Anne Stausboll
Assistant Executive Officer, Member and Benefit Services: Kathie Vaughn
Assistant Executive Officer, Governmental, Administrative & Planning Services: Robert D. Walton
Assistant Executive Officer, Public Affairs: Patricia K. Macht
Chief, Member Services: Darryl Watson
General Counsel: Peter H. Mixon
Auditors: PricewaterhouseCoopers LLP

LOCATIONS

HQ: California Public Employees' Retirement System
Lincoln Plaza, 400 P St., Sacramento, CA 95814
Phone: 916-795-3829   Fax: 916-558-4001
Web: www.calpers.ca.gov

PRODUCTS/OPERATIONS

2003 Assets

	$ mil.	% of total
Cash & equivalents	27,155	16
Bonds	38,080	22
Stocks	86,571	50
Other investments	7,385	4
Real estate	11,596	7
Receivables	2,376	1
Other assets	170	—
Total	173,333	100

Selected Retirement Plans

Defined Benefit Plans
  Judges' Retirement Fund
  Judges' Retirement Fund II
  Legislators' Retirement System
  Public Employees' Retirement Fund
  Volunteer Firefighters' Length of Service Award System
Defined Contribution Plans
  State Peace Officers' and Firefighters' Defined Contribution Plan Fund
Health Care Plans
  Public Employees' Health Care Fund
  Public Employees' Contingency Reserve Fund
Others
  Replacement Benefit Fund
  Public Employees' Long-Term Care Fund
  Public Employees' Deferred Compensation Fund
  Old Age & Survivors' Insurance Revolving Fund

COMPETITORS

A.G. Edwards	Morgan Stanley
Alliance Capital Management	Nationwide Financial
AXA Financial	Principal Financial
Charles Schwab	Putnam
Citigroup Global Markets	Raymond James Financial
FMR	State Street
Franklin Resources	T. Rowe Price
Janus Capital	TIAA-CREF
Legg Mason	UBS Financial Services
Mellon Financial	USAA
Merrill Lynch	VALIC
MFS	Vanguard Group

HISTORICAL FINANCIALS

Company Type: Government-owned

Income Statement

FYE: June 30

	ASSETS ($ mil.)	NET INCOME ($ mil.)	INCOME AS % OF ASSETS	EMPLOYEES
6/03	173,333	—	—	1,687
6/02	162,167	—	—	1,614
6/01	173,717	—	—	1,614
6/00	191,157	—	—	1,594
6/99	172,446	—	—	1,500
6/98	156,643	—	—	1,247
6/97	128,880	—	—	1,089
6/96	102,797	—	—	1,037
6/95	90,417	—	—	1,000
6/94	69,484	—	—	900
Annual Growth	10.7%	—	—	7.2%

Asset History

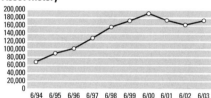

C&S Wholesale

C&S Wholesale Grocers is at the bottom of the food chain — and likes it that way. The company is New England's largest food wholesaler and second in the US (behind SUPERVALU), delivering groceries to approximately 4,000 independent supermarkets, major supermarket chains (including Safeway), mass marketers, and wholesale clubs. The company distributes more than 53,000 items, including groceries, produce, and non-food items. C&S also sells groceries through Grand Union supermarkets. Chairman and CEO Richard Cohen owns the company, which his grandfather started in 1918.

Under pressure from the rapid growth of self-distributing grocery chains (notably Wal-Mart Supercenters), C&S Wholesale has grown by providing outsourced distribution and logistics services to its retailer customers through its logistics service provider ES3. The wholesaler has taken over the facilities and runs distribution and logistics for customers including the Stop & Shop, Pathmark, Safeway's Eastern Division, and the Tops Markets supermarket chains.

To avoid losing one of its top customers, the company, through affiliate GU Markets, bought bankrupt supermarket chain The Grand Union Company's assets in March 2001, expanding C&S Wholesale into retailing. However, C&S Wholesale has since closed or sold off most of Grand Union's 170 stores. The 2002 acquisition of Tops' distribution operations, with facilities in Buffalo, New York, and the Cleveland area, opened up new markets for C&S Wholesale. In keeping with its buying surge, C&S in 2003 purchased parts of the wholesale grocery division of Fleming Companies.

HISTORY

Israel Cohen and Abraham Siegel began C&S Wholesale Grocers in 1918 in Worcester, Massachusetts. Cohen ran the company for more than 50 years after buying out Siegel in 1921. It became a family concern in 1972 when Cohen turned the company over to his son Lester, who soon brought in his sons, Jim and Rick.

C&S Wholesale expanded over the years, growing along with its customers. It had $98 million in sales in 1981, the year its skyrocketing growth began. Also in 1981 Rick, now the company's chairman, president, and CEO, engineered a move to Brattleboro, in southern Vermont, where it had better access to interstate highways and a larger workforce.

After attending a seminar hosted by management whiz Tom Peters, in 1987 Cohen set up self-managed teams of three to eight employees who would act as small business units responsible for a customer's order from the time it was received to when it was delivered. Team members were paid for the amount of time they worked and were given bonuses for error-free operations and penalties for errors or damaged goods. His plan saw an immediate response in terms of increased sales, and by 1992 C&S Wholesale had more than $1 billion in sales. Rick bought out his father in 1989 and the next year became the company's single shareholder when he bought out his brother.

C&S Wholesale started its produce business in 1990 (by 1994 it was the major purchaser of locally grown fruits and vegetables) and began making plans to build an 800,000-sq.-ft. refrigerated warehouse near a scenic highway in Brattleboro. However, it ran up against environmentalists as well as Vermont's Act 250 environmental impact law, and eventually dropped its original plan, opting instead to expand at its headquarters.

In 1992 the wholesaler offered plans for a smaller, revised warehouse, but again met opposition. After a two-year battle, C&S Wholesale gave up and said it would build elsewhere. (Most of its employees and warehouses are now in Massachusetts and New Jersey.)

The following year C&S Wholesale welcomed 127 Grand Union stores and several East Coast Wal-Mart stores as customers. The next year the company picked up another 103 Grand Union stores; Grand Union said it was closing two distribution centers and shifting distribution to C&S Wholesale in a deal worth $500 million a year. A $650 million-per-year contract with Edwards stores was inked in 1996, the year C&S Wholesale's sales topped $3 billion.

The company acquired ice-cream distributor New England Frozen Foods in 1997. Continuing its move toward the mid-Atlantic, C&S Wholesale took over the distribution and supply operations of New Jersey-based grocery chain Pathmark Stores in 1998 for $60 million. In 1999 C&S Wholesale purchased Shaw's Supermarkets' Star Markets' wholesale division and moved into Pennsylvania with a facility in York.

In 2001 the company, through affiliate GU Markets, bought most of the assets of one of its biggest customers, bankrupt The Grand Union Company. C&S acquired about 170 of Grand Union's 197 stores in the purchase. It transferred most of the stores to third-party purchasers, but will continue operating about 20 of them.

In June 2002 C&S Wholesale formed a new holding company, called C&S Holdings, and reorganized its management to better oversee its various businesses. Also that summer the company acquired the grocery distribution operations of Tops Markets, a division of Dutch supermarket giant Royal Ahold.

In 2003 C&S acquired the New England operations of SUPERVALU. In January 2004 president and COO Albertian resigned after three years with the company. He was replaced by Ron Wright, a 20-year veteran with the company.

EXECUTIVES

Chairman and CEO: Richard B. (Rick) Cohen
Vice Chairman: Reuben T. Harris
President, C&S Holdings: Ronald (Ron) Wright
EVP, CFO, General Counsel, and Secretary: Mark Gross
EVP, Distribution and Supply Chain Management:
Nat Silverman
SVP, Chain Sales and Customer Service:
Marilyn Tillinghast
SVP, Finance: Jim Weidenheimer
SVP, Human Resources: Richard S. Burgess
SVP, MIS: Walter Pong
SVP, Merchandising: Michael Papaleo
SVP, Retail Services: Ken Ferrera
SVP, Strategic Planning: William Hamlin
SVP, Supply Chain: George Semanie
Chief Administrative Officer: William C. (Bill) Copacino
Director, Corporate Giving: Gina Goff

LOCATIONS

HQ: C&S Wholesale Grocers, Inc.
7 Corporate Dr., Keene, NH 03431
Phone: 603-354-7000 **Fax:** 603-354-6488
Web: www.cswg.com

C&S Wholesale Grocers has 36 warehouse operations located in 10 US states.

PRODUCTS/OPERATIONS

Selected Customers
A&P Food Mart
Big Y Foods
BJ's Warehouse
Demoulas
Giant Food Stores
Great American
Pathmark
Safeway
SavMart/Foodmax
Shaw's
Stop and Shop

COMPETITORS

Alex Lee
Associated Wholesalers
AWG
Bozzuto's
Di Giorgio
IGA
Krasdale Foods
McLane
Nash Finch
Roundy's
SUPERVALU
Unified Western Grocers
Wakefern Food
White Rose Food

HISTORICAL FINANCIALS

Company Type: Private

Income Statement FYE: September 30

	REVENUE ($ mil.)	NET INCOME ($ mil.)	NET PROFIT MARGIN	EMPLOYEES
9/03	11,300	—	—	10,000
9/02	9,700	—	—	7,500
9/01	8,500	—	—	7,000
9/00	7,000	—	—	5,000
9/99	6,050	—	—	4,000
9/98	5,120	—	—	3,800
9/97	3,665	—	—	3,000
9/96	3,348	—	—	2,850
9/95	2,650	—	—	2,000
9/94	1,837	—	—	1,500
Annual Growth	22.4%	—	—	23.5%

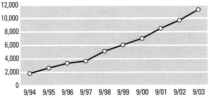

Revenue History

Cargill

Cargill may be private, but it's highly visible. The US's largest private corporation, Cargill's diversified operations include grain, cotton, sugar, and petroleum trading; financial trading; food processing; futures brokering; feed and fertilizer production; and steelmaking. The company is the leading grain producer in the US, and its Excel unit is one of the top US meatpackers. Cargill's brands include Diamond Crystal (salt), Gerkens (cocoa), Honeysuckle White (poultry), and Sterling Silver (fresh meats). Descendants of the founding Cargill and MacMillan families own about 85% of Cargill.

Being private doesn't mean Cargill is cut off from the world. The agribusiness giant has operations in 67 countries throughout the world. Along with its grain and meatpacking businesses, Cargill is a commodity trader and a producer of animal feed and crop fertilizers. It is also a global supplier of oils, syrups, flour, and other products used in food processing.

Cargill also is involved in petroleum trading, financial trading, futures brokering, and shipping. Its North Star subsidiary is a major mini-mill steelmaker in the US. To focus on processing, Cargill sold its seed operations and coffee trading business and is selling part of its steel business. It formed a joint venture with Hormel Foods to market fresh beef, along with pork, under the brand name Always Tender.

In 2003 the company announced a joint venture with Hain Celestial to develop healthy functional foods and beverages using Cargill's isoflavones, inulin, and chondroitin products.

That year Cargill also announced plans to combine its crop-nutrition segment with phosphate fertilizer maker IMC Global to form a new, publicly traded company to be called Mosaic. Cargill will own about 66% of the company.

In 2004 the company announced the discovery of genetic markers in cattle that predict whether or not a specific steer will produce good-tasting meat. It plans to introduce a prototype blood test for the marker and will use it to screen cattle in its feedlots to see if it proves economical.

HISTORY

William W. Cargill founded Cargill in 1865 when he bought his first grain elevator in Conover, Iowa. He and his brother Sam bought grain elevators all along the Southern Minnesota Railroad in 1870, just as Minnesota was becoming an important shipping route. Sam and a third brother, James, expanded the elevator operations while William worked with the railroads to monopolize transport of grain to markets and coal to farmers.

Around the turn of the century, William's son William S. invested in a number of ill-fated projects. William W. found that his name had been used to finance the projects; shortly afterward, he died of pneumonia. Cargill's creditors pressed for repayment, which threatened to bankrupt the company. John MacMillan, William W.'s son-in-law, took control and rebuilt Cargill. It had recovered by 1916 but lost its holdings in Mexico and Canada. MacMillan opened offices in New York (1922) and Argentina (1929), expanding grain trading and transport operations.

In 1945 Cargill bought Nutrena Mills (animal feed) and entered soybean processing; corn processing began soon after and grew with the demand for corn sweeteners. In 1954 Cargill benefited when the US began making loans to help developing countries buy American grain. Subsidiary Tradax, established in 1955, became one of the largest grain traders in Europe. A decade later Cargill began trading sugar by purchasing sugar and molasses in the Philippines and selling them abroad.

Cargill made its finances public in 1973 (as a requirement for its unsuccessful takeover bid of Missouri Portland Cement), revealing it to be one of the US's largest companies, with $5.2 billion in sales. In the 1970s it expanded into coal, steel, and waste disposal and became a major force in metals processing, beef, and salt production.

In the early 1990s Cargill began selling branded meats and packaged foods directly to supermarkets. To placate family heirs who wanted to take Cargill public, CEO Whitney MacMillan, grandson of John, created an employee stock plan in 1991 that allowed shareholders to cash in their shares. He also boosted dividends and reorganized the board, reducing the family's control. MacMillan retired in 1995 and non-family member Ernest Micek became CEO and chairman.

The firm bought Akzo Nobel's North American salt operations in 1997, becoming the #2 US salt company. Cargill bulked up its grain trading business by acquiring the grain export operations of Continental Grain in 1999. Micek resigned as CEO that year and was replaced by Warren Staley. Also in 1999 Cargill fessed up to misappropriating some genetic seed material from rival Pioneer Hi-Bred, killing the $650 million sale of its North American seed assets to Germany's AgrEvo.

Cargill sold its coffee trading unit in 2000. Also, Cargill sold its North American hybrid seed business to Dow Chemical and bought Agribrands International (Purina and Checkerboard animal feeds sold outside the US). In 2001 the company bought family-held turkey and chicken processor Rocco Enterprises.

In 2002 Cargill purchased a 56% stake in Cerestar (starches, syrups, feeds) from Montedison SpA, the Italian agriculture and energy conglomerate. It subsequently purchased the bulk of the company's publicly held stock, increasing its ownership of Cerestar to approximately 97%.

In 2003 Cargill moved into the European industrial chocolate market with the purchase of OCG Cacao S.A., which operates chocolate processing plants in Belgium, France, and the UK.

As part of a joint venture with Mitsubishi Chemical, in 2004 Cargill opened a manufacturing plant for erythritol, a sweetener that is claimed to taste like sugar but contain no calories. It also formed an alliance with Mitsui to distribute erythritol in the Far East.

Entering into the European ingredients market, that year Cargill also acquired The Duckworth Group, a UK flavor company with facilities in Africa, China, India, and the UK. Also in 2004 Cargill bought Agway's feed and nutrition segment; and sold its Brazilian orange juice operations to Citrosuco and Cutrale in separate transactions. Also that year Cargill acquired the German and UK cocoa processing activities of Nestlé and the Brzilian food operations of J.M. Smucker. Later in 2004, Cargill took over Canadian frozen beef-patty maker, Caravelle Foods; it also acquired a 62% interest in Seara Alimentos, a large Brazilian meat producer and intends to buy the remaining interest in 2005.

EXECUTIVES

Chairman and CEO: Warren R. Staley
Vice Chairman and CFO: Robert L. Lumpkins
Vice Chairman: F. Guillaume (Bassy) Bastiaens, age 61
Vice Chairman: David W. Raisbeck, age 56
President and COO: Gregory R. Page
EVP: Fredric W. (Fritz) Corrigan, age 62
EVP: David M. Larson
SVP: David W. Rogers
SVP, Director of Corporate Affairs: Robbin S. Johnson
Corporate VP and President, Excel:
  William A. (Bill) Buckner
Corporate VP: John E. Geisler
Corporate VP: James N. Haymaker
Corporate VP: John D. March
Corporate VP: K. Scott Portnoy
Corporate VP and Controller: Galen G. Johnson
Corporate VP and CTO: Ronald L. Christenson
Corporate VP and Treasurer: William W. Veazey
Corporate VP, General Counsel and Corporate Secretary: Steven C. Euller
Corporate VP, Human Resources: Nancy P. Siska
Corporate VP, Information Technology, and CIO:
  Rita J. Heise
Corporate VP, Procurement: James T. Prokopanko
Corporate VP, Public Affairs: Bonnie E. Raquet
Corporate VP, Transportation & Product Assurance:
  Frank L. Sims, age 53
Director, Stakeholder and Investor Relations:
  Lisa Clemens
Auditors: KPMG LLP

LOCATIONS

HQ: Cargill, Incorporated
  15407 McGinty Rd. West, Wayzata, MN 55391
Phone: 952-742-7575   **Fax:** 952-742-7393
Web: www.cargill.com

Cargill has operations in about 60 countries worldwide.

PRODUCTS/OPERATIONS

Selected Divisions and Products

Agriculture
  Caprock Industries
  Cargill AgHorizons
  Cargill Animal Nutrition
  Cargill Fertilizer
  Cargill Ventures
  Champions Choice
Financial and Risk Management
  Black River Asset Management
  Cargill Financial Markets Group
  Cargill Investor Services (CIS)
  Cargill Value Investment
  Cargill Ventures
Food/Food Processing
  Caravelle Foods
  Cargill Dry Corn Ingredients
  Duckworth Group
  Cargill Foods
  Cargill Foodservice
  Cargill Juice
  Cargill Malt
  Cargill Salt
  Cargill Sweeteners
  Chocolate
  Cocoa Processing
  Excel
  Health and Food Technologies
  Honeysuckle White
  Horizon Milling
  Industrial Oils and Lubricants
  Progressive Baker
  Specialty Food Ingredients
  Sterling Silver Premium Meats
  Starches and Sweeteners
  Sun Valley Foods
  Sunny Fresh Foods
Industrial
  Cargill Industrial Oils
  NatureWax
  Cargill Steel
Trading

Selected Joint Ventures

Ag Partners, L.L.C.
Agrograin Prairie Malt
Banks Cargill Agriculture
Cargill Bottled Oil Europe
Cargill Dow
Horizon Milling
Precept Foods LLC
Renessen
Saskferco
Steel Wind River LLC

COMPETITORS

ADM
Ag Processing
BASF AG
Bunge Limited
Cereol
CHS
COFCO
ConAgra
ContiGroup
Corn Products
  International
Dow Chemical
DuPont
General Mills
Hormel
King Arthur Flour
Koch
Land O'Lakes Farmland
  Feed
Morton Salt
Nippon Steel
Nucor
Perdue
Rohm and Haas
Saskatchewan Wheat Pool
Smithfield Foods
Tate & Lyle
Tyson Foods
Tyson Fresh Meats
United States Steel

HISTORICAL FINANCIALS

Company Type: Private

Income Statement
FYE: May 31

	REVENUE ($ mil.)	NET INCOME ($ mil.)	NET PROFIT MARGIN	EMPLOYEES
5/04	62,907	1,331	2.1%	101,000
5/03	59,894	1,290	2.2%	98,000
5/02	50,826	827	1.6%	97,000
5/01	49,204	358	0.7%	90,000
5/00	47,602	480	1.0%	84,000
5/99	45,697	597	1.3%	84,000
5/98	51,418	468	0.9%	80,600
5/97	56,000	814	1.5%	79,000
5/96	56,000	902	1.6%	76,000
5/95	51,000	671	1.3%	73,300
Annual Growth	2.4%	7.9%	—	3.6%

Net Income History

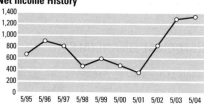

Carilion Health System

Carilion Health System rings true for residents of western Virginia. Founded in 1899 as the Roanoke Hospital Association, the system today includes about 10 hospitals, a nursing home, and a cancer center. Its Medical Center for Children in Roanoke serves as a regional pediatric referral site, and its Carilion Behavioral Health has become one of the most comprehensive psychiatric service networks in its area. Through its 60%-owned, for-profit Carilion Health Plans subsidiary, the system markets its own HMO and point-of-service health care plans.

Carilion has also formed a biomedical research institute together with Virginia Tech and the University of Virginia. Carilion is selling its Carilion Health Plans operation in order to reduce costs.

EXECUTIVES

Chairman: George B. Cartledge Jr.
President and CEO: Edward Murphy
EVP Medical Direction: K. Kellogg Hunt Jr.
EVP Strategic Services: Donald E. Lorton
SVP Human Resources: Brucie Boggs
EVP and President, Western Division: Matt Perry

LOCATIONS

HQ: Carilion Health System
  1212 3rd St., Roanoke, VA 24016
Phone: 540-981-7000   **Fax:** 540-344-5716
Web: www.carilion.com

Carilion Health System operates in Virginia.

Carlson

Carlson Companies began in 1938 as the Gold Bond Stamp Company, but has evolved into a leisure services juggernaut. The company owns 50% of travel giant Carlson Wagonlit (French hotelier Accor owns the rest). It also owns more than 800 hotels under brands such as Radisson, Country Inns & Suites By Carlson, Park Inn, and Park Plaza. Carlson's restaurant empire includes the 700-unit T.G.I. Friday's chain. A specialist in relationship marketing, Carlson Marketing Group offers services such as sales promotion and customer loyalty programs. CEO Marilyn Carlson Nelson and director Barbara Carlson Gage, daughters of founder Curtis Carlson, each own half of the company.

Carlson Companies' travel operations include Carlson Wagonlit Travel, the company's 50/50 joint venture with Accor. One of the largest business travel firms in the world, Carlson Wagonlit counts AT&T, General Electric, and IBM among its clients.

In 2002 the company announced it was building about 20 new hotels, largely Radisson and Country Inns & Suites, in India. Carlson also is active in cruise operations through its Radisson Seven Seas Cruises, which offers one all-suite and five deluxe ships sailing to over 300 destinations.

HISTORY

Curtis Carlson, the son of Swedish immigrants, graduated from the University of Minnesota in 1937 and went to work selling soap for Procter & Gamble in the Minneapolis area. In 1938 he borrowed $55 and formed Gold Bond Stamp Company to sell trading stamps. His wife, Arleen, dressed as a drum majorette and twirled a baton to promote the concept. By 1941 the company had 200 accounts. Business was slowed by WWII but took off in the 1950s. During the 1960s the company began diversifying into other enterprises such as travel, marketing, hotels, and real estate.

In 1962 Gold Bond Stamp bought the Radisson Hotel in Minneapolis and began expanding the chain. The company adopted the Carlson Companies name in 1973. Carlson Companies continued expanding its holdings during the 1970s, buying the 11-unit T.G.I. Friday's chain, as well as Country Kitchen International, a string of family restaurants.

In 1979 Carlson bought First Travel Corp., which owned travel agency Ask Mr. Foster and Colony Hotels. Carlson Companies slowed the pace of its acquisitions in the 1980s. Hired in 1984, Juergen Bartels changed the hospitality division's strategy from building and owning hotels to franchising and managing them. This enabled Carlson to weather the crash that followed the 1980s hotel building boom.

The company took T.G.I. Friday's public to fund expansion in 1983, but it reacquired all outstanding shares in 1989. Carlson launched its cruise ship business in 1992, when the luxury liner SSC *Radisson Diamond* set sail.

The company made a major international advance in 1994 when it formed joint venture Carlson Wagonlit Travel, with France's Accor. In 1997 Carlson expanded into the luxury hotel business when it bought Regent International from Four Seasons. In a nod to its roots, the company also unveiled the Gold Points Reward guest loyalty system to reward customers who frequent its hotels and restaurants.

In 1998 Curtis Carlson appointed his daughter, Marilyn Carlson Nelson, as the company's chief executive (he remained chairman). The following year Carlson Companies merged its UK leisure travel business with UK-based travel and financial services firm Thomas Cook. Founder Curtis Carlson died that year and Nelson added chairman to her title. The company later filed to spin off its T.G.I. Friday's unit as Carlson Restaurants Worldwide.

In 2001 Carlson Companies sold its 22% stake in Thomas Cook Holdings to German tour company C&N (which then changed its name to Thomas Cook AG). In mid-2001 the company bought 52-unit Asian restaurant chain Pick Up Stix. That year it also added a sixth ship to its cruise line.

EXECUTIVES

Chairman and CEO: Marilyn Carlson Nelson, age 64
President and COO: Curtis C. Nelson
EVP and CFO: Martyn R. Redgrave, age 51
SVP and CIO: Stephen S. Brown
SVP and General Counsel: William A. Van Brunt
SVP, Human Resources: Jim Porter
VP and Treasurer: John M. Diracles Jr.
VP, Assurance and Business Risk Management: Vicki Rasmusen
VP, Business Process Improvement: Joseph Dehler
VP, Corporate Human Resources: Charles Montreuil
VP, Enterprise Supply Chain Management: Larry Taylor
VP, Executive Communications: Douglas R. Cody
VP, Finance and Chief Accounting Officer: Robert Kleinschmidt
VP, Human Resources Shared Services: Greg Peters
VP, Legal and Corporate Secretary: Ralph Beha
VP, Strategic Planning and Corporate Development: Peter Hawthorne
VP, Tax: Darrel M. Hamann
COO, CW Government Travel: Scott Guerrero

LOCATIONS

HQ: Carlson Companies, Inc.
701 Carlson Parkway, Minnetonka, MN 55305
Phone: 763-212-1000   **Fax:** 763-212-2219
Web: www.carlson.com

Carlson Companies has operations in more than 140 countries.

PRODUCTS/OPERATIONS

Selected Operations

Cruises
  Radisson Seven Seas Cruises
Hotels
  Country Inns & Suites By Carlson
  Park Inn and Park Plaza hotels
  Radisson Hotels & Resorts
  Regent International Hotels
Management Consulting
  Peppers & Rogers Group
Marketing
  Carlson Marketing Group
  Gold Points Rewards
Restaurants
  Pick Up Stix
  T.G.I. Friday's
Travel
  Carlson Leisure Travel Services
  Carlson Wagonlit Travel (50%)

COMPETITORS

American Express
Applebee's
Brinker
Carnival
Darden
Denny's
Fairmont Hotels
Four Seasons Hotels
Gage Marketing
Hilton
Hyatt
Interpublic Group
Maritz
Marriott
Metromedia
Mitchells & Butlers
O'Charley's
Omnicom
Outback Steakhouse
Ritz-Carlton
Rosenbluth International
Royal Caribbean Cruises
Starwood Hotels & Resorts
Sunterra
TRT Holdings
WorldTravel
WPP Group
Wyndham

PRODUCTS/OPERATIONS

Selected Facilities

Burrell Nursing Center
Carilion Bedford Memorial Hospital
Carilion Franklin Memorial Hospital
Carilion Giles Memorial Hospital
Carilion New River Valley Medical Center
Carilion Roanoke Community Hospital
Carilion Roanoke Memorial Hospital
Carilion Saint Albans Hospital
Smyth County Hospitals
Tazewell Community Hospital
Wythe County Community Hospital

COMPETITORS

American HomePatient
Ascension Health
Bon Secours Health
HCA
Health Management Associates
Inova
Novant Health
Sentara Healthcare
Tenet Healthcare

HISTORICAL FINANCIALS

Company Type: Not-for-profit

Income Statement
FYE: September 30

	REVENUE ($ mil.)	NET INCOME ($ mil.)	NET PROFIT MARGIN	EMPLOYEES
9/03	777	—	—	9,498
9/02	669	—	—	9,609
9/01	1,177	—	—	10,200
9/00	1,080	—	—	10,000
9/99	976	—	—	—
9/98	900	—	—	8,728
9/97	780	—	—	8,500
9/96	701	—	—	7,751
9/95	680	—	—	8,200
9/94	799	—	—	8,000
Annual Growth	(0.3%)	—	—	1.9%

Revenue History

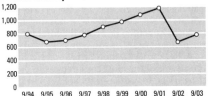

Carlson Wagonlit

History was bunk for Henry Ford, but for Carlson Wagonlit Travel it was a bunk bed. Carlson Wagonlit (pronounced Vah-gon-LEE) Travel descends from Europe's Wagons-Lits (literally, sleeping cars) company, which was founded by the creator of the Orient Express, and from the US's oldest travel agency chain (Ask Mr. Foster). It manages business travel from more than 3,000 travel offices in more than 140 countries. The company is the #2 travel firm in the world behind American Express. It is co-owned by the US firm Carlson Companies (whose US leisure and franchise operations also fall under the Carlson Wagonlit brand) and France's Accor.

Carlson Companies is a service conglomerate with nonbusiness travel operations such as hospitality (it franchises Radisson Hotels, T.G.I. Friday's and Italianni's restaurants, and luxury cruise lines) and marketing services (motivational and incentive programs for businesses). Accor is reaping the benefits of training the company's travel agents in booking Accor hotel rooms. The company's two parents have invested $100 million to get Carlson Wagonlit online with business-to-consumer and business-to-business sites.

The company's joint venture project with China Air Service (51% owned by CAS; 49% Carlson Wagonlit) opened offices in Shanghai and Guangzhou in 2004, further strengthening its position as China's leading corporate travel management company. In March 2004 Carlson Wagonlit agreed to purchase Maritz Travel's US corporate travel subsidiary (MCT).

HISTORY

Belgian inventor Georges Nagelmackers' first enterprise was adding sleeping compartments to European trains in 1872. Nagelmackers later created the Orient Express. Over the years his Wagons-Lits company expanded its mission to become Wagonlit Travel.

While Nagelmackers was establishing his business in Europe, Ward G. Foster was giving out steamship and train schedules from his gift shop facing the stately Ponce de Leon Hotel in St. Augustine, Florida. As legend has it, hotel patrons with travel questions were directed to Foster's shop with: "Ask Mr. Foster. He'll know." In 1888 he founded Ask Mr. Foster Travel (it became the oldest travel agency in the US). By 1913 the company had offices located in pricey department stores and in the lobbies of upscale hotels and resorts throughout the country. After 50 years at the helm, Foster sold his business in 1937, three years before his death.

After suffering hard times during WWII and into the 1950s, the company changed hands again in 1957 when Donald Fisher and Thomas Orr, two Ask Mr. Foster shareholders, bought controlling interests for $157,000. In 1972 Peter Ueberroth (future Major League Baseball commissioner and Los Angeles Olympic Organizing Committee president) bought the company, then sold it in 1979 to Carlson Companies, Inc. In 1990 Ask Mr. Foster became Carlson Travel Network. Also that year Carlson Companies acquired the UK's A.T. Mays, the Travel Agents — a leading UK seller of vacation and tour packages. By 1992 Carlson Companies, besides adding a travel agency a day to the 2,000-plus it already owned, was adding a new hotel every 10 days.

Europe's Wagonlit Travel and the US's Carlson Travel Network joined forces in 1994 to pursue expansion efforts. Under a dual-president ownership, the parent companies owned operations in specific world regions. The two companies began developing new business technology and expanded into new global business markets. In 1994 the venture acquired Germany's Brune Reiseburo travel agency and opened a branch office in Moscow. Through 1995 and 1996 acquisitions targeted the Asia/Pacific region, including Hong Kong's and Japan's Dodwell Travel and the corporate travel business of Singapore's Jetset Travel. It also formed a partnership with Traveland, an Australian travel agency.

In 1997 Wagonlit Travel and Carlson Travel Network finalized the merger of their business activities operations, renamed Carlson Wagonlit Travel. The following year the new company acquired Florida's Travel Agents International, with more than 300 franchised operations and $600 million in annual sales. In 1999 three travel agencies in eastern Canada consolidated under the Carlson Wagonlit Travel brand, creating the largest travel network in that region. Also, Carlson Companies founder and Carlson Wagonlit Travel chairman Curtis Carlson died. In 2000 the company formed a Japan-based joint venture with Japan Travel Bureau (now JTB Corp.). The arrangement increased Carlson Wagonlit's presence in Asia while increasing the number of JTB locations in North America. In 2001 Carlson Wagonlit cut jobs because of a slowdown in business travel.

In 2003 the company formed a joint venture with China Air Service Ltd., creating China's leading corporate travel management company. In 2004 the joint venture project opened offices in Shanghai and Guangzhou.

EXECUTIVES

President and CEO; President, Europe, Middle East, and Africa: Hervé Gourio
Global CFO: Tim Hennessy
EVP Business Travel Services: Dan Miles
EVP Europe, Middle East, and Africa: Liliana Frigerio
EVP Europe, Middle East, and Africa: August Gossewisch
EVP Europe, Middle East, and Africa: Richard Lovell
EVP Global Sales and Marketing: Martin Warner
VP Human Resources: David Moran
President, Asia Pacific and Latin America: Geoffrey Marshall
President, North America: Robin Schleien
EVP and COO, Carlson Wagonlit US: Jack O'Neill
EVP Human Resources, Europe, Middle East, and Africa: Philippe Vinay
EVP Supplier Relations, Industry Relations and Solutions Group, North America: Robert (Rob) Deliberto
VP Finance, North America: Nicholas C. (Nick) Bluhm, age 52
VP Marketing and Support Services, North America: Mark Carter
Global CIO: Loren Brown
CIO, North America: Shawn Smith
Public Relations Specialist: Laurie Alexander

LOCATIONS

HQ: Carlson Wagonlit Travel, Inc.
1405 Xenium Ln. North, Plymouth, MN 55441
Phone: 763-212-4000   **Fax:** 763-212-2219
Web: www.carlsonwagonlit.com

COMPETITORS

American Express
JTB
Kuoni Travel
Maritz
Rosenbluth International
Thomas Cook AG
TUI
World Travel Specialists
WorldTravel

HISTORICAL FINANCIALS

Company Type: Private

Income Statement — FYE: December 31

	ESTIMATED REVENUE ($ mil.)	NET INCOME ($ mil.)	NET PROFIT MARGIN	EMPLOYEES
12/03	6,800	—	—	190,000
12/02	6,700	—	—	180,000
12/01	6,800	—	—	188,000
12/00	9,800	—	—	192,000
12/99	9,800	—	—	188,000
12/98	7,800	—	—	147,000
12/97	6,600	—	—	68,530
12/96	4,900	—	—	65,462
12/95	4,500	—	—	69,000
12/94	3,900	—	—	65,000
Annual Growth	6.4%	—	—	12.7%

Revenue History

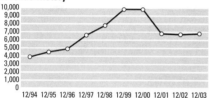

HISTORICAL FINANCIALS

Company Type: Joint venture

Income Statement — FYE: December 31

	REVENUE ($ mil.)	NET INCOME ($ mil.)	NET PROFIT MARGIN	EMPLOYEES
12/03	11,500	—	—	7,047
12/02	10,700	—	—	7,504
12/01	11,000	—	—	8,083
12/00	12,000	—	—	7,702
12/99	11,000	—	—	7,015
12/98	11,000	—	—	20,100
12/97	10,600	—	—	20,000
12/96	9,500	—	—	20,000
Annual Growth	2.8%	—	—	(13.8%)

Revenue History

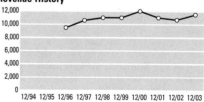

Carlyle Group

Can you say military-industrial complex? The Carlyle Group takes part in management-led buyouts (MBOs), acquires minority stakes, and provides other investment capital for companies. It is particularly hawkish on the aerospace and defense industries, putting to good use the experience of its chairman emeritus Frank Carlucci, a former US secretary of defense. Firms in this arena make up a significant share of the portfolio at Carlyle, one of the world's largest private equity firms. The company has also engineered MBOs and other capital deals for firms in such industries as consumer products, energy, health care, information technology, real estate, beverages, and telecommunications.

Carlyle's directorship reads like George W. Bush's inaugural ball invite list. President Reagan's Treasury Secretary James Baker serves as a senior counselor, and Richard Darman, former director of the Office of Management and Budget under George Bush (the elder), is a managing director. Former President George Bush has served with Carlyle and Colin Powell, before becoming secretary of state, made an appearance on behalf of the firm. There's some former Clinton-era officials on board, too: former FCC chairman William Kennard heads up the firms' telecommunications and media group and former SEC chairman Arthur Levitt is a senior advisor. However, Carlyle is quietly trying to remake its management board less political and a little more entrepreneurial, and recently saw the departure of former British Prime Minister John Major, former president of the Philippines, Fidel Ramos, and Anand Panyarachun, former prime minister of Thailand.

The company has more than $17 billion in assets under management and has invested in such names as United Defense Industries of Crusader artillery fame, Dr Pepper/Seven Up Bottling Group, and MedPointe.

Although the majority of the firm's money is in North America, it is also pushing more intensely overseas, launching funds aimed at Asia, Europe, Latin America, and Russia. One of the company's larger moves overseas is the purchase of the transportation business of The Daiei, Japan's #2 retailer in which the company has a 90% stake. The firm's first European energy deal is now on tap: Carlyle has agreed to buy out Petroplus International, a Dutch oil refiner.

Its moves overseas haven't all been as easy as picking up the phone or as lucrative, however. Carlyle, along with investment firm Welsh, Carson, Anderson & Stowe, bought Dex Media, the yellow pages business of the financially strapped Qwest Communications, but quickly flipped that investment through an IPO less than a year after the acquisition. The firm also returned portions of its European venture capital group funds to investors after the values of its investments lessened and the availability of target acquisitions decreased.

California Public Employees' Retirement System (CalPERS) owns more than 5% of Carlyle.

HISTORY

In 1987 T. Rowe Price director Edward Mathias brought together David Rubenstein, a former aide to President Carter; Stephen Norris and Daniel D'Aniello, both executives with Marriott; William Conway Jr., the CFO of MCI; and Greg Rosenbaum, a VP with a New York investment firm. They pooled their experience along with a load of money from T. Rowe Price Associates, Alex. Brown & Sons (now Deutsche Banc Alex. Brown), First Interstate (now part of Wells Fargo), and Pittsburgh's Mellon family to form a buyout firm.

Named after the Carlyle Hotel in New York, the firm opted to make Washington, DC, its headquarters so it wouldn't get lost in the crowd of New York investment firms. The company spent its first years investing in a mish-mash of companies, using Norris' and D'Aniello's Marriott experience to focus primarily on restaurant and food service companies (including Mexican restaurant chain Chi-Chi's).

In 1989 it wooed the well-connected Frank Carlucci, who had served as President Reagan's secretary of defense, to join the group. Soon thereafter, Carlyle began making more high-profile deals. That year it acquired Coldwell Banker's commercial real estate operations (sold 1996) and Caterair International, Marriott's airline food services (sold 1995).

Carlucci helped redirect the firm's focus to the downsizing defense industry. Among its targets were Harsco (1990), BDM International (1991), and LTV's missile and aircraft units (1992). Carlyle helped overhaul their operations and make them attractive (for the right price) to the industry's elite, including Boeing and Lockheed Martin.

As the company's reputation grew, so did its cast of players. Among its new backers were James Baker and Richard Darman (both Reagan and Bush administration alums) and investor George Soros, who chipped some $100 million into the Carlyle Partners L.P. buyout fund. With the help of its "access capitalists" such as Baker and Saudi Prince al-Waleed bin Talal (whom the firm helped add to his fortune in a 1991 Citicorp stock transaction), Carlyle made deals in the Middle East and Western Europe (including a bailout of Euro Disney) in the mid-1990s.

While the firm continued to be a side in the iron triangle, acquiring such defense companies as aircraft castings maker Howmet in 1995, it picked up a grab bag of holdings, such as natural food grocer Fresh Fields Markets (1994; sold 1996); the quick turnaround helped build Carlyle's war chest. The firm also began investing in industrial-cleanup companies, seeing increased government spending as a major opportunity for profit. In 1999, the firm acquired automobile engine parts manufacturer Honsel International Technologies in Germany's first public-to-private transaction.

As Carlyle's esteem rose, so did the number of its investors. In the late 1990s the firm launched buyout funds targeting Asia (closed 1999), Europe (closed 1998), Russia, and Latin America. At home, it faced a dwindling number of opportunities as the long-running bull market drove up prices and more investors chased fewer deals. Among those was its partnership with Cadbury Schweppes to buy the Dr Pepper Bottling Co. of Texas and merge it with its own American Bottling Co.

Carlyle began the new century by launching Carlyle Asset Management Group, selling its stake in Le Figaro to Socpresse, acquiring Rexnord and a majority stake in CSX Lines.

EXECUTIVES

Chairman: Louis V. Gerstner Jr., age 62
Chairman Emeritus: Frank C. Carlucci, age 74
Founder and Managing Director: William E. Conway Jr., age 54
Founder and Managing Director: Daniel A. D'Aniello
Founder and Managing Director: David M. Rubenstein
Senior Counselor: James A. (Jim) Baker III, age 73
Senior Advisor, Aerospace and Defense, Europe Buyout: Julian Browne
Senior Advisor, Aerospace and Defense, US Buyout: Thomas A. Corcoran, age 59
Senior Advisor, Energy and Power, US Venture, Asia Venture, and Global Energy & Power: Richard G. Darman, age 60
Senior Advisor, US High Yield: Wilfred A. Finnegan
Senior Advisor, Aerospace & Defense, US Buyout: Kent Kresa, age 66
Senior Advisor, Telecom & Media, London: Duncan Lewis
Senior Advisor: Arthur Levitt Jr., age 71
Senior Advisor: Thomas F. (Mack) McLarty III, age 58
Senior Advisor, Technology & Business Services, US Buyout and US Venture: Charles O. Rossotti, age 63
Senior Advisor, US Buyout: David L. Squier
Managing Director and CFO: John F. Harris
VP Corporate Communications: Chris Ullman

LOCATIONS

HQ: The Carlyle Group
1001 Pennsylvania Ave. NW, Ste. 220 South, Washington, DC 20004
Phone: 202-347-2626   **Fax:** 202-347-1818
Web: www.thecarlylegroup.com

PRODUCTS/OPERATIONS

Selected Portfolio Companies

Aerospace and Defense
 Aviall Services, Inc.
 Avio SpA (Italy)
 Firth Rickson (UK)
 Qinetiq (UK)
 Sippican, Inc.
 United Defense Industries, Inc.
 Vought Aircraft Industries, Inc.
Automotive
 Beru AG (Germany)
 Edscha AG (Germany)
 Key Plastics, LLC
 Key Saftey Systems, Inc.
 United Components, Inc.
Consumer & Industrial
 Boto International (artificial Christmas trees, China)
 Custom Alloy (France)
 Dr. Pepper/Seven Up Bottling Group
 Duratek, Inc. (23%, disposal of radioactive materials)
 Groupe Genoyer (France)
 Kito Corp. (cranes and hoists, Japan)
 Kuhlman Electric Corporation
 Messner Eutectic Castolin Group (Germany)
 Otor (Corrugated board and recycled containerboard, France)
 Pacific China Holdings (department stores, China)
 Panolam Industries International, Inc. (decorative laminate paneling)
 Rexnord Corporation
 Tecnoforge Group (Italy)
 Terreal (clay roof tile and bricks, France)
Energy & Power
 CDM Resource Management Ltd.
 Frontier Drilling ASA (Norway)
 InTank, Inc.
 Legend Natural Gas (natural gas and crude oil exploration)
 Magellan Midstream Partners, L.P.
 Seabulk International, Inc. (marine support and transportation services)

Healthcare
  Acufocus, Inc.
  Align Technology, Inc.
  Apteka Holding ZAO (Russia)
  Colin Medical Technology Corporation (Japan)
  ConnectiCare Holdings, Inc.
  Endius, Inc.
  Hertiage Heath Systems, Inc.
  The Innovation Factory
  InteliStaf Group, Inc.
  Medipointe, Inc.
  NeoVista, Inc.
  Primary Health, Inc.
  Sight Resource Corporation
Telecom & Media
  Actelis Networks, Inc.
  Aprovia (business publishing, France)
  Bredbandsbolaget AB (Sweden)
  Casema BV (cable television, The Netherlands)
  LinkAir Communications, Inc. (China)
  Mercury Corporation (South Korea)
  Orthogon Systems (UK)
  Taiwan Broadband Communications
  Verizon Hawaii
  Videótron Telecom (Canada)
  WCI Cable, Inc.
Transportation
  Air Cargo, Inc. (ground transportation services)
  Garrett Aviation Services
  Gemini Air Cargo, Inc.
  Grand Vehicle Works, LLC
  Piedmont Hawthorne Holdings, Inc.
  TrenStar, Inc.

COMPETITORS

Bain Capital
Blackstone Group
Credit Suisse First Boston (USA), Inc.
Forstmann Little
Goldman Sachs
Hicks Muse
Investcorp
J.P. Morgan Partners
KKR
Lehman Brothers
Texas Pacific Group
Thomas Lee

Carpenter

It's a cushy job for Carpenter Co., making polyurethane foam and chemicals and polyester fiber used as cushioning by the automotive, bedding, floor covering, and furniture industries, among others. The company started out making foam rubber; it now manufactures air filter media, expanded polystyrene building materials, and a tire fill product as a replacement for air in off-road construction vehicles. Carpenter has facilities throughout the US, as well as in Canada, Denmark, France, Germany, Spain, Sweden, and the UK. The company also sells consumer products — which include craft fiber products, mattress pads, and pillows — through retailers. Carpenter is owned by Chairman and CEO Stanley Pauley.

EXECUTIVES

Chairman and CEO: Stanley F. Pauley
CFO: Dave Moorman
VP, Sales and Marketing, Consumer Division: Dan Schecter
Director, MIS: Tim Lester
Personnel Recruiter: Tom Newport

LOCATIONS

HQ: Carpenter Co.
  5016 Monument Ave., Richmond, VA 23230
Phone: 804-359-0800 **Fax:** 804-353-0694
Web: www.carpenter.com

Carpenter has manufacturing facilities throughout the US, as well as in Canada, Denmark, France, Germany, Spain, Sweden, and the UK.

PRODUCTS/OPERATIONS

Selected Products
Air filter media
Bedding
Carpet cushion
Chemicals
Chemical systems
Consumer products
Expanded Polystyrene Systems
Flexible foam packaging
Furniture
Polyester fiber
Tire products

COMPETITORS

Acordis
Advanced Materials
British Vita
Foamex
Magnifoam Technology
Owens Corning
PMC Global
Reliance Industries
Sealed Air
Wellman

HISTORICAL FINANCIALS

Company Type: Private

Income Statement FYE: December 31

	REVENUE ($ mil.)	NET INCOME ($ mil.)	NET PROFIT MARGIN	EMPLOYEES
12/02	1,114	—	—	6,000
12/01	1,035	—	—	6,200
12/00	1,075	—	—	6,200
12/99	977	—	—	5,500
12/98	950	—	—	6,500
12/97	879	—	—	6,325
12/96	800	—	—	6,500
12/95	745	—	—	6,900
12/94	691	—	—	6,901
12/93	619	—	—	6,905
Annual Growth	6.7%	—	—	(1.5%)

Revenue History

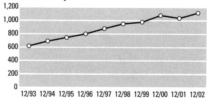

CARQUEST

Searching for a sensor, solenoid, or switches? CARQUEST can steer you in the right direction. The replacement auto parts distribution group is owned by its seven member warehouse distributors (the largest is North Carolina-based General Parts). The CARQUEST group includes a network of about 60 distribution centers serving about 4,000 distributor-owned and independent jobbers in the US and Canada. The company sells its own line of auto parts (made by Moog Automotive, Dana, Gabriel, and others) to the jobbers, as well as wholesalers, for eventual resale to professional repair centers, service stations, dealerships, and, to a lesser degree, do-it-yourself (DIY) customers.

General Parts owns more than 1,200 stores across the US and Canada. The average CARQUEST store carries 18,000 parts, while a distribution center carries 150,000 items.

In order to strengthen ties with service shops, CARQUEST offers the Tech-Net Professional Auto Service program. The program provides a national computer base of more than 600,000 repair records as well as a full guarantee on parts; signage and other marketing tools are also included.

Consolidation in the aftermarket industry has blurred the lines of distribution between wholesalers and retailers, causing all segments of the industry to scramble for ways to gain or maintain market share. CARQUEST focuses on professional mechanics, but it is being squeezed as retailers such as AutoZone look beyond their regular DIY customers for a piece of the commercial pie. At the same time, chains such as The Pep Boys — Manny, Moe & Jack are chipping away at service stations' business by offering parts and service.

HISTORY

Even though he didn't know the auto parts business, Temple Sloan recognized America's infatuation with the automobile and started distributor General Parts in 1961 at age 21. By 1972 he had acquired enough warehouse space to supply the entire state of North Carolina. Determined to get bigger faster, Sloan studied auto parts kingpin Genuine Parts, digging through its annual reports and uncovering tricks of the trade, while working on a few of his own. To compete in what was then a fast-growing industry, Genuine Parts had created a marketing alliance, NAPA, that used mass buying power to garner better pricing and service from manufacturers that often wouldn't recognize individual companies.

Sloan recruited friends and fellow distributors Dan Bock, president of Bobro Products, and Joe Hughes, president of Indiana Parts Warehouse, and together they formed CARQUEST in 1974. The company was designed to help jobbers (middlemen between distributors and mechanics) being threatened by retailers attempting to get a piece of the commercial business market traditionally served by jobbers. CARQUEST began recruiting other distributors and achieved first-year sales of $29 million. In the first five years, almost 1,500 jobbers committed to CARQUEST. Leadership rotated among distributor members until Bock became president in 1984.

As CARQUEST grew, the need for a unifying private-label line became apparent. In the 1970s it developed the Proven Value line of do-it-yourself-oriented products such as oils and filters. The establishment of the CARQUEST brand in the mid-1980s gave the company complete control over quality, coverage, price, and promotions, giving CARQUEST jobbers an advantage in the marketplace. Private-label sales grew from 20%-25% of business to 70% by 1996.

HOOVER'S HANDBOOK OF PRIVATE COMPANIES 2005

That year CARQUEST relocated its national headquarters from Tarrytown, New York, to Lakewood, Colorado, and Peter Kornafel became president and CEO, replacing Bock. Kornafel had been president of Hatch Grinding, a Denver distributor that merged with General Parts in 1996. The next year the firm moved into Canada, as General Parts bought half of the McKerlie-Millen subsidiary of Acklands (more than 400 parts stores). In 1998 CARQUEST launched its TechNet Professional Service program.

Also in 1998 CARQUEST added about 150 new stores to its network when General Parts bought bankrupt APS Holding; it also added 75 stores and eight DCs from Republic Auto. In 1999 General Parts bought The Parts Source, which included 41 Ace Auto Parts stores in Florida.

In January 2000 General Parts bought Acktion Corp's 50% interest in CARQUEST Canada, giving them complete ownership. Later in the year, General Parts also bought St. Louis-based distributor; A.E. Lottes Co. In 2001 the company moved its headquarters to Raleigh, North Carolina, and Art Lottes III succeeded Kornafel as president.

EXECUTIVES

Chairman: Neil Stockel
Vice Chairman, Secretary, and Treasurer: Pete Kornafel
President: A.E. Lottes III
EVP: Todd Hack
CFO, CARQUEST and General Parts: John Gardner
Human Resources Director: Ed Whirty

LOCATIONS

HQ: CARQUEST Corporation
2635 E. Millbrook Rd., Raleigh, NC 27604
Phone: 919-573-3000   **Fax:** 919-573-2501
Web: www.carquest.com

CARQUEST operates some 60 warehouse distribution centers serving about 4,000 stores in the US and Canada.

PRODUCTS/OPERATIONS

Member Warehouse Distributors
Automotive Warehouse, Inc.
BWP Distributors, Inc.
CAP Warehouse
CARQUEST Canada, Ltd. (owned by General Parts)
General Parts, Inc.
Muffler Warehouse
Straus-Frank Co.

Selected Manufacturers of CARQUEST Products
Airtex
Cardone Industries
Dana
Federal Mogul Corporation
Gates
Maremont/Gabriel
Melling
Moog Automotive
NEAPCO
Standard Motor Products
WIX

COMPETITORS

Advance Auto Parts
AutoZone
CSK Auto
Genuine Parts
Hahn Automotive
Pep Boys
Sears
Target
Wal-Mart

HISTORICAL FINANCIALS

Company Type: Private

Income Statement
FYE: December 31

	ESTIMATED REVENUE ($ mil.)	NET INCOME ($ mil.)	NET PROFIT MARGIN	EMPLOYEES
12/03	1,800	—	—	36,500
12/02	2,500	—	—	36,500
12/01	2,200	—	—	36,000
12/00	2,000	—	—	36,000
12/99	2,000	—	—	36,000
12/98	1,400	—	—	35,000
12/97	1,300	—	—	35,000
12/96	1,200	—	—	26,000
12/95	940	—	—	26,000
12/94	860	—	—	—
Annual Growth	8.6%	—	—	4.3%

Revenue History

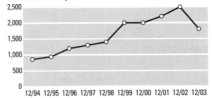

Carrols

You might say Carrols has some quick-service royalty in its blood. Through subsidiary Carrols Corporation, the company is the #1 Burger King franchisee in the US, with more than 350 units in about a dozen states. Carrols Holdings also owns and franchises its own quick-service chains, Taco Cabana and Pollo Tropical. Its 130 Taco Cabana units (about 10 are franchised) offer Tex-Mex and traditional Mexican dishes, such as tacos and quesadillas. The 80-plus-unit Pollo Tropical chain (24 are franchised) serves fresh grilled chicken and Caribbean side dishes. Carrols Holdings, started in 1968 by Herbert Slotnick, is controlled by investment firms BIB Holdings (about 42%) and Madison Dearborn Partners (about 21%).

While more than half the company's sales come from its Burger King operations, Carrols is focused on growing its other two quick-service chains, Taco Cabana and Pollo Tropical.

EXECUTIVES

Chairman and CEO: Alan Vituli, age 62, $550,008 pay
President, COO, and Director: Daniel T. Accordino, age 53, $420,000 pay
VP, CFO, and Treasurer: Paul R. Flanders, age 47, $210,000 pay
VP and Controller: Timothy J. LaLonde, age 47
VP, General Counsel, and Secretary: Joseph A. Zirkman, age 43, $210,000 pay
VP Human Resources: Jerry Digenova, age 46
VP Information Services: John Lukas, age 42
EVP, Pollo Tropical: James E. (Jim) Tunnessen, age 49
EVP, Taco Cabana: Michael A. Biviano, age 47, $234,231 pay
Chief Concept Officer, Hispanic Brands: John W. Haywood, age 40
Auditors: PricewaterhouseCoopers LLP

LOCATIONS

HQ: Carrols Holdings Corporation
968 James St., Syracuse, NY 13203
Phone: 315-424-0513   **Fax:** 315-425-8874
Web: www.carrols.com

2003 Burger King Locations

	No.
New York	145
Ohio	82
North Carolina	40
Michigan	26
South Carolina	21
Pennsylvania	12
Other states	25
Total	**351**

2003 Taco Cabana Locations

	No.
Texas	120
Oklahoma	6
Other states	4
Total	**130**

2003 Pollo Tropical Locations

	No.
US	
Florida	61
International	
Puerto Rico	19
Ecuador	4
Total	**84**

PRODUCTS/OPERATIONS

2003 Sales

	% of total
Burger King	55
Pollo Tropical	28
Taco Cabana	17
Total	**100**

2003 Locations

	No.
Burger King	351
Taco Cabana	
Owned	121
Franchised	9
Pollo Tropical	
Owned	60
Franchised	24
Total	**565**

COMPETITORS

AFC Enterprises
Boston Market
B.T. Woodlipp
California Pizza Kitchen
Checkers Drive-In
Chick-fil-A
CKE Restaurants
Consolidated Restaurant Operations
Dairy Queen
Jack in the Box
McDonald's
Pancho's Mexican Buffet
Subway
Triarc
Wendy's
YUM!

HISTORICAL FINANCIALS

Company Type: Private

Income Statement			FYE: Sunday nearest December 31
	REVENUE ($ mil.)	NET INCOME ($ mil.)	NET PROFIT MARGIN	EMPLOYEES
12/03	645	2	0.4%	15,900
12/02	657	12	1.8%	16,100
12/01	656	(4)	—	16,100
12/00	467	4	0.9%	17,200
12/99	457	1	0.2%	13,200
12/98	417	0	0.1%	12,725
12/97	295	2	0.7%	11,700
12/96	241	3	1.3%	8,400
12/95	226	15	6.6%	7,500
12/94	204	(2)	—	7,800
Annual Growth	13.7%	—	—	8.2%

2003 Year-End Financials

Debt ratio: 1,736.9%
Return on equity: 10.1%
Cash ($ mil.): 2
Current ratio: 0.34
Long-term debt ($ mil.): 364

Net Income History

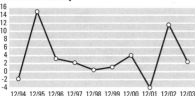

Catholic Health East

Catholic Health East doesn't believe prayers to St. Jude are necessary to continue providing health care to any person in need. Catholic Health East is one of the top religious health systems in the US. The company carries out its mission of serving the poor and the old by offering health care through more than 30 hospitals, about 40 nursing homes, and some 20 independent- and assisted-living facilities, primarily on the East Coast. The network also operates behavioral health facilities and offers adult day care, home health services, and hospice care. Catholic Health East is sponsored by 14 religious communities.

Catholic Health East is governed by a board composed of 10 nuns, eight secular health care professionals, and one reverend.

Like many religious health care systems, Catholic Health East continues to struggle with the problem of keeping both the faith and the bottom line intact. Providing indigent care is becoming increasingly difficult thanks to the ever-rising costs of health care coupled with cuts in reimbursements that have hurt not only the system's hospital services but its nursing home and outpatient services as well. Catholic Health East expanded in mid-2004 when Pennsylvania's Maxis Health joined the organization.

HISTORY

It was three easy pieces that made up Catholic Health East in 1997. Allegany Health System, Eastern Mercy Health System, and Sisters of Providence Health System operated almost entirely in separate, but adjacent, geographic areas on the East Coast, overlapping only in Florida.

Catholic Health East's history goes as far back as 1831, when the Sisters of Mercy was founded in Dublin, Ireland, by Catherine McAuley, who established a poorhouse using her inheritance. Some of the sisters hopped the Pond in 1843, establishing the first Catholic hospital in the US, the Mercy Hospital of Pittsburgh, four years later. Over the years the Sisters of Mercy expanded throughout the US. By 1991 there were 25 Sisters of Mercy congregations; they united that year under the newly formed Institute of the Sisters of Mercy of the Americas.

The Sisters of Providence came from Kingston, Ontario, to found the first hospital in Holyoke, Massachusetts. Having established their own ministry, the sisters in Holyoke became a separate congregation in 1892. The congregation expanded slowly, moving into North Carolina in 1956, eventually forming the Sisters of Providence Health System.

A Polish nun, Mother Colette Hilbert, formed a new congregation in Pittsburgh in 1897 after the other members of her former parish were recalled to Poland. The new congregation entered health care in 1926, establishing a home for the elderly in New York. In honor of Hilbert's favorite saint, the order became the Franciscan Sisters of St. Joseph in 1934.

The Franciscan Sisters of St. Joseph and the Sisters of Mercy united to form the ministry that became Pittsburgh Mercy Health System in 1983. In 1986 the congregations formed Eastern Mercy Health System as a holding company for the health concern. The consolidation served to cut costs, as well as to preserve the organization's religious mission.

The Franciscan Sisters of Allegany congregation got its start in 1859 teaching children in Buffalo, New York. In 1883 the order took over St. Elizabeth Hospital in Boston, expanding its health care services ministry throughout New York, New Jersey, and Florida by the 1930s. In 1986 the sisters organized the operations as Allegany Health System.

In the early 1990s Catholic health care systems underwent a round of consolidation. Allegany Health Systems and Eastern Mercy Health Systems combined services, aiming to lower costs through economies of scale.

The mid-1990s also brought consolidation, but this time operational costs weren't the major problem; Catholic health systems across the nation were facing a shortage of sisters. To have a sufficient number of sisters to keep the "Catholic" in Catholic health care, the three health systems merged in 1997, becoming Catholic Health East.

After the merger, the company continued to build its network through acquisitions, including Mercy Health in Miami (1998) and a suffering, secular Cooper Health System in Camden, New Jersey (1999). In 2000 it gained control of two troubled hospitals in Palm Beach, Florida, only to sell them the following year. Catholic Health East remains focused on reducing costs as it expands.

EXECUTIVES

Chairman: Earle L. Bradford Jr.
President and CEO: Robert V. Stanek
EVP and COO: Mark O'Neil
EVP and CFO: Peter L. (Pete) DeAngelis Jr.
EVP and Chief Administration Officer: Stanley T. Urban
EVP and Chief Medical Officer: Richard F. (Rick) Afable
EVP, Mission Integration: Sister Juliana Casey
EVP, Continuing Care Division: Robert H. Morrow
EVP, Mid-Atlantic Division: Judith M. (Judy) Persichilli
EVP, Northeast Division: Sister Kathleen Popko
EVP, Southeast Division: Howard Watts
VP, Advocacy and Government Relations: Kenneth A. Becker
VP, Strategy Development: Elaine Bauer
VP, Ethics: Philip Boyle
VP, Mission Services: Mary Ann Carter
VP, Quality and Patient Safety: Diane S. Denny
VP, System Communications: Salvatore C. (Sal) Foti
VP, Financial Services, Continuing Care Division: Patricia Gathers
VP, System Compliance and Legal Services and General Counsel: Michael C. Hemsley
VP, Information Technology and CIO: Jack Hueter
VP, Philanthropy: J. William Kingston
VP, Organization Effectiveness and Human Resources: George F. Longshore
VP, Risk Management Services and Chief Risk Officer: Theodore Schlert

LOCATIONS

HQ: Catholic Health East
14 Campus Blvd., Ste. 300,
Newtown Square, PA 19073
Phone: 610-355-2000 **Fax:** 610-355-2050
Web: www.che.org

Divisions

Northeast
  Mercy Health System of Maine (Portland)
  Sisters of Providence Health System (Springfield, MA)
  St. Peter's Health Care Services (Albany, NY)
  Catholic Health System (Buffalo, NY)
  St. James Mercy Health System (Hornell, NY)
Mid-Atlantic
  St. Francis Healthcare Services (Wilmington, DE)
  Our Lady of Lourdes Health System (Camden, NJ)
  St. Francis Medical Center (Trenton, NJ)
  Mercy Health System of Southeastern Pennsylvania (Conshohocken, PA)
  Maxis Health System (Carbondale, PA)
  St. Mary Medical Center (Langhorne, PA)
  Pittsburgh Mercy Health System
Southeast
  BayCare Health Systems (Clearwater, FL)
  Holy Cross Health Ministries (Fort Lauderdale, FL)
  Mercy Hospital (Miami)
  St. Mary's Health Care System, Inc. (Athens, GA)
  Saint Joseph's Health System (Atlanta)
Continuing Care
  Mercy Medical (Daphne, AL)
  Mercy Community Health, Inc. (West Hartford, CT)
  Mercy Uihlein Health Corporation (Lake Placid, NY)
  St. Joseph of the Pines (Southern Pines, NC)

PRODUCTS/OPERATIONS

Supporting Congregations

Franciscan Sisters of Allegany (St. Bonaventure, NY)
Franciscan Sisters of St. Joseph (Hamburg, NY)
Sisters of Charity of Seton Hill (Greensburg, PA)
Sisters of Mercy of the Americas (Albany, NY)
Sisters of Mercy of the Americas (Baltimore)
Sisters of Mercy of the Americas (Orchard Park, NY)
Sisters of Mercy of the Americas (Hartsdale, NY)
Sisters of Mercy of the Americas (Merion, PA)
Sisters of Mercy of the Americas (Pittsburgh)
Sisters of Mercy of the Americas (Portland, ME)
Sisters of Mercy of the Americas (Rochester, NY)
Sisters of Mercy of the Americas (West Hartford, CT)
Sisters of Providence (Holyoke, MA)
Sisters of St. Joseph (St. Augustine, FL)

COMPETITORS

Ascension Health
Bon Secours Health
Catholic Health Initiatives
HCA
Triad Hospitals

HISTORICAL FINANCIALS

Company Type: Not-for-profit

Income Statement — FYE: December 31

	REVENUE ($ mil.)	NET INCOME ($ mil.)	NET PROFIT MARGIN	EMPLOYEES
12/03	5,700	—	—	43,000
12/02	5,000	—	—	43,000
12/01	4,300	—	—	43,000
12/00	4,300	—	—	44,000
12/99	4,300	—	—	45,000
12/98	3,800	—	—	45,000
12/97	3,000	—	—	31,838
12/96	2,700	—	—	—
Annual Growth	11.3%	—	—	5.1%

Revenue History

Catholic Health Initiatives

"And he sent them out to preach the Kingdom of God and to heal the sick" (Luke 9:2). Catholic Health Initiatives (CHI) hopes to make those words the driving force behind its initiative. The giant not-for-profit Roman Catholic health system is one of the largest in the US. CHI operates nearly 70 hospitals and more than 40 long-term care, assisted-living, and residential facilities. Combined, the health system has more than 8,300 beds. The organization is sponsored by 12 different congregations and serves communities in some 20 states, primarily in the Midwest.

CHI is an amalgamation of four Roman Catholic health care systems: Catholic Health Corporation of Omaha, Nebraska; Franciscan Health System of Aston, Pennsylvania; Sisters of Charity Health Care Systems of Cincinnati; and Sisters of Charity of Nazareth Health Care System of Bardstown, Kentucky. As a reflection of its divine purpose in a mundane health care market, the company's governing board is made up of both religious and lay officers.

Catholic Health Initiatives has to deal with the conundrum facing many Catholic health systems: Their religious mission — to care for the "unserved and underserved" (and underinsured) members of its communities — is financially uncompetitive. CHI offsets the expense of its mission by also providing health care to the general public and by making business decisions more often associated with secular business (cutting staff, centralizing functions, and joining with other Catholic health care institutions to drive harder bargains with medical suppliers).

HISTORY

In 1860 the Sisters of St. Francis established a hospital in Philadelphia, laying the foundation for a larger health care organization. In 1981 Franciscan Health System was formally established to be a national holding company for Catholic hospitals and related organizations. By the mid-1990s the system consisted of 12 member and two affiliate hospitals and 11 long-term-care facilities located in the mid-Atlantic states and the Pacific Northwest.

Sisters of Charity of Cincinnati and the Sisters of St. Francis Perpetual Adoration of Colorado Springs co-sponsored The Sisters of Charity Health Care Systems, incorporated in 1979 as a multi-institutional health care network. By the mid-1990s the system included 20 hospitals in Colorado, Kentucky, Nebraska, New Mexico, and Ohio.

Three congregations collaborated to form Catholic Health Corporation in 1980, one of the first such health care partnerships between religious communities within the Roman Catholic Church in the US. By 1996 this coalition operated 100 health care facilities in 12 states.

The development of modern managed care health care systems put pressure on the smaller Catholic hospital operations, so the three systems established Catholic Health Initiatives (CHI) in 1996 as a national entity serving five geographic regions. Patricia Cahill, a lay health care veteran who previously served the Archdiocese of New York, was appointed president and CEO of CHI. The following year CHI absorbed the 10-hospital Sisters of Charity of Nazareth Health Care System, based in Bardstown, Kentucky (founded in a log cabin in 1812).

That year CHI continued to seek new partnerships to improve efficiency. With Alegent Health it formed provider network Midwest Select with nearly 200 hospitals, marketing discounted rates to businesses. CHI allied with the Daughters of Charity to form for-profit joint venture Catholic Healthcare Audit Network to provide operational, financial, compliance, and information systems audits, as well as due diligence reviews. CHI also joined insurance joint venture NewCap Insurance with the Daughters of Charity and Catholic Health East; the firm allowed CHI to operate independently of commercial insurers.

CHI made a secular tie-in with the University of Pennsylvania Health System in 1998, whereby the university's system would offer care through five Catholic hospitals (CHI made plans to transfer these hospitals to Catholic Health East in 2001). The next year CHI announced its first loss, due to lackluster performance in the Midwest. During 2000 the company responded by streamlining operations and changing management, resulting in a positive bottom line. In 2001 it sold three hospitals in Pennsylvania, one in Delaware, and one in New Jersey to Catholic Health East.

EXECUTIVES

President and CEO: Kevin E. Lofton
EVP and COO: Michael T. Rowan
SVP, Human Resources, and Chief Administrative Officer: Michael Fordyce
SVP, Finance and Treasury: Sister Geraldine Hoyler
SVP, Sponsorship and Governance: Sister Peggy Martin
SVP and Chief Medical Officer: Harold E. (Hal) Ray
SVP, Communications: Joyce Ross
SVP, Advocacy: Colleen Scanlon
VP, Strategic Planning: Bob Cook
VP, Strategic Planning and Business Development: John DiCola
Director, Public Policy: Marcia Desmond
Director, Communication Services: Peg O'Keefe
Auditors: Ernst & Young LLP

LOCATIONS

HQ: Catholic Health Initiatives
1999 Broadway, Ste. 2600, Denver, CO 80202
Phone: 303-298-9100   **Fax:** 303-298-9690
Web: www.catholichealthinit.org

PRODUCTS/OPERATIONS

Sponsoring Congregations
Benedictine Sisters of Mother of God Monastery (Watertown, SD)
Congregation of the Dominican Sisters of St. Catherine of Siena (Kenosha, WI)
Franciscan Sisters of Little Falls (Little Falls, MN)
Nuns of the Third Order of St. Dominic (Great Bend, KS)
Sisters of Charity of Cincinnati
Sisters of Charity of Nazareth (Bardstown, KY)
Sisters of the Holy Family of Nazareth (Philadelphia, PA)
Sisters of Mercy of the Americas, Regional Community of Omaha (Omaha, NE)
Sisters of the Presentation of the Blessed Virgin Mary (Fargo, ND)
Sisters of St. Francis of Colorado Springs
Sisters of St. Francis of the Immaculate Heart of Mary (Hankinson, ND)
Sisters of St. Francis of Philadelphia

COMPETITORS

Allina Hospitals
Ascension Health
Baxter Regional Medical Center
Beverly Enterprises
BJC HealthCare
Catholic Healthcare Partners
HCA
Health Management Associates
Life Care Centers
Mayo Foundation
OhioHealth
Presbyterian Healthcare Services
Tenet Healthcare

HISTORICAL FINANCIALS

Company Type: Not-for-profit

Income Statement
FYE: June 30

	REVENUE ($ mil.)	NET INCOME ($ mil.)	NET PROFIT MARGIN	EMPLOYEES
6/03	6,072	203	3.3%	67,000
6/02	5,900	117	2.0%	67,000
6/01	5,742	167	2.9%	66,000
6/00	5,551	97	1.7%	56,100
6/99	5,000	—	—	50,000
6/98	4,500	—	—	44,000
6/97	4,002	—	—	—
6/96	3,755	—	—	—
6/95	3,800	—	—	—
6/94	1,116	—	—	—
Annual Growth	20.7%	28.1%	—	8.8%

2003 Year-End Financials
Debt ratio: 55.0%
Return on equity: 5.5%
Cash ($ mil.): 298
Current ratio: 1.56
Long-term debt ($ mil.): 2,070

Net Income History

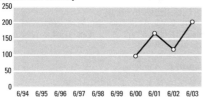

Catholic Health Services of Long Island

Catholic Health Services of Long Island provides faith-based health care services to the people of Long Island. Sponsored by the Diocese of Rockville Centre, the health care system is comprised of five hospitals — Good Samaritan Hospital Medical Center, Mercy Medical Center, St. Catherine of Siena Medical Center, St. Charles Hospital, and St. Francis Hospital — that combined have nearly 1,700 beds. Other operations include three nursing homes, a regional hospice and home care network, and a community-based agency for persons with special needs.

EXECUTIVES

President: James Harden
SVP, Finance and CFO: Terence G. Daly
SVP, Medical Affairs and Chief Medical Officer: Joel Yohai
VP and CIO: Marcy Dunn
VP and Administrator, St. Catherine of Siena Nursing Home: Jeffrey Rogoff
President and CEO, Mercy Medical Center: Martin A. Bieber
President and CEO, St. Catherine of Siena Medical Center: Vincent DiRubbio
President and CEO, Good Shepherd Hospice: Marianne Gillan
President and CEO, Maryhaven Center of Hope: Lewis Grossman
President and CEO, St. Francis Hospital: Alan D. Guerci
President and CEO, Nursing Sisters Home Care: Keith Kertland
President and CEO, Good Samaritan Hospital Medical Center: Richard J. Murphy
Executive Director and CEO, St. Charles Hospital and Rehabilitation Center: James O'Connor
President and CEO, Our Lady of Consolation Nursing and Rehabilitative Care Center: Dennis Verzi
Administrator, Good Samaritan Nursing Home: Michael Quartararo
Auditors: KPMG LLP

LOCATIONS

HQ: Catholic Health Services of Long Island
992 North Village Ave., Rockville Centre, NY 11570
Phone: 516-705-3700 **Fax:** 516-705-3730
Web: www.chsli.org

HISTORICAL FINANCIALS

Company Type: Not-for-profit

Income Statement
FYE: December 31

	REVENUE ($ mil.)	NET INCOME ($ mil.)	NET PROFIT MARGIN	EMPLOYEES
12/03	1,311	—	—	13,500

Catholic Healthcare Partners

Catholic Healthcare Partners offers health care services, primarily in Ohio but also in Indiana, Kentucky, Pennsylvania, and Tennessee through the more than 100 corporations that make up its system. Facilities include about 30 hospitals, more than a dozen stand-alone long-term care facilities, housing sites for the elderly, and wellness centers. The system also offers physician practices, hospice and home health care, and outreach services. Catholic Healthcare Partners is co-sponsored by the Sisters of Mercy communities of Cincinnati and Dallas, Pennsylvania; the Sisters of the Humility of Mary of Villa Maria, Pennsylvania; the Franciscan Sisters of the Poor; and Covenant Health Systems.

Catholic Healthcare Partners organizes its operations into 10 regions to better serve the communities where its facilities are located. In addition to these regions, the system operates Laurel Lake Retirement Community, a senior citizen home in northeast Ohio that offers various levels of care.

The health system will be losing one of its members at the end of 2004: St. Elizabeth Health Partners, which serves northern Kentucky, has announced plans to regain its independence. The loss won't hurt Catholic Healthcare Partners too much since the member's financial assets were never combined with those of its parent.

EXECUTIVES

Chairman: Raymond R. Clark
Vice Chairman: Sister Mildred Ely
President and CEO: Michael D. Connelly
EVP: Jane Durney Crowley
EVP: Susan Smith Makos
EVP: A. David Jimenez
SVP and CFO: William Shuttleworth
SVP and Chief Medical Officer: Donald E. Casey Jr.
SVP and CIO: Rebecca Sykes
SVP and General Counsel: Michael A. Bezney
SVP, Human Resources and Organization Effectiveness: Jon C. Abeles
SVP, Mission and Values Integration: Sister Doris Gottemoeller
Corporate Director, Communications: Greg Smith
Auditors: Ernst & Young LLP

LOCATIONS

HQ: Catholic Healthcare Partners
615 Elsinore Place, Cincinnati, OH 45202
Phone: 513-639-2800 **Fax:** 513-639-2700
Web: www.health-partners.org

PRODUCTS/OPERATIONS

2003 Sales

	$ mil.	% of total
MHP — Northern Region	655.3	22
MHP — Southwest Ohio Region	531.6	17
Humility of Mary Health Partners	426.2	14
West Central Ohio Health Partners	264.4	9
St. Mary's Health Partners	256.0	8
MHP — Northeast Region	210.5	7
Community Health Partners	172.2	6
MHP — Western Ohio Region	164.9	5
MHP — Kentucky/Indiana Region	146.5	5
CHP Home Office	141.3	5
CHP Liability Self Insurance Trust	37.8	1
Other	35.5	1
Adjustments	(167.9)	—
Total	**2,874.3**	**100**

Regions
Community Health Partners (north-central Ohio)
Humility of Mary Health Partners (northeast Ohio)
Mercy Health Partners Kentucky/Indiana Region
Mercy Health Partners Northeast Region (northeast Pennsylvania)
Mercy Health Partners Northern Region (northwest Ohio and southern Michigan)
Mercy Health Partners Southwest Ohio Region
Mercy Health Partners Western Ohio Region
St. Elizabeth Health Partners (northern Kentucky)
St. Mary's Health Partners (eastern Tennessee)
West Central Ohio Health Partners

COMPETITORS

Ascension Health	NeighborCare
Catholic Health Initiatives	OhioHealth
HCA	Tenet Healthcare
Kindred	Universal Health Services

HISTORICAL FINANCIALS

Company Type: Not-for-profit

Income Statement
FYE: December 31

	REVENUE ($ mil.)	NET INCOME ($ mil.)	NET PROFIT MARGIN	EMPLOYEES
12/03	2,874	—	—	30,524
12/02	2,715	—	—	30,524
12/01	2,602	—	—	30,000
12/00	2,373	—	—	27,941
12/99	1,984	—	—	30,800
12/98	1,821	—	—	29,000
12/97	1,778	—	—	23,920
12/96	1,909	—	—	24,000
12/95	2,246	—	—	18,100
12/94	1,045	—	—	15,739
Annual Growth	11.9%	—	—	7.6%

Revenue History

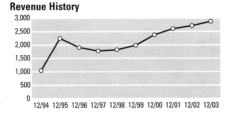

Catholic Healthcare West

Catholic Healthcare West (CHW) has found it takes a lot of nunsense to become one of the largest private, not-for-profit health care providers in the state of California. CHW has a network of some 40 facilities in California, Arizona, and Nevada. CHW's health care system consists of acute care hospitals, skilled nursing facilities, and medical centers. CHW also has an alliance with Scripps, a major San Diego-based health care provider. The organization has nearly 7,100 acute care beds and almost 1,200 skilled nursing beds. CHW is sponsored by seven religious congregations.

With both clergy and laity on its governing board, CHW has grown by consolidating hospitals owned by Roman Catholic women's religious orders. Additional affiliations with non-Catholic institutions have raised some hackles because Catholic doctrine opposes abortion, most forms of birth control, and in vitro fertilization.

In 2004 CHW joined other Catholic hospitals in announcing plans to charge uninsured patients the same rates charged to patients on Medicare, Medicaid, and other government-funded health care programs. The announcement came in part as a response to criticism that hospitals across the country charge uninsured patients much higher rates for services and aggressively seek payment.

The hospital operator is expanding its California presence. CHW bought two hospitals from Universal Health Services: French Medical Center in San Luis Obispo and Arroyo Grande Community Hospital in Arroyo Grande. The two facilities combined have almost 180 beds.

HISTORY

Catholic Healthcare West traces its roots to 1857, when the Sisters of Mercy founded St. Mary's Hospital in San Francisco. The order expanded in that area, and in 1986 two different communities of the Sisters of Mercy merged their hospitals into an organization with one retirement home and 10 hospitals from the Bay Area to San Diego. Declining membership in Roman Catholic religious orders, combined with consolidation in the field, led the orders to see merger as their only route to survival.

Rising medical costs, slow payers, and merger expenses dropped the organization's combined net income to $20 million in 1988 (from nearly $58 million in 1986). One of the hardest-hit CHW affiliates was Mercy Healthcare Sacramento, which lost $4.2 million between 1986 and 1987. In 1988 Mercy Healthcare restructured along regional lines.

The next year the Sisters of St. Dominic brought two hospitals into the alliance. CHW launched the Community Economic Assistance program, which provided $220,000 in grants to 16 human service and health care agencies in its first year.

CHW continued to add facilities, including AMI Community Hospital in Santa Cruz, California, in 1990. Since CHW already owned the area's only other acute care hospital, Dominican Santa Cruz Hospital, CHW in 1993 was ordered not to acquire any more acute care hospitals in Santa Cruz County without FTC approval.

As the trend to managed care became a stampede in the 1990s, CHW moved more into preventive care and began reining in costs through productivity improvement plans. It continued to add hospitals, including tax-supported institutions trying to compete with national for-profit systems.

The network increased its medical clout in 1994 by allying with San Diego-based Scripps, one of the state's largest HMO systems. In 1995 the Daughters of Charity Province of the West realigned its six-hospital operation with CHW. The next year the Dominican Sisters (California), the Dominican Sisters of St. Catherine of Siena (Wisconsin), and the Sisters of Charity of the Incarnate Word allied their California hospitals with CHW. New community hospitals included Bakersfield Memorial, Sierra Nevada Memorial (Grass Valley), Sequoia Hospital (Redwood City), and Woodland Healthcare.

Charity and cost-consciousness clashed in 1996 when union members staged a walkout to protest nonunion outsourcing of vocational nursing, housekeeping, and kitchen jobs. This dispute was settled, but CHW continued to be a target for union organizers, with a bitter battle against the Service Employees International Union (SEIU) starting in 1998.

CHW agreed in 1996 to merge with Samaritan Health Systems (now Banner Health System) in a move that would have made CHW one of the US's top five providers, but the deal fell apart in 1997. In 1998 CHW merged with UniHealth, a group with eight facilities in Los Angeles and Orange counties. Mounting costs forced CHW to post a loss, and in 1999 it cut some managerial positions and reorganized to recover.

The year 2000 brought CHW more problems with labor relations: SEIU argued that the organization was resistant to unionization. Continued losses led the organization to implement major restructuring the following year, as its 10 regional divisions were consolidated into four.

In 2001, CHW stepped up donations, grants, and other sponsorship efforts designed to benefit areas served by its hospitals and clinics. However, the rapid expansion that made the system a name in the California health care industry also left it bloated. Rising health care costs and trouble with its physician management groups cut deeply into earnings. Management casualties occurred as CHW reorganized that year.

Two years later, the company parted ways with one of its sponsoring organizations, the Franciscan Sisters of the Sacred Heart of Frankfort, Illinois. The sponsorship ended when CHW closed St. Francis Medical Center of Santa Barbara. However, the hospital operator that fiscal year posted its first operating profit since 1996.

EXECUTIVES

Chairperson: Diane Grassilli
President and CEO: Lloyd H. Dean
EVP and COO: Michael Erne
EVP and CFO: Michael D. Blaszyk
SVP and Chief Medical Officer: George Bo-Linn
SVP and General Counsel: Derek F. Covert
SVP and Chief Strategy Officer: Charles P. Francis
SVP, Corporate Relations: Alan Iftiniuk
SVP, Sponsorship and Mission Integration:
 Sister Bernita McTernan
SVP and Chief Administrative Officer: Elizabeth Shih
SVP, Human Resources: Ernest (Ernie) Urquhart
SVP, Managed Care: John Wray
President, Marian Medical Center:
 Charles (Chuck) Cova, age 48
CEO, Saint Francis Memorial Hospital: Cheryl Fama
CEO, St. Mary's Medical Center: Ken Steele
President, Mercy Healthcare Sacramento and Mercy San Juan Medical Center: Mike Uboldi, age 51
CIO: Michael O'Rourke
Secretary: Charles H. Chapman
Manager, Workers' Compensation: Barbara Pelletreau
Auditors: Deloitte & Touche LLP

LOCATIONS

HQ: Catholic Healthcare West
 185 Berry St., Ste. 300, San Francisco, CA 94107
Phone: 415-438-5500 **Fax:** 415-438-5724
Web: www.chw.edu

Facilities

Arizona
 Barrow Neurological Institute (Phoenix)
 Chandler Regional Hospital (Phoenix)
 Chandler Regional Medical Center (Phoenix)
 CHW Business Services Center (Phoenix)
 St. Joseph's Hospital and Medical Center (Phoenix)
California
 Arroyo Grande Community Hospital (Arroyo Grande)
 Bakersfield Memorial Hospital (Bakersfield)
 Mercy Southwest Hospital (Bakersfield)
 Mercy Hospital (Bakersfield)
 St. John's Pleasant Valley Hospital (Camarillo)
 Mercy San Juan Medical Center (Carmichael)
 Mercy Hospital of Folsom (Folsom)
 Glendale Memorial Hospital and Health Center
  (Glendale)
 Sierra Nevada Memorial Miners Hospital (Grass Valley)
 St. Mary Medical Center (Long Beach)
 California Hospital Medical Center (Los Angeles)
 St. Dominic's Hospital (Manteca)
 Mercy Medical Center Merced (Merced)
 Mercy Medical Center Mt. Shasta (Mt. Shasta)
 Northridge Hospital Medical Center — Roscoe Blvd.
  Campus (Northridge)
 Oak Valley Hospital District (Oakdale)
 St. John's Regional Medical Center (Oxnard)
 St. Elizabeth Community Hospital (Red Bluff)
 Mercy Medical Center Redding (Redding)
 Sequoia Hospital (Redwood City)
 Mercy General Hospital (Sacramento)
 Methodist Hospital of Sacramento (Sacramento)
 Mark Twain St. Joseph's Hospital (San Andreas)
 Community Hospital of San Bernardino (San
  Bernardino)
 St. Bernardine Medical Center (San Bernardino)
 Saint Francis Memorial Hospital (San Francisco)
 St. Mary's Medical Center (San Francisco)
 San Gabriel Valley Medical Center (San Gabriel)
 French Hospital Medical Center (San Luis Obispo)
 Dominican Hospital (Santa Cruz)
 Marian Medical Center (Santa Maria)
 St. Joseph's Behavioral Health Center (Stockton)
 St. Joseph's Medical Center (Stockton)
 Mercy Westside Hospital (Taft)
 Northridge Hospital Medical Center — Sherman Way
  Campus (Van Nuys)
 Woodland Healthcare (Woodland)
Nevada
 St. Rose Dominican Hospital Rose de Lima Campus
  (Henderson)
 St. Rose Dominican Hospital Siena Campus
  (Henderson)

PRODUCTS/OPERATIONS

2003 Sales

	$ mil.	% of total
Net patient revenue	4,630.0	93
Premiums	346.8	7
Contributions	12.3	—
Total	4,989.1	100

2003 Patient Revenues

	% of total
Contracted rate payors	36
Medicare	36
Medicaid	19
Commercial insurance, self pay & others	9
Total	100

Sponsoring Organizations

Auburn Regional Community of the Sisters of Mercy (Auburn, CA)
Burlingame Regional Community of the Sisters of Mercy (Burlingame, CA)
Congregation of the Dominican Sisters of St. Catherine of Siena of Kenosha (Kenosha, WI)
Congregation of the Sisters of Charity of the Incarnate Word (Houston)
Sisters of St. Dominic, Congregation of the Most Holy Rosary (Adrian, MI)
Sisters of St. Francis of Penance and Christian Charity, St. Francis Province (Redwood City, CA)
Sisters of the Third Order of St. Dominic, Congregation of the Most Holy Name (San Rafael, CA)

COMPETITORS

Adventist Health
Catholic Health Initiatives
HCA
Los Angeles County Health Department
Memorial Health Services
Sutter Health
Tenet Healthcare
Triad Hospitals

HISTORICAL FINANCIALS

Company Type: Not-for-profit

Income Statement

FYE: June 30

	REVENUE ($ mil.)	NET INCOME ($ mil.)	NET PROFIT MARGIN	EMPLOYEES
6/03	4,989	51	1.0%	36,000
6/02	4,502	(51)	—	36,000
6/01	4,807	(87)	—	36,000
6/00	4,513	(47)	—	40,000
6/99	4,200	82	2.0%	38,000
6/98	3,301	73	2.2%	20,000
6/97	2,749	36	1.3%	17,451
6/96	2,688	161	6.0%	21,495
6/95	2,674	99	3.7%	20,000
6/94	2,584	91	3.5%	17,618
Annual Growth	7.6%	(6.3%)	—	8.3%

2003 Year-End Financials

Debt ratio: 111.2%
Return on equity: 2.7%
Cash ($ mil.): 114
Current ratio: 1.62
Long-term debt ($ mil.): 2,116

Net Income History

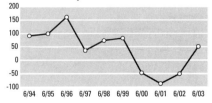

CCA Global

Business is "floor"ishing at CCA Global Partners. Formerly Carpet Co-op, the firm has more than 3,200 locations selling name-brand carpets and floor coverings such as ceramic tile, laminates, and hardwoods. Most stores operate under the Carpet One name; other names include Flooring America, Flooring One, ProSource, and International Design Guild (high-end showrooms). The world's largest floor covering retailer (with stores in the US, Canada, Australia, and New Zealand), Carpet One is the exclusive US marketer of Bigelow and Lees carpet brands. CCA Global has also made forays into mortgage banking, specialty lighting, and men's formalwear. Executives Howard Brodsky and Alan Greenberg founded the co-op in 1984.

CCA Global's Lenders One division operates as an aggregator of mortgage money. Its Lighting One division (bought by CCA in 2001) has about 100 locations selling lamps, ceiling fans, accessories. The flooring group is also looking to increase its market share in the hard window treatment business.

In 2003 CCA Global expanded into formalwear with its acquisition of Tuxedo America Group, a cooperative of more than 300 independently-owned retailers of men's formalwear. Today the independent retailers are known collectively as Sawi Formalwear. The company plans to operate 300 Sawi Formalwear stores by 2006.

EXECUTIVES

Co-Chairman and Co-CEO: Howard Brodsky
Co-Chairman and Co-CEO: Alan Greenberg
Co-COO; President, Carpet One Canada: Charlie Dilks
Co-COO and SVP Marketing: Dean Marcarelli
CFO: Ed Muchnick
VP Hard Surfaces: Randy Gum
President, Carpet One: Sandy Mishkin
President, Tuxedo America: Christopher Ramey
Chief Information Officer: Alan Tortorella
Chief Product Officer: Jim Gould
Director of Human Resources: Lisa Miles

LOCATIONS

HQ: CCA Global Partners
4301 Earth City Expwy., Earth City, MO 63045
Phone: 314-506-0000 **Fax:** 314-291-6674
Web: www.ccaglobal.com

PRODUCTS/OPERATIONS

Selected Companies

US Flooring
  Carpet One
  FloorExpo
  Flooring America
  International Design Guild
  ProSource Wholesale Floorcoverings
  Rug Décor
  Stone Mountain's Carpet Mill Outlet/GCO Carpet Outlet
International Flooring
  Carpet One (Canada, Australia, New Zealand)
  Flooring One (UK)
  Flooring Canada (Canada)
Mortgage Banking
  Lenders One
Specialty Lighting
  Lighting One
Men's Formalwear
  Tuxedo America Group

COMPETITORS

Abbey Carpet
After Hours
Federated
Formal Specialist
Gingiss
Home Depot
L.D. Brinkman
Lowe's
May
Menard

HISTORICAL FINANCIALS

Company Type: Cooperative

Income Statement

FYE: September 30

	REVENUE ($ mil.)	NET INCOME ($ mil.)	NET PROFIT MARGIN	EMPLOYEES
9/03	8,000	—	—	350
9/02	6,000	—	—	550
9/01	5,000	—	—	450
9/00	4,000	—	—	350
9/99	3,100	—	—	300
9/98	2,450	—	—	265
9/97	2,000	—	—	150
9/96	1,600	—	—	—
Annual Growth	25.8%	—	—	15.2%

Revenue History

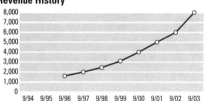

Center Oil

Center Oil is a core petroleum peddler. The company is one of the largest private wholesale distributors of gasoline and other petroleum products to customers primarily in the eastern region of the US. Center Oil owns nine storage terminals capable of storing more than 1.5 million barrels of petroleum product. It also has access to 36 terminals in 10 states, as well as access to the Williams, Texas Eastern, Kinder Morgan Chicago, and Kaneb pipeline systems. Its products are also distributed through a fleet of ships, barges, and trucks. The company was founded in 1986 by president and CEO Gary Parker.

EXECUTIVES

President and CEO: Gary R. Parker
VP and CFO: John R. Niemi
Secretary: Christine K. Moyer
Treasurer: Richard I. (Rick) Powers
Controller: Joseph (Joe) Beck
Finance Manager: Brian Skoff
Sales Manager: Rob Kraeger
Manager Business Development: Chris Pelligreen
Manager Operations and Scheduling: Jerry Jost
Manager Terminal Operations: Ray Idzior
General Counsel: Michael Aufdenspring

LOCATIONS

HQ: Center Oil Company
600 Mason Ridge Center Dr., St. Louis, MO 63141
Phone: 314-682-3500 **Fax:** 314-682-3599
Web: www.centeroil.com

Center Oil operates storage terminals in Baltimore; Chillicothe, Illinois; Cleveland; Hartford; Indianapolis; Madison, Wisconsin; Newark; St. Louis; and Wichita, Kansas.

COMPETITORS

Apex Oil
Colonial Group
George Warren
Gulf Oil
U.S. Oil

HISTORICAL FINANCIALS

Company Type: Private

Income Statement				FYE: December 31
	REVENUE ($ mil.)	NET INCOME ($ mil.)	NET PROFIT MARGIN	EMPLOYEES
12/03	3,400	—	—	50
12/02	2,600	—	—	44
Annual Growth	30.8%	—	—	13.6%

Revenue History

Central Grocers Cooperative

In a city of big stores, Chicago-located Central Grocers Cooperative helps neighborhood markets stay afloat. The co-op distributes name-brand and private-label (Centrella and Silver Cup) food and nonfood merchandise to about 240 member-owner stores in the Chicago area as well as in Indiana and Wisconsin. Founded in 1918, Central Grocers has clung to its independence as national giants have bought up local chains. The cooperative bought stores itself in 1998 rather than lose them as customers. The stores operate under the banners Centrella, Strack and Van Til, Town & Country, and Ultra Foods.

EXECUTIVES

President and CEO: Joseph (Joe) Caccamo
VP and Assistant General Manager:
 Robert J. (Bob) Wagner
Chief Technology Officer: Mark Brandes
Controller: Jane Denges
Director, Meat: Tom Smith
Manager, Human Resources: Annalee Robish
Auditors: Deloitte & Touche LLP

LOCATIONS

HQ: Central Grocers Cooperative, Inc.
11100 Belmont Ave., Franklin Park, IL 60131
Phone: 847-451-0660 **Fax:** 847-288-8710

COMPETITORS

Albertson's
ALDI
Associated Wholesalers
AWG
C&S Wholesale
Certified Grocers Midwest
Dominick's
Kroger
Meijer
Nash Finch
Roundy's
Safeway
Schnuck Markets
SUPERVALU
Wal-Mart

HISTORICAL FINANCIALS

Company Type: Cooperative

Income Statement				FYE: Saturday nearest July 31
	REVENUE ($ mil.)	NET INCOME ($ mil.)	NET PROFIT MARGIN	EMPLOYEES
7/03	973	—	—	—
7/02	967	—	—	—
7/01	919	—	—	—
7/00	739	—	—	350
7/99	695	—	—	300
7/98	581	—	—	400
7/97	458	—	—	—
7/96	465	—	—	280
7/95	443	—	—	285
7/94	412	—	—	260
Annual Growth	10.0%	—	—	5.1%

Revenue History

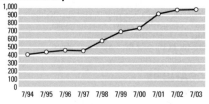

Central National-Gottesman

Got pulp? Central National-Gottesman does. Founded in 1886, the family-owned company distributes pulp, paper, paperboard, and newsprint in about 75 countries worldwide. In addition to its North American operations, the company operates about 25 overseas offices in 22 countries located in Asia, Europe, and Latin America. The Central National-Gottesman network includes the Lindenmeyr family of companies, which specialize in the distribution of fine paper as well as papers for books and magazines. The company's extensive list of suppliers includes paper industry leaders International Paper (#1) and Weyerhaeuser.

EXECUTIVES

President and CEO: Kenneth L. Wallach
Treasurer: Joshua J. (Josh) Eisenstein
VP, Human Resources: Louise Caputo
Marketing Manager: Jay Norris

LOCATIONS

HQ: Central National-Gottesman Inc.
3 Manhattanville Rd., Purchase, NY 10577
Phone: 914-696-9000 **Fax:** 914-696-1066
Web: www.lindenmeyr.com/cng.htm

Central National-Gottesman has operations in the Americas, Asia, Australia, and Europe including 24 overseas sales offices.

COMPETITORS

Clifford Paper
International Paper
Midland Paper
Pope & Talbot
Ris Paper
Smurfit-Stone Container
Unisource

HISTORICAL FINANCIALS

Company Type: Private

Income Statement				FYE: December 31
	ESTIMATED REVENUE ($ mil.)	NET INCOME ($ mil.)	NET PROFIT MARGIN	EMPLOYEES
12/02	1,600	—	—	850
12/01	1,700	—	—	900
12/00	1,825	—	—	900
12/99	1,660	—	—	900
12/98	1,600	—	—	900
12/97	2,000	—	—	900
12/96	2,000	—	—	900
12/95	2,000	—	—	900
12/94	2,000	—	—	900
12/93	1,500	—	—	700
Annual Growth	0.7%	—	—	2.2%

Revenue History

Certified Grocers Midwest

If you shop at a Certi-Saver, you can be certain your groceries came from Certified Grocers Midwest (CGM). CGM is a cooperative wholesaler of baked goods, fresh produce, meat products, and health and beauty aids; it distributes brand-name and private-label goods to member and non-member stores. CGM provides support services such as advertising, market research, site analysis, and financial help to its member stores, some of which operate under the Certi-Saver banner. The cooperative, established in 1940, covers Illinois, Indiana, Iowa, Michigan, and Wisconsin. To attract more Hispanic customers, CGM has expanded its selection of Hispanic items, which include the Gamesa and Los Pericos brands of foods.

EXECUTIVES

President and CEO: Ken R. Koester, age 49
CFO: Ken Lalla
VP, Marketing and Merchandising: Dave Verzak
VP, Produce: Donald Schwer
VP, Retail Sales and Secretary: James Cripe
Director, Advertising: David Laxner
Director, Bakery: Jeff Serritella
Director, Distribution: Mike Swift
Director, Information Technology: Dennis Wszolek
Supervisor, Human Resources: Marcy Meister

LOCATIONS

HQ: Certified Grocers Midwest, Inc.
 1 Certified Dr., Hodgkins, IL 60525
Phone: 708-579-2100 **Fax:** 708-354-7502
Web: www.certisaver.com

COMPETITORS

Albertson's
Central Grocers Cooperative
Dominick's
IGA
Nash Finch
Roundy's
S. Abraham & Sons
Spartan Stores
SUPERVALU

HISTORICAL FINANCIALS
Company Type: Cooperative

Income Statement				FYE: August 31
	REVENUE ($ mil.)	NET INCOME ($ mil.)	NET PROFIT MARGIN	EMPLOYEES
8/03	606	—	—	—
8/02	610	—	—	—
8/01	632	—	—	540
8/00	680	—	—	560
8/99	724	—	—	2,100
8/98	710	—	—	800
8/97	715	—	—	790
8/96	698	—	—	700
8/95	714	—	—	700
8/94	701	—	—	700
Annual Growth	(1.6%)	—	—	(3.6%)

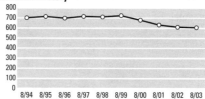

Revenue History

CF Industries

The grass is always greener at CF Industries. Organized in 1946 as Central Farmers Fertilizer Company, CF Industries is an interregional agricultural cooperative that manufactures and markets fertilizers, including nitrogen products (ammonia, granular urea, and UAN solutions), phosphates, and potash (potassium) products to its members in 48 states and two Canadian provinces. The co-op is owned by eight regional agricultural co-ops, including GROWMARK, Land O'Lakes, and Southern States. CF Industries operates nitrogen and phosphate plants, a phosphate mine, and a network of distribution terminals and storage facilities through which it offers products worldwide.

EXECUTIVES

President and CEO: Stephen R. Wilson
SVP and COO: John H. Sultenfuss
SVP and CFO: Ernest Thomas
VP, Sales: Monty R. Summa
VP, General Counsel, and Secretary: Douglas C. Barnard
VP, Human Resources: William G. Eppel
VP, Nitrogen Operations: Lou M. Frey
VP, Phosphate Operations: Herschel E. Morris
VP, Planning and Business Development:
 Stephen Chase
VP, Public Affairs: Rosemary O'Brien
VP, Raw Materials Procurement: Phil P. Koch
VP and Controller: Robert D. Webb
Treasurer: Dennis Baker

LOCATIONS

HQ: CF Industries, Inc.
 1 Salem Lake Dr., Long Grove, IL 60047
Phone: 847-438-9500 **Fax:** 847-438-0211
Web: www.cfindustries.com

CF Industries has facilities in Florida, Illinois, Indiana, Iowa, Louisiana, Minnesota, Missouri, Nebraska, North Dakota, Ohio, and Washington, and in Alberta, Canada.

PRODUCTS/OPERATIONS

Selected Members
CHS, Inc.
Cooperative federee de Quebec
GROWMARK, Inc.
Intermountain Farmers Association
Land O'Lakes, Inc.
MFA Incorporated
Southern States Cooperative, Inc.
Tennessee Farmers Cooperative

Selected Products
Anhydrous ammonia
Diammonium phosphate
Granular triple super phosphate
Granular urea
Monoammonium phosphate
Urea ammonium nitrate

COMPETITORS

Agrium
Koch
Mississippi Chemical
Potash Corporation
Terra Industries

HISTORICAL FINANCIALS
Company Type: Cooperative

Income Statement				FYE: December 31
	REVENUE ($ mil.)	NET INCOME ($ mil.)	NET PROFIT MARGIN	EMPLOYEES
12/03	1,287	—	—	1,444
12/02	1,100	—	—	1,500
12/01	1,087	—	—	1,700
12/00	1,101	—	—	1,474
12/99	1,095	—	—	1,519
12/98	1,200	—	—	1,600
12/97	1,432	—	—	1,652
12/96	1,468	—	—	1,609
12/95	1,383	—	—	1,548
12/94	1,183	—	—	1,471
Annual Growth	0.9%	—	—	(0.2%)

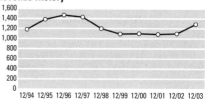

Revenue History

CH2M HILL

CH2M's name is a company (not a chemical) compound derived from the initials of its founders — Cornell, Howland, Hayes, and Merryfield — plus HILL, from its first merger. The group offers engineering consulting related to industrial facility design, transportation, water treatment, and environmental remediation. Specialties include sewer and waste-treatment design, hazardous-waste cleanup, and transportation projects such as highways and bridges. CH2M HILL is also involved in federal nuclear waste cleanup projects, facilities operations and management, and security and emergency management services. Founded in 1946 in Corvallis, Oregon, the firm is employee-owned and operates from about 200 offices worldwide.

CH2M HILL's full range of integrated services enables it to offer clients support for projects throughout several cycles — from concept, planning, and financing through design, implementation, and providing operations and maintenance. The company resides at the top levels of industry rankings of environmental consulting and engineering firms for several sectors: hazardous waste, water, sewer/waste, telecommunications, and transportation. The group is also one of the largest environmental firms to serve state and local governments, as well as federal clients.

It also holds lofty rankings among the US construction management-for-fee firms. CH2M HILL is one of the largest contractors in the nuclear waste, site assessment and compliance, clean air compliance, water treatment plants, and hazardous waste sectors. It is the largest privately held firm in Colorado, as well as one of the largest private construction companies in the US. With its 2003 acquisition of engineering and construction firm Lockwood Greene, the company has enhanced its offerings to the industrial and power markets worldwide. Lockwood Greene has annual revenues of some $600 million and about 2,500 employees.

Although the group was selected as one of FORTUNE's "100 Best Companies to Work For" in 2003, it has also come under fire from union members for its tank-farm cleaning operations at the Hanford nuclear facility in Washington State. The federal government has offered bonuses of up to $2 million for each tank CH2M HILL cleans by the end of its contract in 2006. The site has 177 tanks, holding about 53 million gallons of radioactive and toxic waste from plutonium produced for nuclear weapons. At issue are allegations of worker injuries from tank vapors. Federal and state investigations have been conducted, but the Energy Department's investigation cleared CH2M HILL of any criminal conduct regarding ammonia vapor readings. Despite steps taken by the company to strengthen its safety practices, CH2M workers at Hanford were exposed to higher-than-normal levels of radiation in July 2004 and were not wearing protective leaded gloves. By October 2004, CH2M HILL had identified 52 chemicals of "potential concern" that might pose a threat to workers at the site.

In 2004 the group restructured its operations according to three main client groups: civil infrastructure (state and local governments), federal (US and international governments), and industrial (private-sector clients). Its federal business segment includes environmental and nuclear services and outsourcing services.

EXECUTIVES

Chairman, President, and CEO: Ralph R. Peterson, age 59, $1,069,852 pay
Vice Chairman and SVP: Joseph A. (Bud) Ahearn, age 67
EVP, CFO, and Secretary: Samuel H. (Sam) Iapalucci, age 51, $644,481 pay
EVP: Alan M. Parker
CIO: Robert (Bob) Bullock
SVP Finance and Director: M. Catherine Santee, age 42
SVP and Director; President and CEO, Civil Infrastructure Client Group: Donald S. (Don) Evans, age 53, $613,825 pay
SVP and Director; President and CEO, Federal Client Group and Industrial Client Group: James J. (Jim) Ferris, age 60, $679,429 pay
SVP; President, Industrial Business Group and Industrial Design and Construction: Kenneth F. Durant
SVP and Director; President, Transportation Business Group: Michael D. (Mike) Kennedy, age 54, $514,713 pay
SVP and Director; President, Water Business Group: Thomas G. (Tom) Searle, age 50
VP and Controller: Vern L. Nelson
VP and Treasurer: Stanley W. (Stan) Vinson
VP Human Resources: Robert C. (Bob) Allen
Director Marketing Communications: Cary Baird
Public Relations Team Manager: Patty Keck
Auditors: KPMG LLP

LOCATIONS

HQ: CH2M HILL Companies, Ltd.
 9191 S. Jamaica St., Englewood, CO 80112
Phone: 303-771-0900 **Fax:** 720-286-9250
Web: www.ch2m.com

CH2M HILL Companies operates in more than 30 countries.

PRODUCTS/OPERATIONS

2003 Sales

	$ mil.	% of total
Environmental, energy & infrastructure	1,239.0	58
Water	693.3	32
Industrial	222.0	10
Total	**2,154.3**	**100**

Selected Subsidiaries

CH2M HILL Capital Services, Inc. (CAPCO, infrastructure financing)
CH2M HILL Canada Limited (Canadian division; energy, environment and systems, water, and transportation services)
CH2M HILL Hanford Group, Inc. (prime contractor for US Department of Energy; treating waste at underground tanks at Hanford site in Washington State)
CH2M HILL Inc. (engineering, program management, and construction services)
CH2M HILL International, Ltd. (construction project management outside the US)
Industrial Design and Construction (IDC, high-technology facilities design)
Lockwood Greene Engineers, Inc. (engineering and construction)
Kaiser-Hill Company, LLC (50%, joint venture with Kaiser Group International for closure of Rocky Flats nuclear weapons production site)
Operations Management International, Inc. (OMI, utilities support services and maintenance)

COMPETITORS

AECOM	Jacobs Engineering
Bechtel	MWH Global
Black & Veatch	Parsons
Earth Tech	Parsons Brinckerhoff
ERM	Shaw Group
Fluor	Tetra Tech
Foster Wheeler	URS

HISTORICAL FINANCIALS
Company Type: Private

Income Statement				FYE: December 31
	REVENUE ($ mil.)	NET INCOME ($ mil.)	NET PROFIT MARGIN	EMPLOYEES
12/03	2,154	24	1.1%	14,000
12/02	1,999	30	1.5%	10,600
12/01	1,941	28	1.4%	10,500
12/00	1,707	25	1.4%	10,600
12/99	1,185	14	1.1%	9,200
12/98	932	6	0.6%	7,000
12/97	918	5	0.5%	7,200
12/96	937	5	0.5%	7,026
12/95	805	5	0.7%	6,876
12/94	676	3	0.5%	6,559
Annual Growth	13.7%	24.5%	—	8.8%

2003 Year-End Financials

Debt ratio: 3.5%
Return on equity: 12.5%
Cash ($ mil.): 31
Current ratio: 1.19
Long-term debt ($ mil.): 7

Net Income History

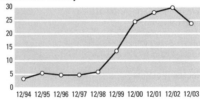

Chapman Automotive

Spend a few hours with a dealer in Vegas and you might lose your shirt — or end up with a new car. Chapman Automotive Group sells more than 17,000 new and used automobiles from about 10 dealerships in Nevada and Arizona. The group sells General Motors, Cross Lander, DaimlerChrysler, BMW, Isuzu, Lincoln, Mercury, and Volkswagen automobiles. The company's dealerships also offer parts and service departments. In addition to selling to individual consumers, Chapman Automotive also supplies cars to fleet buyers. CEO Jerry Chapman founded the group in 1978.

EXECUTIVES

CEO: Jerry B. Chapman
COO: Edward (Eddie) Davault
Controller: Allen Elggren
Internet Manager, Chapman Auto Center: Bill Mansoor
Internet Fleet Manager, Chapman BMW, Chapman Dodge, and Chapman Volkswagen: David Robinson
Internet Fleet Manager, Chapman BMW on Camelback: Ben Majidi
Internet Fleet Manager, Chapman Chevrolet Isuzu: Nick Bruce
Internet Fleet Manager, Chapman Lincoln Mercury: Patrick Heigl

LOCATIONS

HQ: Chapman Automotive Group, LLC
 6601 E. McDowell Rd., Scottsdale, AZ 85271
Phone: 480-970-0740 **Fax:** 480-994-4096
Web: www.chapmanchoice.com

COMPETITORS

AutoNation	Lithia Motors
Findlay Automotive	Tuttle-Click
Fletcher Jones	VT Inc.

HISTORICAL FINANCIALS
Company Type: Private

Income Statement				FYE: December 31
	REVENUE ($ mil.)	NET INCOME ($ mil.)	NET PROFIT MARGIN	EMPLOYEES
12/03	593	—	—	—
12/02	586	—	—	—
12/01	612	—	—	—
12/00	522	—	—	—
12/99	500	—	—	—
12/98	450	—	—	—
12/97	440	—	—	350
12/96	450	—	—	335
Annual Growth	4.0%	—	—	4.5%

Revenue History

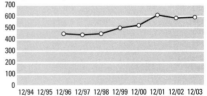

Chas. Levy

Chas. Levy keeps racking up sales. The wholesaler distributes magazines and books throughout the US, primarily in several midwestern states. It is one of four companies that control nearly 90% of single-copy sales at US magazine racks. Having grown through acquisitions of other distributors, Chas. Levy distributes books through its Levy Home Entertainment subsidiary to retail chains including Best Buy, Kmart, Meijer, ShopKo, Stop & Shop, Target, and Wal-Mart. The company has shut down its newspaper distribution operation. Chair Barbara Levy Kipper owns the company her grandfather founded in 1893.

EXECUTIVES
Chairman: Barbara Levy Kipper
Vice Chairman: James (Jim) Levy
President and CEO: Carol G. Kloster
President and COO, Levy Home Entertainment: Howard F. Reese
EVP and COO, Chas. Levy Circulating Company: George Lampros
VP and CFO: William Nelson
Acting Director, HR: John Zilm
Auditors: Deloitte & Touche

LOCATIONS
HQ: Chas. Levy Company LLC
1200 N. North Branch St., Chicago, IL 60622
Phone: 312-440-4400   **Fax:** 312-440-7414
Web: www.chaslevy.com

PRODUCTS/OPERATIONS
Subsidiaries
Chas. Levy Circulating Co. (magazine distribution)
Levy Home Entertainment (book distribution)

COMPETITORS
Advanced Marketing
Anderson News
Baker & Taylor
Hudson News
Ingram Industries
Jim Pattison Group

HISTORICAL FINANCIALS
Company Type: Private

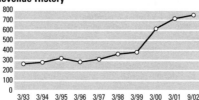

Revenue History

Income Statement			FYE: September 30
	REVENUE ($ mil.)	NET INCOME ($ mil.)	NET PROFIT MARGIN	EMPLOYEES
9/02*	750	—	—	6,500
3/01	715	—	—	6,000
3/00	615	—	—	5,000
3/99	381	—	—	4,500
3/98	362	—	—	4,240
3/97	310	—	—	3,168
3/96	284	—	—	2,234
3/95	320	—	—	2,000
3/94	280	—	—	1,885
3/93	265	—	—	1,800
Annual Growth	12.3%	—	—	15.3%

*Fiscal year change

Charmer Industries

Not easily shaken by competition, Charmer Industries has not stirred from its top spot as New York State's #1 wine and liquor wholesaler. Among its holdings are Connecticut Distributors and Washington (DC) Wholesale Liquor. Charmer Industries is owned by the Merinoff family and run by CEO Herman Merinoff. Charmer Industries is part of the Maryland-based Charmer-Sunbelt Group, the second-largest wine and spirits wholesaler in the US.

EXECUTIVES
Chairman: Charles Merinoff
CEO: Herman I. Merinoff
CFO: Steve Meresmen
Director Human Resources: Annette Perry
Manager, Greater Metropolitan Area: John Paladino

LOCATIONS
HQ: Charmer Industries, Inc.
19-50 48th St., Astoria, NY 11105
Phone: 718-726-2500   **Fax:** 718-726-4428
Web: www.charmer.com

COMPETITORS
Gallo
Johnson Brothers
National Distributing
Peerless Importers
Southern Wine & Spirits

HISTORICAL FINANCIALS
Company Type: Private

Income Statement			FYE: December 31
	ESTIMATED REVENUE ($ mil.)	NET INCOME ($ mil.)	NET PROFIT MARGIN	EMPLOYEES
12/03	700	—	—	1,000
12/02	790	—	—	1,500
12/01	790	—	—	1,500
12/00	790	—	—	1,500
12/99	725	—	—	1,300
12/98	670	—	—	1,300
12/97	675	—	—	1,300
12/96	650	—	—	1,300
12/95	650	—	—	1,000
12/94	605	—	—	1,230
Annual Growth	1.6%	—	—	(2.3%)

Charmer-Sunbelt

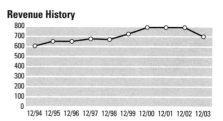

Revenue History

The Charmer-Sunbelt Group has become one of the biggest swigs in its business. A leading wine and spirits wholesaler, the company operates through a number of joint ventures and subsidiaries including Charmer Industries (New York), Premier Beverage (Florida), Reliable Churchill (Maryland), Ben Arnold-Sunbelt Beverage (South Carolina), and others in Alabama, Arizona, Colorado, Connecticut, Mississippi, Pennsylvania, and Washington, DC. Division management bought the group from McKesson (drugs and sundries wholesaler) and took it private in 1988. Herman Merinoff has a majority stake in the company.

The Charmer-Sunbelt Group handles 15% of Southcorp Limited's US wine business and has exclusive rights to Allied Domecq brands in Maryland, Florida, and Washington, DC.

EXECUTIVES
CEO: Charles Merinoff
EVP and CFO: Gene Luciano
VP, Human Resources: Ann Giambusso

LOCATIONS
HQ: The Charmer-Sunbelt Group
60 E. 42nd St., New York, NY 10165
Phone: 212-699-7000   **Fax:** 212-699-7099
Web: www.charmer-sunbelt.com

PRODUCTS/OPERATIONS
Selected Subsidiaries
Bacchus Importers
Been Arnold-Sunbelt Beverage
Capital Wine & Spirits
Charmer Industries
Premier Beverage Company
Reliable Churchill, LLP

COMPETITORS
Bacardi USA
Constellation Brands
Glazer's Wholesale Drug
Johnson Brothers
National Distributing
Southern Wine & Spirits
Young's Market

CHEMCENTRAL

HISTORICAL FINANCIALS
Company Type: Private

Income Statement
FYE: March 31

	ESTIMATED REVENUE ($ mil.)	NET INCOME ($ mil.)	NET PROFIT MARGIN	EMPLOYEES
3/03	2,200	—	—	3,800
3/02	950	—	—	1,700
3/01	910	—	—	1,700
3/00*	850	—	—	1,500
12/99	820	—	—	1,500
12/98	770	—	—	1,700
12/97	700	—	—	1,485
12/96	675	—	—	1,485
12/95	665	—	—	1,485
12/94	660	—	—	1,700
Annual Growth	14.3%	—	—	9.3%

*Fiscal year change

Revenue History

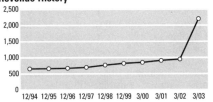

CHEMCENTRAL is in the center of a chemically dependent world. The company is one of the top chemical distributors in North America. It carries products made by BASF, Dow Chemical, DuPont, and others. Key customers for CHEMCENTRAL's more than 8,000 chemical products include companies that manufacture adhesives, caulks, and sealants; cleaning agents; cosmetics and personal care products; inks and paint coatings; and plastic and rubber compounds. Established in 1926 as the William J Hough Company of Chicago, CHEMCENTRAL now has more than 100 warehouse, distribution, and sales units worldwide.

As one of the world's largest private distributors of chemicals, CHEMCENTRAL benefits from economies of scale and wide geographic coverage.

EXECUTIVES
President and CEO: John R. Yanney
VP and CFO: John G. LaBahn
VP and Director of Sales: Phillip A. Scafido
VP, Finance and Treasurer: Lloyd Tarrh
VP, Marketing: William R. Hough
VP, Personnel: Ken Krausz
Director of Corporate Accounts and Business Development: Kris Weigal
Midwest Regional Sales Manager: Scott Obermeier

LOCATIONS
HQ: CHEMCENTRAL Corporation
7050 W. 71st St., Bedford Park, IL 60499
Phone: 708-594-7000 **Fax:** 708-594-6382
Web: www.chemcentral.com

CHEMCENTRAL operates distribution facilities in the US, Canada, and Mexico. The company also has joint ventures in Asia and India and cooperative alliances in Europe.

PRODUCTS/OPERATIONS
Selected Products
Adhesives
Amines
Caulks
Glycerin
Glycols
Paint coatings
Personal care product additives
Polymers
Printing ink products
Rubber and plastic compounds
Sealants
Silicones
Solvents
Surfactants

COMPETITORS
Aceto
Air Products
Arrow-Magnolia
Ashland
Cytec
Dow Chemical
DuPont
HELM U.S.
Hercules
K.A. Steel Chemicals
Nalco
Royal Vopak
Stinnes
Univar
Yule Catto

HISTORICAL FINANCIALS
Company Type: Private

Income Statement
FYE: December 31

	REVENUE ($ mil.)	NET INCOME ($ mil.)	NET PROFIT MARGIN	EMPLOYEES
12/03	895	—	—	970
12/02	885	—	—	1,000
12/01	860	—	—	982
12/00	917	—	—	1,050
12/99	881	—	—	1,000
12/98	880	—	—	918
12/97	875	—	—	870
12/96	825	—	—	865
12/95	850	—	—	897
12/94	745	—	—	834
Annual Growth	2.1%	—	—	1.7%

Revenue History

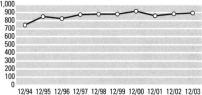

Chevron Phillips Chemical

A coin toss determined which name would go first when Chevron (now ChevronTexaco) and Phillips Petroleum (now ConocoPhillips) formed a new 50-50 joint venture, Chevron Phillips Chemical Company (CP Chem), in 2000. Among the largest US petrochemical firms, CP Chem produces ethylene, propylene, polyethylene, and polypropylene — sometimes used as building blocks for the company's other products such as pipe. CP Chem also produces aromatics such as benzene and styrene, specialty chemicals such as acetylene black (a form of carbon black), and drilling and mining chemicals. The company has formed several petrochemicals joint ventures in the Middle East. Most of CP Chem's operations are located in the US.

After an improved but still unprofitable 2002, CP Chem turned a small profit in 2003 following across-the-board price increases and a particularly good year from Saudi Chevron Phillips Company, in which it has a 50% stake. Still, a low natural gas inventory and the resulting high prices for it, as well as the war in Iraq and the SARS scare in Asia, hampered overall business in 2003.

The company is North America's largest producer of high-density polyethylene (HDPE) — used in blow/injection molding, plastic bags and pipes, and films. CP Chem also is near the top in styrene, ethylene, and aromatics production.

Chevron Phillips Chemical Company LP is the US operating subsidiary of CP Chem, which also includes foreign ventures, mainly those in Asia and the Middle East. Chevron Phillips Chemical Company LP accounts for about 85% of its parent's revenues.

EXECUTIVES
President and CEO: James L. (Jim) Gallogly, age 52, $792,950 pay
SVP, CFO, and Controller: Greg G. Maxwell, age 47
SVP, Aromatics and Styrenics: J. M. (Mike) Parker, age 57, $372,979 pay
SVP, Manufacturing: R. L. (Rick) Roberts, age 49
SVP, Olefins and Polyolefins: Timothy G. (Tim) Taylor, age 50, $418,278 pay
SVP, Planning and Specialty Projects: Greg C. Garland, age 45, $436,725 pay
CIO: Larry R. Frazier
VP, General Counsel, and Secretary: Craig B. Glidden, age 46, $412,552 pay
VP, Human Resources: D.F. (Don) Kremer, age 53
VP and Treasurer: Joseph M. (Joe) McKee, age 53
VP, Environment, Health, and Safety: A. S. (Scott) Meyer
Auditors: Ernst & Young LLP

LOCATIONS
HQ: Chevron Phillips Chemical Company LLC
10001 6 Pines Dr., The Woodlands, TX 77380
Phone: 832-813-4100 **Fax:** 800-231-3890
Web: www.cpchem.com

Chevron Phillips Chemical operates about 30 manufacturing facilities and five research and technical centers, including facilities in Belgium, China, Mexico, Qatar, Saudi Arabia, Singapore, South Korea, and the US.

2003 Sales

	% of total
US	84
Other	16
Total	**100**

PRODUCTS/OPERATIONS

2003 Sales

	$ mil.	% of total
Olefins & polyolefins	4,390	59
Aromatics & styrenics	2,648	36
Specialty products	397	5
Adjustments	(417)	—
Total	**7,018**	**100**

Selected Products

Olefins and Polyolefins
  Ethylene
  Polyethylene
  Polyethylene pipe
  Polypropylene
  Propylene

Aromatics & styrenics
  Benzene
  Cumene
  Cyclohexane
  Paraxylene
  Styrene

Specialty products
  Acetylene black
  Alpha olefins
  Dimethyl sulfide
  Drilling specialty chemicals
  High-purity hydrocarbons and solvents
  Mining chemicals
  Neohexene
  Performance and reference fuels
  Polyalpha olefins
  Polystyrene

Selected Joint Ventures

Chevron Phillips Singapore Chemicals (Private) Limited (50%)
CPChem/BP Solvay Polyethylene (50%)
K R Copolymer Co., Ltd. (60%)
Phillips Sumika Polypropylene Company (60%)
Qatar Chemical Company Ltd. (Q-Chem)
Saudi Chevron Phillips Company (50%)
Shanghai Golden Phillips Petrochemical Co. (40%)

COMPETITORS

BASF AG	KRATON
BP Petrochemicals	NOVA Chemicals
Dow Chemical	Sasol
DuPont	Shell Chemicals
Equistar Chemicals	Sterling Chemicals
ExxonMobil Chemical	Sunoco Chemicals
Jilin Chemical	

HISTORICAL FINANCIALS
Company Type: Joint venture

Income Statement   FYE: December 31

	REVENUE ($ mil.)	NET INCOME ($ mil.)	NET PROFIT MARGIN	EMPLOYEES
12/03	7,018	7	0.1%	5,451
12/02	5,473	(30)	—	5,517
12/01	6,010	(480)	—	6,056
Annual Growth	8.1%	—	—	(5.1%)

2003 Year-End Financials

Debt ratio: 33.9%
Return on equity: 0.2%
Cash ($ mil.): 43
Current ratio: 1.38
Long-term debt ($ mil.): 1,189

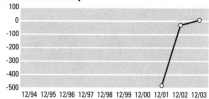

Net Income History

Chevy Chase Bank

Chevy Chase Bank is one of the largest banks serving the Washington, DC, area (including parts of Maryland and northern Virginia), with a branch network of approximately 210 offices and more than 750 ATMs. The savings bank offers traditional retail services such as checking and savings accounts, CDs, and IRAs, in addition to investment management services, insurance, credit cards, and business and private banking. Its loan portfolio is dominated by one- to four-family residential mortgages (almost two-thirds of all loans) and also includes consumer, commercial, and construction loans. Chairman and CEO B. Francis Saul II controls the bank through various companies.

EXECUTIVES

Chairman and CEO: B. Francis Saul II
Vice Chairman: Alexander R.M. Boyle
Vice Chairman: B. Francis Saul III, age 42
EVP and CFO: Stephen R. Halpin
EVP and CIO: Robert H. Spicer II
EVP and Chief Lending Officer: George P. Clancy Jr.
EVP, Retail Banking: W. Scott McSween
EVP and General Counsel: R. Timothy Hanlon
President, Chevy Chase Financial Services:
  Richard L. Clark
Director of Human Resources: Russ McNish
President and CEO, Chevy Chase Trust Company; EVP, Chevy Chase Bank: Peter M. Welber
President and CEO, ASB Capital Management, Inc.:
  Daniel B. Mulvey
President, B.F. Saul Mortgage Company:
  Robert D. Broeksmit

LOCATIONS

HQ: Chevy Chase Bank, F.S.B.
  7501 Wisconsin Ave., Chevy Chase, MD 20814
Phone: 240-497-4101   **Fax:** 240-497-4110
Web: www.chevychasebank.com

PRODUCTS/OPERATIONS

2003 Sales

	$ mil.	% of total
Interest		
Loans	402.4	41
Securities	42.6	4
Other	6.5	1
Noninterest		
Deposit servicing fees	122.5	12
Servicing and securitization	103.4	10
Automobile rental income	235.8	24
Gain on trading securities & sale of loans	41.2	4
Real estate income	6.8	1
Other	30.6	3
Total	**991.8**	**100**

Selected Subsidiaries

Chevy Chase Financial Services Corporation
  Chevy Chase Insurance Agency, Inc.
  Chevy Chase Securities, Inc.

COMPETITORS

Bank of America	Provident Bankshares
BB&T	Riggs National
M&T Bank	Sandy Spring Bancorp
Mercantile Bankshares	SunTrust

HISTORICAL FINANCIALS
Company Type: Private

Income Statement   FYE: September 30

	ASSETS ($ mil.)	NET INCOME ($ mil.)	NET INCOME AS % OF ASSETS	EMPLOYEES
9/03	11,796	80	0.7%	4,000
9/02	11,286	57	0.5%	3,900
9/01	—	61	—	3,517
9/00	11,024	38	0.3%	3,445
9/99	9,173	45	0.5%	3,597
Annual Growth	6.5%	15.5%	—	2.7%

2003 Year-End Financials

Equity as % of assets: 4.9%
Return on assets: 0.7%
Return on equity: 14.3%
Long-term debt ($ mil.): 250
Sales ($ mil.): 992

Net Income History

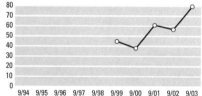

Chick-fil-A

Beloved by bovines, Chick-fil-A operates one of the nation's largest fast-food chains that specialize in chicken dishes. (It is #2 in sales behind YUM! Brands' KFC unit.) With more than 1,100 restaurants, Chick-fil-A serves chicken entrees, sandwiches, and salads, along with its popular waffle fries and fresh-squeezed lemonade. The chain is made up primarily of mall-based stores, but it also includes free-standing units that offer drive-through service as well as dine-in seating. Chick-fil-A also licenses its concept to food service operators for high-traffic areas, such as schools and airports. All of its restaurants are closed on Sundays, a policy insisted upon by founder (and devout Baptist) Truett Cathy.

Unlike most fast-food franchises, Chick-fil-A owns most of its restaurants and licenses franchisees to run the units for a fixed annual income plus a share in the profits. This unique arrangement lowers the initial cost to its franchisees and has resulted in less operator turnover than in other chains.

With more than a third of its restaurants in three states (Florida, Georgia, and Texas) Chick-fil-A has been focusing its expansion efforts on opening more free-standing restaurants — most recently in Southern California — as well as licensed units in non-traditional locations. It has also developed a "lunch counter" design concept for use in office buildings. Overall, Chick-fil-A plans to open about 90 restaurants in 2004.

As part of its marketing strategy, Chick-fil-A is a big sponsor of athletic events, including the annual Peach Bowl college football game. It also supports leadership training and scholarship programs through the WinShape Centre Foundation.

The company also operates two full-service restaurant concepts, Chick-fil-A Dwarf Houses and Truett's Grill.

EXECUTIVES

Chairman: S. Truett Cathy
President and COO: Dan T. Cathy
SVP; President, Dwarf House: Donald M. (Bubba) Cathy
SVP Design and Construction: Perry A. Ragsdale
SVP Finance and CFO: James B. (Buck) McCabe
SVP Marketing and Chief Marketing Officer:
 Steve A. Robinson
SVP Operations: Timothy P. (Tim) Tassopoulos
SVP Public Relations: Don Perry
SVP Real Estate and General Counsel:
 Bureon E. Ledbetter Jr.
VP and CIO: Jon Bridges
VP Brand Development: Woody Faulk
VP Training and Development: Mark Miller
Senior Director of Purchasing: Steve Hester
Senior Director of Real Estate: Alex Dominguez
Director of Development: John H. McCleskey Jr.
Senior Manager of Technical Architecture: Chris Taylor
Corporate Information Systems Manager:
 Mark Brackett
Human Resources Administrator: Renea Boozer

LOCATIONS

HQ: Chick-fil-A Inc.
 5200 Buffington Rd., Atlanta, GA 30349
Phone: 404-765-8038   **Fax:** 404-765-8971
Web: www.chick-fil-a.com

Chick-fil-A operates about 1,125 restaurants in 38 states.

COMPETITORS

AFC Enterprises
Blimpie
Burger King
Captain D's
CKE Restaurants
Dairy Queen
Jack in the Box
KFC
Krystal
McDonald's
Panasonic Mobile Communications
Quizno's
Subway
Triarc
Wendy's
YUM!
Zaxby's

HISTORICAL FINANCIALS
Company Type: Private

Income Statement FYE: December 31

	REVENUE ($ mil.)	NET INCOME ($ mil.)	NET PROFIT MARGIN	EMPLOYEES
12/03	1,534	—	—	46,500
12/02	1,373	—	—	45,000
12/01	1,242	—	—	43,000
12/00	1,082	—	—	40,000
12/99	750	—	—	35,000
12/98	650	—	—	35,000
12/97	672	—	—	28,500
12/96	570	—	—	25,000
12/95	502	—	—	—
12/94	451	—	—	—
Annual Growth	14.6%	—	—	9.3%

Revenue History

Children's Hospital of Philadelphia

In the City of Brotherly Love, sick boys and girls have a place to go to get better. The Children's Hospital of Philadelphia is a leading pediatric hospital and has one of the largest pediatric research programs in the world. The nation's first hospital devoted exclusively to the care of children, it has about 430 beds at its primary facility and operates a pediatric health care network with some 50 affiliated offices, clinics, and research facilities in Delaware, New Jersey, and Pennsylvania. The hospital has been a leader in formal pediatric medical training, pediatric emergency medicine, and adolescent medicine.

In 2003 the hospital claimed for the first time the coveted title of top US pediatric hospital bestowed by *US News & World Report*. Usually it ranked just behind Children's Hospital Boston.

EXECUTIVES

President and CEO: Steven M. Altschuler, $1,475,642 pay
EVP and COO: Jeffrey A. Rivest, $1,540,642 pay
COO: Gavin R. Kerr
SVP and Chief Nursing Officer: Leslie A. Clarke
Executive Director, The e-Transformation and e-Medicine Center: Evan L. Crawford
Director of the Vaccine Education Center and Chief of Infectious Diseases: Paul A. Offit
Director of Recruitment: Lynette Smith
Director of Neurosurgery: Leslie N. Sutton
Controller: Walter Greiner
Chief of Gastroenterology and Nutrition; Co-Director, The Fred and Suzanne Biesecker Pediatric Liver Center: David A. Piccoli
Chief of the Division of Endocrinology and Diabetes: Charles A. Stanley
General Counsel: Bonnie Brier

LOCATIONS

HQ: The Children's Hospital of Philadelphia
 34th St. & Civic Center Blvd.,
 Philadelphia, PA 19104
Phone: 215-590-1000   **Fax:** 215-590-4090
Web: www.chop.edu

COMPETITORS

All Children's Hospital
Catholic Health East
Children's Hospital Boston
Children's Hospital Inc.
Children's Hospital of Pittsburgh
Children's Hospital of The King's Daughters
Children's Hospitals and Clinics
HCA
Miami Children's Hospital
New York City Health and Hospitals
Shriners Hospitals For Children
St. Jude Children's Research Hospital
Tenet Healthcare
Texas Children's Hospital

HISTORICAL FINANCIALS
Company Type: Not-for-profit

Income Statement FYE: June 30

	REVENUE ($ mil.)	NET INCOME ($ mil.)	NET PROFIT MARGIN	EMPLOYEES
6/03	722	—	—	5,100

Choice Homes

Choice Homes is the builder of choice for many first-time buyers and first-time move-up homeowners in Texas and Georgia. The privately held builder of affordable homes and single-family townhomes is one of the largest homebuilders in the Dallas/Fort Worth area. It maintains more than 160 communities in and around Amarillo, Austin, Dallas/Fort Worth, Galveston, Houston, Lubbock, and San Antonio, Texas, and 16 Georgia communities in Atlanta, Gainesville, and Macon. Customers may choose from more than 200 floor plans with a variety of options. The company, which began in 1987, builds about 4,400 homes annually. For five consecutive years *Builder* magazine has ranked it as one of the top 25 builders in the US.

Consistent with its philosophy to share its success with the people who helped make it happen, Choice Homes incorporates a companywide dividend program that divides equally among its employees a percentage of the company's profits each year. The company presented over $1.5 million in performance bonuses to its employees in 2002 and more than $1.2 million in 2003.

The company's plan for growth targets Houston, West Texas, and San Antonio markets, as well as the greater Atlanta area. Choice Homes is expanding into the New Braunfels market in Texas and entered Lubbock in 2004.

EXECUTIVES

President and CEO: Stephen T. (Steve) Wall
VP Finance and CFO: Darris McClure
VP and Real Estate Director: Matthew (Matt) Bilardi
Regional VP, Austin and San Antonio: Frank Prince
Regional VP, Dallas and East Texas: Zack Jones
Regional VP, Houston: Marc Jungers
Regional VP, Tarrant, Parker, Hood, and Denton Counties, Texas: Daniel D. Couture
Regional VP, Georgia: Kelly Dempsey
Director, IT: Andrew Brimberry
Director, Marketing and Advertising: Kristina (Kris) Densing
Public Relations Manager: Erin Kolp

LOCATIONS

HQ: Choice Homes, Inc.
1600 East Lamar Blvd., Arlington, TX 76011
Phone: 817-652-5100   **Fax:** 817-633-2925
Web: www.choicehomes.com

Choice Homes builds in and around Amarillo, Austin, Dallas/Fort Worth, Galveston, Houston, Lubbock, and San Antonio, Texas, and in Atlanta, Gainesville, and Macon, Georgia. It has offices in Arlington (near Dallas/Fort Worth), Houston, San Antonio, and Atlanta.

COMPETITORS

Beazer Homes
Centex
David Weekley Homes
D.R. Horton
KB Home
Kimball Hill Homes
Lennar
Pulte Homes

HISTORICAL FINANCIALS

Company Type: Private

Income Statement   FYE: December 31

	ESTIMATED REVENUE ($ mil.)	NET INCOME ($ mil.)	NET PROFIT MARGIN	EMPLOYEES
12/03	540	—	—	485
12/02	466	—	—	440
Annual Growth	15.9%	—	—	10.2%

Revenue History

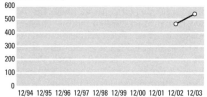

CHRISTUS Health

CHRISTUS has plenty to be merry about. The Catholic health system operates more than 40 hospitals and other health care facilities. The majority of its operations are in Louisiana and Texas, but the organization also has facilities in Arkansas and Utah, as well as in Mexico. CHRISTUS Health's facilities include acute care hospitals, outpatient centers, and long-term acute care facilities (operated by Dubuis Health System), as well as hospice centers and medical education centers. The health system typically operates in midsized markets where it faces little competition from larger health systems.

CHRISTUS was formed through the 1999 merger of Incarnate Word Health System and Sisters of Charity Health System. Both systems have their roots in the religious order Sisters of Charity of the Incarnate Word, founded when three French nuns arrived in Texas in 1866 to care for the poor and sick.

EXECUTIVES

Chairman: Richard S. Blair
President and CEO: Thomas C. (Tom) Royer
SVP and CIO: George Conklin
SVP and Chief Medical Officer: John Gillean
SVP and CFO: Jay Herron
SVP, Human Resource Services and Corporate Integrity Officer: Mary Lynch
SVP, Business, Strategy, and Corporate Development: Peter Maddox
SVP, Communications, Public Affairs, and Philanthropy: Linda McClung
President and CEO, CHRISTUS Gulf Coast Region Division: Patrick B. Carrier
CEO, CHRISTUS St. Joseph Hospital: Jeff Webster
Corporate Controller: Jenny Barnett
President and CEO, CHRISTUS Santa Rosa Health Care: Don A. Beeler
President and CEO, Dubuis Health System: Ellen Smith
Director, Marketing: Heather Boler

LOCATIONS

HQ: CHRISTUS Health
6363 N. Hwy. 161, Ste. 450, Irving, TX 75038
Phone: 214-492-8500   **Fax:** 214-492-8540
Web: www.christushealth.org

Selected Facilities

Mexico
  Hospital Christus Muguerza (Monterrey)
US
  Arkansas
    Magnolia Hospital (Magnolia)
  Louisiana
    CHRISTUS St. Frances Cabrini Hospital (Alexandria)
    CHRISTUS Schumpert Bossier (Bossier City)
    CHRISTUS Coushatta Health Care Center (Coushatta)
    CHRISTUS St. Patrick Hospital (Lake Charles)
    Natchitoches Parish Hospital (Natchitoches)
    CHRISTUS Schumpert Highland (Shreveport)
    CHRISTUS Schumpert St. Mary Place (Shreveport)
  Texas
    CHRISTUS Spohn Hospital Alice (Alice)
    Baptist St. Anthony's Health System (50%, Amarillo)
    CHRISTUS St. Elizabeth Hospital (Beaumont)
    CHRISTUS Spohn Hospital Beeville (Beeville)
    CHRISTUS Spohn Hospital Memorial (Corpus Christi)
    CHRISTUS Spohn Hospital Shoreline (Corpus Christi)
    Rice Medical Center (Eagle Lake)
    CHRISTUS St. Joseph Hospital (Houston)
    CHRISTUS Jasper Memorial Hospital (Jasper)
    CHRISTUS St. Catherine Hospital (Katy)
    CHRISTUS Spohn Hospital Kleberg (Kingsville)
    CHRISTUS St. John Hospital (Nassau Bay)
    CHRISTUS St. Mary Hospital (Port Arthur)
    CHRISTUS Santa Rosa Hospital (San Antonio)
    CHRISTUS Santa Rosa Rehabilitation Hospital (San Antonio)
    CHRISTUS St. Michael Rehabilitation Hospital (Texarkana)
  Utah
    CHRISTUS St. Joseph Villa (Salt Lake City)

COMPETITORS

Baylor Health
Harris County Hospital
HCA
Intermountain Health Care
Memorial Hermann Healthcare
Methodist Hospital System
Sisters of Mercy Health System
St. Luke's Episcopal Hospital
Tenet Healthcare
Vitas Healthcare

HISTORICAL FINANCIALS

Company Type: Not-for-profit

Income Statement   FYE: June 30

	REVENUE ($ mil.)	NET INCOME ($ mil.)	NET PROFIT MARGIN	EMPLOYEES
6/03	2,302	20	0.9%	8,000
6/02	2,378	—	—	8,000
6/01	2,200	—	—	8,000
6/00	2,080	—	—	8,000
6/99	1,884	—	—	—
Annual Growth	5.1%	—	—	0.0%

Revenue History

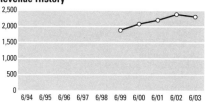

CIC International

Like a veteran goalie, CIC International holds its own on defense. The company makes military equipment and systems for governments and defense industries worldwide. It makes military products for land, sea, and air. The company's main products include night vision and optical devices, munitions, helicopters, and avionics components (jet engines, fuel systems, headup displays). CIC also upgrades tanks and armored personnel carriers. Its naval services include upgrading weapon systems and providing engineering for surface warfare problems. The defense contractor began in 1930 as a silk and fur trader. Company executives and employees control CIC.

EXECUTIVES

Chairman and CEO: Satiris G. Fassoulis
CFO: Robert C. (Bob) Perry
EVP; President, Columbia Technology: Joseph Ceva
VP, CIO/CTO: James Chladek
VP, Human Resources; Customer Service: Robert Volvo
International Operations: Dino Seferian
Legal: Richard Zaroff
Purchasing: Robert Thompson
Secretary; Business Development: Larry Thompson
Treasurer: Marie Couvaras

LOCATIONS

HQ: CIC International Ltd.
5 Marine View Plaza, Hoboken, NJ 07030
Phone: 201-792-1800 **Fax:** 201-792-5755
Web: www.cic-international.com

CIC International has plants in Honolulu and Philadelphia.

PRODUCTS/OPERATIONS

Selected Products and Services

Aerospace
   Avionics
   Control systems
   Escape equipment
   Headup displays
   Hydraulics
   Instruments
   Jet engines
   Power plant and electronic accessories
Communications
   PH-26 Phantom Radio System (handheld, frequency-hopping transceiver)
Defense
   Armored vehicles
   Kits for weapons modernization
Helicopters
   Airborne thermal imaging systems
   Guidance systems and components
   Head-up displays
   Hydra 70 family of rockets
   Laser-guided missiles
   Machine gun pods
   Self-protection systems
   Wire guided ordnance (TOW and HOT)
Munitions
   Ammunition (anti-aircraft, howitzer, tank)
   Bombs
   Detonators
   Elements
   Grenades
   High explosives
   Mines
   Primers
   Projectiles
   Propellants
Naval Support Services
   Amphibious warfare
   Coastal warfare systems
   Gun turrets
   Launchers and simulation devices
   Mechanical and electrical systems
   Mines and mine countermeasures
   Search and track systems
   Ship electromagnetic and electro-optic reconnaissance
   Ship hulls
   Strategic targeting
   Surface ship combat systems
   Surface warfare modeling and analysis
Night Vision
   Goggles (dual and single tubes)
   Units for night surveillance (battlefield and frontier)
   Vehicle-mounted night vision devices

COMPETITORS

Alliant Techsystems
Allied Defense Group
Alvis
Anteon
Ball Aerospace
Elbit Systems
General Dynamics
Lockheed Martin
Lockheed Martin Missiles
Meggitt USA
Napco International
Northrop Grumman
United Defense Industries

HISTORICAL FINANCIALS

Company Type: Private

Income Statement FYE: August 31

	REVENUE ($ mil.)	NET INCOME ($ mil.)	NET PROFIT MARGIN	EMPLOYEES
8/03	781	—	—	726
8/02	773	—	—	735
8/01	709	—	—	624
8/00	563	—	—	514
8/99	505	—	—	502
8/98	438	—	—	252
8/97	426	—	—	—
Annual Growth	10.6%	—	—	23.6%

Revenue History

Cincinnati Children's Hospital

Cincinnati Children's Hospital Medical Center has a special place in its heart for kids — and possibly vice versa. The pediatric health care facility performs a number of organ and tissue transplants each year; procedures include transplants of hearts, blood and marrow, livers, kidneys, and small bowel. Cincinnati Children's Hospital has more than 420 beds and operates more than a dozen outpatient care centers. The hospital also serves as a Level 1 pediatric trauma center for southwestern Ohio, northern Kentucky, and southeastern Indiana. The Cincinnati Children's Hospital Research Foundation seeks new treatments for a variety of ailments that afflict both kids and adults.

EXECUTIVES

President and CEO: James M. Anderson
SVP, Planning and Business Development: Dwight E. Ellingwood
SVP, Finance and CFO: Scott J. Hamlin
SVP, Clinical Care Delivery: William M. Kent
SVP, Patient Services: Dorine R. Seaquist
VP, Family and Community Relations: David Anderson
VP, Inpatient Nursing, Patient Services: Shelley Baranowski
VP, Marketing and Communications: Phyllis Goodman
VP, Facilities Management: Thomas E. Kinman
VP, Quality and Transformation: Uma Kotagal
VP, Medical Affairs, Physician Hospital Organization: Keith Mandel
VP, Outpatient and Home Care Services: Char Mason
VP, Human Resources: Ronald B. McKinley
VP, Information Services: Marianne Speight
VP and General Counsel: Elizabeth A. Stautberg
Chief-of-Staff: Michael K. Farrell

LOCATIONS

HQ: Cincinnati Children's Hospital Medical Center
3333 Burnet Ave., Cincinnati, OH 45229
Phone: 513-636-4200 **Fax:** 513-636-2460
Web: www.cincinnatichildrens.org

HISTORICAL FINANCIALS

Company Type: Not-for-profit

Income Statement FYE: June 30

	REVENUE ($ mil.)	NET INCOME ($ mil.)	NET PROFIT MARGIN	EMPLOYEES
6/03	671	—	—	7,207
6/02	598	—	—	6,235
Annual Growth	12.3%	—	—	15.6%

Revenue History

Cinemark

Cinemark has left its mark on the cinema landscape. The third-largest movie exhibitor in the US (following Regal Entertainment and AMC) has more than 3,000 screens in 294 theaters in the US and several other countries, mostly in Latin America. Cinemark operates multiplex theaters (the ratio of screens to theaters is about 12 to 1) in smaller cities and suburban areas of major metropolitan markets. Some larger theaters operate under the Tinseltown name; others are "discount" theaters, as opposed to those which exhibit first-run films. Chairman and CEO Lee Roy Mitchell owns about 92% of the company's voting stock. Private investment firm Madison Dearborn Partners plans to buy Cinemark for about $1 billion.

All of Cinemark's theaters are multiplexes, many of which sport neon color schemes not found in nature. About 15% of its theaters are "discount" cinemas. The company prefers to build new theaters in midsized markets or in suburbs of major cities where the Cinemark theater is the only game in town. Cinemark's theaters can be found in 33 US states and 14 other countries. Cinemark has also teamed up with Imax Corporation to build 5 Cinemark IMAX Theatres in Colorado, Illinois, New York, Oklahoma, and Texas.

The company spent the late nineties upgrading into one of the most modern and technologically advanced movie chains. (About two-thirds of the current screens have been built since 1996; about 65% of its North American first run screens and 75% of its international screens feature stadium seating — a trend that began in the 1990s.) Cinemark, along with the rest of the movie theater industry, struggled through the late 1990s as numerous bankruptcies abounded thanks to overbuilding. Things seemed to be on the upswing in early 2002, and Cinemark responded by filing an IPO. However, the overall decline of the stock market forced the firm to postpone its offering later that year. Cinemark has since abandoned plans to take the company public in favor of putting itself up for sale.

EXECUTIVES

Chairman and CEO: Lee Roy Mitchell, age 67, $1,335,240 pay
Vice Chairman, EVP, and Assistant Secretary: Tandy Mitchell, age 53
President and COO: Alan W. Stock, age 43, $502,717 pay
SVP Operations and IT: Robert F. Carmony, age 46, $353,880 pay
SVP, Treasurer, CFO, and Assistant Secretary: Robert D. Copple, age 45, $367,081 pay
SVP; President, Cinemark International: Tim Warner, age 59, $407,665 pay
VP, General Counsel, and Assistant Secretary: Michael Cavalier, age 37
VP Construction: Don Harton, age 46
VP Development: Tom Owens, age 46
VP Purchasing: Walter Hebert III, age 58
VP Film Licensing: John Lundin, age 54
VP Real Estate and Assistant Secretary: Margaret E. Richards, age 45
VP Marketing and Communications: Terrell Falk, age 53
Controller: Joe Manzi
Director Human Resources: Brad Smith
Auditors: Deloitte & Touche LLP

LOCATIONS

HQ: Cinemark, Inc.
3900 Dallas Pkwy., Ste. 500, Plano, TX 75093
Phone: 972-665-1000   **Fax:** 972-665-1004
Web: www.cinemark.com

Cinemark has theaters in Argentina, Brazil, Canada, Chile, Colombia, Costa Rica, Ecuador, El Salvador, Honduras, Nicaragua, Mexico, Panama, Peru, the UK, and 33 states in the US.

2003 Sales

	$ mil.	% of total
US and Canada	743.8	78
Brazil	74.9	8
Mexico	70.2	7
Other regions	70.2	7
Eliminations	(1.5)	—
Total	**957.6**	**100**

COMPETITORS

AMC Entertainment	National Amusements
Carmike Cinemas	Pacific Theatres
Famous Players	Rainbow Movies
Hoyts Cinemas	Regal Entertainment
Loews Cineplex	

HISTORICAL FINANCIALS

Company Type: Private

Income Statement
FYE: December 31

	REVENUE ($ mil.)	NET INCOME ($ mil.)	NET PROFIT MARGIN	EMPLOYEES
12/03	958	45	4.7%	12,700
12/02	939	39	4.2%	12,500
12/01	854	(4)	—	8,000
12/00	786	(10)	—	8,000
12/99	713	1	0.1%	8,000
12/98	571	11	1.9%	8,000
12/97	435	15	3.5%	7,000
12/96	342	15	4.3%	6,500
12/95	299	13	4.4%	7,000
12/94	283	7	2.5%	5,500
Annual Growth	**14.5%**	**22.9%**	**—**	**9.7%**

2003 Year-End Financials

Debt ratio: 848.1%   Current ratio: 0.90
Return on equity: 85.5%   Long-term debt ($ mil.): 652
Cash ($ mil.): 107

Net Income History

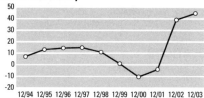

Cingular Wireless

BellSouth *plus* SBC *times* wireless assets *equals* Cingular Wireless. With a name chosen to emphasize unity and the individual customer, the two regional Bell companies have combined assets to create the #2 wireless carrier in the US, behind Verizon Wireless. With 25 million customers, including subscribers to its Mobitex wireless data services network, the joint venture is 60%-owned by SBC and 40% by BellSouth, according to the contributions made by the two companies, which share control. Eleven brand names used by the SBC and BellSouth wireless units have been replaced by the Cingular Wireless brand. Cingular has agreed to buy rival AT&T Wireless.

Cingular won a bidding war with UK-based wireless operator Vodafone Group to acquire AT&T Wireless as part of a long-anticipated consolidation within the mobile phone industry. The cash deal, valued at $41 billion, is subject to shareholder and regulatory approval. If completed, the acquisition will create the leading US wireless carrier with 46 million customers, topping the current leader Verizon Wireless. Prior to the deal, Cingular had formed a joint venture with AT&T Wireless to work on the development of advanced networks. The two wireless carriers use the same network technology.

To accommodate the deal to acquire AT&T Wireless, Cingular has agreed to sell a wireless network in California and Nevada to T-Mobile USA. The deal, valued at $2.5 billion, includes a $200 million payment to T-Mobile USA to end a venture in which the two companies shared each other's networks. Cingular had earlier held merger talks with VoiceStream Wireless, now T-Mobile USA.

The company also has agreed to sell its Cingular Interactive subsidiary, which provides wireless corporate e-mail and messaging services, to a unit of Cerberus Partners.

Cingular Wireless also has acquired additional licenses from bankrupt NextWave Telecom. The deal, valued at $1.4 billion, sent 34 licenses to Cingular for markets that include 83 million potential customers. These markets are primarily areas where Cingular already operates. In another deal, Cingular has completed a swap of some cellular properties in northwest Michigan to Dobson Communications in exchange for properties along the eastern Maryland shore. It also has acquired 16,000 customers in Louisiana, as well as spectrum and operations in Louisiana, Texas, and Arkansas, from US Unwired in a cash deal valued at $27.6 million.

Reports also have suggested that the company will seek an IPO in 2004 to raise money. Some of the proceeds could be used for additional acquisitions.

EXECUTIVES

Chairman: Randall L. Stephenson, age 44
President and CEO: Stanley T. (Stan) Sigman, age 56, $2,776,000 pay
COO: Ralph de la Vega, age 52, $1,126,319 pay (prior to promotion)
CFO: Peter (Pete) Ritcher
EVP and General Counsel, Legal and Regulatory: Joaquin R. Carbonell III, age 51, $600,277 pay
EVP Human Resources: Rickford D. (Rick) Bradley, age 51
SVP Customer Service: Kathleen (Kathy) Dowling
CIO: F. Thaddeus Arroyo, age 40, $678,750 pay
CTO: W.E. (Bill) Clift
Controller: Gregory T. Hall, age 48
President, Cingular Interactive: Charles Nelson
President, Network Operations: Edgar L. (Ed) Reynolds, age 55
Senior Director, Media Relations: Clay Owen
Executive Director, Investor Relations: Kent Evans
Auditors: Ernst & Young LLP

LOCATIONS

HQ: Cingular Wireless LLC
Glenridge Highlands Two, 5565 Glenridge Connector, Atlanta, GA 30342
Phone: 404-236-6000   **Fax:** 404-236-6005
Web: www.cingular.com

PRODUCTS/OPERATIONS

2003 Sales

	$ mil.	% of total
Wireless services		
Local voice service	12,133	78
Roaming	757	5
Data	454	3
Long-distance	171	1
Other services revenues	708	5
Equipment sales	1,260	8
Total	**15,483**	**100**

Selected Services

Analog wireless access
Digital wireless access
Interactive messaging
Short text messaging
Wireless data
Wireless Internet access

Selected Subsidiaries

Cingular Wireless Corporation (managing entity)

COMPETITORS

ALLTEL	Sprint PCS
Arch Wireless	Telephone & Data Systems
AT&T Wireless	T-Mobile USA
Centennial Communications	U.S. Cellular
CenturyTel	Verizon Wireless
Nextel	Western Wireless

HISTORICAL FINANCIALS

Company Type: Joint venture

Income Statement
FYE: December 31

	REVENUE ($ mil.)	NET INCOME ($ mil.)	NET PROFIT MARGIN	EMPLOYEES
12/03	15,483	1,022	6.6%	39,400
12/02	14,727	1,207	8.2%	33,800
12/01	14,108	1,692	12.0%	—
12/00	3,055	127	4.2%	—
12/99	9,042	—	—	—
12/98	7,988	—	—	—
12/97	7,433	—	—	—
Annual Growth	13.0%	100.4%	—	16.6%

2003 Year-End Financials

Debt ratio: 148.4%
Return on equity: 12.8%
Cash ($ mil.): 1,139
Current ratio: 1.04
Long-term debt ($ mil.): 12,592

Net Income History

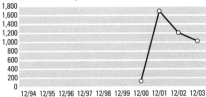

Citation

Citation is forging ahead with a fresh cast of characters. After being taken private by management and investment firm Kelso & Company, the company has altered its primary role as a metal castings supplier and recast itself as a producer of machined and assembled, as well as cast and forged, components. Citation makes a wide range of iron, steel, and aluminum products, primarily for equipment manufacturers and other industrial customers. The company organizes its operating groups around the markets they serve: Aerospace and Technology, Automotive, Industrial Iron, and Industrial Steel. Because of soaring steel prices, Citation filed Chapter 11 bankruptcy protection in 2004.

Some of Citation's customers include makers of cars, trucks, pumps, valves, compressors, engines, and other durable and capital goods. Ford is the company's largest customer. The company produces its iron, steel, and aluminum goods at around 20 locations in eight states and Germany.

Citation depends on its manufacturing technologies, product mix, and engineering prowess to weather the pricing pressures and cyclical downturns of the industries it serves. The automotive industry presents the greatest challenge. In response, Citation has branched into machined and assembled components.

EXECUTIVES

President, CEO, and Director: Ed Buker
CFO and VP Finance: Chuck Bloome
Corporate Director, Human Resources:
  James M. Gordon
Group VP, Automotive Group: John W. Lawson
Group VP - Light Metals and Machining Group:
  Cary B. Wood
Group VP: Tim Roberts
Group VP: Robert (Bob) Simcox
VP, Forging: Jeff Lunsford
VP, Product Engineering and Development:
  Vincent Genise
VP, Quality and Process Improvement: Ratan Ray
VP, Sales and Marketing: Charles A. (Chuck) Pestow
VP, Supply Management: Larry Tackett
Director, Program Management: David Brassell

LOCATIONS

HQ: Citation Corporation
  2700 Corporate Dr., Ste. 100,
  Birmingham, AL 35242
Phone: 205-871-5731 **Fax:** 205-870-5772
Web: www.citation.net

Citation operates facilities in Alabama, California, Illinois, Indiana, Michigan, North Carolina, Tennessee, Texas, Wisconsin, and Düsseldorf, Germany.

PRODUCTS/OPERATIONS

Operating Groups

Aerospace and Technology
  Citation Precision
  Product Engineering and Development

Automotive
  Alabama Ductile
  Bohn Aluminum
  Camden Casting
  Citation Marion
  Dycast
  Southern Aluminum
  Texas Foundries

Industrial Group - Iron
  Castwell Products
  Citation Foam
  Custom Products
  Foundry Service
  Southern Ductile
  Wisconsin Castings

Industrial Group - Steel
  Interstate Forging

COMPETITORS

Grede Foundries
INTERMET
Jay Industries
Jernberg Industries
Lexington Precision
Lufkin Industries
Margate Industries
McWane
Mueller Industries
Precision Castparts
Transportation Technologies
Worthington Industries

HISTORICAL FINANCIALS

Company Type: Private

Income Statement
FYE: Sunday nearest September 30

	REVENUE ($ mil.)	NET INCOME ($ mil.)	NET PROFIT MARGIN	EMPLOYEES
9/03	650	—	—	5,000
9/02	700	—	—	5,600
9/01	750	—	—	6,500
9/00	800	—	—	7,000
9/99	800	—	—	7,000
9/98	724	—	—	6,336
9/97	649	—	—	5,778
9/96	488	—	—	5,155
9/95	308	—	—	3,879
9/94	192	—	—	2,441
Annual Growth	14.5%	—	—	8.3%

Revenue History

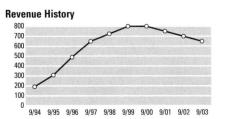

City University of New York

The City University of New York (CUNY) is the big "U" in the Big Apple. The college has 20 campuses in the five boroughs of New York City and is the US's largest urban university system. About 450,000 undergraduate, graduate, and continuing education students (from 145 countries) are enrolled at CUNY. CUNY has 11 senior colleges, six community colleges, a doctoral-granting graduate school, a four-year technical school, and medical and law schools. Its 1,230 programs range from specialized, career-oriented courses to traditional liberal arts curricula. CUNY's 12,000-person faculty is split almost evenly between full- and part-time teachers.

CUNY has made some big changes, including tougher admission standards that critics feared would hurt the university's ethnic diversity, a hallmark of the school (enrollment numbers have proven otherwise). Notable CUNY alumni include novelist Oscar Hijuelos, General Colin Powell, comedian Jerry Seinfeld, and 11 Nobel laureates.

As with many public universities throughout the US, CUNY is enduring tough times economically. In order to free up the money to hire more full-time professors, the university has had to end a 10-year tradition: not charging four-year students for the last semester of their senior year. Tuition and fees account for about 36% of funds for the university.

HISTORY

The New York State Legislature first created a municipal college system in New York City in 1926, when it formed the New York City Board of Higher Education to manage the operations of the City College of New York and Hunter College. City College's roots were established in 1847 when New York passed a referendum creating the Free Academy, a tuition-free school. Hunter College was founded in 1870 as a women's college, and it was the first free teachers college in the US.

The Board of Higher Education authorized City College to create the Brooklyn Collegiate Center (a two-year men's college) in 1926; Hunter established a similar two-year women's branch in Brooklyn. Four years later the schools merged to create the Brooklyn College of the City of New York, the city's first public, coed liberal arts college. Other schools added to the municipal system included Queens College (1937), New York City Community College (1947), Staten Island Community College (1955), Bronx Community College (1957), and Queensborough Community College (1958).

The state legislature renamed New York City's municipal college system The City University of New York (CUNY) in 1961 and ordered its board of trustees to expand the system's facilities and scope. One of the first actions was to create a graduate school. CUNY chartered a number of new schools during the 1960s, including Richmond College (1965), York College (1966), Medgar Evers College (1968), and several community colleges. CUNY took over management of the New York State Institute of Applied Arts and Sciences (renamed New York City Technical College) in 1964 and established the John Jay College of Criminal Justice. CUNY became affiliated with Mount Sinai School of Medicine in 1967.

Despite its expansion, the university system had difficulty keeping up with demand, particularly after 1970, when it established an open admissions policy for all New York City high school graduates. Richmond College and Staten Island Community College became the College of Staten Island in 1976. Both CUNY and the City of New York ran into serious financial problems in the mid-1970s, spelling the end of CUNY's tradition of free undergrad tuition for New York City residents. To increase state financial support for CUNY, the legislature signed the City University Governance and Financing Act in 1979.

The City University School of Law held its first classes in 1983. The following year the state board of regents authorized CUNY to offer a doctor of medicine degree. CUNY's law school received accreditation from the American Bar Association in 1992. Since abandoning the free enrollment policy in the 1970s, the university's tuition continued to increase. In 1992, after presenting a nearly $600 increase in tuition, CUNY initiated its "last semester free" program, whereby four-year students did not have to pay tuition for the last semester of their senior year.

After several years of budget cuts and steadily increasing enrollment, CUNY declared a state of financial emergency in 1995. The following year New York's Governor George Pataki proposed new budget cuts, and in 1997 he called for tuition hikes. CUNY's board of trustees introduced a resolution calling for the elimination of remedial education programs at the senior college level in 1998. The state Board of Regents approved the plan in 1999 (most remedial classes were phased out by 2001). Matthew Goldstein was appointed chancellor in 1999 and has worked to increase CUNY's budget to hire more full-time faculty.

Belt-tightening continued in 2002. The university was forced to begin charging four-year students for the last semester of their senior year in order to earn more money.

EXECUTIVES

Chancellor: Matthew Goldstein
Vice Chancellor for Facilities Planning, Construction, and Management: Emma Espino Macari
Vice Chancellor for Faculty and Staff Relations: Brenda Richardson Malone
Vice Chancellor for University Relations: Jay Hershenson
Interim Vice Chancellor for Budget and Finance: Ernesto Malave
General Counsel and Vice Chancellor for Legal Affairs: Frederick P. Schaffer
University Dean for Student Services and Enrollment Management: Otis Hill
University Dean for Instructional Technology and Information Services: Michael Ribaudo
University Dean for The Executive Office: Robert Ptachik
University Dean for Academic Affairs and Deputy to the Executive Vice Chancellor: John Mogulescu
Special Counsel to the Chancellor: Dave Fields
Auditors: KPMG LLP

LOCATIONS

HQ: The City University of New York
535 E. 80th St., New York, NY 10021
Phone: 212-794-5555 **Fax:** 212-209-5600
Web: www.cuny.edu

The City University of New York has schools serving the Bronx, Brooklyn, Manhattan, Queens, and Staten Island boroughs of New York City.

PRODUCTS/OPERATIONS

Senior Colleges
Bernard M. Baruch College
Brooklyn College
City College
City University School of Law at Queens College
The College of Staten Island
The Graduate School and University Center
Herbert H. Lehman College
Hunter College
John Jay College of Criminal Justice
Medgar Evers College
New York City College of Technology
Queens College
York College

Community Colleges
Borough of Manhattan Community College
Bronx Community College
Hostos Community College
Kingsborough Community College
LaGuardia Community College
Queensborough Community College

HISTORICAL FINANCIALS
Company Type: School

Income Statement — FYE: June 30

	REVENUE ($ mil.)	NET INCOME ($ mil.)	NET PROFIT MARGIN	EMPLOYEES
6/03	1,192	—	—	30,000
6/02	1,041	—	—	30,000
6/01	1,927	—	—	30,000
6/00	1,900	—	—	30,000
6/99	1,873	—	—	28,000
6/98	1,784	—	—	28,000
6/97	1,729	—	—	27,900
6/96	1,756	—	—	25,800
6/95	1,722	—	—	25,800
6/94	1,655	—	—	—
Annual Growth	(3.6%)	—	—	1.9%

Revenue History

Clarian Health Partners

Clarian Health Partners is one of the largest health systems in Indiana. The system includes three major hospitals — Methodist Hospital, Indiana University Hospital, and Riley Hospital for Children — that have more than 1,300 beds total. Two more hospitals — Clarian North Medical Center and Clarian West Medical Center — are under construction. The health system also includes several clinics, family practices, and specialized health facilities. Clarian Health's hospitals are some of the top providers of organ transplant services in the US.

EXECUTIVES

Chairman, President, and CEO: Daniel F. (Dan) Evans Jr., age 55
EVP and Chief Medical Officer: Richard Graffis
EVP and CFO: Marvin Pember
SVP, Values, Ethics, and Pastoral Services: Steve Ivy
SVP, Nursing and Patient Care Services and Chief Nurse Executive: Karlene Kerfoot
VP, Operations: David (Dave) Hesson
VP, Finance: Isadore Rivas
CEO, Clarian West Medical Center: Al W. Gatmaitan
CEO, Clarian North Medical Center: Jonathan R. (Jon) Goble, age 46
President and CEO, Methodist Hospital and Indiana University Hospital: Samuel L. (Sam) Odle
President and CEO, Riley Hospital for Children: Ora Hirsch Pescovitz, age 47
Senior Public Relations Coordinator: Jon Mills

LOCATIONS

HQ: Clarian Health Partners, Inc.
1600 Senate Blvd., Indianapolis, IN 46202
Phone: 317-962-2000 **Fax:** 317-962-4533
Web: www.clarian.org

HISTORICAL FINANCIALS
Company Type: Not-for-profit

Income Statement — FYE: December 31

	REVENUE ($ mil.)	NET INCOME ($ mil.)	NET PROFIT MARGIN	EMPLOYEES
12/03	2,102	—	—	11,088
12/02	1,660	—	—	11,396
Annual Growth	26.7%	—	—	(2.7%)

Revenue History

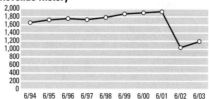

Clark Enterprises

Like Clark Kent, this company holds some super powers. Clark Enterprises, one of the largest private companies in the US, provides ownership, investment, and asset management services to its subsidiaries. It holds interests in real estate, private equities, and commercial, heavy, and residential construction companies. The Clark Construction Group, its main subsidiary, is the largest privately held US contractor and works on commercial, institutional, and heavy construction projects. Other units include residential developer Clark Realty Capital, heavy contractor Atkinson Construction, and highway construction company Shirley Contracting. Chairman and CEO James Clark owns the company, which was founded in 1972.

EXECUTIVES

Chairman and CEO: A. James Clark
President and COO: Lawrence C. Nussdorf, age 57
EVP: Robert J. (Bob) Flanagan, age 47
VP and Treasurer: Sandy R. Garchik
VP: Terri D. Klatzkin
VP and General Counsel: Rebecca L. Owen
Deputy General Counsel: David H. Brody
Chairman, Clark Construction Group: Peter C. Forster
President and COO, Clark Construction Group: Dan T. Montgomery
President, Clark Realty Builders: Glenn Ferguson
President, Clark Realty Management: Douglas Sandor
President and CEO, Atkinson Construction: Scott Lynn
President, Seawright Corp.: D. Stephen Seawright

LOCATIONS

HQ: Clark Enterprises, Inc.
7500 Old Georgetown Rd., 15th Fl., Bethesda, MD 20814
Phone: 301-657-7100 **Fax:** 301-657-7263
Web: www.clarkenterprisesinc.com

PRODUCTS/OPERATIONS

Selected Subsidiaries
Atkinson Construction (heavy contractor)
The Clark Construction Group, Inc.
Clark Realty Capital, LLC (residential development)
Clark Realty Management, LLC (property management)
CNF Investments LLC (private equity investment)
Shirley Contracting (highway and heavy construction)

COMPETITORS

Barton Malow
Bechtel
Bovis Lend Lease
Centex
FaulknerUSA
Fluor
Gilbane
Hensel Phelps Construction
Hunt Construction
Perini
Peter Kiewit Sons'
Skanska
Turner Corporation
Tutor-Saliba
Webcor Builders
Whiting-Turner

HISTORICAL FINANCIALS
Company Type: Private

Income Statement
FYE: December 31

	ESTIMATED REVENUE ($ mil.)	NET INCOME ($ mil.)	NET PROFIT MARGIN	EMPLOYEES
12/03	2,750	—	—	4,200
12/02	2,800	—	—	4,500
12/01	2,500	—	—	4,000
12/00	2,400	—	—	4,500
12/99	1,800	—	—	5,000
12/98	1,500	—	—	5,000
12/97	1,330	—	—	3,500
12/96	1,400	—	—	4,500
12/95	1,500	—	—	5,000
12/94	1,500	—	—	5,000
Annual Growth	7.0%	—	—	(1.9%)

Revenue History

Cleary, Gottlieb

Cleary, Gottlieb, Steen & Hamilton may be a big cheese in the Big Apple, but the law firm also has made a name for itself in the international arena. Cleary, Gottlieb's attorneys work from 11 offices scattered across the globe and are known for specializing in practice areas such as corporate finance, mergers and acquisitions, litigation, and intellectual property. The firm has more than 700 attorneys, with a third of those outside the US. It has represented British Airways and Deutsche Telekom. It was founded in 1946 by former Root Clark Buckner partners George Cleary, Leo Gottlieb, Fowler Hamilton, and Mel Steen.

EXECUTIVES

Managing Partner: Peter Karasz
Administrative Director: John H. Slattery
Director of Finance: Adrienne E. Boan
Director of Administrative Personnel: Nancy J. Roberts
Manager Media Relations: Amy Fantini

LOCATIONS

HQ: Cleary, Gottlieb, Steen & Hamilton
1 Liberty Plaza, New York, NY 10006
Phone: 212-225-2000 **Fax:** 212-225-3999
Web: www.cgsh.com

Cleary, Gottlieb, Steen & Hamilton has offices in Belgium, France, Germany, Hong Kong, Italy, Japan, the UK, and the US.

PRODUCTS/OPERATIONS

Selected Practice Areas
Antitrust and competition
Corporate
Employee benefits
Energy
Environmental law
Individual clients and charitable organizations
Intellectual property
International trade
Litigation
Real estate
Tax
US antitrust and European competition

COMPETITORS

Baker & McKenzie
Clifford Chance
Cravath, Swaine
Davis Polk
Debevoise & Plimpton
Dewey Ballantine
Fried, Frank, Harris
Jones Day
LeBoeuf, Lamb
Morgan, Lewis
Shearman & Sterling
Simpson Thacher
Skadden, Arps
Weil, Gotshal

HISTORICAL FINANCIALS
Company Type: Partnership

Income Statement
FYE: December 31

	REVENUE ($ mil.)	NET INCOME ($ mil.)	NET PROFIT MARGIN	EMPLOYEES
12/03	580	—	—	—
12/02	531	—	—	—
12/01	492	—	—	—
12/00	460	—	—	—
12/99	412	—	—	1,300
12/98	366	—	—	1,400
12/97	341	—	—	1,430
12/96	310	—	—	—
12/95	286	—	—	—
12/94	265	—	—	—
Annual Growth	9.1%	—	—	(4.7%)

Revenue History

ClubCorp

ClubCorp makes its green from the green — the golf green, that is. The world's largest operator of golf courses, country clubs, private business clubs, and resorts, the company owns and operates about 170 properties in the US and three other countries. Its holdings include Mission Hills Country Club near Palm Springs, California, and North Carolina's Pinehurst Resort and Country Club (site of the 1999 US Open). The company has sold its interests in ClubLink, a leading Canadian developer and operator of golf courses, and PGA European Tour Courses, an operator of tournament golf courses across Europe. The family of late founder Robert Dedman owns 43% of ClubCorp.

Striving to stay on top of the game, the company has been acquiring new properties and is building new ones through Bear's Best, a joint venture with golf legend Jack Nicklaus. Robert Dedman, who was named by *Forbes* magazine as one of the 400 wealthiest Americans, died in 2002. His son, Robert Jr., took over as CEO, but passed those duties to president John Beckert in 2004. (Dedman Jr. remains chairman.) ClubCorp's other shareholders include The Cypress Group, which owns about 16%.

HISTORY

Though his childhood in Depression-era Arkansas was dominated by intense poverty, ClubCorp founder Robert Dedman knew how to dream big. At a young age he vowed to become "very, very rich," and the scrappy Dedman embarked on achieving that goal by earning a college scholarship, obtaining a law degree, and eventually launching a flourishing Dallas law practice.

Dedman's law firm was successful, but he realized that it wouldn't bring him the $50 million he wanted to earn by age 50. In 1957 he formed Country Clubs, Inc., to venture into the country club business. At that time, doctors and lawyers working on a volunteer basis were managing most clubs, and Dedman believed his new company could bring professional management expertise to these facilities. The company opened its first country club, Dallas' Brookhaven Country Club, in 1957. Through the subsequent purchase of 20 more clubs, Country Clubs refined its management style, implementing unique practices such as reducing playing time on the golf course and developing specialized training for club staff.

In 1965 the company expanded into city and athletic clubs and assumed the Club Corporation of America name. The expansion drive that followed fueled a 30% growth rate that the company maintained from the 1960s through the 1980s. In 1985 the company was restructured and divided into a handful of separate companies owned by the newly formed Club Corporation International holding company.

In 1988 the company bought an 80% interest in Franklin Federal Bancorp. The bank's club properties had initially caught his eye, but Dedman also believed that the 400,000 members of his clubs might prove fertile ground for the marketing of financial services. In 1996, however, Club Corporation International sold the financial institution to Norwest. Although Franklin Federal was turning a profit, losses from investment in derivatives, coupled with the bank's inability to compete with larger competitors, prompted the company to sell the bank and refocus on its core club and resort business.

In 1996 Japanese cookie-maker Tohato sued the company, claiming that it intentionally mismanaged the Pinewild Country Club. Pinewild was owned by Tohato, managed by Club Corporation International, and located next door to Club Corporation International's Pinehurst Resort and Country Club. Tohato alleged that the company's mismanagement was part of a scheme to eventually buy Pinewild at a reduced price. The case was eventually settled, but the nasty legal wrangling that ensued cast a pall over the impending 1999 US Open at Pinehurst.

In 1998 the company was reincorporated as ClubCorp International, Inc. It expanded its international base that year by purchasing nearly 30% of PGA European Tour Courses. The company also entered into a joint venture with Jack Nicklaus to develop three dozen new golf courses.

The company shortened its moniker to ClubCorp in 1999. Among the additions ClubCorp made to its holdings that year were 22 properties acquired from The Meditrust Companies. The company also increased its ownership of Canadian club developer ClubLink to 25%. An influx of funds for further expansion came in 1999 after investment firm The Cypress Group took a stake. In 2001 the company sold its interests in ClubLink and PGA European Tour Courses.

Robert Dedman died in 2002. His son, Robert Dedman Jr., took over as CEO for a time, but relinquished those duties to president John Beckert in 2004. Dedman Jr. remains chairman.

EXECUTIVES

Chairman: Robert H. Dedman Jr., age 46, $735,000 pay (prior to title change)
President, CEO, and COO: John A. Beckert, age 50, $781,250 pay (prior to promotion)
CFO: Jeffrey P. Mayer, age 47, $569,972 pay
EVP, Secretary, and General Counsel: Thomas T. Henslee, age 44
EVP ClubCorp USA: Douglas T. Howe, age 46
EVP ClubCorp USA: Frank C. Gore, age 54, $453,592 pay
EVP Resorts: Richard N. Beckert, age 47, $517,079 pay
EVP Strategic Operations: Murray S. Siegel, age 58
EVP: Mark W. Dietz, age 50
SVP, Controller, and Chief Accounting Officer: Angela A. Stephens
SVP Business and Sports Division: David B. Woodyard
SVP Human Resources: John Longstreet
SVP Marketing: Lisa H. Kislak
CIO: Colby H. Springer, age 54
President, The Pinehurst Company: Patrick A. (Pat) Corso, age 52, $365,940 pay
Auditors: Deloitte & Touche LLP

LOCATIONS

HQ: ClubCorp, Inc.
3030 LBJ Fwy., Ste. 700, Dallas, TX 75234
Phone: 972-243-6191   **Fax:** 972-888-7700
Web: www.clubcorp.com

ClubCorp has operations in Australia, China, Mexico, and the US.

PRODUCTS/OPERATIONS

Selected Clubs
Aspen Glen Country Club (Colorado)
The Athletic and Swim Club at Equitable Center (New York)
Columbia Tower Club (Washington)
The Hills Country Club (Texas)
Mission Hills Country Club (California)
Pinehurst Resort and Country Club (North Carolina)
Teal Bend Golf Club (California)

COMPETITORS

American Golf
Club Med
Four Seasons Hotels
Golf Trust of America
Hillman
Hilton
Hyatt
Marriott
ResortQuest International
Sandals Resorts
Silverleaf Resorts
Starwood Hotels & Resorts

HISTORICAL FINANCIALS

Company Type: Private

Income Statement
FYE: December 31

	REVENUE ($ mil.)	NET INCOME ($ mil.)	NET PROFIT MARGIN	EMPLOYEES
12/03	912	(105)	—	19,000
12/02	947	(62)	—	20,000
12/01	1,015	(106)	—	23,000
12/00	1,069	(17)	—	24,000
12/99	1,028	12	1.1%	23,000
12/98	851	38	4.5%	21,000
12/97	840	122	14.5%	20,000
12/96	784	29	3.7%	19,000
12/95	761	(11)	—	19,800
12/94	773	15	1.9%	19,200
Annual Growth	1.8%	—	—	(0.1%)

2003 Year-End Financials
Debt ratio: 237.5%   Current ratio: 1.05
Return on equity: —   Long-term debt ($ mil.): 691
Cash ($ mil.): 90

Net Income History

Coca-Cola Bottling Co. United

Coca-Cola Bottling Co. United brings icy-cold Cokes to the sunny South. Founded in 1902, Coke United serves up "the real thing" in The Coca-Cola Company's home turf, reaching consumers from Atlanta, Georgia, to Baton Rouge, Louisiana. It is the #3 Coca-Cola bottler (the world's #1 soft drink) in the US. Brands include Coca-Cola Classic, Diet Coke, Fresca, Sprite, and Vanilla Coke. Its 101-year-old subsidiary, Chattanooga Coca-Cola Bottling Co., is the world's oldest Coca-Cola franchise. The bottler was the subject of a 1987 book, *Coca-Cola Bottling Company United, Inc.: A Pause to Reflect.*

EXECUTIVES

President, Chairman, and CEO: Claude B. Nielsen, age 54
EVP, Administration, General Counsel, and Corporate Secretary: M. Williams Goodwyn Jr.
VP and CFO: Hafiz Chandiwala
VP, Human Resources: Debbie Myles
VP, IT: P. Michael Neighbors
President, Eastern Region: John Sherman
President, Gulf Coast Region: Gary Sligar
Corporate Controller: E. Eric Steadman
Director, Community Relations: Walker Jones

LOCATIONS

HQ: Coca-Cola Bottling Co. United, Inc.
4600 E. Lake Blvd., Birmingham, AL 35217
Phone: 205-841-2653 **Fax:** 205-841-9168

Coca-Cola Bottling Co. serves customers in Alabama, Georgia, Louisiana, Mississippi, South Carolina, and Tennessee.

COMPETITORS

Buffalo Rock
Coca-Cola Bottling Consolidated
Coca-Cola Enterprises
Cott
National Beverage
Pepsi Bottling
PepsiAmericas

HISTORICAL FINANCIALS

Company Type: Private

Income Statement — FYE: December 31

	REVENUE ($ mil.)	NET INCOME ($ mil.)	NET PROFIT MARGIN	EMPLOYEES
12/03	525	—	—	—
12/02	525	—	—	2,900
12/01	500	—	—	2,900
12/00	495	—	—	3,000
12/99	501	—	—	3,000
12/98	450	—	—	3,000
12/97	449	—	—	3,300
12/96	425	—	—	2,600
12/95	425	—	—	2,500
Annual Growth	2.7%	—	—	2.1%

Revenue History

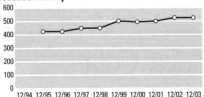

Coinmach

You won't find much dirty laundry at Coinmach. The leading US supplier of coin- and card-operated laundry equipment and related services has helped customers do millions of loads of laundry. Leasing laundry rooms in apartments and dormitories, Coinmach owns and operates more than 870,000 washing machines and dryers at about 80,000 locations nationwide. The company also owns Appliance Warehouse, which rents machines to apartment residents and management companies, and more than 160 Kwik Wash laundromats in Texas and Arizona. Subsidiary Super Laundry designs and builds or retrofits retail laundromats and distributes laundry equipment. GTCR Golder Rauner owns about two-thirds of Coinmach.

The company's LaundriMate service notifies apartment and dormitory residents when machines are available and when laundry is finished.

Coinmach has been rapidly increasing its machine count, which stood at about 55,000 in 1995. Operating in a largely fragmented industry, Coinmach folds newly purchased operations into its national organization to achieve economies of scale. The company maintains more than 60 regional offices in about 20 states.

EXECUTIVES

Chairman and CEO: Stephen R. (Steve) Kerrigan, age 50, $937,620 pay
President and COO: Mitchell Blatt, age 52, $465,753 pay
SVP, CFO, Treasurer, and Secretary: Robert M. (Bob) Doyle, age 47, $346,875 pay
SVP, Corporate Development: John E. Denson, age 65
SVP: Stephen P. Close
SVP and President and Secretary of AWA: Ramon Norniella, age 45, $220,000 pay
SVP: Michael E. Stanky, age 52, $232,100 pay
Human Resources Manager: Cathy Chambers
Investor Relations: Sandra Leach
Auditors: Ernst & Young LLP

LOCATIONS

HQ: Coinmach Service Corp.
303 Sunnyside Blvd., Ste. 70, Plainview, NY 11803
Phone: 516-349-8555 **Fax:** 516-349-9125
Web: www.coinmachservicecorp.com

COMPETITORS

Alliance Laundry
Clean Rite Centers
Dryclean USA
Mac-Gray
SpinCycle
Web Service Company

HISTORICAL FINANCIALS

Company Type: Private

Income Statement — FYE: March 31

	REVENUE ($ mil.)	NET INCOME ($ mil.)	NET PROFIT MARGIN	EMPLOYEES
3/04	531	(6)	—	2,003
3/03	535	(3)	—	1,994
3/02	539	(42)	—	2,049
3/01	528	(34)	—	2,119
3/00	527	(17)	—	2,226
3/99	505	(12)	—	2,045
3/98	325	(15)	—	1,850
3/97	207	(11)	—	1,180
3/96	89	(3)	—	689
3/95	90	(6)	—	—
Annual Growth	21.8%	—	—	14.3%

2004 Year-End Financials

Debt ratio: 1,754.4%
Return on equity: —
Cash ($ mil.): 32
Current ratio: 0.88
Long-term debt ($ mil.): 768

Net Income History

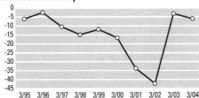

Colliers International

Colliers International Property Consultants is one of the world's largest commercial real estate dealers. With more than 230 offices in about 50 countries, the company is a partnership of more than 40 independently-owned firms. Colliers International agencies provide brokerage, construction consulting, investment sales, and property development and management services to tenants, owners, and investors. Colliers Macauley Nicolls (doing business as Colliers International) is the group's largest member with offices in nearly 90 cities worldwide. Originally founded in 1832, Colliers Jardine represents the Asia/Pacific region. Colliers International firms manage some 333 million sq. ft. of space on six continents.

EXECUTIVES

Chairman, Colliers USA: Mark Burkhart
President and CEO, Colliers USA: Margaret Wigglesworth
President, Colliers Latin America: Chris McLernon
Executive Director, Colliers Europe, Middle East, and Africa: Rob Pearman
President, Colliers Asia Pacific: James W. (Jamie) Horne
COO, Colliers USA: Margaret Kemp Carlson
SVP and Director, Corporate Services Group, Colliers USA: Richard B. Kimball
VP and Director, Research: Ross Moore
CTO, Colliers USA: Joshua Fost
VP and Director, Marketing, Colliers USA: Karen Galvin
VP Corporate Services, Colliers Latin America: Luis Lira
CIO: Richard Secor
Director, Research and Communications, Colliers Latin America: Mario Rivera

LOCATIONS

HQ: Colliers International Property Consultants Inc.
50 Milk St., 20th Fl., Boston, MA 02019
Phone: 617-722-0221 **Fax:** 617-722-0224
Web: www.colliers.com

COMPETITORS

CB Richard Ellis
Cushman & Wakefield
DTZ
Gale Company
Grubb & Ellis
JMB Realty
Jones Lang LaSalle
NRT Inc.
Trammell Crow Company

HISTORICAL FINANCIALS

Company Type: Private

Income Statement — FYE: December 31

	REVENUE ($ mil.)	NET INCOME ($ mil.)	NET PROFIT MARGIN	EMPLOYEES
12/03	995	—	—	8,823
12/02	880	—	—	7,572
12/01	800	—	—	6,600
12/00	1,000	—	—	9,000
12/99	900	—	—	8,000
Annual Growth	2.5%	—	—	2.5%

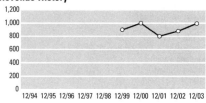

Revenue History

Colson & Colson

Colson & Colson Construction builds retirement communities for senior citizens worldwide. The company primarily develops affordable retirement properties nationwide for Holiday Retirement Corp. (HRC), the #1 owner and manager of retirement homes in the US and Canada; it also operates in France and the UK. Colson & Colson has interests in some 20,000 HRC units. Generally located in a midsized town, the typical property is a traditional retirement facility of about 115 units. The company uses a prefabrication process to speed construction and keep costs down. William Colson is head of both Colson & Colson and HRC. The Colson family owns the majority of Colson & Colson and also holds a significant stake in HRC.

EXECUTIVES
President, CEO, and Managing General Partner: William E. (Bill) Colson, age 62
SVP: Norman Brendan
VP and COO: Barton (Bart) Colson
Secretary and Acquisitions Director: Bruce Thorn
Treasurer: Gregory Tibbot
Director, IS: Steve McDowell
Manager, Human Resources: Linda Livermore

LOCATIONS
HQ: Colson & Colson Construction Company
2250 McGilchrist SE, Ste. 200, Salem, OR 97302
Phone: 503-370-7070   **Fax:** 503-370-4205
Web: www.colson-colson.com

Colson & Colson Construction develops property for Holiday Retirement Corp.'s operations in 39 states in the US, six provinces in Canada, and in France and the UK.

COMPETITORS
Centex
Del Webb
Embree Construction
John Wieland Homes
KB Home
Lennar
Marriott
Morrison Homes
Pulte Homes

HISTORICAL FINANCIALS
Company Type: Private

Income Statement FYE: December 31

	REVENUE ($ mil.)	NET INCOME ($ mil.)	NET PROFIT MARGIN	EMPLOYEES
12/03	857	—	—	7,300
12/02	900	—	—	7,300
12/01	888	—	—	7,100
12/00	690	—	—	6,800
12/99	707	—	—	6,800
12/98	675	—	—	6,500
12/97	600	—	—	6,000
12/96	500	—	—	—
Annual Growth	8.0%	—	—	3.3%

Revenue History

Colt's

The Colt .45 may have won the West, but it took a New York investment firm to save Colt's Manufacturing from a post-Cold War decline in weapons sales and tough foreign competition. Through its subsidiaries, Colt's Manufacturing makes handguns (Cowboy, Defender) and semi-automatic rifles for civilian use and military weapons (M-16, M-4 Carbine) for the US and other governments. The company has distributors throughout Europe, Asia, and Australia. Founded in 1836 by Samuel Colt, the company is about 85%-owned by investment firm Zilkha & Co., who has been reviving the company since 1994 when it bought the firm out of bankruptcy.

With the firearms industry taking cover from safety and health care expense-related lawsuits filed by cities and counties across the US, Colt's is discontinuing a number of handguns it makes for the consumer market. The company spun off its "smart gun" division as iColt but the division closed soon after.

In 2003 the company began reproduction of its classic WWI military sidearm, the 1911. The original 1911 and its descendants have been used by servicemen during WWI and WWII, as well as in Korea and Vietnam.

HISTORY

After waiting four years for a patent, Samuel Colt started the Patent Arms Manufacturing Company in 1836 to make his revolutionary handgun, a revolver. The newfangled gun was slow to catch on (the company went bankrupt in 1842), but it gained fame after being adopted by the Texas Rangers. The US Army delegated Capt. Samuel Walker to work with Colt to improve the design, and sales of the resulting "Walker Colt" enabled Colt to set up a factory in Hartford, Connecticut.

In 1851 the company was the first American manufacturer to open a plant in England. Patent Arms Manufacturing was renamed Colt's Patent Fire Arms Manufacturing Co. four years later. Colt was a millionaire when he died in 1862 at age 47.

Colt's introduced the six-shot Colt .45 Army Model, "the gun that won the West," in 1873. More products followed, including machine guns and automatic pistols designed by inventor John Browning. Colt's widow sold the firm to an investor group in 1901.

Business boomed during both world wars, but by the 1940s labor strife and outmoded equipment began to take a toll, and Colt's lost money during the last years of WWII. In 1955 the struggling firm was acquired by conglomerate Penn-Texas. In 1959 Colt's patented the M-16 rifle; in 10 years it sold a million units to the US military. During the Vietnam War the company flourished, but the 1980s brought low-end competition and shrinking defense orders. Colt's sales were hurt when the US government replaced the Colt .45 as the standard-issue sidearm for the armed forces. A three-year strike prompted the Army to shift its M-16 contract to Belgium's FN Herstal in 1988.

Two years later Colt's was acquired by private investors and a Connecticut state pension fund and was renamed Colt's Manufacturing. Sales remained flat, however, forcing the company to seek bankruptcy protection in 1992. There Colt's remained until New York investment firm Zilkha & Co. bailed it out in 1994, reorganizing the company. The new management made an offer for rival FN Herstal in 1997, but the deal was blocked by the Belgian government and fell through. Late that year the company won a contract to supply M-4 rifles to the Army.

Colt's bought military weapons specialist Saco Defense, maker of MK 19 and Striker grenade launchers, in 1998. Also that year Steven Sliwa succeeded retiring CEO Ronald Stewart.

As US cities began suing Colt's and other makers of firearms in attempts to recover safety and health expenses attributed to gun violence, the company stepped up lobbying in 1999 and said it would increase gun safety efforts, including development of its "smart gun" technology.

A restructuring in 1999 ended most of Colt's consumer handgun business. It also spun off its smart gun technology as a separate company, iColt. Sliwa left to head iColt, and retired US Marine Lieutenant General William Keys was named president and CEO of Colt's. Also in 1999 Colt's bought Ultra-Light Arms, a maker of upscale hunting rifles, and said it would buy Heckler & Koch, a small arms manufacturer based in Germany. By 2000 the company had withdrawn iColt (investors didn't seem interested in a lawsuit laden industry) and stepped away from the Heckler & Koch deal. The company continues to focus on weapons for the military and police, but in 2001 it lost out to CAPCO Inc. in a bid for a contract to upgrade M16 rifles used by the Air Force.

EXECUTIVES
Chairman: Donald Zilkha
President and CEO: William M. (Bill) Keys
CFO: Tom Moore
Director, Commercial and Law Enforcement Sales: Joshua Dorsey
Director, Human Resources: Mike Magouirk
Director, Marketing: Mike Reissig
Director, Materials: John Ibbotson

LOCATIONS
HQ: Colt's Manufacturing Company, LLC
545 New Park Ave., West Hartford, CT 06110
Phone: 860-236-6311   **Fax:** 860-244-1442
Web: www.colt.com

PRODUCTS/OPERATIONS
Selected Products and Brands
Classics
  Anaconda
  Colt 1911 WWI replica
  Python
Commercial rifles
  Colt accurized rifles
  Match target rifles
Law enforcement
  AR15
  Carbine
  Colt accurized rifles
  Commando
  M-16A2
  M203 Grenade Launchers
  M-4 Carbine
  Match target rifles
  Submachine guns
Performance products
  Colt Gunsite Pistol
  Colt XSE Series
  Gold Cup Trophy
  Special Combat Government Competition
Personal protection
  Colt Defender
  M1991A1
Western
  Colt Cowboy
  Model Ps

COMPETITORS
Beretta
Browning
FN Manufacturing
Glock
Marlin Firearms
Mauser-Werke
Remington Arms
Ruger
SIG
Smith & Wesson Holding
Springfield Inc.
U.S. Repeating Arms

HISTORICAL FINANCIALS
Company Type: Private

Income Statement				FYE: December 31
	ESTIMATED REVENUE ($ mil.)	NET INCOME ($ mil.)	NET PROFIT MARGIN	EMPLOYEES
12/03	95	—	—	700
12/02	95	—	—	700
12/01	95	—	—	700
12/00	95	—	—	700
12/99	95	—	—	700
12/98	96	—	—	700
12/97	92	—	—	700
Annual Growth	0.5%	—	—	0.0%

Revenue History
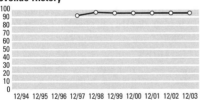

Columbia Forest Products

Columbia Forest Products is a clear-cut leader as North America's largest manufacturer of hardwood plywood, veneer, and laminated products. The employee-owned company makes products used in flooring, cabinets, architectural millwork, and commercial fixtures. Columbia Forest Products specializes in Northern Appalachian hardwoods. Its rotary veneer is used by the cabinetry, door, furniture, and decorative plywood industries. The company sells its products to OEMs, wholesale distributors, and mass merchandisers. Columbia Forest Products began in 1957 with a plywood plant in Oregon and has grown to operate 20 plants throughout the US and Canada.

Columbia Forest Products purchased Weyerhaeuser's Nipigon Multiply hardwood plywood underlayment operation (Ontario, Canada) in 2003; it enlists Weyerhaeuser Building Materials as a sales and distribution agent to its customers in North America. The company also has an exclusive agreement with Halex Corporation to head up sales of the Multiply flooring underlayment to wholesale flooring distributors in North America. (Multiply is three-ply aspen, one-fourth-inch plywood, for use under vinyl, ceramic, and laminate flooring.)

Also in 2003 Columbia acquired Millwood Specialty Flooring Inc., which produces unfinished three-quarter-inch solid hardwood flooring in Ellijay, Georgia.

EXECUTIVES
Chairman: Arnold Curtis
President and CEO: Harry L. Demorest, age 62
EVP and CFO: Clifford (Cliff) Barry
EVP Sales and Marketing: Ed Woods
VP Hardwood Veneer Operations: Ted Jewett
Director, MIS: Frank Leipzig
Director, Organizational Development and Human Resources: Rick Howell
President, Columbia Flooring: David Wootton
Public Relations Manager: John McIsaac

LOCATIONS
HQ: Columbia Forest Products Inc.
222 SW Columbia, Ste. 1575, Portland, OR 97201
Phone: 503-224-5300   **Fax:** 503-224-5294
Web: www.columbiaforestproducts.com

Columbia Forest Products operates manufacturing plants in Arkansas, Georgia, Maine, North Carolina, Oregon, Tennessee, Vermont, Virginia, West Virginia, and Wisconsin in the US, as well as plants in Ontario and Quebec, Canada.

PRODUCTS/OPERATIONS
Selected Products
Flooring
Hardwood plywood
Hardwood plywood flooring underlayment
Hardwood veneers
Veneer raised panels and door inserts

COMPETITORS
Armstrong Holdings
Boise Cascade
Dal-Tile
Georgia-Pacific Corporation
Louisiana-Pacific
Mohawk Industries
Norbord
Plum Creek Timber
Potlatch
Roseburg Forest Products
Shaw Industries
Sierra Pacific Industries
Temple-Inland
West Fraser Timber
Weyerhaeuser

HISTORICAL FINANCIALS
Company Type: Private

Income Statement				FYE: December 31
	ESTIMATED REVENUE ($ mil.)	NET INCOME ($ mil.)	NET PROFIT MARGIN	EMPLOYEES
12/03	900	—	—	3,500
12/02	700	—	—	3,000
12/01	750	—	—	3,300
12/00	800	—	—	3,500
12/99	725	—	—	3,300
12/98	650	—	—	3,214
12/97	600	—	—	3,042
Annual Growth	7.0%	—	—	2.4%

Revenue History
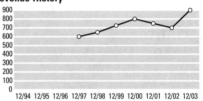

Columbia House

If the house is a-rockin', it's probably Columbia House. Initially a fifty-fifty joint venture between entertainment giants Sony and Time Warner, Columbia House is the top club-based direct marketer (with some 10 million members in the US, Canada, and Mexico) of music, videos, DVDs, and video games in North America. The company sells more than 10,000 music selections and 7,000 video titles via mail order and on-line. The company agreed to merge with online music retailer CDnow in 1999, but the deal was called off in 2000. Merger talks with rental giant Blockbuster are currently underway. Investment firm Blackstone Group bought 85% of Columbia House in June 2002 (Sony and Time Warner retain a 15% stake).

Columbia University

EXECUTIVES

Chairman and CEO: Scott N. Flanders, age 46
President: Brian S. Wood
COO: Terry Dwyer
EVP and CFO: Frank Mergenthaler
SVP and General Manager: Neil Pennington
SVP, Human Resources: Michael E. Pilnick
SVP, Music Club: Jim Litwak
SVP, New Member Marketing: Terry Macko
SVP, Product Development: Marc Zachary
SVP, Video Clubs: Michelle Jehle
SVP, Video Sales and Member Retention: Andy Yost
CIO: Marc Saffer
Chief Administrative Officer and General Counsel: Andrea Hirsch

LOCATIONS

HQ: Columbia House Company
1221 Avenue of the Americas, New York, NY 10020
Phone: 212-596-2000   **Fax:** 212-596-2213
Web: www.columbiahouse.com

COMPETITORS

Amazon.com
barnesandnoble.com
Bertelsmann
Best Buy
Borders
CDnow
EMusic.com
Hastings Entertainment
Indigo Books & Music
Musicland
Netflix
Tower Records
Trans World Entertainment
Wal-Mart

HISTORICAL FINANCIALS

Company Type: Private

Income Statement FYE: December 31

	REVENUE ($ mil.)	NET INCOME ($ mil.)	NET PROFIT MARGIN	EMPLOYEES
12/02	1,200	—	—	4,000
12/01	1,100	—	—	4,000
12/00	1,200	—	—	4,000
12/99*	1,000	—	—	3,000
3/98	1,400	—	—	3,000
Annual Growth	(3.8%)	—	—	7.5%

*Fiscal year change

Revenue History

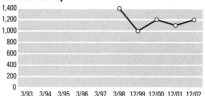

Predating the American Revolution, Columbia University (founded as King's College in 1754) is the fifth-oldest institution of higher learning in the US. With a student population of more than 23,000 students and a campus spread across 36 acres in Manhattan, Columbia's 16 schools and colleges grant undergraduate and graduate degrees in about 100 disciplines, including its well-known programs in journalism, law, and medicine. The Ivy League university's more than 3,000-member faculty has included 69 Nobel laureates and former Vice President Al Gore. Columbia also has a strong reputation for research.

Columbia has forged affiliations with nearby institutions such as Barnard College, Teachers College, Union Theological Seminary, and Jewish Theological Seminary. Columbia-Presbyterian Medical Center, the result of more than 75 years of partnership between Columbia and New York Presbyterian Hospital, helped pioneer the concept of academic medical centers.

Columbia's list of alumni includes such luminaries as Yankee great Lou Gehrig, Supreme Court Justice Ruth Bader Ginsberg, and President Franklin Roosevelt. The university has gone to the alumni well (and others sources) often over the past 10 years, with an endowment valued at $4.3 billion.

HISTORY

Created by royal charter of King George II of England, the university was founded in 1754 as King's College. Its first class of eight students met in a schoolhouse adjacent to Trinity Church (in what is now Manhattan). Some of the university's earliest students included Alexander Hamilton and John Jay. King's College was renamed Columbia College in 1784, a name that symbolized the patriotic mind-set of the age.

The college moved to 49th Street and Madison Avenue in 1849. The School of Law was founded in 1858, followed by the predecessor to the School of Engineering and Applied Science in 1864. The Graduate School of Arts and Sciences was established in 1880, and Columbia became affiliated with Barnard College in 1889.

Columbia College became Columbia University in 1896, and the following year it moved to its present location, the former site of the Bloomingdale Insane Asylum. Columbia continued to expand during the early 20th century. It added the School of Journalism in 1912 with funding from publishing magnate Joseph Pulitzer. Other additions included the School of Business (1916), the School of Public Health (1921), and the School of International and Public Affairs (1946).

Dwight Eisenhower became president of Columbia in 1948, retaining the position until becoming President of the United States in 1953. During the late 1960s Columbia gained a reputation for student political action, and in 1968 students closed down the university for several days in protest of the Vietnam War.

Facing financial woes, an escalating New York City crime rate, and contention among its faculty, Columbia struggled to maintain its reputation during the 1970s and 1980s. With this challenge as a backdrop, the university continued to evolve, welcoming its first coed freshman class in 1983.

Still facing economic pressures and reductions in government research spending, Columbia was forced to cut costs, eliminating its linguistics and geography departments in 1991. George Rupp became Columbia's president in 1993. Columbia took over operation of the controversial Biosphere 2 laboratory in Arizona in 1996 (the university had been associated with the lab since 1994, when it formed a consortium with other universities to overhaul the ailing science experiment).

By the late 1990s Columbia had begun to recover from its financial and academic decline. Under the leadership of president Rupp, the university improved its fund-raising efforts and became more selective in student admissions. Microsoft founder Bill Gates donated $50 million to Columbia's School of Public Health in 1999 for research into the prevention of death and disability from childbirth in developing countries. That year Columbia created Morningside Ventures, a for-profit company focused on producing educational materials.

The university partnered in 2000 with the British Library, Cambridge University Press, London School of Economics, the New York Public Library, and the Smithsonian to form another for-profit venture, Fathom.com, a site offering online access to various scholarly resources from each institution. Although the Web site served more than 65,000 people, Fathom.com discontinued operations in 2003. Columbia refocused its online efforts through its Columbia Digital Knowledge Ventures (DKV), a Web site created in 2000, but updated to include e-learning tools in 2003.

In 2001, the National Science Foundation awarded Columbia a $90,000 grant to gather personal accounts and create an oral history piece on the World Trade Center attacks of September 11. In 2002 Columbia University received a pledge of $8 million from Bernard Spitzer for stem cell research to develop new treatments for Parkinson's disease and other neurological disorders. Also that year Lee Bollinger replaced Rupp as president.

EXECUTIVES

Chairman: David J. Stern, age 62
President: Lee C. Bollinger
Provost: Alan Brinkley
SEVP: Robert A. Kasdin
EVP Communications and External Affairs: Loretta Ucelli
EVP Finance: Albert G. (Al) Horvath
EVP Government and Community Affairs: Emily Lloyd
EVP Health and Biomedical Sciences: Gerald D. Fischbach
EVP Research: David Hirsh
VP Human Resources: Colleen M. Crooker
General Counsel: Elizabeth J. Keefer
Interim Treasurer and Controller: Gail Hoffman
Auditors: Deloitte & Touche LLP

LOCATIONS

HQ: Columbia University
2690 Broadway, New York, NY 10027
Phone: 212-854-1754   **Fax:** 212-749-0397
Web: www.columbia.edu

Columbia University in the City of New York is located in the Morningside Heights section of Manhattan.

PRODUCTS/OPERATIONS

Selected Schools, Colleges, and Programs
Continuing Education
Graduate and Professional Schools
   College of Physicians and Surgeons
      Human Nutrition
      Occupational Therapy
      Physical Therapy
   The Fu Foundation School of Engineering & Applied Science
   Mailman School of Public Health
   School of Architecture, Planning & Preservation
   School of the Arts
   School of Arts and Sciences
   School of Business
      Executive Education Program
      Executive MBA Program
   School of Dental & Oral Surgery
   School of International and Public Affairs
   School of Journalism
   School of Law
   School of Nursing
   School of Social Work
Undergraduate Schools
   Columbia College
   The Fu Foundation School of Engineering and Applied Science
   School of General Studies

HISTORICAL FINANCIALS
Company Type: School

Income Statement — FYE: June 30

	REVENUE ($ mil.)	NET INCOME ($ mil.)	NET PROFIT MARGIN	EMPLOYEES
6/03	2,074	—	—	—
6/02	2,009	—	—	15,300
6/01	1,934	—	—	7,072
6/00	1,790	—	—	15,000
6/99	1,574	—	—	15,000
6/98	1,448	—	—	15,300
6/97	1,339	—	—	17,930
6/96	1,234	—	—	16,300
6/95	1,160	—	—	16,565
6/94	1,103	—	—	14,639
Annual Growth	7.3%	—	—	0.6%

Revenue History

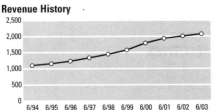

Community Hospitals of Indiana

Community Hospitals of Indiana, doing business as Community Health Network, keeps the residents of central Indiana in excellent health. The health care system includes four acute care hospitals (all operating under the Community Hospital moniker) and The Indiana Heart Hospital, where Hoosiers can go to keep their tickers ticking. The network also includes a number of outpatient and specialty services facilities, including Hook Rehabilitation Center, which offers inpatient and outpatient physical, occupational, and other rehabilitative therapy care.

EXECUTIVES
President and CEO: William E. (Bill) Corley, age 61
COO: Mark Dixon
CFO: Kelly George
Network VP, Medical and Academic Affairs: Glenn J. Bingle
Network VP, Business Development and Marketing: Jack C. Frank
Network VP, Finance and Business Strategy Development: Ted E. Milkey
Network VP, Legal Services and General Counsel: Karen Lloyd
Network VP, Human Resources: Jill Parris
VP and CIO: Ed Koschka

LOCATIONS
HQ: Community Hospitals of Indiana, Inc.
1500 N. Ritter Ave., Indianapolis, IN 46219
Phone: 317-355-1411   **Fax:** 317-351-7723
Web: www.ecommunity.com

HISTORICAL FINANCIALS
Company Type: Not-for-profit

Income Statement — FYE: December 31

	REVENUE ($ mil.)	NET INCOME ($ mil.)	NET PROFIT MARGIN	EMPLOYEES
12/03	812	—	—	8,500

Community Medical Centers

Community Medical Centers keeps California's San Joaquin Valley community healthy. The health system operates three acute care hospitals: Community Regional Medical Center, Community Medical Center-Clovis, and University Medical Center. The hospitals have more than 880 beds. Other facilities include the Fresno Heart Hospital for patients with cardiovascular conditions, a diagnostic imaging center, and the California Cancer Center. Community Medical Centers also operates a few community health care clinics and a handful of long-term care facilities.

EXECUTIVES
President and CEO: J. Phillip Hinton
EVP and COO: Tracy J. Farnsworth
SVP and CIO: Craig S. Castro
SVP, Human Resources: Linzie L. Daniel
SVP and CFO: Wesley H. Qualls
SVP and Chief Medical Officer: Andrew S. Robertson
SVP and Chief Legal Officer: Robert E. Ward
SVP, Physician Services and New Ventures: Scott B. Wells
SVP, Communications: John Zelezny
VP, Managed Care Contracting: Vicki L. Anderson
VP, Clinical Support Services: Phyllis Baltz
VP, Human Resources: Ginny R. Burdick
VP, Santé Management Services Organization: Chris Cheney
VP, Continuum of Care Services: Dawan Haubursin

LOCATIONS
HQ: Community Medical Centers
2823 Fresno St., Fresno, CA 93721
Phone: 559-459-6000   **Fax:** 559-459-2450
Web: www.communitymedical.org

HISTORICAL FINANCIALS
Company Type: Not-for-profit

Income Statement — FYE: August 31

	REVENUE ($ mil.)	NET INCOME ($ mil.)	NET PROFIT MARGIN	EMPLOYEES
8/03	574	—	—	6,522

CompuCom

CompuCom Systems helps businesses piece together the hardware puzzle. The company offers business software applications and software management services, as well as consulting, distribution, help desk support, and other information technology services. It also distributes desktop, mobile, and wireless computers, networking equipment, and peripherals to nearly 6,000 customers. Customers include Continental Airlines, Checker's Restaurants, and Union Pacific Railroad. Buyout specialist Platinum Equity acquired CompuCom through an affiliate holding company in 2004.

As manufacturers of technology products turn increasingly to direct sales in an effort to cut costs, CompuCom Systems has continued to expand the services side of its business largely through acquisitions.

EXECUTIVES
Chairman, President, and CEO: J. Edward (Ed) Coleman, age 52, $1,016,500 pay
SVP, Finance, CFO, Secretary, and Director: M. Lazane Smith, age 49, $612,500 pay
SVP and CTO: David W. Hall
SVP, Human Resources: David A. (Dave) Loeser, age 49, $367,500 pay
SVP, CompuCom Federal Systems and CIO: Suresh V. Mathews
SVP, Sales and Business Development: Thomas (Tom) Ducatelli
SVP, Services: John F. McKenna, age 41, $437,500 pay
VP, Finance, Treasurer, and Controller: Daniel L. (Dan) Celoni

President, Excell Data Corporation:
Richard T. (Rick) Jorgenson
President, CompuCom Federal Systems:
Kenneth (Ken) Dyer
Public Relations: Scott Greenwald
VP, Information Services: Steve Birgfeld
Auditors: KPMG LLP

LOCATIONS

HQ: CompuCom Systems, Inc.
7171 Forest Ln., Dallas, TX 75230
Phone: 972-856-3600   **Fax:** 972-856-5395
Web: www.compucom.com

CompuCom Systems has offices and service centers throughout the US, including Alaska and Hawaii.

PRODUCTS/OPERATIONS

2003 Sales

	$ mil.	% of total
Product	1,158.3	80
Services	296.8	20
Total	**1,455.1**	**100**

Products
Computers
Data storage equipment
Mobile and wireless computing products
Networking equipment
Peripherals
Software

Selected Services
Asset tracking
Configuration
Consulting
Distribution
Field engineering
Help desk support
Network management
Networking support
Product procurement
Software management

COMPETITORS

Accenture	Ingram Micro
Agilysys	Interpharm
ASI Corp.	Merisel
Avnet	MicroAge
Bell Industries	MoreDirect
Bell Microproducts	New Age Electronics
Black Box	Optical Laser
CDW	Pomeroy IT
CompUSA	SARCOM
Computech Systems	Siemens
Computer Sciences	Softmart
CSI Computer Specialists	Software House
DiData	Software Spectrum
EDS	Tech Data
En Pointe	Unisys
GTSI	Vizacom
Hewlett-Packard	Westcon
High Point Solutions	ZT Group
IBM	

HISTORICAL FINANCIALS
Company Type: Private

Income Statement
FYE: December 31

	REVENUE ($ mil.)	NET INCOME ($ mil.)	NET PROFIT MARGIN	EMPLOYEES
12/03	1,455	13	0.9%	3,500
12/02	1,571	19	1.2%	3,437
12/01	1,816	7	0.4%	3,800
12/00	2,711	5	0.2%	4,100
12/99	2,908	12	0.4%	5,000
12/98	2,255	0	0.0%	4,800
12/97	1,950	35	1.8%	4,300
12/96	1,995	31	1.5%	3,700
12/95	1,442	21	1.4%	2,615
12/94	1,256	15	1.2%	1,975
Annual Growth	1.7%	(1.2%)	—	6.6%

2003 Year-End Financials
Debt ratio: 0.0%
Return on equity: 5.3%
Cash ($ mil.): 81
Current ratio: 1.79
Long-term debt ($ mil.): 0

Net Income History

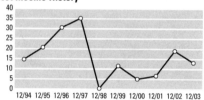

Conair

Counterintelligence has shown that Conair has a place in many bathrooms and kitchens. Personal products by Conair include curling irons, hair dryers, mirrors, shavers, and salon products (Jheri Redding, Rusk) designed for both home and professional salon use. Its small appliances include food blenders, food processors, and other kitchen appliances produced by its Cuisinart and Waring divisions. Conair also sells telephones, answering machines, and Interplak electric toothbrushes. Products are sold at discount chains, department stores, and mass merchants (Bed Bath & Beyond, Target, Wal-Mart) throughout the US. Lee Rizzuto, who founded Conair in 1959 with his parents, pleaded guilty to tax evasion in 2002.

EXECUTIVES

Co-President: Ronald T. Diamond
Co-President: Barry Haber
CFO: Pat Yannotta
SVP Administration: John Mayorek
VP Sales and Marketing: Frank Lindsey

LOCATIONS

HQ: Conair Corporation
1 Cummings Point Rd., Stamford, CT 06904
Phone: 203-351-9000   **Fax:** 203-351-9180
Web: www.conair.com

PRODUCTS/OPERATIONS

Selected Brands
BaByliss
Conair
ConairPro
Cuisinart
Grand Finale
Interplak
Jheri Redding
Pollenex
Rusk
Waring

Selected Divisions and Products
Conair Appliance Manufacturing (worldwide production)
Conair Packaging (health and beauty aid products)
Consumer Electronics (telephones)
Consumer Toiletries (hair care products)
Cuisinart (kitchen appliances)
Interplak (electric toothbrushes)
Personal Care (hair dryers, curling irons, health and wellness appliances)
Professional Products (toiletries and appliances)
Rusk (hair care products)
Waring (kitchen appliances)

COMPETITORS

Alberto-Culver
Applica
Braun GmbH
Gillette
Global-Tech Appliances
Goody
Helen of Troy
John Paul Mitchell
L'Oréal
National Presto Industries
Newell Rubbermaid
Philips Electronics
Philips Oral
Professional Dental Technologies
Rayovac
Revlon
Salton
Stephan
Sunbeam
Water Pik Technologies

HISTORICAL FINANCIALS
Company Type: Private

Income Statement
FYE: December 31

	REVENUE ($ mil.)	NET INCOME ($ mil.)	NET PROFIT MARGIN	EMPLOYEES
12/03	1,277	—	—	4,000
12/02	1,176	—	—	4,373
12/01	1,151	—	—	4,592
12/00	1,082	—	—	4,461
12/99	928	—	—	3,676
12/98	787	—	—	3,898
12/97	716	—	—	3,652
12/96	655	—	—	3,175
12/95	614	—	—	3,431
Annual Growth	9.6%	—	—	1.9%

Revenue History

HOOVER'S HANDBOOK OF PRIVATE COMPANIES 2005

Concentra

Concentra (formerly CONCENTRA Managed Care) concentrates on getting people back to work cheaper. It is the holding company for Concentra Operating Corporation, which provides cost containment and case management services to employers and to occupational, auto, and group health payors throughout the US. Concentra offers specialized cost-containment services for occupational and auto injury cases, preferred provider network management, telephone case management, and medical bill review. The company also operates more than 250 medical centers in about 35 states, providing occupational health care including pre-employment screening, injury care, and loss prevention.

Welsh, Carson, Anderson & Stowe owns nearly 65% of Concentra.

Concentra's health service centers, which provide services such as drug testing, treatment for work related injuries, and physical therapy, account for nearly 50% of the firm's revenue.

Concentra plans to grow by expanding its health services offerings.

EXECUTIVES

Chairman: Paul B. Queally, age 40
CEO and Director: Daniel J. Thomas, age 45, $600,000 pay
President and COO: Fredrick C. Dunlap, age 45, $500,000 pay
EVP, CFO, and Treasurer: Thomas E. Kiraly, age 44, $405,000 pay
EVP, Secretary, and General Counsel: Richard A. Parr II, age 45, $363,500 pay
EVP, Corporate Development: James M. Greenwood, age 43, $295,000 pay
SVP and Chief Medical Officer: W. Tom Fogarty
SVP and Chief Marketing Officer: Andrew R. Daniels, age 46
SVP and Chief Information Officer: Laura Ciavola
SVP, National Sales: Ken Loffredo
Human Resources: Tammy Jackson
Auditors: PricewaterhouseCoopers

LOCATIONS

HQ: Concentra Inc.
5080 Spectrum Dr., Ste. 400W, Addison, TX 75001
Phone: 972-364-8000 **Fax:** 972-387-1938
Web: www.concentra.com

PRODUCTS/OPERATIONS

2003 Sales

	$ mil.	% of total
Health services	511.4	49
Case management services	279.1	26
Network services	260.2	25
Total	**1,050.7**	**100**

Divisions
Concentra Case Management Services
Concentra Health Services
Concentra Medical Examinations
Concentra Preferred Systems
First Notice Systems
FOCUS HealthCare Management

COMPETITORS

CORE
CorVel
Crawford & Company
First Health Group
NDCHealth
Per-Se Technologies
RTW
UnumProvident

HISTORICAL FINANCIALS

Company Type: Private

Income Statement
FYE: December 31

	REVENUE ($ mil.)	NET INCOME ($ mil.)	NET PROFIT MARGIN	EMPLOYEES
12/03	1,051	43	4.1%	10,000
12/02	999	(4)	—	10,254
12/01	843	(10)	—	10,500
12/00	752	(7)	—	8,800
12/99	681	(27)	—	8,800
12/98	617	23	3.6%	7,800
12/97	459	3	0.6%	7,270
12/96	170	11	6.5%	2,725
12/95	109	6	5.6%	2,125
12/94	60	2	3.7%	1,900
Annual Growth	37.5%	39.2%	—	20.3%

2003 Year-End Financials
Debt ratio: 1,486.9%   Current ratio: 1.87
Return on equity: 39.2%   Long-term debt ($ mil.): 654
Cash ($ mil.): 43

Net Income History

Conemaugh Health System

Conemaugh Health System serves western Pennsylvania through Memorial Medical Center, Meyersdale Medical Center, Windber Medical Center, Miners Medical Center, and a network of community and specialized health care facilities. With more than 600 beds in its system, Conemaugh Health offers such services as regional cancer, cardiovascular, and neurosciences centers; home health care and home medical equipment; and specialized facilities for managing pain and wounds that are difficult to heal. Conemaugh Health also operates Penn Highlands Health Plan, a PPO.

The health system's community health network has about a dozen clinics.

EXECUTIVES

CEO and Chief Medical Officer, Conemaugh Health System and Memorial Medical Center: Richard F. (Rich) Salluzzo
CFO: Edward H. DePasquale
VP, Clinical Programs and Special Projects: Thomas M. Kurtz
VP, Office of Community Health: Matt Masiello
VP, Management Information Systems and CIO: Joan M. Roscoe
President, Windber Medical Center and Windber Research Institute: F. Nicholas Jacobs
President, Miners Hospital: Michael K. Lauf, age 33
President, Meyersdale Medical Center: Mary Libengood
President, Conemaugh Health Foundation: Susan Mann
President and Chief Medical Officer, Conemaugh Health Initiatives: Michael Tatarko Sr.
President, Memorial Medical Center and Good Samaritan Medical Center: Steven E. Tucker
Director, Public Affairs: Amy Bradley

LOCATIONS

HQ: Conemaugh Health System
1086 Franklin St., Johnstown, PA 15905
Phone: 814-534-9130   **Fax:** 814-533-3244
Web: www.conemaugh.org

Selected Facilities
Miners Medical Center (Hastings, PA)
Memorial Medical Center (Johnstown, PA)
Meyersdale Medical Center (Meyersdale, PA)
Windber Medical Center (Windber, PA)

PRODUCTS/OPERATIONS

2003 Sales

	$ mil.	% of total
Patient services	296.9	91
Other	30.6	9
Total	**327.5**	**100**

COMPETITORS

Bon Secours Health
Ohio Valley General
UPMC
West Penn Allegheny Health System
Westmoreland-Latrobe Health Partners

HISTORICAL FINANCIALS

Company Type: Not-for-profit

Income Statement
FYE: June 30

	REVENUE ($ mil.)	NET INCOME ($ mil.)	NET PROFIT MARGIN	EMPLOYEES
6/03	328	(5)	—	3,700
6/02	284	(13)	—	3,400
Annual Growth	15.2%	—	—	8.8%

Net Income History

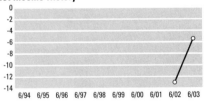

ConnectiCare

To profit or not to profit? That is no longer a question for ConnectiCare. The company, one of the largest HMOs in Connecticut, converted to for-profit status in order to raise capital. In 1979 a group of doctors at Hartford Hospital planted the seeds for what would become ConnectiCare; today, the company's nearly 280,000 members in Connecticut, western Massachusetts, and upstate New York choose from HMO or point-of-service options. The company has a network of nearly 40 hospitals and more than 10,000 care providers. ConnectiCare also established a charitable foundation as part of its reorganization to for-profit status. The company is being acquired by the Health Insurance Plan of Greater New York.

Conservative investment firm The Carlyle Group partnered with private equity firm Liberty Partners to buy ConnectiCare.

The company is expanding into four upstate New York counties via its acquisition of the AmeriHealth Health Plan.

EXECUTIVES

Chairman: Eileen S. Kraus
President and CEO: Marcel L. (Gus) Gamache, age 61
SVP, CFO and Treasurer: Thomas L. Tran
SVP and Chief Medical Officer: Paul A. Bluestein
SVP and Chief Marketing Officer: Paul Philpott, age 53
VP and General Counsel: Gail Bogossian
VP, Network Operations: William F. Carroll
VP, Operations: Ida M. Schnipper
VP, Human Resources: Dick Rogers
Chief Information Officer: Mark Dixon
Director, Public Relations: Deborah Hoyt

LOCATIONS

HQ: ConnectiCare Inc.
175 Scott Swamp Rd., Farmington, CT 06032
Phone: 860-674-5700   **Fax:** 860-674-2030
Web: www.connecticare.com

ConnectiCare operates in Connecticut, and in the Massachusetts counties of Hampden, Hampshire, and Franklin. The company also operates in the New York counties of Orange, Putnam, Rockland, and Westchester.

PRODUCTS/OPERATIONS

Selected Health Plans
ConnectiCare Network USA - PPO
HMO Open Access
HMO Personal Care Plan
Point-of Service Open Access
Point-of-Service Personal Care Plan

Subsidiaries
AmeriHealth Health Plan, Inc.
ConnectiCare Insurance Company
ConnectiCare of Massachusetts, Inc.

COMPETITORS

Aetna
Anthem
Blue Cross
CIGNA
Harvard Pilgrim
Health Net
Oxford Health
Tufts Health Plan
UnitedHealth Group

HISTORICAL FINANCIALS

Company Type: Private

Income Statement
FYE: December 31

	REVENUE ($ mil.)	NET INCOME ($ mil.)	NET PROFIT MARGIN	EMPLOYEES
12/03	708	—	—	550
12/02	626	—	—	550
12/01	654	—	—	540
12/00	541	—	—	530
12/99	440	—	—	450
12/98	354	—	—	450
12/97	291	—	—	400
12/96	264	—	—	—
Annual Growth	15.1%	—	—	5.5%

Revenue History

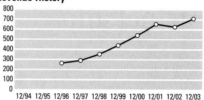

Connecticut Lottery

The Connecticut Lottery gives residents of the Constitution State a chance to amend their incomes. The organization operates a variety of scratch-off instant games and daily numbers games (Cash 5, Nightly Numbers, Play 4). It also offers Classic Lotto twice-a-week jackpot games and the multistate Powerball Lottery. Players who buy Instant Powerball TV Game scratch-off tickets also are eligible to win a chance to get their 15 minutes of fame by competing on *Powerball Instant Millionaire*, a weekly lottery game show operated by the Multi-State Lottery Association. The Connecticut Lottery pays out about 60% of lottery revenue in prizes and about 30% to Connecticut's general fund.

EXECUTIVES

President and CEO: James (Jim) Vance
VP Sales and Marketing: Dennis Chapman
VP Operations: Barabara Porto
Director, Sales: Gloria Donnelly
Drawing Coordinator: Richard Wiszniak
Lottery Ambassador: Bill Hennessey
Auditors: State of Connecticut Auditor of Public Accounts

LOCATIONS

HQ: Connecticut Lottery Corporation
270 John Downey Dr., New Britain, CT 06051
Phone: 860-348-4001   **Fax:** 860-348-4015
Web: www.ctlottery.org

PRODUCTS/OPERATIONS

2004 Allocation of Sales

	% of total
Prizes	59
General fund	31
Retailers	6
Operating costs	4
Total	**100**

Selected Games
Cash 5
Classic Lotto
Mid-day 3
Mid-day 4
Play 4
Powerball
Powerball Instant Millionaire
Scratch-off games

COMPETITORS

Loto-Québec
Mashantucket Pequot Gaming
Massachusetts State Lottery
New Jersey Lottery
New York State Lottery
Pennsylvania Lottery

HISTORICAL FINANCIALS

Company Type: Government-owned

Income Statement
FYE: June 30

	REVENUE ($ mil.)	NET INCOME ($ mil.)	NET PROFIT MARGIN	EMPLOYEES
6/04	912	—	—	120
6/03	858	—	—	120
6/02	850	—	—	120
6/01	840	—	—	120
6/00	838	—	—	120
6/99	871	—	—	120
6/98	806	—	—	115
6/97	772	—	—	105
6/96	707	—	—	100
6/95	671	—	—	—
Annual Growth	3.5%	—	—	2.3%

Revenue History

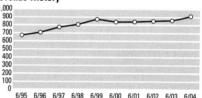

Connell Company

The Connell Company can sell you a boatload of rice or lend you money for that power plant you've been meaning to install. Connell's core business is rice distribution, conducted through subsidiary Connell Rice & Sugar. The company's support operations have grown into full subsidiaries including brokerage of flour and sweeteners, export sales of food manufacturing equipment, commercial real estate development, heavy equipment leasing, exporting, and financial services (such as underwriting airlines' purchases of aircraft). The company has offices in Taiwan, Thailand, and the US. Connell has remained a family-owned business since it was founded in 1926.

EXECUTIVES
President: Grover Connell
CFO: Terry Connell
VP, Human Resources: Maureen Waldron

LOCATIONS
HQ: The Connell Company
1 Connell Dr., Berkeley Heights, NJ 07922
Phone: 908-673-3700   **Fax:** 908-673-3800
Web: www.connellco.com

PRODUCTS/OPERATIONS

Selected Divisions and Subsidiaries
Connell & Co. (flour, sugar brokerage services)
Connell Finance Company, Inc. (financial advisory services)
Connell Equipment Leasing Company
Connell Technologies Company (asset management services)
Connell GATCO Company (heavy equipment distribution)
Connell International Co. (exporting)
Connell Realty & Development Co. (commercial and corporate buildings)
Connell Rice & Sugar Co.

COMPETITORS

American Rice	Man Group
Atlas Copco	Merrill Lynch
Cargill	Riceland Foods
Deere	Riviana Foods

HISTORICAL FINANCIALS
Company Type: Private

Income Statement   FYE: December 31

	REVENUE ($ mil.)	NET INCOME ($ mil.)	NET PROFIT MARGIN	EMPLOYEES
12/01*	2,525	—	—	245
12/00	2,425	—	—	240
12/99	2,300	—	—	220
12/98	2,100	—	—	225
12/97	1,275	—	—	225
12/96	1,300	—	—	220
12/95	1,200	—	—	200
12/94	1,100	—	—	200
Annual Growth	12.6%	—	—	2.9%

*Most recent year available

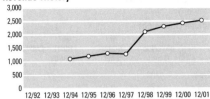

Revenue History

Connell Limited Partnership

Connell Limited Partnership operates companies in the aluminum alloy and industrial equipment businesses. Connell's wholly owned businesses, Wabash Alloys, Danly IEM, and Yuba Heat Transfer, serve customers in the automotive, appliance, aerospace, electronics, and power and process industries. Connell Limited Partnership started operating in 1987, and it claims to have grown companies engaged in the metallurgy and manufacturing of metal products ever since. The company operates some 30 facilities in the US, Mexico, and Canada, and has grown through acquisitions. Connell's investment strategy is to acquire and operate manufacturing sector companies with growth opportunities.

EXECUTIVES
President and CEO: Francis A. (Frank) Doyle, age 55
VP and CFO: Kurt J. Keady
VP, Legal and Environmental: John Curtin
Director, Human Resources: Catherine Gallagher

LOCATIONS
HQ: Connell Limited Partnership
1 International Place, Boston, MA 02110
Phone: 617-737-2700   **Fax:** 617-737-1617
Web: www.connell-lp.com

Connell Limited Partnership has manufacturing plants and other facilities in Canada, Mexico, the UK, and the US.

COMPETITORS

Anchor Lamina
Bethlehem Corporation
Commercial Metals
Envirosource
Harsco
IMCO Recycling
Metallurg
Productivity Technologies
Tang Industries
United States Steel

HISTORICAL FINANCIALS
Company Type: Private

Income Statement   FYE: December 31

	REVENUE ($ mil.)	NET INCOME ($ mil.)	NET PROFIT MARGIN	EMPLOYEES
12/03	1,000	—	—	1,400
12/02	1,100	—	—	1,700
12/01	1,000	—	—	1,700
12/00	1,185	—	—	2,000
12/99	1,160	—	—	3,114
12/98	1,110	—	—	2,836
12/97	1,190	—	—	2,620
12/96	1,238	—	—	3,123
12/95	1,257	—	—	3,000
12/94	1,163	—	—	2,923
Annual Growth	(1.7%)	—	—	(7.9%)

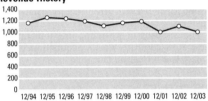

Revenue History

Conrail

Conrail is the holding company for Consolidated Rail, a freight railroad system in the heavily industrialized Northeast. Most of the lines and facilities formerly operated by Conrail have been taken over by the company's owners, railroads CSX (42%) and Norfolk Southern (58%). Conrail, however, continues to operate some lines and facilities in the Philadelphia and Detroit metropolitan areas and in much of New Jersey. To serve customers along those lines, CSX and Norfolk Southern pay Conrail for line access; Conrail acts as the local switching and terminal management agent.

In 2004 Norfolk Southern and CSX reorganized Conrail so that each railroad took direct ownership of the Conrail assets that it operates. Norfolk Southern took over Conrail's former Pennsylvania Lines unit, and CSX took over Conrail's former New York Central Lines unit. Conrail will continue to provide switching and terminal management services.

EXECUTIVES
President and CEO: Ronald L. Batory
VP Finance: Joseph Rogers
VP Human Resources: Anthony Carlini
VP Law, General Counsel, and Secretary: Jonathan M. Broder
VP Taxes and Real Estate: Patrick Rogers
Assistant VP Information Systems: Lawrence J. Davis
Auditors: Ernst & Young LLP; KPMG LLP

LOCATIONS
HQ: Conrail Inc.
2001 Market St., 16th Fl., Philadelphia, PA 19103
Phone: 215-209-2000   **Fax:** 215-209-4819
Web: www.conrail.com

COMPETITORS
Burlington Northern Santa Fe
Canadian National Railway
Canadian Pacific Railway
Genesee & Wyoming
Guilford Transportation
RailAmerica
Union Pacific

HISTORICAL FINANCIALS
Company Type: Private

Income Statement
FYE: December 31

	REVENUE ($ mil.)	NET INCOME ($ mil.)	NET PROFIT MARGIN	EMPLOYEES
12/03	918	203	22.1%	—
12/02	893	180	20.2%	—
12/01	903	174	19.3%	—
12/00	985	170	17.3%	—
12/99	2,200	26	1.2%	—
12/98	3,863	267	6.9%	22,000
12/97	3,765	7	0.2%	22,000
12/96	3,714	342	9.2%	21,280
12/95	3,686	264	7.2%	23,510
12/94	3,733	324	8.7%	24,833
Annual Growth	(14.4%)	(5.1%)	—	(3.0%)

2003 Year-End Financials
Debt ratio: 24.0%
Return on equity: 4.7%
Cash ($ mil.): 18
Current ratio: 0.92
Long-term debt ($ mil.): 1,067

Net Income History
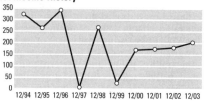

Consolidated Electrical

Electrical equipment wholesaler Consolidated Electrical Distributors (CED) has US distribution wired. With more than 500 locations nationwide, the family-owned business is one of the largest distributors of electrical products in the country. CED supplies load centers, panelboards, transformers, switches, motor controls, drives, and similar products to residential and commercial contractors and industrial customers. Founded in 1957 as The Electric Corporation of San Francisco, the company has grown by acquiring electrical distributors; since it usually keeps the acquired firm's name and management team, CED now does business under about 80 names. The Colburn family owns CED.

EXECUTIVES
President: H. Dean Bursch
VP and CFO: Thomas A. Lullo
Secretary: David C. Verbeck
Treasurer: John D. Parish
Recruiting Coordinator: Marie Lipp

LOCATIONS
HQ: Consolidated Electrical Distributors, Inc.
31356 Via Colinas, Ste. 107,
Westlake Village, CA 91362
Phone: 818-991-9000 **Fax:** 818-991-6842
Web: www.cedcareers.com

Consolidated Electrical Distributors has more than 500 US locations in 44 states.

PRODUCTS/OPERATIONS
Selected Products
Adjustable frequency drives
Circuit breakers
Control transformers
Load centers
Metering equipment
Motor control centers
Open starters/contractors
Panelboards
Power outlet panels
Pushbuttons
Relays
Safety switches
Starters
Switchboards
Switchgear
Timers
Transformers

COMPETITORS
Anixter International
Cameron & Barkley
Electrocomponents
General Cable
Graybar Electric
Hubbell
Hughes Supply
McJunkin
McNaughton-McKay
Rexel Canada
Rexel, Inc.
Sonepar USA
Stuart C. Irby
SUMMIT Electric Supply
Thomas & Betts
WESCO International
W.W. Grainger

HISTORICAL FINANCIALS
Company Type: Private

Income Statement
FYE: December 31

	ESTIMATED REVENUE ($ mil.)	NET INCOME ($ mil.)	NET PROFIT MARGIN	EMPLOYEES
12/02	2,300	—	—	5,000
12/01	2,400	—	—	5,350
12/00	2,500	—	—	5,500
12/99	2,700	—	—	5,000
12/98	2,600	—	—	4,500
12/97	1,925	—	—	4,500
12/96	1,900	—	—	4,000
12/95	1,600	—	—	4,000
12/94	1,600	—	—	3,700
12/93	1,500	—	—	2,800
Annual Growth	4.9%	—	—	6.7%

Revenue History

Consumers Union

Consumers Union of United States (CU) inspires both trust and fear. Best known for publishing *Consumer Reports* magazine (4 million subscribers), the not-for-profit organization also serves as a consumer watchdog through newsletters, books, TV and radio programming, and the *Consumer Reports for Kids Online* site. Its subscriber Web site (more than 1 million paid subscribers) rates products ranging from candy bars to cars. The company tests and rates thousands of products annually. Its Consumer Policy Institute conducts research and education projects on issues such as air pollution, biotechnology, food safety, and right-to-know laws.

It maintains 50 laboratories within its National Testing and Research Center in Yonkers, New York. In addition to conducting its own product testing, CU gathers product information by surveying the readers of its publications.

CU derives revenue from sales of its publications, from car and insurance pricing services, and from contributions, grants, and fees. The company has revamped its *Consumer Reports* publication with additional content and a new look aimed at improving the magazine's layout and organization.

Retailer Sharper Image is suing the CU over an article unflattering to the company's popular air purifier device.

The organization testifies before legislative and regulatory entities and files lawsuits on behalf of consumers. CU is governed by an 18-member board. To preserve its independence, CU accepts no advertising and does not permit its ratings or comments to be used commercially.

HISTORY

In 1926 engineer Frederick Schlink organized a "consumer club" (in White Plains, New York), which distributed lists of recommended and non-recommended products. The lists led to the founding of Consumers' Research and a magazine devoted to testing products.

Schlink moved the group to Washington, New Jersey, in 1933. In 1935 three employees formed a union. Schlink fired them. Faced with another strike that year, Schlink accused the strikers of being "Red" and responded with strikebreakers and armed detectives. The next year the strikers set up their own organization, the Consumers Union of United States (CU).

CU's first magazine, *Consumers Union Reports*, came out three months later and rated products that the fledgling organization could afford to test, such as soap and breakfast cereals. Subsequent issues focused on food and drug regulation and working conditions for women in textile mills.

The organization drew the wrath of both *Reader's Digest* and *Good Housekeeping* (which accused it in 1939 of prolonging the Depression). The next year the House Un-American Activities Committee put CU on its list of suspect organizations. CU cut staff and dropped "Union" from its magazine title, but circulation remained low until after WWII.

By 1950, however, Americans began consuming again, helping to boost circulation to almost 400,000. During the 1950s CU published a series of reports on the health hazards of smoking.

In 1960 CU helped found the International Organization of Consumers Unions (now Consumers International) to foster the consumer movement worldwide. Rhoda Karpatkin was hired as publisher in 1974. During the 1970s CU established consumer advocacy offices in California, Texas, and Washington, DC.

Recession and an increase in not-for-profit mailing rates caused the organization to lose money in the early 1980s. CU looked to its readers, who donated more than $3 million. It was hit by a 13-week strike in 1984 by union members calling for more say in management.

In 1996 CU slapped "not acceptable" ratings on the Isuzu Trooper and the Acura SLX. The next year the National Highway Traffic Safety Administration declared that CU's testing procedure of the Trooper was flawed, but CU stood by its tests of the vehicle.

CU hit another bump in 1998 when it was compelled to retract a story on the nutritional value of Iams and Eukanuba pet food. Admitting its test results were incorrect, CU's retraction of the story was something of a rarity — its last retraction had occurred almost 20 years earlier when the organization retracted a story on condoms.

In 1999 the company defended itself in court against allegations by Isuzu and Suzuki that their companies were defamed through negative reviews by *Consumer Reports*. The following year a jury found CU guilty of falsely reporting on the Isuzu but declined to impose fines on the publisher. Also in 2000 a district court upheld the dismissal of Suzuki's suit against CU (based on CU's 1988 rating of the Suzuki Samurai as "not acceptable" due to rollover risks); Suzuki appealed the decision. Karpatkin announced she would step down as president in 2001. Later that year CU agreed to license its content to Internet portal Yahoo! James Guest, CU's chairman since 1980, took over as president in 2001.

The legal dispute between Suzuki and CU was settled in 2004.

EXECUTIVES

Chairman and President: James (Jim) Guest
CFO: Richard Gannon
SVP, Technical Policy: R. David Pittle
Director, Consumer Policy Institute: Jean Halloran
Senior Director for Advocacy and Public Policy:
  Gene Kimmelman
Director, Southwest Regional Office: Reggie James
Editorial Director: Elizabeth Crow
Project Director, Eco-labeling Project: Urvashi Rangan
Research Associate, Consumer Policy Institute:
  Michael K. Hansen
Senior Scientist: Edward (Ned) Groth
Health Policy Editor, Consumer Reports:
  Trudy Lieberman
Project Leader, Consumers Union Technical Division,
  Public Service Projects: Deborah Wallace
Auditors: KPMG LLP

LOCATIONS

HQ: Consumers Union of United States, Inc.
  101 Truman Ave., Yonkers, NY 10703
Phone: 914-378-2000   **Fax:** 914-378-2900
Web: www.consumersunion.org

Consumers Union of United States performs most product tests at a renovated warehouse in Yonkers, New York. It has consumer advocacy offices in Austin, Texas; San Francisco; and Washington, DC.

PRODUCTS/OPERATIONS

Selected Operations

Auto Services
  CR New Car Price Service
  CR Used Car Price Service
Books and Buying Guides
Auto Books
  New Car Buying Guide
  New Car Preview
  Used Car Buying Guide
  Used Car Yearbook
House and Home
  Best Buys for Your Home
  Buying Guide
  Home Computer Buying Guide
Money
  Consumer Reports Money Book
  How to Plan for a Secure Retirement
Personal and Leisure
  Consumer Drug Reference
  Guide to Baby Products
  Guide to Health Care for Seniors
  Travel Well for Less
Magazines and Newsletters
  Consumer Reports Magazine
TV and Radio
  Consumer Reports on TV (video segments)
  CR Radio (daily radio feature)
Web Sites
  ConsumerReports.org
  Consumer Reports for Kids Online (zillions.org)

COMPETITORS

Consumers' Research
Epinions
Hearst
International Data Group
J.D. Power
National Technical Systems
PRIMEDIA
Reader's Digest
Reed Elsevier Group
Underwriters Labs

HISTORICAL FINANCIALS

Company Type: Not-for-profit

Income Statement   FYE: May 31

	REVENUE ($ mil.)	NET INCOME ($ mil.)	NET PROFIT MARGIN	EMPLOYEES
5/03	157	43	27.1%	450
5/02	151	30	19.6%	450
5/01	161	38	23.5%	450
5/00	140	—	—	450
5/99	140	—	—	482
5/98	140	—	—	475
5/97	135	—	—	461
5/96	136	—	—	451
5/95	129	—	—	453
5/94	124	—	—	451
Annual Growth	2.6%	5.8%	—	(0.0%)

Net Income History

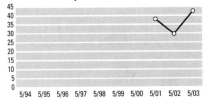

ContiGroup

It's farther up the food chain now, but ContiGroup Companies (CGC, formerly Continental Grain) is still a big name in agribusiness. CGC has exited the grain export business and now operates through ContiBeef (the #2 cattle feedlot operator, behind Cactus Feeders), PSF Group Holdings (the #2 US fresh pork producer, after Smithfield Foods), and Wayne Farms, a major poultry processor. Overseas the company has interests in feed milling, aquaculture, shipping, and energy trading. CGC's investment arm, ContiInvestments, manages diverse holdings. Chairman Paul Fribourg (the founder's great-great-great-grandson) and his family own CGC.

In China, the Caribbean, and Latin America, CGC has interests in flour milling, animal feed, poultry processing, and aquaculture. Despite its size and scope, the company remains genteelly private about its business.

HISTORY

Simon Fribourg founded a commodity trading business in Belgium in 1813. It operated domestically until 1848, when a drought in Belgium caused it to buy large stocks in Russian wheat.

As the Industrial Revolution swept across Europe and populations shifted to cities, people consumed more traded grain. In the midst of such rapid changes, the company prospered. After WWI, Russia, which had been Europe's primary grain supplier, ceased to be a major player in the trading game, and Western countries picked up the slack. Sensing the shift, Jules and Rene Fribourg reorganized the business as Continental Grain and opened its first US office in Chicago in 1921.

Throughout the Depression the company bought US grain elevators, often at low prices. Through its purchases, Continental Grain built a North American grain network that included major locations like Kansas City, Missouri; Nashville, Tennessee; and Toledo, Ohio.

In Europe, meanwhile, the Fribourgs were forced to endure constant political and economic upheaval, often profiting from it (they supplied food to Republican forces during the Spanish Civil War). When Nazis invaded Belgium in 1940, the Fribourgs were forced to flee, but they reorganized the business in New York City after the war.

Following the war, Continental Grain pioneered US grain trade with the Soviets. The company went on a buying spree in the 1960s and 1970s, acquiring Allied Mills (feed milling, 1965) and absorbing many agricultural and transport businesses, including Texas feedlots, a bakery, and the Quaker Oats agricultural products unit.

During the 1980s Continental Grain sold its baking units (Oroweat and Arnold) and its commodities brokerage house. Amid an agricultural bust, it formed ContiFinancial and other financial units.

Michel Fribourg stepped down as CEO in 1988 and was succeeded by Donald Staheli, the first outside CEO. The company entered a grain-handling and selling joint venture with Scoular in 1991. Three years later Staheli added the title of chairman, and Michel's son Paul became president. Continental Grain sold a stake in ContiFinancial (home equity loans and investment banking) to the public in 1996. Also in 1996 the firm formed ContiInvestments, an investment arm geared toward the parent company's areas of expertise.

That year Continental Grain and an overseas affiliate (Arab Finagrain) agreed to pay the US government $35 million, which included a $10 million fine against Arab Finagrain, to settle a fraud case involving commodity sales to Iraq.

Paul succeeded Staheli as CEO in 1997. The company bought Campbell Soup's poultry processing units that year, and in 1998 it bought a 51% stake in pork producer/processor Premium Standard Farms. Meanwhile, ContiFinancial diversified into retail home mortgage and home equity lending.

Continental Grain sold its commodities marketing business in July 1999 to #1 grain exporter Cargill. With its grain operations gone, in 1999 the company renamed itself ContiGroup Companies.

During 2000 ContiFinancial declared bankruptcy, and ContiGroup sold its Animal Nutrition Division (Wayne Foods) to feed manufacturer Ridley Inc. for $37 million. In mid-2000, Premium Standard Farms doubled its processing capacity with the purchase of Lundy Packing Company.

Chairman emeritus Michel Fribourg, the founder's great-great-grandson, died in 2001. That same year ContiSea, the salmon and seafood processing joint venture between ContiGroup and Seaboard, was sold to Norway's Fjord Seafood, giving ContiGroup a significant share of Fjord.

To better focus on its food and agribusiness holdings, in early 2003 ContiGroup sold off its ContiChem LPG business.

EXECUTIVES

Chairman, President, and CEO: Paul J. Fribourg
EVP and COO: Vart K. Adjemian
EVP, Human Resources and Information Systems:
  Teresa E. McCaslin
EVP, Investments and Strategy and CFO; President, ContiInvestments: Michael J. Zimmerman
CEO, ContiBeef: Mike Thoren
CEO, Premium Standard Farms: John M. Meyer
CEO, Wayne Farms: Elton Maddox
SVP and Managing Director, Asian Industries Division:
  Michael A. Hoer
VP and General Manager, ContiLatin: Brian Anderson

LOCATIONS

HQ: ContiGroup Companies, Inc.
  277 Park Ave., New York, NY 10172
Phone: 212-207-5100   **Fax:** 212-207-2910
Web: www.contigroup.com

ContiGroup Companies operates in the Caribbean, China, Latin America, and the US.

PRODUCTS/OPERATIONS

Major Business Units
Asian Industries
  Feed milling (China)
  Pork production (China)
  Poultry production (China)
ContiBeef, LLC
  Cattle feedlots
ContiInvestments, LLC
  Investment management
ContiLatin
  Feed and flour milling
  Poultry operations
  Shrimp farming
PSF Group Holdings, Inc.
  Premium Standard Farms (hog and pork production)
Wayne Farms, LLC
  Poultry production

COMPETITORS

AzTx Cattle
Cactus Feeders
Cargill
CHS
ConAgra
Seaboard
Smithfield Foods
Tyson Foods

HISTORICAL FINANCIALS
Company Type: Private

Income Statement				FYE: March 31
	ESTIMATED REVENUE ($ mil.)	NET INCOME ($ mil.)	NET PROFIT MARGIN	EMPLOYEES
3/04	2,200	—	—	15,500
3/03	2,000	—	—	13,500
3/02	3,300	—	—	14,500
3/01	4,000	—	—	14,500
3/00	10,000	—	—	13,500
3/99	10,500	—	—	14,000
3/98	15,000	—	—	17,500
3/97	16,000	—	—	16,800
3/96	15,000	—	—	16,000
3/95	14,000	—	—	16,000
Annual Growth	(18.6%)	—	—	(0.4%)

Revenue History

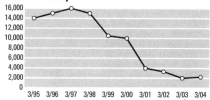

Contran

Give Texas billionaire Harold Simmons a 10-yard penalty, because the company he founded, Contran, is a holding company. Through subsidiaries and affiliations, Valhi, Inc. (a publicly traded company about 90% controlled by Contran) conducts diversified operations in chemicals (NL Industries and Kronos Worldwide), metals (Titanium Metals Corporation), waste management (Waste Control Specialties), computer support systems, and precision ball bearing slides and locking systems (CompX International). Contran also has a controlling interest in Keystone Consolidated Industries, a maker of fencing and wire products. Trusts benefiting Simmons' family (with Simmons as the sole trustee) own pretty much all of Contran.

EXECUTIVES

Chairman, President, and CEO: Harold C. Simmons, age 72
SVP: William J. Lindquist, age 46
VP and Treasurer: Bobby D. O'Brien, age 46
VP and General Counsel: J. Mark Hollingsworth, age 52
VP and Controller: Gregory M. Swalwell, age 47
VP: Robert D. Graham, age 48
VP and Assistant Treasurer: Eugene K. Anderson, age 68
Secretary: A. Andrew R. Louis, age 43
Director, Tax: Kelly D. Luttmer, age 41
Employee Benefits Manager: Keith A. Johnson

LOCATIONS

HQ: Contran Corporation
  Three Lincoln Centre, 5430 LBJ Fwy., Ste. 1700, Dallas, TX 75240
Phone: 972-233-1700   **Fax:** 972-448-1444

COMPETITORS

DuPont
Huntsman
Imperial Chemical Industries
Kerr-McGee
Millennium Chemicals
Minebea
Nachi-Fujikoshi
RTI International Metals
Timken
Waste Management

HISTORICAL FINANCIALS
Company Type: Private

Income Statement				FYE: December 31
	REVENUE ($ mil.)	NET INCOME ($ mil.)	NET PROFIT MARGIN	EMPLOYEES
12/02	1,100	—	—	7,300
12/01	1,100	—	—	7,300
12/00	1,200	—	—	9,000
12/99	1,160	—	—	9,000
12/98	1,077	—	—	8,500
12/97	1,112	—	—	3,800
12/96	1,094	—	—	4,100
12/95	1,125	—	—	4,100
12/94	1,213	—	—	4,000
12/93	1,148	—	—	—
Annual Growth	(0.5%)	—	—	7.8%

Revenue History

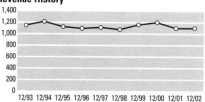

Cook Inlet Energy Supply

Cook Inlet Energy Supply is one of the largest privately owned energy trading companies in the US. The company primarily buys and sells natural gas on the wholesale market, and it provides storage, transportation, hedging, and asset management services. Customers include municipal and regional utilities, power producers, industrial end-users, government and financial institutions, and other energy marketers. Cook Inlet Energy operates in Canada, Mexico, and the US. Inupiat Energy Corporation, which is controlled by Cook Inlet CEO Gregory Craig, owns a majority stake in the company.

EXECUTIVES

CEO: Gregory L. Craig
President: Hans O. Saeby
EVP: Suyen E. Pell
Chief Risk Officer: Neelesh (Neel) Pinge
Controller: Meehee Voelzke
VP Trading: Cindy Khek
Director, Contract Administration: Angela Jones
Director, Quality Control: Aamer Khan
Director, East Coast and Gulf Coast Trading and Marketing: Mark Gazzilli
Director, MidContinent Trading and Marketing: Scott Biscoe
Director, Pacific Northwest and Southwest Trading and Marketing: Sabrina Bienstock

LOCATIONS

HQ: Cook Inlet Energy Supply L.L.C.
10100 Santa Monica Blvd., 18th Fl.,
Los Angeles, CA 90067
Phone: 310-789-3900   **Fax:** 310-789-3901
Web: www.cook-inlet.com

COMPETITORS

Entergy-Koch
Mirant
Sempra Energy Trading

HISTORICAL FINANCIALS

Company Type: Private

Income Statement   FYE: December 31

	REVENUE ($ mil.)	NET INCOME ($ mil.)	NET PROFIT MARGIN	EMPLOYEES
12/03	2,950	—	—	62
12/02	2,870	—	—	58
Annual Growth	2.8%	—	—	6.9%

Revenue History

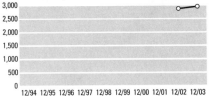

Copley Press

There's no business like the news business for The Copley Press. The newspaper publisher has holdings that include *The San Diego Union-Tribune*, *The Daily Breeze* (Torrance, California), and about 20 other newspapers — mostly in Illinois (the *Journal Star*), Ohio (*The Independent*), and Southern California (the *Borrego Sun*). Its Copley News Service operates six news bureaus in the US and Mexico. In addition, Copley owns the La Casa del Zorro Desert Resort in Borrego Springs, California, and has a stake in a newsprint mill.

The company is owned and operated by descendants of James Copley, adopted son of founder Colonel Ira Copley. In 2001 Helen Copley turned over the day-to-day operations of the company and her title of chairman to her son David. Helen Copley died in 2004 at age 81.

EXECUTIVES

Chairman, President, CEO, and Publisher *San Diego Union-Tribune*: David C. Copley
EVP and COO: Charles F. Patrick
VP and Chief Human Resources Officer: James F. Vargas
VP and Chief Legal Officer: Harold W. Fuson Jr.
VP and CIO: Milton J. Goldwasser Jr.
VP Finance, CFO, and Treasurer: Dean P. Dwyer
Controller: Jessica W. Walker
Manager of Sales and Marketing, Copley News Service: Timothy Cien

LOCATIONS

HQ: The Copley Press, Inc.
7776 Ivanhoe Ave., La Jolla, CA 92037
Phone: 858-454-0411   **Fax:** 858-729-7689
Web: www.copleynewspapers.com

The Copley Press has newspapers in California, Illinois, and Ohio, as well as news bureaus in California, Illinois, Mexico, and Washington, DC.

PRODUCTS/OPERATIONS

Selected Newspapers
Borrego Sun (Borrego Springs, CA)
The Courier (Lincoln, IL)
The Daily Breeze (Torrance, CA)
The Independent (Massillon, OH)
Journal Star (Peoria, IL)
The Register-Mail (Galesburg, IL)
The Repository (Canton, OH)
The San Diego Union-Tribune
The State Journal-Register (Springfield, IL)
The Times-Reporter (New Philadelphia, OH)

Selected Other Operations
Copley News Service (news distribution service)
La Casa del Zorro (resort; Borrego Springs, CA)
Newsprint manufacturing

COMPETITORS

Advance Publications	Hollinger International
Associated Press	Knight-Ridder
Cox Enterprises	Liberty Group Publishing
Dow Jones	Media General
E. W. Scripps	MediaNews
Freedom Communications	New York Times
Gannett	Paddock Publications
Hearst	Pulitzer
Hollinger	Tribune

HISTORICAL FINANCIALS

Company Type: Private

Income Statement   FYE: December 31

	REVENUE ($ mil.)	NET INCOME ($ mil.)	NET PROFIT MARGIN	EMPLOYEES
12/03	573	—	—	—
12/02	530	—	—	—
12/01	534	—	—	4,500
12/00	565	—	—	4,654
12/99	550	—	—	4,700
12/98	500	—	—	4,654
12/97	477	—	—	4,200
12/96	423	—	—	3,800
12/95	398	—	—	3,232
12/94	384	—	—	3,800
Annual Growth	4.5%	—	—	2.4%

Cornell University

To excel at Cornell, you'll need every one of your brain cells. The Ivy League university has been educating young minds since its founding in 1865. Its more than 20,000 students can select from seven undergraduate and six graduate and professional colleges and schools. In addition to its Ithaca, New York, campus the university has medical programs in New York City and Doha, Qatar. Cornell's faculty includes a handful of Nobel laureates, and the university has a robust research component studying everything from animal health to space to waste management; the university's 19 libraries hold more than 7 million volumes. Notable alumni include author E. B. White and US Supreme Court Justice Ruth Bader Ginsburg.

EXECUTIVES

President: Jeffrey S. Lehman
Provost: Carolyn A. (Biddy) Martin
Provost Medical Affairs: Antonio M. Gotto Jr., age 68
Vice Provost: Walter I. Cohen
Vice Provost Diversity and Faculty Development: Robert L. Harris Jr.
Vice Provost Land Grant Affairs and Special Assistant to the President: Francille M. Firebaugh
Vice Provost Life Sciences: Kraig K. Adler
Vice Provost Medical Affairs: Lisa Staiano-Coico
Vice Provost Research: Robert C. Richardson
Vice Provost Undergraduate Education: Isaac Kramnick
Associate Provost Admissions and Enrollment: Doris Davis
VP Administration and CFO: Harold D. Craft
VP Communications and Media Marketing: Thomas W. Bruce
VP Financial Affairs and University Controller: Joanna M. Stefano
VP Human Resources: Mary G. Opperman
University Counsel and Secretary: James J. Mingle
Auditors: KPMG LLP

LOCATIONS

HQ: Cornell University
Cornell University Campus, 305 Day Hall,
Ithaca, NY 14853
Phone: 607-255-2000   **Fax:** 607-255-5396
Web: www.cornell.edu

Revenue History

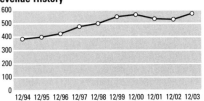

PRODUCTS/OPERATIONS

Selected Undergraduate Colleges and Schools
College of Agriculture and Life Sciences
College of Architecture, Art, and Planning
College of Arts and Sciences
College of Engineering
School of Hotel Administration
College of Human Ecology
School of Industrial and Labor Relations

Selected Graduate and Professional Colleges and Schools
College of Veterinary Medicine
Graduate School
Johnson Graduate School of Management
Law School
Weill Graduate School of Medical Sciences (New York City)
Weill Medical College (New York City and Doha, Qatar)

HISTORICAL FINANCIALS
Company Type: School

Income Statement FYE: June 30

	REVENUE ($ mil.)	NET INCOME ($ mil.)	NET PROFIT MARGIN	EMPLOYEES
6/03	1,903	—	—	13,517
6/02	1,666	—	—	13,319
6/01	1,459	—	—	12,866
6/00	2,352	—	—	12,468
6/99	1,856	—	—	12,207
6/98	1,899	—	—	11,873
6/97	1,709	—	—	11,757
6/96	1,747	—	—	11,481
6/95	1,378	—	—	9,600
6/94	1,315	—	—	9,500
Annual Growth	4.2%	—	—	4.0%

Revenue History

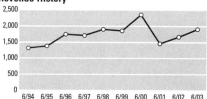

Cornerstone Brands

Cornerstone Brands' foundation is split between six direct marketers. Formed in 1995, the company serves as a holding company for catalog operators: Ballard Designs, Frontgate, Garnet Hill, Smith+Noble, The Territory Ahead (formerly owned by Lands' End), and TravelSmith Outfitters. Cornerstone Brands' companies sell home and leisure goods and casual apparel through catalogs primarily aimed at affluent, well-educated consumers ages 35 to 54. Cornerstone Brands operates a distribution center in Cincinnati and provides customer database management and order fulfillment for its catalog companies. Several investment firms, including Madison Dearborn, own a majority of Cornerstone Brands.

EXECUTIVES
Co-Chairman: Benjamin D. (Ben) Chereskin, age 45
Co-Chairman: Stephen P. Murray
CEO and Director: Richard J. (Dick) Gyde
CFO: John Schaefer
EVP, Business Development: John A. O'Steen, age 59
VP, Corporate Accounting: Doug Dever
VP, Human Resources: Thomas J. (Tom) Wonderly
VP, Information Services: Steve Lamontagne
VP, Treasurer, and Controller: Pat Butler
President, CBI Retail: Marvin B. Cooper
President, Cornerstone Consolidated Services Group: Kent Martin

LOCATIONS
HQ: Cornerstone Brands, Inc.
5568 West Chester Rd., West Chester, OH 45069
Phone: 513-603-1100   **Fax:** 513-603-1124
Web: www.cornerstonebrands.com

PRODUCTS/OPERATIONS
Catalogs
Ballard Designs (home furniture and decorations)
Frontgate (outdoor furniture, pool products, indoor cooking and entertainment goods, organizational products)
  Splash
  The Frontgate Gift Collection
  The Ultimate Grill
Garnet Hill (bedding and bath products, sleepwear, children's and women's apparel)
Smith+Noble (custom-made window treatments)
The Territory Ahead (men's and women's apparel)
  Isabella Bird
TravelSmith Outfitters (travel apparel and accessories)

COMPETITORS

Coldwater Creek	Neiman Marcus
Federated	Saks Inc.
Hanover Direct	Smith & Hawken
J. Crew	Spiegel
Lands' End	Williams-Sonoma
L.L. Bean	

HISTORICAL FINANCIALS
Company Type: Private

Income Statement FYE: Saturday nearest January 31

	REVENUE ($ mil.)	NET INCOME ($ mil.)	NET PROFIT MARGIN	EMPLOYEES
1/03	650	—	—	1,200
1/02	500	—	—	—
1/01	485	—	—	—
1/00	450	—	—	—
1/99	300	—	—	—
1/98	216	—	—	1,380
1/97	106	—	—	—
1/96	61	—	—	—
Annual Growth	40.4%	—	—	(2.8%)

Revenue History

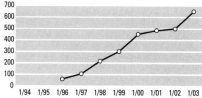

Cornerstone Propane

Propane is the cornerstone of Cornerstone Propane Partners' profits. One of the largest retail propane marketers in the US, Cornerstone sells about 275 million retail gallons of propane a year. It serves more than 420,000 customers in more than 30 states. Burdened by debt, Cornerstone is looking to Chapter 11 protection and restructuring options, including the possible sale of the company. It has sold its Coast Energy Group's crude oil pipeline, gathering, and marketing assets. Utility holding company NorthWestern has disposed of its equity stake in the company.

EXECUTIVES
Chairman: Merle D. Lewis
CEO: Curtis G. (Curt) Solsvig III
CEO: Bill Corbin, age 44
Acting CFO: Robert W. Sundius Jr.
VP Human Resources: Alan Movson
VP Operations: Kevin Cronin
Chief Restructuring Officer: Robert S. Everett, age 40
Director Information Systems: Rod Misaki
Director Organizational Development: Gregory C. (Greg) Gamble
Director Technical Services: Dennis Dukes
Auditors: Marcum & Kliegman LLP

LOCATIONS
HQ: Cornerstone Propane Partners, L.P.
432 Westridge Dr., Watsonville, CA 95076
Phone: 831-724-1921   **Fax:** 831-724-2799
Web: www.cornerstonepropane.com

COMPETITORS

All Star Gas	Piedmont Natural Gas
AmeriGas Partners	Star Gas Partners
Duke Energy	Suburban Propane
Energy Transfer	Williams Companies
Ferrellgas Partners	

HISTORICAL FINANCIALS
Company Type: Private

Income Statement FYE: June 30

	REVENUE ($ mil.)	NET INCOME ($ mil.)	NET PROFIT MARGIN	EMPLOYEES
6/02	1,176	(216)	—	—
6/01	4,206	(14)	—	2,206
6/00	3,727	(10)	—	2,436
6/99	1,155	5	0.5%	2,396
6/98	768	9	1.2%	2,000
6/97	390	6	1.5%	1,881
6/96	99	4	3.7%	1,685
6/95	57	0	0.7%	—
6/94	60	4	5.8%	—
6/93	61	5	7.7%	—
Annual Growth	38.9%	—	—	5.5%

2002 Year-End Financials
Debt ratio: —   Current ratio: 0.09
Return on equity: —   Long-term debt ($ mil.): 27
Cash ($ mil.): 5

Net Income History

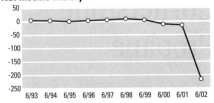

Corporation for Public Broadcasting

This organization is made possible by a grant from the federal government and by support from viewers like you. The Corporation for Public Broadcasting (CPB) is a private, not-for-profit corporation (not a government agency) created by the federal government that receives appropriations from Congress to help fund programming for more than 1,000 member-owned stations of the Public Broadcasting Service, National Public Radio, Public Radio International, and other organizations. The organization's funding is often a political hot potato (frequently a target of Republicans who are opposed to government funding of educational, informational, and cultural programming). CPB was created by Congress in 1967.

Funding was approved through 2003 despite a 1999 investigation that revealed some PBS stations had given their mailing lists to the Democratic party for fundraising purposes. CPB's funding was approved at $350 million for 2002 and $365 million for 2003. Contributions from CPB represent 15% of public broadcasting's revenues. Following those appropriations, the company has received additional funding that will keep it rolling through fiscal 2005.

HISTORY

As commercial radio began to fill the radio dial, the FCC in 1945 reserved 20 channels from 88 FM to 92 FM for noncommercial, educational broadcasts. The first public television station started broadcasting in 1953, and by 1965 there were 124 public TV stations across the country. To help allocate government funds to these public TV and radio stations, Congress created the Corporation for Public Broadcasting (CPB) in 1967. CPB created the Public Broadcasting Service (PBS) in 1969 and National Public Radio (NPR) in 1970.

CPB has always been politically controversial; critics have often charged it with elitism, cultural bias, and liberalism. When Republicans gained control of Congress in 1994, their laundry list of grievances included government cultural spending. They were foiled in their effort to eliminate funding for CPB, however, in part because of public support for public television. Congress still cut funding by $100 million, forcing CPB to reduce its staff by almost 25% and introduce performance criteria for stations seeking grant money, including listenership and community financial support minimums.

Robert Coonrod was promoted to CEO in 1997. The following year Congress approved additional funding to help public television's transition from analog to digital broadcasting. Frank Cruz was appointed chairman of CPB in 1999. At about the same time, increased funding for 2003 (funding is approved two years in advance) was threatened when it was discovered that some PBS stations were giving their mailing lists to the Democratic party for fundraising purposes. Nevertheless, funding for CPB was increased in the 2001 budget.

In late 2001 businesswoman Katherine Milner Anderson was voted in as chairman, taking over for Cruz (who remained on the board). After serving two consecutive terms as chairman, Anderson was replaced by veteran journalist Kenneth Y. Tomlinson in 2003.

In 2004 Coonrod left the company. Former COO Kathleen Cox replaced him as president and CEO.

EXECUTIVES

Chairman: Kenneth Y. Tomlinson
Vice Chairman: Frank H. Cruz
EVP and Senior Adviser to the President:
  Frederick L. DeMarco
President and CEO: Kathleen Cox
SVP Media: Andrew Russell
SVP Radio: Vincent Curren
VP, General Counsel, and Corporate Secretary:
  Donna Coleman Gregg
SVP Television Programming: Michael Pack
VP Business Affairs: Steven J. Altman
VP Education: Cheryl Scott Williams
VP Finance and Administration, Treasurer:
  Elizabeth A. Griffith
VP Government Relations: Deborah K. Kilmer
VP Program Operations: Yoko N. Arthur
SVP, System and Station Development:
  Douglas A. Weiss
VP Television and Digital Media: Terry Bryant
VP Television Program Development: John Prizer
Inspector General: Ken Konz
Director, Information Technology: David Creekmore
Director, Budget: Luis Guardia
Auditors: Deloitte & Touche LLP

LOCATIONS

HQ: Corporation for Public Broadcasting
  401 9th St., NW, Washington, DC 20004
Phone: 202-879-9600   **Fax:** 202-879-9700
Web: www.cpb.org

PRODUCTS/OPERATIONS

Selected Affiliations
American Public Television (programs for public television)
The Annenberg/CPB Projects (telecourses and education programs)
Association of America's Public Television Stations (organization of public TV stations)
Independent Television Service (independent creative programming for public TV)
National Public Radio (radio programming distribution)
Public Broadcasting Service (TV distribution)
Public Radio International (international radio distribution)

HISTORICAL FINANCIALS

Company Type: Not-for-profit

Income Statement FYE: September 30

	REVENUE ($ mil.)	NET INCOME ($ mil.)	NET PROFIT MARGIN	EMPLOYEES
9/03	426	—	—	100
9/02	400	—	—	100
9/01	398	—	—	110
9/00	384	—	—	100
9/99	283	—	—	90
9/98	285	—	—	90
9/97	282	—	—	90
9/96	296	—	—	85
9/95	286	—	—	95
9/94	275	—	—	100
Annual Growth	5.0%	—	—	0.0%

Revenue History

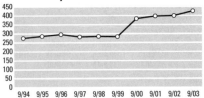

Cox Enterprises

The Cox family has been working at this enterprise for more than 100 years. One of the largest media conglomerates in the US, family-owned Cox Enterprises publishes 17 daily newspapers (including *The Atlanta Journal-Constitution*) and about 25 weeklies and shoppers and owns 15 TV stations through Cox Television. It also owns about 62% of Cox Radio (more than 80 radio stations) and controls 63% of Cox Communications, though the company has announced an $8.5 billion deal to acquire the rest of Cox Communications, which is one of the US's largest cable systems, with more than 6.3 million subscribers in about 20 states. Cox's Manheim runs 115 automobile auctions worldwide and owns a majority stake in AutoTrader.com.

While Cox Communications is the company's biggest revenue generator, Cox Enterprises has been spending a lot of money and time driving on the information superhighway. AutoTrader.com, which the company operates in conjunction with Manheim, is one of the few profitable Internet companies. Manheim is the world's largest used-car auctioneer and the combination of the businesses has proved lucrative for Cox.

However, Cox has also learned the hard lesson that other media companies have been taught as they try to be successful on the Internet. Cox scrapped a plan for an AutoTrader.com IPO in 2000 when the market soured. And in 2002 the company cut about 75 jobs from its interactive unit and dropped a plan to develop a nationwide network of local city Web sites.

Fed up with the demands of running a publicly traded cable company, Cox Enterprises announced in 2004 that it would take Cox Communications private in an $8.5 billion stock deal.

Barbara Cox Anthony (mother of chairman and CEO James Kennedy) and Anne Cox Chambers, daughters of founder James Cox, control 98% of the company. The sisters were recently ranked high on *Forbes'* list of the richest Americans.

HISTORY

James Middleton Cox, who dropped out of school in 1886 at 16, had worked as a teacher, reporter, and congressional secretary before buying the *Dayton Daily News* in 1898. After acquiring the nearby *Springfield Press-Republican* in 1905, he took up politics, serving two terms in the US Congress (1909-1913) and three terms as Ohio governor (1913-1915; 1917-1921). He even ran for president in 1920 (his running mate was future President Franklin Roosevelt) but lost to rival Ohio publisher Warren G. Harding.

Once out of politics, Cox began building his media empire. He bought the *Miami Daily News* in 1923 and founded WHIO (Dayton, Ohio's first radio station). He bought Atlanta's WSB ("Welcome South, Brother"), the South's first radio station, in 1939 and added WSB-FM and WSB-TV, the South's first FM and TV stations, in 1948. Cox founded Dayton's first FM and TV stations (WHIO-FM and WHIO-TV) the next year, and *The Atlanta Constitution* joined his collection in 1950. Cox died in 1957.

The company continued to expand its broadcasting interests in the late 1950s and early 1960s. It was one of the first major broadcasting companies to expand into cable TV when it purchased a system in Lewistown, Pennsylvania, in 1962. The Cox family's broadcast properties were placed in publicly held Cox Broadcasting in 1964. Two years later its newspapers were placed into privately held Cox Enterprises, and the cable holdings became publicly held Cox Cable Communications. The broadcasting arm diversified, buying Manheim Services (auto auctions, 1968), Kansas City Automobile Auction (1969), and TeleRep (TV ad sales, 1972).

Cox Cable had 500,000 subscribers in nine states when it rejoined Cox Broadcasting in 1977. Cox Broadcasting was renamed Cox Communications in 1982, and the Cox family took the company private again in 1985, combining it with Cox Enterprises. James Kennedy, grandson of founder James Cox, became chairman and CEO in 1987.

Expansion became the keyword for Cox in the 1990s. The company merged its Manheim unit with the auto auction business of Ford Motor Credit and GE Capital in 1991. It also formed Sprint Spectrum in 1994, a partnership with Sprint, TCI (now part of AT&T), and Comcast to bundle telephone, cable TV, and other communications services (Sprint bought out Cox in 1999). Then, in one of its biggest transactions, Cox bought Times Mirror's cable TV operations for $2.3 billion in 1995 and combined them with its own cable system into a new, publicly traded company called Cox Communications. The following year it spun off its radio holdings into a public company called Cox Radio.

To expand its online presence, the company formed Cox Interactive Media in 1996, establishing a series of city Web sites and making a host of investments in various Internet companies, including Career Path, ExciteHome, iVillage, MP3.com, and Tickets.com. Cox also applied the online strategy to its automobile auction businesses, establishing AutoTrader.com in 1998 and placing the Internet operations of Manheim Auctions (now just Manheim) into a new company, Manheim Interactive, in 2000.

In 2002 Cox dropped plans to expand its local Internet city guide business nationwide and moved its Interactive Media operations to other parts of the company.

EXECUTIVES

Chairman and CEO: James C. Kennedy, age 56
Vice Chairman: David E. Easterly, age 61
President and COO: G. Dennis Berry, age 59
EVP and CFO: Robert C. (Bob) O'Leary, age 65
SVP Administration: Timothy W. Hughes, age 60
SVP Public Policy: Alexander V. Netchvolodoff, age 67
VP and CIO: Gregory B. Morrison, age 44
VP and General Tax Counsel: Preston B. Barnett, age 57
VP and Treasurer: Richard J. Jacobson, age 46
VP Human Resources: Marybeth H. Leamer, age 46
VP Legal Affairs, General Counsel, and Secretary: Andrew A. Merdek
VP Marketing: John C. Williams, age 56
VP Public Policy: Alexandra M. Wilson, age 44
President and CEO, AutoTrader.com: Victor A. (Chip) Perry III, age 50
President and CEO, Cox Communications: James O. (Jim) Robbins, age 61
President and CEO, Cox Radio: Robert F. Neil, age 45
President and CEO, Manheim: Dean H. Eisner, age 46
President, Cox Newspapers: Jay R. Smith, age 54
President, Cox Television: Andrew S. Fisher, age 55

LOCATIONS

HQ: Cox Enterprises, Inc.
  6205 Peachtree Dunwoody Rd., Atlanta, GA 30328
Phone: 678-645-0000 **Fax:** 678-645-1079
Web: www.coxenterprises.com

PRODUCTS/OPERATIONS

2003 Sales

	$ mil.	% of total
Cable TV	5,800	54
Auctions	2,400	22
Newspapers	1,400	13
TV stations	636	6
Radio stations	426	4
Internet auto classifieds	134	1
Adjustments	(96)	—
Total	**10,700**	**100**

Selected Operations

Cox Broadcasting
  Cox Television
    Harrington, Righter & Parsons (TV ad sales)
    MMT Sales (TV ad sales)
    TeleRep (TV ad sales)
    Television Stations
      KAME (Reno, NV; UPN)
      KFOX (El Paso, TX; FOX)
      KICU (San Francisco/San Jose, CA; Independent)
      KIRO (Seattle, CBS)
      KRXI (Reno, NV; FOX)
      KTVU (Oakland/San Francisco, CA; FOX)
      WAXN (Charlotte, NC; Independent)
      WFTV (Orlando, FL; ABC)
      WHIO (Dayton, OH; CBS)
      WJAC (Johnstown, PA; NBC)
      WPXI (Pittsburgh, NBC)
      WRDQ (Orlando, FL; Independent)
      WSB-TV (Atlanta, ABC)
      WSOC (Charlotte, NC; ABC)
      WTOV (Steubenville, OH; NBC)

Cox Communications (63%, cable system)
Cox Radio (62%)
  Atlanta (WBTS-FM, WSB-AM, WSB-FM)
  Birmingham, AL (WBHJ-FM, WBHK-FM, WZZK-FM)
  Bridgeport/New Haven, CT (WEZN-FM)
  Dayton, OH (WHIO-AM, WHKO-FM)
  Greenville/Spartanburg, SC (WJMZ-FM)
  Honolulu (KRTR-FM, KXME-FM)
  Houston (KLDE-FM)
  Jacksonville (WAPE-FM, WFYV-FM, WKQL-FM)
  Long Island, NY (WBAB-FM, WBLI-FM)
  Louisville, KY (WRKA-FM, WVEZ-FM)
  Miami (WEDR-FM, WHQT-FM)
  New Haven, CT (WPLR-FM)
  Orlando, FL (WHTQ-FM, WWKA-FM)
  Richmond, VA (WKLR-FM)
  San Antonio (KCYY-FM, KISS-FM, KONO-FM)
  Stamford/Norwalk, CT (WEFX-FM, WNLK-AM)
  Tampa (WDUV-FM, WWRM-FM)
  Tulsa, OK (KRAV-FM, KRMG-AM, KRTQ-FM, KWEN-FM)
Cox Newspapers
  Daily Newspapers
    The Atlanta Journal-Constitution
    Austin American-Statesman (Texas)
    Dayton Daily News (Ohio)
    The Daily Advance (Elizabeth City, NC)
    The Daily Reflector (Greenville, NC)
    The Daily Sentinel (Grand Junction, CO)
    The Daily Sentinel (Nacogdoches, TX)
    The Hamilton Journal News (Ohio)
    Longview News-Journal (Texas)
    The Lufkin Daily News (Texas)
    The Middleton Journal (Ohio)
    News Messenger (Marshall, TX)
    Palm Beach Daily News (Florida)
    The Palm Beach Post (Florida)
    Rocky Mount Telegram (North Carolina)
    Springfield News Sun (Ohio)
    Waco Tribune-Herald (Texas)
  Cox Custom Media (commercial newsletters)
  PAGAS Mailing Services
  SP Newsprint (33%)
  Trader Publishing (50%, classified advertising)
  Valpack (direct mail advertisements)
Manheim
  Manheim Interactive (online auto auctions)
    AutoTrader.com (majority owned, online auto sales)
Sports Teams
  Atlanta Beat (women's professional soccer)
  San Diego Spirit (women's professional soccer)

COMPETITORS

Advance Publications
Austin Chronicle
Belo
Clear Channel
Columbus Fair Auto Auction
Comcast
Dow Jones
E. W. Scripps
Gannett
Hearst
Knight-Ridder
Media General
Morris Communications
New York Times
News Corp.
Ticketmaster
Time Warner Cable
Tribune
Viacom
Walt Disney
Washington Post

Cox Health Systems

Cox Health Systems provides health care to locals and tourists alike in the Ozarks. The health care network serves more than 25 counties in southern Missouri and northern Arkansas. Cox Health's network includes three acute care hospitals with more than 1,000 beds and 55 clinics. Centers for cardiac care, cancer treatment, and women's health are among Cox Health's specialized care options. Other services include a long-term care hospital; rehabilitation, behavioral health, and psychiatric facilities; an ambulance service offering both ground and air transportation; and the Oxford HealthCare home health care company.

EXECUTIVES

President and CEO: Robert H. (Bob) Bezansen, age 58
Interim CFO; CFO, Cox HealthPlans: Jacob McWay
VP, Medical Affairs: James Coulter
CIO: John Duff
Director, Public Relations: Laurie Cunningham
Director, Health Information Management and Privacy Officer: Robin Gann

LOCATIONS

HQ: Cox Health Systems
1423 N. Jefferson Ave., Springfield, MO 65802
Phone: 417-269-3000 **Fax:** 417-269-8204
Web: www.coxhealth.com

HISTORICAL FINANCIALS

Company Type: Private

Income Statement
FYE: December 31

	REVENUE ($ mil.)	NET INCOME ($ mil.)	NET PROFIT MARGIN	EMPLOYEES
12/03	10,700	—	—	77,000
12/02	9,900	—	—	77,000
12/01	8,693	—	—	76,000
12/00	7,824	—	—	74,000
12/99	6,097	—	—	61,000
12/98	5,355	—	—	55,500
12/97	4,936	—	—	50,000
12/96	4,591	—	—	43,000
12/95	3,806	—	—	38,000
12/94	2,939	—	—	37,000
Annual Growth	15.4%	—	—	8.5%

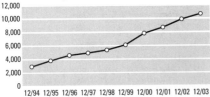

Crete Carrier

Crete Carrier keeps customers' goods moving. The flagship of a group of truckload carriers controlled by chairman Duane Acklie, Crete Carrier provides dry van freight transportation services in the 48 contiguous states. It operates from more than 15 terminals, mainly in the eastern half of the US. The company's Shaffer Trucking unit transports temperature-controlled cargo, and Hunt Transportation (no relation to J.B. Hunt Transport Services) hauls heavy equipment and other cargo on flatbed trailers. Collectively, the companies operate about 5,300 tractors and more than 12,400 trailers.

EXECUTIVES

Chairman: Duane W. Acklie, age 72
President and CEO: Tonn M. Ostergard
CFO: Dean Troester
VP Operations: Lee Hoffman

LOCATIONS

HQ: Crete Carrier Corporation
400 NW 56th St., Lincoln, NE 68501
Phone: 402-475-9521 **Fax:** 402-479-2075
Web: www.cretecarrier.com

COMPETITORS

Celadon
CFI
Covenant Transport
Heartland Express
J. B. Hunt
Landstar System
Schneider National
Swift Transportation
U.S. Xpress
Werner Enterprises

HISTORICAL FINANCIALS

Company Type: Private

Income Statement
FYE: September 30

	REVENUE ($ mil.)	NET INCOME ($ mil.)	NET PROFIT MARGIN	EMPLOYEES
9/03	745	—	—	5,466
9/02	725	—	—	5,000
Annual Growth	2.8%	—	—	9.3%

HISTORICAL FINANCIALS

Company Type: Not-for-profit

Income Statement
FYE: September 30

	REVENUE ($ mil.)	NET INCOME ($ mil.)	NET PROFIT MARGIN	EMPLOYEES
9/03	1,044	—	—	8,799
9/02	954	—	—	8,956
Annual Growth	9.5%	—	—	(1.8%)

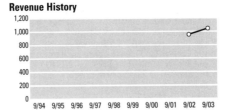

CROSSMARK

CROSSMARK helps its clients in the consumer packaged goods (CPG) industry get its products into stores and then out of stores. The company provides Headquarter sales (securing distribution in retail outlets), in-store merchandising, sales support, and supply chain optimization services for supermarkets, convenience stores, and drug stores, along with other specialty trade channels. CROSSMARK has operations in the US, Australia, Canada, and New Zealand.

EXECUTIVES

CEO: David Baxley
SVP Strategic Alliances: Joe Crafton
Chief Communications Officer: Jeff Rice
COO: Jim Borders
CFO: Don Martin
CIO: Clay Curtis
VP Administrative Services: Robert Browning
VP Human Resources: Rodger Fisher
VP and General Counsel: J. Johnette Oden-Brunson
President, CROSSMARK Retail Services:
  John Thompson
President, CROSSMARK Sales Agency: Ben Fischer

LOCATIONS

HQ: CROSSMARK
5100 Legacy Dr., Plano, TX 75024
Phone: 469-814-1000 **Fax:** 469-814-1355
Web: www.crossmark.com

COMPETITORS

Acosta Sales
Advantage Sales and Marketing
Ferolie Group

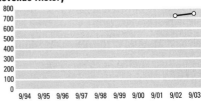

HISTORICAL FINANCIALS

Company Type: Private

Income Statement

	ESTIMATED REVENUE ($ mil.)	NET INCOME ($ mil.)	NET PROFIT MARGIN	EMPLOYEES
2003	550	—	—	10,000

Crowley Maritime

Crowley Maritime has pushed and pulled its way into prominence as one of the largest tug and barge operators in the world. The company transports containers, trailers, petroleum products, and breakbulk (structures that cannot be broken down) by ship. It provides ship assists, towing, logistics, and marine salvage. The company's fleet of nearly 300 vessels includes tugboats, tankers, barges, and specialized cargo carriers. Crowley Maritime has about 100 offices worldwide. CEO Thomas Crowley (grandson of the founder), his family, and employees control the company, which was founded in 1892.

EXECUTIVES

Chairman and CEO: Thomas B. (Tom) Crowley Jr., age 37, $1,467,940 pay
Vice Chairman and EVP: William A. Pennella, age 59, $576,935 pay
SVP and General Counsel: William P. Verdon, age 63, $367,540 pay
SVP and General Manager, Logistics: John Hourihan
SVP and General Manager, Marine Transport: Rockwell (Rocky) Smith
SVP and General Manager, Puerto Rico and Caribbean Services: John Douglass
SVP and General Manager, Latin America Services: Rinus Schepen
VP and Controller: John Calvin
VP Human Resources: Susan Rodgers
VP Tax and Audit: Richard L. Swinton, age 56, $219,180 pay
VP and Treasurer: Albert M. Marucco, age 62, $290,405 pay
Corporate Secretary: Bruce Love
Director of Corporate Communications: Mark Miller
Auditors: Deloitte & Touche LLP

LOCATIONS

HQ: Crowley Maritime Corporation
155 Grand Ave., Oakland, CA 94612
Phone: 510-251-7500 **Fax:** 510-251-7788
Web: www.crowley.com

PRODUCTS/OPERATIONS

2003 Sales

	$ mil.	% of total
Liner	578.6	59
Oil & chemical distribution & transportation	255.5	26
Ship assist & escort	73.7	8
Energy & marine	70.2	7
Total	**978.0**	**100**

Major Subsidiaries

Crowley Liner Services, Inc.
Crowley Logistics Inc.
Crowley Marine Services, Inc.
Crowley Petroleum Transport, Inc.
Marine Transport Corporation
Vessel Management Services, Inc.

COMPETITORS

Alexander & Baldwin
A.P. Møller - Maersk
APL
Compañía Sud Americana de Vapores
Evergreen Marine
Hamburg Süd
Hanjin Shipping
International Shipholding
Kirby
Maritrans
Overseas Shipholding Group
P&O

HISTORICAL FINANCIALS
Company Type: Private

Income Statement
FYE: December 31

	ESTIMATED REVENUE ($ mil.)	NET INCOME ($ mil.)	NET PROFIT MARGIN	EMPLOYEES
12/03	978	13	1.3%	4,000
12/02	978	17	1.8%	3,913
12/01	1,001	20	2.0%	3,800
12/00	799	20	2.5%	5,000
12/99	775	—	—	3,300
12/98	1,100	—	—	5,000
12/97	1,100	—	—	5,000
12/96	1,100	—	—	5,000
12/95	1,100	—	—	5,000
12/94	1,100	—	—	5,000
Annual Growth	(1.3%)	(14.2%)	—	(2.4%)

2003 Year-End Financials

Debt ratio: 142.3%
Return on equity: 4.6%
Cash ($ mil.): 161
Current ratio: 1.73
Long-term debt ($ mil.): 382

Net Income History

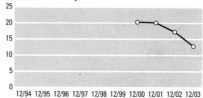

Crown Central Petroleum

Independent oil refiner and marketer Crown Central Petroleum's family jewels includes two refineries in Texas with a total capacity of 152,000 barrels per day, 200 gas stations (most of which were sold in 2004), and 10 product terminals. Crown Central also offers fleet fueling services. Rosemore, the holding company of Henry Rosenberg and his family, took control of Crown Central in 2001 after beating out a competing bid for control from rival Apex Oil. The company has come under attack for a four-year labor lockout at its Houston-area refinery, civil rights violations, and excessive toxic releases. Crown Central is in the process of selling most of its refineries, terminals, and retail assets.

EXECUTIVES

President: Thomas L. Owsley
CFO: John E. Wheeler Jr.
VP, General Counsel and Corporate Secretary: Andrew Lapayowker
Auditors: Ernst & Young LLP

LOCATIONS

HQ: Crown Central Petroleum Corporation
1 North Charles St., Baltimore, MD 21201
Phone: 410-539-7400 **Fax:** 410-659-4747
Web: www.crowncentral.com

Crown Central Petroleum owns two refineries in Texas.

PRODUCTS/OPERATIONS

Products

Diesel fuel
Fleet fueling services
Fuel oil
Gasoline
Heating oil
Jet fuel
Kerosene
Telephone calling cards

COMPETITORS

Apex Oil
BP
ConocoPhillips
Exxon Mobil
George Warren
Giant Industries
Marathon Ashland Petroleum
Motiva Enterprises
Premcor
Sunoco
Valero Energy
Williams Companies

HISTORICAL FINANCIALS
Company Type: Private

Income Statement
FYE: December 31

	REVENUE ($ mil.)	NET INCOME ($ mil.)	NET PROFIT MARGIN	EMPLOYEES
12/02	1,737	—	—	2,600
12/01	1,700	—	—	2,600
12/00	1,961	—	—	2,636
12/99	1,270	—	—	2,695
12/98	1,264	—	—	3,028
12/97	1,603	—	—	2,819
12/96	1,635	—	—	2,900
12/95	1,451	—	—	3,009
12/94	1,319	—	—	2,971
Annual Growth	3.5%	—	—	(1.7%)

Revenue History

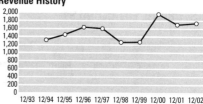

Crown Equipment

Crown Equipment Corporation is a leading maker of electric heavy-duty lift trucks for maneuvering goods in warehouses and distribution centers. The company's products include narrow-aisle stacking equipment, powered pallet trucks, order-picking equipment, and forklift trucks. Its equipment can move four-ton loads and stack pallets nearly 45 feet high. Crown Equipment sells its products globally through retailers. The company, founded in 1945 by brothers Carl and Allen Dicke, originally made temperature controls for coal furnaces. It began making material-handling equipment in the 1950s. The Dicke family still controls Crown Equipment.

EXECUTIVES

Chairman Emeritus: James F. Dicke
Chairman and CEO: James F. Dicke II, age 57
President: James F. Dicke III
SVP: Donald E. Luebrecht
SVP: James D. Moran
VP and General Counsel: John G. Maxa
VP, Branch Operations: James B. Ellis
VP, Design Center: Michael P. Gallagher
VP, Engineering: Timothy S. Quellhorst
VP, Finance: Kent W. Spille
VP, Human Resources: Randy W. Niekamp
VP, Information Services: Mark A. Manuel
Publicity Administrator: David Helmstetter

LOCATIONS

HQ: Crown Equipment Corporation
44 S. Washington St., New Bremen, OH 45869
Phone: 419-629-2311 **Fax:** 419-629-2900
Web: www.crown.com

Crown Equipment has 75 factory-owned sales and service facilities and 150 independent dealers worldwide.

PRODUCTS/OPERATIONS

Selected Products
Counterbalanced trucks
Hand pallet trucks
Narrow-aisle reach trucks
Rider pallet trucks
Stockpickers
Tow tractors
Walkie pallet trucks
Walkie stackers

COMPETITORS

Caterpillar
Hyundai Heavy Industries
Komatsu
NACCO Industries
Toyota Material Handling

HISTORICAL FINANCIALS

Company Type: Private

Income Statement			FYE: March 31	
	REVENUE ($ mil.)	NET INCOME ($ mil.)	NET PROFIT MARGIN	EMPLOYEES
3/03	1,000	—	—	6,500
3/02	966	—	—	6,500
3/01	1,127	—	—	7,290
3/00	1,010	—	—	6,510
3/99	968	—	—	6,440
3/98	855	—	—	6,050
3/97	781	—	—	5,975
3/96	707	—	—	5,800
3/95	607	—	—	5,000
3/94	486	—	—	4,200
Annual Growth	8.3%	—	—	5.0%

Revenue History

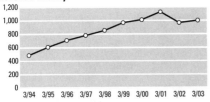

Culligan

"Hey Culligan Man!" To be sure, the phrase made famous by an ad campaign still rings in the ears of Culligan International workers. Formerly a subsidiary of Veolia Environnement, Culligan produces filters for tap water, household water softeners, microfiltration products, desalination systems, and portable deionization services for commercial and industrial users. The franchised "Culligan Man" noted in the advertising phrase delivers bottled water and water systems to consumers and businesses throughout the US and in more than 90 other countries. Besides Culligan, the company's brand names include Everpure, Elga, and Bruner. Buyout firm Clayton, Dubilier & Rice acquired the company for $610 million in 2004.

EXECUTIVES

Chairman: George W. Tamke, age 56
CFO: Joe Morrison
VP Sales: Larry Holzman
Director Human Resources: Gail Wasserstein

LOCATIONS

HQ: Culligan International Company
1 Culligan Pkwy., Northbrook, IL 60062
Phone: 847-205-6000 **Fax:** 847-205-6030
Web: www.culligan.com

Culligan has offices in more than 100 countries in Africa, the Americas, Asia, and Europe.

PRODUCTS/OPERATIONS

Selected Products
Bottled water
Commercial dealkalizers
Commercial deionizers
Commercial reverse osmosis systems
Counter top systems
Drinking water systems
Faucet mount systems
Household filters
Replacement filter cartridges
Softeners

COMPETITORS

AquaCell
BRITA
Calgon Carbon
CUNO
Ionics
Millipore
Pall

HISTORICAL FINANCIALS

Company Type: Private

Income Statement			FYE: June 30	
	REVENUE ($ mil.)	NET INCOME ($ mil.)	NET PROFIT MARGIN	EMPLOYEES
6/04	718	—	—	5,500

Cumberland Farms

Beginning as a one-cow dairy, Cumberland Farms now owns and operates about 650 convenience stores (three-fourths of which sell gasoline) in 11 eastern seaboard states from Maine to Florida. The company has its own grocery distribution and bakery operations to supply its stores. Cumberland Farms owns a two-thirds limited partnership in petroleum wholesaler Gulf Oil, giving it the right to use and license Gulf trademarks in Delaware, New Jersey, New York, most of Ohio, Pennsylvania, and the New England states. The company, the first convenience-store operator in New England, was founded in 1938 by Vasilios and Aphrodite Haseotes. The Haseotes' children, including CEO Lily Haseotes Bentas, own the company.

EXECUTIVES

Chairman, President, and CEO: Lily Haseotes Bentas
EVP and COO: Harry J. Brenner
SVP, Retail Operations: Daniel D. Phaneuf
VP, Human Resources: Foster G. Macrides
VP, Information Technology: John Carroll
VP, Marketing: Alvin (Al) McKay
VP, Wholesale Petroleum: George P. Haseotes
Controller: Kevin Johnson
General Counsel: Michael A. Kelly
Senior Corporate Recruiter: Stephen Dolinich

LOCATIONS

HQ: Cumberland Farms, Inc.
777 Dedham St., Canton, MA 02021
Phone: 781-828-4900 **Fax:** 781-828-9624
Web: www.cumberlandfarms.com

Cumberland Farms operates about 650 convenience stores in Connecticut, Delaware, Florida, Maine, Massachusetts, New Hampshire, New Jersey, New York, Pennsylvania, Rhode Island, and Vermont.

COMPETITORS

7-Eleven
BP
ChevronTexaco
DeMoulas Super Markets
Exxon Mobil
Gate Petroleum
Getty Realty
Golub
Motiva Enterprises
Racetrac Petroleum
Sheetz
Stewart's Shops
Wawa, Inc.

HISTORICAL FINANCIALS

Company Type: Private

Income Statement			FYE: September 30	
	REVENUE ($ mil.)	NET INCOME ($ mil.)	NET PROFIT MARGIN	EMPLOYEES
9/03	2,000	—	—	6,976
9/02	1,700	—	—	6,976
9/01	1,500	—	—	6,545
9/00	950	—	—	6,200
9/99	1,140	—	—	6,900
9/98	1,387	—	—	6,800
9/97	1,469	—	—	7,100
9/96	1,396	—	—	7,100
9/95	1,321	—	—	7,200
9/94	1,188	—	—	7,500
Annual Growth	6.0%	—	—	(0.8%)

Revenue History

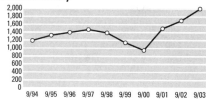

CUNA Mutual

CUNA would soonah eat tuna than make its products available to banks. CUNA Mutual Group offers the more than 9,500 credit unions in the US (as well as those in 30 other countries) a range of products and services, including life insurance, investment advisory, and information technology. Entities that make up the group include CUNA Mutual Insurance Society (accident, health, and life insurance) and CUNA Mutual Mortgage Corporation (mortgage loan origination, purchasing, and servicing). The group also offers customers such technology services as Web site enhancement and automated lending software. CUNA was founded in 1935 by pioneers of the credit union movement and is owned by its credit union policyholders.

Jeffrey Holley moved into the CEO office in 2004 after Mike Kitchen resigned under pressure in relation to allegations of anti-labor union activity.

EXECUTIVES

Chairman: Loretta M. Burd
Vice Chairman: Eldon R. Arnold
Acting President, Acting CEO, and CFO: Jeff Holley
Chief Sales & Marketing Officer: Jim Gowan
CTO: Rick R. Roy
SVP, Human Resources: Keith Williams
Assistant VP, Public Relations: Sydney Lindner
Senior Manager, Media Relations: Rick Uhlmann
Auditors: PricewaterhouseCoopers LLP

LOCATIONS

HQ: CUNA Mutual Group
 5910 Mineral Point Rd., Madison, WI 53701
Phone: 608-238-5851
Web: www.cunamutual.com

PRODUCTS/OPERATIONS

2003 Sales

	$ mil.	% of total
Life & health premiums & deposits	1,221	51
Property & casualty premiums	472	19
Net investment income	357	15
Other income	366	15
Total	**2,416**	**100**

Selected Subsidiaries and Affiliates

CMG Mortgage Assurance Company
CMG Mortgage Insurance Company
CUMIS Insurance Society, Inc.
CUNA Brokerage Services, Inc.
CUNA Mutual Insurance Agency, Inc.
CUNA Mutual Insurance Society
CUNA Mutual Life Insurance Company
CUNA Mutual Mortgage Corporation
MEMBERS Capital Advisors, Inc.
Stewart Associates, Inc.

COMPETITORS

BISYS
Certegy
Equix Financial Services
Intrieve
Lincoln Trust
Online Resources
PrimeVest
SEI
U.S. Central

HISTORICAL FINANCIALS

Company Type: Mutual company

Income Statement
FYE: December 31

	ASSETS ($ mil.)	NET INCOME ($ mil.)	INCOME AS % OF ASSETS	EMPLOYEES
12/03	12,885	134	1.0%	6,000
12/02	11,009	(9)	—	5,000
Annual Growth	17.0%	—	—	9.5%

2003 Year-End Financials

Equity as % of assets: 11.5%
Return on assets: 1.1%
Return on equity: 9.7%
Long-term debt ($ mil.): 6,394
Sales ($ mil.): 2,416

Net Income History

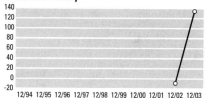

Cushman & Wakefield

Cushman & Wakefield serves the real estate needs of corporations and financial institutions around the globe. The commercial real estate brokerage and services company, founded in 1917 by J. Clydesdale Cushman and Bernard Wakefield, has some 160 offices in about 50 countries. In addition to property management (for about 5,500 properties totaling nearly 300 million sq. ft.) and brokerage services, Cushman & Wakefield also provides research and analysis on 85 major markets worldwide. It has also partnered with Business Integration Group and Yardi Systems to develop Web-based real estate management services software. The Rockefeller Group, a Mitsubishi Estate subsidiary, owns 72% of Cushman & Wakefield.

Cushman & Wakefield focuses its global efforts on European (where it operates as Cushman & Wakefield Healey & Baker) and Asian markets. Domestically, growth plans entail the retail brokerage and multifamily investment businesses.

Cushman & Wakefield's Asian operations have expanded to China via a joint venture with PREMAS International, a Singapore-based firm. Mindful of tenants' security concerns after the terrorist attacks of September 11, 2001, Cushman & Wakefield has also partnered with Kroll to provide security consulting services.

EXECUTIVES

Chairman: John C. Cushman III, age 63
Vice Chairman: Charles R. Borrok
Vice Chairman: John M. Cefaly
Vice Chairman: Louis B. Cushman
Vice Chairman: August A. DiRenzo
Vice Chairman: Donald A. DiRenzo Sr.
Vice Chairman and Area Leader, Texas Region: Timothy D. (Tim) Relyea
Vice Chairman: Edward J. Weiss
President and CEO: Arthur J. Mirante II, age 87
President, US Operations: Bruce Mosler, age 46
EVP and CFO: Thomas P. Dowd
EVP International Operations: John B. Coppedge III
EVP Global Services and Retail Services: David M. Gialanella
EVP Brokerage: Mitchell L. Konsker
EVP Advisory Group: Christopher J. Lowery
EVP Asset Services: John C. Santora
EVP Industrial Brokerage: O. B. (Barney) Upton III
Executive Managing Director, Human Resources: Carolyn F. Sessa
Executive Managing Director and General Counsel: Kenneth P. Singleton
Senior Managing Director, Corporate Communications: Celine T. Clarke

LOCATIONS

HQ: Cushman & Wakefield, Inc.
 51 W. 52nd St., New York, NY 10019
Phone: 212-841-7500 **Fax:** 212-841-7767
Web: www.cushmanwakefield.com

PRODUCTS/OPERATIONS

Selected Projects

American Express Tower, New York (managing agent)
Bank of America, San Francisco (project consultant)
Centro Insurgentes, Mexico City (leasing agent)
Chrysler Building, New York (project management)
Citicorp Center, San Francisco (leasing & managing agent)
Georgia-Pacific, Atlanta (development consultant & later leasing & managing agent)
McGraw Hill, Ryder Court, London (lease negotiation)
Pan Am Building, New York (project management)
Sears Tower, Chicago (project consultant & leasing & managing agent)
World Bank, Washington, DC (strategic planning & advisory services)

COMPETITORS

CB Richard Ellis
Colliers International
Grubb & Ellis
Jones Lang LaSalle
Lend Lease
Trammell Crow Company

HISTORICAL FINANCIALS

Company Type: Private

Income Statement
FYE: December 31

	REVENUE ($ mil.)	NET INCOME ($ mil.)	NET PROFIT MARGIN	EMPLOYEES
12/03	800	—	—	11,000
12/02	750	—	—	11,000
12/01	720	—	—	11,000
12/00	850	—	—	11,500
12/99	700	—	—	9,500
12/98	600	—	—	7,700
12/97	400	—	—	5,500
Annual Growth	12.2%	—	—	12.2%

Revenue History

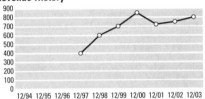

Dairy Farmers of America

Dairy Farmers of America (DFA) are partners in cream. DFA is now the world's largest dairy co-operative, with almost 23,000 members in 48 states. The co-op produces 33% of the US milk supply with an annual pool of about 57 billion pounds of milk. Along with fresh and shelf-stable fluid milk, the co-op also produces cheese, butter, and other products for industrial, wholesale, and retail customers worldwide. DFA is seeking strength in value-added products and joint ventures to distribute its milk and milk-based food ingredients to wider regions.

While DFA is a major supplier to the #1 US milk processor, Dean Foods, it also owns half of what will likely become the #2 US milk processor, National Dairy Holdings. DFA's American Dairy Brands makes and markets Borden cheeses, and its Formulated Dairy Food Products group bottles up Starbucks' Frappuccino coffee drink. In addition, the co-op provides marketing, research and development, and legislative lobbying on behalf of its members.

American dairy farmers have had to come to terms with consolidation in the retail industry, dissolving government milk price supports, and increased foreign competition. To better compete with other dairy processors and soften the swings of the commodity markets, DFA has invested heavily in facilities and joint ventures to process its fluid milk into value-added products and high-end dairy-based ingredients.

HISTORY

Mid-America Dairymen (Mid-Am), the largest of the cooperatives that merged to form Dairy Farmers of America (DFA), was born in 1968. At that time, several Midwestern dairy co-ops banded together to attack common economic problems, such as reduced government subsidies, price drops resulting from a rising milk surplus, dealer consolidation, and improvements in production, processing, and packaging. The merging organizations — representing 15,000 dairy farmers — were Producers Creamery Company (Springfield, Missouri), Sanitary Milk Producers (St. Louis), Square Deal Milk Producers (Highland, Illinois), Mid-Am (Kansas City, Missouri), and Producers Creamery Company of Chillicothe (north central Missouri).

During the early 1970s Mid-Am struggled with internal restructuring. Most dairy farmers and co-ops were hit hard by the energy crisis and the government's decision to allow increased dairy imports in 1973, the same year the US Justice Department filed an antitrust suit against Mid-Am. (A judge cleared the co-op 12 years later.)

In 1974 Mid-Am lost almost $8 million on revenues of $625 million, chalked up to record-high feed prices, a weakened economy, a milk surplus, and a massive inventory loss. Co-op veteran Gary Hanman was named CEO that year. Over the next two years, Mid-Am cut costs, sold corporate frills, downsized management, and began marketing more of its own products under the Mid-America Farms label, thus reducing dependency on commodity sales.

Mid-Am expanded its research and development efforts throughout the 1980s. The co-op opened its services to farmers in California and New Mexico in 1993, and a series of mergers in 1994 and 1995 nearly doubled its size. In 1997 it purchased some of Borden's dairy operations, including rights to the valuable Elsie the Cow and Borden's trademarks.

Wary of falling milk prices, Mid-Am merged with Western Dairymen Cooperative, Milk Marketing, and the Southern Region of Associated Milk Producers at the end of 1997 to form DFA. Hanman moved into the seat of CEO at the new co-op. DFA began a series of joint ventures with the #1 US dairy processor, Suiza Foods.

DFA added California Gold (more than 330 farmers, 1998) and Independent Cooperative Milk Producers Association (730 dairy farmer members in Michigan and parts of Ohio and Indiana, 1999). In another joint venture with Suiza, in early 2000 DFA sold its 50% stake in the US's #3 fluid milk processor, Southern Foods, in exchange for 34% of a new company named Suiza Dairy Group.

After mollifying the government's antitrust fears, DFA acquired the butter operations of Sodial North America in mid-2000. It then molded all its butter businesses into a new entity, Keller's Creamery, LLC. However, another acquisition did not fare as well. In February 2000 DFA acquired controlling interest in Southern Belle Dairy only to have the merger challenged three years later by the Department of Justice. Arguing that the merger formed a monopoly in school milk sales in several states, the Department of Justice filed suit which a federal judge later dismissed.

During 2001 the cooperative went in with Land O'Lakes 50/50 to purchase a cheese plant from Kraft. Later in the year as Suiza Foods acquired Dean Foods (and took on its name), DFA sold back its stake in Suiza Dairy Group to the new Dean Foods. DFA then teamed up with a group of dairy investors to form a new 50/50 joint venture, National Dairy Holdings, which received 11 processing plants from Dean Foods as part of the exchange for Suiza Dairy.

Weak milk prices and a drop in demand during 2002 caused DFA's revenues to slide. DFA has typically grown by inviting smaller dairy co-ops to merge with it, including the Black Hills Milk Producers Cooperative in 2002. However, to better secure milk sources for its customers in the northeastern US, that same year DFA welcomed two regional co-ops, Dairylea and St. Albans, to join as members. The two co-ops remain as separate but affiliated organizations.

EXECUTIVES

Chairman: Tom Camerlo
President and CEO: Gary E. Hanman
CFO: Gerald (Jerry) Bos
EVP: Don H. Schriver
SVP Southeast Area, Mideast Area, and Central Area; COO, Southeast Area: John I. Collins
SVP; COO, Southwest Area, Mountain Area: David C. Jones
Corporate VP, Human Resources & Administration: Harold Papen
Corporate VP, Marketing and Economic Analysis: John J. Wilson
Corporate VP and Legal Counsel: David A. Geisler
VP, Accounting & Information Systems: Joel Clark
VP, Communications and Public Relations: Agnes Schafer
VP; COO, Central Area: Randall S. (Randy) McGinnis
VP; COO, Mideast Area: James F. (Jim) Carroll
VP; COO, Western Area: David L. Parrish
COO, Northeast Area; CEO, Dairylea: Richard P. (Rick) Smith
President, American Dairy Brands; Corporate VP, DFA Dairy Food Products Group: Mark Korsmeyer
President, Dairy Food Products: Sam E. McCroskey
Auditors: Deloitte & Touche LLP

LOCATIONS

HQ: Dairy Farmers of America, Inc.
10220 N. Ambassador Dr., Kansas City, MO 64153
Phone: 816-801-6455   **Fax:** 816-801-6456
Web: www.dfamilk.com

Dairy Farmers of America includes almost 23,000 members from 48 states.

PRODUCTS/OPERATIONS

Selected Products

Butter (Breakstone's, Hotel Bar, Keller's, Plugra)
Cheese dips
Cheeses (Borden)
Coffee creamer
Condensed milk
Cream
Dehydrated dairy products
Infant formula
Nonfat dry milk powder
Shelf-stable nutritional beverages (Sport Shake)
Whey products

COMPETITORS

AMPI
Arla Foods
California Dairies Inc.
Dean Foods
Fonterra
Foremost Farms
Glanbia
Kraft Foods North America
Lactalis
Land O'Lakes
Northwest Dairy
Parmalat
Prairie Farms Dairy
Quality Chekd
Saputo
Schreiber Foods
Unilever
WestFarm Foods

HISTORICAL FINANCIALS
Company Type: Cooperative

Income Statement			FYE: December 31
	REVENUE ($ mil.)	NET INCOME ($ mil.)	NET PROFIT MARGIN	EMPLOYEES
12/03	6,933	56	0.8%	4,000
12/02	6,448	50	0.8%	4,000
12/01	7,902	62	0.8%	4,000
12/00	6,586	39	0.6%	4,000
12/99	7,483	43	0.6%	5,000
12/98	7,284	70	1.0%	5,300
12/97	3,818	26	0.7%	5,300
12/96	4,085	17	0.4%	3,200
12/95	3,681	14	0.4%	3,100
12/94	2,491	12	0.5%	3,000
Annual Growth	12.0%	18.6%	—	3.2%

Net Income History

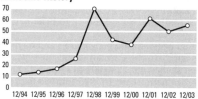

Dairylea

Yes, the farmer takes a wife, then hi-ho, the dairy-o, the farmer takes membership in milk marketing organizations such as Dairylea Cooperative. Owned by more than 2,500 dairy farmers in the northeastern US, Dairylea markets 5.5 billion pounds of milk for its farmers annually to food manufacturers. Its Agri-Services holding company provides members with financial and farm management services as well as insurance. Its Empire Livestock unit operates a livestock auction market. Dairylea, the largest milk marketer in the Northeast, has a joint marketing venture with Dairy Farmers of America.

EXECUTIVES
Chairman and President: Clyde E. Rutherford
CEO: Richard P. (Rick) Smith
COO: Greg Wickham
VP, Finance and Administration: Edward Bangel
VP of Finance: Ellen Gall
Secretary: William Beeman
Treasurer: David R. Chamberlain
Director of Communications: Monica Coleman

LOCATIONS
HQ: Dairylea Cooperative Inc.
  5001 Brittonfield Pkwy., East Syracuse, NY 13057
Phone: 315-433-0100 **Fax:** 315-433-2345
Web: www.dairylea.com

COMPETITORS
Agri-Mark
Dairy Farmers of America
Land O'Lakes

HISTORICAL FINANCIALS
Company Type: Cooperative

Income Statement			FYE: March 31
	REVENUE ($ mil.)	NET INCOME ($ mil.)	NET PROFIT MARGIN	EMPLOYEES
3/04	963	1	0.1%	115
3/03	852	1	0.1%	115
3/02	941	1	0.1%	115
3/01	803	1	0.1%	107
3/00	812	—	—	205
3/99	881	—	—	250
3/98	750	—	—	200
3/97	699	—	—	150
3/96	594	—	—	80
Annual Growth	6.2%	3.6%	—	4.6%

Net Income History

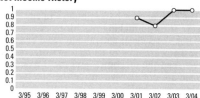

D&H Distributing

D&H could stand for Distributing and How! D&H Distributing sells more than 10,000 computer and electronics products to resellers nationwide. Clients include small to large resellers and retailers, system builders, and college bookstores. D&H also targets local, state, and federal government agencies. Its six divisions include computer products, home entertainment, security, educational resources, government services, and video gaming. Suppliers include Hewlett-Packard, Intel, and Microsoft. Founded in 1918 as a tire retreader, the company entered the electronics business in 1926. D&H has been employee-owned since 1999.

EXECUTIVES
Chairman and CEO: Israel (Izzy) Schwab
President: Gary Brothers
EVP and Treasurer: James F. (Jimmy) Schwab
VP, Sales: Jeff Davis
VP and Controller: Robert J. Miller Jr.
VP, Marketing: Daniel (Dan) Schwab
VP, Purchasing: Michael (Mike) Schwab
Director, Government Services Division: Anne Brennan
Director, Credit and Financial Services: Joe Chaudoin
Director, Inside Sales: Pat Donavan
Director, Purchasing: Rob Eby
Manager, Home Entertainment and Security Products Division: Jeff Stevenson
Manager, National VAR Sales and Systems: Art Steinberg

LOCATIONS
HQ: D&H Distributing Co., Inc.
  2525 N. 7th St., Harrisburg, PA 17110
Phone: 717-236-8001 **Fax:** 717-255-7838
Web: www.dandh.com

D&H Distributing has offices in California, Florida, Illinois, Massachusetts, Pennsylvania, and Texas.

PRODUCTS/OPERATIONS
Divisions
Computer Products
Educational
Government Services
Home Entertainment
Security Products

COMPETITORS
Agilysys
Arrow Electronics
ASI Corp.
Avnet
Elcom International
Ingram Micro
Manchester Technologies
Merisel
New Age Electronics
Sayers Group
SED International
Sirius Computer Solutions
Solarcom
Supercom
Tech Data
ZT Group

HISTORICAL FINANCIALS
Company Type: Private

Income Statement			FYE: April 30
	ESTIMATED REVENUE ($ mil.)	NET INCOME ($ mil.)	NET PROFIT MARGIN	EMPLOYEES
4/04	1,070	—	—	618
4/03	857	—	—	550
4/02	760	—	—	—
4/01	637	—	—	—
4/00	643	—	—	400
4/99	620	—	—	400
4/98	600	—	—	360
4/97	550	—	—	400
4/96	490	—	—	400
4/95	430	—	—	375
Annual Growth	10.7%	—	—	5.7%

Revenue History

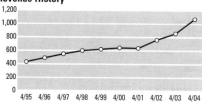

Darcars

Buying a new vehicle in the Washington, DC, area can expose you to the Darcars side of human nature. Darcars Automotive Group, an automobile dealership holding company, has about 30 automobile dealerships in Maryland and Virginia. Its dealerships sell a variety of new and used automobiles, including cars made by DaimlerChrysler, Ford Motor, General Motors, Kia Motors, Mitsubishi, Toyota, Volkswagen, and Volvo. Darcars offers a full range of automotive services, including parts and service departments and car body repair. Darcars Automotive Group was founded in 1977 by John Darvish, whose family still owns and runs the company.

EXECUTIVES

Chairman: John R. Darvish, age 63
CFO: Michael Hancheruk
VP; General Manager, Darcars Toyota: Tammy Darvish, age 38
Finance Director: Mike Quinn
Personnel Director: Sam Bruner

LOCATIONS

HQ: Darcars Automotive Group
    12210 Cherry Hill Rd., Silver Spring, MD 20904
Phone: 301-622-0300   **Fax:** 301-622-4915
Web: www.darcars.com

COMPETITORS

Atlantic Automotive	Ourisman Automotive
AutoNation	Pohanka Automotive
Brown Automotive	Rosenthal Automotive
CarMax	Sheehy Auto
Jim Koons Automotive	Sonic Automotive

HISTORICAL FINANCIALS

Company Type: Private

Income Statement   FYE: December 31

	REVENUE ($ mil.)	NET INCOME ($ mil.)	NET PROFIT MARGIN	EMPLOYEES
12/03	1,070	—	—	1,800
12/02	813	—	—	1,800
12/01	845	—	—	1,800
12/00	783	—	—	1,700
12/99	732	—	—	1,600
12/98	592	—	—	1,500
12/97	546	—	—	1,521
12/96	521	—	—	1,612
12/95	491	—	—	1,245
12/94	446	—	—	1,000
Annual Growth	10.2%			6.7%

Revenue History

Dart Container

Dart Container is a world cup winner — maybe not in soccer, but it is the world's top maker of foam cups and containers, with about half of the global market in cups. The company uses a secret method of molding expandable polystyrene to make its products, which include cups, lids, dinnerware, and cutlery for customers such as hospitals, schools, and restaurants. To cut costs, Dart Container builds its own molding machinery and operates its own distribution trucks. The firm sells its recycled polystyrene to companies that make such items as insulation material and egg cartons. Although often embroiled in litigation, the Dart family continues to own the company.

In terms of Dart's products, the company is moving into foam lid and plastic containers for industrial or retail use.

The company runs four polystyrene-recycling plants and operates in the US and through subsidiaries in Argentina, Australia, Canada, Mexico, and the UK.

The king of cups has a simple strategy — secrecy. The cup-making machine developed by the Darts was never patented to avoid revealing how it works. Most of its factory workers have never seen the machines, and the firm's salespeople are not allowed inside the plants. After years of legal battles, the Darts have reached an agreement regarding alleged discrepancies in the family inheritance. The terms of the settlement are, naturally, secret.

In 2003 Ken Dart added to the family fortune, winning a $700 million lawsuit against Argentina in a dispute over the country's decision to default on its bonds in 1991.

HISTORY

William F. Dart founded a Michigan firm to make steel tape measures in 1937. Dart's son William A. started experimenting with plastics in 1953, and in the late 1950s the two devised a cheap way to mold expandable polystyrene and built a cup-making machine. Dart Container was incorporated in Mason, Michigan, in 1960 and shipped its first cups that year. By the late 1960s the rising demand for plastic-foam products sparked an increase in R&D. In 1970 the company built a plant in Corona, California.

It was a family feud in the making in 1974, as William F. divided the business among his grandsons — Tom, Ken, and Robert — in separate trusts that named William A. trustee for all. Tom branched out in 1975 and founded oil and gas company Dart Energy, which was later absorbed into Dart Container. William F. died the next year. Following the oil market crash of the early 1980s, Tom went through a sticky divorce and admitted to cocaine abuse. His father temporarily removed him as head of Dart Energy in 1982, and the next year the entire family underwent group psychiatric counseling.

The family reorganized its assets in 1986, giving Ken and Robert the cup business and Tom the energy business plus $58 million in cash. In 1987 Ken began to swell the family fortune with a series of successful investments. Better tax rates motivated Dart family members to move to Sarasota, Florida, in 1989. They set up shop in an unmarked building behind a sporting-goods store. By the late 1980s Dart Container commanded more than 50% of the worldwide market for foam cups.

In 1990 the company paid $250,000 to settle a factory worker's minority discrimination lawsuit. The next year Ken bought 11% of the Federal Home Loan Mortgage Corp. (Freddie Mac), as well as portions of Salomon and Brazil's foreign debt. According to Tom, that year Ken also financed brain research in hopes of finding a way to keep his brain alive after the death of his body in an attempt to avoid future estate taxes.

Tom sued his brothers and father in 1992 for allegedly cheating him out of millions in trust money in the 1986 reorganization. Ken turned a $300 million investment into $1 billion by selling the Freddie Mac shares. The next year he and Robert renounced their US citizenship to avoid paying taxes. Ken also made a failed attempt to block the restructuring of Brazil's debt (of which Dart owned 4%). That year Ken's new $1 million Sarasota home was firebombed (the case remains unsolved), and Robert moved to Britain, where he soon filed for divorce.

Ken began hiring bodyguards, and he moved his family to the Cayman Islands in 1994. Dart then shelled out $230,000 to settle yet another discrimination case. In 1995 Tom was fired from Dart Energy, and Ken tried — and failed — to return to the US as a diplomat of Belize. In 1996 Tom accused Judge Donald Owens of being biased in favor of William A. The judge succumbed to the pressure in 1997 and removed himself from the proceedings, only to be ordered back on the case by Michigan's Court of Appeals. The lawsuit was settled in 1998 before going to trial, but the terms were kept secret.

The following year saw yet another series of lawsuits for the container company. In 1999 Dart Container filed an appeal to an IRS demand to pay $31 million in back taxes from 1994 and late penalties. The legal wrangling continued through 2001, but in 2002 the company agreed to pay $26 million to settle the issue. Meanwhile, the company has expanded their foam lid and container products for wholesale industrial or retail use.

EXECUTIVES

Chairman: William Dart
CEO: Kenneth B. Dart
President: Robert C. Dart
CFO and Treasurer: William (Bill) Myers
VP and COO: George Jenkins
VP, Administration and General Counsel: Jim Lammers
VP, Manufacturing: Dan Calkins
VP, Manufacturing: John M. Murray
VP, Technology: Ralph MacKenzie
Director, Human Resources: Mark Franks

LOCATIONS

HQ: Dart Container Corporation
    500 Hogsback Rd., Mason, MI 48854
Phone: 517-676-3800   **Fax:** 517-676-3883
Web: www.dartcontainer.com

Dart Container has four recycling centers in Canada and the US, and manufacturing operations in Argentina, Australia, Canada, Mexico, the UK, and the US.

PRODUCTS/OPERATIONS

Selected Products
Clear containers
Container lids
Deli containers and lids
Dinnerware
Foam cups
Hinged containers
Paper cups and lids
Plastic cups and lids
Plastic cutlery

Selected Services
CARE (Cups Are REcyclable) Program (provides densifier to larger customers to compact their polystyrene, which Dart then picks up)
Foam-Recycling (four plants in Canada, Florida, Michigan, and Pennsylvania and a drop-off site in Georgia)
Recycla-Pak (provides small-volume businesses with cup-shipping containers that double as recycling bins)

COMPETITORS

Berry Plastics
Huhtamäki
NOVA Chemicals
Radnor Holdings
Smurfit-Stone Container
Sonoco Products
Sweetheart
Temple-Inland

HISTORICAL FINANCIALS
Company Type: Private

Income Statement
FYE: December 31

	ESTIMATED REVENUE ($ mil.)	NET INCOME ($ mil.)	NET PROFIT MARGIN	EMPLOYEES
12/02	1,100	—	—	4,950
12/01	1,170	—	—	5,000
12/00	1,200	—	—	5,000
12/99	1,100	—	—	5,000
12/98	1,150	—	—	5,000
12/97	1,000	—	—	5,000
12/96	1,000	—	—	4,300
12/95	1,000	—	—	4,300
12/94	800	—	—	3,600
12/93	600	—	—	3,750
Annual Growth	7.0%	—	—	3.1%

Revenue History
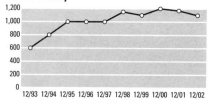

David McDavid Auto Group

David McDavid Auto Group sells plenty of horsepower in the Lone Star State. The company, a part of Asbury Automotive Group, is one of the largest vehicle vendors in Texas, with about a dozen dealerships in Austin, Houston, and the Dallas area. David McDavid Auto Group sells new cars made by Acura, Ford, General Motors, Honda, Kia, and Nissan. It also sells used cars and provides parts and service. The company was originally named for its founder and former CEO, David McDavid, who started his first car dealership in 1962 at age 19; he is a former minority owner of the Dallas Mavericks basketball team. McDavid sold 70% of the company to Asbury in 1998.

EXECUTIVES
President and CEO: Thomas G. McCollum, age 48
CFO: Jay Torda
Human Resources Director: Kelly Atkinson

LOCATIONS
HQ: David McDavid Auto Group
3600 W. Airport Fwy., Irving, TX 75062
Phone: 972-790-6100 **Fax:** 972-986-5689
Web: www.mcdavid.com

COMPETITORS
Allen Samuels Enterprises
Ancira
AutoNation
CarMax
CarsDirect.com
Don Davis Auto Group
Gillman
Group 1 Automotive
Gulf States Toyota
Gunn Automotive
Huffines Automotive Dealerships
McCombs Enterprises
Red McCombs Automotive Group
Sonic Automotive
VT Inc.

HISTORICAL FINANCIALS
Company Type: Private

Income Statement
FYE: December 31

	REVENUE ($ mil.)	NET INCOME ($ mil.)	NET PROFIT MARGIN	EMPLOYEES
12/02	600	—	—	1,100
12/01	700	—	—	1,200
12/00	596	—	—	1,100
12/99	575	—	—	1,050
12/98	550	—	—	1,000
12/97	542	—	—	1,000
12/96	512	—	—	930
12/95	500	—	—	928
12/94	420	—	—	870
Annual Growth	4.6%	—	—	3.0%

Revenue History
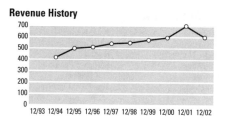

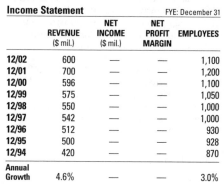

David Weekley Homes

A development home developed to *your* taste? David Weekley Homes will do it. Founded in 1976, it is the second-largest privately owned homebuilder in the US, annually building around 3,500 single-family detached homes that range in size from about 1,500 sq. ft. to more than 4,000 sq. ft. Weekley builds homes from hundreds of floor plans and offers custom upgrades. Prices range from $120,000 to about $650,000. The company builds in its own planned communities in Texas, Colorado, and in the Southeast, as well as on buyers' lots. For the past three years, it has been listed among the "Top 100 Companies to Work for in America" in *FORTUNE* magazine. Founder and chairman David Weekley owns the firm.

EXECUTIVES
Chairman and CEO: David M. Weekley, age 50
President and COO: John Johnson
CFO: Jim Alexander
CIO: Heather Humphrey
VP Design: Bob Rhode
VP Human Resources: Michael (Mike) Brezina
VP Marketing: Natalie Harris
VP Operations: Mike Humphrey
VP Supply Chain: Bill Justus
Communications Coordinator: Cindy Haynes
Communications Coordinator: Alyssa Parrish
Auditors: Ernst & Young LLP

LOCATIONS
HQ: David Weekley Homes
1111 N. Post Oak Rd., Houston, TX 77055
Phone: 713-963-0500 **Fax:** 713-963-0322
Web: www.davidweekleyhomes.com

Markets Served
Atlanta
Austin, TX
Charleston, SC
Charlotte, NC
Dallas/Fort Worth
Denver
Fort Myers, FL
Houston
Jacksonville
Nashville, TN
Orlando, FL
Raleigh, NC
San Antonio
Tampa

David Wilson's Automotive

First Orange County, then the world — or at least Arizona. David Wilson's Automotive Group has its roots in Orange County, California. In 1985 owner David Wilson bought Toyota of Orange, the first of his 12 dealerships, which are all located in California and Arizona and sell Acura, Ford, and Honda cars as well as Toyotas and Lexuses. David Wilson's Automotive Group didn't expand eastward until 1998 when it opened a Honda dealership in Scottsdale, Arizona. The company then added a Toyota location in Arizona in 1999. The dealerships run by David Wilson's Automotive Group also offer parts and service departments; some offer fleet services.

EXECUTIVES
Chairman and CEO: David Wilson
President: Randy Rooney
CFO: Ted Tomasek
EVP: Craig Whetter
VP Human Resources: Vicki Murphy

COMPETITORS
Centex	Pulte Homes
D.R. Horton	Rottlund
Engle Homes	Ryland
KB Home	Standard Pacific
Lennar	Toll Brothers
M/I Homes	Town and Country Homes
NVR	

HISTORICAL FINANCIALS
Company Type: Private

Income Statement — FYE: December 31

	REVENUE ($ mil.)	NET INCOME ($ mil.)	NET PROFIT MARGIN	EMPLOYEES
12/03	948	—	—	1,041
12/02	855	—	—	1,037
12/01	937	—	—	1,037
12/00	828	—	—	1,010
12/99	711	—	—	900
12/98	608	—	—	820
12/97	503	—	—	790
12/96	474	—	—	638
12/95	427	—	—	600
12/94	428	—	—	600
Annual Growth	9.2%	—	—	6.3%

Revenue History

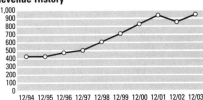

Davis Polk

Founded in 1849, Davis Polk & Wardwell is one of the oldest law firms in the US. Having built a notable corporate practice early on, it helped J. P. Morgan (now J.P. Morgan Chase) form General Electric. With some 650 lawyers, the firm is known for its skill in litigation, securities, and mergers and acquisitions; other practice areas include real estate, tax, and technology. Davis Polk serves such high-profile clients as AT&T (it was involved in the record-breaking stock offering of AT&T's wireless unit in 2000), Comcast, General Motors, RJR Nabisco, and Philip Morris. In addition, more than one-third of the firm's clients are non-US companies or governments. Davis Polk has nine offices in seven countries.

EXECUTIVES
Managing Partner: John R. Ettinger
Director Recruiting: Bonnie Hurry
Business Development Administrator: Kevin Cavanaugh

LOCATIONS
HQ: David Wilson's Automotive Group
1400 N. Tustin, Orange, CA 92867
Phone: 714-639-6750 **Fax:** 714-771-0363
Web: www.preownedautosuperstore.com

COMPETITORS
AutoNation	Penske Automotive
Holman Enterprises	Prospect Motors
Marty Franich	Tuttle-Click

HISTORICAL FINANCIALS
Company Type: Private

Income Statement — FYE: December 31

	REVENUE ($ mil.)	NET INCOME ($ mil.)	NET PROFIT MARGIN	EMPLOYEES
12/03	1,336	—	—	500
12/02	1,094	—	—	450
12/01	1,073	—	—	450
12/00	1,033	—	—	450
12/99	395	—	—	420
12/98	391	—	—	413
12/97	409	—	—	500
12/96	388	—	—	472
12/95	296	—	—	393
12/94	262	—	—	—
Annual Growth	19.8%	—	—	3.1%

Revenue History

LOCATIONS
HQ: Davis Polk & Wardwell
450 Lexington Ave., New York, NY 10017
Phone: 212-450-4000 **Fax:** 212-450-3800
Web: www.dpw.com

Davis Polk & Wardwell has US offices in Menlo Park, California; New York City; and Washington, DC. It has international offices in Frankfurt, Hong Kong, London, Madrid, Paris, and Tokyo.

PRODUCTS/OPERATIONS
Selected Practice Areas
Antitrust
Corporate
Employment
Estate planning
Mergers and acquisitions
Real estate
Securities
Tax
Technology
White-collar crime

COMPETITORS
Baker & McKenzie	Kelley Drye
Cleary, Gottlieb	Proskauer Rose
Coudert Brothers	Simpson Thacher
Cravath, Swaine	Skadden, Arps
Debevoise & Plimpton	Sullivan & Cromwell
Dewey Ballantine	Wachtell, Lipton
Hughes Hubbard	

HISTORICAL FINANCIALS
Company Type: Partnership

Income Statement — FYE: December 31

	REVENUE ($ mil.)	NET INCOME ($ mil.)	NET PROFIT MARGIN	EMPLOYEES
12/03	587	—	—	—
12/02	570	—	—	—
12/01	570	—	—	—
12/00	525	—	—	—
12/99	460	—	—	1,400
12/98	435	—	—	1,400
12/97	390	—	—	1,360
12/96	346	—	—	—
12/95	282	—	—	—
12/94	254	—	—	—
Annual Growth	9.8%	—	—	1.5%

Revenue History

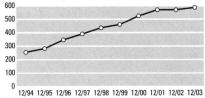

Dawn Food Products

A muffin at Starbucks, a cookie from Mrs. Fields, or a doughnut from Krispy Kreme — all just another day in the kitchen for Dawn Food Products. The company provides pre-baked and fully baked products — as well as bases, equipment, fillings, frozen dough, icings, ingredients, and mixes — to the food industry. Its customers include food service companies, institutional bakeries, restaurants, retail outlets, and supermarkets. Dawn Food Products also offers support services such as merchandising and marketing. In 2004 it acquired the bakery business of Bunge North America. Owned by the Jones family, Dawn Food Products has operations throughout the US and in 13 other countries.

EXECUTIVES

Chairman, President, and CEO: Ronald L. (Ron) Jones
CFO: Jerry Baglieon
EVP; Director of Research and Development and Director: Miles E. Jones
VP, Distribution Services and Sales: Erik Riswick
VP, Europe: Dave Kowal
VP, Operations: Rick Dahlin
President, Dawn Foods North America and Director: John C. Nally
President, Dawn International and Director: Carrie L. Barber
Controller: David Hawkins
Manager, HR: William (Bill) Lambkin

LOCATIONS

HQ: Dawn Food Products, Inc.
2021 Micor Dr., Jackson, MI 49203
Phone: 517-789-4400 **Fax:** 517-789-4465
Web: www.dawnfoods.com

COMPETITORS

Bridgford Foods
Flowers Foods
General Mills
George Weston
Gonnella Baking
International Multifoods
Interstate Bakeries
Maple Leaf Foods
Otis Spunkmeyer
Rich Products
Sara Lee Bakery Group

HISTORICAL FINANCIALS
Company Type: Private

Income Statement
FYE: December 31

	REVENUE ($ mil.)	NET INCOME ($ mil.)	NET PROFIT MARGIN	EMPLOYEES
12/02	750	—	—	2,800
12/01	655	—	—	2,100
12/00	650	—	—	2,100
12/99	649	—	—	2,101
12/98	603	—	—	2,150
Annual Growth	5.6%	—	—	6.8%

Revenue History

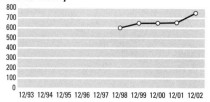

Day & Zimmermann

The Day & Zimmermann Group offers services as distinct as day and night. The company provides engineering and construction, security, munitions products and services, and technical and administrative staffing services worldwide. Day & Zimmermann provides government operations and maintenance services to US and foreign governments and commercial customers. The group has sold three divisions (transportation construction, infrastructure, and public buildings) to integrate its operations and focus on its strategic businesses, particularly technical staffing unit H. L. Yoh Company (Yoh Co.). Founded in 1901, Day & Zimmermann is owned and managed by the Yoh family, which has headed the firm for three generations.

EXECUTIVES

Chairman and CEO: Harold L. (Hal) Yoh III, age 43
VP Finance and CFO: Joseph W. (Joe) Ritzel
EVP Commercial Operations: Joseph J. Ucciferro
SVP Administration: William R. (Bill) Hamm
VP and Executive Committee Member: John Dabek
VP and CIO: Anthony J. Bosco Jr.
VP and Group Controller: Joseph E. McKinney
VP Corporate Marketing and Communications: Sharon Gosdeck
VP Human Resources: Belen J. Acosta
President, Day & Zimmermann Services: Larry Ames
President, H.L. Yoh Company: Lawrence M. Suwak
President and CEO, Yoh Group: William C. (Bill) Yoh
Auditors: Deloitte & Touche

LOCATIONS

HQ: The Day & Zimmermann Group, Inc.
1818 Market St., Fl. 22, Philadelphia, PA 19103
Phone: 215-299-8000 **Fax:** 215-299-8030
Web: www.dayzim.com

The Day & Zimmermann Group operates from more than 150 locations worldwide.

COMPETITORS

Adecco
Alliant Techsystems
AMEC
Bechtel
CDI
Fluor
Foster Wheeler
Halliburton
Jacobs Engineering
Johnson Controls
Louis Berger
Manpower
McCarthy Building
McDermott
Parsons
Peter Kiewit Sons'
URS
Washington Group
WS Atkins

HISTORICAL FINANCIALS
Company Type: Private

Income Statement
FYE: December 31

	REVENUE ($ mil.)	NET INCOME ($ mil.)	NET PROFIT MARGIN	EMPLOYEES
12/03	1,300	—	—	20,000
12/02	1,351	—	—	21,000
12/01	1,300	—	—	20,000
12/00	1,554	—	—	26,000
12/99	1,650	—	—	24,000
12/98	1,080	—	—	16,500
12/97	995	—	—	15,000
12/96	812	—	—	14,000
12/95	766	—	—	13,800
12/94	706	—	—	12,000
Annual Growth	7.0%	—	—	5.8%

Revenue History

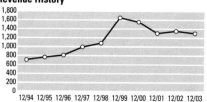

DeBartolo Corporation

Real estate holdings, gambling, horse racing, a felony conviction, and warring siblings surrounded by a storied NFL franchise — sounds like an old episode of *Dallas*. But the story of The DeBartolo Corporation takes place in Youngstown, Ohio (where the company is based), via San Francisco (where the company owns the 49ers football team). The company also provides management services to the Louisiana Downs racetrack in Bossier City. The firm's other interests include a software firm in Tennessee and a few health care companies in Oklahoma and Pennsylvania. DeBartolo Corp. is also trying to bring an Arena Football League team to San Francisco.

The saga of the DeBartolo family concerns chairman Denise DeBartolo York and her brother, former CEO Eddie DeBartolo Jr., children of the company's founder. Eddie's guilty plea to charges of failing to report a felony led to his ouster and a lawsuit from his sister to recover a $94 million debt he owed the company. Eddie countersued, and after much wrangling, the siblings reached an agreement whereby Denise took the company name, the 49ers, and the racetrack (which it later sold but still operates), and Eddie received real estate and the firm's minority stake in Simon Property Group, one of North America's largest public real estate companies.

HISTORY

Edward J. DeBartolo left his stepfather's paving business in 1944 and established the eponymous Edward J. DeBartolo Corporation. DeBartolo's foresight about the growth of the suburbs led him to build one of the first strip-style malls outside California, the Belmont Plaza, near Youngstown, Ohio, in 1949. Over the next 15 years, the company built 45 more strip centers throughout the US. In the 1960s DeBartolo became one of the first to develop large, covered regional malls in many parts of the nation. DeBartolo opened the Louisiana Downs racetrack in 1974 and moved the company into the sports business in 1977 when he helped his son, Edward Jr. (Eddie), buy the San Francisco 49ers.

When the management of Allied Stores asked DeBartolo to help fend off a bid by real estate developer Robert Campeau, DeBartolo thought that control of Allied's department store chains would provide anchor stores for his mall developments and loaned Campeau $150 million for the takeover instead. Two years later DeBartolo borrowed $480 million and lent it to Campeau for his acquisition of Federated Department Stores.

The company reached its zenith in the late 1980s (opening the Rivercenter in San Antonio and Lakeland Square in Florida), but Campeau was in trouble — the highly leveraged Allied and Federated went bankrupt and threatened to take DeBartolo with them. As part of the bankruptcy settlement, DeBartolo took a 60% interest in California-based Ralphs supermarket (since sold) and started selling off assets in 1991 to cover the loan he made to Campeau and the company's own $4 billion debt. The fire sale included his private jet, three malls, two office buildings, a 50% stake in Higbee's department stores, and the Rivercenter.

Edward died in 1994. His daughter, Denise DeBartolo York, became chairman, and his son, Eddie (who was also chairman and CEO of the 49ers) became president and CEO. Eddie reshuffled the company's assets with most of its real estate holdings turned into DeBartolo Realty, a real estate investment trust that went public that year, raising $575 million. Mounting tensions between the siblings intensified in 1995 when Eddie formed DeBartolo Entertainment, his own separate company in the gaming business (Denise tried to distance the family business from Eddie's new company in a press release). DeBartolo Realty merged with Simon Property Group the following year.

Eddie ran into trouble in 1997 when an investigation revealed that he had paid former Louisiana governor Edwin Edwards $400,000 in an effort to obtain a riverboat gambling license for DeBartolo Entertainment. (Before the gambling fraud probe became public, San Francisco voters approved a $100 million bond issue to help finance a $525 million stadium/shopping mall for the 49ers. Those plans were put on ice.) Eddie pleaded guilty to felony charges of concealing wrongdoing the next year, was fined $2 million, and stepped down from DeBartolo Corp. (His later testimony against Gov. Edwards helped lead to the government official's conviction on extortion charges.) The NFL then fined Eddie another $1 million and banned him from the 49ers in 1999. Later that year Denise sued Eddie for debt owed to the company and he countersued. DeBartolo Corp. also sold two of its racetracks (Thistledown and Remington Park).

In 2001 the DeBartolos completed the division of the company's assets between them. DeBartolo York also shortened the company's name to The DeBartolo Corporation.

EXECUTIVES

Chairman: Marie Denise DeBartolo York, age 53
President: John C. York II
President and CEO, San Francisco 49ers: Peter L. Harris, age 60
General Manager, San Francisco 49ers: Terry Donahue, age 60
Head Coach, San Francisco 49ers: Dennis Erickson, age 57

LOCATIONS

HQ: The DeBartolo Corporation
 7620 Market St., Youngstown, OH 44512
Phone: 330-965-2000 **Fax:** 330-965-2077
Web: http://www.49ers.com/team/office.asp

The DeBartolo Corporation has operations in California, Louisiana, Ohio, Oklahoma, Pennsylvania, and Tennessee.

COMPETITORS

Golden State Warriors
Harrah's Entertainment
Oakland Raiders
San Jose Sharks

HISTORICAL FINANCIALS

Company Type: Private

Income Statement — FYE: June 30

	ESTIMATED REVENUE ($ mil.)	NET INCOME ($ mil.)	NET PROFIT MARGIN	EMPLOYEES
6/01*	250	—	—	4,000
6/00	250	—	—	4,000
6/99	254	—	—	4,000
6/98	250	—	—	4,000
6/97	250	—	—	3,000
6/96	220	—	—	3,000
6/95	230	—	—	3,000
6/94	550	—	—	3,800
Annual Growth	(10.7%)	—	—	0.7%

*Most recent year available

Revenue History

DeBruce Grain

Got a few tons of wheat and no place to keep it? DeBruce Grain stores, handles, and sells grain and fertilizer for the agribusiness industry. The company runs 10 grain-handling facilities, 13 grain elevators (with a storage capacity of 60 million bushels), a fertilizer distribution terminal, and seven retail fertilizer operations in five states, as well as an office in Mexico, which serves its international customers. The company also markets both wholesale and retail fertilizer. DeBruce paid a $685,000 fine in relation to the 1998 explosion, which killed seven workers, of its Haysville, Kansas, facility — the largest grain elevator in the world. Owner and CEO Paul DeBruce founded the company in 1978.

EXECUTIVES

CEO: Paul DeBruce
President: Larry Kittoe
CFO: Curt Heinz

LOCATIONS

HQ: DeBruce Grain, Inc.
 4100 N. Mulberry Dr., Kansas City, MO 64116
Phone: 816-421-8182 **Fax:** 816-584-2350
Web: www.debruce.com

PRODUCTS/OPERATIONS

Company Divisons
DeBruce Fertilizer Inc.
DeBruce Grain Inc.
DeBruce Transportation Inc.

COMPETITORS

ADM	Cargill
Ag Processing	CHS
Bartlett and Company	ConAgra
Bunge Limited	Scoular

HISTORICAL FINANCIALS

Company Type: Private

Income Statement — FYE: March 31

	REVENUE ($ mil.)	NET INCOME ($ mil.)	NET PROFIT MARGIN	EMPLOYEES
3/04	2,018	—	—	420
3/03	1,729	—	—	420
3/02	1,378	—	—	400
3/01	1,201	—	—	330
3/00	879	—	—	300
3/99	772	—	—	250
3/98	723	—	—	200
3/97	865	—	—	200
3/96	688	—	—	150
3/95	507	—	—	130
Annual Growth	16.6%	—	—	13.9%

Revenue History

Delaware North

When it comes to corn dogs and nachos, Delaware North makes a lot of concessions. A giant in the food concession industry, the firm has a string of subsidiaries ready to make hungry folks happy. Among the company's holdings are Sportservice (food service at sports stadiums), CA One Services (airport food service), and Delaware North Parks Services (visitor services for national parks and tourist attractions). It also operates Boston's FleetCenter, owns a handful of pari-mutuel racetracks nationwide, and a steamboat firm. Delaware North was founded in 1915 by brothers Charles, Louis, and Marvin Jacobs. The Jacobs family (including CEO Jeremy Jacobs, owner of the NHL's Boston Bruins) still controls the company.

EXECUTIVES

Chairman and CEO: Jeremy M. Jacobs Sr.
Vice Chairman: Richard T. Stephens
President and COO: Charles E. (Chuck) Moran Jr.
EVP; Chairman, Sportservice Corporation: Jeremy Jacobs Jr.
EVP: Louis M. (Lou) Jacobs
CFO: Karen L. Kemp
VP and Controller: Bruce W. Carlson
VP, Corporate Communications and Public Relations: Wendy A. Watkins
VP, Finance and Treasurer: Ellen Ott
VP, General Counsel, and Secretary: Bryan J. Keller
VP, Human Resources: Eileen Morgan
Group President, Contract Services: John Fernbach
Group President, Hospitality and Entertainment: Dennis J. Szefel, age 57

LOCATIONS

HQ: Delaware North Companies, Inc.
40 Fountain Plaza, Buffalo, NY 14202
Phone: 716-858-5000   **Fax:** 716-858-5479
Web: www.delawarenorth.com

Delaware North has operations in Canada, Europe, the Pacific Rim, and the US.

PRODUCTS/OPERATIONS

Selected Operations
American Park 'n Swap (open air markets)
Boston Bruins (pro hockey team)
CA One Services (airport food service operator)
Delaware North Parks Services (visitor services for national parks, state parks, and tourist attractions)
FleetCenter (venue operation)
Sportservice (sports stadium food service)
Sportsystems (pari-mutuel facility operator)
The Delta Queen Steamboat Company (paddlewheel boat trips)

Selected Customers
Boston Celtics
Chicago White Sox
Colonial Stadium (Melbourne)
Grand Canyon
John F. Kennedy International Airport
Kennedy Space Center
Melbourne Zoo
St. Louis Cardinals
Sydney Entertainment Center
Texas Rangers
Yosemite National Park

COMPETITORS

ARAMARK
Compass Group
Creative Host Services
HMSHost
Levy Restaurants
Sodexho
Sodexho Alliance
Volume Services America

HISTORICAL FINANCIALS
Company Type: Private

Income Statement
FYE: December 31

	REVENUE ($ mil.)	NET INCOME ($ mil.)	NET PROFIT MARGIN	EMPLOYEES
12/03	1,600	—	—	28,000
12/02	1,600	—	—	28,000
12/01	1,600	—	—	25,000
12/00	1,500	—	—	25,000
12/99	1,400	—	—	25,000
12/98	1,224	—	—	25,000
12/97	1,200	—	—	25,000
12/96	1,214	—	—	25,000
12/95	1,200	—	—	20,000
12/94	1,165	—	—	20,000
Annual Growth	3.6%	—	—	3.8%

Revenue History

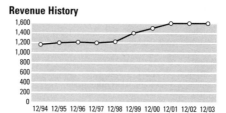

Deloitte

This company is "deloitted" to make your acquaintance, particularly if you're a big business in need of accounting services. Deloitte Touche Tohmatsu (now doing business simply as Deloitte) is one of accounting's Big Four, along with Ernst & Young, KPMG, and PricewaterhouseCoopers. Deloitte offers traditional audit and fiscal-oversight services to a multinational clientele. It also provides human resources and tax consulting services, as well as services to governments and international lending agencies working in emerging markets. (China is an important market.) Units include Deloitte & Touche (the US accounting arm) and Deloitte Consulting. Consulting services account for more than 25% of Deloitte's sales.

Deloitte spent the 1980s and 1990s pursuing a strategy of using accountants and consultants in concert to provide seamless service in auditing, accounting, strategic planning, information technology, financial management, and productivity. Deloitte Consulting became Deloitte's fastest-growing line, offering strategic and management consulting, in addition to information technology and human resources consulting services.

Increasingly, though, Deloitte and its peers were coming under fire for their combined accounting/consulting operations; regulators and observers wondered whether accountants could maintain objectivity when they were auditing clients for whom they also provided consulting services. Criticism mounted after Enron's collapse capsized Arthur Andersen and put the entire accounting industry under scrutiny. (Deloitte picked up new business and members in Andersen's wake.)

Deloitte in 2002 announced it would spin off its consulting business, becoming the last of the big accountants to do so; a year later it called off the split, citing a weakened market for consulting, among other woes.

Deloitte was in the headlines again in late 2003, when auditing client Parmalat filed for bankruptcy in the midst of a $12 billion financial scandal, then dropped Deloitte as its auditor. Parmalat sued Deloitte in 2004, claiming its auditing procedures were inadequate and should have uncovered the fraud at Parmalat earlier.

HISTORY

In 1845 William Deloitte opened an accounting office in London, at first soliciting business from bankrupts. The growth of joint stock companies and the development of stock markets in the mid-19th century created a need for standardized financial reporting and fueled the rise of auditing, and Deloitte moved into the new field. The Great Western Railway appointed him as its independent auditor (the first anywhere) in 1849.

In 1890 John Griffiths, who had become a partner in 1869, opened the company's first US office in New York City. Four decades later branches had opened throughout the US. In 1952 the firm partnered with Haskins & Sells, which operated 34 US offices.

Deloitte aimed to be "the Cadillac, not the Ford" of accounting. The firm, which became Deloitte Haskins & Sells in 1978, began shedding its conservatism as competition heated up; it was the first of the major accountancy firms to use aggressive ads.

In 1984 Deloitte Haskins & Sells tried to merge with Price Waterhouse, but the deal was dropped after Price Waterhouse's UK partners objected.

In 1989 Deloitte Haskins & Sells joined the flamboyant Touche Ross (founded 1899) to become Deloitte & Touche. Touche Ross's Japanese affiliate, Ross Tohmatsu (founded 1968) rounded out the current name. The merger was engineered by Deloitte's Michael Cook and Touche's Edward Kangas, in part to unite the former firm's US and European strengths with the latter's Asian presence. Cook continued to oversee US operations, with Kangas presiding over international operations. Many affiliates, particularly in the UK, rejected the merger and defected to competing firms.

As auditors were increasingly held accountable for the financial results of their clients, legal action soared. In the 1990s Deloitte was sued because of its actions relating to Drexel Burnham Lambert junk bond king Michael Milken, the failure of several savings and loans, and clients' bankruptcies.

Nevertheless, in 1995 the SEC chose Michael Sutton, the firm's national director of auditing and accounting practice, as its chief accountant. That year Deloitte formed Deloitte & Touche Consulting to consolidate its US and UK consulting operations; its Asian consulting operations were later added to facilitate regional expansion.

In 1996 the firm formed a corporate fraud unit (with special emphasis on the Internet) and bought PHH Fantus, the leading corporate relocation consulting company. The next year Deloitte and Thurston Group (a Chicago-based merchant bank) teamed up to form NetDox, a system for delivering legal, financial, and insurance documents via the Internet. In 1997, amid a new round of industry mergers, rumors swirled that a Deloitte and Ernst & Young union had been scrapped because the firms could not agree on ownership issues. Deloitte disavowed plans to merge and launched an ad campaign directly targeted against its rivals.

The Asian economic crisis hurt overseas expansion in 1998, but provided a boost in restructuring consulting. In 1999 the firm sold its accounting staffing service unit (Resources Connection) to its managers and Evercore Partners, citing possible conflicts of interest with its core audit business. Also that year Deloitte Consulting decided to sell its computer programming subsidiary to CGI Group, and Kangas stepped down as CEO to be succeeded by James Copeland; the following year Kangas ceded the chairman's seat to Piet Hoogendoorn.

In 2001 the SEC forced Deloitte & Touche to restate the financial results of Pre-Paid Legal Services. In an unusual move, Deloitte & Touche publicly disagreed with the SEC's findings.

The accountancy put some old trouble to bed in 2003 when it agreed to pay $23 million to settle claims it had been negligent in its auditing of failed Kentucky Life Insurance, a client in the 1980s. Later that year the UK's High Court found Deloitte negligent in audits related to the failed Barings Bank; however, the ruling was considered something of a victory for the accountancy because it essentially cleared Deloitte of the majority of charges against it and effectively limited its financial liability in the matter. Copeland retired from the global CEO's office that year and handed the reins over to Bill Parrett, who had formerly served as managing director for the US and the Americas.

EXECUTIVES

Chairman: Piet Hoogendoorn
CEO; Senior Partner, US: William G. (Bill) Parrett, age 58
CFO and Managing Partner, Global Office: William A. Fowler
CIO: Wolfgang Richter
Global Managing Partner, Reputation, Excellence, and Practice Protection; Managing Partner, Netherlands: Willy A. Biewinga
Global Managing Partner, Innovation and Investment; Managing Partner, Germany and Regional Managing Partner, Europe/Middle East/Africa: Wolfgang Grewe
Global Managing Partner, Client Service Excellence; Tohmatsu Representative to DTT, and Regional Managing Partner, Japan: Shuichiro Sekine
Global Managing Partner, Brand and Eminence; Chief Executive and Managing Managing Partner, Canada and Regional Managing Partner, North America: Colin Taylor
Global Managing Partner, Intellectual Capital, Inclusion, and Development; Chief Executive, France: Philippe Vassor
Global Managing Partner, Financial Advisory Services: Ralph G. Adams
Global Managing Partner, Audit: Stephen Almond
Global Managing Partner, Regulation and Risk: Jeffrey K. (Jeff) Willemain
CEO, Deloitte Consulting: Paul Robinson, age 51
Chairman, Deloitte & Touche LLP: Sharon L. Allen, age 52
Global Managing Partner, Human Resources: Conrad Venter
General Counsel: Joseph J. Lambert

LOCATIONS

HQ: Deloitte Touche Tohmatsu
1633 Broadway, New York, NY 10019
Phone: 212-489-1600 **Fax:** 212-492-4154
Web: www.deloitte.com

Deloitte Touche Tohmatsu operates through about 700 offices in nearly 150 countries.

PRODUCTS/OPERATIONS

Selected Services
Accounting and auditing
Corporate finance
Emerging markets consulting
Forensic services
Human resources, actuarial, insurance, and managed care consulting
Legal services
Management consulting
Outsourcing
Reorganization services
Risk management
Tax advice and planning
Transaction services

Selected Industry Specializations
Aviation and transport services
Banking and securities
Consumer products
Consumer services
Gas and oil
Insurance
Investment management
Manufacturing
Mining
Retail/wholesale and distribution
Technology, media, and telecommunications
Utilities

COMPETITORS

Accenture
BDO International
Booz Allen
Boston Consulting
Capgemini
EDS
Ernst & Young
Grant Thornton International
H&R Block
KPMG
Marsh & McLennan
McKinsey & Company
PricewaterhouseCoopers
Towers Perrin
Watson Wyatt

HISTORICAL FINANCIALS

Company Type: Partnership

Income Statement
FYE: May 31

	REVENUE ($ mil.)	NET INCOME ($ mil.)	NET PROFIT MARGIN	EMPLOYEES
5/03	15,100	—	—	119,237
5/02	12,500	—	—	98,000
5/01	12,400	—	—	95,000
5/00*	11,200	—	—	90,000
8/99	10,600	—	—	90,000
8/98	9,000	—	—	82,000
8/97	7,400	—	—	65,000
8/96	6,500	—	—	63,440
8/95	5,950	—	—	59,000
8/94	5,200	—	—	56,600
Annual Growth	12.6%	—	—	8.6%

*Fiscal year change

Revenue History

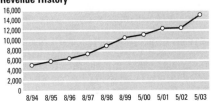

Delta Dental of California

Delta Dental of California (formerly Delta Dental Plan of California) doesn't just help keep the mouths of movie stars clean. A not-for-profit organization, the company is a member of the Delta Dental Plans Association and has affiliates nationwide. Delta Dental of California provides dental coverage through HMOs, preferred provider plans (PPOs), and such government programs as California's Denti-Cal. The company serves some 17 million enrollees in California; its programs cover more than one-third of California residents. Together with Delta Dental of Pennsylvania, Delta Dental of California formed Dentegra Group, a holding company that serves nearly 20 million members throughout the US.

Delta Dental of California also provides information technology services to other Delta Plan affiliates across the nation through its for-profit subsidiary, DeltaNet.

EXECUTIVES

President and CEO: Gary D. Radine, age 54
CFO: Elizabeth Russell
SVP and Chief Administrative Officer: Jerry Holcombe
SVP, and Chief Information Officer: Patrick S. Steele, age 54
SVP and General Manager, California Commercial Business Unit: Anthony S. Barth, age 40
SVP and General Counsel: Robert G. Becker
SVP, State Government Programs: Michael Kaufmann
SVP, Public and Professional Services: Marilyn Belek
SVP, Health Care Affiliates; President, PMI Health Plans: Robert B. Elliot
VP and Controller: Michael J. Castro
VP, Marketing, Underwriting, and Actuarial: Kenneth E. Bernardi
Director, Human Resources: Teri Forestieri

LOCATIONS

HQ: Delta Dental of California
100 1st St., San Francisco, CA 94105
Phone: 415-972-8300 **Fax:** 415-972-8466
Web: www.deltadentalca.org

PRODUCTS/OPERATIONS

Selected Products
DeltaCare (dental plans for groups in more than one state)
DeltaCare USA (group and individual dental HMOs)
DeltaVision (group vision HMO)

COMPETITORS

Aetna
CIGNA
Health Net
MetLife
PacifiCare
SafeGuard Health Enterprises
WellPoint Health Networks

Delta Dental Plan of Michigan

Delta Dental Plan of Michigan is a not-for-profit company that provides dental benefits and related administrative services to about five million members in Michigan, Ohio, and Indiana. Delta Dental Plan of Michigan provides HMO, PPO, and fee-for-service dental plans. Customers include employer groups, trade associations, and unions. The company is Delta Dental Plans Association's second largest affiliate, and operates both Delta Dental Plan of Ohio and Delta Dental Plan of Indiana. Oral health public education and research is provided via the company's Delta Dental Fund.

Delta Dental Plan of Michigan also provides vision plans and vision plan administration services.

EXECUTIVES
Chairperson: Laura O. Stearns
President and CEO: Thomas J. Fleszar
VP, Finance: Mack B. Solomon Jr.
VP and Assistant to the President: Patrick T. Cahill
VP and Actuary: William T. Billard
VP, Marketing: E. Craig Lesley
VP, Sales: Charles D. Floyd
VP, Information Systems and Services: Timothy E. DeWeese
VP, Operations and Human Resources: Sherry L. Crisp
VP, Quality Management and Informatics: Laura L. Czelada
VP, Corporate and Public Affairs: Nancy E. Hostetler

LOCATIONS
HQ: Delta Dental Plan of Michigan Inc
4100 Okemos Rd, Okemos, MI 48864
Phone: 517-349-6000 **Fax:** 517-347-5499
Web: www.ddpmi.com

HISTORICAL FINANCIALS
Company Type: Not-for-profit

Income Statement
FYE: December 31

	REVENUE ($ mil.)	NET INCOME ($ mil.)	NET PROFIT MARGIN	EMPLOYEES
12/03	4,300	—	—	2,500
12/02	4,000	—	—	2,500
12/01	3,300	—	—	2,400
12/00	2,800	—	—	2,400
12/99	2,700	—	—	2,400
12/98	2,440	—	—	2,400
12/97	2,315	—	—	2,115
12/96	2,114	—	—	1,960
12/95	2,145	—	—	1,800
12/94	2,025	—	—	1,649
Annual Growth	8.7%	—	—	4.7%

Revenue History
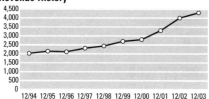

Demoulas Super Markets

Supermarket or soap opera? Demoulas Super Markets runs about 60 grocery stores under the Market Basket and Demoulas Super Market names in Massachusetts and New Hampshire. The firm also has real estate interests. The company was founded in 1954 when brothers George and Mike Demoulas bought their parents' mom-and-pop grocery. The men agreed that, upon one brother's death, the other would care for the deceased's family and maintain the firm's 50-50 ownership. In 1990 George's family alleged that Mike had defrauded them of all but 8% of the company's stock; the 10-year court battle was decided in favor of George's family, giving it 51% of the company. By then Mike had resigned as CEO; the post remains vacant.

PRODUCTS/OPERATIONS
2003 Membership
	Members	% of total
Michigan	3,900,000	77
Ohio	925,000	18
Indiana	263,000	5
Total	**5,088,000**	**100**

Products and Services Provided
DeltaCare (HMO)
DeltaPreferred Option (POS)
DeltaPreferred Option (PPO)
DeltaPremier (fee-for-service)
DeltaUSA (third-party administration services)
DeltaVision (vision plans & TPA services)

COMPETITORS
Aetna
Anthem
CIGNA
UnitedHealth Group

HISTORICAL FINANCIALS
Company Type: Not-for-profit

Income Statement
FYE: December 31

	REVENUE ($ mil.)	NET INCOME ($ mil.)	NET PROFIT MARGIN	EMPLOYEES
12/03	1,326	—	—	670
12/02	1,163	—	—	600
12/01	1,079	—	—	650
Annual Growth	10.8%	—	—	1.5%

Revenue History

EXECUTIVES
EVP: Julien Lacourse
EVP: James Miamis
VP, Finance and Treasurer: Donald Mulligan
VP, Grocery Sales and Merchandising: Joseph Rockwell
VP and Treasurer, Retail Management and Development Inc.: Michael Kettenbach
Corporate Counsel: Sumner Darman
Payroll Administrator: Lucille Lopez

LOCATIONS
HQ: Demoulas Super Markets Inc.
875 East St., Tewksbury, MA 01876
Phone: 978-851-8000 **Fax:** 978-640-8390

COMPETITORS
Big Y Foods	IGA
BJs Wholesale Club	Shaw's
Costco Wholesale	Stop & Shop
Cumberland Farms	SUPERVALU
Golub	Wal-Mart
Hannaford Bros.	

HISTORICAL FINANCIALS
Company Type: Private

Income Statement
FYE: December 31

	ESTIMATED REVENUE ($ mil.)	NET INCOME ($ mil.)	NET PROFIT MARGIN	EMPLOYEES
12/03	1,900	—	—	12,700
12/02	1,900	—	—	12,700
12/01	2,000	—	—	12,700
12/00	1,800	—	—	12,500
12/99	1,800	—	—	12,500
12/98	1,700	—	—	12,350
12/97	1,850	—	—	12,300
12/96	1,760	—	—	11,900
12/95	1,650	—	—	11,700
12/94	1,338	—	—	10,000
Annual Growth	4.0%	—	—	2.7%

Revenue History
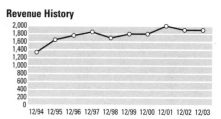

Depository Trust

It's clear that securities trading just wouldn't be the same without The Depository Trust & Clearing Corporation (DTCC), whose subsidiaries provide the infrastructure for clearing, settlement, and custody of most US securities transactions. DTCC was founded in 1999 when operating companies The Depository Trust Company (DTC) and the National Securities Clearing Company (NSCC) — both of which were founded in the 1970s — were combined under a single holding structure. DTC is the world's largest securities depository and a clearinghouse for trading settlement; NSCC processes most broker-to-broker equity, corporate, and municipal bond trades in the US.

DTCC, which has designs on global domination of the securities transaction trade, has expanded its scope. In addition to its mainstays DTC and NSCC, the company has subsidiaries or joint ventures focused on services for fixed-income, international, and emerging-markets products, as well as government and mortgage-backed securities. DTCC is owned by its users, which include banks, brokerages, the NASD, and the NYSE.

EXECUTIVES

Chairman, President and CEO; Chairman and CEO, The Depository Trust Company and National Securities Clearing Corporation: Jill M. Considine, age 59
COO; President and COO, The Depository Trust Company; President, National Securities Clearing Corporation; Vice Chairman and CEO, Fixed Income Clearing Corporation: Donald F. Donahue
CFO: Ellen Fine Levine
CEO, Fixed Income Clearing Corp. and CEO, Emerging Markets Clearing Corp.: Richard R. Macek
President, Fixed Income Clearing Corporation: Thomas Costa
Managing Director, Corporate Communications: Stuart Z. Goldstein
Managing Director and General Auditor: Lori Klebous-Zivny
Managing Director, Marketing: Joan J. Lewis
Managing Director and General Counsel: Richard B. Nesson
Managing Director, Human Resources: Anthony Portannese
Managing Director, Deputy General Counsel, and Secretary: Karen L. Saperstein
Auditors: PricewaterhouseCoopers LLP

LOCATIONS

HQ: The Depository Trust & Clearing Corporation
55 Water St., 49th. Fl., New York, NY 10041
Phone: 212-855-1000   **Fax:** 212-855-8440
Web: www.dtcc.com

PRODUCTS/OPERATIONS

2003 Sales

	$ mil.	% of total
Trading services	548.5	58
Custody services	166.6	18
Interest income	76.5	8
Network services	69.0	7
Equity in Omgeo income	29.8	3
Other income	56.7	6
Total	**947.1**	**100**

Selected Subsidiaries and Affiliates

Emerging Market Clearing Corporation (services for cross-border trades of emerging market debt instruments)
Fixed Income Clearing Corporation
  Government Securities Division (services for government securities)
  Mortgage-Backed Securities Division (services for mortgage-backed securities)
National Securities Clearing Company
Omgeo LLC (joint venture with Thomson Financial to provide global trade management services)
The Depository Trust Company

HISTORICAL FINANCIALS

Company Type: Private

Income Statement
FYE: December 31

	REVENUE ($ mil.)	NET INCOME ($ mil.)	NET PROFIT MARGIN	EMPLOYEES
12/03	947	12	1.2%	3,000
12/02	906	51	5.6%	2,600
12/01	819	5	0.6%	3,250
12/00	914	5	0.5%	3,000
Annual Growth	1.2%	34.8%	—	0.0%

2003 Year-End Financials
Debt ratio: 141.9%
Return on equity: 5.4%
Cash ($ mil.): 4,745
Current ratio: —
Long-term debt ($ mil.): 307

Net Income History

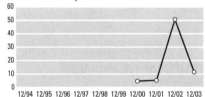

Detroit Medical Center

The seeds for the Detroit Medical Center were planted in 1955, when four Detroit hospitals joined efforts to provide coordination between the hospitals and Wayne State University's medical school. Today the medical center (which became a not-for-profit corporation in 1985) serves patients in southeastern Michigan with more than 2,000 beds and some 3,000 physicians. The center is made up of seven hospitals, more than 100 outpatient facilities, and two nursing centers. The Detroit Medical Center is the teaching and clinical research site for Wayne State, now one of the US's largest medical schools; it is also allied with the Barbara Ann Karmanos Cancer Institute and the Kresge Eye Institute.

EXECUTIVES

Chairman: Chuck O'Brien
President and CEO: Michael E. Duggan
CIO: Michael LeRoy
EVP and CFO: Chris Palazzolo
VP, Human Resources: Ruthann Liagre
Director of Marketing and Communications: Sharyl Smith
President, Detroit Receiving Hospital and University Health Center: Leslie C (Les) Bowman
President, Children's Hospital of Michigan: Larry E. Fleischman
President, Sinai-Grace Hospital: Conrad Mallett Jr.
President, Rehabilitation Institute of Michigan: Terry Reiley
President, Karmanos Cancer Institute: John C. Ruckdeschel
President, Harper University Hospital and Hutzel Women's Hospital: Iris Taylor

LOCATIONS

HQ: Detroit Medical Center
3990 John R. St., Detroit, MI 48201
Phone: 313-578-2000   **Fax:** 313-578-3225
Web: www.dmc.org

PRODUCTS/OPERATIONS

Hospitals
Children's Hospital of Michigan (Detroit)
Detroit Receiving Hospital and University Health Center
Harper Hospital (Detroit)
Huron Valley-Sinai Hospital (Commerce, MI)
Hutzel Hospital (Detroit)
Rehabilitation Institute of Michigan (Detroit)
Sinai-Grace Hospital (Detroit)

Selected Affiliates
Barbara Ann Karmanos Cancer Institute
DMC ComfortCare Home Medical
DMC Health Care Centers
DMC Nursing Centers
International Center
Kresge Eye Institute
Renaissance Home Health Care

COMPETITORS

Ascension Health
Catholic Health Initiatives
HCA
Henry Ford Health System
Trinity Health (Novi)
William Beaumont Hospital

HISTORICAL FINANCIALS

Company Type: Not-for-profit

Income Statement
FYE: December 31

	REVENUE ($ mil.)	NET INCOME ($ mil.)	NET PROFIT MARGIN	EMPLOYEES
12/03	1,600	—	—	14,311
12/02	1,600	—	—	13,000
12/01	1,600	—	—	14,000
12/00	1,600	—	—	16,500
12/99	1,453	—	—	16,500
12/98	1,573	—	—	16,500
12/97	1,448	—	—	16,288
12/96	1,300	—	—	13,879
12/95	1,200	—	—	10,000
12/94	1,161	—	—	12,000
Annual Growth	3.6%	—	—	2.0%

Revenue History

Di Giorgio

Di Giorgio delivers little apples (and other foods) to the Big Apple. Founded in 1920, the firm is a food wholesaler and distributor primarily in New York City, Long Island, New Jersey, and the greater Philadelphia area. It offers more than 21,000 products to food retailers ranging from independents and members of co-ops to regional chains. (Associated Food Stores accounts for 15% of sales.) Although Di Giorgio distributes national brands, it also supplies frozen and refrigerated products under its White Rose brand, a name known in New York for well over a century. Di Giorgio co-chairman and CEO Richard Neff owns approximately 99% of the company, primarily through his sole general partnership in Rose Partners.

Capitalizing on the popularity of ethnic and organic foods, Di Giorgio has launched a new division called DGI Specialty Foods, which offers a complete line of specialty food products including ethnic, gourmet, and organic products. Di Giorgio lost its largest customer A&P in October 2003.

EXECUTIVES

Co-chairman and CEO: Richard B. Neff, age 55, $840,000 pay
Co-chairman, President and COO: Stephen R. Bokser, age 61, $840,000 pay
SVP and CFO: Lawrence S. (Larry) Grossman, age 42, $286,000 pay
EVP, Finance and Treasurer: Robert A. Zorn, age 49, $332,100 pay
SVP, Distribution: Joseph R. DeSimone, age 64
SVP and General Manager, White Rose Dairy Division: Joseph Fantozzi, age 42, $294,000 pay
SVP and General Manager, White Rose Frozen Division: John Annetta, age 52
SVP: John J. Zumba, age 66
VP, General Counsel and Secretary: Harlan Levine, age 42
VP, Logistics: George Conklin, age 43
Auditors: Deloitte & Touche LLP

LOCATIONS

HQ: Di Giorgio Corporation
380 Middlesex Ave., Carteret, NJ 07008
Phone: 732-541-5555   **Fax:** 732-541-3590
Web: www.whiterose.com

PRODUCTS/OPERATIONS

Selected Customers
Associated Foods Stores
Bravo
C-Town
Foodtown
Grande (Puerto Rico)
Gristede's Foods
King Kullen
Kings Super Markets
Met
Pioneer
Scaturros
Shop 'N Bag
Sloans Supermarkets
Super Food
Thristway
Western Beef

COMPETITORS

Associated Wholesalers
Bozzuto's
C&S Wholesale
General Trading
Key Food
Krasdale Foods
SGA Sales & Mktg
SUPERVALU
Wakefern Food

HISTORICAL FINANCIALS

Company Type: Private

Income Statement			FYE: Saturday nearest December 31	
	REVENUE ($ mil.)	NET INCOME ($ mil.)	NET PROFIT MARGIN	EMPLOYEES
12/03	1,544	14	0.9%	1,238
12/02	1,560	13	0.8%	1,288
12/01	1,539	12	0.8%	1,353
12/00	1,488	11	0.7%	1,373
12/99	1,414	10	0.7%	1,275
12/98	1,197	4	0.4%	1,229
12/97	1,072	(3)	—	1,156
12/96	1,050	5	0.5%	1,123
12/95	1,020	—	—	1,135
12/94	934	—	—	1,305
Annual Growth	5.7%	—	—	(0.6%)

2003 Year-End Financials
Debt ratio: 461.8%   Current ratio: 1.74
Return on equity: 47.1%   Long-term debt ($ mil.): 150
Cash ($ mil.): 2

Net Income History

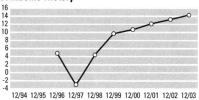

Dick Corporation

Without any help from Tom or Harry, Dick Corp., a general contracting, construction, and construction management company, builds commercial, institutional, power, industrial, bridge, and highway structures. Some of its landmark projects include PNC Park, home of the Pittsburgh Pirates, and the preservation of Fallingwater, a home designed by Frank Lloyd Wright. Current projects include contracts to help construct a military complex at the Navy base at Guantanamo Bay. The firm founded by Noble Dick in 1922 is still owned by his descendants, including co-chairmen Douglas and David Dick.

Dick Corp.'s 1999 acquisition of Fletcher Pacific Construction Co. established a presence for it in Hawaii and the Pacific Rim. Dick Pacific has designed and constructed multifamily housing and institutional and commercial structures. Projects in which it has participated include the Grand Wailea Resort on Maui, the Federal Detention Center on Oahu, and a military facility on Kwajalein.

EXECUTIVES

Co-Chairman: Douglas P. Dick
Co-Chairman: David E. Dick
President: Stephen (Steve) D'Angelo
SVP, Corporate Counsel, and Secretary: Roger J. Peters
SVP; President, National Building Operations: Don F. Cooper
SVP Strategic Planning: Ellsworth F. Vines
VP and General Manager, Bridge and Highway Division: Jeffrey D. Sciullo
VP and General Manager, Construction Management: Gilbert S. Brindley
VP Finance: Bob Coppage
Corporate Communications: David Rearick
Auditors: Deloitte & Touche LLP

LOCATIONS

HQ: Dick Corporation
1900 State Rt. 51, Large, PA 15025
Phone: 412-384-1000   **Fax:** 412-384-1150
Web: www.dickcorp.com

Dick Corporation has offices in the metro areas of Chicago; Fairbanks, Alaska; Honolulu; Las Vegas; Pittsburgh (Large, Pennsylvania); and Washington, DC. It also has offices in Barrigada, Guam, and San Juan, Puerto Rico.

PRODUCTS/OPERATIONS

Markets Served
Airports
Bridges
Commercial buildings
Construction management
Correctional facilities
Education
Entertainment
Government
Health care
Highways
Hospitality
Housing
Industrial/manufacturing
Metals
Military
Power
Retail
Technology
Water/wastewater

COMPETITORS

BE&K
Bechtel
Beck Group
Black & Veatch
Brown and Caldwell
CH2M HILL
Choate Construction
Devcon International
Dyckerhoff & Widmann
Embree Construction
Fluor
Foster Wheeler
Gilbane
Granite Construction
Graycor
Hardin Construction
Hensel Phelps
 Construction
Impregilo
Jacobs Engineering
Louis Berger
Malcolm Pirnie
Michael Baker
MWH Global
Parsons
Peter Kiewit Sons'
Raytheon
TIC Holdings
Turner Corporation
Tutor-Saliba
URS
Washington Group
Zachry

HISTORICAL FINANCIALS

Company Type: Private

Income Statement				FYE: December 31
	ESTIMATED REVENUE ($ mil.)	NET INCOME ($ mil.)	NET PROFIT MARGIN	EMPLOYEES
12/03	919	—	—	—
12/02	1,100	—	—	3,500
12/01	1,100	—	—	3,500
12/00	1,050	—	—	3,000
12/99	689	—	—	5,000
12/98	550	—	—	5,000
12/97	540	—	—	5,000
12/96	550	—	—	5,000
12/95	450	—	—	5,000
12/94	500	—	—	3,000
Annual Growth	7.0%	—	—	1.9%

Revenue History

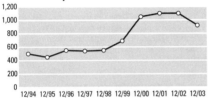

Dierbergs Markets

Dierbergs Markets has a taste of what folks in St. Louis like to eat. Dierbergs operates about 20 upscale supermarkets in the St. Louis area, where rival Schnuck Markets is the market leader. Dierbergs' stores offer food, drugs, photo processing, video centers, as well as cooking schools, banks, self-service checkout, Krispy Kreme donuts, and made-to-order Chinese food at some locations. Dierbergs Florist and Gifts, affiliated with FTD, offers gift baskets and floral services at its stores and over the Internet for local and international delivery. Founded as a trading outpost in 1854, the Dierberg family has owned and operated Dierbergs since 1914.

EXECUTIVES

Chairman, President and CEO: Robert J. (Bob) Dierberg
Vice Chairman: Roger Dierberg
EVP: Gregory (Greg) Dierberg
VP, CFO: Connie Holley
VP, Coprorate Development: Laura Dierberg-Padousis
VP, Human Resources: Linda Ryan
VP, Marketing: John Muckerman
Controller: Laura Schneider
Director, Information Technology: Robert Sanabria
Director, Pharmacy Services: David Meador

LOCATIONS

HQ: Dierbergs Markets Inc.
16690 Swingley Ridge Rd., Chesterfield, MO 63017
Phone: 636-532-8884   **Fax:** 636-532-8759
Web: www.dierbergs.com

COMPETITORS

7-Eleven
ALDI
AWG
IGA
Kmart
Kroger
Schnuck Markets
Shop 'N Save
Walgreen
Wal-Mart

HISTORICAL FINANCIALS

Company Type: Private

Income Statement				FYE: December 31
	REVENUE ($ mil.)	NET INCOME ($ mil.)	NET PROFIT MARGIN	EMPLOYEES
12/02	575	—	—	4,700
12/01	550	—	—	4,500
12/00	525	—	—	4,300
12/99	500	—	—	4,230
12/98	450	—	—	4,200
12/97	475	—	—	4,134
12/96	446	—	—	4,300
Annual Growth	4.3%	—	—	1.5%

Revenue History

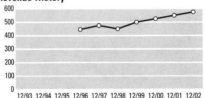

Discount Drug

Drugs are just part of the story at Discount Drug Mart. One of the largest drugstore chains in northeastern Ohio, primarily in the Cleveland area, the company offers pharmacy services, nonprescription medications, and medical supplies, as well as food, housewares, beauty products, video rentals, photo developing, stamps, pet supplies, hardware, and more. Its 60 stores offer, on average, 25,000 sq. ft. of selling space, about twice the size of rival drugstores. Discount Drug also runs mail-order and online prescription services through subsidiary Immediate Pharmaceutical Services. The company is expanding into central Ohio. Chairman and CEO Parviz Boodjeh owns Discount Drug, which was founded in 1970.

Discount Drug Mart is growing cautiously, typically adding four to six stores annually. In 2004, Discount Drug Mart will add three stores in the Columbus, Ohio market. Recent improvements in the chain's warehouse operations will support about 110 stores, giving Discount Drug Mart plenty of room to grow.

EXECUTIVES

Chairman and CEO: Parviz Boodjeh
President: John Gans
VP and CFO: Thomas J. (John) McConnell
COO: Donald Boodjeh
SVP Marketing: David Baytosh
VP Human Resources: Michael Eby
VP Pharmacy: Pete Ratcyz
Treasurer, Chief Administrative Officer:
 Douglas Boodjeh
Director, Home Health Care: Karen Houser
Auditors: Grant Thornton

LOCATIONS

HQ: Discount Drug Mart Inc.
211 Commerce Dr., Medina, OH 44256
Phone: 330-725-2340   **Fax:** 330-722-2990
Web: www.discount-drugmart.com

COMPETITORS

Ahold USA
Costco Wholesale
CVS
Giant Eagle
Kmart
Marc Glassman
Rite Aid
Target
Walgreen
Wal-Mart

HISTORICAL FINANCIALS

Company Type: Private

Income Statement				FYE: March 31
	REVENUE ($ mil.)	NET INCOME ($ mil.)	NET PROFIT MARGIN	EMPLOYEES
3/03	550	—	—	2,450
3/02	480	—	—	2,300
3/01	442	—	—	2,100
3/00	400	—	—	2,100
3/99	400	—	—	2,100
3/98	327	—	—	1,250
Annual Growth	11.0%	—	—	14.4%

Revenue History

Discount Tire

Concerned about that upcoming "re-tirement"? Discount Tire Co., one of the largest independent tire dealers in the US, can provide several options. With more than 500 stores in about 20 states, the company sells such leading brands as Michelin, Goodyear, and Uniroyal, as well as wheels. Discount Tire operates mostly in the Midwest and Southwest. Some of the company's West Coast stores operate as America's Tire Co. because of a name conflict. Customers can search for tires by make and model on the company's Web site. Owner Bruce Halle founded the company in 1960 with six tires — four of them recaps.

EXECUTIVES

CEO: Gary T. Van Brunt
CFO: Christian Roe
EVP and Chief Administrative Officer: Bob Holman
Assistant Vice President, Human Resources and Payroll: Staci Adams

LOCATIONS

HQ: Discount Tire Co. Inc.
  20225 N. Scottsdale Rd., Scottsdale, AZ 85255
Phone: 480-606-6000   **Fax:** 480-606-4401
Web: www.discounttire.com

Discount Tire Co. and America's Tire Co. have stores in Arizona, California, Colorado, Florida, Georgia, Illinois, Indiana, Michigan, Minnesota, Nevada, New Mexico, North Carolina, Ohio, Oregon, South Carolina, Texas, Utah, Virginia, and Washington.

COMPETITORS

BFS Retail & Commercial Operations
Les Schwab Tire Centers
Penske
Pep Boys
Sears
TBC
TCI Tire Centers
Wal-Mart

HISTORICAL FINANCIALS

Company Type: Private

Income Statement
FYE: December 31

	REVENUE ($ mil.)	NET INCOME ($ mil.)	NET PROFIT MARGIN	EMPLOYEES
12/03	1,541	—	—	9,500
12/02	1,417	—	—	8,944
12/01	1,320	—	—	8,415
12/00	1,192	—	—	8,987
12/99	1,031	—	—	8,100
12/98	900	—	—	6,500
12/97	864	—	—	6,200
12/96	739	—	—	5,154
12/95	658	—	—	4,714
12/94	590	—	—	4,200
Annual Growth	11.3%	—	—	9.5%

Revenue History

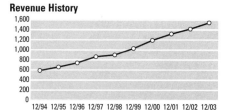

Discovery Communications

Discover science and nature in the comfort of your living room with Discovery Communications (DCI). Reaching more than 86 million households, its Discovery Channel is one of the top-rated cable networks in the US. DCI owns other cable networks as well, including The Learning Channel (with its popular *Trading Spaces* program), Travel Channel, and Animal Planet. DCI also operates Discovery Channel retail stores, and its Internet unit, Discovery.com, houses various nature and science Web sites. Liberty Media Corp. (49%), Cox Communications (25%), and Advance/Newhouse Communications (25%) own DCI.

The company also operates five digital Discovery cable channels focused on specific topics such as science and home and health. In a joint venture, Discovery and The New York Times Company have launched the news-oriented Discovery Times Channel, which took the place of the Discovery Civilization Channel. The company also launched a new digital cable network called Discovery HD Theater, which features high-definition quality television.

Building on its name brand, DCI creates original programming, games, and activities for a series of science and nature Web sites under the Discovery.com name and publishes videos, books, and CD-ROMs. It also operates about 165 Discovery Channel retail stores.

Speculation about whether DCI would be acquired has made headlines in recent times, but founder John Hendricks has denied all reports of a sale. Hendricks did, however, step down as the firm's CEO in mid-2004 (he remains chairman). President Judy McHale replaced him.

HISTORY

John Hendricks, a history graduate who wanted to expand the presence of educational programming on TV, founded Cable Educational Network in 1982. Three years later he introduced the Discovery Channel. Devoted entirely to documentaries and nature shows, the channel premiered in 156,000 US homes. After dodging bankruptcy (it had $5,000 cash and $1 million in debt to the BBC), within a year the Discovery Channel had 7 million subscribers and a host of new investors, including Cox Cable Communications and TCI (now AT&T Broadband). It expanded its programming from 12 hours to 18 hours a day in 1987.

Discovery continued to attract subscribers, reaching more than 32 million by 1988. The next year it launched Discovery Channel Europe to more than 200,000 homes in the UK and Scandinavia. The company began selling home videos in 1990 and entered the Israeli market. The following year Discovery Communications, Inc. (DCI) was formed to house the company's operations, and it bought The Learning Channel (TLC, founded in 1980). The company revamped TLC's programming, and in 1992 introduced a daily, six-hour, commercial-free block of children's programs. The next year it introduced its first CD-ROM title, *In the Company of Whales*, based on the Discovery Channel documentary.

DCI increased its focus on international expansion in 1994, moving into Asia, Latin America, the Middle East, North Africa, Portugal, and Spain. The next year the company introduced its Web site and began selling company merchandise such as CD-ROMs and videos. DCI solidified its move into the retail sector in 1996 with the acquisition of The Nature Company and Scientific Revolution chains (renamed Discovery Channel Store). Also that year it launched its third major cable channel, Animal Planet.

The company continued expanding internationally throughout the mid-1990s, establishing operations in Australia, Canada, India, New Zealand, and South Korea (1995); Africa, Brazil, Germany, and Italy (1996); and Japan and Turkey (1997). DCI also added to its stable of cable channels with the purchase of 70% of Paxson Communications' Travel Channel in 1997 (it acquired the rest in 1999). The company's 1997 original production, "Titanic: Anatomy of a Disaster," attracted 3.2 million US households, setting a network ratings record.

The following year DCI and the British Broadcasting Corporation launched Animal Planet in Asia through a joint venture and agreed to market and distribute new cable channel BBC America. It also bought CBS's Eye on People, renaming the channel Discovery People (DCI shut the channel down in 2000). DCI spent $330 million launching its new health and fitness channel, Discovery Health, in 1999 and formed partnerships with high-speed online service Road Runner (to provide interactive information and services to Road Runner customers) and Rosenbluth Travel (to provide vacation packages based on DCI programming).

DCI reorganized its Internet activities into one unit called Discovery.com in 2000 with plans to eventually take it public. Later that year the Discovery Channel set back-to-back records with the two highest-rated documentaries ever on cable, "Raising the Mammoth" (10.1 million people) and "Walking With Dinosaurs" (10.7 million people). In 2001 the company cut about 50 jobs as part of a restructuring. Later that year Discovery Communications struck a three-year deal to lease time from NBC on Saturday mornings (paying $6 million per season) to show its Discovery Kids programs.

In 2002 the company launched a 24-hour high-definition television network called Discovery HD Theater. Two years later founder John Hendricks relinquished his CEO duties (he remains chairman). President Judy McHale replaced him.

EXECUTIVES

Chairman: John S. Hendricks, age 52
President and CEO: Judith A. McHale, age 57
SEVP Corporate Operations and General Counsel: Mark Hollinger
SEVP Human Resources and Administration: Pandit Wright
SEVP Strategy and Development: Donald A. Baer
EVP and CFO: Barbara (Barb) Bennett
EVP Advertising Sales: Scott McGraw
EVP Discovery Networks US: Clark Bunting
EVP New Media and Network Services: Mona Abutaleb
EVP Research and Planning: Daniel Fischer
EVP and General Manager, Animal Planet, US: Maureen Smith
EVP and General Manager, Discovery Channel: Jane Root
EVP Discovery Education: Steve Sidel
EVP Marketing, Discovery Networks US: Ken Dice
SVP and Chief Information Officer, Technology: Diane Duggan
President, Ad Sales: Joe Abruzzese
President, Affiliate Sales and Marketing: Bill Goodwyn
President, Discovery Consumer Products: Michela A. English, age 54
President, Discovery Networks International: Dawn L. McCall
President, Discovery Networks, US: William M. (Billy) Campbell III

LOCATIONS

HQ: Discovery Communications, Inc.
  1 Discovery Place, Silver Spring, MD 20910
Phone: 240-662-2000   **Fax:** 240-662-1868
Web: www.discovery.com

PRODUCTS/OPERATIONS

Selected Operations
Discovery Consumer Products
  Discovery Channel Catalog (product catalog)
  Discovery Channel Stores (approximately 165
    Discovery Channel retail outlets)
  Discovery Education (educational video productions)
  Discovery.com (online store)
Discovery HD Theater (digital channel featuring high-
  definition TV programming)
Discovery Networks International (33 languages, 154
  countries)
Discovery Networks US
  Animal Planet (115 million households)
  BBC America (35 million households, markets and
    distributes for the BBC)
  Discovery Channel (85 million)
  Discovery en Español (digital)
  Discovery Health Channel (55 million)
  Discovery Kids (106 million)
  Discovery Times Channel (digital)
  The Learning Channel (84 million)
  Travel Channel (70 million)

COMPETITORS

A&E Networks
CPB
Crown Media
E. W. Scripps
Lifetime
National Geographic
NBC
NBC Universal
News Corp.
Oxygen Media
PBS
Space Holdings
Time Warner
Univision
Viacom
Walt Disney

HISTORICAL FINANCIALS

Company Type: Joint venture

Income Statement   FYE: December 31

	REVENUE ($ mil.)	NET INCOME ($ mil.)	NET PROFIT MARGIN	EMPLOYEES
12/03	1,717	—	—	5,000
12/02	1,995	—	—	5,000
12/01	1,800	—	—	4,000
12/00	1,730	—	—	4,000
12/99	1,400	—	—	3,500
12/98	1,100	—	—	3,000
12/97	860	—	—	3,000
12/96	662	—	—	1,900
12/95	452	—	—	500
12/94	200	—	—	400
Annual Growth	27.0%	—	—	32.4%

Revenue History

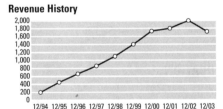

Do it Best

If you're building a house or fixing one up, you might as well Do it Best — at least, that's the hope of the hardware industry's second-largest cooperative (by sales) after Ace Hardware. Do it Best has about 4,100 member-owned stores in the US and about 44 other countries. The stores stock some 70,000 hardware and building products, which are also sold online. (Its Web site offers advice for do-it-yourselfers.) The co-op, whose buying power enables members to get retail products at competitive prices, also offers unifying branding programs using the Do it Best and Do it center names. Do it Best (formerly Hardware Wholesalers) began in 1945; it bought the Our Own Hardware co-op in 1998.

The company's RetailStart program provides market and site analysis, demographic research, project financing, inventory assistance, and project management for retailer-members who want to open more stores.

EXECUTIVES

Chairman: Steve Hawkinson
Vice Chairman: Bruce Ellis
President and CEO: Bob Taylor
EVP and COO: David (Dave) Haist
VP of Finance: David (Dave) Dietz
VP of Hardware Products: Jay Brown
VP of Information Technology: Kay Williams
VP of Lumber and Building Materials: Quent Ondricek
VP of Marketing and International Development:
  William Zielke
VP of Retail Development: Dave Heine
VP of Retail Logistics Services: John Snider
Secretary: Brenda Ward
Treasurer: Myron Andersen
Manager of Communications: Heather Martin
Manager of Human Resources: Nancy Harris

LOCATIONS

HQ: Do it Best Corp.
  6502 Nelson Rd., Fort Wayne, IN 46801
Phone: 260-748-5300   **Fax:** 260-748-5620
Web: www.doitbest.com

COMPETITORS

84 Lumber
Ace Hardware
Home Depot
Lowe's
Menard

Northern Tool
Sears
Sutherland Lumber
TruServ
Wal-Mart

HISTORICAL FINANCIALS

Company Type: Cooperative

Income Statement   FYE: June 30

	REVENUE ($ mil.)	NET INCOME ($ mil.)	NET PROFIT MARGIN	EMPLOYEES
6/03	2,334	0	0.0%	—
6/02	2,308	—	—	1,625
6/01	2,191	—	—	1,350
6/00	2,445	—	—	1,307
6/99	2,215	—	—	1,300
6/98	1,900	—	—	1,250
6/97	1,830	—	—	1,100
6/96	1,620	—	—	1,100
6/95	1,705	—	—	1,100
6/94	1,628	—	—	—
Annual Growth	4.1%	—	—	5.7%

Revenue History

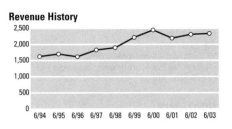

Doane Pet Care

Doane Pet Care has no quibble with kibble. The largest maker of private-label dog and cat food in Europe and North America, the company makes dry (nearly 75% of sales) and semi-moist foods, soft treats, and dog biscuits. Doane also makes products for other pet food companies. Its customers include Wal-Mart (about 40% of sales), mass merchandisers, grocery and pet store chains, and farm and feed stores. The company has expanded into Asia, Europe, and Latin America through acquisitions. Doane is owned by a group of private equity investors, as well as investment companies, including J.P. Morgan Partners, and buyout firm Bruckmann, Rosser, Sherrill.

EXECUTIVES

Chairman: George B. Kelly, age 54
President and CEO: Douglas J. (Doug) Cahill, age 44
VP, Finance and CFO: Philip K. Woodlief, age 50
VP and General Manager, North American Operations:
  David L. Horton, age 43
VP and Managing Director, European Operations:
  Tonny F. Carstensen
VP, Co-Manufacturing and Specialty:
  Richard A. Hannasch, age 50
VP, People: Debra J. Shecterle
VP, Supply Chain, Quality, and CIO: Joseph J. Meyers,
  age 42
Corporate Controller and Principal Accounting Officer:
  Stephen P. Havala
Auditors: KPMG LLP

LOCATIONS

HQ: Doane Pet Care Company
  210 Westwood Place South, Ste. 400,
  Brentwood, TN 37027
Phone: 615-373-7774   **Fax:** 615-309-1187
Web: www.doanepetcare.com

Doane Pet Care has about 25 manufacturing and distribution facilities in Alabama, California, Colorado, Florida, Georgia, Indiana, Iowa, Louisiana, Minnesota, Missouri, New York, Ohio, Oklahoma, Pennsylvania, South Carolina, Tennessee, Texas, Virginia, and Wisconsin. It also has facilities in Austria, Denmark, Italy, Spain, and the UK.

2003 Sales

	$ mil.	% of total
Domestic	758.5	75
International		
Denmark	201.8	20
Spain	38.9	4
UK	14.7	1
Total	**1,013.9**	**100**

Doctor's Associates

You don't have to go underground to catch this subway. Doctor's Associates operates the Subway chain of sandwich shops, the second largest chain behind McDonald's. It boasts more than 21,000 locations in about 75 countries, with more US locations than the Golden Arches. Virtually all Subway restaurants are franchised and offer such fare as hot and cold sandwiches, turkey wraps, and salads. Subways are located in freestanding buildings, as well as in airports, convenience stores, sports facilities, and other locations. The company is owned by co-founders Fred DeLuca and Peter Buck, who opened the first Subway in 1965.

With a low initial franchise cost and simple operations (minimum space requirements and little on-site cooking), Subway has been one of the fastest-growing franchises in the world. Doctor's Associates saw more than 2,000 Subway franchises open in 2003. Its popularity as a healthy alternative to burgers and fries has also increased with the help of an advertising campaign featuring Jared Fogle, a customer who claims to have lost 245 pounds on a diet of Subway sandwiches. Subway now controls about a third of the sandwich market.

The company is focused on increasing its international presence, having opened more than 100 locations in the UK and 400 in Australia. In the US, It is seeking to outpace its competition in key markets, including deli-rich New York City. The chain is also introducing new menu items, such as wrap sandwiches endorsed by Atkins Nutritionals, to satisfy the health concerns of fast-food consumers.

HISTORY

In 1965 17-year-old Fred DeLuca dreamed of becoming a doctor and worked as a stock boy in a Bridgeport, Connecticut, hardware store to earn college tuition. It wasn't enough, so he cornered family friend Peter Buck at a backyard barbecue and asked for advice. Buck, a nuclear physicist, suggested DeLuca open a submarine sandwich shop and put up $1,000 to get him started.

As the summer of 1965 was coming to an end, DeLuca rented a small location in a remote area of Bridgeport, opened Pete's Super Submarines, and there he sold foot-long sandwiches. On the first day the sandwiches were so popular that DeLuca hired his own customers to work behind the counter; by the end of the day, he had sold out of all his supplies. The sandwiches continued to be popular for a while, but within a few months the shop started losing money, and DeLuca and Buck found that selling submarine sandwiches was a seasonal business. They decided they could create an illusion of success by opening a second location and then a third. The third store was finally successful, partly because of its more visible location and increased marketing and partly because of a new name — Subway.

DeLuca and Buck had set a goal of 32 shops opened by 1975, but they had only 16 by 1974. They realized that the only way they could reach their goal in one year was to license the Subway name. The first franchise opened that year in Wallingford, Connecticut, and they opened 32 by the end of 1975. The partners hit 100 by 1978, then 200 by 1983, and DeLuca set a new goal: 5,000 Subway shops by 1994. The first international Subway opened in Bahrain in 1984, and DeLuca achieved his goal of 5,000 shops by 1990.

During the 1990s, DeLuca experimented with several other franchise concepts, including We Care Hair (budget styling salons), Cajun Joe's (spicy fried chicken), and Q Burgers. But none of these ventures fared as well as his sandwich empire. As Subway grew, however, controversy surrounding its treatment of franchisees began to surface. A Federal Trade Commission investigation of the company was dropped in 1993, but Subway continued to battle franchisees complaining about broken contracts, market oversaturation (and, therefore, too much competition and self-cannibalization), and what the franchisees viewed as unreasonably high royalty fees.

In spite of its franchising troubles, Subway kept growing. It expanded into Russia and China in the mid-1990s, and opened its 11,000th restaurant in 1995. In 1997 Subway inked deals with the Army, Navy, and Air Force exchange services to bring Subway units to military bases. Two years later the company opened its 14,000th restaurant in Mount Gambier, Australia, an event that coincided with Subway's renewed push to expand internationally.

The company got some unexpected publicity in 1999 when 22 year-old Jared Fogle claimed that he dropped 245 pounds from his 425-pound frame by subsisting on a diet of Subway turkey sandwiches. Subway helped Fogle extend his 15 minutes of fame by featuring him and his oversized pants in a TV commercial. (The company has since built an entire campaign around Fogle which features other weight watchers attributing their success to Jared and Subway.) Subway introduced its largest menu initiative ever in 2000 when it unveiled its Subway Selects Gourmet Sandwiches, adding 13 items to the menu. In April of 2001 the company opened its 15,000th store.

Also that year, Buck retired as chairman, but stayed on as a member of the board of directors. Becoming one of the fastest growing franchises in the world, Subway expanded from 16,000 locations in 2002 to more than 20,000 stores by the end of 2003.

EXECUTIVES

President: Frederick A. (Fred) DeLuca, age 56
Chief Marketing Officer: Bill Schettini
Controller: David Worroll
Assistant VP: Cindy Eadie
Director of Corporate Communications:
Michele Klotzer
Director of Franchise Sales: Don Fertman
Director of International Development:
Patricia Demarais
Director of Research and Development: Suzanne Greco
Director of Creative Services: Ruth Woyciesjes
Senior National Accounts Manager: Janet Bencivenga
Public Relations Coordinator: Les Winograd

LOCATIONS

HQ: Doctor's Associates Inc.
 325 Bic Dr., Milford, CT 06460
Phone: 203-877-4281 **Fax:** 203-876-6695
Web: www.subway.com

PRODUCTS/OPERATIONS

2003 Sales

	$ mil.	% of total
Dry pet food	740.1	73
Wet, semi-moist & other	182.5	18
Biscuits & treats	91.3	9
Total	**1,013.9**	**100**

Selected Brand Names

Bonkers
Canine Club
Country Prime
Dura Life
Exceed
Hy Vee
Kozy Kitten
Maxximum Nutrition
NutraCare
Ol' Roy
Pathmark
Pet Club
Pet Lovers
PMI-Nutrition
Retriever
Special Kitty
TrailBlazer

COMPETITORS

Colgate-Palmolive
Del Monte Foods
Hartz Mountain
Hill's Pet Nutrition
Iams
Nestlé Purina PetCare
Nutro Products
Royal Canin

HISTORICAL FINANCIALS

Company Type: Private

Income Statement
FYE: December 31

	REVENUE ($ mil.)	NET INCOME ($ mil.)	NET PROFIT MARGIN	EMPLOYEES
12/03	1,014	(68)	—	2,671
12/02	887	15	1.7%	2,707
12/01	896	(22)	—	2,730
12/00	892	(5)	—	3,585
12/99	771	21	2.8%	2,286
12/98	687	(22)	—	2,453
12/97	565	6	1.1%	2,330
12/96	513	(2)	—	—
Annual Growth	10.2%	—	—	2.3%

2003 Year-End Financials

Debt ratio: 1,797.7%
Return on equity: —
Cash ($ mil.): 29
Current ratio: 1.24
Long-term debt ($ mil.): 561

Net Income History

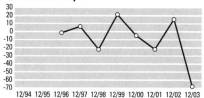

2003 Locations	No.
US	16,518
Canada	1,871
Australia	586
UK	204
Puerto Rico	168
New Zealand	98
Japan	95
Mexico	87
Venezuela	70
Germany	65
South Korea	41
India	31
Taiwan	31
China	29
Philippines	24
Spain	24
United Arab Emirates	20
El Salvador	19
Bahamas	17
Costa Rica	17
Singapore	16
Kuwait	14
Iceland	13
Sweden	13
Other countries	214
Total	**20,285**

COMPETITORS

AFC Enterprises
Blimpie
Burger King
Chick-fil-A
CKE Restaurants
Dairy Queen
Jack in the Box
Jimmy John's
McDonald's
Mr. Goodcents
Quizno's
Triarc
Wendy's
YUM!

HISTORICAL FINANCIALS

Company Type: Private

Income Statement				FYE: December 31
	ESTIMATED REVENUE ($ mil.)	NET INCOME ($ mil.)	NET PROFIT MARGIN	EMPLOYEES
12/03	468	—	—	638
12/02	500	—	—	730
12/01	400	—	—	730
12/00	350	—	—	730
12/99	300	—	—	—
12/98	300	—	—	—
12/97	300	—	—	—
12/96	250	—	—	—
12/95	250	—	—	—
12/94	200	—	—	—
Annual Growth	9.9%	—	—	(4.4%)

Revenue History

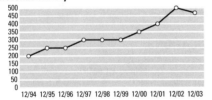

Dole Food

Bananas might be Dole Food's favorite fruit because they have "a-peel," but as the world's largest producer of fresh fruits and vegetables, it grows and markets much more. The company is one of the world's leading producers of bananas and pineapples, and also markets citrus, table grapes, dried fruits, nuts, and fresh-cut flowers. Dole has added value-added products (packaged salads, novelty canned pineapple shapes) to insulate itself from fluctuating commodity markets. Cost-cutting measures, including job cuts, have helped boost Dole's earnings. CEO David Murdock took the company private in 2003.

Along with being the world's largest producer of fresh fruits and vegetables, Dole is also the world leading producer of fresh-cut flowers. The company has been introducing convenience-oriented products such as bagged vegetables, ready-to-eat salads, and individual fruit servings packaged in plastic cups, as well as niche products such as organic bananas. It is adding to its distribution channels, with a significant share of its products now available in drug and convenience stores, club stores, and mass merchandisers.

HISTORY

James Dole embarked on an unlikely career in a faraway land when he graduated from Harvard College in 1899 and sailed to Hawaii. He bought 61 acres of farmland for $4,000 in 1900 and the next year organized the Hawaiian Pineapple Company, announcing that the island's pineapples would eventually be in every US grocery store.

Others had tried and failed to sell fresh fruit to the mainland. Dole decided he would succeed by canning pineapples. He built his first cannery in 1903 and introduced a national magazine advertising campaign in 1908 designed to make consumers associate Hawaii with pineapples (then considered exotic fruits).

In 1922 Dole expanded his production by buying the island of Lanai, where he set up a pineapple plantation. He financed the purchase by selling a third interest in Hawaiian Pineapple to Waialua Agricultural Company, which was part of Castle & Cooke (C&C). Samuel Castle and Amos Cooke, missionaries to Hawaii, formed C&C in 1851 to manage their church's failing depository, which supplied outlying mission posts with staple goods. In 1858 they entered the sugar business and within 10 years served as agents for several Hawaiian sugar plantations and the ships that carried their cargoes.

C&C gained control of Hawaiian Pineapple in 1932 when it acquired an additional 21% interest in the business. The company began using the Dole name on packaging the next year. Dole became chairman of the board of the reorganized company in 1935 but pursued other business interests until he retired in 1948.

Hawaiian Pineapple was run separately until C&C bought the remainder in 1961. The company started pineapple and banana farms in the Philippines in 1963 to supply markets in East Asia. C&C began importing bananas when it purchased 55% of Standard Fruit of New Orleans in 1964. (It purchased the remainder four years later.)

Heavily in debt and limping from two hostile takeover attempts, C&C agreed in 1985 to merge with Flexi-Van, a container leasing company. The merger brought with it needed capital, Flexi-Van owner David Murdock (who became C&C's CEO), and a fleet of ships to transport produce. Murdock began trimming back, leaving C&C with its fruit and real estate operations. He then decided to end all pineapple operations on Lanai to concentrate on tourist properties. (The company took a $168 million write-off on them in 1995, when it spun off its real estate and resort operations as Castle & Cooke.)

C&C became Dole Food in 1991. The company expanded at home and internationally, adding SAMICA (dried fruits and nuts, Europe, 1992), Dromedary (dates, US, 1994), Chiquita's New Zealand produce operations (1995), and SABA Trading (60%, produce importing and distribution, Sweden, 1998).

In 1995 Dole sold its juice business to Seagram's Tropicana Products division, keeping its pineapple juices and licensing the Dole name to Seagram (PepsiCo bought Tropicana in 1998.) Dole entered the fresh-flower trade in 1998 by acquiring four major growers and marketers. It is now the world's largest producer of freshly cut flowers.

A worldwide banana glut, Hurricane Mitch, and severe freezes in California hit the company hard in late 1998. The next year Dole launched cost-cutting measures, which by early 2000 had ripened into better earnings. Nonetheless, cutbacks and disposals continued throughout 2001.

In 2002 Murdock made a cash and debt takeover bid for the company worth about $2.5 billion. However, at least one minority shareholder was dissatisfied with the offer and filed a proposal calling for Murdock's resignation. The company rejected Murdock's $29.50 per share offer and negotiated with him regarding a larger price-per-share offer. In December Dole and Murdock finally signed a merger agreement. The deal, which gave stockholders $33.50 per share in cash, was approved by company stockholders in March 2003 and left Murdock in sole control of the company.

When Maui Land & Pineapple decided to sell off its Costa Rican subsidiary, Dole scooped it up in late 2003, paying $15.3 million for the pineapple-growing and marketing business. In 2004 Lawrence Kern, Dole's president and COO, left the company and Chairman, CEO, and sole owner Murdock took over as president. In July 2004 CFO Richard Dahl became president. Also in 2004 the company acquired frozen fruit manufacturer J.R. Wood, Inc. and fresh berry producer Coastal Berry Company.

EXECUTIVES

Chairman and CEO: David H. Murdock, age 80, $2,336,269 pay
President, COO, and Director: Richard J. Dahl, age 52, $977,615 pay
EVP, Corporate Development, and Director: Scott A. Griswold, age 50
EVP, General Counsel, and Corporate Secretary: C. Michael Carter, age 60, $977,615 pay
EVP and Assistant to the Chairman: Roberta Wieman, age 58
SVP, Human Resources: Sue Hagen
SVP, Strategy: Javier H. Idrovo
VP, Corporate Controller and Chief Accounting Officer: Yoon J. Hugh, age 32
VP, Sales and Marketing, Foodservice: Chris Lock
VP and CFO: Joseph S. Tesoriero
VP and Director, Dole Nutrition Institute: Jennifer Grossman
VP and Treasurer: Beth Potillo, age 43
President, Dole Asia: James Prideaux
President, Dole Fresh Flowers: John T. Schouten
President, Dole North America Tropical Fresh Fruit: Michael J. Cavallero, age 56

President, Dole Worldwide Packaged Foods:
Peter M. Nolan, age 60
President, Dole Worldwide Vegetables:
Eric M. Schwartz, age 44
Director, Corporate Communications: Freya Maneki
Auditors: Deloitte & Touche LLP

LOCATIONS

HQ: Dole Food Company, Inc.
1 Dole Dr., Westlake Village, CA 91362
Phone: 818-879-6600 **Fax:** 818-879-6615
Web: www.dole.com

Dole Food distributes its more than 200 products in more than 90 countries worldwide.

2003 Sales

	$ mil.	% of total
US	2,227.5	47
Europe	1,359.1	28
Asia	743.3	16
Latin America	158.0	3
Other international	285.2	6
Total	**4,773.1**	**100**

PRODUCTS/OPERATIONS

2003 Sales

	$ mil.	% of total
Fresh fruit	3,134.1	66
Fresh vegetables	850.6	18
Packaged foods	587.2	12
Fresh-cut flowers	168.1	4
Other	33.1	—
Total	**4,773.1**	**100**

Divisions and Selected Products

Dried Fruit and Nuts
  Almonds
  Dates
  Pistachios
  Prunes
  Raisins
Fresh Flowers
  Carnations
  Chrysanthemums
  Roses
Fresh Fruit
  Apples
  Bananas
  Cherries
  Cranberries
  Grapefruit
  Grapes
  Kiwi
  Lemons
  Mangoes
  Melons
  Oranges
  Papayas
  Pears
  Pineapples
  Raspberries
  Strawberries
  Tangelos
Fresh Vegetables
  Artichokes
  Asparagus
  Broccoli
  Carrots
  Celery
  Lettuce
  Onions
  Snow peas
  Spinach
Ready-to-Eat Foods
  Coleslaw
  Peeled mini-carrots
  Salad mixes
  Shredded lettuce

Packaged Foods
  Canned mandarin-orange segments
  Canned mixed fruits
  Canned pineapple
  Pineapple juice

COMPETITORS

Blue Diamond Growers
Chiquita Brands
Del Monte Foods
Earthbound Farm
Fresh Del Monte Produce
Fyffes
Geest
Global Berry Farms
John Sanfilippo & Son
Maui Land & Pineapple
Ocean Spray
Seneca Foods
Sun Growers
Sunkist
UniMark Group
United Foods

HISTORICAL FINANCIALS
Company Type: Private

Income Statement
FYE: Saturday closest to December 31

	REVENUE ($ mil.)	NET INCOME ($ mil.)	NET PROFIT MARGIN	EMPLOYEES
12/03	4,773	84	1.8%	59,000
12/02	4,392	36	0.8%	57,000
12/01	4,449	150	3.4%	59,000
12/00	4,763	68	1.4%	61,000
12/99	5,061	49	1.0%	59,500
12/98	4,424	12	0.3%	53,500
12/97	4,336	160	3.7%	44,000
12/96	3,840	89	2.3%	46,000
12/95	3,804	23	0.6%	43,000
12/94	3,842	68	1.8%	46,000
Annual Growth	2.4%	2.4%	—	2.8%

2003 Year-End Financials
Debt ratio: 395.1%
Return on equity: 14.0%
Cash ($ mil.): 33
Current ratio: 1.34
Long-term debt ($ mil.): 1,804

Net Income History

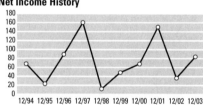

Dot Foods

Dot Foods, the largest food service redistributor in the US, began as a station wagon that hauled dairy goods around as Associated Dairy Products. The company now runs more than 500 trucks (under the name Dot Transportation) that receive groceries, flatware, serve ware, and janitorial supplies from food and equipment makers and redistribute them to food processors and food service distributors. Dot owns facilities in California, Georgia, Illinois, Maryland, and Missouri, and has customers throughout the US. Its edotfoods subsidiary handles Dot's e-commerce. Dot also owns Principle Resource, a provider of marketing services to food manufacturers. Robert and Dorothy Tracy founded the family-owned company in 1960.

EXECUTIVES

CEO: Patrick F. (Pat) Tracy
President: John Tracy
CFO: William (Bill) Metzinger
VP, Administration, Chesterfield Office: John Long
VP, Administration, Headquarters: Dan Koch
VP, Business Development: Mike Buckley
VP, Management Information Systems: Mark Read
VP, Marketing: Scott Stamerjohn
VP, Sales: Mike Duggan
President, Tracy Family Foundation: Jean Buckley
Director, Human Resources: Mike Hulsen
National Sales Manager: Dick Tracy
Manager of Transportation Safety, Dot Transportation Inc.: Scott Bowen

LOCATIONS

HQ: Dot Foods, Inc.
Route 99 South, Mt. Sterling, IL 62353
Phone: 217-773-4411 **Fax:** 217-773-3321
Web: www.dotfoods.com

COMPETITORS

C.D. Hartnett
McLane Foodservice
Purity Wholesale Grocers
SYSCO
U.S. Foodservice

HISTORICAL FINANCIALS
Company Type: Private

Income Statement
FYE: December 31

	REVENUE ($ mil.)	NET INCOME ($ mil.)	NET PROFIT MARGIN	EMPLOYEES
12/03	1,410	—	—	2,000
12/02	1,410	—	—	2,000
12/01	1,500	—	—	1,750
12/00	1,107	—	—	1,607
12/99	986	—	—	1,468
12/98	814	—	—	1,307
Annual Growth	11.6%	—	—	8.9%

Revenue History

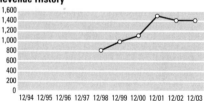

Dow Corning

Break out the streamers and party hats for Dow Corning. In June 2004 the 50-50 joint venture of chemical titan Dow and glass giant Corning emerged from nine years of bankruptcy protection that had come about as a result of thousands of claims alleging the company's silicone-gel breast implants were harmful. Dow Corning produces about 7,000 silicone-based products such as adhesives, insulating materials, and lubricants for aerospace, automotive, and electrical uses. Because silicone does not conduct electricity, it is also used in its hard polycrystalline form (silicon) as the material on which semiconductors are built. With plants worldwide, the company sells more than half its products outside the US.

Having filed for bankruptcy protection in 1995, Dow Corning appeared close to a settlement that would help it emerge from Chapter 11 in 1998. The settlement would provide $2.35 billion for breast implant claims over a 16-year period. A bankruptcy court approved the settlement in 1999 (paving the road for the company's exit from bankruptcy), but the deal fell through when the judge ruled that women who did not agree to the settlement could still sue Dow Corning's corporate parents. Dow Corning and about 94% of the women who had sued it appealed the judge's ruling.

In October 2003 an advisory panel recommended the FDA approve the use of silicone implants made by another company, Inamed, a move that might have protected Dow Corning from further lawsuits. The FDA, though, ruled against that recommendation, keeping the implants illegal except in trials.

Finally, in April 2004, a Bankruptcy Court judge ruled that the re-approved settlement would go through effective June 1. The move allows the money Dow Corning set aside for the settlement to be dispersed to claimants and for the company to exit Chapter 11, which finally occurred June 1.

Corning, Inc., has been suffering from weak sales in telecommunications markets, and Dow Corning's exit from bankruptcy could help Corning back to profitability.

HISTORY

Dow Corning was founded in 1943 as a joint venture between Dow Chemical and Corning Glass Works. Corning, founded by Amory Houghton in 1875, provided Thomas Edison with glass for the first light bulbs. It developed Pyrex heat-resistant glass in 1915.

Corning made its first silicone resin samples in 1938. It teamed with a group of Dow Chemical scientists who were also working on silicone products in 1940. Dow Chemical president Willard Dow and Corning Glass Works president Glen Cole shook hands on the idea of a joint venture in 1942, and 10 months later Dow Corning was formed. Its first product, the engine grease DOW CORNING 4, enabled B-17s to fly at 35,000 feet (a major contribution to the Allied war effort). In 1945 DOW CORNING 35 (an emulsifier used in tire molds) and Pan Glaze (which made baking pans stick-proof and easier to clean) were instant successes on the home front.

Dow Corning expanded rapidly in international markets and in 1960 set up Dow Corning International to handle sales and technical service in markets outside North America. By 1969 the company had operations worldwide.

Dow Corning's first breast implants went on the market in 1964. Since then Dow Corning and other silicone makers have sold silicone breast implants to more than a million women in the US. In the early 1980s breast-implant recipients began suing Dow Corning and other implant makers, claiming that the silicone gel in the implants leaked and caused health problems. Dow Corning, the leading implant maker, defended the devices as safe. Dow Corning stopped making implants in 1992, after the Food and Drug Administration called for a moratorium on silicone-gel implants.

In 1993 Baxter International, Bristol-Myers Squibb, and Dow Corning offered $4.2 billion to settle thousands of claims. The corporation declared bankruptcy in 1995 to buy time for financial reorganization. A federal judge stripped Dow Chemical of its protection from direct liability, and the company was later ordered to pay a Nevada couple $4.1 million in damages (other jurisdictions did not follow suit). Dow Corning sold its Polytrap polymer technology to Advanced Polymer, maker of polymer-based pharmaceutical delivery systems, in 1996. The following year the company sold Bisco Products, its silicone-foam business, to Rogers Corporation for $12 million.

Dow Corning's $3.7 billion bankruptcy reorganization plan, offered in 1997, allowed for $2.4 billion to be set aside to settle most implant lawsuits against the corporation. However, a federal bankruptcy judge found legal flaws in the proposal and refused to allow claimants to vote on it. In 1998 Dow Corning upped the ante to $4.4 billion — $3 billion to the silicone claimants and the rest to creditors.

Both sides later agreed to a $3.2 billion compensation package, and in 1999 the plan received approval from a bankruptcy judge and creditors. However, the settlement stalled when the judge ruled that women who disagreed with the settlement could sue Dow Chemical and Corning (Dow Corning appealed). Despite its court battles, in 2000 the company acquired the 51% of Universal Silicones & Lubricants (high-tech lubricants and silicone sealants) it did not own and renamed the company Dow Corning India. Dow Corning finally emerged from Chapter 11 in mid-2004.

EXECUTIVES

President and CEO: Stephanie A. Burns, age 49
SVP; President, Americas; and General Manager, Specialty Chemicals Industry Business:
Jere D. Marciniak
SVP; General Manager, Construction Industry and Core Products Business Unit: Christopher J. (Chris) Bowyer
VP and CFO: Joseph D. (Don) Sheets
VP and Chief Human Resources Officer:
Derek A. O'Malley-Keyes
VP and Executive Director, Supply Chains:
Alexandre (Alex) Royez
VP, General Counsel, and Secretary: Sue K. McDonnell
VP; General Manager, New Ventures Business Unit:
Jean-Marc Gilson
VP; General Manager, Service Enterprise Unit:
Allan C. (Harry) Ludgate
VP, Geographic Development; President, Asia:
Bruno Sulmon
VP and General Manager, Electronics Business; President, Dow Corning China: Ian Thackwray
CIO and Executive Director: Abbe Mulders
CTO and Executive Director, Science and Technology:
Gregg Zank
President, Hemlock Semiconductor:
Donald (Don) Pfuehler
President, Multibase: Andy Tometich
Executive Director and Chief Communications Officer:
Janet M. Botz
Executive Director, Marketing and Sales:
Scott E. Fuson
Auditors: PricewaterhouseCoopers LLP

LOCATIONS

HQ: Dow Corning Corporation
2200 W. Salzburg Rd., Midland, MI 48686
Phone: 989-496-4000   **Fax:** 989-496-4393
Web: www.dowcorning.com

Dow Corning has about 25 manufacturing sites worldwide. Its principal manufacturing facilities in the US are located in Kentucky and Michigan. Its principal non-US manufacturing facilities are located in Belgium, Germany, Japan, and the UK.

PRODUCTS/OPERATIONS

Selected Products and Applications

Aerospace
   Adhesives
   Encapsulants
   Exotic composite materials
   Greases
   High-purity fluids
   Protective coatings
Automotive
   Brake systems
   Chassis
   Electrical component
   Electronic components
   Engine/drivetrain
   Fuel systems
Chemical and Material Manufacturing
   Agrochemicals
   Auto appearance chemicals
   Industrial release agents
   Materials treatment
   Pulp manufacturing
Cleaning Products
   Dry cleaning
   Laundry detergents
   Polishes and hard surface cleaners
Coatings and Plastics
   Caulks
   Coatings
   Sealants
Electrical/Electronics
   Adhesives and sealants
   Conformal coatings
   High-voltage insulators
   Hyperpure polycrystalline silicon
   Interlayer dielectric and passivation materials
   Liquid transformer fluid
   Silicone encapsulants
   Silicone RTV coating for insulators
   Thermally conductive adhesives
Food and Beverage
   Defoamers
   Packaging
Health care
   Hydrocephalus shunts
   Pacemaker leads
   Tubing for dialysis
Paper Manufacturing & Finishing
   Release coatings for label-backing paper, pressure-sensitive adhesives, and paper coatings
Personal Care
   Materials for deodorants, cosmetics, and lotions
Plastics
Textiles
   Waterproofing agents

COMPETITORS

3M
Asahi Glass
BASF AG
Bayer MaterialScience
Bostik Findley
Crompton
Cytec Engineered Materials
Degussa
Dynea
Eastman Chemical
Formosa Plastics
GE Advanced Materials
Goldschmidt
H.B. Fuller
Hexcel
Honeywell Specialty Materials
Imperial Chemical Industries
National Starch and Chemical
Rhodia
Shin-Etsu Chemical
Wacker

HISTORICAL FINANCIALS
Company Type: Joint venture

Income Statement				FYE: December 31
	REVENUE ($ mil.)	NET INCOME ($ mil.)	NET PROFIT MARGIN	EMPLOYEES
12/03	2,873	177	6.1%	8,200
12/02	2,610	59	2.2%	8,200
12/01	2,438	(23)	—	7,500
12/00	2,751	105	3.8%	9,000
12/99	2,603	110	4.2%	9,000
12/98	2,568	207	8.0%	9,000
12/97	2,644	238	9.0%	9,100
12/96	2,532	222	8.8%	8,900
12/95	2,493	(31)	—	8,500
12/94	2,205	(7)	—	8,300
Annual Growth	3.0%	—	—	(0.1%)

2003 Year-End Financials
Debt ratio: 6.2%
Return on equity: 25.5%
Cash ($ mil.): 462
Current ratio: 2.14
Long-term debt ($ mil.): 52

Net Income History

DPR Construction

From bio labs to wafer fabs, the projects of DPR Construction reflect the diversity of its commercial building. The general contractor/construction manager, one of the largest in the US, focuses on projects for the biotechnology, pharmaceutical, health care, education, and semiconductor markets. DPR also specializes in corporate office and entertainment projects (such as theme parks and studios) and warehouses and distribution centers. Clients have included Apple Computer, Banner Health, Pixar Animation, and PricewaterhouseCoopers. President Doug Woods, CEO Peter Nosler, and secretary/treasurer Ron Davidowski (the D, P, and R) founded the company in 1990. The now employee-owned company has 10 offices in the US.

EXECUTIVES
CEO: Peter C. Nosler
President: Douglas E. (Doug) Woods
CFO: Sandra Waechter
Secretary and Treasurer: Ron J. Davidowski
EVP: Eric Lamb
EVP: Peter A. Salvati
Marketing and Corporate Communications: Yumi Clevenger
Director Human Resources: Jorinne Liberatore

LOCATIONS
HQ: DPR Construction, Inc.
1450 Veterans Blvd., Redwood City, CA 94063
Phone: 650-474-1450 **Fax:** 650-474-1451
Web: www.dprinc.com

DPR Construction has offices in Atlanta; Austin, Texas; Fairfax, Virginia; Newport Beach, Redwood City, Sacramento, San Diego, San Francisco, and San Jose, California; and Phoenix.

COMPETITORS
Alberici
Austin Industries
Beck Group
Devcon Construction
Fluor
Hathaway Dinwiddie Construction
Hensel Phelps Construction
Hoffman Corporation
Jacobs Engineering
Rudolph & Sletten
Skanska USA Building
Swinerton
Turner Corporation
Webcor Builders
Whiting-Turner

HISTORICAL FINANCIALS
Company Type: Private

Income Statement				FYE: December 31
	REVENUE ($ mil.)	NET INCOME ($ mil.)	NET PROFIT MARGIN	EMPLOYEES
12/03	1,271	—	—	—
12/02	1,049	—	—	2,132
12/01	1,800	—	—	3,100
12/00	1,958	—	—	3,100
12/99	1,200	—	—	2,000
12/98	1,300	—	—	2,500
12/97	890	—	—	1,200
12/96	620	—	—	1,149
12/95	257	—	—	656
12/94	175	—	—	350
Annual Growth	24.7%	—	—	25.3%

Revenue History

Dr Pepper/Seven Up Bottling

Dr Pepper/Seven Up Bottling Group (DPSUBG) rings up sweet results for Cadbury Schweppes, the world's #3 soft-drink firm. It is a leading bottler of soft drinks in the US, distributing in 21 states. Besides the Dr Pepper and 7 UP brands (owned by Cadbury Schweppes), it also bottles the lesser-known Big Red and Crush brands. DPSUBG was formed in 1999 when Dr Pepper Bottling Company of Texas and American Bottling merged. Cadbury Schweppes and The Carlyle Group own 40% and 53% of the company, respectively. CEO Jim Turner joined Dr Pepper Bottling Company of Texas in 1982 and built it by acquiring franchises. The company continues to grow by acquiring other bottlers.

EXECUTIVES
President and CEO: Jim L. Turner, age 58
CFO: Holly Lovvorn
EVP, Administration: Tom Taszarek
VP, Human Resources: Kellie Defratus
VP, Information Systems: Gerry Mecca
VP, Sales and Marketing: Guy Mueller

LOCATIONS
HQ: Dr Pepper/Seven Up Bottling Group, Inc.
5950 Sherry Ln., Ste. 500, Dallas, TX 75225
Phone: 214-530-5000 **Fax:** 214-530-5036

COMPETITORS
Buffalo Rock
Coca-Cola
Coca-Cola Bottling Consolidated
Coca-Cola Enterprises
Coke United
Cott
National Beverage
Pepsi Bottling
Pepsi Bottling Ventures
Pepsi MidAmerica
PepsiAmericas
PepsiCo
Philadelphia Coca-Cola

HISTORICAL FINANCIALS
Company Type: Private

Income Statement				FYE: December 31
	REVENUE ($ mil.)	NET INCOME ($ mil.)	NET PROFIT MARGIN	EMPLOYEES
12/02	1,820	—	—	8,800
12/01	1,820	—	—	8,800
12/00	1,900	—	—	8,000
12/99	1,900	—	—	3,000
12/98	878	—	—	2,700
12/97	709	—	—	2,500
12/96	523	—	—	1,567
12/95	496	—	—	1,535
12/94	532	—	—	1,400
12/93	475	—	—	1,320
Annual Growth	16.1%	—	—	23.5%

Revenue History
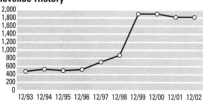

DreamWorks

DreamWorks L.L.C has moguls times three. Created in 1994 by Steven Spielberg (famed film director/producer), Jeffrey Katzenberg (former Disney film executive and animation guru), and David Geffen (recording industry maven), DreamWorks produces animated features (*Shrek*), live action movies (*Catch Me if You Can*), and TV shows (*Las Vegas*). DreamWorks Animation is the studio's Silicon Valley-based computer-animation arm. DreamWorks pulled out of the GameWorks video arcade business it started with SEGA and Universal Pictures, and has sold its music business to Universal Music. The three founders collectively own the majority of DreamWorks; Microsoft co-founder Paul Allen also owns a stake.

The company had once dared to dream of operating a media empire with movie, animation, and television production units, as well as music and Internet holdings. And though its live-action movie unit has generated successes such as *Old School* and *Road to Perdition*, and its animation unit has produced hits including *Chicken Run* and *Shrek* (one of 2001's highest grossing films), DreamWorks has been less successful in other areas. DreamWorks Records, which produced the soundtracks to all Dream-Works films and albums for popular artists, never caught fire and the company sold the unit to Universal Music Group for an estimated $100 million. The company's TV unit has produced only one notable hit (*Spin City*, whose six-year series-run ended in 2002).

The company's DreamWorks Animation division has turned out to be DreamWorks' most successful business. 2004's *Shrek 2* proved to be yet another money-making creation from the division and has surpassed previous records as one of the most successful animated films of all time. The company is spinning off DreamWorks Animation in an initial public offering. Its animated feature *Shark Tale* opened with a splash in 2004.

As far as the company's television operations go, DreamWorks' TV has signed a development pact with NBC. Series under the deal include *Father of the Pride* and *The Contender*, which have been included in NBC's fall 2004 line-up.

The company's history has been marked with other obstacles: its first animated feature (*Prince of Egypt*) and early live-action films (*Amistad, Almost Famous*) flopped at the box office; and DreamWorks scuttled plans for a Web entertainment division. In contrast to its major studio rivals Paramount and Universal that produce about two dozen films annually, the smaller DreamWorks makes eight to ten films a year.

Japanese media firm Kadokawa Holdings has announced plans to invest $100 million in DreamWorks, giving Kadokawa a 3% stake in the studio. Its investment gives Kadokawa exclusive rights to distribute DreamWorks films, videos, DVDs, and other products in Japan.

HISTORY

Before pooling their collective talents in 1994, Steven Spielberg, Jeffrey Katzenberg, and David Geffen had each established an impressive track record. Spielberg had spawned such blockbusters as *Jaws, The Indiana Jones Trilogy,* and *Jurassic Park*. Katzenberg had guided Walt Disney's return to animation (*The Lion King, Aladdin*) before a falling out with Disney CEO Michael Eisner. Music guru Geffen had helped make superstars of the Eagles and Nirvana.

A high-tech who's who embraced the SKG dream. Microsoft invested around $30 million to develop video games, while Microsoft co-founder Paul Allen shelled out nearly $500 million for a stake in the new company. Soon DreamWorks had arranged a $100 million programming deal with ABC, a 10-year HBO licensing agreement worth an estimated $1 billion, and co-founded a $50 million animation studio with Silicon Graphics. DreamWorks then announced plans in 1995 to build the first new studio since the 1930s, just outside of Los Angeles in Playa Vista. In 1996 the company purchased a stake in the Sunnyvale, CA-based computer animation firm PDI to form PDI/DreamWorks.

DreamWorks produced a string of TV flops before finding success with the Michael J. Fox comedy *Spin City* in 1996. Later that year the company released the first record under its new label, a dud from pop star George Michael, and it announced its partnership with SEGA and MCA (now Universal Studios) to develop SEGA GameWorks (video arcade super-centers featuring SEGA titles and games designed by Spielberg). The company finally released its first three movies in 1997 (*The Peacemaker, Amistad,* and *Mouse Hunt*) to mixed critical reviews and mediocre box office performances. Combined with DreamWorks' less-than-stellar offerings in TV and music, buzz circulated that the meeting of the minds at DreamWorks wasn't all it cracked up to be.

But DreamWorks started showing signs of life in 1998 with the comet disaster film *Deep Impact* and Spielberg's Oscar-winning *Saving Private Ryan*, the highest grossing film of the year. It also introduced the first of its animated films that year, which included the successful *Antz*. DreamWorks finished the year with the highest average gross per film of all the major studios.

After facing a multitude of environmental protests, cost overruns, and construction delays, DreamWorks scrapped its Playa Vista studio plans in 1999. Around the same time, Katzenberg settled his high-profile lawsuit against Disney over a bonus owed him when he resigned. Later that year DreamWorks announced a five-picture deal with Academy Award-winning animation firm Aardman Animations, with which it co-produced *Chicken Run* (released in 2000).

DreamWorks and Microsoft sold DreamWorks Interactive, their video game joint venture, to Electronic Arts in 2000. Later that year *American Beauty* took home the Oscar for Best Picture of 1999, and the studio continued its successful box-office run with three films that grossed more than $100 million (*Gladiator*, which scored the studio its second Best Picture Oscar, *Chicken Run*, and *What Lies Beneath*).

The studio won big in 2001 with *Shrek*, which became one of that year's highest grossing films with more than $265 million at the box office. *A Beautiful Mind*, its co-production with Universal Pictures, won one of the company's films yet another Best Picture Oscar. Also that year the company exited the GameWorks venture when the arcades failed to catch on quickly.

In late 2003 the company exited the music business with the sale of DreamWorks records to Universal Music's Interscope Records. DreamWorks scored another hit with the 2004 release of *Shrek 2*.

EXECUTIVES

Principal: David Geffen, age 61
Principal: Jeffrey Katzenberg, age 53
Principal: Steven Spielberg, age 58
COO: Helene Hahn
Co-Head of DreamWorks Television: Justin Falvey
Co-Head of DreamWorks Television: Darryl Frank
Head of Feature Animation: Ann Daly, age 48
Co-Head of Motion Picture Division: Laurie MacDonald
Co-Head of Motion Picture Division: Walter Parkes, age 52
Head of PDI/DreamWorks: Patti Burke
Head of Theatrical Distribution: Jim Tharp
President of Production: Adam Goodman
Head of Animation Technology, PDI/DreamWorks: Andy Hendrickson
Head of International Marketing and Distribution: Stephen Basil-Jones

LOCATIONS

HQ: DreamWorks L.L.C.
1000 Flower St., Glendale, CA 91201
Phone: 818-733-7000   **Fax:** 818-695-7574
Web: www.dreamworks.com

DreamWorks SKG has offices in Glendale, Los Angeles, and Universal City, California.

PRODUCTS/OPERATIONS

Selected Films, Recording Artists, and Television Shows

DreamWorks Pictures
  A Beautiful Mind (2001, co-produced with Universal Studios)
  Almost Famous (2000)
  American Beauty (1999)
  Amistad (1997)
  Antz (1998)
  Catch Me if You Can (2002)
  Chicken Run (2000, co-produced with Aardman Animation)
  Deep Impact (1998, co-produced with Paramount Pictures)
  Galaxy Quest (1999)
  Gladiator (2000, co-produced with Universal Studios)
  House of Sand and Fog (2003)
  The Legend of Bagger Vance (2000)
  Minority Report (2002)
  Mouse Hunt (1997)
  Old School (2003)
  The Peacemaker (1997)
  The Prince of Egypt (1998)
  The Ring (2002)
  Road to Perdition (2002)
  Road Trip (2000)
  Saving Private Ryan (1998, co-produced with Paramount Pictures)
  Shrek (2001)
  Shrek 2 (2004)
  Sinbad: Legend of the Seven Seas (2003)
  Small Time Crooks (2000)
  What Lies Beneath (2000, co-produced with 20th Century Fox)
DreamWorks Television
  Boomtown (2002-2003)
  Freaks and Geeks (1999-2000)
  The Job (2001)
  Las Vegas (2003)
  Oliver Beene (2003)
  Spin City (1996-2002)
  Undeclared (2001)

COMPETITORS

Carsey-Werner
Fox Filmed Entertainment
Lions Gate Entertainment
Lucasfilm
MGM
Miramax
NBC Universal
Paramount Pictures
Pixar
Sony Pictures Entertainment
Universal Pictures
Warner Bros.

HISTORICAL FINANCIALS
Company Type: Private

Income Statement
FYE: December 31

	REVENUE ($ mil.)	NET INCOME ($ mil.)	NET PROFIT MARGIN	EMPLOYEES
12/03	1,250	—	—	1,100
12/02	1,813	—	—	1,600
12/01	2,219	—	—	1,500
12/00	1,873	—	—	1,500
Annual Growth	(12.6%)	—	—	(9.8%)

Revenue History

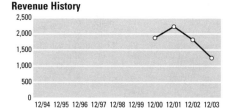

Drees Co.

A family-operated enterprise since its founding by Theodore Drees in 1928, The Drees Co. builds about 3,100 homes annually. Customers may choose from more than 100 floor plans for homes that range in price from about $100,000 to more than $800,000. Drees is a leading homebuilder in Cincinnati. It also builds condominiums, apartments, and commercial buildings through its nine divisions. The company is expanding through acquisitions such as the additions of the homebuilding assets of Zaring National in Cincinnati (Zaring Premier Homes), Indianapolis, and Nashville, and Ausherman Homes in Frederick, Maryland (near Washington, DC). Drees offers financing through its First Equity Mortgage subsidiary.

EXECUTIVES
Chairman: Ralph Drees
President and CEO: David Drees
EVP and CFO: Mark Williams
SVP Marketing: Jack Miller
VP Human Resources: Effie McKeehan
Director, IS: Mike Rulli
Director, Marketing: Barbara Drees
Secretary and Treasurer: Lawrence G. Herbst
President, Midwest Region: Terry Sievers
President, Southern Region: Mike Rubery
President, Dallas Division: Greg Dawson
President, Indianapolis Division: Peter Hils

LOCATIONS
HQ: The Drees Co.
211 Grandview Dr., Ste. 300, Fort Mitchell, KY 41017
Phone: 859-578-4200 **Fax:** 859-341-5854
Web: www.dreeshomes.com

The Drees Co. has operations in Indianapolis, Indiana; northern Kentucky; Frederick, Maryland; Raleigh, North Carolina; Cincinnati, Cleveland, and Dayton, Ohio; Nashville, Tennessee; Austin and Dallas/Fort Worth, Texas; Virginia; and Washington, DC.

Division Office Locations
Austin Division (Austin, Texas)
Cincinnati Division (Ft. Mitchell, Kentucky)
Cleveland Division (North Canton, Ohio)
Dallas Division (Irving, Texas)
Dayton Division (Centerville, Ohio)
Indianapolis Division (Indianapolis, Indiana)
Nashville Division (Brentwood, Tennessee)
Raleigh Division (Raleigh, North Carolina)
Washington, DC, Division (Alexandria, Virginia)

COMPETITORS
Centex
D.R. Horton
Engle Homes
Fischer Homes
KB Home
Lennar
M/I Homes
Pulte Homes
Ryland

HISTORICAL FINANCIALS
Company Type: Private

Income Statement
FYE: March 31

	REVENUE ($ mil.)	NET INCOME ($ mil.)	NET PROFIT MARGIN	EMPLOYEES
3/04	978	—	—	1,200
3/03	822	—	—	1,232
3/02	848	—	—	1,100
3/01	527	—	—	850
3/00	515	—	—	—
3/99	366	—	—	700
3/98	343	—	—	685
3/97	301	—	—	675
3/96	253	—	—	675
3/95	236	—	—	625
Annual Growth	17.1%	—	—	7.5%

Revenue History

Dresser

All dressed up and no place to flow? Not Dresser. The company, formerly Dresser Industries (and once a part of Halliburton), makes flow control products, measurement systems, and power systems. In addition to diagnostic equipment, injection pumps, and valves, Dresser's flow control segment oversees the products once created by the company's measurement systems unit. Dresser's power systems include natural gas-powered engines, rotary blowers, and vacuum pumps bearing the Waukesha and ROOTS brands. First Reserve Corporation, a US-based investment firm, owns more than 90% of Dresser. Morgan Stanley and Credit Suisse First Boston are representing the underwriters for the proposed IPO of the company.

EXECUTIVES
Chairman: Patrick M. Murray, age 61, $747,500 pay
President, CEO, and Director: Steven G. Lamb, age 48, $845,000 pay
EVP and CFO: James A. Nattier, age 43, $345,002 pay
SVP Corporate Development: J. Scott Matthews, age 58
SVP Human Resources: Mark J. Scott, age 50
VP and CIO: Troy D. Matherne, age 41
VP, General Counsel, and Secretary: Frank P. Pittman, age 57
VP Business Reengineering: Brian White, age 44
VP; President, Dresser Flow Solutions: Andrew E. Graves, age 45, $289,872 pay (partial-year salary)
VP; President, Dresser Instruments: John T. McKenna
VP; President, Dresser Wayne: John P. Ryan, age 52, $376,113 pay
VP; President, Waukesha Engine: Thomas J. Laird, age 54
Chief Accounting Officer and Corporate Controller: Thomas J. Kanuk, age 52
Treasurer: Richard T. Kernan
Auditors: PricewaterhouseCoopers LLP

LOCATIONS
HQ: Dresser, Inc.
15455 Dallas Pkwy., Ste. 1100, Addison, TX 75001
Phone: 972-361-9800 **Fax:** 972-361-9929
Web: www.dresser.com

Dresser has manufacturing facilities around the globe.

2003 Sales
	$ mil.	% of total
US	716	43
Europe & Africa	450	27
Canada & Latin America	224	14
Other regions	267	16
Total	**1,657**	**100**

PRODUCTS/OPERATIONS

2003 Sales
	$ mil.	% of total
Flow control	996	60
Measurement systems	391	23
Compression & power systems	277	17
Adjustments	(7)	—
Total	**1,657**	**100**

COMPETITORS
Caterpillar
Cooper Cameron
Danaher
Datamarine
Dover
Emerson Electric
Flowserve
IDEX
ITT Industries
Labfacility
Pentair
Rotork
SPX
Tokheim
Tyco International

HISTORICAL FINANCIALS
Company Type: Private

Income Statement
FYE: December 31

	REVENUE ($ mil.)	NET INCOME ($ mil.)	NET PROFIT MARGIN	EMPLOYEES
12/03	1,657	(45)	—	8,300
12/02	1,589	(23)	—	7,900
12/01	1,546	57	3.7%	8,500
Annual Growth	3.5%	—	—	(1.2%)

2003 Year-End Financials
Debt ratio: —
Return on equity: —
Cash ($ mil.): 149
Current ratio: 1.87
Long-term debt ($ mil.): 941

Net Income History

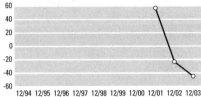

DriveTime

In this story the ugly duckling changes into DriveTime. DriveTime Automotive, formerly known as Ugly Duckling, is a leading used-car dealership chain, primarily targeting low-income customers and those with credit problems. To cater to these subprime customers, the company is a "buy here-pay here" dealer, meaning it finances and services car loans rather than using outside lenders (interest rates range from 20% to 30%). DriveTime operates about 80 dealerships in metropolitan areas in eight states. The cars undergo a 52-point inspection and are run through Experian AutoCheck, an auto history database. The company was taken private by a group led by chairman Ernest Garcia.

EXECUTIVES
Chairman: Ernest C. Garcia II
President and CEO: Gregory B. Sullivan
VP and CFO: Mark G. Sauder
VP, Secretary, and General Counsel: Jon D. Ehlinger, age 44, $160,000 pay
VP and Treasurer: Bill Aguayo
Director, Human Resources: Brandie Anslow
Auditors: KPMG LLP

LOCATIONS
HQ: DriveTime Automotive Group, Inc.
4020 E. Indian School Rd., Phoenix, AZ 85018
Phone: 602-852-6600   **Fax:** 602-852-6686
Web: www.drivetime.com

COMPETITORS
America's Car-Mart
AutoNation
CarMax
Driver's Mart Worldwide
Gillman
Gunn Automotive
Hall Auto World
Red McCombs Automotive Group
Sonic Automotive
VT Inc.

HISTORICAL FINANCIALS
Company Type: Private

Income Statement
FYE: December 31

	REVENUE ($ mil.)	NET INCOME ($ mil.)	NET PROFIT MARGIN	EMPLOYEES
12/03	729	—	—	2,049
12/02	400	—	—	2,100
12/01	434	—	—	2,300
12/00	483	—	—	2,600
12/99	390	—	—	2,700
12/98	288	—	—	2,500
12/97	124	—	—	2,300
12/96	54	—	—	652
12/95	56	—	—	425
12/94	34	—	—	—
Annual Growth	40.7%	—	—	21.7%

Revenue History

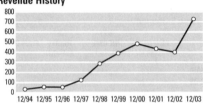

Drummond

Drummond Company is building its business from the ground down. The company's Shoal Creek coal mine in Alabama is one of the US's largest underground mines. Shoal Creek produces more than 4 million tons of coal annually, most of which it sells to electric utility Alabama Power. Drummond also operates a surface coal mine in Colombia. Its ABC Coke unit has an annual capacity of some 750,000 tons. In addition, the company develops housing communities and office parks in Alabama, California, and Florida. Heman Drummond began his namesake company in 1935 on land homesteaded by his mother; eventually his five sons entered the business. The Drummond family still owns and manages the company.

EXECUTIVES
Chairman and CEO: Garry N. Drummond Sr., age 65
Vice Chairman: E. A. (Larry) Drummond
SEVP, External Affairs and Treasurer: Walter F. Johnsey
SVP and CFO: Jack Stilwell
President, ABC Coke Division: John M. Pearson
President, Drummond Coal Sales, Inc.: George E. Wilbanks
President, Drummond, Ltd.: Augusto Jimenez
President, Mining Division: Mike Zervos
VP, Human Resources: Andy Slentz

LOCATIONS
HQ: Drummond Company, Inc.
530 Beacon Pkwy. W., Ste. 900, Birmingham, AL 35209
Phone: 205-945-6500   **Fax:** 205-945-6440
Web: www.drummondco.com

Drummond Company has mining operations in the US (in Alabama) and in Colombia, and a coke facility in Alabama. The company is also involved in real estate projects in Alabama, California, and Florida.

PRODUCTS/OPERATIONS

Selected Operations
ABC Coke (coke plant; Jefferson County, Alabama)
La Loma Mine (coal, Colombia)
Liberty Park (real estate development; Birmingham, Alabama)
Oakbridge (real estate development; Lakeland, Florida)
Rancho La Quinta (real estate development; La Quinta, California)
Shoal Creek Mine (coal; Jefferson County, Alabama)

COMPETITORS
Alliance Resource
Arch Coal
Black Hills
CONSOL Energy
Grupo México
Horizon Natural Resources
Level 3 Communications
Massey Energy
NACCO Industries
Oxbow
Peabody Energy
Penn Virginia
Sherritt International
Walter Industries
Westmoreland Coal

HISTORICAL FINANCIALS
Company Type: Private

Income Statement
FYE: December 31

	REVENUE ($ mil.)	NET INCOME ($ mil.)	NET PROFIT MARGIN	EMPLOYEES
12/03	800	—	—	2,500
12/02	830	—	—	2,500
12/01	850	—	—	2,500
12/00	615	—	—	2,800
12/99	720	—	—	3,300
12/98	734	—	—	2,900
12/97	746	—	—	2,850
12/96	750	—	—	2,800
12/95	725	—	—	3,350
12/94	687	—	—	2,800
Annual Growth	1.7%	—	—	(1.3%)

Revenue History

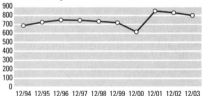

Duane Reade

Duane Reade is the Big Apple of drugstores. Named after the two streets where its first store was located, the company is the market leader in the densely populated Manhattan area. The company operates about 240 stores in New York and New Jersey. More than half of the company's stores are in high-traffic Manhattan (giving the firm more sales per square foot than any other US drugstore chain). Duane Reade's stores vary greatly in size (1,600-14,700 sq. ft.). The company sells prescription drugs, but nearly 60% of sales come from items such as over-the-counter medications, food and beverages, and health and beauty aids. Duane Reade was taken private in mid-2004 by equity group Oak Hill Capital Partners.

Oak Hill Capital is led by Texas investor Robert M. Bass. In return for each share, stockholders received $16.50 in cash for a transaction valued at about $700 million — including debt — for the company.

Burdened in the 1990s by debt and expansion costs, Duane Reade became profitable despite increased competition from rivals CVS and Rite Aid. Since its 1998 IPO, which helped it refinance that debt, the company has been growing rapidly. Much of Duane Reade's growth is through new store openings, including what it terms "planned cannibalization," where new stores are opened near crowded older stores to relieve traffic. The drugstore chain plans to open as many as a dozen stores in 2005.

The firm buys most of its non-pharmacy products directly from manufacturers and distributes those items through its warehouses in New Jersey and Queens. Duane Reade fills about 1,700 called-in prescriptions a day from its midtown central fill station. The company also offers more than 800 private-label products (including its "apt.5" line of cosmetics), which account for about 7% of non-pharmacy sales.

A ruling by the National Labor Relations Board could force the regional drugstore chain to pay out more than $25 million in unpaid benefit contributions to its unionized employees. The ruling is part of an ongoing labor dispute between Duane Reade and 2,600 members of Local 338, which the company no longer recognizes.

EXECUTIVES

Chairman, President, and CEO: Anthony J. Cuti, age 57, $850,000 pay
SVP, Sales and Marketing: Gary Charboneau, age 58, $450,000 pay
SVP, CFO, Assistant Secretary: John K. Henry, age 53, $350,000 pay
SVP, Merchandising: Timothy R. LaBeau, age 49, $385,000 pay
SVP, Store and Pharmacy Operations: Jerry M. Ray, age 55, $350,000 pay
VP, General Counsel and Secretary: Michelle D. Bergman, age 37
VP and Controller: Chris Darrow
VP, Finance: Anthony M. Goldrick
VP, Asset Protection: Mike Knievel
VP, Management Information Systems: Joseph S. Lacko, age 61, $258,536 pay
VP, Human Resources and Administration: James M. Rizzo
Auditors: PricewaterhouseCoopers LLP

LOCATIONS

HQ: Duane Reade Inc.
440 9th Ave., New York, NY 10001
Phone: 212-273-5700 **Fax:** 212-244-6527
Web: www.duanereade.com

Duane Reade operates about 240 drugstores in New York and New Jersey; it also has a central fill station in Manhattan and distribution facilities in North Bergen, New Jersey, and Queens, New York.

PRODUCTS/OPERATIONS

Selected Merchandise and Services
Automated teller machines
Cosmetics
Food and beverage items
Greeting cards
Health and beauty aids
Hosiery
Housewares
Lottery ticket sales
Nutritional products
Over-the-counter medications
Photo supplies
Photofinishing
Prescription drugs
Seasonal merchandise
Tobacco products
Vitamins

COMPETITORS

A&P	Pathmark
CVS	Rite Aid
drugstore.com	Walgreen

HISTORICAL FINANCIALS

Company Type: Private

Income Statement			FYE: Saturday nearest December 31	
	REVENUE ($ mil.)	NET INCOME ($ mil.)	NET PROFIT MARGIN	EMPLOYEES
12/03	1,384	5	0.4%	6,100
12/02	1,275	16	1.2%	6,000
12/01	1,144	25	2.2%	5,100
12/00	1,000	23	2.3%	5,500
12/99	840	41	4.8%	5,000
12/98	587	(5)	—	3,500
12/97	430	(15)	—	2,000
12/96	382	(18)	—	2,000
12/95	337	(18)	—	—
12/94	281	(16)	—	—
Annual Growth	19.4%	—	—	17.3%

2003 Year-End Financials
Debt ratio: 80.8%   Current ratio: 2.98
Return on equity: 1.5%   Long-term debt ($ mil.): 273
Cash ($ mil.): 1

Net Income History

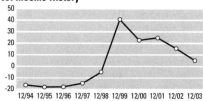

Duchossois Industries

Business is no longer a horse race for holding company Duchossois Industries. The former owner of Chicago's Arlington International Racecourse, Duchossois Industries (pronounced Deshy-swa) sold its interests in the track to Churchill Downs. The Chamberlain Group, a Duchossois subsidiary, is the world's largest maker of residential and commercial door openers, and it is a leading maker of access control products. Duchossois also has interests in the consumer products, transportation, defense, and entertainment industries. Duchossois sold its railroad car unit (Thrall) to Trinity Industries in 2001. Chairman Richard Duchossois and his family own the company; he also holds a 24% stake in Churchill Downs.

EXECUTIVES

Chairman: Richard L. Duchossois, age 82
President and CEO: Craig J. Duchossois, age 59
CFO: Robert L. (Bob) Fealy, age 52
VP and General Counsel: David L. Filkin, age 40
CEO, The Chamberlain Group, Inc.: J. David Rolls
EVP, Administration, The Chamberlain Group, Inc.: Mark Tone
VP, Information and Technology, The Chamberlain Group, Inc.: David Gillhouse
Hiring Manager, The Chamberlain Group, Inc.: Melanie Ditore
Auditors: KPMG

LOCATIONS

HQ: Duchossois Industries, Inc.
845 N. Larch Ave., Elmhurst, IL 60126
Phone: 630-279-3600 **Fax:** 630-530-6091

PRODUCTS/OPERATIONS

Selected Subsidiaries
Automatic Gate Supply
The Chamberlain Group, Inc.
M & S Systems, Inc.
Sentex Systems

COMPETITORS

ACF	Microchip Technology
GE	Nortek
General American Door	Overhead Door
Greenbrier	Stanley Works
Griffon	Trinity Industries

HISTORICAL FINANCIALS

Company Type: Private

Income Statement			FYE: December 31	
	ESTIMATED REVENUE ($ mil.)	NET INCOME ($ mil.)	NET PROFIT MARGIN	EMPLOYEES
12/02	1,000	—	—	8,000
12/01	1,105	—	—	6,500
12/00	1,200	—	—	7,000
12/99	1,500	—	—	8,000
12/98	1,250	—	—	8,000
12/97	1,250	—	—	7,000
12/96	1,260	—	—	8,000
12/95	1,070	—	—	8,000
12/94	1,000	—	—	8,000
12/93	1,000	—	—	8,000
Annual Growth	0.0%	—	—	0.0%

Revenue History

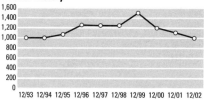

Duke Energy Field Services

Duke Energy Field Services (DEFS) is a midstream maven. Formed when Duke Energy and Phillips Petroleum (later ConocoPhillips) combined their gas gathering, processing, and marketing operations, the firm is one of the largest midstream natural gas operators in the US, with 58,000 miles of gathering pipeline and 56 processing plants. DEFS also owns NGL processing facilities and is the US's #1 NGL producer, at about 365,000 barrels per day. The firm sells about 40% of its NGL production to ConocoPhillips under a long-term contract. Duke Energy owns about 70% of DEFS; ConocoPhillips owns 30%. DEFS is the general partner of TEPPCO Partners, L.P., which owns a network of refined products and crude oil pipelines.

EXECUTIVES

Chairman, President, and CEO:
  William H. (Bill) Easter III, age 54
EVP Gathering and Processing:
  Michael J. (Mike) Bradley, age 49, $478,800 pay
EVP Marketing and Corporate Development:
  Mark A. Borer, age 49, $477,848 pay
SVP Northern Division: Robert F. (Rob) Martinovich, age 46, $428,975 pay
VP and CFO: Rose M. Robeson, age 43
VP, General Counsel, and Secretary: Brent L. Backes, age 44
VP Technical Services: William S. (Bill) Prentice
President, Duke Energy NGL Services:
  William S. (Bill) Waldheim
Human Resources: David Goode
Investor Relations: Tom Long
Auditors: Deloitte & Touche LLP

LOCATIONS

HQ: Duke Energy Field Services, LLC
  370 17th St., Ste. 900, Denver, CO 80202
Phone: 303-595-3331   **Fax:** 303-595-0480
Web: www.defieldservices.com

Duke Energy Field Services operates in Colorado, Kansas, New Mexico, Oklahoma, Texas, and Wyoming, and in northwestern Alberta, Canada. It also operates along the US Gulf Coast and in the Gulf of Mexico.

PRODUCTS/OPERATIONS

2003 Sales

	$ mil.	% of total
Natural gas	8,097	82
NGLs	1,782	18
Adjustments	(1,060)	—
Total	8,819	100

COMPETITORS

ChevronTexaco
Dynegy
El Paso
Enterprise Products
Kerr-McGee
Kinder Morgan Energy
  Partners
Koch
Plains All American
  Pipeline
Western Gas
Williams Companies

HISTORICAL FINANCIALS

Company Type: Joint venture

Income Statement				FYE: December 31
	REVENUE ($ mil.)	NET INCOME ($ mil.)	NET PROFIT MARGIN	EMPLOYEES
12/03	8,819	214	2.4%	3,575
12/02	5,492	(47)	—	3,800
12/01	9,598	364	3.8%	3,600
12/00	9,093	680	7.5%	3,400
12/99	3,458	43	1.3%	2,700
12/98	1,584	2	0.1%	—
12/97	1,802	51	2.8%	—
Annual Growth	30.3%	26.9%	—	7.3%

2003 Year-End Financials

Debt ratio: 82.4%   Current ratio: 0.94
Return on equity: 8.2%   Long-term debt ($ mil.): 2,262
Cash ($ mil.): 43

Net Income History

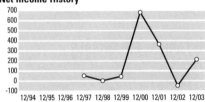

Dunavant Enterprises

King Cotton is alive and well in Memphis. Homegrown Dunavant Enterprises is one of the largest cotton traders in the world. Dunavant was founded in 1960 by William Dunavant, his son Billy (who is allergic to cotton), and Samuel T. Reeves. (The elder Dunavant died shortly after the founding, and Reeves left in 1995 to form Pinnacle Trading.) The company, which grew by selling aggressively to China and the Soviet Union, maintains offices in Africa, Asia, Australia, Europe, Mexico, South America, the former Soviet Union, and the southern US. The company's other business interests include cotton ginning, trucking, and warehousing. Dunavant Enterprises is owned by the Dunavant family and company employees.

EXECUTIVES

Chairman and CEO: William B. (Billy) Dunavant Jr.
President, Dunavant of California: Roger Glaspey
Manager, Human Resources: Mike Andereck

LOCATIONS

HQ: Dunavant Enterprises, Inc.
  3797 New Getwell Rd., Memphis, TN 38118
Phone: 901-369-1500   **Fax:** 901-369-1608
Web: www.dunavant.com

COMPETITORS

Calcot
Cargill Cotton Inc.
J.G. Boswell Co.
King Ranch
Plains Cotton
Southwestern Irrigated Cotton
Staplcotn
Weil Brothers Cotton

HISTORICAL FINANCIALS

Company Type: Private

Income Statement				FYE: June 30
	ESTIMATED REVENUE ($ mil.)	NET INCOME ($ mil.)	NET PROFIT MARGIN	EMPLOYEES
6/03	1,099	—	—	2,000
6/02	1,000	—	—	2,000
6/01	1,030	—	—	2,400
6/00	1,022	—	—	950
6/99	1,065	—	—	700
6/98	1,200	—	—	700
6/97	1,250	—	—	950
6/96	1,300	—	—	920
6/95	1,300	—	—	—
6/94	1,250	—	—	—
Annual Growth	(1.4%)	—	—	11.7%

Revenue History

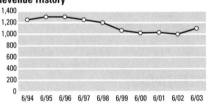

Dunn Industries

Although its beginnings date back to 1924, this company is far from done. Dunn Industries, owned by descendants of founder John E. Dunn, holds the J.E. Dunn Group of construction companies, including flagship J.E. Dunn Construction and Atlanta-based R.J. Griffin & Company. The group builds institutional, commercial, and industrial structures; it also provides construction and program management and design/build services. J.E. Dunn Construction, which ranks among the top 10 US general builders, was one of the first contractors to offer the construction management delivery method. Projects include Sprint's world headquarters near Kansas City, one of the Midwest's largest construction projects.

EXECUTIVES

Chairman Emeritus: William H. Dunn Sr.
Chairman: Stephen D. (Steve) Dunn
Vice Chairman: Robert A. Long
President and CEO: Terrence P. (Terry) Dunn
EVP: William H. Dunn Jr.
SVP Finance: Gordon E. Lansford III
SVP and General Counsel: Casey S. Halsey
SVP Corporate Development:
  Charles J. (Chuck) Cianciaruso
VP Human Resources: Rick Beyer
VP Information Services: Kent Immenschuh
VP Marketing: John Brake
Secretary: Barbara G. Hachey
Financial Analyst and Auditor: John Conley

LOCATIONS

HQ: Dunn Industries, Inc.
929 Holmes, Kansas City, MO 64106
Phone: 816-474-8600 **Fax:** 816-391-2510
Web: www.jedunn.com

COMPETITORS

Alberici
Bovis Lend Lease
Clark Enterprises
Hensel Phelps Construction
Rudolph & Sletten
Skanska USA Building
Turner Corporation
Washington Group

HISTORICAL FINANCIALS

Company Type: Private

Income Statement FYE: December 31

	REVENUE ($ mil.)	NET INCOME ($ mil.)	NET PROFIT MARGIN	EMPLOYEES
12/03	1,655	—	—	3,000
12/02	1,655	—	—	3,000
12/01	1,533	—	—	3,000
12/00	1,311	—	—	3,000
12/99	1,063	—	—	2,000
12/98	871	—	—	2,000
12/97	386	—	—	2,000
12/96	632	—	—	1,700
Annual Growth	14.7%	—	—	8.5%

Revenue History

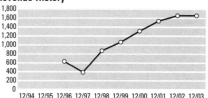

Dyson-Kissner-Moran

Privately held investment firm Dyson-Kissner-Moran, through takeovers and strategic acquisitions, has diversified its holdings to include businesses from manufacturing to arts and crafts. The firm typically uses its own capital to fund acquisitions and usually leaves them intact after the purchase. Founded in the mid-1950s, its purchases have included Household Finance and electronic-parts maker Kearney-National. Dyson-Kissner-Moran is controlled by the family of co-founder Charles Dyson (prominent philanthropist, LBO pioneer, and #5 on Richard Nixon's political enemies list), who died in 1997. His son Robert is the firm's chairman and CEO.

EXECUTIVES

Chairman and CEO: Robert R. Dyson, age 56
President and Chief Operating Officer: Grahame N. Clarke Jr.
VP Corporate Development: Bruce A. Cauley
VP Corporate Transactions: Robert Farley
VP and CFO: Marc Feldman
VP Planning and Analysis: Mark Chamberlin
VP and Treasurer: Lynn McCluskey
Secretary and General Counsel: John FitzSimons
Corporate Controller: Pam Lunny

LOCATIONS

HQ: The Dyson-Kissner-Moran Corporation
565 5th Ave., 4th Fl., New York, NY 10017
Phone: 212-661-4600 **Fax:** 212-986-7169
Web: www.dkmcorp.com

PRODUCTS/OPERATIONS

Selected Investments

Coto Technology (manufacture of reed switches)
Gas Components Group (custom assemblies and components for gas-fired appliances and grills)
Hapco (manufacture of aluminum light poles)
Plaid Creative Group (consumer craft and do-it-yourself products)
Recreational Vehicle Group (manufacture of sanitation and refrigeration systems for recreational vehicles)
Wabash Technologies (automotive sensors and actuators)

COMPETITORS

Advent International
AEA Investors
Blackstone Group
Haas Wheat
Hicks Muse
KKR

HISTORICAL FINANCIALS

Company Type: Private

Income Statement FYE: January 31

	ESTIMATED REVENUE ($ mil.)	NET INCOME ($ mil.)	NET PROFIT MARGIN	EMPLOYEES
1/02	850	—	—	39
1/01	850	—	—	4,600
1/00	800	—	—	4,600
1/99	767	—	—	4,500
1/98	670	—	—	4,400
1/97	660	—	—	4,350
1/96	600	—	—	—
Annual Growth	6.0%	—	—	(61.0%)

Revenue History

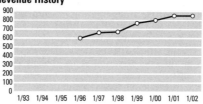

Eagle-Picher

From batteries to boron, Eagle-Picher Industries (EPI) provides products for the automotive, aerospace, telecommunications, pharmaceutical, and food and beverage industries.

EPI's automotive group leads in sales with products that include precision-machined components, rubber-coated parts, and fluid systems. The company's technologies segment makes batteries for satellites, launch vehicles, and missiles, as well as boron for nuclear applications.

Eagle-Picher has sold its machinery segment that made elevating wheel tractor scrapers (exclusively for Caterpillar). Its filtration and minerals segment produces diatomaceous earth and perlite filter aids. Dutch investment firm Granaria Holdings owns EPI.

EXECUTIVES

Chairman: Joel P. Wyler, age 52
President and CEO: John H. Weber, age 48, $225,000 pay
SVP and CFO: Thomas R. Pilholski
SVP, Human Resources: Jeffrey D. Sisson, age 45
VP and Controller: John F. Sullivan, age 59
VP, Director of Taxes: David N. Evans, $215,000 pay
VP, General Counsel, and Secretary: David G. Krall, age 39, $336,666 pay
President, Construction Equipment Division: Randy J. Holloway
President, Eagle-Picher Minerals: James L. Lauria
President, Eagle-Picher Technologies: William E. Long
President, Hillsdale Division: William D. Oeters
President, Wolverine Gasket Division: John (Jay) Pittas
Treasurer: Tom B. Scherpenberg, $165,000 pay
Auditors: Deloitte & Touche LLP

LOCATIONS

HQ: Eagle-Picher Industries, Inc.
3402 E. University Dr., Phoenix, AZ 85034
Phone: 602-794-9600 **Fax:** 602-794-9601
Web: www.epcorp.com

Eagle-Picher Industries has facilities primarily in the US. Other operations are located in Canada, Germany, and Mexico.

PRODUCTS/OPERATIONS

2003 Sales

	$ mil.	% of total
Automotive	413.7	60
Power Group	143.9	21
Filtration and Minerals	78.5	12
Specialty Minerals Group	40.2	6
Pharmaceutical Services	9.1	1
Total	**685.4**	**100**

Selected Divisions and Products

Automotive
  Hillsdale Division (components for engine, transmission, and driveline applications)
  Wolverine Division (sealing solutions for engines, transmissions, and compressors)
Technologies
  Batteries for satellites, launch vehicles, and missiles
  Boron
  Germanium
Minerals
  Diatomaceous earth
  Functional filters
  Industrial absorbants
  Perlite filter aids
  Soil amendments and conditioners

COMPETITORS

Alleghany Corporation
Exide
Federal-Mogul
JCI
Linamar
Newcor
Precision Castparts

HISTORICAL FINANCIALS

Company Type: Private

Income Statement				FYE: November 30
	REVENUE ($ mil.)	NET INCOME ($ mil.)	NET PROFIT MARGIN	EMPLOYEES
11/03	685	3	0.4%	3,900
11/02	697	(37)	—	3,800
11/01	693	(54)	—	4,100
11/00	838	(6)	—	5,400
11/99	913	(18)	—	6,925
11/98	826	—	—	6,600
11/97	906	—	—	6,700
11/96	891	—	—	7,700
11/95	849	—	—	—
11/94	757	—	—	—
Annual Growth	(1.1%)	—	—	(9.3%)

2003 Year-End Financials

Debt ratio: —
Return on equity: —
Cash ($ mil.): 67
Current ratio: 1.60
Long-term debt ($ mil.): 409

Net Income History

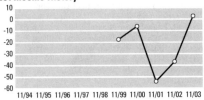

E. & J. Gallo

Let them drink wine! E. & J. Gallo Winery brings merlot to the masses. The world's largest wine maker produces about 30% of the wine sold in the US, thanks in part to its inexpensive jug and box brands Carlo Rossi and Peter Vella. It also makes the fortified Thunderbird brand. The vintner cultivates more than 3,000 acres in the Napa and Sonoma valleys in California. Gallo also makes its own labels and bottles and is the leading US wine exporter. Among its premium wines and imports are those of Gallo of Sonoma and Italian wine Ecco Domani. For those who prefer a little kick to their wine, Gallo distills several lines of brandy. The Gallo family owns E. & J. Gallo.

Gallo once only sold wine in the low-to-moderate price range, but now sells nearly 35 brands over a wide price range, from alcohol-added wines and wine coolers to upscale varietals that fetch more than $50 a bottle. It has successfully expanded premium wines such as Turning Leaf and Gossamer Bay, which don't have the Gallo name on the label. The vintner's strong affiliation with Wal-Mart has boosted wine sales in new Wal-Mart markets such as Germany and the UK.

In addition to using its own grapes, Gallo buys the fruit from other Sonoma County growers. Its 2002 purchase of fellow Sonoma County vintner Louis M. Martini Winery marked the first time Gallo bought another winery rather than land or wine labels. Gallo invested about $1 million in capital improvements at the winery with plans to ramp up production of cabernet under the Martini label.

HISTORY

Giuseppe Gallo, the father of Ernest and Julio Gallo, was born in 1882 in the wine country of northwest Italy. Around 1900 he and his brother, Michelo (they called themselves Joe and Mike), traveled to America seeking fame and fortune in San Francisco. Both brothers became wealthy growing grapes and anticipating the growth of the market during Prohibition (homemade wine was legal and popular).

Giuseppe's eldest sons, Ernest and Julio, worked with their father from the beginning, but their relationship was strained. The father was reluctant to help his sons, particularly Ernest, in business. However, the mysterious murder-suicide that ended the lives of Giuseppe and his wife in 1933 eliminated that problem: the sons inherited the business their father had been unwilling to share.

From then on Ernest ran the business end, assembling a large distribution network and building a national brand, while Julio made the wine and Joe Jr., the third, much younger, brother, worked for them. In the early 1940s Gallo opened bottling plants in Los Angeles and New Orleans, using screw-cap bottles, which then seemed more hygienic and modern than corks. Gallo lagged during WWII, when alcohol was diverted for the military. Under Julio's supervision, it upgraded its planting stock and refined its technology.

In an attempt to capitalize on the sweet wines popular in the 1950s, Gallo introduced Thunderbird, a fortified wine (its alcohol content boosted to 20%), in 1957. In the 1960s Gallo spurred its growth by heavily advertising and keeping prices low. It introduced Hearty Burgundy, a jug wine, in 1964, along with Ripple. Gallo introduced the carbonated, fruit-flavored Boone's Farm Apple Wine in 1969, creating short-term interest in "pop" wines.

The company introduced its first varietal wines in 1974. In the 1970s Gallo field workers switched unions, from the United Farm Workers to the Teamsters. Repercussions included protests and boycotts, but sales were largely unaffected. From 1976 to 1982 Gallo operated under an FTC order limiting its control over wholesalers. The order was lifted after the industry's competitive balance changed.

Through the 1970s and 1980s, Gallo expanded its production of varietals; in 1988 it began adding vintage dates to labels. But it also kept a hand in the lower levels of the market, introducing Bartles & Jaymes wine coolers.

Gallo began a legal battle in 1986 with Joe, who had been eased out of the business, over the use of the Gallo name. In 1992 Joe lost the use of his name for commercial purposes. Julio died the next year when his Jeep overturned on a family ranch.

In 1996 rival Kendall-Jackson sued Gallo for trademark infringement over Gallo's new wine brand, Turning Leaf, claiming Gallo copied its Vintner's Reserve bottle and label. A jury ruled in Gallo's favor in 1997; a federal appeals court supported that decision in 1998.

In May 2000 Gallo announced plans to promote wine-cooler market leader Bartles & Jaymes with a new advertising campaign, although the category continued to wane. The next year Gallo expanded the technological end of the wine business. Gallo's research team patented a number of tools licensed to winemakers around the world; one tool, for example, can diagnose a sick vine in a matter of hours, rather than years.

Gallo bought the Louis M. Martini Winery in Napa Valley in 2002, furthering its expansion into premium wines. It also bought the brand name and stocks of San Jose-based wine producer Mirassou Vineyards, one of the oldest wineries in California.

EXECUTIVES

Chairman: Ernest Gallo
Co-President: James E. Coleman
Co-President: Joseph E. Gallo
Co-President: Robert J. Gallo
EVP and General Counsel: Jack B. Owens
EVP, Marketing: Albion Fenderson
CFO: Tony Youga
VP, Creative Services: Joseph Visola
VP, Human Resources: Mike Chase
VP and CIO: Kent Kushar
VP, Media: Sue McClelland
VP, National Sales: Gary Ippolito

LOCATIONS

HQ: E. & J. Gallo Winery
  600 Yosemite Blvd., Modesto, CA 95354
Phone: 209-341-3111 **Fax:** 209-341-3569
Web: www.gallo.com

E. & J. Gallo Winery has four wineries in the California counties of Fresno, Livingston, Modesto, and Sonoma, and vineyards throughout the region. Its wine is sold throughout the US and in more than 85 countries.

PRODUCTS/OPERATIONS

Selected Products and Labels

Bargain generic and varietals (Carlo Rossi, Livingston Cellars, Peter Vella, Twin Valley, Wild Vines)
Brandy (E & J, E&J Cask & Cream, E&J VSOP)
Flagship (Gallo of Sonoma — County, Estate, and Single Vineyard series)
Fortified and jug (Night Train, Ripple, Thunderbird)
Hospitality industry (Burlwood, Copperidge by E&J Gallo, Liberty Creek, William Wycliff Vineyards)
Imported varietals (Bella Sera, Ecco Domani, McWilliams Hanwood Estate)
Mid-priced varietals (Redwood Creek, Turning Leaf)
Sparkling (André, Ballatore, Indigo Hills, Tott's)
Premium (Anapamu, Frei Brothers Reserve, Indigo Hills, Marcelina, Rancho Zabaco, Turning Leaf Coastal Reserve)

COMPETITORS

Allied Domecq
Asahi Breweries
Bacardi
Bacardi USA
Beringer Blass
Brown-Forman
Chalone Wine
Concha y Toro
Constellation Brands
Diageo
Foster's
GIV
Heaven Hill Distilleries
Jim Beam Brands
Kendall-Jackson
Kirin
LVMH
Pernod Ricard
Premier Pacific
Ravenswood Winery
R.H. Phillips
Robert Mondavi
Sebastiani Vineyards
Taittinger
Terlato Wine
Trinchero Family Estates
UST
Vincor
Wine Group

HISTORICAL FINANCIALS

Company Type: Private

Income Statement
FYE: December 31

	ESTIMATED REVENUE ($ mil.)	NET INCOME ($ mil.)	NET PROFIT MARGIN	EMPLOYEES
12/02	1,800	—	—	4,600
12/01	1,700	—	—	3,500
12/00	1,610	—	—	3,600
12/99	1,520	—	—	5,250
12/98	1,500	—	—	5,000
12/97	1,300	—	—	5,000
12/96	1,200	—	—	5,000
12/95	1,100	—	—	4,000
12/94	980	—	—	4,000
12/93	1,100	—	—	4,000
Annual Growth	5.6%	—	—	1.6%

Revenue History

Earle M. Jorgensen

Earle M. Jorgensen Company (EMJ) is one of the US's largest independent steel distributors. The company sells tubing, pipes, and bar, as well as structural, plate, and sheet metal products. EMJ makes its products from carbon steel, alloy steel, stainless steel, and aluminum.

The company markets to the automotive, agriculture, chemical, medical, oil, defense, food, petrochemical, and machinery-manufacturing industries. EMJ has roughly 35,000 customers in the agricultural, fluid power, industry equipment, machine tools, transportation, and oil and gas industries.

The company operates a cutting center, a tube-honing facility, and 36 service centers throughout North America. Employees own about 25% of EMJ; investment firm Kelso & Company owns most of the rest.

EXECUTIVES

Chairman: David M. Roderick, age 80
President, CEO, COO, and Director:
 Maurice S. Nelson Jr., age 66, $1,003,830 pay
EVP: R. Neil McCaffery, age 54, $379,966 pay
VP, CFO, and Secretary: William S. Johnson, age 47
EVP, Dallas, Houston, and Tulsa Facilities:
 Kenneth L. Henry, age 58, $422,358 pay
VP, Cleveland, Indianapolis, and Cincinnati Facilities:
 James D. Hoffman, age 46, $381,625 pay
VP, Merchandising: Frank D. Travetto, age 51, $418,478 pay
Director, Human Resources: Inger Dickinson
Auditors: Ernst & Young LLP

LOCATIONS

HQ: Earle M. Jorgensen Company
 10650 Alameda St., Lynwood, CA 90262
Phone: 323-567-1122 **Fax:** 323-563-5500
Web: www.emjmetals.com

Earle M. Jorgensen Company operates facilities in Canada and the US.

PRODUCTS/OPERATIONS

2004 Sales

	$ mil.	% of total
Bars		
Carbon & alloy	416.3	40
Stainless	114.4	11
Aluminum	72.8	7
Brass	20.8	2
Tubing		
Carbon & alloy	249.7	24
Aluminum	31.2	3
Stainless	20.8	2
Plate		
Carbon & alloy	31.2	3
Aluminum	20.8	2
Stainless	10.4	1
Other	52.0	5
Total	**1,040.4**	**100**

COMPETITORS

AK Steel Holding Corporation	O'Neal Steel
Alcoa	Reliance Steel
Chaparral Steel	Russel Metals
Dalmine	Ryerson Tull
Gerdau AmeriSteel	Severstal North America
Japan Steel Works	Siderca
Lone Star Technologies	Superior Group
MAXXAM	TXI
Metals USA	Ulbrich Stainless Steels
Nippon Steel	United States Steel

HISTORICAL FINANCIALS

Company Type: Private

Income Statement
FYE: March 31

	REVENUE ($ mil.)	NET INCOME ($ mil.)	NET PROFIT MARGIN	EMPLOYEES
3/04	1,040	15	1.5%	1,616
3/03	920	2	0.3%	1,674
3/02	895	5	0.6%	1,725
3/01	1,060	18	1.7%	2,010
3/00	938	24	2.6%	1,920
3/99	916	25	2.7%	1,900
3/98	1,050	16	1.5%	2,200
3/97	1,024	(27)	—	2,300
3/96	1,026	(29)	—	2,600
3/95	1,023	20	1.9%	2,800
Annual Growth	0.2%	(2.9%)	—	(5.9%)

2004 Year-End Financials

Debt ratio: —
Return on equity: —
Cash ($ mil.): 16
Current ratio: 1.58
Long-term debt ($ mil.): 306

Net Income History

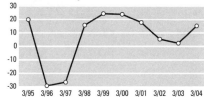

Earnhardt's Auto Centers

Milking the Southwest for all it's worth, Earnhardt's Auto Centers (and its bull-riding founder) sell more than 25,000 new and used vehicles each year. The company's nine auto dealerships in Arizona feature Chrysler, Dodge, Ford, Honda, Hyundai, Jeep, Kia, Mazda, Nissan, Suzuki, and Volkswagen autos. The outlets also operate parts and service departments and offer financing. The company also sells new and used RVs. Earnhardt's Web site allows customers to "build" their next car online: Shoppers can select from a complete list of options before submitting it electronically. Established in 1951 by Tex Earnhardt, the company is family-owned and -operated.

EXECUTIVES

Chairman: Hal J. (Tex) Earnhardt Jr.
President: Hal J. Earnhardt III
CFO: Robbyn McDowell
Secretary and Treasurer: Jim B. Earnhardt
Director of Human Resources: Sue Camrud
Director of Special Finance: Kevin Murphy

LOCATIONS

HQ: Earnhardt's Auto Centers
 1301 N. Arizona Ave., Gilbert, AZ 85233
Phone: 480-926-4000 **Fax:** 480-632-7712
Web: www.earnhardt.com

Earnhardt's Auto Centers has dealerships in Apache Junction, Chandler, Gilbert, Glendale, Mesa, and Tempe, Arizona.

COMPETITORS

Autobytel	David Wilson's
AutoNation	Larry H. Miller Group
AutoTrader	Tuttle-Click
carOrder.com	United Auto Group
CarsDirect.com	VT Inc.
Chapman Automotive	

HISTORICAL FINANCIALS

Company Type: Private

Income Statement
FYE: December 31

	ESTIMATED REVENUE ($ mil.)	NET INCOME ($ mil.)	NET PROFIT MARGIN	EMPLOYEES
12/03	610	—	—	2,000
12/02	650	—	—	2,000
12/01	685	—	—	2,000
12/00	680	—	—	1,500
12/99	800	—	—	1,500
12/98	800	—	—	1,500
12/97	650	—	—	1,400
12/96	560	—	—	1,112
12/95	475	—	—	—
12/94	400	—	—	—
Annual Growth	4.8%	—	—	8.7%

Revenue History

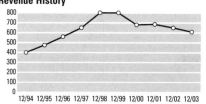

EBSCO

Few portfolios are more diverse than that of EBSCO Industries (short for Elton B. Stephens Company). Among the company's information services, manufacturing, and sales subsidiaries are magazine subscription and fulfillment firms, a fishing lure manufacturer, a rifle manufacturer, a specialty office and computer furniture retailer, and a real estate company. The conglomerate's main businesses revolve around the publishing industry: EBSCO operates a subscription management agency and is one of the largest publishers of information online and on CD-ROM. The family of founder Elton B. Stephens Sr. owns the company.

EBSCO provides bulk subscription services for print and electronic journals, technical reports, books, and other publications to schools, libraries, and professional offices. It offers sales, promotion, telemarketing, and fulfillment services to publishers, and it owns commercial printers and supplies bindery and packaging products.

Among EBSCO's eclectic subsidiaries are promotional products manufacturers Four Seasons and Vitronic; PRADCO, which makes fishing tackle; Valley Joist, which produces steel construction materials; Vulcan Industries, which makes point-of-purchase displays; Knight & Hale, which makes hunting accessories; specialty furniture makers H. Wilson and Luxor; and real estate unit EBSCO Development.

In 2003 EBSCO acquired the European operations of RoweCom, a company that provided libraries with an online service giving subscribers access to more than 240,000 periodicals.

EXECUTIVES

Chairman Emeritus: Elton B. Stephens
Chairman, President, and CEO: James T. (J.T.) Stephens
COO: F. Dixon Brooke Jr.
VP and CFO: Richard L. Bozzelli
VP; General Manager, Administrative Services: Becky Caldarello
VP; General Manager, Information Systems and Services: John R. Fitts
VP; General Manager, EBSCO Information Services: Allen Powell
VP; General Manager, EBSCO Publishing: Timothy R. (Tim) Collins
VP; General Manager, EBSCO Realty: Elton B. Stephens Jr.
VP; General Manager, EBSCO Telemarketing Service: Robert (Bob) Prosise
VP; General Manager, MetaPress: Mark Williams
VP and Director, Marketing: Jack H. Breard Jr.
VP Corporate Communications: Joe K. Weed

LOCATIONS

HQ: EBSCO Industries Inc.
5724 Hwy. 280 East, Birmingham, AL 35242
Phone: 205-991-6600 **Fax:** 205-995-1636
Web: www.ebscoind.com

PRODUCTS/OPERATIONS

Selected Operations
Information Services
  EBSCO Information Services (reference databases, online journals, and subscription services)
  EBSCO Publishing (database publishing and information retrieval services)
  EBSCO Subscription Services (subscription services for libraries and institutions)
Manufacturing
  EBSCO Media (commercial printer)
  Four Seasons (promotional products)
  H. Wilson Co. (audiovisual and computer products and furniture)
  Knight Rifles
  Luxor (specialty furniture for offices, schools, libraries, and health care facilities)
  PRADCO Outdoor Brands (fishing lures, fishing line, and related products)
  Valley Joist (steel joists, girders, and metal decks for the construction industry)
  Vitronic (promotional products)
  Vulcan Industries (point-of-purchase displays)
  Wayne Industries (point-of-purchase advertising and signs)
Sales
  EBSCO Development Co. (real estate development)
  EBSCO Magazine Express (direct-marketing subscription agency)
  EBSCO Realty (real estate broker)
  EBSCO TeleServices (telemarketing services)
  Military Service Company (producer and manufacturers' representative serving military base exchanges)
  NSC International (distribution of binding and laminating systems)
  Publishers' Warehouse (publishers' warehousing and shipping service)
  S.S. Nesbitt & Co. (insurance)
  Vulcan Service (magazine subscription sales)

COMPETITORS

ACI Telecentrics
AMREP
APAC Customer Services
Black Dot Group
Bowne
Brunswick
Dai Nippon Printing
divine
General Binding
HA2003
Johnson Outdoors
McGraw-Hill
Quebecor
Reed Elsevier Group
Roanoke Electric Steel
R.R. Donnelley
Scholastic
Simon Worldwide
SITEL
TeleSpectrum
Thomson Corporation

HISTORICAL FINANCIALS

Company Type: Private

Income Statement
FYE: June 30

	ESTIMATED REVENUE ($ mil.)	NET INCOME ($ mil.)	NET PROFIT MARGIN	EMPLOYEES
6/03	1,400	—	—	4,500
6/02	1,400	—	—	5,000
6/01	1,375	—	—	4,500
6/00	1,375	—	—	4,200
6/99	1,210	—	—	4,200
6/98	1,000	—	—	4,000
6/97	1,000	—	—	4,000
6/96	900	—	—	4,000
Annual Growth	6.5%	—	—	1.7%

Revenue History

Eby-Brown

Eby-Brown makes its money on vices such as munchies and nicotine. The company is a leading convenience-store supplier of more than 11,000 name-brand products, including tobacco, candy, snacks, health and beauty aids, and general merchandise.

The company's eight distribution centers serve 28 states and more than 25,000 stores, including the Speedway and SuperAmerica chains owned by Marathon Ashland Petroleum. Eby-Brown also has a marketing division that offers its customers advertising and promotion services.

The century-old company is family-owned and run. Co-CEOs Tom and Dick Wake succeeded their father, William Wake Jr., in 1983. William died in 2004 at the age of 78.

EXECUTIVES

Co-President and Co-CEO: Richard (Dick) Wake
Co-President and Co-CEO: Thomas G. (Tom) Wake
CFO: Mark Smetana
EVP, Sales: Al Palma
VP, Advertising and Sales Promotions: Ralph Kallmann
VP, Business Development: Ron Coppel
Employment Contact: Joan Nauman
Auditors: Deloitte & Touche

LOCATIONS

HQ: Eby-Brown Company
280 W. Shuman Blvd., Ste. 280, Naperville, IL 60566
Phone: 630-778-2800 **Fax:** 630-778-2830
Web: www.eby-brown.com

Eby-Brown's distribution centers are located in Florida, Georgia, Illinois, Indiana, Maryland, Michigan, Ohio, and Wisconsin.

COMPETITORS

AMCON Distributing
C&S Wholesale
C.D. Hartnett
GSC Enterprises
H.T. Hackney
McLane
Nash Finch
Purity Wholesale Grocers
S. Abraham & Sons
Spartan Stores
SUPERVALU

HISTORICAL FINANCIALS

Company Type: Private

Income Statement
FYE: September 30

	REVENUE ($ mil.)	NET INCOME ($ mil.)	NET PROFIT MARGIN	EMPLOYEES
9/03	3,670	—	—	2,100
9/02*	3,600	—	—	2,100
12/01	3,670	—	—	2,100
12/00	3,400	—	—	2,011
12/99	2,773	—	—	2,011
12/98	1,700	—	—	1,550
12/97	1,650	—	—	1,450
12/96	1,670	—	—	1,395
12/95	1,550	—	—	1,411
12/94	1,450	—	—	1,327
Annual Growth	10.9%	—	—	5.2%

*Fiscal year change

Revenue History

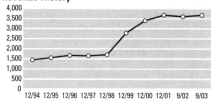

Educational Testing Service

For college-bound high school students, taking the SAT is as much a rite of adulthood as getting a driver's license. Educational Testing Service (ETS), the creator of the Scholastic Assessment Test (SAT), develops and administers more than 12 million achievement, occupational, and admissions tests a year. In addition to the SAT, ETS develops other tests, including the CLEP, GMAT, GRE, and TOEFL.

Founded in 1947, the not-for-profit group is one of the nation's largest testing organizations. The ETS Research unit conducts research projects focusing on education. ETS agreed in 2004 to sell its corporate testing subsidiary Capstar to Thomson Prometric.

ETS plans to release a new Test of English as a Foreign Language (TOEFL) in 2005 that will evaluate a person's ability to use English overall — speaking, listening, reading, and writing.

EXECUTIVES

President and CEO: Kurt M. Landgraf, age 57
CFO: Frank R. Gatti
SVP and General Counsel: Stanford H. von Mayrhauser
SVP and General Manager, Elementary and Secondary Education: John H. Oswald
SVP Higher Education: Mari A. Pearlman
SVP International: Paul A. Ramsey
SVP Operations and Technology: Arthur C. Chisholm
SVP Research and Development: Ida Lawrence
VP and Corporate Secretary: Eleanor V. Horne
VP Communications and Public Affairs:
  Leslie C. Francis

LOCATIONS

HQ: Educational Testing Service
  Rosedale Road, Princeton, NJ 08541
Phone: 609-921-9000   **Fax:** 609-734-5410
Web: www.ets.org

Educational Testing Service administers tests in about 200 countries and has operations in Puerto Rico, the Netherlands, and the US.

PRODUCTS/OPERATIONS

Selected Programs and Services

Capstar services
  Candidate screening
  Certification and licensing examinations
  Job analysis
  Program audits
  Skills assessment
  Test sites and proctors
  Test administration (computer, paper, and online)
  Training needs analysis
  Test development
ETS testing programs
  Advanced Placement (AP)
  College-Level Examination Program (CLEP)
  Graduate Management Admission Test (GMAT)
  Graduate Record Examinations (GRE)
  The Praxis Series: Professional Assessments for Beginning Teachers
  Scholastic Assessment Test Program (SAT)
  Test of English as a Foreign Language (TOEFL)

COMPETITORS

ACT
Harcourt Education
Houghton Mifflin
Kaplan
McGraw-Hill
Princeton Review
Touchstone Applied Science

HISTORICAL FINANCIALS

Company Type: Not-for-profit

Income Statement
FYE: June 30

	REVENUE ($ mil.)	NET INCOME ($ mil.)	NET PROFIT MARGIN	EMPLOYEES
6/03	741	14	1.9%	2,684
6/02	685	10	1.5%	2,500
6/01	572	—	—	2,500
6/00	500	—	—	2,500
6/99	494	—	—	2,100
6/98	496	—	—	2,300
6/97	432	—	—	2,300
6/96	411	—	—	2,300
6/95	386	—	—	2,300
Annual Growth	8.5%	36.5%	—	1.9%

Net Income History

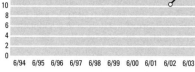

Elder Automotive

Being respectful to Elders is job one at the Elder Ford dealership and other lots in the Elder Automotive Group. It owns a leading Jaguar dealership in North America, Jaguar of Troy, Michigan, as well as Elder Ford; Aston Martin Tampa in Florida; Aston Martin Troy; Jaguar of Tampa; and Saab of Troy. The company sells new and used cars and offers repairs and maintenance through its parts and service departments. Elder Automotive Group was founded in 1967 by the Elder family; Irma Elder, owner and CEO, took over after her husband's death in 1983.

EXECUTIVES

CEO: Irma Elder
President: Tony Elder
Controller: Sue Kvock

LOCATIONS

HQ: Elder Automotive Group
  777 John R. Rd., Troy, MI 48083
Phone: 248-585-4000   **Fax:** 248-583-0815
Web: www.elderautomotivegroup.com

COMPETITORS

AutoNation
March/Hodge
Meade Group
Serra Automotive

HISTORICAL FINANCIALS

Company Type: Private

Income Statement
FYE: December 31

	REVENUE ($ mil.)	NET INCOME ($ mil.)	NET PROFIT MARGIN	EMPLOYEES
12/02	633	—	—	304
12/01	539	—	—	317
12/00	484	—	—	280
12/99	486	—	—	250
12/98	437	—	—	213
12/97	381	—	—	229
Annual Growth	10.7%	—	—	5.8%

Revenue History

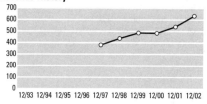

Elkay Manufacturing

Elkay Manufacturing doesn't make everything, but they do make the kitchen sink — along with cabinets, drinking fountains, faucets, water coolers, and water filtration products. The Katz family founded Elkay in the early 1920s to make sinks for butlers' pantries and sculleries. Elkay now sells residential and commercial stainless steel sinks under such names as Celebrity, Lustertone, and Gourmet. The company also offers kitchen accessories (colanders, cutting boards, soap dispensers). Elkay's cabinetmaking holdings include Yorktowne Cabinets, Medallion Cabinetry, and MasterCraft Cabinets.

Elkay is the parent of 10 privately held companies and one joint venture. Chairman Ronald Katz owns Elkay Manufacturing.

EXECUTIVES

Chairman and CEO: Ronald C. (Ron) Katz
President and COO: John P. Edl
EVP Marketing and Sales: John Heilstedt
VP and CFO: Timothy J. (Tim) Bondy
VP Sales: William (Bill) Blaine
VP Human Resources: Walter E. Reilly
Division President: James (Jim) Scott
Division Director, Quality: Jeff Sharp
Manager, Product Planning, Faucets and Accessories: Laura James
Manager, Product Planning, Sinks: Michael (Mike) Gicela
Director, Marketing Services, Elkay Division: Steve Sorensen
Manager, Research and Development: Wally Moran
Director, Marketing Services: Alan Danenberg

LOCATIONS

HQ: Elkay Manufacturing Company
2222 Camden Ct., Oak Brook, IL 60523
Phone: 630-574-8484   **Fax:** 630-574-5012
Web: www.elkay.com

Elkay Manufacturing operates 14 production plants and 24 distribution centers in North America. It also has a joint venture in the Pacific Rim region.

PRODUCTS/OPERATIONS

Selected Products
Drinking fountains
Faucets
Kitchen cabinets
Residential and commercial sinks
Sink accessories (including colanders, cutting boards, drain trays, soap dispensers)
Sink tops, countertops, and drainboards
Water coolers
Water filters

COMPETITORS

American Standard
American Woodmark
AquaCell
Armstrong World Industries
Black & Decker
Jacuzzi Brands
Kohler
MAAX
Masco
MasterBrand Cabinets
Moen
Novar

HISTORICAL FINANCIALS
Company Type: Private

Income Statement
FYE: December 31

	REVENUE ($ mil.)	NET INCOME ($ mil.)	NET PROFIT MARGIN	EMPLOYEES
12/03	575	—	—	3,900
12/02	560	—	—	3,700
12/01	527	—	—	3,700
12/00	515	—	—	3,800
12/99	470	—	—	3,650
12/98	422	—	—	3,300
12/97	370	—	—	2,950
12/96	320	—	—	2,634
12/95	273	—	—	2,260
12/94	264	—	—	2,375
Annual Growth	9.0%	—	—	5.7%

Revenue History

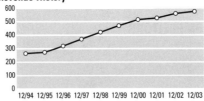

Encyclopaedia Britannica

Encyclopaedia Britannica thinks it knows everything, and it probably does. The company publishes reference works including its flagship 32-volume *Encyclopaedia Britannica* (first published in 1768), *The Annals of America*, and *Great Books of the Western World*. It also publishes a variety of dictionaries (*Merriam Webster's Collegiate Dictionary*, *Merriam Webster's Biographical Dictionary*) through its Merriam-Webster subsidiary. Most of the company's products are available online, as well as on CD-ROM and DVD. Swiss financier Jacob Safra (a nephew of the late banking king Edmond Safra) owns the company.

Its Britannica.com Web site offers access for a fee to its entire collection of encyclopedia articles, an editorially reviewed Web site directory, and third-party content from *The New York Times* and other providers. Britannica's site also features an online store where users can buy its print and interactive products.

After initially being late to the CD-ROM and dot-com party, Encyclopaedia Britannica decided to commit to Britannica.com, a sister firm devoted to electronic content which was to be spun off in an IPO. But the idea turned out to be disastrous (in part because of bad publicity over traffic jams at the site and a downturn in online advertising), and the company has since focused back on its core business with a renewed interest in print products. The company is considering selling its Merriam-Webster subsidiary to raise capital.

Trying a new approach to reach consumers, the company began selling its products on TV home shopping network QVC in 2003.

HISTORY

Engraver Andrew Bell and printer and bookseller Colin Macfarquhar created the first edition of the *Encyclopaedia Britannica* in Scotland, releasing the three-volume set in weekly installments between 1768 and 1771. Benjamin Franklin and John Locke were among early contributors. The second edition, completed in 1784, expanded to 10 volumes; the fourth (1809) contained 20. The ninth edition (1889) captured the scientific spirit of the age with articles by Thomas Henry Huxley and James Clerk Maxwell.

American businessmen Horace Hooper and Walter Jackson purchased the *Encyclopaedia* in 1901 and established the Encyclopaedia Britannica Company in the US. It published the first *Britannica Book of the Year* in 1913. Sears chairman Julius Rosenwald bought the company in 1920 and tried to market *Britannica* through Sears' retail operations, as well as with door-to-door sales. William Benton (of Benton & Bowles Advertising) bought the business from Sears in 1941 and built a nationwide sales force with a hard-sell reputation. Britannica released its first foreign-language encyclopedia, *Enciclopedia Barsa*, in 1957 and acquired dictionary publisher G. & C. Merriam in 1964.

When Benton died in 1974, he bequeathed the operation to the non-profit William Benton Foundation, the sole beneficiary of which was the University of Chicago. Britannica later bought out rival Compton's Encyclopedia in the mid-1970s. The 1989 CD-ROM release of *Compton's MultiMedia Encyclopedia* was a first for the industry, but Britannica sold Compton's NewMedia division to Chicago's Tribune Company in 1993 just before the CD-ROM market exploded. The company also promised not to release a competing multimedia version of Encyclopaedia Britannica for two years. Not realizing that the electronic revolution was upon them and reluctant to change its established and profitable door-to-door sales techniques, the conservative company fell behind challengers who offered CD-ROMs including Microsoft and its *Funk & Wagnalls* product (later relaunched as *Encarta*).

Jacob Safra, a *Britannica* lover since childhood, led a group that paid $135 million for the struggling company in 1996. With book sales dwindling and heavy competition, Britannica cut its prices and ceased its door-to-door marketing that year. It agreed to sell both its CD-ROM and print encyclopedias in retail stores in 1997, and lured publisher Paul Hoffman away from Walt Disney's successful *Discover* magazine. Britannica Internet Guide (BIG), a free Internet search engine, launched that year. Britannica added guest columns and other features to BIG in 1998 and renamed it eBlast (it changed the site's name again to Britannica the following year).

Encyclopaedia Britannica Holdings (Safra's umbrella firm for the publisher) launched a sister firm, Britannica.com, in 1999 to oversee the company's electronic and Internet products and services. CEO Don Yannias resigned his post with the print company and took the reins of the new digital firm, allowing Hoffman to take over as the publisher's president. Britannica.com struggled with the rest of the Internet industry in 2000, laying off almost 25% of its staff.

In 2001 Yannias left the company entirely and was replaced by Ilan Yeshua, an executive from an Israeli educational technology firm. Later that year, the company integrated Britannica.com back into the encyclopedia unit of Encyclopaedia

Britannica, a move that involved severely downsizing the Web staff. Yeshua departed the company in 2003 and was replaced by Britannica executive Jorge Cauz.

EXECUTIVES

Chairman: Jacob E. Safra
President: Jorge Cauz
EVP, Secretary, and General Counsel: William J. Bowe
SVP and Editor: Dale Hoiberg
SVP Corporate Development: Michael Ross
SVP International: Leah Mansoor
SVP Sales and Marketing: Patti Ginnis
VP Operations and Finance: Richard Anderson
President and Publisher, Merriam-Webster: John Morse
Director, Corporate Communications: Tom Panelas
Executive Director, Technology: Tom Lang
Marketing Manager, Consumer Sales: Elizabeth Arnold
Direct Marketing Manager: Christine Hodgson
Auditors: PricewaterhouseCoopers

LOCATIONS

HQ: Encyclopaedia Britannica, Inc.
310 S. Michigan Ave., Chicago, IL 60604
Phone: 312-347-7000   **Fax:** 312-347-7399
Web: corporate.britannica.com

Encyclopaedia Britannica makes its headquarters in Chicago and maintains offices in London, New Delhi, Paris, Seoul, Sydney, Taipei, Taiwan; Tel Aviv, and Tokyo.

PRODUCTS/OPERATIONS

Selected Products

Dictionaries
  Merriam Webster's Biographical Dictionary
  Merriam Webster's Collegiate Dictionary
  Merriam Webster's Collegiate Thesaurus
  Merriam Webster's Dictionary of Law
Encyclopedias
  Britannica First Edition Replica Set
  Encyclopædia Britannica
  The Encyclopedia of Popular Music
Other Reference Works
  The Annals of America
  Gray's Anatomy
  Great Books of the Western World

COMPETITORS

Berkshire Hathaway
Dow Jones
Editis
Franklin Electronic Publishers
Harcourt Education
LexisNexis
McGraw-Hill
Microsoft
National Geographic
Pearson
Random House
Scholastic Library Publishing
Thomson Corporation
Time

HISTORICAL FINANCIALS

Company Type: Private

Income Statement   FYE: December 31

	REVENUE ($ mil.)	NET INCOME ($ mil.)	NET PROFIT MARGIN	EMPLOYEES
12/01*	225	—	—	260
12/00	275	—	—	300
12/99**	279	—	—	350
9/98	300	—	—	400
9/97	325	—	—	400
9/96	375	—	—	700
9/95	400	—	—	800
9/94	453	—	—	900
9/93	540	—	—	1,000
9/92	586	—	—	1,100
Annual Growth	(10.1%)	—	—	(14.8%)

*Most recent year available   **Fiscal year change

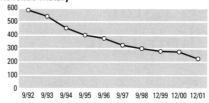

Revenue History

Enterprise Rent-A-Car

This Enterprise is boldly going where it hasn't gone before — the airport. The company, which offers to ferry customers to the rental office, says it is the largest car rental firm in the US. With more than 600,000 cars in its fleet, Enterprise operates in the US, Canada, Germany, Ireland, and the UK. The company targets customers whose own cars are in the shop or who need a rental for short trips; it also has begun serving the airport market. Controlled by founder Jack Taylor and his family, Enterprise has spun off its non-automotive operations (balloons, footwear, a golf course, hotel amenities, and prison supplies) as Centric Group.

The company also leases vehicles and manages fleets for other companies (Enterprise Fleet Services), and when it's ready to refresh its fleet, Enterprise sells its cars (Enterprise Car Sales) through a nationwide program. Potential customers can shop by make and model through the Enterprise Web site.

In March 2004 Enterprise announced plans to hire some 6,500 additional employees over the course of the year, citing new branch openings of about one per business day as the reason. Enterprise opened 300 new locations during 2003.

Founder John Taylor's son Andrew is the company's chairman and CEO.

HISTORY

In 1957 Jack Taylor, the sales manager for a Cadillac dealership in St. Louis, hit on the idea that leasing cars might be an easier way to make money than selling them. Taylor's idea sounded good to his boss, Arthur Lindburg, who agreed to set Taylor up in the leasing business. In return for a 50% pay cut, Taylor received 25% of the new enterprise, called Executive Leasing, which began in the walled-off body shop of a car dealership.

In the early 1960s Taylor started renting cars for short periods as well as leasing them. When his leasing agents expressed annoyance with the rental operation, Taylor turned that business over to Don Holtzman. Holtzman realized that his 17-car rental operation was too little to take on industry giants like Hertz and Avis; instead, he concentrated on the "home city" or replacement market. He offered competitive rates to insurance adjusters who needed to find cars for policyholders whose vehicles were damaged or stolen.

Propelled by court decisions that required casualty companies to pay for loss of transportation, Taylor expanded from his St. Louis base in 1969 with a branch office in Atlanta. Since another car leasing outfit in Georgia was already named Executive, Taylor changed the name of his company to Enterprise Rent-A-Car.

The company expanded into Florida and Texas in the early 1970s, targeting garages and body shops that performed repairs for insured drivers. Oil price shocks of that period compelled Taylor to diversify his operations. In 1974 Enterprise acquired Keefe Coffee and Supply, a supplier of coffee, packaged foods, and beverages to prison commissaries. To service FORTUNE 1000 companies wanting to lease or buy more than 50 vehicles, the company started Enterprise Fleet Services in 1976.

Enterprise acquired Courtesy Products (coffee and tea for hotel guests) in 1980, and the following year sales reached the $100 million mark. It acquired ELCO Chevrolet in 1986, the same year it formed Crawford Supply (hygiene products for prisons). Taylor bought out the Lindburg family's interest in Enterprise the next year. In 1989 Enterprise raised its brand recognition with a national TV campaign that focused on an older and higher-income audience by showing its commercials exclusively on CBS. Also in the late 1980s, the company began targeting "discretionary rentals" to families with visiting relatives or with children home for the holidays.

Taylor's son, Andrew, became CEO of Enterprise in 1991, and sales topped $1 billion for the first time. By 1994 sales had passed $2 billion, and the company had expanded into Canada and the UK. By 1996 Enterprise had a fleet of more than 300,000 vehicles. That year it opened several locations in the UK. In 1997 the company opened locations in Ireland, Germany, Scotland, and Wales.

In 1998 Enterprise battled other rental firms over use of the advertising tagline, "We'll pick you up," which it had trademarked. Rent-A-Wreck lost a court case over the matter; Hertz settled with Enterprise over use of the phrase.

In 1999 the company more than doubled the number of its airport locations in an attempt to woo occasional travelers (rather than hard-core corporate fliers). That year the Taylor family split off their non-automotive operations (including companies involved in prison supplies, hotel amenities, a golf course, mylar balloons, and athletic shoes) as Centric Group.

In 2001 the company's COO, Donald Ross, became the first non-Taylor to be promoted to president after Jack Taylor was named chairman emeritus and Andrew gave up the president title to assume the company's chairmanship while remaining as CEO.

EXECUTIVES

Chairman and CEO: Andrew C. (Andy) Taylor, age 56
Vice Chairman and President: Donald L. Ross
EVP and COO: Pamela M. (Pam) Nicholson, age 44
EVP and CFO: William W. (Bill) Snyder
SVP and CIO: Craig Kennedy
SVP and Chief Administrative Officer: Lee R. Kaplan
SVP, Car Sales: Tim Walsh
SVP, Corporate Strategy: M.W. (Sandy) Rogers
SVP, European Operations: James (Jim) Burrell
SVP, Fleet Services: Steven E. (Steve) Bloom
SVP, Group Operations, Canada and Michigan: Tony Moise
SVP, Group Operations, North Central: John Murray
SVP, Group Operations, Northeast: Rick Allen
SVP, Group Operations, South Central: Randal Narike
SVP, Group Operations, Southeast: Dave Nestor
SVP, Human Resources: Edward (Ed) Adams
SVP, North American Operations: Matthew G. Darrah
SVP, Rental: Jim Runnels
SVP, Vehicle Acquisition: Dan Kirchhoeffer
VP, Marketing Communications: Steve Smith
Auditors: Ernst & Young LLP

LOCATIONS

HQ: Enterprise Rent-A-Car Company
600 Corporate Park Dr., St. Louis, MO 63105
Phone: 314-512-5000 **Fax:** 314-512-4706
Web: www.enterprise.com

Enterprise Rent-A-Car has about 5,500 locations in the US (in all 50 states), Canada, Germany, Ireland, and the UK.

PRODUCTS/OPERATIONS

Operations
ELCO Chevrolet Inc. (car dealership, St. Louis)
Enterprise Car Sales (used car sales)
Enterprise Fleet Services (vehicle leasing)
Enterprise Rent-A-Car

COMPETITORS

Alamo
Avis Europe
Avis Group
Budget
Dollar Thrifty Automotive
Hertz
Rent-A-Wreck
Sixt
Vanguard Car Rental

HISTORICAL FINANCIALS

Company Type: Private

Income Statement
FYE: July 31

	REVENUE ($ mil.)	NET INCOME ($ mil.)	NET PROFIT MARGIN	EMPLOYEES
7/03	6,900	—	—	53,500
7/02	6,500	—	—	50,000
7/01	6,300	—	—	50,000
7/00	5,600	—	—	45,000
7/99	4,730	—	—	40,000
7/98	4,180	—	—	37,000
7/97	3,680	—	—	35,182
7/96	3,127	—	—	28,806
7/95	2,464	—	—	21,703
7/94	2,108	—	—	18,500
Annual Growth	14.1%	—	—	12.5%

Revenue History

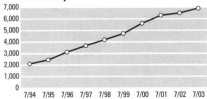

Equistar Chemicals

Polymers are made up of petrochemicals, and Equistar Chemicals — a partnership between Lyondell Chemical (which owns 70.5%) and Millennium Chemicals (29.5%) — is made up of both. Equistar's largest business segment, petrochemicals, makes olefins (ethylene, propylene, and butadiene), oxygenated products (ethylene oxide, ethylene glycol), and aromatics (benzene and toluene). Equistar's polymers segment makes polyolefins (polyethylene, polypropylene) and performance polymers. Polyethylene is used in plastic bags and bottles; polypropylene is used in plastic caps, rigid packaging, automotive components, and carpet. Lyondell recently acquired Occidental's 30% stake in the company.

EXECUTIVES

Co-Chairman: Robert E. (Bob) Lee, age 47
Co-Chairman and CEO: Dan F. Smith, age 57
EVP and COO: Morris Gelb, age 57
SVP, Chemicals and Polymers: Edward J. Dineen, age 49
SVP, Manufacturing: James W. Bayer, age 48
SVP, Fuels and Raw Materials: W. Norman Phillips Jr., age 48, $408,096 pay
VP and Treasurer: Karen A. Twitchell
VP, Sales: Vaughn Deasy
VP, Human Resources: John A. Hollinshead, age 54
VP, Corporate Communications: Susan Moore
Manager, Public Affairs: David Harpole
Manager, Marketing Communications: Eric Stebel
Auditors: PricewaterhouseCoopers LLP

LOCATIONS

HQ: Equistar Chemicals, LP
1221 McKinney St., Ste. 700, Houston, TX 77010
Phone: 713-652-7200 **Fax:** 713-652-4151
Web: www.equistarchem.com

Equistar Chemicals operates around 15 major plants in Illinois, Iowa, Louisiana, New Jersey, Ohio, and Texas.

PRODUCTS/OPERATIONS

2003 Sales

	$ mil.	% of total
Petrochemicals	4,522	69
Polymers	2,023	31
Total	6,545	100

Selected Products

Petrochemicals
  Aromatics
  Olefins
  Oxygenated products
  Specialty products
Polymers
  High-density polyethylene (HDPE)
  Liquid polyolefins
  Linear low-density polyethylene (LLDPE)
  Low-density polyethylene (LDPE)
  Performance polymers
  Polypropylene
  Thermoplastic polyolefins

COMPETITORS

A. Schulman
AEP Industries
BP Petrochemicals
Chevron Phillips Chemical
Dow Chemical
Eastman Chemical
ExxonMobil Chemical
Formosa Plastics USA
Huntsman
Methanex
NOVA Chemicals
PMC Global
PolyOne
PVC Container
Royal Dutch/Shell Group
W. R. Grace

HISTORICAL FINANCIALS

Company Type: Partnership

Income Statement
FYE: December 31

	REVENUE ($ mil.)	NET INCOME ($ mil.)	NET PROFIT MARGIN	EMPLOYEES
12/03	6,545	(339)	—	3,165
12/02	5,537	(1,299)	—	3,400
12/01	5,909	(283)	—	3,400
12/00	7,495	153	2.0%	3,700
12/99	5,436	32	0.6%	4,500
12/98	4,363	143	3.3%	5,000
12/97	365	7	1.9%	4,000
Annual Growth	61.8%	—	—	(3.8%)

2003 Year-End Financials

Debt ratio: 144.5%
Return on equity: —
Cash ($ mil.): 199
Current ratio: 1.67
Long-term debt ($ mil.): 2,314

Net Income History

Equity Group Investments

Equity Group Investments is the apex of financier Sam Zell's pyramid of business holdings. The Chicago-based private investment group controls a multi-billion dollar mix of businesses, including real estate investment trusts (REITs), restaurants, and cruise ships. Zell's REIT portfolio makes him the US's largest owner of property leased by manufactured homeowners (Manufactured Home Communities), office buildings (Equity Office Properties Trust), and apartments (Equity Residential Properties Trust). Sam Zell has a controlling interest in Equity Group Investments.

Equity Office Properties is one of the largest landlords in San Francisco and Seattle. Zell has made his niche — and a lot of money — by purchasing distressed properties and turning them into profitable investments (for which he earned the nickname "Grave Dancer").

Equity Group Investments has rescued many companies floundering in bankruptcy and often buys during downturns. Many acquisitions are made through the Zell/Chilmark Fund. Zell's Equity Residential Properties continues to build its portfolio through acquisitions.

Subsidiary Equity International Properties invests in Latin American commercial and residential real estate. It has established Mexico Retail Partners, a joint venture with the Black Creek Group, to develop big-box retail south of the border.

Zell has made forays into other investments with mixed success. He bought into sugar mills in Mexico that were nationalized by the government. Another holding, American Classic Voyages, suffered a combo of misfortune with the soft Hawaiian cruise industry on one side and the aftermath of September 11 on travel on the other. It is no longer in operation.

HISTORY

Sam Zell's first business endeavor was photographing his eighth-grade prom. In 1953 he graduated to reselling 50-cent *Playboy* magazines to schoolmates at a 200% markup.

While at the University of Michigan in the 1960s, Zell teamed with fraternity brother Robert Lurie to manage off-campus student housing. In graduate school, they invested in residential properties and formed Equity Financial and Management Co. after graduation. Their collection of distressed properties grew in the 1970s as Zell made the deals and Lurie made them work. Zell's hands-off management style had its drawbacks, however. In 1976 Zell and three others (including his brother-in-law) were indicted on federal tax-related charges after selling a Reno, Nevada, hotel and apartment complex. The charges were later dropped against Zell and another defendant (only the brother-in-law was convicted).

In the 1980s tax-law changes led the team to begin buying troubled companies. They started in 1983 with Great American Management and Investment, a foundering real estate manager they turned into an investment vehicle. Other targets included Itel (1984, now Anixter International) and oil and gas company Nucorp (1988, now part of insurer CNA Surety). The true attraction in many of these acquisitions, however, lay in tax-loss carryforwards that could be applied against future earnings.

Lurie died in 1990, after which Zell began to consolidate his power and ease out old friends. (Lurie's estate still owns shares of many Zell enterprises.) That year Zell and David Schulte formed the Zell/Chilmark Fund, which soon owned or controlled such companies as Schwinn (sold 1997), Sealy (sold 1997), and Revco (sold 1997). Among the fund's failures was West Coast retailer Broadway Stores, which Zell bought out of bankruptcy in 1992; when California's slumping economy prevented a rapid turnaround, Zell sold it (once again near bankruptcy) in 1995.

Starting in 1987, Zell formed four real estate funds with Merrill Lynch; six years later, both Equity Residential and Manufactured Home Communities went public. As REITs became popular with investors, more trusts began vying for distressed assets — Zell's traditional lifeblood. In 1997 Zell melded four of his commercial real estate funds into another REIT, Equity Office Properties Trust, and took it public.

In 1998, as investors and financiers looked for fresh opportunities, Zell launched Equity International Properties, a fund targeting acquisitions in Latin America and elsewhere. That year a civil racketeering suit brought against Zell by former executive Richard Perlman shed light on "handshake" loans to top executives and other informal business deals. In 1999 Zell sold Jacor Communications to radio industry consolidator Clear Channel Communications. Equity Group Investments remained diversified, however. That year Equity Office Properties teamed with venture capital firm Kleiner Perkins Caufield & Byers to form Broadband Office to offer Internet and phone services to Zell's tenants and those of other property owners. Not surprisingly, Broadband Office bit the dust in the dot-com blowout.

Equity Office Properties Trust continued its buying into the 21st century, claiming New York-based Cornerstone Properties (2000) and California's Spieker Properties (2001).

Equity International Properties continues to expand its holdings in Mexico and the rest of Latin America, targeting both the commercial and residential sectors.

EXECUTIVES

Chairman: Samuel (Sam) Zell, age 62
President: Donald J. Liebentritt
CFO: Philip Tinkler, age 38
Managing Director: William C. Pate, age 39

LOCATIONS

HQ: Equity Group Investments, L.L.C.
2 N. Riverside Plaza, Ste. 600, Chicago, IL 60606
Phone: 312-454-0100   **Fax:** 312-454-0335

PRODUCTS/OPERATIONS

Selected Affiliates

Angelo & Maxie's, Inc. (38%, restaurants)
Anixter International, Inc. (14%, communications network equipment)
Capital Trust, Inc. (commercial real estate finance)
Davel Communications, Inc. (14%, pay-telephone operator)
Equity International Properties (overseas buyout fund)
Equity Office Properties Trust (4%, office property REIT)
Equity Residential Properties Trust (3%, apartments REIT)
Equity International Properties, Ltd. (Latin American property investment)
Manufactured Home Communities, Inc. (15%, mobile home communities REIT)
Transmedia Network (40%, consumer savings programs)
Zell/Chilmark Fund L.P. (investment vulture fund)

COMPETITORS

Apollo Advisors	JMB Realty
Blackstone Group	KKR
Carlyle Group	Thomas Lee
CD&R	Trump
Goldman Sachs	

Ergon

When it comes to work, Ergon (named after the Greek word for work) has it covered. The diversified company operates in six major business segments: asphalt and emulsions; information technology; oil and gas; real estate; refining and marketing; and transportation and terminaling. In addition to providing a range of petroleum products and services, the company manufactures and markets computer technology services and sells road maintenance systems, including emulsions and special coatings. Ergon also provides truck, rail, and marine transport services and sells residential and commercial real estate properties.

EXECUTIVES

CEO: Leslie B. Lampton Sr.
CFO: A. Patrick Busby
President, Asphalt Division: Bill Lampton
VP Environment, Health, and Safety, Ergon Refining: Paul Young
VP Marine Operations, Magnolia Marine Transport: Roger Harris
Media Relations Manager: Jim Temple

LOCATIONS

HQ: Ergon, Inc.
2829 Lakeland Dr., Ste. 2000, Jackson, MS 39232
Phone: 601-933-3000   **Fax:** 601-933-3350
Web: www.ergon.com

PRODUCTS/OPERATIONS

Major Operations

Asphalt and Emulsions
   Crafco, Inc.
   Ertech
Information Technology
   Diversified Technology, Inc.
Oil and Gas
   Lampton-Love, Inc.
Real Estate
   Ergon Properties, Inc.
Refining and Marketing
   Ergon Refining, Inc.
   Ergon-West Virginia, Inc.
   Lion Oil Company
   Petroleum Specialties Marketing Division
Transportation and Terminaling
   Ergon Rail
   Ergon Terminals
   Ergon Trucking, Inc.
   Magnolia Marine Transport Company

COMPETITORS

AmeriGas Partners	Koch
Ferrellgas Partners	Marathon Oil
Kirby	

HISTORICAL FINANCIALS

Company Type: Private

Income Statement   FYE: December 31

	ESTIMATED REVENUE ($ mil.)	NET INCOME ($ mil.)	NET PROFIT MARGIN	EMPLOYEES
12/02	1,380	—	—	2,000
12/01	1,460	—	—	2,000
12/00	1,900	—	—	2,000
12/99	1,400	—	—	2,000
Annual Growth	(0.5%)	—	—	0.0%

Revenue History

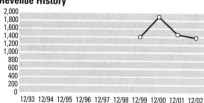

Ernst & Young

Accounting may actually be the *second*-oldest profession, and Ernst & Young is one of the oldest practitioners. Ernst & Young is also one of the world's largest accounting firms, offering auditing and accounting services around the globe. The firm also provides legal services and services relating to emerging growth companies, human resources issues, and corporate transactions (mergers and acquisitions, IPOs, and the like). Ernst & Young has one of the world's largest tax practices, serving multinational clients that have to comply with multiple local tax laws.

After spending decades building their consultancies, the big accountancies have all moved toward shedding them, because of internal and regulatory pressures, as well as the perceived conflict of interest in providing both auditing and consulting services to the same clients. Ernst & Young was the first to split off its consultancy, selling it in 2000 to what is now Cap Gemini Ernst & Young.

Ernst & Young, which gained an impressive amount of weight in former rival Andersen's diaspora, has also boosted its legal services, assembling some 2,000 lawyers in dozens of countries.

Ernst & Young has faced Andersen-style trouble of its own. Federal regulators in 2002 sued the firm for its alleged role in the failure of Superior Bank FSB, and threatened civil charges for purported fraud relating to Cendant. In the UK, insurer Equitable Life in 2003 sued the accountancy for professional negligence related to work performed when Ernst & Young was its auditor. More problems followed with clients Healthsouth and America Online; Ernst & Young faces a lawsuit in relation to its work for the former company.

Rick Bobrow stepped down as the firm's global CEO after just a year on the job; the departure was presumed to have been related to the airing of previously unpublicized Ernst & Young financial information during Bobrow's divorce proceedings.

HISTORY

In 1494 Luca Pacioli's *Summa di Arithmetica* became the first published text on double-entry bookkeeping, but it was almost 400 years before accounting became a profession.

In 1849 Frederick Whinney joined the UK firm of Harding & Pullein. His ledgers were so clear that he was advised to take up accounting, which was a growth field as stock companies proliferated. Whinney became a name partner in 1859 and his sons followed him into the business. The firm became Whinney, Smith & Whinney (WS&W) in 1894.

After WWII, WS&W formed an alliance with Ernst & Ernst (founded in Cleveland in 1903 by brothers Alwin and Theodore Ernst), with each firm operating on the other's behalf across the Atlantic. Whinney merged with Brown, Fleming & Murray in 1965 to become Whinney Murray. In 1979 Whinney Murray, Turquands Barton Mayhew (also a UK firm), and Ernst & Ernst merged to form Ernst & Whinney.

But Ernst & Whinney wasn't done merging. Ten years later, when it was the fourth-largest accounting firm, it merged with #5 Arthur Young, which had been founded by Scotsman Arthur Young in 1895 in Kansas City. Long known as "old reliable," Arthur Young fell on hard times in the 1980s because its audit relationships with failed S&Ls led to expensive litigation (settled in 1992 for $400 million).

Thus the new firm of Ernst & Young faced a rocky start. In 1990 it fended off rumors of collapse. The next year it slashed payroll, even thinning its partner roster. Exhausted by the S&L wars, in 1994 the firm replaced its pugnacious general counsel, Carl Riggio, with the more cost-conscious Kathryn Oberly.

In the mid-1990s Ernst & Young concentrated on consulting, particularly in software applications, and grew through acquisitions. In 1996 the firm bought Houston-based Wright Killen & Co., a petroleum and petrochemicals consulting firm, to form Ernst & Young Wright Killen. It also entered new alliances that year, including ones with Washington-based ISD/Shaw, which provided banking industry consulting, and India's Tata Consulting.

In 1997 Ernst & Young was sued for a record $4 billion for its alleged failure to effectively handle the 1993 restructuring of the defunct Merry-Go-Round Enterprises retail chain (it settled for $185 million in 1999). On the heels of a merger deal between Coopers & Lybrand and Price Waterhouse, Ernst & Young agreed in 1997 to merge with KPMG International. But Ernst & Young called off the negotiations in 1998, citing the uncertain regulatory process they faced.

In 1999 the firm reached a settlement in lawsuits regarding accounting errors at Informix and Cendant and sold its UK and Southern African trust and fiduciary businesses to Royal Bank of Canada (now RBC Financial Group).

In 2000 Ernst & Young became the first of the (then) Big Five firms to sell its consultancy, dealing it to France's Cap Gemini Group for about $11 billion. The following year the UK accountancy watchdog group announced it would investigate Ernst & Young for its handling of the accounts of UK-based The Equitable Life Assurance Society. The insurer was forced to close to new business in 2000 because of massive financial difficulties.

Ernst & Young made headlines and gave competitors plenty to talk about in 2002 when closely held financial records were made public during a divorce case involving executive Rick Bobrow (who in 2003 abruptly retired as global CEO after just a year on the job). The firm in 2002 also formed an alliance with former New York City mayor Rudy Giuliani to help launch a business consultancy and an investment firm bearing the Giuliani name.

EXECUTIVES

Global Chairman and CEO; Chairman for the Americas: James S. (Jim) Turley, age 49
CFO and Global Managing Partner - Finance and Infrastrucure: Norbert R. Becker
COO: Paul J. Ostling
Global Managing Partner - Quality & Risk Management: Michael N.M. Boyd
Global Managing Partner - Markets: Mike Cullen
Global Managing Partner - People: Timothy T. (Tim) Griffy
Global Managing Partner - Practice Integration: Jean-Charles Raufast
Deputy Global Managing Partner - Infrastructure; VC of Knowledge & Technology, Ernst & Young LLP: John G. Peetz Jr.
Global Director - Business Risk Services: Thomas Bussa
Vice Chairman - Strategy: Beth A. Brooke
Vice Chairman - Assurance and Advisory Business Services: James A. Hassett
Vice Chairman - Global Financial Services: Robert W. (Bob) Stein
Vice Chairman - Tax: Karl Johansson
Vice Chairman - Technology, Communications and Entertainment: Stephen E. Almassy
Vice Chairman - Law: Patrick Bignon
Vice Chairman - Sales: Patrick J.P. Flochel
Vice Chairman - Corporate Finance: Francis Small

LOCATIONS

HQ: Ernst & Young International
5 Times Square, New York, NY 10036
Phone: 212-773-3000 **Fax:** 212-773-6350
Web: www.eyi.com

Ernst & Young International has approximately 670 offices in more than 140 countries.

PRODUCTS/OPERATIONS

2003 Sales

	$ mil.	% of total
Assurance & advisory business services	7,736	59
Tax & law services	4,165	32
Transaction advisory services	960	7
Other	275	2
Total	**13,136**	**100**

Selected Services

Assurance and Advisory
  Actuarial services
  Audits
  Accounting advisory
  Business risk services
  Internal audit
  Real estate advisory services
  Technology and security risk services
  Transaction support services
Emerging Growth Companies
  Corporate finance services
  IPO services
  Mergers and acquisitions advisory
  Operational consulting
  Strategic advisory
Human Capital
  Compensation and benefits consulting
  Cost optimization and risk management
  Transaction support services
Law
  Corporate and M&A
  Employment
  Finance
  Information technology services
  Intellectual property
  International trade and anti-trust
  Litigation and arbitration
  Real estate
Tax
  Customs and international trade
  Electronic VAT assurance
  International tax
  Partial exemption evaluation process
  Tax outsourcing
Transactions
  Capital management
  Due diligence and transaction support
  Financial and business modeling
  M&A advisory
  Post-deal advisory
  Strategic finance
  Valuation

COMPETITORS

Bain & Company
BDO International
Deloitte
Grant Thornton International
IBM
KPMG
PricewaterhouseCoopers

HISTORICAL FINANCIALS

Company Type: Partnership

Income Statement — FYE: June 30

	REVENUE ($ mil.)	NET INCOME ($ mil.)	NET PROFIT MARGIN	EMPLOYEES
6/03	13,136	—	—	103,000
6/02	10,124	—	—	87,206
6/01	9,900	—	—	82,000
6/00*	9,500	—	—	88,625
9/99	12,500	—	—	97,800
9/98	10,900	—	—	85,000
9/97	9,100	—	—	79,750
9/96	7,800	—	—	72,000
9/95	6,867	—	—	68,452
9/94	6,020	—	—	61,287
Annual Growth	9.1%	—	—	5.9%

*Fiscal year change

Revenue History

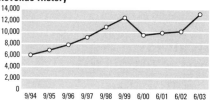

ESPN

ESPN is a superstar of the sports broadcasting world. The company is the leading cable sports broadcaster with seven domestic networks — including its flagship ESPN, ESPN2 (sporting events and news), ESPN Classic (historical sports footage), ESPN HD, and ESPNEWS (24-hour news and information) — that reach more than 88 million US homes. It also reaches another 145 countries through its ESPN International unit. In addition, ESPN creates content for TV and radio and operates one of the most popular sports sites on the Internet. ESPN also has lent its name to a magazine and a chain of eight sports-themed restaurants. ESPN is 80% owned by Walt Disney (through Disney ABC Cable); Hearst has a 20% stake.

After buying domestic rights from the National Basketball Association in 2002, ESPN became the first network ever to have contracts to televise all four professional sports leagues — baseball, football, basketball, and hockey. The company launched a high definition service, called ESPN HD, in spring 2003. In addition to its heavily watched sports wrap-up shows, the company has tried its hand at original programming including movies *Season on the Brink* and *The Junction Boys*.

In 2004 ESPN announced that it would launch a 24-hour channel devoted to college sports called ESPNU in early 2005.

For those curious about the roots of the company's name: the network's original name was the Entertainment and Sports Programming Network when it was formed in 1979. The network adopted the new name — ESPN, Inc. — in 1985.

EXECUTIVES

Chairman and President; President, ABC Sports: George W. Bodenheimer, age 45
President, Disney and ESPN Affiliate Sales and Marketing: Sean H. R. Bratches
President, ESPN/ABC Sports Customer Sales and Marketing: Ed Erhardt
EVP and CFO: Christine Driessen
EVP Advertising Sales, New Media, and Consumer Products: John Skipper
EVP National Sales and Customer Marketing: Lou Koskovolis
EVP National Sales and Event Marketing: David Rotem
EVP Marketing: Lee Ann Daly
EVP Programming and Production: Mark Shapiro
SVP and Executive Editor, ESPN Inc. and ESPN Internet Group: John Walsh
SVP and General Manager, ESPN Enterprises: Rick Alessandri
SVP and Editor In Chief, *ESPN The Magazine*: John Papanek
SVP and Managing Editor: Robert Eaton
SVP Corporate Communications and Outreach: Rosa Gatti

LOCATIONS

HQ: ESPN, Inc.
ESPN Plaza, 935 Middle St., Bristol, CT 06010
Phone: 860-766-2000   **Fax:** 860-766-2213
Web: espn.go.com

ESPN has offices in Bristol, Connecticut, as well as New York City.

PRODUCTS/OPERATIONS

Selected TV Operations
ESPN (sporting events and news channel)
ESPN Classic (archival sports footage channel)
ESPN Deportes (Spanish-language sports network)
ESPN Extra (pay-per-view events)
ESPN HD (high definition channel)
ESPN Now (scheduling information channel)
ESPN Original Programming (original content for cable channels)
ESPN Today (interactive television sports channel)
ESPN2 (sporting events and news channel)
ESPNEWS (24-hour sports news channel)

Web Operations
ESPN.com (sports information site)

Other Operations
BASS (bass fishing organization)
ESPN Outdoors
ESPN Radio
ESPN The Magazine (magazine)
ESPN Wireless
ESPN Zone (sports-themed restaurants)
SportsTicker (provider of sports news and scores)

COMPETITORS

CBS	SportsLine.com
Comcast Spectacor	Turner Broadcasting
Fox Entertainment	Vulcan Sports Media
NBC	Yahoo!

HISTORICAL FINANCIALS

Company Type: Joint venture

Income Statement — FYE: September 30

	REVENUE ($ mil.)	NET INCOME ($ mil.)	NET PROFIT MARGIN	EMPLOYEES
9/03	2,869	—	—	3,400
9/02	2,120	—	—	—
9/01	2,500	—	—	—
9/00	2,600	—	—	2,500
Annual Growth	3.3%	—	—	10.8%

Revenue History

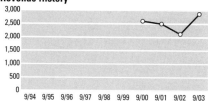

Esselte

Write it, print it, staple it, drop it in a folder, and store it in a filing cabinet — Esselte is there for each step. With more than 30,000 products, the company is the world's top maker of office supplies. Esselte makes paper-based filing and document management items (files, binders, folders, covers), labeling systems (labels, small printers), workspace products (staplers, letter trays), and computer accessories under the DYMO, Esselte, Leitz, Pendaflex, and Xyron brands. Customers range from wholesalers and direct marketers to office superstores and mass retailers. J. W. Childs Associates acquired Esselte in 2002.

The company resumed its acquisition activity in 2003 with the purchase of Scottsdale, Arizona-based Xyron, a binding and laminating company. A year later Esselte acquired EJA CZ in the Czech Republic and Universal Trade Stationers in Ireland.

EXECUTIVES

President and CEO: Magnus Nicolin
SVP and CFO: Richard A. (Rich) Douville
SVP Business Development: Robert Hawes
SVP Human Resources: Jim O'Leary
SVP Supply Chain, Filing Europe: Ulf Brodd
VP and Corporate Controller: Joseph Keyes
VP Global IT: Mark Katz
VP Global Marketing: Bill Mullenix
VP Innovation: Cindi Goldberg
Director, Public Relations and External Communications: Chris Curran
Auditors: Ernst & Young AB

LOCATIONS

HQ: Esselte
44 Commerce Rd., Stamford, CT 06902
Phone: 203-355-9000   **Fax:** 203-355-9071
Web: www.esselte.com

Esselte has operations in 26 countries and its products are sold in more than 120 countries.

PRODUCTS/OPERATIONS

Selected Products
Filing
  Arch files
  Concertina files
  File folders
  Indices
  Plastic pockets
  Presentation folders
  Ring binders
  Suspension files
Labeling
  Printers and labels
  Tools and tape

Workspace
  Binding and lamination equipment
  Desk accessories
  Letter trays
  Magazine files
  Perforators
  Staplers
Other Products
  Computer accessories
  Printer supplies

COMPETITORS

ACCO World
Avery Dennison
Cardinal Brands
MeadWestvaco
Smead
TAB Products

HISTORICAL FINANCIALS
Company Type: Private

Income Statement			FYE: December 31
	REVENUE ($ mil.)	NET INCOME ($ mil.)	NET PROFIT MARGIN	EMPLOYEES
12/03	1,100	—	—	5,900
12/02	1,200	—	—	6,500
12/01	1,027	—	—	6,462
12/00	1,178	—	—	6,398
12/99	1,313	—	—	7,038
12/98	1,694	—	—	10,517
12/97	1,643	—	—	9,223
12/96	1,707	—	—	9,500
12/95	1,826	—	—	9,480
12/94	1,633	—	—	10,166
Annual Growth	(4.3%)	—	—	(5.9%)

Revenue History

Estes Express

Estes Express Lines is a multiregional less-than-truckload (LTL) freight hauler. (LTL carriers consolidate freight from multiple shippers into a single trailer.) The company operates a fleet of about 3,800 tractors and 11,800 trailers from a network of more than 100 terminals, mainly in the eastern half of the US. It provides services to the rest of the US and Canada through its partners in the ExpressLINK regional LTL alliance: G.I. Trucking, Lakeville Motor Express, and TST Overland Express. Estes Express also offers warehousing, domestic airfreight forwarding, truckload transportation, and truck and trailer leasing. Founded by W. W. Estes in 1931, the company is owned and operated by the Estes family.

EXECUTIVES

Chairman: Robey W. Estes Sr.
President: Robey W. (Rob) Estes Jr., age 52
EVP: William T. (Billy) Hupp
VP; General Manager, Southwest Division: John D. Rogers

VP Corporate Communications: Trish Garland
VP Human Resources: Thomas Donahue
VP Maintenance: Ray G. Williams
VP Operations: John T. (Junior) Johnson
VP Pricing: Paul J. Dugent
VP Sales: Chuck Parker
Corporate Secretary: Stephen E. Hupp
Treasurer and CFO: Gary D. Okes
Information Services: Hugh Camden
Auditors: Joyner, Kirkham, Keel & Robertson, P. C.

LOCATIONS

HQ: Estes Express Lines, Inc.
   3901 W. Broad St., Richmond, VA 23230
Phone: 804-353-1900 **Fax:** 804-353-8001
Web: www.estes-express.com

COMPETITORS

Arkansas Best
Con-Way
J. B. Hunt
Old Dominion Freight
Overnite Transportation
Ryder
Schneider National
SCS Transportation
Universal Express
USF
Watkins Associated Industries
Yellow Roadway

HISTORICAL FINANCIALS
Company Type: Private

Income Statement			FYE: December 31
	REVENUE ($ mil.)	NET INCOME ($ mil.)	NET PROFIT MARGIN	EMPLOYEES
12/03	865	—	—	10,027
12/02	800	—	—	9,160
12/01	695	—	—	8,531
12/00	691	—	—	8,000
12/99	603	—	—	7,800
12/98	519	—	—	7,000
Annual Growth	10.8%	—	—	7.5%

Revenue History

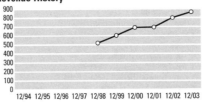

ETMC Regional Healthcare

East Texas Medical Center Regional Healthcare System (ETMC) helps meet the health care needs of residents of rural eastern Texas. The health system operates about a dozen hospitals across the region, along with behavioral, rehabilitation, and home health care services. The system also includes nearly a dozen health clinics and three emergency care facilities around the Tyler area. In addition to its facilities, ETMC operates an emergency ambulance service subsidiary. Another subsidiary, DRL LABS, provides clinical lab services to the care facilities of ETMC.

ETMC's Tyler facility offers specialized care for cancer, cardiovascular conditions, and neurological conditions.

EXECUTIVES

President and CEO: Elmer G. Ellis
COO: Jerry Massey
SVP and CFO: Byron Hale
Administrator and CEO, East Texas Medical Center Tyler: Robert B. Evans
Administrator and CEO, East Texas Medical Center Gilmer: Ken May
VP, DRL LABS: Paula Anthony
Director of Operations, DRL LABS: Todd Hancock
Director of Finance, DRL LABS: Kirk Hopkins
Director of Marketing: Carrol Roge

LOCATIONS

HQ: East Texas Medical Center Regional Healthcare System
  1000 S. Beckham Ave., Tyler, TX 75701
Phone: 903-597-0351 **Fax:** 903-535-6100
Web: www.etmc.org

Hospital Locations
Athens
Carthage
Clarksville
Crockett
Fairfield
Jacksonville
Mt. Vernon
Pittsburg
Quitman
Trinity
Tyler

COMPETITORS

Good Shepherd Health System
HCA
Memorial Health Systems of East Texas
Mother Frances Hospital of Tyler, TX
Tenet Healthcare
Trinity Mother Frances Health System
Woodland Heights Medical Center

HISTORICAL FINANCIALS
Company Type: Not-for-profit

Income Statement			FYE: October 31
	REVENUE ($ mil.)	NET INCOME ($ mil.)	NET PROFIT MARGIN	EMPLOYEES
10/03	676	—	—	2,601

Euromarket Designs

Think you've never bought anything from Euromarket Designs? Think again. The retailer, which does business under the Crate & Barrel name, pioneered the fashionable-yet-homey look for contemporary interiors. It has more than 115 stores (including nearly a dozen outlet stores) in over 20 US states and the District of Columbia. About a third of the merchandise, which includes furniture and housewares, is unique to the chain. Crate & Barrel issues about 15 million catalogs annually and sells merchandise on its Web site. Germany-based Otto GmbH, the world's largest mail-order merchant, owns a majority stake in Euromarket Designs, but co-founder and CEO Gordon Segal still has operating control.

The Crate & Barrel stores carry contemporary furnishings, rugs, tableware, and kitchenware in au courant colors and styles. Its merchandise is stocked in large quantities to give the stores the feel of a well-kept stockroom. In addition to catalog and Internet sales, which account for about 20% of total sales, Euromarket Design's gift registries (in-store and online) represent a substantial chunk of profits, as well. A dozen new Crate & Barrel stores are expected to open in the US over the next two years.

Crate & Barrel's smaller Chicago-based store (called CB2), which targets a younger, less wealthy demographic, has recently proven a success. Two new CB2 stores debuted in Chicago, and plans are being made to open up shop in Boston, Washington, and New York. CB2 has also launched its own Web site and a catalog is in the works. Crate & Barrel also owns a 50% stake in The Land of Nod, a catalog company featuring high-quality furniture and accessories for kids' rooms. The Otto family also controls Spiegel.

EXECUTIVES
CEO: Gordon Segal, age 65
President: Barbara Turf
VP, Finance: Bruce Schneidewind
CIO: Ed Renemann
Director, Catalogs: John Johanson
Director, Human Resources: Susie Muellman
Director, Public Relations: Bette Kahn
Director, Technology: Lou Tucker
Direct Marketing Business Director: John Seebeck

LOCATIONS
HQ: Euromarket Designs Inc.
 1250 Techny Rd., Northbrook, IL 60062
Phone: 847-272-2888   **Fax:** 847-272-5366
Web: www.crateandbarrel.com

Euromarket Designs operates Crate & Barrel stores in Arizona, California, Colorado, Connecticut, Florida, Georgia, Illinois, Indiana, Maine, Maryland, Massachusetts, Michigan, Minnesota, New Jersey, New York, North Carolina, Pennsylvania, Rhode Island, Texas, Virginia, Washington, and Washington, DC.

PRODUCTS/OPERATIONS
Selected Merchandise
Barware
Baskets
Bedding
Candles and candle holders
Dishes
Furniture (dining room, home office, kitchen, living room)
Glassware
Hampers
Kitchenware
Lamps
Picture frames
Pillows
Rugs and mats
Table linens
Tableware
Vases
Wine racks

COMPETITORS
Ashley Furniture
Bed Bath & Beyond
Bombay Company
Container Store
Cost Plus
Ethan Allen
Garden Ridge
Hanover Direct
IKEA
Levitz Furniture
Lillian Vernon
Linens 'n Things
Longaberger
Martha Stewart Living
Pampered Chef
Pier 1 Imports
Restoration Hardware
Smith & Hawken
Spiegel
Target
Tuesday Morning
Urban Outfitters
Williams-Sonoma
Z Gallerie

HISTORICAL FINANCIALS
Company Type: Private

Income Statement
FYE: Last day in February

	REVENUE ($ mil.)	NET INCOME ($ mil.)	NET PROFIT MARGIN	EMPLOYEES
2/03	865	—	—	6,000
2/02*	770	—	—	5,000
1/01	703	—	—	5,000
1/00	598	—	—	5,000
1/99	530	—	—	4,200
1/98	480	—	—	3,800
1/97	374	—	—	2,475
1/96	335	—	—	1,750
1/95	274	—	—	1,400
1/94	232	—	—	—
Annual Growth	15.7%	—	—	20.0%

*Fiscal year change

Revenue History

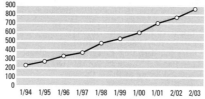

Evanston Northwestern Healthcare

Evanston Northwestern Healthcare provides care to residents of the north side of Chicago and its suburbs through hospitals, home services, and a 300-physician medical group. The 550-bed Evanston Hospital has teaching and research programs, as well as a trauma center, perinatal center, and several mammography centers. The smaller Glenbrook Hospital is also a teaching facility. Highland Park Hospital has nearly 240 beds and is home to the Kellogg Cancer Care Center. The organization's research institute has close ties with Northwestern University Medical School.

The Federal Trade Commission in early 2004 filed suit against the health care system, alleging its 2000 acquisition of Highland Park Hospital violated antitrust laws.

EXECUTIVES
President and CEO: Mark R. Neaman
COO: Jeffrey H. Hillebrand, age 50
EVP, Finance and Treasurer: Thomas H. Hodges
SVP, Corporate Relations: David Loveland
SVP and Chief Administrative Officer, ENH Research Institute: Leopold Selker
SVP, Medical Informatics: Nancy Semerdjian
SVP, Development: Ronald G. Spaeth
President, Evanston Hospital: Raymond Grady
President, Highland Park Hospital: Mary S. O'Brien
President, Glenbrook Hospital: Douglas M. Silverstein
Chief Human Resources Officer:
 William R. (Bill) Luehrs
Senior Director, Corporate Communications:
 Gail Polzin
Auditors: Ernst & Young LLP

LOCATIONS
HQ: Evanston Northwestern Healthcare Corporation
 2650 Ridge Ave., Evanston, IL 60201
Phone: 847-570-2020   **Fax:** 847-570-2940
Web: www.enh.org

COMPETITORS
Advocate Health Care
Central DuPage Hospital
Children's Memorial Hospital
HCA
Provena Health
Rockford Health System
Rush System for Health
Tenet Healthcare
University of Chicago Hospitals

HISTORICAL FINANCIALS
Company Type: Not-for-profit

Income Statement
FYE: September 30

	REVENUE ($ mil.)	NET INCOME ($ mil.)	NET PROFIT MARGIN	EMPLOYEES
9/03	1,793	4	0.2%	7,665
9/02	945	—	—	7,655
Annual Growth	89.7%	—	—	0.1%

Revenue History

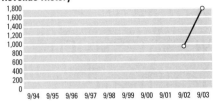

Everett Smith Group

From skins to steel, Everett Smith Group has you covered. The investment firm owns Albert Trostel & Sons, the parent of Eagle Ottawa Leather, which makes upholstery leather for major carmakers. Albert Trostel & Sons also is parent of Trostel, Ltd., a manufacturer of rubber molded seals for the appliance and automotive industries, and Trostel SEG, which makes thermoplastic products for the automotive and hand tool industries. Other Everett Smith investments include OEM Worldwide, which manufactures electronic assemblies for medical and industrial applications, and Maysteel, which makes power distribution equipment and enclosures for the utility industry.

EXECUTIVES
Chairman and CEO: Anders Segerdahl
Vice Chairman: Thomas Hauske Jr.
VP and COO: Randall Perry
VP and CFO: James Orth
VP and General Counsel: Steven Hartung

LOCATIONS
HQ: Everett Smith Group, Ltd.
800 N. Marshall St., Milwaukee, WI 53202
Phone: 414-273-3421 **Fax:** 414-273-1058
Web: www.esmithgroup.com

Everett Smith Group has operations in Argentina, Hungary, Ireland, Mexico, South Africa, the UK, and the US.

PRODUCTS/OPERATIONS
Selected Operations
Albert Trostel & Sons Co.
Maysteel Corp.
Eagle Ottawa Leather Company
OEM Worldwide
Trostel, Ltd.
Trostel SEG

COMPETITORS
Federal-Mogul   JFE Shoji Holdings
Giddings & Lewis   Tandy Brands

HISTORICAL FINANCIALS
Company Type: Private

Income Statement FYE: November 30

	REVENUE ($ mil.)	NET INCOME ($ mil.)	NET PROFIT MARGIN	EMPLOYEES
11/03*	799	—	—	6,115
12/02	723	—	—	5,900
12/01	680	—	—	5,300
12/00	677	—	—	5,300
12/99	635	—	—	6,000
12/98	700	—	—	6,000
Annual Growth	2.7%	—	—	0.4%

*Fiscal year change

Revenue History

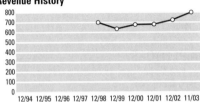

Evergreen International Aviation

Evergreen International Aviation soars through blue skies and travels across green lands. The company's fleet of 747s and DC-9s transports cargo for airlines, freight forwarders, and government agencies. Evergreen also operates a fleet of helicopters that provides fire fighting, construction, and rescue support worldwide. On land, the company provides ground handling services at more than 30 US airports. In addition, Evergreen sells, leases, and repairs aircraft; supplies parts; and runs a plant nursery. Del Smith, a former Air Force pilot and crop duster, founded the company in 1960. Its McMinnville, Oregon, museum houses Howard Hughes' Spruce Goose.

EXECUTIVES
Chairman and CEO: Delford M. (Del) Smith, age 73, $1,433,333 pay
President, Evergreen International Aviation: Timothy G. Wahlberg, age 58, $140,000 pay
Acting CFO, Treasurer, SVP Risk Management, and Director: John A. Irwin, age 48
President, Evergreen Air Center: Trevor VanHorn, age 58, $130,000 pay
President, Evergreen Aviation Ground Logistics Enterprises: Brian T. Bauer, age 36, $124,615 pay
President, Evergreen Helicopters International: James A. Porter, age 57
EVP, Evergreen International Airlines: Anthony E. (Tony) Bauckham, age 51
SVP Sales and Marketing, Evergreen International Airlines: Ranjit Seth, age 39, $165,600 pay
Secretary and Acting In-House Counsel: Gwenna R. Wootress, age 46
VP Personnel: Elsie M. Henry, age 63
Auditors: Deloitte & Touche LLP

LOCATIONS
HQ: Evergreen International Aviation, Inc.
3850 Three Mile Ln., McMinnville, OR 97128
Phone: 503-472-9361 **Fax:** 503-472-1048
Web: www.evergreenaviation.com

PRODUCTS/OPERATIONS
2004 Sales

	% of total
Flight revenue	70
Ground logistics services	19
Sales of aircraft and parts	3
Support services and other	8
Total	**100**

Subsidiaries
Evergreen Agricultural Enterprises, Inc.
Evergreen Air Center, Inc.
Evergreen Aircraft Sales & Leasing Co.
Evergreen Aviation Ground Logistics Enterprises, Inc.
Evergreen Helicopters, Inc.
Evergreen International Airlines, Inc.
Quality Aviation Services, Inc.

COMPETITORS
Air T
Arrow Air
Atlas Air Worldwide
Express One International
Grand Aire
Keystone Helicopter
Mercury Air Group
Offshore Logistics
World Airways

HISTORICAL FINANCIALS
Company Type: Private

Income Statement FYE: February 28

	REVENUE ($ mil.)	NET INCOME ($ mil.)	NET PROFIT MARGIN	EMPLOYEES
2/04	550	—	—	4,354
2/03	574	—	—	4,386
2/02	448	—	—	—
2/01	488	—	—	4,000
2/00	450	—	—	—
2/99	435	—	—	—
2/98	389	—	—	2,500
2/97	256	—	—	—
2/96	189	—	—	—
Annual Growth	14.3%	—	—	9.7%

Revenue History

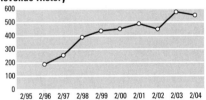

Express Personnel

When you need a worker fast, Express Personnel Services delivers. The professional staffing company provides work for some 225,000 employees from more than 400 offices in Australia, Canada, South Africa, and the US. In addition to temporary staffing, it provides professional placement and contract staffing through Express Professional Staffing and offers workplace services (consulting, training, development) through Express Business Solutions.

The company is owned by founders William Stoller (vice chairman) and Robert Funk (CEO), who also owns the Oklahoma City Blazers hockey team and Express Ranches, one of the nation's largest cattle breeders.

EXECUTIVES

Chairman and CEO: Robert A. Funk
Vice Chairman: William H. Stoller
EVP and CFO: Thomas N. Richards
SVP Franchise Support and Information Services: Terri Weldon
SVP Marketing and Communications: Linda C. Haneborg
SVP Risk Management: J. David Baird
EVP Sales: Bob Fellinger
VP and Controller: Sharon Patric
VP Administration and Personnel: Carol Lane
VP Franchising: Nikki Sells
VP Human Resources: Larry Ferree

LOCATIONS

HQ: Express Personnel Services
  8516 Northwest Expwy., Oklahoma City, OK 73162
Phone: 405-840-5000   **Fax:** 405-717-5669
Web: www.expresspersonnel.com

PRODUCTS/OPERATIONS

Selected Staffing Fields

Express Personnel
  General labor
  Industrial
  Office and clerical
  Technical
Express Professional
  Accounting and financial
  Engineering and manufacturing
  Health care
  Human resources
  Information technology
  Sales and marketing
  Technical

COMPETITORS

Adecco
Administaff
ADP TotalSource
Barrett Business Services
Butler International
Gevity HR
Kelly Services
Manpower
MPS
Randstad
Robert Half
Spherion
Uniforce Staffing
Volt Information

HISTORICAL FINANCIALS

Company Type: Private

Income Statement   FYE: December 31

	REVENUE ($ mil.)	NET INCOME ($ mil.)	NET PROFIT MARGIN	EMPLOYEES
12/03	962	—	—	224,000
12/02	819	—	—	224,000
12/01	781	—	—	224,000
12/00	916	—	—	262,000
Annual Growth	1.6%	—	—	(5.1%)

Revenue History

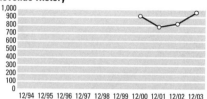

Extended Stay America

Extended Stay America (ESA) wants to be your home away from home. With more than 450 hotels in over 40 states, it offers customers weekly rates under its Extended StayAmerica Efficiency Studios (economy), StudioPLUS Deluxe Studios (mid-price), and Crossland Economy Studios (budget) banners. ESA caters to thrifty business travelers, as well as to professionals who are either relocating or working on temporary assignments. Features include kitchenettes, weekly housekeeping, laundry facilities, voice mail, and Internet access. The company was purchased by investment firm The Blackstone Group in May 2004.

ESA sees opportunity at the lower end of the extended stay lodging market and is on a path of steady growth. It opened about 30 new facilities in 2000 and another 39 in 2001. Due to downturns in the lodging industry and the economy in general, the number of new openings in 2002 and 2003 dropped to about 20.

Prior to being purchased by The Blackstone Group, CEO and co-founder George Johnson Jr. owned about 7% of the company; chairman and co-founder Wayne Huizenga (Blockbuster, AutoNation) owned 11%; and Microsoft founder Bill Gates' Cascade Investment owned 6%.

EXECUTIVES

Chairman: H. Wayne Huizenga, age 66
CEO and Director: George D. Johnson Jr., age 62
President and COO: Corry W. Oakes III, age 37, $288,000 pay
CFO, Secretary, and Treasurer: James A. Ovenden, age 41
VP and Corporate Controller: Patricia K. Tatham
VP, Construction: Daniel A. Fuchs
VP, Development/Legal: Piero Bussani
VP, Human Resources: Marshall L. Dildy
VP, Information Systems: George Rutledge
VP, Marketing: Michael M. Wilson
VP, Operations: Richard A. Fadel Jr.
VP, Real Estate: Todd R. Turner
Auditors: PricewaterhouseCoopers LLP

LOCATIONS

HQ: Extended Stay America, Inc.
  101 Dunbar St., Spartanburg, SC 29306
Phone: 864-573-1600   **Fax:** 864-573-1695
Web: www.extstay.com

Extended Stay America operates more than 450 facilities in 42 states.

PRODUCTS/OPERATIONS

2003 Hotels

	No. of hotels	% of total
Extended Stay	335	72
StudioPLUS	95	20
Crossland	39	8
Total	**469**	**100**

Selected Brands

Crossland Economy Studios (budget)
Extended StayAmerica Efficiency Studios (economy)
StudioPLUS Deluxe Studios (mid-price)

COMPETITORS

Choice Hotels
Hilton
Homestead Village
InterContinental Hotels
Marriott
Prime Hospitality
Suburban Franchise Systems
Sunburst Hospitality

HISTORICAL FINANCIALS

Company Type: Private

Income Statement   FYE: December 31

	REVENUE ($ mil.)	NET INCOME ($ mil.)	NET PROFIT MARGIN	EMPLOYEES
12/03	550	40	7.3%	7,600
12/02	548	57	10.4%	7,250
12/01	542	57	10.6%	6,725
12/00	518	70	13.5%	6,100
12/99	418	47	11.3%	5,600
12/98	274	28	10.2%	4,600
12/97	131	3	2.0%	2,900
12/96	16	3	21.7%	800
12/95	1	(1)	—	65
12/94	1	—	—	—
Annual Growth	99.5%	—	—	81.3%

2003 Year-End Financials

Debt ratio: 95.6%
Return on equity: 3.6%
Cash ($ mil.): 16
Current ratio: 0.51
Long-term debt ($ mil.): 1,098

Net Income History

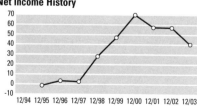

F. Dohmen Co.

The F. Dohmen Co. helps pharmacists with just about everything except interpreting handwriting. The company is one of the largest private pharmaceutical wholesalers in the US. Its Dohmen Medical division distributes brand name and generic products, including medical and surgical supplies. F. Dohmen also makes pharmaceutical management systems that perform an array of services, including prescription processing, physician and insurer information management, and chronic disease management. The company's additional services include advertising assistance; it sells National Brand Equivalent products that permit pharmacies to use their own store labels. German immigrant Frederick Dohmen founded the firm in 1858.

EXECUTIVES
President and CEO: John Dohmen
CFO: Tracy Pearson
CIO: Thomas Farrington
EVP, Human Resources: Robert Dohmen

LOCATIONS
HQ: The F. Dohmen Co.
W194 N11381 McCormick Dr.,
Germantown, WI 53022
Phone: 262-255-0022 **Fax:** 262-255-0041
Web: www.dohmen.com

PRODUCTS/OPERATIONS

Selected Company Divisions
DDN Pharmaceutical Logistics (pharmaceutical distribution)
Dohmen Distribution Partners, LLC (pharmacy management services)
jASCorp (pharmaceutical management systems)
RESTAT (prescription benefits management)

Selected Products
DotConnect (central prescription editing, messaging, and data analysis system)
Encounter Pro (disease management system)
Encounter Rx (prescription processing system)
Enhance Pro (pharmacy counseling system)
HealthCare America Ad Program (advertising assistance)
HealthCare America private labels (National Brand Equivalent products)
Impact (insurer/physician/patient information management system)
Infonet EC (electronic ordering system)
P3 Performance Plan (program that assists pharmacists with marketing and provides product information)

COMPETITORS
AmerisourceBergen
Cardinal Health
D & K Healthcare Resources
Kinray
McKesson
Owens & Minor
QK Healthcare

HISTORICAL FINANCIALS
Company Type: Private

Income Statement FYE: April 30

	REVENUE ($ mil.)	NET INCOME ($ mil.)	NET PROFIT MARGIN	EMPLOYEES
4/03	1,400	—	—	500
4/02	838	—	—	450
4/01	748	—	—	450
4/00	655	—	—	480
4/99	524	—	—	430
Annual Growth	27.8%	—	—	3.8%

Revenue History

Fallon Community Health Plan

Fallon Community Health Plan is a not-for-profit HMO that provides health insurance products and related services to nearly 200,000 members in central and eastern Massachusetts. The company's health insurance offerings include, PPO, Point of Service (POS), Traditional Indemnity, and Medicare. Fallon Community Health Plan also provides third party administration (TPA) services to employers, and wellness services to the community through its Fallon Foundation. Fallon Community Health Plan is a subsidiary of Fallon Health and Life Assurance Company.

EXECUTIVES
President and CEO: Eric H. Schultz
VP and COO: Mark Fisher
VP and CFO: Charles Goheen
VP and Chief Medical Officer: Dennis Batey
VP, and Chief Human Resources Officer: Teena Osgood
VP, Sales and Corporate Communications: William Mazza
VP, Public Affairs and Business Planning: Richard Burke
Assistant VP and Chief Internal Auditor: Robert Vayo
Assistant VP, and Chief Technical Officer: Drew Weng
Director and Special Assistant to the President: Elizabeth Guerra
Director, Strategic Planning and Implementation: Julie Owens

LOCATIONS
HQ: Fallon Community Health Plan Inc.
10 Chestnut St., Worcester, MA 01608
Phone: 508-799-2100 **Fax:** 508-831-1137
Web: www.fchp.org

COMPETITORS
Blue Cross (MA)
Harvard Pilgrim
Tufts Health Plan

HISTORICAL FINANCIALS
Company Type: Not-for-profit

Income Statement FYE: December 31

	ESTIMATED REVENUE ($ mil.)	NET INCOME ($ mil.)	NET PROFIT MARGIN	EMPLOYEES
12/03	678	9	1.3%	500
12/02	184	—	—	480
Annual Growth	268.5%	—	—	4.2%

Revenue History

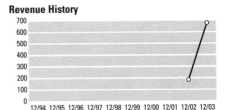

Faulkner Organization

The sound and the fury of Buicks moving off the lot is coming from The Faulkner Organization, one of the Delaware Valley's largest-volume automotive dealers. The company operates more than 20 automobile dealerships in Pennsylvania. Its domestic car franchises include Buick, Cadillac, Chevrolet, Ford, GMC, Mercury, Pontiac, and Saturn; its import franchises sell Toyotas, Hondas, Mitsubishis, and Mazdas. In addition to new and used cars, the company sells auto parts and offers automotive repairs and car financing. Founded in 1932 by Henry Faulkner, the company is still owned and operated by the Faulkner family.

EXECUTIVES
CEO: Gail Faulkner
COO: Bob Lewis
CFO and Director of Human Resources: Bill Sebald
Director of Fixed Operations: Walt Huber

LOCATIONS
HQ: The Faulkner Organization
4437 Street Rd., Trevose, PA 19053
Phone: 215-364-3980 **Fax:** 215-364-0706
Web: www.tobesure.com

COMPETITORS
Asbury Automotive
AutoNation
Brown Automotive
Budget
CarMax
Darcars
Holman Enterprises
Jim Koons Automotive
Ourisman Automotive
Pacifico
Planet Automotive Group
Rosenthal Automotive
Sonic Automotive

HISTORICAL FINANCIALS

Company Type: Private

Income Statement   FYE: December 31

	REVENUE ($ mil.)	NET INCOME ($ mil.)	NET PROFIT MARGIN	EMPLOYEES
12/03	822	—	—	1,100
12/02	804	—	—	1,100
12/01	818	—	—	1,100
12/00	821	—	—	1,100
12/99	806	—	—	1,100
12/98	735	—	—	1,000
12/97	711	—	—	1,000
12/96	630	—	—	1,200
12/95	625	—	—	1,200
12/94	550	—	—	1,100
Annual Growth	4.6%	—	—	0.0%

Revenue History

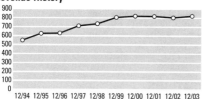

Federal Prison Industries

Some businesses benefit from captive audiences; this company benefits from captive employees. Federal Prison Industries (FPI), known by its trade name UNICOR, uses prisoners to make products and provide services, mainly for the US government. More than 20,000 inmates (about 20% of the total eligible inmate population) are employed in over 100 FPI factories. UNICOR, which is part of the Justice Department's Bureau of Prisons, manufactures products such as office furniture, clothing, beds and linens, electronics equipment, and eyewear. It also offers services including data entry, bulk mailing, laundry services, printing, recycling, and refurbishing vehicle components.

Federal law mandates that government buyers consider UNICOR products first; the company is allowed to sell services (but not products) to the private sector. FPI already produces most of the products the federal government buys, and it is benefiting from a growing prison population and the cheap cost of its labor (pay ranges from 23 cents to $1.15 per hour). The company is also tapping into the commercial market by offering services. Self-supporting, UNICOR is overseen by a governing board that is appointed by the US president.

Legislation was introduced by Rep. Peter Hoekstra that if passed would make UNICOR compete with private companies for government contracts.

HISTORY

FPI was established by President Franklin Roosevelt in 1934 to teach job skills at men's and women's federal prisons. During WWII, 95% of FPI's output was dedicated to the war effort — the company's products included parachutes and munitions. In the late 1950s and early 1960s, FPI built or renovated structures at 18 of the 31 federal prisons. In 1974 it established regional sales offices, and in 1977 it took the name UNICOR.

Although self-supporting, UNICOR remained necessarily inefficient because of its goal to put as many inmates as possible to work. However, as the prison population increased, the company underwent rapid expansion and added skilled services in the 1980s.

UNICOR put its product catalog online in 1996. The next year the Senate authorized a study of ways to make UNICOR more competitive, after private businesses had complained that the booming prison population, low wages (23 cents to $1.15 per hour), and government preferential treatment gave UNICOR an unfair advantage. Legislation to force FPI to bid against the private sector for government contracts was brought before Congress in 1999; at the same time, a bill was introduced to allow the company to offer its products to the private sector. Meanwhile, FPI began selling services such as data entry to private-sector customers.

In 2003 Dell Computer dropped UNICOR as the vendor for its computer recycling program.

EXECUTIVES

CEO: Harley G. Lappin
COO: Steve Schwalb
Controller: Bruce Long
Assistant Director, Human Resources: Keith Hall
Ombudsman: Jan Hynson
Auditors: PricewaterhouseCoopers LLP

LOCATIONS

HQ: Federal Prison Industries, Inc.
320 1st St. NW, Washington, DC 20534
Phone: 202-305-3500   **Fax:** 202-305-7340
Web: www.unicor.gov

Federal Prison Industries operates 112 factories at 71 prisons in the US.

PRODUCTS/OPERATIONS

2003 Sales

	$ mil.	% of total
Clothing & textiles	158.4	22
Electronics	152.4	21
Office furniture	152.0	21
Fleet management	123.3	17
Industrial products	36.7	5
Graphics	23.7	3
Services	12.2	2
Recycling	8.1	1
Other revenue	55.1	8
Total	**721.9**	**100**

Selected Products

Clothing and textiles
   Apparel
   Draperies and curtains
   Embroidery and screen printing on textiles
   Mattresses, bedding, linens, and towels
Electronics
   Electrical cables (both braided and cord assemblies)
   Electrical components and connectors
   Lighting systems
   Wire harness assemblies and circuit boards

Office furniture
   Casegoods and training table products
   Filing and storage products
   Office furniture and accessories
   Office system products
   Packaged office solutions
   Seating products
Fleet management
   Fleet management customized services
   New-vehicle retrofit services
   Rebuilt and refurbished vehicle components
Industrial products
   Custom fabricated industrial products, lockers, and storage cabinets
   Dorm and quarters furnishings
   Industrial racking catwalks, mezzanines, and shelving
   Optical eyewear (safety and prescription)
   Replacement filters
   Security fencing
Graphics
   Custom engraving and printing on awards, promotional gifts, and license plates
   Interior and exterior signs
   Printing and creative design services
   Remanufacturing of toner cartridges
Services
   Assembly and packing services
   Call center and order fulfillment services
   Distribution and mailing services
   Document conversion
   Laundry services
Recycling
   Recycling of electronic components
   Reuse and recovery of usable components for resale

COMPETITORS

Anderson Hickey
Avnet
CPAC
Deere
Federal Signal
Global Furniture
Haworth
Herman Miller
HighPoint Furniture
HNI
Kimball International
Matthews International
Mine Safety Appliances
Molex
Steelcase
Tyco International
WestPoint Stevens

HISTORICAL FINANCIALS

Company Type: Government agency

Income Statement   FYE: September 30

	REVENUE ($ mil.)	NET INCOME ($ mil.)	NET PROFIT MARGIN	EMPLOYEES
9/03	722	2	0.3%	20,274
9/02	717	9	1.3%	21,778
9/01	602	5	0.8%	22,560
9/00	546	(12)	—	21,688
9/99	566	17	2.9%	20,966
9/98	534	(2)	—	21,800
9/97	513	3	0.6%	18,414
9/96	496	12	2.4%	17,379
9/95	459	—	—	16,780
9/94	395	—	—	16,200
Annual Growth	6.9%	(22.6%)	—	2.5%

2003 Year-End Financials

Debt ratio: 6.9%   Current ratio: 2.01
Return on equity: 0.7%   Long-term debt ($ mil.): 20
Cash ($ mil.): 187

Net Income History

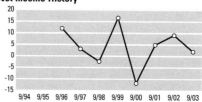

Federal Reserve

Where do banks go when they need a loan? To the Federal Reserve System, which sets the discount interest rate, the base rate at which its member banks may borrow. Known as the Fed, the system oversees a network of 12 Federal Reserve Banks located in major US cities; these in turn regulate banks in their districts and ensure they maintain adequate reserves. The Fed also clears money transfers, issues currency, and buys or sells government securities to regulate the money supply. Through its powerful New York bank, the Fed conducts foreign currency transactions, trades on the world market to support the US dollar's value, and stores gold for foreign governments and international agencies.

The seven-member Board of Governors, chaired by former Ayn Rand compadre Alan Greenspan since the Reagan administration, oversees the Fed's activities. As chairman under four different presidents, Greenspan has wielded more power than perhaps any Fed chief in history and securities markets virtually dangle on his every word.

Fed Members are appointed by the US President and confirmed by the Senate for one-time 14-year terms, staggered at two-year intervals to prevent political stacking. The seven governors comprise the majority of the 12-person Federal Open Market Committee, which determines monetary policy. The five remaining members are reserve bank presidents who rotate in one-year terms, with New York always holding a place. Although the Fed enjoys significant political and financial freedom (it even operates at a profit), the chairman is required to testify before Congress twice a year. National member banks must own stock in their Federal Reserve Bank, though it is optional for state-chartered banks.

By setting the discount rate and the federal funds rate (the rate at which banks borrow from each other), the Fed influences the pace of lending and, many believe, the pace of the economy itself. After slashing the federal funds rate in 2001 to its lowest point in some 40 years via an unprecedented skein of cuts, the Fed cut the rate another half-point in November 2002 to an infinitesimal 1.25% in hopes of fueling growth. The economy showed few signs of rebound by June 2003, so the Fed cut the federal funds rate again, to 1%.

A year later, with the economy in a tentative upturn in June 2004, the Fed raised the federal funds rate for the first time in four years, back up to 1.25%. Still optimistic, it bumped up the rate another quarter of a point in both August and September of that year, to 1.75%.

HISTORY

When New York's Knickerbocker Trust Company failed in 1907, it brought on a panic that was stemmed by J. P. Morgan, who strong-armed his fellow bankers into supporting shaky New York banks. The incident showed the need for a central bank.

Morgan's actions sparked fears of his economic power and spurred congressional efforts to establish a central bank. After a six-year struggle between eastern money interests and populist monetary reformers, the 1913 Federal Reserve Act was passed. Twelve Federal Reserve districts were created, but New York's economic might ensured it would be the most powerful.

New York bank head Benjamin Strong dominated the Fed in the 1920s, countering the glut of European gold flooding the US in 1923 by selling securities from the Fed's portfolio. After he died in 1928, the Fed couldn't stabilize prices. Such difficulty, along with low rates encouraging members to use Fed loans for stock speculation, helped set the stage for 1929's crash.

During the Depression and WWII, the Fed yielded to the demands of the Treasury to buy bonds. But after WWII it sought independence, cultivating Congress to help free it from Treasury demands. This effort was led by chairman William McChesney Martin, with the assistance of New York bank president Alan Sproul (also a rival for the chairmanship). Martin diluted Sproul's influence by governing by consensus with the other bank leaders.

The Fed managed the economy successfully in the postwar boom, but it was stymied by inflation in the late 1960s. In the early 1970s the New York bank also faced the collapse of the fixed currency exchange-rate system and the growth of currency trading. Its role as foreign currency trader became even more crucial as the dollar's value eroded amid rising oil prices and a slowing economy.

The US suffered from double-digit inflation in 1979 as President Jimmy Carter appointed New York Fed president Paul Volcker as chairman. Volcker, believing that raising interest rates a few points would not suffice, allowed the banks to raise their discount rates and increased bank reserve requirements to reduce the money supply. By the time inflation eased, Ronald Reagan was president.

During the 1980s and 1990s, US budget fights limited options for controlling the economy through spending decision, so the Fed's actions became more important. Its higher profile brought calls for more access to its decision-making processes. Alan Greenspan took over as chairman in 1987 after being designated by Reagan (and has since been reappointed by Presidents George H. W. Bush and Bill Clinton).

While the US economy seemed immune to the Asian currency crisis of 1997 and 1998, the Federal Reserve remained relatively quiescent. But when Russia defaulted on some of its bonds in 1998, leading to the near-collapse of hedge fund Long-Term Capital Management, the New York Federal Reserve Bank brokered a bailout by the fund's lenders and investors.

This led in 1999 to new guidelines for banks' risk management. The next year, the Fed faced up to the Internet age, taking a look at e-banking supervision. After raising interest rates to stave off inflation during the go-go late 1990s, the Fed cut rates an unprecedented 11 times in 2001 (to a 40-year low of 1.75%) to help spur the flagging post-boom economy.

EXECUTIVES

Chairman of the Board of Governors: Alan Greenspan, age 78, $171,900 pay
Vice Chairman of the Board of Governors: Roger W. Ferguson Jr., age 52
Member of the Board of Governors: Edward M. Gramlich, age 65
Member of the Board of Governors: Susan Schmidt Bies, age 57
Member of the Board of Governors: Mark W. Olson, age 61
Member of the Board of Governors: Ben S. Bernanke, age 50
Member of the Board of Governors: Donald L. Kohn, age 61
Director of the Division of Consumer and Community Affairs: Sandra F. Braunstein
General Counsel: Scott G. Alvarez
President, Federal Reserve Bank of New York: Timothy F. Geithner, age 43
President, Federal Reserve Bank of Boston: Cathy E. Minehan, age 57
President, Federal Reserve Bank of Philadelphia: Anthony M. Santomero, age 58
President, Federal Reserve Bank of Cleveland: Sandra Pianalto, age 50
President, Federal Reserve Bank of Richmond: Jeffrey M. (Jeff) Lacker, age 49
President, Federal Reserve Bank of Atlanta: Jack Guynn, age 61
President, Federal Reserve Bank of Chicago: Michael H. Moskow
President, Federal Reserve Bank of St. Louis: William Poole, age 67
President, Federal Reserve Bank of Minneapolis: Gary H. Stern
President, Federal Reserve Bank of Kansas City: Thomas M. Hoenig, age 58
President, Federal Reserve Bank of Dallas: Robert D. (Bob) McTeer Jr., age 61
President, Federal Reserve Bank of San Francisco: Janet L. Yellen, age 58
Auditors: PricewaterhouseCoopers LLP

LOCATIONS

HQ: Federal Reserve System
20th Street and Constitution Avenue NW, Washington, DC 20551
Phone: 202-452-3000
Web: www.federalreserve.gov

Federal Reserve Banks
Atlanta
Boston
Chicago
Cleveland
Dallas
Kansas City, Missouri
Minneapolis
New York
Philadelphia
Richmond, Virginia
St. Louis
San Francisco

PRODUCTS/OPERATIONS

2003 Sales

	$ mil.	% of total
Interest		
US government & federal agency securities	22,597	84
Investments denominated in foreign currencies	260	1
Loans to depository institutions	1	—
Noninterest		
Net foreign currency gains	2,695	10
Income from services	887	3
Other	407	2
Total	**26,847**	**100**

HISTORICAL FINANCIALS

Company Type: Government agency

Income Statement — FYE: December 31

	ASSETS ($ mil.)	NET INCOME ($ mil.)	INCOME AS % OF ASSETS	EMPLOYEES
12/03	771,487	23,006	3.0%	20,448
12/02	730,977	26,048	3.6%	21,208
12/01	654,949	28,035	4.3%	22,000
12/00	609,877	29,868	4.9%	23,056
12/99	674,460	26,262	3.9%	—
Annual Growth	3.4%	(3.3%)	—	(3.9%)

Federated Insurance

Federated Insurance is a mutual company with a specific focus. Consistent with its century-old roots as an insurer for Minnesota farm implement dealers, Federated offers group life and health coverage, as well as workers' compensation, automobile, property & casualty, retirement planning, and individual life insurance to a narrow niche of businesses — auto and tire dealers, service stations, building contractors, equipment dealers, machine shops, and printers. Operating nationwide, Federated Insurance markets its policies directly and through an independent sales force.

EXECUTIVES

Chairman, President, and CEO: Al Annexstad
EVP, Insurance Operations, and Director:
  Sarah L. Buxton
EVP, Insurance Operations, and Director: Jock Kinnett
EVP, Insurance Operations, and Director:
  A. Daniel Lewis
EVP, Insurance Operations: Paul F. Droher
EVP, Insurance Operations: Mark D. Scharmer
SVP and General Counsel: Peggy J. Birk
SVP, Accounting: Raymond R. Stawarz
SVP, Actuarial Services: Steven W. Judd
SVP, Insurance Alliances, Assistant Secretary:
  David W. Ramsey
SVP, Investments & Taxes: Gregory J. Stroik
Secretary-Treasurer and Director: Jairus E. Meilahn
Director Human Resources: Bryan Brose
Auditors: KPMG LLP

LOCATIONS

HQ: Federated Insurance Companies
  121 E. Park Sq., Owatonna, MN 55060
Phone: 507-455-5200   **Fax:** 507-455-5452
Web: www.federatedinsurance.com

Federated Insurance Companies operates throughout the US, primarily in the eastern part.

PRODUCTS/OPERATIONS

Selected Subsidiaries
Federated Life Insurance Company
Federated Mutual Insurance Company
Federated Service Insurance Company
Primary Source Insurance Agency, Inc.

2003 Year-End Financials

Equity as % of assets: 2.3%   Long-term debt ($ mil.): 689,757
Return on assets: 3.1%   Sales ($ mil.): 26,847
Return on equity: 133.5%

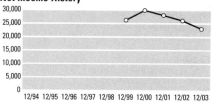

COMPETITORS

ACE Limited
AIG
Allstate
American Financial
Anthem
Blue Cross
CIGNA
CNA Financial
Farmers Group
Kemper Corporation
Liberty Mutual
MetLife
Nationwide
Progressive Corporation
Prudential
Safeco
St. Paul Travelers
State Farm

HISTORICAL FINANCIALS

Company Type: Mutual company

Income Statement   FYE: December 31

	ASSETS ($ mil.)	NET INCOME ($ mil.)	INCOME AS % OF ASSETS	EMPLOYEES
12/03	3,815	80	2.1%	2,900
12/02	3,689	25	0.7%	2,900
12/01	3,476	(21)	—	3,000
12/00	3,216	67	2.1%	3,100
12/99	3,128	80	2.5%	3,100
12/98	3,092	87	2.8%	2,950
12/97	2,920	99	3.4%	2,930
12/96	2,775	68	2.4%	2,749
12/95	—	—	—	2,699
12/94	—	—	—	2,673
Annual Growth	4.7%	2.5%	—	0.9%

2003 Year-End Financials

Equity as % of assets: 30.8%   Long-term debt ($ mil.): 44
Return on assets: 2.1%   Sales ($ mil.): 1,444
Return on equity: 7.2%

Feld Entertainment

A lot of clowning around has helped Feld Entertainment become one of the largest live entertainment producers in the world. The company entertains some 10 million people each year through its centerpiece, Ringling Bros. and Barnum & Bailey Circus, which visits about 90 locations. Feld also produces several touring ice shows, including Disney On Ice shows such as *Beauty and the Beast* and *Toy Story*. Feld's Siegfried & Roy show at The Mirage in Las Vegas closed after Roy Horn was mauled by a tiger in 2003. (The Mirage is replacing it with a Cirque du Soleil show.) Chairman and CEO Kenneth Feld, whose father, Irvin, began managing the circus in 1956, owns the company and personally oversees most of its productions.

Feld has engaged in some high-profile battles lately with animal rights activists. In 2001 a district court judge dismissed a complaint filed against the company by several animal activist groups, who claimed that Feld Entertainment didn't comply with federal regulations regarding the care of Asian elephants. The lawsuit was reinstated in early 2003 due to a procedural technicality.

HISTORY

When five-year-old Irvin Feld found a $1 bill in 1923, he told his mother, "I'm going to buy a circus." He started by working the sideshows of traveling circuses before settling in Washington, DC, in 1940. Feld, who was white, opened the Super Cut-Rate Drugstore in a black section of the segregated city with the backing of the NAACP. In 1944 he opened the Super Music City record store and started his own record company, Super Disc. Feld and his brother Israel also began promoting outdoor concerts. When rock and roll became popular in the 1950s, Feld promoted Chubby Checker and Fats Domino, among others.

Feld came a step closer to his dream in 1956 when he began managing the Ringling Bros. and Barnum & Bailey Circus for majority owner John Ringling North. North's circus traced its roots back to 1871 and P. T. Barnum's Grand Traveling Museum, Menagerie, Caravan, and Circus. Barnum's circus merged with James Bailey's circus in 1881, creating Barnum & Bailey. In 1907 Bailey's widow sold Barnum & Bailey to North's uncles, the Ringling brothers, who had started their circus in 1884.

Among Feld's suggestions to North was moving the circus into air-conditioned arenas, saving $50,000 a week because 1,800 roustabouts were no longer needed to set up tents. Feld continued to promote music acts, but he suffered a serious blow in 1959 when three of his stars — Buddy Holly, Ritchie Valens, and J. P. Richardson (the Big Bopper) — died in a plane crash.

Feld's dream of owning a circus finally was realized in 1967 when he and investors paid $8 million for Ringling Brothers. He fired most of the circus' performers and opened a Clown College to train new ones. Feld bought a German circus the following year to obtain animal trainer Gunther Gebel-Williams (who then spent the next 30 years with Ringling Brothers). Feld split Ringling into two units in 1969, so he could book it in two parts of the country at the same time and double his profits. Feld took the company public that year.

Feld and the other stockholders sold the circus to Mattel in 1971 for $47 million in stock; Feld stayed on as manager and held on to the lucrative concession business, Sells-Floto. He persuaded Mattel to buy the Ice Follies, Holiday on Ice, and the Siegfried & Roy magic show in 1979. Mattel sold the circus back to Feld in 1982 for $22.5 million, along with the ice shows and the magic show. Feld died two years later, and his son Kenneth became head of the company. A chip off the old block, Kenneth fired almost all the circus performers when he took over.

In an attempt to leverage the Barnum & Bailey brand, the company opened four retail store locations in 1990, but the venture failed and the stores were closed two years later. A constant target of animal rights activists, Feld began backing conservation efforts on behalf of the endangered Asian elephant and established the Center for Elephant Conservation in Florida in 1995. The next year the company changed its name to Feld Entertainment.

Under increasing pressure as the company's creative guru and managerial boss, Feld hired Turner Home Entertainment executive Stuart

Snyder as president and COO in 1997, so he could focus on the creative side of the business. That focus produced Barnum's Kaleidoscape in 1999, an upscale version of the original circus, featuring specialty acts, gourmet food, plush seats, and audience interaction. Plus, for the first time since 1956, a Feld circus was performed under a tent. (The company later shut down the tour of the Kaleidoscape, but claims it will return.) Snyder resigned later in 1999.

In an effort to inject new life into the 130-year-old Ringling Bros. and Barnum & Bailey Circus, Feld Entertainment launched two new marketing campaigns (one aimed at adults, the other aimed at children) in 2001.

Feld Entertainment's popular Siegfried & Roy show suffered a tragedy in 2003 when Roy Horn was mauled by a white tiger during a performance. He later suffered a stroke that left him partially paralyzed, and the Siegfried & Roy show is closed indefinitely.

EXECUTIVES

Chairman and CEO: Kenneth Feld, age 55
CFO: Mike Ruch
SVP Field Marketing and Sales, North America: Jeff Meyer
SVP Marketing: Julie Robertson
VP Creative Development: Jerry Bilik
VP International Sales and Business Development: Robert McHugh
VP and Corporate Counsel: Julie Alexa Strauss
Director of Corporate Communications: Catherine Ort-Mabry
Director of Human Resources: Kirk McCoy
Executive Director of Animal Stewardship: John Kirtland
Public Relations, Siegfried & Roy: Frank H. Lieberman
National Director of Public Relations: Mark Riddell

LOCATIONS

HQ: Feld Entertainment, Inc.
8607 Westwood Center Dr., Vienna, VA 22182
Phone: 703-448-4000 **Fax:** 703-448-4100
Web: www.feldentertainment.com

Feld Entertainment produces shows in 48 countries on six continents.

PRODUCTS/OPERATIONS

Selected Attractions
Disney On Ice
 Beauty and the Beast
 The Jungle Book
 The Lion King
 Tarzan
 Toy Story 2
 Walt Disney's 100 Years of Magic
Ringling Bros. and Barnum & Bailey Circus

Other Operations
Feld Consumer Products (concessions operations)
Hagenbeck-Wallace (prop design studio)

COMPETITORS

CIE
Cirque du Soleil
Clear Channel Entertainment
Harlem Globetrotters
HIT Entertainment
On Stage Entertainment
Renaissance Entertainment
Six Flags
TBA
Tom Collins

HISTORICAL FINANCIALS

Company Type: Private

Income Statement — FYE: January 31

	ESTIMATED REVENUE ($ mil.)	NET INCOME ($ mil.)	NET PROFIT MARGIN	EMPLOYEES
1/02	780	—	—	1,550
1/01	776	—	—	2,500
1/00	675	—	—	2,500
1/99	645	—	—	2,500
1/98	630	—	—	2,500
1/97	550	—	—	2,500
1/96	625	—	—	2,500
1/95	600	—	—	2,500
1/94	570	—	—	2,500
1/93	500	—	—	2,500
Annual Growth	5.1%	—	—	(5.2%)

Revenue History

Fellowes

Fellowes (formerly Fellowes Manufacturing Company) produces office products that can organize or obliterate. A leading maker of paper shredders (Powershred, Shredmate), it also makes computer and office accessories, such as ergonomic wrist rests, multimedia storage, and other accessories. As a licensee of Body Glove International (maker of high-tech surf and scuba gear), Fellowes offers fashionable Body Glove cases for mobile phones and iPods. Fellowes' products are sold through office retailers and mass merchants, as well as online. Still owned and run by the Fellowes family, the company was started in 1917 when Harry Fellowes paid $50 for Bankers Box, a maker of storage boxes for bank records.

EXECUTIVES

CEO: James (Jim) Fellowes
President and COO: Jude Rake, age 45
CFO: Joseph T. (Joe) Koch
EVP and Chief Supply Chain Officer: James (Jim) Lewis
VP Human Resources: Lyn Bulman
VP Sales and Planning: Jeff Nielson, age 41
President, Fellowes Europe: Peter Fellowes
President, Fellowes North America: Bob Compagno
Director, Corporate Marketing Communications: Maureen Moore
Corporate Marketing Manager: Julie Garrard

LOCATIONS

HQ: Fellowes, Inc.
1789 Norwood Ave., Itasca, IL 60143
Phone: 630-893-1600 **Fax:** 630-893-1648
Web: www.fellowes.com

Fellowes has operations in Africa, Asia, Australia, Benelux, Canada, France, Germany, Italy, Japan, Latin America, the Middle East, Poland, the UK, and the US.

PRODUCTS/OPERATIONS

Selected Products
Business machines
 Binding machines and supplies
 Laminating machines and supplies
 Paper shredders and supplies
Desktop and office essentials
 Cleaning supplies
 Headsets
 Keyboard managers
 Mice, keyboards, and trackballs
 Monitor and CPU accessories
 Printer stands
 Surge protection
 Tool kits
 Wrist rests
Media labeling and storage
 CD storage
 CD/DVD labeling
 DVD storage
 Multimedia storage
 Video storage
Mobile accessories
 Camera cases
 Cellular accessories
 Laptop accessories
 PDA accessories
 Tablet PC accessories

COMPETITORS

ACCO World   Lane Industries
Cummins-American   Newell Rubbermaid
Esselte   Smead
General Binding

HISTORICAL FINANCIALS

Company Type: Private

Income Statement — FYE: March 31

	REVENUE ($ mil.)	NET INCOME ($ mil.)	NET PROFIT MARGIN	EMPLOYEES
3/03	536	—	—	1,500
3/02	524	—	—	1,750
3/01	559	—	—	1,800
3/00	607	—	—	1,800
3/99	523	—	—	1,773
3/98	500	—	—	1,450
3/97	358	—	—	1,474
3/96	310	—	—	1,461
3/95	220	—	—	1,258
3/94	191	—	—	—
Annual Growth	12.2%	—	—	2.2%

Revenue History

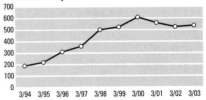

Ferolie Group

A food broker serving the entire US, The Ferolie Group broke into the business on the East Coast in 1948. The company provides sales and marketing services for packaged food and packaged goods companies. Through exclusive area and regional contracts, the group arranges distribution to warehouse stores, drugstores, supermarkets, and mass merchandisers. Some of Ferolie's biggest clients are Gillette's Duracell, Georgia-Pacific's Fort James, Kraft Foods, Unilever's Lipton, and McCormick & Company. The company is affiliated with Advantage Sales & Marketing, a partnership of food brokerages operating across the US. Founded by Joseph Ferolie, the company remains family-owned.

EXECUTIVES

CEO: Lawrence J. Ferolie Sr.
President: Paul Nadel
COO: Tony Scuderi
EVP, Business Teams: Anthony (Tony) Ferolie
EVP, Customer Teams: Frank Tomanelli
SVP, Grocery: Rich Desimone
SVP, Grocery: Tony Fischetta
VP, Finance: Catherine (Cathy) Ross
VP, Human Resources: Julie Shasteen
VP, Sales: Robert (Bob) Martin
VP, Sales Operations: Lawrence J. Ferolie Jr.
CIO: James (Jim) Ferolie
Director, Marketing: Steven Nadel
General Counsel: Daryl Fox

LOCATIONS

HQ: The Ferolie Group
2 Van Riper Rd., Montvale, NJ 07645
Phone: 201-307-9100   **Fax:** 201-782-0878
Web: www.feroliegroup.com

COMPETITORS

Affiliated Foods
Atlantic Mktg
C&S Wholesale
Carrefour
CROSSMARK
Di Giorgio
Nash Finch
Royal Ahold
Wal-Mart

HISTORICAL FINANCIALS

Company Type: Private

Income Statement
FYE: December 31

	ESTIMATED REVENUE ($ mil.)	NET INCOME ($ mil.)	NET PROFIT MARGIN	EMPLOYEES
12/02	2,200	—	—	850
12/01	1,200	—	—	615
12/00	1,100	—	—	615
12/99	1,100	—	—	615
12/98	970	—	—	615
12/97	800	—	—	610
12/96	750	—	—	—
Annual Growth	19.6%	—	—	6.9%

Revenue History

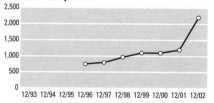

FHC Health Systems

FHC Health Systems is one of the country's largest behavioral health care companies. FHC Health Systems provides behavioral health care services to more than 20 million people through its various subsidiary companies. Employee assistance, substance abuse, and mental health treatment programs are provided by the company's ValueOptions subsidiary. Residential psychiatric care, and case management services are provided by the company's Alternative Behavioral Services subsidiary. Third party administration of behavioral health programs is provided via the company's FirstLab subsidiary.

FHC Health Systems also provides health care software and management information services through its StayStat and CS&O subsidiaries.

EXECUTIVES

Chairman, President, and CEO, FHC Health Systems, and ValueOptions; Chairman and CEO, FirstLab: Ronald I. Dozoretz
CFO, FHC Health Systems and ValueOptions: Thomas E. Oram
VP Human Resources: Carol Dalton Cash
President and CEO, CS&O: Jonathan Ross
President and CEO, FirstLab: David M. Martin
President and CEO, StayStat: Michael Taylor
CEO, Alternative Behavioral Services: Edward C. Irby
COO, ValueOptions: Michele D. Alfano
EVP and Chief Technology Officer, ValueOptions: Bob Esposito
Chief Administrative Officer, ValueOptions: Tom Brown

LOCATIONS

HQ: FHC Health Systems, Inc.
240 Corporate Blvd., Norfolk, VA 23502
Phone: 757-459-5100   **Fax:** 757-459-5219
Web: www.fhchealthsystems.com

PRODUCTS/OPERATIONS

Subsidiaries

ABSolute Integrated Solutions (behavioral health practice management software)
Alternative Behavioral Services (behavioral health services)
Corporation for Standards and Outcomes (CS&O) (outcome & accountability software)
FirstLab (behavioral health third party administration services)
StayStat (physician practice software and services)
ValueOptions (managed behavioral care)

COMPETITORS

Horizon Health
Magellan Health
Mental Health Network

HISTORICAL FINANCIALS

Company Type: Private

Income Statement
FYE: December 31

	ESTIMATED REVENUE ($ mil.)	NET INCOME ($ mil.)	NET PROFIT MARGIN	EMPLOYEES
12/03	1,300	—	—	7,000
12/02	1,188	—	—	8,169
Annual Growth	9.4%	—	—	(14.3%)

Findlay Industries

Revenue History

Findlay Industries doesn't need a room to show off its interior designs. The automotive interiors supplier makes door and sidewall trim panels (quarter-trim panels), seat back and trunk covers, headliners, and sleeper cabs. It makes these components for customers such as General Motors, Ford, BMW, Toyota, and other car and heavy truck makers around the world. Findlay's brands include the ProBond family of molded headliner material. The company has 24 manufacturing facilities in Europe and North America. The company, founded by Philip D. Gardner in 1959, is controlled by Gardner and former president Philip J. Gardner.

EXECUTIVES

CEO: Phil D. Gardner
CFO: Tom Hogan
Marketing Manager: Marc Ingwersen
Human Resources: Geneva Fennell

LOCATIONS

HQ: Findlay Industries, Inc.
4000 Fostoria Rd., Findlay, OH 45840
Phone: 419-422-1302   **Fax:** 419-427-3390
Web: www.findlayindustries.com

Findlay Industries has 24 manufacturing facilities in seven countries throughout North America and Europe.

PRODUCTS/OPERATIONS

Selected Products, Services, and Systems

Aftermarket
Assembly, sequencing, and logistics
Door panel systems
Overhead systems
Rear compartment systems
Seat systems

COMPETITORS

Delphi
Dura Automotive
Faurecia
Honeywell International
Intier
Johnson Controls
Lear
Magna International
Siemens

HISTORICAL FINANCIALS
Company Type: Private

Income Statement				FYE: April 30
	REVENUE ($ mil.)	NET INCOME ($ mil.)	NET PROFIT MARGIN	EMPLOYEES
4/03	555	—	—	3,742
4/02	800	—	—	3,500
4/01	776	—	—	3,400
4/00	845	—	—	5,400
4/99	525	—	—	3,300
Annual Growth	1.4%	—	—	3.2%

Revenue History

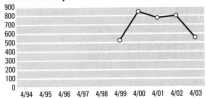

Fletcher Jones

Image is important at Fletcher Jones Management Group. The company holds the title as the US's top Mercedes seller. It rolls out Benzes from a 225,000-sq.-ft. superstore in Las Vegas, an 186,000-sq-ft. store in Newport Beach, California, and another dealership in Chicago. Fletcher Jones also operates five other dealerships in Chicago, another two in Las Vegas and one in Reno, Nevada, selling cars from Audi, Ford, Honda, Infiniti, Lexus, Nissan, Toyota, and Volkswagen. Fletcher Jones Management Group is owned by president and CEO Fletcher Jones Jr., whose father started it in 1954 with one Los Angeles dealership.

EXECUTIVES
President and CEO: Fletcher (Ted) Jones Jr.
COO: Tom Downer
CFO: Shawn Dettrey

LOCATIONS
HQ: Fletcher Jones Management Group
7300 W. Sahara Ave., Las Vegas, NV 89117
Phone: 702-739-9800   **Fax:** 702-739-0486
Web: www.fletcherjones.com

COMPETITORS
AutoNation
Chapman Automotive
Findlay Automotive
Galpin Motors
House of Imports
Lithia Motors
Tuttle-Click
United Auto Group

HISTORICAL FINANCIALS
Company Type: Private

Income Statement				FYE: June 30
	REVENUE ($ mil.)	NET INCOME ($ mil.)	NET PROFIT MARGIN	EMPLOYEES
6/03*	1,103	—	—	1,100
6/99	677	—	—	1,050
6/98	662	—	—	1,047
6/97	584	—	—	1,050
6/96	578	—	—	1,032
6/95	525	—	—	1,419
Annual Growth	16.0%	—	—	(5.0%)

*Irregular reporting interval

Revenue History

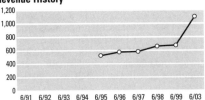

Flint Ink

The world's #2 ink maker (behind Sun Chemical), Flint Ink produces inks and coatings for a variety of applications, including packaging, publication, commercial uses, and digital printing. It operates eight divisions: North America, Latin America, Asia, India/Pacific, Flint-Schmidt (which serves Europe), Jetrion (digital ink and hardware), Precisia (for electronics), and CDR Pigments and Dispersions (colorants used in ink and for other uses). The company's products include sheet-fed and web offset, gravure, ultraviolet and electronic beam (UV/EB) curable, and digital inks. The Flint family owns the company, and Howard Flint II represents the third generation of the family to head the firm.

Flint Ink has plants throughout the world. The company's primary customers include printing facilities that produce magazines, newspapers, catalogs, and packaging materials. Flint Ink also makes specialty inks (for example, for printing lottery tickets) and environment-friendly vegetable oil-based inks.

Although the world's #1 privately held maker of inks, Flint Ink has drawn a bull's-eye on becoming the #1 ink maker, regardless of ownership. The company has been growing through acquisitions, joint ventures, and partnerships. Flint Ink acquired one of Europe's largest ink makers, German-based Gebr. Schmidt GmbH, in 2002.

In 2003 Flint also launched two new subsidiaries. Jetrion is a digital ink manufacturer, and Precisia makes conductive and advanced inks for electronics uses.

H. Howard Flint founded Flint Ink in 1920.

EXECUTIVES
Chairman and CEO: H. Howard Flint II
President: Leonard D. (Dave) Frescoln
COO: Linda J. Welty, age 47
EVP: David B. Flint
SVP, Finance and CFO: Michael J. Gannon
SVP, Research and New Product Development: Joseph W Raksis
VP and General Manager, North American Publication and Commercial Ink Divisions: Susan Kuchta
VP, Human Resources: Glenn T. Autry
VP, Research and Development: Graham Battersby
Director, Corporate Communications: Rita Conrad
Senior Scientist: Walt Zawacki

LOCATIONS
HQ: Flint Ink Corporation
4600 Arrowhead Dr., Ann Arbor, MI 48105
Phone: 734-622-6000   **Fax:** 734-622-6131
Web: www.flintink.com

Flint Ink has operations in Africa, the Americas, Asia, Europe, India/Pacific, and the Middle East.

PRODUCTS/OPERATIONS

Selected Products and Brands
Commercial inks
Digital inks
Flexographic news inks
Flexo/Gravure packaging inks
High-performance inks and coatings
Inkjet inks
Offset news inks
Packaging inks
Publication gravure inks
Sheetfed inks
UV/EB curable inks
Web offset heatset inks

COMPETITORS
Akzo Nobel
Americhem
BASF AG
Cabot
Engelhard
Field Container
INX International Ink
Mitsubishi Chemical America
Sun Chemical

HISTORICAL FINANCIALS
Company Type: Private

Income Statement				FYE: December 31
	REVENUE ($ mil.)	NET INCOME ($ mil.)	NET PROFIT MARGIN	EMPLOYEES
12/03	1,454	—	—	4,600
12/02	1,400	—	—	4,600
12/01	1,400	—	—	4,000
12/00	1,080	—	—	3,700
12/99	1,200	—	—	3,500
12/98	1,216	—	—	3,500
12/97	924	—	—	3,500
12/96	836	—	—	2,730
12/95	875	—	—	2,700
12/94	634	—	—	2,613
Annual Growth	9.7%	—	—	6.5%

Revenue History

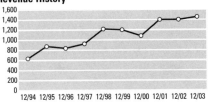

Florida's Natural Growers

Florida's Natural Growers is known for squeezing out profits. The cooperative is one of the largest largest citrus juice sellers in the US, using its 1,100 member-farmers' harvest from their more than 60,000 acres of citrus groves to make juice. The cooperative produces frozen concentrated and not-from-concentrate juices (orange, apple, grapefruit, lemonade, and fruit blends) under the Florida's Natural, Growers' Pride, Growers Style, Donald Duck, and Ruby Red brand names. The company was founded in 1933 by a group of citrus growers in order to process grapefruit.

The co-op's products are sold to the food service, retail, and vending industries, and it exports to more than 40 countries.

EXECUTIVES
CEO: Stephen Caruso
CFO: William (Chip) Hendry
VP, Sales and Marketing: Walt Lincer
Director, Human Resources: Susan Langley

LOCATIONS
HQ: Florida's Natural Growers
20205 US Hwy. 27 North, Lake Wales, FL 33853
Phone: 863-676-1411   **Fax:** 863-676-5744
Web: floridanatural.com

COMPETITORS
Chiquita Brands
Coca-Cola North America
Horizon Organic
Louis Dreyfus Citrus
Naked Juice
National Grape Cooperative
Northland Cranberries
Ocean Spray
Odwalla
Procter & Gamble
Smucker
Sunkist
Tree Top
Tropicana
Vitality Foodservice
Welch's

HISTORICAL FINANCIALS
Company Type: Cooperative

Income Statement
FYE: August 31

	REVENUE ($ mil.)	NET INCOME ($ mil.)	NET PROFIT MARGIN	EMPLOYEES
8/03	528	—	—	1,000
8/02	600	—	—	1,000
8/01	620	—	—	—
8/00	605	—	—	—
8/99	550	—	—	—
8/98	469	—	—	—
Annual Growth	2.4%	—	—	0.0%

Revenue History
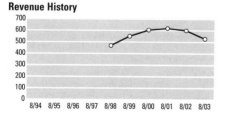

Flying J

Flying J puts out a welcome mat for truckers in North America. From its beginnings in 1968 with four locations, the company is now the #1 distributor of diesel fuel and a leading truck-stop operator in the US — with more than 160 amenity-loaded Flying J Travel Plazas in 41 states and Canada. Flying J and its subsidiaries, including Big West Oil, go beyond the usual truck-stop fare (food, fuel, showers) by offering extra services, including banking, bulk-fuel programs, communications (wireless Internet connections), fuel cost analysis, insurance, and truck fleet sales. The company also owns oil and gas reserves and a 25,000-barrel-a-day refinery. Founder and chairman Jay Call died in a plane crash in 2003.

EXECUTIVES
President and CEO: J. Phillip Adams
Controller and Treasurer: Scott Clayson
SVP, Legal and Secretary: Barre G. Burgon
SVP, Supply & Distribution, and Petroleum Marketing: Richard D. Peterson
SVP, Refining: Jeff Uttley
EVP, Big West Oil (Refining): Fred Greener
VP, Financial and Communications Services: J. J. Singh
VP, Retail Operations: James (Jim) Baker
VP, Real Estate: Ronald R. Parker
VP, Restaurant Operations: Ron DeJuncker
CIO: Bron McCall
Director, Personnel: Jerry Beckman
Director, Marketing: Virginia Parker
Director, Training: Mark Adamson

LOCATIONS
HQ: Flying J Inc.
1104 Country Hills Dr., Ogden, UT 84403
Phone: 801-624-1000   **Fax:** 801-624-1587
Web: www.flyingj.com

Flying J has truck stops in the US and Canada, an oil refinery in Utah, and oil and gas reserves in Montana, North Dakota, Utah, and Wyoming.

PRODUCTS/OPERATIONS
Selected Products and Services
Advertising services
ATMs
Banking
Bulk-fuel programs
Calling cards
Credit cards
Fleet financing
Food
Freight matching
Fuel
Insurance
Laundry facilities
Load and equipment postings
Lube centers
Motels
Restaurants
Showers
Truck washes

COMPETITORS
Exxon Mobil
FFP Operating
Love's Country Stores
Marathon Oil
Petro Stopping Centers
Pilot
Rip Griffin Truck Service Center
Stuckey's
TravelCenters of America

HISTORICAL FINANCIALS
Company Type: Private

Income Statement
FYE: January 31

	REVENUE ($ mil.)	NET INCOME ($ mil.)	NET PROFIT MARGIN	EMPLOYEES
1/04	5,600	—	—	12,000
1/03	4,600	—	—	11,500
1/02	4,200	—	—	11,500
1/01	4,349	—	—	11,000
1/00	2,953	—	—	10,000
1/99	2,344	—	—	9,000
1/98	1,600	—	—	8,000
1/97	1,558	—	—	8,000
1/96	1,282	—	—	7,600
1/95	1,031	—	—	6,952
Annual Growth	20.7%	—	—	6.3%

Revenue History

FM Global

If you're looking to protect your corporation, turn your insurance dial to FM Global. The insurer provides commercial and industrial property insurance and a variety of risk management services, ranging from all-risk programs to specialized products for ocean cargo and machinery equipment, as well as property loss prevention engineering and research. FM Global operates through such subsidiaries as Factory Mutual Insurance, Mutual Boiler Re, Affiliated FM Insurance, and Bermuda-based New Providence Mutual (which offers alternative risk financing for hard-to-find coverage). In addition to the US, the company has offices in Asia, Australia, Canada, Europe, and South America.

EXECUTIVES
Chairman and CEO: Shivan S. Subramaniam
EVP, Staff Operations and Planning: Ruud H. Bosman
EVP and Manager, North American Operations: Brian J. Hurley
SVP, Finance and CFO: Jeffrey A. Burchill
SVP, Commercial Lines: Carol G. Barton
SVP, Underwriting: Robert E. Bean
SVP, Marketing: Roland Bonitati
SVP, Claims: Dennis J. Hedden
SVP, Investments: Paul E. LaFleche
SVP, Research and Approvals: Thomas Lawson
SVP, Information Services: Jeanne R. Lieb
SVP, Law and Governmental Affairs: John J. Pomeroy
SVP, Human Resources: Enzo Rebula
Auditors: Ernst & Young LLP

LOCATIONS

HQ: FM Global
  1301 Atwood Ave., Johnston, RI 02919
Phone: 401-275-3000 **Fax:** 401-275-3029
Web: www.fmglobal.com

PRODUCTS/OPERATIONS

2003 Sales

	$ mil.	% of total
Premiums	2,559	92
Investment income	207	7
Fees	23	1
Total	2,789	100

Selected Subsidiaries
Affiliated FM Insurance
FM Global Research
FM Insurance Company, Limited
Mutual Boiler Re
New Providence Mutual
TSB Loss Control Consultants, Inc.

COMPETITORS

ACE Limited	The Hartford
AIG	Nationwide
Allianz	Royal & SunAlliance USA
CNA Financial	St. Paul Travelers
GE Global Insurance	Zurich Financial Services
Gerling	

HISTORICAL FINANCIALS

Company Type: Mutual company

Income Statement

FYE: December 31

	ASSETS ($ mil.)	NET INCOME ($ mil.)	INCOME AS % OF ASSETS	EMPLOYEES
12/03	8,250	666	8.1%	4,400
12/02	7,189	244	3.4%	4,400
12/01	6,516	(132)	—	4,000
12/00	5,673	345	6.1%	—
Annual Growth	13.3%	24.5%	—	4.9%

2003 Year-End Financials
Equity as % of assets: 36.9%
Long-term debt ($ mil.): 123
Return on assets: 8.6%
Sales ($ mil.): 2,789
Return on equity: 26.0%

Net Income History

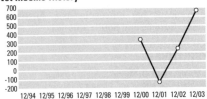

FMR

FMR Corp. is *semper fidelis* (ever faithful) to its core business. The financial services conglomerate, better known as Fidelity Investments, is the world's #1 mutual fund company. Serving some 18 million individual and institutional clients, Fidelity manages nearly 340 funds and has approximately $775 billion of assets under management. Among its notable offerings is the Magellan Fund, which was for many years the US's largest. The founding Johnson family controls most of FMR; Abigail Johnson, CEO Ned's daughter and heir apparent, is the largest single shareholder with about 25%.

Fidelity's nonfund offerings include life insurance, trust services, securities clearing, retirement services, and a leading online discount brokerage. It is one of the largest administrators of 401(k) plans, and the firm continues to grow this segment, which includes other services related to benefits outsourcing.

FMR has major holdings in telecommunications (COLT Telecom Group) and transportation (BostonCoach). Like many institutional investors, Fidelity uses its clout to sway the boards of companies in which it has significant holdings.

HISTORY

Boston money management firm Anderson & Cromwell formed Fidelity Fund in 1930. Edward Johnson became president of the fund in 1943, when it had $3 million invested in Treasury bills. Johnson diversified into stocks, and by 1945 the fund had grown to $10 million. In 1946 he established Fidelity Management and Research to act as its investment adviser.

In the early 1950s Johnson hired Gerry Tsai, a young immigrant from Shanghai, to analyze stocks. He put Tsai in charge of Fidelity Capital Fund in 1957. Tsai's brash, go-go investment strategy in such speculative stocks as Xerox and Polaroid paid off; by the time he left to form his own fund in 1965, he was managing more than $1 billion.

The Magellan Fund started in 1962. The company entered the corporate pension plans market (FMR Investment Management) in 1964, and retirement plans for self-employed individuals (Fidelity Keogh Plan) in 1967. It began serving investors outside the US (Fidelity International) in 1968.

Holding company FMR was formed in 1972, the same year Johnson gave control of Fidelity to his son Ned, who vertically integrated FMR by selling directly to customers rather than through brokers. In 1973 he formed Fidelity Daily Income Trust, the first money market fund to offer check writing.

Peter Lynch was hired as manager of the Magellan Fund in 1977. During his 13-year tenure, Magellan grew from $20 million to $12 billion in assets and outperformed all other mutual funds. Fidelity started Fidelity Brokerage Services in 1978, becoming the first mutual fund company to offer discount brokerage.

In 1980 the company launched a nationwide branch network and in 1986 entered the credit card business. The Wall Street crash of 1987 forced its Magellan Fund to liquidate almost $1 billion in stock in a single day. That year FMR moved into insurance by offering variable life, single premium, and deferred annuity policies. In 1989 the company introduced the low-expense Spartan Fund, targeted toward large, less-active investors.

Magellan's performance faded in the early 1990s, dropping from #1 performer to #3. Most of Fidelity's best performers were from its 36 select funds, which focus on narrow industry segments. FMR founded London-based COLT Telecom in 1993. In 1994 Johnson gave his daughter and heir apparent, Abigail, a 25% stake in FMR.

Jeffrey Vinik resigned as manager of Magellan in 1996, one of more than a dozen fund managers to leave the firm that year and the next. Robert Stansky took the helm of the $56 billion fund, which FMR decided to close to new investors in 1997. Fidelity had a first that year when it went with an outside fund manager, hiring Bankers Trust (now part of Deutsche Bank) to manage its index funds.

FMR did some housecleaning in the late 1990s. It sold its Wentworth art galleries (1997) and *Worth* magazine (1998). Despite continued management turnover, it entered Japan and expanded its presence in Canada.

In 1999 the firm formed a joint venture with Charles Schwab; Donaldson, Lufkin & Jenrette, known now as Credit Suisse First Boston (USA); and Spear, Leeds & Kellogg to form electronic communications network REDIBook ECN (now part of Archipelago) to trade Nasdaq stocks online. That year Fidelity teamed with Internet portal Lycos (now part of Terra Lycos) to develop its online brokerage.

FMR opened savings and loan Fidelity Personal Trust Co. in 2000. That year the Magellan Fund for a time lost its longtime title as the US's largest mutual fund to the Vanguard Index 500 Fund. In 2001 the company teamed up with Frank Russell to offer a new fund for wealthy clients.

EXECUTIVES

Chairman and CEO: Edward C. (Ned) Johnson III, age 71
Vice Chairman and COO: Robert L. (Bob) Reynolds
EVP and CFO: Laura B. Cronin
Chief Administrative Officer: Stephen P. Jonas
Vice Chairman, Fidelity Management & Research: Peter S. Lynch
President, Fidelity Real Estate: Stephen M. Bell
President, Fidelity Investments Tax-Exempt Services: John W. Callahan
President, Fidelity Investments Life Insurance: Melanie Calzetti-Spahr
President, Fidelity Personal Investments: Jeffrey R. Carney
President, Fidelity Money Management: Dwight D. Churchill
President, Fidelity Investments Institutional Brokerage Group: David F. Denison
President, Fidelity eBusiness: Steven E. Elterich
President, Fidelity Investments Systems: Donald A. Haile
President, Fidelity Operations Group: Timothy F. Hayes
President, Fidelity Management & Research: Abigail P. (Abby) Johnson, age 42
President, Fidelity Strategic Investments and Fidelity Capital: Robert A. Lawrence
President, National Financial Services: Norman R. Malo
President, Fidelity Brokerage Company: Ellyn A. McColgan
President, Fidelity Employer Services: Peter J. Smail
EVP, Corporate Affairs: Thomas E. Eidson
EVP, Human Resources: Guy L. Patton
EVP, Risk Oversight: Kenneth A. Rathgeber
EVP, Public Policy and Regional Affairs: David C. Weinstein
SVP and General Counsel: Lena G. Goldberg
Treasurer: Michael B. Fox
Auditors: PricewaterhouseCoopers LLP

LOCATIONS

HQ: FMR Corp.
  82 Devonshire St., Boston, MA 02109
Phone: 617-563-7000 **Fax:** 617-476-6150
Web: www.fidelity.com

FMR has offices in about 70 US cities, as well as in Australia, Bermuda, Canada, France, Germany, Hong Kong, India, Japan, Luxembourg, the Netherlands, Spain, Sweden, Switzerland, Taiwan, and the UK.

Follett

Not all kids like to read, but (fortunately for Follett) by the time they reach college, they don't have a choice. Follett is the #1 operator of US college bookstores with over 680 campus bookstores in 48 states, as well as Canada. The company's business groups, which reach about 60 countries, also provide books and audiovisual materials to grade school and public libraries, library automation and management software, textbook reconditioning, and other services. Its efollett.com Web site sells new and used college textbooks (its database has about 16 million titles). The Follett family has owned and managed the company for four generations.

In addition to books, campus stores sell items such as clothing, school supplies, and software. The company has capitalized on the growing trend of universities farming out operations to independent operators.

HISTORY

Follett began in 1873 as a small bookstore opened by the Rev. Charles Barnes in his Wheaton, Illinois, home. By 1893 a recession had rocked the business, and Barnes sought investment from his wife's family, for which he gave up controlling interest. Sales topped $237,000 in 1899.

Initially hired by Barnes in 1901 to help move the store to a new location in Chicago, 18-year-old C. W. Follett stayed on as both salesman and stock clerk. Barnes retired the following year and left the business to his son William and his father-in-law, John Wilcox, who was a major shareholder. In 1917 C. W. bought into the company when William moved to New York (he started what became one of Follett's biggest competitors, Barnes & Noble), and he renamed it J. W. Wilcox & Follett Company. Wilcox died in 1923, and C. W. bought the Wilcox family shares and shortened the name to Wilcox & Follett.

C. W.'s sons were brought into the business, and each was instrumental in shaping the company's future. Garth created Follett Library Resources, a wholesale service for libraries. Dwight started the elementary textbook publishing division. But Robert would have the most influence: He began wholesaling college textbooks, which led to the establishment of Follett College Stores and Follett Campus Resources.

Wilcox & Follett expanded throughout the Depression. During WWII it began publishing kids' books, which were in demand because of a metal toy shortage. C. W. died in 1952 and Dwight took over. Five years later the firm organized into divisions; Follett was created as the parent company. During the 1960s Follett developed the first multi-racial textbook series. Dwight built the company to $50 million in annual sales by 1977, when he retired. His son Robert succeeded him and led Follett through tremendous growth in the 1980s.

In 1983 the company sold its publishing division to Esquire Education Group; using funds from this sale, it began acquiring college bookstore chains such as Campus Services. In 1989 Follett developed Tom-Tracks, a computerized textbook system for college bookstores. A year later the company acquired Brennan College Service, adding 57 stores to its chain. Robert's son-in-law Richard Traut, named chairman in 1994, was the first person without the Follett name to hold that position. By 1994 Tom-Tracks had been installed in over 500 bookstores across the country. That year Follett introduced Sneak Preview Plus, a CD-ROM product designed to enhance the acquisition process in libraries.

The company acquired used-textbook reseller Western Textbook Exchange (1996), juvenile-book distributor Book Wholesalers (1997), and coursepack printer CAPCO (1998). In early 1998 Follett reorganized its corporate structure by market segments, establishing three divisions: the Elementary/High School Group, the Higher Education Group, and the Library Group. Later that year the Follett Campus Resources unit agreed to pay the University of Tennessee $380,000 after the school discovered that the firm had been underpaying students in a book-buyback program for several years. Adding to its bevy of campus bookstores, it signed a contract the same year to build a $5 million bookstore at the University of Texas at Arlington.

Also in 1998 CFO Kenneth Hull replaced Richard Litzsinger as CEO. Follett launched efollett.com in early 1999 to sell college textbooks online. That year CEO Kenneth Hull became chairman upon Richard Traut's departure. In November 2000 Christopher Traut became CEO; Hull remained chairman.

In April 2001 Hull retired, and Mark Litzsinger succeeded him as chairman.

EXECUTIVES

Chairman: R. Mark Litzsinger
President and CEO: Christopher Traut
EVP Finance and CFO: Kathryn A. Stanton
EVP Human Resources: Richard Ellspermann
President and CEO, School and Library Group: Ross Follett
President, Higher Education Group: Thomas A. (Tom) Christopher
EVP, School and Library Group: Chuck Follett
President, BWI: John Nelson

LOCATIONS

HQ: Follett Corporation
  2233 West St., River Grove, IL 60171
Phone: 708-583-2000   **Fax:** 708-452-9347
Web: www.follett.com

PRODUCTS/OPERATIONS

Company Divisions

Elementary/High School Group
  Follett Educational Services (K-12 textbooks and workbooks)
  Follett Software Company (library automation)
Higher Education Group
Library Group
  Book Wholesalers, Inc. (BWI) (public libraries)
  Follett Library Resources (school libraries)

COMPETITORS

Baker & Taylor
Barnes & Noble College Bookstores
Brodart
Ecampus.com
Educational Development
Ingram Industries
Nebraska Book
Varsity Group
Wal-Mart

PRODUCTS/OPERATIONS

Selected Subsidiaries

Fidelity Capital
Fidelity Financial Intermediary Services
  Fidelity Investments Canada Limited
  Fidelity Investments Institutional Services Company, Inc.
Fidelity International Limited (Bermuda)
Fidelity Investments Institutional Retirement Group
  Fidelity Benefits Center
  Fidelity Group Pensions International
  Fidelity Institutional Retirement Services Company
  Fidelity Investments Public Sector Services Company
  Fidelity Investments Tax-Exempt Services Company
  Fidelity Management Trust Company
Fidelity Investments Life Insurance Company
Fidelity Personal Investments and Brokerage Group
  Fidelity Brokerage Technology Group
  Fidelity Capital Markets
  Fidelity Investment Advisor Group
  National Financial Correspondent Services
Fidelity Technology & Processing Group
Strategic Advisers, Inc.

COMPETITORS

Alliance Capital
American Century
Ameritrade
AXA Financial
Barclays
Charles Schwab
Citigroup
Dow Jones
E*TRADE Financial
Goldman Sachs
John Hancock Financial Services
Lehman Brothers
Marsh & McLennan
MassMutual
Merrill Lynch
MetLife
Morgan Stanley
Northwestern Mutual
Prudential
Putnam
Raymond James Financial
T. Rowe Price
TD Waterhouse
TIAA-CREF
UBS Financial Services
Vanguard Group

HISTORICAL FINANCIALS

Company Type: Private

Income Statement
FYE: December 31

	REVENUE ($ mil.)	NET INCOME ($ mil.)	NET PROFIT MARGIN	EMPLOYEES
12/03	9,200	908	9.9%	29,424
12/02	8,900	808	9.1%	29,000
12/01	9,800	1,320	13.5%	31,033
12/00	11,096	2,170	19.6%	33,186
12/99	8,845	1,008	11.4%	30,000
12/98	6,776	446	6.6%	28,000
12/97	5,878	536	9.1%	25,000
12/96	5,080	423	8.3%	23,300
12/95	4,277	431	10.1%	18,000
12/94	3,530	315	8.9%	14,600
Annual Growth	11.2%	12.5%	—	8.1%

Net Income History

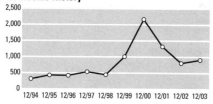

HISTORICAL FINANCIALS

Company Type: Private

Income Statement
FYE: March 31

	REVENUE ($ mil.)	NET INCOME ($ mil.)	NET PROFIT MARGIN	EMPLOYEES
3/03	1,851	—	—	10,000
3/02	1,733	—	—	10,000
3/01	1,554	—	—	8,000
3/00	1,401	—	—	8,000
3/99	1,200	—	—	8,000
3/98	1,073	—	—	7,500
3/97	916	—	—	8,000
3/96	811	—	—	7,500
3/95	713	—	—	7,200
3/94	646	—	—	6,800
Annual Growth	12.4%	—	—	4.4%

Revenue History

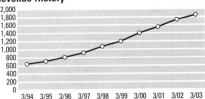

Ford Foundation

As one of the US's largest philanthropic organizations with a more than $9 billion diversified investment portfolio, The Ford Foundation can afford to be generous. The not-for-profit foundation offers grants to individuals and institutions in the US and abroad that meet its stated goals of strengthening democratic values, reducing poverty and injustice, promoting international cooperation, and advancing human achievement. The Ford Foundation's charitable giving covers a wide spectrum, from A (Association for Asian Studies) to Z (Zanzibar International Film Festival).

The Ford Foundation gives to a variety of causes in one of three areas: Asset Building and Community Development (designed to help expand opportunities for the poor and reduce hardship); Peace and Social Justice (promotes peace and the rule of law, human rights, and freedom); and Education, Media, Arts, and Culture (aimed at strengthening education and the arts and at building identity and community). Following the September 11 terrorist attacks in 2001, The Ford Foundation joined other philanthropic organizations in providing disaster relief.

The foundation is governed by an international board of trustees and no longer has stock in Ford Motor Company or ties to the Ford family. Funds are derived from a diversified investment portfolio that includes publicly traded equity and fixed-income securities.

HISTORY

Henry Ford and his son Edsel gave $25,000 to establish The Ford Foundation in Michigan in 1936, followed the next year by 250,000 shares of nonvoting stock in the Ford Motor Company. The foundation's activities were limited mainly to Michigan until the deaths of Edsel (1943) and Henry (1947) made the foundation the owner of 90% of the automaker's nonvoting stock (catapulting the endowment to $474 million, the US's largest).

In 1951, under a new mandate and president (Paul Hoffman, former head of the Marshall Plan), Ford made broad commitments to the promotion of world peace, the strengthening of democracy, and the improvement of education. Early education program grants overseen by University of Chicago chancellor Robert Maynard Hutchins ($100 million between 1951 and 1953) helped establish major international programs (e.g., Harvard's Center for International Legal Studies) and the National Merit Scholarships.

Under McCarthyite criticism for its experimental education grants, the foundation in 1956 granted $550 million (after selling 22% of its Ford shares) to noncontroversial recipients such as liberal arts colleges and not-for-profit hospitals. The organization's money set up the Radio and Television Workshop (1951); public TV support became a foundation trademark.

International work, begun in Asia and the Middle East (1950) and extended to Africa (1958) and Latin America (1959), focused on education and rural development. The foundation also supported the Population Council and research in high-yield agriculture with The Rockefeller Foundation.

In the early 1960s Ford targeted innovative approaches to employment and race relations. McGeorge Bundy (former national security adviser to President John Kennedy), named president of the foundation in 1966, increased the activist trend with grants for direct voter registration; the NAACP; public-interest law centers serving consumer, environmental, and minority causes; and housing for the poor.

The early 1970s saw support for black colleges and scholarships, child care, and job training for women, but by 1974 inflation, weak stock prices, and overspending had eroded assets. Programs were cut, but continued support for social justice issues led Henry Ford II to quit the board in 1976.

Under lawyer Franklin Thomas (named president in 1979), Ford established the nation's largest community development support organization, Local Initiatives Support. Thomas, the first African-American to lead the foundation, was a catalyst in a series of meetings between white and black South Africans in the mid-1980s.

Thomas stepped down in 1996, and new president Susan Berresford, formerly EVP, consolidated the foundation's grant programs into three areas: Asset Building and Community Development; Peace and Social Justice; and Education, Media, Arts, and Culture. In the late 1990s Ford was surpassed by various other foundations and had to relinquish its 30-year title as the biggest charitable organization in the US.

In 2000 the foundation announced its largest grant ever, the 10-year, $330 million International Fellowship Program to support graduate students studying in 20 countries. The Ford Foundation provided aid to people affected by the September 11 attacks in 2001, committing grants of $10 million in New York City and more than $1 million in Washington, DC.

EXECUTIVES

Chair: Kathryn S. Fuller, age 57
President: Susan V. Berresford
EVP, Secretary, and General Counsel: Barron M. Tenny
SVP and Acting VP Communications:
Barry D. Gaberman
VP and Chief Investment Officer: Linda B. Strumpf
VP Asset Building and Community Development:
Pablo Farias
VP Knowledge, Creativity, and Freedom:
Alison R. Bernstein
VP Peace and Social Justice: Bradford K. Smith
Treasurer, and Director Financial Services:
Nicholas M. Gabriel
Director Human Resources: Bruce D. Stuckey
Assistant Secretary and Associate General Counsel:
Nancy P. Feller
Auditors: PricewaterhouseCoopers LLP

LOCATIONS

HQ: The Ford Foundation
320 E. 43rd St., New York, NY 10017
Phone: 212-573-5000   **Fax:** 212-351-3677
Web: www.fordfound.org

The Ford Foundation has representatives in New York City, as well as Beijing; Cairo; Hanoi, Vietnam; Jakarta, Indonesia; Johannesburg; Lagos, Nigeria; Manila, Philippines; Mexico City; Moscow; Nairobi, Kenya; New Delhi; Rio de Janeiro; and Santiago, Chile.

PRODUCTS/OPERATIONS

Program Area Grants

Asset Building and Community Development
  Community and resource development
  Economic development
  Human development and reproductive health
Education, Media, Arts, and Culture
  Education, knowledge, and religion
  Media, arts, and culture
Peace and Social Justice
  Governance and civil society
  Human rights and international cooperation

HISTORICAL FINANCIALS

Company Type: Foundation

Income Statement
FYE: September 30

	REVENUE ($ mil.)	NET INCOME ($ mil.)	NET PROFIT MARGIN	EMPLOYEES
9/03	261	—	—	—
9/02	289	—	—	400
9/01	992	—	—	500
9/00	2,432	—	—	600
9/99	1,785	—	—	576
9/98	1,087	—	—	580
9/97	1,005	—	—	574
9/96	899	—	—	570
9/95	586	—	—	587
9/94	489	—	—	597
Annual Growth	(6.8%)	—	—	(4.9%)

Revenue History

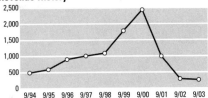

Foremost Farms

No jokes about "herd mentality," please. Foremost Farms USA — owned by about 4,000 dairy farmers in seven Midwestern states, mainly Wisconsin — is a major dairy cooperative in the US. From 25 plants the cooperative churns more than 5 billion pounds of milk into solid and fluid dairy products for industrial, retail, and food-service customers. Foremost's retail brands include Golden Guernsey Dairy and Morning Glory Dairy; it also produces private-label products for retailers. To reduce dependence on commodity products, the co-op is developing new products (flavored milk drinks, pharmaceutical-grade lactose) and has expanded its mozzarella capacity to meet consumer demand.

EXECUTIVES

Chairman: Edward Brooks
President: David (Dave) Fuhrmann
VP, Finance: Duaine Kamenick
VP, Fluid Milk, Employee and Member Services: James (Jim) Kasten
VP, Planning and Marketing Analyst: Curtis Kurth
VP, Cheese Division: Douglas (Doug) Wilke
VP, Fluid Products Division: Joseph Weis
VP, Ingredient Division: James (Jim) Geyer
Director of Communications: Joan Behr
Director, Sales and Marketing: Keith Gretenhart
Marketing Manager: Susan Crane
Auditors: PricewaterhouseCoopers LLP

LOCATIONS

HQ: Foremost Farms USA, Cooperative
E10889A Penny Ln., Baraboo, WI 53913
Phone: 608-355-8700   **Fax:** 608-355-8699
Web: www.foremostfarms.com

Foremost Farms serves farmers in Illinois, Indiana, Iowa, Michigan, Minnesota, Ohio, and Wisconsin.

PRODUCTS/OPERATIONS

2003 Sales

	% of total
Cheese	53
Liquid & condensed milk products	20
Packaged milk products	16
Whey products	7
Butter	2
Juice products	2
Milk powder products	—
Total	**100**

Selected Products

Butter
Cheese
  American
  Asadero
  Brick
  Cheddar
  Colby
  Havarti
  Monterey Jack
  Mozzarella
  Muenster
  Provolone
  Queso Quesadilla
Fluid milk
Grip It. Sip It. (single-serve flavored milk drinks)
Juices
Lactose (pharmaceutical-grade)
Sour cream
Whey protein concentrate (for infant formula)

COMPETITORS

Alto Dairy
AMPI
Century Foods
Dairy Farmers of America
Dairylea
Dean Foods
Horizon Organic
Land O'Lakes
Leprino Foods
MMPA
National Dairy Holdings
Prairie Farms Dairy
Quality Chekd
Saputo
Schreiber Foods

HISTORICAL FINANCIALS

Company Type: Cooperative

Income Statement   FYE: December 31

	REVENUE ($ mil.)	NET INCOME ($ mil.)	NET PROFIT MARGIN	EMPLOYEES
12/03	1,202	8	0.6%	1,509
12/02	1,167	2	0.2%	1,766
12/01	1,332	10	0.8%	1,705
12/00	1,093	10	0.9%	1,646
12/99	1,302	19	1.5%	1,716
12/98	1,376	27	2.0%	1,800
12/97	1,193	5	0.4%	1,750
12/96	1,357	17	1.2%	2,000
12/95	822	13	1.5%	2,000
12/94	548	—	—	1,000
Annual Growth	9.1%	(6.1%)	—	4.7%

2003 Year-End Financials

Debt ratio: 39.0%
Return on equity: 4.7%
Cash ($ mil.): 0
Current ratio: 1.58
Long-term debt ($ mil.): 64

Net Income History

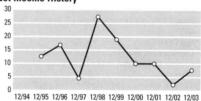

Forever Living

Forever Living Products International might not lead you to immortality, but its aloe vera-based health care products are intended to improve your well-being. The firm sells aloe vera drinks, as well as aloe vera-based aromatherapy products, cosmetics, dietary and nutritional supplements, lotion, soap, and tooth gel products. Owner Rex Maughan also owns aloe vera plantations in the Dominican Republic, Mexico, and Texas; Aloe Vera of America, a processing plant; and Forever Resorts' US resorts and marinas, including Dallas-area Southfork Ranch (of *Dallas* TV show fame).

Forever Living Products, founded in 1978, sells its goods through a global network of independent distributors.

Subsidiary Forever Resorts has more than 20 locations (lodges and marinas) in Alaska, Arizona, California, Colorado, Georgia, Kentucky, Missouri, Nevada, Texas, Washington, and Wyoming. Forever Living's resort subsidiary expanded into Africa in July 2003 when Rex Maughan bought 10 resorts there.

EXECUTIVES

Chairman, President, and CEO: Rex Gene Maughan
Vice Chairman, CFO, General Counsel, and Secretary: Rjay Lloyd
EVP: Navaz Ghaswala
SVP, Human Resources: Glen B. Banks
SVP, Sales: Gregg Maughan
VP, Finance: Dave Hall
VP, Sales: Harold Greene
Director of Customer Service: Marcy Rivera
Director of Information Systems: Steve Itami
Director of Marketing: Aidan O'Hare

LOCATIONS

HQ: Forever Living Products International, Inc.
7501 E. McCormick Pkwy., Ste. 135S, Scottsdale, AZ 85258
Phone: 480-998-8888   **Fax:** 480-998-8887
Web: www.foreverliving.com

Forever Living Products has distributors throughout the US and on all five continents. The company operates two facilities in the Rio Grande Valley area of Texas. One produces raw aloe gel primarily for cosmetics and the second makes aloe juice. From its Dominican Republic plant, Forever Living Products runs one of the largest aloe vera farms in the world.

PRODUCTS/OPERATIONS

Selected Product Categories

Aloe vera drinks
Bee products
Cosmetics
Nutrition
Resorts
Skin care
Weight loss

COMPETITORS

Alticor
Amway
Avon
Body Shop
Burt's Bees
GNC
Herbalife
Mannatech
Nature's Sunshine
NBTY
Shaklee
Sunrider
Whole Foods
Wild Oats Markets

HISTORICAL FINANCIALS

Company Type: Private

Income Statement   FYE: December 31

	REVENUE ($ mil.)	NET INCOME ($ mil.)	NET PROFIT MARGIN	EMPLOYEES
12/03	2,012	—	—	4,100
12/02	1,773	—	—	4,000
12/01	1,489	—	—	2,000
12/00	1,200	—	—	1,901
12/99	1,100	—	—	932
12/98	1,000	—	—	1,700
12/97	950	—	—	1,200
12/96	900	—	—	1,360
12/95	800	—	—	750
12/94	750	—	—	—
Annual Growth	11.6%	—	—	23.7%

Revenue History

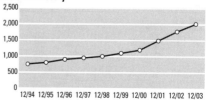

Foster Poultry Farms

As the West Coast's top poultry company, Foster Poultry Farms has a secure place in the pecking order. The company's vertically integrated operations see chickens and turkeys from the incubator to grocers' meat cases (under the Foster Farms brand). In addition to hatching, raising, slaughtering, and processing chickens and turkeys for the grocery and foodservice industries, the company grinds its own feeds. Already #1 in its home state, Foster Poultry Farms bought the chicken operations of local rival Zacky Farms, making it even larger. Max and Verda Foster founded the company in 1939; it is still owned by the Foster family, which also operates sister company Foster Dairy Farms.

EXECUTIVES

Director: Ron Foster
President: Don Jackson
CFO: Larry Keillor
VP Human Resources: Tim Walsh
VP Sales: Bob Kellert
VP Marketing: David Schanzer
Corporate Credit Manager: Suzanne Koch
Director of Corporate Accounting: Troy Mangrum
Auditors: Deloitte & Touche LLP

LOCATIONS

HQ: Foster Poultry Farms
   1000 Davis St., Livingston, CA 95334
Phone: 209-394-7901   **Fax:** 209-394-6342
Web: www.fosterfarms.com

Foster Poultry Farms has operations in Alabama, California, Oregon, and Washington.

COMPETITORS

Cagle's
ConAgra
Gold Kist
Hormel
Murphy-Brown
Pilgrim's Pride
Randall Foods
Tyson Foods
Zacky Farms

HISTORICAL FINANCIALS

Company Type: Private

Income Statement				FYE: December 31
	REVENUE ($ mil.)	NET INCOME ($ mil.)	NET PROFIT MARGIN	EMPLOYEES
12/03	1,520	—	—	—
12/02	1,434	—	—	11,000
12/01	1,269	—	—	11,000
12/00	1,127	—	—	9,500
12/99	1,100	—	—	7,500
12/98	990	—	—	7,000
12/97	1,000	—	—	7,200
12/96	925	—	—	6,800
12/95	825	—	—	6,700
12/94	800	—	—	6,600
Annual Growth	7.4%	—	—	6.6%

Foundation Coal

Revenue History

Foundation Coal Holdings, formerly RAG American Coal, has found a solid footing in the US. The company is one of the largest coal miners in the country, with surface and underground mines in Central Appalachia, Northern Appalachia, Powder River Basin, and the Illinois Basin. Foundation Coal produces about 70 million tons of coal annually and has nearly 2 billion tons of proven coal reserves. It produces steam coal (for electric utilities) and metallurgical coal (for steel manufacturers). German mining giant RAG Aktiengesellschaft sold its RAG American Coal subsidiary to investors in 2004.

EXECUTIVES

Chairman: William E. Macaulay, age 58
President, CEO, and Director: James F. Roberts, age 54, $540,000 pay
SVP and CFO: Frank J. Wood, age 51
SVP Development and IT: James A. Olsen, age 53
SVP Eastern Operations: James J. Bryja, age 48, $279,000 pay
SVP, General Counsel, and Secretary: Greg A. Walker, age 48, $315,879 pay
SVP Human Resources and Safety: Michael R. Peelish, age 43
SVP Planning and Engineering: Klaus-Dieter Beck, age 49
SVP Sales and Marketing: John R. Tellmann, age 54, $352,144 pay
SVP Western Operations: Thomas J. Lien, age 62, $290,000 pay
Auditors: Ernst & Young LLP

LOCATIONS

HQ: Foundation Coal Holdings, Inc.
   999 Corporate Blvd., Ste. 300,
   Linthicum Heights, MD 21090
Phone: 410-689-7600   **Fax:** 410-689-7611

Foundation Coal Holdings has more than a dozen coal mines in Illinois, Pennsylvania, West Virginia, and Wyoming.

PRODUCTS/OPERATIONS

2003 Sales

	$ mil.	% of total
Northern Appalachia	326.4	33
Powder River Basin	303.5	31
Central Appalachia	270.7	28
Other	83.1	8
Total	983.7	100

COMPETITORS

Arch Coal
CONSOL Energy
Fording Canadian Coal
Horizon Natural Resources
Kennecott Energy
Massey Energy
North American Coal
Peabody Energy
Westmoreland Coal

HISTORICAL FINANCIALS

Company Type: Private

Income Statement				FYE: December 31
	REVENUE ($ mil.)	NET INCOME ($ mil.)	NET PROFIT MARGIN	EMPLOYEES
12/03	984	33	3.3%	2,600
12/02	897	33	3.7%	—
12/01	756	26	3.4%	—
Annual Growth	14.1%	11.8%	—	—

2003 Year-End Financials

Debt ratio: 109.6%
Return on equity: 6.4%
Cash ($ mil.): 261
Current ratio: 2.03
Long-term debt ($ mil.): 573

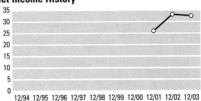

Net Income History

Foxworth-Galbraith Lumber

It might be a mouthful to say, but Foxworth-Galbraith Lumber Company sells more than a handful of building materials to customers in the Southwest. Through about 80 locations in Arizona, Colorado, New Mexico, and Texas, it sells hardware, lumber, paint, plumbing equipment, and tools. Foxworth-Galbraith's main customers are residential and commercial builders; other clients include do-it-yourselfers, retailers, specialty contractors, and federal and state agencies. The company acquired Brookhart's Building Centers in Colorado in 1999. Foxworth-Galbraith is still owned and operated by the families of W. L. Foxworth and H. W. Galbraith, who founded the company in Dalhart, Texas, in 1901.

EXECUTIVES

Chairman and CEO: Walter L. Foxworth
President: Jimmy Galbraith III
COO: Jack Foxworth
EVP and Internet Director: Ted Galbraith
EVP, Strategy and Business Development: Kenneth Black
VP, Commodities Distribution: Corby Biddle
VP, Construction Services: Daniel Brunson
VP, Sales: Ted Sojourner
Human Resources Recruiter: Eileen Nichols

LOCATIONS

HQ: Foxworth-Galbraith Lumber Company
17111 Waterview Pkwy., Dallas, TX 75252
Phone: 972-437-6100   **Fax:** 972-454-4251
Web: www.foxgal.com

PRODUCTS/OPERATIONS

Selected Product Categories
Building materials
Cabinets
Electrical
Hardware
Lawn & garden
Lumber
Paint
Plumbing
Tools

COMPETITORS

84 Lumber
A.C. Houston Lumber
Ace Hardware
Building Materials Holding
Do it Best
Home Depot
Lowe's
McCoy
Sears
Sherwin-Williams
Stock Building Supply
Sutherland Lumber
TruServ

Frank Consolidated Enterprises

Frank Consolidated Enterprises has an old lease on life. Its Wheels subsidiary, which claims to have pioneered the auto leasing concept, provides fleet management services — administrative, management, and financing services to help corporations manage their vehicle fleets. The company manages more than 240,000 vehicles. It operates in the US as Wheels and in other countries through Interleasing, an alliance of international fleet management and leasing companies. Wheels was founded in 1939 by Zollie Frank. Frank's family still owns the parent company; his widow serves as its chair, and son Jim is the president and CEO.

EXECUTIVES

Chairman: Elaine S. Frank
President and CEO: James S. (Jim) Frank
EVP and COO, Wheels: Ford Pearson
SVP, Finance and Operations and CFO, Wheels: Mary Ann O'Dwyer, age 48
SVP, Sales, Marketing, and Account Management, Wheels: Scott Pattullo
VP, IT and CIO, Wheels: Larry Buettner
VP, Human Resources, Wheels: Joan Richards
VP, International Sales, Wheels: Peter Egan
VP, Maintenance Assistance Program Operations, Wheels: John Frank
VP, Sales, Wheels: Michael Christian

LOCATIONS

HQ: Frank Consolidated Enterprises
666 Garland Place, Des Plaines, IL 60016
Phone: 847-699-7000   **Fax:** 847-699-6494
Web: www.wheels.com

COMPETITORS

Donlen
Emkay
Enterprise Rent-A-Car
GE Equipment Services
Holman Enterprises
Jordan Automotive
PHH Arval
Sixt

HISTORICAL FINANCIALS

Company Type: Private

Income Statement
FYE: August 31

	REVENUE ($ mil.)	NET INCOME ($ mil.)	NET PROFIT MARGIN	EMPLOYEES
8/03	1,500	—	—	550
8/02	1,575	—	—	550
8/01	1,500	—	—	600
8/00	1,431	—	—	591
8/99	1,364	—	—	562
8/98	1,181	—	—	574
8/97	1,025	—	—	600
8/96	1,200	—	—	675
8/95	1,165	—	—	675
8/94	1,045	—	—	700
Annual Growth	4.1%	—	—	(2.6%)

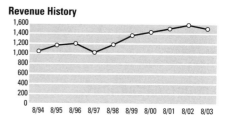

Freedom Communications

Southern California is the real cradle of Freedom. Media conglomerate Freedom Communications owns more than two dozen daily newspapers, including *The Gazette* in Colorado Springs, Colorado, and the company's flagship, California's *Orange County Register,* with a circulation of about 320,000. In addition, the company owns 37 weekly papers and eight television stations (five CBS and three ABC affiliates). Freedom Communications also operates a number of Web sites, which range from online versions of its printed properties to regional information guides.

The family of founder R. C. Hoiles has had some clashes over the company's future. Tim Hoiles, grandson of the company's founder, threatened to sue his relatives if he was not able to cash out his 8.6% share in the company. The company explored selling all or part of the business to raise the amount necessary to buy out certain family shareholders, and big newspaper companies were salivating over the prospect. In the end, Freedom Communications finalized a recapitalization plan in 2004 that allows the company to remain in family hands, while allowing relatives who want to sell their shares to do so.

EXECUTIVES

Chairman Emeritus: R. D. Threshie, age 71
President and CEO: Alan J. Bell, age 70
SVP and CFO: David Kuykendall
VP Human Resources and Organizational Development: Marcy Bruskin
VP and CFO of Shared Services: Jeff Whitton
VP and CIO: Mike Brown
VP and Controller: Nancy Trillo
VP Corporate Affairs and Director: Richard A. Wallace, age 64
VP General Counsel: Rachel Sagan
VP Shareholder Relations: JoAnne Norton
President, Freedom Broadcasting: Doreen Wade
President, Freedom Community Newspapers: Jonathan (Jon) Segal
President, Freedom Metro Newspapers: N. Christian (Chris) Anderson III
Director Corporate Communications and Marketing: Stephanie Miclot
Director Internal Audit: Jon Forte

HISTORICAL FINANCIALS

Company Type: Private

Income Statement
FYE: December 31

	REVENUE ($ mil.)	NET INCOME ($ mil.)	NET PROFIT MARGIN	EMPLOYEES
12/03	545	—	—	2,350
12/02	515	—	—	2,250
12/01	500	—	—	2,500
12/00	540	—	—	2,500
12/99	450	—	—	2,300
12/98	375	—	—	1,550
12/97	350	—	—	1,471
12/96	340	—	—	1,522
12/95	339	—	—	1,479
12/94	350	—	—	1,800
Annual Growth	5.0%	—	—	3.0%

Revenue History

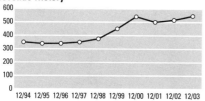

LOCATIONS

HQ: Freedom Communications, Inc.
17666 Fitch Ave., Irvine, CA 92614
Phone: 949-253-2300 **Fax:** 949-474-7675
Web: www.freedom.com

PRODUCTS/OPERATIONS

Selected Newspapers
Brownsville Herald (Texas)
Clovis News Journal (New Mexico)
The Daily News (Jacksonville, NC)
The Gaston Gazette (Gastonia, NC)
The Gazette (Colorado Springs, CO)
The Lima News (Ohio)
The Monitor (McAllen, TX)
The News Herald (Panama City, FL)
Odessa American (Texas)
The Orange County Register (Santa Ana, CA)
The Tribune (Seymour, IN)
Valley Morning Star (Harlingen, TX)

Television Stations
KFDM-TV (Beaumont, TX)
KTVL-TV (Medford, OR)
WLAJ-TV (Lansing, MI)
WLNE-TV (Providence, RI)
WPEC-TV (West Palm Beach, FL)
WRGB-TV (Albany, NY)
WTVC-TV (Chattanooga, TN)
WWMT-TV (Grand Rapids, MI)

COMPETITORS

Advance Publications
Belo
Copley Press
Cox Enterprises
Daily Journal
E. W. Scripps
Gannett
Hearst
Journal Communications
Media General
MediaNews
Meredith
New York Times
Stephens Media Group
Tribune
Young Broadcasting

HISTORICAL FINANCIALS
Company Type: Private

Income Statement
FYE: December 31

	ESTIMATED REVENUE ($ mil.)	NET INCOME ($ mil.)	NET PROFIT MARGIN	EMPLOYEES
12/03	824	—	—	—
12/02	768	—	—	—
12/01	760	—	—	8,000
12/00	850	—	—	8,000
12/99	750	—	—	8,100
12/98	673	—	—	7,000
12/97	645	—	—	7,200
12/96	605	—	—	6,900
12/95	525	—	—	5,500
12/94	501	—	—	6,800
Annual Growth	5.7%	—	—	2.3%

Revenue History
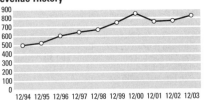

Fry's Electronics

Service may be heavy-handed, but where else can you buy appliances, build a computer, grab some Ho-Ho's or Maalox, and find the latest *Maxim* or *Byte*? The 25-store Fry's Electronics chain offers all that plus low prices, extensive inventory (including vacuums, stereos, TVs, and computer software and hardware), and whimsically themed displays (such as Wild West motifs).

The technogeek's superstore began in 1985 as the brainchild of CEO John Fry (with brothers Randy and Dave) and EVP Kathryn Kolder. The Fry brothers, who got their start at Fry's Food Stores, still own the company. Fry's also owns tech products e-tailer Cyberian Outpost.

Fry's mammoth stores, some swallowing almost 200,000 sq. ft., cater to the intensely technical shopper. Fry's outlets (a regular stop on bus tours) stock more than 50,000 low-priced electronic items and are known for their decor and displays. Each follows a theme, from *Alice in Wonderland* to a UFO crash site. The geek-gaws range from silicon chips to potato chips, from *Byte* to *Playboy*, and high-speed PCs (plus software and peripherals) to No-Doz (and other over-the-counter drugs).

Fry's stores' extensive inventories are said to be the company's strongest draw, unlike its reputation for poor customer service. This reputation, combined with Fry's bemoaned system for returning items, has left the company a target of many gripe-filled Web sites.

HISTORY

The Fry brothers — David, John, and Randy — wear genes stitched of retailing. Their father, Charles, started Fry's Food Stores supermarket chain in the 1950s in South Bay, California. The 40-store chain was sold for $14 million in 1972 before Charles' progeny heard the retail calling.

Charles gave each of his sons $1 million from the sale of the supermarkets. His oldest, John, who had gained technical expertise while running the supermarket's computer system, convinced his siblings of the viability of a hard-core computer retail store. The brothers pooled their funds and in 1985 started the first in Sunnyvale, California, along with Kathryn Kolder (now EVP). They added a store in Fremont in 1988; the Palo Alto store was completed two years later.

John mixed his supermarket sales experience with a sharp marketing acumen, selling prime shelf space at smart prices to suppliers. He stocked the stores with everything for a computer user's survival and slashed prices. The first Los Angeles-area store opened in 1992; a second one opened the following year.

Hiring an ex-Lucasfilm designer, John spent $1 million on each location, decorating stores like medieval castles, Mayan temples, Wild West saloons, and other individual fantasy themes.

In 1994 the Los Angeles computer retail market began to see increased competition from nationwide discount computer superstores. The next year Fry's responded by opening a new store in Woodland Hills with an *Alice in Wonderland* motif. It was the first Southern California Fry's Electronics store to offer appliances and an expanded music department.

The chain continued to gain notoriety for the contempt it seemed to show its customers. Local Better Business Bureaus started ranking Fry's "unsatisfactory" because the stores would not respond to complaints. Patrons with a beef were usually met by security guards, scores of hidden surveillance cameras, and employees who were promised bonuses for talking customers out of cash returns.

Still the company thrived, turning over its inventories twice as fast as competitors. One customer who sued Fry's for injuries allegedly received at the hands of store security guards went back for deals soon thereafter. Fry's went on an expansion frenzy in 1996, opening new California stores in Burbank, San Jose, and Anaheim. Moving beyond its Pacific roots, the company in 1997 spent $118 million to buy six of Tandy's failed Incredible Universe retail mega-outlets in Arizona, Oregon, and Texas. The company also won a legal battle with Frenchy Frys, a Seattle vending machine maker, for the right to own and use the frys.com URL. The company in 1998 continued to restructure its new stores into Fry's outlets.

Fry's opened a new store (complete with gushing oil derricks) in Houston in 2001. That year it pulled out of a deal to acquire all of the assets of technology products marketer Egghead.com and bought competitor Cyberian Outpost instead. In 2003 Fry's set up shop in Las Vegas; the entrance features a two-story neon slot machine.

EXECUTIVES

CEO: John Fry
President: William R. (Randy) Fry
CIO: David (Dave) Fry
EVP, Business Development: Kathryn Kolder
VP, Merchandising and Advertising: Ohmar Siddiqui
Controller: Chris Scheiber
Director, Human Resources: Karen Schultz
Manager, Community Relations: Manuel Valerio

LOCATIONS

HQ: Fry's Electronics, Inc.
600 E. Brokaw Rd., San Jose, CA 95112
Phone: 408-487-4500 **Fax:** 408-487-4741
Web: www.frys.com

Fry's Electronics has stores in Arizona, California, Georgia, Illinois, Nevada, Oregon, Washington, and Texas.

PRODUCTS/OPERATIONS

Selected Products
Appliances (coffeemakers, blenders, vacuums)
Cameras
CD players
Computer components (hard drives, routers)
Computers (PCs, notebooks)
DVD players
DVDs
MP3 players
Office products (printers, copiers, fax machines)
PDAs
Software
Toys
Video games

COMPETITORS

Best Buy
BUY.COM
CDW
Circuit City Stores
CompUSA
Dell
Electronics Boutique
GameStop
Gateway
Good Guys
Office Depot
PC Mall
PC Warehouse
RadioShack
Staples
Tweeter Home Entertainment Group
Zones

HISTORICAL FINANCIALS
Company Type: Private

Income Statement — FYE: December 31

	ESTIMATED REVENUE ($ mil.)	NET INCOME ($ mil.)	NET PROFIT MARGIN	EMPLOYEES
12/02	2,000	—	—	5,650
12/01	1,900	—	—	4,900
12/00	1,500	—	—	4,450
12/99	1,420	—	—	4,100
12/98	1,250	—	—	4,000
12/97	950	—	—	4,000
12/96	535	—	—	2,000
12/95	414	—	—	1,500
12/94	327	—	—	1,500
12/93	250	—	—	1,300
Annual Growth	26.0%	—	—	17.7%

Revenue History

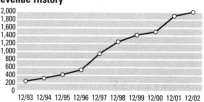

Galpin Motors

Galpin Motors will do just about anything to get you to buy a car, even jolt you with joe at the full-service Starbucks shops attached to its dealerships. Claiming to have sold the first Saturn and ranking as the top Ford dealer in the world, it also sells Aston Martin, Jaguar, Lincoln, Mazda, Mercury, and Volvo models, as well as used cars, from four dealerships and a Web site. It also rents and customizes — or "Galpinizes" — vehicles, such as the Tailgate Party Truck with a built-in stainless steel barbecue and refrigerated beer kegs. The company gave $1 million to Mother Teresa. Founded in 1946, Galpin Motors is owned and run by the Boeckmann family.

EXECUTIVES

President: Herbert F. (Bert) Boeckmann II, age 73
CFO: Phil Marshall
VP: Beau Boeckmann
VP: Brad Boeckmann
VP: Karl Boeckmann
VP and General Counsel: Alan J. Skobin
Director Human Resources: Joyce McNeely
Director, Information Technology: Lynn Shurley

LOCATIONS

HQ: Galpin Motors, Inc.
15505 Roscoe Blvd., North Hills, CA 91343
Phone: 818-787-3800   **Fax:** 818-778-2210
Web: www.gogalpin.com

COMPETITORS

AutoNation
Conant Auto Retail
David Wilson's
Fletcher Jones
Penske Automotive
Santa Monica Ford
Tuttle-Click

HISTORICAL FINANCIALS
Company Type: Private

Income Statement — FYE: December 31

	REVENUE ($ mil.)	NET INCOME ($ mil.)	NET PROFIT MARGIN	EMPLOYEES
12/03	774	—	—	1,000
12/02	724	—	—	800
12/01	666	—	—	750
12/00	655	—	—	750
12/99	616	—	—	741
12/98	550	—	—	715
12/97	533	—	—	682
12/96	502	—	—	675
12/95	434	—	—	620
12/94	394	—	—	595
Annual Growth	7.8%	—	—	5.9%

Revenue History

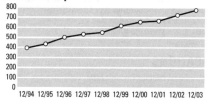

Gate Petroleum

Gate Petroleum swings three ways. The company runs a chain of more than 150 gas stations in seven southeastern states, selling gas and groceries and offering fleet management services. The company is also in the real estate and construction materials businesses. In Florida the company owns three private clubs (the Epping Forest Yacht Club, the Ponte Vedra Inn & Club, and the Ponte Vedra Lodge & Club), office buildings and business parks, and it is developing a huge residential and commercial complex in Jacksonville. Subsidiary Gate Concrete has plants in seven states, making and selling concrete and building materials. CEO Herbert Peyton, who founded the company in 1960, owns the majority of Gate Petroleum.

EXECUTIVES

Chairman and CEO; President, Gate Marketing Co.: Herbert H. (Herb) Peyton, age 72
VP, Finance: P. Jeremy Smith
VP, Human Resources: Marlene Giese
VP, Real Estate; President GL National: Ken Wilson
Chairman, Gate Marketing Co.: Wayne Levitt
President, Gate Marketing Co.: Mitchell Rhodes
VP, Development, Gate Marketing Co.: George Nail
VP, North Division, Gate Marketing Co.: John McMahon
Director, Fleet Services, Gate Marketing Co.: Jim Beck

LOCATIONS

HQ: Gate Petroleum Company
9540 San Jose Blvd., Jacksonville, FL 32257
Phone: 904-737-7220   **Fax:** 904-732-7660
Web: www.gatepetro.com

Gate Petroleum operates gas stations and convenience stores in Florida, Georgia, Kentucky, Louisiana, North Carolina, South Carolina, and Virginia. Gate also operates concrete plants in Alabama, Florida, Georgia, Kentucky, North Carolina, Tennessee, and Texas.

COMPETITORS

7-Eleven
ChevronTexaco
Cumberland Farms
Exxon Mobil
The Pantry
Racetrac Petroleum
Royal Dutch/Shell Group

HISTORICAL FINANCIALS
Company Type: Private

Income Statement — FYE: June 30

	REVENUE ($ mil.)	NET INCOME ($ mil.)	NET PROFIT MARGIN	EMPLOYEES
6/03	634	—	—	4,000
6/02	598	—	—	4,000
6/01	615	—	—	4,000
6/00	550	—	—	3,750
6/99	515	—	—	3,500
6/98	500	—	—	3,800
6/97	465	—	—	3,000
Annual Growth	5.3%	—	—	4.9%

Revenue History

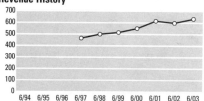

General Parts

Feel free to salute General Parts, distributor of replacement automotive parts, supplies, and tools for every make and model of foreign and domestic car, truck, bus, and farm or industrial vehicle. The largest member of the CARQUEST network, employee-owned General Parts, with more than 1,200 company-owned stores, distributes its products to about 4,000 CARQUEST and other auto parts stores across North America through 35 distribution centers. The company, which has been growing through acquisitions, sells its parts to do-it-yourself mechanics, professional installers, body shops, farmers, and fleet owners (commercial customers account for about 85% of sales). The company owns CARQUEST Canada.

EXECUTIVES

Chairman and CEO: O. Temple Sloan Jr., age 65
Vice Chairman: Joe Owen
President: O. Temple Sloan III
CFO: John Gardner
VP Administration and Accounting: William Kuykendall
VP Human Resources: Ed Whirty
President, Stores Group: Wayne Lavrack

LOCATIONS

HQ: General Parts, Inc.
2635 Millbrook Rd., Raleigh, NC 27604
Phone: 919-573-3000   **Fax:** 919-573-3553

COMPETITORS

Advance Auto Parts
AutoZone
CSK Auto
Genuine Parts
Hahn Automotive
Pep Boys
TBC

HISTORICAL FINANCIALS

Company Type: Private

Income Statement   FYE: December 31

	REVENUE ($ mil.)	NET INCOME ($ mil.)	NET PROFIT MARGIN	EMPLOYEES
12/03	1,600	—	—	13,500
12/02	1,650	—	—	14,000
12/01	1,562	—	—	13,000
12/00	1,459	—	—	12,000
12/99	1,462	—	—	12,700
12/98	1,248	—	—	10,150
12/97	1,060	—	—	6,700
12/96	818	—	—	6,700
12/95	680	—	—	4,700
12/94	612	—	—	4,670
Annual Growth	11.3%	—	—	12.5%

Revenue History

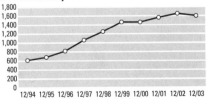

Genlyte Thomas

The marriage between The Genlyte Group and Thomas Industries, which formed Genlyte Thomas Group, is singing a different tune, "Breaking Up Is Hard To Do." The joint venture of which Thomas Industries owned 32% has been sold to the Genlyte Group. Genlyte Thomas' lighting fixtures and controls are used both indoors and outdoors, for decoration, landscaping, and tracking. Brand names include Bronzelite, Capri, Lightolier, and ZED. The company markets to distributors, who resell the products for use in the construction and remodeling of residential, commercial, and industrial facilities. The Genlyte Group now has complete control of the company.

Genlyte Thomas will continue to diversify its lighting interests. Recent acquisitions include the manufacturing and sales divisions of entertainment lighting specialist Vari-Lite Inc. from the US-based VLPS Lighting Services International (formerly Vari-Lite International). The company's Lightolier division is developing new safety lighting products that feature nickel metal hydride batteries for use in the event of power failures. Genlyte Thomas' Canada-based division, Canlyte, has introduced Symmetry Thermoplastic LED Exit emergency signage products.

Genlyte Thomas' flagship Lightolier division is teaming up with Steelcase to develop workplace lighting.

EXECUTIVES

Chairman, President, and CEO: Larry K. Powers, age 61, $200,000 pay
CFO: William G. (Bill) Ferko, age 49
President, Lightolier Division: Zia Eftekhar, age 58
VP, Sales, Central and East Region, Canlyte Division: Pierre Vincent
VP, Sales, Central and West Region, Canlyte Division: Terry Madden
Chief Information Officer: Rick Blanchard
Director, Human Resources: Manny Cadima
Marketing Director, Lightolier Division: Ken Mackenzie
National Account Coordinator: Claudia Saucier
Public Relations, Lightolier: Ken Czech
Auditors: Ernst & Young LLP

LOCATIONS

HQ: Genlyte Thomas Group LLC
10350 Ormsby Park Place, Ste. 601, Louisville, KY 40223
Phone: 502-420-9500   **Fax:** 502-420-9540
Web: www.genlytethomas.com

Genlyte Thomas Group operates facilities in Canada, Mexico, and the US.

PRODUCTS/OPERATIONS

Selected Brands

Bronzelite	Lightolier
Canlyte	Lightolier Controls
Capri	Lite-Energy
Chloride Systems	Lumec
Crescent	Lumec-Schreder
Day-Brite	Matrix
Emco	mcPhilben
ExceLine	Omega
Forecast	Stonco
Gardco	Thomas Lighting
Hadco	Translite
Horizon	Wide-Lite
Ledalite	ZED
Lightguard	

COMPETITORS

Catalina Lighting	Leviton
Cooper Industries	LSI Industries
Dann Dee Display Fixtures	Luminex Lighting
GE	Philips Electronics
Hubbell	Sonepar USA
Jacuzzi Brands	WKI Holding
Juno Lighting	

HISTORICAL FINANCIALS

Company Type: Private

Income Statement   FYE: December 31

	REVENUE ($ mil.)	NET INCOME ($ mil.)	NET PROFIT MARGIN	EMPLOYEES
12/03	1,034	46	4.5%	5,201
12/02	970	41	4.2%	5,076
12/01	985	85	8.6%	5,314
12/00	1,008	36	3.6%	3,317
12/99	978	79	8.1%	1,060
12/98	624	27	4.2%	—
Annual Growth	10.6%	11.8%	—	48.8%

2003 Year-End Financials

Debt ratio: 3.1%   Current ratio: 2.79
Return on equity: 14.2%   Long-term debt ($ mil.): 11
Cash ($ mil.): 82

Net Income History

Genmar Holdings

Genmar Holdings trolls for sales by cruising the pleasure boat market with a line of luxury yachts, recreational powerboats, and fishing boats. The company builds more than 250 different boat models ranging in size from 60-foot yachts (servants not included) to fishing skiffs. Its brands include Glastron, Ranger, and Wellcraft. Genmar markets its boats through independent dealers in the US and 30 other countries. The company, which is a combination of 16 different boat manufacturers acquired over 25 years, is controlled by chairman Irwin Jacobs (investor and former corporate raider). The company sold its Aluminum Boat Companies unit (Crestliner, Lowe, and Lund brands) to fellow boat maker Brunswick in 2004.

EXECUTIVES

Chairman: Irwin L. Jacobs
President and COO: Roger R. Cloutier II
EVP, Operations: David Vigdal
SVP, Marketing: George E. Sullivan
SVP, Purchasing: Ronald V. Purgiel
Corporate Communications: Mark Helgren
Corporate Communications, Aquasport Boats: Chris Wainscott

LOCATIONS
HQ: Genmar Holdings, Inc.
80 S. 8th St., Minneapolis, MN 55402
Phone: 612-337-1965   **Fax:** 612-337-1994
Web: www.genmar.com

Genmar Holdings has manufacturing facilities in Arkansas, Florida, Kansas, Minnesota, North Carolina, Wisconsin, and Canada.

PRODUCTS/OPERATIONS
Selected Brands

Aquasport	Larson
Carver	Ranger
Champion	Seaswirl
Four Winns	Stratos
Genmar by Zodiac	Triumph
Glastron	Trojan
Hydra Sports	Wellcraft

COMPETITORS

Bénéteau	Rodriguez Group
Brunswick	Sea Fox Boats
Cigarette Racing Team	Sea Ray Boats
Duckworth Boat Works	Triton Boats
Fountain Powerboat	Yamaha Motor
Marine Products	

HISTORICAL FINANCIALS
Company Type: Private

Income Statement FYE: June 30

	REVENUE ($ mil.)	NET INCOME ($ mil.)	NET PROFIT MARGIN	EMPLOYEES
6/03	1,100	—	—	6,000
6/02	1,200	—	—	6,500
6/01	990	—	—	7,000
6/00	858	—	—	6,500
6/99	705	—	—	4,600
6/98	586	—	—	4,700
6/97	261	—	—	4,700
6/96	618	—	—	4,900
6/95	549	—	—	5,200
6/94	499	—	—	5,100
Annual Growth	9.2%	—	—	1.8%

Revenue History

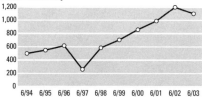

GeoLogistics

GeoLogistics gets goods going, globally. The company's integrated logistics offerings include multimodal freight forwarding, customs brokerage, warehousing and distribution, supply chain management, and trade-show logistics. GeoLogistics provides real-time shipment tracking through its Internet-based GeoVista logistics software system. The company has operations in 140 countries. To focus on core logistics operations, GeoLogistics sold its moving van unit, The Bekins Company. Investment firms Questor Management, William E. Simon & Sons, and Oaktree Capital Management control GeoLogistics, which was founded in 1996.

EXECUTIVES
President and CEO: William J. (Bill) Flynn
EVP and CFO: Stephen P. (Steve) Bishop
SVP and Chief Logistics Officer: Scott T. Brinks
SVP Marketing: Christopher Logan
SVP Operations, GeoLogistics Americas: Ray Loehner
SVP Sales and Marketing, Europe, Middle East, and Africa: Andrew Birtley
VP Finance: Michael Bible
VP and General Counsel: Ronald (Ron) Jackson
President, Matrix International Logistics: Abe Ranish
CIO: Charles Kirk
Director, Human Resources, GeoLogistics Americas: Bob Westman
Auditors: Ernst & Young LLP

LOCATIONS
HQ: GeoLogistics Corporation
1251 E. Dyer Rd., Ste. 200, Santa Ana, CA 92705
Phone: 714-513-3000   **Fax:** 714-513-3120
Web: www.geo-logistics.com

PRODUCTS/OPERATIONS
Selected Services

Air and ocean freight forwarding
Customs brokerage
Distribution and warehousing
Inventory management
Packaging, transportation, unpacking
Packing and crating
Real-time shipment tracking
Trade show and exhibition services

COMPETITORS

APL	EGL
APL Logistics	Exel
BAX Global	Expeditors
C.H. Robinson Worldwide	Panalpina
CNF	Stinnes

HISTORICAL FINANCIALS
Company Type: Private

Income Statement FYE: December 31

	REVENUE ($ mil.)	NET INCOME ($ mil.)	NET PROFIT MARGIN	EMPLOYEES
12/02	1,200	—	—	6,000
12/01	1,000	—	—	6,000
12/00	1,500	—	—	6,000
12/99	1,558	—	—	6,200
12/98	1,600	—	—	6,300
12/97	1,525	—	—	6,000
12/96	1,639	—	—	6,352
Annual Growth	(5.1%)	—	—	(0.9%)

Revenue History

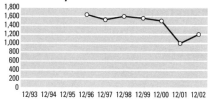

George E. Warren Corporation

By barge, by pipeline, by tank truck, by George, George E. Warren is a major private wholesale distributor of petroleum in the eastern US. Founded in Boston by George E. Warren in 1907 as a coal and oil distributor, it moved to Florida in the early 1990s. The company distributes product mostly by barge and pipeline, though it uses some tank trucks as well. Warren has distribution facilities in the southeastern and southwestern US. It distributes products including ethylene and heating oil to various industries. President and CEO Thomas Corr owns the company.

EXECUTIVES
President and CEO: Thomas L. Corr
CFO and Controller: Michael E. George
Director Human Resources: Martin Paris

LOCATIONS
HQ: George E. Warren Corporation
3001 Ocean Dr., Vero Beach, FL 32963
Phone: 772-778-7100   **Fax:** 772-778-7171
Web: www.gewarren.com

COMPETITORS

Center Oil	Penn Octane
ConocoPhillips	Sun Coast Resources
Crown Central Petroleum	Western Gas
Exxon Mobil	Williams Companies
Martin Resource Management	

HISTORICAL FINANCIALS
Company Type: Private

Income Statement FYE: December 31

	REVENUE ($ mil.)	NET INCOME ($ mil.)	NET PROFIT MARGIN	EMPLOYEES
12/03	2,586	—	—	32
12/02	3,000	—	—	25
12/01	3,200	—	—	25
12/00	2,000	—	—	25
12/99	1,281	—	—	25
12/98	1,406	—	—	25
12/97	2,602	—	—	24
12/96	2,313	—	—	23
Annual Growth	1.6%	—	—	4.8%

Revenue History

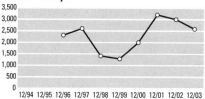

Georgia Crown

Aptly named Fate Leebern may have died for Georgia Crown Distributing, a beverage bottler and distributor. He founded Georgia Crown as Columbus Wine Company Distributor in 1938, the same year Georgia prohibition was repealed. After the first rail shipment of legal liquor was received, someone — reportedly the Dixie Mafia — murdered Leebern. Today the family-owned company distributes beer, wine, liquor, bottled water, juices, and soft drinks to Georgia, Alabama, and Tennessee. The bottler also distributes its brand of bottled water, Melwood Springs. CEO Donald Leebern is the grandson of the company's founder. The Leebern family owns the business.

Georgia Crown is moving its headquarters northeast from Columbus, Georgia, to a $12 million facility in Henry County.

EXECUTIVES

Chairman and CEO: Donald M. Leebern Jr., age 63
President: Donald M. Leebern III
CFO: Orlene Bovaird
VP Human Resources: Mary Beth Gibbon
General Manager, Georgia Crown, Albany: Ray Holder
General Manager, Georgia Crown, Atlanta: Greg Beyer
General Manager, Georgia Crown, Columbus: Brad Bush
General Manager, Georgia Crown, Savannah: Joe Strickland
General Manager, Alabama Crown Distributing, Birmingham: Tom Cubelic
General Manager, Alabama Crown Distributing, Mobile: Richard Rone
General Manager, Alabama Crown Distributing, Montgomery: Greg Rains
General Manager, Tennessee Crown Distributing: Randy Smith

LOCATIONS

HQ: Georgia Crown Distributing Company
7 Crown Cir., Columbus, GA 31907
Phone: 706-568-4580 **Fax:** 706-561-1647
Web: www.georgiacrown.com

Georgia Crown Distributing has facilities throughout Georgia in Albany, Atlanta, Augusta, and Savannah as well as operations in Alabama and Tennessee.

COMPETITORS

Buffalo Rock
Coca-Cola Bottling Consolidated
Coca-Cola Enterprises
Constellation Brands
Gambrinus
Johnson Brothers
National Beverage
National Distributing
Southern Wine & Spirits
Sunbelt Beverage

HISTORICAL FINANCIALS

Company Type: Private

Income Statement
FYE: July 31

	REVENUE ($ mil.)	NET INCOME ($ mil.)	NET PROFIT MARGIN	EMPLOYEES
7/02	730	—	—	1,600
7/01	730	—	—	1,665
7/00	710	—	—	1,600
7/99	700	—	—	1,600
7/98	675	—	—	1,600
7/97	670	—	—	1,600
7/96	656	—	—	1,600
7/95	648	—	—	1,600
7/94	645	—	—	1,600
Annual Growth	1.6%	—	—	(0.0%)

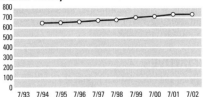

Revenue History

Georgia Lottery

Lottery fans with an eye toward education may have Georgia on their minds. Established in 1993, the Georgia Lottery has contributed more than $6 billion to the state's education coffers. In addition to the HOPE program, which has helped more than 700,000 students attend college with lottery-funded scholarships, the lottery helps finance a pre-kindergarten program and public school capital improvements. More than 7,000 retailers throughout Georgia sell tickets for lottery games, including instant-ticket games, online games, keno-style games, and a Powerball-like game aptly named Mega Millions. In its first year the Georgia Lottery reached $1.1 billion in sales and has been growing ever since.

EXECUTIVES

President and CEO: Margaret R. DeFrancisco
SVP Administration: Joan Schoubert
SVP Corporate Affairs: Cathy Walls
VP Advertising: Jeannie Lin
VP Legal Affairs: Rosemarie Morse
VP Financial Management: Sharman Lomax
VP Security: Mar-D Greer
VP Information Technology: Larry Sipes
VP Systems Development: Daniel Johnson
VP Human Resources: Jeff Martin
Communications Director: J.B. Landroche

LOCATIONS

HQ: Georgia Lottery Corporation
250 Williams St., Ste. 3000, Atlanta, GA 30303
Phone: 404-215-5000 **Fax:** 404-215-8886
Web: www.galottery.com

PRODUCTS/OPERATIONS

Selected Games
Cash 3
Cash 4
Fantasy 5
Lotto South
Mega Millions
Quick Cash

COMPETITORS

Florida Lottery
Multi-State Lottery
Virginia Lottery

HISTORICAL FINANCIALS

Company Type: Government-owned

Income Statement
FYE: June 30

	REVENUE ($ mil.)	NET INCOME ($ mil.)	NET PROFIT MARGIN	EMPLOYEES
6/03	2,604	—	—	250
6/02	2,449	—	—	250
6/01	2,194	—	—	250
6/00	2,310	—	—	250
6/99	2,030	—	—	250
6/98	1,735	—	—	250
6/97	1,720	—	—	250
6/96	1,593	—	—	250
6/95	1,422	—	—	266
6/94	1,127	—	—	—
Annual Growth	9.8%	—	—	(0.8%)

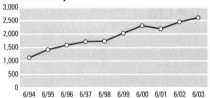

Revenue History

G-I Holdings

G-I Holdings (formerly GAF Corporation) works to keep a roof over your head. It is one of the US's oldest sources for commercial and residential roofing materials, with more than 25 plants. Subsidiary Building Materials Corporation of America makes flashing, vents, and complete roofing systems. Other products include residential shingles (Timberline and Sovereign brands) and GAF CompositeRoof for commercial asphalt roofing. Customers include contractors, distributors, and retail outlets such as The Home Depot. G-I Holdings has filed for bankruptcy protection due to asbestos liability claims. Chairman Samuel Heyman owns 99% of the company and all of affiliate International Specialty Products Inc.

EXECUTIVES

Chairman: Samuel J. Heyman, age 64
Director; EVP, General Counsel, and Secretary, International Specialty Products Inc.: Richard A. Weinberg, age 43
SVP, CFO, and Treasurer: Susan B. Yoss, age 44
VP Human Resources: Gary Schneid

LOCATIONS

HQ: G-I Holdings Inc.
1361 Alps Rd., Wayne, NJ 07470
Phone: 973-628-3000 **Fax:** 973-628-3326

G-I Holdings operates 26 plants throughout the US.

PRODUCTS/OPERATIONS

Selected Residential Products
Laminated shingles (Timberline)
Roofing systems (Weather Stopper)
Specialty shingles (Slateline)
Strip shingles (Sovereign)

COMPETITORS

Bridgestone Americas
Carlisle Companies
ElkCorp
Formica
Johns Manville
NCI Building Systems
Owens Corning

HISTORICAL FINANCIALS

Company Type: Private

Income Statement — FYE: December 31

	REVENUE ($ mil.)	NET INCOME ($ mil.)	NET PROFIT MARGIN	EMPLOYEES
12/03	1,056	—	—	4,300
12/02	1,361	—	—	3,400
12/01	1,293	—	—	3,400
12/00	1,200	—	—	3,500
12/99	1,140	—	—	3,500
12/98	1,088	—	—	3,300
12/97	945	—	—	3,000
12/96	1,568	—	—	5,209
12/95	1,339	—	—	5,400
12/94	1,156	—	—	4,500
Annual Growth	(1.0%)	—	—	(0.5%)

Revenue History

Giant Eagle

With its talons firmly wrapped around western Pennsylvania, Giant Eagle is eyeing new territory. The grocery chain is the #1 food retailer in Pittsburgh, and it has about 140 corporate and 84 franchised supermarkets (about 60,000 sq. ft. in size) throughout Maryland, western Pennsylvania, Ohio, and north central West Virginia. In addition to food, many Giant Eagle stores feature video rental, banking, photo processing, and ready-to-eat meals. Giant Eagle is also a wholesaler to the licensed stores and sells groceries to other retail chains. Chairman and CEO David Shapira is the grandson of one of the five men who founded the company in 1931. The founders' families own Giant Eagle.

As with other birds of the retailing feather, Giant Eagle's stores carry private-label merchandise (Eagle Valley and Giant Eagle brands) and nonfood items; many have pharmacies.

Giant Eagle became the #1 food seller in eastern Ohio through a 1997 acquisition, and the supermarket chain has expanded to Cleveland, Columbus, and Toledo. The company's goal is to grow Giant Eagle food and drug sales through a combination of acquisitions and organic growth to $9 billion by 2007. To that end, in 2002 Giant Eagle launched a successful bid for the remaining assets of bankrupt discount drugstore chain Phar-Mor. It also acquired and converted eight Big Bear grocery stores in the Columbus area from bankrupt supermarket operator Penn Traffic, which has sold off its Big Bear chain.

The company is launching a new convenience store chain called GetGo from Giant Eagle. Of the initial 30 GetGo stores, some are located next to Giant Eagle supermarkets, while others are larger (4,500 sq. ft.) stand-alone structures. Both formats feature fresh foods and sell gas.

The supermarket chain has shifted the start of its weekly sales specials from Sunday to Thursday to match its customers' changing shopping patterns and better compete with nontraditional grocery chains, such as Costco Wholesale and Wal-Mart Supercenters.

HISTORY

When Joe Porter, Ben Chait, and Joe Goldstein sold their chain of 125 Eagle grocery stores in Pittsburgh to Kroger in 1928, the agreement stated that the men would have to leave the grocery business for three years. In retrospect, Kroger should have made the term last for the length of their lives, because in 1931 the three men joined the owners of OK Grocery — Hyman Moravitz and Morris Weizenbaum — and launched a new chain of grocery stores called Giant Eagle. Eventually, the chain would knock Kroger out of the Pittsburgh market.

Although slowed by the Great Depression, the chain expanded, fighting such large rivals as Acme, A&P, and Kroger for Pittsburgh's food shoppers. The stores were mom-and-pop operations with over-the-counter service until they began converting to self-service during the 1940s. Store sizes expanded to nearly 15,000 sq. ft. in the 1950s. During that time Giant Eagle, with about 30 stores, launched Blue Stamps in answer to Green Stamps and other loyalty programs.

It phased out trading stamps in the 1960s in lieu of everyday low prices. To accommodate its growth, in 1968 Giant Eagle acquired a warehouse in Lawrenceville, Pennsylvania, that more than doubled its storage area. Also that year the firm opened its first 20,000-sq.-ft. Giant Eagle store.

During the inflationary 1970s Giant Eagle introduced generic items and began offering the Food Club line, a private-label brand, in conjunction with wholesaler Topco. It continued its expansion, and by 1979 it had become Pittsburgh's #1 supermarket chain, as chains such as Kroger, Acme, and A&P were leaving the city. In 1981 Giant Eagle, with 52 stores, acquired Tamarkin, a wholesale and retail chain in Youngstown, Ohio, part-owned by the Monus family. The purchase moved it into the franchise business, and later that year the first independent Giant Eagle store opened in Monaca (outside Pittsburgh).

The Tamarkin purchase brought together Mickey Monus and Giant Eagle CEO David Shapira, grandson of founder Goldstein. In 1982 they created Phar-Mor, a deep-discount drugstore chain (Wal-Mart's Sam Walton once said it was the only competitor he truly feared). From a single store in Niles, Ohio, Phar-Mor grew rapidly to 310 outlets in 32 states in the early 1990s.

Phar-Mor president Monus helped found the World Basketball League (WBL) in 1987 and became the owner of three teams. In 1992 an auditor discovered two unexplainable Phar-Mor checks to the WBL totaling about $100,000. Investigators soon uncovered three years of overstated inventories and a false set of books; Shapira (who was also CEO of Phar-Mor), Giant Eagle owners (which held a 50% stake in Phar-Mor until 1992), and other investors had been duped of more than $1 billion. Shapira fired Monus and his cronies on July 31, 1992. The next day the WBL folded; about two weeks after that Phar-Mor filed for Chapter 11 bankruptcy. A mistrial in 1994 couldn't save Monus from prison; he was reindicted in 1995 and sentenced to 20 years (later reduced to 12).

Giant Eagle made its largest acquisition in 1997, paying $403 million for Riser Foods, a wholesaler (American Seaway Foods) with 35 company-owned stores under the Rini-Rego Stop-n-Shop banner. The stores were converted to the Giant Eagle banner in 1998 (another 18 independent Stop-n-Shop stores were also converted).

In 2000 Giant Eagle opened several stores in Columbus, Ohio. The grocer moved into Maryland in 2001 when it acquired six Country Market stores in Maryland and Pennsylvania. Also in 2001, the grocer founded ECHO Real Estate Services Co. to develop retail, housing, and golf course projects.

In 2002 Giant Eagle was among the winning bidders for the remaining assets of bankrupt Phar-Mor. The company acquired leases to 10 Phar-Mor stores and the inventory and prescription lists for 27 stores.

The retailer scrapped its plan to sell its transportation business and signed a new five-year contract with its union delivery drivers in September 2003.

EXECUTIVES

Chairman and CEO: David S. (Dave) Shapira, age 62
Vice Chairman: Anthony C. Rego
President and COO: Raymond Burgo
EVP, Business Systems: Jack Flanagan
SVP and CFO: Mark Minnaugh
SVP, Distribution: Larry Baldauf
SVP, Information Services: Russ Ross
SVP, Meat and Seafood: Ed Steinmetz
SVP, Operations: Laura Karet
VP, Marketing: Kevin Srigley
VP, Application Engineering: Mike Krugle
VP, Columbus Operations: David (Dave) Daniel
VP, Logistics: Bill Parry
VP, Pharmacy: Randy Heiser
Director, Communications: Rob Borella
Director, Human Resources Services: Vicki Clites

LOCATIONS

HQ: Giant Eagle, Inc.
101 Kappa Dr., Pittsburgh, PA 15238
Phone: 412-963-6200   **Fax:** 412-968-1617
Web: www.gianteagle.com

2004 Stores

	No.
Pennsylvania	100
Ohio	114
West Virginia	5
Maryland	3
Total	**222**

PRODUCTS/OPERATIONS

Private Labels
Eagle Valley
Giant Eagle

Selected Services

Bakery	Greeting cards
Banking services	Pharmacy
Childcare	Photo developing
Deli department	Ready-to-eat meals
Dry cleaning	Ticketmaster outlet
Fresh seafood	Video rental

COMPETITORS

7-Eleven	Kroger
A&P	Shop 'N Save
Ahold USA	Wal-Mart
Giant Food	Wegmans
Heinen's	Weis Markets
IGA	Whole Foods

HISTORICAL FINANCIALS

Company Type: Private

Income Statement — FYE: June 30

	ESTIMATED REVENUE ($ mil.)	NET INCOME ($ mil.)	NET PROFIT MARGIN	EMPLOYEES
6/03	4,739	—	—	26,000
6/02	4,415	—	—	26,000
6/01	4,435	—	—	25,600
6/00	4,221	—	—	25,600
6/99	4,360	—	—	25,600
6/98	4,050	—	—	25,000
6/97	3,800	—	—	19,200
6/96	2,200	—	—	12,000
6/95	2,100	—	—	7,200
6/94	2,000	—	—	7,200
Annual Growth	10.1%	—	—	15.3%

Revenue History

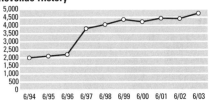

Gibson, Dunn & Crutcher

Gibson, Dunn & Crutcher leans heavily on its mergers and acquisitions work. Founded in Los Angeles in 1890, Gibson, Dunn & Crutcher is one of the top corporate transactions law firms in the US. It also practices in areas such as labor and employment, litigation, real estate, and personal tax and estate planning. The firm has over 800 attorneys in about a dozen US and European offices and a client base of government entities, individuals, commercial and investment banks, multinational corporations, and startups. Gibson, Dunn & Crutcher partner Theodore Olson was selected as solicitor general by President George W. Bush, strengthening the firm's ties to Washington, DC.

EXECUTIVES

Chairman and Managing Partner: Kenneth M. Doran
Chair, European Operations: Bernard Grinspan
Director, Human Resources: Stacy Glover

LOCATIONS

HQ: Gibson, Dunn & Crutcher LLP
  333 S. Grand Ave., Los Angeles, CA 90071
Phone: 213-229-7000   **Fax:** 213-229-7520
Web: www.gdclaw.com

Gibson, Dunn & Crutcher has offices in Century City, Irvine, Los Angeles, Palo Alto, and San Francisco, California; Dallas; Denver; London; Munich; New York City; Paris; and Washington, DC.

PRODUCTS/OPERATIONS

Selected Practice Areas
Antitrust and trade regulation
Business restructuring and reorganization
Corporate tax
Corporate transactions
Intellectual property
International trade and customs
Labor and employment
Personal tax and estate planning
Securities litigation

COMPETITORS

Dewey Ballantine	O'Melveny & Myers
Fried, Frank, Harris	Paul, Hastings
Latham & Watkins	Skadden, Arps
Morrison & Foerster	Willkie Farr

HISTORICAL FINANCIALS

Company Type: Partnership

Income Statement — FYE: October 31

	REVENUE ($ mil.)	NET INCOME ($ mil.)	NET PROFIT MARGIN	EMPLOYEES
10/03	646	—	—	—
10/02	569	—	—	—
10/01	537	—	—	—
10/00	469	—	—	—
10/99	418	—	—	2,400
10/98	374	—	—	2,200
10/97	336	—	—	2,000
10/96	294	—	—	1,800
10/95	277	—	—	1,750
10/94	290	—	—	1,750
Annual Growth	9.3%	—	—	6.5%

Revenue History

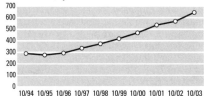

Gilbane

Family-owned Gilbane has been the bane of its rivals for four generations. Subsidiary Gilbane Building provides construction management, contracting, and design and build services to construct office buildings, manufacturing plants, schools, prisons, and more for the firm's governmental, commercial, and industrial clients. Landmark projects include work on the National Air and Space Museum, Lake Placid's 1980 Winter Olympics facilities, and the new WWII memorial in Washington, DC. Another subsidiary, Gilbane Properties, develops and finances public and private projects and acts as a property manager. In 1873 William and Thomas Gilbane founded the firm, which remains family-owned.

EXECUTIVES

Chairman and CEO: Paul J. Choquette Jr., age 65
VP; President and CEO, Gilbane Properties:
  Robert V. Gilbane
VP; President and COO, Gilbane Building Company:
  William J. Gilbane Jr., age 57
VP; Chairman and CEO, Gilbane Building Company:
  Thomas F. Gilbane Jr., age 56
CFO and Treasurer: Ken Alderman
VP, General Counsel, and Secretary: Brad A. Gordon

LOCATIONS

HQ: Gilbane, Inc.
  7 Jackson Walkway, Providence, RI 02903
Phone: 401-456-5800   **Fax:** 401-456-5936
Web: www.gilbaneinc.com

PRODUCTS/OPERATIONS

Selected Markets
Aviation
Corporate
Criminal justice
Education
Government
Health care
Infrastructure
Library
Life sciences
Public assembly
Waste and wastewater

Subsidiaries
Gilbane Building Company
Gilbane Properties, Inc.

COMPETITORS

BE&K	McCarthy Building
Bechtel	Parsons
Black & Veatch	Perini
Bovis Lend Lease	Skanska
Clark Enterprises	Structure Tone
Fluor	Swinerton
Hunt Construction	Turner Corporation
Jacobs Engineering	Whiting-Turner
M. A. Mortenson	

HISTORICAL FINANCIALS

Company Type: Private

Income Statement — FYE: December 31

	REVENUE ($ mil.)	NET INCOME ($ mil.)	NET PROFIT MARGIN	EMPLOYEES
12/02	2,771	—	—	1,700
12/01	2,658	—	—	1,700
12/00	2,388	—	—	1,510
12/99	2,179	—	—	900
12/98	2,200	—	—	1,200
12/97	1,923	—	—	1,148
12/96	1,848	—	—	993
12/95	1,371	—	—	1,000
12/94	1,249	—	—	958
12/93	936	—	—	843
Annual Growth	12.8%	—	—	8.1%

Glazer's Wholesale Drug

Glazer's Wholesale Drug, named during Prohibition when only drugstores and drug wholesalers could deal in liquor, is a wholesale distributor of alcoholic beverages. It is the largest distributor of malts, spirits, and wines in Texas and one of the largest US wine and spirits distributors. It also operates in Arizona (Alliance Beverage), Arkansas, Indiana (Olinger Distributing), Iowa, Kansas, Louisiana, Missouri, and Ohio. The company distributes Robert Mondavi wines, Brown-Forman and Bacardi spirits, and Diageo products. CEO Bennett Glazer and family own Glazer's.

In 2003 Glazer's bought a 50% stake in Union Beverage Co. (a subsidiary of National Wine & Spirits Inc.) to move distribution into Illinois. In June 2003 the company became the sole provider of Diageo brands in Dallas and Houston as part of Diageo's consolidation of its Texas distributors. Glazer's has been acquiring wholesalers and distributors in the Midwest, including Mid-Continent Distributor (Missouri). Glazer's is expanding in Oklahoma, having bought Reliance Wine & Spirits Co. It also has purchased Hirst Imports Co.

EXECUTIVES
Chairman: R.L. Glazer
CEO: Bennett Glazer
President: Jerry Cargill
EVP and COO: Barkley J. Stuart
EVP and Secretary: Mike Glazer
VP and CFO: Cary Rossel
VP, Operations: Jack Westenborg
VP, Business Development: Mike Maxwell
VP, Business and Marketing: George Trilikis
VP and CIO: Mike Adams
VP, Sales and Marketing: Don Pratt
Director of Domaines and Estates: James Gunter
Director of Training: Bill Saul
Director of Human Resources: Rusty Harmount

LOCATIONS
HQ: Glazer's Wholesale Drug Company, Inc.
14860 Landmark Blvd., Dallas, TX 75254
Phone: 972-702-0900 **Fax:** 972-702-8508
Web: www.glazers.com

Glazer's Wholesale Drug operates in 11 US states, including Arizona, Arkansas, Illinois, Indiana, Iowa, Kansas, Louisiana, Missouri, Ohio, Oklahoma, and Texas.

COMPETITORS
Ben E. Keith
Block Distributing
Gallo
Gambrinus
Johnson Brothers
National Distributing
National Wine & Spirits
Southern Wine & Spirits
Tarrant Distributors
Wirtz

HISTORICAL FINANCIALS
Company Type: Private

Income Statement

FYE: December 31

	REVENUE ($ mil.)	NET INCOME ($ mil.)	NET PROFIT MARGIN	EMPLOYEES
12/02	1,750	—	—	3,900
12/01	1,600	—	—	3,600
12/00	1,480	—	—	3,200
12/99	1,110	—	—	2,700
12/98	855	—	—	2,700
12/97	758	—	—	2,500
12/96	670	—	—	1,850
12/95	590	—	—	1,100
12/94	520	—	—	1,000
12/93	470	—	—	1,000
Annual Growth	15.7%	—	—	16.3%

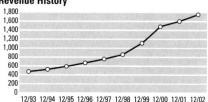

Global Companies

Global Companies imports petroleum products from global sources, but its marketing is mainly regional. Formerly Global Petroleum, the company wholesales heating oil, residual fuel oil, diesel oil, kerosene, and gasoline to customers in the northeastern US. It also sells gasoline and diesel directly to more than 85 branded service stations and makes financing available for upgrades or new construction. The company makes proprietary diesel oil and home heating oil. Its alliance with National Grid USA offers oil, natural gas, and electricity to commercial and industrial customers. Founded in 1933 by CEO Alfred Slifka's father, Global Companies is controlled by Spanish oil company Repsol YPF.

EXECUTIVES
Chairman and President: Alfred A. Slifka
CEO: Julio Gavito
COO: Eric Slifka
SVP Finance and CFO: Thomas McManmon
VP and Controller: Charles Rudinsky
VP; Marketing Manager, Distillates and Gasoline Wholesale: Joe DeStefano
CIO: Jim Shelton
Director Applications: Martha Thayer
Director Human Resources: Barbara E. Rosenbloom
Director Operations: Tom Rizzo
Director Special Projects: Kent Mills
Director Technology: Bill Gifford
Director Telecommunications: Harvey Finstein

LOCATIONS
HQ: Global Companies LLC
800 South St., Waltham, MA 02454
Phone: 781-894-8800 **Fax:** 781-398-4160
Web: www.globalp.com

Global Companies has operations in Connecticut, Maine, Massachusetts, New Hampshire, New Jersey, New York, and Rhode Island.

PRODUCTS/OPERATIONS

Selected Products
Diesel oil
Electricity
Gasoline
Home heating oil
Kerosene
Natural gas

COMPETITORS
Crown Central Petroleum
Exxon Mobil
George Warren
Getty Petroleum Marketing
Gulf Oil
Koch
Tauber Oil
Warren Equities

Golden State Foods

Did somebody say McDonald's? Food processor and distributor Golden State Foods is listening. The firm is the fast-food giant's largest full-line supplier, providing McDonald's with more than 130 products. These include beef patties, the Big Mac sauce (which it helped formulate), buns, ketchup, mayonnaise, and salad dressing. Golden State Foods has 11 distribution centers in the US and overseas (Australia, Egypt, and Mexico) and operates two food processing plants in the US. The company was founded in 1947 by the late William Moore. Investment firm Yucaipa owned a 51% stake in the firm until 2004; Wetterau Associates owns 100%. Also in 2004 investor Ron Burkle sold his stake for some $100 million.

Yucaipa and Wetterau Associates bought Golden State in 1998 from its management, which kept a small stake in the company.

Golden State Foods supplies more than 2,900 McDonald's restaurants throughout the US and worldwide. McDonald's and its suppliers have established a symbiotic relationship. Golden State Foods adheres to McDonald's standards and gears its operations toward furthering the restaurant chain's interests. The company serves McDonald's without the benefit of a long-term, written contract, but McDonald's is known for its loyalty to its suppliers.

EXECUTIVES

Chairman and CEO: Mark S. Wetterau
SEVP, Liquid Products Group: Frank Listi
EVP and CFO: Mike Waitukaitis
VP, Accounting and Information Services:
  Richard D. Moretti
VP, Human Resources: Steve Becker
VP, International: Phillip Crane
**VP, Legal Affairs, General Counsel and Assistant
  Secretary:** Michael J. Hoppe Jr.
President, Distribution: Robert (Bob) Jorge
President, Meat Group: David H. Gilbert
Director of Development: John Walter

LOCATIONS

HQ: Golden State Foods
  18301 Von Karman Ave., Ste. 1100,
  Irvine, CA 92612
Phone: 949-252-2000   **Fax:** 949-252-2080
Web: www.goldenstatefoods.com

Golden State Foods has distribution and processing facilities in Arizona, California, Georgia, Hawaii, New York, North Carolina, Oregon, South Carolina, Virginia, and Washington as well as Australia, Egypt, and Mexico.

PRODUCTS/OPERATIONS

Selected Products

Beef patties	Mayonnaise
Buns	Onions
Ketchup	Salad dressing
Jelly	Sundae toppings
Lettuce	

COMPETITORS

Anderson-DuBose	Reyes Holdings
JR Simplot	Services Group
Keystone Foods	Shamrock Foods
Martin-Brower	SYSCO
MBM	U.S. Foodservice
McLane Foodservice	

HISTORICAL FINANCIALS

Company Type: Private

Income Statement				FYE: December 31
	ESTIMATED REVENUE ($ mil.)	NET INCOME ($ mil.)	NET PROFIT MARGIN	EMPLOYEES
12/03	2,000	—	—	2,400
12/02	1,700	—	—	2,000
12/01	1,800	—	—	2,000
12/00	1,764	—	—	2,000
12/99	1,750	—	—	2,000
12/98	1,600	—	—	1,800
12/97	1,500	—	—	2,000
12/96	1,450	—	—	2,000
12/95	1,340	—	—	1,700
12/94	1,260	—	—	1,700
Annual Growth	5.3%	—	—	3.9%

Revenue History

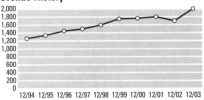

Golub

Supermarket operator The Golub Corporation offers tasty come-ons such as table-ready meals, gift certificates, automatic discount cards, and a hotline where cooks answer food-related queries. Golub operates 100-plus Price Chopper supermarkets in Connecticut, Massachusetts, New Hampshire, upstate New York, northeastern Pennsylvania, and Vermont. It also runs Mini Chopper service stations and convenience stores. Golub has discontinued its HouseCalls home delivery service. Brothers Bill and Ben Golub founded the company in 1932. The Golub family owns 45% of the firm and has turned down offers to sell it. Employees own the remaining 55% of The Golub Corp.

EXECUTIVES

Chairman: Lewis Golub
President and CEO: Neil M. Golub
CFO: John Endres
EVP and COO: Lawrence Zettle
EVP, Secretary and General Counsel: William Kenneally
SVP, Information Systems and CIO, Price Chopper:
  Tom Nowak
SVP, Sales and Merchandising: Tom Robbins
VP, Distribution: Ron Cellupica
VP, Human Resources: Margaret Davenport
VP, Operations: Mark E. Boucher
VP, Real Estate: Don Orlando
VP, Real Estate and Construction: Ron Schleich
VP, Store Operations: David (Dave) Hepfinger
Manager, Public Relations and Consumer Services:
  Mona Golub
Auditors: PricewaterhouseCoopers LLP

LOCATIONS

HQ: The Golub Corporation
  501 Duanesburg Rd., Schenectady, NY 12306
Phone: 518-355-5000   **Fax:** 518-379-3515
Web: www.pricechopper.com

2004 Stores

	No.
New York	68
Massachusetts	14
Vermont	12
Pennsylvania	7
Connecticut	4
New Hampshire	1
Total	**106**

COMPETITORS

7-Eleven
A&P
Big Y Foods
Cumberland Farms
DeMoulas Super Markets
Hannaford Bros.
Penn Traffic
Shaw's
Stop & Shop
Tops Markets
Wal-Mart
Wegmans

HISTORICAL FINANCIALS

Company Type: Private

Income Statement				FYE: April 30
	ESTIMATED REVENUE ($ mil.)	NET INCOME ($ mil.)	NET PROFIT MARGIN	EMPLOYEES
4/03	2,100	—	—	20,000
4/02	2,100	—	—	19,700
4/01	2,000	—	—	19,500
4/00	1,800	—	—	18,500
4/99	1,710	—	—	18,000
4/98	1,610	—	—	18,000
4/97	1,600	—	—	17,500
4/96	1,375	—	—	15,500
4/95	1,200	—	—	9,000
4/94	1,140	—	—	8,000
Annual Growth	7.0%	—	—	10.7%

Revenue History

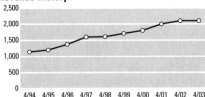

Goodman Manufacturing

Goodman Manufacturing knows how to cool off a hot situation. The company makes air-conditioning, ventilation, and heating equipment for residential and commercial use. Goodman, which sells its products through independent installers and distributors worldwide, is among the top US makers of air conditioners and heaters. Its brands include Amana, Goodman, GmC, Janitrol, and QuietFlex. Goodman is owned by the family of Harold Goodman, who founded the company in 1982.

EXECUTIVES

Chairman: John B. Goodman
President and CEO: Charles A. Carroll
CFO: Larry Blackburn
EVP Human Resources: Donald R. King
SVP Marketing: Gary Clark
President, Company-Owned Distribution:
  James L. Mishler

LOCATIONS

HQ: Goodman Manufacturing Company, L.P.
  2550 N. Loop West, Ste. 400, Houston, TX 77092
Phone: 713-861-2500   **Fax:** 713-861-0772
Web: www.goodmanmfg.com

Goodman Manufacturing operates three manufacturing facilities in Tennessee and Texas.

PRODUCTS/OPERATIONS

Selected Products
Air handlers
Evaporator coils
Gas furnaces
Packaged air conditioners
Packaged gas and electric air conditioners
Packaged heat pumps
Split-system air conditioners
Split-system heat pumps
Through-the-wall air conditioners

COMPETITORS

AAON	Maytag
American Standard	Mestek
Carrier	Mitsubishi Electric
Continental Materials	Paloma Industries
Fedders	Samsung Electronics
GE Consumer & Industrial	United Technologies
Lennox	Whirlpool
LG Electronics	York International

HISTORICAL FINANCIALS

Company Type: Private

Income Statement
FYE: December 31

	ESTIMATED REVENUE ($ mil.)	NET INCOME ($ mil.)	NET PROFIT MARGIN	EMPLOYEES
12/02	1,100	—	—	3,750
12/01	1,150	—	—	3,750
12/00	1,100	—	—	3,750
12/99	2,160	—	—	7,500
12/98	2,055	—	—	7,500
12/97	1,900	—	—	7,500
12/96	1,850	—	—	7,200
12/95	500	—	—	1,700
12/94	450	—	—	1,700
12/93	400	—	—	1,500
Annual Growth	11.9%	—	—	10.7%

Revenue History

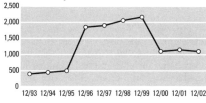

Goodwill

Founded to give those in need of "a hand up, not a handout," Goodwill Industries International supports the operations of about 210 independent Goodwill chapters worldwide. Though known mainly for its some 1,900 thrift stores, Goodwill focuses on providing rehabilitation, training, placement, and employment services for those with disabilities and other barriers to employment. Goodwill is one of the world's largest providers of such services, as well as one of the world's largest employers of the disabled. Funding comes primarily from the retail stores, contract services provided to local employers, and grants. Nearly 85% of revenues go to job training and rehabilitation programs.

EXECUTIVES

President and CEO: George W. Kessinger
VP Operations: Linda Chandler
Director, Contracts and Industrial Services:
  Ellen Brown
Director, Goodwill Global, Inc.: Howard Wallack
Director, Media Relations: Christine Nyirjesy Bragale
Director, Retail and Donated Goods: Renee Weippert
Human Resources Consultant: Ann Morrison
VP Membership Support Services: John Huber
Auditors: Deloitte & Touche

LOCATIONS

HQ: Goodwill Industries International, Inc.
  15810 Indianola Ave., Rockville, MD 20855
Phone: 301-530-6500   **Fax:** 301-530-1516
Web: www.goodwill.org

Goodwill Industries International has about 210 member organizations throughout the US, Canada, and 23 other countries.

HISTORICAL FINANCIALS

Company Type: Not-for-profit

Income Statement
FYE: December 31

	REVENUE ($ mil.)	NET INCOME ($ mil.)	NET PROFIT MARGIN	EMPLOYEES
12/03	2,210	—	—	82,370
12/02	2,055	—	—	140,023
12/01	1,940	—	—	61,766
12/00	1,850	—	—	77,895
12/99	1,650	—	—	60,000
12/98	1,507	—	—	60,000
12/97	1,361	—	—	60,000
12/96	1,200	—	—	60,679
12/95	1,038	—	—	64,403
Annual Growth	9.9%	—	—	3.1%

Revenue History

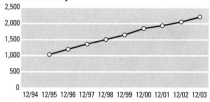

Gordon Food Service

Gordon Food Service (GFS) caters to the tastes of Midwesterners and Canadians alike. A broadline food distributor serving schools, restaurants, and other institutions, GFS boasts more than 14,000 products and some 30,000 customers. The firm also makes its own foods (Triumph Packaging and Ready, Set, Serve) and it sells food in bulk through some 100 GFS Marketplace stores in the Midwest and Florida. GFS acquired the Pacific Division of SERCA Foodservice from Sobeys in 2002 and renamed it Neptune Food Service. The late Isaac VanWestenbrugge (great-grandfather of CEO Dan Gordon) founded the company as a butter and egg distributor in 1897. GFS is still owned and run by the Gordon family.

EXECUTIVES

President and CEO: Dan Gordon
COO: Steve Plakmeyer
CFO: Steve Whitteberry
EVP: Jim Gordon
President, GFS Canada: Frank Geier
Secretary and Treasurer: John Gordon Jr.
Director, Human Resources: David Vickery
Marketing and Communications Manager:
  Marianne Manderfield

LOCATIONS

HQ: Gordon Food Service
  333 50th St. SW, Grand Rapids, MI 49501
Phone: 616-530-7000   **Fax:** 616-717-7600
Web: www.gfs.com

Gordon Food Service has operations in Michigan and Ohio and distributes food across the midwestern US and in Canada (Ontario and Quebec). GFS Marketplace stores are located in Florida, Illinois, Indiana, Michigan, and Ohio.

PRODUCTS/OPERATIONS

Selected Products

Beverage systems	Meats
Dairy	Poultry
Disposables	Sanitation systems
Fresh produce	Seafood
Frozen foods	Tabletop and supplies
Groceries	

Selected Brand Names
GFS
Primo Gusto Italian Specialties
Ready, Set, Serve
Signature Coffee
Triumph Packaging

COMPETITORS

Clark Products	Services Group
ConAgra	Sherwood Food
Costco Wholesale	Sobeys
MBM	SYSCO
McLane Foodservice	U.S. Foodservice
Performance Food	Wal-Mart

HISTORICAL FINANCIALS

Company Type: Private

Income Statement
FYE: October 31

	REVENUE ($ mil.)	NET INCOME ($ mil.)	NET PROFIT MARGIN	EMPLOYEES
10/03	3,000	—	—	5,750
10/02	2,750	—	—	5,000
10/01	2,600	—	—	5,000
10/00	2,150	—	—	4,400
10/99	2,000	—	—	3,600
10/98	1,700	—	—	3,400
10/97	1,600	—	—	3,300
10/96	1,400	—	—	3,000
10/95	1,250	—	—	2,450
10/94	1,115	—	—	2,300
Annual Growth	11.6%	—	—	10.7%

Revenue History

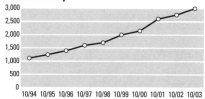

Gores Technology

In the gory aftermath of the tech wreck, Gores Technology Group can probably find a bargain. The company buys and manages software, hardware, technology services, and telecommunications concerns. Targets typically have revenues between $10 million and $1 billion and are often spinoffs of noncore operations from Global 2000 companies. Gores Technology usually takes full ownership. Since its founding by chairman Alec Gores in 1992, it has bought some 35 companies around the world.

Successful turnaround ventures include MPC Computers, the personal computer operations of Micron Electronics (now Interland), enterprise software firm Aprisma Management Technologies, software maker The Learning Company (which subsequently sold its education business to Ireland's Riverdeep software firm) and Verifone (sold to GTCR Golder Rauner).

EXECUTIVES

Chairman: Alec E. Gores, age 51
President and CEO: Vance W. Diggins
CFO: Catherine Babon Scanlon
EVP and General Counsel: Eric Hattler
EVP Marketing and Business Development: Frank V. Stefanik
SVP Finance: Thomas F. Perugini
Group VP, Operations: James A. MacKenzie
VP and Director of Business Development: Daniel J. Gray
VP and Director of Human Resources: Liz Davis
VP and Head of Facilities: David A. Hollenbeck
VP and Group General Counsel: David L. McEvoy
VP Finance: Michael Hirano
VP Technology: Leslie E. Cook

LOCATIONS

HQ: Gores Technology Group, LLC
10877 Wilshire Blvd., Ste. 1805,
Los Angeles, CA 90024
Phone: 310-209-3010 **Fax:** 310-209-3310
Web: www.gores.com

Gores Technology Group has operations in Asia, Europe, South America, and the US.

PRODUCTS/OPERATIONS

Selected Investments
Adventa Control Technologies, Inc.
Anker B.V.
Aprisma Management Technologies, Inc.
Humanic Solutions Inc.
JAMIS Software Corporation
MPC Computers, LLC (formerly MicronPC, LLC)
Omni Tech, End User Division
Pierce Technology Service
Proxicom
QuorTech Solutions, Inc.
Real Software Group
Revere, Inc.
Select Business Solutions, Inc.
Voicecom Telecommunications
Wire One Technology, Inc.

COMPETITORS

Bain Capital
Carlyle Group
CD&R
Forstmann Little
Hicks Muse
KKR
Platinum Equity

HISTORICAL FINANCIALS
Company Type: Private

Income Statement — FYE: December 31

	REVENUE ($ mil.)	NET INCOME ($ mil.)	NET PROFIT MARGIN	EMPLOYEES
12/01*	2,000	—	—	10,000
12/00	1,200	—	—	3,000
12/99	800	—	—	1,200
12/98	300	—	—	900
12/97	200	—	—	850
12/96	150	—	—	700
Annual Growth	67.9%	—	—	70.2%

*Most recent available

Revenue History

Gould Paper

Paper is as good as gold for Gould Paper, one of the largest privately owned distributors of printing and fine papers in the US. The company distributes and sells paper for multiple markets including fine papers, commercial printing, lithography, newsprint, direct mail, catalogs, envelopes, and specialty papers. The Gould North America division oversees business within the US and Canada, while Gould National produces paper rolls (wholesale). Its International Packaging Group makes specialty packaging (paperboard, plastics). Harry Gould Sr. (father of chairman, president, CEO, and owner Harry Gould Jr.) formed the company in 1924. Gould Paper has expanded over the years by acquiring other paper companies.

EXECUTIVES

Chairman, President, and CEO: Harry E. Gould Jr.
EVP and CFO: Carl Matthews
VP and CIO: Robert Bunsick
VP, Secretary, and Treasurer: Pat Mullen
President, Gould National Division: Robert Anderson
President, Gould International Packaging Group: John Curtin
President, Gould Business Products Division: Michael Negri
Chairman, Gould North America: Thomas Ryan
President, Gould North America Division: Robert Kralik
President, Gould Communications & Business Products Division: Robert Simone
President, Gould Distribution: Robert Weil
President, BRW Paper Company: Gale Woellfer
President, Legion Paper Co., Inc.: Len Levine

LOCATIONS

HQ: Gould Paper Corporation
11 Madison Ave., New York, NY 10010
Phone: 212-301-0000 **Fax:** 212-481-0067
Web: www.gouldpaper.com

Gould Paper has divisions and locations in California, Florida, Illinois, Massachusetts, Maryland, New Jersey, and New York.

COMPETITORS

Bradner Central
Clifford Paper
Crane & Co.
International Paper
Midland Paper
National Envelope
Ris Paper

HISTORICAL FINANCIALS
Company Type: Private

Income Statement — FYE: December 31

	REVENUE ($ mil.)	NET INCOME ($ mil.)	NET PROFIT MARGIN	EMPLOYEES
12/02	1,125	—	—	485
12/01	820	—	—	455
12/00	810	—	—	455
12/99	805	—	—	450
12/98	855	—	—	450
12/97	740	—	—	525
12/96	700	—	—	525
12/95	790	—	—	450
12/94	830	—	—	425
12/93	510	—	—	375
Annual Growth	9.2%	—	—	2.9%

Revenue History

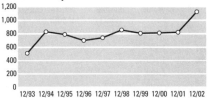

Goya Foods

Whether you call 'em *frijoles* or *habichuelas*, beans are beans, and Goya's got 'em. Goya Foods produces about 1,000 Hispanic and Caribbean grocery items, including canned and dried beans, canned meats, fruit nectars, olives, rice, seasonings and sauces, plantain and yucca chips, and frozen entrees. It sells more than 20 rice products and 30 types of beans and peas. Brands include Goya and Canilla. It also sells beverages such as tropical fruit nectars and juices, tropical sodas, and coffee. Goya is owned by one of the richest Hispanic *familias* in the US, the Unanues, who founded the company in 1936.

Goya has historically served the Hispanic communities in the Northeast and Florida with mostly Cuban, Dominican, and Puerto Rican customers. The company now has products geared toward the tastes of Hispanics in California and the Southwest with roots in Mexico and Central and South America. A growing taste for ethnic foods across the US has fueled Goya's growth beyond its Hispanic roots. In addition, its "all-in-one-aisle" product placement in food stores has proven very successful.

Yet it faces competition from food giants such as Kraft Foods, which have lines of Hispanic specialty products. It's also challenged by food manufacturers from Mexico who are turning north to tap the pocketbooks of US consumers. Goya is one of the largest Hispanic-owned companies in the US.

HISTORY

Immigrants from Spain by way of Puerto Rico, husband and wife Prudencio Unanue and Carolina Casal founded Unanue & Sons in New York City in 1936. The couple imported sardines, olives, and olive oil from Spain, but when the Spanish Civil War (1936-1939) interrupted supply lines, they began importing from Morocco.

In 1949 the company established a cannery in Puerto Rico; the Puerto Rican imports were distributed to local immigrants from the West Indies. Each of the couple's four sons eventually joined the family business, and in 1958 the firm relocated to Brooklyn. The company took its current name, Goya Foods, in 1962 when the family bought the Goya name — originally a brand of sardines — for $1.

The oldest Unanue son, CEO Charles, was fired from Goya in 1969 — and subsequently cut out of Prudencio's will — when he spoke out about an alleged tax evasion scheme. (Legal wrangling between Charles and the rest of the family continued into the late 1990s.) Goya moved to its present New Jersey headquarters in 1974.

Another son, Anthony, died in 1976, as did Prudencio. That year Joseph, another sibling, was named president and CEO. Along with his brother Francisco (Frank), president of Goya Foods de Puerto Rico, he began a cautious expansion campaign by adding traditional products to the company's existing line of Latin Caribbean and Spanish favorites.

Buoyed by the growing popularity of Mexican food, in 1982 Goya began distributing its products in Texas, targeting the region's sizable Mexican and Central American population. At first, the move proved a disaster. Goya's products were not suited to the Mexican palate, which generally preferred spicier food. Likewise, a similar strategy to capture a portion of Florida's huge Cuban market share initially met with only moderate success, but Goya persevered, eventually turning the tables in its favor.

During the 1980s the company also attempted to woo the non-Hispanic market. While Goya's cream of coconut — a key ingredient in piña coladas — found a broader market, its ad campaign featuring obscure actress Zohra Lampert did little to attract a large following of non-Hispanic customers.

Success in that market came in the 1990s. America's interest in the reportedly healthier "Mediterranean diet" boosted sales of Goya's extra-virgin olive oil. Recommendations for low-fat, high-fiber diets prompted the company's launch of the "For Better Meals, Turn to Goya" advertising campaign — its first in English — in 1992.

Three years later the company released a line of juice-based beverages. In 1996 Goya sponsored an exhibition of the works of the Spanish master Goya at the New York Metropolitan Museum of Art. Continuing its efforts to reach out to non-Hispanics and English-dominant Hispanics, in 1997 the company began including both English and Spanish on the front of its packaging.

To lure more snackers, the next year Goya added yucca (a.k.a. cassava) chips to its line. In 1999 Goya began packaging its frozen entrees in microwaveable trays. In 2001 it bought a new factory in Spain.

In 2002 Goya added 12 flavors (including guava, mandarin orange, and tamarind) to its line of Refresco Goya Fruit Sodas, thus joining the beverage industry trend toward offering more diverse flavors. In late 2002, the president of the company's Puerto Rican division, Francisco J. Unanue, died.

In February 2004 long-time chairman, CEO, and president Joseph Unanue and his son, COO Andy Unanue, were forced out of family-owned Goya by Joseph's two nephews, Robert I. and Francisco R. Unanue. Robert is now president and Francisco took over the Florida division of the company.

EXECUTIVES

President: Robert I. Unanue
VP, MIS: David Kinkela
VP, Purchasing: Joseph Perez
VP, Sales & Marketing: Conrad O. Colon
President, Florida Division: Francisco R. Unanue
Controller: Tony Diaz
Director, Finance: Miguel Lugo
Director, Human Resources: Johana Soco
Director, Marketing: Esperanza Carrion
Director, Public Relations: Rafael Toro
Director, Sales: Richard Gonzales
General Counsel: Carlos Ortiz
Deputy Counsel: Ira Matestsky
Corporate Secretary: Maribel Alvarez
Assistant, Public Relations: Evanessa Mangual
General Manager, West Coast Operations: Francisco Javier Ahumada
Manager, Secaucus Plant: Benjamin Spinnickie
President, Goya Foods Great Lakes: Robert Drago

LOCATIONS

HQ: Goya Foods, Inc.
100 Seaview Dr., Secaucus, NJ 07096
Phone: 201-348-4900   **Fax:** 201-348-6609
Web: www.goya.com

PRODUCTS/OPERATIONS

Selected Products

Beverages
  Café Goya
  Coconut Water
  Malta (malt beverage)
  Nectars and juices (apple, apricot, banana, guanabana, guava, mango, passion fruit, papaya, peach, pear, pear/passion, pineapple, pineapple/guava, pineapple/passion, strawberry, strawberry/banana, tamarind, tropical fruit punch)
  Tropical sodas (apple, coconut, cola champagne, fruit punch, ginger beer, grape, guaraná, guava, lemon lime, mandarin orange, pineapple, strawberry, tamarind)

Foods & Other Products
  Beans (black-eyed peas, chick peas, lentils, refried)
  Bouillon
  Cooking sauces
  Cooking wine
  Cornmeal
  Devotional candles
  Flour
  Frozen foods
  Marinades
  Meat (chorizo, corned beef, potted, vienna sausage)
  Olive oil
  Olives
  Pasta
  Plantain chips
  Rice
  Seafood
  Seasonings
  Spices
  Yucca chips

COMPETITORS

American Rice
Authentic Specialty Foods
Bimbo
Chiquita Brands
ConAgra
Del Monte Foods
Dole Food
Frito-Lay
Herdez
Hormel
Kraft Foods
McCormick
Nestlé
Pro-Fac
Riceland Foods
Riviana Foods
Seneca Foods
Unilever

HISTORICAL FINANCIALS

Company Type: Private

Income Statement
FYE: May 31

	REVENUE ($ mil.)	NET INCOME ($ mil.)	NET PROFIT MARGIN	EMPLOYEES
5/04	850	—	—	—
5/03	750	—	—	2,500
5/02	750	—	—	2,500
5/01	715	—	—	2,500
5/00	695	—	—	2,500
5/99	653	—	—	2,200
5/98	620	—	—	3,000
5/97	600	—	—	3,000
5/96	560	—	—	2,200
5/95	528	—	—	2,000
Annual Growth	5.4%	—	—	2.8%

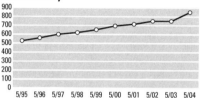

Revenue History

Graham Packaging

Grocery stockers and mechanics handle Graham Packaging's products every day. The company makes blow-molded plastic containers for food and beverages, household and personal care products, and automotive lubricants. Customers such as Hershey Foods, Procter & Gamble, and Pennzoil-Quaker State (SOPUS) use the containers for juices, sauces, teas, fabric and dish detergents, and motor oil. More than 40% of Graham Packaging's manufacturing plants are located on the grounds of its customers' production facilities. The company, which is controlled by Blackstone Group, has postponed its IPO until market conditions improve.

Many of Graham's manufacturing facilities (24 out of 56) are located at its customer's plants — a distinct competitive advantage borne out by the fact that its top twenty customers have been customers for some 15 years on average. The top twenty customers account for 84% of sales. Graham's largest customer, PepsiCo, accounts for more than 15% of annual sales. Dial and Danone together account for about 20% of annual sales.

In 2004 glass manufacturing giant Owens-Illinois sold its blow-molded plastic container operations in North America, South America, and Europe to Graham for about $1.2 billion. Graham hopes this transaction will solidify its presence as one of the global leaders in plastic packaging.

EXECUTIVES

Chairman and CEO: Philip R. Yates, age 56, $528,881 pay
President and COO: Roger M. Prevot, age 44, $356,692 pay
CFO: John E. Hamilton, age 45, $255,544 pay
SVP and General Manager, North America Automotive and South America: G. Robinson Beeson, age 55, $217,232 pay
SVP and General Manager, Household and Personal Care: Scott G. Booth, age 47, $478,492 pay
SVP and General Manager, Europe and North America Food and Beverage Polyolefins: Ashok Sudan, age 50, $217,791 pay
SVP, Global People Resources: George Lane
SVP and General Manager, North America Food and Beverage PET: John A. Buttermore, age 56, $417,565 pay
Investor Relations: Mark Leiden
Auditors: Deloitte & Touche LLP

LOCATIONS

HQ: Graham Packaging Company, Inc.
2401 Pleasant Valley Rd., York, PA 17402
Phone: 717-849-8500 **Fax:** 717-848-4836
Web: www.grahampackaging.com

Graham Packaging Holdings Company has 55 plants in Europe, Latin America, and North America.

2003 Sales

	$ mil.	% of total
North America	809.6	83
Europe	143.9	15
Latin America	25.2	2
Total	**978.7**	**100**

PRODUCTS/OPERATIONS

2003 Sales

	$ mil.	% of total
Food & beverage	573.0	58
Automotive lubricants	214.1	22
Household & personal care	191.6	20
Total	**978.7**	**100**

Selected Products

Food and Beverage Containers
  Frozen juices
  Jellies and jams
  Non-carbonated juice drinks
  Pasta sauce and other sauces
  Soups
  Teas
  Toppings
  Yogurt and nutritional drinks
Household and Personal Care Containers
  Body wash
  Dish care
  Hair care
  Hard surface cleaners
  Liquid automatic dishwashing detergents
  Liquid fabric care
Automotive Lubricant Containers
  Antifreeze
  Motor oils

COMPETITORS

Amcor
Ball Corporation
Chesapeake Corporation
Consolidated Container
Constar International
Owens-Illinois
Pechiney
Plastipak Holdings, Inc.
RPC Group
Silgan

HISTORICAL FINANCIALS

Company Type: Private

Income Statement
FYE: December 31

	REVENUE ($ mil.)	NET INCOME ($ mil.)	NET PROFIT MARGIN	EMPLOYEES
12/03	979	10	1.0%	3,900
12/02	907	8	0.8%	3,900
12/01	923	(44)	—	4,100
12/00	825	(46)	—	4,000
12/99	716	1	0.2%	4,000
12/98	588	(28)	—	—
12/97	522	11	2.0%	—
12/96	460	21	4.6%	—
12/95	467	19	4.0%	—
Annual Growth	**9.7%**	**(7.9%)**	—	**(0.6%)**

2003 Year-End Financials

Debt ratio: — Current ratio: 1.03
Return on equity: — Long-term debt ($ mil.): 1,085
Cash ($ mil.): 7

Net Income History

Grant Thornton International

Grant Thornton International is a kid brother to the Big Four. The umbrella organization of accounting and management consulting firms operates from more than 580 offices around the world, making it one of the top second-tier companies that trail around behind the biggest of the big guys (Deloitte Touche Tohmatsu, Ernst & Young International, KPMG International, and PricewaterhouseCoopers). Grant Thornton International's member firms elect representatives to an international policy board that runs the day-to-day operations of the accounting company.

Industry consolidation prompted Grant Thornton International and other second-tier firms to enter such niche areas as information technology and corporate finance. And while the Big Four focus on large corporations, Grant Thornton locks in on owner-managed companies, helping them with accounting, audit, and tax issues, as well as growth strategies. It is facing new competitors for its target market; such firms as H&R Block and American Express have been adding accounting, tax planning, and consulting services.

With the lowering of trade barriers in Latin America and Europe, Grant Thornton has been focusing on developing business in emerging markets. Member firms have been working to increase cross-border cooperation by pooling resources and cutting costs. The organization also helped pick up the pieces as Andersen crumbled, acquiring employees, offices, and clients from the felled giant.

Like Andersen before it, Grant Thornton felt the red-hot glare of unwanted media attention as Italian food giant Parmalat (a former auditing client) fell into bankruptcy amidst an Enron-style scandal in late 2003. Grant Thornton's Italian unit had remained the auditor for Parmalat subsidiary Bonlat, which played a central role in the unfolding scandal. The Italian affiliate, which has been expelled from Grant Thornton's global network, maintains it was a victim of fraud in the case. Parmalat in 2004 filed suit against the Italian accountancy, claiming two of its partners were involved in the fraud; the two also face criminal charges.

HISTORY

Cameron, Missouri accountant Alexander Grant founded Alexander Grant & Co. in 1924 with William O'Brien. They built their firm in Chicago and concentrated on providing services to midwestern clients.

In the 1950s and 1960s, the firm began expanding both domestically and internationally. Alexander Grant & Co. continued to focus on manufacturing and distribution companies.

In 1973 O'Brien died. In 1979 the company began publishing its well-known (and sometimes controversial) index of state business climates. An attempt to merge with fellow second-tier accounting firm Laventhol & Horwath failed that year. The next year Grant Thornton International was formed when Alexander Grant & Co. and its British affiliate, Thornton Baker, combined their offices around the world to form a network. The UK and US branches, however, kept their respective names.

The 1980s brought turmoil and change for the firm. Financial scandals led investors and the government to hold accounting firms liable for their audits. Along with the (then) Big Six, Alexander Grant & Co. was hit with several lawsuits alleging fraud and cover-ups. One case marred the firm's squeaky-clean image and caused dozens of clients to jump ship: Just days after Alexander Grant issued it a clean audit, a Florida trading firm was shut down by the SEC. Jilted investors sued to reclaim lost money; Alexander Grant settled for $160 million. Chairman Herbert Dooskin and other leaders also left the company; although they denied it was because of the scandal, their departures left Alexander Grant rudderless during a critical time.

Meanwhile, the company merged with Fox & Co. to create the US's #9 accounting firm. With scandal-scared partners leaving (and taking clients), Fox looked to the merger to shore up its reputation. But Alexander Grant's auditing troubles led some Fox partners and clients to flee from the merged company.

After the fallout from the lawsuits and the merger, the company began rebuilding, taking on new clients, reclaiming lost ones, and refocusing on midsized companies. In 1986 both Alexander Grant & Co. and Thornton Baker took the Grant Thornton name.

The early 1990s recession reduced accounting revenues but increased demand for management consulting. As political and economic barriers fell during the decade, Grant Thornton International grew. The firm entered emerging markets in Africa, Asia, Europe, and Latin America. In 1998 the Big Six became the Big Five; Grant Thornton added refugee firms and partners to its global network. In 1999 the firm's US branch entertained merger offers from H&R Block and PricewaterhouseCoopers, but instead announced plans to reposition itself as a corporate services firm to better compete.

In 2000 the company pulled out of its advisory position to companies involved in controversial diamond mining in war-torn portions of Africa. It also agreed to merge its UK operations with those of HLB Kidsons; the merged firm retained the Grant Thornton name.

The following year, after disagreements about strategy, US CEO Dom Esposito resigned. UK partner David McDonnell was named the global CEO. In 2002, Grant Thornton grew by picking up pieces of Andersen that fell away as a result of the Enron scandal. Andersen's fall also winnowed out Grant Thornton's competitors (at least in the numeric sense), as the Big Five became the Big Four.

EXECUTIVES

Chairman: Leonard Brehm
Global CEO: David C. McDonnell
Divisional Director, Asia Pacific: Gabriel Azedo
Divisional Director, Europe, Middle East and Africa: Clive Bennett
Divisional Director, The Americas: Shelley Stein
Worldwide Director, Audit and Quality Control: Barry Barber
Worldwide Director, Client Services: Soren Carlsson
International Director, Marketing Communication: Sue Palmer
Treasurer and Director of Administration: Louis A. Fanchi
Director of Administration: Ricky Lawrence
Director of Human Resources, Grant Thornton LLP: Jill Osborn

LOCATIONS

HQ: Grant Thornton International
175 W. Jackson Blvd., Chicago, IL 60604
Phone: 312-856-0200 **Fax:** 312-602-8099
Web: www.gti.org

Grant Thornton International has offices in 110 countries worldwide.

PRODUCTS/OPERATIONS

Selected Services
Assurance
Corporate finance
Corporate recovery and business reorganization
International tax
PRIMA (people and relationship issues in management)

COMPETITORS

American Express Tax and Business Services
Baker Tilly International
BDO International
Deloitte
Ernst & Young
H&R Block
KPMG
McGladrey & Pullen
McKinsey & Company
Moore Stephens International
Moores Rowland
PricewaterhouseCoopers
RSM McGladrey, Inc.

HISTORICAL FINANCIALS

Company Type: Not-for-profit

Income Statement
FYE: July 31

	REVENUE ($ mil.)	NET INCOME ($ mil.)	NET PROFIT MARGIN	EMPLOYEES
7/03	2,000	—	—	21,500
7/02	1,840	—	—	21,500
7/01	1,700	—	—	21,879
7/00	1,690	—	—	20,300
7/99	1,800	—	—	20,000
7/98	1,600	—	—	20,160
7/97	1,405	—	—	18,562
7/96	1,285	—	—	18,300
Annual Growth	6.5%	—	—	2.3%

Revenue History

Graybar Electric

There's no gray area when it comes to describing Graybar Electric's main business: it's one of the largest distributors of electrical products in the US. Purchasing from thousands of manufacturers, the employee-owned company distributes nearly 1 million types of electrical and communications components, including wire, cable, and lighting products. Its customers include electrical contractors, industrial plants, power utilities, and telecommunications providers. Subsidiary Graybar Financial Services offers equipment leasing and financing, as well as complete project funding.

The construction industry has been the company's traditional market, but changes in telecommunications have prompted it to solidify relationships with major vendors such as GE, Lucent, and Thomas & Betts.

Graybar has reorganized its sales force into regional districts throughout the US. To help bring supply, distribution, and inventory costs down, the company uses electronic data interchange and supplier-assisted inventory management, and urges its suppliers to use bar codes on all products. Graybar Electric has grown by targeting both national and international accounts.

HISTORY

After serving as a telegrapher during the Civil War, Enos Barton borrowed $400 from his widowed mother in 1869 and started an electrical equipment shop in Cleveland with George Shawk. Later that year Elisha Gray, a professor of physics at Oberlin College who had several inventions (including a printing telegraph) to his credit, bought Shawk's interest in the shop, and the firm moved to Chicago, where a third partner joined.

The company incorporated as the Western Electric Manufacturing Co. in 1872, with two-thirds of the company's stock held by two Western Union executives. As the telegraph industry took off, the enterprise grew rapidly, providing equipment to towns and railroads in the western US.

Gray and his company missed receiving credit for inventing the telephone in 1875 when Gray's patent application for a "harmonic telegraph" reached the US Patent Office a few hours after Bell's application for his telephone. However, the telephone and the invention of the light bulb in 1879 opened new doors for Western Electric. The company began to grow into a major corporation, selling and distributing a variety of electrical equipment, including batteries, telegraph keys, and fire-alarm boxes. By 1900 the firm was the world's #1 maker of telephone equipment.

Western Electric formed a new distribution business in 1926, Graybar Electric Co. (from "Gray" and "Barton"), the world's largest electrical supply merchandiser. In 1929 employees bought the company from Western Electric for $3 million in cash and $6 million in preferred stock. During the 1930s it marketed a line of appliances and sewing machines under the Graybar name.

In 1941 the company bought the outstanding shares of stock from Western Electric for $1 million. Graybar Electric was a vital link between manufacturers and US defense needs during WWII. Its men and equipment wired the Panama Canal with telephone cable; it also helped the US military during the Korean conflict and the Vietnam War.

By 1980 Graybar Electric had reached nearly $1.5 billion in sales. Business was hurt when construction slowed in the late 1980s and the early 1990s, and the company reorganized in 1991, closing regional offices and cutting jobs. Rebounding in 1992 as the US economy improved, Graybar acquired New Jersey-based Square Electric Co.

In 1994 the company acquired a minority interest in R.E.D. Electronics, a Canadian data communications and computer networking company, and realigned its operations into two business segments: electrical products and communications and data products.

In 1995 Graybar Electric formed the Solutions Providers Alliance with wholesale distributors Kaman Industrial Technologies, VWR Scientific Products, and Vallen Corporation. In 1996 AT&T's Global Procurement Group named the company as one of only three suppliers for its electrical products. The next year Graybar Electric upped its stake in one of its Canadian operations, Harris & Roome Supply Limited.

Graybar Electric in 1998 opened a subsidiary in Chile and formed a joint venture, Graybar Financial Services, with Newcourt Financial (formerly AT&T Capital). The next year Graybar Electric bought the Connecticut-based electrical wholesaler Frank A. Blesso, Inc., and it expanded its distribution partnership with wire and cable manufacturer Belden Electronics in 2000.

In 2001 Graybar opened a new distribution location in northeastern Pennsylvania. The following year Graybar increased its presence in the telecommunications industry when it inked a deal to distribute products made by Copper Mountain Networks, a US-based broadband equipment manufacturer.

EXECUTIVES

President, CEO, and Chairman: Robert A. Reynolds Jr., age 55, $737,762 pay
SVP, CFO, and Director: Juanita H. Hinshaw, age 59, $371,930 pay
SVP, Sales and Distribution and Director:
Dennis E. DeSousa, age 45, $322,040 pay
SVP, Electrical Business and Director: Charles R. Udell, age 59, $322,113 pay
SVP, Operations and Director:
Lawrence R. (Larry) Giglio, age 49
SVP, Sales and Marketing and Director:
Richard D. Offenbacher, age 53
VP, CIO, and Director: D. Beatty D'Alessandro, age 43
VP, Secretary, General Counsel, and Director:
Thomas F. Dowd, age 60
VP, Human Resources and Strategic Planning and Director: Kathleen M. Mazzarella, age 44
VP, Human Resources and Director: Jack F. Van Pelt, age 65, $333,132 pay
Auditors: Ernst & Young LLP

LOCATIONS

HQ: Graybar Electric Company, Inc.
34 N. Meramec Ave., St. Louis, MO 63105
Phone: 314-573-9200   **Fax:** 314-512-9453
Web: www.graybar.com

Graybar Electric Company has offices and distribution facilities in Canada, Mexico, Japan, Puerto Rico, Saudi Arabia, and the US.

PRODUCTS/OPERATIONS

Selected Products

Ballasts	Industrial fans
Batteries	Lighting
Cable	Lubricants
Conduit	Paints
Connectors	Patch cords
Emergency lighting	Smoke detectors
Enclosures	Testing and measuring
Fiber optic cable	instruments
Fittings	Timers
Fluorescent lighting	Transfer switches
Fuses	Transformers
Hand tools	Utility products
Hangers/fasteners	Wire
Heating and ventilating equipment	

Selected Subsidiaries

Commonwealth Controls Corporation
Distribution Associates, Inc.
Graybar Business Services, Inc.
Graybar Canada Limited
Graybar Commerce Corporation
Graybar Electric Canada Limited
Graybar Electric de Mexico, S. de R.L. de C.V.
Graybar Electric Limited (Canada)
Graybar Financial Services, Inc.
Graybar Foundation, Inc.
Graybar International, Inc.
Graybar Services, Inc.

COMPETITORS

Agilysys	Premier Farnell
Anixter International	Rexel, Inc.
Communications Supply	Siemens
Consolidated Electrical	Sonepar USA
Cooper Industries	SPX
Eaton	SUMMIT Electric Supply
Emerson Electric	Tech Data
GE Supply	Tyco International
Hagemeyer	WESCO International
Matsushita	W.W. Grainger
Molex	

HISTORICAL FINANCIALS

Company Type: Private

Income Statement   FYE: December 31

	REVENUE ($ mil.)	NET INCOME ($ mil.)	NET PROFIT MARGIN	EMPLOYEES
12/03	3,803	9	0.2%	7,900
12/02	3,975	11	0.3%	8,300
12/01	4,815	32	0.7%	9,800
12/00	5,214	66	1.3%	10,500
12/99	4,300	65	1.5%	8,900
12/98	3,744	60	1.6%	7,900
12/97	3,338	53	1.6%	7,200
12/96	2,991	45	1.5%	6,600
12/95	2,765	37	1.3%	6,200
12/94	2,356	19	0.8%	5,500
Annual Growth	5.5%	(8.4%)	—	4.1%

2003 Year-End Financials

Debt ratio: 65.6%   Current ratio: 1.63
Return on equity: 2.2%   Long-term debt ($ mil.): 254
Cash ($ mil.): 19

Net Income History

Great Dane

Great Dane is really going places — the company is one of the largest manufacturers of truck trailers in North America. Great Dane makes refrigerated (reefer) and freight vans and platform trailers. The company has manufacturing plants in the US and sales, parts, and service centers across the US, Canada, Mexico, and South America. It also sells used trailers. Great Dane is a unit of Chicago-based investment group CC Industries, which is controlled by the Henry Crown family. The company started in 1900 as a maker of steel products and switched to trailer making in 1931.

EXECUTIVES

Chairman and Customer Relations:
C. F. (Kit) Hammond III
COO; President, Pines Trailer Division:
Phillip (Phill) Pines
EVP, Administration and Manufacturing: Jim Pines
SVP, Sales and Marketing: Chris Adkins
VP, Business Development, Great Dane Limited Partnership: Tom Czapka
Director, Advertising and Industry Relations:
Brandie Fuller
Dallas Branch Manager: Glen Williams
Savannah Plant Manager: Bruce Long

LOCATIONS

HQ: Great Dane Limited Partnership
602 E. Lathrop Ave., Savannah, GA 31415
Phone: 912-644-2100   **Fax:** 912-644-2166
Web: www.greatdanetrailers.com

Great Dane has nine manufacturing plants in the US.

PRODUCTS/OPERATIONS

Selected Products

Freight Vans	Reefers
Aluminum	Classic aluminum
Customized	Stainless steel
Stainless steel	SuperSeal
Platform Trailers	Thermacube
All steel	
Drop deck	
Extendable platform	
Steel/aluminum combo	

COMPETITORS

Carlisle Companies	RailAmerica
Featherlite	Supreme Industries
Fontaine Trailer	Trailmobile
Hyundai Translead	Utility Trailer
Lufkin Industries	Wabash National

HISTORICAL FINANCIALS

Company Type: Private

Income Statement   FYE: December 31

	ESTIMATED REVENUE ($ mil.)	NET INCOME ($ mil.)	NET PROFIT MARGIN	EMPLOYEES
12/02	1,000	—	—	4,000
12/01	1,000	—	—	3,400
12/00	1,310	—	—	5,000
12/99	1,400	—	—	4,000
12/98	1,000	—	—	4,700
12/97	1,000	—	—	4,715
Annual Growth	0.0%	—	—	(3.2%)

Revenue History

Great Lakes Cheese

Great Lakes Cheese Company understands the power of provolone and the charm of cheddar. The firm manufactures and distributes natural and processed cheeses, including cheddar, Swiss, mozzarella, and provolone. The company packages shredded, chunk, and sliced cheese under retailers' private labels. Additionally it imports cheeses, and produces cheese for deli, bulk, and foodservice sale. The firm has seven plants in New York, Ohio, Utah, and Wisconsin. It sells directly to consumers through a store in its New York plant and its Web site. Hans Epprecht, a Swiss immigrant, founded the company in 1958 as a bulk-cheese distributor in Cleveland. Chairman Epprecht and Great Lakes Cheese employees own the company.

EXECUTIVES
Chairman: Hans Epprecht
President and CEO: Gary Vanic
CFO: Russell (Russ) Mullins
VP, Packaging: John Epprecht
VP, Sales: Bill Andrews
Director of Human Resources: Beth Wendell
Director of Information Services: Ron Barlow

LOCATIONS
HQ: Great Lakes Cheese Company, Inc.
17825 Great Lakes Pkwy., Hiram, OH 44234
Phone: 440-834-2500 **Fax:** 440-834-1002
Web: www.greatlakescheese.com

COMPETITORS
Agri-Mark
AMPI
ConAgra
Dairy Farmers of America
Kraft Foods
Land O'Lakes
Leprino Foods
Lucille Farms
Marathon Cheese
Masters Gallery
Saputo
Schreiber Foods

HISTORICAL FINANCIALS
Company Type: Private

Income Statement FYE: December 31

	REVENUE ($ mil.)	NET INCOME ($ mil.)	NET PROFIT MARGIN	EMPLOYEES
12/03	965	—	—	1,700
12/02	851	—	—	1,300
12/01	843	—	—	1,200
12/00	717	—	—	1,200
12/99	770	—	—	1,200
12/98	700	—	—	1,000
12/97	625	—	—	950
12/96	612	—	—	900
12/95	473	—	—	830
12/94	414	—	—	659
Annual Growth	9.9%	—	—	11.1%

Revenue History

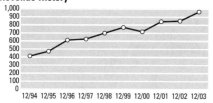

Green Bay Packaging

Green Bay Packaging is always packed and ready to go. The company is an integrated and diversified paperboard packaging manufacturer. In addition to corrugated containers, the company makes pressure-sensitive label stock, folding cartons, linerboard, and lumber products. Its Fiber Resources division in Arkansas manages more than 210,000 acres of company-owned forests and, through contractors, produces lumber, woodchips, recycled paper, and wood fuel. Green Bay Packaging also offers fiber procurement, wastepaper brokerage, and paper-slitting services.

Founded by corrugated paper pioneer George Kress in 1933, the company operates about 30 divisions in 14 states. The Kress family controls Green Bay Packaging.

EXECUTIVES
President: William F. Kress
CFO and Treasurer: Joseph Baemmert
EVP: Thomas M. Herlihy
SVP, Coated Products Operations: Paul Hasemeyer
VP and General Manager: Rich Garber
Director, Quality Management: William Kelley

LOCATIONS
HQ: Green Bay Packaging Inc.
1700 N. Webster Ct., Green Bay, WI 54307
Phone: 920-433-5111 **Fax:** 920-433-5337
Web: www.gbp.com

Green Bay Packaging operates about 30 divisions in 14 states.

PRODUCTS/OPERATIONS
Selected Products and Services
Corrugated containers
Fiber procurement
Folding cartons
Linerboard
Lumber
Paper slitting
Wastepaper brokerage and procurement

COMPETITORS
Caraustar
Chesapeake Corporation
Graphic Packaging
Norampac
Rock-Tenn
Shorewood Packaging
Smurfit-Stone Container
Temple-Inland

HISTORICAL FINANCIALS
Company Type: Private

Income Statement FYE: December 31

	ESTIMATED REVENUE ($ mil.)	NET INCOME ($ mil.)	NET PROFIT MARGIN	EMPLOYEES
12/03	810	—	—	2,687
12/02	800	—	—	2,750
12/01	800	—	—	2,800
12/00	826	—	—	3,025
12/99	738	—	—	3,000
12/98	650	—	—	2,700
12/97	500	—	—	2,700
12/96	650	—	—	2,600
12/95	650	—	—	2,560
12/94	533	—	—	2,557
Annual Growth	4.8%	—	—	0.6%

Revenue History

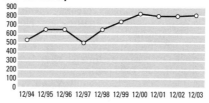

Green Bay Packers

On the frozen tundra of Lambeau Field, the Green Bay Packers battle for pride in the National Football League. The team, founded in 1919 by Earl "Curly" Lambeau, has been home to such football icons as Bart Starr, Ray Nitschke, and legendary coach Vince Lombardi. Current head cheeses include coach Mike Sherman and quarterback Brett Favre. The Packers boast a record 12 championship titles, including three Super Bowl victories. The team is also the NFL's only community-owned franchise, being a not-for-profit corporation with about 111,500 shareholders. The shares do not increase in value nor pay dividends, and can only be sold back to the team. No individual is allowed to own more than 200,000 shares.

After a couple of poor seasons, both athletically and financially, the Packers organization has high hopes for the future. Green Bay voters approved public financing for a $295 million renovation of historic Lambeau Field (which the city owns) in 2000, and the completed project added 10,000 seats to the stadium as well as additional luxury suites. The team's waiting list for season tickets boasts more than 56,000 names.

HISTORY

In 1919 Earl "Curly" Lambeau helped organize a professional football team in Green Bay, Wisconsin, with the help of George Calhoun, the sports editor of the *Green Bay Press-Gazette*. At 20 years old, Lambeau was elected team captain and convinced the Indian Packing Company to back the team, giving the squad its original name, the Indians. The local paper, however, nicknamed the team the Packers and the name stuck. Playing on an open field at Hagemeister Park, the team collected fees by passing the hat among the fans. In 1921 the team was admitted into the American Professional Football Association (later called the National Football League), which had been organized the year before.

The Packers went bankrupt after a poor showing its first season in the league, and Lambeau and Calhoun bought the team for $250. With debts continuing to mount, *Press-Gazette* general manager Andrew Turnbull helped reorganize the team as the not-for-profit Green Bay Football Corporation and sold stock at $5 a share. Despite winning three straight championships from 1929-31, the team again teetered on the brink of bankruptcy, forcing another stock sale in 1935. With fortunes on and off the field dwindling, Lambeau retired in 1950. A third stock sale was called for that year, raising $118,000. City Stadium (renamed Lambeau Field in 1965) was opened in 1957. In 1959 the team hired New York Giants assistant Vince Lombardi as head coach.

Under Lombardi, the Packers dominated football in the 1960s, winning five NFL titles. With players such as Bart Starr and Ray Nitschke, the team defeated the Kansas City Chiefs in the first Super Bowl after the 1966 season. Lombardi resigned after winning Super Bowl II (he died in 1970), and the team again fell into mediocrity. Former MVP Starr was called upon to coach in 1974 but couldn't turn the tide before he was released in 1983.

Bob Harlan, who had joined the Packers as assistant general manager in 1971, became president and CEO in 1989. He hired Ron Wolf as general manager in 1991, who in turn hired Mike Holmgren as head coach early the next year. With a roster including Brett Favre, Reggie White, and Robert Brooks, the Packers posted six straight playoff appearances and won its third Super Bowl in 1997. A fourth stock sale (preceded by a 1,000:1 stock split) netted the team more than $24 million.

After Holmgren resigned in 1999 (he left to coach the Seattle Seahawks), former Philadelphia Eagles coach Ray Rhodes tried to lead the team but lasted only one dismal season. In 2000 Mike Sherman, a former Holmgren assistant, was named the team's 13th head coach. Prompted by falling revenue, the team announced plans to renovate Lambeau Field, and voters in Brown County later approved a sales tax increase to help finance the $295 million project. (The project was completed in 2003.) The next year Wolf retired and coach Sherman was tapped as general manager. The team also signed quarterback Favre to a 10-year, $100 million contract extension.

EXECUTIVES

President and CEO: Robert E. Harlan, age 68
EVP and COO: John M. Jones, age 52
EVP, General Manager, and Head Coach:
  Michael F. (Mike) Sherman, age 49
VP Player Finance and General Counsel:
  Andrew Brandt, age 44
Director of Accounting: Duke Copp
Director of Administrative Affairs: Mark Schiefelbein
Director of College Scouting: John Dorsey, age 44
Director of Corporate Security: Jerry Parins
Director of Marketing and Corporate Sales:
  Craig Benzel
Director of Information Technology: Wayne Wichlacz
Director of Facility Operations: Ted Eisenreich
Director of Finance: Vicki Vannieuwenhoven
Director of Player Development: Edgar Bennett, age 35
Director of Premium Guest Services: Jennifer Ark
Director of Pro Personnel: Reggie McKenzie, age 41
Director of Public Relations: Jeff Blumb
Director of Research and Development: Mike Eayrs, age 53
Director of Retail Operations: Kate Hogan
Director of Ticket Operations: Mark Wagner
Corporate Sales Executive: Jason Hartlund
Executive of Special Events: Dee Geurts-Bengtson
Manager of Community Relations: Cathy Dworak
Marketing Entertainment Coordinator: Kandi Goltz
Marketing and Corporate Sales Coordinator: Shea Greil
Team Historian: Lee Remmel, age 80
Auditors: Wipfli Ullrich Bertelson LLP

LOCATIONS

HQ: The Green Bay Packers, Inc.
  1265 Lombardi Ave., Green Bay, WI 54304
Phone: 920-569-7500   **Fax:** 920-569-7301
Web: www.packers.com

The Green Bay Packers play at Lambeau Field in Green Bay, Wisconsin. The team holds its training camp at St. Norbert College in De Pere, Wisconsin.

PRODUCTS/OPERATIONS

Championship Titles
Super Bowl I (1967)
Super Bowl II (1968)
Super Bowl XXXI (1997)
NFC Championships (1996-97)
NFC Central Division (1972, 1995-97)
NFC North Division (2002-03)
NFL Championships (1929-31, 1936, 1939, 1944, 1961-62, 1965)
NFL Western Conference (1936, 1938-39, 1944, 1960-62, 1965-67)

COMPETITORS

Chicago Bears
Detroit Lions
Minnesota Vikings

HISTORICAL FINANCIALS

Company Type: Not-for-profit

Income Statement				FYE: March 31
	REVENUE ($ mil.)	NET INCOME ($ mil.)	NET PROFIT MARGIN	EMPLOYEES
3/04	179	29	16.2%	150
3/03	153	15	9.9%	150
3/02	132	4	2.9%	150
3/01	124	9	7.0%	140
3/00	109	3	2.5%	95
3/99	103	7	6.3%	95
3/98	82	6	7.7%	92
3/97	75	—	—	90
3/96	70	—	—	82
3/95	62	—	—	80
Annual Growth	12.5%	29.1%	—	7.2%

Net Income History

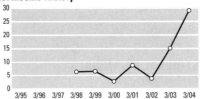

Greenberg Traurig

Show business isn't Greenberg Traurig's only legal business. Greenberg Traurig practices in such areas as corporate securities, information technology, and telecommunications, as well as entertainment. Among its corporate clients are Delta Airlines, Lorimar Pictures, and Metromedia. The firm has more than 1,000 lawyers in its nearly 25 offices. Much of Greenberg Traurig's growth has been achieved through several mergers, including its 1998 pairing with Atlanta entertainment practice Katz, Smith & Cohen, and its 1999 acquisition of Minkin & Snyder. Greenberg Traurig was founded in 1967 by Miami lawyer Mel Greenberg.

EXECUTIVES

Chairman: Larry J. Hoffman
President and CEO: Cesar L. Alvarez, age 56
Director Accounting: Frances M. Wylde
Director Human Resources: Rosalyn Friedman
Director Recruitment: Janet McKeegan
Director Marketing and Recruitment: Sandy Grossman

LOCATIONS

HQ: Greenberg Traurig, LLP
  1221 Brickell Ave., Miami, FL 33131
Phone: 305-579-0500   **Fax:** 305-579-0717
Web: www.gtlaw.com

Greenberg Traurig has offices in Amsterdam; Albany, NY; Atlanta; Boston; Chicago; Dallas; Denver; Los Angeles; Morristown, New Jersey; New York City; Philadelphia; Phoenix; Tyson's Corner, Virginia; Silicon Valley; Washington, DC; Wilmington, Delaware; and Zurich. It has Florida locations in Boca Raton, Fort Lauderdale, Miami, Orlando, Tallahassee, and West Palm Beach.

PRODUCTS/OPERATIONS

Selected Areas of Practice
Alternative dispute resolution
Antitrust
Appellate
Aviation
Corporate and securities
Employment
Entertainment
Environmental
Financial institutions
Governmental and administrative
Health
Immigration
Information technology
Intellectual property
International
International trade
Land use
Litigation
Public finance
Public infrastructure group
Real estate
Reorganization, bankruptcy, and restructuring
Tax
Telecommunications
Trusts and estates

COMPETITORS

Akin Gump	Holland & Knight
Baker & Hostetler	Hughes Hubbard
Baker & McKenzie	Paul, Weiss, Rifkind
Coudert Brothers	Proskauer Rose
Cravath, Swaine	Stroock
Fulbright & Jaworski	Vinson & Elkins

HISTORICAL FINANCIALS

Company Type: Partnership

Income Statement				FYE: December 31
	REVENUE ($ mil.)	NET INCOME ($ mil.)	NET PROFIT MARGIN	EMPLOYEES
12/03	573	—	—	—
12/02	465	—	—	—
12/01	420	—	—	—
12/00	345	—	—	1,250
12/99	213	—	—	1,250
12/98	161	—	—	850
12/97	135	—	—	—
12/96	107	—	—	—
12/95	91	—	—	—
12/94	81	—	—	—
Annual Growth	24.4%	—	—	21.3%

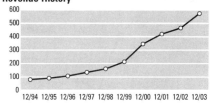

Greenville Hospital System

Greenville Hospital System is a not-for-profit community hospital system serving South Carolina's "Golden Strip" (the I-85 corridor connecting Charlotte, North Carolina, and Atlanta). Founded in 1912 as a community hospital, the system today includes four acute-care hospitals (about 900 beds), as well as a children's hospital, a cancer center, and a nursing home. Greenville Hospital System offers a full range of services, including a primary-care physician network, a health plan, and outpatient care. The company, which also operates a charitable foundation, has teaching affiliations with two medical schools and a research affiliation with Clemson University.

EXECUTIVES

President: Frank D. Pinckney
VP, Financial Services, CFO, and Treasurer: Susan Bichel
CIO: Doran Dunaway
VP Human Resources: Douglas Dorman
Auditors: Ernst & Young LLP

LOCATIONS

HQ: Greenville Hospital System
701 Grove Rd., Greenville, SC 29605
Phone: 864-455-7000   **Fax:** 864-455-6218
Web: www.ghs.org

Greenville Hospital System operates in South Carolina.

PRODUCTS/OPERATIONS

Selected Operations

Allen Bennett Hospital (Greer, acute care)
Greenville Memorial Hospital (acute care)
Hillcrest Hospital (Simpsonville, acute care)
Marshall I. Pickens Hospital (Greenville, psychiatric care)
North Greenville Hospital (Travelers Rest, acute care)
Roger C. Peace Rehabilitation Hospital (Greenville, rehab)
Roger Huntington Nursing Center (Greer, assisted living)

COMPETITORS

Bon Secours Health
Health Management Associates
Novant Health

HISTORICAL FINANCIALS

Company Type: Not-for-profit

Income Statement
FYE: September 30

	REVENUE ($ mil.)	NET INCOME ($ mil.)	NET PROFIT MARGIN	EMPLOYEES
9/03	754	53	7.0%	6,500
9/02	710	33	4.7%	6,500
9/01	691	34	4.9%	6,500
9/00	592	35	5.9%	6,200
9/99	541	10	1.8%	6,000
9/98	494	—	—	5,700
9/97	453	—	—	5,500
9/96	430	—	—	5,500
9/95	399	—	—	5,000
9/94	373	—	—	5,000
Annual Growth	8.1%	52.6%	—	3.0%

2003 Year-End Financials

Debt ratio: 122.2%
Return on equity: 15.9%
Cash ($ mil.): 74
Current ratio: 2.01
Long-term debt ($ mil.): 436

Net Income History

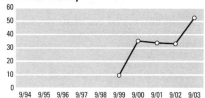

Grocers Supply

Need crackers in Caracas or vanilla in Manila? Grocers Supply Co. distributes groceries near and far. The company (not to be confused with fellow Texas distributor GSC Enterprises) distributes food, health and beauty items, household products, and school and office supplies to more than 1,200 convenience stores, 650 grocery stores, and 200 schools within a 350-mile radius of Houston. Its Grocers Supply International (GSI) division ships supplies to oil company operations, other commercial customers, and US embassies around the world. GSI boasts that it will buy anything to ship anywhere for anyone, including macaroons in Rangoon, or even oleo in Tokyo. Grocers Supply is owned by the Levit family.

The company's subsidiary Bexar County Markets runs 10 Handy Andy Supermarkets in the San Antonio, Texas, area. In 2003 the company acquired the Garland, Texas, division of Fleming Companies when Fleming sold its wholesale distribution business. In 2004 Grocers Supply Co. agreed to acquire Fiesta Mart, Houston's largest ethic grocery chain and its largest customer.

EXECUTIVES

President: Max Levit, age 69
SVP, Accounting: Michael Castleberry, age 46
SVP, Buying: Tom Becker, age 62
SVP, Financial Services: Jim Nelson, age 58
SVP, Operations: Robert Hunt, age 56
SVP, Sales: Dave Hoffman, age 58
VP, Human Resources: Terry Collins, age 48
VP, Management Information Systems: David Bash, age 48
VP, Real Estate: James Arnold, age 58
VP, Sales: Jim Davenport, age 55
President, Bexar County Markets: Terry Warrren
Secretary: Tracy Levit-Larner, age 40
Controller: Bill Stewart, age 52
Auditors: PricewaterhouseCoopers

LOCATIONS

HQ: The Grocers Supply Co., Inc.
3131 E. Holcombe Blvd., Houston, TX 77221
Phone: 713-747-5000   **Fax:** 713-746-5611
Web: www.grocerssupply.com

COMPETITORS

Affiliated Foods	GSC Enterprises	Randall's
AWG	H-E-B	SUPERVALU
Brenham Wholesale	Kroger McLane	Wal-Mart
C.D. Hartnett	Nash Finch	

HISTORICAL FINANCIALS

Company Type: Private

Income Statement
FYE: December 31

	REVENUE ($ mil.)	NET INCOME ($ mil.)	NET PROFIT MARGIN	EMPLOYEES
12/03	1,500	—	—	2,000
12/02	1,500	—	—	2,538
12/01*	1,500	—	—	2,400
5/00	1,400	—	—	2,000
5/99	1,400	—	—	1,800
5/98	1,400	—	—	1,938
5/97	1,300	—	—	1,200
5/96	1,200	—	—	1,200
5/95	1,500	—	—	1,200
5/94	1,450	—	—	1,200
Annual Growth	0.4%	—	—	5.8%

*Fiscal year change

Revenue History

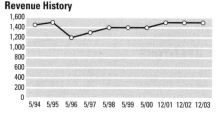

Group Health

Group Health Cooperative of Puget Sound is a not-for-profit managed health care group serving counties in Washington and northern Idaho. Members may participate in HMO, PPO, or point-of-service health plans. The co-op is governed by an 11-person board elected by the organization's members. Specialized services include mental health and substance abuse treatment, hospice services, and HIV/AIDS case management. Group Health Cooperative of Puget Sound has an alliance with Virginia Mason Medical Center (to share medical centers and hospitals), as well as with Kaiser Permanente, one of the nation's largest nonprofit health care systems. The organization is owned by its nearly 540,000 members.

Group Health Cooperative of Puget Sound is one of the largest consumer owned health care companies in the nation.

EXECUTIVES

Chairman: Grant Hendrickson
Vice Chairman: Ruth Ballweg
President and CEO: Cheryl M. Scott, age 54
EVP and CFO: Jim Truess
EVP and COO: Scott Armstrong
EVP and Chief Marketing Officer; President and CEO, Group Health Options: Maureen McLaughlin
EVP, Integrated Group Practice: Peter G. Adler
VP and General Counsel: Rick Woods
VP and Chief Information Officer: Janice Newell
VP Public Affairs and Governance: Pam MacEwan
VP, Human Resources: Brenda Tolbert
Auditors: Deloitte & Touche

LOCATIONS

HQ: Group Health Cooperative of Puget Sound
521 Wall St., Seattle, WA 98121
Phone: 206-448-5600 **Fax:** 206-448-4010
Web: www.ghc.org

PRODUCTS/OPERATIONS

2003 Sales

	$ mil.	% of total
Member dues	1,179.5	60
Other	786.5	40
Total	**1,966.0**	**100**

Selected Services

The Adolescent Center
The Care Center at Kelsey Creek (long-term care)
Center for Attention Deficit Disorders
Consulting Nurse Service
Group Health Credit Union
Group Health Fitness Network
The Group Health Resource Line
The Hear Centers
Language translators
Nutrition Clinics
See Centers/Contact Lens Clinics
Speech, Language and Learning Centers
Take Care stores (wellness products)
Weight Management Programs

COMPETITORS

Aetna
CIGNA
PacifiCare
UnitedHealth Group

HISTORICAL FINANCIALS

Company Type: Cooperative

Income Statement				FYE: December 31
	REVENUE ($ mil.)	NET INCOME ($ mil.)	NET PROFIT MARGIN	EMPLOYEES
12/03	1,966	156	7.9%	9,708
12/02	1,760	—	—	10,519
12/01	1,436	—	—	10,500
12/00	1,400	—	—	9,873
12/99	1,400	—	—	9,746
12/98	1,323	—	—	9,602
12/97	1,016	—	—	8,300
12/96	927	—	—	7,179
12/95	1,039	—	—	7,100
12/94	1,013	—	—	7,100
Annual Growth	7.6%	—	—	3.5%

Revenue History

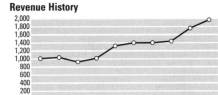

GROWMARK

Retail farm-supply and grain-marketing co-operative GROWMARK can mark its growth by the grain. Through its member-owner co-ops, GROWMARK serves more than 250,000 farmers in the midwestern US and Ontario, Canada. Under the Fast Stop name, the co-op runs fuel stations and convenience stores. Its FS- and NK-brand grains include alfalfa, corn, wheat, and soybeans. GROWMARK also offers fertilizer and buildings such as grain bins. Its Seedway subsidiary markets farm and turf seed. GROWMARK partners with ag giant Archer Daniels Midland, fertilizer maker and distributor CF Industries, pet-food producer PRO-PET, ag company Land O'Lakes, and agribusiness company Syngenta.

EXECUTIVES

Chairman and President: Dan Kelley
CEO: Bill Davisson
CIO and Executive Director, Information Technologies: Tim Piper
VP, Corporate Marketing and Operations: Steve Barwick
VP, Eastern Retail Operations: Steve Buckalew
VP, Finance: Jeff Solberg
VP, Grain: Davis Anderson
VP, Member Services: Dennis Farmer
VP, Strategic Planning and Corporate Services: Vern McGinnis
VP and General Counsel: Steve Carr
Controller: Bill Erlenbush
Auditors: Ernst & Young LLP

LOCATIONS

HQ: GROWMARK, Inc.
1701 Towanda Ave., Bloomington, IL 61701
Phone: 309-557-6000 **Fax:** 309-829-8532
Web: www.growmark.com

COMPETITORS

ADM
Ag Processing
Agricore
Barkley Seed
Cargill
CHS
ConAgra
DeBruce Grain
Pioneer Hi-Bred
Provimi
Rabo AgServices
Sakata Seed
Seminis
Southern States
Terra Nitrogen
Wilbur-Ellis

HISTORICAL FINANCIALS

Company Type: Cooperative

Income Statement				FYE: August 31
	REVENUE ($ mil.)	NET INCOME ($ mil.)	NET PROFIT MARGIN	EMPLOYEES
8/03	1,679	19	1.1%	626
8/02	1,242	18	1.4%	697
8/01	1,461	18	1.3%	745
8/00	1,392	(0)	—	1,000
8/99	1,156	(10)	—	—
8/98	1,300	37	2.8%	966
8/97	1,570	53	3.4%	875
8/96	1,350	—	—	845
8/95	1,100	—	—	900
8/94	950	—	—	—
Annual Growth	6.5%	(15.5%)	—	(4.4%)

2003 Year-End Financials

Debt ratio: 24.9%
Return on equity: 6.1%
Cash ($ mil.): 7
Current ratio: 1.13
Long-term debt ($ mil.): 81

Net Income History

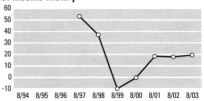

Guardian Industries

Giving its customers a break would never occur to Guardian Industries, one of the world's largest glassmakers. With more than 60 facilities on five continents, Guardian primarily produces float glass and fabricated glass products for the automobile and construction markets. It also makes architectural glass, fiberglass, and automotive trim parts. Through its Guardian Building Products Group, the company operates Guardian Fiberglass, Builder Marts of America, Guardian Building Products Distribution, and Ashley Aluminum. President and CEO William Davidson took Guardian Industries public in 1968 and bought it back for himself in 1985. Davidson is also the managing partner of the Detroit Pistons NBA team.

Guardian has been expanding primarily through international acquisitions and by increasing its already significant position in the building materials business. In 2003 the company expanded to Mexico where it began building a float glass plant.

HISTORY

Guardian Glass began as a small maker of car windshields in Detroit in 1932 during the Great Depression. The company spent the 1930s and 1940s building its business to gain a foothold in glassmaking, historically one of the world's most monopolized industries. In 1949 PPG Industries and Libbey-Owens-Ford (now owned by the UK's Pilkington) agreed to stop their alleged monopolistic activity. William Davidson took over Guardian Glass from his uncle in 1957. As president, he tried to boost the enterprise's standing in the windshield niche, but PPG and Libbey-Owens-Ford refused to sell him raw glass. That year Guardian Glass filed for bankruptcy to reorganize.

The company emerged from bankruptcy in 1960 (the same year Pilkington developed the float process for glassmaking), and in 1965 it was hit with its first patent-infringement lawsuit. Three years later the company went public, changed its name to Guardian Industries, and was refused a license to use Pilkington's float technology. Guardian began an aggressive acquisition strategy in 1969, and in 1970 it hired Ford's top glass man (who knew the float process) and proceeded to build its first float-glass plant in Michigan. PPG sued Guardian in 1972.

Davidson bought the Detroit Pistons in 1974. He applied a do-or-die style that might best be illustrated by the 1979 firing of Piston's coach Dick Vitale, who claims Davidson axed him on his own front doorstep while a curbside limo waited with the motor running.

In 1980 Guardian started making fiberglass and began hiring former workers from insulation maker Manville to duplicate that company's patented technology for fiberglass insulation. Manville successfully sued Guardian in 1981. Guardian opened a Luxembourg plant that year. Pilkington sued Guardian in 1983, but the case was settled out of court three years later. Davidson took Guardian private in 1985, and in 1988 he bought an Indiana auto trim plant. He also built The Palace of Auburn Hills sports arena in 1988.

The 1990s brought more international expansion for Guardian, with plants added in India, Spain, and Venezuela. It also set up a distribution center in Japan, a country known for its tight control of the glass industry. In 1992 Guardian bought OIS Optical Imaging Systems, a maker of computer display screens. Guardian moved its headquarters to Auburn Hills, Michigan, in 1995. Its 1996 purchase of Automotive Moulding boosted its position in the auto plastics and trim market.

Guardian booted its OIS Optical Imaging Systems unit in 1998, citing ongoing losses. That year the company's fiberglass subsidiary bought 50% of building materials buying group Builder Marts of America, giving Guardian a foothold in the markets for lumber and roofing products. Also in 1998 Davidson made a failed attempt to buy the Tampa Bay Lightning hockey team.

In 1999 Guardian bought Siam Guardian Glass Ltd. from Siam Cement Plc, the company's partner in Thailand. The next year Guardian acquired Cameron Ashley Building Products (renamed Ashley Aluminum), a distributor with more than 160 branches in the US and Canada. In 2002 the company expanded to Poland where it built a float glass plant.

EXECUTIVES

President and CEO: William M. (Bill) Davidson, age 81
EVP: Ralph J. Gerson
Group VP, Finance and CFO: Jeffrey A. Knight
President and CEO, Automotive Products Group: D. James Davis
President, Building Products Group: Duane H. Faulkner
President, Glass Group: Russell J. Ebeid
Director of Communications: Gayle A. Joseph

LOCATIONS

HQ: Guardian Industries Corp.
2300 Harmon Rd., Auburn Hills, MI 48326
Phone: 248-340-1800 **Fax:** 248-340-9988
Web: www.guardian.com

Guardian Industries operates worldwide manufacturing and distribution facilities.

PRODUCTS/OPERATIONS

Selected Products and Services

Architectural Glass
  Custom fabrication
  Float glass
  Insulating glass
  Laminated glass
  Mirrors
  Patterned glass
  Reflective coated glass
  Tempered glass
Automotive Systems
  Bodyside (mud flaps, wheel covers)
  Front and rear end (grilles, rub strips)
  Side window (door-frame moldings)
  Windshield (window-surround moldings)
Guardian Building Products
  Aluminum screen doors
  Carports
  Ceiling tile
  Door frames
  Doors
  Fiberglass insulation
  Formica
  Metal roofing
  Patio covers
  Plywood
  Rebar
  Sheetrock
  Storm doors
  Windows
Guardian Fiberglass
  Fiberglass insulation
Retail Auto Glass
  Auto glass
  Auto glass repair and replacement
  Insurance claim processing

COMPETITORS

Apogee Enterprises
Asahi Glass
Corning
CRH
Donnelly
Johns Manville
Nippon Sheet Glass
Owens Corning
Pilkington
PPG
Safelite Group
Saint-Gobain
Vitro

HISTORICAL FINANCIALS

Company Type: Private

Income Statement
FYE: December 31

	ESTIMATED REVENUE ($ mil.)	NET INCOME ($ mil.)	NET PROFIT MARGIN	EMPLOYEES
12/03	4,000	—	—	19,000
12/02	3,950	—	—	19,000
12/01	4,000	—	—	19,000
12/00	4,000	—	—	20,000
12/99	3,650	—	—	15,000
12/98	2,200	—	—	15,000
12/97	2,000	—	—	14,000
12/96	1,900	—	—	13,000
12/95	1,700	—	—	12,000
12/94	1,500	—	—	10,000
Annual Growth	11.5%	—	—	7.4%

Revenue History

Guardian Life Insurance

When your guardian angel fails you, there's Guardian Life Insurance Company of America. The mutual company, owned by its policy holders, offers life insurance, disability income insurance, and — more recently — retirement programs. Guardian Life Insurance Company of America's employee health indemnity plans provide HMO, PPO, and dental and vision plans, as well as disability plans. In the retirement area, Guardian has long offered the Park Avenue group of mutual funds and annuity products, managed by its Guardian Investor Services.

To meet competition in the quickly deregulating financial services area, the company is building its wealth management capabilities to target baby boomers getting ready for retirement. It created broker-dealer Park Avenue Securities and launched Guardian Trust Company to offer trust and investment management services. The company has also added long-term care insurance to its product line.

Guardian has also grown through acquisition, buying complementary firms, such as disability insurance specialist Berkshire Life Insurance.

HISTORY

Hugo Wesendonck came to the US from Germany in 1850 to escape a death sentence for his part in an abortive 1848 revolution. After working in the silk business in Philadelphia, he moved to New York, which was home to more ethnic Germans than any city save Berlin and Vienna.

In 1860 Wesendonck and other expatriates formed an insurance company to serve the German-American community. Germania Life Insurance was chartered as a stock mutual, which paid dividends to shareholders and policy owners. Wesendonck was its first president.

The Civil War blocked the company's growth in the South, but it expanded in the rest of the US and by 1867 even operated in South America.

After the Civil War, many insurers foundered from high costs. Wesendonck battled this by implementing strict cost controls and limiting commissions, allowing the company to continue issuing dividends and rebates on its policyholders' premiums.

In the 1870s Germania opened offices in Europe, and for the next few decades much of the company's growth was there. By 1910, 46% of sales originated in Europe. The company's target clientele in the US decreased between the 1890s and WWI as German immigration slowed, and its market share dropped from ninth in 1880 to 21st in 1910.

During WWI the company lost contact with its German business. Prodded by anti-German sentiment in the US, the company changed its name to The Guardian Life Insurance Company of America in 1917. After WWI the company began winding down its German business (a process that lasted until 1952).

In 1924 Guardian began mutualizing but could not complete the process until 1944 because of probate problems with a shareholder's estate.

After WWII, Guardian offered noncancelable medical insurance (1955) and group insurance (1957). The company formed Guardian Investor Services in 1969 to offer mutual funds; two years later it established Guardian Insurance & Annuity to sell variable contracts. In 1989 it organized Guardian Asset Management to handle pension funds.

In 1993, as indemnity health costs rose, the company moved into managed care via its membership in Private Health Care Systems, a consortium of commercial insurance carriers offering managed health care products and services. This allowed Guardian to offer HMO and PPO products.

Guardian entered a joint marketing agreement in 1995 with HMO Physicians Health Services, which contracts with physicians and hospitals in the New York tri-state area. In 1996 the company acquired Managed Dental Care of California and an interest in Physicians Health Services.

Facing deregulation and consolidation in the financial services area, as well as the demutualization of some of its largest competitors, Guardian in the late 1990s decided to add depth to its employee benefits lines and breadth to its wealth management lines.

In 1999 Guardian formed its broker-dealer subsidiary and received a thrift license to facilitate creation of a trust business. Acquisitions included Innovative Underwriters Services, Fiduciary Insurance Co. of America, and managed dental care companies First Commonwealth and First Choice Dental Network. In 2001 the company moved to boost its disability business with the purchase of Berkshire Life Insurance.

EXECUTIVES

President, CEO, and Director: Dennis J. Manning
EVP and CFO: Robert E. Broatch, age 49
EVP and CIO: Dennis S. Callahan
EVP and Chief Actuary: Armand M. de Palo
EVP and Director: Edward K. Kane
EVP, Risk Management Products: Gary B. Lenderink
EVP, Equity Products: Bruce C. Long
EVP and Chief Investment Officer: Thomas G. Sorell
SVP, Individual Markets: David W. Allen
SVP and Corporate Secretary: Joseph A. Caruso
SVP, Human Resources: James D. (Jim) Ranton
SVP, Corporate Marketing: Nancy F. Rogers
SVP, Group Insurance: Richard A. White
VP, Group Pensions: Dennis P. Mosticchio
VP and General Counsel: John Peluso
VP, Agency Growth and Development: Thomas W. Slack
VP, Reinsurance: Jeremy Starr
Auditors: PricewaterhouseCoopers LLP

LOCATIONS

HQ: The Guardian Life Insurance Company of America
7 Hanover Sq., New York, NY 10004
Phone: 212-598-8000 **Fax:** 212-919-2170
Web: www.guardianlife.com

Guardian Life Insurance Company of America has operations throughout the US.

PRODUCTS/OPERATIONS

2003 Sales

	% of total
Premiums, annuity considerations & fund deposits	81
Net investment income	16
Other income	3
Total	**100**

Selected Subsidiaries and Affiliates

Berkshire Life Insurance Company of America
First Commonwealth, Inc.
Guardian Baillie Gifford Limited
The Guardian Insurance & Annuity Company, Inc.
Guardian Investor Services LLC
Guardian Trust Company, FSB
Innovative Underwriters, Inc.
Managed Dental Care
Managed DentalGuard (New Jersey)
Managed DentalGuard (Texas)
Park Avenue Life Insurance Company
Park Avenue Securities LLC

COMPETITORS

Aetna
AIG American General
Allstate
Anthem
AXA Financial
Charles Schwab
CIGNA
Citigroup
CNA Financial
FMR
General Re
The Hartford
John Hancock Financial Services
Liberty Mutual
Lincoln National
MassMutual
Merrill Lynch
MetLife
Nationwide
New York Life
Northwestern Mutual
Oxford Health
Pacific Mutual
Principal Financial
Prudential
UBS Financial Services
UnitedHealth Group
UnumProvident
USAA
WellPoint Health Networks

HISTORICAL FINANCIALS
Company Type: Mutual company

Income Statement				FYE: December 31
	ASSETS ($ mil.)	NET INCOME ($ mil.)	INCOME AS % OF ASSETS	EMPLOYEES
12/03	21,671	218	1.0%	5,500
12/02	34,074	(283)	—	5,500
12/01	34,333	170	0.5%	6,000
12/00	32,359	563	1.7%	6,000
12/99	31,696	325	1.0%	5,465
12/98	25,854	160	0.6%	—
12/97	22,089	299	1.4%	4,800
12/96	18,196	173	1.0%	5,155
12/95	15,811	125	0.8%	5,322
12/94	13,567	144	1.1%	7,602
Annual Growth	5.3%	4.7%	—	(3.5%)

2003 Year-End Financials
Equity as % of assets: 12.0%   Long-term debt ($ mil.): 15,704
Return on assets: 0.8%   Sales ($ mil.): 6,732
Return on equity: 5.3%

Net Income History

Gulf Oil

Gulf Oil bridges the gap between petroleum producers and retail sales outlets. The petroleum wholesaler distributes gasoline and diesel fuel to about 1,800 Gulf-brand stations in 11 northeastern states. Gulf Oil, which owns and operates 12 storage terminals, also distributes motor oils, lubricants, and heating oil to commercial, industrial, and utility customers. The company has alliances with terminal operators in areas in the Northeast where it does not have a proprietary terminal. Noteworthy for providing the world's first drive-in service station, Gulf Oil was established in 1901 with an oil strike in Spindletop, Texas. The oil company restructured into seven operating companies in the 1970s.

EXECUTIVES

CEO: John Kaneb
President: Gary Kaneb
Controller: Alice Kuhne
Director Human Resources: Karen Channel

LOCATIONS

HQ: Gulf Oil Limited Partnership
90 Everett Ave., Chelsea, MA 02150
Phone: 617-889-9000 **Fax:** 617-884-0637
Web: www.gulfoil.com

Gulf Oil operates in 11 northeastern US states.

PRODUCTS/OPERATIONS

Selected Products

Antifreeze	Kerosene
Gasoline	Synthetic lubricants
Grease	Transmission fluid
Heating oil	Zinc-free oils

COMPETITORS

Amerada Hess
BP
CITGO
Exxon Mobil
Getty Petroleum Marketing
Global Companies
Motiva Enterprises
Premcor
Sunoco

HISTORICAL FINANCIALS
Company Type: Partnership

Income Statement				FYE: September 30
	ESTIMATED REVENUE ($ mil.)	NET INCOME ($ mil.)	NET PROFIT MARGIN	EMPLOYEES
9/03	2,100	—	—	150
9/02	1,680	—	—	150
9/01	1,970	—	—	200
9/00	1,800	—	—	185
9/99	1,808	—	—	185
9/98	1,800	—	—	185
9/97	2,300	—	—	200
9/96	1,900	—	—	200
9/95	2,000	—	—	200
9/94	1,800	—	—	200
Annual Growth	1.7%	—	—	(3.1%)

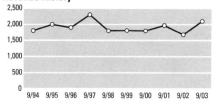

Revenue History

Gulf States Toyota

Even good ol' boys buy foreign cars from Gulf States Toyota. One of only two US Toyota distributors not owned by Toyota Motor Sales (the other is JM Family Enterprises' Southeast Toyota Distributors), the company distributes Toyota cars, trucks, and sport utility vehicles in Arkansas, Louisiana, Mississippi, Oklahoma, and Texas. Founded in 1969 by Thomas Friedkin and still owned by The Friedkin Companies, Gulf States distributes new Toyotas, parts, and accessories to around 150 dealers in its region. Gulf States Toyota has acquired Metrix Holdings in New York.

EXECUTIVES
President and General Manager: Toby Hynes
CFO: Frank Gruen
VP, Human Resources: Dominic Gallo
VP, Marketing: J.C. Fassino
VP, Sales Operations: Tom Bittenbender
Director, Administration: David Copeland
Senior Manager of Marketing Support: Eric Williamson
Scion Marketing Manager: Tom Lauterbach
Technical Capacity Manager: Don Cole

LOCATIONS
HQ: Gulf States Toyota, Inc.
7701 Wilshire Place Dr., Houston, TX 77040
Phone: 713-580-3300 **Fax:** 713-580-3332

COMPETITORS
BMW
DaimlerChrysler
David McDavid Auto Group
Ford
General Motors
Honda
JM Family Enterprises
Kia Motors
Mazda
Nissan North America
Volkswagen
Volvo

HISTORICAL FINANCIALS
Company Type: Private

Income Statement				FYE: December 31
	ESTIMATED REVENUE ($ mil.)	NET INCOME ($ mil.)	NET PROFIT MARGIN	EMPLOYEES
12/02	3,700	—	—	3,000
12/01	3,800	—	—	3,000
12/00	3,250	—	—	1,650
12/99	3,158	—	—	1,600
12/98	2,500	—	—	1,600
12/97	2,300	—	—	1,600
12/96	1,700	—	—	1,500
12/95	1,600	—	—	1,500
12/94	1,800	—	—	1,500
12/93	1,534	—	—	1,500
Annual Growth	10.3%	—	—	8.0%

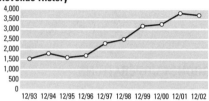

Revenue History

Guthy-Renker

What do Kathie Lee Gifford, Cindy Crawford, Victoria Principal, and Tony Robbins have in common? Each has starred in a program produced by Guthy-Renker, one of the largest infomercial producers in the US. The firm's pitch people hawk a variety of goods and services, including skin care products and cosmetics (the company's primary category), fitness equipment, and motivational tapes. In addition, Guthy-Renker sells *The Dean Martin Celebrity Roasts*. The company also pursues marketing opportunities through direct mail, retail, and telemarketing. Guthy-Renker was founded in 1988 by co-CEOs Bill Guthy and Greg Renker, after being spun off from Guthy's Cassette Productions Unlimited (CPU).

EXECUTIVES
Co-CEO: William Bill Guthy
Co-CEO: Greg Renker
EVP, CFO, and COO: Kevin Knee
EVP Business Affairs and New Development: Ben Van De Bunt

LOCATIONS
HQ: Guthy-Renker Corp.
41-550 Eclectic St., Ste. 200, Palm Desert, CA 92260
Phone: 760-773-9022 **Fax:** 760-733-9016
Web: www.guthy-renker.com

PRODUCTS/OPERATIONS
Selected Infomercials
The Dean Martin Celebrity Roasts
The Dean Martin Variety Show
Comprehensive Formula nutritional products (hosted by Marilu Henner)
Get The Edge motivational (hosted by Tony Robbins)
Meaningful Beauty skin care (hosted by Cindy Crawford)
Natural Advantage skin care (hosted by Kathie Lee Gifford)
Principal Secret skin care (hosted by Victoria Principal)
Pro-Activ Solutions skin care (hosted by Vanessa Williams and Judith Light)
Sheer Cover make-up (hosted by Leeza Gibbons)
Winsor Pilates weight loss (hosted by Daisy Fuentes and Mary Winsor)
Youthful Essence skin care (hosted by Susan Lucci)

COMPETITORS
Aloette
GenesisIntermedia
GT Brands
Hydron
IAC
QVC
Ronco
Thane International
ValueVision Media

HISTORICAL FINANCIALS
Company Type: Private

Income Statement				FYE: December 31
	REVENUE ($ mil.)	NET INCOME ($ mil.)	NET PROFIT MARGIN	EMPLOYEES
12/03	970	—	—	—
12/02	800	—	—	—
12/01	700	—	—	175
12/00	500	—	—	—
12/99	350	—	—	200
12/98	350	—	—	200
12/97	350	—	—	190
12/96	300	—	—	126
12/95	270	—	—	67
12/94	125	—	—	63
Annual Growth	25.6%	—	—	15.7%

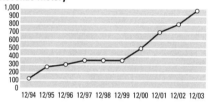

Revenue History

H Group Holding

Owned and operated by the Pritzkers, Chicago's financial super-family, H Group Holding is the holding company for Hyatt Hotels, Conwood tobacco company, and Classic Residence senior communities. Since the death of Jay Pritzker in 1999, family squabbles over their vast $15 billion fortune have led to talks of breaking up the empire and taking Hyatt public. The Pritzker portfolio also includes the Marmon Group (including credit check subsidiary Trans Union), Pritzker Realty, and a stake in the Royal Caribbean cruise ship line. The family is active in philanthropic circles through the Pritzker Foundation.

EXECUTIVES
CEO: Thomas J. Pritzker, age 53
CFO: Frank Borg

LOCATIONS
HQ: H Group Holding Inc.
200 W. Madison St., Ste. 3800, Chicago, IL 60606
Phone: 312-750-1234   **Fax:** 312-750-8550

COMPETITORS
Cendant
Four Seasons Hotels
GE
Henry Crown
Hilton
Host Marriott
ITT Industries
Marriott
Starwood Hotels & Resorts
Swisher International
UST
Wyndham

HISTORICAL FINANCIALS
Company Type: Private

Income Statement			FYE: December 31
	REVENUE ($ mil.)	NET INCOME ($ mil.)	NET PROFIT MARGIN	EMPLOYEES
12/02	2,047	—	—	41,000
12/01	2,000	—	—	41,000
12/00	2,300	—	—	70,000
12/99	2,200	—	—	70,000
12/98	2,000	—	—	70,000
12/97	1,378	—	—	43,000
12/96	869	—	—	—
Annual Growth	15.3%	—	—	(0.9%)

Revenue History

Haggen

Haggen showers shoppers in the Pacific Northwest with salmon, coffee, and other essentials. The area's largest independent grocer, Haggen operates about 30 combination supermarket/drugstores in Washington and Oregon. Most upscale Haggen Food & Pharmacy stores feature specialty departments, while the TOP Food & Drug outlets emphasize savings; however, both may offer such amenities as Starbucks Coffee shops, Blockbuster video outlets, or child-care centers. To keep up with the Joneses of supermarket fame and fortune, Haggen partnered with ShopEaze.com (an e-commerce service provider), which failed, leaving Haggen without an online store. Brothers and co-chairmen Don and Rick Haggen own the chain.

Through its acquisition of a Fairhaven Market on Seattle's South Side, Haggen is experimenting with a smaller, neighborhood grocery store format.

Haggen announced in June 2004 that it was switching suppliers from Minneapolis-based SUPERVALU to Associated Grocers of Seattle.

EXECUTIVES
Co-Chairman: Donald E. (Don) Haggen
Co-Chairman: Richard R. (Rick) Haggen, age 59
President and CEO: Dale C. Henley
SVP, Sales and Merchandising: Dave Norton
Group VP, Administration: Jeff Wood
VP, Center Store: Scott Brown
VP, Finance: Tom Kenney
VP, Marketing: Scott Smith
VP, New Business: Brad Haggen
VP, Perishables: Mike Lobaugh
Controller: Gary Hall
Director, Food Service: Cheryl-Ann Jones
Director, Human Resources and Payroll:
  Derrick Anderson

LOCATIONS
HQ: Haggen, Inc.
2211 Rimland Dr., Bellingham, WA 98226
Phone: 360-733-8720   **Fax:** 360-650-8235
Web: www.haggen.com

Haggen operates Haggen Food & Pharmacy stores in Washington and Oregon and TOP Food & Drug stores in Washington.

PRODUCTS/OPERATIONS

Selected Departments and Services
Bakery
Banking
Blockbuster Video
Cash machines
Deli
Dry cleaning
Full-service floral department
Garden supplies
In-store home economist
Just for Kids child-care center
Library book drop off
Market Street Café
Meat
Orient Express
Parcel pickup
Pharmacy
Produce
Seafood
Service deli catering
Starbucks Coffee shop
Sushi
Wine

COMPETITORS
Albertson's
Brown & Cole Stores
Costco Wholesale
Fred Meyer Stores
Quality Food
Safeway
SAM'S CLUB
Trader Joe's Co
Wal-Mart
WinCo Foods

HISTORICAL FINANCIALS
Company Type: Private

Income Statement			FYE: December 31
	REVENUE ($ mil.)	NET INCOME ($ mil.)	NET PROFIT MARGIN	EMPLOYEES
12/03	780	—	—	4,000
12/02	760	—	—	4,000
12/01	700	—	—	4,000
12/00	666	—	—	4,000
12/99	579	—	—	3,500
12/98	521	—	—	3,200
12/97	450	—	—	2,850
12/96	436	—	—	3,000
12/95	420	—	—	2,600
12/94	400	—	—	2,400
Annual Growth	7.7%	—	—	5.8%

Revenue History

Hallmark

As the #1 producer of warm fuzzies, Hallmark Cards is the Goliath of greeting cards. The company's cards are sold under brand names such as Hallmark, Shoebox, and Ambassador and can be found in more than 42,000 US retail stores (about 4,300 of these stores bear the Hallmark Gold Crown name; the majority of these stores are franchised). Hallmark also owns Binney & Smith (maker of Crayola brand crayons) and portrait studio chain The Picture People. It offers electronic greeting cards and flowers through its Web site, Hallmark.com, and produces television movies through Hallmark Entertainment and its majority-owned Crown Media unit. Members of the founding Hall family own two-thirds of Hallmark.

Not resting on well-engraved laurels, Hallmark has announced its intention to triple its revenue by 2010. While it plans to continue expanding its greeting card empire, the company is also intent on stretching its reach in markets such as personal development and family entertainment. Hallmark is bringing a literary slant to its products with a new line of cards and products developed by Pulitzer Prize nominee and poet Maya Angelou.

Hallmark decided to move some of its IT operations to Affiliated Computer Services in a seven-year deal worth $230 million; the Dallas-based company will open a center near the Hallmark headquarters to handle the work.

The company's Crown Media unit is considering selling its overseas operations as well as foreign rights to its program library.

HISTORY

Eighteen-year-old Joyce Hall started selling picture postcards from two shoe boxes in his room at the Kansas City, Missouri, YMCA in 1910. His brother Rollie joined him the next year, and the two added greeting cards to their line in 1912. The brothers opened Hall Brothers, a store that sold postcards, gifts, books, and stationery, but it was destroyed in a 1915 fire. The Halls got a loan, bought an engraving company, and produced their first original cards in time for Christmas.

In 1921 a third brother, William, joined the firm, which started stamping the backs of its cards with the phrase "A Hallmark Card." By 1922 Hall Brothers had salespeople in all 48 states. The firm began selling internationally in 1931.

Hall Brothers patented the "Eye-Vision" display case for greeting cards in 1936 and sold it to retailers across the country. The company aired its first radio ad in 1938. The next year it introduced a friendship card, displaying a cart filled with purple pansies. The card became the company's best-seller. During WWII Joyce Hall persuaded the government not to curtail paper supplies, arguing that his greeting cards were essential to the nation's morale.

The company opened its first retail store in 1950. The following year marked the first production of *Hallmark Hall of Fame*, TV's longest-running dramatic series and winner of more Emmy awards than any other program. Hall Brothers changed its name to Hallmark Cards in 1954 and introduced its Ambassador line of cards five years later.

Hallmark introduced paper party products and started putting *Peanuts* characters on cards in 1960. Donald Hall, Joyce Hall's son, was appointed CEO in 1966. Two years later Hallmark opened Crown Center, which surrounded company headquarters in Kansas City. Disaster struck in 1981 when two walkways collapsed at Crown Center's Hyatt Regency hotel, killing 114 and injuring 225.

Joyce Hall died in 1982, and Donald Hall became both chairman and CEO. Hallmark acquired Crayola Crayon maker Binney & Smith in 1984. It introduced Shoebox Greetings, a line of nontraditional cards, in 1986. Irvine Hockaday replaced Donald Hall as CEO the same year (Hall continued as chairman).

The company joined with Information Storage Devices in 1993 to market recordable greeting cards. It unveiled its Web site, Hallmark.com, in 1996 and began offering electronic greeting cards. Hallmark's 1998 acquisition of UK-based Creative Publications boosted the company into the top spot in the British greeting card market. The following year the company acquired portrait studio chain The Picture People and Christian greeting card maker DaySpring Cards. Hallmark also introduced Warm Wishes, a line of 99-cent cards. The company also unveiled the Hallmark Home Collection, a line of home furnishings.

The company began testing overnight flower delivery in the US just in time for Valentine's Day 2000. Hallmark Entertainment subsidiary Crown Media went public in that same year. Hockaday retired as president and CEO at the end of 2001; vice chairman Donald Hall Jr. took the additional title of CEO in early 2002.

EXECUTIVES

Chairman: Donald J. Hall
Vice Chairman, President, and CEO: Donald J. (Don) Hall Jr., age 48
EVP and CFO: Robert J. Druten, age 57
EVP Corporate Strategy: Anil Jagtiani, age 42
EVP and Chief Marketing Officer, Hallmark Channel: Chris R. Moseley, age 52
SVP Creative Product Development: Paul Barker
SVP Human Resources: David E. Hall, age 41
SVP Information Technology: Steve Hawn
SVP Public Affairs and Communication: Steve Doyal
SVP Sales: Steve Paoletti
VP Operations: Wayne Herran
VP Trade Development: Vince G. Burke
VP Supermarket Sales: Marc Woodward
Director of Marketing: Jen Weiss
Director of Performance Management and Rewards: Jeff Blair
President and CEO, Binney & Smith: Mark J. Schwab
President and CEO, Crown Media: David J. Evans, age 63
President, Hallmark Canada: Roger Baranowski
President, Hallmark Entertainment; Chairman, Crown Media and Hallmark Entertainment Investments: Robert A. Halmi Jr., age 47
President, Hallmark North America: Donald H. Fletcher
President, Hallmark Loyalty Marketing: Scott Robinette
Manager Corporate Media Relations: Julie O'Dell

LOCATIONS

HQ: Hallmark Cards, Inc.
2501 McGee St., Kansas City, MO 64108
Phone: 816-274-5111 **Fax:** 816-274-5061
Web: www.hallmark.com

Hallmark Cards has operations in Australia, Belgium, Canada, Denmark, Japan, Mexico, the Netherlands, New Zealand, Puerto Rico, Spain, the UK, and the US.

PRODUCTS/OPERATIONS

Selected Product Lines
Ambassador (greeting cards)
Fresh Ink (greeting cards)
Life Mosaic (cards and gifts by poet Maya Angelou)
Hallmark.com (electronic greeting cards, gifts, flowers)
Hallmark Flowers (flower delivery)
Keepsake (holiday ornaments and other collectibles)
Mahogany (products celebrating African-American heritage)
Nature's Sketchbook (cards and gifts)
Shoebox (greeting cards)
Sinceramente (Spanish-language greeting cards)
Tree of Life (products celebrating Jewish heritage)
Selected Subsidiaries
Binney & Smith (Crayola brand crayons and markers)
Crown Center Redevelopment (retail complex)
DaySpring Cards (Christian greeting cards)
Gift Certificate Center (business and consumer certificates)
Hallmark Entertainment (television, movies, and home video production)
Crown Media Holdings (79%, pay television channels)
Halls Merchandising (department store)
Image Arts (discount greeting card distribution)
InterArt (specialized cards)
Irresistible Ink (handwriting and marketing service)
Litho-Krome (lithography)
The Picture People (portrait studio chain)
William Arthur (invitations, stationery)

COMPETITORS

1-800-FLOWERS.COM
American Greetings
Amscan
Andrews McMeel Universal
Blyth
CPI Corp.
CSS Industries
Dixon Ticonderoga
Enesco Group
Faber-Castell
Lifetouch
Nobleworks
Olan Mills
Paramount Cards
Party City
PCA International
SPS Studios
Syratech
Thomas Nelson
Time Warner
Viacom
Walt Disney

HISTORICAL FINANCIALS

Company Type: Private

Income Statement FYE: December 31

	REVENUE ($ mil.)	NET INCOME ($ mil.)	NET PROFIT MARGIN	EMPLOYEES
12/03	4,300	—	—	18,000
12/02	4,000	—	—	18,645
12/01	4,000	—	—	20,000
12/00	4,200	—	—	24,500
12/99	4,200	—	—	21,000
12/98	3,900	—	—	20,945
12/97	3,700	—	—	12,554
12/96	3,600	—	—	12,600
12/95	3,400	—	—	12,100
12/94	3,800	—	—	12,800
Annual Growth	1.4%	—	—	3.9%

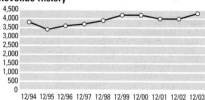

Revenue History

Hampton Affiliates

As a vertically integrated lumber company, Hampton Affiliates knows trees from the seedling to the stud. One of Oregon's top timber firms, Hampton produces about 900 million board feet of lumber annually. The company has more than 180,000 acres of timberland and owns tree farms and mills in Oregon and Washington. Through its Hampton Distribution Companies division, it distributes doors, windows, and other building materials; its Lane Stanton Vance division produces lumber from imported and domestic hardwood. Hampton has added stud lumber and distribution operations to supply home-building centers. L. M. "Bud" Hampton founded the company in 1942, and the Hampton family still owns it.

Hampton Affiliates has grown primarily by adding timberland and increasing its manufacturing capacity and distribution operations. Its plan for future growth includes expanding its resource base, adding manufacturing plants, and investing in new technologies and equipment upgrades. The company also plans to diversify into new market segments and opportunities throughout the Pacific Rim region.

During 2002 the company acquired Darrington Lumber Mills and completed a timberland exchange of 92,000 acres.

EXECUTIVES

Vice Chairman: Ronald C. (Ron) Parker
CEO: Steven J. (Steve) Zika
CTO: Andy McNiece
VP Finance and CFO: Robert Bluhm
VP Manufacturing: Bruce Mallory
Controller: Arvid Lacy
President, HLS: Michael (Mike) Phillips
General Sales Manager: Carter Stinton
Director, Human Resources: Dave Salmon

LOCATIONS

HQ: Hampton Affiliates
9600 SW Barnes Rd., Ste. 200, Portland, OR 97225
Phone: 503-297-7691 **Fax:** 503-203-6607
Web: www.hamptonlumber.com

Hampton Affiliates owns sawmills in Oregon and Washington, and distribution facilities in California.

PRODUCTS/OPERATIONS

Selected Products

Clear and industrial lumber
Dimensional lumber
Domestic and imported hardwood lumber
Engineered wood
Panel products
Residential doors
Siding and trim
Stud lumber
Timbers
Wood windows

Selected Services

Custom milling
Design floor and roof systems
Engineered wood take-offs
Overseas delivery
Rail car delivery
Reloading
Softwood remanufacturing
Truck delivery
Warehousing

COMPETITORS

Boise Cascade
Crown Pacific Partners
Georgia-Pacific Corporation
International Paper
Louisiana-Pacific
Roseburg Forest Products
Sierra Pacific Industries
Simpson Investment
TreeSource
West Fraser Timber
Western Forest Products
Weyerhaeuser

HISTORICAL FINANCIALS

Company Type: Private

Income Statement				FYE: January 31
	REVENUE ($ mil.)	NET INCOME ($ mil.)	NET PROFIT MARGIN	EMPLOYEES
1/04	700	—	—	1,300
1/03	700	—	—	1,300
1/02	700	—	—	1,300
1/01	721	—	—	1,300
1/00	715	—	—	1,100
1/99	525	—	—	900
1/98	500	—	—	800
Annual Growth	5.8%	—	—	8.4%

Revenue History

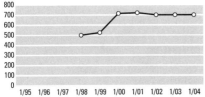

Harbour Group

Troubled manufacturers can seek refuge with Harbour Group Industries, a conglomerate that acquires and consolidates manufacturing companies in fragmented industries. Harbour's current portfolio includes companies in about 30 different industries, including auto accessories, chimney and fireplace products, industrial cleaning, paint sundries, plastics-processing equipment, heat exchangers, and textile machinery. Since its founding in 1976, Harbour Group has acquired about 130 companies; most have been combined with similar acquisitions. New company additions include companies specializing in stain removal, paint removal and wood finishing, and touchscreen entertainment products.

Experts in the acquisition game, the folks at Harbour Group look for companies in mature but fragmented industries, which they build and fortify by continually re-investing in them and combining them with newly acquired complementary companies. In this way Harbour Group creates clusters of companies within a given industry to create operational efficiencies. When the company enters a new business segment, the first acquisition is known as the "platform" company, and from there the buy-and-build strategy begins anew. Harbour Group takes a long-term approach with its acquisitions, retaining existing management and assisting them with operational needs and investments.

In 2002 Harbour Group bought Merit Industries, the largest developer and manufacturer of touch-screen entertainment systems in North America and the worldwide leader in countertop video game systems (card games, trivia, and the like) seen in bars and restaurants. Merit is the platform company of the newly created Entertainment Products Group. Auto Meter Industries, another 2002 purchase, is the platform company for Harbour Group's new Performance Products Group. Auto Meter makes gauges, tachometers, and similar products for the professional auto racing industry as well as your everyday hot rodders.

Other company segments include industrial springs, specialty distribution, and building products. Chairman and CEO Sam Fox controls the company.

EXECUTIVES

Chairman and CEO: Sam Fox, age 73
President and COO: Jeff Fox
Managing Director: Mark Leeker
SVP and CFO: William (Bill) Willhite
VP and Treasurer: Mike Santoni
Corporate Development: Clay Hunter
Office Administrator: Harriet Lovins

LOCATIONS

HQ: Harbour Group Industries, Inc.
7701 Forsyth Blvd., Ste. 600, St. Louis, MO 63105
Phone: 314-727-5550   **Fax:** 314-727-9912
Web: www.harbourgroup.com

PRODUCTS/OPERATIONS

Selected Divisions and Companies

Automotive Accessories
  FloTool Corp.
  Hopkins Manufacturing Corp.
  TAP, Inc.
Building Products Group
  WSI Group
Chimney and Fireplace Products
  Copperfield Chimney Supply, Inc.
Entertainment Products Group
  Merit Industries, Inc.
Heat Exchangers
  Southern Heat Exchanger Corp.
Industrial Cleaning
  C-Tech Industries
  Cuda Corporation
  The Hotsy Corporation
  Landa Water Cleaning Systems
  Rhino Pressure Washers
Industrial Springs
  Hyperco, Inc.
  Matthew Warren Holdings, Inc.
  Peck Spring Co.

Paint Sundries
  Gonzo Corporation
  Homax, Inc.
  JASCO Chemical Corp.
  Magic American Corporation
  Tile Care Products Inc.
Performance Products
  Auto Meter Products, Inc.
Plastics-Processing Equipment
  HydReclaim
  Nelmor
Specialty Distribution Group
  Classic Chevy International Eckler Industries
Textile Machinery
  Ashby Jacumin Engineering & Machine Company
  Marshall and Williams
  RFG Enterprises, Inc.
  Tube-Tex

COMPETITORS

Albert Trostel & Sons
AptarGroup
Baxter
Federal Signal
Flow
Giddings & Lewis
Haskel
Ingersoll-Rand Industrial Solutions
Kennametal
Milacron
Rieter Holding
Swagelok
United States Surgical

HISTORICAL FINANCIALS

Company Type: Private

Income Statement				FYE: December 31
	ESTIMATED REVENUE ($ mil.)	NET INCOME ($ mil.)	NET PROFIT MARGIN	EMPLOYEES
12/02	2,800	—	—	—
12/01	2,800	—	—	—
Annual Growth	0.0%	—	—	—

Revenue History

Harpo

Everyone knows Oprah Winfrey is an exceptional businesswoman; there's no need to Harpo on it. Unrelated to the silent Marx brother, Harpo controls the entertainment interests of talk show host/actress/producer Oprah Winfrey. *The Oprah Winfrey Show* is the highest-rated TV talk show in history, seen in almost every US market and in 110 countries. Winfrey's show has ranked number one among all talk shows for virtually every season of its long run (it is currently in its 19th season). Harpo also produces feature films (*Beloved*, which also starred Winfrey) and made-for-TV movies (*Oprah Winfrey Presents: Tuesdays with Morrie*) and publishes *O, The Oprah Magazine* with Hearst at a circulation of about 2.6 million.

Winfrey is worth about $1 billion according to *Forbes* magazine's list of billionaires. (She is the first black woman to join the ranks.) Her innovative ideas (such as Oprah's Book Club, which sent many previously little known titles to the top of bestseller lists) have earned *The Oprah Winfrey Show* about 39 Emmys. Each week her show has some 23 million viewers in the US, about three-fourths of whom are women. The talk show icon had previously announced that her show would end in 2006, the 20th anniversary of the program; however, she has since signed a new contract to keep it on the air into 2011.

Winfrey also owns about 8% of women's cable company Oxygen Media. The Oxygen network airs her *Oprah After the Show* program, where viewers can see the candid conversations Oprah has with her studio audience.

Winfrey founded Harpo (Oprah spelled backwards) in 1986.

HISTORY

Oprah Winfrey began her broadcasting career in 1973 at age 19 as a news anchor at Nashville's WTVF-TV. She became an evening news co-anchor in Baltimore in 1976, where she was recruited to co-host WJZ-TV's local talk show *People Are Talking*. She moved to Chicago in the early 1980s to host ABC affiliate WLS-TV's *AM Chicago*, which quickly became the city's top morning talk show. It was renamed *The Oprah Winfrey Show* in 1985.

Winfrey's performance in Steven Spielberg's *The Color Purple* in 1985 (her first ever acting role) won her an Oscar nomination and boosted her ratings when *The Oprah Winfrey Show* debuted nationally in 138 cities the following year thanks to a syndication deal with King World Productions secured by her agent (later Harpo's president and COO) Jeffrey Jacobs. Harpo was founded that year.

Winfrey obtained full ownership of her program in 1988. Two years later Harpo Films was created, and Winfrey bought a Chicago studio to produce *Oprah*, becoming only the third woman to own her own production studio (Mary Pickford and Lucille Ball were the others). She introduced the popular Oprah's Book Club in 1996. Also that year Texas cattlemen filed a lawsuit claiming she had caused a drop in beef futures prices after a show on the UK outbreak of mad cow disease (Winfrey didn't emphasize that the disease had not appeared in the US). But jurors ruled in her favor in early 1998. Winfrey also renewed her contract that year until the 2001-2002 TV season.

In 1998 Winfrey agreed to produce original programming for Oxygen, a new cable network for women, in exchange for an equity stake. CBS bought King World in 1999, and the deal gave King World stockholder Winfrey a $100 million stake in CBS (which is now a stake in Viacom following its buy of CBS). The following year Winfrey launched with Hearst her own magazine (*O, The Oprah Magazine*) that focuses on relationships, health, and fashion.

In 2002 the talk show diva decided that Oprah's Book Club would be an occasional, instead of a regular, segment on her TV program (much to the dismay of many book publishers). In addition, a spinoff talk show hosted by Dr. Phil McGraw (a regular on the Oprah show) premiered that year. In 2003 Winfrey announced that she was reviving her book club (with an emphasis on classic literature rather than books authored by contemporary writers). She also signed a contract to keep her TV program on the air into 2008. The next year Winfrey extended the contract even further, striking a deal to keep gabbing until 2011.

EXECUTIVES

Chairman: Oprah Winfrey, age 49
CFO: Doug Pattison
President, Harpo Productions: Tim Bennett
President, Harpo Films: Kate Forte
Director of Media and Corporate Relations: Lisa Halliday
Director of Human Resources: Bernice Smith

LOCATIONS

HQ: Harpo, Inc.
110 N. Carpenter St., Chicago, IL 60607
Phone: 312-633-1000   **Fax:** 312-633-1976
Web: www.oprah.com

PRODUCTS/OPERATIONS

Selected Operations

Harpo Entertainment Group
  Harpo Films
    Beloved (1998)
    Oprah Winfrey Presents: Before Women Had Wings (1997)
    Oprah Winfrey Presents: The Wedding (1998)
    Overexposed (1992)
    There Are No Children Here (1993)
  Harpo Productions
    Oprah Winfrey Presents: Amy & Isabelle (2001)
    Oprah Winfrey Presents: David and Lisa (1998)
    Oprah Winfrey Presents: Tuesdays with Morrie (1999)
    The Oprah Winfrey Show
    The Women of Brewster Place (1989)
  Harpo Video

COMPETITORS

Hallmark	Rainbow Media
iVillage	Sony Pictures
Lifetime	Entertainment
Martha Stewart Living	Time Warner
NBC Universal Television	Viacom
News Corp.	

HISTORICAL FINANCIALS

Company Type: Private

Income Statement   FYE: December 31

	REVENUE ($ mil.)	NET INCOME ($ mil.)	NET PROFIT MARGIN	EMPLOYEES
12/02	225	—	—	240
12/01	200	—	—	221
12/00	180	—	—	200
12/99	170	—	—	200
12/98	162	—	—	190
12/97	150	—	—	175
12/96	140	—	—	176
12/95	130	—	—	166
12/94	120	—	—	141
12/93	110	—	—	135
Annual Growth	8.3%	—	—	6.6%

Revenue History

Harvard University

Many parents dream of sending their children to Harvard; some even dream of being able to afford it at about $27,500 a year (undergrad). Harvard, the oldest institution of higher learning in the US, is home to Harvard College (undergraduate studies) and 10 graduate schools including the John F. Kennedy School of Government and the Harvard Business, Law, and Medical Schools. The Radcliffe Institute for Advanced Study at Harvard was created when Radcliffe College and Harvard University merged in 1999. Harvard has more than 19,500 students, nearly two-thirds of whom are enrolled in graduate programs. Harvard's endowment of more than $19 billion is the largest of any US university (Yale ranks #2).

It's usually a toss-up whether Harvard or one of its Ivy League rivals Princeton or Yale will rank at the top of the list of America's premiere schools or programs, but the university's reputation for academic excellence is well-founded. More than 30 Harvard faculty members have won Nobel Prizes over the years. Additionally, among Harvard's alumni are six US presidents — John Adams, John Quincy Adams, Rutherford B. Hayes, John F. Kennedy, Franklin Delano Roosevelt, and Theodore Roosevelt.

HISTORY

In 1636 the General Court of Massachusetts appropriated 400 pounds sterling for the establishment of a college. The first building was completed at Cambridge in 1639 and was named for John Harvard, who had willed his collection of about 400 books and half of his land to the school. The first freshman class had four students.

During its first 150 years, Harvard adhered to the education standards of European schools, with emphasis on classical literature and languages, philosophy, and mathematics. It established its first professorship in 1721 (the Hollis Divinity Professorship) and soon after added professorships in mathematics and natural philosophy. In 1783 the school appointed its first professor of medicine.

Harvard updated its curriculum in the early 1800s, after professor Edward Everett returned from studying abroad with reports of the modern teaching methods in Germany. The university established the Divinity School in 1816, the Law School in 1817, and two schools of science in the 1840s.

In 1869 president Charles Eliot began engineering the development of graduate programs in arts and sciences, engineering, and architecture. He raised standards at the medical and law schools and laid the groundwork for the Graduate School of Business Administration and the School of Public Health. Radcliffe College was founded as "Harvard Annex" in 1879, 15 years after a group of women had begun studying privately with Harvard professors in rented rooms.

Harvard's enrollment, faculty, and endowment grew tremendously throughout the 20th century. The Graduate School of Education opened in 1920, and the first undergraduate residential house opened in 1930. In the 1930s and 1940s, the school established a scholarship program and a general education curriculum for undergraduates. During WWII Harvard and Radcliffe undergraduates began attending the same classes.

A quota limiting the number of female students was abolished in 1975, and in 1979 Harvard introduced a new core curriculum. Princeton-educated Neil Rudenstine became president in 1991 and vowed to cut costs and to seek additional funding so that no one should be denied a Harvard education for financial reasons.

Harvard made dubious headlines during its 1994-95 academic year, enduring a bank robbery in Harvard Square, three student suicides, and one murder-suicide. The following year Harvard paid a fine of $775,000 after the US Attorney's Office claimed the school's pharmacy had not properly controlled drugs, including antidepressants and codeine cough syrup. The fine was the largest ever paid in the US under the Controlled Substance Act.

In 1998 Harvard's endowment fund acquired insurance services firm White River in one of the largest direct investments ever made by a not-for-profit institution. Also that year the school altered some of its graduation processes and introduced stress-reducing programs in the wake of another student suicide.

In 1999 Radcliffe College merged with Harvard and the Radcliffe Institute for Advanced Study at Harvard was established. In 2000 president Neil Rudenstine announced he would step down in June 2001. Former Treasury Secretary Lawrence Summers replaced him.

EXECUTIVES

President: Lawrence H. (Larry) Summers, age 50
Provost: Steven E. Hyman
VP Administration: Sally H. Zeckhauser
VP Alumni Affairs and Development: Donella Rapier
VP Finance: Ann E. Berman
VP Government, Community, and Public Affairs: Alan Stone
VP and General Counsel: Robert I. Iuliano
Treasurer: James Rothenberg
Auditors: PricewaterhouseCoopers LLP

LOCATIONS

HQ: Harvard University
  Massachusetts Hall, Cambridge, MA 02138
Phone: 617-495-1000 **Fax:** 617-495-0754
Web: www.harvard.edu

PRODUCTS/OPERATIONS

Selected Programs and Schools

Undergraduate
  Harvard College
Graduate
  Graduate School of Arts and Sciences
  Graduate School of Design
  Graduate School of Education
  Harvard Business School
  Harvard Divinity School
  Harvard Law School
  Harvard Medical School
  Harvard School of Public Health
  John F. Kennedy School of Government
  School of Dental Medicine

HISTORICAL FINANCIALS
Company Type: School

Income Statement				FYE: June 30
	REVENUE ($ mil.)	NET INCOME ($ mil.)	NET PROFIT MARGIN	EMPLOYEES
6/03	2,473	—	—	11,000
6/02	2,357	—	—	15,000
6/01	2,228	—	—	15,000
6/00	2,023	—	—	11,360
6/99	1,788	—	—	10,500
6/98	1,679	—	—	9,701
6/97	1,565	—	—	12,782
6/96	1,519	—	—	12,150
6/95	1,467	—	—	11,100
6/94	1,377	—	—	11,000
Annual Growth	6.7%	—	—	0.0%

Revenue History

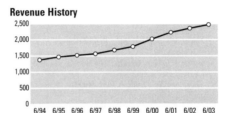

Haskell

Design/build services lie at the heart of Haskell. The company ranks among the US's top design/build firms, which oversee not only the architectural and engineering design but also the construction of a project. Haskell also offers construction management, facility management, interior design, and real estate services. Projects include industrial, commercial, and institutional facilities and range from a Krispy Kreme Doughnuts factory to a federal medium-security prison. Chairman Preston Haskell founded the employee-owned firm in 1965 and also led the establishment of the Design-Build Institute of America in 1993.

The company has more than 160 design professionals on its staff.

Haskell's numerous projects include the corporate headquarters for St. Joe Company in Florida; Jet Aviation's general aviation/fixed-base operations (FBO) and headquarters building in Teterboro, New Jersey; and the Dale Earnhardt Bridge, a pedestrian overpass spanning the eight-lane International Speedway Boulevard in Daytona Beach, Florida.

EXECUTIVES

Chairman: Preston H. Haskell
President and CEO: Steven T. (Steve) Halverson
EVP and CFO; President and CEO, Haskell Enterprise Group: Edward W. (Ted) Mullinix
SVP and Chief Architect: David L. (Dave) Engdahl
SVP Human Resources and Organizational Development: David I. Bogage
SVP, South Florida Office: Robert W. (Bob) Soulby Scheele
VP, Corporate Marketing: H. Lamar Nash

President, Civil Group: John H. Patton
President, Industrial Group: Gregory (Greg) Ferrell
President, Institutional/Commercial Group: James A. (Jim) Gray
Auditors: KPMG

LOCATIONS

HQ: The Haskell Company
  111 Riverside Ave., Jacksonville, FL 32202
Phone: 904-791-4500 **Fax:** 904-791-4699
Web: www.thehaskellco.com

Haskell has offices in the US in Florida and Texas and also in Mexico City. Haskell operates in North America, Latin America, and the Caribbean region.

PRODUCTS/OPERATIONS

Industry Divisions
Aviation
Criminal Justice
Distribution
Diversified
Education
Food & Beverage
General Commercial
Healthcare
Latin America
Manufacturing & Technology
Senior Living
Site
Transportation
Water & Wastewater

COMPETITORS

BE&K
Hensel Phelps Construction
Kimley-Horn and Associates
Parsons
Peter Kiewit Sons'
Skanska USA Building
Stellar Group
Turner Corporation
Washington Group

HISTORICAL FINANCIALS
Company Type: Private

Income Statement				FYE: December 31
	REVENUE ($ mil.)	NET INCOME ($ mil.)	NET PROFIT MARGIN	EMPLOYEES
12/03	630	—	—	1,310
12/02	651	—	—	1,325
12/01	700	—	—	1,300
Annual Growth	(5.1%)	—	—	0.4%

Revenue History

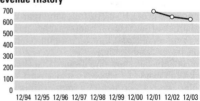

Haworth

Designers at Haworth sit at their cubicles and think about . . . more cubicles. The company is one of the top office furniture manufacturers in the US (behind #1 Steelcase and #2 HNI Corporation, and competing with Herman Miller for #3). Haworth offers a full range of furniture known for its innovative design, including partitions, desks, chairs, tables, and storage products. Brands include Berlin, if, PLACES, and X99. Dilbert and other long-suffering office drones have Haworth to thank for inventing the pre-wired partitions that make today's cubicled workplace possible. Haworth is owned by the family of Gerrard Haworth, who founded the company in 1948.

The company sells its products worldwide through more than 600 dealers. It has about 40 manufacturing locations and 60 showrooms.

Haworth, known as an aggressive competitor, has been expanding its presence in Europe, mostly through acquisitions. Operations include Germany's Roeder, Spain's Kemen, and Canada's SMED and Groupe Lacasse. In late 2003 Haworth agreed to purchase the assets of flooring maker Interface Architectural Resources.

An extended decline in the office furniture industry is forcing the company to consolidate operations, including relocating its US manufacturing from four states (Arkansas, North Carolina, Pennsylvania, and Texas) to three plants in Michigan.

EXECUTIVES

Chairman and CEO: Richard G. Haworth
COO: Franco Bianchi
CFO: Calvin W. (Cal) Kreuze
VP, Architecture and Design:
 Georgianna D. (Georgy) Olivieri
VP, Asia/Pacific: Frank Rexach
VP, European Operations: José Amaral
VP, Global Information Systems: Micheal Moon
VP, Global Manufacturing: Stephen Burkhammer
VP, Global Sales: Al Lanning
VP, Human Resources: Nancy Teutsch
VP, SMED International: Gary Scitthelm
Director, Customer Development: Phil Todd
Manager, Corporate Communications: Susan Wray

LOCATIONS

HQ: Haworth, Inc.
 1 Haworth Center, Holland, MI 49423
Phone: 616-393-3000   **Fax:** 616-393-1570
Web: www.haworth.com

Haworth operates in more than 120 countries throughout the Americas, Asia, the Caribbean, Europe, and the Middle East.

PRODUCTS/OPERATIONS

Products
Desks and casegoods
Files and storage
Seating
Systems
Tables
Work tools

COMPETITORS

Boss Office Products
Falcon Products
Global Group
Herman Miller
HNI
Inscape
Jami
KI
Kimball International
Knoll
Neutral Posture
Skandinavisk Group
Steelcase
Teknion
Trendway
Virco Mfg.

HISTORICAL FINANCIALS
Company Type: Private

Income Statement
FYE: December 31

	REVENUE ($ mil.)	NET INCOME ($ mil.)	NET PROFIT MARGIN	EMPLOYEES
12/03	1,224	—	—	8,525
12/02	1,320	—	—	9,500
12/01	1,710	—	—	10,000
12/00	2,065	—	—	14,500
12/99	1,580	—	—	10,000
12/98	1,540	—	—	10,000
12/97	1,510	—	—	10,000
12/96	1,370	—	—	9,000
12/95	1,150	—	—	8,900
12/94	1,005	—	—	7,400
Annual Growth	2.2%	—	—	1.6%

Revenue History

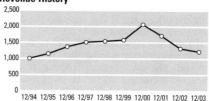

HBE Corporation

HBE derives a healthy business out of designing and building health care facilities. The firm provides planning, architectural, engineering, management, interior design, and construction services throughout the US. Hospital Building & Equipment is the group's chief operating division. HBE also designs and builds financial institutions and hotels and has been engaged in the hospitality industry through its operation and ownership of Adam's Mark Hotels & Resorts properties. However, the company has sold many of its Adam's Mark hotels to concentrate on its core business. HBE is owned by chairman, president, and CEO Fred Kummer, who founded the design/build firm as a small construction company in 1960.

EXECUTIVES

Chairman, President, and CEO: Fred S. Kummer
Vice Chairman and Secretary: June Kummer
EVP and CFO: Gregory Beck
EVP and COO: Matthew E. Nail
EVP Financial Facilities: Paul Barrath
EVP Real Estate/Investments: Richard Miller
VP Hospital Consulting: Stephen G. Dailey
VP Hospital Marketing: Dennis Oerly
VP Hospital Sales: David Ferrell
VP Purchasing: Howard Ackerman
VP Development, Medical Buildings: Michael Parnas
Director Personnel: Jim O'Daniel

LOCATIONS

HQ: HBE Corporation
 11330 Olive Blvd., St. Louis, MO 63141
Phone: 314-567-9000   **Fax:** 314-567-0602
Web: www.hbecorp.com

COMPETITORS

Bovis Lend Lease
Brasfield & Gorrie
Centex
DPR Construction
Gilbane
Hyatt
M. A. Mortenson
Marriott
Pepper Construction
Skanska USA Building
Starwood Hotels & Resorts
Turner Corporation
Walsh Group

HISTORICAL FINANCIALS
Company Type: Private

Income Statement
FYE: December 31

	REVENUE ($ mil.)	NET INCOME ($ mil.)	NET PROFIT MARGIN	EMPLOYEES
12/03	625	—	—	6,000
12/02	625	—	—	9,100
12/01	614	—	—	9,100
12/00	658	—	—	11,000
12/99	650	—	—	10,000
12/98	658	—	—	7,000
12/97	575	—	—	7,000
Annual Growth	1.4%	—	—	(2.5%)

Revenue History

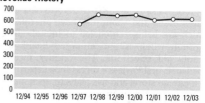

H. E. Butt Grocery

The Muzak bounces between Tejano and country, and the warm tortillas and ribs are big sellers at H. E. Butt Grocery (H-E-B). Texas' largest private company and the #1 food retailer in South and Central Texas, H-E-B owns more than 300 supermarkets, including a growing number of large (70,000 sq. ft.) gourmet Central Market stores in major metropolitan areas and more than 80 smaller (24,000-30,000 sq. ft.) Pantry Foods stores, often in more rural areas. H-E-B also has one store in Louisiana and about 20 upscale and discount stores in Mexico. H-E-B processes some of its own bread, dairy products, meat, and tortillas. The company is owned by the Butt family, which founded H-E-B in Kerrville, Texas, in 1905.

To cement its #1 spot in Central Texas and fend off Wal-Mart, which is expanding in the region, H-E-B recently lowered prices on some 12,000 items in the Austin market. H-E-B also acquired nine stores in Texas from rival Albertson's to bolster its position in the San Antonio market and elsewhere. To answer its supercenter competition, H-E-B is experimenting with a new, larger format called HEB Plus. These stores are 20% larger than average H-E-B outlets and devote considerable space to nonfood items, including furniture.

The Texas grocery chain is investing heavily in the Houston market to add 11 large combination food and drug stores, while closing some of its smaller Pantry supermarkets in the area. The company aims to become a major player in and around Houston, where Kroger is #1. To gain an edge on its competition, H-E-B plans to incorporate aspects of its upscale Central Market format, including cafes, into the new Houston stores.

H-E-B is familiar with the tastes of Latinos as about half of its market is Hispanic. South of the border H-E-B has moved into Monterrey's more affluent neighborhoods, with stores operating under the H-E-B banner and the Economax name (a discount supermarket format). The company plans to have about 40 stores in Mexico by the end of 2004.

More than 40% of the H-E-B stores have gasoline outlets, and about 190 have pharmacies, which are being remodeled to include drive-through windows and enlarged health and beauty aid selections. The retailer recently opened its first Payless Express shoe department in a Laredo store, and has plans to open more.

The grocery chain may lay off about 50 people (many at its San Antonio headquarters) in a reorganization of administrative positions. H-E-B also plans to add about 300 customer service jobs.

HISTORY

Charles C. Butt and his wife, Florence, moved to Kerrville, in the Texas Hill Country, in 1905, hoping the climate would help Charles' tuberculosis. Since Charles was unable to work, Florence began peddling groceries door-to-door for A&P. Later that year she opened a grocery store, C. C. Butt Grocery. However, Florence, a dyed-in-the-wool Baptist, refused to carry such articles of vice as tobacco. The family lived over the store, and all three of the Butt children worked there. The youngest son, Howard, began working in the business full-time in his teens and took over the business after WWI.

By adopting modern marketing methods such as price tagging (and deciding to sell tobacco), the Butts earned enough to begin expanding. In 1927 Howard opened a second store in Del Rio in West Texas, and over the next few years he opened other stores in the Rio Grande Valley. The company gained patron loyalty by making minimal markups on staples. It moved from Kerrville to Harlingen, Texas, in 1928 (it moved to Corpus Christi, Texas, in 1940 and to San Antonio in 1985).

The company began manufacturing foods in the 1930s, and it invested in farms and orchards. In 1935 Howard (who had adopted the middle name Edward) rechristened the chain the H. E. Butt Grocery Company (H-E-B). He put his three children to work for the company, grooming son Charles for the top spot after Howard Jr. took over the H. E. Butt Foundation from his mother.

While other chains updated their stores during the 1960s, H-E-B plodded. Howard Sr. resigned in 1971 and Charles took over, bringing in fresh management. But this was not enough. Studies showed that the reasons for its lagging market share were its refusal to stock alcohol and its policy of Sunday closing; it abandoned these policies in 1976. It also drastically undercut competitors, driving many independents out of business. Winning the price wars, H-E-B emerged the dominant player in its major markets.

H-E-B's first superstore, a 56,000-sq.-ft. facility offering general merchandise, photofinishing, and a pharmacy, opened in Austin, Texas, in 1979, and it concentrated on building more superstores over the next decade. It also installed in-store video rentals and added 35 freestanding Video Central locations (sold to Hollywood Entertainment in 1993).

In 1988 H-E-B launched its H-E-B Pantry division, which remodeled and built smaller supermarkets, mostly in rural Texas towns. Three years later it launched another format, the 93,000-sq.-ft. H-E-B Marketplace in San Antonio, which included restaurants. It also opened the upscale Central Market in Austin with extensive cheese, produce, and wine departments in 1994 (it later opened similar stores in San Antonio and Houston).

Chairman and CEO Charles retired as president in 1996, and James Clingman became the first non-family member to assume the office. That year H-E-B opened its first non-Texas store, in Lake Charles, Louisiana. In 1997 it opened its first Mexican store in an affluent area of Monterrey, followed the next year by a discount supermarket there under the Economax banner. In 1999 the company said it would expand further in Mexico with six to eight new stores per year (it opened seven in 2001). Also in 2001 H-E-B opened its first store — a Central Market — in the Dallas/Ft. Worth area.

In mid-2002 H-E-B opened a new Central Market in Dallas, its seventh Central Market in Texas and the company's 300th store. The company also acquired five San Antonio stores from Albertson's and reopened them as H-E-B stores in August and September.

In early 2004, H-E-B opened its first H-E-B Plus store in San Juan, Texas.

EXECUTIVES

Chairman and CEO: Charles C. Butt
COO: Robert D. (Bob) Loeffler, age 52
Chief Administration Officer and CFO: Jack C. Brouillard
EVP, Food Manufacturing, Procurement, and Merchandising: Steve Harper
SVP, General Manager, South Texas: Jeff Thomas
SVP, General Merchandise, San Antonio Region: Greg Souquette
SVP Grocery Merchandising, Procurement, and Own Brand: Roger Davidson
SVP, Human Resources: Todd Piland
SVP, Information Solutions and Chief Information Officer: Don Beaver
SVP, Supply Chain and Logistics: Kenneth Allen
Group VP, Advertising: Cory J. Basso
Group VP, Public Affairs and Diversity: Winell Herron
VP, Business Intelligence: Birgit Enstrom
VP, E-Commerce: Alan Markert
VP, General Manager of Store Operations: Paul Madura
VP, Meat Merchandising, Procurement and Product Development: Randy Vaclavik
VP, Operations, Central Market, and Dallas-Fort Worth Region: Stephen Butt
VP, Pharmacy: Greg Webb
Innovation Officer; VP, Procurement/Merchandising, Central Market: John Campbell
VP, Quality Assurance and Environmental Affairs: Bill Fry
VP, Selling and Customer Service: Jaren Shaw
President, H-E-B Houston and Central Market Stores: Scott McClelland, age 47

LOCATIONS

HQ: H. E. Butt Grocery Company
646 S. Main Ave., San Antonio, TX 78204
Phone: 210-938-8000 **Fax:** 210-938-8169
Web: www.heb.com

H. E. Butt Grocery Company operates grocery stores and gas stations throughout Texas; and in Louisiana and Mexico. The company also operates bakeries; a photo processing lab; and meat, milk, and ice cream plants.

PRODUCTS/OPERATIONS

Private Labels
H-E-B Own Brand
Hill Country Fare

Store Formats
Central Market (about 70,000 sq. ft., upscale supermarkets with expanded organic and gourmet foods; located in major metropolitan markets)
Economax (discount supermarkets, Mexico)
Gas 'N Go (gas stations)
H-E-B (large supermarkets)
H-E-B Marketplace (large supermarkets with specialty departments)
H-E-B Pantry (24,000-30,000 sq. ft., no-frills supermarkets with basic groceries; often located in rural or suburban areas)

COMPETITORS

7-Eleven
Albertson's
Brookshire Brothers
Chedraui
Comerci
Costco Wholesale
Fiesta Mart
Gerland's Food Fair
Gigante
Grupo Corvi
IGA
Kmart
Kroger
Minyard Food Stores
Randall's
Rice Food Markets
Soriana
Walgreen
Wal-Mart
Wal-Mart de México
Whole Foods
Winn-Dixie

HISTORICAL FINANCIALS

Company Type: Private

Income Statement — FYE: October 31

	REVENUE ($ mil.)	NET INCOME ($ mil.)	NET PROFIT MARGIN	EMPLOYEES
10/03	10,700	—	—	56,000
10/02	9,900	—	—	60,000
10/01	8,965	—	—	60,000
10/00	8,200	—	—	50,000
10/99	7,500	—	—	45,000
10/98	7,000	—	—	45,000
10/97	6,500	—	—	45,000
10/96	5,800	—	—	42,000
10/95	5,137	—	—	25,000
10/94	4,844	—	—	25,000
Annual Growth	9.2%	—	—	9.4%

Revenue History

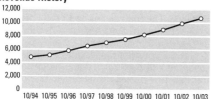

Health Care Service

Health Care Service Corporation (HCSC) has the Blues. HCSC is made up of Blue Cross Blue Shield of Illinois (that state's oldest and largest health insurer), Blue Cross and Blue Shield of Texas, and Blue Cross and Blue Shield of New Mexico. A licensee of the Blue Cross and Blue Shield Association, the mutual company provides a range of group and individual insurance and medical plans to nearly 10 million members, including indemnity insurance and managed care programs. HCSC also offers prescription drug plans, Medicare supplement insurance, dental and vision coverage, life and disability insurance, workers' compensation, retirement services, and medical financial services through subsidiaries.

HCSC also covers federal employees in its three states through the Federal Employee Program, a contract with the US government.

HCSC's strategy for growth consists of making strategic acquisitions of other independent Blue Cross companies, as well as other health and insurance companies that complement the company's core product offerings.

This strategy has allowed HCSC to better compete in the health care industry by benefiting from economies of scale.

HISTORY

The seeds of the Blue Cross organization were sown in 1929, when an official at Baylor University Hospital in Dallas began offering schoolteachers 21 days of hospital care for $6 a year. Fundamental to its coverage was a community rating system, which based premiums on the community's claims experience rather than subscribers' conditions.

In 1935 Elgin Watch Co. owner Taylor Strawn, Charles Schweppe, and other Chicago civic leaders pooled resources to form Hospital Services Corporation to provide the same type of coverage. (The firm adopted the Blue Cross symbol in 1939.) Employees of the Rand McNally cartography company were the first to be covered by the plan.

Soon, four similar plans were launched in other Illinois towns. Between 1947 and 1952, Hospital Services Corp. and these other four joined forces, offering coverage nearly statewide.

Meanwhile, Blue Shield physician's fee plans in several cities were incorporated as Illinois Medical Service. Hospital Services Corp. and Illinois Medical Service operated independently but shared office space and personnel.

A 1975 change in state legislation let the entities merge to become Health Care Service Corp. (HCSC), which offered both Blue Cross and Blue Shield coverage. Following the merger, the company's board of directors (which had been primarily composed of care providers) became dominated by consumers, which helped HCSC become more responsive to its members.

For the next six years, the state denied HCSC any rate increases, leaving it with a frighteningly low $12 million in reserves in 1982.

HCSC achieved statewide market presence in 1982 when it merged with Illinois' last independent Blue Cross plan, Rockford Blue Cross. In 1986, as managed care swept through the health care industry, only 14% of HCSC's members were enrolled in managed care plans. HCSC created its Managed Care Network Preferred point-of-service plan in 1991; the idea caught on with both employers and individuals and enrollment skyrocketed. By 1994 more than two-thirds of the firm's subscribers participated in some sort of managed care plan. That year it picked up Medicare payment processing for the state of Michigan.

In 1995 HCSC and Blue Cross and Blue Shield of Texas (BCBST) formed an affiliation they hoped would culminate in a merger giving the combined company $6 billion in sales and reserves of more than $1 billion. Texas consumer groups objected to the merger, claiming that Texas residents own BCBST and that Texans should be compensated for the transfer of ownership — especially since BCBST had received state tax breaks for decades in exchange for accepting all applicants. (A Texas judge ruled in favor of the merger in 1998.)

Citing high risks and low margins, HCSC in 1997 dropped its Medicare payment processing contract, which it had held for some 30 years. The next year HCSC agreed to pay $144 million after it pleaded guilty to covering up its poor performance in processing Medicare claims.

In 1998 HCSC acquired Blue Cross and Blue Shield of Texas.

In 1999 HCSC agreed to buy Aetna's NylCare of Texas, giving it large, profitable HMOs in Houston and Dallas (completed in 2000). The next year it bested Anthem and Wellmark in wooing the troubled Blue Cross Blue Shield of New Mexico (completed in 2001).

EXECUTIVES

President and CEO: Raymond F. McCaskey
EVP and COO: Sherman M. Wolff
SVP and CFO: Denise A. Bujack
SVP and Chief Information Officer: Patrick E. Moroney, age 48
SVP, Human Resources: Patrick O'Conner
President of Blue Cross and Blue Shield of Illinois: Gail K. Boudreaux, age 43
President, Blue Cross and Blue Shield of New Mexico: Liz Watrin, age 40
President, Blue Cross and Blue Shield of Texas: Patricia A. Hemingway Hall, age 51
VP and Treasurer: Brian A. Kennedy
VP and Actuary: Kenneth Avner
VP, Sales and Marketing Division, Blue Cross and Blue Shield of New Mexico: Dorane Wintermeyer
VP, Member Services Division, Blue Cross and Blue Shield of New Mexico: Linda Amburn
VP, National and Major Accounts: Paul Boulis
VP, Public Affairs and Advertising: John Ori
Director, Human Resources: Robert Ernst
Auditors: Ernst & Young LLP

LOCATIONS

HQ: Health Care Service Corporation
300 E. Randolph St., Chicago, IL 60601
Phone: 312-653-6000   **Fax:** 312-819-1220
Web: www.hcsc.net

PRODUCTS/OPERATIONS

2003 Membership

	Members	% of total
Illinois	5,300,000	64
Texas	2,800,000	34
New Mexico	200,000	2
Total	**8,300,000**	**100**

Selected Products and Services

Dental insurance
Disability insurance
Indemnity insurance
Life insurance
Managed health care plans
Supplemental Medicare coverage
Prescription drug coverage
Retirement plans
Vision insurance
Workers' compensation

Selected Subsidiaries

Group Medical and Surgical Service
Preferred Financial Group
　Colorado Bankers Life Insurance Company
　Fort Dearborn Life Insurance Co.
　Medical Life Insurance Company
Rio Grande HMO, Inc.
Texas Gulf Coast HMO, Inc.
Texas Health Plan, Inc.
West Texas Health Plans, L.C.

COMPETITORS

Aetna
AFLAC
Anthem
CIGNA
Guardian Life
Humana
Kaiser Foundation
Mutual of Omaha
New York Life
Prudential
UnitedHealth Group

HISTORICAL FINANCIALS

Company Type: Mutual company

Income Statement
FYE: December 31

	REVENUE ($ mil.)	NET INCOME ($ mil.)	NET PROFIT MARGIN	EMPLOYEES
12/03	8,190	625	7.6%	13,000
12/02	7,312	246	3.4%	—
12/01	6,198	387	6.2%	—
12/00	10,430	174	1.7%	—
12/99	8,980	111	1.2%	—
12/98	7,819	50	0.6%	—
12/97	5,107	71	1.4%	5,700
12/96	4,478	89	2.0%	5,650
12/95	4,201	139	3.3%	5,600
12/94	3,930	166	4.2%	—
Annual Growth	8.5%	15.9%	—	11.1%

2003 Year-End Financials
Debt ratio: 18.7%
Return on equity: 34.7%
Cash ($ mil.): 502
Current ratio: —
Long-term debt ($ mil.): 400

Net Income History

Health Insurance of New York

This firm says it's HIP to be healthy. Health Insurance Plan of Greater New York (HIP) is a not-for-profit HMO founded in the 1940s to provide low-cost health care to New York City employees; HIP now boasts more than 1 million members, is the largest HMO in the New York metro area, and New York state's biggest Medicare provider. The organization also provides medical, lab, and pharmacy services through some 20,000 physicians and about 100 facilities around New York City. HIP serves more than 10,000 employer groups ranging from small firms to FORTUNE 500 companies.

HIP's efforts in the 1990s to expand out-of-state proved disastrous; its New Jersey effort was closed by regulators, and HIP sold its Florida affiliate after accumulating huge losses. Back home, HIP has faced allegations from regulators of lavish executive lifestyles and too-cozy relationships with contractors.

The company still dominates the New York metro HMO market, and is nationally recognized for its efficient use of information technology to reduce its operating costs and improve patient care.

To expand its presence in the Northeast, HIP acquired ConnectiCare.

EXECUTIVES
Chairman and CEO: Anthony L. Watson, age 63
President and COO: Daniel T. McGowan
EVP, CFO, General Counsel, and Corporate Secretary: Michael D. Fullwood
EVP, Brand Leadership: Thomas J. Mcateer Jr.
EVP, Medical Affairs and Chief Medical Officer: Ronald Platt
EVP, Operations and Chief Information Officer: John H. Steber
SVP, Information Technology and Chief Technology Officer: Pedro Villalba
SVP, Corporate Compliance and Internal Audit: Valerie A. Reardon
SVP, Finance and Corporate Controller: Dominic F. D'Adamo
SVP, Human Resources: Fred Blickman
SVP, Marketing and Sales, and Chief Marketing Officer: Larry G. Posner
SVP, Operations, Public Policy and Regulatory Affairs: David S. Abernethy
SVP, Public Affairs and Operations Advisor to the Chairman: Ronald Maiorana
VP and Treasurer: Michael S. Vincent
VP, Investor Relations: Arthur J. Byrd
Auditors: Deloitte & Touche LLP

LOCATIONS
HQ: Health Insurance Plan of Greater New York
55 Water St., New York, NY 10041
Phone: 212-630-5000
Web: www.hipusa.com

PRODUCTS/OPERATIONS

2003 Sales

	$ mil.	% of total
Premiums	3,325.8	99
Admin services & fees	15.7	—
Investment income	28.4	1
Total	3,369.9	100

Selected Health Plans
HIPaccess I & II (Traditional)
HIP Prime Dental
HIP Prime EPO/PPO
HIP Prime (HMO)
HIP Prime POS (point-of-service)
HIP VIP (Medicare)

COMPETITORS
Aetna
CIGNA
Health Net
Humana
Oxford Health
Prudential
UnitedHealth Group
WellChoice

HISTORICAL FINANCIALS
Company Type: Not-for-profit

Income Statement
FYE: December 31

	REVENUE ($ mil.)	NET INCOME ($ mil.)	NET PROFIT MARGIN	EMPLOYEES
12/03	3,370	275	8.2%	2,000
12/02	2,902	178	6.1%	2,000
12/01	2,600	—	—	2,000
12/00	2,410	—	—	2,000
12/99	2,223	—	—	1,500
12/98	2,000	—	—	1,500
12/97	1,568	—	—	1,483
12/96	1,734	—	—	1,500
12/95	1,777	—	—	1,500
12/94	1,714	—	—	1,485
Annual Growth	7.8%	54.5%	—	3.4%

2003 Year-End Financials
Debt ratio: 0.1%
Return on equity: 45.4%
Cash ($ mil.): 348
Current ratio: 1.85
Long-term debt ($ mil.): 1

Net Income History

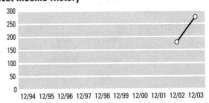

Hearst

Like legendary founder William Randolph Hearst's castle, The Hearst Corporation is sprawling. The company owns 12 daily newspapers (including the San Francisco Chronicle and the Houston Chronicle) and 14 weekly newspapers, 18 US consumer magazines (such as Cosmopolitan and Esquire), TV and radio stations (through 40%-owned Hearst Argyle Television), and a cartoon and features service (King Features). Hearst is also active in cable networks through stakes in A&E, Lifetime, and ESPN; and online services through its 30% stake in iVillage, the Web network aimed at women. The company is owned by the Hearst family, but managed by a board of trustees.

Hearst sold the San Francisco Examiner to the Fang family to satisfy antitrust regulators in conjunction with its 2000 purchase of the larger San Francisco Chronicle. (The Fangs sold the Examiner to Denver billionaire Philip Anschutz in 2004.) Although it no longer owns Hearst Castle (deeded to the State of California in 1951), the company has extensive real estate holdings.

Using the selling power of its popular Cosmopolitan magazine, the company has capitalized with a TV channel in Spain and Portugal based on the magazine. The company then added another one in Latin America and is considering a US launch. Hearst also turned a TV channel into a magazine; the company launched Lifetime magazine in 2003 in a joint venture with women's cable channel Lifetime. Hearst hopes the move takes some of the sting out of its high-profile failure of Talk magazine, a joint venture with movie studio Miramax. Led by Tina Brown, the famous former editor of The New Yorker, the magazine only lasted two years before the partners shut it down, citing the downturn in the economy and poor circulation.

Hearst further expanded its potent stable of magazines in 2003 by purchasing Seventeen magazine from PRIMEDIA. In addition to the magazine, the deal (valued at $182 million) includes the purchase of Teen magazine and school marketing business Cover Concepts.

Upon his death, William Randolph Hearst left 99% of the company's common stock to two charitable trusts controlled by a 13-member board that includes five family and eight non-family members. The will includes a clause that allows the trustees to disinherit any heir who contests the will.

HISTORY

William Randolph Hearst, son of a California mining magnate, started as a reporter — having been expelled from Harvard in 1884 for playing jokes on professors. In 1887 he became editor of the *San Francisco Examiner,* which his father had obtained as payment for a gambling debt. In 1895 he bought the *New York Morning Journal* and competed against Joseph Pulitzer's *New York World.* The "yellow journalism" resulting from that rivalry characterized American-style reporting at the turn of the century.

Hearst branched into magazines (1903), film (1913), and radio (1928). Also during this time it created the Hearst International News Service (it was sold to E.W. Scripps' United Press in 1958 to form United Press International). By 1935 Hearst was at its peak, with newspapers in 19 cities, the largest syndicate (King Features), international news and photo services, 13 magazines, eight radio stations, and two motion picture companies. Two years later Hearst relinquished control of the company to avoid bankruptcy, selling movie companies, radio stations, magazines, and, later, most of his San Simeon estate. (Hearst's rise and fall inspired the 1941 film *Citizen Kane.*)

In 1948 Hearst became the owner of one of the US's first TV stations, WBAL-TV in Baltimore. When Hearst died in 1951, company veteran Richard Berlin became CEO. Berlin sold off failing newspapers, moved into television, and acquired more magazines.

Frank Bennack, CEO since 1979, expanded the company, acquiring newspapers, publishing firms (notably William Morrow, 1981), TV stations, magazines (*Redbook,* 1982; *Esquire,* 1986), and 20% of cable sports network ESPN (1991). Hearst branched into video via a joint venture with Capital Cities/ABC (1981) and helped launch the Lifetime and Arts & Entertainment cable channels (1984).

In 1991 Hearst launched a New England news network with Continental Cablevision. The following year it brought on board former Federal Communications Commission chairman Alfred Sikes, who quickly moved the company onto the Internet. In 1996 Randolph A. Hearst passed the title of chairman to nephew George Hearst (the last surviving son of the founder, Randolph died in 2000). Broadcaster Argyle Television merged with Hearst's TV holdings in 1997 to form publicly traded Hearst-Argyle Television.

In 1999 Hearst combined its HomeArts Web site with Women.com to create one of the largest online networks for women. It also joined with Walt Disney's Miramax Films to publish entertainment magazine *Talk* (shut down in 2001) and Oprah Winfrey's Harpo Entertainment to publish *O, The Oprah Magazine* (launched in 2000). In 1999 the company sold its book publishing operations to News Corp.'s HarperCollins unit. It also agreed to buy the *San Francisco Chronicle* from rival Chronicle Publishing. That deal was called into question over concerns that the *San Francisco Examiner* would not survive and the city would be left with one major paper. To resolve the issue, the next year Hearst sold the *Examiner* to ExIn (a group of investors affiliated with the Ted Fang family and other owners of the *San Francisco Independent*). Also in 2000 Hearst bought the UK magazines of Gruner + Jahr, the newspaper and magazine unit of German media juggernaut Bertelsmann.

The following year Hearst gained a 30% stake in iVillage following that company's purchase of rival Women.com Networks. In mid-2002 Victor Ganzi took over as CEO and president following Bennack's retirement from these positions. Hearst expanded further into entertaining the younger generation with the purchase of *Seventeen* magazine from PRIMEDIA.

EXECUTIVES

Chairman: George R. Hearst Jr., age 76
Vice Chairman: Frank A. Bennack Jr., age 71
President and CEO; Chairman, Hearst-Argyle Television: Victor F. Ganzi, age 57
SVP and CFO: Ronald J. Doerfler
SVP and Chief Legal and Development Officer: James M. Asher
SVP; President, Hearst Newspapers: George B. Irish
SVP; President and Group Head, Hearst Entertainment and Syndication: Raymond E. Joslin
VP and Chief Communications Officer: Debra Shriver
VP and General Counsel: Eve Burton
VP; President and CEO, Hearst Magazines International; EVP, Hearst Magazines: George Green
VP; VP and Deputy Group Head, Hearst Entertainment and Syndication; President, Hearst Entertainment: Bruce Paisner
President and CEO, Hearst-Argyle Television: David J. Barrett, age 56
President, Hearst Business Media: Richard P. Malloch
President, Hearst Interactive Media: Kenneth A. Bronfin, age 44
President, Hearst Magazines: Cathleen P. (Cathie) Black, age 59
EVP, Hearst Newspapers: Steven R. Swartz
VP and General Manager, Hearst Interactive Sudios: Jay Bobowicz
VP, Hearst Interactive Media: Michael Dunn, age 44
VP, Hearst Interactive Media: Scott English

LOCATIONS

HQ: The Hearst Corporation
959 8th Ave., New York, NY 10019
Phone: 212-649-2148   **Fax:** 212-649-2108
Web: www.hearstcorp.com

Hearst newspapers are located throughout the US. Hearst Magazines are distributed in more than 110 countries.

PRODUCTS/OPERATIONS

Selected Operations
Broadcasting
  Hearst-Argyle Television (40%)
Business Publications
  Black Book
  Diversion
  Electronic Products
  First DataBank
  Motor Magazine
Entertainment and Syndication
  A&E Television Networks (37.5%, with ABC & NBC)
    The History Channel
  Cosmopolitan Television Iberia (Spain, Portugal, and Latin America)
  ESPN (20%)
  King Features Syndicate
  Lifetime Entertainment Services (50%, with ABC)
  Locomotion (with Cisneros Group; all animation TV)
  New England Cable News (with Comcast)
  Tevecap (10%, pay-TV; Brazil)
Interactive Media
  Circles (invested in online loyalty solutions company)
  drugstore.com (invested in online pharmacy site)
  Hire.com (invested in career job site)
  iVillage (30%, Internet site geared towards women)
Magazines
  Best (UK magazine)
  Company (UK magazine)
  CosmoGIRL!
  Cosmopolitan
  Country Living
  Country Living GARDENER
  Esquire
  Good Housekeeping
  Harper's Bazaar
  HouseBeautiful
  Lifetime (50%)
  Marie Claire (with Marie Claire Album)
  O, The Oprah Magazine (with Harpo)
  Popular Mechanics
  Prima (UK magazine)
  Redbook
  Seventeen
  She (UK magazine)
  SmartMoney (with Dow Jones)
  Teen
  Town & Country TRAVEL
  Veranda
  Your Home (UK magazine)
  Zest (UK magazine)
Major Newspapers
  Albany Times Union (New York)
  Houston Chronicle
  Huron Daily Tribune (Michigan)
  Laredo Morning Times (Texas)
  Midland Daily News (Michigan)
  San Antonio Express-News
  San Francisco Chronicle
  Seattle Post-Intelligencer
Real Estate
  Hearst Realties
  San Francisco Realties
  Sunical Land & Livestock Division
Other Operations
  Cover Concepts (in-school marketing)

COMPETITORS

Advance Publications
Andrews McMeel Universal
Belo
Bertelsmann
Bloomberg
Cox Enterprises
Dennis Publishing
E. W. Scripps
Emap
Freedom Communications
Gannett
Hachette Filipacchi Médias
IPC Group
Knight-Ridder
Liberty Media
McGraw-Hill
MediaNews
Meredith
New York Times
News Corp.
PRIMEDIA
Reader's Digest
Reed Elsevier Group
Rodale
Seattle Times
Time Warner
Tribune
Viacom
Walt Disney
Washington Post

HISTORICAL FINANCIALS

Company Type: Private

Income Statement				FYE: December 31
	REVENUE ($ mil.)	NET INCOME ($ mil.)	NET PROFIT MARGIN	EMPLOYEES
12/03	4,100	—	—	20,000
12/02	3,565	—	—	17,320
12/01	3,300	—	—	17,170
12/00	3,400	—	—	18,300
12/99	2,740	—	—	14,000
12/98	2,200	—	—	13,555
12/97	2,833	—	—	15,000
12/96	2,568	—	—	14,000
12/95	2,513	—	—	14,000
12/94	2,299	—	—	14,000
Annual Growth	6.6%	—	—	4.0%

Revenue History

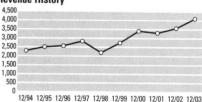

Helmsley

What word rhyming with "itch" describes Leona Helmsley? Rich! Helmsley Enterprises is the repository of the real estate empire amassed by the late Harry Helmsley over a period of 50 years. Helmsley's widow and heir, Leona, has interests in such high-profile properties as Helmsley Park Lane, Carlton House, and the Helmsley Windsor. Other holdings include apartment buildings and millions of square feet of primarily New York real estate, not to mention a lease held on the Empire State Building until 2075.

The portfolio was valued at $5 billion before Harry Helmsley's death in 1997. Leona Helmsley has sold more than $2 billion worth of property since; the company now controls real estate valued at about half that amount.

Helmsley has ended a relatively quiet half-decade of staying out of the limelight. After quietly selling off a number of properties, many at a premium in New York's stratospheric real estate market, the "Queen of Mean" is grabbing headlines again: She appears to have won a public fight with Donald Trump over the terms of the Empire State Building lease (he sold his ownership interest in 2002), but she's lost a lawsuit involving the alleged mistreatment of gay hotel employees (a judge reduced the jury-rewarded damages from $11.1 million to a mere $554,000).

Leona's holdings may be eroding even further; the Helmsley Middletowne is up for sale, Helmsley hotels no longer hold coveted slots on the *Zagat Survey of Top U.S. Hotels*, and occupancy levels are below those of Manhattan's new trendy boutique hotels.

At its apex, Helmsley's real estate empire included interests in more than 25 million sq. ft. of office space, more than 20,000 apartments, some 7,500 hotel rooms, 50 retail projects, warehouse space, land, garages, restaurants, and real estate companies. To keep the money in the family, the properties were managed by Helmsley-Spear (then 99%-owned by Helmsley, sold in 1997) and Helmsley-Noyes.

HISTORY

In 1925 Harry Helmsley began his career as a Manhattan rent collector; the work, then done in person, taught him to evaluate buildings and acquainted him with their owners. During the Depression, Helmsley obtained property at bargain prices. He paid $1,000 down for a building with a $100,000 mortgage and later quipped that he did so to provide a job for his father, whom he hired as superintendent. In 1946 he sold the building for $165,000.

In the late 1940s Helmsley teamed up with lawyer Lawrence Wien. Helmsley located properties; Wien financed them through a device of his own invention, the loan syndicate. Prominent properties Helmsley bought into in the 1950s included the Flatiron (1951), Berkeley (1953), and Equitable (1957) buildings. He moved into management in 1955 with the purchase of Leon Spear's property management firm. In 1961 Helmsley bought the Empire State Building for $65 million and sold it to Prudential for $29 million with a 114-year leaseback (which expires in 2075); a public offering for the newly created Empire State Building Co. made up the balance.

In the mid-1960s Helmsley moved into property development, erecting office buildings and shopping centers. He bought the 30-building Furman and Wolfson trust, borrowing $78 million of the $165 million price on the strength of his reputation — the largest signature loan ever.

In 1969 Spear introduced Helmsley to Leona Roberts, a real estate broker who had sold Spear an apartment. Helmsley hired Leona and promoted her to SVP at his Brown, Harris, Stevens real estate brokerage. He divorced his wife and married Leona in 1971. In 1974 he leased an historic building and delegated the renovation to Leona (who built the company's hotel business). The Helmsley Palace opened in 1980 (now the New York Palace, sold 1993).

As Harry's health began to fail in the 1980s, Leona gained control of the empire. Maintenance deteriorated, bookkeeping went lax, and the couple's lavish spending became notorious. In 1988 they were charged with tax evasion. Harry was ruled incompetent to stand trial, but in 1989 Leona was convicted, fined $7.1 million, and sentenced to jail. She spent 21 months incarcerated, the last part of it in a halfway house.

After her 1994 release, Leona was banned from management of the hotels by laws forbidding felon involvement in businesses that serve liquor. She became more involved in the management of Harry's interests and began reshuffling assets, moving management contracts from Helmsley-Spear to Helmsley-Noyes, and selling buildings.

A 1995 suit brought by Harry's partners in Helmsley-Spear accused Leona of looting the company by depriving it of management contracts and loading it with debt to render worthless their right to buy the company under a 1970 option agreement.

In 1997 Harry died, and Leona announced she would sell the 125-property Helmsley portfolio. Wien's son-in-law Peter Malkin, partner in 13 top-notch Manhattan buildings, contested the control granted to her by Harry's will. They resolved their differences late that year. Leona also settled her differences with the Helmsley-Spear partners in 1997, agreeing to sell them the firm for less than $1 million.

Leona sold her favorite, the Helmsley Building on 230 Park Place, in 1998 to the Bass family on condition the building retain the name. That year, partly to avoid estate taxes, she formed the Harry and Leona Helmsley Foundation, a charity to which she contributed more than $30 million in 1999.

Leona moved closer to a deal in 2000 to buy back the Empire State Building from then-owner Donald Trump and partners. The following year Malkin moved to challenge her, forming a plan to buy the skyscraper himself; Leona vowed to block his proposal. In 2002, Trump agreed to sell the building to Malkin for $57.5 million.

EXECUTIVES

Chairman and CEO: Leona Helmsley, age 82
CFO: Abe Wolf
VP and General Counsel: Harold Meriam
Human Resources Director: Yogesh Mathur
Auditors: Eisner & Lubin LLP

LOCATIONS

HQ: Helmsley Enterprises, Inc.
230 Park Ave., New York, NY 10169
Phone: 212-679-3600 **Fax:** 212-953-2810

Helmsley Enterprises operates primarily in New York City.

PRODUCTS/OPERATIONS

Selected Properties
Empire State Building (office building, New York City)
Helmsley Carlton House (hotel, New York City)
Helmsley Middletowne (hotel, New York City)
Helmsley Park Lane (hotel, New York City)
Helmsley Sandcastle (hotel, Sarasota, Florida)
Helmsley Windsor (hotel, New York City)
Lincoln Building (office building, New York City)
New York Helmsley (hotel, New York City)

COMPETITORS

Accor	Ritz-Carlton
Four Seasons Hotels	Shorenstein
Hyatt	SL Green Realty
JMB Realty	Tishman
Lefrak Organization	Trammell Crow Company
Lincoln Property	Trizec Properties
Macklowe Properties	Trump
Marriott	Vornado Realty Trust

HISTORICAL FINANCIALS

Company Type: Private

Income Statement   FYE: December 31

	ESTIMATED REVENUE ($ mil.)	NET INCOME ($ mil.)	NET PROFIT MARGIN	EMPLOYEES
12/02	1,000	—	—	3,500
12/01	1,000	—	—	3,000
12/00	1,000	—	—	3,000
12/99	1,000	—	—	3,000
12/98	1,000	—	—	7,800
12/97	1,000	—	—	7,800
12/96	1,900	—	—	13,000
12/95	1,770	—	—	13,000
12/94	1,700	—	—	13,000
12/93	1,200	—	—	13,000
Annual Growth	(2.0%)	—	—	(13.6%)

Revenue History

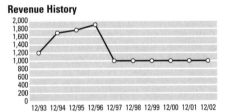

Hendrick Automotive

For megadealer Hendrick Automotive Group, variety is the spice of life. The company sells new and used cars and light trucks from more than 20 automakers, including General Motors, Honda, and Porsche. Hendrick has a network of about 60 dealerships in about 10 states ranging from the Carolinas to California. The company also offers financing, as well as automobile parts, accessories, service, and body repair. Founder Rick Hendrick pleaded guilty in 1997 to mail fraud relating to alleged bribes of American Honda executives; he was later pardoned by President Bill Clinton. Hendrick owns the company, which began in 1976 as a single dealership in Bennettsville, South Carolina.

Rick Hendrick leads the group as chairman, but he is known for granting a large measure of autonomy and ultimate responsibility for results to the general manager of each dealership. His hands-off policy does seem to have achieved results. Hendrick Acura, for instance, has increased its sales count from more than 380 new cars a month in 1997 to more than 1,100 a month in 2003.

EXECUTIVES
Chairman: J.R. (Rick) Hendrick III
CEO: Jim C. Perkins
EVP and CFO: James F. Huzl
VP of Accounting, Audits, and Taxes: Veronica Zayatz
Director of Human Resources: Tim Taylor

LOCATIONS
HQ: Hendrick Automotive Group
6000 Monroe Rd., Charlotte, NC 28212
Phone: 704-568-5550   **Fax:** 704-566-3295
Web: www.hendrickauto.com

Hendrick Automotive Group operates in California, Georgia, Kansas, Missouri, North Carolina, South Carolina, Tennessee, Texas, and Virginia.

COMPETITORS
Asbury Automotive
AutoNation
Bill Heard
CarMax
Holman Enterprises
Morse Operations
Penske
Serra Automotive
Sonic Automotive
United Auto Group
VT Inc.

HISTORICAL FINANCIALS
Company Type: Private

Income Statement				FYE: December 31
	REVENUE ($ mil.)	NET INCOME ($ mil.)	NET PROFIT MARGIN	EMPLOYEES
12/03	2,783	—	—	—
12/02	2,491	—	—	4,700
12/01	2,639	—	—	4,700
12/00	2,483	—	—	4,500
12/99	2,522	—	—	4,500
12/98	2,434	—	—	4,300
12/97	2,455	—	—	4,500
12/96	2,250	—	—	4,500
12/95	2,315	—	—	4,500
12/94	1,800	—	—	4,500
Annual Growth	5.0%	—	—	0.5%

Revenue History
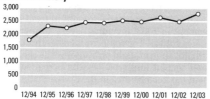

Henry Ford Health System

In 1915 automaker Henry Ford founded the hospital that would be the starting point for southeastern Michigan's not-for-profit Henry Ford Health System (HFHS), a hospital network that is also involved in medical research and education. The system's hospital network includes Henry Ford Hospital, Henry Ford Wyandotte Hospital, and Kingswood Hospital, which specializes in treating mental health patients. HFHS also operates nursing homes, hospice and home health care providers, and a medical supply retailer. The system's Health Alliance Plan of Michigan provides managed care and health insurance to some 560,000 members.

HFHS has a joint venture with Bon Secours Health System, Bon Secours Cottage Health Services, to operate Cottage Hospital and Bon Secours Hospital, both located northeast of Detroit. In 2004 an audit of the joint venture's books revealed its former CFO had misstated revenues and assets for the previous seven years.

The Henry Ford Health Sciences Center Research Institute, the Josephine Ford Cancer Center, and other research centers and affiliated hospitals are also part of the health care system.

After posting a $75 million loss in 2002, the health system began a turnaround initiative that reaped rewards with a profit posted in 2003. To achieve the return to fiscal fitness, HFHS cut more than 1,000 jobs, trimmed some services, and closed one of its facilities. About half of the company's revenue in 2003 came from Health Alliance Plan of Michigan.

EXECUTIVES
President and CEO: Nancy M. Schlichting, age 48
EVP and Chief Medical Officer; CEO, Henry Ford Medical Group: Mark A. Kelley
SVP and CFO: James M. Connelly
SVP, Insurance and Purchaser Relations; President and CEO, Health Alliance Plan of Michigan: Francine (Fran) Parker, age 49
SVP and Chief Administrative Officer: Robert (Bob) Rieny
SVP, Planning and Strategic Development: Vinod K. Sahney
VP, Behavioral Health: Edward Coffey
System VP, Purchasing Supply Chain: Michael F. Whelan
Acting Chairman, Eye Care Services: Paul A. Edwards
Chairman, Heart and Vascular Institute: W. Douglas Weaver
President and CEO, Henry Ford Hospital and Health Network: Anthony (Tony) Armada
CEO, Bon Secours Cottage Health Services: Richard Van Lith
SVP and COO, Henry Ford Hospital and Health Network: Robert Riney
CIO: Arthur Gross
Media Relations Director: Dwight Angell

LOCATIONS
HQ: Henry Ford Health System
1 Ford Place, Detroit, MI 48202
Phone: 313-876-8700   **Fax:** 313-876-9243
Web: www.henryfordhealth.org

PRODUCTS/OPERATIONS
Selected Operations
Bon Secours Cottage Health Services (80%, joint venture with Bon Secours Health System)
Health Alliance Plan of Michigan
Henry Ford Bi-County Community Hospital (osteopathic hospital)
Henry Ford Hospital
Henry Ford Medical Group
Henry Ford Mercy Health Network (joint venture with Trinity Health)
Henry Ford Wyandotte Hospital
Kingswood Hospital (mental health care)
Virginia Park/Henry Ford Hospital Non-Profit Housing Corp.

COMPETITORS
Ascension Health
Blue Cross (MI)
Detroit Medical Center
Healthplus of Michigan
Trinity Health (Novi)
William Beaumont Hospital

HISTORICAL FINANCIALS
Company Type: Not-for-profit

Income Statement				FYE: December 31
	REVENUE ($ mil.)	NET INCOME ($ mil.)	NET PROFIT MARGIN	EMPLOYEES
12/03	2,600	—	—	12,700
12/02	2,400	—	—	12,600
12/01	2,000	—	—	15,000
12/00	1,900	—	—	16,000
12/99	1,229	—	—	16,000
12/98	1,303	—	—	17,000
12/97	2,200	—	—	17,000
12/96	1,980	—	—	17,000
12/95	1,750	—	—	17,000
12/94	1,525	—	—	15,000
Annual Growth	6.1%	—	—	(1.8%)

Revenue History
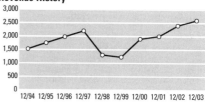

Hensel Phelps Construction

Hensel Phelps Construction builds it all, from the courthouse to the Big House. Launched as a homebuilding firm by Hensel Phelps in 1937, the employee-owned general contractor now focuses on institutional and commercial projects: prisons, airport facilities, hotels, government and corporate complexes, convention centers, sport arenas, and department stores. It also works on mass transportation, educational, residential, and health care projects. Hensel Phelps offers design/build and construction management services. Recent projects include the Hyatt Denver Convention Center Hotel and the new headquarters for Whole Foods Market in Austin, Texas.

EXECUTIVES

President and CEO: Jerry L. Morgensen
EVP and Manager, Eastern Division and Mid-Atlantic District: Robert E. Daniels
EVP and Manager, Western Division; President, Phelps Program Management: Robert J. (Bob) Pesavento
VP Finance and CFO: Stephen J. (Steve) Carrico
VP and General Counsel: Eric L. Wilson
VP, Northern California District: Jon W. Ball
VP, Plains District; EVP, Phelps Program Management (PPM): Ronald G. (Ron) Norby
VP, South Central District: Mark Baugh
VP, Southeast District: Jeffrey (Jeff) Wenaas
VP, Southern California District: Wayne S. Lindholm
VP, Southwest District: Edwin L. Calhoun
Auditors: KPMG LLP

LOCATIONS

HQ: Hensel Phelps Construction Co.
420 6th Ave., Greeley, CO 80632
Phone: 970-352-6565 **Fax:** 970-352-9311
Web: www.henselphelps.com

Hensel Phelps Construction has offices in Arkansas, California, Colorado, Florida, Texas, and Virginia.

PRODUCTS/OPERATIONS

Selected Services
Building operation
Commissioning
Estimating
Feasibility studies
Financing
Land acquisition
Leasing
Moving services
Scheduling
Subcontractor management
Warranty programs
Zoning and code compliance

Selected Projects
Capital Square Office Tower (Sacramento)
Colorado Convention Center Expansion and Renovation Project (Denver)
Denver Center of the Performing Arts
Excelsior Hotel & Convention Center (Little Rock, AR)
J.D. Edwards Corporate Headquarters (Denver)
Neiman Marcus (Palo Alto, CA)
Paseo Nuevo Shopping Center (Santa Barbara, CA)
Pentagon Renovation Wedges 2-5 (Arlington, VA)
Riverport Casino Center (Maryland Heights, MO)
Sahara Hotel and Casino (Las Vegas)
San Antonio International Airport
Sea World New Friends Stadium (San Antonio)
University of Texas at Dallas School of Management
New Midfield Concourse, Washington Dulles Airport
Youth Services Center (Washington, DC)

COMPETITORS

C.F. Jordan
Clark Enterprises
Dick Corporation
Hunt Construction
M. A. Mortenson
McCarthy Building
PCL
Perini
Rooney Holdings
Skanska USA Building
Turner Corporation
Walbridge Aldinger
Walsh Group
Whiting-Turner

HISTORICAL FINANCIALS

Company Type: Private

Income Statement FYE: May 31

	REVENUE ($ mil.)	NET INCOME ($ mil.)	NET PROFIT MARGIN	EMPLOYEES
5/03	1,872	—	—	2,500
5/02	1,771	—	—	2,200
5/01	1,368	—	—	2,200
5/00	1,357	—	—	2,200
5/99	1,165	—	—	2,151
5/98	934	—	—	1,926
5/97	876	—	—	1,535
5/96	726	—	—	1,540
5/95	734	—	—	1,400
5/94	692	—	—	1,650
Annual Growth	11.7%	—	—	4.7%

Revenue History

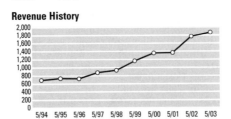

Herb Chambers

Step into the chambers of Herb Chambers Companies and you'll find a wide range of cars. The company runs more than 20 dealerships in New England that sell just about everything from pricey new cars from BMW, Cadillac, Lexus, Mercedes-Benz, and Porsche to more affordable offerings from Honda, Hyundai, Kia, Saturn, and Toyota; dealerships also offer used cars. All of its cars are available online. Herb Chambers also offers parts and service and runs four body shops. Owner and CEO Herb Chambers started his automotive empire with a Cadillac/Oldsmobile dealership in New London, Connecticut, in 1985.

EXECUTIVES

President and CEO: Herbert G. (Herb) Chambers, age 62
CFO: Bruce Spatz

LOCATIONS

HQ: The Herb Chambers Companies
259 McGrath Hwy., Somerville, MA 02145
Phone: 617-666-8333 **Fax:** 617-666-8448
Web: www.chamberscars.com

COMPETITORS

AutoNation
Group 1 Automotive
March/Hodge
Planet Automotive Group
United Auto Group

HISTORICAL FINANCIALS

Company Type: Private

Income Statement FYE: December 31

	REVENUE ($ mil.)	NET INCOME ($ mil.)	NET PROFIT MARGIN	EMPLOYEES
12/03	1,181	—	—	1,000
12/02	1,034	—	—	1,000
12/01	987	—	—	1,000
12/00	974	—	—	1,000
12/99	801	—	—	1,000
12/98	674	—	—	1,000
12/97	607	—	—	822
12/96	562	—	—	798
12/95	461	—	—	703
Annual Growth	12.5%	—	—	4.5%

Revenue History

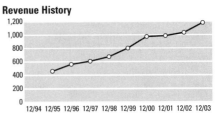

Herbalife

Rooted in the medicinal value provided by Mother Nature, Herbalife International sells more than 160 products containing herbal and other natural ingredients. Products include weight-control mixes and tablets, nutritional supplements specifically designed for men and women, food, shampoos, lotions, sunscreens, and body oils. The multi-level marketer sells its products through a network of independent distributors in more than 50 countries; salespeople earn money from their own efforts, as well as from the sales of those whom they have recruited into the organization.

Distributors in emerging markets in Africa, Asia, and Eastern Europe have been attracted to Herbalife by the low startup costs. After buying promotional materials (average cost: $60), distributors purchase products from Herbalife at a discount of up to 50% and resell them at retail prices.

After founder Mark Hughes passed away in 2000, the company slumped, and was subsequently acquired by a group of venture capital firms including Whitney & Co. and Golden Gate Capital. Striving to reclaim the success it had in the 1980's, the company brought in fresh management in 2003, including several former Disney executives. The company is currently dealing with litigation brought on by users of its ephedra-based weight loss products; the herbal supplement has been banned in the United States.

HISTORY

Mark Hughes' mother's death from an overdose of prescription diet pills was the catalyst for Herbalife. Hughes, a high-school dropout, founded the company with diet supplement maker Richard Marconi in 1980. Herbalife went public in 1986 after rapid growth, but it got into trouble for some of its product claims. Following federal and state investigations and US Senate hearings, Herbalife paid a hefty fine and removed some of its products from the market. Hughes was able to resurrect the firm by taking it overseas. Sales also got a boost from the success of the Thermojetics weight-control systems.

In 1995 Herbalife introduced a line of herbal and botanical skin care products (Dermajetics). In 1997 insider selling of stock prompted a major slide in the price of Herbalife shares. Earnings tanked in 1998 when economic crises hit such big revenue contributors as Russia and Asia.

In 1999 Hughes planned to buy the company's outstanding shares and take the company private; investors sued. In 2000 he dropped the attempt. That year 44-year-old Hughes died in what was ruled an accidental death caused by a combination of alcohol and antidepressant medication. Hughes' longtime associate and former Herbalife COO Christopher Pair moved into the positions of president and CEO. He stepped down a year later after the company's board criticized his management.

Later that year, the Mark Hughes Family Trust turned down a $173 million bid for control of the company from Internet retailer Rbid.com. A group of investment firms bought the company in 2002 and Hughes' hopes to take the company private came to fruition without him.

EXECUTIVES

Chairman: Peter M. Castleman, age 47
Vice Chairman: Henry S. Burdick, age 61
CEO: Michael O. Johnson, age 49
COO: Gregory Probert, age 47
CFO: Richard Goudis
SVP and Managing Director, Herbalife Japan:
 William M. Rahn
SVP, Finance and Treasury: William D. Lowe, age 54
VP, Event Management and Communications:
 Randall (Randy) Brogna
General Counsel: Brett R. Chapman, age 48
Auditors: Deloitte & Touche LLP

LOCATIONS

HQ: Herbalife International, Inc.
 9800 S. La Cienega Blvd., Inglewood, CA 90301
Phone: 866-866-4744 **Fax:** 310-216-5169
Web: www.herbalife.com

Herbalife International's products are available through independent distributors in 58 countries worldwide.

PRODUCTS/OPERATIONS

Selected Products

Nutritional Supplements
 Aminogen
 A.M. Replenishing
 Cell-U-Loss
 Dinomins
 DinoShakes
 Echinacea Plus
 Extreme C
 Florafiber
 Herbal Calmative
 Herbal-Aloe
 Herbalifeline
 Kindermins
 Male Factor 1000
 Male Performance Complex
 P.M. Cleansing
 RoseOx
 Schizandra Plus
 Sleep Now
 Tang Kuei Plus
 Thermo-bond
 Ultimate Prostate Formula
 Woman's Choice
 Women's Advantage
 Xtra-Cal

Weight Management
 Formula 1 Protein Mix
 Thermojetics
 Thermojetics Gold Herbal Supplement Tablets
 Thermojetics Herbal Concentrate
 Thermojetics High-Protein, Low-Carb Program

Personal Care
 Colour cosmetics
 Dermajetics
  AromaVie
  Good Hair Day
  Nature's Mirror
  Parfums Vitessences
  Skin Survival Kit

COMPETITORS

Alticor
GNC
Jenny Craig
Mannatech
Nature's Sunshine
NBTY
Nu Skin
Reliv'
Rexall Sundown
Shaklee
Slim-Fast
Sunrider
Vitamin Shoppe Industries
Weider Nutrition
Whole Living
Wyeth

HISTORICAL FINANCIALS

Company Type: Private

Income Statement
FYE: December 31

	REVENUE ($ mil.)	NET INCOME ($ mil.)	NET PROFIT MARGIN	EMPLOYEES
12/02	1,094	—	—	2,625
12/01	1,020	—	—	2,445
12/00	944	—	—	2,391
12/99	956	—	—	2,170
12/98	867	—	—	1,742
12/97	783	—	—	1,459
12/96	632	—	—	1,180
12/95	489	—	—	1,060
12/94	467	—	—	862
12/93	365	—	—	638
Annual Growth	13.0%	—	—	17.0%

Revenue History

Hicks, Muse, Tate & Furst

These Texas Hicks know an investment pool ain't no cement pond and like to buy, buy & buy. (They sell sometimes, too.) Hicks, Muse, Tate & Furst creates investment pools in the form of limited partnerships. Investors are mostly pension funds but also include financial institutions and wealthy private investors. The leveraged buyout firm assembles limited partnership investment pools, targets underperforming companies in specific niches, builds them up, and uses them to form a nucleus for other investments. Hicks Muse also has holdings in manufacturing and real estate. Thomas Hicks has announced plans to retire in March 2005; co-founder John Muse will replace him at the helm of the firm.

It's "back to basics" for the company — media, branded food, and basic component manufacturing; it reevaluated its investments after some dramatic dot-com era blowouts and a spoiled cinematic adventure with Kohlberg Kravis Roberts (the firms bought Regal Cinemas, but it went bankrupt, leaving a $500 million crater in Hicks Muse's pocket). The firm got out of investing in telecoms and into Europe and Latin America.

Cable television has been in favor with Hicks Muse over the past ten years. The firm bought its first cable company, Marcus Cable, in 1995 and has since bought nearly a dozen. Its latest is Centennial Puerto Rico Cable TV; the deal should close early in 2005.

The company, along with Colorado-based Booth Creek Management, bought a 54% share of ConAgra's meatpacking operations. Hicks Muse also owns the North American assets of bankrupt Vlasic Foods International, including Vlasic pickles, Open Pit barbecue sauces, and Swanson Frozen Food. After bolstering the holdings of Premier International Foods, which bought up troubled, but well-known English food brands from firms like Nestlé, Cadbury Schweppes, and Unilever, it shepherded the company through an IPO, selling off its entire stake.

Recently, the investors Hicks Muse depended on to make its European ventures successful have tightened their purse strings. In order to lure these new and current investors into its new second European investment fund, the firm is sweetening the deal by reducing its fees and making payouts more investor-friendly.

HISTORY

The son of a Texas radio station owner, Thomas Hicks became interested in leveraged buyouts as a member of First National Bank's venture capital group. Hicks and Robert Haas formed Hicks & Haas in 1984; the next year that firm bought Hicks Communications, a radio outfit run by Hicks' brother Steven. (This would be the first of many media companies bought or created by the buyout firm, often with Steven Hicks' involvement.)

Hicks & Haas' biggest coup was its mid-1980s buy of several soft drink makers, including Dr Pepper and Seven-Up. The firm took Dr Pepper/Seven-Up public just 18 months after merging the two companies. In all, Hicks & Haas turned $88 million of investor funding into $1.3 billion. The pair split up in 1989; Hicks wanted to raise a large pool to invest, but Haas preferred to work deal by deal.

Hicks raised $250 million in 1989 and teamed with former Prudential Securities banker John Muse. Early investments included Life Partners Group (life insurance, 1990; sold 1996). In 1991 Morgan Stanley's Charles Tate and First Boston's Jack Furst became partners.

As part of its buy-and-build strategy, Hicks Muse bought DuPont's connector systems unit in 1993, renamed it Berg Electronics, added six more companies to it, and doubled its earnings before selling it in 1998. Not every move was a star in the Hicks Muse crown. Less-than-successful purchases included bankrupt brewer G. Heileman, bought in 1994 and sold two years later for an almost $100 million loss.

The buyout firm's Chancellor Media radio company went public in 1996. That year Hicks Muse gained entry into Latin America with its purchases of cash-starved Mexican companies, including Seguros Commercial America, one of the country's largest insurers. That year also brought International Home Foods (Jiffy Pop, Chef Boyardee) into the Hicks Muse fold.

In 1997 Chancellor and Evergreen Media merged to form Chancellor Media (renamed AMFM in 1999). The next year Hicks Muse continued buying US and Latin American media companies, as well as a few oddities (a UK software maker, a Danish seed company, and US direct-seller Home Interiors & Gifts). Hicks Muse and Kohlberg Kravis Roberts merged their cinema operations to form the US's largest theater chain. The company that year also moved into the depressed energy field (Triton Energy) and formed a $1.5 billion European fund.

Buys in 1999 included UK food group Hillsdown Holdings, one-third of Mexican flour maker Grupo Minsa, and (just in time for millennial celebrations) popular champagne brands Mumm and Perrier-Jouët (it quadrupled its investment when it sold the champagne houses in late 2000). Lured by low stock prices on real estate investment trusts (REITs), the company agreed to buy Walden (formerly Walden Residential Properties) that year.

Hicks Muse, along with UK-based Apax Partners, bought BT's yellow pages firm Yell for roughly $3.5 billion, making it the largest non-corporate LBO in European history. Yell bought US directories publisher McLeodUSA for about $600 million, and floated in 2003.

Hicks Muse spotted a tasty deal and bought Nestlé's Ambient Food Business in 2002, which added well-known UK brands Crosse & Blackwell, Branston Pickle, Chivers (marmalade), Sun-Pat (peanut butter), Gale's (honey), Sarson's (vinegar) and Rowntree's (jelly) to the Premier Foods stable. Unilever's cast-offs Ambrosia (creamed rice and puddings) and Brown & Polson rounded out Premier Foods' portfolio in 2003.

In early 2004, Hicks Muse sold its remaining stake in Yell, and gobbled up #2 UK cereal maker Weetabix. Later that year, it unloaded its stake in Premier Foods.

EXECUTIVES

Chairman and CEO: Thomas O. Hicks, age 58
President: John R. Muse, age 53
COO and Partner: Jack D. Furst, age 45
CFO: Darron Ash
Partner: Dan H. Blanks
Partner: Peter S. Brodsky, age 33
Partner: John P. Civantos
Principal: Marcos A. Clutterbuck
Partner: Joe Colonnetta
Principal: Robert Darwent
Principal: Edward Herring
Partner, Europe: Lyndon Lea
Partner: Eric C. Neuman, age 56
Principal: Eric Lindberg
Partner: Stephan Lobmeyr
Principal: Andrew S. Rosen
Partner: Philippe von Stauffenberg
Principal: Luca Velussi

LOCATIONS

HQ: Hicks, Muse, Tate & Furst Incorporated
200 Crescent Ct., Ste. 1600, Dallas, TX 75201
Phone: 214-740-7300   **Fax:** 214-720-7888

Hicks, Muse, Tate & Furst has offices in Dallas and London.

PRODUCTS/OPERATIONS

Selected Holdings

Cablevision (50%, Argentina)
Claxson Interactive Group (Latin American media and cable)
Glass's Group (automotive information services software)
Grupo Minsa, S.A. de C.V. (32%, corn flour producer, Mexico)
Grupo MVS SA (23%, pay-TV provider and radio station owner, Mexico)
Grupo Vidrio Formas (69%, glass container supplier, Mexico)
Hedstrom Corp. (playground equipment)
Hillsdown Holdings PLC (food production)
Home Interiors & Gifts, Inc. (80%, direct-selling of decorative accessories and gift items)
International Outdoor Advertising (97%; billboards in Argentina, Chile, and Uruguay)
International Wire Holdings Corp. (60%; wire, wire harnesses, and cable)
LIN TV Corp. (46%, television stations)
Pan-American Sports Network (80%, regional cable sports network)
Swift Foods (beef and pork processing)
United Biscuits (Holdings) plc (87%, with Finalrealm; food products; UK)
Viasystems Group (printed circuit boards)
Walden (residential real estate)

COMPETITORS

Bain Capital
Berkshire Hathaway
Boston Ventures
CD&R
CVC Capital Partners
Equity Group Investments
Haas Wheat
Heico
Investcorp
Jordan Company
KKR
Leonard Green
Maseca
Texas Pacific Group
Thomas Lee
Vestar Capital Partners
Vsm Investors
Vulcan Northwest
Wingate Partners

Highmark

Rated as one of the nation's top health plans, Highmark gets an A+ for customer satisfaction. The company provides health-related coverage to some 23 million customers, primarily in Pennsylvania. Highmark offers medical, dental, vision, life, casualty, and other health insurance, as well as such community service programs as the Western Pennsylvania Caring Foundation, which offers free health care coverage to children whose parents earn too much to qualify for public aid but too little to afford private programs. Highmark also processes Medicare claims (Veritus Medicare and HGSAdministrators Medicare Services) and offers administrative and information services (Alliance Ventures).

Highmark continues to operate in western Pennsylvania under the Highmark Blue Cross Blue Shield name, and as Highmark Blue Shield in Central, Eastern and Northeastern Pennsylvania. National subsidiaries include United Concordia Companies (dental coverage) and Highmark Life and Casualty Group (disability and life insurance).

HISTORY

Highmark was created from the merger of Blue Cross of Western Pennsylvania (founded in 1937) and Pennsylvania Blue Shield, created in 1964 when the Medical Service Association of Pennsylvania (MSAP) adopted the Blue Shield name.

The Pennsylvania Medical Society, in conjunction with the state of Pennsylvania, had formed MSAP to provide medical insurance to the poor and indigent. MSAP borrowed $25,000 from the Pennsylvania Medical Society to help set up its operations, and Chauncey Palmer (who had originally proposed the organization) was named president. Individuals paid 35 cents per month, and families paid $1.75 each month to join MSAP, which initially covered mainly obstetrical and surgical procedures.

In 1945 Arthur Daugherty replaced Palmer as president (he served until his death in 1968) and helped MSAP recruit major new accounts, including the United Mine Workers and the Congress of Industrial Organizations. MSAP in 1946 became a chapter of the national Blue Shield association, which was started that year by the medical societies of several states to provide prepaid health insurance plans.

In 1951 MSAP signed up the 150,000 employees of United States Steel, bringing its total enrollment to more than 1.6 million. Growth did not lead to prosperity, though, as the organization had trouble keeping up with payments to its doctors. This shortfall in funds led MSAP to raise its premiums in 1961, at which point the state reminded the association of its social mission and suggested it concentrate on controlling costs instead of raising rates.

MSAP changed its name to Pennsylvania Blue Shield in 1964. Two years later the association began managing the state's Medicare plan and started the 65-Special plan to supplement Medicare coverage. In the 1970s Pennsylvania Blue Shield again could not keep up with the cost of paying its doctors, which led to more rate increases and closer scrutiny of its expenses. Competition increased in the 1980s as HMOs cropped up around the state. Pennsylvania Blue Shield fought back by creating its own HMO plans — some of which it owned jointly with Blue Cross of Western Pennsylvania — in the 1980s.

After years of slowly collecting noninsurance businesses, Blue Cross of Western Pennsylvania changed its name to Veritus in 1991 to reflect the growing importance of its for-profit operations.

In 1996 Pennsylvania Blue Shield overcame physicians' protests and state regulators' concerns to merge with Veritus. The company adopted the name Highmark to represent its standards for high quality; it took a loss as it failed to meet cost-cutting goals and suffered early-retirement costs related to the merger consolidation. To gain support for the merger, Highmark sold for-profit subsidiary Keystone Health Plan East to Independence Blue Cross in 1997.

In 1999 Highmark teamed with Mountain State Blue Cross Blue Shield to become West Virginia's primary licensee. Rate hikes and investment returns helped propel the company into the black as the decade closed.

In 2001 Highmark announced that it had uncovered almost $5 million in health care insurance fraud against the company over the course of the previous year.

EXECUTIVES

Chairman: John N. Shaffer
Vice Chairman: John A. Carpenter
President, CEO, and Director: Kenneth R. Melani, age 48
EVP, Finance and Subsidiary Services, CFO, and Treasurer: Robert C. Gray
EVP, Government Services: David M. O'Brien
EVP, Health Services: James Klingensmith
EVP, Human Resources and Administrative Services: S. Tyrone Alexander
SVP, Corporate Secretary, and General Counsel: Gary R. Truitt
SVP, Corporate Affairs: Aaron A. Walton
SVP and Chief Audit Executive: Elizabeth A. Farbacher
SVP and Corporate Compliance Officer: Michael A. Romano
Assistant Secretary: Carrie J. Pecht
Assistant Treasurer: Joseph F. Reichard
President and CEO, Highmark Life & Casualty Group: Daniel J. Lebish
President, Healthguard of Lancaster: James Godfrey
Auditors: PricewaterhouseCoopers LLP

LOCATIONS

HQ: Highmark Inc.
120 5th Ave., Pittsburgh, PA 15222
Phone: 412-544-7000   **Fax:** 412-544-8368
Web: www.highmark.com

PRODUCTS/OPERATIONS

Selected Health Plans and Divisions
Alliances Ventures
Clarity Vision
Davis Vision
HealthGuard (managed care organization)
HGSAdministrators
Highmark Life & Casualty Group
Insurer Physician Services Organization
Keystone Health Plan Central (HMO; central Pennsylvania)
Keystone Health Plan West (HMO; western Pennsylvania)
United Concordia (dental)
Veritus Medicare Services

COMPETITORS

Aetna
CIGNA
Coventry Health Care
Guardian Life
Humana
New York Life
Prudential
UnitedHealth Group
U.S. Healthcare, Inc.

HISTORICAL FINANCIALS

Company Type: Not-for-profit

Income Statement				FYE: December 31
	REVENUE ($ mil.)	NET INCOME ($ mil.)	NET PROFIT MARGIN	EMPLOYEES
12/03	8,105	76	0.9%	11,000
12/02	7,400	(83)	—	11,000
12/01	6,799	132	1.9%	11,000
12/00	9,000	242	2.7%	11,000
12/99	8,190	69	0.8%	11,000
12/98	7,544	62	0.8%	12,000
12/97	7,405	101	1.4%	12,000
12/96	6,619	(50)	—	10,500
12/95	3,367	43	1.3%	8,000
12/94	3,221	128	4.0%	7,200
Annual Growth	10.8%	(5.7%)	—	4.8%

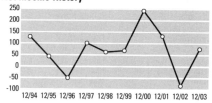

Net Income History

Hines Interests

Hines Interests has been involved in many developments, but none of them include ketchup. Founded by Gerald Hines in 1957, the company is a private commercial real estate development company. Hines handles most aspects of real estate development, including site selection, rezoning, design, construction management, and financing. Its 700-property investment portfolio includes corporate headquarters, industrial facilities, and master-planned residential communities. Hines also manages some 80 million sq. ft. of real estate in the US and 12 other countries. Management services include public relations, tenant relations, and vendor contract-negotiation services. Hines Interests is controlled by the Hines family.

EXECUTIVES

Chairman and CEO: Gerald D. Hines
President: Jeffery C. Hines
CFO: C. Hastings (Hasty) Johnson
SVP and Chief Administration Officer: David LeVrier
EVP, Capital Markets: Charles M. Baughn
SVP Corporate Finance: Kay P. Forbes
EVP Conceptual Construction: John A. Harris
EVP, Western USA and Asia Pacific: James C. (Jim) Buie Jr.
EVP, Eastern USA: Kenneth W. (Ken) Hubbard
EVP, Southwestern USA, Russia, and Mexico: Louis S. Sklar
EVP, Southwestern USA, Russia, and Mexico: E. Staman Ogilvie
EVP, Midwest/Southeast USA and South America: C. Kevin Shannahan
EVP, Europe and Middle East: Michael J. G. Topham
VP Human Resources: Stephanie Fore
VP and CTO: Gerhard Karba
VP Corporate Communications: George C. Lancaster

LOCATIONS

HQ: Hines Interests L.P.
Williams Tower, 2800 Post Oak Blvd., Houston, TX 77056
Phone: 713-621-8000   **Fax:** 713-966-2053
Web: www.hines.com

Hines Interests has offices California, Colorado, Georgia, Illinois, New York, and Texas, and in Argentina, Brazil, China, France, Germany, Italy, Mexico, Poland, Russia, Spain, and the UK.

PRODUCTS/OPERATIONS

Selected Services
Acquisition & Disposition Services
Asset & Property Management Services
Development Services
Marketing & Leasing Services

COMPETITORS

CarrAmerica
CB Richard Ellis
Equity Office Properties
Grubb & Ellis
Jones Lang LaSalle
Lincoln Property
Mack-Cali
Opus
Shorenstein
Staubach
Trammell Crow Company

HISTORICAL FINANCIALS

Company Type: Private

Income Statement				FYE: December 31
	ESTIMATED REVENUE ($ mil.)	NET INCOME ($ mil.)	NET PROFIT MARGIN	EMPLOYEES
12/03	680	—	—	2,800
12/02	750	—	—	2,800
12/01	750	—	—	2,800
12/00	750	—	—	2,800
12/99	750	—	—	2,800
12/98	750	—	—	2,800
12/97	700	—	—	2,700
12/96	650	—	—	2,500
12/95	600	—	—	2,500
12/94	600	—	—	1,300
Annual Growth	1.4%	—	—	8.9%

Revenue History

Hitachi Global Storage

Hitachi Global Storage Technologies manufactures hard disk drives and components for PCs, servers, and electronic devices such as handheld computers and digital cameras. The company was formed in 2003 when Hitachi acquired 70% of IBM's disk drive business; Hitachi plans to acquire IBM's remaining 30% stake by 2005.

EXECUTIVES

CEO: Jun Naruse
COO: Glenn H. Larnerd
CFO: Ryuichi (Dick) Yagi

LOCATIONS

HQ: Hitachi Global Storage Technologies
5600 Cottle Rd., San Jose, CA 95193
Phone: 800-801-4618   **Fax:** 408-256-6770
Web: www.hgst.com

COMPETITORS

Maxtor
Seagate Technology
Western Digital

Hobby Lobby

If something wicker this way comes, Hobby Lobby Stores may be the source. The firm operates more than 330 stores in 27 Southern and Midwestern states and sells arts and crafts supplies, baskets, candles, frames, home-decorating accessories, and silk flowers. The #3 craft retailer (behind Michaels Stores and Jo-Ann Stores), it prefers to set up shop in second-generation retail sites (such as vacated supermarkets and superstores). Sister companies supply Hobby Lobby stores with merchandise, received from its Oklahoma distribution facility. CEO David Green, who owns the company with his wife Barbara, founded the company in 1972 and operates it according to biblical principles, including closing stores on Sunday.

EXECUTIVES

President and CEO: David Green
CFO: John Cargill
EVP: Steve Green
SVP Operations: Ken Haywood
VP Advertising: Bill Hane
VP and Director of Real Estate: Bill Darrow
VP Construction: Steve Seay
VP Legal: Peter Dobelbower
Assistant VP, Real Estate: Scott Nelson
Director of Recruiting: Bill Owens

LOCATIONS

HQ: Hobby Lobby Stores, Inc.
7707 SW 44th St., Oklahoma City, OK 73179
Phone: 405-745-1100   **Fax:** 405-745-1636
Web: www.hobbylobby.com

Hobby Lobby Stores has locations in Alabama, Arkansas, Colorado, Florida, Georgia, Illinois, Indiana, Iowa, Kansas, Kentucky, Louisiana, Michigan, Minnesota, Mississippi, Missouri, Nebraska, New Mexico, North Carolina, North Dakota, Ohio, Oklahoma, South Carolina, Tennessee, Texas, Wisconsin, and Wyoming.

PRODUCTS/OPERATIONS

Selected Products
Arts and crafts supplies
Baskets
Candles
Cards
Furniture
Home accent pieces
Jewelry-making supplies
Memory books
Model kits
Needlework
Party supplies
Picture frames and framing
Rubber stamping supplies
Seasonal items
Sewing materials (fabric, patterns, notions)
Silk flowers

HISTORICAL FINANCIALS
Company Type: Joint venture

Income Statement			FYE: December 31
	REVENUE ($ mil.)	NET INCOME ($ mil.)	NET PROFIT MARGIN	EMPLOYEES
12/03	4,200	—	—	21,000

COMPETITORS

A.C. Moore
Family Christian Stores
Garden Ridge
Hancock Fabrics
HobbyTown USA
Home Interiors & Gifts
Intercraft
Jo-Ann Stores
Kirkland's
Longaberger
Michaels Stores
Old Time Pottery
Rag Shops
Wal-Mart

HISTORICAL FINANCIALS
Company Type: Private

Income Statement				FYE: December 31
	REVENUE ($ mil.)	NET INCOME ($ mil.)	NET PROFIT MARGIN	EMPLOYEES
12/02	1,164	—	—	13,500
12/01	1,015	—	—	15,000
12/00	905	—	—	13,500
12/99	798	—	—	12,000
12/98	664	—	—	11,000
12/97	590	—	—	7,500
12/96	540	—	—	7,500
Annual Growth	13.7%	—	—	10.3%

Revenue History

Hogan & Hartson

One of the most prominent law firms in Washington, DC, Hogan & Hartson helps keep our nation's capital teeming with legal eagles. The firm has a staff of more than 900 attorneys, about 40% of whom conduct corporate, securities, financial, and tax work. In addition to US offices in nine cities, the firm also has garnered recognition as an international advocate, having established offices in Brussels, London, Moscow, Tokyo, and Warsaw. Its practice areas also include energy, government contracts, immigration, and litigation. Founded in 1904, the firm recently served as counsel to Netscape (the Department of Justice's lead witness in the government's antitrust case against Microsoft).

EXECUTIVES

Chairman: J. Warren Gorrell Jr.
Director of Administration: Robert M. Johnston
Director of Finance: Robert (Bob) Bolten
CTO: Mike Lucas
Director of Marketing Strategy: Wendy Taylor
Human Resources Officer: Martha K. Williams

LOCATIONS

HQ: Hogan & Hartson
555 13th St. NW, Washington, DC 20004
Phone: 202-637-5600   **Fax:** 202-637-5910
Web: www.hhlaw.com

Hogan & Hartson has US offices in Baltimore; Boulder, Colorado Springs, and Denver, Colorado; Los Angeles; McLean, Virginia; New York City; Miami; and Washington, DC. The firm has international offices in Berlin, Brussels, Budapest, London, Moscow, Paris, Prague, Tokyo, and Warsaw.

PRODUCTS/OPERATIONS

Selected Practice Areas
Antitrust
Aviation
Business
Communications
Education
Employee benefits
Energy
Environmental
Financial services
Food, drug, medical device, and agriculture
Franchise and distribution
Government contracts
Health
Immigration
International trade
Internet and e-commerce
Labor and employment
Legislative
Litigation
Private equity
Real estate
Real estate securities
Tax
Technology

COMPETITORS

Akin Gump
Arnold & Porter
Baker & McKenzie
Covington & Burling
Jones Day
McDermott, Will
Morgan, Lewis
Skadden, Arps
Williams & Connolly
Wilmer, Cutler

HISTORICAL FINANCIALS
Company Type: Partnership

Income Statement				FYE: December 31
	REVENUE ($ mil.)	NET INCOME ($ mil.)	NET PROFIT MARGIN	EMPLOYEES
12/03	550	—	—	—
12/02	480	—	—	—
12/01	385	—	—	—
12/00	320	—	—	1,644
12/99	262	—	—	1,800
12/98	236	—	—	1,686
12/97	201	—	—	1,457
12/96	165	—	—	—
12/95	140	—	—	—
12/94	135	—	—	—
Annual Growth	16.9%	—	—	4.1%

Revenue History

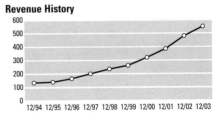

Holiday Companies

Wholesaling and sporting goods retailing have both taken a vacation at Holiday Cos. The firm sold its Fairway Foods distribution business in 2000 and its Gander Mountain sporting goods chain went public in 2004. Holiday Companies now owns about 350 Holiday Stationstores in about a dozen states from Michigan west to Washington and recently moved into Alaska. These stores sell gas supplied by the company's Erickson Petroleum subsidiary as well as Blue Planet gasoline, low-sulfur fuel available in Minnesota. The company was founded in 1928 as a general store in a small Wisconsin town by two Erickson brothers, whose descendants still own and run the company.

Holiday Companies entered the Alaska market in 2004 with the acquisition of about 25 Williams Express gas stations and convenience stores there from the A. T. Williams Oil Co.

Holiday Companies is the former owner of Gander Mountain, a chain of about 65 sporting goods stores, which went public in February 2004.

EXECUTIVES

Chairman and CEO: Ronald A. (Ron) Erickson, age 67
VP, Human Resources: Robert (Bob) Nye
VP, Holiday Stationstores: George Townsend
VP, Petroleum Supply and Distribution, Holiday Stationstores: Dick Mills
President and CEO, Gander Mountain: Mark R. Baker, age 46
CFO, Gander Mountain: Dennis M. Lindahl
EVP, Merchandising and Marketing, Gander Mountain: Allen L. (Al) Dittrich, age 49
EVP, Gander Mountain: Gary Hauger
Regional VP and District Manager, Iowa and Minnesota: Andy Carlin
Controller: Mary Evenson
Director, Food Service, Holiday Stationstores: Larry Hill
Auditors: Ernst & Young LLP

LOCATIONS

HQ: Holiday Companies
4567 American Blvd. West, Bloomington, MN 55437
Phone: 952-830-8700 **Fax:** 952-830-8864
Web: holidaystationstores.com

Holiday Companies operates about 350 Holiday Stationstores in Alaska, Idaho, Iowa, Michigan, Minnesota, Montana, Nebraska, North Dakota, South Dakota, Washington, Wisconsin, and Wyoming.

COMPETITORS

7-Eleven
Casey's General Stores
Exxon Mobil
Galyan's
Kroger
Marathon Ashland Petroleum
QuikTrip

HISTORICAL FINANCIALS

Company Type: Private

Income Statement
FYE: December 31

	ESTIMATED REVENUE ($ mil.)	NET INCOME ($ mil.)	NET PROFIT MARGIN	EMPLOYEES
12/03	1,200	—	—	4,000
12/02	1,250	—	—	6,000
12/01	1,300	—	—	5,500
12/00	1,200	—	—	5,500
12/99	1,100	—	—	5,500
12/98	1,700	—	—	6,000
12/97	1,100	—	—	5,000
12/96	1,000	—	—	5,000
12/95	1,250	—	—	5,100
12/94	1,600	—	—	5,000
Annual Growth	(3.1%)	—	—	(2.4%)

Revenue History

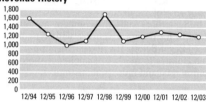

Holland & Knight

Your legal knight in shining armor is just around the corner. Holland & Knight is one of the largest law firms in the US, operating in more than 100 practice areas of law organized into four major departments (business law; litigation; public law; and real estate, environmental, and land use). Holland & Knight was founded in the 1880s and has more than 20 offices in about a dozen US states, with five international offices. The firm has been growing through acquisitions, adding Levine & Associates, a leading firm in Native American affairs; the Los Angeles and Tokyo offices of Whitman Breed Abbott & Morgan; and Gilbert, Segall & Young to its stable of more than 1,200 lawyers.

The firm combined with Chicago-based firm McBride Baker & Coles in August 2002.

EXECUTIVES

Chairman: Martha W. Barnett
Managing Partner: Howell W. Melton Jr.
Executive Director: Herb Albritton
CFO: Carl Culler
CIO: Ralph Barber
Director Human Resources: Andrew Petterson
Director Marketing: Brian Kegelman
Public Relations Manager: Karen Schoening
Auditors: Ernst & Young

LOCATIONS

HQ: Holland & Knight LLP
195 Broadway, 24th Fl., New York, NY 10007
Phone: 212-513-3200 **Fax:** 212-385-9010
Web: www.hklaw.com

Holland & Knight has US offices in California, Florida, Georgia, Illinois, Georgia, Illinois, Maryland, Massachusetts, New York, Rhode Island, Virginia, Washington, and Washington, DC. The firm has international offices in Brazil, Finland, Mexico, and Japan.

PRODUCTS/OPERATIONS

Selected Practice Groups
Business law
Litigation
Public law
Real estate, environmental, and land use

Selected Practice Areas
Agriculture
Appropriations
Bankruptcy
Class action
Communications
Criminal defense
Education
Energy
Estates and trusts
Health care
Native American affairs
Marital and family law
Maritime and shipping
Product liability
REITS
Telecommunications
Trusts and estates
White-collar crime

COMPETITORS

Akin Gump
Foley & Lardner
Greenberg Traurig
Jones Day
Kirkland & Ellis
Latham & Watkins
McDermott, Will
McGuireWoods
Piper Rudnick

HISTORICAL FINANCIALS

Company Type: Partnership

Income Statement
FYE: December 31

	REVENUE ($ mil.)	NET INCOME ($ mil.)	NET PROFIT MARGIN	EMPLOYEES
12/03	532	—	—	2,800
12/02	515	—	—	2,800
12/01	466	—	—	2,722
12/00	364	—	—	—
12/99	298	—	—	2,600
12/98	228	—	—	—
12/97	169	—	—	—
12/96	138	—	—	—
12/95	115	—	—	—
12/94	99	—	—	—
Annual Growth	20.6%	—	—	1.9%

Revenue History

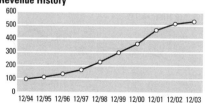

Holman Enterprises

Holman sells a whole lot of cars. Family-owned Holman Enterprises owns about 20 car and truck dealerships in southern New Jersey and southern Florida. Founded in 1924, Holman sells BMW, Ford, Infiniti, Jaguar, Lincoln, Mercury, Rolls-Royce, and Saturn cars, as well as Ford and Sterling trucks. The company also offers collision repair services. Holman's RMP engine and parts distributor sells small parts and engines authorized by Ford. Its Automotive Resources International unit, one of the largest independently owned vehicle fleet leasing management groups in the world, also operates a truck parts and accessories company.

EXECUTIVES
Chairman and CEO: Joseph S. Holman
Vice Chairwoman and President: Mindy Holman
VP: Bill Cariss
VP Finance: Robert Campbell
Director Human Resources: Paul Toepel

LOCATIONS
HQ: Holman Enterprises
7411 Maple Ave., Pennsauken, NJ 08109
Phone: 856-663-5200   **Fax:** 856-665-3444
Web: www.holmanauto.com

COMPETITORS
AMERCO
AutoNation
CarMax
Cendant
Enterprise Rent-A-Car
Hendrick Automotive
JM Family Enterprises
Morse Operations
Penske
Planet Automotive Group
Ryder
Sansone Auto Network
Toresco Enterprises
United Auto Group
Wheels

HISTORICAL FINANCIALS
Company Type: Private

Income Statement				FYE: December 31
	REVENUE ($ mil.)	NET INCOME ($ mil.)	NET PROFIT MARGIN	EMPLOYEES
12/03	2,042	—	—	2,700
12/02	2,483	—	—	2,700
12/01	2,105	—	—	2,600
12/00	2,200	—	—	2,800
12/99	2,146	—	—	2,718
12/98	1,870	—	—	2,700
12/97	1,870	—	—	2,800
12/96	1,800	—	—	2,700
12/95	1,600	—	—	2,500
12/94	1,350	—	—	2,870
Annual Growth	4.7%	—	—	(0.7%)

Revenue History

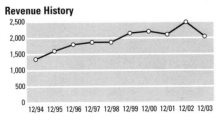

Holmes Group

The Holmes Group makes what it takes to open canned goods, slow-cook meals, and then vacuum seal the leftovers. The company (formerly Holmes Products) makes Bionaire, Family Care, Holmes, and other brands of air purifiers, fans, heaters, and humidifiers. Its Rival kitchen appliances division, which accounts for more than half of Holmes' sales, makes can openers, Crock-Pots, ice cream makers, and more. Holmes has shut down all US manufacturing operations and makes its products in China or buys them from suppliers in the Far East. Holmes' products are sold in the Americas, Asia, and Europe. Together, Wal-Mart, Kmart, and Target ring up about 45% of Holmes' sales.

Investment firm Berkshire Partners owns about 75% of the firm.

In September 2004 the company announced plans to form a joint venture with Wisconsin-based Regal-Beloit. The new partnership will enable Holmes to market its appliance motors to commercial and industrial customers.

EXECUTIVES
Chairman and CEO: Jordan A. (Jerry) Kahn, age 62, $827,944 pay
SVP and CFO: John M. Kelliher, age 52, $343,878 pay
SVP, Human Resources and Organization Performance: Louis F. Cimini, age 49, $257,374 pay
Managing Director, Far East Operations and Director: Woon Fai (Tommy) Liu, age 51, $444,171 pay
Auditors: PricewaterhouseCoopers LLP

LOCATIONS
HQ: The Holmes Group, Inc.
1 Holmes Way, Milford, MA 01757
Phone: 508-634-8050   **Fax:** 508-634-1211
Web: www.theholmesgroup.com

2003 Sales
	$ mil.	% of total
US	521.6	84
Far East	75.7	12
Canada, Europe & Mexico	26.5	4
Total	**623.8**	**100**

PRODUCTS/OPERATIONS

Selected Products
Home environment appliances
  Air purifiers
  Fans
  Heaters
  Humidifiers
  Lighting products
Kitchen appliances
  Deep fryers
  Griddles
  Ice cream makers
  Roaster ovens
  Skillets
  Slow cookers
  Vacuum food sealers

Selected Brands
Bionaire
Crock-Pot
Family Care
Holmes
Patton
Rival
Titan
White Mountain

COMPETITORS
Applica
Craftmade
Fedders
Hamilton Beach/Proctor-Silex
Juno Lighting
Kaz
National Presto Industries
Philips North America
Salton
SEB
Sunbeam
Toastmaster Inc.

HISTORICAL FINANCIALS
Company Type: Private

Income Statement				FYE: December 31
	REVENUE ($ mil.)	NET INCOME ($ mil.)	NET PROFIT MARGIN	EMPLOYEES
12/03	624	52	8.4%	7,500
12/02	609	(58)	—	7,300
12/01	628	(16)	—	7,500
12/00	513	(32)	—	7,500
12/99	507	2	0.4%	7,500
12/98	215	9	4.2%	4,300
12/97	192	4	2.0%	4,150
12/96	194	6	3.2%	—
12/95	178	3	1.8%	—
Annual Growth	17.0%	41.8%	—	10.4%

2003 Year-End Financials
Debt ratio: —
Return on equity: —
Cash ($ mil.): 6
Current ratio: 2.17
Long-term debt ($ mil.): 198

Net Income History

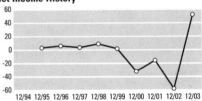

Home Interiors & Gifts

Home Interiors & Gifts is knocking. The company makes decorating accessories, which are sold by nearly 100,000 representatives through home parties in the US, Canada, Mexico, and Puerto Rico. Its product lines include artificial flowers, candles, framed artwork, lighting sconces, mirrors, plaques, and shelves. The firm buys virtually all of its products from subsidiaries such as Dallas Woodcraft Company and Laredo Candle Company. Mary Crowley, sister-in-law of makeup maven Mary Kay Ash, founded Home Interiors in 1957. Executives led by Joey Carter (Crowley's grandson) and buyout firm Hicks, Muse, Tate & Furst recapitalized Home Interiors & Gifts in 1998. Hicks, Muse owns more than 75% of the company.

EXECUTIVES

Chairman and CEO: Donald J. (Joey) Carter Jr., age 43, $725,000 pay
Vice Chairman: Christina L. (Christi) Carter Urschel, age 40
President and CEO: Michael D. (Mike) Lohner, age 41, $1,489,916 pay
SVP Finance, CFO, and Secretary:
 Kenneth J. (Ken) Cichocki, age 51, $347,601 pay
SVP International and Business Development:
 Eugenia B. (Jeannie) Price, age 38, $267,358 pay
SVP Operations: Mary-Knight Tyler, age 42, $181,194 pay
SVP Sales: Nora I. Serrano, age 37, $341,064 pay
VP IT: Alan Boyer
President, Domistyle, Inc.: Charles L. Elsey, age 50
Associate VP Human Resources: Pat Sinclair
Auditors: PricewaterhouseCoopers LLP

LOCATIONS

HQ: Home Interiors & Gifts, Inc.
 1649 Frankford Rd. West, Carrollton, TX 75007
Phone: 972-695-1000   **Fax:** 972-695-1112
Web: www.homeinteriors.com

2003 Sales

	$ mil.	% of total
US	549.5	89
Other countries	67.9	11
Total	**617.4**	**100**

PRODUCTS/OPERATIONS

Selected Products
Artificial floral displays
Candle holders
Candles
Figurines
Framed artwork and mirrors
Planters
Plaques
Sconces
Wall shelves

COMPETITORS

Alticor
Avon
Blyth
Garden Ridge
Hanover Direct
Hobby Lobby
Lancaster Colony
Lillian Vernon
Mary Kay
Michaels Stores
Pier 1 Imports
Pinnacle Frames
Wal-Mart
Yankee Candle

HISTORICAL FINANCIALS

Company Type: Private

Income Statement
FYE: December 31

	REVENUE ($ mil.)	NET INCOME ($ mil.)	NET PROFIT MARGIN	EMPLOYEES
12/03	617	32	5.2%	3,700
12/02	575	36	6.2%	2,400
12/01	462	4	0.8%	1,300
12/00	460	10	2.1%	1,200
12/99	503	52	10.3%	1,400
12/98	490	48	9.9%	1,400
12/97	469	62	13.3%	—
12/96	434	54	12.5%	—
12/95	483	50	10.2%	—
12/94	515	71	13.7%	—
Annual Growth	**2.0%**	**(8.4%)**	—	**21.5%**

2003 Year-End Financials
Debt ratio: —
Return on equity: —
Cash ($ mil.): 37
Current ratio: 1.52
Long-term debt ($ mil.): 312

Honickman

Honickman Affiliates doesn't mind bottling its creative juices. The firm is one of the nation's largest private bottlers — bottling and distributing soft drinks primarily in Maryland, New Jersey, New York, Ohio, and Virginia through more than 10 plants. A major bottler of Pepsi-Cola and Cadbury Schweppes brands including 7 UP, it also sells Canada Dry, Mott's, Snapple, and South Beach Beverage Company's SoBe beverages. It distributes Coors beers in New York and brews up private-label soft drinks. Chairman and owner Harold Honickman started the company in 1957 when his father-in-law built a bottling plant for him.

Net Income History

EXECUTIVES

Chairman: Harold Honickman
CEO: Jeffrey Honickman
CFO: Walt Wilkinson
President of Pepsi-Cola and Canada Dry:
 Robert Brockway
Director of Human Resources: June Raufer
Data Processing: Gwen Dolcemore

LOCATIONS

HQ: Honickman Affiliates
 8275 Rte. 130, Pennsauken, NJ 08110
Phone: 856-665-6200   **Fax:** 856-661-4684

COMPETITORS

Coca-Cola Bottling Consolidated
Coca-Cola Enterprises
Cott
National Beverage
Nestlé
Odwalla
Philadelphia Coca-Cola
Suntory

HISTORICAL FINANCIALS

Company Type: Private

Income Statement
FYE: December 31

	ESTIMATED REVENUE ($ mil.)	NET INCOME ($ mil.)	NET PROFIT MARGIN	EMPLOYEES
12/02	983	—	—	—
12/01	1,100	—	—	5,000
12/00	980	—	—	5,000
12/99	1,000	—	—	5,200
12/98	1,005	—	—	5,200
12/97	1,000	—	—	5,200
12/96	1,000	—	—	5,200
12/95	975	—	—	—
12/94	912	—	—	—
Annual Growth	**0.9%**	—	—	**(0.8%)**

Horizon Blue Cross Blue Shield of New Jersey

Horizon Blue Cross Blue Shield of New Jersey is New Jersey's top not-for-profit health insurance provider, serving nearly 3 million members. The company's insurance plans include traditional indemnity, Horizon HMO, Horizon PPO, and Horizon Direct Access (Open Access). Horizon Blue Cross Blue Shield of New Jersey also offers dental, Medicare, and behavioral health coverage, as well as workers' compensation insurance. The company's Horizon Healthcare Insurance Agency subsidiary provides life, long-term disability, and long-term care coverage. The company's Horizon/Mercy subsidiary participates in the state of New Jersey's Medicaid program.

Although it was once considered a prime candidate for conversion to a for-profit public company (like Anthem, WellChoice, and WellPoint), Horizon Blue Cross Blue Shield of New Jersey has decided to remain not-for-profit.

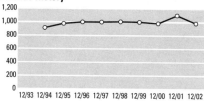

Revenue History

EXECUTIVES

President and CEO: William J. Marino, age 60
SVP, Administration, CFO and Treasurer:
 Robert J. Pures
SVP, General Counsel and Secretary: John W. Campbell
SVP, Healthcare Management: Christy W. Bell
SVP, Information Systems and Chief Information Officer: Charles C. Emery Jr.
SVP, Market Business Units: Robert A. Marino
SVP, Service: Patrick J. Gerghty
VP, Corporate Marketing and Communications:
 Lawrence B. Altman
VP, Actuarial and Chief Actuary: John J. Lynch
VP, Health Affairs and Chief Medical Officer:
 Richard G. Popiel
VP, Human Resources: Carole Czar Soldo
Auditors: PricewaterhouseCoopers LLP

LOCATIONS

HQ: Horizon Blue Cross Blue Shield of New Jersey
 3 Penn Plaza East, Newark, NJ 07101
Phone: 973-466-4000   **Fax:** 973-466-4317
Web: www.horizon-bcbsnj.com

Horizon Blue Cross Blue Shield of New Jersey's operations area includes the state of New Jersey, and ten counties in lower New York state.

PRODUCTS/OPERATIONS

2003 Sales

	$ mil.	% of total
Premiums	4,708.2	93
Administrative service fees	275.5	5
Investments	85.3	2
Other	13.4	—
Total	5,082.4	100

Subsidiaries

Horizon Casualty Services (workers' comp and TPA services)
Horizon Healthcare (managed care plans and services)
Horizon/Mercy (Medicaid HMO)
Horizon Healthcare Dental (managed dental care plans and services)
Horizon Healthcare Insurance Agency (Life, LTD, and LTC)

COMPETITORS

Aetna
CIGNA
UnitedHealth Group

HISTORICAL FINANCIALS

Company Type: Not-for-profit

Income Statement				FYE: December 31
	REVENUE ($ mil.)	NET INCOME ($ mil.)	NET PROFIT MARGIN	EMPLOYEES
12/03	5,082	171	3.4%	4,600
12/02	4,098	114	2.8%	4,600
12/01	3,534	106	3.0%	—
12/00	3,079	117	3.8%	—
Annual Growth	18.2%	13.4%	—	0.0%

2003 Year-End Financials

Debt ratio: 15.6%
Return on equity: 21.2%
Cash ($ mil.): 278
Current ratio: 0.99
Long-term debt ($ mil.): 143

Net Income History

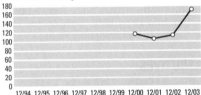

Horizon Natural Resources

Horizon Natural Resources is one of the US's largest producers of steam (bituminous) coal. The company operates mines in four states. It sells mainly to electric utilities in the eastern US. Horizon's Mining Technologies unit makes Addcar-brand highwall mining equipment, while its Mining Machinery subsidiary provides trucking services, major equipment rebuilds, and mining equipment. Horizon's ties to the founding Addington family were severed as part of a reorganization that brought the company out of bankruptcy in 2002; however, later that year it again filed to reorganize under Chapter 11. In 2004 W. L. Ross, through holding company International Coal Group, won the bid for the assets of Horizon.

EXECUTIVES

Acting CEO and Director: Scott M. Tepper, age 42
Financial Advisor: Steven Cohn, age 49
EVP, Human Resources and Administration: Lance G. Sogan, age 56
SVP, Sales and Marketing: Marc R. Merritt, age 50
VP Finance: William Campbell
General Counsel: Daniel L. Stickler, age 57
Auditors: Deloitte & Touche

LOCATIONS

HQ: Horizon Natural Resources Company
2000 Ashland Dr., Ashland, KY 41101
Phone: 606-920-7400 **Fax:** 606-920-7720
Web: www.horizonnr.com

Horizon Natural Resources mines and markets steam coal from mines in Indiana, Illinois, Kentucky, and West Virginia. It also owns subsidiaries that produce mining machinery and offer related services in Kentucky.

PRODUCTS/OPERATIONS

Selected Operations

Mining Machinery (trucking services, equipment and component rebuilding services, equipment rental)
Mining Technologies, Inc. (ADDCAR Highwall Mining System)
Zeigler Coal Holding Company (underground and surface coal mining)

COMPETITORS

Arch Coal
CONSOL Energy
Drummond
Foundation Coal
Ingersoll-Rand
Kennecott Energy
Massey Energy
Peabody Energy
Westmoreland Coal

HISTORICAL FINANCIALS

Company Type: Private

Income Statement				FYE: December 31
	REVENUE ($ mil.)	NET INCOME ($ mil.)	NET PROFIT MARGIN	EMPLOYEES
12/02	1,158	(964)	—	3,500
12/01	1,413	(226)	—	4,000
12/00	1,500	—	—	4,000
12/99	1,331	—	—	4,000
12/98	733	—	—	4,081
12/97	175	—	—	—
12/96	123	—	—	—
Annual Growth	45.3%	—	—	(3.8%)

Net Income History

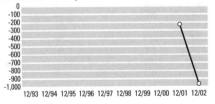

Horseshoe Gaming

Bring your lucky charms to casinos owned by Horseshoe Gaming Holding Corp. The company owns a Horseshoe Casino and Hotel in Bossier City, Louisiana, as well as one in Tunica, Mississippi. In 2001 Horseshoe Gaming sold its Empress Casino riverboat and hotel in Joliet, Illinois, but it retains an Empress location in Hammond, Indiana. Illinois officials denied the company a license to operate the Empress riverboat in Joliet, alleging that owner and CEO Jack Binion failed to comply with state regulations after buying the casino. The company appealed the decision, but later struck a deal that forced it to sell the location to Argosy Gaming. Harrah's Entertainment has acquired Horseshoe for $1.45 billion.

EXECUTIVES

Chairman, CEO, and Secretary: Jack B. Binion, age 67, $1,000,000 pay
Vice Chairperson: Peri N. Howard, age 43, $592,300 pay
President and COO: Roger P. Wagner, age 56, $947,700 pay
SVP, CFO, and Treasurer: Kirk C. Saylor, age 47, $552,800 pay
SVP and CIO: Jon C. Wolfe, age 36
SVP and General Counsel: Dominic F. Polizzotto, age 38, $561,700 pay
SVP Human Resources: David S. Carroll, age 48
SVP Government Affairs: Floyd B. Hannon, age 61, $562,500 pay
SVP Marketing: Christopher Corrado, age 34
Auditors: Deloitte & Touche LLP

LOCATIONS

HQ: Horseshoe Gaming Holding Corp.
9921 Covington Cross Dr., Las Vegas, NV 89144
Phone: 702-932-7800 **Fax:** 702-932-7825
Web: www.horseshoegaming.com

2003 Sales

	% of total
Hammond	41
Bossier City	31
Tunica	28
Total	100

COMPETITORS

Caesars Entertainment
Casino Magic
Isle of Capri Casinos
Lakes Entertainment
Mandalay Resort Group
Pinnacle Entertainment

HISTORICAL FINANCIALS

Company Type: Private

Income Statement				FYE: December 31
	REVENUE ($ mil.)	NET INCOME ($ mil.)	NET PROFIT MARGIN	EMPLOYEES
12/03	848	72	8.4%	7,562
12/02	813	60	7.4%	7,780
12/01	933	232	24.9%	7,843
12/00	1,013	61	6.0%	9,699
12/99	526	32	6.2%	8,920
12/98	461	25	5.4%	—
12/97	335	27	8.2%	—
Annual Growth	16.7%	17.4%	—	(4.0%)

Houchens

2003 Year-End Financials
Debt ratio: 183.7%
Return on equity: 27.5%
Cash ($ mil.): 104
Current ratio: 1.53
Long-term debt ($ mil.): 534

Net Income History

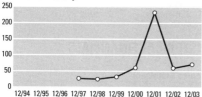

Houchens Industries operates stores for shoppers more interested in supper than super. Eschewing the industry trend toward massive superstores, the company's 40 Houchens Markets in Kentucky average less than 20,000 sq. ft. Its nearly 200 Save-A-Lot stores (licensed from SUPERVALU) offer limited selections and cover 15,000 sq. ft. or less. Houchens has stores in 13 states from eastern Texas to New York. The company also owns more than 40 Jr. Foods convenience stores and 23 Tobacco Shoppe discount cigarette outlets, mostly in Kentucky and Tennessee. It bought cigarette maker Commonwealth Brands in 2001. Founded as BG Wholesale in 1918 by Ervin Houchens, the company is entirely owned by its employees.

Houchens Industries has acquired Food Giant Supermarkets, the operator of 90 Food Giant and Piggly Wiggly supermarkets in eight states. It also plans to acquire Scotty's Contracting & Stone in a stock swap between the two employee-owned companies. Connected with the Scotty's transaction, Houchens also would acquire TS Trucking.

Houchens Industries is a diversified company operating subsidiaries in the construction, insurance, recycling, and warehousing businesses, among others.

EXECUTIVES
Chairman and CEO: James (Jimmie) Gipson
CFO: Mark Iverson
Director of Advertising: Venus Popplewell
Director of Benefits: Sharon Grooms
Information Systems Manager: David Puckett

LOCATIONS
HQ: Houchens Industries Inc.
900 Church St., Bowling Green, KY 42101
Phone: 270-843-3252   **Fax:** 270-780-2877

Houchens Industries has stores in Alabama, Georgia, Illinois, Indiana, Kentucky, New York, North Carolina, Ohio, South Carolina, Tennessee, Texas, Virginia, and West Virginia.

COMPETITORS
7-Eleven
Alliance Tobacco
Cigarettes Cheaper
Cumberland Farms
Delhaize America
Kroger
K-VA-T Food Stores
Meijer
Sheetz
Smokin Joes
Vector
Wal-Mart
Weis Markets
Winn-Dixie

Houghton Mifflin

HISTORICAL FINANCIALS
Company Type: Private

Income Statement — FYE: September 30

	ESTIMATED REVENUE ($ mil.)	NET INCOME ($ mil.)	NET PROFIT MARGIN	EMPLOYEES
9/03	1,913	—	—	7,760
9/02	1,727	—	—	5,850
9/01	820	—	—	5,200
9/00	735	—	—	4,800
9/99	585	—	—	4,200
9/98	515	—	—	3,860
9/97	450	—	—	3,600
9/96	400	—	—	3,100
Annual Growth	25.1%	—	—	14.0%

Revenue History

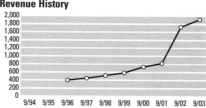

Alice Cooper's 1972 album *School's Out* probably doesn't get much play around the offices of Houghton Mifflin. A top publisher of textbooks for the K-12 and college markets, the company also offers fiction and nonfiction books for adults and children and reference works such as the *American Heritage Dictionary*. Major divisions include McDougal Littell (secondary school textbooks), Riverside Publishing (educational testing), and Great Source Education Group (supplemental school materials for grades K-12). It also operates a digital publishing business. Vivendi Universal Publishing (now Editis), formerly the publishing arm of French media giant Vivendi Universal, sold Houghton to several investment firms in 2002.

The company's trade fiction and nonfiction lines, although small, still produce the occasional best seller (such as 2001's *Fast Food Nation* by Eric Schlosser).

Houghton Mifflin is working on building up the company's college, trade and reference, and workplace assessments units. The publisher currently relies heavily on its K-12 publishing business, which makes up 65% of sales.

After 150 years in business as an independent company, the company has had several changes of ownership in recent years. Houghton Mifflin was acquired by French media giant Vivendi Universal in 2001 for $2.2 billion (which included the assumption of $500 million in debt). Houghton Mifflin was placed under Vivendi Universal's publishing unit, which in 2002 decided to sell off most of its assets as part of Vivendi Universal's $9.8 billion sale of assets. Two investment firms (Thomas H. Lee and Bain Capital) bought Houghton Mifflin.

Parent company HM Publishing Corp. owns Houghton Mifflin.

EXECUTIVES
CEO: Anthony (Tony) Lucki
EVP, CFO, and COO: Stephen Richards
SVP and CIO: Patrick J. (Pat) Meehan
SVP Administration: Gary L. Smith, age 56
SVP, Clerk, Secretary, and General Counsel:
  Paul D. Weaver, age 58
SVP Educational and Governmental Affairs:
  Maureen DiMarco
SVP Human Resources: Gerald T. Hughes, age 44
SVP Trade and Reference: Theresa (Terri) Kelly
VP Corporate Communications: Collin Earnst
Senior Marketing Manager: Carla Gray
Auditors: Ernst & Young LLP

LOCATIONS
HQ: Houghton Mifflin Company
222 Berkeley St., Boston, MA 02116
Phone: 617-351-5000   **Fax:** 617-351-1105
Web: www.hmco.com

PRODUCTS/OPERATIONS

Selected Operations

Education
  Classwell (online pre K-12 educational resources)
  Edusoft (assessment tools)
  Great Source Education Group (supplemental education materials)
  McDougal Littell (secondary textbooks)
  Promissor (test administration technology and services)
  The Riverside Publishing Company (testing materials)
Professional Development
  Calabash (professional development resources)
Trade and Reference Division

COMPETITORS
Educational Testing Service
Everyday Learning
Goodheart-Willcox
Harcourt Education
HarperCollins
John Wiley
McGraw-Hill
Pearson
Random House
Scholastic
Scholastic Library Publishing
Time Warner Book Group
Touchstone Applied Science
Verlagsgruppe Georg von Holtzbrinck
W.W. Norton

HISTORICAL FINANCIALS
Company Type: Private

Income Statement — FYE: December 31

	REVENUE ($ mil.)	NET INCOME ($ mil.)	NET PROFIT MARGIN	EMPLOYEES
12/03	1,264	(72)	—	3,459
12/02	1,195	(790)	—	3,550
12/01	1,129	(26)	—	3,500
12/00	1,028	56	5.4%	3,500
12/99	920	76	8.3%	3,300
12/98	862	64	7.4%	2,830
12/97	797	50	6.2%	2,550
12/96	718	44	6.1%	2,420
12/95	529	(7)	—	2,350
12/94	483	51	10.6%	2,023
Annual Growth	11.3%	—	—	6.1%

2003 Year-End Financials
Debt ratio: 208.4%
Return on equity: —
Cash ($ mil.): 170
Current ratio: 1.87
Long-term debt ($ mil.): 1,134

Net Income History

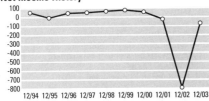

HP Hood

HP Hood is busily trying to cream its competition — with ice cream, sour cream, and whipping cream. The company, one of New England's leading dairies, also produces milk, cottage cheese, and juices. Besides its own brands, HP Hood makes private-label, licensed, and franchise products. It specializes in extended-shelf-life products, which are distributed nationally under licensing agreements. Founded in 1846 by Harvey P. Hood as a one-man milk delivery service, the company still offers home delivery. The family of CEO John Kaneb owns the company. HP Hood bought dairy producers Crowley Foods and Marigold Foods from National Dairy Holdings in 2004.

The purchase brought the Kemp, Heluva, Axelrod, Maggio, Brown's Velvet, and Dairymens brands into the HP Hood fold, among others.

EXECUTIVES

Chairman, President, and CEO: John A. Kaneb
CFO: Gary R. Kaneb
SVP, Sales: James F. Walsh
VP, Human Resources: Bruce W. Bacon
VP, Licensed Marketing: Kevin Donavan
VP, Operations Services: Francis V. Torgerson
VP, Research, Development, and Quality Control:
  Margaret A. Poole
Treasurer: Theresa M. Bresten
Controller: James A. Marcinelli
Director, IS: Jack Billiel
Director, Public Relations and Government Affairs:
  Lynne M. Bohan
General Counsel: Paul F. Beatty

LOCATIONS

HQ: HP Hood Inc.
  90 Everett Ave., Chelsea, MA 02150
Phone: 617-887-3000 **Fax:** 617-887-8484
Web: www.hphood.com

HP Hood has plants in Connecticut, Maine, Massachusetts, New York, Vermont, and Virginia.

PRODUCTS/OPERATIONS

Selected Brands
Axelrod
Booth Brothers
Brown's Velvet
Dairymens
Gillette Milk
Heluva
Hood
Kemp
Lactaid
Maggio
Oak Grove

COMPETITORS

Brigham's
Dean Foods
Dreyer's
Guida's
Organic Valley
Parmalat Canada
Stew Leonard's
Stonyfield Farm
Unilever

HISTORICAL FINANCIALS
Company Type: Private

Income Statement FYE: December 31

	REVENUE ($ mil.)	NET INCOME ($ mil.)	NET PROFIT MARGIN	EMPLOYEES
12/03	1,000	—	—	1,600
12/02	1,000	—	—	1,700
12/01	800	—	—	1,600
12/00	700	—	—	1,439
12/99	600	—	—	1,450
12/98	500	—	—	1,300
12/97	500	—	—	1,200
Annual Growth	12.2%	—	—	4.9%

Revenue History

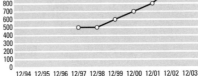

H.T. Hackney

The H.T. Hackney Company began delivering goods to small grocers by horse and buggy in 1891; it now supplies more than 20,000 independent grocers and convenience stores in about 20 states east of the Mississippi. H.T. Hackney distributes more than 25,000 items, including frozen food, tobacco products, health and beauty items, and deli products. In addition it owns Tennessee-based Natural Springs Water Group and has furniture-making operations (Holland House and Volunteer Fabricators). Looking to expand its convenience store business, in 2000 the company acquired six gas stations from Aztex Enterprises and two supply centers from Spartan Stores in 2003. Chairman and CEO Bill Sansom owns H.T. Hackney.

EXECUTIVES

Chairman and CEO: William B. (Bill) Sansom, age 62
VP and CFO: Mike Morton
VP and COO: Dean Ballinger
VP, Administration: Leonard Robinette

LOCATIONS

HQ: H.T. Hackney Company
  502 S. Gay St., Knoxville, TN 37902
Phone: 865-546-1291 **Fax:** 865-546-1501
Web: www.hthackney.com

COMPETITORS

Alex Lee
AMCON Distributing
AWG
C&S Wholesale
Eby-Brown
GSC Enterprises
McLane
Nash Finch
Roundy's
S. Abraham & Sons
Spartan Stores
SUPERVALU

HISTORICAL FINANCIALS
Company Type: Private

Income Statement FYE: March 31

	REVENUE ($ mil.)	NET INCOME ($ mil.)	NET PROFIT MARGIN	EMPLOYEES
3/04	3,500	—	—	3,600
3/03*	3,300	—	—	3,500
12/01	2,500	—	—	3,100
12/00	2,300	—	—	3,100
12/99	2,000	—	—	3,000
12/98	1,818	—	—	2,900
12/97	1,623	—	—	2,643
12/96	1,800	—	—	1,900
Annual Growth	10.0%	—	—	9.6%

*Fiscal year change

Revenue History

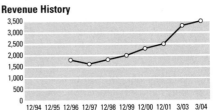

Hunt Consolidated

Hunt Consolidated is a holding company for the oil and real estate businesses of Ray Hunt, son of legendary Texas wildcatter and company founder H.L. Hunt. Founded in 1934 (reportedly with H.L.'s poker winnings), Hunt Oil is an oil and gas production and exploration company with primary interests in North and South America. Hoping to repeat huge discoveries in Yemen, Hunt is exploring in Canada, Ghana, Madagascar, and Oman. It has also teamed up with Repsol YPF and SK Corporation on an exploration project in Peru, and has expanded its Canadian operations through the acquisition of Chieftain International. Hunt Realty handles commercial and residential real estate investment management activities.

EXECUTIVES

Chairman, President, and CEO: Ray L. Hunt, age 60
SVP Financial Operations: Harry Dombroski
SVP Special Projects and New Business Development:
  Thomas A. (Tom) Meurer, age 62
SVP and Tax Counsel: W. Kirk Baker
SVP and General Counsel: Richard A. Massman
VP and CIO: Kevin P. Campbell
VP Global Security: Mike Pritchard
VP Human Resources: Laura S. Weaver

LOCATIONS

HQ: Hunt Consolidated Inc.
  Fountain Place, 1445 Ross at Field, Ste. 1400, Dallas, TX 75202
Phone: 214-978-8000 **Fax:** 214-978-8888
Web: www.huntoil.com

PRODUCTS/OPERATIONS

Selected Subsidiaries and Affiliates
Hunt Oil Company (integrated oil company)
Hunt Oil Company of Canada
Hunt Power L.P. (utility projects and services)
Hunt Private Equity Group
Hunt Realty Corporation (acquires real estate and manages investments)
Hunt Refining Co. Inc.
Hunt Ventures, L.P. (diversified investments)
Yemen Hunt Oil Co.

COMPETITORS

Anadarko Petroleum	Lincoln Property
BP	Murphy Oil
Exxon Mobil	Nexen
Houston Exploration	Royal Dutch/Shell Group
Kerr-McGee	TOTAL

HISTORICAL FINANCIALS

Company Type: Private

Income Statement
FYE: December 31

	REVENUE ($ mil.)	NET INCOME ($ mil.)	NET PROFIT MARGIN	EMPLOYEES
12/02	1,930	—	—	2,500
12/01	1,500	—	—	2,600
12/00	2,000	—	—	2,500
12/99	1,200	—	—	2,600
12/98	700	—	—	2,600
12/97	1,000	—	—	2,600
12/96	1,000	—	—	2,600
12/95	1,000	—	—	2,600
12/94	1,000	—	—	2,600
12/93	1,000	—	—	2,600
Annual Growth	7.6%	—	—	(0.4%)

Revenue History

Huntsman

Huntsman International has gathered together enough business to become the world's largest privately held chemical company (though perhaps not for long). It is among the world's largest makers of basic chemicals and petrochemicals like ethylene and propylene. Huntsman also produces surfactants (used in cleaning and personal care products) and specialty chemicals like polyurethanes, propylene oxides, and propylene glycol. Huntsman also is among the largest makers of titanium dioxide, the most commonly used white pigment, with 15% of the world market.

Though the Huntsman family controls 100% of the company, MatlinPatterson Global Opportunity Partners owns just under half of the business.

In May 2003 Huntsman completed its purchase of four of Imperial Chemical Industries's chemical groups by buying the British chemical giant's 30% stake in Huntsman International for about $400 million. That deal (along with the buyout of the remaining 9% of Huntsman International from JP Morgan Partners and MidOcean Capital Investors) again gave the Huntsman family 100% control of all the Huntsman companies.

However, MatlinPatterson Global Opportunity Partners owns 49.9% equity of the newly created HMP Equity Holdings (which owns Huntsman International and came into being in 2002). The Huntsman family owns the rest and continues to control the company. The agreement with MatlinPatterson saved Huntsman from having to enter bankruptcy. But contingent on Matlin-Patterson's giving full control to the Huntsman family was the eventual move to take the company public. Huntsman International has spent much of 2004 preparing for such a move. The potential IPO would be the chemical industry's largest this decade.

Founder and chairman Jon Huntsman, a cancer survivor, has directed hundreds of millions of dollars of company profits and his own money to educational and charitable causes and medical research. He donated $100 million to fund the Huntsman Cancer Institute at the University of Utah and has pledged an additional $125 to fund research.

His son Jon Huntsman Jr. was elected governor of Utah in November 2004. He was a director of Huntsman International and had been chairman and CEO of Huntsman Family Holding Co., which is one of the larger stakeholders in the Huntsman companies. Jon Huntsman Jr. resigned that position and said that he would place his ownership stake in a blind trust while in office.

HISTORY

First exposed to the use of plastics in the manufacture of egg cartons, Jon Huntsman spent three frustrating years at Dow Chemical. Then he and his brother Blaine raised $300,000 and received a $1 million loan from Hambrecht & Quist to found Huntsman Container in 1970. When chemical supplies began to run short, Huntsman sold the company to Keyes Fiber in 1976.

After six years, half of which had been spent doing missionary work for the Mormon Church, Huntsman took over polystyrene operations and set his sights on an underused Shell plant in Ohio. With oil and gas titan Atlantic Richfield's backing, Huntsman convinced Shell and a bank to lend him the balance of the purchase price and formed Huntsman Chemical in 1982.

With the acquisition of Hoechst Celanese's polystyrene business in 1986, Huntsman became the #1 producer of styrene in the US. In 1987 Huntsman sold 40% of Huntsman Chemical for $52 million and then acquired a New Jersey polypropylene plant from Shell. Huntsman reentered the packaging business in 1989 by acquiring Keyes, the European firm that had once been a part of Huntsman Container.

In 1991 hamburger dynasty McDonald's succumbed to environmentalist pressure and ceased to use the Huntsman-developed polystyrene clamshell containers; as a result, Huntsman lost about 10% of its business. The company acquired packaging assets from Goodyear Tire & Rubber in 1992 and named the new subsidiary Huntsman Packaging. The next year Huntsman bought 50% of Chemplex Australia Limited from Consolidated Press Holdings (controlled by Australian tycoon Kerry Packer).

Huntsman and Packer joined forces again in 1994 to buy most of Texaco's unprofitable petrochemical operations for $1 billion (naming the unit the Huntsman Corporation), which doubled Huntsman's size and added 24 plants in 12 countries. Also that year Huntsman bought Eastman Chemical's worldwide polypropylene business. The next year it formed a joint venture with Texaco to operate Texaco's worldwide lubricant-additives line, and Huntsman reacquired the 17% stake held by Great Lakes Chemical, which had been the only stock in the company held by outsiders at that time.

In 1996 Huntsman placed all of his businesses under a single entity, the Huntsman Corporation. The company bought the last of Texaco's chemicals operations in 1997, moving Huntsman into the propylene oxide market. Huntsman also bought packaging maker Rexene that year.

Huntsman sold its polystyrene and styrene monomer businesses in the US and Europe to NOVA Chemicals in 1998; it retained its expandable polystyrene unit when federal regulators objected to its sale. In 1999 the company doubled its size with the purchase of Imperial Chemical Industries' polyurethane, aromatics, titanium dioxide, petrochemical, and olefins businesses.

In 2000 Huntsman sold Huntsman Packaging to J. P. Morgan Partners in a deal worth $1 billion. Also, Jon Huntsman stepped down as CEO (but remained as chairman). He was succeeded by his son, Peter Huntsman. Late in the year Huntsman acquired Rohm and Haas' thermoplastic polyurethane (TPU) business for about $120 million.

Hamstrung by about $2 billion in debt, higher raw material costs, and a depressed chemicals market, Huntsman stopped paying interest on debt and sought a financial restructuring.

In June 2002 Huntsman restructured its debt through Credit Suisse First Boston's Global Opportunities Partners (now MatlinPatterson Global Opportunity Partners) by creating a holding company that owns Huntsman International and Huntsman Polymers. MatlinPatterson owns 49.9% equity of the newly created HMP Equity Holdings. The Huntsman family owns the rest and continues to run the company.

Also in 2002 Huntsman restructured its business segments. The new categories were: polyurethanes (polyurethanes and PO), base chemicals (olefins and aromatics), pigments (titanium dioxide), and performance products (surfactants, ethyleneamines, and other performance chemicals). The most significant change was the split of the former specialty chemicals segment into two: polyurethanes and performance products. The former tioxide segment was renamed pigments, and the former petrochemicals segment was renamed base chemicals.

EXECUTIVES

Chairman: Jon M. Huntsman Sr., age 66
President, CEO, and Director: Peter R. Huntsman, age 41, $1,348,749 pay
EVP and CFO: J. Kimo Esplin, age 42, $610,775 pay
EVP, General Counsel, and Secretary: Samuel D. Scruggs, age 44, $342,448 pay
EVP: Patrick W. Thomas, $1,006,928 pay (prior to title change)
President, Advanced Materials: Paul Hulme
President, Base Chemicals: Kevin J. Ninow, age 40, $314,213 pay

President, Performance Products: Donald J. Stanutz, age 53
President, Pigments: Thomas J. Keenan, age 51, $436,861 pay (prior to promotion)
President, Polyurethanes: Anthony P (Tony) Hankins
SVP, Environmental, Health, and Safety, and Information Technology: Michael J. Kern, age 54
SVP, Global Public Affairs: Don H. Olsen, age 57
SVP, Purchasing: Brian V. Ridd, age 47
SVP, Pigments: Rob Louw
SVP, Sales and Marketing, Pigments: Wayne Barnacal
VP, Corporate Development: John R. Heskett, age 35
VP, Finance: L. Russell Healy, age 48
VP and Treasurer: Sean Douglas, age 39
VP and Controller: Richard H. Johnigan Jr., age 57
VP, Tax: Kevin Hardman, age 41
Auditors: Deloitte & Touche LLP

LOCATIONS

HQ: Huntsman International LLC
500 Huntsman Way, Salt Lake City, UT 84108
Phone: 801-584-5700 Fax: 801-584-5781
Web: www.huntsman.com

Huntsman International has manufacturing facilities in Africa, Asia, Europe, and North America, and its products are sold throughout the world.

2003 Sales

	$ mil.	% of total
UK	1,927	30
US	1,853	29
Netherlands	1,020	16
Other	1,641	25
Adjustments	(1,195)	—
Total	**5,246**	**100**

PRODUCTS/OPERATIONS

2003 Sales

	$ mil.	% of total
Polyurethanes	2,297	43
Base Chemicals	1,422	26
Pigments	1,010	19
Performance Products	660	12
Adjustments	(143)	—
Total	**5,246**	**100**

Business Segments

Polyurethanes (polyurethanes and propylene oxide)
Base Chemicals (olefins and aromatics)
Pigments (titanium dioxide)
Performance Products (surfactants and other performance chemicals)

Selected Joint Ventures

CONDEA-Huntsman GmbH & Co. KG (automobile parts, boat hulls, and marble bath fixtures; Germany)
Huntsman Chemical Company Australia Limited (joint venture with Consolidated Press Holdings)
Polystyrene Australia (joint venture with Dow Chemical (Australia) Ltd.)
Rubicon, Inc. (manufacturing joint venture with Crompton Corp.)

COMPETITORS

Akzo Nobel	Enichem	Millennium Chemicals
BASF AG	Augusta	
Bayer	Exxon Mobil	Occidental Chemical
BP	Formosa Plastics	
BP Petrochemicals	Hercules	Occidental Petroleum
ChevronTexaco	Houghton Chemical	Owens Corning
Clariant International	Imperial Chemical Industries	PPG
Cognis		Rohm and Haas
Degussa	Kerr-McGee	Sasol
Dow Chemical	Kronos	Shell Chemicals
DuPont	Lyondell	Sinopec
Eastman Chemical		Shanghai Petrochemical
		Teknor Apex

HISTORICAL FINANCIALS

Company Type: Private

Income Statement
FYE: December 31

	REVENUE ($ mil.)	NET INCOME ($ mil.)	NET PROFIT MARGIN	EMPLOYEES
12/03	5,246	89	1.7%	6,300
12/02	4,518	20	0.4%	8,000
12/01	4,575	(61)	—	8,050
12/00	4,448	151	3.4%	6,600
12/99	4,500	—	—	7,500
12/98	4,600	—	—	8,500
12/97	4,750	—	—	9,550
12/96	4,500	—	—	8,000
12/95	4,300	—	—	8,000
12/94	3,400	—	—	8,100
Annual Growth	4.9%	(16.3%)	—	(2.8%)

2003 Year-End Financials

Debt ratio: 253.6% Current ratio: 1.44
Return on equity: 8.0% Long-term debt ($ mil.): 2,925
Cash ($ mil.): 88

Net Income History

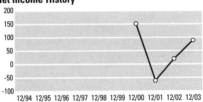

Hyatt

Hyatt is at your service. One of the nation's largest hotel operators, the company (through Hyatt Hotels Corporation) has more than 120 full-service luxury hotels and resorts in North America and the Caribbean. Hyatt International, its overseas branch, operates some additional 80 hotels and resorts in 39 countries. Many of Hyatt's hotels and resorts feature professionally designed golf courses and supervised activities for children (Camp Hyatt). The company also operates gaming (Hyatt Casino) and luxury retirement communities (Classic Residence by Hyatt). Led by chairman and CEO Thomas Pritzker, the company is owned by the wealthy Chicago Pritzker family.

Hyatt caters to business travelers, convention-goers, and upscale vacationers. In addition to the core format, Hyatt Regency, the company operates hotels under the Grand Hyatt (upscale hotels that accommodate large-scale meetings and conventions) and Park Hyatt (smaller luxury hotels that target individual travelers) banners.

The company, through Hyatt International, is doing much of its growing outside the US. It has nearly 20 hotels under construction in places such as China, Korea, Saudi Arabia, Turkey, and Vietnam.

Over the past few years, differences in the Pritzker family have surfaced. Two children of the Hyatt founder are suing the family, claiming they have been cheated out of their inheritance.

HISTORY

Nicholas Pritzker left Kiev for Chicago in 1881, where his family's ascent to the ranks of America's wealthiest families began. His son A. N. left the family law practice in the 1930s and began investing in a variety of businesses. He turned a 1942 investment (Cory Corporation) worth $25,000 into $23 million by 1967. A. N.'s son Jay followed in his father's wheeling-and-dealing footsteps. In 1953, with the help of his father's banking connections, Jay purchased Colson Company and recruited his brother Bob, an industrial engineer, to restructure a company that made tricycles and US Navy rockets. By 1990 Jay and Bob had added 60 industrial companies, with annual sales exceeding $3 billion, to the entity they called The Marmon Group.

The family's connection to Hyatt hotels was established in 1957 when Jay Pritzker bought a hotel called Hyatt House, located near the Los Angeles airport, from Hyatt von Dehn. Jay added five locations by 1961 and hired his gregarious youngest brother, Donald, to manage the hotel company. Hyatt went public in 1967, but the move that opened new vistas for the hotel chain was the purchase that year of an 800-room hotel in Atlanta that both Hilton and Marriott had turned down. John Portman's design, incorporating a 21-story atrium, a large fountain, and a revolving rooftop restaurant, became a Hyatt trademark.

The Pritzkers formed Hyatt International in 1969 to operate hotels overseas, and the company grew rapidly in the US and abroad during the 1970s. Donald Pritzker died in 1972, and Jay assumed control of Hyatt. The family decided to take the company private in 1979. Much of Hyatt's growth in the 1970s came from contracts to manage Hyatt hotels built by other investors. When Hyatt's earnings on those contracts shrank in the 1980s, the company launched its own hotel and resort developments under Nick Pritzker, a cousin to Jay and Bob. In 1988, with US and Japanese partners, it built the Hyatt Regency Waikoloa on Hawaii's Big Island for $360 million — a record at the time for a hotel.

The Pritzkers took a side-venture into air travel in 1983 when they bought bedraggled Braniff Airlines through Hyatt subsidiaries as it emerged from bankruptcy. After a failed 1987 attempt to merge the airline with Pan Am, the Pritzkers sold Braniff in 1988.

Hyatt opened Classic Residence by Hyatt, a group of upscale retirement communities, in 1989. The company joined Circus Circus (now Mandalay Resort Group) in 1994 to launch the Grand Victoria, the nation's largest cruising gaming vessel. The next year, as part of a new strategy to manage both freestanding golf courses and those near Hyatt hotels, the company opened its first freestanding course: an 18-hole, par 71 championship course in Aruba.

President Thomas Pritzker, Jay's son, took over as Hyatt chairman and CEO following his father's death in early 1999. In 2000 Hyatt announced plans to join rival Marriott International in launching an independent company to provide an online procurement network serving the hospitality industry. The following year the company announced plans to build a 47-story skyscraper in downtown Chicago. Construction for the new building, named the Hyatt Center, began at the end of 2002.

EXECUTIVES

Chairman and CEO; Chairman, Hyatt International Corporation: Thomas J. Pritzker, age 53
Vice Chairman; Chairman and President, Hyatt Development Corporation; President, Hyatt Equities: Nicholas J. (Nick) Pritzker
President: Douglas G. Geoga, age 48
Chairman, Classic Residence by Hyatt: Penny S. Pritzker
President, Classic Residence by Hyatt: Randal J. Richardson
President, Hyatt Hotels Corporation: Edward W. Rabin Jr., age 56
President, Hyatt International Corporation: Bernd Chorengel
SVP, Marketing, Hyatt Hotels Corporation: Thomas F. O'Toole, age 46
SVP, Operations, Hyatt Hotels Corporation: Chuck Floyd
VP, Electronic Distribution: Joan Lowell
VP, Finance: Kirk A. Rose
VP, Human Resources, Hyatt Hotels Corporation: Doug Patrick
Divisional VP (Southern), Hyatt Hotels Corporation: Tim Lindgren
Divisional VP (Resorts), Hyatt Hotels Corporation: Victor Lopez, age 53
Divisional VP (Western), Hyatt Hotels Corporation: John Orr
Divisional VP (Central), Hyatt Hotels Corporation: Steve Sokal

LOCATIONS

HQ: Hyatt Corporation
200 W. Madison St., Chicago, IL 60606
Phone: 312-750-1234 **Fax:** 312-750-8550
Web: www.hyatt.com

Hyatt Corporation, through Hyatt Hotels Corporation (North American and Caribbean properties) and Hyatt International (properties on other continents), operate more than 200 hotels and resorts in nearly 40 countries.

PRODUCTS/OPERATIONS

Selected Operations
Camp Hyatt (activities for children)
Classic Residence by Hyatt (upscale retirement communities)
Grand Hyatt (large business and convention hotels)
Hyatt Regency (core hotel format)
Park Hyatt (small luxury hotels)
Regency Casinos (gaming resorts)

COMPETITORS

Accor	Marriott
Four Seasons Hotels	Ritz-Carlton
Hilton	Starwood Hotels & Resorts
InterContinental Hotels	Trump

HISTORICAL FINANCIALS

Company Type: Private

Income Statement				FYE: January 31
	ESTIMATED REVENUE ($ mil.)	NET INCOME ($ mil.)	NET PROFIT MARGIN	EMPLOYEES
1/03	3,600	—	—	40,000
1/02	3,400	—	—	37,000
1/01	3,500	—	—	36,632
1/00	3,950	—	—	80,000
1/99	3,400	—	—	80,000
1/98	3,000	—	—	80,000
1/97	2,900	—	—	80,000
1/96	2,500	—	—	65,000
1/95	1,240	—	—	54,000
1/94	950	—	—	47,000
Annual Growth	16.0%	—	—	(1.8%)

Revenue History

Hy-Vee

Give Hy-Vee a high five for being one of the largest privately-owned US supermarket chains, despite serving some modestly sized towns in the Midwest. The company runs nearly 200 Hy-Vee supermarkets in Illinois, Iowa, Kansas, Minnesota, Missouri, Nebraska, and South Dakota. About half of its supermarkets are in Iowa, as are most of its 25-plus Drug Town drugstores. It distributes products to its stores through several subsidiaries, including Lomar Distributing (specialty foods), Perishable Distributors of Iowa (fresh foods), and Florist Distributing (flowers).

Charles Hyde and David Vredenburg founded the employee-owned firm in 1930. The company's moniker is a combination of the founders' names.

Hy-Vee plans to spend more than $200 million in 2004 to open eight new supermarkets and to relocate or expand about 15 existing stores. It is also acquiring an Osco drugstore in Council Bluffs, Iowa from food-and-drug retail giant Albertson's. That store will become a Drug Town pharmacy.

Going beyond traditional grocery fare, the company has been focusing on adding Hy-Vee Gas units, wine and spirits stores, pharmacies, and Hy-Vee HealthMarket departments. Many Hy-Vee stores also have seasonal garden centers.

EXECUTIVES

Chairman: Ronald D. (Ron) Pearson
President, CEO, and COO: Richard N. (Ric) Jurgens
EVP: Charlie Bell
EVP: Raymond (Ray) Stewart
EVP: Ken Waller
SVP, CFO, and Treasurer: John Briggs
VP, General Merchandise: Jon Wendel
VP, Human Resources: Jane Knaack-Esbeck
VP, Purchasing and Marketing: Ron Taylor
Assistant VP, IT: Cevin Anderson
Assistant VP, Management Information Systems: Ron Waldbillig
Auditors: McGladrey & Pullen, LLP

LOCATIONS

HQ: Hy-Vee, Inc.
5820 Westown Pkwy., West Des Moines, IA 50266
Phone: 515-267-2800 **Fax:** 515-267-2817
Web: www.hy-vee.com

PRODUCTS/OPERATIONS

Selected Subsidiaries
D & D Foods, Inc.
Florist Distributing, Inc.
Hy-Vee Weitz Construction, L.C.
Lomar Distributing
Meyocks & Priebe Advertising, Inc.
Midwest Heritage Bank, FSB
Perishable Distributors of Iowa, Ltd.

COMPETITORS

Albertson's	Nash Finch
AWG	Niemann Foods
Ball's Food	Rite Aid
Casey's General Stores	Roundy's
CVS	SUPERVALU
Dahl's Foods	Target
Fareway Stores	Walgreen
Kmart	Wal-Mart
Kroger	

HISTORICAL FINANCIALS

Company Type: Private

Income Statement				FYE: September 30
	ESTIMATED REVENUE ($ mil.)	NET INCOME ($ mil.)	NET PROFIT MARGIN	EMPLOYEES
9/03	4,230	—	—	46,000
9/02	4,100	—	—	46,000
9/01	3,900	—	—	46,000
9/00	3,600	—	—	44,000
9/99	3,500	—	—	42,900
9/98	3,200	—	—	41,200
9/97	2,900	—	—	38,400
9/96	2,800	—	—	36,000
9/95	2,700	—	—	30,000
9/94	2,480	—	—	30,000
Annual Growth	6.1%	—	—	4.9%

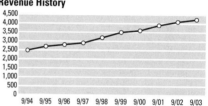

Revenue History

IASIS Healthcare

If you're sick in the suburbs, IASIS Healthcare provides a medical oasis. Formed largely from castoffs of hospital operators Tenet Healthcare and Paracelsus Healthcare (now Clarent Hospital Corporation) and a series of management buyouts in 1999, the company owns and operates 14 acute care hospitals in Arizona, Florida, Texas, and Utah. IASIS also operates three outpatient surgical centers, a behavioral health facility, and Health Choice Arizona, a Medicaid-managed health plan that serves more than 90,000 individuals in Arizona. Private equity firm Joseph Littlejohn & Levy owns more than 85% of the company.

IASIS focuses on building networks of midsized hospitals in growing urban and suburban regions.

EXECUTIVES

Chairman, President, and CEO: David R. White, age 56, $2,142,921 pay
President and COO: Sandra K. McRee, age 47, $952,422 pay
CFO: W. Carl Whitmer, age 39, $792,156 pay
SVP, Development: McKinley D. Moore, age 47

VP and Treasurer: John M. Doyle, age 43
VP, Ethics and Business Practices: Peter Stanos, age 40
VP Communications: Tomi Galin
Chief Information Officer: Lance Smith, age 51
Chief Nursing Officer: Cathy Story
Secretary and General Counsel: Frank A. Coyle, age 39
President, Arizona Market: Dolores Horvath, age 56
President, Florida and Texas Market: Phillip J. Mazzuca, age 44, $427,371 pay
President, Utah Market: Larry D. Hancock, age 45
Director of Human Resources: Russ Follis
Auditors: Ernst & Young LLP

LOCATIONS
HQ: IASIS Healthcare Corporation
113 Seaboard Ln., Ste. A200, Franklin, TN 37067
Phone: 615-844-2747 **Fax:** 615-846-3006
Web: www.iasishealthcare.com

2003 Sales

	$ mil.	% of total
Acute care services	934.2	86
Medicaid health plan	154.0	14
Total	1,088.2	100

Facilities
Hospitals
  Mesa General Hospital Medical Center (Mesa, AZ)
  St. Luke's Medical Center (Phoenix, AZ)
  St. Luke's Behavioral Health Center (Phoenix, AZ)
  Tempe St. Luke's Hospital (Tempe, AZ)
  Memorial Hospital of Tampa (Tampa, FL)
  Palms of Pasadena Hospital (St. Petersburg, FL)
  Town & Country Hospital (Tampa, FL)
  Mid-Jefferson Hospital (Nederland, TX)
  Odessa Regional Hospital (Odessa, TX)
  Park Place Medical Center (Port Arthur, TX)
  Southwest General Hospital (San Antonio, TX)
  Davis Hospital and Medical Center (Layton, UT)
  Jordan Valley Hospital (West Jordan, UT)
  Pioneer Valley Hospital (West Valley City, UT)
  Salt Lake Regional Medical Center (Salt Lake City, UT)
Surgery Centers
  Arizona Diagnostic and Surgery Center (Mesa, AZ)
  Biltmore Surgery Center (Phoenix, AZ)
  Davis Surgical Center (Layton, UT)

COMPETITORS

Ascension Health	HCA
Banner Health	Intermountain Health
Catholic Health East	Care
Catholic Healthcare West	Mayo Foundation
CHRISTUS Health	Tenet Healthcare
Community Health Systems	Triad Hospitals

HISTORICAL FINANCIALS
Company Type: Private

Income Statement — FYE: September 30

	REVENUE ($ mil.)	NET INCOME ($ mil.)	NET PROFIT MARGIN	EMPLOYEES
9/03	1,088	21	1.9%	8,200
9/02	950	(11)	—	8,000
9/01	890	(30)	—	8,000
9/00	815	(15)	—	8,100
9/99*	137	1	0.7%	—
12/98	178	4	2.0%	—
Annual Growth	43.6%	42.5%	—	0.4%

*Fiscal year change

2003 Year-End Financials
Debt ratio: 374.0%   Current ratio: 1.94
Return on equity: 12.4%   Long-term debt ($ mil.): 659
Cash ($ mil.): 101

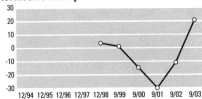
Net Income History

ICON Health

ICON Health & Fitness has brawn as one of the leading US makers of home fitness equipment. Its products include treadmills, elliptical trainers, and weight benches. Brands include HealthRider, NordicTrack, and ProForm. ICON also offers fitness accessories, spas, and commercial fitness gear. It makes most of its products in Utah and sells them through retailers, infomercials, the Web, and its catalog, *Workout Warehouse*. Sears (which accounts for about 40% of ICON's sales) has an exclusive license to sell NordicTrack brand apparel. Bain Capital, Credit Suisse, and founders Scott Watterson and Gary Stevenson collectively own over 90% of ICON. The company plans to license its brands to other manufacturers.

EXECUTIVES
Chairman and CEO: Scott R. Watterson, age 49, $2,072,580 pay
Vice Chairman: Robert C. (Bob) Gay, age 52
President and COO: Gary E. Stevenson, age 49, $1,829,010 pay
President, ICON Canada: Richard Hebert, age 59, $502,473 pay
President, ICON Europe: Giovanni Lato
President, North American Operations: David J. Watterson, age 45, $541,480 pay
SVP, Manufacturing: Jon M. White, age 56
VP, CFO, Chief Accounting Officer, and Treasurer: S. Fred Beck, age 46, $485,480 pay
VP, Design: William T. Dalebout, age 56
VP, Marketing: Colleen Logan
VP, Operations and IT: Joseph Brough, age 40
VP, Product Development: Matthew N. Allen, age 40
Secretary and General Counsel: Brad H. Bearnson, age 50
Corporate Communications: Jay Wright
Auditors: PricewaterhouseCoopers LLP

LOCATIONS
HQ: ICON Health & Fitness, Inc.
1500 S. 1000 West, Logan, UT 84321
Phone: 435-750-5000   **Fax:** 435-750-3917
Web: www.iconfitness.com

ICON has facilities in Canada, China, Europe, and the US.

2004 Sales

	$ mil.	% of total
US	988.9	90
Non-US	106.8	10
Total	1,095.7	100

PRODUCTS/OPERATIONS
Selected Brands

Epic	JumpKing
Free Motion Fitness	NordicTrack
Gold's Gym (licensed)	ProForm
HealthRider	Reebok (licensed)
Image	Weider

COMPETITORS

Bell Sports	Life Fitness
Cybex International	Nautilus Group
Escalade	Precor
Fitness Quest	Soloflex
Keys Fitness	

HISTORICAL FINANCIALS
Company Type: Private

Income Statement — FYE: May 31

	REVENUE ($ mil.)	NET INCOME ($ mil.)	NET PROFIT MARGIN	EMPLOYEES
5/04	1,096	23	2.1%	5,142
5/03	1,012	28	2.8%	4,569
5/02	871	20	2.2%	4,800
5/01	797	13	1.6%	4,200
5/00	733	—	—	3,952
5/99	710	—	—	4,328
5/98	749	—	—	4,200
5/97	836	—	—	5,400
5/96	748	—	—	4,300
5/95	531	—	—	3,437
Annual Growth	8.4%	—	—	4.6%

2004 Year-End Financials
Debt ratio: 227.4%   Current ratio: 1.34
Return on equity: 41.9%   Long-term debt ($ mil.): 153
Cash ($ mil.): 5

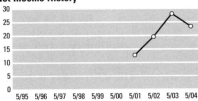
Net Income History

IGA

IGA grocers are independent, but not that independent. The world's largest voluntary supermarket network, IGA has more than 4,000 stores, including members in nearly all 50 states and about 45 other countries. Collectively, its members are among North America's leaders in terms of supermarket sales. IGA (for either International or Independent Grocers Alliance, the company says) is owned by 36 worldwide distribution companies, including SUPERVALU. Members can sell IGA Brand private-label products (2,300 items) and take advantage of joint operations and services, such as advertising and volume buying. Some stores in the IGA alliance, which primarily caters to smaller towns, also sell gas.

The first US grocer in China and Singapore, IGA has moved into Europe with its operations in Poland and Spain. Its international operations account for more than 60% of its total sales. IGA realigned its corporate structure in 2001, setting up IGA North America, IGA Southern Hemisphere/Europe/Caribbean, and IGA Asia, each with its own president.

HISTORY

IGA was founded in Chicago in 1926 by a group led by accountant Frank Grimes. During the 1920s chains began to dominate the grocery store industry. Grimes, an accountant for many grocery wholesalers, saw an opportunity to develop a network of independent grocers that could compete with the burgeoning chains. Grimes and five associates — Gene Flack, Louis Groebe, W. K. Hunter, H. V. Swenson, and William Thompson — created IGA.

Their idea was to "level the playing field" for independent grocers and chain stores by taking advantage of volume buying and mass marketing. IGA originally acted as a purchasing agent for its wholesalers but eventually passed that duty to the wholesalers. The group's first members were Poughkeepsie, New York-based grocery distributor W. T. Reynolds Company and the 69 grocery stores it serviced.

IGA focused on adding distributors and retailers, and it soon added wholesaler Fleming-Wilson (now Fleming Companies) and Winston & Newell (now SUPERVALU). In 1930 it hired Babe Ruth as a spokesman; other celebrity endorsers during the period included Jackie Cooper, Jack Dempsey, and Popeye. IGA also sponsored a radio program called the IGA Home Town Hour.

In 1945 the company introduced the Foodliner format, a design for stores larger than 4,000 sq. ft. The next year IGA introduced the 30-foot-by-100-foot Precision Store — designed so customers had to pass all the other merchandise in the store to get to the dairy and bread sections.

Grimes retired as president in 1951. He was succeeded by his son, Don, who continued to expand the company. Don was succeeded in 1968 by Richard Jones, head of IGA member J. M. Jones Co.

Thomas Haggai was named chairman of the company in 1976. A Baptist minister, radio commentator, and former CIA employee, Haggai had come to the attention of Grimes in 1960 when he praised Christian Scientists in one of his radio broadcasts. Grimes, a Christian Scientist, asked Haggai to speak at an IGA convention and eventually asked him to join the IGA board. Haggai, who became CEO in 1986, tightened the restrictions for IGA members, weeding out many of the smaller, low-volume mom-and-pop stores making up much of the group's network.

Haggai also began a push for international expansion. In 1988 the organization signed a deal with Japanese food company C. Itoh (now ITOCHU) to open a distribution outlet in Tokyo. The 1990s saw expansion into Australia, Papua New Guinea, the Caribbean, China, Singapore, South Africa, and Brazil. IGA also expanded outside the continental US when it entered Hawaii. In 1993 IGA began an international television advertising campaign, a first for the supermarket industry. The next year the company launched its first line of private-label products for an ethnic food market, introducing several Mexican food products. In 1998 the group developed a new format for its stores that included on-site gas pumps.

SUPERVALU signed 54 independent grocery stores (primarily in Mississippi and Arkansas, and Trinidad in the Caribbean) to the IGA banner in August 1999.

With more than 60% of sales coming from international operations, IGA realigned its corporate structure in 2001, setting up IGA Asia, IGA Southern Hemisphere/Europe/Caribbean, and IGA North America, each with its own president.

IGA suffered the loss of Fleming (one of the grocery chain's principal wholesale distributors) and 300 stores in 2003. On the plus side, four Julian's Supermarkets on the Caribbean island of St. Lucia converted to IGA, giving IGA a presence in 45 countries worldwide.

EXECUTIVES

Chairman and CEO: Thomas S. Haggai
EVP and Chief Growth Officer: William (Bill) Benzing
National Accounts Manager: Jim Collins
CFO: Robert (Bob) Grottke
EVP, IGA International, and President, IGA Institute: Paulo Goelzer
VP, Administration, Events and Communication: Barbara G. Wiest
VP, Buying Group Operations, IGA Canada: Randy Huckvale
VP, Information Technology: Nick Liakopulos
VP, Red Oval Family Relations: Thomas (Tom) Zatina
Director, International: Jose Brinson
Director, Marketing Events and Editor-at-large IGA Grocerygram: Patrick Sylvester
Director, Packaging: Tim Considine
Director, Midwest Region: Bill Overman
Director, North Central Area: Ricky St. John
Director, South Central Area: George Beaver
Director, Southeast Area: Doug Blanton
Manager, Events Marketing: Zorona Chapman
Marketing Manager, Southern California: Kendall Hanshaw
IGA Australia, Brand Manager: Neil Vincett
International Coordinator: Jerry Pinney
Consultant, Field: Jim Duban

LOCATIONS

HQ: IGA, Inc.
8725 W. Higgins Rd., Chicago, IL 60631
Phone: 773-693-4520   **Fax:** 773-693-4532
Web: www.igainc.com

IGA has operations in 48 states and about 45 countries, including Anguilla, Antigua, Aruba, Australia, Barbados, Barbuda, Botswana, Brazil, Cambodia, Canada, Cayman Islands, China, the Czech Republic, Dominica, the Dominican Republic, Grenada, Indonesia, Jamaica, Japan, Kenya, Lesotho, Malawi, Malaysia, Mauritius, Mozambique, Namibia, Papua New Guinea, Philippines, Poland, St. Kitts, Singapore, South Africa, South Korea, Spain, St. Lucia, Swaziland, Thailand, Trinidad and Tobago, the Turks and Caicos, Vietnam, Zambia, and Zimbabwe, and is served by 37 independent distribution companies.

PRODUCTS/OPERATIONS

Distributors/Owners
Bozzuto's Inc.
C.I. Foods Systems Co., Ltd. (Japan)
The Copps Corporation
Davids Limited (Australia)
Foodland Associated Limited (Australia)
Great North Foods
IGA Brasil (includes 16 individual companies)
Ira Higdon Grocery Company
Laurel Grocery Company
Martahari Putra Prima Tbk (Indonesia)
McLane Polska (Poland)
Merchants Distributors, Inc.
Metro Cash & Carry (Africa)
Nash Finch Company
NTUC Fairprice (Singapore)
Pearl River Distribution Ltd. (China)
SUPERVALU INC.
Tasmania Independent Wholesalers (Australia)
Tripifoods, Inc.
Villa Market JP Co., Ltd. (Thailand)
W. Lee Flowers & Co., Inc.
WALTERMART SUPERMARKETS (Philippines)

Affiliates
H.Y. Louie (fraternal relationship, Canada)
Sobey's (fraternal relationship, Canada)

Selected Joint Operations and Services
Advertising
Community service programs
Equipment purchase
IGA Brand (private-label products)
IGA Grocergram (in-house magazine)
Internet services
Marketing
Merchandising
Red Oval Family (manufacturer/IGA collaboration on sales, marketing, and other activities)
Volume buying

COMPETITORS

A&P	Ito-Yokado
Albertson's	Kroger
AWG	Meijer
BJs Wholesale Club	Metro Cash and Carry
C&S Wholesale	Penn Traffic
Carrefour	Publix
Casino Guichard	Roundy's
Coles Myer	Royal Ahold
Daiei	Safeway
Dairy Farm International	Spartan Stores
Delhaize	Wakefern Food
George Weston	Wal-Mart
Hannaford Bros.	Winn-Dixie
H-E-B	

HISTORICAL FINANCIALS

Company Type: Holding company

Income Statement
FYE: December 31

	REVENUE ($ mil.)	NET INCOME ($ mil.)	NET PROFIT MARGIN	EMPLOYEES
12/03	21,000	—	—	92,000
12/02	21,000	—	—	92,000
12/01	21,000	—	—	92,000
12/00	21,000	—	—	92,000
12/99	19,000	—	—	92,000
12/98	18,000	—	—	92,000
12/97	18,000	—	—	135,000
12/96	16,800	—	—	128,000
12/95	17,100	—	—	130,000
12/94	17,000	—	—	—
Annual Growth	2.4%	—	—	(4.2%)

Revenue History

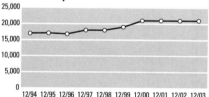

Illinois Lottery

Just because the Cubs can't win in Illinois doesn't mean you can't. Created in 1974, the Illinois Department of the Lottery runs numbers games, including Pick 3 and Pick 4, and participates in the seven-state Big Game in which players can win jackpots starting at $5 million (odds of winning: 1 in 76 million). It also offers instant-win scratch-off games. Of the money collected from ticket sales, 55% is paid in prizes and 35% goes to the state's Common School Fund, which helps finance K-12 public education. The rest covers retailer commissions and expenses. The Illinois Lottery operates through more than 8,400 retail businesses.

EXECUTIVES

Superintendent: Carolyn Adams
Deputy Director Finance: Dave Mizeur
Deputy Director Marketing: Cathy Beres
General Counsel: Kurt Freedlund
Public Information Officer: Anne Plohr Rayhill
Manager Sales: Kris Hanlon
Director Human Resources: Thomas Frescura
Auditors: Martin & Shadid

LOCATIONS

HQ: Illinois Department of the Lottery
  201 E. Madison, Springfield, IL 62702
Phone: 217-524-5157   **Fax:** 217-524-5154
Web: www.illinoislottery.com

PRODUCTS/OPERATIONS

Selected Games
Numbers games
  Big Game (multistate drawing with Georgia, Maryland, Massachusetts, Michigan, New Jersey, and Virginia)
  Little Lotto
  Lotto
  Pick 3
  Pick 4
Scratch-off games
  Add 'Em Up
  Beat Score
  Match 3
  Tic Tac Toe

COMPETITORS

Hoosier Lottery
Kentucky Lottery
Missouri Lottery
Multi-State Lottery
Wisconsin Lottery

HISTORICAL FINANCIALS

Company Type: Government-owned

Income Statement   FYE: June 30

	REVENUE ($ mil.)	NET INCOME ($ mil.)	NET PROFIT MARGIN	EMPLOYEES
6/04	1,799	—	—	151
6/03	1,590	—	—	151
6/02	1,590	—	—	290
6/01	1,550	—	—	—
6/00	1,503	—	—	—
6/99	1,520	—	—	290
6/98	1,577	—	—	284
6/97	1,624	—	—	290
6/96	1,637	—	—	284
6/95	1,630	—	—	281
Annual Growth	1.1%	—	—	(6.7%)

Revenue History

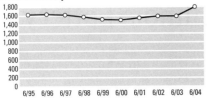

IMG

Show me the money! Founded by the late pioneer of sports marketing Mark McCormack, IMG (previously International Management Group) is the world's largest sports talent and marketing agency. The firm's clients include the hippest athletes of the day, including Tiger Woods, Annika Sorenstam, Peyton Manning, and Venus Williams. In addition to sports idols, IMG represents models and other stars including Elizabeth Hurley and Liv Tyler. IMG also represents corporate clients (Cisco Systems), acts as a literary agent, is active in real estate and golf course design, and produces TV programming through its Trans World International (TWI) division. Forstmann Little & Co. has agreed to acquire IMG for $750 million.

IMG is credited with having invented the field of sports management. While representing VIP clients may be how IMG gained its fame, the company is involved in several other aspects of sports promotion as well. It gives many of its clients venues in which to compete by promoting sporting events, and when athletes need training, they can take advantage of IMG's various sports academies. IMG's television division, TWI, is a leading independent producer and global distributor of sports programming.

The company is active in financial consulting through a joint venture with Merrill Lynch (McCormack Advisors International). IMG continues to expand internationally, organizing sporting events such as basketball, baseball, golf, and rugby across Asia, Australia, and Europe.

After having been in a coma for several months following a heart attack, the 72-year-old McCormack died in 2003. He was replaced by two company executives, Bob Kain and Alastair Johnston, who began a corporate restructuring. As a result, IMG is selling off real estate (including buildings in New York and Sydney, Australia) and discontinuing its Artists Division.

HISTORY

When former amateur golfer Mark McCormack went to Yale Law School in the 1950s, he didn't desert golf entirely. In his free time he set up paid exhibitions for pro golfers he knew from his days on the links, and in 1960 one of these players, Arnold Palmer, asked McCormack to manage his finances so he could concentrate on his game. McCormack went above and beyond the call of duty, signing Palmer to endorsement deals and licensing his name and image. In two years Palmer's annual income skyrocketed from $60,000 to more than $500,000 — a fiscal triumph that would be the bedrock of IMG's business. Throughout the early and mid-1960s, IMG signed up more big-name golfers, as well as stars from other sports such as Jackie Stewart (car racing) and Jean-Claude Killy (skiing).

The addition of foreign stars such as Stewart (Scotland), Killy (France), and Gary Player (South Africa) allowed IMG access to global markets. In the late 1960s, as television began to bring sports and its stars into living rooms around the world, IMG used its clients to promote products and services internationally. In 1967 McCormack created a new division of IMG — a TV production company that filmed and distributed sporting events called Trans World International (TWI). The next year IMG signed a contract with Wimbledon's organizers to coordinate video and television licensing.

IMG's entrepreneurial spirit came to the forefront with a vengeance in the 1980s. In addition to managing athletes, sporting events, and sponsors, the company began to skip the middleman and create the sports event itself. IMG debuted the Skins Game in 1983, a golf invitational featuring four of the sport's top athletes playing for high stakes. IMG also created Saturday afternoon sports staples such as *The Battle of the Network Stars*, shows that featured sports or TV stars competing in a series of events such as tug-o-war and obstacle courses.

By the 1990s McCormack had situated IMG to take advantage of almost every aspect of televised sports events: Typically, an IMG event involved working with the athletes, the sponsor or sponsors, the event itself, and the television distribution rights. The company continued to expand its clientele beyond sports, adding names such as musician Placido Domingo. By 1997 IMG also counted the Rock and Roll Hall of Fame, the Americas Cup, and the Mayo Clinic as clients.

IMG teamed up with Chase Capital Partners (now J.P. Morgan Partners) in 1998 to form IMG/Chase Sports Capital, a private equity fund expected to raise some $200 million to invest in the sports industry. The next year IMG demonstrated a well-honed knack for capitalizing on its clients' appeal by staging a televised golf match between clients Tiger Woods and David Duval, and again in 2000 between Woods and Sergio Garcia. Also that year IMG tried to create a new cable network between TWI and the New York Yankees, but the New York Supreme Court blocked the deal, saying it violated the Yankees' current deal with MSG Network. In 2001 the Yankees broke ties with MSG, paying them $30 million, to do its own network. McCormack died in 2003.

EXECUTIVES

Co-CEO and President, Golf: Alastair Johnston, age 55
Co-CEO: Robert D. Kain, age 54
CEO, TWI: Bill Sinrich
Head of TWI Interactive: Todd McCormack
Senior Corporate VP, Clients: Peter Johnson
Senior International VP, Events and Federations: Julian Brand
Senior Corporate VP, Tennis: Stephanie Tolleson
SVP, Fashion: Chuck Bennett
Senior International VP, Consulting: Andy Pierce
SVP and Director of Academies: Ted Meekma
Senior Staff VP, Licensing: H. Richard Isaacson

LOCATIONS

HQ: IMG
  1360 E. 9th St., Ste. 100, Cleveland, OH 44114
Phone: 216-522-1200   **Fax:** 216-522-1145
Web: www.imgworld.com

IMG has 70 offices in 30 countries.

PRODUCTS/OPERATIONS

Selected Clients
All England Lawn Tennis & Croquet Club (Wimbledon)
Tyra Banks
Jose Carreras
Cisco Systems
Bob Costas
Placido Domingo
David Duval
Sergio Garcia
Wayne Gretzky
Stephen Hawking
International Olympic Committee
Heidi Klum
Nancy Lopez
John Madden
Joe Montana
Colin Montgomerie
Martina Navratilova
Greg Norman
Mark O'Meara
Arnold Palmer
Rugby World Cup
Venus Williams
Tiger Woods
United States Golf Association

Selected Sports Academies
The David Leadbetter Golf Academy
IMG Hockey Academy
International Performance Institute
Nick Bollettieri Tennis Academy
The Soccer and Baseball Academies

Other Operations
IMG Golf Course Services (designs, manages, and markets golf courses worldwide)
Trans World International (sports television production)

COMPETITORS

Brillstein-Grey	Interpublic Group
Bull Run Corporation	Magnum Sports & Entertainment
CAA	Millsport
Clear Channel Entertainment	TBA
Dentsu	United Talent
Elite	William Morris
The Firm	WPP Group
International Creative Management	

HISTORICAL FINANCIALS
Company Type: Private

Income Statement
FYE: December 31

	ESTIMATED REVENUE ($ mil.)	NET INCOME ($ mil.)	NET PROFIT MARGIN	EMPLOYEES
12/03	1,200	—	—	2,200
12/02	1,300	—	—	3,000
12/01	1,300	—	—	2,500
12/00	1,260	—	—	2,900
12/99	1,100	—	—	2,150
12/98	1,100	—	—	2,125
12/97	1,100	—	—	2,000
12/96	1,000	—	—	1,959
12/95	1,000	—	—	1,600
Annual Growth	2.3%	—	—	4.1%

Revenue History
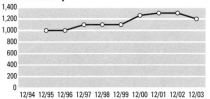

Indiana University

Indiana University has been educating residents of the Hoosier State since its founding in 1820. With a total student population of almost 99,000, the university has eight campuses including flagship institution IU-Bloomington and seven commuter campuses in Fort Wayne, Gary, Indianapolis, Kokomo, New Albany, Richmond, and South Bend. IU-Bloomington offers students more than 100 undergraduate majors. Its graduate schools offer advanced degrees in a variety of areas ranging from business to music to law. IU-Bloomington also is home to a string of centers and institutes including the Advanced Research & Technology Institute and the Center for International Business Education and Research.

EXECUTIVES
President: Adam W. Herbert Jr.
VP and Chief Administrative Officer: J. Terry Clapacs
VP and CFO: Judith G. Palmer
VP Academic Affairs and Chancellor IU Bloomington: Sharon S. Brehm
VP Information Technology and CIO: Michael A. McRobbie
VP Public Affairs and Government Relations: William B. Stephan
VP Student Development and Diversity: Charlie Nelms
Chancellor IU-Perdue University Indianapolis: Charles R. Bantz
Chancellor, IU-Purdue University Fort Wayne: Michael A. Wartell
Chancellor, IU Kokomo: Ruth J. Person, age 59
Chancellor, IU Northwest: Bruce W. Bergland
Chancellor, IU South Bend: Una Mae Reck
Chancellor, IU Southeast: Sandra R. Patterson-Randles
Treasurer: Steven A. Miller
Auditors: Indiana State Board of Accounts

LOCATIONS
HQ: Indiana University
107 S. Indiana Ave., Bloomington, IN 47405
Phone: 812-855-4848 **Fax:** 812-855-7002
Web: www.indiana.edu

Indiana University has campuses in Bloomington, Fort Wayne, Gary, Indianapolis, Kokomo, New Albany, Richmond, and South Bend, Indiana.

PRODUCTS/OPERATIONS

Selected Colleges and Schools
College of Arts and Sciences
Honors College
Graduate School
School of Business
School of Continuing Studies
School of Education
School of Fine Arts
School of Informatics
School of Journalism
School of Library and Information Science
School of Medicine
School of Music
School of Nursing
School of Optometry
School of Public and Environmental Affairs
School of Social Work

HISTORICAL FINANCIALS
Company Type: School

Income Statement
FYE: June 30

	REVENUE ($ mil.)	NET INCOME ($ mil.)	NET PROFIT MARGIN	EMPLOYEES
6/03	1,374	—	—	15,000
6/02	1,261	—	—	16,500
6/01	1,783	—	—	16,070
6/00	1,658	—	—	16,000
6/99	1,541	—	—	15,000
6/98	1,470	—	—	14,458
6/97	1,379	—	—	15,000
6/96	1,280	—	—	17,000
6/95	1,216	—	—	17,000
6/94	1,173	—	—	16,875
Annual Growth	1.8%	—	—	(1.3%)

Revenue History
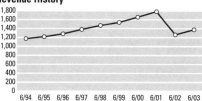

Inductotherm

The heat is on at Inductotherm Industries, the parent of an international group of more than 50 engineering and technology companies that produce a variety of products, primarily for the metals industry. Inductotherm is a leading maker of induction-heating equipment, with more than 10,000 units installed worldwide. Group companies produce welding equipment, electrical components, electronics, engineered products, metal components, and plastic products. Services range from metals fabrication to silkscreen printing. Chairman and majority owner Hank Rowan (namesake of New Jersey's Rowan University) and his late wife Betty financed the company's startup in 1953 from the sale of their home.

EXECUTIVES
Chairman and President: Henry M. Rowan, age 79
President and CEO, Induction and Technology Companies: John H. Mortimer
VP, Finance: Frank D. Manley
VP, Corporate Advertising: Virginia R. Smith
Group VP, Diversified Products and Corporate Development and Treasurer: Manning J. Smith III
Group VP, Electronic Products: Joseph T. Sroka
Group VP, Heating: Byron L. Taylor
VP, Automation Group: William M. Goodlin
VP, Pipe and Tube Technologies Group: Gary A. Doyon
VP, Safety Systems and Communications Group: John O'Meara
VP, Vacuum Furnace Group: William J. Marino
General Counsel and Secretary: L. A. Krupnick
Personnel Director: David L. Braddock
Auditors: KPMG LLP

LOCATIONS

HQ: Inductotherm Industries, Inc.
10 Indel Ave., Rancocas, NJ 08073
Phone: 609-267-9000 **Fax:** 609-267-5705
Web: www.inductothermindustries.com

Inductotherm Industries operates manufacturing plants in Australia, Belgium, Brazil, France, Germany, India, Japan, Mexico, South Korea, Taiwan, Turkey, the UK, and the US.

PRODUCTS/OPERATIONS

Selected Product Groups
Electrical Component Systems Engineering
Electronics
Engineered Products
Heating
Melting
Metal Products and Components
Plastics
Specialized Printing
Welding

COMPETITORS

Astronics
Commercial Metals
Dover
Elgin National Industries
Emerson Electric
Herr-Voss
Illinois Tool Works
Ingersoll-Rand
Invensys
Lincoln Electric
Milacron
Morton Industrial Group
Park-Ohio Holdings
SPX
Tang Industries
Thermadyne Holdings
Watsco

HISTORICAL FINANCIALS

Company Type: Private

Income Statement				FYE: April 30
	REVENUE ($ mil.)	NET INCOME ($ mil.)	NET PROFIT MARGIN	EMPLOYEES
4/02	700	—	—	5,000
4/01	735	—	—	5,048
4/00	750	—	—	5,142
4/99	800	—	—	5,320
4/98	808	—	—	5,334
4/97	779	—	—	5,288
4/96	674	—	—	4,974
4/95	638	—	—	4,823
4/94	552	—	—	4,384
4/93	482	—	—	4,163
Annual Growth	4.2%	—	—	2.1%

Revenue History

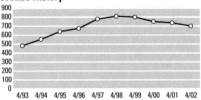

Information Resources

When products fly off the shelves, Information Resources, Inc. (IRI), is watching — and counting. One of the nation's leading market research firms, IRI provides sales data for consumer packaged goods gathered from checkout scanners at 32,000 locations. The company sells the data through subscriptions to its InfoScan service, which offers access to the data as well as analytical software tools. In addition to checkout scanner data, IRI gathers data from more than 50,000 households via consumer panels and offers test marketing services. IRI provides its information and services primarily to packaged goods manufacturers. The company is owned by Symphony Technology Group and Tennenbaum Capital Partners.

A pioneering force in the use of scanner data for market research, IRI has struggled to find and retain new customers as mergers in the packaged goods sector have reduced the number of players in the industry. Meanwhile, the company is competing with larger rival ACNielsen, which can draw from the deep pockets of parent VNU to aggressively expand its product offerings. In 2003 ACNielsen managed to poach Procter & Gamble away from IRI, which led to losses and a call from shareholders to sell the company. IRI was acquired later that year for about $100 million by Tennenbaum and Symphony Technology, two California-based private investment concerns.

In buying the company, Tennenbaum and Symphony Technology have also acquired a share in an ongoing lawsuit in which the settlement could be nearly $1 billion. IRI filed the antitrust suit in 1996 alleging ACNielsen and its affiliates used unfair competition practices in Canada and Europe that hampered IRI's ability to gather retail data. (As part of the acquisition deal, Tennenbaum and Symphony Technology agreed to disburse a percentage of any settlement in the case to former IRI shareholders.)

In 2004 Scott Klein was brought in as CEO to lead IRI through its transition from public to private company. Formerly the head of the consumer industries and retail practice at systems integrator Electronic Data Systems, Klein will oversee a greater emphasis on IRI's value-added services and the development of new products.

EXECUTIVES

Chairman: Romesh Wadhwani, age 51
President and CEO: Scott W. Klein
CFO: Michael S. (Mike) Duffey, age 50
EVP and Corporate Controller: Mary K. Sinclair, age 40
EVP, General Counsel, and Secretary: Monica M. Weed, age 43
EVP Human Resources and Chief People Officer: Gary Newman
CTO and CIO: Marshall Gibbs
Group President, Content - North America: Edward C. (Ed) Kuehnle, age 49
Group President, International Operations: Mark Tims, age 47
President, Global Content Operations: Mark Parise
General Counsel: Robin Bergman
Media Relations: John McIndoe
Auditors: Ernst & Young LLP

LOCATIONS

HQ: Information Resources, Inc.
150 N. Clinton St., Chicago, IL 60661
Phone: 312-726-1221 **Fax:** 312-726-0360
Web: www.infores.com

Information Resources, Inc. has 10 offices in California, Connecticut, Illinois, Massachusetts, Minnesota, New Jersey, North Carolina, Ohio, and Pennsylvania, as well as offices in about 20 other countries.

PRODUCTS/OPERATIONS

Selected Products and Services
Analytic consulting services
Apollo (retail space management software)
CPGNetwork (Web-based business intelligence resource)
InfoScan (retail tracking)
Mosaic InfoForce (retail audit service)
Oracle Sales Analyzer (decision support software)
PowerPlus (data presentation tool)
XLeratePlus (market data presentation tool)

COMPETITORS

Abt Associates
ACNielsen
Catalina Marketing
GfK
IPSOS
Kantar Group
Maritz Research
NFO WorldGroup
NOP World
NPD
Opinion Research
Taylor Nelson

HISTORICAL FINANCIALS

Company Type: Private

Income Statement				FYE: December 31
	REVENUE ($ mil.)	NET INCOME ($ mil.)	NET PROFIT MARGIN	EMPLOYEES
12/03	554	—	—	4,300
12/02	555	—	—	4,350
12/01	556	—	—	4,700
12/00	531	—	—	6,400
12/99	546	—	—	7,100
12/98	511	—	—	7,500
12/97	456	—	—	6,800
12/96	406	—	—	6,300
12/95	400	—	—	6,500
12/94	377	—	—	6,360
Annual Growth	4.4%	—	—	(4.3%)

Revenue History

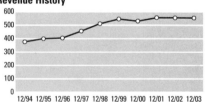

Ingram Entertainment

Companies selling books and CDs might get the star treatment, but Ingram Entertainment doesn't mind a supporting role. Ingram is one of the largest independent video, DVD, and computer game distributors in the US. It also distributes software, audio books, electronics, and used videos and games. From 22 US locations, Ingram serves more than 10,000 video stores, mass retailers, e-tailers, drugstores, and supermarkets (including Blockbuster, Amazon.com, and Circuit City). Ingram offers direct-to-consumer fulfillment services for e-commerce sites and has a majority stake in ad agency Frank, Best & Ingram. Chairman David Ingram owns 95% of the company, which was spun off from family-owned Ingram Industries in 1997.

EXECUTIVES

Chairman and President: David B. Ingram, age 41
EVP and CFO: William D. (Donnie) Daniel
EVP, Purchasing and Operations: Robert W. (Bob) Webb
SVP, Finance and Treasurer: Jeffrey D. (Jeff) Skinner
SVP, Interactive Media: Bob Geistman
SVP, Sales and Marketing: John Reding
VP and CIO: Mark D. Ramer
VP, Human Resources: Andy Grossberg
VP, Sales: Bill Bryant
VP, Sales, Grocery and Drug: Leslie Baker
Auditors: PricewaterhouseCoopers

LOCATIONS

HQ: Ingram Entertainment Holdings Inc.
2 Ingram Blvd., La Vergne, TN 37089
Phone: 615-287-4000 **Fax:** 615-287-4982
Web: www.ingramentertainment.com

PRODUCTS/OPERATIONS

Products
Accessories
  Adapters
  Blank tapes
  Cleaning products
  Controllers
  Head cleaners
  Memory cards
  Repair kits
  Rewinders
  Security tags
  Storage cases
Audio books
DVDs
Electronics
Previously viewed videos
Video games
Videos

Services
Ingram Design Group
Ingram Publications
Internet support services
Marketing programs
Merchandising tools
Studio programs

COMPETITORS

Alliance Entertainment
Baker & Taylor
East Texas Distributing
Handleman
Image Entertainment
KOCH Entertainment
Navarre
Rentrak

HISTORICAL FINANCIALS
Company Type: Private

Income Statement
FYE: December 31

	REVENUE ($ mil.)	NET INCOME ($ mil.)	NET PROFIT MARGIN	EMPLOYEES
12/02	1,070	—	—	980
12/01	871	—	—	928
12/00	1,057	—	—	1,200
12/99	1,155	—	—	1,083
12/98	1,048	—	—	1,030
12/97	914	—	—	1,033
12/96	904	—	—	1,039
12/95	856	—	—	—
12/94	804	—	—	—
12/93	829	—	—	—
Annual Growth	2.9%	—	—	(1.0%)

Revenue History

Ingram Industries

Ingram Industries is heavy into books, boats, and bad drivers. Ingram Book Group is one of the largest wholesale book distributors in the US; it ships more than 175 million books and audiotapes annually, serving some 30,000 retail outlets and 15,000 publishers. Ingram Marine Group operates Ingram Barge and ships grain, ore, and other products through about 3,700 barges and 100 boats. Ingram Insurance Group covers high-risk drivers in seven states through Permanent General Insurance. The Ingram family, led by chairman Martha Ingram (one of America's wealthiest active businesswomen), owns and runs Ingram Industries and controls over 70% of the voting shares of Ingram Micro (a top computer products wholesaler).

Ingram Book Group (operating out of four fulfillment centers) is also a leading distributor to libraries, and the entire book division accounts for over half of Ingram Industries' total sales. Its Lightning Source subsidiary is a leader in print on demand services with over 250,000 titles (including e-books) and a printing count of 12,000 titles a day.

Ingram Industries spun off its largest segment, Ingram Micro, in 1996. Ingram Entertainment (the US's top distributor of videotapes) was spun off the following year and is now owned by Martha's son, David.

HISTORY

Orrin Ingram and two partners founded the Dole, Ingram & Kennedy sawmill in 1857 in Eau Claire, Wisconsin, on the Chippewa River, about 50 miles upstream from the Mississippi River. By the 1870s the company, renamed Ingram & Kennedy, was selling lumber as far downstream as Hannibal, Missouri.

Ingram's success was noticed by Frederick Weyerhaeuser, a German immigrant in Rock Island, Illinois, who, like Ingram, had worked in a sawmill before buying one of his own. In 1881 Ingram and Weyerhaeuser negotiated the formation of Chippewa Logging (35%-owned by up-river partners, 65% by down-river interests), which controlled the white pine harvest of the Chippewa Valley. In 1900 Ingram paid $216,000 for 2,160 shares in the newly formed Weyerhaeuser Timber Company. Ingram let his sons and grandsons handle the investment and formed O.H. Ingram Co. to manage the family's interests. He died in 1918.

In 1946 Ingram's descendants founded Ingram Barge, which hauled crude oil to the company's refinery near St. Louis. After buying and then selling other holdings, in 1962 the family formed Ingram Corp., consisting solely of Ingram Barge. Brothers Bronson and Fritz Ingram (the great-grandsons of Orrin) bought the company from their father, Hank, before he died in 1963, and in 1964 they bought half of Tennessee Book, a textbook distributing company founded in 1935. In 1970 they formed Ingram Book Group to sell trade books to bookstores and libraries.

Ingram Barge won a $48 million Chicago sludge-hauling contract in 1971, but later the company was accused of bribing city politicians with $1.2 million in order to land the contract. The brothers stood trial in 1977 for authorizing the bribes; Bronson was acquitted, but the court convicted Fritz on 29 counts. Before Fritz entered prison (he served 16 months of a four-year sentence), he and his brother split their company. Fritz took the energy operations and went bust in the 1980s. Bronson took the barge and book businesses and formed Ingram Industries.

The new company formed computer products distributor Ingram Computer in 1982 and between 1985 and 1989 bought all the stock of Micro D, a computer wholesaler. Ingram Computer and Micro D merged to form Ingram Micro. In 1992 it acquired Commtron, the world's #1 wholesaler of prerecorded videocassettes, and merged it into Ingram Entertainment.

When Bronson died in mid-1995, his wife Martha (the PR director) became chairman and began a restructuring. Ingram Industries closed its non-bookstore rack distributor (Ingram Merchandising) in 1995 and sold its oil-and-gas machinery subsidiary (Cactus Co.) in 1996. It spun off Ingram Micro in 1996, followed in 1997 by Ingram Entertainment. Ingram Industries purchased Christian books distributor Spring Arbor that year and also introduced an on-demand book publishing service (Lightning Print).

The company in late 1998 agreed to sell its book group to Barnes & Noble for $600 million, but FTC pressure killed the deal in mid-1999. With customers and competitors increasing distribution capacity in the western US, a resulting drop in business led Ingram Industries to cut more than 100 jobs at an Oregon warehouse in 1999.

In early 2000 Ingram renamed Lightning Print as Lightning Source. Also that year Ingram announced plans to distribute products other than books for e-tailers (starting with gifts). In March 2001 Ingram took over the specialty-book distribution for Borders.

In July 2002 Ingram completed its acquisition of Midland Enterprises LLC, a leading US inland marine transportation company that includes The Ohio River Company LLC and Orgulf Transport LLC. In an effort to streamline its distribution network, in mid-2002 Ingram Book Group consolidated its eight distribution centers into four super centers, including a new facility in Pennsylvania.

In late 2003 the company's Lightning Source subsidiary celebrated the printing of its 10 millionth book.

EXECUTIVES

Chairman: Martha Ingram
Vice Chairman; Chairman, Ingram Book Group: John R. Ingram, age 42
President and CEO; Chairman, Ingram Barge Company: Orrin H. Ingram II, age 43
EVP and CFO: Mary K. Cavarra
VP, Human Resources: Dennis Delaney
President and CEO, Ingram Barge: Craig E. Philip
President and CEO, Ingram Book Group: James (Jim) Chandler
President and CEO, Ingram Materials: Charles J. (Buddy) Sanders III
President and CEO, Lightning Source: J. Kirby Best
President and CEO, Permanent General: Randy Parker
President, Ingram Library Services: Peter Clifton
President, Ingram Periodicals: Chris Anderson
President, Tennessee Book Company: John D. Reed III
EVP, Ingram Library Services: Larry C. Price
SVP and COO, Ingram Barge: David G. Sehrt
Company: Randy Collignon

LOCATIONS

HQ: Ingram Industries Inc.
1 Belle Meade Place, 4400 Harding Rd., Nashville, TN 37205
Phone: 615-298-8200 **Fax:** 615-298-8242

PRODUCTS/OPERATIONS

Selected Operations
Ingram Book Group
  Ingram Book Company (wholesaler of trade books and audiobooks)
  Ingram Customer Systems (computerized systems and services)
  Ingram Fulfillment Services (book shipping)
  Ingram International (international distribution of books and audiobooks)
  Ingram Library Services (distributes books, audiobooks, and videos to libraries)
  Ingram Periodicals (direct distributor of specialty magazines)
  Ingram Publisher Relations (publishing services for publishers)
  Lightning Source (on-demand printing and electronic publishing)
  Specialty Retail (book distributor to nontraditional book market)
  Spring Arbor Distributors (product and services for Christian retailers)
  Tennessee Book Company (Tennessee school system textbook depository)
Ingram Insurance Group
  Permanent General Insurance Co. (automobile insurance in California, Florida, Georgia, Ohio, South Carolina, Tennessee, and Wisconsin)
Ingram Marine Group
  Custom Fuel Services (provides midstream fueling services to inland marine operations)
  Ingram Barge (ships grain, ore, and other products)
  Ingram Materials (produces construction materials such as sand and gravel)

COMPETITORS

Advanced Marketing
Allstate
American Commercial Lines
American Financial
Baker & Taylor
Chas. Levy
Follett
Hudson News
Kirby
Media Source
Progressive Corporation
Safeco
State Farm
Thomas Nelson
Times Publishing

HISTORICAL FINANCIALS
Company Type: Private

Income Statement				FYE: December 31
	REVENUE ($ mil.)	NET INCOME ($ mil.)	NET PROFIT MARGIN	EMPLOYEES
12/02	2,200	—	—	6,900
12/01	1,929	—	—	6,148
12/00	2,075	—	—	6,494
12/99	2,135	—	—	6,080
12/98	2,000	—	—	6,500
12/97	1,796	—	—	6,362
12/96	1,463	—	—	5,300
12/95	11,000	—	—	13,000
12/94	8,010	—	—	10,000
12/93	6,163	—	—	9,658
Annual Growth	(10.8%)	—	—	(3.7%)

Revenue History

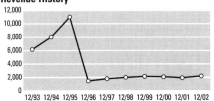

Inova

Inova keeps NoVa (northern Virginia) healthy. Founded in 1956 as a country hospital in Fairfax, Virginia, Inova Health System is a not-for-profit health care provider, offering acute care, long-term care, home health care, mental health, and satellite emergency care services in the northern Virginia suburbs of Washington, DC. Inova's network consists of five hospitals (including a children's hospital) with about 1,400 beds, as well as assisted living centers for seniors and several family practice locations. Through the Inova Health System Foundation, the company coordinates philanthropy programs for the community.

EXECUTIVES

President and CEO: Knox Singleton
EVP and COO: Jolene Tornabeni
SVP and CFO: Richard Magenheimer
SVP, Legal Affairs, and General Counsel: James Hughes
SVP Human Resources: Ellen Menard
Media Relations Manager: Kathleen Thomas

LOCATIONS

HQ: Inova Health System
2990 Telestar Ct., Falls Church, VA 22042
Phone: 703-289-2000 **Fax:** 703-205-2161
Web: www.inova.org

PRODUCTS/OPERATIONS

Selected Facilities
Inova Alexandria Hospital (Alexandria, VA)
Inova Fair Oaks Hospital (Fairfax, VA)
Inova Fairfax Hospital (Falls Church, VA)
Inova Fairfax Hospital for Children (Fairfax, VA)
Inova Mount Vernon Hospital (Alexandria, VA)

COMPETITORS

Bon Secours Health
Carilion Health System
HCA
Johns Hopkins Medicine
Manor Care, Inc.
MedStar Health

HISTORICAL FINANCIALS
Company Type: Not-for-profit

Income Statement				FYE: December 31
	REVENUE ($ mil.)	NET INCOME ($ mil.)	NET PROFIT MARGIN	EMPLOYEES
12/03	1,289	86	6.7%	13,500
12/02	1,248	(15)	—	13,000
12/01	1,154	26	2.2%	13,000
12/00	1,046	139	13.3%	13,000
12/99	963	—	—	13,000
12/98	908	—	—	13,000
12/97	900	—	—	13,000
12/96	700	—	—	9,500
12/95	644	—	—	9,500
Annual Growth	9.1%	(14.8%)	—	4.5%

Net Income History

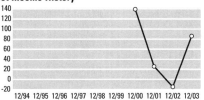

Inserra Supermarkets

The Big Apple need never be short of apples (or oranges, for that matter), thanks to Inserra Supermarkets. Inserra owns and operates more than 20 ShopRite supermarkets and superstores in northern New Jersey and southeastern New York State (most are in Westchester and Rockland counties). Inserra's superstores feature bagel bakeries, cafes, and pharmacies. The company also offers banking services in selected stores through agreements with Poughkeepsie Savings Bank, Statewide Savings Bank, and others. Owned by the Inserra family, the retailer is one of about 40 members that make up cooperative Wakefern Food, the owner of the ShopRite name.

EXECUTIVES

Chairman and CEO: Lawrence R. Inserra
President: Lawrence R. Inserra Jr.
CFO: Theresa Inserra
VP; Director of Operations: Steve Chalas
Director of Human Resources: Marie Larson

LOCATIONS
HQ: Inserra Supermarkets, Inc.
20 Ridge Rd., Mahwah, NJ 07430
Phone: 201-529-5900   **Fax:** 201-529-1189

COMPETITORS
A&P
D'Agostino Supermarkets
Gristede's Foods
Hannaford Bros.
Key Food
King Kullen Grocery
Kings Super Markets
Man-dell Food Stores
Pathmark
Royal Ahold
Trader Joe's Co
Western Beef

HISTORICAL FINANCIALS
Company Type: Private

Income Statement   FYE: December 31

	ESTIMATED REVENUE ($ mil.)	NET INCOME ($ mil.)	NET PROFIT MARGIN	EMPLOYEES
12/03	930	—	—	4,000
12/02	900	—	—	3,900
12/01	800	—	—	3,900
12/00	834	—	—	3,900
12/99	785	—	—	3,500
12/98	750	—	—	4,000
12/97	530	—	—	2,300
12/96	500	—	—	2,300
12/95	500	—	—	2,300
12/94	500	—	—	2,300
Annual Growth	7.1%	—	—	6.3%

Revenue History

Integris Metals

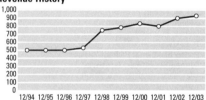

Metals are an integral part of Integris Metals. The company's main operating entity, Integris Metals, Inc., was formed in 2001 as a joint venture between Alcoa and BHP Billiton. The company provides processing services that include cut-to-length leveling, precision blanking, heat treating, polishing, and slitting. Integris Metals sells aluminum, stainless steel, alloy steel, brass and copper, carbon steel, and building products to more than 35,000 customers in the transportation, building and construction, machinery and equipment, and general manufacturing markets. Its products include copper roofing and the AlumaKlad and ColorKlad lines of prepainted architectural metals.

EXECUTIVES
Chairman: Marcus P. Randolph, age 48
President and CEO: Louis F. Terhar, age 54
EVP and CFO: Everett P. Chesley, age 60, $270,169 pay
EVP and VP, Operations: Michael H. Goldberg, age 50, $402,131 pay
SVP and Chief Information Officer: Mark P. Thomson, age 38
VP, Human Resources: John R. Smith, age 49
VP, Information Systems: David Cagle
VP, Sales: Robert V. Bell, age 57
VP, Strategy: Mark D. Irwin, age 36
VP, Supply Chain Management:
  Michael S. Reichenbacher, age 55, $256,040 pay
Auditors: PricewaterhouseCoopers LLP

LOCATIONS
HQ: Integris Metals Corporation
455 85th Ave. NW, Minneapolis, MN 55433
Phone: 763-717-9000   **Fax:** 763-717-7112
Web: www.integrismetals.com

Integris Metals has around 60 facilities in Canada and the US.

2003 Sales

	$ mil.	% of total
US	1,226.8	82
Canada	267.3	18
Total	**1,494.1**	**100**

PRODUCTS/OPERATIONS
2003 Sales

	$ mil.	% of total
Stainless steel	642.5	43
Aluminum	627.5	42
Carbon steel	74.7	5
Other	149.4	10
Total	**1,494.1**	**100**

Selected Products and Processes

Commercial Products
  Alloy steel
  Aluminum
  Brass and copper
  Carbon steel
  Nickel alloys
  Stainless steel
Building Products
  Prepainted architectural metals (AlumaKlad, ColorKlad, and MEGAKlad)
  Roofing copper
Processes
  Cut-to-length leveling
  Flame cutting
  Heat treating
  Polishing
  Precision blanking
  Sawing
  Slitting
  Traverse winding
  Trepanning

COMPETITORS
Metals USA
Reliance Steel
Ryerson Tull
Thyssen Krupp Stahl

HISTORICAL FINANCIALS
Company Type: Joint venture

Income Statement   FYE: Friday nearest December 31

	REVENUE ($ mil.)	NET INCOME ($ mil.)	NET PROFIT MARGIN	EMPLOYEES
12/03	1,494	11	0.7%	2,400
12/02	1,520	10	0.7%	3,000
Annual Growth	(1.7%)	10.1%	—	(20.0%)

2003 Year-End Financials
Debt ratio: 50.0%
Return on equity: 3.4%
Cash ($ mil.): 3
Current ratio: 4.37
Long-term debt ($ mil.): 167

Net Income History

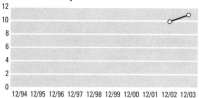

Intelsat

Intelsat's geostationary satellites enjoy a bird's-eye view. The former International Telecommunications Satellite Organization, set up by governments around the world in 1964 and reorganized in 2001 as a private enterprise, provides communications services worldwide over its network of more than 20 satellites. The Intelsat system enables Internet connection, television broadcasting, cellular telephony, and corporate network services. Customers include global communications services provider MCI. Aerospace giant Lockheed Martin owns about 25% of Intelsat. The company has agreed to be acquired by a consortium composed of Apax Partners, Apollo Management, Madison Dearborn Partners, and Permira for $5 billion.

EXECUTIVES
Chairman: John Sponyoe, age 65
CEO and Director: Conny L. Kullman, age 53
COO; President, Intelsat (Bermuda), Ltd.; Managing Director, Intelsat Global Sales & Marketing:
  Ramu V. Potarazu, age 42
CFO: William Atkins
SVP and General Counsel, Intelsat Global Service:
  David B. Meltzer, age 43
SVP and Chief Administration Officer, Intelsat Global Service: Tony A. Trujillo Jr., age 46
VP, Network Infrastructure & CTO Intelsat Global Service Corporation: Khodadad (Ken) Betaharon
VP, Strategy & Global Marketing, Intelsat Global Service Corporation: Amer Khouri
VP, Business Operations: David Sinkfield
VP, Investor Relations, Intelsat Global Service Corporation: Dianne VanBeber
Auditors: KPMG LLP

LOCATIONS
HQ: Intelsat, Ltd.
3400 International Dr. NW, Washington, DC 20008
Phone: 202-944-6800   **Fax:** 202-944-7898
Web: www.intelsat.com

Intelsat has offices in Australia, Bermuda, Brazil, China, France, Germany, India, Singapore, South Africa, the United Arab Emirates, the UK, and the US.

2003 Sales

	% of total
North America & the Caribbean	27
Europe	25
Asia Pacific	17
Sub-Saharan Africa	13
Latin America	11
Middle East & North Africa	7
Total	**100**

HOOVER'S HANDBOOK OF PRIVATE COMPANIES 2005

PRODUCTS/OPERATIONS

2003 Sales

	$ mil.	% of total
Lease services	596.3	63
Channel & carrier services	302.3	32
Managed services	34.6	3
Other	19.6	2
Total	952.8	100

Selected Services
Broadband connectivity
Cellular backhaul
Custom satellite connectivity
Consulting
Internet trunking
Satellite engineering and operations
Testing
Very small aperture satellite (VSAT)
Video transmission
Voice-over-IP

COMPETITORS

APT Satellite
DIRECTV
Eutelsat
FLAG Telecom
Global Crossing
Globalstar
Inmarsat
Level 3 Communications
Loral Space
MCI
Mobile Communications
New ICO
Pasifik Satelit
SES GLOBAL
Tyco Telecommunications

HISTORICAL FINANCIALS

Company Type: Private

Income Statement — FYE: December 31

	REVENUE ($ mil.)	NET INCOME ($ mil.)	NET PROFIT MARGIN	EMPLOYEES
12/03	953	181	19.0%	934
12/02	992	274	27.6%	905
12/01	1,084	499	46.0%	875
12/00	1,097	505	46.0%	792
12/99	977	356	36.5%	750
12/98	1,020	547	53.6%	700
12/97	962	367	38.2%	650
12/96	911	341	37.5%	650
12/95	805	299	37.1%	—
12/94	706	281	39.8%	—
Annual Growth	3.4%	(4.8%)	—	5.3%

2003 Year-End Financials
Debt ratio: 56.2%
Return on equity: 8.1%
Cash ($ mil.): 601
Current ratio: 1.13
Long-term debt ($ mil.): 1,317

Net Income History

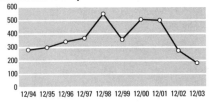

Interactive Brokers

Interactive Brokers Group serves investors wanting to interact with world markets. The company (formerly The Timber Hill Group) executes more than 200,000 trades daily in stocks, options, futures, and foreign exchange. Customers may trade on more than 40 different markets in 16 countries. Interactive Brokers caters to experienced individual and institutional investors who execute their trades via the Internet or with the company's IB Trader Workstation software. The firm's affiliate, Timber Hill LLC, acts as a market maker. Interactive Brokers, the Bourse de Montréal, and the Boston Stock Exchange formed a partnership to launch the Boston Options Exchange (BOX). The company is owned by chairman Thomas Peterffy.

EXECUTIVES

Chairman: Thomas Peterffy
CFO: Paul Brody
CTO: Thomas Frank
VP, Business Development and Marketing: Steve Sanders
Media Relations: Isabelle Clary
Human Resources Manager: Tammy Silby
Auditors: Deloitte & Touche LLP

LOCATIONS

HQ: Interactive Brokers Group LLC
1 Pickwick Plaza, Greenwich, CT 06830
Phone: 203-618-5700   **Fax:** 203-618-5770
Web: www.interactivebrokers.com

In addition to its Greenwich, Connecticut, headquarters, Interactive Brokers Group LLC operates through offices in Chicago, Hong Kong, London, Montreal, Sydney, and Zug, Switzerland.

COMPETITORS

Banc of America Investment Services
Charles Schwab
CIBC World Markets
Citigroup Global Markets
Credit Suisse First Boston
Goldman Sachs
ICAP
Instinet
Jefferies Group
Knight Trading
Lehman Brothers
Man Group
Merrill Lynch
Morgan Stanley
UBS Financial Services
Wachovia Securities
William Blair

HISTORICAL FINANCIALS

Company Type: Private

Income Statement — FYE: December 31

	REVENUE ($ mil.)	NET INCOME ($ mil.)	NET PROFIT MARGIN	EMPLOYEES
12/03	690	—	—	450
12/02	643	—	—	419
12/01	746	—	—	479
12/00	707	—	—	400
Annual Growth	(0.8%)	—	—	4.0%

Revenue History

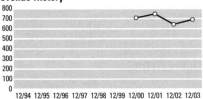

Interbond

The only thing that isn't big about Interbond Corporation of America (which does business as BrandsMart USA) is its geographic scope. The firm runs five BrandsMart USA stores in South Florida and one in Georgia (opened in 2004). BrandsMart USA discount stores sell brand-name consumer electronics, including TVs, DVD players, home theaters, digital cameras, camcorders, and car stereos. BrandsMart also sells appliances, computers, cell phones, music and movies, and offers delivery and installation services. Chairman Robert Perlman founded the company in 1977.

EXECUTIVES

Chairman: Robert Perlman
President: Michael Perlman
CFO: Eric Beazley
EVP: Larry Sinewitz
SVP Merchandising: Richard Wallace
VP Human Resources: Janet Witczak
VP Merchandising: Thomas (Tom) Freeman
VP Operations: Larry Levine
Auditors: Kaufman, Rossin & Co.

LOCATIONS

HQ: Interbond Corporation of America
3200 SW 42nd St., Hollywood, FL 33312
Phone: 954-797-4000   **Fax:** 954-797-4061
Web: www.brandsmartusa.com

COMPETITORS

Best Buy
Circuit City Stores
CompUSA
Home Depot
RadioShack
REX Stores
Sears

HISTORICAL FINANCIALS

Company Type: Private

Income Statement — FYE: August 31

	REVENUE ($ mil.)	NET INCOME ($ mil.)	NET PROFIT MARGIN	EMPLOYEES
8/03	589	—	—	1,500
8/02	571	—	—	1,400
8/01	515	—	—	1,300
8/00	550	—	—	1,300
8/99	520	—	—	1,000
8/98	500	—	—	1,000
8/97	330	—	—	900
Annual Growth	10.1%	—	—	8.9%

Revenue History

Inter-Con Security

There is no conning Inter-Con Security Systems. The company, one of the largest private security consulting firms in the US, provides custom designed security programs for commercial, governmental, and industrial clients in 25 countries on four continents. Its services include security consulting, protection, investigations, and training. It also provides security guard and patrol services. Inter-Con's clients have included NASA, The Academy Awards, and the US government. The company, founded in 1973, is owned by CEO Rick Hernandez and the Hernandez family.

EXECUTIVES

Chairman, President, and CEO:
 Enrique (Rick) Hernandez Jr., age 48
VP Administration: Neil Martau
Client Services Director: Edward (Ed) Ternan
General Manager: Jim Clark

LOCATIONS

HQ: Inter-Con Security Systems, Inc.
 210 S. De Lacey Ave., Pasadena, CA 91105
Phone: 626-535-2200 **Fax:** 626-685-9411
Web: www.icsecurity.com

Inter-Con provides security services to customers in 25 countries on four continents.

COMPETITORS

Gavin de Becker
Guardsmark
Kroll
Securitas Security Services USA
TransNational Security
Vance International

HISTORICAL FINANCIALS
Company Type: Private

Income Statement				FYE: December 31
	ESTIMATED REVENUE ($ mil.)	NET INCOME ($ mil.)	NET PROFIT MARGIN	EMPLOYEES
12/03	1,000	—	—	25,000
12/02	1,000	—	—	25,000
Annual Growth	0.0%	—	—	0.0%

Revenue History

Interline Brands

When something breaks, bursts, or drips, you can call Interline Brands (formerly Wilmar Industries), a national distributor of repair and maintenance products. The company sells more than 45,000 plumbing, hardware, electrical, janitorial, and related products under private labels (including Barnett, Hardware Express, Maintenance USA, Sexauer, U.S. Lock, Wilmar). Interline Brands runs more than 60 distribution centers. In 2003 it acquired Florida Lighting, which distributes specialty lighting and electrical products. Interline Brands is primarily owned by JPMorgan Partners, Parthenon Capital, Sterling Investment Partners, a General Motors pension fund, and management.

EXECUTIVES

Chairman: Ernest K. Jacquet, age 57
President, CEO, and Director: Michael J. Grebe, age 47, $627,558 pay
COO: William E. (Bill) Sanford, age 44, $563,559 pay
SVP and Chief Merchandising Officer: William R. Pray, age 57, $711,540 pay
VP and CFO: Charles Blackmon, age 55
VP and Treasurer: Thomas J. Tossavainen
VP, Corporate Sales: Brian Mendelson
VP, Customer Care and Special Projects: Tony Faralli
VP, Distribution: Jim Spahn
VP, Field Sales: Fred M. Bravo, age 47, $210,903 pay
VP, General Counsel, and Secretary:
 Laurence W. Howard, age 40
VP, Human Resources: Annette A. Ricciuti
VP, Information Systems: Hugh H. Bryan
VP, Marketing: Pamela L. Maxwell, age 39, $209,122 pay
Auditors: Deloitte & Touche LLP

LOCATIONS

HQ: Interline Brands, Inc.
 801 W. Bay St., Jacksonville, FL 32204
Phone: 904-421-1400 **Fax:** 904-358-2486
Web: www.interlinebrands.com

PRODUCTS/OPERATIONS

2003 Sales

	% of total
Plumbing	47
Electrical	13
HVAC, appliances, & parts	12
Security	8
Hardware	7
Other	13
Total	**100**

Selected Brands

AF Lighting	Sexauer
Barnett	SunStar
Hardware Express	U.S. Lock
Maintenance USA	Wilmar

COMPETITORS

Ferguson Enterprises	Noland
Home Depot	Turtle & Hughes
Home Depot Supply	Waxman
Hughes Supply	Wolseley
Lowe's	W.W. Grainger

HISTORICAL FINANCIALS
Company Type: Private

Income Statement			FYE: Last Friday in December
	REVENUE ($ mil.)	NET INCOME ($ mil.)	NET PROFIT MARGIN	EMPLOYEES
12/03	640	7	1.1%	2,200
12/02	638	7	1.1%	2,200
12/01	609	(5)	—	2,200
12/00	382	(10)	—	2,200
12/99	226	13	5.9%	1,338
12/98	193	13	6.5%	903
12/97	151	9	6.1%	764
12/96	101	6	5.9%	606
12/95	61	3	4.6%	361
12/94	48	3	5.9%	327
Annual Growth	33.4%	11.1%	—	23.6%

2003 Year-End Financials
Debt ratio: (126.5%) Current ratio: 2.90
Return on equity: — Long-term debt ($ mil.): 335
Cash ($ mil.): 3

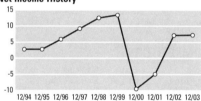

Net Income History

Intermountain Health Care

Intermountain Health Care (IHC) operates some 20 hospitals, more than a dozen home health care agencies, an air ambulance service, and more than 100 physician and urgent care clinics, counseling offices, rehabilitation centers, and other health care facilities in Utah and southern Idaho.

IHC has affiliations with more than 2,000 physicians, including about 400 in its IHC Physician Division. IHC Health Plans offers health insurance programs to large and small employers and to individuals. Affiliate IHC/AmeriNet is a group purchasing organization.

IHC was formed in 1975 when the Church of Jesus Christ of Latter Day Saints (the Mormons) decided to donate 15 of its hospitals to the communities they served.

EXECUTIVES

Chairman: Merrill Gappmayer
Vice Chairman: Kent H. Murdock
President and CEO: William H. (Bill) Nelson
CFO: Everett Goodwin
VP: Greg Poulsen

CEO, Urban South Region: Chris Coons
CEO, Urban North Region: Thomas F. Hanrahan
CEO, Primary Children's Medical Center:
 Joseph R. (Joe) Horton
CEO, IHC Physician Division: Linda C. Leckman
CEO, IHC Health Plans: Sidney C. Paulson
CEO, Urban Central Region: H. Gary Pehrson
Director, Human Resources: Phyllis A. Domm, age 57
General Counsel: Jane Reister

LOCATIONS

HQ: Intermountain Health Care, Inc.
 36 S. State St., Salt Lake City, UT 84111
Phone: 801-442-2000   Fax: 801-442-3327
Web: www.ihc.com

Hospitals
Cassia Regional Medical Center (Burley, ID)
American Fork Hospital (American Fork, UT)
Valley View Medical Center (Cedar City, UT)
Delta Community Medical Center (Delta, UT)
Fillmore Community Medical Center (Fillmore, UT)
Heber Valley Medical Center (Heber City, UT)
Logan Regional Hospital (Logan, UT)
Sanpete Valley Hospital (Mt. Pleasant, UT)
Cottonwood Hospital (Murray, UT)
The Orthopedic Specialty Hospital (Murray, UT)
McKay-Dee Hospital Center (Ogden, UT)
Orem Community Hospital (Orem, UT)
Garfield Memorial Hospital (Panguitch, UT)
Utah Valley Regional Medical Center (Provo, UT)
Sevier Valley Hospital (Richfield, UT)
Dixie Regional Medical Center (St. George, UT)
LDS Hospital (Salt Lake City)
Primary Children's Medical Center (Salt Lake City)
Alta View Hospital (Sandy, UT)
Bear River Valley Hospital (Tremonton, UT)

COMPETITORS

Aetna
Blue Cross
CHRISTUS Health
HCA
Iasis Healthcare
LifePoint
Sierra Health
Trinity Health (Novi)
UnitedHealth Group

HISTORICAL FINANCIALS
Company Type: Not-for-profit

Income Statement   FYE: December 31

	REVENUE ($ mil.)	NET INCOME ($ mil.)	NET PROFIT MARGIN	EMPLOYEES
12/03	3,267	893	27.3%	—
12/02	2,847	—	—	25,000
12/01	2,652	—	—	23,000
12/00	2,552	—	—	23,000
12/99	2,390	—	—	23,000
12/98	2,156	—	—	23,000
12/97	2,009	—	—	22,000
12/96	1,758	—	—	20,000
12/95	1,589	—	—	20,000
12/94	1,380	—	—	19,000
Annual Growth	10.0%	—	—	3.5%

Revenue History

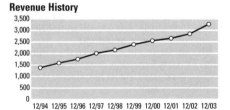

International Data Group

International Data Group (IDG) is a publishing giant with digital appeal. The world's top technology publisher, IDG produces more than 300 magazines and newspapers (including *PC World* and *CIO*) in 85 countries and in dozens of languages. In addition to publishing, IDG provides technology market research through its IDC unit and produces a number of industry events. The company also offers career services through JobUniverse.com and ITcareers.com and operates 400 Web sites featuring technology content. Chairman Patrick McGovern, who founded IDG in 1964, holds a majority stake in the company; an employee stock plan owns the rest.

While a downturn in the economy hurt publishers in 2000 and 2001, IDG weathered the storm in part by concentrating on growing its market research and event marketing businesses. The company's IDC research unit has more than 600 analysts in more than 40 countries, and its industry events include Macworld Expo and the Bio-IT World Conference & Expo.

With traditional business-to-business technology titles still in a slump industry wide, the company is turning to expanding its video games titles and developing additional international titles (for its *PC World* and *ComputerWorld* magazines). In addition, IDG has launched *Digital World*, a "wired home"-type title devoted to consumers with home technology, and *Playlist*, a digital music magazine.

HISTORY

Patrick McGovern began his career in publishing as a paperboy for the *Philadelphia Bulletin*. As a teenager in the 1950s, McGovern was inspired by Edmund Berkeley's book *Giant Brains; or Machines That Think*. He later built a computer and won a scholarship to MIT. There he edited the first computer magazine, *Computers and Automation*. McGovern started market research firm International Data Corporation in 1964 after interviewing the president of computer pioneer UNIVAC. Three years later he launched *Computerworld*, and within a few weeks the eight-page tabloid had 20,000 subscribers. Combined under the name International Data Group, McGovern's company reached $1 million in sales by 1968.

Taking the "International" in its name to heart, IDG began publishing in Japan in 1971 and expanded to Germany in 1975. Following the collapse of communism, the company had 10 publications in Russia and Eastern Europe by 1990. That year two teenage hackers broke into the company's voice mail system and erased orders from customers and messages from writers. The prank cost IDG about $2.4 million. Also in 1990, IDG launched IDG Books Worldwide (renamed Hungry Minds in 2000), which hit it big the next year with *DOS for Dummies*.

With the technology boom of the 1990s, competition in tech publishing heated up. By 1993 several of IDG's magazines, including *InfoWorld*, *Macworld*, and *PC World*, began losing ad pages to rivals Ziff-Davis and CMP Media. To help stem advertiser attrition, IDG started an incentive program tied to its new online service. In 1995 IDG bought a stake in software companies Architect Software (now ExciteHome) and Netscape (now owned by America Online) as part of its move toward Internet-based services.

In 1996 IDG launched *Netscape World: The Web*, a magazine covering the Internet, and introduced more than 30 industry newsletters delivered by e-mail. The company also bought *PC Advisor*, the UK's fastest-growing computer magazine. IDG kicked off its online ad placement service, Global Web Ad Network, in 1997. That year IDG merged *Macworld* with rival Ziff-Davis' *MacUser* in a joint venture called Mac Publishing.

In 1998 IDG pledged $1 billion in venture capital for high-tech startups in China. It also introduced new publications in China, including a Chinese edition of *Cosmopolitan* (with Hearst Magazines) and *China Computer Reseller World*. Later that year the company launched *The Industry Standard* and spun off 25% of IDG Books to the public.

In 1999 it sold a 20% stake in Industry Standard Communications (renamed Standard Media International) to private investors and began laying plans for a possible spinoff in 2000. However, a weakening economy and slowing ad sales in 2000 quieted those plans.

The next year both Standard Media and Hungry Minds announced staff cuts and restructuring. IDG eventually sold its majority interest in Hungry Minds to John Wiley & Sons for about $90 million. Standard Media filed for bankruptcy and liquidated its assets, some of which were bought by IDG. The company also purchased Ziff Davis' 50% stake in their joint venture Mac Publishing. In 2002 IDG CEO Kelly Conlin left the business and was replaced by company executive Pat Kenealy, who had previously founded the now-defunct *Digital News* magazine.

EXECUTIVES

Chairman: Patrick J. (Pat) McGovern, age 66
CEO: Pat Kenealy, age 44
CFO: Ted Bloom
President and CEO, CXO Media: Walter Manninen
President and CEO, IDG International Publishing
 Services: David F. Hill
President and CEO, IDG World Expo: David Korse
President and Publisher, Bio-IT World: Alan Bergstein
President, IDG Communications List Services:
 Deb Goldstein
President, IDG Global Solutions: John P. O'Malley
President, IDG Research Services: Kathy Dinneen
VP Human Resources: Richard Willoughby
VP New Business Development and Operations:
 Colin Crawford
Director, Corporate Communications: Howard Sholkin
Auditors: Deloitte & Touche LLP

LOCATIONS

HQ: International Data Group
 1 Exeter Plaza, 15th Fl., Boston, MA 02116
Phone: 617-534-1200   Fax: 617-423-0240
Web: www.idg.com

International Data Group publishes more than 300 magazines and newspapers in 85 countries.

International Specialty Products

PRODUCTS/OPERATIONS

Selected Operations
IDC (market research)
IDG Communications List Services
IDG Events & Conferences
IDG Global Solutions
IDG Publications (periodical publishing)
IDG Recruitment Solutions (employment services)
IDG Research Services Group
IDG.net (online publications hub)

Selected Events
Bio-IT World Conference & Expo
COMNET Conference & Expo
Demo
The European Telecoms Forum
LinuxWorld Conference & Expo
Macworld Conference & Expo
Storage Forum

Selected Periodicals
Bio-IT World
CIO
CSO
Computerworld
GamePro
InfoWorld
Macworld
Network World
PC World

COMPETITORS

101communications	MediaLive International
CNET Networks	Microsoft
Editis	Pearson
Forrester Research	Penton Media
Freeman Companies	Reed Elsevier Group
Future Network	SYS-CON Media
Gartner	United Business Media
Jupitermedia	VNU
McGraw-Hill	Ziff Davis Media

HISTORICAL FINANCIALS
Company Type: Private

Income Statement
FYE: September 30

	REVENUE ($ mil.)	NET INCOME ($ mil.)	NET PROFIT MARGIN	EMPLOYEES
9/03	2,410	—	—	13,450
9/02	2,580	—	—	13,050
9/01	3,010	—	—	13,200
9/00	3,100	—	—	13,400
9/99	2,560	—	—	12,000
9/98	2,050	—	—	11,500
9/97	1,876	—	—	9,500
9/96	1,700	—	—	8,500
9/95	1,400	—	—	8,200
9/94	1,100	—	—	7,200
Annual Growth	9.1%	—	—	7.2%

Revenue History
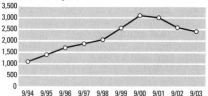

If you're washed, shaved, and groomed, then you've probably shared a chemical experience with the folks at International Specialty Products (ISP). The company — which does business through subsidiary ISP Chemco — makes about 300 types of specialty chemicals, which it breaks into three segments: specialty chemicals (food and pharmaceutical ingredients, personal care and fine chemicals), industrial chemicals (butanediol, for fibers and plastics), and minerals products. ISP also makes waterproofing agents, moisturizers, and preservatives for personal care products such as sunscreen and hair care products. Chairman Samuel Heyman owns ISP; after watching the company's stock dive in 2002, Heyman took ISP private.

After the going-private transaction was complete, ISP went shopping. The company bought Germinal S.A., a South American food ingredients company, and Ameripol Synpol's elastomers plant in Texas.

Heyman and ISP waged and lost, in July 2003, a proxy fight for control of Hercules, Inc., of which ISP owned 10%. ISP sold most of its shares in Hercules in September 2003.

EXECUTIVES
Chairman: Samuel J. Heyman, age 64
President and CEO: Sunil Kumar, age 53, $1,112,555 pay
EVP, Finance and Treasurer: Susan B. Yoss, age 44, $664,230 pay
EVP, General Counsel, and Secretary:
 Richard A. Weinberg, age 43, $765,001 pay
SVP, Corporate Development and Strategy:
 Stephen R. Olsen, age 40, $317,360 pay
SVP and Commercial Director, Americas: Ron Brandt
SVP, Human Resources: Patricia Ippoliti
SVP, Sales and Commercial Director, Europe:
 Roger J. Cope, age 58, $342,780 pay
SVP, Research and Development and Latin America:
 Lawrence Grenner, age 59, $302,125 pay
SVP, Operations: Steven E. Post, age 47
SVP, Sales, and General Manager, Asia: Warren Bishop
Global Marketing Director: Pierre Varin
Auditors: KPMG LLP

LOCATIONS
HQ: International Specialty Products Inc.
 1361 Alps Rd., Wayne, NJ 07470
Phone: 973-628-4000 **Fax:** 973-628-4001
Web: www.ispcorp.com

International Specialty Products has operations in Asia, Canada, Europe, South America, and the US.

2003 Sales
	$ mil.	% of total
North America	434.0	49
Europe	291.8	33
Asia/Pacific	110.4	12
Latin America	56.7	6
Total	**892.9**	**100**

PRODUCTS/OPERATIONS

2003 Sales
	$ mil.	% of total
Specialty chemicals	623.4	70
Industrial chemicals	165.5	18
Mineral products	104.0	12
Total	**892.9**	**100**

Selected Products and Applications
Specialty Chemicals
 Fine chemicals
 Food and beverage
 Performance chemicals
 Personal care
  Hair care
  Skin care
 Pharmaceutical
Industrial Chemicals
 Coatings
 Electronics cleaning
 High-performance plastics
 Lubricating oil and chemical processing
Minerals
 Colored roofing granules (asphalt roofing shingles)

COMPETITORS

3M	GE Advanced Materials
Albemarle	Hercules
BASF AG	Imperial Chemical Industries
Bayer	
BP Petrochemicals	Lyondell Chemical
Cognis	Noveon
CP Kelco	Penford
CPAC	Sigma-Aldrich
Degussa	Stepan
Dow Chemical	Yule Catto
DuPont Canada	

HISTORICAL FINANCIALS
Company Type: Private

Income Statement
FYE: December 31

	REVENUE ($ mil.)	NET INCOME ($ mil.)	NET PROFIT MARGIN	EMPLOYEES
12/03	893	48	5.4%	2,800
12/02	845	(105)	—	2,500
12/01	787	0	0.0%	2,600
12/00	784	94	12.0%	2,600
12/99	787	75	9.5%	2,650
12/98	824	5	0.6%	2,900
12/97	749	93	12.4%	2,675
12/96	717	81	11.3%	2,700
12/95	689	67	9.8%	2,500
12/94	600	45	7.4%	2,400
Annual Growth	4.5%	0.8%	—	1.7%

2003 Year-End Financials
Debt ratio: 157.3%   Current ratio: 2.20
Return on equity: 10.9%   Long-term debt ($ mil.): 620
Cash ($ mil.): 56

Net Income History
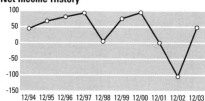

Interstate Battery

Interstate Battery System of America offers a battery of batteries. The company can provide the electrical juice for everything from calculators and radios to automobiles and lawn equipment. Interstate Battery has distributors throughout the US; consumers can purchase Interstate Battery's products at more than 200,000 retail locations, including a growing number of Interstate All Battery Centers. The company is also the official replacement battery for the vehicles of companies such as Land Rover, Subaru, and Toyota. Interstate Battery sponsors the Joe Gibbs Racing team on the NASCAR circuit. Chairman Norm Miller owns the company, which was founded in 1952.

EXECUTIVES

Chairman: Norm Miller
President and CEO: Carlos Sepulveda
VP, Corporate Accounting and Services:
  Lisa Huntsberry
VP, Advertising and Public Relations: Charles Suscavage
VP, All Battery: Mickey Elam
VP, Independent Distributor Development: Jeff Haddock
VP, Information Technology and CIO: Merv Tarde
VP, Interstate Owned Territories: Alex Louis
VP, Interstate Owned Territories: Neal Holford
VP, Human Resources and General Counsel:
  Walter Holmes
VP, Marketing and E-Commerce: Dennis Brown
VP, National Accounts: William (Billy) Norris

LOCATIONS

HQ: Interstate Battery System of America, Inc.
  12770 Merit Dr., Ste. 400, Dallas, TX 75251
Phone: 972-991-1444   **Fax:** 972-458-8288
Web: www.ibsa.com

Interstate Battery System of America has distributors in Canada, the Dominican Republic, Guam, Jamaica, Puerto Rico, and the US.

PRODUCTS/OPERATIONS

Selected Applications

Automotive/truck	Household batteries
Calculators	Lawn and garden
Camcorders	Marine/RV
Cellular phones	Medical equipment
Chargers	Motorcycles
Commercial equipment	Pagers
Computers/laptops	Photo batteries
Cordless phones	Radio batteries
Cordless tools	Sealed lead/SLA
Flashlights	Watches

COMPETITORS

Acme Electric	EnerSys
Battery & Wireless Solutions	Evercel
	Exide
C&D Technologies	Furukawa Electric
Douglas Battery	Imsa
Duracell	Johnson Controls
Eagle-Picher	Rayovac
East Penn	Wilson Greatbatch
Energizer Holdings	

HISTORICAL FINANCIALS
Company Type: Private

Income Statement — FYE: April 30

	REVENUE ($ mil.)	NET INCOME ($ mil.)	NET PROFIT MARGIN	EMPLOYEES
4/04	700	—	—	900
4/03	680	—	—	900
4/02	650	—	—	800
4/01	526	—	—	685
4/00	531	—	—	655
4/99	473	—	—	502
4/98	467	—	—	430
Annual Growth	7.0%	—	—	13.1%

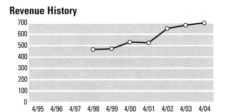
Revenue History

Irvine Company

At The Irvine Company, everything is going according to plan. Master plan, that is. The company creates master-planned communities in well-heeled Orange County, of which the company owns some 50,000 acres (making it California's largest landowner). The company's land is called Irvine Ranch and includes the US's largest planned community, Irvine, with more than 150,000 residents; some 30,000 acres have been set aside for wildlife habitat and open spaces. Its core holdings are derived from the 120,000-acre Irvine Ranch, formed in the mid-1800s when James Irvine bought out the debts of Mexican land-grant holders. Chairman Donald Bren, one of America's wealthiest men, owns the company.

The Irvine Company's portfolio includes Irvine Spectrum, one of the nation's largest high-tech research and business centers, as well as two hotels, four marinas, and three golf courses. Irvine Spectrum encompasses some 40 million sq. ft. and counts some 2,500 companies as tenants. The company's 35 retail centers include Fashion Island and Market Place.

The Irvine Company also owns Irvine Apartment Communities, a residential management firm that owns more than 80 apartment complexes — located on Irvine Ranch as well as in Northern California, San Diego, and Santa Monica, California.

The University of California, Irvine is built on company-donated land.

Chairman Donald Bren has continued the 35-year-old master plan created by the Irvine Foundation (the former parent of The Irvine Company), which calls for gradual development of rigorously planned communities. The plan — which has so far helped form the communities of Laguna Beach, Newport Beach, Orange, and Tustin, as well as centerpiece Irvine — has entered its final phase (set for completion around 2040), but the company faces increasing political opposition to its plans from area residents, who tend to become development-weary after they get their piece of the Irvine Ranch. In a move to prevent unchecked growth, the company has stopped selling desirable Irvine Spectrum land to small commercial building developers.

With most of its developments complete, The Irvine Company has increasingly focused on property investment and management. In 2003 the company took over the management of its industrial and office buildings, and in 2004 started managing its retail properties.

HISTORY

A wholesale merchant in San Francisco during the gold rush, James Irvine and two others assembled vast holdings in Southern California in the mid-1800s by buying out the debts of Mexican and Spanish land-grant holders. Irvine bought his partners' shares in 1876 and passed the ranch of 120,000 acres to his son, James II, upon his death in 1886. Eight years later James II incorporated the ranch as The Irvine Company and began turning it into an agribusiness empire, shifting from sheep ranching to cash crop farming.

James II owned the ranch and company until the 1930s, when the death of his son, James III, prompted him to transfer a controlling interest in the company to the not-for-profit Irvine Foundation. James III's wife, Athalie, and daughter, Joan, inherited 22% of Irvine.

In 1959 company president Myford Irvine, a grandson of James I and uncle to Joan, was found dead from two shotgun wounds. Officials ruled it a suicide, but others weren't so sure.

With Athalie and Joan's encouragement, the firm donated land in the early 1960s for the construction of the University of California, Irvine. The company would continue contributing to educational and philanthropic causes as well as donating property for green space to improve Orange County's suburban areas.

The 1960s also saw the Irvine Foundation forming its definitive master plan for pre-arranged communities and marked the company's entry into the real estate development sector. The plan was designed to anticipate and control growth, with provisions for green space and a mix of pricing levels.

Superrich firebrand Joan, who had long accused Irvine Foundation officers of serving their own interests at the expense of other stockholders, lobbied Congress in the late 1960s to change tax laws pertaining to the foundation. Along with a group of investors led by Donald Bren, Alfred Taubman, and Herbert Allen, Joan trumped a bid by Mobil Oil and in 1977 wrested control of the company from the foundation.

When California's real estate market went sour in 1983, Bren bought out his fellow shareholders, and increased his ownership stake from 34% to 95%. Joan returned to court to protest the price, gaining extra money when the court valued the land at $1.4 billion.

In 1993 Bren sought cash from his holdings by offering apartment developments as a real estate investment trust (REIT), Irvine Apartment Communities.

Orange County's record-setting bankruptcy in 1994 (the county lost $1.7 billion in risky investments) threatened the value of The Irvine Company's property portfolio, most of which is located in Orange County. Thanks in part to a frothy economy and settlements from brokerage firms, Orange County and The Irvine Company were spared another 1983-esque bust.

In 1996 Bren bought the company's remaining stock. As part of its expansion into R&D, retail, and office properties in the Silicon Valley area, The Irvine Company opened an office in San Jose the next year, followed by its Eastgate Technology Park in San Diego in 1998. An industrywide slide in REIT stock prices prompted Bren to take Irvine Apartment Communities private in 1999.

The company continued to expand its retail and office holdings into the aughts — including the purchase of Century City's Fox Plaza. In 2002, the Irvine City Council approved The Irvine Company's plans to develop the last phase of the company's master plan (to be completed in 2040) — bringing over 12,000 homes, 730,000 sq. ft of retail space, and 6.57 million sq. ft. of industrial space to the city's Northern Sphere area.

EXECUTIVES

Chairman: Donald L. Bren, age 72
Vice Chairman and COO: Michael D. McKee, age 58
Group SVP and CFO: Marc Ley, age 40
Group SVP, Environmental Affairs: Monica Florian
Group SVP, Entitlement and Public Affairs: Daniel Young
Group SVP, Corporate Communications: Larry Thomas
Group SVP, Urban Planning and Design: Robert N. Elliott
SVP Capital Markets and Treasurer: Don McNutt
President, Irvine Community Development: Joseph D. Davis
President, Investment Properties Group: Clarence W. Barker
President, Apartment Communities: Max L. Gardner, age 51
President, Office Properties: William (Bill) Halford
President, Resort Properties: L. K. Eric Prevette
President, Retail Properties: Keith Eyrich
SVP Operations, Retail Properties: Russell Lowe
VP, Commercial Land Sales: Larry Williams

LOCATIONS

HQ: The Irvine Company Inc.
550 Newport Center Dr., Newport Beach, CA 92658
Phone: 949-720-2000   **Fax:** 949-720-2218
Web: www.irvinecompany.com

The Irvine Company owns 54,000 acres of land in Orange County, California, including the City of Irvine and parts of Anaheim, Laguna Beach, Newport Beach, Orange, and Tustin. It also owns properties in Los Angeles, San Diego, and San Jose.

PRODUCTS/OPERATIONS

Selected Divisions

Investment Properties Group
  Apartment communities
  Commercial land sales
  Resort properties (hotels, marinas, and golf courses)
  Office properties
  Retail properties
Irvine Community Development

COMPETITORS

Arden Realty	The Koll Company
California Coastal Communities	Majestic Realty
	MBK Real Estate
C.J. Segerstrom & Sons	Mission West Properties
Corky McMillin	Newhall Land
Intergroup	Pan Pacific
KB Home	Rancho Mission Viejo
Kilroy Realty	Tejon Ranch

HISTORICAL FINANCIALS

Company Type: Private

Income Statement

FYE: June 30

	REVENUE ($ mil.)	NET INCOME ($ mil.)	NET PROFIT MARGIN	EMPLOYEES
6/03	2,000	—	—	—
6/02	1,700	—	—	762
6/01	1,500	—	—	470
6/00	1,305	—	—	435
6/99	1,100	—	—	250
6/98	1,000	—	—	236
6/97	816	—	—	200
6/96	710	—	—	190
6/95	700	—	—	200
6/94	800	—	—	200
Annual Growth	10.7%	—	—	18.2%

Revenue History

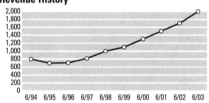

J. Crew

The crews depicted in the flashy catalogs of the J. Crew Group are far from motley. Some 60% of J. Crew's sales come from classic-styled jeans, khakis, and other basic (but pricey) items sold to young professionals through its catalogs and Web site and in nearly 200 retail and factory outlets in the US. It also has about 70 outlets in Japan through a joint venture with ITOCHU. Asian contractors produce about 80% of the company's merchandise. Texas Pacific Group owns more than 60% of J. Crew; Emily Cinader Woods, daughter of founder Arthur Cinader, owns nearly 20%.

Almost two-thirds of J. Crew's sales come from retail and outlet; about 30% of sales are from the 32 catalog editions that reach more than 70 million people each year. Hemmed by the stagnant growth of its catalog operations, the New York City-based company has sold or closed two of its noncore catalog businesses, Popular Club Plan and Clifford & Wills, leaving it with only its namesake operations.

J. Crew has gone through some tough times since the Texas Pacific Group bought a majority stake in the family-run company in 1998. A plan to take the company public was shelved and the company has fallen farther behind rivals such as Abercrombie & Fitch and American Eagle Outfitters. In January 2003, heavy hitter Millard Drexler was brought in as chairman and CEO to try to turn the same successful trick that he did at his former company, The Gap.

Just in time for Fashion Week in 2004, Drexler announced his plans to lead J. Crew down the wedding aisle by introducing an abbreviated (yet J. Crew-style all-American) collection of wedding ensembles for men and women.

EXECUTIVES

Chairman and CEO: Millard S. (Mickey) Drexler, age 59, $700,000 pay
President: Jeff Pfeifle, age 45, $760,000 pay
EVP and CFO: Amanda J. Bokman
EVP, Catalog & e-Commerce: Roxane Al-Fayez, age 47
EVP Merchandising, Planning and Production: Tracy Gardner, age 39
EVP Stores: Michael Dadario, age 45
SVP Manufacturing: Scott D. Hyatt, age 46, $354,000 pay
SVP and CIO: Paul Fusco, age 55
VP and Corporate Controller: Nicholas Lamberti, age 61
VP Human Resources: Linda Marco
Auditors: KPMG LLP

LOCATIONS

HQ: J. Crew Group, Inc.
770 Broadway, New York, NY 10003
Phone: 212-209-2500   **Fax:** 212-209-2666
Web: www.jcrew.com

PRODUCTS/OPERATIONS

2004 Sales

	$ mil.	% of total
J. Crew Retail	406.1	59
J. Crew Direct	172.1	25
J. Crew Factory	82.6	12
Other	27.5	4
Total	**688.3**	**100**

COMPETITORS

Abercrombie & Fitch	Lands' End
Aeropostale	Limited Brands
American Eagle Outfitters	Liz Claiborne
AnnTaylor	L.L. Bean
Benetton	Loehmann's
Burberry	Marks & Spencer
Calvin Klein	May
Chadwick's of Boston	Men's Wearhouse
Coldwater Creek	Nautica Enterprises
Dillard's	Neiman Marcus
Eddie Bauer	new york and company
Esprit Holdings	Nordstrom
Federated	Polo Ralph Lauren
French Connection	Saks Inc.
Gap	Sears
Guess	Spiegel
Hartmarx	Talbots
Inditex	Target
Intimate Brands	Tommy Hilfiger
J. C. Penney	

HISTORICAL FINANCIALS

Company Type: Private

Income Statement

FYE: Saturday nearest January 31

	REVENUE ($ mil.)	NET INCOME ($ mil.)	NET PROFIT MARGIN	EMPLOYEES
1/04	688	(47)	—	5,500
1/03	766	(41)	—	8,200
1/02	778	(11)	—	7,800
1/01	826	22	2.6%	7,600
1/00	717	(7)	—	8,400
1/99	824	(15)	—	8,900
1/98	834	(27)	—	6,200
1/97	809	13	1.5%	6,100
1/96	746	6	0.9%	5,600
1/95	738	15	2.0%	5,413
Annual Growth	(0.8%)	—	—	0.2%

2004 Year-End Financials

Debt ratio: —   Current ratio: 1.49
Return on equity: —   Long-term debt ($ mil.): 517
Cash ($ mil.): 50

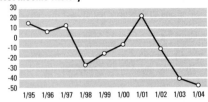

Net Income History

Jefferson Health System

This health care system's freedom-loving namesake might approve of its work to preserve the people's freedom of choice in health care. Jefferson Health System is a not-for-profit alliance of health systems and hospitals serving the Delaware Valley. Members include the Thomas Jefferson University Hospital family (one of the system's founders), Albert Einstein Healthcare Network, Frankford Hospitals, Main Line Health (the other founding organization), and Magee Rehabilitation. The Jefferson network has some 3,100 beds. The health system is affiliated with Thomas Jefferson University.

EXECUTIVES
President and CEO: Joesph T. Sebatianelli
SVP and CFO: Kirk E. Gorman, age 53
SVP, Insurance: Dianne P. Salter
SVP and General Counsel: David F. Simon

LOCATIONS
HQ: Jefferson Health System Inc.
259 N. Radnor-Chester Rd., Ste. 290, Radnor, PA 19087
Phone: 610-225-6200 **Fax:** 610-225-6254
Web: www.jeffersonhealth.org

HISTORICAL FINANCIALS
Company Type: Not-for-profit

Income Statement			FYE: June 30
	REVENUE ($ mil.)	NET INCOME ($ mil.)	NET PROFIT MARGIN	EMPLOYEES
6/03	2,500	—	—	27,000

JELD-WEN

JELD-WEN strives to improve your outlook, whether it's by providing new windows for your home or by offering accommodations at a scenic resort. A leading maker of windows and doors, JELD-WEN owns more than 150 divisions in the Americas, Asia, and Europe. The company manufactures windows (aluminum, vinyl, and wood), interior and exterior doors, garage doors, door frames, moldings, and patio doors. JELD-WEN also sells time-shares at such resorts as Oregon's Eagle Crest and Running Y Ranch. Other interests include specialty wood products (including wood pellets used in fireplaces), real estate, marketing communications, and education. Chairman Richard Wendt and his siblings founded JELD-WEN in 1960.

JELD-WEN is bringing many of the products in its portfolio under the JELD-WEN brand. Products include wood, vinyl, and aluminum windows; wood and wood composite interior doors; and wood, steel, wood composite, and fiberglass exterior doors and entry systems.

EXECUTIVES
Chairman: Richard L. Wendt, age 73
President: Roderick C. (Rod) Wendt
EVP and CFO: Douglas P. (Doug) Kintzinger
EVP: Robert Turner
SVP and Director: William Bernard Early
VP and Controller: Brent Cap
VP and Treasurer: Karen Hoggarth
VP Information Systems: Craig Zemke
VP Door Divisions: Dan Malicki
VP Window Divisions: Barry Homrighaus
VP Marketing: Peter Dempsey
Manager, Corporate Communications: Teri Cline

LOCATIONS
HQ: JELD-WEN, inc.
401 Harbor Isles Blvd., Klamath Falls, OR 97601
Phone: 541-882-3451 **Fax:** 541-885-7454
Web: www.jeld-wen.com

JELD-WEN has divisions and companies in Argentina, Australia, Canada, Chile, France, Indonesia, Japan, Latvia, Lebanon, Malaysia, Morocco, Poland, Singapore, South Korea, Spain, Thailand, Turkey, the UK, and the US.

PRODUCTS/OPERATIONS
Selected Products
Doors
  Exterior (wood, composite, fiberglass, and steel)
  Garage
  Interior (wood, router-carved, molded, and flush)
  Patio (wood, vinyl, and aluminum)
Millwork
  Columns
  Posts
  Spindles
  Stair parts
Windows
  Aluminum clad
  Energy-efficient
  Replacement
  Vinyl
  Wood

Resorts
Eagle Crest Resort (Oregon)
The Running Y Ranch Resort (Oregon)
Silver Mountain Ski Resort (Idaho)
Windmill Inns of America (Arizona, Oregon)

Other Interests
AmeriTitle (real estate)
Creative Media Development, Inc. (marketing communications)
Grossman's (building materials stores)
JELD-WEN Real Estate (buying, selling, leasing, financing, and developing industrial real estate properties)
Paxton/Patterson (turn-key equipment and training solutions and interactive modular learning systems programs)

COMPETITORS
Andersen Corporation
Fairfield Resorts
Guardian Building Products
Lane Industries
Marshfield DoorSystems
Nortek
Owens Corning
Pella
Sierra Pacific Industries
Simonton Windows
Thermal Industries

HISTORICAL FINANCIALS
Company Type: Private

Income Statement			FYE: December 31
	ESTIMATED REVENUE ($ mil.)	NET INCOME ($ mil.)	NET PROFIT MARGIN	EMPLOYEES
12/03	1,878	—	—	21,000
12/02	2,000	—	—	20,000
12/01	2,040	—	—	20,000
12/00	2,000	—	—	20,000
12/99	2,000	—	—	15,000
12/98	1,500	—	—	11,000
12/97	1,400	—	—	10,400
12/96	850	—	—	7,100
12/95	750	—	—	7,050
12/94	800	—	—	7,650
Annual Growth	9.9%	—	—	11.9%

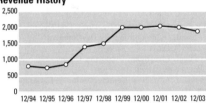

Revenue History

J.F. Shea

J.F. Shea helped construct the Washington, DC, subway system, the Golden Gate Bridge, and the Hoover Dam, and now it wants to build your house. Its Shea Homes division builds single-family houses and planned communities. Flagship unit J.F. Shea Construction is involved in commercial and civil engineering projects and offers design/build services. The group's Heavy Civil Engineering division works on underground projects, including dams and tunnels, and its Redding division produces gravel, asphalt, and concrete products. Other interests include real estate property management, electrical contracting, and concrete guns and pumps. Founded as a plumbing company in 1876, J.F. Shea is still owned by the Shea family.

EXECUTIVES
President and CEO: John F. Shea
COO: Peter O. Shea Jr.
CFO and Secretary: James G. Shontere
EVP; President, J.F. Shea Construction: Peter O. Shea
EVP: Edmund H. Shea Jr.
VP Taxes: Ron Lakey
President, Shea Homes: Bert Selva
Treasurer: Robert R. O'Dell
Senior Technical Manager: Mike Little
Director of Finance: Mike Ciauri

LOCATIONS

HQ: J.F. Shea Co., Inc.
655 Brea Canyon Rd., Walnut, CA 91789
Phone: 909-594-9500   Fax: 909-594-0935
Web: www.jfshea.com

PRODUCTS/OPERATIONS

Major Units

J.F. Shea Construction, Inc. (commercial buildings, subways, and civil engineering projects)
J.F. Shea Heavy Civil Engineering (bridges, tunnels, and transit systems)
Redding Construction (sand, gravel, asphalt, and concrete products; highway construction)
Reed Manufacturing (concrete guns and pumps and concrete-placing equipment)
Shasta Electric, Inc. (full-service electrical contractor for commercial and industrial projects)
Shea Homes (residential units, developed and master-planned communities)
Shea Mortgage (mortgage lender)
Shea Properties (apartment and industrial and commercial building management)
Venture Capital (investment firm)

COMPETITORS

Austin Industries
Bechtel
Black & Veatch
Centex
Del Webb
Dick Corporation
D.R. Horton
Granite Construction
Hyundai Engineering and Construction
KB Home
Lennar
M.D.C. Holdings
Parsons
Peter Kiewit Sons'
Pulte Homes
Ryland
Shapell Industries
Standard Pacific
Tutor-Saliba
Washington Group

HISTORICAL FINANCIALS

Company Type: Private

Income Statement   FYE: December 31

	REVENUE ($ mil.)	NET INCOME ($ mil.)	NET PROFIT MARGIN	EMPLOYEES
12/02	1,994	—	—	2,315
12/01	1,968	—	—	2,288
12/00	1,863	—	—	2,200
12/99	1,794	—	—	2,100
12/98	1,621	—	—	2,000
12/97	1,001	—	—	1,420
12/96	957	—	—	1,200
12/95	687	—	—	1,100
Annual Growth	16.4%	—	—	11.2%

Revenue History

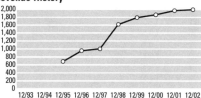

Jim Koons Automotive

Wheelin' and dealin' on the Web, Jim Koons Automotive Companies sells new and used cars the old-fashioned way and through the Internet. Its 10-plus locations in the Washington, DC, area (Virginia and Maryland) offer cars made by DaimlerChrysler, Ford, GM, Mazda, Toyota, and Volvo. Three locations specialize in used cars. Internet customers can obtain quotes, make appointments for parts and service, and access online coupons for oil changes and other services. CEO Jim Koons' father, John Koons Sr., the first auto dealer to enter the Automotive Hall of Fame, founded the company in 1964. The Koons family owns the company.

EXECUTIVES

CEO: James E. Koons
VP: Jim O'Connell
Corporate Controller: Ed Waugh
Systems Administrator: Robert Webb

LOCATIONS

HQ: Jim Koons Automotive Companies, Inc.
2000 Chain Bridge Rd., Vienna, VA 22182
Phone: 703-356-0400   Fax: 703-442-5765
Web: www.koons.com

COMPETITORS

Atlantic Automotive
Brown Automotive
Darcars
March/Hodge
Ourisman Automotive
Rosenthal Automotive

HISTORICAL FINANCIALS

Company Type: Private

Income Statement   FYE: December 31

	ESTIMATED REVENUE ($ mil.)	NET INCOME ($ mil.)	NET PROFIT MARGIN	EMPLOYEES
12/03	1,018	—	—	1,400
12/02	1,022	—	—	1,400
12/01	993	—	—	1,400
12/00	941	—	—	1,400
12/99	800	—	—	1,300
12/98	650	—	—	1,200
12/97	550	—	—	1,200
12/96	550	—	—	1,200
12/95	565	—	—	1,200
12/94	560	—	—	1,100
Annual Growth	6.9%	—	—	2.7%

Revenue History

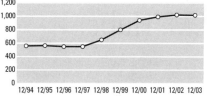

JM Family Enterprises

Founder and honorary chairman Jim Moran and chairman Pat Moran (Jim's daughter) make JM Family Enterprises a family affair. JM, owned by the Moran family, is a holding company (Florida's second-largest private company, in fact, after Publix Super Markets) with about a dozen automotive-related businesses, including the nation's largest-volume Lexus retailer, JM Lexus, in Margate, Florida. JM's major subsidiary, Southeast Toyota Distributors, is the nation's largest Toyota distribution franchise, delivering Toyota cars, trucks, and SUVs to more than 160 dealers in Alabama, Florida, Georgia, and North and South Carolina.

Among JM Family's other subsidiaries, JM&A Group provides insurance and warranty services to retailers nationwide. World Omni Financial handles leasing, dealer financing, and other financial services for US auto dealers.

JM Family Enterprises is one of the largest woman-owned companies in the US.

HISTORY

Jim Moran first became visible as "Jim Moran, the Courtesy Man" in Chicago TV advertisements in the 1950s. At that time he ran Courtesy Motors, where he was so successful as the world's #1 Ford dealer that *Time* magazine put his picture on its cover in 1961.

Moran had entered the auto sales business after fixing up and selling a car for more than three times the price he had paid for it. That profit was much better than what he made at the Sinclair gas station he had bought, so he opened a used-car lot. Later, he moved to new-car sales when he bought a Hudson franchise (Ford had rejected him).

Seeing the promise of TV advertising, in 1948 Moran pioneered the forum for Chicago car dealers, not only as an advertiser and program sponsor but also as host of a variety show and a country/western music barn dance. The increased visibility positioned Moran as Hudson's #1 dealer, but the sales tactics at Courtesy Motors earned an antitrust suit that was settled out of court.

In 1955 Moran started with Ford and, with his TV influence as host of *The Jim Moran Courtesy Hour*, he became the world's #1 Ford dealer in his first month.

He moved to Florida in 1966 after being diagnosed with cancer and given one year to live. Successfully fighting the disease, he bought a Pontiac franchise and later started Southeast Toyota Distributors. In 1969 he formed JM Family Enterprises.

Legal problems cropped up in 1973 when the IRS investigated a Nassau bank serving as a tax haven for wealthy Americans. Moran and three Toyota executives were linked to the bank, and in 1978 Moran was indicted for tax fraud. When an immunity deal fell through, Moran pleaded guilty to seven tax fraud charges in 1984 and was sentenced to two years (suspended), fined more than $12 million, and ordered to perform community service. Moran's legal problems threatened his association with Toyota and were blamed for causing his stroke in 1983.

JM's legal problems continued in the 1980s, partly because of the imposition of auto import restrictions. To get more cars to sell, some Southeast Toyota managers encouraged auto dealers to file false sales reports. Some North Carolina dealers resisted and one sued, settling out of court for $22 million. Other dealers alleged racketeering and fraud on the part of Southeast Toyota, and by the beginning of 1994, JM had paid more than $100 million in fines and settlements for cases stretching back to 1988. In spite of that, Toyota renewed its contract with the company in 1993, a year ahead of schedule.

Pat Moran succeeded her father as JM president in 1992. Between 1991 and 1994 three suits were filed against Jim and Southeast Toyota alleging racism against blacks in establishing Toyota dealerships. All three suits were settled.

Jim teamed with Wayne Huizenga in 1996 to launch a national chain of used-car megastores under the name AutoNation USA, which Jim expected would draw buyers to his own auto dealerships. (AutoNation USA's first store was built just two blocks from JM's Coconut Creek Lexus Dealership.) Jim's interest in AutoNation USA was converted into a small percentage (less than 5%) of Republic Industries stock after Huizenga merged AutoNation into waste hauler Republic Industries (now called AutoNation) in 1997.

In late 1998 JM embarked on a national strategy to expand its presence outside the Southeast, establishing an office in St. Louis that handles indirect consumer leasing.

In 2000 Jim became honorary chairman while Pat was given the chairman position and continued as CEO; COO Colin Brown was named president. Also that year the company was named the 51st Best Company to Work For in the United States by FORTUNE magazine. The company's rank in the Best Company to Work For list rose to 20th place in 2001.

In March 2003 Brown assumed the CEO title, with Pat Moran continuing as chairman.

EXECUTIVES

Honorary Chairman: James M. (Jim) Moran
Chairman: Patricia (Pat) Moran, age 58
President and CEO: Colin Brown, age 53
EVP: Louis Feagles
EVP and CFO: Corliss J. (Corky) Nelson, age 58
EVP, Human Resources: Gary L. Thomas
EVP; President, JM Service Center: Scott Barrett
SVP: Jan Moran
Group VP, Corporate Communications: Tony Stromberg
VP: Larry McGinnes
VP, Aviation: George Kokinakis
VP, Community Relations: Rick Noland
VP, Community Relations and Marine Departments: Kiernan P. Moylanhas
VP and Controller: Mark S. Walter
VP, Corporate Communications: Lisa Kitei
VP, Government Relations: Kienan Moylan
VP, Human Resources: John Heins
VP, Sales and Strategic Alliances, JM&A Group: Mike Casey
VP, Strategic Planning: Harry V. Spanos
Assistant VP and Chief Division Counsel: Caren Snead Williams

LOCATIONS

HQ: JM Family Enterprises, Inc.
100 Jim Moran Blvd., Deerfield Beach, FL 33442
Phone: 954-429-2000 **Fax:** 954-429-2300
Web: www.jmfamily.com

JM Family Enterprises operates auto retail, distribution, leasing, and financing businesses across the US, mainly in Alabama, Florida, Georgia, and North and South Carolina.

PRODUCTS/OPERATIONS

Selected Subsidiaries

Finance and Leasing
 Centerone Financial Services
 World Omni Financial Corp.
Insurance, Marketing, Consulting, and Related Companies
 Courtesy Administrative Services, Inc.
 Courtesy Insurance Company
 Fidelity Insurance Agency, Inc.
 Fidelity Warranty Services, Inc.
 Jim Moran & Associates, Inc.
 JM&A Group (auto service contracts, insurance)
 J.M.I.C. Life Insurance Co.
Retail Car Sales
 JM Lexus
Vehicle Processing and Distribution
 SET Inland Processing
 SET Parts Supply and Distribution
 SET Port Processing
 Southeast Toyota Distributors, LLC

COMPETITORS

CarMax
Gulf States Toyota
Hendrick Automotive
Holman Enterprises
Island Lincoln-Mercury
Morse Operations
United Auto Group

HISTORICAL FINANCIALS

Company Type: Private

Income Statement FYE: December 31

	REVENUE ($ mil.)	NET INCOME ($ mil.)	NET PROFIT MARGIN	EMPLOYEES
12/03	7,700	—	—	3,700
12/02	7,600	—	—	3,500
12/01	7,800	—	—	3,227
12/00	7,100	—	—	3,400
12/99	6,600	—	—	3,304
12/98	6,200	—	—	3,000
12/97	5,400	—	—	2,900
12/96	5,100	—	—	3,000
12/95	4,500	—	—	2,000
12/94	4,200	—	—	2,000
Annual Growth	7.0%	—	—	7.1%

Revenue History

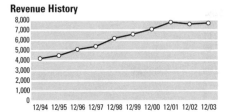

J.M. Huber

As great as toothpaste, paint, and tires are, J.M. Huber claims to make them even better. Hard to believe, we know. Founded in 1883 by Joseph Maria Huber (and still owned by his heirs), the company makes specialty additives and minerals used to thicken and improve the cleaning properties of toothpaste, the brightness and gloss of paper, the strength and durability of rubber, and the flame retardant properties of wire and cable. The diverse company also makes oriented strand board (a plywood substitute). In early 2004 Huber bought out Hercules' minority stake in foodgums maker CP Kelco. Lehman Brothers Banking Partners had owned the remainder of Kelco, though they agreed to sell out to Huber.

Following the purchase of Hercules's portion of CP Kelco, Huber decided to buy out Lehman's 71% of the company and made the sale official at the end of September 2004. Kelco — now 100% owned by Huber — has become a part of Huber Engineered Materials.

Huber also manages a half-million acres of timberland in Maine and the southeastern US, and explores for and produces oil and gas in Texas, Colorado, Utah, and Wyoming.

EXECUTIVES

Chairman, President, and CEO: Peter T. Francis
Director, Corporate Communication: Robert (Bob) Currie
Manager, Human Resources: Gary Crowell
VP and General Manager, Paper, Engineered Materials: John Takerer
President, CP Kelco: Robert B. (Bob) Toth

LOCATIONS

HQ: J.M. Huber Corporation
333 Thornall St., Edison, NJ 08837
Phone: 732-549-8600 **Fax:** 732-549-2239
Web: www.huber.com

J. M. Huber Corporation has operations in Belgium, Canada, Denmark, Finland, France, India, Portugal, Sweden, and the US.

PRODUCTS/OPERATIONS

Selected Operations

CP Kelco (food gums)
Huber Energy (oil and gas acquisition, exploration, and production)
Huber Engineered Materials (engineered minerals and specialty chemicals)
Huber Engineered Woods (high-performance specialty woods, including oriented strand board)
Huber Timber (500,000 acres of timber)
JMH Financial Services (treasury services)
Noviant (carboxymethl cellulose)

COMPETITORS

ADM
Baker Hughes
Boise Cascade
Cabot
Danisco
Degussa
FMC
Georgia-Pacific
Imerys
Ineos Silicas
Kerry Group
Marathon Oil
Minerals Technologies
Occidental Petroleum

HISTORICAL FINANCIALS

Company Type: Private

Income Statement FYE: December 31

	ESTIMATED REVENUE ($ mil.)	NET INCOME ($ mil.)	NET PROFIT MARGIN	EMPLOYEES
12/02	1,231	—	—	3,278
12/01	1,122	—	—	3,003
12/00	1,022	—	—	2,880
12/99	855	—	—	2,699
12/98	1,500	—	—	5,000
12/97	1,500	—	—	5,150
12/96	1,400	—	—	5,000
12/95	1,300	—	—	5,100
12/94	1,300	—	—	5,163
12/93	1,200	—	—	—
Annual Growth	0.3%	—	—	(5.5%)

Revenue History

Jockey International

Jockey International has nothing to do with horses and everything to do with the classic men's brief (its invention). The firm makes men's, women's, and children's underwear and loungewear, sold through some 14,000 department and specialty stores. It licenses and distributes its products in more than 120 countries. Jockey International also holds numerous licensing agreements. Chairman and CEO Debra Waller and her family own the company. Jockey International was founded in 1876 as a hosiery company intended to relieve lumberjacks of blisters and infections resulting from shoddy wool socks.

EXECUTIVES

Chairman and CEO: Debra S. Waller, age 47
President and COO: Edward C. (Ed) Emma
SVP, CFO, CIO: Frank Schneider
EVP, Jockey Brand Merchandising and Sales: John Brody
SVP, Customer Logistics: Edward (Ed) Gill
SVP and General Manager, Jockey Brand: Jim Noble
SVP, Manufacturing and Distribution: Brad Beal
VP, Domestic Licensing: Milou Gwyn
VP, General Counsel, and Corporate Secretary: Mark Jaeger
VP, Human Resources: Michael (Mike) McDermott
VP, Marketing and Advertising: Jamie Lockard
VP, Women's Division: Donna Hunter

LOCATIONS

HQ: Jockey International, Inc.
2300 60th St., Kenosha, WI 53141
Phone: 262-658-8111   **Fax:** 262-658-1812
Web: www.jockey.com

COMPETITORS

Calvin Klein
Danskin
Delta Galil Industries Ltd.
Fruit of the Loom
Maidenform
Sara Lee Branded
Victoria's Secret Stores
Warnaco Group

HISTORICAL FINANCIALS

Company Type: Private

Income Statement
FYE: December 31

	ESTIMATED REVENUE ($ mil.)	NET INCOME ($ mil.)	NET PROFIT MARGIN	EMPLOYEES
12/01*	550	—	—	5,000
12/00	600	—	—	5,000
12/99	600	—	—	5,400
12/98	545	—	—	5,400
12/97	525	—	—	5,400
12/96	500	—	—	5,200
12/95	450	—	—	4,500
12/94	425	—	—	5,000
12/93	450	—	—	—
Annual Growth	2.5%	—	—	0.0%

*Most recent year available

Revenue History

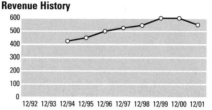

John Paul Mitchell

From pomades to pompadours, John Paul Mitchell Systems offers its best to those who do 'dos. The #1 privately owned hair care firm in the US makes more than 90 different hair care products that sell in about 90,000 hair salons worldwide. John Paul Mitchell was founded in Hawaii in 1980 by John Paul "J. P." DeJoria and the late Paul Mitchell. The company's signature white bottles with distinctive black lettering (because the founders couldn't afford color ink) have attracted the attention of counterfeiters on more than one occasion. Chairman and CEO DeJoria, a former gang member who sports a black ponytail and beard (and is seen in company TV commercials), is a vocal supporter for consumer-product safety.

EXECUTIVES

Chairman and CEO: John Paul (J. P.) DeJoria, age 60
Vice Chairman: Kenin M. Spivak
COO and Human Resources: Luke Jacobellis
VP, Advertising and Public Relations: Nanette Bercu
VP, Finance: Rick Battaglini
VP, Sales: Brent Golden
VP, Sports Marketing: Julie Solwold
CIO: Eric Peterson
Marketing Director, UK: Leslie George Spears
Public Relations Director: Isabelle Smith
Product Security Manager: Vikki Bresnahan
Company Secretary, UK: Peter Derald Barham
Corporate Counsel: Michaelin Re
Senior National Educator: Guadalupe Ovalles-Moore
National Educator: Jodi Bansley

LOCATIONS

HQ: John Paul Mitchell Systems
9701 Wilshire Blvd., Ste. 1205,
Beverly Hills, CA 90212
Phone: 310-248-3888   **Fax:** 310-248-2780
Web: www.paulmitchell.com

PRODUCTS/OPERATIONS

Selected Brands
Modern Elixirs
Paul Mitchell
  Awapuhi
  Baby Don't Cry
  Shampoo One
  Shampoo Two
  Shampoo Three
  Tea Tree
  The Conditioner
  The Cream
  The Detangler
  The Heat
  The Masque
  The Rinse
  The Shine
  The Wash
Paul Mitchell Professional Salon
XTG (Extreme Thickening Glue)

Selected Products
Conditioners
Finish sprays
Shampoos
Styling aids (gel, glaze, foam, lotion, spray, pomade, and wax)

COMPETITORS

Alberto-Culver   SoftSheen/Carson
L'Oréal   Stephan
Modern Organic Products   Unilever
Nexxus Products   Wella

HISTORICAL FINANCIALS

Company Type: Private

Income Statement
FYE: December 31

	ESTIMATED REVENUE ($ mil.)	NET INCOME ($ mil.)	NET PROFIT MARGIN	EMPLOYEES
12/03	800	—	—	—
12/02	700	—	—	—
12/01	600	—	—	100
12/00	600	—	—	100
12/99	600	—	—	97
12/98	200	—	—	110
12/97	185	—	—	100
12/96	165	—	—	89
Annual Growth	25.3%	—	—	2.4%

Revenue History

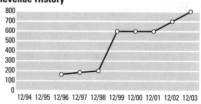

John Wieland Homes

John Wieland Homes and Neighborhoods (JW) develops land and builds cluster homes, townhomes, and more than 100 different types of upscale single-family homes in the Southeast US (in the metropolitan areas of Atlanta, Charleston, Charlotte, Raleigh, and Nashville). The company annually sells about 1,800 homes at an average sales price of $403,000. JW also provides remodeling and landscaping services. In cities where it builds, the company operates New Home Center design centers that provide interior and exterior design services. Wieland Financial Services offers mortgage lending to JW customers and others. Chairman John Wieland owns the firm, which he founded in 1970.

EXECUTIVES

Chairman and Chief Creative Officer: John Wieland
CEO and Director: Terry Russell
President, COO, and Director: Eric Price
EVP, General Counsel, and Director: Richard Bacon
SVP Land Development: Charlie Biele
VP and CFO: Doug Ray
VP Commercial Division: Jack Wieland
VP Organizational Development: Laura McMurrain
President and COO, JW Support Companies: Ron Meehan
President and COO, John Wieland Homes and Neighborhoods, Atlanta - Heritage Division: Michael (Mike) Langella
President, John Wieland Homes and Neighborhoods, Atlanta - Legacy Division: David (Dave) Durham
President, John Wieland Homes and Neighborhoods, Atlanta - Northwest Division: Scott Dozier
VP Human Resources: John Wood
Executive Asst.: Andrea Lofstrand
Auditors: Birnbrey, Minsk & Minsk

LOCATIONS

HQ: John Wieland Homes and Neighborhoods, Inc.
1950 Sullivan Rd., Atlanta, GA 30337
Phone: 770-996-2400   **Fax:** 770-907-3419
Web: www.jwhomes.com

COMPETITORS

Beazer Homes
Centex
Del Webb
D.R. Horton
Engle Homes
M/I Homes
NVR
Oriole Homes
Pulte Homes

HISTORICAL FINANCIALS

Company Type: Private

Income Statement
FYE: September 30

	ESTIMATED REVENUE ($ mil.)	NET INCOME ($ mil.)	NET PROFIT MARGIN	EMPLOYEES
9/04	730	—	—	1,000
9/03	606	—	—	1,000
9/02	500	—	—	900
9/01	502	—	—	900
Annual Growth	13.3%	—	—	3.6%

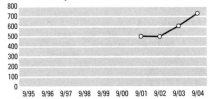

Revenue History

Johns Hopkins Medicine

Hopping John is a recipe for black-eyed peas; Johns Hopkins Medicine is a recipe for Baltimore's health care. The not-for-profit system includes Johns Hopkins University School of Medicine and the Johns Hopkins Health System. Staffed by medical school faculty, the system boasts The Johns Hopkins Hospitals and two other acute care hospitals, as well as facilities that offer long-term care, home care, managed care, and outpatient services. Johns Hopkins Medicine's international division oversees telemedicine programs (that allow remote access to Johns Hopkins physicians) in Europe, across Asia, and in South America.

The Johns Hopkins system also performs clinical research trials and is a leading recipient of federal research funding. About 20% of its revenue comes from research funding. The organization is hoping to boost that funding even as it copes with rising costs and other issues facing health care providers across the US. Johns Hopkins Medicine was created in the mid-1990s to unify the university and health system.

EXECUTIVES

Chairman: Lenox D. Baker Jr., age 62
President, The Johns Hopkins University: William R. Brody, age 60
CEO; CEO and Dean of the Medical Faculty, The Johns Hopkins University School of Medicine: Edward D. Miller Jr., age 61
EVP; President, The Johns Hopkins Hospital and The Johns Hopkins Health System: Ronald R. Peterson, age 56
VP, Corporate Security: Joseph R. Coppola
VP, Corporate Communications: Elaine Freeman
VP, Strategic Planning and Market Research: Toby A. Gordon
VP and CFO: Richard A. (Rich) Grossi
VP and General Counsel: Joanne E. Pollak
VP, Information Services: Stephanie L. Reel
VP, Quality Improvement: Judy A. Reitz
VP, Government Affairs and Community Relations: Linda L. Robertson
VP, Ambulatory Services Coordination and Vice Dean for Administration: Steven J. Thompson
Associate VP, Development and Alumni Affairs: John H. Zeller
Secretary: G. Daniel Shealer Jr.

LOCATIONS

HQ: Johns Hopkins Medicine
720 Rutland Ave., Baltimore, MD 21205
Phone: 410-955-5000   **Fax:** 410-955-4452
Web: www.hopkinsmedicine.org

PRODUCTS/OPERATIONS

2003 Sources of Income

	% of total
Commercial insurance	20
Research	
Government sources	16
Other sources	3
Medicare	17
HMO	14
Medicaid	14
Self-pay	5
Contributions & investment income	4
Other	7
Total	**100**

Selected Operations

Howard County General Hospital
Johns Hopkins at Cedar Lane
Johns Hopkins at Green Spring Station
Johns Hopkins at White Marsh
Johns Hopkins Bayview Medical Center
Johns Hopkins Children's Center
Johns Hopkins Clinical Practice Association
Johns Hopkins Community Physicians
Johns Hopkins HealthCare
Johns Hopkins Home Care Group
The Johns Hopkins Hospital
Johns Hopkins Singapore
Priority Partners
Sidney Kimmel Comprehensive Cancer Center

COMPETITORS

Ascension Health
Bon Secours Health
Christiana Care
Inova
Mayo Foundation
MedStar Health
Memorial Sloan-Kettering
Trinity Health (Novi)

HISTORICAL FINANCIALS

Company Type: Not-for-profit

Income Statement
FYE: June 30

	REVENUE ($ mil.)	NET INCOME ($ mil.)	NET PROFIT MARGIN	EMPLOYEES
6/03	1,600	—	—	25,000
6/02	926	—	—	24,500
6/01	2,500	—	—	24,000
6/00	2,121	—	—	23,550
6/99	1,984	—	—	22,272
6/98	1,661	—	—	20,987
Annual Growth	(0.7%)	—	—	3.6%

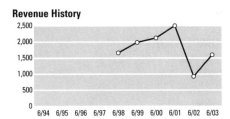

Revenue History

Johnson Brothers

It's safe to say the Johnson brothers put up with "winers." Johnson Brothers Liquor Company is one of the country's top wine and liquor distributors. The company distributes wines and spirits throughout the midwestern and southern US and in Hawaii. Johnson Brothers is a leading distributor of Gallo wines. It also distributes the wines and spirits of Diageo, Robert Mondavi, Constellation Brands, and Kendall-Jackson. Johnson Brothers is owned by the Johnson brothers — CEO Lynn Johnson and President Mitchell Johnson.

EXECUTIVES
CEO: Lynn Johnson
President: Mitchell Johnson
CFO: Scott Belsaas
Director of Human Resources: Susan Ewers

LOCATIONS
HQ: Johnson Brothers Liquor Company
1999 Shepard Rd., St. Paul, MN 55116
Phone: 651-649-5800   **Fax:** 651-649-5894
Web: www.johnsonbrothers.com

COMPETITORS
Georgia Crown
Glazer's Wholesale Drug
National Distributing
National Wine & Spirits
Peerless Importers
Southern Wine & Spirits
Sunbelt Beverage
Wirtz
Young's Market

HISTORICAL FINANCIALS
Company Type: Private

Income Statement
FYE: December 31

	ESTIMATED REVENUE ($ mil.)	NET INCOME ($ mil.)	NET PROFIT MARGIN	EMPLOYEES
12/03	650	—	—	1,280
12/02	618	—	—	1,200
12/01	618	—	—	1,150
12/00	575	—	—	1,100
12/99	550	—	—	1,100
12/98	560	—	—	1,100
12/97	525	—	—	1,100
12/96	520	—	—	1,050
12/95	500	—	—	1,050
12/94	475	—	—	1,100
Annual Growth	3.5%	—	—	1.7%

Revenue History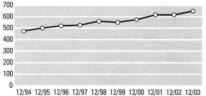

Johnson Publishing

Snubbed by advertisers when he founded his company 60 years ago, John Johnson has pushed his magazine company to the front of the pack. Led by its flagship publication, *Ebony*, family-owned Johnson Publishing Company is the largest black-owned publishing firm in the country. It also publishes *Jet* and operates a book division. In addition, Johnson Publishing produces a line of hair care products (Supreme Beauty) and cosmetics (Fashion Fair) marketed for African-American women, and each year it hosts the Ebony Fashion Fair, a traveling fashion show that raises money for scholarships and charities in cities across the US and Canada.

The company's book division features titles such as *The New Ebony Cookbook* and the more controversial *Forced Into Glory: Abraham Lincoln's White Dream*.

Johnson Publishing is owned and controlled by founder and chairman Johnson and his family. Johnson's daughter, Linda Johnson Rice, handles the day-to-day operations as president and CEO. His wife, Eunice, produces the Ebony Fashion Fair.

HISTORY

John H. Johnson launched his publishing business in 1942 while he was still in college in Chicago. The idea for a black-oriented magazine came to him while he was working part-time for Supreme Life Insurance Co. of America, where one of his jobs was to clip magazine and newspaper articles about the black community. Johnson used his mother's furniture as collateral to secure a $500 loan and then mailed $2 charter subscription offers to potential subscribers. He received 3,000 replies and used the $6,000 to print the first issue of *Negro Digest*, patterned after *Reader's Digest*. Circulation was 50,000 within a year.

Johnson started *Ebony* magazine in 1945 (which gained immediate popularity and is still the company's premier publication) and launched *Jet* in 1951, a pocket-sized publication containing news items and features. In the early days Johnson was unable to obtain advertising, so he formed his own Beauty Star mail-order business and advertised its products (dresses, wigs, hair care products, and vitamins) in his magazines. He won his first major account, Zenith Radio, in 1947; Johnson landed Chrysler in 1954, only after sending a salesman to Detroit every week for 10 years. For 20 years, *Ebony* and *Jet* were the only national publications targeting blacks in the US.

By the 1960s Johnson had become one of the most prominent black men in the US. He posed with John F. Kennedy in 1963 to publicize a special issue of *Ebony* celebrating the Emancipation Proclamation. US magazine publishers named him Publisher of the Year in 1972. Johnson launched *Ebony Jr!* (since discontinued) in 1973, a magazine designed to provide "positive black images" for black preteens. His first magazine, *Negro Digest* (renamed *Black World*), became known for its provocative articles, but its circulation dwindled from 100,000 to 15,000. Johnson retired the magazine in 1975.

Unable to find the proper makeup for his *Ebony* models, Johnson founded his own cosmetics business, Fashion Fair Cosmetics, that year, which carved out a niche beside Revlon (which introduced cosmetic lines for blacks) and another black cosmetics company, Johnson Products (unrelated) of Chicago. By 1982 Fashion Fair sales were more than $30 million.

The company got into broadcasting in 1972 when it bought Chicago radio station WGRT (renamed WJPC; that city's first black-owned station). It added WLOU (Louisville, Kentucky) in 1982 and WLNR (Lansing, Illinois; re-launched in 1991 as WJPC-FM) in 1985. By 1995, however, it had sold all of its stations.

Johnson and the company sold their controlling interest in the last minority-owned insurance company in Illinois (and Johnson's first employer), Supreme Life Insurance, to Unitrin (a Chicago-based life, health, and property insurer) in 1991. That year the company and catalog retailer Spiegel announced a joint venture to develop fashions for black women. The two companies launched a mail-order catalog called *E Style* in 1993 and an accompanying credit card the next year.

Johnson Publishing launched its South African edition of *Ebony* in 1995. Johnson was awarded the Presidential Medal of Freedom in 1996. The next year, however, circulation of *Ebony* fell 7% as mainstream magazines began covering black issues more thoroughly and a host of new titles appeared. In response, the company restructured its ventures and closed its *E Style* catalog. Johnson Publishing retired *Ebony Man* (launched in 1985) in 1998 and *Ebony South Africa* in 2000.

In 2002 John Johnson named his daughter Linda Johnson Rice as CEO of the company; Johnson remains as chairman and publisher.

EXECUTIVES
Chairman and Publisher: John H. Johnson, age 84
President and CEO: Linda Johnson Rice, age 46
Secretary and Treasurer; Producer and Director, EBONY Fashion Fair: Eunice W. Johnson
Executive Editor, EBONY: Lerone Bennett Jr.
SVP and General Counsel: June Acie Rhinehart
SVP Associate Publisher, Advertising: Jeff Burns Jr.
SVP, Fashion Fair Cosmetics: J. Lance Clark
VP and Director of Promotions: Lydia J. Davis Eady
VP Finance: Treka Owens
Director of Circulation: Kenneth C. Brooks
Telecommunications Manager: Sheila Jenkins
Purchasing Manager: Ruth Wagner
Director Human Resources: LaDoris Foster

LOCATIONS
HQ: Johnson Publishing Company, Inc.
820 S. Michigan Ave., Chicago, IL 60605
Phone: 312-322-9200   **Fax:** 312-322-0918

PRODUCTS/OPERATIONS

Selected Operations
Fashion and Beauty Aids
Ebony Fashion Fair (traveling fashion show)
Fashion Fair Cosmetics (color cosmetics, fragrances, skincare)
Supreme Beauty Products (hair care)

Publishing
Books
Magazines
 Ebony
 Jet

COMPETITORS

Advance Publications	Hearst Magazines
Alberto-Culver	LFP
Avon	L'Oréal
BET	Mary Kay
Earl G. Graves	Revlon
Essence Communications	Time
Estée Lauder	Vanguarde Media
Forbes	

HISTORICAL FINANCIALS

Company Type: Private

Income Statement				FYE: December 31
	REVENUE ($ mil.)	NET INCOME ($ mil.)	NET PROFIT MARGIN	EMPLOYEES
12/02	425	—	—	2,076
12/01	412	—	—	2,594
12/00	400	—	—	2,614
12/99	387	—	—	2,657
12/98	372	—	—	2,647
12/97	361	—	—	2,677
12/96	326	—	—	2,702
12/95	316	—	—	2,680
12/94	307	—	—	2,662
12/93	294	—	—	2,600
Annual Growth	4.2%	—	—	(2.5%)

Revenue History

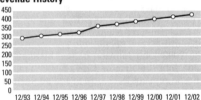

JohnsonDiversey

JohnsonDiversey is the industrial-strength version of S.C. Johnson & Son. Split off from the well-known private company in 1999, JohnsonDiversey consists of two units: Professional and Polymer. Professional provides commercial cleaning, hygiene, pest control, and food sanitation products to retailers, building service contractors, hospitality firms, and food service operators. Polymer produces acrylic resins used in printing, packaging, coatings, and adhesives. The Johnson family controls two-thirds of the company; Unilever controls the rest. The firm changed its name from S.C. Johnson Commercial Markets to JohnsonDiversey in 2002 after acquiring DiverseyLever, Unilever's industrial cleaning business.

The acquisition of DiverseyLever more than doubled the company's sales and made it the #2 industrial and institutional cleaning products firm, behind Ecolab, with a 13% market share. As part of the deal, the company took on considerable debt. JohnsonDiversey has an option to buy out Unilever's stake by 2007.

The company's cleaning products customers include ARAMARK, The Coca-Cola Company, McDonald's, and Wal-Mart; its polymer customers include ink makers Flint Ink and Sun Chemical.

JohnsonDiversey dates back to the 1930s, when S.C. Johnson became involved in commercial sales of cleaning products.

EXECUTIVES

Chairman: Samuel Curtis (Curt) Johnson III, age 48, $1,159,329 pay
President and CEO: Gregory E. (Greg) Lawton, age 53, $1,565,510 pay
EVP, Chief Administrative Officer, Secretary, and General Counsel: JoAnne Brandes, age 50, $635,178 pay
EVP, Corporate Development: Michael J. (Mike) Bailey, age 51, $628,388 pay
SVP and Group President: Mark S. Cross, age 47
SVP, Global Strategy Development: Sanjib Choudhuri, age 55
SVP, Global Supply Chain: Gregory F. Clark, age 50
SVP, Human Resources: Timothy Ransome, age 53
VP and CIO: Sue Leboza, age 49
VP and Treasurer: Francisco Sanchez
VP, Corporate Controller, and Interim CFO: Clive A. Newman, age 40
VP, Global Communications, Public Affairs, and Administrative Services: John Matthews
Regional President, Asia Pacific: Paul A. Mathias, age 59
Regional President, Europe: Graeme D. Armstrong, age 41, $782,602 pay
Regional President, Japan: Morio Nishikawa, age 59, $480,863 pay
Regional President, Latin America: Jean-Max Teissier, age 58
Regional President, North America: Thomas M. Gartland, age 46
Auditors: Ernst & Young LLP

LOCATIONS

HQ: JohnsonDiversey, Inc.
 8310 16th St., Sturtevant, WI 53177
Phone: 262-631-4001   **Fax:** 262-631-4282
Web: www.johnsondiversey.com

JohnsonDiversey has 51 manufacturing facilities in 120 countries.

2003 Sales

	$ mil.	% of total
Europe	1,376.4	46
Americas		
North America	1,012.4	34
Central & South America	128.3	10
Asia		
Japan	278.6	6
Asia-Pacific	170.7	4
Adjustments	(18.6)	—
Total	**2,947.8**	**100**

PRODUCTS/OPERATIONS

2003 Sales

	$ mil.	% of total
Professional	2,681.3	90
Polymer	285.1	10
Adjustments	(18.6)	—
Total	**2,947.8**	**100**

Affiliated Businesses

Austo-C (manufactures commercial warewashing and laundry products)
The Butcher Company (manufactures and markets janitorial supplies)
US Chemical (manufactures labels for specialty cleaning products)
Whitmore Micro-Gen Research Laboratories (manufactures and supplies pesticides and related equipment)

COMPETITORS

Acuity Brands	Dow Chemical
Air Products	Eastman Chemical
Arrow-Magnolia	Ecolab
Avecia	Kimberly-Clark
BASF AG	NCH
Clorox	Procter & Gamble
Colgate-Palmolive	Rohm and Haas
Dainippon Ink	Surface Specialties

HISTORICAL FINANCIALS

Company Type: Private

Income Statement				FYE: December 31
	REVENUE ($ mil.)	NET INCOME ($ mil.)	NET PROFIT MARGIN	EMPLOYEES
12/03	2,948	24	0.8%	13,000
12/02	2,196	30	1.3%	13,530
12/01*	549	11	2.0%	14,500
6/01	1,133	33	2.9%	3,600
6/00	1,028	50	4.8%	3,500
6/99	980	15	1.5%	3,000
Annual Growth	24.6%	10.2%	—	34.1%

*Fiscal year change

2003 Year-End Financials

Debt ratio: 137.4%
Return on equity: 2.6%
Cash ($ mil.): 25
Current ratio: 1.11
Long-term debt ($ mil.): 1,367

Net Income History

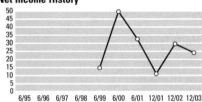

Jones Day

Legal leviathan Jones Day ranks as one of the world's largest law firms, providing counsel to about half of the FORTUNE 500 companies. It has more than 2,000 attorneys in some 30 offices across the US, as well as in Asia, Australia, and Europe. The firm's practice groups include litigation, tax, government regulation, and business. Jones Day has counted Bridgestone/Firestone, General Motors, IBM, RJR Nabisco, and Texas Instruments among its top clients. Other notable clients include America Online and BP Amoco. The firm traces its roots to the Cleveland law partnership founded by Edwin Blandin and William Rice in 1893.

EXECUTIVES

Managing Partner: Stephen J. Brogan
CFO: F. Derald Hunt
Partner-in-Charge International Region:
 David F. Clossey
Partner-in-Charge, New York: Dennis W. LaBarre, age 61
Partner-in-Charge, Paris: Wesley R. Johnson Jr.
Partner-In-Charge, Washington: Mary Ellen Powers
Director of Administration: William Gaskill

LOCATIONS

HQ: Jones Day
Northpoint, 901 Lakeside Ave., Cleveland, OH 44114
Phone: 216-586-3939   **Fax:** 216-579-0212
Web: www.jonesday.com

Jones Day has US offices in Atlanta; Chicago; Cleveland; Columbus, Ohio; Dallas; Houston; Irvine, Los Angeles, Menlo Park, San Diego, and San Francisco, California; New York City; Pittsburgh; and Washington, DC. The firm has international offices in Beijing; Brussels; Frankfurt; Hong Kong; London; Madrid; Milan; Munich; Paris; Shanghai; Singapore; Sydney; Taipei, Taiwan; and Tokyo.

PRODUCTS/OPERATIONS

Selected Practice Areas
Antitrust
Bankruptcy
Environmental
Intellectual property
Labor
Real estate
Securities
Tax

COMPETITORS

Akin Gump
Baker & McKenzie
Cleary, Gottlieb
Clifford Chance
Holland & Knight
Latham & Watkins
Mayer, Brown, Rowe & Maw
Morgan, Lewis
Shearman & Sterling
Sidley Austin Brown & Wood
Skadden, Arps
White & Case

HISTORICAL FINANCIALS

Company Type: Partnership

Income Statement   FYE: December 31

	REVENUE ($ mil.)	NET INCOME ($ mil.)	NET PROFIT MARGIN	EMPLOYEES
12/03	1,035	—	—	—
12/02	908	—	—	—
12/01	790	—	—	—
12/00	675	—	—	3,200
12/99	595	—	—	3,200
12/98	530	—	—	3,200
12/97	490	—	—	3,092
12/96	450	—	—	2,880
12/95	400	—	—	2,800
12/94	384	—	—	468
Annual Growth	11.6%	—	—	37.8%

Revenue History

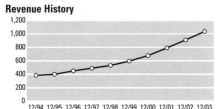

Jones Financial

This is not your father's broker. Well, maybe it is. The Jones Financial Companies is the parent of Edward Jones, an investment brokerage network catering to individual investors. Most of its clients are retired people and small-business owners in rural communities and suburbs. The "Wal-Mart of Wall Street" has thousands of satellite-linked offices in the US, Canada, and the UK. Brokers preach a conservative buy-and-hold approach, offering relatively low-risk investment vehicles such as government bonds, blue-chip stocks, and high-quality mutual funds.

Edward Jones' network of some 9,000 offices — many of them with a single broker — makes it one of the largest brokerage networks in the world. The company also sells insurance and engages in investment banking for such clients as Wal-Mart and public agencies. The firm embraces technology, maintaining one of the industry's largest satellite networks (including a dish for each office).

Preferring to groom brokers internally, the firm accepts applicants with no previous experience, trains them extensively, and monitors investment patterns to prevent account churning and trading in risky low-cap stocks. Before they are given such luxuries as office space or assistants, new brokers must make 1,000 cold calls in their chosen community. Edward Jones' investment in training, backed by what's perceived to be old-school values and strong ethics, seems to be paying off: The firm has repeatedly ranked on *FORTUNE* magazine's "100 Best Companies to Work For."

The company's attempt to embrace old-fashioned traditions has not spared it from some modern-day issues. Edward Jones is one of several brokerage firms under regulatory scrutiny for allegedly failing to disclose the incentives its brokers received for certain mutual fund sales.

The Jones Companies is the only major financial services firm still organized as a partnership, and it has said it has no plans to go public. Meanwhile, the company is plugging away at its goal to have 10,000 locations by the end of 2004, an undertaking that has at least some brokers concerned about competition within the network and market saturation.

HISTORY

Jones Financial got its start in 1871 as bond house Whitaker & Co. In 1922 Edward D. Jones (no relation to the Edward D. Jones of Dow Jones fame) opened a brokerage in St. Louis. In 1943 the two firms merged.

Jones' son Edward "Ted" Jones Jr. joined the firm in 1948. Under Ted's leadership (and against his father's wishes), the company focused on rural customers, opening its first branch in the Missouri town of Mexico in 1955 and beginning its march across small-town America. Ted took over as managing partner in 1968, masterminding the company's small-town expansion. (The Wal-Mart comparison is apt; Ted Jones and Sam Walton were good friends.)

Almost from the start, the firm hammered home a conservative investment message focusing on blue-chip stocks and bonds. It expanded steadily throughout the years, adding offices with such addresses as Cedarburg, Wisconsin, and Paris, Illinois.

In the 1970s Edward D. Jones moved into underwriting with clients including Southern Co., Citicorp, and Humana. (It got burned in the mid-1980s on one such deal, when the SEC accused the company of fraud in a bond offering for life insurer D.H. Baldwin Co., which later filed for bankruptcy.)

The company's technological bent was spurred in 1978 after its Teletype network couldn't handle the demand generated by the firm's 220 offices. As a stopgap, the company nixed use of the Teletype for stock quotes, telling its brokers to call Merrill Lynch's toll-free number instead.

Managing partner John Bachmann took over from Ted Jones in 1980. (Bachmann started at the company as a janitor.) A follower of management guru Peter Drucker, Bachmann inculcated the company's brokers with Drucker's customer- and value-oriented principles.

Edward D. Jones began moving into the suburbs and into less-than-posh sections of big cities in the mid-1980s. In 1986 the company started a mortgage program, but the plan was never successful and was ended in 1988. The company weathered the 1987 stock market crash (many brokerages did not), albeit with thinner profit margins.

In 1990 Ted Jones died. The first half of the decade was a time of great expansion for the company as it doubled its number of offices. In 1993 the company opened an office in Canada.

In 1994 Jones Financial's acquisition of Columbia, Missouri-based thrift Boone National gave it the ability to offer trust and mortgage services to its clients, which helped sales as Jones started facing competition from Merrill Lynch in its small-town niche. The company's rapid expansion and relatively expensive infrastructure (all those one-person offices add up) began to eat at the bottom line, and in 1995 Bachmann stopped expansion so the firm could catch its breath.

In 1997 Edward Jones (which had unofficially dropped its middle "D" to boost name recognition) moved overseas, opening its first offices in the UK, a prime expansion target for the company. The next year the firm teamed up with Mercantile Bank to offer small-business loans. Jones resumed its expansionist push in 1999 and 2000, adding offices in all its markets, but continued to resist online trading.

EXECUTIVES

Managing Partner: Douglas E. (Doug) Hill, age 59, $207,160 pay
Principal, Finance & Accounting: Steven (Steve) Novik, age 54
General Counsel: Lawrence R. Sobol, age 53
Principal, Product and Sales: Brett Campbell
Principal, Compliance: Pam Cavness
Principal, Operations: Norman Eaker
Principal, Internal Audit: Ann Ficken
Principal, Human Resources: Michael R. Holmes, age 45
Principal, Marketing: Dallas Kersey
Principal, United Kingdom Operations: Tim Kirley
Principal, Information Systems: Richie L. (Rich) Malone, age 55, $182,160 pay
Principal, Service Division: Darryl L. Pope, age 64
Principal, Canadian Operations: Gary D. Reamey, $157,160 pay
Principal, Products and Services: Ray Robbins
Principal, Branch Staff Training: Lila Rudolph
Principal, Product and Sales: Dann Timm
Principal, Product and Sales: James D. (Jim) Weddle, $182,160 pay
Chief Market Strategist: Alan F. Skrainka
Auditors: PricewaterhouseCoopers LLP

LOCATIONS

HQ: The Jones Financial Companies, L.L.L.P.
12555 Manchester Rd., Des Peres, MO 63131
Phone: 314-515-2000 **Fax:** 314-515-2622
Web: www.edwardjones.com

The Jones Financial Companies operates more than 9,000 offices in the US, Canada, and the UK.

PRODUCTS/OPERATIONS

2003 Sales

	$ mil.	% of total
Commissions		
Mutual funds	1,088.0	43
Listed	214.0	8
Insurance	226.4	9
OTC	49.8	2
Other	0.6	—
Principal transactions	350.7	14
Investment banking	43.8	2
Interest & dividends	132.0	5
Sub-transfer agent revenue	138.0	5
Mutual fund & insurance revenue	91.8	4
Money market revenue	72.7	3
IRA custodial service fees	58.5	2
Other revenue	72.6	3
Total	**2,538.9**	**100**

Selected Subsidiaries
EDJ Holding Co., Inc.
EDJ Leasing Co., LP
Edward D. Jones & Co. Canada Holding Co., Inc.
Edward D. Jones & Co., LP (broker-dealer)
Edward D. Jones Ltd. (UK)
EJ Insurance Agency Holding LLC
EJ Mortgage LLC
Edward Jones Mortgage (50%)
LHC, Inc.
Unison Capital Corp., Inc.
Passport Research Ltd. (50%, money market mutual fund adviser)
Unison Investment Trust

COMPETITORS

A.G. Edwards	Oppenheimer Holdings
Ameritrade	Piper Jaffray
Charles Schwab	Raymond James Financial
Citigroup	T. Rowe Price
Merrill Lynch	TD Waterhouse
Morgan Stanley	UBS Financial Services
NFP	Wells Fargo

HISTORICAL FINANCIALS
Company Type: Partnership

Income Statement
FYE: December 31

	REVENUE ($ mil.)	NET INCOME ($ mil.)	NET PROFIT MARGIN	EMPLOYEES
12/03	2,539	203	8.0%	29,200
12/02	2,270	149	6.6%	28,469
12/01	2,142	149	7.0%	26,460
12/00	2,212	230	10.4%	23,432
12/99	1,787	187	10.5%	20,541
12/98	1,450	199	13.7%	15,795
12/97	1,135	114	10.1%	13,691
12/96	952	93	9.8%	12,148
12/95	722	58	8.1%	11,717
12/94	661	54	8.2%	7,418
Annual Growth	16.1%	15.9%	—	16.4%

2003 Year-End Financials
Debt ratio: —
Return on equity: —
Cash ($ mil.): —
Current ratio: —
Long-term debt ($ mil.): 40

Net Income History

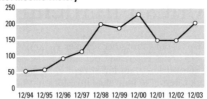

Jordan Industries

It's not related to Michael, but with a name like Jordan Industries, it's no wonder this company does it all. Jordan is involved in markets as diverse as automotive products, bicycle reflector kits, software application development, electric motors, and specialty advertising products. It owns more than 20 companies, which are divided into five business units: Kinetek (electric motors and gears), Jordan Auto Aftermarket (torque converters), Jordan Specialty Plastics (plastic products), Specialty Printing and Labeling (promotional products), and Consumer and Industrial Products (orthopedic supports and gift items). Director David Zalaznick owns 20% of the company; chairman and CEO John W. Jordan II owns 18%.

EXECUTIVES
Chairman and CEO: John W. (Jay) Jordan II, age 56
President, COO, and Director: Thomas H. Quinn, age 56, $1,000,000 pay
SVP, Business Development: Joe Linnen
SVP and Treasurer: Gordon L. Nelson Jr., age 46
VP, Assistant Secretary, and Director: Jonathan F. Boucher, age 47
VP and Controller: Lisa M. Ondrula, age 34
CEO, GramTel USA: Tracy Graham
President, Beemak Plastics, Inc.: Chris Braun
President, Pamco Label Co.: Michael Blechman
President, Sate-Lite Manufacturing: Richard (Dick) Van Deventer
General Counsel, Secretary, and Director: G. Robert Fisher, age 63
Auditors: Ernst & Young LLP

LOCATIONS
HQ: Jordan Industries, Inc.
Arborlake Center, Ste. 550, 1751 Lake Cook Rd., Deerfield, IL 60015
Phone: 847-945-5591 **Fax:** 847-945-0198
Web: www.jordanindustries.com

Jordan Industries has facilities in Canada, China, France, Germany, Italy, Mexico, the UK, and the US.

2003 Sales

	$ mil.	% of total
US	635.3	88
Other countries	84.7	12
Total	**720.0**	**100**

PRODUCTS/OPERATIONS

2003 Sales

	$ mil.	% of total
Kinetek	288.1	40
Jordan Auto Aftermarket	144.9	20
Jordan Specialty Plastics	117.3	16
Specialty Printing & Labeling	100.6	14
Consumer & Industrial Products	69.1	10
Total	**720.0**	**100**

Selected Operations
Kinetek
Jordan Auto Aftermarket
Jordan Specialty Plastics
Specialty Printing and Labeling
Consumer and Industrial Products

COMPETITORS
Aftermarket Technology
Baldor Electric
Bed Bath & Beyond
BorgWarner
Dana
HMI Industries
Multi-Color
Red Man Pipe & Supply
Regal-Beloit
Seven Worldwide
Thomas Nelson
Twin Disc
Tyco International

HISTORICAL FINANCIALS
Company Type: Private

Income Statement
FYE: December 31

	REVENUE ($ mil.)	NET INCOME ($ mil.)	NET PROFIT MARGIN	EMPLOYEES
12/03	720	(33)	—	6,605
12/02	720	(64)	—	7,200
12/01	723	(58)	—	6,500
12/00	807	—	—	6,967
12/99	777	—	—	7,000
12/98	944	—	—	7,092
12/97	707	—	—	6,200
12/96	602	—	—	6,218
12/95	507	—	—	5,150
12/94	424	—	—	3,900
Annual Growth	6.0%	—	—	6.0%

2003 Year-End Financials
Debt ratio: —
Return on equity: —
Cash ($ mil.): 16
Current ratio: 1.70
Long-term debt ($ mil.): 728

Net Income History

Jostens

Are you *sure* you want to remember high school? If so, look to Jostens, the leading US producer of yearbooks and class rings. Class rings are sold on school campuses and through bookstores, retail jewelers, and the Internet, while Jostens' sports rings commemorate professional sports champions (it has made 24 of 36 Super Bowl rings). Other graduation products include diplomas, announcements, caps, and gowns, and it takes and sells class and individual pictures for schools in the US and Canada. In 2003 Jostens was sold to a unit of CSFB. The next year Jostens was recapitalized and became part of a newly created printing and marketing services company co-owned by an affiliate of CSFB and Kohlberg Kravis Roberts.

Yearbooks (for all levels of schools from elementary through college) account for more than 40% of Jostens' sales. Representatives work closely with students and faculty advisors in all phases of yearbook creation — from planning, editing, and layout to production, printing, and distribution. The company also prints books, brochures, and promotional materials. Jostens exited the recognition business in 2001.

In conjunction with Jostens' sale to CSFB in 2003, a newly formed company (controlled by the private equity unit of CSFB), Ring Acquisition Corp., was merged with Jostens; Jostens continued as the surviving corporation. The specialty printing and marketing services company (created in 2004) consists of Jostens, as well as Von Hoffmann Corporation, a leading printer of educational textbooks and supplemental materials, and Arcade Marketing, a printer and manufacturer of sampling products for the fragrance, cosmetics, consumer products, and food and beverage industries.

EXECUTIVES

President and CEO: Michael L. Bailey, age 48, $437,659 pay
SVP and CFO: David A. Tayeh, age 37, $475,190 pay (partial-year salary)
SVP, Operations: John L. (Jack) Larsen, age 46
VP and CIO: Andrew W. Black, age 41, $275,311 pay
VP and Treasurer: Marjorie J. Brown, age 49
VP, General Counsel, and Corporate Secretary: Paula R. Johnson, age 56
VP, Human Resources and Communications: Steven A. Tighe, age 52, $277,792 pay
VP, Marketing: Timothy M. Larson, age 30
VP, Sales: Timothy M. Wolfe, age 43
Director of Communications: Rich Stoebe
Auditors: Ernst & Young LLP

LOCATIONS

HQ: Jostens, Inc.
5501 American Blvd. West, Minneapolis, MN 55437
Phone: 952-830-3300 **Fax:** 952-830-3293
Web: www.jostens.com

Jostens sells its products and services throughout North America through independent and employee sales representatives. It has manufacturing facilities in California, Kansas, Massachusetts, Minnesota, North and South Carolina, Pennsylvania, Tennessee, and Texas, as well as in Canada.

PRODUCTS/OPERATIONS

2003 Sales

	% of total
Yearbooks	41
Class rings	26
Graduation products	25
Photography	8
Total	**100**

Selected Products

Printing and publishing
  Books
  Commercial brochures
  Promotional books and materials
  Yearbooks (elementary, middle, and high schools; college)
Jewelry
  Athletic rings
  Class rings (high school and college)
Graduation products
  Announcements
  Caps and gowns
  Diplomas
Photography
  Class and individual school pictures
  Prom and special events pictures
  Senior portraits
  Student ID cards

COMPETITORS

American Achievement
Herff Jones
Lifetouch
Walsworth

HISTORICAL FINANCIALS

Company Type: Private

Income Statement
FYE: Saturday nearest December 31

	REVENUE ($ mil.)	NET INCOME ($ mil.)	NET PROFIT MARGIN	EMPLOYEES
12/03	788	(26)	—	6,300
12/02	756	30	4.0%	6,700
12/01	737	4	0.6%	6,100
12/00	805	(19)	—	6,500
12/99	782	43	5.5%	6,700
12/98	771	42	5.4%	6,800
12/97	743	57	7.7%	6,500
12/96*	277	(1)	—	6,100
6/96	695	52	7.4%	5,600
6/95	665	50	7.6%	8,000
Annual Growth	1.9%	—	—	(2.6%)

*Fiscal year change

2003 Year-End Financials

Debt ratio: 213.4%   Current ratio: 0.73
Return on equity: —   Long-term debt ($ mil.): 821
Cash ($ mil.): 19

Net Income History

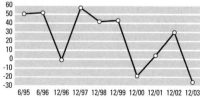

J.R. Simplot

J.R. Simplot hopes you'll have fries with that. Potato potentate J. R. "Jack" Simplot simply shook hands with McDonald's pioneer Ray Kroc in the mid-1960s, and his company's french fry sales have sizzled ever since. The company still remains the major french fry supplier for McDonald's and supplies Burger King and KFC as well. J.R. Simplot produces more than 3 billion pounds of french fries and hash browns annually, making it one of the world's largest processors of frozen potatoes. It offers its potato products mainly to food service and retail customers under its Simplot brand and private labels.

In addition to potatoes, J.R. Simplot also produces fruits and vegetables under the RoastWorks and Simplot Classic labels. The company's spuds sprouted other businesses as well, including cattle ranches and 150,00-head capacity feedlots (which use feed made from potato peels). Its AgriBusiness Group mines phosphates (for fertilizer and feed) and silica. The company's Turf and Horticulture Group produces grass and turf seed and fertilizer.

After being out of the dehydrated potato business for more than 30 years, Simplot acquired the dehydrated potato granule business of Nestlé USA in 2004; in addition it reached an agreement with Idaho Fresh-Pak to distribute that company's dehydrated potatoes.

Officially retired since 1994, J.R. Simplot remains one of the wealthiest Americans. After amassing a mountain of potato money, the spud-illionaire moved on to semiconductors and invested heavily in Boise-based Micron Technology.

HISTORY

J.R. Simplot was born in Dubuque, Iowa, in 1909. His family moved to the frontier town of Declo, Idaho, about a year later. Frustrated with school and an overbearing father, Simplot dropped out at age 14 and moved to a local hotel, where he made money by paying cash for teachers' wage scrip, at 50 cents on the dollar. Simplot then got a bank loan using the scrip as collateral and moved into farming, first by raising hogs and then by growing potatoes. He met Lindsay Maggart, a leading farmer in the area, who taught him the value of planting certified potato seed, rather than potatoes.

Simplot purchased an electric potato sorter in 1928 and eventually dominated the local market by sorting for neighboring farms. By 1940 his company, J.R. Simplot, operated 33 potato warehouses in Oregon and Idaho. The company moved into food processing in the 1940s, first by producing dried onions and other vegetables for Chicago-based Sokol & Co. and later by producing dehydrated potatoes. Between 1942 and 1945 J.R. Simplot produced more than 50 million pounds of dehydrated potatoes for the US military. During the war the company also expanded into fertilizer production, cattle feeding, and lumber. It moved to Boise, Idaho, in 1947.

In the 1950s J.R. Simplot researchers developed a method for freezing french fries. In the mid-1960s Simplot persuaded McDonald's founder Ray Kroc to go with his frozen fries, a handshake deal that practically guaranteed Simplot's success in the potato processing industry. By the end of the 1960s, Simplot was the largest landowner, cattleman, potato grower, and employer in the state of Idaho. He also had established fertilizer plants, mining operations, and other businesses in 36 states, as well as in Canada and a handful of other countries.

During the oil crisis of the 1970s, J.R. Simplot began producing ethanol from potatoes. However, Simplot's empire-building was not without its rough edges. In 1977 he pleaded no contest to federal charges that he failed to report his income, and the next year he was forced to settle charges that he manipulated Maine potato futures.

The company entered the frozen fruit and vegetable business in 1983. Other ventures included using wastewater from potato processing for irrigation and using cattle manure to fuel methane gas plants. Simplot set up a Chinese joint venture in the 1990s to provide processed potatoes to McDonald's and other customers in East Asia.

The company bought the giant ZX cattle ranch near Paisley, Oregon, in 1994. Simplot retired from the board of directors that year to become chairman emeritus; Stephen Beebe was named president and CEO. The 1995 acquisition of the food operations of Pacific Dunlop (now Ansell) led to the creation of Simplot Australia, one of the largest food processors in Australia. Its 1997 stock swap with I. & J. Foods Australia enlarged the subsidiary's frozen food menu.

In 1999 the company sold its Simplot Dairy Products cheese business to France's Besnier Group, and it teamed with Dutch potato processor Farm Frites to enter new markets. In 2000 it launched agricultural Web site planetAg, bought the turf grass seed assets of AgriBioTech, and added the US potato operations of Nestlé to its pantry.

In 2001 the firm said it would build an $80 million potato-processing plant in Manitoba. Also that year the company said it would not increase the value of its contracts with growers struggling amid low prices in a glutted market.

In 2002 Simplot sold its Australian pudding maker Big Sister to the Fowlers Vacola Group and its Agrisource grain company to a private buyer. That same year Beebe retired and Lawrence Hlobik, president of the company's agribusiness unit, was named CEO. The company closed its only meat-processing plant in September 2003.

In 2004 the company began offering zero-gram trans-fat french fries, called Infinity Fries, for the foodservice market.

EXECUTIVES

Chairman Emeritus: J. R. (Jack) Simplot, age 95
Chairman: Scott R. Simplot, age 57
CEO and Director: Lawrence S. (Larry) Hlobik, age 59
SVP, Corporate Secretary, and General Counsel:
  Terry Uhling
SVP, Finance and CFO: Annette Elg
SVP, Human Resources: Mike Vasilenko
SVP, Sales & Marketing Food: Greg Ibsen
SVP, Manufacturing, Logistics, and Wholesale:
  Pat Avery
VP, Business Integration Food: Paul Saras
VP, Public Relations: Fred Zerza
VP, Special Projects: Rick Fisch
VP and CIO: Roger Parks
President, Food Group: James R. Munyon
Director, Energy and Natural Resources: David Hawk
Manager, Customer Focus Marketing: Traci O'Donnell
Manager, Marketing Solutions: Kristi Smith

LOCATIONS

HQ: J.R. Simplot Company
  999 Main St., Ste. 1300, Boise, ID 83702
Phone: 208-336-2110   **Fax:** 208-389-7515
Web: www.simplot.com

In addition to the US, Simplot has operations in Australia, Canada, China, and Mexico.

PRODUCTS/OPERATIONS

Major Operating Groups
AgriBusiness Group
  Nitrogen and phosphate fertilizers
  Phosphate and silica ore mining
Corporate Group
  Corporate Development Department
  Corporate Information Systems
  Simplot Aviation (in-company flight services)
Food Group (Simplot Foods)
  Asparagus, avocados, broccoli, carrots, cauliflower, corn, peas, strawberries
  Fresh potatoes (Blue Ribbon, Golden Classic)
Frozen Fruits and Vegetables
  Frozen potato products (fries, nuggets, patties, sticks)
Roasted Foods
  Roasted vegetables and potatoes
Land and Livestock Group
  Cattle feeding
  Hay, corn, grain production for feedlots

COMPETITORS

ADM
Cargill
ConAgra
ContiGroup
Del Monte Foods
Golden State Foods
Heinz
McCain Foods
Michael Foods
Potash Corporation
Pro-Fac
Seneca Foods

HISTORICAL FINANCIALS

Company Type: Private

Income Statement FYE: August 31

	REVENUE ($ mil.)	NET INCOME ($ mil.)	NET PROFIT MARGIN	EMPLOYEES
8/03	3,100	—	—	12,000
8/02	3,000	—	—	13,000
8/01	3,000	—	—	13,000
8/00	2,700	—	—	12,000
8/99	2,730	—	—	12,000
8/98	2,800	—	—	12,000
8/97	2,800	—	—	12,000
8/96	2,700	—	—	13,000
8/95	2,200	—	—	10,000
8/94	2,100	—	—	10,000
Annual Growth	4.4%	—	—	2.0%

Revenue History

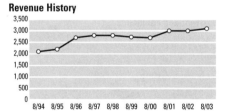

Kaiser Foundation

Kaiser Foundation Health Plan aims to be the emperor of the HMO universe. With more than 8 million members in nine states and the District of Columbia, it is one of the largest not-for-profit managed health care companies in the US. Kaiser has an integrated care model, offering both hospital and physician care through a network of hospitals and physician practices operating under the Kaiser Permanente name. Kaiser also sponsors the Permanente Medical Groups, associations consisting of about 12,000 doctors that provide medical care to Kaiser health plan subscribers. The company also runs a network of thirty Kaiser Foundation hospitals, and more than 430 medical offices.

California is the company's largest market, with more than 75% of its members.

A string of losses due to skyrocketing costs and stiff competition from commercial providers of managed care have prompted Kaiser to raise rates and divest under performing units.

Kaiser's strategy for growth and profitability consists of strengthening its integrated care model via increased use of technology, and construction of new health care facilities.

HISTORY

Henry Kaiser — shipbuilder, war profiteer, builder of the Hoover and Grand Coulee dams, and founder of Kaiser Aluminum — was a bootstrap capitalist who did well by doing good. A high school dropout from upstate New York, Kaiser moved to Spokane, Washington, in 1906 and went into road construction. During the Depression, he headed the consortium that built the great WPA dams.

It was in building the Grand Coulee Dam that, in 1938, Kaiser teamed with Dr. Sidney Garfield, who earlier had devised a prepayment health plan for workers on California public works projects. As Kaiser moved into steelmaking and shipbuilding during WWII (turning out some 1,400 bare-bones Liberty ships — one per day at peak production), Kaiser decided healthy workers produce more than sick ones, and he called on Garfield to set up on-site clinics funded by the US government as part of operating expenses. Garfield was released from military service by President Roosevelt for the purpose.

After the war, the clinics became war surplus. Kaiser and his wife bought them — at a 99% discount — through the new Kaiser Hospital Foundation. His vision was to provide the public with low-cost, prepaid medical care. He created the health plan — the self-supporting entity that would administer the system — and the group medical organization, Permanente (named after Kaiser's first cement plant site). He then endowed the health plan with $200,000. This health plan, the classic HMO model, was criticized by the medical establishment as socialized medicine performed by "employee" doctors.

But the plan flourished, becoming California's #1 medical system. In 1958 Kaiser retired to Hawaii and started his health plan there. But physician resistance limited national growth; HMOs were illegal in some states into the 1970s.

As health care costs rose, Congress legalized HMOs in all states. Kaiser expanded in the 1980s;

as it moved outside its traditional geographic areas, the company contracted for space in hospitals rather than build them. Growth slowed as competition increased.

Some health care costs in California fell in the early 1990s as more medical procedures were performed on an outpatient basis. Specialists flooded the state, and as price competition among doctors and hospitals heated up, many HMOs landed advantageous contracts. Kaiser, with its own highly paid doctors, was unable to realize the same savings and was no longer the best deal in town. Its membership stalled.

To boost membership and control expenses, Kaiser instituted a controversial program in 1996 in which nurses earned bonuses for cost-cutting. Critics said the program could lead to a decrease in care quality; Kaiser later became the focus of investigations into wrongful death suits linked to cost-cutting in California (where it has since beefed up staffing and programs) and Texas (where it has agreed to pay $1 million in fines).

In 1997 Kaiser and Washington-based Group Health Cooperative of Puget Sound formed Kaiser/Group Health to handle administrative services in the Northwest. Kaiser also tried to boost membership by lowering premiums, but the strategy proved *too* effective: Costs linked to an unwieldy 20% enrollment surge brought a loss in 1997 — Kaiser's first annual loss ever.

A second year in the red in 1998 prompted Kaiser to sell its Texas operations to Sierra Health Services. It also entered the Florida market via an alliance with Miami-based AvMed Health Plan. In 1999 Kaiser announced plans to sell its unprofitable North Carolina operations (it closed the deal the following year).

In 2000 Kaiser announced plans to charge premiums for its Medicare HMO, Medicare+Choice, to offset the shortfall in federal reimbursements. Kaiser also responded to rising costs by selling its unprofitable operations in North Carolina (2000) and Kansas (2001). In 2001 the company's hospital division bought the technology and assets of defunct Internet grocer Webvan in an effort to increase its distribution activity. Also that year the son of a deceased anthrax victim sued a Kaiser facility for failing to recognize and treat his father's symptoms.

EXECUTIVES

Chairman and CEO: George C. Halvorson
SVP and CFO: Robert E. Briggs, age 55
SVP, Product and Market Management: Arthur M. Southam
SVP, Chief Information, and Chief Administrative Officer: J. Clifford Dodd
SVP, Communications and External Relations: Bernard J. Tyson
SVP, Community Benefit: Raymond J. (Ray) Baxter
SVP, General Counsel, and Secretary: Kirk E. Miller
SVP, Government Relations and Permanente Partnership Support: Steven (Steve) Zatkin
SVP, Health Plan and Hospital Operations: Leslie A. Margolin
SVP, Hospital Strategy and Operations Support: Christine Malcolm
SVP, Human Resources: Laurence G. O'Neil
SVP, National Contracting Purchasing and Distribution: Joseph W. Hummel
SVP, Quality and Clinical Systems Support: Louise L. Liang
SVP, Research and Policy Development: Robert M. Crane
SVP, Sales and Account Management: Lawrence (Larry) Leisure
SVP and Chief Compliance Officer: Dan Garcia
SVP and Director for Care and Services Quality: Patricia B. Siegel
Auditors: KPMG LLP

LOCATIONS

HQ: Kaiser Foundation Health Plan, Inc.
1 Kaiser Plaza, Oakland, CA 94612
Phone: 510-271-5800 **Fax:** 510-271-6493
Web: www.kaiserpermanente.org

Kaiser Foundation Health Plan operates in California, Colorado, Georgia, Hawaii, Maryland, Ohio, Oregon, Virginia, Washington, and the District of Columbia.

PRODUCTS/OPERATIONS

2003 Membership

	Members	% of total
California	6,224,142	76
Mid-Atlantic states	503,287	6
Oregon/Washington	435,877	5
Colorado	408,194	5
Georgia	269,271	3
Hawaii	235,514	3
Ohio	146,257	2
Total	**8,222,542**	**100**

Selected Operations

Kaiser Foundation Health Plans (health coverage)
Kaiser Foundation Hospitals (community hospitals and outpatient facilities)
Permanente Medical Groups (physician organizations)

COMPETITORS

Aetna
Blue Cross
Catholic Health East
Catholic Health Initiatives
Catholic Healthcare Partners
Catholic Healthcare System
Catholic Healthcare West
CIGNA
HCA
Health Net
Humana
Oxford Health
PacifiCare
Sierra Health
UnitedHealth Group
WellPoint Health Networks

HISTORICAL FINANCIALS

Company Type: Subsidiary

Income Statement
FYE: December 31

	REVENUE ($ mil.)	NET INCOME ($ mil.)	NET PROFIT MARGIN	EMPLOYEES
12/03	25,300	996	3.9%	54,300
12/02	22,500	70	0.3%	47,300
12/01	19,700	681	3.5%	111,000
12/00	17,700	590	3.3%	90,000
12/99	16,841	(6)	—	90,000
12/98	15,500	(288)	—	100,000
12/97	14,500	(270)	—	100,000
12/96	13,241	265	2.0%	90,000
12/95	12,290	550	4.5%	85,000
12/94	12,268	816	6.7%	84,845
Annual Growth	8.4%	2.2%	—	(4.8%)

Net Income History

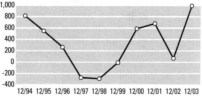

Kaleida Health

Operating five acute-care facilities with some 2,500 beds, Kaleida Health serves the residents of western New York. The health system's hospitals are Buffalo General Hospital, The Women & Children's Hospital of Buffalo, DeGraff Memorial Hospital, Millard Fillmore Gates Circle Hospital, and Millard Fillmore Suburban Hospital. Primary care needs are met through a network of community and school-based clinics. Kaleida Health also operates eight nursing care facilities and provides home health care. Buffalo General Hospital is a teaching affiliate of the State University of New York.

EXECUTIVES

CEO: William D. (Bill) McGuire, age 60
President and COO: James R. (Jim) Kaskie, age 51
EVP and Chief Medical Officer: Cynthia A. Ambres
EVP and CFO: Robert L. (Bob) Glenning
SVP and Chief Learning Officer: Connie Krasinksi
SVP, Public Affairs and Development: Stephen McClellan
SVP, Legal Services and General Counsel; Acting SVP, Human Resources: Robert Nolan
VP, Ambulatory Services and Business Development: Donald Boyd
VP; President, The Women's & Children's Hospital of Buffalo: Cheryl Klass, age 48
VP and General Counsel: Linda J. Nenni
Director, Public Relations: Michael Hughes
Auditors: KPMG LLP

LOCATIONS

HQ: Kaleida Health
100 High St., Buffalo, NY 14203
Phone: 716-859-5600 **Fax:** 716-859-3323
Web: www.kaleidahealth.org

HISTORICAL FINANCIALS

Company Type: Not-for-profit

Income Statement
FYE: December 31

	REVENUE ($ mil.)	NET INCOME ($ mil.)	NET PROFIT MARGIN	EMPLOYEES
12/03	824	2	0.2%	9,724

KB Toys

KB Toys hopes toy buyers will take their haul from the mall. One of the largest toy retailers in the US, KB Toys operates over 750 stores under four main formats: KB Toys mall stores, KB Toy Works neighborhood stores, KB Toy Outlets and KB Toy Liquidator in outlet malls, and KB Toy Express selling closeout toys in malls during the Christmas season. The company (owned by Bain Capital) filed for Chapter 11 bankruptcy in January 2004, resulting in over 350 store closures and about 3,500 layoffs. In March KB Toys sold its KBToys.com Internet business to an affiliate of investment firm D. E. Shaw, which renamed the company eToys Direct. The Web site KBToys.com is now run by eToys Direct via a licensing agreement.

EXECUTIVES

President and CEO: Michael L. Glazer, age 56
EVP and COO: William L. (Bill) McMahon
EVP and CFO: Robert J. Feldman
EVP, Corporate Buying Group: Sal Vasta
SVP, Merchandising: Charles (C.B.) Alberts
SVP, Product Development: Thomas J. (Tom) Alfonsi
VP and Controller: Joel Wiest
VP, Divisional Merchandise Manager:
 Frederick L. (Fred) Hurley
VP, General Counsel, and Secretary: Kenneth A. Grady
VP, Human Resources: Gerry Murray
VP, Loss Prevention: Steve Forgette
VP, Management Information Systems: Keith Porter
VP, Marketing and Advertising: Bonnie Burton
VP, Merchandise Planning: David MacPhee
VP, Real Estate: Steve Dodds
VP, Sales: Pete Lungo

LOCATIONS

HQ: KB Toys, Inc.
100 West St., Pittsfield, MA 01201
Phone: 413-496-3000   **Fax:** 413-496-3616
Web: www.kbtoys.com

KB Toys has distribution and fulfillment centers in Alabama, Arizona, Kentucky, Massachusetts, and New Jersey; it has store locations in the US, Guam, and Puerto Rico.

PRODUCTS/OPERATIONS

Selected Store Formats

KB Toys (mall stores; average size is 3,500 sq. ft.)
 Action figures
 Board games
 Dolls
 Preschool toys
 Video games and equipment
KB Toy Works (neighborhood stores; average size 7,500 sq. ft.)
 Action figures
 Bicycles
 Board games
 Children's sports equipment
 Dolls
 Gift wrap
 Greeting cards
 Preschool toys
 Ride-ons
 Video games and equipment
KB Toy Outlet/Toy Liquidator (outlet mall stores)
 Name-brand close-out merchandise
KB Toy Express (temporary mall stores operating from late October to late December)
 Action figures
 Board games
 Dolls
 Preschool toys
 Video games and equipment

COMPETITORS

Amazon.com
GameStop
Gymboree
Kmart
Sears
Target
Toys "R" Us
Wal-Mart

HISTORICAL FINANCIALS

Company Type: Private

Income Statement   FYE: January 31

	ESTIMATED REVENUE ($ mil.)	NET INCOME ($ mil.)	NET PROFIT MARGIN	EMPLOYEES
1/03	2,000	—	—	24,000
1/02	2,000	—	—	25,000
1/01	2,000	—	—	16,000
1/00	1,767	—	—	13,000
Annual Growth	4.2%	—	—	22.7%

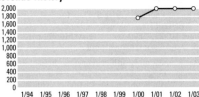

Revenue History

Kellogg Foundation

Charitable grants from W.K. Kellogg Foundation are gr-r-reat! Founded in 1930 by cereal industry pioneer Will Keith Kellogg, the foundation provides more than $200 million in grants each year to programs focused on youth and education, as well as health issues. It also funds many rural development and agricultural projects and works to foster greater volunteerism. Most of its grants go to initiatives in the US, though it also makes grants throughout Latin America and Africa. The foundation's work is funded primarily from its nearly $6 billion trust.

W.K. Kellogg Foundation is guided by its founder's desire "to help people help themselves" and prefers funding programs that offer long-term solutions rather than quick handouts. In 1934 Kellogg donated $66 million in stock to the foundation, which now ranks as one of the largest charitable organizations in the world.

W.K. Kellogg Foundation, which owns nearly a third of the Kellogg Company, is governed by an independent board of trustees.

HISTORY

Born in 1860, Will Keith Kellogg's early jobs included those of stock boy and traveling broom salesman. He also worked as a clerk (and, later, bookkeeper and manager) at the Battle Creek Sanitarium, a renowned homeopathic hospital where his older brother, John Harvey Kellogg, was physician-in-chief. The brothers' experiments to improve vegetarian diets led to a happy accident in 1894 that resulted in the first wheat flakes. In 1906 W.K. Kellogg started the Battle Creek Toasted Corn Flake Company. Through marketing genius and innovative products, Kellogg's company became a leader in the industry.

A philanthropist by inclination, Kellogg established the Fellowship Corporation in 1925 to build an agricultural school and a bird sanctuary, as well as to set up an experimental farm and a reforestation project. He also gave $3 million to hometown causes, such as the Ann J. Kellogg School for disabled children, and for the construction of an auditorium, a junior high school, and a youth recreation center.

After attending a White House Conference on Child Health and Protection, Kellogg established the W.K. Kellogg Child Welfare Foundation in 1930. A few months later he broadened the focus of the charter and renamed the institution the W.K. Kellogg Foundation. That year the foundation began its landmark Michigan Community Health Project (MCHP), which opened public health departments in counties once thought too small and poor to sustain them. In 1934 Kellogg placed more than $66 million in Kellogg Company stock and other investments in a trust to fund his foundation.

During WWII the foundation expanded its programming to Latin America, funding advanced schooling for dentists, physicians, and other health professionals. After the war, it broadened its programming to include agriculture to help war-torn Europe. It funded projects in Germany, Iceland, Ireland, Norway, and the UK. Following Kellogg's death in 1951, the organization began providing support for graduate programs in health and hospital administration, as well as for rural leadership and community colleges.

During the 1970s the foundation lent its support to the growing volunteerism movement and to aiding the disadvantaged, with a special emphasis on programs for minorities. A review of operations in the late 1970s led the Kellogg Foundation to reassert its emphasis on health, education, agriculture, and leadership. The foundation also expanded its programs to southern Africa.

In 1986 The Kellogg Foundation began funding the Rural America Initiative — a series of 28 projects meant to develop leadership, train local government officials, and revitalize rural areas. William Richardson became president and CEO of the foundation in 1995, leaving his post as president of The Johns Hopkins University. Also during the 1990s, the foundation supported the Community-Based Public Health Initiative, which assisted universities in educating public health professionals by presenting community-based approaches to students and faculty.

In 1998 the organization announced a five-year, $55 million plan to bring health care to the nation's poor and homeless. Also that year it gave Portland State University a $600,000 grant to develop its Institute for Nonprofit Management. In 1999 the Kellogg Foundation started its first geographically based program, pledging $15 million in grants for development of Mississippi River Delta communities in Arkansas, Louisiana, and Mississippi. In 2001 the foundation pledged an additional $20 million to support economic growth in the region through the Emerging Markets Partnership. In 2002 the Kellogg Foundation awarded about $2 million in grants to SPARK (Supporting Partnerships to Assure Ready Kids) to help prepare low-income children for starting school. The organization funded a national campaign to improve men's health in 2003.

EXECUTIVES

President and CEO: William C. Richardson, age 63
SVP and Corporate Secretary: Gregory A. Lyman
SVP Programs: Anne C. Petersen
VP and Chief Investment Officer: Paul J. Lawler
VP Finance and Treasurer: La June Montgomery-Tally
VP Programs: Richard M. Foster
VP Programs: Marguerite M. Johnson
VP Programs: Robert F. (Bob) Long
VP Programs: Gail D. McClure
Director Human Resources: Norm Howard
Director Marketing and Communications:
 Karen E. Lake
Director Technology: Tim Dechant
Controller: Gloria Dickerson
General Counsel and Assistant Corporate Secretary:
 Mary C. Cotter
Auditors: Deloitte & Touche LLP

LOCATIONS

HQ: W.K. Kellogg Foundation
  1 Michigan Ave. East, Battle Creek, MI 49017
Phone: 269-968-1611 **Fax:** 269-968-0413
Web: www.wkkf.org

2003 Grants

	$ mil.	% of total
US	161.1	80
Africa	18.0	9
Latin America & the Caribbean	22.3	11
Total	**201.4**	**100**

PRODUCTS/OPERATIONS

2003 Grants

	$ mil.	% of total
Youth and Education	32.1	17
Program Activities	25.1	12
Special Opportunities	25.0	12
Health	24.1	12
Latin America and the Caribbean	22.4	11
Food Systems and Rural Development	22.3	11
Southern Africa	18.0	9
Philanthropy and Volunteerism	16.3	8
Recurring Grants	8.0	4
Greater Battle Creek	7.0	3
Cross Program/Learning Opportunities	1.1	1
Total	**201.4**	**100**

HISTORICAL FINANCIALS

Company Type: Foundation

Income Statement

FYE: August 31

	REVENUE ($ mil.)	NET INCOME ($ mil.)	NET PROFIT MARGIN	EMPLOYEES
8/03	277	—	—	—
8/02	250	—	—	200
8/01	223	—	—	209
8/00	277	—	—	250
8/99	327	—	—	290
8/98	330	—	—	286
8/97	374	—	—	280
8/96	298	—	—	276
8/95	271	—	—	264
8/94	235	—	—	—
Annual Growth	**1.8%**	—	—	**(3.9%)**

Revenue History

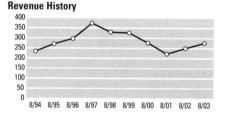

Kentucky Lottery

Kentucky's grass may be blue, but many Kentuckians prefer green — the kind they can stuff into their wallets. For optimists looking to bag some bucks, the Kentucky Lottery offers numbers games (Pick 3, Pick 4, Lotto South) and an array of scratch-off and pull-tab games (One-Eyed Jack, Pool Party, Speed Bingo). Kentucky also participates in the multistate Powerball game. The lottery's proceeds have gone to education, Vietnam veterans, affordable housing, college scholarships, literacy programs, and Kentucky's General Fund. Launched in 1989, the lottery has introduced new games as it struggles with intense competition from nearby casinos.

EXECUTIVES

President and CEO: Arthur L. (Arch) Gleason Jr.
EVP and COO: Margaret (Marty) Gibbs
SVP Finance and Administration: Howard Kline
SVP Information Systems: Harvey Roberts
SVP Marketing and Sales: Steve Casebeer
SVP Security: Bill Hickerson
VP Human Resources: Church Saufley
VP Internal Audit: Gale Vessels
VP Marketing: Betsy Paulley
VP Sales: Robert (Bob) Little
VP Systems Development: Linda Stark
Director Operations: Larry Smith
Director Planning and Research: Larry Newby
General Counsel: Mary Harville

LOCATIONS

HQ: Kentucky Lottery Corporation
  1011 W. Main St., Louisville, KY 40202
Phone: 502-560-1500 **Fax:** 502-560-1670
Web: www.kylottery.com

The Kentucky Lottery Corporation has operations in Bowling Green, Jefferson, Lexington, Louisville, Madisonville, and Prestonsburg, Kentucky.

PRODUCTS/OPERATIONS

Selected Games
Numbers Games
  Kentucky Cash Ball
  Kentucky Powerball
  Lotto South
  Pick 3
  Pick 4
Pull-Tabs
Ace in the Hole
  Cherry Hearts
  Lucky $599
  Wild 7's
Scratch-offs
  Beat the Heat
  Blackjack Attack
  Hot Dice
  In the Bank
  Lucky Queen
  Rake in the Money
  Spin N' Win
  Stinking Rich
  Your Lucky Day

COMPETITORS

Argosy Gaming
Aztar
Churchill Downs
Hoosier Lottery
Illinois Lottery
Trump
Virginia Lottery

HISTORICAL FINANCIALS

Company Type: Government-owned

Income Statement

FYE: July 31

	REVENUE ($ mil.)	NET INCOME ($ mil.)	NET PROFIT MARGIN	EMPLOYEES
7/04	725	—	—	204
7/03	674	—	—	204
7/02*	600	—	—	200
6/01	591	—	—	200
6/00	584	—	—	200
6/99	583	—	—	200
6/98	585	—	—	205
6/97	569	—	—	210
6/96	543	—	—	205
6/95	513	—	—	205
Annual Growth	**3.9%**	—	—	**(0.1%)**

*Fiscal year change

Revenue History

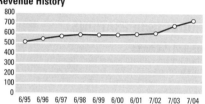

Key Safety Systems

Key Safety Systems (formerly BREED Technologies) is a leading manufacturer of air bags and air bag components. The company also makes steering wheels and seat belts. Key Safety Systems' line of air bag products includes sensors, inflators, driver-side and steering-wheel air bag combinations, and side-impact air bag systems. The company supplies air bag systems to most of the world's carmakers. Key Safety Systems also makes a line of interior trim products including automatic and manual shift knobs, park brake handles, shift and brake boots, armrest covers, pull handles, and other assorted trim components. The Carlyle Group's Key Automotive Group controls the company.

After a mid-1990s buying spree left BREED Technologies awash in debt, the company found itself under bankruptcy protection. The company emerged from Chapter 11 in late 2000 and has been taken private. Carlyle principal B. Edward Ewing became CEO of BREED in early 2003 and soon announced plans to achieve $200 million in cost savings for fiscal 2003. To this end the company plans to cut 3,500 jobs across the company's global operations by the end of 2004 (27% of the workforce), and is seeking price breaks from its suppliers.

The company changed its name to Key Safety Systems in 2003 and was folded into the operations of Key Automotive Group.

EXECUTIVES

Chairman and CEO: B. Edward Ewing
President: Daniel Ajamian
SVP and CFO: Larry Schwentor
SVP, Human Resources: Rick Blough
SVP, Legal: Stuart D. Boyd
VP, Public Relations: Peter McElroy
President, Asia: Jason Luo
President, Europe: Giulio Zambeletti
President, North America: Monti Dickerson

LOCATIONS

HQ: Key Safety Systems, Inc.
7000 Nineteen Mile Rd., Sterling Heights, MI 48314
Phone: 586-726-3800
Web: www.keysafetyinc.com

Key Safety Systems operates facilities in Alabama, California, Tennessee, Texas, and Wisconsin; as well as in China, France, Germany, Italy, Japan, Korea, Mexico, Thailand, and the UK.

PRODUCTS/OPERATIONS

Selected Products
Airbag systems, inflators, and modules
Armrest covers
Electronics (crash sensors)
Park brake handles
Seat-belt systems
Shift and brake boots
Shift knobs
Steering wheels

COMPETITORS

Analog Devices
Autoliv
Denso
Fondmetal
Hi-Shear Technology
Honeywell International
Motorola
Oki Electric
OZ Italy Wheel
PerkinElmer
Robert Bosch
SensoNor
Siemens
Temic
Texas Instruments
Tokai Rika

HISTORICAL FINANCIALS
Company Type: Private

Income Statement				FYE: June 30
	REVENUE ($ mil.)	NET INCOME ($ mil.)	NET PROFIT MARGIN	EMPLOYEES
6/03	1,100	—	—	10,000
6/02	1,100	—	—	16,000
6/01	1,422	—	—	16,000
6/00	1,400	—	—	16,100
6/99	1,400	—	—	16,200
6/98	1,385	—	—	16,300
6/97	795	—	—	11,100
6/96	432	—	—	7,000
6/95	401	—	—	4,800
6/94	278	—	—	3,200
Annual Growth	16.5%	—	—	13.5%

Revenue History

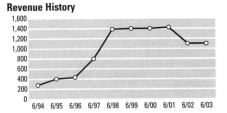

Keystone Foods

Keystone Foods hopes you won't just have the salad. The company is one of the largest makers of hamburger patties and processed poultry. It's a major supplier to McDonald's restaurants; in the 1970s Keystone persuaded McDonald's to switch to frozen beef to reduce the health risks associated with fresh beef. Overseas, operations include McKey Food Services and MacFood Services (some are joint ventures). In addition to its worldwide meat processing plants, which produce millions of burgers daily, Keystone also operates M&M Restaurant Supply, and has begun to supply fresh beef to a US grocery retailer. Chairman and CEO Herb Lotman owns the company, which began as a beef-boning business in the 1960s.

EXECUTIVES

Chairman and CEO: Herbert (Herb) Lotman, age 70
President and COO: Jerry Dean
EVP and CFO: John Coggins
SVP and Controller: Paul McGarvie
VP, Human Resources: Jerry Gotro
VP, Information Systems: Ken Wierman
VP, Quality Assurance and Food Safety: Dane Bernard
Auditors: Ernst & Young LLP

LOCATIONS

HQ: Keystone Foods LLC
300 Barr Harbor Dr., Ste. 600,
West Conshohocken, PA 19428
Phone: 610-667-6700 **Fax:** 610-667-1460
Web: www.keystonefoods.com

Keystone Foods has operations in Asia, Australia, Europe, the Middle East, and the US.

PRODUCTS/OPERATIONS

Selected Products
Beef
  Fajita strips
  Hamburger patties
Chicken
  Breaded patties
  Breast filets
  Diced
  Fajita strips
  Nuggets
  Wings
Fish
Pork

COMPETITORS

Anderson-DuBose
ConAgra
Gold Kist
Golden State Foods
Lopez Foods
Martin-Brower
McLane Foodservice
OSI
Perdue
Pilgrim's Pride
SYSCO
Tyson Foods
Tyson Fresh Meats
U.S. Foodservice

HISTORICAL FINANCIALS
Company Type: Private

Income Statement				FYE: December 31
	ESTIMATED REVENUE ($ mil.)	NET INCOME ($ mil.)	NET PROFIT MARGIN	EMPLOYEES
12/02	2,600	—	—	6,700
12/01	2,700	—	—	6,700
12/00	2,650	—	—	6,700
12/99	2,594	—	—	6,700
12/98	2,342	—	—	4,300
12/97	2,184	—	—	4,300
12/96	1,900	—	—	4,000
12/95	1,700	—	—	2,000
12/94	1,600	—	—	—
12/93	1,500	—	—	—
Annual Growth	6.3%	—	—	18.9%

Revenue History

KI

KI can be found in cubicles, classrooms, cafeterias, and college dorms. Formerly known as Krueger International, KI makes ergonomic seating, cabinets, and other furniture used by businesses, health care organizations, schools, and other institutions. The company offers everything from desks to daybeds, not to mention tables, filing systems, and even trash cans. KI operates manufacturing facilities in Canada, Italy, and the US, and markets its products through sales representatives, furniture dealers, architects, and interior designers. Founded in 1941, KI was bought in the 1980s by its managers, who later allowed the company's employees to buy its stock. KI is now 100% owned by its employees.

EXECUTIVES

President and CEO: Richard J. Resch
CFO and Treasurer: Mark Olsen
EVP Sales and Marketing: Andrew McGregor

LOCATIONS

HQ: KI
1330 Bellevue St., Green Bay, WI 54302
Phone: 920-468-8100 **Fax:** 920-468-0280
Web: www.ki.com

KI has manufacturing facilities in California, Mississippi, North Carolina, and Wisconsin, as well as in Canada.

PRODUCTS/OPERATIONS

Selected Products
Auditorium seating
Bookcases
Carrels
Chairs
Desks
File cabinets
Lecterns
Mobile furniture
Planters
Power and data
 connections
Receptacles
Residence hall furniture
Sleepers
Special events seating
Stools
Tables

COMPETITORS

Allsteel
Boss Office Products
Edsal Manufacturing
Falcon Products
GF Office Furniture
Global Group
Haworth
Herman Miller
HNI
Kimball International
Knoll
La-Z-Boy
SMED International
Steelcase
Trendway
Virco Mfg.

HISTORICAL FINANCIALS

Company Type: Private

Income Statement
FYE: December 31

	REVENUE ($ mil.)	NET INCOME ($ mil.)	NET PROFIT MARGIN	EMPLOYEES
12/03	600	—	—	3,500
12/02	600	—	—	3,500
12/01	625	—	—	3,500
12/00	631	—	—	4,517
12/99	606	—	—	4,500
12/98	550	—	—	4,265
12/97	450	—	—	2,800
12/96	420	—	—	—
Annual Growth	5.2%	—	—	3.8%

Revenue History

Kimball Hill Homes

Chicagoland's GI generation and their offspring, who have long thrived in the 'burbs, can thank lawyer-turned-builder D. Kimball Hill, a pioneer of the city's suburbs and founder of Kimball Hill Homes. The company builds single-family detached homes, townhomes, and condominiums in the Chicago area and in California, Florida, Nevada, Ohio, Oregon, Texas, Washington, and Wisconsin. Kimball Hill Homes mainly targets first-time and move-up buyers, but also builds homes up to 4,100 sq. ft. in size and $800,000 in price. Subsidiary KH Financial offers mortgage financing and refinancing of investment properties in five states. David Hill Jr., CEO and son of the founder, and other Hill family members own the company.

EXECUTIVES

Chairman and CEO: David K. Hill Jr., age 63
President and COO: Isaac Heimbinder
CFO: Gene Rowehl
CIO: Frank Scaramuzza
VP Human Resources: JoAnn Peterson
Director, Sales and Marketing: Ray Wolford
Director, Customer Satisfaction Initiative: Brent Gustafson

LOCATIONS

HQ: Kimball Hill Homes
5999 New Wilke Rd., Ste. 504,
Rolling Meadows, IL 60008
Phone: 847-364-7300   **Fax:** 847-439-0875
Web: www.kimballhill.com

Kimball Hill Homes has principal operations in Austin, Dallas/Ft. Worth, Houston, and San Antonio, Texas; Chicago; Elk Grove, Sacramento, and Stockton, California; Bradenton, Marco Island/Naples, Sarasota, and Tampa, Florida; Las Vegas, Nevada; Cleveland, Ohio; Portland, Oregon; Vancouver, Washington; and Saint Francis (a Milwaukee suburb), Wisconsin.

COMPETITORS

Beazer Homes
Centex
David Weekley Homes
D.R. Horton
KB Home
Lennar
M.D.C. Holdings
Morrison Homes
Neumann Homes
Pulte Homes
Ryland
Schuler Homes
Town and Country Homes

HISTORICAL FINANCIALS

Company Type: Private

Income Statement
FYE: September 30

	REVENUE ($ mil.)	NET INCOME ($ mil.)	NET PROFIT MARGIN	EMPLOYEES
9/03*	800	—	—	700
6/02	700	—	—	654
6/01	673	—	—	546
6/00	580	—	—	510
6/99	490	—	—	427
6/98	410	—	—	320
6/97	296	—	—	280
6/96	224	—	—	240
Annual Growth	19.9%	—	—	16.5%

*Fiscal year change

Revenue History
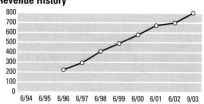

Kinetics Group

Kinetics Group, primarily through its Kinetic Systems division, provides high-purity process systems, primarily to the semiconductor and biopharmaceutical industries. Parent to piping manufacturer Celerity, the group is also one of the leading mechanical contractors in the US. It provides energy infrastructure, pipe and structural steel fabrication, and HVAC (heating, ventilation, and air-conditioning) and electrical installation services. Clients include IBM, Merck, and Genentech. Founded in 1973, Kinetics has operations in Australia, Asia, Europe, Latin America, the Middle East, and the US.

EXECUTIVES

Chairman and CEO: David J. Shimmon, age 45
President and COO: Kurt Gilson
CFO: John Serron
EVP, Biopharm: Michael Lynch
EVP, Electronics: Ian MacLaren
President, East US and Europe/Middle East Region: Robert Pragada

LOCATIONS

HQ: Kinetics Group, Inc.
33225 Western Ave., Union City, CA 94587
Phone: 510-675-6000   **Fax:** 510-675-6187
Web: www.kineticsgroup.com

Kinetics Group has about 40 offices located worldwide.

PRODUCTS/OPERATIONS

Selected Operations
Biopharm (freeze dryers, freezers, water systems)
Electronics (gas piping systems, instrumentation, chemical blend systems)
Industrial & Commercial (commercial HVAC, pipe fabrication, energy services)

COMPETITORS

EMCOR
KeySpan
L'Air Liquide
Southland Industries

HISTORICAL FINANCIALS

Company Type: Private

Income Statement
FYE: December 31

	REVENUE ($ mil.)	NET INCOME ($ mil.)	NET PROFIT MARGIN	EMPLOYEES
12/03	407	—	—	3,000
12/02	580	—	—	3,600
Annual Growth	(29.8%)	—	—	(16.7%)

Revenue History

King Kullen Grocery

How's this for a crowning achievement? King Kullen Grocery Company claims to have been the originator of the supermarket format. Heralding itself as "America's first supermarket," the firm operates nearly 50 supermarkets, mainly on Long Island, New York. King Kullen also owns two Wild By Nature natural foods stores and offers a line of vitamins and supplements under the same name in some King Kullen stores. Most outlets average about 35,000 sq. ft., but it has a 62,000-sq.-ft. upscale market with features such as ethnic fare, catering, and a Wild By Nature section. Started in a Queens, New York warehouse in 1930 by Michael J. Cullen, the firm is owned and operated by Cullen's descendants.

EXECUTIVES
Chairman and CEO: Bernard D. Kennedy
Co-President and Co-COO: Brian C. Cullen
Co-President and Co-COO: J. D. Kennedy
SVP, Finance and Administration: James Flynn
SVP, Operations: Thomas (Tom) Massaro
VP, Government and Industrial Relations: Thomas (Tom) Cullen
VP, Perishables: Joseph Forte
Director, Bakery: Sue Brooks
Director of Human Resources: Thomas Nagle
Director, Produce and Floral: Richard Conger
Produce Coordinator: Guy Savio
Produce Specialist: John Porco
Auditors: Grant Thornton LLP

LOCATIONS
HQ: King Kullen Grocery Company, Inc.
185 Central Ave., Bethpage, NY 11714
Phone: 516-733-7100   **Fax:** 516-827-6325
Web: www.kingkullen.com

COMPETITORS
A&P
Ahold USA
C&S Wholesale
Gristede's Foods
IGA
Kmart
Man-dell Food Stores
Pathmark
Wakefern Food
Wal-Mart

HISTORICAL FINANCIALS
Company Type: Private

Income Statement			FYE: September 30	
	REVENUE ($ mil.)	NET INCOME ($ mil.)	NET PROFIT MARGIN	EMPLOYEES
9/03	800	—	—	—
9/02	790	—	—	4,800
9/01	782	—	—	4,579
9/00	720	—	—	4,400
9/99	714	—	—	4,100
9/98	725	—	—	4,500
9/97	750	—	—	4,400
9/96	724	—	—	4,500
9/95	706	—	—	4,500
9/94	718	—	—	4,500
Annual Growth	1.2%	—	—	0.8%

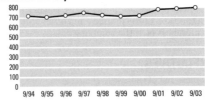

Revenue History

Kingston Technology

Kingston Technology cuts a regal figure in the realm of memory. The company is a top maker of memory modules — circuit boards loaded with DRAM (dynamic random-access memory) or other memory chips that increase the capacity and speed of printers and computers. Kingston also makes flash memory cards used in portable electronic devices such as digital cameras, wireless phones, and personal digital assistants. Kingston has taken on some manufacturing chores for customers through its sister company Payton Technology, which runs a specialized factory that tests and packages memory chips before assembling them into customized memory modules. Founders John Tu (president and CEO) and David Sun (COO) own the company.

Tu and Sun promote a casual atmosphere and treat employees as members of an extended family. (Their work cubicles are identical to their employees'.) Since 1996 they have given over $100 million in bonuses to workers; in some cases the bonuses have amounted to three times the employees' annual salaries.

Kingston is also known for its friendliness to business partners. It is sometimes the first to receive scarce components during shortages, thanks to the relations it enjoys with suppliers.

The company has inked a long-term deal with German chip heavyweight Infineon, under which Infineon is to supply much of Kingston's DRAM needs and Kingston is to provide Infineon with contract manufacturing and engineering services. Kingston has also made a $50 million investment in DRAM maker Elpida Memory.

HISTORY
Kingston Technology was founded in 1987 by Shanghai-born John Tu and Taiwan-born David Sun, both of whom had moved to California in the 1970s. The pair met in 1982 and started a memory upgrade company called Camminton Technology in Tu's garage. Sales had reached $9 million by 1986, when they sold the business to high-tech firm AST Research for $6 million. The two invested their money in stock market futures but suffered heavy losses when the market crashed in 1987.

That year PC makers were producing computers that lacked the memory needed to run the latest, hottest software, so Tu and Sun sprang into action. With just $4,000 in cash, they started another company that converted inexpensive, outdated chips into memory upgrades. Tu, who was educated in Europe, wanted to call the company Kensington after the gardens in London. A mouse pad company had that name, so Kingston was chosen.

Tu had doubts about the new company and bet Sun a Jaguar that it wouldn't survive the first year of operations. Sun won the car (which he later gave to a veteran employee who dreamed of owning one) and within two years the company had sold nearly $40 million worth of products. In 1989 Kingston began making memory system upgrades; a year later it started producing processor upgrades.

The company was #1 on *Inc.* magazine's list of fastest-growing private US companies in 1992. The next year Kingston began marketing networking and storage products. Its vendor-friendly policy paid off that year, when demand for semiconductors far outstripped supply. Suppliers kept shipping to the company even when orders for other buyers were delayed.

In 1996 SOFTBANK paid $1.5 billion for 80% of the company but promised to preserve its culture and retain all management — including Tu and Sun — and employees. Sun and Tu set aside $100 million for employee bonuses.

In 1998 Kingston opened its first foreign manufacturing facilities, in Ireland and Taiwan. Also in 1998, in a unique arrangement suggesting that SOFTBANK overpaid when it bought Kingston, Tu and Sun agreed to forgo SOFTBANK's final $333 million payment. The following year Tu and Sun bought back SOFTBANK's stake for about $450 million. Also in 1999 the company opened a manufacturing plant in Malaysia.

After years of making computer storage devices, Kingston in 2000 formed a separate company, StorCase Technology, which specializes in storage equipment. The next year Kingston discontinued its Peripheral Products Division's offerings.

Also in 2001, Kingston launched a joint venture (and opened a new plant) in China with computer maker China Great Wall Computer Shenzhen Company.

EXECUTIVES
President and CEO: John Tu, age 62
COO: David Sun
CFO: Koichi Hosokawa
SVP, Sales and Marketing: Mike Sager
VP, Administration (HR): Daniel Hsu
Digital Storage Product Manager: Mike Kuppinger

LOCATIONS
HQ: Kingston Technology Company, Inc.
17600 Newhope St., Fountain Valley, CA 92708
Phone: 714-435-2600   **Fax:** 714-435-2699
Web: www.kingston.com

Kingston Technology has operations in Australia, China, France, Germany, Ireland, Malaysia, Taiwan, the UK, and the US.

PRODUCTS/OPERATIONS
Selected Products
Flash memory cards (CompactFlash, DataFlash, MultiMediaCard)
Memory modules and add-on boards
Standard memory modules (ValueRAM)

COMPETITORS

AMD
Amkor
ASE Test Limited
Centon
Elpida
Hynix
Intel
Micron Technology
PNY Technologies
Samsung Electronics
SanDisk
Silicon Storage
SimpleTech
Unigen
Viking Components
Wintec

HISTORICAL FINANCIALS

Company Type: Private

Income Statement — FYE: December 31

	REVENUE ($ mil.)	NET INCOME ($ mil.)	NET PROFIT MARGIN	EMPLOYEES
12/03	1,800	—	—	2,000
12/02	1,450	—	—	1,884
12/01	1,020	—	—	1,900
12/00	1,625	—	—	2,000
12/99	1,400	—	—	2,000
12/98	1,000	—	—	670
12/97	1,000	—	—	663
12/96	2,100	—	—	547
12/95	1,300	—	—	450
12/94	800	—	—	310
Annual Growth	9.4%	—	—	23.0%

Revenue History

Kinray

Kinray, the US's largest privately held wholesale drug distributor, is nothing if not independent. It provides generic, branded, and repackaged drugs, health and beauty products, medical equipment, vitamins and herbals, and diabetes-care products. The company also has a 600-item, private-label program; those products are available under the Preferred Plus Pharmacy brand. The company serves nearly 2,000 pharmacies in seven northeastern US states. The company was founded in 1944 by Joseph Rahr. His son, CEO and president Stewart Rahr, has owned the company since 1975.

Kinray spearheaded the creation of the Wholesale Alliance Cooperative, a group of independent regional drug distributors that aims to help preserve the viability of independent pharmacies (who are customers to the wholesalers).

EXECUTIVES

President and CEO: Stewart Rahr
Director, Human Resources: Howard Hershberg

LOCATIONS

HQ: Kinray Inc.
152-35 10th Ave., Whitestone, NY 11357
Phone: 718-767-1234 **Fax:** 718-767-4388
Web: www.kinray.com

Kinray supplies pharmacies in Connecticut, Delaware, Massachusetts, New Jersey, New York, Pennsylvania, and Rhode Island.

COMPETITORS

AmerisourceBergen
Cardinal Pharmaceutical Distribution
D & K Healthcare Resources
The F. Dohmen Co.
McKesson
QK Healthcare
Quality King

HISTORICAL FINANCIALS

Company Type: Private

Income Statement — FYE: December 31

	REVENUE ($ mil.)	NET INCOME ($ mil.)	NET PROFIT MARGIN	EMPLOYEES
12/02	2,500	—	—	800
12/01	2,000	—	—	600
12/00	1,710	—	—	400
12/99	1,510	—	—	350
12/98	900	—	—	275
12/97	735	—	—	250
12/96	750	—	—	225
12/95	610	—	—	210
12/94	460	—	—	170
12/93	350	—	—	140
Annual Growth	24.4%	—	—	21.4%

Revenue History

Kirkland & Ellis

Kirkland & Ellis is ready to go to court. The litigious law firm — home to former independent counsel Kenneth Starr — has been in the thick of several big courtroom battles, including defending Brown & Williamson Tobacco (it settled with the state of Minnesota for $6.5 billion in 1998). It serves other clients (General Motors, Dow Corning, Motorola) in areas such as intellectual property, antitrust, mergers and acquisitions, tort litigation, and employee benefits. Kirkland & Ellis has more than 950 lawyers in five US offices and one London office. Founded in 1908, the firm rose to prominence with the free speech and libel law strides made by firm namesakes Weymouth Kirkland and Howard Ellis.

EXECUTIVES

Firm Administrator: Douglas McLemore
CFO: Nicholas J. Willmott, age 43
CIO: Steve Novak
Director Human Resources: Wendy Cartland
Senior Marketing Manager: Maria Black
Manager Public Realtions: Brian Pitts

LOCATIONS

HQ: Kirkland & Ellis LLP
Aon Center, 200 E. Randolph Dr., Chicago, IL 60601
Phone: 312-861-2000 **Fax:** 312-861-2200
Web: www.kirkland.com

Kirkland & Ellis has offices in Chicago, Los Angeles, New York City, San Francisco, and Washington, DC, as well as in London.

PRODUCTS/OPERATIONS

Selected Practice Areas
Antitrust
Employee benefits
Energy
Intellectual property
Litigation
Mergers and acquisitions
Real estate
Tax
Trusts and estates
Venture capital
White-collar crime

COMPETITORS

Baker & McKenzie
Cravath, Swaine
Jenner & Block
Jones Day
Mayer, Brown, Rowe & Maw
McDermott, Will
Sidley Austin Brown & Wood

HISTORICAL FINANCIALS

Company Type: Partnership

Income Statement — FYE: January 31

	REVENUE ($ mil.)	NET INCOME ($ mil.)	NET PROFIT MARGIN	EMPLOYEES
1/04	725	—	—	—
1/03	611	—	—	—
1/02	530	—	—	—
1/01	470	—	—	—
1/00	410	—	—	700
1/99	310	—	—	600
1/98	255	—	—	552
1/97	229	—	—	504
1/96	220	—	—	—
1/95	215	—	—	—
Annual Growth	14.5%	—	—	11.6%

Revenue History

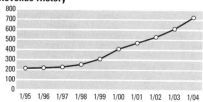

Klaussner Furniture

Klaussner Furniture Industries makes furniture for the couch potato in all of us. A leading US manufacturer of upholstered furniture, Klaussner sells fabric- and leather-upholstered sofas and recliners, chairs, ottomans, occasional tables, home entertainment, and dining furniture under the Distinctions, Realistic, Realistic Motion, Klaussner, and Klaussitalia brand names. Licensed brands include Sealy (sofas, chairs) and Dick Idol ("rustic" home furnishings). Its 20 plants produce items exported to more than 60 countries. Klaussner also owns about 20% of furniture retailer Jennifer Convertibles. Chairman Hans Klaussner has owned the company since 1979; it was founded in 1964 as Stuart Furniture Industries.

EXECUTIVES
Chairman: Hans J. Klaussner
President and CEO: J. B. Davis, age 60
CFO: David O. (Dave) Bryant
SVP Merchandising: Charles Edward Kinney
SVP Sales and Marketing: Jerry L. Bullins
VP Manufacturing: Richard D. Kite
VP Motion/Realistic Merchandising:
  Julian M. (Jay) Foscue
VP Operations: Jerry B. Holder
VP Sales: Stephen M. (Steve) Brower
VP Stationary Merchandising: Jeffery B. Davis
Company Secretary and Controller: Peter O. Brisley
Treasurer: Scott Kauffman
Director Human Resources: Randy Timmerman

LOCATIONS
HQ: Klaussner Furniture Industries, Inc.
  405 Lewallen Rd., Asheboro, NC 27205
Phone: 336-625-6174   **Fax:** 336-626-0905
Web: www.klaussner.com

COMPETITORS

Ashley Furniture	Herman Miller
Bassett Furniture	Hooker Furniture
Berkline/BenchCraft	Jennifer Convertibles
Chromcraft Revington	La-Z-Boy
Ethan Allen	Natuzzi
Flexsteel	Rowe Companies
Furniture Brands	Stanley Furniture
International	Steelcase
Haworth	W. S. Badcock

HISTORICAL FINANCIALS
Company Type: Private

Income Statement				FYE: December 31
	REVENUE ($ mil.)	NET INCOME ($ mil.)	NET PROFIT MARGIN	EMPLOYEES
12/03	915	—	—	7,000
12/02	985	—	—	7,000
12/01	955	—	—	7,000
12/00	1,057	—	—	7,000
12/99	815	—	—	6,800
12/98	750	—	—	6,600
12/97	738	—	—	6,570
12/96	716	—	—	6,900
12/95	717	—	—	6,950
12/94	658	—	—	6,955
Annual Growth	3.7%	—	—	0.1%

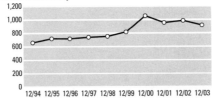

Revenue History

Knoll

Designer cubicles make for happier workers, or so goes the gospel at Knoll. The company makes a variety of distinctively designed, curvilinear office furniture and related accessories, including office systems (a.k.a. cubicles). Its products are sold under such names as Equity, Dividends, and Currents. Other products include ergonomic seating, tables and desks, and filing systems. The company offers an upscale line of designed furniture (KnollStudio), computer and desk accessories (KnollExtra), and fabric and leather upholstery (KnollTextiles). Investment firm Warburg Pincus owns more than 90% of the company.

Some products are created by high-profile architects and designers such as Frank Gehry and Vietnam War Memorial architect Maya Lin. The firm showcases its designs at the Knoll Museum, located in Pennsylvania (near the company's headquarters). In addition, more than 30 Knoll products are included in the permanent Design Collection of New York's Museum of Modern Art.

Knoll markets its products through more than 100 showrooms in the Americas, Asia, and Europe, as well as through its Web site.

EXECUTIVES
Chairman: Burton B. Staniar, age 62, $450,008 pay
CEO and Director: Andrew B. Cogan, age 42, $800,008 pay
President and CEO, Knoll North America, and Director: Kathleen G. (Kass) Bradley, age 55, $800,008 pay
SVP and CFO: Barry L. McCabe, age 57
EVP and Director of Design: Carl G. Magnusson, age 64
SVP, General Counsel, and Secretary:
  Patrick A. Milberger, age 47
SVP, Operations: Stephen A. Grover, age 52, $418,392 pay
SVP, Sales and Distribution: Arthur C. (Art) Graves, age 57, $362,176 pay
VP, Human Resources: S. David Wolfe, age 47
Media Relations: David Bright
Auditors: Ernst & Young LLP

LOCATIONS
HQ: Knoll, Inc.
  1235 Water St., East Greenville, PA 18041
Phone: 215-679-7991   **Fax:** 215-679-1755
Web: www.knoll.com

Knoll has five manufacturing plants in Canada, Italy, and the US (Michigan and Pennsylvania). It has sales outlets worldwide.

2003 Sales

	$ mil.	% of total
US	627.8	90
Europe	50.1	7
Canada	19.3	3
Total	**697.2**	**100**

PRODUCTS/OPERATIONS

Selected Products
Desks and casegoods
Office systems
Seating
Storage solutions and filing cabinets
Tables

COMPETITORS

Boss Office Products	KI
GF Office Furniture	Kimball International
Global Group	Neutral Posture
Haworth	O'Sullivan Industries
Herman Miller	SMED International
HNI	Steelcase
Humanscale	Teknion
Inscape	Trendway
Jami	

HISTORICAL FINANCIALS
Company Type: Private

Income Statement				FYE: December 31
	REVENUE ($ mil.)	NET INCOME ($ mil.)	NET PROFIT MARGIN	EMPLOYEES
12/03	697	36	5.2%	3,518
12/02	773	60	7.7%	3,816
12/01	985	87	8.8%	3,863
12/00	1,164	116	10.0%	4,435
12/99	985	78	8.0%	4,378
12/98	949	93	9.8%	4,061
12/97	811	72	8.8%	3,942
12/96	652	25	3.9%	3,550
12/95	621	29	4.7%	—
12/94	563	(60)	—	—
Annual Growth	2.4%	—	—	(0.1%)

2003 Year-End Financials
Debt ratio: —   Current ratio: 0.85
Return on equity: —   Long-term debt ($ mil.): 300
Cash ($ mil.): 12

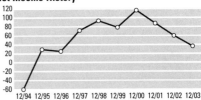

Net Income History

Koch Enterprises

Koch gets straight A's. Koch Enterprises is a diversified company with interests including aluminum, automotive finishing systems, air-conditioning equipment, and adhesives. Subsidiaries include George Koch Sons (engineers, installs, and services a range of finishing systems for the automotive industry), Koch Air (distributes heating and air-conditioning equipment), Gibbs Die Casting (supplies automotive aluminum die-castings products), Brake Supply Company (repairs and replaces brakes and hydraulic systems for the automotive and mining industries), and Uniseal (makes adhesives and sealants for automobile manufactures, as well as connectors for drain and waste pipes). The Koch family owns the company.

EXECUTIVES

President and CEO: Robert L. Koch II, age 65
CFO, Secretary, and Treasurer: Susan E. Parsons
EVP: James H. Muehlbauer, age 61

LOCATIONS

HQ: Koch Enterprises, Inc.
14 S. 11th Ave., Evansville, IN 47744
Phone: 812-465-9800 **Fax:** 812-465-9613
Web: www.kochenterprises.com

Koch Enterprises operates facilities in Florida, Indiana, Kentucky, Michigan, Missouri, Nevada, Texas, Virginia, and Wyoming in the US, as well as in Brazil, Mexico, South Korea, and the UK.

PRODUCTS/OPERATIONS

Selected Subsidiaries
Audubon Metals (51%, aluminum alloy and automobile shredder residue processing)
Brake Supply Co. (brake and hydraulic system repair)
George Koch Sons, LLC (automotive finishing systems)
Gibbs Die Casting (parts manufacturing)
Koch Air LLC (distribution)
Uniseal, Inc. (parts manufacturing)

Selected Products and Services
Aluminum and magnesium die castings
Brake linings
Heating and air-conditioning equipment
Hydraulics
PIPECONX (pipe connectors)
Powder coating systems
Specialty sealants

COMPETITORS

Dana
Graco
Illinois Tool Works
Invensys
Kaiser Aluminum
Sun Hydraulics

HISTORICAL FINANCIALS

Company Type: Private

Income Statement
FYE: December 31

	REVENUE ($ mil.)	NET INCOME ($ mil.)	NET PROFIT MARGIN	EMPLOYEES
12/03	531	—	—	2,700
12/02	550	—	—	3,050
12/01	540	—	—	3,400
12/00	617	—	—	3,400
12/99	561	—	—	3,500
12/98	520	—	—	2,800
Annual Growth	0.4%	—	—	(0.7%)

Revenue History

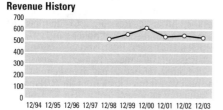

Koch Industries

Koch Industries is the real thing when there's money to be made. Koch (pronounced "coke") is the second-largest private US company, after Cargill. Koch Industries' operations (through its numerous subsidiaries) include asphalt, chemicals, energy, fertilizers, fibers and intermediates, finance, minerals, petroleum, pulp and paper, ranching, securities, and trading. A subsidiary owns three refineries that can process about 787,000 barrels of crude oil daily. Koch subsidiaries also process natural gas liquids, and operate gas gathering systems and pipelines across North America. Brothers Charles and David Koch control the company, which in 2004 acquired INVISTA for $4.2 billion and merged it with its KoSa unit.

Koch's business activities focus on three core competencies: Trading (many Koch companies are well-established traders of a wide range of commodities); Operations (Koch companies strive to be industry-leading, cost-efficient operators of their many plants and facilities); and Investments (Koch has equity investments in a variety of industries).

Koch combined its pipeline system and trading units with the power marketing businesses of electric utility Entergy in 2001 to form Entergy-Koch, a joint venture that ranks among the biggest energy commodity traders in the US.

In 2002 Koch acquired Valero Energy's 40% stake in a Mont Belvieu, Texas, natural gas liquids fractionator, boosting its ownership to 80%.

HISTORY

Fred Koch grew up poor in Texas and worked his way through MIT. In 1928 Koch developed a process to refine more gasoline from crude oil, but when he tried to market his invention, the major oil companies sued him for patent infringement. Koch eventually won the lawsuits (after 15 years in court), but the controversy made it tough to attract many US customers. In 1929 Koch took his process to the Soviet Union, but he grew disenchanted with Stalinism and returned home to become a founding member of the anticommunist John Birch Society.

Koch launched Wood River Oil & Refining in Illinois (1940) and bought the Rock Island refinery in Oklahoma (1947). He folded the remaining purchasing and gathering network into Rock Island Oil & Refining (though he later sold the refineries).

After Koch's death in 1967, his 32-year-old son Charles took the helm and renamed the company Koch Industries. He began a series of acquisitions, adding petrochemical and oil trading service operations.

During the 1980s Koch was thrust into various arenas, legal and political. Charles' brother David, also a Koch Industries executive, ran for US vice president on the Libertarian ticket in 1980. That year the other two Koch brothers, Frederick and William (David's fraternal twin), launched a takeover attempt, but Charles retained control, and William was fired from his job as VP.

The brothers traded lawsuits, and in a 1983 settlement Charles and David bought out the dissident family members for just over $1 billion. William and Frederick continued to challenge their brothers in court, claiming they had been shortchanged in the deal (the two estranged brothers eventually lost their case in 1998, and their appeals were rejected in 2000). In 1987 they even sued their mother over her distribution of trust fund money.

Despite this legal wrangling, Koch Industries continued to expand, purchasing a Corpus Christi, Texas, refinery in 1981. It expanded its pipeline system, buying Bigheart Pipe Line in Oklahoma (1986) and two systems from Santa Fe Southern Pacific (1988).

In 1991 Koch purchased the Corpus Christi marine terminal, pipelines, and gathering systems of Scurlock Permian (a unit of Ashland Oil). In 1992 the company bought United Gas Pipe Line (renamed Koch Gateway Pipeline) and its pipeline system extending from Texas to Florida.

To strengthen its engineering services presence worldwide, Koch acquired Glitsch International (a maker of separation equipment) from engineering giant Foster Wheeler in 1997. It also acquired USX-Delhi Group, a natural gas processor and transporter.

In 1998 Koch bought Purina Mills, the largest US producer of animal feed, and formed the KoSa joint venture with Mexico's Saba family to buy Hoechst's Trevira polyester unit. (Koch acquired the Saba family's stake in KoSa in 2001.) Lethargic energy and livestock prices in 1998 and 1999, however, led Koch to lay off several hundred employees, sell its feedlots, and divest portions of its natural gas gathering and pipeline systems. Purina Mills filed for bankruptcy protection in 1999 (later, it emerged from bankruptcy and held an IPO in 2000, and was acquired by #2 US dairy co-op Land O'Lakes in 2001).

William Koch sued Koch Industries in 1999, claiming the company had defrauded the US government and Native Americans in oil payments on Indian lands. A jury found for William, but he, Charles, and David agreed to settle the case in 2001 — and sat down to dinner together for the first time in 20 years.

In other legal matters, in 2000 Koch agreed to pay a $30 million civil fine and contribute $5 million toward environmental projects to settle complaints over oil spills from its pipelines in the 1990s. The company agreed to pay $20 million in 2001 to settle a separate environmental case concerning a Texas refinery.

EXECUTIVES

Chairman and CEO: Charles G. Koch, age 68
President, COO, and Director: Joseph W. (Joe) Moeller
EVP and Director: David H. Koch, age 64
EVP Operations and Director: Bill R. Caffey
SVP Joint Ventures: Cy S. Nobles
CFO: Steve Feilmeier
VP Business Development: Ron Vaupel
Director of Corporate Compliance: Chris Wilkins
Director of Human Resources: Dale Gibbens
Controller: Kelly Bulloch
CIO: Randal Robison
Public Relations/Corporate Communications: Jay Rosser
President, Flint Hills Resources, LP:
  David L. (Dave) Robertson
President, Koch Capital Markets: Sam Soliman
President and COO, Koch Chemical Technology Group, LLC: John M. Van Gelder
President, Koch Financial Corporation:
  Randall A. (Randy) Bushman

President, Koch Hydrocarbon, LP: Steve Tatum
President, Koch Materials Company: Rob Witte
President, Koch Mineral Services, LLC: Jeff Gentry
President, Koch Nitrogen Company: Steve Packebush
President, Koch Performance Roads, Inc.: Paul Wheeler
President, Koch Pipeline, LLC: Pat McCann
President, Koch Supply and Trading Company, LP:
  Steve Mawer
President, Koch Ventures Inc.: Ray Gary
Chairman and CEO, INVISTA: Jeff Walker
Auditors: KPMG LLP

LOCATIONS

HQ: Koch Industries, Inc.
  4111 E. 37th St. North, Wichita, KS 67220
Phone: 316-828-5500   Fax: 316-828-5739
Web: www.kochind.com

Koch Industries has operations in Argentina, Australia, Belgium, Brazil, Canada, China, the Czech Republic, France, Germany, India, Italy, Japan, Luxembourg, the Netherlands, Poland, South Africa, Spain, Switzerland, the UK, the US, and Venezuela.

PRODUCTS/OPERATIONS

Selected Operations

Flint Hills Resources (formerly Koch Petroleum, crude oil and refined products)
  Koch Exploration Company, LLC
Koch Agriculture Group
  Matador Cattle Co.
Koch Chemicals Group
  INVISTA Inc.
  Koch Chemicals (paraxylene)
  Koch Microelectronic Service Co. (semiconductor chemicals)
  Koch Specialty Chemicals (high-octane missile fuel)
Koch Chemical Technology Group (specialty equipment and services for refining and chemical industry)
  Brown Fintube Company
  Iris Power Engineering, Inc.
  The John Zink Company
  Koch-Glitsch, Inc.
  Koch Membrane Systems Inc.
  Koch Modular Process Systems, LLC
  Tru-Tec Services, Inc.
Koch Energy Group
  Entergy-Koch L.P. (50%)
    Gulf South Pipeline Co. (50%)
Koch Financial Services, Inc.
  Koch Financial Corp.
Koch Gas Liquids Group
Koch Materials Co. (asphalt)
Koch Mineral Services (bulk ocean transportation and fuel supply)
  Koch Fertilizer Storage & Terminal Co.
  Koch Nitrogen Co.
Koch Pipeline Co. LP
Koch Supply & Trading, LLC
Koch Ventures LLC (investment in noncore businesses)

COMPETITORS

ADM	Kerr-McGee
American Electric Power	King Ranch
Aquila	Lyondell Chemical
Ashland	Marathon Oil
Avista	Motiva Enterprises
BP	Occidental Petroleum
Cargill	Peabody Energy
CenterPoint Energy	PEMEX
ChevronTexaco	PG&E
ConocoPhillips	Royal Dutch/Shell Group
ContiGroup	Shell Oil Products
Duke Energy	Southern Company
Dynegy	SUEZ-TRACTEBEL
Enron	Sunoco
Exxon Mobil	Williams Companies
Imperial Oil	

HISTORICAL FINANCIALS

Company Type: Private

Income Statement

FYE: December 31

	REVENUE ($ mil.)	NET INCOME ($ mil.)	NET PROFIT MARGIN	EMPLOYEES
12/03	40,000	—	—	30,000
12/02	40,000	—	—	17,000
12/01	40,000	—	—	11,000
12/00	40,000	—	—	11,500
12/99	33,050	—	—	12,500
12/98	35,000	—	—	16,000
12/97	36,200	—	—	15,600
12/96	30,000	—	—	13,000
12/95	25,200	—	—	12,500
12/94	23,725	—	—	12,000
Annual Growth	6.0%	—	—	10.7%

Revenue History

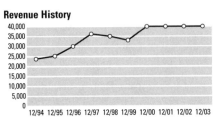

Kohlberg Kravis Roberts

The barbarians at the gate are now knocking politely. The master of the 1980s buyout universe, Kohlberg Kravis Roberts (popularly known as KKR) has shed its hostile takeover image for a kinder, gentler, buy-and-build strategy. KKR assembles funds from institutional and wealthy investors to buy low and sell high. An active investor, the firm supervises or installs new management and revamps strategy and corporate structure, selling underperforming units or adding new ones. KKR profits not only from its direct interest in these companies but also from fund and company management fees. Cousins Henry Kravis and George Roberts are the senior partners in KKR.

KKR's investments include stakes in publishing company PRIMEDIA (*Seventeen*, Channel One) and online mortgage lender Nexstar Financial. Kohlberg Kravis Roberts also has a joint venture with venture capital firm Accel Partners, Accel KKR, to provide support for companies integrating online and brick-and-mortar businesses. Recently, the firm has agreed to acquire PanAmSat from DirecTV and 92% of bedding manufacturer Sealy.

KKR is shopping in Europe, where bloated corporations are shedding non-core operations to streamline. Along with Wendel Investissement, KKR picked up French electrical product maker Legrand from Schneider Electric SA. Other European acquisitions include Motoren und Turbinen Union (MTU), which was completed just a few days before the German government limited foreign interest in aerospace and defense firms to 25%. KKR's Rockwood Specialties Group has agreed to buy Dynamit Nobel, a specialty chemicals firm that is part of German engineering group mg technologies. Additionally, the firm has neatly sewn up a deal with Singer, agreeing to purchase its sewing machine operations.

In a move that has the private equity world talking, KKR has abandoned plans to open a small part of its investment empire to the public markets. It has cancelled the planned IPO of KKR BDC, a business development company. Instead, KKR now has plans to start a private real estate investment trust (REIT) that will invest in mortgage-backed securities and other real estate-related debt.

Since 1976 KKR has invested nearly $120 billion in more than 110 companies, with investors receiving returns of around 23%. As the economy cools, though, the firm is weathering its fair share of tumult. KKR is no longer the top fund raiser in the investment industry and has written off investments in such firms as Birch Telecom, which subsequently slid into bankruptcy.

HISTORY

In 1976 Jerome Kohlberg left investment bank Bear Stearns to form his own leveraged buyout firm; with him he brought protégé Henry Kravis and Kravis' cousin George Roberts. They formed Kohlberg Kravis Roberts & Co. (KKR).

Kohlberg believed LBOs, by giving management ownership stakes in their companies, would yield better results. KKR orchestrated friendly buyouts funded by investor groups and debt. The firm's first buyout was machine-toolmaker Houdaille Industries in 1979.

KKR lost money on its 1981 investment in the American Forest Products division of Bendix. But by 1984 the firm had raised its fourth fund and made its first $1 billion buyout: Wometco Enterprises.

The next year KKR turned mean with a hostile takeover of Beatrice. The deal depended on junk bond financing devised by Drexel Burnham Lambert's Michael Milken and on the sale of pieces of the company. KKR funded the buyouts of Safeway Stores and Owens-Illinois (1986), Jim Walter Homes (1987), and Stop & Shop (1988, sold in 1996).

Unhappy with the firm's hostile image, Kohlberg left in 1987 to form Kohlberg & Co. His suit against KKR over the alleged undervaluing of companies in relation to his departure settlement was resolved for an undisclosed amount.

The Beatrice LBO triggered a rash of similar transactions as the financial industry sought fat fees. The frenzy culminated in 1988 with the $31 billion RJR Nabisco buyout, which brought KKR $75 million in fees. As the US slid into recession in 1989, LBOs dwindled and KKR turned to managing its acquisitions.

The firm also did some bottom feeding. In 1991 KKR joined with FleetBoston to buy Bank of New England. The next year it picked up 47% of what was then Advantica Restaurant Group (now just plain Denny's). It sold that holding in 1997.

KKR made its first international foray in 1993 with Russian truck maker Kamaz; it later stalled when Kamaz refused to pay management fees. The next year it freed itself from the RJR morass by swapping its investment in RJR for troubled food company Borden.

In the latter half of the decade, KKR reaped mixed results on its investments, including what is now Spalding Holdings (sporting goods and Evenflo baby products), supermarket chain Bruno's, and KinderCare Learning Centers. The $600 million KKR had sunk into magazine group

K-III (now PRIMEDIA) between 1990 and 1994 didn't revive interest in the stock, and Bruno's filed for bankruptcy in 1998. Disgruntled investors complained about low returns, and in 1996 KKR booted activist megafund CalPERS from its investor ranks.

In 1998 KKR's niche buying continued when it joined with Hicks, Muse, Tate & Furst to buy Regal Cinemas, which it combined with Act III to form the biggest theater chain in the US. The chain's expansion left it on the brink of bankruptcy, and investor Philip Anschutz bought a chunk of its debt and possible control of the company in 2001.

Focused on Europe, in 2000 the firm claimed the telecommunications business of Robert Bosch (now Tenovis), UK private equity fund Wassall PLC, and Siemens' banking systems unit. Also in 2000, KKR joined with Internet VC firm Accel Partners to form Accel KKR to invest in companies that combine traditional business and Internet assets. It lost its place as the top fund-raiser to Thomas H. Lee, which closed a record-setting $6.1 billion fund in early 2001. Kohlberg acquired major divisions from Laporte for about $1.175 billion in that same year.

After a failed attempt to take Borden Chemical public in 2004, KKR sold the firm to private equity group Apollo Management.

EXECUTIVES

Founding Partner: Henry R. Kravis, age 60
Founding Partner, California: George R. Roberts, age 60
General Partner, London: Edward A. Gilhuly, age 44
General Partner: Perry Golkin, age 50
General Partner, California:
  James H. (Jamie) Greene Jr., age 53
General Partner, California: Robert I. MacDonnell, age 66
General Partner: Michael W. Michelson, age 53
General Partner: Paul E. Raether, age 57
General Partner: Scott M. Stuart, age 44
Managing Director, Europe: Ned Gilhuly
Managing Director, France: Jacques R. Garaïalde
Managing Director, London: Johannes Huth
Chairman, Accel-KKR, Inc.: Paul M. Hazen, age 62
Office Manager: Sandy Cisneros
Auditors: Deloitte & Touche LLP

LOCATIONS

HQ: Kohlberg Kravis Roberts & Co.
  9 W. 57th St., Ste. 4200, New York, NY 10019
Phone: 212-750-8300   **Fax:** 212-750-0003
Web: www.kkr.com

Kohlberg Kravis Roberts & Co. has offices in London; Menlo Park, California; and New York City.

PRODUCTS/OPERATIONS

Selected Investments
Accuride Corporation
Alea Group Holdings AG
Alliance Imaging, Inc.
The Boyds Collection, Ltd.
Bristol West Insurance Group
Broadnet Mediascape Communications AG
Centric Software, Inc.
Demag Holding
  Argillon
  Demag Cranes and Components
  Gottwald Port Technology
  Mannesman Plastics Machinery
  Omnetica
DPL Inc.
DSSI LLC
International Transmission Company
Jazz Pharmaceuticals, Inc.
KinderCare Learning Centers, Inc.
KSL Recreation Corporation

Legrand Holding SA
MedCath Corporation
MTU Aero Engines GmbH
Nexstar Financial Corporation
NuVox Communications (formerly NewSouth Holdings)
Owens-Illinois, Inc.
PRIMEDIA Inc.
Rockwood Specialties Group Inc.
Sealy Corporation
Walter Industries, Inc.
Willis Group Holdings Limited
Wincor Nixdorf International GmbH
Zohne Technologies, Inc.
Zumtobel AG

COMPETITORS

AEA Investors
American Financial
Apollo Advisors
Bear Stearns
Berkshire Hathaway
Blackstone Group
Carlyle Group
CD&R
Citigroup Global Markets
CVC Capital Partners
Equity Group Investments
Forstmann Little
Goldman Sachs
Haas Wheat
Heico
Hicks Muse
Interlaken Investment
Investcorp
Jordan Company
Lehman Brothers
Leonard Green
MacAndrews & Forbes
Merrill Lynch
Texas Pacific Group
Thomas Lee
Veronis Suhler Stevenson
Vestar Capital Partners
Wingate Partners

Kohler

Plumbing powerhouse Kohler may have profits in the toilet, but it's a good thing. Kohler makes bathroom products under the names Hytec, Kohler, and Sterling (plumbing); Ann Sacks (ceramic tile, marble, stone); and Kallista (fixtures). Brands in Europe include Jacob Delafon and Neomediam (plumbing) and Sanijura (cabinetry). Kohler also makes high-end furniture, small engines, generators, and electrical switchgear. Kohler Event Services supplies backup and prime power for events and for emergency support. Kohler owns The American Club resort, Old Course Hotel Golf Resort and Spa (Scotland), and other properties. Chairman Herbert Kohler Jr. and his sister Ruth Kohler, grandchildren of the founder, control Kohler.

Kohler is building a manufacturing facility in Mexico and is expanding some of its US factories. The company's small engines include 4-cycle engines up to 29 hp and power generation systems up to 2800 kW.

Chairman Herbert Kohler Jr. breeds Morgan horses at Kohler Stables in Kentucky. In August 2004 the company hosted the PGA Championship.

HISTORY

In 1873, 29-year-old Austrian immigrant John Kohler and partner Charles Silberzahn founded Kohler & Silberzahn in Sheboygan, Wisconsin. That year they purchased a small iron foundry that made agricultural products for $5,000 from Kohler's father-in-law. In 1880, two years after Silberzahn left the firm, its machine shop was destroyed by fire.

The company introduced enameled plumbing fixtures in the rebuilt factory in 1883. The design caught on, and the business sold thousands of sinks, kettles, pans, and bathtubs. By 1887, when Kohler was incorporated, enameled items accounted for 70% of sales. By 1900 the 250-person company received 98% of its sales from enameled iron products. That year, shortly after John Kohler began building new facilities near Sheboygan (which later became the company village of Kohler), he died at age 56. More trouble followed: Kohler's new plant burned down in 1901, and two of the founder's sons died — Carl at age 24 in 1904 and Robert at age 35 in 1905.

Eldest surviving son Walter built a boarding hotel to house workers and introduced other employee-benefit programs. He also set up company-paid workmen's compensation before the state made it law in 1917.

By the mid-1920s, when Kohler premiered colors in porcelain fixtures and added brass fittings and vitreous china toilets and washbasins to its line, it was the #3 plumbing-product company in the US. As a testament to the design quality of its products, Kohler items were displayed at the New York Museum of Modern Art in 1929. The company also began developing products that would grow in importance in later decades: electric generators and small gasoline engines. During the 1950s Kohler's engines virtually conquered Southeast Asia, where they were used to power boats, drive air compressors, and pump water for rice paddies in Vietnam and Thailand. While strikes against Kohler in 1897 and 1934 had been resolved quickly, a 1954 strike against the firm lasted six years. The strike gave Kohler the dubious honor of enduring the longest strike in US history.

Small-engine use grew in the US in the 1960s, and Kohler's motors were used in lawn mowers, construction equipment, and garden tractors. The founder's last surviving son, Herbert (a child from John Kohler's second marriage), died in 1968. Under the leadership of Herbert's son, Herbert Jr. (appointed chairman 1972), Kohler expanded its operations and began to develop its resort business in the US with the restoration of The American Club hotel (1981); it bought Sterling Faucet (1984), Baker, Knapp & Tubbs (1986), and Jacob Delafon (1986). Subsequent acquisitions have included Sanijura (bathroom furniture, France) in 1993; Osio (enamel baths, Italy) in 1994; Robern (mirrored cabinets) in 1995; Holdiam (baths, whirlpools, and sinks, France) in 1995; and Canac (cabinets, Canada) in 1996.

The company entered a growing plumbing market in China through four joint ventures formed in that country in 1996 and 1997. In 1998 several family and non-family shareholders claimed a reorganization plan unfairly forced them out and undervalued their stock. Legal battles over the stock's fair price continued in 1999, and a settlement was reached in 2000 that granted shareholders a fair price and Herbert Jr. and his sister Ruth gained firm control of the company. Herbert reorganized the company and vowed it would never go public.

In 2001 the company sued Canada-based Kohler International Ltd. for trademark infringement. Also that year Kohler acquired UK-based Mira Showers. Following the tragedy of 9/11, Kohler quickly created a mobile showering unit with nine shower stalls and four sinks within an enormous semi-trailer to provide hot showers for workers and volunteers at the World Trade Center.

In the fall of 2002 Kohler and about 3,450 United Auto Workers (UAW) union members who worked at the company's Village of Kohler and Town of Mosel plants agreed on a five-year labor contract that called for increases in wages and benefits.

Kohler expanded its resort business internationally in 2004 by purchasing the world-renowned Old Course Hotel Golf Resort and Spa in St. Andrews, Scotland, along with Golf Resorts International (GRI), Limited.

EXECUTIVES
Chairman and President: Herbert V. Kohler Jr., age 64
SVP Finance and CFO: Jeffery P. Cheney
SVP Human Resources: Laura Kohler
VP Hospitality and Real Estate: Alice Edland
VP Marketing, Fixtures: Christopher Lohmann
Director; President, Kitchen and Bath Group:
 David Kohler
President, Global Power Group: Richard J. Fotsch, age 48
Manager, Environmental Health and Safety Technology Resources: Paul Kubicek
Marketing Director, Sterling Brand: Mike Chandler
Communications, Kohler Power Systems:
 Stephanie Dlugopolski
Public Relations, Kitchen and Bath Group: Liz Curtis
Public Relations, Kitchen and Bath Group: Todd Weber
Media Relations, Destination Kohler: Scott Silvestri
Auditors: Mancera, S.C.

LOCATIONS
HQ: Kohler Co.
 444 Highland Dr., Kohler, WI 53044
Phone: 920-457-4441   **Fax:** 920-457-1271
Web: kohlerco.com

Kohler Co. operates 44 manufacturing plants, 26 subsidiaries and affiliates, and sales offices worldwide.

PRODUCTS/OPERATIONS
Selected Operations
Engines
 Commercial turf equipment engines
 Consumer lawn and garden equipment engines
 Industrial, construction, and commercial equipment engines
 Recreational equipment engines
Furniture
 Baker Furniture
 McGuire Furniture Company
 Milling Road Furniture
Generators
 Kohler rental power
 Marine generators
 Mobile generators
 On-site power systems
  Automatic transfer switches
  Switchgear
 Residential generators
 Small business generators
Kitchen and Bath Products
 Cabinets and vanities
  Canac (bathroom cabinetry)
  Robern (lighting and mirrored bath cabinetry)
  Sanijura (vanities and other bath furniture)
 Plumbing products
  Jacob Delafon (bathtubs, faucets, lavatories, and toilets)
  Kohler (bath and shower faucets, baths, bidet faucets, bidets, body spa systems, glass showers and shower doors, kitchen and bathroom sinks and faucets, master baths, toilets, toilet seats, vanities, whirlpool baths)
  Kallista (bathroom and kitchen sinks and faucets)
  Sterling (bathing fixtures, faucets, sinks, tub/shower enclosures, vitreous china bath fixtures)
 Tile and stone products
  Ann Sacks (art tile, glazed tile, knobs and pulls, mosaics, terra cotta)

Real Estate and Hospitality (Destination Kohler)
 The American Club (resort hotel)
 Blackwolf Run golf course
 Golf Resorts International, Limited (Scotland)
 Inn on Woodlake
 Kohler Stables
 Kohler Waters Spa
 Old Course Hotel Golf Resort and Spa (Scotland)
 Riverbend (private club)
 River Wildlife
 The Shops at Woodlake Kohler
 Whistling Straits golf course

COMPETITORS
American Standard
Armstrong Holdings
Armstrong World Industries
Bassett Furniture
Black & Decker
Briggs & Stratton
Carlson
Chicago Faucet
Cooper Industries
Crane
Crane Plumbing
Dal-Tile
Dyson-Kissner-Moran
Elkay Manufacturing
Geberit
Geberit Manufacturing
Gerber Plumbing Fixtures
Grohe
Honda
Iberia Tiles
Jacuzzi Brands
Klaussner Furniture
Leggett & Platt
Masco
Moen
Mueller Industries
Newell Rubbermaid
NIBCO
Price Pfister
Samuel Heath
Starwood Hotels & Resorts
Tecumseh Products
TOTO
Villeroy & Boch
Waxman
Yamaha

HISTORICAL FINANCIALS
Company Type: Private

Income Statement   FYE: December 31

	ESTIMATED REVENUE ($ mil.)	NET INCOME ($ mil.)	NET PROFIT MARGIN	EMPLOYEES
12/03	3,005	—	—	25,000
12/02	3,000	—	—	25,000
12/01	3,000	—	—	22,000
12/00	2,700	—	—	20,000
12/99	2,500	—	—	20,000
12/98	2,400	—	—	18,000
12/97	2,210	—	—	18,000
12/96	2,020	—	—	18,000
12/95	1,850	—	—	15,000
12/94	1,600	—	—	14,500
Annual Growth	7.3%	—	—	6.2%

Revenue History

Koppers

Koppers treats wood right. The company (formerly Koppers Industries) makes carbon compounds and treated-wood products for the chemical, railroad, aluminum, utility, construction, and steel industries around the world. Its carbon materials and chemicals unit makes materials for producing aluminum, polyester resins, plasticizers, and wood preservatives. The railroad and utility products unit supplies treated crossties and utility poles and treats wood for vineyard, construction, and other uses. Koppers indirectly owns 50% of KSA Limited Partnership, which produces about 100,000 concrete crossties annually. Koppers was formed in 1988. Private investment firm Saratoga Partners (New York) controls Koppers.

EXECUTIVES
Chairman: Robert Cizik, age 72
President, CEO, and Director: Walter W. Turner, age 57, $744,000 pay
CFO: Brian H. McCurrie
SVP, Administration, General Counsel, and Secretary:
 Steven R. Lacy, age 48, $407,020 pay
 (prior to promotion)
VP, Australasian Operations; Managing Director, Koppers Australia: Ernest S. Byron, age 58
VP, European Operations: David Whittle, age 61, $362,362 pay
VP; General Manager, Carbon Materials and Chemicals:
 Kevin J. Fitzgerald, age 51, $288,400 pay
VP; General Manager, Global Marketing, Sales, and Development Group: Mark R. McCormack, age 44
VP; General Manager, Railroad Products and Services:
 Thomas D. Loadman, age 49, $294,565 pay
VP; General Manager, Utility Poles and Piling Products:
 David T. Bryce, age 56
VP, Safety, Health, and Environmental Affairs:
 Randall D. Collins, age 51
VP, Technology: Robert H. Wombles, age 52
Auditors: Ernst & Young LLP

LOCATIONS
HQ: Koppers Inc.
 436 7th Ave., Pittsburgh, PA 15219
Phone: 412-227-2001   **Fax:** 412-227-2333
Web: www.koppers.com

Koppers operates 39 facilities in Australia, Europe, Malaysia, New Zealand, South Africa, and the US.

2003 Sales

	$ mil.	% of total
US	555.5	66
Australia & Pacific Rim	158.4	19
Europe	129.0	15
Total	**842.9**	**100**

PRODUCTS/OPERATIONS

2003 Sales

	$ mil.	% of total
Carbon Materials & Chemicals	484.1	57
Railroad & Utility Products	358.8	43
Total	**842.9**	**100**

Selected Products

Carbon Materials and Chemicals
 Carbon black
 Carbon pitch
 Coal tar distillates
 Creosote
 Furnace coke
 Phthalic anhydride (PAA)
 Refined tars
 Roofing pitch
Railroad and Utility Products
 Crossties (wood and concrete)
 Pilings
 Track and switch preassemblies
 Utility poles

COMPETITORS

Cabot
Cytec
De Dietrich
Degussa
Kerr-McGee
KMG Chemicals
North American Technologies
Osmose
RailWorks
Stepan
U.S. Plastic Lumber

HISTORICAL FINANCIALS

Company Type: Private

Income Statement
FYE: December 31

	REVENUE ($ mil.)	NET INCOME ($ mil.)	NET PROFIT MARGIN	EMPLOYEES
12/03	843	(37)	—	1,975
12/02	730	17	2.3%	2,057
12/01	708	13	1.9%	2,085
12/00	724	15	2.0%	2,155
12/99	664	24	3.6%	1,904
12/98	671	20	3.0%	1,927
12/97	593	(6)	—	1,990
12/96	589	14	2.4%	1,919
12/95	526	24	4.6%	2,104
12/94	476	11	2.3%	—
Annual Growth	6.5%	—	—	(0.8%)

2003 Year-End Financials

Debt ratio: —
Return on equity: —
Cash ($ mil.): 10
Current ratio: 1.55
Long-term debt ($ mil.): 333

Net Income History

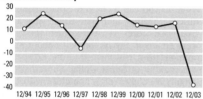

KPMG

Businesses all over the world count on KPMG for accounting. KPMG is the most geographically dispersed of accounting's Big Four, which also includes Deloitte Touche Tohmatsu, Ernst & Young, and PricewaterhouseCoopers. KPMG, a cooperative that operates as an umbrella organization for its member firms, has organized its structure into three operating regions: the Americas, Asia/Pacific, and Europe, Middle East, Africa. Member firms' offerings include audit, tax, and advisory services; KPMG focuses on clients in such industries as financial services, consumer products, government, health care, information, communications, and entertainment. KPMG has discontinued its KLegal International network.

After much regulatory pressure, KPMG separated its accounting and consulting operations; it sold a chunk of the consulting business to networking equipment maker Cisco Systems, then took it public and sold off its shares in 2002. The consulting unit, which in 2002 changed its name to BearingPoint, is buying KPMG's Austrian, German, and Swiss consulting businesses.

In 2003 the SEC charged US member firm KPMG L.L.P. and four partners with fraud in relation to alleged profit inflation at former client Xerox in the late 1990s. A run-in with the US government over tax shelter plans characterized as abusive (costing the US more than $1 billion in tax revenues) led to a shakeup in the US firm's tax services unit in 2004.

Lawsuits over KPMG's work for other former clients hit the accountancy's pocketbook. In 2003 KPMG agreed to pay $125 million to settle a dispute regarding work for Rite Aid. The next year, KPMG's Belgian and US units agreed to a $115 million settlement regarding now-defunct Lernout & Hauspie Speech Products.

HISTORY

Peat Marwick was founded in 1911, when William Peat, a London accountant, met James Marwick during an Atlantic crossing. University of Glasgow alumni Marwick and Roger Mitchell had formed Marwick, Mitchell & Company in New York in 1897. Peat and Marwick agreed to ally their firms temporarily, and in 1925 they merged as Peat, Marwick, Mitchell, & Copartners.

In 1947 William Black became senior partner, a position he held until 1965. He guided the firm's 1950 merger with Barrow, Wade, Guthrie, one of the US's oldest firms, and built its consulting practice. Peat Marwick restructured its international practice as PMM&Co. (International) in 1972 (renamed Peat Marwick International in 1978).

The next year several European accounting firms led by Klynveld Kraayenhoff (the Netherlands) and Deutsche Treuhand (Germany) began forming an international accounting federation. Needing an American member, the European firms encouraged the merger of two American firms founded around the turn of the century, Main Lafrentz and Hurdman Cranstoun. Main Hurdman & Cranstoun joined the Europeans to form Klynveld Main Goerdeler (KMG), named after two of the member firms and the chairman of Deutsche Treuhand, Reinhard Goerdeler. Other members were C. Jespersen (Denmark), Thorne Riddel (Canada), Thomson McLintok (UK), and Fides Revision (Switzerland).

Peat Marwick merged with KMG in 1987 to form Klynveld Peat Marwick Goerdeler (KPMG). KPMG lost 10% of its business as competing client companies departed. Professional staff departures followed in 1990 when, as part of a consolidation, the firm trimmed its partnership rolls.

In the 1990s the then-Big Six accounting firms all faced lawsuits arising from an evolving standard holding auditors responsible for the substance, rather than merely the form, of clients' accounts. KPMG was hit by suits stemming from its audits of defunct S&Ls and litigation relating to the bankruptcy of Orange County, California (settled for $75 million in 1998). Nevertheless KPMG kept growing; it expanded its consulting division with the acquisition of banking consultancy Barefoot, Marrinan & Associates in 1996.

In 1997, after Price Waterhouse and Coopers & Lybrand announced their merger, KPMG and Ernst & Young announced one of their own. But they called it quits the next year, fearing that regulatory approval of the deal would be too onerous.

The creation of PricewaterhouseCoopers (PwC) and increasing competition in the consulting sides of all of the Big Five brought a realignment of loyalties in their national practices. KPMG Consulting's Belgian group moved to PwC and its French group to Computer Sciences Corporation. Andersen nearly wooed away KPMG's Canadian consulting group, but the plan was foiled by the ever-sullen Andersen Consulting group (now Accenture) and by KPMG's promises of more money.

Against this background, KPMG sold 20% of its consulting operations to Cisco Systems for $1 billion. In addition to the cash infusion, the deal allowed KPMG to provide installation and system management to Cisco's customers.

Even while KPMG worked on the IPO of its consulting group (which took place in 2001), it continued to rail against the SEC as it called for relationships between consulting and auditing organizations to be severed. In 2002 KPMG sold its British and Dutch consultancy units to France's Atos Origin.

EXECUTIVES

Chairman; Senior Partner, KPMG UK: Michael (Mike) Rake, age 56
CEO: Robert W. (Bob) Alspaugh, age 57
COO: Colin Holland
Chairman, Americas; Chairman and CEO, KPMG LLP: Eugene D. (Gene) O'Kelly, age 52
Chairman, Europe, Middle East, and Africa: Harald Wiedmann
Chairman, Asia Pacific: John Harrison
Senior Partner/CEO, Switzerland: Jakob Baer
Senior Partner, Brazil: David Bunce
Managing Partner, Singapore: Bobby Chin
President, France: Jean-Luc Decornoy
Senior Partner, Mexico: Guillermo Garcia-Naranjo
Chairman and Senior Partner, South Africa: Tom Grieve
Senior Partner, Italy: Renato Guerini
National Chairman, Australia: Doug Jukes
Managing Partner, Ireland: Jerome Kennedy
Chairman and CEO, Canada: Bill MacKinnon
Senior Partner, Denmark: Finn L. Meyer
Senior Partner, Sweden: Thomas Thiel
Chairman, Board of Management, Netherlands: Ben van der Veer
Senior Partner, Japan: Satoshi Yura
General Counsel: John Shutkin
Secretary: Needra Patel

LOCATIONS

HQ: KPMG International
345 Park Ave., New York, NY 10154-0102
Phone: 212-758-9700 **Fax:** 212-758-9819
Web: www.kpmg.com

KPMG International has offices in nearly 150 countries.

2003 Sales

	$ mil.	% of total
Europe, Middle East, South Asia & Africa	6,290	52
Americas	4,630	38
Asia/Pacific	1,240	10
Total	**12,160**	**100**

PRODUCTS/OPERATIONS

2003 Sales

	$ mil.	% of total
Audit services	5,680	47
Tax services (includes legal services)	3,310	27
Advisory services	3,170	26
Total	**12,160**	**100**

2003 Sales by Customer Type

	$ mil.	% of total
Consumer & industrial markets		
Industrial markets	2,550	21
Consumer markets	1,550	13
Financial services	3,430	28
Infrastructure, government & health care	2,760	23
Information, communications & entertainment	1,870	15
Total	**12,160**	**100**

Selected Services

Audit Services
    Financial statement audit
    Internal audit services
Tax Services
    Corporate & business tax
    Global tax
    Indirect tax
    Personal tax
Advisory Services
    Audit support services
    Financial risk management
    Information risk management
    Process improvement
    Regulatory & compliance

Selected Industry Specializations

Consumer & Industrial Markets
  Consumer Markets
    Consumer products
    Food & beverage
    Retail
  Industrial Markets
    Chemicals & pharmaceuticals
    Energy & natural resources
    Industrial & automotive products
Financial Services
  Banking
  Insurance
Infrastructure, Government & Health Care
  Building, construction & real estate
  Funding agencies
  Government
  Health care
  Transportation
Information, Communications & Entertainment
  Business services
  Communications
  Electronics
  Media
  Software

COMPETITORS

Aon	H&R Block
Bain & Company	Hewitt Associates
Baker Tilly International	Marsh & McLennan
BDO International	McKinsey & Company
Booz Allen	PricewaterhouseCoopers
Deloitte	Towers Perrin
Ernst & Young	Watson Wyatt
Grant Thornton International	

HISTORICAL FINANCIALS
Company Type: Partnership

Income Statement   FYE: September 30

	REVENUE ($ mil.)	NET INCOME ($ mil.)	NET PROFIT MARGIN	EMPLOYEES
9/03	12,160	—	—	100,000
9/02	10,720	—	—	98,000
9/01	11,700	—	—	103,000
9/00	10,700	—	—	108,000
9/99	12,200	—	—	102,000
9/98	10,600	—	—	85,300
9/97	9,200	—	—	83,500
9/96	8,100	—	—	77,000
9/95	7,500	—	—	72,000
9/94	6,600	—	—	76,200
Annual Growth	7.0%	—	—	3.1%

Revenue History

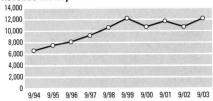

KRATON

KRATON Polymers broke its bonds with Royal Dutch/Shell Group and with Ripplewood Holdings but still has plenty of other bonds — both in the lab and with plastics makers. The company is the leading maker of styrenic block copolymers (SBCs), a kind of polymer used in a variety of plastic, rubber, chemicals, and for improving the stability of asphalt. More specifically, the KRATON family of polymers is used in adhesives, toys, and packaging, and to make shoe soles. The company has six manufacturing facilities in Asia, Europe, and North and South America. Private investment firm Ripplewood bought the company from Shell in 2001 and then sold it to Texas Pacific Group in late 2003.

EXECUTIVES

Chairman: Kelvin Davis
Vice Chairman: Stephen T. (Steve) Wood, age 57
CEO: George Gregory
VP, Americas and Director, KRATON G Polymers: Garret Davies
VP, Asia-Pacific: Issho Nakamura
VP, Europe, Africa, and Middle East and Director, KRATON D Polymers: Roger Morgan
VP, Finance and IT: Gary M. Spitz
VP, Operations: Rick Ott
VP, Technology: Bob Newman
General Legal Counsel: Joseph Waiter
CIO: Paul Yust
Head of Human Resources: Brian Ashcroft

LOCATIONS

HQ: KRATON Polymers LLC
    700 Milam St., North Tower, 13th Fl.,
    Houston, TX 77002
Phone: 832-204-5400   **Fax:** 832-204-5460
Web: www.kraton.com

Manufacturing Facilities
Belpre, Ohio
Berre, France
Kashima, Japan
Paulinia, Brazil
Pernis, the Netherlands
Wesseling, Germany

COMPETITORS

BASF AG	GE Plastics
Bayer MaterialScience	Imperial Chemical Industries
BP Petrochemicals	
Chevron Phillips Chemical	NOVA Chemicals
Dow Chemical	Solvay
DuPont	

HISTORICAL FINANCIALS
Company Type: Private

Income Statement   FYE: December 31

	ESTIMATED REVENUE ($ mil.)	NET INCOME ($ mil.)	NET PROFIT MARGIN	EMPLOYEES
12/02	600	—	—	1,000
12/01	600	—	—	1,000
Annual Growth	0.0%	—	—	0.0%

Revenue History

K-VA-T Food Stores

What do you call a chain of supermarkets in Kentucky, Virginia, and Tennessee? How about K-VA-T Food Stores? K-VA-T is one of the largest grocery chains in the region, with about 85 supermarkets primarily under the Food City banner (and a handful of Super Dollar Supermarkets). Originally a Piggly Wiggly franchise with three stores, K-VA-T was founded in 1955. It has expanded by acquiring stores from other regional food retailers, opening new stores, and adding services such as more than 30 pharmacies, about 20 Gas'N Go gasoline outlets, and banking. Its Mid-Mountain Foods provides warehousing and distribution services. The founding Smith family owns a majority of K-VA-T; employees own the rest of the company.

EXECUTIVES

Chairman: Jack C. Smith
President and CEO: Steven C. Smith, age 46
SVP and COO: Jesse A. Lewis
SVP, Finance and Administration, CFO, Secretary, and Treasurer: Robert L. Neeley
SVP, Marketing: Tom Hembree
EVP, Operations: Jody Helms
EVP, Knoxville Division: John Jones
EVP, Merchandising and Marketing: Richard Gunn
EVP, Tri-Cities Division: Johnny Cecil
VP, Human Resources: Donnie Meadows
VP, Research and Real Estate: Lou Scudere
VP, Store Planning and Development: Don Smith
VP, Community and Government Relations: Bob Southerland
General Counsel and Risk Management: Charlie Fugate
Controller: Anne Overbay

LOCATIONS

HQ: K-VA-T Food Stores, Inc.
    201 Trigg St., Abingdon, VA 24211
Phone: 276-628-5503   **Fax:** 276-628-1592
Web: www.foodcity.com

Land O'Lakes

Land O'Lakes butters up its customers, and shows you what life is like if everyone cooperates. Owned by and serving more than 7,000 dairy farmer members and 1,300 community cooperatives, Land O'Lakes is the #3 dairy co-op in the US (behind Dairy Farmers of America and California Dairies). It provides its members with wholesale fertilizer and crop protection products, seed, and animal feed. Its oldest product, LAND O' LAKES butter, is the #1 butter brand in the US. Land O'Lakes also produces packaged milk, margarine, sour cream, and cheese. The co-op's animal feed division is a leading animal and pet food maker.

In addition to its Land O'Lakes Farmland Feeds and Agriliance agronomy divisions, its Land O'Lakes swine division raises feeder pigs for members and sees the pigs to market. However, it has put this division up for sale.

Land O'Lakes also holds more than half of a joint venture in egg producer MoArk.

The co-op's subsidiary Land O'Lakes Finance provides financing services for beef, dairy, pork, and poultry producers.

In response to changes in the agriculture business and the rapidly consolidating dairy market, Land O'Lakes has positioned itself as a national player. Acquisitions and joint ventures have helped it diversify beyond just butter and dairy commodities.

Outside of the US, Land O'Lakes has taken aim at the largest emerging market: China. The company's sales agent in China is working to establish the Land O'Lakes brand of cheese and cultured dairy products in supermarkets.

HISTORY

In the old days, grocers sold butter from communal tubs and it often went bad. Widespread distribution of dairy products had to await the invention of fast, reliable transportation. By 1921 the necessary transportation was available. That year about 320 dairy farmers in Minnesota formed the Minnesota Cooperative Creameries Association and launched a membership drive with $1,375, mostly borrowed from the US Farm Bureau.

The co-op arranged joint shipments for members; imposed strict hygiene and quality standards; and aggressively marketed its sweet cream butter nationwide, packaged for the first time in the familiar box of four quarter-pound sticks. A month after the co-op's New York sales office opened, it was ordering 80 shipments a week.

Minnesota Cooperative Creameries, as part of its promotional campaigns, ran a contest in 1924 to name that butter. Two contestants offered the winning name — Land O'Lakes. The distinctive Indian Maiden logo first appeared about the same time, and in 1926 the co-op changed its name to Land O'Lakes Creameries. By 1929, when it began supplying feed, its market share approached 50%.

During WWII civilian consumption dropped, but the co-op increased production of dried milk to provide food for soldiers and newly liberated concentration camp victims.

In the 1950s and 1960s, Land O'Lakes added ice cream and yogurt producers to its membership and fought margarine makers, yet butter's market share continued to melt. The co-op diversified in 1970 through acquisitions, adding feeds and agricultural chemicals. Two years later Land O'Lakes threw in the towel and came out with its own margarine. Despite the decreasing use of butter nationally, the co-op's market share grew.

Land O'Lakes formed a marketing joint venture, Cenex/Land O'Lakes Agronomy, with fellow co-op Cenex in 1987. As health consciousness bloomed in the 1980s, Land O'Lakes launched reduced-fat dairy products. It also purchased a California cheese plant, doubling its capacity. Land O'Lakes began ramping up its international projects at the same time: It built a feed mill in Taiwan, introduced feed products in Mexico, and established feed and cheese operations in Poland.

In 1997 the co-op bought low-fat cheese maker Alpine Lace Brands. Land O'Lakes took on the eastern US when it merged with the 3,600-member Atlantic Dairy Cooperative (1997), and it bulked up on the West Coast when California-based Dairyman's Cooperative Creamery Association joined its fold (1998).

During 2000 the co-op sold five plants to Dean Foods with an agreement to continue supplying the plants with raw milk. Also in 2000 Land O'Lakes combined its feed business with those of Farmland Industries to create Land O'Lakes Farmland Feed, LLC, with 69% ownership. That same year Cenex/Land O'Lakes Agronomy and Farmland Industries joined together their agronomy operations to create Agriliance LLC (now 50% owned).

In late 2001 the company spent $359 million to acquire Purina Mills (pet and livestock feeds). Purina Mills was folded into Land O'Lakes Farmland Feed and, as part of the purchase, Land O'Lakes increased its ownership of the feed business to 92%. In 2004 it purchased the remaining 8%.

To take advantage of its nationally recognized brand, Land O'Lakes formed an alliance with Dean Foods in 2002 to develop and market value-added dairy products.

EXECUTIVES

President and CEO: John E. (Jack) Gherty, age 60
EVP; COO Dairy Foods: Chris Policinski, age 46
SVP and CFO: Daniel E. Knutson, age 47
VP, Human Resources: Karen Grabow, age 54
VP, Operations and Supply Chain, Dairy Foods: Fernando Palacios, age 44
VP and General Counsel: Peter Janzen, age 44
VP and Treasurer: Peter Simonse, age 45
President, Land O'Lakes Farmland Feed: Robert D. (Bob) DeGregorio, age 47
Managing Director, Worldwide Foods: James J. Lord
Media Contact: Lydia Botham
Media Contact: Dave Karpinksi
Auditors: KPMG LLP

LOCATIONS

HQ: Land O'Lakes, Inc.
4001 Lexington Ave. North, Arden Hills, MN 55126
Phone: 651-481-2222 **Fax:** 651-481-2000
Web: www.landolakesinc.com

Land O'Lakes operates processing, manufacturing, warehousing, and distribution facilities across the US and internationally.

2003 Stores

	No.
Tennessee	54
Virginia	22
Kentucky	11
Total	**87**

PRODUCTS/OPERATIONS

Selected Departments
Bakery/deli
Café
Dairy
Dry goods
Floral
Frozen foods
Gasoline
Meat
Pharmacy
Produce
Seafood
Video

Selected Services
Banking
Money orders
Party planning
Photo processing
Postage stamps

COMPETITORS

A&P	Kmart
Ahold USA	Kroger
Albertson's	Meijer
Alex Lee	The Pantry
AWG	Ruddick
BI-LO	SUPERVALU
Food Lion	Ukrop's Super Markets
Houchens	Wal-Mart
Ingles Markets	Winn-Dixie

HISTORICAL FINANCIALS

Company Type: Private

Income Statement
FYE: December 31

	REVENUE ($ mil.)	NET INCOME ($ mil.)	NET PROFIT MARGIN	EMPLOYEES
12/03	1,200	—	—	9,500
12/02	1,063	—	—	9,300
12/01	1,000	—	—	8,700
12/00	963	—	—	8,690
12/99	880	—	—	7,100
12/98	760	—	—	6,500
12/97	712	—	—	6,300
12/96	691	—	—	6,000
12/95	634	—	—	4,000
12/94	592	—	—	3,752
Annual Growth	**8.2%**	—	—	**10.9%**

Revenue History

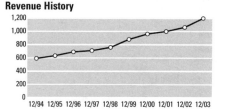

PRODUCTS/OPERATIONS

2003 Sales

	$ mil.	% of total
Dairy foods	2,969.4	47
Feed	2,467.2	39
Seed	479.3	8
Layers	317.8	5
Swine	91.2	1
Adjustments	(4.4)	—
Total	**6,320.5**	**100**

Selected Brands
Alpine Lace (low-fat cheese)
CROPLAN GENETICS (crop seed)
LAND O' LAKES (consumer dairy products)
Land O'Lakes (animal feed)
PMI Nutrition (animal feeds and pet foods)

Dairy Products
Butter
Cheese
Flavored butter
Light butter
Margarine
Milk
Sour cream

COMPETITORS

ADM	Northwest Dairy
AMPI	Parmalat
California Dairies Inc.	Pioneer Hi-Bred
Dairy Farmers of America	Prairie Farms Dairy
Dean Foods	Saputo
Fonterra	Schreiber Foods
Foremost Farms	Unilever
Kraft Foods	WestFarm Foods
National Dairy Holdings	

HISTORICAL FINANCIALS
Company Type: Cooperative

Income Statement
FYE: December 31

	REVENUE ($ mil.)	NET INCOME ($ mil.)	NET PROFIT MARGIN	EMPLOYEES
12/03	6,321	84	1.3%	8,000
12/02	5,847	99	1.7%	8,000
12/01	5,973	72	1.2%	8,600
12/00	5,756	103	1.8%	6,500
12/99	5,613	21	0.4%	6,500
12/98	5,174	69	1.3%	6,500
12/97	4,195	95	2.3%	5,500
12/96	3,486	119	3.4%	5,500
12/95	3,014	121	4.0%	5,500
12/94	2,859	75	2.6%	5,500
Annual Growth	9.2%	1.2%	—	4.3%

2003 Year-End Financials
Debt ratio: 129.9% Current ratio: 1.42
Return on equity: 9.2% Long-term debt ($ mil.): 1,165
Cash ($ mil.): 130

Net Income History
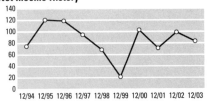

Landmark Communications

Landmark Communications' media properties are all over the map. Owner of cable station The Weather Channel, Landmark is also a leading community newspaper publisher. It publishes three metro newspapers (*The Virginian-Pilot, News & Record,* and *The Roanoke Times*) in North Carolina and Virginia and about 50 daily, semiweekly, and weekly community papers in the East and Midwest. The company also publishes 70 free newspapers and special-interest publications, including some focusing on college sports. Chairman Frank Batten Jr. and his family own the company.

Landmark is 50% owner (with Cox Enterprises) of Trader Publishing, which prints classified advertising for motor vehicles, and owns about 50% of Capital-Gazette Communications, publisher of the *Washingtonian* magazine.

The company also owns CBS-affiliated TV stations in Las Vegas and Nashville, Tennessee. Its Landmark Education Services unit operates a handful of career schools. Shorecliff Communications is a Landmark company focused on trade shows and conferences for the wireless and communications industries.

Landmark sold its stake in Web services company InfiNet to Gannett in 2003.

EXECUTIVES
Chairman and CEO: Frank Batten Jr.
Chairman, Executive Committee: Frank Batten Sr.
Vice Chairman: Richard F. Barry III
President and COO: Decker Anstrom
EVP and CFO: Lemuel E. Lewis
EVP; President, Landmark Publishing Group:
R. Bruce Bradley
EVP, Secretary, and Corporate Counsel: Guy Friddell III, age 53
VP Corporate Development and New Ventures:
Michael W. Alston, age 46
VP Finance: Colleen R. Pittman
VP Human Resources: Charlie W. Hill
President, Landmark Education Services: Dan Sykes
President and CEO, Trader Publishing Company:
Conrad M. Hall
President, The Weather Channel: Debora J. Wilson

LOCATIONS
HQ: Landmark Communications, Inc.
150 W. Brambleton Ave., Norfolk, VA 23510
Phone: 757-446-2010   **Fax:** 757-446-2489
Web: www.landmarkcom.com

Landmark Communications has publications in Arkansas, Colorado, Florida, Illinois, Indiana, Iowa, Kentucky, Maryland, Mississippi, Nebraska, New Mexico, North Carolina, Ohio, Pennsylvania, South Carolina, Tennessee, West Virginia, and Virginia.

PRODUCTS/OPERATIONS

Broadcasting
KLAS-TV (Las Vegas)
Travel network (London)
The Weather Channel Companies
  Pelmorex, Inc. (50%, Canadian weather network)
  The Weather Channel
  weather.com
WTVF-TV (Nashville, TN)

Joint Ventures
Capital-Gazette Communications (49.9%; newspaper and magazine)
Trader Publishing (50% with Cox Enterprises; photo ad guides for vehicles)

Selected Landmark Community Newspapers and Special Interest Publications
Carolina Blue (University of North Carolina sports magazine)
The Carroll County Times (Westminster, MD)
Cats' Pause (University of Kentucky sports magazine)
The Central Kentucky News-Journal (Campbellsville, KY)
Citrus County Chronicle (Crystal River, FL)
Gator Bait (University of Florida sports magazine)
Huskers Illustrated (University of Nebraska sports magazine)
Inside Indiana (University of Indiana sports magazine)
The Kentucky Standard (Bardstown, KY)
The Lancaster News (South Carolina)
Los Alamos Monitor (NM)
News-Enterprise (Elizabethtown, KY)
The Oldham Era (La Grange, KY)
The Roane County News (Kingston, KY)
Sentinel-News (Shelbyville, KY)
The Voice of the Hawkeyes (University of Iowa sports magazine)

Metro Newspapers
News & Record (Greensboro, NC)
The Roanoke Times (VA)
The Virginian-Pilot (Norfolk, VA)

Other Subsidiaries
Landmark Education Services (career schools)
Shorecliff Communications (trade show organizer)

COMPETITORS

Advance Publications	Lamar Advertising
CNN	McClatchy Company
Community Newspaper Holdings	Media General
	Meredith
Cox Enterprises	New York Times
Gannett	Stephens Media Group
Hollinger International	Tribune
Journal Communications	Washington Post
Knight-Ridder	

HISTORICAL FINANCIALS
Company Type: Private

Income Statement
FYE: December 31

	REVENUE ($ mil.)	NET INCOME ($ mil.)	NET PROFIT MARGIN	EMPLOYEES
12/03	743	—	—	—
12/02	728	—	—	—
12/01	732	—	—	5,000
12/00	805	—	—	5,000
12/99	730	—	—	5,000
12/98	650	—	—	4,500
12/97	573	—	—	4,500
12/96	550	—	—	4,500
12/95	501	—	—	4,500
12/94	467	—	—	4,500
Annual Growth	5.3%	—	—	1.5%

Revenue History
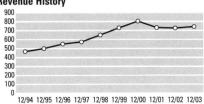

Lane Construction

For more than a century Lane Construction has been a transportation specialist — building everything from lanes for horseless carriages to runways for airports. The heavy civil contractor evolved from a stone-crushing plant opened in 1890 by railroad engineer John S. Lane. The group is known for building highways, roads, bridges, railroads, and mass transit systems, generally on the East Coast and in Texas and Oklahoma. Recent projects include a pedestrian tunnel at Dulles International Airport and an interstate highway in Texas. The company also produces bituminous concrete and aggregates from about 35 plants in the northeastern US. Lane Construction is owned by descendants of Lane and employees.

Lane has expanded through its 2003 acquisition of Rea Construction, a former subsidiary of bankrupt firm J.A. Jones Construction. Now known as Rea Contracting, the Charlotte, North Carolina-based company is a heavy/highway contractor and asphalt producer with a strong presence in the Southeast.

EXECUTIVES

President and CEO: Robert E. (Bob) Alger
EVP and COO, Contracts: Donald M. Cross
EVP and COO, Plants: Frank A. Healy
EVP Administration and Purchasing: Donald P. Dobbs
VP Mechanical: Michael M. Cote
VP: Donald L. Kentzel
VP Finance and Treasurer: Jayne G. Mather
VP: Kirk D. Junco
VP Legal and Safety: Jay S. Cruickshank
Assistant Treasurer and Information Systems Manager: Vincent J. Caiola
Assistant Secretary and Tax Manager: Ann M. Falsey
Chief Engineer: David F. Benton

LOCATIONS

HQ: The Lane Construction Corporation
965 E. Main St., Meriden, CT 06450
Phone: 203-235-3351   **Fax:** 203-237-4260
Web: www.laneconstruct.com

Lane Construction has offices in Connecticut, Florida, Maine, Maryland, Massachusetts, New Hampshire, New York, North Carolina, Pennsylvania, South Carolina, Texas, Vermont, Virginia, and the District of Columbia. It also operates plants in Florida, Maine, Massachusetts, New Hampshire, Pennsylvania, Virginia, and the District of Columbia.

COMPETITORS

Angelo Iafrate
Bechtel
Clark Enterprises
Granite Construction
Modern Continental Companies
O&G Industries
Peter Kiewit Sons'
Skanska USA Civil
Turner Corporation
Tutor-Saliba
Walsh Group
Washington Group

HISTORICAL FINANCIALS
Company Type: Private

Income Statement				FYE: December 31
	REVENUE ($ mil.)	NET INCOME ($ mil.)	NET PROFIT MARGIN	EMPLOYEES
12/03	429	—	—	2,700
12/02	550	—	—	—
12/01	350	—	—	320
Annual Growth	10.7%	—	—	190.5%

Revenue History

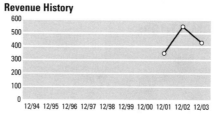

Lane Industries

From the seeds of a humble office machine and supplies manufacturer grew the mighty oak of Lane Industries. The diversified holding company's oldest investment is its nearly two-thirds stake in General Binding, a maker of binding and laminating equipment, marker boards, and paper shredders, founded by William Lane II in 1947. Lane Industries is also active in the lodging industry through Lane Hospitality, which owns or operates about 20 hotels and time-share properties. Lane Industries sold its security monitoring service business, Lane Security, to Integrated Alarm Services Group in 2003. The company is owned by the Lane family.

EXECUTIVES

President and CEO: Forrest M. Schneider, age 56
SVP and CFO: Richard R. Fabbrini
Chairman, President, and CEO, General Binding Corporation: Dennis J. Martin, age 53
President and CEO, Lane Hospitality: Bill DeForrest
Manager, Human Resources: Linda Datz

LOCATIONS

HQ: Lane Industries, Inc.
1200 Shermer Rd., 4th Fl., Northbrook, IL 60062
Phone: 847-498-6789   **Fax:** 847-498-2104

COMPETITORS

Accor
Fellowes
Starwood Hotels & Resorts

HISTORICAL FINANCIALS
Company Type: Private

Income Statement				FYE: December 31
	REVENUE ($ mil.)	NET INCOME ($ mil.)	NET PROFIT MARGIN	EMPLOYEES
12/02	795	—	—	—
12/01	870	—	—	6,350
12/00	1,000	—	—	7,000
12/99	1,000	—	—	8,300
12/98	1,020	—	—	8,650
12/97	890	—	—	7,925
12/96	700	—	—	8,300
12/95	625	—	—	8,300
12/94	553	—	—	7,000
12/93	465	—	—	4,980
Annual Growth	6.1%	—	—	3.1%

Revenue History

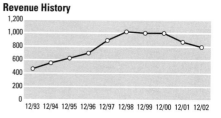

Lanoga

Lanoga is a lumbering giant. The company is one of the top US retailers of lumber and building materials, catering to professional contractors and consumers. Operating more than 300 stores in some 20 states, Lanoga has grown through dozens of small acquisitions. Its divisions include Dixieline (California), the Home Lumber Company (Colorado), Lumbermens Building Centers (Northwest, Arizona, and California), Spenard Builders Supply (Alaska), and United Building Centers (Midwest and Rocky Mountain states). Lanoga was founded in the mid-1850s by the Laird and Norton families, who were cousins. Descendants of the company's founders own Lanoga.

Lanoga acquired some 30 Wickes locations in the Midwest. Lanoga subsidiary Hope Lumber & Supply additionally acquired more than 10 Wickes outlets in the South and Colorado.

EXECUTIVES

Chairman: Paul Brewer
President and CEO: Paul Hylbert
EVP, CFO, Secretary, and Treasurer: William (Bill) Brakken
EVP and COO: Mike Morehouse
VP, Market Development: George C. Finkenstaedt
President and CEO, Dixieline: William S. (Bill) Cowling II
President, Lumbermen's Building Centers: Dave Dittmer
President, Spenard Builders Supply: Ed Waite
President, United Building Centers: Dale Kukowski
IT Manager: Reba Mart

LOCATIONS

HQ: Lanoga Corporation
　17946 NE 65th St., Redmond, WA 98052
Phone: 425-883-4125　　**Fax:** 425-882-2959
Web: www.lanogacorp.com

COMPETITORS

84 Lumber	Lowe's
Ace Hardware	Menard
Building Materials Holding	Stock Building Supply TruServ
Home Depot	Wolohan Lumber

HISTORICAL FINANCIALS

Company Type: Private

Income Statement
FYE: December 31

	REVENUE ($ mil.)	NET INCOME ($ mil.)	NET PROFIT MARGIN	EMPLOYEES
12/02	1,453	—	—	7,009
12/01	1,400	—	—	5,500
12/00	1,300	—	—	5,360
12/99	1,251	—	—	5,125
12/98	1,030	—	—	4,085
12/97	990	—	—	4,147
12/96	842	—	—	3,730
12/95	760	—	—	3,600
12/94	746	—	—	3,400
12/93	657	—	—	2,975
Annual Growth	9.2%	—	—	10.0%

Revenue History

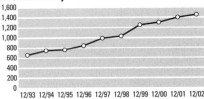

Larry H. Miller Group

You wouldn't hire the Larry H. Miller Group for your late night bebop, but the firm does know a little something about all that jazz. The company operates about 35 auto dealerships in Arizona, Colorado, Idaho, New Mexico, Oregon, and Utah. Its dealerships sell Cadillac, Chevrolet, Honda, Lexus, Toyota, and other makes of cars. The company also owns the Utah Jazz, its home (the Delta Center arena), the WNBA's Utah Starzz, and Salt Lake City TV station KJZZ. In addition the Larry H. Miller Group operates two movie theaters with a total of about 30 screens in Salt Lake City and Sandy, Utah. Also in Sandy the company owns a 10-story office building. Owned by Larry H. Miller, the company was founded in 1979.

EXECUTIVES

CEO: Clark Whitworth
President: Karen G. Miller
COO: Richard Nelson
SVP and Operations Manager: Bryant Henrie
Director of Human Resources: Linda Jeppesen

LOCATIONS

HQ: Larry H. Miller Group
　9350 S. 150 East, Rte. 1000, Sandy, UT 84070
Phone: 801-563-4100　　**Fax:** 801-563-4198
Web: www.lhm.com

COMPETITORS

AutoNation	Phil Long Dealerships
Burt Automotive	Ron Tonkin
DriveTime	United Auto Group
Earnhardt's Auto Centers	VT Inc.

HISTORICAL FINANCIALS

Company Type: Private

Income Statement
FYE: December 31

	REVENUE ($ mil.)	NET INCOME ($ mil.)	NET PROFIT MARGIN	EMPLOYEES
12/03	1,608	—	—	5,700
12/02	1,631	—	—	—
12/01	1,550	—	—	—
12/00	1,367	—	—	—
12/99	1,361	—	—	—
12/98	1,200	—	—	—
12/97	1,019	—	—	3,200
12/96	842	—	—	2,200
12/95	926	—	—	1,700
12/94	700	—	—	1,720
Annual Growth	9.7%	—	—	14.2%

Revenue History

Las Vegas Sands

Rising from the ashes of the bulldozed Sands Hotel, the Venetian Casino Resort (owned and operated by Las Vegas Sands) brings a touch of Venice to the Las Vegas strip. Replete with gondoliers, the colonnades of Doge's Palace, and a replica of the Rialto Bridge, the Venetian offers a 116,000-sq.-ft. casino and a 4,000-suite hotel. The facility also houses a shopping, dining, and entertainment complex. Las Vegas Sands operates the Venetian Congress Center conference facility that links the casino to the nearby Expo Center trade show and convention center (separately owned by an affiliate). The company also operates a casino in Macau, China. Las Vegas Sands chairman and CEO Sheldon Adelson owns 95% of the company.

EXECUTIVES

Chairman, CEO, and Treasurer: Sheldon G. Adelson, age 71, $2,250,000 pay
President, COO, and Director: William P. Weidner, age 59, $2,073,628 pay
EVP: Bradley H. Stone, age 49, $1,658,902 pay
SVP: Robert G. Goldstein, age 49, $1,555,221 pay
VP Finance and Secretary: Harry D. Miltenberger, age 61
VP Advertising: Scott Messinger
VP Casino Marketing: Howie Weiner
VP Hotel Operations: Peter Walterspiel
VP Human Resources, The Venetian Resort: David Newton
VP International Marketing: Rafael Larios
VP Finance, The Venetian Resort: Steve Hauck
VP General Counsel, The Venetian Resort: Tom Smock
VP Sales, The Venetian Resort: Eric Bello
Director of Communications: Kurt Ouchida
Auditors: PricewaterhouseCoopers LLP

LOCATIONS

HQ: Las Vegas Sands, Inc.
　3355 Las Vegas Blvd. South, Las Vegas, NV 89109
Phone: 702-414-1000　　**Fax:** 702-414-4884
Web: www.venetian.com

PRODUCTS/OPERATIONS

2003 Sales

	$ mil.	% of total
Casino	272.8	40
Rooms	251.4	37
Food & beverage	82.9	12
The Grand Canal Shoppes	39.4	6
Retail	8.6	1
Other	31.2	4
Adjustments	(44.8)	—
Total	**641.5**	**100**

COMPETITORS

Boyd Gaming	Mandalay Resort Group
Caesars Entertainment	MGM Mirage
Harrah's Entertainment	

HISTORICAL FINANCIALS

Company Type: Private

Income Statement
FYE: December 31

	REVENUE ($ mil.)	NET INCOME ($ mil.)	NET PROFIT MARGIN	EMPLOYEES
12/03	642	37	5.8%	5,750
12/02	572	(38)	—	4,000
12/01	524	(24)	—	4,000
12/00	590	16	2.7%	4,000
12/99	284	(66)	—	4,000
12/98	1	(30)	—	—
12/97	1	(1)	—	—
Annual Growth	198.9%	—	—	9.5%

2003 Year-End Financials

Debt ratio: (8,395.7%)　　Current ratio: 1.35
Return on equity: —　　Long-term debt ($ mil.): 1,426
Cash ($ mil.): 179

Net Income History

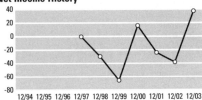

Latham & Watkins

Latham & Watkins' founders Dana Latham and Paul Watkins flipped a coin in 1934 to determine which of their names would go first on the company's shingle. From that coin toss, the law firm has grown into one of the largest in the US. With more than 1,500 lawyers, the firm ranks high in corporate finance, mergers and acquisitions, technology law, and litigation. Latham & Watkins was a key player in the financing for the Venetian Resort Hotel and Casino in Las Vegas and Gemstar's acquisition of TV Guide. Headquartered in Los Angeles, the firm has 21 locations worldwide. Latham & Watkins counts Amgen, Time Warner Inc., Lucent, and Morgan Stanley among its clients.

EXECUTIVES
Chairman and Managing Partner: Robert M. Dell
Executive Director: LeeAnn Black
Director Finance: Grant Johnson
Director Global Human Resources: Mimi Krumholz

LOCATIONS
HQ: Latham & Watkins LLP
633 W. 5th St., Ste. 4000, Los Angeles, CA 90071
Phone: 213-485-1234   **Fax:** 213-891-8763
Web: www.lw.com

Latham & Watkins has offices in Boston; Chicago; Costa Mesa, Los Angeles, Menlo Park, San Diego, and San Francisco, California; Newark, New Jersey; New York City; Reston, Virginia; and Washington, DC; as well as in Brussels; Frankfurt and Hamburg, Germany; Hong Kong; London; Milan; Moscow; Paris; Singapore; and Tokyo.

PRODUCTS/OPERATIONS
Selected Practice Areas
Corporate
Environmental
Finance and real estate
International
Litigation
Tax

COMPETITORS
Baker & McKenzie
Clifford Chance
Davis Polk
Gibson, Dunn & Crutcher
Kirkland & Ellis
Simpson Thacher
Skadden, Arps
Sullivan & Cromwell
Weil, Gotshal

HISTORICAL FINANCIALS
Company Type: Partnership

Income Statement
FYE: December 31

	REVENUE ($ mil.)	NET INCOME ($ mil.)	NET PROFIT MARGIN	EMPLOYEES
12/03	1,032	—	—	—
12/02	906	—	—	—
12/01	770	—	—	—
12/00	643	—	—	2,647
12/99	582	—	—	2,297
12/98	502	—	—	2,287
12/97	421	—	—	—
12/96	363	—	—	—
12/95	300	—	—	—
12/94	263	—	—	—
Annual Growth	16.4%	—	—	7.6%

Revenue History

Lefrak Organization

Horace Greeley said "Go west, young man!" and The Lefrak Organization listened — if you take the famous *New Yorker* comic strip's view that you're in the Midwest once you cross the Hudson. The Lefrak Organization is one of the US's largest private landlords, with more than 70,000 apartments in New York City and New Jersey, another 40,000 units under management, and millions of square feet of commercial space. Owned by the LeFrak family, the company also owns and manages a variety of commercial and retail properties throughout the New York City area, including flagship property 40 West 57th St.; tenants include Nautica, Bank of America, and Infinity Broadcasting.

Lefrak's flagship residential development, the 5,000-unit Lefrak City in Queens, has been home to successive waves of ethnic groups seeking a better life.

The company is concentrating on its Newport development, a 400-acre community of apartments, office towers, and stores on the waterfront in Jersey City across the Hudson River from Manhattan.

Lefrak has built half a dozen office towers (occupied by CIGNA, U.S. Trust, and UBS Financial Services, among others) on the site, and plans for further apartment developments and more office buildings are underway.

The company also has holdings in oil exploration (Lefrak Oil & Gas Organization, or LOGO) and entertainment (Lefrak Entertainment operates LMR, the record label that launched Barbra Streisand). It also owns stage and movie theaters and produces television programs, movies, and Broadway shows.

Chairman Samuel LeFrak, famed for his interpretation of the Golden Rule ("he who has the gold makes the rules"), died in April 2003. He was an active philanthropist, supporting the Guggenheim Museum and the American Museum of Natural History. He also contributed to the oceanographic studies of the late sea explorer Jacques Cousteau.

HISTORY

Harry Lefrak and his father Aaron came to the US from Palestine (or France — there are many conflicting versions of the Lefrak family history — Aaron's father Maurice is said to have been a developer there in the 1840s) around 1900. They began building tenements in Brooklyn's Williamsburg neighborhood to house the flood of immigrants then pouring into New York City.

In 1901, Harry and Aaron started what is now known as The Lefrak Organization. It diversified into glass and for some time provided raw material for the workshops of Louis Comfort Tiffany. After WWI the glass factory was sold, and the company expanded into Brooklyn, where it developed housing and commercial space in Bedford-Stuyvesant, among other areas.

Samuel, Harry's son, began working in the business early, assisting tradesmen at building sites. He then attended the University of Maryland, and shunning a future career in dentistry (family lore claims his left-handedness would have required special tools), returned to the business. Samuel's first project was a 120-unit apartment building in Brooklyn's Midwood — it was 1938, and he was 20 years old and still a university student.

During WWII, the firm built camps and housing for the Army. After the war, business took off, as the company began building low-cost housing. Samuel took over the company in 1948. To keep costs down, Samuel bought clay and gypsum quarries, forests, and lumber mills and cement plants, eventually achieving 70% vertical integration of his operations. This included the creation of in-house architectural, engineering, and construction departments that handled all aspects of building the LeFrak empire's properties — from initial designs to general contracting — from the ground up.

The 1950s building boom was in part spurred by new laws in New York authorizing the issue of state bonds for financing low-interest construction loans, which Lefrak used to build more than 2,000 apartments in previously undeveloped coastal sections of Brooklyn. At its peak, Lefrak turned out an apartment every 16 minutes for rents as low as $21 per room.

In 1960 Lefrak broke ground for Lefrak City, a 5,000-apartment development built on 40 acres in Queens (after four years of negotiations with the trustees of the William Waldorf Astor estate over the sale price — $6 million), which featured air-conditioned units and rented for $40 per room.

The next decade brought a real estate slump that endangered the organization's next project, Battery Park. Lefrak issued public bonds to save it. Samuel also picked up a few more properties during this period, and he capitalized the "F" in his family name but not the company name. (He later said that he did this to distinguish himself from other Lefraks at his club who had been posted for nonpayment of dues, though a conflicting story states that his mother's French-born physician originally capitalized the "F" on Samuel's birth certificate.)

Samuel's son Richard became increasingly involved in the business in the 1980s as the organization began an even bigger project: the 600-acre Newport City development, begun in 1989 with plans for almost 10,000 apartments and retail and commercial space.

Meanwhile, Lefrak City had "turned," as its original Jewish occupants sought greener fields. As occupancy dropped, the company relaxed its tenant screening, and the development deteriorated (it was subsequently tagged "Crack City"). In the 1990s, however, it began attracting a mix of African, Jewish, and Central Asian immigrants, whose tightly knit communities improved the development's safety and equilibrium.

Construction of the company's Newport project continued throughout the 1990s with construction of office buildings, apartments, and a hotel (completed in 2000) on the site. As a tight Manhattan office market drove up lease prices, Lefrak's new offices across the Hudson attracted companies in the finance and insurance sectors. Lefrak filled about 3 million sq. ft. in its Newport development during 1999 and 2000.

In 2001 the company's Gateway complex in Battery Park City was damaged in the World Trade Center terrorist attack. The tenants threatened a rent strike, prompting Lefrak to lower rents to compensate for the difficulties attributed to living near the site.

Samuel LeFrak died in April 2003 at the age of 85.

EXECUTIVES

President, CEO, and COO: Richard S. LeFrak, age 58
EVP and CFO: Richard N. Papert
EVP: Harrison LeFrak
EVP: James (Jamie) LeFrak
SVP Marketing and Public Relations: Edward Cortese
VP Commercial: Marsilia (Marcy) Boyle
VP Commercial: Irwin Granville
VP Construction and Engineering: Anthony Scavo
VP Finance and Administration and Treasurer: Mitchell Ingerman
General Counsel: Arnold S. Lehman
Director, Human Resources: John Farrelly
Director, Residential Leasing: Tom Pichi
Auditors: Lewis Goldberg

LOCATIONS

HQ: The Lefrak Organization
9777 Queens Blvd., Rego Park, NY 11374
Phone: 718-459-9021   **Fax:** 718-897-0688
Web: www.lefrak.com

The Lefrak Organization operates primarily in the New York metropolitan area.

Selected Properties
Commercial Space
  Jersey City, New Jersey
    Newport development
  Manhattan
    40 W. 57th St.
    Gateway Plaza at Battery Park City
    James Tower
Residential Apartments
  Jersey City, New Jersey
    Atlantic
    East Hampton
    James Monroe
    Presidential Plaza
    Riverside
    Southampton
    Towers of America
  Manhattan
    Gateway Plaza at Battery Park City
  Queens
    Lefrak City

Residential Co-op Properties
  Brooklyn
    Bay Ridge
    Bensonhurst
    Flatbush
    Park Slope
    Sheepshead Bay
  Queens
    Elmhurst
    Flushing
    Forest Hills
    Key Gardens
    Rego Park
    Woodside
Retail
  Jersey City, New Jersey
    Newport Centre Mall

PRODUCTS/OPERATIONS

Selected Operations
Energy
  Lefrak Oil & Gas Organization
Entertainment
  Lefrak Entertainment Co.
Real Estate
  Commercial properties
  Residential apartments
  Residential co-op properties
  Retail properties

COMPETITORS

Alexander's
AvalonBay
Boston Properties
Equity Office Properties
Hartz Mountain
Helmsley
Mack-Cali
Macklowe Properties
Port Authority of NY & NJ
Reckson Associates Realty
Related Capital
Silverstein Properties
SL Green Realty
Starrett Corporation
Tishman
Trizec Properties
Trump
Vornado Realty Trust
Witkoff Group

HISTORICAL FINANCIALS
Company Type: Private

Income Statement			FYE: Last Sunday in November
	REVENUE ($ mil.)	NET INCOME ($ mil.)	NET PROFIT MARGIN	EMPLOYEES
11/02	2,800	—	—	16,200
11/01	3,800	—	—	16,200
11/00	3,800	—	—	16,110
11/99	2,500	—	—	16,500
11/98	2,750	—	—	16,000
11/97	3,400	—	—	18,000
11/96	3,500	—	—	17,500
11/95	3,300	—	—	17,400
11/94	3,100	—	—	17,500
11/93	3,200	—	—	18,000
Annual Growth	(1.5%)	—	—	(1.2%)

Revenue History
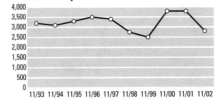

Lenox Hill Hospital

Lenox Hill Hospital provides acute care to patients from facilities located on Manhattan's Upper East Side. The hospital has more than 650 beds and offers such services as cardiac care, high-risk obstetrics, and sports medicine. The facility also serves as a teaching affiliate for NYU Medical Center. Lenox Hill Hospital owns Manhattan Eye, Ear & Throat Hospital, a leading provider of specialty care for vision, hearing, speech, and even swallowing disorders.

EXECUTIVES

President and CEO: Gladys George
EVP and COO: Terence O'Brien
CFO: Thomas Poccio
CIO: Louis Ajamy
Auditors: KPMG LLP

LOCATIONS

HQ: Lenox Hill Hospital
100 E. 77th St., New York, NY 10021
Phone: 212-434-2000   **Fax:** 212-434-2003
Web: www.lenoxhillhospital.org

HISTORICAL FINANCIALS
Company Type: Not-for-profit

Income Statement			FYE: December 31
	REVENUE ($ mil.)	NET INCOME ($ mil.)	NET PROFIT MARGIN	EMPLOYEES
12/03	549	—	—	2,955

Leprino Foods

Don't try to butter up Leprino Foods — it's strictly into mozzarella, and finding things to do with all that leftover whey. The company is the world's largest maker of mozzarella cheese, which it sells to pizza chains (namely Pizza Hut) and food manufacturers. Leprino's other products include whey protein concentrate and lactose for use in animal feeds, baby formula, and baked goods. Supplied by the nation's large dairy co-ops, Leprino hopes to hitch its sales to the rising global popularity of pizza. It has acquired a stake in Glanbia, Europe's largest maker of pizza cheese, as part of a joint venture. Italian immigrant Michael Leprino Sr. founded the company in 1950. It is still owned by the Leprino family.

EXECUTIVES

Chairman: James Leprino
President: Wesley J. Allen
SVP, Administration: Ron Klump
SVP, Business Development: Mike Reidy
VP, Controller: Paul Adams
VP, Dairy Policy and Procurement: Sue Taylor
VP, Human Resources: Tom Deany

LOCATIONS

HQ: Leprino Foods Company
1830 W. 38th Ave., Denver, CO 80211
Phone: 303-480-2600 **Fax:** 303-480-2605
Web: www.leprinofoods.com

Leprino Foods operates plants in California, Colorado, Michigan, Nebraska, New Mexico, and New York.

COMPETITORS

Agri-Mark
Century Foods
Foremost Farms
Great Lakes Cheese
Kraft Foods
Saputo
Schreiber Foods

HISTORICAL FINANCIALS

Company Type: Private

Income Statement				FYE: October 31
	ESTIMATED REVENUE ($ mil.)	NET INCOME ($ mil.)	NET PROFIT MARGIN	EMPLOYEES
10/03	1,900	—	—	3,350
10/02	1,750	—	—	3,000
10/01	1,700	—	—	2,500
10/00	1,650	—	—	2,800
10/99	1,550	—	—	2,800
10/98	1,250	—	—	2,300
10/97	1,000	—	—	2,300
10/96	1,200	—	—	2,200
10/95	1,100	—	—	2,200
Annual Growth	7.1%	—	—	5.4%

Revenue History

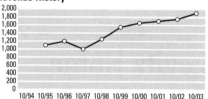

Les Schwab Tire Centers

If you need new tires after heeding Greeley's advice, go to Les Schwab Tire Centers. And it doesn't hurt that the owner wrote the bible of tire retailing: *Pride in Performance — Keep It Going*. Les Schwab Tire Centers prides itself on continued customer service; it sells tires and batteries and does alignment, brake, and shock work at about 365 stores in Alaska, California, Idaho, Montana, Nevada, Oregon, Utah, and Washington. With a story that rivals Moses', founder and chairman Les Schwab was reared in a logging camp and went to school in a converted boxcar. In 1952 he bought a tire shop that grew into Les Schwab Tire Centers. The firm, owned by Schwab and his family, plans to open about 20 stores a year.

EXECUTIVES

Chairman: Les Schwab
President and CEO: Philip (Phil) Wick
CFO: Tom Freedman
EVP: Dick Borgman
VP of Advertising and Marketing: Brian Capp
Director of Human Resources: Larry Smith

LOCATIONS

HQ: Les Schwab Tire Centers
646 NW Madras Hwy., Prineville, OR 97754
Phone: 541-447-4136   **Fax:** 541-416-5208
Web: www.lesschwab.com

COMPETITORS

Advance Auto Parts
AutoZone
BFS Retail & Commercial Operations
Bridgestone Americas
Commercial Tire
CSK Auto
Discount Tire
Goodyear
Pep Boys
Sears
TCI Tire Centers
Wal-Mart

HISTORICAL FINANCIALS

Company Type: Private

Income Statement				FYE: December 31
	ESTIMATED REVENUE ($ mil.)	NET INCOME ($ mil.)	NET PROFIT MARGIN	EMPLOYEES
12/03	1,000	—	—	6,000
12/02	1,000	—	—	6,000
12/01	1,000	—	—	6,000
12/00	800	—	—	6,000
12/99	800	—	—	5,500
12/98	750	—	—	5,300
12/97	850	—	—	5,300
12/96	700	—	—	4,800
12/95	525	—	—	4,225
12/94	500	—	—	4,000
Annual Growth	8.0%	—	—	4.6%

Revenue History

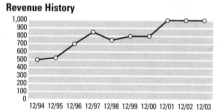

Levi Strauss

Levi Strauss & Co. (LS&CO.) is giving its pants a hike up. LS&CO., the world's #1 maker of brand-name clothing, sells jeans and sportswear under the Levi's, Dockers, and Levi Strauss Signature names in more than 110 countries. Levi's jeans — department store staples — were once the uniform of American youth, but LS&CO. lost touch with the trends in recent years. In response, the company has transformed its product offerings to include wrinkle-free and stain-resistant fabrics used in the making of some of its Levi's and Dockers slacks. The Haas family (relatives of founder Levi Strauss) owns LS&CO.

In late 2002, Levi Strauss overhauled its market strategy and, for the first time since the introduction of Dockers in 1986, rolled out a series of new brands. Varied and tiered in markets rather than relying on its basic one or two styles and brands, Levi's hopes they will help regain some of the market share lost to VF Corporation (makers of Lee and Wrangler) and others over the last decade.

Among a whole roster of new products, Levi's Superlow jeans and Levi Strauss Signature jeans were created for the mass market, though their distribution in the US was short-lived. Dockers Flat Front Mobile pants (with secret pockets for cell phones, PDAs, and other gadgets) and Dockers Go Khaki pants (with Stain Defender, a Teflon treatment preventing stains) target the 25 to 39 age group. Undaunted by a slate of disappointing and short-lived brands (including Levi's Engineered Jeans, the Type 1, and the Superlow), Levi Strauss has revamped a number of its basic products, including Levi's 501, 550, and 515.

In October 2004 the company announced a licensing agreement with Dehli, India-based M&B Footwear to manufacture men's and women's casual shoes and sneakers beginning in 2005. The line will appear in 50 Levi's outlets and M&B's retail stores.

Due to substantial drops in net sales over the last seven years, Levi Strauss has also taken measures to recoup some of its losses, including closing 37 of its factories worldwide and instead using independent contract manufacturers. It has closed its remaining North American manufacturing facilities; San Antonio operations shut down in early 2004 and three Canadian operations are not far behind. The closures will affect some 2,000 employees. In Haiti, Levi Strauss is closing its production facility not because of budget cuts, but labor disputes, an action that will result in the loss of about 700 jobs.

In order to further pare down losses, Levi Strauss announced in 2004 plans to put its popular Dockers brand up for sale; the company quickly took it off the block, however, deciding instead to reinvest in and revitalize the brand. Meanwhile, the company continues to suss out other cost-cutting measures during its internal restructuring process. In mid-2004 Levi Strauss announced plans to close its Spanish manufacturing facilities, resulting in the loss of more than 450 jobs.

HISTORY

Levi Strauss arrived in New York City from Bavaria in 1847. In 1853 he moved to San Francisco to sell dry goods to the gold rushers. Shortly after, a prospector told Strauss of miners' problems in finding sturdy pants. Strauss made a pair out of canvas for the prospector; word of the rugged pants spread quickly.

Strauss continued his dry-goods business in the 1860s. During this time he switched the pants' fabric to a durable French cloth called serge de Nimes, soon known as denim. He colored the fabric with indigo dye and adopted the idea from Nevada tailor Jacob Davis of reinforcing the pants with copper rivets. In 1873 Strauss and Davis produced their first pair of waist-high overalls (later known as jeans). The pants soon became *de rigueur* for lumberjacks, cowboys, railroad workers, oil drillers, and farmers.

Strauss continued to build his pants and wholesaling business until he died in 1902. Levi Strauss & Co. (LS&CO.) passed to four nephews who carried on their uncle's jeans business while maintaining the company's philanthropic reputation.

After WWII Walter Haas and Peter Haas (a fourth-generation Strauss family member) assumed leadership of LS&CO. In 1948 they ended the company's wholesaling business to concentrate on Levi's clothing. In the 1950s Levi's jeans ceased to be merely functional garments for workers: They became the uniform of American youth. In the 1960s LS&CO. added women's attire and expanded overseas.

The company went public in 1971. That year it added a women's career line and bought Koret sportswear (sold in 1984). By the mid-1980s profits declined. Peace Corps veteran-turned-McKinsey consultant Robert Haas (Walter's son) grabbed the reins of LS&CO. in 1984 and took the company private the next year. He also instilled a touchy-feely corporate culture often at odds with the bottom line.

In 1986 LS&CO. introduced Dockers casual pants. The company's sales began rising in 1991 as consumers forsook designer duds of the 1980s for more practical clothes. LS&CO. says seven out of every ten American men own a pair of Dockers. However, LS&CO. missed out on the birth of another trend: the split between the fashion sense of US adolescents and their Levi's-loving, baby boomer parents.

In 1996 the company introduced Slates dress slacks. That year LS&CO. bought back nearly one-third of its stock from family and employees for $4.3 billion. Grappling with slipping sales and debt from the buyout, in 1997 LS&CO. closed 11 of its 37 North American plants, laying off 6,400 workers and 1,000 salaried employees; it granted generous severance packages even to those earning minimum wage.

In 1998, citing improved labor conditions in China, LS&CO. announced it would step up its use of Chinese subcontractors. Further restructuring added a third of its European plants to the closures list that year. LS&CO.'s sales fell 13% in fiscal 1998. The next year LS&CO. closed 11 of 22 remaining North American plants. It also unleashed several new jeans brands that eschewed the company's one-style-fits-all approach of old.

In 1999 Haas handed his CEO title to Pepsi executive Philip Marineau.

In April 2002 LS&CO. announced it would close six of its last eight US plants and cut 20% of its worldwide staff (3,300 workers). In September 2003 it cut another 5% of its worldwide staff (650 workers). Also in September the company opened its first girls-only store located in Paris, France. In December LS&CO. replaced CFO Bill Chiasson with an outside turnaround specialist.

EXECUTIVES

Chairman: Robert D. (Bob) Haas, age 61, $1,148,077 pay
President and CEO: Philip A. Marineau, age 57, $1,450,000 pay
Interim CFO: James P. Fogarty, age 35
SVP and CIO: David G. Bergen, age 48
SVP, General Counsel, and Assistant Secretary: Albert F. Moreno, age 60
SVP; Interim President, Levi Strauss Europe, Middle East and Africa (LSEMA); President, Levi Strauss Asia Pacific: R. John Anderson, age 52, $546,413 pay
SVP and President, Europe Division: Paul Mason, age 42
SVP, Strategy and Commercial Development: Lawrence W. Ruff, age 47
SVP, Worldwide Human Resources: Fred Paulenich, age 39
SVP, World Supply Chain: Paul Harrington, age 42

VP, Global Tax Department: Paul Smith
Director of Internet Marketing: James (Jim) Stone
Director of Marketing (Canada): Julie Klee
U.S. Brand President: Robert Hanson
President, Dockers Brand: Bobbi Stilen
President, Levi Strauss Signature: Scott LaPorta
VP, Marketing, Levi Strauss Signature: Sherri Phillips
Auditors: KPMG LLP

LOCATIONS

HQ: Levi Strauss & Co.
1155 Battery St., San Francisco, CA 94111
Phone: 415-501-6000 **Fax:** 415-501-7112
Web: www.levistrauss.com

Levi Strauss & Co. manufactures and sells its branded jeans, sportswear, and dress pants through retail locations and company-owned outlets in more than 100 countries.

2003 Sales

	$ mil.	% of total
Americas	2,606.3	64
Europe	1,053.6	26
Asia	430.8	10
Total	**4,090.7**	**100**

PRODUCTS/OPERATIONS

2003 Sales

	% of total
Levi's jeans	76
Dockers pants	24
Total	**100**

Selected Brand Names

501	Levi's
505	Levi's Engineered
Dockers	Levi's Red
Dockers K-1	Levi's Silvertab
Dockers Premium	Levi's Type 1
Dockers Recode	ProStyle
Dress Mobile	Pure Blue
Flat Front Mobile	Red Tab
Go Khaki	Superlow

Operating Divisions

Asia Pacific Division
Levi Strauss Europe, Middle East, Africa
Levi Strauss, the Americas
  Levi Strauss & Co. (Canada) Inc.
  Levi Strauss Argentina
  Levi Strauss do Brasil
  Levi Strauss Mexico
  Levi Strauss U.S.

COMPETITORS

Abercrombie & Fitch
American Eagle Outfitters
Benetton
Calvin Klein
Diesel
Eddie Bauer
Fruit of the Loom
FUBU
Gap
Guess
Haggar
J. C. Penney
J. Crew
Jones Apparel
Limited Brands
Liz Claiborne
Nautica Enterprises
OshKosh B'Gosh
Oxford Industries
Polo Ralph Lauren
Tommy Hilfiger
Tropical Sportswear
VF
Warnaco Group

HISTORICAL FINANCIALS

Company Type: Private

Income Statement
FYE: Last Sunday in November

	REVENUE ($ mil.)	NET INCOME ($ mil.)	NET PROFIT MARGIN	EMPLOYEES
11/03	4,091	(349)	—	12,300
11/02	4,137	25	0.6%	12,400
11/01	4,259	151	3.5%	16,700
11/00	4,645	223	4.8%	17,300
11/99	5,140	5	0.1%	30,000
11/98	5,959	103	1.7%	30,000
11/97	6,862	138	2.0%	37,000
11/96	7,136	465	6.5%	37,000
11/95	6,707	735	11.0%	37,700
11/94	6,074	558	9.2%	36,500
Annual Growth	(4.3%)	—	—	(11.4%)

2003 Year-End Financials

Debt ratio: — Current ratio: 1.87
Return on equity: — Long-term debt ($ mil.): 2,651
Cash ($ mil.): 204

Net Income History

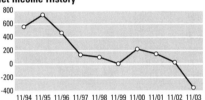

Levitz Home Furnishings

The lamps stay lit at Levitz Home Furnishings, the holding company for Levitz Furniture Incorporated (LFI) and Seaman Furniture. LFI (parent company of the Levitz Furniture Corp. chain) has about 75 stores (half in California), while Seaman has more than 50 stores in the northeastern US. The creation of Levitz Home Furnishings in 2001 allowed LFI to emerge from Chapter 11 bankruptcy (originally filed in 1997), in part by distributing management of its 15 East Coast stores to Seaman. The alliance also combines the two companies' administration, advertising, distribution, merchandising, and warehousing efforts.

Former CEO Alan Rosenberg, credited for taking the Seaman's chain out of bankruptcy and merging it with Levitz (also in bankruptcy), died in November 2003.

EXECUTIVES

Chairman and CEO; CEO, Levitz Furniture Incorporated and Seaman Furniture: Jay Carothers
President and COO: C. Mark Scott
SVP, Finance: Coleen A. Colreavy
Divisional VP, Advertising: Greg Ackerman
CTO: William (Bill) Kelly
Executive Administration: Sybil Handwerker

LOCATIONS

HQ: Levitz Home Furnishings, Inc.
300 Crossways Park Dr., Woodbury, NY 11797
Phone: 516-496-9560 **Fax:** 631-927-1780
Web: www.levitz.com

COMPETITORS

Bombay Company
Cost Plus
Dillard's
Ethan Allen
Euromarket Designs
Federated
IKEA
J. C. Penney
Jennifer Convertibles
La-Z-Boy
Mattress Giant
May
Pier 1 Imports
Sleepy's
Williams-Sonoma

HISTORICAL FINANCIALS

Company Type: Private

Income Statement
FYE: April 30

	REVENUE ($ mil.)	NET INCOME ($ mil.)	NET PROFIT MARGIN	EMPLOYEES
4/03	1,000	—	—	4,000
4/02	915	—	—	4,900
4/01	920	—	—	4,400
Annual Growth	4.3%	—	—	(4.7%)

Revenue History

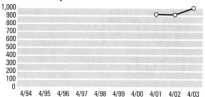

Liberty Mutual

Liberty Mutual wants more liberty. One of the top five property & casualty insurers in the US, the firm gained more flexibility in dealing with rapidly changing markets by reorganizing as a mutual holding company. Liberty Mutual has alliances with health care providers to manage disability care and it also offers homeowners and auto insurance, workers' compensation, retirement products, and group and individual life insurance. Other services include risk-prevention services (analyzing work sites and practices for safety), consulting, rehabilitation case management, and physical rehabilitation centers.

After failing to find a buyer, asset manager subsidiary Liberty Financial sold itself off little by little. Canadian insurer Sun Life acquired Keyport Life Insurance and mutual fund distributor Independent Financial Marketing Group. Liberty Financial's investment management segment (including subsidiaries Crabbe Huston, Stein Roe & Farnham, and Liberty Wanger Asset Management) was snapped up by FleetBoston (now part of the Bank of America empire). The company plans to spend the money it received from the sale of Liberty Financial on new acquisitions. Liberty Mutual has taken what is left of Liberty Financial private and merged it into one of its subsidiaries.

The company's diversification efforts include Liberty International, which provides insurance and occupational health and safety services in such countries as Canada, Japan, Mexico, Singapore, and the UK.

Liberty Mutual saw its results improve in 2003, thanks in part to rising insurance rates and the lack of natural disasters. The company also grew its international presence in areas such as China and southern Europe. Strengthening its personal lines business, Liberty Mutual bought Prudential's domestic property & casualty operations and MetLife's auto business in Spain.

HISTORY

The need for financial aid to workers injured on the job was recognized in Europe in the late 19th century but did not make its way to the US until a workers' compensation law for federal employees was passed in 1908. Massachusetts was one of the first states to enact similar legislation. Liberty Mutual was founded in Boston in 1912 to fill this newly recognized niche.

Liberty Mutual followed the fire insurance practice of taking an active part in loss prevention. It evaluated clients' premises and procedures and recommended ways to prevent accidents. The company rejected the budding industry practice of limiting medical fees, instead studying the most effective ways to reduce the long-term cost of a claim by getting the injured party back to work.

In 1942 the company acquired the United Mutual Fire Insurance Company (founded 1908, renamed Liberty Mutual Fire Insurance Company in 1949). The next year it founded a rehabilitation center in Boston to treat injured workers and to test treatments.

In the 1960s and 1970s, Liberty Mutual expanded its line to include life insurance (1963), group pensions (1970), and IRAs (1975).

Seeking to increase its national presence, the company formed Liberty Northwest Insurance Corporation in 1983. It continued expanding its offerings, with new subsidiaries in commercial, personal, and excess lines and, in 1986, by moving into financial services by buying Stein Roe & Farnham (founded 1958).

The expansion/diversification strategy seemed to work. Earnings between 1984 and 1986 more than tripled. Then came the downturn: Recession was followed by a string of natural disasters, and Liberty Mutual's income fell sharply between 1986 and 1988. In 1992 and 1993 the firm lost suits to Coors and Outboard Marine for failing to back those companies in environmental litigation cases.

Liberty Mutual restructured in 1994, withdrawing from the group health business and reorganizing claims operations into two units: Personal Markets and Business Markets. The next year it gained a foothold in the UK when it received permission to invest in a Lloyd's of London syndicate management company.

The company expanded its financial services operations in 1995 and 1996, merging its Liberty Financial subsidiary with the already-public Colonial Group; it also acquired American Asset Management and Newport Pacific Management.

In a soft workers' compensation market, the company tried to build its position through key market acquisitions. In 1997 Liberty Mutual acquired bankrupt workers' comp provider Golden Eagle Insurance of California; the next year the firm bought Florida's Summit Holding Southeast. Mutual funds were also on the shopping list: Purchases included Société Générale's US mutual funds unit, led by international money dean Jean-Marie Eveillard. The firm also played suitor to high-performance trust fund SIFE; the $450 million proposal was rebuffed as ungenerous. In 1998 the company was slammed by increased claims — many related to a Condé Nast Building construction accident that shut down New York City's Times Square that summer. Liberty Mutual acquired erstwhile competitor Employers Insurance of Wausau that year.

In 1999 the company bought Guardian Royal Exchange's US operations. In a new international initiative that year, Liberty Mutual bought 70% of Singapore-based insurer Citystate Holdings (to be renamed Liberty Citystate) as its foothold in Asia. The following year the company made plans to form a mutual holding company to raise funds for acquisitions.

Slumping property & casualty lines and the events of September 11 (the company paid out some $500 million in claims) hit Liberty Mutual in 2001. The company rebounded nicely in 2002-03, thanks to the rebounding stock market and strategic acquisitions worldwide.

EXECUTIVES

Chairman, President, and CEO: Edmund F. (Ted) Kelly, age 58
EVP, Auto & Home Markets: J. Paul Condrin III
EVP, Commercial Markets: Gary R. Gregg
EVP, Regional Agency Markets: Roger L. Jean
EVP, International Markets: Thomas C. Ramey, age 57
SVP and CFO: Dennis J. Langwell
SVP and CIO: Terry L. Conner
SVP and Chief Investment Officer:
 A. Alexander Fontanes
SVP and General Counsel: Christopher C. Mansfield
SVP and Chief Actuary: Robert T. Muleski
SVP, Human Resources and Administration:
 Helen E. R. Sayles
SVP, Communications: Stephen G. Sullivan
VP and Comptroller: John D. Doyle
VP and Secretary: Dexter R. Legg
VP and Treasurer: Laurance H.S. Yahia
Auditors: Ernst & Young LLP

LOCATIONS

HQ: Liberty Mutual Insurance Company
175 Berkeley St., Boston, MA 02116
Phone: 617-357-9500 **Fax:** 617-350-7648
Web: www.libertymutual.com

Liberty Mutual Insurance has about 800 offices in the US, as well as in Argentina, Australia, Bermuda, Brazil, Canada, China, Colombia, Hong Kong, Ireland, Japan, Malaysia, Mexico, Portugal, Singapore, Spain, Thailand, the UK, and Venezuela.

PRODUCTS/OPERATIONS

2003 Assets

	$ mil.	% of total
Cash & equivalents	1,999	3
Treasury & agency securities	2,717	4
Mortgage & asset-backed securities	11,499	18
State & municipal bonds	718	1
Corporate bonds	17,353	27
Stocks	1,346	2
Receivables	5,238	8
Recoverables	12,227	19
Other	11,325	18
Total	**64,422**	**100**

2003 Sales

	$ mil.	% of total
Premiums	13,956	84
Investment income	1,762	11
Investment gains	373	2
Fees & other revenues	527	3
Total	16,618	100

Selected Product Lines
Annuities
Disability insurance
General liability
Individual and group auto and property insurance
Individual and group life
Investment advice and management
Mutual funds
Workers' compensation

Selected Operating Units
Liberty International
  Liberty ART SA (Argentina)
  Liberty Citystate (Singapore)
  Liberty International Canada
  Liberty International Underwriters
  Liberty Japan
  Liberty Mexico Seguros
  Liberty Mutual Insurance Company (Japan)
  Liberty Mutual Insurance Company (UK) Ltd.
  Liberty Paulista de Seguros (Brazil)
  Liberty Seguros SA (Colombia)
  Liberty Venezuela (merger between Seguros
    Panamerican and Seguros Caracas)
Liberty Mutual Group
  Colorado Casualty
  Golden Eagle Insurance Co.
  Indiana Insurance Company
  Liberty Northwest Insurance Corporation
  Merchants and Businessmen's Insurance Company
  Montgomery Mutual Insurance Company
  Peerless Insurance
  Summit Holding Southeast
  Wausau

COMPETITORS

21st Century	Lincoln National
ACE Limited	MassMutual
AEGON USA	MetLife
AIG	New York Life
Allianz	Northwestern Mutual
Allstate	Progressive Corporation
Charles Schwab	Prudential
CIGNA	Safeco
Citigroup	St. Paul Travelers
CNA Financial	State Farm
COUNTRY Insurance	T. Rowe Price
Fremont General	USAA
GenAmerica	Washington National
The Hartford	Corporation
ING	

HISTORICAL FINANCIALS
Company Type: Mutual company

Income Statement
FYE: December 31

	ASSETS ($ mil.)	NET INCOME ($ mil.)	INCOME AS % OF ASSETS	EMPLOYEES
12/03	64,422	851	1.3%	38,000
12/02	55,877	508	0.9%	35,000
12/01	53,065	(289)	—	35,000
12/00	30,264	403	1.3%	37,000
12/99	55,259	501	0.9%	37,440
12/98	26,254	245	0.9%	24,000
12/97	25,230	412	1.6%	23,000
12/96	22,690	474	2.1%	23,000
12/95	21,791	457	2.1%	23,000
12/94	20,144	451	2.2%	22,000
Annual Growth	13.5%	7.3%	—	6.3%

2003 Year-End Financials
Equity as % of assets: 11.5%   Long-term debt ($ mil.): 1,668
Return on assets: 1.4%   Sales ($ mil.): 16,618
Return on equity: 12.3%

Net Income History

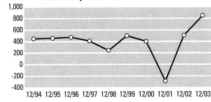

Life Care Centers

Life Care Centers of America is a privately owned operator of retirement and health care centers. The company manages more than 260 facilities in 28 states — including retirement communities, assisted-living facilities, and nursing homes — and provides specialized services such as home health care. Life Care also operates centers specifically for people with Alzheimer's disease or related dementia. Founder Forrest Preston opened his first center in 1970, and the company continues to tout a "corporate culture grounded in the Judeo-Christian ethic." However, Life Care has faced complaints of poor-quality care, part of a problem that plagues the industry overall.

EXECUTIVES
Chairman: Forrest L. Preston
President: Don J. Giardina
CFO: Steve Ziegler
EVP: Beecher Hunter
President, Life Care at Home: Tony E. Oglesby
EVP and Director of Operations, Garden Terrace Associates: Trent Tolbert
SVP, Operations East: Cathy Murray
SVP, Operations West: James W. Scadlock
VP, Life Care at Home: Mary R. Maurer
Director, Public Relations: Sebrena Sawtell
Webmaster: Paul Garner

LOCATIONS
HQ: Life Care Centers of America
  3570 Keith St. NW, Cleveland, TN 37320
Phone: 423-472-9585   **Fax:** 423-339-8337
Web: www.lcca.com

COMPETITORS
Advocat
Assisted Living Concepts
Beverly Enterprises
Kindred
Manor Care
Mariner Health Care
National HealthCare
Sun Healthcare

HISTORICAL FINANCIALS
Company Type: Private

Income Statement
FYE: December 31

	ESTIMATED REVENUE ($ mil.)	NET INCOME ($ mil.)	NET PROFIT MARGIN	EMPLOYEES
12/02	1,460	—	—	30,000
12/01	1,328	—	—	30,000
12/00	1,265	—	—	29,350
12/99	1,210	—	—	26,000
12/98	1,210	—	—	22,000
12/97	1,100	—	—	22,000
12/96	1,000	—	—	22,000
Annual Growth	6.5%			5.3%

Revenue History

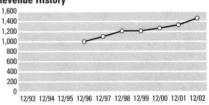

LifeBridge Health

Like a bridge over troubled waters, LifeBridge Health links ailing patients to care and healing. Serving the Baltimore region, the company operates two acute care hospitals — Sinai Hospital of Baltimore and Northwest Hospital Center — and two long-term and subacute care facilities, Levindale Hebrew Geriatric Center and Hospital and Jewish Convalescent & Nursing Home. The health system has more than 1,100 beds total. Other operations include LifeBridge Health & Fitness and three LifeBridge Medical Care Centers.

EXECUTIVES
President and CEO: Warren Green
CFO: Charles Orlando
SVP; President and COO, Northwest Hospital Center:
  Erik G. Wexler
VP, Development: Joel L. Simon
VP, Campus Services: Robert (Bob) Turner
CIO: Karen Barker
Director, Marketing: Jill Bloom

LOCATIONS
HQ: LifeBridge Health, Inc.
  2401 W. Belvedere Ave., Baltimore, MD 21215
Phone: 410-601-9000   **Fax:** 410-601-8492
Web: www.lifebridgehealth.org

HISTORICAL FINANCIALS
Company Type: Not-for-profit

Income Statement
FYE: June 30

	REVENUE ($ mil.)	NET INCOME ($ mil.)	NET PROFIT MARGIN	EMPLOYEES
6/03	672	—	—	5,595

Lifetime

Lifetime Entertainment Services hopes viewers make a long-term commitment to its television programs. The company operates three woman-oriented cable-TV networks (Lifetime, Lifetime Movie Network, Lifetime Real Women) offering original movies, talk shows, and syndicated shows. Its Lifetime channel reaches 87 million US households and is one of the highest-rated cable networks in prime time. The Lifetime Online unit offers information and entertainment on the Web. The firm launched *Lifetime* magazine in 2003, but decided to halt publication in fall 2004. Lifetime was formed by the merger of channels Daytime and Cable Health Network in 1984. It's jointly owned by Walt Disney (via Disney ABC Cable) and Hearst.

EXECUTIVES

President and CEO: Carole Black
EVP and CFO: James Wesley
EVP and General Manager: Rick Haskins
EVP Distribution and Business Development: Louise Henry Bryson
EVP Entertainment: Barbara Fisher
EVP Legal, Business Affairs, and Human Resources: Patricia Langer
EVP Public Affairs and Corporate Communications: Meredith Wagner
EVP Research: Tim Brooks
EVP Sales; EVP and General Manager, Lifetime Television Network: Lynn Picard
SVP Finance: Paul Jennings
SVP Information Technology: Dan Thatte
SVP Operations, Information Systems, and Technology: Gwynne McConkey
SVP Publicity: Carla Princi
VP Corporate Communications: Katherine Urbon
VP Marketing: Catherine Moran

LOCATIONS

HQ: Lifetime Entertainment Services
309 W. 49th St., New York, NY 10019
Phone: 212-424-7000 **Fax:** 212-957-4449
Web: www.lifetimetv.com

PRODUCTS/OPERATIONS

Operations
Lifetime Movie Network
Lifetime Real Women
Lifetime Television Network
Lifetime TV Store

Selected Programming
Any Day Now
Denise Austin
Designing Women
Golden Girls
Intimate Portrait
Lifetime Now
Mad About You
Merge
Strong Medicine

COMPETITORS

A&E Networks
CPB
Crown Media
Discovery Communications
Fox Entertainment
Harpo
iVillage
Martha Stewart Living
NBC
Oxygen Media
Paxson Communications
Rainbow Media
Viacom
Walt Disney

HISTORICAL FINANCIALS
Company Type: Joint venture

Income Statement
FYE: December 31

	REVENUE ($ mil.)	NET INCOME ($ mil.)	NET PROFIT MARGIN	EMPLOYEES
12/03	820	—	—	—
12/02	790	—	—	—
12/01	727	—	—	—
12/00	661	—	—	—
12/99	528	—	—	—
12/98	468	—	—	—
12/97	398	—	—	300
12/96	257	—	—	270
12/95	271	—	—	—
12/94	241	—	—	—
Annual Growth	14.6%	—	—	11.1%

Revenue History

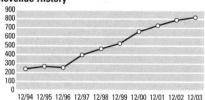

Lincoln Property

Lincoln Property is one of the US's largest diversified real estate companies — honest! Lincoln began by building apartments in the Dallas area, then expanded into commercial and retail projects. It now has residential properties comprising more than 150,000 units and has developed about 140 million sq. ft. of commercial properties nationwide (still managing some 93 million). Lincoln has joint ventures with Lend Lease to develop commercial property and with Sam Zell's Equity Residential Properties to build apartments. Its joint venture with American International Group is active in Central and Western Europe. CEO Mack Pogue cofounded Lincoln in 1965 with Trammell Crow, whose stake Pogue bought out in 1977.

EXECUTIVES

Chairman and CEO: A. Mack Pogue
VP, Secretary, and Treasurer: Nancy Davis
President and CEO, Commercial Division; Chairman, Lincoln Harris: William C. Duvall
President and CEO, Residential Division: J. Timothy Byrne
President, Lincoln Advisory Group: Gary Kobus
President, Lincoln Harris: John Harris
COO, Commercial Division: Gregory S. Courtwright
CFO, Residential Division: Dennis Streit
SVP and General Counsel, Residential Division: Dan M. Jacks
SVP and Operating Partner, Midwest, Residential Division: Brian Byrne
SVP and Operating Partner, Southwest, Residential Division: Jeffrey T. Courtwright
SVP and Operating Parner, Northeast/MidAtlantic, Residential Division: Jeff B. Franzen
SVP and Operating Partner, Midwest, Residential Division: Kevin Keane
SVP and Operating Partner, Southeast, Residential Division: Charles O. Shallat
Human Resources Director: Luanne Hudson

LOCATIONS

HQ: Lincoln Property Company
3300 Lincoln Plaza, 500 N. Akard, Dallas, TX 75201
Phone: 214-740-3300 **Fax:** 214-740-3441
Web: www.lincolnproperty.com

Lincoln Property has US offices in Arizona, California, Colorado, Florida, Georgia, Illinois, Louisiana, Massachusetts, New Jersey, New York, North Carolina, Pennsylvania, Texas, and Washington, DC. It has international offices in the Czech Republic, Germany, Hungary, Italy, Poland, and Spain.

PRODUCTS/OPERATIONS

Services
Corporate Property Services
  Brokerage
  Design & construction management
  Facility management
  Portfolio management
Investment Property Services
  Accounting
  Advisory
  Design & construction management
  Engineering
  Financial
  Leasing
  Property management

COMPETITORS

AIMCO
Archstone-Smith Trust
Boston Properties
CarrAmerica
CB Richard Ellis
Colliers International
Cushman & Wakefield
Duke Realty
Equity Office Properties
Equity Residential
Fairfield Residential
Gale Company
Grubb & Ellis
Hines Interests
Inland Group
JMB Realty
Jones Lang LaSalle
Mack-Cali
New America International
Newmark
Opus
Pinnacle
Related Capital
Rouse
Simon Property Group
Sperry Van Ness
Staubach
Tishman
Trammell Crow Company
Trammell Crow Residential
Transwestern Commercial Services
United Dominion Realty

HISTORICAL FINANCIALS
Company Type: Private

Income Statement
FYE: June 30

	REVENUE ($ mil.)	NET INCOME ($ mil.)	NET PROFIT MARGIN	EMPLOYEES
6/02	1,766	—	—	5,000
6/01	1,352	—	—	4,900
6/00	1,251	—	—	4,900
6/99	1,462	—	—	4,900
6/98	1,399	—	—	4,529
6/97	1,165	—	—	4,054
6/96	1,115	—	—	4,025
6/95	1,100	—	—	4,191
6/94	1,000	—	—	4,200
Annual Growth	7.4%	—	—	2.2%

Revenue History

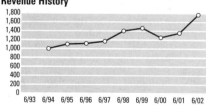

L.L. Bean

With L.L. Bean, you can tame the great outdoors — or just look as if you could. The outdoor apparel and gear maker mails more than 200 million catalogs per year. Products include outerwear, sportswear, housewares, footwear, camping and hiking gear, fishing gear, and the Maine hunting shoe upon which the company was built. L.L. Bean also operates five retail and 16 factory outlets in the US, with nine additional stores in Japan. It also sells online through English- and Japanese-language Web sites. L.L. Bean was founded in 1912 by Leon Leonwood Bean and is controlled by his descendants.

From a pair of waterproof hunting boots in 1911, L.L. Bean's empire is based on catalogs mailed out under 95 different titles and advertising 16,000 products. Catalog sales account for 80% of L.L. Bean's revenue. L.L. Bean's flagship store in Freeport, Maine (known by locals as "the Bean") attracts 3 million visitors annually and is open 24 hours a day, 365 days a year. The company plans to open more retail outlets. Retail sales currently account for 20% of L.L. Bean's revenue; the company would like to see that number eventually rise to 50%. L.L. Bean also plans to scale back the number of catalog titles it offers.

L.L. Bean's famous customer service is exemplified by its liberal return policies and perpetual replacement of the rubber soles of its Maine Hunting Shoe. The company also offers seminars and events on such topics as fly fishing, sea kayaking, and outdoor photography.

In 2004 L.L. Bean pursued legal action against four retailers, including Nordstrom and J. C. Penney. The suit claims trademark infringement on the company's Web site connected with pop-up advertisements redirecting customer traffic to Web sites engineered by the alleged offenders. L.L. Bean claims that the actions of the pop-up advertisements appear to imply endorsement by L.L. Bean. The company hosting the pop-up advertisements filed a counter-suit a few weeks later, claiming that L.L. Bean's suit is frivolous in nature.

HISTORY

Leon Leonwood Bean started out as a storekeeper in Freeport, Maine. Tired of wet, leaky boots, he experimented with various remedies and in 1911 came up with the Maine Hunting Shoe, a boot with rubber soles and feet and leather uppers. It became his most famous product.

From its outset in 1912, Bean's company was a mail-order house. The first batch of boots was a disaster: Almost all of them leaked. But Bean's willingness to correct his product's defects quickly, at his own expense, saved the company.

Maine's hunting licensing system, implemented in 1917, provided the company with a mailing list of affluent recreational hunters in the Northeast, and that year Bean opened a showroom to accommodate the customers stopping by his Freeport workshop.

Bean cultivated the image of the folksy Maine guide, offering durable, comfortable, weather-resistant clothes and reliable camping supplies. In 1920 Bean built a store on Main Street in Freeport. L.L. Bean continued to grow and add products, even during the Depression, and sales reached $1 million in 1937.

During WWII Bean helped design the boots used by the US military, and his company manufactured them, thus remaining afloat as the war years and rationing brought cutbacks in materials and outdoor activities. He began keeping the retail store open 24 hours a day in 1951, noting that he had "thrown away the keys." Bean added a women's department three years later.

Sales rose to $2 million in the early 1960s and were at $4.8 million when Bean died in 1967 at age 94. (He had resisted growing the business bigger, saying, "I'm eating three meals a day; I can't eat four.") The new president was Bean's grandson Leon Gorman, who had started with L.L. Bean in 1960. His early attempts at updating the mailing operations (mailing labels typed by hand and correspondence kept in cardboard boxes) had been vetoed by his grandfather. Gorman brought in new people and made improvements, including automating the mailing systems, improving the manufacturing systems, and targeting new, nonsporting markets (like women's casual clothes).

L.L. Bean continued its transition by targeting more of its classic customer profile — upper-middle-class college graduates — and sales grew about 20% annually for most of the 1980s. By 1989, however, sales had slowed and growth flattened as the national economy slumped and imitators carried away market share.

Unsolicited catalog orders had been coming in from Japan since the late 1980s, so in 1992 L.L. Bean began a joint venture with Seiyu and Matsushita Electric Industrial. Their first store opened that year (the company opened a catalog and service center in Japan in 1995). L.L. Kids began in 1993.

In 1996 the company began an online shopping service. Sparked by the success of its L.L. Kids division, which grew 300% in four years, the company opened a separate children's store in Freeport the next year. The company opened its second full-line store in 2000 near Washington, DC. L.L. Bean plans to continue opening retail stores in the eastern US.

L.L. Bean veteran Chris McCormick was named president and CEO in May 2001; Gorman remained chairman. McCormick is the first person outside of the Bean family to head the company.

In January 2002 L.L. Bean laid off 175 employees (about 4% of its workforce); in early 2003 it cut about 500 more jobs and offered an early retirement program which was accepted by an additional 200 employees.

EXECUTIVES

Chairman: Leon A. Gorman, age 67
President and CEO: Chris McCormick, age 46
Chief Retail Officer: Edward R. (Ed) Howell
SVP and CFO: Mark Fasold
SVP and COO: Bob Peixotto
SVP and General Manager, Retail: Ken Kacere
Senior Systems Analyst: Patrick Carroll
Director of Human Resources: Anne Sowles
Director of IT Operations: Stafford Soule
Senior Product Developer: Sandra Rossi
Advertising Manager: Denise Karkos
PR Spokesman: Rich Donaldson
Director of Logistics: James (Jim) Helming
CIT, Manager of Engineering, Distribution Operations: David Lockman
VP E-Commerce: Mary Lou Kelley
Chief Merchandising Officer: Fran Philip

LOCATIONS

HQ: L.L. Bean, Inc.
Casco Street, Freeport, ME 04033
Phone: 207-865-4761   **Fax:** 207-552-6821
Web: www.llbean.com

L.L. Bean sells through direct-mail catalogs and has retail stores and outlet stores in the US and Japan. It manufactures some of its merchandise in Maine.

PRODUCTS/OPERATIONS

Selected Catalogs
Corporate Sales (custom embroidered clothing and luggage)
Fly Fishing (equipment, outer wear, and accessories)
Home (linens, pillows, and decorating)
L.L. Bean
L.L. Bean Hunting
Outdoor Discovery Schools (classes and symposiums)
Outdoors (seasonal outdoor wear and accessories)
Traveler (clothing, luggage, and accessories)

Selected Products
Home and garden accessories
Men's, women's, and children's casual apparel
Outdoor classes
Outer wear
Shoes and boots
Sports gear and apparel
Travel apparel and luggage

COMPETITORS

Abercrombie & Fitch	Limited Brands
American Eagle Outfitters	May
American Retail	Nautica Enterprises
Bass Pro Shops	Norm Thompson
Cabela's	North Face
Coldwater Creek	Orvis Company
Coleman	OshKosh B'Gosh
Columbia Sportswear	Patagonia
Dillard's	Polo Ralph Lauren
Eddie Bauer	Redcats
Fast Retailing	REI
Federated	Sears
Foot Locker	Spiegel
Gap	Sports Authority
J. C. Penney	Sportsman's Guide
J. Crew	Talbots
J. Jill Group	Target
Johnson Outdoors	Timberland
Lands' End	Tommy Hilfiger
Levi Strauss	

HISTORICAL FINANCIALS

Company Type: Private

Income Statement
FYE: February 28

	REVENUE ($ mil.)	NET INCOME ($ mil.)	NET PROFIT MARGIN	EMPLOYEES
2/03	1,070	—	—	3,800
2/02	1,140	—	—	4,500
2/01	1,100	—	—	4,700
2/00	1,100	—	—	4,000
1/99	1,070	—	—	4,000
2/98	1,068	—	—	3,600
2/97	1,040	—	—	3,500
2/96	1,078	—	—	3,800
2/95	976	—	—	3,800
2/94	867	—	—	3,500
Annual Growth	2.4%	—	—	0.9%

Loews Cineplex

Running a theater chain has its highs and Loews. With more than 2,100 screens in some 200 theaters worldwide, Loews Cineplex Entertainment (the oldest theater circuit in North America) hopes to maintain the highs as one of the world's leading theater chains. It operates the Loews Theatres and Star Theatres brands and has a partnership with Magic Johnson Theaters in the US; it also owns and operates Cineplex Odeon in Canada and Cinemex Theatres in Mexico, as well as stakes in theaters in Spain (Yelmo Cineplex) and South Korea (Megabox Cineplex). Bain Capital, The Carlyle Group, and Spectrum Equity Investors purchased Loews Cineplex from Onex Corporation and Oaktree Capital Management in 2004 for $1.5 billion.

Loews Cineplex had previously struggled in a US market overstuffed with theater seats and had operated under Chapter 11 bankruptcy protection in 2001. The company was not alone — many theater chains filed for bankruptcy protection that year in an industry-wide wave of red ink that was blamed on opening too many multiplex theaters while attendance dwindled at older locations. An investment group led by Onex Corporation acquired Loews Cineplex when it emerged from bankruptcy in 2002.

Later that year the chain filed to go public. However, Loews cancelled its IPO due to unsteady market conditions. It subsequently entered merger discussions with theater chain AMC Entertainment, but talks ended in 2004 with the two companies unable to reach an agreement. Months later the company hired investment banks to help explore strategic alternatives, resulting in a group of buyout firms led by Bain Capital becoming the company's next owners.

HISTORY

Marcus Loew started Loews Theatres in 1904 with a nickelodeon in Ohio. He bought a silent movie production company called Metro and merged it with The Goldwyn Pictures Corporation and Louis B. Mayer Pictures to form MGM in 1924. Loews Theatres continued to show MGM films until 1959, when an antitrust ruling forced studios to give up control of theaters. It changed owners twice in the next 35 years before Sony Corporation acquired it in 1989.

Garth Drabinsky started Cineplex with an 18-screen theater in the basement of a Toronto shopping center in 1979. It did well, but was encumbered by debts. That led him to The Bronfman Group, which invested in the company. Cineplex then bought Canadian Odeon theaters in 1985 and became Cineplex Odeon. MCA (now Universal Studios) took over in 1986. Dramatic expansion coupled with Drabinsky's shaky financial decisions (heavy debt, irregular accounting practices) led to his ouster in 1989. (A decade later Drabinsky was booted from theater company Livent over fraud allegations.)

Loews and Cineplex Odeon merged in 1998, and the new company announced plans to shutter 550 older screens (mostly Cineplex Odeons). In 1999 the company began a joint venture with Aurelio De Laurentiis to build multiplexes in Italy. It struggled with financial problems throughout 2000. In 2001, Onex Corporation led an investment group in an agreement to acquire Loews Cineplex. Also that year Universal Studios (who at the time was operating as Vivendi UNIVERSAL Entertainment) sold its stake in the firm to Goldman Sachs. Onex completed its acquisition in 2002 following Loews' emergence from bankruptcy.

The company celebrated its 100 year anniversary in 2004, and a corporation formed by Bain Capital, The Carlyle Group, and Spectrum Equity Investors acquired the chain from Onex that year.

EXECUTIVES

President and CEO: Travis Reid
President, US Division: Michael P. Norris
President of Cineplex Odeon Corporation, Canada: Sam DiMichele
CEO, Grupo Cinemex: Miguel Angel Davila
SVP, CFO, and Treasurer: John J. Walker
SVP and Coporate Counsel: Michael Politi
SVP and Head Film Buyer: Steven (Steve) Bunnell
SVP and CIO: James (Jim) Fagerstrom
SVP Marketing: John McCauley
SVP Real Estate: Alan Benjamin
VP Finance and Controller: Bryan Berndt
VP Human Resources, US: Allan Fox
Auditors: PricewaterhouseCoopers LLP

LOCATIONS

HQ: Loews Cineplex Entertainment Corporation
711 5th Ave., 11th Fl., New York, NY 10022
Phone: 646-521-6200
Web: www.loewscineplex.com

Loews Cineplex Entertainment Corporation operates theaters in Canada, Mexico, South Korea, Spain, and the US.

PRODUCTS/OPERATIONS

Selected Theater Brands
Cinemex (Mexico)
Cineplex Odeon (Canada)
Magic Johnson Theaters (US)
Megabox Cineplex (South Korea)
Star Theatres (US)
Yelmo Cineplex (Spain)

COMPETITORS

AMC Entertainment
Carmike Cinemas
Century Theatres
Cinemark
Cineplex Galaxy
Famous Players
Hoyts Cinemas
National Amusements
Pacific Theatres
Rainbow Movies
Regal Entertainment

HISTORICAL FINANCIALS

Company Type: Private

Income Statement
FYE: Last day in February

	REVENUE ($ mil.)	NET INCOME ($ mil.)	NET PROFIT MARGIN	EMPLOYEES
2/03	1,772	—	—	—
2/02	856	—	—	16,500
2/01	904	—	—	14,000
2/00	930	—	—	16,300
2/99	851	—	—	16,000
2/98	414	—	—	12,442
2/97	375	—	—	—
2/96	359	—	—	—
2/95	343	—	—	—
2/94	329	—	—	—
Annual Growth	20.6%	—	—	7.3%

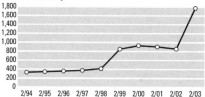

Longaberger

A tisket, a tasket, a Longaberger basket. The Longaberger Company is the #1 maker of handmade baskets in the US, selling nearly 10 million a year. The baskets are sold through in-home shows conducted by Longaberger's more than 70,000 independent sales associates. Baskets account for about half of sales, but the company also sells fabrics, pottery, and wrought-iron home accessories. Longaberger's home office is a seven-story rendition of a basket with two 75-ton handles on top. The company also owns a golf course, a hotel, and Longaberger Homestead (an events area with shops and restaurants). The family-owned firm is run by the daughters of the late Dave Longaberger, who founded the company in 1973.

EXECUTIVES

President and CEO: Tami Longaberger
CFO: Stephanie Imhoff
VP, Operations: Andy Neri
VP, Sales: Andrea Walters-Dowding
President, The Longaberger Foundation: Rachel Longaberger Stukey
CIO: Anne Dunlap
Director, Corporate Communications: Julie Moorehead
Public Relations: Jeanne M. Tiberio

LOCATIONS

HQ: The Longaberger Company
1500 E. Main St., Newark, OH 43055
Phone: 740-322-5000   **Fax:** 740-322-5240
Web: www.longaberger.com

The Longaberger Company has facilities in Dresden, Frazeyburg, Granville, Hartville, Nashport, Newark, and Malta, Ohio.

COMPETITORS

Bed Bath & Beyond
Bombay Company
Cost Plus
Euromarket Designs
Garden Ridge
Hobby Lobby
Kirkland's
Linens 'n Things
Michaels Stores
Pier 1 Imports
Williams-Sonoma

HISTORICAL FINANCIALS

Company Type: Private

Income Statement
FYE: December 31

	REVENUE ($ mil.)	NET INCOME ($ mil.)	NET PROFIT MARGIN	EMPLOYEES
12/03	911	—	—	7,350
12/02	906	—	—	7,300
12/01	970	—	—	7,000
12/00	1,000	—	—	8,000
12/99	819	—	—	7,500
12/98	700	—	—	7,000
12/97	611	—	—	5,800
12/96	520	—	—	5,100
12/95	410	—	—	5,026
12/94	340	—	—	4,500
Annual Growth	11.6%	—	—	5.6%

Revenue History

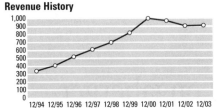

Louis Berger Group

What happens when you combine 100,000 miles of highway, 2,000 miles of railroad, 3,000 bridges, 100 airfields, and numerous environmental and water-supply projects with a bunch of engineers, scientists, economists, and archaeologists? You get The Louis Berger Group, a global engineering firm founded in 1953 by the late Dr. Louis Berger. The company — which provides civil, structural, mechanical, electrical, and environmental engineering services — has worked on high-profile projects such as the Pennsylvania Turnpike, the first toll expressway in the US. It has also won contracts to help rebuild Iraq's communications system, transportation infrastructure, and courthouses.

Among its recent projects in the US is work for the World Trade Center area. The Louis Berger Group, along with Hill International, has been selected by the Port Authority of New York and New Jersey to provide program management services for the engineering, final design, and construction of its Downtown Restoration Program for redevelopment of the World Trade Center and the WTC transportation hub.

Iraq reconstruction contracts awarded to the group include two in 2004 by the U.S. Agency for International Development (USAID) to help restructure and privatize state-owned businesses, promote small businesses, and provide vocational training.

EXECUTIVES

Chairman: Derish M. Wolff
President and CEO: Nicolas J. (Nick) Masucci
CFO: Leon Marantz
EVP and COO; Group VP, International Operations: Michel Jichlinski
IT Director: Randy Morgan
Chief Engineer: Kent Lande
SVP Cultural Resources: John A. Hotopp
SVP Energy Services: Kevin Young
SVP Justice Programs: Robert J. Nardi
SVP Ports, Waterways, and Airports: Isaac Shafran
SVP Transportation Planning, Economics and Environmental Science: Larry Pesesky
Manager Human Resources: Terry Williams
Auditors: PricewaterhouseCoopers

LOCATIONS

HQ: The Louis Berger Group, Inc.
100 Halsted St., East Orange, NJ 07018
Phone: 973-678-1960 **Fax:** 973-672-4284
Web: www.louisberger.com

The Louis Berger Group operates worldwide with offices in more than 60 countries.

PRODUCTS/OPERATIONS

Selected Services

Architecture
Construction management
Cultural resources
Development planning
Economic evaluations
Engineering design
Environmental compliance and analysis
Environmental permitting
Facilities and space planning
Geographic information systems
Maintenance management
Natural resource management
Operations planning and management
Pollution prevention
Privatization studies
Program management
Resident engineering and inspection
Urban planning
Water resources planning

COMPETITORS

AECOM
Black & Veatch
CH2M HILL
Day & Zimmermann
Edwards and Kelcey
HNTB
Hyundai Engineering and Construction
Jacobs Engineering
Kajima
Nishimatsu Construction
Parsons
Parsons Brinckerhoff
URS
VINCI

HISTORICAL FINANCIALS

Company Type: Private

Income Statement
FYE: June 30

	REVENUE ($ mil.)	NET INCOME ($ mil.)	NET PROFIT MARGIN	EMPLOYEES
6/04	541	—	—	4,000
6/03	328	—	—	3,800
6/02	259	—	—	3,782
6/01	398	—	—	3,722
6/00	378	—	—	3,000
6/99	307	—	—	3,000
6/98	312	—	—	2,800
6/97	307	—	—	2,800
6/96	278	—	—	2,800
6/95	170	—	—	—
Annual Growth	13.7%	—	—	4.6%

Revenue History

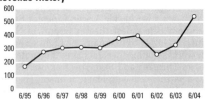

Love's Travel Stops

If you're a trucker or RVer on the road, all you need is Love's. Love's Travel Stops & Country Stores operates more than 80 truck stops throughout a swath of about 23 states from California to Virginia, as well as around 70 convenience stores in Colorado, Kansas, New Mexico, Oklahoma, and Texas. Each travel stop includes a convenience store, a fast-food restaurant, such as Taco Bell or Subway, and gas outlets for cars, trucks, and RVs. The travel stops also provide shower rooms, laundry facilities, game rooms, and mail drops. Love's Travel Stops & Country Stores is owned by the family of CEO Tom Love, who founded the company in 1964.

EXECUTIVES

Chairman and CEO: Tom Love
President and COO, Love's Development Companies: Greg Love
President, Love's Operating Companies: Frank Love
EVP and CFO: Doug Stussi
EVP, Store Operations: Tom Edwards
VP and CIO: Jim Xenos
VP, Construction: Terry Ross
Director, Human Resources: Carl Martincich
Director, Marketing: Mark Romig
Director, Sales: Don Van Curen
Director, Public Relations: Jenny Love Meyer

LOCATIONS

HQ: Love's Travel Stops & Country Stores, Inc.
10601 N. Pennsylvania Ave.,
Oklahoma City, OK 73120
Phone: 405-751-9000 **Fax:** 405-749-9110
Web: www.loves.com

COMPETITORS

7-Eleven	Pilot
Allsup's	Racetrac Petroleum
ChevronTexaco	Rip Griffin Truck Service Center
Exxon Mobil	
E-Z Mart Stores	Royal Dutch/Shell Group
FFP Operating	Stuckey's
Flying J	TravelCenters of America
Marathon Oil	Valero Energy
Petro Stopping Centers	Walgreen

HISTORICAL FINANCIALS

Company Type: Private

Income Statement FYE: December 31

	REVENUE ($ mil.)	NET INCOME ($ mil.)	NET PROFIT MARGIN	EMPLOYEES
12/02	1,300	—	—	3,800
12/01	1,086	—	—	3,200
12/00	894	—	—	3,150
12/99	614	—	—	2,500
Annual Growth	28.4%	—	—	15.0%

Revenue History

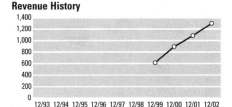

Lucasfilm

The Force is definitely with Emperor George Lucas. With three of the 20 highest-grossing films of all time, Lucasfilm is one of the most successful independent production companies in the history of cinema. Owned by filmmaker George Lucas (the brains behind the *Star Wars* and *Indiana Jones* films), Lucasfilm's productions have won 17 Academy Awards. Its most recent movie is 2002's *Star Wars: Episode II — Attack of the Clones*; Lucasfilm's previous release, 1999's *Episode I — The Phantom Menace*, has grossed more than $920 million worldwide and claims the #4 spot on the all-time list. Other subsidiaries in the Lucas empire are responsible for licensing, special effects, and software. Lucasfilm was created in 1971.

Lucasfilm consists of LucasArts (video games), Lucas Digital (special effects house Industrial Light + Magic and Skywalker Sound), Lucas Licensing (consumer products), and Lucas Online (e-commerce, news, and information). George Lucas also owns educational software firm Lucas Learning.

In 2002 Lucas spun-off digital sound systems firm THX as an independent company. The following year the company formed its Lucasfilm Animation unit to create digitally animated feature films and television productions. The 2003 release of Lucasfilm's *The Adventures of Indiana Jones: The Complete DVD Movie Collection* made record-breaking sales, and the company hit gold again with the DVD release of *The Star Wars Trilogy* in 2004.

The company has also expanded into Asia with the creation of Lucasfilm Animation Singapore. The unit, which will produce digital animation for movies, television, and games, is 75% owned by Lucasfilm. The remainder is held by a Singapore state-led consortium.

Lucasfilm is building a new headquarters and production center at the Presidio, a former Army base in San Francisco. A final sequel to the *Star Wars* series, *Episode III — Revenge of the Sith*, is slated for release in 2005.

HISTORY

After attending film school at the University of Southern California, George Lucas started his career as a documentary filmmaker, chronicling the production of Francis Ford Coppola's *Finian's Rainbow* in 1968. The two men became fast friends and founded American Zoetrope in 1969, which two years later released Lucas' feature film debut, the science-fiction film *THX 1138* (a full-length version of a student film he made at USC). The film flopped, and Coppola went into production on *The Godfather*. Lucas left American Zoetrope and created his own company, Lucasfilm, in 1971.

Two years later Lucas released *American Graffiti* through Universal Pictures (with some financial help from Coppola). The film was a smash hit; it raked in $115 million in the US and made him a millionaire before the age of 30. It also gave him the clout to try and get his most ambitious project off the ground, a space opera called *Star Wars*. Universal, frustrated with cost overruns on *Graffiti*, wanted no part of Lucas' seemingly ridiculous idea, so he went to 20th Century Fox, which agreed to finance the $10 million film. Lucas gave up his directing fee for a percentage of the box-office take and all merchandising rights. He created Industrial Light + Magic (ILM) and Sprocket Systems (later Skywalker Sound) in 1975 to produce the visual and sound effects needed for the film.

Star Wars cost about $12 million, and almost everyone involved was sure it would bomb. Released in 1977, the movie shattered every box-office record, and the merchandising rights Lucas obtained made him a multimillionaire. With his take from *Star Wars*, Lucas was able to finance the film's sequel, *The Empire Strikes Back* (1980), out of his own pocket, meaning he would receive most of the profits (it grossed more than $220 million domestically). Lucasfilm's next production was *Raiders of the Lost Ark* (1981), directed by Lucas' friend Steven Spielberg. It went on to gross more than $380 million worldwide.

The next year Lucas began developing the THX sound system in preparation for the 1983 release of the third *Star Wars* film, *Return of the Jedi* (which hauled in more than $260 million domestically). He also founded LucasArts in 1982 to develop video games. Lucasfilm completed Skywalker Ranch (a facility housing many of its various companies in Marin County, California) in the mid-1980s and filled out the decade with two *Raiders* sequels — *Indiana Jones and the Temple of Doom* (1984, $333 million worldwide) and *Indiana Jones and the Last Crusade* (1989, $495 million worldwide).

Lucasfilm reorganized in 1993 by spinning off LucasArts into a separate company and regrouping ILM and Skywalker Sound into a new company called Lucas Digital. Lucasfilm won local government approval to build an $87 million film studio near Skywalker Ranch in 1996, and the following year it re-released the *Star Wars Trilogy* to theaters with new special effects in celebration of the 20th anniversary, adding another $250 million to its take. Anticipating the release of the first of three prequels to the *Star Wars Trilogy*, Lucasfilm started signing marketing agreements in 1998 (including deals with Hasbro and Pepsi) that resulted in advance licensing of nearly $3 billion.

Star Wars: Episode I — The Phantom Menace opened in May 1999 and has grossed about $920 million worldwide (it finished its initial run second only to *Titanic*). Later in 1999 Lucas announced plans to develop a $250 million digital arts center at the old Presidio army base in San Francisco to house ILM, LucasArts, Lucas Learning, Lucas Online, THX, and the George Lucas Educational Foundation.

The next film in the *Star Wars* series, *Episode II — Attack of the Clones*, opened in May 2002. In early 2003 the company reorganized, bringing in Lucas Digital, LucasArts Entertainment, and Lucas Licensing (which had previously been operating as independent companies) as subsidiaries under the Lucasfilm umbrella.

EXECUTIVES

Chairman and CEO: George W. Lucas Jr.
COO: Micheline Chau, age 50
President, Lucas Digital: Jim Morris
President, Lucas Licensing: Howard Rothman
VP Marketing and Distribution; President, LucasArts: Jim Ward
Director Communications: Lynne Hale

LOCATIONS

HQ: Lucasfilm Ltd.
 5858 Lucas Valley Rd., San Rafael, CA 94946
Phone: 415-662-1800 **Fax:** 415-662-2437
Web: www.lucasfilm.com

PRODUCTS/OPERATIONS

Selected Productions
American Graffiti (1973)
Howard the Duck (1986)
Indiana Jones and the Last Crusade (1989)
Indiana Jones and the Temple of Doom (1984)
Labyrinth (1986)
More American Graffiti (1979)
Radioland Murders (1994)
Raiders of the Lost Ark (1981)
Star Wars: Episode I — The Phantom Menace (1999)
Star Wars: Episode II — Attack of the Clones (2002)
Star Wars: Episode III—Revenge of the Sith (2005)
Star Wars: Episode IV — A New Hope (1977)
Star Wars: Episode V — The Empire Strikes Back (1980)
Star Wars: Episode VI — Return of the Jedi (1983)
Tucker: The Man and His Dream (1988)
Willow (1988)
The Young Indiana Jones Chronicles (1992-96, TV movies)

COMPETITORS

Disney Studios	Paramount Pictures
DreamWorks	Pixar
Fox Filmed Entertainment	Sony Pictures Entertainment
Lions Gate Entertainment	
MGM	Universal Studios
New Line Cinema	Warthog

HISTORICAL FINANCIALS
Company Type: Private

Income Statement				FYE: March 31
	ESTIMATED REVENUE ($ mil.)	NET INCOME ($ mil.)	NET PROFIT MARGIN	EMPLOYEES
3/03	1,200	—	—	1,800
3/02	1,350	—	—	1,900
3/01	1,500	—	—	2,000
3/00	1,100	—	—	1,800
3/99	600	—	—	1,300
3/98	400	—	—	500
3/97	250	—	—	200
3/96	200	—	—	100
3/95	160	—	—	36
3/94	160	—	—	—
Annual Growth	25.1%	—	—	63.1%

Revenue History
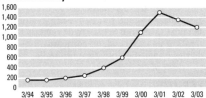

Lumbermens Merchandising

Membership has its privileges. Through Lumbermens Merchandising Corporation (LMC), more than 300 stockholder lumber retailers throughout the US pool their buying resources to leverage volume discounts from vendors and increase their own efficiency. LMC's network of members includes about 1,000 building material dealer locations in 48 states. The cooperative is the largest dealer-owned lumber building materials buying group in the US. It holds members to strict confidentiality, in part to safeguard vendor contracts. In addition to lumber and panel products, LMC also supplies its members with non-wood products, millwork, and hardware.

EXECUTIVES
President and CEO: Anthony J. DeCarlo
SVP Finance and Technology: David J. (Dave) Gonze
SVP Purchasing: John Broomell
Auditors: Hege Kramer Connell Murphy & Goldkamp, P.C.

LOCATIONS
HQ: Lumbermens Merchandising Corporation
137 W. Wayne Ave., Wayne, PA 19087
Phone: 610-293-7000   **Fax:** 610-293-7098
Web: www.lmc.net

PRODUCTS/OPERATIONS
Selected Members
Arch Creek Lumber
Kaufman Lumber
Masten Home Center
Peter Lumber
Short & Paulk Supply Co., Inc.

COMPETITORS
84 Lumber
Ace Hardware
Do it Best
Guardian Building Products
Home Depot
Lowe's
TruServ

HISTORICAL FINANCIALS
Company Type: Cooperative

Income Statement				FYE: September 30
	REVENUE ($ mil.)	NET INCOME ($ mil.)	NET PROFIT MARGIN	EMPLOYEES
9/03	2,300	—	—	200
9/02	2,200	—	—	—
9/01	1,700	—	—	—
9/00	2,100	—	—	—
9/99	1,900	—	—	—
9/98	1,700	—	—	200
9/97	1,666	—	—	—
9/96	1,662	—	—	—
9/95	1,471	—	—	—
Annual Growth	5.7%	—	—	0.0%

Revenue History
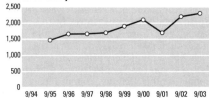

M. Fabrikant & Sons

Diamonds have been around practically forever, and so has M. Fabrikant & Sons, a major US diamond wholesaler. Four generations of the Fabrikant and Fortgang families run the family-owned firm, which claims to be one of the oldest diamond and jewelry companies in the world (it was founded as a loose diamond wholesaler in New York City in 1895). Fabrikant purchases and sells loose and polished diamonds and other precious and semi-precious stones, plus diamond, gold, and silver jewelry. Customers include retailers such as Wal-Mart and major jewelry chains. Affiliates include Susan Fortgang's Royal Asscher Cut branded-diamond company, Japanese joint venture Leer Tokyo Pearl, and about 20% of jeweler Lazare Kaplan.

EXECUTIVES
Chairman: Charles Fabrikant Fortgang
President and CEO: Matthew Fabrikant Fortgang
COO: Michael Shaffet
CFO: Sheldon L. Ginsberg
VP; President, Royal Asscher: Susan Fabrikant Fortgang
VP, Corporate Communications: Susan (Suzy) Boshwit

LOCATIONS
HQ: M. Fabrikant & Sons, Inc.
1 Rockefeller Plaza, 28th Fl., New York, NY 10020
Phone: 212-757-0790   **Fax:** 212-581-3061
Web: www.fabrikant.com

PRODUCTS/OPERATIONS
Selected Stones
Diamonds
Emeralds
Opals
Pearls
Rubies
Sapphires

COMPETITORS
Atlas Pacific
Blue Nile
IWI Holding
Lazare Kaplan
LJ International
Michael Anthony Jewelers

HISTORICAL FINANCIALS
Company Type: Private

Income Statement				FYE: July 31
	REVENUE ($ mil.)	NET INCOME ($ mil.)	NET PROFIT MARGIN	EMPLOYEES
7/03	903	—	—	800
7/02	900	—	—	800
7/01	930	—	—	800
7/00	1,000	—	—	800
7/99	820	—	—	800
7/98	780	—	—	800
7/97	745	—	—	825
7/96	751	—	—	875
7/95	650	—	—	850
7/94	600	—	—	750
Annual Growth	4.6%	—	—	0.7%

Revenue History
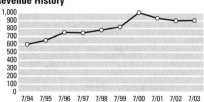

MA Laboratories

If you need a computer part, just ask your MA. Distributor MA Laboratories, one of the largest privately held companies in Silicon Valley, provides computer resellers and systems integrators with more than 3,000 high-tech gadgets and computer items. MA Labs specializes in memory modules but sells just about everything commonly found in or near a computer, including hard drives, motherboards, CD-ROMs, and video cards. Other products include monitors, software, fax modems, network cards, digital cameras, notebook computers, and accessories. Among MA's suppliers are 3Com, Advanced Micro Devices, Hewlett-Packard, IBM, Intel, Microsoft, Sony, and Toshiba. MA Labs was founded in 1983 by owner and CEO Abraham Ma.

EXECUTIVES

President and CEO: Abraham Ma
CFO: Ricky Chow
VP: Michael Ma
Director, Human Resources: Shareen Wu

LOCATIONS

HQ: MA Laboratories, Inc.
2075 N. Capitol Ave., San Jose, CA 95132
Phone: 408-941-0808 **Fax:** 408-941-0909
Web: www.malabs.com

PRODUCTS/OPERATIONS

Selected Products

CD and DVD drives
Computer components (keyboards, cooling fans, and other devices)
Data storage
Digital cameras
Hard drives
Input/output cards
Memory
Modems
Monitors
Motherboards
Multimedia (speakers, scanners, and other devices)
Networking
Notebook computers and accessories
Printers
Processors
Software
Video cards

Services

Technical support

COMPETITORS

Agilysys
Arrow Electronics
Avnet
Bell Microproducts
Ingram Micro
Kingston Technology
Merisel
N.F. Smith
Southland Micro
Supermicro Computer
Tech Data
Viking Components
Wintec

HISTORICAL FINANCIALS

Company Type: Private

Income Statement
FYE: December 31

	REVENUE ($ mil.)	NET INCOME ($ mil.)	NET PROFIT MARGIN	EMPLOYEES
12/03	680	—	—	300
12/02	800	—	—	350
12/01	805	—	—	300
12/00	855	—	—	300
12/99	800	—	—	300
12/98	700	—	—	—
12/97	740	—	—	200
12/96	600	—	—	200
12/95	498	—	—	—
12/94	375	—	—	100
Annual Growth	6.8%	—	—	13.0%

Revenue History

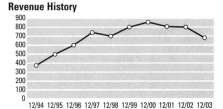

M. A. Mortenson

It's all bricks and mortar for M. A. Mortenson Company, one of the largest builders in the US. The company's services include planning, program and construction management, general contracting and design/build delivery, and maintenance and operations. M. A. Mortenson builds aviation, education, health care, and sports facilities, as well as power plants and dams. It also builds and renovates military housing. Mortenson works primarily in the US, where projects include the FedEx Forum, home of the NBA's Memphis Grizzlies, and the Walt Disney Concert Hall, home of the Los Angeles Philharmonic Orchestra. The family-owned company was founded in 1954 by M. A. Mortenson Sr., whose son now serves as chairman and CEO.

The group, which celebrated its 50th anniversary in 2004, has had clients ranging from Acuity Insurance to Wells Fargo.

EXECUTIVES

Chairman and CEO: M. A. Mortenson Jr.
President and COO: Thomas F. Gunkel
SVP and CFO: Peter A. Conzemius
SVP Administration and Technology: Paul V. Campbell
SVP: Paul I. Cossette
SVP Operations: Bradley C. (Brad) Funk
SVP and Leader, National Healthcare Group:
 Daniel L. (Dan) Johnson
SVP Business Development: Robert J. Nartonis
SVP: John V. Wood
Corporate Secretary: Mark A. Mortenson
Director Human Resources: Daniel R. (Dan) Haag
Communications Manager: Kim Kaisler
Auditors: Deloitte & Touche LLP

LOCATIONS

HQ: M. A. Mortenson Company
700 Meadow Ln. North, Minneapolis, MN 55422
Phone: 763-522-2100 **Fax:** 763-520-3430
Web: www.mortenson.com

M. A. Mortenson has offices in Chicago, Denver, Milwaukee, Minneapolis, and Seattle.

PRODUCTS/OPERATIONS

Selected Services

Construction management
Design/build delivery
Engineering, procurement, and construction (EPC)
General contracting
Maintenance and operations
Planning
Preconstruction services
Program management
Project development
Turnkey construction

COMPETITORS

AMEC, Construction Management
Barton Malow
Bovis Lend Lease
Brasfield & Gorrie
FaulknerUSA
Gilbane
Hensel Phelps Construction
Hoffman Corporation
Hunt Construction
McCarthy Building
Parsons
Perini
Skanska
Turner Corporation
Walbridge Aldinger
Walsh Group
Whiting-Turner
Zachry

HISTORICAL FINANCIALS

Company Type: Private

Income Statement
FYE: December 31

	REVENUE ($ mil.)	NET INCOME ($ mil.)	NET PROFIT MARGIN	EMPLOYEES
12/03	1,103	—	—	1,800
12/02	1,455	—	—	1,800
12/01	1,128	—	—	1,800
12/00	1,080	—	—	2,153
12/99	968	—	—	1,920
12/98	904	—	—	1,873
12/97	803	—	—	1,700
12/96	786	—	—	1,500
12/95	781	—	—	1,650
12/94	775	—	—	1,600
Annual Growth	4.0%	—	—	1.3%

Revenue History

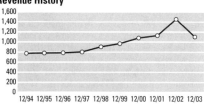

MacAndrews & Forbes

Through MacAndrews & Forbes Holdings, financier Ron Perelman is focused on cosmetics and cash. The holding company has investments in an array of public and private companies, most notably 83%-owned Revlon (the #3 cosmetics company in the US), M&F Worldwide (licorice flavors), and WeddingChannel.com. Perelman is intent on reversing the fortunes of Revlon, which he has controlled since 1985. He made a hefty profit when Consolidated Cigar Holdings (the #1 US cigar maker) was sold to French tobacco maker Seita in 1999. In 2004 Perelman is working on getting behind the wheel of AM General, manufacturer of Humvee and HUMMER vehicles, by acquiring the company through his firm's affiliate, MacAndrews AMG Holdings.

MacAndrews & Forbes' other holdings include the drug-development company TransTech Pharma (in which it is the largest shareholder); 83% of Panavision, the #1 provider of cameras for shooting movies and TV shows; and privately held Allied Security, one of the biggest providers of security guards and systems.

Perelman's holdings have dwindled in value since 1999. Most of the investor's business strategy involves improving his cash position and paying down debt — hence his IPO of Revlon (1996), the sale of The Coleman Company to American Household (formerly Sunbeam Corp., 1998), and the sale of two of Revlon's noncore units. Perelman has committed a $215 million debt-and-equity funding package to rescue Revlon, which is struggling with debt and dwindling market share.

Perelman is still a media curiosity, largely because of his public courtship and wedding to (estranged) wife #4, actress Ellen Barkin.

HISTORY

Ron Perelman grew up working in his father's Philadelphia-based conglomerate, Belmont Industries, but he left at the age of 35 to seek his fortune in New York. In 1978 he bought 40% of jewelry store operator Cohen-Hatfield Industries. The next year Cohen-Hatfield bought a minority stake in MacAndrews & Forbes (licorice flavoring). Cohen-Hatfield acquired MacAndrews & Forbes in 1980.

In 1984 Perelman reshuffled his assets to create MacAndrews & Forbes Holdings, which acquired control of Pantry Pride, a Florida-based supermarket chain, in 1985. Pantry Pride then bought Revlon for $1.8 billion with the help of (convicted felon) Michael Milken. After Perelman acquired Revlon, he added several other cosmetics vendors, including Max Factor and Yves Saint Laurent's fragrance and cosmetic lines.

In 1988 MacAndrews & Forbes agreed to invest $315 million in five failing Texas savings and loans (S&Ls), which Perelman combined and named First Gibraltar (sold to BankAmerica, now Bank of America, in 1993). The next year MacAndrews & Forbes bought The Coleman Company, a maker of outdoor equipment.

With a growing reputation for buying struggling companies, revamping them, and then selling them at a higher price, Perelman bought Marvel Entertainment Group (Marvel Comics) in 1989 and took it public in 1991. That year he sold Revlon's Max Factor and Betrix units to Procter & Gamble for more than $1 billion.

MacAndrews & Forbes acquired 37.5% of TV infomercial producer Guthy-Renker and SCI Television's seven stations and merged them to create New World Television. That company was combined with TV syndicator Genesis Entertainment and TV production house New World Entertainment to create New World Communications Group, which Perelman took public in 1994. That year MacAndrews & Forbes and partner Gerald J. Ford bought Ford Motor's First Nationwide, the US's fifth-largest S&L at that time.

Subsidiaries Mafco Worldwide and Consolidated Cigar Holdings merged with Abex (aircraft parts) to create Mafco Consolidated Group in 1995. Following diminishing comic sales, Perelman placed Marvel in bankruptcy in 1996 and subsequently lost control of the company.

In 1997 First Nationwide bought California thrift Cal Fed Bancorp for $1.2 billion. In addition, Perelman sold New World to Rupert Murdoch's News Corp.

In 1998 Perelman orchestrated a $1.8 billion deal in which First Nationwide merged with Golden State Bancorp to form the US's third-largest thrift. Sunbeam Corp. (now American Household) bought Perelman's stake in Coleman that year, making Perelman a major American Household shareholder. Also in 1998 MacAndrews & Forbes bought a 72% stake in Panavision (movie camera maker, later increased to 91%), invested in WeddingChannel.com, and sold its 64% stake in Consolidated Cigar to French tobacco giant Seita (netting Perelman a smoking $350 million profit).

Still burdened by debt, Revlon sold its professional products business in 2000.

Perelman's stock in American Household was rendered worthless when the company initiated bankruptcy proceedings in February 2001. (It would emerge from bankruptcy, however, in December 2002.) He also was sued by angry shareholders after the board of M&F Worldwide, the licorice company he controls, bought Perelman's stock in Panavision at more than five times its market value. In order to settle the litigation surrounding the purchase, in 2002 M&F agreed to return Pereleman's 83% stake in Panavision to Mafco. Golden State Bancorp also left the MacAndrews fold in 2002 when it was acquired by Citigroup.

MacAndrews & Forbes Holdings acquired Allied Security, the largest independent provider of contract security services and products in the US, from Gryphon Investors in February 2003 for an undisclosed sum.

EXECUTIVES

Chairman and CEO: Ronald O. (Ron) Perelman, age 61
Co-Vice Chairman: Donald G. Drapkin, age 56
Co-Vice Chairman and Chief Administrative Officer: Howard Gittis, age 70
SVP, Corporate Affairs: James T. Conroy
SVP, Corporate Communications: Christine Taylor
VP: Matthew Adam Drapkin, age 31
VP and Controller: Norman J. Ginstling
Auditors: PricewaterhouseCoopers LLP

LOCATIONS

HQ: MacAndrews & Forbes Holdings Inc.
35 E. 62nd St., New York, NY 10021
Phone: 212-688-9000   **Fax:** 212-572-8400

MacAndrews & Forbes Holdings' consumer products operations are principally in the US.

PRODUCTS/OPERATIONS

Selected Holdings

Allied Security (leading provider of security guards and systems)
American Household (about 37%, small appliances and Coleman camping gear)
M&F Worldwide Corp. (32%, licorice extract)
Revlon Inc. (83%, cosmetics and personal care products)
TransTech Pharma (drug development company)
WeddingChannel.com

COMPETITORS

Alberto-Culver
Alticor
Avon
Body Shop
Brunswick
Chattem
Colgate-Palmolive
Dial
Estée Lauder
Guardsmark
Johnson & Johnson
Kellwood
L'Oréal USA
LVMH
Mary Kay
Procter & Gamble
Ulta
Unilever
Wackenhut

HISTORICAL FINANCIALS

Company Type: Private

Income Statement
FYE: December 31

	REVENUE ($ mil.)	NET INCOME ($ mil.)	NET PROFIT MARGIN	EMPLOYEES
12/02	5,700	—	—	19,800
12/01	5,700	—	—	19,800
12/00	5,500	—	—	19,500
12/99	5,400	—	—	19,500
12/98	4,900	—	—	19,500
12/97	6,071	—	—	29,854
12/96	6,196	—	—	30,000
12/95	4,413	—	—	22,800
12/94	3,030	—	—	22,328
12/93	2,748	—	—	23,500
Annual Growth	8.4%	—	—	(1.9%)

Revenue History

Madison Square Garden

Like the city it calls home, Madison Square Garden is the entertainment company that never sleeps. The firm owns some of New York City's iconic institutions such as the NBA's New York Knicks, the NHL's New York Rangers, and their arena, Madison Square Garden, arguably the most famous sports venue in the world. Other holdings include regional sports networks Madison Square Garden Network and Fox Sports Net New York, and Radio City Music Hall, home of the leggy Rockettes. Madison Square Garden is owned by Regional Programming Partners, a joint venture between Cablevision Systems (60%) and Fox Sports Networks (40%). The company also operates outside the Big Apple through Connecticut's Hartford Civic Center.

Madison Square Garden's arena holds about 17,900 seats, and its theater complex contains an additional 5,400 seats. Its Radio City Music Hall fits 5,900 seats. The company cut staff in 2003 due to a decrease in sales thanks to fewer events at the Garden and Radio City, as well as lower Knicks regular season TV revenue.

EXECUTIVES

Chairman: James L. Dolan, age 48
Vice Chairman: Hank J. Ratner, age 45
President and COO, MSG Sports: Steve Mills, age 44
President and General Manager, New York Rangers: Glen Sather, age 61
President, Basketball Operations, New York Knicks: Isiah Thomas, age 43

EVP, MSG Networks: Mike McCarthy
SVP and General Manager, Hartford Civic Center: Martin Brooks
SVP, Communications: Barry Watkins
SVP, Business and Consumer Sales: Joel Fisher
EVP, Finance: Robert Pollichino
SVP, Legal Affairs: Marc Schoenfeld

LOCATIONS

HQ: Madison Square Garden, L.P.
2 Pennsylvania Plaza, Ste. 14, New York, NY 10121
Phone: 212-465-6000 **Fax:** 212-465-6026
Web: www.thegarden.com

PRODUCTS/OPERATIONS

Selected Operations
Fox Sports Net New York (regional sports television network)
Hartford Civic Center (sports and entertainment venue)
Hartford Wolf Pack (minor league hockey team)
Madison Square Garden (sports and entertainment arena)
Theater at Madison Square Garden (entertainment venue)
Madison Square Garden Network (regional sports television network)
New York Knicks (professional basketball team)
New York Liberty (professional women's basketball team)
New York Rangers (professional hockey team)
Radio City Entertainment
Radio City Music Hall (entertainment venue)

COMPETITORS

Clear Channel Entertainment
ESPN
New Jersey Sports and Exposition
New York Giants
New York Islanders
New York Jets

HISTORICAL FINANCIALS

Company Type: Private

Income Statement				FYE: December 31
	REVENUE ($ mil.)	NET INCOME ($ mil.)	NET PROFIT MARGIN	EMPLOYEES
12/03	772	—	—	—
12/02	790	—	—	—
12/01	842	—	—	—
12/00	876	—	—	—
Annual Growth	(4.1%)	—	—	—

Revenue History

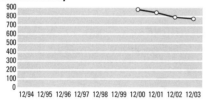

MAGNATRAX

MAGNATRAX Corporation is a holding company for several businesses, including American Buildings Company, that make, sell, and transport engineered steel building products in North America. MAGNATRAX also has regional divisions, which include CBC Steel Buildings, Gulf States Manufacturers, and Kirby Building Systems. The company's VICWEST division provides metal building components; its Polymer Coil Coaters unit provides treated and coated metals. The company sold its Republic Builders Products Company and Windsor Door, Inc., subsidiaries to Desco Capital Partners. MAGNATRAX has restructured and emerged from chapter 11 bankruptcy protection. The company is owned by a group of debt holders and creditors.

EXECUTIVES

Chairman: Jack Hatcher
President, CEO, and Director: Dennis H. Smith
CFO: Allen Capsuto
SVP Sales and Marketing: Maurice Levy
President, American Buildings Company: Larry Hughes
VP Human Resources and Secretary, MAGNATRAX Corporation and American Buildings Company: Peggy S. Woodham

LOCATIONS

HQ: MAGNATRAX Corporation
1220 Old Alpharetta Rd., Windward Chase, Ste. 310, Alpharetta, GA 30005
Phone: 678-455-3360 **Fax:** 678-455-3366
Web: www.magnatrax.com

PRODUCTS/OPERATIONS

Selected Subsidiaries
American Buildings Company
Architectural Metal Systems
CBC Steel Buildings
Gulf States Manufacturers
Kirby Building Systems
Magnatran
Polymer Coil Coaters
Vicwest
Westeel

COMPETITORS

Butler Manufacturing
International Hi-Tech Industries
NCI Building Systems

HISTORICAL FINANCIALS

Company Type: Private

Income Statement				FYE: December 31
	REVENUE ($ mil.)	NET INCOME ($ mil.)	NET PROFIT MARGIN	EMPLOYEES
12/02	693	—	—	3,550

Main Street America Group

Who's your main insurance man? Main Street America Group provides a range of personal and commercial property & casualty products including coverage for small to midsized businesses and auto and homeowners insurance for individuals. The company does the majority of its business through its flagship subsidiary National Grange Mutual Insurance. Information Systems and Services Corporation offers third-party administration services such as broker management, policy processing, and underwriting services. Main Street America Group sells its products through independent agents.

EXECUTIVES

Chairman: Philip D. Koerner
President and CEO: Thomas M. Van Berkel
EVP Finance and Systems: Jeanne H. Eddy
VP and CIO: Joel Gelb
VP, Controller, and Treasurer: Edward J. Kuhl
VP and Secretary: William C. McKenna
VP Marketing: Kelly Stacy
VP: Larry G. Acord
VP: Stephen D. Canty
VP: Scott B. Gerlach
VP: Joseph L. Grauwiler
VP: Richard A. Hyatt
Auditors: Ernst & Young LLP

LOCATIONS

HQ: Main Street America Group
55 West St., Keene, NH 03431
Phone: 603-352-4000 **Fax:** 603-358-1173
Web: www.msagroup.com

Main Street America Group operates in Connecticut, Delaware, Florida, Georgia, Maine, Maryland, Massachusetts, New Hampshire, New York, North Carolina, Pennsylvania, Rhode Island, South Carolina, Tennessee, Vermont, and Virginia.

PRODUCTS/OPERATIONS

Selected Subsidiaries
Main Street America Assurance Company
Main Street America Financial Corporation
Main Street America Holdings, Inc.
MSA — Information Systems and Services Corporation
National Grange Mutual Insurance Company
Old Dominion Insurance Company

COMPETITORS

ACE Limited
AIG
Allstate
American Family Insurance
American Financial
Cincinnati Financial
Farmers Group
Fireman's Fund Insurance
GEICO
The Hartford
Liberty Mutual
Progressive Corporation
Prudential
Royal & SunAlliance USA
Safeco
St. Paul Travelers
State Farm

HISTORICAL FINANCIALS

Company Type: Mutual company

Income Statement — FYE: December 31

	REVENUE ($ mil.)	NET INCOME ($ mil.)	NET PROFIT MARGIN	EMPLOYEES
12/02	583	(24)	—	—
12/01	503	5	1.1%	—
Annual Growth	16.0%	—	—	—

Net Income History

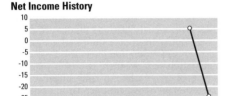

Major League Baseball

It may be the national pastime, but Major League Baseball (MLB) is a big business. MLB runs the game of professional baseball and oversees 30 franchises in 28 cities. Each team operates as a separate business, but each is regulated and governed by MLB. The league sets official rules, regulates team ownership, and collects licensing fees for merchandise. It also sells national broadcasting rights and distributes fees to the teams. (Regional broadcast rights are held by each franchise.) MLB was formed when the rival National and American Leagues joined together in 1903.

Baseball has been riding high on a resurgent wave of popularity since the disastrous players' strike of 1994. The work stoppage, which curtailed the season and led to the cancellation of the World Series, marked a low point in MLB history, but fans returned to the game in record numbers to watch sluggers Mark McGuire and Sammy Sosa chase Roger Maris' single-season home run record in 1998. (McGuire broke the record with 70 long balls, although his mark was broken in 2001 by Barry Bond's 72 home run effort.) The sport's popularity has also given its prosperity a shot in the arm: the league signed a $2.5 billion broadcasting contract with Fox Entertainment in 2000, sold the Japanese television rights to its games to advertising firm Dentsu for $275 million in 2003, and agreed to a $650 million deal with XM Satellite Radio in 2004.

Despite these healthy deals, the league and commissioner Bud Selig have had to make some tough decisions in recent years. The team owners and the league struggled throughout the 2002 season to negotiate a new labor agreement with players, avoiding another strike with a deal signed in late August at the 11th hour. The agreement forces MLB to delay its plans to eliminate two teams until 2006 (the league had planned on contraction as early as 2003) and also places a luxury tax on teams with high payrolls. The money acquired from the tax is distributed to smaller-market teams in an effort to allow those poorer clubs to compete with the high-priced talent of such teams as the New York Yankees. The effects of the luxury tax system can already be seen in higher revenues for smaller market teams.

Even with the threat of strike averted, however, MLB still has image problems that have to be addressed, including allegations that large numbers of players habitually abuse steroids.

HISTORY

The first baseball team to field professional players was the Cincinnati Red Stockings (now the Cincinnati Reds) in 1869. Teams in Boston, New York City, and Philadelphia followed suit. In 1876 eight professional teams formed the National League. Competing leagues sprang up and folded, but Ban Johnson's Western League (formed in 1892) seized on territory abandoned by the National league in 1900 and began luring National League players with higher salaries. Renamed the American League, it also began drawing away fans. The two leagues agreed to join forces in 1903 by having their champions meet in the World Series.

The sport flourished until the "Black Sox" scandal of 1919, in which eight Chicago White Sox players were accused of taking bribes to throw the World Series. The owners hired Judge Kenesaw Mountain Landis as baseball's first commissioner in 1921 to clean up the game's image. He served until his death in 1944. A joint committee of owners and players introduced more reforms in 1947, including a player pension fund.

The players formed the Major League Baseball Players' Association (MLBPA) in 1954 and signed the first collective-bargaining agreement with the owners in 1968. The players called their first strike in 1972, a 13-day walkout that won an improved pension plan. They won the right to free agency in 1976; another seven-week strike interrupted the 1981 season.

Salary increases slowed, and the free agent market dried up in the mid-1980s, prompting the MLBPA to sue the owners for collusion. The owners agreed to a settlement of $280 million in 1990. Baseball's eighth commissioner, Fay Vincent, resigned in 1992 after the owners effectively removed all power from the commissioner's office. An executive council of owners led by Milwaukee Brewers owner Bud Selig took control.

Prompted by the owners' decision to unilaterally restrict free agency and withdraw salary arbitration, the players started a 232-day strike in August 1994 that forced the cancellation of the World Series and stretched into the 1995 season. Revenue and income plummeted. Play resumed in 1995 when the owners and the MLBPA approved a new collective-bargaining agreement. Selig stepped down from the Brewers in 1998 to become the game's ninth commissioner.

Having alienated countless fans, baseball was resuscitated in 1998 by Mark McGwire and Sammy Sosa as they pursued Roger Maris' 37-year-old single-season home run record of 61. (McGwire's record of 70 only lasted until the 2001 season when the San Francisco Giants' outfielder Barry Bonds hit 72 homers.) The next year MLB umpires walked out for higher salaries, but the strategy backfired and 22 umpires lost their jobs. Later that year MLB signed a new six-year, $800 million TV contract with ESPN.

Sweeping changes took place in 2000 when owners, who had voted the previous year to eliminate the American and National league offices (centralizing power with the commissioner's office), also voted to restore the "best interests of baseball" powers to the commissioner, giving Selig full authority to redistribute wealth, block trades, and fine teams and players. The MLB also scored a financial home run when Fox Entertainment agreed to pay $2.5 billion for exclusive rights to televise all postseason contests through the 2006 season.

Due to the consistent financial disparity between large- and small-market teams, the league in 2001 voted to eliminate two teams before the start of the 2003 season. The next year Bob DuPuy was named president and COO of the league. (Former pres Paul Beeston resigned after talks over a new collective bargaining agreement stalled.) Also in 2002 another strike was avoided late in the season. The new labor agreement pushes back the league's contraction plans until 2006 and also places a luxury tax on teams with high payrolls, which is then distributed to small-market franchises.

EXECUTIVES

Commissioner: Allan H. (Bud) Selig, age 70
President and COO: Robert A. (Bob) DuPuy
EVP Administration: John McHale Jr.
EVP Baseball Operations: Richard (Sandy) Alderson
EVP Business: Timothy J. (Tim) Brosnan
EVP Finance and CFO: Jonathan D. Mariner, age 49
EVP Labor Relations and Human Resources: Robert D. (Rob) Manfred Jr.
Chief Legal Counsel: Thomas J. Ostertag
SVP and General Counsel: Ethan Orlinsky
SVP Advertising and Marketing: Jacqueline Parkes
SVP Baseball Operations: Jimmie Lee Solomon
SVP Corporate Sales and Marketing, Major League Baseball Properties: John S. Brody
SVP International Business Operations: Paul Archey
SVP Licensing: Howard Smith
SVP Media Relations: Richard Levin
SVP Security and Facilities Management: Kevin M. Hallinan
VP Broadcasting: Bernadette McDonald
VP Community Affairs: Thomas C. Brasuell
VP Corporate Sales and Marketing: Justin Johnson
VP Domestic Apparel Licensing, Headwear, and Sporting Goods: Steve Armus
VP International Baseball Operations: Lou Melendez
VP Strategic Planning for Recruitment and Diversity: Wendy Lewis
President and CEO, MLB Advanced Media: Robert A. (Bob) Bowman, age 49
Senior Manager of New Technology: Mike Napolitano
Director of Advertising: Jeff Gonyo
Director of Research: Dan Derian
Auditors: Deloitte & Touche LLP

LOCATIONS

HQ: Major League Baseball
245 Park Ave., New York, NY 10167
Phone: 212-931-7800 **Fax:** 212-949-8636
Web: www.mlb.com

Major League Baseball has 30 franchises in 28 cities in the US and Canada.

PRODUCTS/OPERATIONS

Major League Franchises

American League
  Anaheim Angels (1965, California)
    Los Angeles Angels (1961)
  Baltimore Orioles (1954)
    St. Louis Browns (1902)
    Milwaukee Brewers (1901)
  Boston Red Sox (1901)
  Chicago White Sox (1901)
  Cleveland Indians (1915)
    Cleveland Spiders (1889)
  Detroit Tigers (1900)
  Kansas City Royals (1969, Missouri)
  Minnesota Twins (1961, Minneapolis)
    Washington Senators (1901; Washington, DC)
  New York Yankees (1913, New York City)
    New York Highlanders (1903, New York City)
    Baltimore Orioles (1901)
  Oakland Athletics (1968, California)
    Kansas City Athletics (1955, Missouri)
    Philadelphia Athletics (1901)
  Seattle Mariners (1977)
  Tampa Bay Devil Rays (1998)
  Texas Rangers (1972, Arlington)
    Washington Senators (1961; Washington, DC)
  Toronto Blue Jays (1977)

National League
  Arizona Diamondbacks (Phoenix, 1998)
  Atlanta Braves (1966)
    Milwaukee Braves (1953)
    Boston Braves (1912)
    Boston Beaneaters (1883)
    Boston Red Stockings (1871)
  Chicago Cubs (1903)
    Chicago Orphans (1898)
    Chicago Colts (1894)
    Chicago White Stockings (1871)
  Cincinnati Reds (1866)
  Colorado Rockies (1993, Denver)
  Florida Marlins (1993, Miami)
  Houston Astros (1964)
    Houston Colt .45s (1962)
  Los Angeles Dodgers (1958)
    Brooklyn Dodgers (1890, New York)
  Milwaukee Brewers (1970; switched from American League, 1998)
    Seattle Pilots (1969)
  Montreal Expos (1969)
  New York Mets (1962, New York City)
  Philadelphia Phillies (1883)
  Pittsburgh Pirates (1887)
  St. Louis Cardinals (1900)
    St. Louis Brown Stockings (1882)
  San Diego Padres (1969)
  San Francisco Giants (1958)
    New York Giants (1883, New York City)

COMPETITORS

AFL
Indy Racing League
Major League Soccer
NASCAR
NBA
NFL
NHL
Open Wheel Racing
USSF
World Wrestling Entertainment

HISTORICAL FINANCIALS

Company Type: Association

Income Statement
FYE: October 31

	REVENUE ($ mil.)	NET INCOME ($ mil.)	NET PROFIT MARGIN	EMPLOYEES
10/04	4,100	—	—	—
10/03	3,800	—	—	—
10/02	3,547	—	—	—
10/01	3,500	—	—	—
10/00	3,178	—	—	—
10/99	2,838	—	—	—
10/98	3,174	—	—	—
10/97	2,216	—	—	200
10/96	1,847	—	—	200
10/95	1,411	—	—	170
Annual Growth	12.6%	—	—	8.5%

Revenue History

Marc Glassman

Marc Glassman wants to prove that low prices can lead to big things. The retailer operates about 55 drugstores, most of which are Marc's Discount Drug Stores in northeast Ohio, but also a handful of Xpect Discount Drugs in Connecticut. Marc Glassman's no-frills stores (sorry, credit cards not accepted) range in size from 18,000 sq. ft. to 48,000 sq. ft. Most have pharmacies and offer a constantly changing mix of closeout and excess merchandise in some 20 categories, including clothing, cosmetics, housewares, toys, and tools. The company specializes in seasonal products (Christmas, Halloween, lawn and garden). Owner and chairman Marc Glassman founded the company in Middleburg Heights, Ohio, in 1979.

EXECUTIVES

Chairman: Marc Glassman
President and CEO: Kevin Yaugher
CFO: Beth Weiner

LOCATIONS

HQ: Marc Glassman, Inc.
5841 W. 130th St., Parma, OH 44130
Phone: 216-265-7700   **Fax:** 216-265-7737
Web: www.marcs.com

COMPETITORS

Ahold USA
Big Lots
CVS
Discount Drug
Dollar General
Dollar Tree
Family Dollar Stores
Giant Eagle
Kmart
Medic Drug
Rite Aid
Target
Walgreen
Wal-Mart

HISTORICAL FINANCIALS

Company Type: Private

Income Statement
FYE: December 31

	REVENUE ($ mil.)	NET INCOME ($ mil.)	NET PROFIT MARGIN	EMPLOYEES
12/02	799	—	—	6,200
12/01	750	—	—	6,100
12/00	745	—	—	6,150
12/99	645	—	—	6,000
12/98	600	—	—	6,000
Annual Growth	7.4%	—	—	0.8%

Revenue History

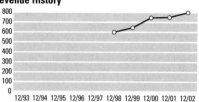

Marian Health System

Patients come to the hospitals of Marian Health System to seek relief from sorrow. The Catholic organization manages four regional health care systems in Kansas, New Jersey, Oklahoma, and Wisconsin. Marian Health System is sponsored by the Sisters of the Sorrowful Mother.

By organizing its operations into regions, the health care provider decentralizes management so its hospitals can better respond to local needs. Via Christi Health System, Marian Health System's operations in Kansas, is co-sponsored by the Sisters of St. Joseph of Wichita.

The system was founded in 1989 as SSM US Health System.

EXECUTIVES

President and CEO, Marian Health System and St. John Health System: Sister M. Therese Gottschalk
President and CEO, Ministry Health Care: Nicholas (Nick) Desien
President and CEO, Saint Clare's Health System: Gary J. Blan
CEO, St. John Medical Center: David Pynn
President and CEO, Via Christi Health System: LeRoy E. Rheault
Director, Accounting: Pat Shearer
Auditors: KPMG LLP

LOCATIONS

HQ: Marian Health System
P.O. Box 4753, Tulsa, OK 74159
Phone: 918-742-9988   **Fax:** 918-744-2716
Web: www.marianhealthsystem.com

Selected Facilities

Ministry Health Care
  St. Elizabeth's Hospital (Wabasha, MN)
  Eagle River Memorial Hospital (Eagle River, WI)
  St. Joseph's Hospital (Marshfield, WI)
  Flambeau Medical Center (Park Falls, WI)
  Sacred Heart/St. Mary's Hospitals (Rhinelander, WI)
  Our Lady of Victory Hospital (Stanley, WI)
  St. Michael's Hospital (Stevens Point, WI)
  Door County Memorial Hospital (Sturgeon Bay, WI)
  Howard Young Medical Center (Woodruff, WI)
Saint Clare's Health System
  Saint Clare's Hospital - Boonton Township Campus (NJ)
  Saint Clare's Hospital - Denville Campus (NJ)
  Saint Clare's Hospital - Dover Campus (NJ)
  Saint Clare's Hospital - Sussex Campus (NJ)
St. John Health System
  Jane Phillips Memorial Medical Center (Bartlesville, OK)
  Jane Phillips Nowata Health Center (Nowata, OK)
  St. John Sapulpa (Sapulpa, OK)
  St. John Medical Center (Tulsa, OK)
Via Christi Health System
  St. Rose Hospital (Hayward, CA)
  Mercy Regional Health Center (Manhattan, KS)
  Mt. Carmel Regional Medical Center (Pittsburg, KS)
  Via Christi Regional Medical Center (Wichita, KS)
  Via Christi Rehabilitation Center/Our Lady of Lourdes Campus (Wichita, KS)
  Via Christi Riverside Medical Center (Wichita, KS)
  Via Christi Oklahoma Regional Medical Center (Ponca City, OK)

COMPETITORS

Catholic Health East
Fairview Health
HealthEast Care System
Hillcrest Healthcare System
North Memorial Health Care
Saint Francis Health System
Stormont-Vail HealthCare

HISTORICAL FINANCIALS

Company Type: Not-for-profit

Income Statement
FYE: September 30

	REVENUE ($ mil.)	NET INCOME ($ mil.)	NET PROFIT MARGIN	EMPLOYEES
9/03	2,805	—	—	4,011
9/02	2,679	—	—	—
Annual Growth	4.7%	—	—	—

Revenue History

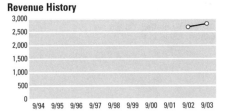

Maritz

Maritz may not be *sending* your employees on business trips, but it will still *motivate* them to go. The company offers employee motivation and marketing services from about 240 offices in more than 40 countries. Its performance improvement and incentive programs help clients improve workforce quality and customer satisfaction. Maritz has phased out its corporate travel business; in 2004 it sold its TQ3 Travel Solutions division (co-owned by TQ3 Maritz Travel Solutions and TUI AG) to Carlson Wagonlit Travel. The Maritz family owns the company.

Maritz's customers include a majority of the *Forbes* 500 (automakers, financial corporations, pharmaceutical and technology companies). In early 2004 Maritz sold Delve, its data collection unit, to Bush O'Donnell Capital Partners.

Chairman and CEO Steve Maritz controls 60% of the company's shares. His brothers Peter and Philip Maritz, who hold the remaining 40%, sued the company in August 2002 and again in 2003; the two have since been seeking a buyer for their shares.

EXECUTIVES

Chairman and CEO: W. Stephen (Steve) Maritz, age 45
SEVP and CFO: James W. Kienker, age 55
VP Community Affairs and Organizational Development: Tom Tener
VP Human Resources: Con McGrath
VP Public Relations and Communications: Beth Rusert
CIO: Gil Hoffman
Business Development: Dennis Hummel
Marketing: Scott Bush
President and CEO, Maritz Automotive Group: Tim Rogers
President and CEO, Maritz Travel Company: Christine Duffy
President, Maritz Incentives: Jane Herod
President, Maritz Research: Michael Brereton

LOCATIONS

HQ: Maritz Inc.
1375 N. Highway Dr., Fenton, MO 63099
Phone: 636-827-4000   **Fax:** 636-827-3312
Web: www.maritz.com

Maritz operates about 240 offices in 42 countries.

PRODUCTS/OPERATIONS

Services

Marketing Research
  Custom marketing research
  Customer satisfaction and customer value analysis
  Data collection (focus groups, telephone interviews)
  Maritz Polls and Maritz Research Reports
  Syndicated buyer research
  Telecommunications research
Performance Improvement
  Communications
  e-Learning
  Fulfillment
  Internet consulting
  Loyalty marketing
  Measurement and feedback
  Rewards and recognition
Travel
  Consulting services
  Corporate travel management
  Group travel services
  Travel award programs

COMPETITORS

ACNielsen
American Express
Carlson
Franklin Covey
Gallup
Harris Interactive
IMS Health
Information Resources
J.D. Power
JTB
Navigant International
NFO WorldGroup
Opinion Research
Rosenbluth International
Thomas Cook AG
WorldTravel

HISTORICAL FINANCIALS

Company Type: Private

Income Statement
FYE: March 31

	REVENUE ($ mil.)	NET INCOME ($ mil.)	NET PROFIT MARGIN	EMPLOYEES
3/03	1,440	—	—	5,700
3/02	1,500	—	—	6,000
3/01	1,318	—	—	6,200
3/00	1,325	—	—	6,500
3/99	2,200	—	—	6,500
3/98	2,170	—	—	6,500
3/97	2,010	—	—	7,500
3/96	1,795	—	—	7,000
3/95	1,078	—	—	6,410
3/94	1,442	—	—	6,080
Annual Growth	(0.0%)	—	—	(0.7%)

Revenue History

Mark IV

Mark IV Industries' engineered components and systems are on the mark when it comes to fluid-handling and power-steering uses. The company's automotive division manufactures idlers, pulleys, belts, power-steering and air-conditioning hoses, manifolds, and water pumps. Mark IV's powertrain division makes diesel and gasoline engines for automotive, industrial, agricultural, and marine uses. Other products include information display systems (for buses, aircraft, and railcars) and intelligent vehicle highway systems (traffic management and electronic toll products). European private equity firm BC Partners controls the company.

Since unloading its Purolator- and Facet-brand air- and fuel-filtration products, Mark IV has concentrated on divesting other product lines to further focus its product mix. The company has sold its Dayco Industrial Power Transmission (belts) unit to Carlisle Companies, and sold Dayco Industrial's fluid transfer and hydraulic hose unit to Parker Hannifin. The company's automotive division accounts for nearly 70% of sales.

EXECUTIVES

President: William P. Montague, age 57
SVP; President, Mark IV Automotive: Kurt J. Johansson
VP, Finance: Mark G. Barberio
VP; EVP, Mark IV Automotive: Giuliano Zucco
VP, Human Resources: Steve Kerns
Director, Communications: Colleen Pibollo

LOCATIONS

HQ: Mark IV Industries, Inc.
501 John James Audubon Pkwy.,
Amherst, NY 14226
Phone: 716-689-4972   **Fax:** 716-689-6098
Web: www.mark-iv.com

Mark IV Industries operates 37 manufacturing plants, 26 distribution and sales facilities, and nine technical centers in 16 countries.

2003 Sales

	% of total
North America	52
Asia, Europe & South America	48
Total	**100**

PRODUCTS/OPERATIONS

2003 Sales

	% of total
Automotive	68
Powertrain applications	17
Information display systems	9
Intelligent vehicle highway systems	6
Total	**100**

Selected Automotive Products

Aftermarket Products
  Automotive service hose
  Belts
  Coolant hoses
  Garage exhaust hoses
  Hydraulic couplings
  Hydraulic hoses
  Pulleys
  Tensioners
OEM Products
  Engine division
    Air-intake systems (ducts, manifolds)
    Belts (poly-rib, raw edge, timing)
    Dampers
    Idlers
    Pulleys
    Tensioners
    Water pumps
  Platform division
    Brake-fluid tanks
    Canisters, fuel lines, and vapor-recovery systems
    Engine and transmission oil-cooling hose and hose assemblies
    Fuel systems and components
    High-technology plastic systems
    Noise tuning
    Power-steering hose and hose assemblies
Powertrain Products
  Diesel engines
  Gasoline engines

COMPETITORS

BorgWarner
Dana
Delphi
Eaton
Gates Rubber
Goodyear
Tesma
Tomkins
Visteon

HISTORICAL FINANCIALS

Company Type: Private

Income Statement
FYE: February 28

	REVENUE ($ mil.)	NET INCOME ($ mil.)	NET PROFIT MARGIN	EMPLOYEES
2/04	1,425	—	—	7,500
2/03	1,300	—	—	7,500
2/02	1,200	—	—	8,000
2/01	2,000	—	—	15,500
2/00	1,994	—	—	15,600
2/99	1,949	—	—	17,000
2/98	2,210	—	—	17,000
2/97	2,076	—	—	15,800
2/96	2,089	—	—	16,000
2/95	1,603	—	—	16,200
Annual Growth	**(1.3%)**	—	—	**(8.2%)**

Revenue History

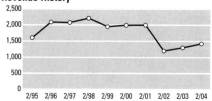

Marmon Group

With more monikers than most, The Marmon Group monitors a melange of more than 100 autonomous manufacturing and service companies. Its manufacturing units make medical products, mining equipment, industrial materials and components, consumer products (including Wells Lamont gloves), transportation equipment, building products, and water-treatment products. Services include marketing and distribution and consumer credit information (Trans Union). Overall, Marmon companies operate 300 facilities in more than 40 countries. Chicago's Pritzker family (owners of the Hyatt hotel chain) owns The Marmon Group.

Each Marmon company works under its own management, and a small corporate office (fewer than 100 employees) oversees and pulls together the conglomerate, acting as combination CFO, tax lawyer, accountant, and broker to member companies.

The group continues to grow through acquisitions, largely to complement existing businesses in fields such as retail display equipment, fasteners and metal products, and consumer credit information.

HISTORY

Although the history of The Marmon Group officially begins in 1953, the company's roots are in the Chicago law firm Pritzker and Pritzker, started by Nicholas Pritzker in 1902. Through the firm the family made connections with First National Bank of Chicago, which A. N. Pritzker, Nicholas' son, used to get a line of credit to buy real estate. By 1940 the firm had stopped accepting outside clients to concentrate on the family's growing investment portfolio.

In 1953 A. N.'s son Jay used his father's connections to get a loan to buy Colson Company, a small, money-losing manufacturer of bicycles, hospital equipment, and other products. Jay's brother, Robert, a graduate of the Illinois Institute of Technology, took charge of Colson and turned it around. Soon Jay began acquiring more companies for his brother to manage.

In 1963 the brothers paid $2.7 million for about 45% of the Marmon-Herrington Company (whose predecessor, Marmon Motor Car, built the car that in 1911 won the first Indianapolis 500). The family now had a name for its industrial holdings — The Marmon Group.

It became a public company in 1966 when it merged with door- and spring-maker Fenestra. However, Jay began to take greater control of the group through a series of stock purchases, and by 1971 The Marmon Group was private once again.

A year earlier, in 1970, the group acquired a promising industrial pipe supplier, Keystone Tubular Service (later Marmon/Keystone). In 1973 Marmon began to acquire stock in Cerro Corp., which had operations in mining, manufacturing, trucking, and real estate; by 1976 the group had bought all of Cerro, thereby tripling its revenues. The brothers sold Cerro's trucking subsidiary, ICX, in 1977 and bought organ maker Hammond Corp., along with Wells Lamont, Hammond's glove-making subsidiary.

Marmon acquired conglomerate Trans Union in 1981. Trans Union brought many operations, including railcar and equipment leasing, credit information services, international trading, and water- and wastewater-treatment systems. Jay acquired Ticketmaster in 1982.

The Pritzkers made a foray into the airline business in 1984 by buying Braniff Airlines. After unsuccessfully bidding for Pan Am in 1987, they sold Braniff in 1988. Disappointments in other Pritzker businesses didn't slow Marmon, which added to its transportation equipment business in 1984 with Altamil, a maker of products for the trucking and aerospace industries.

To mark its 40th anniversary, the company sponsored a car, the Marmon Wasp II, at the 1993 Indianapolis 500. That year the Pritzkers sold 80% of Ticketmaster to Microsoft co-founder Paul Allen but retained a minority interest. Marmon sold Arzco Medical Systems in 1995 and Marmon/Keystone acquired Anbuma Group, a Belgian steel tubing distributor.

The Anbuma purchase and Marmon/Keystone's 1997 acquisition of UK tube distributor Wheeler Group exemplify Marmon's practice of building strength through acquisitions in its established markets. In 1998 Marmon purchased more than 30 companies and opened a business development office in Beijing.

Marmon splashed out more than $500 million in 1999 to make 35 acquisitions, including Kerite (power cables), OsteoMed (specialty medical devices), and Bridport (medical and aviation products). Jay died that year, and the company announced that his title of chairman will not be filled.

In 2000 Marmon spent another $500 million on more than 20 acquisitions, buying operations engaged in the production of retail display equipment, tank containers, and metal products, among others.

Former Illinois Tool Works chief John Nichols took over the Marmon CEO responsibilities from Robert Pritzker in 2001.

EXECUTIVES

President and CEO: John D. Nichols
EVP: Robert C. Gluth
SVP and CFO: Robert K. Lorch
SVP, Secretary, and General Counsel:
 Robert W. (Bob) Webb
SVP: Henry J. (Hank) West
VP Human Resources: Larry Rist
Auditors: Ernst & Young LLP

LOCATIONS

HQ: The Marmon Group, Inc.
 225 W. Washington St., Chicago, IL 60606
Phone: 312-372-9500   Fax: 312-845-5305
Web: www.marmon.com

PRODUCTS/OPERATIONS

Selected Member Companies
Automotive Equipment
 Fontaine Modification Co.
 Fontaine Trailer Co.
 Marmon-Herrington Co.
 Perfection HY-Test Co.
Building Products and Fasteners
 Anderson Copper and Brass Co.
 Atlas Bolt & Screw Company
 Shepherd Caster Corporation
 Shepherd Products Inc.
Consumer Products, Marketing, and Financial Services
 Beijing Huilian Food Co., Ltd.
 Getz Bros. & Co., Inc.
 Great Lakes Consulting Group, Inc.
 MarCap Corp.
 Wells Lamont Corporation
Credit Data and Information Management
 Trans Union LLC
Industrial Products
 Amarillo Gear Co.
 Bridport Aviation
Medical Products
 American Medical Instruments, Inc.
 B.G. Sulzle, Inc.
 Medical Device Technologies, Inc. (MD Tech)
 Pearsalls Limited
 Surgical Specialties Corporation
Metal Products and Materials
 Cerro Copper Products Co.
 Cerro Metal Products Co.
 Penn Aluminum International, Inc.
Pipe and Tube Distribution
 Marmon/Keystone Corporation
  Future Metals, Inc.
  M/K Huron Steel
Railway and Transportation Services
 Exsif Worldwide, Inc.
 Penn Machine Co.
 Railserve, Inc.
 Trackmobile, Inc.
 Union Tank Car Co.
Retail and Food-Service Equipment
 L.A. Darling Co.
 Store Opening Solutions, Inc.
 Thorco Industries, Inc.
Seat Belts and Cargo Restraints
 Am-Safe Inc.
 Bridport Aviation
Water Treatment Systems
 Ecodyne Limited
 EcoWater Systems, Inc.
 Spectrum Labs, Inc.
Wire and Cable Products
 Cable USA, Inc.
 Comtran Corporation
 Hendrix Wire & Cable, Inc.
 The Kerite Co.
 Owl Wire and Cable, Inc.
 Rockbestos-Surprenant Cable Corp.

COMPETITORS

Alcatel
Balfour Beatty
Eaton
Equifax
GE
Illinois Tool Works
Ingersoll-Rand
ITT Industries
LEONI
Masco
Nexans
Pirelli & C.
Superior Essex
Terex
USG
Wolverine Tube

HISTORICAL FINANCIALS
Company Type: Private

Income Statement
FYE: December 31

	REVENUE ($ mil.)	NET INCOME ($ mil.)	NET PROFIT MARGIN	EMPLOYEES
12/03	5,560	—	—	28,000
12/02	5,756	—	—	30,000
12/01	6,414	—	—	35,000
12/00	6,786	—	—	40,000
12/99	6,530	—	—	40,000
12/98	6,032	—	—	35,000
12/97	6,003	—	—	33,000
12/96	5,776	—	—	35,000
12/95	6,083	—	—	30,000
12/94	5,302	—	—	28,000
Annual Growth	0.5%	—	—	0.0%

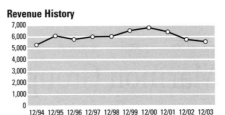

Revenue History

Mars

Mars knows chocolate sales are nothing to snicker at. The company makes such worldwide favorites as M&M's, Snickers, and the Mars bar. Its other products include 3 Musketeers, Dove, Milky Way, Skittles, Twix, and Starburst sweets; Combos and Kudos snacks; Uncle Ben's rice; and pet food under the names Pedigree, Sheba, and Whiskas. Mars also makes drink vending equipment and electronic automated payment systems.

The Mars family (including siblings Forrest Mars Jr., president and CEO John Mars, and VP Jacqueline Badger Mars) owns the highly secretive firm, making the Mars family one of the richest in the US.

Mars makes non-chocolate confections including breath mints such as AquaDrops, and snack foods like Combos and Kudos. It also makes ice-cream versions of several of its candy bars. Mars' Masterfoods USA swallows a large bite of the pet-food market with its Royal Canin, Pedigree, and Whiskas brands. Uncle Ben's and Seeds of Change also come under the Masterfoods umbrella. Mars also owns Flavia Beverage Systems, and its MEI subsidiary makes automated payment systems, including electronic coin-changers and bill-acceptors.

Mars stays virtually debt free and uses its profits for international expansion. It sells its products in more than 100 countries on five continents.

Beginning in 2005, Mars will start phasing out its "king size" candy bars.

HISTORY

Frank Mars invented the Milky Way candy bar in 1923 after his previous three efforts at the candy business left him bankrupt. After his estranged son, Forrest, graduated from Yale, Mars hired him to work at his candy operation. When Forrest demanded one-third control of the company and Frank refused, Forrest moved to England with the foreign rights to Milky Way and started his own company (Food Manufacturers) in the 1930s. He made a sweeter version of Milky Way for the UK, calling it a Mars bar. Forrest also ventured into pet food with the 1934 purchase of Chappel Brothers (renamed Pedigree). At one point he controlled 55% of the British pet food market.

During WWII Forrest returned to the US and introduced Uncle Ben's rice (the world's first brand-name raw commodity) and M&M's (a joint venture between Forrest and Bruce Murrie, son of Hershey's then-president). The idea for M&M's was borrowed from British Smarties, for which Forrest obtained rights (from Rowntree Mackintosh) by relinquishing similar rights to the Snickers bar in some foreign markets. The ad slogan "Melts in your mouth, not in your hand" (and the candy's success in non-air-conditioned stores and war zones) made the company an industry leader. Mars introduced M&M's Peanut in 1954. It was one of the first candy companies to sponsor a television show — *Howdy Doody* in the 1950s.

Forrest merged his firm with his deceased father's company in 1964, after buying his dying half-sister's controlling interest. (He renamed the business Mars at her request.) The merger was the end of an alliance with Hershey, who had supplied Frank with chocolate since his Milky Way inception.

In 1968 Mars bought Kal Kan. (The division now oversees all pet food operations.) In 1973 Forrest, then 69 years old, delegated his company responsibility to sons Forrest Jr. and John. Five years later the brothers, looking for snacks to offset dwindling candy sales from a more diet-conscious America, bought the Twix chocolate-covered cookie brand. During the late 1980s they bought ice-cream bar maker Dove Bar International and Ethel M Chocolates, producer of liqueur-flavored chocolates, a business their father had begun in his retirement.

Hershey passed Mars as the US's largest candy maker in 1988 when it acquired Cadbury Schweppes' US division (Mounds and Almond Joy). In response to the success of Hershey's Symphony Bar, Mars introduced its dark-chocolate Dove bar in 1991.

While Hershey chose to stick close to home, Mars ventured abroad. The company entered the huge confectionery market of India in 1989 by building a $10 million factory there. In 1996 the company opened a confectionery processing plant in Brazil. Back home, the company expanded its Starburst candy line in 1996 and in 1997 launched new ad campaigns, including M&M's spots featuring a trio of animated M&M candies. Mars introduced Uncle Ben's Rice Bowl frozen meals in the late 1990s.

Forrest Sr. died in 1999, spurring rumors that Mars would go public or be sold. Instead, the company dismantled most of its sales force, opting to use less costly food brokers. Also in 1999 Forrest Jr. retired, leaving brother John as president and CEO. Still far behind its rival, Mars received a modest boost in US market share when Hershey experienced computer troubles.

In 2000 the company established a subsidiary, Effem India, to market Mars' products in India. In 2003 Mars acquired French pet food producer Royal Canin. That same year its Mexican subsidiary, Effem Mexico SA de CV, merged with Mexican confectioner Grupo Matre to form a partnership to produce candy for Hispanic markets. Also that year the company began making an energy bar, Snickers Marathon.

The company also acquired Japanese vending machine parts manufacturer Nippon Conlux in 2003. The deal was Mars's first takeover venture in Japan.

Moving into the drink sector, in 2004 Mars licensed its Milky Way, Starburst, and 3 Musketeers brands to Bravo!, which will market vitamin-enhanced milk drinks using the names.

EXECUTIVES

Chairman, President, and CEO: John Franklyn Mars, age 66
VP: Jacqueline Badger Mars, age 64
VP and Secretary: D. M. Newby
VP, Treasurer, and CFO: R. E. Barnes
VP, Chocolate: Mark Mattia
VP, Marketing: Jim Cass
President, Masterfoods South America: Eduardo Senf
President, Masterfoods USA: Bob Gamgort
VP, Marketing Services Masterfoods USA: Peter Littlewood
VP, Marketing Sugar Confectionery Masterfoods: Michael Tolkowsky
Director, In-Store Solutions Masterfoods USA: Dena R. Clem
Director, Licensing Masterfoods USA: Lynn Scott
Director, Marketing Flavia Beverage Systems: Frank LaRusso
Director, Marketing Masterfoods Pet Food: Chris Jones
Director, Marketing Masterfoods USA: Brian Zeug
Director, National Sales Masterfoods USA: Larry Lupo
Director, Science: Harold Schmitz
Manager, Risk: Christopher Dewolfe

LOCATIONS

HQ: Mars, Incorporated
6885 Elm St., McLean, VA 22101
Phone: 703-821-4900 **Fax:** 703-448-9678
Web: www.mars.com

PRODUCTS/OPERATIONS

Selected Products
Candy
  3 Musketeers   Maltesers   Revels
  Bounty   M&M's   Skittles
  Dove   Mars   Snickers
  Ethel M   Milky Way   Starburst
    Chocolates   Opal Fruit   Twix

Ice-Cream Bars
  3 Musketeers
  DoveBars
  M&M Cookie Ice Cream Sandwiches
  Milky Way
  Snickers
  Starburst Ice Bars

Pet Food
  Bounce   Effem   Pedigree
  Brekkies   Frolic   Sheba
  Cesar   KiteKat   Trill
  Chappie   Loyal   Waltham
  Dine   My Dog   Whiskas

Snacks
  Combos
  Kudos

Rice and Other Food and Drinks
  Dolmio sauces
  Flavia drinks
  Masterfoods condiments and sauces
  Suzi Wan Chinese food
  Uncle Ben's Rice

Other Products
  Coin changers
  Flavia office beverage systems
  Klix beverage vending equipment
  Smart card payment systems

COMPETITORS

Barry Callebaut   Heinz
Brach's   Hershey
Butterfields Candy   Kraft Foods
Cadbury Schweppes   Lindt & Sprüngli
Campbell Soup   Meiji Seika
Colgate-Palmolive   Nestlé
ConAgra   Riviana Foods
CSM   Rocky Mountain Chocolate
Doane Pet Care   Russell Stover
Ezaki Glico   See's Candies
Ferrara Pan Candy   Thorntons
Ferrero   Tootsie Roll
General Mills   Unilever
Grupo Corvi   World's Finest Chocolate
Guittard   Wrigley

HISTORICAL FINANCIALS

Company Type: Private

Income Statement FYE: December 31

	ESTIMATED REVENUE ($ mil.)	NET INCOME ($ mil.)	NET PROFIT MARGIN	EMPLOYEES
12/03	17,000	—	—	31,000
12/02	16,200	—	—	30,000
12/01	15,500	—	—	30,000
12/00	15,400	—	—	30,000
12/99	15,200	—	—	28,500
12/98	15,500	—	—	30,000
12/97	14,400	—	—	28,500
12/96	14,000	—	—	28,000
12/95	13,000	—	—	28,000
12/94	12,500	—	—	28,000
Annual Growth	3.5%	—	—	1.1%

Revenue History

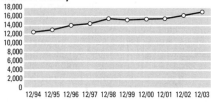

Martin-Brower

The Martin-Brower Company is panning for all the gold(en arches) that McDonald's can offer. It's the largest supplier of distribution services to the McDonald's restaurant chain. The company is the exclusive distributor to about 44% of the McDonald's restaurants in the US and all of its outlets in Brazil, Canada, and Central America, supplying such items as crew hats, first-aid kits, lightbulbs, and trash bags. The company operates about 30 distribution centers (six of which are located in Canada) in seven countries. Martin-Brower changed hands in 1998 when privately owned food and beverage distributor Reyes Holdings purchased the company from UK-based Sygen International (previously PIC International).

EXECUTIVES

Co-Chairman: J. Christopher (Chris) Reyes
Co-Chairman and CEO: M. Jude Reyes
President of US Operations: John Roussel
CIO: Joe Crenshaw
VP, Human Resources: Phil Menzel
President, Martin-Brower of Canada: Peter Hobbes
Information Technology Director: Marcos Hamsi

LOCATIONS

HQ: The Martin-Brower Company, L.L.C.
9500 West Bryn Mawr Ave., Ste. 700,
Rosemont, IL 60018
Phone: 847-227-6500 **Fax:** 847-227-6550

COMPETITORS

Anderson-DuBose   SYSCO
Golden State Foods U.S. Foodservice
Keystone Foods

HISTORICAL FINANCIALS

Company Type: Private

Income Statement FYE: December 31

	REVENUE ($ mil.)	NET INCOME ($ mil.)	NET PROFIT MARGIN	EMPLOYEES
12/03	3,700	—	—	3,000
12/02	3,000	—	—	2,900
12/01	2,800	—	—	2,900
12/00	2,500	—	—	2,200
12/99*	2,400	—	—	2,200
6/98	2,305	—	—	2,200
6/97	2,709	—	—	—
6/96	2,603	—	—	—
Annual Growth	5.2%	—	—	6.4%

*Fiscal year change

Revenue History

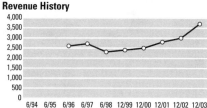

Marty Franich

Fleet customers can sail on into Marty Franich Auto Center dealerships. Founded in 1948, the company consists of two full-service dealerships in Watsonville, California, that sell Chrysler, Dodge, Ford, Jeep, Lincoln, and Mercury vehicles. The dealer also sells used vehicles, and it operates parts and service departments. The company specializes in sales to fleet buyers and sells to rental outfits nationwide, including Hertz and Avis Group.

President and CEO Steven Franich is the son of founder Martin (Marty) Franich, whose family owns the company.

EXECUTIVES

President and CEO: Steven (Rocky) Franich, age 56
Customer Relations Director: Abbie Romandia
Finance Manager: Tim Liebel
General Manager: Doug Inman
General Sales Manager: Leyton Felix
Used Car Manager: Steve Phillips
Internet Sales Manager, Marty Franich Chrysler Dodge Jeep: Jonathan Barr

LOCATIONS

HQ: Marty Franich Auto Center
550 Auto Center Dr., Watsonville, CA 95076
Phone: 831-722-4181   **Fax:** 831-724-1853
Web: www.franichford.com

COMPETITORS

AutoNation
Kuni Automotive
Prospect Motors
Sonic Automotive
Tasha Inc.
United Auto Group

HISTORICAL FINANCIALS

Company Type: Private

Income Statement
FYE: December 31

	REVENUE ($ mil.)	NET INCOME ($ mil.)	NET PROFIT MARGIN	EMPLOYEES
12/02	800	—	—	108
12/01	815	—	—	100
12/00	925	—	—	100
12/99	859	—	—	100
12/98	946	—	—	104
Annual Growth	(4.1%)	—	—	0.9%

Revenue History

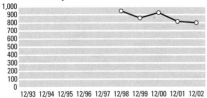

Mary Kay

Celebrating its 40th anniversary in 2003, Mary Kay is in the pink and in Avon's shadow (considering Avon's more than $6.8 billion in revenue in 2003) as the US's #2 direct seller of beauty products. It offers more than 200 products in six categories: body care, color cosmetics, facial skin care, fragrances, nail care, and sun protection. Some 1.3 million independent sales consultants demonstrate Mary Kay products in the US and about 30 other countries. Consultants vie for awards each year, ranging from jewelry to the company's trademark pink Cadillac's (first awarded in 1969). The family of founder Mary Kay Ash owns most of the company.

Founded by a woman for women, Mary Kay has an overwhelmingly female independent sales force. Although the company stands by Mary Kay's original goal of providing financial and career opportunities for women, much of the company's executive population is male. Ash's son Richard Rogers (chairman and CEO) runs the company.

Mary Kay works hard to retain the feel of a small company, despite its more than 1-million-strong independent sales force and the firm's growing international reach. As part of this initiative, each beauty consultant receives the option to buy his or her own Web site to use for selling to clients.

During her lifetime, Mary Kay Ash was known for her religious nature as well as her generosity. She founded the Mary Kay Ash Charitable Foundation in 1996. She suffered a debilitating stroke later that year and died on Thanksgiving Day 2001.

HISTORY

Before founding her own company in 1963, Mary Kay Ash worked as a Stanley Home Products sales representative. Impressed with the alligator handbag awarded to the top saleswoman at a Stanley convention, Ash was determined to win the next year's prize — and she did. Despite that accomplishment and having worked at Stanley for 11 years, a male assistant she had trained was made her boss after less than a year on the job. Tired of not receiving recognition, Ash and her second husband used their life savings ($5,000) to go into business for themselves. Although her husband died of a heart attack shortly before the business opened, Ash forged ahead with the help of her two grown sons.

She bought a cosmetics formula invented years earlier by a hide tanner. (The mixture was originally used to soften leather, but the tanner noticed how the formula made his hands look younger, and he began applying the mixture to his face, with great results.) Ash kept her first line simple — 10 products — and packaged her wares in pink to complement the typically white bathrooms of the day. Ash also enlisted consultants, who held "beauty shows" with five or six women in attendance. Mary Kay grossed $198,000 in its first year.

The company introduced men's skin care products in 1964. Ash bought a pink Cadillac the following year and began awarding the cars as prizes in 1969. (By 1981 orders were so large — almost 500 — that GM dubbed the color "Mary Kay Pink.")

Ash became a millionaire when her firm went public in 1968. Mary Kay grew steadily through the 1970s. Foreign operations began in 1971 in Australia, and over the next 25 years the company entered 24 more countries, including nations in Asia, Europe, Central and South America, and the Pacific Rim.

Sales plunged in the early 1980s, along with the company's stock prices (from $40 to $9 between 1983 and 1985). Ash and her family reacquired Mary Kay in 1985 through a $375 million LBO. Burdened with debt, the firm lost money in the late 1980s. Mary Kay took a number of steps to boost sales and income, doing a makeover on the cosmetics line and advertising in women's magazines again (after a five-year hiatus) to counter its old-fashioned image. The company also introduced recyclable packaging and lipstick in a tube (replacing brush-on palettes). In 1989 Avon rebuffed a buyout offer by Mary Kay, and both companies halted animal testing.

In 1993 Mary Kay opened a subsidiary in Russia, which later became the company's fourth-largest international market (behind Mexico, China, and Canada). Ash suffered a debilitating stroke in 1996.

In 1998 Mary Kay began selling through retail boutiques in China because of a government ban on direct selling. Changing with the times, Mary Kay added a white sport utility vehicle and new shades of pink to its fleet of 10,000 GM cars that year.

Chairman John Rochon was named CEO in 1999. Also in 1999 Mary Kay launched *Women & Success* (a magazine for consultants) and Atlas (its electronic ordering system).

In June 2001 Richard Rogers, the company chairman and son of Ash, replaced Rochon as CEO. A month later Mary Kay introduced the Velocity Products line, targeting girls ages 14 to 24. Ash died on Thanksgiving Day 2001.

Mary Kay Poland, headquartered in Warsaw, became the company's 34th international market in mid-2003.

EXECUTIVES

Chairman and CEO: Richard R. Rogers
President and COO: David B. Holl
President, Global Sales: Tom Whatley
EVP and CIO: Kregg Jodie
EVP, Global Human Resources and Operations: Darrell Overcash
EVP, Global Manufacturing: Dennis Greaney
EVP, Global Marketing/R&D: Myra O. Barker
SVP, Finance: Terry Smith
SVP, General Counsel, and Secretary: Nathan P. Moore
SVP, Marketing: Rhonda Shasteen
VP, Global Corporate Communications: Randall G. Oxford
VP, Government Relations: Anne Crews
VP, Information Technology: Karen Calvert
VP, Sales Development and Administration: Sean Key
President, Mary Kay Europe: Tara Eustance
President, Mary Kay Greater China: Paul Mak
Director, Product Marketing: Lisa Cohorn
Director, Supply Chain Information Services and Technologies: Doug Voss
General Manager, Mary Kay Poland: Ewa Kudlinska-Pyrz
Project Manager, Information Services Technology: Lou Silvey
Corporate Communications: Shannon Summers

LOCATIONS

HQ: Mary Kay Inc.
16251 Dallas Pkwy., Addison, TX 75001
Phone: 972-687-6300   **Fax:** 972-687-1611
Web: www.marykay.com

Mary Kay has an independent sales force of more than 1 million that sells the company's products in more than 33 markets in Asia, Australia, Europe, North America, and South America.

PRODUCTS/OPERATIONS

Selected Product Lines
Body care
Cosmetics
Facial skin care
Fragrances (men's and women's)
Men's skin care
Nail care
Nutritional supplements for men
Nutritional supplements for women
Sun protection

COMPETITORS

Alberto-Culver
Alticor
Avon
Bath & Body Works
BeautiControl Cosmetics
Body Shop
Clarins
Colgate-Palmolive
Coty Inc.
Del Labs
Dial
Estée Lauder
Helen of Troy
Herbalife
Intimate Brands
John Paul Mitchell
Johnson & Johnson
L'Oréal
L'Oréal USA
Merle Norman
Murad, Inc.
New Dana Perfumes
Nu Skin
Perrigo
Procter & Gamble
Reliv'
Revlon
Schwarzkopf & DEP
Scott's Liquid Gold
Shaklee
Shiseido
Sunrider
Unilever

HISTORICAL FINANCIALS

Company Type: Private

Income Statement				FYE: December 31
	REVENUE ($ mil.)	NET INCOME ($ mil.)	NET PROFIT MARGIN	EMPLOYEES
12/03	1,800	—	—	3,600
12/02	1,560	—	—	3,600
12/01	1,300	—	—	3,600
12/00	1,200	—	—	3,600
12/99	1,000	—	—	3,250
12/98	1,000	—	—	3,500
12/97	1,050	—	—	3,500
12/96	1,000	—	—	3,000
12/95	950	—	—	2,800
12/94	850	—	—	2,400
Annual Growth	8.7%	—	—	4.6%

Revenue History

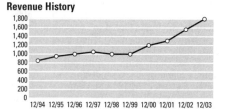

Maryland State Lottery

The Maryland State Lottery Agency offers players a variety of ways to amass a fortune. Among its games of chance are scratch-offs bearing titles such as Betty Boop, High Stakes, Hot Cherries, and Slingo. The agency's numbers games include Lotto, Pick 3, and Pick 4. Maryland State Lottery also participates in the seven-state The Big Game lottery. The agency, which was created in 1973, distributes about 57% of its revenue as prizes; the rest goes to state-funded programs, retailers, and operational expenses. Proceeds from lottery sales helped build Camden Yards, home of Major League Baseball's Baltimore Orioles.

EXECUTIVES

Director: Buddy W. Roogow
Deputy Director and CFO: Gina M. Smith
Deputy Director and CIO: Sandra A. Johnson
Director Communications: Hollis J. (Jimmy) White
Director Creative Services: Jill Q. Baer
Director Human Resources: Lawrence J. Simpson
Director Research and Planning: Tchicaya B. Ellis
Director Sales: Joseph B. Jason
Director Security: Nathaniel (Nate) Smoot
Principal Counsel: Andrea J. Johnson

LOCATIONS

HQ: Maryland State Lottery Agency
1800 Washington Blvd., Ste. 330,
Baltimore, MD 21230
Phone: 410-230-8800   **Fax:** 410-230-8728
Web: www.msla.state.md.us

PRODUCTS/OPERATIONS

Selected Games
Numbers games
  The Big Game
  Keno
  Lotto
  Pick 3
  Pick 4
Scratch-off games
  Betty Boop
  Fire n' Ice
  Hot Cherries
  Pharaoh's Gold
  Riverboat Riches
  Slingo
  Tropical Jackpot
  Vegas

COMPETITORS

Multi-State Lottery
New Jersey Lottery
Pennsylvania Lottery
Virginia Lottery

HISTORICAL FINANCIALS

Company Type: Government-owned

Income Statement				FYE: June 30
	REVENUE ($ mil.)	NET INCOME ($ mil.)	NET PROFIT MARGIN	EMPLOYEES
6/04	1,395	—	—	150
6/03	1,320	—	—	150
6/02	1,300	—	—	150
6/01	1,211	—	—	157
6/00	1,175	—	—	150
6/99	1,080	—	—	150
6/98	1,070	—	—	170
6/97	1,041	—	—	170
6/96	1,112	—	—	160
6/95	1,039	—	—	148
Annual Growth	3.3%	—	—	0.1%

Revenue History

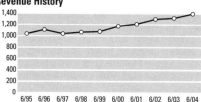

Mashantucket Pequot Gaming

Mashantucket Pequot Gaming Enterprise has propelled the Mashantucket Pequot Tribal Nation (with roughly 600 members) from the depths of intense poverty to its lofty position as the wealthiest Native American tribe in the US. It owns and operates Foxwoods Resort Casino, one of the largest casinos in the world and, many believe, the most profitable. The complex offers more than 6,400 slot machines and 350 gaming tables in six casinos, three hotels (Grand Pequot Tower, Great Cedar Hotel, Two Trees Inn), 24 restaurants, live entertainment, and a string of retail shops.

The Mashantucket Pequot reservation is a sovereign nation, and the Pequot tribe is not obligated to pay local property or business taxes, or reveal all of its finances. However, estimates of Foxwoods' annual revenues exceed $1 billion. The state of Connecticut receives 25% of the casino's slot machine revenues.

In addition to its gaming operations, the Mashantucket Pequot Tribal Nation owns Fox Navigation (high-speed ferry service) and the Pequot Pharmaceutical Network (mail-order and discount pharmaceuticals). It also owns three Connecticut hotels (Hilton Mystic, Norwich Inn & Spa, Randall's Ordinary Inn) and two golf courses (Foxwoods Golf & Country Club at Boulder Hills and Pequot Golf Club). The Mashantucket Pequot Tribal Nation has even established the Mashantucket Pequot Museum and Research Center dedicated to the tribe's life and history.

Two books released in 2000 and 2001, which questioned the authenticity of the Mashantucket Pequot tribe and claimed that the government was duped into giving them more land for their reservation than they were entitled to, sparked a series of lawsuits from neighboring communities. In early 2002 the Mashantucket Pequot tribe announced it had withdrawn its application to annex 165 acres of land close to its Foxwood Resort Casino, ending nearly 10 years of legal battles.

HISTORY

Once a powerful tribe, the Pequots were virtually wiped out in the 17th century by disease and attacks from colonists. More than 350 years later, Richard "Skip" Hayward, a pipefitter making $15,000 a year, led the fight for federal recognition of his nearly extinct Mashantucket Pequot tribe. He was elected tribal chairman in 1975, and the US government officially recognized the tribe in 1983.

The Indian Gaming Regulatory Act of 1988 opened the door for legal gambling on reservations, but tribes still had to negotiate with state governments for authorization. Hayward hired G. Michael "Mickey" Brown as a consultant and lawyer. Brown took the tribe's legal battle to the US Supreme Court, which eventually ruled that the Pequots could build a casino. When some 30 banks turned down the Pequots for a construction loan, Brown introduced Hayward and his tribe to Lim Goh Tong, billionaire developer of the successful Gentings Highlands Casino resort in Malaysia. Tong invested approximately $60 million, and the Foxwoods casino opened in 1992.

Brown brought in Alfred J. Luciani to serve as president and CEO of Foxwoods. Luciani stayed less than a year, however, resigning because of what he called philosophical differences with tribe leadership. Brown took over as CEO in 1993. Although Foxwoods grew rapidly, Brown often wrestled with members of the tribal council over how the business should be run. The next year Brown rehired Luciani to oversee the development of the Grand Pequot Tower hotel.

Brown resigned and Luciani was fired in 1997 after it was revealed that Brown had not fully disclosed his ties with Lim Goh Tong and that, in 1992, Luciani had accepted a $377,000 loan from Gamma International, a vendor that provided keno services to Foxwoods. The Pequots considered these actions to be conflicts of interest. A new management team was brought in, and Floyd "Bud" Celey, a veteran of Hilton Hotels, was appointed CEO.

The Pequots opened the Mashantucket Pequot Museum and Research Center in 1998. When tribal elections were held later that year, Kenneth Reels was elected chairman of the Pequot's tribal governing body, ousting Hayward from the position he had held for more than 20 years. Hayward was elected vice chairman. Mashantucket Pequot Gaming Enterprise concentrated on improving financial accountability in 1999, and the tribe began cutting costs by shuttering unprofitable holdings, including Pequot River Shipworks, its shipbuilding business.

Former COO William Sherlock replaced Celey as CEO in 2000. That year the first of two books (the second was published in 2001), which questioned the tribe's legitimacy, created some controversy for the group. A federal audit in 2000 revealed that the tribe's pharmaceutical firm was giving discount drugs intended for Native Americans to its non-Native American employees. In 2002 the tribe withdrew its application to annex 165 acres of land close to its Foxwood Resort Casino after nearly 10 years of legal battles.

EXECUTIVES

Chairman, Tribal Council: Kenneth Reels
Vice Chairman, Tribal Council: Richard A. (Skip) Hayward
President and CEO: William Sherlock
COO: Robert Sheldon
EVP Marketing: Robert De Salvio
SVP Administration: Bryce Kirchner
SVP Finance: John O'Brien
SVP Human Resources: Joanne Franks
Director, Public Relations: Arthur Henick
Director, Public Relations: Toni Parker-Johnson
Media Relations Manager: Bryce MacDonald

LOCATIONS

HQ: Mashantucket Pequot Gaming Enterprise Inc.
Rte. 2, Mashantucket, CT 06339
Phone: 860-312-3000 **Fax:** 860-312-1599
Web: www.foxwoods.com

The Mashantucket Pequot Gaming Enterprise has holdings in Connecticut and Rhode Island.

PRODUCTS/OPERATIONS

Selected Operations
Foxwoods Resort Casino
  Foxwoods Golf & Country Club at Boulder Hills (Richmond, RI)
  Grand Pequot Tower
  Great Cedar Hotel
  Two Trees Inn

Selected Tribal Holdings
Fox Navigation (ferry service)
Hilton Mystic (Mystic, CT)
Mashantucket Pequot Gaming Enterprise (Foxwoods Resort Casino; Ledyard, CT)
Mashantucket Pequot Museum and Research Center (Mashantucket, CT)
Norwich Inn & Spa (Norwich, CT)
Pequot Golf Club (Stonington, CT)
Pequot Pharmaceutical Network (mail-order and discount pharmaceuticals)
Randall's Ordinary Inn (North Stonington, CT)

COMPETITORS

Aztar
Caesars Entertainment
Connecticut Lottery
Harrah's Entertainment
Kerzner International
Mohegan Tribal Gaming
New York State Lottery
Trump Hotels & Casinos

HISTORICAL FINANCIALS

Company Type: Private

Income Statement
FYE: September 30

	ESTIMATED REVENUE ($ mil.)	NET INCOME ($ mil.)	NET PROFIT MARGIN	EMPLOYEES
9/02	1,000	—	—	11,500
9/01	1,500	—	—	11,500
9/00	1,300	—	—	11,500
9/99	1,200	—	—	11,500
9/98	1,000	—	—	11,500
9/97	1,000	—	—	11,180
9/96	1,100	—	—	12,000
9/95	1,030	—	—	11,000
9/94	1,000	—	—	10,000
9/93	1,000	—	—	9,100
Annual Growth	0.0%	—	—	2.6%

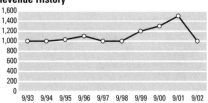

Revenue History

Massachusetts Mutual Life Insurance

After flirting with the possibility of demutualizing, Massachusetts Mutual Life Insurance (MassMutual) has decided to stay the course. Founded in 1851, MassMutual sells individuals and businesses a variety of life insurance and pension products through more than 1,500 US offices, as well as through third parties (financial institutions, brokerages, accountants). MassMutual is active in the retirement and financial products arenas, offering individual and group retirement plans, annuities, and trust services (through The MassMutual Trust Company). Other subsidiaries include OppenheimerFunds (mutual funds), David L. Babson & Co. (investor services), and Cornerstone Real Estate (real estate equities).

Like so many other insurance firms, MassMutual is determined to transform into a financial services firm. However, you won't catch the firm issuing stock to get the job done; the management of MassMutual has decided to keep things collective despite pressure from some policyholders.

MassMutual International is exporting the company's operations worldwide, having established subsidiaries in Asia, Europe, and South America. It focuses on new product development (the majority of sales come from products or channels developed within the last couple of years) and broadened distribution.

HISTORY

Insurance agent George Rice formed Massachusetts Mutual in 1851 as a stock company based in Springfield. The firm converted to a mutual in 1867. For its first 50 years MassMutual sold only individual life insurance, but after 1900 it branched out, offering first annuities (1917) and then disability coverage (1918).

The early 20th century was rough on MassMutual, which was forced to raise premiums on new policies during WWI, then faced the high costs of the 1918 flu epidemic. The firm endured the Great Depression despite policy terminations, expanding its product line to include income insurance. In 1946 MassMutual wrote its first group policy, for Jack Daniel's maker Brown-Forman Distillers. By 1950 the company had diversified into medical insurance.

MassMutual began investing in stocks in the 1950s, switching from fixed-return bonds and mortgages for higher returns. It also decentralized and in 1961 began automating operations. By 1970 the firm had installed a computer network linking it to its independent agents. During this period, whole life insurance remained the core product.

With interest rates increasing during the late 1970s, many insurers diversified by offering high-yield products like guaranteed investment contracts funded by high-risk investments. MassMutual resisted as long as it could, but as interest rates soared to 20%, the company experienced a rash of policy loans, which led to a cash crunch. In 1981, with its policy growth rate trailing the industry norm, MassMutual developed new products, including some that offered higher dividends in return for adjustable interest on policy loans.

In the 1980s MassMutual reduced its stock investment (to about 5% of total investments by 1987), allowing it to emerge virtually unscathed from the 1987 stock market crash.

The firm changed course in 1990 and entered financial services. It bought a controlling interest in mutual fund manager Oppenheimer Management. MassMutual announced in 1993 that, with legislation limiting rates, it would stop writing new individual and small-group policies in New York.

The next year the company targeted the neglected family-owned business niche; in 1995 it sponsored the American Alliance of Family-Owned Businesses and rolled out new whole life products aimed at this segment. That year it bought David L. Babson & Company, a Massachusetts-based investment management firm, and opened life insurance companies in Chile and Argentina.

In 1996 MassMutual merged with Connecticut Mutual. It also acquired Antares Leveraged Capital Corp. (commercial finance) and Charter Oak Capital Management (investment advisory services). The next year MassMutual sold its Life & Health Benefits Management subsidiary.

Still in the mood to merge, the company entered discussions with Northwestern Mutual in 1998, but culture clashes terminated the talks. Also that year the company helped push through legislation that would allow insurers to issue stock through mutual holding companies, a move which MassMutual itself contemplated in 1999.

MassMutual expanded outside the US at the turn of the century. In 1999 it issued securities in Europe, opened offices in such locales as Bermuda and Luxembourg, and bought the Argentina operations of Jefferson-Pilot. A year later it expanded into Asia when it bought Hong Kong-based CRC Protective Life Insurance (now MassMutual Asia). In 2001 the company entered the Taiwanese market, buying a stake in Mercuries Life Insurance (now MassMutual Mercuries Life Insurance) and acquired Japanese insurer Aetna Heiwa Life (a subsidiary of US health insurer Aetna).

EXECUTIVES

Chairman, President, and CEO: Robert J. O'Connell
EVP and CFO: Howard E. Gunton
EVP and Chief Investment Officer; Chairman, President, and CEO, David L. Babson & Company: Stuart H. Reese
EVP, Savings Products, Human Resources, Enterprise Marketing, and Administration: Susan A. Alfano
EVP and General Counsel: Lawrence V. Burkett Jr.
EVP, Retirement Services: Frederick C. Castellani
EVP, Enterprise Services: James E. Miller
EVP; Chairman, President, and CEO, OppenheimerFunds: John V. Murphy
EVP, International, Large Corporate Markets, Mergers & Acquisitions; President and CEO, MassMutual International: Andrew Oleksiw
EVP, Disability Income Insurance, Long-Term Care Insurance, Financial Products Division and Retirement Services: Toby J. Slodden
EVP, Individual Insurance Group, Product, Sales, and Marketing: Matthew E. Winter
Deputy CFO: Michael T. Rollings
SVP, Corporate Tax: Richard D. Bourgeois
SVP; SVP and CEO, MassMutual Asia: Elroy Chan
SVP and Deputy General Counsel, Federal Government Relations: Kenneth S. Cohen
SVP, Corporate Services: Colin C. Collins
SVP, Corporate Communications: Frances B. Emerson
SVP, Investments: Michael D. Hays
SVP and General Auditor: Douglas J. Janik
SVP, Secretary, and Deputy General Counsel: Ann F. Lomeli
SVP, Information Systems: Jonathan Picoult
SVP, Corporate Human Resources: Nancy M. Roberts
Auditors: PricewaterhouseCoopers LLP

LOCATIONS

HQ: Massachusetts Mutual Life Insurance Company
1295 State St., Springfield, MA 01111
Phone: 413-788-8411   **Fax:** 413-744-6005
Web: www.massmutual.com

Massachusetts Mutual Life Insurance operates in Bermuda, Chile, Hong Kong, Japan, Luxembourg, Taiwan, and the US.

PRODUCTS/OPERATIONS

2003 Sales

	$ mil.	% of total
Premium income	13,508	75
Net investment income	4,074	23
Other income	365	2
Total	**17,947**	**100**

Major Subsidiaries

Antares Capital Corporation (commercial finance)
C.M. Life Insurance Company
Cornerstone Real Estate Advisers, Inc. (real estate equities)
David L. Babson and Company, Inc. (institutional investment services)
MassMutual International, Inc.
MassMutual Trust Company, F.S.B.
MML Bay State Life Insurance Company
MML Investors Services, Inc.
OppenheimerFunds, Inc. (mutual funds)

COMPETITORS

AIG	Liberty Mutual
AIG American General	Mellon Financial
Allianz	Merrill Lynch
Allstate	MetLife
American Financial	Nationwide
AXA Financial	New York Life
Charles Schwab	Northwestern Mutual
CIGNA	Principal Financial
Citigroup	Prudential
CNA Financial	Retirement System Group
Conseco	St. Paul Travelers
FMR	State Farm
Genworth Financial	TIAA-CREF
Guardian Life	Torchmark
The Hartford	UBS Financial Services
Jefferson-Pilot	
John Hancock Financial Services	

HISTORICAL FINANCIALS

Company Type: Mutual company

Income Statement   FYE: December 31

	ASSETS ($ mil.)	NET INCOME ($ mil.)	INCOME AS % OF ASSETS	EMPLOYEES
12/03	96,779	461	0.5%	10,000
12/02	84,102	1,408	1.7%	9,000
12/01	78,934	791	1.0%	9,000
12/00	73,739	740	1.0%	8,000
12/99	70,586	441	0.6%	7,900
12/98	66,979	359	0.5%	7,885
12/97	61,069	262	0.4%	—
12/96	55,752	239	0.4%	—
12/95	38,632	159	0.4%	—
12/94	35,720	93	0.3%	—
Annual Growth	11.7%	19.5%	—	4.9%

2003 Year-End Financials

Equity as % of assets: 6.5%   Long-term debt ($ mil.): 50,803
Return on assets: 0.5%   Sales ($ mil.): 17,947
Return on equity: 7.4%

Net Income History

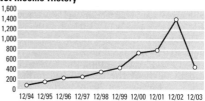

MasterCard

Surpassing Visa in market share — *that* would be priceless. MasterCard is the US's #2 payment system and is owned by its 25,000 financial institution members worldwide. It markets the MasterCard (credit and debit cards) and Maestro (debit cards) brands, provides the transaction authorization network, and collects fees from members. Its cards are accepted at more than 22 million locations around the world. MasterCard also operates the Cirrus ATM network and Mondex International, a chip-based smart card subsidiary. Its European business is conducted primarily through wholly owned subsidiary MasterCard Europe (formerly Europay International).

Citigroup, J.P. Morgan Chase, and BANK ONE each own about 7% of MasterCard.

Long considered more downmarket than Visa, MasterCard is working to add affluent users (the World MasterCard offers 24-hour concierge services).

The company is working amid growing competition to make its electronic smart card (single-use or refillable chip-based cards used as cash) the industry standard through Mondex. Smart cards are common in Europe, but have met consumer resistance in the US. MasterCard is launching smart card initiatives in Asia and moving into wireless e-commerce; it is teaming up with Oberthur Card Systems to develop secure methods to make purchases over wireless devices. And in December 2002 the company initiated a market test of MasterCard PayPass, a new "contactless" radio frequency chip solution enabling users to tap or wave their payment card over a terminal.

MasterCard's quest for market share led to its merger with Europay, the firm's European counterpart, in mid-2002. European members now own about a third of the newly created holding company, MasterCard Inc. While the consolidation of Maestro's ownership (Europay and MasterCard had owned it 50-50) has given MasterCard control of the world's largest debit card network, it continues to trail Visa in credit cards.

Still, the total number of MasterCard cards in circulation worldwide at the end of 2003 was more than 630 million. The company hopes to continue to grow by increasing the number of places MasterCard is accepted, focusing specifically on mobile and electronic commerce, fast-food restaurants, and public sector payments such as taxes, fines, and tolls.

HISTORY

A group of bankers formed The Interbank Card Association (ICA) in 1966 to establish authorization, clearing, and settlement procedures for bank credit card transactions. This was particularly important to banks left out of the rapidly growing BankAmericard (later Visa) network sponsored by Bank of America.

By 1969, ICA was issuing the Master Charge card throughout the US and had formed alliances in Europe and Japan. In the mid-1970s ICA modernized its system, replacing telephone transaction authorization with a computerized magnetic strip system. ICA had members in Africa, Australia, and Europe by 1979. That year the organization changed its name (and the card's) to MasterCard.

In 1980 Russell Hogg became president when John Reynolds resigned after disagreeing with the board over company performance and direction. Hogg made major organizational changes and consolidated data processing in St. Louis. MasterCard began offering debit cards in 1980 and traveler's checks in 1981.

MasterCard issued the first credit cards in China in 1987. The next year it bought Cirrus, then the world's largest ATM network. It also secured Eurocard (now Europay) to supervise MasterCard's European operations and help build the brand.

Hogg resigned in 1988 after disagreements with the board, and was succeeded by Alex Hart. In 1991 the Maestro debit card was unveiled.

The 1990s were marked by trouble in Europe: The Europay pact hadn't resulted in the boom MasterCard had hoped for, customer service was below par, and competition was keen. Alex Hart retired in 1994 and was succeeded by Eugene Lockhart, who tackled the European woes. Lockhart considered ending the relationship but eventually worked things out with Europay. By the end of the decade, Europay was locked in a vicious battle to undercut Visa's market share through lower fees.

MasterCard in 1995 invested in UK-based Mondex International, maker of electronic, set-value, refillable smart cards. But US consumer resistance to cash cards and competition in the more advanced European market delayed growth in this area.

In October 1996 a group of merchants, including Wal-Mart and Sears, filed class-action lawsuits against both MasterCard and Visa, challenging the "honor all cards" rule. Because usage fees are higher, merchants don't want to accept consumers' MasterCard- or Visa-branded off-line, or signature-based debit cards, and claim the card issuers are violating antitrust laws by tying acceptance of debit to that of credit. In a dramatic twist, minutes before the trial was set to begin in 2003, MasterCard announced a settlement (the card issuer is required to pay $125 million in 2003 and $100 million annually from 2004 through 2012). Just months later, armed with the lawsuit's settlement which also freed merchants to pick which credit and debit card services they use, Wal-Mart (along with a handful of others) stopped accepting signature debit cards issued by MasterCard.

Lockhart resigned in 1997 and was succeeded by former head of overseas operations Robert Selander. Yet another management upheaval began in 1999 as the company moved to streamline its organizational structure and shift away from geographical divisions. It also said member banks could boost visibility by putting their logos on card fronts and moving MasterCard's logo to the back.

In 2002 MasterCard merged with Europay, the Belgium-based card company with which it already had close ties. As part of the transaction, holding company MasterCard Inc. was formed; MasterCard International become its main subsidiary and MasterCard Europe (formerly Europay) became its European subsidiary.

EXECUTIVES

Chairman: Baldomero Falcones Jaquotot, age 57
President, CEO, and Director: Robert W. Selander, age 53
COO: Alan J. Heuer, age 62, $1,250,000 pay
CFO: Chris A. McWilton, age 45
Chief Administrative Officer: Michael W. Michl, age 58, $675,000 pay
President, The Americas: Ruth Ann Marshall, age 49
President, Asia/Pacific Region: André Sekulic
President, Canada Region: Walter M. (Walt) Macnee
President, MasterCard Europe: Alexander Labak, age 41
President, Latin America/Caribbean Region: Jean F. Rozwadowski
President, South Asia/Middle East/Africa Region: Sonny Sannon
President, Global Technology and Operations: W. Roy Dunbar, age 43
President, MasterCard Advisors: Keith Stock, age 51
SEVP, Global Development: Christopher D. Thom, age 55, $1,075,000 pay
EVP and Chief e-Business Officer, e-Business and Emerging Technologies: Arthur D. Kranzley
EVP and Chief Marketing Officer, Global Marketing: Lawrence (Larry) Flanagan
EVP and Chief Product Officer, Product Management: John de Lavis
EVP, Global Account Management: Gary Flood
VP, Global Communications and Corporate Public Relations: Sharon Gamsin
General Counsel and Corporate Secretary: Noah J. Hanft, age 51
Auditors: PricewaterhouseCoopers LLP

LOCATIONS

HQ: MasterCard Incorporated
2000 Purchase St., Purchase, NY 10577
Phone: 914-249-2000 **Fax:** 914-249-4206
Web: www.mastercard.com/mcweb

MasterCard has US offices in California, Delaware, Florida, Georgia, Illinois, Missouri, New York, and Washington, DC. It has international offices in Argentina, Australia, Belgium, Brazil, Canada, Chile, China, Colombia, Hong Kong, India, Indonesia, Japan, Malaysia, Mexico, the Philippines, Singapore, South Africa, South Korea, Taiwan, Thailand, the United Arab Emirates, the UK, and Venezuela. It provides services in more than 210 countries.

PRODUCTS/OPERATIONS

Products
Cirrus Card
Debit MasterCard
Debit MasterCard Business Card
Gold MasterCard Card
Maestro Card
MasterCard BusinessCard Card
MasterCard Corporate Card
MasterCard Corporate Executive Card
MasterCard Corporate Fleet Card
MasterCard Corporate MultiCard Card
MasterCard Corporate Purchasing Card
MasterCard Electronic
MasterCard Executive BusinessCard Card
MasterCard travelers cheques
Mondex Card
Platinum MasterCard Card
Standard MasterCard Card
World MasterCard Card

COMPETITORS

American Express
Morgan Stanley
Visa

HISTORICAL FINANCIALS

Company Type: Holding company

	ASSETS ($ mil.)	NET INCOME ($ mil.)	INCOME AS % OF ASSETS	EMPLOYEES
Income Statement				FYE: December 31
12/03	2,901	(386)	—	4,000
12/02	2,261	116	5.1%	4,000
12/01	1,486	142	9.6%	3,300
12/00	1,182	118	10.0%	3,100
12/99	973	86	8.9%	2,700
12/98	841	57	6.8%	2,400
12/97	651	40	6.1%	2,357
12/96	—	72	—	2,025
12/95	—	22	—	2,000
12/94	—	12	—	1,975
Annual Growth	28.3%	—	—	8.2%

2003 Year-End Financials
Equity as % of assets: 24.1%   Long-term debt ($ mil.): 230
Return on assets: —   Sales ($ mil.): 2,231
Return on equity: —

Net Income History

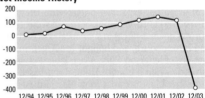

Mayer, Brown, Rowe & Maw

Practicing law is a supreme calling for many attorneys at Mayer, Brown, Rowe & Maw (formerly Mayer, Brown & Platt). One of the largest law firms in the US, Mayer, Brown was one of the first to specialize in arguing cases before the Supreme Court. The firm has over 1,300 lawyers at its 13 offices in the US and Europe, offering their expertise in corporate and securities law and litigation, global trade, and real estate. Founded in 1881 in Chicago, the firm has represented clients such as Dow Chemical, America Online (now Time Warner Inc.), and BMW.

Mayer, Brown is also noted for being one of the first of the top 20 law firms to elect a woman as managing partner (1991) and for having a large percentage of female lawyers.

EXECUTIVES

Chairman: Tyrone C. Fahner
Executive Director: Steven R. Wells
CFO: Alan S. Cohen
Director Human Resources: Coleen Callahan

LOCATIONS

HQ: Mayer, Brown, Rowe & Maw
190 S. LaSalle St., Chicago, IL 60603
Phone: 312-782-0600 **Fax:** 312-701-7711
Web: www.mayerbrownrowe.com

The firm has US offices in Charlotte, North Carolina; Chicago; Houston; Los Angeles; New York City; Palo Alto, California; and Washington, DC. International offices include Brussels; Cologne and Frankfurt, Germany; London and Manchester, UK; and Paris.

PRODUCTS/OPERATIONS

Selected Practice Areas
Bankruptcy
Corporate and securities
Environmental
Government relations
International trade
Labor
Litigation
Real estate
Taxation
Venture capital

COMPETITORS

Baker & McKenzie
Jenner & Block
Jones Day
Katten Muchin
Kirkland & Ellis
Latham & Watkins
McDermott, Will
Sidley Austin Brown & Wood
Skadden, Arps
White & Case
Winston & Strawn

HISTORICAL FINANCIALS

Company Type: Partnership

Income Statement FYE: December 31

	REVENUE ($ mil.)	NET INCOME ($ mil.)	NET PROFIT MARGIN	EMPLOYEES
12/03	813	—	—	—
12/02	705	—	—	—
12/01	573	—	—	—
12/00	534	—	—	1,000
12/99	464	—	—	820
12/98	400	—	—	816
12/97	340	—	—	695
12/96	325	—	—	643
12/95	274	—	—	550
12/94	263	—	—	550
Annual Growth	13.4%	—	—	10.5%

Revenue History

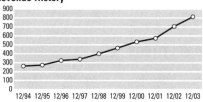

Mayo Foundation

Mayo can whip up a medical miracle. The not-for-profit Mayo Foundation for Medical Education and Research provides health care, most notably for complex medical conditions, through its renowned Mayo Clinic in Rochester, Minnesota. Other clinics are located in Arizona and Florida. The clinics' multidisciplinary approach to care attracts thousands of patients a year, including such notables as the late Ronald and Nancy Reagan and the late King Hussein of Jordan. The Mayo Health System operates a network of affiliated community hospitals and clinics in Minnesota, Iowa, and Wisconsin. The Mayo Foundation also conducts research and trains physicians, nurses, and other health professionals.

In addition to the Mayo Clinics, the foundation operates other hospitals: Saint Marys and Rochester Methodist in Rochester; Mayo Clinic Hospital in Phoenix; and St. Luke's Hospital in Jacksonville. Mayo Health System includes five clinics in Iowa, five hospitals and some 20 clinics in Wisconsin, and nearly 50 facilities in Minnesota. At the University of Minnesota, the foundation's education programs include the Mayo Graduate School of Medicine and the Mayo School of Health-Related Sciences.

With managed care limiting patients' ability to use its facilities, Mayo forms referral alliances with hospital groups, HMOs, and other groups. Its charter prevents it from raising prices to compensate for rising health care costs, so the foundation commercializes medical technology, publishes medical literature, and invests in other medical startups to increase income. Also, affluent patients who can pay — well — for treatment (and who may contribute to the endowment) help subsidize care for those who can't pay.

The Mayo Foundation dates back to a frontier practice launched by William Mayo in 1863.

HISTORY

In 1845 William Mayo came to the US from England. He was a doctor, veterinarian, river boatman, surveyor, and newspaper editor before settling in Rochester, Minnesota, in 1863.

When a tornado struck Rochester in 1883, Mayo took charge of a makeshift hospital. The Sisters of St. Francis offered to replace the hospital that was lost in the disaster if Mayo would head the staff. He agreed reluctantly. Not only were hospitals then associated with the poor and insane, but his affiliation with the sisters raised eyebrows among Protestants and Catholics.

Saint Marys Hospital opened in 1889. Mayo's sons William and Charles, who were starting their medical careers, helped him. After the elder Mayo retired, the sons ran the hospital. Although the brothers accepted all medical cases, they made the hospital self-sufficient, attracting paying patients by pioneering in specialization at a time when physicians were jacks-of-all-medical-trades.

This specialization attracted other physicians, and by 1907 the practice was known as "the Mayo's clinic." The brothers, in association with the University of Minnesota, established the Mayo Foundation for Medical Research (now the Mayo Graduate School of Medicine), the world's first program to train medical specialists, in 1915.

In 1919 the brothers transferred the clinic properties and miscellaneous financial assets, primarily from patient care profits, into the Mayo Properties Association (renamed the Mayo Foundation in 1964). Under the terms of the endowment, all Mayo Clinic medical staff members became salaried employees. In 1933 the clinic established one of the first blood banks in the US. Both brothers died in 1939.

Part of the association's mission was to fund research. In 1950 two Mayo researchers won a Nobel Prize for developing cortisone to treat rheumatoid arthritis. The foundation opened its second medical school, the Mayo Medical School, in 1972.

As insurers in the 1980s pressured to cut hospital admissions and stays, the foundation diversified with for-profit ventures. In 1983 Mayo began publishing the *Mayo Clinic Health Letter*, its first subscription publication for a general audience, and the *Mayo Clinic Family Health Book*. It also began providing specialized lab services to other doctors and hospitals. The addition of Rochester Methodist Hospital (creating the largest not-for-profit medical group in the country) was also a response to financial pressures. Following the money south as affluent folks retired, the foundation opened clinics in Jacksonville (1986); Scottsdale, Arizona (1987); and in nearby Phoenix (1998).

Seeking to expand in its home market, Mayo in 1992 formed the Mayo Health System, a regional network of health care facilities and medical practices. In 1996 former patient Barbara Woodward Lips left $127.9 million to the foundation, the largest bequest in its history.

In the late 1990s the foundation increasingly looked to corporate partnerships to help defray costs and to expand research activities. In 1998 and 1999 Mayo boosted its presence overseas with nonmedical regional offices. Mayo scientists in 2000 announced they had regrown or repaired nerve coverings in mice; this type of damage in humans (caused by such conditions as multiple sclerosis) had been considered irreparable. The Mayo Foundation continues to push for breakthroughs in medical science.

EXECUTIVES

Chairman: Bert A. Getz, age 65
President and CEO: Denis A. Cortese
CFO: Jeffrey W. Bolton
VP; Chairman, Mayo Clinic Rochester: Hugh C. Smith
VP and Chief Administrative Officer: Robert K. Smoldt
Administrator, Mayo Clinic Scottsdale:
  James G. Anderson
Chairman, Mayo Clinic Jacksonville: George B. Bartley
Director, Education: Thomas H. Berquist
Director, Mayo Clinic Cancer Center:
  Franklyn G. Prendergast, age 58
Chairman, Department of Facilities and Systems Support Services: Craig A. Smoldt
Chairman, Mayo Clinic Scottsdale: Victor F. Trastek
Chairman, Information Technology: Abdul Bengali
Chairman, Human Resources: Marita Heller
Secretary and Chairman, Legal Department:
  Jonathan J. Oviatt
Director for Development: James C. Schroeder
Medical Director for Development: David A. Ahlquist
Auditors: Ernst & Young LLP

LOCATIONS

HQ: Mayo Foundation for Medical Education and Research
200 1st St. SW, Rochester, MN 55905
Phone: 507-284-2511 **Fax:** 507-284-0161
Web: www.mayo.edu

Selected Locations

Arizona
  Mayo Clinic Hospital (Phoenix)
  Mayo Clinic Scottsdale
Florida
  Mayo Clinic Jacksonville
  St. Luke's Hospital (Jacksonville)
Iowa
  Amstrong Clinic (Armstrong)
  Decorah Clinic (Decorah)
  Lake Mills Clinic (Lake Mills)
  New Hampton Clinic (New Hampton)
  Franciscan Skemp Healthcare Waukon Clinic (Waukon)
Minnesota
  Albert Lea Medical Center (Albert Lea)
  Austin Medical Center (Austin)
  Cannon Valley Clinic (Faribault)
  Fairmont Medical Center (Fairmont)
  Franciscan Skemp Healthcare Houston Clinic (Houston)
  Lake City Medical Center (Lake City)
  Immanuel St. Joseph's (Mankato)
  Fountain Centers Rochester (Rochester)
  Mayo Clinic Rochester
  Rochester Methodist Hospital
  Saint Marys Hospital (Rochester)
  Springfield Medical Center (Springfield)
  Parkview Care Center (Wells)
Wisconsin
  Barron Medical Center (Barron)
  Bloomer Medical Center (Bloomer)
  Midelfort Clinic (Cameron)
  Luther Midelfort (Eau Claire)
  Red Cedar Medical Center (Menomonie)
  Franciscan Skemp Healthcare Onalaska Clinic (Onalaska)

PRODUCTS/OPERATIONS

2003 Sales

	$ mil.	% of total
Medical services	4,081.3	85
Grants & contracts	222.2	5
Premiums	91.6	2
Contributions	78.1	1
Return on investments	65.2	1
Other	283.8	6
Total	**4,822.2**	**100**

2003 Sales

	% of total
Mayo Clinic Rochester	44
Mayo Health System	21
Mayo Clinic Jacksonville	10
Mayo Clinic Scottsdale	9
Research	5
Mayo Collaborative Services	4
Contributions	2
Investments	1
Other	4
Total	**100**

COMPETITORS

Allina Hospitals	Johns Hopkins Medicine
Ascension Health	Memorial Sloan-Kettering
Catholic Health Initiatives	Methodist Hospital System
Catholic Healthcare Partners	New York City Health and Hospitals
Detroit Medical Center	Rush System for Health
HCA	Scripps
Health Management Associates	SSM Health Care
	Tenet Healthcare
HEALTHSOUTH	Trinity Health (Novi)
Henry Ford Health System	Universal Health Services

HISTORICAL FINANCIALS
Company Type: Not-for-profit

Income Statement FYE: December 31

	REVENUE ($ mil.)	NET INCOME ($ mil.)	NET PROFIT MARGIN	EMPLOYEES
12/03	4,822	349	7.2%	42,620
12/02	4,425	(212)	—	41,527
12/01	4,135	—	—	45,536
12/00	3,710	—	—	44,000
12/99	2,750	—	—	41,265
12/98	2,370	—	—	32,531
12/97	2,566	—	—	30,497
12/96	2,348	—	—	28,671
12/95	2,189	—	—	25,433
12/94	1,873	—	—	21,856
Annual Growth	11.1%	—	—	7.7%

2003 Year-End Financials
Debt ratio: 53.7% Current ratio: —
Return on equity: 14.0% Long-term debt ($ mil.): 1,432
Cash ($ mil.): 22

Net Income History

MBM

What's on the menu at your favorite restaurant? Just ask MBM Corporation, one of the largest privately owned custom food service distributors in the nation. The company specializes in providing food to national restaurant chains such as Arby's, Burger King, Captain D's, Chick-fil-A, and Darden Restaurants (Red Lobster, Olive Garden, Bahama Breeze). MBM fills its customers' orders through its network of about 30 distribution centers across the US. J. R. Wordsworth founded the company about 50 years ago as a retail food distributor. MBM made the transition to its present role in restaurant food distribution after Wordsworth's children bought the business in the 1970s.

Federal safety rules that took effect in January 2004 to reduce driver fatigue are expected to substantially increase trucking rates for MBM Corporation, as well as other large distributors, for the first time in two decades. MBM estimated that it would incur about $10 million in additional expenses to comply with the rules. The firm would need to add to its current fleet of some 800 trucks and 1,800 truck drivers.

EXECUTIVES

Chairman, President, and CEO: Jerry L. Wordsworth
CFO: Jeffrey M. (Jeff) Kowalk
EVP: Jim Sabiston
Executive Director, Human Resources: Tim Ozment
Executive Director, Operations: Andy Blanton
Director, Purchasing: Mitch Brantley
Secretary and Treasurer:
  Debbie Wordsworth-Daughtridge
Controller: Ernest Avent
President Assistant: Doug Martin

LOCATIONS

HQ: MBM Corporation
2641 Meadowbrook Rd., Rocky Mount, NC 27802
Phone: 252-985-7200 **Fax:** 252-985-7241

COMPETITORS

Ben E. Keith	McLane Foodservice
Clark Products	Performance Food
Golden State Foods	Reyes Holdings
Gordon Food Service	Sodexho
Martin-Brower	SYSCO
McLane	U.S. Foodservice

HISTORICAL FINANCIALS
Company Type: Private

Income Statement FYE: December 31

	REVENUE ($ mil.)	NET INCOME ($ mil.)	NET PROFIT MARGIN	EMPLOYEES
12/02	4,236	—	—	3,500
12/01	4,236	—	—	3,500
12/00	3,823	—	—	2,500
12/99	2,700	—	—	2,364
12/98	2,500	—	—	1,600
12/97	2,000	—	—	1,500
12/96	1,800	—	—	—
Annual Growth	15.3%	—	—	18.5%

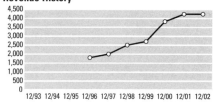

McCarthy Building

A company that was in construction before Reconstruction, McCarthy Building Companies is one of the oldest privately held builders in the US. The general contractor and construction manager has projects worldwide and ranks among the top builders of health care and education facilities in the US. Contracts include heavy construction projects (bridges and water and waste-treatment plants), industrial projects (biopharmaceutical, food processing, and microelectronics facilities), commercial projects (retail and office buildings), and institutional projects (airports, schools, and prisons). Timothy McCarthy founded the firm in 1864. His great-grandson, Michael McCarthy, sold the firm to its employees in 2002.

EXECUTIVES

Chairman and CEO: Michael D. (Mike) Bolen
President and COO: Michael D. Hurst
EVP, CFO, and Treasurer: George F. Scherer
SVP, General Counsel, and Secretary: James A. Staskiel
VP Human Resources: Jan Kraemer
VP Corporate Safety: Gary Amsigner
President, Midwest Division: Karl Kloster
President, Northern Pacific Division: Richard A. Henry
President, Southern California Division:
  W. Carter Chappell, age 50
President, Southwest Division, Las Vegas:
  Randy Highland
President, Southwest Division, Phoenix:
  Robert (Bo) Calbert
President, Texas Division: Michael J. McWay
Director Corporate Communications:
  Michael (Mike) Lenzen
Controller: J. Douglas Audiffred
Auditors: Ernst & Young LLP

LOCATIONS

HQ: McCarthy Building Companies, Inc.
  1341 N. Rock Hill Rd., St. Louis, MO 63124
Phone: 314-968-3300 **Fax:** 314-968-3037
Web: www.mccarthy.com

McCarthy Building Companies has offices in Dallas; Newport Beach, Sacramento, and San Francisco, California; Las Vegas; Phoenix; and St. Louis.

COMPETITORS

Barton Malow
Bechtel
Bovis Lend Lease
Centex
DPR Construction
Gilbane
Hensel Phelps
Perini
Peter Kiewit Sons'
Skanska
Swinerton
Turner Corporation

HISTORICAL FINANCIALS
Company Type: Private

Income Statement — FYE: March 31

	REVENUE ($ mil.)	NET INCOME ($ mil.)	NET PROFIT MARGIN	EMPLOYEES
3/03	1,024	—	—	2,000
3/02	1,050	—	—	2,500
3/01	1,205	—	—	2,500
3/00	940	—	—	2,500
3/99	1,200	—	—	2,000
3/98	1,134	—	—	2,000
3/97	1,059	—	—	1,300
3/96	795	—	—	1,000
3/95	950	—	—	525
3/94	705	—	—	450
Annual Growth	4.2%	—	—	18.0%

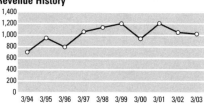

McDermott, Will & Emery

Not only is McDermott, Will & Emery one of the largest law firms in the US, it was also one of the first law firms to admit a female to its partnership ranks. The firm has more than 900 attorneys in eight US offices and international offices in London; and Düsseldorf and Munich, Germany. McDermott, Will & Emery's multiple practice areas include antitrust, corporate, employee benefits, estate planning, health law, intellectual property, international, regulation and government affairs, tax, and trial law. The firm has represented clients such as the City of Anaheim, California (in a case related to Orange County's bankruptcy); Ford; and Chiquita Brands International. E. H. McDermott founded the firm in 1934.

EXECUTIVES

Chairman: Lawrence (Larry) Gerber
Executive Director of Administration: Louis Covotsos
Executive Director of Operations: Lewis Liszt
Director of Finance: David Alexander
Director of Human Resources: Donna Daly
Director of Practice Development: Amy Nigrelli
Director of Professional Development:
  Sharon Abrahams

LOCATIONS

HQ: McDermott, Will & Emery
  227 W. Monroe St., Chicago, IL 60606
Phone: 312-372-2000 **Fax:** 312-984-7700
Web: www.mwe.com

McDermott, Will & Emery has US offices in Boston; Chicago; Irvine, Los Angeles, and Palo Alto, California; Miami; New York City; and Washington, DC. The firm has international offices in London; and Düsseldorf and Munich, Germany.

COMPETITORS

Baker & McKenzie
Hogan & Hartson
Jenner & Block
Jones Day
Katten Muchin
Kirkland & Ellis
Lord, Bissell
Mayer, Brown, Rowe & Maw
Sidley Austin Brown & Wood
Skadden, Arps
Sonnenschein Nath
Winston & Strawn

HISTORICAL FINANCIALS
Company Type: Partnership

Income Statement — FYE: December 31

	REVENUE ($ mil.)	NET INCOME ($ mil.)	NET PROFIT MARGIN	EMPLOYEES
12/03	668	—	—	—
12/02	628	—	—	2,000
12/01	563	—	—	1,970
12/00	503	—	—	2,004
12/99	445	—	—	1,900
12/98	390	—	—	1,831
12/97	334	—	—	2,032
12/96	281	—	—	—
12/95	237	—	—	—
12/94	207	—	—	—
Annual Growth	13.9%	—	—	(0.3%)

McJunkin

It's fitting that McJunkin is a pipeline for many gas and oil companies. The company is a nationwide distributor of steel, pipe, valves and fittings, and drilling, electrical, and mining supplies. Its McJunkin Appalachian unit distributes gas and oil products throughout the Appalachian basin. In addition to providing technical support, McA Target Oil Tools distributes and sells drilling tools. McJunkin Controls provides valve cleaning and rebuilding services. The company operates in Mexico and Latin America through its Trottner-McJunkin joint venture. Clients include power, pulp and paper, mining, and automotive companies. Founded in 1921, the firm is still owned by descendants of the McJunkin family.

The company continues to look for acquisitions that complement its core activities. McJunkin acquired CIGMA LLC in 2003. A joint venture of Vectren Utility Services and Citizens By-Products, CIGMA acts as an integrated supplier and distributor for the utility, pipeline construction, and related industries. The acquisition gives McJunkin a larger gas and oil product presence in its Midwest region. The company will also look to expand its Nigeria and Venezuela operations.

EXECUTIVES

Chairman and CFO: Michael H. Wehrle, age 48
President and CEO: H. Barnard (Bernie) Wehrle III
SVP, National Accounts: Rory Isaac
SVP, Valve and Specialty Products: Gary Ittner
VP, Communications: Lynne Zande
VP, Gas Products Division: David Campbell
VP, Marketing: Scott Vuchetich
CTO: Jim Underhill
National Accounts Manager, Gas Distribution and Gas Transmission Products Group: Terry Boyles
Administrative Assistant, Engineering: Tanya Randoph
Administrative Assistant, Human Resources: Robin Garten
Corporate Accountant: Michael Harper
Credit Support: Diana Haninou
Inventory Analyst: Jessica Newson
Tax Analyst: Nancy Summerfield

LOCATIONS

HQ: McJunkin Corporation
835 Hillcrest Dr., Charleston, WV 25311
Phone: 304-348-5211   **Fax:** 304-348-4922
Web: www.mcjunkin.com

McJunkin Corporation operates through more than 125 locations in Mexico, Nigeria, the US, and Venezuela.

PRODUCTS/OPERATIONS

Selected Products
Carbon Steel Pipe
Carbon Steel and Corrosion Resistant Fittings and Flanges
Electrical Products
Engineered Products
Gas Distribution and Transmission Products
Stainless Steel and Corrosion Resistant Tubular Products
Valves

Selected Subsidiaries and Joint Ventures
McA Target Oil Tools (drilling tool sales and rentals)
McJunkin Controls (valve rebuilding, actuation, and cleaning)
McJunkin-Appalachian (oil-field products)
Trottner-McJunkin (provides supplies to Latin America and Mexico)

COMPETITORS

Amcast Industrial
American Cast Iron pipe
CIRCOR International
Cooper Cameron
McWane
National-Oilwell
Shaw Group
Swagelok
Tyco International
USFilter
Wilson Industries

HISTORICAL FINANCIALS

Company Type: Private

Income Statement — FYE: December 31

	REVENUE ($ mil.)	NET INCOME ($ mil.)	NET PROFIT MARGIN	EMPLOYEES
12/03	800	—	—	1,600
12/02	830	—	—	1,600
12/01	830	—	—	1,600
12/00	741	—	—	1,399
12/99	655	—	—	1,245
12/98	731	—	—	1,600
12/97	700	—	—	1,300
12/96	682	—	—	1,300
12/95	667	—	—	1,300
12/94	627	—	—	1,306
Annual Growth	2.7%	—	—	2.3%

Revenue History

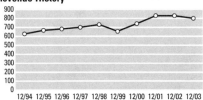

McKee Foods

When Little Debbie smiles up out of your lunch bag, you know you are loved. McKee Foods' Little Debbie is one of the US's leading brands of snack cakes, named for and featuring the smiling face of the company's founders' granddaughter. McKee makes snack cakes, creme-filled cookies, crackers, and candy. It also sells granola bars, fruit snacks, and cereals under its Sunbelt brand. Low prices and family packs of individually wrapped treats have driven sales. McKee Foods is the largest independent bakery in the US. The company started in 1934 with founder O. D. McKee and his wife, Ruth, selling nickel cakes from the back seat of their car. The company is still owned and operated by the McKee family.

The company has a fleet of trucks and brings home extra money through "backhauling" for other customers after delivering Little Debbie products. Employees who have worked for more than two years are eligible for profit-sharing bonuses. New product development is key in the highly competitive snack market, and McKee Foods steadily puts out variations such as its Cosmic Crispy bars with chocolate chips.

Ellsworth and Jack McKee, sons of the founders, are chairman and CEO, respectively. And, while Debbie herself doesn't hold an executive position with the company, third-generation Mike McKee is president.

EXECUTIVES

CEO: Jack C. McKee
President: Mike McKee
CFO: Barry Patterson
VP and General Manager: E. Ray Murphy
Manager, Corporate Communications and Public Relations: Ruth Garren
Manager, Corporate HR: Mark Newsome

LOCATIONS

HQ: McKee Foods Corporation
10260 McKee Rd., Collegedale, TN 37315
Phone: 423-238-7111   **Fax:** 423-238-7101
Web: www.mckeefoods.com

McKee Foods has baking facilities in Arkansas, Tennessee, and Virginia.

PRODUCTS/OPERATIONS

Selected Products
Little Debbie Brand
  Breakfast pastries (coffee cakes, honey buns, muffin loaves)
  Candy (Peanut Cluster, Star Crunch)
  Cookies and pies (Marshmallow Supremes, Nutty Bars, Oatmeal Creme Pies)
  Crackers (Toasty Crackers with Peanut Butter)
  Seasonal snacks (holiday-themed cakes and cookies)
  Snack cakes (Devil Squares, Swiss Cake Rolls)
Sunbelt Brand
  Cereal bars (with fruit filling)
  Cereals (granola, low-fat, fruit & nut)
  Fruit snacks
  Granola bars (chewy, fudge-dipped)

COMPETITORS

Chattanooga Bakery
Flowers Foods
General Mills
Grist Mill Company
Interstate Bakeries
Kellogg
Kellogg Snacks
Lance
Otis Spunkmeyer
Saputo
Tasty Baking
Weston Foods

HISTORICAL FINANCIALS

Company Type: Private

Income Statement — FYE: Friday nearest June 30

	REVENUE ($ mil.)	NET INCOME ($ mil.)	NET PROFIT MARGIN	EMPLOYEES
6/04	1,000	—	—	6,000
6/03	978	—	—	6,500
6/02	970	—	—	6,500
6/01	900	—	—	6,000
6/00	865	—	—	5,450
6/99	855	—	—	5,393
6/98	831	—	—	5,350
6/97	825	—	—	5,346
6/96	735	—	—	5,000
6/95	680	—	—	4,550
Annual Growth	4.4%	—	—	3.1%

Revenue History

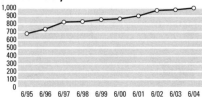

McKinsey & Company

How many McKinsey consultants does it take to screw in a light bulb? None. They would most likely advise rewiring the house. McKinsey & Company is one of the world's top management consulting firms with more than 80 offices in 44 countries. The company provides a full spectrum of consulting services to corporations, government agencies, and foundations, including leadership training, operations analysis, and strategic planning. Its practice areas include such industries as banking, energy, manufacturing, and media, among many others. McKinsey's consultants also dispense their knowledge in an avalanche of articles and books. Founded by James McKinsey in 1926, the company is owned by its partners.

In addition to being one of the largest consulting firms, McKinsey is also one of most well-respected and admired firms. It has earned a reputation for being the best through its accomplishments and history, but it also cultivates a certain mystique through its intense secrecy. Aspiring consultants often list it as the most desirable firm to work for, although McKinsey's rigorous up-or-out weeding process allows only the top 20% of new associates to become partners after five years. Notable McKinsey alumni include former American Express chairman Harvey Golub and former CBS chief Michael Jordan, as well as former Enron CEO Jeff Skilling.

Like its rivals in the consulting industry, McKinsey's business has taken a hit from the downturn in the economy. Many companies are shying away from costly consulting engagements, while bread-and-butter assignments, such as merger and acquisition business, have all but disappeared. Meanwhile, companies such as IBM and Accenture threaten to steal more traditional consulting business from the likes of McKinsey and its brethren. The consulting industry as a whole has also suffered a black eye in the wake of recent corporate scandals, and McKinsey has not been immune: its client list in the 1990s included the likes of Global Crossing, Swissair, and Enron. (The company has never been accused of any improprieties, however.)

Against this backdrop, Ian Davis was elected managing director in 2003 and given the task of leading the firm through uncertain times. A big part of McKinsey's survival could involve a reinforcement of the values of its spiritual leader, the late Marvin Bower, who dictated that the client's interests must come first and that the firm's consultants must be discreet and honest. As more companies seek to assuage regulators and gun-shy investors, an untarnished reputation will become a more valuable asset.

HISTORY

McKinsey & Company was founded in Chicago in 1926 by University of Chicago accounting professor James McKinsey. The company evolved from an auditing practice of McKinsey and his partners, Marvin Bower and A.T. Kearney, who began analyzing business and industry and offering advice. McKinsey died in 1937; two years later, Bower, who headed the New York office, and Kearney, in Chicago, split the firm. Kearney renamed the Chicago office A.T. Kearney & Co. (later acquired by Electronic Data Systems), and Bower kept the McKinsey name and built up a practice structured like a law firm.

Bower focused on the big picture instead of on specific operating problems, helping boost billings to $2 million by 1950. He hired staff straight out of prestigious business schools, reinforcing the firm's theoretical bent. Bower implemented a competitive up-or-out policy requiring employees who are not continually promoted to leave the firm.

The firm's prestige continued to grow during the booming 1950s along with demand for consulting services. Before becoming president in 1953, Dwight Eisenhower asked McKinsey to find out exactly what the government did. By 1959 Bower had opened an office in London, followed by others in Amsterdam; Dusseldorf, Germany; Melbourne; Paris; and Zurich.

In 1964 the company founded management journal *The McKinsey Quarterly*. When Bower retired in 1967, sales were $20 million, and McKinsey was the #1 management consulting firm. During the 1970s it faced competition from firms with newer approaches and lost market share. In response, then-managing director Ronald Daniel started specialty practices and expanded foreign operations.

The consulting boom of the 1980s was spurred by mergers and buyouts. By 1988 the firm had 1,800 consultants, sales were $620 million, and 50% of billings came from overseas.

The recession of the early 1990s hit white-collar workers, including consultants. McKinsey, scrambling to upgrade its technical side, bought Information Consulting Group (ICG), its first acquisition. But the corporate cultures did not meld, and most ICG people left by 1993.

In 1994 the company elected its first managing director of non-European descent, Indian-born Rajat Gupta. Two years later the traditionally hush-hush firm found itself at the center of that most public 1990s arena, the sexual discrimination lawsuit. A female ex-consultant in Texas sued, claiming McKinsey had sabotaged her career (the case was dismissed).

In 1998 McKinsey partnered with Northwestern University and the University of Pennsylvania to establish a world-class business school in India. The following year graduating seniors surveyed in Europe, the UK, and the US named the company as their ideal employer.

Also in 1999 the company created @McKinsey to help "accelerate" Internet startups. The next year it increased salaries and offered incentives to better compete with Internet firms for employees. In 2001 the company expanded its branding business with the acquisition of Envision, a Chicago-based brand consultant.

In 2003 Ian Davis was elected as managing director of the firm, succeeding Rajat Gupta who had served as managing director for nine years. (The firm imposes a term limit on the position.) Davis had previously served as the head of the firm's UK office.

EXECUTIVES

Managing Director: Ian Davis, age 53
Director of the Americas: Michael Patsalos-Fox
Director of Asia: Dominic Barton, age 41
Director of Germany: Jürgen Kluge
Director and Managing Partner, Media and Entertainment Practice: Michael J. Wolf
Director of External Relations, North and South America: Michael Stewart
Director of Personnel: Jerome Vascellaro
Director of McKinsey Global Institute: Diana Farrell
Managing Partner, Australia and New Zealand: Adam Lewis
Practice Manager, Media and Entertainment Practice: Anne Board
Recruiting: Diane Black

LOCATIONS

HQ: McKinsey & Company
55 E. 52nd St., 21st Fl., New York, NY 10022
Phone: 212-446-7000   **Fax:** 212-446-8575
Web: www.mckinsey.com

Selected Office Locations
Amsterdam
Atlanta
Bangkok
Beijing
Boston
Buenos Aires
Dublin
Geneva
Helsinki, Finland
Hong Kong
Kuala Lumpur, Malaysia
London
Los Angeles
Milan
Montreal
Moscow
Paris
Santiago, Chile
Singapore
Sydney
Tokyo
Toronto
Washington, DC
Zurich

PRODUCTS/OPERATIONS

Selected Practice Areas
Automotive and assembly
Banking and securities
Chemicals
Consumer packaged goods
Electric power and natural gas
Healthcare
Insurance
Media and entertainment
Metals and mining
Nonprofit organizations
Petroleum
Pharmaceuticals and medical products
Private equity
Pulp and paper
Retail
Information technology
Telecommunications
Travel and logistics

COMPETITORS

Accenture	Deloitte Consulting
A.T. Kearney	IBM
Bain & Company	Mercer
BearingPoint	PA Consulting
Booz Allen	Perot Systems
Boston Consulting	PRTM
Computer Sciences	Roland Berger

HISTORICAL FINANCIALS
Company Type: Private

Income Statement
FYE: December 31

	REVENUE ($ mil.)	NET INCOME ($ mil.)	NET PROFIT MARGIN	EMPLOYEES
12/02	3,000	—	—	12,000
12/01	3,400	—	—	13,000
12/00	3,400	—	—	13,000
12/99	2,900	—	—	10,500
12/98	2,500	—	—	10,000
12/97	2,200	—	—	8,500
12/96	2,100	—	—	7,100
12/95	1,800	—	—	6,050
12/94	1,500	—	—	6,000
12/93	1,300	—	—	5,560
Annual Growth	9.7%	—	—	8.9%

Revenue History

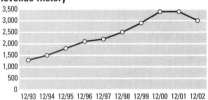

McWane

As a leading manufacturer of fire hydrants, McWane may just be a dog's best friend. Through its many divisions, McWane makes a variety of fluid control devices that include fire hydrants, industrial valves, pipes, and flanges. With the acquisition of Amerex in Trussville, Alabama, McWane has become one of the world's leading makers of fire extinguishers and fire suppression systems. Through its Manchester Tank division, the company also produces gas grills as well as propane tanks for recreational vehicles. Its M&H Valve Company, which makes industrial valves with waste-water applications and fire hydrants, has been in operation since 1854. McWane was founded in 1921 and continues to be family-owned.

Over the years McWane has grown by acquiring troubled companies, and turning them around with infusions of better equipment and streamlined management.

EXECUTIVES

Chairman: C. Phillip McWane, age 46
President: G. Ruffner Page
CFO: Charles (Charley) Nowlin

LOCATIONS

HQ: McWane Corp.
2900 Hwy. 280, Ste. 300, Birmingham, AL 35223
Phone: 205-414-3100 **Fax:** 205-414-3180
Web: www.mh-valve.com

McWane has operations in Alabama, Iowa, New Jersey, New York, Ohio, Texas, and Utah.

PRODUCTS/OPERATIONS

Selected Operations
Amerex Corporation (industrial and commercial fire extinguishers)
Clow Valve Company (fire hydrants and valves)
Clow Water Systems Company (ductile iron pipe and fittings)
Kennedy Valve (fire hydrants and valves)
M&H Valve Company (fire hydrants, gears and casings, stem guides, valves)
McWane Cast Iron Pipe Company
Pacific States Cast Iron Pipe Company (ductile iron pipe)
Tyler Pipe Company (cleanouts, drains, fittings, valves)

COMPETITORS

American Cast Iron pipe
Citation
Henry Technologies
Indeck
INTERMET
Kidde
Margate Industries
McJunkin
Metallurg
Northwest Pipe
Walter Industries

HISTORICAL FINANCIALS
Company Type: Private

Income Statement
FYE: December 31

	ESTIMATED REVENUE ($ mil.)	NET INCOME ($ mil.)	NET PROFIT MARGIN	EMPLOYEES
12/02	1,500	—	—	5,570
12/01	800	—	—	5,200
12/00	630	—	—	5,170
12/99	625	—	—	4,400
12/98	585	—	—	4,350
12/97	575	—	—	5,700
12/96	525	—	—	5,650
12/95	500	—	—	5,500
12/94	475	—	—	5,400
Annual Growth	15.5%	—	—	0.4%

Revenue History

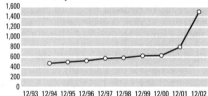

MediaNews

Paper cuts can really hurt, especially when they're made by newspaper group MediaNews Group. Known for ruthlessly cutting staff at unprofitable newspapers, the company publishes more than 40 dailies (including *The Denver Post* and *The Salt Lake Tribune*) and about 65 non-dailies in the US. It also operates Web sites for most of its daily papers and operates a small number of radio and television stations. The company is a joint venture of vice chairman and CEO Dean Singleton and chairman Richard Scudder, who began buying newspapers together in 1983.

Considered one of the nation's top 10 newspaper firms, MediaNews owns newspapers with a combined daily circulation of 2 million. *The Denver Post* is part of the Denver Newspaper Agency, a joint operating agreement (JOA) with E. W. Scripps (owner of the *Rocky Mountain News*) that combines the business operations of both papers. The company's other media holdings include radio stations in Texas and Alaska and a TV station in Anchorage, Alaska (KTVA).

MediaNews focuses on building newspaper clusters in specific geographic regions. Following its strategy, the company has added to its Northern California cluster with multiple newspaper purchases in the region. MediaNews struck a deal with Gannett in 2003 to form the Texas-New Mexico Newspaper Partnership, comprised of six daily and about a dozen non-daily papers.

The Salt Lake Tribune is also run under a similar joint operating agreement with The Deseret News Publishing Company (owner of the *Deseret News*). A legal dispute with the previous owners of *The Salt Lake Tribune* has resulted in a court order forcing the company to offer Utah newspaper back to the McCarthey family.

The families of founders Singleton and Scudder own MediaNews.

EXECUTIVES

Chairman: Richard B. Scudder, age 91
Vice Chairman and CEO: William D. (Dean) Singleton, age 53, $1,022,250 pay
President: Joseph J. (Jody) Lodovic IV, age 43, $724,950 pay
EVP and COO; President and CEO, Los Angeles Newspaper Group: Gerald E. (Jerry) Grilly, age 57, $651,800 pay
SVP Operations: Anthony F. Tierno, age 59, $384,125 pay
VP and CFO: Ronald A. (Ron) Mayo, age 43, $223,100 pay
VP and Controller: Michael J. Koren
VP Human Resources: Charles M. Kamen
President and Publisher, ANG Newspapers: John Schueler
President, MediaNews Group Interactive: Eric J. Grilly, age 33, $290,000 pay
Treasurer: James L. McDougald, age 51
Secretary: Patricia (Pat) Robinson, age 62
Auditors: Ernst & Young LLP

LOCATIONS

HQ: MediaNews Group, Inc.
1560 Broadway, Ste. 2100, Denver, CO 80202
Phone: 303-563-6360 **Fax:** 303-894-9327
Web: www.medianewsgroup.com

MediaNews Group publishes newspapers in Alaska, California, Colorado, Connecticut, Massachusetts, New Mexico, Pennsylvania, Texas, Utah, Vermont, and West Virginia. It also owns a radio station and television station in Alaska and radio stations in Texas.

PRODUCTS/OPERATIONS

2004 Sales

	$ mil.	% of total
Advertising	563.5	75
Circulation	132.5	17
Other	57.8	8
Total	**753.8**	**100**

Operating Divisions

Alaska Broadcasting Group
  Fairbanks Daily News Miner
  Kodiak Daily News
  Radio station (KBYR)
  TV station (KTVA- CBS affiliate)
ANG Newspapers (54%, part of the California Newspapers Partnership)
  Alameda Times-Star
  The Argus
  The Daily Review
  Marin Independent Journal
  The Oakland Tribune
  San Mateo County Times
  Times-Herald
  Tri-Valley Herald
Charleston Newspapers
  Charleston Daily Mail
  Sunday Gazette-Mail
Connecticut Newspapers Group
  Connecticut Post
Denver Newspapers
  The Denver Post
  The Fort Morgan Times
  Journal-Advocate
  Lamar Daily News
Graham Newspapers
  Breckenridge Radio (KLXK, KROO)
  Graham Leader
  Graham Radio (KSWA/KWKQ)
Los Angeles Newspaper Group
  Daily News
  Inland Valley Daily Bulletin
  Long Beach Press-Telegram
  Pasadena Star-News
  Redlands Daily Facts
  San Bernardino County Sun
  San Gabriel Valley Tribune
New England Newspapers Group
  Bennington Banner
  The Berkshire Eagle
  Brattleboro Reformer
  Lowell Sun
  North Adams Transcript
  Sentinel & Enterprise
North Central California Newspaper Group
  Alameda Times-Star
  Chico Enterprise-Record
  The Daily Democrat
  Oroville Mercury-Register
  Red Bluff Daily News
  The Reporter
Northern California Newspapers Group
  Lake County Record-Bee
  Times-Standard
  Ukiah Daily Journal
South Eastern Pennsylvania Newspapers Group
  The Evening Sun
  Lebanon Daily News
  York Daily Record
Texas-New Mexico Newspaper Partnership
  Alamogordo Daily News
  Carlsbad Current-Argus
  The Daily Times
  The Deming Headlight
  Las Cruces Sun-News
Utah Newspaper
  The Salt Lake Tribune

COMPETITORS

Copley Press
E. W. Scripps
Eagle-Tribune Publishing
Freedom Communications
Gannett
Hearst
Hearst Newspapers
Journal Register
Knight-Ridder
Lee Enterprises
Liberty Group Publishing
New Times
New York Times
Pulitzer
SF Newspaper Co.
Tribune
Village Voice Media

HISTORICAL FINANCIALS
Company Type: Private

Income Statement
FYE: June 30

	REVENUE ($ mil.)	NET INCOME ($ mil.)	NET PROFIT MARGIN	EMPLOYEES
6/04	754	28	3.7%	10,000
6/03	739	41	5.5%	10,700
6/02	712	12	1.7%	11,200
6/01	853	25	3.0%	11,200
6/00	947	130	13.8%	8,939
6/99	1,010	—	—	8,997
6/98	850	—	—	8,800
6/97	620	—	—	8,000
6/96	545	—	—	7,000
6/95	375	—	—	4,500
Annual Growth	8.1%	(32.2%)	—	9.3%

2004 Year-End Financials
Debt ratio: 1,053.3%
Return on equity: 37.5%
Cash ($ mil.): 65
Current ratio: 1.60
Long-term debt ($ mil.): 917

Net Income History

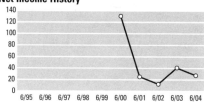

Medical Mutual

Medical Mutual of Ohio (formerly Blue Cross and Blue Shield of Ohio) is a not-for-profit managed care company that provides health insurance products and related services to more than 3 million members in Ohio and Northwestern Pennsylvania. The company's health plans include HMO, PPO, POS, traditional indemnity, and supplemental Medicare. Medical Mutual of Ohio also provides dental, vision, and workers compensation plans, life insurance, and third party administration (TPA) services. Medical Mutual of Ohio is not affiliated with the Blue Cross Blue Shield Association.

Medical Mutual of Ohio is currently expanding into Northwestern Pennsylvania, and eventually plans to extend into Southwestern Pennsylvania.

EXECUTIVES

Chairman, President, and CEO: Kent W. Clapp
EVP and CFO: Susan Tyler
EVP and Chief Information Officer; President, Antares Management Solutions: Kenneth Sidon
EVP, Sales and Customer Relations and Chief Marketing Officer: Errol D. Brick
EVP, Statewide Operations: Linda L. Johnson
EVP: Joseph Krysh
VP, Corporate Communications and Advertising, and Chief Communications Officer: Jared Chaney
VP, Healthcare Finance and National Network Strategy: Michael Taddeo
VP, Pharmaceutical Management and Business Development: Benjamin D. (Ben) Zelman
VP, Broker Sales: Charles Braschwitz
VP, Care Management: Paula Sauer
VP, Claims Operations: James Quiring
VP, Finance: Rick Chiricosta
VP, Underwriting: George Stadtlander
General Counsel and VP, Legal Affairs: John Dorrell

LOCATIONS

HQ: Medical Mutual of Ohio
2060 E. 9th St., Cleveland, OH 44115
Phone: 216-687-7000   **Fax:** 216-687-6044
Web: www.mmoh.com

PRODUCTS/OPERATIONS

Selected Insurance Products
SuperMed Classic (HMO)
SuperMed Dental
SuperMed HMO
SuperMed One (Personal Health Insurance)
SuperMed Plus (PPO)
SuperMed Select (Point-of Service)
SuperMed Vision
Medical Mutual's Greater Miami Valley Health Plan (Dayton Ohio Area Health Plan)

COMPETITORS

Aetna
Anthem
CIGNA
Highmark
Humana
Humana Health Plan of Ohio
UnitedHealth Group

HISTORICAL FINANCIALS
Company Type: Not-for-profit

Income Statement
FYE: December 31

	REVENUE ($ mil.)	NET INCOME ($ mil.)	NET PROFIT MARGIN	EMPLOYEES
12/03	1,600	—	—	2,500
12/02	1,500	—	—	2,500
Annual Growth	6.7%	—	—	0.0%

Revenue History

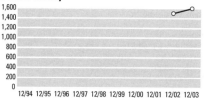

Medline Industries

Medline Industries, a private medical equipment distributor and manufacturer, goes toe-to-toe with the bigger guns, selling more than 100,000 products, such as furnishings for hospital rooms, exam equipment, housekeeping supplies, and surgical gloves and garments. The company manufactures about 70% of its products and then distributes them to such customers as hospitals, extended care facilities, and home health care providers. Marketing efforts are handled by Medline's more than 700 sales representatives and roughly 25 distribution centers. The company is owned by the Mills family, which founded Medline in 1910 as a manufacturer of nurses' gowns.

Medline bought Maxxim Medical's surgical products business consisting of custom procedural trays, drapes, and gowns. Medline also bought Maxxim's medical products business and its vascular products business.

EXECUTIVES

CEO: Charles S. (Charlie) Mills
President: Andy Mills
COO: Jim Abrams
CFO: Bill Abington
VP, Human Resources: Joseph Becker
VP, National Accounts: Steve Heintze
President, Sales: Ray Swaback
President, Operating Room Division: James Spann

LOCATIONS

HQ: Medline Industries, Inc.
1 Medline Place, Mundelein, IL 60060
Phone: 847-949-5500 **Fax:** 800-351-1512
Web: www.medline.com

Medline Industries sells its products in more than 20 countries.

PRODUCTS/OPERATIONS

Selected Product Categories
Bed and bath products
Central supply
Enteral products
Equipment and furnishings
Exam and diagnostics
Gloves
Housekeeping
Incontinence products
Nursing
Rehabilitation
Respiratory
Skin care
Surgery and O.B.
Urology
Wound care

COMPETITORS

Cardinal Medical Products and Services
Hillenbrand
Kimberly-Clark
McKesson
Owens & Minor
Sunrise Medical
Tyco Healthcare

HISTORICAL FINANCIALS

Company Type: Private

Income Statement
FYE: December 31

	REVENUE ($ mil.)	NET INCOME ($ mil.)	NET PROFIT MARGIN	EMPLOYEES
12/02	1,450	—	—	3,800
12/01	1,231	—	—	3,500
12/00	1,016	—	—	3,277
12/99	905	—	—	2,600
12/98	756	—	—	2,300
12/97	655	—	—	2,700
12/96	600	—	—	2,383
12/95	560	—	—	2,200
12/94	476	—	—	2,000
12/93	413	—	—	—
Annual Growth	15.0%	—	—	8.4%

Revenue History

MedStar Health

Whether you've been knocked out and are seeing stars or you're just plain sickly, MedStar Health can cater to you. The not-for-profit organization runs seven hospitals in Baltimore and Washington, DC. With some 2,700 beds and 4,600 affiliated physicians, MedStar offers such services as acute care, rehabilitation, assisted living, hospice, long-term care, and emergency services. Its MedStar Physician Partners contracts with private physicians in the Baltimore/Washington, DC area. MedStar also manages an independent practice association, which includes both primary and specialty care physicians. Its MedStar Research Institute focuses on cardiac care, diabetes, and rehabilitation.

EXECUTIVES

Chairman: James R. Hyde
Vice Chairman: Robert Gladstone
CEO: John P. McDaniel, age 61
President and COO: Kenneth A. Samet
EVP and CFO: Michael J. Curran
EVP, Corporate Services: Michael C. Rogers
EVP, Medical Affairs: William L. Thomas
SVP, Integrated Operations: Steven S. Cohen
SVP and General Counsel: Robert J. (Mike) Ryan
SVP, Strategic Planning: Christine M. Swearingen
SVP, Managed Care: Eric R. Wagner
Corporate Director, Communications and Public Affairs: John A. Marzano
Director of Human Resources: David Noe
Auditors: PricewaterhouseCoopers LLP

LOCATIONS

HQ: MedStar Health
5565 Sterrett Place, 5th Fl., Columbia, MD 21044
Phone: 410-772-6500 **Fax:** 410-715-3905
Web: www.medstarhealth.org

Facilities
Baltimore
   Franklin Square Hospital Center
   Good Samaritan Hospital
   Harbor Hospital
   Union Memorial Hospital
Washington, DC
   Georgetown University Hospital
   National Rehabilitation Hospital
   Washington Hospital Center

COMPETITORS

Ascension Health
Bon Secours Health
Christiana Care
Inova
Johns Hopkins Medicine
Trinity Health (Novi)

HISTORICAL FINANCIALS

Company Type: Not-for-profit

Income Statement
FYE: June 30

	REVENUE ($ mil.)	NET INCOME ($ mil.)	NET PROFIT MARGIN	EMPLOYEES
6/03	2,250	—	—	22,000
6/02	2,110	—	—	22,000
6/01	1,990	—	—	21,700
6/00	1,800	—	—	21,466
6/99	1,600	—	—	21,233
6/98	1,400	—	—	21,000
6/97	643	—	—	7,000
6/96	600	—	—	6,000
6/95	571	—	—	6,500
6/94	522	—	—	—
Annual Growth	17.6%	—	—	16.5%

Revenue History

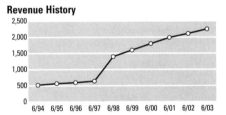

Meijer

Meijer (pronounced "Meyer") is the green giant of retailing in the Midwest. The company operates nearly 160 combination grocery and general merchandise stores; about half are in Michigan, while the rest are in Illinois, Indiana, Kentucky, and Ohio. Its huge stores (which average 200,000 to 250,000 sq. ft. each, or about the size of four regular grocery stores) stock about 120,000 items, including Meijer private-label products. Customers can choose from about 40 departments, including apparel, electronics, hardware, and toys. Most stores also sell gasoline, offer banking services, and have multiple in-store restaurants. Founder Hendrik Meijer opened his first store in 1934; the company is still family owned.

Although the discount superstore format is most often referred to in conjunction with its rival Wal-Mart, Meijer is its pioneer. But that hasn't stopped the world's #1 retailer from muscling in on Meijer's markets. Meijer competes with about 50 supercenters and expects that number to reach 350 by 2007. The company is responding by cutting prices, putting some expansion plans on hold, and renovating some older stores. It is also cutting jobs — eliminating about 1,900 management positions at its stores in January 2004 following a reduction of about 350 positions in 2003 — to become more efficient and competitive. On the plus side, Meijer plans to open five stores in 2004 and another nine in 2005, which the company says will create about 6,500 new jobs. Meijer is also facing increased pressure from warehouse club stores, drugstores, and supermarket chains, like Kroger, that are expanding in its markets.

On the other hand, Kmart's woes have given Meijer a boost. With 35 of Kmart's recent store closings within 10 miles of a Meijer store, the company has begun filling prescriptions for former Kmart customers.

HISTORY

Dutch immigrant and barber Hendrik Meijer owned a vacant space next to his barbershop in Greenville, Michigan. Because of the Depression, he couldn't rent it out. So in 1934 he bought $338.76 in merchandise on credit and started his own grocery store, Thrift Market, with the help of his wife, Gezina; son, Fred; and daughter, Johanna; he made $7 the first day. Meijer had 22 competitors in Greenville alone, but his dedication to low prices (he and Fred often traveled long distances to find bargains) attracted customers. In 1935, to encourage self-service, Meijer placed 12 wicker baskets at the front of the store and posted signs that read, "Take a basket. Help yourself."

A second store was opened in 1942. The company added four more in the 1950s. In 1962 Meijer — then with 14 stores — opened the first one-stop shopping Meijer Thrifty Acres store, similar to a hypermarket another operator had opened in Belgium a year earlier. By 1964, the year that Hendrik died and Fred took over, three of these general merchandise stores were operating. The company entered Ohio in the late 1960s.

In the early 1980s Meijer bought 14 Twin Fair stores in Ohio, 10 in Cincinnati. It sold the stores by 1987, however, after disappointing results. Meijer had greater success in Columbus, Ohio, where it opened one store that year and immediately captured 20% of the market. In 1988 the company began keeping most stores open 24 hours a day.

Meijer annihilated competitors in Dayton, Ohio, in 1991, when it opened four stores that year. The company entered the Toledo market in 1993 with four stores; after one year it had taken 11.5% of the market. A foray into the membership warehouse market was abandoned in 1993, just a few months after they had opened, when Meijer said it would close all seven SourceClubs in Michigan and Ohio.

The company entered Indiana in 1994, opening 16 stores in less than two years; it also reached an agreement with McDonald's to open restaurants in several stores. The first labor strike in Meijer's history hit four stores in Toledo that year, leading to pickets at 14 others. Union officials accused the company of using intimidation tactics by its hiring of large, uniformed men in flak jackets and combat boots as security guards. After nine weeks Meijer agreed to recognize the workers' newly attained union affiliation.

In 1995 the company opened 13 stores, including its first in Illinois. It reentered the Cincinnati market in 1996, announcing the opening of two new stores there by mailing 80,000 videos to residents. By the end of the year, Meijer had a total of five stores in Cincinnati and had entered Kentucky.

Meijer opened a central kitchen in Indiana to prepare deli salads and some vegetables and process orange juice for its stores in 1997. It opened its first two stores in Louisville, Kentucky, the following year. Meijer broke into the tough Chicago-area market with its first store in 1999.

The next year Meijer opened several "village-style" stores — scaled-down versions (about 155,000 sq. ft.) of its larger stores. Later in 2000 Meijer unveiled what it claims is the largest superstore in North America. The 255,000-sq.-ft. behemoth (compared to a Wal-Mart Supercenter, which averages about 183,106 sq. ft.) features a gourmet coffee shop, a card shop, a bank open seven days a week, and restaurants serving pizza and sushi.

In February 2002 co-chairman Hank Meijer was named CEO, succeeding Jim McClean, who had run the company since 1999. The retailer launched a "reinvented superstore format" at six Dayton, Ohio-area stores in late 2002. The makeover emphasizes discount fashion (featuring brands such as Levi's, Dockers, and Gotcha) in a department store atmosphere.

In 2003 Meijer eliminated about 350 jobs to cut costs and opened two new stores.

EXECUTIVES

Chairman Emeritus: Fred Meijer, age 84
Co-Chairman: Doug Meijer, age 50
Co-Chairman and CEO: Hendrik G. (Hank) Meijer, age 52
President and COO: Paul Boyer, age 56
EVP, Store Operations: Larry Zigerelli
SVP, Finance and Administration, and CFO: Jim Walsh
SVP, Human Resources: Wendell (Windy) Ray
SVP, Public and Consumer Affairs: Brian Breslin
Division VP, Foods Merchandising: Dave Perron
Division VP, Hardlines: Terry Griffith
Group VP, Fashions: Rob Gruen
Group VP, Grocery Merchandising: Ralph Fischer
Group VP, Perishables Merchandising: Dave Prostko
VP, Hardlines: Tim Lesneski
VP, Pharmacy: Mike Major
VP, Real Estate: Mike Kinstle
VP, Service Operations: Carole Morgan
Director, Community and Customer Relations: John Zimmerman

LOCATIONS

HQ: Meijer, Inc.
2929 Walker Ave. NW, Grand Rapids, MI 49544
Phone: 616-453-6711 **Fax:** 616-791-2572
Web: www.meijer.com

2004 Stores

	No.
Michigan	78
Ohio	38
Indiana	25
Illinois	9
Kentucky	8
Total	**158**

PRODUCTS/OPERATIONS

Selected Meijer Store Departments

Apparel	Jewelry
Auto supplies	Lawn and garden
Bakery	Music
Banking	Nutrition products
Books	Paint
Bulk foods	Pets and pet supplies
Coffee shop	Pharmacy
Computer software	Photo lab
Dairy	Portrait studio
Delicatessen	Produce
Electronics	Service meat and seafood
Floral	Small appliances
Food court	Soup and salad bar
Gas station	Sporting goods
Hardware	Tobacco
Health and beauty products	Toys
	Wall coverings
Home fashions	Wine

COMPETITORS

A&P	Kohl's
Albertson's	Kroger
ALDI	Marsh Supermarkets
Busch's	Retail Ventures
Costco Wholesale	Roundy's
CVS	SAM'S CLUB
D&W Food Centers	Schnuck Markets
Dollar General	Schottenstein Stores
Dominick's	Spartan Stores
Family Dollar Stores	SUPERVALU
Farmer Jack	Target
Giant Eagle	Walgreen
Home Depot	Wal-Mart
IGA	Whole Foods
Kmart	Winn-Dixie

HISTORICAL FINANCIALS

Company Type: Private

Income Statement

FYE: January 31

	ESTIMATED REVENUE ($ mil.)	NET INCOME ($ mil.)	NET PROFIT MARGIN	EMPLOYEES
1/04	11,100	—	—	75,000
1/03	10,900	—	—	83,402
1/02	10,600	—	—	83,402
1/01	10,000	—	—	80,000
1/00	9,500	—	—	80,000
1/99	8,300	—	—	80,000
1/98	6,900	—	—	77,000
1/97	6,000	—	—	73,000
1/96	5,640	—	—	65,000
1/95	5,160	—	—	70,000
Annual Growth	8.9%	—	—	0.8%

Revenue History

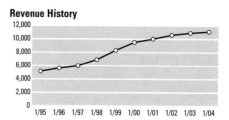

Memec

Active around the world, Memec and its subsidiaries (to be renamed Memec Inc. following its planned IPO) provide logistics and distribution services to international manufacturers and suppliers in the semiconductor industry, including Xilinx, Actel, and Texas Instruments. Memec also provides IT, warehousing, and product packaging services to customers to help streamline their supply chains and lower cost. Each of the Memec group companies focuses on a limited number of suppliers within a specific industry. Investors in the company include London-based buyout firm Permira (68%) and Deutsche Bank (14%). The company may use the proceeds of a planned IPO to pay down debt.

In addition to simply selling products to original equipment manufacturers, Memec works with its OEM customers during their design phases to drive demand for customized products.

EXECUTIVES

Chairman: Peter Smitham, age 62
President, CEO, and Director: David Ashworth, age 42, $707,093 pay
SVP, CFO, and Secretary: Doug Lindroth, age 37, $428,809 pay
SVP and CIO: Gerald (Jerry) Corvino, age 56
SVP, Corporate Development: David Johnson, age 38
SVP, Human Resources: William (Bill) O'Neill, age 47
SVP, Operations; President, Memec United: Gerard (Gerry) Fay, age 45
SVP; President, Memec Americas: Greg Provenzano, age 42, $473,841 pay
SVP; President, Memec Asia-Pacific: Yang-Chiah Yee, age 37, $365,889 pay
SVP; President, Memec EMEA: Chris Page, age 46, $563,338 pay
Auditors: PricewaterhouseCoopers LLP

LOCATIONS

HQ: Memec Group Holdings Limited
3721 Valley Centre Dr., San Diego, CA 92130
Phone: 858-314-8800   **Fax:** 858-314-8850
Web: www.memec.com

Memec has operations in more than 30 countries, including presences in the Americas, Asia, Australia, Europe, and the Middle East.

2003 Sales

	$ mil.	% of total
Americas	774.1	43
Europe, Middle East & Africa	446.4	25
Asia/Pacific		
Japan	138.3	8
Other countries	439.0	24
Total	**1,797.8**	**100**

COMPETITORS

All American Semiconductor	Electrocomponents
Arrow Electronics	Future Electronics
ASCII Group	Jaco Electronics
Avnet	Nu Horizons Electronics
Bell Microproducts	Premier Farnell
Digi-Key	Richardson Electronics
	TTI

HISTORICAL FINANCIALS

Company Type: Private

Income Statement
FYE: December 31

	REVENUE ($ mil.)	NET INCOME ($ mil.)	NET PROFIT MARGIN	EMPLOYEES
12/03	1,798	(86)	—	2,425
12/02	1,609	(85)	—	2,700
12/01	2,065	(25)	—	2,800
12/00	3,700	—	—	—
Annual Growth	(21.4%)	—	—	(6.9%)

2003 Year-End Financials
Debt ratio: —   Current ratio: 1.78
Return on equity: —   Long-term debt ($ mil.): 590
Cash ($ mil.): 42

Net Income History

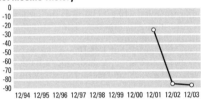

Memorial Hermann Healthcare

Memorial Hermann Healthcare System is a "munster" of an organization. Houston's largest not-for-profit health care system includes about ten hospitals (one is a children's hospital), two long-term nursing facilities, and a retirement community. Through Memorial Hermann Regional Healthcare Services, the company is also affiliated with 19 community hospitals. Subsidiaries include home health care agency Memorial Hermann Home Health and physician practice company Memorial Hermann Health Network Providers.

The company's Memorial Hermann Family Practice Residency Program is affiliated with the University of Texas-Houston Medical School. The organization was formed by the 1997 merger of two smaller systems.

EXECUTIVES

Chairman: A.T. Blackshear Jr.
President and CEO: Daniel J. Wolterman
SVP, Finance: Carrol Aulbaugh
Director, Public/Media Relations: Jamie O'Roark
SVP and CEO, Memorial Hermann Hospital: Juanita Romans
CEO, Memorial Hermann Katy Hospital: Scott Barbe
CEO, Memorial Hermann Fort Bend Hospital: Rod Brace
VP and Interim President, Memorial Hermann Children's Hospital: Craig Cordola
CEO, Memorial Hermann Southeast Hospital: C. David Huffstutler
CEO, Memorial Hermann Northwest Hospital: Keith Parrot
CEO, Memorial Hermann The Woodlands Hospital: Steve Sanders
CEO, Memorial Hermann Southwest Hospital: Chris Vasquez
CEO, Memorial Hermann Memorial City Hospital: Wayne Voss

LOCATIONS

HQ: Memorial Hermann Healthcare System
9401 Southwest Fwy., Houston, TX 77074
Phone: 713-448-5555   **Fax:** 713-448-5665
Web: www.memorialhermann.org

PRODUCTS/OPERATIONS

Selected Facilities
Memorial Hermann Baptist Beaumont Hospital
Memorial Hermann Baptist Orange Hospital
Memorial Hermann Children's Hospital (Houston)
Memorial Hermann Fort Bend Hospital
Memorial Hermann Hospital (Houston)
Memorial Hermann Imaging and Breast Center (Houston)
Memorial Hermann Katy Hospital
Memorial Hermann Memorial City Hospital (Houston)
Memorial Hermann Northwest Hospital (Houston)
Memorial Hermann Rehabilitation Hospital (Houston)
Memorial Hermann Southeast Hospital (Houston)
Memorial Hermann Southwest Hospital (Houston)
Memorial Hermann Spring Shadows Pines (Houston)
Memorial Hermann Sugar Land Health Center
Memorial Hermann The Woodlands Hospital
University Place Retirement Community and Nursing Center (Houston)
Wellness Center (Houston)

COMPETITORS

CHRISTUS Health	St. Luke's Episcopal Hospital
Harris County Hospital	
HCA	Tenet Healthcare
Methodist Hospital System	Triad Hospitals

HISTORICAL FINANCIALS

Company Type: Not-for-profit

Income Statement
FYE: June 30

	REVENUE ($ mil.)	NET INCOME ($ mil.)	NET PROFIT MARGIN	EMPLOYEES
6/03	2,500	—	—	13,000
6/02	2,250	—	—	11,000
6/01	2,000	—	—	11,000
6/00	1,512	—	—	11,000
6/99	1,360	—	—	11,000
6/98	1,003	—	—	12,000
6/97	1,200	—	—	7,500
6/96	973	—	—	7,488
Annual Growth	14.4%	—	—	8.2%

Revenue History

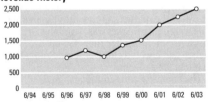

Memorial Sloan-Kettering

Ranked as one of the nation's top cancer centers, Memorial Sloan-Kettering Cancer Center includes Memorial Hospital for Cancer and Allied Diseases for pediatric and adult cancer care and the Sloan-Kettering Institute for cancer research activities. The cancer center specializes in bone-marrow transplants and chemotherapy and offers programs in cancer prevention, treatment, research, and education. Memorial Sloan-Kettering offers inpatient and outpatient services to more than 19,000 patients every year. Other services include pain management, rehabilitation, and psychological programs.

Memorial Sloan-Kettering both gives and receives funding to further the fight against cancer and other diseases. Philanthropic contributions each year typically reach around $100 million.

EXECUTIVES

Chairman: Douglas A. (Sandy) Warner III, age 57
Honorary Co-Chairman: James D. Robinson III, age 68
Vice Chairman; Chairman, Memorial Hospital:
  Richard I. (Dick) Beattie, age 65
Vice Chairman; Chairman, Sloan-Kettering Institute:
  Louis V. Gerstner Jr., age 62
Vice Chairman, Education, Sloan-Kettering Institute:
  Jerard Hurwitz
President and CEO: Harold Varmus
President Emeritus: Paul A. Marks
EVP and COO: John R. Gunn, age 61
SVP, Clinical Program Development:
  Thomas J. Fahey Jr.
SVP, Finance and Assistant Treasurer:
  Michael P. Gutnick
SVP and Hospital Administrator: Kathryn Martin
SVP and General Counsel: Roger N. Parker
SVP, Research Resources Management: James S. Quirk
VP, Human Resources: Michael Browne
VP, Marketing: Ellen Miller Sonet
VP, Public Affairs: Anne Thomas
Director, Communications: Christine Hickey
Secretary: Edwin M. Burke
Treasurer: Clifton S. Robbins

LOCATIONS

HQ: Memorial Sloan-Kettering Cancer Center
  1275 York Ave., New York, NY 10021
Phone: 212-639-2000   **Fax:** 212-639-3576
Web: www.mskcc.org

COMPETITORS

Carilion Health System
Columbia University
Detroit Medical Center
Johns Hopkins Medicine
Mayo Foundation
New York City Health and Hospitals
Partners HealthCare
Rush System for Health
University of Texas

HISTORICAL FINANCIALS

Company Type: Not-for-profit

Income Statement
FYE: December 31

	REVENUE ($ mil.)	NET INCOME ($ mil.)	NET PROFIT MARGIN	EMPLOYEES
12/03	1,318	423	32.1%	8,255
12/02	1,088	(81)	—	7,953
12/01	959	(120)	—	7,609
12/00	876	64	7.3%	7,296
12/99	790	222	28.1%	7,133
12/98	747	204	27.3%	6,618
12/97	694	207	29.8%	6,142
12/96	648	178	27.5%	5,799
12/95	650	191	29.4%	6,050
12/94	637	21	3.4%	6,034
Annual Growth	8.4%	39.3%	—	3.5%

2003 Year-End Financials

Debt ratio: —
Return on equity: 16.6%
Cash ($ mil.): —
Current ratio: —
Long-term debt ($ mil.): —

Net Income History

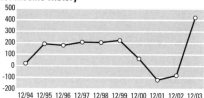

Menard

If sticks and stones break bones, what can two-by-fours and 2-in. nails do? That is what Menard is wondering now that its biggest rivals (#1 home improvement giant The Home Depot and #2 Lowe's) are hammering away at its home turf. The third-largest home improvement chain in the US, Menard has more than 170 stores in Illinois, Indiana, Iowa, Michigan, Minnesota, Nebraska, North and South Dakota, Ohio, and Wisconsin. The stores sell home improvement products, such as floor coverings, hardware, millwork, paint, and tools. Unlike competitors, all the company's stores have full-service lumberyards. Menard is owned by president and CEO John Menard Jr., who founded the company in 1972.

Although Menard outlets are typically smaller than those of Home Depot, they offer a similar selection of products by building large warehouses adjacent to stores and then quickly restocking merchandise when it's sold. The company's products are laid out on easy-to-reach, supermarket-styled shelves. To help keep expenses low and prices cheap, Menard makes some of its merchandise, including doors and trusses.

The company is increasing its average store size to more than 220,000 sq. ft. It has opened its largest store ever — 250,000 sq. ft. — in Minnesota and is expanding 30 to 40 stores. Most of the 20 some stores the company plans to build in 2004 will be more than 200,000 square feet. Besides stocking hardware and building supplies these new megastores will include garden centers and sell a large range of home appliances.

Besides billionaire founder and owner John Menard running the chain, other family members are engaged in its everyday operations. John Menard also owns Team Menard, an Indy car-racing team.

HISTORY

John Menard was the oldest of eight children on a Wisconsin dairy farm. To pay for attending the University of Wisconsin at Eau Claire, he and some fellow college students built pole barns in the late 1950s. Learning that other builders had trouble finding lumber outlets open on the weekends, Menard began buying wood in bulk and selling it to them. He added other supplies in 1960 and sold his construction business in 1970 as building supply revenues became his chief source of income.

He founded Menard in 1972 as the do-it-yourself craze was beginning, but he wanted an operation run more like mass merchandiser Target, with easy-to-reach shelves, wide aisles, and tile floors rather than the cold, cumbersome layout used by lumberyards. To realize that concept, Menard built warehouses and stockrooms behind the stores so he could restock merchandise quickly.

Menard's vision worked, and he began building his Midwestern empire, often acquiring abandoned retail sites that were inexpensive and in good locations. By 1986 Menard was in Iowa, Minnesota, North and South Dakota, and Wisconsin, and by 1990 it had 46 stores. In the early 1990s Menard began enlarging its operations to serve the ever-growing number of stores, opening a huge warehouse and distribution center and a manufacturing facility that made doors, Formica countertops, and other products. Menard entered Nebraska in 1990 and opened its first store in Chicago the next year. By 1992 there were more than 60 stores.

That year Menard made the National Enquirer with a story about the firing of a store manager who had built a wheelchair-accessible home for his 11-year-old daughter with spina bifida, violating a company theft-prevention policy forbidding store managers to build their own homes. The company insisted that the man was fired in part because of poor work performance.

Menard continued to expand to new areas, operating stores in Indiana and Michigan by 1992. As it continued expanding in the Chicago area, it offered varying store formats, ranging from a full line of building materials to smaller Menards Hardware Plus stores. By 1994 Menard had 85 stores, many bigger than 100,000 sq. ft.

In 1995 and 1996 the company was plagued with lawsuits filed by customers charging false arrest and imprisonment for shoplifting. An on-duty police officer apprehending a shoplifting suspect at a store was even stopped and searched. Competition also heated up during that time. The Home Depot's push into the Midwest — including opening several stores directly across the street from Menard — spurred Menard to fight back by lowering prices and opening nearly 40 stores. The fight forced smaller chains like Handy Andy out of business.

In 1997 Menard and his company were fined $1.7 million after dumping bags of toxic ash from its manufacturing facility at residential trash pick-up sites rather than at properly regulated outlets (it had been fined for similar violations in 1989 and 1994). In response to a price war initiated by Home Depot, in 1998 Menard dropped sales prices by 10%.

In 1999 competitor Lowe's began moving into Menard's biggest market, Chicago. Menard began opening larger stores in 2000 (about 162,000 sq. ft., or some 74,000 sq. ft. bigger than the older stores). In 2001 it began beefing up its lines of home appliances, adding more washers, dryers, dishwashers, refrigerators, and ranges.

Menard opened a 225,000 sq. ft. store — larger by 50 sq. ft. than the original — in Indiana in 2003. It then opened a bigger store, at 250,000 sq. ft., in Minnesota in February 2004.

EXECUTIVES
President and CEO: John R. Menard Jr., age 64
CFO and Treasurer: Earl R. Rasmussen
VP of Merchandising: Ed Archibald
VP of Operations: Larry Menard
VP of Real Estate: Marv Prochaska
CTO: Dave Wagner
Payroll Manager: Terri Jain
General Counsel: Dawn M. Sands

LOCATIONS
HQ: Menard, Inc.
4777 Menard Dr., Eau Claire, WI 54703
Phone: 715-876-5911   **Fax:** 715-876-2868
Web: www.menards.com/nindex.html

Menard owns home improvement stores in Illinois, Indiana, Iowa, Michigan, Minnesota, Nebraska, North Dakota, Ohio, South Dakota, and Wisconsin.

PRODUCTS/OPERATIONS

Selected Operations
Menards (home improvement stores)
Midwest Manufacturing (product manufacturing)

Selected Departments
Appliances
Building materials
Electrical (wiring, lighting)
Floor coverings
Hardware
Lumberyard
Millwork (doors, cabinetry, molding)
Plumbing
Seasonal (Christmas, lawn and garden)
Tools
Wall coverings (wallpaper, paint)

COMPETITORS
84 Lumber
Ace Hardware
Carter Lumber
Do it Best
Fastenal
Home Depot
Lanoga
Lowe's
Primus
Sears
Seigle's
Sherwin-Williams
Stock Building Supply
Sutherland Lumber
TruServ
Wal-Mart
Wolohan Lumber

HISTORICAL FINANCIALS
Company Type: Private

Income Statement   FYE: January 31

	ESTIMATED REVENUE ($ mil.)	NET INCOME ($ mil.)	NET PROFIT MARGIN	EMPLOYEES
1/03	5,600	—	—	10,500
1/02	5,300	—	—	9,200
1/01	5,000	—	—	7,600
1/00	4,500	—	—	7,000
1/99	4,000	—	—	7,000
1/98	3,700	—	—	7,000
1/97	3,200	—	—	7,000
1/96	2,700	—	—	6,534
1/95	2,300	—	—	5,800
1/94	1,750	—	—	5,000
Annual Growth	13.8%	—	—	8.6%

Revenue History

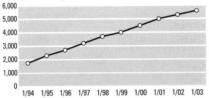

Menasha

Menasha has the whole package. Founded in 1849 as a woodenware business, the holding company now owns businesses that make packaging and paperboard, returnable material handling systems, product labels, and promotional materials. Each company is independently operated. The company's main subsidiaries are Menasha Packaging Company (corrugated packaging), ORBIS Corporation (returnable materials handling products), Poly Hi Solidur (polymers), and Promo Edge Company (printing). It also has investments in other manufacturing companies. Menasha operates nearly 70 facilities across the US and in seven other countries. Descendants of founder Elisha Smith own a majority of Menasha.

Menasha has sold the laminating division of its Menasha Packaging subsidiary and its Thermotech injection molding business as part of its strategy to focus on core operations and distinguish itself from its competition.

In 2004 Menasha's board of directors announced a plan whereby individual directors would be assigned to Menasha's various subsidiaries in active "CEO-like" leadership roles. As a result of these changes, Harold Smethills, president and CEO since 2000, has resigned.

EXECUTIVES
Chairman: Donald C. (Buzz) Shepard III
VP, CFO, and Treasurer: Arthur Huge
VP, General Counsel, and Secretary: James J. Sarosiek
CEO, Menasha Packaging Company: Michael K. Waite
CEO, ORBIS Corporation: David R. (Dave) Schopp
CEO, Poly Hi Solidur, Inc.: R. Jay Finch
CEO, Promo Edge Company: James G. O'Dea
President, ORBIS North America:
  Jerome C. (Jerry) Hessel
COO, Promo Edge: Dennis Pratt
Assistant Secretary: Thomas V. Bender
Assistant Treasurer: Kevin P. Head

LOCATIONS
HQ: Menasha Corporation
1645 Bergstrom Rd., Neenah, WI 54956
Phone: 920-751-1000   **Fax:** 920-751-1825
Web: www.menasha.com

Menasha and its subsidiaries have operations in Australia, Brazil, Canada, France, Germany, India, Japan, Mexico, the Netherlands, Singapore, South Africa, Switzerland, the UK, and the US.

PRODUCTS/OPERATIONS

Selected Operations
Menasha Material Handling Corporation
  Returnable packaging (ORBIS)
  Logistics evaluation and implementation (Menasha Services)
  Operation services (Menasha Services)
  Shipping pallets (ORBIS)
  Storage container systems (LEWISBins+)
Menasha Packaging Company
  Contract carrier truckload services (Menasha Transport)
  Corrugated containers (Menasha Packaging)
  Creative graphic design (Menasha Packaging)
  Fiber material handling containers (Solid Fibre Division)
  Interior protective packaging (Sus-Rap)
  Paperboard
Poly Hi Solidur Group
  Plastic sheets (TIVAR)
  Polyethylene
  Polymer conversion
  Polyvinyl chloride
  Rod and molded parts
Polymer Technologies Group
  Condiment dispensers (Traex)
  Fast food trays (Traex)
Promotional and Informational Graphics Group
  Commercial printing (Neenah Printing)
  Labels and labeling equipment (Promo Edge)
  Printing for pharmaceutical packaging (New Jersey Packaging Division)

COMPETITORS
Boise Cascade
Longview Fibre
Shorewood Packaging
Smurfit-Stone Container
Sonoco Products
Unisource
Valspar

HISTORICAL FINANCIALS
Company Type: Private

Income Statement   FYE: December 31

	REVENUE ($ mil.)	NET INCOME ($ mil.)	NET PROFIT MARGIN	EMPLOYEES
12/03	1,025	—	—	5,283
12/02	1,100	—	—	5,500
12/01	1,100	—	—	5,400
12/00	1,121	—	—	6,046
12/99	991	—	—	5,759
12/98	952	—	—	6,000
12/97	933	—	—	5,759
12/96	915	—	—	5,584
12/95	916	—	—	5,100
12/94	779	—	—	4,900
Annual Growth	3.1%	—	—	0.8%

Revenue History

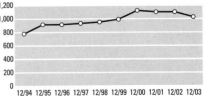

Meridian Automotive Systems

From bumper to bumper, Meridian Automotive Systems has the line on what it takes to keep a vehicle together. The auto parts company operates three business segments: Exterior Composites (body panels, fenders, tailgates); Interiors and Exterior Lighting (floor consoles, fog lamps, instrument panels, signal lamps); and Front and Rear End Modules (bumpers, energy absorbing foam, plastic fascias). Meridian's major customers include Ford, General Motors, and DaimlerChysler. The company operates 20 primary manufacturing plants in North and South America. Meridian is owned by Windward Capital Partners, Capital d'Amerique CDPQ Inc., Credit Suisse First Boston, and Northwestern Mutual Life Insurance.

EXECUTIVES

Chairman: Robert H. Barton III, age 69
President, CEO, and Director: H. H. (Buddy) Wacaser, age 53
EVP and CFO: Richard Newsted, age 45
EVP, Engineering and Product Development: Jon Baker, age 58
SVP, Secretary, and General Counsel: Dean Vanek, age 44
President, FEM/REM Group: Francis I. (Fran) LeVeque, age 44
President, Exterior Composites Group: J. Steve McKenzie, age 45
President, Interior Group: Randall S. (Randy) Wacaser, age 40
VP, Human Resources: Thomas C. (Tom) Eggebeen, age 51
Auditors: PricewaterhouseCoopers LLP

LOCATIONS

HQ: Meridian Automotive Systems, Inc.
550 Town Center Dr., Ste. 475, Dearborn, MI 48126
Phone: 313-336-4182   **Fax:** 313-253-4026
Web: www.meridianautosystems.com

Meridian Automotive Systems has 20 principal manufacturing facilities in Brazil, Canada, Mexico, and the US.

PRODUCTS/OPERATIONS

Selected Products
Exterior Composites
  Body panels
  Fenders
  Grille opening reinforcements
  Hood assemblies
  Midgates
  Pickup truck boxes
  Step assists
  Structural reinforcements
  Tailgates
  Tonneau covers
  Valve covers
Interiors and Exterior Lighting
  Ash trays
  Center high mount stop lamps
  Cupholders
  Decorative trim panels
  Door panels
  Floor consoles
  Fog lamps
  Glove boxes
  Instrument panels
  License lamps
  Park and turn lights
  Signal lamps
  Tail lamps
Front and Rear End Modules
  Chrome-plated and painted stamped steel bumpers
  Energy absorbing foam
  Plastic fascias
  Steel rollform beams

COMPETITORS

A.G. Simpson
Delphi
Dura Automotive
Faurecia
Magnifoam Technology
Tower Automotive

HISTORICAL FINANCIALS

Company Type: Private

Income Statement   FYE: December 31

	REVENUE ($ mil.)	NET INCOME ($ mil.)	NET PROFIT MARGIN	EMPLOYEES
12/03	1,000	—	—	5,600
12/02	1,100	—	—	5,500
12/01	977	—	—	5,900
12/00	803	—	—	—
12/99	468	—	—	—
Annual Growth	20.9%	—	—	(2.6%)

Revenue History

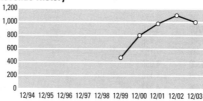

Merrill

Merrill manages documents, lock, stock, and barrel. Merrill Corporation is among the largest document management firms in the US and a leading provider of financial document services, such as preparing and delivering electronic filings to the SEC, producing annual reports, and creating other time-sensitive documents. It also provides business communications-related printing, graphic design, and fulfillment services. Other offerings include facilities management and legal support services. Its DataSite division offers online data rooms for due diligence and discovery. Customers include law firms, real estate companies, financial services corporations, and others.

With its stock price flagging, the company in 1999 agreed to a buyout by affiliates of Donaldson, Lufkin & Jenrette (later acquired by Credit Suisse First Boston). However, a weak market for financial document services seriously impinged the company's ability to pay down its growing debt load in 2000 and Merrill's lenders declared the company in default the next year. A recapitalization plan completed in 2002 helped the company to get back on track.

EXECUTIVES

CEO: John W. Castro, age 55
President and COO: Rick R. Atterbury
EVP and CFO: Robert H. Nazarian
VP and Controller: Dean A. Niehus
VP Human Resources: Brenda Vale
VP Document Services: Peter J. Cawley
VP Document Services Operations: Nancee Ronning
VP DataSite Services: Paul Hartzell
VP Litigation Support Services: Joe Mann
VP Marketing: Leon S. DeMaille
President, Financial Document Services: Mike James
President, Document Management Services: Allen J. (Al) McNee
CTO: John Stolle

LOCATIONS

HQ: Merrill Corporation
1 Merrill Cir., St. Paul, MN 55108
Phone: 651-646-4501   **Fax:** 651-646-5332
Web: www.merrillcorp.com

Merrill has offices in Canada, France, Germany, the UK, and the US.

PRODUCTS/OPERATIONS

Selected Products and Services
Legal
  Compliance and due diligence database
  Electronic discovery
  Securities Law database
Facilities management
  Copy centers
  Mailroom services
  Office services
  Records management
Financial
  Investor Relations services
  SEC documents, filing, and distribution
Printing
  Catalogs
  Corporate communications materials
  Direct mail
  Fulfillment
  Graphic design
  Marketing collateral
  Signage
Supply chain consulting
Translation services
Web-based tools
  MerrillConnect (sales and marketing analysis)
  MerrillReports (report automation for investment funds)
  net:MAIL (newsletters and mailers)
  net: PROSPECT (sales lead management)
Web site hosting
Workgroup Collaboration Web site

COMPETITORS

Banta
Bowne
Bowne Global Solutions
Cenveo
Dai Nippon Printing
Lionbridge
Quad/Graphics
Quebecor World North America
R.R. Donnelley
Service Point
St Ives
Standard Register
Toppan Printing
Workflow Management

HISTORICAL FINANCIALS

Company Type: Private

Income Statement
FYE: January 31

	REVENUE ($ mil.)	NET INCOME ($ mil.)	NET PROFIT MARGIN	EMPLOYEES
1/04	596	8	1.4%	4,200
1/03	582	—	—	4,070
1/02	603	—	—	4,086
1/01	650	—	—	4,100
1/00	588	—	—	4,157
1/99	510	—	—	3,933
1/98	460	—	—	3,838
1/97	354	—	—	2,804
1/96	245	—	—	2,253
1/95	237	—	—	1,739
Annual Growth	10.8%	—	—	10.3%

Revenue History

Mervyn's

Mervyn's is sure hoping that its change in ownership will get it back on target. The company operates about 260 midrange department stores in California and 13 other states, primarily in the west and south. In addition to name-brand apparel and housewares, Mervyn's offers goods under private labels, including Hillard & Hanson. About half of its stores are in regional malls and cater primarily to working moms ages 25 to 49. Mervyn's has been squeezed by upscale department stores as well as discount chains. In 2004 former parent Target sold Mervyn's to an investment consortium of Sun Capital Partners, Cerberus Capital, and Lubert-Adler/Klaff. Its $475 million credit card accounts were sold to GE Consumer Finance.

EXECUTIVES

CFO: Clay Creasey
VP, Human Resources: Janna Adair
VP, Marketing: Lee Walker de Sarvide
VP, Merchandise Planning: Lynn Schirmer
VP, Product Design and Development: Chris Daniel
VP and General Merchandise Manager, Men's: Pete Daleiden
CIO; SVP, Technology Services and CIO, Target Corporation: Paul L. Singer, age 50
Director of Creative Marketing: Robert Raible
Senior Manager, Community Relations: Bernard Boudreaux
Senior Manager, Events Marketing and Licensing: Mark Nawrocki
Marketing and Media Relations: Michele Murphy
Auditors: Ernst & Young LLP

LOCATIONS

HQ: Mervyn's
22301 Foothill Blvd., Hayward, CA 94541
Phone: 510-727-3000   **Fax:** 510-727-2300
Web: www.mervyns.com

2004 Stores

	No.
California	126
Texas	42
Arizona	15
Michigan	15
Washington	13
Colorado	11
Minnesota	9
Utah	8
Nevada	7
Oregon	7
Louisiana	6
New Mexico	3
Oklahoma	3
Idaho	1
Total	**266**

COMPETITORS

American Retail
Burlington Coat Factory
Dillard's
Dress Barn
Federated
Gap
Gottschalks
J. C. Penney
Kmart
Kohl's
Limited Brands
May
Ross Stores
Sears
Target
TJX Companies
Wal-Mart

HISTORICAL FINANCIALS

Company Type: Private

Income Statement
FYE: Saturday nearest January 31

	REVENUE ($ mil.)	NET INCOME ($ mil.)	NET PROFIT MARGIN	EMPLOYEES
1/04	3,553	—	—	29,000
1/03	3,816	—	—	33,000
1/02	4,038	—	—	32,000
1/01	4,152	—	—	29,000
1/00	4,099	—	—	32,000
1/99	4,176	—	—	30,000
1/98	4,227	—	—	29,000
1/97	4,369	—	—	—
Annual Growth	(2.9%)	—	—	0.0%

Revenue History

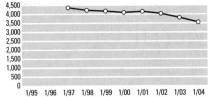

Metaldyne

Whether you're cruising down the highway or being towed, Metaldyne products may be involved. The metal-forming and -machining company's Chassis Group, Engine Group, and Driveline Group make automotive components for passenger cars and commercial vehicles. Products include components and assemblies for engines, noise and vibration control, transmissions, wheels, suspensions, axles, and drivelines. Metaldyne, now part of Heartland Industrial Partners, was formed through the consolidation of MascoTech, Simpson Industries, and Global Metal Technologies.

EXECUTIVES

Chairman, President and CEO: Timothy D. Leuliette, age 54, $2,650,000 pay
Group President, Chassis Group: Joseph Nowak, age 52
Group President, Driveline and Transmission Group: Bruce Swift
Group President, Engine Group: George Thanopoulos, age 39, $537,381 pay
VP and CIO: Dick Lefebvre
VP and Corporate Controller: Jeff Stafeil
VP and Treasurer: Karen A. Radtke, age 49
VP, Corporate Affairs: Myra Moreland
VP, Corporate Development: Thomas Amato
VP, Human Resources: Jim Strahley
VP, Sales and Marketing: Chuck Pestow
VP, Supply Chain Management and Quality: Doug Grimm
Director of Corporate Communications: Kurt Ruecke
Corporate Legal Counsel: Jeff Pollock
Auditors: PricewaterhouseCoopers LLP

LOCATIONS

HQ: Metaldyne Corporation
47603 Halyard Dr., Plymouth, MI 48170
Phone: 734-207-6200   **Fax:** 734-207-6500
Web: www.metaldyne.com

Metaldyne operates more than 50 manufacturing and technology centers in 11 countries.

2003 Sales

	$ mil.	% of total
North America		
US	1,153.6	76
Other countries	58.1	4
Europe	296.5	20
Total	**1,508.2**	**100**

PRODUCTS/OPERATIONS

2003 Sales

	$ mil.	% of total
Driveline	790.8	52
Engine	600.4	40
Chassis	117.1	8
Total	**1,508.2**	**100**

Selected Products

Axles and driveline products
Engine products
Noise, vibration, and harshness products
Transmission and transfer case products
Wheel-End and suspension products

COMPETITORS

American Axle & Manufacturing
ArvinMeritor, Inc.
Dana
Delphi
Eaton
GKN
NGK INSULATORS
Raytech
Remy
Robert Bosch
Sypris Solutions
Visteon

Metromedia

HISTORICAL FINANCIALS
Company Type: Private

Income Statement
FYE: Sunday nearest December 31

	REVENUE ($ mil.)	NET INCOME ($ mil.)	NET PROFIT MARGIN	EMPLOYEES
12/03	1,508	(75)	—	7,900
12/02	1,793	(62)	—	7,100
12/01	2,128	(43)	—	12,500
12/00	1,650	56	3.4%	11,600
12/99	1,680	92	5.5%	9,500
12/98	1,636	98	6.0%	9,200
12/97	922	115	12.5%	9,000
12/96	1,281	52	4.0%	5,100
12/95	1,678	59	3.5%	10,800
12/94	1,702	(220)	—	12,700
Annual Growth	(1.3%)	—	—	(5.1%)

2003 Year-End Financials
Debt ratio: 140.5%
Return on equity: —
Cash ($ mil.): 14
Current ratio: 0.93
Long-term debt ($ mil.): 767

Net Income History
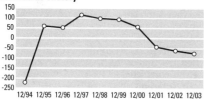

Metromedia Company has a lot of irons in a lot of fires. The global giant is one of the US's largest private companies. Subsidiary Metromedia International Group, a holding company in which Metromedia owns a 20% stake, has interests in telecommunications ventures in Eastern Europe and the former Soviet Union, including wireless and fixed-line phone and cable TV systems. Other Metromedia units include Metromedia Restaurant Group, which owns or franchises Ponderosa, Bennigan's, Bonanza, and Steak and Ale restaurants, and Metromedia Energy, an independent energy marketer. Chairman John Kluge and EVP and partner Stuart Subotnick run Metromedia Company through a partnership.

Eatontown, New Jersey-based Metromedia Energy delivers more than 20 billion cu. ft. per year of commercial and industrial natural gas to customers in the Northeast, Midwest, and Mid-Atlantic US.

In 2003 Metromedia sold a minority stake in its restaurant subsidiary to Irving, Texas-based Apex Restaurant Group, which assumed management of the chain operator.

HISTORY

German immigrant John Kluge, born in 1914, came to Detroit at age eight with his mother and stepfather. He later worked at the Ford assembly line. At Columbia University he studied economics and (to the chagrin of college administrators) poker, building a tidy sum with his winnings by graduation. Kluge worked in Army intelligence during WWII. After the war he bought WGAY radio in Silver Spring, Maryland, and went on to buy and sell other small radio stations.

Kluge began to diversify, entering the wholesale food business in the mid-1950s. In 1959 he purchased control of Metropolitan Broadcasting, including TV stations in New York and Washington, DC, and took it public. He renamed the company Metromedia in 1960.

Metromedia added independent stations — to the then-legal limit of seven — in major markets, paying relatively little compared to network affiliate prices. The stations struggled through years of infomercials but thrived in the late 1970s and early 1980s. Metromedia's stock price rose from $4.50 in 1974 to more than $500 in 1983. The company also acquired radio stations, the Harlem Globetrotters, and the Ice Capades.

In 1983 Kluge bought paging and cellular telephone licenses across the US. He later acquired long-distance carriers in Texas and Florida. In 1984 Metromedia went private in a $1.6 billion buyout and began to sell off its assets in 1985. It sold its Boston TV station to Hearst and its six other TV stations to Rupert Murdoch for a total of $2 billion. In 1986 it sold its outdoor advertising firm, nine of its 11 radio stations, and the Globetrotters and Ice Capades. Kluge then sold most of the company's cellular properties to SBC Communications. In 1990 it sold its New York cellular operations to LIN Broadcasting and its Philadelphia cellular operations to Comcast.

Building what Kluge envisioned as his steak house empire, the firm bought the Ponderosa steak house chain (founded in the late 1960s) in 1988 from Asher Edelman and later added Dallas-based USA Cafes (Bonanza steak houses, founded 1964) and S&A Restaurant Corp. (Steak and Ale, founded 1966; Bennigan's, founded 1976). Also in 1988 Kluge rescued friend Arthur Krim, whose Orion Pictures was threatened by Viacom, by buying control of the filmmaker.

Kluge's grand steak house vision did not come to fruition. Increased competition squeezed profits at Ponderosa and Bonanza. The restaurant group was also plagued by management shake-ups, aging facilities, food-quality issues, and even bad press. (Bennigan's was ranked the worst casual dining chain in the US in a 1992 Consumer Reports poll.)

In 1989 Kluge merged Metromedia Long Distance with the long-distance operations of ITT. Renamed Metromedia Communications in 1991, the company merged with other long-distance providers to become MCI WorldCom. (Kluge sold his 16% of MCI WorldCom to the public in 1995.)

Kluge created Metromedia International Group in 1995 by merging Orion Pictures, Metromedia International Telecommunications, MCEG Sterling (film and television production), and Actava Group (maker of Snapper lawn mowers and sporting goods — sold 2002). Metromedia Restaurant Group announced a $190 million refinancing agreement for S&A Restaurant Corp. in 1998 to expand and refurbish its restaurants; it closed 28 unprofitable restaurants that year and launched a franchise program to grow its Bennigan's and Steak and Ale chains.

Metromedia expanded its Bennigan's units in South Korea in 1999 and the next year announced it would build 65 new restaurants in the US and expand to more than 200 units internationally. In 2001 Verizon Communications invested nearly $2 billion in Metromedia Fiber Network, but the latter company was forced to declare Chapter 11 bankruptcy the following year. It blamed lower than expected demand for its metropolitan Internet services due to stiff competition, which drove down prices.

The company once controlled Metromedia Fiber Network, now known as AboveNet. The company completed reorganization under Chapter 11 bankruptcy protection in 2002, citing a lower than expected demand for broadband connections in large cities and after a primary customer filed for Chapter 11 protection. John Kluge resigned from the Metromedia Fiber Network board that year. He also stepped down from the Metromedia International Group board in 2002.

EXECUTIVES

Chairman and President: John W. Kluge, age 90
EVP; President and CEO, Metromedia International Group: Stuart Subotnick, age 62
SVP Finance and Treasurer: Robert A. Maresca
SVP, Secretary, and General Counsel: David A. Persing
SVP: Silvia Kessel
VP and Controller: David Gassler
VP Financial Reporting: Vincent D. Sasso Jr., age 42
VP: Mario P. Catuogno
Manager Human Resources: Jamie Smith-Wagner
Manager Pension and Profit Sharing: Patti Ann Kletz
CEO, Metromedia Restaurant Group: John J. Todd, age 43
Auditors: KPMG LLP

LOCATIONS

HQ: Metromedia Company
1 Meadowlands Plaza, East Rutherford, NJ 07073
Phone: 201-531-8000   **Fax:** 201-531-2804

PRODUCTS/OPERATIONS

Selected Subsidiaries and Affiliates
Metromedia Energy, Inc. (independent energy marketer)
Metromedia International Group, Inc. (20%, telecommunications holdings)
Metromedia Restaurant Group (51%, Bennigan's, Bonanza, Ponderosa, and Steak and Ale owner and franchisee)

COMPETITORS

Applebee's
AT&T
Brinker
BT
Buffets Holdings
Carlson Restaurants
Darden
Deutsche Telekom
Hellenic Telecommunications
Level 3 Communications
Lone Star Steakhouse
MCI
O'Charley's
Outback Steakhouse
Perkins
Rostelecom
Ryan's
Sprint FON
Verizon
Worldwide Restaurant Concepts

HISTORICAL FINANCIALS
Company Type: Private

Income Statement
FYE: December 31

	ESTIMATED REVENUE ($ mil.)	NET INCOME ($ mil.)	NET PROFIT MARGIN	EMPLOYEES
12/02	1,450	—	—	29,500
12/01	1,400	—	—	28,500
12/00	1,500	—	—	29,500
12/99	1,610	—	—	32,000
12/98	1,500	—	—	62,700
12/97	1,950	—	—	63,000
12/96	1,900	—	—	—
12/95	1,900	—	—	—
12/94	2,000	—	—	—
12/93	1,900	—	—	—
Annual Growth	(3.0%)	—	—	(14.1%)

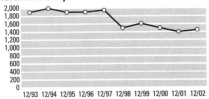

Metromedia Restaurant Group

Make no mistake: Metromedia Restaurant Group (MRG) has a big stake in steak. The company operates and franchises more than 800 casual-dining restaurants, including 480 Bonanza and Ponderosa family steakhouses and about 60 Steak & Ale locations. Bonanza and Ponderosa each feature steak, chicken, and seafood dishes along with an all-you-can-eat salad and soup bar. Steak & Ale offers a broader menu set in the atmosphere of an 18th century English country inn. MRG also owns the Bennigan's Irish American Grill & Tavern chain, with more than 300 locations that offer sandwiches and burgers, as well as ribs, steaks, and seafood. The business is jointly owned by Metromedia Company and Dallas-based APEX Restaurant Group.

Metromedia had announced plans to sell MRG's steakhouse chains in 2003, but that year agreed to turn over management duties for all of its restaurant concepts to APEX, which also acquired a minority stake in MRG. APEX, a private company headed by industry veteran Mark Bromberg (now chairman of MRG) and former Gateway executive John Todd (now CEO), also operates the Semolina chain, as well as Left at Albuquerque and CJ's Roadhouse.

Metromedia acquired the Ponderosa chain 1988 and Bonanza the following year. The Steak & Ale chain and Bennigan's were acquired in 1989 from Grand Metropolitan (now Diageo).

EXECUTIVES

Chairman: Mark L. Bromberg, age 53
CEO: John J. Todd, age 43
CFO: Robin Chamberlain
SVP Human Resources, Ponderosa Steakhouse, Bonanza Steakhouse, and Steak and Ale: Dave Evans
SVP Franchising, Ponderosa Steakhouse and Bonanza Steakhouse: Gary Schneider
VP Finance, Bennigan's Grill & Tavern: Ted Beaman
VP Worldwide Franchising, Bennigan's Grill & Tavern: Nick Flanagan
President, Bennigan's Grill & Tavern: Bill Spae
Regional VP, Steak and Ale: Larry Borgia
Director of International Development, Bennigan's Grill & Tavern: Eric Taylor
Communications Manager: Kathy Doyle

LOCATIONS

HQ: Metromedia Restaurant Group
6500 International Pkwy., Ste. 1000,
Plano, TX 75093
Phone: 972-588-5000 **Fax:** 972-588-5467
Web: www.metromediarestaurants.com

COMPETITORS

Applebee's
Brinker
Buffets Holdings
Carlson Restaurants
Darden
Denny's
Golden Corral
Hooters
Lone Star Steakhouse
O'Charley's
Outback Steakhouse
Perkins
Ruby Tuesday
Ryan's
Western Sizzlin
Worldwide Restaurant Concepts

HISTORICAL FINANCIALS

Company Type: Joint venture

Income Statement — FYE: December 31

	REVENUE ($ mil.)	NET INCOME ($ mil.)	NET PROFIT MARGIN	EMPLOYEES
12/03	719	—	—	—
12/02	755	—	—	—
12/01	766	—	—	—
12/00	764	—	—	—
12/99	749	—	—	—
Annual Growth	(1.0%)	—	—	—

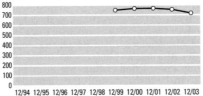

Metropolitan Transportation Authority

No Sigma Chi or Chi Omega chapter has anything on New York City's Metropolitan Transportation Authority (MTA) — it rushes millions of people on an average day. The largest public transportation system in the US, the government-owned MTA moves about 2.4 billion passengers a year. The MTA's New York City Transit Authority runs a fleet of about 4,900 buses in New York City's five boroughs, provides subway service to all but Staten Island, and operates the Staten Island Railway. Other MTA units offer bus and rail service to Connecticut and Long Island and maintains the Triborough system of toll bridges and tunnels.

The MTA, a public-benefit corporation chartered by the New York Legislature, is working to become more self-sufficient. It has attempted to cut expenses through more efficient administration and maintenance. But operating losses have persisted, and the MTA has increased fares and taken advantage of low interest rates to restructure its debt. The MTA also is considering bringing in cash by selling naming rights to subway stations, bus lines, bridges, and tunnels.

In an attempt to better coordinate bus transportation in the city, the MTA has announced plans to take over the operations of seven money-losing private bus lines currently subsidized by New York City.

HISTORY

Mass transit began in New York City in the 1820s with the introduction of horse-drawn stagecoaches run by small private firms. By 1832 a horse-drawn railcar operating on Fourth Avenue offered a smoother and faster ride than its street-bound rivals.

By 1864 residents were complaining that horsecars and buses were overcrowded and that drivers were rude. (Horsecars were transporting 45 million passengers annually.) In 1870 a short subway under Broadway was opened, but it remained a mere amusement. Elevated steam railways were built, but people avoided them because of the smoke, noise, and danger from explosions. Cable cars arrived in the 1880s, and by the 1890s electric streetcars became important.

Construction of the first commercial subway line was completed in 1904. The line was operated by Interborough Rapid Transit (IRT), which leased the primary elevated rail line in 1903 and had effective control of rail transit in Manhattan and the Bronx. In 1905 IRT merged with the Metropolitan Street Railway, which ran most of the surface railways in Manhattan, giving the firm almost complete control of the city's rapid transit. Public protests led the city to grant licenses to Brooklyn Rapid Transit (later BMT), creating the Dual System. The two rail firms covered most of the city.

By the 1920s the transit system was again in crisis, largely because the two lines were not allowed to raise their five-cent fares. With the IRT and BMT in receivership in 1932, the city decided to own and operate part of the rail system and organized the Independent (IND) rail line. Pressure for public ownership and operation of the transit system resulted in the city's purchase of all of IRT's and BMT's assets in 1940 for $326 million.

In 1953 the legislature created the New York City Transit Authority, the first unified system. In 1968, two years after striking transit workers left the city in a virtual gridlock, the Metropolitan Transit Authority began to coordinate the city's transit activities with other commuter services.

The 1970s and 1980s saw the city's transit infrastructure and service deteriorate as crime, accidents, and fares rose. But by the early 1990s a modernization program had begun to make improvements: Subway stations were repaired, graffiti was removed from trains, and service was extended. By 1994 the agency said subway crime was down 50% from 1990, and ridership had increased.

The MTA set up a five-year plan in 1995 to cut expenses by $3 billion. Only 18 months later and already two-thirds of the way to reaching the goal, the authority said it would cut another $230 million and return the savings to customers as fare discounts. The agency agreed in 1996 to sell Long Island Rail Road's freight operations. The next year it began selling its one-fare/free-transfer MetroCard Gold.

In 1998 the MTA capital program completed the $200 million restoration of the Grand Central Terminal. The next year the MTA ordered 500 new clean-fuel buses. But the agency suffered a setback when New York State's $3.8 billion Transportation Infrastructure Bond Act, which included $1.6 billion for MTA improvements, was rejected by voters in 2000.

MTA subway lines in lower Manhattan suffered extensive damage from the September 11, 2001, terrorist attacks that destroyed the World Trade Center's twin towers. The attacks left the MTA, which was already seeking billions of dollars for improvements, faced with $530 million worth of damage.

Confronted with a budget gap for the 2003 fiscal year, the MTA authorized the sale of nearly $2.9 billion worth of transportation bonds — the largest bond issue in the agency's history. The agency had hoped the eventual proceeds from the bonds would help stave off a fare increase, but in 2003 it raised subway and bus fares from $1.50 to $2, among other fare and toll increases.

EXECUTIVES

Chairman: Peter S. Kalikow
Vice Chairman: Edward B. (Ted) Dunn
Vice Chairman: David S. Mack, age 62
Executive Director: Katherine N. Lapp
COO: Thomas J. Savage
CFO: Stephen L. Kessler
Director of Budgets and Financial Management: Gary M. Lanigan
Director of Finance: Patrick J. (Pat) McCoy
Deputy Executive Director, Administration: Linda Kleinbaum
Deputy Executive Director, Corporate and Community Affairs: Christopher P. Boylan
Deputy Executive Director, General Counsel, and Secretary: Catherine A. Rinaldi
Deput Executive Director, Security: William A. Morange
President, MTA Bridges and Tunnels: Michael C. Ascher
President, MTA Capital Construction: Mysore L. Nagaraja
President, MTA Long Island Bus: Neil S. Yellin
President, MTA Long Island Railroad: James J. (Jim) Dermody
President, MTA Metro-North Railroad: Peter A. Cannito
President, MTA New York City Transit: Lawrence G. Reuter
Auditors: Deloitte & Touche LLP

LOCATIONS

HQ: Metropolitan Transportation Authority
347 Madison Ave., New York, NY 10017
Phone: 212-878-7000   **Fax:** 212-878-0186
Web: www.mta.nyc.ny.us

PRODUCTS/OPERATIONS

2003 Sales

	$ mil.	% of total
Passengers & tolls	4,333	96
Other	190	4
Total	**4,523**	**100**

Selected Operating Units

The Long Island Rail Road Company (MTA Long Island Rail Road)
Metro-North Commuter Railroad Company (MTA Metro-North Railroad)
Metropolitan Suburban Bus Authority (MTA Long Island Bus)
New York City Transit Authority (MTA New York City Transit)
Staten Island Rapid Transit Operating Authority (MTA Staten Island Railway)
Triborough Bridge and Tunnel Authority (MTA Bridges and Tunnels)

COMPETITORS

Amtrak
BostonCoach
Coach USA
Laidlaw International
Port Authority of NY & NJ
SuperShuttle International

HISTORICAL FINANCIALS

Company Type: Government-owned

Income Statement FYE: December 31

	REVENUE ($ mil.)	NET INCOME ($ mil.)	NET PROFIT MARGIN	EMPLOYEES
12/03	4,523	651	14.4%	—
12/02	4,053	360	8.9%	64,138
12/01	4,052	390	9.6%	64,169
12/00	4,033	(386)	—	62,800
12/99	5,590	(489)	—	58,000
12/98	5,707	(7)	—	57,551
12/97	5,511	(93)	—	57,563
12/96	5,381	440	8.2%	56,551
12/95	5,005	(154)	—	58,201
12/94	5,189	(156)	—	65,465
Annual Growth	(1.5%)	—	—	(0.3%)

2003 Year-End Financials

Debt ratio: 116.7%
Return on equity: 3.8%
Cash ($ mil.): 88
Current ratio: 1.21
Long-term debt ($ mil.): 20,437

Net Income History

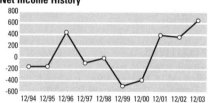

MFA

Begun in 1914 when seven Missouri farmers got together to buy 1,150 pounds of binder twine, agricultural cooperative MFA today ties together 45,000 farmers in Missouri and adjacent states. MFA, the US's oldest regional co-op, supplies its member-owners with manufacturing, distribution, and purchasing services. It runs retail service centers and works with independent dealers. MFA produces and markets beef, dairy, horse, and swine feeds, as well as soybean, corn, wheat, grass, grain, and alfalfa seeds. The co-op also provides crop-protection services, animal-health products, and farm supplies.

EXECUTIVES

Chairman: Lester Evans
Vice Chairman: David Cottrill
President: Don Copenhaver
SVP, Agri Services Division: Bill Streeter
SVP, Corporate Operations: David Jobe
SVP, Corporate and Member Services: Janice Schuerman
SVP, CFO, and Treasurer: Allen Floyd
VP, Corporate Secretary, and General Counsel: J. Brian Griffith
VP Crop Protection, Farm Supply, and Seed Marketing: Ron Utterback
VP, Feed: Alan Wessler
VP, Distribution: Bruce Hanson
VP, Livestock Operations: Kent Haden
VP, Plant Foods Marketing: Charles Cott
Controller: Jane Thompson

LOCATIONS

HQ: MFA Incorporated
201 Ray Young Dr., Columbia, MO 65201
Phone: 573-874-5111   **Fax:** 573-876-5430
Web: www.mfaincorporated.com

COMPETITORS

ADM
Ag Processing
Alabama Farmers Cooperative
Andersons
Cargill
CHS
ConAgra
Gold Kist
GROWMARK
Rabo AgServices
Southern States
Tennessee Farmers Co-op
Wilbur-Ellis

HISTORICAL FINANCIALS

Company Type: Cooperative

Income Statement FYE: August 31

	REVENUE ($ mil.)	NET INCOME ($ mil.)	NET PROFIT MARGIN	EMPLOYEES
8/03	760	9	1.2%	1,450
8/02	692	3	0.4%	1,400
8/01	621	7	1.2%	1,350
8/00	561	8	1.5%	1,300
8/99	563	—	—	1,300
8/98	644	—	—	1,400
8/97	706	—	—	1,800
8/96	667	—	—	1,200
8/95	593	—	—	—
Annual Growth	3.2%	(2.5%)	—	2.7%

2003 Year-End Financials

Debt ratio: 67.2%
Return on equity: 8.4%
Cash ($ mil.): 5
Current ratio: 1.45
Long-term debt ($ mil.): 76

Net Income History

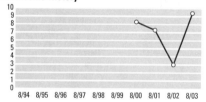

Michael Foods

With the help of willing hens, Michael Foods is the leading US producer of egg products (frozen, pre-cooked, dried). The food processor and distributor has several divisions, but eggs account for 68% of its sales. Its Northern Star division pre-shreds and mashes potatoes. The company also packages cheese and distributes refrigerated foods. Customers include food processors, foodservice distributors, and grocery stores. The company sold its dairy products division (ice cream mixes, coffee creamers) to dairy giant Dean Foods in 2003. In 2003 Thomas H. Lee Partners bought the company from the Michael family and investors for $1.05 billion.

EXECUTIVES

Chairman, President, and CEO: Gregg A. Ostrander, age 51, $1,347,938 pay
COO: James D. Clarkson, age 51, $609,150 pay
EVP and CFO: John D. Reedy, $609,150 pay
President, Crystal Farms: Mark Anderson
CFO, Crystal Farms: Max R. Hoffmann, age 44
CFO, Egg Products and Potato Products: Ronn Seim
Treasurer and Secretary: Mark D. Witmer, age 46
Auditors: PricewaterhouseCoopers LLP

LOCATIONS

HQ: Michael Foods, Inc.
301 Carlson Pkwy., Ste. 400,
Minnetonka, MN 55305
Phone: 952-258-4000 **Fax:** 952-258-4911
Web: www.michaelfoods.com

Michael Foods has production facilities in Canada and the US; it distributes its products in the US, with some sales in the Europe, the Far East, and South America.

PRODUCTS/OPERATIONS

Selected Products

Egg Products
  Dried eggs
  Egg substitutes (Better 'n Eggs, All Whites)
  Extended shelf-life liquid eggs (Easy Eggs, Table Ready)
  Fresh eggs
  Frozen eggs
  Precooked eggs (hard boiled, patties, omelets)
Refrigerated Distribution
  Bagels
  Butter
  Crystal Farms brand cheese
  Eggs
  Juice
  Margarine
  Muffins
  Potato products
Refrigerated Potato Products
  Hash browns
  Mashed potatoes
  Specialty potato products

COMPETITORS

Bob Evans
Cal-Maine Foods
Cargill
ConAgra
Heinz
JR Simplot
Kraft Foods
Land O'Lakes
McCain Foods
Primera Foods
Reser's
Rose Acre Farms
Sargento

HISTORICAL FINANCIALS
Company Type: Private

Income Statement			FYE: Saturday nearest December 31	
	REVENUE ($ mil.)	NET INCOME ($ mil.)	NET PROFIT MARGIN	EMPLOYEES
12/03	1,325	(23)	—	3,806
12/02	1,168	30	2.5%	4,371
12/01	1,161	4	0.4%	4,050
12/00	1,081	45	4.1%	4,100
12/99	1,053	44	4.2%	4,530
12/98	1,021	40	3.9%	4,160
12/97	956	32	3.4%	3,870
12/96	616	(3)	—	2,700
12/95	537	18	3.3%	2,600
12/94	506	15	3.0%	2,700
Annual Growth	11.3%	—	—	3.9%

2003 Year-End Financials
Debt ratio: 272.8%
Return on equity: —
Cash ($ mil.): 46
Current ratio: 1.65
Long-term debt ($ mil.): 785

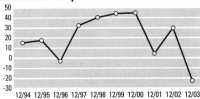

Net Income History

Michigan State University

The Spartan population is still growing today — in Michigan. With a population close to 45,000 students, Michigan State University dominates the small town of East Lansing. It offers more than 150 undergraduate programs among its 15 colleges and schools, with graduate/professional studies that include the arts, business, and law. The university also boasts three on-campus medical schools. MSU was founded in 1855 as a land-grant college and became a full university a century later.

EXECUTIVES

President: M. Peter McPherson, age 63
Provost and VP, Academic Affairs: Lou Anna K. Simon
VP, Finance and Operations, and Treasurer: Fred L. Poston
VP, Governmental Affairs: Steven M. Webster
VP, Legal Affairs and General Counsel: Robert A. Noto
VP, Student Affairs and Services: Lee N. June
VP, University Development: Charles H. Webb
VP, University Relations: Terry Denbow
Assistant VP, CFO, and Controller: David B. Brower
Assistant VP, Human Resources: Denise Anderton
Secretary of Board of Trustees and Executive Assistant to the President: L. Susan (Sue) Carter
Executive Director, MSU Alumni Association: Keith A. Williams
Director, Benefits: Pamela S. Beemer
Senior Adviser to the President for Diversity and Director of Affirmative Action, Compliance, and Monitoring: Paulette Granberry Russell
Auditors: KPMG LLP

LOCATIONS

HQ: Michigan State University
438 Administration Bldg., East Lansing, MI 48824
Phone: 517-355-6550 **Fax:** 517-355-9601
Web: www.msu.edu

HISTORICAL FINANCIALS
Company Type: School

Income Statement			FYE: June 30
	REVENUE ($ mil.)	NET INCOME ($ mil.)	NET PROFIT MARGIN	EMPLOYEES
6/03	1,370	—	—	10,500
6/02	1,295	—	—	—
6/01	1,261	—	—	—
6/00	1,150	—	—	—
6/99	1,088	—	—	—
6/98*	1,034	—	—	—
8/97	973	—	—	—
8/96	946	—	—	—
8/95	902	—	—	—
Annual Growth	5.4%	—	—	—

*Fiscal year change

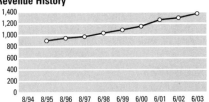

Revenue History

MidAmerican Energy

There's a new kind of twister tearin' up Tornado Alley. MidAmerican Energy Holdings generates, transmits, and distributes electricity to 690,000 customers and distributes natural gas to 670,000 customers in four Midwest states through subsidiary MidAmerican Energy Company. Its UK regional distribution subsidiaries, Northern Electric and Yorkshire Electricity, serve about 3.7 million electricity customers. MidAmerican Energy Holdings also has independent power production, real estate, and gas exploration, production, and pipeline operations. Warren Buffett's Berkshire Hathaway and other investors own the company.

MidAmerican Energy Company distributes electricity in Iowa, South Dakota, and Illinois, and it distributes natural gas in those three states plus Nebraska. It also generates 4,500 MW of electricity (primarily from coal-fired plants) and sells wholesale energy to other utilities and marketers. MidAmerican Energy Holdings' residential real estate brokerage, HomeServices of America (formerly HomeServices.Com), operates in 16 states in the US. Subsidiary CalEnergy has nearly 1,600 MW of capacity from independent power projects in the US and the Philippines.

MidAmerican Energy Holdings, which once focused on building and operating geothermal, hydroelectric, and natural gas power plants worldwide, now gets most of its revenues from its energy distribution operations. While deregulation led many regulated utilities into the independent power production business, MidAmerican Energy Holdings diversified by purchasing regulated utilities in the US and abroad. The company has also expanded its gas transportation operations through acquisitions; it operates nearly 18,000 miles of pipeline.

MidAmerican Energy Holdings was purchased by Warren Buffett's Berkshire Hathaway and other investors in 2000. Because of regulatory restrictions on utility ownership, Berkshire owns the majority of MidAmerican Energy Holdings' stock but has less than 10% of its voting control. Buffett business partner and Berkshire director Walter Scott controls a majority of MidAmerican Energy Holdings' voting rights.

HISTORY

Amid oil shortages, polluted air, and concerns about the safety of nuclear power plants, Charles Condy formed California Energy in 1971 to sell oil and gas partnerships and to consult on the development of geothermal power plants.

In 1978 Congress passed the Public Utility Regulatory Policies Act (PURPA) to wean the US from foreign oil by encouraging efficient use of fossil fuels and development of renewable and alternative energy sources. Grasping the potential of the changing energy environment, CalEnergy signed a 30-year deal with the US government in 1979 to develop the geothermal Coso Project, northeast of Los Angeles. In the 1980s CalEnergy focused entirely on geothermal development and started producing power at the Coso Project in 1987, the year the company went public.

Omaha, Nebraska-based construction firm Peter Kiewit Sons' injected some much-needed capital when it began buying a stake in the company in 1990. CalEnergy restructured in 1991, moving its headquarters from San Francisco to Omaha. It also acquired Desert Peak and Roosevelt Hot Springs geothermal areas in the US and made plans to enter markets in Asia. In 1993 the Philippine government contracted CalEnergy to develop geothermal projects. CalEnergy also obtained the rights to exploit geothermal fields in Indonesia. In 1994 the company opened a geothermal plant in Yuma, Arizona.

In 1996 CalEnergy doubled its size by acquiring rival Magma Power, and it began geothermal projects in the Salton Sea and the Imperial Valley in California. It also took advantage of the growing deregulation trend in the UK by acquiring a controlling stake in Northern Electric, a major British regional electricity company with about 1.5 million customers in northeast England and Wales.

Completing its transformation into a global power player, CalEnergy acquired gas plants in Poland and Australia in 1997. It also attracted 300,000 new gas customers in the UK. The company bought back Kiewit's stake that year. In 1998 CalEnergy subsidiary CalEnergy International Ltd. was part of a consortium (the PowerBridge Group) that won a contract to develop, synchronize, and transmit up to 1,000 MW of electricity from Lithuania to Poland, at an estimated cost of $400 million.

The next year CalEnergy bought MidAmerican Energy Holdings, an electric utility, for about $2.4 billion. CalEnergy then assumed the MidAmerican name and moved its headquarters to Des Moines, Iowa. Subsidiary MidAmerican Realty Services went public as HomeServices.Com; MidAmerican Energy Holdings retained a majority stake. In 2000 Warren Buffett's Berkshire Hathaway led an investor group, which included MidAmerican Energy Holdings CEO David Sokol, in purchasing MidAmerican Energy Holdings for about $2 billion and $7 billion in assumed debt.

In 2001 MidAmerican Energy Holdings bought out minority shareholders in HomeServices.Com, making it a wholly-owned subsidiary. It also traded Northern Electric's electricity and gas retail supply operations for the distribution business of Yorkshire Electricity with Innogy (now RWE npower) in 2001.

The following year the company purchased The Williams Companies' Kern River Gas Transmission subsidiary, which operates a 926-mile interstate pipeline in the western US, in a $960 million deal. Also in 2002 MidAmerican Energy Holdings purchased the Northern Natural Gas pipeline from Dynegy for $928 million plus $950 million in assumed debt.

EXECUTIVES

Chairman and CEO: David L. Sokol, age 47, $3,550,000 pay
President, COO, and Director: Gregory E. Abel, age 42, $2,869,011 pay
SVP and CFO: Patrick J. Goodman, age 37, $558,570 pay
SVP and Chief Administrative Officer; SVP, MidAmerican Energy Company: Keith D. Hartje, age 54, $245,000 pay
SVP and Chief Procurement Officer: P. Eric Connor, age 52
SVP and General Counsel: Douglas L. Anderson, age 45, $510,711 pay
President and CEO, HomeServices of America: Ronald J. (Ron) Peltier
President and COO, CE Electric UK: Mark Horsley, age 44
President, CalEnergy US: Stefan Bird
President, CEGeneration Philippines: David A. Baldwin
President, Kern River Gas: Robert L. Sluder
President, MidAmerican Energy Company: Todd M. Raba, age 47
President, Northern Natural Gas: Mark A. Hewett
VP and Treasurer, MidAmerican Energy Company: Brian K. Hankel, age 41
VP and Controller, MidAmerican Energy Company: Thomas B. Specketer, age 47
VP Operations, Information Technology, and Engineering, Kern River Gas: Michael D. Falk
Director Media Relations: Allan Urlis
Communications Manager: Mark Reinders
Auditors: Deloitte & Touche LLP

LOCATIONS

HQ: MidAmerican Energy Holdings Company
666 Grand Ave., Des Moines, IA 50309
Phone: 515-242-4300   **Fax:** 515-281-2389
Web: www.midamerican.com

MidAmerican Energy Holdings has energy operations in Illinois, Iowa, Nebraska, and South Dakota, and in Australia, the Philippines, Poland, and the UK.

PRODUCTS/OPERATIONS

2003 Sales

	$ mil.	% of total
MidAmerican Energy Co.	2,600	42
HomeServices	1,477	24
CE Electric UK	830	14
CalEnergy Generation		
Foreign	326	5
Domestic	46	1
Northern Natural Gas	482	8
Kern River	260	4
Other	124	2
Total	**6,145**	**100**

Selected Subsidiaries

CalEnergy Generation — Domestic (independent power production)
CalEnergy Generation — Foreign (independent power production, the Philippines)
CE Electric UK Funding
 CalEnergy Gas (Holdings) Limited (exploration and production, Australia, Poland, and the North Sea)
 Northern Electric plc
  Northern Electric Distribution Ltd (NED, electricity distribution, UK)
 Yorkshire Electricity Group plc
  Yorkshire Electricity Distribution plc (YED, electricity distribution, UK)
HomeServices of America, Inc. (formerly HomeServices.Com, real estate brokerage)
Kern River Gas Transmission Company (natural gas pipeline)
MidAmerican Energy Company (electricity and natural gas distribution)
Northern Natural Gas Company (natural gas pipeline)

COMPETITORS

AES
Alliant Energy
Ameren
Aquila
Calpine
Dynegy
Edison International
El Paso
Entergy
International Power
Mirant
National Power
Nebraska Public Power
Nicor
NRG Energy
Peoples Energy
Scottish and Southern Energy
Scottish Power
TXU Europe

HISTORICAL FINANCIALS

Company Type: Private

Income Statement
FYE: December 31

	REVENUE ($ mil.)	NET INCOME ($ mil.)	NET PROFIT MARGIN	EMPLOYEES
12/03	6,145	416	6.8%	11,440
12/02	4,968	380	7.6%	10,985
12/01	5,337	143	2.7%	9,780
12/00	5,103	133	2.6%	9,550
12/99	4,399	167	3.8%	9,700
12/98	2,555	127	5.0%	3,703
12/97	2,166	(84)	—	4,300
12/96	519	93	17.8%	4,400
12/95	355	63	17.9%	593
12/94	155	37	23.8%	278
Annual Growth	**50.6%**	**30.9%**	**—**	**51.1%**

2003 Year-End Financials

Debt ratio: 405.0%   Current ratio: 1.08
Return on equity: 16.4%   Long-term debt ($ mil.): 11,225
Cash ($ mil.): 660

Net Income History

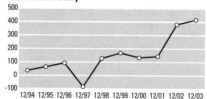

Milliken

Milliken & Company makes textiles and chemicals used in products ranging from art supplies to spacesuits. One of the world's largest textile companies, Milliken produces finished fabrics for rugs and carpets, as well as other synthetic fabrics used in such goods as apparel, automobiles, tennis balls, and specialty textiles. It also makes chemicals and petroleum products. Milliken's colorants infuse products such as Crayola markers, its clarifying agents make plastics clear, and its various other chemical products are used in the automotive, consumer products, and turf markets. Milliken operates about 65 manufacturing operations worldwide. The Milliken family controls the company.

Roger Milliken, a billionaire who is actively campaigning against the US trade policy, has led Milliken since 1947.

HISTORY

Seth Milliken and William Deering formed a company in 1865 to become selling agents for textile mills in New England and the southern US. Deering left the partnership, and in 1869 he founded Deering Harvester (now Navistar).

Milliken set up operations in New York before the turn of the century, began buying the accounts receivable of cash-short textile mill operators, and invested in some of the companies.

In his position as agent and financier, Milliken was able to spot failing mills. He bought out the distressed owners at a discount and soon became a major mill owner himself. In 1905 Milliken and his allies waged a bitter proxy fight and court case to win control of two mills, earning Milliken a fearsome reputation.

H. B. Claflin, a New York dry-goods wholesaler that also operated department stores, owed money to Milliken. When Claflin went bankrupt in 1914, Milliken got some of the stores, which became Mercantile Stores. The Milliken family retained about 40% of the chain (sold to Dillard's in 1998).

Roger Milliken, grandson of the founder, became the president of the company in 1947 and has ruled with a firm hand. He fired brother-in-law W. B. Dixon Stroud in 1955, and none of Roger's children, nephews, or nieces has ever been allowed to work for the company. The workers at Milliken's Darlington, South Carolina, mill voted to unionize in 1956. The next day Milliken closed the plant, beginning 24 years of litigation that ended at the US Supreme Court. Milliken settled with its workers for $5 million.

In the 1960s the company introduced Visa, a finish for easy-care fabrics. Milliken launched its Pursuit of Excellence program in 1981; the program stressed self-managed teams of employees and eliminated 700 management positions. Tom Peters dedicated his 1987 bestseller, *Thriving on Chaos*, to Roger.

Away from that limelight, Milliken is (and has always been) a secretive, closely held business. In 1989 that secrecy and family control were threatened when members of the Stroud branch of the family sued the company in the Delaware courts and then sold a small number of shares to Erwin Maddrey and Bettis Rainsford, executives of Milliken competitor Delta Woodside. The courts ruled in favor of Milliken in 1992; Maddrey and Rainsford were required to sign confidentiality agreements before receiving Milliken information. Roger financially backed opponents of NAFTA in 1993.

Milliken is known by competitors for its unofficial motto: "Steal ideas shamelessly." Wovenfilament maker NRB sued Milliken in 1997 for corporate spying and the following year industrial textile maker Johnston Industries filed a similar lawsuit. Milliken settled both cases out of court.

In 1999 Milliken began using its Millitron dye technology to produce residential carpets and rugs. It also introduced new brands of patterned rugs (including Royal Dynasty, Prestige, American Heritage). In 2000 the company built a manufacturing facility in South Carolina to expand its production of Millard-brand clarifying agents. Milliken announced that it would close its Union and Saluda plants by the first half of 2004.

EXECUTIVES

Chairman and CEO: Roger Milliken, age 88
Vice Chairman: Thomas J. (Tom) Malone
President, COO, and CFO: Ashley Allen
VP, Human Resources: Curtis Pressley
President, Milliken Chemical: John Rekers
Director, Public Affairs: Richard Dillard

LOCATIONS

HQ: Milliken & Company Inc.
920 Milliken Rd., Spartanburg, SC 29304
Phone: 864-503-2020   **Fax:** 864-503-2100
Web: www.milliken.com

Milliken & Company has about 65 manufacturing facilities worldwide, including operations in Australia, Belgium, Brazil, Denmark, France, Germany, Japan, Spain, the UK, and the US.

PRODUCTS/OPERATIONS

Selected Products

Chemicals
  Carpet cleaner (Capture)
  Clarifying agents for plastics (Millard)
  Colorants and tints (ClearTint, Liquitint, Palmer, Reactint)
  Electroconductive powders (Zelec)
  Resin intermediates
  Specialty chemicals
  Textile chemicals (Lubestat, SynFac, SynStat, Versatint)
  Turf maintenance chemicals
Fabrics, Carpet, and Rugs
  Area rugs
  Automotive fabrics
  Carpet and carpet tiles
  Drapery fabrics
  Knit and woven apparel fabrics
  Mats (Milliken KEX)
  Mops (Milliken KEX)
  Pool table cloth
  Table linen fabrics
  Tennis ball felt
  Towels
  Upholstery fabric

COMPETITORS

Asahi Kasei	Galey & Lord
Avondale Incorporated	Guilford Mills
Beaulieu of America	Interface
Burlington Industries	Johnston Textiles
Collins & Aikman	Mohawk Industries
Crompton	Reliance Industries
Dixie Group	Shaw Industries
Dow Chemical	Springs Industries
DuPont	WL Gore

HISTORICAL FINANCIALS

Company Type: Private

Income Statement
FYE: November 30

	ESTIMATED REVENUE ($ mil.)	NET INCOME ($ mil.)	NET PROFIT MARGIN	EMPLOYEES
11/03	3,400	—	—	14,000
11/02	3,600	—	—	14,000
11/01	3,900	—	—	20,000
11/00	4,000	—	—	21,000
11/99	3,500	—	—	18,000
11/98	3,100	—	—	16,000
11/97	3,200	—	—	16,000
11/96	3,000	—	—	15,000
11/95	2,800	—	—	13,500
11/94	2,706	—	—	13,500
Annual Growth	2.6%	—	—	0.4%

Revenue History

Minnesota Mutual

With 10,000 lakes in their state, Minnesotans have learned to be careful. Minnesota Mutual Companies helps them (and customers throughout the US) take care. The company, which does business as Minnesota Life, offers individual and group life and disability insurance and annuities, as well as retirement services and mortgage life insurance. The Advantus Capital Management unit provides mutual funds and institutional asset management services, while affiliated units of Securian Financial offer the company's insurance products, along with financial advisory, trust, and related services. Mutual holding company Minnesota Mutual Companies owns Minnesota Life through private stock company Securian Financial Group.

EXECUTIVES

Chairman, President, and CEO: Robert L. Senkler
EVP and Director: Robert E. Hunstad
EVP, Secretary, and General Counsel: Dennis E. Prohofsky
EVP, Individual Financial Security and Retirement Services: Randy F. Wallake
SVP, Financial Services: John F. Bruder
SVP, Securian Advisor Services: Thomas P. Burns
SVP, Human Resources and Corporate Services: Keith M. Campbell
SVP, Group Insurance: James E. Johnson
SVP, Asset Management: Dianne M. Orbison
SVP, Retirement Services: Bruce P. Shay
SVP and CFO: Gregory S. Strong
VP and CIO: Jean Delaney Nelson
Second VP, Communications and Research: Mark B. Hier
Auditors: KPMG LLP

LOCATIONS

HQ: Minnesota Mutual Companies, Inc.
400 Robert St. North, St. Paul, MN 55101
Phone: 651-665-3500   **Fax:** 651-665-4488
Web: www.minnesotamutual.com

Minnesota Mutual Companies operates nationwide, except in New York.

PRODUCTS/OPERATIONS

2003 Sales

	$ mil.	% of total
Premiums	1,005.3	53
Net investment income	465.8	25
Policy & contract fees	351.7	19
Finance charge income	34.1	2
Other income	18.8	1
Net realized investment losses	(48.6)	—
Total	**1,827.1**	**100**

COMPETITORS

American United
AmerUs
Conseco
Guardian Life
Jefferson-Pilot
MetLife
MONY
National Western
Nationwide Life Insurance
New York Life
Northwestern Mutual
Pacific Mutual
Protective Life
Prudential
Torchmark

HISTORICAL FINANCIALS

Company Type: Private

Income Statement   FYE: December 31

	ASSETS ($ mil.)	NET INCOME ($ mil.)	INCOME AS % OF ASSETS	EMPLOYEES
12/03	20,799	44	0.2%	4,400
12/02	17,695	4	0.0%	4,400
12/01	17,711	70	0.4%	4,400
12/00	17,900	235	1.3%	4,400
12/99	18,354	175	1.0%	4,400
12/98	16,434	163	1.0%	4,400
12/97	14,402	190	1.3%	2,187
12/96	12,443	131	1.0%	1,950
Annual Growth	7.6%	(12.6%)	—	12.3%

2003 Year-End Financials

Equity as % of assets: 9.7%   Long-term debt ($ mil.): 125
Return on assets: 0.2%   Sales ($ mil.): 1,827
Return on equity: 2.3%

Net Income History

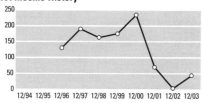

Minyard Food Stores

Everything's bigger in Texas, including regional grocery chains such as Minyard Food Stores. Its 70-plus supermarkets are located primarily in the Dallas/Fort Worth area, one of the nation's most competitive grocery markets. Company banners include nearly 30 Minyard supermarkets, about 20 Sack 'n Save Warehouse Food Stores (low-cost shopping with customers bagging their own groceries), and some 25 Carnival Food Stores, which caters to Hispanics. Minyard also owns 14 On the Go gas stations. The Minyard family started the company in 1932 with a single store in east Dallas. Minyard Food Stores is among the largest US private companies owned and run by women: sisters Elizabeth Minyard and Gretchen Minyard Williams.

Seizing an opportunity presented by the collapse of Texas-based grocery wholesaler Fleming Co., Minyard launched its own wholesale produce distribution business in August 2003. The retailer, which already distributes fruit, vegetables, and deli items to its own stores, now delivers to companies that formerly did business with Fleming.

The company's retail stores range in size from 15,000 sq. ft. to 76,000 sq. ft.

EXECUTIVES

Co-Chairman and Co-CEO: Gretchen Minyard Williams
Co-Chairman and Co-CEO: Elizabeth (Liz) Minyard, age 50
Chairman Executive Committee: Bob Minyard
President and COO: J.L. (Sonny) Williams
SVP, Checks and Fraud: Mary Barber
SVP, Administration and Controller: Jackie Brewer
SVP, Real Estate: James (Jim) Conine
SVP, Retail Operations: Steve Killebrew
SVP, Finance: Mario J. LaForte
SVP, Human Resources: Mary Marvin
SVP, Minyard/Sack 'n Save Food Stores: Ron McDearmon
SVP, Distribution Center: Prudencio Pineda
SVP, Category Management: Gary Price
SVP, Advertising: Randy Shuffield
SVP, Benefits and Insurance: Alan Vaughan
VP, Public Relations: Debbie Krznarich

LOCATIONS

HQ: Minyard Food Stores, Inc.
777 Freeport Pkwy., Coppell, TX 75019
Phone: 972-393-8700   **Fax:** 972-462-9407
Web: www.minyards.com

COMPETITORS

7-Eleven
Albertson's
Brookshire Grocery
Fiesta Mart
H-E-B
Kroger
Randall's
Target
United Supermarkets
Wal-Mart
Whole Foods

HISTORICAL FINANCIALS

Company Type: Private

Income Statement   FYE: June 30

	REVENUE ($ mil.)	NET INCOME ($ mil.)	NET PROFIT MARGIN	EMPLOYEES
6/03	910	—	—	5,440
6/02	910	—	—	6,000
6/01	910	—	—	6,700
6/00	1,000	—	—	7,155
6/99	1,075	—	—	8,000
6/98	1,000	—	—	7,800
6/97	984	—	—	7,500
6/96	938	—	—	5,720
6/95	885	—	—	3,700
6/94	810	—	—	6,500
Annual Growth	1.3%	—	—	(2.0%)

Revenue History

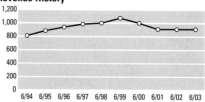

MIT

The Massachusetts Institute of Technology (MIT) really takes the prize. A leading research institution, the school is granted more patents annually than any other university and 57 people associated with MIT are Nobel Prize recipients. Blending that science and engineering acumen with a top business program, MIT graduates have started more than 4,000 companies — Campbell Soup, Hewlett-Packard, and Intel to name just a few. Tuition for MIT's more than 10,000 students runs about $29,000 a year. The faculty of the 35 academic departments includes nearly 1,000 professors. Founded in 1865, MIT is privately endowed.

EXECUTIVES

Chairman, MIT Corporation: Dana G. Mead, age 68
President: Susan Hockfield, age 53
Provost: Robert A. Brown
Chancellor: Phillip L. Clay
EVP: John R. Curry
VP Research and Associate Provost: Alice Gast
VP and Secretary, MIT Corporation: Kathryn A. Willmore
VP Human Resources: Laura Avakian, age 58
VP Information Services and Technology: Jerrold Grochow
VP Resource Development: Barbara Stowe
Treasurer, MIT Corporation: Allan S. Bufferd, age 66
VP Federal Relations: John Crowley
Auditors: PricewaterhouseCoopers LLP

LOCATIONS

HQ: Massachusetts Institute of Technology
77 Massachusetts Ave., Cambridge, MA 02139
Phone: 617-253-1000   **Fax:** 617-258-9344
Web: www.mit.edu

PRODUCTS/OPERATIONS

Selected Schools and Areas of Study

School of Architecture and Planning
   Architecture
   Media Arts and Sciences
   Urban Studies and Planning

School of Engineering
   Aeronautics and Astronautics
   Biological Engineering Division
   Materials Science and Engineering
   Nuclear Engineering
   Ocean Engineering

School of Humanities, Arts, and Social Science
   Economics
   Foreign Languages and Literatures
   History
   Literature
   Music and Theatre Arts
   Political Science

School of Science
   Biology
   Brain and Cognitive Sciences
   Chemistry
   Mathematics
   Physics

Sloan School of Management

Whitaker College of Health Sciences and Technology

Selected Interdisciplinary Laboratories

Artificial Intelligence Laboratory
George Russell Harrison Spectroscopy Laboratory
Haystack Observatory
Laboratory for Financial Engineering
Laboratory for Information and Decision Systems
Laboratory for Manufacturing and Productivity
Lincoln Laboratory
MIT Entrepreneurship Center
Nuclear Reactor Laboratory

HISTORICAL FINANCIALS

Company Type: School

Income Statement
FYE: June 30

	REVENUE ($ mil.)	NET INCOME ($ mil.)	NET PROFIT MARGIN	EMPLOYEES
6/03	1,658	—	—	9,500
6/02	1,665	—	—	9,400
6/01	1,465	—	—	8,700
6/00	2,191	—	—	8,400
6/99	1,549	—	—	6,985
6/98	1,480	—	—	8,500
6/97	1,447	—	—	8,000
6/96	1,360	—	—	8,100
6/95	1,231	—	—	10,000
6/94	1,186	—	—	10,826
Annual Growth	3.8%	—	—	(1.4%)

Revenue History

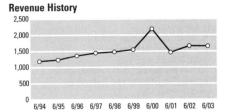

MITRE

The MITRE Corporation may not be able to cut perfect angles, but it can provide some fine systems engineering and information technology (IT) services. The not-for-profit organization develops and protects information systems for the US Department of Defense, the Internal Revenue Service, the Treasury Department, and the Federal Aviation Administration. MITRE's federally funded R&D centers provide such services as systems engineering, systems integration, and IT consulting. Founded in 1958 by a group of former MIT researchers, MITRE also designs reconnaissance systems and provides air traffic management services.

EXECUTIVES

Chairman: James R. Schlesinger, age 75
President and CEO: Martin C. Faga
SVP, CFO, and Treasurer: Lewis Fincke
SVP, Information and Technology: David H. Lehman
SVP and General Manager, Center for Advanced Aviation System Development; Director, FAA FFRDC: Amr A. ElSawy
SVP and General Manager, Center for Air Force Command and Control Systems: Raymond A. Shulstad
SVP and General Manager, Center for Integrated Intelligence Systems: Robert F. Nesbit
SVP and General Manager, IRS FFRDC, Center for Enterprise Modernization: Harlan E. (Gene) Cross
SVP and General Manager, Washington C3 Center: Alfred Grasso
SVP and Director, DOD C3I FFRDC: John S. Quilty
VP, Secretary, and General Counsel: Sol Glasner
VP and Chief Human Resources Officer: Lisa R. Bender

LOCATIONS

HQ: The MITRE Corporation
202 Burlington Rd., Bedford, MA 01730
Phone: 781-271-2000   **Fax:** 781-271-2271
Web: www.mitre.org

PRODUCTS/OPERATIONS

Selected Services

Engineering and integration (Department of Defense)
Strategic, technical, and program management consulting (Internal Revenue Service, Department of the Treasury)
Systems research and development (Federal Aviation Administration)

COMPETITORS

Aerospace Corporation
Battelle Memorial
CACI International
Charles Stark Draper Laboratory
Computer Sciences
EDS
IBM
Research Triangle Institute
SAIC
Southwest Research Institute
SRI International
Titan

HISTORICAL FINANCIALS

Company Type: Not-for-profit

Income Statement
FYE: September 30

	REVENUE ($ mil.)	NET INCOME ($ mil.)	NET PROFIT MARGIN	EMPLOYEES
9/03	785	—	—	5,300
9/02	740	—	—	5,000
9/01	670	—	—	—
9/00	604	—	—	—
9/99	541	—	—	—
9/98	527	—	—	—
9/97	488	—	—	4,300
9/96	454	—	—	4,000
9/95	509	—	—	5,100
9/94	590	—	—	5,800
Annual Growth	3.2%	—	—	(1.0%)

Revenue History

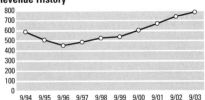

Modern Continental Companies

Modern Continental Companies is a modern concern with Old World values. Italian immigrant Lelio (Les) Marino founded the company in 1967 after he and co-worker Kenneth Anderson left a Boston construction firm. Subsidiary Modern Continental Construction has been a heavy construction leader in New England, focusing on highways, mass transit systems, and other infrastructure projects. Struggling with cashflow problems after work on Boston's Central Artery tunnel wound down, the unit has been restructuring and closing some offices. The company has announced that is is merging with former Massachusetts-based rival Jay Cashman.

EXECUTIVES

President and CEO: Lelio (Les) Marino
CFO: Peter Grela
President, Modern Continental Construction: John H. Pastore
Secretary: Roger J. Berry
Treasurer: Kenneth L. Anderson
Controller: Paul Neenan
Director Marketing: Lorraine Marino
Director Human Resources: Edward Burns
Auditors: Darmody, Merlino & Co.

LOCATIONS

HQ: Modern Continental Companies, Inc.
600 Memorial Dr., Cambridge, MA 02139
Phone: 617-864-6300   **Fax:** 617-864-8766
Web: www.moderncontinental.com

PRODUCTS/OPERATIONS

Selected Construction Operations
- Airports
- Buildings and foundations
- Design/build
- Heavy civil
- Highways and bridges
- Mass transit and rail
- Treatment facilities and utilities
- Tunneling and microtunneling

Selected Subsidiaries and Affiliates
- Boston Harbor Cruises (sightseeing and commuter)
- Boston Yacht Haven (marina complex)
- The Marina at James Landing
- Marino Center for Progressive Health (nonprofit medical clinic)
- Marino Lookout Farm (tourist attraction)
- Modern Health Store (vitamins and health products)
- Paul Revere Transportation (commuter and luxury buses)
- Ristorante Marino (Italian restaurant)

COMPETITORS

Alberici
Bechtel
Bovis Lend Lease
Centex
Clark Enterprises
Fluor
Granite Construction
J.F. White Contracting
Kraus-Anderson
M. A. Mortenson
McCarthy Building
PCL
Perini
Peter Kiewit Sons'
Skanska
Suffolk Construction
Swinerton
TIC Holdings
Turner Corporation
Tutor-Saliba
Walsh Group
Whiting-Turner

HISTORICAL FINANCIALS
Company Type: Private

Income Statement
FYE: June 30

	REVENUE ($ mil.)	NET INCOME ($ mil.)	NET PROFIT MARGIN	EMPLOYEES
6/03	1,098	—	—	4,168
6/02	1,117	—	—	4,823
6/01	1,118	—	—	5,700
6/00	792	—	—	5,200
6/99	665	—	—	4,750
Annual Growth	13.4%	—	—	(3.2%)

Revenue History

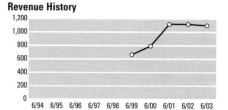

Mohegan Tribal Gaming

The sun also rises at Mohegan Sun Casino, a complex run by the Mohegan Tribal Gaming Authority for the Mohegan Indian tribe of Connecticut. The Native American-themed facility has about 6,100 slot machines, 280 tables, and simulcast horse race wagering. The facility also includes a 1,200-room luxury hotel, a 10,000-seat arena, a 300-seat cabaret, and dozens of stores and restaurants. Gambling revenues go to after-school and cultural programs for the tribe, financial assistance to other tribes, and college education for tribal members; a quarter of the slots revenue goes to the state. The company plans to purchase the Pocono Downs horse racing facility in Pennsylvania from Penn National Gaming for $175 million.

EXECUTIVES

Chairman: Mark F. Brown, age 46
Vice Chairman: Peter J. Schultz, age 49
President and CEO, Mohegan Sun: William J. Velardo, age 48, $1,287,000 pay
EVP Finance and CFO, Mohegan Sun: Jeffrey E. Hartmann, age 41, $720,000 pay
EVP Marketing, Mohegan Sun: Mitchell G. Etess, age 45, $761,000 pay
SVP Administration, Mohegan Sun: Robert J. Soper, age 31
SVP Food and Beverage, Mohegan Sun: Gary S. Crowder, age 53
SVP Hotel Operations, Mohegan Sun: Jon A. Arnesen, age 56, $269,000 pay
SVP Information Systems and CIO, Mohegan Sun: Daniel W. Garrow, age 53
SVP Marketing, Mohegan Sun: Michael W. Bloom, age 45, $291,000 pay
Treasurer: Donald M. Chapman, age 77
Auditors: PricewaterhouseCoopers LLP

LOCATIONS

HQ: Mohegan Tribal Gaming Authority
1 Mohegan Sun Blvd., Uncasville, CT 06382
Phone: 860-862-8000   **Fax:** 860-862-7167
Web: www.mohegansun.com

The Mohegan Tribal Gaming Authority operates the Mohegan Sun Casino in southeastern Connecticut.

PRODUCTS/OPERATIONS

2003 Sales

	$ mil.	% of total
Gaming	1,061.4	83
Food & beverage	87.0	7
Retail & other	79.7	6
Hotel	52.4	4
Adjustments	(91.7)	—
Total	**1,188.8**	**100**

Table Games
Baccarat
Blackjack
Caribbean stud poker
Craps
Pai Gow poker
Roulette

COMPETITORS

Aztar
Caesars Entertainment
Harrah's Entertainment
Mashantucket Pequot Gaming
Trump Hotels & Casinos

HISTORICAL FINANCIALS
Company Type: Private

Income Statement
FYE: September 30

	REVENUE ($ mil.)	NET INCOME ($ mil.)	NET PROFIT MARGIN	EMPLOYEES
9/03	1,189	96	8.1%	11,100
9/02	1,042	100	9.6%	10,203
9/01	787	205	26.0%	7,583
9/00	740	146	19.7%	6,202
9/99	682	(39)	—	5,703
9/98	575	(332)	—	5,065
9/97	466	37	7.9%	4,500
Annual Growth	16.9%	17.3%	—	16.2%

2003 Year-End Financials
Debt ratio: —
Return on equity: —
Cash ($ mil.): 73
Current ratio: 0.53
Long-term debt ($ mil.): 1,102

Net Income History

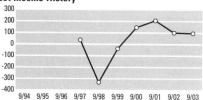

Morgan, Lewis & Bockius

Morgan, Lewis & Bockius is the largest law firm in Philadelphia, but with 19 offices spanning the US, Europe, and Asia, the firm's reach extends far beyond the City of Brotherly Love. The firm's multiple practice areas run the gamut from criminal defense to international trade and include strengths in mergers and acquisitions and employment law, as well as a burgeoning intellectual property practice. It employs more than 1,200 lawyers. Morgan, Lewis & Bockius was founded in 1873 by Charles Morgan Jr. and Francis Lewis.

EXECUTIVES

Chair of the Firm: Francis M. Milone
Managing Partner: Philip H. Werner
Managing Partner, Operations: Thomas J. Sharbaugh
Managing Partner, Practice: Robert A. Dufek
Executive Director: Francis X. Fee
CFO: James M. Diasio
CIO: Andrea Daeubler
Chief Human Resources Officer: Ellen H. Johnston
Director, Marketing: Mona C. Zieberg

LOCATIONS

HQ: Morgan, Lewis & Bockius LLP
1701 Market St., Philadelphia, PA 19103
Phone: 215-963-5000 **Fax:** 215-963-5001
Web: www.morganlewis.com

Morgan, Lewis & Bockius has US offices in Boston; Chicago; Dallas; Harrisburg, Philadelphia, and Pittsburgh, Pennsylvania; Irvine, Los Angeles, Palo Alto, and San Francisco, California; Miami; New York City; Princeton, New Jersey; and Washington, DC. Its international offices are located in Brussels, Frankfurt, London, Paris, and Tokyo.

PRODUCTS/OPERATIONS

Selected Practice Areas
Antitrust
Bankruptcy
Corporate finance
Corporate investigations and criminal defense
Environmental
Government contracts and compliance
Health care
Intellectual property
International
Labor and employment
Litigation
Mergers and acquisitions
Real estate
Securities regulation
Tax

COMPETITORS

Akin Gump
Baker & McKenzie
Cleary, Gottlieb
Davis Polk
Dechert
Gibson, Dunn & Crutcher
Jones Day
Kirkland & Ellis
Latham & Watkins
Mayer, Brown, Rowe & Maw
Pepper Hamilton
Sidley Austin Brown & Wood
Skadden, Arps
White & Case

HISTORICAL FINANCIALS

Company Type: Partnership

Income Statement				FYE: September 30
	REVENUE ($ mil.)	NET INCOME ($ mil.)	NET PROFIT MARGIN	EMPLOYEES
9/03	631	—	—	2,800
9/02	558	—	—	—
9/01	575	—	—	—
9/00	516	—	—	2,670
9/99	430	—	—	2,300
9/98	397	—	—	2,250
9/97	359	—	—	2,300
9/96	320	—	—	—
9/95	296	—	—	—
9/94	242	—	—	—
Annual Growth	11.3%	—	—	3.3%

Revenue History

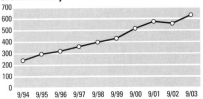

Morris Communications

What we have here is *not* a failure to communicate. Morris Communications' small-market media empire — which stretches from coast to coast and beyond — includes some 60 daily, non-daily, and free community newspapers; more than 30 radio stations; two radio networks; 25 magazines and specialty publications; 27 tourist publications; and a book publisher; as well as online services, outdoor advertising, and printing and marketing operations. Morris has grown through acquisitions, although the company has been selling some newspapers as it consolidates operations. The firm began in 1945 when William Morris Jr. bought *The Augusta Chronicle*, a newspaper founded in 1785. The Morris family owns the company.

EXECUTIVES

Chairman and CEO: William S. (Billy) Morris III, age 69
President: William S. (Will) Morris IV
EVP Newspapers: Carl N. Cannon
EVP Newspapers: James C. Currow
SVP Finance, Secretary, and Treasurer: Craig S. Mitchell, age 45
VP and Controller: Darrel K. Fry
VP and CFO, Newspapers and Shared Services: Steve K. Stone
VP and CIO: Steven B. Strout
VP Advertising: Everton J. Weeks
VP Human Resources: Martha Jean McHaney
VP Newspapers: Michael C. Traynor
Director, Corporate Communications: Jo Ann S. Hoffman

LOCATIONS

HQ: Morris Communications Company LLC
725 Broad St., Augusta, GA 30901
Phone: 706-724-0851 **Fax:** 706-722-7125
Web: www.morriscomm.com

Morris Communications has publishing and broadcasting operations in the US and Europe.

PRODUCTS/OPERATIONS

Book Publishing and Distribution
The Globe Pequot Press (Guilford, CT)

Broadcasting
Anchorage Media Group (Alaska)
Columbia River Media Group (Wenatchee, WA)
Desert Radio Group (Palm Springs, CA)
Grays Harbor Radio Group (Aberdeen, WA)
Kansas
Monaco
Texas

Selected Magazines and Specialty Publications
The Alaska Journal of Commerce
Alaska Magazine
Athens Magazine
Augusta Magazine
Barrel Horse News
Coastal Antiques and Art
Coastal Senior
Gray's Sporting Journal
The Horsetrader
Orlando
Savannah Magazine

Newspaper Publishing

Selected Free Community Papers
The Broadcaster (Vermillion, SD)
Echoland Shopper (Pequot Lakes, MN)
Flashes Shopping Guide (Allegan, MI)
The Jasper Shopper (Ridgeland, SC)
Ridge Shopper (Haines City, FL)
The Shopper's Weekly (Dodge City, KS)
Tip-Off Shopping Guide (Jonesville, VA)
Town & Country News (Oak Grove, MO)
Trade & Transactions (York, NE)
Winter Haven Shopper (FL)

Selected Dailies
Amarillo Globe-News (TX)
Athens Banner-Herald (GA)
The Augusta Chronicle (GA)
The Brainerd Daily Dispatch (MN)
The Daily Ardmoreite (Ardmore, OK)
Dodge City Daily Globe (KS)
The Examiner (Independence, MO)
The Florida Times-Union (Jacksonville)
The Grand Island Independent (NE)
Hannibal Courier-Post (MO)
Juneau Empire (AK)
Log Cabin Democrat (Conway, AK)
Lubbock Avalanche-Journal (TX)
The Morning Sun (Pittsburg, KS)
The Oak Ridger (Oak Ridge, TN)
The St. Augustine Record (FL)
Savannah Morning News (GA)
The Topeka Capital-Journal (KS)
York News-Times (NE)

Selected Non-dailies
Alaska Star (Eagle River, AK)
The Columbia County News-Times (Martinez, GA)
Hardeeville Times (SC)
Homer News (AK)
Jasper County Sun (Ridgeland, SC)
Lake County Echo (Pequot Lakes, MN)
Pine River Journal (MN)
Vermillion Plain Talk (SD)

COMPETITORS

Advance Publications
Clear Channel
Community Newspaper Holdings
Cox Enterprises
Dow Jones
Emmis Communications
Gannett
Hollinger International
Knight-Ridder
Media General
New York Times
Stephens Media Group
Tribune

HISTORICAL FINANCIALS

Company Type: Private

Income Statement				FYE: December 31
	REVENUE ($ mil.)	NET INCOME ($ mil.)	NET PROFIT MARGIN	EMPLOYEES
12/03	533	—	—	—
12/02	530	—	—	—
12/01	570	—	—	6,000
12/00	601	—	—	6,000
12/99	579	—	—	5,800
12/98	539	—	—	5,600
12/97	481	—	—	5,400
12/96	439	—	—	5,400
12/95	425	—	—	5,400
12/94	416	—	—	5,140
Annual Growth	2.8%	—	—	2.2%

Revenue History

Morrison & Foerster

The City by the Bay is home to some pretty steep hills, but San Francisco law firm Morrison & Foerster knows the legal lay of the land. Morrison & Foerster is known for its intellectual property and corporate finance expertise, having lent a hand in some of the most splashy Internet IPOs (EarthWeb, Netscape, uBid). Its nearly 1,000 attorneys also practice in areas such as litigation, labor and employment, and taxation. Morrison & Foerster has 12 US offices, and seven offices in Europe and Asia. The firm traces its roots to a San Francisco law firm founded by Alexander Morrison and Thomas O'Brien in 1883.

EXECUTIVES

Chair: Keith C. Wetmore
Managing Partner: Rachel Krevans
Managing Partner for Operations: Mark Wilmot Danis
Managing Partner for Operations: Laurie S. Hane
Managing Partner for Operations: Frederick Z. Lodge
Managing Partner for Operations: Pamela J. Reed
CFO: William Twomey
CTO: Jo Haraf
VP of Human Resources: Kathleen Dykstra
Communications Manager: Kerry Efigenio
Communications Manager, Europe: Rosemary Hall
Communications Manager, New York: Casey Lawlor

LOCATIONS

HQ: Morrison & Foerster LLP
425 Market St., San Francisco, CA 94105
Phone: 415-268-7000 **Fax:** 415-268-7522
Web: www.mofo.com

Morrison & Foerster has US offices in Denver; Irvine, Los Angeles, Palo Alto, Sacramento, San Diego, San Francisco, and Walnut Creek, California; McLean, Virginia; New York City; and Washington, DC. The firm has international offices in Beijing, Brussels, Hong Kong, London, Shanghai, Singapore, and Tokyo.

PRODUCTS/OPERATIONS

Selected Practice Areas
Communications and mass media
Finance
Financial services
Intellectual property
International
Investment management
Labor and employment
Land use, environmental, and energy
Litigation and dispute resolution
Mergers and acquisitions
Real estate
Tax

COMPETITORS

Baker & McKenzie
Cooley Godward
Fenwick & West
Gray Cary
Heller, Ehrman
Littler Mendelson
Orrick
Pillsbury Winthrop
Skadden, Arps
Wilson Sonsini

HISTORICAL FINANCIALS

Company Type: Partnership

Income Statement FYE: December 31

	REVENUE ($ mil.)	NET INCOME ($ mil.)	NET PROFIT MARGIN	EMPLOYEES
12/03	540	—	—	—
12/02	505	—	—	—
12/01	490	—	—	—
12/00	437	—	—	—
12/99	322	—	—	1,800
12/98	274	—	—	1,664
12/97	242	—	—	1,404
12/96	220	—	—	1,397
12/95	203	—	—	1,358
12/94	200	—	—	1,400
Annual Growth	11.7%	—	—	5.2%

Revenue History

Motiva Enterprises

Making money is a major motive behind Motiva Enterprises, which operates the eastern and southeastern US refining and marketing businesses of Royal Dutch/Shell's Shell Oil unit and Saudi Aramco. The company operates three refineries with a total capacity of 759,000 barrels a day, and it sells fuel at 11,000 Shell and Texaco branded gas stations. In 2004 the company sold its Delaware refining complex to Premcor for $800 million. Motiva and sister company Shell Oil Products US (formerly Equilon), which operates in the West and Midwest, together make up the #1 US gasoline retailer. Motiva is a 50-50 joint venture of Shell and Saudi Aramco.

Motiva was formed in 1998 to combine the eastern and southeastern US refining and marketing businesses of Texaco, Shell Oil, and Saudi Aramco. Texaco and Saudi Aramco each owned 35% of Motiva, and Shell owned 30%. Texaco sold its stakes in Motiva (to Shell and Saudi Aramco) and Equilon (to Shell) to gain regulatory clearance to be acquired by Chevron. In 2002 Shell took full ownership of Equilon, which was renamed Shell Oil Products US.

HISTORY

Although Motiva was not created until the late 1990s, two of its key players, Texaco and Saudi Aramco, had been doing business together in various ventures since 1936. But they had never tried anything on the scale of the Star Enterprise joint venture approved by Texaco CEO James Kinnear and Saudi Oil Minister Hisham Nazer in late 1988. The deal, valued at nearly $2 billion, was the largest joint venture of its kind in the US.

The agreement to create Star Enterprise sprang, in part, from Texaco's tumultuous ride following its purchase of Getty Oil in 1983. Texaco was sued by Pennzoil for pre-empting Pennzoil's bid for Getty, and Pennzoil won a $10.5 billion judgment in 1985. Texaco filed for bankruptcy in 1987 and eventually settled with Pennzoil for $3 billion.

In 1988 Texaco emerged from bankruptcy after announcing a deal with Saudi Aramco at a stockholder meeting. Texaco got a much-needed injection of cash, and Saudi Aramco gained a steady US outlet for its supply of crude. The Saudis had been at odds with their OPEC partners for several years, and in late 1985 then-Saudi Oil Minister Sheikh Yamani and Saudi Aramco began increasing production, leading to an oil price crash in 1986. Nazer replaced Yamani and changed Saudi Aramco's strategy. To secure market share, the Saudis started signing long-term supply contracts.

The deal with Texaco gave Saudi Aramco a 50% interest in Texaco's refining and marketing operations in the East and on the Gulf Coast — about two-thirds of Texaco's US downstream operations — including three refineries and its Texaco-brand stations. In return, the Saudis paid $812 million cash and provided three-fourths of Star's initial inventory, about 30 million barrels of oil. They also agreed to a 20-year, 600,000-barrel-a-day commitment of crude. Each company named three representatives to Star's management.

The new company soon initiated a modernization and expansion program: It acquired 65 stations, built 30 new outlets, and remodeled another 172 during 1989. In 1994 the company began franchising its Texaco-brand Star Mart convenience stores, and by mid-1995 it had sold 30 franchises.

Facing a more competitive oil marketing environment in the US, Shell Oil approached Texaco in 1996 with the possibility of merging some of their operations. In 1998 Shell and Texaco formed Equilon Enterprises, a joint venture that combined their western and midwestern refining and marketing activities.

Later that year Shell and Texaco/Saudi Aramco (Star Enterprises) formed Motiva to merge the companies' refining and marketing businesses on the East Coast and Gulf Coast. Shell and Texaco also formed two more Houston companies as satellite firms for Motiva and Equilon: Equiva Trading Company, a general partnership that provides supplies and trading services, and Equiva Services, which provides support services. Wilson Berry, the former president of Texaco Refining and Marketing, took over as CEO of Motiva.

In 1999 Motiva and Equilon together bought 15 product terminals from Premcor. To boost profits, the Motiva board appointed Texaco downstream veteran Roger Ebert as its new CEO in 2000, replacing Berry, who announced his resignation after a Motiva board meeting.

US government regulators in 2001 required that Texaco sell its Motiva and Equilon stakes in order to be acquired by Chevron. That year Texaco veteran John Boles replaced Ebert (who retired) as CEO. Shell and Saudi Aramco agreed to buy Texaco's stake in Motiva, and Shell agreed to buy Texaco's stake in Equilon. The deals were completed in 2002.

EXECUTIVES

President and CEO: William B. Welte
CFO: Ronald Langan
VP Refining: Rudy Goetzee
VP Commercial Marketing and Distribution: Ralph Grimmer
VP Human Resources and Corporate Services: Elaine Guarrero
VP Services: John Kiappes
VP Supply: Brian Smith
VP Retail: Ian Sutcliffe
Chief Diversity Officer: John Jefferson
General Manager Wholesale: Hugh Cooley
Treasurer and Director of Finance: James B. Castles
General Counsel: Lynda Irvine

LOCATIONS

HQ: Motiva Enterprises LLC
700 Milam St., Houston, TX 77002
Phone: 713-277-8000
Web: www.motivaenterprises.com

Motiva operates gas stations in the northeastern and southeastern US. It has refineries in Convent and Norco, Louisiana; and Port Arthur, Texas.

Major Operations

Alabama	Maryland	Pennsylvania
Arkansas	Massachusetts	Rhode Island
Connecticut	Mississippi	Tennessee
Delaware	New Hampshire	Texas
Florida	New Jersey	Vermont
Georgia	New York	Virginia
Louisiana	North Carolina	

COMPETITORS

7-Eleven
BP
CITGO
Cumberland Farms
Exxon Mobil
Gulf Oil
Marathon Ashland Petroleum
Racetrac Petroleum
Sunoco
Valero Energy
Wawa, Inc.

HISTORICAL FINANCIALS

Company Type: Joint venture

Income Statement				FYE: December 31
	REVENUE ($ mil.)	NET INCOME ($ mil.)	NET PROFIT MARGIN	EMPLOYEES
12/03	19,300	—	—	3,600
12/02	16,700	—	—	3,800
12/01	18,000	—	—	5,000
12/00	19,446	—	—	8,000
12/99	12,196	—	—	6,000
12/98	5,371	—	—	3,750
Annual Growth	29.2%	—	—	(0.8%)

Revenue History

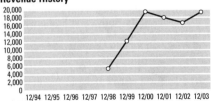

MPC Computers

MPC Computers is a chip off the old Micron block. Once the personal computer division of Micron Electronics (now Interland), MPC (formerly MicronPC) manufactures desktop and notebook PCs, servers, and data storage systems. The company also resells third-party accessories such as Lexmark printers and 3Com networking gear. MPC has found success primarily in government markets, but is focusing on growth in small and medium-sized business, education, and consumer markets. It sells directly and through resellers. Gores Technology Group, a specialist in the acquisition and management of technology companies, bought the company in 2001.

EXECUTIVES

President and CEO: Michael S. Adkins
EVP; General Manager, Sales, Marketing, and Sales Operations: Adam M. Lerner
SVP, Supply Chain Manufacturing: Mark Carrington
VP and CFO: Robb C. Warwick
VP, Corporate Marketing and PR: Ross Ely
VP, Government Sales: Ron Clevenger
VP, Human Resources: Susan Bundgard
VP, Information Technology: Ron Faccio
VP, Legal and General Counsel: Brian Hansen
VP, Product Marketing and Development: Paul R. Petersen
VP, Services and Supply Chain Operations: Jeff Fillmore
VP, SMB and Channel Sales: David McCauley

LOCATIONS

HQ: MPC Computers, LLC
906 E. Karcher Rd., Nampa, ID 83687
Phone: 208-898-3434 **Fax:** 208-898-3424
Web: www.buympc.com

PRODUCTS/OPERATIONS

Selected Products

Desktop computers
Notebook computers
Servers
Storage systems
Third-party accessories

COMPETITORS

Acer	Hewlett-Packard
Apple Computer	IBM
CDW	NEC
Dell	Sony
eMachines	Sun Microsystems
Fujitsu	Toshiba
Gateway	Unisys

HISTORICAL FINANCIALS

Company Type: Private

Income Statement				FYE: August 31
	ESTIMATED REVENUE ($ mil.)	NET INCOME ($ mil.)	NET PROFIT MARGIN	EMPLOYEES
8/03	1,000	—	—	1,000
8/02	1,000	—	—	1,000
8/01	810	—	—	1,000
8/00	1,000	—	—	1,000
Annual Growth	0.0%	—	—	0.0%

Revenue History

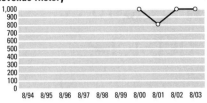

MSX International

MSX International (MSXI) never tires of steering its clients into the driver's seat. The company provides staffing, engineering, and other business services to clients primarily from the auto industry. MSXI generates the majority of its sales by providing services to automotive companies, including DaimlerChrysler, Ford, and GM. Among its offerings are temporary and permanent staffing, executive search, training, product engineering, program management, supply chain management, and custom communications. Citicorp and its affiliates own about 88% of the company.

Although MSXI has concentrated heavily on the auto industry, the company wants to expand its presence in such industries as transportation, financial services, and medical products.

EXECUTIVES

President and CEO: Robert Netolicka, age 56, $233,333 pay
EVP and CFO: Frederick K. (Fred) Minturn, age 47, $310,080 pay
SVP Americas Operations: Park Payne, age 51
SVP European Operations: Wolfgang P. Kurth, age 61
Auditors: PricewaterhouseCoopers LLP

LOCATIONS

HQ: MSX International, Inc.
1950 Concept Dr., Warren, MI 48091
Phone: 248-299-1000 **Fax:** 248-829-6130
Web: www.msxi.com

MSX International has about 60 locations in 25 countries.

2003 Sales

	% of total
US	57
Europe	40
Other	3
Total	**100**

PRODUCTS/OPERATIONS

2003 Sales

	$ mil.	% of total
Business	275.9	39
Staffing	237.5	34
Engineering	192.0	27
Total	**705.4**	**100**

COMPETITORS

Adecco	Kforce
ADP	Lason
Bowne	Manpower
CDI	Monster
EDS	Pininfarina
IBM	Randstad
ICG Commerce	Volt Information
Keane	Xerox
Kelly Services	

HISTORICAL FINANCIALS
Company Type: Private

Income Statement			FYE: Sunday nearest December 31
	REVENUE ($ mil.)	NET INCOME ($ mil.)	NET PROFIT MARGIN	EMPLOYEES
12/03	705	(64)	—	6,149
12/02	807	(63)	—	7,923
12/01	929	1	0.1%	10,142
12/00	1,035	15	1.4%	14,000
12/99	760	10	1.3%	9,594
12/98	1,081	3	0.3%	7,899
12/97	565	(3)	—	—
12/96	228	4	1.7%	—
12/95	216	6	3.0%	—
12/94	185	5	2.9%	—
Annual Growth	16.1%	—	—	(4.9%)

2003 Year-End Financials
Debt ratio: —
Return on equity: —
Cash ($ mil.): 37
Current ratio: 1.03
Long-term debt ($ mil.): 262

Net Income History

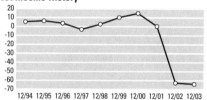

MTS

Whether pop music rocks your world or Broadway tunes set your feet a-tappin', MTS offers a tower of choices. MTS — owner of Tower Records — is one of the largest specialty retailers of music in the US, with nearly 90 company-owned stores. MTS also runs WOW! stores (a joint venture with electronics retailer Good Guys) and its franchise agreements encompass about 10 countries. The company announced in May 2003 that it was selling the Tower Records chain, and in February 2004 (still without a buyer) MTS filed for Chapter 11 bankruptcy, which it emerged from 35 days later. Founder and chairman emeritus Russell "Russ" Solomon and family owned most of MTS before the filing and now own about 15%.

Russell Solomon has described himself as an "aging hippie" who scorns corporate stuffiness and is known for confiscating neckties from visiting executives and displaying them outside his office. MTS was named for his son, Michael T. Solomon.

Though it helped pioneer specialty retailing's superstore concept, MTS has fewer stores than other major music chains; it is known for broad selection and high volume. Unlike other specialty retailers, managers at each store are granted discretion in maintaining the level and mix of their inventories.

The chain has faced increasing competition from discounters such as Wal-Mart, industry consolidation, and online retailers. Big losses prompted the company to adopt a restructuring plan and abandon the idea of going public.

Having emerged from bankruptcy in near record time, a group of creditors including Barclays Bank, AIG Global Investment, and Highland Capital Management now have control of MTS. The company is still up for sale.

EXECUTIVES
Chairman Emeritus: Russell M. (Russ) Solomon, age 75
President and CEO: E. Allen Rodriguez
EVP, CFO, Secretary, and Treasurer: DeVaughn D. Searson
EVP, Sales, Operations, and Product: Kevin Cassidy
SVP, Director, International Operations, Tower Licensing: Bob Kaufman
SVP, Online Operations: Kevin Ertell
VP, Marketing: Russell (Russ) Eisenman
VP, Marketing, Tower Licensing: Mike Jansta
VP, Retail Operations, Tower Licensing: Jason Munyon
Director Human Resources: Shauna Pompei

LOCATIONS
HQ: MTS, Incorporated
2500 Del Monte St., West Sacramento, CA 95691
Phone: 916-373-2500 **Fax:** 916-373-2535
Web: www.towerrecords.com

Tower Records has international franchise locations in Columbia, Ecuador, Hong Kong, Ireland, Israel, Japan, Malaysia, Mexico, the Philippines, and Singapore.

2004 US Locations

	No.
California	44
New York	8
Illinois	4
Pennsylvania	4
Virginia	4
Hawaii	3
Tennessee	3
Arizona	2
Maryland	2
Massachusetts	2
Nevada	2
New Jersey	2
Washington	2
Other states	7
Total	**89**

COMPETITORS

Amazon.com
Barnes & Noble
Best Buy
Books-A-Million
Borders
CDnow
Columbia House
Hastings Entertainment
Kmart
Musicland
Target
Trans World Entertainment
Virgin Group
Wal-Mart

HISTORICAL FINANCIALS
Company Type: Private

Income Statement			FYE: July 31
	REVENUE ($ mil.)	NET INCOME ($ mil.)	NET PROFIT MARGIN	EMPLOYEES
7/02	983	(57)	—	4,828
7/01	1,080	(90)	—	6,795
7/00	1,100	(10)	—	7,158
7/99	1,026	(8)	—	7,500
7/98	1,008	10	1.0%	7,200
7/97	992	4	0.4%	6,800
7/96	1,001	10	1.0%	—
7/95	951	15	1.6%	—
7/94	809	17	2.1%	—
7/93	699	15	2.1%	—
Annual Growth	3.9%	—	—	(6.6%)

2002 Year-End Financials
Debt ratio: —
Return on equity: —
Cash ($ mil.): 37
Current ratio: 0.77
Long-term debt ($ mil.): 116

Net Income History

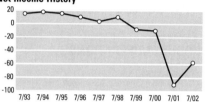

Musicland

The Musicland Group prefers selling the blues, rather than singing them. A former subsidiary of electronics retailer Best Buy, Musicland operates about 965 stores, including about 525 Sam Goody mall-based stores that sell recorded music, videos, and related items. Musicland is the top specialty retailer of prerecorded music and videos in the nation. The firm's stable of stores also includes about 365 Suncoast Motion Picture Company stores (videos, DVDs, and movie-themed apparel), also located in malls. Outside the mall, its over 75 Media Play superstores (and smaller Sam Goody stores in rural areas — formerly known as On Cue) offer music, videos, books, and software. Investment firm Sun Capital owns Musicland.

Musicland has moved beyond its bricks-and-mortar music retail roots to offer books, CD-ROMs, clothing, and DVDs through its Web sites. Media Play superstores average about 45,000 sq. ft., and in addition to their standard fare, sell musical instruments and toys. The Sam Goody rural stores are aimed at smaller markets, primarily at towns with populations between 10,000 to 30,000.

Best Buy bought the company in January 2001 but due to Musicland's declining profits, sold it to Florida-based Sun Capital Partners in June 2003. In December, the company closed about 150 Sam Goody and Suncoast stores and laid off around 900 employees.

EXECUTIVES
President: Michael J. (Mike) Madden
CEO: Eric Weisman
CFO: Craig G. Wassenaar
SVP, Marketing: Laurie A. Clark
SVP, Stores: Tim Sheehan
VP and In-House Counsel: Kristin Peterson LeBre
VP, Distribution and Logistics: John Gilmour
VP, Finance: Jim Muehlbauer
VP, Marketing: Aurora Toth
VP, Planning and Allocation: Rob Willey
VP, Retail Operations: John Pershing
VP, Stores, Sam Goody and Suncoast, and In-Store Technology: Debra Brummer
VP, Visual Merchandising and Space Planning: Flora Delaney
VP and General Manager, Media Play: Bruce Martin
President, Musicland Purchasing Corp.: Lew Garrett

LOCATIONS
HQ: The Musicland Group, Inc.
10400 Yellow Circle Dr., Minnetonka, MN 55343
Phone: 952-931-8000   **Fax:** 952-931-8300
Web: www.musicland.com

Musicland Stores has retail operations in 48 states, the District of Columbia, Puerto Rico, and the US Virgin Islands.

PRODUCTS/OPERATIONS

Selected Stores
Media Play (books, music, videos, computer software, magazines, and other products)
Sam Goody mall (music, videos, and home entertainment products through mall stores)
Sam Goody rural (books, music, videos, computer software, magazines, and other products for smaller markets)
Suncoast Motion Picture Company (videos, DVDs, movie-themed apparel, and other products through mall stores)

COMPETITORS
Amazon.com
Barnes & Noble
Blockbuster
Books-A-Million
Borders
BUY.COM
CDnow
Columbia House
CompUSA
Hastings Entertainment
Hollywood Entertainment
Kmart
Movie Gallery
Target
Tower Records
Trans World Entertainment
Virgin Group
Wal-Mart
Wherehouse Entertainment

HISTORICAL FINANCIALS
Company Type: Private

Income Statement
FYE: February 28

	REVENUE ($ mil.)	NET INCOME ($ mil.)	NET PROFIT MARGIN	EMPLOYEES
2/03	1,727	(441)	—	10,000
2/02*	1,886	—	—	12,500
12/00	1,900	—	—	15,000
12/99	1,892	—	—	15,900
12/98	1,847	—	—	15,600
12/97	1,768	—	—	16,400
12/96	1,822	—	—	15,900
12/95	1,723	—	—	17,000
12/94	1,479	—	—	16,000
12/93	1,182	—	—	13,000
Annual Growth	4.3%	—	—	(2.9%)

*Fiscal year change

Revenue History

Mutual of America

Mutual of America Life Insurance may be the saving grace for a lot of folks in the not-for-profit sector. The company, known as Mutual of America, was founded in 1945 to provide retirement savings to employees of not-for-profit organizations, excluded from Social Security and other retirement programs. The company still serves that market, but also offers its employee-sponsored retirement plans, savings plans, and insurance products to private-sector organizations (typically small to mid-sized businesses); it also offers its products direct to individual investors. Mutual of America sells throughout the US via a network of 36 regional field offices. The company has some $11 billion in assets under management.

EXECUTIVES
Chairman of the Board: William J. Flynn
President, CEO, and Director: Thomas J. Moran
SEVP, CFO and Director; Chairman, President, and CEO, Mutual of America Investment: Manfred Altstadt
SEVP, General Counsel, and Director: Patrick A. Burns
SEVP, Technical Operations and Director: Salvatore R. Curiale
EVP; Chairman and CEO, Mutual of America Securities: William S. Conway
EVP and Treasurer; Chairman, President, and CEO, Mutual of America Institutional Funds: John R. Greed
EVP, Corporate Secretary, and Assistant to the Chairman: Diane M. Aramony
EVP, Technology: William Breneisen
EVP and Chief Actuary: Jeremy J. Brown
EVP, External Affairs: Edward J.T. Kenney
EVP and Internal Auditor: George L. Medlin
EVP, Technology: Joan M. Squires
President and CEO, Mutual of America Capital Management: Richard J. Ciecka
Chairman and CEO, Mutual of America Foundation: Thomas Gilliam
SVP and Corporate Actuary: Walter W. Siegel
SVP, Human Resources: Anne M. Stanard
Auditors: KPMG LLP

LOCATIONS
HQ: Mutual of America Life Insurance Company
320 Park Ave., New York, NY 10022
Phone: 212-224-1600   **Fax:** 212-224-2539
Web: www.mutualofamerica.com

Mutual of America Life Insurance Company has offices in Alaska, California, Colorado, Connecticut, Florida, Georgia, Hawaii, Illinois, Indiana, Kentucky, Louisiana, Maryland, Massachusetts, Michigan, Minnesota, Missouri, New Jersey, New York, Ohio, Pennsylvania, Tennessee, Texas, Virginia, Washington, Wisconsin, and Washington, DC.

PRODUCTS/OPERATIONS

2003 Sales
	% of total
Considerations & premiums	71
Net investment income	26
Separate account investment & administration fees & other income	3
Total	**100**

COMPETITORS
AIG SunAmerica
American United
CitiStreet
MFS
National Life Insurance
Retirement System Group

HISTORICAL FINANCIALS
Company Type: Mutual company

Income Statement
FYE: December 31

	ASSETS ($ mil.)	NET INCOME ($ mil.)	INCOME AS % OF ASSETS	EMPLOYEES
12/03	11,002	30	0.3%	—
12/02	9,944	7	0.1%	—
Annual Growth	10.6%	343.3%	—	—

2003 Year-End Financials
Equity as % of assets: 6.3%
Return on assets: 0.3%
Return on equity: 4.6%
Long-term debt ($ mil.): 5,468
Sales ($ mil.): 1,520

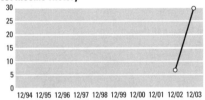

Net Income History

Mutual of Omaha

In the wild kingdom that is today's insurance industry, The Mutual of Omaha Companies wants to distinguish itself from the pack. The company provides individual health and accident coverage (via subsidiary Mutual of Omaha Insurance); its United of Omaha Life Insurance unit offers life insurance and annuities. The firm also offers personal disability coverage, brokerage services, pension plans, mutual funds, and a range of employee benefits products and services. Mutual of Omaha, which is owned by its policyholders, offers its products mainly through agent networks.

In the health insurance arena, traditional indemnity insurers have less power to bargain for low-cost services and consequently have found themselves at a disadvantage against clout-wielding and increasingly cost-minded managed care organizations; state laws mandating coverage for persons regardless of underwriting policy have exacerbated the situation. Mutual of Omaha is exiting the health business in some areas and is adding managed care services. It is focused on growing its health care networks internally, rather than by acquisition, to ensure its standards are met. These networks are largely in underserved rural areas, where the firm has kept a strong presence. The insurer is also working to increase sales of its life insurance and annuities products.

Mutual of Omaha is involved in wildlife conservation and protection. Starting with sponsorship of the long-running *Mutual of Omaha's Wild Kingdom,* this interest has evolved into a grant and scholarship program run by the company's Wildlife Heritage Center.

Focusing on its core individual and employer-based lines, the company is selling its property & casualty and flood insurance operations to Fidelity National Financial.

HISTORY

Charter Mutual Benefit Health & Accident Association got its start in Omaha, Nebraska, in 1909. A year later half of its founders quit, leaving a group headed by pharmaceuticals businessman H. S. Weller in charge. He tapped C. C. Criss as principal operating officer, general manager, and treasurer. Criss brought in his wife, Mabel, and brother Neil to help run the business.

Formed to offer accident and disability protection at a time when there were many fraudulent benefit societies, Charter Mutual Benefit Health faced consumer resistance that slowed growth in its first 10 years. By 1920 it was licensed in only nine states. Experience helped it refine its products and improve its policies' comprehensibility. By 1924 the firm had more than doubled its penetration, gaining licensing in 24 states.

The US was nearing the depths of the Depression when Weller died in 1932. Criss succeeded him as president. The stock crash had brought a steep decline in the value of the firm's asset base, and premium income dropped (accompanied by an increase in claims). Even so, Mutual Benefit Health expanded its agency force, the scope of its benefits, and its operations. It went into Canada in 1935 and began a campaign to obtain licensing throughout the US.

By 1939 the company was licensed in all 48 states. During WWII it wrote coverage for civilians killed or injured in acts of war in the US (including Hawaii) and Canada. With paranoia running high and consumer goods in short supply, the insurance industry boomed during the war (and payouts on stateside act-of-war claims were low to nonexistent). Criss retired in 1949.

Gearing up its postwar sales efforts, in 1950 the company changed its name to Mutual of Omaha and adopted its distinctive chieftain logo. During the 1950s it added specialty accident and group medical coverage. In 1963 it made an advertising coup when it launched *Mutual of Omaha's Wild Kingdom.* Hosted by zoo director Marlin Perkins and, later, naturalist sidekick Jim Fowler, the show was one of the most popular nature programs of all time. Later that decade the company added investment management to its services.

Changes in the health care industry during the 1990s led Mutual of Omaha to de-emphasize its traditional indemnity products in favor of building managed care alternatives. In 1993 it joined with Alegent Health System to form managed care company Preferred HealthAlliance. Mutual of Omaha also stopped writing new major medical coverage in such states as California, Florida, New Jersey, and New York, where state laws made providing health care onerous. This led the company to cut its workforce by about 10% in 1996.

In 1999 it bought out Alegent's interest in their joint venture and entered the credit card business (offering First USA Visa cards). The firm also lifted its $25,000 limit for coverage of AIDS-related illnesses (its standard limit is $1 million); the company had been sued over the policy.

EXECUTIVES

Chairman and CEO, Mutual of Omaha Insurance Company and United of Omaha Life Insurance Company: John W. (Jack) Weekly, age 72
President, Mutual of Omaha Insurance Company and United of Omaha Life Insurance Company: Daniel P. Neary
EVP and Chief Actuary: Cecil D. Bykerk
EVP, Information Services: James L. Hanson
EVP, Corporate Services and Corporate Secretary: M. Jane Huerter
EVP, Group Benefit Services: Daniel Martin
EVP, Government Affairs: William C. Mattox
EVP and General Counsel: Thomas J. McCusker
EVP, Treasurer, and Comptroller: Tommie D. Thompson
EVP, Individual Financial Services: Mike Weekly
EVP and Chief Investment Officer; President, Mutual of Omaha Investor Services: Richard A. (Rick) Witt
SVP of Information Services: Steve Clauson
SVP of Group Health Plans: Joe Connolly
SVP of Special Markets: Gil Peers
SVP of Human Resources: Stacy Sholtz
SVP of Group Specialty Products: Robert Taylor
Auditors: Deloitte & Touche LLP

LOCATIONS

HQ: The Mutual of Omaha Companies
Mutual of Omaha Plaza, Omaha, NE 68175
Phone: 402-342-7600 **Fax:** 402-351-2775
Web: www.mutualofomaha.com

The Mutual of Omaha Companies operate throughout the US.

PRODUCTS/OPERATIONS

Selected Services and Products
401(k) plans
Annuities
Critical illness insurance
Defined benefit plans
Dental insurance
Disability insurance
Health and wellness programs
Health insurance products
Investments
Life insurance
Long-term-care insurance
Medicare supplement insurance
Prescription plans
Property and casualty insurance
Travel insurance

Selected Subsidiaries and Affiliates
Companion Life Insurance Company
innowave Incorporated (water purification products)
Kirkpatrick, Pettis, Smith, Polian Inc. (brokerage)
Mutual of Omaha Insurance Company
Mutual of Omaha Investor Services (mutual funds)
Omaha Property and Casualty Company
United of Omaha Life Insurance Company
United World Life Insurance Company

COMPETITORS

Aetna
Allstate
American National Insurance
Assurant
AXA Financial
Blue Cross
CIGNA
CNA Financial
Guardian Life
John Hancock Financial Services
Liberty Mutual
MassMutual
MetLife
MONY
Morgan Stanley
New York Life
Northwestern Mutual
Prudential
State Farm
USAA

HISTORICAL FINANCIALS

Company Type: Mutual company

Income Statement FYE: December 31

	ASSETS ($ mil.)	NET INCOME ($ mil.)	INCOME AS % OF ASSETS	EMPLOYEES
12/03	18,444	170	0.9%	5,847
12/02	15,203	(14)	—	6,600
12/01	11,533	49	0.4%	6,600
12/00	14,465	156	1.1%	7,000
12/99	13,959	90	0.6%	7,000
12/98	13,231	117	0.9%	7,111
12/97	12,639	181	1.4%	7,309
12/96	11,726	105	0.9%	7,047
12/95	10,659	122	1.1%	8,163
12/94	9,551	82	0.9%	8,330
Annual Growth	7.6%	8.4%	—	(3.9%)

2003 Year-End Financials
Equity as % of assets: 17.5% Long-term debt ($ mil.): —
Return on assets: 1.0% Sales ($ mil.): 3,719
Return on equity: 7.0%

Net Income History

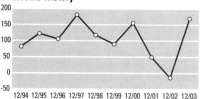

Muzak

The hills are alive with the sound of Muzak. The king of canned music, Muzak offers more than 60 programs delivered via satellite, local broadcast transmission, tapes, and CDs. The company counts retailers, grocery stores, hotels, office buildings, and factories among its 350,000 customers, and an estimated 100 million people hear Muzak tunes each day. In addition to providing music from genres such as classical, country, Latin, oldies, and contemporary, the company also sells, installs, and maintains sound systems, intercoms, telephone messaging systems, closed circuit television, and other communications systems. Investment firm ABRY Partners owns about 64% of the company.

Music delivered via satellite accounts for 75% of Muzak's business. The company made numerous acquisitions in the late 1990s and hopes to restore profitability by renewing its focus on its core services. Radio station giant Clear Channel owns about 21% of Muzak.

HISTORY

George Squier patented a system for transmitting phonograph music over electrical lines in 1922. He sold the rights to utility North American Company, and together they formed a subsidiary to begin testing the system in Cleveland. In 1934 Squier coined the term Muzak ("muz" from music and "ak" from Kodak, his favorite company) before he died that year. The company moved to New York in 1936.

During the 1930s Muzak was used in then-newfangled elevators to calm riders (hence the term "elevator music"). In 1938 Warner Bros. bought the company but sold it the following year to US Senator William Benton. Experiments showed that music could increase productivity, and during WWII Muzak systems were installed in factories.

After the war the company continued to work on "stimulus progression" — the idea of regulating worker productivity through music. In 1972 Teleprompter bought the company and began distributing its music via satellite. Westinghouse bought Teleprompter in 1981 and sold it to Marshall Field V in 1986. Field bought Seattle-based Yesco, a producer of "foreground" music for retailers, and merged the two the next year. Led by Yesco's management, Muzak began updating its sound to appeal to baby boomers. Field sold Muzak to its management and New York investment firm Centre Capital in 1992.

In 1996 the company called off plans to go public. Saddled with debt from the buyout and mounting losses, it ousted CEO John Jester in 1997 and replaced him with Bill Boyd, who refocused Muzak on its core music business. During 1998 the company began buying competitors and its own independent affiliates. In 1999 it merged with Audio Communications Network, a Muzak franchiser owned by media investment firm ABRY Partners, and the Muzak affiliates owned by Capstar (Capstar later became part of AMFM, which was subsequently acquired by radio station owner Clear Channel). Later that year Muzak made a string of acquisitions, including Data Broadcasting's (now Interactive Data Corporation) InStore Satellite Network, a music and ad business.

In 2000 Muzak moved its headquarters to Fort Mill, South Carolina. It continued its acquisition streak with Telephone Audio Productions (audio marketing and messaging) and Muzak franchisee Vortex Sound Communications.

EXECUTIVES

Chairman and CEO: William A. (Bill) Boyd, age 61, $300,023 pay
President: Lon Otremba
COO, CFO, and Treasurer: Stephen P. Villa, age 39, $212,117 pay
SVP Brand: Alvin Collis
SVP Owned Operations: Michael K. (Mike) Hoeltke, age 40, $351,705 pay
SVP Owned Operations and Marketing: Kenneth F. (Kenny) Kahn, age 40, $159,923 pay
SVP Technical Operations: David M. Moore, age 39, $119,995 pay
VP and Secretary: Peni A. Garber, age 41
VP, General Counsel, and Assistant Secretary: Michael F. Zendan II, age 39, $125,000 pay
VP Administration: Page Walker
VP Marketing: Kimberly Wolff
VP Operations: Paul Ziegler
VP Team Member Services (HR): Frank Messana
VP: Royce Yudkoff
Controller: Mark Williams
Financial Reporting Manager: Catherine Walsh
Auditors: PricewaterhouseCoopers LLP

LOCATIONS

HQ: Muzak LLC
3318 Lakemont Blvd., Fort Mill, SC 29708
Phone: 803-396-3000 **Fax:** 803-396-3357
Web: www.muzak.com

Muzak offers its services in 15 countries.

PRODUCTS/OPERATIONS

2002 Sales

	$ mil.	% of total
Music & related services	163.0	75
Equipment & related services	54.8	25
Total	**217.8**	**100**

Selected Products
Audio Architecture (music programming)
Voice (music and messages for phone systems)

Selected Music Genres
Classical
Country
Jazz
Latin
Mature adult
Oldies
Popular contemporary
Popular contemporary instrumental
Specialty
Urban

COMPETITORS

DMX MUSIC
PlayNetwork
Sirius Satellite Radio
TM Century

HISTORICAL FINANCIALS

Company Type: Private

Income Statement
FYE: December 31

	REVENUE ($ mil.)	NET INCOME ($ mil.)	NET PROFIT MARGIN	EMPLOYEES
12/02	218	(30)	—	1,491
12/01	203	(44)	—	1,347
12/00	192	(44)	—	1,395
12/99	130	(22)	—	1,324
12/98	100	(12)	—	1,041
12/97	91	(13)	—	667
12/96	87	(11)	—	751
12/95	87	(6)	—	715
12/94	83	(7)	—	—
12/93	59	(4)	—	—
Annual Growth	15.7%	—	—	11.1%

2002 Year-End Financials
Debt ratio: 249.6%   Current ratio: 1.03
Return on equity: —   Long-term debt ($ mil.): 295
Cash ($ mil.): 2

Net Income History

MWH Global

MWH Global's initials tell the story of this energy and environmental engineering, construction, and water resource management firm formed by the 2001 merger of Montgomery Watson and HARZA Engineering. Montgomery Watson has brought water, wastewater, and environmental specialties to the table, while HARZA has added its expertise in power plant design to the mix. MWH Global offers design, construction, finance, and operations and maintenance services for infrastructure projects in more than 30 countries in the Americas, the Asia/Pacific Rim, Europe, and the Middle East. The new company has deep roots: Montgomery Watson was founded in 1945, and HARZA in 1920. MWH Global employees own the company.

EXECUTIVES

Chairman: Murli Tolaney
Vice Chairman: Refaat A. Abdel-Malek
President and CEO: Robert B. (Bob) Uhler
CFO: David J. D. Harper
Managing Executive, TAG (The Asset Group): Ed Carter
Chief Large Campaign Officer: Skip (Fay) Holland
Chief People and Knowledge Officer: Vic Gulas
Corporate Counsel: David A. Taggart
Chief Planning Officer: Douglas G. Smith
President, MWH Constructors: Mark Swatek
President, MWH Americas: Don Smith
COO, State and Local Government East Operations, MWH Americas: Kevin Kelly
President, MWH Europe, Middle East, Africa, and India: Richard N. (Rich) Wankmuller
President and COO, MWH Soft, Inc.: Paul F. Boulos
COO, Federal Operations, MWH Americas: Gary M. Erickson
COO, Global Energy & Natural Resources: Alan Krause
Director Human Resources: Gary R. Melillo
Auditors: PricewaterhouseCoopers LLP

LOCATIONS

HQ: MWH Global, Inc.
380 Interlocken Crescent, Ste. 200, Broomfield, CO 80021
Phone: 303-533-1900   **Fax:** 303-533-1901
Web: www.mw.com

PRODUCTS/OPERATIONS

Selected Services
Construction
  Bridges
  Office complexes
  Power plants
  Roads
Energy
  Hydropower plant design
  Fossil power plant design
Facilities Development
Government Relations
Water and Environment
  Air quality management
  Aquaculture and aquarium design
  Drainage and flood control
  Environmental planning
  Lab services
  Mining engineering
  Remediation and reclamation
  Solid-waste management
  Wastewater and industrial treatment
  Water distribution
  Water resources

COMPETITORS

AECOM
Bechtel
Black & Veatch
Bouygues
CET Services
CH2M HILL
Dick Corporation
EA Engineering
Earth Tech
Fluor
Foster Wheeler
Halliburton
Jacobs
Engineering
Peter Kiewit Sons'
Severn Trent
SUEZ
Tetra Tech
USFilter
WS Atkins
Zachry

HISTORICAL FINANCIALS

Company Type: Private

Income Statement
FYE: September 30

	REVENUE ($ mil.)	NET INCOME ($ mil.)	NET PROFIT MARGIN	EMPLOYEES
9/03	1,000	—	—	6,100
9/02	856	—	—	6,000
9/01	722	—	—	5,500
9/00	550	—	—	3,500
9/99	510	—	—	3,600
9/98	482	—	—	3,500
9/97	442	—	—	3,200
9/96	433	—	—	3,500
9/95	405	—	—	3,300
9/94	336	—	—	3,100
Annual Growth	12.9%	—	—	7.8%

Revenue History

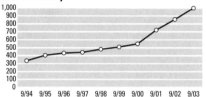

Nalco

Dirty water? Wastewater? Process-stream water? Nalco Holding Company (formerly Ondeo Nalco) treats them all, and now does so as an independent entity. The company — a subsidiary of France's Suez until its fall 2003 sale — is the world's largest maker of chemicals used in water treatment and for industrial processes (in front of #2 GE Water Technologies). Its chemicals help clarify water, conserve energy, prevent pollution, separate liquids from solids, and prevent corrosion in cooling systems and boilers; Nalco also makes oilfield chemicals. Suez sold Nalco in September 2003 to a group of private equity firms that joined to purchase the company for about $4.2 billion.

Nalco's former parent company, Suez, wants to focus on its most profitable businesses, so it began looking to private equity groups as likely suitors. The company announced in September 2003 that it had selected a collection of firms — the Blackstone Group, Apollo Management, and Goldman Sachs Capital Partners — that joined together to buy Nalco for more than $4 billion. Nalco operates as an independent company following the completion of the transaction in November. The acquiring group hired former Hercules CEO William Joyce to take over as chairman and CEO and former Rohm and Haas CFO Bradley Bell for the same position at Nalco.

Customers include municipalities, hospitals, and makers of electronics, chemicals, paper, petroleum, and steel. Nalco also provides water management services and, through its Industrial Solutions unit, maintenance of water treatment operations.

EXECUTIVES

Chairman and CEO: William H. (Bill) Joyce, age 68, $408,545 pay
EVP and COO; President, Industrial and Institutional Services: William J. Roe, age 50, $954,240 pay
EVP and CFO: Bradley J. (Brad) Bell, age 51, $230,000 pay
Group VP; President, Energy Services: Mark L. Bosanko, age 48, $455,160 pay
Group VP; President, Pacific Division: Louis L. (Lou) Loosbrock, age 50, $475,020 pay
Group VP; President, Paper Services: Mark W. Irwin, age 39
Group VP; President, Equipment Division and Managing: Philippe Creteur
VP, General Counsel, and Secretary: Steve Landsman
VP, IT and CIO: William R. Radon
Controller: Bruno Lavandier
Auditors: Ernst & Young LLP

LOCATIONS

HQ: Nalco Holding Company
1601 W. Diehl Rd., Naperville, IL 60563
Phone: 630-305-1000   **Fax:** 630-305-2900
Web: www.nalco.com

Nalco Holding has operations in Africa, Asia, Europe, the Middle East, and North and South America.

2003 Sales

	$ mil.	% of total
US	1,323	48
Other	1,444	52
Total	**2,767**	**100**

PRODUCTS/OPERATIONS

2003 Sales

	$ mil.	% of total
Industrial & Institutional Services	1,186	43
Energy Services	740	27
Paper Services	562	20
Other	279	10
Total	**2,767**	**100**

Selected Products
Lubricants and functional fluids
Process chemicals
Water-treatment chemicals

Selected Markets
Automobile industry
Chemical industry
Commercial buildings (hospitals, hotels)
Electronic industry
Food-processing industry
Paper industry
Petroleum industry
Steel industry
Water-treatment plants

COMPETITORS

Ashland
BASF Corporation
Ciba Specialty Chemicals
Cytec
Ecolab
GE Water Technologies
Great Lakes Chemical
Marmon Group
Rockwood Specialties

HISTORICAL FINANCIALS

Company Type: Private

Income Statement
FYE: December 31

	REVENUE ($ mil.)	NET INCOME ($ mil.)	NET PROFIT MARGIN	EMPLOYEES
12/03	2,767	(182)	—	10,500
12/02	2,644	128	4.9%	10,000
12/01	2,620	(84)	—	10,000
12/00	2,800	—	—	10,000
12/99	1,813	—	—	7,000
12/98	1,574	—	—	7,000
12/97	1,434	—	—	6,900
12/96	1,304	—	—	6,500
12/95	1,215	—	—	6,081
12/94	1,346	—	—	5,935
Annual Growth	8.3%	—	—	6.5%

2003 Year-End Financials
Debt ratio: 305.2%   Current ratio: 1.84
Return on equity: —   Long-term debt ($ mil.): 3,263
Cash ($ mil.): 100

Net Income History

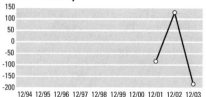

NASCAR

In the race for respectability in the sports world, NASCAR is on the right track. The National Association for Stock Car Auto Racing is one of the fastest-growing spectator sports in the US. NASCAR runs about 90 races each year in 25 states through three racing circuits: the Busch, Craftsman Truck, and its signature Nextel Cup Series (formerly the Winston Cup). The Nextel Cup, featuring popular drivers like Jeff Gordon and Dale Jarrett, alone draws more than 7 million race fans each year. NBC, FOX, and Turner Broadcasting have taken note, paying $2.4 billion for broadcast rights until 2006. NASCAR was founded in 1948 by Bill France Sr. and is still owned by the France family.

Even though the networks have lost money on the first three years of the NASCAR contract, they still have plenty of reason to be optimistic about the future of the partnership. Heading into the 2004 season, NASCAR ratings are second only to the NFL. In addition, as a younger generation of drivers begin to pull in new viewers, the company's popularity has made inroads into parts of the country beyond its traditional fan base of the southern US.

NASCAR has moved races out of some of the smaller markets for the 2004 season, a change that drew loud protests from racetrack owner and rival Speedway Motorsports. The France family also controls publicly traded International Speedway Corporation (ISC), the largest racetrack owner in the US. The reschedulings benefit International Speedway tracks, and a Speedway Motorsports shareholder has filed a lawsuit against NASCAR on antitrust grounds. The parties settled the lawsuit by ISC selling North Carolina Speedway to Speedway Motorsports.

And in a surprise move, R.J. Reynolds dropped out as the sponsor for the title Winston Cup series. The tobacco company's wallet has seen better days thanks to tobacco lawsuits and restricted advertising. Reynolds had been the sponsor of the title race since 1971. Cell phone company Nextel signed a massive 10-year, $750 million deal with NASCAR to become the new sponsor. The agreement has silenced critics who question the racing circuit's longevity, as the Nextel deal is the biggest sports sponsorship deal in history.

HISTORY

Bill France Sr. founded the National Championship Stock Car Circuit (NCSCC) in 1947 as a place for ex-Prohibition-era moonshine runners to show off their driving skills. France, the son of a Washington, DC, banker, was a skilled mechanic and racecar builder. In 1934 he moved his family to Daytona Beach, Florida, which was nirvana for racecar drivers who used the hard beach as a speedway.

The City of Daytona Beach in 1938 approached France, who by then owned a successful gas station and mechanic shop frequented by racers, and asked him to organize a race. France rounded up drivers and solicited local businesses to donate prizes such as beer and cigars. The event drew 4,500 fans. He organized another race the following year and turned a profit of a few thousand dollars.

WWII interfered with France's racing career when he was drafted and sent to work in a shipyard. Upon his return, lacking the money to put another race together in Florida, he sponsored a national championship race for stock cars (cars with standard auto bodies not specially designed for racing) in North Carolina. Since there was no national body governing the races and setting rules, France's championship idea drew little enthusiasm. So in 1947 he formed the NCSCC and set up a point system for drivers and a fund for prize money. Seeking to expand NCSCC's powers, France in 1948 gathered 35 prominent racing figures from all over the US, and they organized to form the National Association for Stock Car Auto Racing (NASCAR), of which France was elected president.

France tirelessly promoted the sport with the help of racetrack owners wanting NASCAR to make their races official, and as a result the sport grew rapidly in the 1950s and 1960s. Racetrack owners began upgrading their facilities or building new ones with paved tracks to replace the older dirt tracks. France in 1957 convinced Daytona Beach to allow him to replace the city's original beach track with a 2.5-mile paved raceway. It opened two years later to a crowd of 42,000.

In 1972, as France got more involved in operating specific tracks and having less time to focus on NASCAR, he passed the business on to his son, Bill France Jr. Bill Jr. signed R.J. Reynolds as a major sponsor in 1971, and NASCAR held the Winston 500 (the first incarnation of today's Winston Cup series) in Talladega, Alabama.

The company's first televised race, the Daytona 500, aired on the CBS Television Network in 1979 and drew about 16 million viewers. Cable sports network ESPN also began airing races in 1981. NASCAR came into its own as a major sports player in 2000 when NBC, Fox, and Turner Broadcasting agreed to pay the company $2.4 billion for the circuit's broadcasting rights until 2006. And the inherent danger of stock car racing began to hit home with the racing related deaths of popular drivers such Adam Petty in 2000 and Dale Earnhardt in 2001.

In 2003 Bill France Jr. handed reins of the company to son Brian France by promoting him to chairman and CEO. Bill Jr. remains vice chairman. Also that year R.J. Reynolds dropped out as the sponsor for the Winston Cup series after more than 30 years with the race. Cell phone company Nextel took over as the new sponsor with the signing of a 10-year, $750 million deal.

The following year NASCAR announced that its Busch racing series would hold a race in Mexico City during the 2005 season, marking the first points-paying international event in about 50 years.

EXECUTIVES

Chairman and CEO: Brian Z. France, age 41
Vice Chairman: William C. (Bill) France Jr., age 70
Vice Chairman, EVP, and Secretary: Jim France
President: Mike Helton
SVP and COO: George Pyne
CFO, NASCAR, NASCAR Broadcasting, and NASCAR Digital Entertainment: R. Todd Wilson, age 41
VP Broadcasting: Paul Brooks
VP Competition: Robin Pemberton, age 48
VP Corporate Administration: Ed Bennett
VP Corporate Communications: Jim Hunter
VP Corporate Marketing: Brett Yormark
VP Finance: Doris Rumery
VP Licensing and Consumer Products: Mark Dyer
VP Research and Development: Gary Nelson
President and CEO, NASCAR Images: Jay Abraham
Corporate Counsel: Gary Crotty
Treasurer: Tom Bledsoe
Director of Human Resources: Starr George

LOCATIONS

HQ: National Association for Stock Car Auto Racing
1801 W. International Speedway Blvd.,
Daytona Beach, FL 32115
Phone: 386-253-0611 **Fax:** 386-681-4041
Web: www.nascar.com

PRODUCTS/OPERATIONS

Selected Races

Busch Series
  Carquest Auto Parts 300
  Food City 250
  Ford 300
  Pepsi 300
  Sam's Town 300
Craftsman Truck Series
  Chevy Silverado 150
  Craftsman Truck Series 200
  Hardee's 200
  MBNA America 200
  Toyota Tundra 200
Nextel Cup Series
  Coca-Cola 600
  Daytona 500
  Gatorade 125
  Pontiac Performance 400
  Subway 500

COMPETITORS

AFL
Indy Racing League
Major League Baseball
NBA
NFL
NHL
World Wrestling Entertainment

HISTORICAL FINANCIALS

Company Type: Private

Income Statement
FYE: December 31

	ESTIMATED REVENUE ($ mil.)	NET INCOME ($ mil.)	NET PROFIT MARGIN	EMPLOYEES
12/02	3,000	—	—	450
12/01	2,500	—	—	400
12/00	2,000	—	—	350
12/99	1,500	—	—	300
12/98	2,000	—	—	—
Annual Growth	10.7%	—	—	14.5%

Revenue History

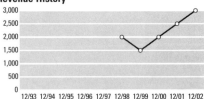

NASD

Bull market or bear, NASD will be there. NASD (formerly The National Association of Securities Dealers) is parent of the #3 US stock market, the American Stock Exchange (AMEX), and former parent of the #2 market, Nasdaq. (Nasdaq was spun off through a series of private sales and now trades OTC; NASD still holds 55% of its stock.) Since Nasdaq's spinoff was completed in 2002, NASD has coped with its emptier nest by concentrating on its regulatory functions. Per SEC orders, NASD Regulation oversees OTC securities trading and disciplines traders; virtually all US securities dealers are members. NASD in 2003 had planned to sell AMEX to GTCR Golder Rauner, but decided to sell AMEX to its members when the deal died.

Even without stock market subsidiaries, NASD has plenty to keep it busy. More than 5,000 brokerages and some 660,000 registered securities representatives are under its jurisdiction. NASD writes rules, conducts investigations, and disciplines firms or individuals that don't comply. NASD also operates arbitration and mediation programs and offers educational services to industry professionals and to investors.

HISTORY

NASD was founded in 1939 as a self-regulating entity for over-the-counter (OTC) securities traders who dealt directly with companies or with market makers authorized to trade their stock. Traders shopped by phone to get the best price from the market makers, and up-to-date OTC quotes were unobtainable. NASD set trading qualifications, administered licensing tests, set standards for underwriting compensation, and disciplined wayward traders.

In 1963 the SEC asked NASD to develop an automated OTC quotations system. Work began in 1968 on facilities in Trumbull, Connecticut, and Rockville, Maryland. The system went online in 1971 and soon turned into an electronic trading medium because it made dealer quotes more competitive and instantly visible. By 1972 volume exceeded 2 billion shares, and two years later the Nasdaq claimed a share volume nearly one-third of the New York Stock Exchange's. By 1980 it reported having almost 60% of the NYSE's volume, although Nasdaq counted both sides of many trades.

In 1975 Congress gave NASD responsibility for regulating the municipal securities market and asked the SEC to develop a national market system for share trading. The SEC handed the task to NASD. The market started trading in 1982 with 40 stocks, establishing a two-tier system: one for the crème de la crème, such as MCI (now WorldCom) and Microsoft, and one for smaller or newer issues. The system is continually updated; new technology made it a model for other markets.

To improve responsiveness to small investors, NASD instituted the SOES (small order entry system) after the 1987 stock crash, when many traders bailed themselves out before executing customer sell orders. So-called SOES bandits (dealers who used the system to make frequent small trades) increased the market's volatility and made Nasdaq vulnerable to NYSE's contention that auction exchanges were fairer to investors. An SEC investigation resulted in a requirement that dealers execute small customer orders along with their own and at the best prices. In 1997 the new rules were phased in and spreads dropped by an average of 35% without affecting volume.

But NASD teetered between appeasing the public and looking out for its own. A 1997 proposal to cap investor arbitration awards at $750,000, regardless of actual damages, met with criticism, since arbitration had been instituted in 1987 because the parties could receive remedies comparable to those available in court.

Reform-minded Wall Streeter Frank Zarb took over in 1997. Nasdaq and the American Stock Exchange (AMEX) merged the next year. NASD reluctantly complied when the SEC asked it to join the NYSE in real-time trade price reporting.

With for-profit, around-the-clock competitors like The Island ECN and Archipelago in mind, NASD prepared in 1999 to spin off Nasdaq as a for-profit market (overwhelmingly approved in 2000). Nasdaq also extended official pricing to 6:30 p.m. (Eastern time) and agreed to share listings with the Hong Kong Stock Exchange.

In 2000 Nasdaq converted stock prices from fractions to decimals, mandated by regulators. That year it joined with SOFTBANK to build Nasdaq Japan, an Internet-based market of primarily Japanese tech companies. In 2001 the flaccid economy led Nasdaq to trim about 10% of its staff — its first job cuts since just after the 1987 crash. Zarb also retired that year.

In the wake of the terrorism attacks that shook Wall Street and the nation in 2001, Nasdaq and the NYSE began discussing a disaster plan under which the two would cooperate should a future incident cripple either market. It also continued to refine its focus toward regulation, with plans to dispose of AMEX, and a series of private stock sales that would ultimately separate Nasdaq from NASD in 2002.

EXECUTIVES

Chairman, President, and CEO: Robert R. Glauber, age 65, $2,100,000 pay
Vice Chairman and President, Regulatory Policy & Oversight: Mary L. Schapiro
President, Regulatory Services & Operations: Douglas H. Shulman
President, Dispute Resolution; EVP and Chief Hearing Officer, Regulatory Policy & Oversight: Linda D. Fienberg
SEVP and Chief Administrative Officer: Michael D. Jones
EVP and General Counsel: T. Grant Callery
EVP and CTO: Martin P. Colburn
EVP and CFO: Todd T. DiGanci
EVP, Member Regulation: Robert C. Errico
EVP and Director of Dispute Resolution: George H. Friedman
EVP, Enforcement: Barry R. Goldsmith
EVP, Market Operations and Information Services: Steven A. (Steve) Joachim
EVP, Registration & Disclosure: Derek W. Linden
EVP, Market Regulation and US Exchange Solutions: Stephen I. Luparello
EVP and General Counsel, Regulatory Policy and Oversight: Marc Menchel
EVP, Member Services: M. Ann Short
EVP, Regulatory Policy & Programs: Elisse B. Walter
SVP and Investment Officer: James R. Allen
SVP and Corporate Controller: Eileen M. Famiglietti
SVP and Deputy General Counsel, Regulatory Policy and Oversight: Patrice M. Gliniecki
SVP, Human Resources: Andrew C. Goresh
SVP, Corporate Communications and Government Relations: Howard M. Schloss
SVP, Enforcement: Roger B. Sherman
SVP, Internal Audit: Daniel S. Shook
SVP and Corporate Secretary: Barbara Z. Sweeney
Auditors: Ernst & Young LLP

LOCATIONS

HQ: NASD
1735 K St. NW, Washington, DC 20006
Phone: 202-728-8000   **Fax:** 202-293-6260
Web: www.nasd.com

NASD has regulation and dispute resolution offices throughout the US.

PRODUCTS/OPERATIONS

2003 Sales

	% of total
Nasdaq	54
NASD	46
Total	**100**

Selected Subsidiaries and Affiliates
NASD Dispute Resolution, Inc.
NASD Regulation, Inc.

COMPETITORS

Bloomberg	Investment Technology
CBOT	Knight Trading
E*TRADE Financial	LaBranche & Co
Goldman Sachs	NYSE
Instinet	

HISTORICAL FINANCIALS

Company Type: Not-for-profit

Income Statement FYE: December 31

	REVENUE ($ mil.)	NET INCOME ($ mil.)	NET PROFIT MARGIN	EMPLOYEES
12/03	1,028	(58)	—	2,000
12/02	1,238	(4)	—	2,087
12/01	1,539	112	7.3%	3,200
12/00	1,555	114	7.3%	3,200
12/99	1,177	154	13.1%	3,000
12/98	740	47	6.4%	2,900
12/97	634	36	5.7%	2,200
12/96	556	55	9.9%	2,218
12/95	438	17	3.9%	2,000
12/94	372	21	5.6%	2,328
Annual Growth	12.0%	—	—	(1.7%)

2003 Year-End Financials
Debt ratio: 22.9%   Current ratio: 2.38
Return on equity: —   Long-term debt ($ mil.): 265
Cash ($ mil.): 333

Net Income History

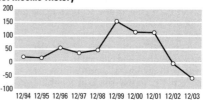

National Basketball Association

The National Basketball Association has shot a lot fewer airballs lately. The 30-team NBA is divided into the Eastern and Western conferences and includes one Canadian team. The league also operates the 13-team WNBA (women's basketball), as well as a six-team development league. After a string of seasons mired by low attendance and ratings, the NBA has seen its popularity rise thanks to the brief return of Michael Jordan with the Washington Wizards in 2001 and a highly rated 2004 championship series between the Detroit Pistons and the Los Angeles Lakers. In 2003 the league also launched NBA TV, a cable channel devoted to all things basketball.

In 2002 the NBA cut a new six-year TV contract with Walt Disney's ABC and ESPN, and Time Warner's Turner Sports worth a reported $4.6 billion. Some fans are unhappy with the new TV contract as it puts a majority of the league's games almost exclusively on cable. The NBA further milked the new TV contract by expanding the first round of the playoffs from a best-of-five to a best-of-seven format.

Expansion is also still very much alive for the NBA. After the Charlotte Hornets moved to New Orleans for the 2002-03 season, the league voted to give the city another franchise that will begin play in 2004-05. Robert Johnson, founder of BET, is the majority owner of the new Charlotte Bobcats. He is the first black owner of a major league sports team. The addition of the Bobcats forced the league to realign into six divisions with five teams each.

The NBA has also decided to rethink its strategy regarding the WNBA. The league has restructured the previous ownership rules for a WNBA franchise that dictated only the current owners of NBA clubs could own a sister team. The move allows the league to expand into cities where there isn't already an NBA franchise. But the new rules also force WNBA teams to find their own corporate sponsors and pay player salaries themselves, which prompted some teams to fold or find new homes. (The Utah Starzz are now the San Antonio Silver Stars and the Orlando Miracle are now the Connecticut Sun. Portland, Miami, and Cleveland ceased operations.)

HISTORY

Dr. James Naismith, a physical education teacher at the International YMCA Training School in Springfield, Massachusetts, invented basketball in 1891. Naismith nailed peach baskets at both ends of the school's gym, gave his students a soccer ball, and one of the world's most popular sports was born.

In the beginning many YMCAs deemed the game too rough and banned it, so basketball was limited to armories, gymnasiums, barns, and dance halls. To pay the rent for the use of the hall, teams began charging spectators fees for admission, and leftover cash was divided among the players. The first pro basketball game was played in 1896 in Trenton, New Jersey.

A group of arena owners looking to fill their halls when their hockey teams were on the road formed the Basketball Association of America in 1946. It merged with the midwestern National Basketball League in 1949 to form the 17-team National Basketball Association (NBA).

Six teams dropped out in 1950. The league got an unexpected boost the next year when a point-shaving scandal rocked college basketball. The bad publicity for the college game made the pros look relatively clean, and it helped attract more fans. Another boost came through innovation when the league introduced the 24-second shot clock in 1954, which sped up the game and increased scoring.

Basketball came into its own in the late 1950s and 1960s, thanks to the popularity of such stars as Wilt Chamberlain, Bill Russell, and Bob Cousy. A rival league, the American Basketball Association (ABA), appeared on the scene in 1967 with its red, white, and blue basketball. Salaries escalated as the two leagues competed for players. The leagues merged in 1976.

By the early 1980s the NBA was suffering major image problems (drugs, fighting, racial issues) and began to wane in popularity. The league was resuscitated by exciting new players such as Magic Johnson, Larry Bird, and Michael Jordan, and, in 1984, a new commissioner, David Stern. Although increased commercialism drove some purists crazy, big-name players and big-time rivalries helped sell the NBA's most important commodity — sport as entertainment.

Stern went to work cleaning up the league's image and financial problems, pushing through a strict anti-drug policy and a salary cap (the first such cap in major US sports). He also signed big marketing deals with such sponsors as Coca-Cola and McDonald's. The NBA added its first two non-US teams in 1995, the Toronto Raptors and the Vancouver Grizzlies. (The Grizzlies moved to Memphis in 2001.) The league also created the Women's NBA (WNBA) in 1996.

On July 1, 1998, the NBA owners voted to lock out players, leading to the first work stoppage in the NBA's 52-year history. The dispute lasted six months, and the NBA's 1998-99 season was pared down to 50 games from the standard 82.

Concerned with the rash of players either leaving college early or skipping it entirely for the NBA, the league announced the formation of a developmental league (akin to baseball's minor leagues) in 2000, which started play in 2001. Also in 2001 the NBA got a much-needed shot in the arm when Michael Jordan came out of retirement for a second time to play for the Washington Wizards.

The following year the league signed a new TV contract. Former game telecaster NBC decided not to pursue the league after its $1.3 billion bid failed to measure up to a six-year, $4.6 billion deal offered by Walt Disney's ABC and ESPN, and Time Warner's Turner Sports.

In 2004 the league launched its 30th franchise, the Charlotte Bobcats. The move forced the league to realign into six divisions with five teams each.

EXECUTIVES

Commissioner: David J. Stern, age 62
Deputy Commissioner and COO: Russell T. Granik
EVP Global Media Properties and Marketing Partnerships: Heidi Ueberroth
EVP Strategic Planning and Business Development: Ed Desser
SVP Basketball Operations: Stu Jackson
SVP Business Affairs: Harvey E. Benjamin
SVP Communications: Timothy P. Andree
SVP Finance: Robert Criqui
SVP Global Merchandising: Sal LaRocca
SVP Interactive Marketing: Brenda Spoonemore
SVP International: Andrew Messick
SVP Marketing and Teams Business Operations: Scott O'Neil
SVP Operations and Technology: Steve Hellmuth
VP Entertainment and Player Marketing: Charlie Rosenzweig
VP Global Media and NBA TV: Steve Justman
VP International Basketball Operations: Kim Bohuny
VP Marketing and Media: Ron Erskine
VP Marketing Partnerships: Jonathan Press
VP Security: Bernie Tolbert
President, National Basketball Development League: Phillip Evans
President and COO, NBA Entertainment: Adam Silver
President, Women's National Basketball Association: Valerie B. Ackerman

LOCATIONS

HQ: National Basketball Association
   Olympic Tower, 645 5th Ave., New York, NY 10022
Phone: 212-826-7000   **Fax:** 212-826-0579
Web: www.nba.com

PRODUCTS/OPERATIONS

Eastern Conference
Atlantic Division
   Boston Celtics
   New Jersey Nets
   New York Knicks
   Philadelphia 76ers
   Toronto Raptors
Central Division
   Chicago Bulls
   Cleveland Cavaliers
   Detroit Pistons
   Indiana Pacers
   Milwaukee Bucks
Southeast Division
   Atlanta Hawks
   Charlotte Bobcats
   Miami Heat
   Orlando Magic
   Washington Wizards

Western Conference
Northwest Division
   Denver Nuggets
   Minnesota Timberwolves
   Portland Trail Blazers
   Seattle SuperSonics
   Utah Jazz
Pacific Division
   Golden State Warriors
   Los Angeles Clippers
   Los Angeles Lakers
   Phoenix Suns
   Sacramento Kings
Southwest Division
   Dallas Mavericks
   Houston Rockets
   Memphis Grizzlies
   New Orleans Hornets
   San Antonio Spurs

COMPETITORS

AFL
Major League Baseball
Major League Soccer
NASCAR
NFL
NHL
PGA
World Wrestling Entertainment

HISTORICAL FINANCIALS

Company Type: Association

Income Statement   FYE: August 31

	REVENUE ($ mil.)	NET INCOME ($ mil.)	NET PROFIT MARGIN	EMPLOYEES
8/00*	2,164	—	—	—
8/99	956	—	—	800
8/98	1,874	—	—	1,000
8/97	1,664	—	—	850
8/96	1,403	—	—	650
8/95	1,259	—	—	550
8/94	1,030	—	—	450
8/93	999	—	—	—
8/92	843	—	—	—
8/91	606	—	—	—
Annual Growth	15.2%			12.2%

*Most recent year available

Revenue History

National Cooperative Refinery

Cooperation is a refined art and refining a cooperative art for the National Cooperative Refinery Association (NCRA), which provides three farm supply cooperatives (Cenex Harvest States, GROWMARK, and MFA Oil) with fuel through its oil refinery in Kansas. In 1943 five regional farm supply cooperatives, tired of wartime fuel shortages, created the NCRA to buy the Globe oil refinery in McPherson, Kansas. The refinery's production capacity is about 75,000 barrels per day. Fuel from the refinery is allocated to member/owners on the basis of ownership percentages. In addition to the refinery, NCRA owns Jayhawk Pipeline, minority interests in two other pipeline companies, and an underground oil storage facility.

EXECUTIVES
President: James Loving
VP Finance: John Buehrle
VP Refining: Rick Leicht
Superintendent of Operations: Allen Wilkerson
Director Human Resources: Jim Richardson
General Manager, Jayhawk Pipeline: Myron Hoover
Auditors: PricewaterhouseCoopers LLP

LOCATIONS
HQ: National Cooperative Refinery Association
1391 Iron Horse Rd., McPherson, KS 67460
Phone: 620-241-2340   **Fax:** 620-241-5531
Web: www.ncrarefinery.com

COMPETITORS
ChevronTexaco
Marathon Ashland Petroleum
Premcor
Valero Energy

HISTORICAL FINANCIALS
Company Type: Cooperative

Income Statement
FYE: August 31

	REVENUE ($ mil.)	NET INCOME ($ mil.)	NET PROFIT MARGIN	EMPLOYEES
8/03	1,285	—	—	560
8/02	962	—	—	534
8/01	800	—	—	560
8/00	700	—	—	600
8/99	700	—	—	600
8/98	700	—	—	560
8/97	773	—	—	540
8/96	760	—	—	560
8/95	596	—	—	—
Annual Growth	10.1%	—	—	0.0%

Revenue History
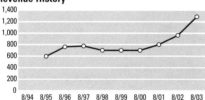

National Distributing

National Distributing Company strives to live up to its name, distributing beverages in Washington, DC, and nine US states. With operations primarily on the East Coast, but also in Colorado, New Mexico, and Ohio, NDC is one of the largest wholesale wine and spirits vendors in the US. A private firm founded in the 1900s by Chris Carlos (joined by Alfred Davis in 1942), NDC distributes brands such as Bacardi rum, Jack Daniels whiskey, Jose Cuervo tequila, Korbel wine, and Finlandia vodka. The Carlos and Davis families own and operate National Distributing.

EXECUTIVES
Chairman and CEO: Jay M. Davis, age 55
Vice Chairman and Secretary: Jerry Rosenberg
Vice Chairman and Treasurer: John A. Carlos
President and COO: Charles Andrews
Chief Accounting Officer: Greg Johnson
EVP: Chris Carlos
SVP and Director of Operations: Steve Feldman
President, Colorado: Jim Smith
President, Florida: Tom White
President, Georgia: Fred Bleiberg
President, Maryland: Pat Vogel
President and General Manager, South Carolina: Charlie Bradford
President and General Manager, Virginia: Joe Gigliotti

LOCATIONS
HQ: National Distributing Company, Inc.
1 National Dr. SW, Atlanta, GA 30336
Phone: 404-696-9440   **Fax:** 404-505-1013
Web: www.ndcweb.com

National Distributing Company operates in Colorado, Florida, Georgia, Maryland, New Mexico, Ohio, South Carolina, Virginia, and Washington, DC.

COMPETITORS
Charmer Industries
Gambrinus
Geerlings & Wade
Georgia Crown
Glazer's Wholesale Drug
Johnson Brothers
Southern Wine & Spirits
Wirtz
Young's Market

HISTORICAL FINANCIALS
Company Type: Private

Income Statement
FYE: December 31

	ESTIMATED REVENUE ($ mil.)	NET INCOME ($ mil.)	NET PROFIT MARGIN	EMPLOYEES
12/03	1,400	—	—	2,600
12/02	1,600	—	—	2,500
12/01	1,700	—	—	2,500
12/00	1,600	—	—	2,500
12/99	1,500	—	—	2,000
12/98	1,300	—	—	2,000
12/97	1,025	—	—	1,700
12/96	995	—	—	1,700
12/95	875	—	—	1,500
12/94	855	—	—	1,500
Annual Growth	5.6%	—	—	6.3%

Revenue History
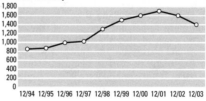

National Envelope

Pushing the envelope is this company's business. National Envelope makes some 160 million envelopes each day, ranging from regular office envelopes to customized envelopes for direct-mail use. Products include envelopes with windows, translucent envelopes, booklet-style envelopes, envelopes with clasps, and presentation folders. National Envelope has manufacturing and distribution locations throughout the US; divisions include New York Envelope, Old Colony Envelope, and Williamhouse. William Ungar, who founded the company in 1952, owns National Envelope; son-in-law Nathan Moser is chairman and CFO.

EXECUTIVES
Chairman and CFO: Nathan F. Moser
CEO: Leslie F. (Les) Stern
EVP Marketing: Bernard M. Matieu
VP Information Technology: Mark Mogul
Director of Human Resources: Karen Schreck

LOCATIONS
HQ: National Envelope Corporation
29-10 Huntserpoint Ave.,
Long Island City, NY 11101
Phone: 718-786-0300   **Fax:** 718-361-3127
Web: www.nationalenvelope.com

National Envelope has more than 20 manufacturing and distribution facilities throughout the US, including locations in California, Colorado, Georgia, Illinois, Kansas, Massachusetts, Missouri, New Jersey, New York, Pennsylvania, Texas, Washington, and Wisconsin, as well as in Ontario, Canada.

PRODUCTS/OPERATIONS

Selected Products
Durable mailers
Envelopes (traditional, translucent, commercial, window, booklet, clasp, jumbo-sized)
Fine papers
Open-end and open-side envelopes
Presentation folders

COMPETITORS
Cenveo
Gould Paper
National Service Industries
Stora Enso Oyj
UPM-Kymmene
Wausau-Mosinee Paper
Workflow Management

HISTORICAL FINANCIALS
Company Type: Private

Income Statement
FYE: December 31

	ESTIMATED REVENUE ($ mil.)	NET INCOME ($ mil.)	NET PROFIT MARGIN	EMPLOYEES
12/03	650	—	—	5,000
12/02	640	—	—	5,000
12/01	625	—	—	5,000
12/00	450	—	—	4,000
12/99	400	—	—	3,500
12/98	350	—	—	2,800
12/97	300	—	—	2,800
12/96	330	—	—	—
12/95	300	—	—	—
12/94	300	—	—	2,800
Annual Growth	9.0%	—	—	6.7%

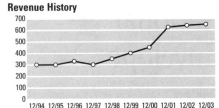

Revenue History

National Football League

In the world of professional sports, the National Football League (NFL) blitzes the competition. The organization oversees America's most popular spectator sport, acting as a trade association for 32 franchise owners. The teams operate as separate businesses but share much of the revenue generated through broadcasting and merchandising. The NFL was founded as the American Professional Football Association in 1920. The league reorganized its two conferences, the AFC and NFC, for the 2002-03 season when the Houston Texans joined the league as the latest, and probably last, expansion team. Fans initially protested the realignment, but quieted once it was clear the reorganization made more geographic sense.

The NFL's primary operations consist of subsidiaries NFL Properties, which generates billions through merchandising and licensing, and NFL Enterprises, the entity that negotiates national broadcasting rights for the teams. The league's current eight-year, $17.6 billion TV contract with FOX, CBS, ESPN, and ABC was struck in 1998. In 2002 the NFL also extended for another five years its exclusive deal with DIRECTV to broadcast NFL Sunday Ticket. The package allows DIRECTV subscribers to view any of the weekly Sunday telecasts, regardless of their local market. The announcement of the $2 billion deal is bad news for some cable channels, which were hoping to gain rights to certain NFL games for national distribution. The NFL has also launched the NFL Network, a 24-hour football network. So far it's distributed primarily through DIRECTV, but Charter Communications and Comcast have struck deals to air the network on their systems.

Other subsidiaries include NFL Charities and NFL Films. The league is also capitalizing on the Internet as a revenue source, signing a four-year $300 million deal with SportsLine.com (in which the league also owns a 9% stake), AOL, and CBS in 2001 to promote and maintain the league's NLF.com site.

The NFL landed in the middle of a scandal during the 2004 Super Bowl when singer Janet Jackson exposed her breast during the halftime show. (Jackson claims the flashing was an accident.) The incident outraged much of the country and the league is rethinking its strategy of producing live entertainment aimed at younger viewers. It also set off a slew of congressional hearings into broadcasting indecency, and the FCC has significantly boosted fines for such violations.

HISTORY

Descended from the English game of rugby, American football was developed in the late 1800s by Walter Camp, a player from Yale University who is generally credited with introducing new rules for downs and scoring. Professional teams sprang up in the 1890s, but football remained relatively unorganized until 1920, when George Halas and college star Jim Thorpe helped organize the American Professional Football Association. The new league featured 14 teams from the Midwest and East, including Halas' Staleys (now the Chicago Bears) and the Racine Cardinals (now the Arizona Cardinals). In 1922 the association changed its name to the National Football League.

The new league suffered many growing pains over the next decade, but by the 1930s the NFL had settled on 10 teams, including the Green Bay Packers (joined in 1921), the New York Giants (1925), and the Philadelphia Eagles (1933). Interest in the game remained somewhat regional, however, until the late 1940s and 1950s. In 1946 the Cleveland Rams moved to Los Angeles, and in 1950 the NFL expanded with three teams joining from the defunct All-American Football Conference. Television showed its potential in 1958 when that year's championship game, the first to be televised nationally, kept audiences riveted with an overtime victory by the Baltimore Colts over the Giants. In 1962 the NFL signed its first league-wide television contract with CBS for $4.65 million.

The 1960s brought a new challenge in the form of the upstart American Football League (AFL). Concerned that the AFL would steal players with higher salaries and draw away fans, NFL commissioner Pete Rozelle negotiated a deal in 1966 to combine the leagues. That season concluded with the first AFL-NFL World Championship Game, which was renamed the Super Bowl in 1969. When the merger was completed in 1970, the new NFL sported 26 teams.

Football's popularity exploded during the 1970s, helped by the rise of franchise dynasties such as the Pittsburgh Steelers (four Super Bowl wins) and the Dallas Cowboys (five NFC titles). In 1982 the Oakland Raiders moved to Los Angeles after a jury ruled against the NFL's attempts to keep the team in Oakland. The decision prompted other teams to relocate in search of better facilities and more revenue. (The Raiders returned to Oakland in 1995.) Rozelle stepped down in 1989 and was replaced by Paul Tagliabue.

During the 1990s the league expanded to 30 teams, adding the Carolina Panthers and Jacksonville Jaguars in 1995. The next year Art Modell moved his Cleveland Browns franchise to Baltimore to become the Ravens (the city of Cleveland held onto the rights to the Browns name and history and the franchise was revived in 1999), and in 1997 the Houston Oilers defected to Tennessee and were later renamed the Titans. The next year brought new television deals worth $17.6 billion over eight years.

The NFL made plans for new expansion in 1999, awarding a franchise to Robert McNair of Houston, who paid a record $700 million franchise fee and $310 million for a new stadium. Named the Houston Texans, the team began play in 2002. (The NFL realigned the NFC and AFC in 2002, shifting to eight divisions with four teams each.) In 2003 the league launched its own television channel, the NFL Network.

EXECUTIVES

Commissioner: Paul J. Tagliabue, age 63
EVP and COO: Roger Goodell
EVP and General Counsel: Jeff Pash
EVP Communications and Government Affairs:
Joe Browne
EVP Finance and Strategic Transactions:
Eric P. Grubman, age 43
EVP Labor Relations; Chairman, NFL Management Council: Harold R. Henderson
SVP Broadcast Planning: Dennis Lewin
SVP Business Affairs: Frank Hawkins
SVP Consumer Products: Mark Holtzman
SVP Finance and NFL Business Ventures:
Kim Williams
SVP Football Operations and Development: Art Shell, age 57
SVP Human Resources and Administration: Nancy Gill
SVP Marketing and Sales: Phil Guarascio
SVP New Media: Christopher J. Russo
SVP Special Events: Jim Steeg
VP Communications: Greg Aiello
VP NFL International: Gordon Smeaton
VP Player and Employee Development: Mike Haynes
VP and Head of Marketing: Shawn Dennis
President, NFL Films: Steve Sabol
Executive Director, NFL Player's Association; Chairman, PLAYERS INC: Gene Upshaw, age 58
Auditors: Deloitte & Touche LLP

LOCATIONS

HQ: National Football League Inc.
280 Park Ave., New York, NY 10017
Phone: 212-450-2000 **Fax:** 212-681-7599
Web: www.nfl.com

The National Football League oversees 32 franchises in 31 cities. It also has six franchises in Europe.

PRODUCTS/OPERATIONS

American Football Conference
Baltimore Ravens (1996)
  Cleveland Browns (1944, joined the NFL from the AAFC in 1950)
Buffalo Bills (1959, joined the NFL from the AFL in 1970, New York)
Cincinnati Bengals (1968, joined the NFL from the AFL in 1970)
Cleveland Browns (1999)
Denver Broncos (1959, joined the NFL from the AFL in 1970)
Houston Texans (2002)
Indianapolis Colts (1984)
  Baltimore Colts (1953)
Jacksonville Jaguars (1995, Florida)
Kansas City Chiefs (1963, joined the NFL from the AFL in 1970, Missouri)
  Dallas Texans (1959)
Miami Dolphins (1966, joined the NFL from the AFL in 1970)
New England Patriots (1971; Foxboro, MA)
  Boston Patriots (1959, joined the NFL from the AFL in 1970)
New York Jets (1959, joined the NFL from the AFL in 1970)
Oakland Raiders (1995, California)
  Los Angeles Raiders (1982)
  Oakland Raiders (1959, joined the NFL from the AFL in 1970)
Pittsburgh Steelers (1940)
  Pittsburgh Pirates (1933)
San Diego Chargers (1961, joined the NFL from the AFL in 1970)
  Los Angeles Chargers (1959)
Tennessee Titans (1998, Nashville)
  Tennessee Oilers (1997, Memphis)
  Houston Oilers (1959, joined the NFL from the AFL in 1970)

National Football Conference
Arizona Cardinals (1994, Phoenix)
   Phoenix Cardinals (1988)
   St. Louis Cardinals (1960)
   Chicago Cardinals (1922)
   Racine Cardinals (1901, Chicago)
   Morgan Athletic Club (1898, Chicago)
Atlanta Falcons (1966)
Carolina Panthers (1995; Charlotte, NC)
Chicago Bears (1922)
   Chicago Staleys (1921)
   Decatur Staleys (1920, Illinois)
Dallas Cowboys (1960)
Detroit Lions (1934)
   Portsmouth Spartans (1930, Ohio)
Green Bay Packers (1919, Wisconsin)
Minnesota Vikings (1961, Minneapolis)
New Orleans Saints (1967)
New York Giants (1925)
Philadelphia Eagles (1933)
St. Louis Rams (1995)
   Los Angeles Rams (1946)
   Cleveland Rams (1937)
San Francisco 49ers (1946, joined the NFL from the AAFC in 1950)
Seattle Seahawks (1976)
Tampa Bay Buccaneers (1976)
Washington Redskins (1937; Washington, DC)
   Boston Redskins (1933)
   Boston Braves (1932)

COMPETITORS

AFL
FIFA
Major League Baseball
Major League Soccer
NASCAR
NBA
NHL
PGA
World Wrestling Entertainment

HISTORICAL FINANCIALS
Company Type: Association

Income Statement
FYE: March 31

	REVENUE ($ mil.)	NET INCOME ($ mil.)	NET PROFIT MARGIN	EMPLOYEES
3/01*	4,200	—	—	450
3/00	3,602	—	—	450
3/99	3,271	—	—	400
3/98	2,448	—	—	400
3/97	2,331	—	—	—
3/96	2,059	—	—	—
3/95	1,730	—	—	—
3/94	1,753	—	—	—
Annual Growth	13.3%	—	—	4.0%

*Most recent year available

Revenue History

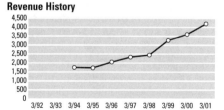

National Geographic

It's not your father's National Geographic Society anymore. Still publishing its flagship *National Geographic* magazine, the not-for-profit organization with more than 7 million members has expanded into an array of venues to enhance our knowledge of the big blue marble. Its National Geographic Ventures subsidiary is fortifying the organization's presence on television and the Web as well as in map-making. The organization owns part of the National Geographic Channel US (a cable channel it operates jointly with FOX), which reaches 48 million households. It also supports geographic expeditions (it has funded more than 7,000 scientific research projects) and sponsors exhibits, lectures, and education programs.

National Geographic has focused on an international expansion strategy, launching its first local-language edition of *National Geographic* magazine for Japan in 1995. The organization now offers 25 local-language editions, with a circulation of more than 2 million. Readers from every country in the world subscribe to the magazine; 40% of readers live outside the US.

The organization also owns part of National Geographic Channels International (NGCI), which is operated jointly with NBC, FOX, and BskyB. NGCI, one of the fastest-growing cable networks around the globe, airs in 145 countries in 26 languages, reaching more than 160 million households. In addition, National Geographic Global Exploration Fun awards grants for international scientific research. Every month the National Geographic Society reaches more than 250 million people worldwide through its National Geographic Channel, magazines, maps, books, videos, and interactive media.

As competition from relative newcomers such as Discovery Communications intensifies, the diversification of the National Geographic Society has been accelerating.

HISTORY

In 1888 a group of scientists and explorers gathered in Washington, DC, to form the National Geographic Society. Gardiner Greene Hubbard was its first president. The organization mailed the first edition of its magazine, dated October 1888, to 165 members. The magazine was clothed in a brown cover and contained a few esoteric articles, such as "The Classification of Geographic Forms by Genesis." The organization's tradition of funding expeditions began in 1890 when it sent geologist Israel Russell to explore Alaska. It began issuing regular monthly editions of *National Geographic* in 1896.

Following Hubbard's death in 1897, his son-in-law, inventor Alexander Graham Bell, became president. Aiming to boost the magazine's popularity, he hired Gilbert Grosvenor (who later married Bell's daughter) as editor. Grosvenor turned the magazine from a dry, technical publication to one of more general interest.

Under Grosvenor the magazine pioneered the use of photography, including rare photographs of remote Tibet (1904), the first hand-tinted colored photos (1910), the first underwater color photos (1920s), and the first color aerial photographs (1930).

The organization sponsored Robert Peary's trek to the North Pole in 1909 and Hiram Bingham's 1912 exploration of Machu Picchu in Peru. National Geographic expanded into cartography with the creation of a maps division in 1915. Grosvenor became president in 1920.

By 1930 circulation was 1.2 million (up from 2,200 in 1900). Grosvenor's policy of printing only "what is of a kindly nature . . . about any country or people" resulted in two articles that were criticized for their kindly portrayal of pre-war Nazi Germany (however, National Geographic maps and photographs were used by the US government for WWII intelligence). That policy eased over the years, and in 1961 a *National Geographic* article described the growing US involvement in Vietnam.

Grosvenor retired in 1954. His son Melville Bell Grosvenor, who became president and editor in 1957, accelerated book publishing with the first edition of *National Geographic Atlas of the World*. In addition, he created a film unit that aired its first TV documentary in 1965. Melville retired in 1967.

Melville's son Gilbert Melville Grosvenor took over as president in 1970. The organization debuted its *National Geographic Explorer* television series in 1985. National Geographic branched into commercial ventures in 1995 when it created subsidiary National Geographic Ventures to expand its presence on television, the Internet, maps, and retail. That same year the *National Geographic* magazine began international circulation.

Grosvenor became chairman in 1996, and Reg Murphy took over as president. Murphy shook up the organization by laying off nearly a quarter of its staff and stepping up its profit-making activities. In 1997 National Geographic branched into cable television when it partnered with Fox, NBC, and BskyB to launch outside the US the National Geographic Channels International (NGCI).

John Fahey replaced Murphy as president in 1998. That same year National Geographic released *Mysteries of Egypt*, its first IMAX-style film. The following year National Geographic unveiled its *Adventure* magazine. The organization began offering *National Geographic* on newsstands for the first time in 1999. In 2000 National Geographic Ventures acquired recreational topographic map company Wildflower Productions. As part of an agreement to buy 30% of travel portal iExplore, National Geographic also agreed to license the use of its name. In 2001 National Geographic Channel US, a cable channel, was launched as a joint venture with FOX.

In 2002 National Geographic began using IBM software and hardware to digitize thousands of its culture and nature images to sell online. That same year *National Geographic World*, a magazine for young people, became *National Geographic Kids*. The organization also began a literacy campaign that included *National Geographic Explorer!* magazine and curriculum materials for classrooms. In 2003 it launched Hungarian, Romanian, Czech, Croation, and Russian-language editions of *National Geographic* magazine.

EXECUTIVES

Chairman: Gilbert M. Grosvenor
Vice Chairman: Reg Murphy
President and CEO: John M. Fahey Jr.
EVP and CFO: Christopher A. Liedel
EVP: Terrence B. Adamson
EVP Mission Programs: Terry D. Garcia

EVP; President, Books and School Publishing Group:
Nina D. Hoffman
EVP; President, Magazine Publishing Group:
John Q. Griffin
EVP, National Geographic Enterprises: Linda Berkeley
SVP and Treasurer: H. Gregory Platts
SVP Communications: Betty Hudson
SVP Human Resources: Thomas A. Sablo
SVP International Licensing and Alliances:
Robert W. Hernandez
VP and Controller: Michael J. Cole
VP and Group Publisher, *National Geographic*:
Steve Giannetti
VP MIS: Bernard B. Callahan
VP, Editor in Chief, *National Geographic Traveler*:
Keith Bellows
VP, Education and Children's Programs: Barbara Chow

LOCATIONS

HQ: National Geographic Society
1145 17th St. NW, Washington, DC 20036
Phone: 202-857-7000   **Fax:** 202-775-6141
Web: www.nationalgeographic.com

PRODUCTS/OPERATIONS

Selected Operations

Books
  Cuba
  Eyewitness to the 20th Century
  Last Climb: The Legendary Everest Expeditions of George Mallory
  Return to Midway
  The World of Islam
Education products
Magazines
  Adventure
  National Geographic
  Traveler
  World
Maps and atlases
Sponsorship of expeditions, lectures, and education programs
Television
  National Geographic Channel
  National Geographic Explorer
  PBS specials
    Really Wild Animals
    Tales from the Wild

COMPETITORS

DeLorme
Discovery Communications
Educational Insights
Encyclopaedia Britannica
ESRI
Lonely Planet
MapQuest.com
Mariah Media
Rand McNally
Time
Time Warner

HISTORICAL FINANCIALS

Company Type: Not-for-profit

Income Statement				FYE: December 31
	REVENUE ($ mil.)	NET INCOME ($ mil.)	NET PROFIT MARGIN	EMPLOYEES
12/03	531	—	—	1,387
12/02	537	—	—	1,337
12/01	550	—	—	1,380
12/00	559	—	—	1,406
12/99	518	—	—	1,294
12/98	510	—	—	1,265
12/97	489	—	—	1,214
12/96	401	—	—	1,300
12/95	423	—	—	1,551
12/94	419	—	—	1,493
Annual Growth	2.7%	—	—	(0.8%)

Revenue History

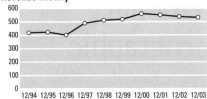

National Grape Cooperative

Well, of course grape growers want to hang out in a bunch! The 1,400 or so grower-owners in the National Grape Cooperative Association grow and harvest purple, red, and white grapes from almost 49,000 acres of vineyards in order to supply its well-known, wholly owned subsidiary Welch Foods. Welch's sells juices, jams, and jellies under the Welch's and BAMA brands. Other products include co-branded candy (with Russell Stover) and fresh grapes (distributed by C.H. Robinson Worldwide). Welch's is the world's #1 marketer of Concord and Niagara grape products.

Though jelly is a slowing market, new juice innovations, new packaging, and single-serving products are driving sales at Welch's. Following the trend of branded fresh produce, the Welch's brand now appears on fresh grapes sold in grocery stores nationwide. Recently publicized antioxidant health benefits of purple grape juice have helped spur sales of what was previously a dusty retail niche. Welch Foods sells its products to retailers in 30 countries.

EXECUTIVES

President and Director: Randolph H. Graham
First VP and Director: Joseph C. Falcone
Second VP: Harold H. Smith
Third VP and Director: James A. Schafer
General Manager, COO, and Treasurer: Brent J. Roggie
Financial and Accounting Officer; SVP, Finance, and CFO Welch Foods, Inc.: Albert B. Wright III
President and CEO, Welch Foods, Inc.: Daniel P. Dillon
Secretary and Assistant Treasurer: Timothy Buss
Assistant Secretary: Vivian S. Y. Tseng
Auditors: KPMG LLP

LOCATIONS

HQ: National Grape Cooperative Association, Inc.
2 S. Portage St., Westfield, NY 14787
Phone: 716-326-5200   **Fax:** 716-326-5494
Web: www.nationalgrape.com

National Grape Cooperative Association's members own almost 49,000 acres in Michigan, New York, Ohio, Pennsylvania, Washington, and Ontario, Canada.

PRODUCTS/OPERATIONS

Selected Products

Bulk Concord grape products (juice, puree, color extract)
Fresh grapes
Fruit juices (bottled, frozen, refrigerated, single-serve, shelf-stable concentrate)
Fruit spreads, jams, jellies, preserves
Juice cocktails (bottled, frozen, refrigerated, single-serve, shelf-stable concentrate)

COMPETITORS

B&G Foods
Cadbury Schweppes
Chiquita Brands
Cliffstar
Coca-Cola
Constellation Brands
Hansen Natural
Nestlé
Northland Cranberries
Ocean Spray
Procter & Gamble
Ralcorp
Smucker
Tropicana

HISTORICAL FINANCIALS

Company Type: Cooperative

Income Statement				FYE: August 31
	REVENUE ($ mil.)	NET INCOME ($ mil.)	NET PROFIT MARGIN	EMPLOYEES
8/03	579	76	13.1%	1,350
8/02	554	65	11.8%	1,264
8/01	650	67	10.4%	1,333
8/00	679	78	11.5%	1,308
8/99	631	71	11.2%	1,241
8/98	600	70	11.6%	1,258
8/97	573	56	9.8%	1,228
8/96	551	58	10.5%	1,224
8/95	509	56	11.1%	1,431
8/94	424	51	12.0%	1,259
Annual Growth	3.5%	4.5%	—	0.8%

2003 Year-End Financials

Debt ratio: 56.4%
Return on equity: 78.4%
Cash ($ mil.): 4
Current ratio: 1.21
Long-term debt ($ mil.): 55

Net Income History

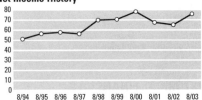

National Hockey League

Hockey is more than a cool sport for serious fans. The National Hockey League is one of the four major professional sports associations in North America, boasting 30 franchises in the US and Canada organized into two conferences with three divisions each. The NHL governs the game, sets and enforces rules, regulates team ownership, and collects licensing fees for merchandise. It also negotiates fees for national broadcasting rights. (Each team controls the rights to regional broadcasts.) In addition, four minor and semi-pro hockey leagues also fly under the NHL banner. The league was organized in Canada in 1917.

Hockey boasts millions of fans throughout North America and the NHL has gone through a tremendous expansion under commissioner Gary Bettman. However, hockey still trails the other top sports in terms of attendance and revenue. Some critics have even suggested that Bettman's plan to add new franchises in the Southern US has hurt the league by spreading talent too thin and too far from hockey's traditional base in Canada. Meanwhile, the remaining Canadian teams (all six of them) are struggling to compete with the deeper pockets of their US competitors.

But Bettman's efforts have at least netted the NHL greater exposure on the national sports stage and greater interest from broadcasters. In 1998 the league agreed to a $600 million TV package with ABC and ESPN that started in 2000. Big ratings for the games (including the Stanley Cup championships) failed to materialize, however, and ABC decided in 2004 to focus on its coverage of the NBA. The league has turned to NBC to take over broadcasting games under a two-year agreement unique in big league sports: the Peacock Network will share revenue from the broadcasts with the NHL instead of paying a large sum of money up front.

The most pressing issue hanging over the head of hockey and its fans, however, is the current labor dispute between players and owners. The collective bargaining agreement between the NHL and the NHL Players Association expired late in the summer of 2004 without a new agreement, leading to a player lockout that threatens to cancel the 2004-05 season. (The last player lockout in 1994 lasted 103 days, cutting the regular season in half.)

HISTORY

The National Hockey League traces its heritage to 1893, when the Stanley Cup (donated by Lord Stanley, Governor General of Canada) was first awarded to the Montreal Amateur Athletic Association hockey club of the Amateur Hockey Association of Canada. The National Hockey Association (NHA) became the first professional league to award the Cup (a large silver chalice with a new layer added each year, passed to the winning team and engraved with the names of that team's players) in 1910.

In the years leading up to WWI, however, disputes began to erupt between owners in the NHA. The onset of war also siphoned away players called up for duty, and with in-fighting intensifying among its owners, the association decided to disband in 1917. Later that year Frank Calder, a British scholar and former sports journalist who came to Canada to be a soccer player, helped form the National Hockey League (NHL) and appointed himself president. The league originally consisted of five teams from the NHA that played a 22-game schedule. (One team, the Montreal Wanderers, disbanded before the end of the first season.)

The league's first dynasty emerged in the form of the original Ottawa Senators (the team went under in 1934; the expansion Senators joined the league in 1992), which won four Cups from 1920 to 1927. The 1920s saw continued expansion — the Boston Bruins became the first US team in the league in 1925 — but the NHL remained amorphous as many teams joined up and dropped out during the decade.

The sport lost most of its talent to the military during WWII, forcing teams to field players who were often too young, too old, or who were barely able to skate. The league almost shut down, but the Canadian government encouraged play to continue, claiming it boosted national morale.

In the post-war years, the NHL consisted of just six teams: the Boston Bruins, the Chicago Blackhawks, the Detroit Red Wings, the Montreal Canadiens, the New York Rangers, and the Toronto Maple Leafs, known as the Original Six. The Canadiens began their three-decade domination of the NHL during this time, winning 17 championships from 1946 to 1979.

The league began expanding in 1967 when six US-based franchises were added to form the West Division, while the Original Six were placed in the East Division. More teams were slowly added through the 1970s and in 1979 the league absorbed four franchises from its rival professional league, the World Hockey Association (founded in 1972).

At the beginning of the 1980s the NHL consisted of 21 teams, including 15 franchises in the US. The NHL's shift towards the US market became more concrete when the league's headquarters moved from Montreal to New York City later in the decade. Trying to gain more US fans, the league tried to put an end to its slugfest image by implementing new rules in 1992, reducing violent play, and emphasizing a quicker game based on skill and style.

Late that year, Gary Bettman, formerly assistant commissioner of the National Basketball Association, was hired as the NHL's first real commissioner. Under his leadership, the NHL began expanding to more southern locations in the US. The league's growth was temporarily slowed in 1994, however, by the first major labor dispute in NHL history. Team owners began a player lockout that delayed the start of the season until early 1995, but they ultimately failed in their goal of implementing a salary cap.

The league's plan to boost popularity by using pro players in the 1998 Winter Olympics games in Nagano, Japan, was thwarted by limited, late-night coverage. Later that year NHL team owners agreed to a $600 million, five-year television contract with Walt Disney's ABC and ESPN starting with the 2000-01 season. That season also marked further expansion as the Minnesota Wild and the Columbus Blue Jackets took to the ice.

In 2003 hockey returned to its roots with the Heritage Classic, an outdoor match between the Edmonton Oilers and the Montreal Canadiens in minus-1 degree weather that drew record crowds.

EXECUTIVES

Commissioner: Gary B. Bettman, age 52
EVP and COO: Jon Litner
EVP and CFO: Craig Harnett
EVP and Chief Legal Officer: William (Bill) Daly
EVP and Director of Hockey Operations: Colin Campbell
SVP and General Counsel: David Zimmerman
SVP Finance: Joseph DeSousa
SVP Hockey Operations: James Gregory
SVP New Business Development and President, NHL Interactive CyberEnterprises: Keith Ritter
SVP Security: Dennis Cunningham
SVP Television and Media Ventures: Doug Perlman
VP Broadcasting and Programming: Adam Acone
VP Communications: Bernadette Mansur
VP Consumer Products Marketing: Jim Haskins
VP Strategic Development: Susan Cohig
Group VP; Managing Director, NHL International: Kenneth (Ken) Yaffe
Group VP Consumer Products Marketing: Brian Jennings
Group VP Corporate Marketing: Andrew Judelson
Group VP Events and Entertainment: Frank Supovitz
Group VP Information Technology: Peter DelGiacco
President, NHL Enterprises: Ed Horne
EVP Legal and Business Affairs and General Counsel, NHL Enterprises: Richard Zahnd
Auditors: Ernst & Young LLP

LOCATIONS

HQ: National Hockey League
1251 Avenue of the Americas, 47th Fl.,
New York, NY 10020
Phone: 212-789-2000 **Fax:** 212-789-2020
Web: www.nhl.com

The National Hockey League has 24 franchises in the US and six in Canada.

PRODUCTS/OPERATIONS

Teams
Atlanta Thrashers (1999)
Boston Bruins (1924)
Buffalo Sabres (1970)
Calgary Flames (1980)
Atlanta Flames (1972)
Carolina Hurricanes (1997)
Hartford Whalers (1975, joined the NHL from the World Hockey League in 1979)
New England Whalers (1971)
Chicago Blackhawks (1926)
Colorado Avalanche (1995)
  Quebec Nordiques (1972, joined the NHL from the World Hockey League in 1979)
Columbus Blue Jackets (2000)
Dallas Stars (1993)
  Minnesota North Stars (1967)
Detroit Red Wings (1926)
Edmonton Oilers (1973, joined the NHL from the World Hockey League in 1979)
  Alberta Oilers (1972)
Florida Panthers (1993)
Los Angeles Kings (1967)
Mighty Ducks of Anaheim (1993)
Minnesota Wild (2000)
Montreal Canadiens (1909)
Nashville Predators (1998)
New Jersey Devils (1982)
  Colorado Rockies (1976)
  Kansas City Scouts (1974)
New York Islanders (1972)
New York Rangers (1926)
Ottawa Senators (1883)
Philadelphia Flyers (1967)
Phoenix Coyotes (1996)
  Winnipeg Jets (1972, joined the NHL from the World Hockey League in 1979)
Pittsburgh Penguins (1967)
San Jose Sharks (1991)
St. Louis Blues (1967)
Tampa Bay Lightning (1992)
Toronto Maple Leafs (1927)
Vancouver Canucks (1947, joined the NHL from the Western Hockey League in 1970)
Washington Capitals (1974)

COMPETITORS

AFL
FIFA
Indy Racing League
Major League Baseball
Major League Soccer
NASCAR
NBA
NFL
PGA

HISTORICAL FINANCIALS

Company Type: Association

Income Statement
FYE: June 30

	REVENUE ($ mil.)	NET INCOME ($ mil.)	NET PROFIT MARGIN	EMPLOYEES
6/04	2,100	—	—	—
6/03	1,996	—	—	—
6/02	1,875	—	—	—
6/01	1,769	—	—	—
6/00	1,566	—	—	—
6/99	1,285	—	—	—
6/98	1,141	—	—	—
6/97	1,105	—	—	—
6/96	936	—	—	—
6/95	568	—	—	—
Annual Growth	15.6%	—	—	—

Revenue History

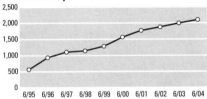

National Life Insurance

One nation, under insurance, with financial security for all. National Life Group, the marketing name for National Life Insurance Company and its affiliated companies, is a mutually owned insurer dating back to 1848. Today, National Life Group offers a range of insurance, investment, and savings products through such subsidiaries and affiliates as The Sentinel Companies (mutual funds), Life Insurance Company of the Southwest (insurance and annuities), National Retirement Plan Advisors, and American Guaranty and Trust (trust and custody services).

National Life's Private Client Group (part of subsidiary NL Capital Management) was spun off to management in 2004 and renamed Maple Capital Management.

EXECUTIVES

Chairman and CEO: Thomas H. MacLeay, age 53
EVP and CFO: Edward J. Bonach
EVP and Chief Investment Officer: Rodney A. Buck
EVP, Corporate Services and General Counsel: Michele S. Gatto
President and CEO, Sentinel Management Company: Kenneth R. Ehinger
VP, Human Resources: Jane Bowman
Auditors: PricewaterhouseCoopers LLP

LOCATIONS

HQ: National Life Insurance Company
1 National Life Dr., Montpelier, VT 05604
Phone: 802-229-3333   **Fax:** 802-229-9281
Web: www.natlifeinsco.com

PRODUCTS/OPERATIONS

2003 Sales

	% of total
Net investment income	52
Insurance premiums	32
Policy & contract charges	8
Mutual fund commission & fee income	5
Other	3
Total	**100**

Selected Subsidiaries
American Guaranty & Trust
Equity Services, Inc.
Life Insurance Company of the Southwest
National Life Insurance Company
National Retirement Plan Advisors Inc.
NL Capital Management, Inc.
The Sentinel Companies

COMPETITORS

AIG American General
AmerUs
AXA Financial
CIGNA
Citigroup
CNA Financial
FMR
John Hancock Financial Services
MassMutual
MetLife
Minnesota Mutual
MONY
Mutual of Omaha
New York Life
Ohio National Financial Services
Pacific Mutual
Principal Financial
Prudential
Sentry Insurance
Utica Mutual

HISTORICAL FINANCIALS

Company Type: Mutual company

Income Statement
FYE: December 31

	ASSETS ($ mil.)	NET INCOME ($ mil.)	INCOME AS % OF ASSETS	EMPLOYEES
12/03	12,034	77	0.6%	1,000
12/02	10,739	26	0.2%	1,000
12/01	10,161	48	0.5%	1,000
12/00	9,618	61	0.6%	950
12/99	9,356	57	0.6%	900
12/98	9,206	20	0.2%	750
12/97	8,814	36	0.4%	750
12/96	8,304	17	0.2%	960
Annual Growth	5.4%	24.1%	—	0.6%

2003 Year-End Financials
Equity as % of assets: 9.3%   Long-term debt ($ mil.): 282
Return on assets: 0.7%   Sales ($ mil.): 1,271
Return on equity: 7.2%

Net Income History

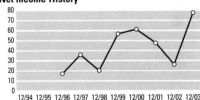

National Rural Utilities Cooperative

Cooperation may work wonders on *Sesame Street*, but in the real world it takes money to pay the power bill. The National Rural Utilities Cooperative Finance Corporation, or CFC, provides financing for electrical and telephone projects throughout the US. Owned by its more than 1,500 members, most of which are electrical cooperatives, the CFC supplements the government loans that traditionally fueled rural electric utilities by selling commercial paper, medium-term notes, and collateral trust bonds for its loans. The CFC was formed in 1969 by the National Rural Electric Cooperative Association, a lobby representing the nation's electric co-ops.

EXECUTIVES

President: Robert A. Caudle, age 59
Governor and CEO: Sheldon C. Petersen, age 51, $622,438 pay
SVP and CFO: Steven L. Lilly, age 54, $378,300 pay
SVP, Corporate Relations: Richard E. Larochelle, age 51
SVP, Credit Risk Management: John M. Borak, age 60
SVP, Member Services, and General Counsel: John J. List, age 57, $327,860 pay
SVP, Operations: John T. Evans, age 54, $327,860 pay
SVP, Rural Telephone Finance Cooperative: Lawrence Zawalick, age 46, $273,637 pay
VP and Controller: Steven L. Slepian
VP: James P. Duncan, age 57
Secretary-Treasurer: Cletus Carter, age 61
Auditors: Deloitte & Touche LLP

LOCATIONS

HQ: National Rural Utilities Cooperative Finance Corporation
2201 Cooperative Way, Herndon, VA 20171
Phone: 703-709-6700   **Fax:** 703-709-6778
Web: www.nrucfc.org

National Rural Utilities Cooperative Finance Corporation provides financing throughout the US.

PRODUCTS/OPERATIONS

Selected Subsidiaries and Affiliates
National Cooperative Services Corporation (debt refinancing and lending to electric co-ops)
Rural Telephone Finance Cooperative (rural telecommunications lending)

COMPETITORS

AgFirst
GE

HISTORICAL FINANCIALS
Company Type: Cooperative

Income Statement
FYE: May 31

	ASSETS ($ mil.)	NET INCOME ($ mil.)	INCOME AS % OF ASSETS	EMPLOYEES
5/04	21,350	(178)	—	218
5/03	20,974	652	3.1%	222
5/02	20,343	107	0.5%	215
5/01	19,999	133	0.7%	200
5/00	17,083	115	0.7%	186
5/99	13,925	76	0.5%	182
5/98	10,683	62	0.6%	164
5/97	9,058	55	0.6%	200
5/96	8,054	49	0.6%	—
5/95	7,081	45	0.6%	—
Annual Growth	13.0%	—	—	1.2%

2004 Year-End Financials
Equity as % of assets: 3.3%
Return on assets: —
Return on equity: —
Long-term debt ($ mil.): 16,659
Sales ($ mil.): 1,006

Net Income History
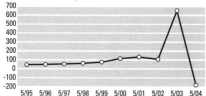

National Service Industries

National Service Industries (NSI) won't throw in the towel when it comes to pushing the envelope. The company operates two segments, linen rental and envelope manufacturing. Its National Linen Service unit rents linens and related products to the restaurant, lodging, and health care industries, primarily in the southeastern US. Its other subsidiary, Atlantic Envelope, makes custom envelopes and other office products. In late 2001 NSI spun off Lithonia Lighting Group (residential, commercial, industrial, and institutional lighting fixtures) and NSI Chemicals Group into a new company named Acuity Brands. NSI merged with NS Acquisition Corp. in 2003 and went private.

Prior to the spinoff, NSI's National Linen Service and Atlantic Envelope units accounted for only about 20% of the company's sales. The much smaller NSI adjusted to its smaller stature by selling its old corporate headquarters building and flattening its hierarchy.

EXECUTIVES
Chairman and CEO: Michael R. Kelly
President and General Counsel: Carol Ellis Morgan
EVP: Nick Spriggs
SVP, CFO, and Treasurer: K. Gene Laminack
SVP, Sales, Operations, and Manufacturing: John Schlich
CIO: Ed Ringer
President and CEO, National Linen Service: Gerry Knotek
Director, Marketing: David Chan
Auditors: PricewaterhouseCoopers LLP

LOCATIONS
HQ: National Service Industries, Inc.
1420 Peachtree St. NE, Atlanta, GA 30309
Phone: 404-853-1000   **Fax:** 404-853-1015
Web: www.nationalservice.com

PRODUCTS/OPERATIONS

Selected Operations
Envelopes (Atlantic Envelope)
  Courier envelopes
  Custom business envelopes
  Specialty filing products
Textile Rental (National Linen Service)
  Bar towels
  Bath towels
  Blankets
  Mats
  Mops
  Napkins
  Restroom supplies
  Scrubs and surgical drapery
  Table and bed linens

COMPETITORS
Angelica
ARAMARK
Cenveo
Cintas
Crothall
G&K Services
National Envelope
Steiner
UPM-Kymmene

HISTORICAL FINANCIALS
Company Type: Private

Income Statement
FYE: August 31

	REVENUE ($ mil.)	NET INCOME ($ mil.)	NET PROFIT MARGIN	EMPLOYEES
8/02	532	(32)	—	7,100
8/01	563	27	4.8%	7,700
8/00	2,566	100	3.9%	20,000
8/99	2,219	124	5.6%	19,700
8/98	2,031	109	5.4%	16,700
8/97	2,036	107	5.3%	16,100
8/96	2,014	101	5.0%	20,600
8/95	1,971	94	4.8%	21,100
8/94	1,882	83	4.4%	22,000
8/93	1,805	75	4.2%	22,200
Annual Growth	(12.7%)	—	—	(11.9%)

2002 Year-End Financials
Debt ratio: 0.5%
Return on equity: —
Cash ($ mil.): 21
Current ratio: 1.78
Long-term debt ($ mil.): 1

Net Income History
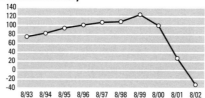

National Textiles

Have you heard the one about National Textiles? Boy, has this company got a yarn to spin. National Textiles makes open-end and ring-spun cotton, cotton-polyester blend yarns, knit fabrics, finished tubular fabrics, and cut parts. Sara Lee (maker of Hanes) is the company's primary customer for use in brands such as Just My Size, Hanes Beefy-Ts, Hanes Her Way, and Champion. It has about 10 production facilities, acquired from Sara Lee, and a cotton distribution center in the southern US; the Georgia location is among the world's largest spinning plants and the Tennessee location is a leading US ring-spun facility. The management bought the company from former chairman Martin J. Granoff in 2003.

EXECUTIVES
President and CEO: Jerry D. Rowland
CFO: Keith G. Huskins
VP, Human Resources: David V. Shirlen
CIO: Barry Markus

LOCATIONS
HQ: National Textiles, L.L.C.
480 Hanes Mill Rd., Winston-Salem, NC 27105
Phone: 336-714-8400   **Fax:** 336-714-8786
Web: www.nationaltextiles.com

National Textiles has plants in Georgia, North Carolina, South Carolina, Tennessee, and Virginia.

Selected Plant Locations
Advance, NC (cotton and yarn warehouse)
China Grove, NC (ring spun)
Eden, NC (knitting)
Forest City, NC (knitting)
Galax, VA (finishing and cutting)
Gastonia, NC (ring spun)
Greenwood, SC (fleece and jersey fabrics)
Mountain City, TN (ring spun)
Rabun Gap, GA (spinning mill)
Sanford, NC (spun yarn)

COMPETITORS
Avondale Incorporated
Galey & Lord
Mount Vernon Mills
Nisshinbo
Parkdale Mills
Toyobo

HISTORICAL FINANCIALS
Company Type: Private

Income Statement
FYE: June 30

	REVENUE ($ mil.)	NET INCOME ($ mil.)	NET PROFIT MARGIN	EMPLOYEES
6/02	700	—	—	4,325
6/01	800	—	—	5,038
6/00	728	—	—	5,157
6/99	727	—	—	4,217
Annual Growth	(1.3%)	—	—	0.8%

Revenue History
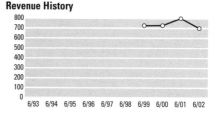

National Waterworks

Before you can hit your high water mark you may need to give National Waterworks a call. The company supplies products such as pipes, fittings, meters, valves, and hydrants to water and wastewater management facilities. JPMorgan Partners, the private equity division of J.P. Morgan Chase & Co., and Boston-based investment firm Thomas H. Lee Partners own National Waterworks.

EXECUTIVES
President and CEO: Harry K. Hornish Jr., age 58
CFO: Mechelle Slaughter, age 47
CIO: Terry Howell, age 40
VP, Human Resources: J. L. Walker, age 57
VP and Controller: Phil Keipp, age 42
VP, Midwest Region: Rob Hickson, age 56
VP, Southwest Region: Ed E. Maczko Jr., age 56
VP, Pacific Region: Ron Hood, age 58
VP, Southeast Region: Jerry L. Webb, age 45
VP, Mid-South Region: Irving B. Welchons III, age 55
VP, Mid-Continent Region: Jack Schaller, age 48
Director, IT: Jack Olson, age 53
Marketing Manager: Judy Barrow
Site Manager, Waco, Texas: Steve Harrup
Auditors: KPMG LLP

LOCATIONS
HQ: National Waterworks, Inc.
200 W. Hwy. 6, Ste. 620, Waco, TX 76712
Phone: 254-772-5355   **Fax:** 254-772-5716
Web: www.nationalwaterworks.com

PRODUCTS/OPERATIONS

2003 Sales

	% of total
Pipes	40
Fittings	15
Valves	12
Meters	9
Service & repair products	7
Fire hydrants	6
Other	11
Total	**100**

COMPETITORS
Emco Corporation
Kelly Pipe Co., LLC
Parker Hannifin

HISTORICAL FINANCIALS
Company Type: Private

Income Statement
FYE: December 31

	REVENUE ($ mil.)	NET INCOME ($ mil.)	NET PROFIT MARGIN	EMPLOYEES
12/03	1,278	34	2.6%	1,447
12/02	1,153	(419)	—	1,460
12/01	1,120	49	4.4%	—
12/00	1,173	49	4.2%	—
Annual Growth	2.9%	(11.6%)	—	(0.9%)

National Wine & Spirits

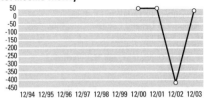

Bartender to the nation's breadbasket, National Wine & Spirits is one of the Midwest's largest wine and liquor distributors. Serving 36,000 locations, the company distributes to restaurants, liquor stores, and retailers in Illinois, Indiana, and Michigan and owns an interest in a Kentucky distributor. Its suppliers include Fortune Brands (Jim Beam), Diageo (Bailey's), and Beringer Blass Wine Estates. The company operates through several wholly owned subsidiaries. CEO James LaCrosse and director Norma Johnston own National Wine & Spirits, which was founded in 1934.

Major changes among suppliers of distilled spirits have National Wine & Spirits and other alcohol distributors across the country re-evaluating how they do business.

For example, Diageo is conducting a state-by-state review to determine the companies that have exclusive rights to distribute its products. In Illinois it has not granted such rights to National Wine & Spirits; two other suppliers, Future Brands and Canandaigua Wine Company, also have ended the company's Illinois distribution rights. As a result, National Wine & Spirits is scaling back operations and about 300 jobs in that state and forming a strategic alliance with Glazer's Wholesale Drug Company.

However, in Michigan and Indiana, National Wine & Spirits does have exclusive rights to distribute Diageo products, which is likely to boost business in those areas.

To broaden its offerings, the company also sells imported and specialty beers through a subsidiary and in some markets sells cigars.

EXECUTIVES
Chairman, President, CEO, and CFO:
James E. LaCrosse, age 71, $409,700 pay
COO, Secretary, and Director: John J. Baker, age 33, $264,519 pay
EVP, Sales and Marketing: Gregory J. Mauloff, age 52, $223,327 pay
EVP and Director: J. Smoke Wallin, age 37, $297,231 pay
VP, Sales, Indiana Fine Wine and Director:
Catherine M. LaCrosse, age 37
VP and General Manager, NWS-Indiana:
Patrick J. Hurrle, age 54, $287,910 pay
President and CEO, US Beverage: Joseph J. Fisch Jr., age 54, $285,000 pay
Treasurer and Corporate Controller: Patrick A. Trefun, age 44
Auditors: Deloitte & Touche LLP

LOCATIONS
HQ: National Wine & Spirits, Inc
700 W. Morris St., Indianapolis, IN 46206
Phone: 317-636-6092   **Fax:** 317-685-8810
Web: www.nwscorp.com

PRODUCTS/OPERATIONS

Selected Subsidiaries
National Wine & Spirits - Indiana
NWS - Illinois, LLC
NWS Michigan, Inc.
United States Beverage, L.L.C.

Selected Brands
Indiana
 Absolut vodka
 Almaden wine
 Beringer wine
 Captain Morgan rum
 Crown Royal whiskey
 Jim Beam whiskey
 Jose Cuervo tequila
 Ravenswood wine
 Seagram's gin
 Smirnoff vodka
 Yellow Tail wine
Kentucky
 Absolut vodka
 Beringer wine
 Jim Beam whiskey
 Kendall-Jackson wine
Michigan
 Absolut vodka
 Captain Morgan rum
 Jim Beam whiskey
 Jose Cuervo tequila
 Smirnoff vodka

COMPETITORS
Glazer's Wholesale Drug
Johnson Brothers
Southern Wine & Spirits

HISTORICAL FINANCIALS
Company Type: Private

Income Statement
FYE: March 31

	REVENUE ($ mil.)	NET INCOME ($ mil.)	NET PROFIT MARGIN	EMPLOYEES
3/04	541	(9)	—	1,388
3/03	713	16	2.2%	1,430
3/02	682	8	1.1%	1,618
3/01	661	15	2.3%	1,521
3/00	626	6	0.9%	1,550
3/99	553	—	—	1,550
3/98	521	—	—	1,517
3/97	491	—	—	—
3/96	443	—	—	—
3/95	427	—	—	—
Annual Growth	2.7%	—	—	(1.5%)

2004 Year-End Financials
Debt ratio: 685.8%   Current ratio: 1.75
Return on equity: —   Long-term debt ($ mil.): 86
Cash ($ mil.): 1

Net Income History
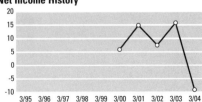

Nationwide

Call it truth in advertising — Nationwide has offices throughout the US. The company is a leading US property & casualty insurer that, though still a mutual firm, operates in part through publicly held insurance subsidiary Nationwide Financial. In addition to personal and commercial property & casualty coverage, life insurance, and financial services, Nationwide offers surplus lines, professional liability, workers' compensation, managed health care, and other coverage. The company sells its products through such affiliates as Farmland Insurance, GatesMcDonald, Scottsdale Insurance, and asset manager Gartmore.

To enhance its focus on personal and small-business lines in the US, Nationwide bought specialty auto insurer THI from Prudential. Nationwide Financial also bought Provident Mutual Life Insurance (now Nationwide Financial Network); the acquisition made it the fourth-largest US provider of variable life insurance.

Although Nationwide Financial and its Strategic Investments segment underperformed in 2002, the company swung to a net profit, helped in part by improved underwriting results by its insurance subsidiaries.

HISTORY

In 1919 members of the Ohio Farm Bureau Federation, a farmers' consumer group, established their own automobile insurance company. (As rural drivers, they didn't want to pay city rates.) To get a license from the state, the company, called Farm Bureau Mutual, needed 100 policyholders. It gathered more than 1,000. Founder Murray Lincoln headed the company until 1964.

The insurer expanded into Delaware, Maryland, North Carolina, and Vermont in 1928 and began selling auto insurance in 1931 to city folks. It expanded into fire insurance in 1934 and life insurance the next year.

During WWII growth slowed, although the company had operations in 12 states and Washington, DC, by 1943. It diversified in 1946 when it bought a Columbus, Ohio, radio station. By 1952 the firm had resumed expansion and changed its name to Nationwide.

The company was one of the first auto insurance companies to use its agents to sell other financial products, adding life insurance and mutual funds in the mid-1950s. Nationwide General, the country's first merit-rated auto insurance firm, was formed in 1956.

Nationwide established Neckura in Germany in 1965 to sell auto and fire insurance. Four years later the company bought GatesMcDonald, a provider of risk, tax, benefit, and health care management services. It organized its property/casualty operations into Nationwide Property & Casualty in 1979.

The company experienced solid growth throughout the 1980s by establishing or purchasing insurance firms, among them Colonial Insurance of California (1980), Financial Horizons Life (1981), Scottsdale (1982), and, the largest, Employers Insurance of Wausau (1985). Wausau wrote the country's first workers' compensation policy in 1911.

Earnings were up and down in the 1990s as the company invested in Wausau and in consolidating office operations. Nationwide set up an ethics office in 1995, a time of increased scrutiny of insurance industry sales practices, and made an effort to hire more women as agents. In 1996 the Florida Insurance Commission claimed the company discriminated against customers on the basis of age, gender, health, income, marital status, and location. Nationwide countered that the allegations originated from disgruntled agents.

In 1997 the company settled a lawsuit by agreeing to stop its redlining practices (it avoided selling homeowners' insurance to urban customers with homes valued at less than $50,000 or more than 30 years old, which allegedly discriminated against minorities). It also dropped a year-old sales quota system that was under investigation.

As the century came to a close, Nationwide began to narrow its focus on its core businesses. It spun off Nationwide Financial Services so the unit could have better access to capital, and it expanded both at home and abroad through such purchases as ALLIED Group (multiline insurance), CalFarm (agricultural insurance in California), and AXA subsidiary PanEuroLife (asset management in Europe). It jettisoned such operations as West Coast Life Insurance, its Wausau subsidiary, and its ALLIED Life operations. The company's discrimination woes came back to haunt it in 1999, and it created a $750,000 fund to help residents of poor Cincinnati neighborhoods buy homes.

At the end of 2000, Nationwide Health Plans asked regulators for permission to exit the profit-poor HMO business. The division plans to maintain its more popular PPO operations. The next year Nationwide's expansion in Europe continued with the purchase of UK fund manager Gartmore Investment Management.

EXECUTIVES

Chairman and CEO: William G. (Jerry) Jurgensen, age 52
President and COO, Nationwide Financial: Mark R. Thresher, age 47
EVP, CFO, and Chief Investment Officer: Robert A. Rosholt, age 53
EVP, General Counsel, and Secretary: Patricia R. (Pat) Hatler, age 49
EVP and Chief Administrative Officer: Terri L. Hill, age 44
EVP and CIO: Michael C. Keller, age 44
EVP and Chief Marketing Officer: Kathleen D. (Kathy) Ricord, age 53
President, Gartmore Group: Paul J. Hondros
President, Nationwide Strategic Investments: Donna A. James, age 46
President and COO, Property and Casualty Insurance Operations: Stephen S. (Steve) Rasmussen, age 51
President and COO, Scottsdale Insurance Companies: R. Max Williamson
Auditors: KPMG LLP

LOCATIONS

HQ: Nationwide
1 Nationwide Plaza, Columbus, OH 43215
Phone: 614-249-7111 **Fax:** 614-249-7705
Web: www.nationwide.com

Nationwide operates in more than 35 countries around the world.

PRODUCTS/OPERATIONS

Selected Subsidiaries and Affiliates
Gartmore Group (UK)
GatesMcDonald
Nationwide Agribusiness
  Farmland Insurance
Nationwide Federal Credit Union
Nationwide Financial
  401k Company
  National Deferred Compensation
  Nationwide Advisory Services
  Nationwide Home Mortgage Company
  Nationwide Retirement Plan Services, Inc.
  Nationwide Retirement Solutions
  PEBSCO Nationwide Retirement Solutions
  Pension Associates, Inc.
  Villanova
Nationwide Global
  PanEuroLife
Nationwide Insurance
  Allied Insurance
  CalFarm Insurance
  Nationwide Health Plans
Nationwide Realty Investors
Scottsdale Insurance

COMPETITORS

ACE Limited	Liberty Mutual
AIG	MassMutual
Allstate	MetLife
American Financial	New York Life
AXA	Northwestern Mutual
AXA Financial	Pacific Mutual
Blue Cross	Principal Financial
CIGNA	Prudential
Citigroup	St. Paul Travelers
CNA Financial	State Farm
Guardian Life	UnitedHealth Group
The Hartford	USAA
John Hancock Financial Services	

HISTORICAL FINANCIALS

Company Type: Mutual company

Income Statement — FYE: December 31

	ASSETS ($ mil.)	NET INCOME ($ mil.)	INCOME AS % OF ASSETS	EMPLOYEES
12/02	117,930	252	0.2%	30,000
12/01	113,463	(295)	—	35,000
12/00	117,040	331	0.3%	35,000
12/99	115,760	526	0.5%	35,000
12/98	98,280	963	1.0%	32,815
12/97	83,214	1,031	1.2%	29,051
12/96	67,624	250	0.4%	33,184
12/95	57,420	183	0.3%	32,949
12/94	47,696	445	0.9%	32,600
12/93	42,213	501	1.2%	32,583
Annual Growth	12.1%	(7.3%)	—	(0.9%)

2002 Year-End Financials

Equity as % of assets: 6.6% Long-term debt ($ mil.): 1,439
Return on assets: 0.2% Sales ($ mil.): 29,421
Return on equity: 3.2%

Net Income History

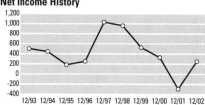

Navy Exchange

Before Old Navy, there was the Navy Exchange Service Command (NEXCOM). Active-duty military personnel, reservists, retirees, and their family members can shop at more than 100 NEXCOM retail stores (brand-name and private-label merchandise ranging from apparel to home electronics), about 190 NEXCOM Ships Stores (basic necessities), and its 100 Uniform Support Centers (the sole source of authorized uniforms). NEXCOM also runs about 40 Navy Lodges in the US and six foreign countries. NEXCOM receives tax dollars for its shipboard stores, but it is otherwise self-supporting. Most of the profits fund morale, welfare, and recreational programs for sailors.

The Bush Administration has proposed merging NEXCOM with Army and Air Force Exchange Service and the Marine Corps Personnel Support service.

EXECUTIVES

Rear Admiral and Commander: Robert E. Cowley
Captain and Vice Commander: J. Richard Trowbridge
COO: Elliott P. Zucker
CFO: Michael P. Good
CIO: Richard Garza
Chief Merchandising Officer: Robert E. McGinty
Controller: Robert Snyder
Marketing Director: Michael Conner
Customer Service Manager: Jim Winn
Legal Counsel: Michael Rigg
Manager, Merchandise Information Systems: Eileen Cook
Vending Branch Manager: Gerard Fantano
Auditors: Deloitte & Touche LLP

LOCATIONS

HQ: Navy Exchange Service Command
3280 Virginia Beach Blvd., Virginia Beach, VA 23452
Phone: 757-463-6200   **Fax:** 757-631-3659
Web: www.navy-nex.com

COMPETITORS

7-Eleven
Best Buy
J. C. Penney
Kmart
Sears
Target
Wal-Mart

HISTORICAL FINANCIALS
Company Type: Government-owned

Income Statement
FYE: January 31

	REVENUE ($ mil.)	NET INCOME ($ mil.)	NET PROFIT MARGIN	EMPLOYEES
1/04	2,100	—	—	15,500
1/03	2,000	—	—	16,000
1/02	1,916	—	—	16,000
1/01	1,974	—	—	16,000
1/00	1,831	—	—	16,000
1/99	1,696	—	—	16,000
1/98	1,661	—	—	17,000
1/97	1,682	—	—	16,194
1/96	1,830	—	—	18,000
1/95	1,947	—	—	21,854
Annual Growth	0.8%	—	—	(3.7%)

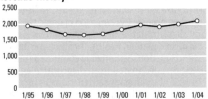

Revenue History

Navy Federal Credit Union

"Once a member, always a member," promises Navy Federal Credit Union (NFCU). This policy undoubtedly helped NFCU become one of the nation's largest credit unions, claiming more than 2 million members. Formed in 1933, NFCU provides US Navy and Marine Corps personnel and their families with checking and savings accounts, mortgages, IRAs, and a variety of loans, including mortgage, auto, and student loans. Members (who can retain their credit union privileges even after discharge from the armed services) get access to ATMs in Visa's PLUS Network and the Armed Forces Financial Network. NFCU has some 90 locations in the US and about 25 more overseas.

EXECUTIVES

Chairman: John A. Lockard
First Vice Chairman: Mary Jane Miller
Second Vice Chairman: Joseph W. Dyer
President, CEO, and Treasurer; Chairman, Navy Federal Financial Group: Brian L. McDonnell
COO: William Earner
SEVP and Chief of Operations: John R. Peden
SEVP, Support Group: Brady M. Cole
President and CEO, Navy Federal Financial Group: Dennis J. Godfrey
Secretary: Kenneth R. Burns
Auditors: PricewaterhouseCoopers LLP

LOCATIONS

HQ: Navy Federal Credit Union
820 Follin Ln., Vienna, VA 22180
Phone: 703-255-8000   **Fax:** 703-255-8741
Web: www.navyfcu.org

PRODUCTS/OPERATIONS

2003 Sales

	$ mil.	% of total
Interest		
Loans to members	908.7	70
Securities	97.3	8
Noninterest		
Sharechek card interchange	52.1	4
Credit card interchange	52.0	4
Net gain on sale of mortgages	50.9	4
Mortgage servicing	35.7	3
Overdrawn Sharechek fees	32.6	2
Other	62.6	5
Total	**1,291.9**	**100**

COMPETITORS

Bank of America
Citibank
USAA
Wachovia
Wells Fargo

HISTORICAL FINANCIALS
Company Type: Not-for-profit

Income Statement
FYE: December 31

	ASSETS ($ mil.)	NET INCOME ($ mil.)	INCOME AS % OF ASSETS	EMPLOYEES
12/03	20,040	314	1.6%	4,000
12/02	17,585	181	1.0%	4,000
12/01	15,107	157	1.0%	4,000
12/00	12,413	185	1.5%	3,500
12/99	11,188	128	1.1%	3,100
12/98	10,793	113	1.0%	3,100
12/97	9,709	95	1.0%	3,597
12/96	8,922	—	—	3,423
12/95	8,723	—	—	3,304
12/94	—	—	—	3,185
Annual Growth	11.0%	22.1%	—	2.6%

2003 Year-End Financials

Equity as % of assets: 89.5%   Long-term debt ($ mil.): 183
Return on assets: 1.7%   Sales ($ mil.): 1,292
Return on equity: 1.9%

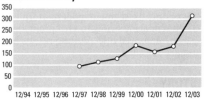

Net Income History

NCH

NCH Corporation has been cleaning up for years, and like everyone else, it's been using soaps and detergents to do so. The company makes and sells about 450 chemical, maintenance, repair, and supply products for customers in more than 60 countries throughout the world. NCH markets its products — including all kinds of cleaners — through a direct sales force to the agricultural, home-improvement, industrial, recreational, and utility industries. Other products include fasteners, welding supplies, plumbing parts, lubricants, and metal working fluids. Descendants of founder Milton Levy own the company.

NCH's cleaning products include hand cleaners, industrial cleaners, and housekeeping supplies. Specialty chemical products, including cleaning and water treatment chemicals, deodorizers, lubricants, paints and paint strippers, patching compounds, and flooring and carpet treatments, account for the majority of sales.

EXECUTIVES

Chairman and President: Irvin L. Levy
EVP: John I. Levy
EVP: Lester A. Levy Jr.
EVP: Robert M. Levy
EVP: Walter M. Levy
SVP, CFO, and Controller: Tom F. Hetzer, age 64
SVP: Earl Nicholson
VP and Treasurer: Glen Scivally
Director, Marketing: Mike Benton
Auditors: Grant Thornton LLP

LOCATIONS

HQ: NCH Corporation
2727 Chemsearch Blvd., Irving, TX 75062
Phone: 972-438-0226 **Fax:** 972-438-0707
Web: www.nch.com

NCH Corporation has roughly 20 manufacturing facilities in Asia, the Americas, and Europe, and office and warehouse facilities in Europe and the Americas.

PRODUCTS/OPERATIONS

Selected Operations and Products

Chemical Specialties
  Cleaning chemicals
  Deodorizers
  Floor and carpet care products
  HVAC products
  Lubricants
  Oil production facility chemicals
  Paint
  Paint removers
  Water-treatment chemicals
Landmark Direct
  First-aid supplies
  Workplace signage and productivity products
Partsmaster Group
  Cutting tools
  Electrical products
  Fasteners
  Welding alloys
Plumbing Products Group
  Plumbing products for new construction
  Plumbing repair and replacement parts

COMPETITORS

Church & Dwight	Illinois Tool Works
Cintas	JohnsonDiversey
Clariant International	Lawson Products
Clorox	Pioneer
Danaher	Quaker Chemical
Detrex	Safety-Kleen
Ecolab	Smart & Final
H.B. Fuller	Snap-on
Hercules	SYSCO
Hughes Supply	WD-40

HISTORICAL FINANCIALS

Company Type: Private

Income Statement
FYE: April 30

	REVENUE ($ mil.)	NET INCOME ($ mil.)	NET PROFIT MARGIN	EMPLOYEES
4/04	684	36	5.2%	6,500
4/03	650	—	—	6,500
4/02	658	—	—	6,500
4/01	680	—	—	8,404
4/00	728	—	—	9,330
4/99	787	—	—	10,093
4/98	784	—	—	10,373
4/97	767	—	—	10,458
4/96	773	—	—	10,543
4/95	735	—	—	10,569
Annual Growth	(0.8%)	—	—	(5.3%)

Revenue History
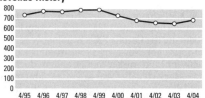

NESCO

NESCO doesn't take diversification lightly. The holding company's operations include industrial equipment manufacturing, real estate investment, and staffing services. NESCO's industrial group includes material handlers Continental Conveyor (conveyor systems for mining) and Goodman Conveyor (bulk conveyor equipment). Other industrial group companies include ACC Automation, which makes dip molding equipment for manufacturing everything from rubber gloves to condoms, Penn Station (copper/aluminum electrical connectors), NESCO Service Co. (staffing), and Rogers Company (trade show exhibits). Founder and president Robert Tomsich owns the company, which is not related to Oklahoma's NESCO, a specialty contactor.

EXECUTIVES

Chairman and President: Robert J. Tomsich
President: John R. Tomsich
VP, Finance: Frank Rzicznek
President and CEO, Continental Conveyor & Equipment: C. E. Bryant Jr.
President, Goodman Conveyor: Doug Markham
EVP, Continental Conveyor & Equipment: James L. (Jim) Smothers

LOCATIONS

HQ: NESCO, Inc.
6140 Parkland Blvd., Mayfield Heights, OH 44124
Phone: 440-461-6000 **Fax:** 440-449-3111
Web: www.nescoinc.com

PRODUCTS/OPERATIONS

Selected Subsidiaries

ACC Automation (custom machinery and engineering systems)
Continental Conveyor & Equipment Co. (conveyor equipment and systems)
Goodman Conveyor Co. (conveyor equipment and systems)
NESCO Service Co. (clerical, industrial, and technical staffing)
Penn Station (electrical connectors)
Rogers Co. (marketing exhibits)

COMPETITORS

Babcock International	Kelly Services
Briggs & Stratton	MAN
FKI	Manpower
Heidelberg	Molex
Ingersoll-Rand	RWE
Jervis B. Webb	Thomas & Betts

HISTORICAL FINANCIALS

Company Type: Private

Income Statement
FYE: December 31

	REVENUE ($ mil.)	NET INCOME ($ mil.)	NET PROFIT MARGIN	EMPLOYEES
12/02	1,050	—	—	9,500
12/01	1,065	—	—	9,500
12/00	1,200	—	—	10,250
12/99	1,100	—	—	10,250
12/98	1,065	—	—	700
12/97	1,000	—	—	10,000
12/96	1,000	—	—	6,000
12/95	420	—	—	3,400
12/94	320	—	—	—
Annual Growth	16.0%	—	—	15.8%

Revenue History
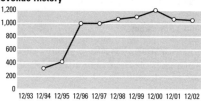

New Balance

New Balance Athletic Shoe's everyman appeal is what gives it a boost. Unlike its rivals, the company shuns celebrity endorsers; its lesser-known athletes show its emphasis on substance versus style. The approach attracts a clientele of aging boomer jocks who are less fickle than the teens chased by other shoe firms. Founded in 1906 to make arch supports, New Balance is known for its wide selection of shoe widths. Besides men's and women's shoes for running, cross-training, basketball, tennis, hiking, and golf, the company offers fitness apparel and kids' shoes and owns leather boot maker Dunham. Owner, chairman, and CEO Jim Davis bought New Balance on the day of the 1972 Boston Marathon.

EXECUTIVES

Chairman and CEO: James S. (Jim) Davis, age 60
President and COO: Jim Tompkins
President Emeritus: John E. Larson
CFO and EVP: John Gardner
EVP Administration: Anne Davis
EVP Manufacturing and Procurement: Herb Spivak
VP and Corporate Controller: John Withee
VP and Group Controller: Alan Rosen
VP Corporate Human Resources: Carol O'Donnell
VP Global Marketing: Paul Heffernan
VP International: Edward (Ed) Haddad
VP International, Pacific/Asia: Joseph (Joe) Preston
VP Manufacturing: John Wilson
VP Sales, US and Canada: Fran Allen

LOCATIONS

HQ: New Balance Athletic Shoe, Inc.
Brighton Landing, 20 Guest St., Boston, MA 02135
Phone: 617-783-4000 **Fax:** 617-787-9355
Web: www.newbalance.com

COMPETITORS

adidas-Salomon
ASICS
Brooks Sports
Converse
Fila USA
K-Swiss
Mizuno
NIKE
PUMA
Reebok
Roots
Saucony

HISTORICAL FINANCIALS

Company Type: Private

Income Statement
FYE: December 31

	REVENUE ($ mil.)	NET INCOME ($ mil.)	NET PROFIT MARGIN	EMPLOYEES
12/02	1,200	—	—	2,400
12/01	1,160	—	—	2,400
12/00	1,100	—	—	2,400
12/99	890	—	—	2,000
12/98	630	—	—	1,600
12/97	560	—	—	1,500
12/96	483	—	—	1,300
12/95	380	—	—	1,200
Annual Growth	17.9%	—	—	10.4%

Revenue History

New NGC

New NGC, Inc., doing business as National Gypsum Company, produces an array of wall supplies and is the second-largest gypsum wallboard manufacturer in the US, behind USG Corporation. The company sells wallboard under the Gold Bond and Durabase brand names. It also produces joint treatment compounds (ProForm), cement board (PermaBase), plaster, and framing systems and tests acoustical, fire, and structural properties of building materials. National Gypsum sells its products worldwide to the construction industry. Delcor Inc., a subsidiary of Golden Eagle Industries, owns the company.

Although National Gypsum never manufactured products that contained asbestos, the company has negotiated an agreement that will, upon federal approval, protect New NGC from any future asbestos liability claims related to its 1993 purchase of assets of Asbestos Claims Management Corporation (ACMC). (ACMC filed for Chapter 11 bankruptcy protection in 2002.)

New NGC will pay $347 million to the NGC Bodily Injury Trust for protection against all asbestos claims related to National Gypsum.

In 2003 president and CEO Thomas Nelson was named vice chairman of the policy advisory board for Harvard University's Joint Center for Housing Studies. Also that year *Occupational Hazards* magazine named National Gypsum as one of "America's Safest Companies."

EXECUTIVES

Chairman: C. D. (Dick) Spangler Jr.
President and CEO: Thomas C. Nelson
SVP, Business Development and Technology: Page Odom
SVP, Operations: Gerard (Jerry) Carroll
SVP, Sales and Marketing: Craig Weisbruch
VP and CFO: William D. (Bill) Parmelee
VP and General Counsel: Sam Schiffman
VP, Human Resources: Nick Rodono
Director, Communications: Nancy H. Spurlock
Director, Marketing: David Drummond
Auditors: PricewaterhouseCoopers LLP

LOCATIONS

HQ: New NGC, Inc.
2001 Rexford Rd., Charlotte, NC 28211
Phone: 704-365-7300   **Fax:** 800-329-6421
Web: www.national-gypsum.com

New NGC operates 31 plants, eight mines and quarries, four paper mills, and two research facilities in Canada and the US.

PRODUCTS/OPERATIONS

Selected Products and Brands
Ceiling systems (Gridstone, Seaspray, and High Strength)
Cement board (PermaBase)
Gypsum wallboard (Gold Bond and Durabase)
Joint compounds, spray textures, and tape
Manufactured housing products (wallboard, ceiling board, spray texture, and construction guides)
Plaster, plaster base, and finishes
Prefinished gypsum wallboard and panels (Durasan)
Shaftwall and area separation wall (H-stud and I-stud systems)
Wallboard and plaster base (Hi-Abuse and Hi-Impact)

COMPETITORS

Eagle Materials
Johns Manville
Lafarge North America
Temple-Inland
USG

HISTORICAL FINANCIALS

Company Type: Private

Income Statement
FYE: December 31

	ESTIMATED REVENUE ($ mil.)	NET INCOME ($ mil.)	NET PROFIT MARGIN	EMPLOYEES
12/03	1,400	—	—	2,700
12/02	1,400	—	—	2,700
12/01	1,300	—	—	2,600
12/00	1,510	—	—	2,650
12/99	1,410	—	—	2,600
Annual Growth	(0.2%)	—	—	0.9%

Revenue History

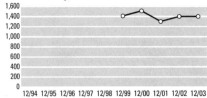

New United Motor Manufacturing

What do you get when a Japanese production process meets a California lifestyle? New United Motor Manufacturing, Inc. (NUMMI), a 50-50 joint venture between General Motors (GM) and Toyota. NUMMI makes Tacoma pickup trucks and Corolla sedans for Toyota. The Tacoma is made only at the NUMMI plant in Fremont, California. The company also makes GM's Pontiac division's Vibe sport wagon. NUMMI can produce 220,000 cars and 150,000 pickups a year. Together GM and Toyota are researching alternative-fuel vehicles. Since its formation in 1984, NUMMI has produced more than 5 million vehicles.

NUMMI began as an experiment to see if Japanese management techniques emphasizing team decision-making would work in the US. The experiment has been a success story. Toyota's strategy to build more vehicles in the markets it serves (rather than transport them) helps the company reduce costs. NUMMI's production methods are considered to be among the world's most efficient.

HISTORY

Rivals General Motors (GM) and Toyota applied the old adage, "If you can't beat 'em, join 'em," in forming their 50-50 joint venture New United Motor Manufacturing, Inc. (NUMMI). During the early 1980s GM was sagging in the small-car market, and Japan's Toyota wanted to build cars in the US to ease trade tension. GM head Roger Smith and Toyota chairman Eiji Toyoda met in 1982 to discuss ways to achieve their goals.

After a year of negotiations, the two companies announced their partnership at GM's plant (which GM had closed in 1982) in Fremont, California. Toyota put up $100 million, and GM provided the plant (valued at $89 million) and $11 million cash. The companies also raised $350 million to build a stamping plant.

To gain FTC approval, the companies agreed to limit the venture to 12 years (extended later), make no more than 250,000 cars a year for GM, and refrain from sharing strategic information. In 1984 the FTC approved the deal and NUMMI was born.

The Fremont plant had a reputation for poor labor relations, and Toyota originally refused to rehire any of the workers from the plant; after prolonged negotiations with the United Auto Workers (UAW), it agreed to hire 50% plus one of the former workers. From the outset NUMMI was different, with fewer management layers and a blurred distinction between blue- and white-collar workers.

NUMMI's first car, a Chevy Nova, rolled off the assembly line in late 1984. The company began producing the Corolla FX, a two-door version of the four-door Nova, in 1986. NUMMI earned kudos for high worker morale and productivity and was selected that year as a case study on positive labor-management relations for the International Labor Organization Conference.

Despite its success on some fronts, NUMMI's sales slid during the late 1980s. It had earned a reputation for high-quality cars, but it struggled with high overhead and weak Nova sales. In 1988 NUMMI halted Nova and Corolla FX production to build Geo Prizm and Corolla sedans.

By late 1989 NUMMI's production numbers had begun to rebound. In 1990 NUMMI began a major expansion as it geared up to build Toyota's half-ton pickup. Its first Toyota 4X2 pickup (the Toyota Hi-Lux) rolled off the assembly line in 1991, followed by the Toyota 4X4 pickup the next year.

In 1993 the FTC approved an indefinite extension of the original 12-year GM-Toyota agreement. Also that year NUMMI began building the Toyota Xtracab (an extended version of Toyota's pickup), and it began constructing a plastics plant to build bumper coverings for Prizms and Corollas. It also expanded the paint, body welding, and assembly plant facilities.

Although Toyota had produced half of its North America-bound pickups in Japan and half in the US for years, it shifted all compact truck production to the NUMMI plant with the 1995 launch of the Tacoma. NUMMI built its 3 millionth vehicle in 1997 and marked the event by donating three vehicles to charitable agencies in the Fremont area.

In 1998 Toyota introduced an updated Tacoma compact pickup, and GM changed the name of the Geo Prizm to the Chevrolet Prizm. The companies agreed in 1999 to a five-year partnership to develop and possibly produce alternative-fuel vehicles.

GM alluded to the possible discontinued production of the Prizm in 2000, and the last one left the NUMMI assembly line in December 2001. The Prizm was replaced with the Pontiac Vibe the following month.

EXECUTIVES

Chairman, President, and CEO: Yuki Azuma
VP, Human Resources and Legal, and Corporate Secretary: Patricia Salas Pineda
VP, Manufacturing Operations: Ernesto Gonzalez-Beltran
General Manager, Purchasing: Linda McColgan
Assistant Manager, Community Relations: Rhonda Rigenhagen

LOCATIONS

HQ: New United Motor Manufacturing, Inc.
45500 Fremont Blvd., Fremont, CA 94538
Phone: 510-498-5500 **Fax:** 510-770-4116
Web: www.nummi.com

PRODUCTS/OPERATIONS

Selected Models
Pontiac Vibe (sport wagon)
Toyota Corolla (sedan)
Toyota Tacoma (pickup)

COMPETITORS

DaimlerChrysler
Fiat
Ford
Fuji Heavy Industries
Honda
Isuzu
Kia Motors
Mack Trucks
Mazda
Nissan
Peugeot Motors of America, Inc.
Saab Automobile
Suzuki Motor
Volkswagen

New York City Health and Hospitals

New York City Health and Hospitals Corporation (HHC) takes care of the Big Apple. HHC has facilities in all five boroughs of New York City. As one of the largest municipal health service systems in the US, HHC operates a health care network consisting of 11 acute care hospitals (including Bellevue, the nation's oldest public hospital), community clinics, diagnostic and treatment centers, long-term care facilities, and a home health care agency. HHC also provides medical services to New York City's correctional facilities and operates MetroPlus, a health maintenance organization.

In recent years HHC has lost paying patients to newer, better-equipped facilities and is left caring for a deluge of medically indigent and Medicaid patients, who tend to be sicker than the general population since they wait longer to seek care.

To streamline, HHC has slashed jobs, worked to reduce the average length of stay of patients, and shuttered unnecessary facilities.

HISTORY

The City of New York in 1929 created a department to manage its hospitals for the poor. During the Depression, more than half of the city's residents were eligible for subsidized care, and its public hospitals operated at full capacity.

Four new hospitals opened in the 1950s, but the city was already having trouble maintaining existing facilities and attracting staff (young doctors preferred private, insurance-supported hospitals catering to the middle class.) Meanwhile, technological advances and increased demand for skilled nurses made hospitals more expensive to operate. The advent of Medicaid in 1965 was a boon for the system because it brought in federal money.

In 1969 the city created the New York City Health and Hospitals Corporation (HHC) to manage its public health care system — and, it was hoped, to distance it from the political arena. But HHC was still dependent on the city for funds, arousing criticism from those who had hoped for more autonomy. A 1973 state report claimed "the people of New York City are not materially better served by the Health and Hospitals Corporation than by its predecessor agencies."

City budget shortfalls in the mid-1970s led to cutbacks at HHC, including nearly 20% of staff. Later in the decade several hospitals closed and some services were discontinued. Ed Koch became mayor in 1978 and gained more control over HHC's operations. Struggles between his administration and the system led three HHC presidents to resign by 1981. That year Koch crony Stanley Brezenoff assumed the post and helped transform HHC into a city pseudo-department.

The early 1980s brought greater prosperity to the system. Reimbursement rates and collections procedures improved, allowing HHC to upgrade its record-keeping and its ambulatory and psychiatric care programs. In the late 1980s sharp increases in AIDS and crack addiction cases strained the system and a sluggish economy decreased city funding. Criticism mounted in the early 1990s, with allegations of wrongful deaths, dangerous facilities, and lack of Medicaid payment controls. HHC lost patients to managed care providers, and revenues plummeted. In 1995 a city panel recommended radically revamping the system.

Faced with declining revenues and criticism from Mayor Rudolph Giuliani that HHC was "a jobs program," the company began cutting jobs and consolidating facilities in 1996. Under Giuliani's direction, HHC made plans to sell its Coney Island, Elmhurst, and Queens hospital centers. In 1997 the New York State Supreme Court struck down Giuliani's privatization efforts, saying the city council had a right to review and approve each sale. In 1998 Giuliani continued to seek to restructure HHC, and the agency itself contended it was making progress toward its restructuring goals, which were aimed at giving HHC more autonomy as well as more fiscal responsibility. In anticipation of a budget shortfall that year, the system laid off some 900 support staff employees. In 1999 the state court of appeals ruled HHC could not legally lease or sell its hospitals.

In 2000 HHC launched an effort to improve its physical infrastructure by beginning the rebuilding and renovation of facilities in Brooklyn, Manhattan, and Queens. The organization also began converting to an electronic (and thus more efficient) clinical information system. In 2001 HHC forged ahead with further restructuring initiatives. It introduced the Open Access plan, a cost-cutting measure designed to expedite the processes involved in outpatient visits.

EXECUTIVES

President and CEO: Benjamin K. Chu, $250,000 pay
SVP, Central Brooklyn Family Health Network; Executive Director, Kings County Hospital Center: Jean G. Leon
SVP, Corporate Planning, Community Health, and Intergovernmental Relations: LaRay Brown
SVP, Finance: Marlene Zurack
SVP and General Counsel: Alan D. Aviles
SVP, Generations Plus Northern Manhattan Health Network; Executive Director, Lincoln Medical and Mental Health Center, and Metropolitan Hospital Center: Jose R. Sanchez
SVP, Medical and Professional Affairs: Van Dunn
SVP, North Bronx Healthcare Network; Executive Director, Jacobi Medical Center and North Central Bronx Hospital: Joseph S. Orlando
SVP, North Brooklyn Health Network; Executive Director, Woodhull Medical and Mental Health Center: Lynda D. Curtis
SVP, Operations: Frank J. Cirillo
SVP, Queens Health Network; Executive Director, Elmhurst Hospital Center: Pete Velez
SVP, South Manhattan Healthcare Network; Executive Director, Bellevue Hospital Center: Carlos Perez
SVP, South Brooklyn and Staten Island Health Network; Executive Director, Coney Island Hospital: William P. Walsh
Corporate Director, Communications and Marketing: Kate McGrath
Auditors: KPMG LLP

LOCATIONS

HQ: New York City Health and Hospitals Corporation
125 Worth St., Ste. 514, New York, NY 10013
Phone: 212-788-3321 **Fax:** 212-788-0040
Web: www.ci.nyc.ny.us/html/hhc

HHC Networks
Central Brooklyn Family Health Network
  Dr. Susan Smith McKinney Nursing and
    Rehabilitation Center
  East New York Diagnostic & Treatment Center
  Kings County Hospital Center
Generations Plus Northern Manhattan Health Network
  Harlem Hospital Center
  Lincoln Medical and Mental Health Center
  Metropolitan Hospital Center
  Morrisania Diagnostic & Treatment Center
  Renaissance Health Care Network Diagnostic &
    Treatment Center
  Segundo Ruiz Belvis Diagnostic & Treatment Center
North Bronx Healthcare Network
  Jacobi Medical Center
  North Central Bronx Hospital
North Brooklyn Health Network
  Cumberland Diagnostic & Treatment Center
  Woodhull Medical and Mental Health Center
Queens Health Network
  Elmhurst Hospital Center
  Queens Hospital Center
South Brooklyn and Staten Island Health Network
  Coney Island Hospital
  Sea View Hospital Rehabilitation Center and Home
South Manhattan Healthcare Network
  Bellevue Hospital Center
  Coler-Goldwater Specialty Care and Nursing Facility
  Gouverneur Healthcare Services

COMPETITORS

Catholic Healthcare System
Columbia University
Cornell University
Memorial Sloan-Kettering
Montefiore Medical
Mount Sinai NYU Health
North Shore-Long Island Jewish Health System
NYU
Saint Vincent Catholic Medical Centers

HISTORICAL FINANCIALS

Company Type: Government-owned

Income Statement
FYE: June 30

	REVENUE ($ mil.)	NET INCOME ($ mil.)	NET PROFIT MARGIN	EMPLOYEES
6/03	4,200	—	—	—
6/02	4,300	—	—	31,544
6/01	4,300	—	—	32,385
6/00	4,100	—	—	33,500
6/99	4,131	—	—	33,403
6/98	3,835	—	—	31,600
6/97	4,069	—	—	33,000
6/96	4,461	—	—	35,000
6/95	4,134	—	—	41,711
6/94	3,949	—	—	45,000
Annual Growth	0.7%	—	—	(4.3%)

Revenue History

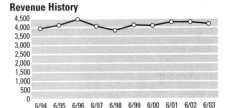

New York Life

New York Life Insurance has been in the Big Apple since it was just a tiny seed. The company (the top mutual life insurer in the US) is adding products but retaining its core business: life insurance and annuities. New York Life has added such products and services as mutual funds for individuals. It also offers its investment management services to institutional investors. Other lines of business include long-term care insurance and special group policies sold through AARP and other affinity groups or professional associations. The company, through New York Life International, is also reaching out geographically, targeting areas where the life insurance market is not yet mature.

After state legislators failed to approve its proposed mutual holding company structure, New York Life announced it would not follow its rivals in demutualizing for fear of being gobbled up in a merger.

The insurer will instead use its considerable war chest to further build its international operations (Asia is a major expansion target) and its investment management operations, which include New York Life Investment Management (mutual funds, group and individual retirement plans, college savings products), NYLIFE Securities (registered broker/dealer), and New York Life Trust Company, FSB (trust, investment management, custody, and administration services).

HISTORY

In 1841 actuary Pliny Freeman and 56 New York businessmen founded Nautilus Insurance Co., the third US policyholder-owned company. It began operating in 1845 and became New York Life in 1849.

By 1846 the company had the first life insurance agent west of the Mississippi River. Although the Civil War disrupted southern business, New York Life honored all its obligations and renewed lapsed policies when the war ended. By 1887 the company had developed its branch office system.

By the turn of the century, the company had established an agent compensation plan that featured a lifetime income after 20 years of service (discontinued 1991). New York Life moved into Europe in the late 1800s but withdrew after WWI.

In the early 1950s the company simplified insurance forms, slashed premiums, and updated mortality tables from the 1860s. In 1956 it became the first life insurer to use data-processing equipment on a large scale.

New York Life helped develop variable life insurance, which featured variable benefits and level premiums in the 1960s; it added variable annuities in 1968. Steady growth continued to the late 1970s, when high interest rates led to heavy policyholder borrowing. The outflow of money convinced New York Life to make its products more competitive as investments.

The company formed New York Life and Health Insurance Co. in 1982. It acquired MacKay-Shields Financial, which oversees its MainStay mutual funds, in 1984. The company's first pure investment product, a real estate limited partnership, debuted that year. (Investors sued New York Life when limited partnerships proved riskier than most insurance customers bargained for; in 1996 the company negotiated a plan to liquidate the partnerships and reimburse investors.)

Expansion continued in 1987 when New York Life bought a controlling interest in a third-party insurance plan administrator and group insurance programs. The company also acquired Sanus Corp. Health Systems.

New York Life formed an insurance joint venture in Indonesia in 1992; it also entered South Korea and Taiwan. The next year it bought Aetna UK's life insurance operations.

In 1994 New York Life grew its health care holdings, adding utilization review and physician practice management units. Allegations of churning (agents inducing customers to buy more expensive policies) led New York Life to overhaul its sales practices in 1994; it settled the resulting lawsuit for $300 million in 1995. Soon came claims that agents hadn't properly informed customers that some policies were vulnerable to interest-rate changes and that customers might be entitled to share in the settlement. Some agents lashed out, saying New York Life fired them so it wouldn't have to pay them retirement benefits.

As health care margins decreased and the insurance industry consolidated, New York Life in 1998 sold its health insurance operations and said it would demutualize — a plan ultimately foiled by the state legislature.

In 2000 the company bought two Mexican insurance firms, including the nation's #2 life insurer, Seguros Monterrey. It received Office of Thrift Supervision permission to open a bank, New York Life Trust Company. Also that year the company created a subsidiary to house its asset management businesses and entered the Indian market through its joint venture with Max India.

In 2002 New York Life entered into a joint life insurance venture with China's Haier Group.

EXECUTIVES

Chairman and CEO: Seymour (Sy) Sternberg, age 60
President: Frederick J. (Fred) Sievert
Vice Chairman; Chairman, New York Life International: Gary G. Benanav, age 58
EVP and Co-Head of Life and Annuity: Phillip J. (Phil) Hildebrand
EVP and Co-Head of Life and Annuity: Theodore A. (Ted) Mathas
EVP and CFO: Michael E. Sproule
EVP; Chairman and CEO, New York Life Investment Management: Gary E. Wendlandt
SVP and Treasurer: Jay S. Calhoun
SVP and CIO: Judith E. Campbell
SVP, Controller, and Chief Accounting Officer: John A. Cullen
SVP and General Counsel: Shelia K. Davidson
SVP: Gregory (Greg) Deavens
SVP, Human Resources: Leonard J. Elmer
SVP: Jonathan (JJ) Jaramillo
SVP and Chief of Staff: Sandra J. Kristoff
SVP, Northeastern Agencies: Mark Pfaff
SVP and Chief Investment Officer: Anne F. Pollack
SVP, Agency Department; President and CEO, NYLEX Benefits: Albert J. (Bud) Schiff
SVP and Chief Actuary: Joel M. Steinberg
SVP, Corporate Secretary, and Deputy General Counsel: Susan A. Thrope
SVP, General Auditor, and Chief Privacy Officer: Thomas J. Warga
Chief Tax Counsel: Michael (Mike) Oleske, age 52
Auditors: PricewaterhouseCoopers LLP

New York Power Authority

Question authority? Well, without question, authority for power lies in the Power Authority of the State of New York (commonly referred to as the New York Power Authority, or NYPA). The company generates and transmits more than 20% of New York's electricity, making it the largest state-owned public power provider in the US. It is also New York's only statewide electricity supplier. NYPA owns hydroelectric and fossil-fueled generating facilities that produce about 5,700 MW of electricity, and it operates more than 1,400 circuit-miles of transmission lines.

The authority sells power to government agencies, municipal systems, rural cooperatives, private companies, private utilities (for resale), and neighboring states. Its clients include some of the largest electricity users in the US, including the New York City government and the Metropolitan Transportation Authority. NYPA receives no state funds or tax credits. Instead, it finances new projects through bond sales.

Following its shift from a regulated monopoly to a competitor in an open power market, NYPA is aiming to grow by reducing the cost of the energy it provides and by developing electric transportation (such as electric cars) and other energy-efficiency projects, such as installing emergency power generators in metropolitan buildings. It is also working to improve the state's transmission grid and increase its generating capacity.

HISTORY

The Power Authority of the State of New York (aka New York Power Authority, or NYPA) was established in 1931 by Gov. Franklin Roosevelt to gain public control of New York's hydropower resources. The utility's major power plants came on line with the opening of the St. Lawrence-Franklin D. Roosevelt Power Project (1958) and the Niagara Power Project (1961). The Blenheim-Gilboa Pumped Storage Power Project opened in 1973.

In the mid-1970s NYPA shifted to nuclear power when it opened the James A. FitzPatrick Nuclear Power Plant (1975) and the Indian Point 3 Nuclear Power Plant (1976). The company then opened gas- and oil-powered plants: the Charles Poletti Power Project (1977) and the Richard M. Flynn Power Plant (1994).

In 1998 the authority allocated low-cost electricity to five companies that planned to invest $104 million in business expansions in western New York. The company suffered a loss in 1999 in part from reduced hydro generation and a drop in investment earnings. In 2000 NYPA sold its two nuclear plants (1,800 MW of capacity) to utility holding company Entergy for $967 million.

The company completed the installation of 11 gas-powered turbines at various locations in New York City and on Long Island in 2001; the program was initiated to prevent against expected energy shortages that summer, but it also helped maintain power in areas of the city during the September 11 terrorist attack.

EXECUTIVES

Chairman: Louis P. Ciminelli
Vice Chairman: Frank S. McCullough Jr.
President and CEO: Eugene W. Zeltmann
EVP, Secretary, and General Counsel: David E. Blabey
EVP Corporate Services and Administration: Vincent C. Vesce
EVP Power Generation: Robert A. Hiney
SVP and CFO: Joseph M. Del Sindaco
SVP Energy Services and Technology: Robert L. Tscherne
SVP Marketing, Economic Development, and Supply Planning: Louise M. Morman
SVP Public and Governmental Affairs: Peter A. Barden
SVP Transmission: H. Kenneth Haase
VP and Controller: Arnold M. Bellis
VP Energy Risk Assessment and Control and Chief Risk Officer: Thomas H. Warmath
VP and Chief Engineer: Charles I. Lipsky
CIO: Dennis Eccleston
VP Ethics and Regulatory Compliance: Anne Wagner-Findeisen
VP Finance: Donald A. Russak
VP Major Accounts Marketing and Economic Development: James H. Yates
Treasurer: Michael Brady
Deputy Secretary and Deputy General Counsel: Carmine J. Clement
Deputy Secretary: Angela D. Graves
Auditors: PricewaterhouseCoopers LLP

LOCATIONS

HQ: Power Authority of the State of New York
    123 Main St., White Plains, NY 10601
Phone: 914-681-6200   **Fax:** 914-681-6949
Web: www.nypa.gov

Selected Operations

Transmission Control Facility
    Frederick R. Clark Energy Center (Oneida County)
Fossil-Fueled Plants
    Charles Poletti Power Project (New York City)
    Richard M. Flynn Power Plant (Suffolk County)
    PowerNow! Turbines (11 units in New York City and Long Island)
Hydropower Plants
    Blenheim-Gilboa Pumped Storage Power Project (Schoharie County)
    Niagara Power Project (Niagara County)
    St. Lawrence-Franklin D. Roosevelt Power Project (St. Lawrence County)
Small Hydropower Plants
    Ashokan Project (Ulster County)
    Crescent Plant (Albany and Saratoga Counties)
    Gregory B. Jarvis Plant (Oneida County)
    Kensico Project (Westchester County)
    Vischer Ferry Plant (Saratoga and Schenectady counties)

PRODUCTS/OPERATIONS

2003 Sales

	$ mil.	% of total
Power sales	1,870	82
Wheeling charges	278	12
Transmission charges	144	6
Total	**2,292**	**100**

COMPETITORS

CH Energy
Con Edison
Dynegy
Enbridge
Energy East
Entergy
KeySpan
Rochester Gas and Electric
TransCanada

HISTORICAL FINANCIALS

Company Type: Government-owned

Income Statement
FYE: December 31

	REVENUE ($ mil.)	NET INCOME ($ mil.)	NET PROFIT MARGIN	EMPLOYEES
12/03	2,292	88	3.9%	—
12/02	2,060	84	4.1%	1,600
12/01	2,016	18	0.9%	1,600
12/00	2,034	170	8.3%	1,531
12/99	1,458	(233)	—	—
12/98	1,484	63	4.2%	—
12/97	1,481	106	7.1%	3,259
12/96	1,430	69	4.8%	3,200
12/95	1,413	—	—	3,300
12/94	1,460	—	—	3,500
Annual Growth	5.1%	3.7%	—	(9.3%)

2003 Year-End Financials
Debt ratio: 128.9%
Return on equity: 5.1%
Cash ($ mil.): 62
Current ratio: 1.37
Long-term debt ($ mil.): 2,264

Net Income History

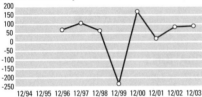

New York State Lottery

Winning the New York State Lottery could make you king of the hill, top of the heap. The New York State Lottery is one of the largest and oldest state lotteries in the US (only New Hampshire's lottery is older). It offers players both instant-win games, as well as the multimillion-dollar jackpots of its lotto games. In addition, the New York lottery operates Quick Draw, a keno-style game in which numbers are picked every five minutes. The lottery sells tickets through more than 15,000 retailers and some 14,000 online terminals (maintained by GTECH Holdings).

The New York State Lottery has raised more than $20 billion for state educational programs (which get 33% of sales) since its inception. In addition to education, proceeds from the lottery have helped pay for the construction of New York City Hall, as well as bridges and roads for the state. The lottery returns more than half the money it takes in as prizes; 2% of sales are used to cover administrative costs, while retailers get 6%.

New York's legislature had resisted approving a multistate game, but finally caved late in 2001 and authorized a bill allowing New Yorkers to buy Powerball tickets. The New York State Lottery joined up with the nine-state Big Game Group in 2002 to launch the Mega Millions game.

HISTORY

In the mid-1960s the New York state legislature succeeded in sending a lottery amendment to voters, and 60% of New Yorkers voted in favor of the amendment in 1966. Lottery sales began in 1967 with a raffle-style drawing game. In its first year of operation, the lottery contributed more than $26 million to the state's education fund.

New York introduced its first instant game in 1976, with sales topping $18 million the first week. The state debuted its six-of-six lotto game two years later. Sales were slow until 1981, when Louie "the Light Bulb" Eisenberg — the state's first lottery celebrity — won $5 million, the largest single-winner prize at that time.

GTECH Holdings won the contract to operate New York's lottery terminal sales in 1987. The Quick Pick option — through which a terminal chooses a player's numbers — was introduced in 1989, as was a new lotto game and the state's first online computer terminal game. Autoworker Antonio Bueti set a record for the largest individual prize, winning $35 million in 1990. A jackpot of $90 million was split among nine players in 1991.

Through the mid-1990s, however, lackluster lottery sales were blamed on the Persian Gulf War, the recession, and poor publicity. During 1993 and 1994 lottery management revamped the state's lottery infrastructure and redesigned some games. The investment paid off in October 1994 when lotto fever pushed a jackpot to $72.5 million. During the height of the frenzy, sales reached $46,000 a minute.

Quick Draw, which lets players choose numbers every five minutes, was added in 1995. Sales of the game topped $1 million on the second day, and soon it was grossing nearly $12 million a week. Real estate mogul Donald Trump unsuccessfully sued to stop Quick Draw, claiming that it was more addictive than (his) casinos and would encourage organized crime. That year the New York State Lottery became the first to reach $3 billion in sales in a single year.

In 1996 the state pulled its Quick Draw advertising after critics complained it encouraged compulsive gambling. Lottery officials replaced enticing ads with advertising stressing the lottery's benefits to state education. The lottery was the subject of a sting operation that year led by Governor George Pataki to crack down on lottery vendors selling tickets to minors. In 1997 the lottery spawned its own game show with the debut of *NY Wired*, a half-hour weekly program pitting vendor representatives against each other for cash prizes given to audience members and schools.

With sales slipping, the state left longtime ad partner DDB Needham Worldwide (now DDB Worldwide) in 1998 and signed a $28 million contract with Grey Advertising. Lottery director Jeff Perlee resigned the next year. He was replaced by Margaret DeFrancisco, who helped drum up sales with Millennium Millions, which paid out a record $100 million prize to Johnnie Ely, a cook from the South Bronx, on the eve of 2000. Two players shared a record $130 million jackpot later in the year.

After holding out for years, the New York legislature in late 2001 authorized a bill that would allow state residents to participate in the multi-state Powerball lottery. In 2002 the New York Lottery joined with the nine-state Big Game Group to launch the Mega Millions game, which replaced the Big Game established in 1996.

EXECUTIVES

Director: Nancy Palumbo
Deputy Director: Susan E. Miller
Director Financial Administration:
Gerald (Jerry) Woitkoski
Director Operations: Daniel J. (Dan) Codden
Director Marketing and Sales:
Cornelia H. (Connie) Laverty
Director Human Resources: Charles Titus
Auditors: KPMG LLP

LOCATIONS

HQ: New York State Lottery
1 Broadway Center, Schenectady, NY 12301
Phone: 518-388-3300 **Fax:** 518-388-3368
Web: www.nylottery.org

PRODUCTS/OPERATIONS

Selected Games

Numbers games
 New York Lotto
 Numbers
 Pick 10
 Quick Draw
 Take Five
 Win 4

Instant-win games
 Blackjack
 Cash Flurries
 Fortune Cookie
 Go for the Green
 Ho Ho Doubler
 Hot Shots
 Loose Change
 Lucky 7s
 Pot o' Gold
 Red Hot Hearts
 Take 5
 Top 10
 Win 4

COMPETITORS

Connecticut Lottery
Massachusetts State Lottery
Multi-State Lottery
New Hampshire Lottery
New Jersey Lottery
Pennsylvania Lottery
Vermont Lottery

HISTORICAL FINANCIALS

Company Type: Government-owned

Income Statement
FYE: March 31

	REVENUE ($ mil.)	NET INCOME ($ mil.)	NET PROFIT MARGIN	EMPLOYEES
3/04	5,848	1,955	33.4%	—
3/03	5,396	1,787	33.1%	—
3/02	5,000	—	—	—
3/01	4,185	—	—	350
3/00	3,674	—	—	350
3/99	3,831	—	—	345
3/98	4,185	—	—	350
3/97	4,136	—	—	340
3/96	3,752	—	—	310
3/95	3,028	—	—	239
Annual Growth	7.6%	5.1%	—	6.6%

Net Income History

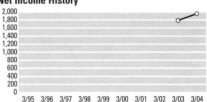

New York Stock Exchange

It's not called the Big Board for nothing: The New York Stock Exchange (NYSE) is one of the US's oldest and the world's largest stock market. The member-owned, not-for-profit group lists nearly 2,800 companies, including most of the largest US corporations; it also recruits foreign companies seeking the liquidity available only in US markets. To better compete with electronic exchanges — such as archrival Nasdaq — the NYSE in mid-2004 said it would break with its long tradition of operating as an auction exchange (where stock prices are set largely by a throng of traders on the exchange floor) and adopt a hybrid system that permits automated trading.

While the NYSE has always touted its people-driven exchange, it has faced some stiff competition, not only from Nasdaq, but also from foreign exchanges and electronic communications networks (ECNs) such as The Island (now owned by Instinet). Even though the NYSE has argued that ECN trades hamper investors' ability to see the big picture, the exchange accommodates brokers making large-block trades off the floor.

The NYSE also has begun offering more and more new products, including ETFs (exchange-traded funds), such as the Qs. It also launched Open Book, a product that offers traders real-time access to specialist firms' buy and sell order information.

The company owns two-thirds of Securities Industry Automation Corporation (SIAC), which provides communications, data processing, and clearing services primarily to the NYSE and to the American Stock Exchange, which owns the remainder of SIAC.

The exchange had also bandied about plans to go public as a for-profit company, but has shelved the idea.

NYSE chairman Richard Grasso, who earned a reputation as something of a hero in the months following the 2001 terrorist attacks on New York City, resigned under fire two years later when his $187 million pay package was revealed. During the furor over Grasso's pay, the SEC launched an investigation, and many officials — including the heads of top pension funds — called for his resignation. Grasso, who had started as a clerk at the exchange in the late 1960s and worked his way up through the ranks, is now being sued by New York Attorney General Eliot Spitzer, who wants Grasso to return several million dollars. Grasso is countersuing, alleging breach of contract and defamation.

Former Citigroup Chairman John Reed was named interim chairman and CEO following Grasso's departure; former Goldman Sachs president John Thain was subsequently tapped for the CEO role.

In November 2003 Reed outlined plans to improve the NYSE's governance (and public image) by jettisoning the exchange's 27-seat board in favor of a smaller one that would be much more independent. In February 2004, Thain — just weeks into his new job — said salaries for some of the NYSE's top executives would be cut by an average of 10% to 20%.

HISTORY

To prevent a monopoly on stock sales by securities auctioneers, 24 New York stockbrokers and businessmen agreed in 1792 to avoid "public auctions," to charge a commission on sales of stock, and to "give preference to each other" in their transactions. The Buttonwood Agreement, named after a tree on Wall Street under which they met, established the first organized stock market in New York. The Bank of New York was the first corporate stock traded under the Buttonwood tree.

Excluded traders continued dealing on the streets of New York until 1921 and later formed the American Stock Exchange.

In 1817 the brokers created the New York Stock & Exchange Board, a stock market with set meeting times. The NYS&EB began to require companies to qualify for trading (listing) by furnishing financial statements in 1853. Ten years later the board became the New York Stock Exchange.

Stock tickers began recording trades in 1867, and two years later the NYSE consolidated with competitors the Open Board of Brokers and the Government Bond Department. Despite repeated panics and recessions in the late 1800s, the stock market remained unregulated until well into the 20th century.

In the 1920s the NYSE installed a centralized stock quote service. Postwar euphoria brought a stock mania that fizzled in the crash of October 1929. The subsequent Depression brought investigation and federal regulation to the securities industry.

The NYSE registered as an exchange in 1934. In 1938 it reorganized, with a board of directors representing member firms, nonmember brokers, and the public; it also hired its first full-time president, member William McChesney Martin. As a self-regulating body, the NYSE policed the activities of its members.

The NYSE began electronic trading in the 1960s; in 1968 it broke 1929's one-day record for trading volume (16 million shares). It became a not-for-profit corporation in 1971.

Despite upgrades, technology was at least partly to blame for the crash of 1987: A cascade of large sales triggered by computer programs fueled the market's fall. NYSE's income suffered, leading to a $3 million loss in 1990.

In 1995 Richard Grasso became the first NYSE staff employee named chairman. The NYSE followed the other US stock markets in 1997 by switching trade increments from one-eighth point to one-sixteenth point (known as a "teenie" by arbitrageurs). New circuit-breaker rules halted trading on October 27 when the Dow Jones Industrial Average dropped 550 points in a day (the NYSE increased the trigger to 1,050 points in 1999).

The NYSE used a veiled threat to move to New Jersey to win itself the promise of some growing space. In 1999 the exchange named Karen Nelson Hackett as its first woman governor.

The Big Board in 2000 announced plans to go public, but the move stalled, then died altogether. It also extended its official pricing until 6:30 p.m. (Eastern). In the wake of the terrorism attacks that shook Wall Street and the nation, the NYSE and Nasdaq in 2001 began discussing a disaster plan that would see the two cooperating should a future incident cripple either market. Also that year the NYSE moved entirely to decimal pricing in accordance with SEC mandates.

EXECUTIVES

Chairman: John S. Reed, age 65
CEO: John A. Thain, age 48
President, and Co-COO: Robert G. (Bob) Britz, age 53, $1,275,000 pay
President, and Co-COO: Catherine R. Kinney, age 52, $1,275,000 pay
EVP and CFO: Amy S. Butte, age 36
CTO: Roger Burkhardt, age 43
Chief Regulatory Officer: Richard G. (Rick) Ketchum, age 53
Chief of Staff, Office of the CEO: David L. Shuler, age 41
EVP, Regulation: Edward A. Kwalwasser, age 63
EVP and General Counsel: Richard P. (Rich) Bernard, age 53, $1,050,000 pay
EVP, Corporate Listings and Compliance: Noreen M. Culhane
EVP, Enforcement: Susan L. Merrill, age 47
EVP, Communications and Government Relations: Margaret Tutwiler
EVP, Member Firm Regulation: Grace B. Vogel, age 48
SVP, Communications: Richard C. (Rich) Adamonis, age 48
SVP, Floor Operations: Anne E. Allen
SVP and Chief Economist: Paul B. Bennett
SVP, Human Resources: Dale B. Bernstein, age 49
SVP and Associate General Counsel: James F. Duffy, age 54
SVP and Controller: Michael (Mike) Ferraro
Corporate Secretary: Darla C. Stuckey, age 44
Auditors: PricewaterhouseCoopers LLP

LOCATIONS

HQ: New York Stock Exchange, Inc.
11 Wall St., New York, NY 10005
Phone: 212-656-3000   **Fax:** 212-656-2126
Web: www.nyse.com

PRODUCTS/OPERATIONS

2003 Sales

	$ mil.	% of total
Listing fees	294.6	27
Data processing fees	224.8	21
Market information fees	172.4	16
Trading fees	157.2	15
Regulatory fees	113.5	11
Facility & equipment fees	60.5	5
Membership fees	10.9	1
Investment and other income	40.2	4
Total	**1,074.1**	**100**

COMPETITORS

AMEX
Archipelago
CBOE
Chicago Mercantile Exchange
Deutsche Börse
E*TRADE Financial
Instinet
Investment Technology
Island ECN
Knight Trading
London Stock Exchange
Nasdaq Stock Market
NYFIX
TRADEBOOK

HISTORICAL FINANCIALS

Company Type: Not-for-profit

Income Statement
FYE: December 31

	REVENUE ($ mil.)	NET INCOME ($ mil.)	NET PROFIT MARGIN	EMPLOYEES
12/03	1,074	50	4.6%	1,500
12/02	1,066	28	2.6%	1,500
12/01	884	32	3.6%	1,500
12/00	815	73	8.9%	1,500
12/99	736	75	10.2%	1,500
12/98	729	101	13.9%	1,500
12/97	639	86	13.5%	1,475
12/96	562	74	13.3%	1,475
12/95	501	57	11.3%	1,450
12/94	452	44	9.7%	1,450
Annual Growth	10.1%	1.3%	—	0.4%

2003 Year-End Financials

Debt ratio: 39.7%
Return on equity: 5.4%
Cash ($ mil.): 11
Current ratio: 2.94
Long-term debt ($ mil.): 378

Net Income History

New York University

Higher education is at the core of this Big Apple institution. The setting and heritage of New York University (NYU) have helped make it one of the nation's most popular educational institutions. With more than 50,000 students attending its 14 schools and colleges, NYU is among the largest private schools in the US. It is well regarded for its arts and humanities studies, and its law school and Leonard N. Stern School of Business are among the best in the country. In addition to a Manhattan campus, NYU has branch campuses in Westchester and Rockland counties. The school was started in 1831. Its alumni include Federal Reserve Chairman Alan Greenspan and film producer Ismail Merchant (*The Remains of the Day*).

With New York City experiencing a renaissance, NYU has become one of the more popular — and picky — schools, with more than 30,000 applicants for its 4,000 freshman seats. (Undergraduate tuition runs about $25,500 per year.) Its stature and location have also helped it attract the largest number of international students of any college in the US. To continue attracting students, NYU has also spent lavishly on facilities and top-notch faculty rather than increasing the size of its endowment (which now stands at about $1 billion).

EXECUTIVES

Chairman Board of Trustees: Martin Lipton
Vice Chairman Board of Trustees: Larry A. Silverstein, age 71
President: John E. Sexton, age 58
Provost: David W. McLaughlin
EVP: Jacob L. (Jack) Lew
SVP, General Counsel, and Secretary: S. Andrew Schaffer
SVP Development and Alumni Relations: Debra A. LaMorte
SVP Finance and Budget: Jeannemarie (Jeanne) Smith
SVP Health: Robert Berne
SVP University Relations and Public Affairs: Lynne P. Brown
SVP Operations and Administration: Cheryl Mills
VP Public Affairs: John Beckman
VP Public Resource Administration and Development: Richard N. Bing
VP Student Affairs: Marc Wais
Vice Provost Faculty Affairs: Sharon L. Weinberg
Vice Provost University Life and Interdisciplinary Initiatives: Linda G. Mills
Associate Provost and Chief Information Technology Officer: Marilyn McMillan
Auditors: KPMG LLP

LOCATIONS

HQ: New York University
70 Washington Sq. South, New York, NY 10012
Phone: 212-998-1212 **Fax:** 212-995-4040
Web: www.nyu.edu

PRODUCTS/OPERATIONS

Selected Schools and Colleges

College of Arts and Science (founded 1832)
College of Dentistry David B. Kriser Dental Center (1865)
Gallatin School of Individualized Study (1972)
Graduate School of Arts and Science (1886)
Leonard N. Stern School of Business (1900)
Robert F. Wagner Graduate School of Public Service (1938)
School of Continuing and Professional Studies (1934)
School of Law (1835)
School of Medicine (1841)
Shirley M. Ehrenkranz School of Social Work (1960)
Tisch School of the Arts (1965)

HISTORICAL FINANCIALS

Company Type: School

Income Statement
FYE: August 31

	REVENUE ($ mil.)	NET INCOME ($ mil.)	NET PROFIT MARGIN	EMPLOYEES
8/03	2,005	—	—	15,010
8/02	1,866	—	—	10,136
8/01	1,692	—	—	13,000
8/00	1,546	—	—	13,000
8/99	1,410	—	—	13,000
8/98	1,296	—	—	12,790
8/97	1,771	—	—	12,937
8/96	1,669	—	—	15,000
8/95	1,524	—	—	15,400
8/94	1,409	—	—	15,300
Annual Growth	4.0%	—	—	(0.2%)

Revenue History

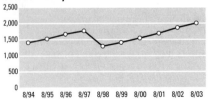

Newark Group

The Newark Group is proof that one man's trash is another man's treasure. The company, founded in 1912, is a major producer of paper products from recycled materials. Its recycled fibers division operates paper mills across the US and converts the 2.5 million tons of wastepaper it collects annually into several grades of paper and fiber products, including envelopes, corrugated cardboard, and newspaper. The paperboard division produces 1.3 million tons of paperboard per year from its 11 US mill sites. Recycled paperboard ends up in such products as books, puzzles, gameboards, and packaging. Brands include BreezeBoard (100% recycled paperboard), NewKote (boxboard), and Stress Relief (separator stock).

EXECUTIVES

Chairman: Fred G. von Zuben
Vice Chairman: Edward K. Mullen
President and CEO: Robert H. Mullen
VP and CFO: Joseph E. Byrne
VP and Controller: Lynn M. Herro
VP and General Counsel: David Ascher
VP, Human Resources: Carl R. Crook
Auditors: Deloitte & Touche LLP

LOCATIONS

HQ: The Newark Group, Inc.
20 Jackson Dr., Cranford, NJ 07016
Phone: 908-276-4000 **Fax:** 908-276-2888
Web: www.newarkgroup.com

The Newark Group operates plants in Canada, France, Spain, and the US. The group sells its products in these countries as well as the Pacific Rim region.

PRODUCTS/OPERATIONS

Selected Products

Recycled Fibers
  Corrugated products
  Envelopes
  Newspapers
  Printing grades
  Roll stock
Recycled Paperboard
  Boxboard
  Clay-coated folding board
  Separator stock
  Tube and core grades

Selected Operations

BCI Book Covers
Newark Europe
Newark Group International
Newark Paperboard Products
Paperboard Mill Division
Recycled Fibers Division

COMPETITORS

Caraustar
Georgia-Pacific Corporation
Green Bay Packaging
International Paper
Oji Paper
Parsons & Whittemore
Rock-Tenn
Smurfit-Stone Container
Sonoco Products
Southern Container
Stora Enso North America
Unipapel
Weyerhaeuser

HISTORICAL FINANCIALS
Company Type: Private

Income Statement
FYE: April 30

	REVENUE ($ mil.)	NET INCOME ($ mil.)	NET PROFIT MARGIN	EMPLOYEES
4/04	788	—	—	3,358
4/03	798	—	—	3,500
4/02	800	—	—	3,700
4/01	883	—	—	4,150
4/00	864	—	—	4,500
4/99	800	—	—	3,900
4/98	715	—	—	3,200
4/97	690	—	—	3,000
4/96	700	—	—	3,000
4/95	700	—	—	2,700
Annual Growth	1.3%	—	—	2.5%

Revenue History

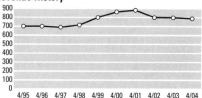

NewYork-Presbyterian Healthcare

NewYork-Presbyterian Healthcare System serves New York City, as well as several counties in New York, Connecticut, and New Jersey. The system, which has nearly 14,200 licensed beds, includes more than 30 hospitals; NewYork-Presbyterian Hospital is the flagship facility. All the hospitals are affiliated with either Columbia University's College of Physicians and Surgeons or Cornell University's Weill Medical College. NewYork-Presbyterian Healthcare System also operates about a dozen nursing homes, health care clinics, and rehabilitation centers.

EXECUTIVES
President and CEO: Herbert Pardes, age 70
SVP and COO: Arthur A. Klein
SVP, CFO, and Treasurer: Phyllis R. F. Lantos
SVP and CIO: Aurelia G. Boyer
VP, Operations: David Alge
VP and Chief Administrative Officer: Laurence J. Berger
VP, Medical Affairs: Eliot J. Lazar
Associate Dean and Director, Office of Affiliations, Weill Cornell Medical College: Oliver T. Fein
System Affairs, Columbia University College of Physicians & Surgeons: Joseph Tenenbaum
Auditors: Ernst & Young LLP

LOCATIONS
HQ: NewYork-Presbyterian Healthcare System
525 E. 68th St., New York, NY 10021
Phone: 212-305-2500 **Fax:** 212-746-8235
Web: www.nypsystem.org

PRODUCTS/OPERATIONS
Facilities
Hospitals
  NewYork-Presbyterian Hospital
  Bassett Healthcare
  The Brooklyn Hospital Center
  Holy Name Hospital
  Hospital for Special Surgery
  Lawrence Hospital Center
  New Milford Hospital
  New York Community Hospital
  New York Hospital Queens
  New York Methodist Hospital
  New York United Hospital Medical Center
  New York Westchester Square Medical Center
  Northern Westchester Hospital
  Nyack Hospital
  Orange Regional Medical Center
  Palisades Medical Center
  The Rogosin Institute
  St. Barnabas Hospital - The Bronx
  St. Luke's Cornwall Hospital
  St. Vincent's Medical Center - Bridgeport
  South Nassau Communities Hospital
  Stamford Health System
  The Valley Hospital
  White Plains Hospital Center
  Winthrop-University Hospital
  Wyckoff Heights Medical Center
Long-Term Care Facilities
  Amsterdam Nursing Home
  Fort Tryon Center for Rehabilitation and Nursing
  Frankin Center for Rehabilitation and Nursing
  Friedwald Center for Rehabilitation and Nursing
  The Harborage at Palisades Medical Center
  Manhattanville Health Care Center
  Menorah Home and Hospital
  New York United Hospital Medical Center Skilled Nursing Pavilion
  St. Barnabas Nursing Home
  St. Mary's Hospital for Children - Queens
  Sea Crest Health Care Center
  Shore View Nursing Home
  The Silvercrest Center for Nursing and Rehabilitation
  Tandet Center for Continuing Care
Other Facilities
  The Burke Rehabilitation Hospital
  Community Healthcare Network
  Gracie Square Hospital
  Helen Hayes Hospital
  New York College of Podiatric Medicine & Foot Clinics of New York

HISTORICAL FINANCIALS
Company Type: Not-for-profit

Income Statement
FYE: December 31

	REVENUE ($ mil.)	NET INCOME ($ mil.)	NET PROFIT MARGIN	EMPLOYEES
12/02	6,580	—	—	53,268

NextiraOne

A next step toward convergence, NextiraOne provides voice and data systems integration, network infrastructure assessment and outsourcing, and call center applications. The company also offers consulting services focusing on technology, business protection, and education advisory services. NextiraOne operates a global network and teams up with such technology partners as Nortel Networks, Cisco Systems, and Alcatel to serve its more than 400,000 clients. The company is owned by Platinum Equity Holdings, which formed NextiraOne in 2001 by combining a group of companies that included the network services unit of Williams Communications Group (now WilTel) and assets from Alcatel.

EXECUTIVES
President and CEO: Michael S. (Mike) Ruley, age 43
EVP and CFO: Robert (Bob) Buhay
EVP, CTO, and Chief Marketing Officer: Chuck Daniels
EVP, Human Resources, and General Counsel: Ted O'Neal
SVP, Business Development and Strategy: Michael Mecham
SVP, Service Operations: Charles Copeland Jr.
VP and CIO: Loren Tobey
Manager, Corporate Communications: Kathy Bradley

LOCATIONS
HQ: NextiraOne, LLC
2800 Post Oak Blvd., Ste 200, Houston, TX 77056
Phone: 713-307-4000 **Fax:** 713-307-4914
Web: www.nextiraone.com

NextiraOne has operations in Houston and Paris.

PRODUCTS/OPERATIONS
Selected Services
Alarm monitoring and notification
Configuration management
Convergence readiness assessment
Data installation
Data network design
LifeCycle services (planning, design, implementation, management, and support)
Network discovery and documentation
Network performance baseline
PBX traffic and security assessment and analysis
Staging and configuration
Strategic consulting
Systems integration
Voice network design

COMPETITORS
Accenture	Greenwich Technology Partners
AT&T	
Avaya	HP Technology Solutions Group
CIBER	
Computer Sciences	IBM
Convergys	Keane
Deloitte Consulting	Perot Systems
Deutsche Telekom	SBC Communications
DiData	Sprint
EDS	Verizon

HISTORICAL FINANCIALS
Company Type: Private

Income Statement
FYE: December 31

	REVENUE ($ mil.)	NET INCOME ($ mil.)	NET PROFIT MARGIN	EMPLOYEES
12/03	2,000	—	—	9,000
12/02	2,500	—	—	13,000
12/01	1,000	—	—	6,500
Annual Growth	41.4%	—	—	17.7%

Revenue History

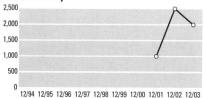

Nikken

Nikken Global has pull. The company buys and sells magnetic therapeutic devices through its global distribution network. Nikken's independent distributors sell its magnetic wellness products (pillows, sleep masks, support wraps, shoe inserts, jewelry, blankets), as well as supplements and skin care products. It also offers pet products, such as blankets and vitamins. The company operates in more than 30 countries in the Asia/Pacific region, Europe, and North America. Nikken Global is owned by Isamu Masuda, who founded the company in Japan in 1975.

EXECUTIVES
Chairman and CEO: Toshizo (Tom) Watanabe
President and COO: Kendall Cho
VP Sales, Nikken North America: Eric Marchant
World Ambassador: Larry Proffit
Managing Director, Nikken UK: Mark Baker
Operations Director, Nikken UK: Anthony Peter Chaplin
Human Resources Manager: Rick Knudson
Accountant, Nikken UK: Ryutaro Oishi

LOCATIONS
HQ: Nikken Global Inc.
52 Discovery Rd., Irvine, CA 92618
Phone: 949-789-2000 **Fax:** 800-669-8856
Web: www.nikken.com

PRODUCTS/OPERATIONS
Selected Products
Magnetic
  Bio-Directed Pet Canine Complete
  Bio-Directed Pet Feline Complete
  Elastomag Headband
  Elastomag Shoulder Wrap
  Intelli-Rest Pillow
  Jewelry
  Kenko Dream Deluxe Mattress
  Kenko Pet Pad
  Kenko Sleep Mask
  KenkoPillow
  Kenkoseat Plus (seat pad)
  KenkoTherm Comforter
  Magsteps (insoles)
  Magstrides (insoles)
  PiMag Water System
  Solitens (TENS - Transcutaneous Electrode Nerve Stimulator)
  ThermoWear Clothing
  Ultra Kenkopad (mattress pad)
Skin Care
  Bio-Directed CM Complex Skin Cream
  Swiss Soflöwer Skin Care products
  ThalassoKea Skin Therapy

COMPETITORS
Amway
Biomagnetics
Magnetherapy
Nautilus Group
Shaklee

HISTORICAL FINANCIALS
Company Type: Private

Income Statement				FYE: December 31
	ESTIMATED REVENUE ($ mil.)	NET INCOME ($ mil.)	NET PROFIT MARGIN	EMPLOYEES
12/03	1,500	—	—	—
12/02	1,500	—	—	—
12/01	1,500	—	—	—
12/00	1,500	—	—	—
12/99	1,500	—	—	—
12/98	1,500	—	—	250
12/97	1,500	—	—	171
Annual Growth	0.0%	—	—	46.2%

Revenue History

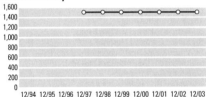

Nortek

Nortek Holdings, parent of Nortek, Inc., and other subsidiaries, makes and distributes building, remodeling, and indoor environmental control products for the residential and commercial construction, do-it-yourself, remodeling, and renovation markets. Products include range hoods and other spot ventilation products, heating and air-conditioning systems, indoor air quality systems, and specialty electronic products. It sells residential HVAC products under such brands as Frigidaire and Tappan. Nortek sold its Hoover Treated Wood Products and Ply Gem Industries (windows, doors, and siding) subsidiaries. Thomas H. Lee Partners, in partnership with company management, agreed in 2004 to acquire Nortek Holdings.

Nortek, Inc., was reorganized as holding company Nortek Holdings in 2002 in order for it to be acquired. Kelso & Company and certain members of Nortek Holdings' management, including chairman and CEO Richard Bready, completed the acquisition in January 2003. Richard Bready's equity interest in the company was reduced from about 35% to 16%. The next year, Nortek Holdings signed an agreement to be purchased by Thomas H. Lee Partners, in partnership with Nortek's management.

Nortek began the search for a buyer for its Ply Gem Industries, Inc. (windows, doors, and vinyl sidings) subsidiary by hiring UBS Securities LLC and Daroth Capital Advisors LLC as its scouts. In February 2004 the company sold the unit for about $560 million to investment vehicles associated with Caxton-Iseman Capital, Inc.

EXECUTIVES
Chairman, President, and CEO: Richard L. Bready, age 58
VP and CFO: Almon C. Hall III
VP, General Counsel, and Secretary: Kevin W. Donnelly
VP and Treasurer: Edward J. Cooney
Director, Human Resources: Jane White
Auditors: Ernst & Young LLP

LOCATIONS
HQ: Nortek Holdings, Inc.
50 Kennedy Plaza, Providence, RI 02903
Phone: 401-751-1600 **Fax:** 401-751-4610
Web: www.nortek-inc.com

Nortek has manufacturing operations in Canada, China, France, Italy, and the US.

PRODUCTS/OPERATIONS
Selected Products and Brands
Exterior Residential Products
  Air conditioners, heat pumps, gas/electric units (Nordyne — Frigidaire, Gibson, Kelvinator, Philco, Tappan)
  Residential gate and door operating systems (OSCO — Operator Specialty Company)
Interior Residential Products
  Cooking ranges (La Cornue, France)
  Indoor-air quality systems (Venmar Ventilation, Canada)
  Range hoods, bath fans, medicine cabinets, door chimes, central vacuum systems, and intercoms (Aubrey and Jensen divisions of the Broan-NuTone Group)
  Wireless security and remote-control products (Linear)
Light Commercial Products
  Access control (Linear)
  Air conditioners, heat pumps, gas/electric units (Nordyne — Frigidaire, Gibson, Kelvinator, Philco, Tappan)
  Exhaust fans, access doors, mailboxes, key keepers, collection boxes, and directories (Broan-NuTone)
  Indoor air quality systems and heat and energy recovery systems (Venmar CES, Canada)
  Residential gate and door operating systems (OSCO — Operator Specialty Company)
  Self-contained V-Cube floor-by-floor units and water source heat pumps (Mammoth)
Commercial Products
  Custom designed commercial HVAC systems and components (Eaton-Williams, UK)

COMPETITORS
AAON
American Standard
Andersen Corporation
Associated Materials
Black & Decker
Bocenor
Carrier
GE Security
Goodman Manufacturing
Groupe Lapeyre
JELD-WEN
Lennox
Masco
Masonite International
MasterBrand Cabinets
Mohawk Industries
NCI Building Systems
Novar
Owens Corning
Pella
Royal Group Technologies
Simpson Manufacturing
Stanley Works
ThermoView Industries
York International

HISTORICAL FINANCIALS

Company Type: Private

Income Statement
FYE: December 31

	REVENUE ($ mil.)	NET INCOME ($ mil.)	NET PROFIT MARGIN	EMPLOYEES
12/03	1,515	12	0.8%	4,139
12/02	1,888	63	3.3%	9,750
12/01	1,856	8	0.4%	9,900
12/00	2,195	42	1.9%	12,200
12/99	1,993	49	2.5%	12,100
12/98	1,738	35	2.0%	9,640
12/97	1,134	21	1.9%	9,262
12/96	970	22	2.3%	6,497
12/95	776	15	1.9%	6,423
12/94	737	18	2.4%	5,317
Annual Growth	8.3%	(4.1%)	—	(2.7%)

2003 Year-End Financials
Debt ratio: 661.6%
Return on equity: 4.8%
Cash ($ mil.): 194
Current ratio: 2.65
Long-term debt ($ mil.): 1,325

Net Income History

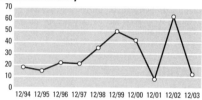

North Carolina Electric

It's a cooperative effort: North Carolina Electric Membership (NCEMC) generates and transmits electricity to 26 of 27 of the state's electric cooperatives. The co-op owns two peaking generators (30 MW of capacity) and a 28% stake in the Catawba Nuclear Station (640 MW) in South Carolina. It also buys power from Progress Energy, American Electric Power, and other for-profit utilities. NCEMC's member cooperatives serve more than 800,000 businesses and homes (or about 2.4 million people) in North Carolina. The wholesale co-op also operates an energy operations center and offers training programs, engineering and construction management, and power supply planning to all 27 cooperatives.

EXECUTIVES
President of the Board of Directors: Curtis Wynn
VP of the Board: J. Ronald McElheney
EVP and CEO: Charles W. (Chuck) Terrill
COO and General Counsel: Robert B. Schwentker
SVP and COO, Strategic Services: Richard K. Thomas
SVP and COO, Material Services Division: Lewis Hobson
SVP Competitive Strategies: Carolyn Watts
SVP Corporate Relations: Nelle P. Hotchkiss
SVP Power Supply: David L. Beam
VP Finance: Lark S. James
VP Project Management: Terrence W. Ryan
Secretary and Treasurer: Buddy G. Creed
Director Corporate Communications: Jane Pritchard
Auditors: Grant Thornton LLP

LOCATIONS
HQ: North Carolina Electric Membership Corporation
3400 Sumner Blvd., Raleigh, NC 27616
Phone: 919-872-0800 **Fax:** 919-878-3970
Web: www.ncemcs.com

PRODUCTS/OPERATIONS

North Carolina Cooperatives
Albemarle Electric Membership Corporation
Blue Ridge Electric Membership Corporation
Brunswick Electric Membership Corporation
Cape Hatteras Electric Cooperative
Carteret-Craven Electric Cooperative
Central Electric Membership Corporation
Edgecombe-Martin County Electric Membership Corporation
EnergyUnited
Four County Electric Membership Corporation
French Broad Electric Membership Corporation
Halifax Electric Membership Corporation
Harkers Island Electric Membership Corporation
Haywood Electric Membership Corporation
Jones-Onslow Electric Membership Corporation
Lumbee River Electric Membership Corporation
Pee Dee Electric Membership Corporation
Piedmont Electric Membership Corporation
Pitt & Greene Electric Membership Corporation
Randolph Electric Membership Corporation
Roanoke Electric Cooperative
Rutherford Electric Membership Corporation
South River Electric Membership Corporation
Surry-Yadkin Electric Membership Corporation
Tideland Electric Membership Corporation
Tri-County Electric Membership Corporation
Union Power Cooperative
Wake Electric Membership Corporation

COMPETITORS
American Electric Power
Dominion Resources
Duke Energy
MEAG Power
Progress Energy
Santee Cooper
SCANA
TVA

HISTORICAL FINANCIALS

Company Type: Cooperative

Income Statement
FYE: December 31

	REVENUE ($ mil.)	NET INCOME ($ mil.)	NET PROFIT MARGIN	EMPLOYEES
12/03	773	—	—	148
12/02	750	—	—	148
12/01	660	—	—	146
12/00	665	—	—	151
12/99	636	—	—	150
12/98	645	—	—	149
12/97	630	—	—	150
12/96	650	—	—	150
12/95	711	—	—	150
Annual Growth	1.0%	—	—	(0.2%)

Revenue History

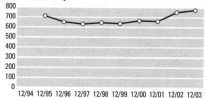

North Pacific Group

Paneling, poles, pilings, pipes and all, North Pacific Group (NOR PAC) is building on the construction industry. The company is one of North America's largest wholesale distributors of building materials. Employee-owned since the 1986 retirement of its founder, Doug David, NOR PAC distributes wood, steel, agricultural, and food products. Wood products, which make up the majority of its business, include lumber, millwork, poles, and logs. NOR PAC sells its products to furniture makers, retailers, and metal fabricators. Its more than 20 subsidiaries and divisions include Saxonville USA, Landmark Building Products, and Cascade Imperial Mills. David founded NOR PAC in 1948.

EXECUTIVES
Chairman: Thomas J. Tomjack
President, CEO, and COO: Jay A. Ross
SVP, Human Resources: Maureen Haggarty
VP, Credit: Larry Carr
COO, Distribution: David Hughes
President, Schultz, Snyder & Steele: Tom LeVere
President, Southern Business Unit: Frank Johnston
EVP, Burns Lumber: John Stembridge
EVP, Hardwood Business Unit: Jack Clark
SVP, Industrial Division: Tom Reynolds
CFO and Treasurer: Christopher D. Cassard
Corporate Secretary: Tacy Lind
Corporate Controller: Pat Norquist
Director, Internal Audit: Kim Johnsen
Auditors: KPMG LLP

LOCATIONS
HQ: North Pacific Group, Inc.
815 NE Davis St., Portland, OR 97232
Phone: 503-231-1166 **Fax:** 503-238-2641
Web: www.north-pacific.com

PRODUCTS/OPERATIONS

Selected Subsidiaries
Allen Timber Co. (wholesales softwoods and hardwoods)
Avalon Specialty Products (wholesales natural and organic food ingredients)
Burns Lumber Company, Inc. (wholesales forest products)
Cascade Imperial Mills, Ltd. (wholesales Canadian wood products)
Castle Pacific Sacramento, Inc. (wholesales hardwood lumber and plywood)
Landmark Building Products, Inc. (sales of forest products and building materials)
Tri-State Lamination (sales of laminated products)
Norte Pacifico de Durango (sales of hardwood products)
North Pacific Composites (sales of fiberglass poles)
Saxonville USA (general partnership that distributes panel products in the northeast US)
Schultz, Snyder & Steele Lumber Company, Inc. (distributes building materials in Michigan, Ohio, and Indiana)

COMPETITORS
ABC Supply
Boise Cascade
Bradco Supply
Georgia-Pacific Corporation
Guardian Building Products
Huttig Building Products
Louisiana-Pacific
MAXXAM
PrimeSource Building
Sierra Pacific Industries
Simpson Investment
Temple-Inland
Weyerhaeuser

Northwestern Mutual

HISTORICAL FINANCIALS
Company Type: Private

Income Statement
FYE: December 31

	REVENUE ($ mil.)	NET INCOME ($ mil.)	NET PROFIT MARGIN	EMPLOYEES
12/02	1,140	—	—	870
12/01	1,100	—	—	850
12/00	1,200	—	—	840
12/99	1,128	—	—	746
12/98	970	—	—	850
12/97	1,126	—	—	860
12/96	1,027	—	—	840
12/95	1,012	—	—	600
12/94	948	—	—	560
12/93	840	—	—	465
Annual Growth	3.5%	—	—	7.2%

Revenue History

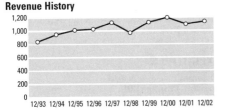

Making sure it's not all quiet on the Northwestern front, Northwestern Mutual's 7,900 agents (meticulously recruited and trained) sell a lineup of life and health insurance and retirement products, including fixed and variable annuities and mutual funds to a clientele of small businesses and prosperous individuals. Other lines of business include institutional asset manager Frank Russell Company, known for the Russell 2000 stock index, and trust services subsidiary Northwestern Mutual Trust. The company in 2004 completed a series of transactions that returned ownership of midwestern investment bank Robert W. Baird & Co. to its employees.

Northwestern Mutual would "enter the 21st century as we left the 19th," according to its former chairman and CEO, John Ericson (who retired in mid-2001).

Well, not exactly. Although the company has resisted the industry trend of demutualizing and remains committed to ownership by its approximately 3 million policyholders, The Quiet Company has begun blowing its own horn — in a diffident, upper Midwest way. Reorganized to highlight its wealth management products, life insurance still accounts for the majority of the company's revenue. The company targets wealthy individuals over 55.

HISTORY

In 1854, at age 72, John Johnston, a successful New York insurance agent, moved to Wisconsin to become a farmer. Three years later Johnston returned to the insurance business when he and 36 others formed Mutual Life Insurance (changed to Northwestern Mutual Life Insurance in 1865). From the beginning, the company's goal was to become better, not just bigger.

The company continued to offer level-premium life insurance in the 1920s, while competitors offered new types of products. This failure to rise to new demands brought a decline in market share that lasted into the 1940s.

Northwestern Mutual automated in the late 1950s. In 1962 it introduced the Insurance Service Account, whereby all policies owned by a family or business could be consolidated into one monthly premium and paid with pre-authorized checks. In 1968 Northwestern Mutual inaugurated Extra Ordinary Life (EOL), which combined whole and term life insurance, using dividends to convert term to paid-up whole life each year. EOL soon became the company's most popular product.

Suffering from a low profile, in 1972 the insurer kicked off its "The Quiet Company" ad campaign during the summer Olympics. Public awareness of Northwestern Mutual jumped. But even in advertising, the company was staid; a revamped Quiet Company campaign made a return Olympic appearance 24 years later in another effort to raise the public's consciousness.

In the 1980s Northwestern Mutual began financing leveraged buyouts, gaining direct ownership of companies. The firm's investments included two-thirds of flooring maker Congoleum (with other investors); it also bought majority interests in Milwaukee securities firm Robert W. Baird (1982) and mortgage guarantee insurer MGIC Investment (1985; later divested).

The firm stayed out of the 1980s mania for fast money and high-risk diversification. Instead, it devoted itself almost religiously to its core business, despite indications that it was a shrinking market.

In the early 1990s new life policy purchases slowed and the agency force declined — ominous signs, since insurers make their premium income on retained policies, and continued sales are crucial to growth. Northwestern Mutual reversed the trend, adding administrative support for its agents, using database marketing to target new customers, and increasing the cross-selling of products among existing customers. The result was a record-setting 1996.

With the financial services industry consolidating, Northwestern Mutual in 1997 moved into the mutual fund business by setting up its Mason Street Funds.

In the 1990s many large mutuals sought to demutualize, and in 1998 Northwestern Mutual, politically influential in Wisconsin, successfully lobbied for legislation to permit demutualization, citing the need to be able to move quickly in shifting markets.

The next year the company acquired Frank Russell Company, a pension management firm. The acquisition gave Northwestern Mutual a foothold in global investment management and analytical services (the Russell 2000 index).

The company followed up with an all-out reorganization, separating the office of president from the duties of chairman and CEO, and naming, for the first time, a marketing officer. In 2001 the firm opened Northwestern Mutual Trust, a wholly owned personal trust services subsidiary.

In 2004 the employees of Robert W. Baird completed a buyback of Northwestern Mutual's stake in the firm.

EXECUTIVES

President and CEO: Edward J. Zore, age 59
COO and Chief Compliance Officer: John M. Bremer, age 56
Chief Insurance Officer: Peter W. Bruce, age 58
EVP, Planning and Technology: Deborah A. Beck, age 56
EVP, Agencies: William H. Beckley, age 56
EVP and Chief Investment Officer: Mason G. Ross, age 60
SVP and CIO: Barbara F. Piehler, age 53
SVP and CFO: Gary A. Poliner, age 50
SVP, Public Markets: Mark G. Doll, age 54
SVP, Life Product: Richard L. Hall, age 58
SVP and Chief Actuary: William C. Koenig, age 56
SVP, Insurance Operations: Gregory C. Oberland, age 46
SVP, Marketing: Marcia Rimai, age 48
SVP, Investment Products and Services: Charles D. Robinson, age 59
SVP, Investment Products and Services and Affiliates: John E. Schlifske, age 44
SVP, Investment Product Operations: Leonard F. Stecklein, age 57
SVP, Corporate and Government Relations: Frederic H. Sweet, age 60
VP, Secretary, and General Counsel: Robert J. Berdan, age 57
VP and Controller: John C. (Chris) Kelly, age 44
VP, Human Resources: Susan A. Lueger, age 50
VP, Communications: Brenda F. Skelton, age 48
Auditors: PricewaterhouseCoopers LLP

LOCATIONS

HQ: The Northwestern Mutual Life Insurance Company
720 E. Wisconsin Ave., Milwaukee, WI 53202
Phone: 414-271-1444
Web: www.northwesternmutual.com

Northwestern Mutual Life Insurance has agents and offices throughout the US.

PRODUCTS/OPERATIONS

2003 Sales

	$ mil.	% of total
Premiums	10,307	62
Net investment income	5,737	35
Other income	501	3
Total	**16,545**	**100**

Selected Subsidiaries and Affiliates

Alexandra International Sales, Inc.
Amber, LLC
Baraboo, Inc.
Bayridge, LLC
Bradford, Inc.
Brendan International Sales, Inc.
Brian International Sales, Inc.
Burgundy, LLC
Carlisle Ventures, Inc.
Cass Corporation
Chateau, Inc.
Coral, Inc.
Diversey, Inc.
Elderwood International Sales, Inc.
Elizabeth International Sales, Inc.
Elizabeth Lakes Associates
Frank Russell Investment Management Company
The Grand Avenue Corporation
Green Room Properties, LLC
Hazel, Inc.
Higgins, Inc.
Highbrook International Sales, Inc.
Hobby, Inc.
INV Corp.
Jack International Sales, Inc.
Justin International FSC, Inc.
JYD Assets, LLC
KerryAnne International Sales, Inc.
Klode, Inc.
Kristiana International Sales, Inc.
Lake Bluff, Inc.
Larkin, Inc.
Logan, Inc.

Lydell, Inc.
Mallon International Sales, Inc.
Maroon, Inc.
Mason & Marshall, Inc.
Mason Street Advisors, LLC
Mitchell, Inc.
Network Planning Advisors, LLC
New Arcade, LLC
Nicolet, Inc.
NML Development Corporation
NML Real Estate Holdings, LLC
NML Securities Holdings, LLC
NML-CBO, LLC
North Van Buren, Inc.
Northwestern Foreign Holdings B.V. (Netherlands)
Northwestern Investment Management Company, LLC
Northwestern Mutual Trust Company
Northwestern Real Estate Partnership Holdings, LLC
Northwestern Reinsurance Holdings N.V. (Netherlands)
Northwestern Securities Holdings, LLC
NW Pipeline, Inc.
Olive, Inc.
Painted Rock Development Corporation
Park Forest Northeast, Inc.
RE Corporation
Regina International Sales, Inc.
Rocket Sports, Inc.
Russell Investment Funds
Russet, Inc.
Saskatoon Centre, Limited (Canada)
Sean International Sales, Inc.
Solar Resources, Inc.
St. James Apartments, LLC
Stadium and Arena Management, Inc.
Summerhill Management, LLC
Summit Mall, LLC
Travers International Sales, Inc.
Tupelo, Inc.
White Oaks, Inc.

COMPETITORS

AEGON USA
AIG
AIG American General
Alliance Capital
Allianz
AXA Financial
CIGNA
Citigroup
CNA Financial
Conseco
FMR
GenAmerica
Genworth Financial
Guardian Life
The Hartford
ING
John Hancock Financial Services
Liberty Mutual
MassMutual
Merrill Lynch
MetLife
MONY
Morgan Stanley
Mutual of Omaha
Nationwide
New York Life
Pacific Mutual
Principal Financial
Prudential
Sun Life
T. Rowe Price
TIAA-CREF

HISTORICAL FINANCIALS

Company Type: Mutual company

Income Statement
FYE: December 31

	ASSETS ($ mil.)	NET INCOME ($ mil.)	INCOME AS % OF ASSETS	EMPLOYEES
12/03	113,822	692	0.6%	4,500
12/02	102,935	158	0.2%	4,200
12/01	98,392	650	0.7%	4,100
12/00	92,125	1,829	2.0%	3,900
12/99	85,985	1,337	1.6%	3,700
12/98	77,995	809	1.0%	4,117
12/97	71,081	689	1.0%	3,818
12/96	62,680	620	1.0%	3,513
12/95	54,876	459	0.8%	3,344
12/94	48,112	279	0.6%	3,300
Annual Growth	10.0%	10.6%	—	3.5%

2003 Year-End Financials
Equity as % of assets: 8.9%
Return on assets: 0.6%
Return on equity: 8.0%
Long-term debt ($ mil.): 5,995
Sales ($ mil.): 16,545

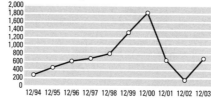

Net Income History

Northwestern University

Near the City of Big Shoulders is a place that shapes broad minds. With its main campus in the Chicago suburb of Evanston, Northwestern University serves its 17,000 students through 11 schools and colleges such as the McCormick School of Engineering and Applied Sciences and the Medill School of Journalism. Its Chicago campus houses the schools of law and medicine, as well as several hospitals of the McGaw Medical Center. Northwestern is home to several research centers, continuing education services, and community outreach programs. The university also supports 19 intercollegiate athletic programs. Founded in 1851, Northwestern is the only private institution in the Big 10 conference.

With tuition and fees running very close to $30,000 a year, about 60% of undergraduates receive some form of financial aid from the school.

Among Northwestern's top-ranked programs are its law school, medical school, and its engineering program. Its J. L. Kellogg Graduate School of Management is ranked first in the nation by *Business Week*. Its journalism and drama programs produced such alumni as Charlton Heston, Gary Marshall, and Julia Louis-Dreyfus. Current US Supreme Court Justice John Paul Stevens is also a former Wildcat.

The school's endowment has swelled to about $3.5 billion, and it has exceeded its original Campaign Northwestern fund-raising goal of $1 billion by more than $15 million. The money will be used to increase endowment for student scholarships and fellowships, to help repair and build facilities, and fund more faculty positions.

HISTORY

Northwestern University's Methodist founders met in 1850 to create an institution of higher learning serving the original Northwest Territory. The university was chartered in 1851, and two years later it acquired 379 acres of property north of Chicago on Lake Michigan. The town of Evanston was later named after John Evans, one of the school's founders.

Classes began in the fall of 1855 with two professors and 10 students. By 1869 Northwestern had more than 100 students and began to admit women. In 1870 Northwestern signed an affiliation agreement with the Chicago Medical College (founded 1859), and three years later it joined with the original University of Chicago (no relation to the current institution) to create the Union College of Law. When the University of Chicago closed in 1886 due to financial difficulties, Northwestern took control of the law school. The university reorganized in 1891, consolidating its affiliated professional schools (dentistry, law, medicine, and pharmacy) into the university.

By 1900 Northwestern had become the third-largest university in the US (after Harvard and Michigan), with an enrollment of 2,700. During the 1920s the university created the Medill School of Journalism, named for Joseph Medill, founder of the *Chicago Tribune*. In 1924 the school's athletic teams adopted the nickname Wildcats, and two years later the university completed the primary buildings that form its Chicago campus. Northwestern suffered a drop in enrollment during the Depression, but after WWII it saw student numbers swell as veterans took advantage of the GI Bill. Expansion continued throughout the 1960s and 1970s.

In 1985 the school and the City of Evanston began developing a research center to attract more high-tech industries to the area. The university's graduate school of business achieved national prominence in 1988 after it was ranked #1 in the US by *Business Week*. In 1995 Henry Bienen, a dean at Princeton, became the school's 15th president. That year Northwestern's football team, forever the doormat of the Big 10, achieved national fame when it won the conference championship.

In 1998 faculty member Professor John Pople won the Nobel Prize in Chemistry, the first Nobel Prize awarded to a faculty member while teaching at the university. To help pay for needed expansion, Bienen launched Campaign Northwestern that year with the goal of raising $1 billion. Northwestern won a significant legal battle in 1998 when a judge ruled that the university was not obligated to pay a faculty member simply because he had been granted tenure.

Encouraged by its successful fund-raising efforts, the college, in 2000, raised its goal to $1.4 billion from $1 billion. The university's dental school closed its doors in 2001, citing the difficulties posed for private schools in providing a competitive dental education.

EXECUTIVES

President: Henry S. Bienen
Provost: Lawrence B. Dumas
SVP Business and Finance: Eugene S. Sunshine
VP and General Counsel: Thomas G. Cline
VP Administration and Planning: Marilyn McCoy
VP Development: Sarah R. Pearson
VP Information Technology and CTO: Morteza A. Rahimi
VP Research: C. Bradley Moore
VP Student Affairs: William J. Banis
VP University Relations: Alan K. Cubbage
Associate VP Human Resources: Guy E. Miller
Director Media Relations: Charles R. Loebbaka
Auditors: Deloitte & Touche LLP

LOCATIONS

HQ: Northwestern University
633 Clark St., Evanston, IL 60208
Phone: 847-491-3741   **Fax:** 847-491-8406
Web: www.nwu.edu

Northwestern University has one campus in Chicago and one in Evanston, Illinois.

PRODUCTS/OPERATIONS

Selected Undergraduate Colleges and Schools
Medill School of Journalism
Robert McCormick School of Engineering and Applied Sciences
School of Communication
School of Education and Social Policy
School of Music
Weinberg College of Arts and Sciences

Graduate and Professional Schools
Feinberg School of Medicine
Interdisciplinary Biological and Life Sciences
J.L. Kellogg School of Management
McCormick School of Engineering and Applied Science
Medill School of Journalism
School of Communication (Speech)
School of Education and Social Policy
School of Law
School of Music

HISTORICAL FINANCIALS
Company Type: School

Income Statement
FYE: August 31

	REVENUE ($ mil.)	NET INCOME ($ mil.)	NET PROFIT MARGIN	EMPLOYEES
8/03	1,055	—	—	6,278
8/02	989	—	—	6,800
8/01	959	—	—	5,700
8/00	875	—	—	5,700
8/99	782	—	—	5,700
8/98	816	—	—	5,985
8/97	721	—	—	5,978
8/96	779	—	—	5,800
8/95	708	—	—	5,800
8/94	676	—	—	5,650
Annual Growth	5.1%	—	—	1.2%

Revenue History

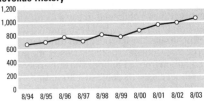

Novant Health

Novant Health is a not-for-profit health system in North Carolina. Formed in 1997 by a merger of Carolina Medicorp, Presbyterian Healthcare System, and Thomasville Medical Center, Novant serves nearly 4 million people in more than 30 counties across North and South Carolina and Virginia. The system includes six hospitals (with about 2,000 beds), three philanthropic foundations, three senior residential facilities, physician clinics, a women's health center, long-term-care facilities, rehabilitation and community outreach programs, and surgical and diagnostic outpatient offices. Novant Health also includes the for-profit PARTNERS National Health Plans of North Carolina, an HMO covering more than 300,000 members.

EXECUTIVES
Chairman: Peter S. Brunstetter
President, CEO, and Trustee: Paul M. Wiles
EVP and CFO: Dean Swindle
President and CEO, Presbyterian Healthcare: Carl Armato
President, Novant Health, Winston-Salem Region; President, Forsyth Medical Center and Affiliates: Gregory J. Beier
EVP; COO, Presbyterian Healthcare: Lynn I. Boggs
SVP, Human Resources: Jacque Gattis

LOCATIONS
HQ: Novant Health, Inc.
2085 Frontis Plaza Blvd., Winston-Salem, NC 27103
Phone: 336-718-5000   **Fax:** 336-718-9258
Web: www.novanthealth.org

PRODUCTS/OPERATIONS

Selected Health Facilities (Charlotte Region)
Buddy Kemp Caring House
Hawthorn Medical Center
Midtown Medical Plaza
Presbyterian Hemby Children's Hospital
Presbyterian Hospital
Presbyterian Hospital Matthews
Presbyterian Medical Tower
Presbyterian NorthPoint
Presbyterian Orthopaedic Hospital
Presbyterian Rehabilitation Center
Presbyterian Wesley Care Center

Selected Health Facilities (Winston-Salem Region)
Forsyth Medical Center
Hawthorne Surgical Center
Medical Park Hospital
Salem MRI Center
Springwood Care Center of Forsyth
The Oaks at Forsyth
Thomasville Medical Center

COMPETITORS

Bon Secours Health
Carilion Health System
Greenville Hospital System
Mid Atlantic Medical
Sentara Healthcare
Wake Forest University Baptist Medical Center

HISTORICAL FINANCIALS
Company Type: Not-for-profit

Income Statement
FYE: December 31

	REVENUE ($ mil.)	NET INCOME ($ mil.)	NET PROFIT MARGIN	EMPLOYEES
12/03	1,350	—	—	14,060
12/02	1,240	—	—	13,726
12/01	1,000	—	—	13,000
12/00	802	—	—	12,000
12/99	764	—	—	12,000
12/98	752	—	—	12,000
12/97	1,100	—	—	13,000
12/96	400	—	—	5,109
12/95	324	—	—	4,716
12/94	383	—	—	4,118
Annual Growth	15.0%	—	—	14.6%

Revenue History

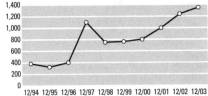

Nypro

Nypro is a real pro when it comes to injection molding. The company makes plastic parts used in devices that range from cell phones, electric razors, and seat belts to inkjet printer cartridges and personal computers. Customers in the electronics and telecommunications industries together account for nearly half of sales. Although custom-precision plastic-injection molding is Nypro's core business, the company also offers assembly services to other manufacturers. US-based computer manufacturer Dell is Nypro's largest customer. Co-chairman Gordon Lankton sold Nypro to employees in 1999 through an employee stock ownership plan.

EXECUTIVES
Co-Chairman: Gordon B. Lankton
Co-Chairman: Nicholas D. (Nick) Aznoian
President and Director: Brian S. Jones
VP, Information Technology, Chief Supply Chain Officer, and Director: Michael C. MacKenty
VP, CFO, and Director: Theodore E. Lapres III
VP and CTO: Rodolfo Archbold
VP and General Manager, East Region: Gregory G. Adams
VP, China and India: James R. Buonomo
VP, Contract Manufacturing: Louis Gaviglia
VP, Engineering: Richard J. Hoeske
VP, Human Resources and Organizational Development: Ann S. Liotta
VP, Marketing and Business Development: Stephen J. Glorioso
Corporate Communications: Al Cotton
Auditors: PricewaterhouseCoopers LLP

LOCATIONS
HQ: Nypro Inc.
101 Union St., Clinton, MA 01510
Phone: 978-365-9721   **Fax:** 978-368-0236
Web: www.nypro.com

Nypro has operations in 27 plants in Asia, Europe, and North and South America.

2003 Sales

	% of total
North America	43
China	23
Latin America	22
Europe	9
Southeast Asia & India	3
Total	**100**

PRODUCTS/OPERATIONS

2003 Sales by Industry

	% of total
Electronics & telecommunications	49
Health care	22
Consumer industrial	13
Automotive	9
Automation, robotics & tooling	7
Total	**100**

COMPETITORS

Atlantis Plastics
Berry Plastics
Carlisle Engineered Products
Deswell Industries
Hoffer Plastics
Omni Industries
Tuthill

Ocean Spray

HISTORICAL FINANCIALS
Company Type: Private

Income Statement
FYE: June 30

	REVENUE ($ mil.)	NET INCOME ($ mil.)	NET PROFIT MARGIN	EMPLOYEES
6/03	605	19	3.2%	11,000
6/02	590	30	5.1%	9,000
6/01	495	32	6.4%	8,000
6/00	591	25	4.3%	7,000
Annual Growth	0.8%	(8.6%)	—	16.3%

2003 Year-End Financials
Debt ratio: 79.0%
Return on equity: 10.9%
Cash ($ mil.): 101
Current ratio: 0.85
Long-term debt ($ mil.): 143

Net Income History
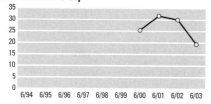

Ocean Spray Cranberries has transformed cranberries from turkey sidekick to the stuff of everyday beverages, cereal, and mixed drinks. Known for its blue-and-white wave logo, the company controls more than half of the US cranberry drink market. A marketing cooperative owned by more than 900 cranberry and citrus growers in the US and Canada, Ocean Spray produces its line of juices by blending the cranberry with fruits ranging from apples to tangerines. It also makes other cranberry products (sauce, snacks), grapefruit juice, and Ocean Spray Premium 100% juice drinks.

In recent years, surplus harvests of cranberries, competition from store brands, and drought in some areas have cut into its market share and forced layoffs. Competition from industry giants such as Coca-Cola and Pepsi, both of which are trying to increase market share in the non-carbonated drinks sector, also have hurt the company.

To expand beyond the berry's traditional role, Ocean Spray has turned the fruit into a chewy snack (Craisins), and cranberries now show up in cobranded cookies and cereal. It has also introduced a "white juice" made from preripened cranberries that have a less tart taste. Promotional efforts have been aided by research showing that cranberry juice can reduce urinary tract infections.

Ocean Spray's Ingredient Technology Group processes fruit into juice ingredients.

In September 2004, Ocean Spray settled an antitrust lawsuit filed by Northland Cranberries and Clermont, Inc. As part of the settlement, Ocean Spray said it would purchase Northland's production plant and would pay $5 million for an option to buy 14 of Northland's cranberry marshes in Wisconsin. As part of the agreement, Ocean Spray will make cranberry concentrate for Northland.

HISTORY

Ocean Spray Cranberries traces its roots to Marcus Urann, president of the Cape Cod Cranberry Company. In 1912 Urann, who became known as the "Cranberry King," began marketing a cranberry sauce that was packaged in tins and could be served year-round. Inspired by the sea spray that drifted off the Atlantic and over his cranberry bogs, Urann dubbed his concoction Ocean Spray Cape Cod Cranberry Sauce.

It didn't take long for other cranberry growers to make their own sauces, and rather than compete, the Cranberry King consolidated. In 1930 Urann merged his company with A.D. Makepeace Company and with Cranberry Products, forming a national cooperative called Cranberry Canners. During the 1940s it added growers in Wisconsin, Oregon, and Washington and, to reflect its new scope, changed its name to National Cranberry Association.

Canadian growers were added to the fold in 1950. Urann retired in 1955, and two years later the co-op introduced its first frozen products. To take advantage of the popular Ocean Spray brand name, in 1959 the company changed its name to Ocean Spray Cranberries.

Two weeks before Thanksgiving that year, the US Department of Health mistakenly announced that aminotriazole, a herbicide used by some cranberry growers, was linked to cancer in laboratory rats. Sales of what consumers called "cancer berries" plummeted, and Ocean Spray nearly folded. However, the US government came to the rescue with subsidies in 1960, and the company stayed afloat.

The scare convinced Ocean Spray it needed to cut its dependence on seasonal demand, and it began to diversify more aggressively into the juice business, introducing a heavily promoted new line of juices blending cranberries with apples, grapes, and other fruits.

Ocean Spray allowed Florida's Indian River Ruby Red grapefruit growers to join the co-op in 1976. The company acquired Milne Food Products, a manufacturer of fruit concentrates and purees, in 1985, and three years later it signed a Japanese distribution deal.

To maintain its edge in a growing but increasingly competitive market, Ocean Spray automated plants and allied with food giants to create cranberry-flavored treats such as cookies (Nabisco, 1993) and cereal (Kraft Foods, 1996). In 1998 it unsuccessfully sued to block PepsiCo's purchase of juice maker Tropicana on grounds that it would interfere with PepsiCo's distribution of Ocean Spray's drinks. Ocean Spray also introduced a line of 100% juice blends to compete with rivals such as former co-op member Northland Cranberries.

Bumper harvests from 1997 through 1999 led to lower cranberry prices. As a result, in 1999 the company announced its third round of layoffs since 1997 (bringing the total to 500, or nearly one-fifth of its workforce). It also suspended its practice of buying back the stock of its growers, who must buy shares to join the co-op.

Amid criticism that it has been unable to compete effectively with for-profit rivals, Ocean Spray hired former Pillsbury executive Robert Hawthorne as CEO in 2000. Grower-owners voted not to explore a sale of the company at its 2001 annual meeting, a vote of confidence for the new management. The company supported a 32% crop reduction to help eliminate the crop surpluses that cause depressed prices. Ocean Spray also sold its interest in Nantucket Allserve (Nantucket Nectars) to Cadbury Schweppes, which folded Nantucket's brands into its Snapple unit. In 2002 Hawthorne resigned. Barbara S. Thomas, a board member and former president of Warner Lambert's consumer health care division, was named interim CEO.

In February 2003 rival Northland Cranberries made a cash and stock bid to take over the juice business of Ocean Spray. The company rejected the offer that same month. Upset by their lack of input in the decision, cranberry growers voted in March to revamp the Ocean Spray board, reducing its size from 15 to 12 members and keeping just three of the board's previous members. Soon after, Ocean Spray laid off about 60 people, including several executives.

In 2004, the cooperative nearly revamped its board a second time in one year to again increase input from membership. As a compromise, the cooperative returned the size of its board back to 15 members. Seven of the members were considered "compromise" candidates that would bring "additional viewpoints" to the Board. In June cooperative members rejected a proposed joint venture with PepsiCo.

EXECUTIVES

Chairman: Robert L. Rosbe Jr.
CEO: Randy Papadellis
SVP and COO: Kenneth G. (Ken) Romanzi, age 44
SVP and COO, Ocean Spray International: Stewart (Stu) Gallagher
SVP and CFO: Tim C. Chan
VP, Operations: Michael Stamatakos
VP, Human Resources: Katie Morey
Group Marketing Manager, New Products: Kelly Reilly
Manager, Public Relations: Cindy Taccini
Auditors: Deloitte & Touche

LOCATIONS

HQ: Ocean Spray Cranberries, Inc.
 1 Ocean Spray Dr., Lakeville-Middleboro, MA 02349
Phone: 508-946-1000 **Fax:** 508-946-7704
Web: www.oceanspray.com

Ocean Spray Cranberries operates four bottling facilities in Nevada, New Jersey, Texas, and Wisconsin and three fruit-processing sites in Florida, Washington, and Massachusetts.

PRODUCTS/OPERATIONS

Selected Products

Cranberry Juice Cocktails
 Cranberry Juice Cocktail
 Cranberry Juice Cocktail with Calcium
Cranberry Juice Drinks
 Cran Apple
 Cran Cherry
 Cran Grape
 Cran Mango
 Cran Raspberry
 Cran Strawberry
 Cran Tangerine
 Juice & Tea
Craisins Sweetened Dried Cranberries
 Cherry Flavor Sweetened Dried Cranberries
 Orange Flavor Sweetened Dried Cranberries
 Original Sweetened Dried Cranberries
Fresh Fruits and Sauces
 Citrus
 Cranberries
 Grapefruit
 Jellied Cranberry Sauce
 Whole Berry Cranberry Sauce
Light Cranberry Juice Drinks
 Light Cranberry Juice Cocktail
 Light Cran Grape
 Light Cran Raspberry
 Light White Cranberry

Premium 100% Cranberry Juices
  Cranberry Blend
  Cranberry and Concord Grape
  Cranberry and Georgia Peach
  Cranberry and Mixed Berry
  Cranberry and Pacific Raspberry
  Cranberry and Red Delicious Apple
  White Cranberry Blend
Premium 100% Grapefruit Juices
  Pink Grapefruit
  Ruby Red Grapefruit
  White Grapefruit
Ruby Grapefruit Juice Drinks
  Ruby Lemonade Grapefruit Juice Drink
  Ruby Mango Grapefruit Juice Drink
  Ruby Red Grapefruit Juice Drink
  Ruby Strawberry Grapefruit Juice Drink
  Ruby Tangerine Grapefruit Juice Drink
White Cranberry Juice Drinks
  White Cranberry
  White Cranberry and Apple
  White Cranberry and Peach
  White Cranberry and Strawberry

COMPETITORS

Altria
Cadbury Schweppes
Cadbury Schweppes Americas
Campbell Soup
Chiquita Brands
Clement Pappas & Co.
Cliffstar
Coca-Cola
Dole Food
Florida's Natural
Hansen Natural
Mott's
National Grape Cooperative
Northland Cranberries
Odwalla
Pepsi-Cola North America
Smucker
Sunkist
Tropicana
Welch's

HISTORICAL FINANCIALS
Company Type: Cooperative

Income Statement				FYE: August 31
	REVENUE ($ mil.)	NET INCOME ($ mil.)	NET PROFIT MARGIN	EMPLOYEES
8/03	1,000	—	—	2,000
8/02	1,068	—	—	2,000
8/01	1,104	—	—	2,200
8/00	1,400	—	—	2,000
8/99	1,360	—	—	2,000
8/98	1,480	—	—	2,350
8/97	1,438	—	—	2,300
8/96	1,433	—	—	2,300
8/95	1,361	—	—	2,300
8/94	1,221	—	—	2,300
Annual Growth	(2.2%)	—	—	(1.5%)

Revenue History

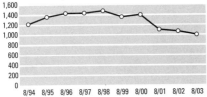

Oglethorpe Power

Not-for-profit Oglethorpe Power Corporation is one of the largest electricity cooperatives in the US, with contracts to supply wholesale power to 39 member/owners (making up most of Georgia's electric distribution cooperatives) until 2025. Oglethorpe Power's member/owners, which also operate as not-for-profits, serve about 1.5 million residential, commercial, and industrial customers. The company, which was formed in 1974, has a generating capacity of more than 4,700 MW from fossil-fueled, nuclear, and hydroelectric power plants. In addition, Oglethorpe purchases power from other suppliers, and it markets power on the wholesale market.

EXECUTIVES

Chairman: Benny W. Denham, age 73
Vice Chairman: J. Sam L. Rabun, age 72
President and CEO: Thomas A. (Tom) Smith, age 49, $416,910 pay
COO: Michael W. (Mike) Price, age 43, $262,867 pay
CFO: Elizabeth Bush (Betsy) Higgins, age 35, $206,750 pay (prior to title change)
SVP, Administration and Risk Management: W. Clayton (Clay) Robbins, age 57, $226,518 pay
SVP, Operations: Clarence D. Mitchell
VP and CIO: Barbara Hampton
VP and Controller: Mark Chesla
VP, External Affairs: Robert D. Steele
VP, Finance: Anne F. Appleby
VP, Human Resources: Jami G. Reusch
Auditors: PricewaterhouseCoopers LLP

LOCATIONS

HQ: Oglethorpe Power Corporation
2100 E. Exchange Place, Tucker, GA 30084
Phone: 770-270-7600 **Fax:** 770-270-7325
Web: www.opc.com

PRODUCTS/OPERATIONS

2003 Sales

	$ mil.	% of total
Members	1,168	97
Non-members	36	3
Total	**1,204**	**100**

2003 Energy Mix

	% of total
Coal	29
Gas & oil	27
Nuclear	22
Hydro	12
Purchased	10
Total	**100**

Member/Owners

Altamaha Electric Membership Corporation
Amicalola Electric Membership Corporation
Canoochee Electric Membership Corporation
Carroll Electric Membership Corporation
Central Georgia Electric Membership Corporation
Coastal Electric Membership Corporation (d/b/a Coastal Electric Cooperative)
Cobb Electric Membership Corporation
Colquitt Electric Membership Corporation
Coweta-Fayette Electric Membership Corporation
Diverse Power Incorporated, an Electric Membership Corporation (formerly Troup Electric Membership Corporation)
Excelsior Electric Membership Corporation
Flint Electric Membership Corporation (d/b/a Flint Energies)
Grady Electric Membership Corporation
GreyStone Power Corporation, an Electric Membership Corporation
Habersham Electric Membership Corporation
Hart Electric Membership Corporation
Irwin Electric Membership Corporation
Jackson Electric Membership Corporation
Jefferson Energy Cooperative, an Electric Membership Corporation
Lamar Electric Membership Corporation
Little Ocmulgee Electric Membership Corporation
Middle Georgia Electric Membership Corporation
Mitchell Electric Membership Corporation
Ocmulgee Electric Membership Corporation
Oconee Electric Membership Corporation
Okefenoke Rural Electric Membership Corporation
Pataula Electric Membership Corporation
Planters Electric Membership Corporation
Rayle Electric Membership Corporation
Satilla Rural Electric Membership Corporation
Sawnee Electric Membership Corporation
Slash Pine Electric Membership Corporation
Snapping Shoals Electric Membership Corporation
Sumter Electric Membership Corporation
Three Notch Electric Membership Corporation
Tri-County Electric Membership Corporation
Upson Electric Membership Corporation
Walton Electric Membership Corporation
Washington Electric Membership Corporation

COMPETITORS

AGL Resources
FPL Group
MEAG Power
Progress Energy
PS Energy
Southern Company
TVA

HISTORICAL FINANCIALS
Company Type: Cooperative

Income Statement				FYE: December 31
	REVENUE ($ mil.)	NET INCOME ($ mil.)	NET PROFIT MARGIN	EMPLOYEES
12/03	1,204	17	1.4%	179
12/02	1,163	18	1.5%	173
12/01	1,139	18	1.6%	175
12/00	1,199	20	1.7%	160
12/99	1,176	20	1.7%	144
12/98	1,144	21	1.8%	125
12/97	1,048	22	2.1%	170
12/96	1,101	22	2.0%	—
12/95	1,150	22	1.9%	—
12/94	1,056	23	2.2%	—
Annual Growth	1.5%	(3.5%)	—	0.9%

2003 Year-End Financials
Debt ratio: 926.8%   Current ratio: 1.62
Return on equity: 4.4%   Long-term debt ($ mil.): 3,657
Cash ($ mil.): 227

Net Income History

Ohio Lottery

The year was 1974 — Nixon resigned, an energy crisis gripped the nation, and Ray Stevens ignited a streaking sensation. But were residents of the Buckeye State paying attention? Maybe not — they had a brand new state lottery to play! Since selling its first lottery ticket that fateful year, the Ohio Lottery Commission has raised more than $12 billion for education in Ohio, the cause to which lottery proceeds are dedicated. The commission offers a variety of instant ticket games (Count Cashula, Fat Cat) and numbers games (Pick 3, Pick 4) for Ohioans' wagering pleasure. Facing slumping sales, in 2000 the Ohio Lottery Commission debuted numbers game Super Lotto Plus, which offered players better odds of winning.

EXECUTIVES

Executive Director: Dennis G. Kennedy
Assistant Director: Constance Miller
Deputy Director, Finance Division: Mark M. Polatajko
Deputy Director, Administration Division: Duane Miller
Deputy Director, Information Technology Division: Michael Petro
Deputy Director, Marketing: Mark Rickel
Deputy Director, Media Relations: Mardele Cohen
Deputy Director, Product Research and Development: Patricia Vasil
Deputy Director, Sales Division: Dan Metelsky
Chief Legal Counsel: Kathleen G. Weiss

LOCATIONS

HQ: Ohio Lottery Commission
615 W. Superior Ave., Cleveland, OH 44113
Phone: 216-787-3200   **Fax:** 216-787-5215
Web: www.ohiolottery.com

PRODUCTS/OPERATIONS

Selected Games

Instant Games
  Best of 3
  Cash and Cars
  Casino Action
  Double Doubler
  Lucky Roll Doubler
  Nifty Fifty
  Poker Royale
  Wild Winnings
Numbers games
  Pick 3
  Pick 4
  Super Lotto

COMPETITORS

Hoosier Lottery
Michigan Lottery
Multi-State Lottery
Pennsylvania Lottery

HISTORICAL FINANCIALS

Company Type: Government-owned

Income Statement
FYE: June 30

	REVENUE ($ mil.)	NET INCOME ($ mil.)	NET PROFIT MARGIN	EMPLOYEES
6/03	2,078	—	—	344
6/02	1,983	—	—	350
6/01	2,000	—	—	350
6/00	2,156	—	—	350
6/99	2,151	—	—	349
6/98	2,195	—	—	351
6/97	2,300	—	—	355
6/96	2,314	—	—	—
Annual Growth	(1.5%)	—	—	(0.5%)

Revenue History

Ohio National Financial

What's round on both ends, high in the middle, and covers millions of people? Ohio National Financial Services! Ohio National Financial Services is the marketing name for Ohio National Life Insurance and affiliated companies, which sell individual and group life insurance, disability insurance, pension plans, and annuities. Other products and services include wholesale and retail brokerage and mutual funds. Ohio National Financial Services sells throughout the US through agents, brokers, affiliated firms, and third parties; the company also sells insurance in Chile. Ohio National converted to mutual holding company structure in 1998.

The insurer is expanding its business in New York through the planned acquisition of Security Mutual Life Insurance Company of New York.

EXECUTIVES

Chairman, President, and CEO: David B. O'Maley, age 57
Vice Chairman: John J. Palmer
EVP, CFO, and Director: Ronald J. Dolan
EVP, Agency and Group Distribution and Director: D. Gates Smith
SVP, Institutional Sales: Thomas A. Barefield
SVP, Administration: Howard C. Becker
SVP, Investments: Michael A. Boedeker
SVP, Information Systems: R. Allen Bowen
SVP, Investments: Christopher A. Carlson
SVP and Actuary: David W. Cook
SVP, Corporate Relations and Communications: Diane S. Hagenbuch
SVP and General Counsel: Michael F. Haverkamp
SVP, PGA Marketing: George B. Pearson Jr.
SVP, Internal Audit and Compliance: James C. Smith
Auditors: KPMG LLP

LOCATIONS

HQ: Ohio National Financial Services
1 Financial Way, Cincinnati, OH 45242
Phone: 513-794-6100   **Fax:** 513-794-4504
Web: www.ohionatl.com

PRODUCTS/OPERATIONS

2003 Sales

	$ mil.	% of total
Net investment income	556.3	58
Net policy fees, charges & premiums	340.2	35
Other income	70.8	7
Total	**967.3**	**100**

Selected Subsidiaries and Affiliates

The O.N. Equity Sales Company
Ohio National Equities, Inc. (wholesale brokerage)
Ohio National Financial Services, Inc.
Ohio National Life Assurance Corporation (ONLAC)
The Ohio National Life Insurance Company (ONLIC)
Ohio National Mutual Holdings, Inc.
Ohio National Seguros de Vida, S.A. (Chile)
Suffolk Capital Management (asset management)

COMPETITORS

AIG	MassMutual
American Family Insurance	MetLife
American United	Midland National Life
AXA Financial	Minnesota Mutual
Great American Financial Resources	National Life Insurance
Guardian Life	Nationwide
The Hartford	New York Life
John Hancock Financial Services	Northwestern Mutual
Lincoln National	Principal Financial
	Prudential
	StanCorp Financial Group

HISTORICAL FINANCIALS

Company Type: Mutual company

Income Statement
FYE: December 31

	ASSETS ($ mil.)	NET INCOME ($ mil.)	INCOME AS % OF ASSETS	EMPLOYEES
12/03	13,573	98	0.7%	750
12/02	11,620	51	0.4%	700
12/01	9,924	76	0.8%	700
12/00	8,092	79	1.0%	700
12/99	7,573	89	1.2%	650
12/98	6,862	68	1.0%	600
12/97	6,331	67	1.1%	575
12/96	5,782	60	1.0%	—
Annual Growth	13.0%	7.3%	—	4.5%

2003 Year-End Financials

Equity as % of assets: 7.9%   Long-term debt ($ mil.): 388
Return on assets: 0.8%   Sales ($ mil.): 967
Return on equity: —%

Net Income History

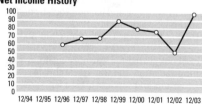

Ohio State University

The first student body of Ohio State University (OSU) had 24 students. Today the university is Ohio's largest institution of higher learning and has the nation's largest single-campus enrollment (about 51,000 students at its Columbus campus). It also has four regional campuses and two agricultural institutes. OSU's approximately 3,000 faculty members offer instruction in more than 170 undergraduate and 200 graduate programs. Its colleges and schools range from the Austin E. Knowlton School of Architecture to the College of Medicine and Public Health to the Fisher College of Business. The school was established in 1870 as Ohio Agricultural and Mechanical College.

Noteworthy university alumni include astronaut Nancy Sherlock Currie, golfer Jack Nicklaus, author John Jakes, and Olympian Jesse Owens.

Near the close of 2000, OSU unveiled a five-year academic plan under which the university will spend $750 million to advance its national academic standing.

HISTORY

In 1870 the Ohio legislature, prompted by Governor Rutherford B. Hayes, agreed to establish the Ohio Agricultural and Mechanical College in Columbus on property provided by the Morrill Act of 1862 (the land-grant institution act, which gave land to states and territories for the establishment of colleges).

After a heated battle over whether the college should teach only agricultural and mechanical arts or foster a broad-based liberal arts curriculum, the college opened in 1873 offering agriculture, ancient languages, chemistry, geology, mathematics, modern languages, and physics courses. Two years later the school appointed its first female faculty member. The Ohio State University became the school's name in 1878; that year it graduated its first class. OSU graduated its first female student the next year.

OSU grew dramatically, adding schools of veterinary medicine (1885), pharmacy (1885), law (1891), and dairy sciences (1895). It awarded its first Masters of Arts degree in 1886.

The university continued to expand in the early 20th century, with enrollment surpassing 3,000 in 1908; by 1923 it had reached 10,000. New schools were added in education (1907), medicine and dentistry (1913), and commerce and journalism (1923). During WWI Ohio State designated part of its campus as training grounds and established the only college schools in the nation for airplane and balloon squadrons. Ohio Stadium was dedicated in 1922.

During the Great Depression Ohio State cut back salaries and course offerings. In the 1940s the school geared for war once again by establishing radiation and war research labs, as well as programs and services for students who were drafted. OSU captured its first national football championship in 1942.

The 1950s ushered in the era of legendary OSU football coach Woody Hayes. Hayes led his beloved Buckeyes to three national championships and nine Rose Bowl appearances before he was discharged for striking a Clemson player in 1978. The 1950s also saw the addition of four regional campuses at Lima, Mansfield, Marion, and Newark.

In the early 1960s the university was engaged in internal free-speech battles. By the end of that decade, enrollment had surpassed 50,000. OSU opened its School of Social Work in 1976.

In 1986 OSU and rival Michigan shared the Big 10 football conference title. Enrollment at OSU topped 54,000 in 1990 but then began declining. In response, the university tried to cut costs and beef up revenues. One way was through alliances: In 1992 it teamed with research group Battelle to develop a testing system for new drugs for the Food and Drug Administration. But when more savings were needed in 1995 and 1996, the university began streamlining operations, merging journalism and communications, and consolidating several veterinary departments. However, it also approved the creation of a new school of public health to provide education in environmental health, epidemiology, and health care management and financing.

But sports were not forgotten, and in 1996 OSU broke ground on the $84 million Schottenstein Center, a multipurpose facility for the university's basketball and ice hockey teams. In 1997 president Gordon Gee announced that he was leaving OSU for Brown University. The next year William Kirwan from the University of Maryland came on board as president.

In 2000 the university's "Affirm Thy Friendship" contribution campaign came to a close. The campaign increased OSU's endowment from $493 million in 1993 to $1.3 billion in 2000. In 2002 William Kirwan stepped down, and Karen Holbrook took over as president. Ohio State won the national football championship in early 2003.

EXECUTIVES

President: Karen A. Holbrook
EVP and Provost: Barbara Snyder
SVP Business & Finance and CFO: Bill Shkurti
SVP Research: Robert T. McGrath
VP Agricultural Administration and University Outreach: Bobby D. Moser
VP Research (Interim): Thomas J. (Tom) Rosol
VP Student Affairs: William H. Hall
Associate VP Human Resources: Larry M. Lewellen
Vice Provost Minority Affairs: Mac A. Stewart
CIO: Ilee Rhimes
Controller: Greta J. Russell
Executive Assistant to the President and General Counsel: Virginia M. (Ginny) Trethewey
Auditors: Deloitte & Touche LLP

LOCATIONS

HQ: The Ohio State University
1800 Cannon Dr., Lincoln Tower, 3rd Fl.,
Columbus, OH 43210
Phone: 614-292-3980   **Fax:** 614-292-0154
Web: www.osu.edu

The Ohio State University has campuses in Columbus, Lima, Mansfield, Marion, and Newark. It has two agricultural centers in Wooster, Ohio.

PRODUCTS/OPERATIONS

Selected Colleges and Schools
Austin E. Knowlton School of Architecture
College of Biological Sciences
College of Dentistry
College of Education
College of Engineering
College of Food, Agricultural, and Environmental Sciences
College of Human Ecology
College of Humanities
College of Law
College of Mathematical and Physical Sciences
College of Medicine and Public Health
College of Nursing
College of Optometry
College of Social and Behavioral Sciences
College of Social Work
College of the Arts
College of Veterinary Medicine
Max M. Fisher College of Business
School of Natural Resources
University College

HISTORICAL FINANCIALS

Company Type: School

Income Statement
FYE: June 30

	REVENUE ($ mil.)	NET INCOME ($ mil.)	NET PROFIT MARGIN	EMPLOYEES
6/04	3,060	—	—	34,000
6/03	2,721	—	—	33,772
6/02	2,000	—	—	33,000
6/01	1,661	—	—	32,000
6/00	1,554	—	—	31,302
6/99	1,923	—	—	29,502
6/98	1,749	—	—	31,268
6/97	1,630	—	—	29,000
6/96	1,531	—	—	29,266
6/95	1,575	—	—	29,500
Annual Growth	7.7%	—	—	1.6%

Revenue History

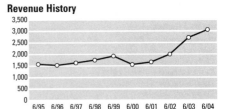

OhioHealth

Operating in more than half of the state's 88 counties, OhioHealth aims to keep Buckeyes healthy. The system operates seven acute care hospitals and is affiliated with about half a dozen more. All told, OhioHealth has more than 2,000 beds.

Additional facilities include outpatient centers, rehabilitation centers, long-term care facilities, diagnostic imaging centers, women's health centers, and sleep centers. Subsidiary HomeReach provides home health care and medical supply services. Its WorkHealth program offers workers' compensation care management and occupational rehabilitation services.

OhioHealth Group, OhioHealth's joint venture with The Medical Group of Ohio, operates the HealthReach PPO.

EXECUTIVES

Chairman: John J. Chester
President and CEO: David P. Blom
SVP, System Advancement: Joan Evans
SVP, Regional Operations and System Development:
  Steven (Steve) Garlock
SVP and CFO: Michael W. (Mike) Louge
SVP and COO: Robert P. (Bob) Millen, age 51
SVP, Human Resources: Debra Plousha Moore
SVP, Medical Affairs and Chief Medical Officer:
  C. David Morehead
VP, Ambulatory Services: Bob Gilbert
**VP, Mission and Ministry Corporate Ethics and
  Compliance Officer:** Rev Keith R. Vesper
System VP and CIO: William E. (Bill) Winnenberg

LOCATIONS

HQ: OhioHealth Corporation
  1087 Dennison Ave., 3rd Fl., Columbus, OH 43201
Phone: 614-544-5424   **Fax:** 614-566-6938
Web: www.ohiohealth.com

PRODUCTS/OPERATIONS

Selected Facilities
Owned
  Doctors Hospital (Columbus)
  Grant Medical Center (Columbus)
  Riverside Methodist Hospital (Columbus)
  Hardin Memorial Hospital (Kenton)
  Marion General Hospital (Marion)
  Doctors Hospital Nelsonville (Nelsonville)
  Southern Ohio Medical Center (Portsmouth)
Affiliated
  Samaritan Regional Health System (Ashland)
  O'Bleness Memorial Hospital (Athens)
  Galion Community Hospital (Galion)
  Grady Memorial Hospital (Delaware)
  Morrow County Hospital (Mt. Gilead)
  Genesis Healthcare System (Zanesville)

COMPETITORS

Catholic Health Initiatives
Catholic Healthcare Partners
HCA
Triad Hospitals
Trinity Health (Novi)

HISTORICAL FINANCIALS

Company Type: Not-for-profit

Income Statement
FYE: June 30

	REVENUE ($ mil.)	NET INCOME ($ mil.)	NET PROFIT MARGIN	EMPLOYEES
6/03	1,036	—	—	15,000
6/02	1,955	—	—	15,000
6/01	2,000	—	—	15,340
6/00	1,200	—	—	15,000
6/99	944	—	—	13,500
6/98	828	—	—	13,400
6/97	800	—	—	10,000
6/96	850	—	—	10,000
6/95	775	—	—	10,000
6/94	747	—	—	8,000
Annual Growth	3.7%	—	—	7.2%

Revenue History

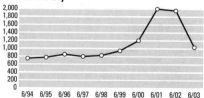

O'Melveny & Myers

O'Melveny & Myers is more than happy to play the role of legal guardian angel. Founded in 1885, O'Melveny & Myers is one of the oldest law firms in Los Angeles, and it has developed strong ties to the media and entertainment industry. Sony Pictures Entertainment, Walt Disney, and Time Warner Inc. are among the firm's clients. It also is known for political clout: Former US Secretary of State Warren Christopher is a senior partner. O'Melveny & Myers' practice areas include labor and employment, litgation, and tax and transactions. The firm is expanding its services for high-tech companies, which include legal advice related to software licensing, intellectual property, and venture capital investments.

EXECUTIVES

Chairman and CEO: Arthur B. Culvahouse Jr.
COO: Bruce Boulware
Director Finance: Joelle Nardone
Director Human Resources: Beth Naples

LOCATIONS

HQ: O'Melveny & Myers LLP
  400 S. Hope St., Ste. 1500, Los Angeles, CA 90071
Phone: 213-430-6000   **Fax:** 213-430-6407
Web: www.omm.com

O'Melveny & Myers has 13 offices worldwide.

PRODUCTS/OPERATIONS

Selected Practice Areas
Asia Practice
Banking and financial institutions
Bankruptcy
Communications
Employee benefits
Entertainment and media
Environmental
Health care
Internet law
Labor and employment
Litigation
Real estate
White-collar crime

COMPETITORS

Akin Gump
Baker & McKenzie
Davis Polk
Gibson, Dunn & Crutcher
Latham & Watkins
Paul, Hastings
Skadden, Arps
Sullivan & Cromwell

HISTORICAL FINANCIALS

Company Type: Partnership

Income Statement
FYE: January 31

	REVENUE ($ mil.)	NET INCOME ($ mil.)	NET PROFIT MARGIN	EMPLOYEES
1/04	658	—	—	—
1/03	563	—	—	2,200
1/02	490	—	—	1,900
1/01	401	—	—	1,500
1/00	373	—	—	1,500
1/99	328	—	—	1,450
1/98	284	—	—	1,400
1/97	260	—	—	1,350
1/96	253	—	—	1,314
1/95	257	—	—	1,334
Annual Growth	11.0%	—	—	6.5%

Revenue History

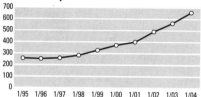

OmniSource

OmniSource lives on scraps. Irving Rifkin founded the private, family-owned scrap-metal processor and trader in 1943 to supply scrap for WWII. OmniSource was a pioneer in adopting formal quality-control programs and in turning scrap into briquettes for foundry and steel-mill furnace use. Today the company rates as one of the largest scrap recycling firms in North America. Through a network of six brokerage offices, it tracks national and international scrap prices and activities. OmniSource operates 32 processing facilities, a secondary aluminum smelting plant, and a heavy-media separation facility. The founder's son, Leonard Rifkin, is chairman and CEO.

EXECUTIVES

Chairman and CEO: Leonard I. Rifkin, age 48
President and COO: Daniel M. Rifkin
EVP and CFO: Gary E. Rohrs
EVP, Administration: Ben A. Eisbart
EVP, Ferrous Group: W. John Marynowski
EVP, Non-Ferrous: Martin Rifkin
EVP, Non-Ferrous: Richard S. Rifkin
SVP, Ferrous Sales: Donald M. Jarrell Sr.
SVP, Industrial Sourcing: Thomas E. Tuschman
Chief Information Officer: Dave Parlette

LOCATIONS

HQ: OmniSource Corporation
  1610 N. Calhoun St., Fort Wayne, IN 46808
Phone: 260-422-5541   **Fax:** 260-423-8528
Web: www.omnisource.com

OmniSource operates 32 facilities in the eastern US and Ontario, Canada.

PRODUCTS/OPERATIONS

Selected Products
Aluminum
Ferrous and nonferrous scrap
Steel briquettes

Selected Services
Metal brokerage

COMPETITORS

Cargill Steel
Commercial Metals
David J. Joseph
International Briquettes
Keywell
Metal Management
Roanoke Electric Steel
Soave
Stelco
Tang Industries

HISTORICAL FINANCIALS
Company Type: Private

Income Statement
*FYE: September 30

	REVENUE ($ mil.)	NET INCOME ($ mil.)	NET PROFIT MARGIN	EMPLOYEES
9/03	1,007	—	—	1,450
9/02	808	—	—	1,350
9/01	691	—	—	1,400
9/00	835	—	—	1,350
9/99	825	—	—	1,500
9/98	680	—	—	1,150
9/97	600	—	—	960
9/96	550	—	—	800
9/95	500	—	—	800
9/94	430	—	—	700
Annual Growth	9.9%	—	—	8.4%

Revenue History

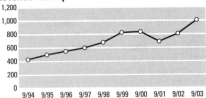

O'Neal Steel

O'Neal Steel has an angle on the steel industry. One of the US's leading private metals service companies, O'Neal sells a full range of metal products — including angles, bars, beams, coil, pipe, plate, and sheet — made from steel, aluminum, brass, and bronze. Its Weldment Fabrication Division makes subassemblies, bracket weldments, and precision parts for the mining and the mobile crane industries. Founded by Kirkman O'Neal in 1922 in Alabama, the company has expanded largely through mergers and acquisitions. It is still owned and run by the O'Neal family.

The company operates around 40 plants in southeastern, Midwestern, Southwestern, and Mountain states, from which it offers such metal-processing services as forming, laser cutting, machining, oxy-fuel and plasma burning, shearing, tube bending, and sawing.

O'Neal's Masonry Arts division was involved in rebuilding the Pentagon after it was destroyed on September 11, 2001, by hijackers. The company provided such supplies as angles, beams, flats, tubing, and aluminum and stainless sheet to assist in completing the project as scheduled.

EXECUTIVES

Chairman: Emmet O'Neal
President and CEO: Bill Jones
COO: Terry Taft
SVP and CFO: Mary Valenta
SVP National Sales: Craft O'Neal
VP Human Resources: Shawn Smith
Director Marketing: Henley Smith
Director Purchasing: Holman Head
IS/IT: Michael Gooldrup
Inside Sales Representative: Susan Gallups

LOCATIONS

HQ: O'Neal Steel, Inc.
744 41st St. North, Birmingham, AL 35222
Phone: 205-599-8000   **Fax:** 205-599-8037
Web: www.onealsteel.com

O'Neal Steel operates metal processing facilities in about 40 locations in the Midwest, Southeast, Southwest, and Mountain areas.

PRODUCTS/OPERATIONS

Selected Products
Alloy bars
Coil
Cold finished bars
Grating
Hot rolled bars
Pipe
Structural shapes
Tubing

Selected Processing Services

Coil processing	Rolling
Cutting	Sawing
Forming	Shearing
Machining	Tube bending
Notching	Welding
Punching and drilling	

COMPETITORS

Canam Manac	Quanex
Cargill Steel	Reliance Steel
Earle M. Jorgensen	Russel Metals
IPSCO	Ryerson Tull
Metalcraft	Worthington Industries
Metals USA	

HISTORICAL FINANCIALS
Company Type: Private

Income Statement
FYE: December 31

	REVENUE ($ mil.)	NET INCOME ($ mil.)	NET PROFIT MARGIN	EMPLOYEES
12/03	770	—	—	2,100
12/02	750	—	—	2,500
12/01	742	—	—	2,500
12/00	941	—	—	2,950
12/99	941	—	—	2,900
12/98	930	—	—	2,675
12/97	755	—	—	2,200
12/96	651	—	—	2,000
12/95	687	—	—	—
12/94	581	—	—	—
Annual Growth	3.2%	—	—	0.7%

Revenue History

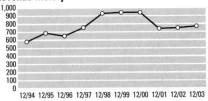

Opus

This Opus can be heard from coast to coast. Founded in 1953 (as Rauenhorst Construction Company), it builds office buildings, warehouses, malls, and business parks for purchase or lease throughout the US. Opus offers architectural and engineering services as well as property management, construction, and financing. The firm has nearly 30 offices across the US. The Gerald Rauenhorst family controls Opus.

EXECUTIVES

Founding Chairman: Gerald (Gerry) Rauenhorst
Chairman: Keith Bednarowski
President and CEO: Mark H. Rauenhorst, age 51
SVP and Chief Investment Officer:
  Andrew C. (Andy) Deckas
SVP and CFO: Ronald W. (Ron) Schiferl
SVP, Secretary, and General Counsel: Dan F. Nicol
SVP Tax: Luz Campa
National Director, Government Programs:
  Tom Olmstead
VP National Account Management, Opus National:
  Julie Kimble
VP, Opus Properties: Wade Lau
VP Human Resources: Janet A. Maistrovich

LOCATIONS

HQ: Opus Corporation
10350 Bren Rd. West, Minnetonka, MN 55343
Phone: 952-656-4444   **Fax:** 952-656-4529
Web: www.opuscorp.com

Opus has offices in Alpharetta, Georgia; Austin, Texas; Columbus, Ohio; Dallas; Denver; Detroit; Fort Lauderdale, Florida; Houston; Indianapolis; Irvine, California; Kansas City, Kansas; Los Angeles; Milwaukee; Minnetonka, Minnesota; Orlando, Florida; Pensacola, Florida; Philadelphia; Phoenix; Plymouth Meeting, Pennsylvania; Portland, Oregon; Rosemont, Illinois; Sacramento, California; San Francisco; Seattle; St. Louis; and Tampa.

PRODUCTS/OPERATIONS

Selected Subsidiaries
Opus Architects & Engineers, Inc.
Opus East, L.L.C.
Opus Military Communities, L.L.C.
Opus National, L.L.C.
Opus North Corporation
Opus North Management Corporation
Opus Northwest Management, L.L.C.
Opus Northwest, L.L.C.
Opus Properties, L.L.C.
Opus South Corporation
Opus South Management Corporation
Opus West Corporation
Opus West Management, L.L.C.

COMPETITORS

Alter
Brookfield Properties
Castle & Cooke
Forest City Enterprises
Hines Interests
Irvine Company
Lincoln Property
Structure Tone
Trizec Properties

HISTORICAL FINANCIALS
Company Type: Private

Income Statement
FYE: December 31

	REVENUE ($ mil.)	NET INCOME ($ mil.)	NET PROFIT MARGIN	EMPLOYEES
12/03	1,100	—	—	1,136
12/02	967	—	—	1,275
12/01	1,200	—	—	1,400
12/00	1,400	—	—	1,250
12/99	1,100	—	—	1,250
12/98	900	—	—	1,250
12/97	575	—	—	1,200
12/96	450	—	—	600
Annual Growth	13.6%	—	—	9.5%

Revenue History

Ormet

Ormet's canny business skills have made it one of the US's leading producers of aluminum. Through its Ormet Primary Aluminum subsidiary, the company smelts aluminum ore (bauxite) and manufactures aluminum ingot, billet (pressed bars), sheet, foil, and other products for the fabrication, extrusion, and conversion markets. The company's Ormet Aluminum Mill Products subsidiary further processes the aluminum into auto trim, cans, gift wrap, packaging, and other products. Ormet operates eight plants, primarily in the midwestern US. In 2004, Ormet filed for Chapter 11 protection in order to reorganize the organization. CEO Emmett Boyle owns the company, which was founded in Hannibal, Ohio, in 1954.

EXECUTIVES

Chairman and CEO: R. Emmett Boyle
President and COO: Michael S. Williams
VP, Finance: Jack Teitz
VP, Primary Operations and Cast Products: Gary Mallett
VP Ormet Aluminum Mill Products Operations:
Ned Damron
Director, Corporate Communications: Laurie Leonard
Director, Personnel: Lisa Riedel
Manager, Hannibal Rolling Mill Division: Steve Jorris
Manager, Primary Division: Dan Roscoe

LOCATIONS

HQ: Ormet Corporation
1233 Main St., Ste. 4000, Wheeling, WV 26003
Phone: 304-234-3900 **Fax:** 304-234-3929
Web: www.ormet.com

Ormet operates in the US from nine facilities in seven states, including sites along the Mississippi and Ohio Rivers.

PRODUCTS/OPERATIONS

Selected Products

Alumina
Aluminum foil
  Capacitor anode and cathode foils
  Standard foil products
Aluminum sheet
  Automotive and appliance trim
  Common alloy non-heat treatable
  Intermediate alloy non-heat treatable
  Lithographic sheet
  Nameplate
  Reroll-hot band
  Standard painted coil sheet
Primary aluminum
  Billet
  Ingot
  Sow

Selected Subsidiaries

Formcast Development (aluminum castings)
Ormet Aluminum Mill Products Corp. (processed aluminum products)
Ormet Primary Aluminum Corp. (smelting; billet, foil, ingot, sheet, and other products)
Specialty Blanks, Inc. (industrial aluminum alloy blanks)

COMPETITORS

Alcan
Alcoa
Corus Group
Hydro Aluminium
Kaiser Aluminum
MAXXAM
Mitsubishi Chemical
Nippon Light Metal
Norsk Hydro
Pechiney
Rio Tinto
SEPI

HISTORICAL FINANCIALS
Company Type: Private

Income Statement
FYE: December 31

	REVENUE ($ mil.)	NET INCOME ($ mil.)	NET PROFIT MARGIN	EMPLOYEES
12/03	600	—	—	2,700
12/02	650	—	—	2,750
12/01	700	—	—	3,000
12/00	700	—	—	3,000
12/99	690	—	—	3,300
12/98	780	—	—	3,300
12/97	910	—	—	3,300
12/96	830	—	—	3,300
12/95	960	—	—	3,300
12/94	880	—	—	3,300
Annual Growth	(4.2%)	—	—	(2.2%)

Revenue History

Ourisman Automotive

Whether your preference is for American or foreign, Ford or Chevy, Ourisman Automotive Enterprises can satisfy your vehicular proclivity. Serving the Washington, DC, area, Ourisman Automotive operates some 15 dealerships throughout Maryland and Virginia. The company's Chevrolet, Chrysler, Dodge, Ford, Honda, Mitsubishi, Suzuki, and Toyota dealerships sell both new and used vehicles. Ourisman Automotive also sells parts and offers service and financing. The Ourisman family, which owns the company, founded Ourisman Automotive Enterprises in 1921.

EXECUTIVES

Chairman: Mandell J. Ourisman, age 77
President: John Ourisman
CFO: Mohamed Reshed
General Manager: Abbas Khademi

LOCATIONS

HQ: Ourisman Automotive Enterprises
4400 Branch Ave., Marlow Heights, MD 20748
Phone: 301-423-4028 **Fax:** 301-423-5725
Web: www.ourisman.com

COMPETITORS

Atlantic Automotive
Brown Automotive
Hall Auto World
Jim Koons Automotive
March/Hodge
Pohanka Automotive
Rosenthal Automotive
Sheehy Auto

HISTORICAL FINANCIALS
Company Type: Private

Income Statement
FYE: December 31

	REVENUE ($ mil.)	NET INCOME ($ mil.)	NET PROFIT MARGIN	EMPLOYEES
12/03	790	—	—	1,100
12/02	762	—	—	1,050
12/01	656	—	—	1,000
12/00	622	—	—	1,000
12/99	549	—	—	950
12/98	535	—	—	973
12/97	520	—	—	1,025
12/96	518	—	—	1,001
12/95	520	—	—	949
12/94	491	—	—	949
Annual Growth	5.4%	—	—	1.7%

Revenue History

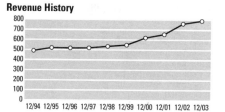

Outsourcing Solutions

Pay now or deal with Outsourcing Solutions (OSI) later. The accounts-receivable management firm provides collection, portfolio purchasing, and outsourcing services to its customers, which include credit card, financial, utility, and health care companies, as well as education, government, and retail clients. The acquisitive company operates some 65 offices in about 25 states; it also offers its services in Canada, Mexico, and Puerto Rico. Services include providing call centers for credit authorization and customer service. OSI also purchases new and delinquent accounts from creditors. OSI, which is majority owned by Madison Dearborn Partners, filed for and emerged from Chapter 11 reorganization in 2003.

The 2003 Chapter 11 filing was primarily due to restructuring debt, rather than any loss in business volume. A major player in the company's rebound was Merrill Lynch, who provided OSI with a helping hand in the form of a $90 million credit facility to strengthen its debt-purchasing arm, OSI Portfolio Services.

EXECUTIVES

President and CEO: Kevin T. Keleghan
EVP and CFO: Gary L. Weller
EVP and President, TSI Business Services Group: Michael A. DiMarco
EVP and President, Financial Services Business Group: Bryan K. Faliero
EVP and President, Telecom/Utilities Business Services Group: Michael B. Staed
EVP, Collections Operations and Specialty Services: Jeffrey S. Wahl
EVP, Sales: Michael G. Meyer
EVP, Business Development and Portfolio Acquisitions: Timothy J. Bauer
SVP and CIO: Russell L. Goldammer
SVP, General Counsel, and Secretary: Eric R. Fencl
SVP, Human Resources: C. Bradford McLeod
Manager, Corporate Communications: Rita Holmes-Bobo
SVP, Operations, Bancard & Pre-Legal: Matt Edmunds
Auditors: Deloitte & Touche LLP

LOCATIONS

HQ: Outsourcing Solutions Inc.
390 S. Woods Mill Rd., Ste. 350, Chesterfield, MO 63017
Phone: 314-576-0022 **Fax:** 314-576-1867
Web: www.osi.to

PRODUCTS/OPERATIONS

Selected Subsidiaries and Affiliates
Coast-to-Coast Consulting, LLC
Greystone Business Group, LLC
Jennifer Loomis & Associates, Inc.
Medical Accounting Service
North Shore Agency, Inc.
OSI Collection Services, Inc.
OSI Education Services, Inc.
OSI Outsourcing Services, Inc.
OSI Portfolio Services, Inc.
Qualink, Inc.
RWC Consulting Group, LLC
Transworld Systems Inc.
University Accounting Services, LLC

COMPETITORS

Asta Funding
BA Merchant Services
Deluxe
Encore Capital Group, Inc.
Equifax
GC Services
IntelliRisk Management
Nationwide Recovery
NCO Group
Portfolio Recovery
Rampart Capital

HISTORICAL FINANCIALS
Company Type: Private

Income Statement
FYE: December 31

	REVENUE ($ mil.)	NET INCOME ($ mil.)	NET PROFIT MARGIN	EMPLOYEES
12/03	488	—	—	6,200
12/02	592	—	—	7,200
12/01	612	—	—	9,000
12/00	543	—	—	7,600
12/99	504	—	—	7,000
12/98	479	—	—	7,000
12/97	272	—	—	5,000
12/96	106	—	—	—
12/95	30	—	—	—
12/94	39	—	—	—
Annual Growth	32.3%	—	—	3.7%

Revenue History
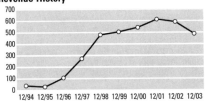

Oxbow

Oxbow is bullish on energy and mining. The diversified firm's Oxbow Carbon & Minerals (OCM) unit produces and markets coke, coal, petroleum, and carbon products. Other company operations include Gunnison Energy, which is developing natural gas sites in Colorado; Oxbow Mining, a coal mine in Colorado; and Oxbow Realty Services, which develops and manages commercial and residential real estate projects. Oxbow is controlled by William Koch, an America's Cup winner who founded Oxbow in 1983 after being ousted from the family business (Koch Industries) by brothers Charles and David. Oxbow nearly doubled in size when its OCM unit acquired Applied Industrial Materials Corporation (AIMCOR) in late 2003.

EXECUTIVES

CEO: William I. (Bill) Koch, age 63
President and COO, Oxbow Carbon and Minerals: Brian Acton, age 53
CFO: Zachary K. Shipley, age 52
VP and General Counsel: Richard P. Callahan, age 59
President, Oxbow Realty Services: Kenneth A. Swanson
EVP, Oxbow Carbon and Minerals: Lawrence H. Black
EVP, Oxbow Realty Services: Russell J. Burke
Director of Corporate Communications: Brad Goldstein
Director of Human Resources: Kathy Flaherty
Director of Operations, Oxbow Realty Services: Kathleen M. Hicks
Director Property Management, Oxbow Realty Services: Chris Maltas
Auditors: PricewaterhouseCoopers LLP

LOCATIONS

HQ: Oxbow Corporation
1601 Forum Place, Ste. 1400, West Palm Beach, FL 33401
Phone: 561-697-4300 **Fax:** 561-640-8747
Web: www.oxbow.com

Oxbow has offices in Australia, Brazil, Canada, China, Egypt, Germany, India, Mexico, the Netherlands, the UK, the US, and Venezuela.

PRODUCTS/OPERATIONS

Selected Operations
Gunnison Energy (development of natural gas resources at North Fork Valley, Colorado)
Oxbow Carbon & Minerals (mining and marketing of coal, petroleum coke, metallurgical coke, steel, gypsum, industrial minerals, and combustion ash)
Oxbow Mining LLC (Elk Creek Mine, located in western Colorado)
Oxbow Realty Services (commercial and residential real estate development and management, primarily in New England)
Oxbow Steel

COMPETITORS

Alliance Resource
Black Hills
Drummond
Duke Energy
Dynegy
Enron
Horizon Natural Resources
Kinder Morgan Energy Partners
Koch
MidAmerican Energy
ONEOK
Sunoco
Westmoreland Coal

HISTORICAL FINANCIALS
Company Type: Private

Income Statement
FYE: December 31

	ESTIMATED REVENUE ($ mil.)	NET INCOME ($ mil.)	NET PROFIT MARGIN	EMPLOYEES
12/03	1,000	—	—	1,000
12/02	450	—	—	500
12/01	450	—	—	500
12/00	450	—	—	500
12/99	440	—	—	500
12/98	475	—	—	800
12/97	500	—	—	700
12/96	450	—	—	900
12/95	425	—	—	900
12/94	720	—	—	1,600
Annual Growth	3.7%	—	—	(5.1%)

Revenue History
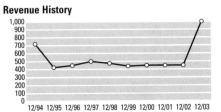

Oxford Automotive

Oxford Automotive, a supplier of metal car and truck components, is riding the sport utility vehicle (SUV) boom all the way to the bank. The company manufactures suspension and structural systems, leaf springs, and other components for the automotive manufacturing industry. A majority of those components roll out on SUVs, minivans, and light trucks made by such companies as GM, Ford, Renault, Peugeot, and DaimlerChrysler. The company's products can be found on Ford's F-Series pickups and on DaimlerChrysler's Ram pickups. After a recapitalization, MatlinPatterson Global Opportunities Partners controls the company.

EXECUTIVES

Chairman: Mark R. Patterson, age 53
CEO: David L. Treadwell
President and COO: Jeffrey W. Wilson
CFO: Patrick Flynn
SVP, Human Resources: Dennis Bemis
VP and Treasurer: Robert R. Krakowiak
Interim President, Europe and Director:
 Hervé Guillaume
Auditors: PricewaterhouseCoopers LLP

LOCATIONS

HQ: Oxford Automotive, Inc.
 850 Stephenson Hwy., Troy, MI 48083
Phone: 248-577-4900   **Fax:** 248-577-4998
Web: www.oxauto.com

Oxford Automotive has operations in Argentina, Canada, France, Germany, Italy, Mexico, Turkey, the US, and Venezuela.

PRODUCTS/OPERATIONS

Selected Products

Mechanisms
 Handbrakes
 Hood and trunk
 Jacks
 Seat latches
 Sliding door mechanisms
Structures
 Body side assemblies
 Cargo doors
 Door assemblies
 Floor plan assemblies
 Front engine compartment
 Radiator yokes
 Rail assemblies (front and rear)
 Rear compartment
 Rear floor members
 Tailgate assemblies
 Toe-to-dash panels
Suspension
 Coil springs
 Control arm subassemblies
 Multi-leaf conventional springs
 Parabolic long taper springs
 Rear suspension modules
 Spring mounting hangers and shackles
 Spring towers

COMPETITORS

Active Tool & Manufacturing
A.G. Simpson
American Axle & Manufacturing
ArvinMeritor, Inc.
Dana
Lear
Magna International
Midway Products Group
SANLUIS
Shiloh Industries
ThyssenKrupp Budd
Tower Automotive
Wagon plc

HISTORICAL FINANCIALS

Company Type: Private

Income Statement
FYE: March 31

	REVENUE ($ mil.)	NET INCOME ($ mil.)	NET PROFIT MARGIN	EMPLOYEES
3/03	1,000	—	—	7,200
3/02	900	—	—	7,000
3/01	824	—	—	7,400
3/00	809	—	—	5,500
3/99	592	—	—	5,100
3/98	410	—	—	3,800
3/97	137	—	—	—
3/96	85	—	—	—
3/95	75	—	—	—
3/94	65	—	—	—
Annual Growth	35.4%	—	—	13.6%

Revenue History

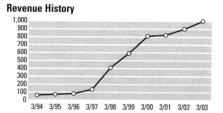

Pabst

The Pabst Brewing Company is a 19th century brewer retooled for the 21st century. Pabst, founded in 1844, today is a "virtual" brewer. It owns no brewery; instead, Pabst pays other brewers, such as Miller and Lion Brewery, to brew the beers, while it retains ownership of the brands (Pabst Blue Ribbon, Pearl, Lone Star, Old Milwaukee, Schlitz, and Colt 45) and markets the products. The Pabst Brewing Company is owned by the Kalmanovitz Charitable Trust.

Pabst's market share can't compare with those of the nation's top brewing giants, but its Pabst Blue Ribbon is enjoying a surge in popularity among rebel beer drinkers who resist the mass marketing of Pabst's rivals. In 2003, Pabst had about 3% of the US beer-drinking market, still exceeding many premium imports such as Heineken and Guinness. The Kalmanovitz Charitable Trust is reportedly interested in selling Pabst.

EXECUTIVES

President and CEO: Brian Kovalchuk
CFO: Brian Bizer
VP and General Counsel: Yeoryios Apallas

LOCATIONS

HQ: Pabst Brewing Company
 121 Interpark Blvd., Ste. 300,
 San Antonio, TX 78216
Phone: 210-226-0231   **Fax:** 210-299-6807
Web: www.pabst.com

COMPETITORS

Adolph Coors
Anheuser-Busch
Constellation Brands
Gambrinus
Heineken
InBev USA
Miller Brewing
Molson
Stone Brewing

HISTORICAL FINANCIALS

Company Type: Private

Income Statement
FYE: June 30

	ESTIMATED REVENUE ($ mil.)	NET INCOME ($ mil.)	NET PROFIT MARGIN	EMPLOYEES
6/03	600	—	—	700
6/02	575	—	—	700
6/01	750	—	—	300
6/00	1,000	—	—	750
6/99	1,200	—	—	700
6/98	500	—	—	1,500
6/97	550	—	—	1,600
6/96	550	—	—	1,604
6/95	600	—	—	1,300
6/94	595	—	—	2,400
Annual Growth	0.1%	—	—	(12.8%)

Revenue History

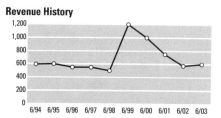

Pacific Mutual

Life insurance is alive and whale at Pacific Mutual Holding. Primary operating subsidiary Pacific Life (whose logo is a breaching whale) is the largest California-based life insurer. Lines of business include life insurance (a variety of products for individuals and small businesses); annuities and mutual funds (also geared to individuals and small businesses); institutional products (including funding agreements, annuities, and guaranteed investment contracts, or GICs) for pension plans and other institutional investors; and group insurance (medical, accident, and health insurance targeted to small and midsized employers).

Major Pacific Mutual subsidiaries include mutual fund and annuities distribution network Pacific Select Distributors; Pacific Asset Funding, which provides trade financing and related services; College Savings Bank, which offers a variety of college savings vehicles; and aircraft leasing operations Aviation Capital Group. Pacific Mutual also has a stake in Allianz Dresdner Asset Management of America (formerly PIMCO Advisors), a major investment management firm majority-owned by insurer Allianz.

Pacific Mutual owns Pacific Life and the other operating subsidiaries through stock company Pacific LifeCorp. Pacific Mutual's conversion from straight mutual ownership to mutual holding company structure gives it more flexibility and the option of an IPO; meanwhile, policyholders retain ownership of the company, but hold no stock.

Pacific Mutual sharpened its focus on individuals and small businesses in 2001 with the sale of its reinsurance unit to what is now Scottish Re; Pacific Mutual holds a minority stake in the reinsurer.

HISTORY

Pacific Mutual began business in 1868 in Sacramento, California, as a stock company. Its board was dominated by California business and political leaders, including three of the "Big Four" who created the Central Pacific Railroad (Charles Crocker, Mark Hopkins, and Leland Stanford) and three former governors (Stanford, Newton Booth, and Henry Huntley Haight). Stanford (founder of Stanford University) was the company's first president and policyholder.

By 1870 Pacific Mutual was selling life insurance throughout most of the western US. Expansion continued in the early 1870s into Colorado, Kentucky, Nebraska, New York, Ohio, and Texas. The company ventured into Mexico in 1873 but sold few policies. It had more luck in China, accepting its first risk there in 1875, and in Hawaii, where it started business in 1877. In 1881 Pacific Mutual moved to San Francisco.

Leland Stanford died in 1893. The eponymous university and Stanford's widow, though rich in assets, found themselves struggling through a US economic depression. The benefit from Stanford's policy kept the university open until the estate was settled.

In 1905 Conservative Life bought the firm. The Pacific Mutual name survived the acquisition just as its records survived the fire that ravaged San Francisco after the 1906 earthquake. Pacific Mutual then relocated to Los Angeles.

The company squeaked through the Depression after a flood of claims on its noncancellable disability income policies forced Pacific Mutual into a reorganization plan initiated by the California insurance commissioner (1936). After WWII, Pacific Mutual entered the group insurance and pension markets.

After 83 years as a stock company and an eight-year stock purchasing program, Pacific Mutual became a true mutual in 1959.

Pacific Mutual relocated to Newport Beach in 1972. During the 1980s it built up its financial services operations, including its Pacific Investment Management Co. (PIMCO, founded 1971). The company was in trouble even before the stock crash of 1987 because of health care costs and over-investment in real estate. That year it brought in CEO Thomas Sutton, who sold off real estate and emphasized HMOs and fee-based financial services.

In the 1990s the firm cut costs and increased its fee income. PIMCO Advisors, L.P. was formed in 1994 when PIMCO merged with Thomson Advisory Group. The merger gave Pacific Mutual a retail market for its fixed-income products, a stake in the resulting public company, and sales that offset interest-rate variations and changes in the health care system.

In 1997 the company assumed the corporate-owned life insurance business of failed Confederation Life Insurance; it also merged insolvent First Capital Life into Pacific Life as Pacific Corinthian Life. That year Pacific Mutual became the first top-10 US mutual to convert to a mutual holding company, thus allowing it the option of issuing stock to fund acquisitions. Because the firm remained partially mutual, however, policyholders retained ownership but got no shares of Pacific LifeCorp, its new stock company.

To compete with such one-stop financial service behemoths as Citigroup, Pacific Mutual began selling annuities through a Compass Bank subsidiary in 1998. The next year it bought controlling interests in broker-dealer M.L. Stern and investment adviser Tower Asset Management. In 2000 the world's #2 insurer, Allianz, bought all of PIMCO Advisors (now Allianz Dresdner Asset Management of America) other than the interest retained by Pacific Mutual when it spun off the investment manager; Pacific Mutual gradually decreased its holdings in the firm through ongoing sales to Allianz.

EXECUTIVES

Chairman and CEO, Pacific Mutual Holding, Pacific LifeCorp, and Pacific Life: Thomas C. Sutton, age 62
President, Pacific Life: Glenn S. Schafer, age 55
EVP and CFO, Pacific Life: Khanh T. Tran, age 46
EVP, Securities Division, Pacific Life: Larry J. Card
EVP, Group Insurance Division, Pacific Life: David W. Gartley
EVP, Institutional Products Division, Pacific Life; EVP and Chief Credit Officer, Pacific Financial Products: Mark W. Holmlund
EVP, Real Estate Division, Pacific Life: Michael S. Robb
EVP, Annuities and Mutual Funds Division, Pacific Life; Chairman and CEO, Pacific Select Distributors: Gerald W. (Bill) Robinson
SVP, Sales Office Marketing, Life Insurance Division, Pacific Life: Michael A. Bell
SVP, Human Resources, Pacific Life: Anthony J. Bonno
SVP, Sales, Annuities and Mutual Funds Division, Pacific Life: Dewey P. Bushaw
SVP and General Counsel, Pacific Life: David R. Carmichael
SVP, Strategic Planning and Development, Pacific Life: Marc S. Franklin
SVP, Public Affairs, Pacific Life: Robert G. Haskell
SVP, Portfolio Management, Securities Division, Pacific Life: Elaine M. Havens
SVP, Administration, Annuities and Mutual Funds Division, Pacific Life: Robert C. Hsu
SVP, Finance, Group Insurance Division, Pacific Life: W. Douglas Lehman
SVP, Risk and Financial Management, Institutional Products Division, Pacific Life, Pacific Life: Henry M. McMillan
SVP, Guaranteed Annuities, Institutional Products Division, Pacific Life: John E. Milberg
SVP, Finance and Administration, Life Insurance Division, Pacific Life: S. Gene Schofield
SVP, Operations, Group Insurance Division, Pacific Life: Christina M. Sumpter
Auditors: Deloitte & Touche LLP

LOCATIONS

HQ: Pacific Mutual Holding Company
700 Newport Center Dr., Newport Beach, CA 92660
Phone: 949-219-3011   **Fax:** 949-219-7614
Web: www.pacificlife.com

Pacific Mutual Holding has insurance operations throughout the US.

PRODUCTS/OPERATIONS

2003 Sales

	$ mil.	% of total
Net investment income	1,804	39
Insurance premiums	1,146	24
Policy fees	932	20
Net realized investment gain	231	5
Commission revenue	220	5
Other income	335	7
Total	**4,668**	**100**

2003 Sales By Segment

	$ mil.	% of total
Life Insurance	1,210	26
Institutional Products	1,069	23
Group Insurance	990	21
Broker-Dealers	776	16
Annuities & Mutual Funds	593	13
Corporate & Other	30	1
Total	**4,668**	**100**

Selected Products and Services

Life Insurance Division
  Interest-sensitive whole life
  Joint and last-survivor life
  Term life
  Universal life insurance
  Variable universal life
Institutional Products Division
  Funding agreements
  Single premium group annuity contracts
  Stable value products
    Floating rate guaranteed interest contracts (GICs)
    Separate account GICs
    Synthetic GICs
    Traditional GICs
  Structured settlement annuities
Group Insurance Division
  Dental and vision insurance
  Disability income insurance
  Life and accidental death and dismemberment insurance
  Medical and prescription drug insurance
  Stop loss contracts
Annuities & Mutual Fund Division
  529 College savings plans
  Fixed annuities
  Mutual funds
  Variable annuities

Selected Subsidiaries and Affiliates

Allianz Dresdner Asset Management of America L.P.
Aviation Capital Group (91%)
College Savings Bank
Pacific Asset Funding, LLC
Pacific Life & Annuity Company
Pacific LifeCorp.
Pacific Life Insurance Company
Pacific Select Distributors, Inc.
Associated Securities Corp.
  M.L. Stern & Co., LLC
  Mutual Service Corporation
  United Planners' Financial Services of America
  Waterstone Financial Group

COMPETITORS

Acordia	MetLife
Aetna	MONY
AXA Financial	Mutual of Omaha
Blue Cross	Nationwide
Charles Schwab	Nationwide Financial Network
CIGNA	New York Life
Citigroup	Northwestern Mutual
GenAmerica	PacifiCare
Great-West Life Assurance	Principal Financial
Guardian Life	Prudential
Hartford Life	St. Paul Travelers
Health Net	StanCorp Financial Group
John Hancock Financial Services	State Farm
Liberty Mutual	USAA
Lincoln National	WellPoint Health Networks
MassMutual	

HISTORICAL FINANCIALS
Company Type: Mutual company

Income Statement
FYE: December 31

	ASSETS ($ mil.)	NET INCOME ($ mil.)	INCOME AS % OF ASSETS	EMPLOYEES
12/03	67,422	418	0.6%	—
12/02	57,305	50	0.1%	3,700
12/01	56,055	247	0.4%	3,600
12/00	54,784	995	1.8%	3,600
12/99	50,123	371	0.7%	3,799
12/98	39,884	242	0.6%	2,700
12/97	34,009	176	0.5%	3,422
12/96	27,065	167	0.6%	2,750
12/95	17,589	85	0.5%	2,700
12/94	14,728	81	0.5%	2,400
Annual Growth	18.4%	20.0%	—	5.6%

2003 Year-End Financials
Equity as % of assets: 7.3%
Return on assets: 0.7%
Return on equity: 9.0%
Long-term debt ($ mil.): 1,166
Sales ($ mil.): 4,668

Net Income History

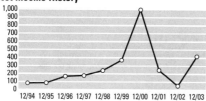

Packard Foundation

One of the wealthiest philanthropic organizations in the US, The David and Lucile Packard Foundation primarily provides grants to not-for-profit entities operating in three areas: conservation and science; children, families, and communities; and population. The foundation has $6 billion in assets and awards about $200 million in national and international grants, with an extra focus on four northern California counties (Monterey, San Mateo, Santa Clara, and Santa Cruz). The late David Packard (co-founder of Hewlett-Packard) and his wife, the late Lucile Salter Packard, created the foundation in 1964. Their children now run the organization.

EXECUTIVES
Chairman: Susan Packard Orr
Vice Chairman: Nancy Packard Burnett
Vice Chairman: Julie E. Packard
President and CEO: Carol S. Larson, age 51
VP and CFO: George A. Vera, age 60
Secretary and General Counsel: Barbara P. Wright, age 56
Director Children, Families, and Communities Program: Lois Salisbury
Director Conservation and Science Program: James Leape
Director Population Program: Sarah Clark
Auditors: Deloitte & Touche LLP

LOCATIONS
HQ: The David and Lucile Packard Foundation
300 2nd St., Los Altos, CA 94022
Phone: 650-948-7658 **Fax:** 650-948-5793
Web: www.packard.org

PRODUCTS/OPERATIONS

Selected Grants
Conservation and Science
  Alaska Conservation Foundation ($450,000)
  American Association for the Advancement of Science ($4,375,000)
  American Indian College Fund ($293,000)
  California Institute of Technology ($625,000)
  Harvard University ($625,000)
  Rice University ($625,000)
Population
  Alan Guttmacher Institute ($900,000)
  California Planned Parenthood Education Fund ($250,000)
  Equilibres & Populations, Paris, France ($325,000)
  Raks Thai Foundation ($10,000)
Children, Families, and Communities
  Action Against Crime and Violence Education Fund ($305,000)
  Afterschool Alliance ($75,000)
  Cabrillo College Foundation ($350,000)
  Children's Defense Fund ($200,000)
  RAND Corporation ($25,000)

HISTORICAL FINANCIALS
Company Type: Foundation

Income Statement
FYE: December 31

	REVENUE ($ mil.)	NET INCOME ($ mil.)	NET PROFIT MARGIN	EMPLOYEES
12/03	1,501	—	—	83
12/02	92	—	—	90
12/01	121	—	—	100
12/00	146	—	—	—
12/99	5,570	—	—	—
12/98	1,017	—	—	—
12/97	663	—	—	100
12/96	462	—	—	100
12/95	907	—	—	—
12/94	289	—	—	—
Annual Growth	20.1%	—	—	(2.6%)

Revenue History

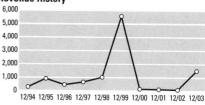

PanAmSat

One of the world's largest communications satellite operators, PanAmSat blankets the globe with 25 in-orbit satellites. The company's satellites provide links for broadcasters, news organizations, and telecommunications companies worldwide. PanAmSat also transmits programming for direct-to-home (DTH) TV services, provides technical support for live broadcasts, and serves private corporate networks using very small aperture terminals (VSATs). The company delivers streaming video to Internet backbone networks for about 50 international ISPs through its network. Private equity firm Kohlberg Kravis Roberts & Co. owns about 80% of PanAmSat.

PanAmSat acquired Sonic Telecom, a provider of videoconferencing services, in 2003 as part of an effort to broaden its array of services. The next year PanAmSat was acquired by a group of private investors including Kohlberg, Kravis, Roberts & Co. and affiliates of The Carlyle Group and Providence Equity Partners.

EXECUTIVES
President, CEO, and Director: Joseph R. (Joe) Wright Jr., $1,395,000 pay
EVP and CFO: Michael J. Inglese, age 43, $492,000 pay
EVP and COO: James B. Frownfelter, age 40, $747,000 pay
EVP, Global Sales and Marketing: Mike Antonovich
EVP, Corporate Development, General Counsel, and Secretary: James W. (Jim) Cuminale, age 51, $608,000 pay
EVP; President, G2 Satellite Solutions: Thomas E. (Tom) Eaton Jr., age 49, $561,000 pay
SVP, Human Resources: Douglas (Max) Reid
Auditors: Deloitte & Touche LLP

LOCATIONS
HQ: PanAmSat Corporation
20 Westport Rd., Wilton, CT 06897
Phone: 203-210-8000 **Fax:** 203-210-9163
Web: www.panamsat.com

The PanAmSat network is capable of reaching more than 98% of the world's population.

2003 Sales

	% of total
US	44
Latin America	19
Asia	15
Africa	9
Other regions	13
Total	**100**

PRODUCTS/OPERATIONS

2003 Sales by Service Area

	% of total
Video	60
Network	25
Government	9
Other	6
Total	**100**

Selected Services

Video
  DTH (transmission of multiple TV channels for household reception)
  Full-time contribution (satellite transmission services for the full-time transmission of programming to network affiliates or broadcast centers)
  Special events (short-term satellite services that provide broadcasters with on-the-scene coverage of sporting events and breaking news)
  Video distribution (full-time transmission of TV programming)
Network
  Carrier services (provided to telecommunications carriers)
  Internet services (provided to content providers and ISPs)
  Private business networks (corporate data networks)
Government
  Fleet redundancy
  Global coverage
  Teleport facilities
Other services
  In-orbit backup services (backup transponder capacity)
  Telemetry, tracking, and control (maintains the proper orbital location and attitude of satellites and monitors on-board systems)

COMPETITORS

Akamai
APT Satellite
Asia Satellite Telecommunications
Eutelsat
Gilat Satellite
Global Crossing
Inmarsat
Intelsat
Level 3 Communications
Lockheed Martin
Loral Space
New Skies
Qwest
Satélites Mexicanos
SES GLOBAL
Tyco Telecommunications

HISTORICAL FINANCIALS

Company Type: Private

Income Statement				FYE: December 31
	REVENUE ($ mil.)	NET INCOME ($ mil.)	NET PROFIT MARGIN	EMPLOYEES
12/03	831	100	12.0%	700
12/02	812	85	10.5%	714
12/01	870	31	3.5%	730
12/00	1,024	126	12.3%	805
12/99	811	122	15.1%	600
12/98	767	125	16.2%	555
12/97	630	113	17.9%	450
12/96	247	62	25.0%	210
12/95	116	18	15.1%	173
12/94	64	18	28.3%	150
Annual Growth	33.0%	20.9%	—	18.7%

2003 Year-End Financials

Debt ratio: 53.4%
Return on equity: 3.2%
Cash ($ mil.): 511
Current ratio: 6.02
Long-term debt ($ mil.): 1,697

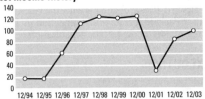

Net Income History

Park Nicollet Health Services

Park Nicollet Health Services serves the Twin Cities area of Minnesota. Its operations include Methodist Hospital, which has some 425 beds and offers a range of general, surgical, and specialty health care. Also part of the health system is Park Nicollet Clinic, a network of 25 facilities in the Minneapolis area that provide primary care as well as specialized services such as vision correction, cancer treatment, rehabilitation, and plastic surgery. The Jane Brattain Breast Center provides mammograms, breast cancer treatment, support and education, and other services. Park Nicollet Institute performs medical research.

EXECUTIVES

CEO: David K. Wessner, age 52
COO: John W. Herman
CFO: David J. Cooke
SVP, Process Management: Michael (Mike) Kaupa
VP, Marketing and Communications: Carol Greenland
VP, Human Resources: Arthur LaPoint
Chief Medical Officer: Samuel E. (Sam) Carlson
CIO: Francis Cheung
Chief Nursing Officer: Kathryn D. Kallas
Director, Media Relations: Jeremiah Whitten

LOCATIONS

HQ: Park Nicollet Health Services
  6500 Excelsior Blvd., St. Louis Park, MN 55426
Phone: 952-993-5000 **Fax:** 952-993-8414
Web: www.parknicollet.com

HISTORICAL FINANCIALS

Company Type: Not-for-profit

Income Statement				FYE: December 31
	REVENUE ($ mil.)	NET INCOME ($ mil.)	NET PROFIT MARGIN	EMPLOYEES
12/03	767	—	—	7,500

Parkdale Mills

Like that nice, soft-spun cotton in your undies? Thank Parkdale Mills. Parkdale, founded in 1916, is the largest independent yarn spinner in the US. The company manufactures cotton and cotton-polyester blend yarns and specializes in spun yarn that winds up in consumer goods such as sheets, towels, underwear, and hosiery. Parkdale has customers worldwide, including Jockey International, Lands' End, Fieldcrest Cannon, L.L. Bean, and Springmaid. The company operates and owns 66% of Parkdale America, a joint venture with polyester and nylon yarn maker Unifi. It also operates mills in Mexico through a joint venture with Burlington Industries. Chairman Duke Kimbrell owns about half of Parkdale.

EXECUTIVES

Chairman: W. Duke Kimbrell, age 79
President and CEO: Anderson D. Warlick, age 47
VP, Weaving Sales: Bill Alfers
VP, Marketing: Charles F. (Charlie) Dickinson
VP, Hosiery Sales: Freddie Harris
VP, Knitting and International Sales: Charles Heilig

LOCATIONS

HQ: Parkdale Mills, Inc.
  P.O. Box 1787, Gastonia, NC 28053
Phone: 704-874-5000 **Fax:** 704-874-5176
Web: www.parkdalemills.com

Parkdale Mills has manufacturing facilities in North Carolina and Virginia. Its fiber distribution facilities are located in North Carolina.

PRODUCTS/OPERATIONS

Selected Products

Hosiery yarns (cotton and cotton heather yarns)
Knitting yarns (cotton and polyester-cotton blends)
Weaving yarns (cotton and polyester-cotton blends)

COMPETITORS

Avondale Incorporated
Burke Mills
Fuji Spinning
Guilford Mills
National Textiles
Nisshinbo

HISTORICAL FINANCIALS

Company Type: Private

Income Statement				FYE: September 30
	ESTIMATED REVENUE ($ mil.)	NET INCOME ($ mil.)	NET PROFIT MARGIN	EMPLOYEES
9/02	900	—	—	2,500
9/01	1,001	—	—	3,650
9/00	1,000	—	—	3,600
9/99	934	—	—	3,600
9/98	850	—	—	3,200
9/97	960	—	—	3,000
9/96	550	—	—	2,600
Annual Growth	8.6%	—	—	(0.7%)

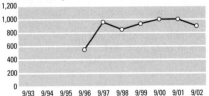

Revenue History

Parsons

Almost evangelically, Parsons carries its message — and its engineering, procurement, and construction management services — worldwide. The company provides design, planning, and construction management through four main operating groups: advanced technologies, commercial technology, infrastructure and technology, and transportation. Among its many projects, Parsons has designed power plants; built dams, resorts, and shopping centers; and provided environmental services such as the cleanup of hazardous nuclear wastes. Parsons has also added improvements to airports and rail systems, bridges, and highways. Customers of the employee-owned company include government agencies and private industries.

The company has diversified in order to compete in every major region of the world. It has even provided vehicle emissions and inspections as part of its advanced technologies offerings. Through its commercial technology group it provides services to a broad range of communications, industrial, and technology customers, such as telecom carriers, equipment manufacturers, state and federal government agencies, pharmaceutical firms, defense contractors, and transportation agencies.

Among Parsons' projects has been its participation since 1998 in the US Army's programs for alternative technologies for chemical weapons disposal. The company established the Parsons Fabrication Facility in Pasco, Washington, to test process systems for chemical weapon and bulk agent disposal. The events of September 11, 2001, prompted the US Army to accelerate the destruction of its chemical weapons, and Parsons' Newport, Indiana, chemical agent disposal facility has been developing a plan for speedy neutralization of the weapons. Parsons has also provided engineering management support for the construction of the Russian Chemical Weapons Destruction Complex.

Parsons has been developing its security services and has been selected to a team of companies that will be providing homeland security services at the Ports of New Jersey and New York to track containers.

Another project is the first major suspension bridge to be built in the US in more than 35 years. Parsons, which has been involved in the design and construction of more than 20 recent suspension bridges, is providing final design and engineering support during construction for the Carquinez Bridge near San Francisco.

In Iraq the company is designing and building military, police, and security sites. It is also designing and building more than 1,000 education and health facilities throughout the war-torn country.

HISTORY

Ralph Parsons, the son of a Long Island fisherman, was born in 1896. At age 13 he started his first business venture, a garage and machine shop, which he operated with his brother. After a stint in the US Navy, Parsons joined Bechtel as an aeronautical engineer. The company changed its name to Bechtel-McCone-Parsons Corporation in 1938. However, Parsons later sold his shares in that company and left in 1944 to start his own design and engineering firm, the Ralph M. Parsons Co., after splitting with partner John McCone (who later headed the CIA).

Parsons Co. expanded into the chemical and petroleum industries in the early 1950s. During that decade it oversaw the building of several natural gas and petroleum refineries overseas, including the world's largest, in Lacq, France.

In the early 1960s the company began working in Kuwait, which later proved to be one of its biggest markets. By 1969 Parsons had built oil refineries for all of the major oil companies, designed launch sites for US missiles, and constructed some of the largest mines in the world. In 1969 the company went public. With annual sales of about $300 million, it ranked second only to Bechtel in the design and engineering field. Ralph Parsons died in 1974.

The company built oil and gas treatment and production plants in Alaska in the 1970s and reorganized itself into The Parsons Corporation and RMP International in 1978. It went private in 1984 as The Parsons Corporation, taking advantage of a new tax law that favored corporations with employee stock ownership plans (ESOPs). Not all employees were happy, though. Several groups sued, maintaining that the plan disproportionately benefited executives, and that the buyout left the ESOP with all of the debt but no decision-making power. A Labor Department investigation later exonerated Parsons executives.

Parsons had just finished work on a power plant in Kuwait when Iraq invaded in 1990. Several employees were detained by the Iraqis but were released shortly before the Persian Gulf War. Two years later the company returned to Kuwait to rebuild some of the country's demolished infrastructure.

James McNulty, who had led the company's infrastructure and technology group, replaced Leonard Pieroni as CEO in 1996 after Pieroni died in the Bosnia plane crash that also claimed the life of US Secretary of Commerce Ronald Brown. Later that year a Parsons-led consortium won a $164.5 million contract for infrastructure projects in Bosnia.

In 1999 Parsons was chosen to manage construction of a $5 billion refinery in Bahrain, a $1.4 billion gas plant in Saudi Arabia, and a $1 billion polyethylene project in Abu Dhabi.

Parsons partnered with TRW in 2000 to create TRW Parsons Management & Operations to bid on the DOE's Yucca Mountain site in Nevada, a potential repository for the US's high-level radioactive waste and spent nuclear fuel. It also was awarded a three-year contract to help rebuild the war-torn Serbian province of Kosovo and the next year was awarded a similar contract for Bosnia-Herzegovina.

In 2001 the company won a US Federal Aviation Agency contract to upgrade air traffic control towers and other equipment and systems, a contract that had been held by rival Raytheon since 1988.

The next year Parsons won a contract from Dallas Area Rapid Transit (DART) to provide systems engineering and construction management services for the second phase of the buildout for the light-rail system, the largest expansion of its kind in North America. In 2003 it also won a contract for final design and construction management of the first light-rail system in Charlotte, North Carolina. In early 2004 the Parsons' joint venture with Kellogg Brown & Root won a controversial defense contract for oil field and refinery engineering, construction, and maintenance in Iraq.

EXECUTIVES

Chairman and CEO: James F. (Jim) McNulty
President and COO: John A. (Jack) Scott
EVP and CFO: Curtis A. Bower
SVP and General Counsel: Gary L. Stone
VP Human Resources: David R. Goodrich
VP Safety: Andrew D. Peters
SVP Government Relations: James E. Thrash
VP Corporate Relations: Erin M. Kuhlman
President, Parsons Advanced Technologies: Clifford C. Eby
President, Parson Commercial Technology: Charles L. (Chuck) Harrington
President, Parsons Infrastructure & Technology Group: Thomas L. (Tom) Roell
President, Parsons Transportation: James R. (Jim) Shappell
President, Parsons Water and Infrastructure Inc. (PWI): David L. Backus
SVP and Manager, International Division, Infrastructure and Technology Group: Earnest O. Robbins II
VP and Director of Project Development, Rail & Transit Systems Division: Sallye Perrin
Principal Transportation Planner, Rail & Transit Systems Division: Peter Smoluchowski

LOCATIONS

HQ: Parsons Corporation
100 W. Walnut St., Pasadena, CA 91124
Phone: 626-440-2000   **Fax:** 626-440-2630
Web: www.parsons.com

Parsons Corporation operates in 46 states in the US and in 37 countries abroad.

PRODUCTS/OPERATIONS

Selected Markets and Services

Parsons Advanced Technologies Group
  Call centers
  Criminal justice
  Energy market data
  Environmental data management
  Revenue collection and management systems
  Transportation data management
  Vehicle inspection and compliance
Parsons Commercial Technology Group
  Cable and component assembly
  Equipment testing and system commissioning
  Network planning and installation
  Physical plants
  Procurement, planning, and logistics
  Project management
  Remediation
  Wireless and wireline network management systems
Parsons Infrastructure and Technology Group
  Commercial and institutional facilities
  Entertainment
  Infrastructure
  Mobile source air quality
  Water resources
Parsons Transportation Group
  Aviation
  Bridges
  Highways
  Railroads
  Systems engineering
  Tunneling
  Urban transport

COMPETITORS

ABB	Jacobs Engineering
AECOM	Lend Lease
BE&K	Louis Berger
Bechtel	M. A. Mortenson
Black & Veatch	Michael Baker
Bouygues	Peter Kiewit Sons'
Day & Zimmermann	Stone & Webster
Fluor	TIC Holdings
Foster Wheeler	Turner Corporation
Gilbane	Tutor-Saliba
Granite Construction	URS
Halliburton	Washington Group
Hyundai Engineering and Construction	

HISTORICAL FINANCIALS

Company Type: Private

Income Statement — FYE: December 31

	REVENUE ($ mil.)	NET INCOME ($ mil.)	NET PROFIT MARGIN	EMPLOYEES
12/02	1,534	—	—	9,800
12/01	1,500	—	—	9,500
12/00	2,400	—	—	13,500
12/99	1,800	—	—	11,000
12/98	1,600	—	—	11,000
12/97	1,263	—	—	10,400
12/96	1,600	—	—	10,000
12/95	1,467	—	—	10,600
12/94	1,597	—	—	9,500
12/93	1,547	—	—	10,000
Annual Growth	(0.1%)	—	—	(0.2%)

Revenue History

Parsons & Whittemore

Parsons & Whittemore is one of the world's largest producers of market pulp, the raw material used in papermaking. It is also a supplier of bleached kraft pulp, which is used to make paper bags, butcher wrap, newsprint, strong bond and ledger paper, and tissue. Parsons & Whittemore has pulp mills in Alabama and in Canada. It also produces newsprint through its Alabama River Newsprint joint venture with Canada's Abitibi-Consolidated, the world's largest newsprint maker. Chairman George Landegger and his family own the company. Landegger's father, Karl, came to the US from Austria in 1938 and bought Parsons & Whittemore, then a small pulp-trading firm founded in 1909.

In mid 2004 the company caused a stir when it closed a pulp mill in New Brunswick, Canada, causing 400 people to lose their jobs. Parsons & Whittemore cited uncertainties in the pulp market and the rising value of the Canadian dollar as reasons for closing the mill.

EXECUTIVES

Chairman, President, and CEO: George Landegger
CFO: Steven Sweeney
Director, Human Resources: Suzanne Henry

LOCATIONS

HQ: Parsons & Whittemore, Incorporated
4 International Dr., Rye Brook, NY 10573
Phone: 914-937-9009   **Fax:** 914-937-2259

Parsons & Whittemore operates pulp mills in Alabama and Canada.

COMPETITORS

Boise Cascade	Potlatch
International Paper	Smurfit-Stone Container
Louisiana-Pacific	Tembec
Pope & Talbot	Weyerhaeuser

HISTORICAL FINANCIALS

Company Type: Private

Income Statement — FYE: March 31

	ESTIMATED REVENUE ($ mil.)	NET INCOME ($ mil.)	NET PROFIT MARGIN	EMPLOYEES
3/02	1,100	—	—	2,500
3/01	1,100	—	—	2,500
3/00	1,045	—	—	2,500
3/99	790	—	—	2,500
3/98	825	—	—	2,500
3/97	780	—	—	2,500
3/96	800	—	—	2,000
3/95	1,600	—	—	2,000
3/94	1,181	—	—	1,800
3/93	870	—	—	1,500
Annual Growth	2.6%	—	—	5.8%

Revenue History

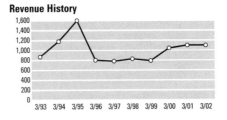

Parsons Brinckerhoff

After converting the US, Parsons Brinckerhoff is spreading its word around the globe. A leading transportation engineering firm, the company provides planning, design, construction and program management, and consulting services for construction projects worldwide. It specializes in transit systems, tunnels, bridges, highways, and airports but also works on telecommunications, energy, and environmental projects. Founded in 1885 by William Barclay Parsons, the firm designed New York City's first subway. Recent projects range from designing Kentucky's William H. Natcher Bridge to recycling stockpiled munitions for the U.S. Army. Employee-owned Parsons Brinckerhoff operates from about 150 offices worldwide.

From its beginnings in rail engineering, the company has expanded its services to encompass all types of infrastructure projects: buildings, enviornment, power, and telecommunications. Since its start more than a century ago, Parsons Brinckerhoff has worked in nearly 80 countries. It has contributed to such landmark projects as the Cape Cod Canal, the Detroit-Windsor Tunnel, and the North American Air Defense Command (NORAD). In the 1890s it helped build the first railroad across China, where the company still works on large infrastructure projects. It also has participated in the design of several of the world's leading public transit systems, including those in Atlanta, San Francisco, Singapore, and Taipei.

Other notable projects in which the globetrotter has been involved include Boston's Central Artery/Tunnel, Kuwait's Sabiya Power Station, Egypt's Greater Cairo Metro, and Spain's Madrid-Barajas International Airport.

EXECUTIVES

Chairman: Morris S. Levy
President and CEO: Thomas J. (Tom) O'Neill
EVP and CFO: Richard A. (Rich) Schrader
EVP and Director Corporate Development; Chairman, PB Consult: Michael I. (Mike) Schneider
EVP and Director Human Resources: John J. Ryan
Director of Operations, Americas: David A. McAlister
Director of Operations, International: Daniel K. (Dan) Mazany
SVP; President, Parsons Brinckerhoff Quade & Douglas: William D. (Bill) Smith
SVP; Chairman, PB Transit & Rail Systems; Northwest District Manager, Parsons Brinckerhoff Quade & Douglas: Anthony Daniels
Chairman, PB Power: Joel H. Bennett
General Counsel and Secretary: Kevin J. Curran
Director Public Relations: Thomas W. (Tom) Malcolm
Auditors: Ernst & Young

LOCATIONS

HQ: Parsons Brinckerhoff Inc.
1 Penn Plaza, New York, NY 10119
Phone: 212-465-5000   **Fax:** 212-465-5096
Web: www.pbworld.com

PRODUCTS/OPERATIONS

Major Operations
Construction management
Engineering
Operations and maintenance
Planning
Program management

Selected Subsidiaries
Parsons Brinckerhoff Construction Services, Inc.
Parsons Brinckerhoff Limited (engineering services for infrastructure projects, the UK)
Parsons Brinckerhoff Quade & Douglas, Inc.
PB Asia (Parsons Brinckerhoff International, Pte. Ltd.)
PB Facilities, Inc.
PB Farradyne Inc. (transportation systems design)
PBConsult Inc. (management consulting services)

COMPETITORS

AECOM	Parsons
BE&K	Skidmore Owings
Black & Veatch	STS Consultants
CH2M HILL	STV
Granite Construction	Tutor-Saliba
HNTB	URS
Jacobs Engineering	Washington Group
Louis Berger	

HISTORICAL FINANCIALS
Company Type: Private

Income Statement				FYE: October 31
	REVENUE ($ mil.)	NET INCOME ($ mil.)	NET PROFIT MARGIN	EMPLOYEES
10/03	1,374	15	1.1%	8,975
10/02	1,286	11	0.9%	9,370
10/01	1,348	16	1.2%	9,280
10/00	1,162	19	1.6%	8,670
10/99	969	17	1.7%	7,870
10/98	760	—	—	7,750
10/97	613	—	—	5,320
10/96	541	—	—	5,024
10/95	493	—	—	4,834
10/94	470	—	—	4,800
Annual Growth	12.7%	(3.3%)	—	7.2%

2003 Year-End Financials
Debt ratio: 0.0%
Return on equity: 13.9%
Cash ($ mil.): 67
Current ratio: 1.47
Long-term debt ($ mil.): 0

Net Income History
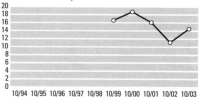

Partners HealthCare

Partners HealthCare System runs Massachusetts' biggest hospital group. The umbrella organization for Brigham and Women's Hospital and Massachusetts General Hospital, Partners HealthCare offers primary and specialist care, acute care hospitals, and other services. Affiliated institutions include the Harvard Medical School, Dana-Farber/Partners CancerCare (a collaboration between the Dana-Farber Cancer Institute and Partners hospitals), and Partners Community HealthCare (a physician network encompassing more than 1,000 practitioners). The organization also sponsors research programs and community health outreach programs.

EXECUTIVES
Chairman: John M. (Jack) Connors Jr.
President and CEO: James J. Mongan
COO: Thomas P. Glynn, age 57
VP, Human Resources: Dennis D. Colling
VP, Managed Care and Market Development: Lynne J. Eickholt
VP and CIO: John P. Glaser
VP and General Counsel: Brent L. Henry
VP, Quality Management and Clinical Programs: Sheridan L. Kassirer
VP, Finance: Peter K. Markell
VP, Research Management: Ronald S. Newbower
VP, Corporate Development and Treasury Affairs: Jay B. Pieper, age 60
VP, Clinical Affairs and Senior Academic Officer for Education: George E. Thibault
Chief of Staff and Secretary: Robin M. Jacoby
Treasurer: Stanley J. Lukowski
Director, Communications: Jennifer A. Watson

LOCATIONS
HQ: Partners HealthCare System, Inc.
Prudential Tower, 800 Boylston St., Ste. 1150, Boston, MA 02199
Phone: 617-278-1000 **Fax:** 617-278-1049
Web: www.partners.org

PRODUCTS/OPERATIONS
Selected Member Institutions
Brigham and Women's Hospital
Faulkner Hospital
Dana-Farber/Partners CancerCare
Massachusetts General Hospital
McLean Hospital
Newton-Wellesley Hospital
North Shore Medical Center
Partners Community HealthCare, Inc.
Rehabilitation Hospital of the Cape and Islands
Spaulding Rehabilitation Hospital Network

COMPETITORS
Baystate Health Systems
CareGroup
HCA
Tenet Healthcare

HISTORICAL FINANCIALS
Company Type: Not-for-profit

Income Statement				FYE: September 30
	REVENUE ($ mil.)	NET INCOME ($ mil.)	NET PROFIT MARGIN	EMPLOYEES
9/03	4,561	86	1.9%	—
9/02	4,218	56	1.3%	30,000
9/01	3,773	32	0.8%	30,000
9/00	3,317	123	3.7%	30,000
9/99	2,873	28	1.0%	20,000
9/98	2,434	54	2.2%	19,407
9/97	2,209	90	4.1%	19,132
9/96	2,107	—	—	24,900
9/95	1,773	—	—	24,878
9/94	1,664	—	—	—
Annual Growth	11.9%	(0.8%)	—	2.7%

2003 Year-End Financials
Debt ratio: 40.7%
Return on equity: 2.9%
Cash ($ mil.): 207
Current ratio: 2.63
Long-term debt ($ mil.): 1,295

Net Income History
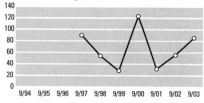

Paul, Hastings

Got a discrimination problem? Paul, Hastings, Janofsky & Walker may suit your needs. The law firm has built a solid reputation in employment law. Paul Grossman, a partner specializing in employment law, co-authored *Employment Discrimination Law* (the official treatise of the American Bar Association). Clients such as UPS and Hughes Aircraft have turned to Paul, Hastings for their expertise in the field. Real estate also is an area of strength for the firm. Other practice areas include business law, litigation, and tax. Founded in 1951, Paul, Hastings has eight offices in the US and five in Europe and Asia.

EXECUTIVES
Chairman: Seth Zachary
Managing Partner: Greg M. Nitzkowski
CFO: Timothy (Tim) Wright
CIO: Stova Wong
Human Resources Officer: Jeanne Gervin

LOCATIONS
HQ: Paul, Hastings, Janofsky & Walker LLP
515 S. Flower St., 25th Fl., Los Angeles, CA 90071
Phone: 213-683-6000 **Fax:** 213-627-0705
Web: www.paulhastings.com

Paul, Hastings, Janofsky & Walker has offices in Atlanta; Costa Mesa, Los Angeles, and San Francisco, California; Stamford, Connecticut; and Washington, DC. It also has offices in Beijing, Hong Kong, London, and Tokyo.

COMPETITORS
Gibson, Dunn & Crutcher
Latham & Watkins
Littler Mendelson
O'Melveny & Myers
Orrick

HISTORICAL FINANCIALS
Company Type: Partnership

Income Statement				FYE: January 31
	REVENUE ($ mil.)	NET INCOME ($ mil.)	NET PROFIT MARGIN	EMPLOYEES
1/04	537	—	—	—
1/03	488	—	—	—
1/02	456	—	—	—
1/01	389	—	—	—
1/00	286	—	—	1,500
1/99	267	—	—	1,500
1/98	219	—	—	1,260
1/97	179	—	—	1,055
1/96	164	—	—	1,100
1/95	157	—	—	1,100
Annual Growth	14.7%	—	—	6.4%

Revenue History
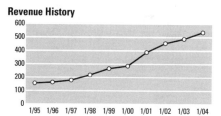

Paul, Weiss, Rifkind

Paul, Weiss, Rifkind, Wharton & Garrison stands in the legal spotlight when it comes to entertainment matters. The law firm, which counts among its clients Oprah Winfrey, employs about 500 attorneys in two US and five international offices. From civil to criminal matters, Paul, Weiss is also known as a high-profile litigator. The firm defended junk bond king Michael Milken and acted as counsel to the Senate in the Iran-Contra hearings. Paul, Weiss offers counsel in other areas, including bankruptcy, mergers and acquisitions, corporate financing, and taxation. The New York-based firm can trace its roots to 1875; it was established in its modern form in 1946.

EXECUTIVES
Chairman: Alfred D. Youngwood
Executive Director: Emil Sommer
Director Finance: Eric Sekler
Director Human Resources: Richard Drankoski
Director Legal Personnel: Joanne Ollman
Director Professional Development and Training: David Cruickshank
Director Information Systems: Andreas Antoniou
Legal Recruitment Manager: Patricia Morrissey
Communications Manager: Madelaine Miller

LOCATIONS
HQ: Paul, Weiss, Rifkind, Wharton & Garrison LLP
1285 Avenue of the Americas, New York, NY 10019
Phone: 212-373-3000 **Fax:** 212-757-3990
Web: www.paulweiss.com

Paul, Weiss, Rifkind, Wharton & Garrison has US offices in New York City and Washington, DC. It has international offices in Beijing, Hong Kong, London, Paris, and Tokyo.

PRODUCTS/OPERATIONS
Selected Practice Areas
Bankruptcy
Entertainment
Environmental
Litigation
Mergers and acquisitions
Personal reputation
Real estate
Securities and corporate finance
Taxation

COMPETITORS
Akin Gump
Cleary, Gottlieb
Cravath, Swaine
Debevoise & Plimpton
Simpson Thacher
Skadden, Arps
Weil, Gotshal
Williams & Connolly

HISTORICAL FINANCIALS
Company Type: Partnership

Income Statement
FYE: December 31

	REVENUE ($ mil.)	NET INCOME ($ mil.)	NET PROFIT MARGIN	EMPLOYEES
12/03	537	—	—	—
12/02	410	—	—	—
12/01	385	—	—	—
12/00	325	—	—	—
12/99	278	—	—	1,100
12/98	230	—	—	1,100
12/97	219	—	—	1,035
12/96	201	—	—	950
12/95	180	—	—	850
12/94	176	—	—	—
Annual Growth	13.2%	—	—	6.7%

Revenue History
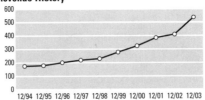

P.C. Richard & Son

P.C. Richard & Son aims to short out Circuit City. Founded in 1909 by Dutch immigrant milkman and jack-of-all-trades Peter Christiään Richard, the family-owned company has nearly 50 stores in the New York City metropolitan area. Once a hardware store, P.C. Richard gets more than half of its sales from home electronics (DVD players, TVs); it also sells computers and appliances (microwaves, vacuum cleaners). The firm is operated by fourth-generation Richard family members. P.C. Richard attempted to go public in 1993 but withdrew its offering after a tepid response. In 2003 the company acquired the name, trademark, and customer lists of bankrupt electronics chain Nobody Beats The Wiz.

EXECUTIVES
Chairman: Alfred J. Richard
President and CEO: Gary Richard
EVP: Peter Richard Sr.
VP and CFO: Tom Pohmer
VP, Merchandising and Operations: Gregg Richard
CTO: Chuck Fichtner
Director, Advertising: Alan Meschkow
Director, Human Resources: Bonni Rondinello

LOCATIONS
HQ: P.C. Richard & Son
150 Price Pkwy., Farmingdale, NY 11735
Phone: 631-843-4300 **Fax:** 631-843-4309
Web: www.pcrichard.com

COMPETITORS
Best Buy
Circuit City Stores
Harvey Electronics
J & R Electronics
Lowe's
REX Stores
Sears
Wal-Mart

HISTORICAL FINANCIALS
Company Type: Private

Income Statement
FYE: January 31

	ESTIMATED REVENUE ($ mil.)	NET INCOME ($ mil.)	NET PROFIT MARGIN	EMPLOYEES
1/03	993	—	—	2,200
1/02	925	—	—	2,134
1/01	880	—	—	2,173
1/00	740	—	—	2,073
1/99	625	—	—	2,000
1/98	520	—	—	1,700
1/97	515	—	—	1,500
1/96	425	—	—	1,500
1/95	400	—	—	1,500
1/94	400	—	—	1,500
Annual Growth	10.6%	—	—	4.3%

Revenue History
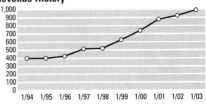

PeaceHealth

Peace out and PeaceHealth, man. PeaceHealth serves residents in southeastern Alaska, coastal regions of Washington, and central portions of Oregon. The health system includes six acute care hospitals: Ketchikan General Hospital (some 85 beds); St. Joseph Hospital (about 250 beds); St. John Medical Center (more than 200 beds); Sacred Heart Medical Center (more than 430 beds); Cottage Grove Community Hospital (about a dozen beds); and Peace Harbor Hospital (about 20 beds). Other operations include physician practices, community health clinics, chemical dependency rehabilitation clinics, and other outpatient care facilities and services.

EXECUTIVES
President and CEO: John Hayward
SVP, Organizational Development and COO: Judy Hodgson
SVP and CFO; Regional VP and CFO, Oregon Region: H.W. (Skip) Kriz
SVP, Health Care Improvement and CIO: John Haughom
SVP and CEO, Whatcom Region: Nancy Bitting
SVP and CEO, Lower Columbia Region: Medrice Coluccio
SVP and CEO, Oregon Region: Alan Yordy
SVP, Legal Services: Stuart Hennessey
VP and CEO, Siuslaw Region: Jim Barnhart
VP and CEO, Southeast Alaska Region: Patrick Branco

LOCATIONS
HQ: PeaceHealth
14432 SE Eastgate Way, Ste. 300, Bellevue, WA 98007
Phone: 425-747-1711 **Fax:** 425-649-3825
Web: www.peacehealth.org

HISTORICAL FINANCIALS
Company Type: Not-for-profit

Income Statement				FYE: June 30
	REVENUE ($ mil.)	NET INCOME ($ mil.)	NET PROFIT MARGIN	EMPLOYEES
6/03	825	—	—	—
6/02	769	—	—	6,230
Annual Growth	7.3%	—	—	—

Revenue History

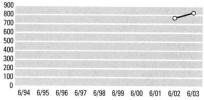

Peerless Importers

Peerless Importers has some of the most beloved liquid assets around. The company, founded in 1943, distributes wine and spirits in New York and Connecticut. Its spirits catalog includes blends, brandy and cognac, cordials and liqueurs (including Baileys Irish Cream), gin, rum, scotch (including J&B), and vodka. Wines are imported from Australia, Chile, and Western Europe. Unfortunately, Peerless Importers does have peers and has, in the past, lost business from liquor giants like Bacardi Limited to New York rivals like Charmer Industries. The Magliocco family (through its Quaker Equities holding company) owns and operates Peerless Importers and its Johnny Barton subsidiary.

Not surprisingly, Peerless Importers opposes the direct sale of out-of-state wine over the Internet. So much so, Peerless and other New York distributors took their views to federal court. A three-judge panel says New York has the right to ban such interstate sales made on the Web.

EXECUTIVES
Chairman: John T. Magliocco
President and CEO: Nino Magliocco
VP: Joseph Magliocco
Controller: Mario Gottesmann
Manager, Human Resources: Debbie Andruk

LOCATIONS
HQ: Peerless Importers, Inc.
16 Bridgewater St., Brooklyn, NY 11222
Phone: 718-383-5500 **Fax:** 718-389-5708

COMPETITORS
Charmer Industries
Fedway Associates
Johnson Brothers

HISTORICAL FINANCIALS
Company Type: Private

Income Statement				FYE: December 31
	REVENUE ($ mil.)	NET INCOME ($ mil.)	NET PROFIT MARGIN	EMPLOYEES
12/02	725	—	—	—
12/01	725	—	—	1,200
12/00	690	—	—	1,200
12/99	660	—	—	1,200
12/98	620	—	—	1,200
12/97	605	—	—	1,200
12/96	590	—	—	1,200
12/95	635	—	—	1,400
12/94	585	—	—	1,200
12/93	535	—	—	1,200
Annual Growth	3.4%	—	—	0.0%

Revenue History

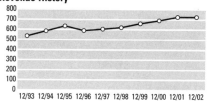

Pella

Window and door maker Pella got out of a jamb by offering its products through retailers. Originally Pella focused on upscale homeowners, builders, and designers, marketing its products through a network of distribution centers and high-end Pella Window Stores retail outlets. The company has expanded its market, allowing do-it-yourselfers to buy its ProLine windows and doors through building supply stores. Pella's products include sliding French and contemporary doors and awning, clad casement, and bay windows. Pella was founded in 1925 as Rolscreen Company (after its first product, a roll-up window screen). The descendants of founder Pete Kuyper own the company.

Pella's plan for growth includes expanding its storm door, entry systems, and window product offerings. The company unveiled its Impervia window and door product line, manufactured from its exclusive Duracast five-layer fiberglass composite material, at the International Builders' Show in January 2003. The material is stated to be nine times stronger than vinyl and twice as strong as aluminum in tensile strength tests. The product line includes single-hung, sliding, and fixed window units.

In 2004, its fifth consecutive year for the award, Pella was distinguished by *FORTUNE* magazine as one of the "100 Best Companies to Work For."

EXECUTIVES
President and CEO: Mel Haught
SVP, CFO, and Secretary: A. Jacqueline (Jackie) Dout, age 49
SVP Finance: Herbert Liennenbrugger
SVP Sales and Marketing: Chris Simpson
VP Human Resources: Karin Peterson
Corporate Public Relations: Kathy Krafka Harkema
Director of Sales and Marketing, Advanced Materials Division: Duane Putz
Marketing Manager, Trade Segment: Carroll Bogard
Installation Engineer: Cordell Burton

LOCATIONS
HQ: Pella Corporation
102 Main St., Pella, IA 50219
Phone: 641-628-1000 **Fax:** 641-628-6070
Web: www.pella.com

Pella has manufacturing plants in Carroll, Pella, Shenandoah, Sioux City, and Story City, Iowa, and in Gettysburg, Pennsylvania.

PRODUCTS/OPERATIONS
Selected Products

Doors	Windows
Entry door systems	Awning
In-swing French	Bow/bay
Out-swing French	Casement
Patio doors	Circlehead
Sliding contemporary	Clad frame
Sliding French	Cornerview
Storm doors	Double-hung
	Replacement
	Single-hung

COMPETITORS

Andersen Corporation	Pacesetter
Atrium	Sierra Pacific Industries
Bocenor	Simonton Windows
HW Plastics	Thermal Industries
International Aluminum	Therma-Tru
JELD-WEN	ThermoView Industries
Marshfield DoorSystems	Tomkins
Nortek	

HISTORICAL FINANCIALS
Company Type: Private

Income Statement				FYE: November 30
	ESTIMATED REVENUE ($ mil.)	NET INCOME ($ mil.)	NET PROFIT MARGIN	EMPLOYEES
11/03	1,000	—	—	7,100
11/02	900	—	—	6,945
11/01	900	—	—	6,800
11/00	910	—	—	6,300
11/99	900	—	—	6,755
11/98	600	—	—	6,000
11/97	600	—	—	4,500
11/96	475	—	—	3,500
11/95	450	—	—	3,500
11/94	425	—	—	3,126
Annual Growth	10.0%	—	—	9.5%

Revenue History

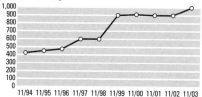

HOOVER'S HANDBOOK OF PRIVATE COMPANIES 2005

Penn Mutual Life Insurance

Founded in 1847, Penn Mutual Life Insurance offers life insurance, annuities, and investment products. The company's major subsidiaries include Penn Insurance and Annuity and brokerages Janney Montgomery Scott and Hornor, Townsend & Kent. Penn Mutual sells its products primarily to high-net-worth individuals, professionals, and business owners. Products include term, whole life, universal life, variable universal life, and disability income insurance policies, as well as a full range of deferred and immediate annuity products. The company also provides trust services and asset management to individuals and institutions.

EXECUTIVES

Chairman and CEO: Robert E. Chappell Jr., age 65
President, COO, and Director: Daniel J. Toran
EVP, Systems and Service: John M. Albanese
EVP, Human Resources: Michael A. Biondolillo
EVP and CFO: Nancy S. Brodie
EVP and Chief Marketing Officer; President and CEO, Hornor, Townsend & Kent: Larry L. Mast
EVP and Chief Investment Officer: Peter M. Sherman
SVP, Market Conduct and General Auditor: Nina M. Mulrooney
SVP, Career Agency System: Ralph L. Crews
SVP, Independence Financial Network: Steven O. Miller
VP, Corporate Communications: Patricia Beauchamp
VP, Independent Broker-Dealer Sales: Frank J. Howell

LOCATIONS

HQ: The Penn Mutual Life Insurance Company
600 Dresher Rd., Horsham, PA 19044
Phone: 215-956-8000   **Fax:** 215-956-8347
Web: www.pennmutual.com

Penn Mutual Life Insurance operates throughout the US.

PRODUCTS/OPERATIONS

2003 Sales

	$ mil.	% of total
Investment income	426.2	37
Premium & other product revenue	315.7	28
Other revenue	403.1	35
Total	**1,145.0**	**100**

Selected Subsidiaries and Affiliates

Hornor, Townsend & Kent, Inc. (NASD broker/dealer)
Independence Capital Management, Inc. (asset management)
Janney Montgomery Scott LLC (stock brokerage)
The Penn Insurance and Annuity Company (life insurance)
The Pennsylvania Trust Company (investment advisory and trust services)

COMPETITORS

Aetna
American National Insurance
AmerUs
AXA Financial
CIGNA
Erie Family Life Insurance
Fidelity & Guaranty Life
The Hartford
Jefferson-Pilot
John Hancock Financial Services
MassMutual
MetLife
Midland National Life
Minnesota Mutual
MONY
Nationwide Financial
Nationwide Financial Network
New York Life
Pacific Mutual
Primerica
Protective Life
Prudential
Security Benefit Group
Sentry Insurance
Union Central

HISTORICAL FINANCIALS

Company Type: Mutual company

Income Statement   FYE: December 31

	ASSETS ($ mil.)	NET INCOME ($ mil.)	INCOME AS % OF ASSETS	EMPLOYEES
12/03	13,065	108	0.8%	1,100
12/02	11,335	73	0.6%	1,100
12/01	10,833	97	0.9%	1,100
12/00	10,708	139	1.3%	950
12/99	10,583	80	0.8%	850
12/98	10,086	58	0.6%	850
12/97	9,367	73	0.8%	848
12/96	8,757	49	0.6%	800
Annual Growth	5.9%	12.0%	—	4.7%

2003 Year-End Financials

Equity as % of assets: 12.7%   Long-term debt ($ mil.): 5,399
Return on assets: 0.9%   Sales ($ mil.): 1,145
Return on equity: 6.7%

Net Income History

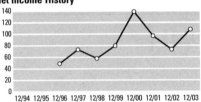

Pennsylvania Lottery

Even if they don't become millionaires, senior citizens in Pennsylvania can still benefit from the state lottery. Established in 1971, Pennsylvania Lottery proceeds are dedicated to programs geared toward seniors (property-tax relief, rent rebates, reduced-cost transportation, co-pay prescriptions). Proceeds also fund more than 50 Area Agencies on Aging across Pennsylvania. State law mandates that at least 40% of lottery proceeds must be awarded in prizes, and at least 30% must be used for benefit programs. Games range from traditional lottery game Super 6 Lotto to daily wagering game Big 4. IGT Online Entertainment Systems (formerly Automated Wagering International) operates the lottery's computer systems.

EXECUTIVES

Executive Director: Robert F. Mars III
Secretary of Revenue: Larry P. Williams
Director Marketing: Kara Sparks
Director Public Relations: Sally Danyluk
Deputy Director of Corporate Accounts: Maria Logan
Personnel: Sabrina Theiss

LOCATIONS

HQ: The Pennsylvania Lottery
2850 Turnpike Industrial Dr., Middletown, PA 17057
Phone: 717-986-4699   **Fax:** 717-986-4767
Web: www.palottery.com

The Pennsylvania Lottery has offices throughout Pennsylvania in Clearfield, Erie, Harrisburg, Lehigh, Middletown, Philadelphia, Pittsburgh, and Wilkes-Barre.

PRODUCTS/OPERATIONS

Selected Games

Instant Games (scratch-off tickets)
  Cash Harvest
  Gold Rush
  Grand-a-Day Holiday
  Harley Davidson USA
  Holiday Package
  Instant Battleship II
  Krazy 8's
  Mistledough Doubler
Numbers Games
  Big 4 (daily)
  Cash 5 (daily)
  Daily Number (daily)
  Super 6 Lotto (twice weekly drawings)

COMPETITORS

Connecticut Lottery
Maryland State Lottery
Multi-State Lottery
New Jersey Lottery
New York State Lottery
Ohio Lottery
Virginia Lottery

HISTORICAL FINANCIALS

Company Type: Government-owned

Income Statement   FYE: June 30

	REVENUE ($ mil.)	NET INCOME ($ mil.)	NET PROFIT MARGIN	EMPLOYEES
6/04	2,352	—	—	—
6/03	2,143	—	—	—
6/02	1,947	—	—	—
6/01	1,803	—	—	—
6/00	1,707	—	—	—
6/99	1,669	—	—	169
6/98	1,682	—	—	152
6/97	1,719	—	—	178
6/96	1,674	—	—	181
6/95	1,592	—	—	135
Annual Growth	4.4%	—	—	5.8%

Revenue History

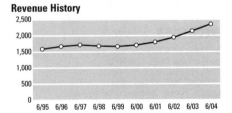

Penske

Penske, headed by race-car legend Roger Penske, seems to be on the right track as a diversified transportation firm. Penske is a partner with GE Equipment Management in Penske Truck Leasing, a commercial truck rental operation with about about 200,000 vehicles at about 1,000 locations. Penske owns more than 40% of publicly traded United Auto Group (UAG), which runs more than 200 franchised dealerships in some 20 states, Brazil, Puerto Rico, and the UK. Through Penske Automotive the company operates five car dealerships in California. Truck-Lite makes safety lights for boats, buses, cars, commercial trucks, construction equipment, and recreational vehicles. Roger Penske is the majority owner of the company.

The company's relationship with Kmart became strained after the retailer filed Chapter 11 early in 2002. Penske eventually responded by closing its 560-plus Penske Auto Centers at Kmart locations nationwide.

Penske just can't seem to resist that new car smell. The company has sold its racetrack interests and upped its stake in the struggling UAG. Roger Penske personally visited most of UAG's dealerships to help return the chain to profitability. He now heads UAG. However, Penske plans to take joint control with DaimlerChrysler of a Detroit Diesel unit in Italy, VM Motori. Penske souped-up its Penske Truck Leasing unit with the purchase of Rollins Truck Leasing, which was the US's third-largest truck rental and leasing player.

Penske is also a lead investment partner in Transportation Resource Partners, which is part of a group that is acquiring Autocam.

HISTORY

As a teen Roger Penske earned money by repairing and reselling cars. At age 21 Penske entered his first auto race; he was running second when his car overheated. His winning ways, however, were soon apparent, and in 1961 *Sports Illustrated* named him race car driver of the year.

Nonetheless, in 1965 Penske went looking for a day job. With a $150,000 loan from his father, he bought a Chevrolet dealership in Philadelphia and retired from racing to avoid loading his balance sheet with steep life-insurance premiums for the CEO. Penske teamed with driver Mark Donohue in 1966 to form the Penske Racing Team. Donohue died in a crash in 1975, but team Penske continued.

In 1969 Penske started a regional truck-leasing business, incorporated under the name Penske. The company established auto dealerships in Pennsylvania and Ohio in the early 1970s. In 1975 the company bought the Michigan International Speedway. Penske and fellow racing team owner Pat Patrick started the race-sponsoring organization Championship Auto Racing Teams (CART) in 1978.

In 1982 Penske's truck-leasing business formed a joint venture with rental company Hertz to form Hertz Penske Truck Leasing. Penske expanded its auto dealerships in the 1980s by acquiring dealerships in California, including Longo Toyota in 1985.

Racing legend Al Unser Sr. surprised Indy 500 watchers in 1987 by driving a car borrowed from an exhibition in a hotel lobby to a first-place finish for the Penske Racing Team.

In 1988 Penske bought 80% of GM's Detroit Diesel engine-making unit, which had a market share of only 3% and had lost some $600 million over the previous five years. Penske trimmed $70 million from the unit's budget by firing 440 salaried employees, streamlining manufacturing processes, and cutting administration expenses. Detroit Diesel's market share doubled in its first two years as a Penske unit. Also in 1988 Penske purchased Hertz's stake in Hertz Penske Truck Leasing, which it later combined with the truck-rental division of appliance maker General Electric to create Penske Truck Leasing.

By 1993 Detroit Diesel's market share had grown to more than 25%. That year the engine maker went public. Penske bought 860 Kmart auto centers for $112 million in 1995. The company's racing business, Penske Motorsports, went public in 1996, but Penske retained a 55% stake in the company. Also that year Penske bought Truck-Lite, Quaker State's automotive lighting unit.

Penske Truck Leasing formed Penske Logistics Europe in 1997 to offer information systems and other integrated logistics services on that continent. The next year it formed a logistics joint venture with Brazil-based Cotia Trading to serve US-based clients in the South American market, and Penske Logistics Europe opened a pan-European transport routing center in the Netherlands.

Penske sold its Penske Motorsports operations, which included racetracks in California, Michigan, North Carolina, and Pennsylvania, to International Speedway in 1999. The same year Penske invested about $83 million for a 38% stake in car retailer United Auto Group and Roger Penske became CEO of Penske. In 2000 the company sold its 48.6% stake in Detroit Diesel to DaimlerChrysler.

The following year Penske Corp. added three additional dealerships. Later in 2001 Penske Truck Leasing acquired Rollins Truck Leasing (then the US's third-largest player behind Ryder and Penske) for $754 million.

After Kmart filed Chapter 11 early in 2002, Penske expressed a "wait and see" strategy about the fate of its Penske Auto Centers business. Later that year Penske's Truck-Lite Industries bought Federal-Mogul's lighting business for $23 million.

Early in April 2002 Penske had waited long enough, and didn't like what it saw. It closed its 560-plus Penske Auto Centers at Kmart locations nationwide.

EXECUTIVES

Chairman and CEO: Roger S. Penske, age 67
President: Robert H. Kurnick Jr., age 42
EVP: Walt Czarnecki
EVP, Administration: Paul F. Walters
EVP and CFO: J. Patrick Conroy
VP: Tim Cindric
VP, Human Resources: Randall W. Johnson
Chairman, Truck-Lite, Inc.; Managing Partner, Birmingham Capital Partners: Richard J. Peters, age 56

LOCATIONS

HQ: Penske Corporation
2550 Telegraph Rd., Bloomfield Hills, MI 48302
Phone: 248-648-2000   **Fax:** 248-648-2005
Web: www.penske.com

Penske operations include Penske Automotive, with five dealerships in California; Penske Truck Leasing, with about 1,000 rental locations in the US and Canada; and United Auto Group, with more than 200 franchise dealerships in some 20 states, Brazil, Puerto Rico, and the UK.

PRODUCTS/OPERATIONS

Selected Subsidiaries and Affiliates

Davco Technologies, LLC (fuel filters and engine accessories)
Penske Automotive Group, Inc. (retail auto sales)
Penske Truck Leasing Co. LP (joint venture with GE Equipment Management, truck rental and leasing)
Truck-Lite Co., Inc. (automotive lighting)
United Auto Group, Inc. (more than 40%, retail auto sales)

COMPETITORS

AMERCO
Asbury Automotive
AutoNation
DaimlerChrysler
Fiat
General Motors
Group 1 Automotive
Isuzu
Mack Trucks
Navistar
PACCAR
Prospect Motors
Ryder
Sonic Automotive
Tasha Inc.
Transport International Pool
Volvo

HISTORICAL FINANCIALS

Company Type: Private

Income Statement

FYE: December 31

	REVENUE ($ mil.)	NET INCOME ($ mil.)	NET PROFIT MARGIN	EMPLOYEES
12/03	14,000	—	—	36,000
12/02	12,000	—	—	36,000
12/01	11,000	—	—	36,000
12/00	10,000	—	—	34,000
12/99	6,400	—	—	34,000
12/98	6,000	—	—	28,000
12/97	5,800	—	—	28,000
12/96	5,200	—	—	25,000
12/95	3,900	—	—	16,700
12/94	3,287	—	—	16,000
Annual Growth	17.5%	—	—	9.4%

Revenue History

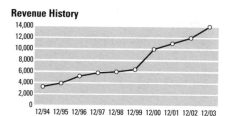

Pepper Construction

Pepper Construction Group sprinkles buildings across the US. The company is the parent of a group of five subsidiaries, including general contractor and construction management subsidiary Pepper Construction Co. The group focuses on commercial, health care, and retail markets, constructing commercial buildings, hospitals, hotels, malls, and schools. It outsources design and engineering tasks but can perform concrete, drywall, masonry, and millwork jobs; it offers hazardous waste services through Pepper Environmental Technologies. Recent projects include constructing a new home for apes at Chicago's Lincoln Park Zoo. Founded by Stanley F. Pepper in Chicago in 1927, the company is owned and run by his family.

EXECUTIVES

Chairman Emeritus: Richard S. Pepper
Chairman, President, and CEO; CEO, Pepper Companies; President, Pepper Construction Pacific: J. David (Dave) Pepper II
CFO: Joel D. Thomason
VP IT: Howie Piersma
EVP and General Counsel: Thomas M. O'Leary
SVP and Secretary; President, Pepper Environmental Technologies, Inc.: Richard H. (Rich) Tilghman
SVP Human Resources: John Beasley
VP and Treasurer: Linda Nila
President and COO, Pepper Construction Co.: Kenneth A. (Ken) Egidi
President, Pepper Construction Co. of Indiana: William J. (Bill) McCarthy
President, Pepper-Lawson Construction Co.: Paul E. Lawson
Director of Communications: Shannon Blagg

LOCATIONS

HQ: Pepper Construction Group, LLC
643 N. Orleans St., Chicago, IL 60610
Phone: 312-266-4700   **Fax:** 312-266-2792
Web: www.pepperconstruction.com

Pepper Construction Group has offices in Barrington, Chicago, and Tinley Park, Illinois; Houston, Texas; Indianapolis; and Irvine, California.

PRODUCTS/OPERATIONS

Selected Subsidiaries
Pepper Construction Company
Pepper Construction Company of Indiana, LLC
Pepper Construction Co. Pacific
Pepper-Lawson Construction, LP
Pepper Environmental Technologies, Inc.

COMPETITORS

AMEC, Construction Management
Barton Malow
Bovis Lend Lease
Centex
Charles Pankow Builders
Clark Enterprises
Gilbane
Graycor
M. A. Mortenson
Power Construction
Turner Corporation
Walbridge Aldinger
Walsh Group

HISTORICAL FINANCIALS
Company Type: Private

Income Statement
FYE: September 30

	REVENUE ($ mil.)	NET INCOME ($ mil.)	NET PROFIT MARGIN	EMPLOYEES
9/03	994	—	—	1,200
9/02	816	—	—	1,250
9/01	834	—	—	1,250
9/00	723	—	—	1,250
9/99	690	—	—	1,257
9/98	623	—	—	1,335
9/97	494	—	—	1,200
9/96	426	—	—	833
9/95	460	—	—	908
9/94	485	—	—	921
Annual Growth	8.3%	—	—	3.0%

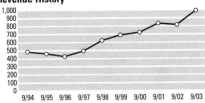
Revenue History

Perdue

James Perdue makes Big Bird nervous. His family's company is one of the largest in the US poultry market, selling more than 48 million pounds of distinctly yellow chicken products and nearly 4 million pounds of turkey products each week. Vertically integrated, Perdue Farms sees its birds from the egg to the supermarket meat case. Perdue is expanding its value-added chicken parts and food service products and has established a plant in China through a joint venture. It also processes grain and makes vegetable oils and pet food ingredients. Founded by Arthur Perdue (James' grandfather) in 1920, the company sells its products in the East, Midwest, and South, and it exports to more than 50 countries.

While the company breeds and hatches the eggs, it ships the chicks off to supervised contract growers, who then send back fully grown birds. The company processes grain to make its own feeds and vegetable oils, and turns poultry by-products into pet food ingredients. In addition, in a joint venture with AgriRecycle, it makes fertilizer from used chicken litter.

James Perdue, who — like his famous father, Frank, had before him — appears in its advertisements. Perdue produces its own breed of chicken, the skin of which is a distinct yellow color, resulting from a diet that includes marigold petals.

HISTORY

If asked which came first, the chickens or the eggs, the Perdue family will tell you the eggs did. Arthur Perdue, a railroad express worker, bought 23 layer hens in 1920 and started supplying the New York City market with eggs from a henhouse in his family's backyard in Salisbury, Maryland. His son Frank joined the business in 1939.

The Perdues sold broiling chickens to major processors, such as Swift and Armour, in the 1940s and pioneered chicken crossbreeding to develop new breeds. The family started contracting with farmers in the Salisbury area in 1950 to grow broilers for them. Frank became president of the company in 1952. The next year it began mixing its own feed.

Frank persuaded his father to borrow money to build a soybean mill in 1961. (Arthur had not willingly gone into debt in his previous 40-plus years in the poultry industry.) The soybean mill was part of Frank's plan to vertically integrate the company — with grain storage facilities, feed milling operations, soybean processing plants, mulch plants, hatcheries, and 600 contract chicken farmers — to counter the threat of processors buying chickens directly from farmers rather than through middlemen like the Perdues. To differentiate their products, the Perdue name was applied to packages on retail meat counters in 1968.

Two years later the company began a breeding and genetic research program. During the following years Frank transformed himself from country chicken salesman to media poultry pitchman when the company decided to use him as spokesperson in its print, radio, and TV ads. Catchy slogans ("It takes a tough man to make a tender chicken") combined with Frank's whiny voice and sincere face helped sales. As Perdue Farms expanded geographically into new eastern markets such as Philadelphia, Boston, and Baltimore, it acquired the broiler facilities of other processors.

In 1983 James Perdue, Frank's only son, joined the company as a management trainee. In 1984 Perdue added processors in Virginia and Indiana and introduced turkey products. Two years later it acquired Intertrade, a feed broker, and FoodCraft, a food equipment maker. However, after enjoying a rising demand for poultry by a health-conscious society in the 1970s and early 1980s, the company found its sales leveling off in the late 1980s. When North Carolina fined Perdue for unsafe working conditions in 1989, the company increased its emphasis on safety.

James, who had become chairman of the board in 1991, replaced his folksy father in 1994 as the company's spokesman in TV ads. In the early 1990s Perdue's management determined future sales growth lay in food service and international sales; therefore, the poultry company quietly began laying the groundwork to support these new markets.

Perdue launched its Cafe Perdue entree meal kits in 1997. The following year it purchased food service poultry processor Gol-Pak and, through a joint venture, opened a poultry processing plant in Shanghai, China.

Settlements to chicken catchers and line workers in 2001 and 2002 cost the company over $12 million in back wages. Also in 2002 Perdue announced it would be shuttering a deboning plant purchased only three years earlier. During 2003 the company started work on a new research and development facility in Salisbury, Maryland. In January 2004 Perdue purchased a poultry processing facility from competitor Cagle's, Inc.

EXECUTIVES

Chairman, CEO, and CFO: James A. (Jim) Perdue
President and COO: Robert (Bob) Turley
SVP of Retail, Sales, and Marketing: Steve Evans
SVP of Supply Chain Management: Larry Winslow
VP, Business Development: Steven M. (Steve) Schwalb

VP, Corporate Research and Development: Dave Owens
VP, Human Resources: Rob Heflin
VP, International Operations: Peggy Vining
President and General Manager, Specialty Foods:
 Randy Day
President and General Manager, Grain and Oilseed Division: Dick Willey
CIO: Don Taylor
Director of Public Relations: Tita Cherrier
Director of Environmental Service: John Chlada

LOCATIONS

HQ: Perdue Farms Incorporated
 31149 Old Ocean City Rd., Salisbury, MD 21804
Phone: 410-543-3000 **Fax:** 410-543-3292
Web: www.perdue.com

Perdue Farms has operations in Alabama, Connecticut, Delaware, Florida, Indiana, Kentucky, Maryland, New Jersey, North Carolina, Pennsylvania, South Carolina, Tennessee, Virginia, and West Virginia.

PRODUCTS/OPERATIONS

Selected Poultry Products and Brands

Fresh Poultry
 Chicken parts (Prime Parts)
 Cornish hens
 Ground chicken
 Roasters and turkeys (Oven Stuffer)
 Seasoned chicken
 Skinless, boneless poultry cuts (Fit 'N Easy)
 Turkey burgers
 Turkey sausage
Fully Cooked Poultry
 Cutlets
 Nuggets (Fun Shapes)
 Rotisserie-style chicken (TenderReady)
 Tenders
Other Products
 Pet food ingredients
 Vegetable oils

Other Brands

Chef's Choice
Cookin' Good
Gol-pak
Shenandoah
Short Cuts

COMPETITORS

AJC International	Hormel
Allen Family Foods	Keystone Foods
Cagle's	Murphy-Brown
Cargill	Pilgrim's Pride
ConAgra	Sanderson Farms
Cooper Farms	Townsends
Gold Kist	Tyson Foods

HISTORICAL FINANCIALS

Company Type: Private

Income Statement FYE: March 31

	REVENUE ($ mil.)	NET INCOME ($ mil.)	NET PROFIT MARGIN	EMPLOYEES
3/04	2,700	—	—	19,000
3/03	2,700	—	—	20,000
3/02	2,700	—	—	20,000
3/01	2,700	—	—	19,500
3/00	2,501	—	—	19,500
3/99	2,515	—	—	20,500
3/98	2,200	—	—	18,000
3/97	2,200	—	—	18,000
3/96	2,100	—	—	19,000
3/95	1,700	—	—	18,600
Annual Growth	5.3%	—	—	0.2%

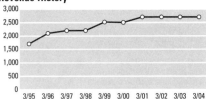

Revenue History

Peter Kiewit Sons'

By building everything from tunnels to highrises, Peter Kiewit Sons' has become a heavyweight in the heavy construction industry. The employee-owned firm is one of the largest general contractors in the US, having projects in nearly 40 states, as well as in Canada and Puerto Rico. A transportation specialist, Kiewit builds bridges, highways, railroads, airports, and mass transit systems. Transportation contracts account for half of Kiewit's sales. It also works on projects such as commercial buildings, mining infrastructure, waste-disposal systems, and telecommunications infrastructure. The company is owned by current and former employees and Kiewit family members.

With most of its contracts dedicated to large-scale transportation projects, the company leads the US in highway construction projects, which have included work for the Winter Olympics in Salt Lake City and for Denver's interstate highway system. It ranks first in dollar volume for federal highway contracts.

The group also ranks highly in the hydropower, water supply, sanitary and storm sewer, and transmission line and cable construction markets. Kiewit specializes in design/build projects and often works through joint ventures. Public contracts account for nearly 65% of total revenues.

The construction business has the undivided attention of Kiewit these days. It has spun off its asphalt and ready-mix concrete business as Kiewit Materials and has created a unit to focus on construction for the offshore drilling industry. The company also continues to provides construction for telephone and data network operator Level 3 Communications, although it divested the telecom business in 1998.

Kiewit Mining Acquisition Co., a subsidiary of the company, has acquired the Buckskin mine in Wyoming from coal producer Arch Coal. The coal mine, in the Powder River Basin near Gillette, was held by Triton Coal Co., a unit of Vulcan Coal Holdings. The sale was contingent upon the approval of Arch's acquisition of Vulcan by the Federal Trade Commission. The addition of the mine, which produced about 18 millions tons of coal in 2003, is part of Kiewit's strategy to expand its coal mining operations. Kiewit Mining Group, which owns or manages six coal mines, is one of the largest coal mining companies in the US.

HISTORY

Born to Dutch immigrants, Peter Kiewit and brother Andrew founded Kiewit Brothers, a brickyard, in 1884 in Omaha, Nebraska. By 1912 two of his sons worked at the yard, which was named Peter Kiewit & Sons. When Peter Kiewit died in 1914, his son Ralph took over, and the firm took the name Peter Kiewit Sons'. Another son, Peter, joined Ralph at the helm in 1924 after dropping out of Dartmouth and later took over.

During the Depression, Kiewit managed huge federal public works projects, and in the 1940s it focused on war-related emergency construction projects.

One of the firm's most difficult projects was top-secret Thule Air Force Base in Greenland, above the Arctic Circle. For more than two years 5,000 men worked around the clock, beginning in 1951; the site was in development for 15 years. In 1952 the company won a contract to build a $1.2 billion gas diffusion plant in Portsmouth, Ohio. It also became a contractor for the US interstate highway system (begun in 1956).

Peter Kiewit died in 1979, after stipulating that the largely employee-owned company should remain under employee control and that no one employee could own more than 10%. His 40% stake, when returned to the company, transformed many employees into millionaires. Walter Scott Jr., whose father had been the first graduate engineer to work for Kiewit, took charge. Scott made his mark by parlaying money from construction into successful investments.

When the construction industry slumped, Kiewit began looking for other investment opportunities, and in 1984 it acquired packaging company Continental Can Co. (selling off non-core insurance, energy, and timber assets). Continental was saddled with a 1983 class action lawsuit alleging that it had plotted to close plants and lay off workers before they were qualified for pensions. In 1991 Kiewit agreed to pay $415 million to settle the lawsuit. In the face of a consolidating packaging industry, the company sold Continental in the early 1990s.

In 1986 Kiewit loaned money to a business group to build a fiber-optic loop in Chicago; by 1987 it had launched MFS Communications to build local fiber loops in downtown districts. In 1992 Kiewit split its business into two pieces: the construction group, which was strictly employee-owned; and a diversified group, to which it added a controlling stake in phone and cable TV company C-TEC in 1993. That year Kiewit took MFS public; by 1995 it had sold all its shares, and the next year MFS was bought by telecom giant WorldCom.

In 1996 Kiewit assisted CalEnergy (now MidAmerican Energy) in a hostile $1.3 billion takeover of the UK's Northern Electric. Kiewit got stock in CalEnergy and a 30% stake in the UK electric company, all of which it sold to CalEnergy in 1998.

That year Kiewit spun off its telecom and computer services holdings into Level 3 Communications. Scott, who had been hospitalized the year before for a blood clot in his lung, stepped down as CEO, and Ken Stinson, CEO of Kiewit Construction Group, took over Peter Kiewit Sons'.

In 1999 Kiewit acquired a majority interest in Pacific Rock Products, a construction materials firm in Canada. Kiewit spun off its asphalt, concrete, and aggregates operations in 2000 as Kiewit Materials. Also that year the company created Kiewit Offshore Services to focus on construction for the offshore drilling industry. In 2001 the company acquired marine construction firm General Construction Company (GCC). The next year it expanded its offshore business further by buying a Canadian subsidiary from oil and gas equipment services company Friede Goldman Halter, which was trying to emerge from bankruptcy.

Kiewit made history in 2002 for the fastest completion of a project of its type when it completed the rebuilding of Webbers Falls I-40 Bridge in Oklahoma at the end of July. The bridge collapsed in May after being hit by a pair of barges, resulting in 14 fatalities.

EXECUTIVES

Chairman Emeritus: Walter Scott Jr., age 72
Chairman and CEO, Peter Kiewit Sons' and Kiewit Construction: Kenneth E. (Ken) Stinson, age 61, $5,058,671 pay
President and COO: Bruce E. Grewcock, age 50, $1,982,100 pay
EVP; EVP, Kiewit Pacific: Richard W. Colf, age 60, $1,468,000 pay
EVP; EVP, Kiewit Pacific: Allan K. Kirkwood, age 60, $903,000 pay
EVP: Douglas E. Patterson, age 53, $717,400 pay
SVP, General Counsel, and Secretary: Tobin A. Schropp
SVP and Division Manager, Midwest Building: Bruce Tresslar
SVP Building Division, Rocky Mountain Region: Robert J. (Bob) Mattuci
SVP, Kiewit Construction; President, Gilbert Industrial Corp.: Scott L. Cassels, age 45
SVP, Kiewit Construction and Kiewit Pacific Co.: Steven Hansen, age 58
SVP, Kiewit Pacific Co.: R. Michael Phelps, age 51
VP, Human Resources and Administration: John B. Chapman, age 58
VP and CFO: Michael J. Piechoski
VP and Treasurer: Ben E. Muraskin, age 40
VP and Associate General Counsel: Norman D. Holly, age 57
VP; President, Kiewit Development Co.: Gerald S. (Jerry) Pfeffer, age 58
VP; Area Manager, Kiewit Pacific: Lawrence J. Cochran, age 48
President, Kiewit Mining Group: Bruce McKay
Controller (Principal Accounting Officer): Michael J. Whetstine
Auditors: KPMG LLP

LOCATIONS

HQ: Peter Kiewit Sons', Inc.
Kiewit Plaza, Omaha, NE 68131
Phone: 402-342-2052   **Fax:** 402-271-2939
Web: www.kiewit.com

Peter Kiewit Sons' has 21 principal operating offices throughout North America.

PRODUCTS/OPERATIONS

2003 Sales

	% of total
Transportation	50
Power, heat & cooling	26
Building	12
Sewage & solid waste	2
Petroleum	2
Water supply/dams	1
Other operations	7
Total	**100**

Selected Subsidiaries

Ben Holt Company
Bibb and Associates, Inc.
Bighorn Walnut, LLC
CMF Leasing Co.
GSC Contracting, Inc.
General Construction Company
Gilbert/CBE Indonesia L.L.C.
Gilbert Central Corp.
Gilbert Frontier, Inc.
Gilbert/Healy, L.P.
Gilbert Industrial Corporation
Gilbert Marine L.L.C.
Gilbert Network Services, L.P.
Gilbert Southern Corp.
Gilbert Texas Corp.
Gilbert Western Corp.
Global Surety & Insurance Co.
Guernsey Construction Company
Gulf Marine Fabricators, Inc.
K-G Leasing Company
K-G-W Leasing Company
KP Leasing Company
KT Mining, LP
KiEnergy, Inc.
Kiewit Alabama Mining Company
Kiewit Construction Company
Kiewit Construction Group Inc.
Kiewit Constructors Inc.
Kiewit Engineering Canada Co.
Kiewit Engineering Co.
Kiewit Finance Group Inc.
Kiewit Industrial Co.
Kiewit Industrial Canada Co.
Kiewit International Inc.
Kiewit International Services Inc.
Kiewit Management Co.
Kiewit Mining Acquisition Company
Kiewit Mining Group Inc.
Kiewit Network Services Co.
Kiewit Offshore Services, Ltd.
Kiewit Pacific Co.
Kiewit Venezuela Inc.
Kiewit Western Co.
Mass. Electric Construction Co.
Midwest Agencies, Inc.
PT Kiewit International
Peter Kiewit Sons Co.
Seaworks, Inc.
Twin Mountain Construction II Company
V. K. Mason Construction Co.
Walnut Creek Mining Company

COMPETITORS

ABB	Kellogg Brown and Root
Balfour Beatty Construction	Lane Construction
	Parsons
Bechtel	Perini
Black & Veatch	Raytheon
Bovis Lend Lease	Skanska USA Civil
Fluor	Turner Corporation
Foster Wheeler	Tutor-Saliba
Granite Construction	Walsh Group
Halliburton	Washington Group
Hubbard Group	Whiting-Turner
ITOCHU	Williams Companies
Jacobs Engineering	

HISTORICAL FINANCIALS

Company Type: Private

Income Statement			FYE: Last Saturday in December	
	REVENUE ($ mil.)	NET INCOME ($ mil.)	NET PROFIT MARGIN	EMPLOYEES
12/03	3,375	157	4.7%	15,000
12/02	3,699	193	5.2%	15,000
12/01	3,871	175	4.5%	16,000
12/00	4,463	179	4.0%	11,146
12/99	4,013	165	4.1%	20,300
12/98	3,403	288	8.5%	16,200
12/97	2,764	155	5.6%	16,200
12/96	2,904	221	7.6%	14,000
12/95	2,902	244	8.4%	14,300
12/94	2,991	110	3.7%	14,000
Annual Growth	1.4%	4.0%	—	0.8%

2003 Year-End Financials

Debt ratio: 2.0%
Return on equity: 14.9%
Cash ($ mil.): 481
Current ratio: 2.13
Long-term debt ($ mil.): 22

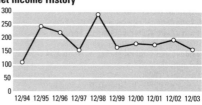

Net Income History

Petro Stopping Centers

Petro Stopping Centers is the center of attention for truckers who need a petro stop. The firm operates about 60 truck stops (about a third of them franchised) in 30 states. Its truck stops sell Mobil-brand diesel fuel, gas, and travel merchandise such as food, toiletries, truck accessories, and electronics. (Fuel accounts for almost 75% of sales.) The centers also provide Petro:Lube facilities (preventive maintenance services), showers, laundry services, game rooms, and Iron Skillet restaurants (home-style cooking). The company is run by chairman and CEO Jack Cardwell, who founded it in 1975, and his son, COO Jim Cardwell. Volvo Petro Holdings owns about 29% of Petro Stopping Centers.

EXECUTIVES

Chairman, President, and CEO:
James A. (Jack) Cardwell Sr., age 72, $570,000 pay
COO and Director: James A. (Jim) Cardwell Jr., age 43, $297,115 pay
CFO, Treasurer, and Secretary: Edward Escudero, age 33, $295,083 pay
VP, Petro:Lube: David Latimer, age 44, $233,366 pay
Executive Director of Fuel/Store Operations: Keith Kirkpatrick, age 43, $152,288 pay
CIO: Richard Tisdale
Director, Engineering: Clark Rudy
Director, Fleet Sales: John Krizak
Director, Franchise Business: Will Bowker
Director of Human Resources: Walter Kalinowski
Director, Marketing: David McClure
Auditors: KPMG LLP

LOCATIONS

HQ: Petro Stopping Centers, L.P.
6080 Surety Dr., El Paso, TX 79905
Phone: 915-779-4711   **Fax:** 915-774-7382
Web: www.petrotruckstops.com

PRODUCTS/OPERATIONS

2003 Sales

	$ mil.	% of total
Fuel	813.1	77
Non-fuel	181.6	17
Restaurant	68.6	6
Total	**1,063.3**	**100**

COMPETITORS

Bowlin Travel Centers
ChevronTexaco
Exxon Mobil
FFP Operating
Flying J
Love's Country Stores
Pilot
Rip Griffin Truck Service Center
TravelCenters of America
Valero Energy

HISTORICAL FINANCIALS

Company Type: Private

Income Statement			FYE: December 31	
	REVENUE ($ mil.)	NET INCOME ($ mil.)	NET PROFIT MARGIN	EMPLOYEES
12/03	1,063	9	0.8%	4,309
12/02	923	7	0.8%	4,202
12/01	914	(14)	—	4,108
12/00	981	(5)	—	4,186
12/99	720	2	0.3%	4,208
12/98	637	(9)	—	3,902
12/97	686	(13)	—	3,691
12/96	637	(9)	—	3,529
12/95	533	4	0.7%	—
Annual Growth	9.0%	10.9%	—	2.9%

2003 Year-End Financials

Debt ratio: 463.0%
Return on equity: 27.8%
Cash ($ mil.): 18
Current ratio: 0.74
Long-term debt ($ mil.): 166

Net Income History

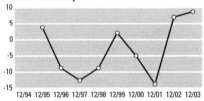

Phil Long Dealerships

The list of car models being sold by Phil Long Dealerships is getting longer. Founded in 1945 by a WWII US Navy pilot, the late Philip Long, the company sells new and used vehicles through about 15 dealerships in Colorado Springs, Denver, and Littleton, Colorado. Makes sold by the dealerships include AUDI, Chrysler, Ford, Hyundai, Kia, Mercedes-Benz, Mitsubishi, Saturn, and Suzuki. In addition, the company allows customers to search for a vehicle, apply for credit, and complete the purchase through its Web site. The dealerships also provide parts and service. The company is owned by a partnership that includes CEO Jay Cimino and other managers.

EXECUTIVES

Chairman, President, and CEO: Jay Cimino
COO: Marvin Boyd
CFO: Tony Basile
CFO: Gene Thomas
CFO: Raymond Turner
VP of Operations: Bob Fenton
VP of Operations: Jim Fynes
Human Resources and Risk Management Director: Scott Arnold
Leadership Development Executive; President, Phil Long Community Foundation: Randy Gradishar
Corporate Communications Manager: Michelle Narron
Human Resources Manager: Linda Bonewell
IT Manager: Shawn Flynn
Risk Management Manager: Cathi Trippe
Corporate Attorney: Joe Bruce
Purchasing Supervisor: Joann Berkhimer

LOCATIONS

HQ: Phil Long Dealerships, Inc.
1212 Motor City Dr., Colorado Springs, CO 80906
Phone: 719-575-7100   **Fax:** 719-575-7837
Web: www.phillong.com

COMPETITORS

AutoNation
Braman Management
Burt Automotive
Germain Motor
Group 1 Automotive
Kuni Automotive
Larry H. Miller Group
MNL, Inc.
Serra Automotive

HISTORICAL FINANCIALS

Company Type: Private

Income Statement			FYE: November 30	
	REVENUE ($ mil.)	NET INCOME ($ mil.)	NET PROFIT MARGIN	EMPLOYEES
11/03	604	—	—	1,500
11/02	653	—	—	1,800
11/01	783	—	—	1,800
11/00	700	—	—	1,500
11/99	639	—	—	1,350
11/98	565	—	—	1,116
11/97	537	—	—	1,100
11/96	501	—	—	1,134
11/95	451	—	—	1,108
11/94	405	—	—	900
Annual Growth	4.5%	—	—	5.8%

Revenue History

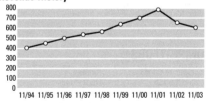

Philip Services

The metal business has tested the mettle of industrial and metals services company Philip Services Corporation (PSC). PSC Metals Services provides scrap charge optimization, inventory management, by-products services, remote scrap sourcing, and industrial scrap removal throughout North America. PSC Industrial Services provides industrial cleaning and maintenance (such as storage tank or offshore vessel cleaning), environmental services (commercial and industrial waste collection and disposal and lab testing), and emergency response to active spills. PSC services small to midsized waste generators. It has sold some outsourcing operations to a unit of Fluor. Businesses owned by investor Carl Icahn control PSC.

EXECUTIVES

CEO: Jon Weber
SVP and CFO: Michael W. Ramirez
VP Sales and Marketing, Industrial Services Group: Chris Maheu
General Counsel: Debbie Huston
Auditors: KPMG LLP

LOCATIONS

HQ: Philip Services Corporation
5151 San Felipe Rd., Ste. 1600, Houston, TX 77056
Phone: 713-623-8777   **Fax:** 713-625-7185
Web: www.contactpsc.com

Philip Services operates from more than 250 locations throughout North America.

COMPETITORS

Clean Harbors
Commercial Metals
David J. Joseph
Envirosource
Headwaters
Infast
Metal Management
Safety-Kleen

HISTORICAL FINANCIALS

Company Type: Private

Income Statement			FYE: December 31	
	REVENUE ($ mil.)	NET INCOME ($ mil.)	NET PROFIT MARGIN	EMPLOYEES
12/03	1,500	—	—	12,000
12/02	1,119	—	—	8,600
12/01	1,510	—	—	10,000
12/00	1,156	—	—	11,400
12/99	1,621	—	—	—
12/98	2,001	—	—	13,000
12/97	1,751	—	—	14,000
12/96	586	—	—	4,000
12/95	537	—	—	1,000
Annual Growth	13.7%	—	—	36.4%

Revenue History

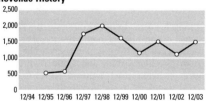

Pilot Travel Centers

Pilot Travel Centers navigates truckers and other drivers to more than 250 Travel Centers in 37 states and 65 convenience stores in Tennessee and Virginia.

In addition to fuel, the travel plazas house fast-food restaurants, including Arby's, Blimpie, McDonald's, Subway, and Wendy's, to name a few. Pilot Travel Centers is expanding its reach through licensing agreements with local travel center operators, most recently Montana-based Town Pump.

The company also plans to expand its commercial truck tire business to some 30 locations nationwide by 2005. The company offers Michelin, BF Goodrich, and Goodyear brand tires. Pilot Travel Centers is a joint venture of Marathon Ashland Petroleum and Pilot Corp.

EXECUTIVES

President and CEO: James A. (Jimmy) Haslam III, age 50
CFO: Mitch Steenrod
EVP Direct Sales and Development: Mark A. Hazelwood
VP, Supply and Distribution: Alan Wright
Director, Restaurant Operations: James (Jim) Barnes
Director, Supply and Distribution: David Dobbins
Wholesale Supervisor: Misty Monday

LOCATIONS

HQ: Pilot Travel Centers, LLC
5508 Lonas Rd., Knoxville, TN 37909
Phone: 865-588-7487 **Fax:** 865-450-2800
Web: www.pilotcorp.com

COMPETITORS

Flying J
Love's Country Stores
Petro Stopping Centers

HISTORICAL FINANCIALS
Company Type: Joint venture

Income Statement				FYE: December 31
	REVENUE ($ mil.)	NET INCOME ($ mil.)	NET PROFIT MARGIN	EMPLOYEES
12/03	5,500	—	—	13,000

Pinnacle Foods

Pinnacle Foods Group (formerly Aurora Foods) has a mouthful of big-name brands. The firm produces grocery store staples such as Mrs. Butterworth's, Log Cabin, and Country Kitchen (syrup, pancake mix); Duncan Hines (baking mixes); Lender's (bagels); Van de Kamp's and Mrs. Paul's (frozen seafood); Chef's Choice (frozen skillet meals); and Celeste (frozen pizza). It has grown by buying well-known brands and then expanding those brand lines by adding new products. Upon its 2004 merger with Pinnacle Foods Holding Corporation, the company renamed itself Pinnacle Foods Group.

The company distributes its products nationwide to supermarket and other retail outlets. It also sells through club stores, as well as private label, military, and foodservice channels. In 2002 Pinnacle's largest customer was Wal-Mart, which accounted for 18% of the company's total sales. It has a product development center in St. Louis.

The merger of Aurora and Pinnacle added Swanson and Hungry-man frozen dinners, Lender's bagels, Open Pit Barbecue sauces, and Vlasic pickles to the company's product list.

EXECUTIVES

Chairman and CEO: C. Dean Metropoulos
Co-President and Co-COO: Eric Brenk, age 39
Co-President and Co-COO: Michael J. Hojnacki
SVP, Productivity and Efficiency: James A. Sieple
VP, Business Development Foodservice: Keith Kandt
VP, Frozen Food: Rick Klauser
VP, National Accounts Foodservice: Mike Lyons
VP, Purchasing: Steve Smiley
VP, General Manager, Lender's Bagels: Patti Gooman
Senior Manager, Business: Michael Ruppe
General Manager, Foodservice: David Keefe
Director, Marketing Breakfast and Pizza: Jason Nibauer
Auditors: PricewaterhouseCoopers LLP

LOCATIONS

HQ: Pinnacle Foods Group, Inc.
6 Executive Campus, Ste. 100, Cherry Hill, NJ 08002
Phone: 856-969-7100 **Fax:** 856-969-7311
Web: www.pinnaclefoodscorp.com

Pinnacle operates facilities in Erie, Pennsylvania; Jackson, Tennessee; Mattoon, Illinois; St. Louis; and Yuba City, California.

PRODUCTS/OPERATIONS

Selected Brand Names
Aunt Jemima (frozen breakfast products only; licensed from The Quaker Oats Company)
Celeste
Chef's Choice (licensed from Perdue Holdings, Inc.)
Country Kitchen
Duncan Hines
Fun Feast
Great Starts
Homestyle Favorites
Hungry-Man
Lender's
Log Cabin
Mrs. Butterworth's
Mrs. Paul's
Open-Pit
Swanson
Van de Kamp's
Vlasic

COMPETITORS

American Seafoods
Campbell Soup
Chelsea Milling
ConAgra
Dulcich
General Mills
Gilster-Mary Lee
Goya
Heinz
International Multifoods
Interstate Bakeries
Kellogg
Kraft Foods
Nestlé
Nestlé USA
Nippon Suisan Kaisha
Red Chamber Co.
Rich Products
StarKist
Thai Union
Trident Seafoods
Unilever

HISTORICAL FINANCIALS
Company Type: Private

Income Statement				FYE: Last Saturday in December
	REVENUE ($ mil.)	NET INCOME ($ mil.)	NET PROFIT MARGIN	EMPLOYEES
12/02	772	(483)	—	1,650
12/01	1,036	(18)	—	2,000
12/00	1,000	(68)	—	2,000
12/99	995	(4)	—	1,850
12/98	789	(45)	—	1,311
12/97	143	1	0.8%	46
Annual Growth	40.1%	—	—	104.6%

2002 Year-End Financials
Debt ratio: 2,582.7%
Return on equity: —
Cash ($ mil.): 13
Current ratio: 0.96
Long-term debt ($ mil.): 1,043

Net Income History

Plains Cotton

Plainly speaking, the Plains Cotton Cooperative Association (PCCA) is one of the nation's largest cotton handlers. The farmer-owned marketing cooperative has about 26,000 members in Oklahoma, Kansas, and Texas. PCCA markets about 3 million bales of cotton each year through TELCOT, its computerized trading system that continually updates cotton prices, buyer data, and other information. The co-op has cotton warehouses in Texas and Oklahoma and denim mills in Texas (Levi Strauss is a major customer). The co-op was formed in 1953 to enable cotton farmers to obtain the most competitive price for their cotton.

EXECUTIVES

Chairman: Eddie Smith
President and CEO: Wallace L. Darneille
VP, Administration and Human Resources: Jim Taylor
VP, Finance: Sam Hill
VP, Information Systems: Joe Tubb
VP, Marketing: Lonnie Winters
VP, Marketing and Fabric Sales: Jack Mathews
VP, Operations: Darryl Lindsey
Secretary and Director, Communications: John Johnson
Personnel Manager: Lee Phenix
Auditors: Robinson Burdette Martin & Cowan, L.L.P.

LOCATIONS

HQ: Plains Cotton Cooperative Association
3301 E. 50th St., Lubbock, TX 79408
Phone: 806-763-8011 **Fax:** 806-762-7333
Web: www.pcca.com

COMPETITORS

Alabama Farmers Cooperative
Avondale Incorporated
Burlington Industries
Calcot
Cargill
Cone Mills
Dan River
Dunavant Enterprises
Greenwood Mills
Parkdale Mills
Staplcotn

HISTORICAL FINANCIALS

Company Type: Cooperative

Income Statement
FYE: June 30

	REVENUE ($ mil.)	NET INCOME ($ mil.)	NET PROFIT MARGIN	EMPLOYEES
6/03	801	—	—	—
6/02	800	—	—	1,000
6/01	620	—	—	1,000
6/00	774	—	—	—
6/99	633	—	—	—
6/98	925	—	—	1,350
6/97	836	—	—	800
6/96	785	—	—	800
6/95	1,014	—	—	800
6/94	798	—	—	800
Annual Growth	0.0%	—	—	2.8%

Revenue History

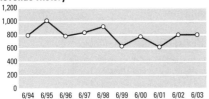

Planet Automotive Group

Expect a lot of iron, glass, and rubber on the surface of Planet Automotive Group. Formerly Potamkin Manhattan, the company coalesced from a network of auto dealerships owned by the Potamkin family. The company's 30-plus dealerships operate primarily in Florida, but also in California, Illinois, Iowa, Massachusetts, New York, Pennsylvania, and Texas. It has grown through acquisitions of new- and used-car dealerships. The company's dealerships also offer parts and service departments. The late Victor Potamkin opened his first dealership in 1946, and his two sons, Robert and Alan, now own and run the company.

EXECUTIVES

Co-Chairman and Co-CEO: Alan Potamkin
Co-Chairman and Co-CEO: Robert Potamkin
President and COO: Joe Herman
CFO: David Yusko
EVP, Mergers and Acquisitions: George McCabe
SVP, Operations: Berry Frieder
SVP, Staff Operations: Andy Pfeifer

LOCATIONS

HQ: Planet Automotive Group, Inc.
2333 Ponce De Leon Blvd., Ste. 600, Miami, FL 33134
Phone: 305-774-7690 **Fax:** 305-774-7697
Web: www.planetautomotive.com

COMPETITORS

AutoNation
Hendrick Automotive
Holman Enterprises
JM Family Enterprises
March/Hodge
Morse Operations
Pacifico
United Auto Group

HISTORICAL FINANCIALS

Company Type: Private

Income Statement
FYE: December 31

	REVENUE ($ mil.)	NET INCOME ($ mil.)	NET PROFIT MARGIN	EMPLOYEES
12/03	1,470	—	—	1,600
12/02	1,604	—	—	1,600
12/01	1,411	—	—	1,600
12/00	1,350	—	—	1,600
12/99	1,306	—	—	1,600
12/98	1,300	—	—	1,800
12/97	1,200	—	—	2,000
12/96	1,218	—	—	2,360
12/95	1,290	—	—	2,500
12/94	1,400	—	—	—
Annual Growth	0.5%	—	—	(5.4%)

Revenue History

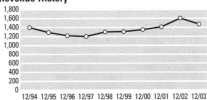

Plastipak Holdings

Plastipak Packaging likes to keep things bottled up. Doing business as Plastipak Packaging, the company manufactures plastic containers for four distinct industries: carbonated and non-carbonated beverages (soft drinks, bottled water, juice drinks, and beer); consumer cleaning (laundry detergent); food and processed juices (coffee creamers, relishes, and vegetable oils); and industrial, automotive, and agricultural (motor oil, antifreeze, windshield washer fluid). Plastipak Packaging makes high-density polyethylene (HDPE) resins and polyethylene terephthalate (PET) at its plants in the US and South America and is an exclusive packaging supplier to Procter & Gamble and Kraft Foods. The Young family owns and runs Plastipak.

The company's two largest business segments, which make containers for carbonated and non-carbonated beverages and the consumer cleaning industries, bring in over 75% of its revenue.

Procter & Gamble is the company's largest customer, accounting for 27% of its sales. Plastipak is the exclusive supplier of plastic containers for Procter & Gamble's liquid laundry detergents (Tide, Cheer, Era, and Gain) and other products like Bounce and Febreze; it is also the largest supplier of plastic containers for Kraft Foods salad dressing, barbecue sauces, and grated cheeses.

The company's Whiteline subsidiary serves 70% of Plastipak's transportation needs with a fleet of 275 tractors and 900 trailers. Its Clean Tech subsidiary, a plastics recycling firm, provides much of the company's raw material needs.

EXECUTIVES

Chairman, President, and CEO: William C. Young, age 63, $1,391,752 pay
VP, Finance; CFO, Treasurer, and Assistant Secretary: Michael J. Plotzke, age 46, $419,675 pay
VP, Controller and Strategic Operation Planning: Pradeep Modi, age 48
VP, International Sales and Marketing: Frank Pollock, age 48
VP, Operations and Manufacturing: William A. Slat, age 53, $390,475 pay
VP, Packaging Development: Richard Darr, age 54
VP, Product Supply: J. Ronald Overbeck, age 55
VP, Sales and Marketing: Gene W. Mueller, age 46, $377,871 pay
CIO: David Daugherty, age 48
President, Clean Tech: Thomas Busard, age 52, $400,892 pay
Corporate Legal Counsel and Secretary: Leann M. Underhill, age 58
Director, Packaging: Thomas L. Schellenberg, age 57
Auditors: Grant Thornton LLP

LOCATIONS

HQ: Plastipak Holdings, Inc.
41605 Ann Arbor Rd., Plymouth, MI 48170
Phone: 734-455-3600 **Fax:** 734-354-7391
Web: www.plastipak.com

Plastipak Holdings has manufacturing facilities in Brazil and the US.

PRODUCTS/OPERATIONS

2003 Sales

	$ mil.	% of total
Carbonated & non-carbonated beverage containers	404.2	45
Consumer cleaning containers	276.3	31
Food and processed juice containers	114.1	13
Industrial, agricultural & automotive containers	49.0	5
Other	54.2	6
Total	**897.8**	**100**

Selected Operations

Package development services
Plastic container manufacturing
  High-density polyethylene (HDPE) resins
  Polyethylene terephthalate (PET)
Technology licensing and equipment
  EXI-PAK preform over-molding process technology (employs multi-layer, barrier, and post-consumer plastic technologies in PET bottles)
  G.E.M. PAK container molding system

COMPETITORS

Amcor
Ball Corporation
Consolidated Container
Constar International
Crown
Graham Packaging
Husky Injection Molding Systems
Liqui-Box
Owens-Illinois
PVC Container
Silgan

HISTORICAL FINANCIALS

Company Type: Private

Income Statement			FYE: Saturday nearest October 31
	REVENUE ($ mil.)	NET INCOME ($ mil.)	NET PROFIT MARGIN	EMPLOYEES
10/03	898	4	0.5%	3,753
10/02	812	9	1.1%	3,700
10/01	810	—	—	3,300
10/00	566	—	—	3,000
Annual Growth	16.6%	(48.8%)	—	7.8%

2003 Year-End Financials
Debt ratio: 935.6%
Return on equity: 11.2%
Cash ($ mil.): 37
Current ratio: 1.36
Long-term debt ($ mil.): 383

Net Income History

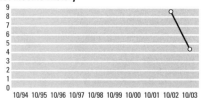

Platinum Equity

Platinum Equity knows "an oldie but a goodie" when it sees one. The information technology investment firm buys underperforming businesses, including units of large corporations. These companies, many of them 20 years old, usually offer legacy products and services and have well-established customer bases and distribution operations. Platinum focuses on companies offering products and/or services in such sectors as call center and help desk operations, data communications and networking, information systems, and software. The firm has operations in the US, Europe, Asia, and South America. Platinum acquired Dallas-based CompuCom Systems, Inc. and Frankfurt (Germany)-based DyStar in 2004.

Platinum is owned by CEO Tom Gores, brother of Alec, who founded investment firm Gores Technology Group.

EXECUTIVES

President and CEO: Tom T. Gores
CFO: Stephen B. Baus
COO: Robert J. Joubran
CTO: David M. Anglin
President, Portfolio Operations: Phil Norment
EVP, Finance and Administration: Douglas E. Johnston Jr.
EVP, Mergers and Acquisitions: Johnny O. Lopez
EVP: John Diggins
EVP: Gary Newton
EVP, Mergers and Acquisitions, Finance: Robert J. Wentworth
EVP and Chief Strategy Officer: Rodica B. Seward
SVP, Mergers, Acquisitions, and Operations: Rob Archambault
SVP, Corporate Communications and External Affairs: Mark Barnhill
SVP, Portfolio Sales and Marketing: Ross Young
VP, General Counsel, and Company Secretary: Eva Kalawski
VP, Human Resources: Kathleen A. Wilkinson
Director of Travel and Purchasing: Kathy Briski

LOCATIONS

HQ: Platinum Equity, LLC
360 North Crescent Dr., Beverly Hills, CA 90210
Phone: 310-712-1850   **Fax:** 310-712-1848
Web: www.platinumequity.com/site/action/home

Platinum Equity has offices in Los Angeles, New York, and Paris.

PRODUCTS/OPERATIONS

Selected Portfolio Companies
Altura Communication Solutions
Axcera LLC
Broadspire Services Inc.
CompuCom Systems, Inc.
Data2Logistics Inc.
David Corporation
DCA Services Inc.
Foresight Software
Gupta Technologies LLC
iET Solutions LLC
Matrix Telecom Inc.
Nextira One
Operator Service Company
Process Software LLC
ProfitKey International LLC
SourceOne Healthcare Technologies Inc.
Tanning Technology
Tesseract Corporation
Vanguard Managed Solutions LLC

COMPETITORS

Apollo Advisors
CD&R
Hicks Muse
Hummer Winblad
KKR
Texas Pacific Group
Thomas Lee

HISTORICAL FINANCIALS

Company Type: Private

Income Statement			FYE: December 31
	REVENUE ($ mil.)	NET INCOME ($ mil.)	NET PROFIT MARGIN	EMPLOYEES
12/03	4,000	—	—	16,000
12/02	3,500	—	—	15,000
12/01	3,000	—	—	15,000
12/00	2,400	—	—	14,900
12/99	792	—	—	10,000
12/98	700	—	—	10,000
Annual Growth	41.7%	—	—	9.9%

Revenue History

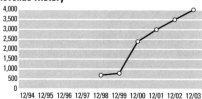

Pliant

Pliant is flexible when it comes to packaging. The company makes flexible packaging products and value-added films for a variety of uses. In the US Pliant produces specialty films used to make diapers, incontinence products, and sterile packaging. It also produces industrial films such as stretch films (used to bundle palletized loads during shipping), PVC films (used to wrap food products), medical films, and converter films. Pliant's International unit sells films in Asia, Canada, Europe, and Mexico. Its Pliant Solutions unit includes the decorative and surface coverings business acquired from Decora Industries. The Durham family and J.P. Morgan Partners own about 28% and 61% of the company, respectively.

In early 2003 Pliant structured its operations into four divisions: Pliant US, Pliant Flexible Packaging, Pliant International, and Pliant Solutions. Pliant US is by far the company's most lucrative division, the main products being a wide array of films: personal care and medical films, converter films, agricultural films, stretch films, and PVC films.

The Pliant Flexible Packaging segment makes and sells printed film and packaging products chiefly in the US. The Pliant Solutions division's products consist largely of the products (decorative and surface coverings) the company inherited from the acquisition of Decora Industries in May 2002.

Through the use of all its manufacturing plants, Pliant churns out an annual film production of roughly 1 billion pounds.

Since August 2003, three EVPs have resigned. President and CEO Harold Bevis hopes to establish a leaner, simpler organizational structure going forward.

EXECUTIVES

Chairman: Edward A. Lapekas, age 60
President, CEO, and Director: Harold C. Bevis, age 44, $78,974 pay
EVP and CFO: Brian E. Johnson, age 48, $315,659 pay
EVP and COO: R. David Corey, age 55, $33,175 pay
SVP and General Manager, Converter Division: Sonny Wooldridge
SVP and General Manager, Industrial Films Division: Robert (Bob) Maltarich
SVP, Human Resources: Lori G. Roberts
SVP, Sales: Paul Franz
SVP, Sales: Glenn Harsh
SVP, Technology and Innovation: Greg Gard
Director, Corporate Communications: John McCurdy
Auditors: Ernst & Young LLP

LOCATIONS

HQ: Pliant Corporation
1475 Woodfield Rd., Ste. 700, Schaumburg, IL 60173
Phone: 847-969-3300   **Fax:** 847-969-3338
Web: www.pliantcorp.com

Pliant Corporation has manufacturing facilities in Australia, Canada, Germany, Mexico, and the US.

PRODUCTS/OPERATIONS

2003 Sales

	$ mil.	% of total
Pliant US	568.7	61
Pliant Flexible Packaging	217.1	23
Pliant International	108.7	12
Pliant Solutions	34.9	4
Total	**929.4**	**100**

COMPETITORS

AEP Industries
Bemis
Griffon
Pactiv
Polymer Group
Printpack
Reynolds Food Packaging
Sealed Air
Spartech

PMC Global

HISTORICAL FINANCIALS
Company Type: Private

Income Statement				FYE: December 31
	REVENUE ($ mil.)	NET INCOME ($ mil.)	NET PROFIT MARGIN	EMPLOYEES
12/03	929	(114)	—	3,250
12/02	879	(43)	—	3,250
12/01	840	(2)	—	3,500
12/00	844	(51)	—	3,150
12/99	814	18	2.2%	3,800
12/98	681	8	1.2%	3,000
Annual Growth	6.4%	—	—	1.6%

2003 Year-End Financials
Debt ratio: —
Return on equity: —
Cash ($ mil.): 3
Current ratio: 1.46
Long-term debt ($ mil.): 783

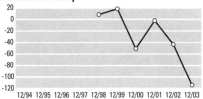
Net Income History

PMC Global

PMC Global makes Bob the Builder's bubble bath *and* the pipe that drains the suds away. The diversified international company produces memory chips, connectors, film, packaging, plastics, plastic-molding equipment, and specialty chemicals, among other things. It operates through more than a dozen specialized divisions such as ASC Group (electronics), Cosrich (children's bath, cosmetics, and toiletry products, including Disney brands), PMC Specialties Group (specialty chemicals), and VCF Films (PVC and acrylic films). CEO Philip Kamins (who owns the company) founded PMC (Plastic Management Corporation) in 1971 as an outgrowth of a small plastics scrap yard he founded in 1964.

EXECUTIVES

President and CEO: Philip E. Kamins
CFO: Thian C. Cheong
EVP and Treasurer: Lori Johnson
President, Austin Semiconductor: Ken Buckley
President, Continental Connector: Michael Sexton
President, Futura Coatings: Charles Zajaczkowski
President, General Plastics Corporation: Robert Scher
President, Komo: Tom Azzarelli
VP, Operations, Austin Semiconductor: Chris Imhof
VP, Sales and Marketing, Austin Semiconductor: Bob Heppel
VP and General Manager, Komo: Michael Verdon
VP, Sales and Marketing, Komo: Jeff Erickson
Controller: Brad Barton
Director, Human Resources: Karen Ferguson

LOCATIONS

HQ: PMC Global, Inc.
12243 Branford St., Sun Valley, CA 91352
Phone: 818-896-1101 **Fax:** 818-897-0180
Web: www.pmcglobalinc.com

PMC Global comprises subsidiaries with operations throughout the US and in Belgium, Canada, France, Germany, Italy, Japan, Luxembourg, the Netherlands, Singapore, Spain, and the UK.

PRODUCTS/OPERATIONS

Selected Operations
ASC Group, Inc. (electronic components)
  Austin Semiconductor (memory chips)
  Continental Connector (electrical connectors)
  Gentape (electrical connectors)
  North Penn Technology (memory packages)
  Secure Communication Systems (ruggedized computers)
Cosrich Group, Inc. (children's bath products and play cosmetics)
Futura Coatings, Inc. (reaction spray elastomers)
General Plastics Group, Inc. (high-performance coatings)
Gusmer Machinery Group, Inc. (equipment for foams, high-performance coatings and elastomers, composites, and fiberglass)
Komo Machine, Inc. (computer numerically controlled routers)
Plastics Color Corporation (color and additive concentrates used in plastics)
Plastic Services & Products, Inc. (polyurethane drainage pipe)
PMC Specialties Group, Inc. (chemical intermediates and specialty products)
PSC Industries, Inc. (design and fabrication of non-metallic materials)
VCF Specialty Films, Inc (PVC and acrylic films)
Winkler Forming, Inc. (PET products)

COMPETITORS

BASF AG
Bayer
BP
Carpenter
Cohesant Technologies
Colgate-Palmolive
Crompton
Dow Chemical
DuPont
E.ON
Huntsman
Inteplast
Johnson & Johnson
Pactiv
Sealed Air
Teknor Apex
TT electronics
Unilever

HISTORICAL FINANCIALS
Company Type: Private

Income Statement				FYE: December 31
	REVENUE ($ mil.)	NET INCOME ($ mil.)	NET PROFIT MARGIN	EMPLOYEES
12/03	600	—	—	—
12/02	600	—	—	4,300
12/01	600	—	—	4,300
12/00	784	—	—	4,300
12/99	877	—	—	5,130
12/98	859	—	—	5,100
12/97	828	—	—	5,125
12/96	876	—	—	4,299
12/95	780	—	—	5,130
12/94	709	—	—	4,100
Annual Growth	(1.8%)	—	—	0.6%

Revenue History

Polaroid

Consumers recognize the Polaroid name in an instant. The company makes instant film and cameras, digital cameras, specialty photo gear (such as lenses and filters), professional imaging equipment, and security ID-card systems. Polaroid's I-Zone instant camera (thumbnail-size images) is the nation's top-selling camera. Following its voluntary bankruptcy filing in 2001 Polaroid emerged as a new, privately held company when One Equity Partners (now part of J.P. Morgan Chase) bought substantially all of its assets (including its trademark name) in 2002, and owns about 65% of Polaroid. The remaining 35% is owned by shell company Primary PDC (representative of the remaining interests in the old Polaroid Corporation).

Business used to be a snap for Polaroid, but these days its life is more complicated. Though its inexpensive I-Zone camera (targeted at the teen market) was key in returning the company to profitability in 1999, Polaroid is now faced with an age when one-hour photo processing and digital imaging have lessened the demand for instant photos. Responding to the digital trend, Polaroid has developed digital kiosks that print as many as 24 digital photos in less than two minutes.

Rising from bankruptcy, a dramatic turnaround for the company seems to be in the works. Polaroid earned more than $50 million in the first half of 2003. The company as it exists today has no legal connection to the Polaroid that went bankrupt, but critics say much of the success of the new Polaroid has come at the expense of rank-and-file employees of the company's predecessor. Those employees had retirement and health care benefits taken away or dramatically devalued as their employer spiraled into bankruptcy.

EXECUTIVES

Chairman: Jacques A. Nasser, age 55
President and CEO: J. Michael Pocock
EVP and CFO: William L. (Bill) Flaherty
VP and Chief Marketing Officer: Jeff Hopper
VP and General Manager, Americas: Robert B. Gregerson
VP and Treasurer: Andra S. Bolotin
VP, European Region Sales and Marketing: Gianfranco Palma
VP, Chief Legal Counsel, and Secretary: Ira H. Parker
VP, Operations: Mark Payne
Senior Marketing Manager, Commercial ID Systems: Audrey J. White
Senior Marketing Manager, Professional Photography: Stuart Strong
Marketing Manager, Healthcare: Amy Hegarty
Director, Corporate Communications: Skip Colcord
Auditors: KPMG LLP

LOCATIONS

HQ: Polaroid Corporation
1265 Main St., Waltham, MA 02451
Phone: 781-386-2000   **Fax:** 781-386-8588
Web: www.polaroid.com

PRODUCTS/OPERATIONS

Selected Products

Close-up cameras
Color film recorders
Conventional film
Digital cameras and printers
Electronics (DVD players, home theater systems, LCD and plasma televisions)
Graphics imaging products
Identification and transaction systems
Instant cameras and films
MP3 players
OEM products (batteries, fiber laser systems, laser diodes)
Passport systems
Photo accessories
Polarizing filters and lenses
Printers
Projectors
Scanners
Scientific cameras
Software for image manipulation and recognition
Sunglasses

COMPETITORS

Agfa	Luxottica
Bausch & Lomb	Nikon
Canon	Philips Electronics
Concord Camera	Ricoh
Eastman Kodak	Sony
Fujifilm	Toshiba
Hewlett-Packard	

HISTORICAL FINANCIALS

Company Type: Private

Income Statement
FYE: December 31

	REVENUE ($ mil.)	NET INCOME ($ mil.)	NET PROFIT MARGIN	EMPLOYEES
12/03	753	71	9.5%	3,400
12/02	364	138	37.9%	3,400
12/01	1,000	—	—	9,000
12/00	1,856	—	—	9,274
12/99	1,979	—	—	8,784
12/98	1,846	—	—	9,274
12/97	2,146	—	—	10,011
12/96	2,275	—	—	10,046
12/95	2,237	—	—	11,662
12/94	2,313	—	—	12,104
Annual Growth	(11.7%)	(5.4%)	—	(13.2%)

2003 Year-End Financials

Debt ratio: 13.6%   Current ratio: 2.18
Return on equity: 39.1%   Long-term debt ($ mil.): 30
Cash ($ mil.): 167

Net Income History

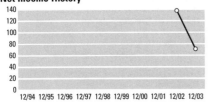

Port Authority of NY and NJ

The Port Authority of New York and New Jersey bridges the often-troubled waters between the two states — and helps with many of the region's other transportation needs. The bi-state agency operates and maintains airports, tunnels, bridges, a commuter rail system, shipping terminals, and other facilities within the Port District, an area surrounding the Statue of Liberty. A self-supporting public agency, the Port Authority receives no state or local tax money but relies on tolls, fees, and rents. The governors of the two states each appoint six of the 12 members of the agency's board and review the board's decisions.

The Port Authority's facilities include such international symbols of transportation and commerce as the George Washington Bridge, the Holland and Lincoln tunnels, and LaGuardia and John F. Kennedy airports. The Port Authority Trans-Hudson (PATH) rapid-transit system provides commuter rail service between New York and New Jersey.

The World Trade Center was among the agency's most visible assets before its twin towers and much of the rest of the complex were destroyed in terrorist attacks on September 11, 2001. The Port Authority is working with other agencies, government officials, and real estate interests on the rebuilding of the 16-acre site in Lower Manhattan. In 2003 it completed the reconstruction and reopening of the PATH rail station located at the World Trade Center site.

Future projects include upgrading the LaGuardia and Newark airports to accommodate anticipated increases in air traffic.

HISTORY

New York and New Jersey spent much of their early history fighting over their common waterways. In 1921 a treaty creating a single, bi-state agency, the Port of New York Authority, was ratified by the New York and New Jersey state legislatures.

The agency struggled at first, although its early projects, such as the Goethals Bridge (1928, linking Staten Island to New Jersey), were far from timid. It merged with the Holland Tunnel Commission in 1930, which brought a steady source of revenue. In 1931 the George Washington Bridge (spanning the Hudson River from Manhattan to New Jersey) was completed. The Lincoln Tunnel (also linking Manhattan to New Jersey) opened in 1937.

After WWII the Port Authority broadened its focus to include commercial aviation. In 1947 the agency took over LaGuardia Airport, and the next year it dedicated the New York International Airport (renamed John F. Kennedy International Airport in 1963).

As trucking supplanted railroads in the late 1950s, The Port Authority experimented with more-efficient ways of transferring cargo. In 1962 it built the first containerport in the world. That year the agency acquired a commuter rail line connecting Newark to Manhattan, which became the Port Authority Trans-Hudson (PATH).

In the early 1970s the Port Authority completed the World Trade Center. The agency changed its name to The Port Authority of New York and New Jersey in 1972 to reflect its role in mass transit between the two states. Critics, however, frequently assailed the agency for inefficiency and pork-barrel politics. In 1993 terrorists detonated a truck bomb in one of the World Trade Center towers, but within a year the building had largely recovered.

George Marlin became executive director in 1995. He cut operating expenses for the first time since 1943 and through budget cuts and layoffs, saved $100 million in 1996 and avoided hikes in tolls and fares. A privatization proponent, Marlin sold the World Trade Center's Vista Hotel to Host Marriott and arranged for the sale of other non-transportation businesses. He stepped down in 1997, and Robert Boyle took the post. That year the agency broke ground on the $1.2 billion Terminal 4 at JFK International Airport.

In 1998 the Port Authority authorized a $930 million design and construction contract for a light-rail line to JFK International Airport. New York City mayor Rudolph Giuliani proposed legislation in 1999 to place the Port Authority's LaGuardia and JFK airports under City Hall jurisdiction.

An 18-month standoff between the governors of New York and New Jersey regarding disputes over leases and agency spending was settled in 2000, which allowed the Port Authority to move forward with projects that had been blocked. Also in 2000 Boyle announced plans to resign. Neil Levin, New York's state insurance superintendent and a former Goldman Sachs vice president, replaced him the next year.

After the Port Authority and Vornado Realty Trust in 2001 failed to finalize an agreement for Vornado to lease the World Trade Center, the Port Authority that year signed a 99-year, $3.2 billion deal to lease portions of the World Trade Center's office space to a group led by Silverstein Properties while leasing the retail space to Westfield America.

Less than two months later, the World Trade Center's twin towers were destroyed when terrorists hijacked passenger jets and flew them into the buildings. Levin was killed, and 83 other Port Authority employees were listed as dead or missing.

The cleanup of the World Trade Center site, known as "Ground Zero," was completed in 2002, eight months after the attacks.

EXECUTIVES

Chairman, Port Authority of New York and New Jersey, Port Authority Trans-Hudson, Newark Legal and Communications Center Urban Renewal, and New York and New Jersey Railroad: Anthony R. Coscia, age 44
Vice Chairman, Port Authority of New York and New Jersey, Port Authority Trans-Hudson, Newark Legal and Communications Center Urban Renewal, and New York and New Jersey Railroad: Charles A. Gargano
Executive Director, The Port Authority of New York and New Jersey; President, Port Authority Trans-Hudson, Newark Legal and Communications Center Urban Renewal, and New York and New Jersey Railroad: Joseph J. Seymour
COO, Port Authority of New York and New Jersey; VP and Secretary, New York and New Jersey Railroad Corporation; VP and General Manager, Port Authority Trans-Hudson Rapid Transit System: Ernesto L. Butcher
VP and Secretary, Newark Legal Center Corporation: Michael Francois
Secretary: Karen E. Eastman
Treasurer: Bruce F. Bohlen
Controller: Michael Fabiano
Director, Audit: John D. Brill

Director, Public Affairs: Kayla Bergeron
General Counsel, Port Authority of New York and New Jersey, Port Authority Trans-Hudson, Newark Legal and Communications Center Urban Renewal, and New York and New Jersey Railroad: Jeffrey S. Green
Auditors: Deloitte & Touche LLP

LOCATIONS

HQ: The Port Authority of New York and New Jersey
225 Park Ave. South, New York, NY 10003
Phone: 212-435-7000   Fax: 212-435-6670
Web: www.panynj.gov

The Port Authority of New York and New Jersey operates primarily in the five boroughs of New York City, four suburban New York counties, and eight counties in northern New Jersey.

PRODUCTS/OPERATIONS

2003 Sales

	$ mil.	% of total
Air terminals	1,617	59
Interstate transportation	796	29
Port commerce	128	5
World Trade Center	126	4
Economic & waterfront development	97	3
Total	**2,764**	**100**

Selected Operations

Air Terminals
  Downtown Manhattan Heliport (New York)
  John F. Kennedy International Airport (New York)
  LaGuardia Airport (New York)
  Newark Liberty International Airport (New Jersey)
  Teterboro Airport (New Jersey)

Interstate Transportation
  Bayonne Bridge (Staten Island to Bayonne, New Jersey)
  George Washington Bridge (Manhattan to Ft. Lee, New Jersey)
  George Washington Bridge Bus Terminal
  Goethals Bridge (Staten Island to Elizabeth, New Jersey)
  Holland Tunnel (Manhattan to Jersey City, New Jersey)
  Lincoln Tunnel (Manhattan to Union City, New Jersey)
  Outerbridge Crossing (Staten Island to Perth Amboy, New Jersey)
  Port Authority Bus Terminal (Manhattan)
  The Port Authority Trans-Hudson System (PATH, rail transportation between New York and New Jersey)

Port Commerce
  Auto Marine Terminal (Bayonne, New Jersey)
  Brooklyn-Port Authority Marine Terminal (New York)
  Elizabeth Marine Terminal (New Jersey)
  Howland Hook Marine Terminal (New Jersey)
  Port Newark (New Jersey)
  Red Hook Container Terminal (New York)

Economic and Waterfront Development
  Bathgate Industrial Park (Bronx, New York)
  Essex County Resource Recovery Center (municipal waste-to-energy electric generation plant; Newark, New York)
  Industrial Park at Elizabeth (Elizabeth, New Jersey)
  Newark Legal & Communications Center (office development; Newark, New Jersey)
  Queens West (mixed-use waterfront development; Queens, New York)
  Hoboken South (mixed-use waterfront development; Hoboken, New Jersey)
  The Teleport (communications center; Staten Island, New York)

COMPETITORS

Amtrak	MTA
Coach USA	Reckson Associates Realty
Covanta	Tishman
Helmsley	Trump
Lefrak Organization	

HISTORICAL FINANCIALS

Company Type: Government agency

Income Statement
FYE: December 31

	REVENUE ($ mil.)	NET INCOME ($ mil.)	NET PROFIT MARGIN	EMPLOYEES
12/03	2,764	883	31.9%	7,000
12/02	2,671	740	27.7%	7,000
12/01	2,715	216	7.9%	7,000
12/00	2,648	372	14.1%	7,000
12/99	2,548	314	12.3%	7,200
12/98	2,361	299	12.7%	7,200
12/97	2,206	282	12.8%	7,500
12/96	2,154	199	9.2%	8,100
12/95	2,083	177	8.5%	9,250
12/94	1,980	153	7.7%	9,200
Annual Growth	3.8%	21.5%	—	(3.0%)

2003 Year-End Financials

Debt ratio: 109.8%   Current ratio: 0.99
Return on equity: 13.9%   Long-term debt ($ mil.): 7,471
Cash ($ mil.): 29

Net Income History

Pricewaterhouse-Coopers

Not merely the firm with the longest one-word name, PricewaterhouseCoopers (PwC) is also one of the world's largest accounting firms, formed when Price Waterhouse merged with Coopers & Lybrand in 1998, passing then-leader Andersen. The accountancy has offices around the world, providing clients with services in three lines of business: Assurance and Business Advisory Services (including financial and regulatory reporting), Tax and Legal Services, and Corporate Finance and Recovery. The company (one of accounting's Big Four, along with Deloitte Touche Tohmatsu, Ernst & Young, and KPMG) serves some of the world's largest businesses, as well as smaller firms.

PwC puts its heft to good use: Non-North American clients make up more than 60% of the firm's sales. Its bottom line, though, changed significantly in 2002, when PwC sold its consulting arm to IBM. A separation had been under consideration for years in light of SEC concerns about conflicts of interest when firms perform auditing and consulting for the same clients. The collapse of Enron and concomitant downfall of Enron's auditor and PwC's erstwhile peer Andersen undoubtedly hastened plans to spin off PwC's consultancy via an IPO, which was scrapped in favor of the IBM deal.

Like the other members of the (now) Big Four, PwC picked up business and talent as scandal-felled Andersen was winding down its operations in 2002. The former Andersen organization in China and Hong Kong joined PwC, accounting for about 70% of the approximately 3,500 Andersen alumni that came aboard.

In 2003 former client AMERCO (parent of U-Haul) sued PwC for $2.5 billion, claiming negligence and fraud in relation to a series of events that led to AMERCO restating its results.

HISTORY

In 1850 Samuel Price founded an accounting firm in London and in 1865 took on partner Edwin Waterhouse. The firm and the industry grew rapidly, thanks to the growth of stock exchanges that required uniform financial statements from listees. By the late 1800s Price Waterhouse (PW) had become the world's best-known accounting firm.

US offices were opened in the 1890s, and in 1902 United States Steel chose the firm as its auditor. PW benefited from tough audit requirements instituted after the 1929 stock market crash. In 1935 the firm was given the prestigious job of handling Academy Awards balloting. It started a management consulting service in 1946. But PW's dominance slipped in the 1960s, as it gained a reputation as the most traditional and formal of the major firms.

Coopers & Lybrand, the product of a 1957 transatlantic merger, wrote the book on auditing. Lybrand, Ross Bros. & Montgomery was formed in 1898 by William Lybrand, Edward Ross, Adam Ross, and Robert Montgomery. In 1912 Montgomery wrote *Montgomery's Auditing,* which became the bible of accounting.

Cooper Brothers was founded in 1854 in London by William Cooper, eldest son of a Quaker banker. In 1957 Lybrand joined up to form Coopers & Lybrand. During the 1960s the firm expanded into employee benefits and internal control consulting, building its technology capabilities in the 1970s as it studied ways to automate the audit process.

Coopers & Lybrand lost market share as mergers reduced the Big Eight accounting firms to the Big Six. After the savings and loan debacle of the 1980s, investors and the government wanted accounting firms held liable not only for the form of audited financial statements but for their veracity. In 1992 the firm paid $95 million to settle claims of defrauded investors in MiniScribe, a failed disk-drive maker. Other hefty payments followed, including a $108 million settlement relating to the late Robert Maxwell's defunct media empire.

In 1998 Price Waterhouse and Coopers & Lybrand combined PW's strength in the media, entertainment, and utility industries, and Coopers & Lybrand's focus on telecommunications and mining. But the merger brought some expensive legal baggage involving Coopers & Lybrand's performance of audits related to a bid-rigging scheme involving former Arizona governor Fife Symington.

Further growth plans fell through in 1999 when merger talks between PwC and Grant Thornton International failed. The year 2000 began on a sour note: An SEC conflict-of-interest probe turned up more than 8,000 alleged violations, most involving PwC partners owning stock in their firm's audit clients.

As the SEC grew ever more shrill in its denunciation of the potential conflicts of interest arising from auditing companies that the firm hoped to recruit or retain as consulting clients, PwC saw the writing on the wall and in 2000 began making plans to split the two operations.

As part of this move, the company downsized and reorganized many of its operations.

The following year PwC paid $55 million to shareholders of MicroStrategy Inc., who charged that the audit firm defrauded them by approving the client firm's inflated earnings and revenues figures.

The separation of PwC's auditing and consulting functions finally became a reality in 2002, when IBM bought the consulting business. (The acquisition took the place of a planned spinoff.)

EXECUTIVES

Global Chairman: Andrew Ratcliffe
Global CEO and Global Board Member:
  Samuel A. DiPiazza Jr., age 54
Global Board Member, France: Pierre B. Anglade
Global Board Member, Netherlands: Paul R. Baart
Global Board Member, US: John J. Barry
Global Board Member, South Africa: Colin Beggs
Global Board Member, UK: M. Clare Bolton
Global Board Member, Australia: Paul V. Brasher
Global Board Member, US: Jay D. Brodish
Global Board Member, Brazil: Raimundo L.M. Christians
Global Board Member, Switzerland: Edgar Fluri
Global Board Member, Germany: Jan Konerding
Global Board Member, US: Keith D. Levingston
Global Board Member, US: Dennis J. Lubozynski
Global Board Member, US: Donald A. McGovern
Global Board Member, Canada: Israel H. Mida
Global Board Member, Ireland: Donal M. O'Connor
Global Board Member, US: Walter G. Ricciardi
Global Board Member, Hong Kong: Silas S.S. Yang
Managing Partner, Global Markets: Willem L.J. Bröcker
Managing Partner, Global Operations:
  Amyas C.E. Morse, age 54
Global General Counsel; Acting US General Counsel:
  Lawrence Keeshan
Global Co-Leader, Human Capital: Richard L. Baird
Global Leader, Tax: Paul Boorman
Global Leader, Assurance and Business Advisory Services: J. Frank Brown, age 45
Global Co-Leader, Human Capital: Marie-Jeanne Chèvremont
Global Leader, Entertainment and Media Practice:
  R. Wayne Jackson
Global Leader, Industries: Alec N. Jones
Global Leader, Assurance: Gerald M. Ward

LOCATIONS

HQ: PricewaterhouseCoopers
  1301 Avenue of the Americas, New York, NY 10019
Phone: 646-471-4000   **Fax:** 646-394-1301
Web: www.pwcglobal.com

PricewaterhouseCoopers has offices in about 140 countries.

2003 Sales

	$ mil.	% of total
Europe	6,655	45
North America & Caribbean	5,431	37
Asia	1,353	9
Australasia & Pacific Islands	565	4
South & Central America	267	2
Middle East & Africa	264	2
Discontinued operations	148	1
Total	**14,683**	**100**

PRODUCTS/OPERATIONS

2003 Sales

	$ mil.	% of total
Assurance & Business Advisory Services	8,983	61
Tax & Legal Services	4,293	29
Corporate Finance & Recovery	1,165	8
Discontinued operations	148	1
Other	94	1
Total	**14,683**	**100**

Selected Services

Audit, Assurance, and Business Advisory Services
  Accounting and regulatory advice
  Attest and related services
  Audit
  Corporate training
  Performance measurement and corporate reporting
  Public services audit and advisory
  Specialized services for growing and middle market companies
Global Risk Management Solutions
  Audit and compliance services
  Behavioral transformation (services related to human resources)
  Operational advisory
  Risk and value management
  Security and technology services
  Sustainability services
Financial Advisory (called Corporate Finance & Recovery outside the US)
  Business recovery services
  Corporate finance
  Dispute analysis and investigations (forensics)
  Specialized services relating to infrastructure, government, and utilities
  Valuation and strategy
Global Tax Services
  Customs and duties
  E-business services
  Finance and treasure
  Global VAT solutions
  Global visa solutions
  International assignment solutions
  Mergers and acquisitions
  Personal financial services
  Tax compliance and outsourcing
  Transfer pricing

Selected Industry Specializations

Consumer and Industrial Products and Services
  Automotive
  Energy and utilities
  Industrial products
  Pharmaceuticals
  Retail and consumer
  Services (including public sector)
Financial Services
  Banking and capital markets
  Insurance
  Investment management
  Real estate
Technology, InfoComm, and Entertainment
  Entertainment and media
  Information and communications
  Technology

COMPETITORS

Bain & Company
BDO International
Booz Allen
Boston Consulting
Deloitte
Ernst & Young
Grant Thornton International
H&R Block
Hewitt Associates
KPMG
Marsh & McLennan
McKinsey & Company
Towers Perrin
Watson Wyatt

HISTORICAL FINANCIALS

Company Type: Partnership

Income Statement FYE: June 30

	REVENUE ($ mil.)	NET INCOME ($ mil.)	NET PROFIT MARGIN	EMPLOYEES
6/03	14,683	—	—	122,820
6/02	13,800	—	—	124,563
6/01	24,000	—	—	160,000
6/00	21,500	—	—	150,000
6/99	15,300	—	—	155,000
6/98	15,000	—	—	140,000
6/97	5,630	—	—	60,000
6/96	5,020	—	—	56,000
6/95	4,460	—	—	53,000
6/94	3,980	—	—	50,122
Annual Growth	15.6%	—	—	10.5%

Revenue History

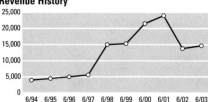

Primus

You Win some, you Win some more. So it goes for Primus, which has invested in some 425 small to medium wholesale distributors in about 40 states that sell plumbing, heating, air-conditioning, electrical, and other supplies to contractors and other professional customers. The companies are easily recognizable by their Win-prefixed names, such as Columbia Winnelson (plumbing products), Salt Lake Windustrial (pipes and valves), and Dayton Winfastener (specialty fasteners). Primus supports these companies, through units Dapsco and Distro, with bulk purchasing, warehousing, accounting, and data processing. Primus is owned by heirs of the investors who founded Primus in 1956.

EXECUTIVES

President: Richard W. Schwartz
CIO/CTO: Jeffrey Dana
Treasurer/Comptroller: Jack W. Johnston
Director, Corporate Communications and Secretary:
  Bruce Anderson
Director, Finance: Ward Allen
Director, Human Resources: Thomas Snow

LOCATIONS

HQ: Primus, Inc.
  3110 Kettering Blvd., Dayton, OH 45439
Phone: 937-294-6878   **Fax:** 937-293-9591
Web: www.winholesale.com

PRODUCTS/OPERATIONS

Selected Businesses
Winair (heating, ventilation, air conditioning, and refrigeration)
Winfastener (specialty fasteners)
Winholesale (piping, commercial valves, and fittings)
Winlectric (electrical supplies and products)
Winpump (pumps and accessories)
Wintronic (electronic parts and equipment)
Winwater Works (waterworks and utility supplies)

Selected Subsidiaries
Dapsco Inc.
Distro Inc.

COMPETITORS

Fastenal
Ferguson Enterprises
Gensco
Groeniger & Company
Hajoca Corporation
Home Depot
Hughes Supply
Johnstone Supply
Lowe's
MSC Industrial Direct
Noland
W.W. Grainger

HISTORICAL FINANCIALS
Company Type: Private

Income Statement
FYE: January 31

	REVENUE ($ mil.)	NET INCOME ($ mil.)	NET PROFIT MARGIN	EMPLOYEES
1/03	1,100	—	—	3,195
1/02	1,001	—	—	3,195
1/01	1,040	—	—	3,093
1/00	931	—	—	3,037
1/99	780	—	—	2,175
Annual Growth	9.0%	—	—	10.1%

Revenue History

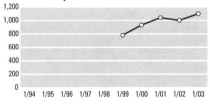

EXECUTIVES

President: Shirley M. Tilghman
Provost: Christopher L. Eisgruber
VP Administration: Mark Burstein
VP Campus Life: Janet Smith Dickerson
VP Development: Brian J. McDonald
VP Facilities: Michael McKay
VP Human Resources: Maureen Nash
VP Information Technology and CIO: Betty Leydon
VP and Secretary: Robert K. Durkee
Treasurer: Christopher McCrudden
General Counsel: Peter G. McDonough
Chief Medical Officer: Daniel Silverman
Auditors: Deloitte & Touche LLP

LOCATIONS

HQ: Princeton University
1 Nassau Hall, Princeton, NJ 08544
Phone: 609-258-3000   **Fax:** 609-258-1301
Web: www.princeton.edu

HISTORICAL FINANCIALS
Company Type: School

Income Statement
FYE: June 30

	REVENUE ($ mil.)	NET INCOME ($ mil.)	NET PROFIT MARGIN	EMPLOYEES
6/03	747	—	—	12,497
6/02	750	—	—	12,238
6/01	639	—	—	11,754
6/00	594	—	—	14,965
6/99	544	—	—	11,169
6/98	519	—	—	11,124
6/97	986	—	—	—
6/96	1,113	—	—	—
6/95	866	—	—	—
6/94	690	—	—	—
Annual Growth	0.9%	—	—	2.4%

Revenue History

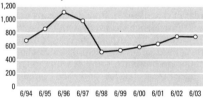

Princeton University

Princeton rules the Ivy League. The highly selective university accepts about 13% of those who apply. Founded in 1746, Princeton is one of the US's richest universities, with an endowment of more than $8.7 billion (behind Harvard, Yale, and Texas). It offers degrees in 35 departments. Princeton's more than 6,600 students pay a tuition that reaches $30,000 a year; more than 50% receive some financial aid. Nobel prize winners associated with Princeton include Woodrow Wilson (who was Princeton's president before becoming US president), writer Toni Morrison, and physicist Richard Feynman. The university also is loosely affiliated with the Institute for Advanced Study where Albert Einstein once taught.

Printpack

Printpack wraps its flexible packaging around salty snacks, confections, baked goods, cookies, crackers, and cereal, as well as tissues and paper towels. The company's packaging includes plastic film, aluminum foil, metallized films and paper with specialized coatings, and cast and blown monolayer and co-extruded films. Customers include Frito-Lay, Georgia Pacific, General Mills, and Quaker Oats. Printpack manufactures packaging materials at about 20 plants in the US, Mexico, and the UK. The founding Love family owns and manages the company, which was founded in 1956.

EXECUTIVES

Chairman: Gay M. Love, age 72
President, CEO, and Director: Dennis M. Love, age 48, $802,674 pay
VP, Finance and Administration: R. Michael Hembree, age 52, $299,706 pay
VP, Human Resources: Nicklas D. Stucky, age 55, $250,633 pay
VP, Engineering: August Franchini Jr., age 58
VP, Technology and Support: Terrence P. Harper, age 43
VP, General Manager, and Director: James E. Love III, age 44, $426,774 pay
VP and General Manager: Michael A. Fisher, age 54
VP and General Manager: James J. Greco, age 57, $443,275 pay
VP and General Manager: William E. Lewis, age 57
VP and General Manager: John N. Stigler, age 53
Corporate Communications Manager: Susan Folds
Auditors: PricewaterhouseCoopers LLP

LOCATIONS

HQ: Printpack, Inc.
4335 Wendell Dr., Atlanta, GA 30336
Phone: 404-691-5830   **Fax:** 404-699-7122
Web: www.printpack.com

Printpack operates 20 manufacturing plants in the US, Mexico, and the UK.

PRODUCTS/OPERATIONS

Selected Customers
Frito-Lay
General Mills
Georgia Pacific
Hershey
Keebler
Kellogg
Mars
Nabisco
Nestle
Quaker Oats

COMPETITORS

AEP Industries
Alcoa
Bemis
Madeco
Pechiney
Pliant
PMC Global
Reynolds Food Packaging
Sealed Air

HISTORICAL FINANCIALS
Company Type: Private

Income Statement
FYE: Saturday nearest June 30

	REVENUE ($ mil.)	NET INCOME ($ mil.)	NET PROFIT MARGIN	EMPLOYEES
6/03	1,053	—	—	3,906
6/02	1,100	—	—	4,300
6/01	1,027	—	—	3,800
6/00	907	—	—	3,800
6/99	846	—	—	3,600
6/98	832	—	—	3,500
6/97	782	—	—	3,500
6/96	443	—	—	2,330
6/95	455	—	—	2,663
6/94	407	—	—	3,000
Annual Growth	11.1%	—	—	3.0%

Revenue History

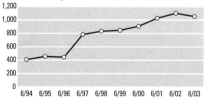

Provena Health

The offspring of a very holy union, Provena Health was created from the merger of Illinois Roman Catholic hospital groups Franciscan Sisters Health Care (Frankfort), ServantCor (Kankakee), and Mercy Center for Health Care Services (Aurora), in an effort to stay competitive in an era of managed care. Provena has six hospitals, 14 nursing homes, nearly 30 clinics, six home health agencies, and its own PersonalCare HMO. It also has a hospice program, and its HealthCare Equipment unit sells a large selection of medical equipment. Provena is sponsored by Franciscan Sisters of the Sacred Heart, Servants of the Holy Heart of Mary, and Sisters of Mercy of the Americas.

EXECUTIVES

Chairman: Guy R. Wiebking
President and CEO: William T. Foley
CFO: Anthony Filer
CIO: Jonathan Manis
VP, Human Resources: Terry S. Solem
VP, Planning and Marketing: Thomas H. Hansen
Public Relations Officer: Clinton Giese
President and CEO, Saint Joseph Medical Center: Jeffrey L. Brickman, age 48
President, Provena Saint Joseph Hospital: William A. Brown
President, Provena St. Mary's Hospital: George N. Miller Jr.
President, Provena Mercy Center: Timothy P. Selz
President, Provena Covenant Medical Center and Provena United Samaritans Medical Center: Mark S. Wiener

LOCATIONS

HQ: Provena Health
19065 Hickory Creek Dr., Ste. 300,
Mokena, IL 60448
Phone: 708-478-6300   **Fax:** 708-478-5960
Web: www.provenahealth.com

Hospitals

Provena Covenant Medical Center (Urbana, IL)
Provena Mercy Center (Aurora, IL)
Provena Saint Joseph Hospital (Elgin, IL)
Provena Saint Joseph Medical Center (Joliet, IL)
Provena Saint Mary's Hospital (Kankakee, IL)
Provena United Samaritans Medical Center (Danville, IL)

COMPETITORS

Advocate Health Care
Alexian Brothers Health System
Ascension Health
BJC HealthCare
Catholic Health Initiatives
Rush System for Health
Sisters of Mercy Health System
University of Chicago

HISTORICAL FINANCIALS
Company Type: Not-for-profit

Income Statement
FYE: December 31

	REVENUE ($ mil.)	NET INCOME ($ mil.)	NET PROFIT MARGIN	EMPLOYEES
12/03	1,200	—	—	10,000
12/02	981	—	—	10,000
12/01	900	—	—	11,000
12/00	869	—	—	11,400
12/99	720	—	—	12,000
12/98	688	—	—	11,500
12/97	634	—	—	11,400
12/96	391	—	—	5,800
12/95	379	—	—	5,750
12/94	369	—	—	—
Annual Growth	14.0%	—	—	7.2%

Revenue History

Providence Health System

Sisterhood is powerful in health care. The order of the Sisters of Providence runs not-for-profit Providence Health System in the Pacific Northwest (with outposts in Alaska and southern California). The system operates about 20 acute care hospitals, some of which offer specialized care centers for cancer and heart disease. Other services include long-term care and assisted-living facilities and primary care centers. All together, the health system has more than 3,700 acute care beds and nearly 1,750 long-term care beds. Providence Health System also offers health plans, low-income housing, and home health, hospice, and various community outreach services.

The Sisters of Providence were founded in 1843 in Montreal. Their work in the US began in 1856, when five members of the order established a mission in what was then Washington Territory.

EXECUTIVES

Chairman: Kay Stepp
President and CEO: John F. Koster, age 53
VP and CFO: Michael (Mike) Butler
VP, Human Resources: Sue Byington
VP, Clinical Excellence and Chief Medical Officer: Rocky Fredrickson
VP, Strategic Development: Claudia Haglund
VP, Government Affairs: Chuck Hawley
VP and Chief Administrative Officer: Jan Jones
VP, Strategic Learning and Leadership Development: Adrienne McDunn
VP and General Counsel: Jeffrey W. (Jeff) Rogers
VP, Information Services and CIO: Rick Skinner
System Director, International Missions: Mark Koenig
System Director, Public Relations: Cheryl Sjoblom

LOCATIONS

HQ: Providence Health System
506 2nd Ave., Ste. 1200, Seattle, WA 98104
Phone: 206-464-3355   **Fax:** 206-464-3038
Web: www.providence.org

Selected Facilities

Alaska
 Providence Alaska Medical Center (Anchorage)
 Providence Kodiak Island Medical Center (Kodiak)
 Providence Seward Medical Center (Seward)
California
 Providence Saint Joseph Medical Center (Burbank)
 Providence Holy Cross Medical Center (Mission Hills)
 San Pedro Peninsula Hospital (San Pedro)
 Little Company of Mary Hospital (Torrance)
Oregon
 Providence Hood River Memorial Hospital (Hood River)
 Providence Medford Medical Center (Medford)
 Providence Milwaukie Hospital (Milwaukie)
 Providence Newburg Hospital (Newburg)
 Providence Portland Medical Center (Portland)
 Providence St. Vincent Medical Center (Porland)
 Providence Seaside Hospital (Seaside)
Washington
 Providence Centralia Hospital (Centralia)
 Providence Everett Medical Center (Everett)
 Providence St. Peter Hospital (Olympia)

COMPETITORS

Adventist Health
Catholic Healthcare West
HCA
Legacy Health System
Los Angeles County Health Department
Memorial Health Services
PacifiCare
Sisters of Charity of Leavenworth
Sutter Health
Tenet Healthcare
Triad Hospitals
UniHealth

HISTORICAL FINANCIALS
Company Type: Not-for-profit

Income Statement
FYE: December 31

	REVENUE ($ mil.)	NET INCOME ($ mil.)	NET PROFIT MARGIN	EMPLOYEES
12/03	3,780	177	4.7%	32,526
12/02	3,529	58	1.6%	33,920
12/01	3,274	95	2.9%	32,929
12/00	3,229	162	5.0%	32,238
12/99	3,000	—	—	27,000
12/98	2,709	—	—	23,000
12/97	2,346	—	—	21,800
12/96	2,137	—	—	20,368
12/95	1,579	—	—	17,956
12/94	1,503	—	—	17,362
Annual Growth	10.8%	16.2%	—	7.2%

2003 Year-End Financials
Debt ratio: 39.7%
Return on equity: 8.4%
Cash ($ mil.): —
Current ratio: —
Long-term debt ($ mil.): 896

Net Income History

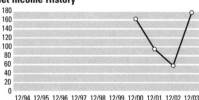

Publix

Publix Super Markets tops the list of privately-owned supermarket operators in the US. By emphasizing service and a family-friendly image rather than price, Publix has grown faster and been more profitable than Winn-Dixie Stores and other rivals. Most of its 800-plus stores are in Florida, but it also operates in Alabama, Georgia, South Carolina, and Tennessee. Publix makes some of its own bakery, deli, and dairy goods, and many stores offer flowers, housewares, pharmacies, and banks. The company also operates four "Pix" convenience stores in the Sunshine State. Founder George Jenkins began offering stock to Publix employees in 1930. Employees own about 30% of Publix, which is still run by the Jenkins family.

Looking for opportunities to expand, Publix has said it will consider acquiring the BI-LO and Bruno's chains from troubled Dutch grocer Royal Ahold.

Publix is expanding into the liquor market with the acquisition of two liquor stores adjacent to a pair of Kash n' Karry outlets in Florida that the company acquired from Delhaize America recently. Publix opens about 30 new supermarkets each year. About 75% of the company's stores are in Florida.

HISTORY

George Jenkins, age 22, resigned as manager of the Piggly Wiggly grocery in Winter Haven, Florida, in 1930. With money he had saved to buy a car, he opened his own grocery store, Publix, next door to his old employer. The small store (named after a chain of movie theaters) prospered despite the Depression, and in 1935 Jenkins opened another Publix in the same town.

Five years later, after the supermarket format had become popular, Jenkins closed his two smaller locations and opened a new, more modern Publix Market. With pastel colors and electric-eye doors, it was also the first US store to feature air conditioning.

Publix Super Markets bought the All-American chain of Lakeland, Florida (19 stores), in 1944 and moved its corporate headquarters to that city. The company began offering S&H Green Stamps in 1953, and in 1956 it replaced its original supermarket with a mall featuring an enlarged Publix and a Green Stamp redemption center. Publix expanded into South Florida in the late 1950s and began selling stock to employees.

As Florida's population grew, Publix continued to expand, opening its 100th store in 1964. Publix was the first grocery chain in the state to use bar-code scanners — all its stores had the technology by 1981. The company beat Florida banks in providing ATMs and during the 1980s opened debit card stations.

Publix continued to grow in the 1980s, safe from takeover attempts because of its employee ownership. In 1988 it installed the first automated checkout systems in South Florida, giving patrons an always-open checkout lane.

Publix stopped offering Green Stamps in 1989, and most of the $19 million decrease in the chain's advertising expenditures was attributed to the end of the 36-year promotion. That year, after almost six decades, "Mr. George" — as founder Jenkins was known — stepped down as chairman in favor of his son Howard. (George died in 1996.)

In 1991 Publix opened its first store outside Florida, in Georgia, as part of its plan to become a major player in the Southeast. Publix entered South Carolina in 1993 with one supermarket; it also tripled its presence in Georgia to 15 stores.

The United Food and Commercial Workers Union began a campaign in 1994 against alleged gender and racial discrimination in Publix's hiring, promotion, and compensation policies.

Publix opened its first store in Alabama in 1996. That year a federal judge allowed about 150,000 women to join a class-action suit filed in 1995 by 12 women who had sued Publix, charging that the company consistently channeled female employees into low-paying jobs with little chance for good promotions. The case, which at the time was said to be the biggest sex discrimination lawsuit ever, was set to go to trial, but in 1997 the company paid $82.5 million to settle and another $3.5 million to settle a complaint of discrimination against black applicants and employees.

Publix promised to change its promotion policies, but two more lawsuits alleging discrimination against women and blacks were filed in 1997 and 1998. The suit filed on behalf of the women was denied class-action status in 2000. Later that year the company settled the racial discrimination lawsuit for $10.5 million. Howard Jenkins stepped down as CEO in mid-2001; his cousin Charlie Jenkins took the helm.

In mid-2002 Publix made an equity investment in Florida-based Crispers, a chain of 13 quick-serve restaurants targeting health-conscious diners. Also that year, Publix entered the Nashville, Tennessee, market with the purchase of seven Albertson's supermarkets, a convenience store, and a fuel center.

In mid-2003 Publix pulled the plug on its online store PublixDirect, which offered delivery service in parts of Florida, citing disappointing sales. However, it added 78 bricks-and-mortar stores in 2003.

In February 2004, Publix acquired three Florida stores from Kash n' Karry, a subsidiary of Belgium's Delhaize Group.

EXECUTIVES

Chairman: Howard M. Jenkins, age 52
Vice Chairman: Hoyt R. (Barney) Barnett, age 60, $322,106 pay
CEO: Charles H. (Charlie) Jenkins Jr., age 60, $544,067 pay
President: William E. (Ed) Crenshaw, age 53, $454,224 pay
CFO and Treasurer: David P. Phillips, age 44, $341,564 pay
SVP and CIO: Daniel M. Risener, age 63
SVP and Director: Tina P. Johnson, age 44
SVP, Supply Chain: James J. (Jim) Lobinsky, age 64, $285,772 pay
VP, Distribution: Richard J. Schuler II, age 48
VP, Facilities: David S. Duncan, age 50
VP, Human Resources and Compliance: James H. Rhodes II, age 59
VP, Human Resources: John T. Hrabusa, age 48
VP, Internal Audit: Linda S. Hall, age 44
VP, Manufacturing: R. Scott Charlton, age 45
VP, Marketing: Mark R. Irby, age 48
VP, Pharmacy: Alfred J. Ottolino
VP, Product Business Development, Fresh Product: David E. Bridges, age 54
VP, Product Business Development, Grocery/Non-Foods: David E. Bornmann, age 46
VP, Public Affairs: M. Clayton Hollis Jr., age 47
VP, Real Estate: John R. Frazier, age 54
VP, Retail Business Development: Dale S. Myers, age 51
VP, Risk Management: Edward T. Shivers, age 64
Director, Consumer Relations and Strategic Communication: Leslie Spencer
General Counsel and Secretary: John A. Attaway Jr., age 45
Auditors: KPMG LLP

LOCATIONS

HQ: Publix Super Markets, Inc.
3300 Airport Rd., Lakeland, FL 33811
Phone: 863-688-1188   **Fax:** 863-284-5532
Web: www.publix.com

Publix Super Markets operates about 800 grocery stores in Alabama, Florida, Georgia, South Carolina, and Tennessee. The company also has three dairy processing plants (Deerfield Beach and Lakeland, Florida, and Lawrenceville, Georgia) and a deli plant and a bakery in Lakeland. Publix operates eight distribution centers in Florida (Boynton Beach, Deerfield Beach, Jacksonville, Lakeland, Miami, Orlando, and Sarasota) and Georgia (Lawrenceville).

2003 Stores

	No.
Florida	600
Georgia	148
South Carolina	34
Alabama	12
Tennessee	7
Total	**801**

PRODUCTS/OPERATIONS

Selected Supermarket Departments

Bakery	Health and beauty care
Banking	Housewares
Dairy	Meat
Deli	Pharmacy
Ethnic foods	Photo processing
Floral	Produce
Groceries	Seafood

Foods Processed
Baked goods
Dairy products
Deli items

COMPETITORS

Albertson's	Nash Finch
ALDI	The Pantry
BI-LO	Rite Aid
Bruno's Supermarkets	Royal Ahold
Costco Wholesale	Ruddick
CVS	Sedano's
Delhaize America	Smart & Final
IGA	Walgreen
Ingles Markets	Wal-Mart
Kerr Drug	Whole Foods
Kmart	Winn-Dixie
Kroger	

HISTORICAL FINANCIALS

Company Type: Private

Income Statement — FYE: Last Saturday in December

	REVENUE ($ mil.)	NET INCOME ($ mil.)	NET PROFIT MARGIN	EMPLOYEES
12/03	16,946	661	3.9%	125,000
12/02	16,027	632	3.9%	123,000
12/01	15,370	530	3.5%	126,000
12/00	14,724	530	3.6%	126,000
12/99	13,069	462	3.5%	120,000
12/98	12,067	378	3.1%	117,000
12/97	11,224	355	3.2%	111,000
12/96	10,431	265	2.5%	103,000
12/95	9,393	242	2.6%	95,000
12/94	8,665	239	2.8%	90,000
Annual Growth	7.7%	12.0%	—	3.7%

2003 Year-End Financials

Debt ratio: 0.0%
Return on equity: 21.4%
Cash ($ mil.): 277
Current ratio: 1.15
Long-term debt ($ mil.): 0

Net Income History

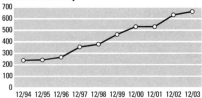

Purdue Pharma

Purdue Pharma makes drugs, not boilers. The company is best known for over-the-counter medicines like Betadine (an antiseptic) and Senokot (a laxative). Purdue concentrates its research and development on pain management and cancer. Prescription drugs include pain relievers MS Contin and OxyContin. It is also developing cardiac and respiratory therapies, as well as inhaled drug delivery systems. The firm markets products from other manufacturers in addition to its own products. Founded in 1892, the firm is part of a network of affiliates with operations in Asia, North and South America, and Europe.

Purdue Pharma also sponsors the pain control organization Partners Against Pain.

The company's OxyContin has been the point of much controversy; the opiate-based drug has received criticism as being too addictive and powerful. The drug has a reputation of illegal use, and the negative publicity has been amplified because of celebrities associated with the drug's use; such as singer and actress Courtney Love, who admitted overdosing on the drug, and radio talk show host Rush Limbaugh, who spent time in rehab battling a reported OxyContin addiction. The company and the FDA have taken numerous steps to curb the abuse of the painkiller, and as patent expiration approaches, Purdue is petitioning the FDA to make sure that any generic manufacturers have in place a risk management program that is equivalent to its own.

EXECUTIVES

President and CEO: Michael Friedman
EVP and CFO: Edward B. Mahony
EVP and Chief Legal Officer: Howard R. Udell
EVP and Counsel to the Board of Directors: Stuart Baker
EVP, Field Operations and Marketing: James Lang
EVP, Worldwide Research and Development and Chief Scientific Officer: Paul D. Goldenheim
SVP, Licensing and Business Development: James Dolan
VP, Corporate Planning: Ron Levine
VP, Corporate Quality: Kathleen Schady
VP, Corporate Security: Aaron Graham
VP, Human Resources: David Long
VP, Information Technology: Larry Pickett
VP, Public Affairs: Robin Hogen
VP, Technical Operations: Fred Sexton
Senior Director, Corporate Communications: Merle Spiegel

LOCATIONS

HQ: Purdue Pharma L.P.
1 Stamford Forum, 201 Tresser Blvd., Stamford, CT 06901
Phone: 203-588-8000   **Fax:** 203-588-8850
Web: www.purduepharma.com

Purdue Pharma operates facilities in Stamford, Connecticut; Cranbury and Totowa, New Jersey; Ardsley, New York; Wilson, North Carolina; and Coventry, Rhode Island.

PRODUCTS/OPERATIONS

Selected Products

Over-The-Counter
  Betadine (antibiotic)
  Colace (laxative)
  Peri-Colace (stool softener)
  Gentlax (laxative)
  Senokot (laxative)
  Senokot-S (laxative)
  Slow-Mag (mineral supplement)
  X-PREP (laxative)
Prescription
  Cerumenex (earwax removal)
  MS Contin (pain management)
  MSIR (pain management)
  OxyContin (pain management)
  OxyFast (pain management)
  OxyIR (pain management)
  Spectracef (anti-infective)
  T-Phyl (asthma and other respiratory ailments)
  Trilisate (pain and inflammation management)
  Uniphyl (asthma and other respiratory ailments)

COMPETITORS

Abbott GmbH
Bayer
Bristol-Myers Squibb
Elan Corporation
Endo Pharmaceuticals
Johnson & Johnson
Merck
Novartis
Pfizer
Sanofi-Aventis

HISTORICAL FINANCIALS

Company Type: Private

Income Statement FYE: December 31

	REVENUE ($ mil.)	NET INCOME ($ mil.)	NET PROFIT MARGIN	EMPLOYEES
12/02	1,551	—	—	5,000
12/01	1,500	—	—	3,000
12/00	1,200	—	—	3,000
12/99	812	—	—	—
12/98	603	—	—	—
Annual Growth	26.6%	—	—	29.1%

Revenue History

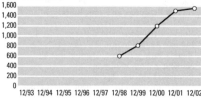

Purity Wholesale Grocers

Purity Wholesale Grocers (PWG) gets the goods to grocers. The company takes advantage of the discounts granted to large wholesalers and retailers (and of the promotional pricing offered in certain regions) by purchasing items and selling them to retailers not privy to those discounts. PWG moves groceries, health and beauty care items, pharmaceutical products, dairy foods, and dry goods to US grocery chains, drugstores, and convenience stores. PWG's marketing network is made up of about a dozen independently operated food distributors, marketers, and transportation firms in the US and Puerto Rico. The company is owned by Jeff Levitetz, who founded PWG in 1982.

EXECUTIVES

Chairman: Jeff Levitetz
President and CEO: Salvatore (Sal) Ricciardi
CFO: Alan Rutner
SVP, Operations: John Tarr
Director, Human Resources: Karen McGrath
Controller: Tom Jankus

LOCATIONS

HQ: Purity Wholesale Grocers, Inc.
5400 Broken Sound Blvd. NW, Ste. 100, Boca Raton, FL 33487
Phone: 561-994-9360   **Fax:** 561-241-4628
Web: www.pwg-inc.com

COMPETITORS

Dot Foods
Eby-Brown
Nash Finch
Spartan Stores
SUPERVALU
SYSCO

HISTORICAL FINANCIALS

Company Type: Private

Income Statement FYE: June 30

	REVENUE ($ mil.)	NET INCOME ($ mil.)	NET PROFIT MARGIN	EMPLOYEES
6/04	1,700	—	—	—
6/03	1,750	—	—	450
6/02	1,600	—	—	490
6/01	1,450	—	—	440
6/00	1,300	—	—	650
6/99	1,500	—	—	650
6/98	1,200	—	—	600
6/97	1,000	—	—	400
6/96	700	—	—	300
6/95	650	—	—	275
Annual Growth	11.3%	—	—	6.3%

Revenue History

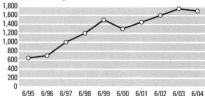

Quad/Graphics

Your mailbox may be filled with Quad/Graphics' handiwork. One of the largest privately held printers in the US, the company prints catalogs, magazines, books, direct mail, and other items. It offers a full range of services, including design, photography, desktop production, printing, binding, wrapping, and distribution. At its printing facilities, five of which are in Wisconsin, the company prints catalogs for the likes of Bloomingdale's and Victoria's Secret, as well as periodicals such as *People*, *Newsweek*, and *Sports Illustrated*. Company employees and relatives of the founding Quadracci family own Quad/Graphics. The company sold its package delivery business Parcel Direct to FedEx in 2004 for $120 million.

Quad is one of the most employee- and community-oriented companies in the industry. The firm has been recognized for its fun work atmosphere, and it provides on-site day care centers, health clubs, and medical clinics. In addition, it sponsors sports leagues (softball, bowling), awards college scholarships to employees' children, and provides interest-free auto loans. Quad/Graphic's Windhover Fund manages the philanthropic distribution of 5% of the company's pretax profit for social, cultural, and educational projects.

HISTORY

Ink runs in Harry V. Quadracci's family. His father, Harry R., founded a printing business — Standard Printing — in Racine, Wisconsin, in 1930, when he was 16. Four years later Quadracci sold out to William A. Krueger. Though he worked to build Krueger into a major regional printer, the elder Quadracci had little equity in the company.

In the 1960s son Harry V. joined Krueger as a company lawyer. Within a few years he had worked his way up to plant manager. Krueger was a union shop, and in those days unions dictated the work rules and often salary levels. In 1970 there was a three-and-a-half-month strike. At odds with new management and reportedly dissatisfied with the way Krueger caved in to union demands and the adversarial relationship between company and union, the younger Quadracci left.

After 18 months of unemployment, in 1971 Quadracci formed a limited partnership with 12 others to get a loan to buy a press, which was installed in a building in Pewaukee, Wisconsin. The next year his father joined the company as chairman. Within two years the partners had recouped their initial investment, but the business' future remained in question until about 1976. One of its most innovative moves was to make its delivery fleet drivers into entrepreneurs by requiring them to find cargo to haul on their return trips.

Working on a shoestring, Quadracci hired inexperienced workers and trained them, moving them up as the company grew. The need to improve fostered a flexibility that Quadracci institutionalized by keeping management layers flat and remaining accessible to his employees. Beginning in 1974, Quadracci rewarded his workers with equity in the company.

In the 1980s Quad/Graphics' commitment to technology enabled it to offer better service than many of its competitors. It was also immune to the merger-and-acquisition fever of the time. Free of acquisition debt, the company had excellent credit and was able to finance equipment upgrades with bank loans. Quad expanded by opening a plant in Saratoga Springs, New York (1985), and buying a plant in Thomaston, Georgia (1989).

But there were missteps, such as its 1985 attempt to break into the newspaper coupon insert business dominated by Treasure Chest Advertising. Quad/Graphics sold that operation three years later. The company could not avoid the national economic downturn that began about that time, which forced it to lay off employees in the late 1980s and early 1990s and prompted it to reduce weekend overtime pay (from double time to time-and-a-half). The firm was also hit when a major customer consolidated its printing outside the Midwest. In response, Quad/Graphics increased its capacity in other regions of the US during the 1990s.

In 1996 the company bought 40% of Argentine printer Anselmo L. Morvillo. Benefiting from the UPS strike and changes in the postal regulations, in 1997 Quad/Graphics expanded its shipping services with Parcel Direct, targeting parcels for large shippers such as catalog merchants, in cooperation with the US Postal Service. Also that year it created a joint venture color printing firm with Brazil's Folha Group.

In 1998 Quad/Graphics expanded its international reach, agreeing to a joint venture in Poland. The next year the company was awarded the pre-press business of Condé Nast magazines. In 2000 it launched a business-to-business portal called Smart Tools. The company was shocked in 2002 when Quadracci died in an accidental drowning at age 66. Quadracci's brother, Tom, was then appointed president.

EXECUTIVES

Chairman: Richard A. Burke
President and CEO: Thomas A. (Tom) Quadracci
SVP Manufacturing: Thomas J. Frankowski
SVP Sales and Administration: J. Joel Quadracci
VP Finance and CFO: John C. Fowler
VP and Controller: Linda Larson
VP Customer Service: Ron Nash
VP East Coast Sales: Bob Wachtendonk
VP Employee Services: Emmy M. LaBode
VP Information Systems: Steve Jaeger
VP Midwest Sales: Timothy Ohnmacht
VP Operations: David Blais
VP West Coast Sales: Renee Lekan
President, QuadCreative Group and Publisher, Milwaukee Magazine: Betty Ewens Quadracci
Director Corporate Purchasing: Arthur W. (Art) Noe
Director Postal Affairs: Joe Schick
Manager Business Development: Chuck DuPont
Manager Credit: Pat Rydzik
Manager Corporate Purchasing: Mike Kaczmarek
Manager Marketing: Claire Ho
General Counsel: Andy Schiesl

LOCATIONS

HQ: Quad/Graphics, Inc.
N63 W23075 State Hwy. 74, Sussex, WI 53089
Phone: 414-566-6000 **Fax:** 414-566-4650
Web: www.qg.com

Quad/Graphics has production plants in Georgia, New York, West Virginia, and Wisconsin. It also operates joint ventures in Argentina, Brazil, and Poland.

PRODUCTS/OPERATIONS

Selected Services
Binding and finishing
Color correction
Design
Desktop production
Direct mailing
Imaging and photography
Ink jetting
Integrated circulation
Mailing and distribution
Mailing list management
Printing
Scanning

COMPETITORS

Arandell	Perry Judd's
Banta	Quebecor World
Brown Printing	R.R. Donnelley
Consolidated Graphics	Spencer Press
Dai Nippon Printing	St Ives US Division
Merrill	Toppan Printing

HISTORICAL FINANCIALS

Company Type: Private

Income Statement
FYE: December 31

	REVENUE ($ mil.)	NET INCOME ($ mil.)	NET PROFIT MARGIN	EMPLOYEES
12/03	2,000	—	—	12,000
12/02	1,800	—	—	11,000
12/01	1,700	—	—	10,500
12/00	1,800	—	—	14,000
12/99	1,500	—	—	13,000
12/98	1,400	—	—	11,000
12/97	1,200	—	—	11,000
12/96	1,042	—	—	9,500
12/95	1,002	—	—	8,444
12/94	801	—	—	7,500
Annual Growth	10.7%	—	—	5.4%

Revenue History

Quality King

Quality King Distributors rules a gargantuan gray market empire. It buys US name-brand products that have been exported to overseas markets, re-imports them, then sells them below suggested retail prices. The practice, deeply disliked by US manufacturers, has been ruled legal by the Supreme Court. Quality King distributes groceries and hair, health, and beauty care products to pharmacy and grocery chains, grocery distributors, and wholesale clubs throughout the US. Bernard Nussdorf and his wife Ruth founded Quality King in 1960 in Queens, New York. The Nussdorf family still owns the company, which has transferred its pharmaceutical distribution business to affiliate QK Healthcare prior to spinning it off.

EXECUTIVES

Chairman and CEO: Glenn Nussdorf
CFO: Dennis Barkey
EVP: Michael W. Katz
VP, Human Resources: Jane Midgal
VP, Data Processing: Marc Garrett

LOCATIONS

HQ: Quality King Distributors Inc.
2060 9th Ave., Ronkonkoma, NY 11779
Phone: 631-737-5555   **Fax:** 631-439-2388
Web: www.qkd.com

The company has warehouse facilities in Ronkonkoma, New York.

COMPETITORS

AmerisourceBergen
Cardinal Health
C.D. Smith Healthcare Inc
D & K Healthcare Resources
Henry Schein
Kinray
McKesson

HISTORICAL FINANCIALS

Company Type: Private

Income Statement
FYE: October 31

	REVENUE ($ mil.)	NET INCOME ($ mil.)	NET PROFIT MARGIN	EMPLOYEES
10/02	2,450	—	—	1,400
10/01	2,400	—	—	1,300
10/00	2,050	—	—	1,200
10/99	1,800	—	—	1,000
10/98	1,400	—	—	1,000
10/97	1,200	—	—	1,000
10/96	950	—	—	900
10/95	880	—	—	700
10/94	850	—	—	660
10/93	860	—	—	650
Annual Growth	12.3%	—	—	8.9%

Revenue History

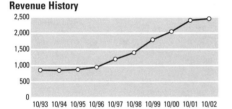

Quexco

Quexco gets the lead out and puts it back in. A leading secondary lead producer, this private holding company recycles scrapped lead acid batteries into refined lead and lead products. Quexco's RSR Corporation subsidiary is one of the largest lead smelters in the US, with operations in California, Indiana, New York, and Texas. Quexco also owns Eco-Bat Technologies plc, a UK-based battery recycler with operations in Europe and South Africa. The company's RSR Technologies subsidiary (formerly its R&D unit) offers technology and product development services to the metals industry. Chairman and CEO Howard Meyers, who also heads Bayou Steel Corporation, controls Quexco.

EXECUTIVES

Chairman, President, and CEO: Howard M. Meyers, age 62

LOCATIONS

HQ: Quexco Incorporated
2777 N. Stemmons Fwy., Dallas, TX 75207
Phone: 214-688-4000   **Fax:** 214-630-5864

Quexco has operations in the US, Europe, and South Africa.

PRODUCTS/OPERATIONS

Selected Operations
Eco-Bat Technologies plc (battery recycling, UK)
    STMC Holdings
RSR Corporation
    Bestolife Corporation (pipe thread compounds and lubricants for the oil exploration industry)
    Quemetco Metals Limited (electro-winning anodes for the copper industry)
    Revere Smelting & Refining (lead recycling)
RSR Technologies Inc. (recycling industry R&D services)
West Morris Properties, Inc.

COMPETITORS

Exide
Noranda
Renco

HISTORICAL FINANCIALS

Company Type: Private

Income Statement
FYE: December 31

	ESTIMATED REVENUE ($ mil.)	NET INCOME ($ mil.)	NET PROFIT MARGIN	EMPLOYEES
12/02	2,000	—	—	7,000
12/01	2,000	—	—	7,000
Annual Growth	0.0%	—	—	0.0%

Revenue History

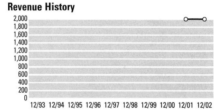

QuikTrip

QuikTrip provides a quick fix for people on the go. QuikTrip (QT) owns and operates 430-plus gasoline and convenience stores primarily in the Midwest. QT stores, which average 4,500 to 5,000 sq. ft., feature the company's own brand of gas, as well as brand-name beverages, candy, and tobacco, and QT's own Quik 'n Tasty and HOTZI lines of sandwiches. QuikTrip travel centers offer CAT scales, food, fuel, showers, and other services for truckers. The company's FleetMaster program offers commercial trucking companies detailed reports showing drivers' product purchases, amounts spent, and odometer readings. QuikTrip was co-founded in 1958 by chairman Chester Cadieux and partners. His son Chet runs the company.

QuikTrip is remodeling stores and expanding its hot and cold beverage selection. The icy "Koolee" introduced in 1963 will be replaced by a frozen carbonated beverage called a Freezoni, available in seven flavors. The drink initiative will be rolled out to all QuikTrip stores by mid-2005.

The company is also testing a high-volume (capable of handling 120 cars per hour) car wash at a location in Tulsa.

EXECUTIVES

Chairman: Chester Cadieux
President and CEO: Chester (Chet) Cadieux Jr.
SVP, Finance: Terry Carter
VP, Marketing: James (Jim) Denny
Treasurer: Paula Cotten
Director, Human Resources: Kimberly (Kim) Owen
Manager, Corporate Sales: Rodney Loyd
Manager, Public and Government Affairs: Mike Thornbrugh

LOCATIONS

HQ: QuikTrip Corporation
4705 S. 129th East Ave., Tulsa, OK 74134
Phone: 918-615-7700   **Fax:** 918-615-7377
Web: www.quiktrip.com

QuikTrip owns stores in Arizona, Georgia, Illinois, Iowa, Kansas, Missouri, Nebraska, Oklahoma, and Texas.

COMPETITORS

7-Eleven
Casey's General Stores
ChevronTexaco
CITGO
Exxon Mobil
E-Z Mart Stores
Krause Gentle
Motiva Enterprises
Racetrac Petroleum

HISTORICAL FINANCIALS

Company Type: Private

Income Statement
FYE: April 30

	REVENUE ($ mil.)	NET INCOME ($ mil.)	NET PROFIT MARGIN	EMPLOYEES
4/03	2,800	—	—	6,663
4/02	3,050	—	—	6,575
4/01	2,929	—	—	6,045
4/00	2,347	—	—	5,248
4/99	1,804	—	—	4,796
4/98	1,830	—	—	4,635
4/97	1,730	—	—	4,400
4/96	1,423	—	—	4,075
4/95	1,195	—	—	2,501
4/94	985	—	—	2,200
Annual Growth	12.3%	—	—	13.1%

Revenue History

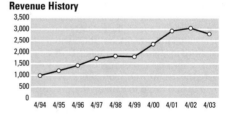

Quintiles Transnational

Quintiles Transnational has plenty to CRO about. One of the world's top contract research organizations (CROs), it provides services to help drug and medical device companies develop and sell their products. The firm's Product Development Services unit offers preclinical research and conducts clinical trials. The CRO's Commercial Services unit offers regulatory consulting, as well as sales and marketing consulting, hiring, and training to get a product to buyers. Quintiles' PharmaBio Development unit teams with emerging health care firms to get new products approved and on the market by exchanging its R&D services for royalties. A group led by chairman Dennis Gillings took the firm private in 2003.

The CRO's Verispan joint venture with McKesson provides health care information products. Verispan, formed in 2002, brought McKesson's Kelly/Waldron unit together with Quintiles-owned Scott-Levin, a preeminent pharmaceutical industry market research company, and SMG Marketing Group. By bringing these marketing services firms under one umbrella, Quintiles can stay involved in a product's life span longer.

Quintiles Strategic Research Services, formed in late 2003, conducts research studies to gather drug data that isn't related to regulatory approval. Types of data generated by these studies can include cost effectiveness, population studies, and other such information. The results, for example, a drugmaker can use to persuade doctors and consumers its drug is safer and more effective than a close competitor's.

Quintiles, which operates in 50 countries, has suffered the double-whammy of pharmaceutical industry consolidation, which has trimmed its client list, and industry cost-cutting efforts. More drugmakers are bringing R&D work in-house to keep down expenses; the firm's top client, Aventis (now Sanofi-Aventis) accounted for less than 10% of sales in 2003.

Its PharmaBio Development and Verispan operations are among the company's attempts to continue to grow, even though they're in the risky business of pinning their hopes on drugs that may not make it onto the market. For instance, PharmaBio inked a deal with Eli Lilly to help market antidepressant Cymbalta, which it thinks could bring in a significant portion of the company's future revenues.

Quintiles ended its nearly 10-year stint as a public company in hopes that once it casts off the burden of meeting and beating Wall Street expectations, the CRO will have the freedom to grow its business as it chooses. The move brought founder Gillings back into the driver's seat; riding shotgun is financial backer BANK ONE's One Equity Partners. The returning CEO envisions Quintiles as an investor in the products it helps develop. However, the company loaded up on debt as part of its leap from NASDAQ.

HISTORY

Quintiles was founded by Dennis Gillings, a British biostatistician who had worked with Hoechst (now part of Sanofi-Aventis) on data analysis in the 1970s. Gillings set up Quintiles (Quantitative Information Technology In The Life and Economic Sciences) in 1982 at the University of North Carolina, where he was then teaching. The company grew as drug companies began outsourcing some of the more irksome tasks of drug development. Quintiles went public in 1994.

Quintiles used the proceeds of the IPO to expand its health economics segment with the purchases of Benefit International (1995) and Lewin Group (1996). These purchases introduced the company to such new clients as governments and HMOs. Quintiles' 1996 purchase of Innovex (unrelated to the computer hardware maker of the same name) made it the world's largest CRO. The buying spree continued in 1997 and 1998. Among the purchases were some intended to strengthen Quintiles' marketing services (Data Analysis Systems Inc., Q.E.D. International, and France-based Serval). The firm also formed new collaborations with such academic research organizations as Johns Hopkins Medicine.

In 1999 Quintiles expanded its marketing arm with the purchase of Pharmaceutical Marketing Services (parent of the leading pharmaceuticals industry research company, Scott-Levin) and jumped headlong into data mining with its purchase of ENVOY — which processed insurance claims. Quintiles found the core business uninspiring and sold it to Healtheon (now WebMD) the next year. But it kept rights to ENVOY's stream of treatment, outcome, and insurance data, gleaned from health care providers, hospitals, payers, and pharmacies — a treasure house of information useful to salespeople and health providers.

The company continued in 2000 to add offices in Europe, Asia, and Latin America. The company also opened additional offices in the US and Europe to help Japanese pharmaceutical companies market their products in those regions. Late in the year, Quintiles bought the clinical development unit of Pharmacia.

In 2001 Quintiles became embroiled in a legal dispute with WebMD involving the availability of data associated with ENVOY; the company challenged WebMD's efforts to withhold such data. The two companies settled the squabble later that year and agreed to sever all ties. Also in 2001 Quintiles streamlined operations and cut about 5% of its workforce.

The future of the CRO came into question at the end of 2002. Gillings presented the company with a buyout offer; he planned to take the company private so he could pursue a new growth strategy Wall Street would surely find risky. The board rejected that offer in October 2002, but it opened up an auction. Some leading equity firms reportedly made offers, but Gillings — with backing from Blackstone Group and BANK ONE's One Equity Partners — placed another offer for Quintiles and won the prize in April 2003. Some five months later, Quintiles went private.

EXECUTIVES

Executive Chairman and CEO: Dennis B. Gillings, age 49, $706,061 pay
CFO: John Ratliff
EVP, General Counsel, and Chief Administrative Officer: John S. Russell, age 49, $1,025,227 pay
EVP, Corporate Development: Ronald J. Wooten, age 44, $1,120,833 pay
SVP, Strategic Planning and Investor Relations: Greg Connors
SVP, Global Business Development: Tracy K. Tsuetaki, age 41
Global VP, e-Clinical Business: Graham Bunn
VP, Medical and Scientific Services: David Frakes
VP, Corporate Communications: Pat Grebe
VP, Biostatistical Services: Stephen C. Smeach
President, Global Product Development: Oppel Greeff, age 55, $1,023,864 pay
Chief Medical and Scientific Officer: Oren Cohen
Senior Medical Director, Medical & Scientific Services Department: Penny Randall
Medical Director, Integrated Cardiac Safety Services: Dhiraj D. Narula
Director, Medical and Scientific Services, North American Clinical Development Services: Ray Dawkins
Director, Medical and Scientific Services: Richard Levine
Auditors: PricewaterhouseCoopers LLP

LOCATIONS

HQ: Quintiles Transnational Corp.
4709 Creekstone Dr., Ste. 200, Durham, NC 27703
Phone: 919-998-2000 **Fax:** 919-998-2094
Web: www.quintiles.com

Quintiles Transnational operates in 50 countries worldwide.

2003 Sales

	% of total
The Americas	
US	35
Other countries	4
Europe & Africa	
UK	28
Other countries	24
Asia/Pacific	
Japan	8
Other countries	1
Total	**100**

PRODUCTS/OPERATIONS

2003 Sales

	$ mil.	% of total
Service revenues	1,498	73
Commercial rights & royalties	152	7
Investments	31	2
Reimbursed service costs	365	18
Total	**2,046**	**100**

Selected Subsidiaries

Action International Marketing Services Limited (UK)
Benefit Holding, Inc.
Clin Data International (PTY) Limited (South Africa)
G.D.R.U. Limited (UK)
Innovex, L.P.
Laboratorie Novex Pharma Sarl (France)
The Lewin Group, Inc.
Medical Informatics KK (Japan)
Minerva Ireland Limited
PharmaBio Development, Inc.
Quintiles (Israel) Ltd.
Quintiles Hong Kong Limited
Source Informatics European Finance, Inc.
Spectral Laboratories Limited (India)
Transforce, S.A. de C.V. (Mexico)
Verispan, L.L.C.

COMPETITORS

Battelle Memorial
Covance
Healthworld Communications
IMS Health
Kendle
Life Sciences Research
NDCHealth
Nelson Communications
PAREXEL
PPD

HISTORICAL FINANCIALS

Company Type: Private

Income Statement
FYE: December 31

	REVENUE ($ mil.)	NET INCOME ($ mil.)	NET PROFIT MARGIN	EMPLOYEES
12/03	2,046	30	1.5%	15,991
12/02	1,992	127	6.4%	15,548
12/01	1,620	(34)	—	17,224
12/00	1,660	419	25.2%	18,219
12/99	1,607	109	6.8%	20,453
12/98	1,188	84	7.0%	15,520
12/97	815	55	6.8%	10,900
12/96	538	4	0.8%	7,375
12/95	156	11	7.2%	2,000
12/94	90	7	7.4%	1,200
Annual Growth	41.5%	18.0%	—	33.3%

2003 Year-End Financials

Debt ratio: 144.6%
Return on equity: 2.8%
Cash ($ mil.): 375
Current ratio: 1.24
Long-term debt ($ mil.): 774

Net Income History

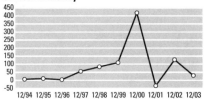

RaceTrac Petroleum

RaceTrac Petroleum hopes it is a popular pit stop for gasoline and snacks in the Southeast. The company operates about 525 company-owned and franchised gas stations and convenience stores in about a dozen states under the RaceTrac and RaceWay names. (RaceWay stores are franchised.) The chain plans to grow by adding between 35 and 45 new locations annually. Carl Bolch founded RaceTrac in Missouri in 1934. His son, chairman and CEO Carl Bolch Jr., moved the company into high-volume gas stations with long, self-service islands that can serve many vehicles at once. RaceTrac's convenience stores also sell fresh deli food, rent videos, and offer some fast-food fare. The Bolch family owns the company.

EXECUTIVES

Chairman and CEO: Carl E. Bolch Jr.
President: Max Lenker
CFO: Robert J. Dumbacher
SVP, Operations: Ben Tison
VP, Human Resources: Allison Moran

LOCATIONS

HQ: RaceTrac Petroleum, Inc.
300 Technology Ct., Smyrna, GA 30082
Phone: 770-431-7600   **Fax:** 770-431-7612
Web: www.racetrac.com

RceTrac Petroleum operates in Alabama, Florida, Georgia, Kentucky, Louisiana, Mississippi, North Carolina, South Carolina, Tennessee, Texas, and Virginia.

COMPETITORS

7-Eleven	Gate Petroleum
ChevronTexaco	Motiva Enterprises
Cumberland Farms	The Pantry
Exxon Mobil	Pilot
E-Z Mart Stores	QuikTrip

HISTORICAL FINANCIALS

Company Type: Private

Income Statement
FYE: December 31

	REVENUE ($ mil.)	NET INCOME ($ mil.)	NET PROFIT MARGIN	EMPLOYEES
12/03	3,200	—	—	—
12/02	3,000	—	—	3,820
12/01	2,942	—	—	3,850
12/00	2,811	—	—	4,932
12/99	1,846	—	—	3,700
12/98	1,500	—	—	3,800
12/97	1,005	—	—	3,612
12/96	1,340	—	—	3,000
12/95	1,056	—	—	2,700
12/94	909	—	—	2,300
Annual Growth	15.0%	—	—	6.5%

Revenue History

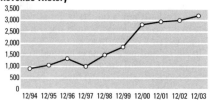

Raley's

Raley's has to stock plenty of fresh fruit and great wines — it sells to the people that produce them. The company operates about 135 supermarkets and larger-sized superstores, mostly in Northern California, but also in Nevada and New Mexico. In addition to its flagship Raley's Superstores, the company operates Bel Air Markets, Nob Hill Foods (an upscale Bay Area chain), and a discount warehouse chain, Food Source. Raley's stores typically offer groceries, natural foods, liquor, and pharmacies. Readers of *Consumer Reports* named Raley's the #1 supermarket chain in the US in 2000. Founded during the Depression by Thomas Porter Raley, the company is owned by Tom's daughter Joyce Raley Teel.

EXECUTIVES

Co-Chairman and Owner: Joyce Raley Teel, age 72
Co-Chairman: James E. (Jim) Teel
President and CEO: William J. (Bill) Coyne
COO: David W. (Dave) D'Arezzo, age 44
EVP and CFO: William Anderson
SVP, Human Resources: Jeffrey D. Szczesny
SVP, Sales and Merchandising: Kevin Curry
VP, Perishables Sales and Merchandising: Steve Hanratty
VP, Superstores: Rick Kaiser
VP, Pharmacy and General Merchandise: Flint Pendergraft
CIO: Eric F. G. Wilson
General Counsel: Jennifer Crabb
Communication Specialist: Jennifer Ortega

LOCATIONS

HQ: Raley's Inc.
500 W. Capitol Ave., West Sacramento, CA 95605
Phone: 916-373-3333   **Fax:** 916-371-1323
Web: www.raleys.com

2003 Stores

	No.
California	113
Nevada	12
New Mexico	9
Total	**134**

PRODUCTS/OPERATIONS

2003 Stores

	No.
Raley's Superstores	83
Nob Hill Foods	26
Bel Air Markets	18
Food Source	7
Total	**134**

COMPETITORS

Albertson's	Save Mart
Costco Wholesale	Trader Joe's Co
Food 4 Less	Wal-Mart
Kroger	Whole Foods
Longs Drug	Wild Oats Markets
Ralphs	WinCo Foods
Safeway	

HISTORICAL FINANCIALS

Company Type: Private

Income Statement
FYE: June 30

	REVENUE ($ mil.)	NET INCOME ($ mil.)	NET PROFIT MARGIN	EMPLOYEES
6/03	3,200	—	—	16,200
6/02	3,200	—	—	17,000
6/01	3,000	—	—	17,000
6/00	2,849	—	—	16,800
6/99	3,000	—	—	15,000
6/98	2,193	—	—	15,000
6/97	1,957	—	—	12,900
6/96	1,912	—	—	11,000
6/95	1,810	—	—	7,500
6/94	1,800	—	—	7,150
Annual Growth	6.6%	—	—	9.5%

Revenue History

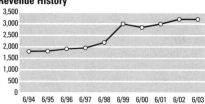

Rand McNally

Rand McNally lets you know where you stand. The largest commercial mapmaker in the world, the company is famous for its flagship Rand McNally Road Atlas —the best-selling product in the history of mapmaking. In addition, the company produces travel-related software (TripMaker, StreetFinder) and educational products for classrooms (globes, atlases). Rand McNally also operates a Web site and makes mileage and routing software for the transportation industry. The company makes maps for the Canadian market through its Rand McNally Canada unit. It sells its products online and through some 50,000 retail outlets across the US, including a handful of Rand McNally stores.

Although it created a Web site in 1996, the company didn't really begin focusing on the Internet until 1999, years later than online rivals such as MapQuest.com. Rand McNally relaunched its Web site and increased its Web and software product offerings in hopes of catching up with its online competitors.

In early 2003 Rand McNally filed for Chapter 11 bankruptcy protection. The company exited bankruptcy within two months, with buyout firm Leonard Green & Partners as its new majority owner with a 60% stake. It has closed some retail stores as part of a new retail strategy.

HISTORY

Rand McNally was founded by William Rand and Andrew McNally in 1856. In 1864 they bought the job-printing department of the *Chicago Tribune* and expanded into printing railroad tickets and schedules. They published their first book, a Chicago business directory, in 1870.

In 1872 the company printed its first map for the *Railway Guide*. Rand McNally later expanded into publishing paperback novels (popular among train travelers), and by 1891 annual sales topped $1 million.

During the 1890s McNally bought Rand's share of the business, and the company branched into printing school textbooks. Rand McNally's first photo auto guide was issued in 1907, and the company introduced its first complete US road atlas in 1924.

When Hitler invaded Poland in 1939, Rand McNally's New York stock of European maps sold out in one day. WWII necessitated the revision of a number of maps — a challenge that the company continued to face throughout the 20th century.

Although the company had abandoned adult fiction and nonfiction in 1914, it reentered the field in 1948 when a company official persuaded explorer Thor Heyerdahl to write a book for the company about his adventures. First published in 1950, Heyerdahl's *Kon-Tiki* sold more than a million copies in its first six years.

Rand McNally produced its first four-color road atlas in 1960, and during the 1970s it began publishing travel guides for Mobil Oil. The next decade the company published several new road atlases to fill the void created when gas stations discontinued their practice of giving away free road maps. Rand McNally sold its textbook publishing business to Houghton Mifflin in 1980, and five years later it began computerizing its cartography operation.

In 1993 the company acquired Allmaps Canada Limited (now Rand McNally Canada). It introduced *TripMaker*, a CD-ROM vacation-planning program, the next year. Also in 1994 Rand McNally won a contract to create maps for a *Reader's Digest* atlas. The company debuted its StreetFinder street-level software in 1995 and created its Cartographic and Information Services division in 1996. It also established a Web site that year.

The next year, as part of a plan to focus on mapmaking and providing geographic information, Rand McNally sold a number of its subsidiaries (Book Services Group, DocuSystems Group). AEA Investors bought a controlling interest in the company later in 1997, bringing an end to more than 140 years of McNally family control (though it did retain a minority stake). While Rand McNally was still profitable, the sale to AEA underscored the challenges facing the company: Growth in earnings had slowed, and technological changes (Internet maps and software) had altered the mapmaking industry.

Rand McNally expanded in 1999 with acquisitions of mapmakers Thomas Bros. Maps and King of the Road Map Service. Later that year Henry Feinberg resigned as chairman and CEO. Richard Davis was appointed CEO, and John Macomber became chairman.

In 2000 the company relaunched its Web site with additional trip planning capabilities. Also that year it became the primary North American distributor of *National Geographic* maps and COO Norman Wells replaced Davis as CEO.

In 2001 Michael Hehir was named CEO, Wells replaced Macomber as chairman, and Macomber remained as a director on the board. In 2003 Hehir left the company and Allstate executive Robert Apatoff was named CEO. Wells was replaced by Peter Nolan, a managing partner at Leonard Green & Partners.

EXECUTIVES

Chairman: Peter J. Nolan, age 46
President and CEO: Robert S. (Rob) Apatoff, age 44
SVP and Chief Marketing Officer: Betsy Owens
SVP and CFO: Norman Smagley, age 42
SVP and CTO: Ken Levin
SVP Vertical Markets: Jim Welch
SVP Geographic Information Services: Joel Minster
SVP Supply Chain Management: Tom Anderson
VP Business Operation: Alan Yefsky
VP Consumer Sales and Distribution: Dennis FitzPatrick
VP Consumer Sales: Jeff Ventura
Director, Educational Publishing: Pat Riley
Director, Retail Stores and Internet: David Rickabaugh
General Manager, Transportation Data Management: Robert (Bob) Simmons
Group Controller: David Jones
Editorial Director: Laurie Borman
Media Relations: Paul Elsberg

LOCATIONS

HQ: Rand McNally & Company
8255 N. Central Park Ave., Skokie, IL 60076
Phone: 847-329-8100   **Fax:** 847-329-6361
Web: www.randmcnally.com

Rand McNally operates in the US and Canada. It has retail stores in California, Massachusetts, and Texas.

PRODUCTS/OPERATIONS

Selected Print Products
Motor Carriers' Road Atlas
Rand McNally Pocket City Atlas
Rand McNally Road Atlas
The Thomas Guides

Selected Sales Channels
Rand McNally (retail stores)
randmcnally.com (e-commerce)

Selected Software
New Millennium World Atlas Deluxe Edition
Rand McNally StreetFinder Deluxe
Rand McNally TripMaker Deluxe

COMPETITORS

AAA
Analytical Surveys
DeLorme
ESRI
Expedia
Globe Pequot
Lonely Planet
MapInfo
MapQuest.com
Michelin
National Geographic
Piersen Graphics
R. L. Polk
TravRoute
Vindigo

HISTORICAL FINANCIALS

Company Type: Private

Income Statement				FYE: December 31
	REVENUE ($ mil.)	NET INCOME ($ mil.)	NET PROFIT MARGIN	EMPLOYEES
12/00*	200	—	—	1,000
12/99	179	—	—	920
12/98	175	—	—	1,000
12/97	175	—	—	1,000
12/96	163	—	—	1,000
12/95	469	—	—	4,650
12/94	438	—	—	4,200
12/93	395	—	—	4,000
12/92	342	—	—	4,000
12/91	307	—	—	4,000
Annual Growth	(4.6%)	—	—	(14.3%)

*Most recent year available

Revenue History

R. B. Pamplin

Founded by a man of the cloth, R. B. Pamplin casts a wide net. The family-owned conglomerate, started in 1957 by minister and company CEO Robert Pamplin Jr. (Robert Sr. is chairman), has operations ranging from entertainment to retail stores to manufacturing interests (asphalt, concrete, and textiles.) The company's Mount Vernon Mills is one of the largest denim producers in the US. Pamplin's entertainment concerns include radio broadcasting, newspapers, and record labels in the northwestern US. The company's other units are as diverse as retail stores offering Christian products to Columbia Empire Farms, which grows berries and grapes used in jams and wine, that are then sold through its Your NorthWest stores.

EXECUTIVES

Chairman: Robert Pamplin Sr.
CFO: David Hastings
President and CEO: Robert Boisseau (Bob) Pamplin Jr.
President and COO, Mount Vernon Mills:
  Roger W. Chastain

LOCATIONS

HQ: R. B. Pamplin Corporation
  805 SW Broadway, Ste. 2400, Portland, OR 97205
Phone: 503-248-1133 **Fax:** 503-248-1175
Web: www.pamplin.org

COMPETITORS

Avondale Incorporated
Burlington Industries
CEMEX
Cone Mills
Gannett
Greenwood Mills
Holcim
Plains Cotton
Salem Communications
Springs Industries
U.S. Concrete
WestPoint Stevens

HISTORICAL FINANCIALS

Company Type: Private

Income Statement
FYE: Saturday nearest Dec. 31

	REVENUE ($ mil.)	NET INCOME ($ mil.)	NET PROFIT MARGIN	EMPLOYEES
12/03	600	—	—	6,270
12/02	800	—	—	8,500
12/01	800	—	—	8,500
12/00*	890	—	—	7,584
5/99	844	—	—	7,500
5/98	843	—	—	7,000
5/97	802	—	—	6,500
5/96	800	—	—	6,500
5/95	835	—	—	6,250
5/94	695	—	—	5,728
Annual Growth	(1.6%)	—	—	1.0%

*Fiscal year change

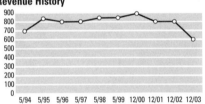

Revenue History

RDO Equipment

RDO Equipment herds Deere in a big way. RDO distributes, sells, rents, services, and finances equipment and new and used trucks to agricultural, construction, manufacturing, transportation, and warehousing industry customers. The company operates about 45 retail stores in nine states, almost 40 of which are Deere stores, making RDO one of the largest Deere dealership networks in North America. New Deere products generate 45% of sales. RDO also sells heavy-duty trucks through Volvo and Mack truck centers. RDO sold its 80%-owned RDO Rental Co. to United Rentals. Chairman Ronald Offutt founded the company in 1968, took it public in 1997, and returned it to private ownership in 2003.

EXECUTIVES

Chairman, President, CEO, and Director:
  Ronald D. Offutt, age 60
COO and Director: Christi J. Offutt, age 33
CFO: Steven B. Dewald, age 42
EVP, Project/Process Management:
  Kenneth J. (Skip) Horner Jr.
SVP, Special Projects: Larry E. Scott
Director, Information Systems: Dave Green
Chief People Officer: Jeff Antonelli
Secretary and Director: Allan F. Knoll, age 59
Treasurer and Asst. Secretary: Thomas K. (Tom) Espel, age 44
General Manager, Phoenix: Steven R. Decker
General Manager, Seattle: Raymond L. Ochsner
General Manager, Southwest Agriculture:
  Terry W. Tolbert
Auditors: PricewaterhouseCoopers LLP

LOCATIONS

HQ: RDO Equipment Co.
  2829 S. University Dr., Fargo, ND 58103
Phone: 701-297-4288 **Fax:** 701-271-6328
Web: www.rdoequipment.com

RDO Equipment has about 45 dealerships in Arizona, California, Minnesota, Montana, Nebraska, North Dakota, South Dakota, Texas, and Washington.

PRODUCTS/OPERATIONS

2003 Sales

	% of total
New equipment & truck sales	51
Used equipment & truck sales	20
Product support (parts & service)	29
Total	**100**

COMPETITORS

AGCO
Bamford Excavators
Caterpillar
CLARK Material
CNH Global
Crown Equipment
DaimlerChrysler
Financial Federal
Ford
Ingersoll-Rand
Kobe Steel
Komatsu
Navistar
Nissan
PACCAR
Ritchie Bros. Auctioneers
Toyota

HISTORICAL FINANCIALS

Company Type: Private

Income Statement
FYE: January 31

	REVENUE ($ mil.)	NET INCOME ($ mil.)	NET PROFIT MARGIN	EMPLOYEES
1/03	535	3	0.6%	1,182
1/02	550	(2)	—	1,325
1/01	680	(19)	—	1,429
1/00	689	7	0.9%	1,602
1/99	579	2	0.3%	1,554
1/98	429	13	3.1%	1,214
1/97	302	11	3.7%	800
1/96	224	5	2.1%	663
1/95	184	10	5.3%	—
1/94	144	6	4.0%	—
Annual Growth	15.7%	(7.1%)	—	8.6%

2003 Year-End Financials

Debt ratio: 5.7%
Return on equity: 3.4%
Cash ($ mil.): 2
Current ratio: 1.41
Long-term debt ($ mil.): 5

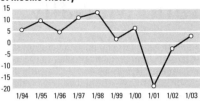

Net Income History

Red Apple Group

Red Apple Group sells apples (and more) in the Big Apple. Subsidiary United Refining, which processes 65,000 barrels of oil a day, distributes fuel to its 372 Country Fair/Red Apple gas stations/convenience stores in New York, Pennsylvania, and Ohio. Red Apple controls Gristede's Foods, a leading New York City supermarket chain. It also has real estate, aircraft leasing, and newspaper operations. CEO John Catsimatidis owns the Red Apple Group, which lost out to Russian oil giant LUKOIL in a bid to acquire East Coast gasoline retailer Getty Petroleum Marketing.

EXECUTIVES

Chairman, President, and CEO, Red Apple Group and Gristede's Foods; Chairman and CEO, United Refining Company: John A. Catsimatidis, age 54
President and COO, United Refining: Myron L. Turfitt, age 51
EVP, CFO, and Director, Gristede's Foods: Kishore Lall, age 56
SVP Marketing, United Refining: Ashton L. Ditka, age 62
VP, Operations; Gristede's Foods: Gallo Balseca

LOCATIONS

HQ: Red Apple Group, Inc.
  823 11th Ave., New York, NY 10019
Phone: 212-956-5803 **Fax:** 212-247-4509
Web: www.jacny.com

The Red Apple Group operates gasoline stations in New York, Ohio, and Pennsylvania. It owns commercial property in Florida, New Jersey, New York, and the Virgin Islands. The company also operates supermarkets in the New York City area.

COMPETITORS

7-Eleven
A&P
Ahold USA
Amerada Hess
D'Agostino Supermarkets
Getty Petroleum Marketing
King Kullen Grocery
Man-dell Food Stores
Motiva Enterprises
Pathmark
Premcor
Sunoco
TOTAL
Wakefern Food

HISTORICAL FINANCIALS
Company Type: Private

Income Statement				FYE: February 28
	ESTIMATED REVENUE ($ mil.)	NET INCOME ($ mil.)	NET PROFIT MARGIN	EMPLOYEES
2/04	3,000	—	—	7,500
2/03	2,100	—	—	7,500
2/02	2,000	—	—	7,000
2/01	1,100	—	—	3,117
2/00	1,000	—	—	3,082
2/99	820	—	—	3,200
2/98	850	—	—	2,700
2/97	2,200	—	—	4,200
2/96	2,150	—	—	4,300
2/95	2,250	—	—	2,425
Annual Growth	3.2%	—	—	13.4%

Revenue History

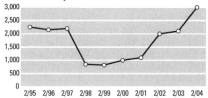

Red Chamber

Red Chamber Co. is part of the Red Chamber Group, one of the largest seafood suppliers in North America (other majors include StarKist and Bumble Bee Seafoods). Red Chamber Co., which started as a small family-owned restaurant in Los Angeles, offers fish, lobster, scallops, surimi, and specialty items like shark fin, octopus, and squid.

EXECUTIVES
Chairperson and CEO: Shan Chun Kou
President and Director: Shu Chin Kou
COO and Director: Ming Bin Kou
EVP and CFO: Ming Shin Kou
SVP: Tony Neves
President, OFI Markesa International: Brent Church
President, Neptune Foods: Howard Choi

LOCATIONS
HQ: Red Chamber Co.
1912 E. Vernon Ave., Vernon, CA 90058
Phone: 323-234-9000 **Fax:** 323-231-8888
Web: www.redchamber.com

COMPETITORS
Bumble Bee
Dulcich
Kyokuyo
Maruha Group
Nichiro
Nippon Suisan Kaisha
StarKist
Trident Seafoods

HISTORICAL FINANCIALS
Company Type: Private

Income Statement				FYE: December 31
	REVENUE ($ mil.)	NET INCOME ($ mil.)	NET PROFIT MARGIN	EMPLOYEES
12/02	680	—	—	—
12/01	680	—	—	—
12/00	665	—	—	—
Annual Growth	1.1%	—	—	—

Revenue History

(bar chart 12/93–12/02, values around 665–680)

Regence Group

The Regence Group is the health care king of the Northwest, operating the largest group of Blue Cross Blue Shield companies in the Northwestern United States. Through its subsidiary companies, Regence BlueCross BlueShield of Oregon, Regence BlueShield, Regence BlueCross BlueShield of Utah, and Regence BlueShield of Idaho, the company provides health insurance products and related services to nearly 3 million members. The company also provides life, disability, and short term medical insurance through its Regence Life & Health Insurance subsidiary.

Although it faces stiff competition, The Regence Group has decided to remain not-for-profit. The company's strategy for remaining competitive consists of consolidating operations, upgrading the company's information technology infrastructure, and deploying new health insurance products.

EXECUTIVES
President and CEO: Mark B. Ganz
EVP; President, Regence BlueShield: Mary O. McWilliams
EVP; President, Regence BlueCross BlueShield of Oregon: Bart McMullan
EVP and Chief Marketing Executive: Mohan Nair
EVP, Health Care Services: Jeffrey A. Robertson
SVP, Strategic Communications and Public Affairs: Kerry Barnett
SVP, Human Resources: Tom Kennedy
VP and CFO: Steve Hooker
VP and Treasurer: Eric Tanaka
Chief Information Officer: Cheron Vail
President, Regence BlueShield of Idaho: John Stellmon
President, Regence BlueCross BlueShield of Utah: D. Scott Ideson
President and CEO, Regence Life & Health Insurance: Kathryn Kremin
Auditors: Deloitte & Touche LLP

LOCATIONS
HQ: The Regence Group
200 SW Market St., Portland, OR 97201
Phone: 503-225-5221 **Fax:** 503-225-5274
Web: www.regence.com

The Regence Group's service area includes the states of Idaho, Oregon, Utah, and Washington.

COMPETITORS
CIGNA
Kaiser Foundation
PacifiCare

HISTORICAL FINANCIALS
Company Type: Private

Income Statement				FYE: December 31
	REVENUE ($ mil.)	NET INCOME ($ mil.)	NET PROFIT MARGIN	EMPLOYEES
12/03	6,700	—	—	6,000
12/02	6,250	—	—	6,600
Annual Growth	7.2%	—	—	(9.1%)

Revenue History

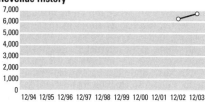

REI

Outdoor gear and clothing from Recreational Equipment, Inc. (REI) outfits everyone from mountain climbers to mall walkers. The company is one of the nation's largest consumer co-operatives, with over 2 million member-owners. Through about 70 outlets in 24 states, REI sells high-end gear, clothing, and footwear (including private-label goods) for adventurous outdoor activities such as climbing, kayaking, and skiing, as well as for hiking, bicycling, and camping. The company also repairs gear, and it sells merchandise online and through occasional catalogs. Its adventure travel service, REI Adventures, offers trips such as cycling the Alps, sea kayaking Costa Rica, and hiking New Zealand.

REI's community and environmental involvement includes youth program support, community service, and designating a portion of its operating budget to environmental restoration projects. Through its partnership with US Bank (a subsidiary of U.S. Bancorp) the company offers members the REI Visa card.

REI stores feature product demonstrations, educational seminars, and gift registries. The company's MSR (Mountain Safety Research) subsidiary makes mountaineering equipment, outdoor clothing, and camping products. Customers can become co-op members by paying a one-time fee; its privileges include getting about 10% of their annual purchases refunded in the form of patronage dividends.

Announced in June 2004, the company's president and CEO, Dennis Madsen, will be retiring after the annual meeting in March 2005. Madsen joined the company as a stockroom clerk when he was 17 years old. Current EVP and COO, Sally Jewell, has been named as his successor.

HISTORY

Lloyd Anderson founded REI in his Seattle garage in 1938 with his wife, Mary, and 23 other mountain climbers looking for high-quality mountaineering equipment at low prices. Uncomfortable about making money off of his friends, Anderson formed a co-op, returning a portion of the profits to its members. REI's first retail location (opened in 1944 in the back of a Seattle gas station) consisted of three shelves of Army surplus items. The company did not hire its first full-time employee until 1953.

Growth was slow yet steady. In 1971 the company operated one store; by 1983 REI had grown to seven stores with several additional product lines and a catalog business. That year Wally Smith became the company's CEO.

REI benefited from the growing interest in outdoor activities, expanding to 17 stores in 13 states in 1987. By 1991, when it built its first distribution center, REI had 27 stores in 16 states. The co-op reached for a new frontier in 1996 when it began selling on the Internet. It launched its REI-Outlet.com Web site in 1998 to sell discounted merchandise, and began a Japanese retail Web site in 1999. Also in 1999 REI decided to scale back its catalog mailings and focus instead on e-commerce. Smith, who grew the company from 9 to 54 stores during his 17-year reign, retired in early 2000 and was replaced by COO Dennis Madsen, a 34-year company veteran.

In 2000, the co-op rankled its rank and file when it moved its manufacturing operations to Mexico and closed its fleece-manufacturing subsidiary, Thaw. Also that year the company opened its first international location in Tokyo, but ended up closing the store and shutting down the Japanese Web site in 2001.

In January of 2003, the company was named to *FORTUNE*'s "100 Best Companies" list for the sixth year in a row. It made the list again in January 2004, ranking 24th.

EXECUTIVES

Chairman: Bill Britt
Vice Chairman: Anne V. Farrell, age 68
President and CEO: Dennis Madsen, age 55
EVP and COO: Sally Jewell
SVP, CFO, and Corporate Treasurer: Brad Johnson
SVP, Merchandising and Logistics: Matt Hyde
SVP, Retail: Brian Unmacht
VP, General Counsel, and Corporate Secretary: Pam Myers
VP, Distribution: Clark Koch
VP, Human Resources: Glen Simmons
VP, Information Services: Brad Brown
VP, Marketing: Atsuko Tamura
VP, Multi-Channel Programs: Joan Broughton
VP, Public Affairs: Michael Collins
VP, Real Estate: Jerry Chevassus
Director, Online Sales: Noel Nelson
Director, Inventory and Logistics: John Strother
Manager, Public Relations: Randy Hurlow

LOCATIONS

HQ: Recreational Equipment, Inc.
6750 S. 228th St., Kent, WA 98032
Phone: 253-395-3780   **Fax:** 253-395-4352
Web: www.rei.com

2003 Stores

	No.
California	16
Washington	9
Colorado	7
Georgia	3
Massachusetts	3
Oregon	3
Texas	3
Arizona	2
Illinois	2
Maryland	2
Michigan	2
Minnesota	2
North Carolina	2
Utah	2
Virginia	2
Wisconsin	2
Other states	8
Total	**70**

PRODUCTS/OPERATIONS

Selected Products and Services
Bicycles and accessories
Books and maps
Camping gear
Canoes, kayaks, and related gear
Climbing gear
Clothing (children's, men's, and women's)
Fitness gear
Footwear
Gift registry
Racks (bike, boat, and ski mounts)
REI repair service
Sleeping bags
Snow sports gear
Tents
Travel accessories

COMPETITORS

Academy	Johnson Outdoors
Bass Pro Shops	Lands' End
Big 5	L.L. Bean
Cabela's	Patagonia
Dick's Sporting Goods	Spiegel
Eastern Mountain Sports	Sport Chalet
Galyan's	Sports Authority
G.I. Joe's	Sportsman's Guide
Hibbett Sporting Goods	

HISTORICAL FINANCIALS

Company Type: Cooperative

Income Statement				FYE: December 31
	REVENUE ($ mil.)	NET INCOME ($ mil.)	NET PROFIT MARGIN	EMPLOYEES
12/03	805	19	2.4%	—
12/02	735	16	2.2%	—
12/01	740	8	1.0%	6,000
12/00	698	(11)	—	7,000
12/99	621	10	1.7%	6,000
12/98	587	14	2.4%	6,000
12/97	536	15	2.8%	5,100
12/96	484	16	3.2%	4,800
12/95	448	13	2.8%	—
12/94	432	14	3.2%	—
Annual Growth	7.2%	3.6%	—	4.6%

2003 Year-End Financials

Debt ratio: 25.3%   Current ratio: 1.30
Return on equity: 8.1%   Long-term debt ($ mil.): 63
Cash ($ mil.): 123

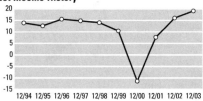

Net Income History

Remy

Carmakers get cranked up with the help of Remy International (formerly Delco Remy International), which manufactures and distributes starters and alternators for carmakers and light- and heavy-duty truck makers. The company, which is owned by Citicorp Venture Capital, also remanufactures engines, fuel systems, starters, and alternators for the automotive aftermarket. Remy's OEM customers include companies such as General Motors, Delphi, Navistar, and Caterpillar; aftermarket customers include O'Reilly, AutoZone, and other automotive parts chains.

Acquisitions boosted Remy's sales, but they failed to do much for the company's stock price, which consistently traded below its IPO price. The company was finally acquired by Citicorp Venture Capital in 2001. Berkshire Hathaway holds about a 20% stake.

EXECUTIVES

Chairman: Harold K. Sperlich, age 74
Vice Chairman: Erwin H. (Bill) Billig, age 76
President, CEO, and Director: Thomas J. Snyder, age 59, $934,900 pay
EVP and CFO: Raj Shah, age 52, $654,400 pay
SVP, Human Resources and Communications: Roderick English, age 52, $430,200 pay
VP, Aftermarket Services: Al Rowley
VP and Corporate Controller: Amitabh Rai, age 43
VP; Managing Director, Europe: Patrick C. Mobouck, age 49
VP, Production Control and Logistics: Tania Wingfield
President, Delco Remy America: Richard L. Stanley, age 46, $488,500 pay
Treasurer: Craig Hart
Auditors: Ernst & Young LLP

LOCATIONS

HQ: Remy International, Inc.
2902 Enterprise Dr., Anderson, IN 46013
Phone: 765-778-6499   **Fax:** 765-778-6404
Web: www.remyinc.com

Remy International has manufacturing facilities in Belgium, Brazil, Canada, Hungary, Mexico, Poland, South Korea, Tunisia, the UK, and the US.

2003 Sales

	$ mil.	% of total
US	871	83
Europe	111	10
Latin America	38	4
Asia Pacific	31	3
Canada	2	—
Total	**1,053**	**100**

PRODUCTS/OPERATIONS

2003 Sales

	$ mil.	% of total
Electrical systems	842	80
Powertrain/drivetrain	146	14
Other	65	6
Total	1,053	100

Selected Products

Alternators
Diesel and marine engines
Fuel systems
Gears
Power steering systems
Rack and pinions
Starters
Water pumps

COMPETITORS

Champion Parts	Mitsubishi Motors
Dana	Motorcar Parts
Federal-Mogul	Prestolite Electric
General Parts	Robert Bosch
Genuine Parts	Valeo
Hahn Automotive	

HISTORICAL FINANCIALS

Company Type: Private

Income Statement — FYE: December 31

	REVENUE ($ mil.)	NET INCOME ($ mil.)	NET PROFIT MARGIN	EMPLOYEES
12/03	1,053	(187)	—	6,159
12/02	1,069	(133)	—	6,338
12/01	1,054	(73)	—	7,422
12/00*	443	10	2.2%	7,424
7/00	1,091	12	1.1%	7,707
7/99	954	28	3.0%	6,845
7/98	815	(4)	—	4,833
7/97	690	(14)	—	4,949
7/96	637	(5)	—	3,000
7/95	573	7	1.2%	3,000
Annual Growth	7.0%	—	—	8.3%

*Fiscal year change

2003 Year-End Financials

Debt ratio: —
Return on equity: —
Cash ($ mil.): 21
Current ratio: 1.23
Long-term debt ($ mil.): 593

Net Income History

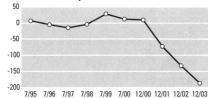

Renco

Renco Group is a holding company for a diverse bunch of businesses. Its AM General subsidiary (which Ronald Perelman's MacAndrews & Forbes Holding is acquiring) makes the HUMVEE, an extra-wide all-terrain vehicle used by the military, and the HUMMER, the HUMVEE's civilian counterpart. Renco Steel and WCI Steel manufacture, fabricate, and distribute steel. Renco was established in 1980 and is owned by industrialist Ira Rennert, a former business consultant whose Long Island, New York, home is double the size of the White House and is said to include 29 bedrooms, 42 bathrooms, a 100-car garage, and an English pub.

Other Renco Group companies include Doe Run, the world's #2 lead smelter; coal miner Rencoal; and Consolidated Sewing Machine, which makes industrial sewing machines.

EXECUTIVES

Chairman, President, and CEO: Ira Leon Rennert, age 68
EVP and COO: Patrick G. Tatom, age 53
EVP: Marvin Koenig
VP Finance; VP Finance and CFO, Renco Steel: Roger L. Fay, age 57
VP Commercial: David A. Howard, age 43
Vice Chairman, President, and CEO, Doe Run: Jeffrey L. Zelms, age 57
President and CEO, WCI Steel: Ed Caine
VP Finance and CFO, Renco Steel: John P. Jacunski, age 38
Secretary and General Counsel: Justin W. D'Atri

LOCATIONS

HQ: Renco Group, Inc.
30 Rockefeller Plaza, New York, NY 10112
Phone: 212-541-6000 **Fax:** 212-541-6197

PRODUCTS/OPERATIONS

Selected Subsidiaries

AM General (manufactures the High Mobility Multipurpose Wheeled Vehicle known as the HUMVEE and the HUMMER, and diesel engines)
Consolidated Sewing Machine Corp. (manufactures industrial sewing machines, specialty machines, cutting machines, and motors)
Doe Run Company (lead smelter)
Renco Steel Holdings, Inc. (steel producer)
Rencoal, Inc. (coal miner)
WCI Steel, Inc. (steel producer)

COMPETITORS

AK Steel Holding Corporation	Oshkosh Truck
ASARCO	Peugeot
Nippon Steel	RSR
Nucor	Singer
	United States Steel

HISTORICAL FINANCIALS

Company Type: Private

Income Statement — FYE: October 31

	REVENUE ($ mil.)	NET INCOME ($ mil.)	NET PROFIT MARGIN	EMPLOYEES
10/03	2,100	—	—	13,500
10/02	2,175	—	—	13,500
10/01	2,150	—	—	14,000
10/00	2,500	—	—	15,000
10/99	2,500	—	—	15,000
10/98	2,550	—	—	11,000
10/97	2,520	—	—	10,500
10/96	1,800	—	—	7,150
10/95	1,650	—	—	6,995
10/94	1,650	—	—	7,000
Annual Growth	2.7%	—	—	7.6%

Revenue History

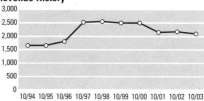

Republic Engineered Products

Republic Engineered Products (formerly Republic Technologies International) has set the bar higher as it leaps ahead into the future. The company is one of the largest makers of special bar quality (SBQ) used to make automobiles, heavy equipment, and similar products. Customers — including DaimlerChrysler, Ford, GM, and their suppliers — turn the company's steel into components such as bearings, crankshafts, and spark plug shells. In December 2003 New York investment firm Perry Capital purchased the company for approximately $277 million.

Republic Engineered Products also has received $200 million in revolving credit from GE Commercial Finance and includes UBS Loan Finance LLC, Bank One, and Merrill Lynch Capital.

EXECUTIVES

President, CEO, and Director: Joseph F. Lapinsky, age 53
EVP and CFO: George E. Strickler, age 56
EVP, Technology and Quality Assurance: John G. Asimou, age 57, $236,250 pay
VP, Human Resources and Corporate Relations: John Willoughby
VP, Commercial: James Ted Thielens Jr.
VP, Finance: Joseph A. Kaczka
VP, Purchasing: John B. George
VP, Sales: Charles T. Cochran
VP and General Manager, Lorain (Ohio) Operations: James T. Kuntz
VP, Hot Roll Bar Operations: Noel J. Huettich
Director, Information Technologies: Michael J. Bodden
Director, Production Planning: Thomas R. Fee
Auditors: Deloitte & Touche LLP

LOCATIONS

HQ: Republic Engineered Products Inc.
3770 Embassy Pkwy., Akron, OH 44333
Phone: 330-670-3000 **Fax:** 330-670-7031
Web: www.republicengineered.com

Republic Engineered Products operates facilities in Indiana, Ohio, and New York.

PRODUCTS/OPERATIONS

Selected Products

Hot-rolled engineered bar
Merchant-quality bar
Reinforcing bar

COMPETITORS

AK Steel Holding Corporation
Arcelor
Chaparral Steel
Corus Group
Gerdau AmeriSteel
Macsteel Service Centers USA
Niagara Corporation
North Star Steel
Nucor
Quanex
Severstal North America
Timken
United States Steel

HISTORICAL FINANCIALS

Company Type: Private

Income Statement — FYE: December 31

	REVENUE ($ mil.)	NET INCOME ($ mil.)	NET PROFIT MARGIN	EMPLOYEES
12/03	900	—	—	2,400
12/02	912	—	—	2,494
12/01	994	—	—	2,500
12/00	1,265	—	—	3,889
12/99	1,033	—	—	5,019
12/98	473	—	—	—
12/97	243	—	—	—
Annual Growth	24.4%	—	—	(16.8%)

Revenue History

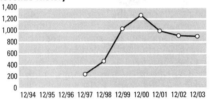

Resolution Performance Products

The name Resolution Performance Products (RPP) is beginning to resin-ate throughout the chemical industry. Once the resins and versatics unit of Shell Chemicals, it was sold to private investment firm Apollo Management in 2000 and renamed. RPP is the world's leading maker of epoxy resins (ahead of Dow and Huntsman), which are used in coatings, adhesives, and printed circuit boards. While RPP gets about two-thirds of its sales from epoxy resins, it also produces versatic acids — used in pharmaceuticals, personal care products, and coatings — and bisphenol-A, a chemical intermediate used in making epoxy resins. Apollo Management owns about 90% of the company; Shell Oil owns nearly 8%.

In August 2004 Apollo bought a portion of Eastman's specialty chemicals business for about $220 million and organized it under the name Resolution Specialty Materials (RSM). Both RSM and Resolution Performance Products are now held by Apollo as affiliates known jointly as the Resolution Group of companies. RPP president and COO Jeff Nodland left the company to lead RSM as its president.

EXECUTIVES

Chairman and CEO: Marvin O. Schlanger, age 55, $150,000 pay
EVP and CFO: David S. Graziosi, age 37
SVP, General Counsel, and Secretary: Mark S. Antonvich, age 43, $182,999 pay (prior to title change)
VP, Major Resins: Wouter W. Jongepier, age 41
VP, Performance Products, Technology, and Development: Douglas B. Rahrig, age 53
VP, Environment, Health, and Safety: Edward Guetens, age 62
VP, Human Resources: Dennis F. White, age 52
VP and Chief Administrative Officer, Europe: Francois Vleugels, age 55
Treasurer: Thomas P. Bausch, age 55
Controller: Roger Wollenberg
Auditors: PricewaterhouseCoopers LLP

LOCATIONS

HQ: Resolution Performance Products LLC
1600 Smith St., Ste. 2400, Houston, TX 77002
Phone: 832-366-2300 **Fax:** 832-366-2584
Web: www.resins.com

2003 Sales

	$ mil.	% of total
Europe and Africa	430	55
US	349	45
Asia/Pacific and Middle East	3	—
Total	782	100

PRODUCTS/OPERATIONS

2003 Sales

	$ mil.	% of total
Resins	499	64
BPA	129	16
Versatics	116	15
ECH	34	4
Other	4	1
Total	782	100

Selected Products
Basic versatic acids
Bisphenol-A (BPA)
Cardura
Epichlorohydrin (ECH)
Epoxy resins
VeoVa

COMPETITORS

Asahi Denka
Ashland Specialty Chemical
Bayer MaterialScience
Dainippon Ink
Dow Chemical
ExxonMobil Chemical
GE Advanced Materials
Huntsman
Mitsubishi Chemical
Mitsui Chemicals
Nan Ya Plastics
Nippon Kayaku

HISTORICAL FINANCIALS

Company Type: Private

Income Statement — FYE: December 31

	REVENUE ($ mil.)	NET INCOME ($ mil.)	NET PROFIT MARGIN	EMPLOYEES
12/03	782	(62)	—	900
12/02	740	(7)	—	994
12/01	863	15	1.7%	940
Annual Growth	(4.8%)	—	—	(2.2%)

2003 Year-End Financials

Debt ratio: —
Return on equity: —
Cash ($ mil.): 49
Current ratio: 2.26
Long-term debt ($ mil.): 674

Net Income History

Retail Brand Alliance

Given a food court and some kiosks, Retail Brand Alliance could open its own shopping mall. The holding company operates more than 1,000 mostly mall-based women's apparel shops in about 45 states under the Casual Corner and Petite Sophisticate banners. The company also owns 160-store chain Brooks Brothers (men's and women's clothing) which is returning to its classic roots and expanding internationally. Carolee Designs (jewelry and accessories) and Adrienne Vittadini, a womenswear designer, are also in the company's portfolio. President and CEO Claudio Del Vecchio owns Retail Brand Alliance, which he acquired from his father's company, Luxottica Group (operator of LensCrafters and Sunglass Hut).

In September 2004 Retail Brand Alliance put its Casual Corner Group up for sale for an asking price of $250 to $300 million. The company additionally announced its plans to sell Carolee Designs for approximately $35 million.

EXECUTIVES

President and CEO: Claudio Del Vecchio
COO: Mark Shulman
CFO: Brian K. Baumann
SVP Stores: Kathy Self
VP Human Resources: Susan Eyvazzadeh
Chief Merchandising Officer: Eraldo Poletto
VP of Management Information System: Stefano Gaggion
Vice President of Planning and Allocation: Denise Albright
VP of Creative Services, Brooks Brothers and Adrienne Vittadini: Michael Glossmeyer

LOCATIONS

HQ: Retail Brand Alliance, Inc.
100 Phoenix Ave., Enfield, CT 06082
Phone: 860-741-0771 **Fax:** 860-745-9714

PRODUCTS/OPERATIONS

Selected Stores
Adrienne Vittadini
August Max
Brooks Brothers
Casual Corner
Carolee Designs
Petite Sophisticate

COMPETITORS

AnnTaylor
Dillard's
Federated
Gap
J. C. Penney
Limited Brands
LVMH
May
Men's Wearhouse
Pinault-Printemps-
 Redoute
Richemont
Saks Inc.
Talbots

HISTORICAL FINANCIALS
Company Type: Private

Income Statement — FYE: July 31

	REVENUE ($ mil.)	NET INCOME ($ mil.)	NET PROFIT MARGIN	EMPLOYEES
7/02	1,500	—	—	10,036
7/01	900	—	—	10,000
Annual Growth	66.7%	—	—	0.4%

Revenue History

Year	1,600 1,400 1,200 1,000 800 600 400 200 0
7/93 7/94 7/95 7/96 7/97 7/98 7/99 7/00 7/01 7/02	

Reyes Holdings

Closely held Reyes Holdings has a grip on two things that are considered complementary — food and beer. Through its subsidiary companies Reyes Holdings distributes products throughout North, Central, and South America. One of these, The Martin-Brower Company, supplies McDonald's restaurants in the US and Canada, as well as serving Brazil, Central America, and Puerto Rico. Reyes Holdings also counts Premium Distributors of Virginia, Chicago Beverage Systems, and California's Harbor Distributing among the wholesalers it owns. The company operates more than 35 distribution centers in the US and six other countries. Chairman Chris Reyes, vice chairman Jude Reyes, and VP David Reyes own the company.

EXECUTIVES
Chairman: J. Christopher (Chris) Reyes, age 50
Vice Chairman: M. Jude Reyes
EVP, Business Development: Dean H. Janke
SVP and CFO: Daniel P. (Dan) Doheny
SVP, Human Resources: Phil Menzel
SVP, IT: Joe Crenshaw
SVP, Operations: Ray Guerin
VP: David K. Reyes

LOCATIONS
HQ: Reyes Holdings LLC
 9500 West Bryn Mawr Ave., Ste. 700,
 Rosemont, IL 60018
Phone: 847-227-6500 **Fax:** 847-227-6550

PRODUCTS/OPERATIONS

Selected Wholesalers
Chicago Beverage Systems
Harbor Distributing
The Martin-Brower Company
Premium Distributors of Virginia

COMPETITORS

Alex Lee
Anderson-DuBose
Ben E. Keith
Clark Products
Golden State Foods
Gordon Food Service
Keystone Foods
MBM
McLane Foodservice
Performance Food
 Services Group
SYSCO
U.S. Foodservice

HISTORICAL FINANCIALS
Company Type: Private

Income Statement — FYE: December 31

	REVENUE ($ mil.)	NET INCOME ($ mil.)	NET PROFIT MARGIN	EMPLOYEES
12/02	4,180	—	—	3,994
12/01*	3,900	—	—	3,877
9/00	3,500	—	—	4,200
9/99	2,375	—	—	—
Annual Growth	20.7%	—	—	(2.5%)

*Fiscal year change

Revenue History

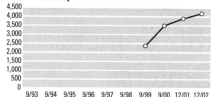

Riceland Foods

Riceland Foods is ingrained in the marketing and milling business. Started in 1921, the cooperative markets rice, soybeans, and wheat grown by its more than 9,000 member-owners in Arkansas, Louisiana, Mississippi, Missouri, and Texas. As one of the world's leading millers of rice, Riceland sells long grain, brown, wild, and flavored rice (under the Riceland name as well as private labels) to grocery, food service, and food manufacturing customers. The co-op also sells oil and shortening products and processes soybeans, edible oils, and lecithin. Riceland markets its products throughout the US and internationally, mainly in the Caribbean, Mexico, the Middle East, South Africa, and Western Europe.

EXECUTIVES
Chairman: Thomas C. (Tommy) Hoskyn
President and CEO: K. Daniel (Danny) Kennedy, age 45
VP, Corporate Communications & Public Affairs:
 Bill J. Reed
VP, International Rice Marketing: Terry Harris
VP, Research: Don McCaskill
VP, Soybeans and Grains: John B. Ruff
Director, Marketing Food Ingredients: Dan Meins
Manager, Sales Private Label: Randy Johnson
Manager, Sales Rice Feed Ingredients: Sherry Brantley

LOCATIONS
HQ: Riceland Foods, Inc.
 2120 S. Park Ave., Stuttgart, AR 72160
Phone: 870-673-5500 **Fax:** 870-673-3366
Web: www.riceland.com

COMPETITORS

Aarhus United
American Rice
CHS
Connell Company
Ebro Puleva
Farmers' Rice Cooperative
Goya
Mars
Producers Rice Mill
Riviana Foods

HISTORICAL FINANCIALS
Company Type: Cooperative

Income Statement — FYE: July 31

	REVENUE ($ mil.)	NET INCOME ($ mil.)	NET PROFIT MARGIN	EMPLOYEES
7/04	951	—	—	1,900
7/03	873	—	—	1,900
7/02	750	—	—	—
7/01	683	—	—	—
7/00	694	—	—	—
7/99	813	—	—	1,850
7/98	804	—	—	1,850
7/97	868	—	—	1,850
7/96	734	—	—	1,850
7/95	737	—	—	1,850
Annual Growth	2.9%	—	—	0.3%

Revenue History

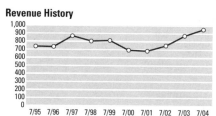

Rich Products

Starting in 1945 with "the miracle cream from the soya bean," Rich Products has grown from a niche maker of soy-based whipped toppings and frozen desserts to a major US frozen foods manufacturer. Since the 1960s the company has developed products, such as Coffee Rich (non-dairy coffee creamer), and expanded to include frozen bakery and pizza doughs and ingredients for the food service and in-store bakery markets, plus RICH-SEAPAK (seafood) and Byron's (barbecue). Rich Products markets more than 2,000 products in about 75 countries. The company, owned and operated by the founding Rich family, also owns Buffalo Bisons, the Jamestown Jammers, and the Wichita Wranglers minor-league baseball teams.

In a move to grow its dessert offerings, Rich acquired Mother's Kitchen (gourmet cakes and cheesecakes) in 2003. Continuing to add to its offerings, that year Rich also acquired Morningstar Foods' brand frozen whipped topping and creamer lines from Dean Foods.

In 2004 Rich announced a joint venture with Grupo Bimbo (called Fripan S.A. de C.V.) to make and sell frozen-dough and fresh-baked specialties to in-store bakery and foodservice companies.

EXECUTIVES

Chairman: Robert E. Rich Sr.
President: Robert E. Rich Jr.
COO: William G. Gisel Jr., age 51
CFO: Charles R. Trego
EVP, Innovation: Mindy Rich
EVP, People Network: Maureen O. Hurley
EVP, Sales and Marketing: Kevin Malchoff
SVP, Human Resources: Brian Townson
VP, Informations Systems and CIO: Paul Klein
President, Food Service: Dennis Janesz
President and COO, Rich Products Canada, Ltd.: Howard Rich
President, Rich Products South Africa: Evan Poulos
Secretary: David E. Rich
Director, Public Relations: Peter Ciotta

LOCATIONS

HQ: Rich Products Corporation
1 Robert Rich Way, Buffalo, NY 14213
Phone: 716-878-8000 **Fax:** 716-878-8765
Web: www.richs.com

Rich's has US manufacturing facilities in California, Illinois, Ohio, and Tennessee; its foreign operations are located in Canada, China, Mexico, and the UK.

PRODUCTS/OPERATIONS

Selected Products

Bagels
Barbecue
Brownies
Cakes
Cheesecakes
Donuts
Dough
  Bread
  Cookie
Dry Mixes
Eclairs and puffs
Fillings
Icings
Mini desserts
Muffins
Pies
Pizza
Pretzels
Pudding
Sweet rolls
Topping
  On-top topping
  Prewhipped topping
  Ready-to-whip topping

Selected Subsidiaries

Casa Di Bertacchi Corporation (Italian food specialties)
Jon Donaire (specialty desserts)
J.W. Allen (cakes, icings, and toppings)
RICH-SEAPAK Corporation (frozen seafood)

COMPETITORS

ConAgra
Dawn Food Products
Flowers Foods
International Multifoods
Kraft Foods
Nestlé
Pinnacle Foods
Schwan's
Unilever

HISTORICAL FINANCIALS

Company Type: Private

Income Statement FYE: December 31

	REVENUE ($ mil.)	NET INCOME ($ mil.)	NET PROFIT MARGIN	EMPLOYEES
12/03	1,800	—	—	—
12/02	1,784	—	—	6,500
12/01	1,702	—	—	6,500
12/00	1,620	—	—	7,000
12/99	1,515	—	—	6,500
12/98	1,400	—	—	6,000
12/97	1,300	—	—	6,000
12/96	1,200	—	—	6,000
12/95	1,100	—	—	6,500
12/94	1,000	—	—	7,000
Annual Growth	6.7%	—	—	(0.9%)

Revenue History

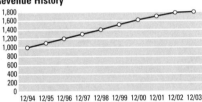

Ritz Camera Centers

Ritz Camera Centers began as a one-man portrait studio and developed into the largest photographic chain in the US. More than 1,200 stores nationwide offer one-hour photofinishing, cameras, film, and related photographic and optical products and services. Stores operate under the Ritz, Camera Shop, Kits, Inkley's, and Wolf names; the company also sells online. Subsidiary Boater's World Marine Centers has more than 100 stores nationwide that offer gear and clothing for fishing and boating. CEO David Ritz owns Ritz Camera, which was founded in 1918. His cousin, Chuck Wolf, owned Wolf Camera (#2 photo chain in the US), which Ritz Camera bought in 2001. Still focused on growth, Ritz bought Camera World in 2002.

EXECUTIVES

Chairman, President; and CEO; Chairman, Ritz Interactive: David M. Ritz
Vice Chairman: Charles R. (Chuck) Wolf
CFO: Jay Sloan
EVP: Richard Tranchida
President and CEO, Ritz Interactive: Fred H. Lerner
VP and Chief Marketing Officer, Ritz Interactive: Andre Brysha
VP and COO, Ritz Interactive: Peter Tahmin
VP and CFO, Ritz Interactive: Scott F. Neamand
Director of Human Resources: Alan MacDonald
Public Relations Manager: Brooke Ritz
Manager, Public Relations and Communications, Ritz Interactive: Mark Malkin

LOCATIONS

HQ: Ritz Camera Centers, Inc.
6711 Ritz Way, Beltsville, MD 20705
Phone: 301-419-0000 **Fax:** 301-419-2995
Web: www.ritzcamera.com

Ritz Camera Centers operates more than 1,200 stores throughout the US. The company also operates more than 100 Boater's World Marine Centers in more than 25 states.

PRODUCTS/OPERATIONS

Selected Merchandise and Services

Boater's World Marine Centers
  Apparel
  Electronics
  Fishing equipment
  Watersports equipment
Ritz Camera Centers
  Albums and frames
  Batteries
  Binoculars
  Camera accessories
  Camera attachments
  Cameras
  Cellular phones
  Darkroom equipment and supplies
  Digital imaging accessories
  Digital imaging services
  Film and processing
  Lenses
  Memory
  One-hour photofinishing
  Personalized photo products
  Printers and scanners
  Projectors and accessories
  Studio lighting and accessories
  Telescopes

COMPETITORS

Best Buy
Circuit City Stores
Costco Wholesale
CVS
MarineMax
MOTO Franchise
PhotoWorks
Travis Boats & Motors
Walgreen
Wal-Mart
West Marine

HISTORICAL FINANCIALS

Company Type: Private

Income Statement FYE: December 31

	ESTIMATED REVENUE ($ mil.)	NET INCOME ($ mil.)	NET PROFIT MARGIN	EMPLOYEES
12/02	1,200	—	—	10,800
12/01	1,350	—	—	12,000
12/00	800	—	—	7,000
12/99	800	—	—	7,000
12/98	650	—	—	6,500
12/97	625	—	—	7,000
Annual Growth	13.9%	—	—	9.1%

Revenue History

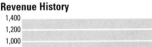

Robert Wood Johnson University Hospital

Robert Wood Johnson University Hospital is the flagship facility of the Robert Wood Johnson Health System (operated by the The Robert Wood Johnson Health Care Corp.). The medical center offers patients acute and tertiary care, including cardiovascular services (at The Heart Center of New Jersey); organ and tissue transplantation; pediatric care (at The Bristol-Myers Squibb Children's Hospital); Level 1 trauma care; cancer treatment; and more. The facility has nearly 570 beds and serves as a teaching center for the Robert Wood Johnson Medical School.

EXECUTIVES

President and CEO, The Robert Wood Johnson Health System and Robert Wood Johnson University Hospital: Harvey A. Holzberg
Treasurer: John J. Ganter
SVP, Medical Affairs and Interim Chief of Staff: Peter S. Amenta
SVP, Corporate Services: Judith E. Burgis
SVP, Operations: Stephen K. Jones
SVP, Development: Bruce D. Newman
SVP, Human Resources: John Regina
SVP, Nursing and Patient Services: Kathi Kendall Sengin
VP, Financial Services: Kevin Dunn
VP, Strategic Planning: Lawrence Garinello
VP, Information Systems: Robert G. Irwin
VP, Public and Community Affairs: Barbara Kerwin Jones, age 48
VP, Support Services: Herman Lindenbaum
VP, Administrative Services: Kevin J. McTernan

LOCATIONS

HQ: Robert Wood Johnson University Hospital
1 Robert Wood Johnson Place,
New Brunswick, NJ 08901
Phone: 732-828-3000   **Fax:** 732-545-6749
Web: www.rwjuh.edu

HISTORICAL FINANCIALS

Company Type: Not-for-profit

Income Statement
FYE: December 31

	REVENUE ($ mil.)	NET INCOME ($ mil.)	NET PROFIT MARGIN	EMPLOYEES
12/03	543	—	—	4,600
12/02	440	—	—	3,354
Annual Growth	23.3%	—	—	37.1%

Revenue History

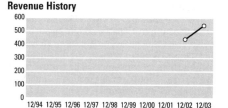

Rockefeller Foundation

The Rockefeller Foundation is one of the nation's oldest private charitable organizations. It supports grants, fellowships, and conferences for programs that try to identify and alleviate need and suffering around the world. These programs (or themes) include initiatives to foster fair implementation of health care, job opportunities for America's urban poor, creative expression through the humanities and arts, and agricultural policies that ensure food distribution to people in developing countries. The foundation's cross theme of global inclusion binds its programs to a global focus, ensuring that globalization gets doled out democratically and helps populations typically alienated from the global economy.

President Gordon Conway has introduced the reorganization focusing on the role of globalization in aiding the poor. The foundation's former divisions — such as Agricultural Sciences, Equal Opportunity, and Health Sciences — now come under the themes of Food Security, Working Communities, and Health Equity. Its non-New York City offices (Bangkok; Mexico City; Nairobi, Kenya; Harare, Zimbabwe; and San Francisco) are taking on increasing responsibility in carrying out the group's global mission. The foundation maintains no ties to the Rockefeller family or its other philanthropies. An independent board of trustees sets program guidelines and approves all expenditures.

HISTORY

Oil baron John D. Rockefeller, one of America's most criticized capitalists, was also one of its pioneer philanthropists. Before founding The Rockefeller Foundation in 1913, he funded the creation of The University of Chicago (with $36 million over a 25-year period) and formed organizations for medical research (1901), the education of southern African-Americans (1903), and hookworm eradication in the southern US.

Rockefeller turned the control of the foundation over to his son John D. Rockefeller Jr. in 1916. The younger Rockefeller separated the foundation from the family's interests and established an independent board. (The board later rejected a proposal from John Sr. to replace school textbooks that he claimed promoted Bolshevism.)

In the mid-1920s the foundation started conducting basic medical research. In 1928 it absorbed several other Rockefeller philanthropies, adding programs in the natural and social sciences and the arts and humanities. During the 1930s the foundation developed the first effective yellow fever vaccine (1935), continued its worldwide battles against disease, and supported pioneering research in the field of biology. Other grants supported the performing arts in the US and social science research. During WWII it supplied major funding for nuclear science research tools (spectroscopy, X-ray diffraction).

After the war, with an increasing number of large public ventures modeled after the foundation (e.g., the UN's World Health Organization) taking over its traditional physical and natural sciences territory, the organization dissolved its famed biology division in 1951. The following year emphasis swung to agricultural studies under chairman John D. Rockefeller III. The organization took wheat seeds developed at its Mexican food project to Colombia (1950), Chile (1955), and India (1956); a rice institute in the Philippines followed (1960). The Green Revolution sprouted 12 more developing-world institutes.

In the 1960s the foundation began dispatching experts to African and Latin American universities in an effort to raise the level of training at those institutions. The long bear market of the 1970s caused the foundation's assets to drop to a low of $732 million (1977).

In 1990 the organization set up the Energy Foundation, a joint effort with the Pew Charitable Trusts and the MacArthur Foundation, to explore alternate energy sources.

In the mid-1990s the Republican-led Congress launched three probes into the foundation and several other not-for-profits over allegations of political activities that could jeopardize their tax status.

In 1998 Gordon Conway, a British agricultural ecologist, became the foundation's 12th (and first foreign) president. He implemented a retooling of the organization's programs in 1999. He also led an effective campaign against bioengineering giant Monsanto's (now part of Pfizer) plan to market "sterile seeds" that do not regenerate. In 2000 James Orr III, a Rockefeller board member and CEO of Boston's United Asset Management Corporation, succeeded Alice Ilchman as chairman of the board of trustees. In 2001 the foundation pledged $5 million for disaster relief efforts in New York City following the September 11 terrorist attacks. The Rockefeller Foundation launched a multi-year initiative to promote fair intellectual property policies to the poor in 2002.

EXECUTIVES

Chairman: James F. Orr III
President: Gordon R. Conway
President: Judith Rodin, age 59
VP, Administration and Communication: Denise Gray-Felder
SVP: Julia I. Lopez
Director Africa Region: John Lynam
Director, Creativity and Culture: Morris Vogel
Director of Food Security: Gary H. Toenniessen
Director, Health Equity: Timothy Evans
Associate Director for Health Equity: Joyce L. Moock
Programme Officer for Food Security: Pat Naidoo
Auditors: Ernst & Young LLP

LOCATIONS

HQ: The Rockefeller Foundation
420 Fifth Ave., New York, NY 10018
Phone: 212-869-8500   **Fax:** 212-764-3468
Web: www.rockfound.org

The Rockefeller Foundation has field offices in Kenya, Mexico, Thailand, Zimbabwe, and the US, and maintains the Bellagio Study and Conference Center in northern Italy.

PRODUCTS/OPERATIONS

Themes

Creativity & Culture (renews and preserves the cultural heritage of people excluded from the globalizing economy; promotes public exchanges of ideas; supports diversity and creativity in humanities and arts)

Food Security (generates agricultural institutions, policies, and innovations to help rural poor in developing countries)

Global Inclusion (seeks to ensure that globalization processes are carried out fair and democratically, benefiting those most in need)

Health Equity (seeks to improve the implementation of health care in developing countries)
Working Communities (seeks to increase employment, improve schools, and encourage democratic participation in poor urban neighborhoods in the US)

HISTORICAL FINANCIALS
Company Type: Foundation

Income Statement
FYE: December 31

	REVENUE ($ mil.)	NET INCOME ($ mil.)	NET PROFIT MARGIN	EMPLOYEES
12/02	93	—	—	—
12/01	104	—	—	250
12/00	127	—	—	230
12/99	680	—	—	220
12/98	388	—	—	150
12/97	510	—	—	149
12/96	413	—	—	152
12/95	319	—	—	130
12/94	21	—	—	137
12/93	208	—	—	147
Annual Growth	(8.6%)	—	—	6.9%

Revenue History

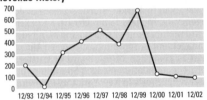

Rockwood Specialties

The more Rockwood Specialties adds, the more it makes. The company gets most of its sales from additives, including wood preservation chemicals, smectite-based chemicals, and additives for water. Additionally, Rockwood Specialties has two other divisions: electronics (specialty chemicals for semiconductors and printed circuit boards) and compounds (subsidiaries AlphaGary and Gomet), which prepare plastics for a variety of uses. A leader or #2 in many of its niches, the firm is Europe's largest silicon wafer recycler. The company was created in 2000 when Kohlberg Kravis Roberts & Co. bought several divisions from Laporte. It added Dynamit Nobel to its collection in April 2004 in a deal worth $2.7 billion.

The overall chemicals industry has lagged behind the general economic recovery of 2003-04, and Rockwood Specialties has been no different really. It wasn't until the latter half of 2003 that the company saw real improvement in most of its businesses. However the strong US construction market has really buoyed its performance additives division, whose products are used in roof tiles, pacing stones, and the like.

Rockwood bought Dynamit Nobel's specialty chemicals businesses, which included titanium dioxide pigments, advanced ceramics for medical applications, and water treatment chemicals. It also made lubricants and sealants.

Among Rockwood's customers are global giants like DuPont, Alcoa, Georgia-Pacific, Motorola, and Rohm and Haas.

EXECUTIVES
Chairman and CEO: Seifi Ghasemi, age 59
VP and CFO: Robert J. Zatta, age 54
VP, Law and Administration: Thomas J. Riordan, age 54
CIO: Mark J. Yankowskas
President, Cyantek: Gary Grossklaus
President, Rockwood Electronic Materials, Electrochemicals: Moenes Elias
President, Water Treatment Chemicals: Stephen M. (Steve) D'Onfro, age 45
President, Specialty Compounds: Robert (Bob) Gingue, age 59
President, Timber Treatment Chemicals: Stephen B. (Steve) Ainscough, age 57
President, Pigments: Ronald L. (Ron) Rapaport, age 59
President, Clay-Based Additives: Vernon (Vern) Sumner, age 52
Auditors: Deloitte & Touche LLP

LOCATIONS
HQ: Rockwood Specialties Group, Inc.
100 Overlook Center, Princeton, NJ 08540
Phone: 609-514-0300 **Fax:** 609-514-8720
Web: www.rockwoodspecialties.com

Rockwood Specialties operates about a dozen units in all, with operations in North America, Asia, and Europe.

2003 Sales

	$ mil.	% of total
North America	533.1	67
Europe	217.4	27
Asia	46.8	6
Total	**797.3**	**100**

PRODUCTS/OPERATIONS

2003 Sales

	$ mil.	% of total
Performance Additives	477.3	60
Specialty Compounds	176.4	22
Electronics	143.6	18
Total	**797.3**	**100**

Selected Operations and Products
Advantis Technologies (pool, spa, and water surface chemicals)
AlphaGary Corp. (compounding of plastics)
American Silicon Products (wafer reclaim)
Chemical Specialties Inc. (CSI, wood preservation chemicals)
Compugraphics (photomasks)
Cyantek (specialty chemicals for semiconductors)
Electrochemicals (chemicals for printed circuit boards)
Exsil, Inc. (silicon test wafers)
Gomet (compounding and molding of plastics)
Mineral Research and Development (MRD)
Rockwood Additives, Ltd. (smectite-based additives)
Rockwood Electronic Materials (ultra-pure chemicals and wafer reclaim)
Rockwood Pigments (iron oxide pigments)
Southern Clay Products (smectite-based additives)
Southern Color Company (pigments for the construction industry)

COMPETITORS

Arch Chemicals	Nalco
BASF Corporation	OM Group
Bayer	Photronics
BioLab	PolyOne
DuPont Photomasks	Rohm and Haas Electronic Materials
Elementis	R.T. Vanderbilt
Ferro	Süd-Chemie Inc.
Kingboard	Trio-Tech
LNP	

HISTORICAL FINANCIALS
Company Type: Private

Income Statement
FYE: December 31

	REVENUE ($ mil.)	NET INCOME ($ mil.)	NET PROFIT MARGIN	EMPLOYEES
12/03	797	(72)	—	2,284
12/02	760	(55)	—	2,500
12/01	800	—	—	2,700
Annual Growth	(0.2%)	—	—	(8.0%)

2003 Year-End Financials
Debt ratio: 233.0% Current ratio: 1.66
Return on equity: — Long-term debt ($ mil.): 824
Cash ($ mil.): 43

Net Income History

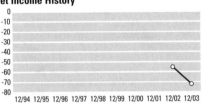

Roll International

Churning out collectible family heirlooms (or flea market fodder) was once the primary business of Stewart and Lynda Resnick's Roll International. The centerpiece of their empire, The Franklin Mint, was at one time the world's largest collectibles company with operations in 15 countries. In 2003 it closed The Franklin Mint Museum (which displayed authentic items such as a Jacqueline Kennedy Onassis necklace and a Princess Diana gown), and shuttered its retail and catalog operations. It now distributes goods via wholesale and the Internet. Other Roll operations include Paramount Farms (largest pistachio and almond farm in California), Paramount Citrus (citrus products), and Teleflora (floral delivery service).

The Franklin Mint (no connection to the US Mint) developed about 1,200 products each year and has sold everything from *Gone With the Wind* figurines and *Star Trek* chess sets to limited-edition Monopoly games and even the Elvis Presley commemorative .45 automatic. Many of its wares are produced under licensing agreements with the likes of the Vatican, The Coca-Cola Company, among others. The company is now focusing on its die-cast cars and airplanes, precision modeling, and its Harley-Davidson-branded items.

On the up and up is the Resnicks' Paramount Farms division. In 1996 the couple began planting 6,000 acres of pomegranate trees, and as the trees begin to bear fruit, so the Resnicks are pushing them to consumers. The fruit is being advertised as a source of antioxidants, and Paramount Farms' ad campaign plays upon the fruit's age-defying attributes, "The pomegranate is 5,000 years old. Drink it and you will be, too." Aside from fruit sales to grocery stores, Paramount Farms' pomegranate drinks, marketed through a company called Pom Wonderful, are becoming quite the rage, even making a debut at a 2003 Victoria's Secret lingerie show where "Sexy Flirts" (sugar-rimmed glasses of Pom and vodka) were served.

EXECUTIVES

Co-Chairman, President, and CEO; Chairman and CEO, The Franklin Mint; Co-Chairman and CEO, Teleflora; President, Paramount Farms: Stewart A. Resnick, age 67
Co-Chairman, Roll International and Teleflora; Vice Chairman, The Franklin Mint: Lynda R. Resnick
SVP Taxes: Neil R. Bersch
President and CEO, Teleflora: Gregg Coccari
Director of Human Resources: Dennis G. Rhyne

LOCATIONS

HQ: Roll International Corporation
11444 W. Olympic Blvd., 10th Fl.,
Los Angeles, CA 90064
Phone: 310-966-5700   **Fax:** 310-914-4747

PRODUCTS/OPERATIONS

Selected Product Categories
Clocks
Collectible knives and weapons
Collector eggs
Die-cast vehicle scale models
Games
Jewelry
Plates
Pocket watches
Porcelain and pewter sculptures
Porcelain and vinyl dolls
Tankards

Selected Franklin Mint Licenses
The Coca-Cola Company
Conservation International
Ford
General Motors
Graceland
Harley-Davidson
House of Fabergé
Mercedes-Benz
Metro-Goldwyn-Mayer
Milton Bradley
National Football League
Oleg Cassini
Paramount
Parker Brothers
Rolls-Royce
Turner Entertainment Co.
Twentieth Century Fox
Universal Pictures
The Vatican
Volkswagen

COMPETITORS

1-800-FLOWERS.COM	Hallmark
Action Performance	John Sanfilippo & Son
AgraQuest	King Ranch
Blue Diamond Growers	Maisto
Boyds Collection	Martha Stewart Living
Brown-Forman	ML Macadamia Orchards
Calcot	RC2
Charisma Brands	Security Capital
Department 56	Sun Growers
Dow AgroSciences	Village Farms
Enesco Group	Zindart
FTD	

HISTORICAL FINANCIALS

Company Type: Private

Income Statement   FYE: December 31

	ESTIMATED REVENUE ($ mil.)	NET INCOME ($ mil.)	NET PROFIT MARGIN	EMPLOYEES
12/01	800	—	—	5,100
12/00	825	—	—	5,100
12/99	700	—	—	5,000
12/98	725	—	—	7,500
12/97	1,511	—	—	7,500
12/96	1,280	—	—	7,500
12/95	1,360	—	—	7,700
12/94	1,300	—	—	7,500
12/93	1,180	—	—	7,500
12/92	960	—	—	7,500
Annual Growth	(2.0%)	—	—	(4.2%)

Revenue History

Rooms To Go

Need that sofa, recliner, table, and lamp in a hurry? Rooms To Go — with about 90 stores in Florida, Georgia, North Carolina, South Carolina, Tennessee, and Texas — has transformed itself into the top-selling furniture retailer in the US. The company markets its limited selection of furniture to brand-conscious, time-pressed customers. It packages low- to moderately priced furniture and accessories and offers discounts for those willing to buy a roomful. Rooms To Go also operates a Rooms to Go Kids chain with nearly 20 stores in the Southeast, Texas, and Puerto Rico. President and owner Jeffrey Seaman and his father, Morty, founded the firm in 1990 after selling Seaman Furniture Company.

EXECUTIVES

President and CEO: Jeffrey (Jeff) Seaman
COO: Steve Buckley
CFO: Lewis Lou Stein
VP Advertising: Richard Scobey
IT Director: Russ Rossen
Director Human Resources: Linda Garcia

LOCATIONS

HQ: Rooms To Go, Inc.
11540 Hwy. 92 East, Seffner, FL 33584
Phone: 813-623-5400   **Fax:** 813-620-1717
Web: www.roomstogo.com

COMPETITORS

Bassett Furniture	J. C. Penney
Bombay Company	La-Z-Boy
Ethan Allen	Pier 1 Imports
Furniture.com	Rowe Companies
Havertys	Sears
IKEA	

HISTORICAL FINANCIALS

Company Type: Private

Income Statement   FYE: December 31

	REVENUE ($ mil.)	NET INCOME ($ mil.)	NET PROFIT MARGIN	EMPLOYEES
12/02	1,300	—	—	5,500
12/01	1,260	—	—	5,500
12/00	1,040	—	—	4,834
12/99	860	—	—	4,000
12/98	720	—	—	3,500
12/97	600	—	—	3,314
12/96	450	—	—	—
Annual Growth	19.3%	—	—	10.7%

Revenue History

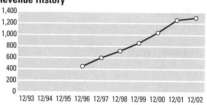

Rooney Holdings

Film star Mickey isn't the only Rooney to have landed big contracts. Rooney Holdings (formerly Rooney Brothers), through Manhattan Construction and other subsidiaries, builds hospitals, government buildings (George Bush Presidential Library in Texas), offices, highways, and sports arenas (Reliant Stadium in Houston). It offers construction management, general contracting, and design/build services across the US and in Mexico and Central America. Rooney Brothers also makes construction materials, operates an insurance agency and lumber and building supply stores, and manufactures electronics. The family-owned group was formed in 1984 to acquire Manhattan Construction, founded by patriarch L. H. Rooney in 1896.

EXECUTIVES

Chairman and CEO: L. Francis Rooney III
President and COO; CEO, Hope Lumber: James (Jim) Cavanaugh
CFO and Chief Administrative Officer: Kevin P. Moore
VP Administration: Jackie Proffitt
VP and Corporate Controller: Paul Vaughn
VP Human Resources: Bill Vogt
VP Information Technology: Duwayn Anderson
Auditors: Hogan & Slovacek

LOCATIONS

HQ: Rooney Holdings, Inc.
649 Fifth Ave. South, Naples, FL 34102
Phone: 239-403-0375   **Fax:** 239-263-2824
Web: www.rooneybrothers.com

Rooney Holdings has offices in Florida and Oklahoma.

PRODUCTS/OPERATIONS

Selected Construction Areas
Airport and aviation
Corporate and commercial
Corrections
Entertainment
Government
Health care
Hospitality and leisure
Institutional and academic
Special projects
Sports and entertainment

Selected Operations
Hope Lumber & Supply Company
Manhattan Construction Company
M.J. Lee Construction
Moore's Lumber Company
OAI Electronics
Rooney Insurance Agency

COMPETITORS

84 Lumber
Austin Industries
Barton Malow
Bechtel
Beck Group
Fluor
Foster Wheeler
Hensel Phelps Construction
Home Depot
Jacobs Engineering
Lowe's
M. A. Mortenson
McCoy
Siemens
Skanska USA Building
Turner Corporation
Washington Group

HISTORICAL FINANCIALS

Company Type: Private

Income Statement
FYE: September 30

	REVENUE ($ mil.)	NET INCOME ($ mil.)	NET PROFIT MARGIN	EMPLOYEES
9/03	1,262	—	—	2,400
9/02	1,201	—	—	2,500
9/01	1,053	—	—	2,400
9/00	1,002	—	—	2,400
9/99	925	—	—	2,400
9/98	769	—	—	2,000
9/97	611	—	—	1,800
9/96	500	—	—	1,800
9/95	230	—	—	750
9/94	214	—	—	—
Annual Growth	21.8%	—	—	15.6%

Revenue History

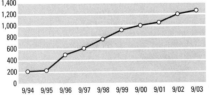

Roseburg Forest Products

With roots in a Depression-era sawmill, Roseburg Forest Products has branched out with a comprehensive line of wood products. The company produces specialty panels (melamine, particleboard, and vinyl laminates), and plywood products such as concrete forming panel and siding. Its standard lumber offerings include pine, Douglas fir, and Hemlock products. Roseburg manages nearly 800,000 acres of land in northern California and southern Oregon. Heirs of philanthropist Kenneth Ford, who established the Ford Family Foundation, own Roseburg Forest Products. Allyn Ford, Kenneth's son, is chairman, president, and CEO of the company.

Roseburg Forest Products laid off 670 employees in Douglas County in 2003 and another 32 in January 2004. The company is the county's largest employer, but a gluttonous market for domestic plywood as well as competing products has hurt it.

EXECUTIVES

Chairman, President, and CEO: Allyn Ford
Controller: Jeff Groom
VP Operations and Manufacturing: Lindsay Crawford
VP Engineering: Bill Randles
VP Information Services: Todd Rask
VP Sales and Marketing: Ray Barbee
VP Human Resources: Hank Snow
Logistics/Transportation Manager: Josh Renshaw

LOCATIONS

HQ: Roseburg Forest Products Co.
Old Hwy. 99 South, Roseburg, OR 97470
Phone: 541-679-3311   **Fax:** 541-679-9543
Web: www.rfpco.com

Roseburg Forest Products has operations and timberlands in California and Oregon.

PRODUCTS/OPERATIONS

Selected Products
Lumber
  Douglas fir
  Hemlock/white fir
  Pine
  Premier stud
Plywood Products
  Concrete forming
  Hardwood plywood
  Industrial grades
  Medium-density overlay
  Sanded fir plywood
  Sheathing
  Siding
  Superply
  Underlayment
Specialty Panels
  Foil overlays
  Melamine
  Particleboard
  Prefinished
  Shelving
  Vinyl laminates

COMPETITORS

Columbia Forest Products
Georgia-Pacific Corporation
Hampton Affiliates
Louisiana-Pacific
MAXXAM
Potlatch
Sierra Pacific Industries
Simpson Investment
Weyerhaeuser

HISTORICAL FINANCIALS

Company Type: Private

Income Statement
FYE: December 31

	ESTIMATED REVENUE ($ mil.)	NET INCOME ($ mil.)	NET PROFIT MARGIN	EMPLOYEES
12/03	800	—	—	3,800
12/02	750	—	—	3,600
12/01	750	—	—	3,600
12/00	730	—	—	3,600
12/99	850	—	—	4,000
12/98	850	—	—	4,000
12/97	775	—	—	3,950
12/96	850	—	—	3,050
12/95	750	—	—	3,300
12/94	620	—	—	3,500
Annual Growth	2.9%	—	—	0.9%

Revenue History

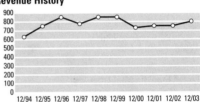

Rosen's Diversified

Rosen's Diversified has the goods to make the grass greener for the cows it slaughters. The agricultural holding company has interests including Rosen's Incorporated which distributes agricultural chemicals, including fertilizers, for farms in the upper Midwest. Its beef-slaughtering operations consist of four meatpacking plants with the capacity to slaughter about 4,000 head of cattle a day. Rosen's Diversified processes meat for restaurants, government customers, and food manufacturers in the US. The company was founded in 1946 by brothers Elmer and Ludwig Rosen. CEO Thomas Rosen (the son of Elmer) and other family members share ownership of Rosen's Diversified.

EXECUTIVES

CEO: Thomas J. Rosen, age 56
CFO: Rob Hovde
General Counsel, Director of Human Resources: Dominick Driano
President, Rosen's Incorporated: Ivan R. Wells

LOCATIONS

HQ: Rosen's Diversified, Inc.
1120 Lake Ave., Fairmont, MN 56031
Phone: 507-238-4201 **Fax:** 507-238-9966
Web: www.rosens.com

COMPETITORS

American Foods
Cargill
Smithfield Foods
Swift
Tyson Foods

HISTORICAL FINANCIALS
Company Type: Private

Income Statement
FYE: September 30

	ESTIMATED REVENUE ($ mil.)	NET INCOME ($ mil.)	NET PROFIT MARGIN	EMPLOYEES
9/03	1,200	—	—	2,200
9/02	950	—	—	2,000
9/01	800	—	—	2,000
9/00	700	—	—	1,800
9/99	620	—	—	1,500
9/98	560	—	—	1,200
9/97	550	—	—	1,200
9/96	500	—	—	900
9/95	500	—	—	900
Annual Growth	11.6%	—	—	11.8%

Revenue History

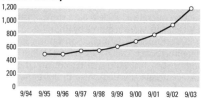

Rosenthal Automotive

A dealer of wheels in a city of wheeler-dealers, Rosenthal Automotive operates about 15 auto dealerships in the Washington, DC, area. Rosenthal's dealerships sell Acuras, Chevrolets, Chryslers, Hondas, Isuzus, Jaguars, Jeeps, Land Rovers, Mazdas, Nissans, Volkswagens, and Volvos. The company also sells used cars. Chairman and owner Robert Rosenthal founded Rosenthal Automotive in 1954 when he opened his first Chevrolet dealership in Arlington, Virginia. In 1997 Rosenthal joined other dealers in the Washington, DC, area to form Capital Automotive REIT, the first automotive-only real estate investment trust in the US.

Robert Rosenthal owns about 11% of Capital Automotive REIT.

EXECUTIVES

Chairman: Robert M. Rosenthal, age 76
President: Don Bavely
CFO: Michael Baron
Director of Human Resources: Jeraldine Mendez

LOCATIONS

HQ: Rosenthal Automotive Organization
1100 S. Glebe Rd., Arlington, VA 22204
Phone: 703-553-4300 **Fax:** 703-553-8435
Web: www.rosenthalauto.com

COMPETITORS

Atlantic Automotive
AutoNation
Brown Automotive
CarMax
Darcars
Jim Koons Automotive
March/Hodge
Ourisman Automotive
Sheehy Auto

HISTORICAL FINANCIALS
Company Type: Private

Income Statement
FYE: December 31

	REVENUE ($ mil.)	NET INCOME ($ mil.)	NET PROFIT MARGIN	EMPLOYEES
12/03	1,013	—	—	1,500
12/02	900	—	—	1,500
12/01	862	—	—	1,500
12/00	825	—	—	1,625
12/99	791	—	—	1,600
12/98	823	—	—	1,600
12/97	786	—	—	1,500
12/96	846	—	—	1,600
12/95	846	—	—	1,600
12/94	785	—	—	1,500
Annual Growth	2.9%	—	—	0.0%

Revenue History

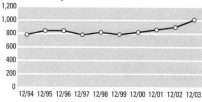

Rotary

The rotary phone may be gone, but Rotary International is still going strong. The service organization addresses issues such as AIDS, hunger, and illiteracy, and includes about 30,000 clubs in more than 160 countries with a membership of nearly 1.2 million (predominantly men, although women are its fastest-growing segment). Its not-for-profit Rotary Foundation invests in international education and humanitarian programs (funds are raised through voluntary contributions). Rotary International also sponsors Interact clubs for secondary school students, as well as a network of more than 6,900 Rotaract clubs for members ages 18-30. It is governed by a 19-member board and maintains offices globally.

Membership in Rotary clubs is by invitation only. Each club strives to include representatives from major businesses, professions, and institutions in its community. The organization's name arose from the early practice of rotating meetings among members' offices. Originally all male, women were first admitted into the organization in 1989.

HISTORY

On February 23, 1905, lawyer Paul Harris met with three friends in an office in Chicago's Unity Building. Inspired by the fellowship and tolerance of his boyhood home in Wallingford, Vermont, Harris proposed organizing a men's club to meet periodically for the purpose of camaraderie and making business contacts. The new endeavor was organized as the Rotary Club of Chicago and had 30 members by the end of the year.

As additional clubs followed, the organization assumed its role as a civic and service organization (the installation of public comfort stations in Chicago's City Hall was one of its first projects). At the first convention of the National Association of Rotary Clubs in 1910, Harris was elected president. International clubs soon followed, and by 1921 there were Rotary clubs on each continent.

In 1932, while struggling to revive a company with financial difficulties, Rotarian Herbert Taylor devised a statement of business ethics that later became the Rotarian mantra. Taylor's "4-Way Test" consisted of the following questions: "Is it the truth? Is it fair to all concerned? Will it build goodwill and better friendships? Will it be beneficial to all concerned?"

During WWI Rotary clubs promoted war relief and peace fund efforts. Following WWII the clubs assisted in efforts to aid refugees and prisoners of war. The extent of Rotarian involvement in international issues became clear when 49 members assisted in drafting the United Nations Charter in 1945.

The first significant contributions to The Rotary Foundation followed Harris' death in 1947. These funds formed the bedrock for the foundation's programs, and in 1965 the foundation created its Matching Grants and Group Study Exchange programs. Rotary International also welcomed younger members in the 1960s by creating its Interact and Rotaract clubs in 1962 and 1968, respectively.

The largest meeting of Rotarians occurred in 1978 when almost 40,000 members attended the organization's Tokyo convention. But controversy was fast approaching the male-only organization. In 1978 a California Rotary club defied the male-only requirement and admitted two women. Claiming that the club had violated the organization's constitution, Rotary International revoked the club's charter. A lengthy court battle ensued, and a series of appeals landed the issue on the docket of the US Supreme Court. In 1987 the court ruled that the all-male requirement was discriminatory. Two years later Rotary International officially did away with its all-male status.

In the 1990s membership in Rotary clubs grew, but at a slower pace than in the organization's past. Mary Wolfenberger was appointed the organization's first female CFO in 1993 (resigned 1997). In 1998 Rotary International joined with the United Nations to launch a series of humanitarian service projects in developing areas. In 1999 the organization spearheaded events to help flood victims in North Carolina and refugees in the Balkans. In 2000 the group created a program specializing in peace and conflict resolution. Rotary International established its first Internet-based Rotary club in early 2002. Also that year the group founded the Rotary Centers for International Studies which selects 70 scholars a year to participate in a master's-level peace studies program.

EXECUTIVES

President: Glenn E. Estess Sr.
President-Elect: Carl-Wilhelm Stenhammar
VP: John F. Germ
General Secretary: Edwin H. Futa
Controller: Mark A. Vieth
Director Human Resources: Carolyn Engblom
Communications Services General Manager:
  Kathy Kessenich
Membership Services General Manager: Theresa Nissen
Rotary Foundation General Manager: Duane Sterling
Corporate Services Manager: Andrew McDonald
Public Relations Manager: Susan Ross
Auditors: Deloitte & Touche LLP

LOCATIONS

HQ: Rotary International
  1 Rotary Center, 1560 Sherman Ave.,
  Evanston, IL 60201
Phone: 847-866-3000 **Fax:** 847-328-8281
Web: www.rotary.org

Rotary International has clubs in more than 160 countries.

PRODUCTS/OPERATIONS

Selected Issues Addressed
AIDS
Concern for the aging
Drug-abuse prevention
Environment
Hunger
Literacy
Polio
Service to women
Urban violence prevention
Youth

Selected Programs
Educational programs
  Ambassadorial Scholarships
  Grants for University Teachers
  Group Study Exchange (GSE)
  Rotary World Peace Scholarships
Humanitarian grants
  Discovery Grants
  Grants for Rotary Volunteers
  Matching Grants
  New Opportunities Grants
  Peace Program Grants
PolioPlus Program
  Polio Eradication Advocacy
  Polio Eradication Private Sector Campaign
  PolioPlus Partners

HISTORICAL FINANCIALS

Company Type: Not-for-profit

Income Statement FYE: June 30

	REVENUE ($ mil.)	NET INCOME ($ mil.)	NET PROFIT MARGIN	EMPLOYEES
6/03	61	—	—	600
6/02	56	—	—	500
6/01	62	—	—	500
6/00	61	—	—	450
6/99	61	—	—	450
6/98	73	—	—	400
6/97	72	—	—	400
6/96	62	—	—	400
6/95	60	—	—	350
6/94	59	—	—	450
Annual Growth	0.3%	—	—	3.2%

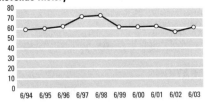

Revenue History

Roundy's

Roundy's rounds up name-brand and private-label goods and distributes them to warehouse and grocery stores throughout the Midwest. Roundy's services about 800 independent and licensee stores. The company also owns 120 retail stores in Wisconsin, Minnesota, and other Midwest locations. Roundy's offers its members and customer stores support services, including accounting and inventory control, advertising, and store financing. Roundy's is a leading Wisconsin food retailer, with supermarket chains operating under the Pick 'N Save and Copps Food Centers banners. Roundy's was founded in 1872. It is owned by the private investment firm Willis Stein & Partners.

Forty-two percent of Roundy's sales come from its distribution business to independent Midwestern grocery stores. To boost its sales and profits, Roundy's has been acquiring independent stores, most recently in June 2003, when it bought 31 Rainbow Foods stores in the Minneapolis/St. Paul metro area from Fleming Companies. In 2004 Roundy's subsidiary Ultra Mart Foods agreed to purchase the seven Wisconsin retail Pick 'N Save grocery stores owned by McAdams Inc.

HISTORY

Migration from the eastern US and overseas was boosting Milwaukee's ranks when William Smith, Judson Roundy, and Sidney Hauxhurst formed grocery wholesaler Smith, Roundy & Co. in 1872. Smith left the firm in 1878 for his first of two terms as Wisconsin's governor, and William Peckham joined the enterprise, which was then renamed Roundy, Peckham & Co. Two years later Charles Dexter joined the company, by then operating in five Midwestern states and running a manufacturing business.

The wholesaler became Roundy, Peckham & Dexter Co. in 1902, following the death of Hauxhurst (Roundy died in 1907). The company introduced its first private-label product — salt — in 1922. In 1929 Dexter (then 84) came up with a plan to publicize the Roundy's name by handing out cookbooks that called for the company's goods.

Roy Johnson, who joined the company in 1912, was named president near the end of the Depression. In the 1940s the wholesaler acquired smaller companies in the region. The company became Roundy's in 1952 when Roundy, Peckham & Dexter was bought by a group comprising hundreds of Wisconsin grocery retailers. Johnson remained head of the new company until his death in 1962. James Aldrich led the company for the next 11 years.

In 1970 Roundy's started Insurance Planners, which offered insurance to retailers. Vincent Little became president of the company in 1973. Two years later Roundy's began a real estate subsidiary (Ronco Realty) and opened its first Pick 'n Save Warehouse Foods store.

The company expanded in the mid-1980s through the purchase of distributors. But expansion hurt profits, and dividends were suspended in 1984 and 1985. In the late 1980s several Pick 'n Save stores opened throughout Wisconsin and other Midwestern states. Owners grew suspicious of Little's accounting practices and the special treatment given a Roundy's-owned store run by his son, and in 1986 they forced him out of his president and CEO positions. John Dickson replaced him.

By 1994 Pick 'n Save had vastly upgraded its image — one store sold $1,000 cognac and featured an $18,000 cappuccino machine. However, sales dropped off for the third straight year. COO Gerald Lestina was named CEO in 1995, replacing Dickson, who continued as chairman. Dickson died later that year.

Roundy's did not pay its members a dividend in 1995 as it made an effort to offset losses in Michigan and Ohio. To ease those losses, in 1997 the company closed 12 poorly performing stores in those states. A year later a fire destroyed its Evansville, Indiana, warehouse; the company rebuilt the facility in 1999. Also in 1999 Roundy's purchased three supermarkets in Indiana from Kroger and The John C. Groub Company.

The Mega Marts and Ultra Mart chains, which together operate 24 Pick 'n Save stores, primarily in Wisconsin, were acquired by Roundy's in 2000. In 2001 Roundy's launched an online grocery shopping service, called Pick 'n Save Online Shopping, in two test stores in Wisconsin (the plan was eventually scuttled). Also in 2001 the company purchased its competitor, The Copps Corporation, acquiring 21 stores in north and central Wisconsin and a wholesale business that distributes to retailers in Wisconsin and northern Michigan. Chicago-based Willis Stein & Partners bought Roundy's in June 2002.

Dale Riley, who had been hired to revitalize Roundy's flagging Rainbow Food chain, resigned in 2004 after a year on the job.

EXECUTIVES

Chairman, President, and CEO: Robert A. Mariano, age 53, $1,211,539 pay
EVP and CFO: Darren W. Karst, age 44, $1,021,963 pay
Group VP, Human Resources: Colleen J. Stenholt, age 53
Group VP, IT and Business Processes: John W. Boyle, age 46
Group VP, Legal, Risk and Treasury; Secretary, and Treasurer: Edward G. Kitz, age 50
Group VP, Marketing: Andrew A. Abraham, age 40, $381,410 pay (partial-year salary)
Group VP, Merchandising and Procurement: Robin S. Michel, age 49
Group VP, Retail Operations and Customer Satisfaction: Gary L. Fryda, age 51, $520,011 pay
Group VP, Supply Chain: Donald S. Rosanova, age 54, $440,577 pay
Group VP, Wholesale Development & Real Estate: Michael J. Schmitt, age 55, $275,250 pay
VP and General Manager, Minnesota Retail: Mark Beaty
Auditors: Ernst & Young

LOCATIONS

HQ: Roundy's, Inc.
875 E. Wisconsin Ave., Milwaukee, WI 53202
Phone: 414-231-5000 **Fax:** 414-231-7939
Web: www.roundys.com

Roundy's distributes its goods from seven wholesale distribution centers located in Illinois, Indiana, Ohio, and Wisconsin to approximately 800 licensee and independent retail operations throughout the Midwest.

PRODUCTS/OPERATIONS

2003 Sales

	% of total
Company-owned stores	42
Independent retailers	42
Licensed Pick 'n Save stores	16
Total	**100**

Selected Private Labels
IGA
Old Time
Roundy's

Product Lines
Bakery goods
Dairy products
Dry groceries
Fresh produce
Frozen foods
General merchandise
Meats

Selected Services
Centralized bakery purchasing
Business development
Financing
Group advertising
Insurance
Inventory control
Market analysis
Merchandising
Ordering assistance
Point-of-sale support
Pricing services
Purchasing reports
Retail accounting
Retail training

COMPETITORS

A&P	Hy-Vee
Albertson's	IGA
ALDI	Kroger
AWG	McLane
Central Grocers Cooperative	Meijer
	Nash Finch
Certified Grocers Midwest	S. Abraham & Sons
Costco Wholesale	Spartan Stores
Dominick's	SUPERVALU
GSC Enterprises	Wal-Mart

HISTORICAL FINANCIALS

Company Type: Private

Income Statement
FYE: Saturday nearest December 31

	REVENUE ($ mil.)	NET INCOME ($ mil.)	NET PROFIT MARGIN	EMPLOYEES
12/03	4,383	55	1.2%	19,999
12/02	3,638	31	0.9%	13,151
12/01	3,450	26	0.7%	13,451
12/00	2,984	21	0.7%	9,071
12/99	2,717	18	0.6%	5,617
12/98	2,579	12	0.5%	5,193
12/97	2,611	11	0.4%	5,071
12/96	2,579	10	0.4%	5,481
12/95	2,488	9	0.4%	4,839
12/94	2,462	7	0.3%	4,775
Annual Growth	6.6%	26.5%	—	17.3%

2003 Year-End Financials
Debt ratio: 153.4% Current ratio: 1.03
Return on equity: 15.1% Long-term debt ($ mil.): 598
Cash ($ mil.): 90

Net Income History

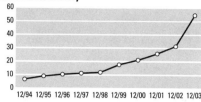

Royster-Clark

Royster-Clark has been spreading it on thick for more than 125 years. The company makes and distributes fertilizer and crop-protection products. It processes seed for other companies and sells seed under its own label. Operations include granulation, blending, and seed-processing plants, 400 retail farm supply centers, and a network of distribution terminals and warehouses. The company operates in the eastern, southern, and Midwestern US. Chairman and CEO Francis Jenkins owns 38% of the company. Investment firm 399 Venture Partners (a Citigroup affiliate) owns 32%. Almost all of the company's sales come from distribution of fertilizers bought from third parties.

EXECUTIVES

Chairman and CEO: Francis P. Jenkins Jr., age 61, $699,990 pay
President and COO: G. Kenneth (Ken) Moshenek, age 52, $485,000 pay
CFO: Paul M. Murphy, age 59, $310,000 pay
Senior Managing Director, International: Max Baer, age 71
Managing Director, Credit and Farm Financing: Michael J. Galvin, age 40
Managing Director, Crop Protection and Seed: Gary L. Floyd, age 49
Managing Director, Environmental, Health, and Safety: J. William (Billy) Pirkle, age 42
Managing Director, Human Resources: Kenneth W. (Ken) Carter, age 58
Managing Director, Information Technology: Robert L. Paarlberg, age 58
Managing Director, Logistics: Greg Hutchison, age 46
Managing Director and Controller: Joel F. Dunbar, age 55
Auditors: KPMG LLP

LOCATIONS

HQ: Royster-Clark, Inc.
1251 Avenue of the Americas, Ste. 900, New York, NY 10020
Phone: 212-332-2965 **Fax:** 212-332-2999
Web: www.roysterclark.com

Royster-Clark operates primarily in the eastern, southeastern, and midwestern US. The company has production facilities in Alabama, Florida, Georgia, Illinois, North Carolina, Ohio, South Carolina, Tennessee, Virginia, and Wisconsin.

PRODUCTS/OPERATIONS

2003 Sales

	$ mil.	% of total
Fertilizer materials	377.7	39
Fertilizer	227.8	24
Crop protection	185.7	19
Seed	75.6	8
Other	93.1	10
Total	**959.9**	**100**

Selected Products
Crop Nutrients
  Bagged and bulk dry fertilizers
  Custom-blended fertilizers
  Fertilizer materials
  Granulated fertilizers
  Lime and landplaster
  Liquid fertilizers
  Specialty fertilizers
Crop Protection
  Fungicides
  Herbicides
  Insecticides
Seeds
  Soybean
  Wheat

Selected Services
Crop Management
Agronomist services
Crop management
Crop protection application
Crop scouting
Custom blending
Custom spreading
Farm delivery
Soil sampling

COMPETITORS

Agrium	FMC
Canpotex	Monsanto
Cargill	Southern States
CHS	Terra Industries
ConAgra	Terra Nitrogen
Dow Chemical	Tractor Supply
DuPont	Wilbur-Ellis

HISTORICAL FINANCIALS

Company Type: Private

Income Statement
FYE: December 31

	REVENUE ($ mil.)	NET INCOME ($ mil.)	NET PROFIT MARGIN	EMPLOYEES
12/03	960	(21)	—	3,120
12/02	898	(5)	—	3,130
12/01	954	(9)	—	3,130
12/00	913	(5)	—	3,130
12/99	715	7	0.9%	—
Annual Growth	7.6%	—	—	(0.1%)

2003 Year-End Financials
Debt ratio: 627.1% Current ratio: 2.31
Return on equity: — Long-term debt ($ mil.): 343
Cash ($ mil.): 1

Net Income History

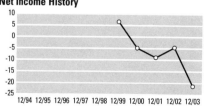

RTM Restaurant Group

RTM Restaurant Group beefs up its operations with a little motivation and a lot of Horsey Sauce. RTM, which stands for Results Through Motivation, operates and franchises more than 800 restaurants in 24 states, and the company is the nation's largest operator of Arby's restaurants. It runs more than 700 units franchised from Triarc. The quick-service restaurants are known for their roast beef sandwiches and other burger alternatives. In addition, the company has a stake in Winners International, the franchisor of Mrs. Winner's Chicken & Biscuits. RTM was founded in 1973 by CEO Russ Umphenour. He retains majority ownership in the company.

RTM intends to expand to 5,000 units by 2020.

EXECUTIVES
Chairman: Dennis Cooper
CEO: Russell V. (Russ) Umphenour Jr.
President: Tom Garrett
SVP and CFO: Linda S. Harty
SVP and CIO: Patti Reilly
SVP: Ray Biondi
SVP: Russ Welch
SVP Accounting and Controller: J. David Pipes
SVP Corporate Communications and Public Relations: John Gray
SVP Development: Devin Keil
SVP Operations: Michael Lippert
VP Employment and Litigation Counsel: Clete McGinty
Chief Administrative Officer and Corporate Secretary: Sharron Barton

LOCATIONS
HQ: RTM Restaurant Group
5995 Barfield Rd., Atlanta, GA 30328
Phone: 404-256-4900   **Fax:** 404-256-7277
Web: www.rtminc.com

COMPETITORS
AFC Enterprises
Blimpie
Burger King
Chick-fil-A
CKE Restaurants
Dairy Queen
Jack in the Box
McDonald's
NPC International
Quizno's
Schlotzsky's
Sonic
Subway
Wendy's
YUM!

HISTORICAL FINANCIALS
Company Type: Private

Income Statement   FYE: May 31

	REVENUE ($ mil.)	NET INCOME ($ mil.)	NET PROFIT MARGIN	EMPLOYEES
5/04	781	—	—	25,000
5/03	751	—	—	25,000
5/02	735	—	—	25,000
5/01	675	—	—	25,000
5/00	605	—	—	25,000
5/99	685	—	—	23,000
5/98	647	—	—	23,000
5/97	405	—	—	20,000
Annual Growth	9.8%	—	—	3.2%

Revenue History
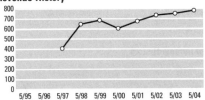

Rudolph and Sletten

Rudolph and Sletten builds on shaky ground in California, but the force is with it. The firm built Lucasfilm's Skywalker Ranch production facility and is a leading player in the Silicon Valley, where it raised corporate campuses for Apple Computer, Microsoft, and Sun Microsystems, among others. Acting as on-site general contractor or construction manager, the company specializes in projects for the health care, high-tech research and manufacturing, biotechnology, and entertainment industries; recent projects include the San Diego Museum of Contemporary Art. Onslow "Rudy" Rudolph, father of president and CEO Allen Ruldoph, founded the company in 1960 and was joined by former chairman Kenneth Sletten in 1962.

EXECUTIVES
President and CEO: Allen A. Rudolph
CFO: James F. (Jim) Evans
COO: Dennis R. Giles
Chief Administrative Officer: Karen M. Rudolph
EVP and Chief of Estimating/Preconstruction: Gary L. Walz
COO, Southern California: Martin B. Sisemore
SVP Estimating: Joseph A. (Joe) Francini
EVP Operations: Richard A. (Rick) Militello
VP and General Counsel: Paul A. Aherne
Controller: Andrew J. Maurer
Director Human Resources: Barbara Duncan
Business Development, Marketing, and Sales Executive: Dianna Wright
Auditors: KPMG LLP

LOCATIONS
HQ: Rudolph and Sletten, Inc.
989 E. Hillsdale Blvd., Ste. 100, Foster City, CA 94404
Phone: 650-572-1919   **Fax:** 650-577-1558
Web: www.rsconstruction.com

Rudolph and Sletten has offices in Foster City, Sacramento, and San Diego, California.

PRODUCTS/OPERATIONS

Selected Customers
3Com
Amgen
Apple Computer
Bayer Corporation
Genentech
Microsoft
Monterey Bay Aquarium
Shaklee Corporation
Stanford Medical Center
Stanford University
Sun Microsystems

Major Markets
Biotechnology
Corporate campuses
Entertainment
Health care
High-tech
Pharmaceutical

COMPETITORS
Beck Group
Clark Construction
Devcon Construction
DPR Construction
Hathaway Dinwiddie Construction
Hensel Phelps Construction
Hoffman Corporation
Kitchell Corporation
S. J. Amoroso Construction
Swinerton
Turner Corporation
Webcor Builders
Whiting-Turner

HISTORICAL FINANCIALS
Company Type: Private

Income Statement   FYE: June 30

	REVENUE ($ mil.)	NET INCOME ($ mil.)	NET PROFIT MARGIN	EMPLOYEES
6/03	700	—	—	—
6/02	1,002	—	—	800
6/01	852	—	—	1,200
6/00	675	—	—	1,200
6/99	565	—	—	1,000
6/98	600	—	—	900
6/97	500	—	—	767
6/96	453	—	—	815
6/95	350	—	—	641
6/94	276	—	—	570
Annual Growth	10.9%	—	—	4.3%

Revenue History
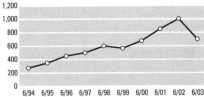

Safelite Group

Safelite Group has the answer to what blew into your windshield. The company, one of the US's largest auto glass retailers, serves more than 2 million customers each year through Safelite AutoGlass, Jiffy Lube, and Pep Boys service centers. It makes its own windshields at a factory in Kansas and another in North Carolina. Safelite also operates four national call centers for auto glass service scheduling and claims processing. Heavy debt led Safelite to file for Chapter 11 bankruptcy in 2000; later that year it emerged from bankruptcy and restructured. Founded in 1947, Safelite merged with rival Vistar in 1997. Safelite is owned by a group of banks and other former creditors.

EXECUTIVES

President and CEO: Dan Wilson
EVP and CFO: Douglas A. (Doug) Herron
EVP and Chief Client Officer: Thomas M. (Tom) Feeney
SVP, Manufacturing, Distribution, and Purchasing: Douglas A. Maehl
SVP, Manufacturing and Fulfillment: Steven B. Micheli
SVP, Marketing, Strategic Planning, and Human Resources: Elizabeth A. Wolszon
VP, Finance: Poe A. Timmons
VP, Marketing, Safelite Glass: Denise Klapper
VP, National Accounts and Field Services, Safelite Solutions: David P. Stagner
CIO/CTO: Tim Plazk
Auditors: Deloitte & Touche LLP

LOCATIONS

HQ: Safelite Group, Inc.
2400 Farmers Dr., 5th Fl., Columbus, OH 43216
Phone: 614-210-9000 **Fax:** 614-210-9451
Web: www.safelite.com

PRODUCTS/OPERATIONS

Selected Subsidiaries
Safelite AutoGlass (auto-glass repair and replacement)
Safelite Glass Corp. (windshield manufacturing)
Safelite Solutions LLC (claims-management outsourcing)
Service AutoGlass (auto-glass wholesaling)

COMPETITORS

Apogee Enterprises
Asahi Glass
Donnelly
Guardian Industries
Pilkington
PPG
Vitro America, Inc.

HISTORICAL FINANCIALS
Company Type: Private

Income Statement			FYE: Saturday nearest March 31	
	REVENUE ($ mil.)	NET INCOME ($ mil.)	NET PROFIT MARGIN	EMPLOYEES
3/03	611	37	6.1%	6,000
3/02	634	33	5.2%	6,000
3/01	725	—	—	6,300
3/00	859	—	—	6,100
3/99	877	—	—	6,300
3/98	214	—	—	6,800
3/97	483	—	—	6,500
3/96	438	—	—	—
3/95	372	—	—	—
3/94	357	—	—	—
Annual Growth	6.1%	—	—	(1.3%)

Net Income History
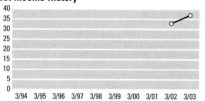

Safety-Kleen

Safety-Kleen Corp. has recycled itself and emerged from bankruptcy as a private company with a new name: Safety-Kleen Holdco. The company's main operating subsidiary is Safety-Kleen Systems. Local auto shops, government agencies, and large corporations turn to Safety-Kleen for industrial waste management services. Safety-Kleen collects, processes, recycles, and disposes of a large range of hazardous and non-hazardous wastes. It also provides specialty services such as parts cleaning and is the largest recovery and recycling company for used oil products in the US. It operates a network of about 250 service and recycling centers throughout North America.

After allegations of improper accounting practices in 2000, Safety-Kleen filed for bankruptcy protection and restated three years of financial results. It emerged from bankruptcy at the end of 2003. Transportation group Laidlaw owned about 44% of Safety-Kleen before both filed for bankrtupcy protection in 2001. Rival Clean Harbors has acquired Safety-Kleen's chemical services operations.

Safety-Kleen has been working to clean up its own financial house. A bankruptcy court confirmed Safety-Kleen's plan of reorganization, which allowed it to enter its final phase of bankruptcy protection. The group obtained $295 million in financing and began repaying its secured creditors through its bankruptcy plan. Turn-around specialist Ron Rittenmeyer has left the company after three years of leading the company's reorganization, which included relocating its headquarters from South Carolina to Texas.

Safety-Kleen and Laidlaw have settled some $27 billion worth of legal claims against each other. Laidlaw, which also emerged from bankruptcy protection in 2003, had written off its investment in Safety-Kleen. The group has also formed a distribution and recycling services pact with waste recycler Veridium.

EXECUTIVES

Chairman: Ronald W. (Ron) Haddock, age 63
President and CEO: Frederick J. (Fred) Florjancic Jr., age 57
EVP and Chief Administrative Officer: Thomas W. (Tom) Arnst
EVP and CFO: Robert (Bob) Gary
EVP Operations: David M. (Dave) Sprinkle
EVP Branch Sales and Service: Steve Grimshaw
SVP Information Technology: Robert Hawkins
VP Human Resources: Michael (Mike) Williams
VP Compensation, Benefits, and HR Information Systems: Toby Todd
Director Corporate Communications and Governmental Relations: John Kyte
Environmental, Health, and Safety Manager: Matt Hedrick
Auditors: Deloitte & Touche LLP

LOCATIONS

HQ: Safety-Kleen Holdco, Inc.
5400 Legacy Dr., Cluster II, Bldg. 3, Plano, TX 75024
Phone: 972-265-2000 **Fax:** 972-265-2990
Web: www.safety-kleen.com

PRODUCTS/OPERATIONS

Selected Services
Automotive recovery
Imaging (recovery of silver from film processing)
Industrial waste collection
Parts washing
Used oil collection and oil re-refining
Vacuum (removal and disposal of sludge from underground separator tanks)
Waste paint recovery

COMPETITORS

Allied Waste
Casella Waste Systems
Clean Harbors
Duratek
Environmental Safeguards
Envirosource
Industrial Services of America
MPW
Philip Services
Republic Services
SUEZ Environnement
Waste Industries USA
Waste Management

HISTORICAL FINANCIALS
Company Type: Private

Income Statement			FYE: August 31	
	REVENUE ($ mil.)	NET INCOME ($ mil.)	NET PROFIT MARGIN	EMPLOYEES
8/03	850	—	—	5,000
8/02	1,100	—	—	7,000
8/01	1,515	—	—	9,216
8/00	1,586	—	—	9,618
8/99	1,686	—	—	9,990
8/98	1,186	—	—	11,500
8/97*	679	—	—	4,500
9/96	241	—	—	1,349
9/95	217	—	—	1,855
9/94	182	—	—	1,295
Annual Growth	18.7%	—	—	16.2%

*Fiscal year change

Revenue History
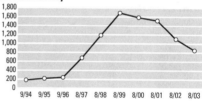

St. Joseph Health System

When young men (and women) heeding the advice to go west find themselves in need of health care, St. Joseph Health System can meet their needs. The health care network operates 15 hospitals, three home health agencies, clinics, hospices, and other health care delivery organizations that operate throughout California and in eastern New Mexico and western Texas. In California, its primary market, the health system has more than 2,100 beds at its nine hospitals. Its Covenant Health System unit operates in Texas and New Mexico with more than 1,300 beds in about 20 owned, leased, or affiliated hospitals.

Salvation Army

EXECUTIVES
Chairman: Sister Katherine (Kit) Gray
President and CEO: Richard J. (Rich) Statuto, age 45
President and CEO: Deborah A. Proctor
SVP, Theology and Ethics: Jack Glaser
SVP and COO: Jeff Flocken
SVP, Planning and Marketing: Jennifer Perry
SVP and CFO: Joseph Randolph
SVP, Sponsorship: Sister Suzanne Sassus
SVP and Chief Medical Officer: Elliot Sternberg
SVP, Human Resources: Cindra Syverson
SVP and General Counsel: Susan Whittaker
SVP and CIO: Ben Williams
VP and Chief Compliance Officer: Tracey A. Calver
VP, Minsitry Leadership: Barb Cox
VP, Theology and Ethics: Johnny Cox
VP, Resource Development: Frank Hall
VP, Finance and Treasurer: Garrett Kop

LOCATIONS
HQ: St. Joseph Health System
500 S. Main St., Ste. 1000, Orange, CA 92868
Phone: 714-347-7500 **Fax:** 714-347-7540
Web: www.stjhs.org

Selected Facilities
California
 St. Mary Medical Center (Apple Valley)
 General Hospital Campus (Eureka)
 St. Joseph Hospital (Eureka)
 Redwood Memorial Hospital (Fortuna)
 St. Jude Medical Center (Fullerton)
 Mission Hospital (Mission Viejo)
 Queen of the Valley Hospital (Napa)
 St. Jospeph Hospital (Orange)
 Petaluma Valley Hospital (Petaluma)
 Santa Rosa Memorial Hospital (Santa Rosa)
Texas
 Covenant Hospital Levelland (Levelland)
 Covenant Children's Hospital (Lubbock)
 Covenant Medical Center (Lubbock)
 Covenant Medical Center Lakeside (Lubbock)
 Covenant Hospital Plainview (Plainview)

COMPETITORS
Catholic Health Initiatives
Catholic Healthcare West
HCA
Kaiser Permanente
Sutter Health

HISTORICAL FINANCIALS
Company Type: Not-for-profit

Income Statement FYE: June 30

	REVENUE ($ mil.)	NET INCOME ($ mil.)	NET PROFIT MARGIN	EMPLOYEES
6/02	2,514	—	—	18,930
6/01	2,378	—	—	18,000
Annual Growth	5.7%	—	—	5.2%

Revenue History

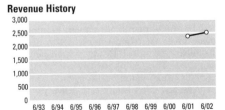

The largest civil army in the land, the Salvation Army is about 2 million strong. Its faith-based programs assist alcoholics, drug addicts, the homeless, the handicapped, the elderly, prison inmates, people in crisis, and the unemployed through a range of services. These include day-care centers, programs for people with disabilities, substance abuse programs, and educational facilities for at-risk students. It also provides disaster relief in the US and abroad. The Salvation Army USA is a national unit of the Salvation Army, an international body based in London, which oversees Army activities in more than 100 countries.

The name Salvation Army may only ring a bell with you around Christmas, but Salvation Army USA is always working. Active as a church and a charity, the organization serves nearly 37 million people a year. It also provides disaster relief in the US and abroad. The Salvation Army usually tops the list of US not-for-profits in terms of donations received: In 2003 contributions reached about $1.4 billion. Also in 2003, the estate of McDonald's heiress Joan B. Croc (widow of McDonald's founder Ray Kroc) donated $1.5 billion to the Salvation Army. The Salvation Army accepted the donation along with the stipulations that half the money be used to build community centers and the other half directed into an endowment that would be used to offset operating expenses.

Along with promoting charity, the Salvation Army seeks to save souls. As an evangelical church, it preaches the message of salvation through Jesus Christ. Before joining the organization and becoming a soldier (a lay member), one must sign an agreement known as the "Articles of War," a commitment to the avoidance of gambling, debt, and profanity and to abstention from alcohol, tobacco, and other recreational drugs. The US organization includes some 450,000 soldiers, more than 1 million volunteers, and nearly 5,400 officers, who are also ordained ministers.

Officers are expected to wear their uniforms at all times and to work full-time for the Salvation Army. They receive no salary; instead, they are provided with room and board and given a limited stipend.

The Salvation Army USA is only one of scores of national Salvation Army organizations around the world, which report to the group's global leader, General John Larsson, at its international headquarters in the UK.

HISTORY

William Booth (1829-1912) started preaching the gospel as a Wesleyan Methodist in the UK, but the church expelled him because he insisted on preaching outside and to everyone, including the poor. In 1865 he moved to the slums of London's East End and attracted large crowds with his volatile sermons. Opposition to his message of universal salvation for drunks, thieves, prostitutes, and gamblers often caused riots. In fact, the first women in the organization wore bonnets designed with a dual purpose in mind — warmth and protection from flying objects.

At a meeting in 1878, a sign was used referring to the "Salvation Army." Booth adopted the reference as both the name and the style of his organization. Members became soldiers, evangelists were officers, and Booth was referred to as "General." Prayers became knee drills, and contributions were called cartridges.

The Salvation Army marched across the Atlantic to the US in 1880, led by seven women and one man. Women have always played an active role in the Salvation Army, both as officers and soldiers. Booth's wife, Catherine Mumford, was a leading suffragette, and Booth advocated equal rights for women.

In 1891 a crab pot, with a sign reading "Keep the Pot Boiling," was placed on a San Francisco street to collect donations. This led to the Salvation Army's annual Christmas kettle program.

During WWI the organization became famous for the doughnuts that it served the doughboys fighting on the front lines. After some internal dissension, the Salvation Army took its only public political stance in 1928 with the endorsement of Herbert Hoover for his support of Prohibition during his presidential campaign. The charity opened its first home for alcoholics in 1939, in Detroit.

After WWII the Salvation Army began using such radio and TV programs as *Heartbeat Theater* and *Army of Stars* to spread its message.

Over the years the Salvation Army has provided assistance to victims of hurricanes, floods, and earthquakes. Volunteers rendered almost 70,000 service hours in the aftermath of the Oklahoma City bombing in 1995, counseling more than 1,600 victims and family members, helping with funeral arrangements, and providing food, clothing, and travel assistance. Indicative of the organization's readiness and extensive reach, its volunteers were helping victims in Guam within minutes of the 1997 Korean Air plane crash. The Salvation Army was quickly on the scene after a Jonesboro, Arkansas, shooting incident in 1998 when four students and one teacher were killed by fellow students. Late that year the organization received the largest donation in its history — $80 million from Joan Kroc, wife of McDonald's co-founder Ray Kroc.

In 2000 General Paul Rader retired, and with incoming General John Gowans the organization initiated its first reform in more than 100 years by allowing officers to marry outside the ranks. Following the September 11 attacks in 2001, the Salvation Army provided assistance to rescue workers and families affected by the tragedy through its Disaster Relief Fund.

In 2003 Joan B. Croc left the Salvation Army a $1.5 billion donation. Receiving one of the largest individual charitable gifts ever was a boon for the Salvation Army's future, but the battles continue. The money is earmarked for community centers and cannot be used to support the Army's existing programs, so ask not for whom the bell tolls.

EXECUTIVES
Chairman National Advisory Board: Edsel Ford
General (International Director): John Larsson
Commissioner (National Commander): W. Todd Bassett, age 64, $28,000 pay
Commissioner (Eastern Territory): Lawrence Moretz
Commissioner (Southern Territory): Philip Needham
Commissioner (Central Territory): Kenneth Baillie
Commissioner (Western Territory): Linda Bond
Commissioner (National President Women's Organizations): Carol Bassett
National Chief Secretary: Larry Bosh

LOCATIONS

HQ: The Salvation Army National Corporation
615 Slaters Ln., Alexandria, VA 22313
Phone: 703-684-5500 **Fax:** 703-684-3478
Web: www.salvationarmyusa.org

Salvation Army USA operates service centers, local churches, and social service programs and facilities throughout the US and provides disaster relief worldwide.

PRODUCTS/OPERATIONS

Selected Services

Alcohol and drug treatment centers
Clinics and hospitals
Convalescent homes
Counseling
Crisis counseling
Food distribution centers
Handicapped housing
Homeless shelters
Institutes for the blind
Leprosy clinics
Military canteens and hostels
Nurseries and day care centers
Occupational centers
Prison ministry
Probation housing
Refugee centers
Science and trade schools
Student housing
Welfare aid

HISTORICAL FINANCIALS

Company Type: Not-for-profit

Income Statement
FYE: September 30

	REVENUE ($ mil.)	NET INCOME ($ mil.)	NET PROFIT MARGIN	EMPLOYEES
9/03	3,040	—	—	42,530
9/02	2,497	—	—	40,000
9/01	2,313	—	—	45,000
9/00	1,803	—	—	45,096
9/99	1,707	—	—	43,318
9/98	2,078	—	—	39,883
9/97	2,525	—	—	40,770
9/96	2,070	—	—	44,626
9/95	1,421	—	—	38,999
9/94	1,355	—	—	39,591
Annual Growth	9.4%	—	—	0.8%

Revenue History

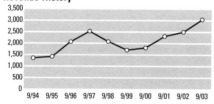

Sammons Enterprises

Sammons Enterprises summons its revenues from several sources. The diversified holding company's interests include insurance (Midland National Life Insurance and North American Company for Life and Health Insurance), and heavy equipment sales and rentals (Briggs Equipment). Sammons Enterprises also owns The Grove Park Inn Resort in Asheville, North Carolina. The late Charles Sammons, an orphan who became a billionaire philanthropist, founded the company in 1962. His estate still owns the company, and his widow, Elaine Sammons, serves as chairman.

Sammons Enterprises continues to expand its horizons. Majority-owned private equity firm Sponsor Investments was launched in 2003; it has invested in North American Technologies Group's TieTek unit and is eyeing the Asia-Pacific region as a potential target area.

EXECUTIVES

Chairman: Elaine D. Sammons
President and CEO: Robert W. Korba
COO: Robert W. Black, age 44
EVP Corporate Development: John Washburn
SVP Finance and Treasurer: Joseph A. Ethridge
VP Organization Development: Bob Kendall
VP Real Estate: Bill Daves
VP, Secretary, and General Counsel: Heather Kreager
VP Taxes: Pamela Doeppe
Chairman and CEO, Sammons Financial Group: Michael M. (Mike) Masterson
President and COO, Sammons Financial Group: John J. Craig II
Controller: Laura Gullo
Auditors: PricewaterhouseCoopers LLP

LOCATIONS

HQ: Sammons Enterprises, Inc.
5949 Sherry Ln., Ste. 1900, Dallas, TX 75225
Phone: 214-210-5000 **Fax:** 214-210-5099
Web: www.sammonsenterprises.com

Sammons Enterprises and its subsidiaries have operations all across the US.

COMPETITORS

CIGNA
MetLife
NationsRent
NES Rentals
Nestlé
New York Life
Principal Financial
Prudential
Suntory
United Rentals
Vermont Pure

HISTORICAL FINANCIALS

Company Type: Private

Income Statement
FYE: December 31

	REVENUE ($ mil.)	NET INCOME ($ mil.)	NET PROFIT MARGIN	EMPLOYEES
12/03	1,969	—	—	3,250
12/02	1,950	—	—	3,200
12/01	1,510	—	—	3,000
12/00	1,934	—	—	3,000
12/99	2,000	—	—	2,300
12/98	1,725	—	—	3,250
12/97	1,580	—	—	2,300
12/96	1,600	—	—	2,300
12/95	1,300	—	—	3,300
12/94	1,300	—	—	1,640
Annual Growth	4.7%	—	—	7.9%

Revenue History

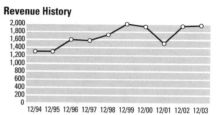

Santa Monica Ford

You can get a new car from Santa Monica Ford if the other Santa doesn't bring one. Santa Monica Ford is one of the top-selling Ford dealers in the US, selling some 40,000 vehicles a year. The dealership sells new Ford cars and trucks, with most of its business from fleet sales (mass quantities to corporate customers). Santa Monica Ford also operates a parts and service department and a body shop. Established in 1948, Santa Monica Ford offers a customer satisfaction program that includes surveys, follow-up phone calls, and keep-in-touch letters. President Ronald Davis owns the company.

EXECUTIVES

President: Ronald (Ron) Davis
Controller: Linda Jordan

LOCATIONS

HQ: Santa Monica Ford
1230 Santa Monica Blvd., Santa Monica, CA 90404
Phone: 310-451-1588 **Fax:** 310-394-8115
Web: www.samoford.com

COMPETITORS

AutoNation
David Wilson's
Galpin Motors

Sonic Automotive
Tuttle-Click

HISTORICAL FINANCIALS

Company Type: Private

Income Statement			FYE: December 31
	REVENUE ($ mil.)	NET INCOME ($ mil.)	NET PROFIT MARGIN	EMPLOYEES
12/03	800	—	—	85
12/02	800	—	—	90
12/01	800	—	—	100
12/00	800	—	—	100
12/99	750	—	—	100
12/98	582	—	—	100
12/97	510	—	—	100
12/96	550	—	—	100
12/95	572	—	—	100
12/94	442	—	—	96
Annual Growth	6.8%	—	—	(1.3%)

Revenue History

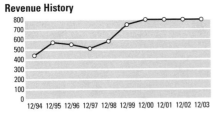

Sargento

Sargento Foods doesn't milk the cows or stir the curds, but it does shred, package, and market mozzarella, cheddar, and other cheeses made to its own specifications. By turning cheese into value-added products such as recipe-ready shredded cheese blends and sliced cheeses for sandwiches, Sargento has been successful in the shadow of cheese giant Kraft Foods, and even offers the official cheese of Lambeau Field. Its foodservice product line includes appetizers, cheese ingredients, and sauces. It also sells high-end specialty cheeses via catalog and the Internet. Historically innovative (it was the first to package shredded cheese), Sargento was founded in 1953 and is owned and operated by the Gentine family.

EXECUTIVES

Chairman and CEO: Louis (Lou) Gentine
CFO: George Hoff
EVP, Operations: Mark Rhyan
SVP, Human Resources: Karri Neils
SVP, Marketing: Brad Flatoff
SVP, New Business Development: Davide Vroom
SVP, Treasurer: Marcy Stanczyk
Chief Customer Officer: Robert (Bob) Clouston
President, Consumer Products Division:
  Michael (Mike) Gordy
President, Food Ingredients Division: Kevin Delahunt
President, Food Service Division: Sam Colson
VP, Controller: James (Jim) Birenbaum
VP, Corporate & Marketing Communications:
  Barbara Gannon

LOCATIONS

HQ: Sargento Foods Inc.
  1 Persnickety Place, Plymouth, WI 53073
Phone: 920-893-8484   **Fax:** 920-893-8399
Web: www.sargentocheese.com

Sargento Foods has four facilities in Wisconsin.

COMPETITORS

Bel/Kaukauna
ConAgra
Kraft Foods
Land O'Lakes
Lucille Farms
Marathon Cheese
Saputo
Schreiber Foods

HISTORICAL FINANCIALS

Company Type: Private

Income Statement			FYE: December 30
	REVENUE ($ mil.)	NET INCOME ($ mil.)	NET PROFIT MARGIN	EMPLOYEES
6/03	534	—	—	1,300
6/02	550	—	—	1,300
6/01	484	—	—	1,100
6/00	400	—	—	1,000
6/99	335	—	—	1,000
6/98	330	—	—	1,000
Annual Growth	10.1%	—	—	5.4%

Revenue History

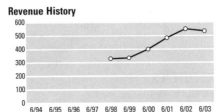

SAS Institute

Don't talk back to this company about business intelligence. SAS (pronounced "sass"), the world's largest privately held software company, leads the market in data warehousing and data mining software used to gather, manage, and analyze enormous amounts of corporate information. Clients such as Maytag, Air France, and the US Department of Defense use its software to find patterns in customer data, manage resources, and target new business. Founded in 1976, SAS also offers industry-specific integrated software and support packages. Chairman, president, and CEO James Goodnight owns about two-thirds of the company; co-founder and EVP John Sall owns the remainder.

The company continues to grow both its revenue (the company has reported some 26 consecutive years of increased sales numbers) and its product offerings. SAS introduced a variety of financial management software packages reflecting the trend, and need, for companies to maintain accurate financial records.

The acquisition of ABC Technologies and event-triggering and behavioral tracking technology from Verbind, as well as the formation of the SAS Performance Management Division in 2002 support the company's goal to lead the growth of the performance management market.

In 2003, SAS acquired OpRisk Analytics and Risk Advisory, providers of risk measurement and management products, to extend its offerings in corporate and consumer risk measurement and reporting.

SAS is also looking to marketing analysis software for future growth. The company created its Marketing & Customer Analytics business unit to develop marketing-analysis software, in addition to its existing SAS Marketing Automation program. Along with its new products, SAS continues to expand its existing business intelligence offerings.

Known for its tight-knit community, SAS offers its employees perks including two on-site child-care centers, atrium-like cafeterias, a gym, a swimming pool, walking trails, a health care center, and free M&Ms in every break room.

EXECUTIVES

Chairman, President, and CEO:
  James H. (Jim) Goodnight
EVP: John Sall
EVP and Chief Administrative Officer:
  W. Greyson Quarles Jr.
SVP and CTO: Keith V. Collins
SVP and Chief Marketing Officer: Jim Davis
VP, General Counsel, and Secretary: John Boswell
CIO and VP, Information Technology: Suzanne Gordon
VP, Financial Services Practice: Mark Moorman
VP, US Commercial Sales, SAS Americas: Kelly Ross
President, SAS International: Art Cooke
Corporate Public Relations: John Dornan

LOCATIONS

HQ: SAS Institute Inc.
  100 SAS Campus Dr., Cary, NC 27513
Phone: 919-677-8000   **Fax:** 919-677-4444
Web: www.sas.com

SAS Institute has 288 offices worldwide and customers in 107 countries.

2003 Sales

	% of total
North America	46
EMEA	43
Asia/Pacific	9
Latin America	2
Total	**100**

PRODUCTS/OPERATIONS

2003 Sales by Industry

	% of total
Business	73
Education	17
Government	10
Total	**100**

Selected Software

Customer relationship management
Data analysis
Data mining
Data warehousing
E-commerce
Enterprise performance management
Experimental design
Financial management
Human resources management
Information technology systems management
Management science
Patent discovery and analysis
Portfolio analysis
Process management
Project planning and management
Quality improvement
Warranty analysis
Risk Management
Statistical analysis
Supplier relationship management
Supply chain analysis
Web traffic analysis

COMPETITORS

Ascential Software	Information Builders
Business Objects	Insightful
Cognos	Microsoft
Computer Associates	MicroStrategy
E.piphany	Oracle
Hummingbird	SPSS
Hyperion	Sybase
IBM	Teradata

HISTORICAL FINANCIALS

Company Type: Private

Income Statement
FYE: December 31

	REVENUE ($ mil.)	NET INCOME ($ mil.)	NET PROFIT MARGIN	EMPLOYEES
12/03	1,340	—	—	9,306
12/02	1,180	—	—	9,023
12/01	1,130	—	—	8,636
12/00	1,120	—	—	8,500
12/99	1,020	—	—	6,400
12/98	871	—	—	5,400
12/97	750	—	—	5,108
12/96	653	—	—	4,500
12/95	562	—	—	4,138
12/94	482	—	—	3,260
Annual Growth	12.0%	—	—	12.4%

Revenue History

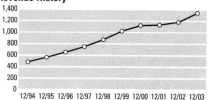

Sauder Woodworking

Sauder Woodworking takes the fear out of furniture and makes furniture for the God-fearing. The firm is the #1 US maker of ready-to-assemble (RTA) furniture (ahead of Bush Industries and O'Sullivan Industries) and, through Sauder Manufacturing, is also a top maker of church furniture and institutional seating. RTA products include computer workstations, desks, entertainment centers, and wardrobes. Subsidiary Archbold Container makes corrugated packaging and displays. Sauder's products are sold through retailers in more than 70 countries. In 2001 Sauder acquired Progressive Furniture, which makes fully assembled furniture. The company was founded in 1934 by Erie Sauder and is still family owned and operated.

EXECUTIVES

Chairman: Maynard Sauder
President and CEO: Kevin Sauder
EVP, Finance and CFO: Arnold Moshier
EVP, Marketing and Sales: John Yoder
EVP, Operations: Garrett Tinsman
VP, Engineering: Myrl Sauder
VP, Human Resources: Steve Webster
VP, Merchandising: Susan Dountas
VP, Sales: Brent Gingerich
VP, Supply Chain Management: David Yoder
Chairman, Progressive: Pete Pilliod
SVP, Operations, Progressive Furniture: Paul Manley

LOCATIONS

HQ: Sauder Woodworking Co.
502 Middle St., Archbold, OH 43502
Phone: 419-446-2711 **Fax:** 419-446-3692
Web: www.sauder.com

PRODUCTS/OPERATIONS

Selected Products

Bedroom
  Armoires
  Chests
  Chifforobes
  Dressers
  Footboards
  Headboards
  Juvenile products
  Mirrors
  Night stands
  Wardrobes
Entertainment
  Audiovisual cabinets
  Corner units
  Entertainment centers and armoires
  TV/VCR carts and stands
Kitchen/Utility
  Buffet storage products
  Chair-side tables
  Cocktail tables
  End tables
  Telephone stands
  Utility carts
Office/Computer
  Computer armoires, carts, and desks
  File cabinets
  Workstations
Shelving/Storage
  Bookcases
  Storage cabinets

COMPETITORS

Bassett Furniture	Herman Miller
Bush Industries	HNI
Chromcraft Revington	IKEA
DMI Furniture	Jami
Dorel Industries	O'Sullivan Industries
Furniture Brands International	Stanley Furniture
Haworth	Steelcase

HISTORICAL FINANCIALS

Company Type: Private

Income Statement
FYE: December 31

	REVENUE ($ mil.)	NET INCOME ($ mil.)	NET PROFIT MARGIN	EMPLOYEES
12/02	700	—	—	3,500
12/01	700	—	—	3,500
12/00	700	—	—	3,950
12/99	565	—	—	3,900
12/98	545	—	—	3,200
12/97	500	—	—	3,300
12/96	500	—	—	3,200
12/95	467	—	—	3,200
12/94	445	—	—	3,200
Annual Growth	5.8%	—	—	1.1%

Revenue History

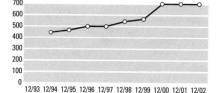

Save Mart

Save Mart Supermarkets is one of the big wheels in the California grocery business. A sponsor of the NASCAR Dodge/Save Mart 350, the company has more than 120 grocery stores in Northern and Central California. Its supermarkets and warehouse stores operate under the S-Mart, Save Mart Foods, and Food Maxx banners. The chain has been trying out different formats, including an upscale prototype with its own coffeehouse and expanded offerings of ethnic and organic foods and its popular private-label salad mix line, Fresh Favorites. Save Mart also owns distributor SMART Refrigerated Transport. CEO Robert Piccinini owns most of Save Mart, which was founded in 1952 by his father, Mike Piccinini, and uncle, Nick Tocco.

Save Mart grew its sales and store count in 2003 with the acquisition of 25 Food 4 Less stores from bankrupt grocery distributor Fleming Companies, which were quickly converted to the Food Maxx banner.

EXECUTIVES

Chairman and CEO: Robert M. (Bob) Piccinini, age 61
President and COO: Bob Spengler
VP, CFO and CIO: Ronald (Ron) Riesenbeck
VP, Human Resources and Law: Mike Silveira
VP, FoodMaxx: Art Patch
VP, Operations: Steve Junqueiro
VP, Real Estate: Jim Watt
Controller: Steve Ackerman
Director, Marketing: Sally Sanborn

LOCATIONS

HQ: Save Mart Supermarkets
1800 Standiford Ave., Modesto, CA 95350
Phone: 209-577-1600 **Fax:** 209-577-3857

COMPETITORS

Albertson's
Costco Wholesale
Kroger
Longs Drug
Raley's
Ralphs
Rite Aid
Safeway
Smart & Final
Trader Joe's
Vons
Wal-Mart

S.C. Johnson

S.C. Johnson & Son helped consumers move from the flyswatter to the spray can. The company is one of the world's largest makers of consumer chemical products. These include Drano-brand drain cleaner, Glade air freshener, Johnson floor wax, OFF! insect repellent, Pledge furniture polish, Raid insecticide, Shout stain remover, Windex window cleaner, and Ziploc plastic bags. The founder's great-grandson and once one of the richest men in the US, Samuel Johnson died in May 2004. His immediate family owns about 60% of S.C. Johnson; descendants of the founder's daughter own about 40%.

Many of S.C. Johnson's products have been and remain top sellers in their market categories. The company has operations in nearly 70 countries and its products are available in more than 100. In 2003 *Working Mother* magazine recognized S.C. Johnson as one of the 100 best companies for working mothers.

The company's commercial products division (Johnson Wax Professional and Johnson Polymer) has been spun off as a private company owned by the Johnson family. The company also has sold most of its personal care line.

HISTORY

Samuel C. Johnson, a carpenter whose customers were as interested in his floor wax as in his parquet floors, founded S.C. Johnson in Racine, Wisconsin, in 1886. Forsaking carpentry, Johnson began to manufacture floor care products. The company, named S.C. Johnson & Son in 1906, began establishing subsidiaries worldwide in 1914. By the time Johnson's son and successor, Herbert Johnson, died in 1928, annual sales were $5 million. Herbert Jr. and his sister, Henrietta Lewis, received 60% and 40% of the firm, respectively. The original section of S.C. Johnson's headquarters, designed by Frank Lloyd Wright and called "the greatest piece of 20th-century architecture" in the US, was finished in 1939.

In 1954, with $45 million in annual sales, Herbert Jr.'s son Samuel Curtis Johnson joined the company as new products director. Two years later it introduced Raid, the first water-based insecticide, and soon thereafter, OFF! insect repellent. Each became a market leader. The company unsuccessfully attempted to diversify into paint, chemicals, and lawn care during the 1950s and 1960s. The home care products segment prospered, however, with the introduction of Pledge aerosol furniture polish and Glade aerosol air freshener.

After Herbert Jr. suffered a stroke in 1965, Samuel became president. In 1975 the firm banned the use of the chlorofluorocarbons (CFCs) in its products, three years before the US government banned CFCs. Samuel started a recreational products division that was bought by the Johnson family in 1986. That company went public in 1987 as Johnson Worldwide Associates, with the family retaining control.

The company launched Edge shaving gel and Agree hair products in the 1970s but had few products as successful in the 1980s. It moved into real estate with Johnson Wax Development (JWD) in the 1970s, but sold JWD's assets in the late 1980s.

S. Curtis Johnson, Samuel's son, joined the company in 1983. In 1986 S.C. Johnson bought Bugs Burger Bug Killers, moving into commercial pest control; in 1990 it entered into an agreement with Mycogen to develop biological pesticides for household use.

In 1993 it bought Drackett, bringing Drano and Windex to its product roster along with increased competition from heavyweights such as Procter & Gamble and Clorox. That year S.C. Johnson sold the Agree and Halsa lines to DEP. In 1996 it launched a line of water-soluble pouches for cleaning products that allow work to be done without touching hazardous chemicals. President William Perez became CEO the next year.

S.C. Johnson bought Dow Chemical's DowBrands unit, maker of bathroom cleaner (Dow), plastic bags (Ziploc), and plastic wrap (Saran Wrap), for $1.2 billion in 1998. It then sold off other Dow brands (cleaners Spray 'N Wash, Glass Plus, Yes, and Vivid) to the UK's Reckitt & Colman to settle antitrust issues.

A year later S.C. Johnson sold its skin care line, including Aveeno, to health care products maker Johnson & Johnson, and spun off its commercial products unit as a private firm owned by the Johnson family. Boosting its home cleaning line, in 1999 it introduced two new products: AllerCare (for dust mite control) and Pledge Grab-It (electrostatically charged cleaning sheets).

In 2000 S.C. Johnson pulled its AllerCare carpet powder and allergen spray from store shelves after some consumers had negative reactions to the fragrance additive in the products. That year H. Fisk Johnson succeeded his father (who became chairman emeritus) as chairman. (Chairman Emeritus Samuel Curtis Johnson died in May 2004.)

In 2001 the company was fined $950,000 for selling banned Raid Max Roach Bait traps in New York after agreeing to pull them from store shelves. Also that year S.C. Johnson's Japanese subsidiary agreed to buy that country's leading drain cleaner brand, Pipe Unish, from Unicharm.

In October 2002 the company acquired the household insecticides unit of German drug giant Bayer Group for $734 million.

HISTORICAL FINANCIALS

Company Type: Private

Income Statement
FYE: March 31

	REVENUE ($ mil.)	NET INCOME ($ mil.)	NET PROFIT MARGIN	EMPLOYEES
3/03	1,655	—	—	7,400
3/02	1,600	—	—	7,300
3/01	1,524	—	—	7,200
3/00	1,468	—	—	7,000
3/99	1,452	—	—	7,200
3/98	1,300	—	—	7,003
3/97	1,200	—	—	6,400
3/96	1,135	—	—	5,864
3/95	1,130	—	—	6,062
3/94	1,130	—	—	6,265
Annual Growth	4.3%	—	—	1.9%

Revenue History

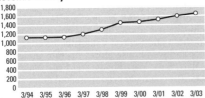

EXECUTIVES

Chairman: H. Fisk Johnson, age 44
President, CEO, and Director: William D. (Bill) Perez, age 56
President, Americas: Pedro Cieza
President, Asia: Steven P. Stanbrook, age 46
President, North America: David L. May
SVP and CFO: W. Lee McCollum, age 54
SVP, General Counsel and Secretary: David Hecker
SVP, Research, Development and Engineering: Richard S. Hutchings
SVP, Worldwide Corporate Affairs: Jane M. Hutterly
SVP, Worldwide Human Resources: Gayle P. Kosterman
SVP, Worldwide Manufacturing and Procurement: Darcy D. Massey
SVP, Worldwide Manufacturing and Procurement: Nico J. Meiland
VP, Corporate Tax Counsel: Robert S. Randleman
VP and Area Director - ASEAN: Frank F. Guerra
VP and CIO: Daniel E. Horton
VP and Corporate Treasurer: William H. Van Lopik
VP and Group Managing Director - Europe: Filippo Meroni
VP, Marketing Services - Worldwide: Ralph D. Perry
VP, North American Sales: Darwin Lewis
Director, Global Public Affairs and Communications: Kelly M. Semrau

LOCATIONS

HQ: S.C. Johnson & Son, Inc.
1525 Howe St., Racine, WI 53403
Phone: 262-260-2000   **Fax:** 262-260-6004
Web: www.scjohnson.com

S.C. Johnson & Son has operations in nearly 70 countries worldwide.

PRODUCTS/OPERATIONS

Selected Products and Brands

Air Care
  Air freshener (Glade, Glade Duet)
  Pillow and mattress covers (AllerCare)
Home Cleaning
  Bathroom/drain (Drano, Scrubbing Bubbles, Vanish, Dow)
  Cleaners (Fantastik, Windex, Windex Multi-Surface Cleaner with Vinegar)
  Floor care (Pledge, Pledge Grab-It, Johnson)
  Furniture care (Pledge, Pledge Wipes, Pledge Grab-it Dry Dusting Mitts)
  Laundry/carpet care (Shout)
Home Storage
  Plastic bags (Ziploc)
  Plastic wrap (Handi-Wrap, Saran Wrap)
Insect Control
  Insecticides (Raid, Raid Max)
  Repellents (Deep Woods OFF!, OFF!, OFF! Mosquito Lamp, OFF! Skintastic)

COMPETITORS

3M
Alticor
Blyth
Church & Dwight
Clorox
Colgate-Palmolive
Dial
DuPont
Gillette
Henkel
IWP International
Procter & Gamble
Reckitt Benckiser
Shaklee
Unilever
United Industries
Yankee Candle

HISTORICAL FINANCIALS

Company Type: Private

Income Statement — FYE: Friday nearest June 30

	ESTIMATED REVENUE ($ mil.)	NET INCOME ($ mil.)	NET PROFIT MARGIN	EMPLOYEES
6/04	6,500	—	—	12,000
6/03	5,370	—	—	12,000
6/02	5,000	—	—	10,700
6/01	4,500	—	—	9,500
6/00	4,200	—	—	9,500
6/99	4,200	—	—	9,500
6/98	5,000	—	—	13,200
6/97	4,300	—	—	12,500
6/96	4,000	—	—	12,100
6/95	4,000	—	—	13,400
Annual Growth	5.5%	—	—	(1.2%)

Revenue History

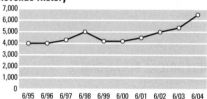

Schneider National

If you think that's the Great Pumpkin behind you, look again. With its signature bright-orange fleet of about 15,000 trucks and 47,000 trailers, Schneider National is one of the top truckload carriers in the US. The company's Schneider National Carriers unit provides truckload service throughout North America, including one-way van, expedited, dedicated, and intermodal offerings, as well as truck brokerage. Schneider Bulk Carriers transports liquid chemicals, and Schneider Specialized Carriers concentrates on the industrial glass industry. The company's Schneider Finance unit sells and leases commercial truck equipment. Schneider Logistics offers supply chain management services.

Not content to rely on its truckload business, Schneider National is expanding its intermodal offerings — freight transportation by a combination of road and rail — through a partnership with Burlington Northern Santa Fe. The company hopes to include other railroads in its intermodal business.

Schneider National is known for being an early adopter of new transportation technology — it was one of the first carriers to link all its trucks by two-way satellite. More recently, the company has invested in an in-cab e-mail system to help drivers stay in touch with their families. Schneider National plans to install global positioning units in its trailers in order to keep closer track of shipments.

Chairman and former CEO Don Schneider, son of the company's founder, is among its shareholders. He doesn't disclose how much of the company he owns.

HISTORY

A. J. "Al" Schneider bought a truck in 1935 with money earned from selling the family car. He drove the truck for three years, got another, and then leased them both to another firm. Becoming general manager of Bins Transfer & Storage in 1938, Schneider bought the company that year and changed the name to Schneider Transport & Storage. In 1944 Schneider stopped storing household goods and continued as an intrastate carrier in Wisconsin through the 1950s, transporting food and household goods. The Interstate Commerce Commission granted its first interstate license to Schneider in 1958.

Al's son Donald joined the company as general manager in 1961, and in 1962 the company dropped "Storage" from its name to become Schneider Transport. The 1960s also saw the first of many acquisitions. Donald became CEO in 1973, overseeing more acquisitions and the creation of Schneider National as a holding company for the organization. Donald also saw to the installation of computerized control systems, the first of many technical innovations Schneider would use in its trucks.

With the Motor Carrier Act's passage in 1980, restrictions eased and interstate shipping opened up. Schneider (and its competitors) saw the sky as the limit and founded Schneider Communications, a long-distance provider, in 1982. Eager to escape the Teamsters' thrall but choosing not to go head-to-head with the powerful union, Schneider formed Schneider National Carriers as a nonunion company out of three 1985 acquisitions, which signed on new recruits, while Schneider Transport remained unionized. Schneider focused on guaranteeing on-time delivery in the deregulated market: In 1988 Schneider became the first trucking company to install a satellite-tracking system in its trucks, setting the industry standard.

Schneider further expanded its services in the 1990s, starting with Schneider Specialized Services for carrying difficult items. It moved into Canada and Mexico in 1991. By 1993 some two-thirds of *FORTUNE* 500 companies used Schneider, and the company formed Schneider Logistics to help companies streamline their shipping operations. It sold Schneider Communications to Frontier Communications in 1995. The company moved into Europe in 1997.

It continued buying other US trucking firms, including Landstar Poole and Builder's Transport (both in 1998), mainly to acquire their drivers for its expanding fleet. In 1999 Schneider acquired the glass-transportation business of A. J. Metler & Rigging.

In 2000 Schneider acquired the freight payment services of Tranzact Systems and further boosted its e-commerce offerings through alliances with ContractorHub.com and Paperloop.com. The company also made plans to spin off Schneider Logistics and sell part of it to the public, but unfavorable market conditions put the IPO on hold. Schneider added expedited services to its portfolio in 2001 to provide time-definite delivery in Canada, Mexico, and the US.

Christopher Lofgren's promotion to president and CEO in 2002 made him the first person outside the founding family to lead the company.

EXECUTIVES

Chairman: Donald J. (Don) Schneider, age 68
President and CEO: Christopher B. (Chris) Lofgren
CFO: Thomas A. (Tom) Gannon
CIO: Steve Matheys
VP Application Development: Bob Grawien
VP Capacity Development and Safety: Don Osterberg
VP Corporate Marketing: Thomas (Tom) Nightingale
VP Human Resources: Tim Fliss
VP Litigation: Frank Stackhouse
VP Technology Services: Paul Mueller
President, Financial Services: Richard Palmieri
President, Schneider Logistics: Thomas I. (Tom) Escott
President, Transportation Services: Scott Arves
VP and General Manager, Intermodal Services: Brian Bowers
VP and General Manager, Schneider Brokerage: Mark Rourke
VP, Schneider Logistics Payment Services: Philip Morse
VP Sales, Transportation Services: Mark DePrey
VP Sales, Mexico: Will Chang
Corporate Counsel: Charlotte Klenke

LOCATIONS

HQ: Schneider National, Inc.
3101 S. Packerland Dr., Green Bay, WI 54306
Phone: 920-592-2000   **Fax:** 920-592-3063
Web: www.schneider.com

PRODUCTS/OPERATIONS

Selected Operating Units

Schneider Finance (commercial financing and leasing services)
Schneider Logistics, Inc. (supply chain management services)
Schneider Bulk Carriers (liquid chemical transport services)
Schneider National Carriers (full-truckload service, including intermodal, brokerage, expedited services, dedicated transport, and one-way van transport)
Schneider Specialized Carriers (open equipment transportation, specializing in industrial glass transport)

COMPETITORS

Burlington Northern Santa Fe	Landstar System
C.H. Robinson Worldwide	Norfolk Southern
CNF	Ryder
Crete Carrier	Swift Transportation
CSX	Union Pacific
J. B. Hunt	U.S. Xpress
	Werner Enterprises

HISTORICAL FINANCIALS

Company Type: Private

Income Statement — FYE: December 31

	REVENUE ($ mil.)	NET INCOME ($ mil.)	NET PROFIT MARGIN	EMPLOYEES
12/03	2,900	—	—	20,733
12/02	2,627	—	—	20,756
12/01	2,388	—	—	19,349
12/00	3,089	—	—	18,775
12/99	3,000	—	—	19,000
12/98	2,711	—	—	17,000
12/97	2,510	—	—	16,500
12/96	2,156	—	—	17,550
12/95	1,700	—	—	15,500
12/94	1,325	—	—	15,300
Annual Growth	9.1%	—	—	3.4%

Revenue History

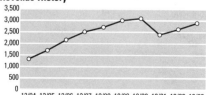

Schnuck Markets

If you'll meet me in St. Louis, then chances are there'll be a Schnuck Market in sight. The region's largest food chain, Schnuck Markets operates about 100 stores, mostly in the St. Louis area, but also in other parts of Missouri and in Illinois, Indiana, Tennessee, and Wisconsin. All stores offer a full line of groceries, and most have pharmacies, video rental outlets, in-store banking, and florist shops. Although most stores operate under the Schnuck banner, the company also runs several Logli supermarkets and a Sentry Drug in Illinois. The company acquired 12 Seessel's stores in Memphis from Albertson's in 2002. Founded in 1939, the company is owned by the Schnuck family.

The regional grocery chain is expanding into Iowa with a 65,000-square-foot store scheduled to open there in 2005.

EXECUTIVES

Chairman and CEO: Craig D. Schnuck, age 55
President and COO: Scott C. Schnuck, age 54
SVP, Logistics, Manufacturing and Information Technology: Robert (Bob) Drury
SVP, Marketing and Merchandising: Randy Wedel
SVP, Store Operations: William (Bill) Bredenkoetter
VP and CFO: Todd R. Schnuck
VP, Deli, Seafood and Carryout: Ed Meyer
VP, Human Resources: William (Bill) Jones
VP, Labor Relations: Robert J. Flacke
VP, Meat Merchandising: Cy Jansen
VP, Produce: Michael (Mike) O'Brien
VP, Shopping Center Development: Mark Schnuck
VP, Supermarket Development: Gordon Lyons
Secretary and General Counsel: Mary Moorkamp
Director, Communication: Lori Willis

LOCATIONS

HQ: Schnuck Markets, Inc.
  11420 Lackland Rd., St. Louis, MO 63146
Phone: 314-994-9900   **Fax:** 314-994-4465
Web: www.schnucks.com

2003 Stores

	No.
Missouri	60
Illinois	21
Tennessee	10
Wisconsin	4
Indiana	5
Total	**100**

COMPETITORS

7-Eleven
AWG
CVS
Dierbergs Markets
Dominick's
Hy-Vee
Kmart
Kroger
Meijer
SUPERVALU
Walgreen
Wal-Mart

HISTORICAL FINANCIALS

Company Type: Private

Income Statement   FYE: October 31

	ESTIMATED REVENUE ($ mil.)	NET INCOME ($ mil.)	NET PROFIT MARGIN	EMPLOYEES
10/03	2,200	—	—	16,500
10/02	2,107	—	—	18,000
10/01	2,000	—	—	16,000
10/00	2,100	—	—	17,000
10/99	2,010	—	—	16,000
10/98	1,800	—	—	16,000
10/97	1,800	—	—	16,000
10/96	1,700	—	—	16,000
10/95	1,600	—	—	15,500
10/94	1,200	—	—	12,000
Annual Growth	7.0%	—	—	3.6%

Revenue History

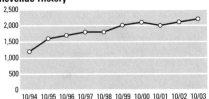

Schreiber Foods

If you order cheese on that burger, you might well get a taste of Schreiber Foods. The cheese processor is a major supplier of the cheese used on hamburgers by US fast-food restaurants. Schreiber primarily produces private-label processed and natural cheese for retailers, food-service distributors, and food manufacturers. Its few retail brands include American Heritage, Cache Valley, and Cooper. The company has bought up smaller cheese operations to expand it geographic reach and is now the leading private-label cream cheese maker. Founded in 1945, Schreiber opted in 1999 to transfer ownership into an employee stock ownership plan.

EXECUTIVES

Chairman: John C. (Jack) Meng, age 59
President and CEO: Larry P. Ferguson
CFO: Brian Liddy
SVP, Information Services: Frederick Parker
VP, Industrial & Regulatory Affairs: Deborah Van Dyk

LOCATIONS

HQ: Schreiber Foods, Inc.
  425 Pine St., Green Bay, WI 54301
Phone: 920-437-7601   **Fax:** 920-437-1617
Web: www.sficorp.com

Schreiber Foods has production facilities in Arizona, Georgia, Missouri, Pennsylvania, Texas, Utah, and Wisconsin, as well as in Germany, Brazil, and Mexico. It has joint ventures with companies in France, India, and Saudi Arabia.

PRODUCTS/OPERATIONS

Subsidiaries
Capri Packaging (packaging films)
Green Bay Machinery (cheese slicing and wrapping equipment)

Brands
American Heritage
Cache Valley
Clearfield
Cooper
Level Valley
Raskas
Schreiber

COMPETITORS

AMPI
Bongrain
Dairy Farmers of America
Foremost Farms
Fromageries Bel
Great Lakes Cheese
Kraft Foods
Land O'Lakes
Leprino Foods
Lucille Farms
Saputo
Sargento
WestFarm Foods

HISTORICAL FINANCIALS

Company Type: Private

Income Statement   FYE: September 30

	ESTIMATED REVENUE ($ mil.)	NET INCOME ($ mil.)	NET PROFIT MARGIN	EMPLOYEES
9/03	2,000	—	—	4,200
9/02	1,450	—	—	4,400
9/01	1,350	—	—	3,100
9/00	1,300	—	—	3,000
9/99	1,160	—	—	2,600
9/98	1,100	—	—	2,600
9/97	1,400	—	—	2,600
9/96	1,375	—	—	2,300
9/95	1,320	—	—	2,400
9/94	1,300	—	—	2,400
Annual Growth	4.9%	—	—	6.4%

Revenue History

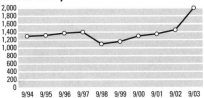

Schwan Food

Frozen pizza is the flashy part of The Schwan Food Company. With well-known pizza brands such as Tony's, Red Baron, and Freschetta, the company is the #2 frozen-pizza maker in the US, behind Kraft Foods. Schwan is also a top supplier to the institutional frozen-pizza market and has operations in Europe. But pizza isn't the only slice of the company's revenue — its core business is a fleet of home-delivery trucks. Schwan delivers casseroles, ice cream, and frozen foods to homes in the continental US. The family of late founder Marvin Schwan owns the company.

With its unintentionally retro-hip freezer delivery trucks, The Schwan Food Company is definitely cool. The company maintains a home-delivery system that brings more than 300 frozen food products directly to customers in 48 mainland states. Orders can include bagels or pancakes, and Schwan's ice cream has a devoted following.

The company's frozen pizza has almost 30% of the US market share (Kraft has almost 40%). Schwan's pizza is aboard Air Force One. In addition to its US pizza market, Schwan sells Freschetta and Chicago Town pizzas in Western Europe and supplies schools and other institutional cafeterias with frozen pizza and sandwiches. Another Schwan unit produces food manufacturing equipment and systems to convert vehicles to using liquid propane.

In conjunction with its Red Baron pizza brand, Schwan owns and operates the #1 civilian airshow act in the world, featuring the Red Baron Stearman Squadron, a formation aerobatics team that performs using vintage Stearman biplanes.

Exploring new customer bases, in 2004 the company started a mail-order delivery operation for sending food gifts under the name Impromptu Gourmet.

The Schwan family is notoriously secretive (Marvin Schwan himself gave no interviews after 1982).

HISTORY

Paul Schwan bought out his partner in their dairy in 1948 and began manufacturing ice cream using his own recipes. His son, Marvin Schwan, made deliveries for the dairy for a few years. After attending a two-year college, Marvin came back in 1950 to work at the dairy full-time. Two years later he began using his delivery experience to take advantage of the increase in homes with freezers. He bought an old truck for $100 and began a rural route selling ice cream to farmers. He quickly developed a loyal customer base and expanded to two routes the following year.

In the 1960s the company diversified with two acquisitions: a prepared sandwich company and a condensed fruit juice company. A new holding company, Schwan's Sales Enterprises, was established in 1964. Schwan's began delivering pizza the next year. Paul died in 1969.

Deciding that frozen pizza was not a fad, Marvin bought Kansas-based Tony's Pizza in 1970 and quickly rose to the top of the new industry. In the late 1970s Schwan's entered the commercial leasing business, and it later added more leasing companies under the Lyon Financial Services umbrella (sold 2000).

The company entered the institutional-pizza market in the mid-1980s and bought out competitors Sabatasso Foods and Better Baked Pizza. Schools liked Schwan's use of their government surplus cheese to make pizzas, which the company then sold to the schools at a discount.

In 1992 the company bought two Minnesota-based food companies: Panzerotti, a stuffed pastry business, and Monthly Market, a specialty retailer that sells groceries to fund-raising groups. It also began selling its pizzas in the UK. The next year Schwan's bought Chicago Brothers Frozen Pizza, a San Diego-based company specializing in deep-dish pizza.

Marvin died of a heart attack in 1993 at age 64, with his worth estimated at more than $1 billion. The previous year he had willed two-thirds of the company's stock to a charitable Lutheran trust, which was to be bought out by Schwan's after his death. In 1994 his brother, Alfred, and Marvin's friend Lawrence Burgdorf made arrangements to have the company repurchase the foundation's shares for a total of $1.8 billion. But Marvin's four children filed a lawsuit in 1995 against their uncle and Burgdorf over the action. They claimed the men did not have the financial health of the company at heart and were divided in their loyalty. The children, on the other hand, were called money-hungry and callous to their father's last wishes. (The case was settled in 1997, but no information was released.)

In 1994 more than 200,000 people in 28 states contracted salmonella food poisoning after eating *E. coli*-tainted Schwan's ice cream. The company's insurance company eventually paid out nearly $1 million to about 6,000 affected customers in exchange for their signing releases promising they would not sue Schwan's.

Lenny Pippin became the company's fourth CEO in 1999, replacing Alfred, who stayed on as chairman. Schwan's exited the Canadian market at the end of 1999 due to perennial losses. In 2000 Schwan's introduced irradiated frozen ground-beef patties, struck an agreement with another company to electronically pasteurize some of its products, and sold the assets and trademarks of its Chicago Brothers food operations.

In mid-2001 Schwan's expanded its offerings by acquiring frozen-dessert maker Edwards Fine Foods from private equity firm Ripplewood Holdings. In early 2002 the company sold off its Orion Food Systems fast-food subsidiary to Kohlberg Investors. That year Schwan joined the food industry trend toward handheld convenience foods by introducing a microwaveable, single-serve pizza slice designed to be eaten on the go.

The company began a reorganization of its business units and changed its name from Schwan's Sales Enterprises to The Schwan Food Company in early 2003.

In April 2003 Schwan acquired the frozen-dessert business of Mrs. Smith's Bakeries from Flowers Foods for $240 million in cash. Flowers retained the frozen bread and roll dough segment of Mrs. Smith. The pies, cakes, cobblers, and pie crusts fits in well with Schwan's other products. Later that year the company launched Impromptu Gourmet, a catalog and Web site for ordering meals by mail.

EXECUTIVES

Chairman: Alfred Schwan
President and CEO: M. Lenny Pippin
EVP, Finance and CFO: Tracy Burr
EVP, Operations: Doug Olsem
EVP, Strategic Development: Dave Bunnell
EVP and COO, Schwan's Consumer Brands North America Inc.: William McCormack
EVP, Administration and General Counsel: Dave Paskach
EVP; President and COO, Food Service: Larry A. Oberkfell
EVP; President and COO, Global Consumer Brands: John Beadle
VP, Food Safety and Quality Assurance: Bill Ludwil
VP, Human Resources: Sue Beary
VP, Information Services, and CIO: Bruce Saugstad
VP and Corporate Controller: Bernadette M. Kruk
Director, Category Management Consumer Brands: Greg Hatfield
Director, E-Commerce and Emerging Channels: Glenn Bader
Director, Fund Raising and Daycare: Ryan Jackson
Brand Manager, Tony's: Laura Daley

LOCATIONS

HQ: The Schwan Food Company
115 W. College Dr., Marshall, MN 56258
Phone: 507-532-3274   **Fax:** 507-537-8226
Web: www.schwans.com

The Schwan Food Company has manufacturing facilities in the US and in Europe; its products are sold in the 48 contiguous states and Western Europe.

PRODUCTS/OPERATIONS

Selected Consumer Brands
Chicago Town (frozen pizza, UK)
Edward's Fine Foods (desserts)
Freschetta
Impromptu Gourmet (mail-order meals)
Larry's (frozen potato side dishes)
Mrs. Smith (bakery)
Pagoda Café (frozen Oriental foods)
Red Baron
Tony's

COMPETITORS

Ben & Jerry's
Blue Bell
Celentano Brothers
Colorado Prime
ConAgra
Domino's
Dreyer's
Kraft Foods
Kraft Foods North America
Little Caesar's
Luigino's
Nation Pizza Products
Nestlé
Omaha Steaks
Papa John's
Pinnacle Foods
SYSCO
YUM!

HISTORICAL FINANCIALS

Company Type: Private

Income Statement				FYE: December 31
	ESTIMATED REVENUE ($ mil.)	NET INCOME ($ mil.)	NET PROFIT MARGIN	EMPLOYEES
12/03	4,000	—	—	24,000
12/02	3,000	—	—	24,000
12/01	3,000	—	—	22,000
12/00	3,100	—	—	6,000
12/99	3,350	—	—	6,000
12/98	2,875	—	—	6,000
12/97	2,900	—	—	6,000
12/96	2,500	—	—	6,000
12/95	2,350	—	—	6,000
12/94	2,200	—	—	6,000
Annual Growth	6.9%	—	—	16.7%

Revenue History

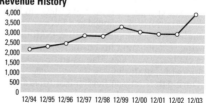

Science Applications International

It definitely pays to have a rich Big Brother, or an Uncle Sam with deep pockets. Science Applications International Corporation (SAIC) provides a variety of systems integration, engineering, and R&D services to the US government, which accounts for about 75% of revenues. SAIC also provides professional services to the commercial sector, including consulting, enterprise resource planning, software implementation, and network engineering as well as data mining and data warehousing services. SAIC is the nation's largest employee-owned research and engineering company.

Following the terrorist attacks of September 11, 2001, the company has seen increased demand for homeland security-related projects, prompting it to install an emergency telecommunications system in New York, develop a training program for US sky marshals, and build a communications network for the US Central Command. SAIC also has its hands in undersea data collection and space systems engineering.

Together with Boeing, SAIC has inked various multi-million-dollar deals with the US Army. Together, those companies are developing practices for the $14.9 billion Future Combat Systems (FCS) program.

In April of 2003 SAIC acquired the rights to various threat-analysis Information Sharing and Analysis Centers (ISACs) from Predictive Systems. The ISACs were created in 1997 to encourage private companies to share information about threats and warnings as a way to reduce their vulnerability to terrorist attacks.

SAIC's Telcordia Technologies subsidiary (formerly the research arm of the Baby Bells) supplies a variety of software and services to the telecommunications sector.

Founder and longtime former CEO Robert Beyster has asserted that employee ownership is key to the company's success, and SAIC has shown little interest in pursuing an IPO. The company last received $200,000 from private investors in 1970.

HISTORY

Physicist Robert Beyster, who worked at Los Alamos National Laboratory in the 1950s, was hired by General Atomic in 1957 to establish and manage its traveling wave linear accelerator. When the company was sold to Gulf Oil in 1968, research priorities changed and Beyster left. He founded Science Applications Inc. (SAI) the following year and built his business from consulting contracts with Los Alamos and Brookhaven National Laboratories.

During the first year Beyster instituted an employee ownership plan that rewarded workers that brought onboard new business with stock in SAI. Beyster's idea was to share the success of SAI and to raise capital.

In 1970 the company established an office in Washington, DC, to court government contracts. Despite a recession, SAI continued to grow during the 1970s, and by 1979 sales topped $100 million. The following year SAI restructured, becoming a subsidiary of Science Applications International Corporation (SAIC), a new holding company.

During the 1980s defense buildup, an emphasis on high-tech weaponry and SAIC's high-level Pentagon connections (directors have included former defense secretaries William Perry and Melvin Laird and former CIA director John Deutch) brought in contracts for submarine warfare systems and technical development for the Strategic Defense Initiative ("Star Wars").

As defense spending slowed with the end of the Cold War, SAIC began casting a wider net. By 1991 computer systems integration and consulting accounted for 25% of sales, which surpassed the $1 billion mark.

SAIC made several purchases during the mid-1990s, including transportation communications firm Syntonic, Internet domain name registrar Network Solutions, Inc. (NSI), and government think tank Aerospace Corp. In 1997 SAIC acquired Bellcore (the research lab of the regional Bells, now Telcordia Technologies), and reduced its stake in NSI through a public offering. SAIC formed several alliances in 1998, including a joint venture with Rolls-Royce to service the aerospace, energy, and defense industries.

The next year SAIC expanded its information technology (IT) expertise with the acquisition of Boeing's Information Services unit. It also acquired the call center software operations of Elite Information Group. SAIC in 2000 realized a significant gain on its $5 million purchase of NSI when e-commerce software maker VeriSign bought the minority-owned (23%) subsidiary for $17 billion.

In 2001 SAIC signed a variety of large contracts, including an outsourcing agreement with BP to manage that company's North American application and hosting services, as well as a $3 billion deal to provide support (in conjunction with Bechtel Group) for the US Department of Energy's civilian radioactive waste management program.

The omnipresent and self-described workaholic Beyster retired as CEO in 2003, turning the position over to former General Dynamics VP Kenneth Dahlberg. Within a few months of joining the company, Dahlberg announced a major reorganization of the company's business into three divisions: commercial, federal, and Telcordia.

EXECUTIVES

Chairman, President, and CEO:
 Kenneth C. (Ken) Dahlberg, age 59, $1,260,000 pay (partial-year salary)
EVP and CFO: Thomas E. Darcy, age 53, $1,069,992 pay
EVP, CTO, and Director: Stephen D. (Steve) Rockwood, age 60
Group President: Carl M. Albero, age 68
Group President and Director: Don H. Foley, age 59
Group President: Mark V. Hughes III, age 59
Group President: Larry J. Peck, age 55
Corporate EVP, Chief Administrative Officer, and Director: John H. Warner Jr., age 63, $985,977 pay
Corporate EVP and Director: Randy I. Walker, age 39
Corporate EVP: William A. Roper Jr., age 58
EVP and Operations Manager, Washington, DC:
 Robert A. Rosenberg, age 69
EVP and Secretary: J. Dennis Heipt, age 61, $1,010,014 pay
EVP Commercial Outsourcing: Art L. Slotkin, age 57
EVP Strategic Initiatives and Director:
 Joseph P. (Joe) Walkush, age 51
EVP Telecommunications Sector: Neil E. Cox, age 54
SVP and Analyst: Lewis A. Dunn
SVP and Controller: Peter N. Pavlics, age 43
SVP, General Counsel, and Secretary: D. E. Scott, age 47
SVP and Treasurer: Steven P. Fisher, age 43
SVP Business Development: Jim Russell
SVP Human Resources: Bernard Theull
President and COO, Federal Business and Director:
 Duane P. Andrews, age 59, $1,204,511 pay
Auditors: Deloitte & Touche LLP

LOCATIONS

HQ: Science Applications International Corporation
 10260 Campus Point Dr., San Diego, CA 92121
Phone: 858-826-6000 **Fax:** 858-826-6800
Web: www.saic.com

Science Applications International has offices in more than 150 cities worldwide.

PRODUCTS/OPERATIONS

2004 Sales

	% of total
Regulated	81
Non-regulated telecommunications	13
Non-regulated other	6
Total	**100**

Selected Practice Areas and Services

Biomedical research
 Biomedical information systems
 Cancer and AIDS research
Criminal justice
 Automated warrants and booking
 Corrections support
 DNA analysis
 Records management
 Training
Customer relationship management
Data mining and warehousing
 Data analysis
 Data management
Distributed enterprise management
E-business systems
 Application development and integration
 Document management systems
 E-learning
 Procurement
Energy
 Oil and gas industries
 Utilities
Enterprise resource planning
Environmental consulting
 Energy management
 Health and safety assessment
 Operations analysis
 Project planning and engineering
 Natural resource management
 Site management and remediation
Financial services
 Financial modeling and analysis
 Lease financing
Imagery
 Global imagery
 Remote sensing
Information security
Information technology
Knowledge management
Maritime systems
 International security
 Submarine telecommunications
National security
 Command and control
 Homeland security
 Policy support
 Training
Outsourcing
 Infrastructure
 Network operations
 Security services
Software development

Space systems
    Applied research and technology
    Design and analysis
    Modeling and simulations
    Operational support
    Safety and reliability
    Space, Earth, and atmospheric sciences
Supply chain management
    Collaborative systems
    Organizational transformation
    Process optimization
    Strategy and operations consulting
Systems integration and program management
Telecommunications
Training programs
    Environmental training
    Software process improvement
    Terrorism response
Transportation
    Asset management
    Aviation management
    Commercial vehicle operations
    Fleet management
    Highway and vehicle research
    Policy analysis
Wireless communications
    Automotive telematics
    Broadband
    Engineering services
    Mobile workforce automation
    Railroad systems

COMPETITORS

Accenture	IBM
Anteon	ITT Industries
Battelle Memorial	Keane
CACI International	Lockheed Martin
Capgemini	ManTech
CapTech	MITRE
Computer Sciences	Northrop Grumman
DIRECTV	Perot Systems
EDS	Titan
General Dynamics	Unisys
Hewlett-Packard	

HISTORICAL FINANCIALS

Company Type: Private

Income Statement
FYE: January 31

	REVENUE ($ mil.)	NET INCOME ($ mil.)	NET PROFIT MARGIN	EMPLOYEES
1/04	6,720	351	5.2%	42,700
1/03	5,903	246	4.2%	38,700
1/02	6,095	19	0.3%	40,400
1/01	5,896	2,059	34.9%	41,500
1/00	5,530	620	11.2%	39,078
1/99	4,740	151	3.2%	35,200
1/98	3,089	85	2.7%	30,300
1/97	2,402	64	2.7%	22,600
1/96	2,156	57	2.7%	21,100
1/95	1,922	49	2.6%	20,500
Annual Growth	14.9%	24.4%	—	8.5%

2004 Year-End Financials
Debt ratio: 56.3%
Return on equity: 16.7%
Cash ($ mil.): 2,365
Current ratio: 2.29
Long-term debt ($ mil.): 1,232

Net Income History
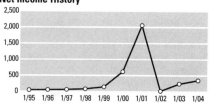

Scott & White

Scott & White serves central Texas. The health care system operates Scott & White Memorial Hospital in Temple and 15 regional clinics throughout the area. Some 500 doctors are associated with the health network. The hospital has some 650 beds and offers acute care as well as such tertiary health care services as cancer treatment, behavioral health, rehabilitation, and eye care. Scott & White Memorial Hospital is a teaching affiliate of Texas A&M University. The organization also owns the Scott & White Health Plan.

EXECUTIVES

President and CEO: Alfred B. Knight
COO: Donny Sequin
CFO: Kenneth (Ken) Johnson
Executive Director, Scott & White Health Plan: Allan Einboden
CFO, Scott & White Memorial Hospital: David Verinder
Controller: Dick Dixon
Director, Marketing Communications: Tracy Brown
Director, Human Resources: Judy White House
Manager, Marketing Communications: Scott Clark
Auditors: Ernst & Young LLP

LOCATIONS

HQ: Scott & White
2401 S. 31st St., Temple, TX 76508
Phone: 254-724-2111   **Fax:** 254-724-8422
Web: www.sw.org

HISTORICAL FINANCIALS
Company Type: Not-for-profit

Income Statement
FYE: August 31

	REVENUE ($ mil.)	NET INCOME ($ mil.)	NET PROFIT MARGIN	EMPLOYEES
8/03	713	—	—	8,000
8/02	673	—	—	8,000
Annual Growth	5.9%	—	—	0.0%

Revenue History
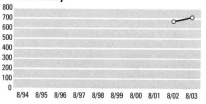

Scoular

The people who grow the wheat aren't usually the ones who grind it. The Scoular Company handles the process that goes on between the two groups. The company is best known for grain marketing, trading more than 400 million bushels of grain and more than one million tons of grain byproducts (used for animal feed) annually throughout North America. Other divisions offer fishmeal products for animal and aquaculture feeds, ingredients for food manufacturing, truck freight brokering, and livestock marketing. Founded in 1892 to run grain elevators, employee-owned Scoular operates elevators in Colorado, Nebraska, and South Dakota.

EXECUTIVES

Chairman: Marshall E. Faith
CEO: Randal L. Linville
CFO: Roger L. Barber
SVP, Administration, Development, and Finance: John M. Heck
SVP, Corporate Development and Shareholder Relations: David M. Faith
SVP, Flourmill Markets: Charles (Chuck) Elsea
SVP, Industrial Marketing: Eric H. Jackson
SVP, Processor Markets: Robert (Bob) Ludington
SVP, Producer Markets: George V. Schieber
SVP, Secretary and General Counsel: Joan C. Maclin
VP, Chief Accounting and Control Officer: Randall Foster
Director, Human Resources: Yvonne Lutz

LOCATIONS

HQ: The Scoular Company
9401 Indian Creek Pkwy., Bldg. 40, Ste. 850, Overland Park, KS 66210
Phone: 913-338-1474   **Fax:** 913-338-2999
Web: www.scoular.com

COMPETITORS

ADM
Ag Processing
Bartlett and Company
Bunge Limited
Cargill
CHS
ConAgra
DeBruce Grain
GROWMARK
Southern States

HISTORICAL FINANCIALS
Company Type: Private

Income Statement
FYE: May 31

	REVENUE ($ mil.)	NET INCOME ($ mil.)	NET PROFIT MARGIN	EMPLOYEES
5/03	1,900	—	—	330
5/02	2,100	—	—	330
5/01	2,098	—	—	400
5/00	2,015	—	—	379
5/99	1,729	—	—	400
5/98	1,606	—	—	267
5/97	1,900	—	—	278
5/96	1,955	—	—	285
5/95	1,130	—	—	225
5/94	1,121	—	—	250
Annual Growth	6.0%	—	—	3.1%

Revenue History
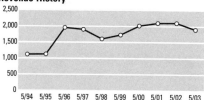

Scripps

Scripps has its lines down cold. The hospital group serves the San Diego area with five acute care hospitals with nearly 1,400 beds and a dozen outpatient clinic locations. The system also offers home health care and operates community outreach programs. Scripps consists of two partners: Scripps Health (overseeing hospitals, clinics, and home health care) and Scripps Physicians (a managed care network of more than 2,600 affiliated physicians). Scripps is affiliated with The Scripps Research Institute, which performs biomedical research; Scripps Foundation for Medicine and Science serves as a fundraiser for both the hospital group and the research institute.

EXECUTIVES

President and CEO: Chris D. Van Gorder
CFO and Treasurer: Richard Rothberger
SVP and Chief Community Health Officer: Clyde (Bud) Beck
VP, Human Resources: Victor Buzacazro
VP, Strategic Planning, Business Development, and Community Benefit: June Komar
VP and Medical Director for Information Services: Joe Traube
CIO: Jean Balgrosky
Chief Medical Officer: A. Brent Eastman
Chief Audit and Compliance Officer: Glen Mueller
General Counsel and Secretary: Richard R. Sheridan

LOCATIONS

HQ: Scripps
4275 Campus Point Ct., San Diego, CA 92121
Phone: 858-678-7000 **Fax:** 858-678-6558
Web: www.scrippshealth.org

PRODUCTS/OPERATIONS

Selected Facilities
Scripps Memorial Hospital Chula Vista
Scripps Memorial Hospital Encinitas
Scripps Green Hospital (La Jolla, CA)
Scripps Memorial Hospital La Jolla
Scripps Mercy Hospital (San Diego)

COMPETITORS

Adventist Health
Children's Hospital and Health Center of San Diego
HCA
Kaiser Permanente
Kindred
Sharp Memorial Hospital
Tenet Healthcare

HISTORICAL FINANCIALS

Company Type: Not-for-profit

Income Statement			FYE: September 30
	REVENUE ($ mil.)	**NET INCOME** ($ mil.)	**NET PROFIT MARGIN**	**EMPLOYEES**
9/03	1,221	—	—	10,000
9/02	1,130	—	—	9,950
9/01	1,004	—	—	10,000
9/00	787	—	—	9,342
9/99	666	—	—	8,500
9/98	653	—	—	8,400
9/97	616	—	—	8,000
9/96	668	—	—	9,596
9/95	600	—	—	9,700
9/94	536	—	—	—
Annual Growth	9.6%	—	—	0.4%

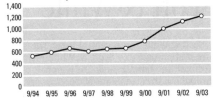

Revenue History

Sealy

Sealy is a slumbering giant. The company, North America's #1 maker of bedding products, manufactures mattresses and box springs and sells them in more than 7,000 stores. Its brands include Sealy, Bassett, and Stearns & Foster. Sealy's customers include sleep shops, furniture and department stores, warehouse clubs, and mass merchandisers, as well as the hospitality industry. Sealy also licenses its name to makers of other bedding products (pads, pillows) and home furnishings (sofas, futons). The company runs about 30 factories worldwide. Sealy, formerly owned by Boston-based investment firm Bain Capital, was bought by Kohlberg Kravis Roberts (KKR) in 2004.

While the majority of Sealy's sales come from the US, the firm also has licensees and sales operations worldwide. Sealy is making acquisitions and building plants to expand its business in the Latin American region.

Sealy's merger agreement with affiliates of KKR, which closed in April 2004, was valued at about $1.5 billion. KKR and Sealy management acquired about 92% of Sealy in the transaction, while existing Sealy shareholders retained 8% of the company.

EXECUTIVES

President and CEO: David J. (Dave) McIlquham, age 48, $636,552 pay
Corporate VP and CFO: James B. (Jim) Hirshorn, age 36
Corporate VP, General Counsel, and Secretary: Kenneth L. Walker, age 54
Corporate VP Human Resources: Jeffrey C. Claypool, age 55, $310,001 pay
Corporate VP Marketing: Mark Hobson, age 43
Corporate VP National Accounts: Charles (Chuck) Dawson, age 47
Corporate VP Operations: G. Michael Hofmann, age 44
Corporate VP Research and Development: Bruce G. Barman, age 57
Corporate VP Sales: Al Boulden, age 56
VP Information Technology: David Twine
President, International Bedding Group: Lawrence J. Rogers, age 54, $371,565 pay
Auditors: PricewaterhouseCoopers LLP

LOCATIONS

HQ: Sealy Corporation
1 Office Pkwy. at Sealy Dr., Trinity, NC 27370
Phone: 336-861-3500 **Fax:** 336-861-3501
Web: www.sealy.com

Sealy has about 30 manufacturing facilities in Argentina, Brazil, Canada, France, Italy, Mexico, Puerto Rico, and 17 US states. It has licensees in Australia, Bahamas, the Dominican Republic, Israel, Jamaica, Japan, New Zealand, Saudi Arabia, South Africa, Thailand, and the UK.

PRODUCTS/OPERATIONS

Brand Names
Advanced Generation Sealy Posturepedic
Bassett
Bed Time
Carrington-Chase
Meyer
Sealy
Sealy Back Saver
Sealy Correct Comfort
Sealy Kids
Sealy Posture Premier
Sealy Posturematic
Sealy Posturepedic
Sealy Posturepedic Crown Jewel
Stearns & Foster

COMPETITORS

Mattress Giant
Premier Bedding Group
Select Comfort
Serta
Simmons
Spring Air
Tempur-Pedic
W. S. Badcock

HISTORICAL FINANCIALS

Company Type: Private

Income Statement			FYE: Sunday nearest November 30
	REVENUE ($ mil.)	**NET INCOME** ($ mil.)	**NET PROFIT MARGIN**	**EMPLOYEES**
11/03	1,190	18	1.5%	6,562
11/02	1,189	17	1.4%	6,480
11/01	1,197	(21)	—	6,410
11/00	1,102	30	2.7%	6,077
11/99	986	16	1.6%	5,460
11/98	891	(34)	—	5,193
11/97	805	7	0.9%	5,456
11/96	698	(1)	—	4,875
11/95	654	20	3.0%	4,520
11/94	698	29	4.2%	4,345
Annual Growth	6.1%	(5.1%)	—	4.7%

2003 Year-End Financials
Debt ratio: —
Return on equity: —
Cash ($ mil.): 101
Current ratio: 1.35
Long-term debt ($ mil.): 700

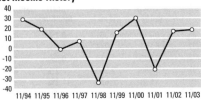

Net Income History

Security Benefit Group

The Security Benefit Group of Companies hopes to soar like a sunflower, not to be as flat as the Kansas plains. The group, which operates through Security Benefit Life Insurance Company and other subsidiaries, offers variable life insurance, annuities, mutual funds, and asset management services to individuals, investment advisors, and plan sponsors. After more than 100 years as a mutual company, the company made plans to convert to stock ownership but never followed through on those plans. Security Benefit's roots go back to the Knights and Ladies of Security, a benefit society begun in 1892 in Topeka, Kansas.

Security Benefit has about $12 billion in assets under management, a figure that will be boosted in the spring of 2004, when the company takes over some 25,000 variable annuity and life insurance accounts it has acquired from Mutual of Omaha, which is exiting the variable annuity business.

EXECUTIVES

Chairman: Howard R. Fricke, age 68
President and CEO: Kris A. Robbins
CFO: Tom Swank
SVP and Chief Marketing Officer: Kal Bakk
SVP and CIO: David (Dave) Keith
SVP and Chief Investment Officer:
  Michael G. (Mike) Odlum
SVP, Human Resources: Craig Anderson
VP, Corporate Communications and Brand Strategy: Michel' Philipp Cole
VP and Portfolio Manager: Mark Mitchell
VP, Marketing and Communications: Jenifer Purvis
VP and Head of Equity Asset Management:
  Cindy Shields
Auditors: Ernst & Young LLP

LOCATIONS

HQ: The Security Benefit Group of Companies
1 Security Benefit Place, Topeka, KS 66636
Phone: 785-438-3000   **Fax:** 785-438-5177
Web: www.securitybenefit.com

PRODUCTS/OPERATIONS

Selected Subsidiaries
Security Benefit Life Insurance Company
Security Distributors, Inc.
Security Management Company, LLC

COMPETITORS

Aetna	Kansas City Life
American United	Mutual of Omaha
Americo	Principal Financial
CIGNA	Prudential
CNA Financial	Thrivent Financial
FMR	UnitedHealth Group
John Hancock Financial Services	

HISTORICAL FINANCIALS

Company Type: Private

Income Statement FYE: December 31

	ASSETS ($ mil.)	NET INCOME ($ mil.)	INCOME AS % OF ASSETS	EMPLOYEES
12/03	9,905	37	0.4%	560
12/02	7,325	6	0.1%	700
12/01	7,463	31	0.4%	600
12/00	7,872	70	0.9%	—
12/99	8,310	69	0.8%	—
12/98	7,429	58	0.8%	—
12/97	6,403	52	0.8%	—
12/96	5,748	44	0.8%	—
12/95	4,914	37	0.8%	—
12/94	4,202	34	0.8%	—
Annual Growth	10.0%	0.9%	—	(3.4%)

2003 Year-End Financials
Equity as % of assets: —   Long-term debt ($ mil.): —
Return on assets: 0.4%   Sales ($ mil.): 2,969
Return on equity: —

SEMATECH

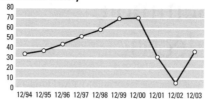
Net Income History

SEMATECH (from "semiconductor manufacturing technology") is more than semantics. The not-for-profit research consortium, which does business as International SEMATECH, pursues advances in design, lithography, interconnect, and other facets of chip manufacturing. It also provides custom wafer processing and publishes technical reports for its members. The group is funded by member dues; employees from its members' companies — Advanced Micro Devices, Freescale Semiconductor, Hewlett-Packard, IBM, Infineon, Intel, Matsushita, Philips, Taiwan Semiconductor, and Texas Instruments — carry out research at its Texas site.

International SEMATECH is credited with updating the equipment used in American factories and helping US chip makers recover their global dominance.

The consortium has lost some of its original US members in recent years — in part because of the US chip industry's return to dominance, in part because of its inclusion of non-US firms — but continues to tackle difficult technological issues related to the shrinking size of chips and use of new materials. The organization has more recently lost two foreign members — Hynix and STMicroelectronics — both citing budgetary reasons.

Amid a harsh downturn in the semiconductor industry and an increasingly difficult funding environment, International SEMATECH is teaming up with other international research organizations, including Selete, its Japanese counterpart. The consortium also announced plans to lay off about 60 employees — a tenth of its workforce — in response to smaller budgets and in the face of a sharp downturn across the semiconductor industry. However the company has established another research campus in Albany, New York — dubbed International SEMATECH North — with funding from New York State and IBM. International SEMATECH has also launched the International SEMATECH Manufacturing Initiative (ISMI), a wholly-owned consortium focused on helping semiconductor makers reduce wafer production costs.

HISTORY

In 1986 Japan surpassed the US to become the leading maker of semiconductors. The Semiconductor Industry Association (SIA), a US chip industry trade group, formed SEMATECH in 1987 with the help of five years' worth of funding from the US Defense Department's Defense Advanced Research Projects Agency, along with another $100 million per year from 14 member companies. Intel co-founder (and chip industry legend) Robert Noyce became the consortium's first CEO.

Former Xerox research executive Bill Spencer became CEO of SEMATECH after Noyce's death in 1990. Despite its technological advances, critics complained that the organization primarily benefited its largest members. In the early 1990s Micron Technology and LSI Logic (its smallest members) and Harris Corp. dropped out.

SEMATECH's government funding was extended (although at a lower level) in 1992. When the US regained its world chip manufacturing title that year, many credited SEMATECH for the turnaround.

In 1994 SEMATECH began phasing out federal backing. Citing the main challenge to US chip makers as technology limits rather than foreign competition, the organization in 1996 invited European and Asian manufacturers to join an initiative to convert semiconductor wafers from eight to 12 inches (300mm). When government funding came to an end in 1996, SEMATECH formed an international branch and increased its dues to cover lost funding.

In 1997 Mark Melliar-Smith was named CEO. (Spencer remained chairman until 2000, when O. B. Bilous succeeded him.) In 1998 five companies from Asia and Europe formed the new International SEMATECH. That year National Semiconductor left SEMATECH, citing financial difficulties.

In 1999 Motorola, concerned about the organization's international push, gave the required two years notice that it would withdraw. Compaq — which had become a member when it acquired Digital Equipment (but not that company's chip operations) in 1997 — also made plans to leave.

SEMATECH and International SEMATECH became a single entity (and began using International SEMATECH as its trade name) by 2000. That year SEMATECH accelerated its international involvement through pacts with Selete, the organization's Japanese counterpart, and Belgium research agency IMEC.

In 2001 Bob Helms, a Texas Instruments engineer and Stanford University emeritus professor, succeeded Melliar-Smith as the consortium's president and CEO. The next year the consortium established a research campus in Albany, New York, with funding from New York State and IBM.

In 2003 Helms stepped down as president and CEO and was replaced by IBM veteran Michael Polcari. The same year International SEMATECH launched International SEMATECH Manufacturing Initiative, a wholly owned consortium focused on reducing semiconductor wafer production costs.

EXECUTIVES

Chairman: O. B. Bilous
President and CEO: Michael R. (Mike) Polcari
VP and COO, Advanced Technology: Betsy Weitzman
VP and COO, Manufacturing Operations and Technology: John Schmitz
Chief Administrative Officer: David Saathoff
General Manager, Advanced Technology Development Facility: Juergen Woehl
Director, Interconnect: Navjot Chhabra
Director, Lithography: Giang Dao
Director, Front End Processes Division:
  Charles Ramiller

Associate Director, Interconnect: Ken Monnig
Associate Director, Lithography: Kevin Kemp
Information Manager, International Technology
 Roadmap of Semiconductors: Linda Wilson
Development Contracts: Tracy Yetter
Media Relations: Dan McGowan
Volunteer Activities and Donations: Christi Cochren
Wafer Processing Services: Lesli Roush
Auditors: PricewaterhouseCoopers LLP

LOCATIONS

HQ: SEMATECH, Inc.
 2706 Montopolis Dr., Austin, TX 78741
Phone: 512-356-3500 Fax: 512-356-3086
Web: www.sematech.org

SEMATECH includes members from Germany, the Netherlands, Taiwan, and the US.

PRODUCTS/OPERATIONS

Research and Development Programs
Advanced technical development facilities and facilities
 design
Front-end processes
Interconnect
Lithography
Manufacturing methods and productivity

SEMATECH Members
Advanced Micro Devices
Hewlett-Packard
IBM
Infineon
Intel
Motorola
Philips
Taiwan Semiconductor Manufacturing Corp.
Texas Instruments

COMPETITORS

IBM
Intel
MIT
Research Triangle Institute
SAIC
Southwest Research
 Institute
SRI International
University of California

HISTORICAL FINANCIALS
Company Type: Consortium

Income Statement				FYE: December 31
	REVENUE ($ mil.)	NET INCOME ($ mil.)	NET PROFIT MARGIN	EMPLOYEES
12/03	125	—	—	500
12/02	160	—	—	600
12/01	—	—	—	600
12/00	—	—	—	600
12/99	—	—	—	600
12/98	—	—	—	600
12/97	—	—	—	800
12/96	—	—	—	800
12/95	—	—	—	800
12/94	—	—	—	841
Annual Growth	(21.7%)	—	—	(5.6%)

Revenue History

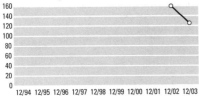

Seminole Electric

This Seminole is not only a native Floridian, but it has also provided electricity in the state since 1948. Seminole Electric Cooperative (SECI) generates and transmits electricity for 10 member distribution cooperatives that serve more than 770,000 residential and business customers in 46 Florida counties. SECI has more than 1,800 MW of primarily coal-fired generating capacity. The cooperative also buys electricity from other utilities and independent power producers, and it owns nearly 350 miles of transmission lines. SECI was formed to aggregate the power demands of its members and is governed by a board of trustees representing the 10 member utilities.

EXECUTIVES

President, Board of Trustees: John W. Drake
VP, Board of Trustees: Mal Green
EVP and General Manager: Richard J. Midulla
VP, Administration: Savino (Al) Garcia
VP, Energy Delivery: Floyd J. Welborn
VP, Energy Production: James R. Duren
VP, Financial Services and Assistant Treasurer:
 John W. Geeraerts
VP, Strategic Services and Assistant Secretary:
 Timothy S. Woodbury
Director, Corporate Planning: Lane T. Mahaffey
Director, Information Systems: William C. Cross
Director, Corporate Compliance: Thomas H. Turke
Director, Operations: Steven R. (Steve) Wallace
Secretary and Treasurer: Robert W. Strickland
Auditors: PricewaterhouseCoopers LLP

LOCATIONS

HQ: Seminole Electric Cooperative, Inc.
 16313 N. Dale Mabry Hwy., Tampa, FL 33618
Phone: 813-963-0994 Fax: 813-264-7906
Web: www.seminole-electric.com

PRODUCTS/OPERATIONS

2003 Sales

	$ mil.	% of total
Members	773.0	97
Non-members	17.1	2
Other	8.6	1
Total	**798.7**	**100**

Members
Central Florida Electric Cooperative
Clay Electric Cooperative
Glades Electric Cooperative
Lee County Electric Cooperative
Peace River Electric Cooperative
Sumter Electric Cooperative
Suwannee Valley Electric Cooperative
Talquin Electric Cooperative
Tri-County Electric Cooperative
Withlacoochee River Electric Cooperative

COMPETITORS

Duke Energy
Florida Public Utilities
FPL Group
JEA
Progress Energy
Southern Company
TECO Energy

HISTORICAL FINANCIALS
Company Type: Cooperative

Income Statement				FYE: December 31
	REVENUE ($ mil.)	NET INCOME ($ mil.)	NET PROFIT MARGIN	EMPLOYEES
12/03	799	2	0.3%	465
12/02	714	2	0.3%	468
12/01	669	2	0.4%	455
12/00	583	—	—	438
Annual Growth	11.1%	0.0%	—	2.0%

2003 Year-End Financials
Debt ratio: 952.1%   Current ratio: 1.98
Return on equity: 3.0%   Long-term debt ($ mil.): 770
Cash ($ mil.): 26

Net Income History

Sentara Healthcare

Health care's a beach for Sentara Healthcare. The not-for-profit organization provides medical services for about 2 million residents of southeastern Virginia and northeastern North Carolina. The system includes six hospitals, nine assisted-living centers, more than 30 primary care offices, an integrated outpatient health care campus, and several fitness centers. Sentara's Optima Health Plan provides HMO coverage to more than 250,000 members. The organization also provides home health services, ground and air medical transport, community health education programs, and mobile diagnostic vans.

EXECUTIVES

CEO: David L. Bernd
President and COO: Howard P. Kern
SVP and CFO: Rob Broerman
EVP, Chief Medical Officer, and Administrator, Sentara
 Norfolk General Hospital: Rod Hochman
VP, Information Technology and CIO:
 Bertram S. (Bert) Reese
VP, Human Resources: Michael Taylor

LOCATIONS

HQ: Sentara Healthcare
 6015 Poplar Hall Dr., Norfolk, VA 23502
Phone: 757-455-7000 Fax: 757-455-7164
Web: www.sentara.com

Sentara operates in northeastern North Carolina and southeastern Virginia.

PRODUCTS/OPERATIONS

Selected Facilities
Sentara Bayside Hospital (Virginia Beach, VA)
Sentara CarePlex Hospital (Hampton, VA)
Sentara Leigh Hospital (Norfolk, VA)
Sentara Norfolk General Hospital (Norfolk, VA)
Sentara Virginia Beach General Hospital (Virginia Beach, VA)
Sentara Williamsburg Community Hospital (Williamsburg, VA)

COMPETITORS

Bon Secours Health
Carilion Health System
Mid Atlantic Medical
Novant Health
Wake Forest University Baptist Medical Center

HISTORICAL FINANCIALS

Company Type: Not-for-profit

Income Statement
FYE: April 30

	REVENUE ($ mil.)	NET INCOME ($ mil.)	NET PROFIT MARGIN	EMPLOYEES
4/04	1,500	—	—	15,000
4/03	1,530	—	—	15,200
4/02	1,600	—	—	15,200
4/01	1,300	—	—	14,000
4/00	1,300	—	—	14,000
4/99	1,100	—	—	11,000
4/98	901	—	—	8,190
4/97	816	—	—	7,734
4/96	726	—	—	7,593
4/95	663	—	—	7,676
Annual Growth	9.5%	—	—	7.7%

Revenue History

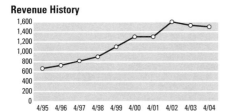

Sentry Insurance

Vigilant for its policyholders, Sentry Insurance (of the famous Minuteman statue logo) offers a variety of insurance coverage, including life, group health, auto, and property/casualty insurance. The mutual company (owned by its policyholders) offers coverage through several subsidiaries. Sentry also provides specialized insurance to small and large businesses, including manufacturers and retailers. The company's Sentry Equity Services offers mutual fund services through its Sentry Fund. Sentry was founded in 1904 to provide insurance to members of the Wisconsin Retail Hardware Association.

EXECUTIVES

Chairman, President, and CEO: Dale R. Schuh
VP and COO: Jim Clawson
VP, Secretary, and General Counsel: William M. O'Reilly
VP, Finance: William J. Lohr
VP, Human Resources: Greg Mox
VP, Investments: Jim Weishan
Senior Director and Controller: Carol Sanders
Auditors: PricewaterhouseCoopers

LOCATIONS

HQ: Sentry Insurance, a Mutual Company
1800 North Point Dr., Stevens Point, WI 54481
Phone: 715-346-6000   **Fax:** 715-346-7516
Web: www.sentry.com

Sentry Insurance has offices throughout the US.

PRODUCTS/OPERATIONS

Selected Subsidiaries
Dairyland County Mutual of Texas
Dairyland Insurance Company
Middlesex Insurance Company
Parker Services, L.L.C.
Patriot General Insurance Company
Sentry Casualty Company
Sentry Equity Services, Inc.
Sentry Life Insurance Company
Sentry Life Insurance Company of New York
Sentry Select Insurance Company

COMPETITORS

AIG	Nationwide
Allstate	New York Life
CIGNA	Prudential
CNA Financial	Reliance Group
Cobalt	State Farm
MetLife	

HISTORICAL FINANCIALS

Company Type: Mutual company

Income Statement
FYE: December 31

	ASSETS ($ mil.)	NET INCOME ($ mil.)	INCOME AS % OF ASSETS	EMPLOYEES
12/03	7,809	180	2.3%	4,400
12/02	6,945	46	0.7%	4,400
12/01	6,587	80	1.2%	4,300
12/00	6,499	217	3.3%	4,200
12/99	6,409	107	1.7%	4,200
12/98	5,782	134	2.3%	4,000
12/97	5,648	147	2.6%	4,479
12/96	5,363	115	2.1%	4,750
12/95	5,162	188	3.6%	3,909
12/94	4,852	—	—	4,041
Annual Growth	5.4%	(0.5%)	—	1.0%

2003 Year-End Financials

Equity as % of assets: 28.0%   Long-term debt ($ mil.): 2,092
Return on assets: 2.4%   Sales ($ mil.): 2,088
Return on equity: 8.7%

Net Income History

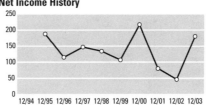

Serta

Serta, the #2 mattress manufacturer in the world (behind Sealy), hopes to keep the competition awake at night. It is the nation's #1 mattress supplier to hotels and motels; its Perfect Sleeper mattress line, which it has been selling since the 1930s, is the best-selling premium mattress in the US. Serta's top-of-the-line mattress collection is sold under the Perfect Night name. Founded in 1931 by 13 mattress makers who licensed the Serta name, the company is now owned by eight independent licensees; each licensee has separate marketing, manufacturing, and sales operations. The group has 26 factories in the US, four in Canada, and another 27 throughout Asia, Europe, the Middle East, and South America.

EXECUTIVES

Chairman, President, and CEO: Edward F. (Ed) Lilly
Group VP and Managing Director, International Division: Al Klancnik
VP and Brand Manager, Masterpiece: Chad Megard
VP and Controller: Kevin Bayer
VP, Information Systems: Mark VanDenburgh
VP, Manufacturing Services: Bob Sabalaskey
VP, Merchandising: Bob Malin
VP, Senior Sales: Jeff Van Tuyle
Chief Brand Officer: Susan Ebaugh

LOCATIONS

HQ: Serta, Inc.
325 Spring Lake Dr., Itasca, IL 60143
Phone: 630-285-9350   **Fax:** 630-285-9330
Web: www.serta.com

COMPETITORS

Nautilus Group	Simmons
Premier Bedding Group	Spring Air
Sealy	Tempur-Pedic
Select Comfort	

HISTORICAL FINANCIALS

Company Type: Private

Income Statement
FYE: December 31

	REVENUE ($ mil.)	NET INCOME ($ mil.)	NET PROFIT MARGIN	EMPLOYEES
12/02	930	—	—	4,800
12/01	870	—	—	4,800
12/00	858	—	—	4,800
12/99	834	—	—	4,800
12/98	764	—	—	4,800
12/97	670	—	—	4,000
12/96	578	—	—	4,000
12/95	552	—	—	2,500
12/94	470	—	—	2,000
12/93	380	—	—	—
Annual Growth	10.5%	—	—	11.6%

Revenue History

Services Group

Although its name is rather vague, Services Group of America specializes in food. Its subsidiary, Food Services of America, is a foodservice distributor that supplies hospitals, restaurants, and schools in 15 western and midwestern states. Its McCabe's Quality Foods business serves fast-food and casual-dining chain restaurants in the western US. Services Group's other operations include fresh fruit and vegetable marketing, commercial real estate development and management, and natural Black Angus beef production and marketing. The firm, formed in 1985, bought the West Coast food-distribution operations of Marriott International, which was absorbed by McCabe's.

EXECUTIVES

Chairman and CEO: Thomas J. (Tom) Stewart
CFO: Peter Smith
VP, Corporate Communications: Gary L. Odegard
Director, Human Resources: Ira Duden
Director, Marketing: Donna Baraya

LOCATIONS

HQ: Services Group of America
4025 Delridge Way SW, Ste. 400, Seattle, WA 98106
Phone: 206-933-5000   **Fax:** 206-933-5283
Web: www.fsafood.com

Services Group of America has operations in Anchorage, Alaska; Billings, Montana; Fargo and Minot, North Dakota; Fresno, California; Everett, Kent, Seattle, and Spokane, Washington; Boise, Idaho; Omaha, Nebraska; and Portland, Oregon.

COMPETITORS

Buckhead Beef	Reyes Holdings
Gordon Food Service	Smart & Final
McLane Foodservice	SYSCO
Performance Food	U.S. Foodservice

HISTORICAL FINANCIALS

Company Type: Private

Income Statement				FYE: January 31
	ESTIMATED REVENUE ($ mil.)	NET INCOME ($ mil.)	NET PROFIT MARGIN	EMPLOYEES
1/03	2,200	—	—	3,500
1/02	1,650	—	—	3,300
1/01	1,480	—	—	3,300
1/00	1,202	—	—	2,900
1/99	1,400	—	—	2,500
1/98	1,350	—	—	2,300
1/97	1,350	—	—	2,500
1/96	1,200	—	—	2,500
1/95	1,030	—	—	2,500
1/94	950	—	—	2,500
Annual Growth	9.8%	—	—	3.8%

Revenue History

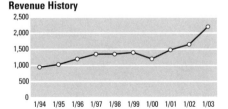

Shamrock Foods

Milk does a business good too. Thanks to that udder delight, Shamrock Foods has fortified itself from a mom-and-pop dairy into the fourth-largest independent foodservice distributor in the US serving supermarkets, convenience stores, restaurants, and institutional clients in 10 states in the West and Southwest, including Southern California, Colorado, and Texas. The company's Shamrock Farms division processes dairy products, including milk, cottage cheese, and sour cream. Production of the company's ice cream is outsourced. Its products are sold under the Shamrock Farms and Sunland brands, as well as under private labels. Started in 1922, Shamrock Foods is owned and run by the founding McClelland family.

EXECUTIVES

Chairman & CEO: Norman McClelland
President and COO: Kent McClelland
SVP and CFO: F. Phillips Giltner III, age 55
VP, Human Resources: Robert (Bob) Beake
Secretary and Treasurer: Frances McClelland

LOCATIONS

HQ: Shamrock Foods Company
2540 N. 29th Ave., Phoenix, AZ 85009
Phone: 602-233-6401   **Fax:** 602-233-2791
Web: www.shamrockfoods.com

Shamrock Foods does business in 10 states: Arizona, California, Colorado, Kansas, Nebraska, Nevada, New Mexico, Texas, Utah, and Wyoming.

PRODUCTS/OPERATIONS

Selected Products
Beverages
Canned goods
Dairy products
Fresh produce
Fresh and frozen meat
Fresh and frozen poultry
Fresh and frozen seafood
Sanitation products
Tabletop and equipment

COMPETITORS

Dairy Farmers of America	McLane Foodservice
Dean Foods	SYSCO
F & L Enterprises	U.S. Foodservice
Land O'Lakes	

HISTORICAL FINANCIALS

Company Type: Private

Income Statement				FYE: September 30
	REVENUE ($ mil.)	NET INCOME ($ mil.)	NET PROFIT MARGIN	EMPLOYEES
9/03	1,186	—	—	2,258
9/02	1,093	—	—	2,143
9/01	1,100	—	—	2,196
9/00	1,177	—	—	2,426
9/99	1,081	—	—	2,337
9/98	995	—	—	2,284
9/97	892	—	—	2,168
9/96	818	—	—	2,064
9/95	703	—	—	1,783
9/94	609	—	—	1,500
Annual Growth	7.7%	—	—	4.6%

Revenue History

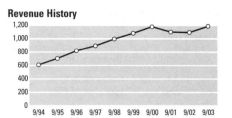

Shapell Industries

Shapell Industries shapes its business around constructing homes for Californians. The real estate development firm builds luxury townhouses and single-family homes in Northern and Southern California that range in price from $400,000 to more than $1 million. Shapell also provides home financing and interior design services for its customers and develops shopping centers and offices near its home communities. The company, which began as S&S Construction Company in 1955, has built more than 60,000 homes since it was founded by Nathan Shapell, his brother David, and brother-in-law Max Webb. A Holocaust survivor, Nathan Shapell constructed homes in Germany for displaced Jews after WWII before he moved to the US.

EXECUTIVES

Chairman and CEO: Nathan Shapell
CFO: Margaret Leong
CTO: Bill Bailey
Human Resources Director: Eileen Ho
Division Manager, Shapell Industries of Northern California: Chris Truebridge
Assistant VP/General Sales Manager, Shapell Industries of Northern California: John Luedemann
Auditors: PricewaterhouseCoopers LLP

LOCATIONS

HQ: Shapell Industries, Inc.
8383 Wilshire Blvd., Ste. 700, Beverly Hills, CA 90211
Phone: 323-655-7330   **Fax:** 323-651-4349
Web: www.shapellnc.com

Shapell Industries has housing communities in Castro Valley, Danville, Gilroy, the San Francisco Bay Area, San Jose, and San Roman in Northern California and in Laguna Niguel, Porter Ranch, Thousand Oaks, and Yorba Linda in Southern California.

PRODUCTS/OPERATIONS

Selected Divisions and Subsidiaries
S&S Construction Co.
Westminster Mortgage Company

COMPETITORS

Barratt Developments	Lennar
Capital Pacific	Pulte Homes
Centex	Ryland
D.R. Horton	Standard Pacific
J.F. Shea	Toll Brothers
KB Home	William Lyon Homes

HISTORICAL FINANCIALS
Company Type: Private

Income Statement			FYE: December 31	
	ESTIMATED REVENUE ($ mil.)	NET INCOME ($ mil.)	NET PROFIT MARGIN	EMPLOYEES
12/02	550	—	—	400
12/01	500	—	—	400
12/00	600	—	—	400
12/99	575	—	—	400
12/98	554	—	—	400
12/97	529	—	—	400
12/96	475	—	—	300
12/95	425	—	—	300
12/94	390	—	—	300
Annual Growth	3.2%	—	—	3.7%

Revenue History

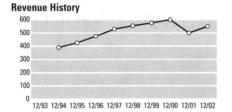

Shearman & Sterling

Law firm Shearman & Sterling has secured its place in history. Founded in 1873, the firm helped railroad baron Jay Gould fight for control of US railroads, aided in brokering a deal to free hostages in Iran, and represented women suing the Citadel military academy for admission. Today Shearman & Sterling has more than 1,000 lawyers in 18 domestic and international offices. Its practice areas include antitrust, bankruptcy, capital markets, intellectual property, litigation, mergers and acquisitions, project development and finance, and tax. Shearman & Sterling clients have included Viacom, Citigroup, and France Telecom.

EXECUTIVES
Senior Partner: David W. Heleniak
Managing Partner: Robert C. Treuhold
Executive Director, New York: Kimberly Gardner
Director Finance, New York: Kenneth W. Johnsen
Director Global Human Resources: Kathleen Weslock
Director Administrative Human Resources: Barbara Gannet
Director Professional Personnel: Halle Schargel

LOCATIONS
HQ: Shearman & Sterling
599 Lexington Ave., New York, NY 10022
Phone: 212-848-4000   **Fax:** 212-848-7179
Web: www.shearman.com

Shearman & Sterling has offices in Menlo Park and San Francisco, California; New York City; and Washington, DC; as well as Abu Dhabi, UAE; Beijing; Brussels; Düsseldorf, Frankfurt, Mannheim, and Munich, Germany; Hong Kong; London; Paris; Rome; Singapore; Tokyo; and Toronto.

PRODUCTS/OPERATIONS
Selected Practice Areas
Antitrust
Bank finance
Executive compensation and benefits
Global capital markets
Intellectual property
International trade
Litigation and dispute resolution
Mergers and acquisitions
Project development and finance
Restructuring and bankruptcy
Tax

COMPETITORS
Cleary, Gottlieb
Clifford Chance
Cravath, Swaine
Davis Polk
Debevoise & Plimpton
Jones Day
Kelley Drye
Milbank, Tweed
Proskauer Rose
Simpson Thacher
Skadden, Arps
Sullivan & Cromwell
Wachtell, Lipton

HISTORICAL FINANCIALS
Company Type: Partnership

Income Statement			FYE: December 31	
	REVENUE ($ mil.)	NET INCOME ($ mil.)	NET PROFIT MARGIN	EMPLOYEES
12/03	731	—	—	—
12/02	700	—	—	—
12/01	620	—	—	—
12/00	590	—	—	—
12/99	491	—	—	1,900
12/98	426	—	—	1,800
12/97	356	—	—	1,760
12/96	324	—	—	—
12/95	284	—	—	—
12/94	268	—	—	—
Annual Growth	11.8%	—	—	3.9%

Revenue History

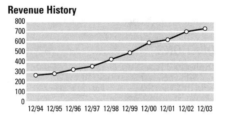

Sheehy Auto

Don't blame Sheehy Auto Stores (formerly VinCo Management) for heavy traffic on the beltway around the nation's capital. Sheehy just sells cars; *people* drive. Sheehy Auto Stores operates more than 10 Sheehy auto franchises in Maryland and Virginia near Washington, DC. The company's dealerships sell new Chevrolet, Dodge, Ford, Honda, Isuzu, Kia, Lexus, Mercury, Mitsubishi, and Nissan vehicles. All Sheehy dealerships sell used cars and offer financing, leasing, and service. Customers can order parts and make service appointments online through the company's Web site.

EXECUTIVES
Chairman: Vincent Sheehy Sr.
President: Vincent A. (Vince) Sheehy Jr., age 45
CFO: Michael Larkin
Sales Operations Manager: Neil Desmond
Marketing Manager: Kevin Scrimgeour
Director of Training Center: Dane Basl

LOCATIONS
HQ: Sheehy Auto Stores, Inc.
12450 Fair Lakes Circle, Ste. 380, Fairfax, VA 22033
Phone: 703-802-3480   **Fax:** 703-802-3481
Web: www.sheehy.com

COMPETITORS
Atlantic Automotive
Brown Automotive
Hall Auto World
Jim Koons Automotive
March/Hodge
Ouriman Automotive
Pohanka Automotive
Rosenthal Automotive

HISTORICAL FINANCIALS
Company Type: Private

Income Statement			FYE: December 31	
	REVENUE ($ mil.)	NET INCOME ($ mil.)	NET PROFIT MARGIN	EMPLOYEES
12/03	758	—	—	—
12/02	671	—	—	—
12/01	600	—	—	—
12/00	500	—	—	—
12/99	368	—	—	—
12/98	292	—	—	—
12/97	343	—	—	1,500
12/96	323	—	—	—
Annual Growth	12.9%	—	—	—

Revenue History

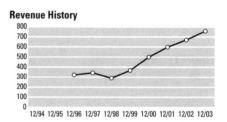

Sheetz

You might say Sheetz is to the convenience store business what Wal-Mart is to discount shopping. Noted for being exceptionally large (stores average 4,200 sq. ft., nearly twice the size of the average 7-Eleven, but new stores are planned to be 4,700 sq. ft.), Sheetz stores sell groceries, fountain drinks, baked goods, and made-to-order sandwiches and salads, self-service car washes, as well as discount gas and cigarettes. The company operates about 300 combination convenience stores and gas stations, mostly in small and midsized towns in Pennsylvania, but also in five other states. Founded in 1952 by Bob Sheetz, the company is owned and run by the Sheetz family.

Sheetz is going beyond traditional convenience store fare at locations in Altoona, Pennsylvania and Raleigh, North Carolina. The two new convenience restaurants are twice the size of a typical Sheetz store and have fried chicken, soups, and salads, in addition to sandwiches, on the menu. The stores seat 48 people. Sheetz hopes to sell beer at the Pennsylvania location.

Sales of the chain's "Made-To-Order" prepared foods dropped following a five-state outbreak of salmonella poisoning linked to food sold at Sheetz convenience stores in July. The company has since switched produce suppliers.

EXECUTIVES
Chairman: Stephen G. Sheetz, age 56
President and CEO: Stanton R. (Stan) Sheetz, age 48
EVP, Marketing: Louie Sheetz
EVP, Operations: Dan McMahon
VP, Finance: Joseph S. Sheetz
VP and General Counsel: R. Michael (Mike) Cortez
VP, Distribution Services: Ray Ryan
VP, Human Resources: Phil Freeman
VP, Marketing: Bill Reilly
VP, Petroleum Supply: Mike Lorenz
VP, Real Estate: Joseph M. Sheetz
Director, Finance and Accounting: Tom Luciano

LOCATIONS
HQ: Sheetz, Inc.
5700 6th Ave., Altoona, PA 16602
Phone: 814-946-3611 **Fax:** 814-946-4375
Web: www.sheetz.com

Sheetz operates about 300 stores in Maryland, North Carolina, Ohio, Pennsylvania, Virginia, and West Virginia.

PRODUCTS/OPERATIONS
Selected Products
Dot'z Bakery items
MTO (Made to Order) sandwiches
Nachos
Salads
Schmuffin breakfast sandwiches

COMPETITORS
7-Eleven
BP
Convenience USA
Cumberland Farms
Exxon Mobil
Giant Eagle
Green Valley
Kroger
Motiva Enterprises
Sunoco
Wawa, Inc.

HISTORICAL FINANCIALS
Company Type: Private

Income Statement				FYE: September 30
	ESTIMATED REVENUE ($ mil.)	NET INCOME ($ mil.)	NET PROFIT MARGIN	EMPLOYEES
9/03	1,900	—	—	9,000
9/02	1,920	—	—	8,500
9/01	1,900	—	—	7,500
9/00	1,620	—	—	7,000
9/99	1,161	—	—	6,200
9/98	952	—	—	4,950
9/97	877	—	—	5,500
9/96	756	—	—	4,900
9/95	750	—	—	4,525
9/94	689	—	—	4,100
Annual Growth	11.9%	—	—	9.1%

Sherwood Food

It doesn't slaughter the cows or grind the sausage, but Sherwood Food Distributors (SFD) will deliver the meat. The company is one of the largest wholesale distributors of meat and poultry in the US. SFD ships more than 12 million pounds of meat from packers such as Cargill, Hormel, and Perdue Farms, and delivers it to grocery retailers, food manufacturers, and food-service distributors in the Midwest and eastern US. The company operates distribution centers in Detroit, Cincinnati, and Cleveland. SFD was formed in 1987 by the merger of the food distribution operations of Orleans International and Regal Packaging, each of which owns half of the company.

To better serve its Kmart Supercenter customers, in 2003 Sherwood began distributing deli and bakery items supplied by Spartan Stores.

EXECUTIVES
Managing Partner: Earl Ishbia
Managing Partner: J. Lawrence (Larry) Tushman
CFO: Lon Makanoff
Operations Director: Phil Walega
Human Resource Manager: Carole Stearn

LOCATIONS
HQ: Sherwood Food Distributors
18615 Sherwood St., Detroit, MI 48234
Phone: 313-366-3100 **Fax:** 313-366-8825
Web: www.sherwoodfoods.com

COMPETITORS
Colorado Boxed Beef
Empire Beef
Gordon Food Service
Stock Yards Packing
Wolverine Packing

HISTORICAL FINANCIALS
Company Type: Private

Income Statement				FYE: October 31
	REVENUE ($ mil.)	NET INCOME ($ mil.)	NET PROFIT MARGIN	EMPLOYEES
10/02	762	—	—	700
10/01	830	—	—	700
10/00	750	—	—	500
10/99	725	—	—	500
10/98	750	—	—	500
10/97	750	—	—	500
10/96	750	—	—	500
10/95	645	—	—	500
10/94	499	—	—	480
10/93	453	—	—	254
Annual Growth	6.0%	—	—	11.9%

Sidley Austin Brown & Wood

Sidley Austin Brown & Wood aims to be a one-stop shop for corporate clients needing legal help. The law firm was created in 2001 by the merger of Chicago-based Sidley & Austin (founded by Norman Williams and John Thompson in 1866) and Wall Street-based Brown & Wood (established in 1914 in New York City). The firm employs more than 1,400 attorneys around the world, including Chicago and five other US cities. International offices are located in Beijing, Geneva, Hong Kong, London, Shanghai, Singapore, and Tokyo. The firm's practices include financial transactions, antitrust, bankruptcy, intellectual property, and taxes. Clients have included AT&T and Citigroup.

EXECUTIVES
Chairman Executive Committee: Thomas A. Cole
Chairman Management Committee: Charles W. Douglas
Vice Chairman Management Committee:
  Thomas R. Smith Jr., age 66
Executive Director: Timothy Bergen
CIO: Nancy Karen
Chief Marketing Officer, Chicago: Nancy Villano
Chief Marketing Officer, New York: Janet Zagorin
Director Human Resources, Firmwide:
  Michael Prapuolenis
Controller: Christian Cooley

LOCATIONS
HQ: Sidley Austin Brown & Wood LLP
Bank One Plaza, 10 S. Dearborn St.,
Chicago, IL 60603
Phone: 312-853-7000 **Fax:** 312-853-7036
Web: www.sidley.com

Sidley & Austin has US offices in Chicago, Dallas, Los Angeles, New York City, San Francisco, and Washington, DC. It has international offices in Beijing, Geneva, Hong Kong, London, Shanghai, Singapore, and Tokyo.

PRODUCTS/OPERATIONS
Selected Practice Areas
Antitrust and trade regulation
Banking and finance
Corporate
Cyberlaw
Employee benefits
Entertainment finance
Environmental
Intellectual property
Litigation
Real estate
Securities
Tax
Telecommunications

Siegel-Robert

Siegel-Robert is molding the future of plastic automotive components. The company is a leading maker of injection-molded plastic products for the automotive industry, as well as a diversified range of other manufacturers. The automotive division makes such items as door handles, emblems, radiator grilles, interior trim components, and side moldings. The company's diversified products division makes items such as texturized computer housings, light housings, and decorative faucet assemblies. Siegel-Roberts also offers chrome plating, painting, and assembly services for the products it makes.

COMPETITORS

Baker & McKenzie
Jenner & Block
Jones Day
Katten Muchin
Kirkland & Ellis
Latham & Watkins
Mayer, Brown, Rowe & Maw
McDermott, Will
Morgan, Lewis
Skadden, Arps
White & Case
Winston & Strawn

HISTORICAL FINANCIALS
Company Type: Partnership

Income Statement				FYE: December 31
	REVENUE ($ mil.)	NET INCOME ($ mil.)	NET PROFIT MARGIN	EMPLOYEES
12/03	926	—	—	—
12/02	831	—	—	2,913
12/01	715	—	—	3,000
12/00	670	—	—	3,000
12/99	446	—	—	2,000
12/98	421	—	—	2,000
12/97	360	—	—	1,952
12/96	303	—	—	1,848
12/95	277	—	—	1,623
12/94	255	—	—	1,606
Annual Growth	15.4%	—	—	7.7%

Revenue History
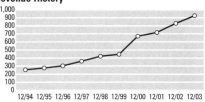

EXECUTIVES

President and CEO: David A. Adams
VP and Treasurer: Robert Bowron
Director, Recruiting: Tom Barry

LOCATIONS

HQ: Siegel-Robert Inc.
12837 Flushing Meadows Dr., St. Louis, MO 63131
Phone: 314-965-2444   **Fax:** 314-544-8472
Web: www.srob.com

Siegel-Robert operates eight manufacturing facilities in Arakansas, Georgia, Kentucky, Missouri, and Tennessee, and maintains sales offices in Mexico, and the UK.

Sierra Pacific Industries

Sierra Pacific Industries (SPI) isn't your run-of-the-mill company. One of the largest landowners in the US, SPI owns 1.5 million acres of California timberlands. SPI produces millwork, lumber, and wood fiber products and aluminum clad and wood patio doors and specialty windows. SPI operates cogeneration plants that recycle wood waste into electricity for powering its plants; excess electricity is sold to local utilities and energy service providers. The company also develops residential and commercial real estate. SPI traces its roots to a company started in the late 1920s by R. H. "Curly" Emmerson, father of CEO "Red" Emmerson. The third generation of the Emmerson family owns and operates Sierra Pacific.

Protests in the 1980s against logging on public land prompted the company to begin buying its own forested areas, a practice the company continues. In 2001 Sierra Pacific sold 30,000 acres of timberland (on the North Fork of the American River) in the Sierra Nevada mountain range to the Trust for Public Land for preservation.

The Sierra Pacific Foundation is a company enterprise that was established and funded in 1979 by "Curly" Emmerson. The foundation annually provides, among other things, more than $367,000 in scholarships to dependent children of SPI employees.

SPI also operates the Eureka Dock facility on Humboldt Bay in Eureka, California, to serve its own shipping needs as well as those of other California sawmills.

SPI is embarking on a new operation — property development. The company has determined that some of its acquired land tracts are better suited for residential or commercial development than for growing trees.

PRODUCTS/OPERATIONS

Selected Products
Automotive Components
  Body side moldings
  Door handles
  Consoles and seat trim
  Emblems
  Exterior mirrors
  Headlamp housings
  Instrument panels
  Interior trim components
  Knobs, levers, and buttons
  Modular front end assemblies
  Nameplates
  Radiator grilles
  Side moldings
  Tail lamp housings
  Wheelcovers
Diversified Products
  Computer housings
  Electrical cable assemblies
  Decorative faucet assemblies
  Decorative nameplates
  Painted furniture fixtures
  Plumbing fixtures
  Shower spray head assemblies

COMPETITORS

A. Schulman
Balda
Collins & Aikman
Donnelly
Dura Automotive
Gentex
Key Plastics
Lacks Enterprises
McKechnie
Nippon Light Metal
Plastic Omnium
Summa Industries
Venture Industries

HISTORICAL FINANCIALS
Company Type: Private

Income Statement				FYE: December 31
	ESTIMATED REVENUE ($ mil.)	NET INCOME ($ mil.)	NET PROFIT MARGIN	EMPLOYEES
12/03	600	—	—	5,000
12/02	550	—	—	4,500
12/01	540	—	—	4,500
12/00	500	—	—	4,000
12/99	500	—	—	3,500
12/98	485	—	—	3,100
Annual Growth	4.3%	—	—	10.0%

Revenue History
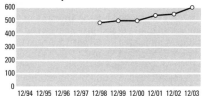

EXECUTIVES

President: A. A. (Red) Emmerson
VP Financial: Mark Emmerson
VP Sales and Marketing: George Emmerson
President, Sierra Pacific Foundation: Carolyn Emmerson Dietz
Data Processing Manager: Steve Gaston
Director, Human Resources: Ed Bond

LOCATIONS

HQ: Sierra Pacific Industries
19794 Riverside Ave., Anderson, CA 96007
Phone: 530-378-8000   **Fax:** 530-378-8109
Web: www.spi-ind.com

Sierra Pacific Industries has operations in Northern and Central California.

PRODUCTS/OPERATIONS

Selected Products
Aluminum-clad windows and doors
Cedar fencing
Chips for pulp mills
Decorative bark
Dimension lumber
Douglas Fir timbers
Millwork
Poles
Shavings for particleboard
Wood windows and doors

COMPETITORS

Atrium	Marshfield DoorSystems
Georgia-Pacific Corporation	MAXXAM
International Paper	North Pacific Group
Louisiana-Pacific	Simpson Investment
	Weyerhaeuser

HISTORICAL FINANCIALS
Company Type: Private

Income Statement
FYE: December 31

	ESTIMATED REVENUE ($ mil.)	NET INCOME ($ mil.)	NET PROFIT MARGIN	EMPLOYEES
12/03	1,400	—	—	3,600
12/02	1,300	—	—	3,900
12/01	1,315	—	—	3,700
12/00	1,500	—	—	3,600
12/99	1,450	—	—	3,600
12/98	1,100	—	—	3,000
12/97	1,000	—	—	3,200
12/96	1,000	—	—	3,200
12/95	950	—	—	3,100
12/94	770	—	—	3,000
Annual Growth	6.9%	—	—	2.0%

Revenue History

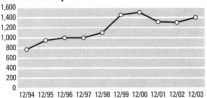

Sigma Plastics

The plastic sheeting and film business is not Greek to Sigma Plastics. Having grown through acquisitions, the company (one of the largest of its kind in North America) produces plastic film and sheet for industrial, institutional, and government markets. The company's Omega Plastics division makes flexible packaging used by the retail, food, and janitorial industries. Its Epsilon Plastics unit makes plastic garment bags. The company manufactures its diverse range of plastic products on 700 extrusion lines at its North American plants. Chairman and CEO Alfred Teo owns Sigma.

EXECUTIVES

Chairman and CEO, Sigma Plastics, Zeta Consumer Products, and Bio Starr; Chairman and Co-CEO, Aargus; Chairman, FlexSol Holding: Alfred S. Teo, age 57
President and COO, Sigma Stretch Film: Robert Nocek
CEO, FlexSol Holding: Brian Stevenson
CFO, Zeta Consumer Products Corp.: John Reier
Director, Human Resources: Debra Barbour

LOCATIONS

HQ: Sigma Plastics Group
Page & Schuyler Ave., Bldg. #8,
Lyndhurst, NJ 07071
Phone: 201-933-6000 **Fax:** 201-933-6429
Web: www.sigmaplastics.com

Sigma has more than 20 manufacturing facilities throughout North America.

COMPETITORS

Bemis	Raven Industries
DuPont	Sealed Air
Huntsman	Sonoco Products
Inteplast	Spartech
Pactiv	Tyco International

HISTORICAL FINANCIALS
Company Type: Private

Income Statement
FYE: October 31

	REVENUE ($ mil.)	NET INCOME ($ mil.)	NET PROFIT MARGIN	EMPLOYEES
10/02	750	—	—	3,100
10/01	765	—	—	3,100
10/00	720	—	—	2,400
10/99	720	—	—	2,400
10/98	765	—	—	3,000
10/97	485	—	—	2,500
10/96	400	—	—	2,150
10/95	325	—	—	1,800
10/94	265	—	—	1,200
10/93	112	—	—	—
Annual Growth	23.5%	—	—	12.6%

Revenue History

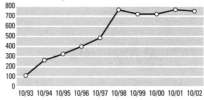

Simpson Investment

Holding company Simpson Investment Company is one of the oldest privately owned forest products companies in the northwestern US. Its Simpson Timber and Simpson Paper subsidiaries make lumber and paper products. Simpson Timber owns timberlands and produces dimension lumber and plywood at its converting facilities in California, Oregon, and Washington; its Simpson Door Company makes stile and rail wood-panel doors. Simpson Paper's Simpson Tacoma Kraft subsidiary makes bleached and unbleached kraft pulp and linerboard used in packaging (boxes and grocery bags); it recycles more than 500 tons of corrugated containers daily to convert into paper. The Simpson family has controlled the firm since its 1890 founding.

EXECUTIVES

Chairman and CEO: Colin Moseley
CFO: Allan F. Trinkwald
VP and General Manager, Simpson Tacoma Kraft Company: Don Johnson
Director, Human Resources: Clifford (Cliff) Slade
Human Resources Assistant: Linda Cronin

LOCATIONS

HQ: Simpson Investment Company
1301 Fifth Ave., Ste. 2800, Seattle, WA 98101
Phone: 206-224-5000 **Fax:** 206-224-5060
Web: www.simpson.com

Simpson Investment Company has operations in the US in California, Oregon, and Washington.

PRODUCTS/OPERATIONS

Selected Products
Doors
Kraft papers
Lumber (Douglas fir, hemlock, and coastal redwood)
Plywood
Recycled cardboard
Wood chip and sawdust products (used to make fuel, landscaping products, and paper)

COMPETITORS

Boise Cascade
Georgia-Pacific Corporation
International Paper
Louisiana-Pacific
North Pacific Group
Rayonier
Roseburg Forest Products
West Fraser Timber
Weyerhaeuser

HISTORICAL FINANCIALS
Company Type: Private

Income Statement
FYE: December 31

	ESTIMATED REVENUE ($ mil.)	NET INCOME ($ mil.)	NET PROFIT MARGIN	EMPLOYEES
12/02	800	—	—	4,300
12/01	800	—	—	4,300
12/00	785	—	—	4,300
12/99	1,400	—	—	4,300
12/98	1,500	—	—	4,500
12/97	1,400	—	—	4,200
12/96	1,500	—	—	4,500
12/95	1,700	—	—	6,600
12/94	2,000	—	—	8,000
12/93	1,100	—	—	7,600
Annual Growth	(3.5%)	—	—	(6.1%)

Revenue History

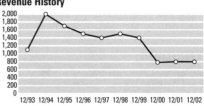

Simpson Thacher

When the urge to merge strikes corporate America, Simpson Thacher & Bartlett is ready to serve. It is one of the largest law firms in New York and a leader in assisting clients in mergers and acquisitions; the firm has had a hand in the Exxon-Mobil merger and America Online's acquisition of Time Warner. Other practice areas include capital markets, government investigations, intellectual property, labor, real estate, and tax. Simpson Thacher, which was founded in 1884, has offices in New York City and Los Angeles and Palo Alto, California, as well as Hong Kong, London, Singapore, and Tokyo.

EXECUTIVES

Chairman of the Executive Committee: Richard I. (Dick) Beattie, age 65
Director of Finance: Christopher Conroy
Director of Legal Employment: Dee Pifer
Business Development: Susan Bussy

LOCATIONS

HQ: Simpson Thacher & Bartlett LLP
425 Lexington Ave., New York, NY 10017
Phone: 212-455-2000 **Fax:** 212-455-2502
Web: www.simpsonthacher.com

PRODUCTS/OPERATIONS

Selected Practice Areas
Antitrust
Capital markets and securities
Credit and banking
Exempt organizations
Government investigations and business crimes
Intellectual property
Labor and employment
Litigation
Mergers and acquisitions
Personal planning
Real estate
Tax

COMPETITORS

Cahill Gordon	Shearman & Sterling
Cleary, Gottlieb	Skadden, Arps
Cravath, Swaine	Sullivan & Cromwell
Davis Polk	Wachtell, Lipton
Debevoise & Plimpton	Weil, Gotshal
Proskauer Rose	

HISTORICAL FINANCIALS
Company Type: Partnership

Income Statement
FYE: December 31

	REVENUE ($ mil.)	NET INCOME ($ mil.)	NET PROFIT MARGIN	EMPLOYEES
12/03	577	—	—	—
12/02	544	—	—	—
12/01	516	—	—	—
12/00	500	—	—	—
12/99	434	—	—	1,500
12/98	386	—	—	1,400
12/97	315	—	—	1,300
12/96	280	—	—	—
12/95	254	—	—	—
12/94	216	—	—	—
Annual Growth	11.5%	—	—	7.4%

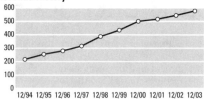

Revenue History

Sinclair Oil

Way out west, where fossils are found, brontosaur signs litter the ground. They belong to Sinclair Oil's more than 2,600 service stations and convenience stores in 22 western and midwestern US states. The company also operates three oil refineries, two pipelines (one jointly owned with ConocoPhillips), exploration operations, and a trucking fleet, all in the western US. It owns the Grand America Hotel, the Little America hotel chain, and two ski resorts (Sun Valley in Idaho and Snowbasin in Utah). Snowbasin was a venue of the 2002 Winter Olympics. The man behind all of this is Earl Holding, whose storied company, founded in 1916 by Harry Sinclair, was a central figure in the infamous Teapot Dome scandal.

EXECUTIVES

President and CEO: R. Earl Holding, age 77
VP Finance and Treasurer: Charles Barlow
VP Government Relations: Clint Ensign
VP: Kevin Brown
General Manager Retail: Larry Rogers
Auditors: PricewaterhouseCoopers LLP

LOCATIONS

HQ: Sinclair Oil Corporation
550 E. South Temple, Salt Lake City, UT 84102
Phone: 801-524-2700 **Fax:** 801-524-2880
Web: www.sinclairoil.com

Sinclair Oil's operations include marketing offices in Colorado, Kansas, Minnesota, Missouri, and Texas; refineries in Oklahoma and Wyoming; trucking terminals in Colorado, Idaho, Iowa, Kansas, Missouri, Nebraska, Oklahoma, and Wyoming; and Little America hotels and resorts in Arizona, California, Idaho, Utah, and Wyoming.

PRODUCTS/OPERATIONS

Selected Operations
Oil and Gas (marketing, pipelines, product terminals, refineries, trucking)
Little America Hotels & Resorts

COMPETITORS

BP
Cendant
ConocoPhillips
Exxon Mobil
Giant Industries
Hilton
Marriott
Royal Dutch/Shell Group
Vail Resorts
Valero Energy
Winter Sports

HISTORICAL FINANCIALS
Company Type: Private

Income Statement
FYE: December 31

	ESTIMATED REVENUE ($ mil.)	NET INCOME ($ mil.)	NET PROFIT MARGIN	EMPLOYEES
12/02	2,290	—	—	6,900
12/01	2,300	—	—	6,900
12/00	1,900	—	—	6,500
12/99	1,200	—	—	5,600
12/98	1,300	—	—	5,600
12/97	1,700	—	—	5,600
12/96	1,400	—	—	5,600
12/95	1,225	—	—	—
12/94	1,050	—	—	—
12/93	1,385	—	—	—
Annual Growth	5.7%	—	—	3.5%

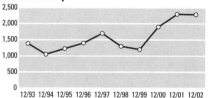

Revenue History

Sisters of Mercy Health System

Not to be confused with the goth rock band of the same name, Sisters of Mercy provides a range of health care and social services through its network of facilities in Arkansas, Kansas, Louisiana, Mississippi, Missouri, Oklahoma, and Texas. Through seven regional health systems units, the organization operates nearly 20 acute care hospitals; it also operates a psychiatric hospital, long-term care facilities, physician practices, and outpatient facilities. Sisters of Mercy Health System also runs several charitable foundations. For-profit subsidiary Mercy Health Plans offers managed care health plans, and third-party administrative services in Missouri, Illinois, and Texas.

Sisters of Mercy Health System was founded by the Sisters of Mercy of the St. Louis Regional Community in 1986.

EXECUTIVES

Chairman: Sister Mary Roch Rocklage
President and CEO: Ronald B. Ashworth, age 56
EVP and COO: John Sullivan
SVP and General Counsel: Bernard A. Duco Jr.
SVP and CFO: James R. Jaacks
EVP: Robert E. (Bob) Schimmel
SVP, Resource Optimization: Lynn Britton
VP, Medical Services: Jolene Goedken
VP, Human Resources: Stephen Isenhower
VP, Mission and Ethics: Brian O'Toole
CIO: Dick Escue
Controller: Julie Burke
Director, Communications: Barb Meyer

LOCATIONS

HQ: Sisters of Mercy Health System
14528 S. Outer Forty Dr., Ste. 100,
Chesterfield, MO 63017
Phone: 314-579-6100 **Fax:** 314-628-3723
Web: www.smhs.com

PRODUCTS/OPERATIONS

Divisions
St John's Mercy Health Care (MO)
St. John's Health System (MO)
Mercy Health System of Kansas
Mercy Health System of Oklahoma
Mercy Health System of Northwest Arkansas
St. Edward Mercy Health Network (AR)
St. Joseph's Mercy Health Center (AR)
Mercy Ministries of Laredo

COMPETITORS

BJC HealthCare
CHRISTUS Health
HCA
Methodist Healthcare
Provena Health
Rush System for Health
Sisters of Charity of Leavenworth
SSM Health Care
Tenet Healthcare
Triad Hospitals

HISTORICAL FINANCIALS

Company Type: Not-for-profit

Income Statement
FYE: June 30

	REVENUE ($ mil.)	NET INCOME ($ mil.)	NET PROFIT MARGIN	EMPLOYEES
6/03	2,722	—	—	26,000
6/02	2,392	—	—	27,800
6/01	2,191	—	—	27,000
6/00	2,200	—	—	26,500
6/99	2,298	—	—	26,000
6/98	2,169	—	—	26,000
6/97	1,970	—	—	25,300
6/96	1,700	—	—	24,000
6/95	1,505	—	—	24,000
6/94	1,046	—	—	16,900
Annual Growth	11.2%	—	—	4.9%

Revenue History

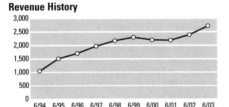

Sithe Energies

Sithe Energies wants to slice through the competition to become a leading independent power producer. Sithe owns stakes in 15 operational facilities in the US with a total generating capacity of about 1,000 MW; it also has a 200 MW facility under construction in Mexico. The firm sells energy to utilities, industrial companies, governments, and other institutions. Sithe is selling some noncore assets; it has sold its Asian and Australian power plant interests. Utility holding company Exelon owns 50% of Sithe; private investment firm Reservoir Capital has purchased the remaining 50% stake.

Exelon exercised its option to buy the remaining 50% of Sithe from other shareholders in 2003; private energy firm Apollo Energy held a 35% stake and Japanese trading firm Marubeni held 15%. Once Exelon completed its call option, it sold the 50% stake in Sithe Energies to Reservoir Capital.

Prior to the deal's completion, Sithe Energies sold seven generating units in the US and Canada (400 MW) to Reservoir Capital and its remaining Asian power generation interests (800 MW) to Marubeni. Sithe sold six power plants in Maine and Massachusetts to Exelon in 2002.

French utility giant Veolia Environnement (formerly Vivendi Environnement) sold its 34% stake in Sithe to Apollo Energy in 2002; Apollo Energy also purchased the 1% stake held by Sithe managers.

EXECUTIVES

Chairman and CEO: William Kriegel
SVP and CFO: Thomas Boehlert
VP Human Resources: Steve Atamanchuk
General Manager, Independence Plant: Bill Fernandez

LOCATIONS

HQ: Sithe Energies, Inc.
335 Madison Ave., 28th Fl., New York, NY 10017
Phone: 212-351-0000 **Fax:** 212-351-0005

Sithe Energies Inc. has power plants in the US in California, Idaho, New York, North Carolina, and Pennsylvania, as well as in Mexico.

COMPETITORS

AES
Calpine
Cogentrix
Duke Energy
Entergy
Mirant
NRG Energy
Reliant Energy
Tenaska

HISTORICAL FINANCIALS

Company Type: Private

Income Statement
FYE: December 31

	REVENUE ($ mil.)	NET INCOME ($ mil.)	NET PROFIT MARGIN	EMPLOYEES
12/03	690	(72)	—	—
12/02	1,000	—	—	—
12/01	1,000	—	—	—
Annual Growth	(16.9%)	—	—	—

Revenue History

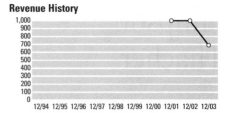

Skadden, Arps

Have you heard about the law firm that sued the business information publisher for a profile that opened with a wickedly clever lawyer joke? Neither have we, and we would like to keep it that way. Skadden, Arps, Slate, Meagher & Flom, the largest US law firm and one of the largest in the world, employs 1,750 attorneys in 21 offices around the world. Founded in 1948, the firm offers counsel for corporate dealings, litigation, and international concerns. Skadden, Arps, Slate, Meagher & Flom has first-rate bankruptcy and securities practices and is a leader in mergers and acquisitions (M&A) work.

Long regarded for its M&A practice, Skadden, Arps is also a very big player in litigation work. In 2003 it defended Cendant Corporation against an investor class action lawsuit and it helped the National Football League in its conflict with Oakland Raiders owner Al Davis over revenue sharing. Embattled corporations WorldCom (now MCI) and HEALTHSOUTH are also among Skadden, Arps' litigation clients. Meanwhile, the firm's M&A practice kept up the pace in 2003, representing clients in more than 70 transactions that were worth more than $100 million.

One area of growth for the firm has been its corporate restructuring practice, which got a big boost from its work on Kmart's history-making bankruptcy and reorganization. The firm is looking to make the same kind of splash in the UK and throughout Europe.

HISTORY

Marshall Skadden, Leslie Arps, and John Slate hung out their shingle in New York City on April Fool's Day, 1948. Skadden and Arps came from a Wall Street law firm, and Slate had been counsel to Pan American World Airways. Without the reputation and connections of the established New York law firms, the firm found work one case at a time from referrals, handling mainly commercial, corporate, and litigations work. Marshall Skadden died in 1958.

Denied the luxury of steady clients, the firm was forced to be innovative and, at times, unorthodox. Joe Flom, who had joined as the firm's first associate, specialized in corporate law and proxy fights. During the 1960s, when tender offers and hostile takeovers increased, many of the more venerable firms referred clients engaged in the undignified corporate raids to Flom to preserve their gentlemanly reputations. With "white shoe" lawyers on Wall Street hesitant to tread into the uncivilized region of corporate takeovers, Skadden, Arps went for it, and the firm virtually pioneered the business of mergers and acquisitions (M&A) under Flom.

When Congress passed the Williams Act in 1968, which "legitimized" tender offers by providing regulation, other law firms started to get in on the act. Skadden, Arps was way ahead of the game, however, and as corporations and lawyers realized that aggressive legal tactics helped win corporate takeover battles, it also became apparent that Joe Flom was the expert. As takeover fights became more frequent in the early 1970s, the firm earned more than just respect. Earnings came not just from some of the highest hourly rates in the industry, but from hefty retainers (now a common practice at many firms) on the theory that association with Flom would scare raiders off. The only other name that could strike such fear in people's hearts was Marty Lipton of rival takeover specialists Wachtell, Lipton, Rosen & Katz. From the late 1970s through the 1980s, Skadden, Arps was involved in almost every important M&A case in the US.

The firm used its success in mergers and acquisitions to build its practice in other areas. In the early 1980s it branched into bankruptcy, product liability, and real estate law. By then it had opened offices in Boston; Chicago; Los Angeles; Washington, DC; and Wilmington, Delaware. Les Arps died in 1987.

With the boom in mergers and acquisitions activity and bankruptcies in the late 1980s, the firm grew to almost 2,000 lawyers by 1989. Then came the recession, and M&A work virtually dried up. Skadden, Arps responded by shedding more than 500 lawyers between 1989 and 1990. It also scrambled to diversify and expand internationally. As takeover activity rebounded in the mid-1990s, the diversification strategy actually began to work against Skadden, Arps because profits didn't skyrocket like those of M&A specialist firms.

The firm opened an office in Singapore in 1995 to coordinate its Asian business, signaling that city's growing importance as a financial center. Two years later two-thirds of the firm's Beijing team defected to a rival firm. Headquarters shrugged it off and flew in replacements. Representing President Bill Clinton, Skadden, Arps won one of its highest-profile cases in 1998 when the sexual harassment suit brought by Paula Jones was thrown out.

With its M&A practice in full swing again, Skadden, Arps was involved in 70 announced M&A deals in 1999, including the $75 billion merger of oil companies Exxon and Mobil. It also became the first US law firm to reach $1 billion in revenue in 2000. The company announced an alliance with Italian law firm Studio Chiomenti the following year and took part in three of the top ten M&A deals of 2002. Skadden, Arps helped struggling discount retailer Kmart emerge from its titanic bankruptcy the next year.

EXECUTIVES

Executive Partner: Robert C. Sheehan
Senior Partner: Joseph H. Flom
Senior Partner, Corporate Practice: Roger S. Aaron
Senior Partner, Litigation: William P. Frank
Finance Director: Carol A. Sawdye
Director of Associate Development: Jodie R. Garfinkel
Director of Human Resources: Laurel J. Henschel
Director of Legal Hiring: Carol Lee H. Sprague
Director of Marketing and Business Development: Sally J. Feldman
Director of Technology: Harris Z. Tilevitz

Managing Partner, Asian Practice: Phyllis G. Korff
Managing Partner, Boston: Louis A. Goodman
Managing Partner, Chicago: Wayne W. Whalen
Managing Partner, European Practice: Bruce M. Buck
Managing Partner, Houston: Lyndon C. Taylor
Managing Partner, Los Angeles: Rand S. April
Managing Partner, New York: Wallace L. Schwartz
Managing Partner, Palo Alto and San Francisco: Kenton J. (Ken) King
Managing Partner, Toronto: Christopher W. Morgan
Managing Partner, Washington, DC: Michael P. Rogan
Managing Partner, Wilmington: Steven J. Rothschild

LOCATIONS

HQ: Skadden, Arps, Slate, Meagher & Flom LLP
4 Times Square, New York, NY 10036
Phone: 212-735-3000   **Fax:** 212-735-2000
Web: www.skadden.com

Selected Office Locations
US
  Boston
  Chicago
  Houston
  Los Angeles
  New York City
  Palo Alto, CA
  San Francisco
  Washington, DC
  Wilmington, DE
International
  Beijing
  Brussels
  Frankfurt
  Hong Kong
  London
  Moscow
  Paris
  Singapore
  Sydney
  Tokyo
  Toronto
  Vienna

PRODUCTS/OPERATIONS

Selected Practice Areas
Antitrust
Banking and institutional investing
Corporate finance
Government affairs
Health care
Insurance
Intellectual property
International trade
Internet and e-commerce
Labor and employment law
Litigation
Mass torts and insurance litigation
Mergers and acquisitions
Real estate
Tax
Trusts and estates
White-collar crime

COMPETITORS

Baker & McKenzie
Cleary, Gottlieb
Clifford Chance
Cravath, Swaine
Davis Polk
Debevoise & Plimpton
Jones Day
Latham & Watkins
Mayer, Brown, Rowe & Maw
Paul, Weiss, Rifkind
Shearman & Sterling
Sidley Austin Brown & Wood
Simpson Thacher
Sullivan & Cromwell
Wachtell, Lipton
Weil, Gotshal
White & Case

HISTORICAL FINANCIALS
Company Type: Partnership

Income Statement
FYE: December 31

	REVENUE ($ mil.)	NET INCOME ($ mil.)	NET PROFIT MARGIN	EMPLOYEES
12/03	1,330	—	—	—
12/02	1,310	—	—	4,490
12/01	1,225	—	—	4,350
12/00	1,154	—	—	4,235
12/99	1,025	—	—	3,600
12/98	890	—	—	3,200
12/97	826	—	—	3,000
12/96	710	—	—	3,150
12/95	635	—	—	3,000
12/94	582	—	—	3,100
Annual Growth	9.6%	—	—	4.7%

Revenue History

Smithsonian

The Smithsonian Institution wears many hats, from the one worn by Harrison Ford in the Indiana Jones Trilogy to the one worn by Abraham Lincoln the night he was assassinated. The world's largest museum, the Smithsonian houses more than 140 million pieces in 17 museums and galleries. More than 35 million people every year come view its exhibits on art, music, TV and film, science, history, and other subjects. Admission to its museums, most of which are located on the National Mall in Washington, DC (two are in New York City), is usually free. The Smithsonian also operates the National Zoo and a handful of research facilities. The Smithsonian receives 57% of its operating revenue from the federal government.

The Smithsonian's exhibits display items such as the Declaration of Independence, the ruby slippers worn by Judy Garland in *The Wizard of Oz*, and the Wright Brothers' first airplane. A board of regents that includes Vice President Richard Cheney, Chief Justice William Rehnquist, six members of Congress, and nine private citizens leads the institution.

HISTORY

English chemist James Smithson wrote a proviso to his will in 1826 that would lead to the creation of the Smithsonian Institution. When he died in 1829, he left his estate to his nephew, Henry James Hungerford, with the stipulation that if Hungerford died without heirs, the estate would go to the US to create "an Establishment for the increase and diffusion of knowledge among men." Hungerford died in 1835 without any heirs, and the US government inherited more than $500,000 in gold.

Congress squandered the money after it was received in 1838, but perhaps feeling pangs of guilt, covered the loss. The Smithsonian was finally created in 1846, and Princeton physicist Joseph Henry was named as its first secretary. That year it established the Museum of Natural History, the Museum of History and Technology, and the National Gallery of Art. The Smithsonian's National Museum was developed around the collection of the US Patent Office in 1858. The Smithsonian continued to expand, adding the National Zoological Park in 1889 and the Smithsonian Astrophysical Observatory in 1890.

The Freer Gallery, a gift of industrialist Charles Freer, opened in 1923. The National Gallery was renamed the National Collection of Fine Arts in 1937, and a new National Gallery, created with Andrew Mellon's gift of his art collection and a building, opened in 1941. The Air and Space Museum was established in 1946.

More museums were added in the 1960s, including the National Portrait Gallery in 1962 and the Anacostia Museum (exhibits and materials on African-American history) in 1967. The Kennedy Center for the Performing Arts was opened in 1971. The Collection of Fine Arts was renamed the National Museum of American Art and the Museum of History and Technology was renamed the National Museum of American History in 1980.

The Smithsonian placed its first-ever contribution boxes in four of its museums in 1993. A planned exhibit featuring the Enola Gay — the plane that dropped the atomic bomb on Hiroshima — created a firestorm in 1994 with critics charging that the exhibit downplayed Japanese aggression and US casualties in WWII. The original exhibit was canceled in 1995, the director of the Air and Space Museum resigned, and a scaled-down version of the exhibit premiered.

Large contributions from private donors continued in the 1990s; the Mashantucket Pequot tribe gave $10 million from its casino operations in 1994 for a planned American Indian museum and prolific electronics inventor Jerome Lemelson donated $10.4 million in 1995. The museum celebrated its sesquicentennial in 1996 amid news that $500 million in repairs were needed over the next 10 years.

California real estate developer Kenneth Behring gave the largest cash donation ever to the museum in 1997 — $20 million for the National Museum of Natural History. Short of funds, the Smithsonian had to cut back on its 150th anniversary traveling exhibit that year. The Smithsonian announced a $26 million renovation for the National Museum of Natural History in 1998. Two years later Kenneth Behring quadrupled his record-breaking 1997 donation of $20 million by giving $80 million to the National Museum of American History. Catherine Reynolds withdrew most of her $38 million gift in 2002 after the Smithsonian Institution refused to implement her ideas for an exhibit at the National Museum of American History.

EXECUTIVES

Secretary: Lawrence M. Small, age 62
Deputy Secretary and COO: Sheila Burke
CFO: Alice Maroni
CEO, Smithsonian Business Ventures: Gary Beer
CIO: Dennis R. Shaw
Treasurer: Sudeep Anand
Director, Communications and Public Affairs: Evelyn S. Lieberman
Director, Government Relations: Penelope (Nell) Payne
Acting Director, Human Resources: James Douglas
Director, National Programs: Herma J. Hightower
Director, Planning, Management, and Budget: Bruce A. Dauer
Director, Policy and Analysis: Carole M. P. Neves
General Counsel: John E. Huerta
Director, American Art Museum and Renwick Gallery: Elizabeth Broun
Director, Hirshhorn Museum and Sculpture Garden: Ned Rifkin
Director, National Air and Space Museum: John R. Dailey
Director, National Museum of American History, Behring Center: Brent D. Glass
Director, National Museum of the American Indian: W. Richard West Jr.
Director, National Museum of Natural History: Cristián Samper
Director, National Portrait Gallery: Marc J. Pachter
Director, National Zoological Park: Lucy H. Spelman, age 41
Director, International Art Museums Division: Thomas W. (Tom) Lentz, age 48

LOCATIONS

HQ: Smithsonian Institution
1000 Jefferson Dr. SW, Washington, DC 20560
Phone: 202-357-2700   **Fax:** 202-786-2377
Web: www.si.edu

The Smithsonian Institution has museums and galleries located in New York City and Washington, DC; its research centers are located in the US and Panama.

PRODUCTS/OPERATIONS

Museums & Research Centers

Anacostia Museum and Center for African American History & Culture
Archives of American Art
Arthur M. Sackler Gallery
Arts and Industries Building
Center for Folklife Programs and Cultural Heritage
Conservation and Research Center
Cooper-Hewitt, National Design Museum (New York City)
Freer Gallery of Art
Hirshhorn Museum and Sculpture Garden
National Air and Space Museum
National Museum of African Art
National Museum of American History
National Museum of Natural History
National Museum of the American Indian (New York City)
National Portrait Gallery
National Postal Museum
National Zoological Park
Smithsonian American Art Museum
Renwick Gallery
Smithsonian Astrophysical Observatory
Smithsonian Center for Latino Initiatives
Smithsonian Center for Materials Research and Education
Smithsonian Environmental Research Center
Smithsonian Institution Building (The Castle)
Smithsonian Marine Station at Fort Pierce
Smithsonian Tropical Research Institute

HISTORICAL FINANCIALS

Company Type: Not-for-profit

Income Statement   FYE: September 30

	REVENUE ($ mil.)	NET INCOME ($ mil.)	NET PROFIT MARGIN	EMPLOYEES
9/03	691	—	—	—
9/02	691	—	—	—
9/01	665	—	—	—
9/00	604	—	—	6,500
9/99	563	—	—	6,400
9/98	775	—	—	—
9/97	729	—	—	6,469
9/96	703	—	—	6,487
9/95	750	—	—	6,600
9/94	605	—	—	6,671
Annual Growth	1.5%	—	—	(0.4%)

Revenue History

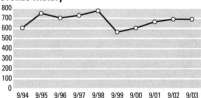

Software House

Software House International (SHI) wants to put software in houses across the globe. The company distributes more than 100,000 hardware and software products from suppliers such as Adobe, Corel, Microsoft, and IBM. SHI also offers professional services such as systems integration and application development through its Software House Enterprise Solutions division. The company counts Agilent, AT&T, Boeing, and Hewlett-Packard among its clients. Founded in 1982, SHI has grown from a company with less than $1 million in annual revenue in 1989, when entrepreneur Thai Lee assumed ownership, to a company with more than $1 billion in annual revenues.

EXECUTIVES

Chairman and Co-CEO: Leo Koguan, age 49
President and Co-CEO: Thai Lee, age 46
CFO: Paul Ng
Human Resources: Anthony Salina

LOCATIONS

HQ: Software House International, Inc.
2 Riverview Dr., Somerset, NJ 08873
Phone: 732-764-8888   **Fax:** 732-764-8889
Web: www.shi.com

Software House International has offices in Canada, France, Hong Kong, the UK, and the US.

PRODUCTS/OPERATIONS

Selected Products
Cameras
Copiers
Fax machines
Motherboards
Notebooks
PCs
Printers
Processors
Scanners
Servers
Software
Storage products
Switchers and routers

Selected Services
Application development
Asset management
Contract staffing
Desktop installation
E-commerce
Network consulting
Security management
Systems integration
Technical support

COMPETITORS

Arrow Electronics
ASI Corp.
Avnet
Bell Microproducts
CDW
CompuCom
GE Access
ICG
Ingram Micro
Merisel
Pacific Magtron
SARCOM
Softmart
Supercom
Tech Data

HISTORICAL FINANCIALS
Company Type: Private

Income Statement				FYE: December 31
	REVENUE ($ mil.)	NET INCOME ($ mil.)	NET PROFIT MARGIN	EMPLOYEES
12/03	1,797	—	—	900
12/02	1,875	—	—	1,000
12/01	1,730	—	—	1,000
12/00	1,390	—	—	1,000
12/99	909	—	—	1,000
Annual Growth	18.6%	—	—	(2.6%)

Revenue History

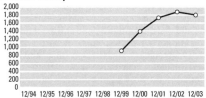

Solo Cup

It looks like Solo Cup has given up the singles life in exchange for a new Sweetheart. The company has agreed to purchase rival SF Holdings, parent company of disposable product maker Sweetheart Cup. It makes disposable cups, plates, cutlery, and the like. Solo Cup's items are sold to major retailers and food-service retailers. The firm's plastic, paper, and foam goods are sold, soiled, and thrown out around the world. Leo J. Hulseman, whose descendants still own the company, founded the Paper Container Manufacturing Company in 1936; it became Solo Cup in 1946, named for the cone-shaped paper cup that made it famous. The company's Sweetheart of a deal was consummated in February 2004.

The marriage of Solo and Sweetheart creates a company with more than 30 manufacturing facilities in North America (more than 20 from the Sweetheart side) and combined sales of $2 billion. Solo also operates factories in England, Japan, and Panama. The deal was helped along by a $220 million investment in Solo from equity firm Vestar Capital Partners in exchange for a minority stake in the new company.

In terms of competition, Dart Container is the largest remaining rival in the North American disposable food service market; the new company would be second to Pactiv Corporation in the injection molding or thermoforming segment.

The sale includes Hoffmaster Tissues and Fonda Brands, two other paper product companies owned by Sweetheart parent SF Holdings Group.

EXECUTIVES

Chairman and CEO: Robert L. Hulseman
President and COO: Ronald L. Whaley
EVP and CFO: Susan Marks
SVP, Global Human Resources: Kathleen Wolf

LOCATIONS

HQ: Solo Cup Company
1700 Old Deerfield Rd., Highland Park, IL 60035
Phone: 847-831-4800   **Fax:** 847-831-5849
Web: www.solocup.com

Solo Cup sells its products in 50 countries around the world. It has distributors in Africa, Asia, the Caribbean, Europe, Latin America, the Middle East, the South Pacific, and the US.

PRODUCTS/OPERATIONS

Selected Products and Brands
Consumer Products Division
  Cozy Cups
  Party Line (plastic plates, bowls, cups)
  SignatureColors (plastic plates, bowls, cups)
  Solo Bathroom Cups
  Solo Kitchen Cups
  Storables (disposable storage containers)
  Ultra Clear (clear and colored plastic cups)
Food Service Products Division
  Cutlery
  Dispensers
  Foam containers
  Paper plates, bowls, cups
  Plastic plates, bowls, cups, lids, deli and food containers
  Straws

COMPETITORS

American Greetings
Amscan
Berry Plastics
Dart Container
EarthShell
Huhtamäki
Pactiv
Rexam
Reynolds Food Packaging

HISTORICAL FINANCIALS
Company Type: Private

Income Statement				FYE: December 31
	ESTIMATED REVENUE ($ mil.)	NET INCOME ($ mil.)	NET PROFIT MARGIN	EMPLOYEES
12/03	900	—	—	4,700
12/02	900	—	—	4,700
12/01	900	—	—	4,700
12/00	833	—	—	4,700
Annual Growth	2.6%	—	—	0.0%

Revenue History

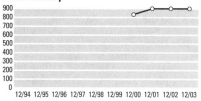

Sony BMG

Hoping to strike all the right chords, Sony BMG Music Entertainment is the world's #2 music company (behind Universal Music). A 50-50 joint venture between Sony Corporation of America and Bertelsmann AG, the company is home to labels such as Columbia (Aerosmith, Dixie Chicks), Epic (Good Charlotte, Jennifer Lopez), RCA (Christina Aguilera, Avril Lavigne), J Records (Alicia Keys, Rod Stewart), LaFace (OutKast, Pink), Sony Classical (Yo-Yo Ma, John Williams), and Jive (Britney Spears, 'N Sync). The newly merged company does not include the music publishing and CD distribution and manufacturing businesses of Sony and Bertelsmann. In conjunction with the merger, Sony BMG expects to cut its staff by about 20%.

While Sony and BMG were previously the third- and fifth-largest record companies in the world, respectively, the merged unit ranks just behind powerhouse Universal, and significantly ahead of Warner Music Group and EMI Group.

Sony has three primary music units: Sony Music (US music operations), Sony Music International (music operations outside the US and Japan), and Sony Classical. Labels under the Sony Music unit include 550 Music, Harmony Records, Legacy Recordings, Loud Records, Razor Sharp, and Untertainment. Among its artists are Aerosmith, Barbra Streisand, and Black Crowes. Sony Music International houses labels such as Mambo, Rubenstein, Dragnet, and Squatt, with artists ranging from Julio Iglesias to Harlem Yu. Artists such as Isaac Stern and Yo-Yo Ma have recorded for Sony Classical, which includes the labels Arc of Light, Masterworks, Sony Broadway, SEON, and Vivarte.

BMG significantly increased its bulk when it purchased Zomba Records for $2.74 billion just a week after buying out Clive Davis' J Records and merging it with RCA. Despite its success, BMG still ranks #5 in worldwide market share and failed to make a profit in 2001. Prior to its announced merger with Sony, BMG parent Bertelsmann negotiated with UK-based EMI Group about a possible merger with BMG in 2000. The deal, however, faced possible opposition by European regulators and talks ended in 2001. BMG joined Warner Music and EMI to form MusicNet in 2001 with RealNetworks. The company unified many of its labels' catalogs through its BMG Heritage label, which develops and markets classics from Elvis, Aretha Franklin, and Willie Nelson, among others. Jive Records accounts for about one-third of BMG's US market share.

In 2004 BMG underwent significant restructuring, expanding its RCA Music Group to include most of Arista's staff and roster. In addition, Zomba Records reorganized to become Zomba Label Group, headed by Jive Records president

Barry Weiss. Zomba has also taken on some of Arista's former staff, and now includes LaFace and So So Def in its family of labels.

On the Sony side, industry veteran Tommy Mottola abruptly resigned as chairman in early 2003 (Sony released him from his contract, which was to expire in 2004), casting further doubt on Sony's stability in a troubled market. Mottola's replacement, former NBC president Andrew Lack, undertook a massive restructuring of the company, eliminating about 1,000 jobs.

EXECUTIVES
Chairman: Rolf Schmidt-Holtz, age 56
CEO: Andrew R. (Andy) Lack, age 57
COO: Michael Smellie
EVP and CFO: Kevin Kelleher
EVP and Chief Marketing Officer: Tim Prescott
EVP and Chief Business and Legal Affairs Officer: Ron Wilcox
SVP, General Counsel, and Secretary: Lisa Weiss
SVP and European Counsel: Jonathan Sternberg
VP Corporate Communications: Keith Estabrook
Chairman and CEO, Sony BMG Music North America: Clive Davis, age 71
Chairman, RCA Nashville: Joe Galante
President and CEO, Sony Music US: Don Ienner
President, Columbia Records Group: Will Botwin

LOCATIONS
HQ: Sony BMG Music Entertainment
550 Madison Ave., New York, NY 10022
Phone: 212-833-8000   **Fax:** 212-833-4818
Web: www.sonybmg.com

Sony BMG Music Entertainment has operations in more than 60 countries.

PRODUCTS/OPERATIONS

Selected Recording Artists

AC/DC	Julio Iglesias
Aerosmith	Justin Timberlake
Alan Jackson	Kenny Chesney
Alicia Keys	Lauryn Hill
Aretha Franklin	Macy Gray
Avril Lavigne	Marc Anthony
Barbra Streisand	Maroon 5
Barry White	Martina McBride
Beyonce	Mary Chapin Carpenter
Bob Dylan	Michael Jackson
Britney Spears	Miles Davis
Bruce Springsteen	Montgomery Gentry
Celine Dion	OutKast
Christina Aguilera	R. Kelly
Clint Black	Sade
Dave Matthews Band	Santana
Destiny's Child	Shakira
Dixie Chicks	Tony Bennett
Foo Fighters	Travis Tritt
Gloria Estefan	Usher
Good Charlotte	Whitney Houston
Jennifer Lopez	Will Smith
Jessica Simpson	Wyclef Jean
John Mayer	Wynton Marsalis
John Williams	Yo-Yo Ma

COMPETITORS
EMI Group
Universal Music Group
Warner Music

Southern States

Founded in 1923 to provide affordable, high-quality seed to Virginia farmers, Southern States Cooperative serves about 321,000 members, mainly in midwestern and southern states. The co-op offers its farmer-owners feed and fertilizer manufacturing, seed processing, grain marketing, and petroleum and propane services, as well as wholesale farm supplies. Its Southern States and GardenSouth stores sell farm supplies, garden products, and fuel through more than 1,100 retail outlets. Other services include GrowMaster Crop Services, sales financing, and an aquaculture program. Southern States Cooperative merged with Michigan Livestock Exchange in 1998 and purchased Agway Inc.'s consumer wholesale dealer business.

With the bankruptcy and subsequent 2004 liquidation of Agway, Southern States became the sole owner of Cooperative Milling Inc. It also obtained various Agway trademarks and its Internet domain name.

EXECUTIVES
Chairman: John Henry Smith
President and CEO: Thomas Scribner
EVP and CFO: Leslie Newton
SVP, General Counsel, and Secretary: N. Hopper Ancarrow Jr.
EVP and COO: Wesley Wright
VP and CIO: Karen Lankford
VP and Controller: Philip Miller
VP, Finance and Treasurer: Fred Jezouit
VP, Human Resources: Jerry Walker
VP, Marketing and Independent Markets: Steve Patterson
Director, Corporate Communications, Member Relations, and Public Affairs: Jim Erickson
Auditors: PricewaterhouseCoopers LLP

LOCATIONS
HQ: Southern States Cooperative, Incorporated
6606 W. Broad St., Richmond, VA 23230
Phone: 804-281-1000   **Fax:** 804-281-1413
Web: www.southernstates.com

Southern States Cooperative has operations in Alabama, Arkansas, Delaware, Florida, Georgia, Indiana, Kentucky, Louisiana, Maryland, Michigan, Mississippi, North Carolina, Ohio, Pennsylvania, South Carolina, Texas, Virginia, and West Virginia.

COMPETITORS

ADM	GROWMARK
Ag Processing	Rabo AgServices
Andersons	Scoular
CHS	Tennessee Farmers Co-op
ConAgra	Tractor Supply

HISTORICAL FINANCIALS
Company Type: Joint venture

Income Statement			FYE: March 31
	ESTIMATED REVENUE ($ mil.)	NET INCOME ($ mil.)	NET PROFIT MARGIN	EMPLOYEES
3/04	8,000	—	—	10,000

HISTORICAL FINANCIALS
Company Type: Cooperative

Income Statement			FYE: June 30
	REVENUE ($ mil.)	NET INCOME ($ mil.)	NET PROFIT MARGIN	EMPLOYEES
6/03	1,311	(55)	—	3,379
6/02	1,463	(68)	—	5,000
6/01	1,739	(15)	—	5,700
6/00	1,547	5	0.3%	5,425
6/99	1,366	(2)	—	6,000
6/98	1,120	11	1.0%	3,800
6/97	1,216	28	2.3%	3,800
6/96	1,123	28	2.5%	3,800
6/95	1,014	18	1.8%	3,800
6/94	950	7	0.8%	3,539
Annual Growth	3.6%	—	—	(0.5%)

2003 Year-End Financials
Debt ratio: 1,613.2%   Current ratio: 1.54
Return on equity: —   Long-term debt ($ mil.): 183
Cash ($ mil.): 18

Net Income History

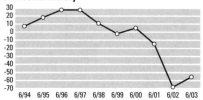

Southern Wine & Spirits

Fueled by alcohol and nicotine, Southern Wine & Spirits of America delivers market dominance. The firm is the #1 US distributor of wine and spirits, serving 12 states. In addition to importing and distributing wine and spirits, it distributes imported brews, such as Grolsch and Steinlager; cigars, such as Don Diego and Montecristo; and nonalcoholic beverages, including Clamato and Rose's Lime Juice. The company also owns large stakes in both Pacific Wine & Spirits (part of Terlato Wine Group) and Romano Bros. Beverage, the largest spirits wholesaler in Illinois; it is also entering new markets elsewhere. Chairman and CEO Harvey Chaplin and his secretive family own more than 50% of the company.

EXECUTIVES
Chairman and CEO: Harvey R. Chaplin
President and COO: Wayne E. Chaplin
EVP and General Manager, Southern Wine & Spirits of California: Ted Simpkins
EVP, Spirits: Rodolfo (Rudy) Ruiz, age 56
SVP, President of Wine Division: Melvin (Mel) Dick
First VP and Treasurer: Steven Becker
VP, Finance and Administration: John R. Preston
VP, Director, National Accounts: Ken Kribel
VP, Sales, National Accounts: Bill Edwards
VP, Marketing, National Accounts: Lisa Barghahn
VP, Systems, National Accounts: Joanne Mitchell
VP, Secretary, and Chief Administrative Officer: Lee F. Hager
Director, Fine Wine: Jimmy Mancbach
National Director, Human Resources: Mark Krauss

LOCATIONS

HQ: Southern Wine & Spirits of America, Inc.
1600 NW 163rd St., Miami, FL 33169
Phone: 305-625-4171 **Fax:** 305-625-4720
Web: www.southernwineandspirits.com

Southern Wine & Spirits of America distributes products from 15 warehouses in Arizona, California, Colorado, Florida, Hawaii, Illinois, Kentucky, Nevada, New Mexico, Pennsylvania, and South Carolina. The company has exclusive rights to distribute Allied Domecq brands in California and Hawaii and a "first choice" agreement with Allied Domecq in South Carolina.

PRODUCTS/OPERATIONS

Selected Products
Beer
Cigars
Nonalcoholic beverages and mixes
Spirits
Wines

COMPETITORS

Altadis
Bacardi
Banfi Vintners
Ben E. Keith
Constellation Brands
Geerlings & Wade
Georgia Crown
Glazer's Wholesale Drug
Johnson Brothers
National Distributing
National Wine & Spirits
Peerless Importers
Rémy Cointreau
Sunbelt Beverage
Synergy Brands
Topa Equities
UST
Wirtz
Young's Market

HISTORICAL FINANCIALS
Company Type: Private

Income Statement   FYE: December 31

	REVENUE ($ mil.)	NET INCOME ($ mil.)	NET PROFIT MARGIN	EMPLOYEES
12/02	4,400	—	—	7,100
12/01	3,750	—	—	5,680
12/00	3,500	—	—	5,600
12/99	3,100	—	—	5,400
12/98	2,600	—	—	4,500
12/97	2,450	—	—	4,500
12/96	2,200	—	—	4,000
12/95	2,125	—	—	4,000
12/94	1,985	—	—	3,925
12/93	1,620	—	—	3,675
Annual Growth	11.7%	—	—	7.6%

Revenue History

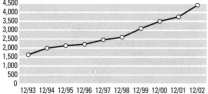

Southwire

Southwire hopes everyone's cable-ready. One of the world's largest cable and wire manufacturers, Southwire makes building wire and cable, utility cable products, industrial power cable, telecommunications cable, copper and aluminum rods, and cord products. The company also provides engineering and machining and fabrication services. Its Forte Power Systems subsidiary provides turnkey services for high-voltage systems using extruded-dielectric cable. Founded in 1950 by Roy Richards Sr. (the chairman's father), Southwire is owned by the Richards family.

Southwire will continue to build on its core operations, as evidenced by its purchase of General Cable Corporation's building wire assets, which made Southwire one of North America's largest producers of building wire. The company is also expanding its base of operations in Asia, such as the copper rod system deal with China's Jiangxi Copper Products Company that includes a furnace system complete with a loader, melter, holder and launder system, casting machine, and automatic metal pouring system.

EXECUTIVES

Chairman: Roy Richards Jr.
Vice Chairman and President, Business Development: Lee Richards
President and CEO: Stuart Thorn
VP, Finance: J. Guyton Cochran Jr.
VP, Information Technology Services: Lee Hunter
VP, Human Resources: Michael R. (Mike) Wiggins
VP, Legal: Stanley Tate
VP, Operations: Jeff Herrin
Manager, Communications: Gary Leftwich

LOCATIONS

HQ: Southwire Company
One Southwire Dr., Carrollton, GA 30119
Phone: 770-832-4242 **Fax:** 770-832-4929
Web: www.mysouthwire.com

Southwire operates manufacturing plants in the US and sales offices in Hong Kong, Mexico City, and Paris.

PRODUCTS/OPERATIONS

Selected Products
Aluminum rod
Building wire
Communication cable
Copper rod
Electrical wire and cable
High-voltage cable
Magnet wire
Specialty wire
Transit cable
Wire-making machinery

COMPETITORS

AFC Cable	Genesis Cable
Alcan	Hitachi Cable
Alcatel	International Wire
Alpine Group	IRCE
Anixter International	Nexans
Balfour Beatty	OFS BrightWave
Belden CDT	Phelps Dodge
Bridon	Pirelli & C.
Capro	Showa Electric Wire & Cable
Carlisle Companies	
Driver-Harris	Sumitomo Electric
Encore Wire	Superior Essex
General Cable	Volex

HISTORICAL FINANCIALS
Company Type: Private

Income Statement   FYE: December 31

	ESTIMATED REVENUE ($ mil.)	NET INCOME ($ mil.)	NET PROFIT MARGIN	EMPLOYEES
12/02	1,400	—	—	3,300
12/01	1,500	—	—	3,300
12/00	1,500	—	—	3,000
12/99	1,300	—	—	4,000
12/98	1,400	—	—	4,500
12/97	1,700	—	—	4,900
12/96	1,700	—	—	5,000
12/95	1,900	—	—	5,200
12/94	1,600	—	—	5,000
12/93	1,300	—	—	5,000
Annual Growth	0.8%	—	—	(4.5%)

Revenue History

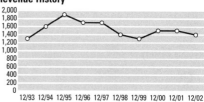

Spectrum Health

Spectrum Health is a regional health system serving western Michigan. The health network features nearly a dozen hospitals, most of which operate under the Spectrum Health name, with more than 2,000 beds. Residents and visitors to the area can also access Spectrum Health through its more than 140 service sites, which include urgent care centers, primary care physician offices, community clinics, rehabilitation and other outpatient facilities, and continuing care residences and services for the elderly. The health system also operates Priority Health, an HMO.

EXECUTIVES

President and CEO: Richard C. (Rick) Breon
EVP and CFO: Michael P. (Mike) Freed
SVP, System Quality: John Byrnes
SVP: John Mosley
SVP, Human Resources: Daniel Oglesby
SVP and CIO: Patrick O'Hare
VP, Operations: Bill Ritscha
VP, Patient Care Services and Chief Nursing Officer: Shawn M. Ulreich
VP, Clinical Operations: Jim Wilson, age 48
General Counsel: David Leonard
Auditors: Ernst & Young LLP

LOCATIONS

HQ: Spectrum Health
100 Michigan St. NE, Grand Rapids, MI 49503
Phone: 616-391-1774 **Fax:** 616-391-2780
Web: www.spectrum-health.org

Hospitals
DeVos Children's Hospital (Grand Rapids)
Spectrum Health Blodgett Campus (Grand Rapids)
Spectrum Health Butterworth Campus (Grand Rapids)
Spectrum Health Kent Community Campus (Grand Rapids)
Spectrum Health United Campus (Greenville)
Spectrum Health Kelsey Campus (Lakeview)
Hackley Hospital (Muskegon)
Spectrum Health Reed City Campus (Reed City)
Hackley Lakeshore Hospital (Shelby)

HISTORICAL FINANCIALS
Company Type: Not-for-profit

Income Statement				FYE: June 30
	REVENUE ($ mil.)	NET INCOME ($ mil.)	NET PROFIT MARGIN	EMPLOYEES
6/04	1,868	—	—	14,000
6/03	1,538	—	—	14,000
6/02	1,373	—	—	—
Annual Growth	16.6%	—	—	0.0%

Revenue History

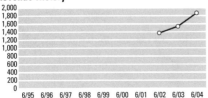

Springs Industries

Springs Industries wants to cozy up in your bedroom. The company makes bath rugs, bedspreads, pillows, sheets, shower curtains, and towels under the Springmaid and Wamsutta brands. Springs also makes baby bedding, fabrics, hardware, infant apparel, and window blinds (Bali, Graber brands). The firm makes private-label items for Wal-Mart and Target, and licensed brands such as Harry Potter and NASCAR. Springs sells through catalogs, department stores, and mass retailers. The Close family, descendants of co-founder Leroy Springs, owns about 55% of Springs. Heartland Industrial Partners, with which the Close family took the firm private, owns the remaining 45%.

Wal-Mart represents about 25% of Springs' sales. The company also sells through about 60 of its own outlet stores. Historically a textile maker for apparel, Springs has spent the last decade refocusing on home fashions through sales and acquisitions. In 2003 Springs acquired Charles D. Owen Manufacturing, the company's blanket supplier.

HISTORY

Springs Industries began in 1887 as Fort Mill Manufacturing Co., a cotton miller organized by Samuel Elliott White and a group of investors, including Leroy Springs, White's future son-in-law. Springs later founded his own cotton mill, Lancaster Cotton Mills, in 1895 and gained control of Fort Mill Manufacturing in 1914, three years after White died.

Leroy's only son, Elliott Springs, became president in 1931 when his father died. Left with massive debt and six aging cotton mills, Elliott rejuvenated the company by modernizing mill equipment and consolidating the plants into the Springs Cotton Mills (1933). During WWII the company's seven mills made fabric for military use.

In 1945 Springs started the Springmaid line of bedding and fabrics. Elliott's satiric, risqué, but effective ads (beginning in 1948) helped the company become a leading producer of sheets.

Elliott died in 1959 and his son-in-law, William Close, became president. With profits sharply declining, the company went public as Springs Mills in 1966.

The first non-family member to be president, Peter Scotese from Federated Department Stores, was hired in 1969. The next year Springs began working with designer Bill Blass. It diversified into synthetic fabrics in 1971 by buying a minority interest in a Japanese textile plant producing UltraSuede for apparel and cars.

Springs acquired Graber Industries (window-decorating products) in 1979 and three years later changed its name to Springs Industries. In 1985 it acquired M. Lowenstein, which made Wamsutta home furnishings; the deal also gave it Clark-Schwebel Fiber Glass (industrial fabrics). Springs added Carey-McFall (Bali blinds) in 1989.

Declining economic conditions throughout the textile industry in the late 1980s and early 1990s forced Springs to close plants and trim its weakened finished-fabrics segment (the downsizing continued into 1993). A $70 million charge in 1990 led to a $7 million loss, its first in 25 years as a public company.

Historically a maker of apparel fabrics, Springs had grown vulnerable to imports and launched a long-term plan to focus on home furnishings through sales and acquisitions. In 1991 the company set up a bath group with the purchase of C. S. Brooks. Springs became a leading seller of home textiles in Canada the next year by buying the marketing and sales units of C. S. Brooks Canada and Springmaid distributor Griffiths-Kerr. A hostile takeover bid for rival Fieldcrest Cannon was rebuffed in 1993.

Expanding in 1995, Springs acquired Dundee Mills (baby and health care products, towels), Dawson Home Fashions (bath accessories, shower curtains), and Nanik Window Coverings (blinds, shutters). In 1996 the company sold its Clark-Schwebel subsidiary and the following year purchased half of American Fiber Industries (pillows, mattress pads, comforters).

Crandall Close Bowles became the eighth president of Springs in 1997. The next year she took over the chairman and CEO posts from Walter Elisha.

To further focus on its home furnishings business, in 1998 the company sold its UltraSuede business (but kept its UltraLeather business) and its industrial products division. In 1999 Springs finally exited the apparel fabrics business when it sold its Springfield division to a management group, then it purchased Regal Rugs (bath and accent rugs) and the remaining 50% of American Fiber Industries.

In April 2001 the Close family agreed to partner with private equity firm Heartland Industrial Partners to take Springs private. In September the deal was completed, increasing the family's stake to 55%, with Heartland owning the remaining 45%.

In March 2002 Springs acquired the rug division of Beaulieu Group, followed in April by its purchase of the sourced quilt division of Ultima Enterprises. In June Springs completed another acquisition, taking control of Burlington Industries' window treatments and bedding consumer products businesses.

In May 2003 Springs completed its acquisition of Charles D. Owen Manufacturing, one of the last remaining blanket makers in the US. The same year Springs acquired Oxford Bath.

EXECUTIVES
Chairman and CEO: Crandall Close Bowles, age 54, $637,504 pay
EVP and CFO: Kenneth E. Kutcher
EVP and CIO: Ray E. Greer
EVP, Operations: Dean Riggs
EVP; President, Marketing Group: Thomas P. (Tom) O'Connor, age 55, $396,672 pay
SVP and President, National Sales: Rick Canter
SVP and Chief Purchasing Officer: John R. Cowart
SVP, General Counsel, and Secretary: C. Powers Dorsett
SVP, Global Sourcing and International Marketing: Charles M. Metzler
SVP, Human Resources: Gracie P. Coleman
VP and Treasurer: Samuel J. Ilardo
VP, Brand Management: Leslie J. Gillock, age 48
VP, Corporate Communications and Public Affairs: Ted Matthews
VP, Corporate Development: Jennifer Scott
VP, Creative Development: Gary Filippone
President, Basic Bedding Strategic Business Unit: Harvey Simon
Director of Juvenile Sales: Thomas McCaffrey
Business Manager, Freestanding Windows: Gary Kitchens
Auditors: Deloitte & Touche LLP

LOCATIONS
HQ: Springs Industries, Inc.
205 N. White St., Fort Mill, SC 29715
Phone: 803-547-1500 **Fax:** 803-547-1636
Web: www.springs.com

Springs Industries operates about 40 manufacturing plants in 12 US states, Canada, and Mexico.

PRODUCTS/OPERATIONS
Selected Products and Brand Names

Home Furnishings (rugs, ceramic bath accessories, comforters, infant bedding, sheets, shower curtains, and towels)
Beaulieu
Daisy Kingdom
Dundee
Regal
Springmaid
Texmade (in Canada)
Wabasso (in Canada)
Wamsutta

Window Furnishings and Related Hardware
Bali
Graber
Maestro
Nanik

COMPETITORS

Avondale Incorporated	Guilford Mills
Burlington Industries	Hollander Home Fashions
Carter's	Hunter Douglas
Coats Holdings	Milliken
Croscill	Mohawk Industries
Crown Crafts	National Textiles
Dan River	Newell Rubbermaid
Galey & Lord	R. B. Pamplin
Gerber Childrenswear	WestPoint Stevens

HISTORICAL FINANCIALS

Company Type: Private

Income Statement				FYE: Saturday nearest December 31
	REVENUE ($ mil.)	NET INCOME ($ mil.)	NET PROFIT MARGIN	EMPLOYEES
12/03	2,500	—	—	17,000
12/02	2,100	—	—	17,000
12/01	1,800	—	—	17,000
12/00	2,275	—	—	18,200
12/99	2,220	—	—	18,500
12/98	2,181	—	—	17,500
12/97	2,226	—	—	19,500
12/96	2,243	—	—	20,700
12/95	2,233	—	—	23,700
12/94	2,069	—	—	20,500
Annual Growth	2.1%	—	—	(2.1%)

Revenue History

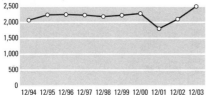

SRI International

Business Week magazine has called SRI International "Silicon Valley's soul." The not-for-profit think tank ponders advances in biotechnology, chemicals and energy, computer science, electronics, and public policy — and ways to commercialize those advances. SRI focuses on technology research and development, business strategies, and issues analysis. It has patents and patent applications in such areas as information sciences, software development, communications, robotics, and pharmaceuticals. Among SRI's clients are Visa, Samsung, NASA, and the US Department of Defense. Originally founded in 1946 as Stanford Research Institute, SRI became fully independent of Stanford University in 1970.

The organization has conceived such innovations as the computer mouse, magnetic encoding for checks, the videodisc, and high-definition television, not to mention some of the foundations of personal computing, the Internet, and stealth technology. Its 1,400 scientists and researchers work at research centers worldwide.

SRI has two for-profit subsidiaries: Sarnoff (formerly a unit of General Electric) specializes in creating and commercializing electronic, biomedical, and information technologies, and SRI Consulting focuses on such issues as organizational management, marketing technologies, and the commercialization of processes. SRI and Sarnoff have together spun off more than 20 companies (*Business Week* has also called SRI "Spin-Off City").

HISTORY

In the 1920s Stanford University professor Robert Swain envisioned a research center devoted to chemistry, physics, and biology. Swain received support from university president Ray Lyman and alumnus Herbert Hoover, but the Great Depression and WWII intervened.

Finally, in 1946, the Stanford Research Institute was formed in conjunction with the university. That year the David Sarnoff Research Center invented the color TV tube under the wing of RCA Laboratories.

During Stanford Research's early years, it worked on such projects as logistics for Disneyland, magnetic ink for character recognition, and strategies for combating air pollution. The think tank was the focus of student protests in the 1960s because of its defense work. In 1969 Stanford Research Institute was one of four nodes on the first computer network, the ARPANET. It became fully independent in 1970 as SRI International.

During the 1960s and 70s, SRI won large contracts from the US Department of Defense for research in such areas as radar, speech recognition, and noise cancellation technologies. It got a tremendous boost in 1987 when longtime client General Electric gave SRI the Sarnoff Research Center (as a tax write-off) plus $250 million in business, along with $65.2 million in cash.

In 1993 SRI founded Pangene to commercialize gene cloning and analysis technology. The next year it founded GeneTrace to develop genetics-related products for biomedical research and Nuance Communications to commercialize speech recognition products. Intuitive Surgical, which develops minimally invasive surgical technologies, was formed in 1995.

SRI developed two key components for use in an improved mail sorting program, which the US Postal Service announced in 1997 it would use to save millions in processing costs. The David Sarnoff Research Center changed its name to Sarnoff Corporation that year. SRI joined Motorola in 1997 to make semiconductors for digital TVs.

In 1998 SRI and the National Science Foundation teamed to develop innovative science and math teaching programs. The following year SRI began working with network equipment leader Cisco Systems and the US Army to develop a voice and multimedia communications system for the military. In 2001 SRI partnered with SPEEDCOM Wireless to co-develop wireless technology.

EXECUTIVES

Chairman: Samuel H. Armacost, age 65
President and CEO: Curtis R. Carlson, age 57
SVP and CFO: Thomas J. Furst
VP Business Development and Marketing: Leonard Polizzotto
VP Corporate and Marketing Communications: Alice R. Resnick
VP Human Resources: Jean E. (Jeanie) Tooker
VP Legal and Business Affairs and General Counsel: Richard Abramson
VP Ventures and Strategic Business Development: Norman D. Winarsky
VP, Biosciences: Glenn Rice
VP, Engineering and Systems: John W. Prausa
VP, Information and Computing Sciences: William Mark
VP, Physical Sciences: Lawrence H. Dubois
VP, Policy Division: Dennis Beatrice
CEO, Sarnoff Corporation: Satyam Cherukuri
Auditors: PricewaterhouseCoopers LLP

LOCATIONS

HQ: SRI International
333 Ravenswood Ave., Menlo Park, CA 94025
Phone: 650-859-2000   **Fax:** 650-859-4111
Web: www.sri.com

SRI International has offices and research centers in Austin, Texas; Centennial, Colorado; Eatontown and Shrewsbury, New Jersey; Helena, Montana; Lexington Park and White Hall, Maryland; Martinez, Georgia; Menlo Park and San Luis Obispo, California; State College, Pennsylvania; and Washington, DC. It also has operations at three US Air Force bases and in Greenland, Japan, and Korea.

Selected Air Force Base Locations
Vandenberg Air Force Base (California)
Eglin Air Force Base (Florida)
Kelley Air Force Base (Texas)

PRODUCTS/OPERATIONS

Selected Research Areas
Automation and robotics
Automotive and commercial equipment technologies
Chemistry, materials, and applied physics
Communications
Defense and intelligence
Homeland defense and national security
Information science and software development
Medical devices
Product engineering
Pharmaceutical services
Policy
Sensors and measurement systems

COMPETITORS

Aerospace Corporation	McKinsey & Company
Andersen	MIT
Battelle Memorial	MITRE
Bayer	PAREXEL
Booz Allen	Quintiles Transnational
CACI International	RAND
Charles Stark Draper Laboratory	Research Triangle Institute SAIC
DaVinci Institute	Southwest Research Institute
DuPont	
Educational Testing Service	Teknowledge
Kendle	University of California
LECG	Wellcome Trust
	Westat

HISTORICAL FINANCIALS

Company Type: Not-for-profit

Income Statement				FYE: December 31
	REVENUE ($ mil.)	NET INCOME ($ mil.)	NET PROFIT MARGIN	EMPLOYEES
12/03	320	—	—	2,800
12/02	318	—	—	2,800
12/01	315	—	—	2,750
12/00	307	—	—	2,700
12/99	330	—	—	2,700
12/98	350	—	—	2,700
12/97	363	—	—	2,783
12/96	326	—	—	2,700
12/95	320	—	—	1,900
12/94	312	—	—	1,973
Annual Growth	0.3%	—	—	4.0%

Revenue History

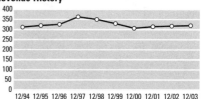

SSA Marine

On a ship, "port" means left, "starboard" means right, and "stevedoring" means heavy lifting, which means a call to SSA Marine, formerly Stevedoring Services of America. The largest marine terminal operator in the US, SSA Marine loads and unloads ships at ports from Seattle to New Zealand. The company also provides rail terminal services, warehousing, and shipment tracking. SSA Marine's Tideworks Technology division offers administrative and operations software and technology services for terminal operators. Founded in the 1880s, SSA Marine has been owned by the Smith and Hemingway families since 1949; president Jon Hemingway is the third generation of his family to head the company.

EXECUTIVES

President and CEO: Jon Hemingway
SVP: Dan Flynn
SVP: Claude Stritmatter
SVP; COO, SSA Terminals: Edward DeNike
SVP, Finance: Charles Sadowski
SVP, Information Technology: Mike Schwank
SVP: Andrew McLauchlan
SVP: David Michou

LOCATIONS

HQ: SSA Marine
  1131 SW Klickitat Way, Seattle, WA 98134
Phone: 206-623-0304   **Fax:** 206-623-0179
Web: www.ssamarine.com

SSA Marine has operations in Africa, the Asia/Pacific region, North America, and South America.

COMPETITORS

Alexander & Baldwin
Associated British Ports
Evergreen Marine
Hutchison Whampoa
Mitsubishi Logistics
P&O
TMM

HISTORICAL FINANCIALS

Company Type: Private

Income Statement FYE: January 31

	ESTIMATED REVENUE ($ mil.)	NET INCOME ($ mil.)	NET PROFIT MARGIN	EMPLOYEES
1/02	1,046	—	—	10,000
1/01	1,000	—	—	6,000
1/00	950	—	—	6,000
1/99	850	—	—	6,000
1/98	850	—	—	7,500
1/97	800	—	—	6,000
1/96	700	—	—	5,000
1/95	500	—	—	4,200
1/94	500	—	—	4,200
Annual Growth	9.7%	—	—	11.5%

Revenue History

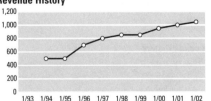

SSM Health Care

The health care mission of SSM Health Care System began with five nuns who fled religious persecution in Germany in 1872 only to arrive in St. Louis in the midst of a smallpox epidemic. They formed their first hospital there in 1877 and later became pioneers in bringing health care to the rural frontier, founding the Oklahoma Territory's first hospital in 1898. Today the not-for-profit, sponsored by the Franciscan Sisters of Mary, owns and operates some 20 acute care hospitals with more than 5,000 licensed beds. The company also operates nursing homes and rehabilitation clinics, and offers home health and hospice care. SSM's facilities are located in Illinois, Missouri, Oklahoma, and Wisconsin.

EXECUTIVES

President and CEO: Sister Mary Jean Ryan
EVP and COO: William C. Schoenhard
SVP Human Resources: Steven M. Barney
SVP, Mission and External Affairs: Dixie L. Platt
SVP Strategic Development: William P. Thompson
SVP, Finance: Kris Zimmer
Regional President and System VP, SSMHC of Oklahoma: Steven L. Hunter
Regional President and System VP, SSMHC of St. Louis: Ronald J. Levy
Regional President and System VP, St. Mary's Good Samaritan, Inc.: James M. Sanger
Regional President and System VP, SSMHC Wisconsin: Mary Starmann-Harrison
President and CIO, SSM Information Center: Thomas K. Langston

LOCATIONS

HQ: SSM Health Care System Inc.
  477 N. Lindbergh Blvd., St. Louis, MO 63141
Phone: 314-994-7800   **Fax:** 314-994-7900
Web: www.ssmhc.com

SSM Health Care operates facilities in Illinois, Missouri, Oklahoma, and Wisconsin.

PRODUCTS/OPERATIONS

Selected Facilities

Illinois
  Good Samaritan Regional Health Center (Mt. Vernon)
  St. Francis Hospital & Health Center (Blue Island)
  St. Mary's Hospital (Centralia)
Missouri
  Pike County Memorial Hospital (Louisiana)
  St. Francis Hospital & Health Services (Maryville)
  St. Mary's Health Center (Jefferson City)
  SSM Cardinal Glennon Children's Hospital (St. Louis)
  SSM DePaul Health Center (Bridgeton)
  SSM St. Joseph Health Center (St. Charles)
  SSM St. Joseph Hospital of Kirkwood
  SSM St. Joseph Hospital West (Lake St. Louis)
  SSM St. Mary's Health Center (St. Louis)
  Villa Marie Skilled Nursing Facility (Jefferson City)
Oklahoma
  Bone & Joint Hospital (Oklahoma City)
  St. Anthony Hospital (Oklahoma City)
Wisconsin
  St. Clare Hospital and Health Services (Baraboo)
  St. Clare Meadows Care Center (Baraboo)
  St. Mary's Care Center (Madison)
  St. Mary's Hospital Medical Center (Madison)

COMPETITORS

Advocate Health Care
Allina Hospitals
BJC HealthCare
Greenville Hospital System
HCA
Mayo Foundation
Rush System for Health
Sisters of Mercy Health System
Tenet Healthcare

HISTORICAL FINANCIALS

Company Type: Not-for-profit

Income Statement FYE: December 31

	REVENUE ($ mil.)	NET INCOME ($ mil.)	NET PROFIT MARGIN	EMPLOYEES
12/03	1,900	—	—	23,300
12/02	1,832	—	—	23,200
12/01	1,705	—	—	22,000
12/00	1,459	—	—	20,500
12/99	1,321	—	—	20,500
12/98	1,285	—	—	20,500
12/97	1,285	—	—	19,439
12/96	2,070	—	—	19,200
12/95	1,856	—	—	19,000
12/94	1,001	—	—	17,000
Annual Growth	7.4%	—	—	3.6%

Revenue History

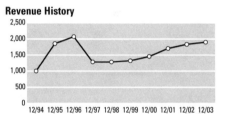

Stanford University

Prospectors panning for gold in higher education can strike it rich at Stanford University. The school is one of the premier educational institutions in the US, boasting respected programs in business, engineering, law, and medicine, among others. Its campus is home to more than 14,000 students as well as 1,700 faculty members. A private institution, Stanford supports its activities through an $8.6 billion endowment, one of the largest in the US. The university was founded in 1885 by Leland Stanford Sr. and his wife, Jane, in memory of their son, Leland Jr.

Stanford is also widely recognized as one of the top US research universities and sports a host of laboratories and research centers, including the Stanford Institute for Economic Policy Research and the Stanford Linear Accelerator Center. Its faculty members include 17 Nobel Prize winners and 21 National Medal of Science winners.

In 2000 the school welcomed its 10th president, former provost John Hennessy, who launched a campaign to raise $1 billion, the largest drive ever undertaken by a university. It quickly reached half that goal thanks to donations from such alumni as Jerry Yang (co-founder of Yahoo!), Charles Schwab, and Texas billionaire Robert Bass. However, its alumni ranks lost a prominent member in 2001 when William Hewlett (of Hewlett-Packard) died.

HISTORY

In 1885 Leland Stanford Sr. and his wife, Jane, established Leland Stanford Junior University in memory of their son Leland Jr., who had died of typhoid at age 15. Stanford made his fortune selling provisions to California gold miners and as a major investor in the Central Pacific Railroad, one of the two companies that built the first transcontinental railway. It was Stanford who connected the tracks laid eastward by Central Pacific and westward by Union Pacific with a gold railway spike in 1869. He also served as California's governor and as a US senator.

The Stanfords donated more than 8,000 acres of land from their own estate to establish an unconventional university, one that was coeducational and nondenominational with a focus on preparing students for a profession. Stanford opened its doors in 1891 to a freshman class of 559 students. It awarded its first degrees four years later, and among the graduates was future US president Herbert Hoover.

Leland Stanford Sr. died in 1893, and in 1903 Jane Stanford turned the university over to the board of trustees. After weathering significant damage in 1906 from the Great San Francisco Earthquake, the university established a law school in 1908, and then five years later, its medical school.

During WWI the university mobilized half of its students into the Students' Army Training Corps. The School of Education was established in 1917, followed by the School of Engineering and Graduate School of Business eight years later. In 1933 a rule limiting the number of women admitted to Stanford was abolished.

Wallace Sterling, who became president of the university after WWII, initiated the transformation of Stanford into a world-class institution with a reputation for teaching and research. Under Sterling the university initiated development on the Stanford Research Park.

In 1958 Stanford opened its first overseas campus (near Stuttgart, Germany), and the Stanford Medical Center was completed the following year. The university created a computer science department in 1965 and two years later opened the Stanford Linear Accelerator Center dedicated to physics research.

Donald Kennedy became president in 1980. The next year students voted to abandon the university's official mascot, the "Indians," in response to concerns raised by Native American students. The nickname "Cardinal" was adopted in its place. The term refers to the school's color, cardinal red.

Also during Kennedy's tenure, it was revealed that Stanford had overcharged the Office of Naval Research for indirect costs associated with research. The scandal led to Kennedy's resignation in 1992, and in 1994 the Office of Naval Research and the university settled a related lawsuit for $1.2 million and a stipulation that Stanford had not committed any wrongdoing. Gerhard Casper succeeded Kennedy as president.

In 1997 Stanford and the University of California at San Francisco combined their teaching hospitals in a public/private merger. Two years later after the controversial experiment had harmed both hospitals' financial picture, the merger was terminated, and the two hospitals agreed to go their separate ways.

In 1999 Casper announced his intention to resign as president. The school tapped provost John Hennessy as his replacement. Soon after his appointment in 2000, Hennessey launched a campaign to raise $1 billion. Former Stanford professor and Netscape co-founder Jim Clark donated $150 million (the largest single donation since its founding grant) later that year to support Stanford's biomedical engineering and sciences program. The school also launched a new company, SKOLAR, which developed an online search engine for the medical industry.

EXECUTIVES

President: John L. Hennessy, age 52
Provost: John W. Etchemendy
VP, Business Affairs and CFO: Randall (Randy) Livingston
VP, Development: John B. Ford
VP, Public Affairs: Gordon Earle
VP and General Counsel: Deborah Zumwalt
CIO: Christopher Handley
Associate VP and Director, University Communications: Alan Acosta
Executive Director, Human Resources: Diane Peck
President, Stanford Alumni Association: Howard Wolf

LOCATIONS

HQ: Stanford University
655 Serra St., Stanford, CA 94305
Phone: 650-723-2300   **Fax:** 650-725-0247
Web: www.stanford.edu

PRODUCTS/OPERATIONS

Selected Schools

Undergraduate
  School of Earth Sciences
  School of Engineering
  School of Humanities and Sciences
Graduate
  School of Business
  School of Earth Sciences
  School of Engineering
  School of Education
  School of Humanities and Sciences
  School of Law
  School of Medicine

Selected Interdisciplinary Research Centers

Alliance for Innovative Manufacturing at Stanford
Center for Computer Research in Music and Acoustics
Center for Integrated Facility Engineering
Center for Integrated Systems

Selected Laboratories, Centers, and Institutes

Center for Research on Information Storage Materials
Center for the Study of Language and Information
Edward L. Ginzton Laboratory
Institute for International Studies
Institute for Research on Women and Gender
Stanford Center for Buddhist Studies
Stanford Humanities Center
Stanford Institute for Economic Policy Research
W.W. Hansen Experimental Physics Laboratory

Selected Medical Research Facilities

Center for Biomedical Ethics
Center for Research in Disease Prevention
Human Genome Center
Richard M. Lucas Center for Magnetic Resonance Spectroscopy & Imaging
Sleep Disorders Center

Other Selected Research Facilities

Hoover Institution on War, Revolution and Peace
Hopkins Marine Station
Martin Luther King, Jr. Papers Project
Stanford Linear Accelerator Center

HISTORICAL FINANCIALS

Company Type: School

Income Statement

FYE: August 31

	REVENUE ($ mil.)	NET INCOME ($ mil.)	NET PROFIT MARGIN	EMPLOYEES
8/01	2,940	—	—	—
8/00	1,957	—	—	—
8/99	1,749	—	—	—
8/98	1,558	—	—	9,535
8/97	1,474	—	—	8,677
8/96	1,416	—	—	8,702
Annual Growth	15.7%	—	—	4.7%

Revenue History

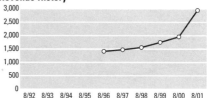

Staple Cotton Cooperative

Wear underwear? Chances are Staplcotn grew the cotton it's made of. Staple Cotton Cooperative Association (Staplcotn) serves approximately 12,000 member-owners in 10 southern states. Founded in 1921 by Mississippi cotton producer Oscar Bledsoe and 10 Delta growers, it sells almost four million bales of cotton annually. Most of the yield is sold to the US textile industry to make men's knit underwear, T-shirts, sheets, towels, and denim. Customers include Fruit of the Loom and Levi Strauss & Co. The co-op's Stapldiscount unit offers members low-interest loans for equipment, buildings, and land. Staple Cotton has 12 regional offices in six states and 15 warehouses in three states.

EXECUTIVES

Chairman; Chairman, Stapldiscount: Ben Lamensdorf
President and CEO; President & CEO, Stapldiscount: Woods E. Eastland, age 59
VP and Treasurer; VP and Treasurer, Stapldiscount: Mack L. Alford
VP and Treasurer: Charles Robertson
VP, Cotton Services: Sterling P. Jones
VP, Human Resources and Secretary; VP Human Resources and Secretary, Stapldiscount: Eugene A. (Gene) Stansel Jr.
VP, Marketing: Meredith B. Allen
VP, Sales Operations: David C. Camp
General Counsel; General Counsel, Stapldiscount: Kenneth E. Downs
Director, Communications and Public Relations: Vicki Wilkey

LOCATIONS

HQ: Staple Cotton Cooperative Association
214 W. Market St., Greenwood, MS 38930
Phone: 662-453-6231   **Fax:** 662-453-6274
Web: www.staplcotn.com

COMPETITORS

Alabama Farmers Cooperative
Calcot
Cargill
Dunavant Enterprises
Plains Cotton
Southern States
Tennessee Farmers Co-op

HISTORICAL FINANCIALS

Company Type: Cooperative

Income Statement FYE: August 31

	REVENUE ($ mil.)	NET INCOME ($ mil.)	NET PROFIT MARGIN	EMPLOYEES
8/04	1,348	—	—	250
8/03	1,024	—	—	250
8/02	1,220	—	—	248
8/01	1,050	—	—	230
8/00	1,041	—	—	230
8/99	850	—	—	200
8/98	705	—	—	197
8/97	657	—	—	156
8/96	640	—	—	—
8/95	664	—	—	—
Annual Growth	8.2%	—	—	7.0%

Revenue History

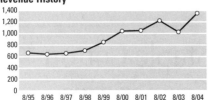

State Farm

Like an enormous corporation, State Farm is everywhere. One of the US's largest personal lines property & casualty companies, State Farm Insurance Companies provides auto insurance, as well as homeowners, nonmedical health, and life insurance through some 17,000 agents. Competition has increased with the fall of barriers between the banking, securities, and insurance industries. State Farm's not-so-secret weapon is a federal savings bank charter (State Farm Financial Services) that offers deposit accounts, CDs, mortgages, and auto and home equity loans by phone and on the Internet.

The company is expanding its financial services, but insurance is still its main source of income. State Farm insures about 20% of the automobiles on US roads; auto insurance accounts for almost 70% of the company's property & casualty premiums. The insurer stopped writing new homeowners policies in some 15 states in an effort to improve profitability.

Although results improved and total revenue increased in 2003, State Farm still experienced an underwriting loss in its flagship auto insurance segment.

Since its founding, the group's companies have been run by only two families, the Mecherles (1922-54) and the Rusts (1954-present).

HISTORY

Retired farmer George Mecherle formed State Farm Mutual Automobile Insurance in Bloomington, Illinois, in 1922. State Farm served only members of farm bureaus and farm mutual insurance companies, charging a one-time membership fee and a premium to protect an automobile against loss or damage.

Unlike most competitors, State Farm offered six-month premium payments. The insurer billed and collected renewal premiums from its home office, relieving the agent of the task. In addition, State Farm determined auto rates by a simple seven-class system, while competitors varied rates for each model.

State Farm in 1926 started City and Village Mutual Automobile Insurance to insure nonfarmers' autos; it became part of the company in 1927. Between 1927 and 1931 it introduced borrowed-car protection, wind coverage, and insurance for vehicles used to transport schoolchildren.

State Farm expanded to California in 1928 and formed State Farm Life Insurance the next year. In 1935 it established State Farm Fire Insurance. George Mecherle became chairman in 1937, and his son Ramond became president. In 1939 George challenged agents to write "A Million or More (auto policies) by '44." State Farm saw a 110% increase in policies.

During the 1940s State Farm focused on urban areas after most of the farm bureaus formed their own insurance companies. In the late 1940s and 1950s, it moved to a full-time agency force.

Homeowners coverage was added to the insurer's offerings under the leadership of Adlai Rust, who led State Farm from 1954 until 1958, when Edward Rust took over. He died in 1985 and his son, Edward Jr., currently holds the top spot.

Between 1974 and 1987 the insurer was hit by several gender-discrimination suits (a 1992 settlement awarded $157 million to 814 women). State Farm has since tried to hire more women and minorities.

In the early 1990s serial disasters, including Hurricane Andrew and the Los Angeles riots, proved costly. The 1994 Northridge earthquake alone generated more than $2.5 billion in claims and contributed to a 72% decline in earnings.

State Farm — the top US home insurer since the mid-1960s — canceled 62,500 residential policies in South Florida in 1996 to cut potential hurricane loss an estimated 11%. In response, Florida's insurance regulators rescinded a previously approved rate hike. That year the company agreed to open more urban neighborhood offices to settle a discrimination suit brought by the Department of Housing and Urban Development, which accused State Farm of discriminating against potential customers in minority-populated areas.

Legal trouble continued. In 1997 State Farm settled with a California couple who alleged the company forged policyholders' signatures on forms declining coverage and concealed evidence to avoid paying earthquake damage claims. That year a policyholder sued to keep State Farm from "wasting company assets" on President Clinton's legal defense against Paula Jones' sexual harassment charges (Clinton held a State Farm personal liability policy).

Relations with its sales force already rocky, State Farm in 1998 proposed to reduce up-front commissions and cut base pay in favor of incentives for customer retention and cross-selling. Reduced auto premiums and increased catastrophe claims from across the US eroded State Farm's bottom line that year. A federal thrift charter obtained in 1998 let the company launch banking operations the next year.

State Farm is appealing a 1999 Illinois state court judgment that it pay $1.2 billion to policyholders for using aftermarket parts in auto repairs. In 2000 the company was hit with a class-action lawsuit about its denial of personal-injury claims; previous suits had been individual cases.

In 2002, State Farm Indemnity withdrew from the New Jersey auto insurance market.

EXECUTIVES

Chairman and CEO: Edward B. (Ed) Rust Jr., age 53
Vice Chairman, President, and COO: Vincent J. Trosino, age 63
SEVP, Chief Administrative Officer, and Director: James E. Rutrough
SEVP, Chief Agency and Marketing Officer, and Director: Charles R. Wright
EVP and General Counsel: Kim M. Brunner
EVP, Financial Services: Jack W. North
EVP: Brian V. Boyden
EVP: Barbara Cowden
EVP: William K. King
SVP, CFO, and Treasurer: Michael L. Tipsord
SVP and Chief Administrative Officer, State Farm Life: Susan D. Waring
SVP, Investments: Paul N. Eckley
SVP: Willie Brown
SVP, Agency: Michael C. Davidson
VP, Corporate Secretary, and Counsel: Laura P. Sullivan
VP, Marketing: Pam El
VP, Fixed Income: Don Heltner
VP, Claims: Susan Hood
VP, Underwriting: Rod Matthews
Auditors: PricewaterhouseCoopers LLP

LOCATIONS

HQ: State Farm Insurance Companies
1 State Farm Plaza, Bloomington, IL 61710
Phone: 309-766-2311   **Fax:** 309-766-3621
Web: www.statefarm.com

State Farm Insurance Companies has operations in Canada and throughout the US.

PRODUCTS/OPERATIONS

2003 Sales

	% of total
Auto	54
Homeowners	21
Other P&C	12
Life	10
Health	2
Banking	1
Total	**100**

Group Companies

State Farm County Mutual Insurance Company of Texas (high-risk auto insurance)
State Farm Federal Savings Bank
State Farm Fire and Casualty Company (homeowners, boat owners, and commercial insurance)
State Farm Florida Insurance Company (homeowners and renters insurance)
State Farm General Insurance Company (property insurance)
State Farm Indemnity Company (auto insurance in New Jersey)
State Farm Life Insurance Company
State Farm Mutual Automobile Insurance Company (auto and health insurance)

COMPETITORS

ACE Limited
AIG
Allstate
American Family Insurance
Berkshire Hathaway
Chubb
CNA Financial
COUNTRY Insurance
GEICO
The Hartford
Liberty Mutual
MetLife
Nationwide
Progressive Corporation
Prudential
Safeco
USAA
Zurich Financial Services

HISTORICAL FINANCIALS

Company Type: Mutual company

Income Statement
FYE: December 31

	ASSETS ($ mil.)	NET INCOME ($ mil.)	INCOME AS % OF ASSETS	EMPLOYEES
12/03	140,611	2,800	2.0%	79,000
12/02	113,043	(2,800)	—	79,400
12/01	117,162	(5,000)	—	79,400
12/00	119,602	408	0.3%	79,300
12/99	80,114	1,033	1.3%	79,300
12/98	88,366	996	1.1%	76,257
12/97	82,296	3,581	4.4%	—
Annual Growth	9.3%	(4.0%)	—	0.7%

2003 Year-End Financials

Equity as % of assets: 36.5%
Return on assets: 2.2%
Return on equity: 6.3%
Long-term debt ($ mil.): —
Sales ($ mil.): 56,100

Net Income History

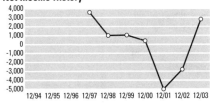

State University of New York

SUNY days are ahead for many New Yorkers seeking higher education. With more than 400,000 students, the State University of New York (SUNY) is running neck-and-neck with California State University for the title of largest university system in the US. The school maintains 64 campuses around New York State, including 13 university colleges and four university centers, 30 community colleges, five technical colleges, and three health centers. Its institutions offer some 6,000 programs of study, including accounting, journalism, bioengineering, and computer science. The university system hands out some 70,000 diplomas each year, including nearly 9,000 post-graduate degrees.

Most students are residents of New York State (about 40% of all New York State high school graduates enroll at SUNY institutions) and pay about $4,400 a year in tuition. SUNY is also top-notch in research, boasting more than $700 million in federal, state, and local grants and contracts. Its laboratories have helped pioneer magnetic resonance imaging, implantable heart pacemakers, and supermarket bar code scanners.

Chancellor Robert King is challenging SUNY administrators and the state to increase levels of funding to help keep the university competitive against other top-flight institutions. New York Governor George Pataki has pledged a $2 billion multi-year construction program for SUNY's facilities.

HISTORY

The State University of New York was organized in 1948, but it traces its roots back to several institutions founded in the 19th century. In 1844 the New York state legislature authorized the creation of the Albany Normal School, which was charged with educating the state's secondary school teachers. Two years later, the University of Buffalo was chartered to provide academic, theological, legal, and medical studies. More normal schools later were founded between 1861 and 1889 in Brockport, Buffalo, Cortland, Fredonia, Geneseo, New Paltz, Oneonta, Oswego, Plattsburgh, and Potsdam.

In the early 1900s the state established several agricultural colleges, including schools in Canton (1907), Alfred (1908), Morrisville (1910), Farmingdale (1912), and Cobleskill (1916). New York also set up several schools as units of Cornell University, including colleges of veterinary medicine (1894), agriculture (1909), home economics (1925), and industrial and labor relations (1945).

After WWII, veterans began to fill US colleges and universities, taking advantage of the GI Bill to secure a college education. The legislature set up SUNY in 1948 to consolidate 29 institutions under a single board of trustees charged with meeting the growing demand. The board coordinated the state colleges into a single body and established four-year liberal arts colleges, professional and graduate schools, and research centers. During the 1950s and 1960s, new campuses were created at Binghamton, Stony Brook, Old Westbury, Purchase, and Utica/Rome, and enrollment began to take off, jumping from 30,000 in 1955 to 63,000 in 1959.

By the early 1970s SUNY had more than 320,000 students at 72 institutions. But budget constraints later that decade led to higher tuition, reduced enrollment goals, and employment cutbacks. In 1975 eight New York City community colleges were transferred to City University. SUNY's enrollment began growing again during the 1980s, reaching more than 400,000 by 1990. Early in the decade, the institution began implementing SUNY 2000, a plan that called for increasing access to education and diversifying undergraduate studies. Following his election in 1994, Governor George Pataki proposed more than $550 million in cuts to the SUNY system.

In 1997 John Ryan replaced Thomas Bartlett as chancellor. The following year SUNY became the exclusive sponsor of The College Channel, a guide to colleges and college life aimed at high school juniors and seniors and broadcast by PRIMEDIA's Channel One. In 1999 the governor's budget director, Robert King, was named chancellor to replace the retiring Bartlett. In 2000 SUNY faced rising budget shortfalls at its teaching hospitals, in part because money was being siphoned off to other areas. That year King announced a set of initiatives to raise an additional $1.5 billion in federal research grants and $1 billion in private donations over five years.

EXECUTIVES

Chancellor: Robert L. King
Provost and Vice Chancellor Academic Affairs: Peter D. Salins
Vice Chancellor and CFO: David Richter
Vice Chancellor and Chief of Staff: Elizabeth D. (Betty) Capaldi
Vice Chancellor Business and Industry Relations: R. Wayne Diesel
University Counsel: D. Andrew Edwards Jr.
Vice Chancellor and Secretary; President, Research Foundation: John J. O'Connor
University Controller: Patrick J. Wiater
University Auditor: C. Kevin O'Donoghue
Assistant Vice Chancellor for Employee Relations: Joyce Villa
Director of Employee Relations: Raymond (Ray) Haines
Auditors: KPMG LLP

LOCATIONS

HQ: State University of New York
State University Plaza, Albany, NY 12246
Phone: 518-443-5500   **Fax:** 518-443-5387
Web: www.suny.edu

PRODUCTS/OPERATIONS

Selected Institutions

Colleges of Technology
  Alfred
  Canton
  Cobleskill
  Delhi
  Morrisville
  University Colleges of Technology
Health Science Centers
  Brooklyn
  Syracuse
Statutory Colleges
  College of Agriculture and Life Sciences at Cornell University
  College of Ceramics at Alfred University
  College of Human Ecology at Cornell University
  College of Veterinary Medicine at Cornell University
  School of Industrial and Labor Relations at Cornell University
University Centers
  Albany
  Binghamton
  Buffalo
  Stony Brook
University Colleges
  Brockport
  Buffalo State
  Cortland
  Empire State
  Fredonia
  Geneseo
  New Paltz
  Old Westbury
  Oneonta
  Oswego
  Plattsburgh
  Potsdam
  Purchase

HISTORICAL FINANCIALS

Company Type: School

Income Statement
FYE: June 30

	REVENUE ($ mil.)	NET INCOME ($ mil.)	NET PROFIT MARGIN	EMPLOYEES
6/03	3,461	—	—	—
6/02	3,476	—	—	—
6/01	5,211	—	—	—
6/00	5,076	—	—	—
6/99	4,629	—	—	65,000
6/98	4,564	—	—	65,000
6/97	4,244	—	—	56,135
6/96	4,136	—	—	55,000
6/95	4,167	—	—	52,000
6/94	4,018	—	—	48,194
Annual Growth	(1.6%)	—	—	6.2%

Revenue History

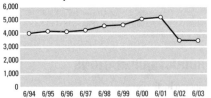

Stater Bros.

Stater Bros. Markets has no shortage of major league rivals, operating in the same Southern California markets as Ralphs, Albertson's, and Safeway-owned Vons. Stater Bros. Holdings has about 160 Stater Bros. Markets, mostly in Riverside and San Bernardino counties. It also has stores in Kern, Los Angeles, Orange, and San Diego counties. In 1999 the company converted about 45 outlets it bought from Albertson's to the Stater Bros. Market name. The grocery chain also owns milk and juice processor Heartland Farms (formerly Santee Dairies), the state's largest milk processor. Stater Bros. is owned by La Cadena Investments, a general partnership consisting of Stater Bros. CEO Jack Brown and other company executives.

Competition from the grocery giants, and the purchase of the stores from Albertson's, has put a strain on the company's profits. To distinguish itself from rivals, the chain refuses to offer promotional games and frequent shopper cards, boasting everyday low prices instead.

Stater Bros. is bracing itself for intense competition from Wal-Mart, which recently opened its first supercenter near Palm Springs and has plans for up to 40 more in Southern California.

Stater Bros. Holdings is the largest privately held supermarket chain in Southern California. The company plans to open three to six new stores per year.

HISTORY

In 1936, at age 23, Cleo Stater and his twin brother, Leo, mortgaged a Chevrolet to make a down payment on a modest grocery store where Cleo had been working for five years in their hometown of Yucaipa, California. Later that year the brothers bought their second grocery in the nearby community of Redlands. Their younger brother, Lavoy, soon joined them to help build the company. In 1938 the brothers opened the first Stater Bros. market in Colton; by 1939 they had a chain of four stores.

The small, family-owned grocery chain continued to grow. In 1948 Stater Bros. opened its first supermarket (which was several times larger than its other stores and had its own parking lot) in Riverside. By 1950 the company had 12 stores.

Stater Bros. consolidated its offices and warehouse in Colton in the early 1960s and continued its expansion into nearby communities. By 1964 it operated 27 supermarkets in 18 cities in Los Angeles, Orange, Riverside, and San Bernardino counties. In 1968 the brothers sold the company's 35 stores to Long Beach, California-based petroleum services provider Petrolane for $33 million. Lavoy succeeded Cleo as president.

As a division of Petrolane, Stater Bros. kept growing. In the 1970s the company introduced a new store design that expanded sales area but required less land and a smaller building. The number of stores more than doubled (to over 80) between 1968 and 1979, when Lavoy retired.

Ron Burkle, VP of Administration for Petrolane, and his father, Joe, president of Stater Bros., attempted to buy the chain for $100 million in 1981. Infuriated by the low bid, Petrolane fired Ron and demoted his father, who left that year. Jack Brown was named president in his place. Petrolane sold the chain in 1983 to La Cadena Investments, a private company that included Brown and other top Stater Bros. executives.

Leo died in 1985. That year the company went public to reduce debt from the 1983 LBO and to provide funds for an extensive expansion plan. It also incorporated as Stater Bros. Inc. In 1986 a proxy fight for control of the company erupted between Brown's La Cadena group and chairman Bernard Garrett, who owned about 41% of Stater Bros. Brown had been suspended as president and CEO (Joe Burkle returned in his place), but Los Angeles-based investment firm Craig Corp. bought Garrett's stake and Brown returned; he was later elected chairman. That year Stater Bros. also became a co-owner in Santee Dairies with Hughes Markets (now part of Kroger).

The next year Craig and Stater Bros. executives took the grocery chain private again. Burkle bought a 9% stake in Craig in 1989 through Yucaipa Capital Partners. Also in 1987 Craig reduced its stake in Stater Bros., transferring some stock to La Cadena. Stater Bros. Holdings was created as a parent company for the grocery chain.

Stater Bros. expressed an interest in buying rival Alpha Beta stores when they were put up for sale, but Yucaipa Companies bought them in 1991. Craig considered selling its stake in Stater Bros. in 1992; it finally sold its half of the company to La Cadena in 1996.

In 1999 Stater Bros. acquired 33 Albertson's and 10 Lucky stores, as well as one store site. (The FTC required Albertson's to sell the stores in order to acquire American Stores, Lucky's parent.) The acquisition and the early retirement of debt resulted in its 1999 losses. In September 2001 company co-founder Cleo Stater died.

In early 2002 the company announced a partnership with Krispy Kreme Doughnuts to offer the treats at selected Stater Bros. supermarkets. In 2003, Stater Bros. introduced Topco private-label brand merchandise in its stores.

In February 2004 Santee Dairies became a wholly-owned subsidiary of Stater Bros. when the grocery chain acquired Kroger's 50% stake in the operation.

Stater Bros. sales rose by about 5% during a four-and-a-half month long strike by employees of rivals Albertson's, Kroger, and Vons. The dispute, which diverted shoppers from those stores to Stater Bros. markets, ended in March 2004. In October Don Baker was promoted to president and COO of Stater Bros. Previously, Baker was EVP and COO of the company.

EXECUTIVES

Chairman and CEO: Jack H. Brown, age 64, $1,260,000 pay
Vice Chairman: Thomas W. Field Jr., age 69
President and COO: Donald I. (Don) Baker, age 62, $515,000 pay
SVP and CFO: Phillip J. (Phil) Smith, age 56, $215,000 pay
SVP, Retail Operations: Edward A. Stater, age 52, $182,000 pay
Group SVP of Marketing: Dennis L. McIntyre, age 43, $240,000 pay
Group SVP of Retail Operations: James W. (Jim) Lee, age 52, $232,000 pay
VP, Construction and Maintenance: Scott Limbacher
VP, Corporate Affairs: Susan Atkinson
VP, Human Resources: Kathy Finazzo
VP, Produce: Roger Schroeder
President and COO, Heartland Farms: Paul Bikowitz
Secretary and Director: Bruce D. Varner, age 67
Property Development Manager: Mike McCasland
Auditors: Ernst & Young LLP

LOCATIONS

HQ: Stater Bros. Holdings Inc.
21700 Barton Rd., Colton, CA 92324
Phone: 909-783-5000   **Fax:** 909-783-3950
Web: www.staterbros.com

Stater Bros. Holdings operates one distribution center and nearly 160 supermarkets in Southern California.

2003 Stores

	No.
San Bernardino County	47
Riverside County	41
Orange County	30
Los Angeles County	27
San Diego County	10
Kern County	2
Total	**157**

PRODUCTS/OPERATIONS

Selected Departments and Products

Bakery
Dairy products
Delicatessen
Fresh produce
Frozen foods
General merchandise
Health & beauty aids
Liquor
Meats
Seafood

COMPETITORS

Albertson's
Arden Group
Costco Wholesale
Longs Drug
Ralphs
Smart & Final
Trader Joe's Co.
Vons
Walgreen
Wal-Mart
Whole Foods

HISTORICAL FINANCIALS
Company Type: Private

Income Statement			FYE: Last Sunday in September
	REVENUE ($ mil.)	NET INCOME ($ mil.)	NET PROFIT MARGIN	EMPLOYEES
9/03	2,754	10	0.4%	13,500
9/02	2,666	12	0.4%	13,400
9/01	2,574	8	0.3%	12,600
9/00	2,418	(6)	—	12,100
9/99	1,830	(9)	—	12,700
9/98	1,726	3	0.1%	8,700
9/97	1,718	14	0.8%	8,900
9/96	1,705	16	0.9%	8,900
9/95	1,580	7	0.4%	9,800
9/94	1,540	9	0.6%	10,000
Annual Growth	6.7%	1.5%	—	3.4%

2003 Year-End Financials
Debt ratio: —
Return on equity: —
Cash ($ mil.): 111
Current ratio: 1.60
Long-term debt ($ mil.): 469

Net Income History
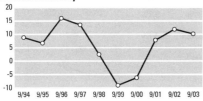

Stewart's Shops

You scream, I scream, we all scream for Stewart's ice cream, especially if we live in upstate New York or Vermont, home to about 315 Stewart's Shops. Stewart's Shops (formerly known as Stewart's Ice Cream Company) runs a chain of convenience stores selling some 3,000 different products, including dairy items, groceries, food to go (chili and soup), beer, gasoline, and, of course, ice cream. Stewart's makes its own ice cream — more than 50 flavors both hand-dipped and packaged — and dairy products, and it has several private-label products. It also sells national brands. The founding Dake family owns about two-thirds of the company; employee compensation plans own the rest of Stewart's Shops.

EXECUTIVES
Chairman: William (Bill) Dake, age 68
President: Gary C. Dake, age 43
SVP: Nancy Trimbur
Treasurer: David A. Farr
Director, HR: Jim Botch
Director, Information Solutions: Rick Cobello
Director, Marketing and Public Relations: Susan Law Dake

LOCATIONS
HQ: Stewart's Shops Corp.
2907 Rte. 9, Balston Spa, NY 12020
Phone: 518-581-1200 **Fax:** 518-581-1209
Web: www.stewartsicecream.com

PRODUCTS/OPERATIONS
Selected Products and Services
Banking terminals
Beer
Dairy products
Food to go
Gasoline
Groceries
Hand-dipped ice cream
Lottery sales
Packaged ice cream
Soda

COMPETITORS
7-Eleven
Allied Domecq
Ben & Jerry's
Brigham's
Cumberland Farms
Exxon Mobil
Golub
Hannaford Bros.
Kroger
Pathmark
Penn Traffic
Royal Ahold
Sunoco
TravelCenters of America

HISTORICAL FINANCIALS
Company Type: Private

Income Statement			FYE: Last Sunday in December
	REVENUE ($ mil.)	NET INCOME ($ mil.)	NET PROFIT MARGIN	EMPLOYEES
12/03	800	—	—	3,300
12/02	730	—	—	3,200
12/01	700	—	—	3,000
12/00	648	—	—	2,990
Annual Growth	7.3%	—	—	3.3%

Revenue History
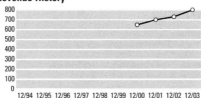

Structure Tone

Structured to set the right tone for its clients, The Structure Tone Organization develops corporate and commercial properties for major clients down the block and around the world. Through four main companies, the group provides general contracting, construction management, and project management services for building construction, interior fit-outs and renovations, and infrastructure upgrades. A top builder in the New York City area (it is a leader in telecommunications projects there as well), the company also works in Asia, Europe, and South America. Structure Tone was founded to focus on building interiors in 1971 by Lou Marino and Patrick Donaghy, whose family now owns the company.

EXECUTIVES
Chairman: James K. Donaghy
Vice Chairman: Brian M. Donaghy
President and COO: Anthony M. Carvette
CFO: Ray Froimowitz
EVP and Secretary: John T. White
SVP Human Resources: Robert (Bob) Yardis
VP Marketing: Kevin Jackson
Director of Management Information Systems: Steven Barber
Director Human Resources: Tony Tursy

LOCATIONS
HQ: The Structure Tone Organization
770 Broadway, 9th Fl., New York, NY 10003
Phone: 212-481-6100 **Fax:** 212-685-9267
Web: www.structuretone.com

The Structure Tone Organization has offices in Florida, Massachusetts, New Jersey, New York, Texas, and Virginia.

PRODUCTS/OPERATIONS
Sectors
Commercial
Convention centers
Correctional facilities
Cultural centers
Educational
Entertainment
Health care
Hospitality
Interiors
Residential
Retail
Sports

COMPETITORS
AMEC, Construction Management
Bovis Lend Lease
Clark Enterprises
Devcon Construction
DPR Construction
Foster Wheeler
Gilbane
HRH Construction
Hunt Construction
Opus
PCL
Perini
Peter Kiewit Sons'
Skanska USA Building
Tishman
Turner Corporation
Walsh Group
Washington Group

HISTORICAL FINANCIALS
Company Type: Private

Income Statement			FYE: October 31
	ESTIMATED REVENUE ($ mil.)	NET INCOME ($ mil.)	NET PROFIT MARGIN	EMPLOYEES
10/03	1,700	—	—	1,500
10/02	2,100	—	—	1,600
10/01	2,100	—	—	1,600
10/00	2,000	—	—	1,300
10/99	1,600	—	—	1,000
Annual Growth	1.5%	—	—	10.7%

Revenue History
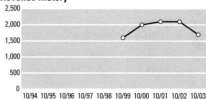

Suffolk Construction

The bricks fly at Suffolk Construction. The firm provides general contracting, construction management, preconstruction, and design/build services to clients in the public and private sectors across the US. Commercial and residential projects include university halls, senior housing, hotels (Marriott, Hilton), corporate offices, and retail facilities. A top Boston contractor, Suffolk Construction is owned by president John Fish and his father Edward, who created Suffolk Construction in 1982. It also operates in Florida and California. The Fish family has been in the construction business for four generations (since the 1890s). Another construction company is owned by John's brother Ted Fish.

EXECUTIVES
Chairman: Edward A. Fish
President and CEO: John F. Fish
EVP and CFO: Michael (Mike) Azarela
EVP and General Manager, Special Projects Division and Suffolk Healthcare: Mark L. DiNapoli
EVP Business Development: Robert (Bob) McCluskey
EVP, Human Resources: Joanna Nikka
SVP Business Development: Frederick M. (Fred) O'Neill
VP Institutional Division: Emil Frei
VP Marketing: Kim Gori
VP and General Counsel: Walter K. McDonough
Auditors: Ziner, Kennedy, & Lehan LLP

LOCATIONS
HQ: Suffolk Construction Company, Inc.
65 Allerton St., Boston, MA 02119
Phone: 617-445-3500   **Fax:** 617-445-2343
Web: www.suffolkconstruction.com

Suffolk Construction has offices in Boston; Irvine and San Francisco, California; and Miami, Naples, and West Palm Beach, Florida. It has projects throughout the US.

COMPETITORS
Bovis Lend Lease
Centex
Clark Enterprises
Kraus-Anderson
McCarthy Building
Modern Continental Companies
Pepper Construction
Perini
Swinerton
Turner Corporation
Walsh Group
Whiting-Turner

HISTORICAL FINANCIALS
Company Type: Private

Income Statement				FYE: August 31
	REVENUE ($ mil.)	NET INCOME ($ mil.)	NET PROFIT MARGIN	EMPLOYEES
8/03	827	—	—	—
8/02	702	—	—	487
8/01	663	—	—	460
8/00	574	—	—	425
8/99	556	—	—	401
Annual Growth	10.4%	—	—	6.7%

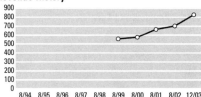

Revenue History

Sullivan & Cromwell

Sullivan & Cromwell has a long and storied history. Founded in 1879 by Algernon Sullivan and William Cromwell, the firm was on hand for the foundation of both General Electric in 1882 and United States Steel in 1901. Today, Sullivan & Cromwell has about 750 lawyers in four US and eight international offices. It focuses on corporate law for industrial, commercial, and financial clients, more than half of which are located abroad. Sullivan & Cromwell's major clients include investment and banking giant Goldman Sachs and Microsoft (which the firm has represented in its antitrust battle with the US Justice Department).

EXECUTIVES
Chairman: H. Rodgin Cohen
Executive Director: Arthur Gurwitz
Director Finance: Robert Howard
Director Legal Personnel: Andrea Locklear
Director Marketing: Charles Osborn

LOCATIONS
HQ: Sullivan & Cromwell LLP
125 Broad St., New York, NY 10004
Phone: 212-558-4000   **Fax:** 212-558-3588
Web: www.sullcrom.com

Sullivan & Cromwell has offices in Los Angeles and Palo Alto, California; New York City; and Washington, DC and internationally in Beijing; Frankfurt; Hong Kong; London; Melbourne; Paris; Sydney; and Tokyo.

PRODUCTS/OPERATIONS
Selected Practice Areas
Commercial real estate
Corporate and financial
  Securities
  Corporate law and counseling
  Asset-based finance
  Bankruptcy and creditors' rights
  International trade and investment
  Privatizations
  Telecommunications
Estates and personal
Litigation
  Anti-trust
  Corporate and securities
  Environmental law
  Arbitration
  Labor and employment
Mergers and acquisitions
  International transactions
Tax

COMPETITORS
Baker & McKenzie
Clifford Chance
Cravath, Swaine
Davis Polk
Jones Day
Latham & Watkins
Skadden, Arps
Wachtell, Lipton
Williams & Connolly

HISTORICAL FINANCIALS
Company Type: Partnership

Income Statement				FYE: December 31
	REVENUE ($ mil.)	NET INCOME ($ mil.)	NET PROFIT MARGIN	EMPLOYEES
12/03	687	—	—	1,800
12/02	624	—	—	1,850
12/01	568	—	—	1,900
12/00	517	—	—	1,950
12/99	474	—	—	2,000
12/98	427	—	—	2,000
12/97	395	—	—	2,000
12/96	346	—	—	—
12/95	318	—	—	—
12/94	298	—	—	—
Annual Growth	9.7%	—	—	(1.7%)

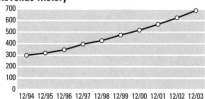

Revenue History

Sunkist

Perhaps the US enterprise least susceptible to an outbreak of scurvy, Sunkist Growers is a cooperative owned by 6,000 citrus farmers in California and Arizona. Sunkist markets fresh oranges, lemons, grapefruit, and tangerines in the US and overseas. Fruit that doesn't meet fresh market standards is turned into juices, oils, and peels for use in food products. The Sunkist brand is one of the most recognized names in the US; through licensing agreements the name also appears worldwide on more than 600 beverages and other products, from vitamins to fruit rolls.

Sunkist is one of the largest marketing cooperatives in America and the largest cooperative in the world's fruit and vegetable industry. Sunkist's biggest export customers are Canada, Hong Kong, Japan, and South Korea. Sunkist has licensing agreements with companies in more than 50 countries.

HISTORY
Sunkist Growers was founded in the early 1890s as the Pachappa Orange Growers, a group of California citrus farmers determined to control the sale of their fruit. Success attracted new members, and in 1893 the Southern California Fruit Exchange was born. The name "Sunkissed" was coined by an ad copywriter in 1908, and it was soon reworked into "Sunkist" and registered as a trademark, becoming the first brand name for a fresh produce item. Even-

tually the co-op renamed itself after its popular brand: It became Sunkist Growers in 1952. Sunkist began licensing its trademark to other companies in the early 1950s.

As early as 1916, efforts to increase citrus consumption included designing and marketing glass citrus juicers and encouraging homemakers to "Drink an Orange." The co-op also promoted the practice of putting lemon slices in tea or water and funded early research on the health benefits of vitamins (vitamin C in particular). In 1925 tissue wrappers gave way to stamping the Sunkist name directly on each piece of fruit.

Although Sunkist pioneered bottled orange juice in 1933, its juice marketing efforts were never as successful as those of its Florida competitors. Florida oranges are drippy and dowdy and thus better suited for juicing. Capitalizing on this aspect, Florida growers dominated the market for fresh and frozen juice.

In 1937 Congress created a system of citrus shipment quotas and limits (known as "marketing orders") that ultimately proved most beneficial to large citrus cooperatives. By the early 1990s the marketing order system was under political attack, and in 1992 the Justice Department filed civil prosecution against Sunkist, alleging that the co-op had reaped unfair extra profits by surpassing its lemon shipment limits. In 1994, after much legal wrangling, the quotas were abolished and the Justice Department dropped its case against Sunkist.

Inconveniently warm weather and increasing competition from imported citrus marked the harvests of 1996. That year the co-op had trouble maintaining discipline among its members; some undercut Sunkist price levels, while others flooded the market to sell their fruit at the higher early market prices, creating a supply surplus. Also that year the co-op relinquished the marketing of all Sunkist juices in North America to Florida-based Lykes Bros. in a licensing agreement.

The co-op agreed in 1998 to distribute grapefruit from Florida's Tuxedo Fruit, providing Sunkist with winter grapefruit supply and increasing its year-round consumer a-peel. Also in 1998 Russell Hanlin, Sunkist president and CEO since 1978, was succeeded by Vince Lupinacci. Lupinacci, who had held positions with Pepsi and Six Flags, became the first person from outside the citrus business to hold Sunkist's top post.

In 1998 the company sold 90 million cartons of fresh citrus — the greatest volume in its history — despite increased competition from imported Latin American, South African, and Spanish crops, a damaging California freeze, and the ill effects of El Nino. The next year production was almost halved because of adverse weather.

Lupinacci resigned in 2000, citing personal and family reasons. Chairman Emeritus James Mast then took the helm as acting president. Although the company grew its market through exports to China in 2000, its profits were squeezed that year by increasing foreign competition, a citrus glut, and lessened demand. In mid-2001 Jeff Gargiulo replaced Mast as Sunkist's president and CEO.

In 2003 Sunkist formed a joint venture with strawberry shipper Coastal Berry Co. to market strawberries under the Sunkist label year-round. Coastal Berry's president and CEO John Gargiulo and Sunkist's president and CEO Jeff Gargiulo are brothers. Also that year Sunkist began offering pre-cut bagged fruit to retail customers and restaurants in order to keep up with a changing market and consumer demand.

EXECUTIVES

Chairman: David W. Krause, age 43
President and CEO: Jeffrey D. (Jeff) Gargiulo
VP and COO: James A. (Jim) Padden
VP and Chief Administration Officer: Jeffrey E. (Jeff) Moxie
VP, Corporate Relations: Michael J. Wootton
VP, Finance and Treasurer: Richard G. French
VP, Domestic Sales: John B. McGuigan
VP, Global Licensing: Greg Combs
VP, International Sales and Sales Operations: Russell L. Hanlin II
VP, Licensing/International Development: Ashok D. Patel
VP, Law and General Counsel: Thomas M. Moore
VP, Marketing and Sales Promotion: Robert J. Verloop
VP, Processed Products, Research/Technical Services: Owen W. Belletto
Director, Human Resources: John R. McGovern
Director, Sales Strawberry: John Corrigan III
Director, Trademark Licensing: Mario Kahn
Manager, Public Relations: Claire H. Smith
Corporate Secretary: Kristen J. Moyer
Auditors: KPMG LLP

LOCATIONS

HQ: Sunkist Growers, Inc.
  14130 Riverside Dr., Sherman Oaks, CA 91423
Phone: 818-986-4800   **Fax:** 818-379-7405
Web: www.sunkist.com

COMPETITORS

Alico
Chiquita Brands
Coca-Cola North America
Dole Food
Florida's Natural
Fresh Del Monte Produce
Louis Dreyfus Citrus
Tropicana
UniMark Group
Vitality Foodservice

HISTORICAL FINANCIALS

Company Type: Cooperative

Income Statement   FYE: October 31

	REVENUE ($ mil.)	NET INCOME ($ mil.)	NET PROFIT MARGIN	EMPLOYEES
10/03	942	27	2.9%	—
10/02	964	(2)	—	—
10/01	993	4	0.4%	—
10/00	847	(4)	—	—
10/99	862	6	0.7%	—
10/98	1,069	6	0.6%	875
10/97	1,075	—	—	813
10/96	1,025	—	—	878
10/95	1,096	—	—	1,150
10/94	1,005	—	—	1,138
Annual Growth	(0.7%)	35.7%	—	(6.4%)

2003 Year-End Financials

Debt ratio: 34.0%
Return on equity: 42.5%
Cash ($ mil.): 6
Current ratio: 1.48
Long-term debt ($ mil.): 26

Net Income History

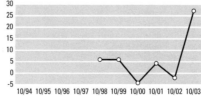

Superior Group

Metal-centric holding company Superior Group makes and sells tubing through subsidiaries Fine Tubes (precision tubing), Superior Tube (small metal tubing), Swepco Tube (corrosion-resistant tubing and pipe), and Western Pneumatic Tube (thin-walled tubing). Its TW Metals subsidiary is a metals distributor and processor for such customers as Air France, FedEx, and United Airlines. Superior's Drever Group designs and sells industrial furnaces to steel mills and metal manufactures, while Sharp Corp. makes consumer-friendly packaging for pharmaceuticals such as carded blister packaging and child-resistant bottles. SGI Capital is Superior's investment arm. Superior is owned by the Warden family, heirs of its founder.

EXECUTIVES

CEO: William G. Warden IV
President: Peter G. Gould
VP Manufacturing, Western Pneumatic Tube: Harland Ostlund
Director Employee Relations: Tom Pezick
Managing Director, Fine Tubes: Roger W. Johnson
Financial Controller, Fine Tubes: David Davies
Sales and Marketing Manager, Fine Tubes: Brian Mercer
President, SGI Capital: Tom Balderston
President and CEO, Sharp: George K. Burke Jr.
VP and CFO, Sharp: David Thomson
VP Sales and Marketing, Sharp: William J. Walker
President, Swepco Tube: Kenneth J. Schultz Jr.
VP Finance, Swepco Tube: Steve Oberhelman
Director Sales and Marketing, Swepco Tube: Philip Lehr
President and CEO, TW Metal: Jack Elrod
VP and CFO, TW Metals: E. Trudy D'Noccia

LOCATIONS

HQ: Superior Group, Inc.
  3 Radnor Corporate Center, Ste. 400,
  Radnor, PA 19087
Phone: 610-964-2000   **Fax:** 610-964-2001
Web: www.superior-group.com

Through its subsidiaries, Superior Group operates more than 40 facilities in Europe and the US.

PRODUCTS/OPERATIONS

Selected Products
Metal Distribution Market
  TW Metals, Inc.
    Fittings
    Pipe
    Tubing
Specialty Market
  Drever Company
    Anneal furnaces
    Bright annealing furnaces
    Continuing annealing furnaces
    Pickle furnaces
    Sintering furnaces
    Tube annealing furnaces
  Sharp Corporation
    Pouches
    Strip packaging
Tube Manufacturing Market
  Fine Tubes Limited
    Coil tube
    Precision tubing
    Small diameter metal tubing
    Straight length tube

Swepco Tube Corporation
  Nickel-based alloys
  Stainless steels
  Structural shapes
  Titanium alloys
  Tubing
  Welded pipe
Western Pneumatic Tube Company
  Light wall welded tubing

COMPETITORS

American Cast Iron Pipe	Lone Star Technologies
Connell Limited Partnership	Maverick Tube
	Novamerican Steel
Earle M. Jorgensen	RPC Group
Field Container	Special Metals
Inductotherm	Wolverine Tube

HISTORICAL FINANCIALS
Company Type: Private

Income Statement
FYE: December 31

	ESTIMATED REVENUE ($ mil.)	NET INCOME ($ mil.)	NET PROFIT MARGIN	EMPLOYEES
12/02	750	—	—	3,400
12/01	800	—	—	3,400
12/00	750	—	—	3,400
Annual Growth	0.0%	—	—	0.0%

Revenue History

Sutter Health

Sutter Health is one of the nation's largest not-for-profit health care systems. It was organized in 1996 through the merger of Sutter Health and California Healthcare System. Today the company caters to residents in more than 100 northern California communities. Its services are provided through the firm's approximately 3,600 affiliated doctors, from facilities of various types, including acute care hospitals, home health/hospice networks, medical groups, occupational health services centers, and skilled nursing facilities. Sutter Health's network also boasts several research institutes.

Almost 40% of Sutter Health's patient services revenues comes from Medicare reimbursement; Medi-Cal, California's Medicaid program, accounts for nearly 15%.

The company's hospitals in northern California might feel a bit of a pinch after about a dozen of them were eliminated from the CalPERS HMO network. The two organizations have fought bitterly over pricing and access, with CalPERS claiming Sutter Health charges 60% to 80% more than other hospitals.

In an effort to reduce costs and errors, Sutter Health announced in 2004 plans to spend some $1.2 billion on IT systems over the next 10 years.

EXECUTIVES

Chairman: Ralph E. Andersen
President, CEO, and Director: Van R. Johnson
EVP and COO: Patrick E. (Pat) Fry
SVP; CEO, Peninsula-Coastal Service Area: David Druker
SVP, Strategy and Organization Development: James Farrell
SVP, Information Services and CIO: John Hummel
SVP, Chief Medical Officer, and Clinical Integration Officer: Gordon C. Hunt Jr.
SVP, Public Affairs: Cyndi Kettmann
SVP and General Counsel: Gary Loveridge
SVP and CFO: Robert D. (Bob) Reed
VP, Communications and Marketing: Bill Gleeson
Communications Manager: Karen Garner
Auditors: Ernst & Young LLP

LOCATIONS

HQ: Sutter Health
  2200 River Plaza Dr., Sacramento, CA 95833
Phone: 916-733-8800   **Fax:** 916-286-6841
Web: www.sutterhealth.org

Hospitals
Sutter Delta Medical Center (Antioch, CA)
Sutter Auburn Faith Hospital (CA)
Alta Bates Medical Center (Berkeley, CA)
Mills-Peninsula Medical Center (Burlingame, CA)
Eden Medical Center (Castro Valley, CA)
Sutter Coast Hospital (Crescent City, CA)
Sutter Davis Hospital (CA)
Marin General Hospital (Greenbrae, CA)
Sutter Amador Hospital (Jackson, CA)
Sutter Lakeside Hospital (Lakeport, CA)
Memorial Hospital Los Banos (CA)
Memorial Medical Center (Modesto, CA)
Novato Community Hospital (CA)
Alta Bates Summit Medical Center (Oakland, CA)
Sutter Roseville Medical Center (CA)
Sutter Medical Center, Sacramento (CA)
Sutter Center for Psychiatry
California Pacific Medical Centers (San Francisco)
St. Luke's Hospital (San Francisco)
San Leandro Hospital (San Leandro, CA)
Sutter Maternity & Surgery Center of Santa Cruz (CA)
Sutter Medical Center of Santa Rosa (CA)
Sutter Warrack Hospital (Santa Rosa, CA)
Sutter Tracy Community Hospital (CA)
Sutter Solano Medical Center (Vallejo, CA)
Kahi Mohala, A Behavioral Healthcare System (Ewa Beach, HI)

COMPETITORS

Adventist Health	Providence Health System
Catholic Healthcare West	Stanford University Medical
HCA	
Memorial Health Services	Tenet Healthcare

HISTORICAL FINANCIALS
Company Type: Not-for-profit

Income Statement
FYE: December 31

	REVENUE ($ mil.)	NET INCOME ($ mil.)	NET PROFIT MARGIN	EMPLOYEES
12/03	5,672	—	—	41,000
12/02	4,931	—	—	39,678
12/01	4,216	—	—	36,000
12/00	3,500	—	—	35,000
12/99	2,919	—	—	35,000
12/98	2,881	—	—	35,000
12/97	2,663	—	—	35,000
12/96	2,453	—	—	35,000
12/95	2,226	—	—	—
12/94	1,940	—	—	—
Annual Growth	12.7%	—	—	2.3%

Revenue History

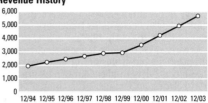

Swagelok

With sales partners worldwide, Swagelok Company has to speak many languages, *fluidly*. The company makes fluid system components, which include plug, pinch, and radial diaphragm valves, sanitary fittings, and welding systems. Its products are used by bioprocessing and pharmaceuticals research companies and in the oil and gas, power, and semiconductor industries. Swagelok has more than 200 manufacturing, research, sales, and distribution facilities worldwide. Founded in 1947 by Fred Lennon in his kitchen, the company requires all prospective sales people and their families to tour company facilities for two months before coming on board. The Lennon family still controls the company.

Swagelok is expanding the product base in its biopharmaceutical line of valves and related supplies through the introduction of new equipment and acquisitions. The company has also expanded its line of pressure gauges. In an attempt to increase Asian customers, Swagelok now has Web sites in traditional and simplified Chinese languages; the company also has French, German, Japanese, and Spanish language sites.

EXECUTIVES

Chairman: Edward A. Lozick
President and CEO: Arthur F. (Art) Anton
CFO: Frank J. Roddy
VP, Corporate Communications: Franziska H. Dacek
VP, Customer Service and Distributor Support: Hans J. Goemans
VP, Engineering: Carl E. Meece
VP, Human Resources: James L. Francis
VP, Information Services: David E. O'Connor
VP, Marketing: Michael R. Butkovic
VP, Operations: Kennan J. Malec
VP, Planning and Development: Michael L. MacKay
VP, Technology and Plastic Business Development: James M. Hanson
Director, Marketing Communications: Jacqueline Ekey

LOCATIONS

HQ: Swagelok Company
  29500 Solon Rd., Solon, OH 44139
Phone: 440-248-4600   **Fax:** 440-349-5970
Web: www.swagelok.com

PRODUCTS/OPERATIONS

Selected Products

Filters	Quick connects
Fittings	Regulators
Gauges	Sample cylinders
Hoses	Tube benders and cutters
Leak detectors	Valves
Lubricants and sealants	Weld systems
Manifolds	

COMPETITORS

Amcast Industrial
CIRCOR International
Crane
Hughes Supply
ITT Industries
Shaw Group
T3 Energy Services
Tyco International
Walter Industries

HISTORICAL FINANCIALS
Company Type: Private

Income Statement
FYE: December 31

	ESTIMATED REVENUE ($ mil.)	NET INCOME ($ mil.)	NET PROFIT MARGIN	EMPLOYEES
12/02	1,000	—	—	3,000
12/01	1,000	—	—	3,000
12/00	1,200	—	—	3,300
12/99	1,050	—	—	2,000
12/98	1,030	—	—	5,000
12/97	1,200	—	—	2,500
12/96	1,100	—	—	2,500
12/95	1,000	—	—	2,500
12/94	1,000	—	—	2,500
12/93	600	—	—	1,900
Annual Growth	5.8%	—	—	5.2%

Revenue History
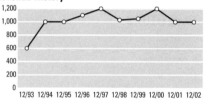

Swedish Health Services

You may find meatballs on the menu in the cafeteria at Swedish Health Services. The health care system serves Seattle and the surrounding area with three acute care hospitals, all branded with the Swedish Medical Center moniker. The three campuses combined have nearly 1,250 beds. Medical specialties include cardiac care, cancer treatment, and neurosurgery. Swedish Health Services also operates a home health services unit and Swedish Physicians, a network of about a dozen community clinics and some 70 medical professionals (not all of whom hail from Sweden).

EXECUTIVES

President and CEO: Richard H. Peterson
COO, Swedish Medical Center/First Hill Campus: Calvin (Cal) Knight
COO, Swedish Medical Center/Providence Campus: Marcel Loh
COO, Swedish Medical Center/Ballard Campus: Lane Savitch
CFO: Ron Sperling
VP, Medical Affairs: Nancy J. Auer
VP, Swedish Physician Division: Kevin Brown
VP, Supply Chain Management: Allen Caudle
VP, Mission, Ethics, and Community Relations: Sister Susanne Hartung
VP, Human Resources: Rena Irwin
VP, Support Services: Mary McHugh
VP, Legal Services: Cindy Strauss
VP, Marketing Communications: Sally Wright

LOCATIONS

HQ: Swedish Health Services
747 Broadway, Seattle, WA 98122
Phone: 206-386-6000 **Fax:** 206-386-2277
Web: www.swedish.org

COMPETITORS

Children's Hospital and Regional Medical Center
Kaiser Permanente
Providence Health System
University of Washington

HISTORICAL FINANCIALS
Company Type: Not-for-profit

Income Statement
FYE: December 31

	REVENUE ($ mil.)	NET INCOME ($ mil.)	NET PROFIT MARGIN	EMPLOYEES
12/03	928	—	—	7,100
12/02	814	—	—	7,116
Annual Growth	13.9%	—	—	(0.2%)

Revenue History

Swinerton

Swinerton is building up the West just as it helped rebuild San Francisco after the 1906 earthquake. The construction group, formerly Swinerton & Walberg, builds commercial, industrial, and government facilities, including resorts, subsidized housing, public schools, Hollywood soundstages, hospitals, and airport terminals. Through its subsidiaries, Swinerton offers general contracting and design/build services, as well as construction and program management. It also provides property management for conventional, subsidized, and assisted living residences. The employee-owned company, which has been expanding in the past decade in the Northwest and Southwest, traces its family tree to 1888.

EXECUTIVES

Chairman and CEO: James R. (Jim) Gillette
President and COO; President, Swinerton Builders: Gordon W. Marks
EVP and CFO: Michael Re
EVP Business Development: Jeffrey C. Hoopes
SVP; Northern California Regional Manager, Swinerton Builders: Charles P. (Charlie) Kuffner
SVP; Southern California Regional Manager, Swinerton Builders: Gary Rafferty
SVP and Colorado Regional Manager, Swinerton Builders: David White
SVP and Seattle Division Manager, Swinerton Builders: Keith M. Henrickson
SVP, Secretary, and General Counsel: Luke P. Argilla
VP and Controller: Linda G. Showalter
Auditors: PricewaterhouseCoopers

LOCATIONS

HQ: Swinerton Incorporated
260 Townsend St., San Francisco, CA 94107
Phone: 415-421-2980 **Fax:** 415-433-0943
Web: www.swinerton.com

Swinerton has offices in California, Colorado, Connecticut, Florida, Hawaii, Oregon, Texas, Utah, and Washington.

PRODUCTS/OPERATIONS

Selected Companies

Bud Bailey Construction (construction management, design/build, and general contracting)
Harbison-Mahony-Higgins Builders, Inc. (HMH, general contracting)
Lyda Swinerton Builders (general contracting)
Swinerton Builders (general contracting)
Swinerton Management & Consulting (property assessment)
Swinerton/Pacific (joint venture)
Swinerton Property Services (property management)
William P. Young Construction (engineering and civil construction)

COMPETITORS

Bechtel
Beck Group
Bovis Lend Lease
Charles Pankow Builders
Cordoba
Devcon Construction
DPR Construction
Gilbane
Hathaway Dinwiddie Construction
Hensel Phelps Construction
J.F. Shea
Kitchell Corporation
Rudolph & Sletten
S. J. Amoroso Construction
Skanska USA Building
Sundt
Turner Corporation
Tutor-Saliba
Webcor Builders
Whiting-Turner

HISTORICAL FINANCIALS
Company Type: Private

Income Statement
FYE: December 31

	REVENUE ($ mil.)	NET INCOME ($ mil.)	NET PROFIT MARGIN	EMPLOYEES
12/03	2,751	—	—	1,331
12/02	1,560	—	—	1,200
12/01	1,549	—	—	1,200
12/00	1,550	—	—	1,450
12/99	1,150	—	—	1,400
12/98	902	—	—	1,500
12/97	792	—	—	1,400
12/96	501	—	—	1,300
12/95	412	—	—	1,000
12/94	389	—	—	1,200
Annual Growth	24.3%	—	—	1.2%

Revenue History
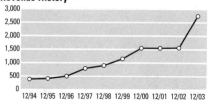

Tang Industries

Although it's not a good source of Vitamin C, Tang Industries *is* a diversified holding company. Its largest subsidiary, National Material, is a metal-fabricating and -distributing company that engages in steel stamping and recycles and trades aluminum and scrap metal. Another subsidiary, SKD Automotive Group, supplies tooling operations aimed at the automobile industry. Tang Industries also has steel operations in China. The company's holdings include real estate, manufacturer GF Office Furniture, and Curatek Pharmaceuticals, which specializes in niche markets overlooked by large drugmakers. The company was founded in 1964 by Chinese immigrant Cyrus Tang after he bought a small metal-stamping shop in Illinois.

EXECUTIVES

Chairman, President, and CEO: Cyrus Tang
VP, Legal and Administration and General Counsel, National Material LP: Vytas Ambutas
Treasurer and Secretary: John Chen
Manager Human Resources: Pam Foster
Assistant Treasurer: Kurt R. Swanson

LOCATIONS

HQ: Tang Industries, Inc.
3773 Howard Hughes Pkwy., Ste. 350N,
Las Vegas, NV 89109
Phone: 702-734-3700   **Fax:** 702-734-6766
Web: www.tangindustries.com

Tang Industries has more than 50 facilities in Canada, China, Mexico, and the US.

PRODUCTS/OPERATIONS

Selected Operations

Curatek Pharmaceuticals
GF Office Furniture, Ltd. (steel and wooden office furniture)
  Office Suites, Inc. (wooden office furniture)
National Material, LP (industrial manufacturing)
  Cox Metal Processing Co.
  Interstate Steel Co.
  National Coating Technology
  National Lamination Co.
  Taber Extrusions
SKD Industries (stamped and welded automotive components)

COMPETITORS

Abbott Labs
Alcoa
Bristol-Myers Squibb
Commercial Metals
Haworth
Herman Miller
Metalcraft
OmniSource
Ryerson Tull
Steelcase

HISTORICAL FINANCIALS

Company Type: Private

Income Statement
FYE: December 31

	ESTIMATED REVENUE ($ mil.)	NET INCOME ($ mil.)	NET PROFIT MARGIN	EMPLOYEES
12/02	1,270	—	—	3,750
12/01	1,250	—	—	3,700
12/00	1,250	—	—	3,700
12/99	1,230	—	—	3,600
12/98	1,200	—	—	3,500
12/97	975	—	—	3,770
12/96	1,100	—	—	4,000
12/95	1,300	—	—	3,800
12/94	1,100	—	—	3,700
12/93	878	—	—	3,500
Annual Growth	4.2%	—	—	0.8%

Revenue History

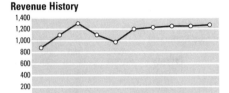

TAP Pharmaceutical Products

TAP Pharmaceutical Products taps into hot drug industry trends. The joint venture between Abbott Laboratories and Takeda Pharmaceutical Company develops and sells drugs in the US and Canada. The company's products target cancer, gastroenterology, gynecology, and urology. TAP's Lupron Depot was developed to treat advanced prostate cancer, but can also treat endometriosis in women and central precocious puberty in children. The company also markets Prevacid, which is used to treat acid reflux disease and ulcers, with Abbott and has gained FDA approval for antibiotic Spectracef.

The company's pipeline includes drugs for hormone replacement therapy, obesity, and gout. Although erectile dysfunction treatment Uprima won European approval, TAP withdrew it from FDA consideration after questions arose over its efficacy and safety. It is continuing to improve the drug for resubmission.

TAP agreed to pay a record-setting $875 million to settle criminal and civil charges over its pricing and marketing of Lupron; a few executives and former executives have been indicted on allegations of criminal conspiracy.

EXECUTIVES

President: Alan MacKenzie, age 51
EVP: Shinji Honda
VP and General Manager, Prevacid and Gastrointestinal Marketing: Brian Luedtke
VP, Ethics and Compliance: L. Stephan Vincze
VP, Human Resources: Denise Kitchen
VP, Research and Development: Xavier Frapaise
Controller: Kevin Dolan
Public Relations: Kim Modory

LOCATIONS

HQ: TAP Pharmaceutical Products Inc.
675 North Field Dr., Lake Forest, IL 60045
Phone: 847-582-2000   **Fax:** 800-830-6936
Web: www.tap.com

TAP Pharmaceutical Products has facilities in California, Georgia, Illinois, New Jersey, and Texas.

PRODUCTS/OPERATIONS

Products

Lupron/Lupron Depot (endometriosis, prostate cancer)
Prevacid (gastric acid inhibitor)
Prevpac (Prevacid plus antibiotics)
Spectracef (antibiotic)
Uprima (erectile dysfunction treatment)

COMPETITORS

AstraZeneca
Bone Care International
GlaxoSmithKline
ICOS
Pfizer
PRAECIS PHARMACEUTICALS
Zonagen

HISTORICAL FINANCIALS

Company Type: Joint venture

Income Statement
FYE: December 31

	REVENUE ($ mil.)	NET INCOME ($ mil.)	NET PROFIT MARGIN	EMPLOYEES
12/03	3,980	1,162	29.2%	3,300
12/02	4,037	1,334	33.0%	3,000
12/01	3,787	668	17.6%	3,000
12/00	3,539	963	27.2%	2,500
12/99	2,928	780	26.7%	2,300
12/98	2,063	533	25.8%	2,000
12/97	1,566	379	24.2%	1,500
12/96	1,129	259	23.0%	1,250
12/95	750	150	19.9%	1,000
Annual Growth	23.2%	29.2%	—	16.1%

2003 Year-End Financials

Debt ratio: 10.5%   Current ratio: 1.50
Return on equity: 163.5%   Long-term debt ($ mil.): 71
Cash ($ mil.): 606

Net Income History

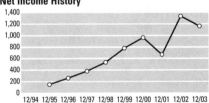

Taylor Corporation

The pleasure of your presence is big business to the Taylor Corporation. The holding company, which owns wedding invitation printer Carlson Craft, operates through some 80 firms in Australia, Europe, and North America. Its subsidiaries print wedding invitations, stationery, business cards, brochures, gift wrap, calendars, and gift items. Taylor owns greeting card company Current, desktop publishing paper maker PaperDirect, and G.Neil, a catalog order business focused on human resources products. The company sells through retail outlets, catalogs, web sites, and local print shops. Chairman Glen Taylor, majority owner of the Minnesota Timberwolves, built the company after buying Carlson Craft in 1975.

One of the largest printing concerns in the US, Taylor Corporation continues to expand its holdings through acquisitions, such as its 2003 purchase of G.Neil — which sells human resources-related business forms, training tools, and software — and its proposed purchase of Executive Greetings.

Taylor is also broadening its Carlson Craft wedding invitation line, offering bolder, contemporary designs and CD wedding invitations, as well as reaching out to the Hispanic market and to mature couples. Its Current greeting card company laid off more than 10% of its workforce in 2002, blaming a downturn in the economy.

EXECUTIVES

Chairman: Glen A. Taylor, age 62
CEO: Bradley (Brad) Schreier, age 52
President: Jean Taylor
COO: Ed Alvarez
CFO: Tom Johnson
CTO: Jeff Eceles
President, Carlson Craft: Keith Herwig
Corporate Communications: Suzanne Spellacy

LOCATIONS

HQ: Taylor Corporation
1725 Roe Crest Dr., North Mankato, MN 56003
Phone: 507-625-2828   **Fax:** 507-625-2988
Web: www.carlsoncraft.com

PRODUCTS/OPERATIONS

Selected Subsidiaries
Apex Business Systems
Carlson Craft Commercial
Current
Direct Marketing Resources
G.Neil
James Tower
Labelworks
Marketing General
Original Smith Printing
Promo Direct
Regency Thermographers
Royal Imprints
Stationery House
Thayer Publishing
Travel Tags
Web Graphics

COMPETITORS

American Achievement
American Greetings
Arandell
BCT International
Black Dot Group
Champion Industries
CSS Industries
Hallmark
Quad/Graphics
Quebecor World
R.R. Donnelley

HISTORICAL FINANCIALS
Company Type: Private

Income Statement   FYE: December 31

	ESTIMATED REVENUE ($ mil.)	NET INCOME ($ mil.)	NET PROFIT MARGIN	EMPLOYEES
12/02	1,269	—	—	14,350
12/01	1,300	—	—	14,000
12/00	1,310	—	—	14,000
12/99	1,300	—	—	11,000
12/98	1,000	—	—	11,000
12/97	900	—	—	12,000
12/96	750	—	—	10,000
12/95	650	—	—	8,000
12/94	600	—	—	6,500
12/93	460	—	—	—
Annual Growth	11.9%	—	—	10.4%

Revenue History

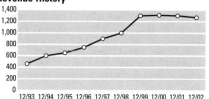

Team Health

Team Health hopes to score some points with its outsourced physician services. It has contracts with some 450 hospitals in about 45 states to provide medical staffing, management, administrative, and other support services. With more than 3,000 physicians in its network, the firm specializes in emergency medicine, radiology, pediatrics, anesthesia, and hospitalists (hospital physicians who coordinate care during patients' stays with their primary physicians and other medical professionals). It operates through physician-managed regional affiliates. A group of emergency physicians founded Team Health in 1979. Cornerstone Equity Investors and Madison Dearborn Capital Partners each own about 40% of the company.

Team Health plans to grow by increasing its presence in the market for staffing military hospitals, and by obtaining business with hospitals that currently do not outsource their hospital staffing functions.

EXECUTIVES

President, CEO, and Director: Lynn Massingale, age 51, $681,063 pay
CFO: David Jones, age 36
EVP and General Counsel: Robert C. (Bob) Joyner, age 56, $286,278 pay
EVP, Billing and Reimbursement: Stephen Sherlin, age 58, $307,064 pay
EVP, Finance and Administration: Robert J. (Bob) Abramowski, age 53, $354,911 pay
SVP, HCFS: Ron Matthews
SVP, Business Integration and Receivables Management: Michael J. Weiner
SVP, Operations and Technology Integration: Randall S. Aguiar
SVP: John Craig
Corporate VP, Human Resources: Lisa Courtney
Chief Information Officer: Harry Herman
Chief Medical Officer: Gar LaSalle
Auditors: Ernst & Young LLP

LOCATIONS

HQ: Team Health, Inc.
1900 Winston Rd., Knoxville, TN 37919
Phone: 865-693-1000   **Fax:** 865-539-8003
Web: www.teamhealth.com

PRODUCTS/OPERATIONS

2003 Sales

	$ mil.	% of total
Fee-for-service	1,041.0	70
Contracts	408.1	28
Other	29.9	2
Total	1,479.0	100

COMPETITORS

EmCare
Per-Se Technologies
RehabCare
Sheridan Healthcare
Sterling Healthcare

HISTORICAL FINANCIALS
Company Type: Private

Income Statement   FYE: December 31

	REVENUE ($ mil.)	NET INCOME ($ mil.)	NET PROFIT MARGIN	EMPLOYEES
12/03	1,479	(3)	—	6,700
12/02	1,231	16	1.3%	6,800
12/01	965	—	—	3,500
12/00	919	—	—	1,804
12/99	852	—	—	1,500
12/98	548	—	—	1,388
Annual Growth	22.0%	—	—	37.0%

2003 Year-End Financials

Debt ratio: (222.1%)   Current ratio: 1.35
Return on equity: —   Long-term debt ($ mil.): 256
Cash ($ mil.): 101

Net Income History

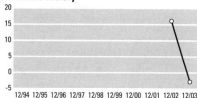

Teamsters

The International Brotherhood of Teamsters is the largest and arguably most (in)famous labor union in the US. With about 1.4 million members, the Teamsters represents 16 trade groups, including truckers, UPS workers, warehouse employees, cab drivers, airline workers, construction crews, and other workers. The union negotiates with employers for contracts that guarantee members fair wages and raises, health coverage, job security, paid time off, promotions, and other benefits. The Teamsters union has about 520 local chapters in the US and Canada.

Elected in 1998, Teamsters chief James P. Hoffa (son of assumed-dead union leader Jimmy Hoffa) is working to shed the union's notorious image and has proposed ethics policies aimed at rooting out internal corruption and ties to organized crime. Hoffa wants the Teamsters to police themselves and put an end to the close governmental supervision under which the union has operated since 1989. He also is working to re-establish the union as a power in national politics, lobbying against plans to allow trucks from Mexico to traverse US highways.

HISTORY

Two rival team-driver unions, the Drivers International Union and the Teamsters National Union, merged to form the International Brotherhood of Teamsters in 1903. Led by Cornelius Shea, the Teamsters established headquarters in Indianapolis. Daniel Tobin (president for 45 years, starting in 1907) demanded that union locals obtain executive approval before striking. Membership expanded from the team-driver base, prompting the union to add Chauffeurs, Stablemen, and Helpers to its name (1909).

Following the first transcontinental delivery by motor truck (1912), the Teamster deliverymen traded their horses for trucks. The union then recruited food processing, brewery, and farm workers, among others, to augment Teamster effectiveness during strikes. It joined the American Federation of Labor in 1920.

Until the Depression the Teamsters was still a small union of predominantly urban deliverymen. Then Farrell Dobbs, a Trotskyite Teamster from Minneapolis, organized the famous Minneapolis strikes in 1934 to protest local management's refusal to allow the workers to unionize. Workers clashed with police and National Guard units for 11 days before management acceded to the workers' demands. The strikes demonstrated the potential strength of unions, and Teamsters membership swelled. Although union power ebbed during WWII, the union continued to grow. It moved its headquarters to Washington, DC, in 1953.

The AFL-CIO expelled the Teamsters in 1957 when Teamster ties to the mob became public during a US Senate investigation. New Teamsters boss Jimmy Hoffa eluded indictment and took advantage of America's growing dependence on trucking to negotiate the powerful National Master Freight Agreement (1964). Hoffa also organized industrial workers. He used a union pension fund to make mob-connected loans and was later convicted of jury tampering and sent to prison. In 1975, four years after his release, Hoffa vanished without a trace and is believed to have been the victim of a Mafia hit.

The Teamsters rejoined the AFL-CIO in 1987 and the following year settled a racketeering lawsuit filed by the US Justice Department by allowing government appointees to discipline corrupt union leaders, help run the union, and oversee its elections. The election of self-styled reformer Ronald Carey in 1991 (he received 49% of the vote) seemed to portend real changes for the union; each of his six predecessors had been accused of or imprisoned for criminal activities. However, membership dropped by 40,000 in both 1991 and 1992.

Carey won re-election as union president in 1996 over rival, and son of former boss Jimmy Hoffa, James P. Hoffa (whom Carey accused of having ties to organized crime). A 15-day strike by the Teamsters' UPS employees in 1997 led to the delivery company's agreement to combine part-time jobs into 10,000 new full-time positions. That year Carey's re-election was overturned amid a campaign finance investigation that netted guilty pleas from three Carey associates, and the Teamsters leader was disqualified from running for re-election in 1998. Carey was officially expelled from the Teamsters by the federal government, and Hoffa won the 1998 election over Tom Leedham (who was backed by the union's reform wing).

Promising to fight corruption, Hoffa hired former federal prosecutor Edwin Stier and several former FBI agents to help him operate Project RISE (respect, integrity, strength, and ethics), a new in-house anti-corruption program. In 2002 the union began lobbying against plans to allow Mexican trucking companies to transport goods across the US.

EXECUTIVES

General President: James P. Hoffa, age 63
General Secretary-Treasurer: C. Thomas (Tom) Keegel
VP At-Large: Randy Cammack
VP At-Large: Fred Gegare
VP At-Large: Carl E. Haynes
VP At-Large: Thomas R. O'Donnell
VP At-Large: Ralph J. Taurone
VP, Canada; President, Teamsters Canada: Robert Bouvier
VP, Canada: Joseph McLean
VP, Canada: Garnet Zimmerman
VP, Central Region: Patrick Flynn
VP, Central Region: Walter Lytle
VP, Central Region: Dotty W. Malinsky
VP, Central Region: Lester A. Singer
VP, Central Region: Philip E. Young
VP, Eastern Region: Jack Cipriani
VP, Eastern Region: Richard K. Hall
VP, Eastern Region: John Murphy
VP, Eastern Region: Richard Volpe
VP, Southern Region: Tyson Johnson
VP, Southern Region: Ken Wood
VP, Western Region: Al Hobart
VP, Western Region: Chuck Mack
VP, Western Region: Jim Santangelo
Director Information Systems: Baker Killam

LOCATIONS

HQ: International Brotherhood of Teamsters
25 Louisiana Ave. NW, Washington, DC 20001
Phone: 202-624-6800 **Fax:** 202-624-6918
Web: www.teamster.org

2003 Membership

	% of total
United States	
Central	32
East	28
West	26
South	7
Canada	7
Total	**100**

PRODUCTS/OPERATIONS

Trade Divisions
Airline
Bakery and Laundry
Brewery and Soft Drink
Building Material and Construction
Carhaul
Dairy
Freight
Industrial Trades
Motion Picture and Theatrical Trade
Newspaper, Magazine, and Electronic Media
Parcel and Small Package
Port
Public Services
Tankhaul
Trade Show and Convention Centers
Warehouse

HISTORICAL FINANCIALS

Company Type: Labor union

Income Statement				FYE: December 31
	REVENUE ($ mil.)	NET INCOME ($ mil.)	NET PROFIT MARGIN	EMPLOYEES
12/03	149	53	35.1%	649
12/02	118	4	3.4%	—
12/01	88	(15)	—	—
12/00	90	—	—	—
12/99	90	—	—	—
12/98	90	—	—	—
12/97	89	—	—	—
12/96	90	—	—	—
12/95	90	—	—	—
12/94	82	—	—	—
Annual Growth	6.9%	—	—	—

Net Income History

Tekni-Plex

Tekni-Plex manufactures packaging, packaging products, and tubing products for the food, health care, and consumer industries. The company's packaging segment makes foam egg cartons, pharmaceutical blister films, poultry and meat processing trays, closure liners, foam plates, and aerosol and pump packaging components. Its tubing products division manufactures irrigation hoses, garden hoses, and pool and vacuum hoses. Tekni-Plex also makes vinyl resins and recycled PET used in a variety of industrial products. Over 85% of the company's sales are in the US. Dr. F. Patrick Smith (chairman and CEO) controls the company through Tekni-Plex Partners.

EXECUTIVES

Chairman and CEO: F. Patrick Smith, age 56, $6,655,000 pay
President, COO, and Director: Kenneth W.R. Baker, age 60, $3,327,500 pay
VP and CFO: James E. Condon, $715,000 pay
VP, Human Resources: Joe Bruno
VP, International Sales and Marketing: Michael Franklin
Corporate Secretary and Director: Arthur P. Witt, age 74
Auditors: BDO Seidman, LLP

LOCATIONS

HQ: Tekni-Plex, Inc.
201 Industrial Pkwy., Somerville, NJ 08876
Phone: 908-722-4800   **Fax:** 908-722-4967
Web: www.tekni-plex.com

Tekni-Plex has manufacturing facilities in the US and abroad in Argentina, Belgium, and Singapore.

2004 Sales

	$ mil.	% of total
US	545.6	86
Europe (primarily Belgium)	72.1	11
Canada	17.9	3
Total	**635.6**	**100**

PRODUCTS/OPERATIONS

2004 Sales

	$ mil.	% of total
Packaging	306.1	48
Tubing products	210.2	33
Other	119.3	19
Total	**635.6**	**100**

Selected Products

Consumer Packaging and Products
   Garden hose
   Irrigation hose
   Precision tubing and gaskets
Healthcare
   Blister packaging
   Cap liners and seals
   Coated film
   Co-extrusions
   Flexible film
   Laminations
   Medical tubing
   Rigid packaging film
   Semi-rigid film
   Vinyl compounds
Food Packaging
   Egg cartons
   Processor trays
Specialty Resins and Compounds
   Vinyl resins

COMPETITORS

Crown
Huntsman
Pactiv
RPC Group
Sealed Air
Smurfit-Stone Container
Sonoco Products
Teknor Apex

HISTORICAL FINANCIALS

Company Type: Private

Income Statement
FYE: Friday nearest June 30

	REVENUE ($ mil.)	NET INCOME ($ mil.)	NET PROFIT MARGIN	EMPLOYEES
6/04	636	(55)	—	3,200
6/03	611	3	0.6%	3,300
6/02	578	(7)	—	3,090
6/01	526	(19)	—	3,000
6/00	507	(21)	—	2,900
6/99	489	15	3.1%	2,950
6/98	310	9	2.8%	2,800
6/97	145	(12)	—	—
6/96	81	1	1.2%	—
6/95	45	0	0.4%	—
Annual Growth	34.3%	—	—	2.3%

2004 Year-End Financials

Debt ratio: —
Return on equity: —
Cash ($ mil.): 30
Current ratio: 3.34
Long-term debt ($ mil.): 732

Net Income History

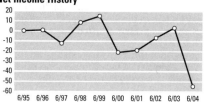

Tenaska

Tenaska is tenacious when it comes to producing and selling energy. The employee-owned company is a top natural gas marketer in the US; it also trades and markets electricity and develops, owns, operates, and maintains power plants, mostly in the Americas. Tenaska has interests in primarily gas-fired and hydroelectric generation facilities (some of which are under construction) that give it 7,600 MW of capacity. It also develops plants for third parties, providing engineering and construction, site development, financing, and management services. Other operations include fuel supply, power transmission, and gas transportation contracting. Tenaska was founded in 1987 by CEO Howard Hawks and VP Thomas Hendricks.

EXECUTIVES

Chairman and CEO: Howard L. Hawks
EVP: Thomas E. Hendricks
EVP and Chief Strategy and Legal Officer: Ronald N. Quinn
EVP and Treasurer: Michael F. (Mike) Lawler
CFO: Jerry K. Crouse
President and CEO, Business Development Group: Darrell W. Bevelhymer
President and CEO, Operations Group: Larry V. Pearson
CEO and Managing Director, Acquisitions Group: Paul G. Smith
President, Tenaska Marketing Ventures and Tenaska Marketing Canada: Fred R. Hunzeker
President, Tenaska Power Services: Trudy A. Harper
VP and Managing Director, Tenaska-Oxy Power Services: Keith E. Emery
Managing Director Acquisition: Daniel E. Lonergan
Managing Director Acquisition: James L. Evans
Corporate Controller: Timothy G. Kudron
EVP Engineering, Construction, and Operations: Michael C. (Mike) Lebens
Director Government and Public Affairs: Jana M. Martin

LOCATIONS

HQ: Tenaska, Inc.
1044 N. 115th St., Ste. 400, Omaha, NE 68154
Phone: 402-691-9500   **Fax:** 402-691-9526
Web: www.tenaska.com

Tenaska owns operating power projects in Alabama, Georgia, Texas, Oklahoma, and Washington in the US, as well as in Bolivia and Pakistan. It also has a plant under construction in Virginia.

PRODUCTS/OPERATIONS

Selected Subsidiaries

Tenaska Energy Holdings, LLC
Tenaska Energy, Inc.
Tenaska Marketing Canada (gas marketing)
Tenaska Marketing Ventures (gas marketing)
Tenaska Operations, Inc. (asset management)
Tenaska Power Fund (acquisitions)
Tenaska Power Services Co. (power marketing)

COMPETITORS

AES
BP
Calpine
ChevronTexaco
Cinergy
ConocoPhillips
Covanta
Edison Mission Energy
El Paso
Exxon Mobil
International Power
Mirant
National Energy & Gas Transmission
NRG Energy
Reliant Energy
Sempra Energy
Shell
Sithe Energies
Texas Genco

HISTORICAL FINANCIALS

Company Type: Private

Income Statement
FYE: December 31

	REVENUE ($ mil.)	NET INCOME ($ mil.)	NET PROFIT MARGIN	EMPLOYEES
12/03	5,600	—	—	475
12/02	2,231	—	—	460
12/01	2,665	—	—	450
Annual Growth	45.0%	—	—	2.7%

Revenue History

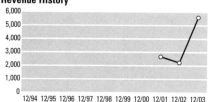

Texas A&M

Everything is bigger in Texas, even its universities. With about 100,000 students at nine institutions, The Texas A&M University System ranks among the largest in the US. Its flagship school at College Station is well-known not only for its programs in engineering and agriculture, but also for its long-held traditions and school spirit. Other system institutions include Tarleton State University and Prairie View A&M. The system also runs state extension agencies and a health sciences center. Texas A&M was founded in 1876 as the Agricultural and Mechanical College of Texas. The A&M system was formed in 1948; it is funded in part by a $7.7 billion state endowment (shared with the University of Texas).

Texas A&M in College Station is the largest campus in the university system, with an enrollment of about 44,000 students.

In the wake of a bonfire collapse which took the lives of 12 students in 1999, Texas A&M has been charged by outsiders with trying to conceal its own involvement in the accident. Still others have called on Texas A&M to loosen some of its traditions. However, the school, students, and alumni have all stood fast against the tide of pressure. Texas A&M has embarked on a 20-year mission to renovate its facilities and secure status as a top public university.

HISTORY

The Texas Constitution of 1876 created an agricultural and mechanical college and stated that "separate schools shall be provided for the white and colored children, and impartial provisions shall be made for both." The white school, the Agricultural and Mechanical College of Texas (later Texas A&M), began instruction that year. Texas A&M was a men's school at first, and membership in its Corps of Cadets was mandatory. The Agricultural and Mechanical College of Texas for Colored Youth (later Prairie View A&M) opened in 1878.

To help fund the agricultural colleges and The University of Texas, the Legislature established the Permanent University Fund in 1876 to hold more than 1 million acres of land in West Texas as an endowment. An additional million acres was added in 1883. The Santa Rita well on the university land struck oil in 1923 and money flowed into the Permanent University Fund's coffers. Under the provisions of the constitution, The University of Texas got two-thirds of the income, and A&M got the rest.

In 1948 The Texas A&M College System was established to oversee Texas A&M, Prairie View A&M, Tarleton State, and Arlington State (which left the system in 1965 and is now The University of Texas at Arlington). By 1963 enrollment system-wide had reached 8,000. That year the system changed its name to The Texas A&M University System, the same year that Texas A&M went co-ed.

By the mid-1980s enrollment had surpassed 35,000 students. The system grew quickly in 1989 when it added Texas A&I University (now Texas A&M University-Kingsville), Corpus Christi State (now Texas A&M University-Corpus Christi), and Laredo State University (now Texas A&M International). West Texas State College in Canyon joined the system in 1990 and became West Texas A&M University in 1993.

The 91-year-old Baylor College of Dentistry (in Dallas) and East Texas State University, well known for training future teachers, joined the A&M system in 1996 (East Texas State was divided into Texas A&M University-Commerce and Texas A&M-Texarkana). In 1997 the system opened the first portion of the $82 million George Bush Presidential Library and Museum.

In early 1998 the system signed an alliance with the private South Texas College of Law in Houston, which was opposed by the Texas Higher Education Coordinating Board. (In 1999 a judge ruled that the two schools had to discontinue their affiliation.) That year Texas Instruments donated $5.1 million to the system (one of the largest donations in the institution's history) for the creation of an analog technology program. Chancellor Barry Thompson announced he would retire in 1999. The system appointed former Army general Howard Graves as the new chancellor (he died in September 2003).

Tragedy struck the College Station campus in 1999 when logs being stacked for the annual bonfire celebrating The University of Texas/Texas A&M football game collapsed and killed 12 people. Clinging to the 90-year tradition, many Aggies past and present insisted the bonfire go on in future years.

Texas A&M University has established "Vision 2020," an initiative to become a consensus top-10 public university by the year 2020.

EXECUTIVES

Chairman, Board of Regents: L. Lowry Mays, age 68
Vice Chairman, Board of Regents: Erle Nye, age 67
Interim Chancellor: A. Benton Cocanougher
Deputy Chancellor: Jerry Gatson
General Counsel: Delmar Cain
Vice Chancellor of Governmental Relations: Stanton C. Calvert
Vice Chancellor of Administration: James A. Fletcher
Vice Chancellor of Business Services: Tom D. Kale
Vice Chancellor of Research and Federal Relations: Kenneth L. Peddicord
Vice Chancellor of Academic and Student Affairs: Leo Sayavedra
Chief Auditor: Catherine A. (Cathy) Smock
Director of Communications: Bob Wright
President, Prairie View A&M University: George C. Wright
President, Tarleton State University: Dennis P. McCabe
President, Texas A&M International University: Ray Keck III
President, Texas A&M University: Robert M. Gates, age 61
President, Texas A&M University-Commerce: Keith McFarland
President, Texas A&M University-Corpus Christi: Robert R. Furgason, age 68
President, Texas A&M University-Kingsville: Rumaldo Juarez
President, Texas A&M University-Texarkana: Stephen R. Hensley
President, West Texas A&M University: Russell Long
Vice Chancellor of Health Affairs; President, The Texas A&M University System Health Science Center: Nancy W. Dickey
Associate Vice Chancellor of Budgets and Accounting: B. J. Crain
Associate Vice Chancellor and Treasurer: Gregory R. Anderson
Comptroller: Sandra K. Brown
Auditors: Texas State Auditor

LOCATIONS

HQ: The Texas A&M University System
A&M System Bldg., 200 Technology Way, Ste. 2043, College Station, TX 77845
Phone: 979-458-6000 **Fax:** 979-458-6044
Web: tamusystem.tamu.edu

PRODUCTS/OPERATIONS

Selected Texas A&M University System Components

Health Science Center
  Baylor College of Dentistry
  College of Medicine
  Graduate School of Biomedical Sciences
  Institute of Biosciences and Technology
  School of Rural Public Health
State Agencies
  Texas Agricultural Experiment Station
  Texas Cooperative Extension
  Texas Engineering Experiment Station
  Texas Engineering Extension Service
  Texas Forest Service
  Texas Transportation Institute
  Texas Veterinary Medical Diagnostic Laboratory
Universities
  Prairie View A&M University
  Tarleton State University
  Texas A&M International University
  Texas A&M University
  Texas A&M University-Commerce
  Texas A&M University-Corpus Christi
  Texas A&M University-Kingsville
  Texas A&M University-Texarkana
  West Texas A&M University

HISTORICAL FINANCIALS

Company Type: School

Income Statement

FYE: August 31

	REVENUE ($ mil.)	NET INCOME ($ mil.)	NET PROFIT MARGIN	EMPLOYEES
8/03	1,257	—	—	38,500
8/02	2,254	—	—	25,000
8/01	1,928	—	—	24,000
8/00	2,620	—	—	23,000
8/99	1,792	—	—	23,000
8/98	1,695	—	—	23,300
8/97	1,550	—	—	22,800
8/96	1,425	—	—	22,600
8/95	1,299	—	—	20,000
8/94	1,287	—	—	16,367
Annual Growth	(0.3%)	—	—	10.0%

Revenue History

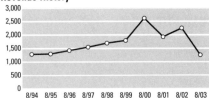

Texas Health Resources

Texas Health Resources is takin' care of Texas with about 25 health care facilities in the Dallas/Fort Worth and North Texas region. Formed by the merger of Harris Methodist Health System, Presbyterian Healthcare System, and Arlington Memorial Hospital Foundation, the not-for-profit system includes more than a dozen tertiary and acute-care hospitals, mental health centers, a retirement community, senior care centers, and home health services. Texas Health Resources' network includes more than 3,000 physicians and some 2,400 beds. The company's Texas Health Research Institute provides clinical studies management, medical device testing, and medical training services.

In order to keep up with the growing population of North Texas, Texas Health Resources is undergoing a $1.5 billion expansion.

EXECUTIVES

President and CEO: Douglas D. Hawthorne
EVP and CFO: Ron Bourland
EVP, Corporate Affairs: Margaret H. Jordan
EVP, Strategy and System Development: Dave Ashworth
EVP, People and Culture: Bonnie Bell
SVP, Regional Operations: Oscar L. Amparan
Chief Information Officer: David S. Muntz
Public Relations Manager: Kent Best

LOCATIONS

HQ: Texas Health Resources Inc.
611 Ryan Plaza Dr., Ste. 900, Arlington, TX 76011
Phone: 817-462-7900 **Fax:** 817-462-6996
Web: www.texashealth.org

Hospitals

Arlington Memorial Hospital (Arlington, TX)
Arlington Memorial South Medical Center (Arlington, TX)
Harris Methodist Erath County (Stephenville, TX)
Harris Methodist Fort Worth
Harris Methodist H-E-B (Bedford, TX)
Harris Methodist Northwest (Azle, TX)
Harris Methodist Southwest (Fort Worth, TX)
Harris Methodist Walls Regional Hospital (Cleburne, TX)
Presbyterian Hospital of Allen
Presbyterian Hospital of Dallas
Presbyterian Hospital of Kaufman
Presbyterian Hospital of Plano
Presbyterian Hospital of Winnsboro

COMPETITORS

Baylor Health
HCA
Triad Hospitals
VHA

HISTORICAL FINANCIALS

Company Type: Not-for-profit

Income Statement
FYE: December 31

	REVENUE ($ mil.)	NET INCOME ($ mil.)	NET PROFIT MARGIN	EMPLOYEES
12/03	1,900	—	—	16,800
12/02	1,700	—	—	16,500
12/01	1,500	—	—	16,000
12/00	1,340	—	—	16,000
12/99	1,291	—	—	15,000
12/98	1,286	—	—	15,000
12/97	1,250	—	—	15,000
Annual Growth	7.2%	—	—	1.9%

Revenue History

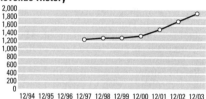

Texas Lottery

The eyes of Texas are watching the lotto jackpot. The Texas Lottery Commission oversees one of the country's largest state lotteries, which has pumped more than $10 billion into state coffers since it was created in 1991. About 57% of lottery sales are paid out in prize money, while more than 30% goes to the state's Foundation School Fund; the remainder covers administration costs and commissions to retailers. The lottery offers four numbers games (Lotto Texas, Pick 3, Cash 5, and Texas Two Step) and several instant-win games sold through retailers around the state. Retailers such as grocery stores, gas stations, and liquor and convenience stores make a small commission on tickets they sell.

The Lone Star lottery seems to be rebounding, with rising sales after two years of losses. The company discontinued its slumping Texas Million lottery game in 2001. It also changed its Lotto Texas game so that customers must match six numbers out of 54 numbers instead of 50. The extra four numbers changed the odds of winning from about one in 16 million to one in 26 million. The game was changed again in 2003 to a two-field game where players first select five numbers out of 44, and then select one number from a second field of 44. The new game has changed the odds of winning the jackpot to one in 48 million, while the odds of winning any prize have changed from one in 71 to one in 57. The commission expects the new game to generate an additional $50 million in revenue.

HISTORY

A state lottery had been an issue in Texas for years before it was discussed in earnest in the mid-1980s. Falling oil and gas revenue had plunged the state into a recession, raising the specter of tax increases. In 1985 the state budget had a shortfall of $1 billion; that figure tripled by 1987. Adding fuel to the fire, the Texas Supreme Court ruled in 1989 that Texas had to change the way it funded public schools to avoid penalizing poor school districts. The ruling forced the state to seek new sources of revenue. In 1991 Governor Ann Richards called a special session of the legislature to deal with the fiscal crisis, and House Bill 54 was passed, creating the state lottery. The measure was approved by 64% of voters.

In May 1992 Richards bought the symbolic first ticket at an Austin feed store (it was not a winner). Fourteen hours later Texans had spent nearly $23 million on tickets — breaking the California Lottery's first-day sales record — and had won $10 million in prizes. More than 102 million tickets were sold the first week. GTECH Holdings was awarded a five-year contract that year for lotto operations. Lotto Texas started in November with a winner taking nearly $22 million. By the end of the year, lotto sales in Texas had topped $1 billion. In its first 15 months, it contributed $812 million to the state's coffers.

In March 1994 five winners split a record $77 million jackpot. By that autumn sales from the lottery's beginning had surpassed $5 billion. In November a Mansfield, Texas, gas station owner picked up the largest single-winner jackpot, $54 million. By the end of 1994, Texas had the largest state lottery in the US. Cumulative sales topped $8 billion in mid-1995. In its first 37 months of operation, the Texas Lottery contributed $2.5 billion to the state's general fund. Cash 5 debuted that year, and instant ticket vending machines were installed at some sites.

In 1996 lottery director Nora Linares was dismissed following allegations that one of her friends received $30,000 from GTECH as a "hunting consultant." When a GTECH official was convicted in New Jersey of taking kickbacks from a lobbyist, questions were raised concerning payments to GTECH's Texas lobbyist, former Texas Lieutenant Governor Ben Barnes. In 1997 Texas canceled its contract with GTECH to operate the lottery through 2002 and reopened bidding; GTECH filed suit to enforce the contract. Executive director Lawrence Littwin later was dismissed by the commission. Littwin sued GTECH, claiming the company had gotten him fired (the case was settled in 1999). Linda Cloud, his replacement, reinstated GTECH's contract. That year the Texas legislature voted to increase the amount going to the state and to reduce prize payouts.

Lottery sales fell sharply in 1998, due in part to the reduced prize money. To combat suffering sales, the legislature reversed itself the next year and restored the level of prize payouts. The commission proposed lengthening the odds of winning to create larger jackpots, but public outcry scuttled the plan. In 2000 the commission agreed to change the wording on its scratch tickets after a San Antonio College professor and his students argued that breaking even is not winning. The following year it introduced its first new lottery game in about three years, Texas Two Step, and discontinued Texas Million following slumping sales. The commission changed its Lotto Texas game in 2003, lengthening the odds to about one in 48 million.

Texas Pacific Group

Yee-hah! Let's round us up some LBOs! Texas Pacific Group (TPG) has staked its claim on the buyout frontier with a reputation for roping in companies other investors wouldn't touch with a ten-foot pole. TPG, an active investor with over $13 billion under management, often takes control of the firms in which it invests. The firm is generally interested in resuscitating well-known consumer and *luxe* brands that have fallen on hard times. TPG is betting on Europe after wrangling the successful turnaround of UK pub chain Punch Taverns and reselling its stake for a tidy $400 million profit. TPG not only profits from the rise in value of its holdings, but also from fund management.

Recent European investments include UK retailer Debenhams (with CVC Capital Partners); restaurant, pub, and hotel chain Scottish & Newcastle (with CVC and Blackstone Group); Gate Gourmet (the world's second largest airline caterer); German bathroom fixtures manufacturer Grohe; and luxury brand Bally.

The firm hasn't completely given up on new investment opportunities in the US — it's currently courting Enron cast-off Portland General Electric. However, in the volatile Latin American market, TPG is curbing the size and pace of its investments.

TPG's other holdings include Burger King, Ducati Motor, J. Crew, Magellan Health Services, Motorola, ON Semiconductor, and Oxford Health Plans. Its venture capital affiliate TPG Ventures invests in telecommunications and technology companies.

It isn't always sunshine and flowers for TPG — the firm has encountered some recent setbacks: Magellan Heath Services' chapter 11 agreement provides for TPG to receive a 2% share in the firm after reorganization; TPG had originally invested some $50 million in the firm. Bally, stunted by a slump in the luxury goods industry, is struggling to return TPG's investment as well.

Co-founder and partner David "Bondo" Bonderman is known for turning around Continental Airlines. TPG usually holds onto a company for at least five years, although consistent moneymakers are likely to be kept indefinitely.

Affiliated funds include the Newbridge partnerships (overseas investments) and Colony Capital (real estate). Newbridge, which is also owned by Blum Capital Partners, is poised to take a share of China-based Shenzhen Development Bank in a landmark foreign investment in mainland China.

HISTORY

The story of Texas Pacific Group is largely the story of David "Bondo" Bonderman. The magna cum laude Harvard law grad — an ardent Democrat and former law professor — built a reputation as an adviser who helped Texas billionaire Robert Bass rack up triple-digit returns.

After a decade with Bass, Bonderman struck out on his own in 1992. James Coulter, recruited to the Bass organization out of Stanford University's business school, went with him. William Price, a former Bain & Company consultant who advised Bonderman on some of his Bass deals, joined them, as did Richard Schifter (airlines background) and David Stanton (technology expertise).

Bonderman raised eyebrows in 1993 when TPG affiliate Air Partners recapitalized Continental Airlines, then in its second bankruptcy. At the time the airline industry was losing billions, and Bonderman was a little-known quantity. After an extensive restructuring and management shakeup, Bonderman turned Continental into the US's #5 airline, logging record profits for four consecutive quarters.

This type of deal would become Bonderman's modus operandi: jumping into troubled waters shunned by others, turning the company around, then (often) selling his interest for a profit. Of the head-rolling that frequently occurs after buyouts, Bonderman once said, "Generally speaking, you like to dance with the girl that brung you, and if you can't, sometimes you have to shoot her." In 1994 Bonderman worked his magic with America West Airlines. As with Continental, TPG sold shares in a second offering that made millions.

While the health care industry was debating reform in 1994, Bonderman seized the opportunity to buy a majority share in managed care company PPOM (sold 1997). In 1995 affiliated fund Colony Capital teamed up with Virgin Group to buy 116 MGM Cinemas and bring the multiplex boom to the UK.

Taking a cue from Robert Mondavi, TPG in 1996 bought Nestlé's debt-ridden Wine World Estates (with help from investment group Silverado Partners), renamed it Beringer Wine Estates Holdings, and took it public in 1997 in an IPO twice as big as Mondavi's.

In 1997 TPG bought clothier J. Crew Group. In an era of falling petroleum prices, the firm gambled on Appalachian energy company Belden & Blake and teamed with Genesis Health Ventures and Cypress Group to buy a stake in ailing elder care operator Multicare. It also bought Del Monte Foods, the world's #1 maker of canned fruits and vegetables (taking it public in 1999).

Bonderman and Air Partners in 1998 sold their interest in Continental to Northwest Airlines. Following its strategy of buying turnarounds, TPG threw lifelines to HMO Oxford Health Plans (1998) and Magellan Health Services (1999). It also built its technology holdings, investing in integrated circuits maker ZiLOG (1998) and leading a management buyout of a Motorola unit that is now ON Semiconductor.

The group jumped into a European investment hotbed, taking a majority stake in Punch Taverns Group, which bought 3,600 pubs from Allied Domecq (TPG sold its Punch stake in 2003). In 1999 TPG bought the Bally fashion house and a stake in Italian scooter maker Piaggio. It failed, however, to turn around Favorite Brands, selling the marshmallow and candy maker to Nabisco. In 2000 TPG said it would buy a stake in French smart-card maker Gemplus and would sell more than 4 million of its 23 million shares of GlobeSpan Virata at about $100 per share. (TPG's original investment was about $850,000.)

In 2002 TPG took off and picked up Gate Gourmet, an airline catering company, from the bankrupt Switzerland-based Swissair Group. It also exited its participation in ZiLOG upon completion of that company's reorganization. TPG dropped its 51% holding of Denbury Resources down to 38% for about $7 million. It also sold about 33% of its stake in motorcycle company Ducati, but it smelled a good deal and bought Burger King Corporation.

EXECUTIVES

Chairman: C. Thomas Clowe
Executive Director: Reagan E. Greer
Financial Administration Director: Lee Deviney
Director Human Resources: Jim Richardson
Director Information Technology: Michael Fernandez
Director Lottery Operations: Michael Anger
Director Marketing: Toni Smith
Director Security: Mike Pitcock
Acting Director Communications: Ed Rogers
General Counsel: Kimberly Kiplin

LOCATIONS

HQ: Texas Lottery Commission
611 E. Sixth St., Austin, TX 78701
Phone: 512-344-5000   **Fax:** 512-344-5080
Web: www.txlottery.org

PRODUCTS/OPERATIONS

2002 Allocation of Sales

	% of total
Prize money	57
Schools	31
Administrative costs	7
Retailers	5
Total	**100**

Selected Games

Lottery Games	
Cash 5	Cold Hard Cash
Lotto Texas	Deal Me In
Pick 3	Deluxe 7-11-21
Texas Two Step	Double Lucky Number
Scratch-off Games	Prairie Dog Dollars
$25,000 Hearts	Ride to Riches
$50,000 Fortune	Star of Texas
Big Bonus Bucks	Texas Trails
Cattle Drive Cash	Treasure Hunt
Round Up	Wild Cash
	Wizard of Odds

COMPETITORS

Georgia Lottery
Multi-State Lottery
New Mexico Lottery Authority

HISTORICAL FINANCIALS

Company Type: Government-owned

Income Statement
FYE: August 31

	REVENUE ($ mil.)	NET INCOME ($ mil.)	NET PROFIT MARGIN	EMPLOYEES
8/02	2,966	64	2.2%	—
8/01	2,826	87	3.1%	—
8/00	2,658	(116)	—	335
8/99	3,156	(118)	—	300
8/98	3,106	1,213	39.0%	335
8/97	3,761	1,421	37.8%	304
8/96	3,449	1,101	31.9%	325
8/95	3,052	1,014	33.2%	325
8/94	2,772	932	33.6%	325
8/93	1,863	660	35.4%	325
Annual Growth	5.3%	(22.8%)	—	0.4%

Net Income History

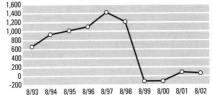

TPG prepared to take flight again in 2003 with a $300 million investment in US Airways once it emerged out of chapter 11, but was upstaged when The Retirement Systems of Alabama stepped in and offered the airline a better deal. TPG raked in a hefty profit in 2003 when Hotwire, in which it held a 30% stake, was acquired by InterActiveCorp. TPG unloaded its 6% stake in Del Monte in 2004.

EXECUTIVES

Managing Partner: David Bonderman, age 62
CFO: Jim O'Brien
VP: John Viola
Managing Director, UK: Stephen Peel
Treasurer: Michelle Reese
General Partner, TPG Ventures for European Investment: Badri Nathan
Human Resources Manager: Jennifer Dixon

LOCATIONS

HQ: Texas Pacific Group
301 Commerce St., Ste. 3300, Fort Worth, TX 76102
Phone: 817-871-4000   **Fax:** 817-871-4001

Texas Pacific Group has offices in Fort Worth, Texas; San Francisco; Washington, DC; and London.

PRODUCTS/OPERATIONS

Selected Holdings
America West Airlines
Bally Management
Burger King Corporation
Ducati Motor SpA
Eutelsat
Gate Gourmet
Genesis Health Ventures Inc.
GlobeSpan
IASIS Healthcare Corporation
J. Crew Group Inc.
Kraton Polymers Corp.
Magellan Health Services Inc.
ON Semiconductor
Oxford Health Plans, Inc.
Paradyne Networks, Inc.
Petco Animal Supplies
Piaggio
Ryanair Holdings

COMPETITORS

AEA Investors
Apollo Advisors
Berkshire Hathaway
Blackstone Group
Carlyle Group
CD&R
Goldman Sachs
Haas Wheat
Heico
Hicks Muse
Jordan Company
Kelso & Company
Keystone
KKR
Oaktree Capital
Sevin Rosen
Thomas Lee
Wingate Partners

Thrivent Financial

The Spirit moved Aid Association for Lutherans (AAL) to merge with Lutheran Brotherhood and form a new entity, christened Thrivent Financial for Lutherans. The fraternal benefit society now includes nearly 3 million members, and brings under one steepled roof some $62 billion in assets under management in mutual funds, bank and trust services (AAL Bank and Trust and LB Community Bank & Trust merged into Thrivent Financial Bank), and other financial services. Thrivent Financial, which operates all over the US, also has more than $150 billion in life insurance in force.

EXECUTIVES

Chairman: John O. Gilbert
President, CEO, and Director: Bruce J. Nicholson, age 58
EVP, Marketing and Products: Pamela J. (Pam) Moret
EVP, Integration: Walter S. Rugland
EVP, Financial Services Operations: Jon M. Stellmacher
CIO: Larry Robbins
SVP and General Counsel: Woodrow E. Eno
SVP, Field Operations: Otis L. Haarmeyer
SVP, Corporate Administration: Jennifer H. Martin, age 56
SVP, Fraternal Operations: Frederick A. Ohlde
SVP, Field Operations: James A. (Jim) Thomsen
SVP, Communications: Marie A. Uhrich
Auditors: Ernst & Young LLP

LOCATIONS

HQ: Thrivent Financial for Lutherans
625 4th Ave. South, Minneapolis, MN 55415
Phone: 800-847-4836
Web: www.thrivent.com

PRODUCTS/OPERATIONS

2003 Sales

	$ mil.	% of total
Net investment income	2,163	51
Premiums	1,253	30
Contract charges	536	13
Realized investment gains	89	2
Other revenue	178	4
Total	**4,219**	**100**

COMPETITORS

American Express
Citigroup
FMR
MetLife
New York Life
Security Benefit Group
State Farm
TIAA-CREF

HISTORICAL FINANCIALS

Company Type: Not-for-profit

Income Statement
FYE: December 31

	ASSETS ($ mil.)	NET INCOME ($ mil.)	INCOME AS % OF ASSETS	EMPLOYEES
12/03	52,667	252	0.5%	2,979
12/02	47,892	(292)	—	3,420
12/01	23,478	139	0.6%	3,733
12/00	22,112	228	1.0%	2,086
12/99	21,158	226	1.1%	3,914
12/98	19,418	134	0.7%	1,751
12/97	17,975	210	1.2%	1,596
12/96	16,671	130	0.8%	1,559
Annual Growth	17.9%	10.0%	—	9.7%

2003 Year-End Financials
Equity as % of assets: 11.9%   Long-term debt ($ mil.): 11,420
Return on assets: 0.5%   Sales ($ mil.): 4,219
Return on equity: 4.2%

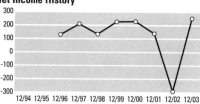

Net Income History

TIAA-CREF

It's punishment enough to write the name once on a blackboard. Teachers Insurance and Annuity Association — College Retirement Equities Fund (TIAA-CREF) is one of the US's largest, if not longest-named, private retirement systems, providing for nearly 3 million members of the academic community and for investors outside academia's ivied confines. It also serves some 15,000 institutional investors. TIAA-CREF's core offerings include financial advice, investment information, retirement accounts, pensions, annuities, individual life and disability insurance, tuition financing, and trust services (through savings bank TIAA-CREF Trust). The system, a nonprofit organization, also manages a line of mutual funds.

TIAA-CREF — one of the nation's heftiest institutional investors, with nearly $315 billion in assets under management — has not been afraid to throw its weight around corporate boardrooms. The organization is known for active and choosy investing and is a vocal critic of extravagant executive compensation packages. With an increasing share of its investment assets overseas, TIAA-CREF is also leading the crusade for global corporate governance standards.

Under the leadership of ex-Merrill Lynch exec Herb Allison, TIAA-CREF is tightening its belt, narrowing its focus on retail funds, and exiting certain business lines, such as group life and disability (sold to StanCorp Financial Group). After a reorganization in 2003, the company also opened its first two retail stores and revealed plans for several more.

HISTORY

With $15 million, the Carnegie Foundation for the Advancement of Teaching in 1905 founded the Teachers Insurance and Annuity Association (TIAA) in New York City to provide retirement benefits and other forms of financial security to educators. When Carnegie's original endowment was found to be insufficient, another $1 million reorganized the fund into a defined-contribution plan in 1918. TIAA was the first portable pension plan, letting participants change employers without losing benefits and offering a fixed annuity. The fund required infusions of Carnegie cash until 1947.

In 1952 TIAA CEO William Greenough pioneered the variable annuity, based on common stock investments, and created the College Retirement Equities Fund (CREF) to offer it. Designed to supplement TIAA's fixed annuity, CREF invested participants' premiums in stocks. CREF and TIAA were subject to New York insurance (but not SEC) regulation.

During the 1950s, TIAA led the fight for Social Security benefits for university employees and began offering group total disability coverage (1957) and group life insurance (1958).

In 1971 TIAA-CREF began helping colleges boost investment returns from endowments, then moved into endowment management. It helped found a research center to provide objective investment information in 1972.

For 70 years retirement was the only way members could exit TIAA-CREF. Their only investment choices were stocks through CREF or a one-way transfer into TIAA's annuity accounts based on long-term bond, real estate, and mortgage investments. In the 1980s CREF indexed its funds to the S&P average.

By 1987's stock crash, TIAA-CREF had a million members, many of whom wanted more protection from stock market fluctuations. After the crash, Clifton Wharton (the first African-American to head a major US financial organization) became CEO; the next year CREF added a money market fund, for which the SEC required complete transferability, even outside TIAA-CREF. Now open to competition, TIAA-CREF became more flexible, adding investment options and long-term-care plans.

John Biggs became CEO in 1993. After the 1994 bond crash, TIAA-CREF began educating members on the ABCs of retirement investing, hoping to persuade them not to switch to flashy short-term investments and not to panic during such cyclical events as the crash.

In 1996 it went international, buying interests in UK commercial and mixed-use property. TIAA-CREF filed for SEC approval of more mutual funds in 1997. Although Federal tax legislation took away TIAA-CREF's tax-exempt status in 1997, the change was made without decreasing annuity incomes for the year.

The status change let TIAA-CREF offer no-load mutual funds to the public in 1998. A trust company and financial planning services were added; all new products were sold at cost, with TIAA-CREF waiving fees. TIAA-CREF in 1998 became the first pension fund to force out an entire board of directors (that of sputtering cafeteria firm Furr's/Bishop's). Also that year TIAA-CREF's crusade to curb "dead hand" poison pills (an antitakeover defense measure) found favor with the shareholders of Bergen Brunswig (now AmerisourceBergen), Lubrizol, and Mylan Laboratories. Late in 1999 the organization sold half of its stake in the Mall of America to Simon Property Group, keeping 27%.

The next year it made a grab for more market share when it launched five new mutual funds.

Biggs retired in 2002 and was succeeded by Herbert Allison.

EXECUTIVES

Chairman, President, and CEO: Herbert M. (Herb) Allison, age 61
EVP and CTO: Susan S. Kozik
EVP and CFO: Elizabeth A. (Betsy) Monrad
EVP, Marketing: Jamie DePeau
EVP and Chief Investment Officer: Scott C. Evans
EVP, Public Affairs: Steven (Steve) Goldstein
EVP, Financial Operations and Facilities: Ira J. Hoch
EVP and Chief Actuary: Harry I. Klaristenfeld
EVP and General Counsel: George W. Madison, age 49
EVP, Risk Management: Erwin W. Martens
EVP, Client Services: Frances Nolan
EVP, Human Resources: Dermot J. O'Brien
EVP, Product Management: Bertram L. Scott, age 52
EVP, Fixed Income Investments: John A. Somers
SVP and Chief Counsel for Corporate Governance: Peter C. Clapman
VP and Corporate Secretary: E. Laverne Jones
Head of Equity Investments: Susan E. Ulick
Head of Global Equity Research: Thomas M. Franks
Auditors: Ernst & Young

LOCATIONS

HQ: Teachers Insurance and Annuity Association — College Retirement Equities Fund
730 3rd Ave., New York, NY 10017
Phone: 212-490-9000   **Fax:** 212-916-4840
Web: www.tiaa-cref.org

Teachers Insurance and Annuity Association — College Retirement Equities Fund (TIAA-CREF) has major offices in Charlotte, North Carolina; Denver; and New York City. It also has dozens of smaller offices throughout the US.

PRODUCTS/OPERATIONS

Selected Subsidiaries and Units
Teachers Personal Investors Services, Inc. (mutual fund management)
TIAA-CREF Individual & Institutional Services, Inc. (broker-dealer)
TIAA-CREF Institute (think tank)
TIAA-CREF Institutional Mutual Funds (investment company)
TIAA-CREF Life Insurance Company (insurance and annuities)
TIAA-CREF Mutual Funds (investment company)
TIAA-CREF Trust Company, FSB (trust services)
TIAA-CREF Tuition Financing, Inc. (state tuition savings program management)

Selected Mutual Funds
Bond Plus
Equity Index
Growth & Income
Growth Equity
High-Yield Bond
Inflation-Linked Bond
International Equity
Large-Cap Value
Managed Allocation
Mid-Cap Growth
Mid-Cap Value
Money Market
Real Estate Securities
Short-Term Bond
Small-Cap Equity
Social Choice Equity
Tax-Exempt Bond

COMPETITORS

Aetna
AIG
AXA Financial
Bank of New York
Berkshire Hathaway
CalPERS
Charles Schwab
CIGNA
Citigroup
FMR
John Hancock Financial Services
J.P. Morgan Chase
MassMutual
Merrill Lynch
MetLife
New York Life
Northwestern Mutual
Principal Financial
Prudential
T. Rowe Price
U.S. Global Investors
USAA
VALIC
Vanguard Group

HISTORICAL FINANCIALS

Company Type: Private

Income Statement				FYE: December 31
	ASSETS ($ mil.)	NET INCOME ($ mil.)	INCOME AS % OF ASSETS	EMPLOYEES
12/03	300,000	—	—	6,000
12/02	261,252	—	—	6,500
12/01	274,390	—	—	6,700
12/00	281,383	—	—	5,000
12/99	289,248	—	—	5,000
12/98	249,715	—	—	5,000
12/97	214,296	—	—	4,920
12/96	182,612	—	—	4,490
Annual Growth	7.3%	—	—	4.2%

Asset History

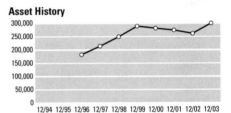

TIC Holdings

TIC Holdings doesn't flinch when it comes to constructing heavy industrial projects. Founded in 1974, the holding company offers services including civil engineering, heavy equipment erection, pipeline construction, and electrical installation. Main subsidiary TIC — The Industrial Company provides industrial construction services in the US through several regional units. Subsidiary Western Summit Constructors focuses on water and wastewater projects. TIC also has an international unit. The management-owned firm ranks among leading contractors in the wastewater, petrochemical, power, refining, mining, and industrial process markets, as well as in the electrical and instrumentation and pulp and paper sectors.

Timex

Branching out from its original "Takes a licking" designs, Timex is strapping on new faces in order to tap new markets worldwide. The US's largest watch producer has expanded its lines from simple, low-cost watches to include high-tech tickers capable of paging or downloading computer data. Its sports watches have gone upscale and gadgety with lines such as Reef Gear and Ironman. (The brightness of its Indiglo watch helped a man lead a group of people down 34 flights of dark stairs after the first World Trade Center bombing in 1993.) Timex also makes watches for Nautica and Guess? under license. Founded in 1854 as Waterbury Clock, Timex is owned by Fred Olsen, whose father bought the company in 1942.

In March 2002, Timex signed a licensing agreement with MEDport, LLC to manufacture and sell medical devices for the home (such as digital thermometers) under the Timex brand name.

Timex closed its last US-based factory in 2001. In 2003 the company dropped its famed "It takes a licking and keeps on ticking" in favor of the more updated "Timex. Life is ticking."

About 15 women who painted glow-in-the-dark dials on watchfaces for the Waterbury Clock Co., dubbed "radium girls," died from radium poisoning during the 1920s and 1930s; dozens of others suffered from crumbling jaws from a technique that required the women to dip their paintbrushes into the glowing paint and then sharpen the brushpoints with their lips.

EXECUTIVES

Chairman: Annette Olsen
President and CEO: Jose Santana
CFO: Edward F. Pytka
General Counsel, Secretary, and SVP Human Resources: Frank Sherer
SVP Marketing and Chief Marketing Officer: Mark Shuster
VP Marketing: Mario Sabatini
VP Licensing: Helen Prial
Director of Advanced Products: Wilson Keithline
Communications Director: Jim Katz
Director of Information Technology: Steve Beaudry
Systems Manager: James Jackson

LOCATIONS

HQ: Timex Corporation
555 Christian Rd., Middlebury, CT 06762
Phone: 203-346-5000 **Fax:** 203-346-5139
Web: www.timex.com

Timex Corporation sells its products worldwide. It has operations in Brazil, China, France, Germany, India, Israel, the Philippines, and the US.

EXECUTIVES

President and CEO: Ronald W. (Ron) McKenzie
VP, CFO, and Treasurer: James F. (Jim) Kissane
CEO, TIC: Gary B. McKenzie
SVP Business Development, TIC: Al Knapp
VP Business Development, TIC: Brad Lawson
VP Business Development, TIC:
  Thomas G. (Tom) Stapleton
Human Resources: Barbara Judd
Public Relations: Gary Bennett

LOCATIONS

HQ: TIC Holdings, Inc.
2211 Elk River Rd., Steamboat Springs, CO 80487
Phone: 970-879-2561 **Fax:** 970-879-6078
Web: www.tic-inc.com

TIC Holdings has offices in California, Colorado, Connecticut, Georgia, Michigan, Minnesota, Oregon, Texas, and Wyoming. It also has an international location in Mexico City and in Edmonton, Canada.

PRODUCTS/OPERATIONS

Selected Subsidiaries

TIC — The Industrial Company
TIC — International, Inc.
TIC — Wyoming, Inc.
Western Summit Constructors, Inc.

COMPETITORS

ABB Lummus Global
Aker Kværner
Bechtel
Black & Veatch
Chicago Bridge and Iron
Day & Zimmermann
Dick Corporation
Earth Tech
Fluor
Foster Wheeler
Gilbane
M. A. Mortenson
McDermott
Parsons
PCL Construction Enterprises
Peter Kiewit Sons'
Shaw Group
Skanska
Turner Corporation
Washington Group
Whiting-Turner
Zachry

HISTORICAL FINANCIALS

Company Type: Private

Income Statement
FYE: December 31

	REVENUE ($ mil.)	NET INCOME ($ mil.)	NET PROFIT MARGIN	EMPLOYEES
12/02	1,221	—	—	7,000
12/01	1,123	—	—	5,000
12/00	998	—	—	6,000
12/99	745	—	—	5,000
12/98	500	—	—	5,000
12/97	516	—	—	5,000
12/96	462	—	—	5,000
12/95	456	—	—	5,000
Annual Growth	15.1%	—	—	4.9%

Revenue History

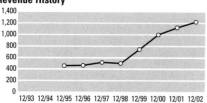

PRODUCTS/OPERATIONS

Selected Products and Brands

Classics
  Bracelets
  Easy Reader
  i-Control
  Multi-function
  Straps
Outdoor
  Timex Expedition
Sports
  Helix
  Reef Gear
  Rush Women's Fitness
  Timex Ironman Triathlon
  Timex/Saturn Pro Cycling Team
Tech
  Beepwear
  Digital Compass
  Digital Heart Rate Fitness System
  Internet Messenger
  Pager Watch
Youth
  TIMEX KIDS
  TMX
Other
  Alarm clocks
  Bathroom scales
  Clock radios
  Eyewear
  Nightlights
  Pens and mechanical pencils
  Pocketwatches
  Stopwatches
  Thermometers
  Timers
  Wall clocks

COMPETITORS

Benetton
Bulova
CASIO COMPUTER
Citizen Watch
E. Gluck
Emerson Radio
Fossil
GE
Measurement Specialties
Movado Group
NIKE
SDI Technologies
Seiko
Swatch
Swiss Army Brands

HISTORICAL FINANCIALS

Company Type: Private

Income Statement
FYE: December 31

	ESTIMATED REVENUE ($ mil.)	NET INCOME ($ mil.)	NET PROFIT MARGIN	EMPLOYEES
12/03	800	—	—	7,500
12/02	600	—	—	5,500
12/01	600	—	—	—
12/00	600	—	—	7,500
12/99	600	—	—	8,000
12/98	600	—	—	8,000
12/97	600	—	—	7,500
12/96	650	—	—	7,500
12/95	650	—	—	—
12/94	650	—	—	—
Annual Growth	2.3%	—	—	0.0%

Revenue History

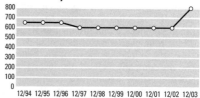

Tishman

Tishman Realty & Construction is an immigrant success story writ large. The company builds office, hospitality, recreational, industrial, and other property for itself and for others. It offers third-party developers a full menu of real estate design, construction, management, and financing services. High-profile projects handled by the company (or its publicly-owned predecessor) include Disney World's EPCOT Center, Madison Square Garden, the ill-fated World Trade Center (as well as its rebuilding), and Chicago's John Hancock Center. The Tishman family — scions of immigrant founder Julius Tishman, who began building tenements in 1898 — own Tishman Realty & Construction.

Tishman's E Walk entertainment and retail development is nearly complete in New York's Times Square district; the project includes the Westin New York hotel (which opened in October 2002), specialty retail shops, restaurants, and entertainment venues. The company is also managing construction of the new structure at 7 World Trade Center. Recently, Tishman took on management of four of Credit Suisse's Manhattan boutique hotels.

Affiliates of Tishman Realty & Construction include Tishman Construction, which carries out development and construction; Tishman Technologies, which equips buildings with data and communications infrastructure; Tishman Real Estate Services, which provides leasing, landlord and tenant representation, and other commercial real estate services; Tishman Hotels, which provides management services to about 160 properties; and Tishman Realty, which finances the firm's activities.

CEO John Tishman has expanded the company beyond its Big Apple origins, most notably through a partnership with the Walt Disney Company to build hotels and theme parks in Florida.

HISTORY

Julius Tishman escaped the Russian pogroms of the late 19th century by emigrating to the US in 1885. Five years later he opened a store in Newburgh, New York. In 1898, as eastern European immigrants inundated New York City, Tishman began building tenements on the Lower East Side. He named his business Julius Tishman & Sons. By the 1920s, the firm had moved uptown and upscale, building luxury apartment buildings. The firm went public in 1928 as Tishman Realty & Construction, with the family retaining an ownership stake. Julius was chairman; son David was CEO.

The pitfalls of going public were soon obvious. The offering raised less than $2 million, not enough to finance projects, and because the stock market favored profit generation over asset appreciation, the company was undervalued. When the Depression hit, David's involvement as a director of the Bank of the United States and the family's participation in bad loans made by the bank forced the firm to sell assets. Tishman's lenders, including insurer Metropolitan Life, took over some of its buildings, leaving the firm to manage them. In the 1930s and 1940s, the company focused mainly on managing its properties. It continued its construction operations on a contract basis for the Federal Housing Authority.

After WWII, Tishman moved away from residential development and into office construction. Meanwhile, David's younger brothers Paul and Norman began jockeying for position to replace him as CEO; in 1948 David chose Norman to succeed him (Paul resigned to form his own construction company). A nephew, John, became head of the firm's construction arm.

By the early 1950s, Tishman had moved into management and leasing services and expanded nationally, opening offices in Chicago and Los Angeles. In 1962 David relinquished his chairmanship to Norman, who was in turn replaced as CEO by his brother Bob. Under Bob's leadership, Tishman divested residential properties to focus on office space, mostly company-owned.

In 1972 the company completed the World Trade Center complex, including twin 110-story towers which were then the tallest buildings in the world. The iconic structures stood more than 1,300 feet above Manhattan until they collapsed as a result of a terrorist attack in 2001.

Tishman was hit hard by recession in the 1970s. In 1976 Bob took the company private again, selling off the firm's New York assets, and split the company into Tishman Speyer Properties (headed by Bob and son-in-law Jerry Speyer); Tishman Management and Leasing (now part of Grubb & Ellis); and Tishman Realty & Construction (headed by John and promptly bought by the Rockefeller Center Corporation).

John Tishman bought back Tishman Realty & Construction in 1980 and steered it into high-profile partnerships with the likes of the Walt Disney Company. He also added project management and real estate financial services to his company's repertoire and continued to take part in highly visible construction projects.

Since the late 1990s, Tishman's major projects have centered around the revitalization efforts of Times Square and 42nd street in New York City — including the construction of 4 Times Square (the Conde Nast building), 3 Times Square (Reuters America headquarters), and E Walk, a mixed-use entertainment and retail center.

EXECUTIVES

Chairman and CEO: John L. Tishman
President and CEO: Daniel R. Tishman
CFO and Treasurer: Larry Schwarzwalder
SVP Public Relations: Richard M. Kielar
SVP and General Counsel: Linda Christensen
Chairman and CEO, Tishman Hotel Corp. and Tishman Realty Corp.: John A. Vickers
President, Tishman Construction Eastern Region: John T. Livingston
President, Tishman Realty Corp.: William J. Sales
President, Tishman Real Estate Services: Joseph J. Simone
COO, Tishman Construction Eastern Region: Jay Badame
EVP, Tishman Real Estate Services: James J. Clark
SVP, Tishman Real Estate Services: Theodore J. Koltis
SVP, Tishman Real Estate Services: Charles A. Wojcik
SVP, Tishman Real Estate Services: Daniel Spiegel
VP, Tishman Real Estate Services: Adam R. Goldberg

LOCATIONS

HQ: Tishman Realty & Construction Co. Inc.
666 5th Ave., New York, NY 10301
Phone: 212-399-3600   **Fax:** 212-397-1316
Web: www.tishman.com

Tishman Realty & Construction has offices in Atlantic City, New Jersey; Boston; Chicago; Los Angeles; Newark, New Jersey; New York City; Orlando, Florida; San Francisco; and Washington, DC.

PRODUCTS/OPERATIONS

Selected Subsidiaries
Tishman Construction Corp. (construction operations)
Tishman Hotel Corp. (hotel development & management)
Tishman Interiors Corp. (interior build-out & renovation)
Tishman Real Estate Management Co. (property management for third-party clients)
Tishman Real Estate Services Co. (real estate consulting & management)
Tishman Research Corp. (building materials research & consulting)
Tishman Technologies Corp. (communication & data systems development)

COMPETITORS

CB Richard Ellis	Lincoln Property
Cushman & Wakefield	Reckson Associates Realty
Gilbane	Starrett Corporation
Grubb & Ellis	Trammell Crow Company
JMB Realty	Trump
Jones Lang LaSalle	Witkoff Group
Lefrak Organization	

HISTORICAL FINANCIALS

Company Type: Private

Income Statement
FYE: June 30

	REVENUE ($ mil.)	NET INCOME ($ mil.)	NET PROFIT MARGIN	EMPLOYEES
6/02	1,980	—	—	900
6/01	1,640	—	—	920
6/00	1,109	—	—	890
6/99	1,005	—	—	800
6/98	937	—	—	650
6/97	650	—	—	620
6/96	580	—	—	600
6/95	572	—	—	575
6/94	540	—	—	575
6/93	527	—	—	510
Annual Growth	15.8%	—	—	6.5%

Revenue History

TNP Enterprises

The sleepy little utility from the Southwest is making big splashes in its industry. TNP Enterprises' regulated utility unit, Texas-New Mexico Power (TNMP), transmits and distributes electricity to 250,000 customers in Texas and New Mexico. Nonregulated subsidiary First Choice Power competes in the Texas retail electric supply market, which was deregulated in 2002. The company has sold its power plant. TNP Enterprises was acquired in 2000 by a private investor group in the first LBO of a US electric utility. Industry veteran William Catacosinos of Laurel

Hill Capital Partners led the buyout and became TNP's CEO. Other investors include CIBC World Markets. The company has agreed to be acquired by PNM Resources.

EXECUTIVES

Chairman and CEO: William J. Catacosinos, age 73, $1,550,000 pay
President and COO: Michael E. Bray, age 57
CFO: Theodore A. (Ted) Babcock, age 49, $283,512 pay
Secretary: Kathleen A. Marion, age 49, $122,567 pay
Treasurer; President, First Choice Power: Manjit S. Cheema, age 49, $495,934 pay
Chairman, President, and CEO, TNMP: Jack V. Chambers Jr., age 54, $656,831 pay
SVP and COO, TNMP: W. Douglas Hobbs, age 60, $397,526 pay
SVP and CFO, TNMP; CFO, First Choice Power: Scott Forbes, age 46, $313,131 pay
VP and Treasurer, TNMP: C. Adam Carte, age 34
VP and Controller, TNMP: Joseph B. (Joe) Hegwood, age 48
VP and General Counsel, TNMP: Michael D. Blanchard, age 53, $318,194 pay
VP Human Resources, TNMP: Melissa D. Davis, age 46, $315,650 pay
Auditors: Deloitte & Touche LLP

LOCATIONS

HQ: TNP Enterprises, Inc.
4100 International Plaza, Tower II,
Fort Worth, TX 76109
Phone: 817-731-0099   **Fax:** 817-737-1343
Web: www.tnpe.com

TNP Enterprises subsidiary Texas-New Mexico Power provides electric service to customers along the Gulf Coast of Texas, north-central and West Texas, and south-central and southwestern New Mexico. Subsidiary First Choice Power operates throughout Texas.

PRODUCTS/OPERATIONS

2003 Sales

	$ mil.	% of total
Nonregulated supply	695.3	74
Regulated transmission & distribution	249.5	26
Adjustments	(109.3)	—
Total	**835.5**	**100**

COMPETITORS

American Electric Power	LCRA
Brazos Electric Power	Pedernales Electric
Cap Rock Energy	PNM Resources
CenterPoint Energy	Reliant Energy
Centrica	TXU
El Paso Electric	

HISTORICAL FINANCIALS
Company Type: Private

Income Statement
FYE: December 31

	REVENUE ($ mil.)	NET INCOME ($ mil.)	NET PROFIT MARGIN	EMPLOYEES
12/03	836	(18)	—	745
12/02	687	32	4.7%	742
12/01	659	9	1.4%	786
12/00	644	1	0.2%	836
12/99	576	30	5.2%	823
12/98	587	19	3.3%	885
12/97	585	30	5.1%	1,305
12/96	503	23	4.6%	935
12/95	486	42	8.5%	894
12/94	478	(17)	—	1,051
Annual Growth	**6.4%**	**—**	**—**	**(3.8%)**

2003 Year-End Financials
Debt ratio: 1,551.4%   Current ratio: 2.30
Return on equity: —   Long-term debt ($ mil.): 809
Cash ($ mil.): 118

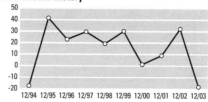
Net Income History

Topa Equities

Holding company Topa Equities casts a wide net. Owned by John Anderson, Topa has about 40 businesses involved in automobile dealerships (Silver Star Automotive), beer distribution, insurance, real estate, and more. Topa's beverage operations include Ace Beverage, Mission Beverages, and Paradise Beverages; the firm dominates the Hawaiian and Caribbean beer markets and serves California. Brands sold include all major US brews and leading US imports Guinness, Heineken, and InBev, among others. Anderson started in 1956 as a distributor of Hamm's beer. UCLA's Anderson School of Business, to which Anderson donated $15 million, is named for him.

EXECUTIVES

Chairman, President, and CEO: John E. Anderson, age 87
CFO: Brenda Seuthe
VP, Office and Retail Leasing: Darren Bell
Director Human Resources: Virginia Flores
IT: Roland Garcia
President and CEO, Topa Insurance Co.: Noshirwan Marfatia
VP, CFO, and Treasurer, Topa Insurance Co.: Daniel Sherrin
VP, Personal Lines, Topa Insurance Co.: H. Edward Good
VP, Claims, Topa Insurance Co.: James Kalupa
Marketing Manager, Topa Insurance Co.: Anita Nevins

LOCATIONS

HQ: Topa Equities, Ltd.
1800 Avenue of the Stars, Ste. 1400,
Los Angeles, CA 90067
Phone: 310-203-9199   **Fax:** 310-557-1837

COMPETITORS

AutoNation	Penske Automotive
Beauchamp Distributing	Prospect Motors
CarrAmerica	Southern Wine & Spirits
CB Richard Ellis	State Farm
Citigroup	Tuttle-Click
Galpin Motors	Young's Market
Nationwide	

HISTORICAL FINANCIALS
Company Type: Private

Income Statement
FYE: December 31

	REVENUE ($ mil.)	NET INCOME ($ mil.)	NET PROFIT MARGIN	EMPLOYEES
12/02	986	—	—	2,025
12/01	946	—	—	1,949
12/00	865	—	—	1,600
12/99	776	—	—	1,400
12/98	754	—	—	1,300
12/97	752	—	—	1,310
12/96	675	—	—	1,300
12/95	656	—	—	1,100
12/94	607	—	—	1,141
12/93	559	—	—	1,179
Annual Growth	**6.5%**	**—**	**—**	**6.2%**

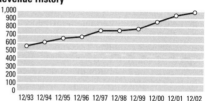
Revenue History

Topco Associates

Topco Associates is principally into private-label procurement. Topco uses the combined purchasing clout of more than 50 member companies (mostly supermarket operators) to wring discounts from suppliers. Serving grocery wholesalers, retailers, and food service firms, Topco markets more than 5,000 private-label items, including fresh meat, dairy and bakery goods, and health and beauty aids. Its brands include Food Club, Shurfine, and a line of "Top" labels such as Top Crest. In 2001 Topco Associates, Inc. merged operations with Shurfine International to form Topco Associates LLC. The new entity is 86%-owned by Topco Holdings, Inc. (formerly Topco Associates).

Holding company Shurfine International owns 14% of the merged entity, which also has members in Israel and Japan. But most of Topco's member companies are in the consolidating US market, where many stores have been bought by giant chains.

In addition to the Shurfine, Food Club, and Top Crest brands, Topco distributes Ultimate Choice and Shurfresh products. Topco also helps members market their own brands. Topco's cost-saving scheme goes beyond product offerings; its buying power cuts costs for its members' stores. Its warehouse equipment purchase and a financial services program also create savings for members.

HISTORY

Food Cooperatives was founded in Wisconsin in 1944 to procure dairy bags and paper products during wartime shortages. A few years later it merged with Top Frost Foods, with which it had some common members. In 1948 the name Topco Associates was adopted (created by combining the word "Top" from Top Frost with the "Co" in Cooperatives). The member companies involved in the merger included Alpha Beta, Big Bear Stores, Brockton Public Market, Fred Meyer, Furr's, Hinky Dinky, Penn Fruit Company, and Star Markets.

Topco initially sold basic commodities to private-label retailers, adding fresh produce in 1958. It expanded its product line further in 1960, moving into general merchandise, health and beauty care items, and store equipment. In 1961, when the company moved its headquarters to Skokie, Illinois, revenues topped the $100 million mark. In the 1960s other leading supermarkets, including Giant Eagle, King Soopers, McCarty-Holman, and Tom Thumb, joined Topco.

Also that decade it came under attack from the Justice Department when it was accused of antitrust activity in granting its members exclusive distribution rights for Topco-branded products. In 1972 the Supreme Court ruled against Topco. It then agreed to sell products under the private labels of its members.

In the late 1970s the company introduced Valu Time, the first nationally marketed line of branded generic products. This concept was then adopted by many US supermarkets. By 1979 Topco surpassed $1 billion in annual revenues.

By the end of the 1980s, Topco's membership had expanded to include Randall's, Riser Foods, Pueblo International, Schnuck Markets, and Smith's Food & Drug Centers. In 1988 it introduced World Classics, a premium line of high-volume, high-margin products promoted as national brands.

During the early 1990s Topco ran through a number of CEOs. In 1990 Robert Seelert replaced 10-year CEO Marcel Lussier. In 1992 John Beggs took over, and the next year Steven Rubow was handed the reins.

The early 1990s also saw rapid growth, with 20 new members bringing the company's total to 46 by 1995 (its membership later declined in number through acquisition and consolidation). Topco also expanded internationally, with the membership of Oshawa Group in Canada and the associate membership of SEIYU in Japan in 1995. Also that year the company lured upscale Kings Super Markets away from distributor White Rose.

Topco began offering members utility accounting and natural gas services through Illinova Energy Partners in 1998. The company expanded its Top Care line of personal care products in 1999, using a variety of packaging designed to resemble several name brands within a single category. CEO Rubow retired late that year and was replaced by Steve Lauer. Topco took aim at consumers who prefer natural foods in 2000, launching the Full Circle line of organically grown items.

In November 2001 Topco combined operations with co-op operator Shurfine International and re-formed as a limited liability company. Topco Associates, Inc., and Shurfine International became holding companies with stakes in Topco Associates LLC. Lauer, the CEO of Topco Associates, Inc., was named president and CEO of the new company. In 2004 IGA became a member of Topco.

EXECUTIVES

Chairman: Joseph V. Fisher
Vice Chairman: Steven C. Smith, age 46
President, CEO, and Director: Steven K. (Steve) Lauer
SVP and Chief Procurement Officer: Jeffrey Posner
SVP and President, Wholesale Channel: John Stanhaus
SVP Center Store: Daniel F. Mazur
SVP Cost Containment Programs/Support Services: Ian Grossman
SVP Member Development: Kenneth H. Guy
SVP Perishables: Russel Wolfe
SVP World Brands: Michael Ricciardi
VP Best Practices, Cost Containment, and Purchasing: David McMurray
VP Brand and Product Innovation: Maryruth Wilson
VP Dairy: Laird Snelgrove
VP Finance: Deborah (Debbie) Byers
VP Grocery: Dennis Dangerfield
VP Non-Foods: Curt Maki
VP Produce: Rob O'Rourke
VP Sales and Marketing, Wholesale Channel: Mike Nugent
Director Creative Services: Karen Vorwald
Director Non-Foods: Norm Spencer
Manager Human Resources: Dennis Pieper
Auditors: KPMG LLP

LOCATIONS

HQ: Topco Associates LLC
7711 Gross Point Rd., Skokie, IL 60077
Phone: 847-676-3030 **Fax:** 847-676-4949
Web: www.topco.com

Topco Associates purchases products on behalf of its members in the US, Israel, Japan, and Puerto Rico.

PRODUCTS/OPERATIONS

Selected Private-Label Brands
Food Club
Full Circle
Pet Club
Price Saver
Savers Choice
Shurfine
Shurfresh
Shurtech
Top Care
Top Crest
Ultimate Choice

Selected Member Companies
Ace Hardware
Acme
Ahold USA
Alex Lee
Associated Grocers, Inc.
Big Y Foods
Blue Square-Israel
Eagle Food Centers
F.A.B. Inc.
Food City
Fred W. Albrecht Grocery Co.
Fresh Brands (Piggly Wiggly)
Furr's Supermarkets
Giant Eagle
Haggen
Harris Teeter
Hy-Vee
IGA, Inc.
Kings Super Markets
K-VA-T Food Stores
Meijer
Penn Traffic Company
Piggly Wiggly Carolina
Pueblo International
Raley's Supermarkets
Schnuck Markets
THE SEIYU
Ukrop's Super Markets
Unipro Food Service
Wegmans
Weis Markets

COMPETITORS

Ahold USA
C&S Wholesale
Kroger
SUPERVALU
SYSCO
Wakefern Food
Wal-Mart

HISTORICAL FINANCIALS

Company Type: Cooperative

Income Statement
FYE: December 31

	REVENUE ($ mil.)	NET INCOME ($ mil.)	NET PROFIT MARGIN	EMPLOYEES
12/03	4,600	—	—	400
12/02	4,000	—	—	300
12/01*	3,300	—	—	300
3/00	3,400	—	—	275
3/99	4,000	—	—	359
3/98	3,900	—	—	365
3/97	3,700	—	—	400
3/96	3,900	—	—	390
3/95	3,700	—	—	375
3/94	3,500	—	—	400
Annual Growth	3.1%	—	—	0.0%

*Fiscal year change

Revenue History

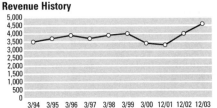

Towers Perrin

Refusing to live in an ivory tower, this company aims to offer practical advice. One of the leading management consulting firms in the world, Towers Perrin serves an extensive list of corporate clients, including more than 700 of the FORTUNE 1000 companies. The firm's core focus is on human resources consulting. Its Tillinghast-Towers Perrin unit focuses on risk management and actuarial services to financial companies, and its Towers Perrin Reinsurance serves clients primarily as a reinsurance intermediary. In addition to consulting, the company produces several publications and surveys investigating business trends and challenges.

After guiding its clients through the downsizing and consolidating 1990s, Towers Perrin has been working to streamline its own operations. The company has pared down its client roster, keeping mainly its biggest customers. At the same time it has been creating new business by expanding into new practice areas, such as public relations and corporate communications.

Towers Perrin was founded by four partners in 1934; it is now owned by more than 630 partners.

EXECUTIVES

Chairman and CEO: Mark Mactas
CFO: Mark L. Wilson
CIO: Tony Candito
Managing Director: Donald L. (Don) Lowman
Managing Director and Chief Administration Officer:
  Garrett L. Dietz
Managing Director, Global Marketing: Sharon Clark
Managing Director, Global Markets:
  Michael (Mike) Ponicall
**Managing Director, Global Retirement Services, Health
  & Welfare, and Administration Services:**
  Robert G. Hogan
Managing Director, Human Resources:
  Anne Donovan Bodnar
**Managing Director, Tillinghast and Towers Perrin
  Reinsurance:** Patricia L. (Tricia) Guinn
General Counsel and Secretary: Kevin Young
Head of Global Consulting Group, UK: Nigel Bateman
Global Consulting Group, UK: Huck Ch'ng
Global Consulting Group, UK: David Finn
Reinsurance Practice, Europe: Amar Shah

LOCATIONS

HQ: Towers Perrin
  1 Stamford Plaza, 263 Tresser Blvd.,
  Stamford, CT 06901
Phone: 203-326-5400   **Fax:** 203-326-5499
Web: www.towers.com

Towers Perrin has about 80 offices in 24 countries worldwide.

PRODUCTS/OPERATIONS

Selected Operations

Tillinghast-Towers Perrin
  Financial Reporting
  Mergers, Acquisitions, and Restructuring
  Products, Markets, and Distribution
    Distribution Strategy, Economics, and Operating
      Solutions
    Market Entry, Analysis, and Positioning
    Product Development and Management
    Group Life and Health Insurance
  Risk Management
    Corporate Risk Management and Self-Insured
      Management
    Insurance and Financial Services
    Health Care Professional Liability
  Value-Based Management
Towers Perrin
  Administration Solutions
  Change Management
  Communication
  Executive Compensation
  Global Databases and Surveys
  Health and Welfare
  HR Delivery Solutions
  Mergers, Acquisitions, and Restructuring
  Retirement Services
  Rewards and Performance Management
  Sales Compensation
  Superannuation in Australia

COMPETITORS

Accenture	Hewitt Associates
Aon	KPMG
A.T. Kearney	Marsh
Bain & Company	Marsh & McLennan
Booz Allen	McKinsey & Company
Boston Consulting	Mercer
Deloitte	PricewaterhouseCoopers
Drake Beam Morin	Right Management
Ernst & Young	Watson Wyatt
Gallup	

HISTORICAL FINANCIALS

Company Type: Private

Income Statement — FYE: December 31

	REVENUE ($ mil.)	NET INCOME ($ mil.)	NET PROFIT MARGIN	EMPLOYEES
12/02	1,441	—	—	9,000
12/01	1,469	—	—	9,009
12/00	1,448	—	—	8,919
12/99	1,338	—	—	8,600
12/98	1,125	—	—	6,314
12/97	1,000	—	—	6,350
12/96	855	—	—	6,361
12/95	822	—	—	5,050
12/94	767	—	—	5,000
12/93	709	—	—	5,000
Annual Growth	8.2%	—	—	6.7%

Revenue History

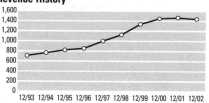

Trader Joe's Co.

When it comes to grocery chains, Trader Joe's isn't your average Joe. With about 215 stores in 18 mostly West and East Coast states, the company offers upscale grocery fare such as health foods, organic produce, and nutritional supplements. To keep costs down, its stores have no service departments and average about 10,000 sq. ft. The company's specialty is its line of more than 2,000 private-label products, including beverages (its signature Charles Shaw brand wine sells for $2 a bottle), soup, snacks, and frozen items. Started by Joe Coulombe as a Los Angeles convenience store chain in 1958, the company was bought in 1979 by German billionaires Karl and Theo Albrecht, who also own the ALDI food chain.

EXECUTIVES

Chairman and CEO: Dan Bane
CFO: Bryan Palbaum
SVP, Operations: Charles J. Pilliter
VP, Real Estate: Doug Yokomizo
VP, Human Resources: Carol Impara
VP, Marketing: Pat St. John
VP, Marketing, Eastern Division: Audrey Dumper
VP, Merchandising: Jon Basalone
Secretary and Treasurer: Mary Genest
Manager, Media Relations: Diane O'Connor

LOCATIONS

HQ: Trader Joe's Company, Inc.
  800 S. Shamrock Ave., Monrovia, CA 91016
Phone: 626-599-3700   **Fax:** 626-301-4431
Web: www.traderjoes.com

Trader Joe's has stores in Arizona, California, Connecticut, Delaware, Illinois, Indiana, Maryland, Massachusetts, Michigan, Nevada, New Hampshire, New Jersey, New York, Ohio, Oregon, Pennsylvania, Virginia, and Washington.

PRODUCTS/OPERATIONS

Selected Private-Label Brands
Charles Shaw (wine)
Trader Giotto's
Trader Ming's

COMPETITORS

A&P	NBTY
Albertson's	Raley's
Arden Group	Royal Ahold
Cost Plus	Safeway
Costco Wholesale	Shaw's
GNC	Smart & Final
Haggen	Stater Bros.
Hannaford Bros.	Stop & Shop
Hickory Farms	Whole Foods
Kroger	Wild Oats Markets

HISTORICAL FINANCIALS

Company Type: Private

Income Statement — FYE: June 30

	ESTIMATED REVENUE ($ mil.)	NET INCOME ($ mil.)	NET PROFIT MARGIN	EMPLOYEES
6/03	2,500	—	—	—
6/02	2,200	—	—	—
6/01	1,900	—	—	7,488
6/00	1,670	—	—	—
6/99	1,460	—	—	—
6/98	1,210	—	—	4,500
6/97	825	—	—	—
6/96	750	—	—	—
6/95	720	—	—	—
6/94	607	—	—	—
Annual Growth	17.0%	—	—	18.5%

Revenue History

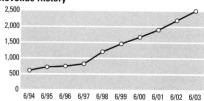

Trader Publishing

Trader Publishing is a leading publisher of classified advertising. It produces dozens of publications such as *Auto Trader*, *Boat Trader*, and *Yacht Trader*. It also publishes real estate listings, employment guides, and discount coupon books. In addition, the company operates companion Web sites for most of its magazines. Founded in 1991, the company is jointly owned by Landmark Communications and Cox Enterprises.

EXECUTIVES

President and CEO: Conrad M. Hall
CFO: Norman Hoffman
Director of Human Resources Information Systems:
  Brooks Stephan
General Manager, EmploymentGuide.com:
  Jamie Clymer
General Manager, ForRent.com: John Wheary
Business Development Manager, RoomSaver.com:
  Brad Petersen
Customer Service Manager, ForRent.com:
  Sandy Damico

LOCATIONS

HQ: Trader Publishing Company
  100 W. Plume St., Norfolk, VA 23510
Phone: 757-640-4000   **Fax:** 757-314-2500
Web: www.traderpublishing.com

PRODUCTS/OPERATIONS

Selected Magazines
Auto Trader
Boat Trader
Distinctive Homes
Employment Guide
For Rent
Harmon Homes
Parenthood
Room Saver
Truck Trader

Selected Web Sites
AeroTraderOnline.com
Ask4hr.com
Autofind.com
Automart.com
BargainTraderOnline.com
BoatTraderOnline.com
CollectorCarTraderOnline.com
CorporateHousing.com
CycleTraderOnline.com
DealerSpecialties.com
Dealsonwheels.com
DistinctHomes.com
EmploymentGuide.com
EquipmentTraderOnline.com
ForRent.com
GetAuto.com
HarmonHomes.com
Parenthood.com
Racingmilestones.com
Roomsaver.com
RVTraderOnline.com
SeniorOutlook.com
Soundingsonline.com
TimeShareSaver.com
TraderOnline.com
Travel Coupon Guides
Travel Saver Guides
Traveler Discount Guide
Truckracecycle.com
TruckTraderOnline.com
US Travel Guide
Walnecks.com
WoodshopNews.com

HISTORICAL FINANCIALS
Company Type: Joint venture

Income Statement
FYE: December 31

	ESTIMATED REVENUE ($ mil.)	NET INCOME ($ mil.)	NET PROFIT MARGIN	EMPLOYEES
12/03	820	—	—	9,400
12/02	998	—	—	
Annual Growth	(17.8%)	—	—	

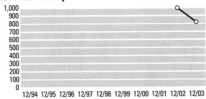

Revenue History

Trammell Crow Residential

Trammell Crow Residential (TCR) builds quite a nest. A builder and manager of upscale apartment complexes, the company operates regionally through national and divisional partners. These partners work with the company to handle the purchase, development, and building of multi-family rental projects. Subsidiary Trammell Crow Residential Services manages more than 60,000 units, with the heaviest concentrations of properties located in Texas, the Southeast, and along the West Coast. The company split off from mammoth Trammell Crow in 1977 but is still associated with the Crow family empire of real estate development firms.

EXECUTIVES

Chairman and CEO: J. Ronald Terwilliger
EVP, Risk Management and Legal Services:
  Thomas J. (Tom) Patterson
EVP and Chief Accounting Officer: Rachel Purcell
EVP, Human Resources and Information Systems:
  Tim Swango
Executive Managing Director, Capital Markets:
  Michael G. Melaugh
Managing Director, Acquisitions: Susan D. Vickery

LOCATIONS

HQ: Trammell Crow Residential
  2859 Paces Ferry Rd., Ste. 1100, Atlanta, GA 30339
Phone: 770-801-1600   **Fax:** 770-801-5395
Web: www.tcresidential.com

Selected Offices
Atlanta
Austin, TX
Costa Mesa, CA
Dallas
Denver
Englewood, CO
Fairfield, CT
Fort Lauderdale, FL
Houston
Kirkland, WA
Morristown, NJ
Nashville, TN
Phoenix
Portland, OR
Raleigh, NC
Rancho Santa Fe, CA
Rockville, MD
San Mateo, CA
San Ramon, CA
Scottsdale, AZ
Winter Park, FL

COMPETITORS

Gables Residential Trust   JPI
Hines Interests   Lincoln Property
Inland Group   Summit Properties

HISTORICAL FINANCIALS
Company Type: Private

Income Statement
FYE: December 31

	REVENUE ($ mil.)	NET INCOME ($ mil.)	NET PROFIT MARGIN	EMPLOYEES
12/03	1,592	—	—	2,300
12/02	2,000	—	—	2,300
12/01	2,000	—	—	2,000
12/00	2,000	—	—	4,000
12/99	1,800	—	—	4,000
12/98	1,617	—	—	3,500
12/97	1,322	—	—	3,000
12/96	920	—	—	2,500
12/95	510	—	—	900
Annual Growth	15.3%	—	—	12.4%

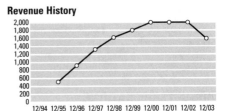

Revenue History

Transammonia

Fertilizer, liquefied petroleum gas (LPG), and petrochemicals form the lifeblood of international trader Transammonia. The company trades, distributes, and transports these commodities around the world. Transammonia's fertilizer business includes ammonia, phosphates, and urea. Transammonia's Sea-3 subsidiary imports and distributes propane to residential, commercial, and industrial customers in the northeastern US and in Florida. The company's Trammochem unit trades in petrochemicals, specializing in aromatics, methanol, methyltertiary butyl ether (MTBE), and olefins. Trammo Petroleum trades oil products including gasoline, heating oil, jet fuel, and naphtha from its office in Houston.

EXECUTIVES

Chairman and CEO: Ronald P. Stanton
VP and CFO: Edward G. Weiner
CIO: Benjamin Tan
Director Human Resources: Marguerite Harrington

LOCATIONS

HQ: Transammonia, Inc.
  350 Park Ave., Ste. 400, New York, NY 10022
Phone: 212-223-3200   **Fax:** 212-759-1410
Web: www.transammonia.com

Transammonia operates offices in 18 countries, with major trading centers in Darien, Connecticut; Tampa; and Houston in the US and in Amman, Jordan; Beijing; Hong Kong, Lachen, Switzerland; London, and Paris.

COMPETITORS

Cargill
CF Industries
ConAgra
Dynegy
HELM
Magellan Midstream
Norsk Hydro
Terra Industries

HISTORICAL FINANCIALS

Company Type: Private

Income Statement
FYE: December 31

	REVENUE ($ mil.)	NET INCOME ($ mil.)	NET PROFIT MARGIN	EMPLOYEES
12/02	2,309	—	—	269
12/01	2,434	—	—	237
12/00	2,447	—	—	218
12/99	1,480	—	—	205
12/98	1,380	—	—	249
12/97	2,100	—	—	262
12/96	2,480	—	—	235
12/95	2,469	—	—	200
12/94	1,330	—	—	207
12/93	1,350	—	—	190
Annual Growth	6.1%	—	—	3.9%

Revenue History

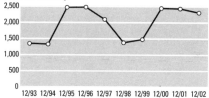

TravelCenters of America

TravelCenters of America is in the food, fuel, and relaxation business for the long haul. The company's network of about 150 interstate highway travel centers in 41 states and Ontario, Canada is the nation's largest. Company-owned and franchised truck stops provide fuel, fast-food and sit-down restaurants (Country Pride, Buckhorn Family), convenience stores, and lodging. With professional truck drivers accounting for most of the customers, some outlets also offer "trucker-only" services such as laundry and shower facilities, telephone and TV rooms, and truck repair. The company was formed in 1992 and is owned by a group of investors led by Oak Hill Capital Partners, Freightliner, and company officers.

The company has agreed to acquire the Rip Griffin chain of 11 truck stops in Arizona, Arkansas, California, Colorado, New Mexico, Texas, and Wyoming, for a purchase price of $120 million. The acquisition is expected to close by the end of 2004.

EXECUTIVES

Chairman and CEO: Edwin P. (Ed) Kuhn, age 61, $875,000 pay
President and COO: Timothy L. Doane, age 46, $577,500 pay
EVP, CFO, and Secretary: James W. (Jim) George, age 52, $551,250 pay
SVP, Sales: Michael H. (Mike) Hinderliter, age 54, $486,750 pay
SVP, Marketing: Joseph A. Szima, age 52
SVP, Development and Franchising: Peter Greene
VP and General Counsel: Steven C. Lee, age 40, $267,880 pay
VP, Human Resources: Bruce Sebera
VP, Shop Marketing: Randy Graham
Director, Advertising and Public Relations: Tom Liutkus
Auditors: PricewaterhouseCoopers LLP

LOCATIONS

HQ: TravelCenters of America, Inc.
24601 Center Ridge Rd., Ste. 200,
Westlake, OH 44145
Phone: 440-808-9100 **Fax:** 440-808-3306
Web: www.tatravelcenters.com

PRODUCTS/OPERATIONS

2003 Sales

	$ mil.	% of total
Fuel	1,513.6	70
Non-fuel	649.5	30
Other	13.1	—
Total	**2,176.2**	**100**

2003 Stores

	No.
Company-owned	126
Leased	14
Total	**140**

COMPETITORS

Bowlin Travel Centers
ChevronTexaco
Exxon Mobil
Flying J
Love's Country Stores
Marathon Ashland Petroleum
Petro Stopping Centers
Pilot
Rip Griffin Truck Service Center
Royal Dutch/Shell Group
Stuckey's

HISTORICAL FINANCIALS

Company Type: Private

Income Statement
FYE: December 31

	REVENUE ($ mil.)	NET INCOME ($ mil.)	NET PROFIT MARGIN	EMPLOYEES
12/03	2,176	9	0.4%	10,500
12/02	1,870	1	0.1%	10,000
12/01	1,935	(10)	—	10,255
12/00	2,060	(38)	—	10,635
12/99	1,455	(25)	—	11,000
12/98	924	(15)	—	9,800
12/97	1,039	(6)	—	8,000
12/96	696	6	0.8%	—
12/95	456	10	2.2%	—
12/94	467	10	2.1%	—
Annual Growth	18.6%	(1.0%)	—	4.6%

2003 Year-End Financials

Debt ratio: 2,012.1%
Return on equity: 44.3%
Cash ($ mil.): 15
Current ratio: 1.37
Long-term debt ($ mil.): 502

Net Income History

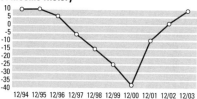

TriMas Corporation

Whether you're hitching your wagon or seeking closure, TriMas' business is always fastenating. The company's Cequent Group unit makes trailers, hitches, and roof racks for SUVs and trucks. TriMas' Rieke Packaging Systems unit makes containers, closures, dispensers, and other packaging items for consumer products. The Industrial Specialties unit manufactures a range of products, including precision tools, gaskets, and tapes. TriMas' Fastening Systems division makes large-diameter bolts used to assemble construction and agricultural equipment. Heartland Industrial Associates controls TriMas; part of Heartland's stake is held by former TriMas parent Metaldyne. Metaldyne is also controlled by Heartland Industrial.

EXECUTIVES

Chairman: Samuel Valenti III, age 58
President, CEO, and Director: Grant Beard, age 43, $1,600,000 pay
CFO: Benson K. Woo, age 49, $162,200 pay (partial-year salary)
President, Cequent Transportation Accessories: Scott Hazlett, age 47, $392,300 pay
President, Industrial Specialties; President, Fastening Systems: Edward L. Schwartz, age 42, $433,100 pay (partial-year salary)
President, Rieke Packaging Systems: Lynn Brooks, age 50, $465,900 pay
VP, Finance and Treasurer: Robert J. Zalupski, age 45
VP, Human Resources: Dwayne Newcom, age 43, $297,500 pay
General Counsel and Secretary: William (Bill) Fullmer, age 44
Corporate Controller: E. R. (Skip) Autry Jr., age 49
Auditors: KPMG LLP

LOCATIONS

HQ: TriMas Corporation
39400 Woodward Ave., Ste. 130,
Bloomfield Hills, MI 48304
Phone: 248-631-5450 **Fax:** 248-631-5455
Web: www.trimascorp.com

TriMas has operations in Australia, Canada, China, Germany, Italy, Mexico, the UK, and the US.

PRODUCTS/OPERATIONS

2003 Sales

	$ mil.	% of total
Cequent Transportation Accessories	427.4	47
Industrial Specialties	217.9	24
Fastening Systems	141.0	16
Rieke Packaging Systems	119.1	13
Total	**905.4**	**100**

Selected Products
Cequent Transportation Accessories
  Cargo liners
  Hitch accessories
  Portable toilets
  Roof racks
  Splash guards
  Tie downs
  Trailer brakes
  Trailer lighting products
  Winches
Industrial Specialties
  Cylinders for acetylene
  Fiberglass facings
  Flame retardant facings
  Heat jacks
  Industrial gaskets
  Precision cutting tools
Fastening Systems
  Blind bolt fasteners
  Large diameter bolts
Rieke Packaging Systems
  Bottle closures and dispensers
  Drum closures and dispensers
  Pail closures and dispensers
  Specialty pumps
  Specialty sprayers

COMPETITORS

AptarGroup
Atwood Mobile Products
Dutton-Lainson
Harsco
Johns Manville
Saint-Gobain Calmar

HISTORICAL FINANCIALS
Company Type: Private

Income Statement				FYE: December 31
	REVENUE ($ mil.)	NET INCOME ($ mil.)	NET PROFIT MARGIN	EMPLOYEES
12/03	905	(31)	—	4,736
12/02	750	(35)	—	3,770
12/01	748	(11)	—	—
Annual Growth	10.0%	—	—	25.6%

2003 Year-End Financials
Debt ratio: 184.5%   Current ratio: 1.46
Return on equity: —   Long-term debt ($ mil.): 732
Cash ($ mil.): 7

Net Income History

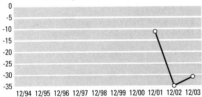

Trinity Health

One needn't believe in the holy trinity to come to Trinity Health. The Catholic health care system runs nearly 50 hospitals and has more than 400 outpatient facilities, as well as long-term care facilities, home health agencies, and hospice programs in seven states. Combined, Trinity Health has some 6,500 acute care and non-acute care beds. Its subsidiary, Trinity Health Plans, operates the Care Choices HMO in about half a dozen southeast Michigan counties. Another subsidiary, Trinity Design, offers health care facility architectural and interior design services. Catholic Health Ministries sponsors the organization.

Trinity Health is really more of a duo than a trio: The not-for-profit company is the result of a coupling between Mercy Health Services and Holy Cross Health System.

EXECUTIVES
Chairman: William Kreykes
President and CEO: Judith C. (Judy) Pelham, age 58
COO: Edgar T. Carlson
CFO: James (Jim) Peppiatt-Combes
EVP, Clinical and Physician Services: M. Narendra Kini
EVP, Eastern Division: Michael A. (Mike) Slubowski
EVP, Western Division: Marsha Casey
SVP and CIO: James (Jim) Elert
SVP and General Counsel: Daniel G. (Dan) Hale
SVP, Human Resources: William (Bill) Anderson
SVP, Mission Integration: Sister M. Gretchen Elliot
SVP, Strategic Planning and Support: Bruce Goldstrom
VP, Corporate Communications and Public Relations: Steve Shivinsky
Auditors: Deloitte & Touche LLP

LOCATIONS
HQ: Trinity Health
27870 Cabot Dr., Novi, MI 48377
Phone: 248-489-5004   **Fax:** 248-489-6039
Web: www.trinity-health.org

Selected Operations
California
  Saint Agnes Medical Center (Fresno)
Idaho
  Saint Alphonsus Regional Medical Center (Boise)
Indiana
  Saint Joseph's Regional Medical Center (South Bend)
Iowa
  Mercy Medical Centers (Clinton, Dubuque, Mason City, New Hampton, Sioux City)
Maryland
  Holy Cross Hospital (Silver Spring)
Michigan
  Saint Joseph Mercy Health System (Ann Arbor)
  Mercy Hospital (Cadillac)
  St. Joseph's Mercy of Macomb (Clinton Township)
  Trinity Design (Farmington Hills)
  Trinity Health International (Farmington Hills)
  Trinity Health Plans (Farmington Hills)
  Saint Mary's Mercy Medical Center (Grand Rapids)
  Mercy Hospital (Grayling)
  St. Mary Mercy Hospital (Livonia)
  Mercy General Health Partners (Muskegon)
  Trinity Continuing Care Services (Novi)
  St. Joseph Mercy Oakland (Pontiac)
  Mercy Hospital (Port Huron)
Ohio
  Mount Carmel Health System (Columbus)
  Ambulatory Management Services (Westerville)

COMPETITORS

Ascension Health
Beverly Enterprises
Blue Cross (MI)
Detroit Medical Center
HCA
Henry Ford Health System
Mayo Foundation
Triad Hospitals
William Beaumont Hospital

HISTORICAL FINANCIALS
Company Type: Not-for-profit

Income Statement				FYE: June 30
	REVENUE ($ mil.)	NET INCOME ($ mil.)	NET PROFIT MARGIN	EMPLOYEES
6/03	4,957	(236)	—	43,900
6/02	4,697	5	0.1%	44,500
6/01	4,500	—	—	45,700
6/00	4,100	—	—	45,700
6/99	3,300	—	—	36,000
6/98	2,534	—	—	26,436
6/97	2,399	—	—	27,510
6/96	2,303	—	—	30,000
6/95	2,201	—	—	26,584
6/94	1,704	—	—	24,362
Annual Growth	12.6%	—	—	6.8%

2003 Year-End Financials
Debt ratio: 67.1%   Current ratio: 1.77
Return on equity: —   Long-term debt ($ mil.): 1,739
Cash ($ mil.): 323

Net Income History

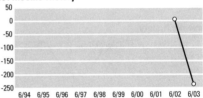

Tri-State Generation and Transmission

Tri-State Generation and Transmission Association supplies wholesale electricity to 44 rural distribution utilities that serve nearly 530,000 customers in Colorado, Nebraska, New Mexico, and Wyoming. The member-owned cooperative has a generating capacity of 1,900 MW from its interests in fossil-fueled power plants, and it operates 5,100 miles of transmission lines. Tri-State also purchases power and sells its excess supply to other utilities. Formed in 1952, Tri-State entered New Mexico through its 2000 acquisition of Plains Electric Generation and Transmission Cooperative.

EXECUTIVES
Chairman: Harold (Hub) Thompson
Vice Chairman: Rick Gordon
EVP and General Manager: J. M. Shafer
SVP and Deputy General Manager: Mike McInnes
SVP and General Counsel: Robert Temmer
SVP Power Management and Generation: Charles (Charlie) Crane
SVP Transmission: Stephen Fausett
VP and CFO: Charles L. (Chuck) Yetzbacher
VP Administration and Human Resources: Sara Rivenburgh
Secretary: Darryl Stout
Auditors: Ernst & Young LLP

LOCATIONS

HQ: Tri-State Generation and
Transmission Association, Inc.
1100 W. 116th Ave., Westminster, CO 80234
Phone: 303-452-6111 **Fax:** 303-254-6007
Web: www.tristategt.org

PRODUCTS/OPERATIONS

2003 Sales

	$ mil.	% of total
Members	491.7	77
Non-members	143.2	22
Other	6.3	1
Total	**641.2**	**100**

Member Systems

Big Horn Rural Electric Company
Carbon Power & Light, Inc.
Central New Mexico Electric Cooperative, Inc.
Chimney Rock Public Power District
Columbus Electric Cooperative, Inc.
Continental Divide Electric Cooperative, Inc.
Delta-Montrose Electric Association
Empire Electric Association, Inc.
Garland Light & Power Company
Gunnison County Electric Association, Inc.
High Plains Power, Inc.
High West Energy, Inc.
Highline Electric Association
Jemez Mountains Electric Cooperative, Inc.
K.C. Electric Association, Inc.
Kit Carson Electric Cooperative, Inc.
La Plata Electric Association, Inc.
Midwest Electric Cooperative Corporation
Mora-San Miguel Electric Cooperative Corporation
Morgan County Rural Electric Association
Mountain Parks Electric, Inc.
Mountain View Electric Association, Inc.
Niobrara Electric Association, Inc.
Northern Rio Arriba Electric Cooperative, Inc.
Northwest Rural Public Power District
Otero County Electric Cooperative, Inc.
Panhandle Rural Electric Membership Association
Poudre Valley Rural Electric Association, Inc.
Roosevelt Public Power District
San Isabel Electric Association, Inc.
San Luis Valley Rural Electric Cooperative, Inc.
San Miguel Power Association, Inc.
Sangre De Cristo Electric Association, Inc.
Sierra Electric Cooperative, Inc.
Socorro Electric Cooperative, Inc.
Southeast Colorado Power Association
Southwestern Electric Cooperative, Inc.
Springer Electric Cooperative, Inc.
United Power, Inc.
Wheat Belt Public Power District
Wheatland Rural Electric Association, Inc.
White River Electric Association, Inc.
Wyrulec Company
Y-W Electric Association, Inc.

COMPETITORS

Aquila
Basin Electric Power
El Paso Electric
Nebraska Public Power
Omaha Public Power
PNM Resources
Xcel Energy

HISTORICAL FINANCIALS

Company Type: Cooperative

Income Statement
FYE: December 31

	REVENUE ($ mil.)	NET INCOME ($ mil.)	NET PROFIT MARGIN	EMPLOYEES
12/03	641	33	5.1%	996
12/02	617	33	5.3%	855
12/01	633	17	2.7%	985
12/00	563	—	—	942
Annual Growth	**4.4%**	**38.5%**	**—**	**1.9%**

2003 Year-End Financials

Debt ratio: 551.3%   Current ratio: 1.16
Return on equity: 13.9%   Long-term debt ($ mil.): 1,388
Cash ($ mil.): 101

Truman Arnold

This jobber jogs petroleum throughout the US. Truman Arnold Companies (TAC) markets and distributes more than 100 million gallons of petroleum products a month to customers located in 48 states in the US through its TAC Energy subsidiary. Through its TAC Air unit, the company offers fixed-base operations (FBO), including aircraft fueling, hanger, and ground transportation services, through ten general aviation facilities in the US. The company also operates convenience stores and provides trucking, real estate, and construction services. The family-owned and -operated company was founded in 1964 by Texarkana businessman Truman Arnold.

EXECUTIVES

Chairman and CEO: Truman Arnold
President and COO: Gregory A. (Greg) Arnold
VP, CFO, and Treasurer: Steve McMillen
VP Administration: James Day
Director Information Technology: Michael Davis
Director Marketing: Cheryl May
Senior Information Technology Administrator:
Josh Lawrence

LOCATIONS

HQ: Truman Arnold Companies
701 S. Robison Rd., Texarkana, TX 75501
Phone: 888-370-8273   **Fax:** 903-831-4056
Web: www.tacenergy.com

Truman Arnold Companies operates in 48 states in the US, as well as in five Canadian provinces.

COMPETITORS

Getty Petroleum Marketing
Gulf Oil
Streicher Mobile Fueling
Sun Coast Resources
Warren Equities

HISTORICAL FINANCIALS
Company Type: Private

Income Statement
FYE: September 30

	REVENUE ($ mil.)	NET INCOME ($ mil.)	NET PROFIT MARGIN	EMPLOYEES
9/03	1,200	—	—	500
9/02	1,150	—	—	400
9/01	1,120	—	—	400
9/00	650	—	—	400
Annual Growth	**22.7%**	**—**	**—**	**7.7%**

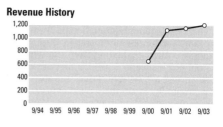

Trump Organization

When it comes to betting on big business, The Donald always pulls out a Trump card. Through The Trump Organization, Donald Trump can claim several pieces of glitzy real estate in the Big Apple, including Trump International Hotel & Tower, Trump Tower (26 floors of it, anyway), and 40 Wall Street. Trump also owns 56% of Trump Hotels & Casino Resorts (THCR), owner and operator of Atlantic City, New Jersey, casinos Trump Taj Mahal, Trump Plaza, and Trump Marina. Other holdings include a Florida resort and 50% of the Miss USA, Miss Teen USA, and Miss Universe beauty pageants (CBS owns the rest). THCR will reorganize under Chapter 11 bankruptcy; Trump's stake in the firm will be reduced to approximately 25%.

Never one to quit in the face of adversity, The Donald continues to excel on the strength of his deal-making prowess. The flamboyant tycoon is renowned for setting up real estate partnerships in which other firms put up most of the cash while he retains most of the control. In the Trump World Tower, for example, he invested $6.5 million, while Korean firm Daewoo pumped in more than $58 million.

Trump also has profited from his famous moniker — which he has trademarked — and his public image: Developers now can pay to co-brand their properties using the Trump name, as long as they meet Trump's super-luxury standard.

Trump dumped his stake in the now-tallest building in New York City. His interest in the Empire State Building leasehold brought in only a paltry $2 million per year. He was also ordered by the courts — after a lengthy legal battle — to sell his 50% stake in the General Motors Building to co-owner Conseco; the two parties agreed to sell the building.

In 2004, Trump renovated New York City's landmark Delmonico Hotel into luxury condos — rechristened Trump Park Avenue — and is planning on providing Canada with its tallest building — Toronto's Trump International Hotel & Tower. Trump's latest proposal is a Las Vegas 64-story hotel and residence; when built it will be that city's tallest building.

Trump is developing the Trump International Hotel & Tower Chicago at the site currently leased by the *Chicago Sun-Times*. Slated to open in 2007, the project has scored a marketing coup: Its construction will be managed by Bill Rancic, the winner of the first season of Trump's hit show *The Apprentice*.

HISTORY

The third of four children, Donald Trump was the son of a successful builder in Queens and Brooklyn. After graduating from the Wharton School of Finance in 1968, his first job was to turn around a 1,200-unit foreclosed apartment complex in Cincinnati that his father had bought for $6 million with no money down. Managing the Cincinnati job gave Trump a distaste for the nonaffluent; he wanted to get to Manhattan to meet all the right people.

Operating as The Trump Organization, he took options on two Hudson River sites in 1975 for no money down and began lobbying the city to finance his construction of a convention center. The center was built, but not by Trump, who nevertheless got about $800,000 and priceless publicity. He and hotelier Jay Pritzker turned the Commodore Hotel near Grand Central Station into the Grand Hyatt Hotel in 1975. Trump married fashion model Ivana Zelnicek two years later.

In 1981 he built the posh Trump Tower on Fifth Avenue and proceeded to wheel and deal himself into 1980s folklore. In 1983 he joined with Holiday Inn to build the Trump Casino Hotel (now Trump Plaza) in Atlantic City using public-issue bonds (he bought out Holiday Inn's interest in 1986), and he bought the Trump Castle from Hilton in 1985. In 1987 he ended up with the unfinished Taj Mahal in Atlantic City, then the world's largest casino, after a battle with Merv Griffin for Resorts International (Griffin won). He bought the Plaza Hotel in Manhattan in 1988, and the Eastern air shuttle (renamed the Trump Shuttle) the next year.

As the 1990s dawned, though, Trump's balance sheet was loaded with about $3 billion in debt. At the same time, his marriage to Ivana broke up in a splash of publicity. Trump's 70 creditor banks consolidated and restructured his debt in 1990. He married Marla Maples in 1993. (They divorced in 1998.)

In 1995 Trump formed Trump Hotels & Casino Resorts and took it public. He also paid a token $10 for 40 Wall St. (now home to American Express). The next year he sold his half-interest in the Grand Hyatt Hotel to the Pritzker family and unloaded more than $1.1 billion in debt by selling the Taj Mahal and Trump's Castle to Trump Hotels. That year Trump bought the Miss Universe, Miss USA, and Miss Teen USA beauty pageants.

In 1997 he published *The Art of the Comeback*, a follow-up to *The Art of the Deal* (1987), and started work on Trump Place, a residential development on New York's Upper West Side. He teamed with Conseco in 1998 to buy the famed General Motors Building for $800 million. In 1999 he began building the Trump World Tower — a 90-story residential building near the United Nations complex. Residents of nearby high rises brought lawsuits in 2000, claiming that the new building would block their view and lower their property value. The court sided with Trump.

The following year Trump and publisher Hollinger International announced plans to transform the former riverfront headquarters of the *Chicago Sun-Times* into a residential and commercial development. Originally planned to be the world's tallest skyscraper, Trump International Hotel & Tower Chicago would have returned the city's lofty title it lost to the Petronas Towers (Kuala Lumpur, Malaysia). Trump decided to scale back the project in the wake of terrorist attacks on the World Trade Center. The hotel and residential project is slated to open in 2007.

In 2004 Trump ventured into reality television as the star and executive producer of *The Apprentice*. A hit with viewers and critics (it garnered four Emmy Award nominations), the show featured candidates competing for a position as a divisional president within The Trump Organization. Riding the wave of fascination with all things Donald, Trump published two more best-selling books (*How to Get Rich* and *Think Like A Billionaire*) that year.

EXECUTIVES

Chairman, President, and CEO: Donald J. Trump, age 57
EVP Operations: Mathew F. Calamari
EVP and CFO: Allen Weisselberg
EVP and General Counsel: Bernard Diamond
EVP Development and Special Projects: Charles (Charlie) Reiss
EVP Golf Course Development: Vincent Stellio
EVP Construction: Andrew Weiss
VP Development: Jill Cremer
VP Development: Russell Flicker
VP Media Relations and Human Resources: Norma Foerderer
VP and Assistant General Counsel: Jason Greenblatt
VP Construction: Micha Koeppel
VP and Controller: Jeffrey McConney
VP Leasing and Insurance: Nathan Nelson
VP Operations and Residential Buildings: Thomas Pienkos
VP Development: Donald J. Trump Jr., age 26

LOCATIONS

HQ: The Trump Organization
725 5th Ave., New York, NY 10022
Phone: 212-832-2000 **Fax:** 212-935-0141
Web: www.trumponline.com

PRODUCTS/OPERATIONS

Trump Hotels & Casino Resorts, Inc.
Indiana Riverboat at Buffington Harbor
Trump 29 Casino (management only)
Trump Marina Hotel Casino
Trump Plaza Hotel and Casino
Trump Taj Mahal Casino Resort

Other Holdings
40 Wall Street
General Motors Building at Trump International Plaza
Mar-A-Lago (private club; Palm Beach, FL)
Miss Teen USA pageant
Miss Universe pageant
Miss USA pageant
Trump Grande Ocean Resort (Sunny Isles Beach, FL)
Trump National Golf Club
Trump International Hotel and Tower
Trump Palace
Trump Parc
Trump Place
Trump Tower
Trump World (Seoul)
Trump World Tower

COMPETITORS

Alexander's
American Real Estate Partners
Aztar
Boston Properties
Caesars Entertainment
Harrah's Entertainment
Helmsley
Hyatt
Lefrak Organization
Marriott
Mashantucket Pequot Gaming
MGM Mirage
Port Authority of NY & NJ
Ritz-Carlton
Rouse
Tishman
Vornado Realty Trust

HISTORICAL FINANCIALS

Company Type: Private

Income Statement
FYE: December 31

	ESTIMATED REVENUE ($ mil.)	NET INCOME ($ mil.)	NET PROFIT MARGIN	EMPLOYEES
12/03	8,500	—	—	15,000
12/02	8,500	—	—	22,000
12/01	8,500	—	—	22,000
12/00	8,000	—	—	22,000
12/99	7,000	—	—	22,000
12/98	6,800	—	—	22,000
12/97	6,500	—	—	22,000
12/96	6,000	—	—	19,000
12/95	4,000	—	—	19,000
12/94	2,750	—	—	15,000
Annual Growth	13.4%	—	—	0.0%

Revenue History

TruServ

To survive against home improvement giants such as The Home Depot and Lowe's, TruServ is relying on pure service. Formed by the merger of Cotter & Company (which was the supplier to the True Value chain) and ServiStar Coast to Coast, the cooperative serves some 6,200 retail outlets, including its flagship True Value hardware stores. The company sells home improvement and garden supplies, as well as appliances, housewares, sporting goods, and toys. Members use the Taylor Rental, Grand Rental Station, Home & Garden Showplace, Induserve Supply, and other banners. TruServ also manufactures its own brand of paints and applicators. TruServ is changing its name to True Value in January 2005.

The merger of Cotter & Company and ServiStar Coast to Coast (operator of Coast to Coast and ServiStar hardware stores, most of which converted to the True Value banner) gave members — many of them mom-and-pop outlets — more buying clout to compete against the do-it-yourself mega-retailers, plus retail advice and advertising support. TruServ has been growing its business in the rental and maintenance, repair, and operation (MRO) arenas, and it plans to begin supplying once again lumber and building materials. (The company had sold its lumber and building materials business in 2000.) At the store level, TruServ has been developing "lite" or smaller versions of its signature programs, such as Platinum Paint Shop, for the co-op's stores (more than half) that are less than 6,000 sq. ft.

Outside the US the company serves about 700 stores in some 70 countries.

HISTORY

Noting that hardware retailers had begun to form wholesale cooperatives to lower costs, John Cotter, a traveling hardware salesman, and associate Ed Lanctot started pitching the wholesale co-op idea in 1947 to small-town and suburban hardware retailers, and by early 1948 they had enrolled 25 merchants for $1,500 each. Cotter became chairman of the new firm, Cotter & Company.

The co-op created the Value & Service (V&S) store trademark in 1951 to emphasize the advantages of an independent hardware store. Acquisitions included the 1963 purchase of Chicago-based wholesaler Hibbard, Spencer, Bartlett, giving Cotter 400 new members and the well-known True Value trademark, which soon replaced V&S signs. Four years later Cotter broadened its focus by buying the General Paint & Chemical Company (Tru-Test paint). The V&S name was revived in 1972 for a five-and-dime store co-op, V&S Variety Stores.

In 1989 Cotter died and Lanctot retired. (Lanctot died in October 2003.) By 1989 there were almost 7,000 True Value Stores. Cotter moved into Canada in 1992 by acquiring hardware distributor and store operator Macleod-Stedman (275 outlets).

Juggling variety-store and hardware merchandise and delivering very small amounts of merchandise to a lukewarm co-op membership did not allow for economies of scale, so in 1995 the company quit its manufacturing operations and its US variety stores (though it still serves variety stores in Canada, operating as C&S Choices), tightened membership requirements, and introduced new services.

Two years later Cotter formed TruServ by merging with hardware wholesaler Servistar Coast to Coast. ServiStar had its origins in the nation's first hardware co-op, American Hardware Supply, which was founded in Pittsburgh in 1910 by M. R. Porter, John Howe, and E. S. Corlett. By 1988, the year it changed its name to ServiStar, the co-op topped $1 billion in sales.

ServiStar expanded in the upper Midwest and on the West Coast in 1990 when it acquired the assets of the Coast to Coast chain (founded in 1928 as a franchise hardware store in Minneapolis); ServiStar brought Coast to Coast out of bankruptcy two years later, making it a co-op. Merging its 1992 acquisition of Taylor Rental Center with its Grand Rental Station stores in 1993 made ServiStar the #1 general rental chain. In 1996 it consolidated Coast to Coast's operations into its own and changed its name to ServiStar Coast to Coast.

President Don Hoye became CEO of the company in 1999. That year TruServ slashed 1,000 jobs and declared it would convert all its hardware store chains to the True Value banner. But TruServ lost $131 million in 1999 over bookkeeping gaffs, and co-op members received no dividends. Of 2,800 ServiStar dealers, only 1,900 raised the True Value flag. Others either declined to switch or were never offered the change because other True Value stores already shared their market area. In addition, stores began deserting the co-op because of inventory and other problems. In late 2000 the company sold its lumber and building materials business.

As competition continued to increase in 2001, the company was facing falling sales, lawsuits from shareholders, and accusations by retailers of unfair practices intended to pressure them into adopting the cooperative's flagship True Value banner. TruServ also had to confront a $200 million loan default. It made cuts in its corporate staff and divested its Canadian interests. In July 2001 Hoye resigned. The company's CFO and COO, Pamela Forbes Lieberman, was named the new CEO that November.

In April 2002 the company reported a net loss of $50.7 million during 2001, which it attributed to restructuring charges, inventory write-downs, and finance fees. Also that month the company announced that it had received $200 million in long-term financing. TruServ, under SEC investigation for alleged inventory, accounting, and other internal-control problems, was one of several companies that failed in August 2002 to meet a government requirement to swear by their past financial results.

In January 2003 TruServ received about $125 million in financing from investment firm W. P. Carey & Co. in a sale-leaseback deal on seven of TruServ's distribution centers. In March 2003 TruServ settled the SEC's allegations, without admitting or denying them, and agreed to follow measures intended to ensure compliance with securities laws.

EXECUTIVES

Chairman: Bryan R. Ableidinger, age 55
President, CEO, and Director:
  Pamela Forbes Lieberman, age 49, $940,156 pay
SVP and CFO: David A. Shadduck, age 43, $457,962 pay
SVP and Chief Merchandising Officer:
  Steven L. Mahurin, age 44
SVP and CIO: Leslie A. Weber, age 47
SVP, Distribution/Logistics and Manufacturing:
  Michael Haining
SVP, General Counsel, and Secretary:
  Cathy C. Anderson, age 54, $370,778 pay (partial-year salary)
SVP, Human Resources and Communications:
  Amy Mysel, age 51
VP and Corporate Treasurer: Barbara L. Wagner
VP, Marketing and Advertising: Carol Wentworth, age 46
VP, Retail Development: Brian Kiernan, age 46
VP, Retail Finance: Jon Johnson
VP, Specialty Businesses: Fred Kirst, age 52
Director, Commodities: Debbie Randall
Director, Corporate Events: Susan Katz
Director, International: Mimi Apelqvist
Director, Member Relations: Dave Feuerhelm
Sales Director, Specialty Businesses: Michelle Finnigan
General Manager, Rental: Tony Sabo
Auditors: PricewaterhouseCoopers LLP

LOCATIONS

HQ: TruServ Corporation
  8600 W. Bryn Mawr Ave., Chicago, IL 60631
Phone: 773-695-5000   **Fax:** 773-695-6516
Web: www.truserv.com

TruServ is a hardware store cooperative serving some 6,200 stores in the US.

PRODUCTS/OPERATIONS

2003 Sales

	$ mil.	% of total
Hardware goods	485	24
Farm and garden	429	22
Electrical and plumbing	353	18
Painting and cleaning	313	15
Appliances and housewares	229	11
Sporting goods and toys	108	5
Other	107	5
Total	**2,024**	**100**

Selected Operations

Grand Rental Station	Induserve Supply
Grill Zone	Party Central
Home & Garden Showplace	Taylor Rental
	True Value

COMPETITORS

84 Lumber	Menard
Ace Hardware	Northern Tool
Akzo Nobel	Réno-Dépôt
Benjamin Moore	Sears
Do it Best	Sherwin-Williams
Fastenal	Stock Building Supply
Hertz	Sutherland Lumber
Home Depot	United Rentals
Kmart	Valspar
Lanoga	Wal-Mart
Lowe's	Wolohan Lumber
McCoy	

HISTORICAL FINANCIALS

Company Type: Cooperative

Income Statement
FYE: December 31

	REVENUE ($ mil.)	NET INCOME ($ mil.)	NET PROFIT MARGIN	EMPLOYEES
12/03	2,024	21	1.0%	3,000
12/02	2,176	21	1.0%	3,200
12/01	2,619	(51)	—	4,000
12/00	3,994	34	0.9%	4,300
12/99	4,502	(131)	—	5,500
12/98	4,328	21	0.5%	6,500
12/97	3,332	43	1.3%	5,800
12/96	2,442	52	2.1%	3,825
12/95	2,437	59	2.4%	4,186
12/94	2,574	60	2.3%	4,200
Annual Growth	(2.6%)	(11.0%)	—	(3.7%)

2003 Year-End Financials

Debt ratio: 2,579.7%   Current ratio: 1.11
Return on equity: 41.2%   Long-term debt ($ mil.): 100
Cash ($ mil.): 9

Net Income History

Trustmark Insurance

Trustmark Insurance was established in 1913 as the Brotherhood of All Railway Employees to provide disability coverage to railroad workers. Trustmark is licensed in all 50 states and covers more than 2.5 million people from all walks of life. Operations include group and individual health coverage (medical, dental, disability, and life insurance) and voluntary insurance products (specialty products through voluntary payroll deductions). Subsidiary Starmark markets health plans to small businesses. Other subsidiaries combat health-care fraud and offer third-party administration and cost management of health care plans. A mutual company, Trustmark is owned by its policyholders.

Trustmark has experienced growth by expanding its third party administration services, and its worksite marketing of voluntary insurance products.

EXECUTIVES
Chairman and CEO, Trustmark Insurance and Trustmark Mutual Holding: J. Grover Thomas Jr.
President and COO, Trustmark Insurance and Trustmark Mutual Holding: David M. McDonough
EVP, Benefits and TPA Services: Mark Schmidt
EVP, Voluntary Products: Christopher J. Martin
SVP and CFO: J. Brink Marcuccili
SVP, General Counsel, and Secretary: Frank G. Gramm III
SVP Investments: Jerry Hitpas
SVP and Chief Marketing Officer, Trustmark Mutual Holding: James K. Derleth
SVP, Managed Care: Julie M. Malida
SVP, Corporate Administration: Warren R. Schreier
VP, Human Resources: Robert R. Worobow

LOCATIONS
HQ: Trustmark Insurance Company
400 Field Dr., Lake Forest, IL 60045
Phone: 847-615-1500 **Fax:** 847-615-3910
Web: www.trustmarkinsurance.com

PRODUCTS/OPERATIONS
Selected Subsidiaries
CoreSource
MultiBenefit Services
The Sentinel Group
Star Marketing and Administration, Inc. (Starmark)
Trustmark Health Resources

COMPETITORS
Aetna
AFLAC
AXA Financial
Blue Cross
CIGNA
Citigroup
CNA Financial
MetLife
Prudential

HISTORICAL FINANCIALS
Company Type: Mutual company

Income Statement   FYE: December 31

	REVENUE ($ mil.)	NET INCOME ($ mil.)	NET PROFIT MARGIN	EMPLOYEES
12/03	1,131	16	1.4%	3,000
12/02	1,100	—	—	3,500
12/01	1,393	—	—	3,400
12/00	1,322	—	—	3,500
12/99	1,167	—	—	3,500
12/98	1,058	—	—	3,300
12/97	972	—	—	2,600
12/96	890	—	—	1,575
12/95	765	—	—	1,555
12/94	711	—	—	1,419
Annual Growth	5.3%	—	—	8.7%

Revenue History

TTI

TTI has a passion for passives. Each year the company distributes more than 1.7 million electronic components, including passive components such as resistors and capacitors, and interconnects such as cables, sockets, and filter connectors. Suppliers of its 160,000 line items include AVX, Tyco Electronics, Molex, KEMET, and Vishay Intertechnology. TTI also offers services such as connector assembly, packaging, testing, and supply chain management. TTI, which owner and CEO Paul Andrews founded in 1971 as a supplier to the military, serves manufacturers of aerospace and defense systems, computers, telecom equipment, medical devices, and industrial products.

Customers in commercial markets account for about three-quarters of sales. The company is expanding its presence in Europe and Asia.

EXECUTIVES
Chairman and CEO: Paul E. Andrews Jr.
SVP, Asia: John Davidson
SVP, Finance: Nick M. Kypreos
SVP, Global Product Marketing: Mike Morton
SVP, Global Sales and Marketing: Craig Conrad
SVP, Information Services: David Minter
SVP, Operations: J. D. Beasley
VP, Northwest Region: Tony Miller
VP, Business Development: David Ryder
VP, Connector Product Marketing: Ernie Schilling Jr.
VP, Passive Product Marketing: Jeff Shafer
VP, TTI Asia: Robin Quek
VP, Sales, North America: Phil Mazzola
Director, Human Resources: Myran Dill
Director, Marketing: Tim Scott
Corporate Communications Coordinator: Cathy Walensky

LOCATIONS
HQ: TTI, Inc.
2441 Northeast Pkwy., Fort Worth, TX 76106
Phone: 817-740-9000 **Fax:** 817-740-5555
Web: www.ttiinc.com

TTI has offices in Austria, Canada, China, Denmark, France, Germany, Hong Kong, Ireland, Italy, Mexico, the Netherlands, Scotland, Singapore, Spain, Sweden, Switzerland, Taiwan, the UK, and the US.

PRODUCTS/OPERATIONS
Selected Products
Capacitors
Circuit protectors
Connectors
Crystals
EMI filters
Magnetics/inductors
Passive integrators
Potentiometers
Relays
Resistors
Resonators
Sensors
Sound components
Switches
Wire and tools

Services
Connector assembly
Connector hot solder dipping
Documentation
Inspecting
Labeling
Lead forming, cutting, and trimming
Marking
Packaging
Parts remarking
Solder testing of passive components
Supply chain management
Taping and reeling
Testing

COMPETITORS
All American Semiconductor
Arrow Electronics
Avnet
Electrocomponents
Future Electronics
Jaco Electronics
N.F. Smith
Nu Horizons Electronics
Premier Farnell
ROHM
Sager Electrical

HISTORICAL FINANCIALS
Company Type: Private

Income Statement   FYE: December 31

	REVENUE ($ mil.)	NET INCOME ($ mil.)	NET PROFIT MARGIN	EMPLOYEES
12/03	525	—	—	1,500
12/02	630	—	—	1,500
12/01	750	—	—	1,550
12/00	955	—	—	1,050
12/99	555	—	—	1,055
12/98	461	—	—	985
12/97	450	—	—	933
12/96	411	—	—	819
Annual Growth	3.6%	—	—	9.0%

Revenue History

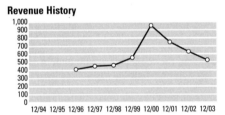

TTX

TTX Company keeps the railroad industry in the US and Canada chugging along by leasing railcars. Rail companies generally prefer to rent railcars as needed rather than buy them because the cars are often switched and traded along the tracks. With 127,000 railcars, TTX's fleet includes three types of railcars (intermodal, autorack, and general use) designed to carry containers, autos, farm and construction equipment, and lumber and steel products.

The company has distribution centers in Illinois and Washington and maintains its fleet through three repair centers (in California, Florida, and South Carolina) and 31 inspection centers in the US. TTX is owned by the largest railroads in the US and Canada.

EXECUTIVES

President and CEO: Andrew F. Reardon
SVP, Equipment: Robert S. Hulick
SVP, Fleet Management: Thomas F. Wells
VP and CFO: Thomas D. (Tom) Marion
VP, Information Technology: John M. Braly
Assistant VP, Human Resources and Administrative Services Department: Michelle Pomeroy
Controller: Frank J. Previti
General Counsel and Corporate Secretary: Patrick Loftus
Assistant Treasurer and Assistant Corporate Secretary: Anthony J. Barton
Auditors: KPMG LLP

LOCATIONS

HQ: TTX Company
101 N. Wacker Dr., Chicago, IL 60606
Phone: 312-853-3223   **Fax:** 312-984-3790
Web: www.ttx.com

TTX Company has distribution centers in Illinois and Washington; division repair facilities in California, Florida, and South Carolina; intermodal terminal repair sites in Alabama, Arkansas, California, Colorado, Florida, Illinois, Maryland, Minnesota, Missouri, New Jersey, Oregon, Tennessee, Texas, Virginia, and Washington; and repair tracks in California, Illinois, Kansas, and Texas.

PRODUCTS/OPERATIONS

Selected Equipment Types
Bi-level auto rack car
Bulkhead flat car
Chain tie-down car
Double-stack container car
General service flat car
Gondola
Plain box car
Tri-level auto rack car

COMPETITORS

Andersons
CIT Capital Finance
GATX
Genesee & Wyoming
Greenbrier
Joseph Transportation
Pacer International
Pioneer Railcorp
XTRA

HISTORICAL FINANCIALS

Company Type: Private

Income Statement
FYE: December 31

	REVENUE ($ mil.)	NET INCOME ($ mil.)	NET PROFIT MARGIN	EMPLOYEES
12/02	918	—	—	1,285
12/01	983	—	—	1,400
12/00	1,020	—	—	1,614
12/99	985	—	—	1,975
12/98	937	—	—	2,000
12/97	880	—	—	2,000
12/96	859	—	—	1,965
12/95	864	—	—	1,985
12/94	810	—	—	2,000
12/93	730	—	—	—
Annual Growth	2.6%	—	—	(5.4%)

Revenue History

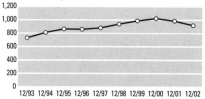

Tube City

Tube City can do just about anything with industrial leftovers. A steel-mill service company, Tube City provides raw materials and services that help mills and foundries profit from their scrap. The company, which has operations in 17 states in the US and three in Europe, primarily processes and brokers steel scrap. Its processing services include burning, breaking, shearing, shredding, and bailing. As a major regional scrap metal broker, Tube City brokers and processes more than 15 million tons of scrap annually. It also provides transportation (trucking and rail), equipment leasing, and maintenance and machine shop services. David Coslov founded the family-owned company in 1926.

EXECUTIVES

Chairman and CEO: Michael Coslov
President and COO: Joseph Curtin, age 57
SVP Finance, Administration, and General Counsel: Tom Lippard
SVP Finance: Daniel Rosati
Human Resources Manager: Jeannie DeCarlo
Marketing Manager: Gary Henkel
SVP Operations and Business Development: Perry VanRosendale

LOCATIONS

HQ: Tube City, LLC
12 Monongahela Ave., Glassport, PA 15045
Phone: 412-678-6141   **Fax:** 412-678-2210
Web: www.tubecity.com

Tube City has operations in Alabama, Arkansas, California, Georgia, Illinois, Indiana, Michigan, Nebraska, New Jersey, Ohio, Oklahoma, Pennsylvania, South Carolina, Tennessee, Texas, and Virginia.

COMPETITORS

Commercial Metals
David J. Joseph
Keywell
Metal Management
OmniSource

HISTORICAL FINANCIALS

Company Type: Private

Income Statement
FYE: December 31

	ESTIMATED REVENUE ($ mil.)	NET INCOME ($ mil.)	NET PROFIT MARGIN	EMPLOYEES
12/03	600	—	—	900
12/02	600	—	—	500
12/01	550	—	—	500
12/00	600	—	—	500
12/99	580	—	—	500
12/98	550	—	—	500
12/97	520	—	—	492
12/96	524	—	—	475
12/95	466	—	—	375
12/94	403	—	—	221
Annual Growth	4.5%	—	—	16.9%

Revenue History

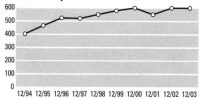

Tufts Associated Health Plans

Managed health care headaches in the New England states have made times tough for Tufts Associated Health Plans. The for-profit company provides administrative, management, advertising and marketing services for its subsidiaries, including not-for-profit Tufts Associated Health Maintenance Organization (TAHMO), and Tufts Insurance Company (life insurance). The company's provider network serves more than 800,000 members. Tufts Associated Health Plans offers HMO, health maintenance organization, PPO, point-of-service, and other health care plans to its customers.

The company also provides third-party administrative services through its Tufts Benefit Administrators subsidiary.

EXECUTIVES

President and CEO: Nancy L. Leaming, age 56
COO: Richard Hallworth
SVP and CFO: Andy Hilbert
SVP and Chief Medical Officer: Philip R. Boulter
SVP and Chief Information Officer: Tricia Trebino
SVP and General Counsel: James Roosevelt Jr.
SVP, Planning and Development: Jon M. Kingsdale
SVP, Sales, Marketing, and Member Services: Kevin J. Counihan
VP and Secretary: Deborah E. Benjamin
VP, Secure Horizons: Patricia Blake
Auditors: Ernst & Young LLP

LOCATIONS

HQ: Tufts Associated Health Plans, Inc.
333 Wyman St., Waltham, MA 02454
Phone: 781-466-9400   **Fax:** 781-466-8583
Web: www.tufts-healthplan.com

PRODUCTS/OPERATIONS

Health Plans
Advantage PPO
Choice CoPay (copay options)
Common Wealth PPO (state employee plan)
EPO (exclusive provider option)
HMO
Liberty Plan (consumer driven plans)
POS (point-of-service)
PPO (preferred provider organization)
Secure Horizons Tufts Health Plan for Seniors (Medicare)

COMPETITORS

Aetna
Blue Cross (MA)
CIGNA
ConnectiCare
Harvard Pilgrim
Prudential
UnitedHealth Group

Turner Industries

HISTORICAL FINANCIALS
Company Type: Private

Income Statement
FYE: December 31

	REVENUE ($ mil.)	NET INCOME ($ mil.)	NET PROFIT MARGIN	EMPLOYEES
12/03	2,300	57	2.5%	2,500
12/02	2,329	—	—	2,500
12/01	2,000	—	—	2,500
12/00	2,000	—	—	3,000
12/99	2,000	—	—	3,000
12/98	1,600	—	—	2,500
12/97	1,210	—	—	2,341
12/96	865	—	—	1,200
12/95	670	—	—	1,128
12/94	542	—	—	—
Annual Growth	17.4%	—	—	10.5%

Revenue History
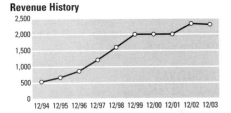

Turner Industries turns out industrial services. Founded in 1961, the company is a top US player in industrial construction, contract maintenance, and outsourcing. Its customers include oil refiners, petrochemical companies, power generators, and pulp and paper mills. Through about a dozen subsidiaries, Turner Industries provides such services as equipment rental, environmental remediation, heavy hauling and rigging, pipe fabrication, and tank cleaning. Turner Industries also offers maintenance and materials management and training workshops and staffing services. Founder and chairman emeritus Bert Turner is principal shareholder of the company.

EXECUTIVES
Chairman Emeritus: Bert S. Turner
Chairman and CEO: Roland M. Toups
President: Thomas H. Turner
VP Finance, CFO, Secretary, and Treasurer: Lester J. (Les) Griffin Jr.
President, Harmony: Donald L. McCollister
President, International Maintenance, National Maintenance, Turner Company, and Turner Industrial Services: Joseph W. Guitreau
President, International Piping Systems: Robert L. Pearson
President, Nichols Construction and Scafco: Davis J. Lauve

LOCATIONS
HQ: Turner Industries, Ltd.
8687 United Plaza Blvd., 5th Fl.,
Baton Rouge, LA 70809
Phone: 225-922-5050 **Fax:** 225-922-5055
Web: www.turner-industries.com

Turner Industries operates from nearly 40 offices in Alabama, Florida, Louisiana, and Texas.

PRODUCTS/OPERATIONS

Selected Services
Bundle extraction
Construction
Contract maintenance
Environmental remediation
Equipment rental
Heavy hauling
Hydroblasting
Painting
Pipe fabrication
Preventive maintenance
Procurement
Rigging
Scaffolding
System integration
Tank cleaning

COMPETITORS
ABB
Aker Kværner
APi Group
Austin Industries
Bechtel
Black & Veatch
Centerline Piping
CH2M HILL
Chicago Bridge and Iron
Fluor
Foster Wheeler
Halliburton
Jacobs Engineering
McDermott
Parsons
Peter Kiewit Sons'
Philip Services
Shaw Group
TIC Holdings
Zachry

HISTORICAL FINANCIALS
Company Type: Private

Income Statement
FYE: October 31

	REVENUE ($ mil.)	NET INCOME ($ mil.)	NET PROFIT MARGIN	EMPLOYEES
10/04	800	—	—	12,000
10/03	800	—	—	12,000
10/02	800	—	—	12,000
10/01	790	—	—	11,000
10/00	741	—	—	12,000
10/99	673	—	—	10,000
10/98	600	—	—	9,800
10/97	553	—	—	10,500
10/96	500	—	—	10,000
10/95	486	—	—	8,100
Annual Growth	5.7%	—	—	4.5%

Revenue History
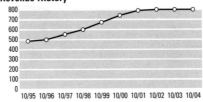

Tuttle-Click

Despite its connections to the Republican Party, Tuttle-Click Automotive Group does sell cars to Democrats. The firm operates about 10 new- and used-car dealerships throughout Orange County, California, and in Tucson, Arizona. The firm's dealerships sell Ford, DaimlerChrysler, Mitsubishi, and Hyundai cars and trucks. The company was founded by Holmes Tuttle, who sold Ronald Reagan a car in 1946 and ended up a prominent GOP fundraiser; he even persuaded Reagan to run for governor of California in 1966. Tuttle's son, co-CEO Robert Tuttle (a White House aide under Reagan), and Arizona-based co-CEO James Click own the company.

EXECUTIVES
Co-CEO: James H. (Jim) Click
Co-CEO: Robert H. (Bob) Tuttle, age 59
CFO: Chris Cotter
Human Resources/Payroll Director: Art Vigil

LOCATIONS
HQ: Tuttle-Click Automotive Group
14 Auto Center Dr., Irvine, CA 92618
Phone: 949-598-4800 **Fax:** 949-830-0980
Web: www.tuttleclick.com

PRODUCTS/OPERATIONS

Selected Automobile Brands
Chrysler
Dodge
Eagle
Ford
Hyundai
Jeep
Mitsubishi
Plymouth

COMPETITORS
AutoNation
David Wilson's
Earnhardt's Auto Centers
Larry H. Miller Group
Lithia Motors
Marty Franich
Prospect Motors
Santa Monica Ford
Sonic Automotive
Southern California Auto Group
Vista

HISTORICAL FINANCIALS
Company Type: Private

Income Statement
FYE: December 31

	REVENUE ($ mil.)	NET INCOME ($ mil.)	NET PROFIT MARGIN	EMPLOYEES
12/03	678	—	—	1,400
12/02	669	—	—	1,400
12/01	687	—	—	1,400
12/00	718	—	—	1,400
12/99	700	—	—	1,380
12/98	665	—	—	1,310
12/97	585	—	—	1,400
12/96	608	—	—	1,400
12/95	582	—	—	1,284
12/94	561	—	—	1,400
Annual Growth	2.1%	—	—	0.0%

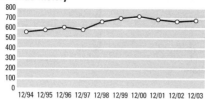

Revenue History

TVA

Although the Tennessee Valley Authority (TVA) may not be an expert on Tennessee attractions like Dollywood and the Grand Ole Opry, it is an authority on power generation. TVA is the largest government-owned power producer in the US, with nearly 32,000 MW of generating capacity. The federal corporation transmits electricity to 158 local distribution utilities, which in turn serve 8.5 million consumers. It also provides power for industrial facilities and government agencies, and it manages the Tennessee River system for power production and flood control.

TVA is the sole power wholesaler, by law, in an 80,000-sq.-mi. territory that includes most of Tennessee and portions of six neighboring states (Alabama, Georgia, Kentucky, Mississippi, North Carolina, and Virginia). Generating and transmitting power to local distribution utilities accounts for 86% of TVA's sales.

Most of TVA's power comes from traditional generation sources, but the company is also exploring alternative energy technologies. It has developed solar, wind, and methane gas facilities, and it is offering green choice options through its distribution affiliates.

TVA has also agreed to produce tritium, a radioactive gas that boosts the power of nuclear weapons, for the US Department of Energy (a first for a civilian nuclear power generator). The company is making modifications at its Watts Bar and Savannah River plants to produce and extract the gas; it plans to begin producing tritium by 2007.

TVA's rates are among the nation's lowest, which would-be competitors attribute to its exemption from federal and state income and property taxes. To prepare for deregulation, the authority is trying to reduce its $25 billion debt.

HISTORY

In 1924 the Army Corps of Engineers finished building the Wilson Dam on the Tennessee River in Alabama to provide power for two WWI-era nitrate plants. With the war over, the question of what to do with the plants became a political football.

An act of Congress created the Tennessee Valley Authority (TVA) in 1933 to manage the plants and Tennessee Valley waterways. New Dealers saw TVA as a way to revitalize the local economy through improved navigation and power generation. Power companies claimed the agency was unconstitutional, but by 1939, when a federal court ruled against them, TVA had five operating hydroelectric plants and five under construction.

During the 1940s TVA supplied power for the war effort, including the Manhattan Project in Tennessee. During the postwar boom between 1945 and 1950, power usage in the Tennessee Valley nearly doubled. Despite adding dams, TVA couldn't keep up with demand, so in 1949 it began building a coal-fired unit. Because coal-fired plants weren't part of TVA's original mission, in 1955 a Congressional panel recommended the authority be dissolved.

Though TVA survived, its funding was cut. In 1959 it was allowed to sell bonds, but it no longer received direct government appropriations for power operations. In addition, it had to pay back the government for past appropriations.

TVA began to build the first unit of an ambitious 17-plant nuclear power program in Alabama in 1967. However, skyrocketing costs forced it to raise rates and cut maintenance on its coal-fired plants, which led to breakdowns. In 1985 five reactors had to be shut down because of safety concerns.

In 1988 former auto industry executive Marvin Runyon was appointed chairman of the agency. "Carvin' Marvin" cut management, sold three airplanes, and got rid of peripheral businesses, saving $400 million a year. In 1992 Runyon left to go to the postal service and was replaced by Craven Crowell, who began preparing TVA for competition in the retail power market.

TVA ended its nuclear construction program in 1996 after bringing two nuclear units on line within three months, a first for a US utility. The next year it raised rates for the first time in 10 years, planning to reduce its debt. In response to a lawsuit filed by neighboring utilities, it agreed to stop "laundering" power by using third parties to sell outside the agency's legally authorized area.

In 1999 the authority finished installing almost $2 billion in scrubbers and other equipment at its coal-fired plants so that it could buy Kentucky coal along with cleaner Wyoming coal. That year, however, the EPA charged TVA with violating the Clean Air Act by making major overhauls on some of its older coal-fired plants without getting permits or installing updated pollution-control equipment. It ordered TVA to bring most of its coal-fired plants into compliance with more current pollution standards. The next year TVA contested the order in court, stating compliance would jack up electricity rates.

TVA was fined by the US Nuclear Regulatory Commission in 2000 for laying off a nuclear plant whistleblower. Crowell resigned in 2001, and Glenn McCullough Jr. was named chairman.

EXECUTIVES

Chairman: Glenn L. McCullough Jr.
President and COO: Oswald J. (Ike) Zeringue
EVP Financial Services and CFO: Michael E. (Mike) Rescoe
EVP and General Counsel: Maureen H. Dunn
EVP Administration: D. LeAnne Stribley
EVP Communications and Government Relations: Ellen Robinson
EVP Customer Service and Marketing: Mark O. Medford
EVP Fossil Power: Joseph R. Bynum
EVP Human Resources: John E. Long Jr.
EVP River System Operations and Environment: Kathryn J. Jackson
EVP Transmission and Power Supply: Terry Boston

SVP Investor Relations and Treasurer: John M. Hoskins
SVP Economic Development: John J. Bradley
SVP Information Services: Diane Bunch
SVP Outage Planning and Execution: Ronald A. (Ron) Loving
SVP Power Resources and Operations Planning: Jack A. Bailey
SVP Strategic Planning and Analysis: Theresa A. Flaim
VP Bulk Power Trading: Amy T. Burns
VP External Communications: Tracy Williams
VP Investor Relations: Sylvia H. (Sissy) Caldwell
Auditors: PricewaterhouseCoopers LLP

LOCATIONS

HQ: Tennessee Valley Authority
400 W. Summit Hill Dr., Knoxville, TN 37902
Phone: 865-632-2101   **Fax:** 865-632-4760
Web: www.tva.gov

The Tennessee Valley Authority's service area covers most of Tennessee and parts of Alabama, Georgia, Kentucky, Mississippi, North Carolina, and Virginia.

PRODUCTS/OPERATIONS

2003 Sales

	$ mil.	% of total
Electric		
Municipalities & cooperatives	5,974	86
Industries directly served	781	11
Federal agencies & other electric	120	2
Other	77	1
Total	**6,952**	**100**

2003 Energy Mix by Net Capacity

	% of total
Fossil	49
Nuclear	18
Hydro	18
Combustion turbine	15
Total	**100**

HISTORICAL FINANCIALS

Company Type: Government-owned

Income Statement
FYE: September 30

	REVENUE ($ mil.)	NET INCOME ($ mil.)	NET PROFIT MARGIN	EMPLOYEES
9/03	6,952	456	6.6%	13,000
9/02	6,835	73	1.1%	13,000
9/01	6,999	(3,311)	—	13,000
9/00	6,762	24	0.4%	13,400
9/99	6,595	119	1.8%	13,322
9/98	6,729	233	3.5%	13,818
9/97	5,552	8	0.1%	14,500
9/96	5,693	61	1.1%	16,021
9/95	5,375	10	0.2%	16,559
9/94	5,401	151	2.8%	19,027
Annual Growth	**2.8%**	**13.1%**	**—**	**(4.1%)**

2003 Year-End Financials

Debt ratio: 1,716.3%   Current ratio: 0.35
Return on equity: 48.9%   Long-term debt ($ mil.): 20,201
Cash ($ mil.): 532

Net Income History

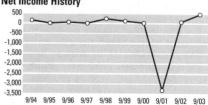

Ty

Take some fabric, shape it like an animal, fill it with plastic pellets, and you, too, could own luxury hotels. That's the lesson taught by Ty Warner, sole owner of Ty Inc., the firm behind Beanie Babies and their worldwide cult following — popular with kids and adults alike. Since 1993 Ty has produced more than 365 different Beanie Babies with colorful names such as Punxsutawney Phil (current) and Cheeks the baboon (retired). Other products include Beanie Buddies (bigger versions of traditional Beanies), Ty Classics (stuffed animals), Beanie Boppers (preteen dolls), and Punkies (squeezable beanbag pals). Beanie bucks enabled Warner to buy three luxury hotels (in New York and California) in recent years.

Ty's marketing smarts have kept Beanies popular for years rather than for a single holiday season, a la Furby or Tickle Me Elmo. The company limits production so that supply never outstrips demand, keeping only 40 or 50 Beanie Babies in circulation at any one time. Ty's "retirement" of a Beanie can cause its price among collectors to skyrocket from its $5-$7 retail debut to hundreds or even thousands of dollars. Rather than flood the market with Beanies through the likes of Toys "R" Us and Wal-Mart, Ty sells them only through specialty toy and gift retailers.

In addition, the firm doesn't advertise, relying instead on the word of mouth that is rampant in Beanie culture. Books, magazines, newsletters, and Web sites stoke collectors' enthusiasm. This collectors' market — which Ty frowns upon (officially, anyway) — shows signs of fading, however.

The company's first ever character licensing agreement is with Paws, Inc., the licensing studio for comic strip cat *Garfield*. The deal consists of a line of Beanies specifically created for the 2004 summer release of *Garfield: The Movie* and includes Garfield, Nermal, Odie, and Arlene.

HISTORY

Ty Warner, the son of a plush-toy salesman, started his toy career selling stuffed animals to specialty shops for stuffed-bear manufacturer Dakin. Warner left Dakin in 1980, moved to Europe for a few years, and in the mid-1980s returned to the US and founded Ty Inc. The company first designed a line of $20, understuffed Himalayan cats.

Beanie Babies first debuted at a 1993 trade show. In January 1994 the first nine Beanies went on sale — at prices low enough for kids to afford — in Chicago specialty stores. As Warner had learned at Dakin, selling stuffed animals through specialty retailers rather than through mass merchandisers meant bigger profits for suppliers and longer-term popularity. By 1995 there were about 30 different Beanies, and Ty's estimated sales were $25 million.

The popularity of Beanies exploded in 1996, first in the Midwest, then along the East Coast, and then across the US. By midyear, Beanies — along with the public's mania for getting them before they sold out — were receiving widespread media coverage. Ty heightened the frenzy among collectors when it started announcing Beanie retirements on its Web site in 1997.

That same year, McDonald's got on the bandwagon: The fast-food giant issued some 100 million "teenie" Beanie Babies in a Happy Meal promotion. McDonald's ran out of the toys and had to end the promotion early, causing a public relations mess. McDonald's doubled its toy order in 1998 and teamed up with Ty again in 1999 and 2000.

In 1998 Warner paid $10 million for a 7% stake in marketing company Cyrk. In return, Cyrk developed the Beanie Babies Official Club, which turned stores that sell Beanies into "official headquarters" offering club membership kits. Ty introduced its Attic Treasures and Beanie Buddies lines that year.

By spring 1998 Beanies had become a customs issue at the Canadian border, where Ty's limit of one imported Beanie per person into the US resulted in tears and fisticuffs. (The company later raised the personal limit to 30.) That summer the crowds at Major League Baseball games featuring Beanie giveaways were 26% bigger than average.

Warner bought the Four Seasons hotel in New York City in 1999. He also provided auditing documents and correspondence to *The New York Post* indicating that Ty had 1998 profits of more than $700 million — more than Hasbro and Mattel combined.

After an August 1999 announcement that it would retire the Beanies at the end of the year, the company held a New Year's vote to determine their fate. In the most shocking outcome since *Rocky IV*, the public voted overwhelmingly in favor of continuing the Beanies. Ty introduced its humanoid Beanie Kids line in early 2000. Later that year Warner bought the Four Seasons Biltmore Hotel and the San Ysidro Ranch — the hostelry where JFK and Jackie honeymooned; both are near Santa Barbara, California.

In 2001 Ty debuted its pre-teen Beanie Boppers (boy and girl dolls designed for kids from 8 to 12 years of age). To round out his Four Seasons Hotels and Coral Casino properties in California, in 2003 Warner purchased nearby Sandpiper Golf Course. Also that year, the Beanie Baby celebrated its 10th anniversary, and Ty marked the event with the introduction of the Decade Beanie Baby.

EXECUTIVES

Chairman and CEO: H. Ty Warner
EVP and CFO: Michael W. Kanzler
EVP, Global Sales and Marketing: John Hong
VP: Tania Lundeen
Director, Human Resources: Nancy Pena

LOCATIONS

HQ: Ty Inc.
 280 Chestnut Ave., Westmont, IL 60559
Phone: 630-920-1515 **Fax:** 630-920-1980
Web: www.ty.com

PRODUCTS/OPERATIONS

Selected Products
Attic Treasures
Baby Ty
Beanie Babies
Beanie Boppers
Beanie Buddies
Beanie Kids
Pluffies
Punkies
Teenie Beanie Boppers
Ty Classics

COMPETITORS

Applause
Boyds Collection
Build-A-Bear
Enesco Group
Gund
Hasbro
Mattel
North American Bear
Russ Berrie
Sanrio
Vermont Teddy Bear

HISTORICAL FINANCIALS

Company Type: Private

Income Statement — FYE: December 31

	ESTIMATED REVENUE ($ mil.)	NET INCOME ($ mil.)	NET PROFIT MARGIN	EMPLOYEES
12/02	750	—	—	600
12/01	750	—	—	650
12/00	850	—	—	1,000
12/99	1,250	—	—	1,000
12/98	1,000	—	—	1,000
12/97	400	—	—	500
12/96	250	—	—	200
12/95	25	—	—	50
Annual Growth	62.6%	—	—	42.6%

Revenue History

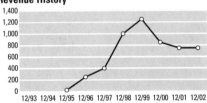

UAP Holding

Keeping varmints out of the fields and ensuring strong and healthy plants, UAP Holding Corp. (formerly United Agri Products) minds the crops. At one time a subsidiary of ConAgra, UAP Holding manufactures and distributes crop production products, ranging from seeds to fertilizers to pest and weed killers. UAP Holding markets its products under the brands ACA, Salvo, Savage, and Shotgun. In 2003 ConAgra sold former UAP Holding units Hacco and Hess & Clark to Neogen Corporation. Later that year, it sold UAP Holding itself to investment firm Apollo Management for about $600 million.

EXECUTIVES

President, CEO, and Director:
 L. Kenneth (Kenny) Cordell, age 46, $286,923 pay
President, Distribution: Bryan S. Wilson, age 43, $88,846 pay
EVP and CFO: David W. Bullock, age 39, $123,365 pay
EVP, Procurement: Dave Tretter, $163,077 pay
EVP, Verdicon: Robert A. Boyce Jr., $162,307 pay
VP, General Counsel, and Secretary: Todd A. Suko, age 37
Director, Human Resources: Phyllis Naibauer
Auditors: Deloitte & Touche LLP

LOCATIONS

HQ: UAP Holding Corp.
7251 W. 4th St., Greeley, CO 80634
Phone: 970-356-4400 **Fax:** 970-347-1560
Web: www.uap.com

COMPETITORS

Agriliance
GROWMARK
Marubeni
Royster-Clark

HISTORICAL FINANCIALS

Company Type: Private

Income Statement			FYE: Last Sunday in February	
	REVENUE ($ mil.)	NET INCOME ($ mil.)	NET PROFIT MARGIN	EMPLOYEES
2/04	2,452	46	1.9%	3,295
2/03	2,664	25	0.9%	3,395
2/02	2,947	(37)	—	—
2/01	2,901	(13)	—	—
Annual Growth	(5.5%)	—	—	(2.9%)

2004 Year-End Financials

Debt ratio: 401.8%
Return on equity: 13.8%
Cash ($ mil.): 173
Current ratio: 1.27
Long-term debt ($ mil.): 309

Net Income History

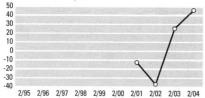

UIS

Once the maker of candy bars *and* car parts, UIS gave up on parts in favor of candy hearts. UIS's operations are now made up of New England Confectionery Company (Sweethearts, NECCO wafers, Clark Bar) and Hurd Millwork (window and patio doors). UIS's automotive subsidiaries included Champion Laboratories (oil filters), Neapco (transmission parts), Wells Manufacturing (ignition and electrical components), and Pioneer (auto specialty supplier) but were sold to The Carlyle Group for $800 million in 2003. Founder Harry Lebensfeld began the company in 1945 with the purchase of an Indiana desk maker. UIS is owned by a trust for Lebensfeld's only child (who is married to EVP Richard Pasculano) and her children.

EXECUTIVES

Chairman, President, and CEO: Andrew E. Pietrini
EVP and Treasurer: Joseph F. Arrigo
EVP: Richard Pasculano

LOCATIONS

HQ: UIS, Inc.
15 Exchange Place, Ste. 1120, Jersey City, NJ 07302
Phone: 201-946-2600 **Fax:** 201-946-9325

PRODUCTS/OPERATIONS

Selected Operations
Hurd Millwork Company, Inc. (window and patio door systems)
New England Confectionery Company (Sweethearts, Necco wafers, Clark Bars)

COMPETITORS

Andersen Corporation
Barry Callebaut
Ben Myerson
Big Red
Brach's
Cadbury Schweppes
Champion Window
Chupa Chups
Cloetta Fazer
Ferrara Pan Candy
HARIBO
Haribo of America
Hershey
Jelly Belly Candy
Mars
Nestlé
Pella
Russell Stover
Spangler Candy
ThermoView Industries
Tootsie Roll

HISTORICAL FINANCIALS

Company Type: Private

Income Statement			FYE: December 31	
	REVENUE ($ mil.)	NET INCOME ($ mil.)	NET PROFIT MARGIN	EMPLOYEES
12/02	1,000	—	—	8,800
12/01	1,056	—	—	8,820
12/00	1,087	—	—	8,910
12/99	1,081	—	—	8,800
12/98	1,020	—	—	8,614
12/97	986	—	—	8,600
12/96	928	—	—	8,300
12/95	871	—	—	8,255
12/94	830	—	—	8,100
12/93	745	—	—	7,258
Annual Growth	3.3%	—	—	2.2%

Revenue History

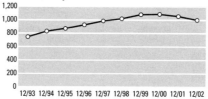

Ukrop's Super Markets

Central Virginia shoppers head to Ukrop's Super Markets for baked goods, prescriptions, to-go meals, even banking services. But they don't go for beer or wine, and they don't go on Sundays. Family-owned Ukrop's is Richmond's #1 supermarket chain, with about 30 Ukrop's Super Markets, a Central Bakery and Kitchen, and a distribution center. Ukrop's owns 51% of First Market Bank (branches in 18 Ukrop's stores and six free-standing locales); National Commerce Bancorporation owns the rest. Joe's Market, a new format featuring gourmet and specialty foods, opened in mid-2001. Joe and Jacquelin Ukrop started the chain in 1937; their sons run it, adhering to Mom's wishes by not stocking alcohol and closing on Sundays.

EXECUTIVES

Chairman: James E. (Jim) Ukrop, age 67
President and CEO: Robert S. (Bobby) Ukrop, age 57
VP and CFO: David J. Naquin
VP and General Counsel: Brian K. Jackson
VP, Operations: Robert S. (Bob) Kelley
VP, Sales and Marketing: Kevin Hade
Director of Human Resources: Jacquelin Aronson
Director of Information Technology: Chellam Manickam
Director, Technical Services: Pat Hadden

LOCATIONS

HQ: Ukrop's Super Markets, Inc.
600 Southlake Blvd., Richmond, VA 23236
Phone: 804-379-7300 **Fax:** 804-794-7557
Web: www.ukrops.com

COMPETITORS

7-Eleven
A&P
CVS
Farm Fresh
Food Lion
Harris Teeter
Kmart
Kroger
SAM'S CLUB
Wal-Mart
Winn-Dixie

HISTORICAL FINANCIALS

Company Type: Private

Income Statement			FYE: July 31	
	ESTIMATED REVENUE ($ mil.)	NET INCOME ($ mil.)	NET PROFIT MARGIN	EMPLOYEES
7/03	613	—	—	5,465
7/02	625	—	—	5,500
7/01	650	—	—	5,500
7/00	575	—	—	5,600
7/99	525	—	—	5,800
7/98	520	—	—	5,600
7/97	500	—	—	5,000
7/96	500	—	—	5,200
7/95	475	—	—	1,750
Annual Growth	3.2%	—	—	15.3%

Revenue History

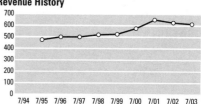

Underwriters Laboratories

Products that pass the muster of this company get the UL symbol of approval. Underwriters Laboratories (UL) is one of the world's leading providers of product safety and certification testing services, performing more than 100,000 product evaluations each year. Products that pass its stringent tests become registered with the company and can bear the UL Mark, which has become a widely trusted symbol for product safety and assurance. Nearly 20 billion products from 70,000 manufacturers bear the UL Mark. UL also offers commercial inspection and regulatory training services, as well as consumer safety advice. The not-for-profit organization was founded by William Merrill in 1894.

In addition to product testing, UL serves as a leader in helping set regulatory and industry standards, promoting conformity among companies and government agencies in setting safety and performance requirements. The company has been actively expanding its international operations and now has offices and affiliates in about two dozen countries serving customers in nearly 100 countries. It also represents US companies in gaining acceptance in foreign markets.

Along with overseas expansion, UL is streamlining its domestic operations in an effort to cut costs and reduce turnaround time on its testing services. As a result the company has cut many jobs at its US testing facilities with more job losses expected in the future.

UL is governed by a board of trustees elected by its corporate members (who are not manufacturers of products subject to UL coverage).

EXECUTIVES
Chairman: Fred R. Marcon
EVP; COO, International: Joe Bhatia
EVP Public Safety and External Affairs:
  Donald A. (Don) Mader
SVP and CFO: Michael Saltzman
SVP and CIO: Mark Sklenar
SVP and CTO: Ted V. Hall
SVP and COO, US and Canada: Gus Schaefer
SVP and Chief Administrative Officer: Ken Melnick
VP Engineering: Jim Beyreis
VP Human Resources: Howard Simon
VP Sales and Marketing: Sara Ulbrich
Media Relations Manager: Paul M. Baker
Acting General Counsel: Stephen Wenc

LOCATIONS
HQ: Underwriters Laboratories Inc.
  333 Pfingsten Rd., Northbrook, IL 60062
Phone: 847-272-8800   **Fax:** 847-272-8129
Web: www.ul.com

Underwriters Laboratories has offices and operations in Argentina, Brazil, Canada, Chile, China, Denmark, France, Germany, India, Italy, Japan, Malaysia, Mexico, the Netherlands, Norway, Portugal, Singapore, South Korea, Spain, Sweden, Switzerland, Taiwan, the UK, and the US.

PRODUCTS/OPERATIONS

Selected Services and Operations
Commercial inspection and testing
Product testing and certification
Training

Selected Product Certifications
Alarm systems
Audio and video equipment
Computers and information technology hardware
Drinking water
Electronic control equipment
Food
Heating, ventilating, and cooling systems
Home appliances
Industrial control equipment
Lasers
Medical equipment and services
Plumbing
Power generating equipment
Software
Telecommunications equipment

COMPETITORS
BSI Group
Bureau Veritas
Canadian Standards Association
Consumers Union
DNV
Exponent
Intertek
J.D. Power
Methode Electronics
National Technical Systems
NSTL
Quality Inspection Services
SGS
Silliker

HISTORICAL FINANCIALS
Company Type: Not-for-profit

Income Statement
FYE: December 31

	REVENUE ($ mil.)	NET INCOME ($ mil.)	NET PROFIT MARGIN	EMPLOYEES
12/03	607	(39)	—	6,023
12/02	553	—	—	5,900
12/01	513	—	—	6,000
12/00	475	—	—	5,938
12/99	425	—	—	5,500
12/98	375	—	—	5,258
12/97	352	—	—	4,200
12/96	320	—	—	4,000
12/95	300	—	—	3,900
12/94	281	—	—	3,900
Annual Growth	8.9%	—	—	4.9%

Revenue History
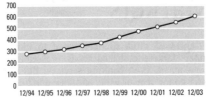

UNICCO Service

UNICCO Service Company isn't afraid to get its hands dirty. The company provides an array of janitorial and other facilities management services to 1,000 industrial, commercial, education, government, and retail clients in the US and Canada. UNICCO's long list of services includes HVAC maintenance, landscaping, lighting design and maintenance, engineering services, administrative support, and plant operation. UNICCO's staff has even been known to plow snow and serve as switchboard operators. Herb Kletjian founded the company in 1949. The Kletjian family (including chairman and CEO Steven Kletjian and vice chairmen Richard and Robert Kletjian) continues to own and operate UNICCO.

EXECUTIVES
Chairman and CEO: Steven C. Kletjian
Vice Chairman: Richard J. Kletjian
Vice Chairman and EVP: Louis J. Lanzillo Jr.
Vice Chairman and VP: Robert P. Kletjian
President and COO: George A. Keches
SVP Operations: John C. Feitor
VP and CFO: James E. (Jim) Lawlor
VP and General Counsel: Walter W. Crow
VP and General Manager, Operations and Business Development: Bruce L. Charboneau
VP Business Development: Michael F. Dunn
VP Business Development, Education: Randy Ledbetter
VP Human Resources: Victor A. Munger
VP Information Technology: Jeffery P. Peterson, age 44
VP Marketing: George R. Lohnes
Auditors: PricewaterhouseCoopers LLP

LOCATIONS
HQ: UNICCO Service Company
  275 Grove St., Newton, MA 02466
Phone: 617-527-5222   **Fax:** 617-969-2210
Web: www.unicco.com

UNICCO Service Company has offices in Boston; Chicago; Detroit; Hartford, Connecticut; Honolulu; Houston; Oklahoma City; Pine Brook, New Jersey; Pittsburgh; Vancouver, Washington; and Washington, DC, in the US and Calgary; Montreal; Ottawa; Toronto; and Vancouver, British Columbia, in Canada.

PRODUCTS/OPERATIONS

Selected Services
Administration
Cleaning
Engineering
Maintenance
Operations management
Route maintenance

COMPETITORS
ABM Industries
ARAMARK
Chemed
Colin Service
Davey Tree
Dwyer Group
Ecolab
Fluor
Healthcare Services
Johnson Controls
Onesource Facility Services
Rentokil Initial
Rollins
ServiceMaster
Sodexho
Swisher

Unified Western Grocers

HISTORICAL FINANCIALS
Company Type: Private

Income Statement
FYE: June 30

	REVENUE ($ mil.)	NET INCOME ($ mil.)	NET PROFIT MARGIN	EMPLOYEES
6/04	690	—	—	20,500
6/03	650	—	—	20,500
6/02	600	—	—	20,500
6/01	590	—	—	20,500
6/00	555	—	—	20,000
6/99	522	—	—	19,000
6/98	491	—	—	19,000
6/97	472	—	—	22,000
6/96	98	—	—	—
6/95	88	—	—	—
Annual Growth	25.7%	—	—	(1.0%)

Revenue History

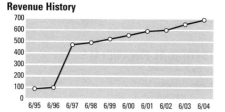

Unified Western Grocers guarantees that food and general merchandise reach mostly independent grocery stores in nine western states and several countries in the South Pacific. The food wholesaler and cooperative supplies a full line of groceries, as well as its own bakery and dairy goods. In addition to name-brand items, its offerings include private labels Better Buy, Cottage Hearth, and Western Family. The co-op also provides member support services such as store remodeling, financing, and insurance. The company was formed in 1999 when Certified Grocers of California merged with United Grocers of Oregon.

Consolidation and the trend toward self-distribution among food retailers has hurt wholesale grocery distributors. Certified Grocers and United Grocers merged to match the buying power afforded to large supermarket chains and wholesalers.

Unified helps independent grocers capture an increasing share of the Hispanic market in places like Los Angeles by supplying ethnic foods and targeted marketing campaigns to its member stores.

HISTORY

Certified Grocers of California evolved from a group of 15 independent Southern California grocers that formed a purchasing cooperative in 1922 to compete against large grocery chains. Certified Grocers of California incorporated in 1925 and issued stock to 50 members.

The co-op merged with a small retailer-owned wholesale company called Co-operative Grocers in 1928. It acquired Walker Brothers Grocery in 1929 and nearly tripled the previous year's sales. By 1938 the co-op had grown to 310 members and 380 stores, and sales passed $10 million.

Certified launched a line of private-label products under the Springfield name in 1947. In the early 1950s it added nonfood items and began processing its own private-label coffee and bean products. The co-op added delicatessen items in 1956. During the 1960s and 1970s, Certified added a meat center, a frozen food and deli warehouse, a produce distribution center, a creamery, a central bakery, and a specialty foods warehouse.

In 1989 the co-op opened several membership warehouse stores called Convenience Clubs. The Save Mart and Boys Markets chains left the fold in 1991. The co-op lost about 30% of its business during the next two years, including the Bel Air and Williams Bros. chains. After disappointing returns, in 1992 Certified sold its warehouse stores, cut staff, and consolidated warehouses.

CFO (and former Atlantic Richfield executive) Al Plamann was appointed CEO in 1994, succeeding Everett Dingwell. In 1996 the co-op began to convert its customers' older retail stores to Apple Markets in Southern California. Revenues began to dip in 1997 as the result of reduced purchases from some supermarkets and the sale the previous year of one of its subsidiaries, Hawaiian Grocery Stores.

Member chain Stumps converted to the Apple Markets banner in 1998. Faced with a declining customer base, in 1999 Certified merged with United Grocers of Oregon to form Unified Western Grocers.

Dr. R. Norton, F. L. Freeburg, and A. C. Brinckerhoff founded United Grocers of Oregon in 1915 as a way for grocers in Portland to cooperate in purchasing merchandise. By the next year the co-op had 35 members. In the 1950s United formed a trucking department and established a general merchandise division. It also grew rapidly in the 1950s through acquisitions, buying Northwest Grocery Company and the Fridegar Grocery Company. In 1963 United formed its frozen food department when it purchased Raven Creamery.

By 1975 the company's Northwest Grocery Company subsidiary had 14 Cash and Carry warehouses that sold goods to small grocers and restaurants. In 1995 United bought California food distributor Market Wholesale. Three years later the company sold its Cash and Carry warehouse-style stores to Smart & Final.

Upon completion of the merger in 1999, Certified's president and CEO, Plamann, was named to head the new organization. Soon after, Unified consolidated warehouse operations, eliminated duplicate personnel, and combined its private labels. Also in 1999 the company acquired California-based Gourmet Specialties.

The next year it bought the specialty foods business of J. Sosnick and Son, another California company, and Central Sales of Washington State. The company attributed net losses during 2001 to delays in moving the source for northern California specialty merchandise from southern to northern California and to the costs of entering the Washington marketplace, among other factors.

In 2002 Unified closed seven retail stores in Northern California and Oregon (under the Apple Markets and SavMax Foods banners) that accounted for sales of about $140 million as part of its plan to reduce debt and focus on wholesaling.

In 2003 the co-op sold or closed all 12 of its company-owned SavMax Foods stores as part of its plan to exit its unprofitable retail business and focus on its wholesale division (99% of total sales).

EXECUTIVES

President and CEO: Alfred A. (Al) Plamann, age 61, $942,555 pay
EVP, Finance and Administration and CFO: Richard J. Martin, age 58, $403,077 pay
EVP, General Counsel, and Secretary: Robert M. Ling Jr., age 46, $446,154 pay
EVP and Chief Marketing and Procurement Officer: Philip S. Smith, age 53, $312,115 pay
SVP, Distribution: Rodney L. VanBebber, age 48
SVP, Retail Support Services; President, SavMax Foods: Daniel J. Murphy, age 57, $291,462 pay
VP, Human Resources: Don Gilpin
VP, Insurance: Joseph A. Ney, age 55
VP and CIO: Gary S. Herman
VP and Controller: William O. Cotè, age 46
VP and Treasurer: Christine Neal
President, Pacific Northwest: Dirk T. Davis
President, Southern California: Luis de la Mata
Director, Distribution Systems and Web Development: Greg Vick
Auditors: Deloitte & Touche LLP

LOCATIONS

HQ: Unified Western Grocers, Inc.
5200 Sheila St., Commerce, CA 90040
Phone: 323-264-5200   **Fax:** 323-265-4006
Web: www.uwgrocers.com

PRODUCTS/OPERATIONS

Selected Co-op Members
Alamo Market
Andronico's Markets
Bales For Food
Berberian Enterprises, Inc.
Bristol Farms Markets, Inc.
Estacada Foods, Inc.
Evergreen Markets, Inc.
Gelson's Markets
Goodwin & Sons, Inc.
Howard's On Scholls
Joe Notrica, Inc.
K. V. Mart Co.
Mar-Val Food Stores, Inc.
Mollie Stone's Markets
Pioneer Super Save, Inc.
Pokerville Select Market
Pro & Son's, Inc.
Sentry Market
Stump's Market, Inc.
Super A Foods, Inc.
Super Center Concepts, Inc.
Sweet Home Thriftway
Tresierras Bros. Corp.
Wright's Foodliner

Selected Support Services
Financing
Information technology
Insurance
Private labels
Real estate development
Store design
Transportation

COMPETITORS

Associated Food
Associated Grocers
Nash Finch
Shurfine International
SUPERVALU
Wal-Mart
WinCo Foods

HISTORICAL FINANCIALS
Company Type: Cooperative

Income Statement			FYE: Saturday nearest September 30	
	REVENUE ($ mil.)	NET INCOME ($ mil.)	NET PROFIT MARGIN	EMPLOYEES
9/03	2,819	5	0.2%	3,000
9/02	2,793	(45)	—	3,600
9/01	2,930	(14)	—	4,200
9/00	3,067	(11)	—	4,000
9/99	1,894	3	0.1%	3,945
9/98	1,832	3	0.2%	2,200
9/97	1,927	2	0.1%	2,400
9/96	1,949	2	0.1%	2,400
9/95	1,823	1	0.0%	2,470
9/94	1,874	(2)	—	2,600
Annual Growth	4.6%	—	—	1.6%

2003 Year-End Financials
Debt ratio: 227.7%
Return on equity: 5.0%
Cash ($ mil.): 17
Current ratio: 1.40
Long-term debt ($ mil.): 232

Net Income History

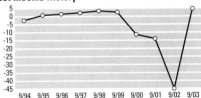

UniGroup

Moving household goods has made many of UniGroup's companies household names. The moving services company transports household goods and other items in more than 100 countries through subsidiaries United Van Lines and Mayflower Transit. Its Total Transportation Services unit sells and leases trucks and trailers and provides moving supplies, and its Vanliner Group offers insurance to movers. Subsidiary UniGroup Worldwide offers relocation management and assistance, and Insite Logistics provides third-party logistics services. Founded in 1987, UniGroup is owned by a 250-person group that includes agents of United Van Lines and Mayflower Transit and company managers.

EXECUTIVES
Chairman and CEO; Chairman, United Van Lines: Gerald P. (Gerry) Stadler
President and COO; COO, United Van Lines: Richard H. (Rich) McClure
CFO: James G. (Jim) Powers
EVP Sales and Marketing: Brian Paluch
VP and Assistant to the President: George Mitsch
CIO: Randall C. (Randy) Poppell
President and CEO, United Van Lines: Patrick (Pat) Larch
President, UniGroup Worldwide: Michael Kranisky
President, Vanliner Group: John Temporiti
Director, Human Resources: Sherry Fagin
Household Goods Central Regional Sales Manager, General Counsel: Jan R. Alonzo
Senior Publications and Public Relations Specialist: Jennifer Bonham

LOCATIONS
HQ: UniGroup, Inc.
1 Premier Dr., Fenton, MO 63026
Phone: 636-326-3100   **Fax:** 636-326-1106
Web: www.unigroupinc.com

COMPETITORS
AMERCO
Atlas World Group
Bekins
Budget
Graebel
Nelson Westerberg
SIRVA

HISTORICAL FINANCIALS
Company Type: Private

Income Statement			FYE: December 31	
	REVENUE ($ mil.)	NET INCOME ($ mil.)	NET PROFIT MARGIN	EMPLOYEES
12/03	1,809	—	—	1,836
12/02	1,708	—	—	1,335
12/01	1,896	—	—	1,400
12/00	2,009	—	—	1,871
12/99	1,878	—	—	1,800
12/98	1,800	—	—	1,600
12/97	1,749	—	—	1,650
12/96	1,626	—	—	1,600
12/95	1,406	—	—	1,000
12/94	995	—	—	950
Annual Growth	6.9%	—	—	7.6%

Revenue History

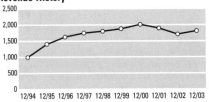

Unimin

Mining company Unimin Corporation produces industrial minerals and provides global transportation services. The company produces aggregates including silica sands, ball clay, bentonite clay, kaolin, dolomite, calcium carbonate, feldspar, and talc. Unimin supplies mineral products to a broad range of industries such as the glass, fiberglass, ceramic, semiconductor, quartz lighting, paint and coatings, fiber-optics, foundry, and oil and gas industries. Unimin has operations in the Americas, Scandinavia, and Australia. The company was founded in 1970.

EXECUTIVES
President: Kevin F. Crawford
EVP: Thomas M. Kilroy Jr.
SVP: Joseph C. Shapiro
VP: H. Frederick Barnard III
VP: Dick Benck
VP: Andrew Bradley
VP: Thomas Hiscox
VP: Craig Johnson
VP: Andrew Kachele

LOCATIONS
HQ: Unimin Corporation
258 Elm St., New Canaan, CT 06840
Phone: 203-966-8880   **Fax:** 203-966-3453
Web: www.unimin.com

PRODUCTS/OPERATIONS
Selected Products
Ball clay
Barium sulfate
Bentonite clay
Calcium carbonate
Dolomite
Feldspar
High-purity quartz
Kaolin
Magnetite
Microcrystalline silica
Nepheline syenite
Olivine
Silica sand
Talc

COMPETITORS
Better Minerals & Aggregates
Lafarge North America
Oglebay Norton

HISTORICAL FINANCIALS
Company Type: Private

Income Statement			FYE: December 31	
	ESTIMATED REVENUE ($ mil.)	NET INCOME ($ mil.)	NET PROFIT MARGIN	EMPLOYEES
12/02	550	—	—	4,000

Union Central Life Insurance

Next stop for insurance, Union Central. Union Central Life Insurance Company is a mutual life insurer operating throughout the US. The company offers a range of individual life and disability insurance, investment products, annuities, and group retirement plans. (Union Central Life in 2003 sold most of its other group products to OneAmerica's American United Life Insurance.) Union Central Life Insurance also offers employee and executive benefit planning, estate planning, and retirement planning. The company was founded in 1867.

EXECUTIVES
Chairman, President, and CEO: John H. Jacobs
EVP, Individual Insurance and Annuities: Gary T. Huffman
EVP, General Counsel, and Secretary: David F. Westerbeck
SVP and Chief Investment Officer; President, Summit Investment Partners: Steven R. Sutermeister
SVP and Corporate Actuary: Dale D. Johnson
SVP and Corporate Compliance Officer; President, Carillon Investments: Elizabeth G. Monsell
SVP: Lisa A. Mullen
SVP: Steven J. Valerius
VP, Human Resources: Stephen K. Johnston
Auditors: Ernst & Young LLP

LOCATIONS

HQ: The Union Central Life Insurance Company
1876 Waycross Rd., Cincinnati, OH 45240
Phone: 513-595-2200 **Fax:** 513-595-5418
Web: www.unioncentral.com

PRODUCTS/OPERATIONS

2003 Sales

	% of total
Net investment income	48
Insurance revenue	40
Net realized gain on investments	6
Other	6
Total	**100**

Selected Subsidiaries and Affiliates
Carillon Investments, Inc.
Payday of America
PRB Administrators, Inc.
Summit Investment Partners

COMPETITORS

AIG American General	Midland National Life
Allstate	New York Life
American National Insurance	Northwestern Mutual
Citigroup	Ohio National Financial Services
FBL Financial	Penn Mutual
John Hancock Financial Services	Principal Financial
Kansas City Life	Protective Life
MassMutual	Prudential
MetLife	Utica Mutual

HISTORICAL FINANCIALS
Company Type: Mutual company

Income Statement — FYE: December 31

	ASSETS ($ mil.)	NET INCOME ($ mil.)	INCOME AS % OF ASSETS	EMPLOYEES
12/03	6,864	33	0.5%	1,100
12/02	6,411	(26)	—	900
12/01	6,119	0	0.0%	900
12/00	5,507	35	0.6%	800
12/99	5,604	19	0.3%	800
12/98	5,088	31	0.6%	800
12/97	4,784	51	1.1%	755
12/96	4,430	39	0.9%	743
12/95	4,091	24	0.6%	750
12/94	3,780	21	0.5%	870
Annual Growth	6.9%	5.3%	—	2.6%

2003 Year-End Financials
Equity as % of assets: 8.9%
Return on assets: 0.5%
Return on equity: 5.5%
Long-term debt ($ mil.): 4,169
Sales ($ mil.): 529

Net Income History

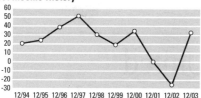

Unisource

Unisource Worldwide has the continent covered in paper, plastic, and packaging. One of the largest distributors of paper products (including Xerox), packaging materials, and maintenance supplies in North America, Unisource distributes printing and imaging products for paper-intensive businesses such as publishers, retail copy centers, and government agencies. The company distributes cleaning supplies (cleaning equipment, trash bags) and packaging systems (pallet systems, shrink packaging systems) to commercial and industrial customers. Bain Capital holds a 60% stake in Unisource; the company remains 40%-owned by Georgia-Pacific.

Other operations include running about 50 Paper Plus retail stores (paper, packaging materials, facility supplies); offering paper order management services (through its Websource division); and converting paper to forms and direct mail products (through its Rollsource division).

Unisource operates about 100 distribution centers in North America. The company's 2003 acquisition of paper broker Graphic Communications further expands Unisource's share of the US paper brokerage market.

EXECUTIVES
CEO: Allan Dragone, age 48
VP and CFO: Matthew Tyser
VP Corporate Diversity: Don Roberts
President, Packaging and Supply Systems: Thomas Pitera
President, Paper: Newell E. Holt, age 57
President, Supply Chain: Tom Shortt
President, Unisource Canada: Yves Montmarquette
Director, Corporate Communications: Michelle Wagner
Director, Talent Acquisition: Amy Ivers
General Counsel and Secretary: Zygmunt Jablonski
Auditors: Ernst & Young LLP

LOCATIONS
HQ: Unisource Worldwide, Inc.
6600 Governors Lake Pkwy., Norcross, GA 30071
Phone: 770-447-9000 **Fax:** 770-734-2000
Web: www.unisourcelink.com

Unisource operates about 50 Paper Plus retail stores and about 100 distribution centers in Canada and the US.

PRODUCTS/OPERATIONS
Selected Products
Envelopes, computer paper, and specialty paper
  Computer paper (blank and proprietary grades)
  Envelopes (mailing, shipping, commercial)
  Specialty products (engineering rolls, labels)
Facility supplies and equipment
  Production supplies (degreasers, work wear)
  Sanitary supplies and equipment (can liners, matting systems)
Packaging
  Case erecting, packaging, and sealing systems (case packers, gummed tapes)
  Case and pallet coding systems (ink jet printers, label materials)
  Packaging Supplies (foam and bubble sheeting)
  Pallet unitization systems (conveyers, stretch films)
  Shrink packaging, bundling, bagging, and overwrapping systems
Printing papers
  Coated and uncoated sheet-fed papers
  Premium text, cover, and writing papers
  Uncoated and coated web papers

Specialty businesses
  Paper Plus (smaller orders of paper, packaging, and supplies)
  Rollsource (paper conversion to forms, direct mail)
  Websource (large web paper orders)

COMPETITORS

Boise Cascade	Katy Industries
Cascades Inc.	Menasha
Central National-Gottesman	Midland Paper
	Nashua
Domtar	Ris Paper
Ecolab	West Coast Paper
International Paper	

HISTORICAL FINANCIALS
Company Type: Private

Income Statement — FYE: Saturday nearest December 31

	REVENUE ($ mil.)	NET INCOME ($ mil.)	NET PROFIT MARGIN	EMPLOYEES
12/02	4,755	—	—	10,000
12/01	6,200	—	—	—
12/00	6,900	—	—	—
12/99*	7,000	—	—	—
9/98	7,417	—	—	13,400
9/97	7,108	—	—	14,200
9/96	7,023	—	—	11,800
9/95	6,987	—	—	11,800
9/94	5,757	—	—	11,200
9/93	4,864	—	—	11,800
Annual Growth	(0.3%)	—	—	(1.8%)

*Fiscal year change

Revenue History

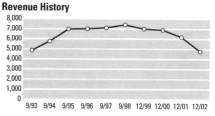

United Industries

Items that usually shouldn't go together (bug killers and pet food) coexist harmoniously within the operations of United Industries. The company's Spectrum Brands unit makes insecticides, insect repellents, lawn and garden pesticides, herbicides, and fertilizers. United Pet Group, acquired in August 2004 for about $360 million, makes pet food and supplies. The Home Depot, Lowe's, and Kmart account for more than 70% of sales. Founded in 1969 as a bolt maker, United acquired Unilever's Chesebrough-Ponds in 1988 and Nu-Gro, a leading Canadian lawn and garden company, in April 2004. The Thomas H. Lee Equity Fund IV owns about 92% of United.

United Industries' products are sold in the US, Canada, and the Caribbean.

In 2002 United Industries bought the Schultz Company (maker of garden fertilizers, potting soils, and plant foods) and WPC Brands (an insect repellent and safety kit maker). United Pet Group has been folded into the company's new pet division.

EXECUTIVES

Chairman, President, and CEO: Robert L. (Bob) Caulk, age 52, $753,375 pay
EVP, CFO, and Director: Daniel J. Johnston, age 45, $469,200 pay
SVP, Business Development: Steven D. Schultz, age 56, $400,945 pay
SVP, Marketing: Kent J. Davies, age 40, $284,316 pay
SVP, Operations: John F. Timony, age 53, $312,228 pay
VP, Corporate Development: Robert S. Rubin, age 37, $306,383 pay
VP, Human Resources: Rick K. Spurlock, age 43
VP, Secretary, and General Counsel: Louis N. Laderman, age 52
Auditors: PricewaterhouseCoopers LLP

LOCATIONS

HQ: United Industries Corporation
2150 Schuetz Rd., St. Louis, MO 63146
Phone: 314-427-0780   **Fax:** 314-253-5978
Web: www.spectrumbrands.com

United Industries has manufacturing plants in Cincinnati and Orrville, Ohio; Sylacauga, Alabama; and Bridgeton and Vinita Park, Missouri. It has distribution centers in Allentown, Pennsylvania; Bridgeton, Missouri; Gainesville, Georgia; Ontario, California; Orrville, Ohio; and Sylacauga, Alabama. It has warehouses in Vinita Park. It has storage facilities in Bridgeton and Vinita Park, Missouri, and Homesville, Ohio.

PRODUCTS/OPERATIONS

2003 Sales

	% of total
Lawn & garden	73
Household	25
Contract	2
Total	**100**

Selected Brands
Aquarium Systems
Atwater Carey (first aid kits)
Cutter (insect repellant)
Dingo
Eight In one
Expert Gardener (fertilizers and controls)
Garden Safe (natural plant care products)
Hot Shot (household insect control)
Jungle Talk
Lazy Pet
Marineland
Multi Cote (plant foods)
Nature's Miracle
No-Pest (household insect control)
Perfecto
Peters (lawn and garden fertilizers)
Potable Aqua (water purification tablets)
Real-Kill (household insect control)
Repel (insect repellent)
Schultz (plant foods and potting soils)
Spectracide (outdoor insecticides and herbicides)
Spectracide Terminate (termite control)
Sting-Eze (insect bite relief sticks)
Vigoro (lawn and garden fertilizers)

COMPETITORS

Bayer
Central Garden & Pet
Del Monte Foods
Doane Pet Care
Hill's Pet Nutrition
Mars
Nutro Products
Procter & Gamble
Royal Canin
S.C. Johnson
Scotts

HISTORICAL FINANCIALS
Company Type: Private

Income Statement FYE: December 31

	REVENUE ($ mil.)	NET INCOME ($ mil.)	NET PROFIT MARGIN	EMPLOYEES
12/03	536	116	21.5%	900
12/02	480	25	5.3%	725
12/01	273	7	2.5%	800
12/00	266	1	0.5%	800
12/99	285	(12)	—	800
12/98	283	47	16.5%	800
Annual Growth	13.7%	19.9%	—	2.4%

2003 Year-End Financials
Debt ratio: 2,581.0%   Current ratio: 2.17
Return on equity: —   Long-term debt ($ mil.): 391
Cash ($ mil.): 11

Net Income History

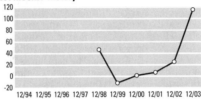

United Space Alliance

USA! United Space Alliance (USA) is a space-race heavyweight (each of the Space Shuttles — Discovery, Atlantis, and Endeavour — weighs 173,000 pounds). A joint venture between Lockheed Martin and Boeing, USA was established in 1996 to consolidate NASA's various Space Shuttle contracts under a single entity. As prime contractor, the company is involved in astronaut and flight controller training, flight software development, Shuttle payload integration, and vehicle processing, launch, and recovery operations. USA also provides training and operations planning for the International Space Station. Its main operations are at the Johnson Space Center (Texas) and Kennedy Space Center (Florida).

As goes the Shuttle program, so goes United Space Alliance. In light of the Columbia disaster of 2003, Shuttle launches will be curtailed for the foreseeable future; at worst, the second disaster in 113 launches (a 1.8% failure rate) could lead to the end of the program as many wonder if it's too costly — in both human and financial terms — to continue. If the current Shuttle program ends, its work will likely be taken up by unmanned rockets, which cost a tiny fraction of a Shuttle launch and risk no lives, and by a next-generation reusable shuttle, which would take advantage of more advanced materials and technologies than do the Shuttles, which were designed in the 1970s.

EXECUTIVES

President and CEO: Michael J. (Mike) McCulley
COO: Brewster Shaw
CFO: Bill Caple
CIO: Kathy Tamer
VP and Program Manager, Space Flight Operations: Howard DeCastro
Space Station Program Manager: James F. Buchli
Director of Security: Ed Wilson

LOCATIONS

HQ: United Space Alliance
600 Gemini St., Houston, TX 77058
Phone: 281-212-6000   **Fax:** 281-212-6177
Web: www.unitedspacealliance.com

United Space Alliance has operations in Alabama, California, Florida (Kennedy Space Center), Texas (Johnson Space Center), and Washington, DC.

PRODUCTS/OPERATIONS

Selected Operations
Astronaut and Flight Controller Training
Flight Operations
Integrated Logistics
Mission Design and Planning
Payload Integration
Software Development and Integration
Vehicle Processing, Launch and Recovery

COMPETITORS

Arianespace
BAE SYSTEMS
EADS
Honeywell Aerospace
Northrop Grumman
Raytheon

HISTORICAL FINANCIALS
Company Type: Joint venture

Income Statement FYE: December 31

	REVENUE ($ mil.)	NET INCOME ($ mil.)	NET PROFIT MARGIN	EMPLOYEES
12/03	1,700	—	—	10,000
12/02	1,690	—	—	10,000
12/01	1,800	—	—	10,000
Annual Growth	(2.8%)	—	—	0.0%

Revenue History

United Supermarkets

From Muleshoe up to Dalhart and on over to Pampa, United Supermarkets keeps the Texas Panhandle well fed. The grocer has about 45 supermarkets, mostly in rural towns. Its stores feature deli, floral, and bakery shops, as well as groceries, pharmacies, and gas at some locales. The company's larger format, Market Street, stocks more specialty foods. United Supermarkets runs its own distribution facility. H. D. Snell founded the firm in Sayre, Oklahoma, in 1916 as United Cash Store. He bucked the norms of the day — when grocers sold on credit — by selling for cash at lower prices. United Supermarkets is owned and run by the Snell family. (President Gantt Bumstead is the great-great-grandson of the founder.)

EXECUTIVES
SVP and CEO: L. Kent Moore
President: Gantt Bumstead
VP and COO: Bert Short
VP and CFO: Keith Mann
VP and CIO: Scott Gilmour
Chief Marketing Officer: Dan Sanders
VP, Center Store: Wes Jackson
VP, Customer and Community Service: Matt Bumstead
VP, Human Resources: Phil Pirkle
VP, Logistics: Kyle Gayler
VP, Perishables: Gerald Critz
Controller: SuzAnn Kirby

LOCATIONS
HQ: United Supermarkets, Ltd.
7830 Orlando Ave., Lubbock, TX 79423
Phone: 806-791-0220   **Fax:** 806-791-7491
Web: www.unitedtexas.com/myunited

PRODUCTS/OPERATIONS
Retail Operations
Market Street
United Supermarkets
United Supermercado

COMPETITORS
Albertson's
H-E-B
Homeland Stores
IGA
Kroger
Minyard Food Stores
Randall's
Wal-Mart

HISTORICAL FINANCIALS
Company Type: Private

Income Statement   FYE: January 31

	ESTIMATED REVENUE ($ mil.)	NET INCOME ($ mil.)	NET PROFIT MARGIN	EMPLOYEES
1/04	900	—	—	7,000
1/03	700	—	—	7,000
1/02	600	—	—	5,000
1/01	575	—	—	5,000
1/00	570	—	—	4,500
1/99	560	—	—	4,000
1/98	520	—	—	4,000
1/97	450	—	—	4,000
1/96	400	—	—	3,300
1/95	350	—	—	3,000
Annual Growth	11.1%	—	—	9.9%

Revenue History

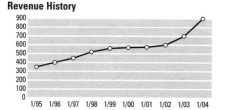

United Way

United Way of America (UWA) has been described as a mutual fund for charitable causes, and with thousands of agencies receiving financial support from UWA's 1,400 local organizations, the epithet seems fitting. The not-for-profit organization focuses on health and human services causes. Its local organizations help to fund a multitude of endeavors, including the American Cancer Society, Big Brothers/Big Sisters, Catholic Charities, Girl Scouts and Boy Scouts, and The Salvation Army. In 2002-2003, UWA raised about $4.4 billion (some 50% from employee contributions and about 23% from corporations). Its administrative expenses average 13% of funds raised.

Each of the local organizations is an independent entity governed by local volunteers, and UWA acts as a national services and training center, supporting the local organizations with services such as national advertising and research. To advance the understanding of its role, UWA has launched an initiative to raise awareness of how it serves local communities.

HISTORY

The first modern Community Chest was created in 1913, laying the foundation for the practice of allocating funds among multiple causes. Five years later, representatives from 12 fundraising organizations met in Chicago and established the American Association for Community Organizations, the predecessor of the present-day United Way. By 1929 more than 350 Community Chests had been established.

Payroll deductions for charitable contributions debuted in 1943. In 1946 the United Way's predecessor organization initiated a cooperative relationship with the American Federation of Labor and the Congress of Industrial Organizations (which merged to become the AFL-CIO in 1955); the two groups agreed to provide services to members of organized labor. (The relationship continues today, with the organizations collaborating on projects such as recruiting members of organized labor to lead health and human services organizations.)

The Uniform Federal Fund-Raising Program was created by order of President Dwight Eisenhower in 1957, enabling federal employees to contribute to charities of their choice. (The program later evolved into the Combined Federal Campaign.) Six years later Los Angeles became the first city to adopt the United Way name when more than 30 local Community Chests and United Fund organizations merged. The national organization, which had been operating under the United Community Funds and Councils (UCFCA) name, adopted the United Way of America (UWA) name in 1970. It established its headquarters in Alexandria, Virginia, the next year.

Congress made its first grant for emergency food and shelter to the private sector in 1983, and UWA was selected as its fiscal agent. UWA created its Emergency Food and Shelter National Board Program the same year. In 1984 UWA created the Alexis de Tocqueville Society to solicit larger donations from individuals (it attracted such members as Bill Gates and Walter Annenberg).

In 1992 William Aramony, UWA's president for more than two decades, resigned after coming under fire for his lavish expenditures. Former Peace Corps head Elaine Chao was tapped to replace him, and in 1995 Aramony was sentenced to seven years in prison for defrauding the organization of about $600,000. Former UWA CFO Thomas Merlo and Stephen Paulachak (former president of a UWA spinoff) were convicted on related charges. After four years spent burnishing UWA's tarnished image, Chao resigned in 1996 and was succeeded the next year by Betty Beene, who had headed UWA operations in Houston and New York City's Tri-State area.

In an effort to stress the manner in which its local organizations benefit their communities, UWA launched a brand-initiative campaign in 1998. The following year UWA's local organization in Santa Clara, California, found itself in serious financial straits when donations began slipping despite its location in the wealthy Silicon Valley. Infoseek (now Walt Disney Internet Group's GO.com) founder Steve Kirsch and Microsoft founder Gates chipped in $1 million and $5 million, respectively, to help keep the organization afloat.

Beene, who drew the ire of some chapters for suggesting a national pledge-processing center and national standards, stepped down in January 2001. That same year UWA began funneling more funds into smaller community projects instead of national charities. In 2002 Brian Gallagher took over as president and CEO.

EXECUTIVES
Chairman, Board of Trustees: Johnnetta B. Cole
President and CEO: Brian A. Gallagher
CFO: Edward J. Christie Jr.
CIO: Michael Schreiber
VP Field and Media Communications: David Albritton
Controller: W. Vernon McHargue Jr.
Director Public Relations: Philip Jones
Legal Counsel: Patti Turner
Human Resources: Evelyn Amador

LOCATIONS
HQ: United Way of America
701 N. Fairfax St., Alexandria, VA 22314
Phone: 703-836-7112   **Fax:** 703-683-7840
Web: national.unitedway.org

United Way of America has 1,400 local organizations across the US.

HISTORICAL FINANCIALS
Company Type: Not-for-profit

Income Statement   FYE: December 31

	REVENUE ($ mil.)	NET INCOME ($ mil.)	NET PROFIT MARGIN	EMPLOYEES
12/03	35	—	—	—
12/02	42	—	—	15,166
12/01	52	—	—	8,500
12/00	41	—	—	—
12/99	92	—	—	—
Annual Growth	(21.5%)	—	—	78.4%

Revenue History

University of California

The University of California (UC) system has approximately 200,000 students at its nine campuses (which include three law schools and five medical schools) located in Berkeley, Davis, Irvine, Los Angeles (UCLA), Riverside, San Diego, San Francisco, Santa Barbara, and Santa Cruz. The schools offer areas of study in more than 150 disciplines ranging from the arts to bioengineering. The university's 10th campus, UC Merced, is scheduled to open in the fall of 2005. UC also operates three US Department of Energy research labs in California and New Mexico.

In the wake of the 1996 approval of California's Proposition 209, which eliminated state affirmative-action programs, enrollment of minorities and the hiring of female faculty both dropped in the UC system. To help restore minority admissions to pre-Prop 209 levels, UC guarantees admission to the top 4% of students at each California high school and operates outreach programs aimed at low-income students.

More than 14% of California high school students were meeting UC's minimum eligibility requirements, a rate higher than the state guideline requiring the school to draw from only the top 12.5%. In 2004 the school agreed to raise the grade point level for students beginning in 2007 in order to shrink its applicants to meet the state guideline. Opponents to the plan argued that the higher standards would unfairly reduce the enrollment of minority and disadvantaged students.

HISTORY

The founders of California's government provided for a state university via a clause in the state's constitution in 1849. The origins of the College of California, opened in Oakland in 1869, date back to the Contra Costa Academy, a small school established by Yale alumnus Henry Durant in 1853. Durant ran Contra Costa, and then the college, until 1872. Women were allowed to enter the school in 1870. The college moved to Berkeley and graduated its first class (12 men) in 1873.

As California's economy and population grew, so did its university system. Renamed University of California (UC) in 1879, it had 1,000 students by 1895. Agriculture, mining, geology, and engineering were among its first fields. A second campus was established at Davis in 1905, followed by campuses in San Diego (1912) and Los Angeles (1919).

The Depression brought cutbacks in funding for UC, but the system rebounded in the 1940s. It opened its fifth campus (Santa Barbara) in 1944, and during WWII it also began gaining recognition for research. Between 1945 and 1965 enrollment quadrupled, spurred by GI Bill-sponsored veterans and a population shift to the West. The state legislature formulated the Master Plan for Higher Education in 1960, which reorganized university administration and established admission requirements. Campuses were established at Irvine and Santa Cruz in 1965.

The first of several important demonstrations in the 1960s at UC Berkeley came in 1964 over the university's attempts to ban political activity on a strip of UC-owned land. The People's Park riot of 1969, touched off when UC tried to close a parcel of land in Berkeley that students had turned into a kind of playground for the counterculture, left one dead and more than 50 wounded.

Aware of the changing demographics of its student body, especially its growing Asian enrollment (28% in 1990), UC Berkeley gave the chancellor's job to Chang-Lin Tien in 1990 — the first person of Asian descent to hold that position at a major US university (Tien served as chancellor until 1997). A California recession in the early 1990s resulted in budget cuts for UC. Strapped for cash, the university launched a for-profit entity in 1992 to tap its extensive library of patents.

UC San Diego chancellor Richard Atkinson succeeded Jack Peltason as UC president in 1995, the same year the UC Board of Regents approved a new campus — the university's 10th — in the San Joaquin Valley. That year it voted to phase out race- and sex-based affirmative action. The board, in an effort to be competitive with other top universities in recruiting faculty, voted to offer health benefits to the partners of gay employees in 1997. Also that year UC created the California Digital Library and began putting its library collection online.

Entrepreneur Alfred Mann donated $100 million to UCLA in 1998 for biomedical research. Also that year admissions of non-Asian-American minorities to the fall freshman classes of UCLA and UC Berkeley fell sharply. The following year the UC system began guaranteeing admission to the top 4% of students in each of the state's high schools. UC took some heat in 1999 and 2000 for two separate instances of security breaches at the Los Alamos National Laboratory.

Robert Dynes, previously chancellor of UC San Diego, became president of the UC system in October 2003.

EXECUTIVES

Chairman: John J. Moores, age 60
President: Robert C. Dynes, $395,000 pay
SVP, Academic Affairs and Provost: M.R.C. (Marci) Greenwood, age 61
SVP, Business and Finance: Joseph P. Mullinix
SVP, University Affairs: Bruce B. Darling
Treasurer and VP, Investments: David H. Russ
VP, Agriculture and Natural Resources: W. R. (Reg) Gomes
VP, Budget: Lawrence C. (Larry) Hershman
VP, Clinical Services Development: William H. Gurtner
VP, Educational Outreach: Winston D. Doby
VP, Financial Management: Anne C. Broome
VP, Health Affairs: Michael V. Drake
VP Laboratory Management: S. Robert Foley
Secretary: Patricia L. (Leigh) Trivette
General Counsel: James E. Holst
Associate VP, Human Resources & Benefits: Judith Boyette
Auditors: PricewaterhouseCoopers LLP

LOCATIONS

HQ: University of California
1111 Franklin St., Oakland, CA 94607
Phone: 510-987-0700 **Fax:** 510-987-0894
Web: www.universityofcalifornia.edu

Campuses

UC Berkeley
UC Davis
UC Irvine
UC Los Angeles (UCLA)
UC Riverside
UC San Diego
UC San Francisco
UC Santa Barbara
UC Santa Cruz

PRODUCTS/OPERATIONS

Department of Energy Laboratories
Ernest Orlando Lawrence Berkeley National Laboratory (Berkeley, CA)
Lawrence Livermore National Laboratory (Livermore, CA)
Los Alamos National Laboratory (New Mexico)

HISTORICAL FINANCIALS

Company Type: School

Income Statement				FYE: June 30
	REVENUE ($ mil.)	NET INCOME ($ mil.)	NET PROFIT MARGIN	EMPLOYEES
6/03	14,166	—	—	118,533
6/02	15,980	—	—	114,282
6/01	15,887	—	—	108,827
6/00	14,048	—	—	103,767
6/99	13,074	—	—	99,890
6/98	9,375	—	—	130,000
6/97	9,022	—	—	130,000
6/96	8,363	—	—	137,874
6/95	7,958	—	—	131,660
6/94	7,895	—	—	132,964
Annual Growth	6.7%	—	—	(1.3%)

University of Chicago

The University of Chicago ranks as one of the world's youngest and most-esteemed major universities. Its undergraduate branch, The College, offers a core curriculum based on the "Great Books." The school is associated with 75 Nobel Prize recipients including Enrico Fermi, Milton Friedman, and Saul Bellow. Undergraduates can major in more than 50 areas. Among the U of C's graduate programs are the University of Chicago Law School and Graduate School of Business, both of which are ranked in the top 10 by U.S. News & World Report. Founded in 1890 by John D. Rockefeller, the university has an endowment of about $3.5 billion. The U of C has 13,000 students and more than 2,100 faculty.

The University of Chicago has steadfastly stood its ground against trendiness in education curricula. All students take courses that expose them to the social, biological, and physical sciences, as well as humanities, mathematics, and language. Rare is the student who is not versed in Thucydides. While the university's list of those who graduated is impressive, the list of those who did not is equally prominent, including Oracle's Larry Ellison and author Kurt Vonnegut.

Students attending the U of C study primarily at its 200-acre main campus on the South Side of Chicago, but the university's Graduate

School of Business also maintains campuses in downtown Chicago; Barcelona, Spain; and Singapore. Among the many institutions affiliated with the U of C are the University of Chicago Medical Center, the Enrico Fermi Institute, the Argonne National Laboratory, and the Yerkes Observatory. The University of Chicago Press publishes 250-300 new titles each year, as well as more than 50 journals, and is the largest university press in the US.

HISTORY

The University of Chicago took its name from the first U of C, a small Baptist school that operated from 1858-1886. The school, incorporated in 1890, was born when William Rainey Harper, the man who was to become the University's first president, convinced Standard Oil's John D. Rockefeller to provide a founding gift of $600,000. Members of the American Baptist Education Society chipped in another $400,000, and department store owner Marshall Field donated the land for the campus.

The university opened in 1892 with a faculty of 103 and 594 students. As it grew, the university took over property that had been used in the Columbian Exposition of 1892-93, eventually surrounding the fair's former midway. (The school's football team later earned the nickname "Monsters of the Midway" while being coached by the legendary Amos Alonzo Stagg; this was before withdrawing from intercollegiate play in 1939.) Legend has it that the university retains the right to rejoin the Big Ten.

Only four years after its founding, the university's enrollment of 1,815 exceeded Harvard's. By 1907, 43% of its 5,000 students were women. Robert Maynard Hutchins, president from 1929 to 1951, revolutionized the university and American higher education by insisting on the study of original sources (the Great Books) and competency testing through comprehensive exams. He organized the college and graduate divisions into their present structure, reaffirming the role of the university as a place for intellectual exploration rather than vocational training. In 1942 the U of C ushered in the nuclear age when Enrico Fermi created the first controlled nuclear chain reaction in the school's abandoned football stadium.

From the 1950s through the 1970s, the university purchased and restored Frank Lloyd Wright's famed Robie House and built the Joseph Regenstein Library (1970). In 1978 Hanna Holborn Gray became the first woman to be named president of a major university. Gray abolished the decade-old Lascivious Costume Ball, a major social event (some would say the only social event) at the university. Hugo Sonnenschein succeeded Gray in 1993. The beginning of his tenure coincided with a period of financial difficulty for the school as increases in costs outpaced revenue growth. In 1996 Sonnenschein announced plans to boost enrollment by as much as 30% in order to invigorate the school's finances.

U of C graduate and former professor Myron Scholes shared the Nobel Prize in economics in 1997. The next year the school announced plans for a $35 million athletics center to be named after Gerald Ratner, a former student who donated $15 million toward construction of the facility. The university later signed an agreement to supply content to Internet distance-learning startup UNext.com, founded by trustee Andrew Rosenfeld. (This agreement was controversial within the university community.) Cardean University, UNext.com's online university, began operating in 2000.

Sonnenschein resigned in 2000 and was replaced by Don Randel, former provost of Cornell University. That year the University of Chicago Graduate School of Business opened a campus in Singapore, and U of C economist James Heckman was awarded the Nobel Prize for his work in microeconomics.

EXECUTIVES

Chairman: James S. Crown, age 50
President: Don Michael Randel, age 63
Provost: Richard P. Saller
VP and CIO: Gregory A. Jackson
VP and Chief Investment Officer: Philip Halpern
VP and Dean of Students in the University: Stephen P. Klass
VP and General Counsel: Beth A. Harris
VP Administration and CFO: Donald J. Reaves, age 55
VP Community and Government Affairs: Henry S. Webber
VP Development and Alumni Relations: Randy L. Holgate
VP Medical Affairs and Dean of BSD/Pritzker School of Medicine: James L. Madara
VP Research and Argonne National Laboratory: Thomas A. Rosenbaum
VP University Relations and Dean College Enrollment: Michael C. Behnke
Comptroller: William J. Hogan Jr.
Auditors: KPMG LLP

LOCATIONS

HQ: The University of Chicago
5801 S. Ellis Ave., Chicago, IL 60637
Phone: 773-702-1234 **Fax:** 773-702-4155
Web: www.uchicago.edu

The University of Chicago has campuses in the Hyde Park area of Chicago; downtown Chicago; Barcelona, Spain; and Singapore.

PRODUCTS/OPERATIONS

Selected Majors at The College (Undergraduate)
African and African American Studies
Ancient Studies
Art History
Biological Chemistry
Cinema and Media Studies
Classical Studies
Early Christian Literature
East Asian Languages and Civilization
English Language and Literature
Geography
Geophysical Sciences
Germanic Studies
History
History, Philosophy, and Social Sciences
International Studies
Jewish Studies
Latin American Studies
Medieval Studies
Music
Near Eastern Languages and Civilizations
Physics
Political Science
Psychology
Public Policy Studies
Religion and the Humanities
Romance Languages and Literatures
Russian Civilization
Sociology
South Asian Languages and Civilizations
South Asian Studies
Tutorial Studies
Visual Arts

Selected Affiliated Institutions
Argonne National Laboratory
Chapin Hall Center for Children and the Laboratory Schools
Enrico Fermi Institute
Oriental Institute

Selected Graduate Schools and Programs
Divinity School
Graduate School of Business
Harris Graduate School of Public Policy Studies
Law School
Pritzker School of Medicine
School of Social Service Administration

HISTORICAL FINANCIALS

Company Type: School

Income Statement FYE: June 30

	REVENUE ($ mil.)	NET INCOME ($ mil.)	NET PROFIT MARGIN	EMPLOYEES
6/03	1,699	—	—	12,623
6/02	1,650	—	—	12,460
6/01	1,617	—	—	12,000
6/00	1,639	—	—	11,900
6/99	848	—	—	11,900
6/98	892	—	—	12,869
6/97	1,377	—	—	12,000
6/96	1,395	—	—	12,000
6/95	1,313	—	—	10,954
6/94	1,217	—	—	11,400
Annual Growth	3.8%	—	—	1.1%

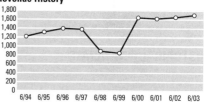

Revenue History

University of Florida

UF students know it's great to be a Florida Gator. Founded in 1853, the University of Florida (UF) is the state's oldest university and one of the largest in the country, with about 48,000 students. UF is a major land-grant research university encompassing 16 colleges offering more than 100 undergraduate majors and nearly 200 graduate programs, including law, dentistry, pharmacy, medicine, and veterinary medicine. It is also a member of the Association of American Universities, a confederation of the top research universities in North America. A founding member of the Southeastern Conference, UF's athletic teams (the Florida Gators) are typically ranked nationally.

EXECUTIVES

President: James B. (Bernie) Machen
SVP Health Affairs: Douglas J. Barrett
VP Development and Alumni Affairs: Paul A. Robell
VP Finance and Administration: John E. (Ed) Poppell
VP Public Relations: Gail F. Baker
VP Research: Winfred M. Phillips
VP and General Counsel: Pamela J. Bernard
VP Student Affairs: Patricia Telles-Irvin, age 48
Controller: Mike McKee
Director of Human Resources: Larry T. Ellis
Community Relations Coordinator:
  Florida Bridgewater-Alford

LOCATIONS

HQ: University of Florida
  226 Tigert Hall, Gainesville, FL 32611
Phone: 352-392-3261 **Fax:** 352-392-9506
Web: www.ufl.edu

PRODUCTS/OPERATIONS

Selected Colleges
College of Agricultural and Life Sciences
College of Dentistry
College of Design, Construction, and Planning
College of Education
College of Fine Arts
College of Health and Human Performance
College of Journalism and Communications
College of Liberal Arts and Sciences
College of Medicine
College of Nursing
College of Pharmacy
College of Public Health and Health Professions
College of Veterinary Medicine
Levin College of Law
Warrington College of Business Administration

HISTORICAL FINANCIALS

Company Type: School

Income Statement FYE: June 30

	REVENUE ($ mil.)	NET INCOME ($ mil.)	NET PROFIT MARGIN	EMPLOYEES
6/03	2,646	—	—	11,996
6/02	1,971	—	—	11,763
6/01	2,782	—	—	11,806
6/00	1,209	—	—	11,528
6/99	1,155	—	—	11,303
6/98	1,062	—	—	11,158
6/97	1,074	—	—	11,445
6/96	933	—	—	11,528
6/95	814	—	—	11,649
6/94	789	—	—	—
Annual Growth	14.4%	—	—	0.4%

Revenue History

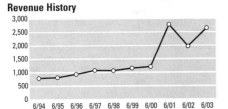

University of Illinois

The log cabins that used to dot the landscape in the Land of Lincoln have given way to the three campuses of the University of Illinois. Established as a land grant institution in 1867, the university has grown to include campuses in Chicago, Springfield, and Urbana-Champaign. Its 67,700 students (more than half of whom study at the Urbana-Champaign campus) can choose from academic fields such as business, fine arts, and medicine. The Urbana-Champaign campus is the site of the National Center for Supercomputing Applications (which developed Mosaic, the basis for popular Internet browsers such as Netscape Navigator); the university's Springfield campus houses the Institute for Public Affairs.

EXECUTIVES

President: James J. Stukel
Chancellor, Chicago Campus: Sylvia Manning
Chancellor, Springfield Campus: Richard D. Ringeisen
Provost and Interim Chancellor, Urbana-Champaign:
  Richard Herman
VP Administration: Steve Rugg
VP Academic Affairs: Chester S. Gardner
VP Economic Development and Corporate Relations:
  David L. Chicoine
Secretary: Michele M. Thompson
Executive Director, Governmental Relations:
  Richard M. Schoell
Executive Director, University Relations: Thomas Hardy
University Counsel: Thomas R. Bearrows
President, Alumni Association: Loren Taylor
President, University of Illinois Foundation:
  Sidney Micek
Auditors: BKD, LLP

LOCATIONS

HQ: University of Illinois
  Henry Administration Bldg., 506 S. Wright St.,
  Urbana, IL 61801
Phone: 217-333-1000 **Fax:** 217-244-2282
Web: www.uillinois.edu

The University of Illinois has campuses in Chicago, Springfield, and Urbana-Champaign, as well as health professions sites and continuing education centers throughout the state.

PRODUCTS/OPERATIONS

Selected Colleges and Instructional Units
College of Agricultural, Consumer and Environmental Sciences
College of Applied Life Studies
College of Commerce and Business Administration
College of Communications
College of Education
College of Engineering
College of Fine and Applied Arts
College of Law
College of Liberal Arts and Sciences
College of Medicine at Urbana-Champaign
College of Veterinary Medicine
Graduate College
Graduate School of Library and Information Science
Institute of Aviation
Institute of Labor and Industrial Relations
School of Social Work

HISTORICAL FINANCIALS

Company Type: School

Income Statement FYE: June 30

	REVENUE ($ mil.)	NET INCOME ($ mil.)	NET PROFIT MARGIN	EMPLOYEES
6/04	2,900	—	—	23,483
6/03	2,850	—	—	24,000
6/02	2,800	—	—	25,000
6/01	2,750	—	—	25,500
6/00	2,722	—	—	26,500
6/99	2,566	—	—	26,667
6/98	2,446	—	—	26,148
6/97	2,285	—	—	26,150
6/96	1,959	—	—	25,105
6/95	1,944	—	—	20,000
Annual Growth	4.5%	—	—	1.8%

Revenue History

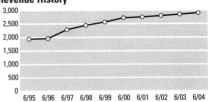

University of Iowa

The University of Iowa Hawkeyes see clearly from their perch as Iowa's largest university. Founded in 1847, the university has nearly 30,000 students (about two-thirds of which are Iowa residents) on its Iowa City campus. The university is home to 11 colleges spanning a variety of majors and disciplines, including distinguished programs in audiology, print making, creative writing, speech pathology, and nursing. Among the University of Iowa's distinguished alumni are Al Jarreau, John Irving, Flannery O'Connor, Gene Wilder, and Tennessee Williams.

EXECUTIVES

President, State of Iowa Board of Regents:
  John D. Forsyth, age 57
President: David J. Skorton, $281,875 pay
Provost: Michael J. Hogan
VP Finance and Operations and University Treasurer:
  Douglas K. True, $240,000 pay
Interim VP Research: William F. (Bill) Decker,
  $179,763 pay
VP Student Services and Dean of Students:
  Phillip E. Jones
Associate VP and Director Human Resources:
  Susan C. (Sue) Buckley, $122,500 pay
Special Assistant to the President for Governmental Relations and Associate VP Research:
  Derek H. Willard Sr.
Assistant VP and CIO: David Dobbins
Interim Assistant VP and CIO: Steve Fleagle
Director Financial Management and Budget and University Secretary: Douglas Young
Controller: Terry L. Johnson
Director University News Services: Linda Kettner
General Counsel: Mark E. Schantz

LOCATIONS

HQ: The University of Iowa
249 IMU, Iowa City, IA 52242
Phone: 319-335-3500   **Fax:** 319-335-0860
Web: www.uiowa.edu

PRODUCTS/OPERATIONS

Selected Colleges and Programs
College of Business
College of Dentistry
College of Education
College of Engineering
College of Law
College of Liberal Arts
College of Medicine
College of Nursing
College of Pharmacy
College of Public Health
Division of Continuing Education
Graduate College
Interdisciplinary Programs
International Programs

HISTORICAL FINANCIALS
Company Type: School

Income Statement   FYE: June 30

	REVENUE ($ mil.)	NET INCOME ($ mil.)	NET PROFIT MARGIN	EMPLOYEES
6/03	1,857	—	—	—
6/02	1,721	—	—	12,000
6/01	1,611	—	—	11,813
6/00	1,531	—	—	16,006
6/99	1,531	—	—	16,576
6/98	1,241	—	—	17,129
6/97	1,344	—	—	28,161
6/96	1,200	—	—	20,000
6/95	1,144	—	—	23,000
6/94	1,119	—	—	22,410
Annual Growth	5.8%	—	—	(7.5%)

Revenue History

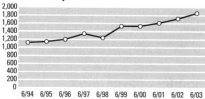

University of Maryland

Students come to Maryland for more than just the crab cakes. The University System of Maryland (USM) operates one of the largest public university systems in the country, serving more than 130,000 students through its 11 campuses. Its flagship university in College Park (founded in 1856) boasts more than 30,000 students and some of the country's top-ranked education programs. The University of Maryland is also known for its successful athletic teams (nicknamed the Terrapins), which compete in the Atlantic Coast Conference. USM's other universities include Townson University and the University of Baltimore; it also operates two major research centers. Maryland established its university system in 1988.

EXECUTIVES

Regents Chairman: Clifford M. Kendall
Regents Vice Chairman: Charles R. Larson, age 67
Chancellor: William E. (Brit) Kirwan, age 66
Vice Chancellor for Administration and Finance:
Joseph F. Vivona
Vice Chancellor for Academic Affairs: Irwin Goldstein
Associate Vice Chancellor and CIO: Donald Z. Spicer
Associate Vice Chancellor for Communications:
Anne Moultrie
Chief of Staff and Secretary: Kathleen M. (Katie) Ryan
Human Resource Officer: Rosario Vandaalen
Auditors: Ernst & Young LLP

LOCATIONS

HQ: University System of Maryland
3300 Metzerott Rd., Adelphi, MD 20783
Phone: 301-445-2740   **Fax:** 301-445-2761
Web: www.usmh.usmd.edu

PRODUCTS/OPERATIONS

Colleges and Research Centers
Bowie State University
Coppin State College
Frostburg State University
Salisbury University
Towson University
University of Baltimore
University of Maryland, Baltimore
University of Maryland, Baltimore County
University of Maryland Biotechnology Institute
University of Maryland Center for Environmental Science
University of Maryland, College Park
University of Maryland Eastern Shore
University of Maryland University College

HISTORICAL FINANCIALS
Company Type: School

Income Statement   FYE: June 30

	REVENUE ($ mil.)	NET INCOME ($ mil.)	NET PROFIT MARGIN	EMPLOYEES
6/03	2,729	—	—	—
6/02	2,657	—	—	32,400
6/01	2,565	—	—	30,901
6/00	2,292	—	—	30,000
6/99	2,592	—	—	27,977
6/98	2,033	—	—	28,115
6/97	1,908	—	—	26,316
6/96	1,713	—	—	25,833
6/95	1,627	—	—	25,690
6/94	1,520	—	—	—
Annual Growth	6.7%	—	—	3.4%

Revenue History

University of Michigan

Michigan — it's shaped like a mitten, and higher education fits the state like a glove. The University of Michigan has been a leader in the state's education effort since its founding in 1817. With about 54,000 students and more than 5,400 faculty members scattered across three campuses in Ann Arbor, Dearborn, and Flint, the university's diverse academic units span such areas of study as architecture, education, law, medicine, music, and social work. Notable alumni include former President Gerald Ford (the university is home to the Gerald R. Ford Library and the Ford School of Public Policy) and playwright Arthur Miller. In addition to state funding, the university is supported by a $3.5 billion endowment.

EXECUTIVES

President: Mary Sue Coleman, age 60
Provost and EVP Academic Affairs: Paul N. Courant
EVP and CFO: Timothy P. Slottow
EVP for Medical Affairs; CEO, U-M Health System:
Robert P. (Bob) Kelch
VP and General Counsel: Marvin Krislov
VP and Secretary of the University: Lisa A. Tedesco
VP Communications: Lisa M. Rudgers
VP Development: Jerry A. May
VP Government Relations: Cynthia H. Wilbanks
VP Research: Fawwaz T. Ulaby
VP Student Affairs: E. Royster Harper
Assistant Provost and Director of Academic Human Resources: Jeffery Frumkin
Associate VP Human Resources and Affirmative Action: Barbara S. Butterfield
Chief Investment Officer: L. Erik Lundberg
Treasurer: Gregory J. Tewksbury
Controller and Director of Financial Operations:
Cheryl L. Soper
Auditors: PricewaterhouseCoopers LLP

LOCATIONS

HQ: The University of Michigan
3074 Fleming Administration Bldg.,
Ann Arbor, MI 48109
Phone: 734-764-1817   **Fax:** 734-764-4546
Web: www.umich.edu

PRODUCTS/OPERATIONS

Selected Academic Units
Architecture and urban planning
Art and design
Business administration
Dentistry
Education
Engineering
Kinesiology
Law
Literature, science, and the arts
Medicine
Music
Natural resources and environment
Nursing
Pharmacy
Public health
Public policy
Social work

HISTORICAL FINANCIALS

Company Type: School

Income Statement
FYE: June 30

	REVENUE ($ mil.)	NET INCOME ($ mil.)	NET PROFIT MARGIN	EMPLOYEES
6/03	3,157	—	—	—
6/02	2,944	—	—	—
6/01	2,696	—	—	—
6/00	4,609	—	—	—
6/99	3,334	—	—	—
6/98	2,881	—	—	23,000
6/97	2,630	—	—	23,000
6/96	2,444	—	—	22,596
6/95	2,348	—	—	—
6/94	2,252	—	—	—
Annual Growth	3.8%	—	—	0.9%

Revenue History

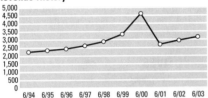

University of Minnesota

More than 65,000 students come seeking higher education in the Land of 10,000 Lakes. One of the country's major land grant university systems, the University of Minnesota (U of M) offers undergraduate and graduate degrees in some 370 academic fields through its four campuses. The school's Twin Cities campus, with nearly 51,000 students, ranks as the second largest in the country (behind the main campus of Ohio State). U of M also serves students though facilities in Crookston, Duluth, and Morris. In addition, the university is a top research institution with numerous research centers and institutes. U of M was founded as a prep school in 1851 and became a land grant institution in 1867.

EXECUTIVES

President: Robert H. (Bob) Bruininks
SVP Academic Affairs and Provost: E. Thomas Sullivan, age 55
SVP Health Sciences: Frank B. Cerra
VP and Chief of Staff: Kathryn F. Brown
VP and Executive Vice Provost, Faculty and Academic Programs: Robert J. Jones
VP Agricultural Policy and Dean of the College of Agricultural, Food, and Environmental Sciences: Charles C. Muscoplat
VP Human Resources: Carol Carrier
VP University Relations: Sandra S. Gardebring
VP University Services: Kathleen O'Brien
Associate VP, CFO, and Treasurer: Richard H. Pfutzenreuter
General Counsel: Mark B. Rotenberg
Director of Communications, University Services: Lori-Anne Williams
Auditors: Deloitte & Touche LLP

LOCATIONS

HQ: University of Minnesota
234 Morrill Hall, 100 Church St. SE,
Minneapolis, MN 55455
Phone: 612-625-5000 **Fax:** 612-626-1693
Web: www.umn.edu

The University of Minnesota has campuses in Crookston, Duluth, Minneapolis-St. Paul, and Morris. It also operates a campus in Rochester through a partnership with Minnesota State University.

PRODUCTS/OPERATIONS

Selected Colleges and Schools
Carlson School of Management
College of Agricultural, Food, and Environmental Sciences
College of Architecture and Landscape Architecture
College of Biological Sciences
College of Continuing Education
College of Education and Human Development
College of Human Ecology
College of Liberal Arts
College of Natural Resources
College of Pharmacy
College of Veterinary Medicine
General College
Graduate School
Hubert H. Humphrey Institute of Public Affairs
Institute of Technology
Law School
Medical School
School of Dentistry
School of Nursing
School of Public Health

HISTORICAL FINANCIALS

Company Type: School

Income Statement
FYE: June 30

	REVENUE ($ mil.)	NET INCOME ($ mil.)	NET PROFIT MARGIN	EMPLOYEES
6/03	1,237	—	—	17,014
6/02	1,131	—	—	—
6/01	2,301	—	—	30,823
6/00	3,224	—	—	34,345
6/99	2,204	—	—	30,304
6/98	2,051	—	—	30,708
6/97	1,872	—	—	33,873
6/96	1,880	—	—	33,000
6/95	2,079	—	—	20,000
6/94	1,898	—	—	18,212
Annual Growth	(4.6%)	—	—	(0.8%)

Revenue History

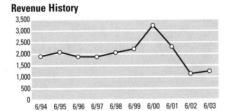

University of Missouri

Education isn't just for show in the "Show Me" state. The University of Missouri, founded in 1839, educates more than 60,000 students at four campuses and through a statewide extension program; some 25% of the students are in graduate or professional programs. Nicknamed "Mizzou," the university's cadre of campuses includes flagship UM-Columbia (home to some 26,000 students, 20 schools and colleges, and the University of Missouri Health Sciences Center), UM-Kansas City, UM-Rolla, and UM-St. Louis. Offering fields of study ranging from journalism to law to fine arts, the university has about 7,200 faculty and research staff members.

EXECUTIVES

President: Elson S. Floyd, age 47
EVP and Director Cooperative Extension: Ronald J. Turner
Chancellor, UM-Kansas City: Martha W. Gilliland
Chancellor, UM-Rolla: Gary Thomas
Chancellor, UM-St. Louis: Thomas F. (Tom) George
VP Academic Affairs: Stephen W. Lehmkuhle
VP Finance and Administration: Natalie R. (Nikki) Krawitz
VP Human Resources: R. Kenneth Hutchinson
VP, Government Relations: Stephen Knorr
Secretary to the Board: Kathleen M. Miller
Treasurer: Shirley S. DeJarnette
Director University Relations: David R. Russell
Director of Planning and Budget: Cuba Plain
General Counsel: Marvin E. (Bunky) Wright
Auditors: Deloitte & Touche LLP

LOCATIONS

HQ: University of Missouri System
321 University Hall, Columbia, MO 65211
Phone: 573-882-2121 **Fax:** 573-882-2721
Web: www.umsystem.edu

The University of Missouri has campuses in Columbia, Kansas City, Rolla, and St. Louis.

PRODUCTS/OPERATIONS

Selected Colleges and Schools
Accountancy
Agriculture
Art
Arts and Science
Business
Education
Engineering
Food Science
Graduate School
Health Professions
Honors College
Human Environmental Sciences
Information Science and Learning Technologies
Journalism
Law
Medicine
Natural Resources
Nursing
Social Work
Veterinary Medicine

Campuses
University of Missouri-Columbia (about 26,000 students)
University of Missouri-Kansas City (about 14,000 students)
University of Missouri-Rolla (about 5,000 students)
University of Missouri-St. Louis (about 15,000 students)

HISTORICAL FINANCIALS
Company Type: School

Income Statement
FYE: June 30

	REVENUE ($ mil.)	NET INCOME ($ mil.)	NET PROFIT MARGIN	EMPLOYEES
6/03	1,252	—	—	26,246
6/02	1,253	—	—	26,316
6/01	1,446	—	—	27,914
6/00	1,356	—	—	32,870
6/99	1,487	—	—	20,000
6/98	1,396	—	—	15,818
6/97	1,336	—	—	15,283
6/96	1,226	—	—	17,400
6/95	1,164	—	—	18,997
6/94	1,060	—	—	20,958
Annual Growth	1.9%	—	—	2.5%

Revenue History
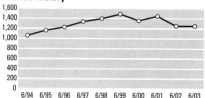

University of Nebraska

The University of Nebraska has sprouted four campuses out in the fields of the Cornhusker State. Founded in 1869, the state university system offers bachelor's, master's, and doctoral degrees in such programs as agriculture, business, education, and engineering at its campuses in Kearney, Lincoln, and Omaha. The university's Medical Center in Omaha trains doctors, performs research, and is affiliated with a 700-bed teaching hospital. The University of Nebraska also operates research and extension services across the state. Nearly 47,000 students attend classes in the university system, which is recovering from a severe 1997 enrollment drop caused by tighter admissions standards.

EXECUTIVES
President: L. Dennis Smith
EVP and Provost: Jay Noren
VP External Affairs and Corporation Secretary: Kim M. Robak, age 48
VP Business and Finance: David E. Lechner
VP and General Counsel: Richard Wood
Chancellor, Kearney Campus: Douglas A. (Doug) Kristensen
Chancellor, Lincoln Campus: Harvey S. Perlman, age 61
Chancellor, Medical Center: Harold M. Maurer
Chancellor, Omaha Campus: Nancy Belck
CIO: Walter Weir
Associate EVP and Provost: Donal Burns
Assistant EVP and Provost: Royce Ballinger
Assistant VP and Director Communications: Joe Rowson
Assistant VP and Director Finance: Michael Justus
Assistant VP and Director Human Resources: Ed Wimes
Auditors: Deloitte & Touche

LOCATIONS
HQ: The University of Nebraska
3835 Holdrege St., Lincoln, NE 68583
Phone: 402-472-2111 **Fax:** 402-472-1237
Web: www.nebraska.edu

PRODUCTS/OPERATIONS

University Campuses
The University of Nebraska at Kearney (6,400 students)
The University of Nebraska-Lincoln (23,000 students)
The University of Nebraska Medical Center (Omaha, 2,800 students)
The University of Nebraska at Omaha (14,500 students)

Selected Colleges and Programs
Agricultural Science and Natural Resources
Architecture
Arts and Sciences
Business Administration
Dentistry (University of Nebraska Medical Center)
Engineering and Technology
Fine and Performing Arts
Graduate Studies
Human Resources and Family Science
Law
Medicine (University of Nebraska Medical Center)
Nursing (University of Nebraska Medical Center)
Pharmacy (University of Nebraska Medical Center)
Teachers College

HISTORICAL FINANCIALS
Company Type: School

Income Statement
FYE: June 30

	REVENUE ($ mil.)	NET INCOME ($ mil.)	NET PROFIT MARGIN	EMPLOYEES
6/03	1,253	—	—	—
6/02	1,133	—	—	11,530
6/01	1,157	—	—	—
6/00	1,071	—	—	—
6/99	1,016	—	—	—
6/98	1,249	—	—	—
6/97	1,270	—	—	16,000
6/96	1,100	—	—	15,000
6/95	1,081	—	—	15,000
6/94	1,145	—	—	—
Annual Growth	1.0%	—	—	(3.7%)

Revenue History
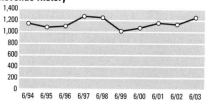

University of Pennsylvania

The University of Pennsylvania was established by Benjamin Franklin when he had a little down time from helping to found our country and experimenting with lightning. Since opening its doors to students in 1751, the Ivy League university has accumulated a notable list of accomplishments, including the creation of the first medical school in the US and the invention of the ENIAC computer. The university's more than 23,200 students pursue their studies in four undergraduate schools and a dozen graduate and professional schools, including the renowned Wharton School and the Annenburg School for Communications.

EXECUTIVES
President: Amy Gutmann
Provost: Robert L. (Bob) Barchi, age 65
Deputy Provost: Peter Conn
SVP Facilities and Real Estate Services: Omar H. Blaik
SVP Finance and Treasurer: Craig Carnaroli
VP Audit and Compliance: Rick N. Whitfield
VP Business Services: Leroy D. Nunery
VP Division of Public Safety: Maureen Rush
VP Government and Public Affairs: Carol R. Scheman
VP Human Resources: John J. Heuer
VP Information Systems and Computing: Robin H. Beck
VP University Communications: Lori Doyle
VP and Chief of Staff: Pedro Ramos
VP and General Counsel: Wendy White
Auditors: PricewaterhouseCoopers LLP

LOCATIONS
HQ: The University of Pennsylvania
3451 Walnut St., Philadelphia, PA 19104
Phone: 215-898-5000 **Fax:** 215-898-9659
Web: www.upenn.edu

PRODUCTS/OPERATIONS

Selected Schools
Annenberg School for Communication
The College at Penn (School of Arts and Sciences)
Graduate School of Education
Graduate School of Fine Arts
Law School
School of Arts and Sciences
School of Dental Medicine
School of Engineering and Applied Science
School of Medicine
School of Nursing
School of Social Work
School of Veterinary Medicine
The Wharton School

HISTORICAL FINANCIALS
Company Type: School

Income Statement
FYE: June 30

	REVENUE ($ mil.)	NET INCOME ($ mil.)	NET PROFIT MARGIN	EMPLOYEES
6/03	3,786	—	—	11,949
6/02	3,563	—	—	—
6/01	3,191	—	—	12,290
6/00	3,007	—	—	—
6/99	2,823	—	—	18,331
6/98	2,602	—	—	20,619
6/97	2,197	—	—	22,934
6/96	1,994	—	—	21,803
6/95	1,778	—	—	20,500
6/94	1,714	—	—	20,000
Annual Growth	9.2%	—	—	(5.6%)

Revenue History
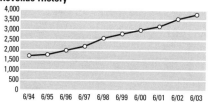

University of Pittsburgh

Now this is a school that really needs a nickname. The University of Pittsburgh of the Commonwealth System of Higher Education (whew! — Pitt for short) has some 34,000 students spread across its five campuses. Its flagship Pittsburgh campus has more than 26,000 students. The Pitt Panthers pursue their studies in 18 schools and colleges, including arts and sciences, engineering, and business. Pitt also is affiliated with the UPMC Health System, which operates a network of hospitals and an insurance company, manages physicians' offices, and offers long-term care and in-home services. The university was founded in 1787 and has an endowment reaching $1.4 billion.

EXECUTIVES

Chairperson: Ralph J. Cappy
Chancellor and CEO: Mark A. Nordenberg, age 55
Executive Vice Chancellor: Jerome Cochran
Senior Vice Chancellor and Provost: James V. Maher
Senior Vice Chancellor Health Sciences: Arthur Levine
Vice Chancellor Budget and Controller: Arthur Ramicone
Vice Provost Academic Affairs: Jack L. Daniel
Vice Provost Academic Planning and Resources Management: Robert F. Pack
Vice Provost Faculty Affairs: Andrew R. Blair
Vice Provost Graduate Studies: Particia Beeson
Vice Provost Research: George E. Klinzing
Associate Vice Chancellor Human Resources: Ronald W. (Ron) Frisch
Director Technology Management: Christopher Capelli
Treasurer: Amy K. Marsh
Auditors: Deloitte & Touche LLP

LOCATIONS

HQ: University of Pittsburgh of the Commonwealth System of Higher Education
4227 5th Ave., Pittsburgh, PA 15260
Phone: 412-624-4141 **Fax:** 412-624-7282
Web: www.pitt.edu

The University of Pittsburgh of the Commonwealth System of Higher Education has campuses in Bradford, Greensburg, Johnstown, Pittsburgh, and Titusville, Pennsylvania.

PRODUCTS/OPERATIONS

Selected Schools and Colleges
Arts and Sciences
Business
Dental Medicine
Education
Engineering
General Studies
Health and Rehabilitation Sciences
Honors College
Information Sciences
Law
Medicine
Nursing
Pharmacy
Public and International Affairs
Public Health
Social Work

HISTORICAL FINANCIALS

Company Type: School

Income Statement
FYE: June 30

	REVENUE ($ mil.)	NET INCOME ($ mil.)	NET PROFIT MARGIN	EMPLOYEES
6/03	1,288	—	—	10,000
6/02	1,146	—	—	10,000
6/01	1,097	—	—	10,000
6/00	1,033	—	—	10,000
6/99	984	—	—	10,000
6/98	888	—	—	9,600
6/97	820	—	—	9,453
6/96	872	—	—	9,621
6/95	844	—	—	9,671
6/94	817	—	—	9,299
Annual Growth	5.2%	—	—	0.8%

Revenue History

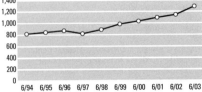

University of Rochester

The buzz about the University of Rochester is music to some ears. The private, upstate New York institution is nationally recognized for its programs in medicine, engineering, and business, and its Eastman School of Music (founded by Eastman Kodak creator George Eastman) is one of the top music schools in the US. The university, which has an endowment of more than $1.1 billion, offers about 175 bachelor's, master's, and doctoral degrees to its more than 8,600 full- and part-time students. Undergraduate tuition runs more than $25,000. Founded as a Baptist-sponsored institution in 1850, the university is nonsectarian today.

EXECUTIVES

President: Thomas H. Jackson
Provost: Charles E. Phelps
SVP Administration and Finance, CFO, and Treasurer: Ronald J. Paprocki
SVP Institutional Resources: Douglas W. Phillips
VP and General Secretary: Paul J. Burgett
Vice Provost and CIO: Amelia Tynan
Auditors: KPMG LLP

LOCATIONS

HQ: University of Rochester
Administration Bldg., Rochester, NY 14627
Phone: 585-275-2121 **Fax:** 585-275-0359
Web: www.rochester.edu

PRODUCTS/OPERATIONS

Selected Schools
Eastman School Campus
  Eastman School of Music
Medical Center
  Eastman Dental Center
  School of Medicine and Dentistry
  School of Nursing
  Strong Memorial Hospital
River Campus
  Margaret Warner Graduate School of Education and Human Development
  William E. Simon Graduate School of Business Administration

Other Operations
C. E. K. Mees Observatory (Bristol Hills, NY)
Center for Optoelectronics and Imaging
Laboratory for Laser Energetics
Memorial Art Gallery
Mt. Hope Campus

HISTORICAL FINANCIALS

Company Type: School

Income Statement
FYE: June 30

	REVENUE ($ mil.)	NET INCOME ($ mil.)	NET PROFIT MARGIN	EMPLOYEES
6/03	1,653	—	—	16,040
6/02	1,427	—	—	11,200
6/01	1,419	—	—	12,242
6/00	1,340	—	—	13,656
6/99	1,160	—	—	12,968
6/98	1,061	—	—	12,568
6/97	865	—	—	11,859
6/96	822	—	—	11,801
6/95	846	—	—	11,956
6/94	804	—	—	11,653
Annual Growth	8.3%	—	—	3.6%

Revenue History

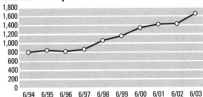

University of Southern California

This Trojan horse, filled with more than 31,000 students, is more than welcome at the University of Southern California (USC). Founded in 1880, the private university (home of the Trojans) grew up with the city of Los Angeles. It offers 77 undergraduate majors and 139 postgraduate degrees. Recognized for distinguished programs in business, engineering, film, law, medicine, public administration, and science, USC boasts two Los Angeles campuses and a string of research centers and health care facilities. The university also supports medical staffs at five Los Angeles hospitals. USC is the largest private employer in Los Angeles.

The university's focus on fund raising under current president Steven Sample has resulted in four individual donations of $100 million or more for his efforts to improve USC's undergraduate programs and medical school, as well as attract top-flight teachers.

EXECUTIVES

President: Steven B. Sample, age 63
SVP Academic Affairs and Provost: Lloyd Armstrong Jr.
SVP Administration: Dennis F. Dougherty
SVP Medical Care: Stephen J. Ryan, age 63
SVP University Advancement: Alan Kreditor
SVP University Relations: Martha Harris
VP and Executive Vice Provost: Michael A. Diamond
VP, General Counsel, and Secretary: Todd R. Dickey
VP Capital Construction: Curtis D. (Curt) Williams
VP External Relations: Carolyn Webb de Macias
VP Health Affairs: Joseph P. Van Der Meulen
VP Student Affairs: Michael L. Jackson
CIO and University Librarian: Jerry D. Campbell
Treasurer and Associate SVP: William C. Hromadka
Executive Director Public Relations Projects: Holly Bridges
Auditors: PricewaterhouseCoopers LLP

LOCATIONS

HQ: The University of Southern California
University Park Campus, Los Angeles, CA 90089
Phone: 213-740-2311   **Fax:** 213-740-5229
Web: www.usc.edu

PRODUCTS/OPERATIONS

Schools and Programs
Annenberg School for Communication
College of Letters, Arts and Sciences
Graduate School
Independent Health Professions
Keck School of Medicine
The Law School
Leonard Davis School of Gerontology
Marshall School of Business
Rossier School of Education
School of Architecture
School of Cinema-Television
School of Dentistry
School of Engineering
School of Fine Arts
School of Pharmacy
School of Policy, Planning, and Development
School of Social Work
School of Theatre
Thornton School of Music

Campuses
Health Sciences Campus
University Park Campus

Health Facilities
Childrens Hospital Los Angeles
Doheny Eye Institute
Los Angeles County+USC Medical Center
USC University Hospital
USC/Norris Comprehensive Cancer Center

HISTORICAL FINANCIALS
Company Type: School

Income Statement
FYE: June 30

	REVENUE ($ mil.)	NET INCOME ($ mil.)	NET PROFIT MARGIN	EMPLOYEES
6/04	1,500	—	—	14,000
6/03	1,568	—	—	17,000
6/02	1,480	—	—	17,000
6/01	1,399	—	—	17,000
6/00	1,186	—	—	17,000
6/99	1,142	—	—	17,000
6/98	1,307	—	—	17,000
6/97	1,239	—	—	17,000
6/96	1,233	—	—	17,100
6/95	1,152	—	—	17,000
Annual Growth	3.0%	—	—	(2.1%)

Revenue History

University of Tennessee

The 200-year-old University of Tennessee (UT), part of the University of Tennessee System, comprises the flagship campus located in Knoxville, the Health Science Center at Memphis, and the Space Institute at Tullahoma. Other UT System institutions are located in Chattanooga and Martin. In all, the UT System campuses provide undergraduate, graduate, and professional academic programs to about 42,000 students; programs include business, engineering, law, pharmacy, medicine, and veterinary medicine. UT was founded in 1794 as Blount College. Notable alumni include former Senate Majority Leader Howard Baker, Nobel Prize-winning economist James Buchanan, and author Cormac McCarthy.

EXECUTIVES

Vice Chair, Board of Trustees: Don C. Stansberry Jr.
President: John D. Petersen
CFO: Emerson H. Fly
Interim Chancellor, UT Chattanooga: Frederick Obear
Chancellor, UT Knoxville: Loren W. Crabtree
Chancellor, UT Martin: Nick Dunagan
EVP: Jack H. Britt
VP, General Counsel, and Secretary: Catherine S. Mizell
VP and Treasurer: Charles M. (Butch) Peccolo
VP Administration and Finance: Sylvia S. Davis
VP Development and Alumni Affairs: Jack E. Williams
VP Equity and Diversity: Theotis Robinson Jr.
VP Operations, UT Knoxville: Philip Scheurer
Auditors: State of Tennessee Department of Audit

LOCATIONS

HQ: University of Tennessee
800 Andy Holt Tower, Knoxville, TN 37996
Phone: 865-974-1000   **Fax:** 865-974-3851
Web: www.tennessee.edu

The University of Tennessee has campuses in Chattanooga, Knoxville, Martin, Memphis, and Tullahoma.

PRODUCTS/OPERATIONS

Selected Colleges, Schools, and Institutes
College of Agricultural Sciences and Natural Resources
College of Allied Health Sciences
College of Architecture and Design
College of Arts and Sciences
College of Business Administration
College of Communication and Information
College of Dentistry
College of Education, Health, and Human Sciences
College of Engineering
College of Graduate Health Sciences
College of Health Science Engineering
College of Law
College of Medicine
College of Nursing
College of Pharmacy
College of Social Work
College of Veterinary Medicine
Graduate School of Medicine
School of Art
School of Music
Space Institute

HISTORICAL FINANCIALS
Company Type: School

Income Statement
FYE: June 30

	REVENUE ($ mil.)	NET INCOME ($ mil.)	NET PROFIT MARGIN	EMPLOYEES
6/03	1,389	—	—	10,787
6/02	1,351	—	—	11,931
6/01	1,324	—	—	11,700
6/00	1,696	—	—	14,004
6/99	1,303	—	—	14,266
6/98	1,232	—	—	14,967
6/97	1,222	—	—	14,993
6/96	1,181	—	—	15,486
6/95	1,165	—	—	15,000
6/94	1,135	—	—	14,980
Annual Growth	2.3%	—	—	(3.6%)

Revenue History

University of Texas

These students are hooked on higher education. The University of Texas System runs nine universities throughout the Lone Star State with a total enrollment of nearly 178,000 students, making it one of the largest university systems in the US. Its flagship school in Austin, with some 50,000 students, ranks as the third-largest campus population in the nation (behind the main campuses at Ohio State and the University of Minnesota). UT also runs six health centers and four medical schools and receives more than $1 billion a year for research. Its $10 billion endowment fund (managed by the University of Texas Investment Management Co.) is the third largest in the country (after Harvard and Yale).

Established in 1876, UT Austin opened in 1883. The UT System was formally organized in 1950.

With the bulging ranks of Generation Y looming on the horizon, the UT System expects its enrollment to swell to 250,000 by the end of the decade. To accommodate the increase, the system has laid out plans for nearly $3 billion in capital spending for new and improved facilities. It also hopes the improvements will put it on par with research institutions such as California State.

HISTORY

The Texas Declaration of Independence (1836) admonished Mexico for having failed to establish a public education system in the territory, but attempts to start a state-sponsored university were stymied until after Texas achieved US statehood and fought in the Civil War. A new constitution in 1876 provided for the establishment of "a university of the first class," and in 1883 The University of Texas (UT) opened in Austin. Eight professors taught 218 students in two curricula: academics and law.

The school's first building opened in 1884, and in 1891 the university's medical school opened in Galveston. By 1894 UT-Austin had 534 students and a football team. UT opened a Graduate School in 1910 and various other colleges over the years. The university added its first academic branch campus when the Texas State School of Mines and Metallurgy (opened in 1914 in El Paso) became part of the system in 1919.

UT's financial future was secured in 1923 when oil was found on West Texas land that had been set aside by the legislature as an education endowment. The income from oil production, as well as the proceeds of surface-use leases, became the Permanent University Fund (PUF), from which only interest and earnings on the revenues can be used: two-thirds by UT and one-third by Texas A&M University. UT continued to grow, thanks to the PUF, which topped $100 million by 1940.

UT sported the black eye of racial prejudice (as did many other institutions at the time) when it refused to admit Heman Sweatt, a black student, to its law school in 1946. The Supreme Court ordered UT to admit him in 1950, the same year the UT System was officially organized. Sixteen years later, in one of the nation's most highly publicized crimes, Charles Whitman killed 14 people and wounded 31 others with a high-powered rifle fired from atop the UT-Austin administration tower. The observation deck wasn't closed until 1975, however, after a series of suicides. (It was later reopened in 1999.)

In the meantime, UT added a medical center in Dallas and several graduate schools in Austin. The 1960s through the 1980s were a time of geographic expansion for the system as it absorbed other institutions, started several new campuses, and expanded its network of medical centers. In 1996 the UT System became the first public university to establish a private investment management company (University of Texas Investment Management Co.) to invest PUF money (by that time over $9 billion) and other funds.

The race issue reared its head again in 1996 when a Federal court ruled in the Hopwood decision (named for the plaintiff) that the UT System could no longer use race to determine scholarships and admissions. Minority enrollments declined the following year, prompting the Texas Legislature to enact a law granting admission to the top 10% of graduates from any Texas high school to the state university of their choice. Chancellor William Cunningham announced plans in 2000 to expand the UT System by 100,000 students over the decade. After he resigned that year, R. D. Burck took over as his successor. In 2001 UT received a $50 million donation, the largest gift in its history, from Texas businessman and Minnesota Vikings owner Red McCombs. The following year Burck stepped down and was replaced by Mark Yudof, former president of the University of Minnesota.

EXECUTIVES

Chairman, Board of Regents: James R. Huffines
Vice Chairman, Board of Regents: Rita C. Clements
Vice Chairman, Board of Regents: Woody L. Hunt
Vice Chairman, Board of Regents: Cindy T. Krier
Counsel and Executive Secretary, Board of Regents: Francie A. Frederick
Chancellor: Mark G. Yudof
Executive Vice Chancellor Academic Affairs: Teresa A. Sullivan
Executive Vice Chancellor Business Affairs: Scott C. Kelley
Vice Chancellor and General Counsel: Cullen M. Godfrey
Vice Chancellor Administration: Tonya M. Brown
Vice Chancellor Community Relations: John De La Garza Jr.
Vice Chancellor External Affairs: Randa S. Safady
Vice Chancellor Federal Relations: William H. Shute
Vice Chancellor for Governmental Relations and Policy: E. Ashley Smith, age 58
Vice Chancellor for Health Affairs: Kenneth I. Shine
Executive Director Public Affairs: Michael L. Warden
Executive Director Special Services: Mary Ellen Oliver
Associate Vice Chancellor and Chief Information Officer: Clair Goldsmith
Associate Vice Chancellor for Business Affairs: Lewis W. Wright III
Associate Vice Chancellor for Finance: Philip R. Aldridge
Assistant Vice Chancellor for Administration: Florence Mayne
Executive Director of Employee Group Benefits: Dan Stewart
Auditors: Texas State Auditor

LOCATIONS

HQ: The University of Texas System
601 Colorado St., Austin, TX 78701
Phone: 512-499-4200 **Fax:** 512-499-4215
Web: www.utsystem.edu

PRODUCTS/OPERATIONS

University of Texas System Component Institutions
Academic Institutions
  The University of Texas at Arlington (established 1895; fall 2003 enrollment 24,979)
  The University of Texas at Austin (1883; 51,438)
  The University of Texas at Brownsville (1991; 10,705)
  The University of Texas at Dallas (1961; 13,725)
  The University of Texas at El Paso (1914; 18,542)
  The University of Texas-Pan American (Edinburg;1927; 15,889)
  The University of Texas of the Permian Basin (Odessa; 1969; 3,044)
  The University of Texas at San Antonio (1969; 24,665)
  The University of Texas at Tyler (1971; 4,783)
Health Institutions
  The University of Texas Health Science Center at Houston (established 1972; fall 2003 enrollment 3,442)
  The University of Texas Health Science Center at San Antonio (1959; 2,785)
  The University of Texas Health Center at Tyler (1947)
  The University of Texas M.D. Anderson Cancer Center (Houston, 1941; 75)
  The University of Texas Medical Branch at Galveston (1891; 2,088)
  The University of Texas Southwestern Medical Center at Dallas (1943; 1,796)

HISTORICAL FINANCIALS

Company Type: School

Income Statement FYE: August 31

	REVENUE ($ mil.)	NET INCOME ($ mil.)	NET PROFIT MARGIN	EMPLOYEES
8/03	5,235	—	—	66,845
8/02	4,806	—	—	65,689
8/01	6,461	—	—	63,054
8/00	5,943	—	—	79,430
8/99	4,131	—	—	78,000
8/98	5,244	—	—	77,112
8/97	4,803	—	—	75,517
8/96	4,624	—	—	74,364
8/95	4,300	—	—	72,395
8/94	4,030	—	—	70,000
Annual Growth	2.9%	—	—	(0.5%)

Revenue History

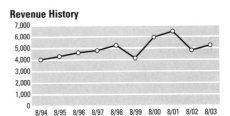

University of Washington

The University of Washington (UW) is Husky indeed, with more than 39,000 students enrolled at its main Seattle campus. Founded in 1861 as the Territorial University of Washington, UW (pronounced "U-dub" by those on campus) also has smaller branches in Tacoma and Bothell. The university maintains 17 schools and colleges for both undergraduate and graduate students (more than 70% of students on the main campus are undergrads). It also operates a health sciences center and an academic medical center, which includes the University of Washington Medical Center and Harborview Medical Center.

EXECUTIVES

President: Mark A. Emmert
EVP: Weldon E. Ihrig
VP Student Affairs: Ernest R. Morris
VP Medical Affairs and Dean School of Medicine:
  Paul G. Ramsey
VP University Relations: Jack H. Faris
VP Computing and Communications:
  Ronald A. Johnson
VP for Minority Affairs: Nancy Barceló
VP Development and Alumni Relations: Connie Kravas
Treasurer of the Board of Regents: V'Ella Warren
Director Human Resources: Elizabeth Coveney
Acting Provost: David Thorud
Auditors: KPMG LLP

LOCATIONS

HQ: University of Washington
  301 Gerberding Hall, Ste. 400, Seattle, WA 98195
Phone: 206-543-2560   **Fax:** 206-543-5651
Web: www.washington.edu

The University of Washington has campuses in Bothell, Seattle, and Tacoma, Washington.

PRODUCTS/OPERATIONS

Schools and Colleges
The College of Architecture and Urban Planning
The College of Arts and Sciences
The College of Education
The College of Engineering
The College of Forest Resources
The College of Ocean and Fishery Sciences
The Graduate School
The Graduate School of Public Affairs
Information School
The School of Business Administration
The School of Dentistry
The School of Law
The School of Medicine
The School of Nursing
The School of Pharmacy
The School of Public Health and Community Medicine
The School of Social Work

Health and Medical Centers
Academic Medical Center
  Alcohol and Drug Abuse Institute
  Center on Human Development and Disability
  Harborview Medical Center
  Institute on Aging
  Regional Primate Research Center
  Research Center in Oral Biology
  University of Washington Medical Center
Warren G. Magnuson Health Sciences Center
  Department of Environmental Health and Safety
  Hall Health Primary Care Center

HISTORICAL FINANCIALS
Company Type: School

Income Statement
FYE: June 30

	REVENUE ($ mil.)	NET INCOME ($ mil.)	NET PROFIT MARGIN	EMPLOYEES
6/03	2,050	—	—	29,077
6/02	1,814	—	—	23,680
6/01	2,647	—	—	23,462
6/00	2,696	—	—	25,917
6/99	2,456	—	—	25,281
6/98	1,748	—	—	34,757
6/97	1,615	—	—	32,080
6/96	1,990	—	—	30,000
6/95	1,785	—	—	22,655
6/94	1,783	—	—	21,536
Annual Growth	1.6%	—	—	3.4%

University of Wisconsin

There is no School of Cheese in the University of Wisconsin System, but there are 13 four-year universities, 13 two-year campuses, and a statewide extension program. The University of Wisconsin System is one of the largest public university systems in the US, with more than 160,600 students. Its top school is the University of Wisconsin at Madison, which offers undergraduate, graduate, and doctoral degrees and regularly ranks as one of the top public schools in the US. It has some 41,600 students and a nationally recognized graduate program in sociology. The system's other major campus is the University of Wisconsin at Milwaukee, with about 26,000 students.

Nearly one-third of the UW System's annual budget comes from state funds. Student fees, federal grants, fund raising, and other sources account for the remainder.

HISTORY

When Wisconsin became a state in 1848, its constitution called for the establishment of a state university. A board of regents was named, and it first established a preparatory school because regents felt Wisconsin's secondary schools were not advanced enough to prepare students for university studies. The school began classes in 1849 with 20 students in the Madison Female Academy Building. The University of Wisconsin's first official freshman class began studies in the fall of 1850. A campus was established a mile west of the state capitol in Madison. By 1854, when it held its first commencement (with two graduates), the school had 41 students.

Enrollment dipped during the Civil War (all but one of the school's senior class joined the army) but soon rebounded, and by 1870 the university had almost 500 students. Meanwhile, it established a school of agriculture (1866) and a school of law (1868). The state established normal schools (teachers colleges) in Platteville (1866), Whitewater (1868), Oshkosh (1871), and River Falls (1874).

There was also a teachers' course for women at the university in Madison. However, when John Bascom became president in 1874, he transformed the university into a truly coeducational institution, putting women "in all respects on precisely the same footing" with the men.

While the university at Madison remained Wisconsin's primary seat of learning, the state continued to establish normal schools. It opened institutions in Milwaukee (1885), Superior (1893), Stevens Point (1894), La Crosse (1909), and Eau Claire (1916). The nine normal schools eventually became a system of state colleges called Wisconsin State Universities.

The university at Madison also continued to grow, and by the late 1920s it had almost 9,000 students. WWII brought a drop in enrollment, but afterward it took off, jumping from about 7,000 in 1945 to over 22,000 by the late 1950s. The University of Wisconsin-Milwaukee branch was founded in 1956. Other branch campuses were established in Green Bay (1965) and Kenosha (1968).

The Madison campus became a focal point for student protests during the Vietnam War. Events came to a head in 1970 when President Fred Harrington resigned during a four-day standoff between students and the National Guard. War protesters also placed a bomb outside Sterling Hall, which housed the Army Math Research Center; the explosion killed one student and injured three others.

The state legislature merged the University of Wisconsin and the Wisconsin State Universities in 1971 to create The University of Wisconsin System. By the early 1980s it had an enrollment of nearly 160,000. Later that decade, however, it tightened admission standards, and enrollment began to fall.

A property-tax reform bill passed by the legislature in 1994 cut into The University of Wisconsin System's funding the next year. The system announced it would cut 500 jobs in 1997, use more part-time instructors, and increase class sizes to deal with the $43 million it lost in the budget cuts.

UW-Madison broke ground on the $22 million Fluno Center for Executive Education in 1998, a 100-room dorm, classroom building, and dining hall rolled into one. The next year enrollment at The University of Wisconsin System's two-year colleges broke 10,000 for the first time in five years. The licensing of technologies invented at the UW-Madison campus was expanded to include all four-year universities in the UW System in 2000. The System's mandatory student-fee policy was ruled unconstitutional later that year. The demand for enrollment for The University of Wisconsin System increased from 2001 to 2002, with the number of applications for undergraduate admissions growing 10%. The UW System raised the price of tuition to help offset cuts in state funding in 2003 and 2004.

EXECUTIVES

President: Kevin Reilly
SVP Academic Affairs: Cora B. Bagley Marrett
SVP Administration: David W. Olien
VP Finance: Deborah A. Durcan
VP University Relations: Linda Weimer
Associate VP Academic and Student Services: Ronald M. Singer
Assistant VP Academic Affairs and Senior Advisor of President for Academic Diversity: Andrea-Teresa (Tess) Arenas
Assistant VP Capital Planning and Budget: Nancy J. Ives
Acting Associate VP Budget and Planning: Freda Harris
Associate VP Human Resources: George H. Brooks
Associate VP Learning and Information Technology: Edward Meachen
Associate VP Policy Analysis and Research: Frank Goldberg
Secretary: Judith Temby
Director, Division of Procurement, UW System Administration: Ellen James
Director of the Office of Budget and Planning: Melissa Kepner
Director Information Services: Nancy Crabb
Director for Operations Review and Audit: Ronald L. Yates
General Counsel: Patricia A. Brady
Auditors: State of Wisconsin Legislative Audit Bureau

LOCATIONS

HQ: The University of Wisconsin System
Van Hise Hall, 1220 Linden Dr., Madison, WI 53706
Phone: 608-262-2321 **Fax:** 608-262-3985
Web: www.uwsa.edu

University Campuses
UW-Baraboo/Sauk County (two-year college, 653 students)
UW-Barron County (two-year college, 434)
UW-Eau Claire (four-year university; 10,643)
UW-Fond Du Lac (two-year college, 679)
UW-Fox Valley (two-year college; 1,633)
UW-Green Bay (four-year university; 5,558)
UW-La Crosse (four-year university; 9,092)
UW-Madison (four-year university; 41,600)
UW-Manitowoc (two-year college,560)
UW-Marathon County (two-year college; 1,189)
UW-Marinette (two-year college, 452)
UW-Marshfield/Wood County (two-year college, 584)
UW-Milwaukee (four-year university; 26,000)
UW-Oshkosh (four-year university; 10,929)
UW-Parkside (four-year university; 5,016)
UW-Platteville (four-year university; 5,511)
UW-Richland (two-year college, 449)
UW-River Falls (four-year university; 5,822)
UW-Rock County (two-year college, 872)
UW-Sheboygan (two-year college, 717)
UW-Stevens Point (four-year university; 8,735)
UW-Stout (four-year university; 7,780)
UW-Superior (four-year university; 2,787)
UW-Washington County (two-year college, 849)
UW-Waukesha (two-year college; 1,976)
UW-Whitewater (four-year university; 10,471)

HISTORICAL FINANCIALS
Company Type: School

Income Statement
FYE: June 30

	REVENUE ($ mil.)	NET INCOME ($ mil.)	NET PROFIT MARGIN	EMPLOYEES
6/03	3,273	—	—	28,030
6/02	3,059	—	—	26,650
6/01	3,160	—	—	24,000
6/00	2,922	—	—	23,981
6/99	2,558	—	—	25,889
6/98	2,543	—	—	25,500
6/97	2,399	—	—	25,399
6/96	2,612	—	—	28,626
6/95	2,556	—	—	30,410
6/94	2,442	—	—	30,341
Annual Growth	3.3%	—	—	(0.9%)

Revenue History
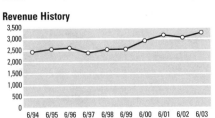

University of Wisconsin Hospital and Clinics

The University of Wisconsin Hospital and Clinics Authority operates University of Wisconsin Hospital and Clinics, which has more than 470 beds. Contained within the hospital is the University of Wisconsin Children's Hospital and a small inpatient psychiatric ward. The hospital offers cancer treatment, ophthalmology, organ transplantation, and a host of other medical services. University of Wisconsin Hospital and Clinics also operates some 80 specialty clinics that provide advanced and emergency health care services. The University of Wisconsin Hospital and Clinics Authority does not receive any financial support from the University of Wisconsin or the state.

EXECUTIVES

President and CEO: Donna K. Sollenberger, age 55
COO: David Entwistle
SVP and CFO: Gary Eiler
Interim SVP, Nursing and Patient Care Services: Jan Feldman
SVP, Medical Affairs: Carl Getto
SVP and General Counsel: James Roberts
VP, Marketing and Public Affairs: Linda Brei
VP and CIO: Dennis Dassenko
VP, Ambulatory Services: Mark Hamilton
VP, Professional and Support Services: Thomas Thielke
VP, Facilities: Terry Wilkerson

LOCATIONS

HQ: The University of Wisconsin Hospital & Clinics Authority
600 Highland Ave., Madison, WI 53792
Phone: 608-263-6400 **Fax:** 608-262-5624
Web: www.uwhospital.org

HISTORICAL FINANCIALS
Company Type: Not-for-profit

Income Statement
FYE: June 30

	REVENUE ($ mil.)	NET INCOME ($ mil.)	NET PROFIT MARGIN	EMPLOYEES
6/03	567	—	—	6,095
6/02	502	—	—	—
Annual Growth	12.8%	—	—	—

Revenue History
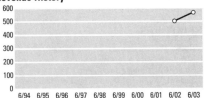

UOP

For UOP, it's not necessarily what you make, it's how you make it. The joint venture of Honeywell and Union Carbide (which is owned by Dow Chemical) develops and licenses technologies for processing chemicals. The technologies mainly are used in oil-derived products and chemicals (such as ethylene and propylene), but also in the manufacture of plastics, detergents, and fibers. About half of the world's biodegradable detergents are produced with UOP technologies. The company has more than 65 licensed processes for companies that process hydrocarbons. UOP also produces catalysts, alumina adsorbents (used to purify gas and dry air), and molecular sieves.

EXECUTIVES

President and CEO: Carlos Guimaraes
VP, Research and Development and CTO: Stanley A. (Stan) Gembicki
VP, Adsorbents and Specialties: Joseph P. Ausikaitis
VP, Catalysts and Advanced Materials: Norman L. Gilsdorf
VP, Process Technology and Equipment: Carlos A. Cabrera
VP, Finance and Accounting: Thomas H. Shears
VP, Human Resources: Rodney A. Smith
VP, Information Technology: Ashis Banerji
VP, Law: John T. Lucking
Director, Six Sigma and Productivity: Allen D. (Al) Arneson
VP, Ventures and Business Development: Richard T. (Rick) Penning
Director, Communications Group: Anita Black

LOCATIONS

HQ: UOP LLC
25 E. Algonquin Rd., Bldg. A, Des Plaines, IL 60016
Phone: 847-391-2000   **Fax:** 847-391-2253
Web: www.uop.com

UOP has six manufacturing sites in the US: Mobile, Alabama; Anaheim, California; McCook, Illinois; Shreveport and Baton Rouge, Louisiana; and Tonawanda, New York. Its foreign manufacturing facilities are located in China, Germany, Italy, Japan, and the UK.

COMPETITORS

BASF AG
International Absorbents
NATCO Group
Süd-Chemie

HISTORICAL FINANCIALS

Company Type: Joint venture

Income Statement
FYE: December 31

	REVENUE ($ mil.)	NET INCOME ($ mil.)	NET PROFIT MARGIN	EMPLOYEES
12/03	932	—	—	3,400
12/02	880	—	—	4,000
Annual Growth	5.9%	—	—	(15.0%)

Revenue History

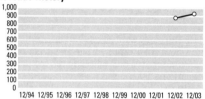

U.S. Can

If any company can manufacture non-beverage containers — U.S. Can. Making steel and plastic non-beverage containers in the US and Europe, U.S. Can's products hold everything from food to paint. Its aerosol containers, which account for the largest portion of sales, are used to package household, automotive, paint, hygiene, and industrial products. Besides standard containers, the company offers custom and specialty products such as decorative tins, stampings, and collectible items like metal signs, as well as containers used to store chemicals. U.S. Can commenced operations in Delaware in 1983, and private investment firm Berkshire Partners owns 77% of the company.

U.S. Can is divided into four business segments: Aerosol Products, International Operations, Paint (Plastic and General Line Products), and Custom and Specialty Products.

U.S. Can's approximately 5,000 customers include Gillette and Sherwin-Williams. The company is the leading seller of aerosol cans in the US and holds the #2 position in Europe.

The company expanded into South America when it bought into a joint venture with a 37% share of Argentina's Fornametal SA, an aerosol can manufacturer.

EXECUTIVES

Co-Chairman and CEO: George V. Bayly, age 61
Co-Chairman: Carl Ferenbach, age 61
EVP and General Manager, Business Units of the Americas: Thomas A. Scrimo, age 55, $287,869 pay
SVP and CFO: Sandra K. Vollman, age 46, $224,792 pay
SVP, International and President, European Operations: Francois J. Vissers, age 43, $341,037 pay
SVP, Metal Manufacturing and Lithography Operations: Larry S. Morrison, age 50, $257,600 pay
SVP, Sales: Sarah T. Macdonald, age 39
VP and CTO: Emil P. Obradovich, age 57
VP and Controller, Financial Planning and Analysis: Robert Burkhardt
VP, Corporate Marketing and CIO: Sheleen Quish, age 55
VP, Human Resources: Thomas J. Olander, age 55
Auditors: Deloitte & Touche LLP

LOCATIONS

HQ: U.S. Can Corporation
700 E. Butterfield Rd., Ste. 250, Lombard, IL 60148
Phone: 630-678-8000   **Fax:** 630-678-8131
Web: www.uscanco.com

U.S. Can has plants in Argentina, Denmark, France, Germany, Italy, Spain, UK, and the US.

2003 Sales

	$ mil.	% of total
US	536.0	65
Europe	286.8	35
Total	**822.8**	**100**

PRODUCTS/OPERATIONS

2003 Sales

	$ mil.	% of total
Aerosol	359.2	44
International	286.8	35
Paint	118.9	14
Custom & Specialty	57.9	7
Total	**822.8**	**100**

Selected Products

Aerosol containers
  Steel aerosol cans
Paint, plastic, and general line cans
  Steel paint and coating containers
  Oblong steel cans (for products such as turpentine and charcoal lighter fluid)
  Plastic pails and other containers for industrial products (such as spackle and dry wall compounds)
  Consumer products (such as swimming pool chemicals and paint)
Custom and specialty containers
  Functional and decorative containers and tins
  Stampings
  Collectible items (such as decorative metal signs and canister sets)

COMPETITORS

Ball Corporation
BWAY
CCL Industries
Crown
Owens-Illinois
Pechiney
Silgan
Sonoco Products

HISTORICAL FINANCIALS

Company Type: Private

Income Statement
FYE: December 31

	REVENUE ($ mil.)	NET INCOME ($ mil.)	NET PROFIT MARGIN	EMPLOYEES
12/03	823	(14)	—	2,300
12/02	797	(72)	—	2,400
12/01	772	(40)	—	2,600
12/00	810	(12)	—	2,700
12/99	714	21	3.0%	3,000
12/98	710	(16)	—	3,195
12/97	739	(32)	—	4,478
12/96	761	12	1.5%	4,065
12/95	627	4	0.6%	3,678
12/94	563	19	3.3%	3,500
Annual Growth	4.3%	—	—	(4.6%)

2003 Year-End Financials

Debt ratio: —
Return on equity: —
Cash ($ mil.): 24
Current ratio: 1.37
Long-term debt ($ mil.): 536

Net Income History

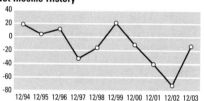

U.S. Central

United credit unions stand in U.S. Central Credit Union, a cooperative "central bank" for a network of about 30 corporate (or regional) credit unions. These, in turn, represent some 10,000 consumer credit unions nationwide. U.S. Central performs a variety of liquidity and cash management functions, such as funds transfer, settlement services, risk management, and custody services. Subsidiary CU Investment Solutions provides investment advisory services to the corporate credit unions, while majority-owned Corporate Network eCom offers bill payment and technology services to the network and its members.

Another subsidiary, Charlie Mac (formerly Network Liquidity Acceptance Company), works as a liquidity facility by purchasing loans originated by the credit union community.

EXECUTIVES

Chairman: Edward J. Fox
Vice Chairman: David A. (Dave) Preter
President and CEO: Dan Kampen
Treasurer and Director: Tom Kuehl
Secretary and Director: Robert W. (Bob) Thurman
SVP, Correspondent Services: Robert Amundson
SVP and CFO: Kathryn (Kathy) Brick
SVP, Asset and Liability Management: David (Dave) Dickens
SVP and General Counsel: François G. Henriquez II
SVP and CIO: Charles Troutman
VP, Research and Development: Scott Burditt
Chief Investment Officer: Connie Loveless
Director, Communications: Roger Dick
Director, Human Resources: Linda Pfingsten
Auditors: Ernst & Young LLP

LOCATIONS

HQ: U.S. Central Credit Union
9701 Renner Blvd., Ste. 100, Lenexa, KS 66219
Phone: 913-227-6000 Fax: 913-227-6250
Web: www.uscentral.org

PRODUCTS/OPERATIONS

2003 Sales

	$ mil.	% of total
Interest		
Investment securities	575.4	81
Securities purchased		
under agreements to resell	39.3	6
Loans	28.1	4
Federal funds sold	24.5	3
Stock of the Central Liquidity Facility	14.0	2
Time deposits		
& other short-term investments	10.9	2
Fee income	17.5	2
Total	**709.7**	**100**

Selected Products and Services
APEX-ACH (automated payment exchange and clearinghouse service)
Automated settlement
CNECS (Internet-based processing system)
eCom's Member Street (portfolio of online financial services for credit unions)
Fixed-callable certificates
Floating rate asset program
International services
Investment strategies and products
Loan purchase and securitization

Selected Subsidiaries and Affiliates
Charlie Mac LLC (formerly Network Liquidity Acceptance Company, correspondent banking)
Corporate Network eCom LLC (87%; electronic billing and technology services)
CU Investment Solutions, Inc. (formerly U.S. Central Capital Markets, Inc.; brokerage and advising services for member credit unions)
Network Financial Services, LLC (common trust fund, file-switching service, and electronic information exchange)

COMPETITORS

A.G. Edwards
Bear Stearns
BISYS
Charles Schwab
CheckFree
DST
EDS
First Data
Fiserv
Fiserv Securities
Jack Henry
Merrill Lynch
NOVA
Online Resources
PBiz
PrimeVest
SEI

HISTORICAL FINANCIALS

Company Type: Cooperative

Income Statement
FYE: December 31

	ASSETS ($ mil.)	NET INCOME ($ mil.)	INCOME AS % OF ASSETS	EMPLOYEES
12/03	35,025	69	0.2%	250
12/02	31,808	59	0.2%	230
12/01	32,221	48	0.1%	200
12/00	22,759	45	0.2%	186
12/99	26,218	43	0.2%	219
12/98	25,709	38	0.1%	190
12/97	18,087	30	0.2%	179
12/96	17,925	29	0.2%	149
12/95	19,305	28	0.1%	151
12/94	18,681	—	—	164
Annual Growth	7.2%	11.9%	—	4.8%

2003 Year-End Financials

Equity as % of assets: 90.2% Long-term debt ($ mil.): 345
Return on assets: 0.2% Sales ($ mil.): 710
Return on equity: 0.2%

Net Income History

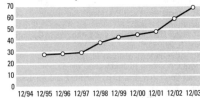

U.S. Oil

U.S. Oil Co. supplies refined oil products to US residents in the Midwest, and does a lot more. In addition to the wholesale distribution of oil products (its largest revenue generator), the company operates gas stations, and installs gas pumps, tanks, and other petroleum-related equipment. It also provides plumbing and heating services, operates a laboratory for environmental analysis, and collects used waste oil to be processed into burner fuel. Founded in the 1950s as Schmidt Oil by the sons of local fuel distributor Albert Schmidt, U.S. Oil Co. is still controlled by the Schmidt family.

EXECUTIVES

President and CEO: Thomas A. Schmidt
CFO and Treasurer: Paul Bachman
Director Human Resources: Gretchen Leverson
Director Information Systems: Fred Pennings
Corporate Secretary: Joe Kaufman
General Counsel: Marjorie Young

LOCATIONS

HQ: U.S. Oil Co., Inc.
425 S. Washington St., Combined Locks, WI 54113
Phone: 920-739-6101 Fax: 920-788-0531
Web: www.usoil.com

U.S. Oil has operations in Illinois, Michigan, Minnesota, Missouri, and Wisconsin.

PRODUCTS/OPERATIONS

Major Operations
Design Air (heating and air conditioning equipment)
Express Convenience Centers (gas stations and car washes)
NEW Energy, LLC, U.S. Oil (fuel oil and gasoline)
U.S. Lubricants (motor oil and related products)
U.S. Petroleum Equipment (petroleum-related equipment installation)
U.S. Petroleum Laboratory (environmental and used oil testing and analysis)
U.S. Petroleum Operations (gasoline, fuel oil, and natural gas)
U.S. Plumbing & Heating (commercial and residential plumbing and heating services)
U.S. Tire & Exhaust (exhaust pipe manufacturing and auto parts distribution)

COMPETITORS

Apex Oil
Motiva Enterprises
Premcor
Sunoco

HISTORICAL FINANCIALS

Company Type: Private

Income Statement
FYE: July 31

	REVENUE ($ mil.)	NET INCOME ($ mil.)	NET PROFIT MARGIN	EMPLOYEES
7/03	1,166	—	—	670
7/02*	753	—	—	730
12/00	765	—	—	850
Annual Growth	23.5%	—	—	(11.2%)

*Fiscal year change

Revenue History

US Oncology

US Oncology wants to get on the frontlines in the war against cancer, having restructured to focus on services more directly related to treating cancer. These services include oncology pharmaceutical management (such as the purchase and distribution of drugs), research and development assistance (such as the supervision of clinical trials), and outpatient cancer center operations. The company serves about 875 cancer physicians and nearly 80 cancer centers in some 32 states. US Oncology was formed from the 1999 merger of American Oncology Resources and Physician Reliance Network. Investment firm Welsh, Carson, Anderson & Stowe purchased the company in 2004.

US Oncology merged with Oiler Acquisition Corp — an affiliate of Welsh, Carson, Anderson & Stowe.

US Oncology plans to grow by providing a wide range of care management support services to medical oncologists.

EXECUTIVES

Chairman, President, and CEO: R. Dale Ross, age 57, $1,465,043 pay
Vice Chairman: Lloyd K. Everson, age 60
EVP and COO: George D. Morgan, age 51, $629,224 pay
EVP, Pharmaceutical Services, CFO and Treasurer: Bruce D. Broussard, age 41, $623,001 pay
EVP, Clinical Affairs: Joseph S. Bailes, age 47, $458,337 pay
EVP, Chief Administrative Officer, and Secretary: Leo E. Sands, age 56, $631,008 pay
SVP, Marketing and Development: Richard J. Hall
VP Human Resources: Robert P. Jordan
President, Cancer Information Research Group: Atul Dhir, age 41, $576,711 pay
General Counsel: Phillip H. Watts, age 38
Chief Information Officer: Todd Schonherz
Director, Public Relations: Steve Sievert
Auditors: PricewaterhouseCoopers LLP

LOCATIONS

HQ: US Oncology, Inc.
16825 Northchase Dr., Ste. 1300,
Houston, TX 77060
Phone: 832-601-8766   Fax: 832-601-6282
Web: www.usoncology.com

US Oncology operates in Alabama, Arizona, Arkansas, California, Colorado, Florida, Illinois, Indiana, Iowa, Kansas, Maryland, Massachusetts, Minnesota, Missouri, Montana, Nebraska, Nevada, New Mexico, New Jersey, New York, North Carolina, Ohio, Oklahoma, Oregon, Pennsylvania, South Carolina, Tennessee, Texas, Virginia, Washington, West Virginia, and Wisconsin.

PRODUCTS/OPERATIONS

2003 Sales

	$ mil.	% of total
Medical oncology services	2,123.2	85
Cancer center services	317.6	13
Other	59.1	2
Amounts retained by practices	(534.2)	—
Total	**1,965.7**	**100**

COMPETITORS

American Healthcare Services
Cancer Treatment Holdings, Inc.
Caremark
Medco Health Solutions
Memorial Sloan-Kettering
Salick Health Care
Sheridan Healthcare
Sterling Healthcare
SurgiCare

HISTORICAL FINANCIALS

Company Type: Private

Income Statement   FYE: December 31

	REVENUE ($ mil.)	NET INCOME ($ mil.)	NET PROFIT MARGIN	EMPLOYEES
12/03	1,966	71	3.6%	8,096
12/02	1,651	(46)	—	8,957
12/01	1,505	46	3.1%	8,254
12/00	1,324	(73)	—	7,716
12/99	1,093	48	4.4%	7,182
12/98	456	30	6.6%	1,293
12/97	322	23	7.1%	1,162
12/96	206	18	8.6%	937
12/95	99	12	11.7%	737
12/94	20	1	5.9%	613
Annual Growth	66.1%	57.3%	—	33.2%

2003 Year-End Financials

Debt ratio: 32.6%
Return on equity: 12.2%
Cash ($ mil.): 125
Current ratio: 1.37
Long-term debt ($ mil.): 188

Net Income History

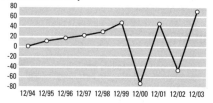

U.S. Postal Service

The United States Postal Service (USPS) handles cards, letters, and packages sent from sea to shining sea. Overall, the USPS delivers more than 200 billion pieces of mail a year to some 141 million addresses. The independent government agency relies on postage and fees to fund operations. Though it has a monopoly on delivering nonurgent letters, the USPS faces competition for services such as package delivery. The US president appoints nine of the 11 members of the board that oversees the USPS. The presidential appointees select the postmaster general, who, along with the deputy postmaster general, is a board member.

A challenge for the agency is the growing use of the Internet, which the USPS expects will cause the volume of "snail mail" to decline. To keep pace, the USPS is launching e-commerce initiatives such as computerized postage. The agency has also tapped into online shopping with its priority mail, merchandise return, and delivery confirmation services. It has formed limited alliances with express delivery companies, including a deal in which FedEx provides air transportation for express mail, priority, and first-class mail shipments (but doesn't deliver the mail).

With an eye on its bottom line, the USPS has scaled down its construction program and accelerated the pace of its rate increases, although officials hope to delay the next increase until 2006. In addition, the agency is reducing its workforce through attrition and cutting hours of operation at some post offices. The strategies worked in 2003: The USPS ended its fiscal year in the black for the first time since 1999.

A commission appointed by President Bush has recommended that the USPS adopt some private-sector management practices in order to ensure the agency's long-term financial health and to preserve universal mail service. The Bush administration expects the commission's recommendations to lead to the most significant revamp of postal operations since the early 1970s.

HISTORY

The second-oldest agency of the US government (after Indian Affairs), the Post Office was created by the Continental Congress in 1775 with Benjamin Franklin as postmaster general. The postal system came to play a vital role in the development of transportation in the US.

At that time, postal workers were riders on muddy paths delivering letters without stamps or envelopes. Letters were delivered only between post offices. Congress approved the first official postal policy in 1792: Rates ranged from six cents for less than 30 miles to 25 cents for more than 450. Letter carriers began delivering mail in cities in 1794.

First based in Philadelphia, in 1800 the Post Office moved to Washington, DC. In 1829 Andrew Jackson elevated the position of postmaster general to cabinet rank — it became a means of rewarding political cronies. Mail contracts subsidized the early development of US railroads. The first adhesive postage stamp appeared in the US in 1847.

Uniform postal rates (not varying with distance) were instituted in 1863, the year free city delivery began. The start of free rural delivery in 1896 spurred road construction in isolated US areas. Parcel post was launched in 1913, and new mail-order houses such as Montgomery Ward and Sears, Roebuck flourished.

The famous pledge beginning "Neither snow nor rain..." — not an official motto — was first inscribed at the main New York City post office in 1914. Scheduled airmail service between Washington, DC, and New York City began in 1918, stimulating the development of commercial air service. The ZIP code was introduced in 1963.

As mail volume grew, postal workers became increasingly militant under work stress. (Franklin's pigeonhole sorting method had barely changed.) A work stoppage in the New York City post office in 1970 spread within nine days to 670 post offices, and the US Army was deployed to handle the mail. Later that year the Postal Reorganization Act was passed. The new law established a board of governors to handle postal affairs and choose the postmaster general, who became CEO of an independent agency, the United States Postal Service (USPS). The next year USPS negotiated the first US government collective-bargaining labor contract. Express mail service began in 1977, and USPS stepped up automation efforts.

In 1995 USPS launched Global Package Link, a program to expedite major customers' shipments to Canada, Japan, and the UK. The next year it overhauled rates, cutting prices for larger mailers who prepared their mail for automation and raising prices for small mailers who didn't.

Postmaster General Marvin Runyon — whose six-year tenure took the agency from the red into the black — retired in 1998 and was succeeded by USPS veteran William Henderson. The next year a one-cent hike in the price of first-class postage took effect. (Another one-cent increase took effect in 2001, and the rate rose once again the following year.) In a nod to the Internet, USPS in 1999 contracted with outside vendors to enable customers to buy and print stamps online.

In 2001 USPS formed a strategic alliance with rival FedEx through which FedEx agreed to provide air transportation for USPS mail, in return for the placement of FedEx drop boxes in post offices.

Henderson stepped down at the end of May 2001, and EVP Jack Potter was named to replace him. That year several postal workers in a Washington, DC, branch office were exposed to anthrax-tainted letters.

EXECUTIVES

Chairman: S. David Fineman
Vice Chairman: John F. Walsh
Postmaster General and CEO: John E. (Jack) Potter
Deputy Postmaster General: John Nolan
EVP and COO: Patrick R. Donahoe
EVP and CFO: Richard J. Strasser Jr.
SVP and Chief Marketing Officer: Anita J. Bizzotto
SVP Government Relations: Ralph Moden
SVP Human Resources: Suzanne Medvidovich
SVP Intelligent Mail and Address Quality:
  Charles E. (Charlie) Bravo
SVP Operations: John A. Rapp

VP and CTO: Robert L. (Bob) Otto
VP and Consumer Advocate: Francia G. Smith
VP Delivery and Retail (Acting): William P. Galligan
VP Diversity Development: Murray Weatherall
VP Emergency Preparedness: Henry A. Pankey
VP Engineering: Thomas G. Day
VP Facilities: Rudolph K. Umscheid
VP Finance and Controller: Donna M. Peak
VP and General Counsel: Mary Anne Gibbons
VP International Business: James P. Wade
VP Labor Relations: Anthony Vegliante
VP Public Affairs and Communications:
 Azeezaly S. Jaffer
VP Sales: Jerry Whalen
VP and Treasurer: Robert J. Pedersen
Chief Postal Inspector: Lee Heath
Auditors: Ernst & Young LLP

LOCATIONS

HQ: United States Postal Service
 475 L'Enfant Plaza SW, Washington, DC 20260
Phone: 202-268-2500 **Fax:** 202-268-4860
Web: www.usps.com

PRODUCTS/OPERATIONS

2003 Sales

	$ mil.	% of total
First-class mail	37,048	54
Standard mail	17,203	25
Priority mail	4,494	7
Periodicals	2,235	3
Package services	2,216	3
International airmail	1,469	2
Express mail	888	1
Certified	624	1
Other services	2,352	4
Total	**68,529**	**100**

COMPETITORS

BAX Global   FedEx
DHL   UPS

HISTORICAL FINANCIALS

Company Type: Government agency

Income Statement FYE: September 30

	REVENUE ($ mil.)	NET INCOME ($ mil.)	NET PROFIT MARGIN	EMPLOYEES
9/03	68,529	3,868	5.6%	826,955
9/02	66,463	(676)	—	854,376
9/01	65,834	(1,680)	—	797,795
9/00	64,540	(199)	—	787,538
9/99	62,726	363	0.6%	800,000
9/98	60,072	550	0.9%	792,041
9/97	58,216	1,264	2.2%	765,174
9/96	56,402	1,567	2.8%	760,966
9/95	54,294	1,770	3.3%	753,384
9/94	49,252	(914)	—	728,944
Annual Growth	3.7%	—	—	1.4%

2003 Year-End Financials

Debt ratio: 0.1%   Current ratio: 0.22
Return on equity: —   Long-term debt ($ mil.): 1
Cash ($ mil.): 2,266

Net Income History

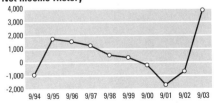

USAA

USAA has a decidedly military bearing. The mutual insurance company serves more than 5 million customers, primarily military personnel and their families. Its products and services include property & casualty (sold only to military personnel) and life insurance, banking, discount brokerage, and investment management. USAA relies largely on technology and direct marketing to sell its products, reaching clients via the telephone and Internet. The company also has a large mail-order catalog business (computers, furniture, jewelry, and home and auto safety items), and it offers long-distance telephone service, travel services, and Internet access to its members.

The company is expecting its membership to continue growing, projecting it to nearly double by 2010. In an attempt to increase revenue, the company has entered new markets by making efforts to target people less affluent than military officers.

Facing rising claims and a decline in value of its investments, USAA has streamlined operations by reducing staff and closing down divisions (including mailing, printing, and information technology offices).

In 2003, USAA increased sales and improved net income thanks to the rebounding stock market and membership growth.

HISTORY

In 1922 a group of 26 US Army officers gathered in a San Antonio hotel and formed their own automobile insurance association. The reason? As military officers who often moved, they had a hard time getting insurance because they were considered transient. So the officers decided to insure each other. Led by Major William Garrison, who became the company's first president, they formed the United States Army Automobile Insurance Association.

In 1924, when US Navy and Marine Corps officers were allowed to join, the company changed its name to United Services Automobile Association. By the mid-1950s the company had some 200,000 members. During the 1960s the company formed USAA Life Insurance Company (1963) and USAA Casualty Insurance Company (1968).

Robert McDermott, a retired US Air Force brigadier general, became president in 1969. He cut employment through attrition, established education and training seminars for employees, and invested in computers and telecommunications (drastically cutting claims-processing time). McDermott added new products and services, such as mutual funds, real estate investments, and banking. Under McDermott, USAA's membership grew from 653,000 in 1969 to more than 3 million in 1993.

During the 1970s, in an effort to go paperless, USAA became one of the insurance industry's first companies to switch from mail to toll-free (800) numbers. In the early 1980s the company introduced its discount purchasing program, USAA Buying Services. In 1985 it opened the USAA Federal Savings Bank. USAA began installing an optical storage system in the late 1980s to automate some customer service operations.

McDermott retired in 1993 and was succeeded by Robert Herres. The following year USAA Federal Savings Bank began developing a home banking system, offering members information and services over advanced screen telephones provided by IBM.

In the early 1990s USAA's real estate activities increased dramatically. In 1995 USAA restructured its interest in the Fiesta Texas theme park in San Antonio in order to focus on previously developed properties in geographically diverse areas. That year Six Flags Theme Parks (now Six Flags, Inc.) assumed operation and management of Fiesta Texas (which purchased it from USAA in 1998).

In 1997 USAA began including enlisted military personnel as members. It also started to experiment with a "plain English" mutual fund prospectus. In 1998 USAA also began offering Choice Ride in Orlando, Florida. For about $1,100 per quarter and a promise not to drive except in emergencies, the pilot program provided 36 round trips and a 90% discount on car insurance, in hopes of keeping older drivers from unnecessarily getting behind the wheel.

Also in 1998, as part of its new Financial Planning Network, USAA began offering retirement and estate planning assistance aimed at 25- to 55-year-olds for a yearly $250 fee. In 1999 claims doubled largely due to the impact of Hurricane Floyd and spring hail storms hitting military communities in North Carolina and Virginia.

USAA also moved in 1999 to consolidate its customers' separate accounts (such as mutual fund holdings, stocks and bonds, and life insurance products) into one main account to strengthen customer relationships and reduce operational costs. The next year, after completing a number of technology projects, it laid off workers for the first time in its history.

In 2002, Robert Herres resigned as chairman and was succeeded by CEO Robert Davis.

EXECUTIVES

Chairman and CEO: Robert G. (Bob) Davis
EVP, Enterprise Business Operations and COO:
 Robert T. Handren
EVP, CFO, and Corporate Treasurer:
 Josue (Joe) Robles Jr., age 57
EVP, Corporate Secretary, and General Counsel:
 Bradford W. Rich
EVP, Corporate Communications: Wendi E. Strong
EVP, Corporate Services: David H. Garrison
EVP, Human Resources: Elizabeth D. Conklyn
EVP, Marketing: Karen B. Presley
President and CEO, Alliance Services Company:
 Dawn M. Johnson
President and CEO, USAA Federal Savings Bank:
 Mark H. Wright
President and CEO, USAA Investment Management:
 Christopher W. Claus
President and CEO, USAA Real Estate:
 Edward B. Kelley
President, USAA Life Insurance: Kristi A. Matus
President, USAA Property and Casualty Insurance:
 Henry Viccellio Jr.
Auditors: KPMG LLP

LOCATIONS

HQ: USAA
 9800 Fredericksburg Rd., San Antonio, TX 78288
Phone: 210-498-2211 **Fax:** 210-498-9940
Web: www.usaa.com

USAA has major regional offices in Arizona, California, Colorado, Florida, Texas, and Virginia. It maintains international offices in London and Frankfurt, Germany.

PRODUCTS/OPERATIONS

2003 Sales

	$ mil.	% of total
Premiums	7,967	75
Fees, sales & loan income	1,342	13
Investment income	831	8
Real estate	218	2
Other	235	2
Total	**10,593**	**100**

Selected Operations
USAA Alliance Services Company (merchandising & member services)
USAA Federal Savings Bank
USAA Investment Management Company (mutual funds, investment and brokerage services)
USAA Property & Casualty (including automobile, home, boat, and flood insurance)
USAA Real Estate Company

COMPETITORS

21st Century	Kemper Insurance
AIG	Liberty Mutual
AIG American General	MassMutual
Allstate	MetLife
American Express	Morgan Stanley
American Financial	Mutual of Omaha
AXA Financial	Nationwide
Berkshire Hathaway	New York Life
Charles Schwab	Northwestern Mutual
Chubb	Pacific Mutual
CIGNA	Prudential
Citigroup	St. Paul Travelers
CNA Financial	State Farm
FMR	T. Rowe Price
Guardian Life	UBS Financial Services
The Hartford	
John Hancock Financial Services	

HISTORICAL FINANCIALS
Company Type: Mutual company

Income Statement — FYE: December 31

	ASSETS ($ mil.)	NET INCOME ($ mil.)	INCOME AS % OF ASSETS	EMPLOYEES
12/03	41,044	1,501	3.7%	21,000
12/02	38,203	500	1.3%	22,000
12/01	33,829	604	1.8%	22,000
12/00	32,794	669	2.0%	22,000
12/99	30,323	765	2.5%	21,795
12/98	28,831	980	3.4%	20,120
12/97	25,007	1,189	4.8%	17,967
12/96	23,622	855	3.6%	16,571
12/95	22,244	730	3.3%	15,677
12/94	19,548	564	2.9%	15,233
Annual Growth	8.6%	11.5%	—	3.6%

2003 Year-End Financials

Equity as % of assets: 22.1%   Long-term debt ($ mil.): 12,870
Return on assets: 3.8%   Sales ($ mil.): 10,593
Return on equity: 17.7%

Net Income History

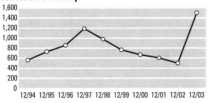

Utica Mutual

Utica Mutual Insurance is native to the Mohawk Valley, but has spread its insurance business across the US since its founding in 1914. The company (which uses the marketing name Utica National Group) specializes in commercial and personal property & casualty insurance; it also offers life insurance and specialty coverage for such groups as printers, schools, and insurance agents. Utica Mutual operates through a host of subsidiaries including Graphic Arts Mutual Insurance, Republic-Franklin Insurance, Utica National Life, and Utica National Insurance Company of Texas. Selling its products nationwide, the company is represented by more than 1,200 independent agents.

EXECUTIVES

Chairman: W. Craig Heston
President and CEO: J. Douglas Robinson
EVP: Brian P. Lytwynec
EVP, CFO, and Treasurer: Anthony C. Paolozzi
SVP and Director of Reinsurance: Richard J. Beidleman
SVP, General Counsel, and Senior Claims Officer: Richard P. Creedon
SVP and Director of Human Resources: Clarke Peterson
SVP and Senior Regional Operations Officer: Albert A. Ritchie
VP and Director of Corporate Communications: Michael C. Austin
VP and Senior Information Services Officer: James P. Carhart
VP and Investment Officer: Cynthia L. Casale
VP and General Auditor: Robert W. Dicks Jr.
VP and Actuary: George T. Dodd
VP and Senior Marketing and Sales Officer: Daniel D. Daly
Auditors: PricewaterhouseCoopers LLP

LOCATIONS

HQ: Utica Mutual Insurance Company
180 Genesee St., New Hartford, NY 13413
Phone: 315-734-2000   **Fax:** 315-734-2680
Web: www.uticanational.com

PRODUCTS/OPERATIONS

Selected Subsidiaries and Affiliates
Graphic Arts Mutual Insurance Company
Republic-Franklin Insurance Company
Uni-Service Excess Facilities Insurance Agency Of New England, Inc.
Uni-Service Excess Facilities, Inc.
Uni-Service Life Agency, Inc.
Uni-Service Operations Corp.
Uni-Service Risk Management Corp.
Utica Lloyd's Of Texas
Utica Lloyd's, Inc.
Utica National Assurance Company
Utica National Insurance Company Of Texas
Utica National Life Insurance Company
Utica Specialty Risk Insurance Company

COMPETITORS

ACE Limited	National Life Insurance
AIG	Penn Mutual
Allstate	PMA Capital
American Financial	Prudential
Amica Mutual	Safeco
AXA Corporate Solutions	St. Paul Travelers
Farmers Group	State Farm
The Hartford	USAA
Kemper Insurance	White Mountains Insurance Group
Liberty Mutual	

HISTORICAL FINANCIALS
Company Type: Mutual company

Income Statement — FYE: December 31

	REVENUE ($ mil.)	NET INCOME ($ mil.)	NET PROFIT MARGIN	EMPLOYEES
12/03	656	—	—	1,435
12/02	643	—	—	1,500
12/01	784	—	—	1,500
Annual Growth	(8.5%)	—	—	(2.2%)

Revenue History

Utility Trailer

Utility Trailer Manufacturing is spreading its own brand of reefer madness. Utility Trailer is one of the US's largest manufacturers of refrigerated trailers, or reefers, as they are known in the business. The company also produces dry freight trailers, flatbeds, and curtain-sided trailers at five plants in the US. Its refrigerated trucks include special designs for the whole food distribution and fast-food markets, such as a truck with separate chambers for frozen and dry goods. The company's trailers are distributed throughout Canada, Mexico, the US, and to a lesser extent in Argentina. Two brothers, H.C. and E.W. Bennett, founded the company in 1914 and their descendants still own it.

EXECUTIVES

CEO: Paul Bennett
CFO: Arthur Goolsbee
SVP, Marketing and Sales: Craig Bennett
Director, Data Processing: Richard Vaughn
Director, Human Resources: John Stanton

LOCATIONS

HQ: Utility Trailer Manufacturing Co.
17295 E. Railroad St., City of Industry, CA 91748
Phone: 626-965-1541   **Fax:** 626-965-2790
Web: www.utilitytrailer.com

Utility Trailer Manufacturing operates seven manufacturing facilities throughout the US.

PRODUCTS/OPERATIONS

Selected Products
Dry freight trailers
Flatbeds
Refrigerated trailers (reefers)
Curtain-sided trailers
Used trailers

ValleyCrest Companies

ValleyCrest Companies hit pay dirt with plant care. The company uses its green thumb to provide landscape construction and maintenance, irrigation, golf course construction, lawn care, nurseries, and site engineering. ValleyCrest grows more than 2 million trees (for relocation), maintains indoor and outdoor gardens, and restores wetlands. It also franchises landscape maintenance services. Co-founder and CEO Burton Sperber and his family control the company, which began operations in 1949.

ValleyCrest purchased the landscape construction operations of TruGreen LandCare in 2001 to expand operations in Maryland, Massachusetts, Illinois, Minnesota, and Texas. In 2004 the company acquired the landscaping division of Omni Facility Services, which will be integrated into ValleyCrest's landscape maintenance division. The acquisition expands ValleyCrest's operations in the eastern US.

COMPETITORS

Fontaine Trailer
Great Dane
Hyundai Translead
J.B. Poindexter
Lufkin Industries
Obsidian Enterprises
RailAmerica
Supreme Industries
Trailmobile
Wabash National

HISTORICAL FINANCIALS

Company Type: Private

Income Statement — FYE: December 31

	REVENUE ($ mil.)	NET INCOME ($ mil.)	NET PROFIT MARGIN	EMPLOYEES
12/03	600	—	—	3,200
12/02	600	—	—	3,200
12/01	650	—	—	3,400
12/00	680	—	—	3,400
12/99	650	—	—	2,900
12/98	584	—	—	2,600
12/97	483	—	—	2,550
12/96	429	—	—	2,500
12/95	515	—	—	—
12/94	400	—	—	—
Annual Growth	4.6%	—	—	3.6%

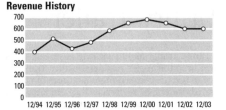
Revenue History

EXECUTIVES

Chairman and CEO: Burton S. (Burt) Sperber
Vice Chairman; CEO, Valley Crest Tree Company: Stuart J. Sperber
President and COO: Richard A. Sperber
EVP and CFO: Andrew J. (Andy) Mandell
SVP Asset and Risk Management: Michael L. (Mike) Dingman
VP and Corporate Controller: Anthony (Tony) Garruto
VP and Corporate Counsel: William N. (Bill) Cohen
VP Customer Satisfaction: Pamela S. (Pam) Stark
VP: Marissa Andrada
VP and Assistant COO: Renu Nallicheri
CIO: John D. Johnston
Corporate Secretary: Anita Legg
Director, Public Relations: Cheryl Steelberg

LOCATIONS

HQ: ValleyCrest Companies
24121 Ventura Blvd., Calabasas, CA 91302
Phone: 818-223-8500 **Fax:** 818-223-8142
Web: www.valleycrest.com

ValleyCrest Companies has operations in Arizona, California, Colorado, Florida, Georgia, Illinois, Indiana, Kentucky, Maryland, Massachusetts, Michigan, Minnesota, Missouri, Nevada, North Carolina, Pennsylvania, Tennessee, Texas, and Virginia.

PRODUCTS/OPERATIONS

Selected Subsidiaries and Operating Divisions
U.S. Lawns
ValleyCrest Landscape Development
ValleyCrest Landscape Maintenance
ValleyCrest Golf Course Maintenance
Valley Crest Tree Company

COMPETITORS

Davey Tree
FirstService
GreenSmart
Griffin Land & Nurseries
Hines Horticulture
OneSource Landscape and Golf Services
Skinner Nurseries
TruGreen Landcare

HISTORICAL FINANCIALS

Company Type: Private

Income Statement — FYE: April 30

	ESTIMATED REVENUE ($ mil.)	NET INCOME ($ mil.)	NET PROFIT MARGIN	EMPLOYEES
4/04	700	—	—	8,000
4/03	620	—	—	8,000
4/02	605	—	—	—
4/01	500	—	—	5,500
4/00	450	—	—	5,000
4/99	400	—	—	4,000
4/98	350	—	—	4,000
4/97	340	—	—	4,100
4/96	300	—	—	4,689
4/95	265	—	—	—
Annual Growth	11.4%	—	—	6.9%

Revenue History

Vanderbilt University

The house that Cornelius built, Vanderbilt University was founded in 1873 with a $1 million grant from industrialist Cornelius Vanderbilt. The university's endowment has grown to about $2 billion, and the school today is a haven for more than 11,000 students and 2,200 full-time faculty. Vanderbilt has 10 schools and colleges; its Owen Graduate School of Management and its medical school rank near the top of national surveys. A major research university, Vanderbilt receives millions of dollars annually in sponsored awards to fund its facilities. Vanderbilt offers undergraduate and graduate programs in areas such as education and human development, engineering, and the arts and sciences.

EXECUTIVES

Chairman: Martha R. Ingram, age 68
Vice Chairman: Darryl D. Berger
Vice Chairman: Dennis C. Bottorff
Secretary: William W. Bain Jr.
Chancellor: E. Gordon Gee, age 60
Vice Chancellor Administration and CFO: Lauren J. Brisky
Vice Chancellor Health Affairs: Harry R. Jacobson, age 57
Vice Chancellor Public Affairs: Michael J. Schoenfeld
Vice Chancellor Investments and Treasurer: William T. Spitz
Vice Chancellor Student Life and University Affairs, General Counsel, and Secretary of the University: David Williams II
Provost and Vice Chancellor Academic Affairs: Nicholas S. Zeppos
Assistant Vice Chancellor Research Finance: Jerry Fife
Assistant Vice Chancellor Management Information Systems: Timothy R. (Tim) Getsay
Associate Vice Chancellor Finance and Controller: Betty Price
Auditors: KPMG LLP

LOCATIONS

HQ: Vanderbilt University
2201 West End Ave., Nashville, TN 37235
Phone: 615-322-7311
Web: www.vanderbilt.edu

PRODUCTS/OPERATIONS

2004 Sales

	$ mil.	% of total
Health care services	1,188.0	60
Government grants & contracts	238.6	12
Tuition, fees, room & board	204.8	10
Endowment distributions	101.9	5
Facilities & administrative costs recovery	87.6	4
Gifts, private grants & contributions	59.5	3
Auxiliary services	45.0	3
Other	45.5	3
Total	**1,970.9**	**100**

Selected Schools and Colleges
Blair School of Music
College of Arts and Science
Divinity School
Graduate School
Law School
Owen Graduate School of Management
Peabody College of Education and Human Development
School of Engineering
School of Medicine
School of Nursing

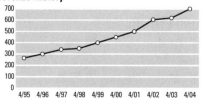

HISTORICAL FINANCIALS

Company Type: School

Income Statement
FYE: June 30

	REVENUE ($ mil.)	NET INCOME ($ mil.)	NET PROFIT MARGIN	EMPLOYEES
6/04	1,971	—	—	18,551
6/03	1,799	—	—	17,700
6/02	1,590	—	—	16,679
6/01	1,419	—	—	15,427
6/00	1,280	—	—	16,532
6/99	1,181	—	—	16,161
6/98	1,246	—	—	13,993
6/97	1,125	—	—	13,739
6/96	1,121	—	—	12,937
6/95	1,021	—	—	12,040
Annual Growth	7.6%	—	—	4.9%

Revenue History

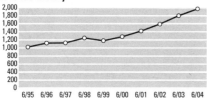

Vanguard Group

If you buy low and sell high, invest for the long term, don't panic, and generally disapprove of those whippersnappers at Fidelity, then you may end up in the Vanguard of the financial market. The Vanguard Group offers individual and institutional investors a line of highly sought-after mutual funds and brokerage services; it is the #2 fund manager after FMR (aka Fidelity), but is closing the gap, claiming some $725 billion of assets under management. Vanguard's fund options include more than 100 stock, bond, mixed, and international offerings, as well as variable annuity portfolios; its Vanguard 500 Index Fund is one of the largest in the US.

The company is known as much for its puritanical thriftiness and conservative investing as for its line of index funds, which track the performance of such groups of stock as the S&P 500. Retired company founder John Bogle is sometimes derisively called "St. Jack" for his zealous criticism of industry practices, but the company's reputation for being squeaky clean appears to have paid off: Vanguard so far remains untainted by the mutual fund industry scandals that began unfolding in late 2003.

Unlike other funds, Vanguard is set up like a mutual insurance company. The funds (and by extension, their more than 18 million investors) own the company, so fees are low to nonexistent; funds are operated on a tight budget so as not to eat into results. The company spends next to nothing on advertising, relying instead on strong returns and word-of-mouth.

And despite its no-broker, no-load background, Vanguard has developed cheap ways to dole out advice, especially through the use of toll-free numbers and the Internet and by quietly touting its online brokerage service.

HISTORY

A distant cousin of Daniel Boone, Walter Morgan knew a few things about pioneering. He was the first to offer a fund with a balance of stocks and bonds, serendipitously introduced early in 1929, months before the stock market collapsed. Morgan's balanced Wellington fund (named after Napoleon's vanquisher) emerged effectively unscathed.

John Bogle's senior thesis on mutual funds impressed fellow Princeton alum Morgan, who hired Bogle in 1951. Morgan retired in 1967 and picked Bogle to replace him. That year Bogle engineered a merger with old-school investment firm Thorndike, Doran, Paine and Lewis. After culture clashes and four years of shrinking assets, the Thorndike-dominated board fired Bogle, who appealed to the mutual funds and their separate board of directors. The fund directors decided to split up the funds and the advisory business.

Bogle named the fund company The Vanguard Group, after the flagship of Lord Nelson, another Napoleon foe. Vanguard worked like a cooperative; mutual fund shareholders owned the company, so all services were provided at cost. The Wellington Management Company remained Vanguard's distributor until 1977, when Bogle convinced Vanguard's board to drop the affiliation. Without Wellington as the intermediary, Vanguard sold its funds directly to consumers as no-load funds (without service charges). In 1976 the company launched the Vanguard Index 500, the first index fund. These measures attracted new investors in droves.

Vanguard rode the 1980s boom. Its Windsor fund grew so large the company closed it, launching Windsor II in 1985. Vanguard weathered the 1987 crash and began the 1990s as the US's #4 mutual fund company. The actively managed funds of FMR (better known as Fidelity), most notably its Magellan fund, led the market then. The retirement of legendary Magellan manager Peter Lynch and the fund's consequential underperformance spurred a rush to index funds. Vanguard moved up to #2.

Vanguard played against type in 1995 when it introduced the Vanguard Horizon Capital Growth stock fund, an aggressively managed fund designed to vie directly with Fidelity's funds.

In 1997 Vanguard added brokerage services and began selling its own and other companies' funds on the Internet to allow clients to consolidate their financial activities. In 1998 Bogle passed the chairmanship to CEO John Brennan, a soft-spoken technology wonk. Walter Morgan died that year at age 100.

Investors were ruffled when 70-year-old Bogle announced that corporate age limits would force him to leave the board of directors at the end of 1999. (Bogle retains an office at Vanguard headquarters, and remains popular on the speaker circuit.)

Despite Vanguard's stated commitment to the little guy, by late 2002 the company was forced to mitigate realities of the economy and started courting investors with bigger bankrolls; it also raised fees for some customers with smaller accounts.

EXECUTIVES

Chairman and CEO: John J. Brennan
Chief Investment Officer: George U. (Gus) Sauter
Managing Director, Legal Department, and General Counsel; Secretary, Vanguard Fiduciary Trust Company: R. Gregory Barton
Managing Director, Investor Programs & Services: James H. Gately
Managing Director, Human Resources: Kathleen C. Gubanich
Managing Director, Client Relationship Group: F. William McNabb III
Managing Director, Planning and Development Group: Michael S. Miller
Managing Director, Finance Group: Ralph K. Packard
Managing Director, IT: Mortimer J. (Tim) Buckley

LOCATIONS

HQ: The Vanguard Group, Inc.
100 Vanguard Blvd., Malvern, PA 19355
Phone: 610-648-6000   **Fax:** 610-669-6605
Web: www.vanguard.com

The Vanguard Group has offices in Malvern, Pennsylvania; Charlotte, North Carolina; and Scottsdale, Arizona; as well as in Brussels, Melbourne, and Tokyo.

PRODUCTS/OPERATIONS

Selected Funds

500 Index Fund
Asset Allocation Fund
Balanced Index Fund
California Intermediate-Term Tax-Exempt Fund
California Long-Term Tax-Exempt Fund
California Tax-Exempt Money Market Fund
Calvert Social Index Fund
Capital Opportunity Fund
Capital Value Fund
Convertible Securities Fund
Developed Markets Index Fund
Dividend Growth Fund
Emerging Markets Stock Index Fund
Energy Fund
Equity Income Fund
European Stock Index Fund
Explorer Fund
Extended Market Index Fund
Federal Money Market Fund
Florida Long-Term Tax-Exempt Fund
Global Equity Fund
GNMA Fund
Growth and Income Fund
Growth Equity Fund
Growth Index Fund
Health Care Fund
High-Yield Corporate Fund
High-Yield Tax-Exempt Fund
Inflation-Protected Securities Fund
Insured Long-Term Tax-Exempt Fund
Intermediate-Term Bond Index Fund
Intermediate-Term Corporate Fund
Intermediate-Term Tax-Exempt Fund
Intermediate-Term Treasury Fund
International Explorer Fund
International Growth Fund
International Value Fund
Large-Cap Index Fund
LifeStrategy Conservative Growth Fund
LifeStrategy Growth Fund
LifeStrategy Income Fund
LifeStrategy Moderate Growth Fund
Limited-Term Tax-Exempt Fund
Long-Term Bond Index Fund
Long-Term Corporate Fund
Long-Term Tax-Exempt Fund
Long-Term Treasury Fund
Massachusetts Tax-Exempt Fund
Mid-Cap Growth Fund
Mid-Cap Index Fund
New Jersey Long-Term Tax-Exempt Fund
New Jersey Tax-Exempt Money Market Fund
New York Long-Term Tax-Exempt Fund
New York Tax-Exempt Money Market Fund
Ohio Long-Term Tax-Exempt Fund
Ohio Tax-Exempt Money Market Fund
Pacific Stock Index Fund
Pennsylvania Long-Term Tax-Exempt Fund
Pennsylvania Tax-Exempt Money Market Fund
Precious Metals Fund
Prime Money Market Fund

PRIMECAP Fund
REIT Index Fund
Selected Value Fund
Short-Term Bond Index Fund
Short-Term Corporate Fund
Short-Term Federal Fund
Short-Term Tax-Exempt Fund
Short-Term Treasury Fund
Small-Cap Growth Index Fund
Small-Cap Index Fund
Small-Cap Value Index Fund
STAR Fund
Strategic Equity Fund
Target Retirement 2005
Target Retirement 2015
Target Retirement 2025
Target Retirement 2035
Target Retirement 2045
Target Retirement Income
Tax-Exempt Money Market Fund
Tax-Managed Balanced Fund
Tax-Managed Capital Appreciation Fund
Tax-Managed Growth and Income Fund
Tax-Managed International Fund
Tax-Managed Small-Cap Fund
Total Bond Market Index Fund
Total International Stock Index Fund
Total Stock Market Index Fund
Treasury Money Market Fund
U.S. Growth Fund
U.S. Value Fund
Value Index Fund

COMPETITORS

AIG
AIM Funds
Alliance Capital Management
American Century
AMVESCAP
AXA Financial
Charles Schwab
FMR
Franklin Resources
Human Resources & Investor Solutions
Janus Capital
Legg Mason
Mellon Financial
Merrill Lynch
MFS
Principal Financial
Putnam
T. Rowe Price
TIAA-CREF
USAA

HISTORICAL FINANCIALS

Company Type: Private

Income Statement				FYE: December 31
	ASSETS ($ mil.)	NET INCOME ($ mil.)	INCOME AS % OF ASSETS	EMPLOYEES
12/03	730,000	—	—	10,000
12/02	560,000	—	—	10,000
12/01	590,000	—	—	11,000
Annual Growth	11.2%	—	—	(4.7%)

Asset History

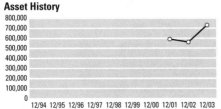

Vanguard Health Systems

Hospitals shouldn't let their guard down with Vanguard Health Systems hanging around the block. The company buys up acute care hospitals and other health care facilities primarily in urban areas. Vanguard acquires hospitals with capital provided by company management as well as various funds controlled by Morgan Stanley Capital Partners. Vanguard seeks to partner with, develop, or convert non-profit hospital systems to investor-owned entities as independent hospitals seek to capitalize on the benefits of becoming part of a larger hospital company. Vanguard also operates a prepaid Medicaid managed health plan called Phoenix Health Plan, serving nearly 70,000 members in Arizona.

EXECUTIVES

Chairman and CEO: Charles N. (Charlie) Martin Jr., age 60, $1,440,000 pay
Vice Chairman: Keith B. Pitts, age 46, $880,000 pay
President, COO, and Director:
 William L. (Larry) Hough, age 51, $880,000 pay
EVP, CFO, Treasurer, and Director:
 Joseph D. (Joe) Moore, age 56, $700,000 pay
EVP, Secretary, General Counsel, and Director:
 Ronald P. (Ron) Soltman, age 57
SVP, Development: Robert E. Galloway, age 58
SVP Operations: Dale St. Arnold, $756,000 pay
SVP, Human Resources: James Johnston, age 59
SVP, Controller, and Chief Accounting Officer:
 Phillip W. Roe, age 42
VP, Investor Relations: Trip Pilgrim
Auditors: Ernst & Young LLP

LOCATIONS

HQ: Vanguard Health Systems, Inc.
 20 Burton Hills Blvd., Ste. 100, Nashville, TN 37215
Phone: 615-665-6000 **Fax:** 615-665-6099
Web: www.vanguardhealth.com

Vanguard operates more than 15 hospitals in the Phoenix (Arizona), Chicago (Illinois), Orange County (California), and San Antonio (Texas) markets.

PRODUCTS/OPERATIONS

Medicare and Medicaid account for about 20% of revenues.

Selected Facilities

Arrowhead Hospital (Phoenix)
Baptist Medical Center (San Antonio)
Huntington Beach Hospital (Orange County)
La Palma Intercommunity Hospital (Orange County)
Louis A. Weiss Memorial Hospital (Chicago)
MacNeal Hospital (Chicago)
Maryvale Hospital (Phoenix)
North Central Baptist Hospital (San Antonio)
Northeast Baptist Hospital (San Antonio)
Paradise Valley Hospital (Phoenix)
Phoenix Baptist Hospital (Phoenix)
Phoenix Memorial Hospital (Phoenix)
Southeast Baptist Hospital (San Antonio)
St. Luke's Baptist Hospital (San Antonio)
West Anaheim Medical Center (Orange County)
West Valley Hospital (Phoenix)

COMPETITORS

HCA
Rush System for Health
Tenet Healthcare
Triad Hospitals

HISTORICAL FINANCIALS

Company Type: Private

Income Statement				FYE: June 30
	REVENUE ($ mil.)	NET INCOME ($ mil.)	NET PROFIT MARGIN	EMPLOYEES
6/03	1,341	17	1.3%	13,500
6/02	911	7	0.7%	8,000
6/01	668	10	1.5%	7,300
6/00	305	(1)	—	—
6/99	92	(5)	—	—
Annual Growth	95.6%	—	—	36.0%

2003 Year-End Financials

Debt ratio: 125.6%
Return on equity: —
Cash ($ mil.): 27
Current ratio: 1.14
Long-term debt ($ mil.): 471

Net Income History

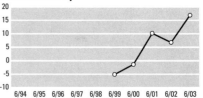

Variety Wholesalers

Variety is not only the spice of life — it's also a major purveyor of deeply discounted retail goods. With about 550 stores in 14 states from Louisiana to Delaware, Variety Wholesalers has survived even Wal-Mart's march through rural America. The company, which has aggressively bought other chains while closing poorly performing stores, tends to set up shop in small towns where the retail giants fear to tread. The company's retail outlets include Bargain Town, Maxway, Rose's, Super 10 (which prices all items at or below $10), Super Dollar, Super Saver, and Value-Mart. Variety Wholesalers was founded in 1932 by James Pope; the Pope family, including chairman and CEO John Pope, owns and leads the company.

EXECUTIVES

Chairman and CEO: John W. Pope Sr.
Vice Chairman, President, and CFO: Art Pope
EVP, Stores and Merchandising: Wilson Sawyer
Controller: Brant Sprunger
Human Resources Manager: Frances Burger

LOCATIONS

HQ: Variety Wholesalers, Inc.
 3401 Gresham Lake Rd., Raleigh, NC 27615
Phone: 919-876-6000 **Fax:** 919-790-5349
Web: www.vwstores.com

COMPETITORS

Big Lots
Bill's Dollar Stores
Dollar General
Dollar Tree
Family Dollar Stores
Fred's
Kmart
Target
Wal-Mart

VarTec

Actors and comedians employed promoting 10-10 calling plans can thank VarTec Telecom, a pioneering provider of "dial-around" long-distance service. VarTec provides residential and business calling plans, as well as Internet access and 800-number service. The company was founded in 1989 by chairman Joe Mitchell and his wife, former company executive Connie Mitchell, along with Ray Atkinson, president of international operations. Holding company Telephone Electronics Corp. owns a majority stake in VarTec, which acquired Dallas-based long-distance retailer Excel Communications in 2002.

EXECUTIVES
Chairman and CEO: A. Joe Mitchell Jr.
COO; President, Consumer Markets: Ron Hughes
EVP Legal and Regulatory Affairs and Chief Legal Officer: Michael Hoffman
President, International Operations Division: Ray Atkinson
Director, Corporate Communications: Paul Thies

LOCATIONS
HQ: VarTec Telecom, Inc.
1600 Viceroy Dr., Dallas, TX 75235
Phone: 214-424-1000   **Fax:** 214-424-1555
Web: www.vartec.com

VarTec Telecom has switching facilities in Atlanta; Chicago; Colorado Springs, Colorado; Dallas; Frankfurt; London; Los Angeles; New York; Orlando, Florida; Pittsburgh; and Seattle.

PRODUCTS/OPERATIONS
Selected Subsidiaries
eMeritus Communications, Inc. (integrated telecommunications services)
EurExcel (integrated telecommunications, UK)
Excel Telecommunications (long-distance reseller)
VarTec Telecom Europe, Ltd. (telecommunications customer services, UK)

COMPETITORS
9278 Communications
AT&T
Matrix Telecom
MCI
McLeodUSA
Qwest
Sprint FON
Talk America

HISTORICAL FINANCIALS
Company Type: Private

Income Statement				FYE: December 31
	REVENUE ($ mil.)	NET INCOME ($ mil.)	NET PROFIT MARGIN	EMPLOYEES
12/03	502	—	—	7,500
12/02	639	—	—	8,300
12/01	650	—	—	8,300
12/00	691	—	—	8,300
12/99	782	—	—	10,100
12/98	820	—	—	10,500
12/97	1,000	—	—	12,000
Annual Growth	(10.9%)	—	—	(7.5%)

Revenue History

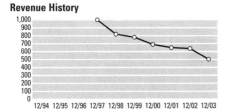

Venture Industries

When it comes to plastic automotive components, Venture Industries is ready for uncharted territory. The company is a leading maker of injection-molded plastic components for automotive OEMs. Products include interior systems, cockpit modules, front-end systems, exterior trim, and closures and panels. Venture Industries also offers design, preproduction, engineering, assembly, tooling, and logistics services to most of the world's automakers. Customers include GM, Ford, DaimlerChrysler, BMW, and Volkswagen. The company offers engineering and technology services in Asia, Australia, Europe, and North America and continues to expand into new regions. CEO Larry Winget owns Venture Industries.

EXECUTIVES
Chairman and CEO: Larry J. Winget Sr., age 59, $509,025 pay
Vice Chairman: Fred L. Hubacker, age 57, $750,584 pay
Vice Chairman: A. James Schutz, age 56
EVP; Chairman, Peguform GmbH: Larry J. Winget Jr., age 41, $432,283 pay
EVP, Interior Operations: Joseph R. Tignanelli, age 40
EVP, Legal, Secretary, and Treasurer: James E. Butler Jr., age 48
EVP, Purchasing: Patricia A. Stevens, age 54
VP and CFO: Michael D. Alexander, age 53
VP, Exterior and Composite Operations: Warren Brown, age 58
VP, Human Resources: Debra Wangurd
President, North American Manufacturing: Gary Woodall, age 59, $390,805 pay
General Counsel: Stephen M. Cheifetz, age 45
Auditors: Deloitte & Touche LLP

LOCATIONS
HQ: Venture Industries
33662 James J. Pompo Dr., Fraser, MI 48026
Phone: 586-294-1500   **Fax:** 586-296-8863
Web: www.ventureindustries.com

Venture Industries operates 63 facilities on five continents.

PRODUCTS/OPERATIONS
Selected Products
Exterior Products
 Body side moldings
 Convertible hardtops
 Doors
 Farings
 Fenders
 Front and rear bumper fascias and systems
 Grille opening panels and reinforcements
 Hatchback doors
 Hoods
 Sunroofs
 Wheel lips
Interior Products
 Airbag covers
 Consoles
 Door panels
 Garnishment molding systems
 Instrument panel systems
 Side wall trim

COMPETITORS
Carlisle Companies
Collins & Aikman
Faurecia
Husky Injection Molding Systems
Johnson Controls
Lacks Enterprises
Lear
Magna International
McKechnie
Meridian Automotive Systems
Plastic Omnium
Siegel-Robert
Textron
ThyssenKrupp Budd
Visteon

HISTORICAL FINANCIALS
Company Type: Private

Income Statement				FYE: December 31
	REVENUE ($ mil.)	NET INCOME ($ mil.)	NET PROFIT MARGIN	EMPLOYEES
12/03	1,300	—	—	3,060
12/02	1,300	—	—	3,200
12/01	1,040	—	—	1,793
12/00	995	—	—	1,276
12/99	960	—	—	2,238
12/98	913	—	—	1,460
12/97	850	—	—	1,200
12/96	470	—	—	—
12/95	125	—	—	—
Annual Growth	34.0%	—	—	16.9%

Revenue History

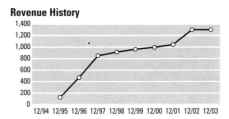

HISTORICAL FINANCIALS (Venture Industries continued)
Company Type: Private

Income Statement				FYE: December 31
	REVENUE ($ mil.)	NET INCOME ($ mil.)	NET PROFIT MARGIN	EMPLOYEES
12/02	1,700	—	—	10,700
12/01	1,860	—	—	18,000
12/00	2,400	—	—	18,000
12/99	2,450	—	—	20,000
12/98	2,500	—	—	10,000
Annual Growth	(9.2%)	—	—	1.7%

Revenue History

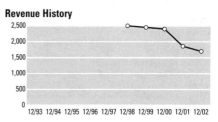

Verizon Wireless

Cellco Partnership, which does business as Verizon Wireless, is the #1 US mobile phone operator serving 40 million customers nationwide. Verizon Wireless began operations in 2000 when Bell Atlantic and Vodafone combined their US wireless assets, including their PrimeCo partnership. Verizon Wireless gained GTE's US wireless operations when Bell Atlantic bought GTE to form Verizon Communications, which owns 55% of the company; Vodafone owns 45%. Plans for an IPO, postponed in 2001, were revived but finally withdrawn in 2003 citing lack of funding needs.

The company is developing third-generation wireless services based on CDMA (code division multiple access) technology. It also has teamed up with Microsoft to develop and market wireless data services.

In late 2002 Verizon Wireless reached an agreement with Northcoast Communications, a unit of Cablevision Systems, to acquire 50 radio wave spectrum licenses in a cash deal valued at $762 million. The licenses cover several lucrative markets, including Boston and New York City, which reach a population of some 47 million. Following the deal's completion in 2003 Verizon Wireless announced plans to introduce a national service in direct competition with rival Nextel's "push to talk" feature.

The company also has announced plans to spend $1 billion over two years on the development of a nationwide broadband wireless Internet data network. It also has agreed to acquire the wireless assets from Qwest Communications in a cash deal valued at about $418 million.

Verizon Wireless hoped to bolster its coverage in the New York metropolitan area by agreeing to acquire licenses held by NextWave Telecom in that company's bankruptcy auction. It later acquired the bankrupt company in a deal valued at $3 billion. At that time NextWave's assets consisted only of spectrum licenses in 23 US markets, including Boston, Los Angeles, New York, and Washington, DC.

EXECUTIVES

Chairman: Ivan G. Seidenberg, age 57
President, CEO, and Director: Dennis F. (Denny) Strigl, age 58, $2,415,000 pay
EVP, COO, and Director: Lowell C. McAdam, age 49, $1,312,950 pay
EVP and CTO: Richard J. (Dick) Lynch, age 55, $837,550 pay
VP and CFO: Andrew N. (Andy) Halford, age 45, $1,073,146 pay
VP and Chief Marketing Officer: John G. Stratton, age 43
VP Business Development: Margaret P. (Molly) Feldman, age 46
VP Corporate Communications: James J. (Jim) Gerace, age 40
VP Enterprise Data Sales: Cindy Patterson
VP Federal Government Wireless Operations: Michael Maiorana
VP Human Resources: Martha Delehanty
VP Information Systems and CIO: Roger Gurnani, age 43
VP Legal and External Affairs, General Counsel, and Secretary: Steven E. Zipperstein, age 44
VP Messaging Services: Todd Buchanan
Auditors: Deloitte & Touche LLP

LOCATIONS

HQ: Cellco Partnership
180 Washington Valley Rd., Bedminster, NJ 07921
Phone: 908-306-7000   **Fax:** 908-306-6927
Web: www.verizonwireless.com

PRODUCTS/OPERATIONS

2003 Sales

	$ mil.	% of total
Service revenues	20,336	90
Equipment & other revenues	2,153	10
Total	**22,489**	**100**

Selected Services
Cellular
Equipment sales
Paging
PCS (personal communications services)
Wireless data and Internet

COMPETITORS

ALLTEL
Arch Wireless
AT&T Wireless
Cingular Wireless
Metrocall
Nextel
SkyTel Communications
Sprint PCS
T-Mobile USA
U.S. Cellular
Western Wireless

HISTORICAL FINANCIALS

Company Type: Joint venture

Income Statement
FYE: December 31

	REVENUE ($ mil.)	NET INCOME ($ mil.)	NET PROFIT MARGIN	EMPLOYEES
12/03	22,489	3,083	13.7%	43,900
12/02	19,260	2,584	13.4%	39,300
12/01	17,393	1,300	7.5%	40,000
12/00	14,222	1,528	10.7%	38,000
12/99	7,659	932	12.2%	32,500
12/98	6,641	906	13.6%	—
12/97	6,196	737	11.9%	—
Annual Growth	24.0%	26.9%	—	7.8%

2003 Year-End Financials

Debt ratio: 19.2%   Current ratio: 0.30
Return on equity: 14.9%   Long-term debt ($ mil.): 4,029
Cash ($ mil.): 137

Net Income History

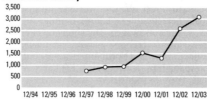

Vermeer

Dig this: Vermeer Manufacturing Company doesn't mind being bored. The company makes, distributes, and rents lawn and heavy construction equipment, such as drilling and pneumatic boring systems. Vermeer also produces other earth-moving equipment like trenching (compactors, plows) and trenchless (vacuum systems) machines for use at construction sites. Other items include a line of landscape products for cutting and edging trees (chippers, cutters). In addition, Vermeer sells ground locating and mapping software for construction use (Atlas Bore Planner, Interragator II). The family of founder Gary Vermeer controls the company.

Vermeer Manufacturing formed a strategic alliance with Lely USA, Inc., in 2003 to market Lely hay and forage equipment in the US. Vermeer will handle the marketing, sales, customer service, logistics and parts support services for Lely products, which include mowers (Splendimo), tedders (Lotus), and rakes (Hibiscus).

EXECUTIVES

Chairman and CEO: Robert (Bob) Vermeer
President and COO: Mary Vermeer Andringa, age 54
CFO: Steve Van Dusseldorp
VP Administration and Human Resources: Vince Newendorp

LOCATIONS

HQ: Vermeer Manufacturing Company
1210 Vermeer Rd. East, Pella, IA 50219
Phone: 641-628-3141   **Fax:** 641-621-7734
Web: www.vermeer.com

Vermeer Manufacturing Company distributes products to dealers throughout the US and Canada.

PRODUCTS/OPERATIONS

Selected Products
Electronics
  Atlas Bore Planner
  FieldCalc System
  Interragator II
  Terrain Mapping
Tree Products
  Brush chippers
  Stump cutters
  Tree spades
  Tub grinders
Trenching
  Compactors
  Concrete cutters
  Lawn plows
  Ride-on trenchers
  Track trenchers
  Vibratory plows
  Walk-behind trenchers
Trenchless
  Horizontal directional drills
  Pneumatic piercing tools
  Rock drilling
  Vacuum systems

COMPETITORS

Bolt Technology
Charles Machine
Deere
Ingersoll-Rand
  Infrastructure
Jacuzzi Brands

Kawasaki Heavy Industries
Kennametal
Sandvik
Scotts
Terex

HISTORICAL FINANCIALS

Company Type: Private

Income Statement				FYE: December 31
	ESTIMATED REVENUE ($ mil.)	NET INCOME ($ mil.)	NET PROFIT MARGIN	EMPLOYEES
12/03	650	—	—	3,000
12/02	350	—	—	1,550
12/01	500	—	—	2,800
Annual Growth	14.0%	—	—	3.5%

Revenue History

Vertis

Although it has changed its name, Vertis still hopes its advertising business will blossom. The company (formerly Big Flower Holdings) provides targeted marketing services from conception through design, production, and distribution for more than 3,000 clients. In 2002 the company unified its three operating units under the Vertis name. Vertis' services include market research, media planning, advertising production, digital production and fulfillment services. Vertis operates the largest digital photography network dedicated to the ad industry and produces newspaper inserts such as color comics, TV magazines, and supplements. An investor group led by Thomas H. Lee Company and Evercore Partners owns Vertis.

In addition to its advertising services Vertis also provides digital services, online marketing, and strategic consulting, as well as direct mailing, response management, Internet integration, and database management. Vertis' customers include grocery stores, retailers, newspapers, consumer good manufacturers, advertising agencies, and any other organization seeking to reach a large number of consumers within certain demographic range.

Vertis has undergone significant restructuring in recent years. It began relying less and less on its traditional commercial printing business in the late 1990s as it expanded into areas of marketing and advertising. Later it consolidated its three primary divisions (all the better to create cross-selling opportunities), took itself private, moved its headquarters from New York City to Baltimore (headquarters of its TC Advertising division), and changed its name from Big Flower Holdings to Vertis. In 2002 the company consolidated all its operations (LTC Group, TC Advertising, and Webcraft) under the Vertis name. The consolidation continued in 2003 as the company realigned operations based on geography rather than marketing discipline.

Vertis' changes were motivated by a desire to streamline operations, cut costs, and ultimately grow revenue. Saddled with debt and with zero to little growth in the advertising sector Vertis' future seems to rely on the economic recovery happening sooner rather than later.

EXECUTIVES

Chairman and CEO: Donald E. (Don) Roland, age 61, $650,000 pay
COO, Vertis North America:
 Herbert W. (Herb) Moloney III, age 53, $480,180 pay
CFO: Dean D. Durbin, age 51, $400,000 pay
SVP and General Counsel: John V. Howard Jr., age 42, $273,000 pay
SVP Finance and Treasurer: Stephen E. Tremblay
SVP Human Resources: Catherine S. Leggett, age 53
SVP National Sales and Marketing: Janice Mayo
VP Creative Services: Meredith Ott
VP Marketing Research: Therese Mulvey
Managing Director, Vertis Europe: Adriaan Roosen, age 52, $302,575 pay
Group President, Vertis North America East:
 Dave Colatriano, age 41
Group President, Vertis North America West:
 Thomas R. Zimmer, $366,401 pay
Auditors: Deloitte & Touche LLP

LOCATIONS

HQ: Vertis Inc.
 250 W. Pratt St., 18th Fl., Baltimore, MD 21201
Phone: 410-528-9800 **Fax:** 410-528-9287
Web: www.vertisinc.com

Vertis operates through more than 120 locations in the US and Europe.

2003 Sales

	$ mil.	% of total
Vertis North America	1,448.5	91
Vertis Europe	137.4	9
Total	**1,585.9**	**100**

PRODUCTS/OPERATIONS

Selected Products and Services

Retail and Newspaper Services
 Ad insert programs for retailer and manufacturers
 Newspaper products including TV magazines, comics, and supplements
 Consumer research
 Creative services for ad insert page layout and design
 Digital advertising design and transmission
 Freight and logistics management
Direct Marketing Services
 Customized one-to-one marketing programs
 Automated digital fulfillment services
 Direct mail production
 Data design, collection, management
 Mailing management services
 Effectiveness measurement
Ad Technology Services
 Digital content management
 Graphic design and animation
 Digital photography, compositing, and retouching
 In-store displays and billboards
 Consulting services
 Newpaper advertisment development
 Media planning and placement software
 Response management, warehousing, and fulfillment services
 Call center and telemarketing services

COMPETITORS

ACG Holdings	News America Marketing
Acxiom	Polestar
ADVO	Quebecor World
Applied Graphics	R.R. Donnelley
communisis	Schawk
Experian	Seven Worldwide
Harte-Hanks	Valassis

HISTORICAL FINANCIALS

Company Type: Private

Income Statement				FYE: December 31
	REVENUE ($ mil.)	NET INCOME ($ mil.)	NET PROFIT MARGIN	EMPLOYEES
12/03	1,586	(96)	—	8,000
12/02	1,675	(120)	—	8,700
12/01	1,851	(55)	—	9,000
12/00	1,986	(25)	—	10,000
12/99	1,800	—	—	10,000
12/98	1,740	—	—	10,000
12/97	1,377	—	—	8,500
12/96	1,202	—	—	6,410
12/95	532	—	—	4,000
12/94	565	—	—	3,200
Annual Growth	12.2%	—	—	10.7%

2003 Year-End Financials

Debt ratio: — Current ratio: 0.81
Return on equity: — Long-term debt ($ mil.): 1,059
Cash ($ mil.): 2

Net Income History

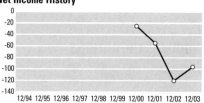

Viasystems

Viasystems counts on manufacturers' desire to build their systems via contract manufacturing. The company makes printed circuit boards (PCBs), backpanel assemblies used to connect PCBs, wire harnesses, custom enclosures, and cable assemblies. Viasystems' products are used in applications such as automotive dashboards, major appliances, data networking and telecom switching equipment, and instrumentation. Customers include General Electric (12% of sales), Delphi, Lucent, and Siemens. Viasystems, which is backed by investment firms Hicks, Muse, Tate & Furst and GSC Partners, has emerged from Chapter 11 bankruptcy a leaner organization.

The company has closed plants and cut jobs in order to streamline operations. Viasystems is, however, expanding its operations in lower cost regions, including China and Mexico. The company's Asian operations account for more than 40% of sales, though customers located in the US continue to make up more than half of sales.

EXECUTIVES

Chairman: Christopher J. Steffen, age 62
CEO and Director: David M. Sindelar, age 46, $1,148,000 pay
President, COO, and Director:
 Timothy L. (Tim) Conlon, age 52, $907,500 pay
President, Asia/Pacific Group: Steven S. L. Tang, age 48, $561,672 pay
SVP and CFO: Joseph S. Catanzaro, age 51, $375,286 pay
SVP, Sales and Marketing: John R. McAlister, age 50
SVP: David J. Webster, age 41, $426,750 pay
SVP, Supply Chain Management: Gerald G. (Jerry) Sax, age 43

VP and CIO: David Egbert
VP and Controller: Bryan Meier
VP, Human Resources: Bailey Hurley
VP, Marketing Communications and Research: John S. Hastings
VP, Sales and Marketing: George Batten
Auditors: PricewaterhouseCoopers LLP

LOCATIONS

HQ: Viasystems Group, Inc.
101 S. Hanley Rd., Ste. 400, St. Louis, MO 63105
Phone: 314-727-2087 **Fax:** 314-746-2233
Web: www.viasystems.com

Viasystems Group has facilities in Canada, China, Mexico, the Netherlands, and the US.

2003 Sales by Destination

	$ mil.	% of total
US	384.8	51
China	101.9	14
Germany	80.4	11
Malaysia	37.7	5
Canada	25.8	3
France	18.4	2
UK	16.0	2
Other countries	86.5	12
Total	**751.5**	**100**

PRODUCTS/OPERATIONS

2003 Sales

	$ mil.	% of total
Printed circuit boards	373.3	50
Wire harnesses & electromechanical solutions	378.2	50
Total	**751.5**	**100**

Selected Products

Backpanel assemblies
Cable assemblies
Custom enclosures
Multilayer printed circuit boards
Single-layer printed circuit boards
Wire harnesses

Services

After-sales support (including repair and upgrades)
Design and prototyping
Full system assembly and test
Packaging and distribution
Supply chain management

COMPETITORS

Benchmark Electronics
Celestica
DDi Corp.
Flextronics
Merix
Photocircuits
Plexus
Sanmina-SCI
SMTC
Solectron
SYNNEX

HISTORICAL FINANCIALS

Company Type: Private

Income Statement

FYE: December 31

	REVENUE ($ mil.)	NET INCOME ($ mil.)	NET PROFIT MARGIN	EMPLOYEES
12/03	752	190	25.3%	22,400
12/02	864	(259)	—	18,000
12/01	1,207	(587)	—	18,800
12/00	1,605	(136)	—	24,700
12/99	1,102	(693)	—	18,500
12/98	1,032	(85)	—	19,350
12/97	900	(35)	—	7,200
12/96	872	(51)	—	7,100
12/95	728	—	—	—
12/94	565	—	—	—
Annual Growth	3.2%	—	—	17.8%

2003 Year-End Financials

Debt ratio: — Current ratio: 1.53
Return on equity: — Long-term debt ($ mil.): 455
Cash ($ mil.): 64

Net Income History

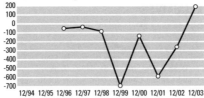

ViewSonic

ViewSonic has a display for every occasion. The company makes CRT and LCD computer displays, including the Professional Series for high-end computer-aided design, desktop publishing, and graphic design; the Graphics and E2 lines for homes and small offices; and the A Series for replacing monitors included in bundled systems. ViewSonic also offers LCD and plasma TVs, wireless networking equipment, LCD projectors, handheld computers, and tablet PCs. CEO James Chu, who founded ViewSonic in 1987, is the company's majority owner. ViewSonic has also received financing from the venture capital arm of chip giant Intel, which partnered with the company to develop inexpensive chipsets for high-definition TV.

A leading provider of displays, ViewSonic has managed to hold its own in an industry where Asian giants such as NEC-Mitsubishi, Samsung, and Sony vie for market share. Viewsonic sells directly and through resellers and distributors to consumer, corporate, government, and education customers.

Viewsonic entered the home networking market in 2004, releasing a line of wireless equipment that includes media gateways and adapters.

EXECUTIVES

Chairman and CEO: James Chu, age 46
CFO: James A. Morlan, age 56
SVP, Business Development and Strategy: Matt Milne
VP, General Counsel, and Secretary: Robert J. Ranucci, age 39
VP; General Manager, Visual Display Group: Y.C. Wu
VP, Human Resources: Timothy Ashcroft
VP, Information Services and CIO: Robert Lee Moon, age 54
VP, Operations: Lorraine Meng
VP, Strategic Planning: Tony Dowzall
VP, Visual Solutions Group: Michael Holstein
Auditors: Deloitte & Touche LLP

LOCATIONS

HQ: ViewSonic Corporation
381 Brea Canyon Rd., Walnut, CA 91789
Phone: 909-444-8888 **Fax:** 909-468-1202
Web: www.viewsonic.com

2003 Sales

	$ mil.	% of total
Americas	668	62
Asia/Pacific	227	21
Europe	180	17
Total	**1,075**	**100**

PRODUCTS/OPERATIONS

2003 Display Sales

	% of total
CRT	49
LCD	42
Other	9
Total	**100**

Selected Products

LCD projectors
Monitors (CRT, LCD)
Personal digital assistants
Tablet PCs
Televisions (high-definition, plasma)
Wireless networking equipment (routers, adapters, access points)

COMPETITORS

Acer
ADI Systems
Apple Computer
BenQ
Daewoo International
Dell
Fujitsu
Gateway
Hewlett-Packard
InFocus
LG Electronics
LG.Philips LCD
Matsushita
Mitsubishi Corporation
NEC
NEC-Mitsubishi Electronics Display
palmOne
Philips Electronics
Philips North America
Planar Systems
Princeton Digital
Samsung Electronics
Sharp
Sony

HISTORICAL FINANCIALS

Company Type: Private

Income Statement

FYE: December 31

	REVENUE ($ mil.)	NET INCOME ($ mil.)	NET PROFIT MARGIN	EMPLOYEES
12/03	1,075	5	0.4%	743
12/02	884	19	2.2%	600
12/01	962	(18)	—	600
12/00	1,371	—	—	800
12/99	1,040	—	—	700
12/98	941	—	—	700
12/97	826	—	—	675
12/96	510	—	—	600
12/95	350	—	—	550
12/94	200	—	—	120
Annual Growth	20.5%	—	—	22.5%

2003 Year-End Financials

Debt ratio: 85.1% Current ratio: 1.28
Return on equity: 7.7% Long-term debt ($ mil.): 55
Cash ($ mil.): 92

Net Income History

Visa

Paper or plastic? Visa International hopes you choose the latter. Visa operates the world's largest consumer payment system (ahead of MasterCard and American Express) with more than 1 billion credit and other payment cards in circulation. The company is owned by 21,000 financial institutions, each of which issues and markets its own Visa products. They all participate in the VisaNet payment system, which provides authorization, transaction processing, and settlement services for purchases from 20 million merchants worldwide. In addition to credit cards, Visa also provides its customers with debit cards, Internet payment systems, value-storing smart cards, and traveler's checks.

Visa International operates through six autonomous regional organizations: Asia Pacific; Canada; Central & Eastern Europe, Middle East & Africa (CEMEA); Europe; Latin America & the Caribbean; and the US. It also owns Inovant, an information technology and processing subsidiary.

Visa is accelerating its push to introduce chip cards over magnetic stripe technology, and it is maneuvering its Open Platform technology into position against the MasterCard-supported Mondex platform and Microsoft's Smart Card for Windows.

Both Visa U.S.A. and MasterCard International were recently in some 4 million retailers' sights. Led by retail giant Wal-Mart, the merchants claimed Visa and MasterCard violated antitrust laws and attempted to monopolize a legally defined market for debit cards. The plaintiffs sought up to $200 billion in damages in their class-action suit. Just as the 1996 lawsuit was to go to trial in early 2003, Visa settled, agreeing to pay $2 billion (twice that of co-defendant MasterCard) over the next decade. Both agreed to pay $25 million immediately, as well as reduce the fee merchants pay for signature-based debit cards. At the time of settlement, some 129 million consumers carried the Visa debit card.

HISTORY

Although the first charge card was issued by Western Union in 1914, it wasn't until 1958 that Bank of America (BofA) issued its BankAmericard, which combined the convenience of a charge account with credit privileges. When BofA extended its customer base outside California, the interchange system controlling payments began to falter because of design problems and fraud.

In 1968 Dee Hock, manager of the BankAmericard operations of the National Bank of Commerce in Seattle, convinced member banks that a more reliable system was needed. Two years later National BankAmericard Inc. (NBI) was created as an independent corporation (owned by 243 banks) to buy the BankAmericard system from BofA.

With its initial ad slogan, "Think of it as Money," the Hock-led NBI developed BankAmericard into a widely used form of payment in the US. A multinational corporation, IBANCO, was formed in 1974 to carry the operations into other countries. People outside the US resisted BankAmericard's nominal association with BofA, and in 1977 Hock changed the card's name to Visa. NBI became Visa USA, and IBANCO became Visa International.

By 1980 Visa had debuted debit cards, begun issuing traveler's checks, and created an electromagnetic point-of-sale authorization system. Visa developed a global network of ATMs in 1983; it was expanded in 1987 by the purchase of a 33% stake in the Plus System of ATMs, then the US's second-largest system. Hock retired in 1984 with the company well on its way to realizing his vision of a universal payment system.

The company built the Visa brand image with aggressive advertising, such as sponsorship of the 1988 and 1992 Olympics, and by co-branding (issuing cards through other organizations with strong brand names, such as Blockbuster and Ford).

In 1994 Visa teamed up with Microsoft and others to develop home banking services and software. Visa Cash was introduced during the 1996 Olympics. Visa pushed its debit cards in 1996 and 1997 with humorous ads featuring presidential also-ran Bob Dole and showbiz success story Daffy Duck.

Visa expanded its smart card infrastructure in 1997. It published, with MasterCard, encryption and security software for online transactions. The gloves came off the next year as the companies vied to convince the world to rally around their respective e-purse technology standards.

During the 1990s, Visa fought American Express' attempts to introduce a bank credit card of its own by forbidding Visa members in the US from issuing the product; the Justice Department responded with an antitrust suit against Visa and MasterCard. The case went to trial in 2000 with the government claiming that Visa and MasterCard stifle competition and enjoy an exclusive cross-ownership structure.

Also that year, the company made a deal with Gemplus, the French smart card company, to enable payments over wireless networks; Visa also inked a billing deal with wireless technology company Aether Systems, as well as e-commerce agreements with telecommunications companies Nokia and Ericsson.

The company continued its technology push in 2000 with a deal with Financial Services Technology Consortium to test biometrics — the use of fingerprints, irises, and voice recognition to identify cardholders. The company also launched a pre-paid card, Visa Buxx, targeted at teenagers.

That year the European Union launched an investigation into the firm's transaction fees, alleging that the fees could restrict competition. The following year Visa International agreed to drop its fee to 0.7% of the transaction value over five years.

EXECUTIVES

Chairman: William P. Boardman, age 63
President and CEO: Christopher J. Rodrigues
CFO: Ken Sommer
EVP and General Counsel: Guy Rounsaville
EVP, Global Marketing Partnerships and Sponsorships: Tom Shepard
EVP, Human Resources: Elizabeth Rounds
SVP, Public Policy: Mark MacCarthy
Manager, Global Brand and Marketing: John Elkins
President, Inovant: John Partridge
President, Visa Asia Pacific: Rupert G. Keeley
President, Visa Canada: Derek A. Fry
President, Visa Central and Eastern Europe, Middle East, and Africa: Anne L. Cobb
President, Visa Europe: Johannes I. (Hans) van der Velde
President, Visa Latin America and Caribbean: Eduardo Eraña
President and CEO, Visa U.S.A.: Carl F. Pascarella, age 61
EVP and CFO, Visa U.S.A.: Victor W. Dahir
EVP, Brand Marketing, Visa U.S.A.: Rebecca (Becky) Saeger, age 47
EVP, Corporate Relations, Visa U.S.A.: Douglas (Doug) Michelman
EVP, General Counsel, and Secretary, Visa U.S.A.: Joshua R. Floum
EVP, Human Resources, Visa U.S.A.: Fred Bauer

LOCATIONS

HQ: Visa International
900 Metro Center Blvd., Foster City, CA 94404
Phone: 650-432-3200 **Fax:** 650-432-7436
Web: www.visa.com

Visa cards are accepted at 20 million merchant locations in 150 countries around the world.

PRODUCTS/OPERATIONS

Products and Services
ATMs (more than 850,000 locations)
Electron (debit card outside of US)
Interlink (debit card)
smartVisa card (computer-chip-embedded card that is accepted worldwide)
Visa Business card (for small businesses and professionals)
Visa Cash (smart cards)
Visa Classic card (credit/debit card issued by Visa's 21,000 member banks)
Visa Corporate card (for travel and entertainment expenses)
Visa Debit card (accesses bank account for immediate settlement of payments)
Visa Gold card (higher spending limits)
VisaNet (electronic transaction processing network)
Visa Purchasing card (for corporate purchases)
Visa Travelers Cheques
Visa TravelMoney (prepaid card in any currency)

COMPETITORS

American Express   MasterCard
Citigroup   Morgan Stanley

HISTORICAL FINANCIALS

Company Type: Private

Income Statement
FYE: September 30

	ESTIMATED REVENUE ($ mil.)	NET INCOME ($ mil.)	NET PROFIT MARGIN	EMPLOYEES
9/03	5,400	—	—	6,000
9/02	4,800	—	—	6,000
9/01	3,600	—	—	6,000
9/00	3,000	—	—	5,000
9/99	2,800	—	—	5,000
9/98	2,550	—	—	5,000
9/97	2,050	—	—	5,000
9/96	1,650	—	—	4,800
9/95	1,330	—	—	4,000
9/94	1,260	—	—	3,500
Annual Growth	17.6%	—	—	6.2%

Revenue History

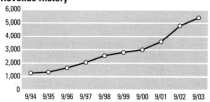

Vision Service Plan

Thanks to Vision Service Plan (VSP), you can see clearly now. One of the top eye care benefits providers in the US (with some 38 million members, more than one in 8 people in the US use the company's services), VSP offers vision coverage ranging from general plans to laser vision correction procedures. VSP has nearly 20,000 clients. The company's Sight for Students program provides uninsured children with vision exams and glasses. The VSP network includes thousands of doctors nationwide that provide both eye exams and eyewear.

VSP's strategy for growth consists of forming alliances with managed care companies, eyeglass makers, and others in order to sell its services. The company expects to do well as aging baby boomers are expected to increase demand for the company's services.

EXECUTIVES

President and CEO: Roger Valine
SVP, Marketing and Corporate Development: Don Yee
SVP, Operations: Gary Brooks
VP and CFO: Patricia Cochran
VP Marketing: Kate Renwick-Espinosa
VP and Legal Counsel: Barclay Westerfeld
VP, Client Services: Mary Ann Cavanagh
VP, Customer Service: Laura Costa
VP, Health Care Services: Cheryl Johnson
VP, Human Resources: Walter Grubbs
VP, Information Systems: Steve Scott
VP, Sales: Ric Steere

LOCATIONS

HQ: Vision Service Plan
3333 Quality Dr., Rancho Cordova, CA 95670
Phone: 916-851-5000 **Fax:** 916-851-4858
Web: www.vsp.com

PRODUCTS/OPERATIONS

Selected Vision Plans
VSP WellVision Plan
Computer VisionCare
Laser VisionCare
Primary EyeCare
Safety EyeCare

COMPETITORS

EyeMed Vision Care
Guardian Life
Kaiser Foundation
Oxford Health
PacifiCare
Spectera
UnitedHealth Group

HISTORICAL FINANCIALS
Company Type: Private

Income Statement				FYE: December 31
	REVENUE ($ mil.)	NET INCOME ($ mil.)	NET PROFIT MARGIN	EMPLOYEES
12/03	1,970	—	—	2,000
12/02	1,860	—	—	2,300
12/01	1,770	—	—	2,300
12/00	1,500	—	—	2,300
Annual Growth	9.5%	—	—	(4.6%)

Vistar/VSA

Vistar/VSA Corporation distributes specialty food products and related supplies to vending and foodservice operations nationwide through its more than 25 warehouses. Vistar/VSA was formed in 1997 through the merger of Multifoods Distribution — specializing in Italian markets — and VSA, which provided vending and office coffee products. Vistar/VSA is owned by Wellspring Capital Management LLC. In 2004 Vistar/VSA acquired Atlanta's pizza, deli, and Italian restaurant supplier Original Brand Foods.

EXECUTIVES

President and CEO: George Holm
EVP: Patrick (Pat) Mulhern
SVP and CFO: Tom McGonagle
VP, Merchandising, Foodservice: Ron Hanson
VP, Merchandising, Specialty Markets: Pat Hagerty
Attorney: Kent Burke

LOCATIONS

HQ: Vistar/VSA Corporation
12650 E. Arapahoe Rd., Centennial, CO 80112
Phone: 303-662-7100
Web: www.vistarvsa.com

COMPETITORS

ARAMARK
compass group north america
Performance Food
Pierre Foods
SYSCO

HISTORICAL FINANCIALS
Company Type: Private

Income Statement				FYE: February 28
	REVENUE ($ mil.)	NET INCOME ($ mil.)	NET PROFIT MARGIN	EMPLOYEES
2/04	2,500	—	—	2,500
2/03	2,400	—	—	2,500
Annual Growth	4.2%	—	—	0.0%

Revenue History

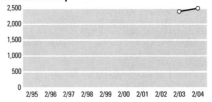

Volunteers of America

Volunteers of America is a national faith-based organization that provides community-level human services. It operates such programs as Camp P.O.S.T.C.A.R.D., which brings at-risk and inner-city children together with police officers, and ASPIRE, a rehabilitation program for former prison inmates. Volunteers of America was organized in 1896 by Ballington and Maud Booth.

EXECUTIVES

National President: Charles W. Gould
CFO: Janie Burks
VP Communications: Steve Abbott
VP External Relations: Jimmie Walton Paschall
VP Program Management: Karen M. Dale
Public Relations Manager: Julie Anderson
Publications Manager: Sally Ruth Bourrie

LOCATIONS

HQ: Volunteers of America, Inc.
1660 Duke St., Alexandria, VA 22314
Phone: 703-341-5000 **Fax:** 703-341-7000
Web: www.volunteersofamerica.org

HISTORICAL FINANCIALS
Company Type: Not-for-profit

Income Statement				FYE: June 30
	REVENUE ($ mil.)	NET INCOME ($ mil.)	NET PROFIT MARGIN	EMPLOYEES
6/03	711	—	—	14,000

Vought Aircraft

The skies are fraught with Vought; Vought Aircraft Industries is one of the world's largest aerostructures subcontractors. Products include fuselage subassemblies (doors and fuselage panels), nacelles, thrust reversers, empennage structures, wings, and other components for military and commercial aircraft. The company's primary customers include Boeing, Gulfstream Aerospace, Lockheed Martin, and Northrop Grumman. Vought also does subcontract work for military cargo planes (C-17), bombers (B-2), and fighters (F-14 and F/A-18). The Carlyle Group owns about 90% of Vought, which also provides spare parts, maintenance, repair, and overhaul services.

EXECUTIVES

President and CEO: Tom Risley
VP and General Counsel: W. Bruce White Jr.
VP, Boeing Commercial Programs:
   Stephen A. (Steve) Davis
VP, Business Management: Randy Smith
VP, Controller, and Treasurer: Cletus C. Glasener Jr.
VP, Human Resources, Administration, and Information Services: Judith W. (Judy) Northup
VP, Materiel: Dan Smartis

Revenue History

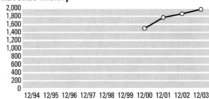

VP, Military and Other Commercial Programs:
Erich G. Smith
VP, Quality, Engineering, and Technology:
Vernon H. (Vern) Broomall
VP, Site Operations: William J. (Bill) McKenna
Director, Corporate Communications: Mike Schwarz

LOCATIONS

HQ: Vought Aircraft Industries, Inc.
9314 W. Jefferson Blvd., Dallas, TX 75211
Phone: 972-946-2011   **Fax:** 972-946-3465
Web: www.voughtaircraft.com

Vought Aircraft Industries has facilities in California, Florida, Georgia, Tennessee, Texas, and Washington.

PRODUCTS/OPERATIONS

Selected Products
Doors
Empennage and flight control surfaces
Fuselage panels
Nacelles
Wings

Selected Commercial Programs
Boeing 737
Boeing 747
Boeing 757
Boeing 767
Boeing 777
Gulfstream IV
Gulfstream V
Hawker 800

Selected Military and NASA Programs
B-2
C-17 Globemaster III
E-2C Hawkeye
E-8C/JSTARS
EA-6B Prowler
F-14 Tomcat/Super Tomcat
F/A-18E/F Super Hornet
Global Hawk
P-3C Orion
S-3A/B Viking
T-38 Talon
V-22 Osprey

COMPETITORS

CPI Aerostructures	Martin-Baker Aircraft
Ducommun	NORDAM
Goodrich	TransTechnology
LMI Aerospace	

HISTORICAL FINANCIALS
Company Type: Private

Income Statement				FYE: December 31
	REVENUE ($ mil.)	NET INCOME ($ mil.)	NET PROFIT MARGIN	EMPLOYEES
12/03	1,201	—	—	6,591
12/02	1,200	—	—	6,290
12/01	1,400	—	—	5,000
12/00	1,000	—	—	5,000
Annual Growth	6.3%	—	—	9.6%

Revenue History
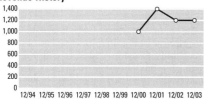

VT

VT is in pursuit of the pole-position as one of the top three US car dealers. The company operates more than 30 dealerships in some 10 states, primarily Texas and Missouri. It offers about 20 brands of new and used cars (and RVs) made by General Motors, Ford, Honda, Isuzu, and Nissan, among others. VT also engages in fleet sales and receives a significant portion of its revenue from back-shop operations such as parts and service and body shop sales. Founder and co-CEO Cecil Van Tuyl began his automotive empire in 1955. He owns the company with son and co-CEO Larry Van Tuyl.

EXECUTIVES

President and Co-CEO: Cecil Van Tuyl
Co-CEO: Larry Van Tuyl
Secretary and Treasurer: Robert J. Holcomb

LOCATIONS

HQ: VT Inc.
8500 Shawnee Mission Pkwy., Ste. 200,
Shawnee Mission, KS 66202
Phone: 913-895-0200   **Fax:** 913-789-1039
Web: www.vanenterprises.com

VT has dealerships in Arizona, Florida, Illinois, Indiana, Kansas, Missouri, Nebraska, New Mexico, and Texas.

COMPETITORS

Asbury Automotive	Hendrick Automotive
AutoNation	Jordan Automotive
CarMax	United Auto Group

HISTORICAL FINANCIALS
Company Type: Private

Income Statement				FYE: December 31
	REVENUE ($ mil.)	NET INCOME ($ mil.)	NET PROFIT MARGIN	EMPLOYEES
12/03	5,229	—	—	—
12/02	5,250	—	—	—
12/01	5,299	—	—	7,000
12/00	4,300	—	—	6,000
12/99	3,600	—	—	5,805
12/98	2,587	—	—	5,000
12/97	2,423	—	—	5,000
12/96	2,075	—	—	4,300
12/95	1,755	—	—	3,950
12/94	1,681	—	—	3,874
Annual Growth	13.4%	—	—	8.8%

Revenue History
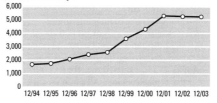

Vulcan

Even with all his Vulcan logic, could Spock invest like *this?* Brainy billionaire Paul Allen organizes his business and charitable ventures under Vulcan (formerly Vulcan Northwest). Vulcan includes Allen's slim stake in the industry-defining juggernaut Microsoft, as well as holdings in dozens of companies providing computer, technology, multimedia, and communications products and services; most recently, biotechnology ventures and real estate have been added to his portfolio. Allen also owns professional sports teams like the NBA's Portland Trail Blazers and the NFL's Seattle Seahawks, as well as stakes in six charitable organizations.

Vulcan's charities support the arts, medical research, land conservation, and other causes. Allen, who co-founded Microsoft with Bill Gates, promotes a "wired world" vision, in which everyone is united through interconnecting communications, entertainment, and information systems. CEO Jody Patton, Allen's sister, oversees both his business and charitable ventures.

Many of Allen's investments in the "wired world" took a beating with the stock market downturn. He even saw his own personal wealth take a dip by a third. The most recent casualty, communications company RCN Corporation, has filed for bankruptcy, rendering Allen's 15% stake essentially worthless.

Allen is finally dumping the last of his unprofitable stakes in tech-boom companies, and has cleaned house in other ways — long-time right-hand man William Savoy has left the firm. Vulcan Ventures, the VC arm of Allen's empire, has started investing in cutting-edge biotechnology firms. Allen has also agreed to acquire energy firm Plains Resources, and he's bought up real estate in Seattle, and is intent on redeveloping it.

HISTORY

Paul Allen and Bill Gates first worked together on computer projects as schoolmates in Seattle. They developed a program to determine traffic patterns and launched Traf-O-Data, an operation that failed because the state provided the information for free. When Allen saw an article on the MITS Altair 8800 minicomputer in 1975, the two realized it needed a simplified programming language to make it useful. They offered MITS a modified version of BASIC they had written for Traf-O-Data. The company set them up in an office in Albuquerque, New Mexico. They then began their biggest collaboration of all: Microsoft. While Gates concentrated on business, Allen focused on technical issues.

They moved to Bellevue, a Seattle suburb, in 1979. The next year IBM asked them to create a programming language for a PC project. Allen bought Q-DOS (quick and dirty operating system) from Seattle Computer; the pair tweaked it and renamed it MS-DOS. Allen and Gates made a key decision to structure their contract with IBM to allow clones. They also helped design many aspects of the original IBM PC.

Allen developed Hodgkin's disease in 1982. Facing his own mortality, he ended his daily involvement in Microsoft (keeping a chunk of the company and a board seat) and began to play more (traveling and playing the electric guitar). With his cancer in remission in 1985, Allen founded multimedia software company

Asymetrix. The next year he set up Vulcan to hold his diversified interests and Vulcan Ventures. He also began helping startups, indulging his interests (buying the NBA's Portland Trail Blazers in 1988 and donating some $60 million to build a museum honoring his musical idol, Jimi Hendrix, and other Pacific Northwest artists). He has also funded Seattle-area civic improvements.

In 1990 Allen hired William Savoy to help organize his finances; Savoy later became president of Vulcan Ventures. Seeing a need for more R&D in the US, Allen in 1992 started Interval Research. He also invested in America Online (sold 1994). In 1993 Allen bought 80% of Ticketmaster (sold 1997), and in 1995 he invested in DreamWorks SKG, the multimedia company of Steven Spielberg, Jeffrey Katzenberg, and David Geffen.

Allen made a rare buy outside the entertainment and high-tech worlds through a 1996 investment in power turbine maker Capstone Turbine. To prevent the Seattle Seahawks from moving to California, Allen bought the team in 1997 and made plans for a new stadium. He consolidated his management operations under Vulcan and dissolved Paul Allen Group (founded 1994), keeping Vulcan Ventures.

Allen moved into cable in 1998 and 1999; his Charter Communications eventually became the #4 US cable firm. In 1999 several Allen investments (Charter Communications, Vulcan Ventures, RCN, High Speed Access, and Go2Net) joined to form wired-world venture Broadband Partners.

In 2000 it was nearly impossible to ignore Allen's influence on Seattle as several major projects took shape or were completed, including the new Seahawks' arena, the Experience Music Project, and the renovation of a 90-year-old train station as part of a complex that will include Vulcan's new headquarters. That year he provided a $100 million infusion to struggling Oxygen Media. In 2001 Vulcan Ventures bought sports games Web site operator Small World Media to boost its sports holdings, which was later folded into the online fantasy sports operations of another Allen holding, *The Sporting News*.

Tech-boom losses accounted for only about 5% of Allen's portfolio, but things looked very bleak indeed in 2002 when the US attorney's office began investigating Charter Communications — for accounting irregularities. Four former executives were later indicted for fraud in 2003.

In late 2003, Allen began to restructure his holdings, dumping remaining unprofitable holdings (including RCN), and laying off many employees, including William Savoy. TechTV was sold to Comcast in 2004; the network was merged in to Comcast's existing gaming and technology network, G4 TV. It is now called G4techTV.

EXECUTIVES

Chairman: Paul G. Allen, age 51
President and CEO: Jo Allen (Jody) Patton, age 46
EVP Investment Management: Lance Conn
VP Tax, Risk, and Asset Management: Joseph Franzi
VP Corporate Communications: Steven C. Crosby
VP Corporate Development and Operations: Denise Wolf
VP Finance and CFO: Nathaniel T. (Buster) Brown
VP Technology: Chris Purcell
VP Investment Management; Managing Director, Vulcan Captial: Nathan Troutman
VP Media Development: Richard E. Hutton
VP Real Estate Development: Ada M. Healey
Managing Director, Private Equity, Vulcan Ventures: Hoon Cho
Managing Director, Venture Capital, Vulcan Ventures: Ralph Derrickson

LOCATIONS
HQ: Vulcan Inc.
505 5th Ave. South, Ste. 900, Seattle, WA 98104
Phone: 206-342-2000   **Fax:** 206-342-3000
Web: www.vulcan.com

PRODUCTS/OPERATIONS

Selected Holdings
Charter Communications (57%, TV system)
Click2learn, Inc. (27%, multimedia development software)
Cytokinetics, Inc. (small molecule drugs)
Dick's Clothing & Sporting Goods (9%, sporting goods retailer)
Digeo, Inc. (interactive television)
DreamWorks SKG (entertainment company)
Microsoft Corporation
Oxygen Media (Internet and television content provider)
Perlegen Sciences, Inc. (genetics research)
Portland Trail Blazers (professional basketball team)
PTC Theraputics, Inc. (small molecule drugs)
Seattle Seahawks (professional football team)
The Sporting News (print and online sports magazine)
Xcyte Therapies, Inc. (cell-based therapies)

COMPETITORS

Accel Partners
Austin Ventures
Benchmark Capital
Boston Ventures
Draper Fisher Jurvetson
Harris & Harris
Hummer Winblad
Institutional Venture Partners
Kleiner Perkins
Matrix Partners
Mayfield Fund
Menlo Ventures
Microsoft
SOFTBANK
Sutter Hill Ventures
Trinity Ventures
US Venture Partners
Venrock Associates
Veronis Suhler Stevenson

Wakefern Food

Started by seven men who each invested $1,000, Wakefern Food has grown into the largest retailer-owned supermarket cooperative in the US. The co-op is now owned by 38 independent grocers who operate more than 200 ShopRite supermarkets in Connecticut, Delaware, New Jersey (where it is a leading chain), New York, and Pennsylvania. More than half of ShopRite stores offer pharmacies. In addition to name-brand and private-label products (ShopRite, Chef's Express, Reddington Farms), Wakefern supports its members with advertising, merchandising, insurance, and other services. Wakefern's ShopRite Supermarkets subsidiary acquired the assets of Florida-based Big V Supermarkets, which filed for bankruptcy in 2000.

The cooperative provides members and other customers with more than 20,000 name-brand items, including groceries, dairy and meat products, produce, frozen foods, and general merchandise. It also sells more than 3,000 items under the ShopRite label. All members are given one vote in the co-op, regardless of size.

HISTORY

Wakefern Food was founded in 1946 by seven New York- and New Jersey-based grocers: Louis Weiss, Sam and Al Aidekman, Abe Kesselman, Dave Fern, Sam Garb, and Albert Goldberg (the company's name is made up of the letters of the first five of those founders). Like many co-operatives, the association sought to lower costs by increasing its buying power as a group.

They each put in $1,000 and began operating a 5,000-sq.-ft. warehouse, often putting in double time to keep both their stores and the warehouse running. The shopkeepers' collective buying power proved valuable, enabling the grocers to stock many items at the same prices as their larger competitors.

In 1951 Wakefern members began pooling their resources to buy advertising space. A common store name — ShopRite — was chosen, and each week co-op members met to decide which items would be sale priced. Within a year, membership had grown to over 50. Expansion became a priority, and in the mid-1950s co-op members united in small groups to take over failed supermarkets. One such group, called the Supermarkets Operating Co. (SOC), was formed in 1956. Within 10 years it had acquired a number of failed stores, remodeled them, and given them the ShopRite name.

During the late 1950s sales at ShopRite stores slumped after Wakefern decided to buck the supermarket trend of offering trading stamps (which could then be exchanged for gifts), figuring that offering the stamps would ultimately lead to higher food prices. The move initially drove away customers, but Wakefern cut grocery prices across the board and sales returned. The company also embraced another supermarket trend: stocking stores with nonfood items.

The co-op was severely shaken in 1966 when SOC merged with General Supermarkets, a similar small group within Wakefern, becoming Supermarkets General Corp. (SGC). SGC was a powerful entity, with 71 supermarkets, 10 drugstores, six gas stations, a wholesale bakery, and a discount department store. Many Wakefern members opposed the merger and attempted to block the action with a court order. By 1968 SGC had beefed up its operations to include department store chains as well as its grocery stores. In a move that threatened to break Wakefern, SGC broke away from the co-op, and its stores were renamed Pathmark.

Wakefern not only weathered the storm, it grew under the direction of chairman and CEO Thomas Infusino, elected shortly after the split. The co-op focused on asserting its position as a seller of low-priced products. Wakefern developed private-label brands, including the ShopRite brand. In the 1980s members began operating larger stores and adding more nonfood items to the ShopRite product mix. With its number of superstores on the rise and facing increased competition from club stores in 1992, Wakefern opened a centralized, nonfood distribution center in New Jersey.

In 1995, 30-year Wakefern veteran Dean Janeway was elected president of the co-op. The company debuted its ShopRite MasterCard, co-branded with New Jersey's Valley National Bank, in 1996. The following year the co-op purchased two of its customers' stores in Pennsylvania, then threatened to close them when contract talks with the local union deteriorated. In 1998 Wakefern settled the dispute, then sold the stores.

The company partnered with Internet bidding site priceline.com in 1999, offering customers an opportunity to bid on groceries and then pick them up at ShopRite stores. Big V, Wakefern's biggest customer, filed for Chapter 11 bankruptcy protection in 2000 and said it was ending its distribution agreement with the co-op. In

July 2002, however, Wakefern's ShopRite Supermarkets subsidiary acquired all of Big V's assets for approximately $185 million in cash and assumed liabilities.

EXECUTIVES
Chairman and CEO: Thomas (Tom) Infusino
President and COO: Dean Janeway
CFO: Ken Jasinkiewicz
EVP, Marketing: Joseph Sheridan
SVP, Administrative Services: Natan Tabak
VP, Corporate and Consumer Affairs: Mary Ellen Gowin
VP, Corporate Merchandising and Advertising: Bill Crombie
VP, Human Resources: Ernie Bell
President and COO ShopRite Supermarkets: Kevin Mannix
Director, Advertising: Karen McAuvic
Manager, Corporate Communications and Media Relations: Karen Meleta

LOCATIONS
HQ: Wakefern Food Corporation
600 York St., Elizabeth, NJ 07207
Phone: 908-527-3300   **Fax:** 908-527-3397
Web: www.shoprite.com

Wakefern Food's 38 members operate more than 200 ShopRite supermarkets in Connecticut, Delaware, New Jersey, New York, and Pennsylvania.

PRODUCTS/OPERATIONS
Major Members
Foodarama Supermarkets
Inserra Supermarkets
Village Super Market

Selected Private Labels
Black Bear (deli items)
Chef's Express
Reddington Farms (poultry)
ShopRite

COMPETITORS
A&P
C&S Wholesale
Di Giorgio
IGA
King Kullen Grocery
Kings Super Markets
Krasdale Foods
Pathmark
Royal Ahold
Shurfine International
Stop & Shop
SUPERVALU
Wal-Mart
White Rose Food

HISTORICAL FINANCIALS
Company Type: Cooperative

Income Statement				FYE: September 30
	REVENUE ($ mil.)	NET INCOME ($ mil.)	NET PROFIT MARGIN	EMPLOYEES
9/03	6,578	—	—	50,000
9/02	6,208	—	—	50,000
9/01	5,900	—	—	—
9/00	5,800	—	—	—
9/99	5,500	—	—	—
9/98	5,000	—	—	—
9/97	4,613	—	—	—
9/96	4,304	—	—	—
9/95	3,700	—	—	—
9/94	3,740	—	—	—
Annual Growth	6.5%	—	—	0.0%

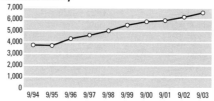
Revenue History

Walbridge Aldinger

The Motor City has been home to Motown Records, Madonna, and . . . Walbridge Aldinger? Walbridge Aldinger, a top US contractor, provides design, engineering, construction management, and plant operation and maintenance. Much of its business is tied to the automotive industry, but the company serves several markets through three groups: commercial, industrial, and heavy civil special projects. Units include rigging and equipment installer Belding Walbridge, automotive construction joint ventures DEVCON Industrial Group and Walbridge Tilbury, and building installation services firm Walbridge Specialty Services. In 1975 the father of CEO John Rakolta, Jr., bought Walbridge Aldinger, which was founded in 1916.

EXECUTIVES
Chairman and CEO: John Rakolta Jr.
Vice Chairman: Ronald L. (Ron) Hausmann
President and COO: Richard J. (Rick) Haller
EVP: Michael R. (Mike) Haller
SVP Business Development: Dave Hanson
VP and CFO: Vince DeAngelis
VP Human Resources: Terry Merritt
VP; General Manager, Belding Walbridge: Joseph (Joe) Margevicius
Group VP Business Development: Mike McIntyre
Group VP: Eric Twigg
General Counsel: Thomas D. (Tom) Dyze
Assistant VP Business Development: Wade Herzig
Auditors: Doeren & Mayhew

LOCATIONS
HQ: Walbridge Aldinger Company
613 Abbott St., Detroit, MI 48226
Phone: 313-963-8000   **Fax:** 313-963-8150
Web: www.walbridge.com

Walbridge Aldinger operates in the US from offices in Chicago; Detroit; Monroe, North Carolina; Tampa, Florida; and Toledo, Ohio. It also has offices in Canada (London and Windsor), Mexico (Mexico City), and the UK (Birmingham).

PRODUCTS/OPERATIONS
Selected Services
Construction management
Consulting
Design/build delivery
General contracting
Ironworker and boilermaker services
Facility management
Machinery and equipment moving and installation
Millwright and machinist services
Program management
Transportation, heavy haul, logistical, and forwarding services

Selected Markets
Airport
Automotive
Commercial
Correctional
Education
Government building
Health care
Hospitality
Office building
Retail and entertainment
Sports and recreation
Surface transportation
Water and wastewater

COMPETITORS
Alberici
Barton Malow
Bechtel
Clark Enterprises
EllisDon Construction
Fluor
Foster Wheeler
Halliburton
Hensel Phelps Construction
Jacobs Engineering
M. A. Mortenson
Parsons
Pepper Construction
Peter Kiewit Sons'
Skanska USA Building
Turner Corporation
Washington Group
Whiting-Turner

HISTORICAL FINANCIALS
Company Type: Private

Income Statement				FYE: December 31
	REVENUE ($ mil.)	NET INCOME ($ mil.)	NET PROFIT MARGIN	EMPLOYEES
12/02	925	—	—	1,500
12/01	810	—	—	1,300
12/00	750	—	—	1,000
12/99	775	—	—	700
12/98	675	—	—	643
12/97	630	—	—	600
12/96	675	—	—	500
12/95	660	—	—	500
12/94	503	—	—	500
12/93	405	—	—	612
Annual Growth	9.6%	—	—	10.5%

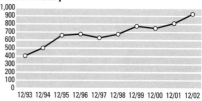
Revenue History

HOOVER'S HANDBOOK OF PRIVATE COMPANIES 2005

Walsh Group

The Walsh Group erects walls, halls, malls, and more. Walsh provides design/build and construction services for industrial, public, and commercial projects throughout the US. Projects range from prisons to skyscrapers to shopping malls. The group consists of Walsh Construction and Archer Western Contractors. Walsh provides complete project management services, from planning and demolition to general contracting and finance. It is a major player in bridge and highway construction and also renovates and restores buildings and provides interior construction and design services. Among its projects is work on Chicago's Millenium Park. The Walsh family still owns the firm, founded in 1898.

EXECUTIVES

Chairman; CEO, Walsh Construction:
Matthew M. Walsh
President; President, Walsh Construction:
Daniel J. Walsh
CFO, Secretary, and Treasurer: Larry J. Kibbon
VP Business Development: Patrick M. Donley
Human Resources Manager: Rhonda Hardwick
Auditors: Wolf & Company, P.C.

LOCATIONS

HQ: The Walsh Group
929 W. Adams St., Chicago, IL 60607
Phone: 312-563-5400   **Fax:** 312-563-5466
Web: www.walshgroup.com

The Walsh Group's Archer Western Contractors has offices in Arlington, Texas; Atlanta; Jacksonville, Florida; Phoenix; San Diego; and Virginia Beach, Virginia. Its Walsh Construction Company has offices in Boston; Chicago; Detroit; LaPorte, Indiana; and Pittsburgh.

PRODUCTS/OPERATIONS

Projects
Apartment complexes
Correctional facilities
Data centers
Education facilities
Health-care facilities
Highways and bridges
Hotels
Industrial parks
Interiors
Laboratories
Parking garages
Renovations
Retail centers
Senior housing
Skyscrapers
Treatment plants

Selected Services
Construction management
Design/build
General contracting
Preconstruction
Project financing
Project and tenant analysis

COMPETITORS

Alberici
Balfour Beatty Construction
Barton Malow
Bechtel
Black & Veatch
Bovis Lend Lease
Brasfield & Gorrie
Dunn Industries
Earth Tech
Fluor
Granite Construction
Hunt Building
Hunt Construction
Jacobs Engineering
Lane Construction
M. A. Mortenson
McCarthy Building
Pepper Construction
Peter Kiewit Sons' Skanska
TIC Holdings
Turner Corporation

HISTORICAL FINANCIALS

Company Type: Private

Income Statement
FYE: December 31

	REVENUE ($ mil.)	NET INCOME ($ mil.)	NET PROFIT MARGIN	EMPLOYEES
12/03	1,600	—	—	—
12/02	1,754	—	—	3,691
12/01	1,450	—	—	3,000
12/00	1,304	—	—	2,600
12/99	1,080	—	—	1,000
12/98	1,170	—	—	3,500
12/97	992	—	—	2,000
12/96	740	—	—	1,500
12/95	604	—	—	1,000
12/94	450	—	—	4,000
Annual Growth	15.1%	—	—	(1.0%)

Revenue History

Warner Music

These records were made to be listened to, not broken. Warner Music Group (WMG) markets a variety of musical artists through its recording labels Atlantic Records Group and Warner Bros. Records. Its roster of more than 800 artists includes Green Day, Madonna, Faith Hill, and Red Hot Chili Peppers. Its Warner/Chappell publishing unit holds the rights to more than a million songs. WMG sold its WEA CD manufacturing unit to Cinram for $1 billion. Warner Music Group has been purchased by a group led by Thomas H. Lee Partners and Edgar Bronfman, Jr., for $2.6 billion.

The long heritage of WMG's labels has produced an impressive back catalog, featuring works by Led Zeppelin, Jimi Hendrix, Van Halen, and the Eagles. The company also distributes works from a number of jointly owned labels, including Maverick (with Madonna), Qwest (run by Quincy Jones), Strictly Rhythm, and Sub Pop (Seattle's once hip rock label). Its Alternative Distribution Alliance offers distribution for independent labels and artists. Warner Music has operations in 70 countries.

Once the biggest music company in the world, WMG has watched its market share erode over the past decade. To catch up to Sony and Universal, it courted the UK's struggling EMI Group in 2000. The deal had to be called off, however, to assuage European regulators in light of America Online's acquisition of Time Warner. Instead, former chairman Roger Ames consolidated ownership of its jointly owned labels and cut staff to create a leaner business unit. The company also began exploring online music distribution by teaming with EMI, BMG, and RealNetworks to launch MusicNet.

In conjunction with his purchase of WMG, Edgar Bronfman, Jr., has lured rap pioneer Lyor Cohen away from Island Def Jam to oversee WMG's US recorded music operations. WMG has also undergone restructuring since the Bronfman purchase, combining its Atlantic, Elektra, and Lava labels under the umbrella of the Atlantic Records Group.

EXECUTIVES

Chairman and CEO: Edgar Bronfman Jr., age 48
Chairman and CEO, US Recorded Music: Lyor Cohen
Acting CFO: Michael Ward
EVP and General Counsel: David H. Johnson
EVP Strategic Planning and Business Development:
Paul J. Vidich
EVP: Kevin Liles, age 36
SVP and CIO: Tsvi Gal
SVP Financial Operations: John Avagliano
SVP Human Resources: James A. (Jim) Blauvelt

LOCATIONS

HQ: Warner Music Group
75 Rockefeller Plaza, New York, NY 10019
Phone: 212-275-2000
Web: www.wmg.com
Warner Music Group has operations in 70 countries.

PRODUCTS/OPERATIONS

Selected Operations and Subsidiaries
Record Labels
  Atlantic Records Group (Atlantic, Elektra, Lava)
  London Records (UK)
  Reprise Records
  Rhino Entertainment
  Warner Bros. Records
  Warner Bros. JazzSpace
  Warner Reprise Nashville
  Word Entertainment
Joint Venture Labels
  143 Records
  Maverick
  Qwest
  RuffNation Records
  Strictly Rhythm Records
  Sub Pop Records

Selected Recording Artists

Bjork
Brandy
Eric Clapton
Clutch
Deftones
Disturbed
Gipsy Kings
Philip Glass
Faith Hill
Chris Isaak
Jewel
Kid Rock
Kronos Quartet
Led Zeppelin
Lil' Kim
Linkin Park
Madonna
Metallica
Pat Metheny
Alanis Morissette
Nick Cave and the Bad Seeds
Tom Petty
Phish
Red Hot Chili Peppers
Lou Reed
R.E.M.
Paul Simon
Staind
Dwight Yoakam
Neil Young

COMPETITORS

Chrysalis Group
DreamWorks
edel music
EMI Group
KOCH Entertainment
Sony BMG
Universal Music Group
Zomba

HISTORICAL FINANCIALS
Company Type: Private

Income Statement
FYE: December 31

	REVENUE ($ mil.)	NET INCOME ($ mil.)	NET PROFIT MARGIN	EMPLOYEES
12/03	3,500	—	—	—
12/02	4,205	—	—	5,300
12/01	4,036	—	—	—
12/00	4,148	—	—	—
12/99	3,834	—	—	—
12/98	4,025	—	—	—
12/97	3,691	—	—	—
12/96	3,949	—	—	—
12/95	4,196	—	—	—
12/94	3,986	—	—	—
Annual Growth	(1.4%)	—	—	—

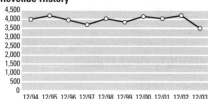

Revenue History

Warren Equities

Warren Equities fills car tanks and stomachs in the US Northeast. The holding company sells fuel and groceries from over 400 Xtra Mart brand service stations and convenience stores from Maine to Virginia. Warren's distribution companies supply those stores, as well as independent outlets, with gasoline, grocery, and tobacco products. Other Warren companies trade and store petroleum, provide environmental testing services, and make promotional signs and clothing. Chairman and owner Warren Alpert founded the company in 1950 after Standard Oil awarded him a distributorship. His foundation gives annual grants to medical researchers; he has donated more than $20 million to Harvard Medical School.

EXECUTIVES

Chairman: Warren Alpert, age 83
Vice Chairman: Edward M. Cosgrove
President and CEO: Herbert Kaplan
CFO and Treasurer: John Dziedzic
EVP: Francis K. La Forge
Controller and Assistant Treasurer: Richard J. Sawicki
Director Human Resources: Thomas Palumbo

LOCATIONS
HQ: Warren Equities, Inc.
27 Warren Way, Providence, RI 02905
Phone: 401-781-9900 **Fax:** 401-461-7160
Web: www.warreneq.com

Warren Equities operates in Connecticut, Maine, Maryland, Massachusetts, New Hampshire, New York, Pennsylvania, Rhode Island, and Virginia.

PRODUCTS/OPERATIONS

Subsidiaries
Auburn Merchandise Distributors, Inc. (wholesale marketing)
Convenient Graphics (promotional products)
Drake Petroleum Company, Inc. (wholesale gasoline)
Kenyon Oil Company, Inc. (retail gasoline and convenience stores)
MidValley Oil Company (retail gasoline and convenience stores)
Warex Terminals Corporation (wholesale marketing)
Xcel Environmental, Inc. (environmental services)

COMPETITORS

7-Eleven
BP
Casey's General Stores
Crown Central Petroleum
Cumberland Farms
Getty Petroleum Marketing
Global Companies
Motiva Enterprises
Sunoco
SUPERVALU
Wawa, Inc.

HISTORICAL FINANCIALS
Company Type: Private

Income Statement
FYE: May 31

	REVENUE ($ mil.)	NET INCOME ($ mil.)	NET PROFIT MARGIN	EMPLOYEES
5/02	1,000	—	—	2,200
5/01	984	—	—	2,200
5/00	797	—	—	2,100
5/99	587	—	—	2,100
5/98	620	—	—	2,100
5/97	700	—	—	2,300
5/96	900	—	—	2,100
5/95	786	—	—	1,600
5/94	701	—	—	1,600
5/93	650	—	—	1,560
Annual Growth	4.9%	—	—	3.9%

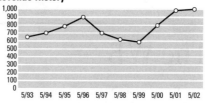

Revenue History

Watkins Associated Industries

Watkins Associated Industries does business over the road, on the ground, and by the sea. Its Watkins Motor Lines subsidiary is a long-haul, less-than-truckload (LTL) carrier that operates throughout the US with a fleet of more than 4,000 tractors and 11,500 trailers. Other Watkins Associated Industries units provide truckload transportation, logistics, and dedicated fleet services. In addition, Watkins owns businesses engaged in real estate development (apartment complexes and shopping centers), door and window manufacturing, and seafood processing (Tampa Maid). Bill Watkins founded the family-owned company in 1932 with a $300 pickup truck.

EXECUTIVES

Chairman and CEO, Watkins Associated Industries and Watkins Motor Lines: John Watkins
President and CFO: Michael L. (Mike) Watkins
Chairman, Tampa Maid Foods: George C. Watkins
CEO, Highway Transport: Greg Watkins
President, Land Span: Roger Reed
President, Watkins Canada Express: Bob Simons
President, Wilwat Properties: Kimberley M. (Kim) Watkins
Secretary and Treasurer: George W. Ready Jr.
VP and Controller: Richard (Dick) Wuori
Office Manager: Milton Eades

LOCATIONS
HQ: Watkins Associated Industries, Inc.
1958 Monroe Dr. NE, Atlanta, GA 30324
Phone: 404-872-3841 **Fax:** 404-872-2812
Web: www.watkins.com

PRODUCTS/OPERATIONS

Selected Operating Companies
Transportation
  Highway Transport (logistics)
  Land Span (truckload freight transportation)
  Sunco Carriers (less-than-truckload freight transportation)
  Watkins Canada Express, Inc. (warehousing and transportation)
  Watkins Fleet Services (dedicated trucking fleet services)
  Watkins Motor Lines (less-than-truckload freight transportation)
Other
  Tampa Maid Foods (seafood processing and marketing)
  Tucker Door and Trim (door and window manufacturing)
  Watkins Associated Developers (real estate development)
  Wilwat Properties (real estate development)

COMPETITORS

Abrams Industries
Arkansas Best
Central Freight Lines
Con-Way
Empress International
FedEx Freight
Mazzetta
Old Dominion Freight
Overnite Transportation
USF
Vitran
Yellow Roadway

HISTORICAL FINANCIALS

Company Type: Private

Income Statement
FYE: December 31

	ESTIMATED REVENUE ($ mil.)	NET INCOME ($ mil.)	NET PROFIT MARGIN	EMPLOYEES
12/03	1,118	—	—	9,000
12/02	1,038	—	—	9,000
12/01	1,050	—	—	9,500
12/00	1,076	—	—	10,000
12/99	982	—	—	10,000
12/98	796	—	—	8,300
12/97	725	—	—	8,000
12/96	600	—	—	6,400
12/95	575	—	—	6,179
Annual Growth	8.7%	—	—	4.8%

Revenue History

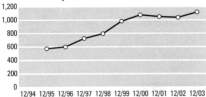

Wawa

It's not baby talk — when folks say they need to go to the Wawa, they need groceries. Wawa runs about 550 Wawa Food Markets in Delaware, Maryland, New Jersey, Pennsylvania, and Virginia. Wawa stores are noted for their coffee and their salad and deli offerings, including hoagie sandwiches; more than 150 stores sell gas. Unlike many convenience store chains, Wawa has its own dairy, supplying Wawa stores and about 1,000 hospitals, schools, and other institutions. The company opened its first store in 1964, but its roots go back to an iron foundry begun in 1803 by the Wood family; food operations began in 1902 when George Wood started a dairy in Wawa, Pennsylvania. The Wood family owns 52% of the company.

EXECUTIVES

Chairman and CEO: Richard D. (Dick) Wood Jr.
President and COO: Howard B. Stoeckel
EVP, Finance and Administration: There du Pont
SVP and Chief Marketing Officer: Rob Price
SVP, Law: Vincent P. Anderson
SVP, Operations: Harry McHugh
VP, Human Resources: Karen Casale
CIO: Neil McCarthy
Director, Food Service: Michael Sherlock
Director IT Architecture: Marty Maglio
Director, Store Operations Technology: John Cunningham
Manager, Public Relations: Lori Bruce

LOCATIONS

HQ: Wawa, Inc.
 260 W. Baltimore Pike, Wawa, PA 19063
Phone: 610-358-8000 **Fax:** 610-358-8878
Web: www.wawa.com

PRODUCTS/OPERATIONS

Selected Products and Private-Label Brands
Bakery (Wawa)
Cold beverages (Wawa)
Hoagies (Built-to-Order, Shorti)
Hot breakfast
 Coffee (Freshly Brewed Coffee)
 Hot breakfast sandwiches (Sizzli)
Party platters
Ready-to-eat foods (Wawa Express)
Sides
Soups

COMPETITORS

7-Eleven
A&P
Albertson's
Amerada Hess
ChevronTexaco
Cumberland Farms
Exxon Mobil
Foodarama Supermarkets
Genuardi's Family Markets
Getty Realty
Green Valley
Kroger
Motiva Enterprises
Rutter's Dairy
Sheetz
Subway
Village Super Market
Warren Equities
Wegmans

HISTORICAL FINANCIALS

Company Type: Private

Income Statement
FYE: December 31

	REVENUE ($ mil.)	NET INCOME ($ mil.)	NET PROFIT MARGIN	EMPLOYEES
12/03	2,819	—	—	15,000
12/02	2,272	—	—	13,400
12/01	2,010	—	—	13,000
12/00	1,500	—	—	13,000
12/99	1,398	—	—	12,000
12/98	1,000	—	—	12,000
12/97	1,010	—	—	12,500
12/96	959	—	—	12,000
12/95	901	—	—	10,000
12/94	838	—	—	—
Annual Growth	14.4%	—	—	5.2%

Revenue History

The WB

The WB Television Network is looking to grow up and get over the teen angst. After catering to Generation Y with hits like *Charmed* and *Smallville*, the upstart network that took to the airwaves in 1995 is trying to combat low ratings by attracting an older audience to new shows such as *Summerland* and *Everwood*. The WB broadcasts prime-time programming six nights a week, and under the guise of Kids' WB!, the network also provides weekday morning, afternoon, and Saturday morning children's programming, including the popular *Pokémon* series. The WB is also producing original movies for the first time to boost non-serialized programming. Turner Broadcasting owns 78% of The WB, Tribune Company owns the rest.

EXECUTIVES

Chairman and CEO: Garth Ancier
President, Entertainment: David Janollari
Co-EVP Comedy Development: Mike Clements
Co-EVP Comedy Development: Tracey Pakosta
EVP Drama Development: Carolyn Bernstein
EVP Finance and Operations: Mitch Nedick
EVP General Counsel: John Maatta
EVP Marketing: Suzanne Kolb
EVP Media Sales: Bill Morningstar
EVP Network Communications: Brad Turell
EVP Talent/Casting: Kathleen Letterie
SVP Affiliate Relations and Communications: Elizabeth Tumulty
SVP Broadcast Standards: Rich Mater
SVP Technology: Hal Protter
Co-President, Marketing: Bob Bibb
Co-President, Marketing: Lew Goldstein
VP Human Resources: Valerie Masterson

LOCATIONS

HQ: The WB Television Network
 4000 Warner Blvd., Bldg. 34R, Burbank, CA 91522
Phone: 818-977-5000 **Fax:** 818-977-6771
Web: www.thewb.com

PRODUCTS/OPERATIONS

Selected Programs
7th Heaven
Blue Collar TV
Charmed
Drew Carey's Green Screen Show
Everwood
Gilmore Girls
Grounded for Life
Jack & Bobby
One Tree Hill
Reba
Smallville
Steve Harvey's Big Time
Summerland
What I Like About You

COMPETITORS

ABC
CBS
FOX Broadcasting
MBC
NBC
UPN

HISTORICAL FINANCIALS

Company Type: Joint venture

Income Statement
FYE: December 31

	REVENUE ($ mil.)	NET INCOME ($ mil.)	NET PROFIT MARGIN	EMPLOYEES
12/03	660	—	—	—
12/02	589	—	—	400
12/01	450	—	—	340
12/00	453	—	—	—
12/99	384	—	—	—
12/98	260	—	—	—
12/97	136	—	—	—
12/96	87	—	—	—
Annual Growth	33.6%	—	—	17.6%

Revenue History

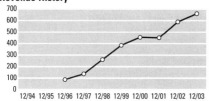

Webcor Builders

The core of Webcor Builders is commercial building in Silicon Valley and Northern California. It constructs mid- and high-rise office buildings, residential and medical facilities, hotels, and parking structures. Known for its focus on high-tech projects, the company has worked on headquarters for Oracle and Adobe Systems and a headquarters compound for Lucas Digital's Industrial Light + Magic and LucasArts Entertainment. The company also provides interior construction and renovation services, seismic upgrades, concrete construction, and telecommunications networking and technology consulting. The surviving entity of a 1994 merger with A.J. Ball Construction, Webcor is owned by president Andrew Ball.

In 2004 Webcor Builders has gained the top ranking for the largest general contractors in California, and it is also one of the top-ranking contractors nationwide. About 88% of its revenue comes from general building projects; the rest is from its interiors operations. Among its recent projects is work on Trinity Plaza in San Francisco and on Broadway 655, the first high-rise building in San Diego in 13 years. Almost all revenues are generated from private-sector contracts.

EXECUTIVES

Chairman: David R. Boyd
President and CEO: Andrew J. (Andy) Ball
EVP: Richard Lamb
SVP and General Counsel: John Bowles
SVP Concrete: Rosser Edwards Jr.
SVP Estimating: Chet Brians
SVP Interiors: Bill Kalff
SVP Business Development: Glenn Gabel
VP Finance: David (Dave) Fisher
CTO: Tommer Catlin
Director Administration and Human Resources: Kaela Hanrahan
Director Marketing: Kerry Boyd
Auditors: S.J. Gallina LLP

LOCATIONS

HQ: Webcor Builders, Inc.
951 Mariners Island Blvd., 7th Fl.,
San Mateo, CA 94404
Phone: 650-349-2727   **Fax:** 650-524-7399
Web: www.webcor.com

Webcor Builders has offices in Anaheim, Hayward, Los Angeles, San Diego, San Francisco, and San Mateo, California.

PRODUCTS/OPERATIONS

Selected Subsidiaries
Webcor Concrete
Webcor Interior Construction Group (ICG)
Webcor Technologies

COMPETITORS

Beck Group
Bovis Lend Lease
Charles Pankow Builders
Clark Enterprises
DPR Construction
Hathaway Dinwiddie Construction
Hensel Phelps Construction
McCarthy Building
Plant Construction
Rudolph & Sletten
S. J. Amoroso Construction
Skanska USA Building
Swinerton
Turner Corporation
Washington Group
Whiting-Turner

HISTORICAL FINANCIALS

Company Type: Private

Income Statement FYE: December 31

	REVENUE ($ mil.)	NET INCOME ($ mil.)	NET PROFIT MARGIN	EMPLOYEES
12/03	1,268	—	—	—
12/02	1,340	—	—	800
12/01	1,155	—	—	800
12/00	760	—	—	840
12/99	636	—	—	400
12/98	541	—	—	377
12/97	526	—	—	337
12/96	411	—	—	203
12/95	83	—	—	250
12/94	69	—	—	255
Annual Growth	38.3%	—	—	15.4%

Revenue History

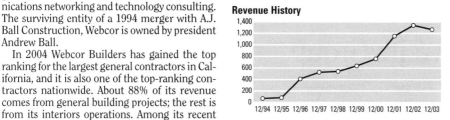

Wegmans

One name strikes fear in the hearts of supermarket owners in New York, Pennsylvania, New Jersey, and now, Virginia: Wegmans Food Markets. The grocery chain owns about 65 stores, but they are hardly typical. Much larger than most supermarkets (up to 120,000 sq. ft.), they offer specialty shops such as huge in-store cafes, cheese shops with some 400 different varieties, and French-style pastry shops. The company is known for its gourmet cooking classes and an extensive employee-training program. Wegmans also runs about 15 Chase-Pitkin Home and Garden home-improvement stores and a restaurant. Founded in 1916, the company is owned by the family of founder John Wegman. His nephew, Robert Wegman, is chairman.

Wegmans opened its first store in Virginia in 2004 and has plans for a second store there. It also plans to build its first store in Maryland.

EXECUTIVES

Chairman: Robert B. Wegman, age 85
President: Daniel R. (Danny) Wegman, age 56
EVP, Operations: Jack DePeters
SVP and CFO: James (Jim) Leo
SVP, Consumer Affairs: Mary Ellen Burris
SVP, Distribution: Mike Bargmann
SVP, Information Technology: Donald (Don) Reeve
SVP, Merchandising: Colleen Wegman, age 32
President, Chase-Pitkin Home and Garden: William (Bill) Strassburg
Secretary and General Counsel: Paul S. Speranza Jr.
Director, B2B: Marianne Timmons
Director, Human Resources: Gerald Pierce
Manager, Media Relations: Jo Natale

LOCATIONS

HQ: Wegmans Food Markets, Inc.
1500 Brooks Ave., Rochester, NY 14624
Phone: 585-328-2550   **Fax:** 585-464-4664
Web: www.wegmans.com

COMPETITORS

A&P
Albertson's
Foodarama Supermarkets
Foodtown
Genuardi's Family Markets
Giant Eagle
Giant Food Stores
Golub
Home Depot
IGA
Pathmark
Penn Traffic
Safeway
SUPERVALU
Tops Markets
Wal-Mart
Wawa, Inc.
Weis Markets

HISTORICAL FINANCIALS

Company Type: Private

Income Statement FYE: December 31

	ESTIMATED REVENUE ($ mil.)	NET INCOME ($ mil.)	NET PROFIT MARGIN	EMPLOYEES
12/03	3,300	—	—	32,000
12/02	3,020	—	—	31,300
12/01	2,920	—	—	29,072
12/00	2,800	—	—	29,826
12/99	2,670	—	—	28,766
12/98	2,450	—	—	25,000
12/97	2,340	—	—	25,000
12/96	2,250	—	—	25,000
12/95	2,130	—	—	—
12/94	2,000	—	—	—
Annual Growth	5.7%	—	—	3.6%

Revenue History

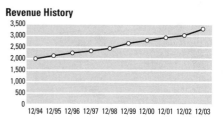

Weil, Gotshal

The seeds of Weil, Gotshal & Manges (WGM) may have been planted in New York City, but its branches have grown globally. Founded in 1931, the law firm has more than 15 offices worldwide. WGM strives to integrate the expertise of its more than 1,000 lawyers across all practice areas for the benefit of clients such as General Electric, Hicks, Muse, Tate & Furst, and CBS. Its office in Washington, DC, for example, lends legislative support and its Silicon Valley office offers technology know-how. WGM is well-known for its business finance and restructuring practice; other practice areas include energy, real estate, tax law, and trusts and estates.

EXECUTIVES

Chairman and Executive Partner: Stephen J. Dannhauser
Executive Director: John W. Neary
CFO: Norman W. LaCroix
CIO: Jim McGinnis
Chief Marketing Officer: Katherine D'Urso
Associate Executive Director: Rob Singer
Associate Relations Director: Brad Scott
Auxiliary Legal Services Director: Kevin Curtin
Human Resources Director: Pat Bowers
Management Information Systems Director: Randy Buckart
Professional Development Director: Victoria Alzapiedi
Library Services Manager: Deborah Cinque
Associate Relations Manager, Diversity: Larry Perkins

LOCATIONS

HQ: Weil, Gotshal & Manges LLP
767 5th Ave., New York, NY 10153
Phone: 212-310-8000   **Fax:** 212-310-8007
Web: www.weil.com

Weil, Gotshal & Manges has U.S. offices in Austin, Dallas, and Houston; Texas; Boston; Miami; New York City; Redwood Shores, California; and Washington, DC. It has international offices in Brussels; Budapest, Hungary; Frankfurt; London; Munich; Paris; Prague, Czech Republic; Shanghai; Singapore; and Warsaw, Poland.

PRODUCTS/OPERATIONS

Selected Practice Areas

Advertising	Litigation
Aviation finance	Mergers and acquisitions
Bankruptcy	Real estate
Business finance and restructuring	Securities
Capital markets	Sports
Corporate	Tax
Energy	Technology
Executive compensation	Trade practices and regulatory law
Health care	Trusts and estates
Intellectual property	

COMPETITORS

Cleary, Gottlieb	Simpson Thacher
Clifford Chance	Skadden, Arps
Cravath, Swaine	Sullivan & Cromwell
Paul, Weiss, Rifkind	Wachtell, Lipton
Proskauer Rose	White & Case
Shearman & Sterling	
Sidley Austin Brown & Wood	

HISTORICAL FINANCIALS

Company Type: Partnership

Income Statement FYE: December 31

	REVENUE ($ mil.)	NET INCOME ($ mil.)	NET PROFIT MARGIN	EMPLOYEES
12/03	801	—	—	
12/02	688	—	—	
12/01	581	—	—	
12/00	506	—	—	
12/99	440	—	—	1,800
12/98	400	—	—	1,700
12/97	354	—	—	1,600
12/96	322	—	—	
12/95	306	—	—	
12/94	311	—	—	
Annual Growth	11.1%	—	—	6.1%

Revenue History

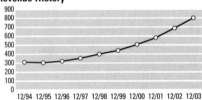

Weitz Group

It took wits for The Weitz Group to become a top US general building contractor. Founded in 1855 by carpenter Charles H. Weitz, the company was run by the Weitz family for four generations before becoming employee-owned. It provides general contracting, construction management, and design/build services, constructing everything from office buildings, industrial plants, senior communities, and schools to hotels, golf courses, supermarkets, and malls. Weitz entered the homebuilding market with its 2001 purchase of Colorado-based Norris Associates, which constructs multimillion-dollar homes in well-heeled resort areas. Weitz builds supermarkets and warehouse/distribution centers through its Hy-Vee Weitz unit.

EXECUTIVES

Chairman, President, and CEO: Glenn H. De Stigter
COO: James (Jim) Simmons
CFO: Craig Damos
CIO: Mark Federle
VP Human Resources: Kris Jensen
VP, Preconstruction Services: Larry Mohr
VP, Weitz Golf International: Tommy Sasser
General Counsel and Secretary: David Strutt
Treasurer: Don Blum
Manager Employee Benefits: Chantry DeVries
Auditors: KPMG Peat Marwick

LOCATIONS

HQ: The Weitz Group, LLC
Capital Square, 400 Locust St., Ste. 300, Des Moines, IA 50309
Phone: 515-698-4260   **Fax:** 515-698-4299
Web: www.weitz.com

The Weitz Group has offices in Arizona, Colorado, Florida, Iowa, Kansas, and Nebraska.

PRODUCTS/OPERATIONS

Selected Clients and Projects
Arizona Biltmore Hotel
The Breakers Hotel
Iowa State University
Rosenblatt Stadium
The Nicklaus Golf Club at LionsGate
The Principal Financial Group
Twentieth Century Fox

COMPETITORS

Barton Malow	H.J. Russell
Bovis Lend Lease	Hunt Construction
Brasfield & Gorrie	Peter Kiewit Sons'
Centex	Skanska
Charles Pankow Builders	Structure Tone
Choate Construction	Sundt
Clark Enterprises	Turner Corporation
David Weekley Homes	Walsh Group
Dunn Industries	Webcor Builders
Gilbane	Whiting-Turner
Graycor	

HISTORICAL FINANCIALS

Company Type: Private

Income Statement FYE: December 31

	REVENUE ($ mil.)	NET INCOME ($ mil.)	NET PROFIT MARGIN	EMPLOYEES
12/03	830	—	—	—
12/02	762	—	—	—
12/01	810	—	—	1,104
12/00	650	—	—	1,322
12/99	657	—	—	1,104
12/98	577	—	—	909
Annual Growth	7.6%	—	—	6.7%

Revenue History

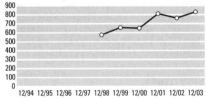

Wells' Dairy

From the five-quart tub of Cherry Nut ice cream to red, white, and blue Bomb Pops, Wells' Dairy spans the frozen treat spectrum. Best known for its Blue Bunny brand of ice cream and frozen novelties, Wells' Dairy sells its products in convenience stores, restaurants, supermarkets, schools, and vending machines. Its Contract Manufacturing Division produces fluid, cultured, and frozen dairy products for third parties. Founded as a small town dairy in 1913 by the late Fred H. Wells, the company grew through acquisitions to become a strong regional ice cream player with a presence in markets across the US and 20 countries. It is still owned and managed by the Wells family.

Already strong in the Midwest, Wells' has its eye on becoming a national brand. The company extended its reach westward by building a plant in Utah and eyeing additional brands to produce.

Wells' has struck a deal with Weight Watchers International to become the sole producer of Weight Watchers brand frozen desserts and novelties. The company has also purchased the FrozFruit and Chill Ice brands of frozen fruit novelties. With the deal came the lease to a facility in New Mexico where the nationally distributed treats are produced.

EXECUTIVES
CEO: Gary M. Wells
President: Dan Wells
COO: Doug Wells
CFO: Larry Heemstra
EVP: Mike Wells
VP, Human Resources: Mac Rothenbuhler
VP, Information Services: Kim Norby
VP, Marketing: Jim Reynolds
VP, Retail Sales: Greg Wells
Director of Public Relations: Dave Smetter
Director of Research and Development:
 Mathew Wolkow

LOCATIONS
HQ: Wells' Dairy, Inc.
 1 Blue Bunny Dr., Le Mars, IA 51031
Phone: 712-546-4000 **Fax:** 712-546-1782
Web: www.wellsdairy.com

Wells' Dairy has production facilities in Iowa, Nebraska, New Mexico, and Utah and additional facilities in Arizona, Kansas, and Texas.

PRODUCTS/OPERATIONS
Selected Products

Cottage cheese	Juice
Fresh yogurt	Milk
Frozen yogurt	Sherbet
Ice cream	Snack dip
Ice cream novelties	Sour cream

COMPETITORS

Allied Domecq QSR	Nestlé
Blue Bell	Quality Chekd
Dairy Farmers of America	Schwan's
Dean Foods	Unilever
Dreyer's	YoCream
Marigold Foods	

HISTORICAL FINANCIALS
Company Type: Private

Income Statement			FYE: December 31	
	REVENUE ($ mil.)	NET INCOME ($ mil.)	NET PROFIT MARGIN	EMPLOYEES
12/03	850	—	—	2,475
12/02	800	—	—	2,475
12/01	650	—	—	2,450
12/00	580	—	—	2,400
12/99	600	—	—	2,200
12/98	525	—	—	2,200
Annual Growth	10.1%	—	—	2.4%

Revenue History

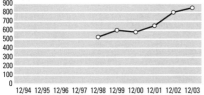

Westcon

The Westcon Group sees more pros than cons in networking equipment. The company's three divisions — Comstor, Westcon, and Voda One — resell networking and communications equipment made by Cisco Systems, Nortel Networks, Avaya, and other top manufacturers. Networking servers, switches, and routers; network security systems; and virtual private network systems top Westcon's product list. The company also provides a variety of support services, including training, network design, and logistical support. South Africa-based networking company Datatec Ltd. owns more than 90% of the company, which has acquired Dutch networking products distributor Landis Group.

The company filed to raise $115 million in an initial public offering in 2004. Philip Raffiani and EVP Thomas Dolan founded Westcon in 1985.

EXECUTIVES
Chairman: John McCartney, age 51
President, CEO, and Director: Thomas (Tom) Dolan, age 50
SVP, Corporate Operations: Brian E. Weisfeld, age 36
VP Finance and CFO: John P. O'Malley III, age 41, $367,273 pay
VP Worldwide Business Operations and Chief Risk Officer: Russ Fein, age 40
VP Marketing and Investor Relations: Jenny Pappas
VP, Worldwide Marketing: Duncan Potter
CIO: Jason Molfetas, age 39
Managing Director, Comstor Europe: Simon J. England, age 39, $312,601 pay
SVP and General Manager, the Americas, Westcon Group North America: Anthony Daley, age 39, $377,456 pay
VP and General Manager, U.S., Westcon Group North America: Carol Rivetti, age 42, $333,692 pay
Auditors: Deloitte & Touche LLP

LOCATIONS
HQ: Westcon Group, Inc.
 520 White Plains Rd., Ste. 100,
 Tarrytown, NY 10591
Phone: 914-829-7000 **Fax:** 914-829-7137
Web: www.westcongroup.com

Westcon Group has operations in Australia, Austria, Belgium, Brazil, Canada, Denmark, France, Germany, Ireland, the Netherlands, Norway, Singapore, South Africa, Spain, Sweden, the UK, and the US.

2003 Sales

	% of total
North America	60
Europe	34
Other regions	6
Total	**100**

PRODUCTS/OPERATIONS
Selected Products
Data caching servers
Integrated communication systems
Internet servers
Network security systems
Network switches and routers
Videoconferencing systems
Virtual private network systems
Wireless network access systems

Selected Services
Inventory management
Logistics
Network design and consulting
Support
Technical services
Training

COMPETITORS
Avaya
CDW
Cisco Systems
CompuCom
En Pointe
Ingram Micro
Nortel Networks
Pomeroy IT
Resilien
ScanSource
Tech Data

HISTORICAL FINANCIALS
Company Type: Private

Income Statement			FYE: Last day in February	
	REVENUE ($ mil.)	NET INCOME ($ mil.)	NET PROFIT MARGIN	EMPLOYEES
2/04	1,885	6	0.3%	1,000
2/03	1,649	(92)	—	1,000
2/02	1,687	16	0.9%	1,000
2/01	2,066	59	2.8%	1,059
2/00*	1,168	21	1.8%	1,057
3/99	587	22	3.7%	—
3/98	334	7	1.9%	—
Annual Growth	33.4%	(1.9%)	—	(1.4%)

*Fiscal year change

2004 Year-End Financials
Debt ratio: 13.2% Current ratio: 1.66
Return on equity: 2.1% Long-term debt ($ mil.): 37
Cash ($ mil.): 114

Net Income History

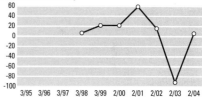

Western Family

From mayo to mops, Western Family Foods supplies private-label products to more than 3,500 independent grocery retailers in 23 mostly western states. It also sells in Asia, Latin America, and Russia. Its main brands are Western Family and Shurfine (no relation to competitor Shurfine International). Western Family coordinates with manufacturers and wholesalers to produce more than 6,000 products. The company helps retailers develop private labels, and it is part of a consortium that buys general merchandise and sells it to independent retailers. Wholesalers Affiliated Foods, Associated Food Stores, Associated Grocers, Olean Wholesale, Unified Western Grocers, and URM Stores own Western Family, founded in 1934.

EXECUTIVES

President and CEO: Ronald S. King
SVP and CFO: Russ Jones
SVP, Procurement: Robert Cutler
SVP Sales and Marketing: David (Dave) Hayden
VP, Information Systems: Gregg Floren
VP, International: Charlie Rotta
VP, Quality Assurance: Roy Besand
Manager, Human Resources: Martina Nilles

LOCATIONS

HQ: Western Family Foods, Inc.
6700 SW Sandburg St., Tigard, OR 97223
Phone: 503-639-6300 **Fax:** 503-684-3469
Web: www.westernfamily.com

In addition to distributing its products in 23 of the United States, Western Family Foods exports to Chile, China, Fiji, Hong Kong, Indonesia, Japan, Malaysia, Mexico, Micronesia, Panama, Guam, the Philippines, Russia, Singapore, South Korea, Taiwan, Thailand, and Vietnam.

PRODUCTS/OPERATIONS

Selected Private Labels
Better Buy
Market Choice
Shur Saving
Shurfine
Western Family

COMPETITORS

Nash Finch
SUPERVALU

HISTORICAL FINANCIALS

Company Type: Private

Income Statement
FYE: April 30

	ESTIMATED REVENUE ($ mil.)	NET INCOME ($ mil.)	NET PROFIT MARGIN	EMPLOYEES
4/03	590	—	—	75
4/02	560	—	—	75
4/01	500	—	—	74
4/00	500	—	—	74
4/99	500	—	—	74
4/98	500	—	—	70
Annual Growth	3.4%	—	—	1.4%

Revenue History

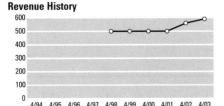

Westfield Group

Westfield Group (formerly Ohio Farmers Insurance) has plowed beyond the crop and cattle biz. Through its affiliates, including First Patriot Insurance, Old Guard Insurance, Westfield Insurance, and Westfield National, the company offers such standard personal lines as auto and homeowners insurance; its niche products include fidelity and surety bonds and specialty coverage for farmers, auto repair shops, and religious organizations. The insurer has opened Westfield Bank, offering personal and business banking services through a referral program involving independent insurance agents in northeastern Ohio.

EXECUTIVES

Chairman and CEO: Robert J. Joyce
CFO and Treasurer: Robert Krisowaty
President, Westfield Bank: Jon Park
Director of Operations, Westfield Financial: Bill Maney
Corporate Secretary: John Batchelder
Controller: Bambi Beshire
Chief Actuary: Stephen Lehecka
Chief Human Resources Officer: Debra Cummings
Chief Investment Officer: John Haney
Chief Solutions Officer: Robert Madden
Corporate Counsel and Secretary: Frank A. Carrino
Senior Executive, Government & Public Relations: Dan Sondles
Senior Executive, Marketing: Kent Daugherty

LOCATIONS

HQ: Westfield Group
1 Park Circle, Westfield Center, OH 44251
Phone: 330-887-0101 **Fax:** 330-887-0840
Web: www.westfield-cos.com

Ohio Farmers Insurance operates in about 20 states nationwide.

PRODUCTS/OPERATIONS

Selected Affiliates
American Select Insurance Company
First Delaware Insurance Company
First Patriot Insurance Company
Ohio Farmers Insurance Company
Old Guard Insurance Company
Old Guard Fire Insurance Company
Westfield Insurance Company
Westfield National Insurance Company

COMPETITORS

AIG
Allstate
CNA Financial
The Hartford
MetLife
Nationwide
New York Life
Prudential
State Farm

HISTORICAL FINANCIALS

Company Type: Private

Income Statement
FYE: December 31

	REVENUE ($ mil.)	NET INCOME ($ mil.)	NET PROFIT MARGIN	EMPLOYEES
12/03	1,300	—	—	2,000
12/02	1,200	—	—	2,000
12/01	745	—	—	2,000
12/00	800	—	—	2,000
12/99	840	—	—	2,000
12/98	854	—	—	2,037
12/97	900	—	—	2,300
12/96	892	—	—	2,290
12/95	856	—	—	2,200
12/94	724	—	—	2,092
Annual Growth	6.7%	—	—	(0.5%)

Revenue History

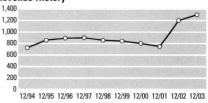

White & Case

What do you call a law firm with some 1,700 lawyers? Well, the safe answer would be White & Case. One of the world's largest law firms, White & Case has buoyed its global reputation by establishing 37 international offices in locations such as Bangkok; Budapest, Hungary; Istanbul, Turkey; London; Paris; Riyadh, Saudi Arabia; and Warsaw, Poland (the firm also maintains six US offices, including its New York City headquarters). Among White & Case's practice areas are bankruptcy, corporate, intellectual property, litigation, project finance, and tax. The firm's client list has included Deutsche Bank and Royal Ahold. White & Case was founded in 1901.

EXECUTIVES

Managing Partner: Duane D. Wall
Administrative Partner: David N. Koschik
CFO: James Latchford
Chief Knowledge Officer: Eugene Stein
Chief Marketing Officer: Liz Pava
Director Media Relations: Roger J. Cohen
Director Administration: Richard M. McKenna
Director Finance: Gregory J. Dolan
Director Human Resources: Jill Connors
Director Marketing, Americas: Helene R. Freymann

LOCATIONS

HQ: White & Case LLP
1155 Avenue of the Americas, New York, NY 10036
Phone: 212-819-8200 **Fax:** 212-354-8113
Web: www.whitecase.com

White & Case has offices in Africa, the Americas, Asia, Europe, and the Middle East.

PRODUCTS/OPERATIONS

Selected Practice Areas
Antitrust
Arbitration and alternative dispute resolution
Bankruptcy and reorganization
Corporate
Employee benefits
Insurance
Intellectual property
Litigation
Mergers and acquisitions
Project finance
Public finance
Tax
Telecommunications

COMPETITORS

Akin Gump
Baker & McKenzie
Clifford Chance
Holland & Knight
Jones Day
Latham & Watkins
Mayer, Brown, Rowe & Maw
Morgan, Lewis
Sidley Austin Brown & Wood
Skadden, Arps
Weil, Gotshal

HISTORICAL FINANCIALS

Company Type: Partnership

Income Statement				FYE: December 31
	REVENUE ($ mil.)	NET INCOME ($ mil.)	NET PROFIT MARGIN	EMPLOYEES
12/03	811	—	—	—
12/02	675	—	—	—
12/01	603	—	—	—
12/00	491	—	—	—
12/99	405	—	—	2,500
12/98	352	—	—	2,300
12/97	318	—	—	2,200
12/96	282	—	—	—
12/95	247	—	—	—
12/94	233	—	—	—
Annual Growth	14.9%	—	—	6.6%

Revenue History

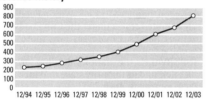

Whiting-Turner Contracting

Whiting-Turner Contracting is a big fish in an ocean of builders. The employee-owned firm provides construction management, general contracting, and design/build services, primarily for large commercial, institutional, and infrastructure projects in the US. It subcontracts about 85% of its volume, but its in-house activities include mechanical and electrical work, concrete forming, and foundation services. A key player in retail construction, the company also undertakes such diverse projects as biotech clean rooms, schools, stadiums, and corporate headquarters for clients like AT&T, General Motors, and the US Army. G. W. C. Whiting and LeBaron Turner founded the company in 1909 to build sewer lines.

Among the group's recent projects is the construction of a defense systems research, development, and test laboratory for the Naval Surface Warfare Center in Dahlgren, Virginia. Projects for its hometown of Baltimore have included the city's convention center and Harborplace.

EXECUTIVES

President and CEO: Willard Hackerman
SEVP Finance and CFO: Charles A. (Chuck) Irish
VP Marketing: David Boucher
Director Human Resources: Edward Spaulding
Auditors: PricewaterhouseCoopers LLP

LOCATIONS

HQ: The Whiting-Turner Contracting Company
300 E. Joppa Rd., Baltimore, MD 21286
Phone: 410-821-1100   **Fax:** 410-337-5770
Web: www.whiting-turner.com

The Whiting-Turner Contracting Company has offices in Allentown, Pennsylvania; Atlanta; Baltimore; Boston; Chantilly, Virginia; Charlotte, North Carolina; Cleveland; Dallas; Fort Lauderdale, Florida; Irvine, California; Las Vegas; New Haven, Connecticut; Newark, Delaware; Orlando, Florida; Richmond, Virginia; San Francisco; Somerset, New Jersey; Tampa, Florida; and Washington, DC.

PRODUCTS/OPERATIONS

Selected Markets
Biotechnology and pharmaceutical
Clean room and high-technology
Education
Entertainment
Health care and senior living
Industrial and manufacturing
Lodging and hospitality
Mission critical facilities
Offices
Parking
Retail
Sports
Transportation
Utility
Warehouse and distribution

COMPETITORS

Barton Malow
Bechtel
Bovis Lend Lease
Choate Construction
Clark Enterprises
DPR Construction
Dunn Industries
Fisher Development
Fluor
Gilbane
Hensel Phelps Construction
Hoffman Corporation
Jacobs Engineering
Kitchell Corporation
McCarthy Building
Perini
Peter Kiewit Sons'
Simon Property Group
Skanska
Suffolk Construction
Swinerton
Turner Corporation
Weitz

HISTORICAL FINANCIALS

Company Type: Private

Income Statement				FYE: December 31
	ESTIMATED REVENUE ($ mil.)	NET INCOME ($ mil.)	NET PROFIT MARGIN	EMPLOYEES
12/02	1,874	—	—	1,335
12/01	2,400	—	—	2,100
12/00	1,646	—	—	2,000
12/99	1,418	—	—	2,000
12/98	1,260	—	—	1,800
12/97	1,050	—	—	1,500
12/96	800	—	—	1,000
12/95	700	—	—	800
12/94	600	—	—	800
12/93	600	—	—	800
Annual Growth	13.5%	—	—	5.9%

Revenue History

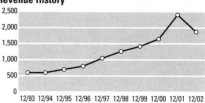

Wilbur-Ellis

Weed 'em and feed 'em could be the motto of Wilbur-Ellis Company. A distributor for major chemical companies, Wilbur-Ellis sells animal feed, fertilizer, insecticides, seed, and machinery through outlets in North America. Subsidiary Connell Brothers exports and distributes chemicals and feed throughout the Pacific Rim. Additionally, Wilbur-Ellis provides consulting, pesticide spraying, and other agriculture-related services. It also owns Knox McDaniels, a supplier of vitamin and mineral premix products in the western US. Brayton Wilbur Sr. and Floyd Ellis founded the company in 1921 as a fish-oil supplier; it is still owned by the Wilbur family.

EXECUTIVES

Chairman: Brayton Wilbur Jr.
Vice Chairman: Carter P. Thacher
President and CEO: Herbert B. Tully
EVP, Agribusiness: Daniel R. Vradenburg
VP, Connell Division: Theodore Eliot
VP, Feed Division: Ron Salter
VP, Strategic Planning and Business Development: John P. Thacher
VP, Treasurer, and CFO: James D. Crawford
Controller: Charles Crume
Director, Information Systems: Jerry Coupe
Director, Human Resources: Mark S. Whitehouse
Director, Credit: Robert Syron
Legal Counsel: Robert Schmalz
Auditors: Hood & Strong

LOCATIONS

HQ: Wilbur-Ellis Company
345 California St., 27th Fl.,
San Francisco, CA 94104
Phone: 415-772-4000   **Fax:** 415-772-4005
Web: www.wilbur-ellis.com

PRODUCTS/OPERATIONS

Selected Products
Agricultural chemicals
Animal feed
Fertilizer
Fungicide
Herbicide
Insecticides
Machinery
Seed protectants
Sprayers

Selected Services
Crop consulting
Fertilizer application
Pesticide application
Product development

COMPETITORS

ADM	ConAgra
Ag Processing	GROWMARK
Agrium	JR Simplot
Cargill	Terra Industries
CF Industries	UAP Holding
CHS	

HISTORICAL FINANCIALS
Company Type: Private

Income Statement
FYE: December 31

	REVENUE ($ mil.)	NET INCOME ($ mil.)	NET PROFIT MARGIN	EMPLOYEES
12/03	1,366	—	—	2,500
12/02	1,223	—	—	2,500
12/01	1,185	—	—	2,500
12/00	1,131	—	—	2,000
12/99	1,300	—	—	2,500
12/98	1,100	—	—	2,500
12/97	1,200	—	—	2,100
12/96	900	—	—	1,900
12/95	870	—	—	1,800
12/94	918	—	—	1,800
Annual Growth	4.5%	—	—	3.7%

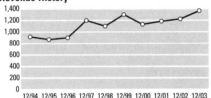

Revenue History

Wilmer Cutler Pickering Hale and Dorr

Law firm Wilmer Cutler Pickering Hale and Dorr LLP was formed from the 2004 merger of two top firms, Wilmer, Cutler, & Pickering (WPC) and Hale and Dorr. The firm boasts over 1,000 lawyers in a dozen offices around the world. Their practice areas include intellectual property, corporate law, international trade, and many others. Founded in 1962, WPC was led by Lloyd Cutler, who has served as counsel to Presidents Jimmy Carter and Bill Clinton. John Pickering, Dick Wilmer and J. Roger Wollenberg. Hale and Dorr began in Boston as a general practice law firm in 1915.

EXECUTIVES
Chairman and Co-Managing Partner: William J. Perlstein
Co-Managing Partner: William F. Lee
CFO: Scot J. Farrell
CTO: Edward MacNamara
Administrative Partner: Carol A. Clayton
Chief Marketing Officer: Christopher C. Quarles III

Director Career Development: Stephen Armstrong
Director Human Resources: Robert J. Dunne
Director Information Services: Jean P. O'Grady
Director Legal Personnel and Recruiting: Christine White
Director Practice Development: Catherine M. Burke
Lawyer Recruitment Administrator: Mary K. Riley

LOCATIONS
HQ: Wilmer Cutler Pickering Hale and Dorr LLP
2445 M St. NW, Washington, DC 20037
Phone: 202-663-6000 **Fax:** 202-663-6363
Web: www.wilmerhale.com

PRODUCTS/OPERATIONS
Selected Practice Areas
Antitrust
Aviation
Bankruptcy
Biotechnology and pharmaceutical industry
Broker-Dealer Compliance
Civil rights and employment litigation and counseling
Class action litigation
Communications
Corporate
Electronic commerce
Employee benefits
Environmental
EU competition
Federal Trade Commission
Financial institutions
Insurance
Intellectual property
Investigations
International
Investment management
Latin America
Legislative
Litigation
Mass media
Product liability
Real estate
Securities
Tax
Telecommunications
White-collar crime

COMPETITORS

Akin Gump	Howrey Simon Arnold & White
Arnold & Porter	
Baker & McKenzie	Skadden, Arps
Covington & Burling	Williams & Connolly
Hogan & Hartson	

HISTORICAL FINANCIALS
Company Type: Partnership

Income Statement
FYE: December 31

	REVENUE ($ mil.)	NET INCOME ($ mil.)	NET PROFIT MARGIN	EMPLOYEES
12/03	659	—	—	—
12/02	297	—	—	—
12/01	235	—	—	1,200
12/00	191	—	—	—
12/99	153	—	—	875
12/98	130	—	—	750
12/97	119	—	—	—
12/96	98	—	—	—
12/95	97	—	—	—
12/94	102	—	—	—
Annual Growth	23.0%	—	—	17.0%

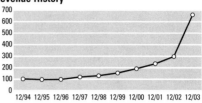

Revenue History

WinCo Foods

WinCo Foods isn't just big on self-service — it's giant. Inside the immense stores (average size is 85,000 sq. ft.) of this mostly employee-owned supermarket chain, customers shop for food in bulk and bag their own groceries. The company's 40-plus stores also feature pizza shops, bakeries, health and beauty products, and organic foods. WinCo Foods, formerly known as Waremart Foods, was renamed as a shortened version of "winning company." The name is also an acronym for its states of operation, which include Washington, Idaho, Nevada, California, and Oregon. Founded in 1968, WinCo Foods formerly operated stores under the Cub Foods and Waremart names. Employees own more than 80% of the company.

SUPERVALU, the nation's leading grocery wholesaler, sold its minority stake in Winco back to the company in April 2003.

EXECUTIVES
Chairman and CEO: William D. (Bill) Long
President and COO: Scott Preece
CFO and Secretary: Gary R. Piva
EVP, Retail Operations: Steve Goddard
VP, Advertising: Sharon Kadell
VP, Engineering: Dick VanderLinden
VP, Information Technology: Glen Reynolds
VP, Labor and Human Resources: Roger Cochell
VP, Loss Prevention & Employment: Linda Nusser
VP, Marketing & Promotions: Dave Strausborger
VP, Public and Legal Affairs: Michael (Mike) Read
VP, Retail Development: Paul Simmons
VP, Transportation: John Reppeto
Controller: Del Ririe

LOCATIONS
HQ: WinCo Foods, Inc.
650 N. Armstrong Place, Boise, ID 83704
Phone: 208-377-0110 **Fax:** 208-377-0474
Web: www.wincofoods.com

2004 Stores

	No.
Oregon	16
California	11
Idaho	8
Washington	6
Nevada	2
Total	**43**

PRODUCTS/OPERATIONS

Selected Store Departments
Bakery
Bulk foods (more than 500 items)
Delicatessen
Fresh meat
Health and beauty aids
Organic products
Pizza shop
Produce
Seafood

COMPETITORS

Albertson's
Associated Food
AWG
Costco Wholesale
Fred Meyer Stores
Haggen
Raley's
Safeway
Stater Bros.
Unified Western Grocers
Wal-Mart

HISTORICAL FINANCIALS

Company Type: Private

Income Statement				FYE: March 31
	REVENUE ($ mil.)	NET INCOME ($ mil.)	NET PROFIT MARGIN	EMPLOYEES
3/04	2,000	—	—	7,000
3/03	1,700	—	—	7,100
3/02	1,540	—	—	6,500
3/01	1,300	—	—	5,300
3/00	1,160	—	—	5,000
3/99	940	—	—	4,900
Annual Growth	16.3%	—	—	7.4%

Revenue History

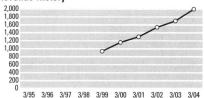

Wirtz

Wirtz does best on ice. Led by CEO William Wirtz, it owns the Chicago Blackhawks hockey team and is partnered with Jerry Reinsdorf, of the Chicago Bulls basketball team, for ownership of the United Center, where both teams play. Wirtz owns liquor distributorships, including Judge & Dolph, the largest in Illinois, and Edison Liquor Co. The firm owns property in Wisconsin, Mississippi, Texas, Nevada, and Florida. Arthur Wirtz (father of William Wirtz) founded the family-controlled empire in 1922.

Wirtz's Judge & Dolph is the exclusive distributor of Allied Domecq brands in Illinois and also has rights to distribute some key Diageo brands such as Crown Royal, Johnny Walker, J&B, and Tanqueray.

The Wirtz family gave thousands of dollars to state lawmakers in 1999 to pass a law protecting liquor distributors by making it difficult for liquor producers to switch distributors (The law later was declared unconstitutional).

EXECUTIVES

CEO: William W. Wirtz
CFO: Max Mohler
President, Judge & Dolph Ltd.: W. R. (Rocky) Wirtz
VP Human Resources: Cindy Krch
VP, Judge & Dolph Ltd.: Julian Burzynski
Controller: Linda Bescalli

LOCATIONS

HQ: Wirtz Corporation
680 N. Lakeshore Dr., 19th Fl., Chicago, IL 60611
Phone: 312-943-7000 **Fax:** 312-943-9017

Wirtz operates liquor distributorships in Illinois, Iowa, Minnesota, Nevada, Texas, and Wisconsin.

PRODUCTS/OPERATIONS

Selected Distribution Companies
DeLuca Liquors (Las Vegas)
Edison Liquor Corp. (Brookfield, Wisconsin)
Griggs, Cooper & Co. (St. Paul, Minnesota)
Judge & Dolph, Ltd. (Wood Dale, Illinois)
Mediterranean Imports Wine Company (Elk Grove, Illinois)
Silver State Distributors (Reno)

COMPETITORS

Columbus Blue Jackets
Detroit Red Wings
Glazer's Wholesale Drug
Johnson Brothers
Nashville Predators
National Distributing
National Wine & Spirits
Southern Wine & Spirits
St. Louis Blues
Young's Market

HISTORICAL FINANCIALS

Company Type: Private

Income Statement				FYE: June 30
	ESTIMATED REVENUE ($ mil.)	NET INCOME ($ mil.)	NET PROFIT MARGIN	EMPLOYEES
6/02	865	—	—	—
6/01	850	—	—	2,000
6/00	880	—	—	2,100
6/99	830	—	—	2,100
6/98	700	—	—	2,100
6/97	675	—	—	2,100
6/96	600	—	—	2,100
6/95	600	—	—	1,800
6/94	410	—	—	1,780
Annual Growth	9.8%	—	—	1.7%

Revenue History

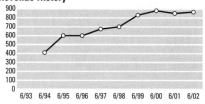

WKI Holding

WKI Holding has cooked up a kitchen kingpin. The holding company's World Kitchen subsidiary (formerly Corning Consumer Products) makes some of the most popular kitchenware and tableware in the US. Its brands, including Corelle, CorningWare, Pyrex, Revere, and Visions, are sold through mass merchants, specialty retailers, and its own factory outlet stores. WKI doubled in size with its 1999 purchases of houseware firms EKCO Group and General Housewares; it adopted the WKI Holding name in 2000. Buyout firm Kohlberg Kravis Roberts bought most of the company in 1998 from high-performance glass maker Corning. WKI Holding filed for Chapter 11 bankruptcy protection in 2002; the firm emerged from Chapter 11 in 2003.

In June 2004 WKI Holding sold its OXO International division (maker of the Good Grips brand of kitchen gadgets) to Helen of Troy for an estimated $275 million.

EXECUTIVES

Chairman: Terry R. Peets, age 59
President, CEO, and Director: James A. (Jim) Sharman, age 44, $1,003,687 pay
SVP and CFO: Joseph W. McGarr, age 52, $793,806 pay
VP, General Counsel, and Secretary: Raymond J. Kulla, age 57, $438,375 pay
VP and CIO: John Conklin
VP and General Manager, Asia Pacific: Jeffrey H. (Jeff) Mei, age 59
VP, Human Resources: Douglas S. (Doug) Arnold, age 49, $331,442 pay
VP, US Sales: Mike Linn
President, Retail Operations: Ken Durrett
Chief Marketing Officer: Nancy Shea
Director, Corporate Communications: Hope Johnson
Auditors: Deloitte & Touche LLP

LOCATIONS

HQ: WKI Holding Company, Inc.
11911 Freedom Dr., Ste. 600, Reston, VA 20190
Phone: 703-456-4700 **Fax:** 607-377-8962
Web: www.worldkitchen.com

WKI Holding has factories and distribution facilities in the US, Canada, and the Asia/Pacific region.

PRODUCTS/OPERATIONS

Selected Brands

Bakeware
  Baker's Secret
  CorningWare
  EKCO
  Pyrex
Cutlery
  Chicago Cutlery
  Regent Sheffield
Dinnerware
  Corelle
Kitchen and Household Tools
  EKCO
Precision Cutting Tools
  Olfa
Rangetop Cookware
  EKCO
  Grilla Gear
  Magnalite
  Revere
  Visions

COMPETITORS

Anchor Hocking
ARC International
Gibson Overseas
Lifetime Hoan
Newell Rubbermaid
Oneida
Pampered Chef
SEB
Tupperware
Waterford Wedgwood
Wilton Industries

HISTORICAL FINANCIALS
Company Type: Private

Income Statement
FYE: December 31

	REVENUE ($ mil.)	NET INCOME ($ mil.)	NET PROFIT MARGIN	EMPLOYEES
12/03	609	(60)	—	2,460
12/02	685	347	50.6%	3,000
12/01	746	(133)	—	4,200
12/00	828	(150)	—	5,200
12/99	618	(35)	—	5,250
12/98	533	(36)	—	3,200
12/97	573	14	2.4%	—
12/96	632	3	0.5%	—
Annual Growth	(0.5%)	—	—	(5.1%)

2003 Year-End Financials
Debt ratio: 550.6%
Return on equity: —
Cash ($ mil.): 10
Current ratio: 2.26
Long-term debt ($ mil.): 362

Net Income History

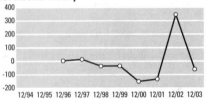

W. L. Gore

W. L. Gore & Associates would like your clothing to take a deep breath. The company makes a variety of fluoropolymer products; best known is its breathable, waterproof, and windproof GORE-TEX fabric. Product uses range from clothing and shoes to guitar strings, dental floss, space suits, and sutures. In addition to its apparel (popular among hikers and hunters), W. L. Gore makes insulated wire and cables, filtration products, and sealants. Fabrics are offered under such brands as GORE-TEX and WINDSTOPPER. The Gore family owns about 75% of the company; Gore associates own the rest.

W. L. Gore is known for its unusual style of management — the lattice system. There is no fixed authority, as the company has "sponsors," not bosses, and all employees are considered associates. Company goals and tasks are determined by consensus.

EXECUTIVES
Chairman: Robert W. Gore
President and CEO: Charles E. Carroll
Associate Chief Information Officer: Justin Kershaw
Director, Human Resources: Sally Gore
Medical Marketing Director: Thom O'Hara

LOCATIONS
HQ: W. L. Gore & Associates, Inc.
555 Papermill Rd., Newark, DE 19711
Phone: 302-738-4880   **Fax:** 302-738-7710
Web: www.gore.com

W. L. Gore & Associates operates manufacturing facilities in China, Germany, Japan, Scotland, and the US, with sales and customer service offices in those countries as well as in Argentina, Australia, Austria, Brazil, Finland, France, Greece, Hong Kong, India, Italy, Korea, Malaysia, the Netherlands, New Zealand, Poland, Russia, Singapore, Spain, Sweden, and Taiwan.

PRODUCTS/OPERATIONS

Selected Divisions, Products, and Brands
Consumer Products
 CleanStream vacuum cleaner filters
 ELIXER guitar strings
 GLIDE dental floss
 ReviveX water and stain repellent
Electronics
 Cable and assembly products
 High data rate cables
 Microwave products
 Electronic packaging and materials
 Conductive adhesives
 EMI/RFI shielding — GORE-SHIELD
 PWB materials
Fabrics
 AIRVANTAGECROSSTECH fabrics
 DRYLOFT fabrics
 GORE WINDSTOPPER fabrics
 GORE-TEX fabrics
 GORE-TEX OCEAN TECHNOLOGY outerwear
Implantable medical devices
 GORE subcutaneous augmentation material
 GORE-TEX DualMesh biomaterial
 GORE-TEX MycroMesh biomaterial
 GORE-TEX regenerative material
 GORE-TEX suture
 GORE-TEX vascular grafts
 PRECLUDE peritoneal membrane
 SEAMGUARD staple line-reinforcement material
Membrane Filtration and Separations
 Cleanroom garments
 CleanStream vacuum cleaner filters
 Filter bags and cartridges
 Liquid filtration tubular filter socks
 Microfiltration filter media
 PRISTYNE UX filter media
Sealants and Fibers Technologies
 GFO fiber packing
 GORE-TEX gasket tape
 GORE-TEX joint sealant
 ONE-UP pump diaphragms
 RASTEX fiber
 SEQUEL fiber packing
 STA-PURE peristaltic pump tubes
 TENARA fiber

COMPETITORS
Belden CDT
Burlington Industries
CardioTech
Donaldson
Kellwood
Malden Mills
Milliken
Superior Essex
Thoratec Corp
Timberland

HISTORICAL FINANCIALS
Company Type: Private

Income Statement
FYE: March 31

	REVENUE ($ mil.)	NET INCOME ($ mil.)	NET PROFIT MARGIN	EMPLOYEES
3/03	1,330	—	—	6,600
3/02	1,230	—	—	6,000
3/01	1,400	—	—	6,600
3/00	1,350	—	—	5,888
3/99	1,280	—	—	7,000
3/98	1,150	—	—	6,600
3/97	1,064	—	—	6,100
3/96	958	—	—	5,860
3/95	825	—	—	5,700
3/94	804	—	—	5,170
Annual Growth	5.8%	—	—	2.8%

Revenue History

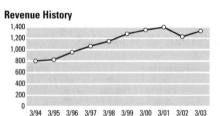

WL Homes

WL Homes, doing business as John Laing Homes, is one of the largest homebuilders in Southern California. John Laing Homes builds homes and communities for first-time to luxury homebuyers. It operates divisions in California and Colorado. The company sells more than 1,800 homes annually. It offers financing through JLH Mortgage. WL Homes was created from the 1998 merger of John Laing Homes (UK) and Watt Homes in the US. In 2001 John Laing Homes (UK) sold more than half of its stake in the company (retaining 22%) to an investor group led by chairman Ray Watt and CEO Larry Webb. *Professional Builder* magazine named John Laing Homes its Builder of the Year in 2004.

EXECUTIVES
Chairman: Ray Watt
CEO: H. Lawrence (Larry) Webb
CFO: Wayne J. Stelmar
EVP Sales and Marketing: William B. (Bill) Probert
VP People: Alejandro Macia
Treasurer: Shahram Gheysari
Region President, Colorado; Division President, Denver: Richard (Rich) Staky
Region President, Northern California: Jack Davidson
Region President, Southern California; Division President, South Coast (Orange County/San Diego, CA): Steve Kabel

LOCATIONS

HQ: WL Homes LLC
  895 Dove St., Ste. 200, Newport Beach, CA 92660
Phone: 949-265-2400 **Fax:** 949-265-2500
Web: www.johnlainghomes.com

WL Homes operates divisions in California (Inland Empire, Los Angeles/Ventura, Orange County/South Coast, Sacramento, San Diego, and Laing Luxury, Southern California, and in Colorado Springs and Denver, Colorado.

COMPETITORS

Brookfield Homes
Centex
D.R. Horton
Hovnanian Enterprises
Lennar
NVR
Pulte Homes
Ryland
Toll Brothers

HISTORICAL FINANCIALS

Company Type: Private

Income Statement
FYE: December 31

	REVENUE ($ mil.)	NET INCOME ($ mil.)	NET PROFIT MARGIN	EMPLOYEES
12/03	744	—	—	—
12/02	701	—	—	—
12/01	600	—	—	—
12/00	603	—	—	—
Annual Growth	7.3%	—	—	—

Revenue History

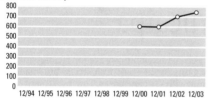

WorldTravel

Instead of phoning home, E.T. could have called WorldTravel BTI. WorldTravel has grown from a small travel agency to #3 in the US (behind American Express and Carlson Wagonlit). Clients include many large US corporations such as PepsiCo, Deloitte Touche, and De Beers. WorldTravel has over 1,600 ticketing locations and more than 50 affiliates across the US; through Business Travel International (BTI) it offers more than 3,000 locations in more than 80 countries. Its WorldTravelNet offers personalized travel information and services, including real-time flight status, hotel rates, weather, and maps. Chairman John Fentener van Vlissingen owns a majority stake in the company through parent company BCD Holdings.

EXECUTIVES

Chairman: John A. Fentener van Vlissingen
CEO: Michael A. (Mike) Buckman, age 54
President: Danny Hood
COO: John Snyder
CFO: Thomas (Tom) Barham
EVP: Dee Runyon
VP Human Resources: Nancy Pavey
VP Information Technology/Network Services:
  Brian Slynn
CEO, BCD N.V.: Joop G. Drechsel
Director Communications and Media Relations:
  Amy Berk

LOCATIONS

HQ: WorldTravel BTI
  1055 Lenox Park Blvd., Ste. 420, Atlanta, GA 30319
Phone: 404-841-6600 **Fax:** 404-814-2983
Web: www.worldtravel.com

PRODUCTS/OPERATIONS

Selected Services
Air Program Manager
BTI Global Hotel Programme
Corporate Fulfillment
Corporate Hotel Program
Leisure Travel
Web-based and Desktop Reporting
WorldTravel BTI Concierges
WorldTravelNet

COMPETITORS

American Express
Carlson Wagonlit
JTB
Kuoni Travel
Maritz
Rosenbluth International
World Travel Specialists

HISTORICAL FINANCIALS

Company Type: Private

Income Statement
FYE: December 31

	REVENUE ($ mil.)	NET INCOME ($ mil.)	NET PROFIT MARGIN	EMPLOYEES
12/02	3,800	—	—	4,500
12/01	3,800	—	—	5,175
12/00	3,800	—	—	5,800
12/99	3,500	—	—	5,000
12/98	3,300	—	—	5,000
12/97	3,000	—	—	5,000
12/96	2,500	—	—	3,000
Annual Growth	7.2%	—	—	7.0%

Revenue History

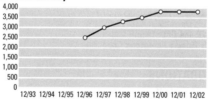

Yale University

What do President George W. Bush, writer William F. Buckley Jr., and actress Meryl Streep have in common? They are all Yalies. Yale University is one of the nation's most prestigious private liberal arts institutions, as well as one of its oldest (founded in 1701). Its $11 billion endowment ranks second only to Harvard's in the US. Yale comprises an undergraduate college, a graduate school, and 10 professional schools. Programs of study include architecture, law, medicine, and drama. Its 12 residential colleges (a system borrowed from Oxford) serve as dormitory, dining hall, and social center. The school has more than 11,200 students and some 3,200 faculty members.

EXECUTIVES

President: Richard C. Levin
Provost: Andrew D. Hamilton
VP and General Counsel: Dorothy K. Robinson
VP and Secretary: Linda Koch Lorimer, age 52
VP Development: Charles J. Pagnam
VP Finance and Administration: John E. Pepper Jr., age 65
VP and Director, New Haven and State Affairs:
  Bruce D. Alexander
Associate VP Human Resources and Chief Human Resources Officer: Robert Schwartz
Director, IT Services and University CIO: Philip Long
Auditors: PricewaterhouseCoopers LLP

LOCATIONS

HQ: Yale University
  246 Church St., New Haven, CT 06520
Phone: 203-432-2331 **Fax:** 203-432-2334
Web: www.yale.edu

PRODUCTS/OPERATIONS

Colleges and Schools
Graduate School of Arts and Sciences
School of Architecture
School of Art
School of Divinity
School of Drama
School of Forestry & Environmental Studies
School of Law
School of Management
School of Medicine
School of Music
School of Nursing
Yale College (undergraduate studies)

HISTORICAL FINANCIALS

Company Type: School

Income Statement
FYE: June 30

	REVENUE ($ mil.)	NET INCOME ($ mil.)	NET PROFIT MARGIN	EMPLOYEES
6/03	2,565	—	—	8,071
6/02	1,467	—	—	7,577
6/01	1,353	—	—	7,398
6/00	1,264	—	—	10,800
6/99	1,150	—	—	10,318
6/98	1,083	—	—	9,685
6/97	992	—	—	10,000
6/96	931	—	—	9,200
6/95	948	—	—	10,000
6/94	902	—	—	9,600
Annual Growth	12.3%	—	—	(1.9%)

Revenue History

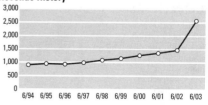

Yates Companies

The Yates Companies is the extended family of W.G. Yates & Sons Construction Company. The commercial and heavy construction builder has been cashing in on casino projects and has won federal contracts for military facilities. Other family members are Mississippi-based JESCO and Tennessee-based Blaine Construction. The group, which operates mostly in the Southeast and along the East Coast, provides a broad range of construction-related services, including engineering, electrical and mechanical construction, millwrighting, and steel fabrication. The company is owned by the Yates family, including president and CEO Bill Yates, who co-founded it in 1964 with his father, the late William Gully Yates.

EXECUTIVES

Chairman, President, and CEO: William G. (Bill) Yates Jr.
CFO and Treasurer: Marvin Blanks III
EVP, Gulf Coast Division, W.G. Yates & Sons: William G. Yates III
VP and General Counsel: Kenny Bush
Controller: Brandon Dunn
President, JESCO: Jerry Stubblefield
President, Blaine Construction: Dorman Blaine
Director of Business Development: Jody Tidwell

LOCATIONS

HQ: The Yates Companies, Inc.
1 Gully Ave., Philadelphia, MS 39350
Phone: 601-656-5411   **Fax:** 601-656-8958
Web: www.wgyates.com

The Yates Companies has offices in Alabama, Florida, Mississippi, and Tennessee.

PRODUCTS/OPERATIONS

Selected Services
Casino construction
Construction management
Corporate
Design/build
Electrical
Engineering
Environmental
Forest products
General construction
Heavy commercial
Hospitality
Industrial
Institutional
Marine
Medical
Processing
Renovation
Resort
Retail
Utility

COMPETITORS

Brasfield & Gorrie
Choate Construction
Clark Enterprises
Dunn Industries
Fluor
Hunt Construction
Jacobs Engineering
Perini
Turner Corporation
Whiting-Turner

HISTORICAL FINANCIALS
Company Type: Private

Income Statement   FYE: December 31

	ESTIMATED REVENUE ($ mil.)	NET INCOME ($ mil.)	NET PROFIT MARGIN	EMPLOYEES
12/02	1,023	—	—	4,100
12/01	750	—	—	3,500
12/00	740	—	—	3,000
12/99	700	—	—	3,000
Annual Growth	13.5%	—	—	11.0%

Revenue History

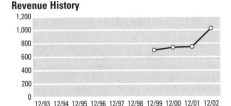

Young's Market

Although no longer young, Young's Market Company is in high spirits. Young's Market is one of the largest distributors of beer, wine, and distilled spirits in the US. The company is a major supplier along the Pacific coast. It also operates in Hawaii through its Better Brands subsidiary. Young's Market distributes products for Bacardi, Brown-Forman, and other distillers and winemakers. It distributes in California wines of the Chalone Wine Group and Brown-Forman's Sonoma-Cutrer Vineyards. John Young founded the company in 1888, which at one time included grocery retailing and specialty food distribution. The Underwood family, relatives of the Youngs, bought Young's Market in 1990.

EXECUTIVES

Chairman and CEO: Vernon O. Underwood
President: Jeffrey Underwood
EVP, Operations: John Klein
EVP and CFO: Dennis J. Hamann
VP, Human Resources: Craig Matsuda

LOCATIONS

HQ: Young's Market Company, LLC
2164 N. Batavia St., Orange, CA 92865
Phone: 714-283-4933   **Fax:** 714-283-6175

Young's Market Company primarily distributes to Alaska, California, Hawaii, Oregon, and Washington.

COMPETITORS

Beauchamp Distributing
Glazer's Wholesale Drug
National Distributing
National Wine & Spirits
Southern Wine & Spirits
Topa Equities
WinterBrook Beverage

HISTORICAL FINANCIALS
Company Type: Private

Income Statement   FYE: February 28

	REVENUE ($ mil.)	NET INCOME ($ mil.)	NET PROFIT MARGIN	EMPLOYEES
2/03	1,200	—	—	1,800
2/02	1,300	—	—	1,700
2/01	1,300	—	—	1,700
2/00	1,100	—	—	1,700
2/99	1,090	—	—	1,600
2/98	1,000	—	—	1,500
2/97	960	—	—	1,400
2/96	1,000	—	—	1,600
2/95	910	—	—	1,650
2/94	900	—	—	1,600
Annual Growth	3.2%	—	—	1.3%

Revenue History

Yucaipa

Yucaipa has a hungry eye for picking out ripe bargains in different industries, but made its name with grocery stores. The investment company forged its reputation as the ultimate grocery shopper, executing a series of grocery chain mergers and acquisitions that put the company on the supermarket map. The Yucaipa Companies owns Jurgensen's, Falley's, and Alpha Beta, among other chains. The company's chairman, billionaire Ron Burkle, is a prominent Democratic activist and fundraiser; former president Bill Clinton and the Rev. Jesse Jackson serve on the company's board.

Yucaipa maintains a link to the food industry through a miniscule stake in Kroger (less than 2%), as well as a minority stake in Simon Worldwide (formerly Cyrk), a promotional marketing company whose largest customer is McDonald's. Yucaipa's portfolio also includes Alliance Entertainment (a distributor of music, videos and games) and TDS Logistics (automotive logistics services).

It sold its 50% stake in McDonald's supplier Golden State Foods to that firm's management and Wetterau Associates in early 2004. Yuciapa has also agreed to purchase distressed and bankrupt restaurant chain Piccadilly Cafeterias and has invested in rapper/mogul Sean "P. Diddy" Combs' clothing line, Sean John.

Some of its investments have run into bumps in the road: Kmart filed for bankruptcy in 2002, and Simon Worldwide faced numerous lawsuits stemming from a scandal after an employee allegedly rigged its client McDonald's Monopoly games and stole the cash.

HISTORY

Ronald Burkle launched his career in the grocery industry as a box boy at his dad's Stater Bros. grocery store. By age 28 Burkle had moved up to SVP of administration, but he was fired after botching a buyout of the company in 1981.

Burkle and former Stater Bros. colleagues Mark Resnik and Douglas McKenzie founded Yucaipa (named after Burkle's hometown of Yucaipa, California) in 1986 when they bought Los Angeles gourmet-grocery chain Jurgensen's. The next year Yucaipa bought Kansas-based Falley's, which had 20 Food 4 Less stores in California.

In 1989 Yucaipa merged with Breco Holding, operator of 70 grocery stores, and bought Northern California's Bell Markets. It acquired ABC Markets in Southern California in 1990. The next year the company bought the 142-store chain Alpha Beta. Thirty-six Yucaipa stores were damaged in the 1992 Los Angeles riots, but Yucaipa rebuilt, working with unions to keep workers employed until the stores were operational.

The company acquired the 28-store Smitty's Super Valu chain (now Fred Meyer Marketplace) in 1994. The following year Yucaipa bought the 70-year-old family-owned chain Dominick's Finer Foods. Later in 1995 Yucaipa's Food 4 Less chain merged with Los Angeles competitor Ralphs Grocery (founded in 1873 by George Ralphs), making Yucaipa #1 in Southern California.

Yucaipa sold Smitty's to Utah-based Smith's in 1996, acquiring a minority stake in Smith's (Burkle became Smith's CEO). Dominick's went public in 1996, and Yucaipa retained a minority stake. The next year Fred Meyer bought Smith's for $1.9 billion. Burkle became the acquired company's chairman, and Yucaipa gained a 9% interest in Fred Meyer.

In 1998 Fred Meyer bought Ralphs and 155-store Quality Food Centers (QFC). Yucaipa and Wetterau Associates, a management firm, bought Golden State Foods, giving Yucaipa a 70% stake in the McDonald's food supplier. Yucaipa sold Dominick's to Safeway.

After Kroger bought Fred Meyer in 1999, Yucaipa turned away from the consolidating grocery industry and moved into cyberspace. That year Burkle and former Walt Disney president Michael Ovitz launched CheckOut Entertainment Network, which operated CheckOut.com, an entertainment Web site at which Web surfers could buy books, music, and videogames. Yucaipa hired Richard Wolpert, former president of Disney Online, to oversee its Internet and technology activities.

Yucaipa added to its portfolio in 1999 by taking stakes in GameSpy (online games), Talk City (later LiveWorld, online chat service), OneNetNow (online communities), ClubMom (Web site for mothers), and Cyrk (now Simon Worldwide, promotional marketing). Yucaipa also bought music, video, and games distributor Alliance Entertainment. The company also holds a minority stake in Simon Worldwide.

Music and video retailer Wherehouse Entertainment became a 50%-owner of CheckOut.com after it merged its online retailing operations with CheckOut.com in 1999. (As the Internet economy faltered, Yucaipa sold CheckOut.com in 2001.)

In 2000 the company digressed from its focus on the Web to invest in Kole Imports, an importer of merchandise sold in discount stores.

Yucaipa sold its stakes in grocery distributor Fleming and discount retailer Kmart in 2001 before both companies crashed and burned into bankruptcy.

EXECUTIVES

Managing Partner: Ronald W. (Ron) Burkle, age 51
CFO: Steve Mortensen
Senior Advisor: William J. Clinton, age 58
Partner: Carlton J. Jenkins, age 48
Partner: Erika Paulson, age 27
Partner: Ed Renwick
Partner: Scott Stedman
Partner: Nick Tasooji
Partner: Ira Tochner
Chief Administration Officer and Human Resources Director: Bill Bailey
Legal: Robert P. Bermingham
Public Relations and Corporate Communications: Ari Swiller
Investor Relations and Business Development: Adrienne Gaines

LOCATIONS

HQ: The Yucaipa Companies LLC
9130 W. Sunset Blvd., Los Angeles, CA 90069
Phone: 310-789-7200   **Fax:** 310-228-2873

PRODUCTS/OPERATIONS

Selected Investments
Alliance Entertainment (music, videos, and game distribution)
Kole Imports (minority stake, discount merchandise importer)
The Kroger Co. (2%, grocery stores)
Simon Worldwide (20%, promotional marketing)

COMPETITORS

Bain Capital
Berkshire Hathaway
Blackstone Group
Carlyle Group
Hicks Muse
KKR
Leonard Green
Texas Pacific Group
Thomas Lee

Zachry

H. B. Zachry began building roads and bridges in 1924, and now his son and grandsons are running the show. Zachry Construction builds and maintains power and chemical plants, steel and paper mills, refineries, roadways, dams, airfields, and pipelines. Operating mostly in Texas and the southeastern US, Zachry has built facilities for companies such as Alcoa, BP Petrochemicals, DuPont, and Samsung. It also works internationally and reconstructed the US Embassy in Moscow. In addition, Zachry owns interests in ranches and in oil exploration, cement, hospitality, and realty companies, as well as a stake in the San Antonio Spurs basketball team. The Zachry family owns the firm.

EXECUTIVES

Chairman: H. Bartell Zachry Jr.
CEO: John B. Zachry
President and COO: David S. Zachry
VP Administration and Accounting: Charles Ebrom
SVP: Edward R. Bardgett
SVP and Controller: Joe J. Lozano
SVP Corporate Business Development: Keith D. Manning
SVP and Manager, Power: Robert J. (Bob) Kalt
SVP Corporate Development: Kenneth A. (Ken) Oleson
SVP Finance: Kirk McDonald
VP, General Counsel, and Secretary: Murray L. Johnston Jr.
VP Employee Relations: Stephen L. (Steve) Hoech
Treasurer: Gonzalo O. Ornelas
Director Public Affairs: Victoria Waddy
Auditors: Ernst & Young

LOCATIONS

HQ: Zachry Construction Corporation
527 Logwood Ave., San Antonio, TX 78221
Phone: 210-475-8000   **Fax:** 210-475-8060
Web: www.zachry.com

Zachry Construction has offices in Arizona, Florida, Louisiana, Texas, and North Carolina. It also has an international office in Saudi Arabia.

COMPETITORS

Aker Kværner
Alberici
APAC
Austin Industries
Barton Malow
Bechtel
Black & Veatch
Dick Corporation
Fluor
Foster Wheeler
Gilbane
Granite Construction
Halliburton
Hensel Phelps Construction
Hoffman Corporation
Holloman
Krupp Polysius
M. A. Mortenson
McCarthy Building
MWH Global
Parsons
Peter Kiewit Sons'
Sumitomo Mitsui Construction
TIC Holdings
Turner Industries
Washington Group

HISTORICAL FINANCIALS

Company Type: Private

Income Statement   FYE: December 31

	REVENUE ($ mil.)	NET INCOME ($ mil.)	NET PROFIT MARGIN	EMPLOYEES
12/03	1,007	—	—	12,000
12/02	1,700	—	—	14,000
12/01	1,940	—	—	14,000
12/00	1,400	—	—	14,000
12/99	1,195	—	—	11,000
12/98	670	—	—	7,500
12/97	660	—	—	7,500
12/96	775	—	—	7,625
12/95	780	—	—	10,100
12/94	750	—	—	10,000
Annual Growth	3.3%	—	—	2.0%

Revenue History

Hoover's Handbook of Private Companies

The Indexes

Index by Industry

INDUSTRY CATEGORIES	
Aerospace & Defense	544
Agriculture	544
Automotive & Transport	544
Banking	544
Beverages	544
Business Services	544
Charitable Organizations	545
Chemicals	545
Computer Hardware	545
Computer Services	545
Computer Software	545
Construction	545
Consumer Products Manufacturers	545
Consumer Services	545
Cultural Institutions	545
Education	545
Electronics	546
Energy & Utilities	546
Environmental Services & Equipment	546
Financial Services	546
Food	546
Foundations	546
Health Care	546
Industrial Manufacturing	547
Insurance	547
Leisure	547
Media	547
Membership Organizations	547
Metals & Mining	547
Pharmaceuticals	548
Real Estate	548
Retail	548
Security Products & Services	548
Telecommunications Equipment	548
Telecommunications Services	548
Transportation Services	548

AEROSPACE & DEFENSE

Aerospace & Defense Maintenance & Service
United Space Alliance 498

Aerospace & Defense Parts Manufacturing
CIC International Ltd. 119
Vought Aircraft Industries, Inc. 524

AGRICULTURE

Agricultural Support Activities & Products
Ag Processing Inc 27
Bartlett and Company 65
The Connell Company 134
DeBruce Grain, Inc. 152
Dunavant Enterprises, Inc. 170
GROWMARK, Inc. 218
MFA Incorporated 333
Plains Cotton Cooperative Association 398
Riceland Foods, Inc. 419
The Scoular Company 439
Southern States Cooperative, Incorporated 454
UAP Holding Corp. 492
Wilbur-Ellis Company 536

Crop Production
Dole Food Company, Inc. 162
National Grape Cooperative Association, Inc. 354
Staple Cotton Cooperative Association 459
Sunkist Growers, Inc. 464

AUTOMOTIVE & TRANSPORT

Auto Manufacturing
New United Motor Manufacturing, Inc. 362

Auto Parts Manufacturing
Eagle-Picher Industries, Inc. 171
Findlay Industries, Inc. 191
Key Safety Systems, Inc. 275
Mark IV Industries, Inc. 308
Meridian Automotive Systems, Inc. 329
Metaldyne Corporation 330
Oxford Automotive, Inc. 383
Remy International, Inc. 416
TriMas Corporation 483
Venture Industries 519

Container Leasing
TTX Company 488

Pleasure Boat Manufacturing
Genmar Holdings, Inc. 202

Rail & Trucking Equipment Manufacturing
ACF Industries, Inc. 20
Great Dane Limited Partnership 214

Truck, Bus & Other Vehicle Manufacturing
Utility Trailer Manufacturing Co. 515

BANKING

Money Center Banks
Federal Reserve System 188

Private Banking
Brown Brothers Harriman & Co. 92

Regional Banks & Thrifts
Chevy Chase Bank, F.S.B. 117

Superregional Banks
Navy Federal Credit Union 360

BEVERAGES

Alcoholic Beverages
E. & J. Gallo Winery 172
Pabst Brewing Company 383

Bottling & Distribution
Charmer Industries, Inc. 115
The Charmer-Sunbelt Group 115
Coca-Cola Bottling Co. United, Inc. 125
Dr Pepper/Seven Up Bottling Group, Inc. 165
Georgia Crown Distributing Company 204
Glazer's Wholesale Drug Company, Inc. 207
Honickman Affiliates 241
Johnson Brothers Liquor Company 267
National Distributing Company, Inc. 351
National Wine & Spirits, Inc 358
Peerless Importers, Inc. 391
Southern Wine & Spirits of America, Inc. 454
Topa Equities, Ltd. 479
Wirtz Corporation 537
Young's Market Company, LLC 540

Non-Alcoholic Beverages
Florida's Natural Growers 193
Ocean Spray Cranberries, Inc. 375

BUSINESS SERVICES

Advantage Sales and Marketing, LLC 22

Muzak LLC 345

Advertising & Marketing
Acosta Sales Company, Inc. 21
CROSSMARK 142
IMG 250
Information Resources, Inc. 252
Vertis Inc. 521

Commercial Cleaning & Facilities Management Services
Asplundh Tree Expert Co. 54
UNICCO Service Company 494
ValleyCrest Companies 516

Commercial Printing
Merrill Corporation 329
Quad/Graphics, Inc. 409
Taylor Corporation 469

Consulting
Bain & Company, Inc. 62
Booz Allen Hamilton Inc. 84
The Boston Consulting Group 87
McKinsey & Company 321
Towers Perrin 480

Legal Services
Akin Gump Strauss Hauer & Feld LLP 29
Baker & McKenzie 62
Cleary, Gottlieb, Steen & Hamilton 124
Davis Polk & Wardwell 150
Gibson, Dunn & Crutcher LLP 206
Greenberg Traurig, LLP 216
Hogan & Hartson 238
Holland & Knight LLP 239
Jones Day 268
Kirkland & Ellis LLP 279
Latham & Watkins LLP 291
Mayer, Brown, Rowe & Maw 317
McDermott, Will & Emery 319
Morgan, Lewis & Bockius LLP 339
Morrison & Foerster LLP 341
O'Melveny & Myers LLP 379
Paul, Hastings, Janofsky & Walker LLP 389
Paul, Weiss, Rifkind, Wharton & Garrison LLP 390
Shearman & Sterling 445
Sidley Austin Brown & Wood LLP 446
Simpson Thacher & Bartlett LLP 449
Skadden, Arps, Slate, Meagher & Flom LLP 450
Sullivan & Cromwell LLP 464
Weil, Gotshal & Manges LLP 532
White & Case LLP 535
Wilmer Cutler Pickering Hale and Dorr LLP 536

Staffing
Allegis Group, Inc. 31
Express Personnel Services 185
MSX International, Inc. 342

INDEX BY INDUSTRY

Technical & Scientific Research Services
The Aerospace Corporation 25
Battelle Memorial Institute 68
The MITRE Corporation 338
SEMATECH, Inc. 441
SRI International 457
Underwriters Laboratories Inc. 494

Uniform Rental & Laundry Services
National Service Industries, Inc. 357

CHARITABLE ORGANIZATIONS
American Cancer Society, Inc. 35
American Heart Association 39
The American Red Cross 39
Goodwill Industries International, Inc. 209
The Salvation Army National Corporation 430
United Way of America 499
Volunteers of America, Inc. 524

CHEMICALS
Agricultural Chemicals
CF Industries, Inc. 113
Royster-Clark, Inc. 427

Basic and Intermediate Chemical & Petrochemical Manufacturing
Chevron Phillips Chemical Company LLC 116
Contran Corporation 137
Equistar Chemicals, LP 178
Huntsman International LLC 245
Koppers Inc. 284

Chemical Distribution
CHEMCENTRAL Corporation 116

Plastic & Fiber Manufacturing
Carpenter Co. 105
Dow Corning Corporation 163
KRATON Polymers LLC 286
Resolution Performance Products LLC 418

Specialty Chemical Manufacturing
Borden Chemical, Inc. 85
Flint Ink Corporation 192
International Specialty Products Inc. 259
J.M. Huber Corporation 264
Nalco Holding Company 347
NCH Corporation 360
PMC Global, Inc. 401
Rockwood Specialties Group, Inc. 422
UOP LLC 510

COMPUTER HARDWARE
Computer Peripherals
ViewSonic Corporation 522

Mass Storage Systems
Hitachi Global Storage Technologies 237

Personal Computers
MPC Computers, LLC 342

COMPUTER SERVICES
Computer Products Distribution & Support
ASI Corp. 53
CompuCom Systems, Inc. 130
D&H Distributing Co., Inc. 147
MA Laboratories, Inc. 302

Software House International, Inc. 452
Westcon Group, Inc. 533

Information Technology Services
Science Applications International Corporation 438

COMPUTER SOFTWARE
Business Intelligence Software
SAS Institute Inc. 432

CONSTRUCTION
Construction & Design Services
AECOM Technology Corporation 24
A. G. Spanos Companies 28
Alberici Corporation 30
American Plumbing & Mechanical, Inc. 39
The Angelo Iafrate Companies 46
APi Group, Inc. 47
Austin Industries, Inc. 60
Barton Malow Company 66
BE&K, Inc. 69
Bechtel Group, Inc. 70
The Beck Group 71
Black & Veatch Holding Company 77
Brasfield & Gorrie, LLC 90
CH2M HILL Companies, Ltd. 113
Choice Homes, Inc. 118
Clark Enterprises, Inc. 124
Colson & Colson Construction Company 127
David Weekley Homes 149
The Day & Zimmermann Group, Inc. 151
Dick Corporation 157
DPR Construction, Inc. 165
The Drees Co. 167
Dunn Industries, Inc. 170
Gilbane, Inc. 206
The Haskell Company 226
HBE Corporation 227
Hensel Phelps Construction Co. 233
J.F. Shea Co., Inc. 262
John Wieland Homes and Neighborhoods, Inc. 266
Kimball Hill Homes 277
Kinetics Group, Inc. 277
The Lane Construction Corporation 289
The Louis Berger Group, Inc. 300
M. A. Mortenson Company 303
McCarthy Building Companies, Inc. 319
Modern Continental Companies, Inc. 338
MWH Global, Inc. 346
Parsons Brinckerhoff Inc. 388
Parsons Corporation 387
Pepper Construction Group, LLC 394
Peter Kiewit Sons', Inc. 395
Rooney Holdings, Inc. 423
Rudolph and Sletten, Inc. 428
Shapell Industries, Inc. 444
The Structure Tone Organization 463
Suffolk Construction Company, Inc. 464
Swinerton Incorporated 467
TIC Holdings, Inc. 476
Turner Industries, Ltd. 490
Walbridge Aldinger Company 527
The Walsh Group 528
Webcor Builders, Inc. 531
The Weitz Group, LLC 532
The Whiting-Turner Contracting Company 535
WL Homes LLC 539
The Yates Companies, Inc. 540
Zachry Construction Corporation 541

Construction Materials
Andersen Corporation 45
Ash Grove Cement Company 52
Associated Materials Incorporated 56
Atrium Companies, Inc. 59
Columbia Forest Products Inc. 128
Elkay Manufacturing Company 176
G-I Holdings Inc. 204
Hampton Affiliates 223
JELD-WEN, inc. 262
Kohler Co. 283
Lumbermens Merchandising Corporation 302
New NGC, Inc. 362
Nortek Holdings, Inc. 370
Pella Corporation 391
Roseburg Forest Products Co. 424
Sierra Pacific Industries 447
Simpson Investment Company 448

CONSUMER PRODUCTS MANUFACTURERS
Apparel
Bill Blass Ltd. 75
Jockey International, Inc. 265
Levi Strauss & Co. 293
New Balance Athletic Shoe, Inc. 361

Appliances
Conair Corporation 131
Goodman Manufacturing Company, L.P. 208
The Holmes Group, Inc. 240

Cleaning Products
JohnsonDiversey, Inc. 268
S.C. Johnson & Son, Inc. 434

Consumer Electronics
Bose Corporation 86

Hand Tools, Power Tools, Lawn & Garden Equipment
United Industries Corporation 497

Home Furniture
Ashley Furniture Industries, Inc. 53
Klaussner Furniture Industries, Inc. 280
Sauder Woodworking Co. 433

Housewares
Jostens, Inc. 271
The Longaberger Company 299
Roll International Corporation 422
WKI Holding Company, Inc. 538

Jewelry & Watch Manufacturing
Timex Corporation 477

Linens
Springs Industries, Inc. 456

Mattress & Bed Manufacturers
Sealy Corporation 440
Serta, Inc. 443

Office & Business Furniture, Fixtures & Equipment
Haworth, Inc. 227
KI 276
Knoll, Inc. 280
Lane Industries, Inc. 289

Office, School, & Art Supplies
Esselte 181
Fellowes, Inc. 190
National Envelope Corporation 351

Personal Care Products
Alticor Inc. 33
Forever Living Products International, Inc. 197
John Paul Mitchell Systems 265

MacAndrews & Forbes Holdings Inc. 303
Mary Kay Inc. 312
Nikken Global Inc. 370

Pet Products
Doane Pet Care Company 160

Photographic & Optical Equipment/Supplies Manufacturers
Polaroid Corporation 401

Sporting Goods & Equipment
Colt's Manufacturing Company, LLC 127
ICON Health & Fitness, Inc. 248

Toys & Games
Ty Inc. 492

CONSUMER SERVICES
Automotive Service & Collision Repair
American Tire Distributors, Inc. 41
Safelite Group, Inc. 428

Car & Truck Rental
Enterprise Rent-A-Car Company 177
Frank Consolidated Enterprises 199

Laundry Facilities & Dry Cleaning Services
Coinmach Service Corp. 126

Travel Agencies & Services
Carlson Wagonlit Travel, Inc. 103
Maritz Inc. 308
WorldTravel BTI 539

CULTURAL INSTITUTIONS
National Geographic Society 353
Smithsonian Institution 451

EDUCATION
Colleges & Universities
Trustees of the California State University 96
The City University of New York 122
Columbia University 129
Cornell University 138
Harvard University 225
Indiana University 251
Michigan State University 334
MIT (Massachusetts Institute of Technology) 337
New York University 368
Northwestern University 373
The Ohio State University 378
Princeton University 405
Stanford University 458
State University of New York 461
The Texas A&M University System 472
University of California 500
The University of Chicago 500
University of Florida 501
University of Illinois 502
The University of Iowa 502
The University of Michigan 503
University of Minnesota 504
University of Missouri System 504
The University of Nebraska 505
The University of Pennsylvania 505
University of Pittsburgh of the Commonwealth System of Higher Education 506
University of Rochester 506
The University of Southern California 507
University of Tennessee 507

INDEX BY INDUSTRY

The University of Texas System 508
University of Washington 509
The University of Wisconsin System 509
University System of Maryland 503
Vanderbilt University 516
Yale University 540

Education & Training Services
Educational Testing Service 175

ELECTRONICS

Contract Electronics Manufacturing
Viasystems Group, Inc. 521

Electrical Products
Consolidated Electrical Distributors, Inc. 135
Graybar Electric Company, Inc. 213
Interstate Battery System of America, Inc. 260

Electronic Components
Memec Group Holdings Limited 326
TTI, Inc. 488

Semiconductors
Kingston Technology Company, Inc. 278

ENERGY & UTILITIES

Ergon, Inc. 179
MidAmerican Energy Holdings Company 334

Electric Utilities
Associated Electric Cooperative Inc. 54
Basin Electric Power Cooperative 67
Bonneville Power Administration 84
Brazos Electric Power Cooperative, Inc. 90
North Carolina Electric Membership Corporation 371
Oglethorpe Power Corporation 376
Power Authority of the State of New York 365
Seminole Electric Cooperative, Inc. 442
Tri-State Generation and Transmission Association, Inc. 484
TVA (Tennessee Valley Authority) 491

Energy Trading & Marketing
Cook Inlet Energy Supply L.L.C. 137
Tenaska, Inc. 471
TNP Enterprises, Inc. 478

Independent/Merchant Power Production
Sithe Energies, Inc. 450

Oil & Gas Exploration & Production
Aera Energy LLC 25
Arctic Slope Regional Corporation 48
Hunt Consolidated Inc. 244

Oil & Gas Refining, Marketing & Distribution
Apex Oil Company, Inc. 47
Center Oil Company 111
Cornerstone Propane Partners, L.P. 139
Crown Central Petroleum Corporation 143
George E. Warren Corporation 203
Global Companies LLC 207
Gulf Oil Limited Partnership 220
Koch Industries, Inc. 281
Motiva Enterprises LLC 341
National Cooperative Refinery Association 350
Red Apple Group, Inc. 414

Sinclair Oil Corporation 449
Transammonia, Inc. 482
Truman Arnold Companies 485
U.S. Oil Co., Inc. 512
Warren Equities, Inc. 529

Oil & Gas Transportation & Storage
Duke Energy Field Services, LLC 170

ENVIRONMENTAL SERVICES & EQUIPMENT

Culligan International Company 144

Remediation & Environmental Cleanup Services
Safety-Kleen Holdco, Inc. 429

Solid Waste Services & Recycling
Philip Services Corporation 397

FINANCIAL SERVICES

Accounting
Deloitte Touche Tohmatsu 153
Ernst & Young International 180
Grant Thornton International 212
KPMG International 285
PricewaterhouseCoopers 403

Asset Management
Alliance Capital Management L.P. 31
CalPERS (California Public Employees' Retirement System) 98
FMR Corp. 194
Mutual of America Life Insurance Company 344
TIAA-CREF 475
U.S. Central Credit Union 511
The Vanguard Group, Inc. 517

Investment Firms
Berwind Group 73
The Carlyle Group 104
The Dyson-Kissner-Moran Corporation 171
Equity Group Investments, L.L.C. 178
Everett Smith Group, Ltd. 184
Gores Technology Group, LLC 210
Hicks, Muse, Tate & Furst Incorporated 235
Kohlberg Kravis Roberts & Co. 282
Texas Pacific Group 474
Vulcan Inc. 525
The Yucaipa Companies LLC 541

Lending
AgFirst Farm Credit Bank 28
AgriBank, FCB 29
MasterCard Incorporated 315
National Rural Utilities Cooperative Finance Corporation 356
Visa International 523

Securities Brokers & Traders
A-Mark Financial Corporation 34
The Depository Trust & Clearing Corporation 155
Interactive Brokers Group LLC 256
The Jones Financial Companies, L.L.L.P. 269

Stock Exchanges
NASD 348
New York Stock Exchange, Inc. 367

Transaction, Credit & Collections
Outsourcing Solutions Inc. 382

Turnaround Specialists & Liquidators
Platinum Equity, LLC 400

FOOD

Candy & Confections
Mars, Incorporated 310
UIS, Inc. 493

Canned & Frozen Foods
Birds Eye Foods, Inc. 76
J.R. Simplot Company 271
Rich Products Corporation 419
The Schwan Food Company 436

Dairy Products
Agri-Mark, Inc. 29
Associated Milk Producers Inc. 56
California Dairies Inc. 96
Dairy Farmers of America, Inc. 146
Dairylea Cooperative Inc. 147
Foremost Farms USA, Cooperative 197
Great Lakes Cheese Company, Inc. 214
HP Hood Inc. 244
Land O'Lakes, Inc. 287
Leprino Foods Company 292
Michael Foods, Inc. 333
Sargento Foods Inc. 432
Schreiber Foods, Inc. 436
Shamrock Foods Company 444
Wells' Dairy, Inc. 533

Fish & Seafood
Red Chamber Co. 415

Food Service
Ben E. Keith Company 73
Delaware North Companies, Inc. 153
Dot Foods, Inc. 163
Golden State Foods 207
Gordon Food Service 209
Keystone Foods LLC 276
The Martin-Brower Company, L.L.C. 311
MBM Corporation 318
Reyes Holdings LLC 419
Services Group of America 444
Vistar/VSA Corporation 524

Food Wholesale Distributors
Affiliated Foods Incorporated 25
Alex Lee, Inc. 31
Associated Food Stores, Inc. 55
Associated Grocers, Inc. 55
Associated Wholesale Grocers, Inc. 57
Associated Wholesalers, Inc. 59
Bozzuto's Inc. 88
C&S Wholesale Grocers, Inc. 99
Central Grocers Cooperative, Inc. 112
Certified Grocers Midwest, Inc. 113
Di Giorgio Corporation 157
Eby-Brown Company 174
The Ferolie Group 191
The Grocers Supply Co., Inc. 217
H.T. Hackney Company 244
Purity Wholesale Grocers, Inc. 408
Roundy's, Inc. 426
Sherwood Food Distributors 446
Topco Associates LLC 479
Unified Western Grocers, Inc. 495
Western Family Foods, Inc. 534

Grains
Dawn Food Products, Inc. 151
McKee Foods Corporation 320
Pinnacle Foods Group, Inc. 398

Meat Products
American Foods Group, Inc. 38
Cargill, Incorporated 100
ContiGroup Companies, Inc. 136
Foster Poultry Farms 198
Perdue Farms Incorporated 394
Rosen's Diversified, Inc. 424

Sauces & Condiments
Goya Foods, Inc. 210

Sugar & Sweeteners
American Crystal Sugar Company 36

FOUNDATIONS

Bill & Melinda Gates Foundation 74
The David and Lucile Packard Foundation 385
The Ford Foundation 196
The Rockefeller Foundation 421
W.K. Kellogg Foundation 274

HEALTH CARE

Health Care Products
Medline Industries, Inc. 324

Health Care Services
Adventist Health 22
Adventist Health System 23
Adventist HealthCare, Inc. 23
Advocate Health Care 23
Alegent Health 30
Allina Hospitals and Clinics 33
Ardent Health Services LLC 49
Arkansas Blue Cross and Blue Shield 49
Ascension Health 51
Banner Health 64
Baptist Health South Florida 64
Baystate Health Systems, Inc. 69
BJC HealthCare 76
Blue Cross and Blue Shield Association 78
Blue Cross and Blue Shield of Massachusetts, Inc. 79
Blue Cross Blue Shield of Michigan 80
Blue Shield Of California 81
BlueCross and BlueShield of Mississippi 82
Bon Secours Health System, Inc. 83
Carilion Health System 101
Catholic Health East 107
Catholic Health Initiatives 108
Catholic Health Services of Long Island 109
Catholic Healthcare Partners 109
Catholic Healthcare West 110
The Children's Hospital of Philadelphia 118
CHRISTUS Health 119
Cincinnati Children's Hospital Medical Center 120
Clarian Health Partners, Inc. 123
Community Hospitals of Indiana, Inc. 130
Community Medical Centers 130
Concentra Inc. 132
Conemaugh Health System 132
ConnectiCare Inc. 133
Cox Health Systems 142
Delta Dental of California 154
Delta Dental Plan of Michigan Inc 155
Detroit Medical Center 156
East Texas Medical Center Regional Healthcare System 182
Evanston Northwestern Healthcare Corporation 183
Fallon Community Health Plan Inc. 186
FHC Health Systems, Inc. 191
Greenville Hospital System 217
Group Health Cooperative of Puget Sound 217
Health Care Service Corporation 229
Health Insurance Plan of Greater New York 230
Henry Ford Health System 233
Highmark Inc. 236

INDEX BY INDUSTRY

Horizon Blue Cross Blue Shield of
New Jersey 241
IASIS Healthcare Corporation 247
Inova Health System 254
Intermountain Health Care, Inc. 257
Jefferson Health System Inc. 262
Johns Hopkins Medicine 266
Kaiser Foundation Health Plan,
Inc. 272
Kaleida Health 273
Lenox Hill Hospital 292
Life Care Centers of America 296
LifeBridge Health, Inc. 296
Marian Health System 307
Mayo Foundation for Medical
Education and Research 317
Medical Mutual of Ohio 323
MedStar Health 324
Memorial Hermann Healthcare
System 326
Memorial Sloan-Kettering Cancer
Center 327
New York City Health and Hospitals
Corporation 363
NewYork-Presbyterian Healthcare
System 369
Novant Health, Inc. 374
OhioHealth Corporation 378
Park Nicollet Health Services 386
Partners HealthCare System, Inc. 389
PeaceHealth 390
Provena Health 406
Providence Health System 406
The Regence Group 415
Robert Wood Johnson University
Hospital 421
St. Joseph Health System 429
Scott & White 439
Scripps 440
Sentara Healthcare 442
Sisters of Mercy Health System 449
Spectrum Health 455
SSM Health Care System Inc. 458
Sutter Health 466
Swedish Health Services 467
Team Health, Inc. 469
Texas Health Resources Inc. 473
Trinity Health 484
Tufts Associated Health Plans,
Inc. 489
The University of Wisconsin Hospital
& Clinics Authority 510
US Oncology, Inc. 512
Vanguard Health Systems, Inc. 518
Vision Service Plan 524

INDUSTRIAL MANUFACTURING

The Marmon Group, Inc. 309

Construction, Mining & Other Heavy Equipment Manufacturing
Vermeer Manufacturing Company 520

Fluid Control Equipment, Pump, Seal & Valve Manufacturing
Dresser, Inc. 167
McJunkin Corporation 319
McWane Corp. 322
National Waterworks, Inc. 358
Swagelok Company 466

Glass & Clay Product Manufacturing
Guardian Industries Corp. 218

Industrial Automation & Industrial Control Products Manufacturing
Duchossois Industries, Inc. 169

Industrial Contract Manufacturing
Federal Prison Industries, Inc. 187

Industrial Machinery & Equipment Distribution
RDO Equipment Co. 414

Industrial Machinery & Equipment Manufacturing
Amsted Industries Incorporated 43
Connell Limited Partnership 134
Harbour Group Industries, Inc. 224
Inductotherm Industries, Inc. 251
Koch Enterprises, Inc. 280
NESCO, Inc. 361

Lighting & Other Fixture Manufacturing
Genlyte Thomas Group LLC 202

Material Handling Equipment Manufacturing
Crown Equipment Corporation 143

Metal Fabrication
Citation Corporation 122
Integris Metals Corporation 255
MAGNATRAX Corporation 305
Tube City, LLC 489

Packaging & Container Manufacturing
BPC Holding Corp. 88
BWAY Corporation 95
Dart Container Corporation 148
Graham Packaging Company,
Inc. 211
Green Bay Packaging Inc. 215
Menasha Corporation 328
Plastipak Holdings, Inc. 399
Pliant Corporation 400
Printpack, Inc. 405
Solo Cup Company 453
Tekni-Plex, Inc. 470
U.S. Can Corporation 511

Paper & Paper Product Manufacturing
Appleton Papers Inc. 48
Central National-Gottesman Inc. 112
Gould Paper Corporation 210
The Newark Group, Inc. 368
Parsons & Whittemore,
Incorporated 388

Rubber & Plastic Product Manufacturing
Nypro Inc. 374
Siegel-Robert Inc. 447
Sigma Plastics Group 448

Textile Manufacturing
Avondale Incorporated 61
Beaulieu of America, LLC 70
Burlington Industries, Inc. 94
Milliken & Company Inc. 336
National Textiles, L.L.C. 357
Parkdale Mills, Inc. 386
R. B. Pamplin Corporation 413
W. L. Gore & Associates, Inc. 538

Wire & Cable Manufacturing
Jordan Industries, Inc. 270
Southwire Company 455

INSURANCE

Life Insurance
American United Mutual Insurance
Holding Company 41
CUNA Mutual Group 145
The Guardian Life Insurance Company
of America 219
Massachusetts Mutual Life Insurance
Company 314
Minnesota Mutual Companies,
Inc. 336
The Mutual of Omaha Companies 344
National Life Insurance Company 356
New York Life Insurance
Company 364
The Northwestern Mutual Life
Insurance Company 372
Ohio National Financial Services 377
Pacific Mutual Holding Company 383
The Penn Mutual Life Insurance
Company 392
Sammons Enterprises, Inc. 431
The Security Benefit Group of
Companies 440
Thrivent Financial for Lutherans 475
The Union Central Life Insurance
Company 496

Property & Casualty Insurance
American Family Insurance Group 37
Amerisure Mutual Insurance
Company 42
Amica Mutual Insurance Company 43
Atlantic Mutual Companies 59
Auto-Owners Insurance Group 61
Federated Insurance Companies 189
FM Global 193
Liberty Mutual Insurance
Company 295
Main Street America Group 305
Nationwide 359
Sentry Insurance, a Mutual
Company 443
State Farm Insurance Companies 460
Trustmark Insurance Company 487
USAA 514
Utica Mutual Insurance Company 515
Westfield Group 534

LEISURE

Carlson Companies, Inc. 102
Madison Square Garden, L.P. 304

Entertainment
Cinemark, Inc. 120
Feld Entertainment, Inc. 189
Loews Cineplex Entertainment
Corporation 299

Gambling
Connecticut Lottery Corporation 133
Georgia Lottery Corporation 204
Horseshoe Gaming Holding Corp. 242
Illinois Department of the
Lottery 249
Kentucky Lottery Corporation 275
Las Vegas Sands, Inc. 290
Maryland State Lottery Agency 313
Mashantucket Pequot Gaming
Enterprise Inc. 313
Mohegan Tribal Gaming
Authority 339
New York State Lottery 366
Ohio Lottery Commission 377
The Pennsylvania Lottery 392
Texas Lottery Commission 473

Lodging
Extended Stay America, Inc. 185
Hyatt Corporation 246

Restaurants & Cafes
Buffets Holdings, Inc. 92
Burger King Corporation 93
Carrols Holdings Corporation 106
Chick-fil-A Inc. 117
Doctor's Associates Inc. 161
Metromedia Restaurant Group 332
RTM Restaurant Group 428

Sports & Recreation
24 Hour Fitness Worldwide Inc. 16
American Golf Corporation 38
AMF Bowling Worldwide, Inc. 42
ClubCorp, Inc. 124
The DeBartolo Corporation 151
The Green Bay Packers, Inc. 215
Major League Baseball 306
NASCAR (National Association for
Stock Car Auto Racing) 347
National Basketball Association 349
National Football League Inc. 352
National Hockey League 354

MEDIA

Cox Enterprises, Inc. 140
The Hearst Corporation 230

Film & Video
DreamWorks L.L.C. 166
Lucasfilm Ltd. 301

Information Collection & Delivery
The Associated Press 57
Bloomberg L.P. 78
EBSCO Industries Inc. 174

Music
BMI (Broadcast Music, Inc.) 82
Sony BMG Music Entertainment 453
Warner Music Group 528

Publishing
Advance Publications, Inc. 21
Consumers Union of United States,
Inc. 135
The Copley Press, Inc. 138
Encyclopaedia Britannica, Inc. 176
Freedom Communications, Inc. 199
Hallmark Cards, Inc. 222
Houghton Mifflin Company 243
International Data Group 258
Johnson Publishing Company,
Inc. 267
Landmark Communications, Inc. 288
MediaNews Group, Inc. 322
Morris Communications Company
LLC 340
Rand McNally & Company 413
Trader Publishing Company 481

Television
A&E Television Networks 17
Corporation for Public
Broadcasting 140
Discovery Communications, Inc. 159
ESPN, Inc. 181
Guthy-Renker Corp. 221
Harpo, Inc. 224
Lifetime Entertainment Services 297
The WB Television Network 530

MEMBERSHIP ORGANIZATIONS

AARP 17
AFL-CIO 26
ASCAP (American Society of
Composers, Authors and
Publishers) 51
Rotary International 425
Teamsters (International Brotherhood
of Teamsters) 470

METALS & MINING

Aluminum Production
Ormet Corporation 381

Coal Mining & Processing
Drummond Company, Inc. 168
Foundation Coal Holdings, Inc. 198
Horizon Natural Resources
Company 242
Oxbow Corporation 382

Industrial Metals & Minerals
Quexco Incorporated 410
Unimin Corporation 496

INDEX BY INDUSTRY

Metals Distribution
Earle M. Jorgensen Company 173
Tang Industries, Inc. 468

Steel Production
American Cast Iron Pipe Company 36
California Steel Industries, Inc. 97
OmniSource Corporation 379
Renco Group, Inc. 417
Republic Engineered Products Inc. 417
Superior Group, Inc. 465

Steel Service Centers
O'Neal Steel, Inc. 380

PHARMACEUTICALS

Biotechnology
Quintiles Transnational Corp. 411

Pharmaceuticals Distribution & Wholesale
Bellco Health Corp. 73
The F. Dohmen Co. 186
Kinray Inc. 279
Quality King Distributors Inc. 409

Pharmaceuticals Manufacturers
Herbalife International, Inc. 234
Purdue Pharma L.P. 408
TAP Pharmaceutical Products Inc. 468

REAL ESTATE

Commercial Property Investment
H Group Holding Inc. 221
Helmsley Enterprises, Inc. 232
The Trump Organization 485

Commercial Real Estate Brokerage
Colliers International Property Consultants Inc. 126
Cushman & Wakefield, Inc. 145

Commercial Real Estate Development
Hines Interests L.P. 237
The Irvine Company Inc. 260
Opus Corporation 380
Tishman Realty & Construction Co. Inc. 478

Residential Property Investment
The Lefrak Organization 291

Residential Property Management
Lincoln Property Company 297

Residential Real Estate Development
Trammell Crow Residential 482

RETAIL

Apparel & Accessories Retail
J. Crew Group, Inc. 261
L.L. Bean, Inc. 298
Retail Brand Alliance, Inc. 418

Auto Parts Retail
CARQUEST Corporation 105
Discount Tire Co. Inc. 158
General Parts, Inc. 202

Automobile Dealers
ANCIRA 45
Bill Heard Enterprises 75
Bob Rohrman Auto Group 83
Braman Management Association 89
Burt Automotive Network 95
Chapman Automotive Group, LLC 114
Darcars Automotive Group 148
David McDavid Auto Group 149
David Wilson's Automotive Group 150
DriveTime Automotive Group, Inc. 168
Earnhardt's Auto Centers 173
Elder Automotive Group 175
The Faulkner Organization 186
Fletcher Jones Management Group 192
Galpin Motors, Inc. 201
Gulf States Toyota, Inc. 221
Hendrick Automotive Group 232
The Herb Chambers Companies 234
Holman Enterprises 240
Jim Koons Automotive Companies, Inc. 263
JM Family Enterprises, Inc. 263
Larry H. Miller Group 290
Les Schwab Tire Centers 293
Marty Franich Auto Center 312
Ourisman Automotive Enterprises 381
Penske Corporation 393
Phil Long Dealerships, Inc. 397
Planet Automotive Group, Inc. 399
Rosenthal Automotive Organization 425
Santa Monica Ford 431
Sheehy Auto Stores, Inc. 445
Tuttle-Click Automotive Group 490
VT Inc. 525

Building Materials Retail & Distribution
84 Lumber Company 16
ABC Supply (American Builders & Contractors Supply Co., Inc.) 18
Bradco Supply Corp. 89
Builders FirstSource 93
Foxworth-Galbraith Lumber Company 198
Interline Brands, Inc. 257
Lanoga Corporation 289
North Pacific Group, Inc. 371
Primus, Inc. 404
TruServ Corporation 486

Camera & Optical Goods Retail
Ritz Camera Centers, Inc. 420

Computer & Software Retail
Fry's Electronics, Inc. 200

Consumer Electronics & Appliances Retail
Interbond Corporation of America 256
P.C. Richard & Son 390

Convenience Stores & Truck Stops
Cumberland Farms, Inc. 144
Flying J Inc. 193
Gate Petroleum Company 201
Holiday Companies 239
Love's Travel Stops & Country Stores, Inc. 300
Petro Stopping Centers, L.P. 396
Pilot Travel Centers, LLC 398
QuikTrip Corporation 410
RaceTrac Petroleum, Inc. 412
Sheetz, Inc. 445
Stewart's Shops Corp. 463
TravelCenters of America, Inc. 483
Wawa, Inc. 530

Department Stores
Belk, Inc. 72
Boscov's Department Store 86
Mervyn's 330

Discount & Variety Retail
Variety Wholesalers, Inc. 518

Drug Stores & Pharmacies
Discount Drug Mart Inc. 158
Duane Reade Inc. 168
Marc Glassman, Inc. 307

Floor & Window Coverings Retail
CCA Global Partners 111

Grocery Retail
Bashas' Inc. 66
Big Y Foods, Inc. 74
Brookshire Brothers, Ltd. 91
Brookshire Grocery Company 91
Demoulas Super Markets Inc. 155
Dierbergs Markets Inc. 158
Giant Eagle, Inc. 205
The Golub Corporation 208
Haggen, Inc. 222
H. E. Butt Grocery Company 228
Houchens Industries Inc. 243
Hy-Vee, Inc. 247
IGA, Inc. 248
Inserra Supermarkets, Inc. 254
King Kullen Grocery Company, Inc. 278
K-VA-T Food Stores, Inc. 286
Meijer, Inc. 324
Minyard Food Stores, Inc. 337
Publix Super Markets, Inc. 407
Raley's Inc. 412
Save Mart Supermarkets 433
Schnuck Markets, Inc. 436
Stater Bros. Holdings Inc. 462
Trader Joe's Company, Inc. 481
Ukrop's Super Markets, Inc. 493
United Supermarkets, Ltd. 498
Wakefern Food Corporation 526
Wegmans Food Markets, Inc. 531
WinCo Foods, Inc. 537

Hobby & Craft Retail
Hobby Lobby Stores, Inc. 238

Home Furnishings & Housewares Retail
Cornerstone Brands, Inc. 139
Euromarket Designs Inc. 183
Home Interiors & Gifts, Inc. 240
Levitz Home Furnishings, Inc. 294
Rooms To Go, Inc. 423

Home Improvement & Hardware Retail
Ace Hardware Corporation 19
Do it Best Corp. 160
Menard, Inc. 327

Jewelry & Watch Retail
M. Fabrikant & Sons, Inc. 302

Military & Government Exchange Retail
Army and Air Force Exchange Service 50
Navy Exchange Service Command 360

Music, Video, Book & Entertainment Retail
Alliance Entertainment Corp. 33
Baker & Taylor Corporation 63
Barnes & Noble College Bookstores, Inc. 65
Chas. Levy Company LLC 115
Columbia House Company 128
Follett Corporation 195
Ingram Entertainment Holdings Inc. 253
Ingram Industries Inc. 253
MTS, Incorporated 343
The Musicland Group, Inc. 343

Office Products Retail & Distribution
Unisource Worldwide, Inc. 497

Sporting & Recreational Equipment Retail
Academy Sports & Outdoors, Ltd. 19
Bass Pro Shops, Inc. 67
REI (Recreational Equipment, Inc.) 415

Toys & Games Retail
KB Toys, Inc. 273

SECURITY PRODUCTS & SERVICES

Security Services
Inter-Con Security Systems, Inc. 257

TELECOMMUNICATIONS EQUIPMENT

Telecommunications Equipment Distribution & Support
Brightstar Corp. 90

TELECOMMUNICATIONS SERVICES

Metromedia Company 331
NextiraOne, LLC 369

Cable & Satellite Services
Intelsat, Ltd. 255
PanAmSat Corporation 385

Fixed-line Voice Services Providers
VarTec Telecom, Inc. 519

Wireless Communications Services
Cingular Wireless LLC 121
Verizon Wireless (Cellco Partnership) 520

TRANSPORTATION SERVICES

Air Cargo Services
Evergreen International Aviation, Inc. 184

Airport Management Services
The Port Authority of New York and New Jersey 402

Logistics Services
GeoLogistics Corporation 203

Marine Shipping
Crowley Maritime Corporation 143

Port, Harbor & Marine Terminal Management
SSA Marine 458

Postal Services
United States Postal Service 513

Rail Infrastructure Management Services
Conrail Inc. 134

Railroads
AMTRAK (National Railroad Passenger Corporation) 44
Metropolitan Transportation Authority 332

Trucking
Averitt Express, Inc. 61
Crete Carrier Corporation 142
Estes Express Lines, Inc. 182
Schneider National, Inc. 435
UniGroup, Inc. 496
Watkins Associated Industries, Inc. 529

Index by Headquarters

ALABAMA

Birmingham
American Cast Iron Pipe Company 36
BE&K, Inc. 69
Brasfield & Gorrie, LLC 90
Citation Corporation 122
Coca-Cola Bottling Co. United, Inc. 125
Drummond Company, Inc. 168
EBSCO Industries Inc. 174
McWane Corp. 322
O'Neal Steel, Inc. 380

ALASKA

Anchorage
Arctic Slope Regional Corporation 48

ARIZONA

Chandler
Bashas' Inc. 66

Gilbert
Earnhardt's Auto Centers 173

Phoenix
Banner Health 64
DriveTime Automotive Group, Inc. 168
Eagle-Picher Industries, Inc. 171
Shamrock Foods Company 444

Scottsdale
Chapman Automotive Group, LLC 114
Discount Tire Co. Inc. 158
Forever Living Products International, Inc. 197

ARKANSAS

Little Rock
Arkansas Blue Cross and Blue Shield 49

Stuttgart
Riceland Foods, Inc. 419

CALIFORNIA

Anderson
Sierra Pacific Industries 447

Artesia
California Dairies Inc. 96

Bakersfield
Aera Energy LLC 25

Beverly Hills
John Paul Mitchell Systems 265
Platinum Equity, LLC 400
Shapell Industries, Inc. 444

Burbank
The WB Television Network 530

Calabasas
ValleyCrest Companies 516

City of Industry
Utility Trailer Manufacturing Co. 515

Colton
Stater Bros. Holdings Inc. 462

Commerce
Unified Western Grocers, Inc. 495

El Segundo
The Aerospace Corporation 25

Fontana
California Steel Industries, Inc. 97

Foster City
Rudolph and Sletten, Inc. 428
Visa International 523

Fountain Valley
Kingston Technology Company, Inc. 278

Fremont
ASI Corp. 53
New United Motor Manufacturing, Inc. 362

Fresno
Community Medical Centers 130

Glendale
DreamWorks L.L.C. 166

Hayward
Mervyn's 330

Inglewood
Herbalife International, Inc. 234

Irvine
Advantage Sales and Marketing, LLC 22
Freedom Communications, Inc. 199
Golden State Foods 207
Nikken Global Inc. 370
Tuttle-Click Automotive Group 490

La Jolla
The Copley Press, Inc. 138

Livingston
Foster Poultry Farms 198

Long Beach
Trustees of the California State University 96

Los Altos
The David and Lucile Packard Foundation 385

Los Angeles
AECOM Technology Corporation 24
Cook Inlet Energy Supply L.L.C. 137
Gibson, Dunn & Crutcher LLP 206
Gores Technology Group, LLC 210
Latham & Watkins LLP 291
O'Melveny & Myers LLP 379
Paul, Hastings, Janofsky & Walker LLP 389
Roll International Corporation 422
Topa Equities, Ltd. 479
The University of Southern California 507
The Yucaipa Companies LLC 541

Lynwood
Earle M. Jorgensen Company 173

Menlo Park
SRI International 457

Modesto
E. & J. Gallo Winery 172
Save Mart Supermarkets 433

Monrovia
Trader Joe's Company, Inc. 481

Newport Beach
The Irvine Company Inc. 260
Pacific Mutual Holding Company 383
WL Homes LLC 539

North Hills
Galpin Motors, Inc. 201

Oakland
Crowley Maritime Corporation 143
Kaiser Foundation Health Plan, Inc. 272
University of California 500

Orange
David Wilson's Automotive Group 150
St. Joseph Health System 429
Young's Market Company, LLC 540

Palm Desert
Guthy-Renker Corp. 221

Pasadena
Inter-Con Security Systems, Inc. 257
Parsons Corporation 387

Rancho Cordova
Vision Service Plan 524

Redwood City
DPR Construction, Inc. 165

Roseville
Adventist Health 22

Sacramento
CalPERS (California Public Employees' Retirement System) 98
Sutter Health 466

San Diego
Memec Group Holdings Limited 326
Science Applications International Corporation 438
Scripps 440

San Francisco
Bechtel Group, Inc. 70
Blue Shield Of California 81
Catholic Healthcare West 110
Delta Dental of California 154
Levi Strauss & Co. 293
Morrison & Foerster LLP 341
Swinerton Incorporated 467
Wilbur-Ellis Company 536

San Jose
Fry's Electronics, Inc. 200
Hitachi Global Storage Technologies 237
MA Laboratories, Inc. 302

San Mateo
Webcor Builders, Inc. 531

San Rafael
Lucasfilm Ltd. 301

San Ramon
24 Hour Fitness Worldwide Inc. 16

Santa Ana
GeoLogistics Corporation 203

Santa Monica
A-Mark Financial Corporation 34
American Golf Corporation 38
Santa Monica Ford 431

Sherman Oaks
Sunkist Growers, Inc. 464

Stanford
Stanford University 458

Stockton
A. G. Spanos Companies 28

Sun Valley
PMC Global, Inc. 401

Union City
Kinetics Group, Inc. 277

Vernon
Red Chamber Co. 415

Walnut
J.F. Shea Co., Inc. 262
ViewSonic Corporation 522

Watsonville
Cornerstone Propane Partners, L.P. 139

INDEX BY HEADQUARTERS LOCATION

Marty Franich Auto Center 312

West Sacramento
MTS, Incorporated 343
Raley's Inc. 412

Westlake Village
Consolidated Electrical Distributors, Inc. 135
Dole Food Company, Inc. 162

COLORADO

Broomfield
MWH Global, Inc. 346

Centennial
Burt Automotive Network 95
Vistar/VSA Corporation 524

Colorado Springs
Phil Long Dealerships, Inc. 397

Denver
Catholic Health Initiatives 108
Duke Energy Field Services, LLC 170
Leprino Foods Company 292
MediaNews Group, Inc. 322

Englewood
CH2M HILL Companies, Ltd. 113

Greeley
Hensel Phelps Construction Co. 233
UAP Holding Corp. 492

Steamboat Springs
TIC Holdings, Inc. 476

Westminster
Tri-State Generation and Transmission Association, Inc. 484

CONNECTICUT

Bristol
ESPN, Inc. 181

Cheshire
Bozzuto's Inc. 88

Enfield
Retail Brand Alliance, Inc. 418

Farmington
ConnectiCare Inc. 133

Greenwich
Interactive Brokers Group LLC 256

Mashantucket
Mashantucket Pequot Gaming Enterprise Inc. 313

Meriden
The Lane Construction Corporation 289

Middlebury
Timex Corporation 477

Milford
Doctor's Associates Inc. 161

New Britain
Connecticut Lottery Corporation 133

New Canaan
Unimin Corporation 496

New Haven
Yale University 540

Stamford
Conair Corporation 131
Esselte 181
Purdue Pharma L.P. 408

Towers Perrin 480

Uncasville
Mohegan Tribal Gaming Authority 339

West Hartford
Colt's Manufacturing Company, LLC 127

Wilton
PanAmSat Corporation 385

DELAWARE

Newark
W. L. Gore & Associates, Inc. 538

DISTRICT OF COLUMBIA

Washington
AARP 17
AFL-CIO 26
Akin Gump Strauss Hauer & Feld LLP 29
The American Red Cross 39
AMTRAK (National Railroad Passenger Corporation) 44
The Carlyle Group 104
Corporation for Public Broadcasting 140
Federal Prison Industries, Inc. 187
Federal Reserve System 188
Hogan & Hartson 238
Intelsat, Ltd. 255
NASD 348
National Geographic Society 353
Smithsonian Institution 451
Teamsters (International Brotherhood of Teamsters) 470
United States Postal Service 513
Wilmer Cutler Pickering Hale and Dorr LLP 536

FLORIDA

Boca Raton
Purity Wholesale Grocers, Inc. 408

Coral Gables
Baptist Health South Florida 64

Coral Springs
Alliance Entertainment Corp. 33

Daytona Beach
NASCAR (National Association for Stock Car Auto Racing) 347

Deerfield Beach
JM Family Enterprises, Inc. 263

Gainesville
University of Florida 501

Hollywood
Interbond Corporation of America 256

Jacksonville
Acosta Sales Company, Inc. 21
Gate Petroleum Company 201
The Haskell Company 226
Interline Brands, Inc. 257

Lake Wales
Florida's Natural Growers 193

Lakeland
Publix Super Markets, Inc. 407

Miami
Braman Management Association 89
Brightstar Corp. 90
Burger King Corporation 93
Greenberg Traurig, LLP 216
Planet Automotive Group, Inc. 399
Southern Wine & Spirits of America, Inc. 454

Naples
Rooney Holdings, Inc. 423

Seffner
Rooms To Go, Inc. 423

Tampa
Seminole Electric Cooperative, Inc. 442

Vero Beach
George E. Warren Corporation 203

West Palm Beach
Oxbow Corporation 382

Winter Park
Adventist Health System 23

GEORGIA

Alpharetta
MAGNATRAX Corporation 305

Atlanta
American Cancer Society, Inc. 35
BWAY Corporation 95
Chick-fil-A Inc. 117
Cingular Wireless LLC 121
Cox Enterprises, Inc. 140
Georgia Lottery Corporation 204
John Wieland Homes and Neighborhoods, Inc. 266
National Distributing Company, Inc. 351
National Service Industries, Inc. 357
Printpack, Inc. 405
RTM Restaurant Group 428
Trammell Crow Residential 482
Watkins Associated Industries, Inc. 529
WorldTravel BTI 539

Augusta
Morris Communications Company LLC 340

Carrollton
Southwire Company 455

Columbus
Bill Heard Enterprises 75
Georgia Crown Distributing Company 204

Dalton
Beaulieu of America, LLC 70

Monroe
Avondale Incorporated 61

Norcross
Unisource Worldwide, Inc. 497

Savannah
Great Dane Limited Partnership 214

Smyrna
RaceTrac Petroleum, Inc. 412

Tucker
Oglethorpe Power Corporation 376

IDAHO

Boise
J.R. Simplot Company 271
WinCo Foods, Inc. 537

Nampa
MPC Computers, LLC 342

ILLINOIS

Bedford Park
CHEMCENTRAL Corporation 116

Bloomington
GROWMARK, Inc. 218
State Farm Insurance Companies 460

Chicago
Amsted Industries Incorporated 43
Baker & McKenzie 62
Blue Cross and Blue Shield Association 78
Chas. Levy Company LLC 115
Encyclopaedia Britannica, Inc. 176
Equity Group Investments, L.L.C. 178
Grant Thornton International 212
H Group Holding Inc. 221
Harpo, Inc. 224
Health Care Service Corporation 229
Hyatt Corporation 246
IGA, Inc. 248
Information Resources, Inc. 252
Johnson Publishing Company, Inc. 267
Kirkland & Ellis LLP 279
The Marmon Group, Inc. 309
Mayer, Brown, Rowe & Maw 317
McDermott, Will & Emery 319
Pepper Construction Group, LLC 394
Sidley Austin Brown & Wood LLP 446
TruServ Corporation 486
TTX Company 488
The University of Chicago 500
The Walsh Group 528
Wirtz Corporation 537

Deerfield
Jordan Industries, Inc. 270

Des Plaines
Frank Consolidated Enterprises 199
UOP LLC 510

Elmhurst
Duchossois Industries, Inc. 169

Evanston
Evanston Northwestern Healthcare Corporation 183
Northwestern University 373
Rotary International 425

Franklin Park
Central Grocers Cooperative, Inc. 112

Highland Park
Solo Cup Company 453

Hodgkins
Certified Grocers Midwest, Inc. 113

Itasca
Fellowes, Inc. 190
Serta, Inc. 443

Lake Forest
TAP Pharmaceutical Products Inc. 468
Trustmark Insurance Company 487

Lombard
U.S. Can Corporation 511

Long Grove
CF Industries, Inc. 113

Mokena
Provena Health 406

Mt. Sterling
Dot Foods, Inc. 163

INDEX BY HEADQUARTERS LOCATION

Mundelein
Medline Industries, Inc. 324
Naperville
Eby-Brown Company 174
Nalco Holding Company 347
Northbrook
Culligan International Company 144
Euromarket Designs Inc. 183
Lane Industries, Inc. 289
Underwriters Laboratories Inc. 494
Oak Brook
Ace Hardware Corporation 19
Advocate Health Care 23
Elkay Manufacturing Company 176
River Grove
Follett Corporation 195
Rolling Meadows
Kimball Hill Homes 277
Rosemont
The Martin-Brower Company, L.L.C. 311
Reyes Holdings LLC 419
Schaumburg
Pliant Corporation 400
Skokie
Rand McNally & Company 413
Topco Associates LLC 479
Springfield
Illinois Department of the Lottery 249
Urbana
University of Illinois 502
Westmont
Ty Inc. 492

INDIANA

Anderson
Remy International, Inc. 416
Bloomington
Indiana University 251
Evansville
BPC Holding Corp. 88
Koch Enterprises, Inc. 280
Fort Wayne
Do it Best Corp. 160
OmniSource Corporation 379
Indianapolis
American United Mutual Insurance Holding Company 41
Clarian Health Partners, Inc. 123
Community Hospitals of Indiana, Inc. 130
National Wine & Spirits, Inc 358
Lafayette
Bob Rohrman Auto Group 83

IOWA

Des Moines
MidAmerican Energy Holdings Company 334
The Weitz Group, LLC 532
Iowa City
The University of Iowa 502
Le Mars
Wells' Dairy, Inc. 533

Pella
Pella Corporation 391
Vermeer Manufacturing Company 520
West Des Moines
Hy-Vee, Inc. 247

KANSAS

Kansas City
Associated Wholesale Grocers, Inc. 57
Lenexa
U.S. Central Credit Union 511
McPherson
National Cooperative Refinery Association 350
Overland Park
Ash Grove Cement Company 52
The Scoular Company 439
Shawnee Mission
VT Inc. 525
Topeka
The Security Benefit Group of Companies 440
Wichita
Koch Industries, Inc. 281

KENTUCKY

Ashland
Horizon Natural Resources Company 242
Bowling Green
Houchens Industries Inc. 243
Fort Mitchell
The Drees Co. 167
Louisville
Genlyte Thomas Group LLC 202
Kentucky Lottery Corporation 275

LOUISIANA

Baton Rouge
Turner Industries, Ltd. 490

MAINE

Freeport
L.L. Bean, Inc. 298

MARYLAND

Adelphi
University System of Maryland 503
Baltimore
Crown Central Petroleum Corporation 143
Johns Hopkins Medicine 266
LifeBridge Health, Inc. 296
Maryland State Lottery Agency 313
Vertis Inc. 521
The Whiting-Turner Contracting Company 535
Beltsville
Ritz Camera Centers, Inc. 420
Bethesda
Clark Enterprises, Inc. 124

Chevy Chase
Chevy Chase Bank, F.S.B. 117
Columbia
MedStar Health 324
Hanover
Allegis Group, Inc. 31
Linthicum Heights
Foundation Coal Holdings, Inc. 198
Marlow Heights
Ourisman Automotive Enterprises 381
Marriottsville
Bon Secours Health System, Inc. 83
Rockville
Adventist HealthCare, Inc. 23
Goodwill Industries International, Inc. 209
Salisbury
Perdue Farms Incorporated 394
Silver Spring
Darcars Automotive Group 148
Discovery Communications, Inc. 159

MASSACHUSETTS

Bedford
The MITRE Corporation 338
Boston
Bain & Company, Inc. 62
Blue Cross and Blue Shield of Massachusetts, Inc. 79
The Boston Consulting Group 87
Colliers International Property Consultants Inc. 126
Connell Limited Partnership 134
FMR Corp. 194
Houghton Mifflin Company 243
International Data Group 258
Liberty Mutual Insurance Company 295
New Balance Athletic Shoe, Inc. 361
Partners HealthCare System, Inc. 389
Suffolk Construction Company, Inc. 464
Cambridge
Harvard University 225
MIT (Massachusetts Institute of Technology) 337
Modern Continental Companies, Inc. 338
Canton
Cumberland Farms, Inc. 144
Chelsea
Gulf Oil Limited Partnership 220
HP Hood Inc. 244
Clinton
Nypro Inc. 374
Framingham
Bose Corporation 86
Lakeville-Middleboro
Ocean Spray Cranberries, Inc. 375
Methuen
Agri-Mark, Inc. 29
Milford
The Holmes Group, Inc. 240
Newton
UNICCO Service Company 494

Pittsfield
KB Toys, Inc. 273
Somerville
The Herb Chambers Companies 234
Springfield
Baystate Health Systems, Inc. 69
Big Y Foods, Inc. 74
Massachusetts Mutual Life Insurance Company 314
Tewksbury
Demoulas Super Markets Inc. 155
Waltham
Global Companies LLC 207
Polaroid Corporation 401
Tufts Associated Health Plans, Inc. 489
Worcester
Fallon Community Health Plan Inc. 186

MICHIGAN

Ada
Alticor Inc. 33
Ann Arbor
Flint Ink Corporation 192
The University of Michigan 503
Auburn Hills
Guardian Industries Corp. 218
Battle Creek
W.K. Kellogg Foundation 274
Bloomfield Hills
Penske Corporation 393
TriMas Corporation 483
Dearborn
Meridian Automotive Systems, Inc. 329
Detroit
Blue Cross Blue Shield of Michigan 80
Detroit Medical Center 156
Henry Ford Health System 233
Sherwood Food Distributors 446
Walbridge Aldinger Company 527
East Lansing
Michigan State University 334
Farmington Hills
Amerisure Mutual Insurance Company 42
Fraser
Venture Industries 519
Grand Rapids
Gordon Food Service 209
Meijer, Inc. 324
Spectrum Health 455
Holland
Haworth, Inc. 227
Jackson
Dawn Food Products, Inc. 151
Lansing
Auto-Owners Insurance Group 61
Mason
Dart Container Corporation 148
Midland
Dow Corning Corporation 163
Novi
Trinity Health 484

INDEX BY HEADQUARTERS LOCATION

Okemos
Delta Dental Plan of Michigan Inc 155

Plymouth
Metaldyne Corporation 330
Plastipak Holdings, Inc. 399

Southfield
Barton Malow Company 66

Sterling Heights
Key Safety Systems, Inc. 275

Troy
Elder Automotive Group 175
Oxford Automotive, Inc. 383

Warren
The Angelo Iafrate Companies 46
MSX International, Inc. 342

MINNESOTA

Arden Hills
Land O'Lakes, Inc. 287

Bayport
Andersen Corporation 45

Bloomington
Holiday Companies 239

Eagan
Buffets Holdings, Inc. 92

Fairmont
Rosen's Diversified, Inc. 424

Marshall
The Schwan Food Company 436

Minneapolis
Allina Hospitals and Clinics 33
Genmar Holdings, Inc. 202
Integris Metals Corporation 255
Jostens, Inc. 271
M. A. Mortenson Company 303
Thrivent Financial for Lutherans 475
University of Minnesota 504

Minnetonka
Carlson Companies, Inc. 102
Michael Foods, Inc. 333
The Musicland Group, Inc. 343
Opus Corporation 380

Moorhead
American Crystal Sugar Company 36

New Ulm
Associated Milk Producers Inc. 56

North Mankato
Taylor Corporation 469

Owatonna
Federated Insurance Companies 189

Plymouth
Carlson Wagonlit Travel, Inc. 103

Rochester
Mayo Foundation for Medical Education and Research 317

St. Louis Park
Park Nicollet Health Services 386

St. Paul
AgriBank, FCB 29
APi Group, Inc. 47
Johnson Brothers Liquor Company 267
Merrill Corporation 329
Minnesota Mutual Companies, Inc. 336

Wayzata
Cargill, Incorporated 100

MISSISSIPPI

Greenwood
Staple Cotton Cooperative Association 459

Jackson
BlueCross and BlueShield of Mississippi 82
Ergon, Inc. 179

Philadelphia
The Yates Companies, Inc. 540

MISSOURI

Chesterfield
Dierbergs Markets Inc. 158
Outsourcing Solutions Inc. 382
Sisters of Mercy Health System 449

Clayton
Apex Oil Company, Inc. 47

Columbia
MFA Incorporated 333
University of Missouri System 504

Des Peres
The Jones Financial Companies, L.L.L.P. 269

Earth City
CCA Global Partners 111

Fenton
Maritz Inc. 308
UniGroup, Inc. 496

Kansas City
Bartlett and Company 65
Black & Veatch Holding Company 77
Dairy Farmers of America, Inc. 146
DeBruce Grain, Inc. 152
Dunn Industries, Inc. 170
Hallmark Cards, Inc. 222

Springfield
Associated Electric Cooperative Inc. 54
Bass Pro Shops, Inc. 67
Cox Health Systems 142

St. Charles
ACF Industries, Inc. 20

St. Louis
Alberici Corporation 30
Ascension Health 51
BJC HealthCare 76
Center Oil Company 111
Enterprise Rent-A-Car Company 177
Graybar Electric Company, Inc. 213
Harbour Group Industries, Inc. 224
HBE Corporation 227
McCarthy Building Companies, Inc. 319
Schnuck Markets, Inc. 436
Siegel-Robert Inc. 447
SSM Health Care System Inc. 458
United Industries Corporation 497
Viasystems Group, Inc. 521

NEBRASKA

Lincoln
Crete Carrier Corporation 142
The University of Nebraska 505

Omaha
Ag Processing Inc 27
Alegent Health 30
The Mutual of Omaha Companies 344
Peter Kiewit Sons', Inc. 395
Tenaska, Inc. 471

NEVADA

Las Vegas
Fletcher Jones Management Group 192
Horseshoe Gaming Holding Corp. 242
Las Vegas Sands, Inc. 290
Tang Industries, Inc. 468

NEW HAMPSHIRE

Keene
C&S Wholesale Grocers, Inc. 99
Main Street America Group 305

NEW JERSEY

Avenel
Bradco Supply Corp. 89

Basking Ridge
Barnes & Noble College Bookstores, Inc. 65

Bedminster
Verizon Wireless (Cellco Partnership) 520

Berkeley Heights
The Connell Company 134

Carteret
Di Giorgio Corporation 157

Cherry Hill
Pinnacle Foods Group, Inc. 398

Cranford
The Newark Group, Inc. 368

East Orange
The Louis Berger Group, Inc. 300

East Rutherford
Metromedia Company 331

Edison
J.M. Huber Corporation 264

Elizabeth
Wakefern Food Corporation 526

Hoboken
CIC International Ltd. 119

Jersey City
UIS, Inc. 493

Lyndhurst
Sigma Plastics Group 448

Mahwah
Inserra Supermarkets, Inc. 254

Montvale
The Ferolie Group 191

New Brunswick
Robert Wood Johnson University Hospital 421

Newark
Horizon Blue Cross Blue Shield of New Jersey 241

Pennsauken
Holman Enterprises 240
Honickman Affiliates 241

Princeton
Educational Testing Service 175
Princeton University 405
Rockwood Specialties Group, Inc. 422

Rancocas
Inductotherm Industries, Inc. 251

Secaucus
Goya Foods, Inc. 210

Somerset
Software House International, Inc. 452

Somerville
Tekni-Plex, Inc. 470

Wayne
G-I Holdings Inc. 204
International Specialty Products Inc. 259

NEW YORK

Albany
State University of New York 461

Amherst
Mark IV Industries, Inc. 308

Astoria
Charmer Industries, Inc. 115

Balston Spa
Stewart's Shops Corp. 463

Bethpage
King Kullen Grocery Company, Inc. 278

Brooklyn
Peerless Importers, Inc. 391

Buffalo
Delaware North Companies, Inc. 153
Kaleida Health 273
Rich Products Corporation 419

East Syracuse
Dairylea Cooperative Inc. 147

Farmingdale
P.C. Richard & Son 390

Ithaca
Cornell University 138

Long Island City
National Envelope Corporation 351

New Hartford
Utica Mutual Insurance Company 515

New York
A&E Television Networks 17
Alliance Capital Management L.P. 31
ASCAP (American Society of Composers, Authors and Publishers) 51
The Associated Press 57
Atlantic Mutual Companies 59
Bill Blass Ltd. 75
Bloomberg L.P. 78
BMI (Broadcast Music, Inc.) 82
Brown Brothers Harriman & Co. 92
The Charmer-Sunbelt Group 115
The City University of New York 122
Cleary, Gottlieb, Steen & Hamilton 124
Columbia House Company 128
Columbia University 129
ContiGroup Companies, Inc. 136
Cushman & Wakefield, Inc. 145
Davis Polk & Wardwell 150
Deloitte Touche Tohmatsu 153

INDEX BY HEADQUARTERS LOCATION

The Depository Trust & Clearing
  Corporation 155
Duane Reade Inc. 168
The Dyson-Kissner-Moran
  Corporation 171
Ernst & Young International 180
The Ford Foundation 196
Gould Paper Corporation 210
The Guardian Life Insurance Company
  of America 219
Health Insurance Plan of Greater New
  York 230
The Hearst Corporation 230
Helmsley Enterprises, Inc. 232
Holland & Knight LLP 239
J. Crew Group, Inc. 261
Kohlberg Kravis Roberts & Co. 282
KPMG International 285
Lenox Hill Hospital 292
Lifetime Entertainment Services 297
Loews Cineplex Entertainment
  Corporation 299
M. Fabrikant & Sons, Inc. 302
MacAndrews & Forbes Holdings
  Inc. 303
Madison Square Garden, L.P. 304
Major League Baseball 306
McKinsey & Company 321
Memorial Sloan-Kettering Cancer
  Center 327
Metropolitan Transportation
  Authority 332
Mutual of America Life Insurance
  Company 344
National Basketball Association 349
National Football League Inc. 352
National Hockey League 354
New York City Health and Hospitals
  Corporation 363
New York Life Insurance
  Company 364
New York Stock Exchange, Inc. 367
New York University 368
NewYork-Presbyterian Healthcare
  System 369
Parsons Brinckerhoff Inc. 388
Paul, Weiss, Rifkind, Wharton &
  Garrison LLP 390
The Port Authority of New York and
  New Jersey 402
PricewaterhouseCoopers 403
Red Apple Group, Inc. 414
Renco Group, Inc. 417
The Rockefeller Foundation 421
Royster-Clark, Inc. 427
Shearman & Sterling 445
Simpson Thacher & Bartlett LLP 449
Sithe Energies, Inc. 450
Skadden, Arps, Slate, Meagher & Flom
  LLP 450
Sony BMG Music Entertainment 453
The Structure Tone Organization 463
Sullivan & Cromwell LLP 464
TIAA-CREF 475
Tishman Realty & Construction Co.
  Inc. 478
Transammonia, Inc. 482
The Trump Organization 485
Warner Music Group 528
Weil, Gotshal & Manges LLP 532
White & Case LLP 535

North Amityville
Bellco Health Corp. 73

Plainview
Coinmach Service Corp. 126

Purchase
Central National-Gottesman Inc. 112
MasterCard Incorporated 315

Rego Park
The Lefrak Organization 291

Rochester
Birds Eye Foods, Inc. 76
University of Rochester 506
Wegmans Food Markets, Inc. 531

Rockville Centre
Catholic Health Services of Long
  Island 109

Ronkonkoma
Quality King Distributors Inc. 409

Rye Brook
Parsons & Whittemore,
  Incorporated 388

Schenectady
The Golub Corporation 208
New York State Lottery 366

Staten Island
Advance Publications, Inc. 21

Syracuse
Carrols Holdings Corporation 106

Tarrytown
Westcon Group, Inc. 533

Westfield
National Grape Cooperative
  Association, Inc. 354

White Plains
Power Authority of the State of New
  York 365

Whitestone
Kinray Inc. 279

Woodbury
Levitz Home Furnishings, Inc. 294

Yonkers
Consumers Union of United States,
  Inc. 135

NORTH CAROLINA

Asheboro
Klaussner Furniture Industries,
  Inc. 280

Cary
SAS Institute Inc. 432

Charlotte
Baker & Taylor Corporation 63
Belk, Inc. 72
Hendrick Automotive Group 232
New NGC, Inc. 362

Durham
Quintiles Transnational Corp. 411

Gastonia
Parkdale Mills, Inc. 386

Greensboro
Burlington Industries, Inc. 94

Hickory
Alex Lee, Inc. 31

Huntersville
American Tire Distributors, Inc. 41

Raleigh
CARQUEST Corporation 105
General Parts, Inc. 202
North Carolina Electric Membership
  Corporation 371
Variety Wholesalers, Inc. 518

Rocky Mount
MBM Corporation 318

Trinity
Sealy Corporation 440

Winston-Salem
National Textiles, L.L.C. 357
Novant Health, Inc. 374

NORTH DAKOTA

Bismarck
Basin Electric Power Cooperative 67

Fargo
RDO Equipment Co. 414

OHIO

Akron
Republic Engineered Products
  Inc. 417

Archbold
Sauder Woodworking Co. 433

Cincinnati
Catholic Healthcare Partners 109
Cincinnati Children's Hospital Medical
  Center 120
Ohio National Financial Services 377
The Union Central Life Insurance
  Company 496

Cleveland
IMG 250
Jones Day 268
Medical Mutual of Ohio 323
Ohio Lottery Commission 377

Columbus
Battelle Memorial Institute 68
Borden Chemical, Inc. 85
Nationwide 359
The Ohio State University 378
OhioHealth Corporation 378
Safelite Group, Inc. 428

Cuyahoga Falls
Associated Materials Incorporated 56

Dayton
Primus, Inc. 404

Findlay
Findlay Industries, Inc. 191

Hiram
Great Lakes Cheese Company,
  Inc. 214

Mayfield Heights
NESCO, Inc. 361

Medina
Discount Drug Mart Inc. 158

New Bremen
Crown Equipment Corporation 143

Newark
The Longaberger Company 299

Parma
Marc Glassman, Inc. 307

Solon
Swagelok Company 466

West Chester
Cornerstone Brands, Inc. 139

Westfield Center
Westfield Group 534

Westlake
TravelCenters of America, Inc. 483

Youngstown
The DeBartolo Corporation 151

OKLAHOMA

Oklahoma City
Express Personnel Services 185
Hobby Lobby Stores, Inc. 238
Love's Travel Stops & Country Stores,
  Inc. 300

Tulsa
Marian Health System 307
QuikTrip Corporation 410

OREGON

Klamath Falls
JELD-WEN, inc. 262

McMinnville
Evergreen International Aviation,
  Inc. 184

Portland
Bonneville Power Administration 84
Columbia Forest Products Inc. 128
Hampton Affiliates 223
North Pacific Group, Inc. 371
R. B. Pamplin Corporation 413
The Regence Group 415

Prineville
Les Schwab Tire Centers 293

Roseburg
Roseburg Forest Products Co. 424

Salem
Colson & Colson Construction
  Company 127

Tigard
Western Family Foods, Inc. 534

PENNSYLVANIA

Altoona
Sheetz, Inc. 445

East Greenville
Knoll, Inc. 280

Eighty Four
84 Lumber Company 16

Glassport
Tube City, LLC 489

Harrisburg
D&H Distributing Co., Inc. 147

Horsham
The Penn Mutual Life Insurance
  Company 392

Johnstown
Conemaugh Health System 132

Large
Dick Corporation 157

Malvern
The Vanguard Group, Inc. 517

Middletown
The Pennsylvania Lottery 392

Newtown Square
Catholic Health East 107

Philadelphia
Berwind Group 73
The Children's Hospital of
  Philadelphia 118

INDEX BY HEADQUARTERS LOCATION

Conrail Inc. 134
The Day & Zimmermann Group, Inc. 151
Morgan, Lewis & Bockius LLP 339
The University of Pennsylvania 505

Pittsburgh
Giant Eagle, Inc. 205
Highmark Inc. 236
Koppers Inc. 284
University of Pittsburgh of the Commonwealth System of Higher Education 506

Radnor
Jefferson Health System Inc. 262
Superior Group, Inc. 465

Reading
Boscov's Department Store 86

Robesonia
Associated Wholesalers, Inc. 59

Trevose
The Faulkner Organization 186

Wawa
Wawa, Inc. 530

Wayne
Lumbermens Merchandising Corporation 302

West Conshohocken
Keystone Foods LLC 276

Willow Grove
Asplundh Tree Expert Co. 54

York
Graham Packaging Company, Inc. 211

RHODE ISLAND

Johnston
FM Global 193

Lincoln
Amica Mutual Insurance Company 43

Providence
Gilbane, Inc. 206
Nortek Holdings, Inc. 370
Warren Equities, Inc. 529

SOUTH CAROLINA

Columbia
AgFirst Farm Credit Bank 28

Fort Mill
Muzak LLC 345
Springs Industries, Inc. 456

Greenville
Greenville Hospital System 217

Spartanburg
Extended Stay America, Inc. 185
Milliken & Company Inc. 336

TENNESSEE

Brentwood
Doane Pet Care Company 160

Cleveland
Life Care Centers of America 296

Collegedale
McKee Foods Corporation 320

Cookeville
Averitt Express, Inc. 61

Franklin
IASIS Healthcare Corporation 247

Knoxville
H.T. Hackney Company 244
Pilot Travel Centers, LLC 398
Team Health, Inc. 469
TVA (Tennessee Valley Authority) 491
University of Tennessee 507

La Vergne
Ingram Entertainment Holdings Inc. 253

Memphis
Dunavant Enterprises, Inc. 170

Nashville
Ardent Health Services LLC 49
Ingram Industries Inc. 253
Vanderbilt University 516
Vanguard Health Systems, Inc. 518

TEXAS

Addison
Concentra Inc. 132
Dresser, Inc. 167
Mary Kay Inc. 312

Amarillo
Affiliated Foods Incorporated 25

Arlington
Choice Homes, Inc. 118
Texas Health Resources Inc. 473

Austin
SEMATECH, Inc. 441
Texas Lottery Commission 473
The University of Texas System 508

Carrollton
Home Interiors & Gifts, Inc. 240

College Station
The Texas A&M University System 472

Coppell
Minyard Food Stores, Inc. 337

Dallas
American Heart Association 39
Army and Air Force Exchange Service 50
Atrium Companies, Inc. 59
Austin Industries, Inc. 60
The Beck Group 71
Builders FirstSource 93
ClubCorp, Inc. 124
CompuCom Systems, Inc. 130
Contran Corporation 137
Dr Pepper/Seven Up Bottling Group, Inc. 165
Foxworth-Galbraith Lumber Company 198
Glazer's Wholesale Drug Company, Inc. 207
Hicks, Muse, Tate & Furst Incorporated 235
Hunt Consolidated Inc. 244
Interstate Battery System of America, Inc. 260
Lincoln Property Company 297
Quexco Incorporated 410
Sammons Enterprises, Inc. 431
VarTec Telecom, Inc. 519
Vought Aircraft Industries, Inc. 524

El Paso
Petro Stopping Centers, L.P. 396

Fort Worth
Ben E. Keith Company 73
Texas Pacific Group 474
TNP Enterprises, Inc. 478
TTI, Inc. 488

Houston
David Weekley Homes 149
Equistar Chemicals, LP 178
Goodman Manufacturing Company, L.P. 208
The Grocers Supply Co., Inc. 217
Gulf States Toyota, Inc. 221
Hines Interests L.P. 237
KRATON Polymers LLC 286
Memorial Hermann Healthcare System 326
Motiva Enterprises LLC 341
NextiraOne, LLC 369
Philip Services Corporation 397
Resolution Performance Products LLC 418
United Space Alliance 498
US Oncology, Inc. 512

Irving
CHRISTUS Health 119
David McDavid Auto Group 149
NCH Corporation 360

Katy
Academy Sports & Outdoors, Ltd. 19

Lubbock
Plains Cotton Cooperative Association 398
United Supermarkets, Ltd. 498

Lufkin
Brookshire Brothers, Ltd. 91

Plano
Cinemark, Inc. 120
CROSSMARK 142
Metromedia Restaurant Group 332
Safety-Kleen Holdco, Inc. 429

Round Rock
American Plumbing & Mechanical, Inc. 39

San Antonio
ANCIRA 45
H. E. Butt Grocery Company 228
Pabst Brewing Company 383
USAA 514
Zachry Construction Corporation 541

Temple
Scott & White 439

Texarkana
Truman Arnold Companies 485

Tyler
Brookshire Grocery Company 91
East Texas Medical Center Regional Healthcare System 182

Waco
Brazos Electric Power Cooperative, Inc. 90
National Waterworks, Inc. 358

The Woodlands
Chevron Phillips Chemical Company LLC 116

UTAH

Logan
ICON Health & Fitness, Inc. 248

Ogden
Flying J Inc. 193

Salt Lake City
Associated Food Stores, Inc. 55
Huntsman International LLC 245
Intermountain Health Care, Inc. 257
Sinclair Oil Corporation 449

Sandy
Larry H. Miller Group 290

VERMONT

Montpelier
National Life Insurance Company 356

VIRGINIA

Abingdon
K-VA-T Food Stores, Inc. 286

Alexandria
The Salvation Army National Corporation 430
United Way of America 499
Volunteers of America, Inc. 524

Arlington
Rosenthal Automotive Organization 425

Fairfax
Sheehy Auto Stores, Inc. 445

Falls Church
Inova Health System 254

Herndon
National Rural Utilities Cooperative Finance Corporation 356

McLean
Booz Allen Hamilton Inc. 84
Mars, Incorporated 310

Norfolk
FHC Health Systems, Inc. 191
Landmark Communications, Inc. 288
Sentara Healthcare 442
Trader Publishing Company 481

Reston
WKI Holding Company, Inc. 538

Richmond
AMF Bowling Worldwide, Inc. 42
Carpenter Co. 105
Estes Express Lines, Inc. 182
Southern States Cooperative, Incorporated 454
Ukrop's Super Markets, Inc. 493

Roanoke
Carilion Health System 101

Vienna
Feld Entertainment, Inc. 189
Jim Koons Automotive Companies, Inc. 263
Navy Federal Credit Union 360

Virginia Beach
Navy Exchange Service Command 360

WASHINGTON

Bellevue
PeaceHealth 390

Bellingham
Haggen, Inc. 222

Kent
REI (Recreational Equipment, Inc.) 415

INDEX BY HEADQUARTERS LOCATION

Redmond
Lanoga Corporation 289

Seattle
Associated Grocers, Inc. 55
Bill & Melinda Gates Foundation 74
Group Health Cooperative of Puget Sound 217
Providence Health System 406
Services Group of America 444
Simpson Investment Company 448
SSA Marine 458
Swedish Health Services 467
University of Washington 509
Vulcan Inc. 525

WEST VIRGINIA

Charleston
McJunkin Corporation 319

Wheeling
Ormet Corporation 381

WISCONSIN

Appleton
Appleton Papers Inc. 48

Arcadia
Ashley Furniture Industries, Inc. 53

Baraboo
Foremost Farms USA, Cooperative 197

Beloit
ABC Supply (American Builders & Contractors Supply Co., Inc.) 18

Combined Locks
U.S. Oil Co., Inc. 512

Eau Claire
Menard, Inc. 327

Germantown
The F. Dohmen Co. 186

Green Bay
American Foods Group, Inc. 38
Green Bay Packaging Inc. 215
The Green Bay Packers, Inc. 215
KI 276
Schneider National, Inc. 435
Schreiber Foods, Inc. 436

Kenosha
Jockey International, Inc. 265

Kohler
Kohler Co. 283

Madison
American Family Insurance Group 37
CUNA Mutual Group 145
The University of Wisconsin System 509
The University of Wisconsin Hospital & Clinics Authority 510

Milwaukee
Everett Smith Group, Ltd. 184
The Northwestern Mutual Life Insurance Company 372
Roundy's, Inc. 426

Neenah
Menasha Corporation 328

Plymouth
Sargento Foods Inc. 432

Racine
S.C. Johnson & Son, Inc. 434

Stevens Point
Sentry Insurance, a Mutual Company 443

Sturtevant
JohnsonDiversey, Inc. 268

Sussex
Quad/Graphics, Inc. 409

Index of Executives

A

Aamodt, Patsy 48
Abbott, Steve 524
Abdel-Malek, Refaat A. 346
Abel, Gregory E. 335
Abeles, Jon C. 109
Abernethy, David S. 230
Abfalter, Dan 16
Abington, Bill 324
Ableidinger, Bryan R. 487
Abraham, Andrew A. 426
Abraham, Jay 348
Abramowski, Robert J. 469
Abrams, Jim 324
Abramson, Richard 457
Abruzzese, Joe 159
Abutaleb, Mona 159
Accordino, Daniel T. 106
Achtenberg, Roberta 97
Ackerman, Greg 294
Ackerman, Howard 227
Ackerman, Steve 433
Ackerman, Valerie B. 350
Ackley, Roberta L. 25
Acklie, Duane W. 142
Acone, Adam 355
Acord, Larry G. 305
Acosta, Alan 459
Acosta, Belen J. 151
Acton, Brian 382
Adair, Janna 330
Adamonis, Richard C. 367
Adams, Carolyn 250
Adams, Clint B. 49
Adams, David A. 447
Adams, Derick W. 42
Adams, Edward 178
Adams, Gregory G. 374
Adams, J. Phillip 193
Adams, Jacob 48
Adams, Mike (Bechtel) 71
Adams, Mike
  (Glazer's Wholesale Drug) 207
Adams, Paul 292
Adams, Ralph G. 154
Adams, Richard C. 68
Adams, Staci 159
Adams, Stan 22
Adamson, James 50
Adamson, Mark 193
Adamson, Terrence B. 353
Adelson, Sheldon G. 290
Ademe, Maurice 20
Adjemian, Vart K. 137
Adkins, Chris 214
Adkins, Michael S. 342
Adler, Kraig K. 138
Adler, Peter G. 218
Afable, Mark V. 37
Afable, Richard F. 107
Agostinelli, D. D. 60
Agres, Robert E. 64
Aguayo, Bill 168

Aguiar, Randall S. 469
Ahearn, Joseph A. 114
Aherne, Paul A. 428
Ahlquist, David A. 318
Ahmaogak, Mary Ellen 48
Ahrold, Robbin 82
Aiello, Greg 352
Ainscough, Stephen Steve 422
Aitchison, Kenneth 23
Ajamian, Daniel 276
Ajamy, Louis 292
Al-Fayez, Roxane 261
Albanese, John M. 392
Albarian, Mark 34
Alberici, John S. 30
Albero, Carl M. 438
Alberts, Charles 274
Albright, Denise 418
Albritton, David 499
Albritton, Herb 239
Alderman, Ken 206
Alderson, Richard 306
Aldridge, Philip R. 508
Alessandri, Rick 181
Alexa Strauss, Julie 190
Alexander, Bruce D. 539
Alexander, Jim
  (David Weekley Homes) 149
Alexander, Jimmy (Ace Hardware) 20
Alexander, John 51
Alexander, Laurie 103
Alexander, Michael D. 519
Alexander, S. Tyrone 237
Alfano, Michele D. 191
Alfano, Susan A. 315
Alfers, Bill 386
Alfonsi, Thomas J. 274
Alford, Mack L. 459
Alge, David 369
Alger, Robert E. 289
Allen, Andrew W. 52
Allen, Anne E. 367
Allen, Ashley 336
Allen, David W. 220
Allen, Fran 361
Allen, James R. 349
Allen, Kenneth 228
Allen, Matthew N. 248
Allen, Meredith B. 459
Allen, Paul G. 526
Allen, Rick 178
Allen, Robert C. 114
Allen, Sharon (Arkansas Blue Cross
  and Blue Shield) 50
Allen, Sharon L. (Deloitte) 154
Allen, Ward 404
Allen, Wesley J. 292
Allison, Dirk 49
Allison, Herbert M. 476
Allison, Linda 92
Almassy, Stephen E. 180
Almond, Stephen 154
Alonzo, Jan R. 496
Alpert, Warren 529

Alspaugh, Robert W. 285
Alston, Michael W. 288
Altendorf, Michael J. 20
Altherr, Jack R. Jr. 62
Altman, Lawrence B. 241
Altman, Steven J. 140
Altschuler, Steven M. 118
Altstadt, Manfred 344
Alvarez, Cesar L. 216
Alvarez, Ed 469
Alvarez, Maribel 211
Alvarez, Scott G. 188
Amador, Evelyn 499
Amaral, José 227
Amato, Thomas 330
Ambler, Michael 95
Ambres, Cynthia A. 273
Amburn, Linda 229
Ambutas, Vytas 468
Amenita, Chris 51
Amenta, Peter S. 421
Amerson, Leon T. 28
Ames, Larry 151
Ammon, Donald R. 22
Amparan, Oscar L. 473
Amsigner, Gary 319
Amundson, Robert 511
Anand, Sudeep 452
Ancarrow, N. Hopper Jr. 454
Ancier, Garth 530
Ancira, Ernesto Jr. 45
Andereck, Mike 170
Andersen, Myron 160
Andersen, Ralph E. 466
Andersen, Sarah J. 46
Anderson, Brian (Allina Hospitals) 33
Anderson, Brian (ContiGroup) 137
Anderson, Bruce 404
Anderson, Cathy C. 487
Anderson, Cevin 247
Anderson, Chris 254
Anderson, Craig 441
Anderson, David
  (Cincinnati Children's Hospital) 120
Anderson, David R.
  (American Family Insurance) 37
Anderson, Davis 218
Anderson, Derrick 222
Anderson, Douglas L. 335
Anderson, Duwayn 423
Anderson, Eugene K. 137
Anderson, Gregory R. 472
Anderson, J. William 92
Anderson, James G.
  (Mayo Foundation) 318
Anderson, James M.
  (Cincinnati Children's Hospital) 120
Anderson, John E. 479
Anderson, Julie 524
Anderson, Kathy 47
Anderson, Kenneth L. 338
Anderson, Lee R. Sr. 47
Anderson, Mark 334
Anderson, N. Christian III 199

Anderson, R. John 294
Anderson, Richard 177
Anderson, Robert 210
Anderson, Ross B. 29
Anderson, Tom 413
Anderson, Vicki L. 130
Anderson, Walter 21
Anderson, William 412
Anderton, Denise 334
Andoga, James R. 60
Andrada, Marissa 516
Andree, Timothy P. 350
Andrews, Bill 215
Andrews, Charles 351
Andrews, Duane P. 438
Andrews, Paul E. Jr. 488
Andrews, R. Michael Jr. 92
Andruk, Debbie 391
Angel Davila, Miguel 299
Angell, Dwight 233
Anger, Michael 474
Anglade, Pierre B. 404
Anglin, David M. 400
Annastas, Tom 82
Annetta, John 157
Annexstad, Al 189
Anslow, Brandie 168
Anson, Mark J.P. 98
Anstrom, Decker 288
Anthony, Paula 182
Anton, Arthur F. 466
Antonelli, Jeff 414
Antonovich, Mike 385
Antonvich, Mark S. 418
Apallas, Yeoryios 383
Apatoff, Robert S. 413
Apelqvist, Mimi 477
Apperson, Kevin 31
Appleby, Anne F. 376
Appleby, C.G. 85
Aramony, Diane M. 344
Archambault, Rob 400
Archbold, Rodolfo 374
Archey, Paul 306
Archibald, Ed 328
Arenas, Andrea-Teresa 510
Argilla, Luke P. 467
Ark, Jennifer 216
Armacost, Samuel H. 457
Armada, Anthony 233
Armato, Carl 374
Armour, Peter A. 21
Armstrong, Graeme D. 268
Armstrong, Lloyd Jr. 507
Armstrong, Murray 20
Armstrong, Scott 218
Armus, Steve 306
Arnesen, Jon A. 339
Arneson, Allen D. 510
Arnold, Douglas S. 537
Arnold, Eldon R. 145
Arnold, Elizabeth 177
Arnold, Gregory A. 485
Arnold, James 217

INDEX OF EXECUTIVES

Arnold, Scott 397
Arnold, Truman 485
Arnst, Thomas W. 429
Aronson, Jacquelin 493
Arrigo, Joseph F. 493
Arroyo, F. Thaddeus 121
Arthur, Yoko N. 140
Arves, Scott 435
Ascher, David 368
Ascher, Michael C. 333
Ash, Darron 236
Ashcroft, Brian 286
Ashcroft, Timothy 522
Asher, James M. 231
Ashley, Roger 22
Ashworth, Dave
  (Texas Health Resources) 473
Ashworth, David (Memec) 326
Ashworth, Ronald B. 449
Asimou, John G. 417
Asplundh, Christopher B. 54
Asplundh, Scott M. 54
Astor, Janet 92
Astrup, Tom 36
Atamanchuk, Steve 450
Atkins, Kelly 55
Atkins, William 255
Atkinson, Anne 17
Atkinson, Kelly 149
Atkinson, Ray 519
Atkinson, Susan 462
Attaway, John A. Jr. 407
Atterbury, Rick R. 329
Audiffred, J. Douglas 319
Auer, Nancy J. 467
Aufdenspring, Michael 111
Aulbaugh, Carrol 326
Ausikaitis, Joseph P. 510
Austin, Michael C. 515
Austin, Wanda M. 25
Autry, E. R. Jr. 483
Autry, Glenn T. 192
Avagliano, John 528
Avakian, Laura 337
Avent, Ernest 318
Avery, Pat 272
Aviles, Alan D. 363
Avner, Kenneth 229
Ayers, Vic 35
Azarela, Michael 464
Azedo, Gabriel 213
Aznoian, Nicholas D. 374
Azuma, Yuki 363
Azzarelli, Tom 401

B

Baart, Paul R. 404
Babcock, Theodore A. 479
Bachman, Paul 512
Backes, Brent L. 170
Backman, Wayne 67
Backus, David L. 387
Bacon, Bruce W. 244
Bacon, Richard 266
Badame, Jay 478
Bader, Glenn 437
Baemmert, Joseph 215
Baer, Donald A. 159
Baer, Jakob 285
Baer, Jill Q. 313
Baer, Max 427
Bagley Marrett, Cora B. 510
Baglieon, Jerry 151
Bagne, Conrad 48
Bahlmann, Jerome R. 68
Bahr, Mark A. 66
Bailes, Joseph S. 512
Bailey, Bill (Shapell Industries) 444
Bailey, Bill (Yucaipa) 541
Bailey, Jack A. 491

Bailey, Michael J.
  (JohnsonDiversey) 268
Bailey, Michael L. (Jostens) 271
Baillie, Kenneth 430
Bain, Mark 34
Bain, William W. Jr. 516
Baird, Cary 114
Baird, J. David 185
Baird, Richard L. 404
Baker, David H. 52
Baker, Dennis 113
Baker, Donald I. 462
Baker, Gail F. 502
Baker, James (Flying J) 193
Baker, James A. III (Carlyle Group) 104
Baker, John J.
  (National Wine & Spirits) 358
Baker, Jon
  (Meridian Automotive Systems) 329
Baker, Joseph P. 38
Baker, Kenneth W.R. 471
Baker, Lenox D. Jr. 266
Baker, Leslie 253
Baker, Mark (Nikken) 370
Baker, Mark R.
  (Holiday Companies) 239
Baker, Paul M. 494
Baker, Stuart 408
Baker, W. Kirk 244
Bakk, Kal 441
Baldauf, Larry 205
Balderston, Tom 465
Baldwin, David A. 335
Balgrosky, Jean 440
Balik, Barbara 33
Ball, Andrew J. 531
Ball, J. Fred 58
Ball, Jon W. 234
Ballenger, Keith 23
Ballhaus, Wiliam F. Jr. 25
Ballinger, Dean 244
Ballinger, Royce 505
Ballweg, Ruth 218
Balseca, Gallo 414
Baltagi, Salim 93
Baltz, Jeffrey D. 47
Baltz, Phyllis 130
Bane, Dan 481
Banerji, Ashis 510
Bangel, Edward 147
Banis, William J. 373
Banks, Glen B. 197
Banos, Leonard C. 62
Bansley, Jodi 265
Bantz, Charles R. 251
Baranowski, Roger 223
Baranowski, Shelley 120
Baraya, Donna 444
Barbe, Scott 326
Barbee, Ray 424
Barber, Barry 213
Barber, Carrie L. 151
Barber, Mary 337
Barber, Ralph 239
Barber, Roger L. 439
Barber, Steven 463
Barber, Tina 51
Barberio, Mark G. 309
Barbour, Debra 448
Barceló, Nancy 509
Barchi, Robert L. 505
Barclay, Richard 53
Barden, Peter A. 365
Bardgett, Edward R. 541
Barefield, Thomas A. 377
Barghahn, Lisa 454
Bargmann, Mike 531
Barham, Peter Derald 265
Barham, Thomas 539
Barker, Clarence W. 261
Barker, Karen 296
Barker, Myra O. 312
Barker, Paul 223

Barkey, Dennis 410
Barlow, Charles 449
Barlow, Ron 215
Barman, Bruce G. 440
Barnacal, Wayne 246
Barnard, Douglas C. 113
Barnard, H. Frederick III 496
Barnes, James 398
Barnes, R. E. 311
Barnes, William Page 49
Barneson, Dale 53
Barnett, Hoyt R. 407
Barnett, Jenny 119
Barnett, Kerry 415
Barnett, Martha W. 239
Barnett, Preston B. 141
Barney, Isabel 33
Barney, Steven M. 458
Barnhart, Jim 390
Barnhill, Mark 400
Baron, Michael 425
Barone, Robert J. 82
Barr, Jonathan 312
Barr, Thomas V. 85
Barrath, Paul 227
Barrera-Moses, Sylvia 19
Barrett, David J. 231
Barrett, Douglas J. 502
Barrett, Scott 264
Barrow, Judy 358
Barry, Clifford 128
Barry, John J. 404
Barry, Richard F. III 288
Barry, Tom 447
Bartels, Robert 18
Barth, Anthony S. 154
Barthels, Trudy C. 52
Bartholomew, Dana 60
Bartholomew, Kevin 73
Bartlett, Paul D. Jr. 65
Bartley, George B. 318
Barton, Anthony J. 489
Barton, Brad 401
Barton, Carol G. 193
Barton, Dominic 321
Barton, John R. 41
Barton, R. Gregory 517
Barton, Robert H. III 329
Barton, Sharron 428
Barwick, Steve 218
Basalone, Jon 481
Bash, David 217
Basha, Edward N. Jr. 66
Basil-Jones, Stephen 166
Basile, Tony 397
Basl, Dane 445
Bassett, Carol 430
Bassett, W. Todd 430
Basso, Cory J. 228
Bastiaens, F. Guillaume 101
Basye, George 25
Batchelder, John 534
Bateman, Nigel 481
Batey, Dennis 186
Batory, Ronald L. 134
Battaglia, Joseph C. 34
Battaglini, Rick 265
Batten, Frank Jr.
  (Landmark Communications) 288
Batten, Frank Sr.
  (Landmark Communications) 288
Batten, George 522
Battersby, Graham 192
Bauckham, Anthony E. 184
Bauer, Brett C. 88
Bauer, Brian T. 184
Bauer, Elaine 107
Bauer, Fred 523
Bauer, Timothy J. 382
Baugh, Mark 234
Baughn, Charles M. 237
Bauman, William J. 20
Baumann, Brian K. 418

Baus, Stephen B. 400
Bausch, Thomas P. 418
Bavely, Don 425
Baxley, David 142
Baxter, Joanne 64
Baxter, Raymond J. 273
Bayer, James W. 178
Bayer, Kevin 443
Bayly, George V. 511
Baytosh, David 158
Beadie, William M. 47
Beadle, John 437
Beake, Robert 444
Beal, Brad 265
Beal, David 26
Beam, Craig T. 39
Beam, David L. 371
Beaman, Ted 332
Bean, Robert E. 193
Beard, Grant 483
Bearnson, Brad H. 248
Bearrows, Thomas R. 502
Beary, Sue 437
Beasley, J. D. 488
Beasley, John 394
Beatrice, Dennis 457
Beattie, Richard I.
  (Memorial Sloan-Kettering) 327
Beattie, Richard I.
  (Simpson Thacher) 449
Beatty, Paul F. 244
Beaty, Mark 426
Beauchamp, Patricia 392
Beaudry, Steve 477
Beaver, Don 228
Beaver, George 249
Beazley, Eric 256
Bechel, Brad 47
Bechtel, Riley P. 71
Bechtel, Stephen D. Jr. 71
Beck, Clyde 440
Beck, Deborah A. 372
Beck, Gregory 227
Beck, Henry C. III 71
Beck, Jim 201
Beck, Joseph 111
Beck, Klaus-Dieter 198
Beck, Robin H. 505
Beck, S. Fred 248
Becker, Howard C. 377
Becker, Joseph 324
Becker, Kenneth A. 107
Becker, Norbert R. 180
Becker, Norman P. 49
Becker, Robert G. 154
Becker, Russell 47
Becker, Steve 208
Becker, Steven 454
Becker, Tom 217
Beckert, John A. 125
Beckert, Richard N. 125
Beckley, William H. 372
Beckman, Jerry 193
Beckman, John 368
Beckman, Richard D. 21
Beckmann, James K. Jr. 52
Bednarowski, Keith 380
Beeler, Don A. 19
Beeler, Ralph Brent 88
Beeman, William 147
Beemer, Pamela S. 334
Beer, Gary 452
Beeson, G. Robinson 212
Beeson, Particia 506
Beeson, Thomas 87
Beggs, Colin 404
Beha, Ralph 102
Behnke, Michael C. 501
Behr, Joan 197
Beidleman, Richard J. 515
Beier, Gregory J. 374
Belck, Nancy 505
Belek, Marilyn 154

HOOVER'S HANDBOOK OF PRIVATE COMPANIES 2005

INDEX OF EXECUTIVES

Belk, H. W. McKay 72
Belk, John R. 72
Belk, Thomas M. Jr. 72
Bell, Alan J. 199
Bell, Bonnie 473
Bell, Bradley J. 347
Bell, Charlie 247
Bell, Christy W. 241
Bell, Darren 479
Bell, Ernie 527
Bell, Michael A. 384
Bell, Robert V. 255
Bell, Stephen M. 194
Bellando, John 21
Belletto, Owen W. 465
Bellis, Arnold M. 365
Bello, Eric 290
Bellows, Keith 354
Belsaas, Scott 267
Bemis, Dennis 383
Benanav, Gary G. 364
Bencivenga, Janet 161
Benck, Dick 496
Bender, Bill 98
Bender, Lisa R. 338
Bender, Thomas V. 328
Bengali, Abdul 318
Benjamin, Alan 299
Benjamin, Deborah E. 489
Benjamin, Harvey E. 350
Benjamin, James 64
Bennack, Frank A. Jr. 231
Bennett, Barbara 159
Bennett, Chuck 250
Bennett, Clive 213
Bennett, Craig 515
Bennett, Ed (NASCAR) 348
Bennett, Edgar
  (Green Bay Packers) 216
Bennett, Gary 477
Bennett, Joel H. 388
Bennett, Lerone Jr. 267
Bennett, Paul (Utility Trailer) 515
Bennett, Paul B. (NYSE) 367
Bennett, Ruth B. 84
Bennett, Tim 225
Bennington, Graham 48
Benson, Robert K. 43
Benton, David F. 289
Benton, Mike 360
Benton, W.D. 36
Benzel, Craig 216
Benzing, William 249
Bercu, Nanette 265
Berdan, Robert J. 372
Berenson, Marvin 82
Beres, Cathy 250
Berg, David A. 36
Berg, Thomas G. 43
Bergen, David G. 294
Bergen, Timothy 446
Berger, Darryl D. 516
Berger, Jeff H. 71
Berger, Laurence J. 369
Bergeron, Kayla 403
Bergland, Bruce W. 251
Bergman, Larry 86
Bergman, Marilyn 51
Bergman, Michelle D. 169
Bergman, Robin 252
Bergstein, Alan 258
Berk, Amy 539
Berkeley, Linda 354
Berkhimer, Joann 397
Berman, Ann E. 226
Bermingham, Robert P. 541
Bernandes, Ricardo 97
Bernanke, Ben S. 188
Bernard, Dane 276
Bernard, Pamela J. 502
Bernard, Peter J. 83
Bernard, Richard P. 367
Bernardi, Kenneth E. 154

Bernd, David L. 442
Berndt, Bryan 299
Berndt, Ellen G. 85
Berne, Robert 368
Bernecker, Bill 59
Berner, Mary G. 21
Bernhard, Alexander 87
Bernick, Alan 46
Berning, Mel 17
Bernstein, Alison R. 196
Bernstein, Carolyn 530
Bernstein, Dale B. 367
Bernstein, Robert E. 89
Berquist, Thomas H. 318
Berresford, Susan V. 196
Berry, G. Dennis 141
Berry, Roger J. 338
Berry, William E. 41
Berry Pigott, Carol 82
Bersch, Neil R. 423
Bertolino, Margaret H. 29
Berube, S. Neal 55
Besand, Roy 534
Bescalli, Linda 537
Beshire, Bambi 534
Best, J. Kirby 254
Best, Kent 473
Betaharon, Khodadad 255
Bettman, Gary B. 355
Bevelhymer, Darrell W. 471
Bevilaqua, Joseph P. 85
Bevis, Harold C. 400
Beyer, Greg 204
Beyer, Rick 170
Beyreis, Jim 494
Bezansen, Robert H. 142
Bezney, Michael A. 109
Bhatia, Joe 494
Bianchi, Franco 227
Bibb, Bob 530
Bible, Michael 203
Bichel, Susan 217
Biddle, Corby 199
Bieber, Martin A. 109
Biele, Charlie 266
Bienen, Henry S. 373
Bienstock, Sabrina 138
Biewinga, Willy A. 154
Bignon, Patrick 180
Bikowitz, Paul 462
Bilardi, Matthew 119
Bilik, Jerry 190
Billard, William T. 155
Billet, Van 74
Billiel, Jack 244
Billig, Erwin H. 416
Bilotti, Gary 43
Bilous, O. B. 441
Bing, Richard N. 368
Bingle, Glenn J. 130
Binion, Jack B. 242
Biondi, Ray 428
Biondolillo, Michael A. 392
Bird, Stefan 335
Birenbaum, James 432
Birgfeld, Steve 131
Birk, Peggy J. 189
Birtley, Andrew 203
Bisciotti, Steve 31
Biscoe, Scott 138
Bishop, Stephen P. 203
Bishop, Warren 259
Bitner, Livia 64
Bittenbender, Tom 221
Bitting, Nancy 390
Biunno, Susan 89
Biviano, Michael A. 106
Bizer, Brian 383
Bizzotto, Anita J. 513
Blabey, David E. 365
Black, Andrew W. 271
Black, Anita 510
Black, Carole 297

Black, Cathleen P. 231
Black, Diane 321
Black, Gail 90
Black, Kenneth 199
Black, Lawrence H. 382
Black, Maria 279
Black, Robert W. 431
Blackburn, Gene 26
Blackburn, Larry 208
Blackmon, Charles 257
Blackshear, A.T. Jr. 326
Blackwell, Ron 26
Blagg, Shannon 394
Blaik, Omar H. 505
Blaine, Dorman 540
Blaine, William 176
Blair, Andrew R. 506
Blair, Jeff 223
Blair, Richard S. 119
Blais, David 409
Blake, Patricia 489
Blan, Gary J. 307
Blanchard, A. J. 19
Blanchard, Michael D. 479
Blanchard, Rick 202
Blandon, Betty Ann 94
Blanks, Dan H. 236
Blanks, Marvin III 540
Blanton, Andy 318
Blanton, Doug 249
Blaszyk, Michael D. 110
Blatt, Mitchell 126
Blauvelt, James A. 528
Blechman, Michael 270
Bledsoe, Tom 348
Blei, Peter 33
Bleiberg, Fred 351
Blickman, Fred 230
Blom, David P. 379
Blom-Antonio, La Donna R. 23
Blood, Charles H. 92
Bloom, Jill 296
Bloom, Kenneth L. 56
Bloom, Michael W. 339
Bloom, Steven E. 178
Bloom, Ted 258
Bloomberg, Michael R. 78
Bloome, Chuck 122
Blough, Rick 276
Bluestein, Paul A. 133
Bluhm, Nicholas C. 103
Bluhm, Robert 223
Blum, Don 532
Blumb, Jeff 216
Blundin, John L. 32
Bo-Linn, George 110
Board, Anne 321
Boardman, William P. 523
Bobowicz, Jay 231
Bodaken, Bruce G. 81
Bodden, Michael J. 417
Bodenheimer, George W. 181
Bodzewski, Michael C. 20
Boe, Ralph 70
Boeckmann, Beau 201
Boeckmann, Brad 201
Boeckmann, Herbert F. II 201
Boeckmann, Karl 201
Boedeker, Michael A. 377
Boehlert, Thomas 450
Bogage, David I. 226
Bogard, Carroll 391
Bogardas, Joe 79
Bogdanov, Vladmir 33
Boggs, Brucie 101
Boggs, Lynn I. 374
Bogossian, Gail 133
Bohan, Lynne M. 244
Bohlen, Bruce F. 402
Bohuny, Kim 350
Bokas, Deno G. 44
Bokman, Amanda J. 261
Bokser, Stephen R. 157

Bolch, Carl E. Jr. 412
Bolen, Michael D. 319
Boler, Heather 119
Bollinger, Lee C. 129
Bolotin, Andra S. 401
Bolten, Robert 238
Bolton, Jeffrey W. 318
Bolton, M. Clare 404
Bonach, Edward J. 356
Bond, Ed 447
Bond, Linda 430
Bonderman, David 475
Bondy, Timothy J. 176
Bonewell, Linda 397
Bong, Francis S. Y. 24
Bonham, Jennifer 496
Bonitati, Roland 193
Bonno, Anthony J. 384
Bonow, Robert O. 39
Boodjeh, Donald 158
Boodjeh, Douglas 158
Boodjeh, Parviz 158
Book, Eric 81
Boorman, Paul 404
Booth, Scott G. 212
Boots, Ira G. 88
Boozer, Renea 118
Borak, John M. 356
Borba, George 96
Borders, Jim 142
Bordovsky, Khaki 90
Borella, Rob 205
Borer, Mark A. 170
Borg, Frank 222
Borgia, Larry 332
Borgman, Dick 293
Borman, Laurie 413
Bornmann, David E. 407
Borrok, Charles R. 145
Boruch, Daniel M. 57
Bos, Gerald 146
Bosanko, Mark L. 347
Bosch, Scott 64
Boschulte, R.D. 37
Bosco, Anthony J. Jr. 151
Boscov, Albert R. 86
Bose, Amar G. 87
Bosh, Larry 430
Boshwit, Susan 302
Bosman, Ruud H. 193
Bossmann, Lori L. 20
Boston, Terry 491
Boswell, John 432
Botch, Jim 463
Botham, Lydia 287
Bottorff, Dennis C. 516
Botwin, Will 454
Botz, Janet M. 164
Bouche, Ron 38
Boucher, David 535
Boucher, Jonathan F. 270
Boucher, Mark E. 208
Bouckaert, Carl M. 70
Boudreaux, Bernard 330
Boudreaux, Gail K. 229
Boulden, Al 440
Boulenger, Bo 64
Boulis, Paul 229
Boulos, Paul F. 346
Boulter, Philip R. 489
Boulware, Bruce 379
Bouma, Brian 16
Bourgeois, Richard D. 315
Bourland, Ron 473
Bourrie, Sally Ruth 524
Bouvier, Robert 470
Bovaird, Orlene 204
Bowe, William J. 177
Bowen, David 81
Bowen, R. Allen 377
Bowen, Scott 163
Bower, Curtis A. 387
Bowers, Brian 435

INDEX OF EXECUTIVES

Bowker, Will 396
Bowles, Debra 81
Bowles, John 531
Bowman, Jane 356
Bowman, Leslie C 156
Bowman, Robert A. 306
Bowron, Robert 447
Bowyer, Christopher J. 164
Boyce, Robert A. Jr. 492
Boyd, David R. 531
Boyd, Donald 273
Boyd, Kerry 531
Boyd, M. Delen 62
Boyd, Marvin 397
Boyd, Michael N.M. 180
Boyd, Stuart D. 276
Boyd, William A. 346
Boyden, Brian V. 460
Boyer, Alan 241
Boyer, Aurelia G. 369
Boyer, Edward 83
Boyer, Paul 325
Boyette, Judith 500
Boylan, Christopher P. 333
Boyle, Alexander R.M. 117
Boyle, John W. 426
Boyle, Marsilia 292
Boyle, Peter 51
Boyle, Philip 107
Boyle, R. Emmett 381
Boyles, Terry 320
Bozzelli, Richard L. 174
Bozzuto, Michael A. 88
Brabec, Todd 51
Brace, Rod 326
Bracken, Wayne 64
Brackett, Mark 118
Braddock, David L. 251
Bradford, Charlie 351
Bradford, Earle L. Jr. 107
Bradley, Amy 132
Bradley, Andrew 496
Bradley, Connie 51
Bradley, John J. 491
Bradley, Kathleen G. (Knoll) 280
Bradley, Kathy (NextiraOne) 369
Bradley, Michael J. 170
Bradley, R. Bruce 288
Bradley, Rickford D. 121
Bradshaw, Les 96
Brady, Michael 365
Brady, Patricia A. 510
Brake, John 170
Brakken, William 289
Braly, John M. 489
Braman, Norman 89
Branco, Patrick 390
Brand, Julian 250
Brandes, Mark 112
Brandt, Andrew 216
Brandt, David H. 124
Brandt, Kate 52
Brandt, Ron 259
Brandt, Sandy 20
Brantley, Mitch 318
Brantley, Sherry 419
Braschwitz, Charles 323
Brasher, Paul V. 404
Brassell, David 122
Brasuell, Thomas C. 306
Bratches, Sean H. R. 181
Braun, Chris 270
Braunstein, Sandra F. 188
Bravo, Charles E. 513
Bravo, Fred M. 257
Bray, Michael E. 479
Bready, Richard L. 370
Breard, Jack H. Jr. 174
Bredenkoetter, William 436
Brehm, Leonard 213
Brehm, Sharon S. 251
Brei, Linda 510
Bremer, John M. 372
Bren, Donald L. 261

Brendan, Norman 127
Breneisen, William 344
Brenk, Eric 398
Brennan, Anne 147
Brennan, John J. 517
Brenneman, Gregory D. 94
Brenner, Harry J. 144
Breon, Richard C. 455
Brereton, Michael 308
Breslin, Brian 325
Bresnahan, Vikki 265
Bress, Joseph M. 44
Bresten, Theresa M. 244
Brett, James 46
Brettingen, Tom 57
Brewer, Bob 55
Brewer, Jackie 337
Brewer, Paul 289
Brewster, James 22
Brezina, Michael 149
Brians, Chet 531
Brick, Errol D. 323
Brick, Kathryn 511
Brickman, Jeffrey L. 406
Brickman, Linda 89
Bridges, David (Arkansas Blue Cross
  and Blue Shield) 50
Bridges, David E. (Publix) 407
Bridges, Holly 507
Bridges, Jon 118
Bridgewater-Alford, Florida 502
Briede, Michelle 16
Brier, Bonnie 118
Briggs, John 247
Briggs, Robert E. 273
Bright, David 280
Brill, John D. 402
Brimberry, Andrew 119
Brindley, Gilbert S. 157
Brinkley, Alan 129
Brinks, Scott T. 203
Brinson, Jose 249
Briski, Kathy 400
Brisky, Lauren J. 516
Brisley, Peter O. 280
Bristol, Walter D. Jr. 39
Britt, Bill 416
Britt, Jack H. 507
Britton, Lynn 449
Britz, Robert G. 367
Broatch, Robert E. 220
Brock, Dan 88
Brockway, Robert 241
Brodd, Ulf 181
Broder, Jonathan M. 134
Brodie, Nancy S. 392
Brodish, Jay D. 404
Brodsky, Howard 111
Brodsky, Peter S. 236
Brody, David H. 124
Brody, John (Jockey International) 265
Brody, John S.
  (Major League Baseball) 306
Brody, Paul 256
Brody, William R. 266
Broeksmit, Robert D. 117
Broerman, Rob 442
Brogan, Stephen J. 268
Brogna, Randall 235
Bromberg, Mark L. 332
Bronfin, Kenneth A. 231
Bronfman, Edgar Jr. 528
Brooke, Beth A. 180
Brooke, F. Dixon Jr. 174
Brooks, Edward 197
Brooks, Gary 524
Brooks, George H. 510
Brooks, Kenneth C. 267
Brooks, Lynn 483
Brooks, Martin 305
Brooks, Paul 348
Brooks, Sue 278
Brooks, Tim 297

Brookshire, Brad 92
Brookshire, Britt 92
Brookshire, Bruce G. 92
Brookshire, Mark 92
Brookshire, Tim 92
Broomall, Vernon H. 525
Broome, Anne C. 500
Broomell, John 302
Brose, Bryan 189
Brosnan, Timothy J. 306
Brothers, Gary 147
Brough, Joseph 248
Broughton, Joan 416
Brouillard, Jack C. 228
Broun, Elizabeth 452
Broussard, Bruce D. 512
Brover, Barry 65
Brower, David B. 334
Brower, Stephen M. 280
Brown, Brad (Austin Industries) 60
Brown, Brad (REI) 416
Brown, Colin 264
Brown, Daniel K. 41
Brown, Dennis 260
Brown, Ellen 209
Brown, J. Frank 404
Brown, Jack H. 462
Brown, Jay 160
Brown, Jeremy J. 344
Brown, Kathryn F. 504
Brown, Keith 38
Brown, Kevin (Sinclair Oil) 449
Brown, Kevin
  (Swedish Health Services) 467
Brown, Loren 103
Brown, Lynne P. 368
Brown, Marjorie J. 271
Brown, Mark F. 339
Brown, Mike (Arkansas Blue Cross
  and Blue Shield) 50
Brown, Mike
  (Freedom Communications) 199
Brown, Nancy A.
  (American Heart Association) 39
Brown, Nancy G.
  (Borden Chemical) 85
Brown, Nathaniel T. 526
Brown, Paul F. 79
Brown, Robert A. 337
Brown, Sandra K. 472
Brown, Scott 222
Brown, Stephen S. 102
Brown, Tom 191
Brown, Tonya M. 508
Brown, Tracy 439
Brown, Vincent P. 99
Brown, Warren 519
Brown, William A.
  (Provena Health) 406
Brown, Willie
  (State Farm Insurance) 460
Brown Garrity, Deborah 95
Browne, Joe 352
Browne, Julian 104
Browne, Michael 327
Browne, Sherry L. 52
Browning, Robert 142
Bruce, Jessica 57
Bruce, Joe 397
Bruce, Nick 114
Bruce, Peter W. 372
Bruce, Thomas W. 138
Bruder, John F. 336
Bruehl, Edna V. 23
Bruininks, Robert H. 504
Brummer, Debra 344
Brunelle, David 74
Bruner, Sam 148
Brunner, Kim M. 460
Bruno, Joe 471
Brunson, Daniel 199
Brunstetter, Peter S. 374
Bruskin, Marcy 199

Bryan, Hugh H. 257
Bryant, Bill 253
Bryant, C. E. Jr. 361
Bryant, David O. 280
Bryant, Del 82
Bryant, Terry 140
Bryce, David T. 284
Bryja, James J. 198
Brysha, Andre 420
Bryson, Louise Henry 297
Bröcker, Willem L.J. 404
Buchanan, Todd 520
Buchli, James F. 498
Buck, Rodney A. 356
Buckalew, Steve 218
Buckley, Jean 163
Buckley, Ken 401
Buckley, Mike 163
Buckley, Mortimer J. 517
Buckley, Steve 423
Buckley, Susan C. 502
Buckman, Michael A. 539
Buckner, William A. 101
Buehrle, John 351
Buenrostro, Fred R. Jr. 98
Buettner, Larry 199
Buffenbarger, R. Thomas 26
Bufferd, Allan S. 337
Buhay, Robert 369
Buhl, Jay 42
Buhr, James 66
Buie, James C. Jr. 237
Bujack, Denise A. 229
Buker, Ed 122
Bulger, Michael 85
Bullins, Jerry L. 280
Bulloch, Kelly 281
Bullock, David W. 492
Bullock, Robert 114
Bulman, Lyn 190
Bumstead, Gantt 499
Bumstead, Matt 499
Bunce, David 285
Bunch, Diane 491
Bundgard, Susan 342
Bunn, Graham 411
Bunnell, Dave 437
Bunnell, Ron 64
Bunnell, Steven 299
Bunsick, Robert 210
Bunting, Clark 159
Buonomo, James R. 374
Burchill, Jeffrey A. 193
Burd, Loretta M. 145
Burdick, Ginny R. 130
Burdick, Henry S. 235
Burditt, Scott 511
Burger, Frances 518
Burgess, Richard S. 100
Burgett, Paul J. 506
Burgher, Cedric W. 94
Burgis, Judith E. 421
Burgo, Raymond 205
Burgon, Barre G. 193
Burish, Thomas G. 35
Burke, Edwin M. 327
Burke, George K. Jr. 465
Burke, Julie 449
Burke, Kent 524
Burke, Patti 166
Burke, Richard (Fallon Community
  Health Plan Inc.) 186
Burke, Richard A. (Quad/Graphics) 409
Burke, Russell J. 382
Burke, Sheila 452
Burke, Vince G. 223
Burkett, Lawrence V. Jr. 315
Burkhammer, Stephen 227
Burkhardt, Robert 511
Burkhardt, Roger 367
Burkhart, Mark 126
Burkle, Ronald W. 541
Burks, Janie 524

HOOVER'S HANDBOOK OF PRIVATE COMPANIES 2005

INDEX OF EXECUTIVES

Burnell, Karen 48
Burnett, Mark 38
Burnett, Nancy Packard 385
Burns, Allen L. 84
Burns, Amy T. 491
Burns, Donal 505
Burns, Edward 338
Burns, Jeff Jr. 267
Burns, Jerry N. 36
Burns, Kenneth R. 360
Burns, Patrick A. 344
Burns, Robert E. 60
Burns, Stephanie A. 164
Burns, Thomas P. 336
Burr, Tracy 437
Burrell, James 178
Burrin, Stephen E. 25
Burris, Mary Ellen 531
Bursch, H. Dean 135
Burstein, Mark 405
Burt, Rick 71
Burton, Bonnie 274
Burton, Cordell 391
Burton, Eve 231
Burzynski, Julian 537
Busby, A. Patrick 179
Bush, Brad 204
Bush, Kenny 540
Bush, Scott 308
Bushaw, Dewey P. 384
Bushman, Randall A. 281
Buss, Timothy 354
Bussa, Thomas 180
Bussani, Piero 185
Bussy, Susan 449
Butcher, Ernesto L. 402
Buth, Douglas P. 48
Butkovic, Michael R. 466
Butler, Gary 92
Butler, James E. Jr. 519
Butler, Michael 406
Butler, Pat 139
Butt, Charles C. 228
Butt, Stephen 228
Butte, Amy S. 367
Butterfield, Barbara S. 503
Buttermore, John A. 212
Buxton, Sarah L. 189
Buzacazro, Victor 440
Byers, Deborah 480
Byington, Sue 406
Bykerk, Cecil D. 345
Bynum, Joseph R. 491
Byrd, Arthur J. 230
Byrne, Brian 297
Byrne, J. Timothy 297
Byrne, Joseph E. 368
Byrnes, John 455
Byron, Ernest S. 284
Bürkner, Hans-Paul 87

C

Cabe, Robert 50
Cabrera, Carlos A. 510
Caccamo, Joseph 112
Cadieux, Chester (QuikTrip) 410
Cadieux, Chester Jr (QuikTrip) 410
Cadima, Manny 202
Caesar, Christopher F. 42
Caffey, Bill R. 281
Cagle, David 255
Cahill, Douglas J. 160
Cahill, Patrick T. 155
Cain, Delmar 472
Caine, Ed 417
Caiola, Vincent J. 289
Calamari, Mathew F. 486
Calbert, Robert 319
Caldarello, Becky 174
Caldera, Louis E. 97
Caldwell, Sylvia H. 491

Calhoun, Edwin L. 234
Calhoun, Jay S. 364
Calhoun, Kendra 33
Calkins, Dan 148
Call, Jeff 47
Callahan, Bernard B. 354
Callahan, Bob 47
Callahan, Dennis S. 220
Callahan, John W. 194
Callahan, Richard P. 382
Callaway, Harold 26
Callery, T. Grant 349
Calver, Tracey A. 430
Calvert, Bruce W. 32
Calvert, Karen 312
Calvert, Stanton C. 472
Calvin, John 143
Calzetti-Spahr, Melanie 194
Camacho, Donna J. 28
Camden, Hugh 182
Camerlo, Tom 146
Cammack, Randy 470
Camp, David C. 459
Campa, Luz 380
Campagna, George 33
Campbell, Brett 269
Campbell, Colin 355
Campbell, David 320
Campbell, James 33
Campbell, Jerry D. 507
Campbell, John (H-E-B) 228
Campbell, John B. (Ag Processing) 27
Campbell, John W.
 (Horizon Blue Cross Blue Shield
 of New Jersey) 241
Campbell, Judith E. 364
Campbell, Keith M. 336
Campbell, Kevin P. 244
Campbell, Paul V. 303
Campbell, Robert 240
Campbell, William
 (Horizon Natural Resources) 242
Campbell, William M. III
 (Discovery Communications) 159
Campion, Janet 30
Campsey, David 26
Camrud, Sue 173
Candela, Bob 51
Candilora, Vincent 51
Candio, Vince 29
Candito, Tony 481
Cannito, Peter A. 333
Cannon, Carl N. 340
Cannon, Fred 82
Cannon, Robert W. 77
Canter, Rick 456
Canty, Stephen D. 305
Cap, Brent 262
Capaldi, Elizabeth D. 461
Capelli, Christopher 506
Caple, Bill 498
Caporale, Michael J. Jr. 56
Capp, Brian 293
Cappy, Ralph J. 506
Capsuto, Allen 305
Caputo, Louise 112
Carbonell, Joaquin R. III 121
Card, Larry J. 384
Cardwell, James A. Sr.
 (Petro Stopping Centers) 396
Cardwell, James A. Jr.
 (Petro Stopping Centers) 396
Cargill, Jerry 207
Cargill, John 238
Carhart, James P. 515
Cariss, Bill 240
Carl, David 58
Carlin, Andy 239
Carlini, Anthony 134
Carlos, Chris 351
Carlos, John A. 351
Carlson, Bruce W. 153
Carlson, Christopher A. 377

Carlson, Curtis R. 457
Carlson, Margaret Kemp 126
Carlson, Samuel E. 386
Carlson Nelson, Marilyn 102
Carlsson, Soren 213
Carlton, Craig K. 55
Carlucci, Frank C. 104
Carmen, Robert G. 22
Carmichael, David R. 384
Carmony, Robert F. 121
Carnaroli, Craig 505
Carnes, Debbie 26
Carney, Christopher M. 83
Carney, Jeffrey R. 194
Carothers, Jay 294
Carpenter, John A. 237
Carr, Larry 371
Carr, Steve 218
Carrico, Stephen J. 234
Carrier, Carol 504
Carrier, Patrick B. 119
Carrington, Mark 342
Carrino, Frank A. 534
Carrion, Esperanza 211
Carroll, Charles A.
 (Goodman Manufacturing) 208
Carroll, Charles E. (WL Gore) 538
Carroll, David S. 242
Carroll, Gerard 362
Carroll, James F. 146
Carroll, John (Cumberland Farms) 144
Carroll, John F. (Amsted) 43
Carroll, Kathleen 57
Carroll, Matt 64
Carroll, Patrick 298
Carroll, William F. 133
Carrosino, John L. 55
Carson, Russell L. 49
Carstensen, Tonny F. 160
Carte, C. Adam 479
Carter, C. Michael 162
Carter, Cletus 356
Carter, Donald J. Jr. 241
Carter, Ed 346
Carter, Kenneth W. 427
Carter, L. Susan 334
Carter, Mark 103
Carter, Mary D. 46
Carter, Mary Ann 107
Carter, Rosalind Clay 17
Carter, Terry 410
Carter, William H. 85
Carter Urschel, Christina L. 241
Cartin, James 59
Cartland, Wendy 279
Cartledge, George B. Jr. 101
Caruso, Joseph A. 220
Caruso, Stephen 193
Carver, Dan 93
Carvette, Anthony M. 463
Casale, Cynthia L. 515
Casebeer, Steve 275
Casey, Donald E. Jr. 109
Casey, Mike 264
Casey, Sister Juliana 107
Cash, Carol Dalton 191
Cass, Jim 311
Cassady, Ed 69
Cassard, Christopher D. 371
Cassels, Scott L. 396
Cassidy, Kevin 343
Castellani, Frederick C. 315
Castleberry, Michael 217
Castleman, Peter M. 235
Castles, James B. 342
Castro, Craig S. 130
Castro, John W. 329
Castro, Michael J. 154
Catacosinos, William J. 479
Catanzaro, Joseph S. 521
Cathy, Dan T. 118
Cathy, Donald M. 118
Cathy, S. Truett 118

Catlin, Tommer 531
Catsimatidis, John A. 414
Catuogno, Mario P. 331
Caudle, Allen 467
Caudle, Robert A. 356
Caughran, Carl W. 76
Cauley, Bruce A. 171
Caulk, Robert L. 498
Cauz, Jorge 177
Cavalier, Michael 121
Cavallero, Michael J. 162
Cavanagh, Mary Ann 524
Cavanaugh, James 423
Cavanaugh, Kevin 150
Cavarra, Mary K. 254
Cavness, Pam 269
Cawley, Peter J. 329
Cecil, Johnny 286
Cefaly, John M. 145
Cellupica, Ron 208
Celoni, Daniel L. 130
Cerra, Frank B. 504
Ceva, Joseph 119
Ch'ng, Huck 481
Chalas, Steve 254
Chall, Craig 46
Chamberlain, David R. 147
Chamberlain, Robin 332
Chamberlin, Mark 171
Chambers, Cathy 126
Chambers, Herbert G. 234
Chambers, Jack V. Jr. 479
Chan, David 357
Chan, Elroy 315
Chan, Thomas 23
Chan, Tim C. 375
Chandiwala, Hafiz 125
Chandler, James 254
Chandler, Linda 209
Chandler, Mike 284
Chaney, Jared 323
Chang, Will 435
Channel, Karen 220
Chaplin, Anthony Peter 370
Chaplin, Harvey R. 454
Chaplin, Wayne E. 454
Chapman, Brett R. 235
Chapman, Byrne W. 37
Chapman, Charles H. 110
Chapman, Dennis 133
Chapman, Donald M. 339
Chapman, Jerry B. 114
Chapman, John B. 396
Chapman, Zorona 249
Chappell, Robert E. Jr. 392
Chappell, W. Carter 319
Chappie, Patricia 98
Charboneau, Bruce L. 494
Charboneau, Gary 169
Charlton, R. Scott 407
Chartrand, Gary 21
Chase, Mike 172
Chase, Stephen 113
Chastain, Roger W. 414
Chau, Micheline 301
Chaudoin, Joe 147
Chavez, Lloyd G. Sr.
 (Burt Automotive) 95
Chavez, Lloyd G. Jr.
 (Burt Automotive) 95
Chavez-Thompson, Linda 26
Cheema, Manjit S. 479
Cheifetz, Stephen M. 519
Chen, Eric 24
Chen, John 468
Cheney, Chris 130
Cheney, Jeffery P. 284
Chenkin, Lonnie 33
Cheong, Thian C. 401
Chereskin, Benjamin D. 139
Cherrier, Tita 395
Cherry, C. William 40
Cherry, Steve 16

INDEX OF EXECUTIVES

Cherukuri, Satyam 457
Chesla, Mark 376
Chesley, Everett P. 255
Chester, John J. 379
Cheung, Francis 386
Chevassus, Jerry 416
Chhabra, Navjot 441
Chicoine, David L. 502
Child, George L. 23
Child, Wayne L. 67
Chin, Bobby 285
Chiricosta, Rick 323
Chisholm, Arthur C. 175
Chlada, John 395
Chladek, James 119
Cho, Hoon 526
Cho, Kendall 370
Choi, Howard 415
Choquette, Paul J. Jr. 206
Chorengel, Bernd 247
Choudhuri, Sanjib 268
Chow, Barbara 354
Chow, Ricky 303
Chrestman, Flossie 48
Christensen, Linda 478
Christenson, Ronald L. 101
Christian, Michael 199
Christians, Raimundo L.M. 404
Christianson, Robert A. 39
Christie, Edward J. Jr. 499
Christman, Craig 50
Christmas, Bradley 30
Christopher, Thomas A. 195
Chu, Benjamin K. 363
Chu, James 522
Chubb, Sarah 21
Church, Brent 415
Churchill, Dwight D. 194
Chvala, Vicki L. 37
Chwat, Anne 94
Chèvremont, Marie-Jeanne 404
Cialone, Henry J. 68
Cianciaruso, Charles J. 170
Ciauri, Mike 262
Ciavola, Laura 132
Cichocki, Kenneth J. 241
Ciecka, Richard J. 344
Cien, Timothy 138
Cieza, Pedro 434
Ciminelli, Louis P. 365
Cimini, Louis F. 240
Cimino, Jay 397
Cindric, Tim 393
Cinotti, Carolyn 87
Ciolino, Paul T. 43
Ciotta, Peter 420
Cipriani, Jack 470
Cirillo, Frank J. 363
Cisneros, Sandy 283
Civantos, John P. 236
Cizik, Robert 284
Clancy, George P. Jr. 117
Clanton, Mark 35
Clapacs, J. Terry 251
Clapman, Peter C. 476
Clapp, Kent W. 323
Clark, A. James 124
Clark, Gary 208
Clark, Gregory F. 268
Clark, J. Lance 267
Clark, Jack 371
Clark, James J. (Tishman Realty
  & Construction) 478
Clark, Jim (Inter-Con Security) 257
Clark, Joel 146
Clark, Laurie A. 344
Clark, O. B. 54
Clark, Raymond R. 109
Clark, Richard L. 117
Clark, Sarah 385
Clark, Scott 439
Clark, Sharon 481
Clarke, Celine T. 145

Clarke, Grahame N. Jr. 171
Clarke, Leslie A. 118
Clarkeson, John S. 87
Clarkson, James D. 334
Clary, Isabelle 256
Claure, R. Marcelo 91
Claus, Christopher W. 514
Clauson, Steve 345
Clawson, Jim 443
Clay, Phillip L. 337
Claypool, Jeffrey C. 440
Clayson, Scott 193
Clayton, William R. 28
Clem, Charles 50
Clem, Dena R. 311
Clemens, Lisa 101
Clement, Carmine J. 365
Clements, Mike 530
Clements, Rita C. 508
Clevenger, Ron 342
Clevenger, Yumi 165
Click, James H. 490
Clift, W.E. 121
Clifton, Peter 254
Cline, Teri 262
Cline, Thomas G. 373
Clinton, William J. 541
Clites, Vicki 205
Close, Stephen P. 126
Close Bowles, Crandall 456
Clossey, David F. 268
Clouston, Robert 432
Cloutier, Roger R. II 202
Clowe, C. Thomas 474
Clutterbuck, Marcos A. 236
Clymer, Jamie 482
Cobb, Anne L. 523
Cobello, Rick 463
Cocanougher, A. Benton 472
Coccari, Gregg 423
Coceo, Cecily A. 81
Cochell, Roger 536
Cochran, Charles T. 417
Cochran, J. Guyton Jr. 455
Cochran, Jerome 506
Cochran, Lawrence J. 396
Cochran, Patricia 524
Cochren, Christi 442
Cockrell, Mel 73
Codden, Daniel J. 366
Cody, Douglas R. 102
Cody, John 82
Coe, George 64
Coffee, Patrick 60
Coffee, Tammie 26
Coffey, Edward 233
Cogan, Andrew B. 280
Coggins, John 276
Cognetta, Gary 21
Cohen, H. Rodgin 464
Cohen, Kenneth S. 315
Cohen, Lyor 528
Cohen, Mardele 377
Cohen, Oren 411
Cohen, Richard B. 100
Cohen, Robert 88
Cohen, Roger J. 534
Cohen, Steven L. (A.G. Spanos) 28
Cohen, Steven S. (MedStar Health) 324
Cohen, Walter I. 138
Cohen, William N. 516
Cohig, Susan 355
Cohn, Steven 242
Cohorn, Lisa 312
Colatriano, Dave 521
Colbourne, William 79
Colburn, Martin P. 349
Colcord, Skip 401
Cole, Brady M. 360
Cole, Diane M. 29
Cole, Don 221
Cole, Johnnetta B. 499
Cole, Michael J. 354

Cole, Michel' Philipp 441
Cole, Thomas A. 446
Coleman, Cy 51
Coleman, Gracie P. 456
Coleman, J. Edward 130
Coleman, James E. 172
Coleman, John 87
Coleman, Mary Sue 503
Coleman, Monica 147
Coleman, Robert C. 96
Colf, Richard W. 396
Collignon, Randy 254
Colling, Dennis D. 389
Collins, Colin C. 315
Collins, Jim 249
Collins, John I. 146
Collins, Keith V. 432
Collins, Michael 416
Collins, Randall D. 284
Collins, Terry 217
Collins, Timothy R. 174
Collins, William J. 29
Collis, Alvin 346
Collum, Chip 56
Colon, Conrad O. 211
Colonna, Ken 39
Colonnetta, Joe 236
Colreavy, Coleen A. 294
Colson, Barton 127
Colson, Sam 432
Colson, William F. 127
Coluccio, Medrice 390
Combs, Greg 465
Compagno, Bob 190
Compton, Ronnie D. 50
Condon, James E. 471
Condrin, J. Paul III 295
Conger, Richard 278
Conine, James 337
Conklin, George
  (CHRISTUS Health) 119
Conklin, George (Di Giorgio) 157
Conklin, John 537
Conklyn, Elizabeth D. 514
Conley, John 170
Conlon, Timothy L. 521
Conn, Lance 526
Conn, Peter 505
Connell, Grover 134
Connell, Terry 134
Connelly, James M. 233
Connelly, Michael D. 109
Conner, Michael 360
Conner, Terry L. 295
Conniff, George 71
Connolly, Joe 345
Connor, Charles D. 40
Connor, P. Eric 335
Connors, Greg 411
Connors, Jill 534
Connors, John M. Jr. 389
Conrad, Craig 488
Conrad, Rita 192
Conroy, Christopher 449
Conroy, J. Patrick 393
Conroy, James T. 304
Conroy, John 63
Considine, Jill M. 156
Considine, Tim 249
Conway, Gordon R. 421
Conway, William E. Jr.
  (Carlyle Group) 104
Conway, William S.
  (Mutual of America) 344
Conzemius, Peter A. 303
Cook, Bob 108
Cook, David W. 377
Cook, Eileen 360
Cook, J. M. 36
Cook, Julie 47
Cook, Leslie E. 210
Cooke, Art 432
Cooke, David J. 386

Cooley, Christian 446
Cooley, Hugh 342
Cooney, Edward J. 370
Coons, Chris 258
Cooper, Dennis 428
Cooper, Don F. 157
Cooper, Marvin B. 139
Cooper, Richard 50
Cooper, Walter L. 36
Copacino, William C. 100
Cope, Roger J. 259
Copeland, Charles Jr. 369
Copeland, David 221
Copenhaver, Don 333
Copley, David C. 138
Copp, Duke 216
Coppage, Bob 157
Coppedge, John B. III 145
Coppel, Ron 174
Copple, Robert D. 121
Coppola, Joseph R. 266
Corbin, Bill 139
Corcoran, Elizabeth 62
Corcoran, Thomas A. 104
Cordell, L. Kenneth 492
Cordola, Craig 326
Corey, R. David 400
Corley, Terry B. 50
Corley, William E. 130
Cornell, Greg L. 61
Corr, Thomas L. 203
Corrado, Christopher 242
Corrigan, Fredric W. 101
Corrigan, John III 465
Corso, Patrick A. 125
Cortese, Denis A. 318
Cortese, Edward 292
Cortez, R. Michael 446
Corvino, Gerald 326
Coscia, Anthony R. 402
Cosgrove, Edward M. 529
Coslov, Michael 489
Cossette, Paul I. 303
Costa, Laura 524
Costa, Thomas 156
Cota, Bob 26
Cote, Michael M. 289
Cott, Charles 333
Cotta, Richard 96
Cotten, Paula 410
Cotter, Chris 490
Cotter, Mary C. 274
Cotton, Al 374
Cottrell, Michael W. 83
Cottrill, David 333
Cotè, William O. 495
Coulter, James 142
Counihan, Kevin J. 489
Coupe, Jerry 535
Courant, Paul N. 503
Courter, Craig 63
Courtney, Lisa 469
Courtwright, Gregory S. 297
Courtwright, Jeffrey T. 297
Couture, Daniel D. 119
Couvaras, Marie 119
Cova, Charles 110
Coveney, Elizabeth 509
Covert, Derek F. 110
Cowart, John R. 456
Cowden, Barbara 460
Cowley, Robert E. 360
Cowling, William S. II 289
Cox, Barb 430
Cox, Johnny 430
Cox, Kathleen 140
Cox, Neil E. 438
Coyle, Frank A. 248
Coyne, Frank 79
Coyne, William J. 412
Crabb, Jennifer 412
Crabb, Nancy 510
Crabtree, Loren W. 507

INDEX OF EXECUTIVES

Craft, Harold D. 138
Crafton, Joe 142
Craig, Gregory L. 138
Craig, John (Team Health) 469
Craig, John J. II
  (Sammons Enterprises) 431
Crain, B. J. 472
Crandell, Bert 34
Crane, Charles 484
Crane, Kelly 90
Crane, Phillip 208
Crane, Robert M. 273
Crane, Susan 197
Crawford, Colin 258
Crawford, Evan L. 118
Crawford, James D. 535
Crawford, Kevin F. 496
Crawford, Lindsay 424
Creasey, Clay 330
Creed, Buddy G. 371
Creedon, Richard P. 515
Creekmore, David 140
Cremer, Jill 486
Crenshaw, Joe (Martin-Brower) 311
Crenshaw, Joe (Reyes Holdings) 419
Crenshaw, William E. 407
Creteur, Philippe 347
Crews, Anne 312
Crews, Ralph L. 392
Cripe, James 113
Criqui, Robert 350
Crisp, Sherry L. 155
Critz, Gerald 499
Crockard, Craig S. 62
Crombie, Bill 527
Cronin, Kevin 139
Cronin, Laura B. 194
Cronin, Linda 448
Crook, Carl R. 368
Crooker, Colleen M. 129
Crosbie, William L. 44
Crosby, Steven C. 526
Crosland, Philip 51
Cross, C. Douglas 60
Cross, Donald M. 289
Cross, Harlan E. 338
Cross, Mark S. 268
Cross, William C. 442
Crotty, Gary 348
Crouse, Jerry K. 471
Crow, Elizabeth 136
Crow, Walter W. 494
Crowder, Gary S. 339
Crowell, Gary 264
Crowley, Jane Durney 109
Crowley, John 337
Crowley, Thomas B. Jr. 143
Crown, James S. 501
Cruickshank, Jay S. 289
Crume, Charles 535
Cruz, Frank H. 140
Cubbage, Alan K. 373
Cubelic, Tom 204
Culhane, Noreen M. 367
Cullen, Brian C. 278
Cullen, John A. 364
Cullen, Mike 180
Cullen, Thomas 278
Culler, Carl 239
Culvahouse, Arthur B. Jr. 379
Cuminale, James W. 385
Cummings, Debra 534
Cummings, Des D. Jr. 23
Cunningham, Dennis 355
Cunningham, Laurie 142
Curiale, Salvatore R. 344
Curley, Tom 57
Curran, Chris 181
Curran, Kevin J. 388
Curran, Michael J. 324
Curren, Vincent 140
Currence, Cynthia 35
Currie, Robert 264

Currow, James C. 340
Curry, John R. 337
Curry, Kevin 412
Curry, Thomas 82
Curtin, John
  (Connell Limited Partnership) 134
Curtin, John (Gould Paper) 210
Curtin, Joseph 489
Curtis, Arnold 128
Curtis, Clay 142
Curtis, James H. 84
Curtis, Liz 284
Curtis, Lynda D. 363
Cushman, John C. III 145
Cushman, Louis B. 145
Cuti, Anthony J. 169
Cutler, Robert 534
Czapka, Tom 214
Czarnecki, Walt 393
Czech, Ken 202
Czelada, Laura L. 155

D

D'Adamo, Dominic F. 230
D'Agostino, Sue 33
D'Alessandro, D. Beatty 214
D'Amour, Charles L. 74
D'Amour, Donald H. 74
D'Amour-Daley, Claire H. 74
D'Angelo, Stephen 157
D'Aniello, Daniel A. 104
D'Arezzo, David W. 412
D'Atri, Justin W. 417
D'Noccia, E. Trudy 465
D'Onfro, Stephen M. 422
Dabek, John 151
Dacek, Franziska H. 466
Dadario, Michael 261
Dahir, Victor W. 523
Dahl, Richard J. 162
Dahlberg, Kenneth C. 438
Dahlin, Rick 151
Dailey, John R. 452
Dailey, Stephen G. 227
Dake, Gary C. 463
Dake, William 463
Dale, Karen M. 524
Dale, Kenneth 57
Dalebout, William T. 248
Daleiden, Pete 330
Daley, Anthony 533
Daley, Deborah 40
Daley, Laura 437
Dalton, Ken F. 24
Dalton, William 35
Daly, Ann 166
Daly, Daniel D. 515
Daly, Lee Ann 181
Daly, Michael J. 69
Daly, Terence C. 109
Daly, William 355
Damico, Sandy 482
Damos, Craig 532
Damron, Ned 381
Dana, Jeffrey 404
Danenberg, Alan 176
Dangerfield, Dennis 480
Daniel, Chris 330
Daniel, David 205
Daniel, Jack L. 506
Daniel, Karen L. 77
Daniel, Kip 71
Daniel, Linzie L. 130
Daniel, William D. 253
Daniels, Andrew R. 132
Daniels, Anthony 388
Daniels, Bob 73
Daniels, Chuck 369
Daniels, Robert E. 234
Danis, Mark Wilmot 341
Danyluk, Sally 392

Dao, Giang 441
Darby, Cliff 60
Darcy, Thomas E. 438
Darling, Bruce B. 500
Darman, Richard G. 104
Darman, Sumner 155
Darneille, Wallace L. 398
Darrah, Matthew G. 178
Darrow, Bill 238
Darrow, Chris 169
Dart, Kenneth B. 148
Dart, Robert C. 148
Dart, William 148
Darvish, John R. 148
Darvish, Tammy 148
Darwent, Robert 236
Dassenko, Dennis 510
Datz, Linda 289
Dauer, Bruce A. 452
Daugherty, Kent 534
Davatzes, Nickolas 17
Davault, Edward 114
Davenport, Jim 217
Davenport, Margaret 208
Daves, Bill 431
Davidowski, Ron J. 165
Davids, Daniel E. 17
Davidson, Jack 538
Davidson, John 488
Davidson, Michael C. 460
Davidson, Roger 228
Davidson, Shelia K. 364
Davidson, William M. 219
Davies, David 465
Davies, Garret 286
Davies, Kent J. 498
Davis, Anne 361
Davis, Bradley T. 27
Davis, Clive 454
Davis, D. James 219
Davis, Dirk T. 495
Davis, Doris 138
Davis, Ian 321
Davis, J. B. 280
Davis, James S. (New Balance) 361
Davis, Jay M. 351
Davis, Jeff (D&H Distributing) 147
Davis, Jeffery B.
  (Klaussner Furniture) 280
Davis, Jim (SAS Institute) 432
Davis, Joseph D. 261
Davis, Kelvin 286
Davis, Lawrence J. 134
Davis, Liz 210
Davis, Melissa D. 479
Davis, Michael 485
Davis, Nancy 297
Davis, R. Denay 30
Davis, Robert G. 514
Davis, Ronald 431
Davis, Stephen A. 524
Davis, Sylvia S. 507
Davis Eady, Lydia J. 267
Davison, J. Scott 41
Davisson, Bill 218
Dawkins, Ray 411
Dawson, Charles 440
Dawson, Greg 167
Dawson, Peter 71
Day, James 485
Day, Randy 395
Day, Teresa M. 22
Day, Thomas G. 514
De La Garza, John Jr. 508
de la Mata, Luis 495
de la Vega, Ralph 121
de Lavis, John 316
de Palo, Armand M. 220
De Salvo, Robert 314
De Stigter, Glenn H. 532
Dean, Jerry 276
Dean, Lloyd H. 110
DeAngelis, Peter L. Jr. 107

DeAngelis, Vince 527
Deany, Tom 292
Deasy, Vaughn 178
Deavens, Gregory 364
DeBartolo York, Marie Denise 152
DeBerry, Ron 50
DeBiase, Lou 33
DeBiasi, Glenn 31
DeBruce, Paul 152
DeCarlo, Anthony J. 302
DeCarlo, Jeannie 489
DeCastro, Howard 498
Dechant, Tim 274
Deckas, Andrew C. 380
Decker, Steven R. 414
Decker, William F. 502
Decornoy, Jean-Luc 285
Dedman, Robert H. Jr. 125
Deegan, Michael 94
DeForrest, Bill 289
DeFrancisco, Margaret R. 204
Defratus, Kellie 165
DeGenova, Paul 76
DeGregorio, Robert D. 287
DeHaven, Michael A. 77
Dehler, Joseph 102
Deininger, Scott A. 41
DeJarnette, Shirley S. 504
DeJoria, John Paul 265
DeJuncker, Ron 193
DeKuyper, Mary H. 40
del Monte, Rick 71
Del Sindaco, Joseph M. 365
Del Vecchio, Claudio 418
Delahunt, Kevin 432
Delaney, Dennis 254
Delaney, Flora 344
Delaney, Gregory 21
Delaney, Katy 68
DeLano, David H. 53
Deleenheer, Ronald V. 52
Delehanty, Martha 520
DelGiacco, Peter 355
Deliberto, Robert 103
Delk, Mary R. 72
Dell, Robert M. 291
DeLuca, Frederick A. 161
DeMaille, Leon S. 329
Demarais, Patricia 161
DeMarco, Frederick L. 140
Demmert, William J. 43
Demorest, Harry L. 128
Dempsey, Kelly 119
Dempsey, Peter 262
DeNarvaez, Denny 33
Denbow, Terry 334
Denges, Jane 112
Denham, Benny W. 376
DeNike, Edward 458
Denison, David F. 194
Dennis, Marlene M. 25
Dennis, Shawn 352
Denny, Diane S. 107
Denny, James 410
Densing, Kristina 119
Denson, John E. 126
DePasquale, Edward H. 132
DePeau, Jamie 476
DePeters, Jack 531
Depies, John R. 48
DePrey, Mark 435
Derian, Dan 306
Derleth, James K. 488
Dermody, James J. 333
Derrickson, Ralph 526
DeSalvo, Daniel R. 37
Desien, Nicholas 307
DeSimone, Joseph R. 157
Desimone, Rich 191
Desmond, Marcia 108
Desmond, Neil 445
DeSousa, Dennis E. 214
DeSousa, Joseph 355

INDEX OF EXECUTIVES

Desser, Ed 350
DeStefano, Joe 207
DeStefano, Kenneth B. 23
DeSutter, Steven C. 94
Dettmer, Dennis 96
Dettrey, Shawn 192
DeVelder, Donn 56
Dever, Doug 139
Deviney, Lee 474
DeVos, Doug 34
DeVries, Chantry 532
Devries, Tim 70
Dewald, Steven B. 414
DeWeese, Timothy E. 155
Dewing, Merlin E. 64
Dewolfe, Christopher 311
Dhir, Atul 512
Diamond, Bernard 486
Diamond, Michael A. 507
Diamond, Ronald T. 131
Diaz, Tony 211
DiBitetto, Robert 17
Dice, Ken 159
Dick, David E. 157
Dick, Douglas P. 157
Dick, Melvin 454
Dick, Roger 511
Dicke, James F.
 (Crown Equipment) 144
Dicke, James F. II
 (Crown Equipment) 144
Dicke, James F. III
 (Crown Equipment) 144
Dickens, David 511
Dickerson, Gloria 274
Dickerson, Janet Smith 405
Dickerson, Monti 276
Dickey, Nancy W. 472
Dickey, Todd R. 507
Dickinson, Charles F. 386
Dickinson, Inger 173
Dicks, Robert W. Jr. 515
DiCola, John 108
Diderrich, John 47
Diehm, Russell C. 86
Dierberg, Gregory 158
Dierberg, Robert J. 158
Dierberg, Roger 158
Dierberg-Padousis, Laura 158
Diesel, R. Wayne 461
Dieterle, Michael M. 42
Dietz, David 160
Dietz, Garrett L. 481
Dietz, Mark W. 125
DiGanci, Todd T. 349
Digenova, Jerry 106
Diggins, John 400
Diggins, Vance W. 210
Dildy, Marshall L. 185
Dilks, Charlie 111
Dill, Myran 488
Dillard, Richard 336
Dillon, Daniel P. 354
DiMarco, Maureen 243
DiMarco, Michael A. 382
DiMento, Douglas 29
DiMichele, Sam 299
DiMuccio, Robert A. 43
DiNapoli, Mark L. 464
Dineen, Edward J. 178
Dingman, Michael L. 516
Dinneen, Kathy 258
Dionisio, John M. 24
DiPiazza, Samuel A. Jr. 404
Diracles, John M. Jr. 102
DiRenzo, August A. 145
DiRenzo, Donald A. Sr. 145
DiRubbio, Vincent 109
Ditka, Ashton L. 414
Ditore, Melanie 169
Dittmer, Dave 289
Dittrich, Allen L. 239
Divoll, Mark 43

Dixon, Dick 439
Dixon, Jennifer 475
Dixon, Mark (Community Hospitals
 of Indiana) 130
Dixon, Mark (ConnectiCare) 133
Dlugopolski, Stephanie 284
Doane, Timothy L. 483
Dobbins, David
 (Pilot Travel Centers) 398
Dobbins, David
 (University of Iowa) 502
Dobbs, Donald P. 289
Dobelbower, Peter 238
Doby, Winston C. 500
Dodd, George T. 515
Dodd, J. Clifford 273
Dodds, Larry D. 22
Dodds, Steve 274
Doeppe, Pamela 431
Doerfler, Ronald J. 231
Doheny, Daniel P. 419
Dohmen, John 186
Dohmen, Robert 186
Dolan, Gregory J. 534
Dolan, James (Purdue Pharma) 408
Dolan, James L.
 (Madison Square Garden) 304
Dolan, Kevin 468
Dolan, Ronald J. 377
Dolan, Thomas 533
Dolceamore, Gwen 241
Dolinich, Stephen 144
Doll, Mark G. 372
Domansky, Edward C. 24
Dombroski, Harry 244
Dominguez, Alex 118
Dominguez, Frank 25
Domm, Phyllis A. 258
Donaghy, Brian M. 463
Donaghy, James K. 463
Donaghy, Kelly 40
Donahoe, John J. 62
Donahoe, Patrick R. 513
Donahue, Donald F. 156
Donahue, Terry 152
Donahue, Thomas 182
Donaldson, A. Gregory 35
Donaldson, Philip 46
Donaldson, Rich 298
Donavan, Kevin 244
Donavan, Pat 147
Donlan, Joseph P. 92
Donley, Patrick M. 528
Donna, James M. 57
Donnelly, Gloria 133
Donnelly, Kevin W. 370
Donohoo, Christine 18
Donohue, Mike 33
Donovan Bodnar, Anne 481
Doran, Dennis 33
Dorfi, Klaus G. 59
Doria, Susan 64
Dorman, Douglas 217
Dornan, John 432
Dorrell, John 323
Dorsett, C. Powers 456
Dorsey, John 216
Dorsey, Joshua 127
Dotta, Jim 53
Dotterer, Herbert T. 74
Dougherty, Dennis F. 507
Dougherty, Michael E. 33
Doughty, Dennis O. 85
Douglas, Charles W. 446
Douglas, James 452
Douglas, Sean 246
Douglass, John 143
Douglass, Lee 50
Douglass, Raymond J. 86
Dountas, Susan 433
Dout, A. Jacqueline 391
Douville, Richard A. 181

Dowd, Thomas F.
 (Graybar Electric) 214
Dowd, Thomas P.
 (Cushman & Wakefield) 145
Dowling, Kathleen 121
Downer, Tom 192
Downey, Todd 48
Downs, Kenneth E. 459
Dowzall, Tony 522
Doyal, Steve 223
Doyle, Francis A. 134
Doyle, John D. (Ascension Health) 52
Doyle, John D. (Liberty Mutual) 295
Doyle, John M. (Iasis Healthcare) 248
Doyle, Kathy 332
Doyle, Lori 505
Doyle, Robert M. 126
Doyon, Gary A. 251
Dozier, Scott 266
Dozoretz, Ronald I. 191
Drago, Robert 211
Dragone, Allan 497
Drake, John W. 442
Drake, Linda R. 25
Drake, Michael V. 500
Drapkin, Donald G. 304
Drapkin, Matthew Adam 304
Drasher, Glenn D. 92
Drechsel, Joop G. 539
Drees, Barbara 167
Drees, David 167
Drees, Ralph 167
Drennan, Jerry M. 25
Dressing, Julie 30
Drexler, Millard S. 261
Driano, Dominick 424
Driessen, Christine 181
Droher, Paul F. 189
Drost, Gary C. 67
Druker, David 466
Drummond, David 362
Drummond, E. A. 168
Drummond, Garry N. Sr. 168
Drury, Robert 436
Druten, Robert J. 223
Duban, Jim 249
Dubinsky, John 76
Dubois, Lawrence H. 457
Dubreuil, Ray 98
Ducatelli, Thomas 130
Duchossois, Craig J. 169
Duchossois, Richard L. 169
Duco, Bernard A. Jr. 449
Duden, Ira 444
Dudley, Bill 71
Duerwachter, Steven S. 43
Duff, Brian 55
Duff, John 142
Duffey, Michael S. 252
Duffy, Christine 308
Duffy, James F. 367
Dugent, Paul J. 182
Duggan, Diane 159
Duggan, Michael E.
 (Detroit Medical Center) 156
Duggan, Mike (Dot Foods) 163
Dukes, Dennis 139
Dumas, Lawrence B. 373
Dumbacher, Robert J. 412
Dumper, Audrey 481
Dunagan, Nick 507
Dunavant, William B. Jr. 170
Dunaway, Doran 217
Dunbar, Joel F. 427
Dunbar, W. Roy 316
Duncan, Barbara 428
Duncan, David S. 407
Duncan, James P. 356
Dunlap, Anne 299
Dunlap, Fredrick C. 132
Dunn, Brandon 540
Dunn, Edward B. 333
Dunn, Kevin 421

Dunn, Lewis A. 438
Dunn, Marcy 109
Dunn, Maureen H. 491
Dunn, Michael (Hearst) 231
Dunn, Michael F.
 (UNICCO Service) 494
Dunn, Stephen D. 170
Dunn, Terrence P. 170
Dunn, Van 363
Dunn, William H. Sr.
 (Dunn Industries) 170
Dunn, William H. Jr.
 (Dunn Industries) 170
DuPont, Chuck 409
Dupuis, Patrick 77
DuPuy, Robert A. 306
Durant, Kenneth F. 114
Durbin, Dean D. 521
Durcan, Deborah A. 510
Duren, James R. 442
Durham, David 266
Durkee, Robert K. 405
Durrett, Ken 537
Duvall, William C. 297
Dworak, Cathy 216
Dwyer, Dean P. 138
Dwyer, Joseph P. 54
Dwyer, Terry 129
Dyer, Joseph W. 360
Dyer, Kenneth 131
Dyer, Mark 348
Dykstra, Kathleen 341
Dynes, Robert C. 500
Dyson, Robert R. 171
Dyze, Thomas D. 527
Dziedzic, John 529

E

Eades, Milton 529
Eadie, Cindy 161
Eagleson, Thomas 95
Eaker, Norman 269
Earle, Gordon 459
Early, William Bernard 262
Earner, William 360
Earnhardt, Hal J. Jr.
 (Earnhardt's Auto Centers) 173
Earnhardt, Hal J. III
 (Earnhardt's Auto Centers) 173
Earnhardt, Jim B. 173
Earnst, Collin 243
Easter, William H. III 170
Easterly, David E. 141
Eastland, Woods E. 459
Eastman, A. Brent 440
Eastman, Karen E. 402
Eaton, Robert 181
Eaton, Thomas E. Jr. 385
Eayrs, Mike 216
Ebaugh, Susan 443
Ebeid, Russell J. 219
Ebrom, Charles 541
Eby, Clifford C. 387
Eby, Michael 158
Eby, Rob 147
Eccleston, Dennis 365
Eceles, Jeff 469
Eck, Patricia A. 83
Eckley, Paul N. 460
Eddy, Jeanne H. 305
Edl, John P. 176
Edland, Alice 284
Edmonds, Bryson 69
Edmunds, Matt 382
Edwards, Alan 67
Edwards, Bill 454
Edwards, D. Andrew Jr. 461
Edwards, Paul A. 233
Edwards, Rosser Jr. 531
Edwards, Tom 300
Efigenio, Kerry 341

INDEX OF EXECUTIVES

Eftekhar, Zia 202
Egan, Peter 199
Egbert, David 522
Eggebeen, Thomas C. 329
Egidi, Kenneth A. 394
Ehinger, Kenneth R. 356
Ehlinger, Jon D. 168
Eickholt, Lynne J. 389
Eidson, Thomas E. 194
Eiler, Gary 510
Einboden, Allan 439
Eisbart, Ben A. 379
Eisenman, Russell 343
Eisenreich, Ted 216
Eisenstein, Joshua J. 112
Eisgruber, Christopher L. 405
Eisner, Dean H. 141
Ekey, Jacqueline 466
El, Pam 460
Elam, Mickey 260
Elcano, Mary S. 40
Elder, Irma 175
Elder, Tony 175
Eldridge, James F. 37
Elg, Annette 272
Elggren, Allen 114
Elias, Moenes 422
Eliot, Theodore 535
Elise, Lori 60
Elkins, John 523
Elko, Ed 86
Ellingwood, Dwight E. 120
Elliot, Robert B. 154
Elliott, Robert N. 261
Ellis, Bruce 160
Ellis, Elmer G. 182
Ellis, James B. 144
Ellis, Larry T. 502
Ellis, Tchicaya B. 313
Ellspermann, Richard 195
Elmer, Leonard J. 364
Elrod, Jack 465
ElSawy, Amr A. 338
Elsberg, Paul 413
Elsea, Charles 439
Elsey, Charles L. 241
Elterich, Steven E. 194
Ely, Mildred 109
Ely, Ross 342
Emerson, Frances B. 315
Emery, Charles C. Jr. 241
Emery, Keith E. 471
Emma, Edward C. 265
Emmerson, A. A. 447
Emmerson, George 447
Emmerson, Mark 447
Emmerson Dietz, Carolyn 447
Emmert, Mark A. 509
Enderson, Dan E. 23
Endres, John 208
Engblom, Carolyn 426
Engdahl, David L. 226
England, Simon J. 533
English, Michela A. 159
English, Roderick 416
English, Scott 231
Eno, Woodrow E. 475
Ensign, Clint 449
Enstrom, Birgit 228
Entwistle, David 510
Eppel, William G. 113
Epprecht, Hans 215
Epprecht, John 215
Eraña, Eduardo 523
Ergas, Jean-Pierre M. 95
Erhardt, Ed 181
Erickson, Dennis 152
Erickson, Gary M. 346
Erickson, Jeff 401
Erickson, Jim 454
Erickson, Paula 20
Erickson, Ronald A. 239
Erlenbush, Bill 218

Erne, Michael 110
Ernst, Robert 229
Errico, Robert C. 349
Erskine, Ron 350
Ertell, Kevin 343
Ertell, Thomas I. 435
Escudero, Edward 396
Escue, Dick 449
Espel, Thomas K. 414
Espino Macari, Emma 123
Esplin, J. Kimo 245
Esposito, Bob 191
Estabrook, Keith 454
Estes, Howell M. III 25
Estes, Robey W. Sr. (Estes Express) 182
Estes, Robey W. Jr. (Estes Express) 182
Estess, Glenn E. Sr. 426
Esvelt, Terence G. 84
Etchemendy, John W. 459
Etess, Mitchell G. 339
Ethridge, Joseph A. 431
Ettinger, John R. 150
Euller, Steven C. 101
Eustance, Tara 312
Evanich, Craig 46
Evans, Daniel F. Jr. 123
Evans, Dave
 (Metromedia Restaurant Group) 332
Evans, David J. (Hallmark) 223
Evans, David N. (Eagle-Picher) 171
Evans, Donald S. 114
Evans, James F.
 (Rudolph & Sletten) 428
Evans, James L. (Tenaska) 471
Evans, Joan 379
Evans, John T. 356
Evans, Kent 121
Evans, Lester 333
Evans, Marsha J. 40
Evans, Phillip 350
Evans, Robert B. 182
Evans, Scott C. 476
Evans, Steve 394
Evans, Timothy 421
Evdoe, Brian 20
Evens, Ronald G. 76
Evenson, Mary 239
Everett, Robert S. 139
Everson, Lloyd K. 512
Ewers, Susan 267
Ewing, B. Edward 276
Eyre, Harmon J. 35
Eyrich, Keith 261
Eyvazzadeh, Susan 418

F

Fabbrini, Richard R. 289
Fabiano, Michael 402
Fabrizio, Joseph M. 86
Faccio, Ron 342
Fadel, Richard A. Jr. 185
Faga, Martin C. 338
Fagerstrom, James 299
Fagin, Sherry 496
Fahey, John M. Jr. 353
Fahey, Thomas J. Jr. 327
Faith, David M. 439
Faith, Marshall E. 439
Faklis, Nick 28
Falcone, Joseph C. 354
Falcones Jaquotot, Baldomero 316
Faliero, Bryan K. 382
Falk, Michael D. 335
Falk, Terrell 121
Falsey, Ann M. 289
Falvey, Justin 166
Fama, Cheryl 110
Famiglietti, Eileen M. 349
Fanchi, Louis A. 213
Fantano, Gerard 360
Fantini, Rick J. 48

Fantozzi, Joseph 157
Faralli, Tony 257
Farbacher, Elizabeth A. 237
Farias, Pablo 196
Faris, Jack H. 509
Farley, Robert 171
Farmer, Dennis 218
Farmer, Scott 88
Farnsworth, Tracy J. 130
Farr, David A. 463
Farrar, George 85
Farrell, Anne V. 416
Farrell, Diana 321
Farrell, James 466
Farrell, Michael K. 120
Farrelly, John 292
Farrington, Thomas 186
Farrow, Randy 33
Fasold, Mark 298
Fassino, J.C. 221
Fassoulis, Satiris G. 119
Faulk, Woody 118
Faulkner, Duane H. 219
Faulkner, Gail 186
Fausett, Stephen 484
Fay, Gerard 326
Fay, Roger L. 417
Fay, Sharon E. 32
Feagles, Louis 264
Fealy, Robert L. 169
Feckner, Rob 98
Fedak, Marilyn G. 32
Feder, Chris 16
Federle, Mark 532
Fee, Thomas R. 417
Feeney, Michael 17
Feeney, Thomas M. 429
Feilmeier, Steve 281
Fein, Oliver T. 369
Fein, Russ 533
Feinberg, Steven 89
Feitor, John C. 494
Feld, Alan D. 30
Feld, Kenneth 190
Feldman, Jan 510
Feldman, Marc 171
Feldman, Margaret P. 520
Feldman, Robert J. 274
Feldman, Steve 351
Feldner, Ronald A. 75
Felix, Leyton 312
Felker, G. Stephen 62
Feller, Nancy P. 196
Fellinger, Bob 185
Fellowes, James 190
Fellowes, Peter 190
Felton, Douglas A. 29
Fencl, Eric R. 382
Fenderson, Albion 172
Fennell, Geneva 191
Fenener van Vlissingen, John A. 539
Fenter, Tom 82
Fenton, Bob 397
Fenton, Ken 47
Fenwick, Lex 78
Ferenbach, Carl 511
Ferguson, Betty 45
Ferguson, Fred 55
Ferguson, Glenn 124
Ferguson, Karen 401
Ferguson, Larry P. 436
Ferguson, Roger W. Jr. 188
Ferko, William G. 202
Fernandez, Bill 450
Fernandez, Michael 474
Fernbach, John 153
Ferolie, Anthony 191
Ferolie, James 191
Ferolie, Lawrence J. Sr.
 (Ferolie Group) 191
Ferolie, Lawrence J. Jr.
 (Ferolie Group) 191
Ferraro, Michael 367

Ferree, Larry 185
Ferrell, David 227
Ferrell, Gregory 226
Ferrera, Ken 100
Ferrie, Elaine 89
Ferrie, John 87
Ferris, James J. 114
Fertman, Don 161
Fetherston, Richard A. 37
Fetter, Lee F. 76
Fetzer, Ronald 75
Feuerhelm, Dave 487
Fichtner, Chuck 390
Ficken, Ann 269
Field, Thomas W. Jr. 462
Fields, Dave 123
Fienberg, Linda D. 349
Fife, Jerry 516
Filer, Anthony 406
Filios, George 28
Filippone, Gary 456
Filkin, David L. 169
Fillmore, Jeff 342
Finazzo, Kathy 462
Finch, R. Jay 328
Fincke, Lewis 338
Fine, Peter S. 64
Fineman, S. David 513
Finkenstaedt, George C. 289
Finn, David 481
Finnegan, Wilfred A. 104
Finnigan, Michelle 487
Finstein, Harvey 207
Firebaugh, Francille M. 138
Fisch, Joseph J. Jr. 358
Fisch, Rick 272
Fischbach, Gerald D. 129
Fischer, Ben 142
Fischer, Daniel 159
Fischer, Paul F. 43
Fischer, Ralph 325
Fischer, Robert H. 24
Fischer, Tom 67
Fischetta, Tony 191
Fish, Edward A. 464
Fish, John F. 464
Fisher, Andrew S. 141
Fisher, Barbara 297
Fisher, David 531
Fisher, G. Robert 270
Fisher, Joel 305
Fisher, John W. 61
Fisher, Joseph V. 480
Fisher, Mark 186
Fisher, Michael A. 405
Fisher, Rodger 142
Fisher, Steven P. 438
Fishkin, Lee 41
Fitts, John R. 174
Fitzgerald, Kevin J. 284
Fitzgerald, Sean 96
FitzPatrick, Dennis 413
FitzSimons, John 171
Flack, Robert J. 27
Flacke, Robert J. 436
Flaherty, Kathy 382
Flaherty, William L. 401
Flaim, Theresa A. 491
Flamholz, Sam 86
Flanagan, Jack 205
Flanagan, Kevin 91
Flanagan, Lawrence 316
Flanagan, Nick 332
Flanagan, Robert J. 124
Flanders, Paul R. 106
Flanders, Scott N. 129
Flatoff, Brad 432
Fleagle, Steve 502
Fleischman, Larry E. 156
Flenard, Donna 20
Fleszar, Thomas J. 155
Fletcher, Donald H. 223
Fletcher, James A. 472

INDEX OF EXECUTIVES

Flicker, Russell 486
Flint, David B. 192
Flint, H. Howard II 192
Fliss, Tim 435
Flochel, Patrick J.P. 180
Flocken, Jeff 430
Flood, Gary 316
Floren, Gregg 534
Flores, Virginia 479
Florian, Monica 261
Florjancic, Frederick J. Jr. 429
Floum, Joshua R. 523
Flowers, Jacki 40
Floyd, Allen 333
Floyd, Charles D.
   (Delta Dental Plan of Michigan) 155
Floyd, Chuck (Hyatt) 247
Floyd, Elson S. 504
Floyd, Gary L. 427
Fluri, Edgar 404
Fly, Emerson H. 507
Flynn, Charlene 28
Flynn, Dan 458
Flynn, James 278
Flynn, Patrick
   (Oxford Automotive) 383
Flynn, Patrick (Teamsters) 470
Flynn, Shawn 397
Flynn, William J. (GeoLogistics) 203
Flynn, William J.
   (Mutual of America) 344
Foerderer, Norma 486
Fogarty, James P. 294
Fogarty, W. Tom 132
Folds, Susan 405
Foley, Don H. 438
Foley, S. Robert 500
Foley, William T. 406
Follett, Chuck 195
Follett, Ross 195
Follis, Russ 248
Fong, Holly 99
Fontanes, A. Alexander 295
Forbes, Kay P. 237
Forbes, Scott 479
Forbes Lieberman, Pamela 487
Ford, Allyn 424
Ford, Edsel 430
Ford, John B. 459
Ford, Judith V. 27
Fordyce, Michael 108
Fore, Stephanie 237
Forestieri, Teri 154
Forgette, Steve 274
Forier, René-Paul 48
Forster, Peter C. 124
Forsyth, John D. 502
Forte, Jon 199
Forte, Joseph 278
Forte, Kate 225
Fortenberry, Kevin 26
Fortgang, Charles Fabrikant 302
Fortgang, Matthew Fabrikant 302
Fortgang, Susan Fabrikant 302
Foscue, Julian M. 280
Fost, Joshua 126
Foster, Kent 71
Foster, Pam 468
Foster, Randall 439
Foster, Richard M. 274
Foster, Ron 198
Foti, Salvatore C. 107
Fotsch, Richard J. 284
Fowler, John C. 409
Fowler, June McAllister 77
Fowler, William A. 154
Fox, Allan 299
Fox, Brent 90
Fox, Daryl 191
Fox, Edward J. 511
Fox, Jeff 224
Fox, Len 25
Fox, Michael B. 194

Fox, Mitchell 21
Fox, Randy 98
Fox, Sam 224
Foxworth, Jack 199
Foxworth, Walter L. 199
Frabotta, Joe 96
Frakes, David 411
France, Brian Z. 348
France, Jim 348
France, William C. Jr. 348
Franchini, August Jr. 405
Francini, Joseph A. 428
Francis, Charles P. 110
Francis, James L. 466
Francis, Leslie C. 175
Francis, Peter T. 264
Franco, Robert M. 56
Francois, Michael 402
Franich, Steven 312
Frank, Darryl 166
Frank, Elaine S. 199
Frank, Fran 89
Frank, Gregory L. 68
Frank, Jack C. (Community Hospitals of
   Indiana) 130
Frank, James S. 199
Frank, John
   (Frank Consolidated Enterprises) 199
Frank, Thomas 256
Franklin, Marc S. 384
Franklin, Michael 471
Frankowski, Thomas J. 409
Franks, Joanne 314
Franks, Mark 148
Franks, Thomas M. 476
Franz, Paul 400
Franzen, Jeff B. 297
Franzi, Joseph 526
Frapaise, Xavier 468
Frazier, Eric 16
Frazier, John R. 407
Frazier, Larry R. 116
Frazier-Coleman, Christie 66
Frederick, Francie A. 508
Fredrickson, Rocky 406
Freed, Butch 50
Freed, Michael P. 455
Freedlund, Kurt 250
Freedman, Tom 293
Freeland, Tom 69
Freeman, Elaine 266
Freeman, Jim 33
Freeman, Phil 446
Freeman, Randall J. 90
Freeman, Thomas 256
Frei, Emil 464
French, Richard G. 465
Frennea, Robert 19
Freschi, Joseph 16
Frescoln, Leonard D. 192
Frescura, Thomas 250
Frey, James E. 30
Frey, Lou M. 113
Freymann, Helene R. 534
Fribourg, Paul J. 137
Fricke, Howard R. 441
Friddell, Guy III 288
Frieder, Berry 399
Friedman, George H. 349
Friedman, Joel 65
Friedman, Mark 38
Friedman, Michael 408
Friedman, Rosalyn 216
Frigerio, Liliana 103
Frisch, Ronald W. 506
Froeschle, Thomas 87
Froimowitz, Ray 463
Frommer, Andrew J. 62
Frownfelter, James B. 385
Frumkin, Jeffery 503
Fry, Bill 228
Fry, Darrel K. 340
Fry, David 200

Fry, Derek A. 523
Fry, John 200
Fry, P. Amy 59
Fry, Patrick E. 466
Fry, William R. 200
Fryda, Gary L. 426
Fuchs, Daniel A. 185
Fugate, Charlie 286
Fuhrmann, David 197
Fulks, Gary L. 54
Fuller, Brandie 214
Fuller, Kathryn S. 196
Fullmer, William 483
Fullwood, Michael D. 230
Fulton, Susan 39
Fumagali, Oscar 91
Funk, Bradley C. 303
Funk, Robert A. 185
Furgason, Robert R. 472
Furnari, Jack 21
Furst, Jack D. 236
Furst, Thomas J. 457
Furth, Mark 56
Furumasu, Brian 84
Fusco, Paul 261
Fuson, Harold W. Jr. 138
Fuson, Scott E. 164
Futa, Edwin H. 426
Futterman, Joel 95
Fynes, Jim 397

G

Gabel, Glenn 531
Gaberman, Barry D. 196
Gabriel, Jack 91
Gabriel, Nicholas M. 196
Gabriele, Antonio 88
Gadiesh, Orit 62
Gafford, Ronald J. 60
Gaggion, Stefano 418
Gagnon, Dave 94
Gaines, Adrienne 541
Gaither, J. Michael 41
Gal, Tsvi 528
Galante, Joe 454
Galbraith, Jimmy III 199
Galbraith, Ted 199
Galin, Tomi 248
Galinson, Murray L. 97
Gall, Ellen 147
Gallagher, Brian A. 499
Gallagher, Catherine 134
Gallagher, Michael P. 144
Gallagher, Stewart 375
Galligan, William P. 514
Gallo, Dominic 221
Gallo, Ernest 172
Gallo, Joseph E. 172
Gallo, Robert J. 172
Gallogly, James L. 116
Galloway, Robert E. 518
Gallups, Susan 380
Galvin, Karen 126
Galvin, Michael J. 427
Gamache, Marcel L. 133
Gamble, Gregory C. 139
Gamgort, Bob 311
Gammarino, Steve W. 79
Gamsin, Sharon 316
Gann, Robin 142
Gannet, Barbara 445
Gannon, Barbara 432
Gannon, Michael J. 192
Gannon, Richard 136
Gannon, Thomas A. 435
Gans, John 158
Ganter, John J. 421
Gantt, Michael 66
Ganz, Mark B. 415
Ganzi, Victor F. 231
Gappmayer, Merrill 257

Garaïalde, Jacques R. 283
Garber, Peni A. 346
Garber, Rich 215
Garchik, Sandy R. 124
Garcia, Dan 273
Garcia, Ernest C. II 168
Garcia, Linda 423
Garcia, Roland 479
Garcia, Savino 442
Garcia, Terry D. 353
Garcia-Naranjo, Guillermo 285
Gard, Greg 400
Gardebring, Sandra S. 504
Gardner, Chester S. 502
Gardner, John (CARQUEST) 106
Gardner, John (General Parts) 202
Gardner, John (New Balance) 361
Gardner, Kimberly 445
Gardner, Max L. 261
Gardner, Phil D. 191
Gardner, Tracy 261
Gargano, Charles A. 402
Gargiulo, Jeffrey D. 465
Garinello, Lawrence 421
Garland, Greg C. 116
Garland, Jerry 58
Garland, Karla 26
Garland, Trish 182
Garlington, Dub 26
Garlock, Steven 379
Garner, Karen 466
Garner, Paul 296
Garofalo, Donald L. 46
Garrard, Julie 190
Garren, Bob 95
Garren, Ruth 320
Garrett, Lew 344
Garrett, Marc 410
Garrett, Tom (Brasfield & Gorrie) 90
Garrett, Tom
   (RTM Restaurant Group) 428
Garrison, David H. 514
Garrow, Daniel W. 339
Garruto, Anthony 516
Garten, Robin 320
Gartland, Thomas M. 268
Gartley, David W. 384
Gary, Ray 282
Gary, Robert 429
Garza, Richard 360
Garza, Tim 99
Gaskill, William 268
Gassler, David 331
Gast, Alice 337
Gaston, Maury D. 36
Gaston, Steve 447
Gately, James H. 517
Gates, Robert M. 472
Gates, William H. III 75
Gathers, Patricia 107
Gatmaitan, Al W. 123
Gatson, Jerry 472
Gatti, Frank R. 175
Gatti, Rosa 181
Gattis, Jacque 374
Gatto, Michele S. 356
Gaufin, Shirley 97
Gaviglia, Louis 374
Gavito, Julio 207
Gay, Robert C. 248
Gayler, Kyle 499
Gazzilli, Mark 138
Gee, E. Gordon 516
Geeraerts, John W. 442
Geffen, David 166
Gegare, Fred 470
Gehle, Sean 52
Geier, Frank 209
Geisler, David A. 146
Geisler, John E. 101
Geistman, Bob 253
Geithner, Timothy F. 188
Gelb, Joel 305

HOOVER'S HANDBOOK OF PRIVATE COMPANIES 2005

INDEX OF EXECUTIVES

Gelb, Morris 178
Gembicki, Stanley A. 510
Genest, Mary 481
Genise, Vincent 122
Gentine, Louis 432
Gentry, Jeff 282
Geoga, Douglas G. 247
George, Boyd L. 31
George, Gladys 292
George, James W. 483
George, John B. 417
George, Kelly 130
George, Michael E. 203
George, Starr 348
George, Thomas F. 504
Gerace, James J. 520
Gerghty, Patrick J. 241
Gerlach, Scott B. 305
Germ, John F. 426
Gerson, Ralph J. 219
Gerstner, Louis V. Jr.
 (Carlyle Group) 104
Gerstner, Louis V. Jr.
 (Memorial Sloan-Kettering) 327
Getsay, Timothy R. 516
Getto, Carl 510
Getz, Bert A. 318
Geurts-Bengtson, Dee 216
Geyer, James 197
Ghasemi, Seifi 422
Ghaswala, Navaz 197
Gherty, John E. 287
Gheysari, Shahram 538
Gialanella, David M. 145
Giambusso, Ann 115
Giannetti, Steve 354
Giardina, Don J. 296
Gibbens, Dale 281
Gibbon, Mary Beth 204
Gibbons, Mary Anne 514
Gibbs, Margaret 275
Gibbs, Marshall 252
Gibson, Denise 91
Gicela, Michael 176
Giese, Clinton 406
Giese, Marlene 201
Gifford, Bill 207
Giglio, Lawrence R. 214
Gigliotti, Joe 351
Gijsen, Rob 63
Gilbane, Robert V. 206
Gilbane, Thomas F. Jr. 206
Gilbane, William J. Jr. 206
Gilbert, Bob 379
Gilbert, David H. 208
Gilbert, John O. 475
Giles, Deborah 26
Giles, Dennis R. 428
Gilhuly, Edward A. 283
Gilhuly, Ned 283
Gill, Adrienne 71
Gill, Edward 265
Gill, Nancy 352
Gillan, Marianne 109
Gillean, John 119
Gillespie, Mary Ellen 50
Gillette, James R. 467
Gillhouse, David 169
Gilliam, Thomas 344
Gilliland, Martha W. 504
Gillings, Dennis B. 411
Gillock, Leslie J. 456
Gilmour, John 344
Gilmour, Scott 499
Gilpin, Don 495
Gilsdorf, Norman L. 510
Gilson, Jean-Marc 164
Gilson, Kurt 277
Giltner, F. Phillips III 444
Gingerich, Brent 433
Gingue, Robert 422
Ginnis, Patti 177
Ginsberg, Sheldon L. 302

Ginstling, Norman J. 304
Gipson, Craig 83
Gipson, James 243
Gisel, William G. Jr. 420
Gittis, Howard 304
Gjellstad, Clifford G. 67
Gladstone, Robert 324
Glasener, Cletus C. Jr. 524
Glaser, Jack
 (St. Joseph Health System) 430
Glaser, John P.
 (Partners HealthCare) 389
Glaser, Raymond H. 85
Glasnapp, J. 46
Glasner, Sol 338
Glaspey, Roger 170
Glass, Brent D. 452
Glassman, Marc 307
Glauber, Robert R. 349
Glazer, Bennett 207
Glazer, Michael L. (KB Toys) 274
Glazer, Mike
 (Glazer's Wholesale Drug) 207
Glazer, R.L. 207
Gleason, Arthur L. Jr. 275
Gleason, Bradley J. 37
Gleberman, Joseph H. 88
Gleeson, Bill 466
Glenn, J. Thomas 20
Glenn, Richard 48
Glenning, Robert L. 273
Glidden, Craig B. 116
Gliniecki, Patrice M. 349
Glisson, Karen 75
Glorioso, Stephen J. 374
Glossmeyer, Michael 418
Glover, Susan L. 23
Gluth, Robert C. 310
Glynn, Thomas P. 389
Go, Phil 66
Goble, Jonathan R. 123
Gochman, David 19
Goddard, Steve 536
Godfrey, Cullen M. 508
Godfrey, Dennis J. 360
Godfrey, James 237
Goedken, Jolene 449
Goelzer, Paulo 249
Goemans, Hans J. 466
Goetzee, Rudy 342
Goff, Gina 100
Goheen, Charles 186
Goit, Whitney II 17
Goldammer, Russell L. 382
Goldberg, Adam R. 478
Goldberg, Cindi 181
Goldberg, Frank 510
Goldberg, Lena G. 194
Goldberg, Michael H. 255
Golden, Brent 265
Goldenheim, Paul D. 408
Goldfield, H. P. 77
Goldrick, Anthony M. 169
Goldsmith, Barry R. 349
Goldsmith, Clair 508
Goldstein, Allen P. 99
Goldstein, Brad 382
Goldstein, Deb 258
Goldstein, Irwin 503
Goldstein, Lew 530
Goldstein, Matthew 123
Goldstein, Neal 73
Goldstein, Robert G. 290
Goldstein, Steven 476
Goldstein, Stuart Z. 156
Goldwasser, Milton J. Jr. 138
Golkin, Perry 283
Golston, Allan C. 75
Goltz, Kandi 216
Golub, Lewis 208
Golub, Mona 208
Golub, Neil M. 208
Gomes, Jim 96

Gomes, Keith 96
Gomes, W. R. 500
Gonyo, Jeff 306
Gonzales, Richard 211
Gonzalez-Beltran, Ernesto 363
Gonze, David J. 302
Gooch, Everett 22
Good, H. Edward 479
Good, Michael P. 360
Goode, David 170
Goodell, Roger 352
Goodlin, William M. 251
Goodman, Adam 166
Goodman, John B. 208
Goodman, Patrick J. 335
Goodman, Phyllis 120
Goodnight, James H. 432
Goodrich, David R. 387
Goodrich, T. Michael 69
Goodwin, Everett 257
Goodwin, Ted E. 48
Goodwyn, Bill 159
Goodwyn, M. Williams Jr. 125
Gooldrup, Michael 380
Goolsbee, Arthur 515
Gooman, Patti 398
Gordon, Brad A. 206
Gordon, Cynthia 82
Gordon, Dan 209
Gordon, James M. (Citation) 122
Gordon, Jim
 (Gordon Food Service) 209
Gordon, John Jr. 209
Gordon, Mark R. 32
Gordon, Rick 484
Gordon, Suzanne 432
Gordon, Toby A. 266
Gordy, Michael 432
Gore, Frank C. 125
Gore, Robert W. 538
Gore, Sally 538
Gores, Alec E. 210
Gores, Tom T. 400
Goresh, Andrew C. 349
Gorga, Joseph L. 95
Gori, Kim 464
Gorman, Kirk E. 262
Gorman, Leon A. 298
Gorrell, J. Warren Jr. 238
Gorrie, M. James 90
Gorrie, M. Miller 90
Gosdeck, Sharon 151
Gossewisch, August 103
Gotro, Jerry 276
Gottemoeller, Doris 109
Gottesmann, Mario 391
Gotto, Antonio M. Jr. 138
Gottschalk, M. Therese 307
Goudis, Richard 235
Gould, Charles W. 524
Gould, Harry E. Jr. 210
Gould, Jim 111
Gould, Peter G. 465
Gourio, Hervé 103
Gowan, Jim 145
Gowin, Mary Ellen 527
Grabow, Karen 287
Gradishar, Randy 397
Grady, Daniel A. 87
Grady, Kenneth A. 274
Grady, Raymond 183
Graffis, Richard 123
Graham, Aaron 408
Graham, George E. Jr. 54
Graham, Phillip R. 82
Graham, Randolph H.
 (National Grape Cooperative) 354
Graham, Randy
 (TravelCenters of America) 483
Graham, Robert D. 137
Graham, Tracy 270
Gramlich, Edward M. 188
Gramm, Frank G. III 488

Granik, Russell T. 350
Granville, Irwin 292
Grassilli, Diane 110
Grasso, Alfred 338
Grauer, Peter T. 78
Grauwiler, Joseph L. 305
Graves, Andrew E. 167
Graves, Angela D. 365
Graves, Arthur C. 280
Grawien, Bob 435
Gray, Carla 243
Gray, Daniel J. 210
Gray, Don 36
Gray, James A. 226
Gray, John 428
Gray, Katherine 430
Gray, Robert C. 237
Gray-Felder, Denise 421
Graziosi, David S. 418
Greaney, Dennis 312
Grebe, Michael J. 257
Grebe, Pat 411
Greco, James J. 405
Greco, Suzanne 161
Greed, John R. 344
Greeff, Oppel 411
Green, Charlie 29
Green, Dan 64
Green, Dave (RDO Equipment) 414
Green, David (Hobby Lobby) 238
Green, George 231
Green, Jeffrey S. 403
Green, Judith 63
Green, Lorraine A. 44
Green, Mal 442
Green, Steve 238
Green, Warren 296
Greenaway, Roger 51
Greenberg, Alan 111
Greenberg, Lawrence T. 25
Greenblatt, Jason 486
Greene, Harold 197
Greene, James H. Jr. 283
Greene, Peter 483
Greener, Fred 193
Greenland, Carol 386
Greenlee, David 73
Greenspan, Alan 188
Greenwald, Scott 131
Greenwalt, Rodgers K. 88
Greenwood, James M. 132
Greenwood, M.R.C. 500
Greer, Mar-D 204
Greer, Ray E. 456
Greer, Reagan E. 474
Gregerson, Robert B. 401
Gregg, Donna Coleman 140
Gregg, Gary R. 295
Gregory, George 286
Gregory, James 355
Gregory, Stephen (Amsted) 43
Gregory, Steve (BlueCross BlueShield of
 Mississippi) 82
Greig, Andy 71
Greil, Shea 216
Greiner, Walter 118
Grela, Peter 338
Grenner, Lawrence 259
Gretenhart, Keith 197
Grevious, Jarvio A. 99
Grewcock, Bruce E. 396
Grewe, Wolfgang 154
Grieve, Tom 285
Griffin, John Q. 354
Griffin, Lester J. Jr. 490
Griffin, Mark 26
Griffith, Elizabeth A. 140
Griffith, J. Brian 333
Griffith, Ray A. 20
Griffith, Terry 325
Griffy, Timothy T. 180
Grigaliunas, Ben 24
Grilly, Eric J. 322

INDEX OF EXECUTIVES

Grilly, Gerald E. 322
Grimes, Tom 47
Grimm, Doug 330
Grimmer, Ralph 342
Grimshaw, Steve 429
Grissom, Stacey 40
Grist, Walter W. 92
Griswold, Scott A. 162
Grizzle, Charles 90
Grochow, Jerrold 337
Groom, Jeff 424
Grooms, Sharon 243
Gross, Arthur 233
Gross, Mark 100
Grossberg, Andy 253
Grossi, Richard A. 266
Grossklaus, Gary 422
Grossman, Ian 480
Grossman, Jennifer 162
Grossman, Lawrence S. 157
Grossman, Lewis 109
Grossman, Sandy 216
Grosvenor, Gilbert M. 353
Groswirth, Jill 24
Groth, Edward 136
Grottke, Robert 249
Groveman, Michael 75
Grover, Stephen A. 280
Grubbs, Walter 524
Grubman, Eric P. 352
Gruen, Frank 221
Gruen, Rob 325
Gruosso, Gerard 17
Guajardo, Beto 34
Guarascio, Phil 352
Guardia, Luis 140
Guarrero, Elaine 342
Gubanich, Kathleen C. 517
Guerci, Alan D. 109
Guerin, Ray 419
Guerini, Renato 285
Guerra, Elizabeth 186
Guerra, Frank F. 434
Guerrero, Scott 102
Guest, James 136
Guetens, Edward 418
Guge, Brett 97
Guido, Bob 20
Guillaume, Hervé 383
Guimaraes, Carlos 510
Guinn, Patricia L. 481
Guitreau, Joseph W. 490
Gulas, Vic 346
Gullo, Laura 431
Gum, Randy 111
Gunby, Steven H. 87
Gunkel, Thomas F. 303
Gunn, David L. 44
Gunn, John R. 327
Gunn, Richard 286
Gunter, James 207
Gunton, Howard E. 315
Gurnani, Roger 520
Gurtner, William H. 500
Gurwitz, Arthur 464
Gustafson, Brent 277
Gustafson, Carl 64
Guthy, William Bill 221
Gutmann, Amy 505
Gutnick, Michael P. 327
Guy, Kenneth H. 480
Guynn, Jack 188
Gwyn, Milou 265
Gyde, Richard J. 139

H

Haag, Daniel R. 303
Haarmeyer, Otis L. 475
Haas, Richard J. 37
Haas, Robert D. 294
Haase, H. Kenneth 365

Haber, Barry 131
Hachey, Barbara G. 170
Hachten, Richard A. II 31
Hack, Todd 106
Hackerman, Willard 535
Haddad, Edward 361
Hadden, Pat 493
Haddock, Jeff 260
Haddock, Ronald W. 429
Hade, Kevin 493
Haden, Kent 333
Haertel, Valerie 32
Hagale, James 67
Hagans, Robert R. Jr. 18
Hagen, Doug 38
Hagen, Sue 162
Hagenbuch, Diane S. 377
Hager, Lee F. 454
Hager, W. Douglas 59
Hagerty, Pat 524
Haggai, Thomas S. 249
Haggarty, Maureen 371
Haggen, Brad 222
Haggen, Donald E. 222
Haggen, Richard R. 222
Haglund, Claudia 406
Hahn, Helene 166
Haile, Donald A. 194
Haines, Raymond 461
Haining, Michael 487
Haist, David 160
Hale, Byron 182
Hale, Ellen 57
Hale, Lynne 301
Hale, Richard J. 82
Halford, Andrew N. 520
Halford, William 261
Hall, Almon C. III 370
Hall, Conrad M. 288, 482
Hall, Dave
 (Forever Living Products) 197
Hall, David E. (Hallmark) 223
Hall, David W. (CompuCom) 130
Hall, Donald J. (Hallmark) 223
Hall, Donald J. Jr. (Hallmark) 223
Hall, Frank 430
Hall, Gary 222
Hall, Gerri Mason 44
Hall, Gregory T. 121
Hall, J. Edward 92
Hall, Keith 187
Hall, Linda S. 407
Hall, Richard J. (US Oncology) 512
Hall, Richard K. (Teamsters) 470
Hall, Richard L.
 (Northwestern Mutual) 372
Hall, Rosemary 341
Hall, Sue 63
Hall, Ted V. 494
Hall, William H. 378
Hallam, Howard 73
Hallam, Robert 73
Haller, Michael R. 527
Haller, Richard J. 527
Halliday, Lisa 225
Hallinan, Kevin M. 306
Hallman, Lesly 40
Halloran, Jean 136
Hallworth, Richard 489
Halmi, Robert A. Jr. 223
Halpern, Philip 501
Halpin, Chip 89
Halpin, Stephen R. 117
Halsey, Casey S. 170
Halverson, Steven T. 226
Halvorson, George C. 273
Hamann, Darrel M. 102
Hamann, Dennis E. 540
Hamilton, Andrew D. 539
Hamilton, Ann M. 37
Hamilton, John E. 212
Hamilton, Mark 510
Hamlin, Scott J. 120

Hamlin, William 100
Hamling, James L. 74
Hamm, William R. 151
Hammond, C. F. III 214
Hampton, Barbara 376
Hampton, Claudette 64
Hamrick, Chris (Angelo Iafrate) 46
Hamrick, Chris (Blue Cross) 79
Hamsi, Marcos 311
Hancheruk, Michael 148
Hancock, Larry D. 248
Hancock, Todd 182
Handley, Christopher 459
Handren, Robert T. 514
Handwerker, Sybil 294
Hane, Bill 238
Hane, Laurie S. 341
Haneborg, Linda C. 185
Hanes, Ray 28
Haney, John 534
Hanft, Noah J. 316
Haninou, Diana 320
Hank, John L. Jr. 47
Hankel, Brian K. 335
Hankins, Anthony P 246
Hanlan, Tom 83
Hanlin, Russell L. II 465
Hanlon, Kris 250
Hanlon, R. Timothy 117
Hanman, Gary E. 146
Hannasch, Richard A. 160
Hanneman, Mike 47
Hannon, Floyd B. 242
Hannon, Trish 69
Hanrahan, Kaela 531
Hanrahan, Thomas F. 258
Hanratty, Steve 412
Hansen, Brian 342
Hansen, Christopher W. 18
Hansen, Michael K. 136
Hansen, Steven 396
Hansen, Thomas H. 406
Hanshaw, Kendall 249
Hanson, Bruce 333
Hanson, Dave 527
Hanson, James L.
 (Mutual of Omaha) 345
Hanson, James M. (Swagelok) 466
Hanson, Robert 294
Hanson, Ron 524
Hara, Patty 95
Haraf, Jo 341
Harden, James 109
Harding, Dick 55
Hardison, Matt 44
Hardman, Kevin 246
Hardwick, Rhonda 528
Hardy, Charles 60
Hardy, Joseph A. Sr. 16
Hardy, Richard 55
Hardy, Thomas 502
Harkema, Kathy Krafka 391
Harlan, Robert E. 216
Harmount, Rusty 207
Harnett, Craig 355
Harper, David J. D. 346
Harper, E. Royster 503
Harper, Michael 207
Harper, Ronald R. 67
Harper, Steve 228
Harper, Terrence P. 405
Harper, Trudy A. 471
Harpole, David 178
Harrigan, Sean 98
Harrington, Charles L. 387
Harrington, Marguerite 482
Harrington, Paul 294
Harris, Beth A. 501
Harris, Freda 510
Harris, Freddie 386
Harris, John (Lincoln Property) 297
Harris, John A. (Hines Interests) 237
Harris, John F. (Carlyle Group) 104

Harris, Martha 507
Harris, Nancy 160
Harris, Natalie 149
Harris, Peter L. 152
Harris, Reuben T. 100
Harris, Robert L. Jr. 138
Harris, Roger 179
Harris, Terry 419
Harrison, Alfred 32
Harrison, John 285
Harrison, Mark G. 33
Harrup, Steve 358
Harsh, Glenn 400
Hart, Craig 416
Hartgraves, John 90
Hartje, Keith D. 335
Hartlund, Jason 216
Hartman, Stewart Jr. 59
Hartman, William 64
Hartmann, Jeffrey E. 339
Hartner, Keith E. 54
Harton, Don 121
Hartung, Steven 184
Hartung, Susanne 467
Harty, Linda S. 428
Hartzell, Paul 329
Harville, Mary 275
Hasbrouck, Gail D. 24
Hasemeyer, Paul 215
Haseotes, George P. 144
Haseotes Bentas, Lily 144
Hash, Thomas F. 71
Haskell, Preston H. 226
Haskell, Robert G. 384
Haskins, Jim 355
Haskins, Rick 297
Haslam, James A. III 398
Hass, John R. 92
Hassan, Jad 16
Hassett, James A. 180
Hastie, Jeffrey 57
Hastings, David 414
Hastings, John S. 522
Hatchell, Dennis G. 31
Hatcher, Jack 305
Hatfield, Greg 437
Hatlen, Roe H. 92
Hatler, Patricia R. 359
Hattler, Eric 210
Haubursin, Dawan 130
Hauck, Loran D. 23
Hauck, Steve 290
Hauger, Gary 239
Haughom, John 390
Haught, Mel 391
Haumesser, John F. 56
Hauske, Thomas Jr. 184
Hausmann, Audrey 59
Hausmann, Ronald L. 527
Havala, Stephen P. 160
Havens, Elaine M. 384
Haverkamp, Michael F. 377
Hawes, Robert 181
Hawk, Carl J. 95
Hawk, David 272
Hawkins, Daryl 16
Hawkins, David 151
Hawkins, Frank 352
Hawkins, Robert 429
Hawkinson, Steve 160
Hawks, Howard L. 471
Hawley, Chuck 406
Hawn, Steve 223
Haworth, Richard G. 227
Hawthorne, Douglas D. 473
Hawthorne, Peter 102
Hayden, David 534
Hayden, Stuart 38
Hayes, Timothy F. 194
Hayford, Warren F. 95
Haymaker, James N. 101
Haynes, Carl E. 470
Haynes, Cindy 149

INDEX OF EXECUTIVES

Haynes, Mike 352
Hays, Michael D. 315
Hayward, John 390
Hayward, Richard A. 314
Haywood, John W. 106
Haywood, Ken 238
Hazelwood, Mark A. 398
Hazen, Paul M. 283
Hazlett, Scott 483
Head, Holman 380
Head, Kevin P. 328
Healey, Ada M. 526
Healy, Frank A. 289
Healy, L. Russell 246
Heard, Bob 50
Heard, William T. 75
Hearst, George R. Jr. 231
Heath, Lee 514
Heberstreit, James B. 65
Hebert, Richard 248
Hebert, Walter III 121
Heck, John M. 439
Hecker, David 434
Hedden, Dennis J. 193
Hedemann, G. Christian 77
Hedrick, Matt 429
Heemstra, Larry 533
Heffernan, Paul 361
Heffington, Joe 96
Heffley, Kathleen 63
Heflin, Rob 395
Hegarty, Amy 401
Heggelke, Steve 88
Heggie, Colin 16
Hegwood, Joseph B. 479
Heigl, Patrick 114
Heilig, Charles 386
Heilman, Leigh 56
Heilstedt, John 176
Heimbinder, Isaac 277
Heine, Dave 160
Heins, John 264
Heintze, Steve 324
Heinz, Curt 152
Heipt, J. Dennis 438
Heise, Rita J. 101
Heiser, Randy 205
Held, John 95
Heleniak, David W. 445
Helgren, Mark 202
Heller, Marita 318
Hellmuth, Steve 350
Helming, James 298
Helms, Jody 286
Helms, Robin 95
Helmsley, Leona 232
Helmstetter, David 144
Heltner, Don 460
Helton, Mike 348
Helwick, Christine 97
Hembree, R. Michael 405
Hembree, Tom 286
Hemingway, Jon 458
Hemingway Hall, Patricia A. 229
Hemphill, Neil 49
Hemsley, Michael C. 107
Henderschedt, Robert R. 23
Henderson, Harold R. 352
Hendrick, J.R. III 233
Hendricks, Diane M. 18
Hendricks, John S. 159
Hendricks, Kenneth A. 18
Hendricks, Kevin 18
Hendricks, Thomas E. 471
Hendrickson, Andy 166
Hendrickson, Grant 218
Hendrix, W. Blake 27
Hendry, William 193
Henick, Arthur 314
Henkel, Gary 489
Henkel, Laurie 89
Henkel, Robert J. 52
Henley, Dale C. 222

Hennessey, Bill 133
Hennessey, Stuart 390
Hennessy, John L. 459
Hennessy, Tim 103
Henrickson, Keith M. 467
Henrie, Bryant 290
Henriquez, François G. II 511
Henry, Brent L. 389
Henry, Elsie M. 184
Henry, Jack (Big Y Foods) 74
Henry, John K. (Duane Reade) 169
Henry, Kenneth L. 173
Henry, Richard (AARP) 18
Henry, Richard A.
 (McCarthy Building) 319
Henry, Suzanne 388
Hensing, John 64
Henslee, Thomas T. 125
Hensley, Stephen R. 472
Hepfinger, David 208
Heppel, Bob 401
Herbert, Adam W. Jr. 251
Herbst, Lawrence G. 167
Herdrich, William J. 88
Herlihy, Thomas M. 215
Herman, Gary S. 495
Herman, Harry 469
Herman, Joe 399
Herman, John W. 386
Herman, Richard 502
Hermanns, Robert P. 55
Hernandez, Enrique Jr. 257
Hernandez, Robert W. 354
Herod, Jane 308
Herran, Wayne 223
Herrin, Jeff 455
Herring, Edward 236
Herro, Lynn M. 368
Herron, Douglas A. 429
Herron, Jay 119
Herron, Winell 228
Hershberg, Howard 279
Hershenson, Jay 123
Hershman, Lawrence C. 500
Hertling, Richard J. 59
Hertog, Roger 32
Herwig, Keith 469
Herzig, Wade 527
Heskett, John R. 246
Hessel, Jerome C. 328
Hesser, Gregory T. 30
Hesson, David 123
Hester, Steve 118
Heston, W. Craig 515
Hetzer, Tom F. 360
Heubner, Jay 20
Heuer, Alan J. 316
Heuer, John J. 505
Hewett, Mark A. 335
Hexner, Thomas S. 32
Heyman, Samuel J. (G-I Holdings) 204
Heyman, Samuel J.
 (International Specialty Products) 259
Heymann, Thomas 17
Hiatt, Jonathan 26
Hickerson, Bill 275
Hickey, Christine 327
Hickok, Steven G. 84
Hicks, Kathleen M. 382
Hicks, Lucky 58
Hicks, Thomas O. 236
Hickson, Rob 358
Hier, Mark B. 336
Higgins, Elizabeth Bush 376
Highland, Randy 319
Highley, Duane D. 54
Hightower, Herma J. 452
Hilbert, Andy 489
Hildebrand, Phillip J. 364
Hill, Charlie W. 288
Hill, David F.
 (International Data Group) 258

Hill, David K. Jr.
 (Kimball Hill Homes) 277
Hill, Douglas E. 269
Hill, Edwin D. 26
Hill, Larry 239
Hill, Otis 123
Hill, Paul W. 60
Hill, Robert 21
Hill, Sam 398
Hill, Terri L. 359
Hillebrand, Jeffrey H. 183
Hils, Peter 167
Hinderliter, Michael H. 483
Hines, Gerald D. 237
Hines, Jeffery C. 237
Hiney, Robert A. 365
Hinshaw, Juanita H. 214
Hinton, J. Phillip 130
Hipp, Frederick R. 42
Hirano, Michael 210
Hirsch, Andrea 129
Hirsh, David 129
Hirshorn, James B. 440
Hiscox, Thomas 496
Hitpas, Jerry 488
Hlis, John 86
Hlobik, Lawrence S. 272
Ho, Claire 409
Ho, Eileen 444
Hobart, Al 470
Hobbes, Peter 311
Hobbs, W. Douglas 479
Hobson, Lewis 371
Hobson, Mark 440
Hoch, Ira J. 476
Hochman, Rod 442
Hockfield, Susan 337
Hockle, Mary 47
Hodge, Edmund F. 23
Hodges, Thomas H. 183
Hodgson, Christine 177
Hodgson, Judy 390
Hodnik, David F. 20
Hoech, Stephen L. 541
Hoeg, Thomas E. 42
Hoeltke, Michael K. 346
Hoenig, Thomas M. 188
Hoer, Michael A. 137
Hoeske, Richard J. 374
Hoff, George 432
Hoffa, James P. 26, 470
Hoffman, Dave 217
Hoffman, Gail 129
Hoffman, Gil 308
Hoffman, James D. 173
Hoffman, Jo Ann S. 340
Hoffman, Larry J. 216
Hoffman, Lee 142
Hoffman, Michael 519
Hoffman, Nina D. 354
Hoffman, Norman 482
Hoffmann, Max R. 334
Hofmann, G. Michael 440
Hogan, Kate 216
Hogan, Michael J. 502
Hogan, Robert G. 481
Hogan, Tom 191
Hogan, William J. Jr. 501
Hogberg, David E. 76
Hogen, Robin 408
Hoggarth, Karen 262
Hoiberg, Dale 177
Hojnacki, Michael J. 398
Holbrook, Karen A. 378
Holcomb, Robert J. 525
Holcombe, Jerry 154
Holder, Jerry B. 280
Holder, Ray 204
Holding, R. Earl 449
Holdsworth, Raymond W. 24
Holets, Thomas D. 33
Holford, Neal 260
Holgate, Randy L. 501

Holl, David B. 312
Holland, Colin 285
Holland, Skip 346
Hollander, Ellie 18
Hollenbeck, David A. 210
Holley, Connie 158
Holley, Jeff 145
Hollinger, Mark 159
Hollingsworth, J. Mark 137
Hollinshead, John A. 178
Hollis, Byron 79
Hollis, M. Clayton Jr. 407
Holloway, Randy J. 171
Holly, Norman D. 396
Holm, George 524
Holman, Bob 159
Holman, Joseph S. 240
Holman, Mindy 240
Holmes, Michael R. 269
Holmes, Walter 260
Holmes-Bobo, Rita 382
Holmlund, Mark W. 384
Holst, James E. 500
Holstein, Michael 522
Holt, Newell E. 497
Holtzman, Mark 352
Holwill, Richard 314
Holzberg, Harvey A. 421
Holzman, Larry 144
Homer, John 18
Homrighaus, Barry 262
Honce, Tom 56
Honda, Shinji 468
Hondros, Paul J. 359
Hong, John 492
Honickman, Harold 241
Honickman, Jeffrey 241
Hood, Danny 539
Hood, Ron 358
Hood, Susan 460
Hoogendoorn, Piet 154
Hook, Gregory 30
Hooker, Steve 415
Hoopes, Jeffrey C. 467
Hoover, George L. 27
Hoover, Myron 351
Hopfield, John J. 68
Hopkins, Kirk 182
Hopp, Beverly 50
Hoppe, Michael J. Jr. 208
Hopper, Jeff 401
Hopping, Jamie E. 49
Horder-Koop, Robin 34
Horn, Charles L. 93
Horne, Ed 355
Horne, Eleanor V. 175
Horne, James W. 126
Horner, Kenneth J. Jr. 414
Hornish, Harry K. Jr. 358
Horsley, Mark 335
Horton, Daniel E. 434
Horton, David L. 160
Horton, Joseph R. 258
Horvath, Albert G. 129
Horvath, Dolores 248
Horvath, James J. 36
Hoskins, John M. 491
Hoskyn, Thomas C. 419
Hosokawa, Koichi 278
Hostetler, Nancy E. 155
Hostetter, David B. 42
Hotchkiss, Nelle P. 371
Hotopp, John A. 300
Hough, William L.
 (Vanguard Health Systems) 518
Hough, William R.
 (CHEMCENTRAL) 116
Houle, Patricia S. 88
Houmann, Lars D. 23
Hourihan, John 143
House, Mark 71
Houser, Karen 158
Hovde, Rob 424

INDEX OF EXECUTIVES

Howard, David A. 417
Howard, John V. Jr. 521
Howard, Laurence W. 257
Howard, Norm 274
Howard, Peri N. 242
Howard, Robert 464
Howe, Douglas T. 125
Howe, Michael W. 33
Howell, Edward R. 298
Howell, Frank J. 392
Howell, Rick 128
Howell, Terry 358
Hower, Matthew J. 43
Howlett, Lori R. 66
Hoyler, Geraldine 108
Hoyt, Deborah 133
Hrabusa, John T. 407
Hradil, Joe 89
Hromadka, William C. 507
Hsu, Daniel 278
Hsu, Robert C. 384
Hubacker, Fred L. 519
Hubbard, Clint 70
Hubbard, Kenneth W. 237
Hubbard, Skip 83
Huber, John 209
Huber, Walt 186
Huckvale, Randy 249
Hudgins, Clifton T. 67
Hudson, Betty 354
Hudson, Luanne 297
Huerta, John E. 452
Huerter, M. Jane 345
Hueter, Jack 107
Huettich, Noel J. 417
Huff, Wynelle J. 22
Huffines, James R. 508
Huffman, Gary T. 496
Huffstutler, C. David 326
Huge, Arthur 328
Hugh, Yoon J. 162
Hughes, David 371
Hughes, Gerald T. 243
Hughes, James 254
Hughes, Larry 305
Hughes, Mark V. III 438
Hughes, Michael (Kaleida Health) 273
Hughes, Michael C. (Bechtel) 71
Hughes, Ron 519
Hughes, Timothy W. 141
Huizenga, H. Wayne 185
Hulick, Robert S. 489
Hull, Jeff L. 60
Hull, Keith M. 62
Hulme, Paul 245
Hulseman, Robert L. 453
Hulsen, Mike 163
Humes, Ed 39
Hummel, Dennis 308
Hummel, John 466
Hummel, Joseph W. 273
Humphrey, Heather 149
Humphrey, James E. (Amsted) 43
Humphrey, James E.
 (Andersen Corporation) 46
Humphrey, Mike 149
Hunstad, Robert E. 336
Hunt, F. Derald 268
Hunt, Gordon C. Jr. 466
Hunt, K. Kellogg Jr. 101
Hunt, Ray L. 244
Hunt, Robert 217
Hunt, Woody L. 508
Hunter, Beecher 296
Hunter, Clay 224
Hunter, Donna 265
Hunter, Jim 348
Hunter, Lee 455
Hunter, Stephanie A. 24
Hunter, Steven L. 458
Huntley, Lee 64
Huntsberry, Lisa 260
Huntsman, Jon M. Sr. 245

Huntsman, Peter R. 245
Hunzeker, Fred R. 471
Huon, Jean-Claude 75
Hupp, Stephen E. 182
Hupp, William T. 182
Hurley, Bailey 522
Hurley, Brian J. 193
Hurley, Frederick L. 274
Hurley, Maureen O. 420
Hurlow, Randy 416
Hurrle, Patrick J. 358
Hurry, Bonnie 150
Hurst, Michael D. 319
Hurwitz, Jerard 327
Huskins, Keith G. 357
Huston, Debbie 397
Hutchings, Richard S. 434
Hutchinson, R. Kenneth 504
Hutchison, Greg 427
Hutchison, Heather T. 24
Huth, Johannes 283
Hutterly, Jane M. 434
Hutton, Richard E. 526
Huzl, James F. 233
Hyatt, Jim 94
Hyatt, Richard A. 305
Hyatt, Scott D. 261
Hyde, James R. 324
Hyde, Matt 416
Hylbert, Paul 289
Hyman, Steven E. 226
Hynes, Toby 221
Hynson, Jan 187

I

Iafrate, Angelo E. Sr.
 (Angelo Iafrate) 46
Iafrate, Angelo E. Jr.
 (Angelo Iafrate) 46
Iafrate, Dominic 46
Iapalucci, Samuel H. 114
Ibbotson, John 127
Ibsen, Greg 272
Icahn, Carl C. 20
Ideson, D. Scott 415
Idrovo, Javier H. 162
Idzior, Ray 111
Ienner, Don 454
Iftiniuk, Alan 110
Ihrig, Weldon E. 509
Ilardo, Samuel J. 456
Imesch, Dave 66
Imhof, Chris 401
Imhoff, Stephanie 299
Immenschuh, Kent 170
Impara, Carol 481
Incaudo, Joseph A. 24
Indgjer, Lisa 18
Infusino, Thomas 527
Ingerman, Mitchell 292
Ingevaldson, Paul M. 20
Inglese, Michael J. 385
Ingram, David B. 253
Ingram, John R. 254
Ingram, Martha
 (Ingram Industries) 254
Ingram, Martha R.
 (Vanderbilt University) 516
Ingram, Orrin H. II 254
Ingulsrud, Brian F. 36
Ingwersen, Marc 191
Inman, Doug 312
Inserra, Lawrence R.
 (Inserra Supermarkets) 254
Inserra, Lawrence R. Jr.
 (Inserra Supermarkets) 254
Inserra, Theresa 254
Ippoliti, Patricia 259
Ippolito, Gary 172
Irby, Edward C. 191
Irby, Mark R. 407

Irish, Charles A. 535
Irish, George B. 231
Irvine, Lynda 342
Irwin, John A. 184
Irwin, Mark D. (Integris Metals) 255
Irwin, Mark W. (Nalco) 347
Irwin, Rena 467
Irwin, Robert G. 421
Isaac, Rory 320
Isaacson, Dean B. 27
Isaacson, H. Richard 250
Iseman, Frederick J. 92
Isenhower, Stephen 449
Ishbia, Earl 446
Itami, Steve 197
Ittner, Gary 320
Iuliano, Robert I. 226
Ivers, Amy 497
Iverson, Marilyn 50
Iverson, Mark 243
Ives, Nancy J. 510
Ivy, Steve 123

J

Jaacks, James R. 449
Jablonski, Zygmunt 497
Jaccodine, Catherine 21
Jacks, Dan M. 297
Jackson, Brian K. 493
Jackson, Don 198
Jackson, Eric H. 439
Jackson, Gregory A. 501
Jackson, James 477
Jackson, Kathryn J. 491
Jackson, Kevin 463
Jackson, Loyd 90
Jackson, Michael L. 507
Jackson, R. Wayne 404
Jackson, Ronald 203
Jackson, Ryan 437
Jackson, Stu 350
Jackson, Tammy 132
Jackson, Thomas H. 506
Jackson, Wes 499
Jacobellis, Luke 265
Jacobs, F. Nicholas 132
Jacobs, Irwin L. 202
Jacobs, Jeremy Jr.
 (Delaware North) 153
Jacobs, Jeremy Sr.
 (Delaware North) 153
Jacobs, John H. 496
Jacobs, Louis M. 153
Jacobs, Seth 81
Jacobson, Harry R. 516
Jacobson, Richard J. 141
Jacoby, Robin M. 389
Jacquet, Ernest K. 257
Jacunski, John P. 417
Jaeger, Mark 265
Jaeger, Steve 409
Jaffer, Azeezaly S. 514
Jagtiani, Anil 223
Jain, Terri 328
Jakubowicz, Donna 66
James, Donna A. 359
James, Ellen 510
James, Lark S. 371
James, Laura 176
James, Mike 329
James, Reggie 136
Janesz, Dennis 420
Janeway, Dean 527
Janik, Douglas J. 315
Janiszewski, Charles A. 27
Janke, Dean H. 419
Jankus, Tom 408
Janollari, David 530
Jansen, Cy 436
Jansson, Dwain 53
Jansta, Mike 343

Janzen, Peter 287
Jaramillo, Jonathan 364
Jarchow, Edward R. 66
Jarrell, Donald M. Sr. 379
Jarvis, Jeff 21
Jasinkiewicz, Ken 527
Jason, Joseph B. 313
Javier Ahumada, Francisco 211
Jean, Roger L. 295
Jefferson, John 342
Jehle, Michelle 129
Jenkins, Carlton J. 541
Jenkins, Charles H. Jr. 407
Jenkins, Francis P. Jr. 427
Jenkins, George 148
Jenkins, Howard M. 407
Jenkins, Sheila 267
Jennings, Brian 355
Jennings, Paul 297
Jensen, Carolyn 51
Jensen, Kris 532
Jeppesen, Linda 290
Jernigan, Donald L. 23
Jewell, Sally 416
Jewett, Ted 128
Jezouit, Fred 454
Jichlinski, Michel 300
Jimenez, A. David 109
Jimenez, Augusto 168
Jimenez, Tony 39
Joachim, Steven A. 349
Jobe, David 333
Jochem, David J. 88
Jochem, Marcia C. 88
Jodie, Kregg 312
Johanson, John 183
Johansson, Karl 180
Johansson, Kurt J. 309
Johnigan, Richard H. Jr. 246
Johnsen, Kenneth W. 445
Johnsen, Kim 371
Johnsey, Walter F. 168
Johnson, Abigail P. 194
Johnson, Andrea M. 313
Johnson, Brad (Bloomberg) 78
Johnson, Brad (REI) 416
Johnson, Brian E. 400
Johnson, C. Hastings 237
Johnson, Cheryl 524
Johnson, Craig 496
Johnson, Dale D. 496
Johnson, Daniel (Georgia Lottery) 204
Johnson, Daniel L.
 (M. A. Mortenson) 303
Johnson, David (Memec) 326
Johnson, David H. (Warner Music) 528
Johnson, Dawn M. 514
Johnson, Don
 (Simpson Investment) 448
Johnson, Donny
 (Brookshire Brothers) 91
Johnson, Edward C. III 194
Johnson, Eunice W. 267
Johnson, Galen G. 101
Johnson, George (Averitt Express) 61
Johnson, George D. Jr.
 (Extended Stay America) 185
Johnson, Grant 291
Johnson, Greg 351
Johnson, H. Fisk 434
Johnson, Hope 537
Johnson, J. Brent 37
Johnson, James E. 336
Johnson, Jerry 91
Johnson, John
 (David Weekley Homes) 149
Johnson, John (Plains Cotton) 398
Johnson, John H.
 (Johnson Publishing) 267
Johnson, John T. (Estes Express) 182
Johnson, Jon (TruServ) 487
Johnson, Justin 306
Johnson, Keith A. 137

HOOVER'S HANDBOOK OF PRIVATE COMPANIES 2005

INDEX OF EXECUTIVES

Johnson, Kenneth 439
Johnson, Kevin 144
Johnson, Linda L. 323
Johnson, Lori 401
Johnson, Lynn 267
Johnson, Marguerite M. 274
Johnson, Mark W. 92
Johnson, Michael O. 235
Johnson, Mitchell 267
Johnson, Paula R. 271
Johnson, Peter 250
Johnson, Randall W. (Penske) 393
Johnson, Randy
  (American Crystal Sugar) 36
Johnson, Randy (Riceland Foods) 419
Johnson, Ray F. 25
Johnson, Richard P. 41
Johnson, Rob 66
Johnson, Robbin S. 101
Johnson, Roger W. 465
Johnson, Ronald A. 509
Johnson, Samuel Curtis III 268
Johnson, Sandra A.
  (Maryland State Lottery) 313
Johnson, Sandra K.
  (Adventist Health System) 23
Johnson, Steve 33
Johnson, Terry L. 502
Johnson, Tina P. 407
Johnson, Tom 469
Johnson, Tyson 470
Johnson, Van R. 466
Johnson, Wesley R. Jr. 268
Johnson, William S. 173
Johnson Rice, Linda 267
Johnson-Winegar, Anna 35
Johnston, Alastair 250
Johnston, Daniel J. 498
Johnston, Douglas E. Jr. 400
Johnston, Frank 371
Johnston, Jack W. (Primus) 404
Johnston, James 518
Johnston, John D.
  (ValleyCrest Companies) 516
Johnston, Murray L. Jr. 541
Johnston, Paul P. 29
Johnston, Robert M. 238
Johnston, Stephen K. 496
Jonas, Stephen P. 194
Jonckowski, Dave 55
Jones, Alec N. 404
Jones, Angela 138
Jones, Barbara Kerwin 421
Jones, Bill 380
Jones, Brian S. 374
Jones, Cheryl-Ann 222
Jones, Chris 311
Jones, David (Rand McNally) 413
Jones, David (Team Health) 469
Jones, David C.
  (Dairy Farmers of America) 146
Jones, David D.
  (Bon Secours Health) 83
Jones, Donald G. 23
Jones, E. Laverne 476
Jones, Fletcher Jr. 192
Jones, Jan 406
Jones, John (K-VA-T Food Stores) 286
Jones, John M.
  (Green Bay Packers) 216
Jones, Mark 90
Jones, Michael D. 349
Jones, Miles E. 151
Jones, Philip (United Way) 499
Jones, Phillip E.
  (University of Iowa) 502
Jones, Robert J. 504
Jones, Ronald L. 151
Jones, Russ 534
Jones, Stephen K. 421
Jones, Sterling P. 459
Jones, Walker 125
Jones, William 436

Jones, Zack 119
Jongepier, Wouter W. 418
Jordan, John W. II 270
Jordan, Linda 431
Jordan, Margaret H. 473
Jordan, Robert P. 512
Jorge, Robert 208
Jorgenson, Richard T. 131
Jorris, Steve 381
Joseph, Gayle A. 219
Joseph, Robert H. Jr. 32
Joslin, Raymond E. 231
Jost, Jerry 111
Joubran, Robert J. 400
Joyce, Robert J. 534
Joyce, Stephen 52
Joyce, William H. 347
Joyner, David S. 81
Joyner, Robert C. 469
Juarez, Rumaldo 472
Judd, Barbara 477
Judd, Steven W. 189
Judelson, Andrew 355
Juengling, Craig S. 23
Jukes, Doug 285
June, Lee N. 334
Jungers, Marc 119
Junqueiro, Steve 433
Junco, Kirk D. 289
Jura, James J. 54
Jurgens, Richard N. 247
Jurgensen, William G. 359
Justman, Steve 350
Justus, Bill 149
Justus, Jerry 50
Justus, Michael 505

K

Kabeche, Elias J. 91
Kabel, Steve 538
Kacere, Ken 298
Kachele, Andrew 496
Kaczka, Joseph A. 417
Kaczmarek, Mike 409
Kadell, Sharon 536
Kahle, Rita D. 20
Kahn, Bette 183
Kahn, Jordan A. 240
Kahn, Kenneth F. 346
Kahn, Mario 465
Kain, Robert D. 250
Kaiser, Rick 412
Kaisler, Kim 303
Kalawski, Eva 400
Kale, Tom D. 472
Kalff, Bill 531
Kalikow, Peter S. 333
Kalinowski, Walter 396
Kallas, Kathryn D. 386
Kallmann, Ralph 174
Kalt, Robert J. 541
Kalupa, James 479
Kalvani, Bimal A. 88
Kamen, Charles M. 322
Kamenick, Duaine 197
Kamins, Philip E. 401
Kammlah, Ross 90
Kampen, Dan 511
Kamps, Trudy 38
Kandt, Keith 398
Kane, Edward K. 220
Kaneb, Gary (Gulf Oil) 220
Kaneb, Gary R. (HP Hood) 244
Kaneb, John (Gulf Oil) 220
Kaneb, John A. (HP Hood) 244
Kanuk, Thomas J. 167
Kanzler, Michael W. 492
Kaplan, Herbert 529
Kaplan, James I. 92
Kaplan, Lee R. 178
Kappitt, Mike 94

Karba, Gerhard 237
Karch, Paul J. 48
Karen, Nancy 446
Karet, Laura 205
Karkos, Denise 298
Karnei, Clifton B. 90
Karpinksi, Dave 287
Karst, Darren W. 426
Kasdin, Robert A. 129
Kaskie, James R. 273
Kassirer, Sheridan L. 389
Kasten, James 197
Katz, Jim 477
Katz, Mark 181
Katz, Michael W. 410
Katz, Ronald C. 176
Katz, Susan 487
Katzenberg, Jeffrey 166
Kauffman, Scott 280
Kaufman, Bob 343
Kaufman, Joe 512
Kaufmann, Michael 154
Kaupa, Michael 386
Keady, Kurt J. 134
Keane, Kevin 297
Keches, George A. 494
Keck, Patty 114
Keck, Ray III 472
Keefe, David 398
Keefer, Elizabeth J. 129
Keegel, C. Thomas 470
Keeley, Brian E. 64
Keeley, John 88
Keeley, Rupert G. 523
Keenan, Thomas J. 246
Keeshan, Lawrence 404
Kegelman, Brian 239
Keil, Devin 428
Keillor, Larry 198
Keipp, Phil 358
Keith, David 441
Keithline, Wilson 477
Keitt, John 57
Kelch, Robert P. 503
Keleghan, Kevin T. 382
Kelleher, Kevin 454
Keller, Bryan J. 153
Keller, Michael C. 359
Kellert, Bob 198
Kelley, Dan 218
Kelley, Edward B. 514
Kelley, Mark A. 233
Kelley, Mary Lou 298
Kelley, Robert S. 493
Kelley, Scott C. 508
Kelley, William 215
Kelliher, John M. 240
Kellogg, Cal 50
Kelly, Edmund F. 295
Kelly, George B. 160
Kelly, Henry G. 60
Kelly, John C. 372
Kelly, Kevin 346
Kelly, Michael A.
  (Cumberland Farms) 144
Kelly, Michael R.
  (National Service Industries) 357
Kelly, Stephen E.
  (Battelle Memorial) 68
Kelly, Steve (Battelle Memorial) 68
Kelly, Theresa 243
Kelly, William 294
Kemp, Karen L. 153
Kemp, Kevin 442
Kendall, Bob 431
Kendall, Clifford M. 503
Kenealy, Pat 258
Kenneally, William 208
Kennedy, Bernard D. 278
Kennedy, Brian A. 229
Kennedy, Craig 178
Kennedy, Dennis G. 377
Kennedy, J. D. 278

Kennedy, James (Associated Press) 57
Kennedy, James C.
  (Cox Enterprises) 141
Kennedy, Jerome 285
Kennedy, K. Daniel 419
Kennedy, Lee 16
Kennedy, Michael D. 114
Kennedy, Paul 55
Kennedy, Tom 415
Kenney, Edward J.T. 344
Kenney, Tom 222
Kent, David 88
Kent, James R. 92
Kent, William M. 120
Kentzel, Donald L. 289
Kepner, Melissa 510
Kerfoot, Karlene 123
Kern, Howard P. 442
Kern, Kevin C. 96
Kern, Michael J. 246
Kernan, Richard T. 167
Kerns, David E. 77
Kerns, Steve 309
Kerr, Gavin B. 118
Kerr, Robert K. Jr. 72
Kerrigan, Stephen R. 126
Kersey, Dallas 269
Kershaw, Justin 538
Kertland, Keith 109
Keskey, Bob 33
Kessel, Silvia 331
Kessenich, Kathy 426
Kessinger, George W. 209
Kessler, Stephen L. 333
Ketchum, Richard G. 367
Ketola, Todd 66
Kettenbach, Michael 155
Kettmann, Cyndi 466
Kettner, Linda 502
Key, Sean 312
Keyes, Joseph 181
Keys, William M. 127
Khademi, Abbas 381
Khan, Aamer 138
Khek, Cindy 138
Khouri, Amer 255
Kiappes, John 342
Kibbon, Larry J. 528
Kidder, C. Robert 85
Kiehnau, Michael 46
Kielar, Richard M. 478
Kienker, James W. 308
Kiernan, Brian 487
Killam, Baker 470
Killebrew, Steve 337
Killian, Jim 74
Killian, Rex P. 52
Kilmer, Deborah K. 140
Kilroy, Thomas M. Jr. 496
Kimball, Richard B. 126
Kimble, Julie 380
Kimbrell, W. Duke 386
Kimmelman, Gene 136
King, Donald R. 208
King, Robert L. 461
King, Ronald S. 534
King, Sonny 22
King, Thomas S. 37
King, Tim 92
King, William K. 460
Kingsdale, Jon M. 489
Kingston, J. William 107
Kinkela, David 211
Kinman, Thomas E. 120
Kinnan, R. Douglas 42
Kinnett, Jock 189
Kinney, Catherine R. 367
Kinney, Charles Edward 280
Kinser, Dennis 58
Kinstle, Mike 325
Kintzinger, Douglas P. 262
Kiplin, Kimberly 474
Kiraly, Thomas E. 132

INDEX OF EXECUTIVES

Kirchhoeffer, Dan 178
Kirchner, Bryce 314
Kirk, Charles 203
Kirkpatrick, Keith 396
Kirkwood, Allan K. 396
Kirley, Tim 269
Kirst, Fred 487
Kirtland, John 190
Kirwan, William E. 503
Kislak, Lisa H. 125
Kissane, James F. 477
Kitchen, Denise 468
Kitchens, Gary 456
Kite, Richard D. 280
Kitei, Lisa 264
Kittoe, Larry 152
Kitz, Edward G. 426
Klancnik, Al 443
Klapper, Denise 429
Klaristenfeld, Harry I. 476
Klass, Cheryl 273
Klass, Stephen P. 501
Klatzkin, Terri D. 124
Klauser, Rick 398
Klausner, Richard D. 75
Klaussner, Hans J. 280
Klebous-Zivny, Lori 156
Klee, Julie 294
Klein, Arthur A. 369
Klein, John 540
Klein, Paul 420
Klein, Russ 94
Klein, Scott W. 252
Klein, Sharon 67
Kleinbaum, Linda 333
Kleinschmidt, Robert 102
Klenke, Charlotte 435
Kletjian, Richard J. 494
Kletjian, Robert P. 494
Kletjian, Steven C. 494
Kletz, Patti Ann 331
Kline, Howard 275
Klingensmith, James 237
Klinzing, George E. 506
Kloster, Carol G. 115
Kloster, Karl 319
Klotzer, Michele 161
Kluge, John W. 331
Kluge, Jürgen 321
Klump, Ron 292
Knaack-Esbeck, Jane 247
Knapp, Al 477
Knedlik, Ronald W. 31
Knee, Kevin 221
Knievel, Mike 169
Kniffen, Craig 38
Knight, Alfred B. 439
Knight, Calvin 467
Knight, George F. 85
Knight, Jeffrey A. 219
Knights, Amy 94
Knittel, Monty 22
Knobbe, Michael J. 27
Knoll, Allan F. 414
Knorr, Stephen 504
Knotek, Gerry 357
Knudson, Rick 370
Knutsen, Nancy 51
Knutson, Daniel E. 287
Knutson, Ronald J. 20
Kobus, Gary 297
Koch, Charles G. 281
Koch, Clark 416
Koch, Dan 163
Koch, David H. 281
Koch, Gary 58
Koch, Joseph T. 190
Koch, Phil P. 113
Koch, Robert L. II 281
Koch, Suzanne 198
Koch, William I. 382
Koenig, Mark 406
Koenig, Marvin 417

Koenig, William C. 372
Koeppel, Micha 486
Koerner, Philip D. 305
Koester, Ken R. 113
Koguan, Leo 452
Kohler, David 284
Kohler, Herbert V. Jr. 284
Kohler, Laura 284
Kohn, Donald L. 188
Kohrt, Carl F. 68
Kokinakis, George 264
Kolb, Suzanne 530
Kolder, Kathryn 200
Kolp, Erin 119
Koltis, Theodore J. 478
Komar, June 440
Komodikis, Maria 17
Konerding, Jan 404
Konsker, Mitchell L. 145
Kontos, Mark W. 68
Konz, Ken 140
Koons, James E. 263
Koop, Al 34
Kop, Garrett 430
Korba, Robert W. 431
Koren, Michael J. 322
Korn, Allan M. 79
Kornafel, Pete 106
Korse, David 258
Korsmeier, Gary L. 96
Korsmeyer, Mark 146
Koschik, David N. 534
Koschka, Ed 130
Koskovolis, Lou 181
Koster, John F. 406
Kosterman, Gayle P. 434
Kotagal, Uma 120
Kou, Ming Bin 415
Kou, Ming Shin 415
Kou, Shan Chun 415
Kou, Shu Chin 415
Kourafas, Jim 28
Kovalchuk, Brian 383
Kowal, Dave 151
Kowalk, Jeffrey M. 318
Kozicz, Gregory J. 30
Kozik, Susan S. 476
Kraeger, Rob 111
Kraemer, Jan 319
Kraft, Ron 99
Krakowiak, Robert R. 383
Kralik, Robert 210
Krall, David G. 171
Kramnick, Isaac 138
Kramp, Kerry A. 92
Kranisky, Michael 496
Kranzley, Arthur D. 316
Krasinksi, Connie 273
Kratochvil, James M. 88
Kraus, Eileen S. 133
Krause, Alan 346
Krause, David W. 465
Krauss, Cheryl 62
Krauss, Mark 454
Krausz, Ken 116
Kravas, Connie 509
Kravis, Henry R. 283
Krawitz, Natalie R. 504
Krch, Cindy 537
Kreager, Heather 431
Kreditor, Alan 507
Kremer, D.F. 116
Kremin, Kathryn 415
Kresa, Kent 104
Kress, William F. 215
Kreuze, Calvin W. 227
Krevans, Rachel 341
Kribel, Ken 454
Kriegel, William 450
Krieger, Burton C. 86
Krier, Cindy T. 508
Krislov, Marvin 503
Krisowaty, Robert 534

Kristensen, Douglas A. 505
Kristoff, Sandra J. 364
Kriz, H.W. 390
Krizak, John 396
Kropiunik, Frank C. 30
Krueger, James 40
Krugle, Mike 205
Kruk, Bernadette M. 437
Krumholz, Mimi 291
Krupnick, L. A. 251
Krysh, Joseph 323
Krznarich, Debbie 337
Kubicek, Paul 284
Kuchta, Susan 192
Kudlinska-Pyrz, Ewa 312
Kudrle, Venetia 33
Kudron, Timothy G. 471
Kuehl, Tom 511
Kuehne, Carl W. 38
Kuehnle, Edward C. 252
Kuffner, Charles P. 467
Kuhl, Edward J. 305
Kuhlman, Erin M. 387
Kuhn, Edwin P. 483
Kuhne, Alice 220
Kukowski, Dale 289
Kulla, Raymond J. 537
Kullman, Conny L. 255
Kumar, Sunil 259
Kummer, Fred S. 227
Kummer, June 227
Kunberger, Ken 95
Kuntz, James T. 417
Kunz, Heidi 81
Kuppinger, Mike 278
Kurnick, Robert H. Jr. 393
Kurth, Curtis 197
Kurth, Wolfgang P. 342
Kurtz, Thomas M. 132
Kurushima, Masakazu 97
Kushar, Kent 172
Kutcher, Kenneth E. 456
Kuykendall, David 199
Kuykendall, William 202
Kvock, Sue 175
Kwalwasser, Edward A. 367
Kypreos, Nick M. 488
Kyte, John 429

L

La Forge, Francis K. 529
LaBahn, John G. 116
Labak, Alexander 316
LaBarre, Dennis W. 268
LaBeau, Timothy R. 169
LaBode, Emmy M. 409
Lack, Andrew R. 454
Lacker, Jeffrey M. 188
Lacko, Joseph S. 169
Lacourse, Julien 155
LaCrosse, Catherine M. 358
LaCrosse, James E. 358
Lacy, Arvid 223
Lacy, Steven R. 284
Laderman, Louis N. 498
Ladner, Sherman 30
LaFleche, Paul E. 193
LaForte, Mario J. 337
Laird, Thomas J. 167
Lake, Karen E. 274
Lakey, Ron 262
Lakin, Edwin A. 86
Lakin, Kenneth S. 86
Lakin, Maralyn 86
Lakin, Peter 86
Lall, Kishore 414
Lalla, Ken 113
LaLonde, Timothy J. 106
Lamb, Eric 165
Lamb, Richard 531
Lamb, Steven G. 167

Lamb, Therese B. 84
Lambert, Joseph J. 154
Lamberti, Nicholas 261
Lambkin, William 151
Lamensdorf, Ben 459
Laminack, K. Gene 357
Lammers, Jim 148
Lamontagne, Steve 139
LaMorte, Debra A. 368
Lampros, George 115
Lampton, Bill 179
Lampton, Leslie B. Sr. 179
Lancaster, Bill 58
Lancaster, George C. 237
Lande, Kent 300
Landegger, George 388
Landgraf, Kurt M. 175
Landis, Gregory 88
Landroche, J.B. 204
Landsman, Steve 347
Lane, Carol 185
Lane, George 212
Laney, David M. 44
Lang, James 408
Lang, Tom 177
Langan, Ronald 342
Langdon, James C. Jr. 30
Lange, Cliff 81
Langella, Michael 266
Langer, Patricia 297
Langley, Susan 193
Langston, Thomas K. 458
Langwell, Dennis J. 295
Lanigan, Gary M. 333
Lankford, George 26
Lankford, Karen 454
Lankton, Gordon B. 374
Lanning, Al 227
Lansford, Gordon E. III 170
Lantos, Phyllis R. F. 369
Lanzillo, Louis J. Jr. 494
Lapayowker, Andrew 143
Lapekas, Edward A. 400
Lapinsky, Joseph F. 417
LaPoint, Arthur 386
LaPorta, Scott 294
Lapp, Katherine N. 333
Lappin, Harley G. 187
Lapres, Theodore E. III 374
Larch, Patrick 496
Larios, Rafael 290
Larkin, Michael 445
Larnerd, Glenn H. 237
LaRocca, Sal 350
Larochelle, Richard E. 356
Larsen, John L. 271
Larson, Carol S. 385
Larson, Charles R. 503
Larson, David M. 101
Larson, Eric 84
Larson, John E. 361
Larson, Linda 409
Larson, Marie 254
Larson, Timothy M. 271
Larsson, John 430
LaRusso, Frank 311
LaSalle, Gar 469
Laspa, Jude 71
Latchford, James 534
Latimer, David 396
Lato, Giovanni 248
Lau, Wade 380
Lauer, Steven K. 480
Lauf, Michael K. 132
Laurendeau, Jack 21
Lauria, James L. 171
Laurila, Duane 46
Lauterbach, Tom 221
Lauve, Davis J. 490
Lavandier, Bruno 347
LaVanway, D. Keith 56
Laverty, Cornelia H. 366
Lavrack, Wayne 202

INDEX OF EXECUTIVES

Law Dake, Susan 463
Lawler, Michael F. 471
Lawler, Paul J. 274
Lawlor, Casey 341
Lawlor, James E. 494
Lawonn, Ken 31
Lawrence, Ida 175
Lawrence, Josh 485
Lawrence, Ricky 213
Lawrence, Robert A. 194
Lawson, Brad 477
Lawson, John W. 122
Lawson, Paul E. 394
Lawson, Ralph 64
Lawson, Thomas 193
Lawton, Gregory E. 268
Laxner, David 113
Lazar, Eliot J. 369
Lea, Lyndon 236
Leach, Sandra 126
Leamer, Marybeth H. 141
Leaming, Nancy L. 489
Leape, James 385
Leavitt, Oliver 48
Lebens, Michael C. 471
Leber, Jeff 82
Lebish, Daniel J. 237
Leboza, Sue 268
Lechner, David E. 505
Leckman, Linda C. 258
Ledbetter, Bureon E. Jr. 118
Ledbetter, Randy 494
Lee, James W. 462
Lee, Randy 64
Lee, Robert E. 178
Lee, Steven C. 483
Lee, Thai 452
Leebern, Donald M. Jr.
 (Georgia Crown) 204
Leebern, Donald M. III
 (Georgia Crown) 204
Leeker, Mark 224
Lefebvre, Dick 330
LeFrak, Harrison 292
LeFrak, James 292
LeFrak, Richard S. 292
Leftwich, Gary 455
Legg, Anita 516
Legg, Dexter R. 295
Leggett, Catherine S. 521
Lehecka, Stephen 534
Lehman, Arnold S. 292
Lehman, David H. 338
Lehman, Jeffrey S. 138
Lehman, W. Douglas 384
Lehmkuhle, Stephen W. 504
Lehnhard, Mary Nell 79
Lehr, Philip 465
Leicht, Rick 351
Leiden, Mark 212
Leipzig, Frank 128
Leisure, Lawrence 273
Lekan, Renee 409
Leleux, Paul 39
Lembke, Mark L. 36
Lemoine, Paul 28
Lenderink, Gary B. 220
Lenker, Max 412
Lentz, Thomas W. 452
Lenzen, Michael 319
Leo, James 531
Leon, Jean G. 363
Leonard, David 455
Leonard, Laurie 381
Leong, Margaret 444
Leprino, James 292
Lerch, Marie 85
LeResche, Steve 52
Lerner, Adam M. 342
Lerner, Fred H. 420
LeRoy, Michael 156
Lescoe, Daniel 74
Lesley, E. Craig 155

Lesneski, Tim 325
Lester, Tim 105
Letterie, Kathleen 530
Leuliette, Timothy D. 330
LeVeque, Francis I. 329
LeVere, Tom 371
Leverson, Gretchen 512
Levin, Ken 413
Levin, Richard
 (Major League Baseball) 306
Levin, Richard C. (Yale University) 539
Levine, Arthur 506
Levine, Ellen Fine 156
Levine, Harlan 157
Levine, Larry 256
Levine, Len 210
Levine, Richard 411
Levine, Ron 408
Levingston, Keith D. 404
Levister, Tony 50
Levit, Max 217
Levit-Larner, Tracy 217
Levitetz, Jeff 408
Levitt, Arthur Jr. 104
Levitt, Wayne 201
LeVrier, David 237
Levy, Irvin L. 360
Levy, James 115
Levy, John I. 360
Levy, Lester A. Jr. 360
Levy, Maurice 305
Levy, Morris S. 388
Levy, Robert M. 360
Levy, Ronald J. 458
Levy, Shari 33
Levy, Susan Nestor 52
Levy, Walter M. 360
Levy Kipper, Barbara 115
Lew, Jacob L. 368
Lewellen, Larry M. 378
Lewin, Dennis 352
Lewis, A. Daniel 189
Lewis, Adam 321
Lewis, Bob 186
Lewis, Daniel C. 85
Lewis, Darwin 434
Lewis, Duncan 104
Lewis, James 190
Lewis, Jesse A. 286
Lewis, Joan J. 156
Lewis, Lemuel E. 288
Lewis, Merle D. 139
Lewis, Wendy 306
Lewis, William E. 405
Lewox, Hugh F. 90
Ley, Marc 261
Leydon, Betty 405
Liagre, Ruthann 156
Liakopulos, Nick 249
Liang, Christine 53
Liang, Louise L. 273
Liang, Marcel 53
Libby, Jay 46
Libengood, Mary 132
Liberatore, Jorinne 165
Liddy, Brian 436
Lieb, Jeanne R. 193
Liebel, Tim 312
Liebentritt, Donald J. 179
Lieberman, Evelyn S. 452
Lieberman, Frank H. 190
Lieberman, Gerald M. 32
Lieberman, Trudy 136
Liedel, Christopher A. 353
Lien, Thomas J. 198
Liennenbrugger, Herbert 391
Liles, Kevin 528
Lilly, Edward F. 443
Lilly, Steven L. 356
Limbacher, Scott 462
Lin, Jeannie 204
Lincer, Walt 193
Lind, Tacy 371

Lindahl, Dennis M. 239
Lindberg, Eric 236
Linden, Derek W. 349
Lindenbaum, Herman 421
Lindgren, Tim 247
Lindholm, Wayne S. 234
Lindley, Michael 26
Lindner, Sydney 145
Lindquist, William J. 137
Lindroth, Doug 326
Lindsey, Darryl 398
Lindsey, Frank 131
Linehan, Maureen 33
Ling, Robert M. Jr. 495
Linklater, William J. 63
Linn, Mike 537
Linnen, Joe 270
Linton, Tom 96
Linville, Randal L. 439
Liotta, Ann S. 374
Lipp, Marie 135
Lippard, Tom 489
Lippert, Michael 428
Lipsky, Charles I. 365
Lipstein, Steven H. 76
Lipton, Martin 368
Lira, Luis 126
List, John J. 356
Listi, Frank 208
Litner, Jon 355
Little, Mike 262
Little, Robert 275
Littlewood, Peter 311
Litwak, Jim 129
Litzsinger, R. Mark 195
Liu, Woon Fai 240
Liutkus, Tom 483
Livermore, Linda 127
Livingston, David WM. 39
Livingston, John T. 478
Livingston, Randall 459
Lloyd, Emily 129
Lloyd, Karen 130
Lloyd, Rjay 197
Loadman, Thomas D. 284
Lobaugh, Mike 222
Lobinsky, James J. 407
Lobmeyr, Stephan 236
Lobsinger, Jean 28
Lock, Chris 162
Lockard, Jamie 265
Lockard, John A. 360
Locklear, Andrea 464
Lockman, David 298
Lodge, Frederick Z. 341
Lodovic, Joseph J. IV 322
Loebbaka, Charles R. 373
Loeffler, Robert D. 228
Loehner, Ray 203
Loeser, David A. 130
Loffredo, Ken 132
Lofgren, Christopher B. 435
LoFrumento, John 51
Lofstrand, Andrea 266
Lofton, Kevin E. 108
Loftus, Patrick 489
Logan, Christopher 203
Logan, Colleen 248
Logan, Maria 392
Loh, Marcel 467
Lohman, Gordon R. 43
Lohmann, Christopher 284
Lohner, Michael D. 241
Lohnes, George R. 494
Lohr, William J. 443
Lomax, Sharman 204
Lomeli, Ann F. 315
Lommel, Ken 47
Lomniczi, Carlos 91
Lonergan, Daniel E. 471
Long, Bruce (Great Dane) 214
Long, Bruce (UNICOR) 187
Long, Bruce C. (Guardian Life) 220

Long, David 408
Long, Eric W. 60
Long, John (Dot Foods) 163
Long, John E. Jr. (TVA) 491
Long, Philip 539
Long, Robert A. (Dunn Industries) 170
Long, Robert F.
 (Kellogg Foundation) 274
Long, Russell 472
Long, Tom 170
Long, William D. (WinCo Foods) 536
Long, William E. (Eagle-Picher) 171
Longaberger, Tami 299
Longaberger Stukey, Rachel 299
Longshore, George F. 107
Longstreet, John 125
Loosbrock, Louis L. 347
Looyenga, Roger L. 61
Lopez, Johnny O. 400
Lopez, Julia I. 421
Lopez, Lucille 155
Lopez, Victor 247
Lorch, Robert K. 310
Lord, James J. 287
Lorenz, Mike 446
Lorimer, Linda Koch 539
Lorton, Donald E. 101
Loscocco, Peter 85
Lotman, Herbert 276
Lottes, A.E. III 106
Louge, Michael W. 379
Louis, A. Andrew R. 137
Louis, Alex 260
Louttit, Gordon J. 25
Louw, Rob 246
Love, Bruce 143
Love, Dennis M. 405
Love, Frank 300
Love, Gay M. 405
Love, Greg 300
Love, James E. III 405
Love, Tom 300
Love Meyer, Jenny 300
Loveland, David 183
Loveless, Connie 511
Lovell, Richard 103
Loveridge, Gary 466
Loving, James 351
Loving, Ronald A. 491
Lovins, Harriet 224
Lovoy, Cynthia 36
Lovstad, John E. 29
Lovvorn, Holly 165
Lowe, Russell 261
Lowe, William D. 235
Lowell, Joan 247
Lowery, Christopher J. 145
Lowman, Donald L. 481
Lowrey, F. A. 28
Loyd, Rodney 410
Lozano, Joe J. 541
Lozick, Edward A. 466
Lubozynski, Dennis J. 404
Lucas, George W. Jr. 301
Lucas, Mike 238
Luciano, Gene 115
Luciano, Tom 446
Luck, David A. 18
Lucki, Anthony 243
Lucking, John T. 510
Ludgate, Allan C. 164
Ludington, Robert 439
Ludwil, Bill 437
Luebrecht, Donald E. 144
Luedemann, John 444
Luedtke, Brian 468
Lueger, Susan A. 372
Luehrs, William R. 183
Lugo, Miguel 211
Lukas, John 106
Lukowski, Stanley J. 389
Lullo, Thomas A. 135
Lumpkins, Robert L. 101

INDEX OF EXECUTIVES

Lund, Constance E. 41
Lund, Jay 46
Lundberg, L. Erik 503
Lundeen, Tania 492
Lundin, John 121
Lungo, Pete 274
Lunny, Pam 171
Lunsford, Jeff 122
Luo, Jason 276
Luparello, Stephen I. 349
Lupo, Larry 311
Luse, Bob 64
Luttmer, Kelly D. 137
Lutz, Anne 83
Lutz, Yvonne 439
Lyall, Lynn 34
Lyman, Gregory A. 274
Lynam, John 421
Lynch, John J. 241
Lynch, Mary 119
Lynch, Michael (Atrium) 60
Lynch, Michael (Kinetics Group) 277
Lynch, Peter S. 194
Lynch, Richard J. 520
Lynn, Scott 124
Lyons, Gordon 436
Lyons, Mike 398
Lytle, Walter 470
Lytwynec, Brian P. 515
López Carbajal, Diego G. 91

M

Ma, Abraham 303
Ma, Michael 303
Maatta, John 530
Mac Donald, Martin 67
Macaulay, William E. 198
MacCarthy, Mark 523
MacDonald, Alan 420
MacDonald, Bryce 314
MacDonald, Laurie 166
Macdonald, Sarah T. 511
MacDonnell, Robert I. 283
Macek, Richard R. 156
MacEwan, Pam 218
Machen, James B. 502
Macht, Patricia K. 99
Macia, Alejandro 538
Mack, Chuck 470
Mack, David S. 333
MacKay, Michael L. 466
MacKenty, Michael C. 374
MacKenzie, Alan 468
MacKenzie, James A. 210
Mackenzie, Ken 202
MacKenzie, Ralph 148
MacKenzie, Robert 43
MacKinnon, Bill 285
Macko, Terry 129
MacLaren, Ian 277
MacLeay, Thomas H. 356
Maclin, Joan C. 439
Macnee, Walter M. 316
MacPhee, David 274
Macrides, Foster G. 144
Mactas, Mark 481
Maczko, Ed E. Jr. 358
Madara, James L. 501
Maday, Charles 17
Madden, Michael J. 344
Madden, Robert 534
Madden, Terry 202
Maddox, Elton 137
Maddox, Peter 119
Mader, Donald A. 494
Madia, William J. 68
Madison, George W. 476
Madison, Thomas F. 64
Madsen, Dennis 416
Madura, Paul 228
Maehl, Douglas A. 429

Magenheimer, Richard 254
Magerko, Maggie Hardy 16
Magliocco, John T. 391
Magliocco, Joseph 391
Magliocco, Nino 391
Magnusson, Carl G. 280
Magouirk, Mike 127
Magruder, Joan R. 77
Mahaffey, Lane T. 442
Mahan, Lt. Gen. Charles S. Jr. 50
Mahar, Dulcy 84
Maher, James V. 506
Maher, Mark W. 84
Maheu, Chris 397
Mahony, Edward B. 408
Mahurin, Steven L. 487
Maibach, Ben C. III 66
Maibach, Sheryl B. 66
Maiden, Benjamin G. 68
Maiorana, Michael 520
Maiorana, Ronald 230
Maistrovich, Janet A. 380
Majidi, Ben 114
Majka, Lawrence J. 24
Major, Mike 325
Major, Paul 38
Mak, Paul 312
Makanoff, Lon 446
Maki, Curt 480
Makos, Susan Smith 109
Malave, Ernesto 123
Malchoff, Kevin 420
Malcolm, Christine 273
Malcolm, Thomas W. 388
Malec, Kennan J. 466
Malicki, Dan 262
Malida, Julie M. 488
Malin, Bob 443
Malinsky, Dotty W. 470
Malkin, Mark 420
Mallery, Gilbert O. 44
Mallett, Conrad Jr. 156
Mallett, Gary 381
Malloch, Richard P. 231
Mallory, Bill 66
Mallory, Bruce 223
Malmskog, David L. 36
Malo, Norman R. 194
Malone, Richie L. 269
Malone, Thomas J. 336
Maloney, Bill 65
Maloy, Lisa M. 36
Maltarich, Robert 400
Maltas, Chris 382
Mancbach, Jimmy 454
Mandel, Keith 120
Mandell, Andrew J. 516
Manderfield, Marianne 209
Maneki, Freya 163
Maney, Bill 534
Manfred, Robert D. Jr. 306
Mangrum, Troy 198
Mangual, Evanessa 211
Manickam, Chellam 493
Manis, Jonathan 406
Manley, Frank D. 251
Manley, Mark R. 32
Manley, Paul 433
Mann, Joe 329
Mann, Keith 499
Mann, Neil 31
Mann, Susan 132
Manninen, Walter 258
Manning, Dennis J. 220
Manning, Keith D. 541
Manning, Kristin 88
Manning, Sylvia 502
Manning, Wendy 79
Mannix, Kevin 527
Mansfield, Christopher C. 295
Mansoor, Bill 114
Mansoor, Leah 177
Mansour, John 82

Mansur, Bernadette 355
Manuel, Mark A. 144
Manzi, Joe 121
Maranell, Michael L. 27
Marantz, Leon 300
Marcarelli, Dean 111
March, John D. 101
Marchant, Eric 370
Marcinelli, James A. 244
Marciniak, Jere D. 164
Marco, Linda 261
Marcon, Fred R. 494
Marcuccili, J. Brink 488
Maresca, Robert A. 331
Marfatia, Noshirwan 479
Margevicius, Joseph 527
Margolin, Leslie A. 273
Mariano, Robert A. 426
Marineau, Philip A. 294
Mariner, Jonathan D. 306
Marino, Lelio 338
Marino, Lorraine 338
Marino, Robert A. 241
Marino, William J. (Horizon Blue Cross Blue Shield of New Jersey) 241
Marino, William J. (Inductotherm) 251
Marion, Kathleen A. 479
Marion, Thomas D. 489
Maritz, W. Stephen 308
Mark, William 457
Markell, Peter K. 389
Markett, Alan 228
Markham, Doug 361
Markoff, Steven C. 34
Marks, Gordon W. 467
Marks, Paul A. 327
Marks, Sheila 75
Marks, Susan 453
Markus, Barry 357
Marley, Brian T. 72
Maroni, Alice 452
Marovich, Jim 98
Marrett, Phillip E. 41
Marrie, Mike 19
Mars, Jacqueline Badger 311
Mars, John Franklyn 311
Mars, Robert F. III 392
Marsh, Amy K. 506
Marsh, Doug 61
Marshall, Geoffrey 103
Marshall, Jonathan 71
Marshall, Pamela J. 84
Marshall, Phil 201
Marshall, Ruth Ann 316
Mart, Reba 289
Martau, Neil 257
Martens, Erwin W. 476
Martin, Bruce 344
Martin, Carolyn A. 138
Martin, Charles N. Jr. 518
Martin, Christopher J. 488
Martin, Daniel 345
Martin, David M. 191
Martin, Dennis R. 289
Martin, Don 142
Martin, Doug 318
Martin, Heather 160
Martin, Jana M. 471
Martin, Jeff 204
Martin, Jennifer H. 475
Martin, Kathryn 327
Martin, Keith 58
Martin, Kent 139
Martin, Peggy 108
Martin, Richard J. 495
Martin, Robert 191
Martincich, Carl 300
Martinez, Martha 98
Martinovich, Robert F. 170
Marucco, Albert M. 143
Marvin, Mary 337
Marynowski, W. John 379
Marzano, John A. 324

Masiello, Matt 132
Maslowe, Philip L. 42
Mason, Char 120
Mason, Paul 294
Massaro, Thomas 278
Massey, Darcy D. 434
Massey, Jerry 182
Massey, Marvin 92
Massingale, Lynn 469
Massman, Richard A. 244
Mast, Larry L. 392
Masters, Seth J. 32
Masterson, Michael M. 431
Masterson, Valerie 530
Mastrov, Mark S. 16
Masucci, Nicolas J. 300
Mater, Rich 530
Matestsky, Ira 211
Mathas, Theodore A. 364
Mather, Jayne G. 289
Matherne, Troy D. 167
Mathews, Jack 398
Mathews, Suresh V. 130
Mathews, Sylvia 75
Matheys, Steve 435
Mathias, Paul A. 268
Mathur, Yogesh 232
Matieu, Bernard M. 351
Matre, Bjorn 87
Matsuda, Craig 540
Matthews, B. Frank II 72
Matthews, Carl 210
Matthews, J. Scott 167
Matthews, James L. (American Tire Distributors) 41
Matthews, Jim (Bill Heard) 75
Matthews, John 268
Matthews, Rod 460
Matthews, Ron 469
Matthews, Ted 456
Mattia, Mark 311
Mattox, William C. 345
Mattuci, Robert J. 396
Matus, Kristi A. 514
Maughan, Gregg 197
Maughan, Rex Gene 197
Mauk, Melissa L. 90
Mauloff, Gregory J. 358
Maurer, Andrew J. 428
Maurer, Harold M. 505
Maurer, Mary R. 296
Mawer, Steve 282
Maxa, John G. 144
Maxwell, Greg G. 116
Maxwell, Mike 207
Maxwell, Pamela L. 257
May, Bruce 69
May, Cheryl 485
May, David L. 434
May, Jerry A. 503
May, Ken 182
May, Shannon 16
Mayer, Jeffrey P. 125
Mayer, Marc O. 32
Mayne, Florence 508
Mayo, Janice 521
Mayo, Ronald A. 322
Mayorek, John 131
Mays, L. Lowry 472
Mazany, Daniel K. 388
Mazur, Daniel F. 480
Mazza, William 186
Mazzarella, Kathleen M. 214
Mazzola, Phil 488
Mazzuca, Phillip J. 248
McAdam, Lowell C. 520
McAleenan, Donald F. 93
McAlister, David A. 388
McAlister, John R. 521
Mcateer, Thomas J. Jr. 230
McAuvic, Karen 527
McCabe, Barry L. 280
McCabe, Dennis P. 472

INDEX OF EXECUTIVES

McCabe, George 399
McCabe, James B. 118
McCaffery, R. Neil 173
McCaffrey, Thomas 456
McCall, Bron 193
McCall, Dawn L. 159
McCann, Pat 282
McCann, Paul 48
McCarthy, Mike 305
McCarthy, William J. 394
McCartney, John 533
McCarty, Jim 92
McCaskey, Raymond F. 229
McCaskill, Don 419
McCasland, Mike 462
McCaslin, Teresa E. 137
McCauley, David 342
McCauley, John 299
McClain, Jackie 97
McClellan, Stephen 273
McClellan Upicksoun, Alma 48
McClelland, Frances 444
McClelland, Kent 444
McClelland, Norman 444
McClelland, Scott 228
McClelland, Sue 172
McClerkin, Hays C. 50
McCleskey, John H. Jr. 118
McClone, Tom 38
McClung, Linda 119
McClure, Darris 119
McClure, David 396
McClure, Gail D. 274
McClure, Richard H. 496
McCluskey, Lynn 171
McCluskey, Robert 464
McColgan, Ellyn A. 194
McColgan, Linda 363
McCollister, Donald L. 490
McCollum, Thomas G. 149
McCollum, W. Lee 434
McCombs, David 83
McConkey, Gwynne 297
McConnell, Allen 19
McConnell, Michael W. 92
McConnell, Thomas J. 158
McConney, Jeffrey 486
McCoole, Robert F. 30
McCormack, Mark R. 284
McCormack, Todd 250
McCormack, William 437
McCormick, Chris 298
McCoy, John B. Jr. 68
McCoy, Kirk 190
McCoy, Marilyn 373
McCoy, Patrick J. 333
McCroskey, Sam E. 146
McCrudden, Christopher 405
McCullars, Art 92
McCulley, Michael J. 498
McCullough, Frank S. Jr. 365
McCullough, Glenn L. Jr. 491
McCullough, Gordon L. 39
McCurdy, John 400
McCurrie, Brian H. 284
McCurry, R. Alan 40
McCusker, Thomas J. 345
McCutcheon, Stephanie S. 83
McDaniel, John P. 324
McDearmon, Ron 337
McDermott, James E. Jr.
 (Amica Mutual) 43
McDermott, James H. (Appleton) 48
McDermott, Michael 265
McDonald, Andrew 426
McDonald, Bernadette 306
McDonald, Brian J. 405
McDonald, John 71
McDonald, Kirk 541
McDonald, Robert P. 40
McDonald, Scott 96
McDonnell, Brian L. 360
McDonnell, David C. 213

McDonnell, Sue K. 164
McDonough, David M. 488
McDonough, Maureen 46
McDonough, Peter G. 405
McDonough, Walter K. 464
McDougald, James L. 322
McDowell, Robbyn 173
McDowell, Steve 127
McDunn, Adrienne 406
McElheney, J. Ronald 371
McElroy, Peter 276
McElveen-Hunter, Bonnie 40
McEvoy, David L. 210
McFarland, Keith 472
McGarr, Joseph W. 537
McGarvie, Paul 276
McGill, Jean B. 35
McGinnes, Larry 264
McGinnis, Randall S. 146
McGinnis, Vern 218
McGinty, Clete 428
McGinty, Robert E. 360
McGonagle, Tom 524
McGovern, Donald A. 404
McGovern, John R. 465
McGovern, Patrick J. 258
McGowan, Dan (SEMATECH) 442
McGowan, Daniel T.
 (Health Insurance of New York) 230
McGrath, Con 308
McGrath, Karen 408
McGrath, Kate 363
McGrath, Robert T. 378
McGraw, Scott 159
McGregor, Andrew 276
McGuigan, John B. 465
McGuire, John F. III 40
McGuire, Maureen 52
McGuire, William D. 273
McHale, John Jr. 306
McHale, Judith A. 159
McHaney, Martha Jean 340
McHargue, W. Vernon Jr. 499
McHugh, Joseph H. 44
McHugh, Mary 467
McHugh, Robert 190
McIlquham, David J. 440
McIndoe, John 252
McInnes, Mike 484
McIntyre, Dennis L. 462
McIntyre, Mike 527
McIsaac, John 128
McKay, Alvin 144
McKay, Bruce 396
McKay, Michael 405
McKee, Jack C. 320
McKee, Joseph M. 116
McKee, Michael D.
 (Irvine Company) 261
McKee, Mike (McKee Foods) 320
McKee, Mike
 (University of Florida) 502
McKeegan, Janet 216
McKeehan, Effie 167
McKenna, John F. (CompuCom) 130
McKenna, John T. (Dresser) 167
McKenna, Richard M. 534
McKenna, William C.
 (Main Street America Group) 305
McKenna, William J.
 (Vought Aircraft) 525
McKenzie, Gary B. 477
McKenzie, J. Steve 329
McKenzie, Reggie 216
McKenzie, Ronald W. 477
McKinley, Ronald B. 120
McKinney, Joseph E. 151
McKinstry, Harry 20
McLarty, Thomas F. III 104
McLauchlan, Andrew 458
McLaughlin, David W. 368
McLaughlin, James 94
McLaughlin, Laura 33

McLaughlin, Maureen 218
McLean, Joseph 470
McLean, R. Bruce 30
McLean, Tom 93
McLean-Shinaman, Keith 69
McLemore, Douglas 279
McLeod, C. Bradford 382
McLernon, Chris 126
McMahon, Dan 446
McMahon, John 201
McMahon, William L. 274
McManmon, Thomas 207
McMillan, Henry M. 384
McMillan, Marilyn 368
McMillen, Steve 485
McMullan, Bart 415
McMurrain, Laura 266
McMurray, David 480
McNabb, F. William III 517
McNee, Allen J. 329
McNeely, Joyce 201
McNiece, Andy 223
McNish, Russ 117
McNulty, James F. 387
McNutt, Don 261
McPherson, M. Peter 334
McPherson, Robert 97
McRee, Sandra K. 247
McRobbie, Michael A. 251
McSally, Mike 31
McSween, W. Scott 117
McTeer, Robert D. Jr. 188
McTernan, Bernita 110
McTernan, Kevin J. 421
McWane, C. Phillip 322
McWay, Jacob 142
McWay, Michael J. 319
McWilliams, Mary O. 415
McWilton, Chris A. 316
Meachen, Edward 510
Mead, Dana G. 337
Meador, David 158
Meadows, Donnie 286
Meath, Michael 28
Mecca, Gerry 165
Mecham, Michael 369
Medford, Mark O. 491
Medlin, George L. 344
Medvidovich, Suzanne 513
Meece, Carl E. 466
Meehan, Patrick J. 243
Meehan, Ron 266
Meek, Sarah 46
Meekma, Ted 250
Megard, Chad 443
Mei, Jeffrey H. 537
Meier, Bryan 522
Meier, Tim 31
Meijer, Doug 325
Meijer, Fred 325
Meijer, Hendrik G. 325
Meilahn, Jairus E. 189
Meiland, Nico J. 434
Meins, Dan 419
Meister, Marcy 113
Melani, Kenneth R. 237
Melaugh, Michael G. 482
Melendez, Lou 306
Meleta, Karen 527
Melillo, Gary R. 346
Mellinger, Kristin 48
Melnick, Ken 494
Melton, Howell W. Jr. 239
Meltzer, David B. 255
Menard, Ellen 254
Menard, John R. Jr. 328
Menard, Larry 328
Menchel, Marc 349
Mendelson, Brian 257
Mendez, Jeraldine 425
Mendez, Lincoln 64
Mendoza, Charles J. 18
Meng, John C. 436

Meng, Lorraine 522
Menuet, Beth 19
Menzel, Phil 311, 419
Mercer, Brian 465
Merdek, Andrew A. 141
Meredith, Mimi 66
Meredith, W. George 68
Meresmen, Steve 115
Mergenthaler, Frank 129
Meriam, Harold 232
Merinoff, Charles 115
Merinoff, Herman I. 115
Merks, Nic A. 87
Meroni, Filippo 434
Merrill, Susan L. 367
Merritt, Marc R. 242
Merritt, Terry 527
Meschkow, Alan 390
Messana, Frank 346
Messick, Andrew 350
Messinger, Scott 290
Metelsky, Dan 377
Metropoulos, C. Dean 398
Metzinger, William 163
Metzler, Charles M. 456
Meurer, Thomas A. 244
Meyer, A. S. 116
Meyer, Alan E. 37
Meyer, Barb 449
Meyer, Calvin J. 27
Meyer, Donna 16
Meyer, Ed 436
Meyer, Finn L. 285
Meyer, Jeff 190
Meyer, John M. 137
Meyer, Mark 22
Meyer, Michael G. 382
Meyers, Howard M. 410
Meyers, Joseph J. 160
Miamis, James 155
Micek, Sidney 502
Michael, Dave 46
Michael, J. Christopher 59
Michel, Robin S. 426
Micheli, Steven B. 429
Michelman, Douglas 523
Michelson, Michael W. 283
Michl, Michael W. 316
Michou, David 458
Miclot, Stephanie 199
Mida, Israel H. 404
Midgal, Jane 410
Midgley, Ben 16
Midulla, Richard J. 442
Milberg, John E. 384
Milberger, Patrick A. 280
Miles, Dan 103
Miles, Lisa 111
Miles, Mark 88
Militello, Richard A. 428
Milkey, Ted E. 130
Millen, Robert P. 379
Miller, Carol 40
Miller, Constance 377
Miller, Duane 377
Miller, Edward D. Jr. 266
Miller, George N. Jr. 406
Miller, Guy E. 373
Miller, Jack 167
Miller, James E. 315
Miller, Karen G. 290
Miller, Kathleen M. 504
Miller, Kirk E. 273
Miller, Mark (Chick-fil-A) 118
Miller, Mark (Crowley Maritime) 143
Miller, Mary Jane 360
Miller, Michael M.
 (Associated Electric) 54
Miller, Michael S.
 (Vanguard Group) 517
Miller, Neil 38
Miller, Norm 260
Miller, Philip 454

INDEX OF EXECUTIVES

Miller, Richard (Barton Malow) 66
Miller, Richard (HBE Corporation) 227
Miller, Robert J. Jr. 147
Miller, Steven A.
  (Indiana University) 251
Miller, Steven O. (Penn Mutual) 392
Miller, Susan E. 366
Miller, Toni (Bass Pro Shops) 67
Miller, Tony (TTI) 488
Milliken, Roger 336
Mills, Andy 324
Mills, Charles S. 324
Mills, Cheryl 368
Mills, Dick 239
Mills, Jon 123
Mills, Kent 207
Mills, Linda G. 368
Mills, Nick 21
Mills, Patrick L. 54
Mills, Steve 304
Milne, Matt 522
Miltenberger, Harry D. 290
Milton, Gene C. 23
Minehan, Cathy E. 188
Miner, Steve 55
Mingle, James J. 138
Minnaugh, Mark 205
Minster, Joel 413
Minter, David 488
Minturn, Frederick K. 342
Minyard, Bob 337
Minyard, Elizabeth 337
Minyard Williams, Gretchen 337
Mirante, Arthur J. II 145
Misaki, Rod 139
Misenhimer, Holly 96
Mishek, Mark G. 33
Mishkin, Sandy 111
Mishler, James L. 208
Mitchell, A. Joe Jr. 519
Mitchell, Clarence D. 376
Mitchell, Craig S. 340
Mitchell, George K. 50
Mitchell, H. Thomas 92
Mitchell, Joanne 454
Mitchell, Lee Roy 121
Mitchell, Mark 441
Mitchell, Tandy 121
Mitchusson, Bob 26
Mitsch, George 496
Mixon, Peter H. 99
Mizell, Catherine S. 507
Mizeur, Dave 250
Mobouck, Patrick C. 416
Moden, Ralph 513
Modory, Kim 468
Moeller, Joseph W. 281
Mog, Steve 46
Mogul, Mark 351
Mogulescu, John 123
Mohamad, Michael 17
Mohler, Max 537
Mohr, Larry 532
Mohr, Michael 34
Moise, Tony 178
Molendorp, Dayton H. 41
Molfetas, Jason 533
Moloney, Herbert W. III 521
Monday, Misty 398
Mongan, James J. 389
Monnig, Ken 442
Monrad, Elizabeth A. 476
Monsell, Elizabeth G. 496
Montague, William P. 309
Montgomery, Dan T. 124
Montgomery, Robert 76
Montgomery-Tally, La June 274
Montmarquette, Yves 497
Montreuil, Charles 102
Monty, Richard L. 85
Moock, Joyce L. 421
Moon, James 50
Moon, Micheal 227

Moon, Robert Lee 522
Moore, C. Bradley 373
Moore, Darnell 37
Moore, David M. 346
Moore, Debra Plousha 379
Moore, Joseph D. 518
Moore, Kevin P. 423
Moore, L. Kent 499
Moore, Maureen 190
Moore, Nathan P. 312
Moore, Ross 126
Moore, Susan 178
Moore, Thomas M. (Sunkist) 465
Moore, Tom (Colt's Manufacturing) 127
Moorehead, Julie 299
Moores, John J. 500
Moorkamp, Mary 436
Moorman, Dave 105
Moorman, Mark 432
Moran, Allison 412
Moran, Catherine 297
Moran, Charles E. Jr. 153
Moran, David 103
Moran, James D.
  (Crown Equipment) 144
Moran, James M.
  (JM Family Enterprises) 264
Moran, Jan 264
Moran, Patricia 264
Moran, Thomas J. 344
Moran, Wally 176
Morange, William A. 333
Morant, Felicia 28
Morehead, C. David 379
Morehouse, Mike 289
Moreland, Myra 330
Moreno, Albert F. 294
Moret, Pamela J. 475
Moretti, Richard D. 208
Moretz, Lawrence 430
Morey, Katie 375
Morgan, Carol Ellis
  (National Service Industries) 357
Morgan, Carole (Meijer) 325
Morgan, Eileen 153
Morgan, George D. 512
Morgan, Randy 300
Morgan, Roger 286
Morgensen, Jerry L. 234
Morgenstern, Jay 51
Morlan, James A. 522
Morman, Louise M. 365
Morningstar, Bill 530
Moroney, Patrick E. 229
Morris, Ernest R. 509
Morris, Gregory K. 24
Morris, Herschel E. 113
Morris, Jim 301
Morris, John L. 67
Morris, William S. III
  (Morris Communications) 340
Morris, William S. IV
  (Morris Communications) 340
Morrison, Ann 209
Morrison, Craig O. 85
Morrison, Gregory B. 141
Morrison, Joe 144
Morrison, John M. 33
Morrison, Larry S. 511
Morrow, Robert H. 107
Morse, Amyas C.E. 404
Morse, John 177
Morse, Philip 435
Morse, Rosemarie 204
Mortensen, Steve 541
Mortenson, M. A. Jr. 303
Mortenson, Mark A. 303
Mortimer, John H. 251
Morton, C. Hugh 85
Morton, Mike (H.T. Hackney) 244
Morton, Mike (TTI) 488
Moseley, Chris R. 223
Moseley, Colin 448

Moseley, Peggy 83
Moser, Bobby D. 378
Moser, Nathan F. 351
Mosey, Ed 84
Moshenek, G. Kenneth 427
Moshier, Arnold 433
Moskow, Michael H. 188
Mosler, Bruce 145
Mosley, John 455
Mostert, Thomas J. Jr. 22
Mosticchio, Dennis P. 220
Motel, George 88
Mott, Daniel C. 36
Moultrie, Anne 503
Movson, Alan 139
Mox, Greg 443
Moxie, Jeffrey E. 465
Moyer, Christine K. 111
Moyer, Kristen J. 465
Moyer, Laura 71
Moylan, Kienan 264
Moylanhas, Kiernan P. 264
Muchnick, Ed 111
Muckerman, John 158
Mudd, John O. 52
Muehlbauer, James H.
  (Koch Enterprises) 281
Muehlbauer, Jim (Musicland) 344
Mueller, Glen 440
Mueller, Guy 165
Mueller, Paul 435
Muellman, Susie 183
Muir, David 39
Mulders, Abbe 164
Muleski, Robert T. 295
Mulhern, Patrick 524
Mullen, Dennis M. 76
Mullen, Edward K. 368
Mullen, Lisa A. 496
Mullen, Pat 210
Mullen, Robert H. 368
Mullenix, Bill 181
Mulligan, Donald 155
Mullinix, Edward W. 25
Mullinix, Joseph P. 500
Mullins, Russell 215
Mulrooney, Nina M. 392
Mulvey, Daniel B. 117
Mulvey, Therese 521
Munger, Victor A. 494
Muntz, David S. 473
Munuz, Erol 87
Munyon, James R. 272
Munyon, Jason 343
Muraskin, Ben E. 396
Murchison, Bradley D. 64
Murdock, David H. 162
Murdock, Kent H. 257
Murphy, Daniel J. 495
Murphy, David 90
Murphy, E. Ray 320
Murphy, Edward 101
Murphy, Jeremiah T. 28
Murphy, John (Teamsters) 470
Murphy, John V. (MassMutual) 315
Murphy, Kevin 173
Murphy, Michele 330
Murphy, Paul M. 427
Murphy, Reg 353
Murphy, Richard J. 109
Murphy, Vicki 150
Murray, Cathy 296
Murray, Gerry 274
Murray, John
  (Enterprise Rent-A-Car) 178
Murray, John M. (Dart Container) 148
Murray, Kathy 18
Murray, Patrick M. 167
Murray, Stephen P. 139
Muscoplat, Charles C. 504
Muse, John R. 236
Myer, David F. 20
Myers, Dale S. 407

Myers, Pam 416
Myers, William 148
Myles, Debbie 125
Myrick, Bill 16
Mysel, Amy 487

N

Nadel, Paul 191
Nadel, Steven 191
Nagaraja, Mysore L. 333
Nagle, Thomas 278
Naibauer, Phyllis 492
Naidoo, Pat 421
Nail, George 201
Nail, Matthew E. 227
Nair, Mohan 415
Nakamura, Issho 286
Nakis, Dominic J. 24
Nallicheri, Renu 516
Nally, John C. 151
Naples, Beth 379
Napolitano, Mike 306
Naquin, David J. 493
Nardi, Robert J. 300
Nardone, Joelle 379
Narea, Jaime 91
Narike, Randal 178
Narron, Michelle 397
Nartonis, Robert J. 303
Narula, Dhiraj D. 411
Naruse, Jun 237
Nash, H. Lamar 226
Nash, Maureen 405
Nash, Ron 409
Nasser, Jacques A. 401
Natale, Jo 531
Nathan, Badri 475
Nattier, James A. 167
Nauman, Joan 174
Nawrocki, Mark 330
Nazarian, Robert H. 329
Neal, Christine 495
Neal, Elise 19
Neaman, Mark R. 183
Neamand, Scott F. 420
Neary, Daniel P. 345
Nedick, Mitch 530
Needham, Philip 430
Neeley, Robert L. 286
Neenan, Paul 338
Neff, Richard B. 157
Negri, Michael 210
NeGron, Larry 91
Neighbors, P. Michael 125
Neil, Robert F. 141
Neils, Karri 432
Nelms, Charlie 251
Nelsestuen, Rodney A. 29
Nelson, Charles 121
Nelson, Corliss J. 264
Nelson, Curtis C. 102
Nelson, Elaine E. 60
Nelson, Gary 348
Nelson, Gordon L. Jr. 270
Nelson, Jean Delaney 336
Nelson, Jim 217
Nelson, John 195
Nelson, Linda 76
Nelson, Maurice S. Jr. 173
Nelson, Nathan 486
Nelson, Noel 416
Nelson, Richard 290
Nelson, Scott 238
Nelson, Thomas C. (AARP) 18
Nelson, Thomas C. (New NGC) 362
Nelson, Vern L. 114
Nelson, William (Chas. Levy) 115
Nelson, William H.
  (Intermountain Health Care) 257
Nenni, Linda J. 273
Neri, Andy 299

INDEX OF EXECUTIVES

Nesbit, Robert F. 338
Nesson, Richard B. 156
Nestor, Dave 178
Netchvolodoff, Alexander V. 141
Netolicka, Robert 342
Neuman, Eric C. 236
Neuvirth, Stephanie 22
Neves, Carole M. P. 452
Neves, Tony 415
Nevins, Anita 479
Newbower, Ronald S. 389
Newby, D. M. 311
Newby, Larry 275
Newcom, Dwayne 483
Newell, Janice 218
Newendorp, Vince 520
Newhouse, Donald E. 21
Newhouse, Samuel I. Jr. 21
Newman, Bob 286
Newman, Bruce D. 421
Newman, Clive A. 268
Newman, Gary 252
Newman, Richard G. 24
Newport, Tom 105
Newsome, Mark 320
Newson, Jessica 320
Newsted, Richard 329
Newton, David 290
Newton, Gary 400
Newton, Leslie 454
Ney, Joseph A. 495
Ng, Paul 452
Nibauer, Jason 398
Nichlos, Kenneth L. 20
Nichols, Eileen 199
Nichols, John D. 310
Nicholson, Bruce J. 475
Nicholson, Earl 360
Nicholson, James B. 42
Nicholson, Pamela M. 178
Nicol, Dan F. 380
Nicolin, Magnus 181
Niehus, Dean A. 329
Niekamp, Randy W. 144
Nielsen, Claude B. 125
Nielson, Jeff 190
Niemi, John R. 111
Nightingale, Thomas 435
Nikka, Joanna 464
Nikol, Eleonora 63
Nila, Linda 394
Nilles, Martina 534
Ninow, Kevin J. 246
Nishikawa, Morio 268
Nissen, Theresa 426
Noble, Jim 265
Nobles, Cy S. 281
Nocek, Robert 448
Noe, Arthur W. 409
Noe, David 324
Nokels, Kevin 31
Nolan, Frances 476
Nolan, John 513
Nolan, Peter J. (Rand McNally) 413
Nolan, Peter M. (Dole Food) 163
Nolan, Robert 273
Noland, Jon 36
Noland, Rick 264
Norby, Kim 533
Norby, Ronald G. 234
Nordenberg, Mark A. 506
Noren, Jay 505
Norman, Paul E. 84
Norment, Phil 400
Norniella, Ramon 126
Norquist, Pat 371
Norris, Jay 112
Norris, Michael P. 299
Norris, William 260
North, Jack W. 460
Northup, Judith W. 524
Norton, Dave 222
Norton, Tom 38

Nosler, Peter C. 165
Noto, Robert A. 334
Novak, Steve 279
Novelli, Bob 81
Novelli, William D. 18
Novelly, Paul Anthony 47
Novik, Steven 269
Nowak, Joseph 330
Nowak, Tom 208
Nowlin, Charles 322
Nugent, Mike 480
Nunemaker, Richard A. 43
Nunery, Leroy D. 505
Nussdorf, Glenn 410
Nussdorf, Lawrence C. 124
Nusser, Linda 536
Nye, Erle 472
Nye, Robert 239
Nyirjesy Bragale, Christine 209

O

O'Brien, Bobby D. 137
O'Brien, Chuck 156
O'Brien, David M. 237
O'Brien, Dermot J. 476
O'Brien, J. Michael 36
O'Brien, Jim 475
O'Brien, John 314
O'Brien, Kathleen 504
O'Brien, Mary S. 183
O'Brien, Michael 436
O'Brien, Rosemary 113
O'Brien, Terence 292
O'Connell, Jeffrey M. 96
O'Connell, Jim 263
O'Connell, Laurence J. 24
O'Connell, Robert J. 315
O'Conner, Patrick 229
O'Connor, David E. 466
O'Connor, Diane 481
O'Connor, Donal M. 404
O'Connor, James 109
O'Connor, John J. 461
O'Connor, Thomas P.
 (Springs Industries) 456
O'Connor, Tom (Allina Hospitals) 33
O'Daniel, Jim 227
O'Dea, James G. 328
O'Dell, Julie 223
O'Dell, Robert R. 262
O'Donnell, Carol 361
O'Donnell, Thomas R. 470
O'Donnell, Traci 272
O'Donoghue, C. Kevin 461
O'Dwyer, Mary Ann 199
O'Hara, Thom 538
O'Hare, Aidan 197
O'Hare, Patrick 455
O'Keefe, Peg 108
O'Kelly, Eugene D. 285
O'Leary, Jim 181
O'Leary, Robert C. 141
O'Leary, Thomas M. 394
O'Maley, David B. 377
O'Malley, John P.
 (International Data Group) 258
O'Malley, John P. III (Westcon) 533
O'Malley-Keyes, Derek A. 164
O'Meara, John 251
O'Meara, Kevin P. 93
O'Neal, Craft 380
O'Neal, Emmet 380
O'Neal, Ted 369
O'Neil, Laurence G. 273
O'Neil, Mark 107
O'Neil, Scott 350
O'Neill, Frederick M. 464
O'Neill, Jack 103
O'Neill, Thomas J. 388
O'Neill, William 326
O'Reilly, William M. 443

O'Roark, Jamie 326
O'Rourke, Michael 110
O'Rourke, Rob 480
O'Steen, John A. 139
O'Sullivan, Patrick 50
O'Toole, Brian 449
O'Toole, Thomas F. 247
Oakes, Corry W. III 185
Obear, Frederick 507
Oberhelman, Steve 465
Oberkfell, Larry A. 437
Oberland, Gregory C. 372
Obermeier, Scott 116
Obradovich, Emil P. 511
Ochsner, Raymond L. 414
Oddo, David 60
Odegard, Gary L. 444
Oden-Brunson, J. Johnette 142
Odgers, David N. 24
Odgren, Ruth 69
Odle, Samuel L. 123
Odlum, Michael G. 441
Odom, Page 362
Oeltjen, Ed 43
Oerly, Dennis 227
Oeters, William D. 171
Offenbacher, Richard D. 214
Offit, Paul A. 118
Offutt, Christi J. 414
Offutt, Ronald D. 414
Ogilvie, E. Staman 237
Ogilvie, Scott 71
Oglesby, Daniel 455
Oglesby, Tony E. 296
Ohlde, Frederick A. 475
Ohnmacht, Timothy 409
Oishi, Ryutaro 370
Okes, Gary D. 182
Olander, Thomas J. 511
Oldenkamp, Curtis 31
Oleksiw, Andrew 315
Olemaun, Forrest 48
Oleske, Michael 364
Oleson, Kenneth A. 541
Olien, David W. 510
Oliver, Mary Ellen 508
Olivieri, Georgianna D. 227
Olmstead, Tom 380
Olmsted, Daniel H. 59
Olsem, Doug 437
Olsen, Annette 477
Olsen, Don H. 246
Olsen, James A. 198
Olsen, Mark 276
Olsen, Stephen R. 259
Olson, Claire M. 67
Olson, D. Joseph 42
Olson, Jack 358
Olson, Mark W. 188
Olson, Steven E. 30
Ondricek, Quent 160
Ondruch, Michael 19
Ondrula, Lisa M. 270
Opperman, Mary G. 138
Oram, Thomas E. 191
Orbison, Dianne M. 336
Orbuch, David B. 33
Orfanos, Natalia 28
Ori, John 229
Orlando, Charles 296
Orlando, Don 208
Orlando, Joseph S. 363
Orlinsky, Ethan 306
Ornelas, Gonzalo O. 541
Orr, James F. III 421
Orr, John 247
Orr, Susan Packard 385
Ort-Mabry, Catherine 190
Ortega, Jennifer 412
Orth, James 184
Ortiz, Carlos 211
Ortiz, Robert 66
Osborn, Charles 464

Osborn, Jill 213
Osborne, Burl 57
Osgood, Teena 186
Osterberg, Don 435
Ostergard, Tonn M. 142
Ostertag, Thomas J. 306
Ostling, Paul J. 180
Ostlund, Harland 465
Ostrander, Gregg A. 334
Oswald, John H. 175
Otremba, Lon 346
Ott, Ellen 153
Ott, Meredith 521
Ott, Rick 286
Ott, Ron 77
Otto, Robert L. 514
Ottolino, Alfred J. 407
Ouchida, Kurt 290
Ourisman, John 381
Ourisman, Mandell J. 381
Ovalles-Moore, Guadalupe 265
Ovenden, James A. 185
Overbay, Anne 286
Overcash, Darrell 312
Overman, Bill 249
Oviatt, Jonathan J. 318
Owen, Clay 121
Owen, Joe 202
Owen, Kimberly 410
Owen, Rebecca L. 124
Owens, Betsy 413
Owens, Bill 238
Owens, Dave 395
Owens, Jack B. 172
Owens, Julie 186
Owens, Tom 121
Owens, Treka 267
Owsley, Thomas L. 143
Oxford, Randall G. 312
Ozaki, Joseph P. 34
Ozment, Tim 318

P

Paarlberg, Robert L. 427
Pachter, Marc J. 452
Pack, Michael 140
Pack, Robert F. 506
Packard, Julie E. 385
Packard, Ralph K. 517
Packebush, Steve 282
Padden, James A. 465
Page, Chris 326
Page, G. Ruffner 322
Page, Gregory R. 101
Pagnam, Charles J. 539
Paisner, Bruce 231
Pakosta, Tracey 530
Palacios, Fernando 287
Paladino, John 115
Palazzolo, Chris 156
Palbaum, Bryan 481
Palm, Craig 55
Palma, Al 174
Palma, Gianfranco 401
Palmer, John J. 377
Palmer, Judith G. 251
Palmer, Sue 213
Palmieri, Richard 435
Paluch, Brian 496
Palumbo, Nancy 366
Palumbo, Thomas 529
Pamplin, Robert Sr.
 (R. B. Pamplin) 414
Pamplin, Robert Boisseau Jr.
 (R. B. Pamplin) 414
Panagopoulos, Jim 28
Pandey, Ratish 87
Panelas, Tom 177
Pankey, Henry A. 514
Pannebaker, Kevin 59
Paoletti, Steve 223

INDEX OF EXECUTIVES

Paolozzi, Anthony C. 515
Papadellis, Randy 375
Papaleo, Michael 100
Papanek, John 181
Papen, Harold 146
Papert, Richard N. 292
Pappas, Jenny 533
Paprocki, Ronald J. 506
Pardes, Herbert 369
Parins, Jerry 216
Paris, Martin 203
Parise, Mark 252
Parish, John D. 135
Park, Jon 534
Parker, Alan M. 114
Parker, Chuck 182
Parker, Dale E. 48
Parker, Daniel 24
Parker, Francine 233
Parker, Frederick 436
Parker, Gary R. 111
Parker, Ira H. 401
Parker, J. M. 116
Parker, Jack 21
Parker, John 79
Parker, Randy 254
Parker, Roger N. 327
Parker, Ronald C.
 (Hampton Affiliates) 223
Parker, Ronald R. (Flying J) 193
Parker, Virginia 193
Parker-Johnson, Toni 314
Parkes, Jacqueline 306
Parkes, Walter 166
Parkinson, Bradford W. 25
Parkinson, Richard A. 55
Parks, Roger 272
Parlette, Dave 379
Parli, Laura 20
Parmelee, William D. 362
Parnas, Michael 227
Parr, Richard A. II 132
Parrett, William G. 154
Parris, Jill 130
Parrish, Alyssa 149
Parrish, David L. 146
Parrot, Keith 326
Parry, Bill 205
Parsons, John R. 25
Parsons, Susan E. 281
Partin, Sam 50
Partridge, John 523
Pascarella, Carl F. 523
Pasculano, Richard 493
Pash, Jeff 352
Paskach, Dave 437
Pastore, John H. 338
Patch, Art 433
Pate, William C. 179
Patel, Ashok D. 465
Patel, Kal 19
Patel, Needra 285
Paterson, Brian 53
Patric, Sharon 185
Patrick, Charles F. 138
Patrick, Doug 247
Patsalos-Fox, Michael 321
Patterson, Barry 320
Patterson, Cindy 520
Patterson, Douglas E. 396
Patterson, Kimberly S. 69
Patterson, Mark R. 383
Patterson, Steve 454
Patterson, Thomas J. 482
Patterson-Randles, Sandra R. 251
Pattison, Doug 225
Patton, Guy L. 194
Patton, Jo Allen 526
Patton, John H. 226
Pattullo, Scott 199
Paulenich, Fred 294
Pauley, Stanley F. 105
Paulley, Betsy 275

Paulson, Erika 541
Paulson, Sidney C. 258
Pava, Liz 534
Pavey, Nancy 539
Pavlics, Peter N. 438
Payne, Mark 401
Payne, Park 342
Payne, Penelope 452
Payne, William R. 34
Peak, Donna M. 514
Pearlman, Mari A. 175
Pearman, Rob 126
Pearson, Ford 199
Pearson, George B. Jr. 377
Pearson, John M. 168
Pearson, Kermit 67
Pearson, Clarke 515
Pearson, Larry V. 471
Pearson, Robert L. 490
Pearson, Ronald D. 247
Pearson, Sarah R. 373
Pearson, Tracy 186
Peccolo, Charles M. 507
Pecht, Carrie J. 237
Peck, Diane 459
Peck, Larry J. 438
Peddicord, Kenneth L. 472
Peden, John R. 360
Pedersen, Robert J. 514
Peel, Stephen 475
Peelish, Michael R. 198
Peers, Gil 345
Peets, Terry R. 537
Peetz, John G. Jr. 180
Pehrson, H. Gary 258
Peixotto, Bob 298
Pell, Suyen E. 138
Pellegrino Puhl, Frances 58
Pelletreau, Barbara 110
Pelligreen, Chris 111
Peltier, Ronald J. 335
Peluso, John 220
Pember, Marvin 123
Pemberton, Robin 348
Pena, Nancy 492
Pendergraft, Flint 412
Pendleton, David E. 30
Pennella, William A. 143
Penning, Richard T. 510
Pennings, Fred 512
Pennington, Neil 129
Pennington, Skip 90
Penske, Roger S. 393
Pepper, J. David II 394
Pepper, John E. Jr. 539
Pepper, Richard S. 394
Perdue, James A. 394
Perelman, Ronald O. 304
Perez, Carlos 363
Perez, Joseph 211
Perez, Nelson 33
Perez, William D. 434
Perkins, Jim C. 233
Perlman, Doug 355
Perlman, Harvey S. 505
Perlman, Michael 256
Perlman, Robert 256
Pernotto, Stephen J. 72
Perrin, Sallye 387
Perron, Dave 325
Perry, Annette 115
Perry, Don 118
Perry, Jennifer 430
Perry, Matt 101
Perry, Ralph D. 434
Perry, Randall 184
Perry, Robert C. 119
Perry, Victor A. III 141
Pershing, John 344
Persichilli, Judith M. 107
Persing, David A. 331
Person, Ruth J. 251
Perugini, Thomas F. 210
Pesavento, Robert J. 234

Pescovitz, Ora Hirsch 123
Pesesky, Larry 300
Pestow, Charles A. (Citation) 122
Pestow, Chuck (Metaldyne) 330
Peterffy, Thomas 256
Peters, Andrew D. 387
Peters, Greg 102
Peters, Richard J. 393
Peters, Roger J. 157
Petersen, Anne C. 274
Petersen, Brad 482
Petersen, John D. 507
Petersen, Paul R. 342
Petersen, Sheldon C. 356
Peterson, Carl 29
Peterson, Clarke 515
Peterson, Eric 265
Peterson, Jeffery P. 494
Peterson, Karin 391
Peterson, Ralph R. 114
Peterson, Richard D. (Flying J) 193
Peterson, Richard H.
 (Swedish Health Services) 467
Peterson, Ronald K.
 (American Crystal Sugar) 36
Peterson, Ronald R.
 (Johns Hopkins Medicine) 266
Peterson LeBre, Kristin 344
Petro, Michael 377
Petrovich, Steven C. 49
Petterson, Andrew 239
Pettingill, Richard R. 33
Peyton, Herbert H. 201
Pezick, Tom 465
Pfaff, Mark 364
Pfeffer, Gerald S. 396
Pfeifer, Andy 399
Pfeifle, Jeff 261
Pfingsten, Linda 511
Pfuehler, Donald 164
Pfutzenreuter, Richard H. 504
Phaneuf, Daniel D. 144
Phelps, Charles E. 506
Phelps, R. Michael 396
Phenix, Lee 398
Philip, Craig E. 254
Philip, Fran 298
Phillips, Bethany 63
Phillips, David P. 407
Phillips, Douglas W. 506
Phillips, Gary 58
Phillips, Jack 41
Phillips, Michael 223
Phillips, Sherri 294
Phillips, Steve 312
Phillips, W. Norman Jr. 178
Phillips, Winfred M. 502
Philpott, Paul 133
Pianalto, Sandra 188
Pibollo, Colleen 309
Picard, Lynn 297
Piccinini, Robert M. 433
Piccoli, David A. 118
Pichi, Tom 292
Pickett, Larry 408
Picoult, Jonathan 315
Piechoski, Michael J. 396
Piehler, Barbara F. 372
Pienkos, Thomas 486
Pieper, Dennis 480
Pieper, Jay B. 389
Pierce, Andy 250
Pierce, Edwin S. 52
Pierce, Gerald 531
Pierce, Harvey R. 37
Pierce, James 19
Pierce, Phil 61
Piersma, Howie 394
Pietrini, Andrew E. 493
Pifer, Dee 449
Piland, Todd 228
Pilgrim, Trip 518
Pilholski, Thomas R. 171

Pilla, Linda 87
Pilliod, Pete 433
Pilliter, Charles J. 481
Pilnick, Michael E. 129
Pimentel, Cedrick 47
Pinckney, Frank D. 217
Pineda, Patricia Salas 363
Pineda, Prudencio 337
Pines, Jim 214
Pines, Phillip 214
Pinge, Neelesh 138
Pinney, Jerry 249
Pinson, Robert 69
Piper, Tim 218
Pipes, J. David 428
Pippin, M. Lenny 437
Pirkle, J. William 427
Pirkle, Phil 499
Pitcock, Mike 474
Pitera, Thomas 497
Pitner, James 92
Pittas, John 171
Pittle, R. David 136
Pittman, Colleen R. 288
Pittman, David 19
Pittman, Frank P. 167
Pitts, Brian 279
Pitts, Keith B. 518
Pitts, Ralph A. 72
Piva, Gary R. 536
Plain, Cuba 504
Plakmeyer, Steve 209
Plamann, Alfred A. 495
Plaszcz, Robert 33
Platt, Dixie L. 458
Platt, Ronald 230
Platts, H. Gregory 354
Plazk, Tim 429
Plohr Rayhill, Anne 250
Plummer, Al 98
Plunkett, Dennis A. 25
Poccio, Thomas 292
Pocock, J. Michael 401
Pogue, A. Mack 297
Pohmer, Tom 390
Polatajko, Mark M. 377
Polcari, Michael R. 441
Poletto, Eraldo 418
Policinski, Chris 287
Poliner, Gary A. 372
Politi, Michael 299
Polizzotto, Dominic F. 242
Polizzotto, Leonard 457
Polk, Anthony J. 40
Pollack, Anne F. 364
Pollak, Joanne E. 266
Pollichino, Robert 305
Pollock, Jeff 330
Poltorak, Anne-Marie 66
Polzin, Gail 183
Pomeroy, John J. 193
Pomeroy, Michelle 489
Pomeroy, Tom 46
Pompei, Shauna 343
Pong, Walter 100
Ponicall, Michael 481
Poole, Margaret A. 244
Poole, William 188
Pope, Art 518
Pope, Darryl L. 269
Pope, John W. Sr. 518
Popiel, Richard G. 241
Popko, Kathleen 107
Poppell, John E. 502
Poppell, Randall C. 496
Popplewell, Venus 243
Porco, John 278
Portannese, Anthony 156
Porter, James A. (Evergreen
 International Aviation) 184
Porter, Jim (Carlson) 102
Porter, Keith 274
Porter, Thomas 66

INDEX OF EXECUTIVES

Portnoy, K. Scott 101
Porto, Barabara 133
Posner, Jeffrey 480
Posner, Larry G. 230
Post, Steven E. 259
Poston, Fred L. 334
Potamkin, Alan 399
Potamkin, Robert 399
Potarazu, Ramu V. 255
Potillo, Beth 162
Potter, Duncan 533
Potter, John E. 513
Poulos, Evan 420
Poulsen, Greg 257
Povich, Lon 87
Powell, Allen 174
Powers, Earl L. 76
Powers, James G. 496
Powers, Larry K. 202
Powers, Mary Ellen 268
Powers, Richard I. 111
Pragada, Robert 277
Prapuolenis, Michael 446
Pratt, Dennis 328
Pratt, Don 207
Pratt, Steven H. 52
Prausa, John W. 457
Pray, William R. 257
Preece, Scott 536
Prendergast, Franklyn G. 318
Prentice, William S. 170
Prescott, Tim 454
Presley, Karen B. 514
Press, Jonathan 350
Pressley, Curtis 336
Pressley, Debra L. 50
Preston, Forrest L. 296
Preston, Frances W. 82
Preston, John R. 454
Preston, Joseph 361
Preston, William 64
Preter, David A. 511
Prevette, L. K. Eric 261
Previti, Frank J. 489
Prevot, Roger M. 212
Prial, Helen 477
Price, Betty 516
Price, Eric 266
Price, Eugenia B. 241
Price, Gary 337
Price, Kevin 36
Price, Larry C. 254
Price, Michael W. 376
Prideaux, James 162
Priest, Patricia P. 71
Prince, Frank 119
Princi, Carla 297
Pritchard, Jane 371
Pritchard, Mike 244
Pritzker, Nicholas J. 247
Pritzker, Penny S. 247
Pritzker, Thomas J. 222, 247
Prizer, John 140
Probert, Gregory 235
Probert, William B. 538
Prochaska, Daniel C. 20
Prochaska, Marv 328
Proctor, Deborah A. 430
Proctor, John 82
Proffit, Larry 370
Proffitt, Jackie 423
Prohofsky, Dennis E. 336
Prokopanko, James T. 101
Prosise, Robert 174
Prostko, Dave 325
Protter, Hal 530
Proulx, Mike 66
Provenzano, Greg 326
Prusiecki, Drew 21
Pryor, David B. 52
Ptachik, Robert 123
Puckett, David 243
Puhrmann, Gene 55

Purcell, Chris 526
Purcell, Rachel 482
Pures, Robert J. 241
Purgiel, Ronald V. 202
Purnell, Kirk 73
Purvis, Jenifer 441
Putz, Duane 391
Pyne, George 348
Pynn, David 307
Pytka, Edward F. 477

Q

Quadracci, Betty Ewens 409
Quadracci, J. Joel 409
Quadracci, Thomas A. 409
Qualls, Wesley H. 130
Quarles, W. Greyson Jr. 432
Quartararo, Michael 109
Queally, Paul B. 132
Quek, Robin 488
Quellhorst, Timothy S. 144
Quilty, John S. 338
Quinn, Mike 148
Quinn, Ronald N. 471
Quinn, Thomas H. 270
Quinten, Bobby 93
Quiring, James 323
Quirk, James S. 327
Quish, Sheleen 511

R

Raba, Todd M. 335
Rabin, Edward W. Jr. 247
Rabun, J. Sam L. 376
Rachey, Loren 47
Radcliffe, R. Stephen 41
Radine, Gary D. 154
Radon, William R. 347
Radtke, Karen A. 330
Raether, Paul E. 283
Rafferty, Gary 467
Raffo, Charlie 28
Rager, Gary 20
Ragona, Philip J. 60
Ragsdale, Perry L. 118
Rahimi, Morteza A. 373
Rahn, William M. 235
Rahrig, Douglas B. 418
Rai, Amitabh 416
Raible, Robert 330
Rains, Greg 204
Raisbeck, David W. 101
Rake, Jude 190
Rake, Michael 285
Rakolta, John Jr. 527
Raksis, Joseph W 192
Raley Teel, Joyce 412
Rambach, Ralph 79
Ramer, Mark D. 253
Ramey, Christopher 111
Ramey, Thomas C. 295
Ramicone, Arthur 506
Ramiller, Charles 441
Ramirez, Michael W. 397
Ramleth, Geir 71
Ramm, Casey 19
Ramos, Pedro 505
Ramsey, David W. 189
Ramsey, Paul A.
 (Educational Testing Service) 175
Ramsey, Paul G.
 (University of Washington) 509
Rand, Mike 58
Randall, Debbie 487
Randall, Penny 411
Randel, Don Michael 501
Randleman, Robert S. 434

Randles, Bill 424
Randolph, Joseph 430
Randolph, Marcus P. 255
Randoph, Tanya 320
Rangan, Urvashi 136
Ranish, Abe 203
Ransome, Timothy 268
Ranton, James D. 250
Ranucci, Robert J. 522
Rapaport, Ronald L. 422
Rapier, Donella 226
Rapp, John A. 513
Raquet, Bonnie E. 101
Rask, Todd 424
Rasmusen, Vicki 102
Rasmussen, Earl R. 328
Rasmussen, Stephen S. 359
Ratcliffe, Andrew 404
Ratcyz, Pete 158
Rathbun, Paul C. 23
Rathgeber, Kenneth A. 194
Ratliff, John 411
Ratner, Hank J. 304
Rauenhorst, Gerald 380
Rauenhorst, Mark H. 380
Raufast, Jean-Charles 180
Raufer, June 241
Raven, Abbe 17
Ravenscraft, Jim 26
Ray, Doug 266
Ray, Harold E. 108
Ray, Jerry M. 169
Ray, Ratan 122
Ray, Wendell 325
Rayford, Rick 92
Razouk, Rami R. 25
Re, Michael 467
Re, Michaeline 265
Read, Mark 163
Read, Michael 536
Ready, George W. Jr. 529
Reagan, Martin P. 27
Reamey, Gary D. 269
Reardon, Andrew F. 489
Reardon, Valerie A. 230
Rearick, David 157
Reaves, Benjamin F. 23
Reaves, Donald J. 501
Rebok, Douglas E. 22
Rebula, Enzo 193
Reck, Una Mae 251
Record, Edward J. 72
Redel, Mark 47
Redgrave, Martyn R. 102
Reding, John 253
Redman, Chuck 71
Redmon, John W. 69
Reed, Bill J. 419
Reed, Charles B. 97
Reed, Gary 41
Reed, John D. III
 (Ingram Industries) 254
Reed, John S. (NYSE) 367
Reed, Michael C. 27
Reed, Pamela J. 341
Reed, Robert D. 466
Reed, Roger 529
Reedy, John D. 334
Reel, Stephanie L. 266
Reels, Kenneth 314
Reese, Bertram S. 442
Reese, Howard F. 115
Reese, Michelle 475
Reese, Stuart H. 315
Reeve, Donald 531
Reeves, Sam 73
Regina, John 421
Rego, Anthony C. 205
Reich, Ronald E. 99
Reich, Steve 55
Reichard, Joseph F. 237
Reichenbacher, Michael S. 255
Reid, Douglas 385

Reid, John 57
Reid, Travis 299
Reidy, Mike 292
Reier, John 448
Reiley, Terry 156
Reilly, Bill 446
Reilly, James G. 32
Reilly, Kelly 375
Reilly, Kevin 510
Reilly, Patti 428
Reilly, Walter E. 176
Reinders, Mark 335
Reiss, Charles 486
Reissig, Mike 127
Reister, Jane 258
Reitz, Judy A. 266
Rekers, John 336
Rekowski, Jerry G. 37
Relyea, Timothy D. 145
Remboldt, Darwin 22
Remmel, Lee 216
Renemann, Ed 183
Renker, Greg 221
Rennert, Ira Leon 417
Renshaw, Josh 424
Renwick, Ed 541
Renwick-Espinosa, Kate 524
Reppeto, John 536
Resch, Richard J. 276
Rescoe, Michael E. 491
Reshed, Mohamed 381
Resnick, Alice R. 457
Resnick, Lynda R. 423
Resnick, Stewart A. 423
Ressler, Rickie 33
Reum, W. Robert 43
Reusch, Jami G. 376
Reuter, Lawrence G. 333
Revello, Joe 89
Rexach, Frank 227
Reyes, David K. 419
Reyes, J. Christopher 311, 419
Reyes, M. Jude 311, 419
Reynolds, Edgar L. 121
Reynolds, Glen 536
Reynolds, Jim 533
Reynolds, Robert A. Jr.
 (Graybar Electric) 214
Reynolds, Robert L. (FMR) 194
Reynolds, Terry 39
Reynolds, Tom 371
Rhimes, Ilee 378
Rhinehart, June Acie 267
Rhode, Bob 149
Rhodes, James H. II 407
Rhodes, Mitchell 201
Rhyan, Mark 432
Rhyne, Dennis G. 423
Ribaudo, Michael 123
Ricciardi, Michael 480
Ricciardi, Salvatore 408
Ricciardi, Walter G. 404
Ricciuti, Annette A. 257
Rice, Alan J. 22
Rice, Glenn 457
Rice, J. Craig 43
Rice, Jeff 142
Rich, Bradford W. 514
Rich, David E. 420
Rich, Howard 420
Rich, Mindy 420
Rich, Nancy 92
Rich, Robert E. Sr. (Rich Products) 420
Rich, Robert E. Jr. (Rich Products) 420
Richard, Alfred J. 390
Richard, Gary 390
Richard, Gregg 390
Richard, Peter Sr. 390
Richards, Joan 199
Richards, Lee 455
Richards, Margaret E. 121
Richards, Roy Jr. 455
Richards, Stephen 243

INDEX OF EXECUTIVES

Richards, Thomas N. 185
Richardson, Barbara J. 44
Richardson, Jim (National Cooperative Refinery Association) 351
Richardson, Jim (Texas Lottery) 474
Richardson, Randal J. 247
Richardson, Robert C. 138
Richardson, William C. 274
Richardson Malone, Brenda 123
Richey, Robert C. 39
Richey, Van L. 36
Richter, David 461
Richter, Wolfgang 154
Rickabaugh, David 413
Rickel, Mark 377
Ricord, Kathleen D. 359
Ridd, Brian V. 246
Riddell, Mark 190
Riedel, Lisa 381
Rieny, Robert 233
Rienzi, Michael J. 44
Riesenbeck, Ronald 433
Rifkin, Daniel M. 379
Rifkin, Leonard I. 379
Rifkin, Martin 379
Rifkin, Ned 452
Rifkin, Richard S. 379
Rigenhagen, Rhonda 363
Rigg, Michael 360
Riggio, Leonard S. 65
Riggs, Dean 456
Riley, Pat 413
Riley, W. Patrick 46
Rimai, Marcia 372
Rinaldi, Catherine A. 333
Riney, Robert 233
Ringeisen, Richard D. 502
Ringer, Ed 357
Riordan, Thomas J. 422
Ripp, Bob 89
Rippley, Robert 59
Ririe, Del 536
Risan, Michael 67
Risener, Daniel M. 407
Risley, Tom 524
Rissman, Paul C. 32
Rist, Larry 310
Riswick, David M. 151
Ritcher, Peter 121
Ritchie, Albert A. 515
Ritscha, Bill 455
Ritter, Keith 355
Ritz, Brooke 420
Ritz, David M. 420
Ritzel, Joseph W. 151
Rivas, Isadore 123
Rivenburgh, Sara 484
Rivera, Marcy 197
Rivera, Mario 126
Rivest, Jeffrey A. 118
Rivetti, Carol 533
Rizzo, James M. 169
Rizzo, Tom 207
Roach, Mike 73
Roach, Randy A. 84
Robak, Kim M. 505
Robb, Michael S. 384
Robbins, Clifton S. 327
Robbins, Earnest O. II 387
Robbins, James O. 141
Robbins, Kris A. 441
Robbins, Larry 475
Robbins, Ray 269
Robbins, Tom 208
Robbins, W. Clayton 376
Robell, Paul A. 502
Roberts, Bryon 66
Roberts, Don 497
Roberts, George R. 283
Roberts, Harry 86
Roberts, Harvey 275

Roberts, James (University of Wisconsin Hospital and Clinics) 510
Roberts, James F. (Foundation Coal) 198
Roberts, Lori G. 400
Roberts, Max J. 65
Roberts, Nancy M. 315
Roberts, R. L. 116
Roberts, Skip 89
Roberts, Tim 122
Robertson, Andrew S. 130
Robertson, Charles 459
Robertson, David L. 281
Robertson, Dennis 50
Robertson, Jeffrey A. 415
Robertson, Julie 190
Robertson, Linda L. 266
Robertson, Rose Marie 39
Robertson, William G. 23
Robeson, Rose M. 170
Robinette, Leonard 244
Robinette, Scott 223
Robinson, Carol 40
Robinson, Charles D. 372
Robinson, David 114
Robinson, Dorothy K. 539
Robinson, Ellen 491
Robinson, Gerald W. 384
Robinson, J. Douglas 515
Robinson, James D. III 327
Robinson, Patricia 322
Robinson, Paul 154
Robinson, Ronnie 90
Robinson, Steve A. 118
Robinson, Theotis Jr. 507
Robish, Annalee 112
Robison, Randal 281
Robles, Josue Jr. 514
Robson, Glenn R. 24
Roche, Pat N. 28
Rock, Rex A. Sr. 48
Rocklage, Mary Roch 449
Rockwell, Joseph 155
Rockwell, Larry 40
Rockwood, Stephen D. 438
Roddy, Frank J. 466
Roderick, David M. 173
Rodgers, Sharon L. 62
Rodgers, Susan 143
Rodin, Judith 421
Rodman, Leonard C. 77
Rodono, Nick 362
Rodrigues, Christopher J. 523
Rodriguez, E. Allen 343
Roe, Christian 159
Roe, Phillip W. 518
Roe, William J. 347
Roell, Thomas L. 387
Roessler, Kenneth M. 95
Roge, Carrol 182
Rogers, David W. 101
Rogers, Dick 133
Rogers, Ed 474
Rogers, Jeffrey W. 406
Rogers, John D. 182
Rogers, Joseph 134
Rogers, Larry (Sinclair Oil) 449
Rogers, Lawrence J. (Sealy) 440
Rogers, M.W. 178
Rogers, Michael C. 324
Rogers, Nancy F. 220
Rogers, Patrick 134
Rogers, Richard R. 312
Rogers, Tim 308
Rogge, Ronald T. 30
Roggenbaum, Douglas R. 42
Roggie, Brent J. 354
Rogoff, Jeffrey 109
Rohrman, Bob 83
Rohrs, Gary E. 379
Rojek, Kenneth J. 24
Roland, Donald E. 521

Roland, Mike 67
Roller, Mark 41
Rollings, Michael T. 315
Rolls, J. David 169
Romandia, Abbie 312
Romano, Michael A. 237
Romans, Juanita 326
Romanzi, Kenneth G. 375
Romero, Elsie 94
Romig, Mark 300
Romley, Bill 66
Rondinello, Bonni 390
Rone, Kenneth J. Jr. 52
Rone, Richard 204
Ronning, Nancee 329
Ronson, Steve 17
Roogow, Buddy W. 313
Rooney, L. Francis III 423
Rooney, Randy 150
Roosen, Adriaan 521
Roosevelt, James Jr. 489
Root, Jane 159
Roper, William A. Jr. 438
Rosanova, Donald S. 426
Rosati, Daniel 489
Rosbe, Robert L. Jr. 375
Roscoe, Dan 381
Roscoe, Joan M. 132
Rose, Kirk A. 247
Rosen, Alan 361
Rosen, Andrew S. 236
Rosen, Michael 78
Rosen, Richard D. 68
Rosen, Thomas J. 424
Rosenbaum, Thomas A. 501
Rosenberg, Jerry 351
Rosenberg, Robert A. 438
Rosenbloom, Barbara E. 207
Rosencrans, Robert D. 79
Rosenthal, Robert M. 425
Rosenzweig, Charlie 350
Rosholt, Robert A. 359
Rosol, Thomas J. 378
Ross, Catherine 191
Ross, Donald L. 178
Ross, Jay A. 371
Ross, John H. III (Ash Grove Cement) 52
Ross, Jonathan (FHC Health Systems) 191
Ross, Joyce 108
Ross, Kelly 432
Ross, Mason G. 372
Ross, Michael 177
Ross, R. Dale 512
Ross, Russ 205
Ross, Susan 426
Ross, Terry 300
Ross, Wilbur L. Jr. 95
Rossel, Cary 207
Rossen, Russ 423
Rosser, Jay 281
Rossi, Sandra 298
Rossotti, Charles O. 104
Rotem, David 181
Rotenberg, Mark B. 504
Roth, Jade 65
Rothberger, Richard 440
Rothenberg, James 226
Rothenbuhler, Mac 533
Rother, John 18
Rothing, Frank 20
Rothman, Howard 301
Rotta, Charlie 534
Rotunno, Greg 39
Rounds, Elizabeth 523
Rounsaville, Guy 523
Rourke, Mark 435
Roush, Lesli 442
Roussel, John 311
Rowan, Henry M. 251
Rowan, Michael T. 108
Rowehl, Gene 277

Rowland, Jerry D. 357
Rowley, Al 416
Rowson, Joe 505
Roy, Rick R. 145
Royer, James R. 24
Royer, Thomas C. 119
Royez, Alexandre 164
Rozanski, Horacio 85
Rozolis, Keith 18
Rozwadowski, Jean F. 316
Rubar, W. H. 69
Rubenstein, David M. 104
Rubery, Mike 167
Rubin, Robert S. 498
Ruch, Mike 190
Ruckdeschel, John C. 156
Rucker, Clyde 94
Rucker, Womack H. Jr. 23
Rudgers, Lisa M. 503
Rudinsky, Charles 207
Rudolph, Allen A. 428
Rudolph, Karen M. 428
Rudolph, Lila 269
Rudy, Clark 396
Ruecke, Kurt 330
Ruff, John B 419
Ruff, Lawrence W. 294
Rugg, Steve 502
Rugland, Walter S. 475
Ruiz, Rodolfo 454
Ruley, Michael S. 369
Rulli, Mike 167
Rumery, Doris 348
Runnels, Jim 178
Runyon, Dee 539
Ruppe, Michael 398
Rusert, Beth 308
Rush, Maureen 505
Russ, David H. 500
Russak, Donald A. 365
Russell, Andrew 140
Russell, David R. 504
Russell, Elizabeth 154
Russell, Greta J. 378
Russell, Jim 438
Russell, John S. 411
Russell, Paulette Granberry 334
Russell, Richard F. 42
Russell, Terry 266
Russo, Christopher J. 352
Russo, Vincent 73
Rust, Edward B. Jr. 460
Rutherford, Clyde E. 147
Ruthruff, Todd 42
Rutledge, George 185
Rutledge, Valinda 83
Rutner, Alan 408
Rutrough, James E. 460
Ryan, John J. (Parsons Brinckerhoff) 388
Ryan, John P. (Dresser) 167
Ryan, Kathleen M. 503
Ryan, Linda 158
Ryan, Mary Jean 458
Ryan, Ray 446
Ryan, Robert J. 324
Ryan, Stephen J. 507
Ryan, Terrence W. 371
Ryan, Thomas 210
Ryder, David 488
Rydzik, Pat 409
Ryser, Karl S. Jr. 33
Rzicznek, Frank 361

S

Saathoff, David 441
Saba, Ed 66
Sabalaskey, Bob 443
Sabatini, Mario 477
Sabiston, Jim 318
Sablo, Thomas A. 354

INDEX OF EXECUTIVES

Sabo, Tony 487
Sabol, Steve 352
Sacks, Lee B. 24
Sadowski, Charles 458
Saeby, Hans O. 138
Saeger, Rebecca 523
Safady, Randa S. 508
Saffer, Marc 129
Safra, Jacob E. 177
Sagan, Rachel 199
Sager, Mike 278
Sahney, Vinod K. 233
Sakai, Stephen P. 48
Sakura, Sumiyoshi 87
Salandra, Mike 31
Sales, William J. 478
Salina, Anthony 452
Salins, Peter D. 461
Salisbury, Lois 385
Sall, John 432
Saller, Richard P. 501
Salluzzo, Richard F. 132
Salmon, Dave 223
Salter, Dianne P. 262
Salter, Ron 535
Saltzman, Michael 494
Salvati, Peter A. 165
Salzwedel, Jack C. 37
Samet, Kenneth A. 324
Sammons, Elaine D. 431
Samper, Cristián 452
Sample, Steven B. 507
Samson, Tom 36
Samuel, Bill 26
Sanabria, Robert 158
Sanborn, Sally 433
Sanchez, Francisco 268
Sanchez, Jose R. 363
Sanchez, Rafael 94
Sanders, Carol 443
Sanders, Charles J. III 254
Sanders, Dan 499
Sanders, Lewis A. 32
Sanders, Steve
 (Interactive Brokers) 256
Sanders, Steve
 (Memorial Hermann Healthcare) 326
Sandor, Douglas 124
Sands, Dawn M. 328
Sands, Leo E. 512
Sanford, William E. 257
Sanger, James M. 458
Sannon, Sonny 316
Sansom, William B. 244
Santana, Jose 477
Santangelo, Jim 470
Santee, M. Catherine 114
Santomero, Anthony M. 188
Santoni, Mike 224
Santora, John C. 145
Santos, John 55
Santulli, William P. 24
Saperstein, Karen L. 156
Sapp, G. David 41
Saras, Paul 272
Sarno, John N. 74
Sarosiek, James J. 328
Sasser, Gary D. 61
Sasser, Tommy 532
Sasso, Vincent D. Jr. 331
Sassus, Suzanne 430
Sather, Glen 304
Satterwhite, George 26
Saucier, Claudia 202
Sauder, Kevin 433
Sauder, Mark G. 168
Sauder, Maynard 433
Sauder, Myrl 433
Sauer, Paula 323
Saufley, Church 275
Saugstad, Bruce 437
Saul, B. Francis II
 (Chevy Chase Bank) 117

Saul, B. Francis III
 (Chevy Chase Bank) 117
Saul, Bill 207
Sauter, George U. 517
Savage, Thomas J. 333
Savio, Guy 278
Savitch, Lane 467
Sawicki, Richard J. 529
Sawtell, Sebrena 296
Sawyer, Wilson 518
Sax, Gerald G. 521
Sayavedra, Leo 472
Sayles, Helen E. R. 295
Saylor, Kirk C. 242
Scadlock, James W. 296
Scafido, Phillip A. 116
Scanlon, Catherine Babon 210
Scanlon, Colleen 108
Scaramuzza, Frank 277
Scavo, Anthony 292
Schach, Mark 36
Schady, Kathleen 408
Schaefer, Gus 494
Schaefer, John 139
Schafer, Agnes 146
Schafer, Glenn S. 384
Schafer, James A. 354
Schaffer, Frederick P. 123
Schaffer, S. Andrew 368
Schaller, Jack 358
Schantz, Mark E. 502
Schanzer, David 198
Schapiro, Mary L. 349
Schargel, Halle 445
Scharmer, Mark D. 189
Schecter, Dan 105
Scheff, Artie 17
Scheiber, Chris 200
Scheman, Carol R. 505
Schenkel, Fred 93
Schepen, Rinus 143
Scher, Robert 401
Scherer, George F. 319
Scherpenberg, Tom B. 171
Schettini, Bill 161
Scheurer, Philip 507
Schick, Joe 409
Schieber, George V. 439
Schiefelbein, Mark 216
Schiesl, Andy 409
Schiferl, Ronald W. 380
Schiff, Albert J. 364
Schiffman, Sam 362
Schilling, Ernie Jr. 488
Schimmel, Robert E. 449
Schirmer, Lynn 330
Schlanger, Marvin O. 418
Schleich, Ron 208
Schleien, Robin 103
Schlert, Theodore 107
Schlesinger, James R. 338
Schlich, John 357
Schlichting, Nancy M. 233
Schlifske, John E. 372
Schloss, Howard M. 349
Schmalz, Robert 535
Schmidt, Mark 488
Schmidt, Thomas A. 512
Schmidt Bies, Susan 188
Schmidt-Holtz, Rolf 454
Schmitt, Michael J. 426
Schmitz, Harold 311
Schmitz, John 441
Schneid, Gary 204
Schneider, Donald J. 435
Schneider, Forrest M. 289
Schneider, Frank 265
Schneider, Gary 332
Schneider, Laura 158
Schneider, Michael I. 388
Schneider, Phill 74
Schneidewind, Bruce 183
Schnipper, Ida M. 133

Schnuck, Craig D. 436
Schnuck, Mark 436
Schnuck, Scott C. 436
Schnuck, Todd R. 436
Schnug, Tony 33
Schoell, Richard M. 502
Schoenfeld, Marc 305
Schoenfeld, Michael J. 516
Schoenhard, William C. 458
Schoening, Karen 239
Schofield, S. Gene 384
Schonherz, Todd 512
Schopp, David R. 328
Schoubert, Joan 204
Schouten, John T. 162
Schrader, Richard A. 388
Schranz, Jim 60
Schreck, Karen 351
Schreiber, Michael 499
Schreier, Bradley 469
Schreier, Warren R. 488
Schriver, Don H. 146
Schroeder, James C. 318
Schroeder, Roger 462
Schropp, Tobin A. 396
Schubert, Tim 20
Schueler, John 322
Schuerman, Janice 333
Schuh, Dale R. 443
Schuldt, Dave 38
Schuler, Richard J. II 407
Schulty, Kyle 97
Schultz, Daniel R. 37
Schultz, Eric H. 186
Schultz, Karen 200
Schultz, Kenneth J. Jr. 465
Schultz, Peter J. 339
Schultz, Steven D. 498
Schumacher, Mary J. 46
Schuss, Eric 73
Schutz, A. James 519
Schwab, Daniel 147
Schwab, Israel 147
Schwab, James F. 147
Schwab, Les 293
Schwab, Mark J. 223
Schwab, Michael 147
Schwab, Steve 187
Schwalb, Robert L. 336
Schwalb, Steven M. 394
Schwan, Alfred 437
Schwaninger, Tom 40
Schwank, Mike 458
Schwartz, Edward L. 483
Schwartz, Eric M. 163
Schwartz, Jack 47
Schwartz, Richard W. 404
Schwartz, Robert 539
Schwarz, Jay 31
Schwarz, Mike 525
Schwarzwalder, Larry 478
Schweitzer, Jeff 36
Schwentker, Robert B. 371
Schwentor, Larry 276
Schwer, Donald 113
Scitthelm, Gary 227
Sciullo, Jeffrey D. 157
Scively, Glen 360
Scobey, Richard 423
Scott, Bertram L. 476
Scott, C. Mark 294
Scott, Cheryl M. 218
Scott, D. E. 438
Scott, James 176
Scott, Jennifer 456
Scott, John A. 387
Scott, Larry E. 414
Scott, Lynn 311
Scott, Mark J. 167
Scott, Peter G. 59
Scott, Steve 524
Scott, Tim (TTI) 488
Scott, Timothy N. (AMF Bowling) 42
Scott, Walter Jr. 396

Scribner, Thomas 454
Scrimgeour, Kevin 445
Scrimo, Thomas A. 511
Scruggs, Samuel D. 245
Scudder, Richard B. 322
Scudere, Lou 286
Scuderi, Tony 191
Seaman, Jeffrey 423
Seandeven, Dave 31
Seaquist, Dorine R. 120
Searle, Thomas G. 114
Seawright, D. Stephen 124
Seay, Steve 238
Sebald, Bill 186
Sebatianelli, Joesph T. 262
Sebera, Bruce 483
Secor, Richard 126
Seebeck, John 183
Seferian, Dino 119
Seffrin, John R. 35
Segal, Barry 89
Segal, Bradley 89
Segal, Gordon 183
Segal, Jonathan 199
Segerdahl, Anders 184
Sehrt, David G. 254
Seidenberg, Ivan G. 520
Seim, Ronn 334
Sekine, Shuichiro 154
Sekulic, André 316
Selander, Robert W. 316
Self, Joe 26
Self, Kathy 418
Selig, Allan H. 306
Selig, Philip A. 36
Selker, Leopold 183
Sells, Nikki 185
Selva, Bert 262
Selz, Timothy P. 406
Semanie, George 100
Semerdjian, Nancy 183
Semler, Jerry D. 41
Semprini, Mark 59
Semrau, Kelly M. 434
Sener, Stephen F. 35
Senf, Eduardo 311
Sengin, Kathi Kendall 421
Senkler, Robert L. 336
Sensor, Wayne A. 31
Sepulveda, Carlos 260
Sequin, Donny 439
Serfaty, Alicia M. 44
Serota, Scott P. 79
Serrano, Nora I. 241
Serritella, Jeff 113
Serron, John 277
Sessa, Carolyn F. 145
Seth, Ranjit 184
Seuthe, Brenda 479
Seward, Rodica B. 400
Sewell, Craig 50
Sewell, John 82
Sexton, Fred 408
Sexton, John E. 368
Sexton, Michael 401
Seymour, Joseph J. 402
Seymour, Laura 47
Shadduck, David A. 487
Shafer, J. M. 484
Shafer, Jeff 488
Shaffer, John N. 237
Shaffet, Michael 302
Shafran, Isaac 300
Shah, Amar 481
Shah, Raj 416
Shailor, Barbara 26
Shaker, John 82
Shalett, Lisa A. 32
Shallat, Charles O. 297
Shannahan, C. Kevin 237
Shapell, Nathan 444
Shapira, David S. 205
Shapiro, Joseph C. 496

INDEX OF EXECUTIVES

Shapiro, Mark 181
Shappell, James R. 387
Sharman, James A. 537
Sharp, Jeff 176
Sharp, Kim 83
Shasteen, Julie 191
Shasteen, Rhonda 312
Shaum, Jack 55
Shaw, Brewster 498
Shaw, D. W. 43
Shaw, Dennis R. 452
Shaw, Greg 75
Shaw, Jaren 228
Shaw, Ray 21
Shaw, Terry D. 23
Shay, Bruce P. 336
Shea, Edmund H. Jr. 262
Shea, John F. (J.F. Shea) 262
Shea, John K. (Atlantic Mutual) 59
Shea, John T. (Bon Secours Health) 83
Shea, Nancy 537
Shea, Peter O. Jr. (J.F. Shea) 262
Shea, Peter O. (J.F. Shea) 262
Sheaffer, Dean 86
Shealer, G. Daniel Jr. 266
Shearer, Pat 307
Shears, Thomas H. 510
Shecterle, Debra J. 160
Sheehan, Tim 344
Sheehy, Vincent Sr. (Sheehy Auto) 445
Sheehy, Vincent A. Jr.
 (Sheehy Auto) 445
Sheets, Joseph D. 164
Sheetz, Joseph M. (Sheetz) 446
Sheetz, Joseph S. (Sheetz) 446
Sheetz, Louie 446
Sheetz, Stanton R. 446
Sheetz, Stephen G. 446
Sheff, Richard 50
Shelby, Charlie Jr. 71
Sheldon, Robert 314
Shell, Art 352
Shelton, Jim 207
Shepard, Donald C. III 328
Shepard, Tom 523
Sherer, Frank 477
Sheridan, Joseph 527
Sheridan, Richard R. 440
Sherlin, Stephen 469
Sherlock, William 314
Sherman, Floyd F. 93
Sherman, John 125
Sherman, Michael F. 216
Sherman, Peter M. 392
Sherman, Roger B. 349
Sherrin, Daniel 479
Sherry, Karen 51
Shields, Cindy 441
Shih, Elizabeth 110
Shimmon, David J. 277
Shine, Kenneth I. 508
Shipley, Zachary K. 382
Shirk, Gary M. 64
Shirk, Michael B. 76
Shirlen, David V. 357
Shirtcliff, Christine 69
Shivers, Edward T. 407
Shkurti, Bill 378
Sholkin, Howard 258
Sholtz, Stacy 345
Shontere, James G. 262
Shook, Daniel S. 349
Shoptaw, Robert L.
 (Arkansas Blue Cross
 and Blue Shield) 50
Shoptaw, Robert L. (Blue Cross) 79
Short, Bert 499
Short, M. Ann 349
Short, Steve 50
Shortt, Tom 497
Showalter, Linda G. 467
Shrader, K. Michael 92
Shrader, Ralph W. 85

Shriver, Debra 231
Shuffield, Randy 337
Shuler, David L. 367
Shulman, Douglas H. 349
Shulman, Mark 418
Shulstad, Raymond A. 338
Shurley, Lynn 201
Shuster, Mark 477
Shute, William H. 508
Shutkin, John 285
Shuttleworth, William 109
Sicilia, Terry 40
Siddiqui, Ohmar 200
Sidel, Steve 159
Sidon, Kenneth 323
Siegel, Murray S. 125
Siegel, Patricia B. 273
Siegel, Walter W. 344
Sieple, James A. 398
Sievers, Terry 167
Sievert, Frederick J. 364
Sievert, Steve 512
Sigman, Stanley T. 121
Silby, Tammy 256
Silva, Enrique 94
Silveira, Mike 433
Silver, Adam 350
Silverman, Daniel 405
Silverman, Mike 57
Silverman, Nat 100
Silverstein, Arthur 21
Silverstein, Douglas M. 183
Silverstein, Larry A. 368
Silvestri, Scott 284
Silvey, Lou 312
Simcox, Robert 122
Simmonds, Mary 35
Simmons, Glen 416
Simmons, Harold C. 137
Simmons, James 532
Simmons, Paul 536
Simmons, Robert 413
Simon, David F. 262
Simon, Harvey 456
Simon, Howard 494
Simon, Joel L. 296
Simon, Lou Anna K. 334
Simone, Joseph J. 478
Simone, Robert 210
Simons, Bob 529
Simons, Hugh 87
Simonse, Peter 287
Simpkins, Ted 454
Simplot, J. R. 272
Simplot, Scott R. 272
Simpson, Chris 391
Simpson, Lawrence J. 313
Sims, Frank L. 101
Sinclair, Mary K. 252
Sinclair, Pat 241
Sindelar, David M. 521
Sinewitz, Larry 256
Singer, Lester A. 470
Singer, Paul L. 330
Singer, Ronald M. 510
Singh, J. J. 193
Singh, Suk 94
Singleton, Kenneth P. 145
Singleton, Knox 254
Singleton, William D. 322
Sinkfield, David 255
Sinrich, Bill 250
Sipes, Larry 204
Sisemore, Martin B. 428
Siska, Nancy P. 101
Sisson, Jeffrey D. 171
Sjoblom, Cheryl 406
Skelton, Brenda F. 372
Skelton, Johnny 92
Skilton, Gary C. 23
Skinner, Jeffrey D. 253
Skinner, Michael 69
Skinner, Rick 406

Skipper, John 181
Sklar, Louis S. 237
Sklenar, Mark 494
Skobin, Alan J. 201
Skoff, Brian 111
Skogsbergh, James H. 24
Skorton, David J. 502
Skrainka, Alan F. 269
Slack, Thomas W. 220
Slade, Clifford 448
Slaughter, Mechelle 358
Slaughter, Thomas E. 57
Slentz, Andy 168
Slepian, Steven L. 356
Slifka, Alfred A. 207
Slifka, Eric 207
Sligar, Gary 125
Slizewski, Bea 76
Sloan, Jay 420
Sloan, O. Temple III 202
Sloan, O. Temple Jr. 202
Slodden, Toby J. 315
Slotkin, Art L. 438
Slottow, Timothy P. 503
Sluder, Robert L. 335
Slynn, Brian 539
Smagley, Norman 413
Smail, Peter J. 194
Small, Francis 180
Small, Lawrence M. 452
Smalley, Diane 31
Smartis, Dan 524
Smeach, Stephen C. 411
Smeaton, Gordon 352
Smellie, Michael 454
Smetana, Mark 174
Smetter, Dave 533
Smiley, Steve 398
Smith, Alison 82
Smith, Bernice 225
Smith, Brad (Cinemark) 121
Smith, Bradford K.
 (Ford Foundation) 196
Smith, Brian 342
Smith, Bruce 24
Smith, Claire H. 465
Smith, Clyde M. 69
Smith, Corrine 77
Smith, D. Gates 377
Smith, Dan F.
 (Equistar Chemicals) 178
Smith, Daniel E.
 (American Cancer Society) 35
Smith, Delford M. 184
Smith, Dennis H. 305
Smith, Don (K-VA-T Food Stores) 286
Smith, Don (MWH Global) 346
Smith, Don A. (Amerisure) 42
Smith, Douglas G. 346
Smith, E. Ashley 508
Smith, Eddie 398
Smith, Ellen 119
Smith, Erich G. 525
Smith, F. Patrick 471
Smith, Francia G. 514
Smith, Gary L. 243
Smith, Gina M. 313
Smith, Greg 109
Smith, Harold H. 354
Smith, Henley 380
Smith, Howard 306
Smith, Hugh C. 318
Smith, Isabelle 265
Smith, Jack C.
 (K-VA-T Food Stores) 286
Smith, James C. 377
Smith, Jay R. 141
Smith, Jeanmarie 368
Smith, Jim 351
Smith, John Henry
 (Southern States) 454
Smith, John R. (Integris Metals) 255
Smith, Kristi 272

Smith, L. Dennis 505
Smith, Lance 248
Smith, Larry (Kentucky Lottery) 275
Smith, Larry
 (Les Schwab Tire Centers) 293
Smith, Lloyd C. 39
Smith, Lynette 118
Smith, M. Lazane 130
Smith, Manning J. III 251
Smith, Marie F. 18
Smith, Maureen 159
Smith, P. Jeremy 201
Smith, Paul (Levi Strauss) 294
Smith, Paul G. (Tenaska) 471
Smith, Pete (Burger King) 94
Smith, Peter (Services Group) 444
Smith, Philip S.
 (Unified Western Grocers) 495
Smith, Phillip J. (Stater Bros.) 462
Smith, Randy (Georgia Crown) 204
Smith, Randy (Vought Aircraft) 524
Smith, Richard P. 146, 147
Smith, Robert W. Jr. 68
Smith, Rockwell 143
Smith, Rodney A. 510
Smith, Roland C. 38
Smith, Scott 222
Smith, Sharyl 156
Smith, Shawn (Carlson Wagonlit) 103
Smith, Shawn (O'Neal Steel) 380
Smith, Stan 60
Smith, Steve
 (Enterprise Rent-A-Car) 178
Smith, Steven C.
 (K-VA-T Food Stores) 286
Smith, Steven C.
 (Topco Associates) 480
Smith, Steven M. (AMPAM) 39
Smith, Terry 312
Smith, Thomas A.
 (Oglethorpe Power) 376
Smith, Thomas R. Jr.
 (Sidley Austin Brown & Wood) 446
Smith, Tom
 (Central Grocers Cooperative) 112
Smith, Toni 474
Smith, Virginia R. 251
Smith, William D. 388
Smith Tunney, Kelly 57
Smith-Wagner, Jamie 331
Smitham, Peter 326
Smock, Catherine A. 472
Smock, Tom 290
Smoldt, Craig A. 318
Smoldt, Robert K. 318
Smoluchowski, Peter 387
Smoot, Nathaniel 313
Smothers, James L. 361
Snead Williams, Caren 264
Snelgrove, Laird 480
Snider, John 160
Snider, Richard 66
Snow, Hank 424
Snow, Thomas 404
Snyder, Barbara 378
Snyder, P. Brent G. 23
Snyder, David M. 93
Snyder, John 539
Snyder, Robert 360
Snyder, Thomas J. 416
Snyder, William W. 178
Sobol, Lawrence R. 269
Soco, Johana 211
Sogan, Lance G. 242
Sojourner, Ted 199
Sokal, Steve 247
Sokol, David L. 335
Solberg, Jeff 218
Soldo, Carole Czar 241
Solem, Terry S. 406
Soliman, Sam 281
Solimine, Stephen P. 42
Sollenberger, Donna K. 510

INDEX OF EXECUTIVES

Solleveld, Ron 82
Solomon, Charles M. 60
Solomon, Jimmie Lee 306
Solomon, Mack B. Jr. 155
Solomon, Russell M. 343
Solomon, William T. 60
Solsvig, Curtis G. III 139
Soltman, Ronald P. 518
Solwold, Julie 265
Somers, John A. 476
Sommer, Ken 523
Sondles, Dan 534
Sones, Randy 31
Sonet, Ellen Miller 327
Sonnett, Judith A. 85
Soper, Cheryl L. 503
Soper, Robert J. 339
Soraci, Joe 94
Sorell, Thomas G. 220
Sorensen, Steve 176
Sorenson, Steve 56
Sorkin, Barbara 95
Sorrentino, Peter 65
Soulby, Robert W. 226
Soule, Stafford 298
Souquette, Greg 228
Southam, Arthur M. 273
Southerland, Bob 286
Sowles, Anne 298
Spackler, J. Keith 27
Spae, Bill 332
Spaeth, Ronald G. 183
Spahn, Jim 257
Spain, Wayne 61
Spangler, C. D. Jr. 362
Spann, James 324
Spanos, Alexander Gus 28
Spanos, Dean A. 28
Spanos, Harry V. 264
Spanos, Michael A. 28
Sparks, Carol 36
Sparks, Kara 392
Spatz, Bruce 234
Spaulding, Edward 535
Spaulding, Steve 50
Spears, Leslie George 265
Specketer, Thomas B. 335
Speight, Marianne 120
Spelce, Byron D. 43
Spellacy, Suzanne 469
Spelman, Lucy H. 452
Spence, David S. 97
Spencer, Christopher S. 37
Spencer, Leslie 407
Spencer, Norm 480
Spencer, Robert S. 63
Spengler, Bob 433
Spenst, Brett 22
Speranza, Paul S. Jr. 531
Speranzo, Anthony J. 52
Sperber, Burton S. 516
Sperber, Richard A. 516
Sperber, Stuart J. 516
Sperlich, Harold K. 416
Sperling, Ron 467
Spicer, Donald Z. 503
Spicer, Robert H. II 117
Spiegel, Daniel 478
Spiegel, Merle 408
Spielberg, Steven 166
Spille, Kent W. 144
Spilman, Pat 67
Spinnickie, Benjamin 211
Spitz, Gary M. 286
Spitz, William T. 516
Spivak, Herb 361
Spivak, Kenin M. 265
Splayt, Richard 26
Sponyoe, John 255
Spoonemore, Brenda 350
Spraggins, T. Wayne 62
Spriggs, Nick 357
Springer, Colby H. 125
Sprinkle, David M. 429
Sproule, Michael E. 364
Sprunger, Brant 518
Spurlock, Nancy H. 362
Spurlock, Rick K. 498
Squier, David L. 104
Squires, Joan M. 344
Srigley, Kevin 205
Srnecz, Jean 64
Sroka, Joseph T. 251
St. Arnold, Dale 518
St. John, Pat 481
St. John, Ricky 249
Stack, Karen 50
Stackhouse, Frank 435
Stacy, Joe 89
Stacy, Kelly 305
Stadler, Gerald P. 496
Stadnick, Patricia 43
Stadtlander, George 323
Staed, Michael B. 382
Stafeil, Jeff 330
Stager, Diana 83
Stagner, David P. 429
Staiano-Coico, Lisa 138
Staky, Richard 538
Staley, Warren R. 101
Stamatakos, Michael 375
Stamerjohn, Scott 163
Stammer, Richard W. 29
Stanard, Anne M. 344
Stanbrook, Steven P. 434
Stanczyk, Marcy 432
Stander, Stephen 17
Stanek, Robert V. 107
Stanhaus, John 480
Staniar, Burton B. 280
Stanky, Michael E. 126
Stanley, Aurelia C. 35
Stanley, Charles A. 118
Stanley, Richard L. 416
Stanos, Peter 248
Stansberry, Don C. Jr. 507
Stansel, Eugene A. Jr. 459
Stansfield, David A. 31
Stanton, John 515
Stanton, Kathryn A. 195
Stanton, Ronald P. 482
Stanutz, Donald J. 246
Stapleton, Thomas G. 477
Stark, Linda 275
Stark, Pamela S. 516
Starkey, Steve 49
Starmann-Harrison, Mary 458
Starr, Jeremy 220
Staskiel, James A. 319
Stater, Edward A. 462
Statler, Don 46
Statton, Tim 71
Statuto, Richard J. 430
Stausboll, Anne 99
Stautberg, Elizabeth A. 120
Stawarz, Raymond R. 189
Steadman, E. Eric 125
Stearn, Carole 446
Stearns, Laura O. 155
Stebel, Eric 178
Steber, John H. 230
Stecklein, Leonard F. 372
Stedman, Scott 541
Steeg, Jim 352
Steelberg, Cheryl 516
Steele, Ken 110
Steele, Kevin 16
Steele, Patrick S. 154
Steele, Robert D. 376
Steele, Susan M. 69
Steen, Ray 40
Steenrod, Mitch 398
Steere, Ric 524
Stefanik, Frank V. 210
Stefano, Joanna M. 138
Steffen, Christopher J. 521
Steier, Larry J. 27
Stein, Eugene 534
Stein, Lewis Lou 423
Stein, Robert W. 180
Stein, Shelley 213
Steinberg, Art 147
Steinberg, Joel M. 364
Steinberg, Michael 82
Steinblatt, Jim 51
Steinmetz, Ed 205
Stellio, Vincent 486
Stellmacher, Jon M. 475
Stellmon, John 415
Stelmar, Wayne J. 538
Stembridge, John 371
Stenhammar, Carl-Wilhelm 426
Stenholt, Colleen J. 426
Stephan, Brooks 482
Stephan, William B. 251
Stephens, Angela A. 125
Stephens, Elton B. (EBSCO) 174
Stephens, Elton B. Jr. (EBSCO) 174
Stephens, James T. 174
Stephens, Richard T. 153
Stephenson, Randall L. 121
Stepp, Kay 406
Sterling, Duane 426
Stern, Carl 87
Stern, David J. 129, 350
Stern, Gary H. 188
Stern, Leslie F. 351
Sternberg, Elliot 430
Sternberg, Jonathan 454
Sternberg, Seymour 364
Stevens, Patricia A. 519
Stevenson, Brian 448
Stevenson, Gary E. 248
Stevenson, Jeff 147
Stewart, Bill 217
Stewart, Dan 508
Stewart, Katie 49
Stewart, Mac A. 378
Stewart, Michael 321
Stewart, Raymond 247
Stewart, Thomas J. 444
Steyn, David A. 32
Stickler, Daniel L. 242
Stier, Jeffrey K. 84
Stigler, John N. 405
Stilen, Bobbi 294
Stilwell, Jack 168
Stinson, Kenneth E. 396
Stinton, Carter 223
Stock, Alan W. 121
Stock, Keith 316
Stockel, Neil 106
Stoebe, Rich 271
Stoecker, Michael E. 30
Stokes, Jack 57
Stolle, John 329
Stoller, William H. 185
Stone, Alan 226
Stone, Bradley H. 290
Stone, Gary L. 387
Stone, James 294
Stone, Jeffrey I. 90
Stone, Mike 38
Stone, Steve K. 340
Stonesifer, Patricia Q. 75
Story, Cathy 248
Story, Kendra A. 18
Story, Roger 92
Stout, Darryl 484
Stowe, Barbara 337
Strahley, Jim 330
Strange, Donald E. 83
Strassburg, William 531
Strasser, Richard J. Jr. 513
Stratton, John G. 520
Straus, Joe M. 25
Strausborger, Dave 536
Strauss, Cindy 467
Strauss, Robert S. 30
Streeter, Bill 333
Streit, Dennis 297
Streit, Gary J. 35
Streitman, Fran 52
Streurer, John 21
Stribley, D. LeAnne 491
Strickland, Joe 204
Strickland, Robert W. 442
Strickland, Samuel R. 85
Strickler, George E. 417
Strigl, Dennis F. 520
Stritmatter, Claude 458
Strobel, Dennis 96
Stroik, Gregory J. 189
Stromberg, Leroy J. 30
Stromberg, Tony 264
Strong, Gregory S. 336
Strong, Stuart 401
Strong, Wendi E. 514
Strother, John 416
Strout, Steven B. 340
Strumpf, Linda B. 196
Strutt, David 532
Stuart, Barkley J. 207
Stuart, Scott M. 283
Stubblefield, Jerry 540
Stuckey, Bruce D. 196
Stuckey, Darla C. 367
Stucky, Nicklas D. 405
Stukel, James J. 502
Stump, David P. 54
Stussi, Doug 300
Subotnick, Stuart 331
Subramaniam, Shivan S. 193
Sudan, Ashok 212
Suko, Todd A. 492
Sukut, Paul 67
Sullivan, E. Thomas 504
Sullivan, George E. 202
Sullivan, Gregory B. 168
Sullivan, John (AARP) 18
Sullivan, John
 (Sisters of Mercy Health System) 449
Sullivan, John F. (Eagle-Picher) 171
Sullivan, Laura P. 460
Sullivan, Mark E. 87
Sullivan, Maureen 79
Sullivan, Mike 26
Sullivan, Stephen G. 295
Sullivan, Teresa A. 508
Sulmon, Bruno 164
Sultenfuss, John H. 113
Summa, Monty R. 113
Summerfield, Nancy 320
Summers, Lawrence H. 226
Summers, Shannon 312
Sumner, Vernon 422
Sumpter, Christina M. 384
Sun, David 278
Sunderland, Charles T. 52
Sunderland, James P. 52
Sunderland, Kent W. 52
Sunderland, Mike 22
Sundius, Robert W. Jr. 139
Sunshine, Eugene S. 373
Supovitz, Frank 355
Suscavage, Charles 260
Sutcliffe, Ian 342
Sutermeister, Steven R. 496
Sutton, Leslie N. 118
Sutton, Thomas C. 384
Suwak, Lawrence M. 151
Swaback, Ray 324
Swalwell, Gregory M. 137
Swango, Tim 482
Swank, Tom 441
Swanson, Kenneth A. 382
Swanson, Kurt R. 468
Swanson, Tom 66
Swanson, William R. 87
Swartz, Steven R. 231
Swatek, Mark 346
Swearingen, Christine M. 324

INDEX OF EXECUTIVES

Sweeney, Barbara Z. 349
Sweeney, Dawn 18
Sweeney, John J. 26
Sweeney, Steven 388
Sweet, Frederic H. 372
Swenson, Doug 85
Swenson, Paul 81
Swier, Ryan 54
Swift, Bruce 330
Swift, Mike 113
Swiller, Ari 541
Swindle, Dean 374
Swinton, Richard L. 143
Sykes, Dan 288
Sykes, Rebecca 109
Sylvester, Patrick 249
Syron, Robert 535
Syverson, Cindra 430
Szczesny, Jeffrey D. 412
Szefel, Dennis J. 153
Szima, Joseph A. 483
Szmyt, Ann Marie 69

T

Taarud, Terese A. 37
Tabak, Natan 527
Tabolt, David 63
Taccini, Cindy 375
Tackett, Larry 122
Tackett, Valerie 45
Taddeo, Michael 323
Taft, Terry 380
Taggart, David A. 346
Tagliabue, Paul J. 352
Tahmin, Peter 420
Takerer, John 264
Talin, Patricia A. 43
Talley, Joseph J. 36
Tamai, Tashiyuki 97
Tamer, Kathy 498
Tamke, George W. 144
Tamura, Atsuko 416
Tan, Benjamin 482
Tanaka, Eric 415
Tang, Cyrus 468
Tang, Steven S. L. 521
Tarde, Jerry 21
Tarde, Merv 260
Tarr, John 408
Tarr, Tom 79
Tarrh, Lloyd 116
Tartikoff, Peter 35
Tasooji, Nick 541
Tassopoulos, Timothy P. 118
Taszarek, Tom 165
Tatarko, Michael Sr. 132
Tate, Michael 91
Tate, Stanley 455
Tatham, Patricia K. 185
Tatom, Patrick G. 417
Tatum, Steve 282
Taurone, Ralph J. 470
Tayeh, David A. 271
Taylor, Andrew C. 178
Taylor, Bob 160
Taylor, Byron L. 251
Taylor, Chris (Bloomberg) 78
Taylor, Chris (Chick-fil-A) 118
Taylor, Christine
 (MacAndrews & Forbes) 304
Taylor, Colin 154
Taylor, Don 395
Taylor, Eric 332
Taylor, Glen A. 469
Taylor, Iris 156
Taylor, Jean 469
Taylor, Jim 398
Taylor, Larry 102
Taylor, Loren 502
Taylor, Michael
 (FHC Health Systems) 191

Taylor, Michael
 (Sentara Healthcare) 442
Taylor, Robert 345
Taylor, Ron 247
Taylor, Sue 292
Taylor, Thomas A. 43
Taylor, Tim (Hendrick Automotive) 233
Taylor, Timothy G.
 (Chevron Phillips Chemical) 116
Taylor, Wendy 238
Tedesco, Lisa A. 503
Teel, James E. 412
Teeter, Thomas C. 59
Teissier, Jean-Max 268
Teitz, Jack 381
Telles-Irvin, Patricia 502
Tellmann, John R. 198
Temby, Judith 510
Temmer, Robert 484
Temple, Jim 179
Temporiti, John 496
Tenenbaum, Joseph 369
Tener, Tom 308
Tennent, Wayne T. 42
Tenny, Barron M. 196
Teo, Alfred S. 448
Tepper, Scott M. 242
TerHaar, Rich 93
Terhar, Louis F. 255
Ternan, Edward 257
Terrill, Charles W. 371
Terry, Tim 26
Tersigni, Anthony R. 52
Terwilliger, J. Ronald 482
Tesoriero, Joseph S. 162
Teutsch, Nancy 227
Tewksbury, Gregory J. 503
Thacher, Carter P. 535
Thacher, John P. 535
Thackwray, Ian 164
Thain, John A. 367
Thanopoulos, George 330
Tharani, Haresh T. 75
Tharp, Jim 166
Thatte, Dan 297
Thayer, Martha 207
Theiss, Sabrina 392
Theull, Bernard 438
Theuninck, Donald W. 29
Thibault, George E. 389
Thiel, Thomas 285
Thiele, Mike 71
Thielens, James Ted Jr. 417
Thielke, Thomas 510
Thies, Paul 519
Thom, Christopher D. 316
Thomas, Anne 327
Thomas, Daniel J. 132
Thomas, Ernest 113
Thomas, Gary
 (University of Missouri) 504
Thomas, Gary L.
 (JM Family Enterprises) 264
Thomas, Gene 397
Thomas, Isiah 304
Thomas, J. Grover Jr. 488
Thomas, Jeff 228
Thomas, Kathleen 254
Thomas, Larry 261
Thomas, Mark 31
Thomas, Patrick W. 245
Thomas, Peter J. 74
Thomas, Richard K. 371
Thomas, William L. 324
Thomason, Joel D. 394
Thompson, Dale 26
Thompson, Harold 484
Thompson, Jane 333
Thompson, John 142
Thompson, Larry 111
Thompson, Michele M. 502
Thompson, Phil 39
Thompson, Robert 119

Thompson, Steven J. 266
Thompson, Tommie D. 345
Thompson, William P. 458
Thomsen, James A. 475
Thomson, Dale 26
Thomson, David 465
Thomson, Mark P. 255
Thone, William J. 29
Thoren, Mike 137
Thorn, Bruce 127
Thorn, Stuart 455
Thornbrugh, Mike 410
Thornton, Tom 31
Thorud, David 509
Thrash, James E. 387
Thresher, Mark R. 359
Threshie, R. D. 199
Thrope, Susan A. 364
Thurman, Neal 77
Thurman, Robert W. 511
Tibbot, Gregory 127
Tiberio, Jeanne M. 299
Tidwell, Jody 540
Tierno, Anthony F. 322
Tiesenga, Donald 59
Tighe, Steven A. 271
Tignanelli, Joseph R. 519
Tilghman, Richard H. 394
Tilghman, Shirley M. 405
Tillinghast, Marilyn 100
Tillman, George 85
Timm, Dann 269
Timmerman, Randy 280
Timmons, Marianne 531
Timmons, Poe A. 429
Timony, John F. 498
Tims, Mark 252
Tinkler, Philip 179
Tinsman, Garrett 433
Tipsord, Michael L. 460
Tisdale, Richard 396
Tishman, Daniel R. 478
Tishman, John L. 478
Tison, Ben 412
Tisserand, Joseph W. 37
Titus, Charles 366
Tobey, Loren 369
Tochner, Ira 541
Todd, John J. 331, 332
Todd, Phil 227
Todd, Toby 429
Toenniessen, Gary H. 421
Toepel, Paul 240
Toft, Paul 56
Tolaney, Murli 346
Tolbert, Bernie 350
Tolbert, Brenda 218
Tolbert, Terry W. 414
Tolbert, Trent 296
Tolkowsky, Michael 311
Tolleson, Stephanie 250
Tolosky, Mark R. 69
Tomanelli, Frank 191
Tomasek, Ted 150
Tometich, Andy 164
Tomjack, Thomas J. 371
Tomlinson, Kenneth Y. 140
Tompkins, Jim 361
Tomsich, John R. 361
Tomsich, Robert J. 361
Tone, Mark 169
Tooker, Jean E. 457
Topham, Michael J. G. 237
Toran, Daniel J. 392
Torbert, Ronald J. 66
Torda, Jay 149
Torgerson, Francis V. 244
Tornabeni, Jolene 254
Toro, Rafael 211
Tortorella, Alan 111
Tossavainen, Thomas J. 257
Toth, Aurora 344
Toth, Robert B. 264

Toub, Christopher M. 32
Toups, Roland M. 490
Townsend, Charles H. 21
Townsend, George 239
Townson, Brian 420
Towsey, M. Stewart 43
Tracy, Dick 163
Tracy, John 163
Tracy, Patrick F. 163
Tran, Khanh T. 384
Tran, Thomas L. 133
Tranchida, Richard 420
Trastek, Victor F. 318
Traube, Joe 440
Traut, Christopher 195
Travetto, Frank D. 173
Traynor, Michael C. 340
Treadwell, David L. 383
Trebino, Tricia 489
Trefun, Patrick A. 358
Trego, Charles R. 420
Tremblay, Stephen E. 521
Tremmel, Kevin 89
Tresslar, Bruce 396
Trethewey, Virginia M. 378
Tretter, Dave 492
Treuhold, Robert C. 445
Tricamo, Frank 58
Trifone, John 82
Trilikis, George 207
Trillo, Nancy 199
Trimble, T. L. 23
Trimbur, Nancy 463
Trinkwald, Allan F. 448
Tripp, Scott A. 30
Trippe, Cathi 397
Trivette, Patricia L. 500
Troester, Dean 142
Trosino, Vincent J. 460
Troutman, Charles 511
Troutman, Nathan 526
Trowbridge, J. Richard 360
True, Douglas K. 502
Truebridge, Chris 444
Truess, Jim 218
Truitt, Gary R. 237
Trujillo, Tony A. Jr. 255
Trumka, Richard L. 26
Trump, Donald J. (Trump) 486
Trump, Donald J. Jr. (Trump) 486
Tscherne, Robert L. 365
Tseng, Vivian S. Y. 354
Tsuetaki, Tracy K. 411
Tu, John 278
Tubb, Joe 398
Tuchman, Alan 33
Tucker, Lou 183
Tucker, Steven E. 132
Tully, Herbert B. 535
Tumulty, Elizabeth 530
Tunnessen, James E. 106
Turell, Brad 530
Turf, Barbara 183
Turfitt, Myron L. 414
Turke, Thomas H. 442
Turley, James S. 180
Turley, Robert 394
Turner, Bert S. 490
Turner, Bruce 55
Turner, Gerry L. 69
Turner, Jim L. 165
Turner, Patti 499
Turner, Paul 69
Turner, Raymond 397
Turner, Robert (JELD-WEN) 262
Turner, Robert (LifeBridge Health) 296
Turner, Ronald P. 504
Turner, Ryan 83
Turner, Thomas H. 490
Turner, Todd R. 185
Turner, Walter W. 284
Tursy, Tony 463
Tuschman, Thomas E. 379

INDEX OF EXECUTIVES

Tushman, J. Lawrence 446
Tuttle, Robert H. 490
Tutwiler, Margaret 367
Twigg, Eric 527
Twine, David 440
Twitchell, Karen A. 178
Twomey, Gerri 64
Twomey, William 341
Tyler, Mary-Knight 241
Tyler, Susan 323
Tynan, Amelia 506
Tyser, Matthew 497
Tyson, Bernard J. 273

U

Uboldi, Mike 110
Ucciferro, Joseph J. 151
Ucelli, Loretta 129
Udell, Charles R. 214
Udell, Howard R. 408
Ueberroth, Heidi 350
Uhler, Robert B. 346
Uhling, Terry 272
Uhlmann, Rick 145
Uhrich, Marie A. 475
Ukrop, James E. 493
Ukrop, Robert S. 493
Ulaby, Fawwaz T. 503
Ulbrich, Sara 494
Ulick, Susan E. 476
Ulijasz, Pamela 63
Ullman, Chris 104
Ulreich, Shawn M. 455
Umphenour, Russell V. Jr. 428
Umscheid, Rudolph K. 514
Unanue, Francisco R. 211
Unanue, Robert I. 211
Underhill, Jim 320
Underwood, Jeffrey 540
Underwood, Vernon O. 540
Unmacht, Brian 416
Upchurch, Joy M. 28
Upshaw, Gene 352
Upton, O. B. III 145
Urban, Stanley T. 107
Urbon, Katherine 297
Urlis, Allan 335
Urquhart, Ernest 110
Utterback, Ron 333
Uttley, Jeff 193

V

Vaclavik, Randy 228
Vahldiek, Lissa Walls 57
Vail, Cheron 415
Vale, Brenda 329
Valenta, Mary 380
Valenti, Samuel III 483
Valerio, Manuel 200
Valerius, Steven J. 496
Valine, Roger 524
Van Andel, Steve 34
Van Berkel, Thomas M. 305
Van Brunt, Gary T. 159
Van Brunt, William A. 102
Van Curen, Don 300
Van De Bunt, Ben 221
Van Den Brandt, Bill 48
Van Der Meulen, Joseph P. 507
van der Veer, Ben 285
van der Velde, Johannes I. 523
Van Deventer, Richard 270
Van Dusseldorp, Steve 520
Van Dyk, Deborah 436
Van Gelder, John M. 281
Van Gorder, Chris D. 440
Van Hise, Martha 59
Van Lith, Richard 233

Van Lopik, William H. 434
van Maldeghem, Todd 95
Van Pelt, Jack F. 214
Van Trease, Sandra A. 77
Van Tuyl, Cecil 525
Van Tuyl, Larry 525
Van Tuyle, Jeff 443
VanBebber, Rodney L. 495
VanBeber, Dianne 255
Vance, James 133
Vance, Ralph B. 35
Vandaalen, Rosario 503
VanDenburgh, Mark 443
Vander Ark, Tom 75
VanderLinden, Dick 536
Vandewater, David T. 49
Vanek, Dean 329
VanHorn, Trevor 184
Vanic, Gary 215
Vannieuwenhoven, Vicki 216
VanRosendale, Perry 489
Vargas, Arlene 91
Vargas, James F. 138
Varin, Pierre 259
Varmus, Harold 327
Varner, Bruce D. 462
Vascellaro, Jerome 321
Vasil, Patricia 377
Vasilenko, Mike 272
Vasquez, Chris 326
Vassor, Philippe 154
Vasta, Sal 274
Vaughan, Alan 337
Vaughan, Brad 77
Vaughn, Doug 88
Vaughn, Kathie 99
Vaughn, Paul 423
Vaughn, Richard 515
Vaupel, Ron 281
Vayo, Robert 186
Veazey, William W. 101
Vegliante, Anthony 514
Velardo, William J. 339
Velez, Maroa 92
Velez, Pete 363
Velussi, Luca 236
Venter, Conrad 154
Ventura, Jeff 413
Vera, George A. 385
Veranth, Joseph 87
Verbeck, David C. 135
Verdon, Michael 401
Verdon, William P. 143
Verinder, David 439
Verloop, Robert J. 465
Vermeer, Robert 520
Vermeer Andringa, Mary 520
Verzak, Dave 113
Verzi, Dennis 109
Vesce, Vincent C. 365
Vesper, Keith R. 379
Vessels, Gale 275
Viccellio, Henry Jr. 514
Vick, Greg 495
Vickers, John A. 478
Vickery, David 209
Vickery, Susan D. 482
Vidich, Paul J. 528
Vieth, Mark A. 426
Vigdal, David 202
Vigil, Art 490
Villa, Joyce 461
Villa, Stephen P. 346
Villalba, Pedro 230
Villamizar, Javier 91
Villano, Nancy 446
Vinay, Philippe 103
Vincent, Michael S. 230
Vincent, Pierre 202
Vincent, Susan Gailey 42
Vincett, Neil 249
Vincze, L. Stephan 468
Vines, Ellsworth F. 157

Vining, Peggy 395
Vinson, Stanley W. 114
Viola, John 475
Viscomi, Ralph 29
Visola, Joseph 172
Vissers, Francois J. 511
Vituli, Alan 106
Vivatson, Robert 36
Viveen, William J. Jr. 34
Vivona, Joseph F. 503
Vleugels, Francois 418
Voeller, John G. 77
Voelzke, Meehee 138
Vogel, Ben 53
Vogel, Charles 53
Vogel, Grace B. 367
Vogel, Morris 421
Vogel, Pat 351
Vogt, Bill 423
Voiland, Eugene A. 25
Volk, Jay 66
Vollbracht, Michael 75
Vollman, Sandra K. 511
Volpe, Richard 470
Volvo, Robert 119
Vomvas, Art 17
von Juergensonn, Janine 65
von Mayrhauser, Stanford H. 175
von Stauffenberg, Philippe 236
von Zuben, Fred G. 368
Vorderstrasse, Samuel C. 50
Vorwald, Karen 480
Voss, Doug 312
Voss, Terry J. 27
Voss, Wayne 326
Vradenburg, Daniel R. 535
Vroom, Davide 432
Vuchetich, Scott 320

W

Wacaser, H. H. 329
Wacaser, Randall S. 329
Wachtel, David 78
Wachtendonk, Bob 409
Waddy, Victoria 541
Wade, Doreen 199
Wade, James P. 514
Wadhwani, Romesh 252
Waechter, Sandra 165
Wagenknecht, Jerry A. 24
Wagner, Barbara L. 487
Wagner, Dave 328
Wagner, Eric R. 324
Wagner, Jack W. 23
Wagner, Mark 216
Wagner, Meredith 297
Wagner, Michelle 497
Wagner, Robert J. 112
Wagner, Roger P. 242
Wagner, Ron 20
Wagner, Ruth 267
Wagner, Ted 42
Wagner-Findeisen, Anne 365
Wahl, Jeffrey S. 382
Wahlberg, Timothy G. 184
Wai, Samuel S. M. 36
Wainscott, Chris 202
Wais, Marc 368
Waite, Ed 289
Waite, Michael K. 328
Waiter, Joseph 286
Waitukaitis, Mike 208
Wake, Richard 174
Wake, Thomas G. 174
Waldbillig, Ron 247
Walden, David A. 36
Waldheim, William S. 170
Waldron, Anne 63
Waldron, Maureen 134
Walega, Phil 446
Walensky, Cathy 488

Walker, Cecil L. 82
Walker, David 25
Walker, Donald R. 25
Walker, Greg A. 198
Walker, J. L. 358
Walker, Jeff 282
Walker, Jerry 454
Walker, Jessica W. 138
Walker, John B. (AMF Bowling) 42
Walker, John J. (Loews Cineplex) 299
Walker, Kenneth L. 440
Walker, Page 346
Walker, Randy I. 438
Walker, Robert C. 58
Walker, William J. 465
Walker de Sarvide, Lee 330
Walkush, Joseph P. 438
Wall, Duane D. 534
Wall, Kathy 79
Wall, Stephen T. 119
Wallace, Al 51
Wallace, Deborah 136
Wallace, Richard
  (BrandsMart USA) 256
Wallace, Richard A.
  (Freedom Communications) 199
Wallace, Steven R. 442
Wallach, Dan 16
Wallach, Kenneth L. 112
Wallack, Howard 209
Wallake, Randy F. 336
Waller, Debra S. 265
Waller, Ken 247
Wallin, J. Smoke 358
Wallis, Dale E. 25
Walls, Cathy 204
Walls, David B. 60
Walsh, Catherine 346
Walsh, Daniel J. 528
Walsh, James F. (HP Hood) 244
Walsh, Jim (AMPI) 56
Walsh, Jim (Meijer) 325
Walsh, John (ESPN) 181
Walsh, John F.
  (U.S. Postal Service) 513
Walsh, Matthew M. 528
Walsh, Tim
  (Enterprise Rent-A-Car) 178
Walsh, Tim (Foster Farms) 198
Walsh, William P. 363
Walter, Elisse B. 349
Walter, John 208
Walter, Mark S. 264
Walters, Paul F. 393
Walters-Dowding, Andrea 299
Walterspiel, Peter 290
Walton, Aaron A. 237
Walton, Robert D. 99
Walton Paschall, Jimmie 524
Walz, Gary L. 428
Wanek, Ronald G. 53
Wanek, Todd 53
Wangurd, Debra 519
Wankmuller, Richard N. 346
Ward, Brenda 160
Ward, Gerald M. 404
Ward, Jim 301
Ward, Michael 528
Ward, Robert E. 130
Warden, Michael L. 508
Warden, William G. IV 465
Warga, Thomas J. 364
Waring, Susan R. 460
Warlick, Anderson D. 386
Warlick-Jarvie, Lois 76
Warmath, Thomas H. 365
Warner, Douglas A. III 327
Warner, Floyd 73
Warner, H. Ty 492
Warner, John H. Jr. 438
Warner, Martin 103
Warner, Tim 121
Warren, V'Ella 509

INDEX OF EXECUTIVES

Warrin, Catherine 74
Warrren, Terry 217
Wartell, Michael A. 251
Warwick, Robb C. 342
Washburn, John 431
Wasley, Susan 69
Wassenaar, Craig G. 344
Wasserstein, Gail 144
Watanabe, Toshizo 370
Waterman, Rita 22
Watkins, Barry 305
Watkins, George C. 529
Watkins, Greg 529
Watkins, John 529
Watkins, Kimberley M. 529
Watkins, Michael L. 529
Watkins, Wendy A. 153
Watrin, Liz 229
Watson, Anthony L. 230
Watson, Darryl 99
Watson, Jennifer A. 389
Watt, Jim 433
Watt, Ray 538
Watterson, David J. 248
Watterson, Scott R. 248
Watts, Carolyn 371
Watts, Emily 91
Watts, Howard 107
Watts, Phillip H. 512
Waugh, Ed 263
Weatherall, Murray 514
Weaver, J. Warren 59
Weaver, Laura S. 244
Weaver, Paul D. 243
Weaver, W. Douglas 233
Webb, Charles H. 334
Webb, Greg 228
Webb, H. Lawrence 538
Webb, Jerry L. 358
Webb, Robert
  (Jim Koons Automotive) 263
Webb, Robert D. (CF Industries) 113
Webb, Robert W.
  (Ingram Entertainment) 253
Webb, Robert W. (Marmon Group) 310
Webb de Macias, Carolyn 507
Webber, Henry S. 501
Weber, John H. (Eagle-Picher) 171
Weber, Jon (Philip Services) 397
Weber, Leslie A. 487
Weber, Todd 284
Webster, Bill 65
Webster, David J. 521
Webster, Jeff 119
Webster, Steve
  (Sauder Woodworking) 433
Webster, Steven M.
  (Michigan State University) 334
Weddle, James D. 269
Wedel, Randy 436
Weed, Joe K. 174
Weed, Monica M. 252
Weekley, David M. 149
Weekly, John W. 345
Weekly, Mike 345
Weeks, Everton J. 340
Wegman, Colleen 531
Wegman, Daniel R. 531
Wegman, Robert B. 531
Wehrle, H. Barnard III 320
Wehrle, Michael H. 320
Wehtje, Rodney 22
Weidenheimer, Jim 100
Weiderhold, Fred E. 44
Weidner, William P. 290
Weigal, Kris 116
Weil, Robert 210
Weimer, Linda 510
Weinberg, Richard A.
  (G-I Holdings) 204
Weinberg, Richard A.
  (International Specialty Products) 259
Weinberg, Sharon L. 368

Weinberger, Michael L. 89
Weinberger, Peter 21
Weiner, Beth 307
Weiner, Edward G. 482
Weiner, Howie 290
Weiner, Michael J. 469
Weinstein, David C. 194
Weippert, Renee 209
Weir, Walter 505
Weis, Harry 22
Weis, Joseph 197
Weisbruch, Craig 362
Weisfeld, Brian E. 533
Weishan, Jim 443
Weisman, Eric 344
Weiss, Andrew 486
Weiss, David A. 77
Weiss, Douglas A. 140
Weiss, Edward J. 145
Weiss, Jen 223
Weiss, Kathleen G. 377
Weiss, Lisa 454
Weisselberg, Allen 486
Weitzman, Betsy 441
Welber, Peter M. 117
Welborn, Floyd J. 442
Welch, Jim 413
Welch, Russ 428
Welchons, Irving B. III 358
Weldon, Terri 185
Weller, Gary L. 382
Wellington, Robert D. 29
Wells, Betty 28
Wells, Dan 533
Wells, Doug 533
Wells, Gary M. 533
Wells, Greg 533
Wells, Ivan R. 424
Wells, Mary Ellen 33
Wells, Mike 533
Wells, Scott B. 130
Wells, Thomas F. 489
Welsh, Thomas S. 28
Welte, William B. 342
Welty, Linda J. 192
Wenaas, Jeffrey 234
Wenc, Stephen 494
Wendel, Jon 247
Wendell, Beth 215
Wendlandt, Gary E. 364
Wendt, Richard L. 262
Wendt, Roderick C. 262
Weng, Drew 186
Wentworth, Carol 487
Wentworth, Robert J. 400
Werner, Thomas L. 23
Wesley, James 297
Weslock, Kathleen 445
Wessler, Alan 333
Wessner, David K. 386
West, Henry J. 310
West, Richard P. 97
West, W. Richard Jr. 452
Westcott, Michael 31
Westenborg, Jack 207
Westerbeck, David F. 496
Westerfeld, Barclay 524
Westman, Bob 203
Westrich, Vernon 49
Wetmore, Keith C. 341
Wetterau, Mark S. 208
Wexler, Erik G. 296
Whalen, Ann M. 48
Whalen, Jerry 514
Whaley, Ronald L. 453
Whatley, Earl 90
Whatley, Tom 312
Wheary, John 482
Wheeler, Arnie 65
Wheeler, John E. Jr. 143
Wheeler, M. Cass 39
Wheeler, Paul 282
Whelan, Michael F. 233

Whetstine, Michael J. 396
Whetter, Craig 150
Whirty, Ed 106, 202
White, Audrey J. 401
White, Brian 167
White, David (Swinerton) 467
White, David R. (Iasis Healthcare) 247
White, Dennis F. 418
White, Hollis J. 313
White, Jane 370
White, John T. (Structure Tone) 463
White, Jon M. (ICON Health) 248
White, Kristin M. 30
White, Mark 50
White, Richard A. 220
White, Tom 351
White, W. Bruce Jr. 524
White, Wendy 505
White House, Judy 439
Whitehouse, Mark S. 535
Whitely, Larry 67
Whitesell, Shirley J. 43
Whitfield, Rick N. 505
Whitmer, W. Carl 247
Whittaker, Susan 430
Whitteberry, Steve 209
Whitten, Jeremiah 386
Whittle, David 284
Whitton, Jeff 199
Whitworth, Clark 290
Wiater, Patrick J. 461
Wichlacz, Wayne 216
Wick, Philip 293
Wickham, Greg 147
Widerlite, Paula S. 23
Wiebking, Guy R. 406
Wiedenhoft, Charles T. 52
Wiederkeht, Lee 50
Wiedmann, Harald 285
Wieland, Jack 266
Wieland, John 266
Wieman, Roberta 162
Wiener, Mark S. 406
Wierman, Ken 276
Wiest, Barbara G. 249
Wiest, Joel 274
Wiggins, Michael R. 455
Wigglesworth, Margaret 126
Wight, Marshall A. 64
Wightman, Lori 33
Wilbanks, Cynthia H. 503
Wilbanks, George E. 168
Wilbur, Brayton Jr. 535
Wilcox, Ron 454
Wiles, Paul M. 374
Wilke, Douglas 197
Wilkerson, Allen 351
Wilkerson, Terry 510
Wilkey, Vicki 459
Wilkins, Chris 281
Wilkinson, Kathleen A. 400
Wilkinson, Walt 241
Willard, Derek H. Sr. 502
Willard, Judith 66
Willemain, Jeffrey K. 154
Willey, Dick 395
Willey, Rob 344
Willhite, William 224
Williams, Ben 430
Williams, Cheryl Scott 140
Williams, Curtis D. 507
Williams, David II 516
Williams, Glen 214
Williams, J.L. 337
Williams, Jack E. 507
Williams, Jamey 26
Williams, John C. 141
Williams, Kay 160
Williams, Keith (CUNA Mutual) 145
Williams, Keith A.
  (Michigan State University) 334
Williams, Kim 352
Williams, Larry (Irvine Company) 261

Williams, Larry P.
  (Pennsylvania Lottery) 392
Williams, Lori-Anne 504
Williams, Mark (Drees) 167
Williams, Mark (EBSCO) 174
Williams, Mark (Muzak) 346
Williams, Martha K. 238
Williams, Michael (Safety-Kleen) 429
Williams, Michael S. (Ormet) 381
Williams, Nick 50
Williams, Ray G. 182
Williams, Terry 300
Williams, Tracy 491
Williamson, Eric 221
Williamson, Maribeth 43
Williamson, R. Max 359
Willis, Lori 436
Willis, Richard 64
Willmore, Kathryn A. 337
Willmott, Nicholas J. 279
Willoughby, John 417
Willoughby, Richard 258
Willson, Mary Anne 83
Wilmoski, Scott 58
Wilner, Eddie 33
Wilson, Alexandra M. 141
Wilson, Bryan S. 492
Wilson, Dan 429
Wilson, David 150
Wilson, Debora J. 288
Wilson, Ed 498
Wilson, Eric F. G. (Raley's) 412
Wilson, Eric L.
  (Hensel Phelps Construction) 234
Wilson, James (California Steel) 97
Wilson, Jeffrey W. 383
Wilson, Jim (Spectrum Health) 455
Wilson, John (New Balance) 361
Wilson, John J.
  (Dairy Farmers of America) 146
Wilson, Ken 201
Wilson, Lawrence A. 71
Wilson, Linda 442
Wilson, Lowell D. 27
Wilson, Mark L. 481
Wilson, Maryruth 480
Wilson, Michael M. 185
Wilson, R. Todd 348
Wilson, Roger G. 79
Wilson, Stephen R. 113
Wimberley, Carl 39
Wimes, Ed 505
Winarsky, Norman D. 457
Winett, Rob 59
Winfrey, Oprah 225
Winget, Larry J. Sr.
  (Venture Industries) 519
Winget, Larry J. Jr.
  (Venture Industries) 519
Wingfield, Tania 416
Winkler, Gary 19
Winkler, Matthew 78
Winn, Jim 360
Winnenberg, William E. 379
Winograd, Les 161
Winslow, Larry 394
Winter, Matthew E. 315
Wintermeyer, Dorane 229
Winters, Lonnie 398
Wirtz, W. R. 537
Wirtz, William W. 537
Wise, Joan 18
Wiszniak, Richard 133
Witczak, Janet 256
Withee, John 361
Withey, Howard C. 77
Witmer, Mark D. 334
Witt, Arthur P. 471
Witt, Richard A. 345
Witte, Rob 282
Witty, Tim E. 27
Woehl, Juergen 441
Woellfer, Gale 210

HOOVER'S HANDBOOK OF PRIVATE COMPANIES 2005

INDEX OF EXECUTIVES

Woitkoski, Gerald 366
Wojcik, Charles A. 478
Wolf, Abe 232
Wolf, Charles R. 420
Wolf, Denise 526
Wolf, Howard 459
Wolf, Kathleen 453
Wolf, Michael J. 321
Wolfe, Jon C. 242
Wolfe, Russel 480
Wolfe, S. David 280
Wolfe, Timothy M. 271
Wolff, Derish M. 300
Wolff, Kimberly 346
Wolff, Sherman M. 229
Wolford, Ray 277
Wolkow, Mathew 533
Woll, Ed 27
Wolle, Darrell 39
Wollen, Foster 71
Wollenberg, Roger 418
Wolman, Jonathan P. 57
Wolszon, Elizabeth A. 429
Wolterman, Daniel J. 326
Wombles, Robert H. 284
Wonderly, Thomas J. 139
Wong, John 87
Woo, Benson K. 483
Wood, Brian S. 129
Wood, Cary B. 122
Wood, David 87
Wood, Frank J. 198
Wood, Jeff 222
Wood, John (John Wieland Homes) 266
Wood, John V. (M. A. Mortenson) 303
Wood, Ken (Teamsters) 470
Wood, Kenneth F.
  (Blue Shield of California) 81
Wood, Richard 505
Wood, Robert H. 88
Wood, Stephen T. 286
Woodall, Gary 519
Woodbury, Timothy S. 442
Woodfill, John H. 52
Woodham, Peggy S. 305
Woodlief, Philip K. 160
Woods, Douglas E. 165
Woods, Ed 128
Woods, Rick 218
Woodward, Marc 223
Woodward, Ralph 66
Woodyard, David B. 125
Wooldridge, Sonny 400
Wooten, Ronald J. 411
Wootress, Gwenna R. 184
Wootton, David 128
Wootton, Michael J. 465

Wordsworth, Jerry L. 318
Wordsworth-Daughtridge, Debbie 318
Wories, John Jr. 43
Wormington, John R. 25
Worobow, Robert R. 488
Worroll, David 161
Woyciesjes, Ruth 161
Wray, John 110
Wray, Susan 227
Wright, Alan 398
Wright, Albert B. III 354
Wright, Barbara P. 385
Wright, Bob 472
Wright, Charles R. 460
Wright, Dianna 428
Wright, George C. 472
Wright, Jay 248
Wright, Joseph R. Jr. 385
Wright, Lewis W. III 508
Wright, Mark H. 514
Wright, Marvin E. 504
Wright, Pandit 159
Wright, Patricia 82
Wright, Ronald 100
Wright, Sally 467
Wright, Stephen J. 84
Wright, Vicente 97
Wright, Wesley 454
Wszolek, Dennis 113
Wu, Shareen 303
Wu, Y.C. 522
Wuori, Richard 529
Wyatt, Bob 66
Wylde, Frances M. 216
Wyler, Joel P. 171
Wynkoop, Roger 20
Wynn, Curtis 371

X

Xenos, Jim 300

Y

Yaffe, Kenneth 355
Yagi, Ryuichi 237
Yaha, Laurance H.S. 295
Yahn, Charles 59
Yancer, Deborah A. 23
Yang, Silas S.S. 404
Yankowskas, Mark J. 422
Yanney, John R. 116
Yannotta, Pat 131
Yarber, Jeff 73
Yardis, Robert 463

Yates, James H. 365
Yates, Philip R. 212
Yates, Ronald L. 510
Yates, William G. Jr.
  (Yates Companies) 540
Yates, William G. III
  (Yates Companies) 540
Yaugher, Kevin 307
Yee, Don 524
Yee, Yang-Chiah 326
Yefsky, Alan 413
Yellen, Janet L. 188
Yellin, Neil S. 333
Yetter, Tracy 442
Yetzbacher, Charles L. 484
Yoder, David 433
Yoder, John 433
Yoh, Harold L. III 151
Yoh, William C. 151
Yohai, Joel 109
Yokomizo, Doug 481
Yordy, Alan 390
York, John C. II 152
York, Johnny A. 90
Yormark, Brett 348
Yoss, Susan B. 204, 259
Yost, Andy 129
Youga, Tony 172
Young, Daniel 261
Young, Douglas 502
Young, Kevin (Louis Berger) 300
Young, Kevin (Towers Perrin) 481
Young, Marjorie 512
Young, Paul 179
Young, Philip E. 470
Young, Ross 400
Youngman, Dwight R. 31
Yows, J. Thomas Jr. 90
Yuan, Crystal 53
Yudkoff, Royce 346
Yudof, Mark G. 508
Yura, Satoshi 285
Yusko, David 399
Yust, Paul 286

Z

Zaccaria, Adrian 71
Zachary, Marc 129
Zachry, David S. 541
Zachry, H. Bartell Jr. 541
Zachry, John B. 541
Zacks, David M. 35
Zagorin, Janet 446
Zahnd, Richard 355
Zajaczkowski, Charles 401

Zalupski, Robert J. 483
Zambeletti, Giulio 276
Zande, Lynne 320
Zank, Gregg 164
Zaroff, Richard 119
Zatina, Thomas 249
Zatkin, Steven 273
Zatta, Robert J. 422
Zawacki, Walt 192
Zawalick, Lawrence 356
Zayatz, Veronica 233
Zeckhauser, Sally H. 226
Zelezny, John 130
Zell, Samuel 179
Zeller, John H. 266
Zelman, Benjamin D. 323
Zelms, Jeffrey L. 417
Zeltmann, Eugene W. 365
Zemke, Craig 262
Zendan, Michael F. II 346
Zeno, Randy 76
Zeppos, Nicholas S. 516
Zeringue, Oswald J. 491
Zervos, Mike 168
Zerza, Fred 272
Zettle, Lawrence 208
Zeug, Brian 311
Ziegler, Paul 346
Ziegler, Steve 296
Zielke, William 160
Zigerelli, Larry 325
Zika, Steven J. 223
Zilkha, Donald 127
Zilm, John 115
Zimmer, Kris 458
Zimmer, Thomas R. 521
Zimmerman, David 355
Zimmerman, Garnet 470
Zimmerman, John 325
Zimmerman, Michael J.
  (ContiGroup) 137
Zimmerman, Mike
  (American Foods) 38
Ziolkowski, Jim 42
Zipperstein, Steven E. 520
Zirkman, Joseph A. 106
Zore, Edward J. 372
Zorn, Robert A. 157
Zucco, Giuliano 309
Zucker, Elliott P. 360
Zulkey, Edward J. 63
Zumba, John J. 157
Zumwalt, Deborah 459
Zurack, Marlene 363
Zurek, Thomas M. 41
Zwettler, Joseph J. 37